The Rebellion Record

A diary of American events, with Document, Narratives, Illustrative Incidents, Poetry, etc.

(Volume VII)

Frank Moore

Alpha Editions

This edition published in 2019

ISBN : 9789353804954

Design and Setting By
Alpha Editions
email - alphaedis@gmail.com

THE

REBELLION RECORD:

A Diary of American Events,

WITH

DOCUMENTS, NARRATIVES, ILLUSTRATIVE INCIDENTS,
POETRY, ETC.

EDITED BY

FRANK MOORE,

AUTHOR OF "DIARY OF THE AMERICAN REVOLUTION."

SEVENTH VOLUME.

WITH FOURTEEN PORTRAITS ON STEEL, AND VARIOUS MAPS AND DIAGRAMS.

NEW-YORK:
D. VAN NOSTRAND, PUBLISHER, 192 BROADWAY.
1864.

JOHN A. GRAY & GREEN,
PRINTERS, STEREOTYPERS, AND BINDERS,
Cor. Frankfort and Jacob Sts.,
New-York.

REBELLION RECORD.

CONTENTS OF THE SEVENTH VOLUME.

LIST OF ILLUSTRATIONS.

DIARY OF EVENTS.

GEN. SAMUEL K. ZOOK

DIARY.

JUNE 1, 1863.

MAJOR-GENERAL BANKS, at Port Hudson, La., issued an order forbidding the passage of steamers from New-York past the quarantine at New-Orleans, without a special order, unless they should be mail steamers or others transporting stores for the Government. This regulation was made necessary by the continued "refusal to transport the soldiers' mails, except upon inadmissible conditions." The provost-marshal was charged with the execution of the order. —AN expedition into Tappahannock, Va., was made by a party of Union soldiers, who succeeded in destroying a large quantity of stores belonging to the rebels, besides carrying off a number of negroes.—*Richmond Enquirer, June* 6.

—AT Philadelphia, Pa., a meeting was held to protest against the arrest of C. L. Vallandigham. Judge Ellis Lewis was appointed chairman, and speeches were made by Messrs. Bigler, Biddle, and Charles J. Ingersoll. The latter counselled obedience to the laws and the constitutional authorities, but resistance to any attempt to control the elections.—GOVERNOR DAVID TOD, of Ohio, appeared before the Court of Common Pleas of Fairfield County, in obedience to his recognizance, to answer the charges filed against him by Dr. Edson B. Olds, when the case was continued to the next term of the court.

—A GOOD deal of publicity has been given to a rumor that General Lee is preparing for a forward movement, from which the newspapers in the United States infer that it is only a *ruse* to cover a demonstration in some other quarter, since they affect to believe that we would be more reticent if an advance were really in contemplation. The month of June, upon which we have this day entered, will unravel the mystery. In the mean time, the confederate army and people can well afford to possess their souls in patience, and to leave their cause in the hands of that kind Pro-

vidence which has guided us thus far through this bloody wilderness.—*Savannah Republican.*

—AN expedition, under the command of Colonel James Montgomery, ascended the Combahee River, S. C., and succeeded in destroying a large quantity of rebel stores and other property. —(*Doc.* 1.)

—THE bombardment of Vicksburgh continued. All the guns in position opened fire at midnight, and continued their fire until daylight this morning. After a short cessation the firing was renewed, and kept up all day.—THE second party of recalcitrants left St. Louis for the South. They numbered seventeen, among whom were the wife and two daughters of Trusten Polk.

—A LARGE meeting, to procure funds to send supplies to the wounded at Vicksburgh, was held at Chicago, Ill., at which nearly six thousand dollars were raised.—THE schooner Echo was captured yesterday, in the Gulf of Mexico, by the United States steamer Sunflower.—A FIGHT took place at Clinton, La., between the Union forces under the command of Colonel Grierson, and the rebel forces stationed in that town, resulting in the loss of twenty-one killed and wounded of the rebels, and a number of the Nationals.

June 2.—The circulation of the newspapers, Chicago *Times* and New-York *World*, was prohibited, in the Department of the Ohio, by a general order from Major-General Burnside, their "repeated expressions of disloyal and incendiary sentiments" being "calculated to exert a pernicious and treasonable influence."—AT Nashville, Tenn., C. F. Jones was arrested for writing treasonable correspondence to the *Freeman's Journal* of New-York.—F. H. PIERPONT, Governor of Virginia, issued a proclamation, calling upon the commandants of the State militia to hold their regiments in readiness for the field at an hour's warning, as "the enemies of their liberty and

prosperity were again threatening their homes."
— The Twenty-fourth regiment of New-York volunteers returned to Oswego.—The city government of Portsmouth, Va., was organized. —West-Point, Va., was evacuated by the Union troops.—The ship Amazonian was captured in latitude 11° 15', longitude 34° 30', by the rebel privateer, Alabama.

June 3.—Col. Kilpatrick returned from an expedition through the country situated between the Rappahannock and York Rivers, in Virginia, having been entirely successful.—(*Doc.* 3.)

—A meeting was held at Sheffield, England, under the presidency of Mr. Alderman Saunders, at which the following resolution was adopted :

"That this meeting has heard with profound regret of the death of Lieutenant-General Thomas Jefferson Jackson, of the confederate States of North-America ; a man of pure and upright mind, devoted as a citizen to his duty, cool and brave as a soldier, able and energetic as a leader, of whom his opponents say he was 'sincere and true and valiant.' This meeting resolves to transmit to his widow its deep and sincere condolence with her in her grief at the sad bereavement, and with the great and irreparable loss the army of the confederate States of America have sustained by the death of their gallant comrade and general." It was decided to request Mr. Mason to transmit the resolution to Mrs. Jackson and the troops lately commanded by the deceased General. —Ashepoo, S. C., was destroyed by the National forces, under the command of Colonel Montgomery, of the Second South-Carolina colored volunteers.—(*Doc.* 55.)

—Admiral Du Pont ordered Lieutenant Commander Bacon to proceed with the Commodore McDonough on an expedition against Bluffton, on the May River, S. C., a stream emptying into the Calibogue.

The army forces were landed near Bluffton, by the gunboat Mayflower and an army transport, under the protection of the Commodore McDonough, and took possession of the town, the rebels having retreated. By the order of Colonel Barton, the town was destroyed by fire, the church only being spared ; and though the rebel troops made several charges, they were driven back by the troops, and the shells and shrapnel of the Commodore McDonough. Bluffton being destroyed, the soldiers reëmbarked without casualties, and returned to Hilton Head.—(*Doc.* 54.)

June 4.—Joseph A. Gilmore was inaugurated

Governor of New-Hampshire. In his message he stated that over eighteen thousand troops had been furnished for the war, and continued : " In such a contest as that in which we are now involved, I am unable to discriminate between the support of the Government and the support of the National Administration. It is no time now to speculate upon the causes of the rebellion. The only facts which we need are that it exists, and that it is our duty to put it down. It was a remark made to me, by a former Governor of this State, the late venerable Isaac Hill, in which I fully concur, that 'a man who will not stand by his Government is a coward and a traitor.' "

—Prince Gortchakoff, in a dispatch to Mr. Clay, the American Minister at St. Petersburgh, after expressing the satisfaction of the Emperor at the reply of Secretary Seward to the proposal of France to join the diplomatic intervention in favor of Poland, remarks: "Such facts draw closer the bonds of sympathy between Russia and America. The Emperor knows how to appreciate the firmness with which Mr. Seward maintains the principle of non-intervention."

—Major-General Stahl sent the following dispatch to the War Department, from his headquarters at Fairfax Court-House, Va. : "All is quiet along our lines and in front, on the Orange and Alexandria Railroad. This morning, when the relief passed, our pickets were attacked on Sawyer's road by guerrillas. Colonel Gray at once started, with about one hundred and twenty men, in pursuit of them, but could find nothing of them in the woods. He then went on to scout the whole country, and when he passed Frying-Pan, his rear-guard was attacked by about one hundred rebels, who were hidden in a thick wood. Colonel Gray turned his column, and charged the rebels, who fled in great haste through the woods. He followed them up to Aldie, and from there returned, *via* Drainesville. Our entire loss is three, and some horses wounded. We captured their surgeon, Dr. Alexander."

—An expedition left Yorktown, Va., proceeding to West-Point, and thence to Walkerstown, by way of the Mattapony. Thence it proceeded to Aylette's Warehouse, about ten miles from the point of landing. At this place, the iron foundry, machine-shops, cotton mills, lumber-yard, and four government warehouses, containing large quantities of corn and grain, were burned ; also a large mill owned by Colonel

Aylette, of the rebel army, with six thousand bushels of grain. The Colonel made his escape, although in the vicinity. The surgeon of the Fourth Delaware captured his horse, which was ready, saddled and bridled. A great number of barns, containing stores for the rebels, such as grain, corn, whisky, cotton goods, etc., were destroyed.—(Doc. 56.)

— A LARGE and enthusiastic Union meeting was held at Chicago, Ill., this evening, at which speeches were made by Senators Trumbull and Doolittle and others.—COLONEL A. BAIRD, in command of the garrison at Franklin, Tenn., was attacked by a force of rebels under General Forrest, and driven into his intrenchments, but being reënforced by a brigade of infantry sent by General Granger, he succeeded in repulsing the enemy with a heavy loss. At the same time an attack was made on Triune, but the rebels were driven off with a loss of two hundred men, four hundred horses, and a large quantity of camp and garrison equipage.—(Doc. 4.)

—GENERAL BURNSIDE's order suppressing the circulation of the Chicago Times was revoked.— THE Twenty-second regiment N. Y. S. V., under the command of Colonel Phelps, returned to Albany from the seat of war.

—A FIGHT took place at Sartoria, Miss., between a body of National troops, under General Nathan Kimball, and two thousand rebels commanded by General Wirt Adams, resulting in the defeat and rout of the latter after a contest of half an hour. The National loss was one killed and seventeen wounded, while the rebels lost over one hundred taken prisoners, and a number killed and wounded.—SIMMSPORT, on the Atchafalaya River, La., was destroyed by the Union ram Switzerland, under the command of Lieut.-Colonel John A. Ellet.—(Doc. 53.)

—THE rebel General Wheeler, with a body of cavalry, made an attack upon the National troops on the Shelbyville road, near Murfreesboro, Tenn., and skirmishing was kept up the whole day. The Second Indiana cavalry, on picket-duty, was first attacked, but being reënforced by the Thirty-ninth Indiana, under the command of Colonel Thos. J. Harrison, they succeeded in putting the rebels to rout, with a loss of several killed and wounded. The National loss was one killed and a number wounded.

June 5.—Contrabands in the vicinity of Suffolk, Va., having signified their intention of serving the United States as armed soldiers, orders were issued by Major-General Peck to Captain John Wilder, "to recruit a company of colored troops, subject to no molestation in removing those so recruited to the place of rendezvous, at Craney Island."—A SQUADRON of the Sixth New-York Cavalry, commanded by Major William P. Hall, on an expedition from Yorktown, Va., to Warwick River, succeeded in destroying twenty-three boats and one schooner belonging to the rebels.—BRIGADIER-GENERAL ALEXANDER P. STEWART, of the rebel army, having been promoted to the rank of Major-General, took leave of his brigade, and assumed command in the corps of General Hardee, at Wartrace, Tenn. —Chattanooga Rebel, June 7.

—THE steamer Isaac Smith, which was captured by the rebels on the first of February last, was sunk while trying to run the blockade of Charleston, S. C., by the national gunboat Wissahickon.—THE rebel privateer Alabama, in latitude 14° S., longitude 34° W., captured and destroyed the ship Talisman.—THE Second division of the Sixth army corps, under the command of General A. P. Howe, crossed the Rappahannock River at Deep Run, on a reconnoissance. During the passage of the river, the rebel sharp-shooters made some opposition, and after the division had crossed there was some brisk skirmishing, the rebel rifle-pits were carried, and over thirty prisoners captured. The National casualties were six killed and thirty-five wounded, among the former Captain Charles E. Cross, of the engineers.—(Doc. 5.)

June 6.—THE rebel General J. E. B. Stuart held a grand review of the forces under his command, at his camp near Culpeper, Va., preparatory to his advance into Maryland and Pennsylvania.—NEAR Nicholasville, Ky., a locomotive exploded, killing six and wounding three soldiers belonging to the Thirty-fifth Massachusetts, Seventh Rhode Island, Fifty-first New-York, and Ninth New-Hampshire regiments.—THE schooner Statesman, loaded with cotton, was captured by the National gunboat Tahoma, under the command of Lieutenant Commander Semmes.—SHAWNEETOWN, Johnson County, Kansas, was sacked and burned by a force of rebel bushwhackers, under Cy Gordon and Dick Yeager. They plundered a number of Union men, and killed four, who resisted. When they had obtained all the plunder possible, they fired the village in several places, and left by the light of the flames.—The bark Whistling Wind, in latitude 33° 38′, longitude 71° 29′, was captured and burned by the rebel privateer Coquette.— Guerrillas destroyed portions of the railroad track, near Germantown, Tenn.—General Sibley's command left St. Paul, Minn., for an expedition against the Sioux. There were two columns employed in this expedition. One started from Sioux City, Iowa, and consisted of three thousand cavalry, one battery of artillery, and a proportionate amount of infantry, under command of Brigadier-General Sully. The other column was under command of Brigadier-General H. H. Sibley, and numbered three full infantry regiments, one battery mountain howitzers, and one thousand two hundred mounted rangers. The two divisions will meet at a given rendezvous in Dacotah. The object in sending a part of the force up the Missouri is to cut off the retreat in that direction of the Indians.

—The ship Southern Cross was captured and burned in latitude 1° 34′ south, longitude 36° west, by the rebel privateer Florida.—Major-General John C. Fremont addressed a letter to the Secretary of War, on the subject of the ranking officer in the army of the United States.— A skirmish took place near Berryville, Va.— (Doc. 57.)

—The battle of Milliken's Bend commenced this day.—(Docs. 5, 8 and 27.)

—General Foster, in command of the Union forces at Newbern, N. C., received instructions from the authorities at Washington, to place in close confinement all rebel officers captured by him.—The rebel steamer Lady Walton, was surrendered by her crew. She was engaged in the carrying trade for the Confederacy up Arkansas River, and left Little Rock under orders to proceed through the cut-off into White River, thence up that river for a load of corn. On reaching White River, her Captain, Moses Pennington, a native of Illinois, and W. H. Caldwell, another of the crew, put in execution, with the concurrence of the rest of those on board, being three white men and six negroes, a scheme they had long meditated, and, instead of going *up* White River, turned her head *down*-stream, and coming into the Mississippi, under a flag of truce, delivered her over to the officers of the first gunboat they met, which was near Island No. 82.

June 7.—The expedition under General F. P. Blair, sent out from Haines's Bluff to the Big Black River, on the twenty-seventh of May last, returned to-day. The captures made during the expedition amount to five hundred head of cattle, five hundred horses and mules, one hundred bales of cotton, and ten thousand pounds of bacon, together with a number of small articles, taken by the soldiers and never accounted for. All bridges were either burned or demolished and the forage destroyed.—Partisan guerrillas burned the railroad bridge over the Little Harpeth River, at Brentwood, Tenn.—The battle of Milliken's Bend was concluded this day. After a most desperate fight, the rebels were repulsed, and retired, leaving over one hundred dead on the field. The Union loss was three hundred and ten killed and wounded.—(Doc. 8 and 27.)

—The plantation of Jefferson Davis was visited by a party of Union troops, who "rifled it completely, destroying every implement of husbandry, all his household and kitchen furniture, defacing the premises, and carrying off every negro on the place. The plantation of Joe Davis, brother of the President, was treated in the same way, if we except four or five domestic servants which the robbers left."—*Jackson Mississippian, June* 11.

—The schooner Alfred H. Partridge, belonging to Gloucester, Mass., was captured by the rebel privateer Clarence.

June 8.—Governor Yates, of Illinois, adjourned the Legislature of that State, fully believing "that the interests of the State will be best subserved by a speedy adjournment, the past history of the present Assembly, holding out no reasonable hope of beneficent results to the citizens of the State, or the army in the field, from its further continuance."

—A Convention of Editors was held at New-York, to consult upon the rights and duties of the public press in the present war crisis. After an interchange of opinions, the general sentiment was expressed in a series of resolutions affirming the duty of fidelity to the Constitution, the Government, and the laws; that treason and rebellion are crimes nowhere so culpable as in a republic, where every man has a voice in the administration; that while journalists have no right to incite or aid rebellion or treason, they have the right to criticise freely and fearlessly the acts of public officers; that "any limitation of this right created by the necessities of war should be confined to localities wherein hostilities actually exist or are imminently threatened, and we deny the right of any military officer to suppress the issue or forbid the general circulation of journals printed far away from the seat of war."

—COLONEL MONTGOMERY, with four companies of the Second South-Carolina colored regiment, on board the Harriet A. Weed and the John Adams, ascended Turtle River to within a short distance of Brunswick, Ga., and after throwing a few shells into the place, discovered that it was entirely deserted. The Harriet A. Weed getting aground, and the John Adams drawing too much water, it was deemed advisable not to occupy the city, or proceed further up the river.

Captains Apthorp and Adams, desiring not to return without accomplishing something, took a skiff with six men, rowed up to the bridge of the Savannah and Brunswick Railroad, fired it in four different places, and had the satisfaction of seeing it totally destroyed before they returned.

On their return to the steamer, they were fired upon from a thicket by some fifteen or twenty rebels, but with the exception of Sergeant Leonard, who received a slight flesh-wound in the arm, not a man was hit.

After shelling the woods by the John Adams, the party returned to St. Simon's Island.

—THE Thirty-seventh and Thirty-eighth regiments N. Y. S. V., returned to New-York from the seat of war, and were welcomed home by thousands of their fellow-citizens.

June 9.—The tow-boat Boston was captured by a party of rebels under the command of Captain James Duke, while towing the ship Jenny Lind up the Mississippi River. The capture took place at a point about three miles from the Pass à l'Outre lighthouse.—(*Doc.* 63.)

—A MAGAZINE at Fort Lyon, near Alexandria, Va., exploded, killing twenty and wounding fourteen men belonging to the Third New-York artillery.—THE Union cavalry, under General Mitchell, at Triune, Tenn., were attacked this morning by a large body of rebels under General Forrest. After a severe fight, the rebels were routed and pursued over five miles, losing over one hundred in killed, wounded, and prisoners.—A PETITION to Earl Russell, concerning the departure from English ports of vessels intending to commit depredations upon the commerce of the United States, prepared and signed by a number of shipping merchants of Liverpool, was made public.—(*Doc.* 59.)

—GENERAL FOSTER, in command at Newbern, N. C., issued the following order:

"The Commanding General orders that all white male citizens between the ages of eighteen and thirty-five, within the lines of this Department, shall be at once enrolled, and the rolls forwarded to these headquarters. Commanders of districts will appoint enrolling officers, and take such steps as may be necessary to fully and promptly carry out this order."

—A FIGHT took place near Monticello, Ky., between the National cavalry under Colonels Carter and Kautz, and the rebels under Pegram, resulting in the rout of the latter, and the occupation of Monticello by the National troops.—(*Doc.* 60.)

—THE Savannah *Republican*, of this date, says: "The movements of Rosecrans still continue clouded in mystery, and it is not known whether he has sent off any of his force or not. It is very difficult to obtain any information of his movements, as he has established a chain of patrols, and it is well-nigh impossible for scouts and spies to penetrate his lines. Rosecrans appears better informed of our movements. Late Yankee papers publish a list of forces which Bragg has sent to Mississippi."—THE brig Mary Alvina was captured and burned by the confederate privateer Coquette.—THE Military Departments of the Monongahela and the Susquehanna were created; Major-General Wm. T. H. Brooks being assigned to the former, and Major-General Darius N. Couch to the latter.—BRIGADIER-GENERAL PLEASANTÓN, in command of a cavalry force numbering about six thousand, supported by the column of infantry under the command of Generals Russell and Ames, had a severe engagement near Brandy Station, Va., with the enemy's cavalry, estimated at twelve thousand men, in which he so seriously crippled the enemy that they were unable to follow him, when, at the close of the day, he returned to the north side of the Rappahannock. General Pleasanton's men behaved in the most gallant manner, handsomely driving back superior forces of the enemy. Over two hundred prisoners and one battle-flag were captured.—(*Docs.* 10 *and* 62.)

—THE Military Districts "of the Frontier," and "of the Border," were created by order of Major-General Schofield; the former under the command of General J. G. Blunt, headquarters at Fort Scott, Indian Territory; and the latter under Brigadier-General Thomas Ewing, Jr., head-quarters at Kansas City.—Colonel LAWRENCE WILLIAMS ORTON, formerly Lawrence Williams, of the Second United States cavalry, one time on General Scott's staff, and late General Bragg's Chief of Artillery, and Lieutenant Dunlop, of the rebel army, were arrested and hung as spies at Franklin, Tenn.—(*Doc.* 61.)

June 10.—Governor Bradford, of Maryland, issued a proclamation, calling upon the citizens of Baltimore and the people of the State to rally for defence against the rebels under General Lee. —A CONVENTION took place at the Cooper Institute in New-York, at which an address and resolutions, urging peace in the strongest manner, and denouncing the administration of President Lincoln, were adopted. Speeches were made by Fernando Wood, Judge J. H. McCunn, and others. —GENERAL BRAXTON BRAGG, of the rebel army, was confirmed at Chattanooga by Bishop Elliot of the Episcopal Church.—THE Democratic Convention of Ohio, by acclamation, nominated C. L. Vallandigham for Governor of that State; the same time refugees reported that Mr. Vallandigham had been imprisoned by the rebels.—DEPUTY PROVOST-MARSHAL STEVENS and a Mr. Clayfield, and an enrolling officer who accompanied them, were fired upon near Manville, Rush County, Indiana, when the former was instantly killed. Mr. Clayfield was mortally wounded, and soon after died. The outrage was committed by persons opposed to the draft.—THE Forty-fourth regiment of Massachusetts volunteers returned to Boston from Newbern, N. C.—THE Assistant Secretary of the Navy stated that the whole number of vessels captured or destroyed by the National blockading fleet up to June first, was eight hundred and fifty-five.—THE enrolment met with resistance in Fulton County, Pa. Officers of the Government were shot at by parties concealed in the woods, and the houses of the enrolling agents burned.—THIRTY mounted Indians attacked a coach at a point thirty miles west of Salt Lake, and killed and scalped the driver and another employé of the route. After opening the mail-bags and committing other depredations, the savages retired, taking with them the horses belonging to the stage.—THE bark Lenox was captured and destroyed by the rebel pirates on board the tow-boat Boston, captured yesterday near Pass à l'Outre, Mississippi River.

—CLARK's (rebel) Diary of the War for Separation has the following estimate of killed, wounded, and missing, from the commencement of the war to the first of January, 1863 :

Federals—Killed, 43,874 ; wounded, 97,027 ; prisoners, 68,218—total, 209,115. Died from disease and wounds, 250,000.

Confederates—Killed, 20,893; wounded, 69,615; prisoners, 22,169—total; 102,677. Died from disease and wounds, 136,000.

—THE steamer Maple Leaf, *en route* from Fortress Monroe to Fort Delaware, with a large number of rebel prisoners, was taken possession of and run ashore about eight miles from Cape Henry Lighthouse, when a greater portion of the prisoners escaped.

June 11.—Peter Everitt, with a body of three hundred rebels, attacked a portion of the Fourteenth Kentucky cavalry at Slate Creek, near Mount Sterling, Ky. A severe engagement, lasting three hours, ensued, when the Nationals retreated, fighting as they withdrew.—TRIUNE, Tenn., was again attacked by the rebel cavalry, under General Forrest, who was repulsed with a loss of twenty-one killed, sixty prisoners, and ten wounded. The Union loss was six killed, among them Lieutenant N. C. Blair, of the Fourth Indiana cavalry.—A DEBATE occurred in the British House of Commons on the slave-trade, and the independence of the rebels.—THE blockade-runner Havelock was sunk by the blockading fleet off Charleston, S. C., while attempting to enter the harbor.—FIVE companies of the Fourteenth New-York cavalry, Colonel Thaddeus B. Mott, doing out-post duty near Port Hudson, were captured by a cavalry raid of rebels, under the command of Colonel Logan, of Bragg's command, while encamped within three miles of General Banks's headquarters. The capture was owing to the negligence of the officer, who should have posted and attended to the picket-guard. It seems that the guard were either never posted, or were at the time fast asleep, for in the middle of the night the rebels rode into the Union camp, surrounded the Unionists, roughly awakened them, ordered them to saddle up, and run off five companies of the cavalry, with all their horses, arms, and equipments. The rebels made them ride at speed for eighty-three miles, making but one stop in that distance. When a horse gave out, they entered a farmer's premises and impressed another. At the journey's end, the soldiers were thrown into a black hole, where they were under close confinement.

The companies were: company G, under com-

GEN. GEORGE STONEMAN

mand of Captain Porter; company A, under Lieutenant Nolan; company C, under Lieutenant Leroy Smith; company F, under Captain Thayer, who himself alone escaped, and the greater part of company E, under Captain Ayers. Lieutenant Vigel was also captured with Lieutenant Smith's men. These five companies were under command of Major Mulvey, who was taken with his little boy, twelve years old.—*Chicago Tribune.*

—The Sixth regiment N. Y. S. V., Wilson's Zouaves, returned to New-York from the seat of war in Louisiana.—Port Hudson was thoroughly invested by the Union troops under General Banks.—Darien, Ga., was visited and burned by a body of National troops under the command of Colonel Montgomery, of the Second South-Carolina colored volunteers. At the same time the schooner Pet, loaded with a cargo of cotton, was captured.—(*Doc.* 66.)

—The steamer Calypso was captured off Frying-Pan Shoals, thirty miles south-east of Wilmington, N. C., by the Union gunboat Florida.—(*Doc.* 65.)

—A new army corps, denominated the reserve corps, was created in the Department of Cumberland, and placed under the command of Major-General Gordon W. Granger, with its headquarters at Triune, to be composed of three divisions, commanded by Brigadier-Generals J. D. Morgan, R. S. Granger, and A. Baird.

—A party of rebel cavalry, numbering about two hundred and fifty, crossed the Potomac River this morning, and attacked a company of the Sixth Michigan cavalry stationed at Seneca, Md. The Nationals being outnumbered, gradually fell back, fighting, to within three miles of Poolesville, when the enemy retired across the river, after burning the camp at Seneca. The Unionists lost four men killed and one wounded. The rebels left a lieutenant and one man dead on the field.

June 12.—The bark Tacony, in latitude 37° 18', longitude 75° 4', was captured by the Clarence, tender to the privateer Florida. Captain Munday gave the following account of the capture:

"On the twelfth of June, at six o'clock A.M., when about forty miles off Cape Virginia, I was spoken by the brig Clarence, of Baltimore, who said she was short of water, and wished for a day's allowance. Of course I hauled to on this appeal to humanity, and their boat, with an officer and six men, immediately came aboard. They told me they were fifty-five days from Rio Janeiro,

were bound to Baltimore, and were entirely out of water, and would assist me in passing it to the boat. While taking the after-hatch off, I was confronted by the officer of the boat, who presented a pistol at my head, and stated that my vessel was his prize—a prize to the confederate States, and ordered me to leave for New-York. Immediately after, or while transferring my crew, the schooner M. A. Shindler came up, and was hauled to and captured. While transferring the crew of the latter, the schooner Kate Stewart came along, but she having several lady passengers on board, and being an old vessel, was ransomed on giving bonds in the sum of seven thousand dollars. We were then all transferred on board the Kate Stewart. The pirates then transferred their guns, ammunition, supplies, etc., from the brig Clarence to the bark Tacony, and set fire to the former vessel, as well as to the schooner M. A. Shindler. We were then released, the pirate standing off to the south-east.—Major-General Darius N. Couch assumed command of the Department of the Susquehanna, and established his headquarters at Chambersburgh, Pa.—Governor Andrew G. Curtin issued a proclamation calling upon the people of Pennsylvania to rally for their defence against the rebels who were approaching under General Lee.—General Michael Corcoran, with twelve thousand men, left Suffolk, Va., on a reconnoissance to the Blackwater.—The reply of President Lincoln to the resolutions adopted by the Democrats at Albany, N. Y., on the sixteenth of May, relative to the arrest of Mr. Vallandigham, and the vindication of free speech, was made public.—(*Doc.* 67.)

—Major-General David Hunter was relieved of the command of the Department of the South, and Brigadier-General Quincy A. Gillmore assigned to the same.—Governor Oliver P. Morton issued a proclamation to the people of Indiana, warning all persons against resistance to the Government in any form, or hindering the Federal officers in the enforcement of the enrolment laws of the United States.—A skirmish occurred near Middletown, Va., between the Thirteenth Pennsylvania cavalry and Eighty-seventh infantry, with one section of artillery, and a body of about four hundred rebel cavalry. Eight of the latter were killed, a number wounded, and thirty-seven, including a captain and two lieutenants, were taken prisoners.—(*Doc.* 11.)

June 13.—The battle of Winchester, Va., between the National forces under General R. H.

Milroy, and the rebel General Ewell, ended this day.—(*Doc.* 11.)

—CAPTAIN HARE, of the Mounted Provost-Guard, attacked Hine's guerrillas at Wilson's Creek, near Boston, Ky., killing four and capturing five prisoners and twenty-five horses, and a lot of rifles and equipments. The rebels fled. There was no loss on the National side.—THE army of the Potomac commenced its march for the relief of Maryland and Pennsylvania, these States being threatened by a large body of rebels under General Lee.—THE negroes of Pennsylvania were called upon by Governor Curtin to furnish troops for the defence of the Government.—A PARTY of rebel cavalry intercepted the cars at Elizabethtown, Ky., capturing sixty horses and committing other depredations.—THE town of Eunice, ——, was destroyed by the National gunboat Marmora.—THE bark Good Hope, in lat. 22° 49' south, long. 42° 09' west, was captured and burned by the rebel privateer Georgia.—THE schooner Fashion, from Mobile, was captured "off the island of Cuba," by the United States steamer Juniata.—A PUBLIC meeting was held in Montgomery County, Indiana, at which a resolution was passed, declaring that no enrolment of militia in that county should take place, and a committee was appointed, who waited on the Commissioner and read the resolution, and notified him that an attempt to enroll would be at his peril.—BERRYVILLE, Va., was evacuated by the Union troops under Colonel Andrew T. McReynolds, it having been ascertained that Rodes's division of General Ewell's corps of rebels was advancing upon that place.

June 14.—The ship Red Gauntlet was captured by the rebel privateer Florida in lat. 7° 35' north, long. 35° 40'. She was of and from Boston for Hong Kong, with a cargo of ice. The Florida put a prize crew on board and kept in company, taking a large amount of provisions and a supply of coal. She was burned on the twenty-sixth in lat. 29° 23', long. 47° 12'.—(*Doc.* 68.)

—MARTINSBURGH, Va., was occupied by the rebel General Rodes, who succeeded in capturing one hundred and fifty men, several cannon and a quantity of stores. The rebel loss was one killed and two wounded.—THE English steamer Neptune was captured by the National gunboat Lackawanna, in lat. 25° 42' north, long. 85° 32' west.—GENERAL HOOKER marched from Falmouth, Va., and without any interruption

from the rebels established his headquarters at Fairfax Court-House.—THE brig Umpire, in lat. 37° 37', long. 69° 57' was captured and burned by the privateer Tacony.

—GENERAL BANKS, having established his batteries within three hundred yards of the rebel works at Port Hudson, after a vigorous cannonade, summoned General Frank Gardner, in command, to surrender. On his refusal, an assault was made, which ended in the repulse of the Nationals with heavy losses in killed and wounded.—(*Doc.* 13.)

—HAGERSTOWN, Md., was occupied by the rebel troops advancing into Pennsylvania.

June 15.—Great excitement and anxiety existed in Baltimore, Md., on account of the invasion of the State by the rebels.—GENERAL BANKS from his headquarters before Port Hudson, issued the following order :

"The Commanding General congratulates the troops before Port Hudson upon the steady advance made upon the enemy's works, and is confident of an immediate and triumphant issue of the contest. We are at all points upon the threshold of his fortifications. One more advance, and they are ours. For the last duty that victory imposes, the Commanding General summons the bold men of the corps to the organization of a storming column of a thousand men, to vindicate the flag of the Union and the memory of its defenders who have fallen.

"Let them come forward. Officers who lead the column of victory in this last assault may be assured of a just recognition of their services by promotion; and every officer and soldier who shares its perils and its glory shall receive a medal fit to commemorate the first grand success of the campaign of eighteen hundred and sixty-three for the freedom of the Mississippi. His name shall be placed in General Orders upon the roll of honor. Division commanders will at once report the names of the officers and men who may volunteer for this service, in order that the organization of the column may be completed without delay."

—By order of Major-General Grant, Major-General John A. McClernand was relieved of the command of the Thirteenth army corps, and Major-General E. O. C. Ord was appointed thereto.—A DEBATE was held in the House of Lords on the seizures of British ships by the cruisers of the United States, in which the Marquis of Clanricarde and Earl Russell took part, the latter defending the action of the American Government.—The Fifteenth regiment of New-York Engineers, under the command of Clinton G. Colgate, returned to New-York after having served two years in the army in Virginia.—General Erasmus D. Keyes, in command of a small force of National troops, occupied New-Kent Court-House, within fifteen miles of Richmond, Va., creating considerable excitement in that vicinity.—The Twenty-first regiment of New-Jersey volunteers returned to Trenton from the seat of war.—The United States enrolling officer in Boone County, Indiana, was captured by a party of men and held while the women pelted him with eggs.—Governor A. G. Curtin, of Pennsylvania, issued a proclamation calling on all people of the State capable of bearing arms to enrol themselves for the public defence; State records and other public archives were removed from Harrisburgh.—Greencastle, Pa., was occupied by a small body of rebel troops belonging to the forces of General Ewell.

—In the Missouri State Convention Charles D. Drake offered the following :

Resolved, That it is expedient that an ordinance be passed by the Convention, providing first for the emancipation of all slaves in the State on the first of January next; second, for the perpetual prohibition of slavery in the State after that date; and third, for a system of apprenticeship for slaves so emancipated for such period as may be sufficient to avoid any serious inconvenience to the interest connected with the State labor, and to prepare the emancipated blacks for complete freedom; fourth, for submitting said ordinance to a vote of the people on the first Monday of next August.

—Great excitement existed at Pittsburgh, Pa., on account of the rumored approach of the rebels under General Lee. The merchants and mechanics organized themselves into military companies for the defence of the city; business was suspended, all "the bars, restaurants, and drinking-saloons were closed, and the sale or giving away of liquors stopped."—Chambersburgh, Pa., was entered by one thousand eight hundred rebel cavalry under General Jenkins, who sacked the town and its vicinity.—(*Doc.* 33.)

—The army of the Potomac, on its march to intercept the rebels in Pennsylvania, reached Bull Run, Va.—The rebel forces at Richmond, Miss., numbering four thousand, under the command of Major-General Walker, were attacked and driven from the town by the Union troops under Brigadier-General Ellet.—(*Doc.* 14.)

—President Lincoln issued a proclamation announcing that the rebels were threatening Maryland, Pennsylvania, and Ohio, and calling for troops for their defence.—(*Doc.* 69.)

—At nine o'clock this morning, on the return of the gunboat Lackawanna toward Mobile, in company with the steamer Neptune, captured yesterday, the black smoke of a steamer was seen ahead, for which the ship, as well as the Neptune, gave chase. She was not brought to until a shot struck her, which did no injury, however, and she was captured after having been chased twenty-six miles. She was the rebel steamer Planter, of Mobile, of three hundred and thirteen tons, and left Mobile Bay on the night of June thirteenth for Havana, with a cargo of six hundred and twenty-five bales of cotton and one hundred and twenty-four barrels of rosin. During the chase between sixty and eighty bales of cotton were thrown overboard and several barrels of rosin burned.—*Captain Marchand's Report.*

June 15.—Governor David Tod, of Ohio, in accordance with the proclamation of President Lincoln, issued an order calling out thirty thousand volunteers for the defence of the border.—(*Doc.* 70.)

June 16.—The troops to operate against the Sioux moved from their rendezvous at Camp Pope, under command of General Sibley. The force numbered fully three thousand men, all recruited in Minnesota, and more or less accustomed to frontier life. A pontoon train accompanied it; also three hundred wagons and several hundred head of beef cattle.—The Third Massachusetts regiment from Newbern, N. C., returned to Boston, and were received with enthusiasm.—F. H. Pierpont, Governor of West-Virginia, in view of the approach of the rebels, issued a proclamation, calling upon the commandants of the militia, to convene their regiments and companies to be held in readiness to go to the field at a moment's warning.—Governor Joel Parker, of New-Jersey, issued a proclamation, calling upon the citizens of the State to rally for the defence of Pennsylvania.—(*Doc.* 73.)

—Governor Curtin, of Pennsylvania, made the following appeal :

To the People of Philadelphia:

For nearly a week past it has been publicly known that the rebels in force were about to enter Pennsylvania. On the twelfth instant an urgent call was made on the people to raise a departmental army corps for the defence of the State. Yesterday, under the proclamation of the President, the militia were called out. To-day, a new and pressing exhortation has been given to furnish men to repel the invasion.

Philadelphia has not responded—meanwhile the enemy is six miles this side of Chambersburgh, and advancing rapidly.

Our capital is threatened, and we may be disgraced by its fall, while the men who should be driving the outlaws from our soil are quibbling about the possible term of service for six months.

It never was intended to keep them beyond the continuance of the emergency. You all know this by what happened when the militia were called out last autumn. You then trusted your Government and were not deceived. Trust it again now. I will accept men without reference to the six months' term. If you do not wish to bear the ignomiry of shirking from the defence of your State, come forward at once. Close your places of business and apply your hearts to the work. Come in such organizations as you can form. General Couch has appointed Lieutenant-Colonel Ruff to superintend your organizations.

Report to him immediately.

—BRIGADIER-GENERAL FREDERICK S. WASHBURN, of the Iowa Ninth infantry, died at his home in Waterloo. Captain Washburn was wounded at Vicksburgh, on the twenty-second of May, and just before he left for home was promoted from Captain to rank of Brigadier-General.

—THE rebels under General Lee, in the invasion of Pennsylvania, reached Scotland, a few miles east of Chambersburgh. At Harrisburgh the excitement was intense. A correspondent at that place, describing the scene, says:

"It is difficult to convey an exact idea of the state of affairs here to-night, not only on account of the confusion existing, but in consequence of the danger of trenching on what may be contraband ground. During the morning a perfect panic prevailed, extending to all classes of people, and resulting in the grandest demand for railroad tickets ever witnessed in this city. The enemy were supposed to be just over the river,

or, at any rate, at Carlisle, and every woman in the place seemed anxious to leave for safer regions. Trunks were piled up at the depots six feet in height, for nearly a square, and hundreds if not thousands of people eagerly waited the hour of the departure of the various trains.

"In the mean while, the State Capitol had been completely denuded of every thing of value, from the portraits of the governors to the books in the library. The books, papers, paintings, and other valuables were packed in freight-cars, and made ready for instant departure in case of decided signs of danger to the city.

"Measures were taken yesterday to rouse the people to the danger at hand, and during to-day about one thousand persons were earnestly at work on the other side of the Susquehanna, throwing up a bastioned redoubt, for the protection of Harrisburgh. The work was kept up all day, and far into the evening, and late to-night we saw files of laborers returning from their unwonted toil.

"There were but few regular soldiers in town to-day, the principal display being made by three companies of invalids from the military hospitals at York. They arrived during the afternoon, and when drawn up on Third street, they looked as if there was considerable fight in them yet.

"During the entire afternoon, Market street was occupied with army wagons from Milroy's division, which rumbled across the old bridge, and from thence past the railroad depot and out to a camp ground on the other side of the canal. These wagons were mostly drawn by four horses, though there were some mule-teams among them. Dust was the prevailing feature of the vehicles, from the ears of the horses to the hat-rims of the teamsters. Some of the wagons were filled with hay and some with tents, while from many peeped the black faces, grinning mouths and white teeth of contrabands, large and small, of both sexes. For several hours this wagon-train completely filled Market street, giving the spectators a far better idea of the dust, turmoil, and fatigue of war than they could get in any other way."

—JEFFERSON DAVIS, at Richmond, Va., called upon the States of the "Confederacy" to furnish troops for home defence, in order to replace those, who were then, under the command of General Lee, invading the North.—LITTLESTOWN, eleven miles from Gettysburgh, Pa., was occupied by rebel cavalry.—Rebel salt-works, in Princess Ann County, Va., were destroyed by Major Murray, having under his command one hundred men, belonging to the One Hundred and Forty-eighth regiment of New-York volunteers. —(*Doc.* 72.)

—Governor A. W. Bradford, of Maryland, issued a proclamation calling upon the citizens of Baltimore and people of Maryland to rally to defend their soil from invasion.

As there was no organized militia force in the State, he announced that he would fall back upon the recent enrolment for the draft; but he hoped there is patriotism sufficient among the people to raise the force needed from voluntary enlistments.

—A fight occurred in Fleming County, Ky., between the Fifteenth regiment of Michigan volunteers and a superior force of the rebels, which resulted in the repulse of the latter with a heavy loss. The National casualties were fifteen killed and thirty wounded.

—Yesterday, in latitude twelve degrees north, longitude thirty degrees, the rebel privateer Florida captured the ship B. F. Hoxie, of Mystic, Ct., from Mazatlan for Falmouth, England, with a cargo of logwood, silver bars and thirty tons of silver ore; the bars were valued at five hundred thousand dollars, and the ore at a similar amount. The bars were conveyed on board the Florida, and the ore was sunk in the ship to-day.

—Harper's Ferry, Va., was invested by the rebels, while the National troops held Maryland Heights in large force.—The Councils of Baltimore, Md., appropriated four hundred thousand dollars for bounties.—Colonel De Courcey, with parts of the Tenth and Fourteenth Kentucky, and Seventh and Ninth Michigan cavalry, cut off at Triplett's Bridge, Ky., the body of rebel cavalry that made the attack on Maysville, and after a severe fight routed them, killing and wounding a large number and taking over one hundred prisoners, including one captain and two lieutenants.—(*Doc.* 16.)

June 17.—A body of rebels crossed the Ohio River and advanced on Corydon, Paoli, and Orleans, Indiana. At the latter place they were met by the Paoli home guards, who dispersed and drove them back to the Ohio River, where, being prevented recrossing by the presence of an armed steamer, the whole band was captured.—(*Doc.* 12.)

—A Union mass meeting was held at Concord, N. H., probably not less than twenty thousand people being present. A procession composed of military and civic organizations and the citizens of the State generally, with numerous bands of music, marched through the principal streets to State House Square, where the meeting organized by choosing Ira Perley, President, with twenty Vice-Presidents.

A series of resolutions were adopted, pledging support to the Government in putting down the rebellion. The fourth resolve was as follows:

"That the men of the loyal States, who, by word or deed, directly or indirectly, under whatever pretence or disguise, discourage the recruiting and maintaining of our army and navy, or in any other way lend their aid to schemes calculated to embarrass the Government in this crisis of the national life, ally themselves with the rebellion and are traitors at heart."

Eloquent addresses were made by Major-General Butler, Montgomery Blair, General Hamilton, Ira Perley and others.

—The Seventh, Eighth, and Seventy-first regiments of New-York State militia, left New-York for the seat of war in Maryland and Pennsylvania.—Robert Toombs delivered a speech at Sparta, Ga., on "The state of the country."—General Blunt issued an order forbidding the circulation of the *Caucasian, Chicago Times, Columbus Crisis, Cincinnati Enquirer* and *New-York World* in his department.—A fight took place at Aldie, Va., between the National cavalry under General Gregg, and the rebels under General J. E. B. Stuart.—(*Doc.* 74.)

—A body of rebel cavalry crossed the Potomac near the Point of Rocks, and moved upon that place, at which there was no force of defence, except Captain Means's irregular local cavalry. All these were captured, including the Captain himself.

Simultaneously another body of the enemy, mounted, crossed the river higher up, and attacked Major Coles's cavalry at Catoctin Station, about seven or eight miles east of Harper's Ferry.

About the same time a part of the enemy's cavalry charged upon a military train, and succeeded in its capture. It consisted of one first-class locomotive and about twenty-three cars, returning from Harper's Ferry to Baltimore, after having carried provisions to supply the garrison during the day. Fortunately this was the last train of a convoy of five, the others having just preceded it in safety, and all reached Baltimore. Of the captured train were several cars loaded with produce that was being rescued from danger from the vicinity of Harper's Ferry, also some fifteen passengers who took advantage of the train either to escape, or else business connected with the army required them to come down the road.—*Baltimore American, June* 18.

—The iron-clad gunboat Chattahoochee, belonging to the rebels, was destroyed at Chattahoochee, Florida, by the bursting of her boiler. A correspondent of the *Charleston Courier* gives the following account of the affair:

"The schooner Fashion, at anchor in the Chattahoochee River, twenty-five miles above Apalachicola, was loading with cotton, and intended to run the blockade. She had received sixty bales of Sea-Island cotton, and was awaiting for another arrival from ——, when a spy or some traitorous person conveyed the fact to the enemy's fleet blockading. The result was, that the enemy sent nine launches with armed men, captured the schooner with the cotton on board, and took her to the fleet. When the news reached Chattahoochee, Lieutenant Guthrie, commanding the confederate States ironclad gunboat Chattahoochee, ordered steam to be raised, and was determined to pass the obstructions in the river, if possible, with a view of attacking the United States steamer, and endeavor to relieve the Fashion. Just as the steamer was leaving her anchorage, her boilers exploded, and twelve persons were killed, while several others were badly scalded."

—A portion of two companies of the Ninth regiment of Kansas volunteers, numbering seventy men, while on the march from Paola to Kansas City, were fired on at a point about four miles south-west of Westport, Mo., by a large party of rebels in ambush, and suffered a loss of ten killed and seventeen wounded and missing. The National troops who were under the command of Captain Fletcher, were obliged to fall back to Olathe.

—H. Pinkney Walker, Her Britannic Majesty's Vice Consul, at Charleston, S. C., having submitted to the Secretary of State satisfactory evidence of his appointment as Acting Consul for the States of North and South-Carolina, is recognized as such by the government of the confederate States.—*Lynchburgh Republican, June* 18.

—The rebel ram Atlanta was captured in Warsaw Sound, Ga., by the National monitor Weehawken, under the command of Captain John Rodgers.—(*Doc.* 18.)

—Cumberland, Maryland, was occupied during a portion of the day by a party of Imboden's rebel cavalry, who visited the various stores in town, and made large purchases of boots, shoes, and clothing, paying for the same in rebel scrip, at a heavy discount. Several young men belonging to the town joined the rebels and left with them on their departure, which took place at an early hour in the forenoon.—*Cumberland Union, June* 20.

June 18.—Middleburgh and Philomont, Va., were occupied by the National cavalry.

—It having been ascertained that a heavy force of the rebels was about to advance through Northern Mississippi upon the railroad, for the purpose of destroying the bridges near Pocahontas, Lieutenant-Colonel Phillips, of the Ninth Illinois, was despatched to meet, and, if possible, check their movement. He had with him his own regiment, the third battalion of the Fifth Ohio cavalry, Major Smith, and a part of the Eighteenth Missouri, all mounted. When near Ripley he found the rebels in force, and began to fall back, drawing them north toward Pocahontas.

After a little feint of this kind, Colonel Phillips turned and went toward the enemy. At Rocky Crossing, of the Tallahatchie, he came up with General Ruggles, with a force of two thousand infantry, one battery, and a large force of cavalry. Although Colonel Phillips had but six hundred men all told, and no artillery, yet he offered battle, and fought the enemy with such determination as to check his intended movement northward to the railroad. The Nationals suffered a loss of seven killed and twenty-eight wounded. The loss of the enemy was thirty-five killed and one hundred wounded. Lieutenant-Colonel Phillips returned to Pocahontas, bringing with him thirty prisoners, taken in the battle, including one lieutenant-colonel. The Fifth Ohio cavalry fought splendidly on this oc-

GEN. J. E. B. STUART.

casion, under the leadership of Major Smith.—
Cincinnati Gazette.

—The Thirty-seventh, Twenty-second, and
Eleventh regiments of New-York militia, left
New-York for the scene of operations in Pennsylvania.—The Mechanic Light Infantry left
Salem, Mass., for the seat of war.—The steamer
Platte Valley was fired into at Bradford's Landing on the Mississippi, and two persons were
killed and a number wounded.—The English
schooner Harriet was captured at Tampa Bay,
Florida, by the national gunboat Tahoma; about
the same time she destroyed the schooner Mary
Jane.—A detachment of the First Missouri and
Fifth Ohio cavalry under Major Henry, of the
Fifth Ohio, four hundred strong, while on a reconnoissance, was surrounded near Fernando,
Miss., by General Chambers, with two thousand
rebels. They were routed and most of them
captured or killed. Major Henry was taken
prisoner.

—Fletcher Freeman, the National enrolling
officer of Sullivan County, Indiana, was shot and
instantly killed, while riding along a country
road.—Chambersburgh, Pa., was evacuated by
the rebels under Jenkins, who took up his line
of march to Hagerstown.—A company of negroes arrived at Harrisburgh, Pa., from Philadelphia, but their services were declined by General Couch, on the ground that no authority had
been granted by the War Department for the
muster of colored troops into the service of the
United States for a less period than three years.—
Three hundred rebel cavalry under the command
of Colonel Phillips, made a descent on Plaquemine, La,, and destroyed four steamers and a
large quantity of cotton.

June 19.—A committee from the planters of
Louisiana, made a formal application to the
President of the United States, for readmission
into the Union.—(*Doc.* 75.)

—General Gregg, with his cavalry, met the
rebel line of skirmishers in a piece of wood a
short distance west of Middleburgh, Va., and
forced them back about five miles on the road
leading to Ashby's Gap, where the enemy had
two brigades of infantry. Artillery was used
occasionally on both sides, but most of the time
the fight was more of an Indian warfare than
any thing else. Nearly all the charges made
were in woods where the enemy fought from behind trees, stone walls and natural rifle-pits. A
large number of the Nationals were dismounted,
and they proved themselves to be quite as great
adepts in the Indian style of warfare as the enemy. As the latter were driven out of one piece
of timber, they would retreat into another, and
thus the contest was kept up, from early morning
until four o'clock P.M., almost without intermission.

During the early portion of the day the brigade commanded by Colonel Gregg was alone engaged. During the day, General Kilpatrick's
command came up, and, at a late hour, the regular
cavalry, which had been sent up the Snicker's
Gap road, made a sudden dash upon the left
flank of the rebels, creating quite a panic. As
the regulars passed up the Snicker's Gap pike, a
squadron of the First cavalry was placed to
guard the bridge across Goose Creek. The
main column had been gone only a short time,
when the guard was attacked by a superior
force, and driven away, when the bridge was set
on fire. The First Maine, Tenth, Second, and
Fourth New-York, Fourth and Sixteenth Pennsylvania did most of the skirmishing. The
First Maine made five charges under the most
unfavorable circumstances, and added new laurels to their fame. The National loss in killed
and wounded, yesterday and to-day, will probably not exceed fifty, and of the whole number
there are not half a dozen wounds of a serious
character. On the other hand, at the close of the
day, there were thirty of the enemy's dead and
wounded at the hospital, a majority of the wounds
being of a serious character. Some forty prisoners
were captured, including six officers, a lieutenant-colonel, a major, a captain and three lieutenants. When the Tenth New-York entered Middleburgh yesterday, they found five of the missing First Rhode Island troopers locked up in a
store, their captors not having an opportunity
even to parole or carry them off, so sudden was
the charge into the town made.

—The rebels at Williamsport carried all their
stores to the north side of the Potomac River,
with the purpose of making that their base of
operations for raids into Pennsylvania.—Boonesboro, Md., was evacuated by the rebels, who
carried off a number of horses and some other
property.—The Seventy-fourth and Sixty-fifth
regiments of New-York militia, left Buffalo, for
Harrisburgh, Pa.—Two members of the staff
of General Hooker, Major Sterling and Captain
Fisher, were captured by guerrillas near Fair-

fax, Va.—Horatio Seymour, Governor of New-York, issued an order organizing the National Guard of the State.—The Fifty-sixth and Fifth regiments of New-York militia, left home for Harrisburgh, Pa.—The ship Conrad, was captured by the privateer Alabama.

—A detachment of Jenkins's rebel force on their retreat from Chambersburgh, entered McConnellsburgh, Pa., surprising the citizens and capturing a large number of horses and cattle, besides helping themselves to such provisions and wearing apparel as they could find in the stores. After thoroughly rifling the town, they left, taking the road to Hancock, Maryland.—The brig Isabella Thompson, having on board a cargo of turpentine and cotton, was captured by the Union gunboat United States, commanded by R. W. Mead, Jr.—The British schooner Glenn, of Yarmouth, N. S., from Matamoras for Nassau, being six hundred miles out of her course, was overhauled by the National steamer Cumbria, and her papers not being satisfactory, a prize crew was put on board, and she was ordered to New-York.

June 20.—The First regiment of New-York cavalry encountered a portion of Jenkins's rebel force near Greencastle, Pa., and after a short skirmish defeated them, capturing twenty prisoners.—Extracts from the *World*, *Express*, and *Caucasian*, published in New-York, the *Cincinnati Enquirer* and *Chicago Times*, were suppressed within the limits of the Eighth army corps, by order of General Schenck.—The fishing-boat L. A. Macomber, of Noank, Ct., while at anchor at a point twenty-two miles south-east of the South Shoal light, Mass., was boarded by the privateer Tacony, and afterward burned.—The rebel schooner Hattie was captured while attempting to run the blockade of Wilmington, N. C., by the National gunboat Florida.

—A part of General Lee's army is already in the valley of Virginia, and a part probably in Maryland. The rest will probably follow on. At all events, Richmond is about to be uncovered of the defence afforded by the proximity of his troops. They will be removed to some more distant point, whence they cannot be brought instantly and readily to our assistance, if assistance we should need. This summer's campaign cannot be conducted efficiently, if large numbers of our regular troops are detailed to guard and protect our cities, and other assailable points.

In country and in town we must protect ourselves against raiding parties by means of the militia and of volunteer associations for home defence.

We learn from the United States papers that it is proposed in Pennsylvania to call out the militia up to sixty years of age, to repel apprehended invasion. Shall we do less to repel actual invasion? If she be ready to make such sacrifices to subjugate us, should we not be willing to make greater sacrifices to defend ourselves? Boys, from twelve to eighteen, are excellent marksmen, and although it might demoralize their principles, injure their characters, and endanger their health, to enlist them regularly in the army and expose them to the hardships of the camp, of long marches, and of indifferent diet, yet they may be drilled more readily than old men, and made efficient soldiers in a sudden emergency to aid in the defence of the city and its environs.—*Richmond Sentinel*, *June* 20.

—The expedition that left Suffolk, Va., on the eleventh instant, returned to-day. Its leading object was to investigate the strength of, and destroy the three leading strongholds of the rebels on the Blackwater River, all of which were within a distance of twenty-five miles from Suffolk.—The citizens of Pittsburgh, Pa., held a mass meeting, at which martial law was called for and skulkers denounced. A general suspension of business and the raising of volunteer companies for defence were strenuously advocated.

—The ship Isaac Webb, in lat. 40° 35′, long. 68° 45′, was captured by the rebel privateer Tacony, and released on giving bonds for forty thousand dollars; the crew and passengers of the brig Umpire, which was captured and destroyed by the Tacony on the sixteenth instant, in lat. 37°, long. 69° 57½′, were put on board the Isaac Webb to be carried to New-York.—A. J. Boreman was inaugurated as the first Governor of the State of West-Virginia.—The resistance to the enrolment in Holmes County, Ohio, ended.—A spirited engagement took place at Lafourche Crossing, La., this afternoon. Nearly two thousand rebels attacked the National forces who were guarding the bridge and were repulsed.—Frederick, Md., was occupied by the rebels under J. E. B. Stuart.

June 21.—At Baltimore, Md., as a matter of precaution against rebel demonstrations, earthworks were erected around the north and west sides of the city. The Council appropriated a large sum of money, and a very large force of laborers (mostly contrabands) were impressed into the service. A line of barricades, composed of tobacco hogsheads and empty sugar and molasses hogsheads, filled with brick and sand, was erected within the city, extending from the high ground on the east to the south-western extremity. "These, if the rebels should come," said a participant, "will be defended by the Union League men, who are being armed by General Schenck, and should a cavalry force manage to dash past the batteries, they would here meet a formidable resistance.' The Union men are entirely confident that should the rebels be so rash as to attempt a raid in this direction, they will be able to effectually defeat them."

—The Aëronautic corps of the army of the Potomac was dispensed with, and the balloons and inflating apparatus were sent to Washington.

—The fight at Lafourche Crossing, La., was renewed this day, and ended in the defeat of the rebels with a loss of sixty killed, two hundred and forty wounded, and seventy prisoners. The Union loss was eight killed and sixteen wounded.—*New-Orleans Era, June 23.*

—Major-General Pleasanton, with his cavalry, attacked the rebels, under General Stuart, at Middleburgh, Va., and after driving them over eight miles, succeeded in capturing two pieces of artillery, and sixty prisoners, besides killing and wounding over one hundred men.—(*Doc.* 77.)

—The ship Byzantium and bark Goodspeed were captured and burned by the rebel privateer Tacony off the coast of Massachusetts.—On the approach of the rebels toward Shippensburgh, Pa., the proprietor of the *Union* Hotel in that town blurred his sign over with brown paint.— The steamer Victory was captured off Cuba by the gunboat Santiago de Cuba, and the English schooner Frolic off Crystal Run, Florida, by the gunboat Sagamore.—This afternoon a party of the First Maryland cavalry, under Major Cole, dashed into Frederick, Md., driving out the rebels and capturing one. On the retirement of the Nationals, however, the rebels returned and reöccupied the town.

June 22.—Three steamers laden with military stores, and convoyed by two Union gunboats, were fired into by rebels at Cypress Bend, on the Mississippi River, and a number of persons were killed and wounded. The rebels were finally driven off by the gunboats.—The correspondence between James M. Mason, the rebel commissioner at London, and Moncure D. Conway, was made public.—The rebels were driven out of Cumberland, Md., by the National forces under General B. F. Kelley.—The schooners Marengo and Florence, and the fishing-vessels Elizabeth Ann Thomas, Rufus Choate, and Ripple, were captured by the confederate privateer Tacony.—At Acquia Creek, Va., the quartermaster's buildings, left standing by the Union troops on the evacuation of that place, were burned by the rebels.—Mr. Vallandigham, who was banished to the Southern States for a stated period, arrived at Bermuda in the confederate steamer Lady Davis, from Wilmington. It was reported that Mr. Vallandigham was on his way to Canada, and there to await coming events.—*Bermuda Royal Gazette, June 23.*

—The case of the seizure of the suspected gunboat Alexandra, at Liverpool, England, was announced in the Court of the Queen's Bench at London, before Chief Baron Pollock.—(*See Supplement,* Vol. II.)

June 23.—The State of New-York responded nobly to the call for troops to drive the rebels from the soil of Pennsylvania and Maryland. Twenty regiments at this time had been armed, equipped, and supplied with subsistence and transportation, and had gone to Harrisburgh and Baltimore. Sixteen of these regiments moved from New-York, two from Brooklyn, and two from Buffalo. The following is a list of the regiments that had left: The Seventh, Eleventh, Twelfth, Thirteenth, Twenty-second, Twenty-third, Twenty-eighth, Thirty-seventh, Forty-seventh, Fifty-second, Sixty-ninth, Sixth, Seventy-fourth, Seventy-first, Sixty-fifth, Fifty-sixth, Fifth, Thirty-second, Fifty-fifth, Fourth artillery, and a consolidated regiment from Staten Island.

—The Raleigh (N. C.) *Standard* of this date favored a convention of all the States, to procure peace, either by reconstruction of the Union or by peaceable separation.—Rev. R. I. Graves, of Hillsboro, N. C., who was committed on the fourth of February last, on the charge of treason to the rebel government, was discharged, through the efforts of W. A. Graham.—The London *Times* publishes an elaborate article against the employment of negroes, as soldiers, in the army of the United States.

—In the Missouri State Convention, Governor Gamble, Chairman of the Committee on Emancipation, presented the following ordinance from the majority of the committee: ·

First. That the first and second clauses of the Twenty-sixth Section of the Third Article of the Constitution be abrogated.

Second. That slavery, or involuntary servitude, except for the punishment of crime, shall cease to exist in Missouri on the fourth of July, 1876; and that all the slaves within this State on that day be hereby declared free.

Third. That all slaves hereafter brought into the State, not now belonging to citizens of the State, shall thereupon be free.

Fourth. That all slaves, removed by the consent of their owners to any seceded State, after the passage of the ordinance of secession, and hereafter brought into this State by their owners, shall thereupon be free.

Fifth. The General Assembly shall have no power to pass laws to emancipate slaves without the consent of their owners.

A minority report was also submitted, abrogating some clauses of the Constitution as above, declaring slavery abolished on the first of January, 1864, provided they and their issue be apprenticed to their former owners until the fourth of July, 1876; requiring the Legislature to pass laws regulating the relation between said apprentices and their masters, to secure them humane treatment, necessary education, and providing against importation or emigration of any negro or mulatto in the State. No future assessment of slave property shall be collected, nor shall the right to the services of apprentices be subject to taxation. Provisions were also made to submit the ordinance to a vote of the people.

—Colonel S. H. Saunders returned to Boston, Kentucky, from the expedition sent by General Burnside, into East-Tennessee, and reported as follows:

"I arrived here with my command at eleven o'clock this morning. I struck the railroad at Lenoir, destroyed the road up to Knoxville, made demonstrations against Knoxville, so as to have the troops drawn from above, destroyed the track, and started for Strawberry Plains; burnt Slate Creek Bridge, three hundred and twelve feet long, and the Strawberry Plain Bridge, one thousand six hundred feet long, and also Mossy Creek Bridge, three hundred and twenty-five feet long. I captured three pieces of artillery, some two hundred boxes artillery ammunition, over five hundred prisoners, ten thousand stand of arms, destroyed a large amount of salt, sugar, flour, meal, saltpetre, and one saltpetre works, and other stores. My command is much fatigued. We have had but two nights' sleep since leaving Williamsburgh. The force in East-Tennessee was larger than I had supposed. I did not attack Loudon Bridge, for reasons that I will explain. At Mossy Creek I determined to return. In the mountains I had very great difficulties that were unexpected. I found the gaps, through which I intended to return, strongly guarded with artillery and infantry, and blockaded with fallen timber. A force was also following in our rear. I determined to cross at Smith's Gap, which I did."

—Chambersburgh, Pa., was reöccupied by the rebels, under General Rodes; and the National troops, commanded by General Knipe, retreated to the main body.

—The rebel sloop, John Wesley, which had evaded the blockade of St. Mark's, Fla., on the thirteenth, was captured by the Union steamer Circassian.—The Fifth regiment of Massachusetts volunteers, whose term of service had expired, arrived at Fortress Monroe, from Newbern, N. C., and again volunteered their services to General Dix.—The Union gunboat Sumter was sunk off Cape Henry.—Several wagons, with ammunition, forage, and other articles belonging to the National troops, were destroyed by a party from Mosby's rebel cavalry, on the Chantilly road, near Bull Run, Va.—The sloop Kate, from Nassau, N. P., was captured in Indian River, Fla., by the Union bark, Pursuit.

June 24.—McConnellsburgh, Pa., was occupied by the rebel cavalry this evening, after a short resistance by the Twelfth Pennsylvania cavalry.—Great excitement existed at Harrisburgh, Pa., on the approach of the rebels, who were "slowly advancing on Carlisle;" many merchants packed up their goods ready for shipment, and martial law was proposed, "to prevent all the able-bodied men from leaving the city." The Mayor issued an order, calling upon the people to stand firm, and prohibiting the sale of all liquors.—The Eleventh New-York artillery left Rochester, for Harrisburgh.

—Shippensburgh, Pa., was evacuated by the National troops, and immediately occupied by rebel cavalry.—At Shelbyville, Tenn., the rebels were defeated by the National troops, under General Mitchell.—(*Docs.* 84 *and* 112.)

—Tʜᴇ following General Orders were issued from the War Department at Washington:

I. By direction of the President, that part of the Middle Department west of Hancock, including the adjacent counties of Ohio, will constitute the Department of West-Virginia. Brigadier-General B. F. Kelley is placed in command of the Department of West-Virginia.

II. Major-General W. S. Hancock, U. S. volunteers, is, by direction of the President, assigned to the command of the Second army corps, in place of Major-General D. N. Couch, transferred to another command.

—Tʜᴇ rebel General R. S. Ewell, at Chambersburgh, Pa., issued the following order:

First. The sale of intoxicating liquors to this command, without written permission from a major-general, is strictly prohibited.

Second. Persons having liquor in their possession are required to report the fact to the provost-marshal, or the nearest general officer, stating the amount and kind, that a guard may be placed over it, and the men prevented from getting it.

Third. Any violation of Part I. of these Orders, or failure to comply with Part II., will be punished by the immediate confiscation of all liquors in the possession of the offending parties, besides rendering their other property liable to seizure.

Fourth. Citizens of the country, through which the army may pass, who are not in the military service, are admonished to abstain from all acts of hostility upon pain of being dealt with in a summary manner. A ready acquiescence to the demands of the military authorities will serve to lessen the rigors of war.

—Tʜᴇ army of the Cumberland, excepting the division under General Van Cleve, commenced a forward movement from Murfreesboro, marching by the Shelbyville and Manchester Roads, and skirmishes took place at Guy's, Liberty, and Hanover Gaps, Tenn.—(*Docs.* 37, 112, *and* 120.)

—Cᴏʟᴏɴᴇʟ J. K. Mɪᴢᴇɴᴇʀ returned to La Grange, Tenn., from an extensive cavalry expedition south, from the same point, and reported as follows: He broke up the command under General George, at Panola; destroyed the railroad bridge at the Yocokaway, and the trestle-work just beyond, and a portion of the road from there north.

He then crossed the Tallahatchie, coming north, and pursued Chalmers beyond Coldwater, on the

Helena Road. He made for the Tallahatchie to cross, and at the mouth of the Coldwater he killed fifteen or twenty of Chalmers's men, and took forty prisoners. He paroled all the sick at Panola, brought away and destroyed all the army supplies, workshops, mills, tanneries, and depots.

He passed within three miles of Austin and Commerce, destroying an immense amount of forage and subsistence, took from six to eight hundred horses and mules, and five hundred head of cattle. He sent detachments north and north-east, from Panola, to destroy or bring away all subsistence, forage, horses, and mules. He passed through five counties, travelled two hundred miles, and crossed three streams.

Chalmers had with him Stokes's, Slemmer's, and Blythe's men, nine hundred, with three pieces of artillery. The remainder of his force, nine hundred, fled south, *via* Charleston, under General George. He destroyed all the ferries at Panola and Coldwater, and lost one man killed and five wounded.

—Cᴏʟᴏɴᴇʟ Wɪʟᴅᴇʀ, with his mounted infantry, had a sharp skirmish at Beech Grove, Tenn., with a body of rebel infantry, and succeeded in killing and disabling a large number of them, with a loss of forty of his own men.—(*Doc.* 120.)

June 25.—This afternoon, a fight occurred at Liberty Gap, Tenn., between a rebel division under General Cleburn, and the Nationals, commanded by Generals Willich, Wilder, and Carter, resulting in the rout of the rebels, who fled, leaving their dead and wounded in the hands of the Nationals. The loss of the Nationals was forty killed and one hundred wounded.—(*Doc.* 112.)

—Tʜᴇ ship Constitution, in sight of the Island of Trinidad, latitude 20° 31', longitude 29° 16', was captured by the rebel privateer Georgia.—Fᴀɪʀғᴀx Cᴏᴜʀᴛ-Hᴏᴜsᴇ, Va., having been evacuated by the National troops, was occupied by a rebel guerrilla party during the evening.—Aɴ expedition under the command of Colonel S. P. Spear, of the Eleventh Pennsylvania cavalry, reached a point within six miles of Richmond, Va., creating a great panic in that place.—(*Doc.* 35.)

—Aɴ assault was made on the rebel works at Vicksburgh, by General McPherson's corps, which ended in the capture of one of the forts.—(*Doc.* 36.)

—Tʜᴇ English steamer Britannia, was captured by the Union gunboat St. Jago de Cuba, at a point one hundred and fifty miles from Abaco, having run the blockade of Charleston, South-Carolina.

June 26.—Andrew G. Curtin, Governor of Pennsylvania, issued a proclamation, calling for sixty thousand men to serve for three months, or the period of the rebel invasion.—(*Doc.* 79.)

—BRASHEAR CITY, La., was captured by the rebel forces under Generals Green and Mouton.—(*Docs.* 19, 26, *and* 80.)

—THE Twenty-first regiment of New-York militia, under the command of Colonel Nugent, left Poughkeepsie for Baltimore, Md.—THE Fifth regiment of Massachusetts volunteers returned to Boston, and were welcomed by an imposing and enthusiastic demonstration.—McCONNELLS-BURGH, Pa., was evacuated by the rebels under General Stuart.—REAR-ADMIRAL A. H. FOOTE died at New-York City.—By direction of President Lincoln, Major-General N. J. T. Dana was assigned to the organization and command of the militia and volunteer forces and defences of Philadelphia, Pa.—FREDERICK, Md., was occupied by the National cavalry.

June 27.—A squadron of Scott's Nine Hundred cavalry, under Major Remington, on their way to Centreville, Va., this morning, encountered, near Fairfax, the Sixth Virginia cavalry, and dashed at them with the sabre. The Major made two charges, and drove the rebels for three miles into a wood, and there encountered a superior force, that checked him with the fire of carbines. The fight, from the beginning to the end, was fierce. Major Remington, after having had his horse shot twice, cut his way out and made his escape with eighteen men. Eighty were reported missing. Among them were Captain Dagwell, Captain Campbell, and Lieutenant Hazleton. The companies were B and C.

—CARLISLE, Pa., was abandoned by the Union forces, and soon after occupied by the rebels advancing on Gettysburgh.—A LARGE number of rebel cavalry under command of Fitz-Hugh Lee, made a dash into Annandale, Va., capturing several sutlers who were in the vicinity, and burning a number of hospital stores and sutlers' wagons.

—THE Maryland Club-house at Baltimore, having "degenerated into a resort for those who are disaffected toward the Government, and hostile to its legally constituted authorities," was

closed by order of Major-General Schenck.—MANCHESTER, Tenn., was entered and occupied by the Union forces under General J. J. Reynolds.—SHELBYVILLE, Tenn., was occupied by General Granger.—JOEL PARKER, Governor of New-Jersey, on the reception of a message from Governor Curtin, informing him of the second entrance of the rebels into Pennsylvania, renewed his call upon the citizens of the State to hold themselves in readiness for immediate service.—YORK, Pa., was occupied by the rebels under General Gordon.—(*Doc.* 81.)

—THE schooner Varnum H. Hill was captured by the rebel privateer Florida, in latitude 30° north, longitude 48° 50', but was released on a bond, on condition her master would take to Bermuda, the prisoners captured by the privateer, from the ships lately destroyed by her.—A SKIRMISH occurred on the Walnut Bottom road, at a point five miles from Carlisle, near the Stone Farm, between a detail of Pennsylvania militia under Captain Murray, and a party of rebels, in which ten of the militia were captured and one wounded.—THE rebel schooner Archer, a tender to the privateer Tacony, entered the harbor of Portland, Me., and captured the revenue cutter Caleb Cushing.—(*Doc.* 21.)

June 28.—A skirmish occurred at Oyster Point, about four miles from Harrisburgh, Pa., between the rebels and the Seventy-first regiment of New-York militia and E. Spencer Miller's Philadelphia battery, resulting in the retreat of the Union troops to the intrenchments around Harrisburgh. —THE manufacturers of Morristown, Pa., resolved to close their works until the rebels were driven from the State, and raised ten thousand dollars to pay the wages of all who volunteer during their absence.—MECHANICSBURGH, Pa., was given up to the rebels this morning. On their arrival they pulled down the National flag, which was flying in the square, and raised the rebel colors in its stead.

—THE ship City of Bath was captured by the rebel pirate Georgia in latitude 20° 30' south, longitude 29° 30' west, off the Island of Trinidad.

—MAJOR-GENERAL GEORGE GORDON MEADE assumed command of the army of the Potomac.— A FIGHT took place between a regiment of Pennsylvanians, under the command of Colonel Frick, and a force of rebels who were advancing on Wrightsville, opposite Columbia, Pa. After a sharp contest, Colonel Frick was obliged to retire

across the Susquehanna and burn the bridge.—
(*Doc.* 81.)

—MAJOR-GENERAL DIX, at Fortress Monroe,
sent the following despatch to the War Department
at Washington:

"Colonel Spear, of the Eleventh Pennsylvania
cavalry, whom I sent out two days ago, completely
destroyed the bridge over the South-Anna,
captured General W. F. Lee, Colonel Hearsable,
four captains, five lieutenants, and one hundred
privates, and brought them in. He has also
brought in thirty-five wagons, with six mules
each, and one hundred and fifty mules in addition,
and from seventy-five to one hundred horses.
He took fifteen thousand dollars in confederate
bonds, just issued, from an agent of the authorities
at Richmond. This is all public property.
No private property has been touched. Colonel
Spear's loss is three killed and eight wounded."—
(*Doc.* 87.)

—DONALDSONVILLE, La., was attacked by the
rebel forces under General Green, who succeeded
in gaining possession of the Union intrenchments.
Soon after, the gunboats, commanded by Rear-
Admiral Farragut, opened a flanking fire above
and below the works, and driving back the supporting
party of the rebels, captured the rebels
who had entered them.—*Admiral Farragut's
Report.*

—GENERAL MITCHELL's division of the army
of the Cumberland left Triune, Tenn., this day.
When about eight miles out on the Eagleville
road, the rebel pickets were met and pursued
five miles to Rover, when they made a stand with
infantry, cavalry, and artillery, and a sharp fight
ensued, continuing over two hours, and resulting
in the flight of the rebels, with a slight loss.
The National loss was seven wounded.

June 29.—At Philadelphia, Pa., there was much
excitement on account of the approach of the rebels
toward Gettysburgh. Business was suspended,
and the people prepared themselves for defence.—
(*Doc.* 85.)

—AT Sykesville, Marriottsville, and other points
in Maryland, the rebels appeared and committed
depredations on public and private property.—
COLUMBIA, Pa., was placed under martial law, and
Captain Samuel J. Randall, of the Philadelphia
City Troop, was appointed Provost-Marshal; the
citizens of the town were seized and sent to work
on the intrenchments.—WRIGHTSVILLE, Pa., was
evacuated by the rebels.—THE Forty-fifth regi-

ment of Massachusetts volunteers, returned to
Boston from Newbern, N. C.—NATIONAL troops
enforced the enrolment, and arrested deserters,
in Sullivan and Green counties, Ind.—CAPTAIN
JONES, with a detachment of the First New-York
cavalry, had a sharp engagement with a party of
rebel horsemen belonging to the command of
General Imboden, at McConnellsburgh, Pa., defeating
them and driving them out of the town.—
(*Doc.* 85.)

—GENERAL BRAGG abandoned his fortifications
on the north side of Duck River, Tenn., and made
a hasty retreat toward Tullahoma.—THE rebels
approached to a point on the Reistertown road
seven miles from Baltimore, Md., creating a great
excitement in that city.—A RESOLUTION calling on
President Lincoln to restore General McClellan to
command, passed the Common Council of Philadelphia.—A
PARTY of Colonel Sharpe's scouts,
nine in number, headed by Sergeant M. W. Kline,
dashed into Hagerstown, Md., this morning, in the
very rear of the enemy, and captured ten prisoners
and a large rebel mail, which was on its way
from the South to Lee's army.—AT Westminster,
Md., a fight took place between a portion of the
First regiment of Delaware cavalry and the rebel
cavalry belonging to General Stuart's division.
About half-past three o'clock in the afternoon, a
citizen informed the Nationals that the rebels
were approaching, and the men were rapidly put
in position. Lieutenant Clark, with twelve men,
advanced to reconnoitre; he found about three
hundred rebels coming down the Washington
road, and heard that as many more had crossed
from said road toward the rear of the Delaware
encampment. The reconnoitring party then fell
back to the main body and formed in front of the
first platoon. Major Knight, who was in command
of the Federal force, gave the order to
charge, which was obeyed in gallant style. The
rebels were driven back on the Washington road
about two hundred yards. The fight lasted some
fifteen or twenty minutes, sabres and pistols being
freely used, when the Federals, overpowered
by superior numbers, were in turn forced back.
Just then it was discovered that a large force
was coming up from the rear, and the order was
given to retreat. Major Knight, Lieutenant Clark,
and Adjutant Lobdell remained behind to the
last, covering and directing the retreat. Clark
had a ball pass through the rim of his hat, and
one of his arms was very much bruised by the
side-stroke of a sabre. These officers, with a

number of men, reached Baltimore shortly after midnight. There were about ninety-five men engaged on the Union side, consisting of Captain Corbett's and Lieutenant Churchman's companies. Captain Corbett had his horse shot, was wounded and taken prisoner. Lieutenant Churchman and Surgeon Shields were also captured. The Nationals had two killed, seven wounded, and thirty-eight missing. The names of the killed and wounded were as follows: killed, Daniel Welch and Wm. Vandegraft; wounded, Joseph Wilson, Samuel Bigler, James Newkirk, Frank Stewart, Dickinson Meredith, Theodore Jones, and Robert Machin. Of the rebels, two lieutenants and one private were killed, and fifteen wounded. The rebel dead were buried by the Union troops after Stuart left Westminster. Their wounded were left behind.—*Baltimore American.*

—General Shepley, Military Governor of Louisiana, issued an order calling upon the citizens of New-Orleans for a brigade of volunteers to serve for sixty days in defence of the city.— This day Rear-Admiral Porter, being informed by General Dennis, commanding the post at Young's Point, on the Mississippi River, that the National negro troops at Goodrich's Landing had been attacked by the rebels, directed General Ellet to proceed with the Marine Brigade to the scene of action, and remain there until every thing was quiet. The hindmost vessel of the brigade, the John Haines, arrived there as the rebels were setting fire to the Government plantations, and supposing her to be an ordinary transport, they opened fire on her with field-pieces, but were much surprised to have the fire returned with shrapnel, which fell in among them, killing and wounding a number. The result was a retreat on the part of the rebels, and the escape of a number of negroes whom they had imprisoned. The gunboat Romeo also came up the river about this time, and hearing the firing, hurried to the scene of action. The commander soon discovered the rebels setting fire to the plantations, and commenced shelling them. This he kept up for a distance of fifteen miles, chasing them along—the rebels setting fire to every thing as they advanced. The result was an almost total destruction of houses and property along the river front in that vicinity. The rebels carried off about one thousand two hundred negroes, who were employed in working upon the Government plantations. General Ellet landed his forces, and in company with a black brigade, proceeded to chase the rebels, who were making a hasty retreat. The General found the road strewn with broken carts and furniture, which the rebels left in their haste to get away from his forces. He pursued them as far as Tensas River, where they had crossed. They burned the bridges, and intrenched themselves for a battle. This was soon offered them. The Union artillery opened on them and put them to flight. General Ellet, not knowing the country very well, and having only a small force with him, deemed it proper not to pursue them much further. He sent two hundred infantry across the bayou, and found they were retreating to Delhi, leaving their plunder strewn along the road.

June 30.—Maryland Heights were evacuated by the National troops, after the removal of the Government property and the demolition of the fortifications.—At Cincinnati, Ohio, a meeting to devise means for the defence of the city was held, Major-General Burnside presiding.—General O. B. Wilcox issued a general order against secret political societies and other organizations in Indiana and Michigan.—(*Doc* 88.)

—The Twenty-second and Thirty-seventh regiments of New-York militia, left camp, opposite Harrisburgh, Pa., taking only their arms and canteens, and started out to reconnoitre for a few hours. After scouring the country for ten miles they met the rebels, drawn up in line of battle at Sporting Hill, awaiting their approach. Colonel Roome, of the Thirty-seventh, being senior officer, took the right, and Colonel Aspinwall the left. They then advanced on the rebels, and were forcing them back, when the latter opened on the militia with two pieces of artillery; but a section of an independent Philadelphia battery coming up, soon silenced their guns, when they retreated with a loss of thirteen killed and twenty wounded.

—Major-General Meade, from his headquarters, army of the Potomac, issued the following circular:

"The Commanding General requests that previous to the engagement soon expected with the enemy, corps and all other commanding officers address their troops, explaining to them the immense issues involved in the struggle. The enemy is now on our soil. The whole country looks anxiously to this army to deliver it from the presence of the foe. Our failure to do so will leave us no such welcome as the swelling of millions of hearts with pride and joy at our success would give to every soldier of the army. Homes, firesides, and domestic altars are involved. The army has fought well heretofore. It is believed that it will fight more desperately and bravely than ever if it is addressed in fitting terms. Corps and other commanders are authorized to order the instant death of any soldier who fails to do his duty at this hour."

—A BATTLE took place at Hanover, Pa., between the National forces under Generals Pleasanton, Custer, and Kilpatrick, and the rebels under J. E. B. Stuart, resulting in the defeat of the latter with a heavy loss.—(Doc. 32.)

—COLONEL WILDER's cavalry expedition to the rear of Bragg's army at Tullahoma, returned to Manchester, Tenn. With his brigade of mounted infantry he started on Sunday, the twenty-eighth instant, went to Hillsboro, thence to Decherd, swam Elk River, and crossed with his howitzers on a raft, making fifty miles the same day. He tore up the track, burned the cars, and the dépôt full of stores, and destroyed the trestle work. At daylight on Monday he started up to the Southern University, where he divided his force.

One portion was sent to strike the railroad at Tantalon, while Wilder went to strike it at Anderson. There he found Buckner's whole division and a train of cars going up from Knoxville to Tullahoma, and fell back, in the mean while tearing up the railroad from Cowan to Jersey City. The rebels, meanwhile, having sent a powerful force to intercept him, he struck through the mountain and returned to Manchester, which he reached to-day. He took and paroled a number of prisoners and captured a lot of mules. The damage done to the railroad is very serious, but would have been more so if the rivers had not been so high. The expedition made one hundred and twenty-six miles in two days and a half.—(Doc. 37.)

—IN the British House of Commons an animated debate was held on the subject of the recognition of the rebel government.—HANOVER and York, Pa., were occupied by the National troops, the rebels concentrating near Gettysburgh.—BALTIMORE, Md., was placed under martial law by General Schenck.—(Doc. 86.)

July 1.—Carlisle, Pa., was occupied by the Union troops under the command of General W. F. Smith. Soon after the occupation, the rebels returned and demanded a surrender of the town, which was refused, when a bombardment by the rebels was commenced, and the United States arsenal was set on fire, and other buildings were destroyed.—A BODY of cavalry belonging to the command of General Crittenden, in pursuit of General Bragg from Tullahoma, Tenn., fell in with the rebel cavalry on the road between Pelham and Winchester, and had a fight which resulted in the defeat of the rebels, and the wounding, mortally, of Lieutenant-Colonel Webb, of the Fifty-first regiment of Alabama mounted infantry.—CAPTAIN DAHLGREN, with twenty men, and Captain Kline, of the Third Indiana cavalry, visited Greencastle, and captured the orderly of General Lee and his entire escort, who had very important despatches from Jefferson Davis to General Lee, together with orders to the various generals of Lee's army, muster and pay-rolls, and other military matter.—THE Missouri ordinance of freedom passed the State Convention, in session at Jefferson City, by a vote of eighty yeas against thirty noes.—(Doc. 90.)

—A TRAIN of cars on the road between Louisville and Frankfort, Ky., was thrown off the track, the rails having been removed by the rebel guerrillas.—GENERAL JOHN F. REYNOLDS, with the First and Second corps of the army of the Potomac, checked the advance of Longstreet and Hill, near Gettysburgh, after a desperate and bloody engagement, in which General Reynolds was killed.—(Docs. 20 and 118.)

—TULLAHOMA, Tennessee, was occupied by the advance of General Rosecrans's army, the rebels having fled, taking the road toward Winchester. Strong fortifications, a quantity of stores, and three siege-guns were captured by the Nationals.—(Doc. 115.)

—THE new rebel gunboat Virginia was launched from Rocket's ship-yard at Richmond, Va.—THE question of rank between the major-generals of the United States army was decided by the board of officers convened for that purpose at Washington, D. C.—(Doc. 91.)

—GENERAL GETTY with his brigade, left White House, Va., for the purpose of destroying the bridges over the South-Anna River, that were not burned by Colonel S. P. Spear, in his late raid. At Baltimore Cross-Roads he met a large force of rebels, and after a brisk engagement retired, having lost two killed and five wounded. He did considerable damage, destroying some miles of railroad track and a dépôt.—THE following notice was published by the rebel Bureau of Conscription at Richmond:

"To answer numerous inquiries, and to correct errors not uncommon, the following notice is published to all concerned:

"1. Under the recent call of the President, extending the conscript age, all substitutions have ceased to be valid if the substitute be less than forty-five years old, and is not otherwise exempt by law.

"2. Membership, whether as officer or private, of local organization for home defence or special service, confers no claim to exemption from confederate service; neither does service in the militia, unless in the case of officers actually in commission who have duly qualified.

"3. Hereafter any one furnishing a substitute will become liable in his own person whenever the services of the substitute are lost to the government from any cause other than the casualties of war.

"4. Applications for exemption, on any ground whatever, must first be addressed to the local enrolling officer, who, if he has not power to act, or is in doubt, will refer them to higher authority, with report of the facts. All such addressed direct to higher authority will necessarily and invariably be referred back for local examination and report; and the applicants will thus have uselessly lost time and prolonged suspense."

—THE public debt of the United States, at this date, amounted to $1,097,274,403.

July 2.—The *Richmond Whig* of this date contained the following: "If it be true that the confederate forces occupy Harrisburgh, the attention of the commanding general will no doubt be directed to the coal-fields, which lie within forty or fifty miles of that city. His first aim will be to cut all the railroad connections, and thus put a stop to the transportation of fuel. His next will be to destroy the most costly and not easily replaced machinery of the pits. Whether he would stop at this is questionable. He might set fire to the pits, withdraw the forces sent out on this special duty, and leave the heart of Pennsylvania on fire, never to be quenched until a river is turned into the pits, or the vast supply of coal is reduced to ashes. The anthracite coal is found in large quantities in no other part of the world but Pennsylvania. Enormous quantities are used in the United States navy, the countless workshops and manufactories of

the North, in the river boats, and even upon locomotives. It cannot well be replaced by any other fuel. The bituminous coal which is found near Pittsburgh would not answer the purpose, even if it would bear the cost of transportation. Our troops already hold the railroads and canals leading from the Cumberland coal-fields. All that is needed is to seize the anthracite fields, destroy the roads and the machinery of the pits, set fire to the mines, and leave them. Northern industry will thus be paralyzed at a single blow.

"These views may have induced General Lee to move upon Harrisburgh. We doubt whether he would fire the mines, but the destruction of the Mauch Chunk Railroad and pit implements would be as legitimate as blowing up tunnels and aqueducts or burning bridges. Of one thing we may be sure, that whatever is best to be done will be done by General Lee, and if he thinks fit to destroy the Pennsylvania mines they will certainly be destroyed. Should he leave them untouched, it will be for the best of reasons. But it is impossible not to indulge the hope that he will avail himself of the tremendous power which the possession of the coal-fields, even temporarily, would confer."

—A SKIRMISH occurred near Bottom's Bridge, Va., in which Sergeant Barnett, of company C, Fifth Pennsylvania cavalry, was killed. There were no other casualties. The Fifth Pennsylvania captured twenty-five prisoners. — THE United States steamer Maumee was launched at Brooklyn, N. Y.

—GENERAL NEAL DOW was captured by a party of rebel scouts at a private residence near Clinton, La., and sent to Richmond, Va.—THE rebel blockade-runner Britannia was captured by the National gunboat Santiago de Cuba.—AT Baltimore, Md., the following order was issued by the General Commanding:

"Until further orders, the citizens of Baltimore city and county are prohibited from keeping arms in their houses unless enrolled in volunteer companies for the defence of their homes." The dwellings of citizens were visited by the Provost-Marshal and the police, for arms, in accordance with this order.

—GENERAL WILLIAM JACKSON, with one thousand seven hundred men, and two pieces of artillery, attacked the Union troops at Beverly, Va., but was repulsed and routed with some loss. The rebels expected to make an easy prize of the garrison, which contained the Tenth Virginia infantry, Captain Ewing's battery, and one company of cavalry, under the command of Colonel Harris, of the Tenth Virginia, who was ordered by General Averill to hold the place until he could reach him with reënforcements, which he did; but before their arrival, the rebels were repulsed and the Nationals were in pursuit.—THE battle of Gettysburgh was resumed at early daylight this morning.—(*Docs.* 20 *and* 118.)

—THE rebel Impressment Commissioners of the several States, met in convention at Atlanta, Ga., to-day. Virginia, North-Carolina, and Florida were not represented, and the other States only partially. Consequently the Convention adjourned to the twenty-seventh instant for a full attendance.

—A PICKED force of infantry, artillery, and cavalry, under General Foster in person, left Newbern, N. C., on an expedition inland.—THE battle of Cabin Creek, Indian Territory, ended on this day.—(*Doc.* 30.)

July 3.—The following "commendable appeal" to the foreign residents of Richmond, Va., appeared in the *Enquirer*, published in that city, to-day:

To British Subjects:

FELLOW-COUNTRYMEN: If you desire to protect your homes, and the homes of your friends, from the touch of the ruthless invader; if you believe, as we do, in the justice of the Southern cause, and desire its success; if you have interests here to defend, then it is manifestly your duty, as brave and chivalrous men, to take up arms at this crisis. The history of our past precludes the possibility of our being cowards; but let us here, and now, in this righteous struggle for constitutional law and liberty, add another laurel to our ancestral history.

Those of you who are willing to offer yourselves, for either temporary or permanent duty, should report at once to the undersigned: Sydney H. Davis, Lieutenant H. B. M., Sixteenth regiment, Arlington House. F. L. Buxton, Lieutenant Royal Berks volunteers, Mrs. Duval's, corner Fourteenth and Ross streets.

—AT Vicksburgh, Miss., at eight o'clock this morning, flags of truce appeared before A. J. Smith's front, when the rebels, Major-General Bowen and Colonel Montgomery, were led blindfolded into the Union lines. They bore a communication from General Pemberton, of the following purport:

"Although I feel confident of my ability to resist your arms indefinitely, in order to stop the further effusion of blood, I propose that you appoint three commissioners, to meet three whom I shall select, to arrange such terms as may best accomplish the result."

General Grant replied in these words:

"The appointment of commissioners is unnecessary. While I should be glad to stop any unnecessary effusion of blood, the only terms which I can entertain are those of unconditional surrender. At the same time, myself and men, and officers of this army, are ready to testify to the distinguished gallantry with which the defence of Vicksburgh has been conducted."

At eleven o'clock the messengers returned. This afternoon General Grant met General Pemberton between the lines, and after an hour's consultation settled the surrender of the place. —(*Docs.* 25, 36, *and* 146.)

—THE National Guards, Colonel Wright commanding, composed of the most substantial citizens of Newbern, N. C., received their arms and equipments and entered upon duty at the garrison of that place.

—MAJOR-GENERAL FRENCH sent a force toward Williamsport, Md., which was successful in capturing and destroying the pontoon train of the rebels. The guard, consisting of a lieutenant and only thirteen men, were taken.—*General French's Despatch.*

—THE following orders were issued at New-Orleans, La., by Brigadier-General Emory: "Hereafter no public assemblages, except for public worship under a regular, commissioned priest, will be allowed in this city for any purpose or on any pretence whatever, by white or black, without the written consent of the Commander of the defences of New-Orleans; and no more than three persons will be allowed to assemble or congregate together upon the streets of the city. Whenever more than that number are found together by the patrol, they shall be ordered to disperse, and failing to do so, the offenders shall be placed in arrest.

"All bar-rooms, coffee-houses, stores, and shops of every description, will be closed at nine o'clock P.M.

"All club-rooms and gambling-houses are hereby closed until further orders.

"No citizens or other persons, except the police and officers in the United States service, or soldiers on duty or with passes, are to be allowed in the streets after nine o'clock P.M."—

The United States transport boat Zephyr was fired into, at a point six miles below Donaldsonville, La, and two men were wounded.—A FIGHT occurred at Fairfield, Pa., between the Sixth United States cavalry, under Major Samuel H. Starr, and two brigades of rebel cavalry, under Generals Robinson and Jones.— *Philadelphia Enquirer.*

—THE battle of Gettysburgh was concluded this day. Repulsed at every point, General Lee withdrew in the night, leaving General Meade master of the field.—(*Docs.* 20 *and* 118.)

—SUFFOLK, Va., was evacuated by the Union troops.—A CIRCULAR letter was issued from the Treasury Department by Secretary Chase, regulating the disposition of abandoned, captured and confiscable property in the rebel districts.

July 4.—The rebel gunboat Torpedo, formerly the Dragon, came down the James River, Virginia, having on board Alexander H. Stephens, Vice-President of the rebel government. By flag of truce it was reported that Stephens was the bearer of a letter from Jefferson Davis to President Lincoln, and he requested permission to go to Washington in the Torpedo, to present the letter to President Lincoln in person. This request was declined by the President and Cabinet, but before their determination could be communicated, the Torpedo had left its moorings and proceeded up the James River, without waiting for an answer.—(*Docs.* 23 *and* 34.)

—VICKSBURGH, Miss., was surrendered to the National forces under the command of Major-General Grant.—(*Docs.* 25, 36, 94, *and* 141.)

—ABRAHAM LINCOLN, President of the United States, "announces to the country, that the news from the army of the Potomac to ten P.M. of the third, is such as to cover the army with the highest honor and promise a great success to the cause of the Union, and to claim the condolence of all for the many gallant fallen, and that for this he especially desires, on this day, that He whose will, not ours, should ever be done, be everywhere remembered with the profoundest gratitude."

—THE battle of Helena, Ark., was fought this day, by the National troops under the command of Major-General B. M. Prentiss, and the rebels under Generals Marmaduke, Price, and Holmes.— (*Docs.* 24 *and* 111.)

—GENERAL SHERIDAN's division of Rosecrans's army, in pursuit of General Bragg, crossing the Elk River, Tenn., was thrown forward toward Dechard and Cowan, after reöccupying Winchester. This day he sent his cavalry force, under Colonel Watkins of the Sixth Kentucky, toward the mountains. Near University Place, they encountered the rebel cavalry, killed and wounded forty, routed and drove them three miles up the side of the mountain, and returned with the loss of twelve men. The rebels' flight was so precipitate, that they threw away every thing which could at all impede them, and their course could be traced for miles by their cast-off equipments and accoutrements.

—CAPTAIN TURNER, the Commandant at the Libby Prison, at Richmond, Va., received the following order:

"HEADQUARTERS DEPARTMENT OF HENRICO, }
"July 4, 1863. }

"SPECIAL ORDER, No. 160.—Captain T. N. Turner, commanding confederate States prison, is hereby commanded to select, by lot, from among the Federal Captains now in his possession, two of that number for execution.

"JOHN H. WINDER,

"*Major-General Commanding.*"

Captain Turner at once proceeded to carry out the order, and caused all the captains, seventy-five in number, to be assembled in the large room on the first floor. The order commanding the selection of two of them for execution was then read aloud in their presence, by the Captain, and the seventy-five names deposited in a box placed upon a table. Captain Turner inquired if they would designate any particular person to draw from the box, and explained that the two first names drawn would be the parties selected. There was a deep silence for some moments, when one of the captains spoke and named Rev. Mr. Brown, Chaplain of the Fifth Maryland (Yankee) regiment, as their choice. Mr. Brown here stepped forward, from three chaplains in the room, and, evincing considerable emotion, drew the first name from the box, written upon a piece of paper.

Without glancing at the card, he handed it to Captain Turner, who read out: "Henry Washington Sawyer, Captain First New-Jersey cavalry." Then it was a singular coïncidence struck every one present, for Sawyer was the party who named Mr. Brown for the unpleasant duty he was then discharging. Great drops of sweat beaded Sawyer's brow, as he stepped out from the ranks. The next name was drawn and read out, as before, "John Flinn, Fifty-first Indiana re-

Com. JOHN RODGERS.

giment;" and Flinn took his place with Sawyer. The drawing over, the balance of the officers were returned to their quarters, and Sawyer and Flinn taken from the prison to the office of General Winder. Sawyer was talkative, and said if it was his fate, he would stand it. Flinn said but little.—*Richmond Examiner, July 8.*

—THE First North-Carolina (Union) volunteers, Colonel McChesney, returned to Newbern, N. C., from an expedition up the Pungo River, where the regiment captured two large schooners heavily laden with rebel supplies, large numbers of prisoners, horses, cattle, negroes, and several thousand bushels of corn. This regiment effected a landing near Wade's Point, and moved with great celerity at midnight, taking the enemy everywhere by surprise. Several thousand dollars' worth of rebel commissary stores were also destroyed.

—ORLANDO H. MOORE, Colonel of the Twenty-fifth regiment of Michigan infantry, commanding at Green River Bridge, Kentucky, was summoned to surrender, by the rebel General John Morgan, when he replied, "that the Fourth day of July was no day to entertain such a proposition," and immediately after, a fight was commenced by the rebels, which resulted in their defeat and the loss of over fifty killed and two hundred wounded.—(*Doc.* 44.)

July 5.—This evening, General Kilpatrick captured a rebel train and a large number of prisoners, at a point near Monterey Gap, Va., and in the afternoon he defeated the rebel cavalry under J. E. B. Stuart, at Smithsburgh, Va.—(*Doc.* 32.)

—A SMALL party of rebel cavalry entered Mechanicstown, Md., and after committing some depredations, retired, taking with them a quantity of flour and several horses.—THE following order was officially promulgated at the headquarters of the army at Washington:

Commanding Officer Fort Monroe, Colonel Ludlow, Agent for the Exchange of Prisoners of War:

The President directs that you immediately place W. H. Lee and another officer selected by you, not below the rank of captain, prisoners of war, in close confinement and under strong guards; and that you notify Mr. R. Ould, confederate agent for exchange of prisoners of war, that if Captain H. W. Sawyer, First New-Jersey volunteer cavalry, and Captain John Flynn,

Fifty-first Indiana volunteers, or any other officers or men in the service of the United States, not guilty of crimes punishable with death by the laws of war, shall be executed by the enemy, the afore-mentioned prisoners will be immediately hung in retaliation. It is also directed, that immediately on receiving official or other authentic information of the execution of Captain Sawyer and Captain Flynn, you will proceed to hang General Lee and the other rebel officer designated, as herein above directed, and that you notify Robert Ould, Esq., of said proceedings, and assure him that the Government of the United States will proceed to retaliate for every similar barbarous violation of the laws of civilized war.

H. W. HALLECK, General-in-Chief.

—THE steamer Harriet Pinckney, from Bermuda, arrived at Halifax, N. S., having on board C. L. Vallandigham.—AT seven o'clock this morning, John Morgan, with four thousand cavalry, attacked the Twentieth Kentucky infantry, four hundred strong, under Colonel Hanson, at Lebanon, Kentucky. After a seven hours' fight, Morgan's forces commenced burning the town, setting fire to the railroad depot and six or seven houses. Colonel Hanson then surrendered, and Morgan's forces left in the direction of Springfield.—(*Docs.* 47 and 103.)

—A BATTLE took place near Bolton, Miss., between the National forces under General W. T. Sherman, and the rear-guard of the rebels under Joe Johnston, in which the latter were compelled to surrender their entire force. The Union loss was very slight, while the number of rebels captured amounted to over two thousand.—GENERAL JAMES G. BLUNT, having under his command portions of the Second and Sixth Kansas, Third Wisconsin, and Fourteenth Kansas regiments, left Fort Scott for the seat of war in the far West.

July 6.—Portions of the Tenth Kentucky and First Ohio, under the command of Major Brown, made an expedition through Pound Gap, Ky., into South-western Virginia, and succeeded in surprising the rebels, capturing one hundred and twenty-five prisoners, killing thirty, and wounding about the same number. The National loss was one killed and fourteen wounded.—THE English schooner Lady Maria, was captured off Mobile Bay, by the National gunboat De Soto.

—A FIGHT took place near Quaker Bridge, on the Trent River, N. C., in which the rebels were defeated by a force under the command of General Heckman.—THE case of the British prize ship Peterhoff, was opened before Judge Betts, sitting in prize court at New-York.—THE cavalry battles of Hagerstown and Williamsport, Md., were fought this day.—(*Doc.* 32.)

—KNIGHTS of the Golden Circle entered the depot at Huntington Indiana, at an early hour this morning, and seized and distributed among themselves a quantity of guns and ammunition.— A LARGE amount of money and other necessaries, in aid of the wounded at Gettysburgh, was raised throughout the loyal States.—At New-York City a conspiracy to resist the draft was discovered, and precautionary measures were taken to thwart it.

—So much of the order, issued by Brigadier-General Emory, at New-Orleans, on the third instant, as prohibited peaceable citizens from being out after nine o'clock P.M., provided that they are not in parties of more than three, was rescinded.—GENERAL LEE's army was in full retreat, the Nationals following rapidly. Hopes were entertained that the whole army of rebels would be captured.—At Frederick, Md., a rebel spy, named Wm. Richardson, about fifty years old, was hung this morning. He was captured yesterday at Oxford, Md. He had been previously captured, and made his escape. He admitted the charge, and said that he had been in the business a long time. Important communications between Lee and Ewell were found on his person.—MAJOR-GENERAL OGLESBY resigned command of the left wing, Sixteenth army corps, army of the Tennessee, in consequence of the effects of a severe wound which he received in the battle at Corinth, in October last.—THE *Richmond Sentinel* published an elaborate article, setting forth the plan of General Lee for his movement into Pennsylvania. The "most important part of it was to quit the defensive and assume the offensive toward the enemy."

July 7.—The Richmond *Enquirer*, speculating upon the probabilities and terms of a peace, continues:

"The confederate States, when victorious and about to propose terms of peace, will have nothing more to demand than they would have proposed before the fall of Sumter, except indemnification for those outrages committed by the enemy against every law of civilized warfare.

"The acknowledgment of the independence of every State now in the Confederacy, and the free choice of the people of Maryland to determine whether they will elect the Confederacy or the United States, will form the first of the 'conditions.' Kentucky and Missouri are already members of the Confederacy, and, upon the hypothesis of confederate success, must remain members of the Confederacy unless their people determine otherwise. With their future destiny the United States can have nothing whatever to do, and will not be permitted to exercise any authority or exert any influence upon their people.

"The navigation of the Mississippi, though lost to the United States by the trial of battle, may yet be theirs by the 'conditions of peace.' Its advantages are reciprocal, and will be readily yielded to the United States.

"The return of all negroes deported by the Yankees, or payment of their value, will be another of the 'conditions of peace.' The laws of war were violated in letter and spirit by the running off of these negroes, and the destruction of the property of private, unarmed citizens—payment will be a condition of peace.

"Trade relations will also form a part of these conditions—what their nature or character may be it is impossible to speculate upon. But as they are mutual in their advantages, and exist by treaty between all nations, they will doubtless arise, despite the animosity engendered by the war.

"With such conditions of peace accepted by the United States, in what particular will they have sustained damages by separation which justified this war?

"The people of the United States have been kept in ignorance of the real demands of the confederate States; they have been taught to believe a pro-slavery propaganda, involving the conquest and conversion to slavery of the States of the Union, to be the purpose and designs or the Confederacy.

"The conditions of peace that the victorious confederates will propose are simple, and we believe will, in the course of time, prove advantageous to both nations.

"The people of the confederate States believe that their future destiny can be better accomplished in separate nationality than under the Federal Union.

"To attest the honesty of this belief, they have maintained a war which has desolated much of their territory, sacrificed many of the bravest and best of their people, and endured all the privations and cruelties inflicted by the enemy.

They have demonstrated their determination never again to live in union with the people of the United States; and they have illustrated their power to defy the enemy's efforts by a series of victories unparalleled in the annals of war. Their conditions of peace will involve no humiliation of the enemy; no loss of power except such as is incidental to our separate nationality.

"If the enemy are unwilling to accept these conditions of peace, so let it be. The war is and will remain in Pennsylvania, and further North."

—THE ship Sunrise, commanded by Captain Richard Luce, was captured and bonded by the privateer Florida, in lat. 40° N., long. 68° W.

—A CAVALRY expedition sent from Newbern, N. C., on the third inst., under Colonel Lewis of the Third New-York cavalry, returned to that point, having successfully accomplished their mission without loss. They destroyed (twisting rails, etc., by General Haupt's plan) two miles of the railroad at Warsaw; also, for five miles more, all the culverts, as well as the telegraph. At Kenansville, an armory was destroyed; large quantities of small-arms and quantities of commissary and quartermaster stores were burnt. About one hundred and fifty animals, and thirty prisoners, were captured by them; and some one hundred men and about three hundred women and children, negroes, followed them in.—General Foster's Report.

—THE Twenty-seventh regiment of Maine volunteers, Colonel Wentworth, passed through Boston, Mass., on their return from the seat of war.—THE steamers Alice Dean, and J. S. McCombs, were captured by a party of rebels, at Brandenburgh, Kentucky. — COLONEL WILLIAM BIRNEY opened an office in Baltimore, Md., for the recruiting of negro troops.—AT Washington, the victories at Gettysburgh and Vicksburgh were celebrated with great enthusiasm. Speeches were made by President Lincoln, Secretaries Stanton and Seward, General Halleck, Senator Wilson of Massachusetts, and Representatives E. B. Washburne and Arnold, of Illinois.

—THE expedition sent out from White House, Va., by General Dix, on the first instant, returned. — COLONEL RODDY, with eleven companies of rebel cavalry, made an attack upon a "corral for convalescent horses and mules," near Corinth, Tenn., and succeeded in carrying off over six hundred animals. The "corral" was guarded by one company of the Thirty-ninth Iowa, under

Captain Loomis. The attack was made just at daylight, and the picket was captured after a slight resistance. The rest of the company made a stout defence, until they were surrounded, when some escaped; the captain and twenty of his men were taken prisoners. The rebel loss was two killed; the National, one slightly wounded.—THE Sixth regular cavalry, under Captain Chaflant, made a reconnoissance near Boonsboro, Md., and had a sharp fight, in which they lost eight or nine men.—(Doc. 32.)

—A BATTLE took place near Fort Halleck, Idaho Territory, between a party of Ute Indians and Union soldiers belonging to the Fort, under the command of Lieutenants Brundley and Williams, of the Seventh Kansas volunteers. The battle lasted two hours, when the Nationals, led by Lieutenant Williams, charged upon the Indians, who fled to the mountains, and gave up the contest. The Nationals lost one killed and several wounded, while the Indians' loss was twenty-one killed, and thirty-nine wounded.— SALUTES were fired, and celebrations were held throughout the loyal States, in honor of the victories at Vicksburgh and Gettysburgh. — THE rebel army of the Tennessee, under the command of General Bragg, on its retreat before the army of General Rosecrans, reached Lookout Mountain, near Chattanooga, Tenn.

July 8.—An engagement occurred at Boonsboro, Md., between the National cavalry, under Generals Buford and Kilpatrick, and the rebels, under Generals J. E. B. Stuart, Hampton, and Jones, resulting in the defeat of the latter.— (Doc. 32.)

—THE brig W. B. Nash, in latitude 40°, longitude 70°, was captured and burned by the rebel privateer Florida.—AT Louisville, Ky., a meeting of the citizens was held to take measures for the defence of that city, then threatened by the rebels, supposed to be under Generals Morgan and Buckner. A resolution was adopted: "That all male citizens between the ages of eighteen and forty-five be enrolled into companies for service, if required, and that all such who refuse shall be sent to the North."

—GENERAL BURNSIDE, at Cincinnati, Ohio, issued a general order, giving directions for the conduct of the military affairs of his department in cases of habeas corpus.—A COMPANY of General Stahel's cavalry under Colonel Wynkoop, on a reconnoissance near Hagerstown, Md., succeeded in capturing a rebel company, consisting of two officers and fifty men, who were sent to Carlisle, Pa.—Two rebel schooners were destroy-ed at the Rio Grande, Texas, by a party of men, belonging to the National gunboat Scioto.—A DETACHMENT of National cavalry, under the com-mand of Captain Greenfield and Lieutenant Kelley, of General Kelley's command, captured a train of fifteen wagons, sixty mules, two officers and twenty men, with their horses, at a point four miles from Williamsport, Md.—THERE was a heavy freshet in the Potomac River, which, it was supposed, would prevent the crossing of the retreating army under the rebel General Lee.— GENERAL DABNEY H. MAURY, commanding the rebel department of the Gulf, at Mobile, Ala., issued the following to the citizens of that place and its vicinity :

"The calamity which has befallen our arms at Vicksburgh has a peculiar significance for you. Mobile may be attacked within a very short time, and we must make every preparation for its suc-cessful defence.

"All able-bodied men within the limits of the city and county must at once organize into com-panies, and report for duty in defence of this po-sition. Owners of able-bodied slaves are urged to send them immediately to work on the fortifi-cations.

"Brigadier-General Slaughter will receive the reports of the companies which may be organiz-ed, have arms issued to such as have none, give orders for their instruction, and assign them to their stations.

"Reports of slaves for labor on the defences may be made to Brigadier-General Leadbetter, who has made arrangements for their good treat-ment while in his employ."—PORT HUDSON, La., was surrendered to the Union General Banks, by the rebel commander Frank Gardner. — (Docs. 88 and 89.)

July 9.—Charles Macbeth, the Mayor of Charleston, S. C., noticing the preparations being made by the Nationals for the attack on Morris Island, issued the following proclamation to the citizens of that city and its vicinity :

"Whereas, the enemy by land and sea have appeared in large force on the islands and neigh-borhood of the city, and in consultation with General Beauregard, he expressed the opinion that an attack upon our city is imminent, and with the concurrence of General Beauregard, I advise and earnestly request all women and

children, and other non-combatants, to leave the city as soon as possible."

This was followed by two other proclamations, calling on citizens to close their places of busi-ness, and ordering the arrest of all free negroes in the city, as they were wanted to work on some unfinished defences on Morris Island. During the day some five or more transports ap-peared off the harbor, and the National gunboats in Stono River were occupied in shelling two points on James's Island.

—CORYDON, Ind., was captured and plundered by the rebel forces under General John Morgan. —(Doc. 47.)

—A SHORT engagement took place at Aransas Pass, Texas, between the gunboat Scioto and the rebel batteries at that place, without important results or loss of life.—GENERAL ABNER DOUBLE-DAY published an order, returning his thanks to the Vermont brigade, the One Hundred and Fifty-first Pennsylvania volunteers, and the Twentieth New-York State militia, for their gal-lant conduct in resisting in the front line the main attack of the enemy at Gettysburgh, after sustaining a terrific fire from seventy-five to one hundred pieces of artillery.—MR. WOLFF, a can-didate for Congress in Kentucky, was arrested in Owen County, and sent to General Burnside, at Cincinnati, in consequence of the following words, used in a speech to the people of Owen : "This is a John Brown raid—a war against sla-very, and he hoped every true Kentuckian would rise in arms in opposition to it. He was for se-cession, separation, or any thing against it."— THE National troops marched into Port Hudson, Louisiana.

July 10.—Lord Palmerston, in a speech in the House of Commons, requesting Mr. Roebuck to submit to a postponement of the debate on the question of the recognition of the confederate States, declared anew his hostility to the policy of recognition, and the unchanged sentiments of "Her Majesty's Government" on the subject. His language was :

"It is not likely, I think, that the House would agree either to the motion of the honor-able and learned member for Sheffield, or to the amendment which has been moved to it; and, indeed, I think it very disadvantageous to the public service that any such resolution should be adopted. Therefore the discussion, as far as any practicable results may have been expected by those who are in favor of the motion, would have no important effect. I can assure the House, whereas now it is plainly acknowledged by every body, that the wishes of the Emperor of the French to find a fitting opportunity for advising the reëstablishment of peace in America are not changed, that, on the other hand, her Majesty's Government do not see that that opportunity has arisen."

—The expedition under General J. G. Blunt reached Cabin Creek, fifty-five miles from Fort Gibson.—Thirty-one battle-flags captured by the National forces at Gettysburgh, were sent to the War Department by Major-General Meade.—(*Doc.* 92.)

—The siege of Jackson, Miss., was commenced this day by the Union forces under General Grant. It began by skirmishing on the Clinton road with musketry and artillery; shells were thrown into the city, and several persons were killed and wounded.—*Mobile Advertiser, July* 18.

—An artillery and cavalry battle took place at a point on the road from Boonsboro to Hagerstown, Md., between the Union forces under Generals Buford and Kilpatrick, and the rebels belonging to the army of General Lee.—(*Doc.* 32.)

—Major-General Schenck, from his headquarters at Baltimore, issued an order regulating the treatment of rebel prisoners in his department.—The Mayor of Lynchburgh, Va., issued a proclamation to the citizens of that place, requesting them to suspend business on Friday afternoons, in order that the members of the different military organizations might have an opportunity of attending regularly the drills of their respective companies. . . . . "It is high time," said he, "that we should act, and act at once, toward putting ourselves in readiness for any emergency."

—General Joseph E. Johnston, at Jackson, Miss., issued the following battle order to the troops of his army. It "was read along the line amid deafening shouts : "

"Fellow-Soldiers : An insolent foe, flushed with hope by his recent success at Vicksburgh, confronts you, threatening the people, whose homes and liberty you are here to protect, with plunder and conquest. Their guns may even now be heard as they advance.

"The enemy it is at once the duty and the mission of you brave men to chastise and expel from the soil of Mississippi. The Com-

manding General confidently relies on you to sustain his pledge, which he makes in advance, and he will be with you in the good work even unto the end.

"The vice of 'straggling' he begs you to shun, and to frown on. If needs be, it will be checked by even the most summary remedies.

"The telegraph has already announced a glorious victory over the foe, won by your noble comrades of the Virginia army on Union soil; may he not, with redoubled hopes, count on you while defending your firesides and household gods to emulate the proud example of your brothers in the East ?

"The country expects in this, the great crisis of its destiny, that every man will do his duty."

General Johnston ordered all pillagers to be shot, the guard to shoot them wherever found.

—Martial law was declared at Louisville, Ky.—The letter of William Whiting, Solicitor to the National War Department, to the members of the Fremont League, was published.—Salem, Ind., was visited and sacked by the rebel forces under John Morgan; the railroad bridge over the Blue River was also destroyed by the same parties.—(*Doc.* 47.)

—The National forces under the command of General Q. A. Gillmore, at five o'clock this morning, made an attack upon the rebel fortifications on the south end of Morris Island, in the harbor of Charleston, S. C., and after an engagement of over three hours, captured all the strongholds in that part of the Island, and pushed forward their infantry to within six hundred yards of Fort Wagner. The attacking party was gallantly led by Brigadier-General George C. Strong. It landed from small boats under cover of the National batteries on Folly Island, and four monitors, led by Rear-Admiral Dahlgren, which entered the main channel abreast of Morris Island, soon after the Union batteries opened. The monitors continued their fire during the rest of the day, principally against Fort Wagner.—*General Gillmore's Report.*—(*Doc.* 147.)

July 11.—This morning at daybreak the National forces on Morris Island, under the command of General Gillmore, attempted to carry Fort Wagner by assault. The parapets were gained, but the supports recoiled under the fire to which they were exposed, and could not be got up. Captain S. H. Gray, commanding two companies of the Seventh Connecticut regiment, gives the following report of the affair: After the success of yesterday "we bivouacked for the night under easy range of Fort Wagner. About half-past two A.M., General Strong came and called the Lieutenant-Colonel out. He soon returned and said: 'Turn out! we have got a job on hand.' The men were soon out and into line, but rather slow to time, as they were tired with the work the day before.

"The programme was to try to take Fort Wagner by assault; we were to take the lead, and to be supported by the Seventy-sixth Pennsylvania and Ninth Maine. Silently we moved up to the advance-line of our pickets, our guns loaded and aimed, and bayonets fixed. We were then deployed into line of battle, (we had one hundred and ninety-one men and officers, all told,) reached and crossed the neck of land that approached the Fort, our right resting on the beach. We were deployed and ready for the start. Our orders were to move steadily forward until the pickets fired, then follow them close and rush for the works, and we were promised ready support. General Strong gave the order: 'Aim low, and put your trust in God. Forward the Seventh!' And forward we went, being not over five hundred yards from the Fort when we started.

"We had not gone far before the picket fired, and then we took the double-quick, and with a cheer rushed for the works. Before we reached the outer work, we got a murderous fire from the riflemen behind the works. A few fell— a check in the line. An encouraging word from the officers, and right gallantly we reached the outer works; over them with a will we went; down the opposite side, across the moat—there being about one foot of water in it—right up to the crest of the parapet; and there we lay, anxiously waiting for our support to come up so far as to make it a sure thing for us to rise up and go over with a bound; our men in the mean time busying themselves by picking off the sharpshooters and gunners. We lay so near the top that one had to put his head up and point across the parapet to kill his man.

"As near as I can ascertain, we were in this position from ten to twenty minutes, when both of the regiments that were to support us broke and fled, leaving us to take care of ourselves as best we might. As soon as the regiment in front broke and ran, they paid particular attention to our case. They threw hand-grenades over the parapet, and soon sent men into the flank of a bastion, which commanded the front upon which we lay. They had us there at a great disadvantage. The question was whether we should surrender as prisoners, attempt to carry the works, and to be entirely annihilated, (as they greatly outnumbered us,) or take the back-track and run the gauntlet for our lives.

"Upon consulting the Lieutenant-Colonel, he reluctantly gave the order to retreat. Lieutenant Phillips exclaimed: 'For God's sake, don't let us retreat.' As if by magic, the order was recalled, and although some had started, they returned; but the order had to be repeated, and down in and across the moat we went over the works. They had a perfect enfilading fire of small-arms for a thousand yards — besides, their pieces were giving us grape and canister. They fell on all sides of me, and I alone of four captains was spared, and out of one hundred and ninety-one officers and men that marched out to attack the foe, only eighty-eight returned safe to camp; and ever let it be said, to the credit of the Seventh Connecticut volunteers, that not one straggler could be discovered. Fifteen minutes after we got in camp, the roll was called, and but one man came in afterwards, and he was delayed in assisting a wounded comrade.

"Met General Strong coming off, and with tears in his eyes he said we had done our whole duty, and covered ourselves all over with glory, and if the support had come in time, that 'we should have taken the works,' and without a doubt we should have done so. But our loss is great. We had eleven officers in our mess. Now we have but four. It is hard, but such is the fate of war.

"Our attack on the tenth July was a fearful surprise to them. They had but few troops on this Island. Had they five thousand infantry here, the natural defences are of such a character, that we never could have taken it."

The National losses in the actions of yesterday and to-day, were one hundred and fifty killed, wounded, and missing. Eleven pieces of heavy ordnance and a large quantity of camp equipage was taken from the rebels, who lost two hundred men in casualties.—*General Gillmore's Report.*

—AT New-York the draft was begun and carried on without any disturbance.—THE First National Bank of Pennsylvania announced business

GEN. JAMES LONGSTREET

at Philadelphia.—LIEUTENANT A. L. SANBORN, of the First regiment of colored volunteers, was killed at Norfolk, Va., by Dr. David M. Wright, a prominent rebel physician of that place.—A GRAND torchlight procession took place at New-Orleans in honor of the capture of Port Hudson and Vicksburgh, and "to celebrate the redemption of the South-West from treason and rebellion."—VERNON, Indiana, was visited by the rebels under John Morgan.—(*Doc.* 47.)

—THE rebels evacuated Hagerstown, Md., last evening, but returned to the town again to-day.— A SHARP engagement took place on the Hagerstown road, resulting in the defeat and pursuit of the rebels to Funkstown, where a strong rebel position was found.—WILLIAM McKEE, one of the proprietors of the St. Louis *Democrat*, was put under arrest by order of General Schofield, for the publication of the letter of President Lincoln to General Schofield, explaining the reasons for the removal of General Curtis, and for refusing to state in what manner such letter came into his hands.—THE rebel forces under John Morgan reached Vienna, Indiana, at one o'clock this morning, and burned the dépôt and bridge belonging to the Jefferson Railroad at that place.— (*Doc.* 47.)

July 12.—This morning a portion of the fleet blockading the port of Wilmington, N. C., ran a rebel vessel on shore, close in by the edge of Smith's Island. While trying to get her off, the rebels in Fort Fisher despatched a steamer with a battery on board to prevent it. She had been at Smith's Island but a short time when a fire was opened from the National fleet on the eastern side of the shoals. At the same time a party of rebels was discovered approaching with a piece of artillery. Upon this, the fleet on the western side of the shoals opened fire to prevent the reënforcement of the rebels, and finally succeeded. The firing was continued until four o'clock, when the Union fleet returned to its station.—THE blockade-runner Emma was captured by the Union transport steamer Arago.— HAGERSTOWN and Funkstown, Md., were occupied by the Union forces after a slight engagement.— (*Doc.* 32.)

—NATCHEZ, Miss., was occupied by a detachment belonging to General Grant's army.

July 13.—A fight took place at Donaldsonville, La., between the rebels and a force of National troops under the command of Brigadier-General Dudley and Colonel Morgan, resulting in the re-

treat of the Nationals with a loss of four hundred and fifty killed and wounded, and two guns.

—PRESIDENT LINCOLN wrote the following letter to Major-General Grant:

"MY DEAR GENERAL: I do not remember that you and I ever met personally. I write this now as a grateful acknowledgment for the almost inestimable service you have done the country. I wish to say a word further. When you first reached the vicinity of Vicksburgh, I thought you should do what you finally did, march the troops across the neck, run the batteries with the transports, and thus go below; and I never had any faith, except a general hope that you knew better than I, that the Yazoo Pass expedition, and the like, could succeed. When you got below and took Port Gibson, Grand Gulf, and vicinity, I thought you should go down the river and join General Banks; and when you turned northward, east of the Big Black, I thought it was a mistake. I now wish to make the personal acknowledgment that you was right and I was wrong."

—THE funeral of Brigadier-General Samuel K. Zook, who was killed at the battle of Gettysburgh, took place at New-York City.—GENERAL GEORGE G. MEADE issued a proclamation in reference to depredations committed by citizens, or rebel soldiers in disguise, and announced the punishment therefor.—A RIOT was threatened in Newark, N. J.—D. H. HILL, the rebel Major-General, was appointed Lieutenant-General, and assigned to command by Jefferson Davis.—WILLIAMSTON, on the Roanoke River, was bombarded by four National gunboats under Captain Flusser, the bridge across Gardner's Creek destroyed, and the rebels driven entirely from the river.—THE case of Clement L. Vallandigham was elaborately discussed in the New-York *World*.—FORT POWHATAN, on the James River, Va., was taken possession of by the National fleet under Admiral Lee. The rebels had removed the guns before evacuating the Fort.—THE draft was resisted, and a riot broke out in New-York City. The offices of the provost-marshals were burned, the machinery for the drawing destroyed, telegraph wires cut, railroad tracks torn up, private houses sacked, the Colored Orphan Asylum burned, and a number of the police force badly injured, among them Superintendent Kennedy.—(*See Supplement.*)

—THE rebel army under General Lee crossed the Potomac River at Williamsport, and escaped. —(*Doc.* 95.)

—Yazoo City, Miss., was captured by a combined naval and military National force. Rear-Admiral D. D. Porter, hearing that General Johnston was fortifying the place and gathering troops there for the purpose of obtaining supplies for his army from the Yazoo country, and that the remainder of the rebels' best transports were there, consulted with Major-General Grant, and determined to send an expedition to capture and destroy them. The Baron de Kalb, National, Renwood, and Signal, were despatched, under command of Lieutenant Commander John G. Walker, with a force of troops, numbering five thousand, under Major-General Frank J. Herron. Pushing up to the city, the Baron de Kalb engaged the batteries, which were all prepared to receive her, and after finding out their strength dropped back to notify General Herron, who immediately landed his men, and the army and navy made a combined attack on the enemy's works. The rebels soon fled, leaving every thing in the possession of the Nationals, and set fire to four of their finest steamers that ran on the Mississippi. The army pursued the enemy and captured their rear-guard of two hundred and sixty men. Six heavy guns and one vessel, formerly a gunboat, fell into the hands of the Union troops, and all the munitions of war. Unfortunately, while the Baron de Kalb was moving slowly along she ran foul of a torpedo, which exploded and sunk her. There was no sign of any thing of the kind to be seen. While she was going down another exploded under her stern. No lives were lost on the National side.—*Admiral Porter's Despatch.*

July 14.—At Indianapolis, Ind., while the Twelfth Michigan battery was marching through the streets, a caisson exploded, instantly killing three soldiers and the driver.—The draft riot continued in New-York; business was suspended; loyal citizens were called upon by the Mayor to enroll themselves as special policemen for the restoration of law and order; General Wool issued a call to the veteran volunteers to tender their services to the Mayor; severe conflicts were carried on between the rioters and the soldiery; Colonel O'Brien was killed; negroes were hanged and burned; travelling was suspended, and the operations of the railroads arrested; Governor Seymour made a speech to the rioters at the City Hall, and issued a proclamation calling "upon all persons engaged in these riotous proceedings to retire to their homes and employments, declaring to them that unless they do so at once, I shall use all the power necessary to restore the peace and order of the city."—(*See Supplement.*)

—A reconnoissance was made from Donaldsonville, La., down the La Fourche River by the National troops under Generals Weitzel and Grover. The rebels were met in strong force, and the Nationals were obliged to retire with the loss of one section of the First Maine battery.—Riots occurred at Troy, N. Y., and Boston, Mass., both of which were suppressed without much trouble. —(*Doc.* 128.)

—General Thomas's corps of the army of the Cumberland, following in the rear of General Bragg's retreating forces, reached Elk River, and encountered a portion of General Buckner's division of infantry and artillery together with a part of Wheeler's cavalry, whom they dispersed after a short skirmish.—The rebels under General Morgan reached Miamiville, on the Little Miami road, this morning, tore up the track and committed other outrages.—(*Doc.* 47.)

—Joe Hart, the rebel guerrilla, was killed near Chillicothe, Mo., by a detachment of militia under Lieutenant Gibbs, of the Fourth Provisional regiment.—The cavalry belonging to General Meade's army occupied Falling Waters, having overtaken and captured a brigade of infantry one thousand five hundred strong, two guns, two caissons, two battle-flags, and a large number of small-arms.— (*Docs.* 97 *and* 104.)

July 15.—Foreigners of every age and sex crowded the office of the provost-marshal, in Richmond, "anxious to get passports to go North, by way of the blockade. The Jew, whose ample pockets were stuffed with confederate money; the Germans, with hands on pockets tightly pressed; Italians, with the silvery jargon; and the Irish woman, with 'nine children and one at the breast,' all beset the office and wanted passports to leave the country." This was on account of the late conscription proclamation of Jefferson Davis. "It is not fair," said the *Richmond Enquirer*, "that those who have drained the very life-blood of our people, should be let off thus quietly, and not made to shed the first, at least, if not the last, drop of blood for the Government which protected them in the collection of their hoarded pelf."—Vallandigham arrived at Niagara Falls, Canada West, and issued an address to the people of Ohio.— (*Doc.* 129.)

—General John G. Parke, with a body of National troops, was attacked by a legion of South-Carolina troops, near Jackson, Miss. After an engagement of half an hour the rebels retreated with a loss of three hundred, leaving the Nationals in possession of the field.

—The draft riot continued at New-York City. Mayor Opdyke issued a proclamation announcing that the riot, which for two days had disgraced the city, had been in a good measure subjected to the control of the public authorities.—Drafting commenced in New-Haven, Ct., Springfield, Mass., and Philadelphia, and passed off quietly.—The National cavalry overtook and engaged the rebels on their retreat, near Charlestown, Va., and captured near one hundred prisoners.—A riot broke out at Portsmouth, N. H., but was suppressed without casualty.

A party of rebel cavalry entered Hickman, Kentucky, and pillaged all the stores in the town.—Joel Parker, Governor of New-Jersey, owing to the excitement consequent upon the draft, issued a proclamation calling upon the citizens of the State "to avoid angry discussions, to discourage large assemblies of the people, and use every effort to preserve the peace."—Great excitement was caused among the rebels in Central Mississippi, by the movements of General Sherman, with the National forces. Large numbers of negroes, cattle, horses and mules were run across the Tombigbee River, at every ferry.

—Jefferson Davis issued a proclamation calling out, under the rebel conscription act, all white men between the ages of eighteen and forty-five, to serve for three years, under penalty of being punished for desertion in case of disobeying the call. They were offered the privilege of joining volunteer organizations before the enrolment. The *Columbus* (Ga.) *Times* estimated ninety-five thousand, three hundred and twenty-four, as the number that would be obtained under this proclamation.—(*Doc. 39.*)

July 16.—Major-General Dix, preparatory to assuming command of the Eastern Department, relinquished the command of the Department of Virginia, to Major-General J. G. Foster.—General Heckman returned to his quarters at Morehead City, N. C., having been absent four days on a reconnoissance toward Swansboro. The objects of the expedition were

Vol. VII.—Diary 3

fully accomplished without casualty.—Jackson, Miss., was evacuated by the rebels.—(*Doc. 98.*)

—The steamboat Imperial arrived at New-Orleans, La., from St. Louis, Mo., the first boat between the cities for more than two years.—The rebels made an attack on General Terry's brigade on James Island, S. C., but were repulsed. The monitors and mortar-boats kept up an almost constant fire upon Fort Wagner all day, but most of them withdrew at night.

—A force of National troops visited the salt works, near St. Mark's, Florida, and succeeded in destroying them completely, besides carrying off fifteen slaves.—The rebel forces under General Morgan passed through Piketon, Ohio.—The Colored Convention of the State of New-York, met at Poughkeepsie, and issued a manifesto and call to the colored population, defining their position.—The draft riot continued in New-York.—A sharp cavalry fight occurred near Shepherdstown, Va.—(*Doc. 145½.*)

July 17.—J. J. Pettigrew, of the rebel army, died at the residence of Mr. Boyd, at Bunker Hill, Va., from the effects of a wound received at the battle of Falling Waters, Va.—The attack on Fort Wagner, by the monitors and mortar-boats, was continued.—At New-York the riot was suppressed, quiet was restored and business resumed. — Provost-Marshal General J. B. Fry ordered the enforcement of the draft in New-England and the Middle States, by the aid of the military.—Edwin Hides and Henry Light, at York, England, were sentenced to imprisonment for counterfeiting the circulating notes of the United States.—The battle of Elk Creek, Kansas, was fought this day, by the National forces under General Blunt, and the rebels under General Cooper.—(*Docs. 100 and 109.*)

—The cavalry battle near Shepherdstown, Va., was fought this day. (*Doc. 145½.*)—Major-General Stanley, in command of the National forces, entered Huntsville, Alabama, without opposition, capturing six hundred horses, two hundred of them having contraband riders.—Many of the most prominent and influential lawyers of the cities of Brooklyn and New-York, "sensible of the wrongs inflicted during the late riots upon the colored inhabitants of these cities and vicinity, offered their professional advice and assistance, free of charge, to aid such persons in recovering compensation for the damages inflicted upon them by riotors."—COR-INTH, Miss., was occupied by the advance of the National forces under the command of General Hurlbut.

—GENERAL RICHARDSON, the notorious guerrilla, returned to his former field of operations in the neighborhood of Hickory, Wythe, Galloway's Station and Belmont, in the counties of Tipton, Shelby, and Fayette, Tenn. Richardson had a force of about two hundred men. These were, like himself, destitute of all principle save that of self-interest. Richardson was aided by the Rev. Captain Burrow and Captain Murray. One thing very remarkable was, that each of these men once laid claim to sanctimoniousness. Richardson was once a great exhorter among the Methodist friends in Memphis. Burrow was a minister of the Cumberland Presbyterian Church, while Murray was a very sanctimonious elder of the same denomination with Burrow.—*Memphis Bulletin, July 17.*

July 18. — General Beauregard, from his headquarters at Charleston, S. C., issued the following address: "While the Commanding General regrets that the enemy have succeeded in effecting a landing upon Morris Island, he acknowledges with satisfaction the conduct of the troops in their brave and prolonged resistance against a force largely their superior in numbers; and he is especially gratified by the spirit and success with which the garrison of Battery Wagner, and the troops under Colonel Graham, repelled the assaults on that fortification, as it gives the assurance that he can rely upon the conduct and courage of both officers and men to check the progress of the enemy." — GENERAL GEORGE C. STRONG, with a column of General Gillmore's forces, made an assault upon Fort Wagner. The storming party was led by the Fifty-fourth regiment of Massachusetts, (colored,) under Colonel Robert G. Shaw. After gaining an angle of the Fort, and holding it for some time, they were repulsed with terrible slaughter. Colonels Shaw and Putnam were killed, and General Strong severely wounded.—*(Doc. 41.)*

—GEORGE W. L. BICKLEY, supposed to be the originator of the order of the Knights of the Golden Circle, was arrested at New-Albany, Ind. —THE draft in New-Haven, Ct., was concluded.— THE expedition into North-Carolina, under the command of Brigadier-General Potter, left New-bern.—*(Doc. 101.)*

—JOHN A. ANDREW, Governor of Massachusetts, delivered an eloquent speech at Boston, on the occasion of the presentation of four flags, the gift of the women of Ohio, to the Fifty-fifth regiment Massachusetts colored volunteers. — ONE hundred guns were fired at Cambridge, Mass., in honor of the fall of Port Hudson.

—THE rebel steamers, James Battle and James Bagaley, were captured off Mobile, Alabama. —AT Baltimore, Md., an order was issued by General Schenck, directing all officers in the military service of the United States, residing at Barnum's City Hotel, to leave that establishment without delay.—WYTHEVILLE, Va., was captured by the National forces, under Colonel Toland.— *(Doc. 132.)*

—AT Yates' Point, on the Potomac River, an action took place between a party of rebels on shore, and the gunboats Jacob Bell, Resolute, and Teaser, and mortar-boat Dan. Smith. While the firing was going on, a party of Nationals was sent on shore, and the rebels were put to flight. —MAJOR-GENERAL JOHN G. FOSTER assumed command of the Department of Virginia, in addition to that of North-Carolina.

July 19.—At Charleston, S. C., a large side-wheel steamer, endeavoring to run into the harbor, was chased by the Canandaigua, and other outside blockaders, and finally driven upon the shoals by Commander George W. Powers, of the Kaatskill, then anchored abreast of Fort Wagner, on picket-duty. The steamer was fired by her crew, and was totally destroyed.—*Rear-Admiral Dahlgren's Report.*

—GREENVILLE and Sparta, N. C., were visited by the National forces, under the command of Brigadier-General Potter, and every thing at those places belonging to the rebel government destroyed.—*(Doc. 101.)*

—JAMES B. FRY, Provost-Marshal General, issued the following circular: "Existing laws make a distinction in the matter of pay, bounties, or other allowances, between soldiers of African descent and other soldiers in the service of the United States. Men of African descent can only be accepted as substitutes for each other, under the Enrolment Act."—THE battle of Buffington Island, Ohio, was fought this day.—*(Doc. 47.)*

—AT Cleveland, Ohio, Bishop Rappe preached a sermon in the cathedral, on the subject of riots in New-York. He was unsparing in bitter denunciation of the mob that had committed such outrages. He warned his hearers against any act that tended in any degree to provoke like scenes there. He said that the laws must be obeyed, and the conscription law quietly submitted to among the rest. He urged the members of his flock to attend strictly to their business, and not even to discuss the question of the draft. If any of them were drafted, and could not procure exemption, they must do their duty to the country as soldiers. If the drafted man was poor, and no provision had been made by the city or county for the relief of his family, they should be cared for by the Church.

He warned them not to ill-treat the colored people. A colored man had as much right to live and to labor for his living as a white man had, and their right must be respected. It was cowardly and sinful to molest these people, because their skin was of a different color.

He also spoke against the practice of demanding extortionate wages. It was wrong and wicked to extort from employers more than the fair price of their labor.

Finally, he warned them not to provoke a breach of peace in any manner, and said that he had pledged his word, as a Catholic Bishop, to the citizens of Cleveland, that there should be no disturbance from the Catholic Irish, and he looked to them that his pledge should not be broken.

July 20. — The Chamber of Commerce, at Cincinnati, Ohio, at a business meeting, expelled thirty-three members of their body for refusing to take the oath of allegiance.—At New-York City a large meeting of merchants was held, to adopt measures for the relief of the negro sufferers by the riots. Speeches were made by Jonathan Sturges, Richard Warren, A. F. Dow, and others; and resolutions were adopted, pledging the protection of the merchants to the negroes, in pursuing their customary avocations.

—Colonel Bussey, Chief of Cavalry of the army under General Sherman, returned to Jackson, from an expedition to Canton and beyond. At Canton, on the eighteenth, he met Jackson's rebel cavalry division, four thousand strong, with three pieces of artillery, and, after a severe engagement, drove him across the Pearl River. The National force consisted of four thousand cavalry, under Bussey, and one thousand infantry, commanded by Colonel Wood, of the Seventy-eighth regiment of Ohio. They destroyed the railroad bridge over the Big Black, one mile of trestle-work between the Big Black and Canton,

burning Way's Bluff Station, destroying six miles of the track of the Jackson and New-Orleans and Mississippi Central Railroad, five locomotives, fifty cars, thirteen large manufacturing establishments and railroad buildings; completely destroyed the Dixie Works, and burned a large quantity of lumber. At Canton, they also destroyed the railroad, burned two locomotives, twenty-five cars, the dépôt, and a large lot of cotton. At Calhoun, they destroyed a pontoon-bridge, the ferry at Grant's Mills, and several railroad bridges. They captured nearly one hundred prisoners, and lost twenty in killed and wounded.—(*Doc*, 138.)

July 21.—The Fifty-fifth regiment (colored) of Massachusetts, left Boston for Newbern, N. C. —A party of thirty bushwhackers early this morning, made a descent upon a settlement on Indian Creek, near Olathe, Kansas, and after plundering several of the inhabitants, retired, taking with them a large quantity of stock, and several men.—The schooner Revenge was captured and destroyed at a point near the Sabine Pass, by the Union gunboat Owasco, under the command of Lieutenant Commander J. Madigan, Jr.—The Forty-third regiment of Massachusetts, returned to Boston from the seat of war.—The Twelfth regiment, of Rhode Island, returned to Providence, and was received by the military of that place.—General Rosecrans, from his headquarters at Tullahoma, Tenn., issued a circular regulating the circulation of newspapers in his army.

July 22.—Major-General John G. Foster, pursuant to instructions from the War Department, commenced the enlistment of colored troops within the lines of the Department of Virginia and North-Carolina; and the unoccupied land on Roanoke Island was set apart for the use of the families of negro soldiers and other contrabands in the service of the United States.—The rebel privateer Florida was at Bermuda, being delayed there by the refusal of the naval authorities to furnish her with coal.

July 23.—The enrolment was resisted in the vicinity of Jarrettsville, Harford County, Md.— The First regiment of colored United States volunteers was completed at Philadelphia, Pa., and Colonel Benjamin Tilghman appointed to the command.—The draft took place in Auburn, N. Y., and every thing passed off with the best of order. The occasion, instead of being one of rioting, arson, and murder, was rather one of rejoicing and demonstrations of loyalty. The drafted men formed in procession, with a band of music, and marched through the streets cheering for the draft, the Union, etc., and in the evening listened to patriotic speeches from the Provost-Marshal, the Mayor and others.

July 24.— General John Morgan, with his guerrillas, was attacked at Washington, Ohio, by a party of National troops under Major Krouse, and driven from the town.—The blockade-runner Emma, in latitude 33° 41′, longitude 76° 13′, was captured by the National transport steamer Arago, under the command of Captain Gadsden.—The bombardment of Charleston was renewed this morning, and continued all day, except for a short time, during which a flag of truce visited the rebel authorities and perfected an exchange of prisoners.—Brashear City, La., was occupied by the National forces.—A fight took place at Wapping Heights, near Manassas Gap, Va., between a brigade of National troops under the command of General Spinola, and a brigade of rebels under General Wright, resulting in the defeat and rout of the latter.—(*Doc.* 104.)

—The battle of Big Mound, Dakotah, was fought this day.—(*Doc.* 110.)

—Major-General J. G. Foster, at Newbern, N. C., made the following report to headquarters at Washington:

"I have the honor to report that the cavalry raid, having for its object the destruction of the railroad bridge at Rocky Mount, has returned completely successful. The expedition consisted of the Third regiment New-York cavalry and a squadron of the Twelfth, and of Mix's men, (cavalry,) and one company of the North-Carolina regiment, and was under the command of Brigadier-General Edward E. Potter, Chief-of-Staff.

"The bridge over the Tar River, at Rocky Mount, a station on the Wilmington and Weldon Railroad, was completely destroyed. The bridge was three hundred and fifty feet long, and the trestle-work over one hundred more. A cotton-mill, filled; a flouring-mill, containing one thousand barrels of flour and large quantities of hard bread; a machine-shop, containing shells, gunpowder, and every munition of war; a large dépôt, offices, etc.; an engine and a train of cars; a wagon-train of twenty-five wagons, filled with stores and munitions; an armory and machine-shop, with the machinery and materials,

and eight hundred bales of cotton, were all destroyed.

"At Tarboro, two steamboats and one large and fine iron-clad in process of construction, a saw-mill, a train of cars, one hundred bales of cotton, and large quantities of subsistence and ordnance stores, were destroyed; about one hundred prisoners taken, and some three hundred animals, (horses and mules.)

"Some three hundred contrabands followed the expedition into Newbern. The force had constant fighting with the enemy, who made great endeavors to intercept their return, but in every case the enemy's position was either turned or they were compelled to retire. Our loss in killed, wounded, and missing, will not exceed twenty-five men."—(*Doc.* 101.)

—A slight resistance to the draft occurred at Lancaster, Pa.—Alexander H. Stephens, the Vice-President of the rebel government, delivered a speech at Charlotte, N. C., expressing entire confidence in the ability of the rebels to maintain their cause and achieve independence.—(*Doc.* 42.)

July 25.—The rebel steamers Merrimac and Lizzie were captured by the National gunboat Iroquois, they having run the blockade of Wilmington, N. C., the evening previous. — The rebel steamer Beauregard, after attempting to run the blockade of Charleston, S. C., returned to Nassau, N. P.—Jefferson Davis, "regarding the furloughs granted the paroled prisoners from Vicksburgh of too great duration in the present condition of the country, with the exception of those of men most distant" from the camp of General Pemberton, at Demopolis, ordered that they be reduced, and an order to that effect was issued by General Pemberton.

July 26.—General R. E. Lee, from his headquarters, army of Northern Virginia, issued the following order:

"All officers and soldiers now absent from this army, who are able to do duty and are not detached on special service, are ordered to return immediately. The Commanding General calls upon all soldiers to rejoin their respective regiments at once. To remain at home in this the hour of our country's need is unworthy the manhood of a Southern soldier. While you proudly boast that you belong to the army of Northern Virginia, let it not be said that you deserted your comrades in a contest in which every thing you hold dear is at stake. The Commanding Gen-

C.C. Washburn
Maj Genl

eral appeals to the people of the States to send forth every man able to bear arms to aid the brave soldiers who have so often beaten back our foes, to strike a decisive blow for the safety and sanctity of our homes, and the independence of our country."

JOHN J. CRITTENDEN died at Frankfort, Ky., at half-past three o'clock this morning.—GENERAL JOHN H. MORGAN, with Colonel Cluke and about four hundred of his men, was captured at a point four miles south of New-Lisbon, Ohio, by the National forces under Colonel J. M. Shackleford.—(*Doc.* 114.)

The National gunboat Sagamore, accompanied by the steamer Oleander, mortar-schooner Para, and schooner Beauregard, on an expedition into Mosquito Inlet, Florida, succeeded in destroying the town of Smyrna, and capturing two schooners, one of which was loaded with cotton. An attempt was made to capture another schooner loaded with cotton, when the rebels set fire to the vessel, and it was totally destroyed. The expedition returned to Key West, having met with no casualties.

July 27.—Brigadier-General Saxton, commanding the department of South-Carolina, at Beaufort, issued the following to the colored soldiers and freedmen in his department: "It is fitting that you should pay a last tribute of respect to the memory of the late Colonel Robert Gould Shaw, Colonel of the Fifty-fourth regiment of Massachusetts volunteers. He commanded the first regiment of colored soldiers from a Free State ever mustered into the United States service.

"He fell at the head of his regiment, while leading a storming party against a rebel stronghold. You should cherish in your inmost hearts the memory of one who did not hesitate to sacrifice all the attractions of a high social position, wealth and home, and his own noble life, for the sake of humanity—another martyr to your cause that death has added, still another hope for your race. The truths and principles for which he fought and died, still live, and will be vindicated. On the spot where he fell, by the ditch into which his mangled and bleeding body was thrown, on the soil of South-Carolina, I trust that you will honor yourselves and his glorious memory by appropriating the first proceeds of your labor as free men toward erecting an enduring monument to the hero, soldier, martyr — Robert Gould Shaw."

—GOLD was sold at Atlanta, Ga., at twelve dollars and eleven cents rebel currency for one dollar.—THE Twenty-seventh regiment of Connecticut volunteers returned to New-Haven.— A SALUTE of one hundred guns was fired at Boston, Mass., in honor of the victories at Port Hudson, Vicksburgh, and the opening of the Mississippi River.

July 28.—Secretary Stanton ordered the formation of a Bureau of Cavalry to be attached to the War Department of the United States.— Colonel Rowett, of the Seventh Illinois infantry, in command of a force from Corinth, Miss., fell upon a party of rebels, belonging to Roddy's force, near Lexington, Tenn., and in a skirmish which followed, captured Colonel Campbell and Captain Clark, together with another captain, two lieutenants, and twenty-five men.

—THE steamboat Imperial, the first boat from New-Orleans since the opening of the Mississippi River, arrived at St. Louis, Mo., and was welcomed with great enthusiasm. — THE National forces under Colonel Sanders, at Richmond, Ky., were attacked by a large body of rebels, and driven back to a point within five miles of Lexington, the rebels closely following. Lexington was placed under martial law, and all able-bodied citizens between the ages of eighteen and forty-five were ordered to report for duty.—AT Richmond, Va., the demolition of the street railroads was completed, the track having been torn up and the iron sent to the mill to be rolled into mail for a gunboat.

July 29.—Numerous depredations and outrages having been committed by citizens and rebel soldiers in disguise, harbored and concealed by citizens residing on the route of the Orange and Alexandria Railroad, orders were issued by General Halleck authorizing the arrest of every citizen against whom there was sufficient evidence of his having been engaged in these practices.—A SKIRMISH took place at St. Catherine's Creek, near Natchez, Miss., between a party of rebels belonging to the command of General Logan, and the Seventy-second Illinois regiment, under the command of Captain James, in which the former were routed with a loss of fifty prisoners and seventy-five horses.—A FORCE of rebels, numbering about two thousand, under the command of General Pegram, made an attack upon the National troops at Paris, Ky., and after a severe engagement, lasting over two hours, were repulsed and routed.—THE Eighth regiment of

Massachusetts volunteers returned to Boston from the seat of war.—BRIGADIER-GENERAL INNIS N. PALMER was ordered to the command of the Eighteenth army corps at Newbern, N. C., and of the posts and districts occupied by that corps. —At Lynchburgh, Va., the rebel government officials were busily engaged in pressing horses for artillery service in General Lee's army. The pressure was general, exempting only the horses in the employment of the government and those belonging to countrymen. — THE British ship Banshee was captured off New-Inlet, N. C.— QUEEN VICTORIA's speech, delivered to Parliament to-day, contained the following: "The civil war between the Northern and Southern States of the American Union still unfortunately continues, and is necessarily attended with much evil, not only to the contending parties, but also to nations which have taken no part in the conflict. Her Majesty, however, has seen no reason to depart from the strict neutrality which Her Majesty has observed from the beginning of the contest."— COLONEL RICHARDSON, the rebel guerrilla, issued an order requiring all men of West-Tennessee, between the ages of eighteen and forty-five, to report to his camp under the rebel conscription law. The following instructions were issued to govern them in carrying out the order:

"If a man should absent himself from home to avoid the order, burn his house and all his property, except such as may be useful to this command.

"If a man resists this by refusing to report, shoot him down and leave him dying.

"If a man takes refuge in his house and offers resistance, set the house on fire, and guard it, so he may not get out."

—WILLIAM L. YANCEY, a member of the rebel Senate from Alabama, who died yesterday, was buried at Montgomery.

July 30.—A brief skirmish occurred at Irvine, Estelle County, Ky., between the Union forces of Colonel Lilly, commanding two squadrons of the Fourteenth Kentucky cavalry, and the rebels. The latter, under Colonel Scott, after their failure to take Lexington and Paris, commenced beating a hasty retreat for Irvine. They were hotly pursued by the Federal forces. Skirmishing commenced at or near Winchester, and continued for a long distance. Irvine is some thirty miles from Winchester, where the Fourteenth were stationed. The rebels came upon them unawares, but this not discomfit them in the least, nor did they

stop to calculate how far they were outnumbered, which they were, fully four to one. As soon as the attack was made by the rebels, the Fourteenth was ready for them, and gave them such a battle as they have cause long to remember. Every assault was bravely met and withstood, and notwithstanding the enemy gained some little advantage at one point, and captured some of the Nationals, the tide of battle was soon turned again, and the Nationals recaptured, together with eighty odd prisoners of the enemy, and their whole force driven across the Kentucky River, with the loss of all their wagons and stolen mules. At this point the pursuers came up and crossed the river and continued the pursuit. The Union loss was four killed, fifteen wounded, and ten prisoners. The rebel loss was seven killed, from sixteen to eighteen wounded, and seventy-five prisoners.—THE Fifty-second regiment of Massachusetts volunteers, under the command of Colonel Greenleaf, arrived at Cairo, Ill., *en route* to Boston, to be mustered out of the service.— PRESIDENT LINCOLN issued a proclamation declaring that the United States would protect its troops of all colors.—(*Doc.* 137.)

—IN Saline County, Mo., Captain Cannon, with about seventy-five men of the Fourth enrolled Missouri militia, attacked a band of sixty-three bushwhackers, under one Captain Blunt, and supposed to belong to Quantrell's command. The militia lost two men killed and one wounded, and a horse killed. The rebels had several men wounded, and Blunt's horse received a fatal shot. The militia then retreated, and the enemy fell back to the brush, cheering for Quantrell as they retired. The rebels next attacked a smaller party of militia, fifteen in number, belonging to the First enrolled Missouri militia, acting as a guard to a paymaster, who had about fifty thousand dollars. The money escaped observation, but two militiamen were captured and paroled, and seven of the best horses belonging to their comrades taken. The enrolled Missouri militia squad finally got safe within a brick church, and were not again molested.—THE rebel guerrilla Mosby entered Fairfax Court-House this evening, and captured a number of sutlers' wagons, together with stores and other property valued at nearly ninety thousand dollars.—GENERAL GRANT, from his headquarters at Vicksburgh, Miss., issued a general order regulating the transportation on the river steamboats.—THE bombardment of Fort Wagner was continued to-day, by the Ironsides and two monitors. Two men were killed in the Fort.

July 31.—A party of rebels captured Stanford, Ky., but they were soon after compelled to evacuate the place with considerable loss, by a force of National cavalry, who pursued them in their retreat toward the Cumberland River.—THE rebel guerrilla Mosby, who was retiring from Fairfax Court-House with the property captured there last night, was overtaken by Colonel Lowell with a detachment of the Second Massachusetts cavalry, and compelled to relinquish the capture, and retreat, with a loss of twenty horses.—MAJOR-GENERAL HALLECK having ordered that "every guerrilla and disloyal man be driven out of the country between the Potomac, Rappahannock, and Blue Ridge," Major-General Pleasanton directed that, under that order, "every man takes the oath of allegiance or be arrested and sent in." —THE rebel steamer Kate was captured while endeavoring to elude the blockade of Charleston, by the Union gunboat Iroquois.—KENTUCKY being invaded by a rebel force with the avowed intention of overawing the judges of elections, intimidating loyal voters, and forcing the election of disloyal candidates at the election to take place on the third of August, General Burnside issued an order placing the State under martial law, and commanding the military to aid the constituted authorities of the State in the support of the laws and the purity of suffrage.

August 1.—Jefferson Davis issued an address to the people of the States in rebellion, calling upon them to hasten to the camps of the rebel armies, all persons who had absented themselves without leave, and granting an amnesty to all who should return to duty before the expiration of twenty days. (*Doc.* 113.)—THE English steamer Peterhoff was condemned at New-York, by the United States Prize Court, for carrying contraband of war at the time of capture.—A PARTY of rebels made an attack upon one of the new Union batteries, in course of erection on Morris Island, S. C., and were repulsed with considerable loss.

—THE funeral of Brigadier-General George. C. Strong, who fell in the attack on Fort Wagner, July eighteenth, took place at New-York City.— THE monitor Canonicus was successfully launched from the works of Harrison Loring, at East-Boston, Mass.—THE Fourth and Seventh United States army corps were discontinued by order of the Secretary of War.

—THIS morning General Buford's cavalry division crossed the Rappahannock River, at the Rappahannock Station, and shortly afterward encountered a brigade of Stuart's rebel cavalry, which they attacked, The rebels were soon reenforced by the balance of General Stuart's command, who fought with obstinacy, but they were driven back to within one mile of Culpeper. Here a division of infantry made its appearance, and the Union troops, finding they were in danger of being outflanked, slowly fell back, followed by the enemy's artillery, cavalry, and infantry. General Buford soon secured an eligible position, and for some hours held the whole rebel force at bay.

The fighting was obstinate, and the loss on both sides severe. The Union troops, although greatly outnumbered, heroically held their position, and repulsed every assault of the enemy. General Buford was shortly afterward reenforced by the First corps of our army, and the combined force soon compelled the rebels to cease their attack. The loss of the Nationals was one hundred and forty, sixteen of whom were killed.

—THE *Richmond Sentinel* published the following this day: " A lecture at the Bethel meeting-house, Union Hill, to-morrow forenoon, is announced. The subject is, ' The Northern States of America the most likely location of the Lake of Fire and Brimstone, in which the Beast and the False Prophet will be tormented.' The lecturer will have the prejudices of his audience on his side."

August 2.—Five hundred rebel prisoners were taken by four companies of the "Lost Children," New-York volunteers, on an island in the rear of Folly Island, in Charleston harbor.

August 3.—The exigencies under which one hundred thousand militia, for six months' service, from the States of Maryland, Pennsylvania, Ohio, and West-Virginia were called out by the President's proclamation of June fifteenth, 1863, having passed, it was ordered by the President that enlistments under that call be discontinued.— HORATIO SEYMOUR addressed a letter to President Lincoln, requesting him to suspend the draft for troops in New-York, and elaborately setting forth his reasons therefore.—THE lighthouse on Smith's Island, in the Chesapeake Bay, was destroyed by a party of rebels.

August 4.—The draft in Philadelphia, Pa., and Oswego, N. Y., was completed this day.—THE launch of the National steamer Wabash, containing a crew of twenty-two men, under the command of Acting Master E. L. Haines, of the gunboat Powhatan, and carrying a twelve-pound howitzer, was captured by the rebel blockade-runner Juno, near Cummings Point, in Charleston Harbor.—A FORCE of rebel cavalry attacked General Buford's pickets, near Rappahannock Station, but were repulsed and driven back beyond Brandy Station, with slight loss. The National loss was one killed and two wounded.—THE steamer Ruth, with two million five hundred thousand dollars in funds, belonging to the United States, was burned on the Mississippi River.

August 5.—Major-General Foster, with the iron-clad Sangamon and the gunboats Commodore Barney, General Jessup, and Cohasset made an expedition up the James River. At a point seven miles from Fort Darling, near Dutch Gap, a torpedo was exploded under the bows of the Commodore Barney, by a lock-string connected with the shore. The explosion was terrific. It lifted the gunboat's bows full ten feet out of the water, and threw a great quantity of water high into the air, which, falling on the deck, washed overboard fifteen of the crew. Among them was Lieutenant Cushing, the Commander of the Commodore Barney. Two sailors were drowned. All the rest were saved. Major-General Foster was on board the boat when the explosion took place.

The rebels then opened upon them from the shore with a twelve-pound field-piece. The Barney was penetrated by fifteen shots, beside a great number of musket-balls; but not a man was injured except the paymaster, who was slightly wounded by splinters. The gunboat Cohasset received five twelve-pound shots, one of which passed through her pilot-house and instantly killed her Commander, Acting Master Cox, striking him in the back.—A BRISK skirmish took place near Brandy Station, Va., between a party of National troops nnder the command of General Merritt and Colonel Davis, and a large number of rebels, resulting in the retreat of the latter, with a loss of two killed and one wounded. The National loss was one killed and two wounded.

August 6.—Eight sutlers' wagons, returning from the front, were captured by Mosby's rebel guerrillas, at a point between Washington, D. C., and Fairfax Court-House, Va.—THANKSGIVING was celebrated throughout the loyal States; business was generally suspended and religious exercises were held in the various churches.—AT Richmond, Va., "enough of companies composed of youths below the conscript age will speedily be formed to take the place of veteran troops now doing guard-duty in Richmond.

"Captain Figner is enrolling a company of youth between the ages of fifteen and eighteen for Major Munford's battalion, and they are specially designed to take the place of a North-Carolina company stationed here. The enrolling quarters of the company are corner of Third and Broad streets. Only a few more youths are wanted to complete the organization."—*Richmond Examiner.*

—A DISTURBANCE between a party of secessionists and the National soldiers stationed at the place, occurred at Visalia, a town in Tulare County, California, during which one soldier was killed and several secessionists wounded.—THE ship Francis B. Cutting was captured and bonded, in latitude 41° 10′, longitude 44° 20′, by the rebel privateer Florida.

August 7.—The Twenty-first and Twenty-fifth regiments of Maine volunteers, passed through Boston, Mass., on their return from the seat of war.—PRESIDENT LINCOLN declined to suspend the draft in the State of New-York, in accordance with the request given by Governor Seymour in his letter of August 3.

August 8.—To secure and preserve discipline, provide against disaster from the elements or attack by the enemy, an order was issued from the War Department, compelling the organization of troops on board government transports, and regulating their transportation.—GOVERNOR HORATIO SEYMOUR, of New-York, replied to the letter of President Lincoln, relative to the draft.

—THIS morning, the rebel steamer Robert Habersham, which had been occupied in watching the Union advance movement up the Savannah River, was entirely destroyed by an explosion of her boiler, while lying off Scrieven's Ferry. The entire crew were either killed or mortally injured.

—A SPECIAL order was issued by Brigadier-General Mercer, in command at Savannah, Ga., impressing into the rebel service, one fifth of the able-bodied male slaves in Eastern, Southern, and South-western Georgia. for the purpose of erecting additional fortifications for the defence of Savannah. "Transportation will be furnished them and wages paid at the rate of twenty-five dollars per month. The Government will be responsible for the value of such negroes as may be killed by the enemy or may in any manner fall into his hands."

—THE gunboat Sagamore captured the sloop Clara Louisa, and schooners Southern Rights, Shot, and Ann, while endeavoring to evade the blockade of Key West, Florida.

August 9.—A reconnoissance under Major Warden, of General Ransom's staff, to Woodville, seventy miles from Natchez, Miss., destroyed five locomotives, forty-three platform and twelve passenger cars; and burned a rebel cotton factory at Woodville, and also cotton and manufacturing goods to the value of two hundred thousand dollars.

—JOHN L. CHATFIELD, Colonel of the Sixth regiment of Connecticut volunteers, died at Waterbury, from wounds received in the assault on Fort Wagner, of July eighteenth.

August 10.—MAJOR-GENERAL GRANT, at his headquarters at Vicksburgh, Miss., issued an order, establishing camps "for such freed people of color as are out of employment at all military posts within his department, where slavery had been abolished by the proclamation of the President of the United States;" and setting forth rules for their government.

—AT Chicago, Ill., the City Council unanimously passed an ordinance providing for an appropriation for raising bounties for volunteers, to act as substitutes for the drafted men who were unable to leave their homes or raise three hundred dollars for exemption.

August 11.—A meeting of the citizens of North-Carolina, representing every county in the First and Second Congressional districts and a portion of the Third, was held at Washington, N. C. The First North-Carolina Union regiment, stationed at that point, participated in the meeting.

Addresses were made and resolutions adopted expressing sympathy with the great conservative movement of North-Carolina, declaring an energetic prosecution of the war in that department to be the only means by which the Union sentiment in the interior of the State could be made practically useful in restoring her to the national jurisdiction, asking the Government for reënforcements for this purpose, accusing the con-

federate government of perfidy and cruelty toward North-Carolina, declaring that her people were therefore absolved from any further obligations to sustain it, placing the responsibility for the destruction of slavery upon Jefferson Davis and his co-conspirators against the Union, expressing the belief that North-Carolina would, notwithstanding, find ample compensation in the blessings of free labor for the present inconveniences of emancipation, rejoicing in the recent Union victory at the Kentucky election, denouncing copperheadism at the North, and commending the ability and patriotism of the Administration in the conduct of the war, and especially in the sound national currency originated by the Secretary of the Treasury.—PRESIDENT LINCOLN closed the correspondence with the Governor of New-York relative to the draft.

August 12.—The One Hundred and Twenty-third Illinois regiment, mounted infantry, under command of Lieutenant-Colonel Biggs, returned to Winchester, Tenn., from a trip into Alabama, with the aim of disbanding a party of bandits, near the junction of Larkin's Fork and Point Rock River. About three hundred of the Eleventh Texas regiment were encountered and driven back, being closely followed a considerable distance down Point Rock River. A number of prisoners were taken, and refugees, issuing from their hiding-places among the mountains, poured in continually until Colonel Biggs's command withdrew toward Winchester.

—THE United States steamer Wateree was launched at Chester, Pa., this morning.

August 13.—A gunboat reconnoissance from Clarendon, up the White River, Ark., was made by the steamers Lexington, Cricket, and Mariner, under the command of Captain Bodie. They returned in the evening, bringing as prizes the steamers Tom Suggs and Kaskaskia. They also destroyed two mills used by the rebel army for grinding corn, and a pontoon-bridge across the Little Red River. The casualties on the Union side were five men wounded, two of whom died.

—AN expedition under the command of Lieutenant-Colonel Phillips, of the Ninth Illinois infantry, left La Grange, Tennessee, for Central Mississippi.—MAJOR-GENERAL BURNSIDE issued an order regulating the employment and subsistence of negro laborers.

—THIS night a party of rebel cavalry made a descent upon a signal station, located on Water Mountain, near Warrenton, Va., capturing every thing except the officers and one glass. Sixteen horses, several wagons, the camp equipage, together with a number of telescopes, fell into the hands of the rebels. The officers had sufficient warning to enable them to escape before the enemy reached them, but their private property was lost.—THE first full regiment of colored men, raised in Pennsylvania, left Philadelphia by steamer for Morris Island, S. C., to reënforce the army under General Gillmore.

—COLONEL CATHERWOOD, commanding the Sixth Missouri cavalry, sent the following despatch to headquarters, from his camp at Pineville, Mo.:

"Colonel Coffee attacked me to-day, and was completely routed, with over thirty killed and wounded. We have a large number of prisoners, all his ammunition wagons, commissary stores, arms, horses, cattle, etc. We scattered all his force except two hundred with himself. Our force is following him closely. My horses are so worn down that they cannot move further until rested. Colonel Hirsch, just in, reports that he killed thirty-five and wounded a large number."

August 14.—Major-General Warren assumed temporary command of the Second army corps of the army of the Potomac. — A SMALL party of rebels made a descent upon Poolesville, Md., capturing the telegraph operator and his instruments, and destroying the wires. After robbing the merchants in the village, they retired.—BRIGADIER-GENERAL THOMAS WELCH, commanding the First division of the Ninth army corps, died at Cincinnati, Ohio.

August 15.—Major-General Rosecrans issued an order, holding the citizens in the Department of the Cumberland responsible for guerrilla operations.—(*Doc.* 150.)

August 16. — The rebel steamer Cronstadt, from Wilmington, N. C., for Nassau, N. P., was captured by the Union gunboat Rhode Island, at a point forty miles from Abaco.—THE letter from President Lincoln to the Union Convention at Springfield, Ill., was made public. It is remarkable for its plain strong sense, and for directness of purpose and clearness of language. — BRIDGEPORT, Alabama, was evacuated by the rebel forces.—THE rebel blockade-runner, Alice Vivian, was captured by the United States steamer, De Soto, under the command of Captain William M. Walker.

August 17.—The bombardment of Fort Sum-

ter commenced this morning at daybreak, by the siege-batteries, and the naval shore battery, under General Gillmore, assisted by the Ironsides and the entire monitor fleet, led by Admiral Dahlgren. Fort Gregg, the innermost battery of the rebels on Morris Island, and Fort Wagner, were silenced. A shot from the latter fort struck the monitor Catskill, and, forcing off a portion of the interior lining of the ship, instantly killed Commander Rodgers and Paymaster Woodbury. —(*See Supplement.*)

—MAJOR-GENERAL DIX, from his headquarters at New-York, issued an address to the citizens of that place, in view of the enforcement of the draft, about to take place, imploring them to preserve order.

—ROBERT TOOMBS, of Georgia, addressed the following letter to Dr. A. Bees of Americus, in the same State:

"MY DEAR SIR: Your letter of the fifteenth instant, asking my authority to contradict the report that 'I am in favor of reconstruction,' was received this evening. I can conceive of no extremity to which my country could be reduced in which I would for a single moment entertain any proposition for any union with the North on any terms whatever. When all else is lost, I prefer to unite with the thousands of our own countrymen who have found honorable deaths, if not graves, on the battle-field. Use this letter as you please."

—THE rebel steamer Nita, having sailed from Havana, on the thirteenth, was captured by the Union steamer De Soto, in lat. 29° 45′, long. 86° 40′, while attempting to violate the blockade. —THE Fourth Massachusetts and Twenty-eighth Maine regiments passed through Buffalo, New-York, *en route* for home.—AN order, regulating the discharge of prisoners, was issued from the War Department.

—CAPTAIN WM. S. HOTCHKISS, commander of the Union gunboat General Putnam, was killed while engaged in an expedition up the Piankatank River, Va., by a party of guerrillas.

August 18.—Lieutenant Bross, with a detachment of the Engineer regiment, on an expedition about twelve miles south of Pocahontas, Ark., was attacked by Colonel Street's company, at a point where defence was difficult. After a brief skirmish, Lieutenant Bross drew his men in line of battle, and charged upon the rebels, who broke and ran. They were chased for five miles, when four were captured, with several of their horses and mules. Colonel Street was among those pursued. He was subsequently discovered and chased, and pressed so hard, that he jumped from his horse, and hid himself in a swamp and undergrowth. In Street's saddle-bags were found the pay-roll of a company of the First Mississippi militia, as follows: One hundred and fifty men all told, twenty-two prisoners of war, forty-two absent without leave, and nine turned over to another company, leaving his present strength seventy-one men. — The British steamer Hebe was run ashore near New-Inlet, N. C., and afterward destroyed by the United States steamer Niphon. One of the Niphon's boats was swamped, and her crew captured by the rebels, who lined the shore, firing on the boats charged with the destruction of the Hebe.—The Forty-seventh regiment of Massachusetts volunteers, under the command of Colonel Marsh, returned to Boston, from the seat of war.—The bombardment of Fort Sumter was continued.

August 19.—Drafting commenced in New-York City, and was conducted without any disturbance. Governor Seymour issued a proclamation, counselling peace and submission to the draft, and repeating his determination to test the constitutionality of the law under which the draft was made.

August 20.—Acting Brigadier-General B. F. Onderdonk, First New-York Mounted Rifles, and two companies of the Eleventh Pennsylvania cavalry, returned to Portsmouth, Va., from a raid into North-Carolina. They passed through Edenton, N. C., and opened communication with Captain Roberts, in command at South-Mills. Thence they proceeded to Pasquotank and Hertford, and while about half-way between the two places, were attacked by the guerrillas, and in the skirmish lost two mounted riflemen. They killed thirty guerrillas, and drove several into the Dismal Swamp, where they were drowned; captured ninety horses, thirty mules, and other cattle.—(*Doc.* 159.)

—Colonel Wilder's cavalry, the advance of the army of the Cumberland, reached the eastern base of Waldon's Ridge, *en route* to Chattanooga.—General Beauregard, at Charleston, S. C., issued an order relative to the observation of fast-day, appointed by Jefferson Davis.

August 21.—Roger A. Pryor, a brigadier-general in the rebel army, resigned his commission. —Lawrence, Kansas, was invaded and pillaged by a band of rebel guerrillas, under the command of the chief Quantrell.—(*Doc.* 119.)

—General Gillmore, having rendered Fort Sumter untenable as a fortification, demanded its surrender, together with the rebel forts on Morris Island, threatening to shell Charleston, should his demand not be complied with.—(*See Supplement.*)

—The United States ship Bainbridge foundered in a storm off Cape Hatteras, and seventy-nine of the crew were lost.

—Chattanooga was shelled by the National forces under Colonel Wilder. The cannonade commenced at ten o'clock in the morning, and continued at intervals until five o'clock in the afternoon. Every piece from which the rebels opened was eventually silenced, although they fired with not less than nineteen guns. The only casualty on the Union side was the wounding of one man, Corporal Abram McCook, belonging to Lilly's battery.—General Meade issued an order regulating the circulation of newspapers in the army of the Potomac.—The rebel steamer Everglade, while endeavoring to run out of Savannah River, was overhauled and sunk near Tybee Island. Twenty-two of her passengers and crew were captured.

August 22.—The bombardment of Fort Sumter was continued and finally reduced to a ruin, although not captured by the Nationals. Six hundred and four shots were fired at the Fort during the day, of which four hundred and nineteen struck inside and outside. The east wall was crushed and breached so that the shot swept through the Fort, the parapet was undermined, the north-west wall knocked down, and all the guns dismounted.—(*See Supplement.*)

—A detachment of the Twelfth Pennsylvania cavalry, under command of Captain Gerry, were ordered by Acting Brigadier-General L. B. Pierce on a reconnoissance from Martinsburgh, Va. Going to Bunker Hill, and thence to Leetown, they encountered the enemy, and captured a number of the rebel Gillmore's men, one lieutenant and one horse, and returned to camp this afternoon without loss.

—No attention having been paid to General Gillmore's demand for the surrender of Fort Sumter, and other rebel works in Charleston harbor, heavy rifled shells were thrown into Charleston, from a battery located in a marsh five miles distant from that city—a range, before that time never attained by any piece of artillery known to the world; General Beauregard protested against the bombardment as "inhuman and unheard of."

—The United States gunboats Satellite and Reliance were captured to-night off the mouth of the Rappahannock River, by a party of rebels, under the command of Lieutenant Commander J. Taylor Wood, of the rebel navy.—Colonel Wilder, with a force belonging to the army of the Cumberland, crossed the Tennessee River, opposite Shell Mound, and burned the railroad bridge over the Nicojack, destroying for the time all communication between the rebels at Chattanooga and those in the vicinity of Bridgeport, Ala.—A riot occurred at Danville, Ill., in which three citizens were killed and a number wounded.—The schooner Wave, having run the blockade at San Luis Pass, near Galveston, Texas, was captured by the National gunboat Cayuga.

—The expedition to Central Mississippi, which left La Grange, Tenn., on the thirteenth instant, returned this day, having met with the greatest success. The force consisted of detachments of the Third Michigan, Second Iowa, Eleventh Illinois, Third Illinois, Fourth Illinois, and Ninth Illinois cavalry, and a part of the Ninth Illinois mounted infantry, all under the command of Lieutenant-Colonel Phillips, of the Ninth Illinois infantry. They left the line of the Memphis and Charleston Railroad, and proceeded by different routes to Oxford, Miss., where the force united and moved on to Grenada, via Water Valley and Coffeeville, meeting with but little opposition till the seventeenth instant, when within eight miles of Grenada. Here the rebels began to oppose their further progress. But they pushed steadily forward, driving the enemy before them and compelling him to fly from behind his fortifications at Grenada, and the victorious troops entered the town with the loss of but one man. The rebel loss is unknown. Several of their wounded were found in the hospital at that place. The Unionists captured quite a number of prisoners. During the evening Colonel Phillips was joined by a force of eight hundred cavalry from Vicksburgh, under the command of Colonel Winslow, of the Fourth Iowa cavalry. The result of the capture was that the Unionists came into possession of sixty-five locomotives and five hundred cars.

As the enemy had destroyed the railroad bridges across the Tallabusha River before he retreated from the town, it was wholly impracticable to run the stock North, and so it was given over to the flames, together with the large railroad buildings belonging to the Mississippi Central and Mississippi and Tennessee railroads, which form a junction at that place. Probably the value of the property destroyed was not less than three millions of dollars, and the loss to the rebels is wholly irreparable. The forces of Colonel Winslow and Lieutenant-Colonel Phillips were joined together here, and proceeded northward on the line of the Mississippi and Tennessee Railroad, meeting with but little opposition on the route. After crossing the Tallahatchie River at Panola, the forces separated, and the Vicksburghers proceeded to Memphis, and the rest of the forces to their respective camps on the Memphis and Charleston Railroad.

August 23.—Fort Fisher, situated below Wilmington, N. C., was bombarded by the National frigate Minnesota.

August 24.—A party of Missouri cavalry, under the command of Colonel R. G. Woodrow, made a descent upon Pocahontas, Ark., and succeeded in routing and capturing a number of rebels, among whom was Brigadier-General Jeff Thompson.—(*Doc.* 154.)

General Gillmore, in a despatch from his headquarters on Morris Island, S. C., reported the partial demolition of Fort Sumter, as the result of seven days' bombardment of that work.—Charleston was again shelled by the troops under General Gillmore.—(*See Supplement.*)

—A meeting of a portion of the people of Cumberland County, Va., was held this day, at which the following resolutions were unanimously adopted:

Resolved, That we heartily approve of the action of our Governor in calling an extra session of the Legislature for the purposes designated.

Resolved, That whereas we are engaged in a war for the maintenance of principles dear to every freeman, and that we are firmly resolved to prosecute this war under all circumstances and through whatever disasters may befall us, until our independence is established; therefore, we do request our representatives in the Senate and House of Delegates to advocate the passage of a bill for the enrolment, organization, and drilling, for home defence, of all capable of rendering such service, who are not already subject to military duty.

W. B. Hazen
Brig Gen

Resolved, That the said representatives be requested to advocate all measures having for their object the vigorous prosecution of this war.

Resolved, That we look with abhorrence on the idea of the reconstruction of the Union with the United States.

Resolved, That these proceedings be published in any Richmond papers.

—A SKIRMISH took place at Coyle's Tavern, on Little River turnpike, near Fairfax, Va., between a detachment of the Second Massachusetts cavalry and Mosby's guerrillas. The Nationals, numbering only twenty-five, were attacked front and rear at the same time, but fought manfully. Their loss was two killed, three wounded, and nine taken prisoners, together with all the horses they had in charge, fifteen of which, however, were afterward recaptured, leaving eighty-five still in the hands of the enemy. The loss of the enemy was one captain and one lieutenant killed, and one lieutenant and three privates wounded. Mosby was himself wounded in two places, side and thigh. Colonel Lowell pursued the enemy from Centreville as far as Snicker's Gap, but they succeeded in making their escape by reason of having constant remounts of fresh horses.—FITZ-HUGH LEE, with a rebel cavalry force, crossed the Rappahannock River near Corbin's Neck, six miles below Fredericksburgh, but was soon driven back by the brigade of General Custer, with a loss in prisoners of three engineer officers, and a number of privates killed and wounded. The Union loss was slight.—THE Richmond *Whig* of this day contained the following: "A Southern paper, some weeks ago, threw out a suggestion that the Confederacy should arm some five or six hundred thousand negroes, and precipitate them upon the Yankees. The suggestion was doubtless to frighten the Yankees; but it has imposed upon a few of our own people. The proposition is too preposterous for serious discussion. It is enough to say it would be exchanging a profitable laborer for a very unprofitable soldier. Let the Yankees have negro armies. Nothing but their cowardice could have betrayed them into such a folly. They use the poor creatures as breastworks, but thus far with very little advantage. The Southern people are willing to employ their slaves in any way that would tell best against the enemy. But it has yet to appear that they can do so in any manner so effective as in raising food for our armies. Some may be occasionally used in ditching and throw-

ing up breastworks, and it is possible a limited number might be advantageously substituted for teamsters; though, in respect to the last, there may be doubts. In the main, no doubt, the most useful function compatible with their capacities is that to which they are accustomed—food-raising."

August 25.—Early this morning, Deputy Marshal Taylor of Coshocton County, Ohio, with a squad of five men, went to a house near Chili, in Crawford Township, to arrest two men, Wens and J. Lour, Germans, who were drafted last fall, but had, up to that time, evaded the authorities. Not finding them at the house, they approached the barn to search it, when Wens and Lour came out of it, armed, and fired. Taylor and his men closed upon them to secure them, when a hand-to-hand fight occurred. Stafford, one of the Marshal's men, fell dead, pierced with nine balls. One other of the Marshal's men was severely wounded, and Wens and Lour, the two drafted men, both killed.—*Cincinnati Gazette.*

—THE advance-guard of General Steele's army, under General Davidson, consisting of five thousand men, arrived in front of Brownsville, Arkansas, and immediately opened fire upon the town. A sharp fight was kept up for about fifteen minutes, when the rebels commenced a retreat, evacuating the town and leaving, in the hands of the Nationals, General Burbridge and a number of privates.

August 26.—A fight took place near Perryville, Arkansas, between the rebel forces under Cabell, who were retreating from Camp Stand Watie, and the National troops belonging to the army of General Blunt, in which the former were routed with considerable loss.—MAJOR JOHN J. STEVENSON, Lieutenant D. H. Chambers, and sixty men of Rober's Third Pennsylvania artillery, left Fortress Monroe, Va., last Sunday night, on the armed steamboat C. P. Smith, and reached the Chickahominy River the next morning. They proceeded about ten miles up, landing scouting-parties at different points along the shore, and destroying a number of small boats. When about nine miles up the Chickahominy, they met a detached party of thirty rebel cavalry, belonging to Robinson's regiment. The latter were repulsed, without any injury being sustained. They then shelled and destroyed the building used as the headquarters of Colonel Robinson, of the rebel army. Two men were captured, who were released after all the information that could be obtained from them was received. The expedition returned to Fortress Monroe this afternoon, having succeeded in the reconnoissance, with the most satisfactory results.—THE steamer Live Oak was captured at Berlin, Mo., by a gang of guerrillas, who, having plundered the boat and passengers, released them.—THE rifle-pits of the rebels at Vinegar Hill, on Morris Island, S. C., in front of Fort Wagner, were assaulted and captured by the troops of General Gillmore's army, with a loss of ten killed and seventeen wounded.—THE battle at White Sulphur Springs, Va., was fought this day.—(Doc. 157.)

August 27.—John B. Floyd, a General in the rebel service, died at Abington, Virginia.—A PORTION of Colonel Wilder's cavalry, belonging to the army of the Cumberland, encountered a rebel force at Hanover, Ala., and succeeded in defeating them, killing three, and capturing one. —A GOVERNMENT train of twenty-eight wagons was captured by a party of rebel guerrillas, at a point about six miles from Philippi, on the road to Beverly, Va.—THE battle at Bayou Metea, Ark., between a large infantry and cavalry force of rebels, and General Davidson's division of National cavalry, took place this day.—(Doc. 156.)

August 28.—The Board of Supervisors of the city of New-York devoted two millions of dollars to exempt the firemen, the militia, and the police, and to provide for the families of drafted men in indigent circumstances.—By direction of Jefferson Davis, Lieutenant-General W. J. Hardee assumed command of the paroled rebel prisoners, captured at Vicksburgh and Port Hudson.—(Doc. 158.)

—SAMUEL JONES, a Major-General in the rebel service, issued an order from his headquarters at Dublin, Va., thanking the home guard and other citizens for their services in the action at White Sulphur Springs.—A PARTY of rebel guerrillas attacked the mail-carriers from a cavalry division of the army of the Potomac, stationed at Harwood Church, Va., killing one man and capturing four others, together with the mail.

August 29.—Five deserters, belonging to the Fifth corps of the army of the Potomac, were executed according to sentence.—GENERAL WISTAR's cavalry returned to Yorktown, Va., from an expedition to Bottom's Bridge. The force engaged were parts of the First New-York Mounted Rifles, Colonel Onderdonk, and of the Fifth Pennsylvania cavalry, Lieut.-Colonel Lewis. They left Williamsburgh on the twenty-sixth instant, and pushed through New-Kent Court-House, directly to Bottom's Bridge. At the latter place, they found one regiment of infantry in rifle-pits, supported by a squadron of cavalry. A charge was immediately made, which carried the rifle-pits, and drove the enemy across the bridge, which they took up. The Union troops lost one killed, and one wounded. They captured five prisoners from the enemy, who left dead on the ground one officer, one sergeant, and two men, besides those they carried off. The bridge being rendered impassable, and the object of the expedition being entirely accomplished, the troops returned.—(Doc. 159.)

—CORRESPONDENCE between Major-General Dix and Governor Seymour, relative to the draft, was made public.

August 30.—LIEUT.-COLONEL CLARK, with the Ninth Kansas cavalry, returned to Kansas City, from the pursuit of Quantrell, through Jackson, Cass, and Johnson Counties, Missouri, having killed, during his expedition, forty of the perpetrators of the Lawrence massacre.

August 31.—The rebel transport, Sumter, having on board the Twentieth regiment of South-Carolina volunteers, and the Twenty-third regiment of Georgia, was sunk in Charleston harbor by the guns of Fort Moultrie. The Twenty-third Georgia had been on duty at the rebel Battery Wagner, and, being "relieved, went on board the steamer to go to Fort Johnson. The tide being low, they could not go the usual course, but steamed off in the direction of Sullivan's Island. The watch at Moultrie, supposing it to be a Yankee monitor, awakened the gunners, when they opened a spirited fire on the defenceless vessel. Every means possible were employed to signal to them, both from Sumter and the boat, but they recognized no signal.

"The third and fourth shots sunk the boat, yet they kept firing until a small boat was sent to tell them who we were. This was about three o'clock A.M. The men were panic-struck, and leaped off into the water by fifties and hundreds, and it seemed for a while that nearly all would be either killed or drowned; but the cool conduct of Major Ballinger, the Commandant of the Twenty-third Georgia, and a sand-bar on the left of the boat, covered by some four or five feet of water, saved them from a watery grave.

" By nine o'clock, the whole regiment was once more on dry land, and, miraculous as it was, not a single life has been lost by the dangerous wreck. But guns, blankets, oil-cloths, haversacks, canteens, boots and shoes, and, in fact, all kinds of clothing, were left upon the rugged waters of the boiling deep."—*Atlanta Intelligencer.*

—THE sloop Richard, loaded with cotton, was captured off the coast of Florida, by the United States bark Gem of the Sea.

September 1.—A fight took place at Barbee's Cross-Roads, Va., between a patrol of forty-nine men belonging to the Sixth Ohio cavalry, under the command of Major John Cryor, and a party of rebel guerrillas, in which the former lost two killed, four wounded, and twenty-four prisoners.

— THOMAS E. BRAMLETTE was inaugurated as Governor of Kentucky, to-day. In his inaugural address he contends that the revolted States did not change their status by rebelling; that all that is necessary for them to do is to return to their fealty, and take their position as States; that the rebellion did not remit them to a territorial state.

He says we have now, and will have before the rebellion closes, the identical Constitution which extremists seek to destroy, the one by innovation, the other by force. It is not a restored Union, not a reconstructed Union that Kentucky desires, but a preserved Union and a restored peace upon a constitutional basis.

The Governor strongly objects to the arming of negro regiments, and asks what is to be done with such soldiers at the end of the war. He points to the result of the recent election as a proof that Kentucky will not fraternize with rebellion, either open or covert, and declares that Kentucky ever has been, and now is, and always will be, loyal to the Government of our fathers.

—A GENERAL engagement took place in Charleston harbor, between the iron-clads, and Forts Wagner, Sumter, and Moultrie. Fleet-Captain Oscar C. Badger, the successor of Captain Rodgers, was injured by the explosion of a shell.

—AN engagement took place at the Devil's Back-Bone, a point sixteen miles from Fort Smith, Arkansas, between a portion of the army of General Blunt, under Colonel Cloud, and the rebel forces under Cabell, in which the latter was routed with a loss of twenty-five killed and forty wounded. The National loss was two killed and twelve wounded and missing.—FORT SMITH, Ark.,

was captured by the Union forces under General Blunt.—(*Doc.* 179.)

— A FORCE of rebel cavalry crossed the Upper Potomac, at Edwards's Ferry, Va., and captured a large number of cattle, which, however, they were unable to carry off, being pursued by the National forces.—SIX hundred persons, chiefly heads of families, and resident in Kansas City and vicinity, who were believed to be aiders and abettors of the rebellion, or strong sympathizers with it, were ordered to remove from the district, by General Ewing.

September 2.—Kingston, Tenn., was occupied by a portion of General Burnside's army, under the command of General Minty.—THE gunboats Satellite and Reliance, which were captured by the rebels on the twenty-second of August, were destroyed by the Union forces under the command of General Kilpatrick, at Port Conway, Va.—THE guerrilla Hughes, with one hundred rebels, appeared in Burksville, Ky.

—A JOINT committee of the Alabama Legislature reported a resolution in favor of the proposition to employ slaves in the military service of the confederate States, which proposition was favored by many of the presses of Mississippi and Alabama. After discussion in the Alabama House, the resolution was adopted by a vote of sixty-eight yeas to twelve nays, after striking out the words "military" before service, and "soldiers" at the end of the resolution. The resolution was amended and reads as follows:

" That it is the duty of Congress to provide by law for the employment in the service of the confederate States of America, in such situations and in such numbers as may be found absolutely necessary, the able-bodied slaves of the country, whether as pioneers, sappers and miners, cooks, nurses and teamsters."—*Savannah News,* September 2.

September 3.—The battle of White Stone Hill, D. T., was fought this day.—(*Doc.* 161.)

—THE expedition under Acting Brigadier-General B. F. Onderdonk, which left Gloucester Point, Va., on the twenty-sixth of August, returned to the point from which it started, having been perfectly successful in accomplishing its object.—(*Doc.* 159.)

September 4.—Knoxville, Tenn., was occupied by the National forces under Major-General Burnside. " The East-Tennesseans were so glad to see the Union soldiers that they cooked every thing they had, and gave it to them freely, not asking pay, and apparently not thinking of it. Women stood by the roadside with pails of water, and displayed Union flags. The wonder was, where all the Stars and Stripes came from. Knoxville was radiant with flags. At a point on the road from Kingston to Knoxville sixty women and girls stood by the road-side waving Union flags and shouting: 'Hurrah for the Union.' Old ladies rushed out of their houses, and wanted to see General Burnside and shake hands with him, and cried: 'Welcome, welcome, General Burnside! welcome to East-Tennessee!'"—(Doc. 168.)

—THE women of Mobile, Ala., rendered desperate by their sufferings, met in large numbers on the Spring Hill road, with banners on which were printed such devices as "Bread or Blood," on one side, and "Bread and Peace," on the other, and, armed with knives and hatchets, marched down Dauphine street, breaking open the stores in their progress, and taking for their use such articles of food or clothing as they were in urgent need of.

September 5.—Major E. W. Stephens, with a portion of the First West-Virginia volunteer infantry, was surprised in his camp at Moorefield, Va., by a party of rebels under the command of Imboden and Jones.—(Doc. 141.)

—FORTS Wagner and Gregg, in Charleston harbor, were furiously bombarded by the National fleet and land batteries, under the command of Admiral Dahlgren and General Gillmore. The firing began at daylight and continued until dark. —(*See Supplement.*)

—THE *Charleston Mercury* of this date contained the following:

"Although carefully covered over with the mantle of secrecy by Congress, enough has been disclosed by stern realities to show the total incompetency of President Davis to govern the affairs of the Confederacy. He has lost the confidence of both the army and the people; and if an election to-morrow was to come off for the Presidency, we believe that he would not get the vote of a single State in the Confederacy. Yet, if the Provisional Congress had done its duty — if the present Congress would do its duty—President Davis could readily be driven into a course of efficiency. He is President of the confederate States for six years. The constitution has not been proved to be inadequate to

rectify his imbecilities. He can be controlled and directed, as the King of Great Britain is. That government is a constitutional monarchy, having coördinate branches. In Great Britain, no policy of the government, no cabinet advisers, can stand against the expressed opinion of the House of Commons. Are the people less potent in the confederate States through their representatives in Congress, than the people of Great Britain in Parliament? We do not believe it. Parliament has no power, like that of Congress, to pass a law in spite of the King's veto; yet no King, since 1688, has dared to veto a bill passed by Parliament. No King has dared to defy public opinion in the appointment of the national counsellors and the commanders of the armies, setting up personal favoritism and partisanship above efficiency.

". . . . The legislative power which Congress possesses, as to measures and men, can control the government and force efficiency into the administration whether in the appointment of cabinet officers, commanders of armies and bureau officers, or in the management of our diplomacy, our finances, our military operations, our naval preparations, and the efficiency of our bureaus of conscription, commissary stores and quartermaster stores. But this can never be done by those who look upon President Davis as 'our Moses.' Congress must assume its duties under the constitution, as an independent element of power. It must abandon the idea that it is only a secret body for registering the will of the President. It must be the people, standing forth in the light of day, clothed with the whole legislative power of the government, and with their agent, the President, instrumental for their deliverance. That our cause will ultimately triumph we do not doubt, in spite of the incompetency of President Davis and his silly and most disastrous policy, by which the confederate States have been deluged with blood, and covered over with suffering and misery. His inefficiency and Yankee efficiency will both be overcome.

"But if President Davis is to be treated as 'our Moses' we really do not see the use of Congress. If the people, through their representatives in Congress, are to exercise no power but at the bidding of the executive, Congress is a nonentity. It is worse; it is a tool of the executive, by which the constitution is practically overthrown and a military dictatorship established in its stead; characterized by a base assumption of power on the part of the executive,

O. B. Willcox
Brig Genl Vols

and a baser betrayal of trust on the part of Congress."

—THE United States troops encamped within the city of New-York for the preservation of order during the draft, were removed by order of Brigadier-General Canby.—R. R. Belshaw, in a letter to Earl Russell, sets forth a series of outrages committed upon himself and other British subjects, by the rebel government in the States of Alabama and Tennessee, and asks for redress.—SIX privates and one of the telegraph operators, belonging to the army of General Rosecrans, were captured at Running Water Bridge, near Chattanooga.—A FIGHT occurred in Dacotah Territory, near the battle-ground of White Stone Hill, between a party of hostile Indians and the Second regiment of Nebraska volunteers, belonging to the command of General Sully.—(Doc. 161.)

September 6.—A fight took place at Brandy Station, Va., in which the rebel cavalry, under General Stuart, were driven back four miles beyond Culpeper Court-House, on the road to Richmond, and two pieces of horse artillery were captured from the rebels by the Union forces, under the command, in person, of General Custar, who was slightly wounded.

—THE bombardment of Forts Wagner and Gregg, in Charleston harbor, was continued during the day. Last night battery Gregg was assaulted by the National forces, who were repulsed.

—FORTS Wagner and battery Gregg were evacuated by the rebels in accordance with the orders of General Beauregard, and seventy-five men and twenty-one guns were left in the hands of the National forces.—(See Supplement.)

September 7.—Cumberland Gap, Tenn., which had been well fortified and occupied by the rebels for the year past, surrendered to the Union forces under the command of General Shackelford, without firing a gun. The garrison consisted of four regiments, namely, Fifty-fifth Georgia, Sixty-fourth Virginia, Sixty-second and Sixty-fourth North-Carolina, a portion of Leyden's artillery, Captain Barnes's company, of Georgia; also Fain's Tennessee battery, commanded by Lieutenant Conner.—A CAVALRY force belonging to General Herron's army, under Major Montgomery, on a reconnoissance from Morgan's Bend, La., met a party of rebel pickets about three miles from the river and commenced skirmishing with them,

continuing all day, the rebels constantly falling back, the Unionists following until the rebels had crossed the Atchafalaya River, twelve miles from the position where the skirmishing commenced. Here the rebels made a stand, and crossing the river being impracticable, the Unionists fell back and encamped for the night, with a loss of one killed and eight wounded.—THIS evening the monitor Weehawken went aground midway between Forts Sumter and Moultrie, in Charleston harbor. Several attempts were made to get her off, but each proved ineffectual. Toward evening the Ironsides, with the monitors Nahant, Montauk, Patapsco, and Lehigh commenced a vigorous bombardment of Fort Moultrie, withdrawing at dark.

September 8.—The United States gunboats Clifton and Sachem were captured by the rebels at Sabine Pass, La., being disabled by the fire from the fortifications on shore. They were operating for the landing of a column of United States troops under Major-General Franklin, to be employed in a movement against Louisiana and Texas. In consequence of the failure at this point, the movement was abandoned.—(Docs. 125 and ,165.)

—CHATTANOOGA was evacuated by the rebels, who retreated to the south.—THE bombardment of Fort Moultrie, by the monitors Nahant, Montauk, Patapsco, and Lehigh, was renewed and continued during the first half of the day. A house on Sullivan's Island was set on fire by the shells.—THE Washita River expedition, consisting of the greater part of General Logan's old brigade, a regiment of cavalry, and a battery of artillery, returned to Vicksburgh from the portion of Louisiana lying adjacent to Washita River. No organized force of the rebels could be found. The detour was made to the north-west, in direction of the village of El Dorado, Ark. A large number of rebel soldiers came voluntarily into the Union lines and surrendered.—A FORCE of National troops assaulted Fort Sumter, but were repulsed, leaving in the hands of the rebels a large number of prisoners.—(See Supplement.)

—THE National forces at Bath, Va., composed of a portion of two companies of Colonel Wynkoop's Seventieth Pennsylvania cavalry, were attacked this morning at three o'clock by a party of rebels, numbering over two hundred, who were repulsed and driven off.—AT Baltimore, Md., General Schenck issued an order suppressing the substitute business in Maryland and in his department, it having been found that the agencies for procuring substitutes to go out of the State and department interfered with the operation of the draft and recruiting.

September 9.—Chattanooga, Ga., was occupied by the National forces belonging to the army of General Rosecrans.—Colonel Cloud, with his division, belonging to the army of General Blunt, attacked a body of over one thousand rebels at Dardanelle, Ark., and defeated them, capturing their entire camp and a large amount of stores.—Lieutenant-Colonel Hays, with companies A, B, H, and parts of E and F, of the One Hundredth Ohio regiment, was attacked near Telford, Tenn., ninety-three miles up the railroad, by one thousand eight hundred rebels, under Jackson, and fought them gallantly for two hours, losing heavily in killed and wounded, but was finally compelled to surrender to overpowering numbers. National loss by the affair was about three hundred — killed, wounded, and prisoners — of which an undue proportion were commissioned officers.—The bombardment of Fort Moultrie, S. C., was continued.

September 10.—Major-General S. A. Hurlbut, from his headquarters at Memphis, Tenn., issued general orders causing reprisals to be made for all rebel outrages committed within his lines, by levying assessments upon the wealthiest and most notorious sympathizers with the rebellion, adding fifty per cent to the amount of damages proven.—Last night a party of soldiers, belonging to General Benning's rebel brigade, robbed the office of the *Standard* newspaper, at Raleigh, N. C., and this morning a crowd of citizens "gathered and rushed upon the office of the *State Journal*, in the same place, and totally destroyed the furniture and printing materials."— (*Doc.* 166.)

—Little Rock, Arkansas, was captured by the National forces under the command of General Steele.—(*Docs.* 124 *and* 145.)

—Major-General James G. Blunt, from his headquarters at Fort Smith, issued the following address to the people of Arkansas:

"The flag that two and a half years ago was struck, when a weak garrison of United States troops were compelled to abandon this post, before a superior number of maddened and infuriated men, who had resolved upon the overthrow of the best Government upon earth, now floats in triumph over Fort Smith. In reply to the many inquiries made, "Is the occupation of this post by Federal troops to be permanent?" I answer yes. The flag that floats from yonder staff, shall continue to wave its folds to the breeze, never again to be desecrated by treason's foul pollution. The whole of the Indian Territories and Western Arkansas are now in my possession, and under my control. All the rebel hordes, except a few guerrillas, have been driven beyond the Red River. The most obnoxious of the rebel citizens have followed the army with their families to seek the '*last ditch*.' It is for you, who have chosen to remain at your homes, to elect whether you will have peace or war.

"From the unfeigned joy manifested by thousands of your citizens upon the occupation of this city and the neighboring city of Van Buren— from the reports of delegations who have visited me from over one hundred miles in the interior, south of the Arkansas River, as also from the fact that hundreds of true men have come from the mountains to swell the Union ranks in the last few days, and still continue to come from whither they have been driven and hunted like beasts of prey by confederate soldiers—gives assurance that the love and attachment for the Union is not yet extinct in Western Arkansas. Moreover, the bleached and crumbling bones of hundreds of Arkansians who, in this locality, have recently been hung upon the gibbet, by a fiendish and merciless crew of confederate murderers, for no other reason than that they loved the old flag, and would not bow their necks to the behests of treason, is evidence that they were true and devoted heroes, worthy a better fate.

"Many applications have been made by citizens for safeguards. None will be issued. The best safeguard you can have is the American flag suspended over your premises, and to deport yourselves as becomes good and loyal citizens. Your conduct must be your safeguard. If it shall be your desire to disenthral yourselves from the tyranny and oppression to which you have been subjected, and organize a civil government, under the auspices of the United States authority, every facility will be afforded you to accomplish this purpose. I leave the matter with you, trusting that wise counsels may prevail."

—The Eleventh regiment of Kentucky mounted infantry, commanded by Colonel Love, in pursuit of the rebel guerrillas under Colonel O. P. Hamilton, overtook them at Brimstone Creek, Tenn., where a brisk skirmish occurred, the guerrillas mounting their horses and making off. Hamilton, who was recognized, rode boldly up to within one hundred and fifty yards of the Union advance, and delivered his fire, then turned and dashed into the bush. He was followed by a volley and retreated to the hills. The morning report of their Adjutant was captured, showing four hundred and eighty men for duty. Four of the guerrillas were killed and found in the brush. Two prisoners were taken, who acknowledged that seven were wounded. The rebels, who had bushwhackers in the hills assisting them, so completely blockaded the road by felling trees, that it was found impossible to pursue them. Colonel Love withdrew, and under orders from Colonel Harney, halted at Ray's Cross Roads.

The following proclamation was found posted on a tree at Tompkinsville, given literally:

HEAD QRS HAMILTONS BATTALION
TOMKINSVILLE Ky
Sept 7 1863

I Now Give Notice to Citizens and Soldiers to all Concerned that the principle of Burning and Pilaging must be Stopt as I am ordered to retaliate in Every respect Let us fight and not make war on the Women and Children I am Roundly opposed to Burning and Plundering But I am Compelled to Retaliate tharefore I am Desireous that the Burning and Pilaging may be stopt if it *Does not stop* I will Certainly Retaliate I will Certainly Regard Citizens if the Citizens of the South is Regarded. I am your Humble Servt

O. P. HAMILTON
Col. Comdg
The Cavalry!

—MATHEW F. MAURY addressed a letter to the London *Times*, on the reports and war-plans of the National Government.—A FIGHT occurred at Ringgold, Ga., between the National forces under Colonel Wilder and General Van Cleve, and a portion of the rebel army which was retreating from Chattanooga, resulting in the expulsion of the latter from the town, with a loss of three killed and eighteen taken prisoners. The Union loss was three men wounded of the Ninety-third Illinois regiment.—MAJOR-GENERAL ROSECRANS entered Chattanooga.

—B. H. RICHARDSON and his son, Frank A. Richardson, and Stephen J. Joyce, proprietors of the Baltimore, Md., *Republican,* were to-day arrested by order of General Schenck, for publishing in their paper of yesterday evening a piece of poetry entitled the "Southern Cross." The three were sent across our lines this morning. The proprietors of the *Republican* were frequently warned by the authorities against the publication of disloyal sentiments in their paper.

September 11.—The steamer Sir William Peel was captured at the mouth of the Rio Grande, by the United States steamer Seminole.

September 12.—About three o'clock to-day, a prowling band of guerrillas, some three hundred strong, supposed to be a part of the rebel Colonel Freeman's men, at Salem, Mo., attacked the Union forces, consisting of one company of the Fifth M. S. M., under command of Captain Whyback, resulting in the greatest confusion and slaughter among the rebels. The rebels had laid their plans to surround the soldiers, and in attempting to carry out their projects—the strong wind blowing the dust in thick clouds round about—they became literally entangled among themselves, and supposing a part of their own men to be Nationals, commenced a most deadly engagement, resulting in great slaughter. In the mean time the militia were "keeping cool," watching the sport, and at the proper time charged upon the confused foe, raking them down in every direction, putting their vastly superior number to flight, hotly pursued by the undaunted boys of the gallant Fifth, who scattered death and terror to the rebels in their hasty retreat, a distance of eighteen miles. Their loss was not less than twenty killed in the chase. There was not a man of the Fifth killed, and only three wounded. A more complete victory over guerrillas has not been accomplished in Missouri for many months.—*Rollo Express, September* 19.

—THE blockade-runner Alabama was chased ashore on the Chandeleur Islands, Mississippi, and captured, by the United States flag-ship San Jacinto; during the afternoon the rebel steamer Fox was driven ashore by the United States steamers Genesee, Calhoun, and Jackson, and afterward burned by the rebels.—FITZ-HUGH LEE, a brigadier-general in the rebel service, relinquished the command of his brigade, having received promotion to a major-generalship.—As the second battalion of the Sixty-third Indiana regiment was returning from Terre Haute to Indianapolis, this day, an attempt was made to hang D. W. Voorhees, who was reëlected to Congress from Indiana at the last election. Mr. Voorhees was travelling as a passenger in the same train with the soldiers. He was rescued by the officers, but compelled by the soldiers to leave the train at Greencastle.—THE national salute was fired at noon to-day from the Fort at Sandy Hook, Fort Lafayette, Castle William, and Fort Schuyler, New-York, in honor of the Union victories at Morris Island, Knoxville, and Chattanooga.—THE schooner Flying Scud was captured by the National steamer Princess Royal. She was from Brazos, Texas, and was loaded with cotton.

September 13.—A portion of rebel guerrillas belonging to the band of the Chief Biffles, amounting in number to over one hundred and ten, was surrounded by a detachment of Missouri cavalry and a company of mounted infantry from Paducah, Ky., near Paris, Tenn., and six of them killed, twenty-one wounded, and the rest captured.—THE Clyde-built side-wheel steamer Jupiter, a noted blockade-runner, one hundred and eighty-four feet long, nineteen feet beam, formerly a passenger-boat on the Clyde, was captured by the United States steamer Cimarron, at half-past three o'clock this morning, in attempting to run the blockade into Savannah, by the way of Warsaw Sound. She had for passengers four officers of the Royal Navy, an agent of the Confederacy named Weaver, and a commercial agent. Also Nassau and Savannah pilots.—A CAVALRY fight took place near Culpeper Court-House, Va., between the Nationals, under General Kilpatrick, and the rebels, under General Lomas and Colonel Beale, of the Ninth Virginia cavalry, resulting in a complete rout of the rebels, with considerable loss in killed, wounded, and prisoners.—(*Doc.* 169.)

—THE National troops stationed at Salem, Dent County, Mo., were attacked by four hundred rebels, who were repulsed, with a loss of twenty killed and a number wounded.—THE expedition against the Sioux Indians, commanded by General H. H. Sibley, returned to Fort Snelling.—THE United States steamer Genesee, and gunboats Calhoun and Jackson, shelled the rebel iron-clad Gaines near the fort at Grant's Pass, below Mobile, and compelled her to retire behind the fort, together with another vessel belonging to the rebel fleet. After the retreat of the rebel iron-clad and the transport steamer behind the fort, the shelling was directed solely against the latter. Twenty-two shells from the Genesee alone, fell inside the fort, and the firing from the other boats was remarkably accurate. Sand, stones, logs of wood, etc., were sent flying upward in great quantities, and before the action terminated every gun was dismounted, and, it is

believed, disabled. One large gun in particular was knocked completely end over end, as could be plainly seen from the vessels, and the achievement drew forth hearty cheers from the gallant tars.—AN expedition composed of sailors and marines from the Navy-Yard and frigate Potomac, was organized at Pensacola, Florida, and sent up the Blackwater River to destroy a ferry and bridges used by the rebel troops in passing from Alabama into Florida, for the purpose of annoying our garrisons and stealing supplies. Lieutenant Houston, United States Marine corps, employed the captured steamer Bloomer, and accomplished his mission with a loss of two men, namely, Corporal Enderly, marine guard, killed; private ——, Potomac guard, wounded.

September 14.—This evening three squadrons of the First Maryland cavalry, commanded by Major Russell, were ordered to the front to relieve the Sixth Ohio, then engaged with the rebels at Rapidan Station. When it reached the battle-ground the enemy was forming for a charge. One squadron was immediately dismounted and deployed as skirmishers, and the other two formed in line of battle. Scarcely were they formed when the enemy charged with a full regiment upon the line of skirmishers. These two squadrons promptly charged the enemy and drove him back. The enemy soon rallied and charged again; but Major Russell had his men well in hand, and met the enemy the second time and drove him back again, capturing one officer and one private. The enemy was satisfied with charging. All this time the rebels had four batteries playing at cross-fires upon the Unionists, and yet, strange to say, the only casualties in the regiment of First Maryland cavalry are Captain Joseph Cook, company D, slightly wounded; Corporal Jno. McCowhen, company G, killed; private John Otto, company F, wounded; private John Schmits, company A, wounded, and three privates missing. Never did men charge more gallantly, or behave better than did these squadrons. They met more than double their number, and twice drove them back and held the field. Lieutenant Bankard, company A, distinguished himself by his cool and gallant conduct.

—THE following circular was issued this day from the headquarters of the army of the Potomac, by command of Major-General Meade:

I. Newspaper correspondents will be admonished to hold no communication with prisoners of war, whether on their way to headquarters or

temporarily detained in the custody of any guard, or to seek any information from guides, scouts, or refugees, coming from beyond the lines.

II. No newspaper correspondent or civilian, not connected with the army, will be permitted to accompany or remain with cavalry serving in the front, or on the flank of the army.

—The cavalry advance of the army of the Potomac, under the command of General Pleasanton, reached the Rapid Ann River, at Raccoon Ford, after considerable heavy skirmishing between Culpeper and that point. No rebel infantry had been met with, though a strong force of rebel cavalry had been constantly driven back by the National forces.

—This morning, at about six o'clock, a regiment of Texas Rangers, the Second Texas cavalry, two hundred and fifty strong, under command of Colonel George Madison, charged on the Union picket stationed about one mile south of the town of Vidalia, La., on the road leading along the levee, near the river. The picket—only one lieutenant and six men strong — had to fall back against such an overwhelming power. The musketry firing was distinctly heard in town, where only two companies of the Thirtieth Missouri regiment were stationed. Colonel Farrar, who happened to be present, at once ordered all his men to "fall in," and was in a few minutes at the place of attack, having only about twenty men, who were first under arms, along with him, the whole force at Vidalia who were fit for duty consisting only of about fifty men. In the double-quick he rushed forward, and was received by a heavy fire of the enemy, who had taken possession of a pontoon train encamped in the southern part of the town, and were just preparing to burn up the wagons loaded with the pontoons. The Union skirmishers opened a brisk fire on the enemy, who was covered by a live hedge, and could not be seen by the men, though the distance was only about twenty yards. Colonel Farrar seeing that the object of the enemy's attack was the destroying of the pontoon trains, ordered a charge at once, and with cheers his men rushed to the guard, where a lively skirmish for about fifteen minutes took place, and he succeeded in driving the enemy back. The Unionists lost two men killed and four wounded. The enemy lost six killed, eleven wounded, and two prisoners, among whom was a Lieutenant Skinner, of the Twenty-sixth Tennessee cavalry, who stated

that the strength of his regiment was two hundred and fifty, and that Brigadier-General Majors, with a body-guard of thirty men from a Louisiana cavalry regiment, was near, but did not take part in the charge; that his regiment had crossed Black River near Trinity City, La., on the evening of the thirteenth, to charge on Vidalia for the purpose of burning down the pontoon train; that besides his regiment there were two Texas cavalry regiments, under command of Colonels Stone and Lane, at Black River, seventeen miles distant, and also one Louisiana and one Arkansas cavalry regiment, all under command of Brigadier-General Majors. Colonel Farrar, who had sent notice to Natchez about the attack, at once prepared to have his men mounted to follow up the enemy as quick as reënforcements came. At about eight o'clock two regiments of infantry and a few companies of cavalry had crossed the river and come to his assistance. The enemy was followed up closely and overtaken at Black River, where another skirmish took place, lasting until dark. The enemy was forced to cross the river, and the National forces returned to camp, where they arrived at eleven o'clock P.M.

September 15.—Rear-Admiral D. D. Porter, writing to the Navy Department from Cairo, Ill., under this date, says:

"The river below seems quiet. There has been but one attempt made to obstruct commerce or transportation. A party of guerrillas attacked the gunboat Champion from behind the levee while she was convoying a body of troops below. The troops passed on safely, and the Champion stopped and fought the rebels until she made them retire, losing some of their men—report says fifty-seven. They have not been heard of since, excepting that they were falling back on Alexandria, General Herron having given them a chase with his division. As I came up, I overtook a part of the Marine Brigade under Colonel Curry. He reported to me that he had just captured at Bolivar three rebel paymasters with two million two hundred thousand dollars in confederate money to pay off the soldiers at Little Rock. He also captured the escort consisting of thirty-five men. This will not improve the dissatisfaction now existing General Price's army, and the next news we hear will be that General Steele has possession of Little Rock. The gunboats pick up deserters every day, who say the rebels do not intend to fight in Arkansas, and that with proper steps she will be in the Union again in forty days. Lieutenant Bache captured a Colonel Mattock, who was on a conscription expedition, and it gave unusual satisfaction to all the people."

—At Richmond, Va., three Irishwomen were charged with buying a load of mush-melons in the Second Market, with intent to retail them, and were fined five dollars, and the melons were ordered to be confiscated.

It is well the attention of the efficient clerk of the Second Market has been called to these creatures. They swarm through the market every morning, and buy up the major part of the fruit brought in by the country people, and take it to their houses to retail. As they understand the world, a jug of whisky and a half-dozen melons, and a dozen hard-boiled eggs, constitute a respectable store.—*Richmond Examiner.*

—M. LARUE HARRISON, commanding a force of National troops three hundred strong, attacked the combined forces of the rebels Coffee and Brown at Seneca Station, one mile west of Enterprise, at the mouth of Buffalo Creek, Indian Territory, at ten o'clock this morning, and after an engagement of two hours, completely routed them, driving them southward in disorder. As the engagement occurred in a dense grape-vine thicket, it was impossible to estimate the loss of the rebels; five were ascertained to have been killed, among them a Captain W. R. Johnson. Colonel Harrison lost none, either in killed, wounded, or missing.—A MAGAZINE on James Island, S. C., belonging to the rebels, exploded, killing a lieutenant and six men.—PRESIDENT LINCOLN issued a proclamation suspending the writ of *habeas corpus* in certain cases.—(*Doc.* 171.)

September 16.—The rebel steamer Lizzie Davis, from Havana, for Mobile, Ala., was captured in latitude 25° 58′ north, longitude 85° 11′ west, by the National flag-ship San Jacinto.—THE rebel forces made an attempt to recross the Rapid Ann River, but were foiled by the National artillery and cavalry. They advanced in three columns, with artillery, toward the river, but being opposed by the Union troops on the north side, soon fell back.—A SPIRITED skirmish took place at White Plains, Va., in which the rebels were dispersed in disorder.

September 17.—The steamer Marcella was seized and plundered by rebel guerrillas, in the vicinity of Dover Landing, ten miles below Lexington, Mo. Four soldiers of company A, Fifth M. S. M.—Edwin Ross, Chris. Sele, Martin Fisher, and Charles Waggoner—were on the steamer visiting their homes at the latter place, on furloughs. They were taken out and marched off with the assurance that they were to be exchanged for other prisoners or paroled. When the rebels had marched about two miles, they stopped and divided the plunder and money, which employed them about an hour, after which the prisoners were put in line, and instantly the order was given to fire, at which Ross, Sele, and Fisher fell dead, but young Waggoner, finding himself unhurt, sprang away for safety, and though shot after shot rattled past him, he finally made his way uninjured to the brush, and went into Lexington.

—A REBEL raid was made upon a collection of vessels on the eastern shore of Virginia. The schooners Ireland and John J. Houseman were taken out to sea, plundered, and set adrift. The schooner Alexandria was also plundered, and the government schooner Alliance, loaded with stores valued at thirty thousand dollars, was captured.

September 18.—General Schofield, in command in Missouri, issued a General Order, stating that martial law would be enforced throughout his department against all persons who should in any manner encourage military insubordination, or endeavor to create disaffection among the troops and against all persons who should publish or utter publicly words calculated to excite insurrection, lawless acts among the people, or who should publish falsehoods or misrepresentations of facts, calculated to embarrass or weaken the military authorities, or in any way interfere with the men in the discharge of their duties. Any person guilty of either of the offences above mentioned, should be punished by fine and imprisonment at the discretion of a military commission, and any newspaper which might contain said publications in violation of this order would be suppressed.

—A PARTY of soldiers, belonging to the Eighty-third Illinois regiment, were attacked, about five miles above Fort Donelson, Tenn., by a party of rebel guerrillas, led by the notorious George Hinson. The guerrillas were secreted in bushes, from which they fired a volley, killing two of the soldiers, named John Pickerel and A. P. Wolfe, of company E. The guerrillas escaped after the firing. The soldiers sent a man to the fort for an ambulance, removed a short distance from the road, and hid in the bushes. The guerrillas soon returned, when the soldiers fired on them five rounds. Hinson was shot in the head. The rest fled.

—Major-General Dix issued general orders, thanking the troops quartered in the city of New-York, during the difficulties consequent upon the draft, for their admirable discipline and soldierly deportment.—Colonel Trusten Polk, formerly United States Senator from Missouri, with his wife and daughter, was captured at Bolivar Landing, Arkansas, and delivered to General Buford, commanding at Helena. Colonel Polk was General Holmes's Judge-Advocate General, and was with the rebels at New-Madrid.

September 19.—A party belonging to the command of General Buford, swam the Rapid Ann River, near Raccoon Ford, and after capturing a considerable number of prisoners, returned to their camp in safety.—The battle of Chickamauga, Ga., between the Union forces under General Rosecrans, and the rebels under General Bragg, commenced this day.—(*Docs.* 43, 105, *and* 123.)

September 20.—Lieutenant Earl, of the Fourth Wisconsin regiment, in command of a squad of forty cavalry, marched from Baton Rouge, La., as far as Comite River, and captured fourteen prisoners, with their arms, horses, and equipments. Among the prisoners were Colonel Hunter and Captain Perry, notorious guerrilla chiefs.

September 21.—Twenty-one persons, exiled for various degrees and offences of disloyalty, accompanied by nine ladies, who went by permission of the War Department to rejoin their families, permanently residing at the South, left St. Louis, Mo., in charge of Captain Edward Lawler, of the First Missouri infantry. They were sent within the rebel lines in accordance with orders of the National War Department, of April twenty-fourth, 1863.—James M. Mason, the rebel commissioner in England, informed Earl Russell, at the Court of St. James's, that his commission was at an end, and that he was ordered by Jefferson Davis to remove from the country.— The British schooner Martha Jane, was captured by the gunboat Fort Henry's tender Annie, off Bayport, Florida.

—The revenue steamer Hercules, while lying off the Virginia shore, was attacked by a large party of rebel guerrillas, but they were driven off after a fight of about twenty minutes, without inflicting any serious damage to the steamer or her crew.—The battle of Chickamauga, Ga., was concluded by the Union forces falling back on Chattanooga, after a gallant fight by General Thomas's corps.—(*Docs.* 43, 105, 123, *and* 184.)

September 22.—General Buford, with a portion of his division, drove the rebel pickets through Madison Court-House, Va. Three miles beyond he encountered a strong force of the enemy's cavalry, and after a spirited fight he forced them to retreat, and drove them across the Rapidan at the point where the Gordonsville Railroad intercepts the river. The National casualties were one killed and about twenty wounded. Forty-five prisoners were taken; among them Lieutenant-Colonel Delaney, of Cobb's Georgia Legion, Lieutenant Boyce, and two privates of North-Carolina regiments, who were seriously wounded. Unionists wounded include Lieutenant Hines, of the Fifth New-York cavalry, and Lieutenant G. W. Bullock, of the Ninth; also, R. Minshall, of the Third Indiana, and Sergeants Dunning, Cummings, and Bell, and Corporal Bell, all of the Eighth Illinois, and J. Ingmonson, of the Twelfth Illinois, (the last-named a bugler.) B. F. Soder, of the Third Indiana, was killed.

—A scout of the Sixth Provisional regiment, E. M. M., commanded by Captain Holloman, attacked a party of guerrillas in Arkansas, killing four, wounding four, and capturing one—the wounded also being prisoners.—The steamer Leviathan, which was captured at an early hour this morning by the crew of the rebel yacht Teaser, was recaptured by the National gunboat De Soto, soon after she had left the mouth of the Mississippi River.—The battle of Blountville, Tenn., was fought this day between the Union forces under the command of Colonel Foster, and the rebels under Carter.—(*Doc.* 173.)

—The English steamer Juno, which had run the blockade of Wilmington the night previous, was captured by the National gunboat Connecticut.—A body of rebel cavalry crossed into Upper Maryland, a few miles from Rockville, but had not proceeded far before they were met by a portion of Scott's "Nine Hundred" cavalry and an infantry force. A fight ensued, and thirty-four rebels were killed and wounded. Among their killed was Captain Frank Kilgore, (of Maryland,) the commander of the enemy's forces. The rebels finding they were contending with superior numbers, retreated.

September 23.—The blockade-running steamer Phantom was chased ashore near Rich Inlet, N. C., by the Union gunboat Connecticut, and afterward deserted by her crew, who set her on fire before leaving; in the afternoon, men were sent on shore from the Connecticut, to destroy the boats of the steamer that had been drawn up on the beach. While in the act of destroying them, the men were attacked by a party of concealed rebels, who succeeded in driving them back to the gunboat with a loss of one killed and one wounded.—LIEUTENANT-GENERAL LONGSTREET issued General Orders to his troops, congratulating them on the brilliant victory which had crowned their heroic efforts at Chickamauga.— AT one o'clock this morning, a raid was made upon a telegraph office opposite Donaldsonville, La., by a band of rebel guerrillas, who captured and carried off fourteen men of the Fourteenth regiment of New-York cavalry and the telegraph operator.—THE English steamer Diamond, while attempting to run the blockade, was captured by the United States steamer Stettin, off St. Simon's Sound, Ga.—A SECRET expedition from Beaufort, S. C., to the mainland, under Captain J. E. Bryant, of the Eighth Maine volunteers, and consisting of two companies of colored troops, the chaplain of Colonel Higginson's regiment, a telegraph operator, and a lieutenant of the Fourth South-Carolina volunteers, returned with only partial success. The expedition started by order of General Gillmore, with the view, not of cutting the rebel telegraph between Charleston and Savannah, but of attaching a wire and receiving their despatches. Owing to the carelessness of the operator, the wire, instead of being hid behind the pole, was allowed to hang in plain sight, and was discovered by the passengers in the first passing train; not, however, until some very important messages had been received, and among others a telegram to the commander of the rebel troops in Savannah from Beauregard, ordering all his forces to Charleston, to engage in an attack on Folly Island.

September 24.—General Robert E. Lee issued an order announcing to the rebel army in Virginia, "with profound gratitude to Almighty God, the victory achieved at Chickamauga by the army of Braxton Bragg," and calling upon his soldiers to "emulate the heroic example of our brethren in the South, until the enemy shall be expelled from our borders, and peace and independence be secured."—BETWEEN eight and nine

o'clock this morning a squad of twenty-one guerrillas made a raid at Wood Station Number Thirteen, on the line of the Orange and Alexandria Railroad, Va., about twelve miles from the latter place, stealing nine mules. Sergeant Highland, of Pennsylvania, who started in the direction of the plunderers, was taken prisoner.—PRESIDENT LINCOLN issued a proclamation raising the blockade of the port of Alexandria, Va.—(*Doc.* 175.)

September 25.—The English steamer William Penn, which was captured near the Rio Grande, arrived at New-Orleans. — SPENCER KELLOGG BROWN, condemned by the rebels as a spy, was hung at Richmond, Va.—A FIGHT took place near Upperville, Va., between Major Cole's command of National cavalry, and about one hundred and fifty guerrillas belonging to Mosby's gang, in which the latter were defeated and put to flight. Major Cole recaptured seventy-five horses and mules, and one man belonging to the Nineteenth New-York cavalry, besides killing one of the guerrillas and capturing nine. — A PARTY of guerrillas attacked the Union garrison at Donaldsonville, La., but were repulsed, and compelled to retire with slight loss.

September 26.—E. Kirby Smith, Lieutenant-General in the rebel army, commanding in the South-West, issued the following address to the people of Louisiana, Arkansas, and Texas:

"Your homes are in peril. Vigorous efforts on your part can alone save portions of your State from invasion. You should contest the advance of the enemy, thicket, gully, and stream; harass his rear and cut off his supplies. Thus you will prove important auxiliaries in any attempt to reach him in front, and drive him, routed, from our soil. Determination and energy only can prevent his destruction of your homes. By a vigorous and united effort you preserve your property, you secure independence for yourselves and children—all that renders life desirable. Time is our best friend. Endure awhile longer; victory and peace must crown our efforts. The amended regulations governing the formation of corps for local defence are published for your information, and I call upon you to organize promptly under its provisions."

September 27.—Captain Parker, of the First Arkansas infantry, with seventy-five men, was attacked near Moffat's Store, in Franklin County, Arkansas, by Shelby's rebel cavalry. His loss was two killed, two wounded, and fifteen prisoners. The rebel loss was five killed and twenty wounded—among the latter, Shelby, their commander.

September 28.—President Lincoln directed that the Twentieth and Twenty-first army corps be consolidated and called the Fourth army corps, and that Major-General Gordon Granger be the commander of this consolidated corps. He also directed that a Court of Inquiry be convened to inquire into and report upon the conduct of Major-Generals McCook and Crittenden in the battles of the nineteenth and twentieth instant. These officers were relieved from duty in the army of the Cumberland, and were ordered to repair to Indianapolis, Ind., reporting their arrival by letter to the Adjutant-General of the army.—LIEUTENANT EARL and thirty men, belonging to the Fourth Wisconsin cavalry, captured a party of rebel guerrillas and cavalrymen, in the neighborhood of the junction of the Amite and Comite Rivers, La., and safely conducted them into Baton Rouge. Among the prisoners were Colonel Hunter (Ten-Mile Bob) and Captain Penny, the leaders in the raids and attacks on the river steamboats in that vicinity.—FORT SUMTER, S. C., was bombarded by the National batteries on Morris Island.—MR. —— SPENCE, of London, England, ceased to be the financial agent of the rebel government.—*Richmond Despatch, Sept.* 29.

—AN engagement took place at McMinnville, Tenn., in which the rebels were repulsed with a loss of a large number of prisoners.—THE rebel steamer Herald was captured by the gunboat Kearny, and carried into Key West, Fla.—MAJOR-GENERAL GRANT, from his headquarters at Vicksburgh, issued Special Orders authorizing the issuing of rations to such families only, as should " take an oath to support the Government of the United States, and to withdraw all support and countenance from the so-called confederate government."—THE entire cotton crop in South-Carolina was seized by order of Brigadier-General Rufus Saxton, by virtue of authority vested in him as Military Governor of the Department of the South.—GENERAL Orders were issued by Major-General Banks, at New-Orleans, La., authorizing the Commanding-General of the Corps d'Afrique " to detail from the line an additional staff-officer, with the rank and pay of captain, to be designated ' Corps Instructor,' whose duty it shall be to superintend in garrison, and, as far as may be consistent with military duty, in the field, the education of men engaged in the Corps d'Afrique."

September 29.—The *Cincinnati Enquirer* of this day contained the following :

" It is now stated that a bill has been prepared and will be placed before the next Congress, declaring Lincoln President while the war lasts. Thus the mad fanatics are plotting against our liberties, and if we do not speak right soon through the ballot-box, the last vestige of our republican government will have been swept away."

—THE gunboat Bombshell, Captain Brinkerhoff, left Newbern a few days ago, under sealed orders, and made a reconnoissance of Pasquotank River, which empties into Albemarle Sound. Landing a boat's crew near Elizabeth City, the men were captured by rebels, when Captain Brinckerhoff opened a vigorous fire on the town, doing considerable damage.—A SLIGHT skirmish took place at Moor's Bluff on the Big Black River, Miss., resulting in the retreat of the Union forces. —A BATTLE took place at Morganza, La.—(*Doc.* 177.)

September 30.—Colonel Rowett, with the Seventh Illinois and Seventh Kansas regiments of cavalry, had a fight with the rebel guerrillas under Newsome, at Swallow's Bluff, on the Tennessee River. Colonel Rowett came up with the rebels while they were crossing the river. About one hundred had already crossed with the horses and baggage, leaving a major and twenty men on this side. The rebels were sheltered by the bluff, and defended by their comrades on the other side, who were in supporting distance, but the Unionists dashed in and captured the whole party with the loss of one killed and two wounded.—THE bombardment of Forts Sumter, Johnson, and Simpkins, in Charleston harbor, was continued all day, Forts Moultrie and Simpkins alone replying.—(*See Supplement.*)

—LEONIDAS POLK, a Lieutenant-General in the rebel service, being relieved from his command "in consequence of an unfortunate disagreement between himself and the commander-in-chief of the rebel department of the Mississippi," issued his farewell order.

October 1.—The rebel General Wheeler, with a large body of mounted men, crossed the Tennessee River at Washington, at a point thirteen miles above Chattanooga, and passed down the Sequatchie Valley. He captured fifty wagons belonging to one of General Rosecrans's trains, at the foot of the mountain, near Anderson's Cross-

Roads, burning a number of them, and killing about three hundred horses and mules. The train was laden with ammunition, clothing, and rations. Forty wagons carrying medical and sanitary stores, and about fifty sutlers' teams were also lost.

—The loyal men and women of De Kalb County, Ill., and adjoining counties, met in mass meeting at De Kalb, to renew to each other their solemn pledges to stand by the Government in the vigorous prosecution of the war, "till this accursed rebellion and its cause shall be buried in one common grave."

October 2.—The *Natchez Courier* of this day contained the subjoined editorial:

The following communication appears in the *Columbia* (S. C.) *Guardian:*

To His Excellency Governor Bonham: The stream of negro emigration from Mississippi has commenced flowing into this State, having been prohibited in Georgia and Alabama. The heavy rains of the summer have so damaged the corn crops that the question of subsistence for another year may be of great importance, and it becomes doubly so from the influx of consumers. Would it not be well for this State also to adopt some precautionary measures before it is too late? This suggestion is only thrown out to catch the attention of the proper authorities, the writer having every confidence that if any thing ought to be done in the premises, it will not be overlooked. Very respectfully,

Citizen.

To this the *Augusta Constitutionalist* replies:

It is untrue that either Georgia or Alabama have refused refuge and domicil to the unfortunate fugitives from Mississippi. Our people are incapable of so outrageous a breach of hospitality.

We have before alluded to this matter of emigration, and we do so again more in sorrow than anger. Although the people of Alabama and Georgia perhaps have not formally protested against Mississippians flying to those States, several of the press have spoken out against it. At the time we alluded to this matter, it was done with the view of presenting to the Mississippi citizen his true position in the present crisis.

If he emigrates with his family and negroes, he is denounced by some of the journals as a coward, for surrendering his home. Where he stays at home, endeavoring to pursue the even tenor of his way in raising crops for the support of his family, he is by other prints stigmatized as a submissionist; and cavalry squads are sent out by the confederates to subsist on his already diminished supplies, and with a view to make him miserable and poor indeed, his little crop of cotton is burnt to cap the climax of trouble.

This is no fancy sketch—it is a reality, as almost any planter on the Mississippi River can testify. When the planter is thus made poor and even destitute, does the confederate government come to his relief? Never! Instead of this, the confederate force gradually falls back toward the Alabama River, leaving the property of Mississippians almost a total wreck.

How shall the resident of Mississippi act under this state of things? If he takes refuge further East, he is censured for leaving home; and if he remains home to raise another crop in the confederate lines, as soon as the Union army again presses forward, his supplies will once more be taken by the confederate cavalry, and his cotton committed to the flames again!

Mississippians! by staying on your places and cultivating the soil, in our humble opinion, you are doing much good for yourselves and those around you. Though given the "cold shoulder" occasionally of those who appear to think themselves entirely safe from the ravages of war in the mountains of Alabama and Georgia, by remaining at home you will have the consolation of knowing that you have been tried in the fire and have done the best for your country.

Unto the new order of things instituted by the military authority of the United States, it behooves us all to assimilate; and as its lines extend, if we have not realized all our hopeful visions, we can have the blessed consolation of knowing that we have been discreet, law-abiding citizens.

For our part, we look forward with daily renewed hope to that time when our internal strifes shall end, when brother shall cease to be arrayed against brother, and when the Constitution and Union of our fathers shall be revered by every one on American soil.

—General Rosecrans issued an order, thanking his soldiers for their patience, perseverance, and courage, displayed in the campaign against General Bragg.—(*Doc.* 183.)

—Colonel Edward McCook, with the First Missouri and Second Indiana cavalry, attacked Wheeler's rebel force, four thousand strong, at Anderson's Cross-Roads, Tenn., and whipped

them badly, killing and wounding one hundred and twenty, taking eighty-seven prisoners and recapturing all the Government property, including eight hundred and nine mules, and the prisoners taken from the Nationals yesterday.

Among the prisoners was a major on Wheeler's staff, commander of the escort; a major on General Martin's staff, Colonel Russell, commanding a brigade, and nine other officers. The enemy was completely routed and driven ten miles. — GREEK fire-shells were thrown into Charleston, S. C., from the batteries of General Gillmore, on Morris Island. — THE English schooner Florrie was captured six miles from Matagorda, Texas, having on board a cargo of medicines, wines, saddles, and other stores.—A CAVALRY skirmish occurred near Franklin, La., between the Union troops under Colonel Davis, and the rebels commanded by Captain Squires. The rebels were defeated at the first fire, Squires being mortally wounded. Colonel Davis captured one piece of artillery.

October 3.—McMinnville, Tenn., was captured by the rebels under General Wheeler. Major Patterson, who was taken prisoner with a portion of the Fourth Tennessee infantry, relates the following history of the capture: He had with him seven companies, mostly fragments. On the second instant he sent out scouts, who returned and reported no enemy. On the next day he sent Lieutenant Farnsworth with twenty scouts, who were cut off. He then sent out Lieutenant Allen, who passed the pickets a quarter of a mile and returned, reporting the rebels in force. Major Patterson drew up his command, four hundred and four in all, and fifty convalescents from the hospital. Skirmishing followed for an hour and a quarter, during which the rebels were repulsed in three charges. Wheeler then sent in a flag of truce, with a verbal demand for a surrender, which Major Patterson refused, saying he would not surrender until he was compelled to do so. In half an hour Colonel Hodge of the Kentucky brigade brought a demand for surrender in writing.

Major Patterson, after consulting with his officers, deeming it useless to contend against an enemy so greatly superior in numbers, surrendered. Wheeler had four divisions of cavalry, artillery, and ten brigades, and said he had ten thousand men. The Union loss was seven killed and thirty-one wounded and missing. The rebels admitted a loss of twenty-three killed and

wounded. After the surrender Major Patterson's trunk was broken open, and one hundred and fifty dollars stolen out of it, while his men were generally robbed of their money, watches, knives, and other valuables. The prisoners were all paroled. While two of them were going on the Carthage road they were halted by a Dr. Fain, who drew his pistol on them, and cocking it, ordered one of them to pull off his boots and give them up. Protestation and pleas of sore feet and a long journey were of no avail, and the valiant highway robber rode off with the boots which he had taken from a defenceless paroled prisoner."

—PRESIDENT LINCOLN issued a proclamation designating the twenty-sixth of November as a day of general thanksgiving.—(*Doc.* 182.)

October 4.—The steamers Chancellor, Forest Queen, and Catahoula, were destroyed by rebel incendiaries at St. Louis, Mo.—INFORMATION having reached Colonel William L. Utley, commanding the Union forces at Murfreesboro, Tenn., that that post would soon be attacked by the rebels, the following order was issued:

"Non-combatants, women, and children will, immediately on the approach of the enemy, repair to the fortifications or elsewhere for safety. All that portion of the city lying adjacent to the railroad will be shelled immediately upon the occupation of the city by the rebels. The remainder of the city will be shelled at the expiration of five (5) hours after the entrance of the enemy. Every possible facility will be afforded the citizens to get to a place of safety. It is to be hoped that there will be no unnecessary alarm, as every precaution will be taken against false rumors, and the citizens will be warned in time."

—A SLIGHT skirmish took place near Newtown, La., between a party belonging to the Union forces under General Banks, and a body of rebels, who had ambushed themselves until they had fired one volley upon the Union advance; they then fell back, being pursued. National loss was one killed and four wounded.

October 5.—Great excitement prevailed at Nashville, Tenn., in consequence of the rebel General Forrest, with a force of over three thousand mounted men, having made a descent upon the railroad between that place and Bridgeport. Skirmishing occurred in the neighborhood of Murfreesboro, a railroad bridge at a point south of that place being destroyed by the rebels.—A BAND of guerrillas, under the chief White, of Loudon County, Va., made a raid into Langley, six miles above Georgetown, D. C., driving in the pickets, without any casualty. — COLONEL CLOUD, in a message to General Blunt, dated at Fort Smith, Ark., said he had just returned from a raid in the Arkansas Valley. Near Dardanelles he was joined by three hundred "mounted Feds," as the Union Arkansians are called, and with them and his own force routed the rebels, one thousand strong. They fled in confusion, leaving tents, cooking utensils, wheat, flour, salt, sugar, and two hundred head of beef cattle behind. They reported as they ran that "Old Blunt, with his whole army, was after them." Several hundred Union men offered their services as a home guard regiment. Colonel Cloud authorized them to enrol and offer their services to the Military Governor, when appointed. He left garrisons there and at Clarksville.—THE batteries on Lookout Mountain, and at points all along the rebel lines, opened fire upon Chattanooga. The Unionists under Rosecrans, replied from their works on Moccasin Point, the Star Fort, and other works. The Tennessee River rose rapidly during the day.—A PARTY of Captain Bean's cavalry on a scouting expedition near Harper's Ferry, Va., encountered a number of rebel cavalry belonging to the command of Colonel Imboden. A skirmish ensued, when the Union forces were repulsed, with a loss of one killed, three wounded, and ten captured. Two of the Unionists cut their way out and returned to camp, although severely wounded.

October 6.—General Blunt and his escort were attacked at Baxter's Springs, near Fort Scott, Mo., and nearly all of them were massacred.—(*Doc.* 190.)

—GENERAL MITCHELL, with a body of National troops, overtook the rebels below Shelbyville, Tenn., and attacked them with great spirit, putting them to a complete rout. They did not stop for their wounded, and left over one hundred dead upon the field.—AN attempt was made to blow up the United States iron-plated frigate Ironsides, in Charleston Harbor, by means of a torpedo. The instrument of destruction was suspended from the bow of a small cigar-shaped steamer, which was driven against the Ironsides at full speed. A tremendous explosion followed, which threw a large body of water on the deck of the Ironsides, but did no serious damage to

the vessel. Lieutenant Glassett, the commander of the rebel steamer, was taken prisoner, having been thrown overboard by the force of the explosion. On board the Ironsides, Ensign Charles Howard was killed by a musket-shot fired by Glassett, as his steamer was approaching the frigate.

October 7.—Colonel Harrison's force of West-Tennessee cavalry were attacked at Como, Mississippi, by rebel guerrillas, under Colonels Faulkner and Wilson, and was forced to retreat after an engagement of two hours, with a loss of thirty-seven men. The rebel loss was large, Colonel Wilson being among the killed.—A FIGHT took place at Farmington, Tenn., between the Union forces under General Crook and the rebels commanded by General Wharton.—(*Docs.* 181 and 191.)

—ACTING VOLUNTEER LIEUTENANT JAMES P. COUTHOUY, having received information that a rebel steamer was tied up to the bank on Red River, fitted out an expedition, under charge of Acting Chief-Engineer Thomas Doughty, with twenty men and Mr. Hobbs, who crossed over from the Mississippi to Red River, and after great labor in getting through the entanglements of the bushes and other undergrowth, got a sight of the steamer lying at the bank. They managed to get up to her and capture her. A few moments afterward they were enabled to capture another one, and found themselves in possession of two steamers and nine prisoners. One of the prisoners was an aid to the rebel General Taylor, who had been sent up expressly for the last steamer.—*Admiral Porter's Despatch.*

October 8.—Last night the garrison at Harper's Ferry, Va., were alarmed by an attack, and the cavalry and two regiments of infantry started out to meet the enemy. Near Charlestown a force of between three hundred and four hundred cavalry, commanded by Imboden, were posted. The rebels had a large portion of their force dismounted and in ambuscade. Captain Somers, with his company of cavalry, had advanced to hunt up the enemy. He met a company of rebel cavalry, who charged upon him and were repulsed. They purposely retreated, Captain Somers and his company pursuing until they entered the fatal ambuscade. At the first fire Captain Somers and ten men were killed, as many more wounded, and nearly all the others captured. The few who escaped carried the information into camp, and the rest of the cavalry start-

ed in pursuit, but were unable to come up with the rebels.—THE following order was issued at Richmond, Va., by the rebel Adjutant-General Cooper: "The Chief of the Nitre and Mining Bureau is directed, through the officers of his bureau, to impress copper, coal, and such other minerals as may be needed for the use of the government."—A FIGHT occurred near Salem, Miss., between four thousand rebels, under General S. D. Lee, and five thousand Nationals, under McCullis and Phillips, resulting in the defeat of the rebels with a loss of fifteen killed and wounded.—A MOB at Jackson, N. H., burned the hotel where the Deputy Provost-Marshal was stopping while serving notices on drafted men.— CARTHAGE, Mo., was burned by the rebel troops. —A PARTY of one hundred guerrillas, under command of Captain Richardson, at two o'clock this afternoon, placed obstructions on the track of the Lebanon Branch Railroad, at New-Hope, Ky., twenty miles from the junction, threw the train off the track, and fired into it, but did no damage to the passengers. They then captured the train, burned two passenger-cars, baggage and express cars, destroyed the locomotive, robbed the passengers of money and clothing, and decamped.

October 9.—Two iron-plated rams, built on the Mersey, England, by the Lairds for the use of the rebel government, were seized by order of the British government, upon a charge of an intention to evade the neutrality laws.—MAJOR-GENERAL J. G. FOSTER sent the following despatch to the National War Department: "I have the honor to report that the expedition sent out on Sunday, under General Wistar, to break up or capture the guerrillas and boats' crews organized by the enemy in Matthews County, has returned, having in the main accomplished its object. Four rebel naval officers, twenty-five men, and twenty-five head of cattle belonging to the Confederacy, together with horses, mules, and arms, are the results. A large number of rebel boats were destroyed. Our loss was one man killed. General Wistar reports the Fourth United States infantry (colored) making thirty miles in one day, with no stragglers."

—FORT JOHNSON, in Charleston harbor, S. C., was again silenced. A well-directed shot from the Union batteries entered an embrasure and dismounted the gun.—ONE of the two-hundred pounder batteries on Morris Island, that had been silent for a week, opened on Fort Sumter and the other rebel forts.

October 10.—Early this morning one of General Kilpatrick's cavalry brigades, consisting of four regiments, attempted a reconnoissance on the south side of Robertson's River, when they were met by a large body of Stuart's rebel cavalry. A fight ensued, which lasted about an hour, when the Union cavalry fell back upon the infantry reserves. Another severe conflict ensued, which resulted in the giving way of the Union infantry and the capture of a considerable number of them. A detachment of the cavalry afterward made a dash upon the rebels and recaptured all, excepting fifteen or twenty, of the infantry. The entire National force were then pushed back toward Culpeper, skirmishing all the way.—(*Doc.* 196.)

—ZOLLICOFFER, Tenn., was captured by the Union forces under General Shackelford.— (*Doc.* 198.)

—LIEUTENANT-COLONEL G. W. LEE has recently returned from his deserter-hunting trip into the mountains of North-Carolina. He has captured between three hundred and four hundred deserters and tories. Their leader, Colonel Busty, notorious for his daring outrages, was said to have about six hundred men under him. They were not, however, in a body, but scattered through the country, engaged in their treasonable work of stealing and destroying the property of the people, and carrying off cattle fattening for the army. With two hundred men, Colonel Lee pursued and drove him to Loudon, and captured fifty prisoners, among them two Yankee recruiting officers, and about seventy-five fine beef cattle.—*Richmond Whig, October* 10.

—A LARGE and enthusiastic meeting of mechanics was held in Richmond, Va., at which the following resolution, among others, was adopted:

Resolved, That, awakened to a sense of the abject posture to which labor and we who labor have been reduced, and to the privileges which as citizens and people the institutions of our country rest in us, we will not sleep again until our grasp has firmly clenched the rights and immunities which are ours as Americans and men, until our just demands have been met by the concessions of all opposing elements.

—THE National forces under General Burnside defeated the rebels at Blue Springs, Tenn.— (*Doc.* 192.)

October 11.—The English steamer Spaulding was captured by the steam transport Union whilst attempting to run the blockade of Charleston, S. C.—THE blockade-running steamer Douro was run ashore and afterward burned by the National gunboat Nansemond, under the command of Lieutenant Lamson.—A BATTLE occurred near Culpeper, Va., the rebels losing four hundred, and the Nationals one hundred and fifty in killed, wounded, and missing.—(Doc. 196.)

October 12.—Jefferson Davis, accompanied by General Bragg and staff, visited the battle-field of Chickamauga. He complimented the General in the highest terms, remarking that "his soldiers were entitled to the gratitude of the country for their heroism, and promising them that the green fields of Tennessee would shortly again be theirs."—THE Union cavalry, under Colonel Hatch, in pursuit of the rebels, who were retreating from the battle-field of Colliersville, overtook them at Ingham's Mills, a point on Coldwater River, three miles from Byhalia, Miss. The rebels were posted in a strong position, but were compelled to retreat after a fight of two hours, with a loss of over fifty in killed and wounded.

October 13.—A fight took place at Wyatts, a town on the Tallahatchie River, Miss., between a party of rebels retreating from Colliersville, Tenn., and the National cavalry under Colonel Hatch. The place had previously been fortified and was surrounded by a deep trench. By the aid of pontoon-bridges the rebels had succeeded in crossing their horses and stores, so that their whole force was rendered available for repelling the Union troops. They had upward of three thousand men, with nine pieces of artillery, and were sheltered by the log-houses of which the town was composed ; the Union force was less than two thousand five hundred, with eight pieces of artillery. The fight commenced at three o'clock in the afternoon, by the enemy attempting to force back the Union left. In this they failed. They next massed their forces to break the centre, but were driven back. Slowly Colonel Hatch advanced his line, driving the enemy back, step by step. Thus the afternoon wore away, till night, dark and rainy, closed the scene. The rebels, taking advantage of the darkness, succeeded in crossing by means of their bridges, though many of them were killed by the artillery. The Union loss in the engagement was less than forty in killed and wounded. It was impossible correctly to estimate the loss of the confederates, as they succeeded in carrying off

all, of their wounded and many of their dead. Fifteen dead rebels were found and buried. Colonel Hatch captured seventy-five prisoners, among whom was a rebel chief of artillery.

—A REBEL force, under the command of Colonel William L. Jackson, attacked the outpost of General B. F. Kelley's army, at Bulltown, Braxton County, Va., this morning, and after a severe fight were compelled to retreat with heavy loss. They were pursued by the Union cavalry. The Union force in the engagement consisted of detachments of the Sixth and Eleventh Virginia regiments, numbering about four hundred, commanded by Captain William H. Mattingly, of the former regiment. He was dangerously wounded. The other casualties were slight. The rebel loss was sixty wounded and nine killed.—*General Kelley's Despatch.*

—A FIGHT took place near Merrill's Crossing, Mo., between the Union troops under General Brown and the rebels under Shelby, in which the latter was defeated.—(Doc. 195.)

October 14.—Jefferson Davis, issued an address to the soldiers of the army of Tennessee, thanking them for the "glorious victory on the field of Chickamauga."—A FIGHT took place at Salt Lick, Va., between the rebels under Colonel William M. Jackson, who were retreating from the battle-field of Bulltown, and a party of Virginia cavalry under Major Howe and Captain Harrison, resulting in a complete rout of the rebels.—AN expedition to the interior of Mississippi left Vicksburgh, under the command of General McPherson.

—THE battle of Bristoe Station, Va., was fought this day.—(Doc. 188.)

October 15.—A fight took place at McLean's Ford, on Bull Run, Va., between the rebels and the New-Jersey brigade of the Third corps of the army of the Potomac, in which the former lost sixty in killed and wounded, and the latter two killed and twenty-five wounded.—*Philadelphia Inquirer, October* 22.

—CANTON, Miss., was captured by the Union forces under General McPherson, after a severe engagement, in which the rebels lost two hundred in killed, wounded, and prisoners.

—AT a special meeting of the Richmond, Va., City Council this evening, a report was adopted appointing a board, consisting of five members of the Council and three citizens, to purchase articles for sale at cost, under their direction, at depots to be established by them, one in each ward. The Council also made an appropriation of fifty thousand dollars for the relief of the poor, and authorized the Finance Committee to sell that amount of confederate State bonds in the city treasury.—THE British steamer Mail, having on board a large quantity of cotton and other merchandise, was captured by the United States steamer Honduras, in latitude 27° 57', longitude 83° 9'.—AN entire company of thirty-seven men and three officers, belonging to Gillmore's rebel battalion, was captured near Hedgesville, Va. Day before yesterday, Colonel L. D. Pierce, commanding the forces at Martinsburgh, was informed that Gillmore and his battalion were in the habit of holding frequent picnics through Back Creek Valley, principally for the object of plunder. He accordingly detailed a picket of six men, supplied them with a field-glass, and stationed them upon a prominent point of lookout in the mountains, there to watch, and advise him of any movement that this force might make in that direction. This morning one of the pickets came in and reported the enemy in sight, and a citizen immediately afterward reported a force, numbering from forty to sixty, concealed in the mountains, some two miles from Hedgesville—their intention being to remain there during the day, and burn Back Creek bridge, on the Baltimore and Ohio Railroad, to-night. Colonel Pierce at once despatched a detachment of forty men of the Twelfth Pennsylvania cavalry, under Captain George W. Henrie, on the Pughtown road, and another of fifty, of the First New-York, under Captain Richard Pendegrass, on the Hedgesville road; the one to flank them on the right, the other on the left. This they did, forming a junction, and very cunningly arranging their lines so as to form two sides of a triangle; while, in the mean time, a company of the One Hundred and Sixteenth Ohio infantry were sent out from North Mountain Station, with orders to attack the enemy directly in front and drive them into the trap so ingeniously laid by the cavalry. The whole scheme worked charmingly. Upon reaching the woods, the infantry deployed as skirmishers and advanced. They proceeded but a short distance before they came upon the enemy's camp, and, finding them all napping, with their horses tied to the trees, broke in upon their peaceful slumbers with a very unceremonious volley of musketry, that started a gymnasium among the "rebs," such as is rarely witnessed in ordinary country shows, the principal feat performed being one known among the chivalry as "right smart git." They scattered in all directions, leaving their horses behind them, and, in many cases, their hats and arms. The moment the infantry commenced firing, the cavalry closed in upon them, and the whole party permitted themselves to be captured, offering scarcely any resistance. Lieutenant Pierson, of the Twelfth Pennsylvania cavalry, captured nine, including one lieutenant, with no other assistance than that of his sabre.

The officers captured gave their names as Captain William Digges, First Lieutenant John Blackford, and Second Lieutenant Eugene Reed. The prisoners frankly admitted that it was a portion of their programme to burn Back Creek bridge, and do such other damage to the railroad as might come under the head of their mission. No casualties occurred on the Union side. The enemy reported from three to four killed and two wounded.—*Baltimore American.*

October 16.—General Bragg, in command of the rebel army of the Tennessee, issued the following General Orders from his headquarters at Missionary Ridge, Ga. :

"In order to augment the strength of the army, and to give to our brave soldiers an opportunity to visit home and provide for their families during the coming winter, the following rule is adopted :

"1. A furlough of not exceeding forty days will be granted to every non-commissioned officer and private who secures a recruit for his company.

"2. The recruit must be received and mustered into service, and be doing duty in the company before the application for furlough is forwarded.

"3. In all applications made in pursuance of section first, the commanding officer of the company will certify that the applicant has obtained an approved recruit who has been mustered into the service, and is present with the company, doing duty."

October 17.—This morning a squad of guerrillas made a descent on the Alexandria Railroad at Acotink, Va., and carried off fifteen men belonging to the One Hundred and Twentieth regiment of New-York, who were posted at that point.—A PARTY of the Thirteenth New-York cavalry, stationed at Stuart's, near Chantilly, Va., were surprised and surrounded by Mosby's guerrillas, and six were captured. — GENERAL BUFORD's division of cavalry crossed the Rapid Ann River at Germania Ford on Saturday evening, and, following the river to Hunter's Ford, surprised the enemy in their fortifications, and captured sixty of them. General Buford occupied these works till Sunday morning, when he received orders to return, and recrossed the Rapid Ann, followed by a large force of Stuart's cavalry and some mounted infantry, whom he gallantly fought, although greatly outnumbered, as he fell back through Stevensburgh to Brandy Station, where he joined Kilpatrick's forces. The whole cavalry command then slowly retired across the Rappahannock. This action was one of the most gallant and brilliant in the history of the Union cavalry.—THE rebel steamer Scottish Chief, and sloop Kate Dale, were destroyed in Hillsborough River, Fla., by the Union gunboats Tahoma and Adela.—(*Doc.* 200.)

October 18.—This morning, General Imboden, with a portion of his rebel forces, having surrounded Charlestown, Va., garrisoned by the Ninth regiment of Maryland loyal volunteers, under Colonel Simpson, demanded its surrender. The demand was refused, and soon after another was sent in, informing the Colonel that time would be given to remove the women and children. The rebels then commenced the attack, throwing shells into the town, killing one man and severely wounding the adjutant of the regiment. In a short time the Nationals surrendered and the town was occupied by Imboden's forces. As soon as information of the capture reached General Sullivan, in command at Harper's Ferry, he despatched a force under Colonel G. D. Wells, of the Thirty-fourth Massachusetts, who succeeded in routing and driving the rebels from the town, with a loss of thirty killed and wounded, and twenty-one prisoners. The Union loss was ten killed, three wounded, and three hundred and seventy-nine captured.—(*Doc.* 188.)

—THIRTEEN officers belonging to General Sedgwick's corps were captured in detail this afternoon, while strolling in the woods near headquarters, by rebels concealed in the undergrowth.—JEFFERSON DAVIS arrived at Selma, Ala., this evening, and was welcomed by the citizens *en masse.* "An immense crowd gathered in front of the hotel. The President congratulated the people on meeting them under such favorable circumstances, and spoke in glowing terms of the gallantry of Alabamians on every battle-field. He

said if the non-conscripts of Alabama would gather their guns and go to the rescue, by guarding Courtland and other points, thereby relieving regular soldiers, who are now from necessity discharging that sort of duty, such blows would be dealt the enemy as he would find it difficult to recover from. In this way most effective aid could be given the gallant men and officers who are carrying out the plans of the noble Longstreet under the supervision of the heroic Bragg. In this way the President was confident that Rosecrans could be crushed to dust. It was only by force of arms that the Yankees could be brought to reason and their plans for our subjugation defeated. Self-reliance and energy was now our duty. We should not look to Europe for aid, for such is not to be expected now. Our only alternative was to sustain ourselves with renewed energy and determination, and a little more sacrifice upon the part of the people, and the President firmly believed that next spring would see the invader driven from our borders. Then farmers, who are now refugees, could return to their families and pursue their business undisturbed as heretofore. In fact, he believed that the defeat of Rosecrans would practically end the war."—*Mobile Register, October* 19.

October 19.—The grand-jury of Twiggs County, Georgia, Supreme Court, requested the Court to order a record, called the "Black Roll," in which the names of all who refuse to take confederate bills, bonds or notes in payment for any debt shall be recorded on this recommendation, and that of each succeeding grand-jury, that the names of such malcontents may be officially handed down to posterity, and their ultimate reward insured.—MAJOR-GENERAL W. S. ROSECRANS relinquished the command of the Department of the Cumberland, and issued a farewell address to his "brothers in arms." General George H. Thomas succeeded to the command.—THE result of the draft made in July, was made known by Provost-Marshal Fry.

October 20.—Colonel Spencer's expedition into Alabama, which left Corinth, Miss., yesterday, returned to-day on account of high water from heavy rains in the mountains. It penetrated to within fifteen miles of Jasper, over one hundred and fifty from Corinth. The whole cavalry force of Tuscumbia Valley was concentrating to cut him off. While endeavoring to press his command, which was about five hundred strong, between them, Colonel Spencer encountered a force of from one thousand to one thousand three hundred, under General Ferguson, in the south-east corner of Tishomingo County, Mississippi, and was quite roughly handled. Colonel Spencer formed a square of three lines of battle. As one position after another was outflanked, and the regiment becoming disordered and surrounded, he led it into the woods, where the rebels were held in check until night, when it broke up into squads, the men being all intimately acquainted with the country, and coming out the best way they could.

Captains Chanler, Pulo, and Stemberg, of Joliet, Ill., were killed; also, Lieutenant Perry, of company I, First Alabama cavalry. Lieutenant Swift, of Ottawa, was mortally wounded, and about ten privates were killed.

The rebel loss was more severe, as they rushed in large numbers upon the Nationals, who were under cover.

—THE Union forces under Colonel Wolford, were captured at Philadelphia, Tenn.—(Doc. 203.)

October 21.—This morning the United States steamer Nansemond, Lieutenant R. H. Lamson, commanding, captured and destroyed the rebel steamer Venus, from Nassau to Wilmington, with a cargo of lead, drugs, clothing, coffee, and bacon for the rebels. The Venus was one of the very finest and fastest steamers engaged in running the blockade. She was two hundred and seventy feet long, one thousand tons burthen, and had the finest engines of any steamer in this trade, and could run sixteen knots per hour. The Nansemond fired one shell through her foremast, another burst in the centre, a third passed through forward, killing one man, (this is the first man killed running the blockade,) and a fourth struck under the guard, near the water-line, knocking in an iron plate, which forced her to run ashore to keep from sinking. She was boarded so quickly that her captain, officers, and most of her crew were captured. As she could not be got off, she was entirely destroyed, under a heavy fire from the rebel batteries ashore.—(Doc. 204.)

—WARRENTON, Va., was entered and occupied by the National cavalry.—AN engagement took place at Cherokee Station, Alabama, between the National forces under General Osterhaus, who was moving eastward from Corinth, and the rebels under Generals S. D. Lee, Roddy, and Richardson, numbering over four thousand. The

fight lasted an hour, when the rebels were driven back with severe loss.—(Doc. 205.)

—OPELOUSAS, La., was entered by General Franklin's column of General Banks's army at noon to-day. The rebels made a stand at a point about five miles in front of the town, with a body of troops composed of infantry, cavalry, and artillery, but they were quickly driven from the field. At Vermillion Bayou, where the rebels held a strong position, an engagement might have been expected; but the threats made on their rear by General Dana's forces compelled the rebel commander to divide his troops, and so weakened the force on the bayou, that it was easily turned.

October 22. — Colonel Gregg, commanding the Second brigade of Gregg's division, sent out the Second Pennsylvania cavalry, under Lieutenant-Colonel Brinton, from the vicinity of Fayetteville, Va., to establish the picket-line from Freeman's to Kelly's Ford, the former some miles above and the latter some miles below Rappahannock Station. At Liberty (a few miles from Bealton, on the road between that place and Sulphur Springs) they met the enemy's pickets, and the First Maine cavalry being sent to their support, drove them in and followed them up rapidly along the road leading to the different fords. The party which took the direction of Rappahannock Crossing turned and made a stand when approaching their infantry supports, and for some time the fighting was quite brisk. In this encounter the Second regiment lost six men wounded, among them Major Taggart, who was struck while gallantly leading a charge on the enemy's line.

October 23.—A supply train which left Nashville, Tenn., this morning, under a guard of thirty men belonging to the Seventieth Indiana regiment, commanded by Lieutenant Campbell, was thrown from the track, at a point five miles below Tullahoma, the rails having been removed by a band of rebels. The members of the train had but a moment's time to reflect upon the state of things, when the rebels charged upon them with a terrific fire. The assault was bravely met by the guard, and the assailants were compelled to retire in confusion after an engagement of fifteen minutes.—DR. D. W. WRIGHT, of Norfolk, Va., was executed this morning for the murder of Lieutenant Sanborn.

October 24.—An order from the rebel War Department at Richmond went into effect, subjecting to conscription and enrolment all clerks who entered upon clerkships at the several departments, after October 1862.—ADAIR, Ky., was visited by a band of guerrillas under the chief Dillsbury, who, after plundering the inhabitants, returned into Tennessee.

October 25.—Colliersville, Tenn., was again attacked by the rebels, who were repulsed and driven off.—ONE hundred and fifty armed guerrillas crossed White River, Ark., going north to operate against steamers at Council Bend.—THE battle of Pine Bluff, Ark., was fought this day. —(*Doc.* 207.)

October 26.—Heavy skirmishing took place near Bealton, Va.—COLONEL GEORGE E. SPENCER, commanding five hundred men of the First regiment of Alabama (native) cavalry, on an expedition through Northern Alabama and Mississippi, was attacked and defeated by the rebel forces, "in the extreme south-east corner of Tishomingo County, Miss."—A FIGHT occurred at Tuscumbia, Ala.—(*Doc.* 209.)

October 27.—A detachment of National troops, under the command of General William F. Smith, surprised and routed a large body of rebels at Brown's Ferry, opening communication with Bridgeport.—(*Docs.* 96, 210, *and* 211.)

—AT Charleston, S. C., four monitors opened fire upon Fort Sumter, at a distance of one mile, and continued the bombardment until late in the afternoon. At eleven o'clock in the morning solid shot were thrown into the city of Charleston, one of which struck the building occupied by the Union Bank.

October 28.—Major-General Benjamin F. Butler, by direction of the President of the United States, was appointed to the command of the Eighteenth army corps, and of the Department of Virginia and North-Carolina.—A HEAVY fire was kept up on the sea face of Fort Sumter during the whole of last night, by the monitors and two guns at battery Gregg, and this morning the bombardment of the rebel works was renewed with great vigor.—CORRESPONDENCE in relation to the depredation of rebel privateers upon the commerce of the United States, passed between the merchants of New-York and Secretary Welles of the National Navy Department.—THE battle of Lookout Mountain took place this day.—(*Doc.* 211.)

October 29.—Major-General George H. Thomas sent the following dispatch to the headquarters of the United States army, from his camp at Chattanooga, Tenn.:

"In the fight last night the enemy attacked General Geary's division, posted at Wauhatchie, on three different sides, and broke into his camp at one point, but was driven back in most gallant style by a part of his force, the remainder being held in reserve. General Howard, whilst marching to Geary's relief, was attacked in flank. The enemy occupying in force two commanding hills on the left of the road, he immediately threw forward two of his regiments and took both of them at the point of the bayonet, driving the enemy from his breastworks and across Lookout Creek. In this brilliant success over their old adversary, the conduct of the officers and men of the Eleventh and Twelfth corps is entitled to the highest praise."—(*Doc.* 211.)

—THE flag of truce boat arrived at Annapolis, Md., from City Point, Va., with one hundred and eighty-one paroled men, eight having died on the passage from actual starvation. A correspondent says:

"Never, in the whole course of my life, have.I ever seen such a scene as these men presented; *they were living skeletons;* every man of them had to be sent to the hospitals, and the surgeon's opinion is, that more than one third of them must die, being beyond the reach of nourishment or medicine.

"I questioned several of them, and all state that their condition has been brought on by the treatment they have received at the hands of the rebels. They have been kept without food, and exposed a large portion of the time without shelter of any kind. To look at these men, and hear their tales of woe and how they have been treated, one would not suppose they had fallen into the hands of the Southern chivalry, but rather into the hands of savage barbarians, destitute of all humanity or feeling. If human means cannot be brought to punish such treatment to prisoners, God, in his justice, will launch his judgments upon the heads of any people who will so far forget the treatment due to humanity.

"It seems to be the policy of the South to keep the Union prisoners until they are so far worn out as ever to be unfit for service again, and then send them off to die; while the men captured by the Nationals are returned to them

well clothed and well fed, ready to go into the field the moment they arrive within their lines."

—JEFFERSON DAVIS sent the following letter to Lieutenant-General Polk, who had been relieved of his command, upon a charge of mismanagement at the battle of Chickamauga:

"After an examination into the causes and circumstances attending your being relieved from command with the army commanded by General Bragg, I have arrived at the conclusion that there is nothing to justify a court-martial or court of inquiry, and I therefore dismiss the application.

"Your appointment to a new field of duty, alike important and difficult, is the best evidence of my appreciation of your past services and expectation of your future career."

October 30.—Unconditional Unionists, representing twenty counties of Western Arkansas, held a convention at Fort Smith, at which patriotic speeches were made, resolutions adopted, and Colonel ——— Johnson of the First Arkansas infantry, nominated to represent that district in the Congress of the United States.—THE National forces which occupied Loudon, Tenn., retired to the north bank of the river, and established themselves upon the heights commanding the town.

—THE *Richmond Whig* of this date contained the following:

"Beef ought to be selling now at sixty-five to seventy cents a pound, in accordance with the proposed arrangements between the butchers and the government. It is quoted in yesterday morning's report of the markets at a dollar to a dollar and a half a pound. The butchers say they are unable to get cattle, and may be compelled to close their stalls for want of meat to sell."

October 31.—A. W. Bradford, Governor of Maryland, addressed a letter to President Lincoln, upon the subject of military interference in the election in his State.—THE Texas expedition, under the command of General Banks, landed at Brazos.

DOCUMENTS AND NARRATIVES.

EXPEDITION UP THE COMBAHEE.

COLONEL MONTGOMERY'S OFFICIAL REPORT.

BY TELEGRAPH FROM BEAUFORT, S. C., }
Dated June 3, 1863. }

To Major-General D. Hunter, Commanding Tenth Army Corps, Department of the South:

GENERAL: I have the honor to report that, in obedience to your orders, I proceeded up the Combahee River, on the steamers John Adams and Harriet A. Weed, with a detachment of three hundred (300) men of the Second South-Carolina volunteer regiment, and a section of the Third Rhode Island battery, commanded by Captain Brayton. We ascended the river some twenty-five (25) miles, destroyed a ponton bridge, together with a vast amount of cotton, rice, and other property, and brought away seven hundred and twenty-seven slaves, and some fine horses. We had some sharp skirmishes, in all of which, the men behaved splendidly. I hope to report more fully in a day or two.

I have the honor to be, General,
Your most obedient servant,
JAMES MONTGOMERY,
Colonel Commanding S. C. V.

A NATIONAL ACCOUNT.

PORT ROYAL, S. C., June 6, 1863.

We have at last received accurate intelligence of Col. Montgomery's expedition, which was most brilliant in its success. It was composed of five companies of the Second South-Carolina volunteers, (colored troops,) and a section of battery C, Third Rhode Island artillery, Captain Brayton, all under command of Colonel Montgomery, and left Beaufort on transports about nine o'clock last Monday evening, *en route* for Combahee River. It had proceeded as far as St. Helena Sound, when one of the transports having run aground, quite a delay was occasioned in transferring the troops from her to the other transports. This having been successfully accomplished, the expedition pushed rapidly on to its destination, and arrived at the mouth of the Combahee at half-past two o'clock A.M.

The enemy were entirely unconscious of the approaching danger, and Colonel Montgomery, without being discovered, ascended the river and landed a portion of his troops, under command of Captain Thompson, at Field's Point, which is

twenty-five miles up the river. A rebel picket was stationed here, but they fled without firing a gun, and Captain Thompson's company occupied the deserted breastworks which were found at this point, while the rest of the expedition proceeded up the river to Tar Bluff, two miles above Field's Point. Here another company was landed, Captain Carver's, who occupied the deserted rifle-pits of the enemy. The remaining two steamers moved on, and having arrived at Nichols's plantation, two miles above, the Weed was left behind, and the John Adams pushed on to the Combahee Ferry.

Across this ferry was a very fine ponton bridge, which had been built for the benefit of the rebels, and as the Adams came in sight of it a rebel cavalry company was seen galloping over it with great haste. The temptation could not be resisted, and so the artillery on the Adams threw a few shells at them, by way of warning to hurry over. The cavalry succeeded, however, in crossing safely, and the Adams having reached the bridge, it was taken up and destroyed, and formed the first prize of the expedition. Want of transportation was the reason for its not being brought away. After this exploit, the Adams attempted to proceed further up the river, but was prevented by the obstructions which had been placed in the channel by the rebels.

Colonel Montgomery, while the ponton bridge was being destroyed, sent Captain Hoyt's company up the right bank of the river, for the purpose of destroying property and confiscating negroes. This little expedition covered itself with glory. Having reached Green Pond, they found the rebel Colonel Heyward's splendid plantation, with its large and elegantly furnished mansion house. Colonel Heyward avoided capture, making his escape, not, however, being able to carry any thing with him. Even his sabre and horses were confiscated, so great had been his haste to leave. Our troops then proceeded to destroy the growing crops, burn the rice-mills, storehouses, and cotton warehouses, which were all large and well filled. Many thousand dollars' worth of crops was thus given to the flames, and, to crown all, the mansion house, with all its out-buildings, was burned to the ground. Having accomplished thus much, our soldiers started back for the expedition.

As Captain Hoyt's company was returning, rebel cavalry and sharp-shooters appeared and pressed hard upon our men. Captain Hoyt, how ever, nothing daunted, drew up his company across the road, and making a bold stand, defied the approaching force, which, though not large, was quite respectable in numbers. The enemy pressed forward, confident of making our colored troops run by such a display of chivalry; but they were disappointed, as the negroes behaved well and kept up a sharp and effective fire for over half an hour, until the John Adams came to the rescue; and dispersed the rebels with a few well-directed shells. During this skirmish one of Colonel Heyward's horses was shot, and our men left his carcass upon the field to solace the enemy. The other horse was brought away in safety. They were both valuable animals, as was seen from the bill of sale found by our troops in the Colonel's house. The horses had been imported, and cost one thousand dollars. Captain Hoyt's company all returned to the John Adams in safety.

At the same time that Captain Hoyt started up the right bank, Captain Brayton, with his battery section, proceeded up the left bank of the river, and was equally successful. The rebel pickets did not fall back upon a large force of the rebels stationed on the Ashapoo River, but hurried around in hot haste to the different plantations, notifying owners and overseers of the coming of negro troops. Captain Brayton destroyed every building within reach, and cotton and rice crops gathered and growing, mills, storehouses, and residences, were burned to the ground. He also captured a large number of horses, mules, and cattle, but owing to our lack of transportation, they were left behind. It is a matter of regret that this question of transportation had not received more attention before the expedition started, as by this means we should have brought away much valuable property.

The shores were lined with slaves of all sizes, ages, and descriptions, who rushed down to the banks, hailing our troops with delight, and praying to be taken on board. The transports, however, could only accommodate about seven hundred of them, not near the number that sought deliverance, or stood upon the banks cheering the Stars and Stripes. This was the saddest sight of the whole expedition—so many souls within sight of freedom, and yet unable to attain it. But the transports were filled to their utmost capacity; they looked more like slavers than the harbingers of liberty; and as they turned away from the river-banks, and started homeward bound, moist eyes were on those decks, for they saw in the distance those whom a cruel fate had left behind. The song of liberty floated upon the river, but the wail of despair went up from the dismal shore.

During the absence of the main part of the expedition, under Colonel Montgomery, the rebels attacked both Captains Carver's and Thompson's companies, stationed at the above-named points. Our forces, however, held the enemy in check, though outnumbered and subjected, as Captain Carver was, to the fire of a rebel field-piece, when his own ammunition was nearly exhausted. Our men, however, boldly stood their ground, and

awaited the arrival of the John Adams, which, coming up in the nick of time, dispersed the enemy with a brisk shelling. None of our men were injured.

The expedition returned to Beaufort, and received a grand reception. The captured slaves, as they marched through the streets, attracted much attention, and were overwhelmed with the congratulations of their brethren who have been enjoying liberty for some time. They were quartered in one of the Beaufort churches, but will soon be provided with quarters. The males will be put into the Second South-Carolina regiment, and are numerous enough to make two large companies.

This expedition reflects great credit upon Col. Montgomery and the men of his command. He has destroyed property of the enemy estimated at a million of dollars, proved himself a capable commander, and that the negro troops can be made efficient soldiers. He has also provided his regiment with two additional companies, deprived the rebels of seven hundred and twenty-seven negroes, and accomplished the most successful raid in this department.

—Philadelphia Inquirer.

Doc. 2.

GENERAL BURNSIDE'S ORDER.

HEADQUARTERS DEPARTMENT OF OHIO,
CINCINNATI, OHIO, June 3, 1863.

GENERAL ORDER No. 90.

THE General Commanding directs that General N. C. McLean, Provost-Marshal General, at once institute an investigation into the cases of all citizen prisoners now confined in this department, and in all such cases as do not clearly show premeditated disloyalty on the part of the accused, or when a desire is manifested to atone for past faults by future good conduct, the prisoners will be released on taking the oath of allegiance and giving bonds for a strict observance thereof. The General Commanding is convinced that a large majority of the men arrested have been misled by dishonest and designing politicians, and he prefers to strike at the sources of the evil, and allow those who have been led astray to return to their loyalty and allegiance, if they have seen the folly and sin of opposing the Government.

The United States, in striving to put down a rebellion unparalleled in history, requires that every man, at home or in the field, shall each in his sphere be enlisted in the cause. The necessity demands a sacrifice from all. In responding to this call, the devotion of the citizen soldier stands foremost, and his sacrifice is the greatest. He gives up all that is dear to the citizen—his home, his freedom of speech and action, the prospect of gain, and often gives his life. He exacts no conditions, but surrenders himself wholly to his country, as represented by the constituted authorities placed over him.

But while he thus yields up his civic rights so entirely to his country, he is none the less a citizen; he waives them temporarily to give greater efficiency to his efforts, and looks forward to the time when, the authority of the Government restored, he shall again exercise the rights he has patriotically laid down.

While the duties of a citizen are of a more peaceful and less exacting character, he is none the less a soldier, and it becomes him to appreciate the grandeur and entireness of the devotion of his brethren in the field, and to remember that he too has sacrifices to make; but the country's demand upon him is comparatively but small. The country requires from him no physical sacrifice, no personal hardships; it merely asks that he shall imitate the loyal example of the soldiers in the field, so far as to abate somewhat of that freedom of speech which they give up so entirely. The citizen would be unjust to the soldier, as well as unfaithful to his country, if, while enjoying the comforts of home, he were unwilling to give up a portion of a privilege which the soldier resigns altogether. That freedom of discussion and criticism which is proper in the politician and the journalist in time of peace, becomes rank treason when it tends to weaken the confidence of the soldier in his officers and his Government. When this insidious treason, striking at the very root of that military power which is for the time being the country's protection, makes its appearance, it is the bounden duty of the Commanding General to expel it from his lines, with a heavier hand than he would drive from his camp the villain who would scatter a material poison that would enervate and decimate his soldiers.

The General Commanding desires to again call the attention of all officers, Provost-Marshals, and others in authority to the necessity of great care in the making of arrests, which should in all instances be founded on full affidavits sustaining distinct charges, except when the exigencies of the case demand instant action. Carelessness in this respect is only less censurable than negligence in the detection and punishment of crime.

With the exercise of scrupulous care and sound discretion on the part of officers, and a candid consideration on the part of all citizens of the relations of the people and the army to each other as above set forth, the General Commanding is full of hope that mutual coöperation in putting down the rebellion will become more hearty and effective. The necessity for arrests will be diminished, and the tendency to factious opposition to the Government, and hurtful criticisms of its measures be removed.

By command of
Major-General A. E. BURNSIDE.
LEWIS RICHMOND,
Assistant Adjutant-General.
Official: W. P. ANDERSON,
Assistant Adjutant General.

Doc. 3.

COLONEL KILPATRICK'S EXPEDITION.

WASHINGTON, Thursday, June 4, 1863.

THE cavalry raid of General Stoneman's command was concluded yesterday by Colonel Kilpatrick's brigade in one of the most brilliant acts of the war. He left Gloucester Point on Saturday last, and passing in a north-easterly direction through Gloucester County, crossed the Dragon River at Saluta, and thence through Middlesex County to Urbanna, on the Rappahannock; crossing that river to Union Point, Colonel Kilpatrick proceeded through Westmoreland and King George counties to near the headquarters of General Hooker without losing a single man of his command. The rebels had divined that this force was to attempt to rejoin the command of General Stoneman, and therefore took special pains to capture it. The command was composed of about nine hundred men in all, the Second New-York (Harris Light cavalry) and the Twelfth Indiana cavalry. No difficulty whatever was encountered in Gloucester County, but upon reaching Dragon River it was found the rebels had destroyed all the bridges, and a superior force of cavalry, under General Stuart, had assembled at a higher point up the river, with the intention, no doubt, of forcing the command to cross the Rappahannock at Leeds, a narrow place, where the enemy themselves have been in the habit of fording without opposition whenever occasion required; but Colonel Kilpatrick was prepared for just such an emergency, and his pioneers without any unnecessary delay constructed a bridge, over which the Dragon River was crossed without difficulty. The bridge was then destroyed. Here, to foil the enemy, the command moved forward in several columns. The principal one on the right, under Colonel Hasbrouck Davis, took a southerly direction, and went to Pine Tree, in the lower part of Middlesex County. The people of this hitherto unrivalled region were completely taken by surprise; they did not deem it possible that the much hated Yankees would dare visit that spot; in fact, it was a place so secluded that some of the large planters near Richmond had sent their negroes here for safety. The house of Colonel Jones, who commands and controls all the bushwhackers in that section of the State, was approached so suddenly that the redoubtable Colonel was himself captured, and last night slept on one of the boats of the Potomac flotilla at Acquia Creek. He will probably extend his visit to the National capital to-day. No opposition whatever was met with in this direction, and but few armed men were seen, and these were bushwhackers, armed principally with double-barrelled shot-guns. They fled precipitately, however, at sight of the blue coats, and as the country thereabouts is covered with a thick growth of pines, they succeeded generally in making good their escape. On the road the carrier of a rebel mail was overtaken. An inspection of the mail matter was forthwith instituted. The letters for the most part were of a private nature, and some of them were addressed to persons residing within the loyal States. Their cases will doubtless be attended to by the proper authorities in due season. One letter, however, attracted particular attention. It was signed by the veritable General Stuart, and was addressed to Colonel Jones, who a few hours before had been taken prisoner, in response to an appeal of the inhabitants to be protected from the very cavalry force then in their midst. General Stuart in the letter promised the protection called for, and stated that he would be there on Sunday, the day the mail was captured. He was not there, however—at all events was not seen in that vicinity by our troops. He had laid a trap, as stated above, into which he expected the Yankee Colonel would fall without hesitation, but in this he was fortunately mistaken. This portion of the command reached Urbanna Sunday evening, having captured a large number of horses and mules, and being followed by a motley group of contrabands of all ages and both sexes. Among the captures by this portion of the command was a confederate agent, with thirteen thousand dollars in Georgia and Missouri money.

The left wing of the command went in a north-easterly direction, and reached the road north of Urbanna Sunday evening. Here the picket of the enemy, which was to annihilate the whole force, was encountered. A detachment charged and drove this force in a north-westerly direction across the Dragon River, at Church's Mill—the only bridge they had not destroyed. They here fell back upon their reserves, strongly intrenched. The pursuing party, having accomplished the object of their mission, set fire to the bridge and slowly retired. They were not pursued. Monday morning the whole command was in front of Urbanna, ready to cross the river. To protect this part of the movement, Lieutenant Commander McGaw, of the Potomac flotilla, was present. He left Acquia Creek on Saturday evening with the following named vessels, and was at the rendez-vous the very moment when ordered: Tallaca, (ferry-boat,) Star, William W. Frazer, Long Branch, (light-draught steamboats to transport the troops across the river,) and the gunboats Yankee, Freeborn, Anacosta, Currituck, Primrose, Ella, and Satellite. Capt. Moffet, of the Ninety-fourth New-York volunteers, with one hundred picked men, was also taken down, and Captain J. C. Paine, chief signal officer stationed at Acquia Creek. The gunboats were immediately put in readiness for action. Captain Moffet's command was landed at Urbanna, and were at once deployed outside of the town as skirmishers. Captain Paine secured an eligible position just north of the town, the direction from which an attack was anticipated. A detachment of the Fifty-second New-York volunteers (engineers) speedily constructed a bridge across the mouth of Urbanna creek, and repaired a wharf on the opposite side of the Rappahannock, so that the boats could receive the troops on one side and land them on the other without difficulty. These arrangements perfected, the crossing was commenced at nine o'clock Monday morning, but it was not until Tuesday morning that the whole of Col. Kilpatrick's command was landed on the opposite shore, a distance of six miles from the point of embarkation. Col. Kilpatrick immediately moved forward, and was met by a cavalry force which had been sent down from headquarters to welcome him and afford any assistance that might be necessary. Difficulty was anticipated at Reed's Ford, but the rebels doubtless repented of their threat to annihilate the command, and therefore did not attempt to interfere further.

Colonel Kilpatrick has thus made the complete circuit of the most formidable army the rebels have in the field, destroying millions of dollars' worth of property in the shape of railroads and material; captured hundreds of horses and mules; brought away at least one thousand of the producing class of the South, and by his visit so demoralized those who remain behind, that even the rebels will not hereafter be willing to say that property mounted on two legs is the most desirable to be had. More than this, he has visited some benighted regions of the Confederacy, where the people believed that the Yankees were any thing but civilized beings.

Among other articles captured was the flag of the Twelfth Virginia regiment.

While the wants of the soldiers were supplied on the road, the strictest orders were given to protect the rights of those not in arms against the Government. Horses and mules, and whatever the soldiers and horses required to eat, were taken, but in all other respects the citizens have no cause to complain. Indeed the citizens at several points, and especially in the largest village, Urbanna, expressed their gratification at the good conduct of the soldiers generally.

The country was almost entirely deserted of able-bodied men, and only the old and decrepid of the male sex were to be seen. These, as well as the women, believing the exaggerated reports of their own soldiery, believed that the Yankee troops never showed any mercy to any one in rebeldom, and therefore were filled with apprehension upon our approach, expecting as they did to be murdered. One family, consisting of a widow woman and three daughters, all highly cultivated, concealed themselves in the woods, and when found by an officer, it was with difficulty he could induce them to return to their house. They fully expected to be murdered, but afterward expressed much satisfaction at the conduct of the Union troops.

On Monday night one of our advanced pickets from Urbanna saw in the dim distance a force of some kind approaching. The picket made the usual challenge, but there was no response, and he fired. The object fired at continuing to advance, the picket fell back upon the reserve. On came the mysterious foe, and preparations were being made by the reserve for a severe contest, when one man with stronger eyesight than the rest saw that the approaching force was composed of negroes. Sure enough, it proved that thirty or forty negroes were coming up in one gang. When asked why they did not halt after being fired upon, the leader said they thought the safest way was to rush in and give themselves up; they believed this to be the way soldiers surrendered in battle.

The immediate benefit of this raid, aside from

the good effect upon our own men, is the capture of two hundred horses and mules, forty wagons loaded with provisions, one thousand contrabands, and the demoralization of the blacks in three or four counties—two of which have never been penetrated before by our troops—and undeceiving the inhabitants as to the real character of the Union soldiers.

To all appearances the residents of the counties passed through are better supplied with the necessaries of life than in any other portion of the State yet visited; economy in the consumption of food, however, is everywhere exercised, to enable each land proprietor to supply the army agents with large quantities of food. To this end, by a special order from Jeff Davis, the negro's ration has been reduced one third, so that a field-hand barely receives enough to sustain him. Regular rations, in fact, are no longer furnished the slaves. Twice a day a small piece of corn bread and meat is dealt out to them, and at night a piece of corn bread alone.

That a force not exceeding nine hundred men could have passed from Gloucester Point across two rivers not fordable, in the presence, in fact, of much superior force, without having a man killed, is one of the remarkable events of this war.

Doc. 4.

FIGHT AT FRANKLIN, TENN.

FRANKLIN, TENN., June 7, 1863.

EARLY on Thursday morning, June fourth, the enemy left his cantonments at Spring Hill, and advanced upon this post, anticipating an easy victory. Our force consisted of one regiment of cavalry (Seventh Kentucky) and about a regiment of infantry, under the command of Colonel Baird, of the Eighty-first Illinois, who was commandant of the post. The force of the enemy consisted of the brigades of Armstrong and Jackson, and the cavalry division of the late Van Dorn, now commanded by Starnes, the whole under the control of Forrest. About two o'clock P.M. his advance-guards commenced skirmishing with our cavalry pickets, and immediately afterwards heavy columns made their appearance upon the Lewisburgh, Columbia, and Carter's Creek roads. Such being the superiority of the enemy in point of numbers, our cavalry videttes retired slowly, hotly contesting every inch of ground, and expecting to be supported by the infantry reserves. The latter, however, seeing the futility of making a stand against so overwhelming a force of mounted troops, retired to the fortifications on the north bank of the river, leaving the handful of cavalry (about sixty in number) to come out of a tight fix in the best manner they could.

About this time, probably a half-hour after the first gun was fired, Colonel Faulkner was ordered to move his regiment, the Seventh Kentucky cavalry, over the river, and keep the enemy from obtaining possession of the town. The boys went in with a yell, and the battalions,

severally commanded by Lieutenant-Colonel Vimont, and Majors Bradley and Collier, succeeded in repulsing the enemy at every point, and for some three hours held the town against every odds brought to bear against it. After the enemy commenced sweeping the streets of the town with round shot and grape, the Seventh only retired to the north of Harpeth, after being repeatedly ordered to do so by the post commandant. Some of the most brilliant cavalry exploits it has ever been my lot to witness were performed by these gallant Kentuckians during this unequal contest. Infantry officers who carefully watched every movement from the fort with glasses, describe the conduct of the Seventh Kentucky as deserving of all praise.

When it became apparent that the enemy was massing his forces to make an irresistible dash upon Colonel Faulkner and his gallant command, he was ordered to retire to the north side of the river. He drew off his men in admirable order, while the enormous shells from the heavy siege-gun of the fort held the mass of the enemy in check, and scattered a portion of his forces in every direction. As the evening wore apace, it became evident that the enemy had crossed the river east of town, and was moving in a northerly direction for the purpose of attacking our left. Lieutenant Gruelle, of the Seventh, was dispatched with a small reconnoitring force to ascertain his numbers and position. He discovered a column of about one thousand five hundred (Second Kentucky and First Tennessee) taking position in the dense woods upon the old Murfreesboro road, which force was being constantly augmented by the arrival of fresh detachments. Having reported the state of affairs in that direction, Major Collier was ordered to take a force to the support of Gruelle, and hold the chain of hills on the left of camp at all hazards until nightfall. Shortly after Collier had taken his position, heavy volleys were heard immediately in front, and riderless horses and panic-stricken rebels emerged from the woods and made for the river in hot haste. They had been surprised and attacked on their flank and rear by the Fourth Kentucky, (Colonel Cooper,) Sixth Kentucky, (Colonel Watkins,) Ninth Pennsylvania, (Colonel Jordan,) and Second Michigan, (Colonel Campbell.) The hottest and heaviest work fell to the the lot of the Fourth Kentucky, whose gallant and intrepid leader, Colonel Wickliffe Cooper, was disabled by his horse falling while he was heading a charge. The animal was going at full speed, and fell upon the Colonel's right leg, terribly bruising and otherwise injuring that member. All these regiments performed their duty as soldiers should. Everywhere the enemy was broken and disorganized by their impetuous charges. When the shades of night fell upon the hard-fought field, the enemy had been driven to his original position among the hills south of town.

Next morning, Friday, Brownlow's East-Tennessee regiment was ordered to cross the river and feel the enemy's position, which had evidently been shifted during the course of the night. He was accompanied by Colonel Faulkner, of the Seventh Kentucky. About two miles from town, on the Columbia pike, the enemy was discovered drawn up in line of battle, a force of four or five hundred occupying a commanding eminence, protected at all points by heavy stone fencing. Colonel Faulkner obtained permission to take two companies of the Fourth Kentucky cavalry, under command of Major Welling, and charge the height. The boys responded gallantly to his call, and never was a hill quicker or more cleanly swept. It was decidedly the prettiest cavalry dash of the war. It was here that Colonel Faulkner received his severe and painful wound. Our pardonable exultation at an unmistakable victory over an enemy of eight or ten times our strength was considerably dampened by this casualty. Two of our most dashing leaders (Cooper and Faulkner) were placed *hors du combat*, and our entire little army joined in heartily in the grief of their commands. As the news spread from mouth to mouth that Faulkner was killed, (such being at first the erroneous report,) it seemed as though the hearer felt as if his own brother had been stricken down in battle. Tears sprang to eyes unused to weeping, and cheeks that all the dangers of battle could not pale, "grew as white as my lady's hand." I am glad that his wound, at first believed to be mortal, turns out not to be so serious as we supposed. He and Colonel Cooper are both at Nashville, and, when heard from this morning, were improving fast.

The enemy has about disappeared from our front. He burned the railroad bridge near Brentwood this morning. Our loss in the battles, in killed, wounded, and missing, will not exceed twenty-five. The enemy's loss is not far off one hundred and fifty. General Armstrong was severely wounded, some prisoners say killed, and Starnes is among their missing. A flag of truce approached our outposts this morning to inquire if he had fallen into our hands.　KENTUCKY.

ANOTHER NARRATIVE.

CAMP NINTH PENNSYLVANIA CAVALRY, }
TRIUNE, June 7, 1863. }

Major-General Gordon Granger having been ordered by General Rosecrans to move the main portion of the right wing of the army of the Cumberland from Franklin to Triune, we marched there on June third, leaving a small force at Franklin under Colonel Baird, of the Eighty-fifth Indiana, to hold the fortifications. The rebel forces in front, at Spring hill, having been foiled in their two attacks under Van Dorn, thinking that "now or never" was their time to capture it, made a desperate dash, with some five or six thousand cavalry and some artillery under General Forrest, on Thursday, the fourth instant. We heard the cannonading of the rebels and the replies of the heavy fortification guns at Triune at three P.M. Signals having been passed here at half-past three, General Granger ordered Colonel A. P. Campbell, of the Second Michigan, command-

ing the First cavalry brigade, to hasten with his troops to the relief of Franklin. He galloped out at four o'clock with his cavalry in the following order: Sixth Kentucky cavalry, Colonel Watkins commanding; Fourth Kentucky cavalry, Colonel Cooper commanding; Second Michigan cavalry, Major Godley commanding; Ninth Pennsylvania cavalry, Colonel Jordan commanding.

Nearing Franklin, we found the rebels had possession of part of the town, and had planted their artillery in the outskirts, had surrounded the fortifications on the north side of the Harpeth with his cavalry, having his heaviest forces on the left, between Franklin and Triune. After a severe march of fourteen miles over a very rocky and partially red-cedared country, we came in sight of the enemy's pickets about sunset. The Sixth Kentucky, Colonel Watkins, (in advance,) were ordered by Colonel Campbell to charge the enemy on a by-road. They fled at the dash, to the left, without showing fight, and crossed the Harpeth in great disorder at Hughs's Mill and Ford, and were followed by Colonel Watkins to the Lewisburgh pike, who captured and brought up a rebel ammunition wagon. The Fourth Kentucky (being now in front) came up with a second force of the enemy, at two miles this side the forts. (Colonel Cooper's horse, in the gallop over, had fallen with him on the rocky, slippery road, and seriously injured him.) Major Gwynne, now commanding the Fourth, was ordered to deploy to the left and present front. The Second Michigan, marching in column on the road, were attacked by the enemy in force on the flank. They were instantly prepared to fight as dragoons on foot, and engaged the enemy, Colonel Campbell ordering Colonel Jordan with the Ninth Pennsylvania to support them in column on each flank with drawn sabre for a charge, which was promptly done. The fighting was very severe here for an hour between the forces. The rebels appeared to be determined to hold their ground as if they intended to hold the battle-field, and continue the Franklin attack in the morning, but they were compelled to give way after our force got fairly to work, and they fled toward the fords in much confusion.

The Ninth Pennsylvania were now ordered down the Murfreesboro road to turn the enemy's left flank. The enemy rallied after a short flight, and drew up in a very fair line of battle, but it was of no use, the blood of our men was now up, and the rebels were unable to stand the deadly fire of our revolving rifles of the Second Michigan. He was pressed so closely at this point that General Armstrong's battle-flag and four of his escort were captured by the first battalion, Second Michigan, Captain Smith, and he left lying here eighteen killed and wounded. The Fourth Kentucky charged on the right, capturing half a score. The enemy broke once more and the eager troopers of the Second, Fourth, and Ninth pursued him through the now darkened woods and brushes and fields, and over the stone walls and fences lighted up by the flashes of the carbines. He divided his forces in the general "sauve qui peut," part dashing over the Harpeth at McGavoch's Ford to the Lewisburgh pike, and part running clear round the forts and crossing the Nashville pike between them and Brentwood, crossed the Harpeth below Franklin and reached their camp. It was most unfortunate that we could not have had an hour more of daylight, and have gotten a haul of prisoners of some moment, including the general commanding. Our cavalry were gathered together by sound of bugle and marched near the fort on their old camping-ground, and lay down for the night in a drenching rain-storm, shelterless and supperless. The rebels had drawn off their forces from the attack of the forts when they heard the cavalry firing on the Triune road.

The town of Franklin, lying in direct range between the forts and where the rebel artillery was posted, was in a dangerous position, and the most of the terrified inhabitants fled to the cellars or the country. A score of the inhabitants brought their families over the pontoons into the fort, and manfully took up arms against the rebels, proving that there *are* men in Middle Tennessee who will yet fight for their country when the iron yoke of the Confederacy is relieved from their necks. Several of the houses were fired in the artillery engagement, but they were extinguished — many of them had balls and shells through them, but fortunately none of the inhabitants were injured.

At eight P.M. General Granger ordered a brigade of infantry and a battery of artillery from Triune to Franklin. Marching through the storm and darkness, they arrived at daylight on the fifth. There were reconnoissances made by the infantry and some artillery and a small force of cavalry on the fifth, and there was some little skirmishing, but the enemy had withdrawn his forces to Spring Hill at two P.M. and the dropping shots ceased. The troops that had marched from Triune to the relief of Franklin returned to camp here on the sixth.

The Federal cavalry loss was three killed and four wounded. The rebel loss was twenty-five men and three officers killed and wounded in our hands, (besides those who escaped wounded,) and twenty-five prisoners.

The rebel surgeon who came over to look after their wounded said that General Armstrong acknowledged himself badly whipped, and that it was only the darkness that enabled him to draw off his forces, they having a thorough knowledge of the country.

In the reconnoissance of the fifth, Colonel Faulkner, commanding the Seventh Kentucky, (being part of Colonel Baird's forces,) most unfortunately got severely wounded in the thigh and scrotum by a musket-ball.

Colonel Campbell complimented the officers and men of his command very highly for their efficiency and bravery; also for the "vim" and willingness with which the officers instantly executed his commands.

Colonel Watkins, with the Sixth Kentucky, was ordered to return from the Lewisburgh pike, but failed to get back and participate in the engagement with his regiment on the evening of the fourth.

The next time the rebs "try it on" Franklin, "may we be there to see," as Cowper says in his Johnny Gilpin. "LOCHIEL."

Doc. 5.

CROSSING THE RAPPAHANNOCK.

JUNE 5, 1863.

HEADQUARTERS ARMY OF THE POTOMAC, Saturday, June 6, 1863.

FOR the third time in six months, the Rappahannock has been successfully crossed by our brave men, with slight loss.

Yesterday morning the Engineer brigade was ordered to proceed to the river, with a pontoon train sufficient for two bridges. Howe's splendid fighting division of the Sixth corps was selected for the work of crossing, and the point for laying the bridges was just below the mouth of Deep Run, at the identical spot where we have crossed twice before.

Our infantry and artillery, as well as the engineers, began to debouch on the open plain opposite the crossing soon after noon, but, for some reason, active operations were not commenced until about five o'clock. During the afternoon the pickets of the enemy lounged on the opposite bank, apparently filled with astonishment at the preparations of this "demoralized and weakened" army, which were going on right under their noses. Save this picket of the enemy, no other force was visible, and the impression was strong that the enemy had left.

About five o'clock the engineers drove their teams down to the river-bank, and commenced unloading. The rebels at once betook themselves to the rifle-pits, and commenced firing. Their rifle-pit here is a very strong one, and our men were within very close range. Quite a number of the engineers were soon wounded, and it was evident that the old and successful method of pushing men across in boats would have to be adopted.

General Howe at once ordered the Twenty-sixth New-Jersey, Colonel Morrison, of the Vermont brigade, to man the boats, push over and storm the rifle-pits.

Six of the batteries of the Sixth corps, namely, Williston's, Butler's, Haines's, McCartney's, Cowan's, and McCarthy's, were placed in position on the plain, and for nearly two hours shelled the rifle-pits, and the flanks of our position very vigorously. Their practice was excellent, the rifle-pits being almost demolished, yet the casualties among the enemy by shells were few. The rebels stuck to their position until the gallant Jerseymen set foot on the south side of the river, at about half-past six o'clock, when, notwithstanding the shower of canister sent after them, they fled before the rapid charge of our men. Indeed, they could not well leave before, for our guns completely swept the plain, and the rifle-pit was by far the safest place for them. The Twenty-sixth New-Jersey was soon followed by the Vermont regiments, and that whole brigade crossed in the boats. Skirmishers were immediately deployed, and we at once advanced in the direction of the Bowling Green road, covering Deep Run on our right, and a point below Mansfield on our left. Some sixty or seventy prisoners were soon brought in, being the main part of the force which had occupied the rifle-pit. They belonged chiefly to the Second Florida regiment. By dark our skirmishers had advanced nearly to the edge of the timber beyond the Bowling Green road, without having met the enemy in force. Pickets, skirmishers, and scouts were plenty, however, and in the direction of Fredericksburgh the rifle-pits seemed to be full of men. The enemy used no artillery against us, and none was seen. A few wagons hastily moved down the Telegraph road, and a few tents were seen south of Fredericksburgh. At eight o'clock last night, when I left the spot, these were all the indications that had been discovered.

The prisoners give but little information relative to the enemy. Enough was learned, however, to convince us that a large portion of the enemy's force is still in the neighborhood of Salem Church and Chancellorsville, apparently on the watch for our movements, rather than on any offensive demonstration of their own.

The charge of the New-Jersey regiment (Twenty-sixth) is deserving of especial praise. Almost any other regiment would have done the same, doubtless, but they are nine months' men and their time is out in three days. They thus go home crowned with the glory of this additional achievement, and thus add to the lustre of the arms of that State already won on many a battle-field.

The conduct of all our men was most admirable. The Fifteenth and Fiftieth New-York, and the regular battalion behaved manfully, and withstood a murderous fire at close range. Our casualties are five or six killed, and thirty-five to forty wounded. Among the former we have to lament Captain Charles E. Cross of the regular Engineers, shot through the brain, while at the river-bank, in charge of the bridge details. He was a gallant and accomplished officer, and his loss is deeply regretted. He had rendered valuable services at every former crossing, and was promptly at his post again, when he was struck by the fatal bullet.

ANOTHER ACCOUNT.

HEADQUARTERS ARMY OF THE POTOMAC,
Saturday, June 6, 1863.

An order was issued to the army yesterday to be in readiness to march at a moment's notice with three days' rations, while all baggage, stores, etc., were ordered to the rear. At eight o'clock the pontoon train moved down toward Franklin Crossing, halting behind the ridge near the river, where they remained till late in the afternoon. Howe's division of the Sixth corps was ordered to take the advance, when it moved forward, and

halted a short distance from the river, where the men lay on their arms for several hours. At half-past five P.M. our batteries were brought into position near the bank of the river on the flats, and opened a brisk fire on the rifle-pits opposite. The guns were handled with skill, many of the shells bursting directly over the heads of the rebels. A company of the Second Florida was stationed in these pits, and they kept up a brisk fire, endeavoring to pick off our gunners, but they were not very successful.

After an hour's cannonading, the pontoons having been laid in the mean time, our troops were ordered to cross the river, and take the rifle-pits. This was done with alacrity, the Fifth Vermont taking the lead. As our men approached the rebels almost ceased firing, the majority throwing down their arms and surrendering themselves, while a few retreated into an open field in the rear, when our troops followed, keeping up a running fire, which in connection with some shells thrown by our batteries beyond, compelled them to turn and give themselves up rather than run the gauntlet of both fires. Not more than a dozen got away.

Several regiments having crossed by this time, they formed in line of battle and advanced about a mile, skirmishers being thrown out in front. On the Richmond road to the left of the field, a line of pickets were stationed, who opened fire on our forces, but were soon silenced. Our men then advanced toward a piece of woods directly opposite the crossing, but the enemy seemed to have left, no firing coming from that place. Another force advanced toward Fredericksburgh, the rebel pickets firing and retreating under cover of trees and houses. Numbers were seen leaving for the woods in rear of the town. It was now getting dark, and the action ceased for the night. Captain Cross of the Fiftieth New-York was killed, with three or four others, and some ten or twelve wounded.

The loss of the enemy was not ascertained. We took fifty-five prisoners—all of the Second Florida regiment. Some of them say that Lee has fallen back, while others report that he only fell back behind the hills, and is waiting for our advance. Twenty mules loaded with baggage were also captured and brought over just before dark.

This morning at six A.M. our skirmishers advanced past the Richmond road, and soon drew the rebel fire. Both lines are still engaged (ten A.M.) with little damage on either side, each line maintaining its position.

About a division of the enemy were seen at seven A.M. crossing the ridge toward St. Mary's Heights from the left, and shortly after one regiment returned on the same route. Our thirty-two-pounders opened and our shell was thrown into their line, which made them scatter in short order. These guns are very valuable, throwing shells a distance of about three miles with great precision. The rebels say they are the only ones they are afraid of.

Doc. 6.

THE BRITISH CONSUL AT RICHMOND, VA.

LETTERS PATENT REVOKING EXEQUATUR OF GEORGE MOORE, HER BRITANNIC MAJESTY'S CONSUL AT RICHMOND.

Jefferson Davis, President of the Confederate States of America:

To ALL WHOM IT MAY CONCERN: Whereas, George Moore, Esq., Her Britannic Majesty's Consul for the port of Richmond and State of Virginia, (duly recognized by the Exequatur issued by a former government, which was, at the time of the issue, the duly authorized agent for that purpose of the State of Virginia,) did recently assume to act as consul for a place other than the city of Richmond, and a State other than the State of Virginia, and was, thereupon, on the twentieth day of February last, 1863, requested by the Secretary of State to submit to the Department of State his consular commission, as well as any other authority he may have received to act in behalf of the government of Her Britannic Majesty before further correspondence could be held with him as Her Majesty's Consul at the port of Richmond; and whereas, the said George Moore has lately, without acceding to said request, entered into correspondence, as Her Majesty's Consul, with the Secretary of War of these confederate States, thereby disregarding the legitimate authority of this government.

These, therefore, are to declare that I do no longer recognize the said George Moore as Her Britannic Majesty's Consul in any part of these confederate States, nor permit him to exercise or enjoy any of the functions, powers, or privileges allowed to the consuls of Great Britain. And I do wholly revoke and annul any *Exequatur* heretofore given to the said George Moore by the government which was formerly authorized to grant such *Exequatur* as agent of the State of Virginia, and do declare the said *Exequatur* to be absolutely *null* and *void* from this day forward.

In testimony whereof, I have caused these letters to be made patent, and the seal of the confederate States of America to be herewith affixed.

Given under my hand this *fifth* day of [SEAL.] June, in the year of our Lord one thousand eight hundred and sixty-three.

By the President: JEFFERSON DAVIS.

J. P. BENJAMIN,
Secretary of State.

Doc. 7.

GENERAL FREMONT'S LETTER.

NEW-YORK, June 6, 1863.

To the Hon. Edwin M. Stanton, Secretary of War:

SIR: I received from the War Department on the twenty-third ultimo, a copy of Gen. Butler's demand to be declared the ranking officer of the army of the United States, regular and volunteer. By your order I am informed that his demand will be referred for decision to a board of officers, and I am invited to submit any remarks which I desire to make upon the subject, and am allowed for this purpose fifteen days from the date of your order.

In reply, I have to say that I do not think the question open to discussion. This is a case involving the acts of the Government, which have a binding and conclusive force, the bare statement of which is sufficient for a decision.

The strength of Gen. Butler's argument rests upon the assumption that it was the President's "intention" to make him the senior Major-General, in consideration of his "meritorious services rendered in the service of the United States, etc.". But the President did not make his recognition of these services public and effective. He did not carry out any such "intention" by nominating General Butler to the ranking position, but did so nominate Generals McClellan and Fremont, and gave Gen. Butler an inferior date, placing him in what was then, and has always been, considered a distinct and separate branch of the military service. The Senate confirmed these nominations accordingly, and by their act constituted Generals McClellan and Fremont Major-Generals of the regular army "to rank as such from the fourteenth day of May, 1861," and General Butler a Major-General in the United States volunteer forces, to rank from the sixteenth day of May, 1861.

The act of the Senate fixes the time at which the rank shall begin, and the usage of the War Department has been in conformity to it from the foundation of the Government to the present day. Our respective commissions were conferred upon us by that authority which the Constitution makes alone competent to give them, and no inferior tribunal can, by any possibility, alter or modify the direct meaning and effect of the terms in which those commissions are given. I am, therefore, not willing to submit my commission held under this authority to the revision of any board of officers, nor can I for a moment, by any act, admit the right of Gen. Butler to call it into question. But, while entering this protest, I will, in deference to your request, make some remarks upon General Butler's argument.

And in making these remarks I confine myself strictly to the law and the established usage of the War Department, holding that stability and good order in the army, and the security of those who belong to it, can be found only in their rigid observance. I take the facts as they are, and in making any distinction between classes and branches of the service, I do so because the law makes them, and with no disposition to discriminate otherwise in favor of either. Certainly in no profession can fixity of rights and duties and clearly defined authority be more essential than in the military service. It seems superfluous to assert a fact which the experience and practice of the world confirm.

Such a question could not occur in any European service, certainly not in Continental Europe; but in ours, under the present extraordinary circumstances, there necessarily already exists an uncertainty and confusion, greatly perplexing to officers and injurious to the public interest. To destroy the precision of authority fixed by date would unsettle all commissions, and seriously disturb the whole economy of the army. The fact that it required a special act of Congress to enable the President to disregard the date in the employment of officers shows both the usage itself and the force of it.

General Butler claims, first, that the rank dates from the day on which the letter of appointment is received, and not from the day fixed in the commission.

The statement of the point carries the refutation with it. The letter of appointment is simply a letter of information, setting out the rank which is offered and the date from which that rank shall be held to take effect, if consented to by the Senate. The rank and date of it are fixed by the President and the Senate together, and the form in which they are both expressed is the commission itself, and the official record of the Army Register, which classifies officers under the head "date of commission," and knows nothing of any letters of appointment or oaths of office, but rests solely on the date of commission. The files and papers of the War Department must be held to be authentic history of all public acts relative to that branch of the Government. In this sense I understand Gen. Butler to use the term "form," and if he relies on these forms he has no case, for as here presented, "law, fact, and form," are combined on one side against Gen. Butler's individual opinions on the other.

2. That "in consideration of meritorious services performed in the service of the United States, etc.," the President "intended" to give him seniority of the rank.

But the President did not do so in the only public and official way which could give validity or binding force to his alleged intention. "For every thing the Executive does there must be the warrant of law;" the relative positions of General Butler and the other Major-Generals are fixed under this "warrant," and it would be unprecedented to say that any unfulfilled intentions of the President are sufficient of themselves to render void a deliberate and final act of the Government to which he himself was a principal party.

Upon the retirement of Lieut.-Gen. Scott all the officers whose rank is called in question by Gen. Butler being then in active service, the President placed in chief command Gen. McClellan of the regular army, one of the two officers ranking first by date of commission. At that time the resolution of April fourth, 1862, authorizing the President to disregard seniority of rank in assigning command had not been passed, and he would have felt required to give General Butler the chief command, which would have been his of right, if he were the senior Major-General. Whatever the President's intentions might have been before the issuance of the respective commissions, his acts on this occasion show conclusively his construction of their effect as to relative rank after they were issued.

3. Gen. Butler, in support of his claim, cites the fifth paragraph of the Army Regulations, which applies only to the case of commissions of even date. He admits that this "would hardly seem to cover" his case, but at the same time proceeds to apply it precisely as if it did. Arguing under this head, he proceeds to assume that the major-generals of the army constitute a corps, and assuming at the same time that he is of even date with Generals McClellan and Fremont, and that he is of the same corps with them, he draws the conclusion that this fifth paragraph of the Army Regulations decides the question in his favor under every clause. To this I have to reply:

1. That the major-generals of the army do not constitute a corps.

2. And if they did, General Butler would not belong to the same corps with Major-Generals McClellan and Fremont.

3. And if he did belong to the same corps with them, the fifth paragraph does not apply to him in any of its specifications, because his date is subsequent to theirs.

The major-generals in the service belong to a grade and constitute a class—they do not constitute a corps. In 1857, the date of the Army Regulations quoted by General Butler, there was but one major-general in the service, and he could not very well be construed into a corps.

The Articles of War use the word corps in the sense of a portion of the army organized by law, with a head and members, or any other military body having such organization, as the marine corps. A regiment is a corps, an independent company is a corps, a body of officers, with one head, is a corps, as the Topographical Engineers. Detachments of parts of regiments, or of whole regiments, united for a particular purpose, whether for a campaign or a part campaign, are not corps in the sense of the Rules and Articles of War; for such bodies have neither head nor members commissioned in the particular body temporarily so united, but the officers with such detachments hold commissions either in the corps composing the detachment, in the army at large, in the marine corps or militia. (Scott's Military Dictionary.)

The same work, under the word "line," gives an extract from General Order Number 51 of the series of 1851, in which President Fillmore explains the rule regulating seniority of rank among officers of different corps, and concludes by remarking that when a major-general or brigadier-general is present, "no question can arise as to the right to command, because the general officer, not belonging to any corps, takes command by virtue of a general rule of superiority in rank."

Generals McClellan and Fremont were commissioned major-generals in the regular or permanent army of the United States, and General Butler in the volunteer or temporary force raised for the suppression of the rebellion. Generals McClellan and Fremont were commissioned under section three of the act approved July twenty-ninth, 1861, entitled, "An Act to increase the present military establishment of the United States," and beginning, "That there shall be added to the regular army," etc. Under this act the regular army was increased to thirty regiments, namely, nineteen of infantry, six of cavalry, and five of artillery. Section three reads: "That there shall be added to the army of the United States the following general officers, namely, four major-generals," etc. The four major-generals appointed under this act—Generals McClellan, Fremont, Halleck, and Wool—all had been or were in the regular army.

The whole current of the debate in the Senate upon the passage of this law is unfavorable to General Butler's claim. Among the amendments strongly pressed was one to the effect that no officer should be appointed to the increased regular army above the rank of colonel, unless he should have previously served at least ten years in the regular or volunteer service. General Butler had served two months in the volunteer service when appointed major-general; General McClellan, twelve years continuously in the regular army, resigning with the rank of captain; General Fremont, ten years continuously in the regular army, resigning with the rank of lieutenant-colonel.

General Butler was commissioned under section four of an act approved July twenty-second, 1861, entitled, "An act to authorize the employment of volunteers," etc. The fourth section reads, "That the President shall be authorized to appoint, by and with the advice and consent of the Senate, for the command of the forces provided for in this act, a number of major-generals, not exceeding six, etc." Section three of an additional act, approved July twenty-fifth, 1861, entitled, "An act in addition to the act to authorize the employment of volunteers, etc," says, "That the President shall be authorized to appoint, by and with the advice and consent of the Senate, for the command of the volunteer forces, such number of major-generals as may in his judgment be required for their organization," using nearly the same terms as in the previous act.

These three acts indisputably show that Congress held the regular army and the volunteer forces to be distinct bodies, and that Generals McClellan and Fremont belong to a separate military establishment, and not in any sense to the same "corps" with General Butler. It requires an act of Congress and reörganization to bring these two bodies into one. Section five of an act approved June twenty-sixth, 1812, entitled, "An act for the more perfect organization of the army of the United States," enacts "that the military establishment authorized by law previous to the twelfth day of April, 1808, and the additional military force raised by virtue of the act of April twelfth, 1808, be, and the same are hereby incorporated," etc.

While upon this subject of distinct corps it may be pertinent to make the following observation: The appointments of Generals McClellan, Fremont, Butler, Banks, and Dix were virtually all made in May, and were made generally known in the public journals of that month.

At that time, under the law (see ninety-eighth Article of War) and under immemorial usage, offi-

cers of the regular army ranked those of the militia or volunteers, and this usage was carried out through all the details of service. The regular troops as a body were always placed on the right ranking position, the marine corps next in order, and in the extreme left the militia or volunteers.

If when he made these appointments the President intended to give General Butler the position of ranking general in the armies of the United States, regular and volunteer, why did he not place him in the ranking body? And why did he, on the contrary, place him in that branch of the military service where law and usage positively made him junior in rank to every other officer of the same grade in the other branch of the service?

In point of fact, none of these appointments made before the passage of the acts of July twenty-second, twenty-fifth, and twenty-ninth, gave any legal status. The act of the President in making the appointments was merely provisional, and out of the necessity of the case. Upon the enactment of these laws the President submitted his appointments to the consideration of the Senate, and after they had been confirmed by this body the commissions were issued conformably.

But admitting that military usage and the laws did not expressly operate against General Butler's claim to belong to the same corps with Generals McClellan and Fremont, the fifth paragraph of the Army Regulations does not apply to him in any of its specifications, because the decree of the Senate completing the respective commissions and fixing the character and the extent of the authority conferred, positively assign him an inferior and subsequent date. Therefore, the Regulations, which interpret—they enact nothing—which interpret and formalize the acts of Congress, and make another branch of what must be understood by the term "form," do not in any way sustain General Butler's position in derogation of the two first generals named in the Register.

It is a peculiarity of the argument brought forward under the fifth paragraph, that throughout it is based upon an assumption of facts which General Butler himself, in his preliminary remarks, declares do not exist, namely, a priority of date in his own commission, and its consequent coïncidence with the commissions of the general officers whom he thereby holds to come "in order of seniority" with himself. With the fact constantly in view that the argument rests on an imaginary basis, it is a sort of anomaly to the understanding to follow it in detail through the outside points presented by General Butler.

In his concluding remarks he affirms that "there is no act of Congress which has or can settle seniority of rank." But certainly there are many precedents which go to show that they can and do settle such questions. The Act of August sixth, 1861, made General Butler senior to brigadier-generals appointed on or after July twenty-second, 1861, and gave him his only claim to seniority upon the ground of superior rank when appointed.

General Butler adds, that "questions of seniority now are only useful in points of etiquette and service upon courts-martial." But these questions involve something more than etiquette; they are questions of rank, and of rank under such circumstances as often to convey the most positive control and command. The resolution of April fourth, 1862, authorizing the President "to assign the command of troops in the same field or department to officers of the same grade, without regard to seniority," does not vitiate the right to command, which is given by superiority of rank, except in those cases when it is specially so ordered by the President.

I rest here my remarks on the subject, concluding briefly. General Butler demands that the commissions of Generals McClellan and Fremont be in part set aside in his favor, upon the ground that, in consideration of his services in the department of Annapolis, the President intended to give him the position now legally held by one of those two officers. To this I desire, finally, to reply that the act of the President and Senate which conferred on them their commissions was constitutional and binding in all its terms, and I respectfully submit that there is no authority competent to modify it.

Very respectfully, your obedient servant,

JOHN C. FREMONT,
Major-General U. S. A.

Doc. 8.

FIGHT AT MILLIKEN'S BEND, MISS.

ACCOUNT BY AN EYE-WITNESS.

MILLIKEN'S BEND, June 13.

FIRST allow me to describe the ground occupied by our troops. The camp is along the bank of the Mississippi River, and at this point the levee is not more than one hundred and fifty yards from the river. The encampment is between the levee and the river. Breastworks have been thrown up on the right and left, and a few rifle-pits dug along the levee; and this constituted our defensive work. The levee is about eight feet high at this point, and back of it is a plantation covered with hedges, fruit and ornamental trees, in the immediate vicinity of our camp and to the rear. For some days previous to the attack we had known that a force of rebels were in the vicinity, estimated from one thousand five hundred to ten thousand strong. The colored troops were only partially organized regiments and had all been armed within a week to meet this emergency. With such raw material you may be sure a battle was any thing but desirable to the officers of the colored regiments.

Our force consisted of the Ninth Louisiana, Colonel Scibs; the Eleventh, Colonel Chamberlain; and the First Mississippi, only one hundred and fifty men, and one hundred and sixty from the Twenty-third Iowa.

Our entire force engaged was about one thousand four hundred, of which one thousand two hundred and fifty were colored.

About three o'clock in the morning our pickets were driven in, and fifteen minutes later the enemy appeared and formed in line of battle on our left front. They formed for bayonet-charge three lines deep with a reserve. Six regiments were brought into action, commanded, as we learn, by McCulloch, brother of Ben McCulloch, killed at Pea Ridge. With yells that would make faint hearts quail, on double-quick they charged our little band. They met the shock like heroes, reserving their fire until the foe was within one hundred yards, then a terrible volley broke the first line of the enemy, and made the whole column tremble for a moment, but rallied by their officers, with redoubled yells onward they rushed. A hedge at the base of the levee furnished a screen, behind which for a moment they halted, closed their lines and then rushed up the levee. Our men stood up bravely to the work, but were overpowered by numbers. At this moment the conflict was terrible. The whiz of bullets made the air vocal with dread music. Whoever has been in battle knows well the fiendish scream. In ten minutes not less than three hundred of our brave men were either killed or wounded.

Our own fallen covered the levee on one side, and the enemy on the other. For a few moments our men held their own ground, but the enemy were three to our one, and our left were compelled to fall back. This they did, continuing the fire, which prevented the enemy following us up. Our right held the works at that point and opened a raking fire on the enemy. The left and centre fell back to the river one hundred and fifty yards and opened fire from the cover of the river-bank. Thus posted, the battle continued from four to eleven A.M. Soon after our forces fell back, the gunboat Choctaw opened on the enemy with shell. The range, however, was short, and for some time all the damage done to the enemy was the arousing of their fears. Soon, however, on our right a flanking movement was disconcerted by a few well-directed shells. The gunboat doubtless did much to save the day. About eleven o'clock our men on the left were rallied to a charge, and the whole line of the enemy gave way. The gunboat now threw shell thick and fast into their retreating ranks, and soon their retreat became a rout and they ran for shelter to hedges and timber in the rear. At half-past eleven o'clock the battle was ended and the work of gathering in the dead and wounded commenced.

I was on the field during the whole time of the engagement, and watched with interest the conduct of officers and their commands. It was a fight for which we were all unprepared, and hence concert of action could not be expected. Each regiment, and I may add, each company and man fought on his own hook. Had our forces been drilled men, we would have called them whipped in detail, the work wasn't done, and the enemy were repulsed with heavy loss. I will speak of the officers of the Eleventh Louisiana, as I was with this regiment. Every officer, so far as I can learn, did his duty on that trying day. The Colonel brought his command into action, when the enemy were pressing with his whole force upon our line. For a little time he held the enemy in check, but the number of the enemy and the exposed position of his men, the enemy now occupying our left, made it necessary for him to fall back to the river. In falling back his horse was shot, and he was injured in the hip. He remained, however, a half-hour longer on the field, and then went on board the gunboat and gave direction for throwing their shells. The Lieut.-Colonel, Cyrus Sears, commanded the right and held his position and remained on the field during the battle. The Major William Cotton, a brave officer, was mortally wounded, early in the engagement, and borne from the field. The Adjutant, Thomas Free, conducted himself most praiseworthily, and as he is a citizen of Tama County, I may speak freely of him. He was in the thickest of the fight executing orders and cheering on the men to duty. It is a marvel how he passed through the battle of that day untouched, but so it is, save a few bullet-holes in his clothes. He is a brave, spirited, efficient young officer of whom Tama County may feel proud. The line officers without exception did their duty, and to this fact I attribute our success. Tauntingly it has been said that negroes won't fight. Who say it, and who but a dastard and a brute will dare to say it, when the battle of Milliken's Bend finds its place among the heroic deeds of this war? This battle has significance. It demonstrates the fact that the freed slaves will fight. The enemy were at least three thousand strong, mostly Texan troops, infantry, while we were but one thousand four hundred, and yet for eight long hours we contested the field, and finally drove the enemy in such hot haste that he had left one hundred and fifteen of his dead for us to bury. Could we have had a small cavalry force, we might have added many prisoners to the successes of the day; as it was, we only took a few. Our many dead and wounded shall tell how bravely they fought, how dearly they won the battle-field of Milliken's Bend on the seventh of June, 1863.

Allow me to say, that the Twenty-third Iowa honored itself and the State it represented on this bloody field. Iowa has never been dishonored on the field of battle. May her proud fame remain untarnished! The Twenty-third Iowa had one hundred and sixty men in battle, lost twenty-five killed, twenty-six wounded, three missing.

Now come the colored regiments; they are yet unorganized, only eight companies having been mustered in, and may be considered raw material. The Ninth Louisiana went into action with about five hundred men; killed sixty, wounded one hundred fifteen. Eleventh Louisiana went into action with about six hundred; killed forty, wounded one hundred and twenty-five, missing one hundred and thirty-one. First Mississippi went into action with one hundred and fifty; killed two, wounded twenty-one, missing three. I believe there were a few

men of the Thirteenth Louisiana in the engagement, mixed with the other regiments.

Total engaged, (colored,) one thousand two hundred and fifty; (white,) one hundred and sixty; killed, one hundred and twenty-seven; wounded, two hundred and eighty-seven; missing, one hundred and thirty-seven; whole number engaged, one thousand four hundred and ten. Total loss, five hundred and fifty-one.

Here is a total loss of near forty per cent and a loss in killed and wounded of thirty per cent nearly, and yet the battle is won. Now let the friend and the enemy of the colored man figure up the per cent loss of the great battles of this war, and decide each for himself, whether Milliken's Bend shall find a place among the records of heroic deeds and battle-fields.

Our figures are our arguments that colored men will fight, and they need no comment. We leave them as the battle-field gave them, mournfully brave.

The enemy's loss as ascertained from prisoners was not less than two hundred killed and four hundred to five hundred wounded. In the charge when the struggle was terrific, they had the open field while our forces occupied the breastworks. It is but reasonable to suppose therefore that their loss would exceed ours. Then again when they retreated the gunboat shelled them for a mile and a half, and a number were killed and wounded by shell. I think their loss will exceed seven hundred, and I base my estimate on statements of prisoners and others.

A prisoner said the rebel commander expected to capture the post with ease, and was severely chagrined at being defeated. He said it was the severest fight he had ever been in.

It is rumored that Kirby Smith commands the rebel force and that he said he would take the d—d nigger camp or wade in blood to his knees. It was first reported that the rebels shot all the prisoners taken when they got to Richmond, ten miles from here. We have since learned that the proposition was made and the Louisiana troops were for executing it, but that the Texan troops drew up in line of battle and declared it could not be done while they bore arms. Good for Texans. The threat is not executed. The officers are kept in close confinement and the prisoners are treated with rigor. I understand, however, they will be regarded as prisoners and exchanged the same as white soldiers. A rebel force is still hovering about the vicinity of Richmond, said to be six thousand strong. We may be attacked again, but I doubt not we will give a good account of ourselves if so. Two additional regiments have come into this camp since the battle, and in several particulars we are better prepared to inspect rebel troops. Yours, G. G. EDWARDS.

ANOTHER ACCOUNT.

CAIRO, June 15, 1863.

The battle of Milliken's Bend occurred on Saturday and Sunday, the sixth and seventh inst., the first attack having been made on the afternoon of Saturday, closing with the retreat of the rebels before nightfall. I gather the following in regard to the affair from an officer of the steamer Dunleith, just from the scene of action.

It would appear that the Union forces at Milliken's Bend were under the command of a colonel of Iowa volunteers — supposed to be the Twenty-third — and his force consisted of two Iowa regiments and one or two colored regiments, new in the service, and short in point of numbers, and no heavy or even light artillery of any importance with which to repel an attack. But hearing early on Saturday that the rebels, under General Henry McCulloch, brother of Ben McCulloch, were concentrating near him, with a menacing front, toward Milliken's Bend, the commander sent out some cavalry with orders to reconnoitre and report.

The cavalry dashed out from the works early in the day, and soon returned with a full confirmation of the report previously brought in, in regard to the proximity of the rebels and their designs upon the little garrison at the Bend. The rebels were said to be about five thousand strong, and late from Alexandria, La., but more recently at Richmond upon the Shreveport Railroad. This force of from five to six thousand, it was supposed, General McCulloch had divided into three parts, sending one part to Young's Point, another to Lake Providence, and with the third was about to attack the Union forces holding Milliken's Bend. This third force was estimated at some three thousand.

The approach of the rebels, momentarily expected — and prepared for as well as the limited supply of ammunition and arms would permit — at last became apparent. Pickets, thrown out for the purpose, came in saying an immense army was coming. The commander sent out detachments of white troops to repel their approach, detailing a regiment of negroes to act as reserves, the orders being, if the white troops could not stem the current, to fall back upon the support of the colored troops, and then unitedly oppose the advance until no longer able to withstand the men brought against them.

This programme, in a measure, was most promptly carried out. The troops advanced, met the enemy, engaged him in force and with effect with musketry, and, as the colonel had anticipated, found that our strength was not adequate to the undertaking, being greatly outnumbered by the rebels. But both fought for an hour most stubbornly. The Iowa troops were loth to retreat at all and obtain the support of their colored reserves, and the loss on the rebel side, said to have been one hundred in this early affray, attests their valor and efficiency. But the rebels pressed our men gradually back, in good order, however, until the blacks were reached, when they came in with a will. The spirits of the retreating and outnumbered Iowans were raised; they rallied, they stood their ground; the negroes came up with volley after volley, delivered with good effect and rapidity; and after a short battle, in which the blacks lost a number — but the rebels more — the rebels fell back, finally broke, and retreated in disorder. The Union forces were in too small number to pursue, and had no cannon with which to cut up their then rear guard. Hence, the retrograde was made without great loss to the enemy. After the last of the rebels had disappeared, it being night, pickets were placed, scouts sent out, and every preparation made to be ready in the event of a return of the rebels. It was rightly supposed that, having felt their strength, and knowing that our men were without guns and in small force, the enemy would not long delay a second attempt to occupy Milliken's Bend. But this was the end of the attack for that day. A steamer from below chanced to come in sight just at dark, going to Helena. She was hailed, informed of the attack, and sent back for aid of some kind. Just at the break of day, the dark sides, huge wheel-houses, and yawning ports of the gunboat Choctaw were discerned by the guard. Here was help, indeed. With such support the garrison could never be taken without immense loss to the captors. The Choctaw took her position with reference to the point from which the rebels must necessarily attack, and remained until sunrise, awaiting in ominous silence the expected advance.

Sunday morning had hardly been ushered in, and the sun had been out of his eastern bed but half an hour, when the scouts and pickets of the garrison came in in great haste to report that the enemy had again commenced an advance movement, headed toward the Bend. On this occasion, understanding well his strength, and conscious of the support his iron-clad helpmate would bring, the commander of the post gradually drew in all his pickets, not leaving a man outside of his hastily built earthworks. When the advance of the rebels made their appearance there was not a man to be seen — all that confronted them was silence and apparently deserted breastworks and rifle-pits. But, fearful of deception, the rebel commander had recourse to a *ruse* for the comparative protection of his advance upon the works. All the mules belonging to his command, and all he could steal from adjoining planters along the route, were brought to the front. Extending from the centre to each wing of the approaching host, covering the soldiers from the bullets of the Yankees — from the sight of their sharp-shooters — was a line of living, moving breastworks — the bodies of the devoted mules. As they drew nigh the Union defences the enemy opened heavily with musketry. Their first volley was the signal for the Iowans and the colored regiments to make their appearance. They rose as though by magic from behind their protection, took deliberate aim wherever a rebel could be seen, and dropped their bullets surely and certainly into the bodies of such as were foolish enough to disdain a shield of mule muscle and mule bone; and yet the living line kept up its snakelike advance. Taking the hint, perhaps, from the rebel commander at the siege of Lexington — when the gallant Colonel Mulligan and his Irish brigade were defeated by the approach of men behind revetted bales of hay, which they rolled before them as they neared the Union ranks — McCulloch expected to gain Milliken's Bend by substituting mules for hay. If so, he nearly set himself down an ass in the estimation of those he proposed attacking. A bale of cotton or hay might make a breastwork of considerable value, but the mules, unless moved forward sidewise—and the animal is known to be stubborn—presented but slight obstacle to the sharp eye of an experienced rifleman. Hence the rebels fell in considerable numbers from the first volleys of our troops. Still they advanced. But now came the turn of the rebels to be surprised. When within a short distance of the works the gunboat, until the moment partially concealed by the smoke of the battle, opened with heavy guns, sending a continuous line of ten-inch shell into the serried columns of the enemy. It was an astonisher. It was worse than the negro reserves of the previous day. It was paralyzing. To make the matter worse, the same negro regiments, taking advantage of their surprise, were again upon them, scaling the works from within, rushing down upon the mules, frightening them out of the little sense nature had endowed them with, and in turn attacking the soldiers with bayonet and clubbed musket, came the black besom of destruction, like unto a small, dark colored, mighty, destructive hurricane. Rebel nerve could never withstand all of this. After a few volleys — after an ineffectual attempt to drive back the negro assailants—after imploring his men in vain to stand up to it and fight or "die in the last ditch," McCulloch, if it were McCulloch, was compelled to sound the retreat and withdraw, leaving a heap of dead men and mules lying stark upon the field. The colored regiment had thus far not met with any considerable loss. But with great lack of caution their colonel led them forward in pursuit of the fleeing foe, until they were in full range of the guns of the Choctaw, and, sad to relate, a goodly number of the brave blacks, who had literally saved the fortunes of the day for the Federal arms, were cut down and instantly killed by our own shell. A signal stopped the firing as quickly as possible, but not until dreadful havoc had been made.

But the rebels were, it is now supposed, most effectually whipped, and so badly crippled by loss of dead and wounded, that they would not return to the attack. Our loss is put down at about one hundred, killed, wounded, and missing, during the two fights. That of the rebels was twice the number. Had it not been for the unfortunate occurrence of the Choctaw, our loss would have been very small indeed. Over one hundred dead were left by the enemy unburied, unattended to, upon the field. They took off nearly all their wounded.

ANOTHER ACCOUNT.

TWENTY-SECOND DAY IN REAR OF VICKSBURGH, June 9, 1863.

Two gentlemen from the Yazoo have given me the following particulars of the fight at Milliken's Bend, in which negro troops played so conspicuous a part:

My informant states that a force of about one thousand negroes, and two hundred men of the Twenty-third Iowa, belonging to the Second brigade, Carr's division, (the Twenty-third Iowa had been up the river with prisoners, and was on its way back to this place,) was surprised in camp by a rebel force of about two thousand men. The first intimation that the commanding officer received was from one of the black men, who went into the colonel's tent, and said: "Massa, the secesh are in camp." The colonel ordered him to have the men load their guns at once. He instantly replied: "We have done did dat now, massa." Before the colonel was ready, the men were in line, ready for action. As before stated, the rebels drove our force toward the gunboats, taking colored men prisoners and murdering them. This so enraged them that they rallied and charged the enemy more heroically and desperately than has been recorded during the war. It was a genuine bayonet charge, a hand-to-hand fight, that has never occurred to any extent during this prolonged conflict. Upon both sides men were killed with the butts of muskets. White and black men were lying side by side, pierced by bayonets, and in some instances transfixed to the earth. In one instance, two men, one white and the other black, were found dead, side by side, each having the other's bayonet through his body. If facts prove to be what they are now represented, this engagement of Sunday morning will be recorded as the most desperate of this war. Broken limbs, broken heads, the mangling of bodies, all prove that it was a contest between enraged men; on the one side from hatred to a race, and on the other, desire for self-preservation, revenge for past grievances, and the inhuman murder of their comrades, One brave man took his former master prisoner, and brought him into camp with great gusto. A rebel prisoner made a particular request, that *his own* negroes should not be placed over him as a guard. Dame Fortune is capricious! His request was *not* granted. Their mode of warfare does not entitle them to any privileges. If any are granted, it is from magnanimity to a fellow-foe.

The rebels lost five cannon, two hundred men killed, four hundred to five hundred wounded, and about two hundred prisoners. Our loss is reported to be one hundred killed and five hundred wounded; but few were white men.

Doc. 9.

THE NATIONAL ENROLMENT.
SOLICITOR WHITING'S OPINION.

WAR DEPARTMENT, OFFICE PROVOST-MARSHAL GENERAL, June 9.

THE following opinion of Hon. William Whiting, solicitor of the War Department, has been ordered to be published by the Secretary of War:

The National forces, liable to perform military duty, include all able-bodied male citizens of the

United States, and persons of foreign birth who have declared their intention to become citizens according to law, being between twenty and forty-five years of age. Certain persons are excepted, divided into eight classes. No persons but such as are therein excepted shall be exempt. (Sec. 2d.)

It is declared the duty of the enrolling officers to enroll all persons subject to military duty, (Sec. 9.) All persons thus enrolled shall be subject for two years after July first succeeding the enrolment, to be called into the military service, (Sec. 11.) The national forces (not now in the military service) enrolled under the act shall be divided into two classes, etc., (Sec. 3.)

Those of the second class shall not be called out until those of the first class shall have been exhausted.

Thus it seems, by the true construction of this act, while all persons coming within its provisions are to be enrolled in the national forces, nevertheless, under the first enrolment, those who were in the military service at the time the act went into effect are not to be included in that class which is subject to the first draft.

Several provisions of this statute are inconsistent to the idea that persons then in the service were to be treated as liable to draft from the first class.

Thus it is provided in the seventh section that regulars, volunteers, militiamen, or persons called into the service under this or any other act of Congress, were to be arrested as deserters, wherever they might be found, by the provost-marshal, and to be sent to the nearest military post, thus admitting a plain distinction between these different classes of persons, namely, those who were then in the service and those who were to be drafted in.

The same distinction between those who were in the service and those who were to be drafted in is recognized in Sec. 18, which provides bounties to those who being then in the service should volunteer to reënlist.

The statute providing for the classification of troops from which drafts are to be made enacts as follows: (Sec. 3d.) That the national forces of the United States, *not now in the military service*, enrolled under this act, shall be divided into two classes. Thus those who are "now" (that is to say, on the third of March, 1863) in the military service, are not to be included in either of these classes. And as those *then* (March third) in the service were not included in either of these two classes, they may be said to constitute a class of persons to be enrolled under the provisions of this act.

As between the first and second class the law (Sec. 3) requires that the second class shall not in any district be called into the service of the United States until those of the first shall have been thus called in.

Volunteers or regulars who had been in the service, and who had been discharged therefrom, or had resigned prior to the third day of March, 1863, are liable to be drafted in the same manner as if they had never been in the service; no regard is to be paid to their former period of service or to the length or brevity of the period between the date of their discharge and that of the draft.

Volunteers who were in the service of the United States on the third of March, 1863, and have since that time been discharged, are not therefore included in the first class from which the first draft is intended to be made, and are therefore not now liable to be called on by a draft, which is to be made from that class of the forces of the United States under the provisions of this act. WILLIAM WHITING,
Solicitor of the War Department.

JAMES B. FRY,
Provost-Marshal General.

WAR DEPARTMENT,
PROVOST-MARSHAL GENERAL'S OFFICE,
WASHINGTON, D. C., June 6.

The following opinion of Hon. William Whiting, solicitor of the War Department, has been ordered to be published by the Secretary of War:

OPINION.

It is made the duty of provost-marshals "to obey all lawful orders and regulations of the provost-marshal general, and such as shall be prescribed by law concerning the enrolment and calling into service of the national forces." (Act March 3, 1863. Sec. 7.)

The twenty-fifth Section of the same act provides that "if any person shall resist any draft of men enrolled under the act into the service of the United States, or shall counsel or aid any person to resist any such draft, or shall assault or obstruct any officer in making such draft, or in the performance of any service in relation thereto, or shall counsel any person to assault or obstruct any such officer, or shall counsel any drafted man not to appear at the place of rendezvous, or wilfully persuade them from the performance of military duty, as required by law; such person shall be subject to summary arrest by the provost-marshal, and shall be forthwith delivered to the civil authorities, and upon conviction thereof shall be punished by a fine not exceeding five hundred dollars, or by imprisonment not exceeding two years, or by both of said punishments."

To do any act which will prevent or impede the enrolment of the national forces (which enrolment is preliminary and essential to the draft) is to prevent or impede the draft itself.

The enrolment is a service to be performed by the provost-marshal in relation to the draft. It is not the act of drawing ballots out of a ballot-box itself, but it is "in relation to it," and is the first step that must by law be taken preparatory to the draft. It is therefore clearly within the duty of the provost-marshal to subject all persons who obstruct the enrolment, the meeting of the board, or any other proceeding which is preliminary and essential to the draft, to summary arrest, according to the provisions of Section 25.

There are many ways of obstructing officers in

the performance of their services or duties in making, or in relation to, the draft, without employing physical force. The neglect or refusal to do an act required by law to be done may itself be such an obstruction as to subject the offender to arrest. Suppose a person to be found standing in a passage through which the drafting officers are required to enter into a place designated by law as the place for the draft ; and suppose that his standing in that place would prevent access by these officers to the place of draft. If they request him to move away and he neglects or refuses to do so for the purpose of preventing the draft, the non-performance of the act of removal would be of itself an "obstruction of the draft, or of an officer in the performance of his duty in relation to it."

Standing mute in civil courts is, under certain circumstances, a punishable offence. And so if a person, with intent to prevent the draft, refuses to give his true name when lawfully requested so to do by an officer whose legal duty it is to ASCERTAIN and ENROLL it, it is an obstruction of that officer in the performance of one of his duties in relation to the draft. So also is the giving of false names with the same illegal intent ; and the offender will in either case be subject to summary arrest by the provost-marshal.

WILLIAM WHITING,
Solicitor of the War Department.
JAMES B. FRY,
Provost-Marshal General.

Doc. 10.

FIGHT AT BEVERLY'S FORD, VA.

NATIONAL ACCOUNTS.

IN BIVOUAC AT BEALETON, VA.,
ORANGE AND ALEXANDRIA RAILROAD,
Tuesday Evening, June 9, 1863.

THIS has truly been an exciting day. An hour since I sent you the mere skeleton of the day's operations, which scarcely affords any idea of the extent or character of our achievements. I informed you by letter on Monday what might be expected to-day, and I have now the result to record.

About the middle of last week, information of a pretty positive character was received at headquarters, concerning the massing and drilling of a large force of the enemy's cavalry in the vicinity of Culpeper. Numerous reports had been received before, but they were more or less conflicting, especially that portion of them which concerned the movement of the rebel infantry forces in a westerly direction. In my letter of Monday I gave in substance such information as I had concerning the strength and character of the enemy's augmented cavalry force. It was in the main correct, but in the light of to-day's operations I can give you the details as specifically as you can desire ; for, beside defeating the enemy in a severe battle, we have ravaged his camp, ascertained his strength to a figure, and frustrated a bold plan, the execution of which *was* to have begun to-morrow morning at daylight.

VOL. VII.—DOC. 2.

The bold reconnoissance across the Rappahannock on Friday last, below Fredericksburgh, which we rightly thought would startle the indifferent public, had more than one object. Its first object was to discover the exact whereabouts of the rebel army, which was accomplished Saturday morning. Its second object was to remain where it was as a diversion, while we hastily gathered together a force to feel of and if prudent to attack this threatening mass of cavalry opposite our extreme right flank.

General Hooker conceived the whole plan very quickly, and caused its execution to be begun with that rapidity and secrecy for which he is noted.

Saturday evening the composition of the force was determined upon, and all the cavalry that could be made immediately available was detailed for the work under command of Gen. Pleasanton, (Gen. Stoneman having been relieved,) assisted by Generals Buford and Gregg and Col. Dufie, as subordinate commanders. In addition, two small brigades of picked infantry, under General Ames, of the Eleventh corps, and Gen. Russell, of the Sixth corps, were detailed to accompany the expedition. A detail of artillery was made in the proportion of one battery to each brigade, the horse-batteries with the cavalry being in charge of Capt. Robertson, chief of artillery on General Pleasanton's staff.

The infantry force selected challenged particular admiration. The regiments were small, but they were reliable—such, for instance, as the Second, Third, and Seventh Wisconsin, Second and Thirty-third Massachusetts, Sixth Maine, Eighty-sixth and One Hundred and Twenty-fourth New-York, and one or two others of like character.

The force when completed did not, by several thousand, reach the reported number of the enemy, from twelve to fifteen thousand ; but then as far as cavalry was concerned, we sent all that could be spared, and as far as infantry was concerned, the sequel proved that fully as much was sent as could be used to advantage. And then there was a strong supposition that the force of the enemy had been exaggerated.

Gen. Pleasanton's cavalry rendezvoused during Saturday and Sunday at Catlett's Station and Warrenton Junction, getting supplies of forage and food from both places, by the Orange and Alexandria Railroad. General Ames's infantry moved Saturday evening to the Spotted Tavern, and on Sunday to near Bealeton Station. Gen. Russell's brigade moved on Sunday to Hartwood Church, and on Monday to Kelly's Ford. The plan was to rendezvous the command at the two points on the Rappahannock, Beverly's Ford on the right and Kelly's Ford on the left, the two being six miles apart, and then move the column forward toward Culpeper on roads converging at Brandy Station, where a junction of the forces was to be formed, or sooner if necessary.

On Monday evening, therefore, Gen. Buford's column left Warrenton Junction, and followed by General Ames from Bealeton, bivouacked for the night near the Bowen mansion, about one mile from Beverly's Ford. General Gregg, taking his own and Colonel Dufie's command, moved to the left from the Junction, and encamped for the night in close proximity to Kelly's Ford, where Gen. Russell had already arrived. No fires were allowed, and a vigilant watch was kept to prevent disturbances or any thing which might give any indication of our presence.

The orders were to arouse the commands at three A.M., and to make the passage of the river as soon as it was daylight.

At dawn Gen. Buford's command was in motion. Col. Davis's brigade, led by two squadrons of the Eighth New-York, and supported by the Eighth Illinois and Third Indiana, had the advance. The morning was cool and pleasant, a thick mist hung over the river, and objects on the other side were rather indistinct. Our cavalry soon reached the river, dashed in, dashed up the bank, and were well on the opposite side before the rebels in their fortifications were aware of their presence. The suddenness of the movement completely surprised them, and they at once broke for the first friendly timber, which was about one fourth of a mile in their rear. Our cavalry followed rapidly, and in these woods the first severe skirmish occurred, in which we speedily lost one of the most valued officers of the command, Col. B. F. Davis, of the Eighth New-York cavalry, and Captain in the First regular cavalry, and the same gallant officer who led the gallant charge out of Harper's Ferry last fall, and captured Longstreet's ammunition-train. When the rebels, who were dismounted, reached the woods, they began to skirmish, and detained our force there long enough to give the alarm to Jones's brigade, they being encamped just beyond in the outer edge of the woods. Though their horses were grazing in the fields, yet they speedily fell in, and in a very short time two or three squadrons came charging down the road and through the timber. Hurling their force upon the Eighth New-York, they broke it and forced it back, and killed and wounded quite a number. Col. Davis, who was gallantly leading the advance, turned to rally them, and waving his sword to the Eighth Illinois, shouted, "Come on, boys," when a rebel rode out in front of him, and fired three shots from his pistol at him, the last one taking effect in his forehead, and inflicting a mortal wound. Quick as thought Lieut. Parsons, acting Assistant Adjutant-General to Col. Davis, was at the side of the rebel, and rising in his stirrups, with one well-directed blow of his sabre, he laid his head open midway between eyes and chin, and the wretch fell dead in the dust at his horse's feet. Parsons is but a youth; his adversary was a strong, athletic man, yet the former, though young in years and slight in stature, nobly avenged his commander's fall.

By this time the gallant Eighth Illinois, though meeting with a hot reception, in which Captain Clark and Captain Forsyth were both wounded, had charged upon the rebels, and driven them back upon the main body of the enemy, who were now engaged in deploying and forming in the rear of the woods and just beyond their camp, nearly two miles from the river.

Major Whiting's command now came up to the support of the Illinois and Indiana troops. Gen. Ames also brought his infantry over, and deployed them on the left of the road as skirmishers, and then pushed them out in line of battle to the edge of the woods, in front of which the enemy was drawn up by squadrons, with artillery at the intervals, which omitted no opportunity to shell every thing in sight that had motion to it. Thus far the enemy evidently had but one brigade at hand, and a few prisoners taken said they belonged to the Sixth, Seventh, and Twelfth Virginia cavalry, of General Jones's brigade. When asked if he was "Jones, the guerrilla," they indignantly denied the imputation; nevertheless, he was. Gen. Pleasanton now directed General Buford to make preparations to charge this force in the flank, while the infantry and artillery engaged it in front. It was desirable to do this as soon as possible, as the enemy might be getting reënforcements at any moment. General Buford having driven the enemy's pickets and skirmishers in the open fields on the right of the road, sent in the Sixth Pennsylvania, supported by the Fifth and Sixth regulars, to charge this line on the flank. The Pennsylvanians came up to their work in splendid style. This is the regiment formerly known as the "Lancers," and they had a matter of pride to settle in this charge. Steadily and gallantly, they advanced out of the woods in excellent order, and then dashed across the open field in an oblique direction toward the enemy's guns. They went up almost to their very muzzles, through a storm of canister and shell, and would have taken them, when suddenly there dashed out of the woods on their right flank, in almost the very spot from which they themselves had issued, two whole regiments of the enemy, on the full charge. Retreat was almost cut off, but the regiments, now subjected to a fire in front and on both flanks, charged back, cutting their way out with considerable loss. The Sixth regulars came to the rescue, but the fire was so severe that even these veterans could not stand it, and they fell back with some loss. In this charge we lost about the only prisoners captured by the enemy during the day. Major Morris, of the Sixth Pennsylvania, was seen to fall from his horse, and is probably wounded and a prisoner. Captain Davis, of the same regiment, was killed. Capt. Lieper was wounded, and Major Hazeltine had his horse shot under him. Capt. Dahlgren, of General Hooker's staff, a model of cool and dauntless bravery, charged with the regiments, and his horse was shot in two places. He describes the charge as one of the finest of the war.

The enemy was now being reënforced very rapidly, and in a short time Gen. Pleasanton found that Buford's small division was opposed by three strong brigades of rebels, with artillery to match.

After the repulse of the Sixth Pennsylvania, the rebels made two rapid attempts to gain our rear and the approaches to the ford, both on our right and on our left, but particularly on the right. But they were handsomely foiled by Buford, and for two hours there was very sharp skirmishing, rapid shelling, and admirable manœuvring by both sides, in the open and undulating fields on our extreme right. A brigade of the enemy's cavalry came down the road which branches off to the right from Beverly's, and made a dash for the ford, but they were too late. A couple of squadrons and a section of artillery interposed. They never got nearer than a mile to the point, and during the two hours that they remained in position they suffered severely from our shells and skirmishers.

At this stage of the engagement, General Pleasanton plainly saw that the division under Gen. Buford was far outnumbered, and much anxiety was expressed to hear from General Gregg, whose column was considerably stronger than Buford's. Word had been received from him at eight o'clock, saying that he had crossed with scarce any opposition, and that he was driving the enemy before him, but his guns had not yet been heard. Matters thus remained in *statu quo* until twelve o'clock, nothing being done save some artillery practice, which was pretty accurate on both sides. We dismounted one gun of a section that the enemy had on the extreme right, and compelled the enemy to move the other. During this interim the skirmishers of each party would frequently become very annoying. General Ames formed his skirmish line, and they picked off the rebel officers without mercy. Although our infantry were masked by the timber, yet the enemy seemed to know what we had, and always refused to meet them, save by dismounted cavalry as skirmishers against skirmishers. They were very profuse of their shells and canister, however, and opened whenever any of our cavalry approached near enough. Many of our men were wounded by canister-shot, a thing almost heretofore unknown in cavalry fighting.

At one time, on the left of General Ames's brigade, the rebel cavalry skirmishers had advanced and concealed themselves in some bushes, where they were annoying a body of the Ninth New-York. Major Martin, of that regiment, was finally ordered to take a squadron and drive them out. This he most gallantly did, though it was right in the teeth of the enemy's artillery, and he was met by a perfect storm of canister. He captured fifty prisoners, but owing to the severity of the enemy's fire, could bring but a portion of them away. The gallant Major was himself wounded in the shoulder.

About one o'clock Buford again began to press the enemy, and this time he showed evident signs of uneasiness, and soon withdrew his force from our right flank as though he had a fire in the rear. About the same time we heard Gregg's guns, and some prisoners taken from Robinson's North-Carolina brigade just then reported General Russell's infantry advancing through the woods on their right flank and rear. General Gregg, from the sound of the firing, was evidently in the vicinity of Brandy Station. Pleasanton now pushed forward, but the rebels soon gave way, and

fell back rapidly. They were in a bad predicament — for Gregg was almost directly in their rear, Russell was on their right flank, and Buford on their front. They therefore made a hasty retreat, abandoning their old camp entirely, part of which we had already occupied, and two regiments were very near being cut off, as Kilpatrick moved off toward the right, to make connection with Buford. They had but a narrow strip of land, not covered by our force, through which to escape.

General Pleasanton's headquarters were moved forward to where the rebel commander's had been, and the lines of the two columns were soon connected.

General Gregg reported that his two brigades, under Kilpatrick and Wyndham, had been hotly engaged all the morning, but had driven the enemy uniformly from the river back to Brandy Station. Our troops, especially the First New-Jersey, First Maine, and Tenth New-York, fought most gallantly, and repulsed the enemy in repeated charges, though losing heavily themselves. The artillery with General Gregg also suffered considerably, and the Sixth New-York battery was almost totally disabled. It did excellent service, however. In the charges by General Gregg's column, a stand of colors and over one hundred and fifty prisoners were taken. Colonel Wyndham's brigade captured the heights commanding Brandy Station, and there discovered rebel infantry being brought up by the cars. A portion of it drew up and fired a volley at our cavalry. Another correspondent will give you further particulars about the gallant fighting of this column. Col. Wyndham was shot through the calf of the leg by a bushwhacker, but his wound is not serious, and he still keeps the saddle.

While a junction was being effected with Gregg's column on the left, Buford and Ames were pushing out on the right, and, with Vincent's battery, Buford had by two o'clock carried all the crests occupied by the enemy during the forenoon, and had forced him back over three miles from the river. In these exploits the regulars, especially the Second and Fifth regiments, distinguished themselves by their intrepidity. The Third Wisconsin skirmishers also won praise by the accuracy of their fire, which was fatal to many a rebel.

The fact that the enemy were now falling back upon strong infantry supports, and we being already numerically inferior to them, induced Gen. Pleasanton to consult with his subordinates, and it having been left discretionary with the former to advance or return, it was finally deemed prudent to return, and at four o'clock our forces began falling back. The enemy was not inclined to "pick a fight" on the return, and, save some slight skirmishing, we were not molested. Buford's division fell back to Beverly Ford, and Gregg's division to Rappahannock Ford, a mile and a half below. We brought off all our dead and wounded, and also some of the enemy's, while many of the latter were still remaining on the field when we retired. By dark our forces were all over the river, and the wounded of Buford's division all loaded in the cars and on the way to Washington. The loss in his division is about one hundred and eighty, and in Gregg's about the same. The rebel prisoners report their loss as heavier than ever before, and express admiration of the gallantry of our cavalry. The total number of prisoners taken is about two hundred and twenty-five, and we lost about fifty.

Though our force was not large enough to thoroughly defeat the rebels, yet they received a sound thrashing, and it will result in postponing their "grand raids" into the North for some time, if not indefinitely; for, beside chastising them, we have gained full information of their strength, character and designs. Witness the following letter captured on the battle-field, which I have copied from the original verbatim:

CAMP NEAR BRANDRETH STATION, CULPEPER }
COURT-HOUSE, June 8, 1863. }

DEAR BROTHER: We have made another change of base. We left Dayton one week ago to-day, and after five days of marching we encamped at this place. We have had two grand reviews of five brigades of cavalry, about twelve thousand in number, under General Stuart. The first took place on Saturday, when we were inspected by Stuart; and I have just now returned from the second, when we were inspected by Lieutenant-General Robert E. Lee in person. He was a fine-looking man, but very gray-haired. We are now in a battery numbering about sixteen pieces, under the command of Major Beckham. Longstreet's division passed us on Saturday. The Wise artillery was along. You can look out for some small fighting before a week. We are now about two miles from the Rappahannock, at Beverly Ford. I expect, from the preparations that is being made, that we are going to make a grand raid toward the Potomac as soon as the valley is cleared. . . .

You must excuse the shortness of this letter, as I have just returned from the review, and I feel tired from riding so much. Direct your letter to Chero's battery, Jones's cavalry brigade.

Please write immediately, as we may leave in a couple of days.

Your affectionate brother,   J. M. D.

I leave the name blank for the sake of the writer. This confirms all the information we previously had. Fitz-Hugh Lee, W. F. Lee, G. W. Jones, Robertson of North-Carolina, and Field of Virginia, commanded the brigades. In the latter's brigade is all the mounted infantry they had—reported at eight hundred men.

An order was found from General Stuart, dated June sixth, ordering the commands to be held in readiness to move at fifteen minutes' notice.

A captain, who was taken prisoner, said they were under orders to move on Wednesday morning at daylight. They moved a day sooner, and backward at that.

The prompt manner in which these plans of the enemy have been baffled will elicit the admi-

ration of every one. A day longer, and it would have been too late. Their plans are now known, and we can prepare accordingly. Pennsylvania and Maryland will awake to the importance of the occasion, and make all needful preparations to receive this horde of raiders. They will probably only defer, not abandon, their designs, and such a body of cavalry once loose in a defenceless State, they can take the whole of i   But General Hooker has unmasked them, and given time for preparation. Shortly he will be fully ready himself to take them thoroughly in hand.

L. L. CROUNSE.

OFFICIAL REPORT OF COLONEL WYNDHAM.

HEADQUARTERS SECOND BRIGADE, }
THIRD DIVISION CAVALRY CORPS. }

Captain H. C. Weir, Assistant Adjutant-General Third Division Cavalry Corps:

CAPTAIN: I have the honor to make the following report of the part my command took in the action of yesterday. After crossing the river and coming up with Colonel Duffie, I turned to the right, and, in obedience to orders from the general commanding, pushed on rapidly to Brandy Station. On arriving at that place I found the enemy strongly posted in the rear and on the right of the station, with batteries planted on the heights near the Barber House.

I immediately formed my command into line of battle, and had the section of artillery attached to it placed in position, and opened on their battery in front of the Barber House.

Observing the enemy breaking away on the left, I ordered a portion of the First Maryland cavalry, led by Major Russell, to charge on the station, which they did in fine style, capturing a number of the enemy, and bringing away an ambulance and four horses, captured by our advance-guard. I next ordered the section of artillery to advance, as they had completely silenced the battery they had been firing upon, and at the same time ordered the First New-Jersey to charge on a battery stationed in the rear of the Barber House, and the First Pennsylvania reserve corps and the balance of the First Maryland to charge the heights on which the house stands. The whole command moved gallantly forward and nobly accomplished the work assigned them.

The First Maryland, which consisted of little more than a squadron, led by Lieutenant-Colonel Deems, charged first, but were met by fully a regiment of the enemy, posted behind the buildings and drawn up in the garden and orchard, and, after a spirited fight, were compelled to fall back. The First Pennsylvania, coming up, charged next. Col. Taylor, leading part of the regiment, struck the enemy in front, while Lieut.-Colonel Gardiner, with the balance, dashed on his flank next to the house, forcing him back at both points, cutting him off from the house, and gaining his rear, drove him from his cover into the open plain below, where he was again met by the First Maryland cavalry, which had rallied. Thus assailed on both sides, his force was completely scattered, a large number being killed, wounded or captured. The charge of the First New-Jersey on the battery in the rear of the house I led in person, aided by Lieut.-Colonel Broderick. At the first onset the enemy were driven from their guns. The support coming up was met, and in a few minutes also driven back. Reënforced, it returned, and was again repulsed.

My command being now much scattered by the charges it had made, Colonel Duffie not coming up to my support, as I expected, and seeing the enemy strongly reënforced, advancing from several points, I was compelled to withdraw. This was done by the greatest part of the command forming on the Brandy Station road, while I collected the balance at the station, and forming them into a rear-guard, remained till the field was cleared. The enemy here charged upon my line twice, but were repulsed each time by my carbineers with heavy loss. Having checked the enemy's advance on my retreating column, I then took across the field to join the head of my command, when a squad of the enemy's cavalry concealed in the woods fired, wounding me through the leg. I still retained command until five o'clock P.M., when orders were given to retreat, when, becoming very much exhausted from loss of blood, I turned over the command to Colonel Taylor, of the First Pennsylvania reserve cavalry, and left the field. He reports that shortly afterward he received orders to report to General Buford, and assisted in covering the withdrawal of his command across the river.

In closing my report it affords me no small degree of pleasure to be able to say that all of my command that followed me on the field behaved nobly, standing unmoved under the enemy's artillery fire, and when ordered to charge dashing forward with a spirit and determination that swept all before them. I cannot speak too highly of the manner in which the field officers of my command acted, without exception gallantly and efficiently performing every duty assigned them; and of the line officers I can say the same. I lament to say that Lieutenant-Colonel Broderick and Major Shelmire, of the First New-Jersey cavalry, were wounded and captured, and Major W. T. McEwen, First Pennsylvania cavalry, wounded; Captain Creager, of First Maryland, killed; Captain Sawyer, of First New-Jersey, missing, and seven other officers wounded or missing, whose names are reported in the list of casualties. Two hundred and seven enlisted men are reported killed, wounded, and missing.

Major January, who was doing duty as field officer of the day, and Captain H. S. Thomas, Acting Quartermaster-General; Lieutenant W. P. Lloyd, Acting Assistant Adjutant-General; Lieutenant Gremlee and Lieutenant Parry, Acting Aid-de-camp of my staff, all rendered invaluable service by the prompt and efficient manner in which they had every order executed, and the assistance they afforded in rallying and re-forming the different portions of the command. Respectfully submitted,

PERCY WYNDHAM,
Commanding Brigade.

CASUALTIES IN THE FIRST NEW-JERSEY CAVALRY.

The following is a complete list of the casualties in the First New-Jersey cavalry, near Brandy Station, Va., June ninth, 1863:

Colonel Sir Percy Wyndham, wounded; Lieutenant-Colonel V. Brodrick, wounded and missing; Major J. H. Shelmire, wounded and missing; Captain Henry Sawyer, wounded; Lieutenant Hyde Crocker, wounded and missing; John Black, company A, missing; E. Crossdale, company A, missing, Charles E. Wilson, company A, missing; Henry Clark, company A, missing; Joseph Howard, company B, killed; Aaron Rake, company B, wounded; Sergeant S. P. Crossman, company B, missing; John Tynon, company B, John Casler, company B, missing; Thos. Boyle, company C, missing; William McCune, company C, missing; Josiah Buchain, company D, wounded; Joseph Crane, company D, missing; Octave Antonio, company D, missing; Sergeant George W. Stewart, company E, wounded and missing; Sergeant James H. Palmater, company E, missing; Corporal Robert Williams, missing; T. L. Clement, missing; Daniel McCormick, missing; George Polston, company E, killed; Sergeant Samuel Rainear, company F, killed; Corporal Amos Poinsett, company F, wounded; Charles Cadot, company F, wounded; Nathan Moore, company F, missing; John C. Danty, company F, missing; Daniel Oliver, company F, missing; Sergeant Joseph Thibesdeau, company F, missing; Corporal R. S. Asay, company F, missing; R. Darnstad, company G, killed; A. A. Ringlop, company G, killed; Sergeant J. P. Brower, company G, wounded and missing; Sergeant B. G. Joline, company G, wounded and missing; W. P. Brown, company G, missing; John Finnigan, company G, missing; F. Craus, company G, missing; J. H. Stubbs, company G, wounded and missing; M. Summers, company G, wounded and missing; Corporal John Scaffer, company H, missing; W. H. H. Jackson, company H, missing; Douglass Grey, company H, missing; Timothy Mahoney, company H, wounded; Sergeant Chas. Earley, company I, wounded and missing; Sergeant F. Schall, company I, wounded; Philip Ham, company I, missing; Sergeant Robert Tuthill, company K, wounded and missing; Sergeant Richard Decker, company K, wounded; Jno. Hendershot, company K, wounded; John Hanley, company K, missing; James Linley, company M, missing; Horace Van Orden, company M, missing. Total—officers, five; men fifty-two—fifty-seven. Carried into action, twenty-two officers and two hundred and eighty-one men.

E. A. PAUL'S ACCOUNT.

RAPPAHANNOCK RIVER, Wednesday, June 10, 1863.

In justice to the gallant men who have fallen, to those who are still suffering from injuries received, as well as to the brave men who passed through the terrible ordeal of yesterday unscathed, and to-day stand ready at a moment's notice to meet the enemies of their country in deadly strife again, I shall endeavor to give a more detailed account than you have yet received, of the movements and conduct of Gen. Gregg's command, with such scenes and incidents occurring in the whole of Gen. Pleasanton's command as came under my own observation, and as I have obtained from sources which I deem reliable.

Gen. Gregg moved from Warrenton Junction on Monday, the eighth, encamping that night near Kelly's Ford, a fording place on the Rappahannock River, six miles below the Orange and Alexandria Railroad bridge. His command consisted of the Second and Third divisions of cavalry, a section of artillery attached to each, and a force of one thousand five hundred foot-soldiers, the latter under the command of Gen. Russell. The movement across the river was commenced on Tuesday morning, at about six o'clock, the Second division, commanded by Col. Duffie, taking the advance, closely followed by Gen. Gregg's own division, the Third, and the infantry. By nine o'clock the whole force was safely on the right bank of the river, no opposition to the crossing having been met except such as could be given by a rebel picket of twenty badly scared men, who ran away at the very sight of a blue coat. Here the command was divided into three columns. Col. Duffie, with the Second division and a section of Tidball's old battery, commanded by Lieut. ——, occupied the extreme left, and at once moved forward to Stevensburgh, where a regiment of the enemy was discovered, supporting a section of artillery stationed to oppose the advance of our troops. A brief but sanguinary struggle took place, resulting in the capturing of one hundred and fifty prisoners, and dispersing the balance of the force in front. Gen. Gregg, though sending frequently for this command, did not see it again until the movement to join Gen. Buford, who, as stated in a previous letter, had crossed the river at Beverly Ford, and was engaged with a superior force of the enemy. The Third division occupied the centre, and took a road leading to Brandy Station, and the infantry occupying the right, moved along near the river—the object being to unite the two wings of Gen. Pleasanton's command, on either side of the railroad. This was not effected, however, owing to the stubborn resistance of the enemy, they being present in large force, until after the fight at Brandy Station, some account of which will be given in the proper place. The Third division occupied the centre, and as it participated in some of the severest cavalry fighting of the war, I shall endeavor to give its movements somewhat in detail. The First brigade of this division, commanded by Col. Kilpatrick, was composed of his own regiment, the Second New-York cavalry, (Harris's Light,) First Maine cavalry, Col. Douty, and Tenth New-York cavalry, Lieut.-Col. Irvine. The Second brigade was commanded by Colonel Wyndham, and consisted of his own regiment, the First New-Jersey cavalry, First Maryland cavalry, Lieut.-Col. Deems, and First Pennsylvania cavalry, Lieut.-Col. Taylor. Each brigade was formed in three columns by squadrons, the First brigade on the right, and the Second on the left.

The ground between Kelly's Ford and Brandy Station is rolling, interspersed with clumps of trees, and not the most desirable for cavalry operations; nevertheless the men of the different regiments succeeded in keeping in excellent order. The division moved toward Brandy Station. The first indication of the enemy in force was the discovery of a signal station on a hill to the right by Capt. J. W. Kester, Aid to Gen. Gregg. Just previous to this, and one mile from the station, a picket of two men was captured. Gen. Gregg, upon being satisfied by the working of the signal-flag that a force of the enemy was near by, ordered Col. Wyndham to advance with his brigade, find the enemy, and attack him. Col. Wyndham moved promptly forward, and when arrived nearly opposite, and to the south of the signal station, a two-gun battery was opened upon the command at short-range. The two guns attached to the brigade were soon in position and at work, and two or three squadrons were sent forward to secure the railroad—a train loaded with infantry was coming up from Culpeper. Our men turned a switch, and the train was run off the track; another train soon followed, but the enemy then had possession of the railroad, having forced the troops occupying the ground to retire. Captain Martin's two guns, with the First brigade, were ordered forward, and took a position south-east of Telegraph Hill. The rebels were soon forced to withdraw their battery, and they moved it across the railroad track to the vicinity of a house, in which it was subsequently ascertained were the rebel Gens. Stuart, Hampton, and Jones, the latter having just arrived from Winchester (the rebel prisoners say) to make arrangements to join the proposed expedition into Pennsylvania and Maryland. Upon this point it appears two rebel colums were approaching. The advance, Colonel Wyndham had attacked and driven back. Following up the advantage thus gained, the First Maryland was ordered to charge, which they did in the most gallant manner, surrounding the house in which the notorious rebel chieftains were plotting. The enemy fought desperately at this point, and several hand-to-hand conflicts took place. Our men were gaining the advantage, when a large rebel force advanced, and they were forced to retire. As soon as the First Maryland had got a little scattered in the mélée, the First New-Jersey, Lieut.-Col. Broderick at their head, charged, and was followed in turn by the First Pennsylvania, led by Lieut.-Col. Taylor. At first, as each regiment came charging into the fight, the enemy were forced back, and though their force was much larger than ours, they continued to fall back until largely reënforced. On a rise just at the rear of the house before referred to, Colonel Wyndham's brigade captured two guns. When forced back to near Brandy Station, the guns were dragged along and placed with a section of our own artillery. The enemy dashed upon this battery, commanded by Capt. Martin, with great fury, and killed and wounded nine of the men at the guns with their sabres. By the order of Gen. Gregg, Capt. Kester placed a two-gun battery so as to rake the position, and the rebels were forced to retire into the woods, when our men again got possession of the guns. The enemy was again reënforced, and another desperate conflict was had over the guns. One had burst, and another was rendered useless by a ball being rammed home in the excitement without a cartridge. Nearly all of the horses had been killed by the rebel sharp-shooters, and it was impossible to drag the remaining two guns away by hand. The enemy, again reënforced, made a final charge upon the guns, and succeeded in holding the position. In this *mélée*—one of the most exciting and desperate that has occurred during the whole war—the sword, for the most part, was the only weapon used. Col. Wyndham, more conspicuous than the rest of the officers who mingled in the fight, by his dress and general appearance, was evidently recognized and made a target of, both by swordsmen and carbineers. He escaped with a ball in the calf of his right leg.

Gen. Gregg and staff advanced and ordered Col. Kilpatrick to support Col. Wyndham on the right. As the first regiment, Tenth New-York, Lieut.-Col. Irvine, emerged from the woods, they charged upon the rebels formed near the railroad, and were closely followed by the Harris Light cavalry, (Second New-York,) Lieut.-Col. Davies. They met with such firm resistance that they became somewhat scattered, and were ordered back—only a portion of them having crossed the railroad. At this juncture, the First Maine cavalry, commanded by Col. C. S. Douty, came upon the field. It was a critical moment. A line of skirmishers had been advanced to the railroad, a section of artillery thrown forward on the right; a superior force of the rebels had driven our forces from the hill on the left so gallantly taken by the Second brigade, the Tenth being on the left of the First brigade—the whole command rising in echelon, was ordered to charge and drive the enemy from the hill and hold it, when the whole line was threatened by a superior force. It was here Col. Irvine was seen to fall. Col. Davies, of the Harris Light cavalry, was ordered to attack the enemy in flank—their movements were checked by two columns of the enemy just beyond the railroad—and both regiments were thrown into some confusion, and they were called back to rally. It was just at this point that Colonel Douty emerged from the woods, when he was made aware of the attitude of affairs, and was called upon to charge the enemy in flank—the two previous attempts having proved failures. The force in front outnumbered ours two to one—but onward the sons of Maine swept, with drawn sabres and plumes waving in the air—a grander sight was seldom ever witnessed; across the railroad they dashed and drove every thing before them, and in a very few minutes the hill at the rear of Stuart's headquarters was carried; two cannon, a flag, and a large number of prisoners were captured. As the First Maine arrived at Stuart's quarters, the first battalion, under Lieut.-Col. Smith, passed to the left of the house, and Major Boothby, with the second battalion, swept round to the right

over the hill; and on they rode for about three quarters of a mile beyond where the regiment was again formed. Here was another critical position; there was no one coming to their support, and they were not only to lose what they had, by their daring valor, gained, but there was a fair prospect of being cut off; the enemy were closing in upon them near the railroad, and to escape they had to pass between two sections of artillery and a cross-fire of carbines. The position was taken in at a glance—a dash was made toward one of the batteries, as if to take it, when on a sudden a detour was made, and the whole command passed around the rebels and rejoined the brigade. The section of artillery captured by this regiment could not be taken away, but the horses were all killed.

The several divisions then fell back toward Kelly's Ford, united and moved up the right of the Rappahannock, across the railroad, until the left of General Buford's command was reached some time during the afternoon. The fact that the rebels did not make a step toward following the command, though vastly superior in numbers, indicates very clearly that they had had quite enough of the Yankees for one day.

During the afternoon, the main object of the reconnoissance having been accomplished, our forces gradually recrossed the river at Beverly Ford—two miles above the Orange and Alexandria Railroad bridge—the rear covered by the Eighth Illinois cavalry and Fifty-sixth Pennsylvania infantry. The enemy kept up a desultory fire, but little damage was done. The troops retired at their leisure and in good order—every man, though fatigued, feeling fully satisfied with the result of the contest.

Just at dark, a rebel regiment made its appearance near the Rappahannock Railroad Station. One regiment crossed the river to see what they wanted, but the enemy ran away so fast they did not ascertain the special object of the untimely visit.

This being really the first cavalry fight in force which has been indulged in during the present war, it becomes a matter of interest to all to know how our troopers thus massed conducted themselves. As one who travelled quite extensively over the extended field while the troops were the most hotly engaged—from five o'clock A.M. until one o'clock P.M.—I can say with pleasure that I neither saw myself or heard of any thing but what was creditable alike to their manhood and the cause in which they were engaged. In two instances, squadrons were broken while charging and suddenly and unexpectedly coming upon superior forces. In one of these cases, two thirds of the men engaged were recruits, and had never been in a fight before. In the other instance, they were momentarily thrown into a panic by the death of their leader. Both of these commands quickly rallied, and subsequently, by their gallant conduct, wiped away whatever stigma any one might consider as having been attached to them for previous conduct. One or two regiments also got somewhat scattered after a charge, but they were speedily in line again, and a few moments afterward fully retrieved their previously well-earned reputation. These exceptions are always to be met with on every battle-field, and are liable to occur with the most experienced troops.

Of individual acts of gallantry I could write columns, if time permitted. One of the most remarkable, perhaps, was a dash made by Major Martin, of the Ninth New-York cavalry, in Gen. Buford's command. In front of their line were two belts of timber, extending from the main forest, the whole of which was occupied by the enemy in force, the line of skirmishers extending from one point of woods to the other. Major Martin was ordered to sweep in this line of skirmishers. He did so by making one of the most brilliant and daring dashes on record. First sending a detachment, commanded by Capt. Hanley, to clear one point of the woods of the enemy's carbineers, Major Martin, with three companies, dashed across the open space, in rear of the skirmishers, and forced in as prisoners nearly the whole line of rebel skirmishers, extending across the open space between the two belts of timber. The spot was covered by artillery and the carbines of an immense rebel force. Major Martin had two men killed and several wounded. He escaped with a severe flesh-wound in the right shoulder. Capts. Ayres and Dickson, and Lieutenants Burroughs, Bailey, and Herrick, who participated in this attack, were not injured.

Major Gasten, of the First Pennsylvania cavalry, attached to Gen. Gregg's staff, was captured, and his captors, while taking him to the rear, commenced to draw lots for his clothing and equipments. His horse being a fast walker, he got a little ahead of his captors, when he turned about, bid them good day, and escaped.

Men often resort to curious expedients to escape being captured. A sergeant of the Harris cavalry got within the enemy's lines. To escape being captured he climbed a tree, and remained there until the enemy had fallen back. A little bugler attached to the First Maine was captured, but during the night escaped and regained his regiment, then across the river.

A member of company M, First Maine, captured a mounted rebel, fully armed. In making the capture, he pointed an empty pistol at the head of Mr. Reb, who surrendered at discretion. On the way to the rear the same man took another rebel prisoner in the same way.

Lieut. Taylor, company M, First Maine, captured a man on foot. The rebs pursued, and he made the man run before his horse. When the man gave out he made him take hold of his horse's tail and run along. He saved himself and prisoner.

In no single instance during the day did a rebel stand in single combat. The moment one of our men approached one of the enemy standing alone, invariably the enemy fled. This is no vain boasting, but a fact which was illustrated in my presence a number of times, and can be vouched for by hundreds of persons engaged in the conflict.

A negro held a position in the rebel line of skirmishers on the extreme left, directly in front of the Sixth Pennsylvania cavalry. He was making some excellent shots when the Pennsylvania boys concluded to put a stop to him. One man fired while another stood ready to shoot the negro as he raised to fire again. The plan succeeded, and the negro was killed.

In a previous letter the noble conduct of Lieut. Parsons in avenging the death of Col. Davis, of the Eighth New-York, was recorded. A similar case occurred in the death of Captain Foot, of the Eighth New-York. A skirmisher had fired three shots at the Captain, the third striking his horse. He dismounted to see how much the animal was injured, and had just placed one foot in the stirrup to remount, when the same man fired again. The ball this time struck the Captain in the back, he raised one hand and fell to the ground dead. A private in Capt. Foot's company, named Cruthers, watched his opportunity and killed the man who had shot his captain.

Among the captures was a rebel flag, belonging to a North-Carolina regiment. Corporal Drew, company A, First Maine, captured a rebel battle-flag in the fight near the house occupied by Stuart. A negro servant in the Sixth New-York cavalry got hold of a gun and fought valiantly in a line of skirmishers. The loss sustained by Gen. Gregg's command, so far as at present ascertained, will not exceed two hundred and twenty-five. In addition to the casualties already forwarded, I send you the following:

Capt. Davis, Sixth New-York cavalry—killed.

Lieutenant Halliday, Sixth New-York cavalry—missing.

Major Maurice, Sixth New-York cavalry—prisoner.

J. W. Ross, Third Virginia (rebel)—wounded in thigh.

David Lowes, One Hundred and Twenty-fourth New-York volunteers—ankle.

Thos. Lee, Sixth United States cavalry—right arm.

Soloman Grath, Fifty-sixth Pennsylvania—left leg.

O. D. Hess, Eighth Illinois cavalry—arm.

O. Richard, Sixth Pennsylvania cavalry—back.

C. Oleus, Fifth United States cavalry—back.

Lieut. Wade, Sixth United States cavalry—head, slight.

Lieut. Flynn, Second United States cavalry—slight.

Lieut. Phillips, Sixth New-York—right leg amputated.

Major Robins, one of General Pleasanton's staff, had two horses shot under him.

Capt. Sawyer, of the First New-Jersey cavalry, is missing; as also Major Forbes, commissary of Colonel Kilpatrick's brigade.

E. A. PAUL.

ANOTHER ACCOUNT.

HEADQUARTERS FIRST MARYLAND CAVALRY, }
WARRENTON JUNCTION, June 11, 1863. }

You are already informed of the cavalry battle which took place between General Pleasanton's and Stuart's cavalry, at Beverly Ford, on the ninth instant, but it must certainly be of great interest to know how Maryland was represented by the behavior of its First regiment of cavalry, now commanded by Lieutenant-Colonel James Deems. Let me tell you what part this gallant regiment played. The regiment, a part of the Second brigade, commanded by Colonel Wyndham, of the Third cavalry division, commanded by General Gregg, left Warrenton Junction on the eighth instant, and crossed Kelly's Ford at three o'clock A.M., on the ninth instant. Continual cannonading was heard on our right ever since five o'clock; it was at Beverly's Ford, where General Buford had engaged parts of Fitz-Hugh Lee's and Wade Hampton's divisions. After crossing the ford the whole division marched rapidly on the road leading to the right to Culpeper, and was near Brandy Station within an hour and a half. Coming out of the woods the enemy had placed several guns to the right of the road behind an embankment, and at once commenced shelling our column with great precision and in rapid succession. Their cavalry, supporting the artillery, was stationed behind several ruins of old farm-houses and the gardens and bushes surrounding them, close in rear of their guns. A section of the Sixth New-York artillery was immediately brought up, placed opposite, and opened a rapid succession of shells, but their firing, although effective, was not very precise. After a short artillery duel of this kind, the order was given to charge, and Colonel Deems at once ordered his squadrons forward. The men, eager for the fight, would have rushed on with fury, but he quieted them, and gave them orders to walk, draw sabre, then a slow trot, and finally a gallop charge, and on went our brave Maryland boys, jumping two fences, and not one shrinking back or wavering. Colonel Deems and all the officers most bravely ahead charged and met the enemy on the other side of the defences. The sabre was to decide, not the pistol; and, although the rebs fired their volleys in rapid succession, the cold steel blade decided. They were driven back. Following the retiring foe, their allies rushed out of the woods by thousands, and our brave boys retired. At the time the charge was made the enemy was trying to run off a railroad train, wagons, and ambulances. Colonel Deems at once ordered the third squadron, composed of companies H, E, and K, Lieutenant R. Norwood, of company K, commanding, toward Brandy Station. When about a hundred yards distant, Colonel Deems commanded a gallop, and accompanied the squadron a short distance beyond the station, where he halted with six men and sent eleven prisoners, captured by the squadron, to the rear. The remainder of the squadron, led by Major Russell, charged gallantly out the different roads leading from the station after the flying rebels. They were too late for the trains; but our gallant Major Russell, with a few men, captured an ambulance with General Stuart's plan of the intended raid which was to have been made into Maryland and Pennsylvania; also many other valuable papers were captured and secured.

This squadron, led by Major Russell, was repeatedly charged upon by squads of rebels; but by charging them in return and ordering reënforcements with loud voice (although none were very near) their overwhelming numbers were checked, or else they would have annihilated it. With the remainder of the squadron Major Russell and Lieutenant Norwood captured thirty-five prisoners, and in bringing them to the rear were entirely cut off by the advance of two rebel regiments, who retook twenty-two of the prisoners. Major Russell and Lieutenant Norwood made their way around the right flank of the enemy with the remaining thirteen prisoners. Major Russell here met the Hon. John Minor Botts, and shook hands with him.

The first squadron, commanded by Captain J. Hancock, and composed of companies F, G, and L, proceeded, by order of Colonel Wyndham, on the road to Germania Ford. When they came within a mile of the Culpeper and Fredericksburgh roads, they met the rebel pickets, and learned that since the sixth instant no force had passed up from Fredericksburgh. Captain Hancock, after a general reconnoissance, returned safely with his squadron, and joined in other useful operations on the road. Part of company A, in charge of Lieutenant Charles R. Bankard, by order of Major Russell, patroled the Fredericksburgh road, and the balance, with Lieutenant John Axer, who commanded the first platoon of the fourth squadron, took part in the charges toward Brandy Station.

Company B, belonging to the second squadron, commanded by First Lieutenant Henry Appel and Second Lieutenant C. E. Lyman, behaved with great valor throughout the whole engagement. This company, like company D, is composed entirely of Germans from the city of Baltimore. They behaved very gallantly, and really deserve praise. Company D, commanded by First Lieutenant Henry C. Erich, formed the centre of the second squadron, commanded by Captain John K. Buckley. Every member was at his post from the beginning to the end of the fight. Our forces suffering severely from a battery on a hill near Brandy Station, the attempt was made to take it. All acted with coolness and gallantry to the last of the fight. The rebels tried hard to take the flag from the color-bearer, Corporal Michael Karman, but the brave German defended it most furiously, now sticking its point into the enemy, then knocking one over the head with it, changing into the other hand, hitting with the butt one on the other side; and although hundreds of shots were fired at him, he remained unhurt, and the flag was carried off by him in triumph. The wounded in this company were comparatively few. Mortally wounded was private John Aich—a ball from a shrapnel struck his breast. Lieutenant Henry C. Erich received two light wounds from pistol-balls, and his horse was shot through the mouth. He was near being killed by a rebel who approached him in the rear, and he was just about splitting his head with a sabre when private Klein, of company B, shot the rebel through the heart; he dropped the sabre, and falling back, his horse galloped off with the dying man. Corporal Richard Klein and private Daniel Gnord, of this company, are reported missing.

Captain John K. Buckley, of company C, commanding second squadron, composed of companies B, C, and D, was ordered by Colonel Wyndham to charge upon and take a battery on the hill facing the railroad. Captain Buckley ordered "draw sabre," and onward they went. As soon as the rebels saw our men charge, they pulled the guns out of their position, and a brigade of rebel cavalry moved quickly in front of their guns, meeting our second squadron with drawn pistols. The fury with which our men charged broke the rebel line and turned the whole of their column, and drove them from the top of the hill, our men holding it for fifteen minutes. Captain Buckley was first on top of the hill, and waving his sabre cheered the men on, who bravely followed their gallant commander. Lieutenant-Colonel Broaderick, of the First New-Jersey, charged immediately, following with three squadrons on the left of our second squadron; but the enemy then brought up new forces, and, by overwhelming numbers, made our men retire, when they fell back on our battery, which was unsupported. Following our men, they took Captain Buckley and Colonel Deems prisoners, but both soon made their escape, our men having in the intermediate time rallied, and re-charged the enemy. As a strange instance it is worth mentioning that the sabre taken from Captain Buckley was an hour afterward recaptured by some colonel and handed back to the Captain.

Corporal James A. Campbell deserves great credit for charging on the rebels with his guidon, which he used as a lance, dealing severe blows on the enemy after he was twice severely wounded. Exhausted from the loss of blood, clasping his guidon, he finally fell from his horse, and has not been heard from since.

To company I was assigned the duty of supporting the brigade battery, which it did nobly, standing unflinchingly under a heavy artillery fire. After all the rest of the regiment had charged, and were being forced back by the very weight of men and horses brought against them, Colonel Wyndham ordered this company to charge the pursuing foe. The gallant and lamented Frank M. Creager led them, and they drove the enemy back until a fresh regiment was hurled against them. They fell back and rallied for a second charge with drawn sabres. Just as they were about to charge, Captain Creager fell, pierced by a bullet in the left breast. The command then devolved on Second Lieutenant R. J. Kimble. He fearlessly led them into the second charge; they were forced back. Again he rallied and led them to their third and last charge, on which they lost two privates killed, six wounded, and eight taken prisoners. Those of the latter

were recaptured. Colonel Wyndham then gave the order to retire, but in retiring the gallant company I brought twenty prisoners off the field. While they were falling back Sergeant Hiseshew, whose horse had been wounded, was captured. A rebel officer raised his pistol to shoot him, when, seeing his gray trowsers he said: "Oh! you are all right, give them ——." "Indeed I will," said the Sergeant, and he charged with the officer, and kept on charging until he reached our lines. Sergeant Embry was captured, and escaped by virtue of a gray blouse. Bugler S. W. Long received two sabre-cuts on the head whilst bravely fighting. The gallant bearing of Lieutenant Kimble throughout the whole affair cannot be too highly lauded.

Here I cannot forbear mentioning that when Major Russell captured General Stuart's ambulance, he and Corporal Brown Austin, of company H, were charging neck and neck. The Corporal succeeded in getting back to the regiment in time to join in the second charge, when again the dashing soldier pierced the rebel lines, firing in all directions, and wheeling his horse, he charged through their lines again and joined the regiment in perfect safety, although hundreds of bullets were discharged at him, and notwithstanding all these perils, our friend Brown still maintained his dignity. Although I might mention a number of instances of personal bravery, I forbear. In conclusion I wish to mention our excellent surgeon, T. J. Dunott, who did his best to care for our wounded and make them as comfortable as possible.

REBEL REPORTS AND NARRATIVES.

GENERAL LEE'S DESPATCH.

CULPEPER, June 9, 1863.

To General S. Cooper:

The enemy crossed the Rappahannock this morning at five o'clock, at the various fords from Beverly's to Kelly's, with a large force of cavalry, accompanied by infantry and artillery. After a severe contest, till five P.M., General Stuart drove them across the river.   R. E. LEE.

LYNCHBURGH REPUBLICAN ACCOUNT.

LYNCHBURGH, June 11.

The forces engaged on our side were Generals W. H. F. Lee's, Hampton's Legion, Jones's and Robertson's brigades, with the Beauregard battery from this city, and one other company of artillery. Our total force numbered about four thousand. The enemy had, it is estimated, about ten thousand cavalry, seven regiments of infantry, and six batteries, the whole under command of General Pleasanton.

The enemy commenced to cross the Rappahannock simultaneously at Beverly's and Kelly's Fords, and at other intermediate points, about daylight on Tuesday morning, both of their main columns pushing forward toward Brandy Station, five miles below Culpeper Court-House, with the design of getting in the rear of our forces, who were between the court-house and station. They captured our pickets, and thus prevented early intelligence of their movements being reported. The fight commenced at seven o'clock, and about ten o'clock our forces were all brought in position, and from that time until two o'clock the fight raged with terrific fierceness, our men gradually driving the enemy before them toward the Rappahannock bridge. About two o'clock the enemy commenced retreating up the Rappahannock, when Colonel Munford, commanding Fitz Lee's brigade, whose camp was near Oak Shade, crossed the Hazel River and attacked them in their front. The fight continued to rage until six o'clock, when the discomfited enemy effected a recrossing of the Rappahannock at Beverly's and fords adjacent.

The enemy fought hand to hand for a time, but relied principally upon their cavalry, dismounted and used as infantry, and their artillery. Our brave troops made many desperate charges, and were often driven back by sheer force of numbers. They as often rallied, and finally succeeded in forcing the enemy to commence to retreat, leaving many of their dead and wounded in our hands.

Our losses are heavy, and among them some of our best officers. We took a large number of prisoners, three hundred and thirty-six of whom have already arrived, including two majors. Thirty prisoners also arrived at Richmond from Winchester. These were captured by the forces of General Albert G. Jenkins.

RICHMOND SENTINEL ACCOUNT.

RICHMOND, June 12.

The cars on yesterday evening brought down three hundred and two prisoners of war, cavalrymen and artillerymen, captured by Stuart's cavalry in the fight near Brandy Station on Tuesday. Twelve of the number were commissioned officers—including one colonel, one major, and sundry captains and lieutenants. Twenty prisoners, captured in the Valley, accompanied those above named.

The bodies of Colonel Hampton, of Hampton's cavalry brigade, and Colonel Williams of South-Carolina, were received by the same train, and escorted by the Virginia State Guard to the capitol. It is to be conveyed South for sepulture. The gallant Colonel was one of the slain in the battle.

From passengers and other sources of information, we present the following details :

The cavalry of the enemy numbered, it is supposed, eight thousand to ten thousand. It was accompanied and supported by two thousand or three thousand dismounted men and artillery.

The enemy's force crossed in one place, it is said, at a ford prepared by them for the occasion. They thus eluded our pickets, got in their rear and captured them, and pressed on rapidly to our camps. This was at an early hour in the morning.

The First South-Carolina and Fourth Virginia, which were on picket, lost many men captured in these early operations.

The enemy's column next fell on General Jones's brigade, which they found in the act of forming, with guns and pistols not yet loaded. Taking them at this advantage, they pierced and broke our line, and forced our men to fall back. They gained so much ground as to capture General Stuart's headquarters, near Brandy ; also Brandy Station, and, we understand, some stores there.

Our men, recovering from their surprise, now rapidly came forward and threw themselves, sabre in hand, upon the enemy. These were driven, in their turn, nearer to the river, with the loss of a number of prisoners, beside the killed and wounded.

The fight fluctuated throughout the day, lasting from five to five—twelve long hours. It was doubtless the severest and most extensive cavalry fight of the war. The scene lay chiefly on the farm owned by the late John S. Barbour, Sen. The enemy made much use of their sharp-shooters, who, from the shelter of the adjacent timber, did us considerable damage. But the hand-to-hand encounters of cavalry and the crossing of sabres were the principal features of the fight. Many of our own wounded bear the evidence of this on their persons ; while the slain and wounded of the enemy prove it still more conspicuously. Our being caught with unloaded fire-arms, left them, indeed, no other resource at first.

During the conflict the enemy charged and captured our horse artillery ; but it was quickly recaptured by the desperate determination of our troops. We learn that we amply retaliated afterward by capturing and holding a battery of four or five guns belonging to the enemy.

The battle at last settled decisively in our favor. The enemy, repulsed and driven at all points, fell back to the Rappahannock, and recrossed it.

We captured from them in the fight and on the retreat three hundred and two prisoners, already received in this city. Beside these, between fifty and sixty more were brought to Culpeper Court-House yesterday morning, and they were still coming.

Our own loss is variously stated. The information at the provost's office at Culpeper Court-House, yesterday morning, was that about two hundred of our men were prisoners. Our killed and wounded are supposed to reach several hundred. Some put the figures higher and some lower.

The loss of the enemy in killed and wounded is believed to be considerably greater than ours. This is usually the case with the army that is defeated.

Among our slain are Lieutenant-Colonel Hampton of General Hampton's brigade, and Colonel Saul Williams of the Second North-Carolina regiment. Colonel Butler of South-Carolina had his foot shot off, and has suffered amputation. General W. H. F. Lee received a painful but not dangerous flesh-wound in the thigh. He came down yesterday to Colonel Wickham's in Hanover. Colonel A. W. Harman of the Twelfth Virginia cavalry was wounded, but not seriously, in the neck.

The forces engaged on our side were the brigades of Generals Hampton, W. H. F. Lee, and Jones.

We understand that the Yankees burned Kelly's Mill.

The fight, on the whole, may be said to have begun in a surprise and ended in a victory. The latter is what we are accustomed to hear of confederate soldiers; the former we trust never to hear again.

THE REBEL PRESS ON THE FIGHT.

RICHMOND, June 12.

The more the circumstances of the late affair at Brandy Station are considered, the less pleasant do they appear. If this was an isolated case, it might be excused under the convenient head of accident or chance. But this much puffed cavalry of the army of Northern Virginia has been twice, if not three times, surprised since the battles of December, and such repeated accidents can be regarded as nothing but the necessary consequences of negligence and bad management. If the war was a tournament, invented and supported for the pleasure and profit of a few vain and weak-headed officers, these disasters might be dismissed with compassion. But the country pays dearly for the blunders which encourage the enemy to overrun and devastate the land with a cavalry which is daily learning to despise the mounted troops of the Confederacy. It is high time that this branch of the service should be reformed.

The surprise on this occasion was the most complete that has occurred. The confederate cavalry was carelessly strewn over the country, with the Rappahannock only between it and an enemy who has already proven his enterprise to our cost. It is said that their camp was supposed to be secure, because the Rappahannock was not believed to be fordable at the point where it was actually forded. What! do Yankees then know more about this river than our own soldiers, who have done nothing but ride up and down its banks for the last six months. They knew at least that the weather was dry, the water low, and that fifteen or twenty thousand horse, confident from impunity and success, were on the other side. They could not have failed to know this much; and they were surprised, caught at breakfast, made prisoners on foot, with guns empty and horses grazing. Although the loss was insignificant, the events of that morning were among the least creditable that have occurred. Later some of the best officers sacrificed their lives to redeem the day. A very fierce fight ensued, in which, it is said, for the first time in this war, a considerable number of sabre-wounds were given and received. In the end the enemy retired, or was driven, it is not yet clearly known which, across the river. Nor is it certainly known whether the fortunate result was achieved by the cavalry alone or with the assistance of confederate infantry in the neighborhood. As the Southern troops remained masters of the field, and as they are believed to

have taken at least as many prisoners toward the close of the day as they lost in the morning, they may be considered victors.

But it is a victory over which few will exult. It resembles that other victory won at Kelly's Ford on the seventeenth of March. Both would have been well merited defeats if valor had not paid the price of conceit and carelessness. The ease with which the enemy outwitted the guard of the river on the first occasion was the prompter of Stoneman's incursion at the head of ten thousand horse into the heart of the State, which he accomplished without the slightest interference from the confederate cavalry. It is with pain that these reflections are made. They occur at this moment, not only to the present writer, but also to the whole public, and their utterance may have a wholesome effect. Events of this description have been lately too frequent to admit of the supposition that they are the results of hazard. They are the effects of causes, which will produce like effects while they are permitted to operate, and they require the earnest attention both of the chiefs of the government and the heads of the army. The enemy is evidently determined to employ his cavalry extensively, and has spared no pains or cost to perfect that arm. The only effective means of preventing the mischief it may do is to reörganize our own forces, enforce a stricter discipline among the men, and insist on more earnestness among the officers in the discharge of their very important duty.

—*Richmond Examiner.*

Doc. 11.

EVACUATION OF WINCHESTER.

MAJOR-GENERAL MILROY'S REPORT.

BALTIMORE, June 30, 1863.

COLONEL: I have been compelled by the exigencies of public duties connected with my late command to defer until this time a report of the recent operations about Winchester. Having no reports from brigade commanders and not even an opportunity of conferring with them, I am still unable to give a detailed report. A sense of duty to myself and to the officers and soldiers which I had the honor to command requires that I should submit some general statements.

I occupied Winchester with my command on the twenty-fifth of December last; and continued in its occupancy until Monday morning, the fifteenth instant, when, for reasons which will appear in the sequel of this report, I was compelled to evacuate it. When I first occupied Winchester, the valley of the Shenandoah, from Staunton to Strasburgh, was occupied by the rebel General Jones, with a force variously estimated at from five to six thousand men, and constituted principally of cavalry. Imboden at the same time occupied the Cacapon Valley with a force composed of infantry, cavalry, and artillery, estimated at one thousand five hundred men. These were the only forces by which I was in danger of being assailed, unless by a force from Lee's army, which it was supposed would be prevented from hostile demonstrations in my direction by the army of the Potomac. The object in occupying Winchester was to observe and hold in check the rebel forces in the valley and to secure the Baltimore and Ohio Railroad against depredations. Late in March, in pursuance of an order issued upon my own suggestion, I stationed the Third brigade of my division, consisting of the Sixth regiment Maryland volunteer infantry, Sixty-seventh regiment Pennsylvania volunteer infantry, First regiment New-York volunteer cavalry, and the Baltimore battery, at Berryville, Colonel McReynolds, of the First New-York cavalry, commanding. My instructions to Col. McReynolds were to keep open our communication with Harper's Ferry, and to watch the passes of the Blue Ridge (Snicker's and Ashby's Gaps) and the fords of the Shenandoah River known as Snicker's and Berry's. To this end he was to cause to be diligently scouted, the country between him and those localities, and as far south as Millwood. I was expressly instructed to undertake no offensive operations in force. Acting in accordance with these instructions, I kept my forces well in hand in the vicinities of Berryville and Winchester, except that during the expedition of General Jones into West-Virginia, by order from your headquarters, I sent portions of them into that State. During my occupancy of Winchester, I almost continually kept out heavy cavalry scouts on the Front Royal road as far as Front Royal, and on the Strasburgh road as far as Strasburgh. My cavalry frequently drove the enemy's pickets as far up the valley as Woodstock, and I held almost undisputed possession of the valley as far as Strasburgh until about the first of June. By means of these cavalry expeditions, and information furnished me by Union citizens, I kept continually posted as to the rebel forces in the valley under Jones and Imboden, and was at no time deceived as to their numbers or movements. About the first of June the enemy became bolder, and small detachments of his cavalry were met as far down the valley as Middletown. On Friday, the twelfth day of June, for the purpose of ascertaining whether there had been any accumulation of rebel forces in my front, I sent out two strong reconnoitring parties, one on the Strasburgh and the other on the Front Royal road. The one on the Strasburgh road consisted of the Eighty-seventh Pennsylvania volunteer infantry, Thirteenth Pennsylvania volunteer cavalry, and one section of battery L, Fifth regiment artillery, under command of Col. Shawl, of the Eighty-seventh regiment Pennsylvania volunteer infantry. This reconnoissance was conducted with energy, in pursuance of instructions, and its results were in every way satisfactory. The expedition proceeded up the valley, the cavalry in advance, but within supporting distance of the infantry and artillery, until it had arrived within two miles of Middletown, at which place a messenger from Major Kerwin, who was in command of the cavalry, announced to Colonel

Shawl that a superior force of cavalry of the enemy had been discovered in line of battle immediately north of Middletown. The infantry and artillery were immediately concealed, the former in a dense grove to the right and within one hundred yards of the road, and the latter behind a ridge. Our cavalry retired skirmishing with the enemy, until he was drawn within reach of the fire of the infantry. Upon the first fire of our infantry, the enemy retreated precipitately, followed by our cavalry, which pursued beyond Middletown.

In this affair the enemy lost fifty (as has since been ascertained) in killed and wounded, and we took thirty-seven prisoners. Colonel Shawl remained on the ground an hour, during which time his cavalry scoured the country in every direction, but could detect no traces of an accumulation of rebel forces. The prisoners taken all belonged to the Maryland battalion and Fourteenth regiment Virginia cavalry, troops which had been in the valley and on picket-duty during the whole period of my occupancy of Winchester. Besides, separate examinations of the prisoners disclosed that there was no accumulation of rebel forces there. Col. Shawl made his report to me about seven o'clock in the evening, and it relieved me from all apprehensions of an attack from the Strasburgh road. It is now known that no portion of Lee's army approached Winchester from that direction.

The reconnoissance of the Front Royal road was abortive. The expedition consisted of the Twelfth Pennsylvania cavalry, about four hundred strong, under command of Lieut.-Col. Moss. It returned to Winchester about three o'clock in the afternoon of Friday. Its commanding officer reported, that at Cedarville, a place twelve miles from Winchester, he had encountered a large force of the enemy, composed of cavalry, infantry, and artillery. It did not appear, however, that he had placed himself in a position to ascertain the number or character of the force which he had encountered, or exercised the usual and necessary efforts to obtain that essential information. Officers of his command and reliable scouts, who were present, gave contradictory reports.

This report was discredited by myself and by Gen. Elliott my second in command. There was nothing in the report which indicated the presence of Gen. Lee's army. It was supposed that the force on the Front Royal road could not be other than the enemy which we had faced during the occupancy of Winchester, or that the anticipated cavalry raid of Gen. Stuart was in progress, against either or both of which combined I could have held my position. I deemed it impossible that Lee's army, with its immense artillery and baggage trains, could have escaped from the army of the Potomac and crossed the Blue Ridge through Ashby's, Chester, and Thornton gaps in concentric columns. The movement must have occupied five or six days, and notice of its being in progress could have been conveyed to me from General Hooker's headquarters in five minutes; for telegraphic communication still existed between Baltimore and Winchester.

On Friday night I doubled my pickets and kept out strong cavalry patrols on the leading roads, and I also sent a messenger to Colonel McReynolds at Berryville notifying him that the enemy was reported to be in considerable force in the Front Royal road. I instructed him to keep a strong party of observation in the direction of Milwood; to place his command in readiness to move at a moment's warning; if attacked by a superior force, to fall back upon Winchester by the route which he might deem most practicable, and that if his command should be needed at Winchester he would be notified by four discharges from the large guns at the main fort at Winchester.

The whole forces under my command at this time were: First brigade, Brigadier-General Elliott commanding: One Hundred and Tenth regiment O. V. I., Col. Keifer; One Hundred and Sixteenth regiment O. V. I., Colonel Washburn; One Hundred and Twenty-second regiment O. V. I., Col. Ball; One Hundred and Twenty-third regiment O. V. I., Col. Wilson; Thirteenth regiment Pennsylvania cavalry, Col. Gallagher; Twelfth regiment Pennsylvania cavalry, Lieut.-Col. Moss; battery L, Fifth regiment artillery, First Lieut. Randolph. Second brigade, Colonel Ely, Eighteenth Connecticut, commanding: Eighty-seventh regiment Pa. V. I., Colonel Shawl; Twelfth regiment Va. V. I., Col. Klunk; Eighteenth regiment Conn. V. I., Lieut.-Col. Nichols; Fifth regiment Md. V. I., Capt. Holton; battery D, First Virginia artillery, Capt. Carlin; company K, First Virginia cavalry, Lieut. Dawson; companies D and E, Third Virginia cavalry, Capt. White.

The composition of the Third brigade, Colonel McReynolds commanding, is above given.

The heavy guns of the principal fort, consisting of four twenty-pound Parrotts and two twenty-four-pound howitzers, were served by a company of the Fourteenth Massachusetts heavy artillery, commanded by Captain Martin.

The command numbered, according to Friday morning's return, six thousand nine hundred men. On Saturday morning, at a few minutes before eight o'clock, my cavalry patrols on the Front Royal road reported that the enemy was approaching in force.

Deeming it advisable that under the circumstances the whole command should be united at Winchester, I gave Colonel McReynolds the concerted signal above stated. I immediately sent forward on the Front Royal and Strasburgh roads forces to observe and report the forces and movements of the enemy. That on the Front Royal road consisted of the Twelfth Pennsylvania cavalry, Eighty-seventh Pennsylvania infantry, Eighteenth Connecticut infantry, Fifth Maryland infantry, and one section of battery L Fifth regiment artillery, Col. Ely commanding. A little over a mile from Winchester this force encountered a battery of the enemy located in a wood at the right of the Front Royal road. After a short artillery skirmish, Col. Ely retired his command to near the junction of the Front Royal and Strasburgh roads, immediately south and adjoining Winchester. The enemy did not pursue in force. Occasionally, during the day, small detachments of rebel cavalry approached from that direction, but were driven off by our infantry pickets, which were well protected and directed to remain at their posts and act as skirmishers.

The force on the Strasburgh road consisted of the One Hundred and Tenth and One Hundred and Twenty-third Ohio and Twelfth Virginia infantry, and Thirteenth Pennsylvania volunteer cavalry, and Carlin's battery, Brig.-Gen. Elliott commanding.

A little to the west and adjoining Winchester is a high ridge, which extends from the town south for over a mile to Mill Creek, which is known as Applepie Ridge. Around the southern terminus of this ridge the creek and a mill-race wind across the Strasburgh road, and from thence in a northern direction across the Front Royal road, and north of that road to the Hollingsworth mills, where the race terminates and the creek takes an abrupt eastern course. The whole length of the race is about two miles. The creek and race combined afford a strong protection against cavalry, and for that reason, and the additional one that stone fences and other covers abound in its vicinity, they had been adopted as a portion of my infantry picket-line. The force above designated, except two sections of Carlin's battery stationed on the southern extremity of the ridge above described, proceeded up the Strasburgh road to within a short distance of Kearnstown, where it remained, encountering no enemy, except occasional parties of skirmishers, until about two o'clock P.M., when Brig.-General Elliott, through Lieut. Alexander, of his staff, reported to me at the place where two sections of Carlin's battery were in position, that he could find no enemy in his front, but that there were indications that the enemy was massing his forces on our left, in the vicinity of the Front Royal road. I then directed Gen. Elliott to retire his force on the Strasburgh road back of the creek and race above described, so as to put it in a position to support Col. Ely on the Front Royal road, or the forces at the forts, as exigency might require. While this order was being executed, and when Gen. Elliott's command had arrived at within six hundred yards of the creek and race, a considerable force of the enemy's infantry, in two lines of battle, displayed itself to our right, with the apparent intention to flank and cut off our retiring troops. I estimated the force of the enemy then in sight at two thousand. The two sections of Carlin's battery on the ridge as above stated commanded the position of the enemy, and immediately opened on him with sufficient effect to throw him into confusion, when the One Hundred and Tenth regiment Ohio volunteer infantry, Col. Keifer, and One Hundred and Twenty-third regiment Ohio volunteer infantry, Col. Wilson, charged upon him and drove him back in disorder, with considerable loss. Simultaneously the Twelfth Virginia infantry, Col. Klunk, engaged a large body of the enemy's skirmishers in a wood south of the ridge, and on the opposite side of the creek and race, and after holding them in check two hours, being outflanked and greatly outnumbered, retired. Our whole force which had been advanced on the Strasburgh road, retired behind the creek and race above described. That creek and race then constituted the line of our forces in front of the town, and was held by Col. Ely, with a portion of his brigade, on the Front Royal road, and by Gen. Elliott, with a portion of his brigade, on the Strasburgh road. The remainder of my forces were in the forts immediately north of the town.

Immediately after our forces had retired from the Strasburgh road to the Winchester side of the creek and race, the enemy advanced his skirmishers, and brisk skirmishing ensued until dark. About five o'clock in the evening the enemy advanced and took possession of a picket post surrounded by a stone wall on the south, east, and west, and which commanded the Strasburgh road, from which they were dislodged by two companies of the Twelfth Virginia volunteer infantry. In this affair, which occurred about six o'clock in the evening, we captured a prisoner, from whom I learned that he belonged to Hay's Louisiana brigade, which was a part of Ewell's corps, the whole of which, and also that of Longstreet, was in our immediate vicinity. A deserter, who came in shortly afterward, confirmed his statement. This was the first intimation that I received that Lee's army had quietly retired before the lines of the army of the Potomac and performed a five or six days' march. Telegraphic communication with my headquarters continued until twelve o'clock M. on Saturday. The Blue Ridge screened the operations of Lee's army from me. I had always relied with implicit confidence upon receiving timely notice by telegraph of its advance in my direction. On Saturday, under the cover of night, I withdrew my forces on the Strasburgh and Front Royal roads, in front of Winchester, to the southern suburbs of the town, under orders to retire to the forts north of the town at two o'clock in the morning. Colonel McReynolds arrived with his command between nine and ten o'clock P.M., and was assigned to the star fort, immediately north of the main fortification. At this time it was evident that at least two corps of Lee's army, numbering not less than fifty thousand men, and abundantly supplied with artillery, were in my immediate vicinity, and that my retreat by the Martinsburgh and Berryville roads was cut off.

I still hoped that there had been some corresponding action of the army of the Potomac, and that if I could sustain myself for twenty-four hours I would be relieved.

Early on Sunday morning detachments of cavalry were sent out on the Berryville and Martinsburgh roads, but were driven back by the enemy's skirmishers and sharp-shooters. From seven o'clock on Sunday morning until four o'clock in the afternoon detachments from the Eighteenth Connecticut, Fifth Maryland, and Eighty-seventh Pennsylvania volunteer infantry, under the direction of Colonel Ely, continually skirmished with the enemy in front of the forts and east of the town, between the Front Royal and Martinsburgh roads. During this skirmishing the rebels took possession of a large brick dwelling, surrounded by dense shrubbery, on the Berryville road, about half a mile from Winchester. Our skirmishers attacked and carried the house, killing one officer and five men, and capturing eleven prisoners. At one time during the day the rebels in considerable numbers appeared in the town, but were driven out by the Eighteenth Connecticut and Eighty-seventh Pennsylvania volunteer infantry. On Sunday morning General Elliott, with a portion of his brigade, Carlin's battery, and the Twelfth Virginia volunteer infantry, took position on the ridge above described, about a quarter of a mile south of the Romney road. He had frequent and sometimes severe skirmishes. The enemy did not, however, at any time appear before him in force.

In consequence of the overwhelming masses of the enemy about me, I kept my forces during the day well in hand, and in immediate connection with the forts. As early as Saturday evening, after I learned the presence of Lee's army in force, I made up my mind to act entirely on the defensive, economize my forces, wait until the enemy had massed himself for the final attack, and then, unless relieved, force my way through what *might appear* to be the weakest portion of his lines.

My belief was superinduced by the manœuvres of the enemy on Saturday, and by the grounds that the real attack would come from the Romney road. Early on Sunday morning I ordered Captain Morgan, of the Twelfth Pennsylvania cavalry, with a detachment of two companies of that regiment, to proceed out the Pughtown road as far as Pughtown, if practicable, thence across to the Romney road, and by that road back to the forts. I instructed him to carefully observe the disposition and forces of the enemy, if any, in that direction. That officer returned with his command to the forts about two o'clock P.M., and reported that he had made the round indicated without meeting or detecting any traces of an enemy in that direction. Immediately west of and parallel with the ridge on which the main fortification is constructed, and about two thousand yards distant therefrom, is another range, known as Flint Ridge, on which there was in process of construction a line of earthworks which commanded the Pughtown and Romney roads, and all the approaches from the west. These works were occupied on Sunday by the One Hundred and Tenth and part of the One Hundred and Sixteenth Ohio volunteer infantry, and battery L, Fifth regiment artillery, under Colonel Keifer. The report of Captain Morgan relieved me from all apprehension of an immediate attack in that direction, and induced me to turn my attention to the approaches in other directions. I am still at a loss to know how Captain Morgan could have made the tour which he reported without seeing or encountering the enemy, for within two hours after he made the report the enemy opened upon me from the west with at least four full batteries, some of his guns being of the longest range, under cover of which fire he precipitated a column at least ten thousand strong upon the outwork held by Colonel Keifer, which, after a stubborn resistance, he carried. This outwork was commanded by the guns of the main and star forts, which were immediately brought to bear upon the enemy, driving him from the position and affording a protection to Colonel Keifer's command, under which it retreated, with small loss, to the main fort. The guns at the fort, and the Baltimore battery, Captain Alexander, at the star fort, and Carlin's battery, immediately south of the main fort, engaged the enemy's guns, and an artillery contest ensued which was maintained with energy on both sides until eight o'clock in the evening. During its progress I massed my troops in the main and star forts, and in the rifle-pits in front of them. To my regret, the enemy made no effort to take my position by assault. About nine o'clock in the evening I convened a council of war, consisting of Brigadier-General Elliott, commanding First brigade, Colonel Ely, commanding Second brigade, and Colonel McReynolds, commanding Third brigade.

Before stating the result of this council, it is proper that I should state the circumstances by which we were surrounded. It was certain that Lee had eluded the army of the Potomac, and was at liberty to use his whole force against us without hindrance from any source. Our position at Winchester, although affording facilities for defence which would enable an inferior to maintain itself against a superior number for a limited time, could not be successfully defended by the limited means at my command against such an army as surrounded me. Six principal roads, known in the army as the Romney, Pughtown, Martinsburgh, Berryville, Front Royal, and Strasburgh roads, lead into the town. The names of these roads indicate their courses. They are all intersected and connected by cross-roads in close proximity to the town. Cavalry and artillery can approach the town and the forts from any direction. We had but one day's rations left, and our artillery ammunition was almost entirely expended. On Monday morning the enemy could have brought one hundred guns to bear on us, to which we could have made no reply. Precedents which have occurred during this rebellion and in other countries would have justified a capitulation; but I thought, and my comrades in council thought, that we owed our lives to the Government rather than make such a degrading concession to rebels in arms against its authority.

The propositions concluded upon in that council were, that in consequence of the entire exhaustion of artillery ammunition, it was impossible to hold the forts against the overwhelming forces of the enemy, and that a further prolongation of the defence could only result in sacrificing the lives of our soldiers without any practical benefit to the country; that we owed it to the honor of the Federal arms to make an effort to force our way through the lines of the beleaguering foe; that the artillery and wagons should be abandoned, and the division, brigade, and regimental quartermasters instructed to bring away all public horses; and that the brigades, in the order of their numbers, should march from the forts at one o'clock in the morning, carrying with them their arms and the usual supply of ammunition. The Thirteenth Pennsylvania cavalry was attached to the Third brigade. The forts were evacuated at the time designated, and immediately thereafter the cannon spiked, and the ammunition which could not be carried by the men thrown into the cisterns of the forts. The column proceeded through a ravine, avoiding the town of Winchester, about one mile, until it struck the Martinsburgh road. It then proceeded up the Martinsburgh road to where a road leads from it to Summit Station, about four miles and a half from Winchester, when I received a message from General Elliott that he was attacked by the enemy's skirmishers. I had heard the firing and was riding forward. The enemy was on elevated ground, in a wood east of the road and a field east of and adjoining the wood. This occurred between three and four o'clock in the morning. General Elliott immediately filed the One Hundred and Twenty-third, the One Hundred and Tenth, and One Hundred and Twenty second Ohio regiments to the left, and formed them in line of battle west of and in front of the woods in which the enemy was posted. He then advanced the One Hundred and Tenth Ohio, Col. Keifer, into the woods to feel of the enemy. This regiment soon became actively engaged, and was immediately supported with the One Hundred and Twenty-second Ohio, which promptly took its position on the right of the One Hundred and Tenth. It soon became evident that the enemy was present in considerable force, with at least two batteries of artillery. It was evident, however, that a retreat could not be effected except under cover of a heavy contest with him. The One Hundred and Tenth and One Hundred and Twenty-second Ohio maintained the contest for over an hour, occasionally falling back, but in the main driving the enemy. They captured one of the enemy's caissons, and silenced two of his guns by killing his gunners and artillery horses. Although immediately under the guns of the enemy, they preserved their lines, and kept up an incessant, heavy, and murderous fire of musketry, under the effect of which the enemy's right flank fell into disorder and recoiled. During this contest Colonel Keifer especially distinguished himself by the display of the qualities of a brave soldier and a judicious and skilful officer.

About the time the contest commenced on my left, by my orders, the Eighty-seventh Pennsylvania volunteer infantry, Colonel Shawl, advanced against the enemy's left, but was soon driven back. I then supported the Eighty-seventh by the Eighteenth Connecticut, and the two regiments, under Colonel Ely, again advanced into the woods, but were again driven back. I then supported Colonel Ely with the One Hundred and Twenty-third Ohio, and again advanced the line, but it was repulsed with inconsiderable loss, the range of the enemy's guns being so elevated as to render his artillery inefficient. At this time a signal gun fired at Winchester announced the approach of the enemy in my rear. Colonel Ely's command was again rallied and formed in line of battle west of the Martinsburgh road, and that officer again directed to engage the enemy. At this time the One Hundred and Tenth and One Hundred and Twenty-second Ohio volunteer infantry regiments were still maintaining their fire on the left with unabating energy. I then gave instructions that my forces unengaged and trains should retreat under cover of the contest, taking the Martinsburgh road for a short distance and then turning to the right. I instructed my staff-officers, except Captain Baird, who was engaged with the One Hundred and Tenth and One Hundred and Twenty-second Ohio volunteer infantry on my left, to diligently carry these instructions. They were conveyed to Colonel Washburn, commanding the One Hundred and Sixteenth Ohio volunteer infantry; Col. Klunk, commanding the Twelfth Virginia volunteer infantry; Major Adams, commanding First New-York cavalry; and Major Titus, commanding Twelfth Pennsylvania cavalry. These forces immediately marched, but instead of taking the road indicated, took a road which leads to the left through Bath, in Morgan County. They were followed by considerable bodies of the Eighteenth Connecticut and Eighty-seventh Pennsylvania, and some stragglers from the One Hundred and Twenty-third, One Hundred and Tenth, and One Hundred and Twenty-second Ohio volunteer infantry. Colonel Ely was instructed to fall back and retreat as soon as the troops had passed his rear. Major McGee and Captain Palmer, of my staff, who were at different times, despatched to Colonel McReynolds with his instructions, each separately reported that they could not find that officer or any part of his command, except Major Adams, with the First New-York cavalry. It was supposed that during the battle he had retreated to the right of the Martinsburgh road. About the time that I had given the directions above indicated, my horse was shot from under me. Some time intervened before I could be remounted. When remounted, I went in the direction of the One Hundred and Tenth and One Hundred and Twenty-second Ohio volunteer infantry, and met them falling back by the Martinsburgh road. The retreat was now in full progress, the two columns by different routes, and it was impossible to unite them. I proceeded with the One Hundred and Tenth and One Hundred and Twenty-second Ohio volunteer infantry regiments, and fragments of other regiments which followed after them. This portion of the command, by way of Smithfield,

arrived at Harper's Ferry late in the afternoon of Monday. I was not pursued. The column that proceeded in the direction of Bath crossed the Potomac at Hancock, and subsequently massed at Bloody Run, in Bedford County, Pa., two thousand seven hundred strong.

Having no report from Col. McReynolds, I am unable to state the operations of his brigade on Monday morning. That officer arrived at Harper's Ferry about twelve M. on Monday, unaccompanied by any considerable portion of his command.

The Sixth Maryland infantry regiment, attached to his brigade, arrived at that place Monday evening, almost intact. His other infantry regiment, the Sixty-seventh Pennsylvania, was principally captured. I have learned that while Colonel Ely was endeavoring to retreat in pursuance of directions, he was surrounded and compelled to surrender, with the greater portion of the command which he led in the last charge.

The force which we encountered on Monday morning in our front was Johnson's division of Ewell's corps, from eight to ten thousand strong. The whole number of my division which have reported at Harper's Ferry and Bloody Run and other places exceeds five thousand. The stragglers scattered through the country are perhaps a thousand. My loss in killed and wounded cannot be large. It is not my object at this time to bestow praise or cast censure, but I feel it to be my duty to say, that during the late operations near Winchester, generally the officers and men under my command conducted themselves with distinguished gallantry, and deserve well of the country. If they could be again united (as they should be) under their appropriate brigade and regimental organizations, they would be formidable on any field. It is proper that I should here refer again to the instructions under which I occupied Winchester. They were not materially changed from those above given, until Thursday, twelve o'clock at night, when I received from Colonel Piatt, at Harper's Ferry, the following telegram:

In accordance with orders from Halleck, received from headquarters, at Baltimore, to-day, you will immediately take steps to remove your command from Winchester to Harper's Ferry. You will, without delay, call in Colonel McReynolds, and such other outposts not necessary for observation at the front. Send back your heavy guns, surplus ammunition and subsistence, retaining only such force and arms as will constitute what General Halleck designates as a lookout, which can readily and without inconvenience, fall back to Harper's Ferry.   Don Piatt,
                    Lieutenant-Colonel and Chief of Staff.

I immediately telegraphed to Major-General Schenck, as follows:

I have the place well protected, and am well prepared to hold it, as General Tyler and Colonel Piatt will inform you, and I can, and would hold it, if permitted to do so, *against any force the rebels can afford to bring against me*, and I exceedingly regret the prospect of having to give it up. It will be cruel to abandon the loyal people in this country to the rebel fiends again.

R. H. MILROY,
Major-General.

Early on Friday morning, the twelfth of June, I received this telegram:

"BALTIMORE, June 12, one o'clock A.M., 1863.
Major-General R. H. Milroy:

Lieutenant-Colonel Piatt, as I learn by copy of despatch sent me, which he forwarded to you from Harper's Ferry, misunderstood me, and somewhat exceeded his instructions. You will make all the required preparations for withdrawing, but hold your position in the mean time. Be ready for movement, but await further orders. I doubt the propriety calling in McReynolds's brigade at once. If you should fall back to Harper's Ferry, he will be in part on the way and cover your flank. But use your discretion as to any order to him. Below, I give you a copy of the telegram of the General-in-Chief. Nothing heard since. Give me constant information.

ROBERT C. SCHENCK,
Major-General, Commanding.

COPY OF GENERAL HALLECK'S TELEGRAM.

Harper's Ferry is the important place. Winchester is of no importance other than a look-out. The Winchester troops, except enough to serve as a look-out, should be withdrawn to Harper's Ferry. No large amount of supplies should be left in any exposed position.

H. W. HALLECK,
General-in-Chief.

Late on Friday evening I received a despatch from General Schenck, which is lost, but which was in substance as follows: A dispatch just received from Colonel Don Piatt says, "I read Halleck's last despatch by the light of his of the thirtieth April, and considered it a positive order to fall back to Harper's Ferry, and I so ordered Milroy. I have been on the ground and gave it advisedly. Milroy cannot move from his present position in presence of the enemy. He has not transportation enough to move in face of the enemy, and he has not cavalry he can rely upon, to scout beyond Strasburgh." What are your facilities for transportation?

This telegram I immediately answered as follows:

I can at any time, if not cut off from Martinsburgh, have sufficient transportation to take all public stores from here in six hours.

R. H. MILROY,
Major-General.

Late on Friday night, June the twelfth, perhaps about ten o'clock, I sent Major-General Schenck this despatch, to wit:

The Twelfth Pennsylvania cavalry had a slight skirmish with a rebel cavalry force of about five hundred, twelve miles from here, on the Front Royal road, this afternoon. The Thirteenth Penn-

sylvania cavalry and Eighty-seventh Pennsylvania infantry, with one section of artillery, had a splendid little skirmish with some four hundred rebel cavalry this side of Middletown, at the same time. The Thirteenth skirmished with the rebels a short time, and drew them into an ambuscade of the Eighty-seventh and artillery. Eight of the rebels were killed, and a number wounded, and thirty-seven, including a captain and two lieutenants, taken prisoners. No casualties on our side. *The enemy is probably approaching in some force.* Please state specifically whether I am to abandon this place or not.

R. H. MILROY,
Major-General.

To this communication no reply was received.* It is clear that I received no order to evacuate Winchester, except that of Colonel Piatt, which was annulled by the telegram of Major-General Schenck, received on Friday, the twelfth. The telegram above copied of the General-in-Chief was before me, but that is advisory in its tone, and I, in common with General Schenck, did not construe it as amounting to an order, or as indicating that immediate compliance was intended. I rather considered it as indicating the course which should be pursued upon an emergency yet to happen. This telegram, although sent as late as Thursday, the eleventh, must have been written in the absence of all knowledge of the impending emergency; otherwise language calculated to hasten my action would have been used. The language contained in my telegram, expressive of my confidence in my ability to hold Winchester was used with reference to any contingency which would probably happen. I did not mean that I could hold it against such an army as that which I knew to be at the disposal of General Lee, and it was no part of my duty to watch the movements of that army. My limited cavalry force did not enable me to scout beyond the Blue Ridge.

That army was faced, however, by the army of the Potomac, between the headquarters of which and my own, by way of Washington, a continuous line of telegraphic communication existed. I believed that Lee could not move his large army with its immense artillery and baggage trains, and perform a six days' march in my direction unless I received timely notice of the important fact. The immense cavalry force at the disposal of General Hooker strengthened this confidence. Therefore, on Friday, when I perceived indications of the approach of the enemy in some force on the Front Royal road, I felt confident that it was composed of the forces which I had faced, or that the expected cavalry expedition of General Stuart was in progress. Acting upon this belief, I regarded it as my duty to remain at my post at Winchester.

Lee's army in parallel columns once across the passes of the Blue Ridge from the direction of

* My telegraph operator at Winchester had just commenced receiving a cipher despatch Saturday, the thirteenth, when the wire was cut between that and Martinsburgh by the rebels, and nothing could be made of what was received.

I have since learned from General Schenck that that despatch was an order to me to fall back immediately to Harper's Ferry.

R. H. MILROY, Major-General.

Front Royal, it was impossible for me to retreat upon either Martinsburgh or Harper's Ferry without encountering it. I could not at any time after Friday, have retreated without encountering it. And I had no knowledge of its presence, as above stated, until late on Saturday, when I learned it from prisoners. After all, it may well be doubted, whether the three days' delay, and the loss which my presence at Winchester occasioned the rebel army, were not worth to the country the sacrifice which they cost it.

I am, Colonel, very respectfully,
Your most obedient servant,
R. H. MILROY,
Major-General.

Lieutenant-Colonel DON PIATT,
Chief of Staff, Eighth A. C.

LIEUTENANT H. E. ALEXANDER'S ACCOUNT.

BALTIMORE, June 18, 1863.

As there have been conflicting accounts relative to the termination of the fight at Winchester, I beg to give a statement which I think may be relied on, as what I shall relate came either under my personal observation, or from first hands.

On Saturday morning the rebels were reported by our scouts as marching on Berryville. The brigade commanded by Colonel McReynolds, consisting of the Sixth Maryland regiment, Sixty-seventh Pennsylvania, First New-York cavalry, and one battery, immediately fell back toward Winchester, as ordered by General Milroy, proceeding by way of Smithfield and Martinsburgh road.

I was placed with my section, supported by part of the Sixth Maryland infantry and the cavalry, in one of the fortifications on the south side, which had been erected by Captain Alexander, and was fortunate enough to hold them in check for two hours, giving the advance time to get ahead. We then moved off, and, marching fast, caught up to them.

The rebel cavalry pursued us, and came up at the Opequon, eight miles from Winchester, after marching twenty miles. Here we had a skirmish. The formation of the road would not permit us to fire until they were within fifty yards, and so the fire was more destructive.

We succeeded in beating them back, and some prisoners captured by the cavalry stated that the two discharges of canister had killed a dozen and wounded over thirty. We arrived in Winchester at night unmolested, and camped in the star fort on the north side of the town, a small work about two hundred feet in diameter.

There had been heavy fighting at Winchester during the day. The rebels made five charges and were repulsed.

On Sunday there was skirmishing all around the town, but the rebels appeared in very small force, leading us to believe that they intended to march for Martinsburgh.

One of the sections of the battery was out during the whole day, under Lieutenant Leary, supported by two regiments, the whole under General Elliott, and kept back the entire line of rebel skirmishers by a display of scientific practice which called forth General Elliott's admiration.

To understand the battle of Sunday evening, it will be necessary to state that there are three ranges of hills on the north of Winchester. The first range was occupied by three forts. That to the left was the main fort, with twenty-pounder Parrotts, where General Milroy was with most of the command.

The middle was the star fort, where our brigade was, and on the right, on the hill, commanding all the others, was an unfinished work. Had this last been finished, the whole rebel force could not have taken us. The second range of hills was occupied by battery D, First Virginia artillery, Captain Carsen, on the left, and battery L, Fifth United States regulars, Lieutenant Randolph commanding.

The latter was on the hill immediately opposite us, and was supported by the Fifth Maryland regiment. On the third range the rebels were. As the men and horses of battery L were feeding, at nine P.M., the rebels opened upon them with two batteries, one of which was twenty-pounders.

They fought for half an hour, and then the rebels charged with a large body of men and drove the Fifth Maryland back. The Fifth Maryland behaved with great bravery. They formed half-way down the hill, and charged up and drove the rebels back again some distance.

We could see the whole, as we were within one thousand five hundred yards, and yet could not render assistance. The rebels, however, drove them back, and Randolph spiked three of his five guns. Nearly all his horses were shot. As soon as the coast was clear we opened on them with at first two guns and then four guns.

There was not space on one side of the fort to work more. They answered the large fort for some time, but then brought their whole four batteries, amounting to twenty-four guns, to bear upon us, and then the fighting began. This was about seven P.M. We fired as accurately as we could.

They attempted three times to take a position, and each time we drove them away, blowing up at one time a limber, then a caisson, and dismounting two guns. They had an excellent range, and fired well.

The balls came flying all around the fort and over our heads, but only one man was wounded, and one man flung down by the wind of a ball. We lost five horses. We returned the compliment as well as we could, and succeeded by half-past nine P.M. in causing them to cease firing.

Shortly after that they tried to storm the large fort, but were repulsed. We expected them to storm our works, and the infantry were drawn up inside and in the rifle-pits outside, and I don't think ten thousand men could have taken us, from the calmness and firmness which the Sixth Maryland evinced.

I cannot speak too highly of the coolness and bravery of the men of the battery. Though it was the first time they had been under fire, not a man flinched, but they fought without excitement, and as coolly and regularly as if on drill, jesting and talking as if it were mere pastime.

About this time it became too dark to see, and we ceased firing. We found that we had not more than twenty rounds per gun left, and no more could be had. Our scouts also reported that the rebels were moving their heaviest guns around through the hollow to the high ground on the right, where they could command us, and shell us out easily.

The other batteries were in the same want of ammunition, and General Milroy determined to spike the guns and mount the cannoneers on the off-horses, and cut our way through. The other two brigades started first, and the third brigade brought up the rear. When we got five miles from Winchester the rebels opened on us with four pieces of artillery.

Our infantry and cavalry moved up and charged them desperately. As our cannoneers were unarmed, our captain ordered them to move up as close as they could safely, and then to take to the woods separately and make for the Ferry or any point on the river.

The First New-York cavalry, a fine organization, charged upon the guns. Finally the infantry and cavalry succeeded in capturing two guns, which were turned upon the others and drove them back. As they could not be carried off, they were disabled.

Our men rode up behind the cavalry through the open field, under the fire of the artillery, and then broke from the cover of the woods. We all thus became separated.

ANOTHER ACCOUNT.

BLOODY RUN, PA., June 22, 1863.

Permit me, sir, if you please, to lay before your readers a true account of the recent battles around Winchester, Va. I have carefully watched the accounts written by different correspondents thus far, and am utterly surprised at the vagueness of some, the falsity of others, and the imperfection of all. The battles of Winchester were of no small moment, deciding as they did the fate of the Great Valley, as well as the fate of Western Virginia, Pennsylvania, and Maryland. Could Winchester and neighboring towns have still been held in spite of the desperate courage and efforts of the enemy, Martinsburgh and Cumberland, Pennsylvania and Maryland, the railroads, canals, and public buildings would have been likewise secure. How immense the stakes we were playing for at Winchester! Then it is important as a matter of public interest and historic record that the true history of the whole matter be published. The skirmishing in front of our works opened the ball on Friday evening, June twelfth. Saturday morning it was resumed, and kept up hotly all day, the enemy still showing themselves, in small force only, in a sort of semicircle in front. A part of our forces were then at Berryville, and

were signalled to return to Winchester, Saturday morning. They succeeded in reaching us late Saturday evening. By this time fighting had commenced at Bunker Hill, eleven miles north-east of Winchester, on the Martinsburgh road. Here Major W. T. Morris was commanding detachments from the One Hundred and Sixteenth Ohio V. I., Eighty-seventh Pennsylvania, and First New-York cavalry. There, at about five o'clock Saturday evening, the scouts came in and reported the advance of a large force of rebels. Our force there was securely lodged in a large brick church, and were less than two hundred strong. But they immediately marched forth to meet the enemy, and met him shortly in such numbers as they never expected.

Instead of finding it to be only the advance-guard of the enemy, as they at first supposed, they came upon a force of over two thousand infantry and cavalry together. The fight immediately commenced, and our handful of heroes fought with a stubborn energy and determination unsurpassed in any action of like magnitude. Judge of the numbers of the respective parties, when it is actually the case that company A, of the One Hundred and Sixteenth O. V. I., lost forty-seven men in killed, wounded, and missing within half an hour's time. The loss of gallant company I, of the same regiment, was hardly less. The whole party fought well, as their losses prove. Three commissioned officers and over one hundred men were left on the field, when the shattered remnants were forced to retreat. They were soon safe within the brick church, and from port-holes they had made through the walls of the sacred edifice they poured death and dismay into the ranks of the enemy who had crowded up and striven in vain to gain admission. The doors were effectually barricaded. Every volley from within sent some wretches quivering to their dread account, while the rebel bullets pattered as harmlessly against the strong walls of the holy citadel as the drops of rain that come down silently at night upon the homestead roof. But death lurked around them. The night was setting in. Milroy had left them to shift for themselves. Morning would bring destruction. Escape seemed impossible. What was to be done? The coolness and courage of Major Morris saved them. When the firing had ceased, in the stillness and darkness of the midnight hour, the brave old Major led his men out as silently as a funeral train, and brought them safely to Winchester on Sunday morning. I have seen no parallel for this action and retreat in the history of the whole war, and yet, such is the partiality or ignorance of some, not a single word has before been written concerning these almost Spartan heroes.

By Sunday morning the forces had arrived from Berryville, Bunker Hill, and intermediate points. They had all to fight their way through to Winchester. The dark woods in the direction of Strasburgh and Front Royal were turning gray with the hordes of rebels who were pouring in upon us. Whatever officers may have thought, the men were convinced by this time, of two things—namely, that we were surrounded, and that the force was overwhelming. Before this, every one said, "It was only Jenkins or Imboden;" but when we considered all these things, and had the additional evidence of the regiments which skirmished with the enemy Sunday forenoon, we had no doubt that the brave desperate legions of Stonewall Jackson were again in the valley. Deserters had come in as early as Friday, and reported that even then we were skirmishing with the advance-guard of a rebel corps numbering over thirty thousand. General Milroy ought to have known this. Who can say that he had any right to rest satisfied with partial information concerning a force sufficient to overwhelm and destroy him? I care not what others say; I know our effective force was less than eight thousand. Why, we had only ten regiments of infantry, and some of these the merest fragments. Of the cavalry, here or elsewhere, I have nothing to say. That some of them, especially the First New-York, did their duty, I will not deny, but that they deserve the fulsome praise that has been so copiously lavished upon them, I most emphatically deny.

On Sunday, it will be remembered that the enemy never fired a single cannon during the forenoon, and not even till late in the afternoon. Every one was in suspense all day. That this dread silence meant something, all deeply felt, but what was the strategy progressing none seemed able to discover. One sharp, discerning glance then would have done more harm to the enemy than the fire of a whole brigade. One sharp eye then would have been of more value than a battery. But alas for us! no such eye was there so to glance for us.

The Ohio regiments have hardly been mentioned in connection with the skirmishing in front. The One Hundred and Twenty-second, One Hundred and Twenty-third, and One Hundred and Tenth, all took a large share, indeed, the principal part in the fighting of Saturday and Sunday. These noble regiments manœuvred from morning till night, during two successive days, driving the enemy at the point of the bayonet out of their rifle-pits, and from behind stone-fences. It was as close hand-to-hand work as could be, sometimes skirmisher to skirmisher, and at others two whole brigades driving like two mad streams together. Ohio lost severely in men in all the fights in front, but she gained new lustre and renown for her already glorious history. Sunday evening, at half-past four o'clock, the "main fort" had four heavy siege-guns working effectually upon the enemy wherever he dared to show himself. The "star fort" had a battery of smaller but well-managed guns; while away over to the right and west the "regular battery" was stationed, firing occasionally as opportunity was afforded. This fort was supported by company C, of the One Hundred and Sixteenth O. V. I., and the One Hundred and Tenth O. V. I. Below the fort, west, and beyond a ravine, was a wood, and in that lurked a secret danger of which

no one yet even dreamed. The flag was floating proudly above the "main fort;" the brave and dauntless form of Milroy could now be seen resting fifty feet up on the flag-pole—an exhibition of coolness and courage unsurpassed in the annals of all history. There, too, had he been for two days. Away down the valley in front heavy skirmishing was going on. Every eye was turned that way, when on a sudden came a boom of cannon, and a rush of shell, as if hell itself had burst its bolts and bars and was bringing fire and tempest on the world. Every eye was turned west. Twenty rebel cannon were throwing shot and shell into the regular battery. In less than five minutes the roar of cannon was exchanged for the sharp rattle of musketry, as we saw the fort stormed, taken, and the rebel flag floating over it!

If an angel had descended from heaven, and told us of this five minutes before, we would not have believed it. As quick as thought the new position was bristling with cannon, and then commenced a fire of artillery, such as your correspondent never beheld before. Now came an order from General Milroy for the One Hundred and Sixteenth Ohio volunteer infantry and Eighth Pennsylvania to go to the support of our battery, (meaning the one just taken,) and when Colonel Washburn told the officer who brought the order that the fort was taken, "Go anyhow!" was the answer, and we started, right across the fields, in the face of the enemy's guns, for half a mile, the two regiments proceeded, and the order to charge the batteries had been given, when, to the surprise of every one, General Milroy ordered us to march back, and up into the main fort.

Railroad iron, shells, and musketry followed us thickly, clear across the field, but, *mirabile dictu*, not a man was hurt. All the force was now gathered into the main fort, except small detachments left to guard the star fort, and battery D, First Virginia artillery. The whole fire of the enemy was now directed, with very little interruption, toward our main fort. There still sat the intrepid but unfortunate General upon his elevated seat, the shells shrieking and whistling around him, and yet as calm and unmoved as if he were quietly taking his siesta at home. The firing all the evening was like the mingled roar of ten thousand thunders, and only closed when night set in. Every one knows now what followed—the retreat, in the darkness of night, with every thing left behind except men and animals; hundreds of wagons, immense commissary and government stores, some dozen large sutler stores, all the private baggage, books and papers of both officers and men; in a word, provisions enough to feed ten thousand men for two months, and clothing enough for the same number for six months. I feel confident that the above estimates are correct.

The attack on the Martinsburgh road, our defeat and retreat, have been so variously reported, that at this late day I feel no disposition to contradict any of them. Gross injustice has been done the Ohio regiments which were engaged in that desperate and unequal fight. I have seen scarcely any mention of them, and yet the One Hundred and Twenty-second, One Hundred and Twenty-third, and One Hundred and Tenth Ohio were all in the thickest of the fight, charged the enemy repeatedly, and came out in good order, but with heavy loss. Why, the whole three regiments are not now as large as any one of them before the fight. Colonel Washburn, of the One Hundred and Sixteenth Ohio, deserves all credit for the good order with which he brought off his regiment. While you might have seen some colonels and majors straggling hither and thither, the whole field and staff of the One Hundred and Sixteenth Ohio came through as they should. Thus it will be seen that Ohio did take some part in the fight. The One Hundred and Sixteenth Ohio had three companies completely destroyed; while the other three Ohio regiments took the most conspicuous places in the fight.

J. M. D.

LETTER TO THE PRESIDENT OF THE UNITED STATES,

Explanatory of the Evidence before the Court of Inquiry relative to the Evacuation of Winchester, Va., by the Command of Major-General R. H. Milroy.

To His Excellency Abraham Lincoln, President of the United States:

SIR: Under Special Order No. 346, from the War Department, a court of inquiry was detailed, by your authority, "to inquire into the facts and circumstances connected with the recent evacuation of Winchester." This order was subsequently so amended as to make it the duty of the court to report the facts without expressing any opinion upon them.

As I was in command of the forces which evacuated Winchester, my reputation and usefulness may be affected by the result of this investigation. Right and justice, therefore, require that you the Commander-in-Chief of the army of the United States, should read the brief remarks which I now have the honor to submit, in explanation of the testimony taken before the Court of Inquiry.

The evacuation of Winchester took place about two o'clock, on the morning of Monday, June fifteenth, 1863, and "the facts and circumstances" connected with that event were all comprised within the three preceding days, beginning with Friday, the twelfth.

Whether Winchester was or was not an important post, was a question not submitted to my judgment. It was determined by my superior officer, whose orders it was my duty to obey.

The orders received by me on Friday morning, June twelfth, 1863, from Major-General Schenck, my immediate commander, were as follows: "You will make all required preparations for withdrawing, *but hold your position in the mean time. Be ready for movement*, BUT AWAIT FURTHER ORDERS."

This emphatic command irresistibly implied that, in case of necessity, further orders would be given; and it now appears, by the testimony of Major-Gen. Schenck, that on Saturday night he did attempt to give me the proper orders; but as the lines had been cut, the despatch was not received. Gen. Schenck testifies distinctly that I did not disobey any of his commands.

In the same order above quoted, Gen. Schenck further says: "I doubt the propriety of calling in McReynolds's brigade at once. If you should fall back to Harper's Ferry, he will be in part on your way, and cover your flank. *But use your discretion as to any order to him.*" In the exercise of this discretion, I ordered Col. McReynolds, on Saturday morning, June thirteenth, to join me at Winchester. At this time there was no information of the approach of Lee's forces, nor any thought of evacuating the post. The object was to concentrate, in order to repel an attack either of the forces under Imboden, Jones, and Jenkins, or of Stuart's cavalry, then expected to appear in the valley. Colonel McReynolds left Berryville on the morning of the thirteenth, and, by a circuitous route of thirty miles, reached Winchester about ten o'clock that night. In the mean time, at about six o'clock that afternoon, I learned from prisoners and deserters that Ewell's and Longstreet's corps of Lee's army were in front of me. This was the first intimation I had received of the fact, and it brought to my mind, for the first time, the consideration of the necessity of evacuating the post. To have left with my forces before the arrival of Col. McReynolds would have exposed the whole Third brigade to capture, and would certainly have brought me into conflict with the enemy in the absence of one third of my command. Thus divided, my forces would have been destroyed or captured in detail. The enemy had followed Colonel McReynolds in force, and on the same day had attacked our forces at Bunker's Hill, on the Martinsburgh road.

My line of communication with Major-General Schenck was not cut until some time on Saturday evening. Down to that moment he could at any time have ordered me to retreat, and might have communicated any information which he deemed important. As his orders of the day before were not changed in any particular, while it was all the time in his power to have modified them, I had the *continuing command* of my superior officer *to remain at Winchester*, at least down to the time when communication by telegraph was cut off.

Every thing is necessarily left to the discretion of a commander when suddenly and unexpectedly surrounded on all sides by the enemy in overwhelming force, and with no orders adapted to the emergency. Colonel McReynolds found the Berryville road occupied by the enemy on Saturday, so that he could not march directly to Winchester. He had been followed also on his circuitous route, and the enemy was probably on the Martinsburgh road. It is doubtful whether I could have marched by either of those roads on Saturday night without a serious engagement under great disadvantages. But even if I could have done so, I did not and could not know why

General Schenck had withheld any orders during Friday and Saturday, while the telegraph was in operation. Was it not reasonable for me to suppose that General Hooker would intercept the march of Lee's army, or that General Schenck would in some way provide for relieving me? No one could have anticipated, as I certainly did not, that Lee's army could have escaped the army of the Potomac, and penetrated the Shenandoah valley as far as Winchester, without timely notice of it being given to me through General Schenck at Baltimore. It is in proof that my small force of cavalry was most actively and industriously engaged in reconnoitring; but it was impossible for them to push their reconnoissances beyond the Blue Ridge, and they had no suspicion of the presence of any other enemy but those under Imboden, Jones, and Jenkins, whom they had long watched and thwarted in the valley.

Under these circumstances, I deemed it wise and prudent to await the developments of Sunday, the fourteenth. If I should not during that day receive orders, or be relieved, I knew that the enemy would be compelled to reveal his purposes, and in some measure to mass his forces, so that I could then best determine how and when to cut my way through his lines. Accordingly, on Sunday night, after the enemy had massed his forces, and made an attack from the west, a council of war was held by my order; and it was therein resolved that the Martinsburgh road, being commanded by the guns of the forts, and being apparently open, offered the best route for a retreat upon Harper's Ferry, and that it was indispensable for the safety of the command to evacuate the place during the night, or in the early morning. But the enemy's pickets were within two hundred yards of our lines; and in order to escape without his notice, it was necessary to abandon the guns and wagons, which could not have been brought away, without so much noise in descending the rocky hills from the forts as to defeat the indispensable purpose of secrecy. The precautions adopted by the council of war were successful. We eluded the enemy, who surrounded us on three sides, and marched four and a half miles before encountering any of his forces. Then, after a sharp engagement of one hour, we succeeded in passing the enemy, and most of my forces escaped.

A single view of the situation will make the matter too clear for a moment's doubt.

On Friday, I had the plain, clear, direct, and positive order of General Schenck, commanding me to remain at Winchester, and await further orders. There was no known change of circumstances, after I received that order, until Saturday afternoon, when the prisoner was taken. But at that time the Third brigade, under a signal given in the morning, was on the march to Winchester, and reached that place at ten o'clock at night. They had then marched thirty miles on Saturday, and required all Saturday night for rest and refreshment. I could not have left Winches-

ter, at the earliest possible date, till Sunday morning, and then it would have been improper to do so by daylight. I waited, therefore, till Sunday night, and then called a council of war. We left at two, in the morning of Monday; and as we left in darkness, so we had to do so in quietness, as the one was as essential as the other to effect our escape. We, therefore, left every thing that went on wheels. Weighed against the lives of my brave men, they were less than nothing.

I do not suppose it necessary to defend the act of finally retreating from Winchester, although I had no orders to do so. It is now apparent to all men, that the alternative was between retreating or remaining to surrender. The only matter upon which there can be any inquiry, is as to the manner of the retreat—the energy, the watchfulness, the skill and success with which it was conducted. The severe fighting of Sunday, vigorously maintained through the whole day, had checked, if not crippled the enemy, and had doubtless served to mislead him as to my designs. He fully expected to find me in Winchester on Monday morning. Having succeeded in making this impression upon him, and thus allayed his suspicions as well as his vigilance, that time was the most favorable that could possibly have been selected for the retreat. No skill or precaution on my part, however, could have enabled me to evade the enemy where we met him on Monday morning. He was posted in a position to command both roads, at the point where the one leading to Summit Point diverges from the Martinsburgh road. Here we fought him until we heard a signal gun in the direction of Winchester, and two sections of the enemy's artillery, on the road from that place, were seen in hot pursuit of us. I then ordered the march to be continued, and the larger part of my forces went in different directions from the field of battle.

The result of this engagement would have been far different if my orders had been obeyed, or my example followed. When the retreat commenced, we anticipated the attack from the rear. But as soon as I heard the firing in front, I hastened to the scene of action. In passing along the line I found Colonel McReynolds some distance in advance of his brigade, and ordered him to return and hurry up his forces to the front. It was not my intention to continue the engagement longer than was necessary to enable all my forces to pass away. While I was actively engaged in front, I sent back no less than three different orders for the Third brigade to come up; but neither of my aids could find Colonel McReynolds on the field, nor any part of his command, except the First New-York cavalry. In consequence of this failure—waiting for the Third brigade to come up—I held my forces in the fight longer, and lost more men of the First and Second brigades than would have been necessary, if my orders had been promptly obeyed. The regiments of the Third brigade were separated, and though they were not in the engagement, they lost as many as the other brigades, and escaped by different routes from the scene of this action. Whatever irregularities and losses occurred during the march are attributable to the failure on the part of this brigade to respond to my commands. You will find the testimony sufficiently clear on this point; although, I regret to say, the court denied my request to summon and examine two of the colonels commanding regiments in the Third brigade, who allege that their commanding officer gave them no orders, and was not seen by them on the field.

Notwithstanding this unfortunate occurrence at the critical moment of my retreat, by which my plans were somewhat thwarted, out of the six thousand nine hundred brave and effective men who started from Winchester, upward of six thousand have been ascertained by General Schenck to be now on duty. Upward of two thousand men have been paroled by the enemy; but these consist of the sick and disabled who were left at Winchester, in addition to those who were taken in the engagement on the morning of the retreat.

A great misapprehension has existed in the public mind, and has been promoted by reckless correspondents of the public press, in reference to the amount of public property abandoned and lost on the retreat from Winchester. You will see by the testimony that the stores on hand were extremely small. My ammunition was nearly exhausted, the men were on half-rations, and a large portion of the wagons had already been sent away in pursuance of my orders, to be prepared for evacuation. It was my intention, and orders were given accordingly, to keep always on hand five days' supply of ammunition and subsistence. Fortunately the latest requisitions of my ordnance officer, for some reason unknown to me, had not been filled, and even this small amount was saved to the Government.

If the investigation made by the Court of Inquiry has not been full and satisfactory upon all points, it is not from any deficiency on my part. Anxious to lay open the whole transaction, even to its minutiæ, I earnestly urged the Court to summon and examine many other officers, who bore a conspicuous part in the retreat from Winchester, as well as others who could throw light on the general subject. The Court refused to grant my application, doubtless because they were satisfied that I had made my justification complete. I think I may assume that no Court would refuse to hear the testimony of some of the principal actors in the events under examination, so long as any room for censure remained against him who desired additional evidence.

So far, I may have no right to complain of the decision of the Court; but in another rejected application, I think I have. At the commencement of the investigation, immediately upon the organization of the Court, the General-in-Chief of the army sent in, as testimony, copies of several telegrams, addressed by him to Major-General Schenck, in which he speaks of me most disrespectfully and unjustly, and with imputations not true in fact. I asked the Court to summon Major-General Halleck; and as they required a statement of what a witness was expected to prove, I filed the paper, which, with others of

the same kind, will be found appended to this letter. These papers were all indorsed and returned to me, as will be seen, with a refusal to hear the testimony.

If it was admissible for the General-in-Chief to introduce his telegrams, charging me at some time with having been "on a stampede," it was certainly legitimate for me to call that officer, and inquire the occasion to which he referred, in order that I might prove, as I certainly could, the falsity of his information. The imputation conveyed in the words of Gen. Halleck, and perpetuated in the record of this Court, is highly disreputable to a soldier; and the most obvious principles of justice require that I should be permitted to refute it. If the substance of these telegrams be not a proper subject of investigation by the Court, then the introduction of them was calculated to serve no other purpose but to create a prejudice, and do me a wrong which I could have no opportunity to repel.

In another telegram put in evidence before the Court, I am charged with "madness" by the General-in-Chief, for sending part of my forces on a certain expedition in the valley. I could easily show that this "madness" would have resulted in the capture of the enemy's camp, with a large amount of supplies, which had been left exposed by the withdrawal of his forces into Western Virginia. But this affair had no connection with the evacuation of Winchester, and the incorporation of this telegram into the record is calculated unjustly to injure my reputation, without serving any public purpose.

In another telegram, likewise made a part of the record, I am charged with a failure to protect the Baltimore and Ohio Railroad at Harper's Ferry, when I never had any command there; also with incompetency in this respect, when, with my forces at Winchester, I successfully guarded that road for six months, so that during that period the enemy never touched it, within the limits of my command.

Gen. Halleck's telegram, of the fifteenth June, containing another ungenerous thrust at me, might well have been omitted from the record, inasmuch as it was written after the evacuation, and could not have the slightest bearing on the investigation. But it is quite as legitimate as the others, its only possible effect being to throw into the scale against me the weight of General Halleck's personal enmity.

On the twenty-seventh of June last, I was placed in arrest by order of the General-in-Chief. No charges have been preferred against me, unless the splenetic and censorious telegrams of that officer, above referred to, can be considered such. Since the commencement of this war, no officer of my rank has been subjected to the indignity of an arrest, without the exhibition of charges to justify it. I have not yet been relieved from this arrest; and the peculiar phraseology of the articles of war seems to render it doubtful whether the expiration of the time limited for making charges operates to give me that relief. I entered the army at the beginning of the war; and, until my arrest, I have never asked for leave of absence, nor been one day off duty. It has been my greatest pleasure continuously and faithfully to perform a soldier's part in defence of my country. I confess the humiliation, I feel, that the first period of rest allowed me has been one of implied censure, if not of disgrace.

I am very confident that an impartial examination of the record of this Court will show nothing to justify the treatment I have received. But, at all events, I have the proud satisfaction of knowing that I have not failed, in any instance, to give my best energies of mind and body to the service. Even in the defence and final evacuation of Winchester, (although, with timely and correct information, I would have acted differently,) yet I am sure that the holding of that place, and the engagement there, gave us the information we could not otherwise have obtained, developed the plans and purposes of the enemy, checked and delayed his advance into Maryland for three days, and by these means enabled the army of the Potomac to follow with timely resistance, and to prevent the loss of millions of property, which would otherwise have fallen into his hands. The inconsiderable loss suffered at Winchester was a trifle compared with these advantages; and so far from feeling that I am chargeable with any error in judgment, or failure in duty, I shall ever, in my own bosom, enjoy a conscience without self-reproach, and wholly void of any just offence to my country.

I have caused this letter to be printed for your convenience, and ask the privilege of publishing it, together with my official report made to Major-General Schenck, which has not yet been permitted to be made public.

I have the honor to be, with great respect, your obedient servant,   R. H. MILROY,
Major-General U. S. V.

JOHN JOLLIFFE,
FRED. P. STANTON,
Counsel.
WASHINGTON CITY, D. C., Sept. 10, 1863.

APPENDIX.

Major-General Milroy requests the Court to summon, in his behalf, Major-General Joseph Hooker, who, at the time of the evacuation of Winchester, was in command of the army of the Potomac.

The facts expected to be proved by this witness are: First, That he communicated information of the enemy's movements toward the valley of Virginia as early as the twenty-eighth May last to the General-in-chief, and suggested the propriety of sending General Stahl's cavalry to that valley. Secondly, The value and importance of the check given to the enemy by the holding of Winchester during the twelfth, thirteenth, and fourteenth of June, and its effect in saving Harrisburgh, and probably other important cities of the Union. It is believed that the testimony will clearly show that the aforesaid holding of Win-

chester was of far greater value than the amount of any losses incurred in the defence and evacuation of that post.   R. H. MILROY,
Major-General U. S. V.
August 22, 1863.

Indorsed: The Court does not feel authorized by the order under which it is acting to enter into the investigation suggested by the within communication.   ROBERT N. SCOTT,
Captain Fourth U. S. Infantry, Judge-Advocate.
April 29, 1863.

To Brig.-Gen. Barry, President of the Court of Inquiry, convened under Order No. 346.

I have learned directly from Colonel Horn, and indirectly from Colonel Staunton, that neither of those officers received any orders from Colonel McReynolds at the time of the engagement, on the morning of the fifteenth June last. I respectfully ask that they may be examined, together with some officer of the Thirteenth Pennsylvania cavalry.   R. H. MILROY,
Major-General U. S. Vols.
September 7, 1863.

The Court is of the opinion that the testimony above alluded to is not requisite to enable it to comply fully with the orders under which it is now acting.   ROBERT N. SCOTT,
Captain Fourth U. S. Infantry, Judge-Advocate.
September 7, 1863.

To the Court of Inquiry convened by Order No. 346.

Major-General Milroy supposing that the change of order under which the Court is acting may in some measure modify its views of the testimony to be received, again asks that Major-General Hooker may be summoned to give evidence upon the points already stated.

He also asks that Major-General Halleck, General-in-Chief of the army, may be summoned for the purpose of explaining the telegrams introduced at the beginning of the examination, in which he suggests that Major-General Milroy is on "another stampede." It is proper that the General-in-Chief should be required to say when and where Major-General Milroy was guilty of *stampeding.* Other similar insinuations are contained in the said telegrams, which a due regard to the military reputation of General Milroy requires should be explained. It is also desired that Major-General Halleck shall testify as to the failure to communicate information of the approach of Lee's army, with peremptory orders for the evacuation of Winchester.
R. H. MILROY,
Major-General U. S. Vols.
September 3, 1863.

Indorsed: Respectfully returned to Major-General Milroy. This Court of Inquiry does not consider that the order under which it is acting authorizes the investigation suggested by this communication.   ROBERT N. SCOTT,
Captain Fourth U. S. Infantry, Judge-Advocate.
September 3, 1863.

Doc. 12.

REBEL RAID INTO INDIANA.

New-Albany, Indiana, June 20, 1863.

Last week a raid was made into Elizabethtown, Kentucky, by what was then supposed to be a force of guerrillas. They did little damage except to plunder the stores, and help themselves to whatever portable property struck their fancy. Horses suffered particularly, they being a self-moving article of plunder. Medicines, wearing apparel, and boots and shoes were also much in demand. After a stay of a few hours in the town the rebels moved off to the southward, and it was supposed they had retired to the Cumberland River. They stated that they belonged to Captain Hind's company of the Second Kentucky cavalry, and were attached to Morgan's brigade. They were well armed with sabres, carbines, and revolvers, and uniformed in the regular uniform of rebel cavalry. They were estimated from eighty to one hundred and thirty strong — probably much nearer the former number.

After leaving Elizabethtown nothing more was heard from them until, on Thursday last, word was brought that five hundred rebels were crossing the Ohio, near Leavenworth, sixteen miles below this point. Hardly had the news become circulated before another messenger arrived confirming the statement of the crossing, but placing the rebel strength at three instead of five hundred. The Ohio is now quite low, and at Leavenworth it spreads out for nearly a mile in width and becomes very shallow. It is at this point that boats frequently run aground during low stages of water.

After crossing the river the rebels made no delay, but pushed rapidly forward for a raid into the river counties. Crawford, Orange, and Washington counties lay before them, and into these they pushed as rapidly as possible. They moved in a compact body, throwing out scouts on each side for the double purpose of guarding against surprise and bringing in any good horses that might be found. This portion of Indiana abounds in good horses, and from indications the rebels had been well apprised of this fact. They knew the names of such farmers as had fine stock, and were earnest in their inquiries for a Mr. Braxton, who resided near Paoli, in Orange county. On reaching Paoli, about six o'clock on Friday evening, they immediately commenced a search for horses and medicines, and before leaving they ransacked every store, taking whatever they wanted. They found Mr. Braxton, and, not content with taking his best horses, made him a prisoner.

Most of their own horses were thin and broken down, and as fast as they found fresh ones they changed saddles and abandoned their former steeds. Nearly all the horses they left bore the brand of "M. C.," such as is placed upon all the animals of Morgan's cavalry. They had evidently seen hard service.

Before arriving at Paoli the rebels entered the town of Vallini, Orleans County, the first that lay in their route after leaving the river. Here they demanded food of the citizens, and threatened to burn the town in case the demand was not complied with. The citizens were not prepared to accommodate such a large number of guests, and the delay in the preparation of dinner incensed the rebels so that they fulfilled their threat of setting the town on fire. As soon as they had done so they moved off, and by the exertions of the citizens a portion of the village was saved from destruction.

From Paoli the rebels moved toward Orleans, keeping up their system of stealing as they proceeded. Shortly after leaving Paoli they made a halt of several hours for the purpose of gathering in horses from places some distance from the road. News of their movements had spread like wildfire, and their numbers were magnified to a wonderful extent. The home guard in all the larger towns had been assembled, and made ready to meet them. Two companies from Mitchell, about one hundred strong, started as soon as they could be got together, and reached Orleans about one o'clock yesterday morning. At that time the rebels had completed their halt, and were moving toward Orleans. Hearing of their advance the Mitchell home guard moved out from Orleans to meet them. About three o'clock they encountered them three miles out from Orleans, and a brisk skirmish ensued. For fresh troops, the home guards fought well, but their enemies had the advantage of long service. The home guards were repulsed, with a loss of three wounded and twelve captured. The skirmish lasted about an hour.

The encounter with the force from Mitchell convinced the rebels that their movements were known, and they beat a retreat in the direction of Salem, without attempting to enter Orleans. Shortly after the fight they met Mr. Williams, a respectable elderly gentleman, well known in Orleans County. Mr. Williams was riding a fine horse, which the rebels coveted. They ordered him to dismount and give up his horse, and on his refusal to do so he was shot through the head and left dead in the road.

The Mitchell home guard rallied and attempted to pursue the retreating rebels; but as they were on foot their pursuit was of little avail. A full company of home cavalry from Crawford County, led by Major Woodbury, started from Leavenworth in pursuit as soon as he could muster his men. By daylight yesterday the rebels passed through Hardinsburgh, in Washington County, and, after plundering the stores in that place, left for King's Mills, in the direction of the Ohio River. Two hours after they had departed Major Woodbury came up, and, without halting, pushed on in pursuit, in the hope of overtaking the marauders at the crossing of the river. At King's Mills the latter delayed a half-hour to plunder a store, and on arriving there in pursuit Major Woodbury found he was only a half-hour behind his game.

The place where the rebels crossed the Ohio on their entrance into the State, was at Blue Island, in sight of Leavenworth. They reached this point about two o'clock yesterday. They had left several of their men on the opposite bank of the river, and the plan as arranged was for the latter to be at Blue Island at daybreak this morning with a ferry-boat to take them across. The reception by the inhabitants and the pursuit by Major Woodbury not having been looked for, hastened their departure about fifteen hours, and consequently the ferry-boat was not ready at the crossing-place. At the ford they discovered a force of home guards, so strongly posted that their hope of crossing by that means was cut off. The steamer Izetta had just reached Leavenworth, and the home guard at once placed a piece of artillery on board, and moved up the stream. They opened fire on the rebels and forced them to go still higher up, where the water was deeper. A small boat happened to be passing down at the time, and the rebels hailed her in the hope of capturing her, thus obtaining means to cross the stream. As the Izetta was firing on the rebels, the descending boat suspected their character, and refused to land.

At the same time the land force of home guards moved up the bank of the river, so as to get in the rear of the rebels. These home guards were from Leavenworth, and were commanded by Major Clendenin, a resident of that place, who served in one of the earlier Indiana regiments. As soon as the rebels saw the approach of Major Clendenin's force they at once plunged into the river and attempted to reach the island by swimming. The Izetta opened upon them with her artillery, and with her small arms as soon as she came within range. At the first fire of the latter four of the rebels were killed outright, and as many more wounded, so that they were unable to swim, and were drowned in consequence.

Major Clendenin's men were not long in reaching the scene of action, and opening fire, they added to the havoc caused by the Izetta, and as the boat passed between the island and the rebels, the latter saw there was no hope of escape. They turned their horses' heads toward the Indiana shore, and threw up their hands in token of surrender. One of their number produced what had once been a white handkerchief, and waved it vigorously until he reached dry land. The leader of the band took off his sword and advanced, holding it by the belt, as he looked around for some one to whom he could deliver it. The entire mob, seventy in number, were models of dripping meekness. One only of the entire party crossed the river to the Kentucky shore. He was welcomed by a citizen of that State, who at once took him prisoner.

Just as Major Clendenin was receiving his prisoners and taking an account of the captured property, Major Woodbury with his cavalry made his appearance. They were deeply chagrined at not having been present at the capture to which they had so largely contributed. The honor of the affair is to be divided equally between Major Clendenin, Major Woodbury, and the home guard from Mitchell. The latter by their resistance,

and Major Woodbury by his pursuit, completely broke up the plans of the rebels. By driving them to the river fifteen hours before the appointed time, they threw them out of the plan that had been made for crossing, and enabled Major Clendenin to complete the capture.

Five horses were lost in the attempt to cross the river, but the remainder fell into our hands. Those that were stolen from the citizens are being returned to them. The captured arms were loaded upon the Izetta, and will arrive here to-night.

The prisoners are now here, but will be sent to Louisville. They say that if their plans had succeeded, they would have broken the railway between New-Albany and Mitchell.

There is some dispute as to whether they will be held as regular prisoners of war or as guerrillas. They claim to belong to the Second Kentucky cavalry, and properly attached to the rebel army. The matter will be decided at Louisville.

Doc. 13.

SIEGE OF PORT HUDSON.

ATTACK OF JUNE 14, 1863.

MAJOR-GENERAL AUGUR'S HEADQUARTERS, BEFORE
PORT HUDSON, Monday, June 15, 1863.

HERE we are still, among these grand old magnolia forests, with the almost incessant roar of artillery and musketry in our ears; the desultory firing, kept up night and day, being enough to keep the beleaguered rebels, one would imagine, perpetually without rest. They must certainly attach a deep importance to this stronghold, or human endurance could scarcely hold out against the dreadful ordeal to which we have subjected them for the past two or three weeks.

Since the twenty-seventh, on which day occurred the attacks of which I have sent you an account, there has been nothing going on here of a nature to be made public, or which could be said to go beyond mere preparations for future operations, and investing the enemy more closely than ever. The bloody results of that day taught us what the people of the North are not always ready to believe, namely, that it is far easier to *talk* of taking a strongly-fortified place than to *do* it, and our brave fellows are now paying the dear penalty of that insane supineness which ever *permitted* such a fortress as Port Hudson to be built, when we could at one time have prevented it with scarcely more than a corporal's guard.

All that the twenty-seventh of May left us we not only retain, but have gone far beyond. Along our whole line, from the extreme right to the extreme left, we have been gradually gaining upon the enemy, dismounting their guns as fast as they are remounted, picking off, by our splendid sharp-shooters, every man who dared to show his head above their ramparts, and by these means rendering their armaments almost useless, as we steal up closer and closer to them. In some places we have got our batteries to within three hundred yards of them, and it is really terrible to peep through the embrasures of one of them, and almost look down the throats of the enemy's missiles, so close to us in front.

Thus matters continued until yesterday, when the Commanding General, deeming the time had arrived to give the rebels another strong dose, gave the order for one more simultaneous attack.

It was as late as ten P.M., of Saturday, June thirteenth, that General Augur, who had just returned from the headquarters of General Banks, told his staff that they were to be in motion at three A.M. of the next day. We all immediately hurried off to snatch a few hours' rest, and when I awoke at three o'clock, I found the General and his staff already at breakfast. In half an hour afterward they were all off to the field, whither I speedily followed them.

Before dawn the most terrific cannonading commenced along our whole line that ever stunned mortal ears. The shells bursting over Port Hudson, mingled with their own firing and that of our fleet, and the dense clouds of our artillery, gave the place the appearance of one vast conflagration just about to burst into flame.

After two hours of this dreadful cannonading there was a comparative lull, and the sharp and continuous rattle of musketry told where the work of death was going on most furiously. This was at the right, where General Grover's division was placed, and under him those gallant and fearless soldiers, Generals Weitzel and Paine.

If Weitzel had the larger share in the work of the twenty-seventh, that duty seemed to-day to fall upon the command immediately under General Paine.

The forces of the latter consisted of the Eighth New-Hampshire, Captain Barrett, and the Fourth Wisconsin, under Captain Moore, who were in advance as skirmishers. Behind these came five companies of the Fourth Massachusetts and the One Hundred and Tenth New-York, under Captain Bartlett, followed by four companies of the Third brigade. Closely upon these came the Third brigade, under Colonel Gooding, and composed of the Thirty-first Massachusetts, Lieutenant-Colonel Hopkins, Thirty-eighth Massachusetts, Major Richardson, Fifty-third Massachusetts, Colonel Kimball, One Hundred and Fifty-sixth New-York, Colonel Sharpe, and One Hundred and Seventy-fifth New-York, Colonel Bryan, who was killed. Then the Second brigade, under Colonel A. Fearing, and composed of the One Hundred and Thirty-third New-York, Colonel Currier, and the One Hundred and Seventy-third New-York, Major Galway, the rest of this brigade being detailed as skirmishers. After the Second came the First brigade, under Colonel Ferris, of the Twenty-eighth Connecticut, and composed of the Twenty-eighth Connecticut, the Fourth Massachusetts, Colonel Walker, and four companies of the One Hundred and Tenth New-York, under Major Hamilton. These were all followed up by the necessary number of pioneers and Nim's Massachusetts battery.

At half-past three A.M. of Sunday, June fourteenth, the column formed on the Clinton road and commenced moving. At about four A.M. the skirmishers moved right up to the scene of action, General Paine being with them in advancing, and the deadly work commenced, the enemy pouring in upon them the most terrible volleys, and our dauntless men combating their way right up to the enemy's breastworks. For hours the carnage continued furiously; our determined soldiers, in spite of their General being seriously wounded, and in spite of the fearful odds against them of fighting against men snugly screened behind their barriers, keeping up the fight with the most indomitable bravery. It was impossible for any men, under their circumstances, to show more reckless disregard of death.

But Port Hudson was destined not to be carried this time—at that point—at any rate. Owing to the horrible inequalities of the ground, and the impediments which the overwhelming slaughter of our advance had created, the whole column was not able to come up as expected, and late in the afternoon our troops had to be withdrawn. During the intensest part of the struggle, it is only fair to say that Colonel Kimball, of the Fifty-third, and Colonel Currier, of the One Hundred and Thirty-third New-York, advanced most gallantly with their men to reënforce those in front.

It is impossible to overrate the courage and endurance which General Paine showed on this occasion. Although so severely wounded in the leg as to be quite disabled, he would not consent to leave the field, but remained there during the long sultry day, to cheer on his men, at the momentary risk of being killed by some rebel shot.

Various efforts were made by his men to get him off the field, or at least to get refreshment to him, and two gallant fellows, on two separate occasions, lost their lives in the attempt. One was E. P. Woods, private, of company E, Eighth New-Hampshire, and the other John Williams, company D, Thirty-first Massachusetts. I happened to be at the hospital when the latter poor fellow was brought in. He had been shot clean through the breast, and lingered but a few minutes after his arrival there.

While at this hospital, witnessing the horrible spectacle of the wounded being brought in — something more painful to contemplate than the battle-field itself—a personal incident occurred to me which was deeply impressive. I was dismounting from my horse, when a soldier, who was gazing at me most intently, said, "The owner of that saddle is dying within a few feet of you, over there"—pointing to where two or three dozen men were lying on the shady greensward, in all forms of mutilation. "Do you know me?" I asked. "No; but I know that saddle was Lieutenant Bond's. I've sat in it too often not to know it." Hurrying to the spot indicated, I found it was indeed too true. There lay the young and gallant Lieutenant N. F. Bond, of company D, Thirty-first Massachusetts, flat on his back, and—as if proud of his wound, as he well may be—with his broad, manly bosom bared, and showing a rifle-shot wound in the centre of his right breast.

Learning from his attendants, who were bending over and fanning him, that he was still conscious and might be spoken to, I bent forward and took his cold, clammy hand in mine. "Who is it?" he inquired, looking up languidly. "A friend—don't you remember who bought that saddle of you near the sugar-house?" "Yes, I remember. Ah! sir, you will have to set me down among the items." "Oh! no, Lieutenant, I hope not," I replied, although my heart belied my speech, for death seemed stamped upon every lineament. I left him as another glorious martyr to his country's cause; but I am glad to say that, at this moment of writing, I hear the ball has been extracted, that he is doing well, and hopes are entertained of his recovery. Judging from what his own men say of him, (and I find this one of the surest tests of merit,) a braver young man does not live in the United States service. Before leaving this hospital, I cannot refrain from bearing my testimony to the unceasing and faithful attention toward the wounded which I noticed on the part of Surgeon L. C. Hartwell, Medical Director of the Third division.

Before General Paine was wounded, he had succeeded in getting five regiments within three or four rods of the enemy's works—some of the skirmishers actually getting inside.

Our loss on this occasion was very great—the killed, wounded and missing of Paine's command reaching to nearly seven hundred. A number of officers and privates (among them Captain Stamyard, of the Eighth New-Hampshire, Lieutenant Harsley and Lieutenant Newell, of the same) being wounded, were ordered in as prisoners, under threat of being shot from the enemy's works. General Paine was shot below the knee of the left leg, shattering both bones, but hopes are still entertained of saving his leg. He was not brought off the field till night-time, when his wound was dressed and he immediately conveyed to New-Orleans.

While this was going on in one portion of General Grover's command, the remainder, if not so hotly pressed, were scarcely less actively engaged.

At two A.M. the troops under General Weitzel's immediate command got into motion from their present locality, (which they so gallantly won on the twenty-seventh of May, and have held ever since,) and advanced round to the left to Colonel Dudley's front, leaving five companies on picket-line. The attack—for assaults these demonstrations can scarcely be called—was made by two columns in two different places. The column on the right was composed of Grover's division and Weitzel's brigade, under command of General Weitzel, while the left was composed of General Emory's division, under command of General Paine—whose doings I have just recorded. Colonel Dudley's brigade, of Augur's division, was held in reserve.

The forces under General Weitzel comprised his own brigade, formed of the Eighth Vermont, Lieutenant-Colonel Dillingham; Twelfth Connecticut, Lieut.-Colonel Peck; Seventy-fifth New-

York, Lieutenant-Colonel Babcock; One Hundred and Fourteenth New-York, Lieutenant-Colonel Perlee, and two regiments of Grover's division—the Twenty-fourth Connecticut and Fifty-second Massachusetts.

The history of the action on the part of General Weitzel would be but a counterpart of that of General Paine—the same obstacles to overcome, the same indomitable bravery in opposing them, the same temporary suspension of hostilities in the face of opposition too elaborately difficult to be surmounted for the moment.

Of what was going on at the extreme left, under General Dwight, I am not yet so well informed, for correspondents cannot be omnipresent, though many would have them so, and I would rather tell your readers nothing than give them incorrect information. I therefore do not feel myself in a position either to support or oppose the rumors which I hear everywhere—and among officers of very high rank—that the right wing did not come up as promptly to the mark as it was supposed they would have to do, if we would divide the enemy and keep them from concentrating their power, as they certainly did, upon our valorous and devoted right wing. The very same complaint was made—with what amount of truth time alone will decide—against our left wing in the great attack of our right wing on the twenty-seventh May.

To whatever cause it may be attributed, it is certainly lamentable to see any thing like a want of complete coöperation in moments of such intense consequence to the nation. Go where we will, do what we may, it seems to be our everlasting fate to be allowing ourselves to suffer for want of concentration and coöperation. The very same portion of the enemy who were so desperately contending with our right wing under Weitzel, on the twenty-seventh May, are actually asserted to have—at a later hour of the day—opposed us at other portions of our line, which could not have been possible had our movements been simultaneous. With a plan so well concocted, it is quite impossible to suppose that such an oversight could have formed part of the scheme, and therefore we are driven—in both events of the twenty-seventh May and the fourteenth June—to ascribe failure to some lack of punctuality in carrying out directions, somewhere or other. All I can answer for is that that portion of the line which had been most immediately under my own observation, (I mean Major-General Augur's,) on both those occasions, came squarely up to the orders given to it.

NEW-YORK HERALD ACCOUNT.

NEAR PORT HUDSON, June 17, 1863.

At early dawn on Sunday, the fourteenth instant, we commenced another advance movement on Port Hudson, with a force which was thought to be equal to any emergency, but which, as the result will show, was entirely insufficient to accomplish the object of the original plan.

As I have before indicated, in speaking of the conjunction of our right and left, the rebel defences form nearly a right angle, both the lines of which extend to the river, inclosing a sharp bend in the stream by which our gunboats found it so difficult to pass. The most accessible approach apparently to the rebel earthworks is over a clear field, about six hundred yards in width, and which at first sight presents the appearance of an almost perfectly level piece of ground. This spot, however, since our last assault, has been determined to be, although the most inviting, the most treacherous place along the entire line of rebel defences. Our soldiers in their charge found it to be filled with deep, narrow gullies, too small to cover a large body of troops, and too large to make a passage over them, even for infantry barely possible. Horses are out of the question, and were not used at this point. These artificial ravines are completely covered with fallen trees and vines; which are so arranged as to nearly obscure them from sight, and make an advance over them a matter of extreme difficulty. In our charge upon the enemy's lines at this spot it was impossible for our soldiers to keep in regular order of battle. Frequently whole squads of men would sink out of sight only to be resurrected by the assistance of their comrades. Down the right line of the enemy's works all approach to the fortifications is made exceedingly difficult by high bluffs and deep, irregular gullies. The enemy's rifle-pits are, although bearing the appearance of very wide constructions, built upon the most approved modern engineering skill. Here, again, fallen trees have been so arranged as to make it impossible to move artillery or troops in line of battle. The entire distance of rebel works presented for our reduction are nearly eight miles in extent.

Last Saturday evening the order of attack was determined upon at headquarters and communicated to the Generals who were to command the assaulting columns. Most of the details were arranged by General Grover The point of attack was the extreme north-easterly angle of the enemy's breastworks. Five or six days previous to the assault several pieces of the enemy's artillery, which had been in position behind their fortifications immediately in our front, were dismounted by our guns and abandoned. Those still in position were rendered useless to the rebels by our sharp-shooters. . Rebel deserters and prisoners brought into camp speak of our artillery practice as splendid, and say that they were not able to fire a gun more than five or six times before they had to move it, as the accuracy of our range would work it certain destruction. As before mentioned, we commenced preparations for the attack while yet it was scarcely daylight. The plan of the assault was briefly as follows: The Seventy-fifth New-York, under command of Captain Cray, and the Twelfth Connecticut, led by Lieutenant-Colonel Peck, were detailed as skirmishers, forming a separate command under Lieutenant-Colonel Babcock, of the Seventy-fifth New-York. The Ninety-first New-York, Colonel Van Zandt, commanding—each soldier carrying a five-pound hand grenade, with his musket thrown over his shoul-

der—followed next in order. The skirmishers were to creep up and lie on the exterior slope of the enemy's breastworks, while the regiment carrying the grenades were to come up to the same position and throw over the grenades into the enemy's lines, with a view to rout them and drive them from behind their works. The Twenty-fourth Connecticut, Colonel Mansfield, with their arms in like manner to the grenade regiment, followed, carrying sand-bags filled with cotton, which were to be used to fill up the ditch in front of the enemy's breastworks, to enable the assaulting party the more easily to scale them and charge upon the rebels. Following these different regiments came, properly speaking, the balance of General Weitzel's whole brigade, under command of Colonel Smith, of the One Hundred and Fourteenth New-York. This command consisted of the Eighth Vermont, Lieutenant-Colonel Dillingham, the One Hundred and Fourteenth New-York, Major Morse, and the One Hundred and Sixteenth New-York, Lieutenant-Colonel Van Petten. Next came Colonel Kimble's and Colonel Morgan's brigades, the last of which, with another brigade, (the name of which I was unable to learn,) was under the general command of Colonel Birge. This force was held to support the assaulting column, which was under the immediate command of General Weitzel, who made the attack on the right. General Emory's old division moved in conjunction with General Weitzel on the left, forming a separate column. The two divisions— General Weitzel's and General Paine's—were under command of General Grover, who, as has been before stated, planned the whole assault after General Banks's order to advance was received by him. Hence the mode of attack was entirely his own. General Weitzel's division was expected to make a lodgment inside of the enemy's works, and in that manner prepare the way for General Paine's division. After the inside of the enemy's fortifications had been reached, skirmishers were to push forward and clear the way, while both columns were to be deployed in line of battle and move toward the town of Port Hudson, where a grand citadel, which forms the last means of rebel defence, is situated.

I have thus far been speaking of General Grover's command exclusively, and the plan above given is applicable only to his movements, as determined upon at the time of its adoption.

About daylight the Seventy-fifth New-York, which had been slowly advancing, approached the enemy's works sufficiently near to see his fire. Previously the columns of the main body of General Grover's command were formed in the woods skirting the enemy's breastworks. The Twelfth Connecticut, during the night, had lost its way in the woods, and the Ninety-first New-York was ordered by General Weitzel to take the place that had been assigned to it and follow immediately in the rear of the Seventy-fifth New-York. After the advance of the Seventy-fifth and Ninety-first regiments, General Weitzel's entire command commenced moving forward. Several days previous our army engineers had been preparing a covered way, which extended from the woods where our troops lay up to within about one hundred and fifty yards of the enemy's position. Through this covered way our troops marched in single file up to the point where the first line of battle was formed. It should be remarked that the covered way spoken of was relied upon as being sufficiently deep to afford protection to our soldiers. It turned out, however, to be of no considerable consequence, owing to some fault in its construction. After the advance had arrived at the end of the covered way, they began slowly to push over the innumerable barriers that had been planted by the rebels to obstruct their march. The difficulties that I have before spoken of concerning the open field, immediately facing the enemy's works, were here experienced. The deep gullies, covered over by brush and creeping vines, were completely obscured from sight, and were only known to exist after our soldiers had plunged into them. Part of our skirmishers deployed to the right while suffering severely from the enemy's fire, and a portion of the advance took up a position on the left of the point to be attacked. They were immediately followed by General Weitzel's column, General Paine in the mean time advancing toward the enemy's works with his command further on the left. It should be stated that our troops, as soon as they had left the cover of the woods, which were scarcely three hundred yards from the enemy's breastworks, were subject to the constant fire of the rebel infantry. A portion of our artillery, which was planted some distance in the rear of our advancing forces, kept up a continuous fire at the rebel works. Captain Terry, of the Richmond, with his battery of eight-inch Dahlgren guns, and Captain McLaflin, with his battery, a portion of the Twenty-first Indiana artillery, did good execution. These batteries served very much to protect our troops as they were advancing to the attack. After our skirmishers had picked their way up to within about thirty yards of the enemy's works, they sprang into the ditch, expecting to be able to shelter themselves under the cover of the rebel fortifications, and keep the enemy down while the regiment with the hand-grenades should advance and perform their part of the work in driving the rebels from their position. The portion of the Seventy-fifth which succeeded in reaching the ditch were immediately repulsed, and nearly all of them were either killed or wounded. The ditch was so enfiladed that it was impossible for men to live long under the murderous fire of the enemy. The question may be asked why all this was not known before; but I have no time to comment.

In consequence of the repulse of the portion of Seventy-fifth that succeeded in reaching the ditch, the hand-grenaders could accomplish but little. In fact, although they made many desperate and gallant attempts to be of service, they rather damaged than benefited our prospects of success; for as they threw their grenades over the rebel breastworks, the rebels actually caught them and hurled them back among us. In the mean time, while the skirmishers were nobly endeavoring to sustain themselves in their position, General Weitzel's column moved up as rapidly as possible, and made a series of desperate assaults on the enemy's works, which for bravery and daring the history of the war can hardly furnish a parallel. At this time the sun having fairly risen, the fight became general. A fog, which had partially obscured the contending armies, lifted and revealed their respective positions. The enemy were fully prepared for us, and they lined every part of their fortifications with heavy bodies of infantry. The battle had begun in earnest, and General Paine's column, as well as General Weitzel's, was actively engaged. Before proceeding further with the details of the fight of General Grover's command, it will be necessary to mention a fact that I have previously omitted—namely, that under the general plan of attack, as directed by General Banks, Generals Augur and Dwight were to make feints on the extreme left of General Grover's position, to distract the attention of the enemy from the main assault. Accordingly, before the engagement became general between General Grover's command and the enemy, Generals Augur and Dwight had attacked the enemy, as before indicated, on General Grover's extreme left. It was not the intention that the last-named of these forces should storm the rebel works, but hold the enemy in check while General Grover was performing his part of the work according to the original plan, which, had he been successful, would have opened the way for the advance of our entire army on Port Hudson proper, which is surrounded, it is understood, by a series of fortifications more impregnable than any we have yet assaulted. The fight on the part of General Dwight's command was exceedingly severe, and scarcely less so with General Grover's. General Dwight's loss in killed and wounded will probably exceed two hundred. General Augur's loss will fall considerably short of that number. Under General Grover's command probably the most desperate fighting was done by General Weitzel's old brigade. Colonel Smith, leading these veterans, the heroes of many fights, fell early in the action, mortally wounded. The ball pierced his spine and passed around to the right side. The Colonel still lingers, but his death is hourly expected. The charges made on the rebel works by our brave soldiers showed a determination to carry them at all hazards; but human bravery on this occasion was not adequate to the accomplishment of their object. The most formidable obstacle that presented itself as a barrier to our success, was the rebel glacis, which at the point attacked had been constructed in such a manner as to make every bullet tell that was fired from the rebel breastworks while our troops were endeavoring to make the ascent. In fact the great natural advantages and engineering ability at Port Hudson have been rather under than overrated. Immediately upon the fall of Colonel Smith, Lieutenant-Colonel Von Petten, of the One Hundred and Sixtieth New-York, took command of the brigade, and gallantly led the charge until all further hope of driving the rebels from their position was gone. Brigade after brigade followed in rapid succession, storming the rebel works until compelled to fall back under the terrible fire of the enemy. Conspicuous among the brigades that did the most desperate fighting, were those under the command of Colonels Kimball, Morgan, and Birge. They were all, however, eventually repulsed with great slaughter.

The fighting ceased at eleven o'clock in the morning. We having been repulsed in every assault, our soldiers, under command of their officers, laid themselves down under the shelter of the gullies, trees, covered way, in fact, every thing that could afford them protection, and waited for the day to pass and darkness come on. Many of our wounded who were accessible were carried from the field by squads detailed for that purpose. It is a shameful reflection on humanity that a large number of our soldiers, carrying the wounded and dying from the field on stretchers, were shot down by the enemy, and in several instances the wounded were killed while being borne from the field. At nightfall, however, we commenced the burial of our dead, and succeeded before the morning in carrying most of our wounded from the battle-field.

The enemy's hospitals, after the battle began, seemed to grow as rapidly as mushrooms in the dark. I counted no less than twelve hospital flags within a square of a quarter of a mile. I strongly suspect the protection afforded by them was not in every case legitimate, for on one occasion I saw firing in the immediate locality of one of the tents.

NEW-YORK, June 28.

The *Herald* has advices from Port Hudson to the twentieth instant. General Banks on the fifteenth instant issued a congratulatory order to his troops over their steady advance upon the enemy's works, stating that he is confident of an immediate and triumphant issue of the conflict, and says we are at all points upon the threshold of his fortifications. One more advance and they are ours. He then will summons the organization of a storming column of one thousand men to vindicate the flag of the Union and the memory of its defenders, who have fallen, promising promotion to the officers, and a medal to officers and privates.

A letter of the twentieth reports no material change in the position of affairs. The camp rumors about assaults by volunteers and general attacks have proved unfounded. We are steadily advancing. Our first parallel which completely incloses the outer line of rebel breastworks and our skirmishers are behind rifle-pits—within twenty yards of the rebel intrenchments. There are nightly skirmishes without definite results. Battery No. Seven, to be mounted with twelve thirty-two-pounders, has been erected, commanding the entire series of the enemy's river works. One heavy shot from the enemy had pierced the heavy plating of the Essex. The gun which effected this has been dismounted by battery No. Seven. The citadel on which it was mounted was expected to be soon reduced.

It was rumored and generally believed that an assault would take place on the night of the twentieth, to be led by Gen. Grierson and Col. Von Petten, of the One Hundred and Sixteenth New-York. The assaulting party was to be supported by General Weitzel's old brigade and that of Colonel Dudley.

A rebel bearer of despatches had been captured with, it is said, a despatch from Johnston, who promises to reënforce Port Hudson and capture Banks's entire army, if the place would hold out until the following Tuesday. This may be a ruse, however, to induce Banks to make an immediate assault, that he may be repulsed, and arrest the slow process of starvation which stares the rebels in the face.

Deserters report a consultation of rebel officers, who unanimously requested General Gardner to surrender. He replied that large reënforcements would arrive within a week, and if they would only hold out a few days longer, the siege would result favorably to them. The disaffected officers returned to their camps and told the men if the General did not surrender in a week they would compel him to.

Another deserter reports that the rebels have but forty head of cattle left to feed on.

BOSTON "TRAVELLER" ACCOUNT.

NEW-ORLEANS, June 19, 1863.

It is not with much pleasure or satisfaction that I undertake to narrate the momentous events in this department for the past week. Most prominent among them is the second unsuccessful assault on Port Hudson, last Sunday, the fourteenth. Since the first assault, on the twenty-seventh May, our forces have held the position gained by them then, our infantry in many places being very near the enemy's works, so that easy conversation can be carried on by the belligerents.

The country about Port Hudson is very uneven, cut by deep ravines, especially on the north and east, so that in these ravines one can approach very close to the enemy unseen. Our army has been very strongly posted in these places, scooping out sleeping-places in the sides of the banks, and making breastworks on top. Here they rested eighteen days. In the mean time our artillery had been pouring an almost unceasing shower of shot and shell into the devoted city. Each day had been added a siege-gun or mortar, till on the thirteenth every thing was in position, when for a few hours the very earth shook from their rapid discharges.

Having given them many tons of iron, the firing ceased, and Gen. Banks sent, by a flag of truce, an order to surrender, which his persistence, Gen. Gardner, refused to do, saying he should hold out as long as he had a man left. The firing was then resumed, and kept up till half-past three the next morning, when the assault was to have been made. The right wing, commanded by Brig.-Gen. Grover, and composed of Emory's old division, under General Paine, and Grover's old division and Weitzel's brigade, under Weitzel, started promptly.

These two divisions were to make two separate assaults. In front of Gen. Paine, two hundred yards, were thrown out as skirmishers the Eighth New-Hampshire and Fourth Wisconsin regiments, both then very much reduced and almost without officers, from the affair of the twenty-seventh. These were followed by the Fourth Massachusetts, bearing hand-grenades, which were to have been thrown over the works as soon as they got near enough; then the Fifty-third Massachusetts, each man carrying a sack stuffed with cotton, with which to fill the moat, that the main body might pass easily over.

Then came the column, company front, until they could deploy on the open space before the works. This would have been a dangerous experiment if it had not previously been ascertained that the enemy had no artillery bearing on this point. At the head of the column was Colonel Currie, with the One Hundred and Thirty-third New-York regiment, as fine a body of soldiers as are in the department. Scarcely had the brave fellows of the two regiments, little more than companies, deployed, when the musket-balls and buckshot of the enemy commenced to whistle their requiems about their heads.

They heeded them not, never even stopping to bind up the wounds of their comrades or carry off their dead, but rapidly loaded and discharged their faithful rifles and hurried on to almost certain death. It was but a short distance across the space they had to go—an old cotton-field, selected because it was more easily passed over—but when they arrived at the enemy's works, so as to be sheltered by them, they found that they had left two thirds of their numbers on the field, either killed or wounded.

The hand-grenades had not come up, with the exception of a dozen or so; the cotton-bags were not in sight, and the column, which should have been but two hundred yards behind, was not visible, except Col. Currie, with a part of his regiment in good order. Then Lieut. Jewett, of the Fourth Wisconsin, one of the bravest of the brave, drew his sword, and calling upon his men to follow him, leaped into the ditch, followed by about thirty men, climbed the work, and jumped down on the inside.

Then, if there had been five hundred men to have followed, the work could have been carried; but for some cause, unaccountable except on the hypothesis of the want of pluck of some of our regiments, there was nobody to go in, and this brave band of heroes were murdered; so that when Col. Currie came up in a few minutes, the work was bristling again with bayonets and belching lead like hail. He fell badly wounded in each arm, and his men took position under a slight hill and waited for assistance.

Previous to this time, Gen. Paine, at the head of his column, and while cheering on his men by word and action, had been wounded by a ball, which broke both bones of his leg just below the knee. He fell on the field, and his column with-

ered before the shower of balls. If they had followed sooner the line of skirmishers, they would have suffered less, for the enemy took advantage of our delay to mass their forces to receive us. The column became broken. A part went no further, and a part forced its way on till it was around by the hill spoken of.

But the bags of cotton were gone, so there was no easy way of crossing the ditch, and the enemy now could send from their safe place an irresistible storm of bullets. Thus ended Gen. Paine's charge. If he had not been wounded so soon, I think he would have forced his way through.

In the mean time, Gen. Weitzel's skirmishers had advanced to the very ditch, but for some unaccountable cause the cotton-bags had been intrusted to those who cared not to risk their lives for fame.

Weitzel's old brigade, then commanded by Col. Smith, of the One Hundred and Fourteenth New-York, was at the head of his column, but Colonel Smith being mortally wounded very early, it had fallen into confusion, and although a fighting brigade, it became powerless, yet it was badly cut up. General Weitzel's assault was to have been made in the woods, so the Seventy-fifth New-York and Twelfth Connecticut, his skirmishers, were not so badly cut up as Paine's, though they lost nearly one half their men. Weitzel, finding it impossible to carry the works without losing nearly all his command, rested them in the numerous ravines.

For some cause the charge on the left was not vigorously sustained, and the loss there was very trifling. I was unable to ascertain the cause of their failure.

Many of the wounded on the right had to remain on the field of battle all day, suffering from loss of blood, for want of water, and the hot sun pouring down on them. They were in easy musket-range, and if one approached to carry them off or relieve their suffering, they were shot. Gen. Paine, wounded early in the morning, was not brought off till after dark, when his wound was alive with maggots.

This was also the condition of many others. He lay between two rows of an old cotton-field, on his back, and he said if he attempted to cover his face with his cap, a shower of balls would fall around him. His wound is now doing well, and it is hoped his leg may be saved. He is cared for most tenderly by his wife, who is fortunately here, and by the Sisters of Charity, in whose hospital, the Hotel Dieu, he is treated. Just across the hall from him is Gen. Sherman, wounded on the twenty-seventh, who has just had his leg amputated to save his life, and who is now doing very well.

Our forces remained in the position I have described till after dark Sunday night, when they were withdrawn, and occupy the same places they did for the eighteen days previous.

Our whole loss, killed, wounded, and missing, was about seven hundred and fifty. But a very small proportion were killed, and many are very slightly wounded, the enemy not opening at all with artillery. Among the killed are Colonels Holcomb, First Louisiana; Galway, One Hundred and Seventy-third New-York; Bryan, One Hundred and Seventy-fifth New-York; and Smith, of the One Hundred and Fourteenth New-York, mortally wounded.

ACCOUNT BY A PARTICIPANT.

BIVOUAC OF THE "THOUSAND STORMERS," }
BEFORE PORT HUDSON, June 22. }

Some days since I wrote and sent to New-Orleans by a friend, a few lines, which I hope are ere now in your hands. From them you will know of my whereabouts. I know the date line of this letter will seem queer to you, but the order inclosed will explain it. [General Banks's call for a thousand volunteers to storm the fort.] I have thus far been spared, but I fear now that this is my last letter for a long time, if not forever. On the fourteenth we stormed the works again and were repulsed with much loss.

Our regiment lost sixty out of two hundred and fifty. I lost just half my company, (killed and wounded,) and was slightly hurt on the left wrist by an unexploded shell, which cut the flesh, and the concussion lamed the arm badly. However, I am on duty, and have commanded the regiment since then till yesterday A.M., Colonel B. being in command of the brigade, and Lieutenant-Colonel B. being sick. Poor Major Bogart was killed in the charge — struck in the hip by a shell before it exploded and almost cut in two. The same one killed Sergeant Lord and Corporal Newman, of my company — then exploded and wounded several men. I have been in many battles, but I never saw, and never wish to see, such a fire as that poured on us on June fourteenth. It was not terrible—it was HORRIBLE.

Our division (Second) stormed about a mile from the Mississippi. We left our camp where I wrote you last at twelve o'clock midnight, on the thirteenth, and proceeded to the left, arriving just at daylight, where the balance of our brigade (Second) awaited us.

Colonel Benedict arrived from opposite Port Hudson on the twelfth, and our regiment was transferred from the First to the Second brigade, and he placed in command. The movement to the left took all by surprise; but we got in shape behind a piece of woods which concealed the enemy's works and rested. The First brigade went in first and we followed—the Third brigade being a reserve. I saw the First brigade file left and move on, but saw no more of it. When the order came to move on, we did so in "column of company," at full distance. Ask some good military man what he thinks of a brigade moving to a charge in that manner. The One Hundred and Sixty-second leading, the One Hundred and Seventy-fifth (Bryan's) after us, then the Forty-eighth Massachusetts and Twenty-eighth Maine. We were in a road parallel to the enemy's works, and had to change direction to or file left round the corner of the woods, and then started forward by a road leading up. The ground rose gradually, and away above, the rebel works were in plain sight. The moment we turned into the road, shot, shell, grape, and canister, fell like hail in amongst and around us. But on we went. A little higher, a new gun opened on us. Still farther, they had a cross-fire on us—oh! such a terrible one; but on we went, bending, as, with sickening shrieks, the grape and canister swept over us. Sometimes it fell in and about us; but I paid no heed to it.

After the first, my whole mind was given to the colors, and to keep my men around them; and they did it well. I wonder now, as I think of it, how I did so. I walked erect, though from the moment I saw how they had us, I was sure I would be killed. I had no thought (after a short prayer) but for my flag. I talked and shouted. I did all man could do to keep my boys to their "colors." I tried to draw their attention from the enemy to it, as I knew we would advance more rapidly. The brave fellows stood by it, as the half-score who fell attest. The "color-bearer" fell, but the "flag" did not. Half the guard fell, but the "flag" was there. Ask (if I never come home) my colonel or lieutenant-colonel if any one could have done better than I did that day. I do not fear their answer. When about three hundred yards from the works, I was struck. The pain was so intense that I could not go on. I turned to my second lieutenant, who was in command of company C, as he came up to me, and said: "Never mind me, Jack; for God's sake jump to the colors." I don't recollect any more, till I heard Colonel B. say: "Up, men, and forward." I looked, and saw the rear regiments lying flat to escape the fire, and Colonel B. standing there, the shot striking all about him, and he never flinching. It was grand to see him. I wish I was of "iron nerve," as he is. When I heard him speak, I forgot all else, and, running forward, did not stop till at the very front and near the colors again. There, as did all the rest, I lay down, and soon learned the trouble. Within two hundred yards of the works was a ravine parallel with them, imperceptible till just on the edge of it, completely impassable by the fallen timber in it. Of course we could not move on. To stand up was certain death; so was retreat. Naught was left but to lie down with what scanty cover we could get. So we did lie down, in that hot, scorching sun. I fortunately got behind two small logs, which protected me on two sides, and lay there, scarcely daring to turn, for four hours, till my brain reeked and surged, and I thought I should go mad. Death would have been preferable to a continuance of such torture. Lots of poor fellows were shot as they were lying down, and to lie there and hear them groan and cry was awful. Just on the other side of the log lay the gallant Colonel Bryan, with both legs broken by shot. He talked of home, but bore it like a patriot. Near him was one of my own brave boys, with five balls in him. I dared not stir, my hand pained so, and it would have been death also. Well, the Colonel got out of pain sooner than some, for he died after two hours of intense agony. Bullets just grazed me as they passed over, and one entered the ground within an inch of my right eye. I could not go that. Our boys had run back occasionally, but got a volley as they did so from the rebels, who would curse them. I waited till our cannon fired a round at them, then up and ran across the road, and fell flat behind some low bush or weeds, and well I did. They saw my sword and fired several volleys after me. As my hand was very lame, I crawled several rods back, then under a big log, got behind it, and, for the first time in five hours, sat up. I bathed my hand, and after a while made my way to the rear, got it dressed, and was on my way back, when I learned that the men were to work in, by one and twos, so I staid. I then learned of poor Bryan's fate, and one by one came the tidings of my own men, and when the word came of them I cried like a child. Some of them passed me on the way to have their wounds dressed, and blessed me as they passed by. When night came, the troops came in and line was formed, and a small one we had. The Major's body was brought in to be sent home, and my pet favorite, Sergeant Fred. Mitchell, (who, as a favor to me, Colonel Benedict had made an acting lieutenant — he was so good a soldier and handsome and talented,) who, the last I saw of him, was his sword flashing in the sunlight as he urged the men forward; but he was brought in with half his head torn off, and it was hard to recognize him. But God bless him! He was true, for his right hand grasped his sword firmly in death. I have it stored to be sent to his friends. Colonel B. and Lieutenant-Colonel B. came out safe. The Lieutenant-Colonel had been sick for some time, and this finished him. So I took command of the regiment, brought it to the mortar battery, and bivouacked for the night.

On the eighteenth came the call from General Banks for a thousand stormers, and four officers and fifty men of our regiment responded to it. Yesterday our regiment went to Springfield Landing to guard against a raid, (it is our base,) and the "Stormers" came here to camp. The thousand are here, and we storm on Weitzel's front, on the extreme right.

The first officer in our brigade was myself, my Second Lieutenant is another, and Colonel Benedict leads us. It is, as you will perceive, in spite of the flattering order, "a forlorn hope." Our position is critical. Something must be done. I am confident this will succeed. I pray earnestly it may, though I live not to know it. You will wish to know why I came when our regiment is so short of officers, and I am so easily fixed now. I came on principle. I did not come for the reward or promotion, but because I deemed it my duty to come.

Bold men are wanted. If I am not bold, God will make me so. I came, and am to have the honor of leading a company in this charge. If I am wounded, I shall come home at once, and I know you will not be ashamed of me or my conduct. If I die, you will think of me as one whose short life was not wholly without a purpose. I hope to come to you with honor — with the medal on my breast. WILLIE.

Doc. 14.

THE CAPTURE OF RICHMOND, LA.

ADMIRAL PORTER'S REPORT.

UNITED STATES MISSISSIPPI SQUADRON,
FLAG-SHIP BLACK HAWK, NEAR VICKSBURGH,
Thursday, June 18, 1863.

SIR: I have the honor to inform you, that, hearing the enemy had collected a force of twelve thousand men at Richmond, in Louisiana, nine miles from Milliken's Bend, I sent General Ellet to General Mowry, at Young's Point, to act in conjunction to wake them up. General Mowry promptly acceded to the request, and, with about one thousand two hundred men in company with the Marine brigade, General A. W. Ellet commanding, proceeded to Richmond, where they completely routed the advance-guard of the rebels, consisting of four thousand men and six pieces of artillery, captured a lot of stores, and the town was completely destroyed in the mêlée. This duty was handsomely performed by the different parties connected in it. DAVID D. PORTER,
Assistant Rear-Admiral.

BRIGADIER-GENERAL ELLET'S REPORT.

HEADQUARTERS M. B. BRIGADE,
FLAG-SHIP AUTOCRAT, ABOVE VICKSBURGH, June 17, 1863.

ADMIRAL: I have the honor to inform you, that, in accordance with your consent, I landed my forces at Milliken's Bend on the morning of the fifteenth instant, and proceeded toward Richmond, La.

At the forks of the road, within three miles of Richmond, I met General Mowry's command, and we proceeded forward together, my forces being in advance.

We met the enemy about a mile from the town, who opened upon our advance line of skirmishers, from behind hedges and trees and gullies, but they fled before our advance, and took shelter behind the levee on the opposite side of the bayou, near the town. The position was a good one, and very defensible. I deemed it imprudent to advance our lines across the open field without any cover for my men against an enemy superior in numbers and well intrenched. I therefore ordered the artillery to the front, and opened upon their position; and, after a vigorous cannonade of nearly an hour with all our guns, advanced our infantry through the woods on the right, with the intention of turning the enemy's left wing. They returned the fire of our artillery very vigorously for a time, but soon it slackened, and finally ceased altogether. When I arrived at the left of their position, I found it abandoned and the enemy fled. He had destroyed the bridges over the bayou to prevent our following. We found three of the enemy dead upon the field, two mortally wounded, and captured eleven prisoners and about sixty stand of small arms.

The enemy was commanded by Major-General Walker, was a part of Kirby Smith's command, and consisted of two brigades, containing seven regiments, four thousand strong, with six pieces of artillery. They retreated toward Delhi, where General McCulloch is said to be posted with a command about equal in strength to the one we encountered. This was the same force that attacked the negro regiment at Milliken's Bend, a week before, and was repulsed.

Our entire loss was three men wounded, one only dangerously.

Gen. Mowry's command participated throughout most vigorously, and I feel indebted to the General for his prompt coöperation and advice, and his skilful manner of handling his forces.

A. W. ELLET,
Brigadier-General Commanding M. B. Brigade.

A NATIONAL ACCOUNT.

CHICKASAW BAYOU, Thursday, June 18, via Cairo, Wednesday, June 24.

On the sixteenth, the rebel General Anderson, with a division belonging to the command of Major-General Dick Taylor, marched from Richmond toward Lake Providence, where Gen. Reid was stationed with a small Federal force, consisting of the First Kansas and Sixteenth Wisconsin regiments, with some negro troops, less than one thousand five hundred in all.

Richmond is eight miles from Young's Point, on the Louisiana side, at a point where the Shrevesport road crosses the Tensas. It is about twelve miles from Milliken's Bend, and thirty from Lake Providence, and an important point, from the fact that from it those places are easily accessible by good road, and for the enemy it would be an exceedingly offensive position toward us.

General Reid went out to meet him, and destroyed the bridge over the Tensas, a short distance from the head of Lake Providence. The rebels opened on him with a six-pounder, damaging our forces at first considerably, but his men succeeded in silencing the gun and preventing the rebels from crossing, also pouring in a terrible fire of musketry upon them as they pressed up to the river. Thinking our force larger than it was, the enemy retreated, with heavy loss.

On the same day, General Mower marched on Richmond, from Sherman's Landing, with his brigade of infantry and Taylor's old Chicago battery, under command of Capt. Barrett. On reaching the Tensas, he met the rebel pickets and drove them in. The rebels burned the bridges, and undertook to make a stand. Capt. Barret opened fire, well supported by infantry.

Such was the combined shower of shell and bullets, that, though fighting well, they were obliged to fall back with what cavalry force they had. Gen. Mower then pursued the flying enemy, succeeding in capturing forty-two prisoners.

The affair was perfected with signal vigor and promptness—our troops, in their impetuosity and daring, overcoming the disparity in numbers on the part of the enemy. It is likely, from indications, that the entire force of Gen. Dick Taylor (who, by the way, is a son of old Zack) has skedaddled to the Red River country.[*]

Doc. 15.

REBEL VIEWS OF PEACE.

"TWO YEARS HENCE."

RICHMOND, June 16.

IN two years, as many persons hope, we may possibly have peace—that is, always provided we continue to repulse and defeat the invading enemy. The Yankee "democracy" is certainly rousing itself and preparing for a new struggle (at the ballot-box) in the great cause of the "spoils," or, as they call it, the cause of constitutional liberty. Those Democrats are evidently beginning to raise a peace platform for their next Presidential election; and if they have the good luck to be helped on and sustained by more and more serious disasters of the Yankee army in the field, there is no doubt that the present devourers of the said spoils at Washington may soon be so discredited and decried that our enemy's country would be ripe for such peaceful ballot-box revolution.

It is sincerely to be hoped that those earnest champions of constitutional freedom will be helped on and sustained in the manner they require, namely, by continued and severe reverses in the field, and it is the first and most urgent duty of our countrymen so to help and sustain that Democratic party. It is nothing to us which of their factions may devour their "spoils;" just as little does it signify to us whether they recover or do not recover that constitutional liberty which they so wantonly threw away in the mad pursuit of Southern conquest and plunder. But it is of the utmost importance to us to aid in stimulating disaffection among Yankees against their own government, and in demoralizing and disintegrating society in that God-abandoned country. We can do this only in one way—namely, by thrashing their armies and carrying the war to their own firesides. Then, indeed, conscientious constitutional principles will hold sway; peace platforms will look attractive; arbitrary arrests will become odious, and habeas corpus be quoted at a premium. This is the only way we can help them. In this sense and to this extent, those Democrats are truly our allies, and we shall endeavor to do our duty by them.

But they evidently look for other and further help at our hands, and of quite a different sort. No doubt they are pleased for the present with the efficient aid which the confederate army is affording them. Chancellorsville was a godsend to them, and the tremendous repulse at Port Hudson is quite a plank in their platform. Yet they understand very well that no matter how soundly their armies may be happily beaten; no matter how completely Lincoln's present

---

[*] For further accounts of this affair, see Supplement.

war policy may be condemned by its results, yet all this will not be enough to enable the unterrified Democracy to clutch the "spoils"—or, as they phrase it, to restore the Constitution of their fathers. This, of itself, would never give them a peace Democrat President and Cabinet: it would only result in another abolitionist administration, with a new Secretary of War and a new Commander-in-Chief, and a slightly different programme for "crushing the rebellion." These Black Republicans are in power, after long waiting, pining, intriguing in the cold shade of the opposition, and they have now the numerical preponderance so decidedly that they both can and will hold on to the office with a clutch like death. The Democrats can do absolutely nothing without "the South," as they persist in terming these confederate States, and they cannot bring themselves to admit the thought that we would refuse to unite with them (as alas! we used to do) in a grand universal Presidential campaign for a Democratic President with a peace platform, and "the Constitution as it is." In fact, this whole two years' war, and the two years' more war which has yet to be gone through, is itself, in their eyes, only a Presidential campaign, only somewhat more vivacious than ordinary.

This explains the Vallandigham peace meetings in New-York and New-Jersey, and the "manly declarations" of Mr. Horatio Seymour and other patriots. "Do not let us forget," says Fernando Wood, writing to the Philadelphia meeting, "that those who perpetrate such outrages as the arrest and banishment of Mr. Vallandigham do so as necessary war measures. Let us, therefore, strike at the cause, and declare for peace and against the war."

This would sound very well if the said "declaring for peace" could have any effect whatever in bringing about peace. If a man in falling from a tower could arrest his fall by declaring against it, then the declarations of Democrats against the war might be of some avail. As it is, they resemble that emphatic pronouncement of Mr. Washington Hunt: "Let it be proclaimed upon the house-tops that no citizen of New-York shall be arrested without process of law." There is no use in bawling from the house-tops what every body knows to be nonsense. Or this resolution of the New-Jersey meeting:

"*Resolved*, That in the illegal seizure and banishment of the Hon. C. L. Vallandigham, the laws of our country have been outraged, the name of the United States disgraced, and the rights of every citizen menaced, and that it is now the duty of a law-respecting people to demand of the Administration that it at once and forever desist from such deeds of despotism and crime. (Enthusiasm.)"

Demand, quotha? The starling that Mr. Sterne saw in the cage said only: "I can't get out." It would have been more "manly" to scream—"I demand to get out; I proclaim on the house-tops that I will get out."

Another of the New-Jersey resolutions throws an instructive light upon this whole movement and its objects:

"*Resolved*, That we renew our declaration of attachment to the Union, pledging to its friends, wherever found, our unwavering support, and to its enemies, in whatever guise, our undying hostility, and that, God willing, we will stand by the Constitution and laws of our country, and under their sacred shield will maintain and defend our liberty and rights, 'peaceably if we can, forcibly if we must.' (Great cheering.)"

This phrase, "wherever found," implies that there are friends of the Union in this Confederacy, and the resolution obligingly pledges to them the support of the New-Jersey Democracy—not surely without an equivalent return.

To the same meeting General Fitz-John Porter writes a letter, declaring, of course, for the Constitution and resistance to despotism, and ending thus:

"The contest of arms, however, will not be required; the certain and peaceful remedy will be found in the ballot-box. Let us all possess our souls in patience. The remedy is ours."

General Fitz-John knows well that the remedy is not theirs, unless "the South" consent to throw its votes into that same ballot-box; and it is for this, and this only, that the Democratic hook is baited with "peace." But in a speech of Senator Wall, of New-Jersey, before a Democratic club of Philadelphia (which we find printed in the *Sentinel*,) is a passage more fully expounding the Democratic plan than any other we have seen. He says:

"Subjugation or annihilation being alike impossible, I am in favor of an immediate cessation of hostilities—for an armistice—that 'mid the lull of the strife, the heat of passion shall have time to cool, and the calm, majestic voice of reason can be heard. In the midst of such a calm I am for endeavoring to learn from those in arms against us what their demands may be, and inviting their coöperation in the name of a common Christianity, in the name of a common humanity, to some plan of reconciliation or reconstruction by which the sections may unite upon a more stable basis—a plan in which the questions upon which we have differed so long may be harmoniously adjusted; and each section, by virtue of the greatness developed in this war, may profit by the experience. If it shall be found that sectional opinions and prejudices are too obstinate, and the exasperations of this war have burned too deep to settle it upon the basis of reconciliation or reconstruction, then I know that separation and reconstruction are inevitable."

Here is the whole plan: an armistice, and then "inviting our coöperation." During that armistice they hope that the "calm majestic voice of reason" and a "common Christianity" might do something considerable. The game, as they calculate, would then be on the board, with stakes so tempting. Mr. Wall would endeavor to "learn from us what our demands are."

Any thing in reason he would be prepared to grant us; but if we replied, our demands are that you bring away your troops from every inch of our soil, that you leave the Border States free to decide on their own destiny, that you evacuate all our forts and towns which you now hold, and make us rid of you and the whole breed of you forever, then Mr. Wall would exclaim: What! do you call that the calm majestic voice of reason? Is that your common Christianity? He would say, when I spoke of the calm majestic, etc., I meant the spoils; when I said a common Christianity, I meant money. Let us talk rationally—how much common Christianity will you take?

In vain is a net spread in the sight of any bird. We are aware of them; and we will watch them well, and the friends of the Union, "wheresoever found." Our views go a little further than theirs. We have to so disorganize and disintegrate society in their country that they will rush into armed revolution and anarchy. We spit upon their ballot-box. We care not what they "demand" in resolutions, nor what helpless trash they proclaim on the house-tops. We do not believe in their power to attain so much as an armistice for two years to come. If an armistice, indeed, were offered, and the invading troops were withdrawn, of course we should not object to it, and good use could be made of it.

But mark well, ye armistice mongers! During that suspension of hostilities all negotiations must be between government and government. Our lines should be more strictly guarded than ever. No negotiations or fraternization of parties by public meetings or private conferences; no bargaining with the "calm voice of reason;" no secret pocketing of Wall's "common Christianity.".

But armistice there will be none, and we are glad of it. Our sovereign independence is already won and paid for with treasures of brave blood. It shall not be sold by peddlers, to be built into a Yankee platform.—*Richmond Inquirer.*

Doc. 16.

DEFEAT OF EVERETT'S GUERRILLAS.

CAMP TENTH KENTUCKY VOLUNTEER CAVALRY, }
MOUNT STERLING, KY., June 17. }

THE expedition against Pete Everett's gang of guerrillas has returned. They were the Eighth and Ninth Michigan cavalry, and the Tenth Kentucky cavalry, the two former under Colonel De Courcy, the latter under Major Foley. The rebels were about two hundred and fifty strong. They immediately, after committing their depredations at Maysville, broke for the mountains. The Tenth, under Major Foley, went as far as Fleminsburgh, and finding that they had escaped, pushed on to overtake them. In the mean time the Eighth and Ninth Michigan cavalry had gone by the way of Owingsville to cut them off. The Tenth overtook them at Triplitt's Bridge last evening, some twenty miles east of the former place. In the mean time Colonel De Courcy, with the Eighth and Ninth regiments, had got on

before them and formed in a line of battle on the bluff facing the bridge across the creek.

The rebels being ignorant of the force in their front, and supposing those in their rear to be home guards, left two companies just this side of the bridge, formed on the hill-side in the bushes, intending when they came up to bushwhack them to pieces. But they were mistaken in their game. The two companies in front, companies E and F, on being fired upon, charged right and left, clearing the hill at one sweep, capturing all their horses and some eight or ten prisoners. The rest fell back on the bridge, the Tenth following close on them.

At the moment the latter appeared on top of the hill, our men, the Eighth and Ninth Michigan cavalry, opened on them; also with two pieces of artillery. The Tenth, seeing the mistake of Colonel De Courcy, made signs to inform them and stop the firing, which was, for about ten minutes, terrific. But they "couldn't see it," and the Tenth were compelled to fall back behind the hill. The rebels, profiting by this unfortunate mistake, crossed the bridge in front of the Eighth and Ninth, and filing off under the bluff, escaped up a ravine. Night coming on, the only means left was to send a regiment around to one of the gaps to cut them off. The Eighth Michigan was accordingly despatched on this business. We lost, singular to say, but one man killed—William West, company C—and two wounded—Joseph Blair and James Hicks—all of the same company. West was shot in the forehead by a Minie ball, and fell fighting bravely. The prisoners number about forty; among the number Captain James White, of Maysville.

The Eighth Michigan cavalry, which was left on the field, it is expected will capture the greater part of the remainder. The rebel surgeon came in with their wounded and gave himself up; he reported that Pete Everett, the commander, was killed in the charge by company C. About two thousand dollars' worth of property of every description was picked up on the field by our boys.

To conclude, I think that guerrillaing has very near played out in this section of the country, especially as long as a man remains in the

TENTH.

Doc. 17.

MAJOR-GEN. M'CLERNAND'S REPORT.

DETAILING THE MARCH OF THE THIRTEENTH ARMY CORPS FROM MILLIKEN'S BEND TO VICKSBURGH, MISSISSIPPI, ETC.*

HEADQUARTERS THIRTEENTH ARMY CORPS, }
BATTLE-FIELD, NEAR VICKSBURGH, MISS., June 17, 1863. }

Lieutenant-Colonel J. A. Rawlins, Assistant Adjutant-General, Department of the Tennessee:

COLONEL: I have the honor to submit the following report of the principal operations of the forces with me, since the thirtieth of last March, in compliance with orders from department headquarters.

* See page 637 Docs., Vol. VI. R. R.

These forces consist of a portion of the Thirteenth army corps, and comprise four divisions, organized as follows:

NINTH DIVISION—Brigadier-General P. J. Osterhaus commanding:

First Brigade—Brigadier-General T. T. Garrard commanding, consisting of the Forty-eighth and Sixty-ninth Indiana, One Hundred and Twentieth Ohio, One Hundred and Thirteenth Illinois, and Seventh Kentucky.

Second Brigade—Colonel L. A. Sheldon (Forty-second Ohio) commanding, consisting of the Sixteenth, Forty-second, and One Hundred and Fourteenth Ohio, Fifty-fourth Indiana, and Twenty-second Kentucky.

Artillery—First Wisconsin and Seventh Michigan batteries.

Cavalry—Companies A and K Third Illinois cavalry.

TENTH DIVISION—Brigadier-General A. J. Smith commanding:

First Brigade—S. G. Burbridge commanding, consisting of the Sixteenth, Sixtieth, and Sixty-sixth Indiana, Eighty-third and Ninety-sixth Ohio, and Twenty-third Wisconsin.

Second Brigade—Col. W. J. Landrum (Nineteenth Kentucky) commanding, consisting of the Nineteenth Kentucky, Seventy-seventh, Ninety-seventh, One Hundred and Eighth, and One Hundred and Twentieth Illinois, and Forty-eighth Ohio.

Artillery—Chicago Mercantile and Seventeenth Ohio batteries.

Cavalry—A company of the Fourth Indiana cavalry.

TWELFTH DIVISION—Brigadier-General A. P. Hovey commanding:

First Brigade—Brigadier-General G. F. McGinnis commanding, consisting of the Eleventh, Twenty-fourth, Thirty-fourth, and Forty-sixth Indiana, and Twenty-ninth Wisconsin.

Second Brigade—Colonel J. R. Slack (Forty-seventh Indiana) commanding, consisting of the Forty-seventh Indiana, Twenty-fourth and Twenty-eighth Iowa, and Fifty-sixth Ohio.

Artillery—Peoria light artillery, Second and Sixteenth Ohio, and First Missouri batteries.

Cavalry—Company C First Indiana cavalry.

FOURTEENTH DIVISION—Brigadier-General E. A. Carr commanding:

First Brigade—Brigadier-General W. P. Benton commanding, consisted of the First U. S. infantry, Eighth and Eighteenth Indiana, and the Thirty-third and Ninety-ninth Illinois.

Second Brigade—Brigadier-General M. K. Lawler commanding, consisting of the Eleventh Wisconsin, and Twenty-first, Twenty-second, and Twenty-third Iowa.

Artillery—First Indiana battery.

Cavalry—Companies E and F Third Illinois cavalry.

Detachments of the Second and Third Illinois and Sixth Missouri cavalry, also formed part of my immediate command.

MARCH FROM MILLIKEN'S BEND TO PORT GIBSON.

After several fruitless attempts to penetrate the State of Mississippi above Vickburgh, and to turn the rear of that city, it became a question of the highest importance, whether a point below on the Mississippi River, might not be reached, and a way thus opened to the attainment of the same end.

My corps, happily, was in favorable condition to test this question. It was inspired by an eager desire to prove its usefulness, and impatiently awaited an opportunity to do so. Sharing in this feeling, I was more than rejoiced in permission to essay an effort to cross the peninsula opposite Vicksburgh, from Milliken's Bend to New-Carthage.

Accordingly, on the twenty-ninth of March, I ordered Gen. Osterhaus to send forward a detachment of infantry, artillery, and cavalry to surprise and capture Richmond, the capital of Madison Parish, La. On the morning of the thirtieth, Colonel Bennett, with the Sixty-ninth Indiana, a section of artillery, and a detachment of the Second Illinois cavalry, took up the line of march in execution of this order. By two o'clock P.M. he had marched twelve miles over a miry road and reached the bank of Roundaway Bayou, opposite Richmond.

Artillery first, and infantry next, opened fire upon the small force garrisoning the town, and immediately dislodged it. A portion of the cavalry dismounting from their horses, sprang into the small boats brought along on wagons, and paddling them across the bayou with the butts of their carbines, hastened to occupy the town. Hot pursuit of the fugitive enemy was soon after made by another portion of cavalry, who swam their horses over the bayou. Seven of the enemy were wounded, four of whom fell into our hands.

This spirited and successful attack was consummated under my own observation, and effectually cut off the supplies which were wont to be transported through Richmond from the rich tracts traversed by the Tensas River and Bayou Macon to Vicksburgh.

On the night of the third a bridge two hundred feet in length, made of logs taken from houses, was thrown across Roundaway Bayou at Richmond, by the pioneer corps, under Capt. Patterson. This was the work of twenty-four hours, and a way being thus opened, the remainder of General Osterhaus's division was rapidly moved forward and so disposed as to cover and hold the only practicable land route between Milliken's Bend and Smith's plantation, two miles north of New-Carthage.

Meantime, many obstacles were overcome—old roads were repaired, new ones made, boats constructed for the transportation of men and supplies; twenty miles of levee sleeplessly guarded day and night, and every possible precaution used to prevent the rising flood from breaking through the levee and engulfing us.

Other obstacles were also encountered. Harrison's rebel cavalry, supported by a detachment of infantry, were active and vigilant to oppose our advance, but after having been repeatedly repulsed, on the fourth fled across Bayou Vidal, and returned to their camp at Perkins's plantation, on the Mississippi, six miles below Carthage.

On the same day, embarking in a skiff at Smith's plantation, and accompanied by General Osterhaus and a few members of our respective staffs, I made a reconnoissance, terminating only a half-mile from Carthage and the river, and in full view of both. We discovered the country to be deluged from Smith's plantation, where Bayous Vidal and Roundaway unite, and whence they communicate by a common channel with the Mississippi to Carthage. Also, that the levee extending from Bayou Vidal to Carthage and the Mississippi was broken and crossed by rapid currents at three different places. Upon our approach to the last crevasse, a half-mile from Carthage, we were fired upon by the enemy, and our skiff stopped, but not until we had ascertained that steamers could pass from the Mississippi to Smith's plantation, and that by such means our forces could be transferred from Smith's to the Mississippi shore.

Having thus determined this important point, on the fifth a flat-boat was wrested from the enemy on Bayou Vidal, eight miles below Smith's, and brought to the latter place. On the sixth, after the boat had been hastily prepared to receive them, a party with two mountain howitzers were embarked and moved forward to dislodge the enemy at Carthage.

Upon the approach of the boat the enemy hastily evacuated Carthage and took refuge a mile and a half below, among a number of buildings on James's plantation. Rapidly disembarking, the party pursued and again dislodged him, killing a rebel lieutenant and taking possession of the buildings.

On the seventh, Gen. Osterhaus pressed his advantages by sending forward artillery and shelling the woods beyond Bayou Vidal, in the neighborhood of Dunbar's plantation, and dislodging the enemy's sharp-shooters.

In turn, on the eighth, the enemy took the offensive and sought to dislodge the detachment at James's. For this purpose he opened two twelve-pound howitzers upon it, but after an hour had been spent in fruitless endeavors again fell back to Perkins's.

On the eighth, Lieut. Stickel, with a company of the Second Illinois cavalry, while scouring the country westward toward the Tensas, fell in with a recruiting party of the enemy, and succeeded in capturing three officers and one private.

Having been considerably strengthened by reenforcements supposed to have been sent from Grand Gulf, on the east bank of the Mississippi, the enemy on the fifteenth sought to reinstate his line between Perkins's and Dunbar's—the latter place being eight miles from Perkins's, and the same distance from Smith's. For this purpose he divided his force, directing one portion across Mill Bayou against our rear in the neighborhood of Dunbar's and the remainder against the detachment at James's.

Our pickets near Dunbar's upon the approach of the enemy fell back upon their reserves, who being rapidly reënforced promptly attacked and forced the enemy to recross Mill Bayou, taking two prisoners; our own loss being one man killed and one wounded, of the Second Illinois cavalry. Thus failing at this point, that portion of the enemy operating in front of James's retreated.

Up to this time I had been restrained from throwing any considerable portion of my forces upon the river, for want of any other means than a few skiffs and small boats; and because, in the absence of gunboats to protect them, while limited by the flood to the occupancy of the Mississippi levee, they would have been exposed to destruction by the gunboats of the enemy, then supposed to be cruising near New-Carthage.

To supply the means of moving my forces from Smith's to Carthage and across the Mississippi to some point from which operations could be directed against Vicksburgh, and also to afford them needed protection against river attack, I ventured earnestly to urge the pressing and transcendent importance of forwarding steam transports and gunboats from their moorings above Vicksburgh below to Carthage.

Happily, on the seventeenth, my recommendation was responded to by the appearance of five transports and seven gunboats, and on the twenty-second by three more transports, all of which had run the blockade.

A number of barges having started in tow of the transports and been cut loose on the way, were caught and brought to by parties from Gen. Osterhaus's division, who went out in skiffs for that purpose. Nor should I omit to add that during the advance of my forces from Milliken's Bend, they subsisted in large part upon the country through which they passed, and seized and sent back as a forfeiture to the United States a large quantity of cotton owned by the rebel government.

The increased facilities afforded by the transports and barges alluded to, hastened the removal of the Ninth division from Smith's to Carthage.

The Fourteenth division followed from Milliken's Bend to the same place; also, the Tenth division to Smith's, and a part of it to Carthage. The rest of the Tenth division rested near Smith's until a land route had been opened ten miles from there to Perkins's. The Twelfth division, which only arrived at Milliken's Bend on the fourteenth, followed to Smith's, and was followed from there to Perkins's by the rest of the Tenth, a large part of the trains of the whole corps, and afterward by the Seventeenth and Fifteenth army corps.

The last five miles of the route from Smith's to Perkins's, was obstructed by numerous bayous. To accelerate the general movement, Gen. Hovey undertook the experiment of overcoming these obstacles. In order to do so, he constructed near two thousand feet of bridging out of material created for the most part on the occasion. This he did within the short space of three days and nights, thus extending and completing the great military road across the peninsula from the Mississippi River above to the Mississippi River forty miles below Vicksburgh. The achievement is one of the most remarkable occurring in the annals of war, and justly ranks among the highest examples of military energy and perseverance.

On the twenty-second, receiving a communication from Admiral Porter, informing me that he would attack the enemy at Grand Gulf on the following morning, and requesting me to send an infantry force to occupy the place when he had silenced the enemy's guns, I directed Gen. Osterhaus immediately to embark his division on all available boats, and to coöperate with the gunboats in carrying into effect the purpose mentioned.

In prompt execution of my order, General Osterhaus embarked his division during the night of the twenty-second, but Admiral Porter informing me in the morning, that the enemy was in much stronger force than he first supposed, and that more extensive preparations on the part of our land and naval forces were required than could be immediately made, the contemplated attack was postponed.

On the twenty-third, accompanied by General Osterhaus, I made a personal reconnoissance of the enemy's works and position at Grand Gulf, on board the gunboat General Price, which had been kindly placed at my disposal for that purpose by Admiral Porter, and found them very strong. On the twenty-fourth in obedience to my order, General Osterhaus sent a detachment of the Second Illinois cavalry, under Major Marsh, and the Forty-ninth Indiana, and the One Hundred and Fourteenth Ohio infantry, together with a section of artillery, all under command of Colonel Kaigwin, to reconnoitre the country between Perkins's and the mouth of Bayou Pierre, and to examine into the practicability of expediting the general movement by marching troops across the country to the mouth of that stream. The expedition was frequently interrupted by rebel cavalry, but not until reaching a point on the west side of Bruin's Lake did it meet any considerable resistance.

Here the cavalry of the enemy, six or seven hundred strong, with several pieces of masked cannon, drawn up in line of battle on the opposite side of Choctaw Bayou, made a resolute stand. A desultory fight, however, of four hours served to dislodge him and leave us master of the field. Thence the detachment continued its march to Hard Times, fifteen miles below Perkins's, and three miles above Grand Gulf. Thence the cavalry marched across Coffee Point to D'Schron's plantation, three miles below Grand Gulf, and on to a point opposite Bruinsburgh, the landing for Port Gibson, twelve miles below Grand Gulf, thus demonstrating the existence of a practicable land route from Perkins's to a point opposite Bruinsburgh. The whole or a portion of the Seventeenth army corps, afterward followed to D'Schron's, and so the Fifteenth, as far as Hard Times.

Having concentrated my whole corps at Per-kins's, on the twenty-eighth, without wagons, baggage, tents, or officers' horses, which were left behind for want of transportation, the whole of it except the detachment at Hard Times and two regiments ordered to remain at Perkins's as a garrison, embarked on steamers and barges including the gunboat General Price, for Grand Gulf. Arriving at Hard Times that evening, they rested there during the night on boats and on shore.

On the morning of the twenty-ninth the gunboats steamed three miles down the river to Grand Gulf, and closely approaching, the enemy's batteries opened fire upon them. The Ninth, Tenth, and Twelfth divisions of my corps followed on transports, casting anchor in full view of the Gulf, and holding themselves in readiness to push forward and disembark the moment the enemy's water-batteries should be silenced and a footing for them thus secured. General Carr's division remained at Hard Times, waiting for the return of transports to bring them on too.

At the termination of a daring and persistent bombardment of five and a half hours, the principal batteries had not been silenced, several of the gunboats had been crippled, and all of them were drawn off.

Returning to Hard Times, the Ninth, Tenth, and Twelfth divisions disembarked, and together with the Fourteenth division, crossed over the point opposite Grand Gulf that evening and night to D'Schron's. The same night the gunboats, transports, and barges ran the blockade at Grand Gulf, and landed at D'Schron's.

If the attack upon Grand Gulf had succeeded, it would have secured either or both of two objects. First, a base for operations against the rear of Vicksburgh; second, safety in reënforcing General Banks at Port Hudson; but failing, it became important to gain a footing at some other favorable point. The reconnoissance made by my cavalry, in pursuance of Major-General Grant's order, indicated Bruinsburgh to be the point. Hence, embarking on the morning of the thirtieth my corps immediately proceeded to that place, and disembarked before noon.

Only halting long enough to draw and distribute three days' rations, at four o'clock all my corps, except the cavalry on the opposite side of the river, took up the line of march agreeably to Major-General Grant's instructions, for the bluffs some three miles back. Reaching the bluffs some time before sunset, and deeming it important to surprise the enemy if he should be found in the neighborhood of Port Gibson, and if possible to prevent him destroying the bridges over Bayou Pierre, on the roads leading to Grand Gulf and to Jackson, I determined to push on, by a forced march, that night as far as practicable.

BATTLE OF PORT GIBSON.

About one o'clock, on the morning of the first of May, upon approaching Magnolia Church, thirteen miles from Bruinsburgh, and four miles from Port Gibson, General Carr's division leading the advance was accosted by a light fire of the enemy's infantry, and soon after by the fire of his artillery. Harris's brigade, the command of which had devolved upon Colonel Stone, of the Twenty-second Iowa, in consequence of the illness of the former, was immediately formed in line of battle. Griffith's and Klaus's batteries brought up and the enemy's fire briskly replied to and silenced. The division rested upon its arms at Shaiffer's plantation during the short remnant of the night.

Coming up about day-dawn in the morning, I learned from a fugitive negro, that the two roads diverging at Shaiffer's led to Port Gibson—one to the right by Magnolia Church, and the other to the left, passing near Bayou Pierre, where it is spanned by a rail and earth road bridge; also that the greatest distance between the roads was only some two miles; that the space between and for miles around was diversified by fields, thick woods, abrupt hills, and deep ravines, and that the enemy was in force in front and intended to accept battle. Immediately proving the general correctness of this information by further inquiry and by personal reconnoissance, I determined to advance my forces upon the chord of the rude ellipse formed by the roads, resting my reserve back near the fork of them.

After the smoke of the previous engagement and the glimmering of the rising sun had ceased to blind our view, I ordered General Osterhaus to move his division on the road to the left to relieve a detachment of General Carr's division, which had been sent to watch the enemy in that direction, and to attack the enemy's right. The object of this movement was to secure whatever direct advantage might result from attacking the enemy's line at a point supposed to be comparatively weak, and to make a diversion in favor of my right preparatory to its attack upon the strong force understood to be in its front.

The first brigade of General Osterhaus's division hastening forward in execution of this order, at half-past five A.M. encountered the enemy in considerable force a short distance from Shaiffer's house. The position of the enemy was a strong one, and he seemed determined to maintain it, yet after a hard struggle for more than an hour he was forced to yield it and seek temporary safety at a greater distance, under cover of ravines and houses.

The splendid practice of Lanphere's and Foster's batteries disabled two of the enemy's guns, and contributed largely to this success.

Communicating with General Osterhaus, I offered him reënforcements, but his second brigade having now come up, he declined them until more urgent occasion should arise. Thus strengthened he pressed forward, until insurmountable obstacles in the nature of the ground and his exposure to the fire of the enemy arrested his progress and proved the impracticability of successful front attack. It was now two o'clock P.M., and about this time General J. E. Smith's brigade of General Logan's division came up, and attempting to carry the enemy's position, by such an attack, failed to do so, thus demonstrating the

correctness of General Osterhaus's admonition upon that point.

A flank movement had been resolved on by General Osterhaus, to accomplish the same object. With a view to deceive the enemy, he caused his right centre to be threatened, and taking advantage of the effect, rapidly moved a strong force toward his extreme right, and personally leading a brilliant charge against it, routed the enemy, taking three pieces of cannon.

A detachment of General Smith's brigade joined in the pursuit of the enemy, to a point within a half-mile of Port Gibson.

At a quarter-past six o'clock A.M. when sufficient time had elapsed to allow Osterhaus's attack to work a diversion in favor of my right, I ordered General Carr to attack the enemy's left. General Benton's brigade promptly moved forward to the right of the main road to Port Gibson. His way lay through woods, ravines, and a light canebrake, yet he pressed on until he found the enemy, drawn up behind the crest of a range of hills, intersected by the road. Upon one of these hills, in plain view, stood Magnolia Church. The hostile lines immediately opened on each other, and an obstinate struggle ensued. Meanwhile Stone's brigade moved forward on and to the left of the road into an open field, and opened with artillery upon the enemy's left centre.

The action was now general except at the centre, where a continuation of fields extending to the front of my line for more than a mile separated the antagonists. The enemy had not dared to show himself in these fields, but continued to press my extreme right with the hope, as I subsequently learned, of crushing it and closing his concave line around me.

General Hovey came up at an opportune moment and reporting his division to be on the ground, I immediately ordered him to form in two lines near the fork of the two roads, and to hold it there for further orders. About the time it had been thus formed, General A. J. Smith's division came up, and General Hovey was ordered to advance his division to the support of General Carr's. In the execution of this order General McGinnis's brigade moved to the right front in support of Benton's, encountering the same obstacles that had been overcome by the latter. Colonel Slack's brigade moved by the flank near the main road, and without much difficulty gained its proper position to the left of McGinnis.

During the struggle between Benton's brigade and the enemy the former moved to the right to secure its flank, and left a considerable gap between it and Stone's. This gap was immediately filled up by a portion of Hovey's division, upon its arrival upon the ground assigned to it. The enemy's artillery was only one hundred and fifty yards in front, and was supported by a strong line of infantry which it was reported had just been reënforced, and was the occasion of the shouting of the enemy distinctly heard about this time.

To terminate a sanguinary contest which had continued for several hours, General Hovey ordered a charge, which was most gallantly executed, and resulted in the capture of four hundred prisoners, two stands of colors, two twelve-pounder howitzers, three caissons, and a considerable quantity of ammunition. A portion of General Carr's division joined in this charge. About this time I heard that Major-General Grant had come up from Bruinsburgh, and soon after had the pleasure of meeting him on the field.

Determined to press my advantages, I ordered Generals Carr and Hovey to push the enemy with all vigor and celerity. This they did, beating him back over a mile, and frustrating all his endeavors to make an immediate stand. For particular mention of the regiments, companies, officers, and men who distinguished themselves in this daring charge, I would refer to the reports of these Generals.

Returning to bring up the narrative of other operations: General Smith's division came up to Shaiffer's about seven o'clock A.M., and just before General Hovey moved to the support of General Carr. The four divisions of my corps were now upon the field, three of them actually engaged and the fourth eager to be. The last was immediately moved into the field, in front of Shaiffer's house, and together with a portion of Osterhaus's division held the centre, and at the same time formed a reserve.

The second position taken by the enemy on my right front was stronger than the first. It was in a creek bottom, covered with trees and underbrush, the approach to which was over open fields, and ragged and exposed hill slopes. Having advanced until they had gained a bald ridge overlooking the bottom, General Hovey's and Carr's divisions again encountered the enemy's fire. A hot engagement ensued, in the course of which, discovering that the enemy was moving a formidable force against my right front with the evident design to force it back and turn my right flank, I ordered General Smith to send forward a brigade to support that flank. Burbridge's brigade rapidly moved forward for that purpose. Meanwhile General Hovey massed his artillery on the right and opened a partially enfilading and most destructive fire on the enemy. The effect of these combined movements was to force the enemy back with considerable loss upon his centre.

Here with a large concentration of forces, he renewed the attack, directing it against my right centre. General Carr met and returned it, both with infantry and artillery, with great vigor. At the same time Landrum's brigade of General Smith's division, reenforced by a detachment from General Hovey's division, forced its way through cane and underbrush and joined in Carr's attack. The battle was now transferred from the enemy's left to his centre, and after an obstinate struggle he was again beaten back upon the high ridge on the opposite side of the bottom, and within a mile of Port Gibson.

General Stevenson's brigade of General Logan's division came up in time to assist in consummating this final result. The shades of night soon after closed upon the stricken field which the valor of our men had won and held, and upon which they found the first repose since they had left D'Schron's Landing twenty-four hours before.

At day-dawn, on the morning of the second, Smith's division, leading the advance, and followed by the rest of my corps, triumphantly entered Port Gibson, through which place and across the south branch of Bayou Pierre the enemy had hastily fled the night before, burning the bridge across that stream in his rear.

This, the battle of Port Gibson or Bayou Pierre, was one of the most admirably and successfully fought battles, in which it has been my lot to participate since the present unhappy war commenced. If not a decisive battle, it was determinate of the brilliant series of successes that followed. It continued twelve hours, and cost us eight hundred and three men killed and wounded; of which the Ninth division lost thirty-seven killed and one hundred and seventy-six wounded; the Tenth division, two killed and sixteen wounded; the Twelfth division, forty-two killed and two hundred and sixty-six wounded; and the Fourteenth division, forty-two killed and two hundred and twenty-two wounded, making the aggregate above named, including eight reported missing.

The loss of the enemy was three stands of colors, four pieces of cannon, three caissons, a quantity of ammunition, a number of small arms and ammunition-wagons, and five hundred and eighty prisoners. His loss in killed and wounded is not known, but it must have been considerable.

Remaining at Port Gibson, on the second of May my corps assisted in constructing a bridge across the south branch of Bayou Pierre, under the direction of Lieutenant-Colonel Wilson, Engineer and Aid-de-camp on Major-General Grant's staff; reconnoitred the country east and north of that stream, and skirmished with a detachment left by the enemy on the north side of it, to watch our movements.

On the night of the second the fugitive enemy was met by reenforcements reported to be on their way from Grand Gulf and Vicksburgh, and communicating their fears to the latter, the whole fled across Big Black. The panic also extended to the garrison at Grand Gulf, only seven miles from Port Gibson, who spiked their guns and hastily abandoning the place, also fled across the same river. Next day a naval force took possession of the place without resistance.

On the same day Brigadier-General Lawler, having reported to me for duty under Major-General Grant's order, was assigned to the command of the Second brigade of General Carr's division.

MARCH FROM PORT GIBSON TO CHAMPION HILL.

On the third, agreeably to your instructions, my corps, save Lawler's brigade, which was left behind temporarily to garrison Port Gibson, marched on the Raymond road to Willow Springs; on the sixth to Rocky Spring; on the eighth to Little Sand; and on the ninth to Big Sand.

General Osterhaus led the advance from Little to Big Sand, and upon arriving at the latter creek, immediately threw a detachment of infantry, preceded by the Second Illinois cavalry, over it, toward Hall's Ferry, on Big Black. Finding a detachment of the enemy in front of the ferry, a company of cavalry, under Lieutenant Stickel, dashed forward and dispersed it before it had time to form, killing twelve men, and capturing thirty prisoners.

Resuming its march on the eleventh, my corps moved to Five-Mile Creek, and on the tenth to Fourteen-Mile Creek. During the last thirteen days it subsisted on six days' rations, and what scanty supply the country in the immediate vicinity of the road afforded; was wholly without tents and regular teams, and almost without cooking utensils; yet was cheerful and prompt in the discharge of duty.

General Hovey's division led the advance to Fourteen-Mile Creek, followed by General Carr's and General Osterhaus's. General Smith's division moved by the way of Hall's Ferry on Big Black River, and leaving a detachment there to guard that crossing, passed on to Montgomery's bridge on Fourteen-Mile Creek, three miles below the point of General Hovey's approach.

An outpost of the rebel force at Edwards's Station, concealed in the thick woods and underbrush lining the creek, was first encountered by General Hovey's advance-guard, consisting of a detachment of the Second Illinois cavalry, under Lieutenant-Colonel Bush, and soon after by his artillery and infantry, which were boldly advanced across the open fields for that purpose. Overcoming the resistance of the enemy and driving him from his cover, General Hovey pushed forward a portion of his command beyond the creek, and secured the crossing.

My loss in this skirmish was four men wounded. The loss of the enemy is unknown, but must have been greater. On the same day General Sherman seized the crossing of Turkey Creek, a few miles to the right, and General McPherson, after a sharp skirmish, seized Raymond, still further to the right.

The flight of the enemy from Raymond left the way open to Jackson, the capital of Mississippi, and General Grant determined to march his army in that direction. This involved a change in the direction of his movements. Up to this time Edwards's Station, to which I had been leading the advance, was the objective point. Here it was known the enemy had concentrated a considerable force, and intended to accept battle when offered. Jackson now became the objective point.

On the night of the twelfth, I was ordered by Major-General Grant to move on the following morning on the north side of Fourteen-Mile Creek to Raymond. At this time my corps rested within four miles of Edwards's Station, with an outpost only three and a picket only two miles from that place. The outpost of the enemy had been driven back from the creek, and he was fully advised of the fact and of our proximity.

The movement ordered was a delicate and hazardous one, but was calculated to deceive the enemy as to our design. To insure it against casualties as far as possible, I ordered General Hovey to advance his division early on the morning of the thirteenth a mile on the main road to Edwards's Station, and form it in line of battle across the road.

The movement was happily executed, and had the effect to throw the enemy upon his defence against apprehended attack. Meanwhile General Osterhaus's and Carr's divisions crossed the creek, and filing by the flank to the rear, and under cover of Hovey's line, crossed Baker's Creek a mile eastward, on the road to Raymond, and halted. Hovey's division followed in successive detachments, under cover of the woods. The movement was discovered by the enemy too late to allow him to prevent or embarrass it. His attack upon the rear-guard was hesitating and feeble, and was promptly and completely repulsed. All were now safely beyond Baker's Creek.

On the same morning General Smith's division, after destroying Montgomery's bridge, hastened back on the south side of the creek, in pursuance of Major-General Grant's order, to Old Auburn, to guard and bring forward to Raymond the army's trains. That night the same division rested at Old Auburn; while the three remaining divisions rested on the Raymond road between Turkey Creek and Raymond.

The morning of the fourteenth found General Osterhaus's division in Raymond, which, in pursuance of Major-General Grant's direction, I ordered to garrison that place. On the same day, in pursuance of like direction, General Carr's and Hovey's divisions marched through Raymond in a heavy rain-storm—the former to Forest Hill Church, within six miles of General Sherman's position, at Jackson—the latter to a creek within four miles of General McPherson's position, at Clinton. This was the most fatiguing and exhausting day's march that had been made.

That night I received a despatch from Major-General Grant, informing me that the enemy had retreated from Jackson, and was probably attempting to reach Vicksburgh in advance of us, and ordering me immediately to move my corps eight miles north to Bolton Station, to frustrate the design. Corresponding orders were immediately issued by me to commanders of divisions, and by nine and a half o'clock on the fifteenth, General Osterhaus's division had seized Bolton Station, capturing several prisoners, and driving the balance of the enemy's picket away. General Hovey's division soon after came up from Clinton, and both divisions were disposed to meet any attack that might come from the enemy known to be in front. During the day an active reconnoissance was pushed by Colonel Mudd, chief of cavalry of my corps, up to the enemy's picket-line, and at some points beyond. General Lee, who had reported for duty that morning, and had kindly volunteered his service as Aid-de-camp, until he could be assigned to a command, also displayed great enterprise and daring. Indeed, every effort was made by myself, personally, and by others, to acquire familiar knowledge of the ground and roads for seven miles west to Edward's Station.

It was found three roads led from the Raymond and Bolton road to Edwards's Station—one diverging a mile and a half north of Raymond, a second three miles and a half, and a third seven and a half miles north of Raymond and one mile south of Bolton and the railroad. These roads may be designated as the northern, middle, and southern roads to Edwards's Station, and united some two miles east of that place.

Night found Generals Hovey's, Osterhaus's, and Carr's divisions in the order stated at the entrance of these several roads, prepared to receive a threatened attack, or to move forward upon converging lines against Edwards's Station. General Smith's division came up during the night, and bivouacked north of Raymond, near General Carr's. General Blair's division of General Sherman's corps bivouacked at Raymond.

This disposition of my corps but anticipated events. During the evening of the fifteenth, I received a despatch from Major-General Grant, advising me that the entire force of the enemy at Vicksburgh had probably crossed the Big Black and taken position at Edwards's Station, and ordering me to feel the enemy without bringing on a general engagement, and to notify General Blair what to do.

BATTLE OF CHAMPION HILL.

It only remained to execute what has already been intimated. Hence, on the night of the fifteenth, orders were issued by me to commanders of divisions, to move forward on the following morning. General Smith advanced on the southern road at five o'clock A.M., on the sixteenth, followed and supported by General Blair. General Osterhaus, on the middle road at six o'clock, followed and supported by General Carr and General Hovey, at the same hour on the northern road. The starting of the different divisions at different hours, was in consequence of the difference in the distances they had to march, and was designed to secure a parallel advance of the different columns. Each division was instructed to keep up communication with that or those next to it.

Believing that General Hovey's division also needed support, I sent a despatch on the fifteenth to Major-General Grant, requesting that General McPherson's corps, then arrived in rear of General Hovey's division, should also move more forward, and early on the morning of the sixteenth, I rode over to General McPherson's head-quarters and suggested the same thing to him—urging among other things, that if his corps should not be needed as a support, it might, in the event I should beat the enemy, fall upon his flank and rear, and cut him off. Assurances altogether satisfactory were given by the General, and I felt confident of our superiority on the right.

I went forward with the centre, formed by Generals Osterhaus and Carr. At half-past seven o'clock A.M., when my whole line had approached within five miles of Edwards's Station, General Smith's division on my left, encountered the enemy's skirmishers, who retired. A half-mile further on they encountered the fire of the enemy's artillery, which was briskly replied to until it ceased.

At the moment these demonstrations commenced, there was strong reason to believe (corroborated by subsequent information) that the enemy was moving in large force on the Raymond road with the hope of turning my left flank and gaining my rear; but the sudden appearance of my forces in that direction foiled the design, and threw his right back in some confusion toward his centre and left.

Hearing the report of artillery on the left, General Osterhaus pushed forward through a broad field to a thick wood which covered a seeming chaos of abrupt hills and yawning ravines. From the skirt of this wood he drove a line of skirmishers, and continuing his advance until he discovered the enemy in strong force, commenced feeling him.

Early notifying Major-General Grant and Major-General McPherson what had transpired on the left, I requested the latter to coöperate with my forces on the right, and directed General Hovey to advance promptly but carefully.

At forty-five minutes past nine o'clock A.M. I received a despatch from General Hovey informing me that he had found the enemy strongly posted in front; that General McPherson's corps was behind him, that his right flank would probably encounter severe resistance, and inquiring whether he should bring on the impending battle.

My whole command was now about four miles from Edwards's Station, and immediately informing Major-General Grant, whom I understood to be on the field, of the position of affairs, I inquired whether General McPherson could not move forward to the support of General Hovey, and whether I should bring on a general engagement? A despatch from the General, dated thirty-five minutes past twelve P.M., came, directing me to throw forward skirmishers as soon as my forces were in hand, to feel and attack the enemy in force, if opportunity occurred, and informing me that he was with Hovey and McPherson, and would see that they fully coöperated.

Meanwhile a line of skirmishers had connected General Osterhaus and Smith's divisions, closing up the narrow space between them. General Blair had moved a brigade further to the right to support the skirmishers and the proximate flanks of Osterhaus and Smith. General Ransom's brigade of the Seventeenth army corps had been ordered to hasten up from the neighborhood of Raymond, and skirmishing along my left and centre, particularly the latter, was quite brisk.

These measures, in part, had been taken in compliance with General Grant's orders, based on information of which he had advised me, that the enemy was in greatest strength in front of my centre and left, and might turn my left flank and gain my rear. This, doubtless, as already explained, had been the tendency of the enemy early in the morning, but had been counteracted by General Smith's operations. Later information was brought by an aid-de-camp of General Smith, and communicated by me to Major-General Grant, of the absence at that time, of the danger apprehended.

Instantly, upon the receipt of Major-General Grant's order to attack, I hastened to do so—ordering Generals Smith and Osterhaus to "attack the enemy vigorously and press for victory"—General Blair to support the former and General Carr the latter, holding Lawler's brigade in reserve.

At ten o'clock A.M. General Hovey resumed his advance, and approaching in plain view of the enemy, disposed his forces for battle along a skirt of wood and across the road of his approach. General McGinnis's brigade was formed on the right and Colonel Slack's on the left. General Logan's division of General McPherson's corps was between the railroad and my right, and about half a mile from the latter.

A mile in front stood a hill some sixty or seventy feet high, covered with thick wood. In this wood the enemy was drawn up in strong force, doubtless augmented by his tendency to his right above noticed. This hill is indifferently called Midway or Champion Hill, from the fact of its being half-way between Jackson and Vicksburgh, and the reputed property of a citizen by the name of Champion. The space between the hill and my right was composed of undulating fields, exposed to the enemy's fire, while the ground to its left and front was scarred by deep ravines and choked with underbrush, thus making a further advance extremely difficult.

Undaunted the brave men of the Twelfth division pressed on under a galling fire. By eleven o'clock A.M. the engagement became general all along the hostile lines, and continued to rage with increasing fury until twelve o'clock M. Meantime the enemy had been driven back with great slaughter, quite six hundred yards, leaving in our hands three hundred prisoners and eleven pieces of cannon.

Rallying in his desperation, and bringing forward fresh troops, he poured down the road, and with superior numbers renewed the conflict. Not daring to cross the open field in the direction of General McPherson, who had handled him roughly on the extreme right, his main force was directed against General Hovey. A crisis had come. Struggling heroically against the adverse tide, that officer called for the support of a division of General McPherson's corps, hard by, which had not been engaged, but did not get it until his line was being borne back. The support finally came, and was also borne back. Slowly and stubbornly, however, our men retired, contesting every inch of ground lost with death, until they had neared the brow of the hill.

Here, under partial cover, they rallied and checked the advance of the enemy; but a bold and decisive blow was necessary to retrieve the day in this part of the field. This was happily struck by General Hovey. Massing his artillery,

strengthened by Dillon's Wisconsin battery, upon elevated ground, beyond a mound to his right, he opened an enfilading fire upon the enemy, which, challenging the cheers of our men, went crashing through the woods with deadly effect. The enemy gave way, and the fortune of the day in this part of the field was retrieved.

Gens. Hovey's and Crocker's divisions pushed forward to the crest of the hill, while General Logan's division, falling upon the flank of the broken foe, captured many prisoners. Five of the enemy's guns that had been captured by General Hovey, and had not been brought off, again fell into our hands. The carnage strewing the field literally stamped Midway as the Hill of Death. General Hovey had lost nearly one third of his men — killed and wounded. It was now about half-past two o'clock P.M.

As already mentioned, General Osterhaus's division early advanced to feel the enemy—General Garrard's brigade on the right and General Lindsey's on the left. The sharp skirmish that followed upon the receipt of my orders to attack was pressed until the centres of the opposing lines became hotly engaged. The battle was raging all along my centre and right.

In front of my centre, as well as my right, the enemy appeared in great numbers. Garrard's brigade was hard pressed, and General Osterhaus requested that it should be supported. Support was afforded by Benton's brigade of Carr's division, which promptly moved forward in obedience to my order, and joined the former in the conflict. All of Lawler's brigade of the same division, except a reserve of one regiment, also advanced to support Lindsey's, who had pushed a charge near the mouth of a battery. Lawler's brigade here cast the trembling balance in our favor. Himself narrowly escaping the effect of a shell, his men joined Lindsey's, and both dashed forward, shooting down the enemy's artillery horses, driving away his gunners, and capturing two pieces of cannon.

This success on the left centre, forcing a portion of the enemy to the right, increased the resistance offered to my right centre, and caused it to be continued until the flight of the enemy on my extreme right had communicated its effects to the centre.

The enemy, thus beaten at all points, fled in confusion—the main body along the road to Vicksburgh—a fragment to the left of that road. General Carr's division taking the advance, hotly pursued the former, and Lindsey's and Burbridge's brigades the latter, until night closed in; each taking many prisoners. The rebel General Tighlman is reported to have been killed by a shot from General Burbridge's batteries.

At eight o'clock P.M. General Carr arrived at Edwards's Station, where flames were consuming a train of cars and a quantity of stores, which the enemy had fired. Both, to a considerable extent, were saved by the activity and daring of his men. During the same night General Carr's division was joined by General Osterhaus's. Generals Blair's and Smith's divisions rested some three miles south-east of Edwards's Station, and General Hovey's division at Midway, under orders to care for the wounded and bury the dead.

The loss sustained by my corps attests the severity of this memorable battle. General Hovey's division lost two hundred and eleven killed, eight hundred and seventy-two wounded, and one hundred and nineteen missing; General Osterhaus's division, fourteen killed, seventy-six wounded, and twenty missing; General Smith's division, twenty-four wounded and four missing; making an aggregate of one thousand three hundred and thirty-four. Of General Blair's loss I am not advised, not having received a report from him.

Besides the capture already mentioned, a large number of small arms were taken. The field was strewn with the dead and wounded of the enemy, and his loss must have been very great.

BATTLE OF BIG BLACK RIVER.

At half-past three o'clock on the morning of the seventeenth my corps again resumed the advance—General Carr's division leading, and General Osterhaus's closely following on the road to Black River bridge, six miles distant. On the way General Carr's division captured a number of prisoners, which were sent to the rear, and upon nearing a skirt of wood masking the enemy's position, encountered and drove back his picket. Passing to the further edge of the wood, the enemy was discovered in force, strongly intrenched in elaborate defences, consisting of a series of works for artillery and two lines of breastworks, the inner one about a half-mile in length, the outer about a mile; both resting their extremities upon Big Black, and forming the segment of a rude circle. Outside of the latter was a deep miry slough, the approach to which from the line of my advance was across a field connecting with others that widened on the right and left.

General Carr's division having entered the wood mentioned, was immediately formed in obedience to my order, General Lawler's brigade on the right, resting its flank near Big Black, and General Benton's brigade on its left and the right of the railroad. A section of Foster's battery and two regiments of Osterhaus's division were ordered to the right and rear of Lawler to support him, and to counteract any approach through the forest to the opposite bank of the river.

Osterhaus's division was ordered to form to the left of the road, Lindsey's brigade in front, and the remaining two regiments of Garrard's brigade obliquely on the left and rear of Lindsey's, to counteract any movement in that direction.

Two sections of Foster's battery were brought forward, and, while being posted in the centre of the two divisions under the personal direction of General Osterhaus, was opened on by the enemy's artillery. General Osterhaus and Captain Foster were both wounded, one man killed and a limber-box exploded by a shell. The command

of the division, by my order, immediately devolved upon General Lee.

A brisk action had continued for a half-hour or more, when General Smith's division came up and was ordered by me to extend and support my left, in which direction it was reported that the enemy was moving in large numbers. After this disposition had been made, my right centre and left engaged the enemy with increased effect, and General Lawler, aided by this diversion, and availing himself of information obtained by Colonel Mudd, chief of cavalry, of the practicability of making a near approach under partial cover on the extreme right, dashed forward under a heavy fire across a narrow field, and, with fixed bayonets, carried the enemy's works, capturing many prisoners and routing him. This feat was eminently brilliant, and reflects the highest credit upon the gallant officers and men of General Lawler's and Osterhaus's commands who achieved it. It was determinate of the success of the day. Fleeing toward a steamer, which formed a bridge across the Big Black near the railroad bridge, most of the enemy escaped to the commanding bluff on the opposite side, while others, hotly pressed by Benton's brigade and the right of Lindsey's, were cut off from that escape, and driven to the left and down the river upon the left of Lindsey's and the front of Burbridge's brigades, and fell into their hands.

A victory could hardly have been more complete. The enemy burnt the bridge over which he had passed, two other steamers and the railroad bridge. About one thousand five hundred prisoners and stands of arms fell into our hands, eighteen pieces of cannon, and a considerable quantity of ammunition and cotton. A number of the enemy were found dead upon the field, but nothing now is certainly known of his loss in killed and wounded.

The loss on our part was limited to my own forces, which alone were engaged. The Ninth division lost ten killed, nineteen wounded, and one missing. The Fourteenth division, nineteen killed, two hundred and twenty-three wounded, and one missing; making in all three hundred and seventy-three killed, wounded, and missing. Among the killed is Colonel Kinsman, Twenty-first Iowa, who fell mortally wounded while leading his regiment in the charge upon the enemy's works.

Driven across the river, the enemy made a feeble stand to cover his trains and retreat upon Vicksburgh, but several hours before sunset was dislodged by my forces, leaving tents and a considerable quantity of clothing and other stores, together with a large number of small arms, a smoking ruin.

During the following night and morning a bridge was thrown across the Big Black by the pioneer corps, under Captain Patterson.

On the morning of the eighteenth I crossed with General Osterhaus's, Smith's and Carr's divisions of my corps, and took up the line of march for Vicksburgh, twelve miles distant. General Smith's division led, followed by Generals Oster-

haus's and Carr's, on the Jackson and Vicksburgh road to St. Alban's; and thence by a cross
road and Baldwin's Ferry road to Four-Mile
Creek, arriving there about sunset, and resting
there for the night, four miles from Vicksburgh.
Several prisoners and wagons were captured during the march.

General Osterhaus resumed command of the
Ninth division on the west bank of the Big Black,
and General Lee was assigned the command of
the First brigade of that division, during the absence of General Garrard, who had been ordered
to report to General Prentiss, at Helena. Early
on the morning of the nineteenth, accompanied
by my staff, I made a personal reconnoissance to
the brow of a long hill overlooking a creek two
miles from Vicksburgh. This hill runs north
and south, and conforms very much to the line
of Vicksburgh's defences, in plain view, on a similar range, a mile west. The creek is called Two-
Mile Creek, because it is only two miles from
Vicksburgh. Colonel Mudd came very near being
shot by one of the enemy's pickets during the
reconnoissance. The intervening space between
these two ranges consists of a series of deep hollows separated by narrow ridges, both rising near
the enemy's works and running at angles from
them, until they are terminated by the narrow
valley of Two-Mile Creek. The heads of the hollows and ridges were entirely open; nearer their
termination, they were covered with a thicket of
trees and underbrush.

At this time the picket and skirmishers of the
enemy were in this thicket, watchful to discover
and obstruct our advance.

The enemy's defences consisted of an extended
line of rifle-pits, occupied by infantry and covered
by a multitude of strong earthworks, occupied by
artillery, so arranged as to command not only
the approaches by the ravines and ridges, in
front, but each other.

THE SIEGE OF VICKSBURGH.

Since four o'clock A.M., my command had been
under orders to be in readiness to move forward
and commence the investment of the city. By
half-past six o'clock A.M., it came up, and in obedience to my order, formed behind the crest of
the hill upon which I had been waiting—General
Smith's division on the right of the Vicksburgh
road, General Osterhaus's on the left, and General Carr's along the base of the hill as a reserve.
Skirmishers were thrown forward, who engaged
the enemy's skirmishers, and artillery was opened
from the most commanding positions upon the
enemy's works, and a body of infantry observed
between them and Burbridge's brigade on my
right.

In a short time the enemy's skirmishers fell
back, and my line advanced across Two-Mile
Creek to the hills on the opposite side.

About this time, (half-past ten o'clock A.M.,)
an order come from Major-General Grant, directing corps commanders to gain as close a position as possible to the enemy's works until two
o'clock P.M., at that hour to fire three volleys from

all their pieces in position, when a general charge
of all the corps along the whole line should be
made.

By two o'clock, with great difficulty, my line
had gained a half-mile, and was within eight hundred yards of the enemy's defences. The ground
in front was unexplored, and commanded by his
works, yet at the appointed signal my infantry
went forward, under such cover as my artillery
could afford, and bravely continued a severe conflict until they had approached within five hundred yards of the enemy's lines, and exhaustion
and the lateness of the evening intermitted it.

An advance had been made by all the corps
and the ground gained was firmly held, but the
enemy's works were not carried.

A number of brave officers and men fell, killed
or wounded, and among the latter, General Lee,
who had signalized his brief command by equal
activity, intelligence, and gallantry. The command of his brigade devolved on Colonel Kaigwin, an able and worthy successor.

On the twentieth General Hovey brought up
Colonel Slack's brigade of the Twelfth division,
from Champion Hill, and supported General Osterhaus's on the left. General Carr supported
General Smith on the right. Lively skirmishing
continued during the twentieth and twenty-first,
and nearer approach to the enemy's works was
made, where it could be done. On the evening
of the twenty-first I received an order from Major-General Grant of the same date, in material
part as follows:

"A simultaneous attack will be made to-morrow at ten o'clock A.M., by all the army corps of
this army. During the day army corps commanders will have examined all practical routes over
which troops can possibly pass. They will get
in position all the artillery possible, and gain all
the ground they can with their infantry and skirmishers.

"At an early hour in the morning a vigorous
attack will be commenced by artillery and skirmishers. The infantry, with the exception of
reserves and skirmishers, will be placed in column of platoons, or by a flank, if the ground
over which they may have to pass will not admit
of a greater front, ready to move forward at the
hour designated. Promptly at the hour designated all will start, at quick-time, with bayonets
fixed, and march immediately upon the enemy,
without firing a gun until the outer works are
carried.

"Skirmishers will advance as soon as possible
after heads of columns pass them and scale the
walls of such works as may confront them."

General Carr's division relieved General Smith's
on the same day, and now formed the advance
on the right, supported by the latter. On the
left, dispositions continued as before. Communicating Major-General Grant's order to division
commanders, during the same evening, as far as
practicable every thing was done calculated to
insure success.

On the morning of the twenty-second I opened
with artillery, including four thirty, six twenty

and six ten-pounder Parrotts; in all, thirty-nine guns, and continued a well-directed and effective fire until ten o'clock — breaching the enemy's works at several points, temporarily silencing his guns and exploding four rebel caissons.

Five minutes before ten o'clock the bugle sounded the charge, and at ten o'clock my columns of attack moved forward, and within fifteen minutes Lawler's and Landrum's brigades had carried the ditch, slope and bastion of a fort. Some of the men, emulous of each other, rushed into the fort, finding a piece of artillery, and in time to see the men who had been serving and supporting it, escape behind another defence commanding the interior of the former.

All of this daring and heroic party were shot down except one, who, recovering from the stunning effect of a shot, seized his musket, and captured and brought away thirteen rebels, who had returned and fired their guns. The captor was Sergeant Joseph Griffith, of the Twenty-second Iowa, who, I am happy to say, has since been promoted. The colors of the Thirteenth Illinois were planted upon the counterscarp of the ditch, while those of the Forty-eighth Ohio and Seventy-seventh Illinois waved over the bastion.

Within fifteen minutes after Lawler's and Landrum's success, Benton's and Burbridge's brigades, fired by the example, rushed forward and carried the ditch and slope of a heavy earthwork, and planted their colors on the latter. Crowning this brilliant feat with a parallel to Sergeant Joseph Griffith's daring, Captain White, of the Chicago Mercantile battery, carried forward one of his pieces, by hand, quite to the ditch, and double-shotting it, fired into an embrasure, disabling a gun in it ready to be discharged, and scattering death among the rebel cannoneers. A curtain connected the works forming these two points of attack.

Men never fought more gallantly; nay, more desperately. For more than eight long hours they maintained their ground with death-like tenacity. Neither the blazing sun nor the deadly fire of the enemy shook them. Their constancy and valor filled me with admiration. The spectacle was one never to be forgotten.

A portion of the United States infantry under Major Malony, serving heavy artillery, added to their previous renown. Neither officers nor men could have been more zealous and active. Being in the centre, they covered, in considerable part, the advance of Benton's and Lawler's brigades, and materially promoted their partial success.

Meantime Osterhaus's and Hovey's forces, forming the column of assault on the left, pushed forward under a severe fire upon a more extended line until an enfilading fire from a strong redoubt on their left front, and physical exhaustion, compelled them to take shelter behind a ridge. Here they could distinctly hear the words of hostile command. Their skirmishers, however, kept up the conflict.

Alarmed for his safety, and the assault of the corps on my left having failed, the enemy early hastened to mass large numbers from his right

and left in my front. Thus reënforced, he renewed his efforts with increased effect. All my forces were now engaged. Failure and loss of my hard-won advantages became imminent.

Advising General McArthur (who was on his way from Warrenton) of the state of affairs, I requested reënforcements and notified Major-General Grant of the fact. At eleven o'clock A.M. I also informed him that I was hotly engaged; that the enemy was massing upon me from his right and left, and that a vigorous blow, by Gen. McPherson, would make a diversion in my favor. Again, at twelve M., that I was in partial possession of two forts, and suggested whether a vigorous push ought not to be made all along our lines.

Responsively to these despatches, Major-General Grant directed me to communicate with General McArthur; to use his forces to the best advantage, and informed me that General Sherman was getting on well. This despatch was dated half-past two o'clock P.M., and came to hand half-past three o'clock P.M. About the same time I received information that General Quimby's division was coming to my support.

Hastening to acknowledge the receipt of this welcome intelligence, I replied that I had lost no ground; that prisoners had informed me that the works in which I had made lodgments were commanded by strong defences in their rear, but that with the divisions promised, I doubted not that I would force my way through the hostile lines, and with many others, I doubt it not yet.

But obstacles intervened to disappoint. General McArthur's division being several miles distant, did not arrive until next day. Colonels Boomer's and Sandburn's brigades, of General Quimby's division, moving in the direction of my position, and in view of the enemy, prompted the latter to concentrate additional forces in my front, and to make a sortie, which was promptly repelled. Coming up late in the evening, much exhausted, night set in and terminated the struggle before either of these brigades could be fully applied; indeed, before one of them was entirely formed. Colonel Boomer fell early after his arrival while leading his men forward, lamented by all. About eight o'clock P.M., after ten hours' continuous fighting, without food or water, my forces withdrew to the nearest shelter, and rested for the night, holding by a strong picket most of the ground they had gained.

My loss during this memorable day, comprised full three fourths of my whole loss before Vicksburgh. My whole loss was one thousand four hundred and eighty-seven, of which General Osterhaus's was thirty-five killed, two hundred and thirty-three wounded, and one missing; General Smith's, sixty-nine killed, four hundred wounded, and thirty missing; General Hovey's, forty-two killed and wounded; and General Carr's one hundred and nine killed, and five hundred and sixty-eight wounded.

To say that the Thirteenth army corps did its whole duty manfully and nobly, throughout this arduous and eventful campaign, is only to say what historical facts abundantly establish. They opened and led the way to the field of Fort Gibson, and had successfully fought that battle for several hours before reënforcements came. They led the way to Champion Hill, and bore the brunt of that battle. Unassisted they fought and won the battle of Big Black. They made the first if not the only lodgment in the enemy's works at Vicksburgh, retaining their advantage longest, withdrawing last, and probably sustaining the greatest loss.

That their officers are subject to no just reproach is equally true. On the contrary, that my officers, generally, have borne themselves faithfully and gallantly, is attested by conspicuous and incontrovertible facts. Their success is a conclusive testimonial of their merit.

While referring to the reports of division, brigade and regimental commanders for particular notice of the officers of their commands most distinguishing themselves, it is proper as commander of the corps, that I should recommend Brigadier-Generals Hovey, Carr, and Osterhaus, for promotion; also, Colonels Slack, Stone, Kaigwin, Landrum, Lindsey, and Mudd. The skill, valor, and services of those officers entitle them to it.

Not having received the reports of Generals Blair, Smith, and Quimby, I have been unable to furnish a more particular account of the operations of these commands.

To the members of my staff I am largely indebted for zealous and valuable assistance. Colonel Mather, acting chief of staff of artillery and of ordnance; Colonel Mudd, Chief of Cavalry; Lieutenant-Colonel Pardee, acting Inspector-General; Lieutenant-Colonel Warmoth, Aid-de-camp; Lieutenant-Colonel Scates, A. A. General, and Major Butler, Provost-Marshal—all have been active and eminently useful in their respective spheres of duty.

Lieutenant-Colonel Warmoth, while by my side, during the assault of the twenty-second ultimo, was severely wounded. Lieutenants Haine, Chief Engineer of the corps, McComas, Jayne, and Mason, have commended themselves by ability, activity, and diligence. Lieutenant-Colonel Taggart, Chief Commissary, and Lieutenant-Colonel Dunlap and Captain Garber, Quartermasters, have administered their affairs with an energy and success commanding my hearty approbation. Major Forbes, Medical Director, has done every thing that could be expected of an officer of rare talent, intelligence, and various experience in his department.

Sympathizing with the General commanding the noble army of the Tennessee in the loss of so many brave men, killed and wounded, I cannot but congratulate him in my thankfulness to Providence upon the many and signal successes which have crowned his arms in a just cause.

JOHN A. McCLERNAND,
◦ Major-General Commanding Thirteenth Army Corps.

Doc. 18.
CAPTURE OF THE ATLANTA.
REPORTS OF ADMIRAL DU PONT.

FLAG-SHIP WABASH,
PORT ROYAL HARBOR, S. C., June 17, 1863.

Hon. Gideon Welles, Secretary of Navy, Washington:

SIR: Having reason to believe the Atlanta and other rebel iron-clads at Savannah were about attempting to enter Warsaw Sound by Wilmington River, for the purpose of attacking the blockading vessels there and in the sounds further south, I despatched some days ago the Weehawken, Captain John Rodgers, from this port, and the Nahant, Commander J. Downes, from North-Edisto, to Warsaw, where the Cimerone, Commander Drake, was maintaining the inside blockade. I have the satisfaction to report to the department this morning that the Atlanta came down by Wilmington River into Warsaw Sound, and was captured. This information has just been received in a telegram from Fort Pulaski, sent by Captain John Rodgers.

Very respectfully, your obedient servant,
S. F. DU PONT,
Rear-Admiral Commanding South-Atlantic Blockading Squadron.

FLAG-SHIP WABASH,
PORT ROYAL HARBOR, S. C., June 17, 1863.

Hon. Gideon Welles, Secretary of the Navy:

SIR: I have the honor to inform the Department that since mailing my despatch, No. 316, I have received further details of the capture of the Atlanta, sent, through the kindness of Colonel Barton, by telegraph from Fort Pulaski.

The Atlanta, Captain William Webb, came down this morning, *via* Wilmington River, to attack our vessels in Warsaw Sound, accompanied by two wooden steamers, filled, it is said, with persons as spectators. The Weehawken, Captain John Rodgers, at once engaged her, firing in all five shots, three of which took effect, penetrating her armor, and killing or wounding the crews of two guns. Two or three of the pilots were also badly wounded, and the pilot-house broken up, whereupon the vessel grounded and immediately after surrendered.

The armament of the Atlanta was two seven-inch and two six-inch guns. She is but slightly injured.

Very respectfully, your obedient servant,
S. F. DU PONT,
Rear-Admiral Commanding South-Atlantic Blockading Squadron.

P. S.—The officers and crew of the Atlanta numbered one hundred and sixty-five persons.
S. F. D.

FLAG-SHIP WABASH,
PORT ROYAL, S. C., June 19, 1863.

SIR: I have the honor to forward herewith, marked No. 1, the interesting report of Captain John Rodgers, of the Weehawken, of the capture, on the seventh instant, of the confederate iron-clad steamer Atlanta, better known as the Fingal, as well as the report of Commander Downes, of the Nahant, who participated in the capture, marked No. 2.

The Fingal, in a dense fog, ran the blockade of Savannah a few days after the Port Royal forts were taken, in November, 1861. She has been closely watched ever since, and as in the case of the Nashville, the long and ceaseless vigilance of my officers has been rewarded. The Atlanta is now in Port Royal, under the American flag, having unaided steamed into this harbor from Warsaw.

The department will notice in this event how well Captain Rodgers has sustained his distinguished reputation, and added to the list of the brilliant services which he has rendered to the country during the rebellion. It will be my duty to recapitulate those services which have taken place during his connection with my command in another communication.

Commander Downes, with his usual gallantry, moved as rapidly as possible toward the enemy, reserving his fire until he could get into close action, but lost the opportunity, from the brief nature of the engagement, of using his battery.

I have been told that the confederate government considered the Atlanta as the most efficient of their iron-clads.

The officers and crew of the Atlanta, with the exception of the wounded and one of the surgeons, have been transferred to the United States steamer James Adger, to be conveyed to Fortress Monroe. A list is herewith inclosed, marked No. 3.

I cannot close this despatch without calling the attention of the department to the coolness and gallantry of Acting Master Benjamin W. Loring, especially recommended by Captain Rodgers. I trust that the department will consider his services as worthy of consideration.

I forward herewith, marked Nos. 4, 5, and 6, the list of the officers and crews of the Weehawken, Nahant, and Cimerone.

Very respectfully, S. F. Du Pont,
Rear-Admiral Commanding South-Atlantic Blockading Squadron.
To Hon. Gideon Welles,
Secretary of the Navy.

REPORT OF CAPTAIN RODGERS.

United States Steamer Weehawken,
Warsaw Sound, Ga., June 17, 1863.

Sir: I have the honor to report that this morning, at ten minutes past four, an iron-clad vessel was discovered coming down at the mouth of Wilmington River; also two other steamers, one a side-wheel and the other a propeller. Beat to quarters and commenced clearing the ship for action. At twenty minutes past four shipped the cable and steamed slowly down toward the north-east end of Warsaw Island. At thirty minutes past four turned and stood up the sound, heading for the iron-clad, which at this time was discovered to have the rebel flag flying. The Nahant, having no pilot, followed in our wake. At five minutes of five the enemy, being about one and a half miles distant, fired a rifle-shot, which passed across our stern and struck near the Nahant.

At this time the enemy was lying across the channel, waiting our attack. At a quarter-past five o'clock, being distant from him about three hundred yards, we commenced firing. At half-past five o'clock the enemy hauled down his colors and hoisted the white flag, we having fired five shots. Steamed near the iron-clad and ordered a boat to be sent alongside.

At a quarter to six o'clock Lieutenant Alexander came on board to surrender the rebel iron-clad Atlanta. He reported the vessel aground on the sand-spit that makes to the south-east from Cabbage Island. Shortly afterward Captain W. A. Webb came on board and delivered up his sword. Sent a prize crew to take charge of the vessel, under the command of Lieutenant Commander D. B. Harmony, of the Nahant. Sent also Lieutenant Commander J. J. Cornwell, of this vessel, and acting First Assistant Engineer J. G. Young to take charge of the engine.

On examination it was found that the enemy had been struck four times—first on the inclined side by a fifteen-inch coned shot, which although fired at an angle of fifty degrees with her keel, broke in the armor and wood backing, strewing the deck with splinters, prostrating about forty men by the concussion, and wounding several by broken pieces of armor and splinters. One man has since died. The second shot (eleven-inch solid) struck the edge of the overhung knuckle, doing no damage except breaking a plate or two. The third shot (a fifteen-inch coned) struck the top of the pilot-house, knocking it off, wounding two pilots and stunning the men at the wheel. The fourth shot, supposed to be eleven-inch, struck a port-stopper in the centre, breaking it in two and shattering it very much, and driving many fragments in through the port.

At twenty minutes past eight the engine of the Atlanta was secured by Engineer J. G. Young, and the vessel backed off into deep water, when she was brought to an anchor.

The wounded, sixteen in number, were removed to the steamer Island City, which had been kindly brought over from Fort Pulaski by Colonel Barton, United States army. The officers of the vessel were sent to the tug Oleander, and a portion of the crew to the United States steamer Cimerone, for transportation to Port Royal.

The Atlanta was found to have mounted two six-inch and two seven-inch rifles, the six-inch in broadside and the seven-inch working on a pivot, either as broadside or bow and stern guns. There is a large supply of ammunition for these guns, and other stores, said to be of great value by some of the officers of the vessel.

There were on board at the time of capture, as per muster roll, twenty-one officers and one hundred and twenty-four men, including twenty-eight mariners. The captured rebel officers told me that they thought we should find the speed of the Atlanta reach ten knots. They believe her the strongest iron-clad in the Confederacy, and confidently anticipated taking both the Nahant and Weehawken.

The behavior of the officers and crew was admirable. Lieutenant Commander J. J. Cornwall did his duty zealously and efficiently. Acting Master Benjamin W. Loring, whom I recommend for promotion for gallant behavior under the fire of Fort Darling, served the guns admirably, as the result shows. His energy and coolness were every thing that could be wished. Executive officer Lieutenant Commander J. J. Cornwell informs me that on the berth deck the powder and shell divisions, under Acting Master O. C. Kingsbury, wore the aspect of exercise so completely, that no one would have thought the vessel was in action. The engine under the direction of Acting Assistant Engineer James George Young, always in beautiful order, was well worked. Mr. Young has, I hope, by his participation in this action, won the promotion for which, on account of his skill and valuable services, I have already recommended him. In a word, every man in the vessel did his duty.

I have the honor to be your obedient servant,
      JOHN RODGERS,
         Captain.
To Rear-Admiral S. F. DU PONT,
Commanding South-Atlantic Blockading Squadron.

REPORT OF COMMANDER DOWNES.

UNITED STATES IRON-CLAD STEAMER NAHANT, }
  WARSAW SOUND, June 18, 1863. }

SIR: I have the honor to submit the following statement of the participation of this vessel in the capture of the rebel iron-clad steamer Atlanta, captured by the Weehawken and Nahant yesterday morning in these waters:

The Atlanta was first discovered at early dawn, about three miles distant, standing toward us, coming out from the Wilmington River, and rapidly approaching. At first she was mistaken for our usual visitor, a steamer that had reconnoitred us daily at about this hour; but a few moments sufficed to show us the true character of the vessel, and we instantly commenced weighing anchor and clearing ship for action.

The Weehawken, slipping her cable, passed us standing out seaward. At about forty-five minutes past four A.M. cleared ship for action, and in a few moments, our anchor being weighed, we followed in her wake. At this time the Atlanta fired the first shot, which passed close to our pilot-house. The Weehawken having at this time turned, was approaching the enemy, who continued, however, to direct his fire upon us, though without effect. At five A.M. the Weehawken closed with the enemy, and opened fire on him with accuracy, this vessel approaching at the time with the intention of running him abroad before delivering fire; but at the fourth fire of the Weehawken the enemy struck, and hoisted the white flag, the firing ceasing after one more shot from the Weehawken, this vessel not having the satisfaction of expending one shot in reply to the enemy's fire, which had been directed exclusively at her.

Lieutenant Commander Harmony proceeded on board the prize at half-past five A.M., taking possession and hoisting the American ensign.

During the action two of the enemy's armed steamers were in sight up the river, crowded with people, apparently observing the progress of events, who steamed up the river when the result was attained.

The behavior of officers and men was, as usual, every thing that could be desired. Acting Ensign Clarke, though quite sick, and under the doctor's charge, proceeded to his station at the first call, and remained there until the affair was decided.

I am, respectfully, your obedient servant,
      JOHN DOWNES,
        Commander.
To Captain JOHN RODGERS,
Senior Officer present, United States Steamer Weehawken.

REPORT OF ADMIRAL LEE.

NEWPORT'S NEWS, June 22, 1863.
Hon. Gideon Welles, Secretary of the Navy:

Your telegram just received. Admiral Du Pont sent the Weehawken, Captain John Rodgers, and Nahant down to Warsaw Sound, to look out for the Atlanta. June seventeenth, at six A.M., the Atlanta came down, accompanied by two gunboats. The engagement was exclusively between the Weehawken and Atlanta. The latter mounted four of the Brooke rifles—two of seven-inch on the bow and stern pivots, and two of six-inch on each end. She could fight two of the former and one of the latter on a side. Rodgers engaged the rebel at close quarters. The first fifteen-inch shot, fired by himself, took off the top of the Atlanta's pilot-house and wounded two of her three pilots. Another fifteen-inch shot struck halfway up her roof, iron-plated, four inches thick, killing one and wounding seventeen men. Eleven shots were fired in all; five by the Weehawken and six by the Atlanta. The latter got aground and surrendered. The fight was short, the victory signal. The Weehawken sustained no injury of any sort.

The Atlanta steers well, and made six knots against a head sea going to Port Royal. She was completely provided with instruments and stores for a regular cruise. She had a ram, a saw, and a torpedo on her bow. Ex-Lieutenant W. A. Webb commanded her. Her complement was one hundred and sixty-five souls. The Atlanta is said to have come down confident of capturing the monitors easily, and her consorts, filled with spectators, were prepared to tow them to Savannah. She will soon be ready for service under the flag of the Union. S. P. LEE,
       Acting Rear-Admiral.

SECRETARY WELLES TO CAPTAIN RODGERS.

NAVY DEPARTMENT, June 25, 1863.
SIR: Your despatch of the seventeenth instant, announcing the capture of the rebel iron-clad steamer Fingal, alias Atlanta, has been received. Although gallantly sustained by Commander John Downes, of the Nahant, the victory, owing to the brevity of the contest, was yours, and gives me unaffected pleasure to congratulate you upon the result. Every contest in which the iron-clads have been engaged against iron-clads has been

instructive, and affords food for reflection. The lessons to be drawn are momentous.

On the eighth of March, 1862, there were lying at anchor in Hampton Roads the first-class steam frigates Roanoke and Minnesota, the sailing frigates Congress and St. Lawrence, the razee Cumberland, and several gunboats. In the presence of this formidable force, representing the highest offensive power of the wooden navy, boldly appeared the rebel iron-clad steamer Merrimac, and notwithstanding the broadsides poured into her by, and the heroic defence of, the Congress and the Cumberland, these two wooden vessels were easily destroyed, and the fate of the others was only reserved for the morrow. During the night, however, the Monitor, the first vessel of her class, arrived, and on the ninth of March, when the morning mists lifted and showed the Merrimac and her wooden consorts approaching to complete the work of destruction, our defence consisted, not in the great ships that were still afloat and their numerous heavy guns, but in a single small iron-clad vessel, armed with two guns. History has recorded the courage and skill of Commander John L. Worden, who, disappearing in the smoke of the advancing fleet, dispersed and put to flight their wooden steamers, turned at bay the Merrimac, grappled with that formidable monster, and drove her back into Norfolk, and kept her there until the evacuation of that place led the rebels to destroy their famous iron-clad rather than encounter and risk her capture by her puny antagonist.

The lessons of that contest taught us the inadequacy of wooden vessels and our existing ordnance to meet armored ships. For inland operations the Monitor turret was immediately adopted, and the fifteen-inch gun of Rodman, being the only gun of greater weight than the eleven-inch yet tested, was ordered to be placed in the turret of the vessels that were constructing. The result of this policy is developed in the action through which you have just passed. In fifteen minutes, and with five shots, you overpowered and captured a formidable steamer, but slightly inferior to the Merrimac, a vessel that the preceding year had battled, with not very serious injury to herself, against four frigates, a razee, and for a time with one Monitor armed with eleven-inch guns, thus demonstrating the offensive power of the new and improved Monitors, armed with guns of fifteen-inch calibre.

Your early connection with the Mississippi flotilla, and your participation in the projection and construction of the first iron-clads on the Western waters; your heroic conduct in the attack on Drury's Bluff; the high moral courage that led you to put to sea in the Weehawken upon the approach of a violent storm, in order to test the sea-going qualities of these new craft, at the time when a safe anchorage was close under your lee; the brave and daring manner in which you, with four associates, pressed the iron-clads under the concentrated fire of the batteries of Charleston harbor, and there tested and proved the endurance and resisting power of these vessels, and your crowning, successful achievement in the capture of the Fingal, alias Atlanta, are all proofs of a skill and courage and devotion to the country and the cause of the Union, regardless of self, that cannot be permitted to pass unrewarded. To your heroic, daring, and persistent moral courage, beyond that of any other individual, is the country indebted for the development, under trying and varied circumstances on the ocean, under fire from enormous batteries on land, and in successful encounter with a formidable antagonist, of the capabilities and qualities of attack and resistance of the monitor class of vessels and their heavy armament. For these heroic and serviceable acts I have presented your name to the President, requesting him to recommend that Congress give you a vote of thanks, in order that you may be advanced to the grade of Commodore in the American Navy.

Very respectfully, etc.,
GIDEON WELLES,
Secretary of the Navy.
Captain JOHN ROGERS,
United States Navy, commanding United States Steamer Weehawken, South-Atlantic Squadron, Port Royal, S. C.

PHILADELPHIA "INQUIRER" ACCOUNT.

PORT ROYAL, S. C., June 19, 1863.

Now that the smoke of the late brilliant naval action in this vicinity has cleared away, and the Atlanta, flying the Stars and Stripes, is riding safely at anchor in this harbor, within hailing distance of the Wabash and other respectable United States sea-dogs, I am able, from a personal inspection of the craft, as well as from an account which I have gathered from eye-witnesses, to furnish your readers with an intelligible description of the capture of the Atlanta by the Weehawken. And, first, we may as well settle the nativity of said vessel, as much discussion has already arisen here as to whether she is, or was, the Fingal, the Georgia, or the Atlanta.

You will recollect, that upon the twelfth of November, 1861, the Fingal, an English, Clyde-built steamer, ran our blockade, and carried a valuable cargo of arms and ammunition in to the rebels at Savannah. She had aboard of her also several batteries of the celebrated Armstrong guns, which the rebels immediately mounted in Fort Pulaski, and which fell into our hands when we captured that fort. In the following January, the rebels having loaded the Fingal with a cargo of one thousand bales of cotton, endeavored to re-run the blockade, but were detected by our cruisers, and driven back up the Savannah River. After this occurrence the idea seemed to occur to them that the Fingal might be converted into an iron-clad, and to this result they have industriously devoted themselves for the last fourteen months. After she was near completion her name was changed to the Georgia, and subsequently she received a new christening as the Atlanta, which name she has borne for over six months.

From a perusal of her log-book, which was captured, together with her other valuables, I learn, by an entry made on the twenty-fourth day of January, 1863, that the Atlanta, then having been fully completed, was ordered to engage our blockading squadron and Fort Pulaski, and in the general fire run out to sea. In accordance with this programme she was fully manned and equipped for her voyage, and her sides slushed for action. But Admiral Du Pont, having been advised of this intended movement by deserters from Savannah, immediately adopted such precautions that the Atlanta's officers, seeing that their plans had been betrayed, immediately gave up their adventure, although their craft was in sight both of the blockading fleet and Pulaski. She returned to Savannah, and attempted nothing serious until lately, which adventure is the subject of the present letter.

On the seventh instant, it was announced that the Atlanta was about to achieve the most signal victory of the war, and properly christen the newly-adopted confederate flag. The people in Savannah were jubilant, and assembled *en masse* upon the wharves to bid her a suitable farewell. The Atlanta, owing to her drawing fifteen feet of water when loaded for the intended cruise, and St. Augustine's Creek not being deep enough to float her in this condition, she only took on board her crew at Savannah, and steamed down the river, drawing but eleven feet of water. Her provisions and stores followed her upon some gunboats belonging to Tatnall's mosquito fleet, and when she had successfully passed through St. Augustine's Creek, which runs from Cranston's Bluff to the head of the Wilmington River, she then received on board all her stores, provisions, ammunition, etc., and was made ready for action. It occupied six days in getting her down safely from Savannah to the head of Wilmington River.

We were fully apprised of this intended excursion by deserters, who, from time to time, have escaped from the Atlanta, and unbosomed their hearts to Admiral Du Pont. From these chivalric sons, Admiral Du Pont learned that the Atlanta was about to assume the offensive, and imitate her worthy predecessor, the Merrimac. Accordingly, ten days ago he sent the Weehawken, Captain John Rodgers commanding, and the Nahant, Commander Downes, to watch the Atlanta, and give her every satisfaction which she might demand. The Weehawken and Nahant proceeded to Warsaw Sound, and took up their positions near the mouth of the Wilmington River, which empties into this sound.

Captain Rodgers stationed a picket-boat every night up the river, in order that he might not be taken unawares, and the two monitors rode at anchor, anxiously awaiting an introduction to their mutual enemy. On the morning of the seventeenth, the picket-boat, as was its wont, had returned to the Weehawken, and the men having reported no suspicious-looking steamer, turned into their bunks, where the rest of the crew were already enjoying themselves in a sleep undisturbed except, perhaps, by the vision of a sinking ram. When the picket returned, it was about five o'clock A.M., and hardly had they "bunked," before the Atlanta was seen coming down the river some three miles distant. She was coming at a rapid rate, and was followed by two Worden gunboats.

No time was to be lost, and the monitors were ready for action in less time than I can describe it. Owing to its being flood-time the monitors were not "bow on," that is, their sterns were toward the Atlanta, and it was necessary for proper action that they should turn around and face the enemy. For fear, on account of the shallowness of the water, that he might run aground in executing this manœuvre, Captain Rodgers steamed down the Sound, as also did the Nahant, to deep water, and having successfully turned, he steamed up with all haste to meet the Atlanta, which was coming down upon him with full speed, intending, beyond a doubt, fight.

In order that you may fully appreciate the sequel to this rebel adventure, I will here, while the Atlanta and the monitors are approaching each other, narrate, as I have it from the officers themselves, the object and intention of their expedition. The following was their plan: They were fully aware of the presence of the Weehawken and Nahant in Warsaw Sound, but they intended to engage these monitors, and having captured them, to send them up in tow of their gun-boats to Savannah. If on engaging our monitors they found themselves unable to whip and capture them, then they intended to run past them, and put out to sea. Having gained the ocean, they were to proceed immediately to Charleston harbor, and engage the blockading fleet there, in conjunction with the rebel rams at Charleston, which were to come down to our fleet upon certain signals, which had already been agreed upon, being made by the Atlanta. Our blockaders having been annihilated, the Atlanta and her consorts would proceed to Wilmington, and raise our blockade there in a similar manner. After these important victories had been gained, then an indiscriminate raid upon the Northern seaboard towns and cities was to be made, and general havoc ensue upon the land and sea. This was their intention; let us see how

"The best laid schemes of men and mice gang aft aglee."

But, before detailing the engagement, I would, for the amusement of your female readers, state that the two wooden gunboats which accompanied the Atlanta were crowded with Savannah ladies, who had come down to see the abominable Yankees receive a severe castigation, and wave their perfumed cambrics at the victorious Atlanta as she proudly steamed out to sea covered with glory, while they would escort back to Savannah our disabled monitors.

But we left the Atlanta steaming down upon our monitors, while the latter, especially the Weehawken, was making counter advances. The Nahant, for some reason or other, did not seem to get along very well, and the Weehawken soon left her some distance astern. The Atlanta, when she arrived within six hundred yards of the Weehawken, ran aground, but succeeded in immediately backing off, and regaining her course. But again, as if some strange fatality attended her, she ran aground the second time, and in this condition opened fire upon the Weehawken, which was then within four hundred yards of her. Our officers, however, did not know that the Atlanta was aground until the action was over. The first shot which the Atlanta fired was from her pivot gun, but it fell short of the Weehawken, and demonstrated that the gunner who sighted that shot was a novice in the art.

Captain Rodgers himself, anxious as ever for a good beginning, sighted his fifteen-inch gun, loaded with a solid shot, and away went this huge missile against the shutter of the starboard aft port-hole, and shivering it as well as the iron and wood-work adjoining, fell off into the water without doing further injury. The Atlanta, in reply, fired another shot from her pivot gun, which, like its predecessor, fell short.

Captain Rodgers again sighted his fifteen-inch pet, and the solid shot hurled through the air, carrying away, in its fearful passage, the pilot-house of the Atlanta. The falling iron and wood-work wounded severely two out of the three pilots, so that the Atlanta was not only with but one pilot, but also minus her pilot-house.

Nothing daunted, however, she returned the fire from her fore starboard gun, but alas! for the aim, the shot failed to hit the Weehawken. Rodgers again sighted, and grazed the wreck of the pilot-house. The Atlanta did not return the fire, and again the Weehawken sent forth a fifteen-inch, which went completely through the Atlanta's smoke-stack. To this the Atlanta replied with her pivot gun, and her shot fell within two feet of the Weehawken. When within a hundred yards of the rebel craft, Captain Rodgers, wishing to encourage such a laudable ambition on the part of the Atlanta's guns, sighted his gun for the fifth shot, and crash went the solid fifteen-inch ball against the Atlanta's side, just aft of the starboard fore port-hole. You can judge of the velocity of this shot when I tell you that it completely bent in a wrought-iron armor four inches thick, and shivered into fragments a four-inch thickness of live oak plank and a four-inch thickness of Georgia pine plank. These flying fragments struck the men working the larboard fore gun, killing one and wounding thirteen of them. The force of the blow was so great, that every man working the pivot gun fell to the deck completely stunned. The ball itself rolled off from the Atlanta's side, and fell into the water. •

This last shot of the Weehawken caused all visions of the blockade, Charleston, and Wilmington, to rapidly fade from the mental vision of the Atlanta's officers, and immediately the white flag was seen waving from the wreck of her pilot-house. The action was only of fifteen minutes' duration, and she fell a prize to the Weehawken's prowess in twenty-six minutes from the time she appeared in sight, and as the white flag fluttered from her deck, the Savannah ladies were seen rapidly going up Wilmington River, to bear to the people of Savannah not the glorious news of victory, but the sad tidings of defeat.

Upon seeing the white flag our men cheered most lustily, and Captain Rodgers immediately despatched Captain Harmony, of the Weehawken, in a small boat to the Atlanta, to receive her commander's sword and take possession of her in the name of the Navy of the United States. As soon as Captain Harmony arrived on board he received the sword of Captain Webb, hauled down the new confederate flag which was flying at her stern, and ran up our own victorious ensign. He then went forward and was ordering his men to cast anchor, when Captain Webb exclaimed: "For God's sake, Captain, don't cast off these anchors; we have a torpedo underneath this bow." Captain Harmony turned to him with the utmost *nonchalance*, and said: "I don't care any thing about your torpedoes, I can stand them if you can, and if you don't wish to be blown up with me, you had better tell me how to raise the torpedo."

To this Captain Webb readily assented, and, calling some of his men, pulleys were attached to a large iron rod which ran out from the prow, and soon there appeared coming out of the water a huge torpedo attached to the end of this rod, which projected thirty feet beyond the bow. Captain Harmony ordered his men to carefully remove the cap from the torpedo, and then fill it with water, in order that the powder might be destroyed. This was done, and the torpedo, holding fifty pounds of powder, was raised aloft on this rod, and was secured at an angle of about forty-five degrees from the deck.

A remarkable circumstance in this affair is the fact that Captain William Webb, formerly a lieutenant in our navy, and commanding the Atlanta, is an old class-mate of Captain John Rodgers, who commands the Weehawken. Captain Harmony also found that the other officers were old and intimate acquaintances of his before the rebellion occurred. I have no doubt but that these discoveries lent an additional zest to the victory.

Captain Webb, after surrendering his vessel, summoned the crew on deck, and addressed them as follows: "I have surrendered our vessel because circumstances, over which I had no control, have compelled me to do so. I know that you started upon this expedition with high hopes, and you have been disappointed. I most earnestly wish that it had happened otherwise, but Providence, for some good reason, has interfered with our plans, and we have failed of success. You all know that if we had not run aground that the result would have been different, and now that a regard for your lives has influenced me in this surrender, I would advise you to submit quietly to the fate which has overtaken us. I hope that we all may soon be returned to our homes, and meet again in a common brotherhood."

At the conclusion of this speech, Captain Webb became so affected that he fainted. What a contrast this speech presents to the one which the same man had delivered, upon that same deck, to the same crew, but an hour previous, when he promised them, in a grandiloquent oration, that, "Before breakfast we will have in tow the Yankee monitors."

One cannot imagine a more villainous-looking set of men than this same Atlanta crew. They are all Georgia "crackers," the poorest "white trash" of Georgia, without education, or any thing, in fact, which would entitle them to be called men, except that they have the human form. Not one man among them is a sailor, but they are all soldiers. The officers, being perfect gentlemen, compared strangely with this gang of cut-throats. The men, however, were grievously disappointed, and loudly declaimed against their ill-luck.

Fourteen officers and fifty men, including those wounded, were transferred to the steamer Island City, and the remainder of the officers and crew were placed on board of the Oleander. They were all brought up to this place yesterday morning, and again transferred to the United States steamship Vermont, and the wounded properly cared for. This afternoon they were all put aboard the United States gunboat James Adger, which will carry them to New-York. The entire crew, officers and men, number one hundred and sixty-five, and a more dejected looking set of naval heroes never trod the deck of our gunboat before.

Upon examining our prize, Captain Rodgers found that she had an immense stock of provisions and stores. These, at the least calculation, were amply sufficient for a two months' cruise, and of the best quality. The clothing found on her was of a superior make and texture, and sufficient to keep the crew well clothed for a year. Her chronometers and sextants, of which she had a large number, were very choice and valuable. The officers' quarters were fitted up very luxuriously, and revealed a well-selected stock of liquors, segars, tobacco, etc. Every thing about her, in fact, indicated not only that she was a pet of the rebels, but that her unfortunate voyagers had started upon a long cruise.

The Atlanta is armed with six guns, one seven-inch pivot gun fore and aft, and two six-inch guns on each broadside. These guns are all the Brooks guns, which, you will recollect, made such good execution against our iron-clads, in the late attack on Charleston. They are, also, all rifled, and throw that long steel-pointed missile of English manufacture. The Atlanta has two magazines, one fore and one aft, well protected, and, upon opening one of them, five hundred rounds of ammunition were found in it. The other magazine is supposed to contain the same amount, and, indeed, her officers say that she has on board one thousand rounds. When you consider that one hundred rounds is a ship's regular armament, you cannot but conclude that the Atlanta's cruise intended some damage. She had also, in addition, a plentiful supply of torpedoes, cutlasses, boarding-pikes, guns, revolvers, etc. Her armament is truly gigantic.

She has inside three decks; first, the gun-deck, two hundred feet long by forty wide; immediately below this is a deck two hundred and eighty feet long, which is subdivided into the captain's cabin, aft, the ward-room, the petty officers' quarters, and forward the men's quarters. Below this deck is the third, the orlop deck, in which are stored all the stores, provisions, etc. Immediately fore and aft of this deck are the magazines. The engines and their necessary complements, of course, occupy the centre of the vessel. These engines are the same which were in her when she ran the blockade as the old Fingal. They were built on the Clyde, and are models for their beauty and action.

First and on the outside were wrought-iron bars, six inches wide by two inches thick, running perpendicularly with her sides, and properly secured, both above and below, by rivets and bolts. Across these bars, horizontally, and on the inside, ran bars of like material and pattern, fastened to the outside layer by the strongest rivets. Within this layer, and fastened to it, were two thicknesses of live oak, two-inch plank also, running perpendicularly and horizontally, and again within these were two more similar thicknesses of Georgia pine plank, forming the last series of her armor. You will thus see that her armor is twelve inches thick, and presenting all the solidity which could be given it by four inches of wrought-iron, four inches of live oak, and four inches of Georgia pine.

Her port-holes, however, were made especially strong. Extra layers of iron and plank, so that the embrasure measures from the inside to the outside forty inches. These port-holes were a foot and a half long by one foot in width, and were protected by wrought-iron shutters, formed by two transverse layers of iron bars, of the same dimensions as those which compose her armor. These shutters hung upon a pivot, firmly adjusted over the port-hole, and were raised or lowered by a small chain which, being attached to the side of each shutter, ran through a small aperture into the gun-deck.

Forward of the smoke-stack was an elevation on the top-deck, to all appearances like as a cone; upon this cone was a small square look-out, just large enough on the inside to allow a man's head to turn with freedom. On each side of this look-out were two small apertures, in the shape of parallelograms, slanting toward the interior, and presenting to the pilot's optics in the look-out two look-outs, an inch and a half long by an inch wide. This look-out was of wrought-iron four inches thick, and the cone upon which it stood was the same thickness, with this additional strength, however, that the interior of the pilot-house being square, the interstices between the sides of the upper part of the pilot-house and the concave surface of the cone were filled with eight-inch, square, live-oak blocks. From the top of the look-out to the base of the cone was but two feet and a half, so that the pilot exposed only about one third of his person, the rest of the pilot-house being within the body of the ship and reached by a step-ladder from the gun-deck. The second shot from the Weehawken, although it was a glancing one, wrenched off this look-out and smashed in the cone. From this pilot-house were seven speaking-tubes connecting with their appropriate rooms below, and all properly lettered and numbered, so that the man at the wheel can readily communicate with those below.

Her length from bow to stern-post is a small fraction over three hundred feet. The gun-deck covering is at its base two hundred feet long and forty feet in width, and at its top one hundred feet in length by fourteen feet in breadth. You will thus see that her roof does not slope all the way up, but has a very respectable top-deck. From the gun-deck to the roof the perpendicular height is six feet, and the sides of the roof sloping at an angle of forty-five degrees, the standing height is eight feet. The lower edge of the roof is twenty inches above water-mark, so that she stands above the water about eight feet. From her aft roof edge it is fifty feet to the stern-post, and from her fore roof edge it is also fifty feet to her bow. The distance from her gun-deck to her keel is sixteen feet and a fraction over. Her steering apparatus is perfect and her rudder completely submerged in the water, thereby being in the safest place imaginable. Her iron-plating extends two feet below the water-line.

It is evident that the rebels have taught us a good lesson on the torpedo subject, as connected with iron-clads, from which we may well afford to learn. It has been a question how a torpedo could be safely carried in front of a vessel without interfering with its steering and other movements, and be at the same time secure from explosion until the proper time. The Atlanta's torpedo gearing solves the question. The forward part of the ram of the Atlanta is solid iron, twenty feet in length, and so overlaid by steel bars, with their ends protruding below the cut-water that a huge steel saw is formed, which would cut any wooden gun-boat in existence. This ram at its bow-end comes to a point, if I may so call it, about two inches square.

From the deck of this iron ram, just ahead of its juncture with the vessel, arises a strong iron bar with a pivot at its top, to which is attached a massive iron boom which runs just over the ram's prow, and then forming an elbow, it descends three feet below the water-line, where it forms another elbow, and then running out some two feet it forms at its end a powerful socket or ring. In this socket is firmly inserted another iron boom, which extends beyond the socket twenty-eight feet, and at its end is hung the torpedo, all capped and ready for the explosion. From this cap runs an insulated wire along the boom and ending in the pilot-house, where are the necessary electrical arrangements with which the pilot could explode the torpedo as soon as it was run under a vessel. You can hardly conceive of a more perfect or efficient engine of destruction than such a torpedo, and thus carried. The iron ram also is savage enough in its appearance, and would saw a hole in a wooden vessel without much difficulty.

Such is but a feeble description of the rebel ram Atlanta, which Captain John Rodgers has the honor to present to the Government. She is certainly superior, in many respects, to any ram which has yet been built; and, as Webb said, if she had not run aground, the result would have been different. She is a very fast vessel. When she came into the harbor, yesterday, she was making, in a heavy sea, seven knots an hour; and our officers, as well as her own, say that she can, under full speed and in ordinary weather, make eleven knots easily. This speed is much greater than that of any of our monitors, and she might, if she had not run aground, steamed away from them, defying pursuit. As it was, Providence interfered in our behalf, and the Atlanta, immovable in the mud, became an easy prey. It was a remarkably short engagement; only nine shots in all being fired—five by the Weehawken, and four by the Atlanta.

The Nahant did not get up to the scene of action until the surrender had been made, so that, much to the regret of Commodore Downes, he was not able to contribute in a positive manner to the victory, although he made every endeavor to bring the Nahant up into action. Admiral Du Pont pronounces the Atlanta the most perfect iron-clad, with the exception of her penetrability, that he has ever seen, and she is certainly the most valuable prize taken by our navy during the war. Her loss, also, to the rebels is as severe as that of the Merrimac, which she resembles very much, both in her appearance and construction, although she has many improvements upon the old terror of Hampton Roads. By this victory Captain Rodgers has endeared himself more than ever to a loyal and anxious people, and I cannot close this letter without expressing a desire, that I know will be cordially responded to throughout the North—long life and success to Captain Rodgers, and the valiant crew of the Weehawken.

PROVIDENCE "JOURNAL" ACCOUNT.

PORT ROYAL, S. C., June 17, 1863.

The work commenced so well in this section in the burning of the Nashville by the Montauk, in February last, has been continued by the iron-clad Weehawken.

The routine of affairs in this harbor was somewhat disturbed this morning by the reception of news from shore to the flag-ship Wabash, through the signal code, that the Weehawken had captured the rebel iron-clad steamer and ram Atlanta, in Warsaw Sound, and that the officers and men of the rebel ram would soon be in Port Royal. Captures and rumors of captures are so much in vogue in these latter days that we hardly knew how much confidence to have in the aforesaid despatch, and yet, inasmuch as it came to the flag-ship in so legitimate a manner, we thought it must indeed be true, and a few hours brought "confirmations strong as proofs of holy writ."

You remember the Atlanta (originally the Anglo-rebel blockade-runner Fingal) came into Savannah last spring, with an immensely valuable cargo of arms and munitions of war. The excitement occasioned by this accession to their supplies, and the running of the Fingal through our fleet, was very great; but the reduction and occupation of Fort Pulaski by the Union forces in this vicinity, participated in by part of the Third Rhode Island regiment, commanded by your efficient young townsman, Colonel Rogers, put an effectual stop to the continuance of such affairs, and the only way to sea left open to the denizens of Savannah was by the inlet or passage to Warsaw Sound, which has been used to a certain extent, only, however, to a point in the north-west of Warsaw Sound, where there is a rebel work called Thunderbolt battery.

It was, however, soon after the arrival of the Fingal that it was determined to convert her into a rebel ram-of-war, and steps were immediately taken for the prosecution of the plan. She was a fine ship, with powerful engines, about seven hundred tons burthen, and the only fault was her draught of water, which was nearly sixteen feet. Her upper works were cut away, and she was under process of remodelling after the pattern of the Merrimac. Months ago it was supposed she must be nearly ready for sea, and the sudden appearance of her black roof, coming into this harbor, would hardly have been a matter of surprise. But every preparation was made for such a possible occurrence, and the result has proved that if she had come in, she would have met with such a reception that she probably would never have gone out again. In January the Montauk was sent to Ossabaw, and the Passaic to Warsaw, and at that time it was understood the Fingal, which had now been remodelled and rebuilt, and was christened the Atlanta, would make an attempt to go to sea notwithstanding the iron-clads. But, in fact, she was not ready, and only wanted completion to make the attempt.

The iron-clad Weehawken has been lying in this harbor since the fight at Charleston, and on Saturday was ordered to Warsaw. Sunday morning the iron-clad Nahant left her anchorage in Edisto for the same destination. This morning, after so long waiting, the attempt was made with all rebel assurance, and resulted in a grand failure. The news was received here at ten o'clock this forenoon, and at four o'clock P.M., the steamer, with the officers and the wounded men, came into the harbor, and alongside the store-ship Vermont. The officers, numbering thirteen, and the men, numbering one hundred and thirty-seven, had been amply provided for on the Vermont.

The wounded consisted of sixteen men, one of whom, by the name of Barrett and belonging to Georgia, was so severely wounded that he died on the passage to Port Royal. The wounds of the others were various in their character; one had his shoulders and head lacerated and bruised, one was so severely wounded that amputation of one or more limbs may be necessary, while the other wounds were flesh-wounds of no dangerous character. Mr. Thurston, the Lieutenant of Marines, was knocked down by a splinter, and another officer, Mr. Wragg, the master, was struck over the left eye with a piece of iron broken off the rebel armor; those were the only officers injured.

The commander of the vessel is an old officer in the Union service, by the name of W. A. Webb, and appears to be a gentlemanly, mild man. He is the third officer that has commanded the vessel. The first assigned was named McBlair, and it is said he was relieved because he did not run by the Yankees and go to sea. That, however, must be a mistake. The next commander was a St. Clair, and he died not long since.

The executive officer, Mr. Alexander, is an old officer in our service, as is also Mr. Barbot, second officer and "lieutenant for the war," and the third lieutenant, Mr. Arledge. The surgeon, Dr. Freeman, and the assistant surgeon, Dr. Gibbs, are old naval officers. The officers all appear to be gentlemen, and are much chagrined to think of their capture.

It seems the Atlanta left Savannah about two weeks ago, intending to go to sea via Warsaw Sound, proceed to Port Royal, and do such destruction as might be permitted her, and then push on to Charleston, where she was to make a foray upon the fleet and then enter the city, although it was not understood in Charleston that this was intended.

Monday morning last found the iron-clads Weehawken and Nahant in Warsaw Sound. The Atlanta had come in the mean time to Thunderbolt battery, where she lay at anchor. Finding that the iron-clads were there caused no disarrangement of plans, except so far as the destruction of them was determined upon, before proceeding to sea, for, as they say, they had no doubt at all of their ability to destroy both the Weehawken and Nahant, considering their own armor proof against eleven-inch or even fifteen-inch shot. At half-past two o'clock yesterday morning the Atlanta got under way from her anchorage, which was about four miles from the iron-clads, and stood down the passage from the battery to the Sound. A temporary grounding delayed her somewhat, but she got off, and was soon in sight of the iron-clads, which were undoubtedly a little surprised to receive so early a call. She steamed on toward the Weehawken, and her officers were astonished to see every thing so still on board the Weehawken, and no attention paid to their approach. Still she steamed on, and firing from her rifle elicited no response from the Weehawken. She was now only one hundred and fifty yards from the iron-clad, when a column of fire issued from the iron turret, and a fifteen-inch went crashing through and through the rebel armor, completely prostrating the whole crew of one gun, (sixteen men,) and, in the language of the officers, "filling and covering the deck with splinters of iron and wood." An eleven-inch shot immediately followed from the Weehawken's small gun, which in like manner passed through and through, but doing less damage. Again a fifteen-inch was fired at them, which struck on what they call the "knuckle" of the armor, (where the armor of the angular side, which slopes to the water, makes a turn down and in toward the hull,) crushing in iron and wood and every thing before it, indeed, making a hole completely through, yet not passing in itself, but glancing up the side it struck the bottom and projecting side of the pilot-house, passing into and demolishing it, and wounding the two pilots within. It was useless to continue a conflict so one-sided, and after seeing the effect of the iron-clad projectiles, they hauled down their new flag and surrendered their vessel. The action lasted but forty-five minutes. The officers seem completely astounded at the effect of the fifteen-inch shot, and had all confidence that their four-inch plate armor would prove impenetrable, that they should capture both iron-clads, and do as they pleased generally, which confidence proves to have been misplaced. The officers seemed pleased to have got out of such a difficulty so easily, are communicative and sociable, and evidently feel relieved. They are in what I suppose should be called uniform, but it's rather a hard-looking uniform. It is of the universal gray, and bears the devices pertaining to each particular rank, in gilt lace or red cord embroidery, and to some extent resembles our own method of naval uniform trimming. The rank of the executive officers is signified by a gilt shoulder-strap filled with blue, with a single star, like a brigadier-general. A commander has two stars, and so on.

Most of their coat-buttons are our own naval buttons, with a frequent sprinkling of army buttons among them, especially on the cuffs. Some of them have buttons with the coat-of-arms of Virginia, South-Carolina, or some other State, upon them. They have a button of their own adoption, an anchor with crossed cannon, but it is not generally worn yet. Most of the uniforms look "home-made" enough, and are faded and rusty.

The marine officer has a sword, and a fine one it is, with equipments, made by Firman & Sons, 153 Strand and 13 Conduit street, London.

The officers say that it was almost intolerable on board the Atlanta, there being no method of ventilation, and the heat was intense. It was continually dark below, candles having to be used both night and day. Some of the officers are new, and all of them think that if confined on board the vessel or at sea they would not be able to live long. They speak of all the arrangements of the steamer as being exceedingly inconvenient. They say that the Fingal, or Atlanta, has been but recently finished, and could steam ten knots an hour. Her engines are unusually fine ones, and of Glasgow make. From her bow there projected a torpedo, fastened on the end of a spar fixed to the steamer's bow, the spar being twenty feet long and five feet below the surface. This they intended to run against the iron-clad, so that the torpedo should strike the hull and explode against it. From experiments made in Savannah they had no doubt that the explosion would have destroyed the iron-clad.

The officers were all allowed to retain their side-arms and personal effects, and will probably leave the Vermont soon for a passage North. They say that the defences of Charleston are more complete now than ever, and that the gun which caused so much harm to the iron-clads in the recent fight at Fort Sumter is of their own make, and not an English gun. They call it the Brooke gun, as it was invented by one of their ordnance officers of that name. They also say that but few guns, little ammunition, and little of any of the material of war come to them from foreign sources, as they are able to manufacture for themselves. They speak of a lack of some of the necessaries of life through the Confederacy, and of the high prices of all articles. One of them, showing a confederate one dollar bill, made the remark: "It takes six of them to get a dollar in gold." The James Adger has been ordered to take them North, we understand. I send a list of the officers:

Commander—William A. Webb, of Virginia.

First Lieutenant and Executive Officer—J. W. Alexander, of North-Carolina.

Second Lieutenant (for the war)—Alphonso Barbot, of Louisiana.

Third Lieutenant—J. H. Arledge, of Florida.

Surgeon—R. J. Truman, of Virginia.

Assistant Surgeon—R. R. Gibbes, of South-Carolina.

Lieutenant Marines—R. G. Thurston, of South-Carolina, wounded.

Paymaster—W. B. Nicon, of Virginia.

Master—T. L. Wragg, of Virginia, wounded.

Chief Engineer—Edward J. Johnson, of Florida.

Second Assistant—George W. Tennent, of Georgia.

Third Assistant—Joseph J. West, of Virginia.

Third Assistant—William J. Morrill, of Alabama.

Gunner—Thomas B. Travers, of Virginia.

Passed Midshipman—William R. Dalton, of Alabama.

Midshipman—J. A. G. Williamson, of Virginia.

June 18.

The Atlanta arrived this afternoon at four o'clock, and came to anchor near the flag-ship. She is quite a formidable looking craft, resembling the Merrimac, or, as she is called in Dixie, the Virginia. S. B. T.

Doc. 19.

CAPTURE OF BRASHEAR CITY.

PRIVATE LETTERS FROM A MEMBER OF THE ONE HUNDRED AND SEVENTY-SIXTH NEW-YORK VOLUNTEERS, (IRONSIDES.)

BRASHEAR, June 22, 1863.

DEAR ———: I write, as the Irishman would say, to tell you that you need not be surprised if you do not get this letter, as all communication is cut off. We, that is, the remnant still left of the once gallant One Hundred and Seventy-sixth, are in hourly expectation of being taken prisoners, yet strange to say the general tendency is to laugh and joke over our interesting situation, and to regard rather the comical than the lugubrious side of the question. I will, however, commence the history from the beginning, and proceed as far as the progress of events will allow me, leaving the still dubious conclusion for another edition.

Yesterday morning at three o'clock, our men were waked up for an expedition; as I have already written to you, we have had an enormous number of false alarms and bogus expeditions of late, and there being fair reason to suppose that this affair belonged to the same category, every one staid behind who could possibly find a pretext for doing so, and those who had to go turned out growling at nervous commandants in general, and at Lieutenant-Colonel Stickney, of "Bosting," in particular. The troops were marched down to the depot, and shortly afterward we heard the train bearing them eastward. Pretty soon followed another, loaded with our rivals, the Twenty-third Connecticut. You will perhaps remember Bayou Lafourche, one of the largest in the parish, about midway between Brashear and Algiers; Thibodeau, the capital of the parish, lies three. miles to the north of the railroad, on this bayou.

The first news we heard, was that a body of rebel cavalry, from two thousand to three thousand strong, had taken Thibodeau, defeating the provost-guard, (company D,) and capturing the Provost-Marshal, Captain Howe. This has been mostly confirmed. The rebels then marched upon the railroad bridge at Lafourche, where were stationed three Connecticut companies, and two or three field-pieces. It was at this time that our men were sent for from Brashear, and they arrived in time to take part in the battle fought for the possession of the bridge, which continued about all day. As soon as these telegrams were received, of course many of the officers and men who had managed to remain behind when they thought the affair was a mere sham, were anxious to join their companies, and have their share of the fun. I obtained permission to go down with them, and shouldered a musket, and strapped on accoutrements for the first time in seven or eight months. Even the drummers caught the infection, and borrowing sick men's guns, fell into the ranks. Woful was the disappointment when we found that all the available rolling stock had already been sent off, and that we could not get down. Meanwhile the wires were cut; the last news received from our operator at Lafourche being, that the fight was still progressing, and that our men were doing well. Rumors of course came in thick and fast, and all speaking of defeat and disaster.

A cautious locomotive was sent down in the afternoon on a scouting trip, and came back with the intelligence that the stronghold at Terre Bonne had fallen, and that Lieutenant Lyon was a prisoner; that the bridge at Lafourche was burnt, and our forces were on the New-Orleans side of the bayou; that the artillery there had been taken, and was on its way up to assist in the reduction of Brashear; that in consequence we were cut off from all assistance by land, and unless we could get reënforcements by water, would be compelled to evacuate the place, and skedaddle on our tug-boat. This latter, however, is not big enough to hold us all, and would probably be riddled before she reached the Gulf. So the Quartermaster's hair stood up on end, as usual, and Shelly, Beveridge and I went to packing, in case boats should come around to take us off in a hurry.

.   .   .   .

There are one million five hundred thousand dollars' worth of United States stores in this place, consisting in rations, tents, guns, ammunition, etc. To protect them we have about a hundred and twenty available men in our two regiments, two or three hundred convalescents, a small gunboat, and two or three pieces of artillery. Most of the men are, however, sick, and all are fagged out with extra guard-duty. At Bayou Bœuf, ten or twelve miles below, we have two or three companies, and two guns.

All the regular drum-calls were beat yesterday, to give the "rebs" on the other side the idea that we still had men in camp; it was comical to see the drummers go through dress parade alone. Last night we burnt Berwick, the town opposite us, and as I was on guard all night, I had a fine opportunity of witnessing the blaze. A boat's crew from the gunboat applied the torches, exchanging volleys with some hidden rascals as they did so. There was a high wind, and the sight was magnificent. The dry frame buildings blazed like tinder, throwing up enormous piles of flame and smoke, that must have been visible in Thibodeau. The sight would probably not improve the state of rebel temper toward us. The houses have long been empty, and are by the Confiscation Act the property of Uncle Sam, so the measure was not so barbarous as the rebel papers will probably represent, although I am by no means sure that it was necessary.

Colonel Duganne is sick, and we have a live major of cavalry in command of the post, and I expect if there is a resistance to be made, he will make it.

To-day, Sunday, it has rained heavily all day, probably impeding the rebel advance, especially if they have field-pieces to drag. I have my "duds" all ready to move at a moment's notice, and have arranged a plan to blow up my twenty-eight thousand rounds cartridge and forty rifles, if the rascals succeed in gaining a foothold on the island. I will await the developments of the morrow, before continuing my letter.

Monday, June 23.

This morning we sent down a skirmishing train to investigate things. Two dirt-cars were rendered defensible by parapets of logs, and filled with about fifty sharp-shooters. I tried hard to get off, but had to confess I was not much of a shot, and was rejected with about fifty other aspirants to glory. "Never mind, boys," said Major Anthony, "we will soon have work for you all." The Major, who belongs to a cavalry regiment, is a good fellow, and we have great confidence in him.

We sent our train off with a "God speed," with instructions to go as far as they could, and investigate *statu quo*. They got through to Terre Bonne without mishap, and were there hospitably welcomed by the two guns which once belonged to that miserable stockade. The twenty-four pounders whistled about the locomotive, and as our boys were not prepared to resist artillery, they were obliged to put back. They described Terre Bonne as well garrisoned by the rebels, but as to the state of the road beyond, or what has become of our regiment at Lafourche, they can of course say nothing.

One thing is evident — that we are isolated, blocked in, and that unless we can get a seaworthy boat from New-Orleans, we must either fight our way through, starve, or surrender.

This afternoon, having nothing better to do, we took a tug, and to the number of fifteen, plus half a dozen negroes, started down the bay to look for rebels and molasses. The former were not to be seen, but we obtained eight or ten casks of half-boiled syrup from a deserted sugar-house. We had got the stuff about half on board when an alarm was raised from the upper deck, that the rebels were advancing through the woods, and I was ordered to take five or six men and see if the rascals really were there. So I deployed my little force as skirmishers, and we advanced across the clearing as fast as the swampy ground and tall grass would permit, expecting every moment to be fired at from the woods. Nothing was found, however, but the glistening edges of the palmetto leaves, which the boat's captain had mistaken for bayonets, so we loaded our syrup, and steamed back to port, covered with glory and mud.

In the sugar-house, a dirty, dilapidated old shed, a poor family had taken shelter when Berwick was first shelled, and had night before last seen their home there burnt to ashes. There was a mother, down with the fever, two very pretty girls between sixteen and twenty, four or five little ones, and a sickly-looking father, with no work and no money. They were, according to their own account, good unionists, and had suffered at the hands of the "rebs" in consequence, and now were losing their last remaining property by the hands of the Federals. The husband had done some work for the United States, but had, as usual, received no pay, for you must know it is the very hardest thing in the world to get pay from the Government for stray jobs. The quartermasters are supposed to discharge such bills, but are seldom provided with funds for the purpose, so that the poor applicant may wait and want a long time before he gets his due. Persecuted and hunted like dogs by the rebels, suspected, worried, and cheated by the Federals, and plundered by both sides and the darkeys, the fate of the Union men of the South is not one to be envied.

I am writing down this account of the occurrences of each day, rather because, every thing

being packed, and the regiment absent, I have nothing else to do, than in the thought that such details can be of much interest to you, however important they may be to me. The grand *denouement* is what you will want to hear, and that I may be able to give you in to-morrow's journal. Good night:

July 1, 1863.

. . . .

Although we had a week of suspense and anticipation, the shock was still a great one. The Ironsides regiment is no more; its officers are killed and captured, its men cut to pieces and prisoners on parole. The post given us to hold is in the hands of the rebels, and the lone star of Texas floats over the road from Brashear almost to Algiers.

I write in durance vile, and in considerable doubt whether my letter will ever reach its destination. I will now attempt to relate how the above unfortunate state of affairs was brought about.

We were awakened at dawn on the morning of the twenty-third by the screeching of shells, and the whistling of Minie balls, and soon found that our camp and town was being bombarded from the other side. There was naturally considerable excitement at this discovery, an excitement differing somewhat from that which you had an opportunity of witnessing, for I assure you there is a great difference between being shelled and shelling. The two guns that yet remained to us had been placed in position down the railroad, as we expected the attack from the direction of Terre Bonne, but they were speedily brought back and brought into action, and our men in camp, taking advantage of trees, little embankments, corners of houses, etc., for shelter, commenced using their muskets with considerable effect. By the united efforts of our artillery and infantry, after a sharp interchange of fire of a couple of hours, the rebels were fairly driven from their guns, with a loss, by their own admission, of from ten to fifteen men, while we had lost but one.

I fired two or three shots, but am ignorant whether or not I am guilty of manslaughter. I was principally exercised to get my ammunition into a place of safety, for if a shell had struck it, the results might have been most disastrous.

Almost all our darkeys had fled on the mules when the first shot was fired, and I could get hold of but one team, and would you believe it, . . . but I managed to stow the official papers into the cart, and off he rode, and I didn't see him for a day or two, till he was brought back a prisoner.

Our men were still drawn up in a straggling line along the shore answering the rebel musketry, when shot were suddenly poured in upon us from behind, and from the orange grove on the left, while the firing from the other shore redoubled in vigor.

Our men thus hemmed in between three fires, naturally broke and fell into disorder, which moment the Texans improved by charging with the bayonet, yelling and whooping at the tops of their voices as they did so. Captain Thomason, the only officer excepting our sick Colonel left in camp, succeeded in forming a line in front of the Twenty-third Connecticut camp along the road, but after delivering two or three volleys, it was found impossible to stand under the concentrated fire, and then it was *sauve qui peut*. The cooler heads retired slowly, stopping behind each tree to deliver a shot at the advancing enemy, and loading as they ran. One little squad, commanded by a corporal of the One Hundred and Fourteenth, especially distinguished themselves by the steadiness with which they retreated, delivering their fire in two directions at once. A large portion, however, rushed pell-mell down the road to the depot, offering as they passed a fair mark both to the guns from the other side, and to the rebels already occupying a parallel road but a few hundred feet distant.

Our Colonel, nerved to exertion by the exigency of the moment, managed to mount his horse, and calling to those nearest to follow him, started for the depot, intending to make a stand there, or if that were impossible, to run a locomotive through to Bayou Bœuf, and escape with the men there on the gunboat. His strength was not equal to his will, however; he fainted and fell from his horse on reaching the hospital, after passing through a perfect hail-storm of bullets unharmed. As soon as I heard the shouts behind us, I concluded we were lost, and tried with Shelly to get the ammunition into the bay.

But the boxes were heavy, and there were too many of them, and we could get no help, so after moving a couple we gave it up. I then piled up some straw, and set fire to the building, and seeing the Colonel start off, took my gun and followed, when he fell, struck as I thought by a bullet. Seeing that all was lost, and finding it impossible to reach the depot, as we were being fired upon from there by our own men, I turned into the camp of the Fourth Massachusetts, and surrendered myself to the first half-dozen of ragged rascals who ran up..

The prisoners were marched back to our camp as they were picked up, and I was provoked to find that my fire had blazed out, and the small stores and cartridges were still unharmed. Perhaps the most gallant stand of the day was made by a portion of the provost-guard defending our twenty-four pounder. Out of the five defenders, four, including the Lieutenant (L. W. Stephenson) and the Sergeant (Deming) were shot down; it is hoped all will recover. Captain Cutter, who, on account of illness had his quarters in the village, came out on hearing the tumult, and on being told to deliver up his sword, replied, "I never surrender," and fell immediately, shot through the head.

He was one of the best men among our officers, a gentleman, a scholar, and a soldier, and his loss is much deplored by all who knew him.

We lost from the portion of our regiment here, five or six killed, and fifteen or eighteen wounded; from the whole post about fifty killed and wounded. The larger part of this loss occurred in the convalescent camp, as it was on that side that the attack was made; and although the men there were partly unarmed, had no officers, were all more or less sick, and made no resistance, they were for the first few moments shot down without mercy, from a misapprehension on the part of the rebels as to the nature of the camp.

Our regiment and the remnant of the One Hundred and Fourteenth were the only ones which did any fighting at all, the Twenty-Third Connecticut and the Fourth Massachusetts succumbing almost immediately.

After the town had been captured, the fort of course could make no resistance, as it has no defences on the land side; and the guns, being mounted *en barbette*, could not be turned against the assailing party. It was surrendered unconditionally. After the prisoners had been collected in our camp, we were marched up to the fort, and huddled up within the narrow precincts of the camp there. They numbered in all about one thousand two hundred, of whom full eight hundred were sick. Our own regiment lost about two hundred. Our captors were the most ragged, dirty-looking set of rascals I had ever seen. There was plenty of pluck and spirit among them, but a great want of order and discipline. The only thing uniform about them was dirt—shirts, pants, and skin being all of a fine mud color. They all carried pistols and dirks, but while the greater number had Enfields, the rest were armed with carbines and buck-shot guns. The officers had little or nothing to distinguish them from the privates, though sometimes a suit of gray made its appearance. There appeared, however, to be a great abundance of them, as every third man was addressed as captain or lieutenant, and at least every tenth as major or colonel. They formed the advanced-guard of a force of four brigades, ten thousand men, under General Moerton, which occupied a couple of days in coming up and crossing. There was a very large proportion of cavalry, for as one of the men said to me: "Texans won't walk." They were on the whole, a good-natured, jolly set of country boys, many of them only just entered into the service, and they treated us with considerable kindness and humanity, although our fare was for some days four hard tacks per diem, and our beds the bare ground. However, they gave us what they had, and enjoyed little better quarters themselves.

The party which had attacked us behind had passed over Flat Lake in scows and small boats, and lay concealed in the swamp in the rear of the camps a day or two, until they heard their guns open upon us from the other side. They were to have made the attack at four in the morning, in which case the carnage would have been much greater. As it was, our surprise was complete, for the swamps had been pronounced by our engineers to be impassable, (and so I believe they would be to any but Texans,) and we feared nothing in the rear, except from down the railroad in case Bayou Bœuf should be taken by force in possession of Terre Bonne. As it was, with our men scattered through half-a-dozen camps, the greater part sick, and without organization or officers, I don't know that we could have done much better than we did, though if we had had a little more time we could have destroyed the stores. But although our regiment was not disgraced, it was a sad sight to see the Stars and Stripes trailing in the dust, and our regimental colors carried off in triumph, and many of our men vowed they would have another crack at the rascals, and avenge the insult before going home.

The privates and non-commissioned officers were paroled, while the commissioned were taken off to a Dixian prison, probably in Houston, Texas.

Getting tired of doing nothing at the "prisoners' camp," I volunteered with three or four others to help nurse our sick and wounded at the hospital, as nurses were much needed. I expected only to stay till the paroled men were sent across our lines, but when they left, the Doctor pressed me so hard to remain, that I decided I ought to do so, only hesitating at the thought that you would be anxious at not hearing from me.

Having expected to go till the last moment, I had not even time to send a line by a friend, and don't know when you will get this.

The Colonel had deputed me to bear the intelligence of the capture of the post to General Emory, and to give the General such information as I could about the numbers and designs of the enemy. He had also requested me to write an account of the affair to Mr. B—— for publication. These two commissions I regretted much not to be able to fulfil; but as almost all our nurses seized the opportunity to go, I didn't like to desert our wounded, and with two others, decided to stay.

Our doctors have worked like Trojans the whole time. The balls whistled through the house during the engagement, as our red hospital flag was mistaken for an ordnance flag, and two sick men and one negro woman were killed, but the two doctors went on amputating and cutting out balls with perfect *sang froid* during the whole storm; and their work was capitally done, and all our wounded are now in a fair way for recovery. The Surgeon of the Fourth Massachusetts ran away early in the action, and the confederate doctors are a lazy, and, I believe, an ignorant set, so that all the work is thrown upon the hands of our men.

Nursing is quite new work for me, and I can't say I like the occupation, but I am getting used to it, and it is better than doing nothing in a parole camp.

Bayou Bœuf, surrounded on all sides, fell without a struggle, which added Colonel Duganne, two Lieutenants, and company I, to the number of prisoners. I had almost forgotten the Quartermaster, who was also taken there.

The men at Lafourche succeeded in repulsing the rebels three times, with considerable loss, but the fourth attack being made with a larger force, the place was taken and the One Hundred and Seventy-Sixth regiment wiped out of existence. Although it has not achieved the triumphs that fond friends hoped for it, it has not fallen ingloriously, but remained at its post to the last, and was lost not through the fault of its men or officers, but owing to the mistaken generalship which left it a prey to a much superior force.

We know not as yet what friends or comrades we have lost at the battle of Lafourche, but according to all accounts the carnage was great. The enemy was again repulsed at Raceland, but after repeated efforts, succeeded in storming the place. From thence they made an attack yesterday on Donaldsonville, where they were defeated. I understand they intend to make a dash at New-Orleans, and they are confident that Banks will be compelled to raise the siege of Port Hudson in order to save the capital of his department.

Of further movements you will be better informed than I, as I can hear but little here, and that through rebel sources.

I must not forget to tell you that Mrs. —— has been unremitting in her attentions to our sick and wounded, and comes almost every day with Miss —— to the hospital, with sheets, drawers, shirts, socks, etc., which are much needed. She is certainly a most kind-hearted woman. I lost almost all my personal baggage, but she has given me a mattress, mosquito-bar, pillows, socks, etc., so that I can get along pretty well. Her husband is home, and has been placed in charge of the road, so she is happy, but she has seen enough of fighting. Several bullets passed through her house, and two or three men were killed in the garden. I was under severe fire two or three times, but escaped unhurt, and am in a fair state of health.

BRASHEAR CITY, LA., July 7, 1863.

DEAR MOTHER: I managed to send off a long letter to M—— about a week ago, relating the sad capture of this place, and the complete disorganization of our regiment, in consequence of the loss of its officers and the cutting up and capture of our men. I also stated that I had remained behind to help care for our wounded, instead of proceeding with the rest of our paroled men to our own lines.

I have now been two weeks here in the hospital, and matters have changed but little. The gunboats have not yet arrived to recapture the place, nor has the flag of truce boat come to bear us all to New-Orleans. We can hear but little of what is occurring between us and the city, but there are indistinct murmurs to the effect that the rebel advance has received a severe check at Donaldsonville, about fifty miles from New-Or leans, and has halted there, awaiting reënforcements. The stake the rebels are playing for is the capture of the Crescent City itself, and to effect this, they are rapidly massing all their forces upon the one point. The Texan brigades were poured rapidly across the frontier and thrown against our feeble defences along this railroad, with what effect I have already told you. We delayed their advance one week, however, according to their own account, by the bold front put on by our almost empty camps, and by fortifying Bayou Bœuf and other places along the road. A fragment of the One Hundred and Seventy-sixth, assisted by a part of the Twenty-third Connecticut, held them at bay four or five days more at Lafourche, a little further down the road, with considerable loss of life on both sides. So that we did our share toward resisting the invasion of the Vandals; and if New-Orleans is not prepared, it is not our fault.

A column of eight thousand men, from the rebel army in Arkansas, is daily expected to cross at this place and support the Texans, while General Kirby Smith is said to be advancing down the east bank of the Mississippi with the troops from Mississippi and Alabama. According to their own accounts they have risked all on this last attempt, and are bound to regain possession of the Department of the Gulf or perish in the struggle. I think they are in earnest, and I do hope Banks and his advisers are aware of and are equal to the exigency of the moment.

Our wounded have not been badly treated by our captors; they give them what they have, but that is often very little. The weather has been very hot for the last few days, and the poor fellows have suffered much, and we have lost several.

To-day little Newlan died; he was a German boy, not more than seventeen years old, but a good soldier and a brave fellow.

He, with three others and a lieutenant, stood by one of our two cannons till the last moment.

Three of the five were struck down, and his comrades, scattered by the fire, fled to the depot and called upon him to follow, but he would not leave his lieutenant. In another moment they fell together; Lieutenant S—— with a bullet through his foot, and poor little Newlan with his arm fractured, a ball through his body, and a charge of buckshot in the head.

He stood his wounds bravely, but this hot weather proved too much for him, and he died in great pain, babbling about his home in the "vaterland."

There are many other pitiful cases in our hospital, and it makes one's heart sick to witness so much misery. But I suppose it is good discipline for a man.

We did not, as you may suppose, pass a very joyous Fourth. I never expected to celebrate it in captivity, where, among greater troubles, champagne and fire-crackers are an impossibility. Yesterday our colonel, lieutenant-colonel, and two lieutenants, who have been here on the sick list, were carried off up to Franklin, a town far-

ther inland, where there is less danger of recapture.

Colonel Nott was as dignified, graceful, and self-possessed as ever, and appeared confident that this reverse was but temporary, and that our arms would soon recover their ascendency.

Brashear looks dreary enough at present; our long line of deserted and pillaged encampments, the closed and empty houses, the vacant railroad depot, once so busy, the cars standing idly on the track, the cessation of all business, the desolation and disorder everywhere apparent, contrast most painfully with the animation, busy life, and neatness of the scene a fortnight ago.

The view from my window of those fatal woods, of the disaster-bringing orange groves, and of the ruins of our once beautiful camp, is hateful to me, and it will be an immense relief to get rid of it.

One of the most melancholy features of the recapture I have omitted to notice—the hundreds of poor negroes who, taken with our troops, are doomed to a harsher fate, to a worse captivity than they ever before experienced. Oh! it is bitter to see them look half-reproachfully, half-imploringly to us, as they are driven off like sheep to the slaughter, as if to say: "How could you betray us, promising us liberty and safety, and now abandoning us to slavery and misery worse than death?" It makes my blood boil to see (as I saw yesterday) three cowardly ruffians driving before them a poor tottering old woman, and not to be able to strike a blow in her defence; to see my own faithful and intelligent servitor, lame and unfit for work, led off, separated from his wife, to hard labor, and to be obliged to disregard his appealing glance for help; to see able-bodied men on horseback driving before them at the point of the bayonet old and young, sick and well, all weary and starving so that they can hardly stand.

God _must_ give us strength and victory to rescue these poor creatures, and I believe yet, in spite of the dark clouds about us, that he _will_ do it.

During the attack many of the negroes escaped to the swamps, and some of the men probably succeeded in getting through to our lines. Many, however, as I was told by eye-witnesses, were shot down like dogs by the rebel pickets; and others, old women and mothers with babes in their arms, unable longer to stand the pangs of hunger and want of rest, have come in day after day, covered with mud, emaciated, and in rags, and surrendered themselves to the Texans. If you had seen these swamps, and could picture to yourself the horrors of exposure to the darkness, mire, alligators, snakes, flies, and mosquitoes, the wandering without food and without hope, you would form some idea of the fear with which these poor creatures regard their former masters, which induces them to dare all dangers rather than be again enslaved.

July 11.—I am still a prisoner and a hospital nurse, and shall hail with relief being freed from both positions, which I hope soon to be. My duties as nurse are not as arduous now as they were at first, as those of my comrades most severely wounded have died, while the others are rapidly approaching recovery, and can almost take care of themselves. I am too seldom reminded that I am a prisoner, and as the hospital is not wholly destitute of books, I am able to while away the leisure hours. Besides several novels and English reviews, I have found a "Life of Jefferson," which is, under the circumstances, a treasure. I also have had opportunities of talking with the rebel doctors, officers, and privates, and find it interesting to hear their side of the question, while at the same time I am by no means backward in stating and defending ours. One of the rebel captains appeared to take quite a fancy to me, and wanted me to go home with him to Texas, where he said he would direct my energies and my spunk into better courses than the defence of abolitionism. He thought I must have been raised in a perfect hot-bed of radicalism, which is a compliment to you and father.

I find these Southern champions are more doughty in the use of the sword than of the tongue, and their logic is easy to controvert. Unfortunately, this very want of logic renders them unable to see when they are discomfited, and by dint of frequent reiterations in a loud tone of voice, interrupting their opponent whenever he is about to say any thing provoking, and breaking off the contest with the sound of their own voice still ringing in their ears, they often leave off with the impression that they have been very successful.

This mode of arguing does not arise so much from want of courtesy as from ungovernable impetuosity of temperament.

M—— may have mentioned to you, one of the reasons given her for secession is "the President's Emancipation Proclamation." Ridiculous as it may seem, I have heard that and similar reasons assigned by many men who ought to know better. Many of the privates have very confused ideas of what they are fighting for, and in fact, being illiterate in the first degree, they have few opportunities of information, and have to believe what their officers tell them about the North and the war. One Texas captain to whom I offered some books told me there was not a man in his company could read. Testaments are almost unknown amongst them, and I have heard of but one regiment that had a chaplain. (Better even to have no chaplain than have one like ours.)

Both officers and men of course talk very confidently about their prospects in the war before us, but now and then, when caught off their guard, they don't speak so boldly, admit that it is impossible for them to fill up their ranks further, that they are short of clothing, food, and accoutrements, and that there is more or less discontent among their men. Many of the privates say openly they would give much if some accommodation could be made, in order to bring the war to an end, and give them a chance to see

their homes again. We can only hear rumors of what is going on between Banks and Taylor, at Vicksburgh, on the Cumberland, and in Virginia, and the want of reliable news from the army and the impossibility of communicating with home are the principal causes of the irksomeness of our present position.

Yesterday a little fellow died whom I had had under my especial care, and whose loss is much felt by all of us. He was hardly eighteen, and had one of the purest, most beautiful faces I ever saw on a boy. He came from New-Haven, and spoke much of his happy home and good mother. Although he was severely wounded, he was always patient, and even cheerful. I think I hardly ever saw a boy who had gone through the temptations of camp life so unstained as he seemed to have done. He must have been well brought up, and I am afraid his mother will feel his loss deeply, as he was an only son—and such a lovable son! I wrote to her a few lines, which will be a softer way of breaking the news to her than the dry hospital report.

It is hard to think how many such lives have been lost in this cruel war, and it is fearful to think of the possibility of their being thrown away, of no great and good object being gained by this expenditure, of the war being a failure, and this carnage murder. I cannot believe that God will permit it. The longer the war lasts the more impossible does it seem that it should not be intended for the regeneration of the land. May God grant that such may be the result!

July 16.—I remember some years ago reading aloud to you "Eothen," which I then considered a very dull book, and the only thing that struck me as sprightly was an account of a dervish who arrogated to himself the power of raising the devil at his will. Undertaking the experiment, however, before a large audience, he proved unsuccessful, and actually died of mortification. The comment of Sir Francis was: "As the mountain wouldn't come to Mohammed, Mohammed went to the mountain."

It is even so with our captor, General Taylor, who, as his supporting force does not come up, must needs fall back to see what has become of it, and it is also so in another sense with us prisoners, who, as we can't go to our lines, are going to have the pleasure of seeing our lines come to us.

The simple truth is, that the rebels, discouraged by the loss of their two great strongholds on the Mississippi, and by the checks they received at Lafourche and Raceland, and their total defeat at Donaldsonville, have relinquished their ambitious designs upon the Crescent City, and are retreating bag and baggage toward Texas, pursued by Banks's victorious forces. Yesterday and to-day they have been crossing over their heavy stores and artillery, and in two or three days this place will be entirely evacuated. I only hope Banks comes up before they get through their work here and bags some of them. If they go, they leave our sick and wounded here, and will only be too glad to be rid of them; but it is to be hoped there will be no long intermission between the pulling down of the stars and bars and the hoisting of the Stars and Stripes, for we should stand a fair chance of starving.

Of course, situated as we are, the news that we hear is vague and unsatisfactory, and it is only worth noting down in order to compare with the "original Jacobs," of which we hope in a few days to be in possession.

It is probable that you, even as I write, know more of the campaign of the last month than I, who have been an actor in it. It is a fact that no one knows so little about a war, or even a great battle, as the soldier engaged.

We are told that Port Hudson fell on the twenty-seventh of June, the works being stormed by a last desperate charge of our men; and it is this sudden release of Banks's troops, the energy with which they have been brought down the river, and the non-arrival of the rebel force from Arkansas, which have put an end to Gen. Taylor's plans. Vicksburgh, according to the rebel account, was surrendered on the fourth of July, not to Grant, but to Admiral Farragut, and if one of the reported conditions be true, the worthy Admiral could not have acted with his usual judgment. I refer to the rebel officers being released on their parole, instead of being detained, as ours have been. We have a large number of officers in rebel hands, and, especially now that they are threatening to hang those belonging to negro regiments, it is important that we should be in a condition to retaliate if necessary.

Such are the reports of the day; to-morrow may witness a dashing of our hopes. Still the presentiment is strong with all of us that before many days we shall again be under the "good old flag."

July 19.—This waiting and watching, now having our hopes fed by the downcast countenances and whispered rumors of disaster among the rebels about us, again having our fears excited by their triumphant and exaggerated reports of successes, is beginning to have an effect upon our nerves, especially with such of us who are not well. Every shock of thunder seems to herald the approach of our victorious gunboats, every drum-tap in the night is magnified by the excited fancy to the once dreaded, now longed-for sound of the "long roll," and at every accidental gunshot from the neighboring camps we listen to the continuous fire of the attack of which it is hoped to be the alarm.

That the rebels are expecting an attack here in their rear is very evident, but whether they will try to evade it, or prepare to meet it, is still a question. Their sick, as fast as they are brought from their forces down the railroad, are moved up the Bayou Teche to Franklin and New-Iberia. The number is very considerable, and our surgeon gives it as his opinion that many of the men are merely shamming, to escape the toils of the campaign.

This Louisiana climate, however, seems to sicken Texans as fast or faster than it acts upon Northern troops, and loud and deep are the curses of the "Lone Star" men upon this "God-forsaken land." Then the exposure to the heavy showers of this month, their utter want of cleanliness, and often of a change of clothing, and their poorly cooked food, must have damaging effects upon their constitutions. We have still fifty sick here, who are all doing well, but are still unable to travel without transportation; and that the rebels can't furnish us. These rascals have pretty well cleaned out poor Lafourche Parish of all that is worth having — negroes, cattle, wagons, tools, etc., and if they escape without punishment, their raid may be termed a most successful one. But they have strong fears that they will not escape so freely. Our forces are reported to have reoccupied the Red River (which the late rains have swollen most opportunely) and cut off their retreat to Texas, and in that case, unless they can cut their way through, there is no resource but surrender.

Meanwhile they are occupied night and day in crossing over their ill-gotten plunder upon two or three antiquated-looking steamboats, which escaped capture when the country was first occupied by running far up the Red River. Horses are carried over in barges or flat-boats, while the cattle are compelled to swim the stream. This last sight is novel and amusing. A drove is collected where the bank is a little steep, and, if possible, the water deep. The cattle are then whipped up and spurred on from behind, and driven with much clamor into the water. Then it is the task of boats to keep behind and along the flanks of the drove, keeping their noses directed toward the opposite shore, and goading up the stragglers with sharp sticks and long whips. Sometimes, when the other shore is not far distant, and the leaders are old soldiers, and know it is useless to rebel, they swim over quietly *en masse*. But oftener, frightened at the broad expanse before them, they will scatter, and the greater fear overcoming the less, shove aside the boats and poles, make for the shore they have left, charge up the bank, scattering and upsetting the drivers, and gallop off to enjoy their temporary liberty. The whole scene is accompanied by the shouts, yells, and war-whoops, without which the true Texan can neither work nor fight; and add to this the roaring and lowing of the herd, the cracking of the enormous whips and the splashing of the water, and you have a very respectable hubbub. I have been told that this method was employed once or twice on dark nights, to victual Port Hudson during the late siege, but they must have made less noise about it.

It is at last, it seems, an established fact that Vicksburgh and Port Hudson are ours.

The capture of the first was the way old U. S. Grant took to celebrate the Fourth, while the last surrendered on the eighth to General Banks, just as the lists of volunteers for the morrow's storming party had been made up. Brave as those volunteers must have been, it was undoubtedly a great relief to them to be spared the murderous duty. These two successes have placed thirty-three thousand prisoners in our hands, and released Grant's army just when it is most needed.

I can't help here recording what it seems to me he ought to do, in order to be able hereafter to compare my dictum with what he does do. After leaving a sufficient garrison in Vicksburgh, he should send fifteen thousand men to reënforce General Banks's worn-out army, by which means Banks could capture or annihilate Taylor and Sibley, and render his authority secure through the whole department.

Second. He should advance with the remainder of his army to attack Bragg in his rear, acting in coöperation with Rosecrans. Together they should be able to finish up Bragg, and then, while Grant was left to protect the Tennessee frontier and finish up the States of Mississippi and Alabama, Rosecrans should advance through West-Tennessee with all the troops that could be spared into Virginia, and, in coöperation with Dix and Hooker, put an end to the war there. Meanwhile, Grant, advancing through Alabama, could communicate by a cavalry raid with Hunter, and together they could overcome Georgia and South-Carolina, and take Savannah and Charleston. This would be the final stroke. Isn't that a fine plan? I only hope some part of it may be accomplished. Our rebel friends are telling us strange stories about the annihilation of Hooker, the capture of Philadelphia, etc., and although we don't believe them, of course, still we feel uneasy and anxious.

If Lee has penetrated into the Keystone State, I have faith enough in the militia of New-York, New-Jersey, and Pennsylvania, to trust that he will have to pay the piper dearly before he gets out again; and then it may be to find Richmond occupied by Dix and Foster, and Virginia no longer a secession State.

One of our negro girls has just come in, and informed me, in a cautious whisper, that the Yankees have advanced as far as "Bayou Bœuf," only eight miles below here.

The crisis is coming, and something has got to burst.

July 22.—Yesterday the rebels completed their evacuation, and left us alone in our glory. The last able-bodied darkey was grabbed, the last straggling cattle swam over, the last crew of "ragged riders" embarked. As fast as they arrived on the west side of the bay they were sent off in long trains toward New-Iberia, and by two P.M. both shores were deserted, the last tent was struck, the last gun on the march, and the steamboats, having finished their work, were steaming up toward their former place of safety.

The cars that had been captured were burnt, and the locomotive sent under full head of steam into the burning train. The concussion was tremendous, and the ruin complete.

They left for our hospital five days' rations, a large portion of which were stolen, and sold by the cooks before the evacuation was over. They took all our negro nurses and cooks, as well as the cooking-stove, and even the wash-basins. As the doctor was sick, there was but one well man left in the building to do every thing, so he had rather a hard time of it. (I had been *hors du combat* myself for ten or twelve days.) Almost every atom of medicine, and even the bandages and lint, were cabbaged by the confederate doctors, so that our sick were left quite destitute. Fortunately, by this morning, we had obtained a reënforcement of darkeys, who had hid themselves in the swamps to escape being carried off, so that the work of the establishment can again be carried on. I could not help laughing at our situation, cast adrift, as it were, between the two armies, unable to help ourselves, and anxiously awaiting whatever fortune the surging tide of war might cast upon us. For a few hours the placid waters and deserted shores of the bay remained undisturbed by any thing warlike, when suddenly from behind the point, far down the bay, a puff of smoke was seen, and "boom!" a shell fell in the water a quarter of a mile below us, and then another, at a higher elevation, screeched over our heads and exploded in the woods behind us. "The gunboat!" was the general exclamation, and the gunboat it proved to be. A white flag was quickly run up on the tower of the dépôt, to show that there was no opposition in the place, and shortly afterward a boat landed, and Lieutenant ——, of the gunboat Sachem, took possession of the town in the name of Uncle Sam. Four hours after the "lone star" had been hauled down, the Stars and Stripes waved triumphantly over the town. The rebel occupation had just lasted four weeks. The gunboat had been trying for two or three days to cross the bar, but for want of a pilot, had only just succeeded.

The most cheering news we had heard for a long time was that Washington and Philadelphia, which the rebels had assured us were taken, were still safe, and that Lee had been defeated instead of being overwhelmingly victorious. Hurrah for Meade! General Weitzel, with the advance of Banks's army, is expected here this afternoon.

A word before I close this epistle about the Texans, whose prisoners we had been for a month. I have called them half savages, and it is about true, but they have some of the noblest qualities of savages. They are brave to rashness, and will endure with patience any amount of exposure and suffering to accomplish their end. They are generous, good-natured, and treat their prisoners with much kindness. They are splendid horsemen, fine marksmen, and can go for days with but a morsel of uncooked food to eat. They are cheap troops to support, because they don't care for tents, will wear any kind of clothing, and will live on bacon and hoecake, or forage for themselves and their horses.

But though brave, they are perfectly undisciplined and regardless of orders, and will fight every man on his own hook, breaking ranks as soon as they commence firing. So that, although they are excellent bushwhackers, they are often scattered and routed in the open field. They consider themselves the equals of their officers, and it is a risky matter to punish them for insubordination. When there is no fighting going on they soon tire of the restraints of camp-life, and often leave for home, coming back when it suits them. Then they will steal, even from their own officers; they will brag beyond all the bounds of truth, and they won't wash themselves or their shirts. They don't consort readily with the Louisianians, whom they call "lazy, cowardly Creoles," and by whom they are cordially hated and termed "Camanches and thieves," and both charges have, I expect, some foundation. To give you an example of the Texan way of doing things: Two or three days ago some of them broke into the stores of their post quartermaster, and came riding past our hospital decked out with their spoils — captured Federal clothing. One long, lank country boy had a hat and a cap on his head and another cap in his hand. One of our wounded men, looking over the balcony, called out: "I wish you would give me one of those caps; I haven't got any!" Not expecting, however, that his request would be granted. "All right," cried Texas, and chucked the cap up; it fortunately proved a good fit.

On the whole, I don't know as we could have fallen into better hands, and our month of captivity passed pretty pleasantly, considering the circumstances of our position.

I am staying at present at Mrs. ——'s, who, since her husband has left, was desirous of having some one in the house to protect it from the thieves and prowlers who always infest an evacuated town. She and Miss ——, her niece, have been very kind to our sick and wounded, and if any property should be protected, hers should.

The arrangement is a very pleasant one for me, as I am not well, and a comfortable bed and well-cooked meals are a great "desideratum."

July 27.—The first detachment of our troops has at length arrived, and their fagged out and tattered appearance was a sufficient excuse for their not coming earlier. That fearful struggle at Port Hudson has worn out Banks's forces, and unless he is speedily reënforced he will have to rest on his oars for a while. It was right pleasant, after such a long dose of "Dixie" and the "Bonnie Blue Flag," to hear the splendid band of the Twelfth Connecticut playing "John Brown." We heard, too, some good news about our boys. They were, it seems, not taken prisoners at Lafourche, but retreated in good order, after repulsing the rebels twice, and they were the first regiment to reöccupy Thibodeaux after the rebel evacuation. Hurrah for the Ironsides! their honor is not lost, though their flags are.

I have the opportunity of sending this by the transport Crescent to New-Orleans, but it may be some days on the road.

Your son,

———

Doc. 20.

THE BATTLES OF GETTYSBURGH.

CINCINNATI "GAZETTE" ACCOUNT.*

AFTER THE INVADERS.

WASHINGTON, June 29, 1863.

I. GETTING A GOOD READY.

"WOULD like you (if you feel able) to equip yourself with horse and outfit, put substitutes in your place in the office, and join Hooker's army in time for the fighting."

It was a despatch, Sunday evening, from the manager, kindly alluding to a temporary debility that grew out of too much leisure on a recent visit west. Of course I felt able, or knew I should by to-morrow. But, alas! it was Hooker's army no longer. Washington was all a-buzz with the removal. A few idol-worshippers hissed their exultation at the constructive disgrace; but for the most part, there was astonishment at the unprecedented act and indignation at the one cause to which all attributed it. Any reader who chanced to remember a few paragraphs in a recent number of the *Gazette*, alluding to the real responsibility for the invasion, must have known at once that the cause was—Halleck. How the cause worked, how they quarrelled about holding Harper's Ferry, how Hooker was relieved in consequence, and how, within an hour afterward, Halleck stultified himself by telling Hooker's successor to do as he pleased concerning this very point, all this will be in print long before this letter can get west.

For once, Washington forgot its *blasé* air, and, through a few hours, there was a genuine, old-fashioned excitement. The two or three Congressmen who happened to be in town were indignant, and scarcely tried to conceal it; the crowds talked over the strange affair in all its phases; a thousand false stories were put in circulation, the basest of which, perhaps, was that Hooker had been relieved for a fortnight's continuous drunkenness; rumors of other changes, as usual, came darkening the very air.

Never before, in the history of modern warfare, had there been such a case. A General had brought his army by brilliant forced marches face to face with the enemy. They were at the very crisis of the campaign; a great battle, perhaps the battle of the war, was daily if not hourly impending. No fault of generalship was alleged, but it happened that a parlor chieftain, in his quiet study, three score miles from the hourly-changing field, differed in judgment on a single point from the General at the head of the troops. The latter carefully examined anew the point in issue, again satisfied himself, and insisted on his conviction, or on relief from responsibility for a course he felt assured was utterly wrong. For this he was relieved—and within five hours was vindicated by his own successor.

But a good, perhaps a better general was put in his place—except from the unfortunate timing

---

* Special correspondence of Mr. Whitelaw Reid to the Cincinnati *Gazette*, from the army of the Potomac.

of the change, we had good reason to hope it would work at least no harm. There was little regret for Hooker personally; it was only the national sense of fair play that was outraged.

Presently there came new excitement. Stuart had crossed the Potomac, twenty-five miles from Washington, had captured a train within twelve or thirteen miles, had thrown out small parties to within a mile or two of the railroad between Baltimore and Washington. In the night the road would certainly be cut, and for a few hours, at any rate, the Capital isolated from the country. We had need to make haste, or it might be difficult "to join Hooker's army."

It was not to be a solitary trip. Samuel Wilkeson, the well-known brilliant writer on the New-York *Tribune*, lately transferred to the *Times*; and U. H. Painter, chief Washington correspondent of the Philadelphia *Inquirer*, a miracle of energy in such a sphere, were to go; and Coffin of the Boston *Journal*, known through all New-England as "Carleton," had telegraphed an appointment to meet me in the army.

Monday morning Washington breathed freer, on learning that the Baltimore trains had come through. Stuart had failed, then? But we counted too fast.

A few hasty purchases to make up an outfit for campaigning along the border, and at eleven we are off. Unusual vigilance at the little block-houses and embankments at exposed points along the road; soldiers out in unusual force, and every thing ready for instant attack; much chattering of Stuart and his failure in the train; anxious inquiries by brokers as to whether communication with New-York was to be severed; and so we reach Baltimore.

"Am very sorry, gentlemen; would get you out at once if I could; would gladly run up an extra train for you; but—the rebels cut our road last night, this side of Frederick, and we have no idea when we can run again." Thus Mr. Prescott Smith, whom every body knows, that has ever heard of the Baltimore and Ohio Railroad.

And so Stuart had *not* failed—we were just one train too late and were cut off from the army!

There was nothing for it but to wait; and so—ill-satisfied with this "Getting a Good Ready"—back to Washington.

II. OFF.

FREDERICK, MD., Tuesday evening, June 30.

Washington was again like a city besieged, as after Bull Run. All night long, troops were marching; orderlies with clanking sabres clattering along the streets; trains of wagons grinding over the bouldered avenue; commissaries were hurrying up their supplies; the quartermaster's department was like a bee-hive; every thing was motion and hurry. From the War Department came all manner of exciting statements; men were everywhere asking what the President thought of the emergency. Trains had again come through regularly from Baltimore, but how long could it continue? Had not Stuart's cavalry been as near as the old Blair place at Silver Springs, and might

they not cut the track any moment they chose? Might they not, indeed, asked the startled bankers, might they not indeed charge past the forts on the Maryland side, pay a hurried visit to the President and Cabinet, and replenish their army chests from *our* well-stored vaults?

In the midst of all this there came a blistering sight that should blacken evermore every name concerned. With cries for reënforcements from the weakened front, with calls for volunteers and raw militia to step into the imminent breach and defend the invaded North, with everywhere urgent need for every man who knew how to handle a musket, there came sprucely marching down the avenue, in all their freshness of brilliant uniforms and unstained arms, with faultlessly apparelled officers and gorgeous drum-major, and clanging band, and all the pomp and circumstance of glorious war, (about the Capital,) with banners waving and bayonets gleaming in the morning sunlight, as with solid tramp that told of months of drill they moved down the street—in such bravery of peaceful soldiering there came a New-England nine months' regiment, mustering over nine hundred bayonets, whose term of service that day expired! With Stuart's cavalry swarming about the very gates of the Capital, with the battle that was to decide whether the war should henceforth be fought on Northern or Southern soil hourly impending, these men, in all the blazonry of banners and music, and glittering uniforms, and polished arms, were marching—home! They had been implored to stay a fortnight, a week—three days even; but, with one accord, they insisted on starting *home!* Would that Stuart *could* capture the train that bears them!

Another exciting ride over a yet unmolested track, and we are again in Baltimore. Mr. Prescott Smith gave us the cheering assurance that the road was open again to Frederick; that nobody knew where Stuart had gone, but that in any event they would send us out in the afternoon.

For the rest there was news of more dashing movements by our army. The rebels were reported concentrating at York, Pennsylvania. Our army had already left Frederick far in the rear, and spreading out like a fan to make use of every available road, it was sweeping splendidly up to meet them. There was no fear of their not fighting under Meade. He was recognized as a soldier, brave and able, and they would follow him just as readily as Hooker—some of them, indeed far more willingly. But there was sore need for every musket. Lee at least equalled us in numbers, they thought.

Baltimore had been in a panic. Monday evening some rebel cavalry had ventured up to within a few miles of the city, and frightened persons had rushed in with the story that great squadrons of horse were just ready to charge down the streets. Alarm-bells rang, the Loyal Leagues rushed to arms, the thoroughfares were thronged with the improvised soldiery, and within an hour thousands of bayonets guarded every approach.

It was worthy the new life of Baltimore. Here, thank God, was an eastern city, able and ready at all times to defend itself.

Stuart did not come—if he had, he would have been repulsed.

General Tyler (former Colonel of the Seventh Ohio) had been hastily summoned here to assume command of the defences of Baltimore. This display of citizen soldiery was part of the work he had already done.

But those "defences!" "Small boy," exclaimed W., as we sauntered through the street and passed an urchin picking pebbles out of a tar barrel to fling at a passing pig, "small boy," and he uttered it with impressive dignity, "You must stop that, sir! You are destroying the defences of Baltimore!" And indeed he was. Single rows of tar-barrels and sugar hogsheads, half filled with gravel, and placed across the streets, with sometimes a rail or two on top, after the fashion of a "stake and rider" fence, constituted the "defences." They were called barricades, I believe, in some official paper on the subject. Outside the city, however, were earthworks, (to which additions had been made in the press of the emergency,) that would have afforded considerable resistance to an attack; and if cavalry had succeeded in getting into the city, the "barricades" might have been of some service in checking their charges.

In the afternoon, Stuart's cavalry was heard from, making the best of its way, by a circuitous route, on the rear and flank of our army, to join Lee in Southern Pennsylvania. Baltimore, then, was safe; and Stuart had made the most ill-advised raid of the war. He had worn out his horses by a terrible march, on the eve of a desperate battle, when, in the event of a retreat, he was especially needed to protect the rear and hold our pursuit in check; and in return he had gained—a few horses, a single army train, which he could only destroy, eighteen hours' interruption of communications by rail between the Capital and the army, and a night's alarm in Washington and Baltimore.

Our own army was now reported to be concentrating at Westminster, manifestly to march on York. To reach this point, we must take the Western Maryland road, but this had been abandoned in terror by the Company, and the rolling stock was all in Philadelphia. There was nothing for it but to hasten to Frederick, then mount and follow the track of the army.

As our party stepped into the train a despatch brought Hooker's vindication, as against Halleck. He had been relieved for insisting on withdrawing the troops from Harper's Ferry, and using them in the active operations of the army. Precisely that thing his successor had done! All honor to Meade for the courage that took the responsibility!

It was a curious ride up the road. Eighteen hours ago the rebels had swarmed across it. The public had no knowledge that they were not yet in its immediate vicinity, and might not attack the very train now starting; yet here were cars crowded to overflowing with citizens and their wives and daughters, willing to take the risks rather than lose a train. Mr. Smith had been good enough to provide a car for our party, but the press was so great we had to throw open the doors to make room for women and children, recklessly ready to brave what they supposed the dangers of the ride.

Frederick is Pandemonium. Somebody has blundered frightfully; the town is full of stragglers, and the liquor-shops are in full blast. Just under my window scores of drunken soldiers are making night hideous; all over the town they are trying to steal horses, or sneak into unwatched private residences, or are filling the air with the blasphemy of their drunken brawls. The worst elements of a great army are here in their worst condition; its cowards, its thieves, its sneaks, its bullying vagabonds, all inflamed with whiskey, and drunk as well with their freedom from accustomed restraint.

III. THE REAR OF A GREAT ARMY.

TWO TAVERNS P. O., PA., July 1.

Our little party broke up unceremoniously. Both my companions thought it better to go back to Baltimore and up to Westminster by rail on the expected Government trains; I thought differently, and adhered to the original plan of proceeding overland. I have already good reasons to felicitate myself on the lucky decision.

An hour after breakfast sufficed for buying a horse and getting him equipped for the campaign.

Drunken soldiers were still staggering about the streets, looking for a last drink or a horse to steal, before commencing to straggle along the road, when a messenger for one of the New-York papers, who had come down with despatches, and myself were off for headquarters. We supposed them to be at Westminster, but were not certain.

South-Mountain, historic evermore, since a previous rebel invasion faded out thence to Antietam, loomed up on the left amid the morning mists; before us stretched a winding turnpike, upheaved and bent about by a billowy country that in its cultivation and improvements began to give evidence of proximity to Pennsylvania farmers. The army had moved up the valley of the Monocacy through Walkersville, Woodbury, and Middleburgh—all pleasant little Maryland villages—where, in peaceful times, Rip Van Winkle might have slumbered undisturbed. The direction seemed too far north for Westminster, and a courier, coming back with despatches, presently informed us that headquarters were not there, but at Taneytown, a point considerably farther north and west. Evidently there was a change in our plans. We were not going to York, or headquarters would not be at Taneytown; and it was fair to suppose that our movements to the north-west were based upon news of a similar concentration by the rebels. The probabilities of a speedy battle were thus immensely increased, and we hastened the more rapidly on.

From Frederick out the whole road was lined with stragglers. I have heard General Patrick highly spoken of as an efficient Provost-Marshal General for the Potomac army; but if he is responsible for permitting such scenes as were witnessed to-day in the rear, his successor is sadly needed.

Take a worthless vagabond, who has enlisted for thirteen dollars a month instead of patriotism, who falls out of ranks because he is a coward and wants to avoid the battle, or because he is lazy and wants to steal a horse to ride on instead of marching, or because he is rapacious and wants to sneak about farm-houses and frighten or wheedle timid countrywomen into giving him better food and lodging than camp-life affords — make this armed coward or sneak or thief drunk on bad whisky, give him scores and hundreds of armed companions as desperate and drunken as himself—turn loose this motley crew, muskets and revolvers in hand, into a rich country, with quiet, peaceful inhabitants, all unfamiliar with armies and army ways — let them swagger and bully as cowards and vagabonds always do, steal or openly plunder as such thieves always will — and then, if you can imagine the state of things this would produce, you have the condition of the country in the rear of our own army, on our own soil, to-day.

Of course these scoundrels are not types of the army. The good soldiers never straggle—these men are the *debris*, the offscourings from nearly a hundred thousand soldiers.

There is no need for permitting these outrages. An efficient Provost-Marshal, such as General Patrick has been called, would have put a provost-guard at the rear of every division, if not of every regiment and brigade, and would have swept up every man that dared to sneak out of ranks when his comrades were marching to meet the enemy. The rebels manage these things better. Death on the spot is said to be their punishment for straggling, and in the main it is a just one.

The army itself had done surprisingly little damage to property along their route. Breaking off the limbs of cherry trees to pick the ripe cherries, seemed to be about the worst of their trespasses. I have never before seen the country so little injured along the line of march of a great army.

But every farm-house was now filled with drunken loafers in uniform; they swarmed about the stables, stealing horses at every opportunity, and compelling farmers to keep up a constant watch; in the fence-corners groups of them lay, too drunk to get on at all.

As we neared the army a new phase of the evil was developed. A few mounted patrols seemed to have been sent out to gather up the stragglers, and some of them had begun their duty by getting drunk, too.

In one fence-corner we passed a drunken trio in fierce altercation with a gay-looking, drunken patrol, with a rose jauntily worn in his buttonhole, and a loaded and cocked revolver carelessly playing in his hand. "These fellows are d-dr-drunk," he explained to us, "and ac'ly talk about sh-shootin' me for or'rin 'em to go to camp." One of the stragglers had his musket cocked and handsomely covering the red rose on the patrol's breast.

A few yards further on was another drunken party under the trees. A patrol, trying to get them started, was just drunk enough to be indiscreetly brave and talkative. "You're cowardly stragglers, every rascal of you," he roared, after a few minutes' unavailing efforts at coaxing. "You're lyin' scoune'rl," was the thick-tongued response; and the last we saw of the party as we galloped on, two of the stragglers were rushing at the patrol, and he was standing at a charge bayonets, ready to receive them. They probably halted before they reached the bayonet-point.

As we stopped at a farm-house by the roadside to feed our horses and get dinner, we passed a party of stragglers in the yard. After dinner, to our amazement we discovered that my luckless "rebel look," and an indignant reply about straggling to some impertinent question they had asked, had well-nigh got us into trouble. The rascals, drunk enough to half believe what they said, and angry enough at being called stragglers to do us any mischief they were able, had held a court on our cases while we were eating, had adjudged us rebel spies, and had sentenced us to — have our horses confiscated! Luckily my companion strolled down to the stable after dinner, just as the fellows were getting the horses out to make off with them! They announced their conclusion that we were spies, and their sentence, and insisted on the horses, but a judicious display of a hearty disposition on his part to knock somebody down, induced them to drop the reins, and allow him to put the horses back in the stable.

We had small time, as we galloped through, to appreciate the beauties of Taneytown, a pleasant little Maryland hamlet, named in honor of the Chief-Justice of the United States, (who has a country-seat in the vicinity,) and like him now somewhat fallen into the sere and yellow leaf. Army trains blocked up the streets; a group of quartermasters and commissaries were bustling about the principal corner; across on the hills, and along the road to the left, far as the eye could reach, rose the glitter from the swaying points of bayonets, as with steady tramp the columns of our Second and Third corps were marching northward. They were just getting started — it was already well on in the afternoon. Clearly something was in the wind.

Half a mile further east, splashed by the hoofs of eager gallopers. A large, unpretending camp, looking very much like that of a battalion of cavalry — we turn in, without ceremony, and are at the headquarters of the army of the Potomac.

At first all seems quiet enough, but a moment's observation shows signs of movement. The slender baggage is all packed, every body is ready to take the saddle at a moment's notice. Engineers are busy with their maps; couriers are coming in with reports; the trustiest counsellors on the staff are with the General.

In a plain little wall-tent, just like the rest, pen in hand, seated on a camp-stool and bending over a map, is the new "General Commanding" for the army of the Potomac. Tall, slender, not ungainly, but certainly not handsome or graceful, thin-faced, with grizzled beard and moustache, a broad and high but retreating forehead, from each corner of which the slightly-curling hair recedes, as if giving premonition of baldness—apparently between forty-five and fifty years of age—altogether a man who impresses you rather as a thoughtful student than as a dashing soldier—so General Meade looks in his tent.

"I tell you, I think a great deal of that fine fellow Meade," I chanced to hear the President say, a few days after Chancellorsville. Here was the result of that good opinion. There is every reason to hope that the events of the next few days will justify it.

A horseman gallops up and hastily dismounts. It is a familiar face—L. L. Crounse, the well-known chief correspondent of the *New-York Times*, with the army of the Potomac. As we exchange hurried salutations, he tells us that he has just returned from a little post-village in Southern Pennsylvania, ten or fifteen miles away; that a fight, of what magnitude he cannot say, is now going on near Gettysburgh, between the First corps and some unknown force of the enemy; that Major-General Reynolds is already killed, and that there are rumors of more bad news.

Mount and spur for Gettysburgh is, of course, the word. Crounse, who is going too, acts as guide. We shall precede headquarters but a little. A few minutes in the Taneytown tavern porch, writing despatches to be forthwith sent back by special messenger to the telegraph office at Frederick; then in among the moving mass of soldiers, and down the Gettysburgh road at such speed as we may. We have made twenty-seven miles over rough roads already to-day; as the sun is dipping in the woods of the western hill-tops, we have fifteen more ahead of us.

It is hard work, forcing our way among the moving masses of infantry, or even through the crowded trains, and we make but slow progress. Presently aids and orderlies begin to come back, with an occasional quartermaster or surgeon, or commissary in search of stores. C. seems to know every body in the army, and from every one he demands the news from the front. "Every thing splendid; have driven them five or six miles from Gettysburgh." "Badly cut up, sir, and falling back." "Men rushed in like tigers after Reynolds's death, and swept every thing before them." (Rushing in like tigers is a stock performance, and appears much oftener in the newspapers than on the field.) "Gettysburgh burnt down by the rebels." "Things were all going wild, but Hancock got up before we were utterly defeated, and I guess there's some chance now." "D—d Dutchmen of the Eleventh corps

broke and ran like sheep, just as they did at Chancellorsville, and it's going to be another disaster of just the same sort." "We still hold Gettysburgh, and every thing looks favorable." "Wadsworth's division cut to pieces; not a full regiment left out of the whole of it; and half the officers killed." "We've been driven pell-mell through Gettysburgh, and things look bad enough, I tell you."

This is the substance of the information we gain, by diligent questioning of scores. It is of such stuff that the "news direct from the battle-field," made up by itinerant liars and "reporters" at points twenty or thirty miles distant, and telegraphed thence throughout the country, is manufactured. So long as the public, in its hot haste, insists on devouring the news before it is born, so long must it expect such confusion and absurdity.

Riding through the columns became more and more difficult as we advanced; and finally, to avoid it, we turned off into a by-way on the right. We were fortunately well supplied with maps, and from these we learned that but a few miles to the right of the Taneytown road, up which we had been going, ran the great Baltimore turnpike to Gettysburgh; and a Dutch farmer told us that our by-path would bring us out, some miles ahead, on this pike. It was certain to be less obstructed, and we pushed on.

Across the hills to the left we could see the white-covered wagons slowly winding in and out through the forests, and the masses of blue coats toiling forward. In either direction, for miles, you could catch occasional glimpses of the same sight through the openings of the foliage. The shades of evening dimmed and magnified the scene till one might have thought the hosts of Xerxes, in all the glory of modern armor, were pressing on Gettysburgh. To the front and right lay broad, well-tilled farms, dotted here and there with mammoth, many-windowed barns, covered with herds and rustling with the ripening grain.

Selecting a promising-looking Dutch house, with a more than usually imposing barn in its rear, we stopped for supper. The good-man's "woman" had gone to see the soldiers on the road, but whatever he could get for us "you pe very heartily welcome to." Great cherry trees bent before the door under their weight of ripe fruit; the kitchen garden was crowded with vegetables; contented cattle stood about the barn; sleek horses filled the stables; fat geese hissed a doubtful welcome as we came too near them; the very farm-yard laughed with plenty.

We put it on the ground of resting our horses and giving them time for their oats; but I fear the snowy bread and well-spread table of the hearty farmer had something too to do with the hour that we spent.

Then mount and spur again. It was dark in the woods, but our by-path had become a neighborhood wagon-road, and the moon presently cast us occasional glances from behind the clouds. The country was profoundly quiet; the Dutch farmers seemed to have all gone to bed at dark, and only their noisy house-dogs gave signs of life as we passed. Once or twice we had to rouse a sleeping worthy out of bed for directions about the road. At last camp-fires gleamed through the woods; presently we caught the hum of soldiers' talk ahead; by the roadside we passed a house where all the lights were out, but the family were huddled on the door-step, listening to the soldiers. "Yes, the army's right down there. If you want to stay all night, turn up by the school-house. 'Squire Durboraw's a nice man."

"Right down there" was the post-village of Two Taverns—thronged with soldiers—the women all in the streets, talking and questioning and frightening themselves at a terrible rate. A corps general's headquarters had been there to-day, but they were now moved up to the front. That didn't look like serious disaster. We were four miles and a quarter or a half from the line of battle. Ewell had come down from York, and we had been fighting him to-day. A. P. Hill was also up, coming by way of Chambersburgh or Hagerstown. Longstreet was known to be on the way, and would certainly be here to-morrow. The reserves were on their way. In short, Lee's whole army was rapidly concentrating at Gettysburgh, and to-morrow, it seemed, must bring the battle that is to decide the invasion. To-day it had opened for us—*not* favorably.

"'Squire Durboraw *is* a nice man." We roused him out of bed, where he must have been for two or three hours. "Can you take care of us and our horses till morning?" "I will do it with pleasure, gentlemen." And no more words are needed. The horses are housed in one of those great horse-palaces these people build for barns; we are comfortably and even luxuriously quartered. If the situation is as we hope, our army must attack by daybreak. At any rate, we are off for the field at four in the morning. AGATE.

II. THE REPULSE ON WEDNESDAY, FIRST JULY.

FIELD OF BATTLE, NEAR GETTYSBURGH, July 2.

TO THE FRONT.

We were in the saddle this morning a little after daybreak. The army was cut down to fighting weight; it had shaken off all retainers and followers—all but its fighters; and the road was alive with this useless material.

My companion and myself were forcing our way as fast as possible through the motley crowd toward the front, where an occasional shot could already be heard, and where we momentarily expected the crash of battle to open, when I was stopped by some one calling my name from a little frame dwelling, crowded with wounded soldiers. It proved to be Colonel Stephenson, the librarian of Congress. He had run away from his duties in the Capital, and all day yesterday, through a fight that we now know to have been one of the hottest in the war, had been serving most gallantly as aid on General Meredith's staff. Congress should make an example of its runaway official!

The lower story of the house was crowded with wounded from the old "Iron Brigade," of Wadsworth's division; in a little upper room was their General. He had been grazed on the head with a fragment of shell, his horse had been shot under him, and had fallen upon him; he had been badly bruised externally and worse internally, and there was little prospect of his being ready for service again for months. He spoke proudly of the conduct of his men, almost tearfully of their unprecedented losses.

Half a mile further on, through crowds of slightly wounded, and past farm-houses converted into hospitals, a turn to the right through a meadow, up the slope of an exposed hill, and by the side of a smouldering camp-fire. Stretched on the ground, and surrounded by his staff, lies General Wadsworth, (late Republican candidate for Governor of New-York,) commander of the advance division in yesterday's fight. He, too, kindles as he tells the story of the day, its splendid fighting, and the repulse before overwhelming numbers.

Batteries are all about us; troops are moving into position; new lines seem to be forming, or old ones extending. Two or three general officers, with a retinue of staff and orderlies, come galloping by. Foremost is the spare and somewhat stooped form of the Commanding General. He is not cheered, indeed is scarcely recognized. He is an approved corps General, but he has not yet vindicated his right to command the army of the Potomac. By his side is the calm, honest, manly face of Howard. An empty coat-sleeve is pinned to his shoulder—memento of a hard-fought field before, and reminder of many a battle-scene his splendid Christian courage has illumined. They are arranging the new line of battle. Howard's dispositions of the preceding night are adopted for the centre; his suggestions are being taken for the flanks. It is manifest already that we are no longer on the offensive, that the enemy has the initiative.

THE POSITION.

A little further forward, a turn to the left, we climb the slope of another hill, hitch our horses half-way up, under cover of the woods, make our way through frowning batteries and by long rows of tombstones, stop for an instant to look at the monument of a hero from Fair Oaks, and are startled by the buzzing hiss of a well-aimed Minie, from the foes that fought us at Fair Oaks, above our heads; move forward to an ambitious little gate-keeper's lodge, at the entrance of the cemetery.

In front, on a gradual declivity, an orchard of gnarled old leafy trees; beyond the valley, a range of hills but little lower than that on which we stand; on this slope, half hidden among the clusters of trees, a large cupola-crowned brick building—a theological seminary; between this and us half a dozen spires, roofs of houses, distinguishable amid the luxuriant foliage, streets marked by the lines of trees—Gettysburgh!

No sound comes up from the deserted town, no ringing of bells, no voices of children, no hum of busy trade. Only now and then a blue curl of smoke rises and fades from some high window; a faint report comes up, and perhaps the hiss of a Minie is heard; the houses are not wholly without occupants.

We are standing on Cemetery Hill, the key to the whole position the enemy occupies, the centre of our line and the most exposed point for a concentration of the rebel fire. To our right, and a little back, is the hill on which we have just left General Wadsworth; still farther back, and sweeping away from the cemetery almost like the side of a horse-shoe from the toe, is a succession of other hills, some covered with timber and undergrowth, others yellow in the morning sunlight, and waving with luxuriant wheat; all crowned with batteries that are soon to reap other than a wheaten harvest. To the left, our positions are not so distinctly visible; though we can make out our line stretching off in another horse-shoe bend, behind a stone fence near the cemetery—unprotected, farther on; affording far fewer advantageous positions for batteries, and manifestly a weaker line than our right. An officer of General Howard's staff pointed out the positions to me, and I could not help hazarding the prediction that there on our left wing would come the rebel attack we were awaiting.

General Howard's headquarters were on this very Cemetery Hill—the most exposed position on the whole field. He had now returned and was good enough, during the lull that still lasted, while we awaited the anticipated attack, to explain the action of yesterday as he saw it.

THE BATTLE OF WEDNESDAY.

I have now conversed with four of the most prominent generals employed in that action, and with any number of subordinates. I am a poor hand to describe battles I do not see, but in this case I must endeavor to weave their statements into a connected narrative. The ground of the action is still in the enemy's hands, and I have no knowledge of it save from the descriptions of others, and the distant view one gets from Cemetery Hill.

We had been advancing toward York. It was discovered that the rebels were moving for a concentration farther south, and we suddenly changed our own line of march. The First corps, Major-General Reynolds, had the advance; next came the unfortunate Eleventh corps, with a new record to make that should wipe out Chancellorsville, and ready to do it.

Saturday they had been at Boonesboro, twelve or fifteen miles to the north-west of Frederick; by Tuesday night, the First corps lay encamped on Marsh Creek, within easy striking distance of Gettysburgh. The Eleventh corps was ten or twelve miles farther back. Both were simply moving under general marching orders, and the enemy was hardly expected yet for a day or two.

At an early hour in the forenoon the First corps was filing down around Cemetery Hill in solid column, and entering the streets of Gettysburgh. In the town our skirmishers had met pickets or scouts from the enemy and had driven them pell-mell back. The news fired the column, and General Reynolds, with little or no reconnoissance, marched impetuously forward. Unfortunate haste of a hero, gone now to the hero's reward!

It was fifteen minutes past ten o'clock. The fire of the rebel skirmishers rattled along the front, but, shaking it off as they had the dew from their night's bivouac, the men pushed hotly on.

Meantime General Reynolds, on receiving his first notice an hour ago from Buford's cavalry, that the rebels were in the vicinity of Gettysburgh, had promptly sent word back to General Howard, and asked him, as a prudential measure, to bring up the Eleventh corps as rapidly as possible. The Eleventh had been coming up on the Emmetsburgh road. Finding it crowded with the train of the First, they had started off on a by-way, leading into the Taneytown road, some distance ahead; and were still on this by-way eleven miles from Gettysburgh, when Reynolds's messenger reached them. The fine fellows, with stinging memories of not wholly merited disgrace at Chancellorsville, started briskly forward, and a little after one their advance brigade was filing through the town to the music of the fire above. General Reynolds's corps consists of three divisions—Wadsworth's, Doubleday's, and Robinson's. Wadsworth's (composed of Meredith's and Cutler's brigades—both mainly Western troops) had the advance, with Cutler on the right and Meredith on the left. Arriving at the Theological Seminary, above the town, the near presence of the enemy became manifest, and they placed a battery in position to feel him out, and gradually moved forward.

An engagement, of more or less magnitude, was evidently imminent. General Reynolds rode forward to select a position for a line of battle. Unfortunate—sadly unfortunate again—alike for him, with all a gallant soldier's possibilities ahead of him, and for the country, that so sorely needed his well-tried services. He fell, almost instantly, pierced by a ball from a sharp-shooter's rifle, and was borne, dying or dead, to the rear. General Doubleday was next in command.

The enemy were seen ready. There was no time to wait for orders from the new corps commander; instantly, right and left, Cutler and Meredith wheeled into line of battle on the double-quick. Well-tried troops, those; no fear of *their* flinching; veterans of a score of battles—in the war some of them from the very start; with the first at Philippi, Laurel Hill, Carrick's Ford, Cheat Mountain and all the Western Virginia campaign; trusted of Shields at Winchester, and of Lander at Romney and Bloomery Gap; through the campaign of the Shenandoah Valley, and with the army of the Potomac in every march to the red slaughter sowing that still had brought no harvest of victory. Meredith's old Iron Brigade was the Nineteenth Indiana, Twenty-fourth Michigan, Sixth and Seventh Wisconsin—veterans all, and well mated with the brave New-Yorkers whom Wadsworth also led.

Cutler, having the advance, opened the attack; Meredith was at it a few minutes later. Short, sharp fighting, the enemy handsomely repulsed, three hundred rebel prisoners taken, General Archer himself reported at their head—such was the auspicious opening. No wonder the First determined to hold its ground.

Yet they were ill-prepared for the contest that was coming. Their guns had sounded the tocsin for the Eleventh, but so they had too for—Ewell, already marching down from York to rejoin Lee. They were fighting two divisions of A. P. Hill's now—numerically stronger than their dwindled three. Their batteries were not up in sufficient numbers; on Meredith's left—a point that especially needed protection, there were none at all. A battery with Buford's cavalry stood near. Wadsworth cut red tape and in an instant ordered it up. The captain, preferring red tape to red fields, refused to obey. Wadsworth ordered him under arrest, could find no officer for the battery, and finally fought it under a sergeant. Sergeant and captain there should henceforth exchange places.

The enemy repulsed, the First advanced their lines and took the position lately held by the rebels. Very heavy skirmishing, almost developing at times into a general musketry engagement, followed. Our men began to discover that they were opposing a larger force. Their own line, long and thin, bent and wavered occasionally, but bore bravely up. To the left, where the fire seemed the hottest, there were no supports at all, and Wadsworth's division, which had been in the longest, was suffering severely.

About one one o'clock Major-General Howard, riding in advance of his hastening corps, arrived on the field and assumed command. Carl Schurz was thus left in command of the Eleventh, while Doubleday remained temporarily Reynolds's successor in the First.

The advance of the Eleventh soon came up and was thrown into position to the right of the First. They had little fighting immediately—but their time was coming. Meantime the First, that had already lost its General commanding and had held its ground against superior numbers, without supports, from ten till nearly two, took fresh courage as another corps came up, and all felt certain of winning the day.

But alas! the old, old game was playing. The enemy was concentrating faster than we. Perhaps no one was to blame for it; no one among the living at least, and the thickly clustering honors that fitly crown the hero's grave bar all criticism and pardon all mistakes, if mistakes they were.

About half-past two that afternoon, standing where we now stand, on Cemetery Hill, one might have seen a long, gray line, creeping down the pike and near the railroad on the north-east side of the town. Little pomp in their march, but much haste; few wagons, but the ammunition trains all up; and the battle-flags that float over their brigades are not our flags. It is the road from *York*—these are Stonewall Jackson's men— led now by Stonewall Jackson's most trusted

and loved Lieutenant. That gray serpent, bending in and out through the distant hills, decides the day.

They are in manifest communication with Hill's corps, now engaged, fully advised of their early losses, and of the exact situation. They bend up from the York road, debouch in the woods near the crest of the hill, and by three o'clock, with the old yell and the old familiar tactics, their battle-line comes charging down.

Small resistance is made on our right. The Eleventh does not flee wildly from its old antagonists, as at their last meeting, when Stonewall Jackson scattered them as if they had been pigmies, foolishly venturing into the war of the Titans. It even makes stout resistance for a little while; but the advantage of position, as of numbers, is all with the rebels, and the line is forced to retire. It is done deliberately and without confusion, till they reach the town. Here the evil genius of the Eleventh falls upon it again. To save the troops from the terrible enfilading fire through the streets, the officers wheel them by detachments into cross-streets, and attempt to march them thus around one square after another, diagonally, through the town. The Germans are confused by the manœuvre; perhaps the old panic at the battle-cry of Jackson's flying corps comes over them; at any rate they break in wild confusion, some pouring through the town a rout, and are with difficulty formed again on the heights to the southward. They lose over one thousand two hundred prisoners in twenty minutes. One of their Generals, Schempelfennig, an old officer in the Russian service in the Crimean war, is cut off, but he shrewdly takes to cover, conceals himself somewhere in the town, and finally escapes.

But while our right is thus suddenly wiped out, how fares it with the left—Robinson, and Doubleday, and sturdy Wadsworth, with the Western troops? Sadly enough.

By half-past three, as they counted the time, the whole of A. P. Hill's corps, acting in concert now with Ewell, precipitated itself upon their line. These men are as old and tried soldiers as there are in the war, and they describe the fire that followed as the most terrific they have ever known. In a single brigade, (Cutler's,) in twenty minutes, every staff-officer had his horse shot under him, some of them two and three. In thirty minutes not a horse was left to General or staff, save one, and that one—as if the grim mockery of war there sought to outdo itself—had his tail shot off! General Cutler himself had three horses shot under him.

Few troops could stand it. All of the First corps could not. Presently the thin line of fire began to waver and bend and break under those terrible volleys from the dark woods above. The officers, brave almost always to a fault, sought to keep them in. One—his name deserves to be remembered—Captain Richardson, of the Seventh Wisconsin, seized the colors of a retreating Pennsylvania regiment, and strove to rally the men around their flag. It was in vain; none but troops that have been tried as by fire can be re-formed under such a storm of death; but the captain, left alone and almost in the rebels' hands, held on to the flaunting colors of another regiment, that made him so conspicuous a target, and brought them safely off.

The right of the corps gave way. The fierce surge of Ewell's attack had beaten up to their front, and, added to Hill's heavy fire, forced them slowly back.

Wadsworth still holds on—for a few minutes more his braves protract the carnival of death. Doubleday managed to get three regiments over to their support; Colonel Biddle's Pennsylvania regiment came in and behaved most gallantly. Colonel Stephenson, who all the day had been serving in the hottest of the fight as aid to Meredith, relieved a wounded colonel, and strove to rally his regiment. Meredith himself, with his Antietam wound hardly yet ceasing to pain him, is struck again, a mere bruise, however—on the head, with a piece of shell. At the same instant his large, heavy horse falls, mortally wounded, bears the General under him to the ground, and beats him there with his head and shoulders in his death convulsions.

It is idle fighting Fate. Ewell turned the scale with the old, historic troops; brave men may now well retire before double their number equally brave. When the Eleventh corps fell back, the flank of the First was exposed; when the right of the First fell back, Wadsworth's flank was exposed; already flushed with their victory, rebels were pouring up against front and both flanks of the devoted brigades. They had twice cleared their front of rebel lines; mortal men could now do no more. And so, "slowly and sullenly firing," the last of them came back.

Meantime, the fate of the army had been settled. It was one of those great crises that come rarely more than once in a lifetime. For Major-General Howard, brave, one-armed, Christian fighting hero, the crisis had come.

His command—two corps of the grand army of the Potomac—were repulsed, and coming back in full retreat, a few sturdy brigades in order, the most in sad confusion. One cavalry charge, twenty minutes' well-directed cannonading, might wipe out nearly a third of the army, and leave Meade powerless for the defence of the North. These corps must be saved, and saved at once.

General Howard met and overmastered the crisis. The Cemetery Hill was instantly selected. The troops were taken to the rear and re-formed under cover. Batteries hurried up, and when the rebel pursuit had advanced half-way through the town a thunderbolt leaped out from the whole length of that line of crest and smote them where they stood. The battle was ended, the corps were saved.

The last desperate attack lasted nowhere along the line over forty minutes; with most of it hardly over half so long. One single brigade, that "iron" column that held the left, went in one thousand eight hundred and twenty strong. It came out with seven hundred men. A few were prisoners; a few concealed themselves in houses and escaped—near a thousand of them were killed and wounded. Its fellow brigade went in one thousand five hundred strong; it came out with forty-nine officers and five hundred and forty-nine men killed and wounded, and six officers and five hundred and eighty-four men missing and their fate unknown. Who shall say that they did not go down into the very valley of the Shadow of Death on that terrible afternoon?   AGATE.

III. THURSDAY'S DOUBTFUL ISSUE—FRIDAY'S VICTORY.

FIELD OF BATTLE NEAR GETTYSBURGH, }
PA., July 4.   }

Two more days of such fighting as no Northern State ever witnessed before, and victory at last! Victory for a fated army, and salvation for the imperilled country!

It were folly for one unaided man, leaving the ground within a few hours after the battle has died fitfully out, to undertake a minute detail of the operations on all parts of the field. I dare only attempt the merest outline of its leading features—then off for Cincinnati by the speediest routes.

I have been unable even to learn all I sought concerning the part some of our own Ohio regiments bore—of individual brigades and regiments and batteries I can in the main say nothing. But what one man, not entirely unfamiliar with such scenes before, could see, passing over the ground before, during, and after the fight, I saw; for the rest I must trust to such credible statements by the actors as I have been able to collect.

THE BATTLE-FIELD.

Whoever would carry in his mind a simple map of our positions in the great battles of Thursday and Friday, the second and third, at Gettysburgh, has but to conceive a broad capital A, bisected by another line drawn down from the top and equi-distant from each side. These three straight lines meeting at the top of the letter are the three roads along which our army advanced, and between and on which lay the battle-field. The junction of the lines is Gettysburgh. The middle line, running nearly north and south, is the road to Taneytown. The right-hand line, running south-east, is the Baltimore pike. That on the left is the Emmetsburgh road.

Almost at the junction of the lines, and resting on the left-hand side of the Baltimore pike, is the key to the whole position—Cemetery Hill. This constitutes our extreme front, lies just south of Gettysburgh, overlooks and completely commands the town, the entire valley to right and left, the whole space over which the rebels advanced to attack our centre, and a portion of the woods from which the rebel lines on their centre debouched.

Standing on this hill and facing north (toward the town) you have, just across the Baltimore pike, another hill, almost as high, and crowned like the Cemetery with batteries that rake the centre front. Farther to the right and rear, the country is broken into a series of short, billowy ridges, every summit of which affords a location for a battery. Through these passes the little valley of Rock Creek, crossing the Baltimore turnpike a couple of miles or so from town, and thus affording a good covered way for a rebel movement to attempt (by passing down the valley from the woods beyond this range of hills) to pierce our right wing, and penetrate to the rear of our centre.

On the left the hills are lower, afford fewer eligible positions for batteries, and are commanded by the heights on the rebel side.

The space between these lines is rolling, and in parts quite hilly; partially under cultivation, the rest lightly timbered; passable nearly everywhere for infantry and cavalry, in most parts for artillery also.

OUR LINE OF BATTLE.

The reader can now in an instant trace for himself our line of battle on the bisected A. Near the apex, the Cemetery, of course; batteries around the crest; infantry in line of battle down the declivity, in the orchard, and sweeping over the Taneytown road and up to that to Emmetsburgh. Then along the stone fence which skirts the hither side of the Emmetsburgh road for say half a mile. Then, bending in from the road a little, leaving its possession to our skirmishers alone, and so passing back for a mile and a half farther, in a line growing more and more distant from the Emmetsburgh road, and nearer that to Taneytown. These are the lines of centre and left. Beginning at the Cemetery again, our right stretches *across* the Baltimore pike and along the range of hills already described, in a direction that grows nearly parallel with the pike, (at a distance from it of a quarter to half a mile,) and down it a couple of miles. Measuring all its sinuosities, the line must be about five miles long.

THE REBEL LINES AND ORDER OF BATTLE.

All the country fronting this remarkable horseshoe line is virtually in the hands of the rebels. It will be seen that their lines must be longer than ours, and that in moving from one point to another of the field they are compelled to make long *detours*, while our troops can be thrown from left to right, or from either to centre, with the utmost ease, and by the shortest routes.

Take the crescent of the new moon, elongate the horns a little, turn the hollow side toward our positions, and you have the general direction the rebels were compelled to give their line of battle. As was seen in Wednesday's fight, Jackson's old corps, under Ewell, formed their left — opposite our right; while A. P. Hill held their centre, and Longstreet, who arrived early Thursday morning, their right.

OUR ORDER OF BATTLE.

On our front the line of battle was arranged by General Meade, at an early hour on Thursday morning, as follows: On the centre, holding Cemetery Hill and the declivity in its front, Major-General Howard, with his Eleventh corps.

Across the pike, on the adjacent hill to the right, what was left of the First corps. Next to it, and stretching to our extreme right, Major-General Slocum, with his Twelfth corps. Beginning again at the Cemetery Hill, and going toward the left, we have first, next to Howard, the Second corps, Major-General Hancock; next to it, the Third, Major-General Sickles; and partly to the rear of the Third, and subsequently brought up on the extreme left, the Fifth corps, Major-General Sykes. The Sixth corps, Major-General Sedgwick, was kept near the Taneytown pike, in the rear, and constituted the only reserve of the army.

CORPS AND DIVISION COMMANDERS.

General readers are scarcely likely to be interested in minute details of the organization of the army, but perhaps it will be convenient to have a roster by corps and divisions, at least.

FIRST CORPS—MAJOR-GENERAL REYNOLDS.

After General Reynolds's death, General Newton was assigned by General Meade to the command of this corps.
First division, ... Gen. Wadsworth.
Second division, ... Gen. Doubleday.
Third division, ... Gen. Robinson.

SECOND CORPS—MAJOR-GENERAL HANCOCK.

First division, ... Gen. Caldwell.
Second division, ... Gen. Gibbons.
Third division, ... Gen. Hayes.

THIRD CORPS—MAJOR-GENERAL SICKLES.

First division, ... Gen. Ward.
Second division, ... Gen. Humphrey.

FIFTH CORPS, (LATELY MEADE'S,) MAJOR-GEN. SYKES.

First division, ... Gen. Barnes.
Second division, ... Gen. Sykes.

ELEVENTH CORPS—MAJOR-GENERAL HOWARD.

First division, ... Major-Gen. Carl Schurz.
Second division, ... Brigadier-Gen. Steinwehr.
Third division, ... Brigadier-Gen. Barlow.

TWELFTH CORPS—MAJOR-GENERAL SLOCUM.

First division, ... Gen. Geary.
Second division, ... Gen. Green.
Third division, ... Gen. Williams.

Of Sedgwick's splendid Sixth corps, which only became engaged as reserves, were brought in on Friday, I cannot give the division commanders now, (there have been such changes since Fredericksburgh,) with any assurance of accuracy.

OUR CONCENTRATION AT GETTYSBURGH.

Our troops were not concentrated so early as those of the rebels, and but for their caution in so long feeling about our lines before making an attack, we might have suffered in consequence. Sedgwick's corps did not all get up till nearly dark Thursday evening, having been sent away beyond Westminster with a view to the intended movement on York. The Twelfth corps had arrived about sunset, Wednesday evening, a couple of hours or more after our repulse beyond Gettysburgh; the Second and Third during that night, and the Fifth about ten Thursday morning. For Thursday's fight the Fifth constituted the only reserve.

THURSDAY TILL FOUR O'CLOCK.

All Thursday forenoon there was lively firing between our skirmishers and those of the enemy, but nothing betokening a general engagement. Standing on Cemetery Hill, which, but for its exposed position, constituted the best point of observation on the field, I could see the long line of our skirmishers stretching around centre and left, well advanced, lying flat on the ground in the meadows or corn-fields and firing at will as they lay. The little streak of curling smoke that rose from their guns faded away in a thin vapor that marked the course of the lines down the left. With a glass the rebel line could be even more distinctly seen, every man of them with his blanket strapped over his shoulder—no foolish "stripping for the fight" with these trained soldiers. Occasionally the gray-coated fellows rose from cover, and with a yell rushed on our men, firing as they came. Once or twice in the half-hour that I watched them, they did this with such impetuosity as to force our skirmishers back, and call out a shell or two from our nearest batteries—probably the very object their officers had in view.

Toward noon I rode over to general headquarters, which had been established in a little, square, one-story, white-washed frame house, to the left and rear of the cemetery, and just under the low hill where our left joined the centre. No part of the line was visible from the spot, and it had been chosen, I suppose, because while within a three minutes' gallop of the Cemetery, or the hither portion of the left, it seemed comparatively protected by its situation. The choice was a bad one. Next to the Cemetery, it proved the hottest point on the field.

General Meade had finished his arrangement of the lines. Reports of the skirmishing were coming in; the facts developed by certain reconnoissances were being presented; the trim, well-tailored person of Major-General Pleasanton was constantly passing in and out; the cavalry seemed to be in incessant demand. General Williams and Major Barstow, the Adjutant-Generals, were hard at work sending out the orders; aids and orderlies were galloping off and back; General Warren, acting Chief of Staff, was with the General Commanding, poring over the maps of the field which the engineers had just finished; most of the staff were stretched beneath an apple tree, resting while they could.

It seemed that a heavy pressure had been brought to bear for an attack on the enemy, by the heads of columns in divisions, pouring the whole army on the enemy's centre, and smashing through it after the old Napoleonic plan; but Meade steadily resisted. The enemy was to fight him where he stood, was to come under the range of this long chain of batteries on the crests. **Wisely decided,** as the event proved.

The afternoon passed on in calm and cloudless splendor. From headquarters I rode down the left, then back to Slocum's headquarters, on a high hill, half or three quarters of a mile south from the Cemetery, on the Baltimore pike. Everywhere quiet, the men stretched lazily on the ground in line of battle, horses attached to the caissons, batteries unlimbered and gunners resting on their guns.

The thunderbolts were shut up, like Æolus' winds; it seemed as if the sun might set in peace over all this mighty enginery of destruction, held in calm, magnificent reserve.

THE REBEL ATTACK ON THE LEFT.

But unseen hands were letting loose the elements. General Meade had not failed to see the comparatively exposed position of our left; and between three and four the order was sent out for the extreme left—then formed by Sickles's (Third) corps—to advance. If the enemy was preparing to attack us there, our advance would soon unmask his movements.

It did. The corps moved out, spiritedly, of course—when, even in disastrous days, did it go otherwise to battle?—and by four o'clock had found the rebel advance. Longstreet was bringing up his whole corps—nearly a third of the rebel army—to precipitate upon our extreme left. The fight at once opened, with artillery first, presently with crashing roars of musketry, too. Rebel batteries were already in position, and some of them enfiladed Sickles's line. Our own were hastily set to work, and the most dangerous of the rebel guns were partially silenced. Then came a rebel charge, with the wild yell and rush; it is met by a storm of grape and canister from our guns, depressed to rake them in easy range. The line is shattered and sent whirling back on the instant. Long columns almost immediately afterward begin to debouch from the woods to the rear of the rebel batteries—another and a grander charge is preparing. General Warren who, as Chief of Staff, is overlooking the fight for the Commanding General, sends back for more troops. Alas! Sedgwick's corps is not yet available. We have only the Fifth for the reserves. Howard and Hancock are already at work on the centre and left centre. But Hancock advances, and the fire grows intenser still along the whole line of the left.

Meantime, Cemetery Hill is raked at once from front and left, and the shells from rebel batteries on the left carry over even into the positions held by our right. The battle rages on but one side, but death moves visibly over the whole field, from line to line, and front to rear. Trains are hurried away on the Baltimore pike; the unemployed *débris* of the army takes alarm, a panic in the rear seems impending. Guards thrown hastily across the roads to send the runaways back, do something to repress it.

The rebel lines we have seen debouching behind their batteries on Sickles's front slowly advance. The fight grows desperate, aid after aid is sent for reënforcements; our front wavers, the line of flame and smoke sways to and fro, but slowly settles backward. Sickles is being — not driven — but pushed back. At last the reserve comes in; the advance of the brigades of the Fifth wind down among the rocks and enter the smoke, the lines braces up, advances, halts soon, but comes no more back. The left is not over-powered yet. We have had two hours of ex-ceedingly severe artillery and musketry fighting. The enemy still holds a little of the ground we had, but the chances seem almost even.

ONE PHASE — A TYPE OF MANY.

I cannot trace the movements further in de-tail; let me give one phase of the fight, fit type of many more. Some Massachusetts batteries— Captain Bigelow's, Captain Phillips's, two or three more under Captain McGilvry of Maine — were planted on the extreme left, advanced now well down to the Emmetsburgh road, with in-fantry in their front — the first division, I think, of Sickles's corps. A little after five, a fierce rebel charge drove back the infantry and me-naced the batteries. Orders are sent to Bigelow on the extreme left, to hold his position at every hazard short of sheer annihilation, till a couple more batteries can be brought to his support. Reserving his fire a little, then with depressed guns opening with double charges of grape and canister, he smites and shatters, but cannot break the advancing line. His grape and can-ister are exhausted, and still, closing grandly up over their slain, on they come. He falls back on spherical case, and pours this in at the shortest range. On, still onward comes the artillery-de-fying line, and still he holds his position. They are within six paces of the guns—he fires again. Once more, and he blows devoted soldiers from his very muzzles. And still mindful of that solemn order, he holds his place. They spring upon his carriages and shoot down his horses! And then, his Yankee artillerists still about him, he seizes the guns by hand, and from the very front of that line drags two of them off. The caissons are further back — five out of the six are saved.

That single company, in that half-hour's fight, lost thirty-three of its men, including every ser-geant it had. The Captain himself was wounded. Yet it was the first time it was ever under fire! I give it simply as a type. *So* they fought along that fiery line!

The rebels now poured on Phillips's battery, and it, too, was forced to drag off the pieces by hand when the horses were shot down. From a new position it opened again; and at last the two reënforcing batteries came up on the gallop. An enfilading fire swept the rebel line; Sickles's gallant infantry charged, the rebel line swept back on a refluent tide — we regained the lost ground, and every gun just lost in this spendid fight.

Once more I repeat, this is but a type.

RE-ENFORCEMENTS CALLED IN FROM THE RIGHT.

Slocum, too, came into the fight. The reserves were all used up; the right seemed safe. It was believed from the terrific attack that the whole rebel army, Ewell's corps included, was massed on our centre and left; and so a single brigade was left to hold the rifle-pits constructed through the day along the whole line of the Twelfth, on the right; and the rest of the corps came across the little neck of land to strengthen our weakening line. Needful, perhaps, but perilous in the extreme.

THE CLOSE.

At six the cannonade grew fiercer than ever, and the storm of death swept over the field from then till darkness ended the conflict. In the main our strengthened columns held the line. At points they were forced back a little; a few prisoners were lost. On the whole the rebels were unsuccessful, but we had not quite held our own.

Some caissons had been blown up on either side; a barn on the Emmetsburgh road was fired by the rebel shells, and its light gave their sharp-shooters a little longer time at that point to work. Both sides lay on their arms exhausted, but in-satiate, to wait for the dawning.

RESULTS AND DOUBTFUL ISSUE.

The Third and Second corps were badly shat-tered. The Eleventh had not been quite so much engaged — its artillery had kept the rebels at a greater distance — but it had behaved well. Sic-kles was wounded — a leg shot off; Gen. Zook was killed; our own old townsman, Col. Cross, was killed; the farm-houses and barns for miles were filled with the wounded. The rebels had left us Barksdale, dying; what other losses they had met we could only conjecture from the piles of dead the last rays of the sun had shown along their front.

And so, with doubtful prospects, darkness came like a wall between us, and compelled na-ture's truce.

From the right there came sudden, sharp vol-leys of cheers; Ewell had *not* gone; a hasty rush had carried some of Slocum's rifle-pits, pro-tected only by the long-drawn-out line of a single brigade. It was a gloomy close. That was our strongest point, where Jackson's men had gained this fortified foot-hold.

Now, indeed, if ever, may the nation well wres-tle with God in prayer. We have fought but three hours and a half; have lost on both flanks; have called every reserve we had on the field into action, and with daybreak must hold these shat-tered columns to the work again. Well may the land take up the refrain of Boker's touching hymn for the Philadelphia Fourth.

"Help us, Lord, our only trust!
We are helpless, we are dust!
All our homes are red with blood;
Long our grief we have withstood;
Every lintel, each door-post,
Drips, at tidings from the host,
With the blood of some one lost.
Help us, Lord, our only trust!
We are helpless, we are dust!"

THE OPENING, FRIDAY MORNING.

I must be pardoned some egotism in what remains. It is easiest to narrate what one has seen, and undue prominence may thus come to be given to certain points, for time and space press me more and more.

At daybreak crashing volleys woke the few sleepers there were. A fusilade ran along the line—each had felt the other, then came cautious skirmishing again.

But on the right there was no cessation. Ewell's men were in possession of part of our rifle-pits, and sought to gain the remainder; Slocum must defend the one part and regain the other at every hazard. They were fighting Stonewall Jackson's men—it might well be desperate work.

I had gone down the Baltimore pike at night to find a resting-place—coming up between four and five, I heard clearly on the right the old charging cheer. Once, twice, three times I counted it, as my horse pushed his way for less than a mile through the curious or coward throng that ebbed and flowed along the pike. Each time a charge was made, each time the musketry fire leaped out from our line more terrific than before, and still the ground was held. To the left and centre, firing gradually ceased. All interest was concentred on this fierce contest on the right; the rest of the line on either side was bracing itself for still more desperate work.

From four to five there was heavy cannonading also, from our batteries nearest the contested points, but the artillery fire diminished and presently ceased. The rebels made no reply; we were firing at random, and it was a useless waste of ammunition. A cloud of smoke curled up from the dark woods on the right; the musketry crash continued with unparalleled tenacity and vehemence, wounded men came back over the fields, a few stragglers were hurried out to the front, ammunition was kept conveniently near the line.

In the fields to the left of the Baltimore pike stood the reserve artillery, with horses harnessed to the pieces and ready to move on the instant. Cavalry, too, was drawn up in detachments here and there. Moved over already within supporting distance of Slocum's line stood a part of Sedgwick's corps, (the reserve of to-day,) ready for the emergency that seemed likely soon to demand it. Occasional bullets from the rebel front spattered against the trees and fences. Now and then a Minie went over with its buzzing hiss, but the pike was too nearly out of range to be cleared of the watching throng.

GENERAL SICKLES.

Through this throng, with slow tread, there came a file of soldiers, armed, but marching to the rear. It was a guard of honor for one who well deserved it. On a stretcher, borne by a couple of stout privates, lay General Sickles—but yesterday leading his corps with all the enthusiasm and dash for which he has been distinguished—to-day with his right leg amputated, and lying there, grim and stoical, with his cap pulled over his eyes, his hands calmly folded across his breast, and *a cigar in his mouth!* For a man who had just lost a leg, and whose life was yet in imminent jeopardy, it was cool indeed. He was being taken to the nearest railroad line, to be carried to some city where he could get most careful attendance; and the guard that accompanied him showed that already there were some apprehensions for the rear.

There was reason for it. Less than an hour later orders were issued from Pleasanton's head-quarters, a mile or so further back on the Baltimore pike, for Gregg to take his cavalry force and guard against a dash down the valley of Rock Creek into the rear and centre. The rebels met the preparation and drew back to try it soon again further out the line.

THE BATTLE ON THE RIGHT.

I rode up the high hill where General Slocum's headquarters were established; but though it afforded an excellent view of most of our positions, the fight going on was concealed by a mask of woods on the distant hills. The Rodman guns on the hill were all manned, and the gunners were eager to try their range, but it still seemed useless. Firing in the woods, they were as likely to hit friend as foe. Signal-officers here were in communication with general headquarters, with Howard on Cemetery Hill, Hancock next him on the right, and one or two of the headquarters on the left. There was no fear of lack of certain communication between the different portions of the field, let the fortunes of the day go what way they would.

As I rode down the slope and up through the wheat-fields to Cemetery Hill, the batteries began to open again on points along our outer line. They were evidently playing on what had been Slocum's line of yesterday. The rebels, then, were there still, in our rifle-pits. Presently the battery on Slocum's hill gained the long-sought permission, and opened, too, aiming apparently in the same direction. Other batteries along the inner line, just to the left of the Baltimore pike, followed the signal, and as one after another opened up, till every little crest between Slocum's headquarters and Cemetery Hill began belching its thunder, I had to change my course through the wheat-fields to avoid our own shells.

Still no artillery response from the rebels. Could they be short of ammunition? Could they have failed to bring up all their guns? Were they, perhaps, massing artillery elsewhere, and only keeping up this furious crash of musketry on the right as a blind?

By eight o'clock I had reached Cemetery Hill. Yesterday's conflict was more plainly inscribed on the tombstones than the virtues of the buried dead they commemorated. Shells had ploughed up lately sodded graves; round shot had shattered marble columns; dead horses lay about among the monuments, and the gore of dead men soaked the soil and moistened the roots of flowers on the old graves.

This morning it was comparatively quiet again.

Sharp-shooters from the houses in the town were picking off officers who exposed themselves along the crest. They knew that we did not want to shell the place, and presumed upon the forbearance of our artillery. The annoyance had at last become too serious, and one of our guns had been directed to dislodge a nest of the most audacious and the surest aimed by battering down the house from which they were firing. It was the only house in Gettysburgh we harmed throughout the battles.

To the front skirmishers were still at work, but in a desultory way. All eyes were turned to the right; where now that our artillery had taken its share in the contest, its intensity seemed but redoubled by Ewell's men. Distinctly, even amid all this roar, there came up the sound of another of those ominous cheers; and the hurricane of crashing sound that followed seemed tearing the forest trees and solid hillside asunder. It was another rebel charge. Standing by the gate-keeper's lodge, with a glass I could distinctly see our shattered line swinging irregularly and convulsively back from those death-bearing woods. The rebel yells redoubled, but so did our artillery fire, now that the gunners saw exactly where to throw. The retreat lasted for but a moment, the line straightened, rallied, plunged into the woods again.

A TRIED GENERAL.

All this while—the fire gradually getting a little hotter on the hill, and an occasional shell from the rebel guns, now beginning to open, coming over—General Howard was calmly reclining against a hillock by a grave-stone, with his staff about him. One or two he kept constantly watching the right, and occasionally sweeping the whole rebel line with their glasses; the rest were around him, ready for instant service. I have seen many men in action, but never one so imperturbably cool as this General of the Eleventh corps. I watched him closely as a Minie whizzed overhead. I dodged, of course; I never expect to get over that habit; but I am confident he did not move a muscle by the fraction of a hair's breadth.

PROGRESS ON THE RIGHT.

About a quarter after nine the conflict in the woods to the right seemed to be culminating. Clouds of smoke obscured the view, but beyond that smoke we knew that our noble line—the Twelfth and a part of the First, with some reserves, were now engaged—was holding its ground; the direction of the sound even seemed to indicate that it was gaining, but of course that was a very uncertain test. "Ride over to General Meade," said Howard to one of his aids, "and tell him the fighting on the right seems more terrific than ever, and appears swinging somewhat toward the centre, but that we know little or nothing of how the battle goes, and ask him if he has any orders." In a few minutes the aid galloped back. "The troops are to stand to arms, sir, and watch the front."

Meantime there was a little diversion away down

toward the extreme right. A brigade had been thrown east of Rock Creek to watch the possible attempt at repeating the effort to get down the valley into our rear. Finding a good opportunity, it began to pour in its volleys upon Ewell's flank. The audacity of a single brigade attempting such a thing was beyond rebel suspicion; they naturally thought a heavy force was turning their flank, and were less inclined to push on Slocum's sorely pressed men in front.

Nothing seemed to come of Howard's "watching the front;" the fire of skirmishers revived occasionally, and then died away again; and finally, about a quarter before ten, I started over to general headquarters. In descending the Cemetery Hill, and crossing the intervening fields, I noticed that some bullets were beginning to come over from our left, but supposed them of course to be merely stray shots from the rebel skirmishers.

THE COMMANDER-IN-CHIEF AT HEADQUARTERS.

Headquarters presented a busy scene. Meade was receiving reports in the little house, coming occasionally to the door to address a hasty inquiry to some one in the group of staff-officers under the tree. Quick and nervous in his movements, but calm, and as it seemed to me, lit up with the glow of the occasion, he looked more the General, less the student. Polished, fashionable-looking Pleasanton, riding-whip resting in the leg of one of his jack-boots, and neatly-fitting kids drawn over his hands, occasionally put in some earnest remark. Warren, calm, absorbed, earnest as ever, was constantly in consultation with the Commander.

In all matters of detail, Williams or Major Barstow was referred to as to an encyclopedia. Orderlies and aids were momentarily dashing up with reports and off with orders; the signal-officers were bringing in the reports telegraphed by the signal-flags from the different crests that overlooked the fight. The rest of the staff stood ready for any duty, and outside the little garden-fence a great group of horses stood hitched.

HEADQUARTERS UNDER FIRE.

W., my original companion from Baltimore, was up at last, and very sad. His son, a gallant young lieutenant of regular artillery, had had his leg shot off in Wednesday's disastrous fight, and whether living now or dead he could not tell; he was a prisoner (or a corpse) in Gettysburgh.

We walked around to the east of the little house and lay down on the grass. Others were there; there was much comparison of views, talk of probabilities, gossip of the arrival of militia from Harrisburgh. The fight still raged furiously on the right. Headquarters were under a slight fire. The balls from the left seemed to increase a little in number; a few came over from the front; we saw no damage that any of them did.

Close by our heads went one, evidently from some kind of small arm that had an unfamiliar sound. "That," said W., æsthetic always, or nothing, "that is a muffled howl; that's the exact phrase to describe it." We discussed the question.

Wh-r-sh-shhh! A sudden exclamation and start all around the group. "Jove!" exclaims one, impulsively; "those fellows on the left have the range of headquarters exactly." It was a round shot that had passed not two feet from the door and buried itself in the road three or four yards in front of us. In an instant there was another and another. General Meade came to the door, told the staff that they manifestly had our range, and that they had best go up the slope fifteen or twenty yards to the stable. As they started, a couple of shells came, then more from a different direction, and a sharp fusilade broke out just behind us on the left. Two rebel batteries clearly had our range, and the fight seemed opening up on the field of last night's bitterest contest.

A few minutes before, I had been talking of going down to look at Barksdale's corpse—there was other work to do than looking at dead men now. Leaving the late headquarters to the shells, I galloped out the Taneytown road along the left. For three quarters of a mile the fire was bursting out.

The air was alive with all mysterious sounds, and death in every one of them. There were "muffled howls" that seemed in rage because their missile missed you, the angry buzz of the familiar Minie, the *spit* of the common musket-ball, hisses, and the great whirring rushes of shells. And then there came others that made the air instinct with warning, or quickened it with vivid alarm; long wails that fatefully bemoaned the death they wrought; fluttering screams that filled the whole space with their horror, and encompassed one about as a garment; cries that ran the diapason of terror and despair.

RISE AND EBB OF THE TIDE OF BATTLE.

It had been a sudden concentration of terrific artillery fire, on our left, with a view to silence our batteries, and sweep resistance from the slopes before they charged. But they did not find us unprepared. The tornado of death that swept over the fields levelled much before it, but not all. After an hour or two it was found that the obstinate defenders still clung to their positions; and the rebels saw they must reserve their energies for the more determined and persistent effort the afternoon was to bring. On it, as on the last toss of the dice, they had staked their all. In an hour or two the left was silent again; on the centre there were but the accustomed straggling shots.

THE RIGHT VICTORIOUS.

Meantime on the right, the fierceness of Ewell's attack had dashed itself out, and but feeble surges came up now against our line. Leaving the left as the attack there was dying away, I rode over again to Slocum's Hill, on the Baltimore pike. From this high eminence we could only make out that the line seemed in its old place, and so the officers said it was. The rifle-pits had been regained; Ewell's corps had been substantially repulsed. The musketry still flickered sharply up occasionally, but the fire had gone out of it. We were practically victorious on the right. It was a quarter-past eleven—seven hours and a quarter of desperate fighting! The old Jackson corps had not given up without an obstinate struggle.

CAVALRY—A LULL.

Away down from the extreme right, and apparently beyond it, there came a ripple of musketry. It was said to be Smith's division from Couch's Harrisburgh force, coming in on Ewell's flank or rear. I have not yet been able to satisfy myself whether the report was true or not.

A quarter of an hour later Pleasanton's scouts reported rebel cavalry coming in on the Bonaughtown road, on the right, to strike the Baltimore pike in our rear. Gregg was instantly sent off to meet them, with orders merely to hold them in check, and not to bring on a close engagement if he could avoid it. At the same time Kilpatrick was ordered to the extreme left to harass the enemy's flank and rear and look after his trains. "Good!" exclaimed Kilpatrick, rubbing his hands, and in a moment was hurrying gleefully to execute the order.

Gregg threw his force up a little brook that comes down between Rock Creek and the post village of Two Taverns. The rebel cavalry no sooner saw their plan detected than they retired. But their effort was not over, and fortunately Gregg understood it. Under cover of the woods, they moved still further south, in a direction parallel with the Baltimore pike; but Gregg was moving too, and when they started out toward the pike, they were again confronted. There was a little carbine firing now, and some sharp shelling, and the rebels again retired. Once more they came out, almost opposite Two Taverns, late in the afternoon, but Gregg was still on the watch for them, and they at once and finally retired without a shot.

There was a lull from a quarter-past eleven to about one. Fitful firing broke out and died away again, here and there, but the lines were mainly silent. The rebels were not yet defeated—except for the hour's sharp work on the left, two of their corps with their reserves had not been engaged at all to-day. Some final, desperate effort must be maturing. Shrewd officers predicted that it would be a massing of all their troops on the left. But Ewell's corps could not possibly be brought over in time for that; its work for the day must be nearly done.

THE LAST DESPERATE ATTACK.

Pretty soon the attack came—sooner, indeed, and wider than was expected. About one the rebel movement was developed in a thunder of cannonading that rolled over our army like doom. They had concentrated immense quantities of artillery—"two hundred and fifty pieces, at least," some of General Meade's staff-officers said, on our centre and left, and those devoted lines were to bear the last, fiercest shock, that, staunchly met, should leave the exhausted rebel army drifting back from its supreme effort, a defeated host. Longstreet and A. P. Hill were to support and follow up the artillery attack, and the reserves were with them.

Soon, from the Cemetery hill, (I did not see this, but tell it as actors in it told me,) could be seen the forming columns of Hill's corps. Their batteries had already opened in almost a semicircle of fire on that scarred hill-front. Three cross-fires thus came in upon it, and to-day the tracks of shells ploughing the ground in as many directions may be seen everywhere among the graves. Howard never moved his headquarters an inch. There was his Eleventh corps, and there he meant to stay, and make them do their duty if he could. They did it well.

When the fierce cannonade had, as they supposed, sufficiently prepared the way, down came the rebel lines, "dressed to the right" as if for a parade before some grand master of reviews. To the front they had a line of skirmishers, double or treble the usual strength, next the line of battle for the charge, next another equally strong in reserve, if the fierce fire they might meet should melt away the first.

Howard sent orders for his men to lie down, and for a little our batteries ceased firing. The rebels thought they had silenced us, and charged. They were well up to our front when that whole corps of concealed Germans sprang up and poured out their sheet of flame and smoke, and swiftly-flying death; the batteries opened—the solid lines broke, and crisped up into little fragments, and were beaten wildly back. Our men charged; company after company, once at least a whole regiment, threw down their arms and rushed over to be taken prisoners and carried out of this fearful fire.

Simultaneously, similar scenes were enacting along the front of the Second, Third, and Fifth corps. Everywhere the rebel attack was beaten back, and the cannonade on both sides continued at its highest pitch.

When this broke out, I had been coming over from the neighborhood of Pleasanton's headquarters. Ascending the high hill to the rear of Slocum's headquarters, I saw such a sight as few men may ever hope to see twice in a lifetime. Around our centre and left, the rebel line must have been from four to five miles long, and over that whole length there rolled up the smoke from their two hundred and fifty guns. The roar, the bursting bombs, the impression of magnificent power, "all the glory visible, all the horror of the fearful field concealed," a nation's existence trembling as the clangor of those iron monsters swayed the balance—it was a sensation for a century!

About two the fire slackened a little, then broke out deadlier than ever, till, beaten out against our impenetrable sides, it ebbed away, and closed in broken, spasmodic dashes.

The great, desperate, final charge came at four. The rebels seemed to have gathered up all their strength and desperation for one fierce, convulsive effort, that should sweep over and wash out our obstinate resistance. They swept up as before, the flower of their army to the front, victory staked upon the issue. In some places they literally lifted up and pushed back our lines, but, that terrible "position" of ours!—wherever they entered it, enfilading fires from half a score of crests swept away their columns like merest chaff. Broken and hurled back, they easily fell into our hands, and on the centre and left the last half-hour brought more prisoners than all the rest.

So it was along the whole line; but it was on the Second corps that the flower of the rebel army was concentrated; it was there that the heaviest shock beat upon and shook and even sometimes crumbled our line.

We had some shallow rifle-pits, with barricades of rails from the fences. The rebel line, stretching away miles to the left, in magnificent array, but strongest here—Pickett's splendid division of Longstreet's corps in front, the best of A. P. Hill's veterans in support—came steadily and as it seemed resistlessly sweeping up. Our skirmishers retired slowly from the Emmetsburgh road, holding their ground tenaciously to the last. The rebels reserved their fire till they reached this same Emmetsburgh road, then opened with a terrific crash. From a hundred iron throats, meantime, their artillery had been thundering on our barricades.

Hancock was wounded; Gibbons succeeded to the command—approved soldier, and ready for the crisis. As the tempest of fire approached its height, he walked along the line, and renewed his orders to the men to reserve their fire. The rebels—three lines deep—came steadily up. They were in point-blank range.

At last the order came! From thrice six thousand guns there came a sheet of smoky flame, a crash, a rush of leaden death. The line literally melted away; but there came the second, resistless still. It had been our supreme effort—on the instant we were not equal to another.

Up to the rifle-pits, across them, over the barricades—the momentum of their charge, the mere machine strength of their combined action swept them on. Our thin line could fight, but it had not weight enough to oppose to this momentum. It was pushed behind the guns. Right on came the rebels. They were upon the guns, were bayoneting the gunners, were waving their flags above our pieces.

But they had penetrated to the fatal point. A storm of grape and canister tore its way from man to man and marked its track with corpses straight down their line! They had exposed themselves to the enfilading fire of the guns on the western slope of Cemetery Hill; that exposure sealed their fate.

The line reeled back—disjointed already—in an instant in fragments. Our men were just behind the guns. They leaped forward upon the disordered mass; but there was little need for fighting now. A regiment threw down its arms, and, with colors at its head, rushed over and surrendered. All along the field smaller detachments did the same. Webb's brigade brought in eight hundred taken in as little time as it requires to write the simple sentence that tells it. Gibbons's old division took fifteen stand of colors.

Over the fields the escaped fragments of the charging line fell back—the battle there was over. A single brigade, Harrow's, (of which the Seventh Michigan is part,) came out with fifty-four less officers, seven hundred and ninety-three less men than it took in! So the whole corps fought—so too they fought further down the line.

FINIS.

It was fruitless sacrifice. They gathered up their broken fragments, formed their lines, and slowly marched away. It was not a rout, it *was* a bitter crushing defeat. For once the army of the Potomac had won a clean, honest, acknowledged victory.

Yet we were very near defeat. Our ammunition had grown scant; the reserve ammunition-train had been brought up and drained; but for that we should have been left to cold steel.

Brigade after brigade had been thrown forward to strengthen the line; as the rebel attack drifted back over the fields there stood in the rear just one single brigade that constituted the entire reserve of the army of the Potomac. Forty thousand fresh troops to have hurled forward upon that retreating mass would have ended the campaign with the battle; but, for forty thousand we had that one wasted brigade! The rebels were soon formed again, and ready for defence—the opportunity was lost!

Shells still dropped over the Cemetery, by the headquarters and in the wheat-fields toward the Baltimore pike; but the fight was over.

Headquarters were established anew under the trees in a little wood near Slocum's Hill. General Meade rode up, calm as ever, and called for paper and aids; he had orders already to issue. A band came marching in over the hill-side; on the evening air its notes floated out—significant melody—"Hail to the Chief."

"Ah! General Meade," said W., "you're in very great danger of being President of the United States." "No," said another, more wisely, as it seems. "Finish well this work so well begun, and the position you have is better and prouder than President."   AGATE.

IV. AFTER THE BATTLE.

Our campaign "after the invaders" was over. There was brief time for last glances at the field, last questions after the dead and dying—then the hurried trip west, and the misery of putting together, from the copious notes taken on the field, on swaying railroad cars, and amid jostling crowds, the story of the day.

The morning after the battle was as sweet, and fresh as though no storm of death had all the day before been sweeping over those quiet Pennsylvania hills and valleys. The roads were lined with ambulances, returning to the field for the last of the wounded; soldiers exchanging greetings after the battle with their comrades, and comparing notes of the day; officers looking after their wounded men, or hunting up the supplies for their regiments. Detachments of rebel prisoners, every few moments, passed back under guard; the woods inside our line had been full of them all night, and we were just beginning to gather them up. Every body was in the most exuberant spirits. For once this army had won a real victory—the soldiers felt it, and the sensation was so novel, they could not but be ecstatic.

THE FIELD.

Along the lines on the left a sharp popping of skirmishers was still kept up. I rode down over the scene of yesterday's fiercest conflict, and at the cost of some exposure, and the close passage of a couple of Minie balls, got a view of the thickly strewn rebel corpses that still cast up to heaven their mute protest against the treason that had made them what they were. But the details of these horrible scenes are too sickening, and alas! too familiar; I must be excused from their description.

AT HEADQUARTERS.

Headquarters—still over in the woods near Slocum's Hill—were in bivouac. The General had a little wall-tent, in which he was dictating orders and receiving despatches; General Ingalls, the Chief Quartermaster, had his writing-table in the open end of a covered wagon; the rest, majors, colonels, generals and all, had slept on the ground, and were now standing about the camp-fires, hands full of fried pork and hard bread, making their breakfasts in a style that a year ago would have astonished the humblest private in the army of the Potomac.

The cavalry generals were again in request, and heavy reconnoissances were ordered. The bulk of the rebel army was believed to be in full retreat; one strong corps could still be seen, strongly posted on well-chosen heights to the northward, and drawn up in line of battle, to repel any attempt at direct pursuit.

The casualties on the staff were wonderfully small. General Warren, acting Chief of Staff, had a remarkable escape. A Minie ball passed directly under his chin, cut his throat in a little line that, with half an inch's motion in his head, or change in the direction of the ball, would have been converted into a deathly wound. As it was, his shirt was stained with the blood that trickled down, but he did not think the wound worth binding up.

It has been telegraphed, and re-telegraphed, and telegraphed again from headquarters, that General Butterfield was badly wounded. He received a slight blow on the back, Friday afternoon, from a spent fragment of shell, I believe; but it did not even break the skin.

These, with the wounding of Lieutenant-Colonel Dickinson, Aid to General Meade, constituted the only casualties on the staff.

Major Barstow, the efficient Adjutant-General, received fragments of shells on both sides of his saddle, but escaped unhurt.

THE FIRE AT HEADQUARTERS.

It was not, however, because they had little exposure that their losses were small. How we were nearly all driven away from headquarters Friday forenoon by the furious cannonade, has already been told; but my friend and companion on that morning, Mr. Samuel Wilkeson, of the New-York *Times*, has so vividly described the scene, that I must be allowed to reproduce it:

"In the shadow cast by the tiny farm-house, sixteen by twenty, which General Meade had made his headquarters, lay wearied staff-officers and tired correspondents. There was not wanting to the peacefulness of the scene the singing of a bird, which had a nest in a peach tree within the tiny yard of the white-washed cottage. In the midst of its warbling, a shell screamed over the house, instantly followed by another and another, and in a moment the air was full of the most complete artillery prelude to an infantry battle that was ever exhibited. Every size and form of shell known to British and to American gunnery, shrieked, whirled, moaned, and whistled and wrathfully fluttered over our ground. As many as six in a second, constantly two in a second, bursting and screaming over and around the headquarters, made a very hell of fire that amazed the oldest officers. They burst in the yard—burst next to the fence on both sides, garnished as usual with the hitched horses of aids and orderlies. The fastened animals reared and plunged with terror. Then one fell, then another—sixteen lay dead and mangled before the fire ceased, still fastened by their halters, which gave the expression of being wickedly tied up to die painfully. These brute victims of a cruel war touched all hearts. Through the midst of the storm of screaming and exploding shells, an ambulance driven by its frenzied conductor at full speed, presented to all of us the marvellous spectacle of a horse going rapidly on three legs. A hinder one had been shot off at the hock. A shell tore up the little step at the headquarters cottage, and ripped bags of oats as with a knife. Another soon carried off one of its two pillars. Soon a spherical case burst opposite the open door—another ripped through the low garret. The remaining pillar went almost immediately to the howl of a fixed shot that Whitworth must have made. During this fire the horses at twenty and thirty feet distant were receiving their death, and soldiers in Federal blue were torn to pieces in the road, and died with the peculiar yells that blend the extorted cry of pain with horror and despair. Not an orderly—not an ambulance—not a straggler was to be seen upon the plain swept by this tempest of orchestral death, thirty minutes after it commenced. Were not one hundred and twenty pieces of artillery trying to cut from the field every battery we had in position to resist their purposed infantry attack, and to sweep away the slight defences behind which our infantry were waiting? Forty minutes—fifty minutes—counted watches that ran, oh! so languidly! Shells through the two lower rooms. A shell into the chimney, that daringly did not explode. Shells in the yard. The air thicker and fuller and more deafening with the howling and whirring of these infernal missiles. The Chief of Staff struck—Seth Williams—loved and respected through the army, separated from instant death by two inches of space vertically measured. An aid bored with a fragment of iron through the bone of the arm. And the time measured on the sluggish watches was one hour and forty minutes."

HOW THE CORRESPONDENTS FACED DEATH.

To this vivid description, in justice to its author, let me add that Mr. Wilkeson staid at the house during this whole terrible cannonade. Mr. Frank Henry, also of the *Times*, likewise stood it out. Their accounts may well be said to have the smell of fire upon them!

C. C. Coffin, of the Boston *Journal*, and L. L. Crounse, of the New-York *Times* as well as several other journalists of whom I knew less, were at different times under almost equally heavy fire. Mr. Crounse had his horse shot under him during Thursday's engagement. Such perils are they compelled to face who would be able to say something more of a battle than what those who are first out of it, can tell.

ONCE MORE ON CEMETERY HILL—DEPARTURE.

We could linger no longer on the field. My companion for the last day or two, Mr. Coffin, and myself, resolved on reaching Baltimore that night. The Northern Central Railroad was still broken, and from Baltimore my shortest road west lay *via* Philadelphia. With such a circuitous route ahead, there was no time to spare.

We rode up the Cemetery hill, for a last look at the field. It was ploughed and torn in every direction by the fierce cross-fires of artillery that had spent their force upon it. Dead men, decently laid out, were in the gate-keeper's lodge. Upturned, swollen horses lay among the tombs, where the sudden shot or shell had stricken them down. Batteries still frowned from the crest; away to the front the rebel line (a strong rear-guard only now) could still be distinctly seen. Howard, Carl Schurz, Steinwehr, and two or three others of lesser rank, were watching the movements through their glasses, and discussing the probabilities.

There was a rush of letters to be mailed and telegraph messages to be sent. Among the number came Henry Ward Beecher's son, a bluff, hearty-looking youth. He had a despatch to Mrs. Stowe he wanted me to send, announcing that her son, too, was among the wounded, and would soon be sent home to her.

On an old grave, that a shell had rudely torn, while a round shot had battered down the iron railing about it, were still blooming the flowers affection's hand had planted in more peaceful times—not a petal shaken off by all this tempest that had swept and whirled and torn about them. Human blood watered the roots—patriot blood, that made them doubly sacred. I stooped and gathered them—roses and columbine, and modest, sweet-scented pinks, mingled with sprigs of cypress—they are my only trophy from that glorious field.

Good-by to Gettysburgh—a mad gallop to Westminster, (which brought our day's ride up to nearly fifty miles,) to catch a train that after all, loaded with wounded soldiers as it was, spent the whole night backing and hauling on side tracks and switches; and so at last to Baltimore; and out of the field once more. May it be forever. AGATE.

GAZETTE OFFICE, July 8.

MAJOR-GENERAL MEADE'S REPORT.

HEADQUARTERS ARMY OF THE POTOMAC, October 1, 1863.

GENERAL: I have the honor to submit herewith a report of the operations of this army during the month of July, including details of the battle of Gettysburgh, which have been delayed by failure to receive the reports of the several corps and division commanders, who were severely wounded in battle.

On the twenty-eighth of June I received orders from the President, placing me in command of the army of the Potomac.

The situation of affairs was briefly as follows: The confederate army, which was commanded by Gen. R. E. Lee, was estimated at over one hundred thousand strong. All that army had crossed the Potomac River and advanced up the Cumberland Valley. Reliable intelligence placed his advance thus: Ewell's corps on the Susquehanna, Harrisburgh, and Columbia; Longstreet's corps at Chambersburgh; and Hill's corps between that place and Cashtown.

The twenty-eighth of June was spent in ascertaining the positions and strength of the different corps of the army, but principally in bringing up the cavalry which had been covering the rear of the army in its passage over the Potomac, and to which a large increase had just been made from the force previously attached to the defences of Washington.

Orders were given on this day to Major-General French, commanding at Harper's Ferry, to move with seven thousand men to occupy Frederick and the line of the Baltimore and Ohio Railroad, with the balance of his force, estimated at four thousand, to remove and escort public property to Washington.

On the twenty-ninth the army was put in motion, and on the evening of that day it was in position, the left at Emmetsburgh and the right at New-Windsor. Buford's division of cavalry was on the left flank, with his advance at Gettysburgh. Kilpatrick's division was in the front at Hanover, where he encountered this day General Stuart's confederate cavalry, which had crossed the Potomac at Seneca Creek, and passing our right flank, was making its way toward Carlisle, having escaped Gregg's division, which was delayed in taking position on the right flank by the occupation of the roads by a column of infantry.

On the thirtieth the right flank of the army was moved up to Manchester, the left still being at Emmettsburgh, or in that vicinity, at which place three corps, First, Eleventh, and Third, were collected under the orders of Major-General Reynolds.

Gen. Buford having reported from Gettysburgh the appearance of the enemy on the Cashtown road in some force, Gen. Reynolds was directed to occupy Gettysburgh.

On reaching that place, on the first day of July, General Reynolds found Buford's cavalry warmly engaged with the enemy, who had debouched his infantry through the mountains on Cashtown, but was being held in check in the most gallant manner by Buford's cavalry. Major-General Reynolds immediately moved around the town of Gettysburgh, and advanced on the Cashtown road, and without a moment's hesitation deployed his advanced division and attacked the enemy, at the same time sending orders for the Eleventh corps, General Howard, to advance as promptly as possible.

Soon after making his dispositions for attack, Major-Gen. Reynolds fell mortally wounded, the command of the First corps devolving on Major-General Doubleday, and the command of the field on Major-Gen. Howard, who arrived about this time (half-past eleven A.M.) with the Eleventh corps, then commanded by Major-Gen. Schurz. Major-Gen. Howard pushed forward two divisions of the Eleventh corps to support the First corps, now warmly engaged with the enemy on a ridge to the north of the town, and posted his third division, with three batteries of artillery, on the Cemetery ridge, on the south side of the town.

Up to this time the battle had been with the forces of the enemy debouching from the mountains on the Cashtown road, known to be Hill's corps. In the early part of the action the success was on the enemy's side. Wadsworth's division of the First corps having driven the enemy back some distance, captured numerous prisoners, among them Gen. Archer, of the confederate army.

The arrival of reënforcements to the enemy on the Cashtown road, and the junction of Ewell's corps coming in on the York and Harrisburgh roads, which occurred between one and two o'clock P.M., enabled the enemy to bring vastly superior forces against both the First and Eleventh corps, outflanking our line of battle, and pressing it so severely that, about four o'clock P.M., Major-General Howard deemed it prudent to withdraw these two corps to the Cemetery ridge, on the south side of the town, which operation was successfully accomplished — not, however, without considerable loss in prisoners, arising from the confusion incident to portions of both corps passing through the town, and the men getting confused in the streets.

About the time of the withdrawal, Major-Gen. Hancock arrived, whom I had despatched to represent me on the field, on hearing of the death of General Reynolds. In conjunction with Major-Gen. Howard, Gen. Hancock proceeded to post the troops on Cemetery ridge, and to repel an attack that the enemy made on our right flank. This attack was not, however, very vigorous; the enemy, seeing the strength of the position occupied, seemed to be satisfied with the success he had accomplished, desisting from any further attack this day.

About seven o'clock P.M. Major-Gens. Slocum and Sickles, with the Twelfth corps and part of the Third, reached the ground and took post on the right and left of the troops previously posted. Being satisfied, from reports received from the field, that it was the intention of the enemy to support, with his whole army, the attack already made, and reports from Major-Gens. Hancock and Howard on the character of the position being favorable, I determined to give battle at this point, and early in the evening first issued orders to all corps to concentrate at Gettysburgh, directing all trains to be sent to the rear at Westminster at eleven P.M. first.

I broke up my headquarters, which till then had been at Taneytown, and proceeded to the field, arriving there at one A.M. of the second. So soon as it was light I proceeded to inspect the position occupied and to make arrangements for posting several corps as they should reach the ground.

By seven A.M. the Second and Fifth corps, with the rest of the Third, had reached the ground, and were posted as follows: The Eleventh corps retained its position on Cemetery ridge, just opposite to the town; the First corps was posted on the right; the Eleventh on an elevated knoll connecting with the ridge and extending to the south and east, on which the Twelfth corps was placed, the right of the Twelfth corps resting on a small stream at a point where it crossed the Baltimore pike, and which formed on the right flank of the Twelfth something of an obstacle.

Cemetery ridge extended in a westerly and southerly direction, gradually diminishing in elevation till it came to a very prominent ridge called "Round Top," running east and west. The Second and Third corps were directed to occupy the continuation of Cemetery ridge, on the left of the Eleventh corps and Fifth corps; pending their arrival the Sixth corps was held in reserve. While these dispositions were being made, the enemy was massing his troops on an exterior ridge, distant from the line occupied by us from a mile to a mile and a half.

At two P.M. the Sixth corps arrived, after a march of thirty-two miles, which was accomplished from nine P.M. of the day previous. On its arrival being reported, I immediately directed the Fifth corps to move over to our extreme left, and the Sixth to occupy its place as a reserve for the right.

About three P.M. I rode out to the extreme left to await the arrival of the Fifth corps and post it, when I found that Major-General Sickles, commanding the Third corps, not fully apprehending my instructions in regard to the position to be occupied, had advanced, or rather was in the act of advancing his corps some half-mile or three quarters of a mile in the front of the line of the Second corps on a prolongation which it was designed his corps should rest.

Having found Major-General Sickles, I was ex-plaining to him that he was too far in the advance, and discussing with him the propriety of withdrawing, when the enemy opened upon him with several batteries in his front and his flank, and immediately brought forward columns of infantry, and made a vigorous assault. The Third corps sustained the shock most heroically. Troops from the Second corps were immediately sent by Major-General Hancock to cover the right flank of the Third corps, and soon after the assault commenced.

The Fifth corps most fortunately arrived, and took a position on the left of the Third, Major-General Sykes commanding, immediately sending a force to occupy "Round Top" ridge, where a most furious contest was maintained, the enemy making desperate but unsuccessful efforts to secure it. Notwithstanding the stubborn resistance of the Third corps, under Major-General Birney, (Major-General Sickles having been wounded early in the action,) superiority in numbers of corps of the enemy enabling him to outflank its advanced position, General Birney was counselled to fall back and re-form, behind the line originally desired to be held.

In the mean time, perceiving the great exertions of the enemy, the Sixth corps, Major-General Sedgwick, and part of the First corps, to which I had assigned Major-General Newton, particularly Lockwood's Maryland brigade, together with detachments from the Second corps, were all brought up at different periods, and succeeded, together with a gallant resistance of the Fifth corps, in checking and finally repulsing the assault of the enemy, who retired in confusion and disorder about sunset, and ceased any further efforts on our extreme left.

An assault was, however, made about eight P.M. on the Eleventh corps, from the left of the town, which was repelled by the assistance of troops from the Second and First corps. During the heavy assault upon our extreme left, portions of the Twelfth corps were sent as reënforcements.

During their absence the line on the extreme right was held by a very much reduced force. This was taken advantage of by the enemy, who, during the absence of Geary's division of the Twelfth corps, advanced and occupied part of the line.

On the morning of the third July, General Geary having returned during the night, attacked at early dawn the enemy and succeeded in driving him back and reoccupying his former position. A spirited contest was maintained all the morning along this part of the line. General Geary, reënforced by Wheaton's brigade of the Sixth corps, maintained his position and inflicted very severe losses on the enemy.

With this exception, our lines remained undisturbed till one P.M. on the third, when the enemy opened from over one hundred and twenty-five guns, playing upon our centre and left. This cannonade continued for over two hours, when, our guns failing to make any reply, the enemy ceased firing, and soon his masses of infantry became visible, forming for an assault on our left and left centre.

An assault was made with great firmness, directed principally against the point occupied by the Second corps, and was repelled with equal firmness by the troops of that corps, supported by Doubleday's division and Stannard's brigade of the First corps. During this assault both Major-General Hancock, commanding the left centre, and Brigadier-General Gibson, commanding the Second corps, were severely wounded.

This terminated the battle, the enemy retiring to his lines, leaving the field strewed with his dead and wounded, and numerous prisoners in our hands.

Buford's division of cavalry, after its arduous service at Gettysburgh, on the first, was, on the second, sent to Westminster to refit and guard our trains. Kilpatrick's division, that on the twenty-ninth, thirtieth, and first had been successfully engaging the enemy's cavalry, was, on the third, sent out on our extreme left, on the Emmetsburgh road, where good service was rendered in assaulting the enemy's line and occupying his attention.

At the same time General Gregg was engaged with the enemy on our extreme right, having passed across the Baltimore pike and Bonaughtown roads, and boldly attacked the enemy's left and rear.

On the morning of the fourth the reconnoissances developed that the enemy had drawn back his left flank, but maintained his position in front of our left, apparently assuming a new line parallel to the mountain.

On the morning of the fifth it was ascertained that the enemy was in full retreat by the Fairfield and Cashtown roads. The Sixth corps was immediately sent in pursuit on the Fairfield road, and the cavalry on the Cashtown road, and by Emmetsburgh and Monterey passes.

The fifth and sixth of July were employed in succoring the wounded and burying the dead.

Major-General Sedgwick, commanding the Sixth corps, having pushed on in pursuit of the enemy as far as Fairfield Pass in the mountains, and reporting that pass as very strong, and one in which a small force of the enemy could hold in check and delay for a considerable time any pursuing force, I determined to follow the enemy by a flank movement, and accordingly leaving McIntosh's brigade of cavalry and Neill's brigade of infantry to continue harassing the enemy, I put the army in motion for Middletown, Maryland.

Orders were immediately sent to Major-General French, at Frederick, to reöccupy Harper's Ferry, and to send a force to occupy Turner's Pass, in South-Mountain. I subsequently ascertained that Major-General French had not only anticipated these orders in part, but had pushed his cavalry force to Williamsport and Falling Waters, where they destroyed the enemy's ponton-bridge and captured its guard. Buford was at the same time sent to Williamsport and Hagerstown.

The duty above assigned to the cavalry was most successfully accomplished, the enemy being greatly harassed, his trains destroyed, and many captures in guns and prisoners made. After halting a day at Middletown to procure necessary supplies and to bring up trains, the army moved through South-Mountain, and by the twelfth of July was in front of the enemy, who occupied a strong position on the heights of Marsh Run, in advance of Williamsport.

In taking this position, several skirmishes and affairs had been had with the enemy, principally by cavalry, from the Eleventh and Sixth corps.

The thirteenth was occupied in making reconnoissances of the enemy's position and preparations for attack, but on advancing on the morning of the fourteenth, it was ascertained he had retired the night previous by a bridge at Falling Waters and a ford at Williamsport.

The cavalry in pursuit overtook the rear-guard at Falling Waters, capturing two guns and numerous prisoners.

Previous to the retreat of the enemy, Gregg's division of cavalry had crossed at Harper's Ferry, and coming up with the rear of the enemy at Charlestown and Shepherdstown, had a spirited contest, in which the enemy were driven to Martinsburgh and Winchester, and pressed and harassed in his retreat.

Pursuit was resumed by a flank movement of the army, crossing the Potomac at Berlin, and moving down Loudon Valley. Cavalry were immediately pushed into several passes of the Blue Ridge, and having learned from scouts of the withdrawal of the confederate army from the lower valley of the Shenandoah, the Third corps, Major-General French in advance, was moved into Manassas Gap, in the hope of being able to intercept a portion of the enemy.

The possession of the gap was disputed so successfully as to enable the rear-guard to withdraw by way of Strasburgh, the confederate army retiring to the Rapid-Ann. Position was taken with this army on the line of the Rappahannock, and the campaign terminated about the close of July.

The result of the campaign may be briefly stated in the defeat of the enemy at Gettysburgh, their compulsory evacuation of Pennsylvania and Maryland, and withdrawal from the upper valley of the Shenandoah, and the capture of three guns, forty-one standards, and thirteen thousand six hundred and twenty-one prisoners. Twenty-four thousand nine hundred and seventy-eight small arms were collected on the battle-field.

Our own losses were very severe, amounting, as will be seen by the accompanying return, to two thousand eight hundred and thirty-four killed, thirteen thousand seven hundred and nine wounded, and six thousand six hundred and forty-three missing—in all twenty-three thousand one hundred and eighty-six.

It is impossible, in a report of this nature, to enumerate all the instances of gallantry and good conduct which distinguished our success on the hard-fought field of Gettysburgh. The reports of corps commanders and their subordinates, herewith submitted, will furnish all information upon this subject.

I will only add my tribute to the heroic bravery of the whole army, officers and men, which, under the blessing of Divine Providence, enabled the crowning victory to be obtained, which I feel confident the country will never cease to bear in grateful remembrance.

It is my duty, as well as my pleasure, to call attention to the earnest efforts and coöperation on the part of Major-General D. N. Couch, commanding the department of the Susquehannah, and particularly to his advance of four thousand men under Brigadier-General W. F. Smith, who joined me at Boonsboro, just prior to the withdrawal of the confederate army.

In conclusion, I desire to return my thanks to my staff, general and personal, to each and all of whom I was indebted for unremitting activity and most efficient assistance.

Very respectfully, your obedient servant,
GEO. G. MEADE,
Major-General Commanding.
Brigadier-General L. THOMAS,
Adjutant-General U. S. A.

GENERAL R. E. LEE'S REPORT.

HEADQUARTERS ARMY NORTHERN VIRGINIA, }
July 31, 1863. }

General S. Cooper, Adjutant and Inspector-General, Richmond, Va.:

GENERAL: I have the honor to submit the following outline of the recent operations of this army for the information of the department:

The position occupied by the enemy opposite Fredericksburgh being one in which he could not be attacked to advantage, it was determined to draw him from it. The execution of this purpose embraced the relief of the Shenandoah Valley from the troops that had occupied the lower part of it during the winter and spring, and, if practicable, the transfer of the scene of hostilities north of the Potomac.

It was thought that the corresponding movements on the part of the enemy, to which those contemplated by us would probably give rise, might offer a fair opportunity to strike a blow at the army therein, commanded by General Hooker; and that, in any event, that army would be compelled to leave Virginia, and possibly to draw to its support troops designed to operate against other parts of the country. In this way it was supposed that the enemy's plan of campaign for the summer would be broken up, and part of the season of active operations be consumed in the formations of new combinations, and the preparations that they would require.

In addition to these advantages, it was hoped that other valuable results might be attained by military success.

Actuated by these and other important considerations that may hereafter be presented, the movement began on the third June. McLaws's division, of Longstreet's corps, left Fredericksburgh for Culpeper Court-House, and Hood's division, which was encamped on the Rapidan, marched to the same place.

They were followed on the fourth and fifth by Ewell's corps, leaving that of A. P. Hill to occupy our lines at Fredericksburgh.

The march of these troops having been discovered by the enemy on the afternoon of the fifth, and the following day he crossed a force, amounting to about one army corps, to the south side of the Rappahannock, on a pontoon-bridge laid down near the mouth of Deep Run. General Hill disposed his command to resist their advance, but as they seemed intended for the purpose of observation rather than attack, the movements in progress were not arrested.

The forces of Longstreet and Ewell reached Culpeper Court-House by the eighth, at which point the cavalry, under General Stuart, was also concentrated.

On the ninth a large force of Federal cavalry, strongly supported by infantry, crossed the Rappahannock at Beverly's and Kelly's Fords, and attacked General Stuart. A severe engagement ensued, continuing from early in the morning until late in the afternoon, when the enemy was forced to recross the river with heavy loss, leaving four hundred prisoners, three pieces of artillery and several colors in our hands.

General Jenkins, with his cavalry brigade, had been ordered to advance toward Winchester to coöperate with the infantry in the proposed expedition into the lower valley, and at the same time General Imboden was directed, with his command, to make a demonstration in the direction of Romney, in order to cover the movement against Winchester, and prevent the enemy at that place from being reënforced by the troops on the line of the Baltimore and Ohio Railroad. Both of these officers were in position when General Ewell left Culpeper Court-House on the sixteenth.

Crossing the Shenandoah near Front Royal, he detached Rodes's division to Berryville, with instructions, after dislodging the force stationed there, to cut off the communication between Winchester and the Potomac. With the divisions of Early and Johnson, General Ewell advanced directly upon Winchester, driving the enemy into his works around the town on the thirteenth. On the same day the troops at Berryville fell back before General Rodes, retreating to Winchester. On the fourteenth General Early stormed the works at the latter place, and the whole army of General Milroy was captured or dispersed. Most of those who attempted to escape were intercepted and made prisoners by General Johnson. Their leader fled to Harper's Ferry with a small party of fugitives.

General Rodes marched from Berryville to Martinsburgh, entering the latter place on the fourteenth, where he took seven hundred prisoners, five pieces of artillery and a considerable quantity of stores. These operations cleared the valley of the enemy, those at Harper's Ferry withdrawing to Maryland Heights. More than four thousand prisoners, twenty-nine pieces of artillery, two hundred and seventy wagons and ambulances, with four hundred horses, were captured, besides a large amount of military stores. Our loss was small. On the night that Ewell appeared at Winchester the Federal troops in front of A. P. Hill, at Fredericksburgh, recrossed the Rappahannock, and the next day disappeared behind the hills of Stafford.

The whole army of General Hooker withdrew from the line of the Rappahannock, pursuing the roads near the Potomac, and no favorable opportunity was offered for attack. It seemed to be the purpose of General Hooker to take a position which would enable him to cover the approaches to Washington City. With a view to draw him further from his base, and at the same time to cover the march of A. P. Hill, who, in accordance with instructions, left Fredericksburgh for the valley as soon as the enemy withdrew from his front, Longstreet moved from Culpeper Court-House on the fifteenth, and advancing along the east side of the Blue Ridge, occupied Ashby's and Snicker's Gaps. His force had been augmented while at Culpeper by General Pickett, with three brigades of his division.

The cavalry, under General Stuart, was thrown out in front of Longstreet to watch the enemy, now reported to be moving into Loudon. On the seventeenth his cavalry encountered two brigades of ours, under General Stuart, near Aldie, and was driven back with loss. The next day the engagement was renewed, the Federal cavalry being strongly supported by infantry, and General Stuart was in turn compelled to retire.

The enemy advanced as far as Upperville, and then fell back. In these engagements General Stuart took about four hundred prisoners and a considerable number of horses and arms.

In the mean time, a part of General Ewell's corps had entered Maryland, and the rest was about to follow. General Jenkins with his cavalry, who accompanied General Ewell, penetrated Pennsylvania as far as Chambersburgh. As these demonstrations did not have the effect of causing the Federal army to leave Virginia, and as it did not seem disposed to advance upon the position held by Longstreet, the latter was withdrawn to the west side of the Shenandoah, General Hill having already reached the valley.

General Stuart was left to guard the passes of the mountains, and observe the movements of the enemy, whom he was instructed to harass and impede as much as possible should he attempt to cross the Potomac. In that event, General Stuart was directed to move into Maryland, crossing the Potomac east or west of the Blue Ridge, as in his judgment should be best, and take position on the right of our column as it advanced.

By the twenty-fourth, the progress of Ewell rendered it necessary that the rest of the army should be in supporting distance, and Longstreet and Hill marched to the Potomac. The former crossed at Williamsport, and the latter at Shepherdstown. The columns reünited at Hagerstown, and advanced thence into Pennsylvania, encamping near Chambersburgh on the twenty-seventh.

No report had been received that the Federal army had crossed the Potomac, and the absence of the cavalry rendered it impossible to obtain accurate information. In order, however, to re-

tain it on the east side of the mountains after it should enter Maryland, and thus leave open our communication with the Potomac through Hagerstown and Williamsport, General Ewell had been instructed to send a division eastward from Chambersburgh, to cross the South-Mountains. Early's division was detached for this purpose, and proceeded as far east as York, while the remainder of the corps proceeded to Carlisle.

General Imboden, in pursuance of the instructions previously referred to, had been actively engaged on the left of General Ewell during the progress of the latter into Maryland. He had driven off the forces guarding the Baltimore and Ohio Railroad, destroying all the important bridges on that route from Cumberland to Martinsburgh, and seriously damaged the Chesapeake and Ohio Canal. He subsequently took position at Hancock, and after the arrival of Longstreet and Hill at Chambersburgh, was directed to march by way of McConnellsburgh to that place.

Preparations were now made to advance upon Harrisburgh; but on the night of the twenty-ninth information was received from a scout that the Federal army, having crossed the Potomac, was advancing northward, and that the head of the column had reached the South-Mountain. As our communications with the Potomac were thus menaced, it was resolved to prevent his further progress in that direction by concentrating our army on the east side of the mountains. Accordingly Longstreet and Hill were directed to proceed from Chambersburgh to Gettysburgh, to which point General Ewell was also instructed to march from Carlisle.

General Stuart continued to follow the movements of the Federal army south of the Potomac after our own had entered Maryland, and in his efforts to impede its progress advanced as far eastward as Fairfax Court-House. Finding himself unable to delay the enemy materially, he crossed the river at Seneca, and marched through Westminster to Carlisle, where he arrived after General Ewell had left for Gettysburgh. By the route he pursued the Federal army was interposed between his command and our main body, preventing any communication with him until his arrival at Carlisle.

The march toward Gettysburgh was conducted more slowly than it would have been had the movements of the Federal army been known.

The leading division of Hill met the enemy in advance of Gettysburgh, on the morning of the first of July. Driving back these troops to within a short distance of the town, he there encountered a large force, with which two of his divisions became engaged. Ewell, coming up with two of his divisions by the way of the Heidlersburgh road, joined in the engagement. The enemy was driven through Gettysburgh with heavy loss, including about five thousand prisoners and several pieces of artillery.

He retired to a high range of hills south and east of the town. The attack was not pressed that afternoon, the enemy's force being unknown, and it being considered advisable to await the arrival of the rest of our troops. Orders were sent back to hasten their march, and, in the mean time, every effort was made to ascertain the numbers and positions of the enemy, and find the most favorable point of attack. It had not been intended to fight a general battle at such a distance from our base, unless attacked by the enemy; but finding ourselves unexpectedly confronted by the Federal army, it became a matter of difficulty to withdraw through the mountains with our large trains.

At the same time, the country was unfavorable for collecting supplies, while in the presence of the enemy's main body, as he was enabled to restrain our foraging parties by occupying the passes of the mountains with regular and local troops. A battle thus became, in a measure, unavoidable. Encouraged by the successful issue of the engagement of the first day, and in view of the valuable results that would ensue from the defeat of the army of General Meade, it was thought advisable to renew the attack.

The remainder of Ewell's and Hill's corps having arrived, and two divisions of Longstreet's, our preparations were made accordingly. During the afternoon intelligence was received of the arrival of General Stuart at Carlisle, and he was ordered to march to Gettysburgh, and take position on the left. A full account of these engagements cannot be given until the reports of the several commanding officers shall have been received, and I shall only offer a general description.

The preparations for attack were not completed until the afternoon of the second.

The enemy held a high and commanding ridge along which he had massed a large amount of artillery. General Ewell occupied the left of our line, General Hill the centre, and General Longstreet the right. In front of General Longstreet the enemy held a position, from which if he could be driven, it was thought that our army could be used to advantage in assailing the more elevated ground beyond, and thus enable us to reach the crest of the ridge. That officer was directed to endeavor to carry this position, while General Ewell attacked directly the high ground on the enemy's right, which had already been partially fortified. General Hill was instructed to threaten the centre of the Federal line, in order to prevent reënforcements being sent to either wing, and to avail himself of any opportunity that might present itself to attack.

After a severe struggle, Longstreet succeeded in getting possession of and holding the desired ground. Ewell also carried some of the strong positions which he assailed, and the result was such as to lead to the belief that he would ultimately be able to dislodge the enemy. The battle ceased at dark.

These partial successes determined me to continue the assault next day. Pickett, with three of his brigades, joined Longstreet the following morning, and our batteries were moved forward to the position gained by him the day before.

The general plan of attack was unchanged, except that one division and two brigades of Hill's corps were ordered to support Longstreet.

The enemy in the mean time had strengthened his line with earthworks. The morning was occupied in necessary preparations, and the battle recommenced in the afternoon of the third, and raged with great violence until sunset. Our troops succeeded in entering the advanced works of the enemy, and getting possession of some of his batteries; but our artillery having nearly expended its ammunition, the attacking columns became exposed to the heavy fire of the numerous batteries near the summit of the ridge, and after a most determined and gallant struggle were compelled to relinquish their advantage, and fall back to their original positions with severe loss.

The conduct of the troops was all that I could desire or expect, and they deserved success so far as it can be deserved by heroic valor and fortitude. More may have been required of them than they were able to perform, but my admiration of their noble qualities, and confidence in their ability to cope successfully with the enemy, has suffered no abatement from the issue of this protracted and sanguinary conflict.

Owing to the strength of the enemy's position and the reduction of our ammunition, a renewal of the engagement could not be hazarded, and the difficulty of procuring supplies rendered it impossible to continue longer where we were. Such of the wounded as were in condition to be removed, and part of the arms collected on the field, were ordered to Williamsport. The army remained at Gettysburgh during the fourth, and at night began to retire by the road to Fairfield, carrying with it about four thousand prisoners. Nearly two thousand had previously been paroled, but the enemy's numerous wounded that had fallen into our hands after the first and second days' engagements were left behind.

Little progress was made that night, owing to a severe storm, which greatly embarrassed our movements. The rear of the column did not leave its position near Gettysburgh until after daylight on the fifth.

The march was continued during that day without interruption by the enemy, except an unimportant demonstration upon our rear in the afternoon, when near Fairfield, which was easily checked. Part of our train moved by the road through Fairfield, and the rest by way of Cashtown, guarded by General Imboden. In passing through the mountains, in advance of the column, the great length of the train exposed them to attack by the enemy's cavalry, which captured a number of wagons and ambulances; but they succeeded in reaching Williamsport without serious loss.

They were attacked at that place on the sixth by the enemy's cavalry, which was gallantly repulsed by General Imboden. The attacking force was subsequently encountered and driven off by General Stuart, and pursued for several miles in the direction of Boonsboro. The army, after an arduous march, rendered more difficult by the rains, reached Hagerstown on the afternoon of the sixth and morning of the seventh July.

The Potomac was found to be so much swollen by the rains, that had fallen almost incessantly since our entrance into Maryland, as to be unfordable. Our communications with the south side were thus interrupted, and it was difficult to procure either ammunition or subsistence, the latter difficulty being enhanced by the high waters impeding the working of neighboring mills. The trains with the wounded and prisoners were compelled to await at Williamsport the subsiding of the river and the construction of boats, as the pontoon-bridge left at Falling Waters had been partially destroyed.

The enemy had not yet made his appearance, but, as he was in condition to obtain large reënforcements, and our situation for the reasons above mentioned was becoming daily more embarrassing, it was deemed advisable to recross the river. Part of the pontoon-bridge was recovered, and new boats built, so that by the thirteenth a good bridge was thrown over the river at Falling Waters.

The enemy in force reached our front on the twelfth. A position had been previously selected to cover the Potomac from Williamsport to Falling Waters, and an attack was awaited during that and the succeeding day. This did not take place, though the two armies were in close proximity, the enemy being occupied in fortifying his own lines. Our preparations being completed, and the river, though still deep, being pronounced fordable, the army commenced to withdraw to the south side on the night of the thirteenth.

Ewell's corps forded the river at Williamsport, those of Longstreet and Hill crossed upon the bridge. Owing to the condition of the roads, the troops did not reach the bridge until after daylight on the fourteenth, and the crossing was not completed until one P.M., when the bridge was removed. The enemy offered no serious interruption, and the movement was attended with no loss of material except a few disabled wagons and two pieces of artillery, which the horses were unable to move through the deep mud. Before fresh horses could be sent back for them, the rear of the column had passed.

During the slow and tedious march to the bridge, in the midst of a violent storm of rain, some of the men lay down by the way to rest. Officers sent back for them failed to find them in the obscurity of the night, and these, with some stragglers, fell into the hands of the enemy.

Brig.-General Pettigrew was mortally wounded in an attack made by a small body of cavalry, which was unfortunately mistaken for our own, and permitted to enter our lines. He was brought to Bunker Hill, where he expired in a few days afterward. He was a brave and accomplished officer and gentleman, and his loss will be deeply felt by the country and the army.

The following day the army marched to Bunker Hill, in the vicinity of which it encamped for several days. The day after its arrival, a large force of the enemy's cavalry, which had crossed the Potomac at Harper's-Ferry, advanced toward Martinsburgh. It was attacked by General Fitz Lee, near Kearneysville, and defeated with heavy loss, leaving its dead and many of its wounded on the field.

Owing to the swollen condition of the Shenandoah River, the plan of operations which had been contemplated when we recrossed the Potomac could not be put in execution, and before the waters had subsided the movements of the enemy induced me to cross the Blue Ridge and take position south of the Rappahannock, which was accordingly done.

As soon as the reports of the commanding officers shall be received, a more detailed account of these operations will be given, and occasion will then be taken to speak more particularly of the conspicuous gallantry and good conduct of both officers and men.

It is not yet in my power to give a correct statement of our casualties, which were severe, including many brave men, and an unusual proportion of distinguished and valuable officers. Among them I regret to mention the following general officers: Major-Generals Hood, Pender, and Trimble severely, and Major-General Heth slightly wounded.

General Pender has since died. This lamented officer has borne a distinguished part in every engagement of this army, and was wounded on several occasions while leading his command with conspicuous gallantry and ability. The confidence and admiration inspired by his courage and capacity as an officer, were only equalled by the esteem and respect entertained by all with whom he was associated, for the noble qualities of his modest and unassuming character. Brigadier-Generals Barksdale and Garnett were killed, and Brigadier-General Semms mortally wounded, while leading their troops with the courage that always distinguishes them. These brave officers and patriotic gentlemen fell in the faithful discharge of duty, leaving the army to mourn their loss and emulate their noble examples.

Brigadier-Generals Kemper, Armistead, Scales, G. T. Anderson, Hampton, J. M. Jones, and Jenkins, were also wounded. Brig.-General Archer was taken prisoner. General Pettigrew, though wounded at Gettysburgh, continued in command until he was mortally wounded near Falling Waters.

The loss of the enemy is unknown, but from observations on the field, and his subsequent movements, it is supposed that he suffered severely. Respectfully submitted,

R. E. LEE,
General.

RICHMOND "ENQUIRER" ACCOUNT.

IN CAMP, NEAR HAGERSTOWN, MD., July 8, 1863.

I proceed to-day to give you a hasty sketch of the movements of this army since we crossed the Potomac. As I was not with our advance, under Lieutenant-General Ewell, I shall not be able to give you as full and reliable reports of the movements of his corps up to the battle of Gettysburgh as of the main body of the army, which crossed the Potomac two days after his corps. I learn that Ewell's crossed on the twenty-second June—one portion at Shepherdstown and another at Williamsport, and that the two columns united at Hagerstown. From the latter place, one division—Rhodes's, I think—was pushed on through Greencastle and Chambersburgh to Carlisle, making at all three of these places considerable captures of army supplies—hats, shoes, clothing, and medical stores. Another division—Early's—turned to the right from Chambersburgh and moved on York, on the Northern Central Railroad, when, after a short and inconsiderable engagement with a body of Pennsylvania militia, in which quite a number were taken prisoners, the town surrendered. Early then pushed on to Wrightsville, on the south side of the Susquehanna, where was posted a small body of militia, who fled precipitately at his approach across the river, and burned the bridge. Some few prisoners were taken at Carlisle—two or three hundred—all militia, and they, as also those captured at York and Wrightsville, were immediately paroled and discharged.

On the morning of June twenty-fourth, A. P. Hill's corps (the Third) crossed the Potomac at Boteler's Mill, one mile below Shepherdstown, Anderson's division being in the advance. That night the head of Hill's corps reached Boonsboro, which latter place was occupied by Wright's brigade of Anderson's division. From this place we moved on Chambersburgh, via Funkstown, Hagerstown, and Middleburgh, reaching the former on the twenty-seventh. Passing through Chambersburgh on the twenty-seventh, we pushed on to Fayetteville, five miles from Chambersburgh, on the Baltimore and Philadelphia turnpike. Here we halted until Tuesday, the thirtieth, waiting for the rear of the corps and our supply trains to come up. In the mean time Longstreet's corps had turned up the river from Millwood, and, passing through Martinsburgh, crossed the river at Williamsport, and, falling into our line of advance at Hagerstown, followed it to Fayetteville, reaching the latter place on Monday, the twenty-ninth. Having now concentrated our army, except Ewell's corps, whose operations have already been given, on Tuesday, the thirtieth, General Lee ordered the line of march to be taken up for Gettysburgh, twenty miles distant in an easterly direction. In this movement Hill's corps was in the advance, and in the following order: Heth's division, Pender's division, Anderson's division; then Longstreet's corps, McLaws's division, Hood's division—Pickett's division being left at Chambersburgh to protect our rear and convoy the reserve trains. Two miles from Fayetteville we crossed the South-Mountain at Stephens's (Thaddeus) iron works, all of which were completely destroyed. Owing to the narrow road through the mountain pass, only two divisions of Hill's corps crossed the mountain on the thirtieth. Early on Wednesday Hill's remaining division (Anderson's) and Longstreet's corps moved on after Hill's advance.

At ten o'clock A.M. on the first instant, Heth's division being ahead, encountered the enemy's advance line—the Eleventh corps—about three miles west of Gettysburgh. Here a sharp engagement began, our men steadily advancing and driving the enemy before them to the town and to a range of hills or low mountains running out a little east of south from the town. Late in the evening two divisions—Early's and Rhodes's, of Ewell's corps—came up on our left from Carlisle and York, and, falling upon the enemy's right flank, drove him with great slaughter upon and through the town to the heights on the south. In the mean time Pender's division (of Hill's corps) had moved up to the support of Heth on the right, and opened a hot fire upon the enemy, which drove them back upon the low mountain range already alluded to. Anderson's division got up too late to participate in the day's engagement, owing to its having been unnecessarily halted for more than three hours on the eastern slope of the South-Mountain, at a small village called Cashtown. This halt was made while the division was not only hearing the fire of the battle, but was actually in sight. From its position the men could see each discharge of our own and the enemy's guns—could see that Heth was driving him slowly but steadily. If Anderson had pushed on, it is more than probable that the whole Yankee force would have been captured; for up to this time (Wednesday evening) the enemy had not brought up his main force. The addition of Anderson's force to that already engaged on our side would have enabled us to get possession of the mountain range upon which the subsequent battles were fought by the enemy. Had our army succeeded in getting possession of this range, there can be no doubt that the whole Yankee army would have been destroyed. As it was, the delay of Anderson prevented Heth and Pender from taking possession of this important position, and permitted it to fall into the enemy's hands. I have no hesitation in saying that this fatal blunder was fraught with the most disastrous consequences to our arms. I learn that all the brigadier commanders in Anderson's division were anxious to advance, but the Major-General would not consent. I have heard no reason given for this delay, and presume that General Lee will have the whole matter investigated. It is due to himself and his noble army that it should be done—that the country and army should know why seven or eight thousand men were kept idle in sight of a terrible and important battle, without being allowed to fire a gun. The result of the day's fight may be summed up thus: We had attacked a superior force; had driven him over three miles; captured three thousand prisoners, and killed and wounded five or six thousand. Our own loss was not heavy, though a few brigades suffered severely. The conduct of Gordon's and Hays's brigades is said to have been very fine. It was these two brigades of Early's division which drove the enemy through the town of Gettysburgh. All of our troops behaved well that were engaged.

Late in the evening Anderson's division, and McLaws's division, of Longstreet's corps, got up to within a mile or two of the town, and bivouacked for the night. Early next (Thursday) morning, the second, Hood's division also got up, and our line of battle was formed. The enemy during the night had succeeded in getting up his entire force—some one hundred and thirty thousand to one hundred and fifty thousand men—and took up a strong position on a low mountain range, or ridge, which runs nearly south from Gettysburgh. The town is situated on the northern slope of this range, and about one and a half or two miles from its summit. The western slope of this range is in cultivation, except small "patches," where the mountain side is so precipitous as to defy the efforts of the farmer to bring it into subjection to the ploughshare; these "patches" are covered with small timber and undergrowth. At the foot of the mountain is a narrow valley, from a mile to two miles in width, broken in small ridges running parallel with the mountain. On the western side of the valley rises a long, high hill, mostly covered with heavy timber; but greatly inferior in altitude to the mountain range upon which the enemy had taken position, but running nearly parallel with it. The valley between this ridge and the mountain is in cultivation, and the fields were yellow with the golden harvest. About four or five miles south from Gettysburgh the mountain rises abruptly to an altitude of several hundred feet, presenting a sharp, rugged, and almost perpendicular peak, covered with original forest growth. Upon this peak the enemy rested his left flank, his right being upon the crest of the range, about a mile or a mile and a half from Gettysburgh. Our line of battle was formed along the western slope of the second and inferior ridge described above, and in the following order: Ewell's corps on the left, beginning at the town, with Early's division, then Rhodes's division. On the right of Rhodes's division was the left of Hill's corps, commencing with Heth's, then Pender's, and Anderson's divisions. On the right of Anderson's division was Longstreet's left, McLaws's division being next to Anderson, and Hood on the extreme right of our line, which was opposite the peak upon which the enemy's left rested. A brisk skirmish-firing was kept up during the entire morning; but no general engagement took place until late in the afternoon. It will be seen that in the order of battle given above, neither Johnson's division, of Ewell's corps, or Pickett's division, of Longstreet's corps, had a place. Up to Thursday noon neither of these divisions had come up. Pickett had been left at Chambersburgh to protect our rear, and escort our reserve train, and Johnson had been operating on the Susquehanna, in the direction of Harrisburgh. At one time, early in the morning, Hays's brigade, of Early's division, made an attack upon the enemy on the south side of the town, and, charging up the northern slope of the mountain, soon

got possession of the enemy's first line, driving them from a strong position on the Cemetery Hill. It is thought that if adequate support had been near at hand, he might have dislodged the enemy from his strong position on the right. Gordon's brigade, which was in the town, was double-quicked to his support, moving promptly and rapidly; but, owing to the great distance they had to traverse, Hays was compelled to fall back before his support reached him. In this charge of Hays's, it is said that his men clubbed their guns, and had a desperate hand-to-hand conflict with a very superior force of the enemy, and that the slaughter of the Yankees was fearful.

About the middle of the afternoon orders were issued to the different commanders to prepare for a general attack upon the enemy's centre and left. Longstreet was to commence the movement, which was to be followed up on his left in quick succession by the respective divisions of Hill's corps. As Anderson's division, or at least a portion of it, took a conspicuous part in this movement, I have ascertained, and now give you, the order of its different brigades: On the extreme right of Anderson's division, connecting with McLaws's left, was Wilcox's brigade, then Perry's, Wright's, Posey's, and Mahone's. At half-past five o'clock, Longstreet commenced the attack, and Wilcox followed it up by promptly moving forward; Perry's brigade quickly followed, and Wright moved simultaneously with him. The two divisions of Longstreet's corps soon encountered the enemy posted a little in rear of the Emmetsburgh turnpike, which winds along the slope of the range upon which the enemy's main force was concentrated. After a short but spirited engagement, the enemy was driven back upon the main line upon the crest of the hill. McLaws's and Hood's divisions made a desperate assault upon their main line, but owing to the precipitate and very rugged character of the slope, were unable to reach the summit. The enemy's loss on this part of the line was very heavy. I have heard several officers say that they have never seen the enemy's dead cover the ground so thickly, not even at the first Fredericksburgh fight, as they did on that portion of the field over which McLaws's troops fought. While the fight was raging on our right, Wilcox and Wright of Anderson's division, were pressing the enemy's centre. Wilcox pushed forward for nearly a mile, driving the enemy before him and up to his very guns, over and beyond his batteries, several guns of which he captured, and nearly up to the summit of the hill. Wright had swept over the valley, under a terrific fire from the enemy's batteries, posted upon McPherson's heights, had encountered the enemy's advance line, and had driven him across the Emmetsburgh pike to a position behind a stone wall or fence, which runs parallel with the pike, and about sixty or eighty yards in front of the batteries on the heights, and immediately under them. Here this gallant brigade had a most desperate engagement for fifteen or twenty minutes; but charging rapidly up the almost perpendicular side of the mountain, they rushed upon the enemy's infantry behind the stone wall, and drove them from it at the point of the bayonet. Now concentrating their fire upon the heavy batteries (twenty guns) of the enemy on the crest of the heights, they soon silenced them, and rushing forward with a shout, soon gained the summit of the heights, capturing all the enemy's guns, and driving their infantry in great disorder and confusion into the woods beyond.

We now had the key to the enemy's stronghold, and, apparently, the victory was won. McLaws and Hood had pushed their line well up the slope on the right; Wilcox had kept well up on his portion of the line; Wright had pierced the enemy's main line on the summit of McPherson's heights, capturing his heavy batteries, thus breaking the connection between their right and left wings. I said that, apparently, we had won the victory. It remains to be stated why our successes were not crowned with the important results which should have followed such heroic daring and indomitable bravery. Although the order was peremptory that all of Anderson's division should move into action simultaneously, Brigadier-General Posey, commanding a Mississippi brigade, and Brigadier-General Mahone, commanding a Virginia brigade, failed to advance. This failure of these two brigades to advance is assigned, as I learn upon inquiry, as the reason why Pender's division, of Hill's corps, did not advance — the order being, that the advance was to commence from the right and be taken up along our whole line. Pender's failure to advance caused the division on his left—Heth's—to remain inactive. Here we have two whole divisions, and two brigades of another, standing idle spectators of one of the most desperate and important assaults that has ever been made on this continent — fifteen or twenty thousand armed men resting on their arms, in plain view of a terrible battle, witnessing the mighty efforts of two little brigades, (Wright's and Wilcox's, for Perry had fallen back overpowered,) contending with the heavy masses of Yankee infantry, and subjected to a most deadly fire from the enemy's heavy artillery, without a single effort to aid them in the assault, or to assist them when the heights were carried. Perry's brigade, which was between Wilcox and Wright, soon after its first advance, was pressed so heavily as to be forced to retire. This left an interval in the line between Wright and Wilcox, and which the enemy perceiving, he threw a heavy column in the gap then made, deploying a portion of it in Wilcox's left flank, while a large force was thrown in rear of Wright's right flank. The failure of Posey and Mahone to advance upon Wright's left enabled the enemy to throw forward a strong force on that flank, and to push it well to his rear along the Emmetsburgh pike. It was now apparent that the day was lost—lost after it was won—lost, not because our army fought badly, but because a large portion did not fight at all.

My narrative left Wright's little brigade of Georgians in the enemy's intrenchments upon the heights. Let us return to this little Spartan band, who this day covered themselves with glory—alas! how vainly! Perceiving, after getting possession of the enemy's works, that they were certainly isolated — more than a mile from support; that Perry's brigade had been driven back on their right; that no advance had been made on their left, and just then seeing the enemy's flanking columns on their right and left flanks rapidly converging in their rear, these noble Georgians faced about, abandoning all the guns they had captured, and prepared to cut their way through the enemy who had now almost entirely surrounded them. Springing with alacrity down the hill to the stone fence, they were halted, and delivered a well-directed fire upon the enemy then passing along the pike road. Following this discharge by a charge over the stone wall and through the enemy's ranks, they soon gained the foot of the slope, when the lately abandoned guns upon the heights opened a most destructive fire of grape and canister upon them. Here their loss was very severe. But although more than one half their number had fallen — although every field officer but one had been killed or wounded — with their comrades falling in heaps on every side, this little handful of choice spirits retired in tolerable order until they reached the bottom of the second slope, where they were halted, faced to the front, and re-formed to await the approach of the enemy, now seen advancing about three hundred yards distant. The Yankees perceiving that our men had re-formed for a fight, prudently withdrew without firing a gun. During this time, Wilcox, who had driven the enemy well up the side of the mountain, capturing several of his guns, found his left exposed by the flank movement of the enemy, heretofore mentioned, and was compelled to retire, abandoning his captured guns. On our right, McLaws and Hood continued to press the enemy until night set in and ended the sanguinary conflict. The enemy's loss during this day's fight was very heavy, particularly on that portion of the field where Benning's brigade, (of Hood's division,) Barksdale's and Wofford's, (of McLaws's,) and Wilcox's and Wright's, (of Anderson's division,) were engaged. Our own loss was slight, except in Wright's and Wilcox's brigades, in both of which it was very heavy, amounting to more than half of the forces engaged.

Early next morning — Friday, the third — preparations were made for a general attack along the enemy's whole line, while a large force was to be concentrated against his centre, with the view of retaking the heights captured and abandoned the day before by Wright. Lieut.-Gen. Longstreet massed a large number of long-range guns—fifty-five in number—upon the crest of a slight eminence just in front of Perry's and Wilcox's brigades, and a little to the left of the heights, upon which they were to open. Lieut.-Gen. Hill massed some sixty guns along the hill in front of Posey's and Mahone's brigades, and almost immediately in front of the heights. At twelve o'clock the signal-gun was fired, and the cannonading commenced. The fire of our guns was concentrated upon the enemy's line on the heights stormed on the day before by Wright's brigade. Our fire drew a most terrific one from the enemy's batteries, posted along the heights from a point near Cemetery Hill to the point in their line opposite to the position of Wilcox. I have never yet heard such tremendous artillery firing. The enemy must have had over one hundred guns, which, in addition to our one hundred and fifteen, made the air hideous with most discordant noise. The very earth shook beneath our feet, and the hills and rocks seemed to reel like a drunken man. For one hour and a half this most terrific fire was continued, during which time the shrieking of shells, the crash of falling timber, the fragments of rock flying through the air shattered from the cliffs by solid shot, the heavy mutterings from the valley between the opposing armies, the splash of bursting shrapnel, and the fierce neighing of wounded artillery horses, made a picture terribly grand and sublime, but which my pen utterly fails to describe. After the firing had continued for little more than an hour, the enemy's guns began to slacken, and finally all were silenced save some six or eight, which were in a clump of woods a little to the left of the stone fence.

Now the storming party was moved up, Pickett's division in advance, supported on the right by Wilcox's brigade and on the left by Heth's division, commanded by Pettigrew. The left of Pickett's division occupied the same ground over which Wright had passed the day before. I stood upon an eminence and watched this advance with great interest; I had seen brave men pass over that fated valley the day before; I had witnessed their death-struggle with the foe on the opposite heights; I had observed their return with shattered ranks, a bleeding mass, but with unstained banners. Now I saw their valiant comrades prepare for the same bloody trial, and already felt that their efforts would be vain unless their supports should be as true as steel and brave as lions. Now they move forward, with steady, measured tread they advance upon the foe. Their banners float defiantly in the breeze, as onward in beautiful order they press across the plain. I have never seen since the war began (and I have been in all the great fights of this army) troops enter a fight in such splendid order as did this splendid division of Pickett's. Now Pettigrew's command emerge from the woods upon Pickett's left, and sweep down the slope of the hill to the valley beneath, and some two or three hundred yards in rear of Pickett. I saw by the wavering of this line as they entered the conflict that they wanted the firmness of nerve and steadiness of tread which so characterized Pickett's men, and I felt that these men would not, could not stand the tremendous ordeal to which they would be soon subjected. These were mostly raw troops, which had been recently brought from the South, and who had, perhaps, never been under fire — who certainly had never been in any very severe fight—and I trembled for their conduct. Just as Pickett was getting well under the enemy's fire, our batteries ceased firing. This was a fearful moment for Pickett and his brave command. Why do not our guns reöpen their fire? is the inquiry that rises upon every lip. Still our batteries are silent as death! But on press Pickett's brave Virginians; and now the enemy open upon them, from more than fifty guns, a terrible fire of grape, shell, and canister. On, on they move in unbroken line, delivering a deadly fire as they advance. Now they have reached the Emmetsburgh road, and here they meet a severe fire from the heavy masses of the enemy's infantry, posted behind the stone fence, while their artillery, now free from the annoyance of our artillery, turn their whole fire upon this devoted band. Still they remain firm. Now again they advance; they storm the stone fence; the Yankees fly. The enemy's batteries are, one by one, silenced in quick succession as Pickett's men deliver their fire at the gunners and drive them from their pieces. I see Kemper and Armistead plant their banner in the enemy's works. I hear their glad shout of victory!

Let us look after Pettigrew's division. Where are they now? While the victorious shout of the gallant Virginians is still ringing in my ears, I turn my eyes to the left, and there, all over the plain, in utmost confusion, is scattered this strong division. Their line is broken; they are flying, apparently panic-stricken, to the rear. The gallant Pettigrew is wounded, but he still retains command, and is vainly striving to rally his men. Still the moving mass rush pell-mell to the rear, and Pickett is left alone to contend with the hordes of the enemy now pouring in upon him on every side. Garnett falls, killed by a Minie ball, and Kemper, the brave and chivalrous, reels under a mortal wound, and is taken to the rear. Now the enemy move around strong flanking bodies of infantry, and are rapidly gaining Pickett's rear. The order is given to fall back, and our men commence the movement, doggedly contending for every inch of ground. The enemy press heavily our retreating line, and many noble spirits who had passed safely through the fiery ordeal of the advance and charge, now fall on the right and on the left. Armistead is wounded and left in the enemy's hands. At this critical moment the shattered remnant of Wright's Georgia brigade is moved forward to cover their retreat, and the fight closes here. Our loss in this charge was very severe, and the Yankee prisoners taken acknowledge that theirs was immense. Anticipating that a renewal of the attack would be made on this point in his line, Meade had concentrated a very heavy force of infantry in support of his batteries, and the fire of our artillery was said to have been very destructive to them, lying, as they were, in heavy masses just in rear of their own guns. I have stated that just after Pickett commenced the attack our batteries ceased firing, and upon inquiry I learn that they had exhausted all their ammunition, and were thus compelled to withdraw. This is most remarkable, and would seem to demand investigation.

During the attack made by Pickett, McLaws had been actively engaged on our right, but with no decisive results. Ewell, also on our extreme left, had been threatening the enemy in his position on Cemetery Hill; but these were mere feints, to cover and divert attention from our main attack upon the centre. You will see that twice we took the McPherson heights — the real key to the enemy's whole position — once by a single brigade, on Thursday, and again by a single division on Friday, and that in both instances we lost it by the failure of proper supports to the attacking parties. On whom the blame rests for the second failure I shall not attempt to say. The most careless reader will be at no loss to discover the responsible party. Of the failure to send in support in the first assault (on Thursday) the conviction is general in this army that Major-General Anderson should be held responsible. It was a portion of his division that made the assault and successful charge, and two of his strongest brigades, although on the field, were not put in action. Why this was so, I presume and hope he will be able to explain when he comes to make his official report.

Nothing further transpired during the afternoon and night of Friday. On Saturday we were engaged with strong working parties burying our dead and caring for the wounded.

It is now apparent that the enemy's position was almost impregnable. It was further made known that the three days' fighting had nearly exhausted our ammunition. There had been indications the night before (Friday) that the enemy were moving off; but all Saturday morning the atmosphere was so hazy that nothing could be seen, and from noon until night the rain poured in such torrents as to utterly preclude any accurate observations being made. During the whole of the day our wounded—at least such as were able to bear it, were being sent toward Hagerstown, and late in the afternoon our artillery and wagon-trains also commenced moving in the same direction. At dark our whole army were put in motion, taking the road to Fairfield, and crossing South-Mountain at Waterloo Gap. Our falling back was orderly and without loss of men or guns. All our artillery was brought off, and very few, if any, stragglers fell into the enemy's hands. Having crossed the mountain, we moved on to Hagerstown, where we arrived on Monday, the sixth. Here we took position and calmly awaited the approach of the enemy. On Tuesday his advance got as near to us as Funkstown, four miles south of Hagerstown, and on Wednesday and Thursday his whole command confronted us. We were anxious for him to commence the attack, and hourly expected the ball to open. During Friday, Saturday, Sunday, and Monday we lay face to face; but the enemy refused to accept our wager of battle. On Monday night, finding that the enemy had no idea of offering us battle, but had gone to work intrenching and fortifying, General

Lee determined to recross the river. I have no doubt the continued and heavy rains, and consequent rapid rising of the Potomac, had some influence on this movement. We are now all on the "sacred soil of old Virginia," in fine spirits and good health, and fully prepared to meet the Yankee army whenever it shall get ready to move upon us. No one in the army has had his confidence in General Lee in the slightest degree impaired by the last month's campaign. He had difficulties to contend with which impartial history will duly record, and his fair fame will not receive a single blot by this campaign. I shall at some future moment, when I have leisure, give you some more full particulars of the campaign and what we accomplished. Our loss in the three days' fighting at Gettysburgh will fall below ten thousand in killed, wounded, and missing. The enemy's loss is at least thirty, thousand killed and wounded, and ten thousand prisoners. Some of the prisoners, indeed, most of them, were paroled in Pennsylvania; the balance have been sent on to Richmond.

THE CHARGE OF PICKETT'S DIVISION.

The sun rises, clouds obscure its brightness as if loth to look upon the scene to witness such inhumanity, but from which no people are exempt who ever left a history or benefited the human race. The conflict began ere Tubal Cain first worked in brass, and will continue till a higher virtue than man has ever reached shall govern events. Soon the division leaves the main road, makes a detour to the right, winds over hill and through wood, toward the right of our line of battle. The morning is now wearing away—at times a cannon-shot breaks the quiet, and a shell comes screaming through the air—now and then the skirmishers break forth, varying from the sharp, quick crack of a single rifle, to perfect volleys. Hour after hour thus passes, and the battle is not yet begun. Our troops are taking position—Ewell is on the left. Hill holds the centre, and Longstreet on the right. Long lines of men are moving across yonder fields, or marching through that piece of wood. Batteries of artillery occupy this hillock and that mound, whilst along the low range of hills just back of Gettysburgh, at intervals, are batteries unlimbered and ready for action. Toward the left a body of cavalry are slowly moving. It is now nearly noon, the clouds break away, the air is warm and sultry. The signal flags are waving fast intelligence along our lines; presently the shrill sound of a Whitworth awakes the silence, then batteries slowly open from this point and that. The enemy reply with vigor. The fire on either side rapidly increases; dense columns of smoke hang over the beautiful valley, and, rising upward, slowly float away. From that point a new battery belches forth—another and still another joins in the awful chorus, the very air seems filled with hissing, screaming, bursting shells. The lurid flame leaps madly from the cannon's mouth—each moment the roar grows more intense—now chime in volleys of small arms. But where is that division which is to play so conspicuous a part in this day's tragedy? They are in line of battle, just fronting that frowning hill, from which heavy batteries are belching forth shell and shrapnel with fatal accuracy. The men are lying close to the ground; hours pass, and the deadly missiles come thick and fast on their mission of death. See that shattered arm; that leg shot off; that headless body, and here the mangled form of a young and gallant lieutenant, who had braved the perils of many battles. That hill must be carried to rout the enemy; a terrible chastisement has been inflicted upon him; with immense loss he had been driven from his position two days previous—this is his stronghold. This captured, rout is inevitable; exceedingly strong by nature, but rendered more so by the works thrown up the night before. It is a moment of great emergency; if unshrinking valor or human courage can carry those heights, it will be done. General Pickett receives the order to charge those batteries at the opportune moment. The cannonade still goes on with intense fury; our batteries are handled with great skill. This battery and that limber up, advance to the front, wheel into action, and again the roar of cannon becomes almost deafening. Our shells seem to burst with terrible accuracy; now a caisson of the enemy's is blown up—quickly another follows—their fire slackens—the order comes to advance. That flag which waved amid the wild tempest of battle at Gaines's Mill, Fraser's Farm, and Manassas, never rose more proudly. Kemper, with as gallant men as ever trod beneath that flag, leads the right; Garnett, with his heroes, brings up the left; and the veteran Armistead, with his brave troops, move forward in support. The distance is more than half a mile. As they advance the enemy fire with great rapidity; shell and solid shot give place to grape and canister; the very earth quivers beneath the heavy roar; wide gaps are made in this regiment and that brigade; yet they quickly close up and move steadily onward. That flag goes down. See how quickly it again mounts upward, borne by some gallant man who feels keenly the honor of his old Commonwealth in this hour which is to test her manhood. The line moves onward, straight onward—cannons roaring, grape and canister plunging and ploughing through the ranks—bullets whizzing as thick as hailstones in winter, and men falling as leaves fall when shaken by the blasts of autumn. In a double-quick, and with a shout which rises above the roar of battle, they charge. Now they pour in volleys of musketry—they reach the works—the contest rages with intense fury—men fight almost hand to hand—the red cross and gridiron wave defiantly in close proximity—the enemy are slowly yielding—a Federal officer dashing forward in front of his shrinking columns, and, with flashing sword, urges them to stand. General Pickett, seeing the splendid valor of his troops, moves among them as if courting death by his own daring intrepidity. The noble Garnett is dead, Armistead wounded, and the brave Kemper, with hat in hand, still cheering on his men, falls from his horse into the ranks of the enemy. His men

rush forward, rescue their General, and he is borne mortally wounded from the field. Where is the gallant Williams? The First is there, but his clear voice is no longer heard—he has fallen lifeless, and there goes his horse now riderless. There stand the decimated ranks of the Third; and Mayo, though struck, stands firm with his faithful men, animating them to yet more daring deeds; but Callcott, the Christian soldier, who stood unmoved amid this carnival of death, has fought his last battle; no sound shall awake him to glory again, till the summons of the great Judge, announcing to him the reward of the faithful soldier, who has fought the good fight. Patton, Otey, and Terry, who, but a moment since, stood at their respective regiments, are wounded. The brave Hunton, hero of Leesburgh, most worthy successor of the noble Garnett, Stewart, and Gant, lies wounded. Carrington, his gallant regiment shattered, stands firmly, flaunting defiantly his colors in the very face of the enemy. Allen and Ellis killed. Hodges, too, has fallen, and the modest, chivalrous Edmunds lies numbered with the noble dead; Aylett wounded, and Magruder has gone down in the shock of battle. The fight goes on—but few are left; and the shrinking columns of the enemy gain confidence from the heavy reenforcements advanced to their support. They, too, are moving in large force on the right flank. This division, small at first, with ranks now torn and shattered, most of its officers killed or wounded, no valor able to rescue victory from such a grasp, annihilation or capture inevitable, slowly, reluctantly fell back. It was not given to these few remaining brave men to accomplish human impossibilities. The enemy dared not follow them beyond their works. Such was the fate of the general and regimental officers—longer is the list of junior officers, and still longer the roll of the "unknown dead"—men who endured privations without murmur, hardships difficult to realize till actually experienced without complaint, with few opportunities of realizing any distinction which ambition might covet as the reward of meritorious conduct, save a soldier's grave; and yet they bore them all, and willingly would they have submitted to a severer lot in vindication of their country's liberty. The Confederacy can find no reward worthy the noble bearing of its private soldiers.

Night now approaches; the wounded are being borne off to their respective hospitals; many with slight wounds plodded along, leaving the ambulances to their less fortunate comrades. With night the battle closed, our army holding the same position from which it had driven the enemy two days previous. One by one the stars came out in the quiet sky, and over that field of carnage hung the sweet influences of the Pleiades. In the series of engagements a few pieces of artillery and eight thousand prisoners were captured by our army. Our loss in killed, wounded, and missing, supposed about ten thousand, whilst the enemy, we understand, acknowledges a loss of thirty thousand. The army of Northern Virginia—with zeal unabated, courage intrepid, devotion unchilled, with unbounded confidence in the wisdom of that great chieftain who has so often led them to victory—stands ready to advance their standards farther into the enemy's country, or repel any new invasion of the Confederacy. Though many a Virginia home will mourn the loss of some noble spirit, yet, at the name of Pickett's division and the battle of Gettysburgh, how the eye will glisten and the blood course quicker, and the heart beat warm, as among its noble dead is recalled the name of some cherished one. They bore themselves worthy of their lineage and their State. Who would recall them from their bed of glory? Each sleeps in a hero's grave!

FROM ANOTHER CORRESPONDENT.

I regret to have to inform your readers of the death of Brigadier-General Pettigrew, who was wounded in the re-crossing on Tuesday last, and who died at Bunker Hill, last evening. His remains have arrived here, but cannot at present be carried further. They would have been taken to Staunton and encased in a metallic coffin, but decomposition has been too rapid. A brave man and a faithful soldier, he has sealed his devotion to his flag by his works on the field of battle. Let his country mourn the loss of her brave departed son.

General Paul J. Semms, who died at Martinsburgh, has been interred there. His remains were attended to their last resting-place by a large number of soldiers, and by a number of the Southern sympathizers of the place. His funeral sermon was preached by the Rev. Dr. W. J. Hoge, and is said to have been fully up to his best pulpit efforts. It must have been a touching discourse, for never had man a better theme in the person of his fellow than in General Semms. He was brave, patriotic, and high-toned; almost without a fault. Georgia, the land of his birth, and the Confederacy, for whom he has surrendered his life, should render their tributes of gratitude to the fallen hero.

The plans and purposes of the enemy are not yet developed. It is currently reported that they are crossing at Harper's Ferry in force. Their prisoners, taken in a cavalry skirmish below Charlestown, on Thursday evening, so say. It is also reported that their cavalry is near Martinsburgh, and that they are coming across at Williamsport. You may, however, feel quite sure that if Meade would not attack Lee with the raging Potomac in his rear, he will not push right ahead and give Lee the advantage of the river intervening between him and his (Meade's) base of supplies.

I have taken some pains to ascertain the number of prisoners captured, and am credibly informed that in all we must have taken about nine thousand prisoners, exclusive of the wounded, numbering about three thousand five hundred, which we captured and paroled in Gettysburgh. Of the nine thousand captured you will probably receive about four thousand in Richmond, the rest, I am told, were paroled on or near the battle-fields.

Our own loss in prisoners, I am inclined to believe, must reach, but will not much exceed five thousand. . . .

Winchester is very much crowded. There are many persons here looking after their friends and relatives. Some, too, have doubtless been drawn by a desire to indulge in speculation. But, thank heaven, the door is closed to these gentry.

Several distinguished clergymen are now here, among them Drs. John A. Broaddus, J. Lansing Burrows, W. J. Hoge, and Rev. Dr. Wilmer, of the Episcopal Church. A series of meetings of a religious character are in progress.

In closing, I may say that every day is adding to the strength and efficiency of the army, and that by the close of another week I sincerely believe that its *morale* will be fully up to if not in advance of its spirit at any time during the past twelve months. The country can rely upon the army of Northern Virginia, and Robert E. Lee, its chosen general.

During the retreat from Gettysburgh, Ewell lost nearly all his forges, and Hill some five or six. This was when the enemy attacked the trains.

Lieutenant-Colonel Christie, a gallant officer, died here, I am informed, last night.   X.

NEW-YORK "WORLD" ACCOUNT.

THE PRELIMINARY CAMPAIGN.

HEADQUARTERS ARMY OF THE POTOMAC,
NEAR GETTYSBURGH, Saturday evening, July 4.

The campaign which has practically terminated in the rout whose last sullen echoes are now dying away among the hills beyond Gettysburgh, was the most significant and remarkable of the war. It has solved more riddles; it has taught more lessons; it has been a brighter advantage to the cause of the Union, and a more signal disaster to that of the rebellion than any victory won by the Federal armies since McClellan hurled back the rebel legions to Virginia from the memorable field of Antietam. The army of the Potomac, under the cloud since the slaughter at Fredericksburgh and the blunder at Chancellorsville, has redeemed itself in the eyes of the nation and the world, to a level with its standard of the days when it was led to victory by the leader whose heart may well leap within him as he contemplates this last achievement of his beloved old-time comrades. Theories of its inferiority, born of the mistakes of Pope, Burnside, and Hooker, and nurtured by the contrast of its failures with the recent victories of western troops, are effectually shattered. It has shown to the public—it has always been evident to military judges—that this army has the capacity for fight, the endurance, the *élan*, and the energy to render it invincible in the hands of a cool and skilful General.

The first movement toward the invasion of Pennsylvania was opened soon after the battle of Chancellorsville by a cavalry movement, which was met and quashed at Brandy Station by General Pleasanton, about the first of June. On the thirteenth ultimo, General Milroy was attacked at Winchester by the advance of Lee's army under

General Ewell, and fled disgracefully, after a short conflict, to Harper's Ferry, abandoning all his stores and cannon to the rebels. This opened the way for the advance of the foe across the Potomac. Another force of its cavalry crossed the upper Potomac on the fifteenth, causing great consternation in Maryland and Lower Pennsylvania. It entered Chambersburgh and Mercersburgh in the evening. The alarm caused by this raid was unnecessarily great, for the main army of Lee had not yet reached the south side of the Potomac. The Union garrison at Frederick, Md., fell back to the Relay House on the sixteenth. A detachment of the enemy attacked Harper's Ferry the same day, but was shelled back by General Tyler from Maryland Heights. Ten thousand rebel infantry crossed the Potomac at Williamsburgh in the night, beginning in earnest the great invasion which was now fully shown to be intended. The fights at Aldie on the eighteenth and nineteenth were between General Pleasanton's and a body of the enemy's cavalry, which is supposed to have flanked their rear. More rebels constantly poured across the Potomac, and on the nineteenth Ewell's entire division occupied Sharpsburgh, in Maryland. By this time Pennsylvania, New-York, and New-Jersey began their great effort to repel Lee's advance from the North. Hooker, reposing in pastoral quiet at Fairfax Station, in Virginia, did not disturb himself with any such activity. He watched, waited, and was puzzled. Milroy's stampede, the clamor of which, it seems, might have come to him from over the western mountains; the cries of help from Harrisburgh, Pittsburgh, Carlisle, and minor Pennsylvania towns; the tremulous appeals from Philadelphia and Baltimore—all these did not serve to arouse him from his lethargy, or give him the least idea of where his enemy was. It was not until a voice of command from Washington, inspired, it is believed, from the midst of his own army, came sounding in his ears like a fire-bell in the night, that he ordered up his tent-stakes and began *his* march northward over the Potomac. Meanwhile, General Couch had commenced the organization of a militia force at Gettysburgh to check the twenty thousand men under Ewell, who were raiding like banditti through the country. The main rebel army was entirely across the Potomac below Williamsburgh on the twenty-sixth, moved northward *via* McConnellsburgh and Chambersburgh, and began in partially scattered columns its advance through Pennsylvania in the direction of Philadelphia and Baltimore. The rashness and audacity of this movement seemed to confound the General then in command of this army. Every mile over which Lee now marched lengthened his lines of communication in such degree as would have imperiled it beyond peradventure had Hooker seen fit to improve his advantage. Forty thousand troops and a hundred pieces of rebel artillery passed through Chambersburgh on the twenty-ninth. On Sunday York was occupied by General Early, who made his famous levy on its citizens. Harrisburgh, long threatened, was not yet attacked.

General Meade took command of this army on Sunday, the twenty-eighth ultimo. At that time his headquarters were at Frederick, and Lee's at Hagerstown. It will be seen that he was in the south-west, and consequently in the rear of the foe, imminently threatening his line of retreat. The army of the Potomac began its campaign from that moment. Orders were issued to the several corps to move early in the evening, and on the morning of the twenty-ninth our whole brilliant and hopeful host was in motion toward Pennsylvania. The First, Third, and Eleventh corps encamped on Tuesday at Emmetsburgh; the Second and Twelfth also pitched their tents near by. The Sixth corps marched to Carlisle Wednesday morning, the first day of this month forever memorable. The First corps, under Major-General Reynolds, and the Eleventh, under Major-General Howard, started for Gettysburgh, Reynolds in command, where they arrived at ten o'clock A.M. The First corps, in the advance, marched directly through the town. The enemy was discovered posted in a wood to the westward, near the Lutheran Theological Seminary. The beginning of the three days' conflict was at hand.

THE BATTLE OF WEDNESDAY.

One who has been in the presence, who now sits among the echoes, and whose brain teems with rushing memories of a conflict so recent and so vast, may well pause before attempting to indicate its magnitude or describe its progress. Rash as the advance of General Reynolds has been pronounced by many brother officers who now lament his death, I question whether it was not after all for the best. It served at once as a reconnoissance showing the enemy's exact position and probable force, and as a check upon any offensive movement which that enemy might have been intent upon. It secured the army of the Potomac the commanding position on Cemetery Hill, from which the battles of the two succeeding days were chiefly fought, and which, had the rebel commander anticipated the engagement, he would doubtless have secured for himself. Not less, perhaps, than the skill of the generals who directed the battle on our side, gave us the victory. When, therefore, the heroic First corps and its fated commander placed themselves in the terrible dilemma of Wednesday morning, they won a knowledge by their sacrifice worth all the world to us thereafter. The corps marched in the following order: First division, under General Wadsworth; Third division, under General Doubleday; five full batteries, under Colonel Wainwright; Fourth division, under General Robinson.

A portion of our artillery took position half a mile south of the seminary. The enemy opened fire upon it with such fierceness as forced the batteries to retire, which they commenced doing in good order. General Wadsworth immediately came to their aid; two of his regiments, the Second Wisconsin and the Twenty-fourth Michigan, charged the rebel infantry, forcing them in turn to retire. The batteries assumed an excellent position further in the rear, which they held during the day. General Reynolds now rode forward to inspect the field and ascertain the most favorable line for the disposal of his troops. One or two members of his staff were with him. The enemy at that instant poured in a cruel musketry fire upon the group of officers; a bullet struck General Reynolds in the neck, wounding him mortally. Crying out, with a voice that thrilled the hearts of his soldiers, "Forward! for God's sake, forward!" he turned for an instant, beheld the order obeyed by a line of shouting infantry, and falling into the arms of Captain Wilcox, his aid, who rode beside him, his life went out with the words: "Good God, Wilcox, I am killed."

The command of the corps devolved upon General Doubleday, who hurried to the front, placed it in position, and awaited a charge which it was seen the rebels were about to make. An eminence whereon stood a piece of woods was the important point thenceforth to be defended. The rebels advanced and opened fire from their entire line. They were instantly charged upon by Meredith's Western brigade, who, without firing a shot, but with a tremendous cheer, dashed forward with such swiftness as to surround nearly six hundred of the foe, who were taken prisoners. A strong column immediately advanced against us from the woods, and, though volley after volley was poured into them, did not waver. Their proximity and strength at last became so threatening that the brigades of the Second division were ordered to make another charge, which was even more successful that the first. Their momentum was like an avalanche; the rebels were shot, bayoneted, and driven to partial retreat, more than two regiments falling into our hands alive. Our ranks suffered fearfully in this demonstration, and it was evident that such fighting could not long go on. The Eleventh corps now made its appearance, and its General (Howard) assumed command of the forces. Steinwehr was ordered to hold Gettysburgh and Cemetery Hill—all his artillery being placed in the latter position. The other two divisions of the Eleventh corps, under Schurz and Barlow, then supported the First corps, on the right, in time to resist two desperate charges by Ewell's troops. A third charge was now made by the entire rebel force in front, which comprised the corps of Hill and Ewell, sixty-two thousand strong. The shock was awful. The superior numbers of the foe enabled them to overlap both our flanks, threatening us with surrounding and capture. Their main effort was directed against our left wing, and notwithstanding the gallant fighting done by our soldiers at that point, they at last obtained such advantage that General Howard was forced to retire his command through the town to the east, which was done in good order, the compliments of the rebels meanwhile falling thick among it, in the shape of shells, grape, and canister. The two corps were placed in line of battle on Cemetery Hill at evening, having withstood during the entire day the assaults of an enemy outnumbering them three to one. Not without grief, nor without misgiving, did the officers and soldiers of those corps contemplate the day's engagement and await the onset they believed was to come. Their comrades lay in heaps beyond the village whose spires gleamed peacefully in the sunset before them. Reynolds the beloved and the brave, was dead, and Zook slumbered beside him. Barlow, Paul, many field and scores of line officers had been killed. The men of the First corps alone could in few instances turn to speak to the ones who stood beside them in the morning without meeting with a vacant space. The havoc in that corps was so frightful as to decimate it fully one half, and that in the Eleventh corps—nobly rescued from the suspicion which rested upon it before—was scarcely less great. Yet the little army flinched not, but stood ready to fall as others had fallen even to the last man. With what a thrill of relief General Howard, who had sent messenger after messenger during the day to Slocum and Sickles, saw in the distance at evening the approaching bayonets of the Third and Twelfth corps, only they can tell who fought beside him. Those corps arrived and assumed positions to the right and left of the First and Eleventh on the heights about Cemetery Hill at dusk. The enemy made no further demonstration that night. General Meade and staff arrived before eleven o'clock. The commander then examined the position, and posted the several corps in the following order: The Twelfth (Slocum) on the right; the Eleventh, (Howard,) next; the Second, (Hancock,) First, (Doubleday,) and Third, (Sickles,) in the centre; the Fifth, (Sykes,) on the extreme left. The situation was brilliant, commanding. For almost the first time in the history of this army's career belonged the advantage in the decisive battles which ensued.

The heights on which our troops were posted sloped gently downward from our front. The line stretched in a semi-circle—its convex centre toward Gettysburgh, the extremes toward the south-west and south. Ledges on the interior sides gave our soldiers in some instances a partial shelter from artillery. Every road was commanded by our cannon, and the routes by which Lee might otherwise soonest retreat in case of his defeat, were all in our possession. At every one weaker than others reserves were judiciously posted, and the cavalry—an arm of the service scarcely brought into play in some recent and destructive battles—protected both our flanks in immense numbers.

Thus the great army lay down to sleep at midnight, and awoke on the morn of a day more sanguinary than the last.

THE BATTLE OF THURSDAY.

On what a spectacle the sun of Thursday rose, the memory of at least that portion of our forces who witnessed it from Cemetery Hill will linger forever. From its crest the muzzles of fifty cannon pointed toward the hills beyond the town. From the bluffs to the right and left additional artillery frowned, and away on either side, in a graceful and majestic curve, thousands of infantry moved into battle line, their bayonets gleaming like serpents' scales. The roofs of Gettysburgh in the valley below, the rifts of woodland along the borders of Rock Creek, the orchards far down on the left, the fields green and beautiful, in which the cattle were calmly grazing, composed a scene of such peace as it appeared was never made to be marred by the clangor of battle. I strolled out to the Cemetery ere the dew was yet melted from the grass, and leaned against a monument to listen to the singing of birds. One note, milder than the rest, had just broken from the throat of an oriole in the foliage above me when the sullen rattle of musketry on the left told that skirmishing had begun. Similar firing soon opened along the entire rebel line, and although no notable demonstration was made during the forenoon, it was apparent that the enemy was feeling our strength preliminary to some decisive effort.

The day wore on full of anxious suspense. It was not until four o'clock in the afternoon that the enemy gave voice in earnest.

He then began a heavy fire on Cemetery Hill. It must not be thought that this wrathful fire was unanswered. Our artillery began to play within a few moments, and hurled back defiance and like destruction upon the rebel lines. Until six o'clock the roar of cannon, the rush of missiles, and the bursting of bombs filled all the air. The clangor alone of this awful combat might well have confused and awed a less cool and watchful commander than General Meade. It did not confuse him. With the calculation of a tactician and the eye of an experienced judge, he watched from his headquarters on the hill whatever movement under the murky cloud which enveloped the rebel lines might first disclose the intention which it was evident this artillery firing covered. About six o'clock P.M., silence, deep, awfully impressive, but momentary, was permitted, as if by magic, to dwell upon the field. Only the groans, unheard before, of the wounded and dying, only the murmur—a morning memory—of the breeze through the foliage, only the low rattle of preparation for what was to come, embroidered this blank stillness. Then, as the smoke beyond the village was lightly borne to the eastward, the woods on the left were seen filled with dark masses of infantry, three columns deep, who advanced at a quickstep. Magnificent! Such a charge by such a force—full forty-five thousand men, under Hill and Longstreet—even though it threatened to pierce and annihilate the Third corps, against which it was directed, drew forth cries of admiration from all who beheld it. General Sickles and his splendid command withstood the shock with a determination that checked, but could not fully restrain it. Back, inch by inch, fighting, falling, dying, cheering, the men retired. The rebels came on more furiously, halting at intervals, pouring volleys that struck our troops down in scores. General Sickles, fighting desperately, was struck in the leg and fell. The Second corps came to the aid of his decimated col-

umn. The battle then grew fearful. Standing firmly up against the storm, our troops, though still outnumbered, gave back shot for shot, volley for volley, almost death for death. Still the enemy was not restrained. Down he came upon our left with a momentum that nothing could check. The rifled guns that lay before our infantry on a knoll were in danger of capture. General Hancock was wounded in the thigh, General Gibbon in the shoulder. The Fifth corps, as the First and Second wavered anew, went into the breach with such shouts and such volleys as made the rebel column tremble at last. Up from the valley behind another battery came rolling to the heights, and flung its contents in an instant down in the midst of the enemy's ranks. Crash! crash! with discharges deafening, terrible, the musketry firing went on; the enemy, re-forming after each discharge with wondrous celerity and firmness, still pressed up the declivity. What hideous carnage filled the minutes between the appearance of the Fifth corps and the advance to the support of the rebel columns of still another column from the right, I cannot bear to tell. Men fell as the leaves fall in autumn before those horrible discharges. Faltering for an instant, the rebel columns seemed about to recede before the tempest. But their officers, who could be seen through the smoke of the conflict galloping and swinging their swords along the lines, rallied them anew, and the next instant the whole line sprang forward as if to break through our own by mere weight of numbers. A division from the Twelfth corps on the extreme right reached the scene at this instant, and at the same time Sedgwick came up with the Sixth corps, having finished a march of nearly thirty-six consecutive hours. To what rescue they came, their officers saw and told them. Weary as they were, barefooted, hungry, fit to drop for slumber as they were, the wish for victory was so blended with the thought of exhaustion that they cast themselves in turn *en masse* into line of battle, and went down on the enemy with death in their weapons and cheers on their lips. The rebel camel's back was broken by this "feather." His line staggered, reeled, and drifted slowly back, while the shouts of our soldiers lifted up amid the roar of musketry over the bodies of the dead and wounded, proclaimed the completeness of their victory. Meanwhile, as the division of Slocum's corps on the extreme right left its post to join in this triumph, another column of the enemy, under command of General Ewell, had dashed savagely against our weakened right wing, and as the failure to turn our left became known it seemed as if determination to conquer in this part of the field overcame alike the enemy's fear of death, and his plans for victory elsewhere. The fight was terrific, and for fifteen minutes the attack to which the three divisions of the Twelfth corps were subjected was more furious than any thing ever known in the history of this army. The Sixth corps came to their support, the First corps followed, and from dusk into darkness, until half-past nine o'clock, the battle raged with varied fortune and unabated fury. Our troops were compelled by overpowering numbers to fall back a short distance, abandoning several rifle-pits and an advantageous position to the enemy, who, haughty over his advantage and made desperate by defeat in other quarters, then made a last struggling charge against that division of our right wing commanded by General Geary. General Geary's troops immortalized themselves by their resistance to this attempt. They stood like adamant, a moveless, death-dealing machine, before whose volleys the rebel column withered and went down by hundreds. After a slaughter inconceivable the repulse of Ewell was complete, and he retired at ten o'clock P.M., to the position before referred to. The firing from all quarters of the field ceased soon after that hour, and no other attack was made until morning.

THE BATTLE OF FRIDAY.

As one who stands in a tower and looks down upon a lengthy pageant marching through a thoroughfare, finds it impossible at the close to recall in order the appearance and the incidents of the scene, so I, who sit this evening on a camp-stool, beside the ruins of the monument against which I leaned listening to the robin of yesterday, find it impossible to recall with distinctness the details of the unparalleled battle just closed. The conflict, waged by one hundred and sixty thousand men, which has occupied with scarce an interval of rest the entire day, from four A.M. until six o'clock this evening, contains so much, so *near*, and such voluminous matter of interest as one mind cannot grasp without time for reflection.

This last engagement has been the fiercest and most sanguinary of the war. It was begun at daylight by General Slocum, whose troops, maddened by the loss of many comrades, and eager to retrieve the position lost by them on the preceding evening, advanced and delivered a destructive fire against the rebels under Ewell. That General's entire force responded with a charge that is memorable even beyond those made by them yesterday. It was desperation against courage! The fire of the enemy was mingled with yells, pitched even above its clangor. They came on, and on, and on, while the National troops, splendidly handled and well posted, stood unshaken to receive them. The fire with which they did receive them was so rapid and so thick as to envelope the ranks of its deliverers with a pall that shut them from sight during the battle which raged thenceforward for six dreary hours. Out of this pall no straggler came to the rear. The line scarcely flinched from its position during the entire conflict. Huge masses of rebel infantry threw themselves into it again and again in vain. Back, as a ball hurled against a rock, these masses recoiled, and were re-formed to be hurled anew against it with a fierceness unfruitful of success—fruitful of carnage, as before. The strong position occupied by General Geary, and that held by General Birney, met the first and hard-

est assaults, but only fell back a short distance before fearful odds, to readvance, to reassume and to hold their places in company with Sykes's division of the Fifth corps and Humphrey's (Berry's old division) of the Third, when, judiciously reënforced with artillery, they renewed and continued the contest until its close. It seemed as if the gray uniformed troops, who were advanced and readvanced by their officers up to the very edge of the line of smoke in front of our infantry, were impelled by some terror in their rear, which they were as unable to withstand as they were to make headway against the fire in their front. It was hard to believe such desperation voluntary. It was harder to believe that the courage which withstood and defeated it was mortal.

The enemy gradually drew forward his whole line until in many places a hand-to-hand conflict raged for minutes. His artillery, answered by ours, played upon our columns with frightful result, yet they did not waver. The battle was in this way evenly contested for a time, but at a moment when it seemed problematical which side would gain the victory, a reënforcement arrived and were formed in line at such a position as to enfilade the enemy and teach him at last the futility of his efforts. Disordered, routed, and confused, his whole force retreated, and at eleven o'clock the battle ceased, and the stillness of death ensued. This silence continued until two P.M. At this moment the rebel artillery from all points, in a circle radiating around our own, began a terrific and concentrated fire on Cemetery Hill, which was held, as I have previously stated, by the Eleventh and Second corps. The flock of pigeons, which not ten minutes previous had darkened the sky above, were scarcely thicker than the flock of horrible missiles that now, instead of sailing harmlessly above, descended upon our position. The atmosphere was thick with shot and shell. The storm broke upon us so suddenly that soldiers and officers—who leaped, as it began, from their tents, and from lazy siestas on the grass—were stricken in their rising with mortal wounds and died, some with cigars between their teeth, some with pieces of food in their fingers, and one at least—a pale young German, from Pennsylvania—with a miniature of his sister in his hands, that seemed more meet to grasp an artist's pencil than a musket. Horses fell, shrieking such awful cries as Cooper told of, and writhing themselves about in hopeless agony. The boards of fences, scattered by explosion, flew in splinters through the air. The earth, torn up in clouds, blinded the eyes of hurrying men; and through the branches of the trees and among the grave-stones in the cemetery a shower of destruction crashed ceaselessly. As, with hundreds of others, I groped through this tempest of death for the shelter of the bluff, an old man, a private in a company belonging to the Twenty-fourth Michigan, was struck scarcely ten feet away by a cannon-ball, which tore through him, extorting such a low, intense cry of mortal pain as I pray God I may never again hear. The hill, which seemed alone devoted to this rain of death, was clear in nearly all its unsheltered places within five minutes after the fire began.

Our batteries responded immediately. Three hours of cannonading ensued, exceeding in fierceness any ever known. Probably three hundred cannon were fired simultaneously until four o'clock, when the rebel infantry were again seen massing in the woods fronting our centre, formed by the First and Second corps. General Doubleday's troops met this charge with the same heroic courage that had so often repelled the enemy in his desperate attempts. The charge was made spiritedly but less venomously than before. General Webb, commanding the Second brigade, Second division of the Second corps, met the main fury of the attack with a steady fire that served to retard the enemy's advance for a moment. That moment was occupied by the rebel General Armistead in steadying his troops behind the fence. General Webb immediately ordered a charge, which was made with such eagerness and swiftness, and supported by such numbers of our troops, as enabled us partially to surround the enemy, and capture General Armistead and three thousand of his men. The carnage which accompanied this charge, and the terror inspired by it, were so great as to reduce numbers of the foe to actual cowardice. They fell upon their knees and faces, holding forward their guns and begging for mercy, while their escaped comrades, panic-stricken, and utterly routed, rushed down across the ditches and fences through the fields and through Gettysburgh. Not a column remained to make another start. The triumph sought for during these three terrible days belonged at last to the noble army of the Potomac.

With a pen that falters, with a hand and a heart heavy even in the presence of this great conquest; saddened by the death of not a few friends, and sick of the sights and sounds that have so long shocked my eyes and numbed my thoughts; with a vision deceived, perhaps, in many instances, by the mere tumult of the conflict; and with ears filled by divers reports and estimates of officers and surgeons, I cannot, I dare not attempt to give you an account or opinion of our losses. They are great. But compared with those of the enemy they are like as pebbles to grains of sand along the shore.

BONAPARTE.

REPORT OF DR. DOUGLAS.

F. Law Olmstead, General Secretary Sanitary Commission.

SIR: When the army of the Potomac broke camp at Falmouth, to commence the campaign which terminated in the battle of Gettysburgh, the operations of the Commission in connection with this army again assumed a most active and laborious character. The evacuation of Acquia necessitated the withdrawal of its large stock of stores, accumulated at that place and at Fal-

mouth; and the instantaneous removal of the thousands of sick and wounded from the corps hospital at Potomac Creek, called for an unusual amount of labor from its relief corps.

I have already reported, in a communication to the executive committee, dated June seventeenth, that all our stores had been safely removed to this city from Acquia, by means of our transport the steamer Elizabeth, and that we had furnished substantial food to over eight thousand sick and wounded soldiers at Lodge No. 5, of the Commission, situated at Sixth Street wharf, where all of the transports brought the inmates of the corps hospitals on their way to the general hospitals of this District. This work of transportation began Saturday, June thirteenth, and continued unceasingly until Monday night, the fifteenth. Coffee, bread, hot beef-soup, lemonade, were provided in quantities to meet the demands of all, and on the arrival of the boats, each invalid was questioned as to his wants, and his wishes complied with. The continuous labor of these two days severely taxed the strength of those engaged in it.

While a portion of our force was thus occupied in removing the stores, and another portion in dispensing refreshments to the arriving thousands, a third party was engaged in following the marching columns, ready to lend assistance whenever it might be needed.

The short halt made by the army in the vicinity of Fairfax Court-House permitted us to accumulate stores at that point. When the march was again resumed, our wagons with a replenished stock continued to follow in the rear of the column.

Dr. Alex. McDonald, who was temporarily in charge of our station at Acquia, as soon as he had reported the removal of our stores from that point, rejoined the corps in the field. I quote from his report a *résumé* of our operations with the army, until it crossed the Potomac at Edwards's Ferry.

"On Monday, the twenty-second instant, (June,) two wagons loaded with hospital stores, in care of Messrs. Bush and Scandlin, and accompanied by Mr. Bellows, were sent to Fairfax Court-House; on Tuesday, another load, accompanied by Messrs. Hoag, Paige, Holbrook, and myself, proceeded to the same point, arriving at four P.M., and on Wednesday, a mule train with forage was sent in charge of Mr. Clampitt.

"Our intention was to leave one wagon with relief agent and storekeeper at Fairfax, to send a similar force to Centreville and Thoroughfare Gap, and another to Gum Springs and Aldie; but on arriving at Fairfax, we were advised by General Sedgwick to remain where we then were, as the roads were not safe without an escort. Acting on this advice, we remained at Fairfax, issuing stores to the hospitals of the Sixth and cavalry corps, which were much in need of such supplies as we then had.

"Found the cavalry hospital located on a slightly elevated hill, well shaded, with good water, though not in large quantity, well drained, clean, raised beds, and the men in a very comfortable condition; but few severe cases; camp was well policed and neatly laid out; surgeons active and efficient; good nurses; clean, well-ventilated tents; every thing in good order, but in want of supplies.

"The hospital of the Sixth corps was established on a new plan—the men being kept in the ambulances, ready for immediate transportation. This plan was still an experiment, and had not been fully tested, but so far as one could judge from observation and the experience and statements of surgeons in charge, should deem it a good one, and well worthy a more extended trial. Ambulances were well parked on a gently sloping piece of ground, kept in good order, and the men seemed to be very comfortably situated, except that they needed more blankets.

"We supplied each of these and some of the regimental hospitals from our stock, and at a time when there were no other means of their obtaining the much-needed articles. The issues at Fairfax were to such an extent as to enable us to pack nearly all the remaining stock in two wagons, and send one nearly empty with the mule train to Washington to be reloaded.

"Thursday morning visited headquarters, and was there advised to send empty wagons and mules to Washington, to start with loaded wagons, and follow in the train of the reserve artillery. . . . Moved with train and camped at night on top of a hill this side of Edwards's Ferry, placed a guard over our stores and horses, and lay down to rest, most of us having been on the road thirty-one hours without food or sleep, except such as we could catch during the halts.

"Saturday, moved on to Poolesville, where we arrived at ten A.M. This point having been designated as a good one for an issue-station, a room was engaged, and before the wagons were unloaded two requisitions came in, the surgeons being very glad to get something for their men. All stores in the town were closed by order of the General Commanding, and the Commission was the only source from which they could obtain any thing."

For the purpose of keeping our stock up, another wagon-load was sent up from Washington Friday afternoon, to intercept our train at Poolesville, Dr. McDonald having informed us from Fairfax that he should make that point. This wagon succeeded in getting through safely, although the road was very insecure, a long government train being seized a few hours after our wagon had passed a certain point in the road by a body of Stuart's cavalry. It reached Poolesville, accompanied by Major Bush and Mr. Clampitt, Saturday afternoon. One wagon was then returned to Washington for repairs. Sunday morning, the army and trains moving on rapidly, our stores were again packed, and the wagons proceeded together to Frederick, arriving there the same evening.

It will be remembered that just previous to this time, before our forces had crossed the Po-

tomac, the enemy had attacked and routed General Milroy's command at Winchester, and the forces at Harper's Ferry and vicinity had been withdrawn into the intrenchments on Maryland Heights, where they were in some respects beleaguered.

"On the eighteenth of June," writes Dr. L. H. Steiner, our Chief Inspector with the army of the Potomac, "I received a telegram from Dr. C. F. H. Campbell, Surgeon U. S. Vols., Medical Director, General Kelley's command, stating that he needed 'lint, stimulants, and bandages.' This telegram was sent in answer to an inquiry made by me, whether I could aid him. Securing the use of a wagon and mule team from Alfred F. Brengle, of Frederick, I despatched, June nineteenth, quite a large quantity of brandy, sherry, whiskey, chocolate, condensed milk, tea, lint, and bandages, to Maryland Heights. James Gall, Jr., relief agent, accompanied the stores, and Mr. Brengle drove the team. They reached their destination safely. Mr. Gall remained on the Heights with his stores. Mr. Brengle was seized by some of the enemy's cavalry on his return, his team and wagons were confiscated, and himself seized as a prisoner, and sent to Richmond. He still remains a prisoner."

The menacing attitude of the enemy, pointing toward another invasion of Maryland, and possibly of Pennsylvania, necessitated a rapid concentration of an opposing force in its front. The President called for one hundred thousand militia for this purpose. The first troops under this call left New-York on the seventeenth June. In anticipation of the accumulation of a large body of troops in the neighborhood of Harrisburgh, I despatched, on the seventeenth, Dr. Wm. F. Swalm, Inspector of the Sanitary Commission, with Mr. Isaac Harris, relief agent, to that point. They arrived at Harrisburgh before any troops, and made diligent preparation to lend such assistance as might be required. They remained on the ground till the enemy had recrossed the Potomac into Virginia, and the militia had been recalled to their several States. They advanced with our advancing columns to Carlisle, Shippensburgh, Chambersburgh, and Boonsborough, visiting camps and hospitals, and pushing forward such extra governmental supplies as were found wanting. The accompanying reports exhibit the activity, and the relief afforded by Dr. Swalm and Mr. Harris to the hurriedly constructed hospital organizations of the militia forces.

The main body of the enemy having crossed the Potomac near Williamsport, about the twenty-seventh of the month, the design and direction of the movement began to be apparent. Our own army was at this time in the vicinity of Frederick City, Maryland, and was moving northward, as rapidly as possible, to meet the equally rapid advance of the opposing forces.

Our Chief Inspector, Dr. Lewis H. Steiner, was at Frederick. Dr. Alexander McDonald had joined him. The wagons of the Commission, which had followed in the train of the army, had reached

Frederick and reported to Dr. Steiner. It was still doubtful where the collision between the opposing forces would take place. We were prepared to do our work in the front and in the rear, but the emergency might arise in an unexpected point, and we wished to be prepared.

A demonstration of the enemy upon the Northern Central Railroad (Baltimore and Harrisburgh) determined me to send out a relief agent in that direction. Accordingly, Mr. James Gall, who had returned from Maryland Heights, was, on the twenty-seventh June, ordered to proceed along the line of that road, to push forward in whatever direction he should learn that a conflict was impending, to acquaint himself with the position of affairs, and to keep the Central office informed of the necessity of forwarding supplies and agents.

Mr. Gall was enabled to proceed only to Parkton by rail, from thence he walked to York, a distance of twenty-eight miles. Upon entering the town, he found it, to his surprise, in possession of the enemy. The following observations, made by Mr. Gall, upon the condition and appearance of the soldiers composing the division of the rebel troops occupying York, I quote from his report:

"Believing that a battle would take place at or near York, I determined — as there was no other means of getting there — to push forward on foot. I started from Parkton at nine o'clock on Sunday morning, and reached York at four o'clock in the afternoon, and found, to my surprise and regret, that the city was already in the possession of the rebel troops. The force occupying York was General Early's division, of Ewell's corps, consisting of five brigades of infantry, three batteries of artillery, and part of two regiments of cavalry — in all about nine thousand men, and eighteen pieces of artillery. Gordon's brigade, accompanied by a battery of artillery, and part of a regiment of cavalry, passed through the city, and pushed on in the direction of Wrightsville. Post's brigade, composed chiefly of North-Carolina men, was quartered near the barracks, and did guard duty near the city. Two batteries of artillery were parked in a field called the 'Fair Grounds.' The other three brigades were camped outside the city, and commanding the various roads leading to it. . . . . . .

"On entering the town, General Early made a levy upon the citizens, promising in the event of its being complied with promptly, to spare all private property in the city; otherwise he would allow his men to take such things as they needed, and would not be responsible for the conduct of his men while they remained in the city. The beef, flour, and other articles, and twenty-eight thousand dollars in money were speedily collected, and handed over to the rebels. The General expressed himself satisfied with what he had received, and scrupulously kept his word in regard to the safety of private property. Nothing belonging to any citizen was touched; no one was molested in the streets; all was as quiet and orderly as if there were no soldiers there.

"On Monday the rebels were busy in carting off the levied articles. About four P.M., Gordon's brigade returned from Wrightsville, bringing with them some horses and cattle which they had picked up on the way. They had about eight supply and ammunition wagons, and twelve ambulances with them. Many of the latter were marked U. S. The ambulances were all filled with men, who had apparently given out on the way. Physically, the men looked about equal to the generality of our own troops, and there were fewer boys among them. Their dress was a wretched mixture of all cuts and colors. There was not the slightest attempt at uniformity in this respect. Every man seemed to have put on whatever he could get hold of, without regard to shape or color. I noticed a pretty large sprinkling of blue pants among them, some of those, doubtless, that were left by Milroy at Winchester. Their shoes, as a general thing, were poor; some of the men were entirely barefooted. Their equipments were light as compared with those of our men. They consisted of a thin woollen blanket, coiled up and slung from the shoulder in the form of a sash, a haversack slung from the opposite shoulder, and a cartridge-box. The whole cannot weigh more than twelve or fourteen pounds. Is it strange, then, that with such light loads they should be able to make longer and more rapid marches than our men? The marching of the men was irregular and careless; their arms were rusty and ill-kept. Their whole appearance was greatly inferior to that of our soldiers.

"During Monday I visited the 'Fair Grounds,' as also the camp of a Louisiana brigade, situated about a mile from the city. The supply wagons were drawn up in a sort of straggling hollow square, in the centre of which the men stacked their arms in company lines, and in this way formed their camp. There were no tents for the men, and but very few for the officers. The men were busy cooking their dinner, which consisted of fresh beef, (part of the York levy,) wheat griddle-cakes raised with soda, and cold water. No coffee or sugar had been issued to the men for a long time. The meat was mostly prepared by frying, and was generally very plentifully salted. The cooking is generally done in squads, or messes of five or six, and on the march the labor of carrying the cooking utensils is equally divided among them. The men expressed themselves perfectly satisfied with this kind of food, and said they greatly preferred the bread prepared in the way they do it, to the crackers issued to the Union soldiers. I question if their bread is as healthy and nourishing as the army biscuit. I asked one of the men how he got along without a shelter-tent. His answer was: 'First rate.' 'In the first place,' said he, 'I wouldn't *tote* one, and in the second place, I feel just as well, if not better, without it. 'But how do you manage when it rains?' I inquired. 'Wall,' said he, 'me and this other man has a gum-blanket atween us; when it rains we spread one of our woollen blankets on the ground to lie on, then we spread the other woollen blanket over us, and the gum blanket over that, and the rain can't tech us.'

And this is the way the rebel army (with the exception of a few of the most important officers) sleeps. Every thing that will trammel or impede the movement of the army is discarded, no matter what the consequences may be to the men. In conversation with one of the officers, I mentioned about the want of tents in his army, and asked whether any bad effects were apparent from it. He said he thought not. On the contrary, he considered the army in better condition now than ever before. Granting the truth of what the officer said about the condition of the rebel army, I very much doubt the correctness of his conclusions. The present good condition of the rebel army is more likely to be due to the following circumstances: First, the army has been lying still all winter, under good shelter; has been tolerably well fed and clothed, and in this way has had a chance to recuperate after the fatiguing campaigns of last summer. Second, most of the weakly men, who could not stand a day's march without being sent to the rear, have been either discharged or have died, thus leaving a smaller portion of those remaining liable to disease. Third, since that portion of the rebel army (Ewell's corps) moved from behind Fredericksburgh, on the fourth of June last, it has been favored with remarkably fine weather; has been stimulated with almost uninterrupted success in its movements; has been marching through a rich and fertile country, and, by levying on the inhabitants of which, the soldiers have been able to procure an abundance of good wholesome food, better, perhaps, than they had for many months. These, and not the want of tents, are probably the causes which give to the rebel army its present healthy tone. Under ordinary circumstances, I have no doubt the want of shelter would prove rather a detriment to the army than otherwise.

"In further conversation with the Louisiana officer, I ascertained that this was the corps which moved down through the Shenandoah Valley, surprised Milroy at Winchester, and was the first to cross the Potomac at Shepherdstown into Maryland. He informed me that his own and the North-Carolina brigade were armed entirely with Enfield rifles taken at Winchester after Milroy's retreat. In speaking of our soldiers, the same officer remarked: 'They are too well fed, too well clothed, and have far too much to carry.' That our men are too well fed I do not believe, neither that they are too well clothed; that they have too much to carry I can very well believe, after witnessing the march of the army of the Potomac to Chancellorsville. Each man had eight days' rations to carry, besides sixty rounds of ammunition, musket, woollen blanket, rubber blanket, overcoat, extra shirt, drawers, socks, and shelter-tent, amounting in all to about sixty pounds. Think of men, (and boys too,) staggering along under such a load, at the rate of fifteen to twenty miles a day.

"About nine o'clock Monday night, the guards were withdrawn from the hotels and liquor-shops,

and the whole of the North-Carolina brigade shortly after left the city in the same direction as Gordon's brigade. On Tuesday morning, about four o'clock the last remaining brigade passed through the city with flags flying and band playing, and took the road to Carlisle. The other two brigades it was supposed had gone off in the direction of Gettysburgh.

"The city was now clear of rebels, except some stragglers who purposely staid behind, or were too drunk to go with their commands.

"While General Early scrupulously kept his agreement with the citizens of York, as to the protection of private property in the city, he did not prevent his troopers from visiting the farms outside the city and taking such horses and mules as they required. The rebel cavalry, as a general thing, are splendidly mounted, better, I think, than the Union cavalry, and their free and easy manner of procuring fresh horses explains it."

Mr. Gall not being able to communicate with us by telegraph, except from Baltimore, reported in person, and was immediately ordered to join Dr. Steiner at Frederick.

The anticipated battle was now near at hand. Supplies were accumulated at New-York, Philadelphia, Baltimore, and Washington. Mr. Knapp was at Philadelphia, and Mr. O. C. Bullard at Baltimore, both with efficient assistants ready to respond to all demands.

The supply train following the army had reached Frederick City, and was under the orders of Dr. Steiner. Its subsequent operations during the battle week I give in the words of Dr. Steiner from his report already referred to.

"*June* 28.—The supply train, with stores from Washington, reported to me during the day, being in charge of Messrs. Bush, Hoag, and Clampitt. Desiring to retain Clampitt to assist me in my work in Frederick, I detached him from the train, which then started off, accompanied by Messrs. Hoag and Bush. The benefits afforded by these supplies to the wounded, to whom they were distributed under fire, during the battles of Gettysburgh, July second and third, by Mr. Hoag, cannot be expressed in words, and the receipted requisitions of the surgeons who employed these stores on that occasion, are sufficient evidence of the utility of being prepared for such emergencies.

"On Saturday, July fourth, two wagons reported to me from Washington, being accompanied by Dr. Alexander McDonald, (Sanitary Inspector,) and Messrs. James Gall, Junior, and Rev. Mr. Scandlin, (relief agents.) Having been informed that a car-load of supplies had been forwarded to Westminster, Maryland, I ordered one wagon, under the direction of Mr. Gall, to that place, with the view of having it then filled with supplies and thence to proceed to Gettysburgh. The second wagon was loaded from the Frederick storehouse, and despatched under the charge of Dr. McDonald, *via* Emmetsburgh to Gettysburgh. Dr. McDonald was provided with instructions to take charge of our operations in the field, and was supplied with discretionary powers. Rev. Mr. Scandlin accompanied the second wagon. The first wagon safely reached Gettysburgh, the second was seized by a party of the enemy's cavalry, in or near Emmetsburgh, its stores and the horses of the party confiscated, and Dr. McDonald, Mr. Scandlin, Leonard Brink, (the teamster,) with a colored boy, Moses Gardner, were taken to Richmond, where they are held as prisoners."

The report of the first pitched engagement of the contending forces, on the first July, reached us the following morning. A freight car (No. 816) was immediately loaded and despatched to Westminster, leaving Washington in the night, in charge of Mr. S. Bacon. Mr. Hovey followed the next morning in passenger train, and reached Westminster about noon July third. Owing to a delay at Baltimore of the government freight train, the car was thirty hours *en route*.

On Sunday, the fifth July, another car, (No. 1499,) loaded with assorted supplies, was sent to Westminster, in charge of Mr. George G. Edgerly, and a third car-load to Frederick, to the care of Dr. Steiner.

These were the supplies which reached the army immediately subsequent to the battle, before the railway leading direct to Gettysburgh was put in repair, and before any communication was open, except through the long and tedious process of hauling by wagons.

What was done by our force in the field, during and immediately after the battle, up to the time when I arrived at Gettysburgh, I shall give in the words of those who performed the labor.

Mr. Hoag, who was in charge of the wagons, sent out by Dr. Steiner from Frederick, gives the following account :

"I left Frederick City in charge of two wagons, well loaded, June twenty-ninth. We fell in with the Twelfth army corps supply-train ; but owing to its moving slowly, did not get more than six miles before we were obliged to put up for the night.

"Tuesday we moved more rapidly, passed through Taneytown, and out on the road to Emmetsburgh, overtook the Third corps in camp, on the banks of the Monocacy. Next morning, Wednesday, I obtained permission to bring my wagons in just behind the headquarters' teams, and kept with them to or near Gettysburgh, where we arrived about nine o'clock P.M. All was quiet until four o'clock P.M., Thursday, when a heavy firing commenced on our left, where the 'rebs' were trying a flank movement. As soon as the wounded began to come in, I started out with the wagons to distribute the stores. We reached five different hospitals, which were all we were able to find that night, and early in the morning three others, which exhausted our stores. We were just in time to do the most good possible, as the Government wagons had been sent back ten miles, and many of the hospitals were not supplied with material sufficient for immediate use. (The hospitals supplied were division hospitals of the First, Second, Third, Fifth, Eleventh, and Twelfth corps.)

"On telling the surgeons that I was on hand with sanitary stores, I was almost invariably greeted with expressions like the following, 'You could never have come at a better time,' and once on mentioning sanitary stores, I received two hearty welcome slaps on the shoulder, one from the medical director of the corps, and the other, the surgeon of the division."

Major Bush, who accompanied Mr. Hoag, gives his account in the following words :

"Monday morning, June twenty-ninth. Mr. Hoag and myself left Frederick with two wagon loads, in connection with the train of the Twelfth corps, by order of General Williams to Dr. Steiner. Reached Taneytown, Maryland, Tuesday, P.M., June thirtieth.

"Wednesday morning, July first, and first day of the battle, I was informed, while at General Meade's headquarters, by an orderly just arrived from this place, (Gettysburgh,) that an attack and a battle was expected here that day, as the cavalry with the First and Eleventh corps had already reached this place. I left Mr. Hoag and our wagons in the train of headquarters, (to which they had been transferred from that of the Twelfth army corps,) and rode to Littlestown, Pennsylvania, thence to this place, arriving at 'Cemetery Hill,' where a portion of our batteries were situated, about eleven P.M., just as the rebel prisoners who were captured by our cavalry and the Eleventh corps, in the first engagement of that day were approaching said hill. The battle soon commenced between the First corps and General Hill's, (rebel,) south-west of the Seminary, which was fought steadily and bravely by the First corps, until it finally retreated with severe loss between two and three P.M. Its commander, General Reynolds, was among the killed.

"The rebels then rallied in the rear of the Seminary and College Hill, during which time the Eleventh corps formed a line between the college and the town, making the fences their line of defence. The rebel forces advanced over this hill in mass about four P.M., formed in line of battle, when they marched firmly toward the Eleventh corps, which retired into the town without making any formidable resistance, and the rebel troops took possession of Gettysburgh, when the fighting of the first day ceased. I now made search for our wagons, but in the vast concourse I was unable to find them that night. (Most of the wounded of this day's fight, were carried into the churches and public buildings of the town, under the organization of the First and cavalry corps, and were prisoners at the close of the day.)

"The Third and Twelfth corps arrived during the afternoon, but too late to enter into battle.

"Thursday, July second, and second day of the battle. The Second corps arrived by the Taneytown road, below Cemetery Hill, at daybreak. The Fifth corps arrived two miles from town, on the Baltimore pike, about ten A.M. One division of the Sixth corps on the same pike from Westminster, at two P.M.

"The battle opened about four P.M. Found our wagons early in the afternoon. As soon as the surgeons had decided upon the different points where the corps hospitals were to be formed, Mr. Hoag moved the wagons to them at once, and commenced to issue our stores, which consisted chiefly of concentrated beef-soup, stimulants, crackers, condensed milk, concentrated coffee, corn-starch, farina, shirts, drawers, stockings, towels, blankets, quilts, bandages, and lint. We hastened from one hospital to another, as rapidly as possible, issuing to each a proportion of our stores, until the supply was nearly exhausted, when, upon consultation with Mr. Hoag, it was decided that I should start for the nearest point from which a telegram could be sent to Washington, ordering up more supplies. Frederick was spoken of, but upon inquiry at different points, it was considered unsafe to go there, as the rebel cavalry were in possession of the roads in that direction. I then decided to go to Westminster, learning that several of the New-York newspaper reporters were about starting for the same place, and learning that the telegraph was in operation from that place to Baltimore. I left the battle-field late in the evening, arrived in Westminster early in the morning of Friday, and soon learned, to our disappointment, that no telegraph was there, and the first train did not leave for Baltimore till twelve M. Arrived in Baltimore just in time to take the express-train to Washington. Found that a car had already been loaded with stores and started for Westminster, under the direction of Messrs. Hovey and Bacon.

"This car arrived at Westminster Saturday, July fourth, when Mr. Hovey procured three government wagons, and that evening started with three full loads of stores, arriving early next morning, (Sunday,) at the First, Second, and Third corps hospitals. By your orders I left Washington by the eleven A.M. train, July fourth, arriving at Relay in time for the two P.M. train for Westminster. Owing to a misunderstanding between the two conductors on the road, the trains waited for each other at either end of the road, so that we did not get started from the Relay until eight o'clock Sunday morning, arriving at Westminster at ten A.M., where I found Mr. Bacon in charge of the remainder of the car-load of stores. About noon our four-mule team came in from Frederick, in charge of Mr. Gall. It was immediately loaded, and early in the morning I left with it, in company of Mr. Gall, Mr. Bacon still remaining in charge at Westminster.

"A school-house was taken on the Baltimore pike, near the different corps hospitals, and about three miles out from Gettysburgh, and from it our stores were thereafter issued, until the opening of the railroad permitted our reaching the field by that route, when, on Tuesday morning, July seventh, a store-house was taken in town, and the school-house closed."

In the mean time, Mr. Hoag had been to Fred-erick with the two wagons, and had returned with full loads to the school-house, where the stores brought by him were issued.

Mr. Hovey, after delivering his loads to the three corps hospitals, returned to Westminster and took three more loads, and Mr. Gall made a second trip with the four-mule team, which took the remainder of the first car-load sent from Washington.

Twelve wagon-loads of extra governmental supplies were therefore taken on to the battle-field previous to the opening of the railroad to Gettysburgh, and before they could reach the wounded from any other direction. Of these, eight wagon-loads were taken from Westminster, and four from Frederick, including the two which were on the field during the battle, and the supplies from which were issued under fire, and to the hospitals the nearest to the line of battle. The last of these stores were given to a hospital to the left of our line, just in the rear of Weed's Hill, where General Weed fell.

The second car-load, sent up in care of Mr. Edgerly, was by him transferred to Mr. Bacon, who, after unloading it, had it reloaded, and by the advice of Major Painter, Post-Quartermaster, sent around by rail to Gettysburgh.

On Monday, July sixth, I left Washington for Baltimore to meet yourself and Mr. Knapp. Upon consultation, it was deemed advisable that I should proceed at once to Gettysburgh. In company, therefore, with Mr. Bullard, Mr. Murray, Mr. Barton, and two Germans, sent to our aid by Mr. Hitz, of Washington, I left Baltimore on Monday evening, upon a freight-train, containing two loaded cars for the Commission.

Heavy trains, heavy grades, delays of all kinds, prevented us from reaching Gettysburgh before late Tuesday afternoon. The temporary terminus of the railway was then over a mile from the town, and to this terminus crowds of slightly wounded men came, limping, dragging themselves along, silent, weary, worn. The moment the cars stopped, the crowd of weary and wounded soldiers accumulated there, indicated that point as a place for a relief lodge. I immediately had two of our largest tents, together capable of sheltering seventy-five men, pitched, stoves erected, and a lodge established. The wise foresight of Mr. Knapp had included these articles among the first invoice. The two Germans, whose names I have unfortunately lost, volunteered as cooks. That night our tents were full, and we had the great satisfaction of not only affording shelter and attention to the wounded, but also supplying good nutritious food to those within our tents, and those who had taken refuge on the cars.

While our tents were being raised, Mr. E. B. Fairchild rode down from the village to ascertain if there had been any arrivals by the train, and found us in the midst of our preparations. He reported the arrival of Dr. Bellows and Dr. Agnew from Harrisburgh, the position of our field-station at the school-house, and the presence of Messrs. Johnson, Biddle, Edgerly, Hoag, Gall, Paige, and Hovey, (relief agents,) at our store-house in the town. The lodge established, I left it in charge of Mr. O. C. Bullard, who was assisted by Mr. Murray and Mr. Barton, and the Germans from Washington, and reported to Dr. Bellows.

The next day our store-house was given up to the Provost-Marshal, and another room on Baltimore street was by his permission taken. The latter place, the store of Messrs. Fahnestock and Company—the largest in the town—became the centre of the busiest scene which I have ever witnessed in connection with the Commission. Car-load after car-load of supplies were brought to this place, till shelves and counter and floor up to the ceiling were filled, till there was barely a passage-way between the piles of boxes and barrels, till the sidewalk was monopolized, and even the street encroached upon. These supplies were the outpourings of a grateful people. This abundant overflow of the generous remembrance of those at home, to those in the army, was distributed in the same generous manner as it was contributed. Each morning the supply-wagons of the division and corps hospitals were before the door, and each day they went away laden with such articles as were desired to meet their wants. If the articles needed one day were not in our possession at the time, they were immediately telegraphed for, and by the next train of cars thereafter they were ready to be delivered. Thus, tons of ice, mutton, poultry, fish, vegetables, soft bread, eggs, butter, and a variety of other articles of substantial and delicate food were provided for the wounded, with thousands of suits of clothing of all kinds, and hospital furniture in quantity to meet the emergency. It was a grand sight to see this exhibition of the tender care of the people for the people's braves. It was a bit of home feeling, of home bounty, brought to the tent, put into the hand of the wounded soldier. I feel grateful that I was permitted to participate in this work.

Mr. H. P. Dechert was placed in charge of this store-house, and was assisted permanently by Messrs. Edgerly, Bacon, Murray, and Bowers, with a detail of four soldiers. To this force, at first, were added Messrs. Johnson, Biddle, Gall, and Paige. These latter gentlemen were afterward hospital visitors, for a few days, when they left to join the army of the Potomac in its advance, as relief agents.

The accompanying tabulated statement of the issues to the different hospitals, as prepared by Mr. Dechert, will exhibit the amount and character of the articles supplied.

The lodge, which was established at the temporary terminus of the railway on Tuesday, was continued there until Friday, when the burned bridge which had prevented the cars from running into town was replaced by a new structure, and the cars resumed their regular runnings to the station. On Thursday I had a tent and fly erected near the depot in preparation for the change in the terminus of the road, and on Saturday the lodge out of town was discontinued and the tents used there added to those near the depot. This second lodge was in successful operation on Friday, though it was not generally made use of till Saturday.

Between Tuesday and Saturday noon we provided at our first lodge good beef-soup, coffee, and fresh bread, for over three thousand slightly wounded soldiers whose injuries did not prevent them from walking to this point, while we sheltered each night about fifty more serious cases, which had been brought down by ambulance, and whose wounds required the attention of a surgeon. We were fortunate in having during these days the volunteer aid of Dr. Hooper, from Boston, who devoted himself to this latter work. Mr. Clark, from New-Hampshire, Mr. Hawkins, from Media, Pa., and Mr. Shippen, from Pittsburgh, also lent their assistance, and all these gentlemen materially aided us at this and at the second lodge until it was fully organized.

With the transfer of our material to town, the irregular organization was changed to a permanent working basis. Dr. W. F. Cheney, who arrived on the tenth, was placed in charge of the camp. He brought with him seven assistants, Messrs. Latz, Cooley, McGuinness, Chesebro, Blakeley, Sherwin, Freshoner, from Canandaigua, N. Y. To these were added Messrs. Reisinger and Hall, from Baltimore, and four detailed soldiers. Cooks had arrived, a large shed for a kitchen had been erected, and full preparations were made for feeding any number. Every facility was granted us by the medical officers of the post and by the commissary. Additional tents were erected, drains made, straw procured, and shelter prepared for one hundred and fifty men. A store-tent was placed near the hospital tents, and given into the charge of two New-York ladies, whose long experience on the Commission's transports during the Peninsular campaign of last summer had made them familiar with all the requirements of this camp. The cars stopped immediately in front of our camp, and distant but a few feet from it.

During the ten days subsequent to the establishment of this lodge over five thousand soldiers (Union and rebel) received food either in our tents or on the cars, and an average of over one hundred remained in our tents each night and had their wounds dressed and more or less clothing distributed to them.

This lodge was continued until all the wounded capable of being removed were transferred from the corps hospitals to the general hospitals of New-York, Philadelphia, Baltimore, Harrisburgh, and York.

When the general field hospital was decided upon for the reception of all those whose serious wounds prevented them from being removed, I asked for a place to be assigned us in the plan, and before leaving Gettysburgh saw two of our tents erected in the camp, one for our stores, the other for the ladies who would be in charge. This design has been effectually carried out.

Our plan of operation and our labors were in Gettysburgh as they have been elsewhere, divided into those of inquiry and relief. The latter, from our experience, was subdivided into general and special relief. The first of these was to be extended by issues from our store-house directly to corps hospitals, in bulk, according to the ascertained necessities, and the latter took the direction of attending to those of the wounded—by far the greater number—who, capable of being transported from the field of battle, were daily removed, until only the more serious cases remained. I have already given the history of the store-house and lodge. The tabulated statement of the issues from the former, and the number assisted and relieved at the latter, will tell how well the organization worked. Few left the region of Gettysburgh without receiving some material aid from us, either in food or clothing.

Our trained permanent corps rendered this work easy and immediate. This would not have been possible, in the same time, with a body of men unaccustomed to and ignorant of the work. The large number of volunteers who came to our assistance, under the direction of those already familiar with the work, fell readily into the line of duty, and soon became efficient co-workers.

The labor of inquiry required the daily visitation of the hospitals, consultation with the medical officers as to the most efficient manner in which we could aid them, the character and quantity of the supplies most needed, the daily movement in the population of the hospitals under their command, with the character and severity of the injuries, and all such information in relation to the disposition of the wounded as would assist us in making our preparations.

Beside the visits of inquiry to the hospitals, a list of the names and wounds of all the inmates of each hospital was taken and forwarded to the office of the Hospital Directory in Washington, and we held ourselves in readiness to attend to messages of inquiry sent to us from any direction, in regard to any wounded man in these hospitals. This work was performed by Mr. Dooley, from the Directory office. Messrs. Stille, Struthers, Hazlehurst, Dullus, Beitler, and Tracy, from Philadelphia, and Messrs. Hosford, Myers, and Braman, from New-York, assisted in this labor, as well as at the lodge, and in attending to special cases.

The duty of visiting the confederate hospitals was assigned to Dr. Gordon Winslow, who reported to me soon after I arrived. The following communication, addressed by him to me, will give briefly the result of his inquiries:

"Gettysburgh, July 22, 1863.

"Sir: Agreeably to your instructions, I have inspected the several confederate hospitals in the vicinity of Gettysburgh, and have indicated, on the accompanying map, the locality, division, general who was in command, surgeon in charge, and number of wounded.

"It appears that the aggregate of wounded, at the time of my visits, was five thousand four hundred and fifty-two, occupying some twenty-four (24) separate camps, over an area of some twelve miles. The wounds, in a large proportion of cases, are severe.

"Amputations and resections are frequent. The corps of confederate surgeons are, as a body, intelligent and attentive. The hospitals are generally in barns, outhouses, and dilapidated tents. Some few cases are in dwelling. I cannot speak favorably of their camp police. Often there is a deplorable want of cleanliness. Especially in barns and outhouses, vermin and putrid matter are disgustingly offensive. As fast as means of transportation can be had, those who are capable of being removed will be placed in more comfortable quarters. Some hundreds are being removed daily. Every provision is made by the Sanitary Commission for their comfort during their stay at the depot lodge, and those who are placed directly in the cars are furnished wholesome food. I am pleased to report that the surgeons have in every instance spoken in the highest terms of praise of the efforts made for their relief and comfort."*

In this connection, I may state that subsequent to these visits, Dr. Winslow procured the signature of every confederate surgeon to a petition to General Lee for the immediate and unconditional release of Dr. McDonald, Mr. Scandlin, Mr. Brengle, Leonard Brink, and Moses Gardner, who had been taken prisoners while acting in their humane office, as non-combatants, and ready to extend assistance to all wounded alike. This petition has been forwarded through the proper authorities, with the advice and consent of our own officers for the exchange of prisoners. A month has elapsed, but so far no notice has been taken by the confederate officers of the wishes of their surgeons in our hands.

The hospitals containing our own wounded were visited by Messrs. Johnson, Biddle, Murray, Paige, Gall, Fairchild, and myself. Some of them were also visited by yourself and Mr. Knapp, who separately came to Gettysburgh, and accompanied me in my rounds.

The hospital organizations were mostly in tents, taking some farmer's house and barn as a nucleus.† For several days immediately succeeding

* The hospitals visited by Dr. Winslow were situated as below, and contained the number of wounded as indicated in the following table:

Location.		Division.	Surgeon.	No.
Cashtown,		Gen. Parine's,	Dr. Wilson,	171
On Chambersburgh Road,	"	Porcher's,	Dr. Ward,	700
On Mummasburgh Road,	"	Rhodes's,	Dr. Hayes,	800
In Penn. College,	"	Heth's,	Dr. Smiley,	700
Hunterstown Road,	"	Johnson's,	Dr. Whitehead,	311
Fairfield,				50
Fairfield Road,	Part of Gen. Johnson's,		Dr. Stewart,	135
" "		" Early's,	Dr. Potts,	259
" "		" Anderson's,	Dr. Mines,	111
" "		" McLaws's,	Dr. Patterson,	700
" "		" Hood's,	Dr. Means,	515

Total, ... 5452

† The First corps hospital was divided. A portion was in the town, occupying several churches and the court-house. These buildings contained the wounded of the battle of July first. The number estimated, including those in private houses, was four hundred to four hundred and fifty. The second portion was about two and a half miles from the town on the Baltimore pike. The First division was in and about the White church and Lightner's house; the Second division in and about Peter Conover's house; and the Third division had Jonathan Young's house for its centre. There were in these divisions two thousand three hundred and seventy-nine wounded, of whom two hundred and sixty were confederates. Dr. Ward was the surgeon in charge.

the battle, there was a great deficiency in tents, and a sad want of most of the necessities of a hospital both in food and furniture. This latter we attempted to fill so far as our limited resources would go. The want was incident to the campaign, and not the result of neglect. Another difficulty, inseparable from the campaign, was the small number of medical officers left upon the ground to take charge of the large number of wounded. The battle ended and the enemy on the retreat, the advance of our forces required the presence of a large proportion of the medical officers to meet the demands of another battle which seemed imminent. Those left behind had to divide their attention among our own wounded and those of the enemy who had fallen into our hands, the number of confederate surgeons left behind being inadequate to their care. In previous battles there has always been a full quota, if not the entire medical corps of the army, to attend to the wounded.

The labor, the anxiety, the responsibility imposed upon the surgeons after the battle of Gettysburgh, were from the position of affairs, greater than after any other battle of the war. The de-

The Second corps hospital was situated on the banks of Rock Creek, in tents, about eighty rods north of the house indicated on the map as that of Isaac Schriever. It contained about four thousand five hundred wounded, of whom one thousand were rebels. Dr. Justin Dwinelle was the surgeon in charge. There were three divisions consolidated.

The Third corps hospital was on high ground south of Schwartz's house, about one hundred rods above the junction of White's Creek with Rock Creek, on Schwietzel's farm. It contained two thousand five hundred and fifty wounded; of these, two hundred and fifty-nine were rebels. Dr. Hildreth was surgeon in charge. There were two divisions only, under separate organization, but remote from each other only by a narrow ravine.

The Fifth corps hospital was in three divisions. The first division was on Mr. Little's farm, north of the house and south of White's Creek, and about one hundred rods east of Third corps. The second division was south of Mrs. Jesse Clapsaddle's house, across Lousy run, about one hundred rods south of White's Creek. The third division was about half a mile west of Two Taverns, on Jesse Werley's farm. This division hospital was the most remote of all the Union hospitals from the town of Gettysburgh. They contained together one thousand four hundred wounded, including seventy-five rebels. Dr. Clark, surgeon in charge.

The three divisions of the Sixth corps hospital were, the first, about the house of John Frastle, near Peach Orchard, and the Second and Third divisions in tents near by. There were three hundred inmates. Dr. Chamberlain, surgeon in charge.

The Eleventh corps hospital occupied the house and farm of George Spangler. The divisions were consolidated under the charge of Dr. Armstrong. It contained one thousand nine hundred wounded, of whom one hundred were said to be confederates.

The Twelfth corps hospital was under the charge of Dr. Ernest Goodman. Its three divisions, under separate organizations, were together around the house of George Bushman. It contained one thousand one hundred and thirty-one wounded, including one hundred and twenty-five rebels.

The cavalry corps hospital was in town, and occupied the Presbyterian church on Baltimore street, and the two school-houses in the immediate vicinity. It was under the charge of Dr. Rulison, and the three buildings contained three hundred of our wounded.

These figures are approximative only, as that was all we sought for at the time. The number of wounded whose wants—beyond those that a beneficent government cared for—we were anxious to supply, can be stated briefly as follows:

1st	Corps (2 portions)	2,519 Union,	260 confederates,	2,779
2d	"	3,500	"	1000	"	4,500
3d	"	2,300	"	250	"	2,550
5th	"	1,325	"	75	"	1,400
6th	"	300	"	..		300
11th	"	1,800	"	100	"	1,900
12th	"	1,006	"	125	"	1,131
Cavalry	"	300	"	..		300
	Total..........	13,050		1810		14,860

votion, the solicitude, the unceasing efforts to remedy the defects of the situation, the untiring attentions to the wounded upon their part, were so marked as to be apparent to all who visited the hospitals. It must be remembered that these same officers had endured the privations and fatigues of the long forced marches with the rest of the army; that they had shared its dangers, for one medical officer from each regiment follows it into battle, and is liable to the accidents of war, as has been repeatedly and fatally the case; that its field hospitals are often, from the changes of the line of battle, brought under the fire of the enemy, and that while in this situation, these surgeons are called upon to exercise the calmest judgment, to perform the most critical and serious operations, and this quickly and continuously. The battle ceasing, their labors continue. While other officers are sleeping, renewing their strength for further efforts, the medical are still toiling. They have to improvise hospitals from the rudest materials, are obliged to make "bricks without straw," to surmount seeming impossibilities. The work is unending, both by day and night, the anxiety is constant, the strain upon both the physical and mental faculties unceasing. Thus, after this battle, operators had to be held up while performing the operations, and fainted from exhaustion the operation finished. One completed his labors to be seized with partial paralysis, the penalty of his over-exertion.

While his duties are as arduous, his exposure as great, and the mortality from disease and injury as large as among staff-officers of similar rank, the surgeon has no prospect of promotion, of a brevet, or an honorable mention, to stimulate him. His duties are performed quietly, unostentatiously. He does his duty for his country's sake, for the sake of humanity. The consciousness of having nobly performed this great duty is well nigh his only, as it must ever be his highest reward. The medical corps of the army is well deserving of this slight tribute.

Respectfully, J. H. DOUGLAS,
Associate Secretary Sanitary Commission.
WASHINGTON, D. C., August 15, 1863.

Doc. 21.

CAPTURE OF THE "CALEB CUSHING,"

IN THE HARBOR OF PORTLAND, ME., JUNE 27, 1863.

PORTLAND, June 29, 1863.

SINCE the fight between the Enterprise and Boxer, in our waters, during the last war with Great Britain, there has not been so much excitement in this city as there was last Saturday.

Early in the morning it was reported that the revenue cutter Caleb Cushing had been surreptitiously taken out of the harbor. Various rumors were afloat respecting it. One was that Lieut. Davenport, who is a Georgian by birth, had run away with her. The cutter had been seen between five and six o'clock in the morning, proceeding outward, through Hussey's Sound, towed by boats, as the wind was very light, and from the Observatory all her movements could distinctly be seen.

Mr. Jewett, Collector of the Port, was informed of the circumstances a little after eight o'clock, and before nine o'clock he had three steamers employed in searching for the vessel, and discovering her position. Without any delay, he chartered the steamers Forest City, of the Portland and Boston line, the steamer Casco, the steam-tug Tiger, and the steamer Chesapeake, of the Portland and New-York line. Two rifled twelve-pounders were placed on board the Forest City, obtained from Fort Preble, and two six-pounders from the Arsenal, by Mayor McLellan, on board the Chesapeake. A detachment of soldiers from the Seventh Maine, under command of Adjutant Nickerson, was placed on board the tug. A detachment of the Seventeenth United States regulars from Fort Preble was placed on board the Forest City, and a detachment of the Seventh Maine on board the Chesapeake, the latter being accompanied by Colonel Mason and Captain Henry Warren. Hundreds of our citizens volunteered to go in the steamers, who were furnished with arms by the Mayor; among them the Rev. Mr. Lovering, of Park street church.

The Forest City left Fort Preble about a quarter before eleven o'clock. She was watched from the Observatory, which was crowded with citizens, by Mr. Moodey, who watched all her movements, as well as those of the cutter, the latter being seen hauling off south by west. At a quarter before twelve o'clock the first flash was seen to come from the thirty-two-pounder of the cutter, and in fifty seconds the report was distinctly heard. The cutter and the Forest City were off Bangs's Island, about ten miles distant. Several more guns were fired by the cutter, but they seemed to have no effect upon the steamer, as she kept steadily on, approaching the cutter.

In the mean time the Chesapeake had got under way, and was fast steaming down to the scene of the conflict. As she approached it, the Forest City let off steam, and waited for her to come up, when arrangements were made between the steamers to board the cutter. The cutter kept up her firing for a short time, when, finding that she would be carried by boarding, she was deserted, after being set on fire. She burned some time before the flames reached the magazine, and about a quarter before two o'clock blew up with a loud explosion, which shook buildings in the city. The Chesapeake, as she bore down upon the cutter, fired her two guns at her without effect.

Captain Liscomb, of the Forest City, reports that his steamer came within gunshot of the cutter about half an hour before the Chesapeake got along. The cutter fired at her six times without showing any flag. The Forest City then laid to, waiting for the Chesapeake to come up. When the latter arrived, after consultation, it was agreed to board the cutter, the Chesapeake being a propeller, and being protected by cotton bales on deck, to lead the way. On proceeding to carry this plan into execution, the rebels discovered

the purposes of the steamers, became frightened, and abandoned the cutter, after setting fire to her. They went in two boats, sending the cutter's crew, who were in irons, off in a separate boat. The two boat-loads of rebels steered for Harpswell, but were pursued and picked up by the Forest City. There were twenty-three persons in the two boats. The Forest City also picked up a small boat containing Mr. Bibber, who had been set adrift from the cutter—he having been captured with his partner from a small fishing-boat Friday off Damascove Island. Mr. Bibber informed Captain Liscomb that he was captured by the schooner Archer, of Southport, which vessel was in possession of a rebel crew from the pirate Tacony. That the schooner came in Friday, and anchored below Munjoy, intending to burn the two new gunboats, and to cut out the revenue cutter and the steamer Forest City. This they found themselves unable to do, but at two o'clock Saturday morning they boarded the cutter quietly, seized the small portion of her crew aboard, put them in irons, and made their way out of the harbor through Hussey's Sound, thus avoiding the fire of the forts.

Learning this, Captain Liscomb immediately pursued the Archer, which was making her way to the eastward as rapidly as the light breeze would permit, and captured her, finding three rebels and Mr. Bibber's partner on board. She was towed up to the city by the Forest City.

Captain Bibber reports that, in his opinion, there are three or more schooners upon the coast with rebel crews, destroying our fishermen. The Archer had only a howitzer on board, and the schooners are probably lightly armed. He also reports a rebel steamer on the coast. The Forest City passed a suspicious black steamer off Cape Porpoise at two o'clock Saturday morning, when coming from Boston, which first made for the Forest City, but afterward kept away to the south-west.

The Forest City arrived up about half-past four o'clock Saturday afternoon. She, as well as the Chesapeake, was received with great enthusiasm by the citizens. She was armed with two rifled twelve-pounders, with thirty soldiers from Fort Preble, and one hundred volunteer armed citizens. She did not get near enough to hit the cutter, and the cutter's shots, though coming very close, fell a little short.

The steamers would undoubtedly have carried the cutter by boarding, had the rebels not deserted and blown her up, as all on board the steamers—sailors, soldiers, and citizens—were anxious for the hand-to-hand fight, having nothing to match the big guns on board the cutter.

The rebel prisoners, twenty-three in number, were landed at Fort Preble. The crew of the cutter were brought up in the Chesapeake, and are held until the matter can be investigated.

The search on board the Archer revealed the fact that the rebel crew was none other than that of the Tacony. The Archer was captured by her on the twenty-fifth, and the Tacony was burned soon afterward, all her armament and stores being removed to the Archer.

By the log-book of the Tacony, which was found on board the Archer, it appears that the Tacony was captured June tenth, latitude thirty-four degrees twenty-one minutes, longitude seventy-six degrees forty-nine minutes.

On the twenty-third of June, the log-book states that she burned four vessels, and sent all the prisoners to New-York.

"*June* 24.—Burned ship ——, from Liverpool, for New-York, with passengers, and kept charge of her during the day.

"*25th.*—Burned the ship, and let her go. At half-past seven captured the schooner, (Archer.) At nine A.M., removing from the bark to the schooner. Finish at two A.M., every body being on board, burnt the bark Tacony. Stood to the N.W."

This is the last entry in the Tacony's log. There is also a journal of the C. S. corvette Florida Number Two, commencing May sixth, which says:

"At four P.M. the brig Clarence was put in commission as the Florida Number Two. The following is a list of the officers and crew: Second Lieutenant, C. W. Read, commanding; Second Assistant Engineer, E. H. Brown; Quartermaster, J. E. Billaps; Quarter Gunner, N. B. Boyd; Captain, A. G. J. W. Matheuson; Crew: Joseph Mayer, Charles Lawson, J. P. Murphy, Robert Muller, James McLeod, J. Robertson, A. L. Drayton, George Thomas, Alex. Stewart, Michael Gorman, Robert Murray, C. W. Dolvin, Hugh McDaniels, Frederick Walton, Jas. Coffer, Daniel Morse, John McNary.

"Received from steamer Florida one howitzer complete, six rifles, thirteen revolvers, ten pistols."

A memorandum-book was found, containing instructions, which reporters were not allowed to see, as it is thought to contain important evidence for Government. An account-book was also found, containing in the back part a list of vessels, probably captured by the rebels, as follows: Jacob Bell, Star of Peace, Oneida, Commonwealth, Kate Dyer, Lapwing, Colcord, Henrietta, Clarence, Estelle, Windward, Carrie Ann, Aldebaran, Byzantium, Isaac Webb, Shatemuc, Whistling Wind, Tacony, Goodspeed, Mary Alvina, Arabella, Umpire, Maringo, Florence, Ripple, Elizabeth Ann, Rufus Choate, Ada, Alfred Partridge, M. A. Shindler, Kate Stuart, Archer, a sloop, Wanderer.

The following is a list of chronometers found on board schooner Archer: Bark Tacony, going; bark Whistling Wind, run down; brig Umpire, going; brig Clarence, going; ship Byzantium, going; bark Goodspeed, going.

It appears from the memorandum-book that Lieutenant Read and crew went on board the Tacony about the fourteenth of May. On the twenty-fifth of June he seems to have burned the Tacony and gone on board the Archer. The last memorandum of the Lieutenant says:

"It is my intention to go along the coast with the view of burning the shipping in some exposed harbor or cutting out some steamer."

On discharging the cargo of the Archer Saturday evening the twelve-pounder brass howitzer which was on board the Tacony was found on board, together with arms and ammunition. The officers in command of the vessel were Second Lieutenant C. W. Read, who has a commission in the confederate navy, dated October twenty-third, 1862; Third Assistant Engineer Eugene H. Brown, who appears to have reported to Admiral Buchanan on board the Florida, October sixteenth, 1862.

An examination of the crew of the cutter disclosed the following facts:

Between one and two o'clock Saturday morning, two boats filled with armed men boarded the cutter on both quarters simultaneously. They were armed with revolvers and cutlasses. The watch on deck, when they heard the oars approaching, called Lieutenant Davenport, who was asleep in the cabin. He was overpowered by four men and ordered below; the watch was also ordered below, and the men below turned out of their hammocks and placed in irons, rebels standing over them with revolvers and threatening them with death if they made any noise. One of the crew tried to escape through the fore hatch to swim ashore and give the alarm, but was caught and secured. The rebels at once proceeded to make sail, hove up the anchors, and placing two boats ahead, towed her out through Hussey's Sound, thus avoiding the Forts. The Lieutenant and crew of the cutter, twenty in number, were kept below in irons until they were ready to set fire to her, when they were put into one of the cutter's boats with their irons on; but on being requested, the rebels threw the keys of the hand-cuffs on board the boat, and thus enabled the sailors to release themselves, and pull away from the cutter. The stores, flags, armament, etc., of the Tacony were on board the Archer. Among the flags was a burgee with the name of Tacony upon it.

Lieutenant Merryman, who was appointed to take command of the cutter, arrived here Friday evening. He went down in the Forest City to assist in the rescue of the vessel from the rebels.

Company A, State guards, in twenty minutes' time from receiving orders, were ready to go on board the tug.

It was fortunate for the prisoners that they were landed at Fort Preble, for such was the indignation of our citizens that they would have been murdered had they been brought up to the city.

When the rebel Lieutenant Read went on board the Forest City he was all of a tremor, and so nervous that he could scarcely do or say any thing. The rebel crew were rather stoical in appearance and action.

No communication was allowed on Saturday with the prisoners at Fort Preble, as by order of Government they are kept in strict confinement. A posse of police officers went down Saturday night for the purpose of bringing up the prisoners and placing them in jail, but the Commandant of the Fort refused to give them up, and stated that they were confined there by United States authority.

On board the Chesapeake, William F. Laighton, Naval Inspector, took command of the vessel. The guns were under the direction of George J. Barry, United States Naval Engineer, and the soldiers and armed citizens under command of Colonel Mason. Captain Willett, who commands the steamer, was as active and earnest as any one on board. It was all excitement from the time the first gun was fired at the Forest City by the cutter. Two guns were fired from the Chesapeake at the cutter.

When the Chesapeake picked up the regular crew of the cutter, it was with difficulty the armed men on board the steamer were restrained from firing into them, so strongly did they believe that the cutter had been carried off by them. A few moments' conversation with the crew satisfied them they were guiltless.

Among the volunteers on board the Chesapeake was an old tar who had been a gunner on board Farragut's fleet. After the Chesapeake fired at the cutter, making a very good shot for a small piece, this old tar rushed up, embraced the gun and affectionately patted her as though she was a pet child, with a hearty expression of approval for her good shot.

When it was concluded between the two steamers that the Chesapeake should lead off in boarding the cutter, Mr. Laighton stated that the question was, whether they should sink the cutter or the cutter should sink them, and then called for a vote upon the question. It was unanimously voted, with rousing cheers, to run the cutter down. A full head of steam was put on, and she bore down upon the cutter at the rate of fifteen knots. She had proceeded but a short distance, however, before it was discovered that the cutter was on fire and abandoned by the rebel crew.

Both boats having a considerable amount of freight on board deemed the risk too great to attempt to extinguish the flames.

The Archer was stripped Saturday night, and her stores, armament, etc., were placed in the Custom-House.

. The boat of the cutter was secured, after the painter had burned off, by Captain Warren, of the Seventh Maine, Mr. Haile, of the *Argus*, and Mr. Edward Pickett. They named her the Trio, and brought her up to the city and placed her in the boat-house of the North Star Boat Club.

There was no communication with the shore by any of the officers or crew of the rebels after they arrived in the harbor Friday evening. So Lieutenant Read states, and he is corroborated by the crew.

Mr. Berry, Agent of the Associated Press, visited Fort Preble yesterday afternoon, saw the prisoners and got an account of the cruise from Lieutenant Read, who courteously answered all questions. He collated his report with all important memorandums from his private note-book furnished the Commandant, namely:

Lieutenant Read reported on board the Florida in Mobile at the close of 1862. He describes her as a small sloop-of-war, eight rifled guns, and one hundred and twenty men. January sixteenth, left Mobile Bay with steam and every sail set to topmast studding sail, making fourteen and a half knots. On the seventeenth, at daylight, saw a big sloop-of war, supposed to be the Brooklyn, which passed within half a mile, showed three lights, and passed to the northward. Nineteenth, burned brig Estella. Early on the morning of the twenty-second, left Havana and steamed to the eastward; burned the brig Windward, letting the crew go in a small boat. Off Cardenas light burned the Corris Ann, and she drifted into Cardenas harbor. Thirty-first, was chased by a Federal gunboat, but had the heels of her. February twelfth, captured the clipper ship Jacob Bell; showed the Yankee flag in hailing her, and burned her on the thirteenth. March sixth, captured the ship Star of Peace, and burned her at four P.M. Thirteenth, captured the schooner Aldebaran. Twenty-eighth, captured the bark Lapwing; christened her the C. S. corvette Oreto, and she captured the ship Commonwealth seventeenth of April, bonding her. The Lapwing was afterward burned. March twenty-ninth, captured bark M. J. Colcord, and burned her the fifteenth of April. April twenty-third, burned bark Henrietta. Twenty-fourth, burned ship Oneida. May sixth, latitude 5.34 south, longitude 34.23 west, captured brig Clarence, and christened her C. S. corvette Florida No. 2.

Lieutenant Read states that the Florida captured fourteen in all up to this time. The Kate Dyer was one, the others I could not learn. Lieutenant Read was transferred to brig Clarence, with the crew as before reported. She was then off Cape St. Roque and ran up north till June sixth, when off Cape Hatteras she burned the bark Whistling Wind, with coal for the United States Navy. Seventh, captured schooner Alfred H. Partridge and bonded her. Ninth, burned brig Mary Alvina, loaded with commissary stores. Twelfth, latitude 37 north, longitude 75.30 west, captured bark Tacony, but finding her faster than the Clarence, transferred every thing and burned the Clarence. They christened the Tacony *Bark Florida*, which accounts for the steamer Florida being reported off our coast. Same day captured schooners M. A. Shindler and Kate Stuart; bonded the Kate Stuart in seven thousand dollars and sent all prisoners aboard and burned the M. A. Shindler. Same day captured and bonded brig Arabella with neutral cargo, and passed a gunboat without being noticed. Fifteenth, latitude 37.42, longitude 70.30, burned brig Umpire. Twentieth, latitude 40.50, longitude 69.04, bonded ship Isaac Webb with seven hundred and fifty passengers, wild Irishmen. Three P.M., burned fishing sloop, name unknown. Twenty-first, latitude 41, longitude 69.10, burned ship Byzantium and enlisted three men from her belonging to New-Orleans; same day burned bark Goodspeed. Twenty-second, burned fishing schooner Marengo and captured schooner

Florence and put all the prisoners aboard her, seventy-six in number, including the crews of schooners Elizabeth Ann, Rufus Choate, and Ripple, which were captured and burned the same day. Twenty-third, burned schooners Ada and Wanderer. Twenty-fourth, latitude 45.10, longitude 67.43, captured packet ship Shatemuc, from Liverpool for Boston, with three hundred and fifty passengers. Was anxious to burn her, being loaded with iron plates, etc. Tried to catch schooners to put the passengers aboard, but failed and had to let her go, bonding her for one hundred and fifty thousand dollars. Same day captured the schooner Archer, chased the Shatemuc and put the Archer's crew aboard.

Hearing that Federal cruisers were after the Tacony, and fearing recognition, burned Tacony, transferring every thing to the Archer. Thence came direct to Portland. Picked up two fishermen for pilots, but they would not serve. Took positions from coast survey charts. Got in at sunset and anchored below Munjoy. Had no communication with the shore. Waited until half-past twelve midnight, when moon went down, then rowed direct to cutter Caleb Cushing in two boats with muffled oars. Boarded one on each side, seized her crew without resistance and ironed them. Captured Lieutenant Davenport as he came on deck. Weighed anchor, being unable to slip the cable, and started at three A.M., going out by Hussey's Sound. Towed out by two boats ahead, followed by the Archer as fast as the light wind would permit. Laid to outside waiting for the Archer. When the steamers attacked us could only find five round shots, and were obliged to fire stones and pieces of iron.

Lieutenant Read belongs in Mississippi, near Vicksburgh, and graduated from Annapolis in 1860. He came in with the intention of burning the shipping and two gunboats which he learned were building, from a coal-laden English schooner from Pictou to New-York. He also intended to catch the steamer Forest City and burn her.

All the Tacony's crew came out of Mobile in the Florida except three taken from the Byzantium. The Tacony passed many steamers during her cruise. On the day the Byzantium and Goodspeed were burned, a large steamer, showing French flag, sailed around the burning vessels, examined them and passed on.

Too much credit cannot be given to Mr. Collector Jewett for the promptness with which he acted on this occasion. He received the following despatch on the evening of the occurrence.

J. Jewett: WASHINGTON, June 27.

SIR: Your prompt and efficient action in relation to the cutter Cushing merits my warmest approval. Cause all the parties implicated who may be arrested, to be placed in close confinement. Report the facts in detail for further instructions.   S. P. CHASE.

—*Portland Press, June 29.*

DEPOSITION OF ALBERT P. BIBBER, ONE OF THE FISH-ERMEN CAPTURED BY THE ARCHER.

I, Albert P. Bibber, of Falmouth, in the District and State of Maine, on oath, depose and say, that on the twenty-fifth day of June, A.D. 1863, between ten and eleven o'clock A.M., I was in my row-boat, about eight miles to the southeast of the Damariscove Island, hauling my trawl, aided by Elbridge Titcomb. We had about twenty-five lines to our trawl, and we had underseen all but two lines. There were no other boats near us, except one about half a mile off. The nearest land was Pumpkin Island, and that about five miles off. I saw a fishing vessel running down to us about half a mile distant, bearing about south-west. The persons on board hailed us: "Boat ahoy. Come alongside." I replied: "I cannot do it." They ordered me alongside again, and I told them I could not come, that I was under my trawl. They replied: "Cut it." I replied I shouldn't do it. The vessel then stood off a short distance and hove to, put out a boat with five men in it, and the boat soon came alongside my boat. The man in charge of the boat told me that I was taken by the confederate privateer Alabama, that is, as near as I can recollect. I think a part had pistols and all had side-knives. Two of them got into my boat and ordered me and my partner alongside their vessel, the two strangers rowing as well as my partner and myself. I went aboard with my partner, and we were both left to go about as we choose.

The vessel was a fishing schooner of about ninety tons, all fitted and found for the Banks. I did not see more than eight or nine men on board, besides myself and Titcomb. I don't remember what, if any thing, was said before I was ordered into the cabin. Titcomb was ordered in first, and he left when I went in. I had been on board an hour or more, when I was ordered into the cabin. I took a seat, and the person I took for the captain asked me where I belonged. I told him I belonged near by Portland. He asked me about the war, the fishery, the steamboats, and the cutter. He seemed principally to want to know the news about the war. I told him I had been fishing some time, that I had not heard of any late news, and I had not heard any thing that was going on. I told him all I knew about the steamboats and the hours they run, but I told him I was not very well posted about them. He seemed to want to know most about what time English boats run. I told him I could not tell where the cutter was, but I saw a topsail schooner go into Boothbay harbor that morning that I took for her. I told him that the last I knew, her complement of men was thirty, but that I had not known any thing about her for a long time. I don't recollect that he asked any thing about her guns. He got up, and started to go out of the cabin, saying: "All I want of you is to take this vessel in and out of Portland." I made no answer. That was all he said to me for the day, that I recollect of. I went upon deck, and staid there most of the time until we came to anchor in Portland harbor. He did not call upon me to take the vessel in, and I did not assist in the least in taking her into Portland harbor.

We finally came to anchor to the eastward of Pomeroy's rock, off Fish Point, Portland harbor, about a quarter of a mile from the rock. It was, I should judge, at the time we anchored about half-past seven or near sunset of said Friday, and I remained upon deck until about nine o'clock. In that time, they passed on deck, out of the cabin, ten or twelve clothes-bags. All the persons on board were at the time they took me, and remained all the time I was with them, in fishermen's clothes, except the person I have called the Captain. He had on blue or black pants and a blue frock coat. He had nothing on that looked like uniform, either naval or military, After they got into the harbor of Portland, the men put on their belts, pistols and cutlasses, and most of them were so armed before nine o'clock. My partner was with me most of the time. He did not assist at all in piloting the vessel into the harbor, and neither was called upon for that purpose. About nine o'clock Titcomb and myself were ordered below into the cabin and fastened up, and one man was left at the gangway, as near as we could judge. From the time that I went on board until we were put below, no boat left the vessel, and no person left it. When we were thus put into the cabin, we lay down in the berths. A man came down and said: "Men, don't attempt to come upon deck to-night. Make no noise or resistance, and it will be all the better for you." I said: "Ay, ay, sir." From the time we went on board the vessel until we went below as just stated, no boat came to the vessel, and no person communicated with any one on board. I was on deck constantly, excepting the time I was in the cabin first, as before stated, and the time I spent in eating dinner.

After being left alone, I heard noise of hoisting and a stir about deck, until twelve or half-past twelve o'clock, I should judge. I did not sleep a wink, and I heard nothing afterward but the tread of the watchman on deck until about daybreak. Then I heard a noise alongside. Men got upon deck and opened the companion-way and ordered us upon deck. Titcomb and myself both went on deck. The vessel was where she was when I went below at night. Both Titcomb and myself were ordered into our own boat alongside. I hesitated a moment. The order came, "Hurry up, men; hurry up, men," and so I went aboard. Three or four men got into the boat and rowed us alongside the cutter. It was daylight, and I could see the cutter near us, with all sail on and two boats towing. She was about an eighth of a mile east of Fish Point. When we got alongside I was ordered on board, and I think one man got out with me, an officer, I think.

Nothing was said to me for an hour, I should think, when one of the men said to me: "What do you think of this? Did you think of this when we came in last night?" I replied that I

did not. He asked me if I did not think it was well done, to take the cutter out, with all hands aboard, without any trouble. I told him I thought it was a very daring act. He said he would have done a good deal more had he had a good wind when he commenced. He asked me if I was acquainted through the way the cutter was going. I told him I was. He said: "Is there plenty of water?" I told him it was a very shallow place at low water. He said: "I shall go out this way." We were then to the northward of Fort Gorges. I don't recollect that he said any thing further, except: "Don't get this vessel aground." I made no reply whatever. I was on the main deck; I had made no remark about the course or direction of the vessel, and had been asked no questions. A man was at the wheel, but I had not spoken to him or been near him. A man was ordered by the officer to heave the lead. Don't know that I heard what depth was reported. We were then being towed to the northeast. There was no wind. We kept on until we got abreast the passage between Cow Island and Hog Island. I was then asked if the cutter would not go through that passage. I told him it was a very bad passage. He said he should go through, and told the man at the wheel to keep her off. She was kept off and taken through that passage. No questions were asked me about the course, and we went through it very quick, as a breeze sprang up just as we entered the passage. I gave no directions as to the course, and was not asked to give any. After getting through there, the cutter was in an open sea-way, and kept right out to sea.

Before we got to the Green Islands I asked the captain if he would not let me go. He said he should not. I saw two men, that looked like the cutter's crew, come up with irons on, and their irons were taken off while they went to the waterspout, and then they were ironed again and taken below. Beside those, I saw no other persons aboard except those I had seen the day previous in the schooner. After getting three miles beyond the Green Islands, I asked again to be let go. He told me no; he would stand off a little further, then he would heave-to and wait for the schooner to come up.

When out past Cod Ledge we saw steamers coming, and when they were within about two miles I asked again to be let go. He told me he didn't care; I might take either of the little boats alongside. I got into the boat as soon as the word was given, and rowed off. One of the men said I had better row a little quartering, for they should fire soon. I finally reached the steamer Forest City, and was taken aboard, and related all the circumstances to the officers. I told the captain that the schooner was somewhere between Portland and Jewell Island. He hesitated a few minutes, and under my direction ran for her. I remained on board the Forest City until I was landed at Fort Preble, where I am now detained. When I was taken on board the schooner I supposed it was a drunken crew of fishermen on a frolic, and I saw nothing suspicious until nearly half-way to Portland, when I saw them passing arms out of the hold for inspection, and it was while I so supposed that they were fishermen that they asked me about the steamboats, the cutter, and other things I have before mentioned as being inquired about.　ALBERT P. BIBBER.

LETTER FROM LIEUT. READ, OF THE PRIVATEER FLORIDA.

FORT PREBLE, PORTLAND, ME., }
July 1, 1863. }

MY DEAR BARBOT: As I have just noticed your arrival at Fort Lafayette, in company with the officers and crew of the late ram Atlanta, I have concluded to drop you a few lines, informing you of my being bagged, and nicely closeted, in a well-built fort in "Old Abe's" dominions.

As you have, perhaps, heard nothing definite of the Florida since she left Mobile Bay, I will give you a brief account of her exploits, and of my cruise since leaving her.

She left Mobile Bay on a clear, starlight night, a stiff breeze blowing from the north-west. We dashed by the blockaders at full speed, and although blue and flash Drummond lights turned night into day, we were not fired at. Next morning the Oneida, Brooklyn, and Cuyler, were in chase, but they soon dropped far astern. The breeze was strong, and we carried all the canvas the Florida could bear. The main-topsail yard was carried away, and the fore-topsail yard sprung. I never saw any vessel make better speed. The Florida is a splendid sea-boat. She will outsail any clipper, and steams thirteen knots. She can fight three heavy rifles directly aft; and as it is in her power always to bring on a stern chase, she can never be captured. With English oak and Southern hearts, she has no superior.

The Florida proceeded to Havana, thence to Nassau and Barbadoes. On the sixth of May she was off Cape St. Roque, and had captured fourteen sail, all valuable vessels. On the sixth of May we captured the brig Clarence, from Rio to Baltimore. I proposed to take her and make a raid on the United States coast. My proposition was acceded to, and I was given twenty-two men and one twelve-pound howitzer. We captured three transports off Cape Henry, and a fine clipper bark called the Tacony. As the latter vessel was a much better sailer than the Clarence, we burned the Clarence and took the bark. With the Tacony we destroyed fifteen sail. On the twenty-third of June we burned the Tacony, and took a small fore-and-aft schooner of seventy tons, with the view of cutting out a better vessel.

On the morning of the twenty-sixth we made Portland light; at sunset we entered the harbor; at half-past one we boarded the revenue cutter Cushing, and took her with but little difficulty. The wind was very light, and it was seven o'clock in the morning before we got out of range of the forts. At ten A.M. we were about fifteen miles from the city, when the wind died and left us becalmed. At eleven, three steamers were discovered approaching us; we cleared for action, but the ordnance department of the cutter, as usual, was in a deplorable condition and we were unable to do as much as we otherwise would have done. The cutter had one thirty-two pounder amidships and one twenty-four pounder howitzer forward. There was but one cartridge for the thirty-two, and but five rusty round shot and a few stand of grape. The attacking steamers were filled with armed men, and their machinery protected by bales of rags and cotton. We fired away all our ammunition, set fire to the cutter, and surrendered in our small boats.

It was my intention, when I came into Portland, to cut out a sea-going steamer, but, strange to say, at the decisive moment, Mr. Brown (whom you will remember in connection with the breaking down of the Arkansas engine) declared himself incompetent to work the engines of the steamer, unless he had another engineer to coöperate with him. All my plans were then crushed, and I was compelled to take the cutter out as a _dernier ressort_. If there had been a breeze, we would have been far out to sea before daylight, having committed considerable destruction in the harbor of Portland.

We have been kindly treated by our captors. I expect we will be sent either to New-York or Boston in a few days. As they have commenced exchanging again, I hope we all may be sent into Dixie before long. My kindest regards to Travers and Williamson. Write to me.

Sincerely, etc., your friend,
Lieut. A. BARBOT,　　　　C. W. READ.
Confederate States Navy, Fort Lafayette, N. Y.

Doc. 22.

THE ARMY OF THE POTOMAC.

THE CHANGE OF COMMANDERS.

GENERAL HOOKER was relieved of the command of the army at his own request. In taking leave of his soldiers, he issued the following address:

HEADQUARTERS ARMY OF THE POTOMAC, }
FREDERICK, MD., June 28, 1863: }

GENERAL ORDER No. 65.

In conformity with the orders of the War department, dated June twenty-seventh, 1863, I relinquish the command of the army of the Potomac. It is transferred to Major-General George G. Meade, a brave and accomplished officer, who has nobly earned the confidence and esteem of the army on many a well-fought field. Impressed with the belief that my usefulness as the commander of the army of the Potomac is impaired, I part from it, yet not without the deepest emotion. The sorrow of parting with the comrades of so many battles is relieved by the conviction that the courage and devotion of this army will never cease nor fail; that it will yield to my successor, as it has to me, a willing and hearty support. With the earnest prayer that the triumph of its arms may bring successes worthy of it and the nation, I bid it farewell.

JOSEPH HOOKER,
Major-General.

S. F. BARSTOW,
Acting Adjutant-General.

GENERAL MEADE'S ADDRESS ON TAKING COMMAND.

HEADQUARTERS OF THE ARMY OF THE POTOMAC, }
June 28, 1863. }

GENERAL ORDER No. 66.

By direction of the President of the United States, I hereby assume command of the army of the Potomac. As a soldier, in obeying this order, an order totally unexpected and unsolicited, I have no promises or pledges to make. The country looks to this army to relieve it from the devastation and disgrace of a hostile invasion. Whatever fatigues and sacrifices we may be called upon to undergo, let us have in view constantly the magnitude of the interests involved, and let each man determine to do his duty, leaving to an all-controlling Providence the decision of the contest. It is with just diffidence that I relieve in the command of this army an eminent and accomplished soldier, whose name must ever appear conspicuous in the history of its achievements; but I rely upon the hearty support of my companions in arms to assist me in the discharge of the duties of the important trust which has been confided to me. GEORGE G. MEADE,
Major-General Commanding.

S. F. BARSTOW,
Assistant Adjutant-General.

Doc. 23.

THE MISSION OF A. H. STEPHENS.

THE following is the correspondence relating to the mission of Alexander H. Stephens and Robert Ould at Fortress Monroe:

FORTRESS MONROE, July 4, 1863, }
U. S. STEAMER MINNESOTA, two P.M. }

Hon. Gideon Welles, Secretary of the Navy:

The following communication is just received from Alexander H. Stephens, who is in the flag of truce boat, anchored above. I shall inform Mr. Stephens that I await your instructions before giving him an answer. S. H. LEE,
Admiral, etc.

CONFEDERATE STATES STEAMER TORPEDO, }
JAMES RIVER, July 4, 1863. }

SIR: As a military commissioner, I am the bearer of a communication in writing from Jeff Davis, Commander-in-Chief of the land and naval forces of the confederate States, to Abraham Lincoln, Commander-in-Chief of the land and naval forces of the United States. Hon. Robert Ould, confederate States Agent of Exchange, accompanies me as secretary for the purpose of delivering the communication in person and conferring upon the subject to which it relates. I desire to proceed directly to Washington in the steamer Torpedo, commanded by Lieutenant Hunter Davidson of the confederate States navy; no person being on board but the Hon. Mr. Ould, myself, the boat's officers and crew.

Yours most respectfully,
ALEXANDER H. STEPHENS.

To S. H. LEE,
Admiral, etc.

NAVY DEPARTMENT, July 4, 1863.

To Acting Rear-Admiral Lee, Hampton Roads:

The request of Alexander H. Stephens is inadmissible. The customary agents and channels are adequate for all needful communication and conference between the United States forces and the insurgents. GIDEON WELLES,
Secretary of the Navy.

Doc. 24.

THE BATTLE AT HELENA, ARK.

OFFICIAL DESPATCHES.

HEADQUARTERS SIXTEENTH ARMY CORPS, }
MEMPHIS, TENN., July 5. }

Major-Gen. H. W. Halleck, General-in-Chief:

GENERAL Prentiss was attacked in force by the rebels, under Holmes and Price, at Helena yesterday. He estimated the force at fifteen thousand. I think nine thousand will cover their strength. General Prentiss sustained their attack until three P.M., from daylight, when the rebels were repulsed at all points, leaving one thousand two hundred prisoners.

Their loss in killed and wounded is about from five to six hundred. General Prentiss lost about fifty. He has already sent me eight hundred and sixty prisoners, which I send to Alton to-day, (Sunday noon.) S. A. HURLBUT,
Major-General Commanding.

HEADQUARTERS DISTRICT EAST-ARKANSAS, }
HELENA, July 4, three A.M. }

To Major-General S. A. Hurlbut, Commanding Fifteenth Army Corps:

GENERAL: We have been hard pressed since daylight by the combined forces of Price, Holmes, Marmaduke, Parsons, Carter, Dobbins, and others. Thus far we have held our own, and have captured several hundred prisoners, whom I send to you by Major Wright, of the Twenty-fourth Iowa, on board the steamer Tycoon.

The enemy are now evidently preparing for a renewed attack in force.

Send another gunboat if possible. The Tyler has done good service to-day.

In great haste, your obedient servant,
B. M. PRENTISS,
Major-General.

HEADQUARTERS DISTRICT EAST-ARKANSAS, }
HELENA, July 4, three P.M. }

Major-General S. A. Hurlbut, Commanding Sixteenth Army Corps:

GENERAL: We have repulsed the enemy at every point, and our soldiers are now collecting their wounded.

We have taken in all one thousand two hundred prisoners, and their loss in killed and wounded will reach five hundred or six hundred; but although the rebels are badly whipped, there is no doubt whatever they will renew the attack at an early moment, and that they are now massing their troops for that purpose. My force is inferior to the rebels. With the aid I expect from you and the gunboats, the rebel army may be severely beaten. The Tyler has been to-day a valuable auxiliary. I remain, General,

Your obedient servant,

B. M. PRENTISS,
Major-General.

COLONEL BENTON'S OFFICIAL REPORT.

HELENA, ARKANSAS, July 6, 1863.

*Editor Nonpareil :**

I send you herewith, for publication a copy of my official report of the part taken by the Twenty-ninth Iowa infantry, in their engagement of the fourth instant, at this place. I would also request that all the papers in our portion of the State, copy for the information of our friends.

I feel proud of the conduct of the Twenty-ninth. They came up to the work promptly and coolly, and stuck to it with unyielding fidelity. The enemy came upon us with a rush and a shout, followed by repeated volleys of small arms and occasionally a little grape, by which several of our men were killed and wounded. It was a critical moment. Had they faltered, serious disaster was inevitable. They stood firm and gave the enemy more than they bargained for, and soon had a portion of his dead and wounded within our lines. The sight of the wounded and dying seemed to inspire them with fresh courage. I advanced several times to the brow of the hills, where I could get a better view of the contending forces. I found our boys in various attitudes—standing, kneeling, half bent, and flat on the ground—loading and firing, and occasionally advancing as deliberately and systematically as a mountaineer after an antelope. Our fire was well aimed. The obstructions behind which the enemy were concealed, after they fell back, were thoroughly peppered with our Enfield balls. By making a sudden dash, we could have taken one of their guns, but prudence dictated that we should not risk an ambuscade for the sake of getting possession of a gun which was no longer doing us any harm.

The respective companies were disposed of as follows: Deployed as skirmishers, A, B, C, E, F, G, H, and K. Held as a reserve, D and I. The following officers were in the engagement: Lieutenant-Colonel Patterson, Major Shoemaker, and Adjutant Lyman; Captain Gardner and Second Lieutenant Kirkpatrick, of company A; Captain Andrews and Second Lieutenant Sheldon, of company B; Captain Bacon, First Lieutenant Hedge, and Second Lieutenant Stocker, of company C; First Lieutenant Stewart and Second Lieutenant Munn, of company D; First Lieutenant Mitchell and Second Lieutenant Ellifritz, of company E; First Lieutenant Turner, of company F; First Lieutenant Johnston and Second Lieutenant McFarland, of company G; Captain Myers and Second Lieutenant Elliott, of company H; First Lieutenant Lenon and Second Lieutenant Muxley, of company I; and First Lieutenant Dale and Second Lieutenant Chantry, of company K. Were I to attempt a eulogy on their conduct, I could not say more than that embraced in the truthful assertion, they did their whole duty.

* Council Bluffs (Iowa) *Nonpareil*, August 1, 1863.

Captains Bower, of company E, and Davis, of company D, were absent on sick leave. Captains Huggins, of company G, and Nash, of company F, were sick and unable to leave their quarters. Time has shown that my selection of Adjutant was a happy one. In the office or in the field he is every inch a soldier, recognizing no deviation from the stern laws that govern a military organization.

Assistant-Surgeons Nicholson and Eakin were on the field, and were active and vigilant in their attentions to the wounded.

A section of the Third Iowa battery (from Dubuque) commanded by Lieutenant Wright, was posted on our right, and did good service, and rendered the position of the enemy very uncomfortable.

I would like to give you the details of the general engagement, but have not time, and you will doubtless see them elsewhere. Suffice it to say that the battle was hotly contested on both sides. The rebels fought well, and yielded only to the superior force of our arms. Our entire effective force, according to the official reports of the day previous, was three thousand eight hundred. That of the enemy, according to their own statement, was between fifteen and twenty thousand, which corroborates the estimates made from our own observation. Our entire loss in killed, wounded, and missing is less than two hundred and fifty. That of the enemy not less than two thousand five hundred. In estimating their loss we have the facts to govern us. We took over one thousand prisoners during the action and a good many stragglers since. We buried some two hundred and seventy-five of their dead on the field, and found the graves of over one hundred buried by themselves. We have had possession of about four hundred of their wounded, some of whom were left at farm-houses a few miles west of the town on their retreat. From the nature of the wounds our surgeons assure us that their dead will not fall short of six hundred. It is fair to presume that they had the usual proportion of slightly wounded, who were taken with them. The rebels were under the leadership of Holmes, Price, and Marmaduke, the former in command. Our forces were commanded by Brigadier-General F. Salomon, brother of Governor Salomon, of Wisconsin.

The limited number of our killed and wounded in a contest against such fearful odds, seems almost incredible. The secret is, that we were not surprised. For the last six weeks we had been vigilant day and night, patrolling the country with scouts, constructing fortifications and digging intrenchments. The hills in the vicinity of our batteries were literally covered with rifle-pits, and the principal roads blockaded with fallen timber. General Salomon deserves great credit for these precautionary steps. The enemy had doubtless ascertained with considerable accuracy our numerical strength, but he was badly deceived as to the extent of our preparations—one of the most important items in modern warfare. They doubtless expected to find us engrossed with a Fourth of July celebration, and totally unprepared for their approach; but for once they were caught in a trap, and did not realize their mistake until the deadly volleys from our rifle-pits began to mow them down. Our little army was drawn up in line of battle at daylight in the respective camps, an hour before the enemy attacked our pickets, awaiting orders from the General Commanding, and in a few minutes after the signal gun was fired, each detachment was in the position assigned it, and a general fire was opened upon the invading foe. Our pickets behaved gallantly. They fell back steadily, loading and firing until they reached our intrenchments. The gunboat Tyler, the lucky boat of the war, was at anchor in front of the town and joined in the action.

The battle, though overshadowed by the brilliant achievements at Vicksburgh, is nevertheless an important one. I think it has given a final quietus to "Price's army," about which we have heard so much during the war. It is to be regretted that our force was too limited to admit of pursuit. We could have wiped out the whole concern. The rebel wounded were treated with the greatest kindness. They were brought into our hospitals during the engagement, and every facility was afforded by our surgeons, assisted by their own, to make them comfortable. We started six hundred and fifty prisoners up the river on the steamer Tycoon before the engagement closed. They left the landing amid the incessant roar of artillery and small arms, laughing, cheering, and swearing. The enemy were well armed, and provided with ammunition of an excellent quality.

Our brigade was commanded by Colonel Rice, of the Thirty-third Iowa. He acquitted himself well. Most of our wounded have been sent North, and it is painful to add that some of them cannot recover, even with the most favorable treatment.

Yours truly,

THOMAS H. BENTON, Jr.

OFFICIAL REPORT.

HEADQUARTERS TWENTY-NINTH REGIMENT
IOWA VOLUNTEER INFANTRY,
HELENA, ARK., July 6, 1863.

COLONEL: I have the honor to make the following report of the part taken in the engagement of the fourth instant, by my regiment. My men were drawn up in line of battle at daylight, in obedience to a standing order of Brig.-Gen. F. Salomon, commanding forces in the field, and at half-past four o'clock A.M., in pursuance of orders from Col. Samuel A. Rice, of the Thirty-third Iowa infantry, commanding Second brigade, we marched westward across the bottom at double-quick, to a position on the Sterling road. Upon reaching the point designated, I found that the enemy occupied the crests of the hills with their skirmishers north of "battery A," commanding my position. I immediately sent forward two companies of skirmishers to dislodge and drive them back; but finding them too strongly posted, and being directed by Col. Rice to hold the position at all hazards, I continued to reënforce the line until eight companies were deployed.

In the mean time the enemy had placed a battery of two guns in position, with which they opened a brisk fire of shell and grape, and moved rapidly upon us, cheering and exulting as they advanced, being partially shielded from view by a fog which covered the hills at that moment. Our skirmishers met them with a galling and incessant fire, under which they gradually fell back, resolutely contesting every inch of ground as they retired. Our skirmishers advanced steadily and cautiously, and having gained the crest of the hill previously occupied by the enemy, compelled him to abandon his guns, which, after several ineffectual attempts, he subsequently recovered and withdrew, leaving one caisson on the field.

My men were under a severe fire for more than five hours, and it affords me the greatest pleasure to speak of both officers and men in terms of the highest commendation for their coolness and bravery during the entire action. I saw no flinching or wavering during the day. It is proper to add that several of my officers and quite a number of my men, who were excused from duty in consequence of physical debility, left their quarters and joined their respective companies when the signal gun was fired.

Any invidious distinctions among the members of my command would not be admissible in this report, but I would not do justice to an accomplished officer should I fail to acknowledge the efficient services of Lieut.-Col. R. F. Patterson during the action, and the special obligations I am under for the thorough instruction previously given by him to both officers and men in the responsible duties and obligations of the soldier, the importance of which was so forcibly illustrated on the fourth instant.

My regiment was promptly supported by the Thirty-sixth Iowa infantry, commanded by Col. C. W. Kittridge, and was relieved by him a short time before the enemy left the field. The enemy's force in front of our line, so far as I have been able to ascertain, from the most reliable information within my reach, was one brigade of five regiments of infantry, one battery and two regiments of cavalry in reserve, under command of Colonel McCrea.

I regret to have to report that during the engagement the loss in my regiment was seven killed and twenty-four wounded—some of them mortally (two of whom have since died) and many of them severely—among the number some of my best and bravest men. The enemy's loss it is not possible to state definitely, as he succeeded in removing many of them from the field. We buried fourteen of his dead and found the graves of seventeen more buried by himself, and brought one of his wounded from the field.

I have the honor to be, Colonel,

Very respectfully, your obedient servant,

THOMAS H. BENTON, Jr.,
Colonel Twenty-ninth Iowa Infantry.

To Colonel SAMUEL A. RICE,
Commanding Second Brigade, Thirteenth Division of Thirteenth Army Corps.

LIEUT.-COLONEL PASE'S REPORT.

HEADQUARTERS FIRST INDIANA CAVALRY, }
HELENA, July 6, 1863. }

M. W. Benjamin, A. A. A. G., Headquarters Colonel Clayton, Commanding Cavalry Brigade, Helena, Arkansas:

SIR: In obedience to orders, I herewith transmit a list of killed and wounded of my command, First Indiana cavalry, together with a statement of the part the regiment took in the attack on Helena on the fourth of July, 1863.

A little before four o'clock on the morning of the fourth of July, two messengers came in from the picket-post on the Little Rock road, bringing word that the enemy were advancing, driving in the pickets before them. I immediately ordered the bugle to sound to horse, and, forming the regiment, moved up the levee near town, and awaited orders.

Soon received orders from you, through your Adjutant, to move tents and baggage within the line of fortifications as rapidly as possible, leaving part of the command to guard the train, and with the rest to form line of battle behind the Fifth Kansas, which was already drawn up in the open flats just above town. I immediately ordered Major Owen to take two companies, with one piece of our small rifled guns, and cover the rear of the train, and with the balance of my command I took positions as ordered.

General Prentiss then ordered our guns some distance in front up the levee, and companies M and L were dismounted and sent forward as a support. Our battery was commanded by Lieut. Leffler, of company B. For the bravery shown and the terrible execution done by them, you are best able to judge, they having been under your immediate command.

By this time Major Owen came up with his detachment, and fell in line with the regiment.

Captain Wethers, Aid to General Salomon, now came up with word that the enemy had captured a battery on the heights in the rear of General Salomon's headquarters, driving our infantry from their rifle-pits, and were rapidly advancing into town; and I was ordered to take my regiment under the walls of Fort Curtis, dismount them, and check their further advance. I did so, taking the regiment on the top of the hill to the left of General Salomon's headquarters.

On the crest of the hill opposite was the battery the enemy had just captured, and over the breastworks from which our infantry had been driven, they were pouring one dark, continuous stream. The boys wheeled into line, and with loud yells, commenced firing, pouring in such a storm of bullets that they soon retreated, with the exception of their sharp-shooters, which, to the number of several hundred, took possession of a ravine running up the side of the hill, which was filled with fallen timber and stumps, from behind which they poured a continuous and deadly fire. Soon ten or twelve daring spirits now rushed down the hill-side and up the steep ascent in front, getting a position on the enemy's left flank, just above them, occupying ground from which we had driven them. They held their position for some time, doing terrible execution, but were finally compelled to fall back, bringing with them quite a number of splendid English rifles which they had captured from the enemy's sharp-shooters. Another detachment of our men soon went over, accompanied by some infantry, a company of which had come up on the hill where my regiment was stationed. (It may be proper to state here, that several companies of infantry were at the foot of the hill to our right, around General Salomon's headquarters, who did good service, acting in concert with us.)

The enemy, finding himself flanked, and having no chance of escape, as every one attempting to run up the hill-side was sure to fall, raised the white flag, and about one hundred surrendered.

Quite a number still held out, seemingly determined to die before they would become prisoners.

Here more than half the regiment threw away their carbines, (many of them being unserviceable, having been condemned by a U. S. inspecting officer some time since,) and supplied themselves with Enfield rifles captured from the enemy.

General Salomon now sent orders for us to charge and retake the battery. Two hills more had to be crossed before reaching it, the sides of which were covered with logs and brush. The hills were several hundred feet steep, almost perpendicular; but, at the word "forward," they were accompanied by two companies of infantry, and where it was too step to walk the boys would crawl on their hands and knees. The enemy did not wait to receive us, but left their works.

I was now compelled to beat a hasty retreat in consequence of the shells from the gunboat Tyler dropping in all around us, and we fell back and resumed our former position.

The men were now much exhausted from charging over the hills and back. The sun was shining out intensely hot, and I ordered the regiment to the foot of the hill, under the trees around headquarters, (the fighting was now over, with the exception of some occasional shots)—after being engaged for five hours under a continued and severe fire.

My killed, wounded, and missing number as follow: Killed—A. Brokan, company A, shot in head; William Stark, company H, shot in breast. Wounded mortally—Robert Smith, company D, shot in abdomen; James Carter, company F, shot in the breast. Wounded severely—Frank Bennett, company F, shot in knee; Thomas Adams, company F, right arm shot off; Frederick Lewis, company F, shot through hand and wrist; Geo. Barter, company H, right thumb shot off. Wounded slightly—John Carter, company B, in head; James H. Campbell, in leg. Missing—Benjamin Happy, company M.

The officers and men all conducted themselves so as to meet my highest approbation. Such being the case, I find it impossible to name particular ones as deserving of notice for their bravery, without doing injustice to the rest. To Major Brewer, however, I am particularly indebted for the valuable aid and assistance he rendered me in carrying out the different orders I received, and for his coolness and bravery. Lieutenant Kelso, Commissary, deserves notice for his timely aid in furnishing food and water to the men while they were engaged. Lieutenant Craig, Quartermaster, also did his whole duty in his department, and B. J. Kilpatrick, Ordnance Sergeant, was always on hand with ammunition for the regiment and battery. Many of the men fired over one hundred rounds. Yours, etc.,

THOS. N. PASE,
Lieutenant-Colonel Commanding First Indiana Cavalry.

NAVAL REPORTS.

UNITED STATES MISSISSIPPI SQUADRON,
FLAG-SHIP BLACK HAWK, OFF VICKSBURGH, July 11, 1863.

SIR: I have the honor to inclose you a full report of the late affair at Helena, where the gunboat Tyler saved the day, and enabled our little band of soldiers to capture a number of the enemy.

I remain, very respectfully, your obedient servant,
DAVID D. PORTER,
A. R. Admiral Commanding Mississippi Squadron.
Hon. GIDEON WELLES,
Secretary of the Navy, Washington.

U. S. IRON-CLAD RAM EASTPORT,
HELENA, ARKANSAS, July 8, 1863.

A. R. Admiral David D. Porter, U. S. Navy, Commanding Mississippi Squadron:

SIR: General Holmes, with a reported force of eighteen thousand rebels, attacked this place at daylight on the morning of the fourth instant, and was repulsed, after a hard contested fight of several hours' duration.

The enemy attacked the centre of the defences and carried the rifle-pits, and a battery upon the crest of the hills in the rear, which commanded not only Helena itself, but also all the other defensive works, including Fort Curtis. After possessing himself of that position, he pushed large forces down the slope of the ridge into the gorges, and his sharp-shooters began the work of driving the artillerists from the guns in the main fort. Rebel guns, both above and below the town, had been planted upon commanding positions, and opened fire upon the lines of defensive works across the river-bottom, about one thousand yards in width, and his troops were in force near them to secure the advantages the capture of the works upon the hills would offer for closing upon the town from both directions along the river-bottom. The Tyler had been covering the approach by the old town road; but Captain Pritchett discovered the enemy pressing down the hill-side after the capture of the battery in the centre, and took up such a position that, while his broadside guns poured a destructive fire upon the slopes and enfiladed the ravines, his stern guns effectually silenced the rebel battery below, and his bow guns played simultaneously upon the upper one. The slaughter of the enemy at this time was terrible, and all unite in describing the horrors of that hillside and the ravines after the battle as baffling

description, the killed being literally torn to pieces by shell, and the avenging fire of the gunboat pursued the enemy two or three miles to his reserve forces, creating a panic there which added not a little to the end of victory.

The enemy's loss is very heavy. Our forces have buried three hundred and eighty of his killed, and many places have been found where he had himself buried his dead. His wounded number one thousand one hundred, and the prisoners also are one thousand one hundred. Our cavalry forces are hourly discovering dead and wounded in the surrounding country, and are bringing in stragglers and deserters. Boats passing up the river for two days after the battle were continually hailed by deserters from the rebel ranks wishing to get on board to escape.

An examination of the field and the reports I hear convince me that the Tyler contributed greatly to the defeat of the enemy, and the terrible slaughter in his ranks is largely hers. It is due to Captain Pritchett to add that he took up an admirable position, and used his battery in a manner alike creditable to himself and to his officers and men.

First at Belmont, then at Pittsburgh Landing, and now here, the Tyler has been of inestimable value, and has saved the fortunes of the day. The garrison, numbering but three thousand three hundred men, with lines entirely too extensive for such a force, evidently fought with a courage and determination without superior example in this war.

Our loss in killed and wounded is about one hundred and eighty.

I am, respectfully, your obedient servant,
S. L. PHELPS,
Lieutenant Commander,
Commanding Second Division, Mississippi Squadron.
To Acting Rear-Admiral DAVID D. PORTER,
Commanding Mississippi Squadron.

HEADQUARTERS DISTRICT OF EASTERN ARKANSAS,
HELENA, ARK., July 9, 1863.

ADMIRAL: I take pleasure in transmitting to you my testimony concerning the valuable assistance rendered me during the battle at this place on the fourth instant, by Lieutenant Commander James M. Pritchett, of the gunboat Tyler. I assure you, sir, that he not only acquitted himself with honor and distinction during the engagement proper, but, with a zeal and patience as rare as they are commendable, when informed of the probabilities of an attack on this place, he lost no time and spared no labor to make himself thoroughly acquainted with the topography of the surrounding country. And I attribute not a little of our success in the late battle to his full knowledge of the situation, and his skill in adapting the means within his command to the end to be obtained. Nor can I refrain from mentioning that after the engagement, and while we were expecting a renewal of the attack, Commander Pritchett, commanding a division of your fleet, was unusually efficient in procuring timely reënforcements.

Permit me to add, sir, that I can conceive of

no case wherein promotion would be more worthily bestowed than in the case of Commander Pritchett, and it will afford me much pleasure to learn that his services have received a proper reward. I write this communication, sir, quite unsolicited and without the knowledge of Commander Pritchett.

I have the honor to be, sir, with much respect, your obedient servant. B. M. PRENTISS,
Major-General.

To DAVID D. PORTER,
Rear-Admiral, Commanding Mississippi Squadron.

ST. LOUIS "DEMOCRAT" ACCOUNT.

HELENA, ARK., July 12, 1863.

At last we have been attacked by Missouri's favorite general, under the direction of the laggard Holmes. At four o'clock A.M., on the fourth day of July, the siege-gun, which was to give the signal of attack, belched forth its startling alarm to the little garrison, and immediately infantry, cavalry, and artillery were in motion to take up the various positions assigned them. For two nights we had been under arms at two o'clock A.M., and it was but a few moments' work to place all in readiness.

To give some idea of the position, let us say that Helena lies upon flat ground, upon the western bank of the Mississippi River. About a quarter of a mile from the river, and running parallel to it, high ridges command the city and approaches, ravines, opening toward the river, and raked by the guns of Fort Curtis, (which is lower than all the ridges, and centrally located,) being between these ridges. Before the departure of General Gorman, Fort Curtis was readily commanded from all the ridges about the city. Generals Ross and Salomon conceived the plan of placing strong batteries upon these hills as an advanced line, and connecting each battery by rifle-pits. This plan was executed by Lieutenant James G. Patton, of the Thirty-third Missouri, and results have demonstrated the correctness of his judgment, and the wisdom of the general plan. Making the city our base, battery A is upon our right running on next to B, C, and D, (which is on the left.) Between the ridges (above and below the town) and the river there is low, flat ground, protected by rifle and cavalry-pits, and flanking batteries of ten-pounder Parrotts, and six and twelve-pounder brass pieces.

"The enemy are in force on the old town road," was the first intimation of the plan of attack. This was on the left of our line, and a strong force of cavalry, with a brigade of infantry and four pieces of artillery, was there. Next came word that the old St. Francis road was occupied in force, and that an assault was being attempted upon battery A. Scarcely was this report in, when news came that batteries C and D were annoyed by sharp-shooters, who were supported by heavy columns, in which could be distinguished the rumbling of wheels, supposed to be artillery moving into position. Cavalry could be seen in front of battery B. So much for the dispositions of the enemy. They were

planned and timed by a master-mind, the pickets being driven at all points at almost the same moment.

On both flanks the enemy's artillery opened with some spirit but no effect, being replied to rapidly with good success. The exchanges were principally at long-range for light pieces, and the design was evidently to make a diversion simply, while the centre was attacked in strong force, thus driving through our long line of defences and falling simultaneously upon the rear of both flanks. The success of this plan would have given them Fort Curtis and the whole wharf, entirely cutting off our retreat by means of the transports. It will be seen that their plan entirely ignored the presence of the gunboat, which they were not expecting to find at our landing. No batteries were opened upon our centre, as they failed, on account of ravines, to obtain favorable positions. Their infantry was relied upon for this work. Lieutenant-General Holmes personally directed the attack upon battery D, which was made by Fagan's Arkansas brigade, while Major-General Price directed that upon battery C. At half-past four A.M., a regiment moved from cover to attack D, advancing in four ranks upon a bridge perpendicular to the line of that work and flanked by the guns of C, which opened upon them with shell as soon as the full length of their line was exposed.

The guns of D opened upon them at the same moment, the guns of both batteries having excellent range, and creating a panic among the enemy, which soon increased to a rout, the regiment drawing off in great disorder. At once they were reënforced, their sharp-shooters pressing closer and annoying the gunners of C so much that the guns had to be turned upon them with canister. One gun of this battery, however, was used to assist D, and again the enemy were checked, taking cover in the ravines and fallen timber. At this time a heavy fog fell upon the ridges and batteries, lasting some three quarters of an hour and causing a cessation of hostilities for that time. When the fog raised, the force in front of battery D appeared to have been weakened; while crossing low ridges between that and battery C, appeared a brigade of three distinct regiments.

When discovered, this brigade (Parsons's) was entirely concealed from the range of guns of C, but exposed to that of D, which accordingly opened upon them with shell from both guns, frequently breaking the column, but only to see it closed again and pressing forward. The first line of pits in front of C was flanked and the company compelled to retreat upon the battery, where they again stood. In front and upon both flanks the enemy charged this work, not in regular lines, but swarming upon our gallant fellows like locusts. Two companies in the pits upon the left of the guns broke and fled in the greatest confusion; two companies with the guns, and two in the pits to the right of them, held their ground steadily, firing double charges of canister and pouring Minie balls into the assailants with the most terrible effect. They were overmatched, however, and the guns could not be saved. The captain of the battery spiked one of his guns as the enemy reached his parapet, and his gunners, with rare presence of mind, secured all the friction-primers, so rendering the battery utterly useless to the enemy. Part of the stragglers rallied at the foot of the hill, between batteries C and D, and made a firm stand, where they were promptly supported by parts of two regiments, and the remainder retired to Fort Curtis to act as sharp-shooters in protecting the gunners.

In possession of battery C, and flushed with apparent certain victory, the enemy turned the captured guns upon our main fort, and loaded them with shell. Then gathering together his scattered companies, who were pillaging the camp of the two companies that garrisoned the battery, with one wild, self-confident yell he charged down the hill immediately in front of Fort Curtis; charged, not in line or in column, not with fixed bayonet showing a glittering line of polished steel, not as the "Old Guard" charged at Waterloo, but charged *en masse*, or worse yet, *en mobbe*, every man being in himself a small host with a leader of its own.

The crest of the hill was six hundred yards from Fort Curtis, and the base five hundred. Five twenty-four pounder siege-guns, and one thirty-two pounder columbiad swept the entire base of the hill, from crest to base. Although the enemy had loaded our captured guns with shell, he could not use them; there were no slow matches, no friction-tubes, and the guns were so much useless brass. Without well-posted artillery, how could they hope to live upon the hill with the light guns of A, B, and D, playing upon their flanks and rear, and the big guns playing upon their front?

Nothing but madness could have driven them on; nothing short of omnipotence could have saved them from destruction. Yet, with the howl of demons, the last mad, defiant, impotent howl of baffled but still determined traitors, exposed to history, to nations, and to themselves; whipped, naked and hungry, on they came, cursing, firing, rushing, like the "Light Brigade," "into the gates of death, into the mouth of hell."

No hurrying, no excitement, and yet no hesitation in the Fort and batteries, but steadily the shell, case, grape, and canister flew, with the swiftness of lightning and the precision of fate, straight in the faces of the infuriate mob. Heads, trunks and limbs hurled asunder by bursting iron, flew into the air, nauseating and sickening all who must witness the horrible sight. No body of men on earth could long endure such a tornado of iron as was hurled upon them. Their shots all fell short, or passed harmlessly over the gunners of the Fort. Not a man was even wounded. Slow to receive convictions, but at last satisfied of the hopelessness of their assault, the mob turned about, as if by common consent,

and broke into squads of twenty, ten, two, and at last each man for himself, "and devil get the hindmost."

Grape-shot and canister, round-shot and shell, followed them mercilessly, bore them down and battered them to pieces. Still they had not enough, but once more sought to approach through a ravine, protected by flanking sides from artillery fire. As they passed from the battery to this ravine, one point which the line must cross was exposed to fire. The guns succeeded shortly in getting such perfect range of this point that nothing could pass it. The regiment, and more, that had passed into the ravine, could not return, and the brigade could not pass in to its support. A Federal regiment of infantry was so posted at the mouth of the ravine as to rake its length, another took a position on a ridge on the enemy's right flank, and the two poured in their fire. Cross-fires from the Fort and batteries, aided by the gunboat, broke and scattered what of the brigade remained upon the ridges, compelling them in their precipitation to leave the guns they had captured uninjured, and the gallant regiment that had led the second charge, with their arms, officers and colors, prisoners of war.

Not less than three hundred killed and wounded, besides nearly four hundred prisoners, were left by the enemy in the vicinity of this battery.

Shortly after the attack was commenced upon battery C, a second and similar one was made by Fagan's brigade in strong force upon battery D. As at the first battery, only a portion of the brigade succeeded in passing through our lines. The remainder were driven back by a murderous fire from the guns of the work, and also from our sharp-shooters, who were in greater force than at C, and well protected by rifle-pits, which almost entirely concealed them from the enemy. Those who succeeded in getting through, took position in a ravine to the left of the battery, out of range of its guns, but raked from the mouth by part of another battery and the reserve of an infantry regiment.

They made a short fight, when they threw down their arms and were formally surrendered. While they were still fighting, a Lieutenant-Colonel, who commanded the rebels, was standing upon a log waving his sword and cheering his men. The captain of battery D called out to him: "What in —— do you keep swinging that sword for? Why don't you surrender?" "By what authority do you demand my surrender?" asked the confederate officer. "By authority of my twelve-pound howitzer," replied the Captain. The confederate looked about him, and could see no chance of escape, so passing his sabre-blade into his right hand, he held it out, humbly saying: "Very well, sir, I surrender." Perhaps at that moment it would have been very difficult to cite a more competent authority upon the question of surrenders than that under which the cool captain claimed to act.

The enemy lost at this battery nearly two hundred and fifty killed and wounded, and between three and four hundred prisoners, with arms, officers, and colors.

At half-past ten o'clock A.M., the enemy had drawn off entirely, and the firing ceased as the white flag was run up at Vicksburgh.

Our total loss in killed, wounded, and missing, has been two hundred and thirty; that of the enemy at least two thousand. They estimate their own loss at two thousand two hundred, among them the entire field and staff of two or three regiments.

Doc. 25.

THE SIEGE OF VICKSBURGH, MISS.

GENERAL GRANT'S OFFICIAL REPORT.*

HEADQUARTERS DEPARTMENT OF THE TENNESSEE,
VICKSBURGH, MISS., July 6, 1863.

COLONEL: I have the honor to submit the following report of the operations of the army of the Tennessee, and coöperating forces, from the date of my assuming the immediate command of the expedition against Vicksburgh, Mississippi, to the reduction of that place.

From the moment of taking command in person, I became satisfied that Vicksburgh could only be turned from the south side, and, in accordance with this conviction, I prosecuted the work on the canal, which had been located by Brigadier-General Williams, across the peninsula, on the Louisiana side of the river, with all vigor, hoping to make a channel which would pass transports for moving the army and carrying supplies to the new base of operations thus provided. The task was much more herculean than it at first appeared, and was made much more so by the almost continuous rains that fell during the whole of the time this work was prosecuted. The river, too, continued to rise and make a large expenditure of labor necessary to keep the water out of our camps and the canal.

Finally, on the eighth of March, the rapid rise of the river and the consequent great pressure upon the dam across the canal, near the upper end, at the main Mississippi levee, caused it to give way and let through the low lands back of our camps a torrent of water that separated the north and south shores of the peninsula as effectually as if the Mississippi flowed between them. This occurred when the enterprise promised success within a short time. There was some delay in trying to repair damages. It was found, however, that with the then stage of water, some other plan would have to be adopted for getting below Vicksburgh with transports.

Captain F. L. Prime, Chief Engineer, and Colonel G. G. Pride, who was acting on my staff, prospected a route through the bayous which run from near Milliken's Bend on the north, and New-Carthage on the south, through Roundaway Bayou into the Tansas River. Their report of the practicability of this route determined me to

* Official reports of the various battles, etc., mentioned in this report will be found under their proper dates in the previous volumes of the RECORD.

commence work upon it. Having three dredge-boats at the time, the work of opening this route was executed with great rapidity. One small steamer and a number of barges were taken through the channel thus opened, but the river commencing about the middle of April to fall rapidly, and the roads becoming passable between Milliken's Bend and New-Carthage, made it impracticable and unnecessary to open water communication between these points.

Soon after commencing the first canal spoken of, I caused a channel to be cut from the Mississippi River into Lake Providence; also one from the Mississippi River into Coldwater, by way of Yazoo Pass.

I had no great expectations of important results from the former of these, but having more troops than could be employed to advantage at Young's Point, and knowing that Lake Providence was connected by Bayou Baxter with Bayou Macon, a navigable stream through which transports might pass into the Mississippi below, through Tansas, Wachita, and Red Rivers, I thought it possible that a route might be opened in that direction which would enable me to coöperate with General Banks at Port Hudson.

By the Yazoo Pass route I only expected at first to get into the Yazoo by way of Coldwater and Tallahatchie with some lighter gunboats and a few troops, and destroy the enemy's transports in that stream and some gunboats which I knew he was building. The navigation, however, proved so much better than had been expected, that I thought for a time of the possibility of making this the route for obtaining a foothold on high land above Haines's Bluff, Mississippi, and small-class steamers were accordingly ordered for transporting an army that way. Major-General J. B. McPherson, commanding Seventeenth army corps, was directed to hold his corps in readiness to move by this route; and one division from each of the Thirteenth and Fifteenth corps were collected near the entrance of the Pass to be added to his command. It soon became evident that a sufficient number of boats of the right class could not be obtained for the movement of more than one division.

While my forces were opening one end of the Pass, the enemy was diligently closing the other end, and in this way succeeded in gaining time to strongly fortify Greenwood, below the junction of the Tallahatchie and Yallobusha. The advance of the expedition, consisting of one division of McClernand's corps, from Helena, commanded by Brigadier-General L. F. Ross, and the Twelfth and Seventeenth regiments Missouri infantry, from Sherman's corps, as sharp-shooters on the gunboats, succeeded in reaching Coldwater on the second day of March, after much difficulty, and the partial disabling of most of the boats. From the entrance into Coldwater to Fort Pemberton, at Greenwood, Mississippi, no great difficulty of navigation was experienced, nor any interruption of magnitude from the enemy. Fort Pemberton extends from the Tallahatchie to the Yazoo, at Greenwood. Here the two rivers come within a few hundred yards of each other. The land around the Fort is low, and at the time of the attack was entirely overflowed. Owing to this fact, no movement could be made by the army to reduce it, but all depended upon the ability of the gunboats to silence the guns of the enemy, and enable the transports to run down, and land troops immediately on the Fort itself. After an engagement of several hours, the gunboats drew off, being unable to silence the batteries. Brigadier-General J. F. Quimby, commanding a division of McPherson's corps, met the expedition under Ross, with his division on its return, near Fort Pemberton, on the twenty-first of March, and being the senior, assumed the command of the entire expedition, and returned to the position Ross had occupied.

On the twenty-third day of March, I sent orders for the withdrawal of all the forces operating in that direction, for the purpose of concentrating my army at Milliken's Bend.

On the fourteenth day of March, Admiral D. D. Porter, commanding Mississippi squadron, informed me that he had made a reconnoissance up Steele's Bayou, and partially through Black Bayou toward Deer Creek, and so far as explored, these water-courses were reported navigable for the smaller iron-clads. Information given mostly, I believe, by the negroes of the country, was to the effect that Deer Creek could be navigated to Rolling Fork, and that from there through the Sunflower to the Yazoo River there was no question about the navigation. On the following morning I accompanied Admiral Porter in the ram Price, several iron-clads preceding us, up through Steele's Bayou, to near Black Bayou.

At this time our forces were at a dead-lock at Greenwood, and I looked upon the success of this enterprise as of vast importance. It would, if successful, leave Greenwood between two forces of ours, and would necessarily cause the immediate abandonment of that stronghold.

About thirty steamers of the enemy would been destroyed or fallen into our hands. Seeing that the great obstacle to navigation, so far as I had gone, was from overhanging trees, I left Admiral Porter near Black Bayou, and pushed back to Young's Point for the purpose of sending forward a pioneer corps to remove these difficulties. Soon after my return to Young's Point, Admiral Porter sent back to me for a coöperating military force. Sherman was promptly sent with one division of his corps. The number of steamers suitable for the navigation of these bayous being limited, most of the force was sent up the Mississippi River to Eagle's Bend, a point where the river runs within one mile of Steele's Bayou, thus saving an important part of this difficult navigation. The expedition failed, probably more from want of knowledge as to what would be required to open this route than from any impracticability in the navigation of the streams and bayous through which it was proposed to pass. Want of this knowledge led the expedition on until difficulties were encountered, and then it would become necessary to send back to Young's Point for the means of removing them. This gave the enemy time to move forces to effectually checkmate further progress, and the expedition was withdrawn when within a few hundred yards of free and open navigation to the Yazoo.

All this may have been providential in driving us ultimately to a line of operations which has proven eminently successful.

For further particulars of the Steele's Bayou expedition, see report of Major-General W. F. Sherman, forwarded on the twelfth of April.

As soon as I decided to open water communication from a point on the Mississippi near Milliken's Bend to New-Carthage, I determined to occupy the latter place, it being the first point below Vicksburgh that could be reached by land at the stage of water then existing, and the occupancy of which, while it secured to us a point on the Mississippi River, would also protect the main line of communication by water. Accordingly, the Thirteenth army corps, Major-General J. A. McClernand commanding, was directed to take up its line of march on the twenty-ninth day of March for New-Carthage, the Fifteenth and Seventeenth corps to follow, moving no faster than supplies and ammunition could be transported to them.

The roads, though level, were intolerably bad, and the movement was therefore necessarily slow. Arriving at Smith's plantation, two miles from New-Carthage, it was found that the levee of Bayou Vidal was broken in several places, thus leaving New-Carthage an island.

All the boats that could be were collected from the different bayous in the vicinity, and others were built, but the transportation of an army in this way was found exceedingly tedious. Another route had to be found. This was done by making a further march around Vidal to Perkins's plantation, a distance of twelve miles more, making the whole distance to be marched from Milliken's Bend to reach water communication on the opposite side of the point, thirty-five miles. Over this distance, with bad roads to contend against, supplies of ordnance stores and provisions had to be hauled by wagons with which to commence the campaign on the opposite side of the river.

At the same time that I ordered the occupation of New-Carthage, preparations were made for running transports by the Vicksburgh batteries with Admiral Porter's gunboat fleet.

On the night of the sixteenth of April, Admiral Porter's fleet, and the transports Silver Wave, Forest Queen, and Henry Clay, ran the Vicksburgh batteries. The boilers of the transports were protected as well as possible with hay and cotton. More or less commissary stores were put on each. All three of these boats were struck more or less frequently while passing the enemy's batteries, and the Henry Clay, by the explosion of a shell or by other means, was set on fire and entirely consumed. The other two boats were somewhat injured, but not seriously disabled. No one on board of either was hurt.

As these boats succeeded in getting by so well, I ordered six more to be prepared in like manner for running the batteries. These latter, namely, Tigress, Anglo-Saxon, Cheeseman, Empire City, Horizonia, and Moderator, left Milliken's Bend on the night of the twenty-second of April, and five of them got by, but in a somewhat damaged condition. The Tigress received a shot in her hull below the water-line, and sunk on the Louisiana shore soon after passing the last of the batteries. The crews of these steamers, with the exception of that of the Forest Queen, Captain D. Conway, and the Silver Wave, Captain McMillan, were composed of volunteers from the army. Upon the call for volunteers for this dangerous enterprise, officers and men presented themselves by hundreds, anxious to undertake the trip. The names of those whose services were accepted will be given in a separate report.

It is a striking feature, so far as my observation goes, of the present volunteer army of the United States, that there is nothing which men are called upon to do, mechanical or professional, that accomplished adepts cannot be found for the duty required in almost every regiment.

The transports injured in running the blockade were repaired by order of Admiral Porter, who was supplied with the material for such repairs as they required, and who was and is ever ready to afford all the assistance in his power for the furtherance of the success of our arms. In a very short time five of the transports were in running order, and the remainder were in a condition to be used as barges in the movement of troops. Twelve barges loaded with forage and rations were sent in tow of the last six boats that run the blockade; one half of them got through in a condition to be used.

Owing to the limited number of transports below Vicksburgh, it was found necessary to extend our line of land travel to Hard Times, La., which, by the circuitous route it was necessary to take, increased the distance to about seventy miles from Milliken's Bend, our starting-point.

The Thirteenth army corps being all through to the Mississippi, and the Seventeenth army corps well on the way, so much of the Thirteenth as could be got on board the transports and barges were put aboard and moved to the front of Grand Gulf on the twenty-ninth of April. The plan here was that the navy should silence the guns of the enemy, and the troops land under cover of the gunboats, and carry the place by storm.

At eight o'clock A.M. the navy made the attack, and kept it up for more than five hours in the most gallant manner. From a tug out in the stream I witnessed the whole engagement. Many times it seemed to me the gunboats were within pistol-shot of the enemy's batteries. It soon became evident that the guns of the enemy were too elevated and their fortifications too strong to be taken from the water-side. The whole range of hills on that side were known to be lined with rifle-pits; besides, the field-artillery could be moved to any position where it could be made useful in case of an attempt at landing. This determined me to again run the enemy's batteries, turn his

position by effecting a landing at Rodney, or at Bruinsburgh, between Grand Gulf and Rodney. Accordingly, orders were immediately given for the troops to debark at Hard Times, La., and march across to the plain immediately below Grand Gulf. At dark the gunboats again engaged the batteries, and all the transports ran by, receiving but two or three shots in the passage, and these without injury. I had some time previously ordered a reconnoissance to a point opposite Bruinsburgh, to ascertain, if possible, from persons in the neighborhood, the character of the road leading to the highlands back of Bruinsburgh. During the night I learned from a negro man that there was a good road from Bruinsburgh to Port Gibson, which determined me to land there.

The work of ferrying the troops to Bruinsburgh was commenced at daylight in the morning, the gunboats as well as transports being used for the purpose.

As soon as the Thirteenth army corps was landed, and could draw three days' rations to put in haversacks, (no wagons were allowed to cross until the troops were all over,) they were started on the road to Port Gibson. I deemed it a matter of vast importance that the highlands should be reached without resistance.

The Seventeenth corps followed as rapidly as it could be put across the river.

About two o'clock on the first of May, the advance of the enemy was met eight miles from Bruinsburgh, on the road to Port Gibson. He was forced to fall back, but as it was dark, he was not pursued far until daylight. Early on the morning of the first I went out, accompanied by members of my staff, and found McClernand with his corps engaging the enemy about four miles from Port Gibson. At this point the roads branched in exactly opposite directions, both, however, leading to Port Gibson. The enemy had taken position on both branches, thus dividing, as he fell back, the pursuing forces. The nature of the ground in that part of the country is such that a very small force could retard the progress of a much larger one for many hours. The roads usually run on narrow, elevated ridges, with deep and impenetrable ravines on either side. On the right were the divisions of Hovey, Carr, and Smith, and on the left, the division of Osterhaus, of McClernand's corps. The three former succeeded in driving the enemy from position to position back toward Port Gibson steadily all day.

Osterhaus did not, however, move the enemy from the position occupied by him on our left until Logan's division of McPherson's corps arrived.

McClernand, who was with the right in person, sent repeated messages to me before the arrival of Logan to send Logan and Quimby's divisions of McPherson's corps to him.

I had been on that as well as all other parts of the field, and could not see how they could be used there to advantage. However, as soon as the advance of McPherson's corps (Logan's division) arrived, I sent one brigade, Brigadier-General J. E. Smith commanding, to the left to the assistance of Osterhaus.

By the judicious disposition made of this brigade, under the immediate supervision of McPherson and Logan, a position was soon obtained giving us an advantage which soon drove the enemy from that part of the field, to make no further stand south of Bayou Pierre.

The enemy was here repulsed with a heavy loss in killed, wounded, and prisoners. The repulse of the enemy on our left took place late in the afternoon. He was pursued toward Port Gibson, but night closing in, and the enemy making the appearance of another stand, the troops slept upon their arms until daylight.

In the morning it was found that the enemy had retreated across Bayou Pierre, on the Grand Gulf road, and a brigade of Logan's division was sent to divert his attention while a floating bridge was being built across Bayou Pierre, immediately at Port Gibson. This bridge was completed, eight miles marched by McPherson's corps to the north fork of Bayou Pierre, that stream bridged, and the advance of this corps commenced passing over it at five o'clock the following morning.

On the third the enemy was pursued to Hawkinson's Ferry, with slight skirmishing all day, during which we took quite a number of prisoners, mostly stragglers from the enemy.

Finding that Grand Gulf had been evacuated, and that the advance of my forces was already fifteen miles out from there, and on the road, too, they would have to take to reach either Vicksburgh, Jackson, or any intermediate point on the railroad between the two places, I determined not march them back, but taking a small escort of cavalry, some fifteen or twenty men, I went to the Gulf myself, and made the necessary arrangements for changing my base of supplies from Bruinsburgh to Grand Gulf.

In moving from Milliken's Bend, the Fifteenth army corps, Major-General W. T. Sherman commanding, was left to be the last to start. To prevent heavy reënforcements going from Vicksburgh to the assistance of the Grand Gulf forces, I directed Sherman to make a demonstration on Haines's Bluff, and to make all the *show* possible. From information since received from prisoners captured, this *ruse* succeeded admirably.

It had been my intention, up to the time of crossing the Mississippi River, to collect all my forces at Grand Gulf, and get on hand a good supply of provisions and ordnance stores before moving, and, in the mean time, to detach an army corps to coöperate with General Banks on Port Hudson, and effect a junction of our forces.

About this time, I received a letter from General Banks giving his position west of the Mississippi River, and stating that he could return to Baton Rouge by the tenth of May; that by the reduction of Port Hudson he could join me with twelve thousand men.

I learned, about the same time, that troops were expected at Jackson from the Southern cities, with General Beauregard in command. To

delay until the tenth of May, and for the reduction of Port Hudson after that, the accession of twelve thousand men would not leave me relatively so strong as to move promptly with what I had. Information received from day to day of the movements of the enemy also impelled me to the course pursued. While lying at Hawkinson's Ferry, waiting for wagons, supplies, and Sherman's corps, which had come forward in the mean time, demonstrations were made, successfully I believe, to induce the enemy to think that route and the one by Hall's Ferry above, were objects of much solicitude to me. Reconnoissances were made to the west side of the Big Black to within six miles of Warrenton. On the seventh of May an advance was ordered, McPherson's corps keeping the road nearest Black River to Rocky Springs, McClernand's corps keeping the ridge road from Willow Springs, and Sherman following with his corps divided on the two roads. All the ferries were closely guarded until our troops were well advanced. It was my intention here to hug the Black River as closely as possible with McClernand's and Sherman's corps, and get them to the railroad, at some place between Edward's Station and Bolton. McPherson was to move by way of Utica to Raymond, and from thence into Jackson, destroying the railroad, telegraph, public stores, etc., and push west to rejoin the main force. Orders were given to McPherson accordingly. Sherman was moved forward on the Edward's Station road, crossing Fourteen Mile Creek at Dillon's plantation; McClernand was moved across the same creek, further west, sending one division of his corps by the Baldwin's Ferry road as far as the river. At the crossing of Fourteen Mile Creek, both McClernand and Sherman had considerable skirmishing with the enemy to get possession of the crossing.

McPherson met the enemy near Raymond two brigades strong, under Gregg and Walker, on the same day engaged him, and after several hours' hard fighting, drove him with heavy loss in killed, wounded, and prisoners. Many threw down their arms and deserted.

My position at this time was with Sherman's corps, some seven miles west of Raymond, and about the centre of the army.

On the night of the twelfth of May, after orders had been given for the corps of McClernand and Sherman to march toward the railroad by parallel roads — the former in the direction of Edward's Station, and the latter to a point on the railroad between Edward's Station and Bolton — the order was changed, and both were directed to move toward Raymond.

This was in consequence of the enemy having retreated toward Jackson after his defeat at Raymond, and of information that reënforcements were daily arriving at Jackson, and that General Joe Johnston was hourly expected there to take command in person. I, therefore, determined to make sure of that place, and leave no enemy in my rear.

McPherson moved on the thirteenth to Clinton,

destroyed the railroad and telegraph, and captured some important despatches from General Pemberton to General Gregg, who had commanded the day before in the battle of Raymond. Sherman moved to a parallel position on the Mississippi Springs and Jackson road; McClernand moved to a point near Raymond.

The next day Sherman and McPherson moved their entire forces toward Jackson. The rain fell in torrents all the night before, and continued until about noon of that day, making the roads at first slippery and then miry. Notwithstanding, the troops marched, in excellent order without straggling and in the best of spirits, about fourteen miles, and engaged the enemy about twelve o'clock M., near Jackson. McClernand occupied Clinton with one division, Mississippi Springs with another, Raymond with a third, and had Blair's division of Sherman's corps, with a wagon train, still in the rear near New-Auburn, while McArthur, with one brigade of his division, of McPherson's corps, was moving toward Raymond on the Utica road. It was not the intention to move these forces any nearer Jackson, but to have them in a position where they would be in supporting distance if the resistance at Jackson should prove more obstinate than there seemed reason to expect.

The enemy marched out the bulk of his force on the Clinton road, and engaged McPherson's corps about two and a half miles from the city. A small force of artillery and infantry took a strong position in front of Sherman, about the same distance out. By a determined advance of our skirmishers these latter were soon driven within their rifle-pits just outside the city. It was impossible to ascertain the strength of the enemy at this part of the line in time to justify an immediate assault; consequently, McPherson's two divisions engaged the main bulk of the rebel garrison at Jackson without further aid than the moral support given them by the knowledge the enemy had of a force to the south side of the city, and the few infantry and artillery of the enemy posted there to impede Sherman's progress. Sherman soon discovered the weakness of the enemy by sending a reconnoitring party to his right, which also had the effect of causing the enemy to retreat from this part of his line. A few of the artillerists, however, remained in their places, firing upon Sherman's troops until the last moment, evidently instructed to do so, with the expectation of being captured in the end. On entering the city it was found that the main body of the enemy had retreated north, after a heavy engagement of more than two hours with McPherson's corps, in which he was badly beaten. He was pursued until near night, but without further damage to him.

During that evening I learned that General Johnston, as soon as he had satisfied himself that Jackson was to be attacked, had ordered Pemberton peremptorily to march out from the direction of Vicksburgh and attack our rear. Availing myself of this information, I immediately issued orders to McClernand and Blair, of

Sherman's corps, to face their troops toward Bolton, with a view to reaching Edward's Station, marching on different roads converging near Bolton. These troops were admirably located for such a move. McPherson was ordered to retrace his steps early in the morning of the fifteenth on the Clinton road. Sherman was left in Jackson to destroy the railroads, bridges, factories, work-shops, arsenals, and every thing valuable for the support of the enemy. This was accomplished in the most effectual manner.

On the afternoon of the fifteenth I proceeded as far west as Clinton, through which place McPherson's corps passed to within supporting distance of Hovey's division of McClernand's corps, which had moved that day on the same road to within one and a half miles of Bolton. On reaching Clinton, at forty-five minutes past four P.M., I ordered McClernand to move his command early the next morning toward Edward's Depot, marching so as to feel the enemy, if he encountered him, but not to bring on a general engagement unless he was confident he was able to defeat him; and also to order Blair to move with him.

About five o'clock on the morning of the sixteenth, two men, employes on the Jackson and Vicksburgh Railroad, who had passed through Pemberton's army the night before, were brought to my headquarters. They stated Pemberton's force to consist of about eighty regiments, with ten batteries of artillery, and that the whole force was estimated by the enemy at about twenty-five thousand men. From them I also learned the positions being taken up by the enemy, and his intention of attacking our rear. I had determined to leave one division of Sherman's corps one day longer in Jackson, but this information determined me to bring his entire command up at once, and I accordingly despatched him, at half-past five A.M., to move with all possible speed until he came up with the main force near Bolton. My despatch reached him at ten minutes past seven A.M., and his advance division was in motion in one hour from that time. A despatch was sent to Blair, at the same time, to push forward his division in the direction of Edward's Station with all possible despatch. McClernand was directed to establish communication between Blair and Osterhaus, of his corps, and keep it up, moving the former to the support of the latter. McPherson was ordered forward, at forty-five minutes past five A.M., to join McClernand, and Lieut.-Colonel Wilson, of my staff, was sent forward to comunicate the information received, and with verbal instructions to McClernand as to the disposition of his forces. At an early hour I left for the advance, and on arriving at the crossing of the Vicksburgh and Jackson Railroad with the road from Raymond to Bolton, I found McPherson's advance and his pioneer corps engaged in rebuilding a bridge on the former road that had been destroyed by the cavalry of Osterhaus's division that had gone into Bolton the night before. The train of Hovey's division was at a halt, and blocked up the road from further advance on the Vicksburgh road. I ordered all quartermasters and wagon-masters to draw their teams to one side, and make room for the passage of troops. McPherson was brought up by this road. Passing to the front, I found Hovey's division of the Thirteenth army corps at a halt, with our skirmishers and the enemy's pickets near each other. Hovey was bringing the troops into line, ready for battle, and could have brought on an engagement at any moment. The enemy had taken up a very strong position on a narrow ridge, his left resting on a height where the road makes a sharp turn to the left approaching Vicksburgh. The top of the ridge and the precipitous hillside to the left of the road are covered by a dense forest and undergrowth. To the right of the road the timber extends a short distance down the hill, and then opens into cultivated fields on a gentle slope and into a valley extending for a considerable distance. On the road and into the wooded ravine and hillside Hovey's division was disposed for the attack. McPherson's two divisions — all of his corps with him on the march from Milliken's Bend (until Ransom's brigade arrived that day after the battle)—were thrown to the right of the road, properly speaking, the enemy's rear. But I would not permit an attack to be commenced by our troops until I could hear from McClernand, who was advancing with four divisions, two of them on a road intersecting the Jackson road about one mile from where the troops above described were placed, and about the centre of the enemy's line; the other two divisions on a road still north and nearly the same distance off.

I soon heard from McClernand through members of his staff and my own whom I had sent to him early in the morning, and found that by the nearest practicable route of communication he was two and a half miles distant. I sent several successive messages to him to push forward with all rapidity. There had been continuous firing between Hovey's skirmishers and the rebel advance, which, by eleven o'clock, grew into a battle. For some time this division bore the brunt of the conflict; but finding the enemy too strong for them, at the instance of Hovey, I directed first one and then a second brigade from Crocker's division to reënforce him. All this time Logan's division was working upon the enemy's left and rear, and weakened his front attack most wonderfully. The troops here opposing us evidently far outnumbered ours. Expecting McClernand momentarily, with four divisions, including Blair's, I never felt a doubt of the result. He did not arrive, however, until the enemy had been driven from the field, after a terrible contest of hours, with a heavy loss of killed, wounded, and prisoners, and a number of pieces of artillery. It was found afterward that the Vicksburgh road, after following the ridge in a southerly direction for about one mile and to where it intersected one of the Raymond roads, turns almost to the west, down the hill and across the valley in which Logan was operating on the rear of the enemy. One brigade of Logan's division had, unconscious

of this important fact, penetrated nearly to this road, and compelled the enemy to retreat to prevent capture. As it was, much of his artillery and Loring's division of his army was cut off, beside the prisoners captured. On the call of Hovey for more reënforcements, just before the rout of the enemy commenced, I ordered McPherson to move what troops he could by a left flank around to the enemy's front. Logan rode up at this time and told me that if Hovey could make another dash at the enemy he could come up from where he then was and capture the greater part of their force. I immediately rode forward and found the troops that had been so gallantly engaged for so many hours withdrawn from their advanced position and were filling their cartridge-boxes. I desired them to use all despatch and push forward as soon as possible, explaining to them the position of Logan's division. Proceeding still further forward, expecting every moment to see the enemy, and reaching what had been his line, I found he was retreating. Arriving at the Raymond road, I saw to my left and on the next ridge a column of troops which proved to be Carr's division and McClernand with it in person; and to the left of Carr, Osterhaus's division soon afterward appeared with his skirmishers well in advance. I sent word to Osterhaus that the enemy was in full retreat, and to push up with all haste. The situation was soon explained, after which I ordered Carr to pursue with all speed to Black River and across it if he could, and to Osterhaus to follow. Some of McPherson's troops had already got into the road in advance, but having marched and engaged the enemy all day they were fatigued and gave the road to Carr, who continued the pursuit until after dark, capturing a train of cars loaded with commissary and ordnance stores and other property.

The delay in the advance of the troops immediately with McClernand was caused, no doubt, by the enemy presenting a front of artillery and infantry, where it was impossible, from the nature of the ground and the density of the forest, to discover his numbers. As it was, the battle of Champion's Hill, or Baker's Creek, was fought mainly by Hovey's division of McClernand's corps, and Logan's and Quimby's divisions (the latter commanded by Brigadier-General M. M. Crocker) of McPherson's corps.

Ransom's brigade, of McPherson's corps, came on to the field where the main battle had been fought immediately after the enemy had begun his retreat.

Word was sent to Sherman, at Bolton, of the result of the day's engagement, with directions to turn his corps toward Bridgeport; and to Blair to join him at this latter place.

At daylight, on the seventeenth, the pursuit was renewed, with McClernand's corps in the advance. The enemy was found strongly posted on both sides of the Black River. At this point on Black River the bluffs extend to the water's edge on the west bank. On the east side is an open, cultivated bottom of near one mile in width, surrounded by a bayou of stagnant water, from two to three feet in depth, and from ten to twenty feet in width, from the river above the railroad to the river below. Following the inside line of the bayou the enemy had constructed rifle-pits, with the bayou to serve as a ditch on the outside and immediately in front of them. Carr's division occupied the right in investing this place, and Lawler's brigade the right of his division. After a few hours' skirmishing, Lawler discovered that by moving a portion of his brigade under cover of the river bank, he could get a position from which that place could be successfully assaulted, and ordered a charge accordingly. Notwithstanding the level ground over which a portion of his troops had to pass without cover, and the great obstacle of the ditch in front of the enemy's works, the charge was gallantly and successfully made, and in a few minutes the entire garrison with seventeen pieces of artillery were the trophies of this brilliant and daring movement. The enemy on the west bank of the river immediately set fire to the railroad bridge and retreated, thus cutting off all chance of escape for any portion of his forces remaining on the east bank.

Sherman, by this time, had reached Bridgeport, on Black River above. The only pontoon train with the expedition was with him. By the morning of the eighteenth he had crossed the river, and was ready to march on Walnut Hills. McClernand and McPherson built floating bridges during the night, and had them ready for crossing their commands by eight A.M. of the eighteenth.

The march was commenced by Sherman at an early hour by the Bridgeport and Vicksburgh road, turning to the right when within three and a half miles of Vicksburgh, to get possession of Walnut Hills and the Yazoo River. This was successfully accomplished before the night of the eighteenth. McPherson crossed Black River above the Jackson road, and came into the same road with Sherman, but to his rear. He arrived after nightfall with his advance to where Sherman turned to the right. McClernand moved by the Jackson and Vicksburgh road to Mount Albans, and there turned to the left to get into Baldwin's Ferry road. By this disposition the three army corps covered all the ground their strength would admit of, and by the morning of the nineteenth, the investment of Vicksburgh was made as complete as could be by the forces under my command.

During the day there was continuous skirmishing, and I was not without hope of carrying the enemy's works. Relying upon the demoralization of the enemy in consequence of repeated defeats outside of Vicksburgh, I ordered a general assault at two P.M. on this day.

The Fifteenth army corps, from having arrived in front of the enemy's works in time on the eighteenth to get a good position, were enabled to make a vigorous assault. The Thirteenth and Seventeenth corps succeeded no further than to gain advanced positions, covered from the fire of the enemy. The twentieth and twenty-first were spent in perfecting communications with our supplies. Most of the troops had been marching and fighting battles for twenty days, on an average of about five days' rations, drawn from the Commissary department. Though they had not suffered from short rations up to this time, the want of bread to accompany the other rations was beginning to be much felt. On the twenty-first my arrangements for drawing supplies of every description being complete, I determined to make another effort to carry Vicksburgh by assault. There were many reasons to determine me to adopt this course. I believed an assault from the position gained by this time could be made successfully. It was known that Johnston was at Canton with the force taken by him from Jackson, reënforced by other troops from the east, and that more were daily reaching him. With the force I had, a short time must have enabled him to attack me in the rear, and possibly succeeded in raising the siege. Possession of Vicksburgh at that time would have enabled me to have turned upon Johnston and driven him from the State, and possess myself of all the railroads and practical military highways, thus effectually securing to ourselves all territory west of the Tombigbee, and this before the season was too far advanced for campaigning in this latitude. I would have saved Government sending large reënforcements, much needed elsewhere; and, finally, the troops themselves were impatient to possess Vicksburgh, and would not have worked in the trenches with the same zeal, believing it unnecessary, that they did after their failure to carry the enemy's works. Accordingly on the twenty-first orders were issued for a general assault on the whole line, to commence at ten A.M. on the twenty-second. All the corps commanders set their time by mine, that there should be no difference between them in movement of assault. Promptly at the hour designated, the three army corps then in front of the enemy's works commenced the assault. I had taken a commanding position near McPherson's front, and from which I could see all the advancing columns from his corps, and a part of each of Sherman's and McClernand's. A portion of the commands of each succeeded in planting their flags on the outer slopes of the enemy's bastions, and maintained them there until night. Each corps had many more men than could possibly be used in the assault, over such ground as intervened between them and the enemy. More men could only avail in case of breaking through the enemy's line, or in repelling a sortie. The assault was gallant in the extreme on the part of all the troops, but the enemy's position was too strong, both naturally and artificially, to be taken in that way. At every point assaulted, and at all of them at the same time, the enemy was able to show all the force his works could cover. The assault failed, I regret to say, with much loss on our side in killed and wounded; but without weakening the confidence of the troops in their ability to ultimately succeed.

No troops succeeded in entering any of the enemy's works, with the exception of Sergeant

Griffith, of the Twenty-first regiment Iowa volunteers, and some eleven privates of the same regiment. Of these, none returned except the Sergeant and, possibly, one man. The work entered by him, from its position, could give us no practical advantage, unless others to the right and left of it were carried and held at the same time.

About twelve M. I received a despatch from McClernand, that he was hard pressed at several points; in reply to which I directed him to reënforce the points hard pressed from such troops as he had that were not engaged. I then rode round to Sherman, and had just reached there, when I received a second despatch from McClernand, stating positively and unequivocally that he was in possession of and still held two of the enemy's forts; that the American flag then waved over them; and asking me to have Sherman and McPherson make a diversion in his favor. This despatch I showed to Sherman, who immediately ordered a renewal of the assault on his front. I also sent an answer to McClernand, directing him to order up McArthur to his assistance, and started immediately to the position I had just left, on McPherson's line, to convey to him the information from McClernand by this last despatch, that he might make the diversion requested. Before reaching McPherson I met a messenger with a third despatch from McClernand, of which the following is a copy:

HEADQUARTERS THIRTEENTH ARMY CORPS, } IN THE FIELD, NEAR VICKSBURGH, MISS., May 22, '63. }

GENERAL: We have gained the enemy's intrenchments at several points, but are brought to a stand. I have sent word to McArthur to reënforce me if he can. Would it not be best to concentrate the whole or a part of his command on this point? JOHN A. McCLERNAND,
Major-General Commanding.

Major-General U. S. GRANT.

P.S.—I have received your despatch. My troops are all engaged, and I cannot withdraw any to reënforce others. McC.

The position occupied by me during most of the time of the assault gave me a better opportunity of seeing what was going on in front of the Thirteenth army corps than I believed it possible for the commander of it to have. I could not see his possession of forts, nor necessity for reënforcements, as represented in his despatches, up to the time I left it, which was between twelve M. and one P.M., and I expressed doubts of their correctness, which doubts the facts subsequently, but too late, confirmed. At the time I could not disregard his reiterated statements, for they might possibly be true; and that no possible opportunity of carrying the enemy's stronghold should be allowed to escape through fault of mine, I ordered Quimby's division, which was all of McPherson's corps then present, but four brigades, to report to McClernand, and notified him of the order. I showed his despatches to McPherson, as I had to Sherman, to satisfy him of the necessity of an active diversion on their part to hold as much

force in their fronts as possible. The diversion was promptly and vigorously made, and resulted in the increase of our mortality list full fifty per cent, without advancing our position or giving us other advantages.

About half-past three P.M. I received McClernand's fourth despatch, as follows:

HEADQUARTERS THIRTEENTH ARMY CORPS, } May 22, 1863. }

GENERAL: I have received your despatch in regard to General Quimby's division and General McArthur's division. As soon as they arrive I will press the enemy with all possible speed, and doubt not I will force my way through. I have lost no ground. My men are in two of the enemy's forts, but they are commanded by rifle-pits in the rear. Several prisoners have been taken, who intimate that the rear is strong. At this moment I am hard pressed.

JOHN A. McCLERNAND,
Major-General Commanding.

Major-General U. S. GRANT,
Department of the Tennessee.

The assault of this day proved the quality of the soldiers of this army. Without entire success, and with a heavy loss, there was no murmuring or complaining, no falling back, nor other evidence of demoralization.

After the failure of the twenty-second, I determined upon a regular siege. The troops now being fully awake to the necessity of this, worked diligently and cheerfully. The work progressed rapidly and satisfactorily until the third of July, when all was about ready for a final assault.

There was a great scarcity of engineer officers in the beginning, but under the skilful superintendence of Captain F. E. Prime, of the Engineer corps, Lieutenant-Colonel Wilson, of my staff, and Captain C. B. Comstock, of the Engineer corps, who joined this command during the siege, such practical experience was gained as would enable any division of this army hereafter to conduct a siege with considerable skill in the absence of regular engineer officers.

On the afternoon of the third of July a letter was received from Lieutenant-General Pemberton, commanding the confederate forces at Vicksburgh, proposing an armistice, and the appointment of commissioners to arrange terms for the capitulation of the place. The correspondence, copies of which are herewith transmitted, resulted in the surrender of the city and garrison of Vicksburgh at ten o'clock A.M., July fourth, 1863, on the following terms: The entire garrison, officers and men, were to be paroled, not to take up arms against the United States until exchanged by the proper authorities; officers and men each to be furnished with a parole, signed by himself; officers to be allowed their side-arms and private baggage, and the field, staff, and cavalry officers one horse each; the rank and file to be allowed all their clothing, but no other property; rations from their own stores sufficient to last them beyond our lines; the necessary cooking utensils for preparing their food; and thirty wagons to transport such articles as could not well be carried. These terms I regarded more favorable to the Government than an unconditional surrender. It saved us the transportation of them North, which at that time would have been very difficult, owing to the limited amount of river transportation on hand, and the expense of subsisting them. It left our army free to operate against Johnston, who was threatening us from the direction of Jackson; and our river transportation to be used for the movement of troops to any point the exigency of the service might require.

I deem it proper to state here, in order that the correspondence may be fully understood, that after my answer to General Pemberton's letter of the morning of the third, we had a personal interview on the subject of the capitulation.

The particulars and incidents of the siege will be contained in the reports of division and corps commanders, which will be forwarded as soon as received.

I brought forward during the siege, in addition to Lauman's division and four regiments previously ordered from Memphis, Smith's and Kimball's divisions of the Sixteenth army corps, and assigned Major-General C. C. Washburne to command of the same. On the eleventh of June, Major-General F. J. Herron's division from the department of the Missouri arrived; and on the fourteenth two divisions of the Ninth army corps, Major-General J. G. Parke commanding, arrived. This increase in my force enabled me to make the investment most complete, and at the same time left me a large reserve to watch the movements of Johnston. Herron's division was put in position on the extreme left south of the city, and Lauman's division was placed between Herron and McClernand. Smith's and Kimball's division and Parke's corps were sent to Haines's Bluff. This place I had fortified to the land side and every preparation made to resist a heavy force. Johnston crossed Big Black River with a portion of his force, and every thing indicated that he would make an attack about the twenty-fifth of June. Our position in front of Vicksburgh having been made as strong against a sortie from the enemy as his works were against an assault, I placed Major-General Sherman in command of all the troops designated to look after Johnston. The force intended to operate against Johnston, in addition to that at Haines's Bluff, was one division from each of the Thirteenth, Fifteenth, and Seventeenth army corps, and Lauman's division. Johnston, however, not attacking, I determined to attack him the moment Vicksburgh was in our possession, and accordingly notified Sherman that I should again make an assault on Vicksburgh at daylight on the sixth, and for him to have up supplies of all descriptions ready to move upon receipt of orders, if the assault should prove a success. His preparations were immediately made, and when the place surrendered on the fourth, two days earlier than I had fixed for the attack, Sherman was found

ready, and moved at once with a force increased by the remainder of both the Thirteenth and Fifteenth army corps, and is at present investing Jackson, where Johnston has made a stand.

In the march from Bruinsburgh to Vicksburgh, covering a period of twenty days, before supplies could be obtained from government stores, only five days' rations were issued, and three days' of those were taken in haversacks at the start, and were soon exhausted. All other subsistence was obtained from the country through which we passed. The march was commenced without wagons, except such as could be picked up through the country. The country was abundantly supplied with corn, bacon, beef and mutton. The troops enjoyed excellent health, and no army ever appeared in better spirit or felt more confident of success.

In accordance with previous instructions, Major-General S. A. Hurlbut started Colonel (now Brigadier-General) B. H. Grierson, with a cavalry force, from La Grange, Tennessee, to make a raid through the central portion of the State of Mississippi, to destroy railroads and other public property, for the purpose of creating a diversion in favor of the army moving to the attack on Vicksburgh. On the seventeenth of April this expedition started, and arrived at Baton Rouge on the second of May, having successfully traversed the whole State of Mississippi. This expedition was skilfully conducted, and reflects great credit on Colonel Grierson and all of his command. The notice given this raid by the Southern press confirms our estimate of its importance. It has been one of the most brilliant cavalry exploits of the war, and will be handed down in history as an example to be imitated. Colonel Grierson's report is herewith transmitted.

I cannot close this report without an expression of thankfulness for my good fortune in being placed in coöperation with an officer of the navy who accords to every move that seems for the interest and success of our arms his hearty and energetic support. Admiral Porter and the very efficient officers under him have ever shown the greatest readiness in their coöperation, no matter what was to be done or what risk to be taken, either by their men or their vessels. Without this prompt and cordial support my movements would have been much embarrassed, if not wholly defeated.

Captain J. U. Shirk, commanding the Tuscumbia, was especially active and deserving of the highest commendation for his personal attention to the repairing of the damage done our transports by the Vicksburgh batteries.

The result of this campaign has been the defeat of the enemy in five battles outside of Vicksburgh; the occupation of Jackson, the capital of the State of Mississippi, and the capture of Vicksburgh and its garrison and munitions of war; a loss to the enemy of thirty-seven thousand (37,000) prisoners, among whom were fifteen general officers; at least ten thousand killed and wounded, and among the killed Generals

Tracy, Tilghman, and Green, and hundreds and perhaps thousands of stragglers, who can never be collected and reörganized. Arms and munitions of war for an army of sixty thousand men have fallen into our hands, besides a large amount of other public property, consisting of railroads, locomotives, cars, steamboats, cotton, etc., and much was destroyed to prevent our capturing it.

Our loss in the series of battles may be summed up as follows:

	Killed.	Wounded.	Missing.
Port Gibson,	130	718	5
Fourteen-Mile Creek, (skirmish,)	4	24	—
Raymond,	69	341	32
Jackson,	40	240	6
Champion's Hill,	426	1,842	189
Big Black Railroad Bridge,	29	242	2
Vicksburgh,	245	3,688	303

Of the wounded many were but slightly wounded, and continued on duty; many more required but a few days or weeks for their recovery. Not more than one half of the wounded were permanently disabled.

My personal staffs and chiefs of departments have in all cases rendered prompt and efficient service.

In all former reports I have failed to make mention of company A, Fourth regiment Illinois cavalry volunteers, Captain S. D. Osband commanding. This company has been on duty with me as an escort company since November, 1861, and in every engagement I have been in since that time rendered valuable service, attracting general attention for their exemplary conduct, soldierly bearing and promptness. It would not be overstating the merits of this company to say that many of them would fill with credit any position in a cavalry regiment.

For the brilliant achievements recounted in this report, the army of the Tennessee, their comrades of the Ninth army corps, Herron's division of the army of the frontier, and the navy coöperating with them, deserve the highest honors their country can award.

I have the honor to be, Colonel, very respectfully, your obedient servant,

U. S. GRANT,
Major-General U. S. A. Commanding.

Col. J. C. KELTON,
Assistant Adjutant-General, Washington, D. C.

OFFICIAL CORRESPONDENCE.

HEADQUARTERS, VICKSBURGH, July 3, 1863.

Major-Gen. Grant, Commanding U. S. Forces:

GENERAL: I have the honor to propose to you an armistice for —— hours, with a view to arranging terms for the capitulation of Vicksburgh. To this end, if agreeable to you, I will appoint three commissioners to meet a like number to be named by yourself at such place and hour today as you may find convenient. I make this proposition to save the further effusion of blood, which must otherwise be shed to a frightful extent, feeling myself fully able to maintain my position for a yet indefinite period. This communication will be handed you under a flag of truce by Major-General James Bowen.

Very respectfully, your obedient servant,

J. C. PEMBERTON.

To this General Grant replied as follows:

HEADQUARTERS, DEPARTMENT OF TENNESSEE,
IN THE FIELD, NEAR VICKSBURGH, July 3, 1863.

Lieut.-General J. C. Pemberton, Commanding "Confederate" Forces, etc.:

GENERAL: Your note of this date, just received, proposes an armistice of several hours, for the purpose of arranging terms of capitulation through commissioners to be appointed, etc. The effusion of blood you propose stopping by this course, can be ended at any time you may choose, by an unconditional surrender of the city and garrison. Men who have shown so much endurance and courage as those now in Vicksburgh, will always challenge the respect of an adversary, and I can assure you, will be treated with all the respect due them as prisoners of war. I do not favor the proposition of appointing commissioners to arrange terms of capitulation, because I have no other terms than those indicated above.

I am, General, very respectfully,
Your obedient servant,

U. S. GRANT,
Major-General.

General Bowen, the bearer of General Pemberton's letter, was received by General A. J. Smith. He expressed a strong desire to converse with General Grant, and accordingly, while General Grant, declining this, requested General Smith to say that if General Pemberton desired to see him, an interview would be granted between the lines in McPherson's front at any hour in the afternoon which General Pemberton might appoint. A message was soon sent back to General Smith appointing three o'clock as the hour, General Grant was there with his staff, and with Generals Ord, McPherson, Logan, and A. J. Smith. General Pemberton came late, attended by General Bowen and Colonel Montgomery. He was much excited, and impertinent in his answers to General Grant. The conversation was held apart between General Pemberton and his officers, and Generals Grant, McPherson, and A. J. Smith. The rebels insisted on being paroled and march beyond our lines, officers and men all with eight days' rations drawn from their own stores, the officers to retain their private property and body-servants. General Grant heard what they had to say, and left them at the end of an hour and a half, saying that he would send in his ultimatum in writing, to which General Pemberton promised to reply before night, hostilities to cease in the mean time.

General Grant then conferred at his headquarters, with his corps and division commanders, and sent the following letter to General Pemberton, by the hands of General Logan and Lieutenant-Colonel Wilson:

HEADQUARTERS, DEPARTMENT OF TENNESSEE,
NEAR VICKSBURGH, July 3, 1863.

Lieut.-General J. C. Pemberton, Commanding Confederate Forces, Vicksburgh, Miss.:

GENERAL: In conformity with the agreement of this afternoon, I will submit the following propositions for the surrender of the city of

Vicksburgh, public stores, etc. On your accepting the terms proposed, I will march in one division as a guard, and take possession at eight A.M. to-morrow. As soon as paroles can be made out and signed by the officers and men, you will be allowed to march out of our lines, the officers taking with them their regimental clothing, and staff, field and cavalry officers one horse each. The rank and file will be allowed all their clothing, but no other property. If these conditions are accepted, any amount of rations you may deem necessary can be taken from the stores you now have, and also the necessary cooking utensils for preparing them, and thirty wagons also, counting two two-horse or mule teams as one. You will be allowed to transport such articles as cannot be carried along. The same conditions will be allowed to all sick and wounded officers and privates, as fast as they become able to travel. The paroles for these latter must be signed, however, whilst officers are present authorized to sign the roll of prisoners.

I am, General, very respectfully,
Your obedient servant,
U. S. GRANT,
Major-General.

The officers who received this letter stated that it would be impossible to answer it by night, and it was not till a little before peep o' day that the proposed reply was furnished:

HEADQUARTERS, VICKSBURGH, July 3, 1863.

Major-Gen. Grant, Commanding U. S. Forces:

GENERAL: I have the honor to acknowledge the receipt of your communication of this date, proposing terms for the surrender of this garrison and post. In the main your terms are accepted; but in justice both to the honor and spirit of my troops, manifested in the defence of Vicksburgh, I have the honor to submit the following amendments, which, if acceded to by you, will perfect the agreement between us at ten o'clock to-morrow. I propose to evacuate the works in and around Vicksburgh, and to surrender the city and garrison under my command, by marching out with my colors and arms and stacking them in front of my present lines, after which you will take possession; officers to retain their side-arms and personal property, and the rights and property of citizens to be respected.

I am, General, yours, very respectfully,
J. C. PEMBERTON,
Lieutenant-General.

To this General Grant immediately replied as follows:

HEADQUARTERS DEPARTMENT OF TENNESSEE,
BEFORE VICKSBURGH, July 4, 1863.

Lieut.-General Pemberton, Commanding Forces in Vicksburgh:

GENERAL: I have the honor to acknowledge your communication of the third of July. The amendments proposed by you cannot be acceded to in full. It will be necessary to furnish every officer and man with a parole signed by himself, which, with the completion of the rolls of prisoners, will necessarily take some time. Again, I

can make no stipulation with regard to the treatment of citizens and their private property. While I do not propose to cause any of them any undue annoyance or loss, I cannot consent to leave myself under restraint by stipulations. The property which officers can be allowed to take with them will be as stated in the proposition of last evening—that is, that officers will be allowed their private baggage and side-arms, and mounted officers one horse each. If you mean by your proposition for each brigade to march to the front of the lines now occupied by it, and stack their arms at ten o'clock A.M., and then return to inside and remain as prisoners until properly paroled, I will make no objections to it. Should no modification be made of your acceptance of my terms by nine o'clock A.M., I shall regard them as having been rejected, and act accordingly. Should these terms be accepted, white flags shall be displayed along your lines to prevent such of my troops as may not have been notified from firing upon your men.

I am, General, very respectfully,
Your obedient servant,
U. S. GRANT,
Major-General U. S. A.

To this the subjoined answer this moment has been received:

HEADQUARTERS, VICKSBURGH, July 4, 1863.

Major-General U. S. Grant, Commanding U. S. Forces:

GENERAL: I have the honor to acknowledge the receipt of your communication of this date, and in reply to say that the terms proposed by you are accepted.

Very respectfully, your obedient servant,
J. C. PEMBERTON,
Lieutenant-General.

REAR-ADMIRAL PORTER'S DESPATCH.

U. S. MISSISSIPPI SQUADRON, FLAG-SHIP BLACK HAWK,
VICKSBURGH, July 4, 1863.

Hon. Gideon Welles, Secretary of the Navy:

SIR: I have the honor to inform you that Vicksburgh has surrendered at last to the United States forces, after a desperate but vain resistance.

That she has not done so sooner has not been for want of ability on the part of our military commanders, but from the magnitude of the defences, which were intended to repulse any force the Government could possibly send there.

What bearing this will have on the rebellion remains yet to be seen, but the magnitude of the success must go far toward crushing out this revolution, and establishing once more the commerce of the States bordering on this river. History has seldom had an opportunity of recording so desperate a defence on one side, with so much courage, ability, perseverance, and endurance on the other; and if ever an army was entitled to the gratitude of the nation, it is the army of the Tennessee and its gallant leaders.

The navy has necessarily performed a less conspicuous part in the capture of Vicksburgh than the army. Still, it has been employed in a manner highly creditable to all concerned. The gunboats have been constantly below Vicksburgh shelling the works, and with success, coöperating heartily with the left wing of the army. The mortar-boats have been at work for forty-two days without intermission, throwing shells into all parts of the city, even reaching the works in the rear of Vicksburgh and in front of our troops, a distance of three miles.

Three heavy guns placed on scows, a nine-inch, ten-inch, and a one hundred pound rifle, were placed in position a mile from the town, and commanded all the water batteries. They have kept up an accurate and incessant fire for fourteen days; doing all the damage that could be done by guns under such circumstances. Five eight-inch, two nine-inch, two forty-two pounder rifles, and four thirty-two pounder shell-guns have been landed, at the request of the different generals commanding corps, from the gunboats, and mounted in the rear of Vicksburgh; and whenever I could spare the officers and men from our small complement, they were sent to manage the guns — with what ability I leave to the General commanding to say.

In the mean time, I stationed the small class of gunboats to keep the banks of the Mississippi clear of guerrillas, who were assembling in force, with a large number of cannon, to block up the river and cut off the transports, bringing down supplies, reënforcements, and ammunition for the army. Though the rebels on several occasions built batteries, and with a large force attempted to sink or capture the transports, they never succeeded, but were defeated by the gunboats with severe loss on all occasions.

Without a watchful care over the Mississippi, the operations of the army would have been much interfered with; and I can say honestly that officers never did their duty better than those who patrolled the river from Cairo to Vicksburgh. One steamer only was badly disabled since our operations commenced, and six or seven men were killed and wounded.

While the army have had a troublesome enemy in front, behind them, the gunboats, Marine brigade, under General Ellet, and a small force of troops, under Generals Dennis and Mower, have kept at bay a large force of rebels, over twelve thousand strong, accompanied by a large quantity of artillery; and though offered battle several times, and engaged, they invariably fled, and satisfied themselves by assaulting half-disciplined and unarmed blacks.

The capture of Vicksburgh leaves us a large army and our naval forces free to act all along the river, and I hope soon to add to my department the vessels which have been temporarily lost to the service, namely, the Indianola and Cincinnati. The effect of this blow will be felt far up the tributaries of the Mississippi. The timid and doubtful will take heart, and the wicked will, I hope, cease to trouble us for fear of the punishment which will sooner or later overtake them.

There has been a large expenditure of ammunition during the siege. The mortars have fired seven thousand mortar-shells, and the gunboats

four thousand five hundred. Four thousand five hundred shots have been fired from naval guns on shore, and we have supplied over six thousand to the different army corps.

I have the honor to remain, very respectfully, your obedient servant, DAVID D. PORTER,*
Acting Rear-Admiral Commanding Mississippi Squadron.

MAJOR-GENERAL SHERMAN'S REPORT.

HEADQUARTERS FIFTEENTH ARMY CORPS,
WALNUT HILLS, MISS., May 24, 1863.

SIR: In order to make a connected history of events preceding the final issue of this campaign, I avail myself of this the first leisure hour to give substantially the operations of the Fifteenth army corps since the movement began.

General Grant's orders for an advance by way of Grand Gulf were dated April twentieth, 1863, and gave McClernand's corps the right, McPherson's the centre, and mine the left; the movement being by the right flank.

I had made all preparations for the movement when, on the twenty-sixth, I received Gen. Grant's letter from Smith's plantation, near Carthage, describing the road as so very difficult that he ordered me to delay until the roads improved or the system of canals then in process of construction could be finished.

Subsequently, on the twenty-eighth of April, I received his letter fixing the time when he proposed to attack Grand Gulf, and saying that a simultaneous feint on the enemy's batteries on the Yazoo, near Haines's Bluff, would be most desirable, provided it could be done without the ill-effect on the army and the country of the appearance of a repulse. Knowing full well the army could distinguish a feint from a real attack by succeeding events, and assured the country would in due season recover from the effect, I made the necessary orders, and embarked on ten steamboats my second division, Blair's, and about ten A.M., on the twenty-ninth April, proceeded to the mouth of the Yazoo, where I found the flag-boat Black Hawk, Capt. Breese, United States Navy, with the Choctaw (just arrived) and De Kalb, ironclads, with the Tyler and several smaller wooden boats of the fleet all ready, with steam up, prepared to cooperate in the proposed demonstration against Haines's Bluff. Capt. Breese fully comprehended the purpose of the movement, and managed the fleet admirably.

We at once proceeded up the Yazoo in order, and lay for the night of April twenty-ninth at the mouth of Chickasaw, and early next morning proceeded up within easy range of the enemy's batteries. The Choctaw led, followed by the De Kalb, she by the Tyler, she by the Black Hawk, and the fleet in order behind.

The Choctaw at once engaged the batteries at very fair range, and the De Kalb manœuvred so as to use her batteries with as little risk to her unarmored part as the circumstances warranted. The Tyler and Black Hawk also came into action, and for four hours a very pretty demonstration was kept up, when the boats engaged were called

* See General McClernand's Report, page 54 Docs. ante.

out of range. The Tyler had received one shot and the Choctaw some fifty, but strange to say, no men were hurt. Waiting till toward evening I ordered the division of troops to disembark in full view of the enemy, and seemingly prepare to assault, but I knew full well that there was no road across the submerged field that lay between the river and the bluff. As soon as the troops were fairly out on the levee, the gunboats resumed their fire and the enemy's batteries replied with spirit. We could see them moving guns, artillery and infantry, back and forth, and evidently expecting a real attack. Keeping up appearances until night, the troops were reëmbarked. During the next day similar movements were made, accompanied by reconnoissances of all the country on both sides of the Yazoo.

Whilst there I received Gen. Grant's orders to hurry forward toward Grand Gulf. Despatching orders to the divisions of Steele and Tuttle at once to march for Grand Gulf, *via* Richmond, I prolonged the demonstration till night, and quietly dropped back to our camp at Young's Point. No casualties were sustained, save a slight wound from a splintered rail by a man of the Eighth Missouri.

Reaching Young's Point during the night of May first, the next morning Blair's division broke camp, and moved up to Milliken's Bend; at the same time Steele's division marched from Milliken's Bend, and Tuttle's from Dockport, Blair's division remaining as a garrison until relieved by troops ordered from Memphis.

The march from Milliken's Bend to the plantation of Hard Times, on the west bank of the Mississippi, four miles above Grand Gulf, occupied until noon of May sixth, distance sixty-three miles. We crossed over the river during the night of the sixth and day of the seventh, and on the eighth marched eighteen miles out to Hankinson's Ferry, across the Big Black, relieving Crocker's division of McPherson's corps. At noon of the tenth, by order of General Grant, the floating bridge across the Black was effectually destroyed, and the troops marched forward to Big Sandy. On the eleventh we marched to Auburn, and on the morning of the twelfth, at Fourteen Mile Creek, first met opposition. The Fourth Iowa cavalry, Lieut.-Colonel Swan, commanding, leading the advance, was fired on as it approached the bridge across the creek. One man was killed, and the horse of Major Winslow was shot under him. Lieut.-Colonel Swan dismounted the men armed with carbines, (about one hundred,) and began to skirmish with the enemy, which afterward proved to be Wirt Adams's cavalry, but the bushes were so dense that nothing could be seen but the puffs of smoke from their guns.

The bridge also was burning; arriving at the head of the column, I ordered Landgraeber's battery forward to give the bushes a few quick rounds of canister, and Wood's brigade of Steele's division to cross over, its front well covered with skirmishers. This disposition soon cleared the way; and the pioneer company was put to work to make a crossing in lieu of the burned bridge.

This affair delayed us about three hours, when we crossed over just in time to see the enemy's cavalry disappear over the hill.

General Grant in person was with my column at the time, and ordered me to camp there one division (Steele's) on the Edward's Depot road, and the other (Tuttle's) toward Raymond. Whilst there we heard that the enemy had met General McPherson near Raymond, and was defeated.

Next morning we marched to Raymond, and passed on to Mississippi Springs, where we surprised a cavalry picket, capturing them, and on the following day, namely, May fourteenth, pushed on to Jackson by the lower road, McPherson's corps following the Clinton road.

We communicated during the night, so as to arrive at Jackson about the same hour. During the day it rained in torrents, and the roads, which had been very dusty, became equally muddy, but we pushed on, and about ten A.M., were within three miles of Jackson. Then we heard the guns of McPherson to the left, and our cavalry advance reported an enemy to our front at a small bridge at the foot of the ridge along which the road we travelled led.

The enemy opened on us briskly with a battery. Hastily reconnoitring the position, I ordered Mower's and Matthie's brigades of Tuttle's division to deploy forward to the right and left of the road, and Buckland's to close up. Waterhouse's and Spoore's batteries were placed on commanding ground and soon silenced the enemy's guns, when he retired about half a mile into the skirt of woods in front of the intrenchments at Jackson. Mower's brigade followed him up, and he soon took refuge behind the intrenchments.

The stream, owing to its precipitous banks, could only be passed on the bridge, which the enemy did not attempt to destroy, and forming the troops in similar order beyond the bridge, only that Mower's brigade, from the course he took in following the enemy, occupied the ground to the left of the road, and Matthie's brigade to the right, the two batteries in the centre, and Buckland's brigade in reserve.

As we emerged from the woods to our front, and as far to the left as we could see, appeared a line of intrenchments, and the enemy kept up a pretty brisk fire with artillery from the points that enfiladed our road. In order to ascertain the nature of the flanks of this line of intrenchments, I directed Captain Pitzmann, acting Engineer, to take a regiment of the reserve, namely, the Ninety-fifth Ohio, and make a detour to the right, to see what was there. While he was gone, Steele's division closed up. About one P.M. Captain Pitzmann returned, reporting he found the enemy's intrenchments abandoned at the point where they crossed the railroad, and he had left the Ninety-fifth Ohio there in possession. I at once ordered General Steele to lead his whole division into Jackson by that route, and as soon I heard the cheers of his men, Tuttle's division was ordered in by the main road. The enemy's infantry had escaped to the north by the Canton road, but we captured about two hundred and fifty prisoners, with all the enemy's artillery (eighteen guns) with much ammunition and valuable public stores.

Disposing the troops on the outskirts of the town, in obedience to a summons from General Grant, I met him and General McPherson at the hotel near the State House, and received orders to at once occupy the line of rifle-pits, and on the following day to destroy effectually the railroad tracks in and about Jackson, and all the property belonging to the enemy. Accordingly, on the morning of the fifteenth of May, Steele's division was set to work to destroy the railroad and property to the south and east, including Pearl River bridge, and Tuttle's division that to the north and west. This work of destruction was well accomplished, and Jackson, as a railroad centre or government depot of stores and military factories, can be of little use to the enemy for six months. The railroads were destroyed by burning the ties and warping the iron. I estimate the destruction of the roads—four miles east of Jackson, three south, three north, and ten west.

In Jackson the arsenal buildings, the government foundry, the gun-carriage establishment, including the carriages for two complete six-gun batteries, stable, carpenter, and paint-shops, were destroyed. The penitentiary was burned, I think by some convicts which had been set free by the confederate authorities, also a very valuable cotton factory. This factory was the property of the Messrs. Greene, who made strong appeals based on the fact that it gave employment to very many females and poor families, and that, although it had woven cloth for the enemy, its principal use was in weaving cloth for the people. But I decided that machinery of that kind could so easily be converted into hostile uses, that the United States could better afford to compensate the Messrs. Greene for their property and feed the poor families thus thrown out of employment than to spare the property. I therefore assured all such families if want should force them, they might come to the river, where we would feed them until they could find employment or seek refuge in some more peaceful land. Other buildings were destroyed in Jackson by some mischievous soldiers (who could not be detected) which was not justified by the rules of war, including the Catholic church, and the confederate hotel—the former resulting from accidental circumstances and the latter from malice.

General Mower occupied the town with his brigade and two companies of cavalry, and maintained as much order as he could among the mass of soldiers and camp followers that thronged the place during our short stay there; yet many acts of pillage occurred that I regret, arising from the effect of some bad rum found concealed in the stores of the town.

On the morning of the sixteenth I received a note from General Grant, written at Clinton, reporting the enemy advancing from Edward's Depot, and ordering me to put in motion one of my divisions toward Bolton, and to follow with the other as soon as I had completed the work of destruction ordered.

Steele's division marched at ten A.M., and Tuttle's followed at noon. As the march would necessarily be rapid, I ordered General Mower to parole the prisoners of war and to evacuate Jackson as the rear of Tuttle's division passed out. I paroled these prisoners because the wounded men of McPherson's corps had been left in a hospital in charge of Surgeon Hewitt to the mercy of the enemy, that I knew would reënter Jackson as we left. The whole corps marched from Jackson to Bolton, near twenty miles, that day, and next morning resumed the march by a road lying to the north of Baker's Creek, reaching Bridgeport on the Big Black at noon. There I found Blair's division and the pontoon train. The enemy had a small picket on the west bank in a rifle-pit, commanding the crossing, but on exploding a few shells over the pit they came out and surrendered, a lieutenant and ten men. The pontoon-bridge was laid across under the direction of Captain Freeman, and Blair's and Steele's divisions passed over that night, Tuttle's following next morning. Starting with the break of day we pushed rapidly, and by half-past nine A.M., of May eighteenth, the head of the column reached the Benton road, and we commanded the Yazoo, interposing a superior force between the enemy at Vicksburgh and his forts on Yazoo. Resting a sufficient time to enable the column to close up, we pushed forward to the point where the road forks, and sending forward on each road the Thirteenth regulars to the right, and the Eighth Missouri to the left, with a battery at the forks, I awaited General Grant's arrival. He came up very soon and directed me to operate on the right, McPherson on the centre, and McClernand on the left. Leaving a sufficient force on the main road to hold it till McPherson came up, I pushed the head of my column on this road till the skirmishers were within musket-range of the defences of Vicksburgh. Here I disposed Blair's division to the front, Tuttle's in support, and ordered Steele's to follow a blind road to the right till he reached the Mississippi. By dark his advance was on the bluffs, and early next morning he reached the Haines's Bluff road, getting possession of the enemy's outer works, his camps, and many prisoners left behind during their hasty evacuation, and had his pickets up within easy range of the enemy's new line of defences, so that by eight A.M. of May nineteenth, we had compassed the enemy to the north of Vicksburgh, our right resting on the Mississippi River, with a plain view of our fleets at the mouth of Yazoo and Young's Point; Vicksburgh in plain sight, and nothing separated us from the enemy but a space of about four hundred yards of very difficult ground, cut up by almost impracticable ravines and his line of intrenchments. I ordered the Fourth Iowa cavalry to proceed rapidly up to Haines's Bluff and secure possession of the place, it being perfectly open to the rear. By four P.M. the cavalry was on the high bluff behind, and Colonel Swan being assured that the place had been evacuated, despatched Captain Peters to go in and secure the place.

I inclose Colonel Swan's report, with one from Lieut. Clark, from which you will see that the Fourth Iowa cavalry first got possession of the enemy's battery, (evacuated, of course, when we were in full possession of the Benton road,) and delivered it over with its guns, magazine (filled) and material to the gunboat De Kalb, at the time (four P.M., May nineteenth) lying two miles below in Yazoo River. Also on that day communication was opened with our fleet at Young's Point and the mouth of the Yazoo, and bridges and roads made to bring up ammunition and provisions from the mouth of the Chickasaw, to which point supply-boats had been ordered by General Grant. Up to that time our men had literally lived upon the country, having left Grand Gulf May eighth with three days' rations in their haversacks, and received little or nothing until after our arrival here on the eighteenth.

The several corps being in position on the nineteenth, General Grant ordered a general assault at two P.M. At that hour Blair's division moved forward, Ewing's and Giles Smith's brigade on the right of the road, and Kirby Smith's brigade on the left of the road, artillery disposed on the right and left to cover the point where the road enters the enemy's intrenchments. Tuttle's division was held on the road, Buckland's brigade deployed in line to the rear of Blair, and the other two brigades in the road under cover. At the appointed signal the line advanced, but the ground to the right and left of the road was so impracticable, cut up in deep chasms, filled with standing and fallen timber, that the line was slow and irregular in reaching the trenches. The Thirteenth regulars, on the left of Giles Smith, reached the works first, planted its colors on the exterior slope; its commander, Captain Washington, was mortally wounded, and five other officers were wounded more or less severely. Seventy-seven out of two hundred and fifty are reported killed or wounded. Two other regiments reached the same position about the same time—the Eighty-third Indiana, Colonel Spooner, and the One Hundred and Twenty-seventh Illinois, Colonel Eldridge. They held their ground and fired upon any head that presented itself above the parapet; but it was impossible to enter. Other regiments gained position to the right and left close up to the parapet; but night found them outside the works unsuccessful. As soon as night closed in, I ordered them back a short distance, where the shape of the ground gave them partial shelter, to bivouac for the night.

The twentieth and twenty-first instant were consumed in perfecting our system of supplies, opening roads, and putting our artillery in new and more commanding positions, but we could see the enemy similarly employed. During these days our pickets were kept up close, and the enemy was kept uneasy by the appearance of assault at several points. On the twenty-first General Grant issued his orders for a general as-

sault by all the army, at ten A.M., on the twenty-second, the assault to be rapid, by the heads of columns. I placed Blair's division at the head of the road, Tuttle's in support, and left General Steele to make his attack at a point in his front about half a mile to the right. The troops were grouped so that the movement could be connected and rapid. The road lies on the crown of an interior ridge, rises over comparatively smooth ground along the edge of the ditch of the right face of the enemy's bastion, and enters the parapet at the shoulder of the bastion. No men could be seen in the enemy's works, except occasionally a sharp-shooter would show his head and quickly discharge his piece. A line of select skirmishers was placed to keep them down. Also a volunteer storming party of about one hundred and fifty men carrying boards and poles to cross the ditch. This, with a small interval, was followed by Ewing's brigade, his by Giles Smith's and Kirby Smith's bringing up the rear of Blair's division.

All marched by the flank, following a road selected the night before, by which the men were partially sheltered, until it was necessary to take the crown of the ridge and expose themselves to the full view of the enemy, known to be lying concealed behind his well-planned parapet. At the very minute named in General Grant's orders, the storming party dashed up the road at the double-quick, followed by Ewing's brigade, the Thirtieth Ohio leading. The artillery of Wood's, Barrett's, Waterhouse's, Spoor's, and Hart's batteries kept a concentric fire on the bastion, which was doubtless constructed to command this very approach.

The storming party reached the salient of the bastion, and passed toward the sally-port, when rose from every part commanding it a double rank of the enemy that poured on the head of the column a terrific fire. It halted, wavered, and sought cover. The rear pressed on, but the fire was so terrific that very soon all sought cover.

The head of the column crossed the ditch on the left face of the bastion, and clamb upon the exterior slope where the colors were planted, and the men burrowed in the earth to shield themselves from the flank fire. The leading brigade of Ewing being unable to carry that point, the next brigade of Giles Smith was turned down a ravine, and by a circuit to the left, found cover, formed line, and threatened the parapet about three hundred yards to the left of the bastion, and the brigade of Kirby Smith deployed on the off slope of one of the spurs, where, with Ewing's brigade, they kept up a constant fire against any object that presented itself above the parapet.

About two P.M. General Blair reported to me that none of his brigades could pass the point of the road swept by the terrific fire encountered by Ewing's, but that Giles Smith had got a position to the left in connection with General Ransom, of McPherson's corps, and was ready to assault.

I ordered a constant fire of artillery and infantry to be kept up to occupy the attention of the enemy in our front. Under these circumstances, Ransom's and Giles Smith's brigades charged up against the parapet, but also met a staggering fire, before which they recoiled under cover of the hillside. At the same time, while McPherson's whole corps was engaged, and having heard General McClernand's report to General Grant, that he had taken three of the enemy's forts, and that his flags floated on the stronghold of Vicksburgh, I ordered General Tuttle to send directly to the assault one of his brigades. He detailed General Mower's, and whilst General Steele was hotly engaged on the right, and I could hear heavy firing all down the line to my left, I ordered their charge, covered in like manner by Blair's division deployed on the hillside, and the artillery posted behind parapets within point-blank range.

General Mower carried his brigade up bravely and well, but again arose a fire more severe, if possible, than that of the first assault, with a similar result. The colors of the leading regiment, the Eleventh Missouri, were planted by the side of that of Blair's storming party, and remained there till withdrawn after nightfall by my orders.

McClernand's report of success must have been premature, for I subsequently learned that both his and McPherson's assaults had failed to break through the enemy's line of intrenchments, and were equally unsuccessful as my own. At the time we were so hotly engaged along the road, General Steele, with his division, made his assault at a point about midway from the bastion and Mississippi River—the ground over which he passed was more open and exposed to the flank fire of the enemy's batteries in position, and was deeply cut up by gullies and washes. Still his column passed steadily through this fire and reached the parapet, which was also found to be well manned and defended by the enemy. He could not carry the works, but held possession of the hill-side till night, when he withdrew his command to his present position. These several assaults, made simultaneously, demonstrated the strength of the natural and artificial defences of Vicksburgh, that they are garrisoned by a strong force, and that we must resort to regular approaches. Our loss during the day was severe, and the proportion of dead to wounded exceeds the usual ratio. The loss in my corps for the attack of May twenty-second will not fall much short of six hundred killed and wounded. Our skirmishers still remain close up to the enemy's works, while the troops are retired a short distance in the ravines which afford good cover. Strong working parties are kept employed in opening roads to the rear, and preparing covered roads to the front. By taking advantage of the shape of the ground I think we can advance our works to within a hundred yards of the redoubt which commands the road, after which the regular "sap" must be resorted to. Captain Jenney, engineer on my staff, has organized the parties and will set to work immediately at two distinct

poins, one in Blair's, and the other in Steele's front. Our position is now high, healthy, and good. We are in direct and easy communication with our supplies, and the troops continue to manifest the same cheerful spirit which has characterized them throughout this whole movement. I have as yet received no detailed reports of my division commanders; indeed our means of transportation have been so limited, and our time so constantly employed, that but little writing has been done; but as soon as possible I will supply you with accurate reports of all the details of events herein sketched with names of killed and wounded, and the names of such officers and men as deserve mention for special acts of zeal and gallantry.

I have sent in about five hundred prisoners, with lists of their names, rank, regiment, etc., and now inclose the papers relating to those paroled at Jackson, Mississippi.

I have the honor to be, your obedient servant,
W. T. SHERMAN,
Major-General Commanding.

Lieutenant-Colonel JOHN A. RAWLINS,
Assistant Adjutant-General, Department of the Tennessee.

GENERAL McPHERSON'S CONGRATULATORY ADDRESS.

GENERAL ORDERS, NO. 20.

HEADQUARTERS SEVENTEENTH ARMY CORPS,
DEPARTMENT OF THE TENNESSEE,
VICKSBURGH, MISS., July 4, 1863.

SOLDIERS OF THE SEVENTEENTH ARMY CORPS: Again I rejoice with you over your brilliant achievements and your unparalleled successes.

Hardly had your flag floated to the breeze on the capitol of Mississippi, when, springing to the call of our noble commander, you rushed upon the defiant columns of the enemy at Champion Hills and drove him in confusion and dismay across the Big Black to his defences within the stronghold of Vicksburgh.

Your assaulting columns, which moved promptly upon his works on the twenty-second of May, and which stood for hours undaunted under a withering fire, were unsuccessful only because no men could take the position by storm.

With tireless energy, with sleepless vigilance, by night and by day, with battery and with rifle-pit, with trench and mine, you made your sure approaches, until, overcome by fatigue and driven to despair in the attempt to oppose your irresistible progress, the whole garrison of over thirty thousand men, with all their arms and munitions of war, have, on this, the anniversary of our national independence, surrendered to the invincible troops of the army of the Tennessee.

The achievements of this hour will give a new meaning to this memorable day, and "Vicksburgh" will brighten the glow in the patriot's heart which kindles at the mention of "Bunker Hill" and "Yorktown."

This is indeed an auspicious day for you. The God of battles is with you; the dawn of a conquered peace is breaking upon you; the plaudits of an admiring world will hail you wherever you may go, and it will be an ennobling heritage surpassing all riches to have been of the Seventeenth army corps on the fourth of July, 1863.

JAS. B. McPHERSON,
Major-General.

W. T. CLARK,
Assistant Adjutant-General.

A NATIONAL ACCOUNT.

LATE HEADQUARTERS OF LIEUTENANT-GENERAL
PEMBERTON, IN THE CITY OF VICKSBURGH,
Anniversary Day, July 4.

I. A SPLENDID VICTORY.

Vicksburgh has fallen! After forty-seven days of steady siege, the stronghold has succumbed! We are now in peaceable possession of the place; the enemy, as prisoners of war, are being paroled. His colors, his guns, his stores, are left in our hands. As an earnest of the good things to follow, fifty steamers lie quietly at the landing, and a few days will doubtless see fleet after fleet floating grandly on their peaceful missions from Cairo to New-Orleans.

So great, so proud an event comes opportunely on the glorious anniversary of our national independence. The rush of bombs is exchanged for the rush of rockets; the flare of heavy guns for the flash of Roman candles, and the crackle of musketry turned to the sputter of Chinese crackers and pyrotechnic novelties.

They who were yesterday taking deadly sight at each other, are now fraternizing over common comforts, and the din and war of battle is lost in the loud laugh of merriment, and the hum of anxious congratulation.

It is, indeed, a "glorious victory"—not without the attendant woes of war. Six thousand sick lie huddled and crowded in the narrow limits. Nearly every house is a hospital. Soldier and civilian are glad to be relieved from the terrible ordeal that has so long hovered over them. Exhausted, weary, gaunt, and soiled, the garrison rests at last in security and shade, while the victors, flushed with no more than brightening enthusiasm, greet their vanquished foe, as becomes brave men to a brave but fallen enemy. We, too, are glad to cease the labor, the danger, the watch and ward over the place, happy in the fact that the reward of all our endeavors and hopes is rich and commensurate with the toil.

THE FOURTH OF JULY.

The day is celebrated with all the internal warmth at least, that marks it as one of the most illustrious in all history. Our brave army of the South-West has this day consummated a victory more glorious and more pregnant than any which has thus far blessed our arms. The names of General Grant and his coadjutors are again in all mouths. The praises of the soldiers and sailors are being spoken in unstinted terms. The fatigues, hardships, perils, and trials of the campaign are at an end. Twenty-seven thousand prisoners, among which are nineteen general officers; a hundred and twenty cannon, and standards innumerable, are among the substantial trophies of victory.

II. THE SIEGE OF VICKSBURGH.

It was on the eighteenth day of May, 1862, that our fleet, under Admiral Farragut, after his capture of New-Orleans, first made his appearance before Vicksburgh. The confederates had foreseen the danger to their western territory from the loss of New-Orleans, and made haste to fortify some point higher up. Vicksburgh, being accessible by railway, offered the best facilities, besides being situated on a point naturally strong. At that time we held Baton Rouge, on the one end, and menaced Fort Pillow, at the other end of the river. At that time there were five heavy guns mounted. Farragut made a demand for the city, when the Mayor made his famous reply that—"Mississippians do not know how to surrender." The sailor had no force that he could land from his three vessels, and time had not developed then the relative merits of war-vessels and land batteries.

THE FAILURE LAST SUMMER.

That the citadel could have been taken by a slight effort at that time, is admitted by the enemy; but after the return of the ships every nerve was strained to strengthen it. On the fourth of March, Columbus had fallen; on the fourth of June, Pillow was abandoned, leading to the possession of Memphis. Meanwhile, Farragut had returned, and was witness to the labors of the engineers. The first force to approach it from above was the fleet of Colonel Ellet, on the fourteenth of June, and on the twentieth he was followed by Commodore Davis. General Butler had, in the mean while, despatched General Williams with a brigade of troops to coöperate with the navy. After several ineffectual efforts to land, their energies were turned to digging a canal across the peninsula which lies opposite the city, which would have sent the river, if successful, away from the city.

The river fell twenty feet, and the engineers had laid out their canal so unskilfully, that it soon became hopeless. The heat of summer, together with the miasma of the low grounds, wrought sad sickness among both soldiers and sailors, and the close of July saw both fleets depart as they had come; not without considerable excitement from the daring trip of the Arkansas to this landing, and the equally brave feat of Farragut in running by the batteries with his fleet.

In the next two months but little was done on our side, more than to make a reconnoissance to the point above. The rebels, however, were busy, still strengthening their works. Their five guns had been increased to forty-five, pits and trenches were being dug all round. Haines's Bluff was fortified, commanding the Yazoo River, and the powerful steamers above were being converted into war-steamers and rams.

The next attempt was made in the winter. General Grant having reached the Yallabusha on his way through Central Mississippi, sent General Sherman, with a large corps of the army to coöperate with him, by seizing Vicksburgh while he seized Jackson. The skilful movement of Van Dorn to the rear of Grant's invading column seems to have upset this programme. Notwithstanding this, General Sherman moved up the Yazoo River, and attempted to reach the rear of Vicksburgh by the road leading from Chickasaw Bayou. After a desperate assault, our forces were repelled, and the army obliged to retreat with considerable loss. The natural advantages of the position, and the superior handling of the rebels, proved too much for the impetuosity of our troops. The expedition was placed under command of General McClernand, and turned back on Arkansas Post, where it obtained a substantial victory.

The next effort to reduce Vicksburgh commenced in February of the present year, when General Grant, withdrawing his army from the interior, embarked and landed opposite Vicksburgh, making Young's Point his dépôt of supplies. The efforts of General Williams in the previous summer, the example of Pope at Island Number Ten, and the inviting appearance of the high water, gave rise to a series of extraordinary canalling projects. First, it was attempted to reöpen the original ditch across De Soto Point. Several weeks of fruitless labor were spent on it in vain. Another at Lake Providence was then tried, with the same view, to reach the Mississippi, below Vicksburgh, but with no better success. A third, gaining entrance into the Coldwater and Tallahatchie, was next tried, but thwarted by a rebel fort at the head of the Yazoo. Another still, through Steele's Bayou and Rolling Fork, was then essayed, which beat a hasty retreat, and was lucky in escaping.

Lastly, a canal leading from Duckport to New-Carthage, which was successful so far that one small steamer did barely pass through. The fall of the waters and the approaching summer put a stop to the era of aqueducts and bayous, and the general pressure of political events indicated that some more immediate and more practical plan should be adopted.

We had endeavored to force a passage to the rear of Vicksburgh by the north or Yazoo route, and had failed. The formidable water-batteries proved too dangerous for us to run unmailed vessels by the batteries. There was one other method to be tried—to march down the west bank and assail the enemy's railroad communication. This was eminently successful, as all know. Landing at Bruinsburgh, the corps of General McClernand marched to Port Gibson, where it was met by a division of General Bowen, and obtained a signal victory, leading to the evacuation of Grand Gulf, a fortified position.

Our land forces united, then pushed on toward Raymond and Jackson, and when at Champion Hills, near Bolton, were again met by the concentrated enemy, who was again defeated and pursued. One column of our troops, at the heels of one of the enemy's, entered Jackson, while another turned toward Vicksburgh, encountering a force near Big Black Bridge, and, after a sharp and decisive fight, captured many guns and drove their foes within Vicksburgh. Our various columns moved upon the city, General McClernand taking the lead and deflecting southward, General McPherson to the centre, and General Sherman to the right, touching the Yazoo River at Haines's Bluff, which the enemy had abandoned in his terror. On the eighteenth of May, just a year after it had been first menaced, the place was approached and our lines drawn around it—it was, in a word, invested.

In this order were the lines drawn round them: Admiral Porter, with the separated portions of his fleet, guarding the river above and below the city. A new base of supplies was established, leading from the Yazoo directly to the rear. Guns were planted in opposition to the long, fortified series of works of the rebels. On the nineteenth the division of General Blair and a brigade of General Sherman's division assaulted what was thought to be a weak place in the enemy's line of defence, but which proved to be immensely strong, and which repelled the little force. On the twenty-second a more concerted attack was ordered by General Grant, and the whole line was bombarded by cannon. At an early hour the left, under McClernand, had gained a foothold in two of the enemy's forts. Had the attack been made in column, or had our whole force been thrown to the left, it is probable that the place might have been carried by assault. The result was different, we suffering a loss of some two thousand five hundred men disabled.

The attempt to take the place by storm seems to have been abandoned after this. It is just to add, now that the affair is over, that our army was then so much reduced by the casualties of the campaign, death, wounds, and absence, that only a wreck of an army was left, possessing, it is true, all the spirit, though lacking in numbers. It has not been generally known that at the time of our first investment our army numbered less than thirty thousand men, eighteen only of which were fit for duty. With this then attenuated line of troops the rebels, with equal numbers, were kept nearly silent, though behind formidable works. It was therefore determined to reduce the position by siege and parallel works. Reënforcements and detachments arrived, the line of supplies was shortened, and the men concentrated. Fort was erected against fort, and trench dug against trench. The enemy had seized the most eligible sites for their guns, yet our batteries were soon enabled to drive them back, and even to build them under the eyes of the enemy. Our sappers constructed their corridors, and passages, and pits, amid a blazing fire of hostile musketry, and the fiercest rays of the summer sun, with a fortitude which has no parallel in history, and is equalled only by that of the Vicksburgh garrison. Day after day—forty-six in all—did this process continue, one half of our force digging, while the other picked off the rebels who were endeavoring to interrupt them.

In this way were we enabled to sap the very foundation of their works, their cannon were silenced, their sharp-shooters taking only a furtive chance shot, and now and then a mortar-shell at long-range. The health and spirits of the men improved. Our camps were right on the hills around the city. The advantage of shade was with us, though the fighting and digging was almost all done in the sun.

On the twenty-fifth ultimo we blew up the first mine, under one of the enemy's principal forts, in the centre. A struggle ensued for the possession of the fort, in which we were only partially successful, after the loss of several brave men. Three days afterward the other side of the work was blown up, and the enemy had been obliged to fall back a few feet. The mines were already being put under other forts, and it was evident that if this process should continue long enough, the place would be blown to pieces.

The enemy, in their turn, kept running counter-saps, so as to meet and cross ours, so that in two or three instances a thin wall of earth only separated the combatants. The object of these mining operations was to break into and seize upon the prominent points of the enemy's line of fortifications, and thereby force them back by degrees to the river. Many days ago it was evident that the Vicksburgh garrison was short of provisions, and that it must in the end surrender of famine. The work upon the mines was then relaxed, a sufficient demonstration upon the lines being kept up with rifle and cannon to annoy the inmates.

Besides the investing line at the land side of the town, stretching from Haines's Bluff to Warrenton, we had a line of infantry stretched across the base of the peninsula, which Vicksburgh overlooks. The gunboat Choctaw and the flagship Black Hawk lay far out of range above the town; the Benton, Mound City, and Switzerland below. The Cincinnati was sunk by the upper batteries, having descended the bend to assist General Steele's advance. The principal weapons of offence in use on the river front were the mortars, (thirteen-inch.) Six of these, mounted on rafts built for the purpose, lay moored in front of the city, on the upper side of the peninsula, so sheltered by the high bank that the hostile shells passed harmlessly over. These mortars, which proved to be of such signal service in the reduction of Forts Jackson and St. Philip, have proved far less effective at Vicksburgh, as also at Island Number Ten.

Besides the mortars were two one hundred pounder Parrott guns, also mounted on rafts. These guns having an extreme range of three and a half miles, were enabled to direct shells with tolerable accuracy to any building within sight.

On the lower side of the peninsula, that is, immediately in front of the city, a battery was erected on the levee, consisting of one twenty-pounder, one ten-pounder Parrott, and one twelve-pounder brass rifled piece. This battery, manned by a portion of the Marine brigade under Lieutenant-Colonel Curry, was successful in harassing the rebel troops, and in destroying the foundry in which they were casting shot and shells.

The number of mortar-shells thrown into the city from the front is enormous. Many of them never exploded, and in general they were comparatively harmless. If they burst in the air there was but little danger from them, and still less if they exploded when buried twenty feet in the soil.

The particulars of the siege you already know up to within three days of the surrender. On the first instant the firing was mainly confined to the firing of heavy guns for an hour or two in the morning, a lull during the heat of the day, and as night set in a random fire from the batteries in front.

On Friday it was quieter than ever. Our men were busily engaged in getting up full supplies of ammunition. Every thing was being prepared for a battle of some kind, most likely an attack. There was a suspicion that the captured despatch (already published) saying that "the garrison could hold out for ten days from the twenty-fourth, and that unless sooner relieved they would be obliged to surrender," was true. All the indications proved it, although in every attempt to seize any advantage of position they steadily resisted. There was on the left some skirmishing between the pickets, but otherwise all was usually quiet up to the morning of the third.

The disposition of our forces at the time of the surrender was as follows: The three corps of the army of the Tennessee rested on the investing line, the right under Major-General W. T. Sherman, the centre under Major-General J. B. McPherson, and the left under Major-General E. O. C. Ord. The position of the divisions was as follows: On the extreme right, the post of honor, the division of Major-General Frederick Steele; next him General Thayer's division, and on his left that of Major-General Frank P. Blair, Junior. On the right of centre was the division of Major-General John A. Logan; to his left again was that of General John E. Smith; further to the left were General A. J. Smith's and General Carr's divisions. On the left wing were General Hovey's division, General Lanman's, and lastly that of Major-General F. Herron.

General Osterhaus, with a division of the reserve, was posted at Big Black Bridge. General Washburne, with another division was at Haines's Bluff, and part of the Ninth army corps, under Major-General Banks, stretching between Haines's Bluff and Osterhaus's position.

As there was some anticipation that Johnston might make a dash into the rear for moral effect, General Sherman was therefore despatched to the reserve to meet him. General Steele, in his absence commanded the right wing.

Perhaps the only noticeable feature of the last day of siege was the fact that along the lines of intrenchment flags were hoisted, and the rebels and our men were chatting together on the parapet of their works in a friendly way. Admiral Porter, perhaps scenting what was in the wind, commenced a more furious bombardment by the mortars. The rebels in the trenches minded it not, and it was not until four in the afternoon that General Grant sent word over to Porter to request him to cease firing, as the rebels had sent out a flag of truce.

III.—THE SURRENDER.

Things were in this ominous stillness on Friday morning, the third instant, when at about eight o'clock a flag of truce was displayed by the rebels on their works in front of General A. J. Smith's division. A party was sent forward to learn their pleasure, when it turned out to be a communication from General Pemberton to General Grant, borne by Major-General Bowen and Colonel Montgomery, of Pemberton's staff. The two officers were then blindfolded and led to the quarters of General Burbridge, where they were entertained until the letter was despatched to General Grant. Correspondence on the subject continued during the day, and was not finally concluded until nine o'clock the next morning, the ever-memorable Fourth of July. General Pemberton afterward came out and had a personal interview with Grant in front of General Burbridge's line, where the two great captains sat for an hour and a half in close parley. Grant was silent, and smoking, while Pemberton, equally cool and careless in manner, was plucking straws and biting them as if in merest chit-chat.

The communications kept passing as rapidly backward and forward during the night as the circumstances allowed. General Grant gave orders for our men not to fire as directed at daylight, and sent the last note to Pemberton, in which he said that if no other communication was received from them he should construe it into an acquiescence with his terms and proceed to occupy the town. Pemberton then sent his last note saying that he must accept those terms.*

It will be observed that the rebel General pleaded hard for some terms less galling than those of the famous "unconditional surrender." He was first anxious to be allowed to march out with arms, flags, and property, which was refused; then he tried the *ruse* of inserting a proviso that they should be allowed to take out with them *eight days' rations.* This, upon entering, we found to be mere deception, as they had no such store in hand. Then followed the negotiation about "property," in which it is evident the rebels were anxious to save their negroes. General Grant resolutely set his face against any such assumption, and stated that they would be allowed to take their clothing, side-arms, one horse to each mounted officer, and thirty wagons of provisions.

General Grant was induced to grant these terms upon natural and justifiable motives. They were given as acts of magnanimity to a brave foe, not extorted as necessities to hasten the capitulation. It is asserted by the rebel officers that any thing less than this would not have been accepted by them, and the consequences would have been a desperate conflict to escape through our lines. The present adjustment has this advantage, that

* See page 151 *ante.*

it rids us of a large and encumbering load of prisoners whom we should have to feed, clothe, and tend, and to transport them three thousand miles at enormous expense. Besides, it is very properly estimated that these men returning to their homes and to their camps will work more demoralization to the rebel cause than a confinement in Northern prisons. It has been mooted among us that many of these men will be found fighting against us in a few days in violation of their paroles. This may be to some extent. Yet we firmly believe that half of the number will never carry musket in behalf of the Confederacy more if they can help it. A fourth of the whole number would take the oath of allegiance if permitted.

The causes which have led to this stupendous result may be briefly summoned up as follows: the Vicksburgh garrison was in round numbers thirty thousand at the commencement of the siege. It was driven within the walls of the city after a hopeless attempt to protect their line of railroad communication with Jackson. Defeated, dispirited, and worn, they retired within their line of intrenchments, and at once set to work to repair their shattered organization and perfect their defences. In the two or three days which elapsed before our arrival they rallied. They had there provisions for thirty days left. Unless they could drive off the besiegers within that time they were inevitably doomed.

Johnston, who had arrived in Central Mississippi in season to find the fragments of a demoralized army, found a herculean task in restoring it to shape and spirit. He was short of artillery, transportation, and cavalry, and his supplies he had to draw from great distances.

The insuperable difficulty was the strength of our army, and the great advantage of our position. Once on the top of the Chickasaw Ridge, and we were almost impregnable, with our flanks defended by gunboats. The prime cause of the rebel defeat lies with the war department at Richmond, in draining the South to sustain the Virginia army. The second cause was a mistake in venturing beyond the Big Black River to give battle. This was Pemberton's blunder. The next fault is chargeable to Johnston. As a military man, he should have known the utmost limit of resistance which the garrison could reach, and should have relieved it without fail. Had he attempted it, he would certainly have failed, and thus it proves that what General Grant remarked after the battle of Champion Hills was true. Vicksburgh was virtually won then, and the great battle decisive of the fate of the Mississippi Valley was then delivered and won by our Western troops.

The stock of provisions was getting short. Already they were reduced to the offal and dregs of their commissaries. Mule meat, while not eaten as a necessity, had become preferable to their pickled beef. Pork was all gone, flour used up. Corn, unground for the most part, was left in limited supply. But the worst difficulty was that of ammunition. Only ten percussion caps to the man were found in their pouches. Originally short, they had received forty-two thousand through the lines since the investment. Of cartridges they had very few.

Their medicines were scanty. Nearly six thousand men in hospital and continually exposed to the dangers of plunging shells; delicate women and tender children crying for bread and wailing for the loss of friends around them. It must have been a strong heart that could have held out longer.

One cause for determining the time was undoubtedly the apprehension that on the Fourth General Grant would attack. The result would be the sack and pillage of the city and great slaughter. The capitulation avoided all without loss of honor.

At nine in the morning of the Fourth accordingly, General McPherson was sent into the lines to receive the surrender. He met General Pemberton at an old stone house about half a mile from the lines, and had conversed some minutes when General Grant rode upon the ground. After a brief consultation they rode into the town. Major-General Logan had already received orders to march into the town and establish a provost-guard. This was, perhaps, a fitting token of the appreciation of that officer's wonderful earnestness and gallantry in the siege. Lieutenant-Colonel Strong and Colonel Coalbagh, aids to General McPherson, rode on in advance with the National flag, which was hoisted over the Court-House, and its folds flung to the breeze at half-past eleven o'clock. The crowd which followed them sung out in stirring tones the well-known song, "Rally round the Flag," and as the last echoes died away the town clock chimed the hour of noon. The ceremony was complete, the majesty of the national emblem was vindicated in the midst of its erratic and rebellious children.

The arms were stacked on the ground where the men were encamped, and as our forces entered the men sat or stood in mute amazement at the movements of our troops. There was no conflict and but very little visible excitement beyond the cheering of our troops. The day was dusty and hot, and the roads were in places literally a fine powder to the depth of ten inches.

At noon an order was received at Chickasaw Bayou for the steamers to be in readiness to leave for Vicksburgh, and before three o'clock a long line of steamers filed down to the wharf.

General Ellet, with the Marine brigade, was the first to land, Admiral Porter next, then the lower fleet, and finally the long line of transports, commissary boats, tugs, barges, etc., from the Yazoo River. Such a fleet of steamers of all dimensions the city has never seen at its levee before.

The first fruits of the victory are, as nearly as they can be estimated in the confusion attendant upon our entry, as follows: An officer on the staff of General Pemberton informs me that they had upon their last morning reports twenty-seven thousand and odd, officers and men. The officer who applied to our commissary for rations stated that he would require rations for thirty-one thousand soldiers. The latter is nearer the number we shall be called on to parole. Of these there are in the hospitals five thousand six hundred under medical treatment. Not more than fifteen thousand of them have been or are able for duty. Many of them are crawling about in what should be convalescent camps. Weakness from fatigue, short rations, and heat have left thousands decrepit. Four thousand citizens and negroes, besides the twenty-seven thousand soldiers, include all the souls within these walls.

Of public property there is little of any value beyond the cannon and ammunition. Thirty siege-guns, a hundred and two field-pieces, and fifty thousand stand of arms and equipments are among the captures. Eighty stand of colors, most of which, we regret to say, have been seized and torn to shreds as trophies by the excited troops. Of ammunition there is about one hundred rounds for each heavy gun, and twelve for light field-pieces. Of cartridges there is a limited quantity. Some of the guns are very superior; one, an English gun, six and a half inch diameter, rifled. Another, three inches and sixty-seven hundredths, a Brooks gun of great range, besides the old-fashioned ten-inch columbiad. It is surprising that there are so few heavy guns, but this is explained by the rebels in the loss of a great number at Grand Gulf, Haines's Bluff, Fort Pemberton, and Big Black. Two of their heavy guns have burst during this siege, and many of their field-pieces are disabled by our shot.

A considerable quantity of molasses, sugar, and tobacco was discovered, but of all other stores the quantity was quite limited.

IV.—THE CITY.

The appearance of the city after such an unparalleled bombardment, was naturally a point of much curiosity. We expected to see awful havoc from shells and the mortar-bombs. The first sight is a disappointment. The place is not damaged so much as might have been expected. Nearly every house has been shot through, it is true, but a hole made by a cannon-ball is in comparison but a small matter. Here and there were buildings with a corner blown out, and some with a bulge in the walls. Huge craters were to be seen in the streets, where the thirteen-inch shells had burst, the pillars of house-porches split and shattered to splinters. There is not, perhaps, a whole pane of glass within five miles of the Court-House. One church was riddled, while another near by was only scratched.

Hospital flags were stuck up on houses all over the city. There are not less than three hundred houses occupied as hospitals.

A very large fire occurred about three weeks previous to our entrance in a block of stores on Washington street. The stores are said to have contained flour and other commodities, which the owner was holding at exorbitant rates, and which the citizens or soldiers had set on fire. The Court-House, the most conspicuous building in the place, was shattered by several shells. A turreted white house at the lower end of the city, belonging to a St. Louis lawyer, but recently occupied by General Pemberton's headquarters, was also an object of interest, as the garden-grounds were ploughed up by shells of all sizes. Some of the inhabitants had amused themselves by piling up in front of the house the fragments of iron and whole shells. We estimate that some of them had a ton of iron, which had fallen within the grounds. All of the horses and most of the mules are wretchedly poor. Scarcely a single horse could be found in serviceable condition.

Vicksburgh has been called the City of a Hundred Hills. We fancy that is the number included within the limits of the fortifications. Never was place better calculated for field fortifications. It abounds in good sites for batteries, and the earth has just that degree of cohesiveness which makes it work easily. The place is full of steep ravines; two little streams enter the river at either end of the town, but the inhabitants use cistern water.

The works describe a crescent shape around the city, with one point curved inward. The circuit is eight miles. There are along the line a hundred cannon, stationed behind small elevations, of all sizes, from six to twenty-four-pounders, and further to the rear are a few guns of heavy calibre. The terrible havoc of our storm of shells is visible in the torn and gashed parapets, the little craters formed in the banks, and the fragments of shell lying in profusion.

Perhaps the greatest curiosities, as they are novelties in warfare, were half a dozen little wooden mortars, turned out of a wooden block, and resembling somewhat a wagon-hub. These had been invented as a safe and easy method of tossing over the twelve-pounder shells into our saps and mines, where we had supposed them to be thrown by hand. They were charged with about an ounce of powder, the lanyard pulled from a rat-hole, and all danger from a premature explosion avoided. The charge of the powder was so graduated as just to throw the shell outside the work.

The trenches and pits, though originally very elaborately designed, were neither so large nor so well constructed as our own. In fact, they seem to have been engaged, for the most part, in constructing nooks and caves in which to avoid our shots and the explosion of our shells, which at times covered them with earth and dust.

Among the prisoners are one lieutenant-general, four major-generals, fifteen brigadiers, and eighty staff-officers. The names of the former are as follows:

Lieutenant-General John C. Pemberton, Pa.; Major-General Stevenson, Ala.; Major-General Martin Luther Smith, La.; Major-General Forney, Ala.; Major-General Bowen, Mo.; Brigadier-General Lee, ——; Brigadier-General Moore, La.; Brigadier-General Hebert, La.; Brigadier-General Abraham Buford, Ky.; Brigadier-General Schoepff; Brigadier-General Baldwin; Brigadier-General Harris, Tenn.; Brigadier-General

Vaughan, Mo.; Brigadier-General Taylor; Brigadier-General Cummings; Brigadier-General Gardner; Brigadier-General Barton; Brigadier-General Withers, La.

Pemberton, as is well known, is a Philadelphian by birth, who early in life married a Southern lady, and has since cast his lot with that section. He has been a trusted friend of Jeff Davis, and was by him intrusted with the special defence of Vicksburgh. He denies having made the speech attributed to him about "the last dog," etc. It must have been invented probably by Johnston, and published to raise the hopes of his army.

General Forney is an Alabamian, but has failed to distinguish himself very favorably. Stevenson is the next officer in rank to Pemberton, and Smith next to Stevenson. General Bowen was formerly an architect in St. Louis, and was a captured officer at Camp Jackson. Brigadier-General Tracy, of the rebel army, was wounded at Port Gibson, and has since died. Brigadier-General Martin Green, of Mo., was killed on the twenty-fifth ult. Brigadier-General Baldwin is wounded in hospital. Colonel Jacob Thompson, of Mississippi, acting as aid-de-camp on the staff of General Pemberton, and who has been one of his chief counsellors, is missing, and is supposed to have made his escape during the siege or since the surrender. A very strict watch has been thrown around the prisoners now, however.

The officers and men will be paroled at once, and allowed to march out with their side-arms and three days' provisions, on the Jackson road. Their destination is said to be a parole-camp at Talladega, Alabama. The following is the form of parole administered to the prisoners:

VICKSBURGH, MISSISSIPPI, July —, 1863.

To All Whom it May Concern, Know Ye That: I, A—— B——, of company —, regiment —— volunteers, C. S. A., being a prisoner of war in the hands of the United States forces, in virtue of the capitulation of the city of Vicksburgh and its garrison, by Lieutenant-General John C. Pemberton, C. S. A., commanding, on the fourth day of July, 1863, do, in pursuance of the terms of said capitulation, give this my solemn parole under oath:

That I will not take up arms again against the United States, nor serve in any military, police, or constabulary force in any fort, garrison, or field-work held by the confederate States of America, against the United States of America; nor as guard of prisons, depots, or stores, nor discharge any duty usually performed by soldiers against the United States of America, until duly exchanged by the proper authorities.

Sworn to and subscribed before me, at Vicksburgh, on the — day of July, 1863.

———————————— and Paroling Officer.

In the thirty-one thousand inhabitants, there were three thousand citizens and a thousand negroes. Their status is not defined, it would appear from the correspondence, but it is understood that they will be required to take either the oath of allegiance or leave the city soon. In the mean time they will have to be fed. Of food there is very little left. Even the secret hoards had all been brought out before the surrender. Something of their sufferings may be understood when we discover that flour was actually sold at ten dollars per pound or two hundred dollars a barrel; sugar, one dollar and seventy-five cents; corn, ten dollars a bushel; bacon, five dollars a pound; rum, one hundred dollars a gallon, and other things in proportion.

General Pemberton, it is said, refused to allow the citizens to draw from the army stores, insisting that the private stock in the city should be used for that purpose. Mr. Genella, a prominent merchant in this city, being accused of extortion in this matter, publishes a card in vindication of his character.

The principal part of the female population is composed of the wives and families of the foreign population, the husbands and supporters of which have long ago been forced into the rebel army. Numbers of these undoubtedly drew rations from the army stores. Beside them were a few ladies of good family, the wives of officers, and a few of the residents of the town. These were not free of their presence after our occupation. We met a few who were unbroken in spirit, and seemed to call down maledictions upon the pestilent Yankees. The most of them appeared to be stricken with all the sadness of adversity, and crushed beneath a weight of suffering and sorrow.

When we consider that these people—men, women, and children—have, for a month and a half, been in daily terror of their lives, never being able to sleep a night at their homes, but crawling into caves, unable to move except in the few peaceful intervals in the heat of the day, we may appreciate what a life of horror was theirs.

These caves, indeed, are among the most curious features of this life in a besieged city. In several places the streets are cut through the bluff, and in the walls rows of caverns have been hewn, resembling somewhat the appearance of a burrow of rabbits. Most of these are shaped like the letter Y, the stem forming the main entrance, and branching out some seven feet. Into these subterranean pits the inhabitants would crawl so often as the guns and mortars opened out what promised to be a heavy fire. As many as twenty-five have been crowded into one hole. The sight of these poor creatures flying

"With blanket in the alarm of fear caught up,"

was both ludicrous and melancholy. The cry would go up from the irreverent soldiers, "Rats, to your holes," as women and children huddled into the bank. The men generally remained outside, or sought shelter in the bombproofs and magazines nearer the batteries.

It is surprising that the injuries to the citizens have not been greater. The incessant rain of shells and balls, which at times resembled the fall of hail, seems for the most part to have fallen hurtless into the ramparts of solid earth.

About three thousand wounded are to be found in the hospitals. About four hundred and fifty have been buried by the rebels.

Among the principal sufferers are General Green, who was killed, General Baldwin wounded, Colonel Erwin killed, Major Hoadley killed, Lieutenant-Colonel Griffin killed.

Of the citizens, Mike Donovan wounded, and the following ladies: Mrs. Cisco killed, Mrs. C. W. Peters killed, Mrs. Major T. B. Reed, Mrs. W. S. Hazard, Mrs. W. H. Clements, Miss Lucy Rawlings, and Miss Ellen Canovan wounded, and Miss Holly killed. A child of Mrs. Jones's was killed by a shell while sitting in the entrance of the cave. One of the most wonderful things of the siege is the fact that ladies, following the example of the men, have actually promenaded the streets in numbers during the bombardment, priding themselves on their ability to dodge the shells.

Some of the most remarkable escapes are reported. Persons have been buried with the shower of dirt thrown up by shells in front of them. Others have had their clothing torn from them, their faces blackened with powder, and other strange escapes. Perhaps the most noticeable case is that of a shell which fell through the *Citizen* office while the power press was running, and although the shell burst under a room full of people no one was hurt.

Indeed, the coolness of these people under the terrible fire is most astonishing. They have become as familiar with the sound and symptom of bomb, Parrott, and columbiad as to be able to designate them and their course with unerring certainty. Such a fire-baptism has given them something of the salamandrine character. As one of them described the philosophy to me: If you see a shell burst above you, stand still, unless it is very high; if it be the sound of a Parrott, the shot has passed before you heard it; alarm is needless, and so on. No men in the world have ever been called upon to endure so heavy a fire, and none we fancy would now prove such splendid artillerists.

Vicksburgh was, in the outbreak of the rebellion, a city containing some very rabid secessionists, and also some very staunch Union men. Two years and a half of revolutionary misrule has left the city half destroyed, the people beggared, and the adjacent country ruined. These miserable agitators have brought upon themselves a heavy vengeance. Now their sentiments, such of them as remain and have any reason left, see to what a sad extremity they are reduced, and we make free to say that they are glad to be restored once more to the dominion of the national authority. Of all the rest, the blessings of our advent will convert them to the cause. Neither Nashville, nor Memphis, nor New-Orleans, underwent the scourge which Vicksburgh has felt. We predict the love of these few remaining people will be all the more ardent for the Union that they have so long defied its army and navy, and have suffered so profound a humiliation. A few of them pretend to see a five years' vengeance for this stroke; we, however, see, if it were possible, five years taken from the length of the war at a single blow.

We have seen no conflict between the two parties, the victors and the vanquished, as yet. All day to-day and yesterday, the knots of soldiers have been busily engaged in discussing the merits of their respective battles, and the old, old issue of the right of their rebellion. Many of our men are offering their haversacks and canteens to the rebels. Many of the steamboat men recognize old acquaintances. Here are loyal and disloyal Missourians fraternizing, (and in one case fighting,) and a few brothers and cousins are greeting each other with a strange sense of their relationship.

Upon one point the rebel officers are complaining. In their negotiations they show the anxiety to save their negro servants as "personal property," but this our leader could not yield. No sooner were we in, than the recruiting officers commenced their unique system of recruiting, much to the chagrin of the rebels. In one or two cases, appeals have been made to General Grant, who replies that these men are free to go or remain, upon a fair understanding of their new state in life.

V. THE CAMPAIGN IN THE SOUTH-WEST.

The first grand result of this step is the consequent fall of Port Hudson and the reëstablishment of the supremacy of our arms the entire length of the Mississippi. General Grant has some days since despatched an offer of assistance to General Banks in anticipation of this result. It is probable that a few days more will see a fleet of transports moving toward that point if the news does not sooner reach us that it has shared the same fate as Vicksburgh.

Every effort of the enemy thus far to interrupt the line of communication by the river has failed. Our magnificent transports still steam proudly up and down in almost the same security as before. The guerrillas have proved to be a humbug, and there is now a probability that they will unite their numbers and cross to the east side to help out the desperate fortunes of Johnston. At any rate we can now spare leisure and force to assail them.

The next business in hand is to drive off Johnston, and already Sherman is on the way to meet him with a strong army. We entertain no doubt but that Johnston will be obliged to fall back beyond Canton. All the rolling stock now collected between Jackson and Panola must fall into our hands or be destroyed. The six locomotives and fifty cars captured at Vicksburgh will be put to use, and it would not be astonishing if Jackson were held. After Port Hudson shall have fallen, Mobile will probably be invested from the land side. Rosecrans by that time may have reached the Tennessee River; the area of the rebellion will thereby be reduced to one third of its dimensions. Johnston is shown to be an ordinary mortal, and Sherman is quite able to take care of him.

The conclusion of so brilliant a campaign naturally suggests the idea that it is due in great part to the superior management and energy of the superior commander. It is true that General Grant is one of the steadiest and hardest workers in the army. For two years he has been almost constantly in the field, and in the last twelve months has had no respite, not having been further north than Cairo. His pushing, resolute qualities, together with the invincible bravery of his troops, have given him victory over his enemy, where more cautious and more finished officers would have faltered. He is deservedly high in the esteem of the entire army.

He has been ably seconded in his efforts by Generals Sherman and McPherson, the former by his tireless brain and the latter by his executive dash. The navy, under Admiral Porter, has always coöperated with him when asked to do so. It does not appear, however, that the opportunities for distinction have been so favorable as during the command of the lamented Admiral Foote.

DIARY OF A CITIZEN IN VICKSBURGH DURING THE SIEGE.

Sunday, May seventeenth, 1863, opened on Vicksburgh with a forbidding and threatening aspect. On the day previous the Federal forces had overthrown General Pemberton's army, and driven it back to the trenches immediately in the rear of Vicksburgh. Great consternation prevailed among the inhabitants of the city of a hundred hills, as the defeated and demoralized remnant of the confederate army was straggling back to town in disorder and confusion, dismayed and discouraged. Their loss had been heavy, having suffered from a continued series of disasters since the landing of the Federal army. They had been on a continued march, and had gone through a succession of fights for the two preceding weeks, fatigued, disheartened, suffering from hunger and from the want of water. As General Pemberton, with his escort, arrived in town from the battle-field at Big Black, a general feeling of distrust was expressed in his competency, and the place was regarded as lost. Every one expected General Grant's army to march into Vicksburgh that night, while there was no means of defence and no spirit in the troops. General Pemberton set to work in reörganizing the army for the last desperate struggle. General Baldwin went out to review the line of defences, and discovering that the first assault would be made on the left wing, he petitioned the Commanding General to be assigned to hold that position with his veteran troops, upon whose fidelity and courage he could depend, and with whom he felt fully confident of holding the point, and was accordingly assigned to that position.

Monday, June 18.—It was in this deplorable condition that the morning of the anniversary which first brought the enemy under Admiral Farragut in sight of the city one year ago, found us on this occasion. Things did not look encouraging in the least—the enemy was no doubt between Vicksburgh and Big Black River—the troops were scattered and dismayed—General Pemberton was both chagrined and provoked at the previous disaster, and declared that he would "sink Vicksburgh and his army together." The people regarded the place as already at the mercy of the enemy, and for the first time since the siege did they lose their hope of holding the city. The army was placed in position on the lines, and placed in the ditches, with General Baldwin on the left and General Lee on the right. The centre was held by Generals Pemberton, Smith, and Forney. The morning of the day was quiet, and no indications of the enemy's approach were visible until three o'clock P.M., when guns were heard toward the left. The firing soon became more rapid, and extended further along the line as night approached. The Federal forces were engaged with their light artillery in shelling the ditches. Several charges were made and successfully repulsed, and the sharpshooters continued firing through the greater part of the night. In the mean time the confederate lines were strengthened, the army recruited, and confidence restored.

Tuesday, May nineteenth, every thing opened bright and cheerfully; full and universal confidence was now entertained by the whole army that the place could be held until succor arrived. Now all was hope and encouragement. Having held the enemy at bay on the day previous, no one feared the final issue. Early in the morning the enemy again advanced and made a desperate attempt to charge, but were repulsed with heavy loss. Again and again did the serried ranks approach the ditches which were spitting forth death and destruction in their midst. The struggle finally extended along the whole line, with but trivial loss to the men in the trenches. The loss of the enemy could not be ascertained. At the close of the day, the firing ceased along the lines, and quiet was restored. At one o'clock at night one of the gunboats below engaged the lower batteries, and continued firing until daylight. The battery sustaining no damage, remained silent until morning, when a few shots were exchanged, and the boat withdrew.

Wednesday morning, May twentieth, the Federal sharp-shooters again opened a promiscuous and random fire along the whole extent of the lines. There being no occasion for the confederates to waste ammunition without effecting any thing, they reserved their fire and kept silent. Several charges were made on the right, occupied by General Lee's division, but all resulted in a failure to storm the works. It had been suspected on the evening before, from the movements of the fleet, that preparations were making to attack the city in front, and the mortars brought into position during the night. A Parrott gun also devoted some time to shelling the city from the rear. In the morning the sharpshooters again opened the fight, and the light artillery soon joined in the boisterous demonstration; and the mortars which were placed in position during the night, and the Parrott gun in

the rear opened on the city in opposite directions; thus the non-combatants were placed between two fires. This, however, did not interfere with the men in the ditches. The shelling in front also was harmless, and did not prevent the women and children from going about their usual avocations. About the hour of midnight the gunboat again attacked the lower batteries, and a heavy artillery duel was kept up till morning.

Thursday, May 21.—This morning the strife again opened pretty much in the same manner as the previous three days. But little artillery firing was heard until late in the afternoon, and the firing was more confined to the centre than before. The attacking party had changed the position of some of their guns—charges were also made. A vigorous storm of severe wind and rain came up in the afternoon, allaying the intolerable dust and cooling the atmosphere. This seemed only to increase the rapidity of the firing, and toward night the artillery practice was remarkably brisk. One gunboat also engaged the lower battery at long-range for some hours. About four o'clock P.M. the mortars on the opposite side of the city opened, and being located at a very eligible point, they were enabled to throw their shells to every quarter of the city, and the town became virtually untenable. The main target of the mortars seemed to be General Pemberton's headquarters. Further and further the deadly missiles reached over the devoted city, and the people began to look about for places of safety. Many had provided themselves with places of shelter by means of caves which had been dug under the hundred hills of the city. As night approached, the scene became more boisterous and furious. The lower gunboats also opened on the batteries, and, in conjunction with the mortars, kept up an incessant and tumultuous shelling, creating a noise and confusion worse confounded. In the mean time the battle raged in all its fury around the breastworks in the rear.

Friday, May 22.—The morning of this day opened in the same manner as the previous one had closed. There had been no lull in the shelling all night, and as daylight approached it grew more rapid and furious. Early in the morning, too, the battle began to rage in the rear. A terrible onslaught was made on the centre first, and then extended further to the left, where a terrific struggle took place, resulting in the repulse of the attacking party. Four gunboats also came up to engage the batteries. At this time the scene presented an awfully sublime and terrific spectacle—three points being attacked at once, to wit, the rifle-pits by the army in the rear, the city by the mortars opposite, and the batteries by the gunboats. Such cannonading and shelling has perhaps scarcely ever been equalled, and the city was entirely untenable, though women and children were on the streets. It was not safe from behind or before, and every part of the city was alike within range of the Federal guns. The gunboats withdrew after a short engagement, but the mortars kept up the shelling, and the armies continued fighting all day. Several desperate charges were made in force against the lines without accomplishing their object. It would require the pen of a poet to depict the awful sublimity of this day's work—the incessant booming of cannon and the banging of small arms, intermingled with the howling of shells, and the whistling of Minie balls, made the day truly most hideous.

Saturday, May 23.—In the morning there was a good deal of shelling from the mortars and gunboats for an hour or two, after which every thing was silent. The firing along the lines, which began right lively in the morning, also became feeble, and ceased almost entirely toward the middle of the day. In the afternoon shelling commenced again by the mortars, and continued throughout the entire night. The range of the shells appeared to extend over the whole city, and three mortars were employed in throwing the missiles. In the night Commodore Porter started a barge loaded with coal from the upper fleet to the boats below, which was discovered on passing by Vicksburgh and secured at the wharf.

Sunday, May 24.—On this morning firing commenced early toward our right and continued at slow intervals through the forenoon. Later in the day the mortars played upon the city with great fury. A continual war was kept up to the close of the day, and through the night until next morning.

Monday, May 25.—The same boisterous and belligerent demonstrations were still going on and presented nothing different from the preceding six days. Along the lines every thing was quiet, which was occasioned by a flag of truce to bury the dead. At five P.M. the mortars again commenced with a fury heretofore unknown, and rained a perfect storm of shells for some fifteen minutes, when it ceased, and every thing became quiet.

Tuesday, May 26.—The sharp-shooters were again at work at an early hour, and considerable artillery firing was also heard on the lines. In front the mortars remained silent up to nine A.M., when they began with a liveliness that indicated a general demolition of the City of a Hundred Hills. This lasted about two hours, and then slacked off until about ten P.M., when they again commenced and continued up to night, shelling over the whole extent of the city. Along the lines there was not much firing until toward night, when a brisk artillery duel was heard. During the night the shelling was continued at intervals until next morning.

Wednesday, May 27.—Nothing different from the preceding day was observable this morning. The mortars were shelling the city, and the sharpshooters were popping away along the line. Four gunboats again attacked the lower batteries at long-range. At the same time the gunboat Cincinnati came down to engage the upper waterbatteries, which resulted in her destruction. After this adventure the firing ceased along the lines as well as on the river.

Thursday morning, May 28—Was ushered in by the chop, chop, chop of the sharp-shooters, whose performances resembled the continual cutting of wood by a hundred choppers. Artillery firing was quite rapid early in the morning, but the mortars were silent. Most of the day was passed in silence, and only an occasional shell was hurled into the city. Toward night a slight rain passed over, which caused a cessation of firing for a short time, after which the mortars again commenced with great rapidity, throwing a great number of shells into the heart of the city. In the night the firing was slow and only at long intervals. Very little damage was done to the houses.

Friday, May 29.—About four o'clock A.M. the Federals opened a terrible fire along the line, and their shells all over the city. The air was filled with missiles of death, and so many were overhead at once that the report of the guns could not be heard from the continual roaring and whirring of the shells through the air. The affair lasted about two hours, after which quietness was restored, and but little annoyance was experienced during the remainder of the day, until five P.M., when another fire was opened similar to the attack in the morning. The artillery roared savagely and continued about one hour. In the night the boats again attacked the lower batteries, and kept up the engagement about one hour. The mortars also made night hideous with the roaring and bursting of shells. On this night the courthouse was struck for the first time, killing two men and wounding four.

Saturday, May 30.—This morning opened contrary to expectations, as all looked for another shelling from the lines; but the morning came and brought no shelling with it. Only an occasional bomb was thrown during the forenoon, and but little firing was heard on the lines. About seven P.M. the mortars commenced shelling the town very rapidly, and continued nearly the whole night. The gunboats were also engaged in shelling the lower batteries. In the night a party of confederate soldiers made a trip to the sunken gunboat Cincinnati, and succeeded in setting fire to her.

Sunday, May 31.—On this morning the Federal artillerists were put to work at an early hour, having opened their batteries at three A.M., with great fury, which was continued about one hour. As the morning advanced silence was restored. The day was very quiet, and religious services were performed in all the houses of worship. As the shades of night spread over the earth, the mortars again opened on the city, casting once in a minute, which was continued during the whole night.

Monday, June 1.—Hostilities again became rampant at three o'clock A.M., and the firing was kept up with about the same rapidity as on the previous mornings. A general attack was expected, had been expected during the night, and General Pemberton was on the lines in person all night. After night the mortars again commenced, as well as the batteries on the lines, and shelled the pits with merciless ferocity. In the middle of the night an incendiary applied the torch to the store of **J.**

A. Peale & Co., on Washington street, and the flames, communicating to the adjoining buildings, consumed nearly the whole block. No shell had fallen in that part of the town, and the fire originated from incendiarism. Supplies were held by speculators in the buildings.

Tuesday, June 2.—A large concourse of people had gathered on Washington street to witness the scene of conflagration during the night. The mortars were also engaged in their usual employment of shelling the city. As the day advanced, the sun grew excessively hot, and the firing from the mortars became feeble and slow. The day was rather more quiet than any previous twenty-four hours for the last two weeks. At night the mortars again resumed their work, and threw a shell at first every ten minutes, and afterward one in every thirty minutes, which was kept up throughout the entire night.

Wednesday, June 3.—This morning was another spell of rest and quietness, and the usual annoyance of artillery firing on the lines was dispensed with. With the exception of the continued shelling from the mortars, there was no interruption of the prevailing quiet.

Thursday, June 4.—Active artillery firing along the lines announced that the contending forces were again at work. The sharp-shooters also were engaged at an early hour. As the day advanced the artillery firing extended all along the lines, and toward night a brisk skirmish occurred to the right of the centre. The cannonading was kept up all night.

Friday June 5.—Some firing with small arms and light artillery was heard soon in the morning. A gunboat came down and exchanged a few shots with Major Hoadley's battery, and then retired beyond the range. The batteries on the lines continued busy all day, and never ceased until nine o'clock at night. No mortar-shells were thrown all day, and the silence could not be accounted for.

Saturday, June 6.—Early in the morning the artillery was again busy on the line, and it was also ascertained that a battery had been erected on the peninsula, and the guns opened on the city early in the morning. There was no indication of the presence of any mortars on the opposite shore. A good deal of cannonading was heard all along the lines, and continued all day.

Sunday, June 7.—The morning opened quietly after a boisterous night. About nine o'clock the mortars again commenced shelling the city, and the hopes that these nuisances had been removed were thus dispelled. The old style of mortar firing was again resumed, and the shells were thrown at intervals varying from one to fifteen minutes. On the lines there was continual firing, but not very heavy nor rapid. Toward night the business in gunpowder became more active, both on the lines and from the mortars.

Monday, June 8.—The mortars were still playing upon the city, and an occasional cannon was heard on the lines. The day was neither very quiet nor very boisterous. Toward the close of the day there was more activity displayed. Heavy musketry was heard in the night, occasioned by a skirmish between the pickets. The mortars kept busy all night.

Tuesday, June 9.—Heavy shelling and artillery firing being the order of the day, it can scarcely be said that one day differs much from another. The never-ceasing popping of musketry greets the ear from morning till night, and from night till morning. In the night there was always more energy manifested, both on the line and by the mortars, than in daytime.

Wednesday, June 10.—This morning opened with a terrible rain, drenching the earth, washing in caves, and deluging all the low lands with a great flood. The pelting rain, the rolling thunder, the roaring of shells, the crash of the mortars and the sharp bang of field artillery rendered the scene truly terrific. The rain continued at intervals all day, and firing also continued until night. The mortars kept up their work till next morning.

Thursday, June 11.—The weather is still threatening more rain. The mortars are still engaged in shelling the city. They have changed the range to the lower portion of the city, and keep sending in about the usual number of shells. Along the line there was considerable artillery and musketry, and in the night the discharge of ammunition appeared to be unusually heavy.

Friday, June 12.—About daylight there was heavy cannonading on the line, but no small arms were heard. As the day advanced the mortar firing and cannonading became general, and continued till night. The distinguishing feature of the fighting now is the heavy artillery — ten-inch columbiads and ten-inch mortars being constantly engaged along the lines. The shelling continued all night.

Saturday, June 13.—Early in the morning there was very heavy firing along the lines, and the town was under a terrible cross-fire for about two hours, and the air was filled with shells and missiles of all kinds. After this heavy spell ceased, the firing became more moderate, but continued all day, and the mortars also kept pouring in their shells. The people are getting familiar with mortar-shells, and pay but little attention to them. After night the shelling became more active, both on the lines and by the mortars.

Sunday, June 14.—Sunday morning opened with a continuation of the artillery and mortar practice. One mortar was engaging the upper water-battery, and another was shelling the city. The Federal sharp-shooters on the peninsula came down to the bank of the river, and commenced firing their small arms. The shelling was directed more to the front of the city than before. At night the shelling became more furious, and the water-batteries were employed in shelling the woods opposite. A number of incendiary shells were thrown in the night, but failed in igniting any thing.

Monday, June 15.—Another boisterous morning opened upon us. The mortars had succeeded in obtaining a position during the night previous, from which they got a cross-fire with shells upon the city. It was decidedly uncomfortable under this state of affairs to be in any part of the city. The shelling was quite severe about six o'clock in the morning, but became more moderate as the day advanced.

Tuesday, June 16.—This morning presented the same spectacle as the foregoing day, and an unusual number of small shells and solid shot were picked up all over town, showing that the Federals had been busy at work during the night. The tumult continued through the day as usual, without any material change. One mortar had dropped further down the river, toward our upper batteries, and the front part of the city was being visited by shells more frequently than agreeably.

Wednesday, June 17.—Heavy firing on the lines, and the air vocal with the reports of cannon, and whistling of missiles was the remarkable feature of this morning. In the evening there was a brisk engagement between some of the batteries on the right wing. The sharp-shooters also commenced their occupation, created considerable noise, and lasted about one hour.

Thursday, June 18.—Parrott guns, which had been planted behind the timber on the peninsula opposite, opened on the city. The shells from these guns were much more dreaded than the bomb-shells from the mortars. The latter remained silent in the morning, but opened again in the afternoon with more energy than ever. Minie balls from the lines also came into the city and wounded some of the citizens. In the night there was heavy artillery firing on the lines, but the mortars did not operate very actively.

Friday, June 19.—The morning opened with the same old story of shells, shells in all directions—shells everywhere. The Parrott guns were most engaged in shelling the Catholic church, and nine small shells entered the building on this day. From the position which the batteries held they appeared to have a cross and an enfilading fire over the whole city. As usual, the shelling was much more serious at night than in daytime.

Saturday, June 20.—This morning the furies seem to have broken loose on the Federal lines. The shells came with a fiendish rapidity, and the air was so full of the missiles that the unbroken stream of their music drowned the sound of the guns from which they were fired. About three hours did this furious assault continue, but afterward ceased, and the lines became quiet for the remainder of the day.

Sunday, June 21.—On this morning there was quite an unusual relief from the daily annoyance, and the shelling was not so heavy as on the three or four days previous. Some light artillery firing took place on the lines early in the morning, and sharp-shooters were also engaged at their works. Information had been received during the night from General Joseph E. Johnston, and great hopes were entertained that he would come to the relief of the beleaguered city. Public worship was had in the different churches, and but little annoyance was experienced.

Monday, June 22.—Again does a bright and smiling morning open without the terrible accompaniment of bombshells. But little artillery was heard on the lines, and the sharp-shooters did not excite much attention, though the popping of their guns was incessant. The mortars had remained almost totally silent for the past two days. Only an occasional shot warned the people of their continued presence. The day was passed without any unusual interruption of its prevailing quiet, and nothing indicative of any approaching storm was apparent. Early in the night there was an extraordinary uproar among the Federals on their extreme right, but without any apparent cause.

Tuesday, June 23.—On this morning the citizens were treated to a spell of very heavy cannonading, which lasted for several hours, but ceased as the sun began to show his face, and during the remainder of the day but little firing was heard. Only an occasional spell of artillery and slight skirmish among the sharp-shooters was all that could be heard. The day was very hot, and the mortars did not operate. These have now maintained their silence for nearly three days. Later in the day the Parrott guns on the peninsula again raked the city, and were intolerably annoying and dangerous. At ten P.M., the mortars again opened with great severity, and simultaneously with it the fire on the lines was opened by the enemy, and a charge was made.

Wednesday, June 24.—This morning opened with a continuation of mortar-shells and Parrott firing. The former were thrown mostly over the city, and the latter also went to the further end. The elements threatened rain in the morning, and but little was heard of small arms. During the day the artillery practice became brisk, both along the lines and from across the river. The mortars played with great energy, as did also the Parrott guns from the land batteries. The gunboats below took part in the work, and there was regular, continuous, and heavy cannonading all day, but in the night it became quiet.

Thursday, June 25.—This morning was ushered in by the sharp cracking of small arms and the roar of the mortar-shells as they seemed to be chasing each other over the city. A beautiful morning it was to behold the work of strife and death going on, but the serene and lovely skies had no effect in quelling the angry tumult. The gunboats below were busy shelling the lower works. At five P.M. a terrible artillery assault was made on the right wing, and the air was filled with the noise of the thundering cannon for about one hour, after which quiet was again restored.

Friday morning, June 26.—On this morning there appeared to be no disposition to disturb the repose of nature. An occasional shell from the mortars, accompanied by the Parrotts, was hurled into the city from across the river. The riflemen on the opposite bank also were engaged in shooting over, and succeeded in driving away the teams which were hauling water from the river. During the night every thing remained quiet.

Saturday morning, June 27.—No firing was heard this morning from the mortars, and only an occasional Parrott shell. But little sharp-shooting was heard on the lines. There was no effort made during the day to annoy the city further than the riflemen on the opposite shore of the river.

Sunday, June 28.—This was the anniversary of the great bombardment one year ago, and, contrary to expectation, every thing opened silently. A few Parrott shells were thrown into the city early in the morning, and several persons attending worship in the Catholic church were badly mangled. Later in the day the firing ceased altogether. Along the lines there appeared to be but little doing with small arms. The day was unusually dull and quiet, and only an occasional shell disturbed the worshippers in the different churches.

Monday, June 29.—This was another as bright and beautiful a day as ever gladdened the heart of man. The sun shone out in all its brilliancy and splendor, and the absence of firing of any kind gave the beautiful morning the resemblance of times of peace, in a secluded rural district, where the noise and horrors of a bombarded city are unknown. The day became very warm and quiet, and only a moderate number of shells were thrown. In the night the mortars played with more activity, and considerable firing was discovered on the extreme right.

Tuesday, June 30.—This morning opened more lively, and firing was heard along the whole line; but it soon settled down into quietness, and in the middle of the day the firing ceased altogether. The night was also passed without the usual disturbance of bomb-shells. The difficulty of getting provisions becomes greater than ever. This day we heard of the first mule meat being eaten. Some of the officers, disgusted with the salt junk, proposed to slaughter some of the fat mules as an experiment; as, if the siege lasted, we must soon come to that diet. The soup from it was quite rich in taste and appearance. Some of the ladies ate of it without knowing the difference.

Wednesday morning, July 1—was as serene as if Vicksburgh had never known what war was. The day opened out with a very hot sun, and no firing was heard on the lines, nor shells from the mortars. The gunboats below were engaged for several hours in shelling the woods, but toward noon ceased firing, and an unusual and almost oppressive silence prevailed. In the middle of the day some active artillery practice was heard on the river, but was of short duration. At night a number of mortar-shells were thrown.

Thursday, July 2.—On the morning of this day there was quite a stir in the lines of the enemy, and a number of bad shells were thrown in from the rear, while the mortars and Parrott guns from opposite the river were also very active, and for an hour or two the shelling was quite furious. Later in the day it settled down into the usual state of quietude, and remained so until night, when the mortars and Parrotts again opened with great fury, and kept up the annoyance until next morning.

Friday morning, July 3.—This day opened with promise of intolerable heat. Early in the morning there was a little firing on the land side. About eight o'clock it ceased, and the report spread through town of a flag of truce being sent out. Some construed it to mean a surrender of the city. Others that the Federals were demanding the surrender. Some supposed that the women and children, of which we had great numbers, were to be sent out, as there was considerable expectation of a bloody battle on the next day. The navy mortars kept up an increased fire upon the town, but in the rear all was quiet. Rumors kept flying about the town to various ends. At four o'clock the mortars ceased, and, for what proved to be a lasting spell, we were once more permitted to breathe without fear. Some degree of disquietude was felt by the citizens and army in regard to the flag of truce that had been passed on this day, and it leaked out that a surrender was in contemplation.

Saturday, July 4.—It became known that the surrender had been made, and that the alleged cause was starvation. The people were divided on this matter—some insisting on an abundance of supplies, while others maintained that they were exhausted. The result will prove that our provisions are exhausted, our men weak in body but undaunted in spirit; whosoever may be chargeable for this calamity, it cannot be laid to the brave and suffering garrison.

Among the casualties during the siege were three women and three children and four men. Among the troops the casualties were greater. Most of these were sick or wounded, and in the hospitals. A number were severely injured, and numerous limbs were lost. Some most remarkable and ludicrous escapes were made. One man had his head blown off while in the act of picking up his child. One man had a shell to explode close by him, and lifted him some distance in the air. Many strange escapes and incidents are spoken of—so many that they have not been specially noticed.

One shell fell and exploded between two officers as they were riding together on the street, and lifted both horses and riders into the air without hurting either man or beast. One woman had just risen from her chair when a shell came through the roof, took her seat and shattered the house without injuring the lady; and a hundred others of similar cases. A little girl, the daughter of Mr. Jones, was sitting at the entrance of a cave, when a Parrott shell entered the portal and took her head right off. Surely this is terrible warfare which dooms the innocent lambs to inhuman slaughter.

THE DIARY OF JOHN W. SATTENWHITE, COMPANY A, SIXTH MISSOURI VOLUNTEERS, C. S. A., BEGINNING WITH THE FIRST DAY OF THE SIEGE OF VICKSBURGH.

May 18, 1863.—This beautiful morning finds us among the hills of Vicksburgh surrounded by breastworks. About six o'clock this evening we took our position in the outside intrenchments to meet the enemy. We skirmished with them until dark. During the night we moved our position and fell back to the next, second line of works.

May 19.—This morning the fight commenced with vigor, heavy fighting all day. The enemy attempted to charge, but were repulsed with heavy loss; we captured five stands of colors. We are held in reserve, moving from one position to another. We lay all night on the extreme left. Went to the support of some Tennessee troops. We had several wounded to-day.

May 20.—Our regiment moved this morning and took position as reserve on the left of the centre. The enemy attempted to turn our right, but were gallantly repulsed by our boys.

May 21.—The firing commenced this morning at daylight. Heavy firing all day. Several wounded in our regiment to-day. A heavy shower of rain fell this evening.

May 22.—About twelve o'clock to-day the heaviest firing of artillery and musketry ever heard by our troops; the earth trembled and the air was filled with missiles of death. The enemy were repulsed. The firing continued all day. We changed our position. We were called upon to go to the assistance of the Louisiana troops, which we did under a heavy fire. We took our position to the left of Fort Beauregard.

May 23.—The firing was confined principally to heavy skirmishing. They have gained some very advantageous positions for artillery. Our confidence is still growing stronger each hour. General Green's brigade crossed the works last night, charged the advance of the enemy, captured some prisoners and arms, together with a great many ditching-tools. (Gallant conduct.)

May 24.—Skirmishing very heavy. The enemy made no attempt to charge, but were discovered to be undermining our works for the purpose of blowing them up. They were driven off, however, by hand-grenades thrown by our boys. They were very destructive.

May 25.—Heavy skirmishing all day with artillery and small arms continued until about four o'clock, when the enemy sent in a flag of truce, asking for permission to bury their dead. Hostilities ceased for the night. The mortar-boats were also engaged in shelling the city and camps. We hear that Johnston has defeated General McClernand's Federal command. Small loss on our lines to-day.

May 26.—The enemy made no attempt to charge our works. Firing heavy from the line of skirmishing. Our brigade was moved this evening to the extreme right fronting the river, where several mortars are engaged in shelling. As we came through the city the shells flew thick and fast. One hundred and twelve prisoners, captured by our forces, came in to-day. No firing in front of us. Day very warm. We have no shelter from the sun. We have been on half-rations of coarse corn-bread and poor beef for ten days.

May 27.—This morning a portion of our brigade was ordered into the ditches on the right fronting the river; about twelve o'clock the lower fleet came up and opened fire upon us without any injury. The gunboat Cincinnati, from the upper fleet, attempted to run by our batteries, but failed, and was sent to the bottom. Afterward the lower fleet moved back down the river; we were then ordered out of the ditches. About four o'clock we took up the line of march, moved to the centre, and took our position in the ditches at Fort Beauregard, to the left of the Jackson road, where we were exposed to a very heavy artillery fire, the first that we have been in in the ditches.

May 28.—The enemy has made no attempt to charge our works, but we are under a heavy fire of artillery, and a strong line of skirmishers still lying in the ditches. One man mortally wounded in our regiment. The mortar-boats have been very diligent to-day.

May 29.—The enemy opened the whole line of artillery at half-past seven o'clock; continued one and a half hours with great vigor, after which every thing was quiet until half-past five in the evening, when the artillery again opened, and continued their fire for one hour. The entire earth seemed to yield to their thundering. You might have seen rebels hugging the ground as close as moles. The fleet was also engaged in front of the city. All quiet now, except an occasional Minie ball, which makes not a very pleasant noise.

May 30.—This morning our company was ordered to take position in the front ditches, immediately in range of eight pieces of artillery, which opened upon us; the firing continued until near dark, the fiercest I ever heard. Shell flew in every direction, exploding immediately over the ditch to the right and left, tearing away the banks in many places, and completely covering us with dust. We lost four killed and three wounded in our regiment. None of our company hurt, fortunately.

May 31.—This morning, about three o'clock, the enemy commenced a very heavy cannonading; the heavens were perfectly checkered with the fuses in the shells; it lasted about one hour and a half. The remainder of the day was unusually quiet. We hear that General Johnston is at Jackson with a heavy force. Two men killed in our regiment to-day.

Monday, June 1.—Early in the day firing light; about half-past six in the evening eight or ten heavy guns opened upon us, which shook the earth and were very frightful; but our brave boys never flinched. Every man was at his post ready for any emergency. Three killed and two wounded in our regiment. We are now eating bean-bread, and half-rations at that. The mortar-boats are engaged in shelling the city.

June 2.—The firing in the early part of the day was moderate; at half-past six o'clock in the evening a most terrific bombardment commenced. Not less than fifteen pieces of artillery were playing upon us. Our regiment was very fortunate—not a man hurt. Rebels hugged the ground very close. The mortar-boats were busy the whole time shelling the city. Half-rations of pea-bread and poor beef constitute our living — hard fare. Our regiment was relieved to-night by the Thirty-eighth Mississippi; we moved to the right of the Jackson road; kept as reserve; good night's rest.

June 3.—We are laying to the right of the Jackson road. Heavy firing all day. We lost to-day Lieut. Yancey, of company K. Our rations are changed; we now get one half rations bread, rice and corn-meal mixed. We hear again that Johnston is advancing in force. It's our only hope.

June 4.—The firing is more moderate to-day. The fleet has kept up a pretty continued fire all day; the firing upon the ditches has been confined to skirmishers. The loss of our brigade since the eighteenth of May in killed and wounded is two hundred and seventy-five. We are still in reserve.

June 5.—The weather is very warm. The bombardment with artillery is heavy; both land and water-batteries are engaged; the mortar-boats are reported to have been moved from the front of the city. Rumor says that Price occupies Helena, but not credited.

June 6.—Day warm; firing moderate all day; the enemy can be seen moving to the left. We hear that Loring engaged them at Black River.

June 7.—Very warm; we hear the engagement of the upper fleet; supposed to be at Milliken's Bend. The mortar-boats are at work; the artillery kept up a fire the entire night.

June 8.—The mortar-boats have been engaged all day; the land firing was unusually moderate; occasionally a shell would make us hunt our holes. Secesh lay very close to the ground.

June 9.—The firing heavier than usual. The *grapevine* brings us the news that two divisions of Bragg's army have arrived at Memphis. The mortar-boats were very quiet during the day, but kept up a heavy fire during the entire night.

Appendix.—The report of the orderly sergeant of this company (company A, Sixth Missouri) shows a loss of sixty-eight men killed, wounded, and missing; six commissioned officers killed and wounded.

June 10.—Heavy rain fell to-day; it had no effect upon the firing; it continued heavy. A wetter, dirtier, muddier lot of rebels were never seen; but we kept our powder dry. Our beef gave out to-day. We are now drawing one quarter of a pound of bacon to the man.

June 11.—The morning cloudy, but cleared about noon. About four o'clock we were ordered to arms; we moved up about six hundred yards, and took our position in rear of the Twenty-seventh Louisiana regiment, to the right of the Jackson road, where we laid under a heavy fire of artillery all night; it was thought the enemy were preparing to make an assault at that point.

June 12.—We occupied the position we took on yesterday evening until nine o'clock this morning, when all fear subsided, and we returned to our old position. Day pleasant. About four o'clock this evening our mortar opened, which has just been put into position; it attracted the entire line of the enemy's guns; they all opened upon her, and the firing was, for about two hours, very heavy.

June 13.—The morning beautiful. I have just finished my breakfast of half rations coarse corn-bread and a slice of raw bacon, with a cup of bean coffee. Regiment moved this morning, and relieved Green's brigade in the ditches. No loss in regiment to-day.

June 14.—Day very warm; the firing to-day heavier than usual, both front and rear. We hear that Johnston is crossing Black River, and Loring is at Hawkins's Ferry. Our regiment in the ditches.

June 15.—Day pleasant; slight fall of rain in the morning; the firing very heavy. Sergeant Ed. Payne of our company had two fingers shot off the right hand. One man killed, five wounded in our regiment. Three of our companies were compelled to leave the ditches, in consequence of an enfilading fire. I visited the hospitals in town to-day. Had a very interesting chit-chat with the Yankees to-night.

June 16.—Our regiment remained in the ditches until dark, when General Green relieved us. The firing to-day was very heavy; loss to-day, one killed. We lay in the hollow in the rear of the ditches we had just left, all night.

June 17.—We moved this morning, and took our position in the hollow as reserves, in rear of the Third Louisiana, and to the left of the Jackson road, to reënforce, if necessary, what is called Fort Beauregard, which point the enemy are undermining. We made ourselves safe by digging holes in the ground for protection. We hear that three divisions of the Federal army have been defeated at McMinnville. The day pleasant.

June 18.—Firing very heavy all day. We lost three men wounded, S. N. Petcher, of our company, among them. Our rations changed: one quarter of a pound of flour, one quarter of a pound of bacon to the man, quite light. No news from the rear.

June 19.—C. R. Marion, of our company, was killed this morning, while sharp-shooting. A Minie ball penetrated his right eye; came out at the top of the head. A braver man never fell. The firing was heavy all day. We still hear of Johnston's advance. Very still to-night; an occasional shot is all that is heard.

June 20.—The firing commenced this morning with great vigor, continued heavy for eight hours, when it was reduced to the scale of moderation. About four o'clock we were called into line, moved up to the parapet; a false alarm; we returned to our holes after about two hours, which we spent in waiting for Yanks, but they failed to come. Captain Norwood slightly wounded; Dugan killed in camp at the time.

June 21.—The firing more moderate than usual. It is reported that a great many of the enemy's guns have been removed. No loss in our regiment to-day.

June 22. — Firing moderate; weather fine.

James Dye went to hospital sick; three wounded in the regiment. We continue to get news of Johnston's approach.

June 23.—Firing not heavy, but very steady. A very refreshing rain fell during the night. Two wounded in regiment. The firing was very heavy on the right during the night. Captain Sawe wounded to-day in camp. The mortar-boats have been very quiet for several days.

June 24.—Firing heavy, front and rear. We hear Lee has gained another victory in Virginia, and threatens Maryland and Pennsylvania. The enemy are advancing rapidly on our works; we are looking for a blow-up every hour.

June 25.—And one mingled with many distressing events. All was quiet until about four o'clock P.M., when the train which was prepared by the enemy to blow up our works was fired. The explosion was terrific. They then attempted to mount our works, but were kept back. The firing was confined mostly to small arms, which was very heavy. Continued all night; we were up with arms in hand and without sleep all night. Colonel Erwin killed; also Lieutenant W. S. Lipscomb, Viers, J. M. Good, Alf. Eaton, D. S. Lipscomb, and George N. Ferrel, wounded. Jack Satterwhite, slightly. The hand-grenades thrown by the enemy were very destructive. Twenty-four killed and wounded in our regiment.

June 26.—The firing continued heavy all day; the enemy have made no further attempt to mount our works; the throwing of hand-grenades was indulged in by both parties. The Fifth Missouri came to our assistance last night. Day very warm; the enemy can be seen working in front of us; we have repaired that portion of the works blown up by the enemy; all right again. The fleet engaged our batteries to-day, with what effect we have not learned; firing very heavy. We had a good night's rest.

June 27.—Firing moderate to-day. We were relieved at twelve o'clock, for six hours only, by the Fifth Missouri; at six o'clock in the evening we returned to the ditches; were relieved at twelve o'clock at night. Elisha Viers, of our company, died to-day, from wounds received on the twenty-fifth. Lee's victory confirmed. Five killed and three wounded in regiment to-day. David Sigman, of our company, killed; James Parker wounded.

June 28.—Returned to the ditches; relieved by the Fifth Missouri; forty-two killed and wounded since the twenty-fifth; no loss to-day; weather pleasant; no news from the outside. The enemy are working vigorously; we throw a great many hand-grenades among them.

June 29.—Firing very moderate; we are digging to meet the undermining foe. The Second, Fifth, and Sixth Missouri are guarding the threatened point. We relieve each other every six hours. Weather pleasant; no loss to-day.

June 30.—Firing moderate; we threw among them to-day, a keg containing one hundred pounds of powder, with a fuse in it—we are not apprised of the damage it done. Our muster-rolls were ordered to be made out to-day; no loss.

July 1.—This day is long to be remembered. The firing in the morning was light. Our regiment went into the ditches at twelve o'clock; about three o'clock the mine which had been prepared by the enemy under our works was fired; great was the explosion. Lieutenants Crenshaw and Roseberry were buried alive, together with several others. Lieutenant Burr, Geo. Ferrell, Ed. Eaton, and Dunlap of our company wounded. Lieutenant Brather of company B lost his leg. Day very warm. The enemy made no attempt to charge.

July 2.—Firing moderate. The troops are becoming very much disheartened. All seem to be of the opinion that we will be compelled to surrender.

July 3.—This evening about three o'clock, our authorities sent out a flag of truce, to make arrangements to surrender the place. The firing ceased—every thing as still as death. We all knew that the fatal hour had arrived; the preliminaries were not agreed upon, and the flag returned, firing commencing again.

July 4.—To-day the place and its contents was surrendered to the Federal authority—a sore stroke to the Confederacy. The enemy came into town in small numbers, about twelve o'clock. They put their fireworks into operation after dark, by the way of celebrating the Fourth, but were very civil, and treated us with a great deal of kindness. The army will all be paroled and move out. Officers will retain and carry out their side-arms.*

Doc. 26.

CAPTURE OF BRASHEAR CITY.

A REBEL ACCOUNT.†

FRIDAY morning last the courier from below brought cheering and important news. The effect on our good people was palpable, and at once every one was impatient for our extra, giving to the public the account of the glorious victory won by the prowess of our arms in the Teche country. We are now able to lay before our readers the full particulars.

General Taylor, with Walker's division, fought the enemy at Ashland, in North-Louisiana, on the seventh of June.

Before starting on this expedition he had despatched one of his staff-officers to South-west Louisiana to keep him advised of matters in that direction. Information he received about this time determined him to make the movement which has resulted so gloriously to our arms. In half an hour he was in the saddle. In this way and in ambulance he travelled through from Richmond, La., to Alexandria in three days, hardly paused for rest, pushed on with relays of

* Further accounts of this siege are given in the Supplement
† *Louisiana* (Alexandria) *Democrat*, July 1. See page 75 Documents, *ante.*

horses, overtook Colonel Majors, commanding a brigade of cavalry, on the Atchafalaya, and instantly unfolded to him his plan of campaign, in which that gallant young officer was to play such a conspicuous part. Majors was to push boldly through the Grosse Tete, Marangoin, and Lafourche country, to Donaldsonville, thence to Thibodeaux, cut off the railroad and telegraph communication, then push rapidly to the Bœuf River, in the rear of Brashear City, and at the first sound of Mouton's and Green's guns, attack them at that place.

After seeing Colonel Majors well on his way, General Taylor returned *via* Washington and Opelousas, and pushed on rapidly to General Mouton and Green's headquarters, to superintend in person the attack on Brashear City and its forts. Orders had been already given them to make this attack. Advice of Majors's movements, and directions to open communication with him *via* the lakes, so that they could make a combined movement.

Two of General Taylor's staff had been urging on preparations for crossing the troops over the bay. Lieutenant Avery particularly had used every exertion, under direction of Brigadier-General Green, in the construction of skiffs and flats. Major-General Taylor arrived at General Mouton's headquarters on the morning of the twenty-first. Generals Mouton and Green had not been idle in carrying out their orders.

For a few days previous they had organized the different corps and their positions in the impending attack. Shortly after General Taylor's arrival at Mouton's headquarters, one of his staff brought up from General Green's headquarters a despatch of twelve M. the previous day, from Colonel Majors; that daring commander had already arrived at Thibodeaux, after a triumphant campaign throughout the whole Lafourche—had captured Plaquemine, with one hundred and fifty prisoners, destroyed three large sea-going vessels loaded with valuable stores—had taken Donaldsonville with its garrison—had attacked that same day the enemy at Thibodeaux, driven him with Pyron's Texan infantry, at the point of the bayonet, from his strong position—had charged and routed his cavalry by charging him with Lane's, Stone's, and Phillips's Texan cavalry, and was now ready to coöperate with us in our movement to-morrow.

At six P.M. on the evening of the twenty-first, a "forlorn hope," composed of volunteers from the different regiments, embarked in the skiffs and sugar-coolers prepared for them. Theirs was the proud privilege of storming the almost impregnable fort on the opposite side of the bay at dawn the following morning, while Generals Green and Mouton occupied them at different points in their front.

It was a hazardous mission—to cross that Lake (twelve miles) in these frail barks—to land at midnight on the enemy's side, in an almost impenetrable swamp, and await the dawn of day to make the desperate attempt which would insure them victory or a soldier's death; but they seemed to treat it as a holiday frolic as they were rowing away, waving their hats to General Taylor and General Mouton, who were on the bank watching their departure.

The boat expedition having left, Generals Taylor and Mouton proceeded below Pattersonville, to arrange for the other movements. Mouton, with the Seventh Texas, Fourth Texas, and Second Arizona regiments, stood post at Gibbons Point, on the island of the name, and immediately opposite Fort Buchanan. From this place his sharp-shooters could sweep the gunners from their positions at the heavy guns in the Fort. General Green with his old regiment, (Fifth Texas,) Walker's battalion, Second Louisiana cavalry, Valverde and Nichols's batteries, took position just before day in Berwick City, ready to open on all their camp, (which extended up and down the opposite bank for two miles,) also to keep in check their gunboats. Every matter of importance being now ready, Major-General Taylor waited with confidence for the boom of Green's artillery, which was to be the signal of attack.

Immediately after daylight General Green fired the first gun from the Valverde battery at a gunboat of the enemy which was standing up the bay in the direction of the upper fort, (Buchanan.) Instantly the whole bay was in a blaze; all of our guns first played upon the immense line of tents of the enemy, which were occupied by about one thousand Yankees. They were completely surprised—they had not imagined an enemy in twenty miles of them on this side of the bay, (their prisoners admit this.) Their heavy guns from the three forts now opened on Green, at the same moment the sharp crack of Mouton's thousand Enfield rifles is heard continually from Gibbons Point, sweeping their gunners from their places like a whirlwind would dash the sand of the desert; all are anxious to hear the roar of Majors's guns. The worthy pupil of old Stonewall strains his ear for the signal. If Majors has arrived at the Bœuf crossing, we have bagged them all; still we do not hear them, although the cannonade has been going on without intermission for one and a half hours. What has become of the storming party? They have not yet attacked; there is no sign of them; presently we hear one, two, and then the long, distant sound of artillery from the Bœuf. Majors is there! Their communication is cut off completely. Just at this moment, to add to the enemy's confusion and disaster, the long looked-for "forlorn hope" made its appearance in the edge of the woods; with a real Texas yell they dashed at once, with bayonets fixed and pistols drawn, full at the threatening walls of the proud forts. In twenty minutes they had climbed its walls, dispersed its garrison, torn down the stars and stripes, and hoisted the "bonnie blue flag" over its ramparts. Leaving a small band to take care of the Fort, the gallant Hunter rushed on to the camps below, the affrighted enemy throwing down their arms and surrendering indiscriminately, until he had swept the whole place. Green, in the mean time, had engaged their gunboat with the Valverde and

Nichols batteries, and after a hotly contested duel of half an hour, drove it shamefully away.

In half an hour Generals Taylor, Mouton, and Green, with their respective staffs, had their headquarters in the city of Brashear.

Captured 1800 prisoners and thirty-three commissioned officers; $3,000,000 commissary stores; $1,500,000 quartermaster's stores; $250,000 ordnance stores; $100,000 medical stores; twenty-three garrison and regimental flags; 1000 tents; 2000 horses and mules; between 6000 and 7000 negroes; sixteen guns; 7000 stand of small arms, and a position of as much importance to this country (trans-Mississippi,) as Port Hudson and Vicksburgh; in fact, the *key* to Louisiana and Texas. This brilliant campaign of General Taylor had another great object in view and one of *vast* importance, namely: A diversion to force the enemy to raise the siege of Port Hudson. He now has his choice, to lose New-Orleans or to abandon his operations against Port Hudson, and retire with his beaten and demoralized army into that city.

Doc. 27.

BATTLE AT MILLIKEN'S BEND.

OFFICIAL REPORT OF GENERAL DENNIS.

HEADQUARTERS DEPARTMENT OF THE TENNESSEE, NEAR VICKSBURGH, June 16, 1863.

GENERAL: Herewith I have the honor of inclosing Brigadier-General E. S. Dennis's report of the battle of Milliken's Bend, Louisiana, fought on the seventh day of June, 1863, together with the list of casualties. In this battle most of the troops engaged were Africans, who had but little experience in the use of fire-arms. Their conduct is said, however, to have been most gallant, and I doubt not, with good officers, they will make good troops.

Very respectfully, your obedient servant,
U. S. GRANT,
Major-General.

To Brig.-General THOMAS,
Adjutant-General of the Army.

HEADQUARTERS N. E. DISTRICT LOUISIANA, YOUNG'S POINT, LA., June 12, 1863.

COLONEL: I have the honor to report that, in accordance with instructions received from me, Colonel Leib, commanding Ninth Louisiana A. D., made a reconnoissance in the direction of Richmond on June sixth, starting from Milliken's Bend at two o'clock A.M.

He was preceded by two companies of the Tenth Illinois cavalry, commanded by Captain Anderson, whom he overtook three miles from the Bend.

It was agreed between them that the Captain should take the left side of Walnut Bayou, and pursue it as far as Mrs. Ames's plantation, while Colonel Leib proceeded along the main Richmond road to the railroad dépôt, three miles from Richmond, where he encountered the enemy's pickets and advance, which he drove in with but little opposition, but anticipating the enemy in strong force, retired slowly toward the bend.

When about half-way back a squad of our cavalry came dashing up in his rear, hotly pursued by the enemy. Colonel Leib immediately formed his regiment across an open field, and with one volley dispersed the approaching enemy. Expecting the enemy would contest the passage of the bridge over Walnut Bayou, Colonel Leib fell back over the bridge, and from thence to Milliken's Bend, from whence he met a messenger informing me of the success of the expedition, and reported the enemy to be advancing.

I immediately started the Twenty-third Iowa volunteer infantry to their assistance, and Admiral Porter ordered the gunboat Choctaw to that point. At three o'clock the following morning the enemy made their appearance in strong force on the main Richmond road, driving the pickets before them. The enemy advanced upon the left of our line, throwing out no skirmishers, marching in close column by division, with a strong cavalry force on his right flank.

Our forces, consisting of the Twenty-third Iowa volunteer infantry and the African brigade, in all one thousand and sixty-one men, opened upon the enemy when within musket-shot range, which made them waver and recoil, a number running in confusion to the rear. The balance pushing on with intrepidity, soon reached the levee, when they were ordered to charge with the cries of "No quarter!"

The African regiments being inexperienced in the use of arms, some of them having been drilled but a few days, and the guns being very inferior, the enemy succeeded in getting upon our works before more than one or two volleys were fired at them. Here ensued a most terrible hand-to-hand conflict of several minutes' duration.

Our men using the bayonet freely, and clubbing their guns with fierce obstinacy, contesting every inch of ground until the enemy succeeded in flanking them, and poured a murderous enfilading fire along our lines, directing their fire chiefly to the officers, who fell in numbers.

Not till they were overpowered and forced by superior numbers, did our men fall back behind the bank of the river, at the same time pouring volley after volley into the ranks of the advancing enemy. The gunboat now moved into position, and fired a broadside into the enemy, who immediately disappeared behind the levee, but all the time keeping up a fire upon our men.

The enemy at this time appeared to be extending his line to the extreme right, but was held in check by two companies of the Eleventh Louisiana infantry A. D., which had been posted behind cotton-bales, and part of the old levee. In this position the fight continued until near noon, when the enemy suddenly withdrew.

Our men, seeing this movement, advanced upon the retreating column, firing volley after volley at them while they remained within gunshot. The gunboat Lexington then paid her compliments to the flying foe, in several well-directed shots, scattering them in all directions.

I here desire to express my thanks to the officers and men of the gunboats Choctaw and Lexington, for their efficient services in the time of need. Their services will long be remembered by the officers and men of the African brigade, for their valuable assistance on that dark and bloody field.

The officers and men deserve the highest praise for their gallant conduct, and especially Colonel Glasgow, of the Twenty-third Iowa, and his brave men, and also to Colonel Leib, of the Ninth Louisiana A. D., who, by his gallantry and daring, inspired his men to deeds of valor, until he fell, seriously though not dangerously wounded.

I regret to state that Colonel Chamberlain, of the Eleventh Louisiana A. D., conducted himself in a very unsoldier-like manner. The enemy consisted of one brigade, numbering about two thousand five hundred, in command of General McCulloch, and two hundred cavalry. The enemy's loss is estimated at about one hundred and fifty killed, and three hundred wounded.

It is impossible to get any thing near the loss of the enemy, as they carried killed and wounded off in ambulances. Among their killed is Colonel Allen, Sixteenth Texas. Inclosed please find tabular statements of killed, wounded, and missing, in all six hundred and fifty-two. Nearly all the missing blacks will probably be returned, as they were badly scattered.

The enemy, under General Hawes, advanced upon Young's Point, whilst the battle was going on at Milliken's Bend, but several well-directed shots from the gunboats compelled them to retire.*

Submitting the foregoing, I remain yours respectfully,

ELIAS S. DENNIS,
Brigadier-General Commanding District N. E. Louisiana.
JOHN A. RAWLINS,
Assistant Adjutant-General.

Doc. 28.

EXPEDITION UP THE SOUTH-EDISTO, S. C.

OFFICIAL REPORT OF COLONEL HIGGINSON.

ON BOARD STEAMER JOHN ADAMS, }
July 11, 1863. }

Brigadier-General Saxton:

GENERAL: I have the honor to submit a report of an expedition up the South-Edisto River, undertaken with your consent and that of General Gillmore, commanding department.

I left Beaufort on the afternoon of the ninth, with the armed steamer John Adams, the transport Enoch Dean, and the small tug Governor Milton. I had with me two hundred and fifty officers and men of my regiment, and a section of the First Connecticut battery, under command of Lieutenant Clinton.

By four o'clock the next morning we anchored before Wiltown, twenty-one miles up the river,

* See page 12, Docs. *ante.*

and engaged a three-gun field-battery there stationed. After three shots they ceased firing, and, landing with Lieutenant West and thirty men, I took possession of the bluff, where the clothing, equipments, and breakfast-fires left behind betrayed a very hasty departure. This bluff affords the key to the river, and we held it all day until sunset, though with constant skirmishing between my pickets and those of the enemy.

We found, as we expected, a row of spiles across the river at Wiltown, and a prisoner whom we had taken affected great terror of torpedoes. None, however, appeared, and the able engineering of Captain Trowbridge, in three hours effected a passage for the two small vessels. This was too late for the tide, and we were obliged to wait till noon before ascending farther.

At the first attempt to ascend with the flood-tide the Governor Milton went aground, and the Dean going about a mile further, had another engagement with the same battery, and again drove it back. She also running aground, we were compelled to wait an hour longer for the tide, when the two small vessels ascended together. We met with no further interruption (the rice-fields on each side being indefensible) till within two miles of the railroad bridge. Here the Dean unluckily grounded again, and all efforts to get her off being fruitless, I signalled Major Strong, on board the tug, to proceed upward to the bridge. He soon found himself under the fire, at two hundred and fifty yards, of a six-gun field-battery planted that morning on the shore, and, after a severe engagement, in which my vessel could render but little aid, our little consort was compelled to withdraw; and when at last the Dean was got off, the tide rendered it necessary to abandon the attempt. We were at this time more than thirty miles from the mouth of the river, and about twenty miles from Charleston.

Descending the river, the Dean had another fight with her old enemies, apparently reënforced, who shelled us very severely from a point near Wiltown. We passed the spiles successfully, but regretted to find the Milton aground upon them. The John Adams tried in vain to pull her off, and the officers on board were reluctantly compelled to abandon her, as the tide was rapidly falling. I was drawing in the pickets and taking them on board the Dean when this decision was made and acted upon, and it was then too late for me to do any thing but order the little vessel to be set on fire, which was accordingly done, the few men on board having been safely removed.

After this we met with no further incident, except one more artillery fight on the way down the river, making five in all. I am happy to say that in all these engagements the artillerists, both white and black, did themselves much credit, as indeed did all my command. I must especially mention companies K (Captain Whitney) and G (Lieutenant Sampson) upon whom very exposed duty devolved, in the way of skirmishing.

We brought away about two hundred contrabands, six bales of cotton of the best quality, and two prisoners, F. Hall (Sixth cavalry) and G.

Henry Barnwell, of the Rebel Troop, one of the well-known family of that name. Both were captured by my skirmishers, with their horses and full equipments. For want of transportation, we left behind a number of fine horses. We destroyed large quantities of rice, by burning the rice-houses, and cut the dams of the rice-fields. No private property not amenable to military rules was burned or pillaged, though there was abundant opportunity for so doing.

My command reports two killed, private July Green, company A, and Wm. S. Verdier, company C, and one wounded, myself not severely, in the side, from the concussion of a shell. Beside these the engineer of the Milton was killed, (Mr. Mills,) and one contraband, name unknown. One sailor was slightly wounded in the foot, and one contraband lost a leg. Considering the number of shells that exploded in and near the vessels—fifteen having passed through the Enoch Dean alone—I am surprised that the list is no larger.

The loss of the enemy is unknown, but the prisoners stated that one of our first shots dismounted a gun and killed three men.

I have the honor to be, General, very respectfully your obedient servant,

T. W. HIGGINSON,
Colonel Commanding.

A NATIONAL ACCOUNT.

CAMP FIRST REGIMENT S. C. VOLUNTEERS, }
BEAUFORT, S. C., July 16, 1863. }

Thinking perhaps that you would like to hear of an expedition made by a detachment of the First S. C. volunteers, I will proceed to give you a few items.

The expedition left Beaufort on the ninth of July, at four P.M., and arrived at Wiltown Bluff next morning about three A.M. The expedition was composed of four companies of the First regiment S. C. volunteers—companies A, B, G, and K—with a detachment of twenty men from company C, who nobly and fearlessly worked the guns on board the gunboat Enoch Dean. The little steamer Governor Milton, commanded by Major Strong, First S. C. V., was armed with two brass twelve-pounder Armstrongs from the Connecticut battery, commanded by Lieutenant Clinton, First Connecticut battery. The John Adams had on board two twenty-four pounder rifles and two twenty-four pounder howitzers, commanded by Mr. Edward Herron and Lieutenant Walker, First S. C. V. The Enoch Dean had two guns, one ten-pounder Parrott and one six-pounder howitzer, commanded by Captain George Dally, First S. C. V. On arriving near the bluff a contraband was seen on shore and a boat sent for him. He reported a battery of three guns on the bluff. The John Adams fired one gun and was answered by one gun from the bluff, when the rebels retired. Companies K, Captain Whitney, and G, Lieutenant Simpson, landed at the bluff and deployed their companies as skirmishers. After marching about one mile they encountered about one company of cavalry and a company of sharpshooters, when they had a brisk skirmish and succeeded in driving the rebel cavalry and infantry, capturing one lieutenant and one private belonging to the Sixth S. C. While the skirmishing was going on, the John Adams was employed in removing some spiling that extended across the river. The work was done under the supervision and engineering of Captain Trowbridge, First S. C. V., and was done with despatch, opening a breach wide enough for the boats to pass up the river. The little Milton and the Dean passed through the breach and proceeded up the river for about a mile and a half, and encountered a battery of two guns. The Dean exchanged a few shots with the battery, when the battery retired. The Milton meanwhile got aground, when the rebels posted a battery of two guns on the opposite bank and commenced a brisk fire on the Milton. A few well-directed shots from Lieutenant Clinton's guns on board the Milton caused them to retire. The Dean went on about a mile further and encountered two more rebel guns, one on each side of the river. A few shots drove them back. Owing to the draft of the Dean she was obliged to return to the spiling. I almost forgot to mention a detachment of Captain Rogers's company, (F,) who accompanied the expedition and were landed below the bluff, and proceeded about a mile to some extensive rice-mills containing about fifteen thousand bushels of rice, and burned them all. We were detained about two hours for the tide to rise, so that we could fulfil the object of our mission. We then weighed anchor, and the Milton and the Dean proceeded up the river to burn the bridge about fifteen miles from the spiling. When about six miles from the spiling the Dean got aground, and Colonel Higginson ordered the Milton to proceed up the river, but when about twenty rods from the Dean the Milton was fired at from the shore by a three-gun battery. One shell hit the Milton about midships, and exploded, injuring her machinery and killing her engineer. The Milton was obliged to turn back, leaving the Dean aground and exposed to two batteries—one on each side of the river. The Dean was hit with eleven shots from the rebels while aground. One shell burst quite near Colonel Higginson, injuring him severely by the concussion. Another shell passed through the bows of the Dean, killing one gunner and injuring three deck-hands severely. Captain Dolly expended all his ammunition for his ten-pounder rifle, and had only his six-pounder howitzer to fight with. The Dean managed to get afloat by using tar to get up steam, and proceeded down the river and encountered a battery of five guns about four miles from the piles, which riddled the Dean completely with shot and canister. The Milton had meanwhile run down the river, and, by mistake, run headlong on the spiles. Being unable to get her off, she was abandoned and burned. The machinery of the Dean was now disabled, and she was taken in tow by the John Adams.

We then proceeded down the river; but it would be well to mention another brisk skirmish which occurred before embarking, between the rebels and company K, Captain Whiting, and company G, Lieutenant Lampson, with a detachment of company B, under Lieutenant Parker, and a detachment of company A, under Lieutenant Trowbridge. As they were about to embark, the rebels dashed down upon them with a force five hundred strong, consisting of cavalry and infantry. A brisk skirmish ensued, and braver men never used a musket than our boys proved themselves to be on that occasion. They fought with admirable bravery, and the rebels fled before them. The extent of the damage to the rebel side is not yet known. Our troops then embarked, and we proceeded down the river about a mile and a half, and then encountered another battery of four guns, which opened a brisk fire upon us. Two balls struck the John Adams, one of which killed two men. The Enoch Dean was struck seventeen times with shot and shell, beside the grape and canister. The boats then proceeded back to Beaufort. The rebel lieutenant who was captured was taken by a negro, who, after firing his gun without effect, seized the horse by the bridle, and with his other hand grasped firmly the rebel, who was armed with sabre and carbine, and pulled him off his horse.

Doc. 29.

MEDALS OF HONOR TO SEAMEN.

NAVY DEPARTMENT, July 10, 1863.

GENERAL ORDER, No. 17.

THE following-named petty officers and others have been recommended to the Department, agreeably to the requirements of General Order No. 10, of April third, 1863, in such terms as, in the opinion of the Secretary of the Navy, to entitle them to the "Medal of Honor," authorized by an act of Congress approved December twenty-first, 1861, to be bestowed upon "such petty officers, seamen, and marines as shall most distinguish themselves by gallantry in action and other seamanlike qualities during the war."

George Bell, captain of the after-guard, United States frigate Santee, was pilot of the boat engaged in cutting out the rebel armed schooner Royal Yacht from Galveston Bay, November seventh, 1861, and evinced more coolness in passing the four forts and the rebel steamer General Rusk than was ever before witnessed by his commanding officer. Although severely wounded in the encounter, displayed extraordinary courage under the most painful and trying circumstances.

William Thompson, Signal Quartermaster, United States steamer Mohican, in the action at Hilton Head, November seventh, 1861, steered the ship with a steady hand and a bold heart under the batteries; was wounded by a piece of shell, but remained at his station until he fell from loss of blood. Leg since amputated.

John Williams, Boatswain's Mate, United States steamer Mohican, in the action at Hilton Head, November seventh, 1861. Captain of eleven-inch gun; was conspicuous for his cool courage, and

pleasant, cheerful way of fighting, losing few shots and inspiring his gun's crew with his manner.

Matthew Arthur, Signal Quartermaster, United States steamer Carondelet, at the reduction of Forts Henry and Donelson, February sixth and fourteenth, 1862, and other actions, most faithfully, effectively, and valiantly performed all the duties of a Signal Quartermaster and captain of rifled bow-gun, and conspicuous for valor and devotion.

John Mackie, Corporal of Marines, United States steamer Galena, in the attack on Fort Darling, at Drury's Bluff, James River, May fifteenth, 1862, particularly mentioned for his gallant conduct and services and signal acts of devotion to duty.

Matthew McClelland, first-class fireman; Joseph E. Vantine, first-class fireman; John Rush, first-class fireman; John Hickman, second-class fireman, United States steamer Richmond, in the attack on the Port Hudson batteries, March fourteenth, 1863, when the fire-room and other parts of the ship were filled with hot steam from injury to the boiler by a shot, these men, from the first moment of the casualty, stood firmly at their posts, and were conspicuous in their exertions to remedy the evil by hauling the fires from the injured boiler—the heat being so great from the combined effects of fire and steam that they were compelled, from mere exhaustion, to relieve each other every few minutes until the work was accomplished.

Robert Anderson, Quartermaster in the United States steamers Crusader and Keokuk, exhibited in the former vessel, on all occasions, in various skirmishes and fights, the greatest intrepidity and devotion. In the latter vessel, during the attack on Charleston, was stationed at the wheel, and when the shot penetrated, scattering the iron, desired to cover his commanding officer with his person.

Peter Howard, Boatswain's Mate; Andrew Brinn, seaman; P. R. Vaughn, Sergeant of Marines, United States steamer Mississippi, in the attack on the Port Hudson batteries, night of March fourteenth, 1863. Commended for zeal and courage displayed in the performance of unusual and trying services, whilst the vessel was aground and exposed to a heavy fire.

Samuel Woods, seamen, United States steamer Minnesota, but temporarily on board the United States steamer Mount Washington, Nansemond River, April fourteenth, 1863, fought his gun with the most determined courage; plunged into the stream and endeavored to save a shipmate who had been knocked overboard by a shell, and was conspicuous for his tender care of the wounded.

Henry Thielberg, seaman, United States steamer Minnesota, but temporarily on board the United States steamer Mount Washington, Nansemond River, April fourteenth, 1863, conducted himself with the highest coolness and courage, and volunteered to go upon the pilot-house to watch the movements of the enemy, which position he did not leave until ordered down, although the balls flew thick around him, and three s'ruck within a few inches of his head.

Robert B. Wood, Cockswain, United States steamer Minnesota, but temporarily on board the United States steamer Mount Washington, Nansemond River, April fourteenth, 1863, behaved with a courage and coolness that could not be surpassed; did not leave his post, although he had received a severe contusion on the head from a partially spent ball, and ventured in an open boat to carry a hawser under a heavy fire.

Robert Jourdan, Cockswain, United States steamer Minnesota, but temporarily on board the United States steamer Mount Washington, Nansemond River, April fourteenth, 1863. Performed every duty with the utmost coolness and courage, and showed an unsurpassed devotion to the service.

Thomas W. Hamilton, Quartermaster, United States steamer Cincinnati, in an attack on the Vicksburgh batteries, May twenty-seventh, 1863, was severely wounded while at the wheel, but afterward returned to "lend a hand," and had to be sent below.

Frank Bois, Quartermaster, United States steamer Cincinnati, in an attack on the Vicksburgh batteries, May twenty-seventh, 1863. Coolness in making signals, and in nailing the flag to the stump of the forestaff under a heavy fire.

Thomas Jenkins, seaman; Martin McHugh, seaman; Thomas E. Corcoran, landsman; Henry Dow, Boatswain's Mate, United States steamer Cincinnati, in an attack on the Vicksburgh batteries, May twenty-seventh, 1863. All conspicuous for coolness and bravery under a severely accurate fire. "These were no ordinary cases of performance of duty."

John Woon, Boatswain's Mate, United States steamer Pittsburgh, in an engagement with the batteries at Grand Gulf, April twenty-ninth, 1863, had been confined to his hammock several days from sickness, yet insisted on and took command of the gun of which he was captain, fought it for over two hours, and only left it when no longer able to stand. Conduct uniformly good.

Christopher Brennen, seaman, United States steamer Mississippi, (but belonging to the Colorado,) in the capture of Forts St. Philip and Jackson, and New-Orleans, April twenty-fourth and twenty-fifth, 1862, by his courageous example to those around him, attracted the particular attention of his commanding officer; was the life and soul of the gun's crew.

Edward Ringold, Cockswain, United States steamer Wabash, in the engagement at Pocataligo, October twenty-second, 1862, solicited permission to accompany the howitzer corps, and performed his duty with such gallantry and presence of mind as to attract the attention of all around him. Knowing there was a scarcity of ammunition, he came up through the whole line of fire with his "shirt slung over his shoulders and filled with fixed ammunition, which he had brought two miles from the rear."

A "Medal of Honor" is accordingly awarded to each of the persons above named, which will be transmitted upon application being made through their commanding officers respectively.

GIDEON WELLES,
Secretary of the Navy.

Doc. 30.

FIGHT AT CABIN CREEK, I. T.

A NATIONAL ACCOUNT.

LEAVENWORTH, KANSAS, Monday, July 20, 1863.

THE news from the district of the frontier is quite cheering. We hope soon to have intelligence of that triumph which has always followed in the path of General Blunt. A small Federal force has gained quite a triumph over a rebel command of equal numbers, posted in a very advantageous position.

Let me give the particulars as I glean them from letters and persons who were eye-witnesses to the conflict, and such knowledge of the ground as I possess.

A subsistence train with paymasters and sutlers, numbering over three hundred wagons in all, left Fort Scott for Colonel Phillips's command, at Fort Blunt, on or about the twenty-fifth ultimo. The escort consisted of three companies of the Third Wisconsin cavalry, one company Sixth Kansas cavalry, company I, Ninth Kansas cavalry, Captain Stewart, (escort to the paymasters,) and six companies of the Second Colorado volunteer infantry, a part of which was temporarily mounted on horses and mules, being taken to Fort Blunt for the purpose of replacing the stock captured several weeks since in the rebel attack upon Phillips's position. The Colorado volunteers were under Lieutenant-Colonel Dodd, and train escort under Captain Moore, Third Wisconsin. This force, with the centre section of the Second Kansas battery, Captain Smith, and a twelve-pound mountain howitzer attached to the cavalry, numbering about eight hundred men, composed the escort. At Neosho, Mo., they were met by Major Forman, Third regiment Indiana brigade, with five hundred Indians, sent by Colonel Phillips to escort the train. At Baxter's Spring, the First regiment Kansas colored volunteers, with two guns, served by detailed negro soldiers, under Captain A. J. Armstrong, company D, joined the train. The regiment numbers eight hundred men, under Colonel J. M. Williams. By the way, the guns attached to the regiment and now served by the negroes, were formerly used by the rebels against us, being a couple of those captured by Grant at Fort Donelson. This addition made our force about one thousand six hundred strong, with four twelve-pounders, two of them rifled, and two howitzers, Major Forman's command having brought one.

On the thirtieth of June the train reached a point seven miles from Cabin Creek, a branch of the Grand, on Neosho River. The advance, composed of the Indians, came suddenly upon a scouting-party of thirty Texans. A fight ensued. The rebels stood their ground, not seeing any force but Indians. After the loss of three killed, four wounded, and three captured, they concluded to leave, which they did before our reënforcements arrived.

From the prisoners we learned that Colonel Stand Waitie, the Cherokee rebel leader, with one thousand two hundred men, about half of whom were Texans and the remainder Indians, was posted on the south bank of Cabin Creek, in a most advantageous position. From this information and other we learned that the movement had been planned for the purpose of cutting off this train. Stand Waitie crossed the Arkansas River, above the mouths of the Grand and Verdigris Rivers, and took position at the Creek. General Cabell was to and did leave Arkansas with two thousand men and six guns, and moving across the Territory, until he got in the rear of our train, which Stand Waitie was to hold at the crossing of Cabin Creek. The plan was well laid, but sufficient margin was not made for contingencies. Cabell got to the Grand River on the night of the thirtieth ultimo, but was not able to cross on account of the high water.

After the picket fight the train encamped for the night. Colonel Williams sent scouting-parties forward to the creek. They found the rebel pickets strongly posted in the timber on the north of the creek. The main body were very advantageously posted behind high banks on the south side. The timber is about a mile across, the larger portion being on the north.

On the morning of the first of July, the train advanced to the edge of the timber and corraled. The cavalry was pressed forward, and a portion of the First colored regiment deployed as skirmishers. The north side of the river was found clear, but when the troops reached the stream the fire became so warm as to cause the cavalry to fall back hastily. The skirmishers, taking positions behind trees, etc., continued the fight. The negroes made their mark, and whenever a head showed they blazed away. Their fire had effect, according to the report of the prisoners taken on the next day. The stream was deep and swift, and the crossing under the heavy rebel fire impracticable. The artillery was placed in position, a section on each flank and the howitzers in the centre. The south bank was then shelled, the fire being rapid and heavy. Under this shelling and the effective fire of the colored skirmishers, Colonel Williams directed the advance of the Third Wisconsin cavalry, for the purpose of attempting the crossing of the stream.

A little incident occurred at this stage, showing the pluck and *elan* of the negro soldiers. The officer in command of the troopers was a Pro-Slavery Democrat, and thought it would be more appropriate to send "the —— niggers or Injuns" to do the work. But in obedience to orders he started out to the bank of the creek, and hastily retreated under the sharp fire of the enemy. On reporting to Colonel Williams, that officer, who is well known as brave even to rashness, declared that "*he* would find men to make the attempt." Five companies of the colored regiment moved on the double-quick to the creek, and under the fire of the opposing forces dashed into the stream with their Colonel at the head. But they could not cross; the stream was too deep. The men followed their leader till they commenced to swim, when Colonel Williams reluctantly ordered them to fall back. All the time, while the bullets spattered on the water like hail, the negroes preserved the most perfect order, and re-formed on the bank of the creek.

The remainder of the day was consumed in skirmishing, with occasional shelling of the rebel position. On the morning of the second, the stream having fallen considerably in the night, it was determined to attempt the crossing. Major Fòrman assumed command of the party, which consisted of the Indians, five companies of the colored regiment, the mounted men of the Colorado Second, and Captain Stewart's company, Ninth Kansas. They moved down to the creek, and, under cover of the shells and musketry, prepared to cross. Major Forman, followed by Captain Gritz, of the Third Indian, advanced into the stream, with the view of ascertaining its depth. In the attempt, he was severely wounded in the back and neck.

Colonel Williams took command of the column, and, at the head of the troops, dashed into the stream. The water was above the waist of the infantry, yet the men, holding their guns and cartridge-boxes above their heads, followed their gallant leader, who, with waving sword and ringing shouts, was cheering on his men. They got across with little loss, and charged on the rebel position. They fled from the centre precipitously when the negroes and Colorado boys charged, leaving arms and accoutrements scattered as they went. To Captain Stewart was intrusted the attack on the right of the enemy's position, where their fire was the best sustained. As our cavalry advanced, the enemy fell back from the timber to the edge of the prairie, when they fired as our men advanced. The Texans numbered four hundred, and their firing was deadly and rapid. Captain Stewart, ordering his men to draw revolvers and reserve their fire, rode rapidly upon the foe. His whole force was less than one hundred. When within thirty or forty yards, the order to fire was given, and volley after volley came crashing from their heavy dragoon Colts. On they rode, and the Texans fled in disorder, leaving eighteen dead, and three prisoners. The wounded got off. Captain Stewart had fifteen men wounded and two killed in that dashing charge. Five of the negroes were severely wounded, and this, with Major Forman's wound, completed our casualties. Forty of the enemy were buried on the field, and nine prisoners taken. These stated that three wagons were loaded with those wounded by our shells, and removed the night before. About half the force had fallen back, and the Texans, numbering seven hundred, were left to contest our advance.

The enemy's position was found to be formidable, and well chosen for its purpose. The ground was uneven and thickly wooded, affording shelter for the men. All the approaches to the road and ford were covered by rude rifle-pits, made by felling trees or piling up the loose stones and brush. These were all along the bank, and along the road. The trees had been thinned so as to make rifle-lanes, if I may use the term, bearing upon the way in which our troops must approach. One of these lanes was continued through the thick underbrush for several hundred yards, and at short intervals were rude abatis and pits. Had it not been for our shells, the advance would have been very fatal.

The defeat of the rebels was disheartening and disastrous. Stand Waitie fled, and with only two companions crossed the Arkansas and returned to the rebel camp near Fort Gibson. So we were informed by their pickets on the sixth. Our trains moved on after burying the dead, and reached Fort Gibson on the morning of the fifth. Their advent was hailed with delight by the garrison and its commander. Supplies were short and the fresh troops much needed. Every body was in good spirits. General Blunt arrived on the twelfth, having been met at Cabin Creek on the tenth by the returning train. He will soon dispose of the rebel force in that vicinity at an early day, make a sweep on Fort Smith, and ere he return to Fort Scott, wake up the Red River valley.

Doc. 31.

BRIG.-GENERAL CONNER'S REPORT

OF OPERATIONS IN THE DISTRICT OF UTAH.

HEADQUARTERS OF THE DISTRICT OF UTAH, }
CAMP DOUGLAS, U. T., June 2, 1863. }

COLONEL: I have the honor to report to the General commanding the department that, on the fifth of May ultimo, company H, Third infantry, California volunteers, Captain Black, left this post, pursuant to my orders, *en route, via* Box Elder, Bear River, Cache and Marsh Valleys, for a point at or near the Great Bend or Bear River, known as Soda Springs, Idaho Territory, for the purpose of establishing a new post in that region for the protection of the overland emigration to Oregon, California, and the Bannock City mines.

Accompanying this expedition, and under its protection, were a large number of persons, heretofore residents of this territory, seceders (under the name of Morrisites) from the Mormon Church.

Many, if not all of them, having been reduced by the long-continued persecutions of the Mormons to the most abject poverty, have for some time past claimed and received the protection of the forces under my command.

Prudential reasons, applying as well to this command as to the Morrisites themselves, rendered it advisable that they should be removed from the vicinity of this camp, and beyond the evil influences and powers of the Mormon hierarchy.

Regarding the expedition to Soda Springs, Idaho Territory, as presenting a favorable opportunity for this purpose, I ordered transportation to be provided for the most indigent, and the distribution of provisions, both *en route* and after arrival at the new post, until such time as, by industry and well-directed effort, these impoverished and persecuted people should be able to support themselves.

Some of them were able to furnish their own teams and wagons; most of them gathered up their household goods and provided themselves with a scanty supply of provisions for their sustenance. They numbered in all one hundred and sixty souls, composed of fifty three families, seven single men, and four widows. On the next day, May sixth, I followed with company H, Second cavalry, California volunteers, Lieut. Clark commanding, and overtook the main train and infantry twenty-five miles north of this city.

Proceeding thence by easy marches of from ten to eighteen miles per day, along the eastern shore of Great Salt Lake, the entire command arrived at Brigham City, (or Boxelder,) sixty miles north, May eighth. Here leaving the infantry and train to proceed by the old beaten road through Cache and Marsh Valleys, and across the mountains, *via* "Sublett's Cut-off," I took the cavalry to a less frequented road, crossing Bear River at the lowest ferry, thence up the plateau lying between the Malade and Bear Rivers, over the mountains dividing the waters of the Great Basin from those of Snake and Columbia Rivers; thence down the westerly side of the north valley. crossing Fort Noeuff River north of Sublett's Cut-off, and down the east and right bank of that river to Snake River ferry, a distance of two hundred miles from this post, arriving at this point May thirteenth. Our general course to the ferry was a little east of due north, passing through a series of valleys well watered and with light timber along the streams and on the mountain-sides.

The luxuriant vegetation at this early season of the year, furnishing good grass for the animals, as well as the evidences of last year's growth, bespoke the fertility of the soil, and its adaptation to agriculture.

This remark more especially applies to Marsh Valley, lying due north of and adjoining Cache Valley; the latter being already thickly settled by Mormons, whose most northerly settlements extend within fifteen or twenty miles of the first-mentioned valley, the Bear River and a low ridge dividing the two valleys.

After leaving Brigham City the command performed two night-marches, the first of twelve and the second of thirty-five miles, as I had reason to believe that wandering bands of hostile savages, remnants of the Shoshones engaged or connected with those who took part in the battle of Bear River, (January twenty-ninth last,) were in the neighborhood, and might be surprised and punished for repeated and recent outrages on emigrants and settlers.

In this expectation, however, I was disappointed, few if any traces of Indians being found, and thenceforward the command proceeded by daily marches. In Fort Nocuff Valley we came across two lodges of Indians, (Shoshones,) who came unhesitatingly into camp with their squaws, satisfactorily answered all questions propounded, and gave evidence of friendly disposition toward the whites.

Giving them to understand the determination of the Government to punish summarily all bad Indians, and receiving assurances of future good conduct on their part, I passed on without molesting these Indians. At Snake River ferry were several large trains of emigrants bound north to the mines, and here recruiting their animals. Here also was an encampment of several lodges of Shoshones (or Snake) Indians, numbering in all, including those who came in the next day, two hundred and fifty or three hundred. They were well mounted, and had grazing in the vicinity a considerable quantity of stock. These Indians were reliably represented to me as friendly and peaceable, and have been living at the ferry during the past winter.

Being accompanied by Judge Doty, Superintendent of Indian Affairs for Utah, a conference was held with the Indians on the night of our arrival, attended by the chiefs, old and young men, and squaws. Through an interpreter many questions were asked as to the locality of hostile chiefs and their bands, and the power of Government duly impressed upon them. They were informed that the troops had been sent to this region to protect good Indians and whites, and equally to punish bad Indians and bad white men. That it was my determination to visit the most summary punishment, even to extermination, on Indians who committed depredations upon the lives and property of emigrants or settlers.

They were also assured that if bad whites trespassed upon their rights, the report of the facts to me or my officers would be followed by punishment on the malefactors, and a prompt remedy of all grievances to the extent of my power.

After the customary smoking with the chiefs, and a grand dance by men and squaws, I ordered the distribution among them of a small quantity of bacon, flour, and sugar. The conference was satisfactory, and the exhibition of the force at my command in that far-off region, as well as our safe march through a country rarely travelled by whites, had a good effect. I learned from them that Pocotello, the great chief of the hostile Shoshones, had gone a large distance off on the Lower Snake, probably in the vicinity of the Humboldt, and that Sagnitch, one of the leaders, who escaped wounded from the battle of Bear River, was somewhere in the south, near the Mormon settlements of Cache Valley, and San Pitch was still further east.

The region immediately about the Snake River, at this ferry (which is about ten miles east of old Fort Hall) is a dry, barren, sand plain, the road to the ferry being exceedingly heavy and difficult to travel. Grass, of tolerable quality and quantity, is to be found several miles to the eastward, on the Blackfoot Creek, which here empties into the Snake, after running, perhaps, thirty miles parallel with and not far from the river. The Snake here is a rapid stream, two hundred and fifty yards in width, and at this season is twenty feet in depth, and is seldom or never fordable at this point.

Beyond and to the northward the plain of sage and greasewood extends some fifty miles to a high range of mountains, three high buttes in the midst of the plain, forming a prominent landmark.

The distance from Soda Springs to this ferry *via* Fort Bridger and Fort Hall emigrant road, is upward of seventy miles, pursuing a north-westerly course. Emigrants from the East *via* this road for the new mines, leaving the ferry, travel up the Snake River in nearly an easterly direction about seventy miles to a point nearly due north of Soda Springs along two sides of a triangle, either of which is seventy miles along, and a distance of one hundred and forty miles.

The infantry, with the settlers, not having yet arrived, detachments under Lieutenants Bradley and Ustick were despatched north and south to explore the country, and find a route for a direct and practicable wagon-road to the settlement in Cache Valley, and to report on the character of the country explored.

On the twentieth, company II, Third infantry, arrived, after a long and tedious trip, accompanied by their charge, the settlers for the new town. A suitable spot was selected on the north bank of the Bear River, near the Great Bend, and four miles east of where the Soda Springs Valley opens into old Crater Valley, and striking Snake River seventy miles above and east of the present ferry.

At this point a ferry has been established, and in a short time a good boat will be in running order. With the main body of the cavalry, train, etc., I left the Blackfoot about fifteen miles east of the ferry, and pursuing a south-easterly course across the divide, on a good natural road, arrived at Soda Springs on the seventeenth of May, passing through large and fertile valleys, lying along Ross's fork of Snake River and the North branch of the Fort Noeuff.

With the design of finding a practicable route for a wagon-road through some pass in the mountains, whereby a more direct course could be made, I sent Lieutenant Clark with a detachment of twenty-five men, with five days' rations, and orders to cross the Blackfoot near its source at the base of the Foot Hills, and proceeding up the Snake River for sixty or seventy-five miles, turn to the south, seek out such pass, and join the command at Soda Springs.

His expedition was eminently successful, finding a good pass for a road along the base of the triangle before mentioned; the latter is some fifty miles in length and twenty in breadth.

The site was surveyed immediately east of the Springs, as was, also, one square mile for a military reservation, adjoining on the east the town site, in latitude about forty-two and a half degrees north, and longitude one degree eleven and a half minutes west. The water is good and abundant, as well from the river as from numerous mountain streams, easily directed for purposes of irrigation.

Back of the town, and north, wood for fuel is abundant, while on the opposite side of the river timber of large growth, suitable for building purposes, is found at a distance of less than two miles.

The soil, judging from the growth of the native grasses, and the appearance of the ground, is susceptible of cultivation and the raising of valuable crops.

The shortness of the season and the altitude of the place alone renders this at all doubtful. The settlers were allotted building lots of fair size, and proceeded immediately to the erection of shelters for themselves and families.

After remaining at this point for six days, and establishing the infantry at the new post, and looking to the present and immediate future wants of the settlers, on the thirtieth of May I returned to this post *via* the Mormon settlements in Cache Valley.

The explorations above referred to satisfied me of the fertility of the country surrounding Soda Springs, and of the entire practicability of making, at a small expense of labor, a good wagon-road from the northern settlements of Cache Valley, crossing Bear River at or near the battle-ground, through a gap in the mountains, and thence northerly along the western bank of Bear River to Soda Springs.

The road will be much more direct than the old road traversed by the infantry company, and the distance can be reduced from two hundred miles, as at present, to about one hundred and fifty or one hundred and sixty miles. This road connecting with the new road explored by Lieutenant Clark, north from Soda Springs to Bannock City, will render the distance from the latter place to this point not more than three hundred and fifty miles.

The new road north from Soda Springs to Snake River will shorten the route of emigrants from the East *via* Fort Bridger, not less than seventy miles, as well as present a route well watered and furnishing good feed for animals, with an abundance of game.

The expedition has travelled in a direct line about five hundred miles, and has carefully explored a region of country over one thousand miles in extent, heretofore little known, and concerning which only the most vague and crude ideas were held.

Before leaving Soda Springs I sent a detachment of twenty men over the mountains to pass through Bear Lake Valley, in hopes of finding the band of Sagnitch supposed to be roaming in that direction.

The detachment was unsuccessful in its object, and it joined the command a few days after at Franklin, the most northern settlement in Cache Valley, having thoroughly searched the region through which it passed. In this connection, I

may add that, having occasion to send an empty train to Carson for quartermaster's stores, I furnished to one hundred and fifty Morrisites transportation to that point, and they have already arrived safe at their destination.

Very respectfully, your obedient servant,
P. EDW. CONNER,
Brigadier-General U. S. Vols., Commanding District.
Lieutenant-Colonel R. C. DRUM,
Assistant Adjutant-General U. S. A., Department of Pacific, San Francisco, Cal.

Doc. 32.

THE UNION CAVALRY SERVICE.

DETAILS OF THE OPERATIONS DURING THE CAMPAIGN AGAINST LEE, JUNE AND JULY, 1863.

FALLING WATERS, MARYLAND, }
Wednesday, July 15, 1863. }

IN addition to the battles of Beverly Ford, Aldie, Middleburgh and Upperville, now matters of history, I have to record fifteen more engagements of our cavalry with the enemy, in thirteen of which cavalry was exclusively used, with flying artillery—all within sixteen days. I have already furnished you with brief accounts of these battles as they have transpired—such as could be hastily prepared when prostrated by fatigue produced by physical exertion and the loss of sleep, and laboring under the depressing effect of a relapse from the wildest excitement and while seated on the wet grass or under a dripping tree—valuable time, in which companions sought repose. But how describe fifteen battles in sixteen days? To do the subject justice would require the pen of a Victor Hugo and as much time as was consumed in the preparation of *Les Miserables*. Surrounded as I am at this moment by all the paraphernalia of actual war, deadly contest still raging within hearing, ay, within full sight of my temporary abode, fully expecting the enemy to force me upon the road at any moment, should our arms meet with but a temporary and even the slightest reverse—it is impossible to describe with that minuteness of detail desirable, the scenes of strife that have passed under my own observation in the brief space of time mentioned. The whole scene, as reviewed at this time, seems more like a dream than a reality. Fighting by day, and marching and sometimes fighting at night, in thunder-storms, crossing mountains, and fording swollen rivers—with a wily, relentless foe both in front and flank, made desperate by his situation—a river in his rear, with only one pontoon and almost without a train, and a large victorious army in front pressing him into his lair.

In attempting to write this *résumé*, I am prompted quite as much to the task by a desire to do justice to the noble dead who sleep in a soldier's grave, to those now suffering from wounds received, to the survivors who have passed through these terrible ordeals unscathed, and last to the cavalry arm of the service, as I am with any hope of presenting any thing particularly new. Shame! shame! that while our volunteers are freely laying their lives upon the altar of their country—fighting battles and suffering all the trials and exposure incident to active military life—that now, when death and disease has thinned their ranks, and the necessities of the country require more men, there can be found those at home who have the effrontery to resist the means adopted to secure so desirable an end. Could the men engaged in the recent disturbance in New-York have heard the indignation expressed by our soldiers when they first read of the riot in New-York, from newspapers scattered along the column to-day, and the wish that they could be led against that mob, they would never dare look a soldier in the face again.

On the twenty-fifth of June, after the battles of Aldie, Middleburgh, and Upperville, the cavalry moved forward to Leesburgh, thence across the Potomac at Edwards's Ferry to Poolesville, passing through Seneca Mills, Middlebrook, Doub's Station, Jefferson, to Frederick City. At this point the force was divided, and went in different directions. As General Kilpatrick was placed in command of the largest division, and being a man of fertile genius, whose heart is in the cause in which he is engaged—and withal one of the most dashing cavalry officers in the United States or any other service, the writer concluded that his duty to the paper he represented required him to proceed with a command which promised so much. For once his judgment was not at fault. The experience of the last ten days has proved quite conclusively that the Third division of the cavalry is the place for representatives of newspapers in search of either news, fatigue, or fighting.

Leaving Frederick on Sunday, the twenty-eighth, Walkerville, Mount Pleasant, Liberty, Johnsville, Middleburgh, Taneytown, and Littletown were passed through, without any important event to record; and, on the thirtieth, (Tuesday,) Hanover was reached. As the troops crossed the line into Pennsylvania, their spirits seemed to be revived by the fertile fields and homelike scenes around them. Cheerfully they moved on—many of them, alas! too soon, to their last resting-place.

THE BATTLE AT HANOVER.

At about midday, General Kilpatrick, with his command, was passing through Hanover, in York County, Pennsylvania—a town containing three thousand inhabitants—and when the rear of General Farnsworth's brigade had arrived at the easterly end of the place, General Custer's brigade having advanced to Abbottsville, General Stuart made a simultaneous attack upon his rear and right flank. The attack was entirely a surprise, as no enemy had been reported in the vicinity; and under any ordinary general, or less brave troops, so sudden and impetuous was the first charge, the whole command would have been thrown into the wildest confusion, and, as a necessary consequence, suffered a severe loss and a disastrous defeat. The force was in the hands of a master. Speedily making his dispo-

sitions, the General hurled upon the insolent and advancing enemy the Fifth New-York cavalry—a regiment never known to falter in an emergency. General Stuart in person led the charging column, and the Fifth was led by General Farnsworth and Major Hammond. For some time the contest hung in the balance, but General Custer's brigade returning after a severe struggle, which lasted nearly four hours, the enemy was forced to retire. They lost in this engagement a stand of colors, fifty men—ten of whom were killed—and included among the latter was Captain James Dickenson, of Baltimore, attached to the Tenth Virginia cavalry. Lieutenant-Colonel Payne, of the same regiment was taken prisoner, together with forty others—officers of the line, non-commissioned officers and privates. It was in this fight that the Adjutant of the Fifth New-York, Lieutenant Gaul, lost his life while gallantly leading his men.

As the cavalry by the battles at Aldie and Upperville, prevented the rebel Stuart from marching his column through Maryland and Pennsylvania by the way of Edwards's Ferry and Boonsboro, so did the whipping of him at Hanover prevent further marauding excursions toward the centre of the State.

Stuart and Early, the marauding chiefs of the rebel army, when they heard that Kilpatrick was on their track, abandoned the disgraceful work they were engaged in, and began to look about them for a safe exit from the State.

These legalized Dick Turpins had demanded tribute in almost every town visited by them, and threatened to destroy the towns unless their demands were promptly met. In some towns the citizens nobly refused to comply, but prepared rather to sacrifice their property than to yield to the invader. In many places, I regret to say, the reverse of all this was acted upon. At York, a town of twelve thousand inhabitants, the chief burgomaster, a man named Small, rode seven miles to surrender the town, and before any demand had been made for its surrender. General Early condescended to say, that if in the course of his peregrinations York was visited, he would consider the surrender as an ameliorating circumstance. Visiting the place, he demanded a ransom of one hundred thousand dollars and a supply of provisions and clothing for his whole command. A committee of citizens was actually formed, and forty-five thousand dollars in greenbacks and the required provisions were turned over to the Early aforesaid, who magnanimously offered to spare the town then, provided the balance of the money demanded was paid upon his return, which he said would be within a few days. Fortunately, General Kilpatrick's troops frightened this pink of generals away, and the citizens of York and vicinity were saved the opportunity of further humiliating themselves.

On the Saturday previous to arriving in Hanover, one hundred and fifty of Stuart's cavalry entered that place, and did pretty much as they pleased, not one of the three thousand inhabitants daring to remonstrate or raise a finger in self-defence.

In fact, it appears they met more friends than enemies—for they found those who gave them information as to the movements of our troops, and were thereby enabled to make the sudden attack they did upon the rear of General Farnsworth's brigade the following Tuesday. Indeed, I have had in my possession a letter written by Fitz-Hugh Lee, and addressed to General Stuart on the very morning of the attack, giving a correct account of General Kilpatrick's movements, "obtained," he says, "from a citizen, and is reliable." There was no "reliable citizen" in all Pennsylvania to inform General Kilpatrick of the approach of General Stuart upon the rear of General Farnsworth's brigade; and our commanders throughout the campaign in that State, labored under almost as many disadvantages as if campaigning in an enemy's country. Indeed, not until we arrived near Gettysburgh, could any valuable information as to the enemy's movements be obtained. In conversation with the editor of a paper in Hanover, whom I accidentally met, after showing him the letter of Fitz-Hugh Lee, I made the remark that the rebels appeared to have a great many sympathizers in that vicinity. He replied: "I don't know as to that, but you see this is a very strong Democratic county, and the Democrats were opposed to the removal of McClellan!" Leading and active Union men were pointed out by the traitors, who seek to mask their treason under the garb of Democracy in this town, that they might be plundered by the marauders. One man, a jeweller, was thus pointed out, and his stock in trade, though concealed, was unearthed, and divided among the rebel soldiers. In Hanover, and at other points, particularly in York County, the enemy found warm friends ready to welcome them, and actually received some recruits for their army. Women at the Washington Hotel in York degraded themselves by waving their handkerchiefs in token of welcome to the rebel troops, and there were a number of citizens who spread tables for the officers, and invited them to their houses. At Mechanicsville, one "Democrat" was so buoyant, that he mounted a sword, and guided the rebel column to the railroad junction, where they destroyed a large amount of property. There seemed to be a perfect understanding between the enemy and men whose loyalty had been questioned before. One of this class recovered nine horses from Stuart; "*they were taken by mistake.*" The keeper of a hotel in Abbotstown, who, I regret to say, was once a leading "Wide Awake" also manifested his pleasure at receiving a visit from the rebels. Fortunately, even the Democrats of York County have seen all they wish of rebels—a column of whom can be smelled as far as a slave-ship. A majority of the women in Hanover and elsewhere are truly loyal. They cared for the wounded—even taking them from the streets while bullets were flying around promiscuously. They furnished provisions to the soldiers, and in most instances, positively refusing to receive any pay. In one instance, a citizen

voluntarily exchanged horses with a scout to enable the latter to escape.

While our troops were engaged at Hanover, another rebel force made a dash at Littlestown, with a view of capturing a train near that place. Lieutenant-Colonel Alexander and Captain Armstrong happened to be near the spot at the time, and repulsed the enemy with the Fifth and Sixth Michigan regiments.

Before visiting Pennsylvania, there is not a shade of doubt but what the rebels expected to secure a large acquisition to their force as soon as the State was invaded; seventy-five thousand, men was the number they everywhere, in Maryland and Virginia, told the citizens, as they passed along, would join them. But your Copperhead is a man of words, and when asked to fight, many of them, at least, suddenly began to love the Union. The enemy lost more men by desertion in Pennsylvania than they received in recruits.

A little boy named Smith, twelve years of age, who came out as bugler in the First Maine cavalry, was active in the fight, and had a horse killed under him at Hanover. Since that time he has been adopted as an aid by General Kilpatrick, and is always to be seen near the General, whether in a charge or elsewhere. Since Hanover he has had another horse killed under him, and one wounded.

Wednesday, July second, General Kilpatrick made a forced march to the vicinity of Heidlersburgh, to intercept Stuart, who was moving toward the main body of the rebel army. Unfortunately, the information of this movement came too late; the enemy had passed the point indicated two hours before the head of the column reached it. In the then jaded condition of the horses, it was impossible to continue the pursuit, and the command fell back several miles, and bivouacked for the night.

THE BATTLE AT HUNTERSTOWN.

Thursday, July second, General Kilpatrick moved his whole command upon Hunterstown, and driving in the enemy's pickets, attacked the left flank of the army. General Gregg's command had the day before been fighting the enemy at Gettysburgh, and held the hill west of the town until driven from it by the artillerymen attached to the Eleventh corps—a position which cost many valuable lives to retake.

The column did not reach Hunterstown until four o'clock P.M., when a squadron of the Eighteenth Pennsylvania cavalry, headed by Captain Estes, charged through and drove the enemy back upon his reserve on the Gettysburgh road. After surveying the position, General Farnsworth's brigade was ordered on a road to the right leading to Cashtown, and General Custer's brigade was placed to the left. Company A, Captain Thompson, of the Sixth Michigan, was ordered to charge upon the rebel force then in sight; at the same time two companies of the Sixth were deployed as skirmishers in a wheatfield obliquely to the road, so as to pour in a raking fire upon the enemy should the force sent forward be repulsed. The charge ordered was made, General Custer and Captain Thompson leading it. The company was repulsed, and the enemy came charging down the road at a fearful rate, yelling like fiends. But their tune was soon changed. Two shells from Elder's battery, together with a flank fire from the Michiganders in the wheat-field, soon brought them to an about face. Pennington's battery was soon in position, and a regular artillery duel commenced, and was continued until after nightfall. Our fire was very destructive to the enemy, as prisoners of rank have since admitted. Captain Thompson was severely wounded, two men were killed, and some twenty-five were wounded. The enemy's loss must have been very severe, for they left three dead lieutenants on our hands and a dozen or more of their wounded. In the charge made, a boy named Churchill, of the First Michigan, took an active part, and succeeded in killing a man who was trying to kill General Custer, whose horse had been shot in the *mêlée*.

Having repulsed the enemy, General Kilpatrick received orders to join the main command at Two Taverns, which place was reached at about four o'clock, Friday morning, July third. Three hours afterward the whole command was again in motion, and, by eleven o'clock, made a dash upon the right flank of the enemy, with a view of destroying his train, if possible, and, at all events, creating a diversion. Owing to a misunderstanding, one brigade (General Custer's) of this division went to the right, and, consequantly, the first object mentioned was not accomplished, but the second was fully. It was known that the enemy would mass his forces on Friday, for the purpose of breaking our right. The sudden and unexpected attack of General Kilpatrick on his own right caused the enemy to fear a flank movement in that direction, and changed the character of the battle from attack to simply defensive. Unexpectedly hearing heavy firing, and receiving a brisk attack on the right flank and rear, the enemy sent forward a large force of infantry to coöperate with the cavalry, then being pressed back. Having had their skirmishers driven from the woods, the enemy took a strong position behind two stone and rail fences, one a few rods in the rear of the other, and a similar fence on the flanks. General Kilpatrick was anxious to carry this position, because, if successful, the enemy's ammunition train could be reached. Every means had been used to start the enemy for a charge, but unsuccessfully. The First Vermont, Colonel Preston; First Virginia, Major Copeland; and the Eighteenth Pennsylvania cavalry, Colonel Brinton, were in position to charge. The First Vermont, First Virginia, and a squadron of the Eighteenth Pennsylvania, led by General Farnsworth, dashed forward at the word until the stone wall was reached. A few men pulled the rail fence away from the top of the wall. General Farnsworth leaped his horse over, and was followed by the First Vermont—the enemy breaking before them

and taking a position behind the second fence. The few rods between the two fences where our men crossed was a fearfully dangerous place, the little fence receiving the concentrated fire of three lines, from front and both flanks. The witnesses of the movement stood in breathless silence—their blood running cold as the chargers gained the second fence. Man after man was seen to fall—General Farnsworth among the rest. "He is killed!" gasped many a one, looking at that fatal spot; but no—that tall form and slouched hat are his—he lives—and all breathe again. His horse had been killed; a soldier gives him his horse; the General again mounts and dashes on. The enemy here make a more formidable stand, but are driven away, and the whole force go dashing, reeling over the fence in a whirlpool of shot and shell, such as is seldom ever witnessed by soldiers. The constant roar of musketry and artillery on the main field gave to the scene a peculiar grandeur. It was fearfully grand. The second fence crossed, and new fires were opened upon this brave band. To retreat at that point was certain death, and the only chance of safety was to advance, and advance they did for between one and two miles, to the rear of the rebel army, in sight of the coveted train—but at what a cost! Dispersing, the men returned under a galling fire as best they could. A few did not get back to their command for hours—many never came. The list of missing gradually lessened, and hope led us to look anxiously for the return of General Farnsworth; and when, with the morning's dawn, no tidings from him were heard, then hope said he was wounded—a prisoner—he has been left seriously, perhaps dangerously, wounded at some house by the roadside. Vain hope! Messengers were sent in every direction to search for the missing spirit. It did not seem possible that he could be dead; and yet, so it was. He fell just after crossing the second fence, his bowels pierced by five bullets. There some of the Vermont boys, left behind at the hospital, found his body two days after the fight, and saw it decently interred. The brave, noble, and generous Farnsworth has gone to his last rest, and the sod that covers his grave has been wet by the tears of those who loved and honored him while living. His name will ever be held in remembrance by every member of the Third division.

Of the three squadrons of the Vermont regiment in the advance in this charge, there were fifteen killed, fifteen wounded, and twenty or more are missing. The regiment lost seventy-five men during the fight.

This was the last charge of the day at this point. It caused the enemy to concentrate a still larger force upon his right flank until their whole line fell back. Night soon came on, and with it a drenching shower, in which the cavalry, exhausted with the labors of the day, retired two miles and sought such repose as could be obtained in an open field.

The day had been exceedingly hot and many men were prostrated by the heat. The Fifth New-York supported a battery which was exposed to a very hot fire. A shell passed through the body of Daniel Hurley, company C, killed a horse, and wounded John Buckley, of the same company.

Saturday morning, July fourth, it became known that the enemy was in full retreat, and General Kilpatrick moved on to destroy his train and harass his column. A heavy rain fell all day, and the travelling was any thing but agreeable. We arrived at Emmetsburgh—one of the strongest secesh villages to be found—about mid-day, during a severe storm. After a short halt the column moved forward again, and at Fountaindale, just at dark, we commenced ascending the mountain. Imagine a long column of cavalry winding its way up the mountain, on a road dug out of the mountain side, which sloped at an angle of thirty degrees—just wide enough for four horses to march abreast—on one side a deep abyss and on the other an impassable barrier, in the shape of a sleep embankment; the hour ten o'clock at night, a drizzling rain falling, the sky overcast, and so dark as literally not to be able to see one's own hand if placed within a foot of the organs of vision; the whole command, both men and animals, worn out with fatigue and loss of sleep; then imagine that, just as the head of this tired, hungry and sleepy column nears the crest of the mountain, a piece of cannon belches forth fire and smoke and destructive missiles directly in front. Imagine all this, and a little more, and the reader can then form some idea of what occurred to General Kilpatrick's command, on Saturday night, July fourth, as it ascended the mountain to the Monterey Gap, and so across to Waterloo on the western slope. The column commenced to ascend the mountain at about dark, and arrived near the Monterey House, at the top, between nine and ten o'clock. The enemy had planted a piece of artillery near this spot, so as to command the road, and also had sharp-shooters on the flanks. It was intended to make a strong defence here, as one half-mile beyond the enemy's train was crossing the mountain on the Gettysburgh and Hagerstown pike. The Fifth Michigan cavalry was in advance, and although on the look-out for just such an occurrence, it startled the whole column; a volley of musketry was fired by a concealed force at the same time at the head of the column; the first squadron of the Fifth broke, fell back upon the second and broke that—but there was no such thing as running back a great ways on that road; it was jammed with men and horses. The broken squadron immediately rallied, and skirmishers were posted on the most available points, and the First Virginia, Major Copeland, was ordered to the front, and upon arriving there was ordered to charge; and charge they did at a rapid gait down the mountain side into the inky darkness before them, accompanied by a detachment of the First Ohio, Captain Jones. As anticipated, the train was struck, just in rear of the centre, at the crossing one half-mile west of the Monterey House. A volley is fired as the train is reached. "Do you surrender?" "Yes," is the

response, and on the First Virginia dash to Ring-gold, ordering the cowed and frightened train-guard to surrender, as they swept along for eight miles, where the head of the train was reached. Here the two hundred men who started on the charge had been reduced to twenty-five, and seizing upon a good position the rebels made a stand. As the force in front could not be seen, Major Copeland decided not to proceed further, but to await daylight and reënforcements. Both came and the enemy fled. Arriving at Gettysburgh pike, the Eighteenth Pennsylvania was placed there as a guard; for protection a barricade was hastily thrown up. No sooner was this done than cavalry was heard charging down the road. "Who comes there, etc. ?" calls out the officer in charge at the barricade. "Tenth Virginia cavalry!" was the reply. "To —— with you, Tenth Virginia cavalry," and the squadron fired a volley into the darkness. That was the last heard of the Tenth Virginia cavalry that night, until numbers of the regiment came straggling in and gave themselves up as prisoners of war. Other cavalry moved up and down the road upon which the train was standing, and some most amusing scenes occurred. The train belonged to Ewell's division, and had in it also a large number of private carriages and teams, containing officers' baggage. Four regiments were doing guard-duty, but as they judged of the future by the past, they supposed our army would rest two or three months after winning a battle, and magnanimously permit the defeated enemy to get away his stores and ordnance, and have a little time also to recruit, and therefore the attack was a complete surprise. A thunderstorm was prevailing at the time, and the attack was so entirely unexpected that there was a general panic among both guard and teamsters. I am not surprised at this, for the howling of the storm, the rushing of water down the mountain-side, and the roaring of the wind, altogether were certainly enough in that wild spot to test the nerves of the strongest. But when is added to this a volley of pistol and carbine shots occasionally, a slap on the back with the flat of a sword, and a hoarse voice giving the unfortunate wight the choice of surrendering or being shot, then added to this the fearful yells and imprecations of the men wild with excitement, all made up a scene certainly never excelled before in the regions of fancy. Two rebel captains, two hours after the train had been captured, came up to one of the reserve commands and wanted to know what regiment that was—supposing it belonged to their own column. They discovered their mistake when Lieutenant Whittaker, of General Kilpatrick's staff, presented a pistol and advised them to surrender their arms. Several other officers who might have easily escaped came in voluntarily and gave themselves up. Under so good subjection were the enemy that there was no necessity of making any change in teamsters or drivers—they voluntarily continuing right on in Uncle Sam's service as they had been in the confederate service, until it was convenient to relieve them. At first the prisoners were coralled near the Monterey House. When the number had got to be large they were driven down the mountain toward Waterloo. A gang started off in this direction at about midnight—it was not prudent to wait until morning, for daylight might bring with it a retreating column of the enemy, and then all the prisoners would have been recaptured; finally, when near the Gettysburgh road crossing, a band of straggling rebels happened to fire into the head of the party from a spur of the mountain overlooking the road. Here was another panic, which alike affected guards and prisoners. The rain was falling in torrents, and the whole party, neither one knowing who this or the other was, rushed under the friendly shelter of a clump of trees. All of these prisoners might have, at that time, escaped. Hundreds did escape before daylight dawned.

It is impossible to tell the number of vehicles of all descriptions captured; the road was crowded with them for at least ten miles; there were ambulances filled with wounded officers and privates from the battle-field of Gettysburgh; ambulances containing Ewell's, Early's, and other officers' baggage; ambulances filled with delicacies stolen from stores in Pennsylvania; four and six mule and horse teams; some filled with barrels of molasses, others with flour, hams, meal, clothing, ladies' and childrens' shoes and underclothing—mainly obtained from the frightened inhabitants of York County and vicinity; wagons stolen from Uncle Sam with the "U. S." still upon them; wagons stolen from Pennsylvania and loyal Maryland farmers; wagons and ambulances made for the confederate government, (a poor imitation of our own;) wagons from North-Carolina and wagons from Tennessee—a mongrel train—all stolen, or what is still worse—paid for in confederate notes, made payable six months after the recognition of the Southern Confederacy by the United States Government—or in other words—never. After daylight a lot of the wagons were parked and burnt at Ringgold; hundreds were burned in the road where captured. Our men filled their canteens with molasses and replenished their stock of clothing, sugar, salt, and bacon. Some very expensive confederate uniforms were captured; several gold watches and articles of jewelry were found. A few of the captured wagons (the best) were saved, and to the balance, with contents, the torch was applied. The road here is more like the bed of a rocky river, the dirt having been washed away by the heavy rains, left large boulders exposed; where there were no boulders, there was mud and water. Over this road the troopers dashed and splashed in the midnight darkness, yelling like demons. Is it to be wondered at that the confederate soldiers unanimously declare that they never will visit Pennsylvania again?

The Fifth New-York was pushed forward to Smithsburgh early on Sunday morning, but found only a small picket to interrupt their progress, and this ran away upon their approach. This town was held by the Fifth until the arrival of the main column, at a late hour in the day.

When the First Vermont, Lieutenant-Colonel Preston, had reached the Monterey House Saturday night, it was detached to aid in the main object of the expedition, by intercepting a portion of the rebel train which it was believed might possibly be in the advance. At the Mountain House, at about twelve o'clock midnight, Colonel Preston took the left-hand road, and moving in a south-westerly direction down the mountain, passed through Smithsburgh and Lightersburgh to Hagerstown, arriving there soon after daylight, without meeting with any team, and scarcely meeting an armed enemy. A drove of cattle and something like one hundred rebel soldiers, stragglers, were captured, and were brought into the main column Sunday night.

The head of the column, as I have said before, reached Ringgold at about daylight—the whole command, horses as well as men, tired, hungry, sleepy, wet, and covered with mud. Men and animals yielded to the demands of exhausted nature, and the column had not been at a halt many minutes before all fell asleep where they stood. Under the friendly protection of the dripping eaves of a chapel, a gay and gallant brigadier could have been seen enjoying in the mud one of those sound sleeps only obtained through fatigue, his long golden locks matted with the soil of Pennsylvania. Near him, in the mud, lay a dandyish adjutant, equally oblivious and unmindful of his toilet, upon which he generally bestows so much attention. Under a fence near at hand is reclining a well-got up major, whose stylish appearance and regular features have turned the heads of many fair damsels on Chestnut street; here a chaplain, there a trooper, a Commanding General, aids, orderlies, and servants, here for the nonce meet on a level. The faithful trooper lies by his horse, between whom there seems to exist an indescribable community of feeling. Two hours are thus passed in sleep— the provost-guard only on duty—when word is passed that "the column has all closed up," which is the signal to move on again. The indefatigable Estes shakes himself and proceeds to shake the Commanding General to let him know that the object for which the halt was made had been accomplished; that it is time to move. Five minutes more all are in the saddle again and marching for Smithsburgh. A body of armed men, mailed in mud! what a picture. Smithsburgh was reached by nine o'clock A.M. The reception met with there made all forget the trials of the night—made them forget even their fatigue. It was Sunday. The sun shone forth brightly; young misses lined the street-sides singing patriotic songs; the General was showered with flowers, and the General and troops were cheered until reechoed by the mountain sides; young ladies and matrons assailed the column with words of welcome and large plates heaped up with pyramids of white bread spread with jelly and butter, inviting all to partake. While the young sang, the old shed tears and wrung the hands of those nearest to them. The little town was overflowing with patriotism and thankfulness at the arrival of their preservers. While these things were detaining the column, the band struck up "Hail Columbia," followed by the "Star-Spangled Banner." Many eyes unused to tears were wet then. The kind reception met with here did the command more good than a week's rest. Even the horses—faithful animals—seemed to be revived by the patriotic demonstration. No one who participated in the raid of Saturday night, July fourth, 1863, can ever forget the reception met with at Smithsburgh. It was like an oasis in the desert—a green spot in the soldier's life. May God prosper the people of Smithsburgh!

THE BATTLE AT SMITHSBURGH.

Here General Kilpatrick decided to let his command rest until evening. But the enemy were on the alert, and seemed determined not to let the troops rest. At about two o'clock P.M., Assistant Adjutant-General Estes, accompanied by scout McCullough and a correspondent, started out to carry despatches to the headquarters of the army, then near Gettysburgh. It was known that the enemy's pickets and patrols were scattered about promiscuously, and a considerable degree of caution was necessary to avoid being captured. At the suggestion of the scout, a route passing a little north of Emmetsburgh was selected as being the most practicable. The trio started off in good spirits, and had gone about six miles up into the mountain when suddenly they came to within one hundred yards of seven armed rebels—the advance, as it suddenly proved to be, of a large column of cavalry and mounted infantry in pursuit of General Kilpatrick. The rebels ordered the trio to surrender, and at the same moment fired. Instead of surrendering, the party wheeled their horses and dashed off down the rocky mountain road at a breakneck speed, the rebels following them. For nearly four miles the race was continued, sometimes the pursued gaining a little and sometimes the pursuing party. The race was interrupted by meeting one of our cavalry patrols. A squadron, and then a regiment, was thrown out to keep the enemy in check, until the prisoners who had been started on this road could be sent off on another toward Boonsboro. While this was going on, another column was reported to be approaching from a north-easterly direction, on the road which the Vermont cavalry had passed over at an early hour in the morning. General Kilpatrick, having got his prisoners off in safety, was in his element, and declared his intention not to leave town until the time agreed upon—evening—notwithstanding the force confronting him was much larger than his own. The enemy had evidently intended to attack him from two points simultaneously, but upon trying at one point, and seeing what splendid disposition General Kilpatrick had made of his force they undoubtedly arrived at the conclusion that the town could be taken only by a greater sacrifice of life

than the result to be attained thereby warranted. They opened a battery on a hill commanding the town, several shells from which struck houses in town during the engagement, doing considerable damage. Elder's battery was opened to respond. The attack was kept up until nightfall, when the enemy, having failed in several attempts to charge into the town, suspended operations, and General Kilpatrick slowly retired, and reached Boonsboro the same night. In this contest the enemy displayed their usual cunning. They, it has since been ascertained, had picked up about seventy-five of our men—stragglers and men whose horses had given out. While the fight was going on at Smithsburgh, these men were exposed in an open field with the avowed intention of attracting our fire. It was the only force thus openly exposed.

In the affair at Smithsburgh, in the disposition of his troops, General Kilpatrick displayed generalship of a high order. Nearly surrounded by a much superior force, he so arranged his command that he could concentrate just so many as might be required to repel an attack at any point, and still from no one point of the field could one fourth of his command be seen. The enemy being on the mountain side, had a better view, and they did not like it.

At dusk the prisoners having got well away, General Kilpatrick moved off slowly, and at eleven o'clock that night reached Boonsboro. The enemy did not follow.

On this march a sad affair occurred. A private of the Fifth New-York, who was much intoxicated, deliberately and without cause killed Lieutenant Williamson, of Elder's battery, by shooting him with a pistol. The men in the vicinity immediately killed the offending trooper. Lieutenant W. was an excellent officer, and much respected in the command.

THE BATTLE OF HAGERSTOWN AND WILLIAMSPORT.

Early on Monday morning, July sixth, General Kilpatrick hearing that the enemy had a train near Hagerstown, moved upon that place. The enemy's pickets were met near the edge of the town. A squadron of the Eighteenth Pennsylvania cavalry, under Captain Lindsey, and led by Lieutenant-Colonel Brinley, of the Eighteenth, and accompanied by Captains Dahlgren, late of General Hooker's staff, and Chauncey, Russell, and Snyder, of General Kilpatrick's staff, and a scout, charged into the town.

The enemy's advance was commanded by Colonel Davis, of the Tenth Virginia cavalry, who was captured. The party charged up the first street into town fifty rods, to where it enters Potomac street. The scout was a little in advance. Colonel Davis, likely to escape, by the superior fleetness of the horse he rode, the scout fired and killed the horse. The main portion of the party turned to the right, up Potomac street, and charged through the town, through the square, past the market, running the gauntlet of a shower of bullets fired from streets, alleys, and houses. Of this party, Captain Snyder, of the Eighteenth, was wounded and taken prisoner. Lieutenant Campbell, of the Eighteenth, had his horse killed; the scout had the end of his nose grazed by a ball; Thomas Hogan, standard-bearer, kept up with the advance, and was killed; Isaac Anderson was killed. Thomas Adams, company B, Eighteenth; Sergeant J. B. Gordon, company A, Eighteenth; Lieutenant David McKay, and others, were wounded.

Captains Dahlgren and Lindsey turned to the left as they entered Potomac street, in pursuit of five men. The men took the first street to the right, and were closely followed. One took deliberate aim at Captain Lindsey and killed him. Captain Dahlgren immediately split the man's head open with his sabre, and so the fight was kept up for some time.

Soon after the first charge a second charge was made by a second squadron of the Eighteenth, under Captains Cunningham and Pennypacker. Of this party only one returned that day. Captain Elder then opened his battery on the outskirts of the town and began an effective fire. While the battery was not in use he went on a reconnoissance to a piece of woods at his right and captured twenty troopers, the advance of a party attempting to make a flank movement and capture his pieces. Captain Elder had his horse killed. Deployed in the gardens and fields in the outskirts of the town, were portions of the First Virginia and First Vermont cavalry. A squadron of the First Virginia, numbering fifty-six men, under Captain W. C. Carman, lost twenty-six men; one officer, Lieutenant Swintzel, was killed, and several others were wounded. To the right of the First Virginia was the First Vermont, deployed as skirmishers, and still further on the right was General Custer's brigade, the First, Fifth, Sixth, and Seventh Michigan regiments. Two companies—D, Lieutenant Cummings, and A, Lieutenant Edwards of the First Vermont, were deployed as skirmishers in the town. They advanced through a wheat-field, drove the enemy from a fence on their front, when they were recalled to form in the rear-guard. They lost fourteen men. Companies L, E, and F, under Captain Schofield and Lieutenant Newton, were deployed to the right of the town, company I, Lieutenant Caldwell, acting as a reserve force. L and E made one charge in skirmish line, and carried a house from behind which the enemy had annoyed our line seriously. These four companies lost fifteen men. The remainder of the Vermont regiment was held in reserve. It appears that the head of one of the enemy's columns, composed of infantry, cavalry, and artillery, had just entered Hagerstown as General Kilpatrick reached there. When the attack commenced, the fact was speedily discovered that there was a large force present, and it would be useless therefore to attempt to strike the train at this point, and General Kilpatrick decided to move rapidly to Williamsport. This was a difficult movement to execute, but was successfully accomplished. Leaving the First Vermont and Fifth New-York with Elder's bat-

tery to protect the rear, the balance of the command was hurried forward. This rear-guard had one of the sharpest fights of the campaign. Taking a position on the Williamsport road, they awaited the approach of the enemy. They were not kept long in suspense, for in less than half an hour the enemy advanced two columns of infantry and one of cavalry, each column numbering more men than the whole force ordered to hold them in check. Of course, it was an easy matter to flank our troops with such a command; but the rebels paid dearly for the advantage gained. The enemy had advanced through the line as our skirmishers retired. Our rear-guard held their first position full half an hour after being attacked. The enemy advanced skirmishing, and made a dart for Elder's guns. They got so near that one gunner knocked a rebel down with his rammer. Elder gave them grape and canister, and the Fifth New-York sabres, while the First Vermont used their carbines. The repulse was complete, but owing to the superior force of the enemy, our men were compelled reluctantly to fall back. At the second position taken there was another desperate contest, against odds. Here one of the bravest spirits fell—Lieutenant Woodward, son of the Chaplain of the First Vermont. At one time companies B and H, First Vermont, Captain Beeman, were entirely cut off, and they were ordered to "surrender!" "I don't see it," replied Captain Beeman. "Who are you talking to?" screamed the rebel officer. "To you," was the response, when the Captain, leaping a fence, was followed by the squadron, and nearly all escaped. Falling back again, two of the Vermont companies were preparing to charge an advancing force; they yelled so loud that a portion of the force engaged at Williamsport supposed them to be rebels, and fired a couple of shells into their ranks. This mistake caused the charge to be abandoned, and our men fell back upon the main body. The officers and men of this rear-guard behaved nobly, and many really shed tears because they could not carry out their orders to the letter. The First Vermont lost fifty men in this retreat. Lieutenant Stuart, of company G; Lieutenant Caldwell, of company I, and Sergeant Hill, of company C, were among the wounded. Stuart and Hill were left upon the field.

It was four o'clock P.M. when General Kilpatrick, with the main column, reached the crest of the hill overlooking Williamsport, on the Boonsboro pike. General Buford's command had been engaged with the enemy two or three miles to the left for two or more hours; Major Medill, of the Eighth Illinois, had already fallen mortally wounded. Two pieces of Pennington's battery were placed on the brow of the hill to the right of the pike, and the other pieces to the left. A squadron of Fifth Michiganders had previously charged down the pike, driving in the enemy's picket and a battalion which occupied an advanced position. The First Michigan, Colonel Towne, was deployed as skirmishers to the right, and ordered to drive the enemy from a brick house a little in advance and to the right of the artillery. Several unsuccessful attempts were made to obey this order; but before it could be done, the brisk firing of the rear-guard warned the Commanding General that his force occupied a dangerous position. Never was a command in a more critical situation; never before was a man cooler, or did one display more real generalship than General Kilpatrick on this occasion. Tapping his boot with his whip, and peering in the direction of the rapidly approaching rear-guard, he saw it falling back apparently in some disorder. Not a moment was to be lost; inaction or indecision would have proved fatal, and the moral effect of a successful campaign destroyed in an hour. Fortunately General Kilpatrick was cool and defiant, and felt the responsibility resting upon him. This made him master of the situation, and by a dashing movement, saved the cavalry corps from disaster. Seeing his rear-guard falling back, he bethought himself of what force could be withdrawn from the front in safety. The enemy were pressing his front and rear—the crisis had arrived; he ordered the Second New-York (Harris's Light) to charge upon the exultant foe then coming like an avalanche upon his rear. Nobly did this band of heroes perform their task. They fell into the breach with a yell, and, sword in hand, drove back the enemy, relieving the exhausted rear-guard, and holding the enemy in check until the whole command was disposed of so as to fall back, which they did in good order, fighting as they went. For three miles, over one of the worst roads ever travelled by man, was this retreat conducted, when the enemy, dispirited at their want of success in surrounding and capturing the whole command, halted, and the cavalry corps went into camp, men and officers, exhausted from the labors of the day, falling to sleep in the spot where they halted. Colonel Devins's brigade, of General Buford's command, had relieved the rear-guard, and were harassed by the enemy all night. Several times an advance was attempted, but on each occasion they were handsomely repulsed, in which work the Ninth New-York cavalry took a conspicuous part. On this day Colonel Devins's advance destroyed twenty wagons between Williamsport and Falling Waters. When Pennington's battery was being placed in the first position on the hill above Williamsport, the enemy, by concentrating their fire upon that spot, endeavored to drive the battery away. A perfect shower of shot and shell fell in and around it. There was no flinching, however. Pennington was there, General Kilpatrick was there. Had they succeeded in this attempt, our force, by the enemy advancing in overwhelming numbers, would have been scattered to the four winds.

THE BATTLES AT AND NEAR BOONSBORO, FUNKTOWN, AND ANTIETAM CREEK.

Tuesday morning, July seventh, the cavalry force moved back to Boonsboro, the enemy following closely the rear-guard, and at intervals there was brisk skirmishing between General Buford's command and the enemy. The same was true of the night. The Sixth cavalry, (regulars,) under Captain Chaflant, made a reconnoissance at night and had a brisk fight, in which they lost eight or nine men. Wednesday morning there were indications that the enemy were present in large force, and by ten o'clock the "fandango" opened in real earnest, in which both Buford's and Kilpatrick's troops participated. The enemy were forced back to the Antietam Creek. Thursday the fight was renewed, and again on Friday, when Funktown was occupied. Saturday the enemy was again forced back, and on Saturday General Kilpatrick's command again moved upon Hagerstown.

THE SECOND BATTLE AT HAGERSTOWN.

When within two miles of the town, the enemy's skirmishers were met. The main features of this battle, and those that took place between Boonsboro and Hagerstown, I have before pretty fully described, and therefore I shall now only record some incidents in connection with them, omitted in the haste of the moment in my previous reports. After fighting for an hour the town was fully occupied, and the enemy fell back to the crest of the hill, one and a half miles west of the town. The streets picketed by the enemy were barricaded, and the troops were disposed of outside of town so as to resist an attack. In clearing the outskirts of the town of skirmishers, the One Hundred and Fifty-seventh New-York infantry, of General Ames's brigade, (Eleventh corps,) rendered material assistance. Upon entering the town, the hearts of our troops were made glad by finding between thirty and forty Union soldiers who had been missing since the Monday before, a majority of whom were supposed to be dead. A few were wounded; all had been concealed by citizens, and had been treated well. Captain Snyder, reported killed, was found wounded at the Franklin Hotel, carefully attended by a bevy of lovely damsels. The ball entered at the right side of the abdomen, and was taken out on the left side. The wound, though severe, is not a mortal one. He also received a severe sabre-cut on the top of his head. Captain Snyder rode some three hundred yards after he was shot, and used his sabre freely, when he fell to the pavement near the hotel, where he was taken in and kindly cared for by the proprietor. Captain Carman, of the First Virginia cavalry, was also concealed. He was skirmishing with his company on Monday, and suddenly a whole regiment of infantry rose before his command; they had been concealed in a field of wheat. He lost five men on the first volley, when those remaining sought a place of safety. Captain Carman fell flat on the ground in a potato patch, and was passed by unnoticed. Captain Macquillet, of the same regiment, was wounded, but managed to conceal himself, was found by a rebel, who robbed him of two hundred dollars, watch, etc., and was finally taken into the house of a citizen. Captain McMasters, of General Kilpatrick's staff, had his horse killed here. A large majority of the citizens of this town are loyal, and they were much gratified when the Union troops reöccupied the place. The rebels treated the citizens the same as they had done people in Pennsylvania—that is, took every thing they could carry away. Not satisfied with taking articles for their own immediate use, the officers as well as men went so far as to steal dresses, hoop-skirts, and other articles of clothing for their wives and sweethearts.

On Monday, the thirteenth, General Kilpatrick was anxious to make an advance, but could not obtain orders. Some of the Pennsylvania militia were placed at his disposal, and he thought he would try one regiment under fire. The Philadelphia Blues was selected, and, accompanied by the First Vermont cavalry, a demonstration was made on our right—the enemy then occupying a fortified position. The militia were then deployed, and it was somewhat interesting to see how different individuals acted as they came under fire for the first time. Some laughed, others cracked jokes; many were serious, and wore a determined aspect. For new troops, however, they acted creditably. The General desired them to move to the crest of a knoll, where the bullets were flying pretty lively. There was some hesitancy at first, whereupon the battle-flag presented to the division by the ladies of Boonsboro was sent to the front. Sergeant W. Judy, bearer of the flag, cried out: "This is General Kilpatrick's battle-flag, follow it!" The militia obeyed the summons promptly. Judy was wounded, and fell some distance in front of the line, and it was supposed for some time that the enemy had captured the flag; but at night, when Judy was brought in on a litter, he proudly waved the battle-flag. The novelty of being under fire for the first time was keenly felt by the militia. About the first man touched had the top of his head grazed just close enough to draw blood. He halted, threw down his musket, truly an astonished man. One or two officers and a dozen or more privates also ran up to see what the matter was. Running both hands over his pate, and seeing blood, he exclaimed, "A ball, I believe," while the others stood agape with astonishment, until the shrill voice of the General sounded in their ears: "Move on there!" Another man's throat was so closely grazed by a ball as to raise a large bunch, but without breaking the skin. A council was held to ascertain whether he was hit by a ball or not. Despite the danger, these and similar acts caused much amusement to the men more used to exposure.

General Kilpatrick was much annoyed at the restraint he was under all day Monday and Tuesday; he desired to move on, believing that the enemy, while making a show of force, was crossing the river. This subsequently proved to be correct. Had the army advanced on Tuesday morning, Lee's whole army would either have been captured or dispersed. When, on Wednesday morning, an advance was made without orders, the fact was then ascertained that the enemy commenced falling back when the attack was

made by the First Vermont and Pennsylvania militia the day before, the enemy believing that it was the initiatory movement of a general advance. Such was the panic among the rebel troops that they abandoned wagons, ammunition, arms, tents, and even provisions. Hundreds of rebels, fearing Kilpatrick's men, fled to the right and left to avoid their terrific charges, and subsequently surrendered themselves. One strapping fellow surrendered to a little bugler, who is attached to General Custer's brigade. As he passed down the line, escorting his prisoner, a Colt's revolver in hand, he called out: "I say, boys, what do you think of this fellow?" "This fellow" looked as if he felt very mean, and expected he would be shot by his captor every moment for feeling so. All along the road to Williamsport prisoners were captured, and their rear-guard was fairly driven into the river. The Fifth Michigan charged into the town, and captured a large number of soldiers, as they were attempting to ford the river. From thirty to fifty of the rebels were drowned while attempting to cross; twenty-five or thirty wagons and a large number of mules and horses were washed away. A regiment of cavalry was drawn up on the opposite bank, but a few of Pennington's pills caused them to skedaddle. They fired a few shells in return, but no harm was done.

Hearing that a force had marched toward Falling Waters, General Kilpatrick ordered an advance to that place. Through some mistake, only one brigade—that of General Custer's—obeyed the order. When within less than a mile of Falling Waters, four brigades were found in line of battle, in a very strong position, and behind half a dozen Eleventh corps or crescent-shaped earth-walls. The Sixth Michigan cavalry was in advance. They did not wait for orders, but a squadron—companies D and C, under Captain Royce (who was killed) and Captain Armstrong—were deployed as skirmishers, while companies B and F, led by Major Weaver, (who was killed,) made the charge. The line of skirmishers was forced back several times, but the men rallied promptly, and finally drove the enemy behind the works. A charge was then made, the squadron passing between the earthworks. So sudden and spirited was the dash, and so demoralized were the enemy, that the first brigade surrendered without firing a shot. The charging squadron moved directly on, and engaged the second brigade, when the brigade that had surrendered seized their guns, and then commenced a fearful struggle. Of the one hundred who made this charge, only thirty escaped uninjured. Seven of their horses lay dead within the enemy's works. Twelve hundred prisoners were here captured, and the ground was strewn with dead and wounded rebels. Among the killed was Major-General Pettigrew, of South-Carolina. A. P. Hill was seated, smoking a pipe, when the attack commenced; it came so suddenly that he threw the pipe away, mounted his horse, and crossed the river as speedily as possible. Three battle-flags were captured, two of them covered with the names of battles in which the regiments owning them had been engaged. Prisoners were captured all along the road between Williamsport and Falling Waters, in which service the First Ohio squadron, under Captain Jones, acting as body-guard, as usual, took an active part. Sergeant Gillespie, of company A, being in advance, overtook a party of men trying to get off with a Napoleon gun; the horses baulked, and the Sergeant politely requested the men to surrender, which order they very cheerfully obeyed. Seven men and four horses were taken with the gun. The caissons were filled with ammunition, and Captain Hasbrouck, of the General's staff, at once placed it in position, and used it upon the enemy—a whole brigade being then in sight. Another Napoleon gun was abandoned, and taken in charge by the Eighteenth Pennsylvania cavalry, Lieutenant-Colonel Brinton. Captain Royce, of the Sixth Michigan, was with the skirmishing party, and was shot twice; the first time through the leg, and the second ball went through his head. Company C, of the skirmishers, lost fifteen men, ten of whom were wounded, namely: First Lieutenant Potter, wounded in head, and captured; John Demay, wounded in breast, and captured; Sergeant Reynolds, foot; Corporal Gibson, leg; William Sweet, Sidney Meagher, slightly; —— Daniels, M. McClure, Jacob Lain, Patrick McQuirk, and Corporal J. Dodge, missing; Sergeant John Pettis, Michael Gibbins, Frederick Williams, prisoners.

Just at the close of the fight General Buford's command came up and pursued the flying foe to the river, capturing four hundred and fifty prisoners. The enemy succeeded in destroying their pontoon-bridge, however, and thus effectually prevented immediate pursuit.

THE LEFT AT WILLIAMSPORT.

Leaving Frederick City on the sixth, General Buford made a short halt at Boonsboro, and then moved upon Williamsport, where he arrived on the seventh. General Merritt's brigade (regulars) opened the fight first on the right, while Colonel Gamble's brigade formed the left. The Third Indiana charged into Falling Waters, and captured seventeen wagons and several prisoners. The Eighth Illinois was deployed as skirmishers, and soon drew the fire of three regiments of infantry, strongly posted behind fences, walls, and trees. Tibball's battery was opened with effect, and joined with our skirmishers. The rebels could not stand the fire and ran. While the Eighth Illinois was charging a barn near this point, Major Medill fell, mortally wounded, while gallantly leading his men. This brigade was relieved by the one commanded by Colonel Devins.

THE RIGHT AT GETTYSBURGH.

But little has been said of the part taken by the cavalry on the right at Gettysburgh, Friday, July third. General Gregg's division, assisted by General Custer's brigade, of General Kilpatrick's division, rendered an important service

here. The enemy seemed determined to capture our batteries and turn the flank. The movement was only prevented through the stubborn bravery of the troops. The Seventh Michigan, a new regiment, charged up to a stone wall under a front and flank fire from a concealed enemy — charging in column by company, closed *en masse*. When the first company reached the wall, and was brought to a sudden stand-still, the balance of the column, being in a very exposed position, was thrown into some confusion. The regiment was recalled, when the First Michigan, Colonel Linne, made a more successful charge. A colonel of the rebel army, who was subsequently captured, told me that the artillery firing at this point (Pennington's battery) was the best he ever witnessed. At one battery, he says, six of the eight gunners at each gun were either killed or wounded in less than twenty minutes.

DEVINS'S BRIGADE AT GETTYSBURGH.

General Devins's brigade, of General Pleasanton's division, reached Gettysburgh Tuesday, June thirtieth, drove the enemy out, and were most cordially received by the people. The following morning the brigade took a position at the west of the town, when skirmishing was immediately commenced. At this point, Captain Hanley, of the Ninth New-York, with one hundred men, held the enemy's skirmishers at bay for two hours, and finally drove them. Unfortunately, soon after this, as the enemy reinforced, advanced again, one of the unfortunate mistakes occurred; a battery opened upon our own men, and by the combined attack, front and rear, the position was lost.

RECONNOISSANCES.

On Tuesday, June thirtieth, Captain Dahlgren applied at the headquarters of the army for permission to make a reconnoissance. He asked for one hundred men, but could only obtain ten. With these he hovered around the enemy's line of communication, and was at one time in sight of the enemy's ammunition-train. If the one hundred men had been furnished him he could have destroyed this train, and the enemy would have been out of ammunition at Gettysburgh. Capturing a messenger of Jeff Davis, and destroying a pontoon-bridge at Williamsport, Captain Dahlgren returned to headquarters. Then one hundred men from the Sixth New-York cavalry were furnished him, and he started out immediately again. At Greencastle and Waynesboro Captain Dahlgren had several fights with the enemy. At the latter place he arrived just in time to prevent the citizens from paying tribute to Stuart's men, under Jenkins. He captured four hundred men and two pieces of artillery, when the enemy came upon him in superior force, recaptured all except twenty-two prisoners and the two guns. Capt. Dahlgren had his horse killed, and escaped by crawling into the bushes. He made the citizens arm themselves and assist in defending the place, and when the enemy reappeared, the citizens conducted the prisoners to a place of safety in the mountains. At Waynesboro, when Jenkins made a demand to see the authorities, they referred him to Capt. Dahlgren, who, with his men, were drawn up in line of battle in another part of the town. Jenkins sent word that he would hang Captain Dahlgren and his men if they did not leave. They did not leave, however; a fight ensued, resulting in Jenkins being driven back six miles. Jenkins had five times as many men as Dahlgren. On this reconnoissance Captain Dahlgren destroyed one hundred and seventy-six loaded wagons, captured one wagon, two captains, and eleven men.

July second, Captain Coffin, of the Ninth New-York, with eighty men, was sent from near Gettysburgh up the Hagerstown pike on an important mission, which he successfully accomplished. He ascertained the exact position of the enemy and the whereabouts of his train, which would have been destroyed but for the error made in the movements of one of General Kilpatrick's brigades.

In sixteen days, one division of our cavalry has had fifteen battles, with infantry in nearly all to contend against, captured and destroyed nearly or quite one thousand loaded wagons, and between three and four thousand horses and mules; taken between four and five thousand rebel prisoners, destroyed one half of the rebel General Stuart's cavalry force, and so demoralized the balance that when a green (or blue) militia regiment, (the Philadelphia Blues,) with a regiment of Green Mountain Boys, attacked them while posted behind earth-works at Hagerstown, the whole command fled panic-stricken—or at Williamsport, where Custer's brigade of Michiganders, with Pennington's battery, captured more than man for man from an enemy whose force consisted of four times their numbers, and strongly located behind earth-works. This is cavalry fighting, the superior of which the world never saw. The cavalry also contributed largely to the success of our arms at Gettysburgh.

In claiming these results for the cavalry arm of the service, the flying artillery with it must not be forgotten. I speak more particularly of Pennington's and Elder's batteries, because circumstances have placed me in the way of realizing their worth. These batteries have contributed materially to the successes of the cavalry. Both the officers who command these batteries and the officers under them, are peculiarly well qualified to fill their positions, by reason of their experience, combined with a thorough knowledge of their branch of the profession of arms, and also from the fact that their hearts are in the work they have in hand.

This letter has already become too lengthy, or I would refer to the able surgeons attached to the cavalry command, of the skill and untiring industry of which this branch of the service can boast, as demonstrated in the persons of Pancost, Capehart, Phillips and others; of the patriotic ladies in the towns through which this command has passed during the last three weeks—especially the ladies of Boonsboro—who

with their own fair hands made and presented flags to the commanders of several brigades; but these matters must be reserved for a more fitting occasion.

The following named persons were in the Washington Hotel Hospital, Hagerstown, July fourteenth:

Sergeant J. W. Woodbury, First Vermont cavalry—wounded in leg.

W. Judy, First Ohio, color-bearer to General Kilpatrick's body-guard—thigh.

J. S. Merritt, First Vermont cavalry—arm.

P. Welsh, First Michigan cavalry—back.

Daniel Horton, Eighteenth Pennsylvania cavalry—shoulder.

J. M. Austin, Seventh Michigan cavalry—scalp.

S. M. Conklin, Eighteenth Pennsylvania cavalry—shoulder.

George S. Spofford, First Vermont cavalry—arm.

Albert Shew, Philadelphia Blue reserves—shoulder.

Robert McNutt, Philadelphia Blue reserves—breast.

John Agin, Philadelphia Blue reserves—left hand.　　　　E. A. PAUL.

Doc. 33.

JENKINS'S RAID INTO PENNSYLVANIA.

CHAMBERSBURGH "REPOSITORY" ACCOUNT.

On Sunday evening, June fourteenth, the dark clouds of contrabands commenced rushing upon us, bringing the tidings that General Milroy's forces at Martinsburgh had been attacked and scattered, and that the rebels, under General Rhodes, were advancing upon Pennsylvania. With due allowance for the excessive alarm of the slaves, it was manifest that the rebels were about to clear out the Shenandoah valley, and, that once done, the Cumberland, with all its teeming wealth, would be at rebel mercy. On Sunday night our people were much excited, and the question of protection became one of paramount interest. To inquiries, the authorities at Washington answered that the aspect of the war just at present rendered it unwise to divide or weaken the army of the Potomac, and that Pennsylvania must furnish her own men for her defence. A call from the President was issued to that effect, which is noticed elsewhere.

On Monday morning the flood of rumors from the Potomac fully confirmed the advance of the rebels, and the citizens of Chambersburgh and vicinity, feeling unable to resist the rebel columns, commenced to make prompt preparation for the movement of stealable property. Nearly every horse, good, bad, and indifferent, was started for the mountains as early on Monday as possible, and the negroes darkened the different roads northward for hours, loaded with household effects, sable babies, etc., and horses and wagons and cattle crowded every avenue to places of safety. About nine o'clock in the morning the advance of Milroy's retreating wagon-train dashed into town, attended by a few cavalry, and several affrighted wagon-masters, all of whom declared that the rebels were in hot pursuit; that a large portion of the train was captured, and that the enemy was about to enter Chambersburgh. This startling information, coming from men in uniform, who had fought valiantly until the enemy had got nearly within sight of them, naturally gave a fresh impetus to the citizens, and the skedaddle commenced in magnificent earnestness and exquisite confusion. Men, women, and children, who seemed to think the rebels so many cannibals, rushed out the turnpike, and generally kept on the leading thoroughfares as if they were determined to be captured, if the rebels were anywhere within range and wanted them. We watched the motley cavalcade rush along for a few hours, when it seems to have occurred to some one to inquire whether the rebels were not some distance in the rear; and a few moments of reflection and dispassionate inquiry satisfied the people that the enemy could not be upon us for several hours at least. The railroad men were prompt and systematic in their efforts to prepare for another fire, and by noon all the portable property of the company was safely under control, to be hauled and moved at pleasure. The more thoughtful portion of our people, who felt it a duty to keep out of rebel hands, remained until the cutting of telegraph communication south, and the reports of reliable scouts rendered it advisable to give way to the guerrilla army of plunderers.

Greencastle being but five miles north of the Maryland line, and in the direct route of the rebels, was naturally enough in the highest state of excitement on Sunday night and Monday morning. Exaggerated rumors had of course flooded them, and every half-hour a stampede was made before the imagined rebel columns. Hon. John Rowe at last determined to reconnoitre, and he mounted a horse and started out toward Hagerstown. A little distance beyond he was captured by a squad of rebels, and held until General Jenkins came up. Jenkins asked Rowe his name, and was answered correctly. He subsequently asked Mr. ——, who was with Rowe, what Rowe's name was, and upon being told that the name had been given to him correctly, he insisted that the Major had been an officer in the United States service. Mr. —— assured Jenkins that the Major had never been in the service, and he was satisfied. (Jenkins had evidently confounded Major Rowe with his son, the gallant Lieutenant-Colonel Rowe, of the One Hundred and Twenty-sixth.) Jenkins then asked Mr. —— whom he had voted for at the last Presidential election. He answered that he had voted for Lincoln. To which Jenkins gave the following chaste and classic reply: "Get off that horse, you — abolitionist." The horse was surrendered, and the same question was propounded to Major Rowe, who answered that he had voted for Douglas, and had scratched every Breckinridge man off his ticket. Jenkins answered: "You can ride your horse as long as you like—I voted for Douglas myself." He then demanded to know what forces were in Greencastle, and what fortifications. Major Rowe told him that the town was defenceless; but Jenkins seemed to be cautious lest he might be caught in a trap. He advanced cautiously, reconnoitred all suspicious buildings, and finally being fully satisfied that there was not a gun in position, and not a man under arms, he resolved upon capturing the town by a brilliant charge of cavalry. He accordingly divided his forces into two columns, charged upon the vacated streets, and reached the centre of the town without the loss of a man! This brilliant achievement, so soon after entering Pennsylvania, seemed to encourage the gallant guerrilla chief to still more daring deeds, and he immediately commenced to empty stables and capture every article within his reach that seemed to suit the fancy of his men. He announced in terms unfit for ears polite that he had come to burn and destroy, and that he would begin at Greencastle. Major Rowe informed him that he could burn Greencastle, but that he would end his depredations and his mundane career at about that point. Jenkins pondered as he blustered, and Jenkins didn't burn and destroy. He probably forgot to apply the torch. Generous teaching of memory!

The rebels were evidently under the impression that forces would be thrown in their way at an early hour, and they pushed forward for Chambersburgh. About eleven o'clock on Monday night they arrived at the southern end of the town, and the same intensely strategic movements exhibited at Greencastle were displayed here. Several were thrown forward cautiously to reconnoitre, and a few of our brave boys captured them and took their horses. This taste of war whetted the appetite of Jenkins, and he resolved to capture the town by a brilliant dash, without so much as a demand for surrender. He divided his forces into several columns— about two hundred in advance as a forlorn hope, to whom was assigned the desperate task of charging upon the empty undefended streets, store-boxes, mortar-beds, etc., of the ancient village of Chambersburgh. Every precaution that strategy could invent was taken to prevent failure. Men were detailed to ride along the columns before the charge was made, bawling out as loudly as possible to plant artillery at different points, although the redoubtable Jenkins had not so much as a swivel in his army. The women and children having been sufficiently frightened by the threatened booming of artillery, and all things being in readiness, the forlorn hope advanced, and the most desperate charge ever known in the history of war—in Chambersburgh at least—was made. Down the street came the iron clatter of hoofs, like the tempest with a thousand thunderbolts; but the great plan had failed in one particular, and the column recoiled before it reached the Diamond. A mortar-bed on the street, in front of Mr. White's new building, had not been observed in the reconnoitring of the town, nor had willing copperheads advised him of it. His force was hurled against it; down went some men and bang went a gun. To strike a mortar-bed and have a gun fired at the same time was more than the strategy of Jenkins had bargained for; and the charge was broken and fell back. A few moments of fearful suspense, and the mortar-bed was carefully reconnoitred, and the musket report was found to be an accidental discharge of a gun in the hand of one of his own men, who had fallen. With a boldness and dash worthy of Jenkins, it was resolved to renew the attack without even the formality of a council of war. Again the steeds of war thundered down the street, and, there being nothing in the way, overcame all opposition, and the borough of Chambersburgh was under the rule of Jenkins. Having won it by the most determined and brilliant prowess, Jenkins resolved that he would be magnanimous, and would allow nothing to be taken from our people—excepting such articles as he and his men wanted.

Jenkins had doubtless read the papers in his day, and knew that there were green fields in the "Green Spot;" and what is rather remarkable, at midnight he could start for a forty-acre clover-patch belonging to the editor of the *Repository* without so much as stopping to ask where the gate might be found. Not even a halt was called to find it; but the march was continued until the gate was reached, when the order "File right!" was given, and Jenkins was in clover. Happy fellow thus to find luxuriant and extensive clover as if by instinct. By way of giving the devil his due, it must be said that, although there were over sixty acres of wheat, and eighty acres of corn and oats in the same field, he protected it most carefully, and picketed his horses so that it could not be injured. An equal care was taken of all other property about the place, excepting half a dozen of our fattest Cottswell sheep, which were necessary, it seems, to furnish chops, etc., for his men. No fences were wantonly destroyed, poultry was not disturbed, nor did he compliment our blooded cattle so much as to test the quality of their steak and roasts. Some of his men cast a wistful eye upon the glistening trout in the spring; but they were protected by voluntary order, and save a few quarts of delicious strawberries, gathered with every care, after first asking permission, nothing in the gardens or about the grounds was taken. Having had a taste of rebel love for horses last October, when General Stuart's officers first stole our horses, and then supped and smoked socially with us, we had started to the mountains slightly in advance of Jenkins's occupation of the town, and, being unable to find them, we are happy to say that General Jenkins didn't steal our new assortment.

However earnest an enemy Jenkins may be, he don't seem to keep spite, but is capable of being very jolly and sociable when he is treated hospitably. For prudential reasons the editor was not at home to do the honors at his own table; but Jenkins was not particular, nor was his appetite impaired thereby. He called upon the ladies of the house, shared their hospitality, behaved in all respects like a gentleman, and expressed very earnest regrets that he had not been able to make the personal acquaintance of the editor. We beg to say that we reciprocate the wish of the General, and shall be glad to make his acquaintance personally—"when this cruel war is over." Colonel French and Surgeon Bee spent much of their time with Mrs. McClure, and the former showed his appreciation of her hospitality by taking her revolver from her when he left. An order having been made for the citizens to surrender all the guns and pistols they had, Colonel French took the pistol of his hostess. How many rifles he didn't get that were in her keeping, we "dinna choose to tell."

Horses seemed to be considered contraband of war, and were taken without the pretence of compensation; but other articles were deemed legitimate subjects of commerce even between enemies, and they were generally paid for after a fashion. True, the system of Jenkins would be considered a little informal in business circles; but it's his way, and our people agreed to it perhaps, to some extent, because of the novelty, but mainly because of the necessity of the thing. But Jenkins was liberal—eminently liberal. He didn't stop to higgle about a few odd pennies in making a bargain. For instance, he took the drugs of Messrs. Miller, Spangler, Nixon, and Heyser, and told them to make out a bill, or if they could not do that, to guess at the amount, and the bills were paid. Doubtless our merchants and druggists would have preferred greenbacks to confederate scrip that is never payable, and is worth just its weight in old paper; but Jenkins hadn't greenbacks, and he had confederate scrip, and such as he had he gave unto them. Thus he dealt largely in our place. To avoid the jealousies growing out of rivalry in business, he patronized all the merchants, and bought pretty much every thing he could conveniently use and carry. Some people, with the antiquated ideas of business, might call it stealing to take goods and pay for them in bogus money; but Jenkins calls it business, and for the time being what Jenkins calls business, was business. In this way he robbed all the stores, drug-stores, etc., more or less, and supplied himself with many articles of great value to him.

Jenkins, like most doctors, don't seem to have relished his own prescriptions. Several horses had been captured by some of our boys, and notice was given by the General Commanding that they must be surrendered or the town would be destroyed. The city fathers, commonly known as the town council, were appealed to in order to avert the impending fate threatened us. One of the horses, we believe, and some of the equipments were found and returned, but there was still a balance in favor of Jenkins. We do not know who audited the account, but it was finally adjusted by the council appropriating the sum of nine hundred dollars to pay the claim. Doubtless Jenkins hoped for nine hundred dollars in "greenbacks," but he had flooded the town with confederate scrip, pronouncing it better than United States currency, and the council evidently believed him; and, desiring to be accommodating with a conqueror, decided to favor him by the payment of his bill in confederate scrip. It was so done, and Jenkins got just nine hundred dollars worth of nothing for his trouble. He took it, however, without a murmur, and doubtless considered it a clever joke.

Sore was the disappointment of Jenkins at the general exodus of horses from this place. It limited his booty immensely. Fully five hundred had been taken from Chambersburgh and vicinity to the mountains, and Jenkins's plunder was thus made just so much less. But he determined to make up for it by stealing all the arms in the town. He therefore issued an order requiring the citizens to bring him all the arms they had, public or private, within two hours; and search and terrible vengeance were threatened in case of disobedience. Many of our citizens complied with the order, and a committee of our people was appointed to take a list of the persons presenting arms. Of course very many did not comply, but enough did so to avoid a general search and probable sacking of the town. The arms were assorted—the indifferent destroyed, and the good taken along.

On Tuesday a few of Milroy's cavalry, escaping from Martinsburgh, were seen by the redoubtable Jenkins hovering in his front. Although but thirteen in number, and without the least appetite for a battle with his two thousand men, he took on a fright of huge proportions, and prepared to sell his command as dearly as possible. Like a prudent general, however, he provided fully for his retreat. The shrill blast of the bugle brought his men to arms with the utmost possible alacrity; his pickets were called in to swell the ranks; the horses and baggage, consisting principally of stolen goods, were sent to the rear, south of the town; the surgeon took forcible possession of all our buildings, houses, barns, sheds, etc., to be used as hospitals, and especially requested that their wounded should be humanely treated in case of their sudden retreat without being able to take them along. The hero of two brilliant cavalry charges upon undefended towns was agitated beyond endurance at the prospect of a battle; and instead of charging upon a little squad of men, who were merely observing the course of his robberies, he stood trembling in battle array to receive the shock. No foe was nearer than the State capital, over fifty miles distant, and there the same scene was being presented. Jenkins in Chambersburgh, and the militia at Harrisburgh, were each momentarily expecting to be cut to pieces by the other. But these armies, alike terrible in their heroism, were spared the deadly clash of arms, inasmuch as even the most improved ordnance is not deemed fatal at a range of fifty miles. Both armies, as the usual reports go, "having

accomplished their purpose retired in good order."

As a rule, we believe that private houses were not sacked by Jenkins's forces; but there were some exceptions. The residences of Messrs. Dengler and Gipe, near Chambersburgh, were both entered (the familes being absent) and plundered of clothing, kettles, and other articles. Bureaus and cupboards were all emptied of their contents, and such articles as they wanted were taken. We have not learned of any instances of the kind in town.

A very few of our citizens exhibited the craven spirit of the genuine copperhead, but Jenkins and his men, in no instance, treated them with even courtesy. That they made use of some such creatures to obtain information, cannot be doubted; but they spurned all attempts to claim their respect because of professed sympathy with their cause. To one who desired to make fair weather with Jenkins, by ardent professions of sympathy with the South, he answered: "Well, if you believe we are right, take your gun and join our ranks." It is needless to say that the cowardly traitor did not obey. To another he said: "If we had such men as you in the South we would hang them." They say, on all occasions, that there are but two modes of peace — disunion or subjugation, and they stoutly deny that the latter is possible. Lieutenant Reilly had just returned from West-Point the day the rebels reached here, and of his presence and residence they were minutely advised, for they called at the house and compelled his sister to go with them into every room to search for them. General Jenkins also had the fullest information of the movements of the editor of this paper. He told at our own house, when we had left, the direction we had gone, and described the horse we rode, and added that there were people in Chambersburgh sufficiently cowardly and treacherous to give such information of their neighbors. When it was suggested that such people should be sent within the rebel lines, he insisted that the South should not be made a Botany Bay for Northern scoundrels.

Quite a number of negroes, free and slave — men, women, and children — were captured by Jenkins and started South to be sold into bondage. Many escaped in various ways, and the people of Greencastle captured the guard of one negro train and discharged the negroes; but, perhaps, full fifty were got off to slavery. One negro effected his escape by shooting and seriously wounding his rebel guard. He forced the gun from the rebel and fired, wounding him in the head, and then skedaddled. Some of the men were bound with ropes, and the children were mounted in front or behind the rebels on their horses. By great exertions of several citizens some of the negroes were discharged.

The southern border of this county has been literally plundered of every thing in the stock line, excepting such as could be secreted. But it was difficult to secrete stock, as the rebels spent a full week in the county, and leisurely hunted out horses and cattle without molestation. The citizens were unable to protect themselves, and owing to the want of promptness of our citizens elsewhere to respond to the call for troops, aid could not be had. We have not sufficient data to estimate the loss sustained by this county, but it cannot fall short of a quarter of a million of dollars. It is a fearful blow to our people, coming as it does in the throngest season of the year, and many croppers, who had little else than their stock, have been rendered almost if not entirely bankrupt by the raid. If the people of Pennsylvania will not fight to protect the State from invasion, the sufferers have a right to claim compensation from the common treasury of the State. The State professes to protect its citizens in the enjoyment of all their rights, and there is no justice in withholding the common tribute from individual sufferers. Among the many unfortunate, perhaps the greatest sufferer is ex-Sheriff Taylor, from whom the rebels captured a drove of fat cattle in Fulton County. His loss is some seven thousand dollars.

The route of Jenkins was through the most densely populated and wealthiest portion of the county. From this point he fell back to Greencastle and south of it, thence he proceeded to Mercersburgh, from where a detachment crossed the Cove Mountain to McConnellsburgh and struck down the valley from there. The main body, however, was divided into plundering parties, and scoured the whole southern portion of the county, spending several days in and about Greencastle and Waynesboro, and giving Welsh Run a pretty intimate visitation.

The rebels seemed omnipresent according to reports. They were on several occasions since their departure from this place just about to re-enter it, and the panic-stricken made a corresponding exit at the other side. On Thursday, the eighteenth, they were reported within two miles of here, in large force, and a general skedaddle took place. And again on Sunday, the twenty-first, they were reported coming with re-enforcements. A few ran off, but most of our people, knowing that there was a military force to fall back upon between this and Scotland, shouldered their guns and fell into ranks to give battle. Prominent among these we noticed Rev. Mr. Niccoll, whose people missed a sermon in his determination to pop a few rebels.

One of the first acts done by the rebels here was to march down to the railroad bridge at Scotland and burn it. The warehouse of Mr. Criswell and several cars were spared upon satisfactory assurance that they were private property. As soon as the rebels fell back the railroad company commenced to rebuild the bridge, and on Sunday evening, the twenty-first, trains passed over it again. The only other instance of firing property that has reached us was the warehouse of Oaks and Linn. It was fired just as they left the town, but the citizens extinguished it.

We had not the felicity of a personal interview with the distinguished guerrilla chief, but our special reporters took his dimensions and autobiography with general accuracy. He was born of his mother at a very early age, and is supposed to be the son of his father. He was flogged through school in his boyhood years much as other children; and may have startling traditions touching his early character, such as the hatchet and cherry-tree which proved that Washington could not lie; but it is for the present regarded as doubtful. He subsequently graduated at Jefferson College in this State, in the same class, we believe, with J. McDowell Sharpe, Esq., and gave promise of future usefulness and greatness. His downward career commenced some five years ago, when in an evil hour he became a member of Congress from Western Virginia, and from thence may be dated his decline and fall. From Congress he naturally enough turned fire-eater, secessionist, and guerrilla. He is of medium size, has a flat but good head, light brown hair, blue eyes, immense flowing beard of a sandy hue, and rather a pleasant face. He professes to cherish the utmost regard for the humanity of war, and seemed sensitive on the subject of his reputation as a humane military leader. He pointed to the raids of the Union troops, who left in many instances widespread and total desolation on their tracks, and expressed the hope that henceforth the Union raids would do no more damage to citizens than he does. He takes horses, cattle, and articles necessary for the army, as both sides treat them as contraband of war, and help themselves on every occasion offered. He pointed with bitter triumph at the raid of Montgomery in South-Carolina, and at the destruction of Jacksonville, Fla., and Jackson, Miss., by our troops, and reminded us that his actions were in accordance with civilized warfare, while those referred to of our troops were barbarous.

We do not learn of any one who was able to count Jenkins's forces accurately, but from the best information we can gather he had about two thousand men. They were clad, as rebel soldiers usually are, in the Southern butternut cloth, and without any regard to uniformity. They carried pistols, rifles, and sabres, and are classed as mounted infantry, or independent guerrillas, although they are recognized as part of the rebel army. We believe that the plunder became their own private property, instead of the property of the rebel authorities, as is the case with their regular troops. They have thus a double incentive to plunder.

We have heard much complaint of our people for not rushing to arms and driving the invaders away. It must be remembered that the entire southern half of our county, embracing two thirds of our population, was occupied by the rebels, who had heavy supporting columns at Williamsport. Every man of ours was threatened hourly at his own door, and concentration was impossible.

Our people generally did their duty, but they were required in their respective neighborhoods to picket and protect, in some degree, their stock. A concentration of our men at Chambersburgh, or Greencastle, or Mercersburgh would have left twenty-five thousand people with their property entirely defenceless. In the valley the citizens were under arms, and had the roads barricaded for defence, but the southern portion of the county is open and unsuited to defence by small parties.

On Sunday, the twenty-eighth, the Eighth New-York militia arrived here, having marched from Shippensburgh, and they were received with the wildest enthusiasm. Considering that they are on our border in advance of any Pennsylvania regiments, they merit, as they will receive, the lasting gratitude of every man in the border.

The old men of the town organized a company, headed by Hon. George Chambers, for the defence of the town. None were admitted under forty-five. On Monday every man capable of bearing arms had his gun, and was in some organization to resist the rebels.

Doc. 34.

THE MISSION OF A. H. STEPHENS.

OFFICIAL CORRESPONDENCE.*

RICHMOND, 2 July, 1863.

Hon. A. H. Stephens, Richmond, Va. :

SIR: Having accepted your patriotic offer to proceed as a Military Commissioner, under a flag of truce, to Washington, you will receive herewith your letter of authority to the Commander-in-Chief of the army and navy of the United States.

This letter is signed by me, as Commander-in-Chief of the confederate land and naval forces.

You will perceive, from the terms of the letter, that it is so worded as to avoid any political difficulties in its reception. Intended exclusively as one of those communications between belligerents which public law recognizes as necessary and proper between hostile forces, care has been taken to give no pretext for refusing to receive it on the ground that it would involve a tacit recognition of the independence of the Confederacy.

Your mission is simply one of humanity, and has no political aspect.

If objection is made to receiving your letter, on the ground that it is not addressed to Abraham Lincoln, as *President,* instead of Commander-in-Chief, etc., then you will present the duplicate letter, which is addressed to him as President, and signed by me as President. To this letter objection may be made on the ground that I am not recognized to be President of the Confederacy. In this event, you will decline any further attempt to confer on the subject of your mission, as such conference is admissible only on the footing of perfect equality.

My recent interviews with you have put you so fully in possession of my views that it is scarcely necessary to give you any detailed instructions,

* See Doc., 23, page 135 *ante.*

even were I, at this moment, well enough to attempt it.

My whole process is, in one word, to place this war on the footing of such as are waged by civilized people in modern times, and to divest it of the savage character which has been impressed on it by our enemies, in spite of all our efforts and protests. War is full enough of unavoidable horrors, under all its aspects, to justify, and even to demand, of any Christian ruler who may be unhappily engaged in carrying it on, to seek to restrict its calamities, and to divest it of all unnecessary severities. You will endeavor to establish the cartel for the exchange of prisoners on such a basis as to avoid the constant difficulties and complaints which arise, and to prevent, for the future, what we deem the unfair conduct of our enemies in evading the delivery of the prisoners who fall into their hands; in retarding it by sending them on circuitous routes, and by detaining them, sometimes for months, in camps and prisons, and in persisting in taking captive non-combatants.

Your attention is also called to the unheard of conduct of Federal officers in driving from their homes entire communities of women and children, as well as of men, whom they find in districts occupied by their troops, for no other reason than because these unfortunates are faithful to the allegiance due to their States, and refuse to take an oath of fidelity to their enemies.

The putting to death of unarmed prisoners has been a ground of just complaint in more than one instance, and the recent execution of officers of our army in Kentucky, for the sole cause that they were engaged in recruiting service in a State which is claimed as still one of the United States, but is also claimed by us as one of the confederate States, must be repressed by retaliation if not unconditionally abandoned, because it would justify the like execution in every other State of the Confederacy, and the practice is barbarous, uselessly cruel, and can only lead to the slaughter of prisoners on both sides, a result too horrible to contemplate without making every effort to avoid it.

On these and all kindred subjects you will consider your authority full and ample to make such arrangements as will temper the present cruel character of the contest, and full confidence is placed in your judgment, patriotism, and discretion, that, while carrying out the objects of your mission, you will take care that the equal rights of the Confederacy be always preserved.

Very respectfully,

JEFFERSON DAVIS.

RICHMOND, July 8, 1863.

His Excellency Jefferson Davis:

SIR: Under the authority and instructions of your letter to me on the second instant, I proceeded on the mission therein assigned without delay. The steamer Torpedo, commanded by Lieutenant Hunter Davidson, of the navy, was put in readiness as soon as possible, by order of the Secretary of the Navy, and tendered for the service. At noon, on the third, she started down James River, hoisting and bearing a flag of truce after passing City Point. The next day, (the fourth,) at about one o'clock P.M., when within a few miles of Newport News, we were met by a small boat of the enemy, carrying two guns, which also raised a white flag before approaching us.

The officer in command informed Lieutenant Davidson that he had orders from Admiral Lee, on board the United States flag-ship Minnesota, lying below, and then in view, not to allow any boat or vessel to pass the point near which he was stationed, without his permission. By this officer I sent to Admiral Lee a note stating my objects and wishes, a copy of which is hereunto annexed, marked A. I also sent to the Admiral, to be forwarded, another in the same language, addressed to the officer in command of the United States forces at Fortress Monroe. The gunboat proceeded immediately to the Minnesota with these despatches, while the Torpedo remained at anchor. Between three and four o'clock P.M., another boat came up to us, bearing the Admiral's answer, which is hereunto annexed, marked B.

We remained at or about this point in the river until the sixth instant, when, having heard nothing further from the Admiral, at twelve o'clock M. on that day I directed Lieutenant Davidson again to speak the gunboat on guard, and to hand to the officer in command another note to the Admiral. This was done; a copy of the note is appended, marked C. At half-past two o'clock P.M. two boats approached us from below, one bearing an answer from the Admiral to my note to him of the fourth. This answer is annexed, marked D.

The other boat bore the answer of Lieutenant-Colonel W. H. Ludlow to my note of the fourth, addressed to the officer in command at Fort Monroe. A copy of this is annexed, marked E. Lieutenant-Colonel Ludlow also came up in person in the boat that brought his answer to me, and conferred with Colonel Ould, on board the Torpedo, upon some matters he desired to see him about in connection with the exchange of prisoners. From the papers appended, embracing the correspondence referred to, it will be seen that the mission failed from the refusal of the enemy to receive or entertain it, holding the proposition for such a conference "inadmissible."

The influences and views that led to this determination after so long a consideration of the subject, must be left to conjecture. The reason assigned for the refusal by the United States Secretary of War, to wit, that "the customary agents and channels" are considered adequate for all needful military "communications and conferences," to one acquainted with the facts, seems not only unsatisfactory, but very singular and unaccountable; for it is certainly known to him that these very agents, to whom he evidently alludes, heretofore agreed upon in a former conference in reference to the exchange of prisoners, (one of the subjects embraced in your letter to

me,) are now, and have been for some time, distinctly at issue on several important points. The existing cartel, owing to these disagreements, is virtually suspended, so far as the exchange of officers on either side are concerned. Notices of retaliation have been given on both sides.

The effort, therefore, for the very many and cogent reasons set forth in your letter of instructions to me, to see if these differences could not be removed, and if a clearer understanding between the parties as to the general conduct of the war could not be arrived at before this extreme measure should be resorted to by either party, was no less in accordance with the dictates of humanity than in strict conformity with the usages of belligerents in modern times. Deeply impressed as I was with these views and feelings, in undertaking the mission, and asking the conference, I can but express my profound regret at the result of the effort made to obtain it, and I can but entertain the belief that if the conference sought had been granted, mutual good could have been effected by it; and if this war, so unnatural, so unjust, so unchristian, and so inconsistent with every fundamental principle of American constitutional liberty, "must needs" continue to be waged against us, that at least some of its severer horrors, which now so eminently threaten, might have been avoided.

Very respectfully,
ALEXANDER H. STEPHENS.

Doc. 35.

COLONEL SPEAR'S EXPEDITION.

IN THE FIELD, WHITE HOUSE, VIRGINIA,
Sunday Night, June 28, 1863.

THIS (Sunday) morning Colonel Spear returned to White House after a most brilliant, dashing, and successful cavalry exploit.

On Thursday last, the twenty-fifth instant, Colonel Spear, commanding the Eleventh Pennsylvania cavalry, accompanied by a detachment of two companies of the Second Massachusetts, and two companies of the Twelfth Illinois, left White House, on the Pamunkey River—the whole comprising a force one thousand strong. The undertaking had for its object spoliation, destruction of property, and the discomfiture of all rebels whom they might meet in the direction of Richmond, added to the obtaining of all the information of the number of the forces at present in and around the so-called confederate capital. At about ten o'clock Thursday A.M., the twenty-fifth, the expedition took up its line of march in the direction of Tunstall Station, a squad of the Second Massachusetts cavalry acting as the advance-guard. As there was nothing to be accomplished at Tunstall Station, a movement on Barrett, a point ten miles from Richmond, was made, where the forces encamped for the night. At daylight the next morning the expedition moved with the utmost celerity to Hanover Court-House, a distance of twenty-four miles from White House, and a point directly north of Richmond, reaching there at nine o'clock in the morning. Just here "the plot thickened" in an admirable and spirited charge made by a squad of the Second Massachusetts and company A of the Eleventh Pennsylvania, under command of Captain Ringland, Lieutenants Barkely and Blake, with Lieutenant Titus in the somewhat anomalous, though useful capacity of acting aid. The charge was made upon the adjacent station and was successful, resulting in its capture, together with a train of one hundred wagons and the destruction of the telegraph line. From this point a movement having in view the destruction of an important bridge on the Pamunkey, and in which company A, Spear's cavalry, (Eleventh Pennsylvania,) held the advance, was made. When within a mile of the bridge, Lieutenant F. A. Blake, with his extreme advance, charged upon and captured the advance picket of the enemy, consisting of a lieutenant, whose name is not known, and six men. On moving further down the river, the rebels showing themselves in considerable force, Colonel Spear ordered the Second Massachusetts riflemen to dismount, and companies A and G of his regiment to move forward in support of a couple of Eleventh Pennsylvania howitzers. Sharp and decisive firing caused the enemy, who appeared to be about three hundred strong, to retreat in "skedaddling" confusion. As they did so, our troops occupied a block-house and several lines of earthworks running close to the bridge, and on both sides of the railroad track. At this time the carabineers of the Second Massachusetts, and a few men of Colonel Spear's command, with howitzers, moved down to the edge of the river, and engaged the enemy with great sharpness. Lieutenant Blake, with his advanced-guard, proceeding further down the river, discovered a ford about half a mile below the bridge. On reporting this fact to Colonel Spear, he immediately ordered companies A and G of his command to cross and attack the enemy in the rear, which they did. Upon charging the earthworks, these companies were temporarily repulsed and driven back a short distance, whereon Colonel Spear instantly ordered companies E and M to move up in reënforcement. Under command of Major Stratton, who ordered line of battle to be formed on two sides of the enemy's works, at the same time directing Lieutenant Hope, of company E, to take a few dismounted carabineers, and moving along the river bank, attack the enemy on the river flank. So soon as these preliminary arrangements were completed, Major Stratton ordered Captain Skelly to charge the enemy's works with his command. This feature of the reconnoissance was one of the most creditable of any similar one since the inauguration of hostilities. It was, indeed, gallantly done. The carabineers at the same time charged the block-house from the river side, under the auspices of Colonel Spear. Lieutenant Roper, Adjutant Menzies, Captain Roberts, and several other officers were with the carabineers. The struggle here was intense in its character, being a terrific hand-to-hand conflict. Victory

crowned our side. In this attack First Sergeant McFarlane, of company B, Eleventh Pennsylvania cavalry, fell while gallantly fighting, pierced through the heart by a hostile bayonet. Sergeant McFarlane was ever brave, ever dutiful, and ever ready to die for his country. His name must be added to the long list of the Union heroes who have nobly sacrificed their lives for their country. The conflict lasted about ten minutes, and in it several lives were lost. The enemy lost nine killed and twenty wounded. I may not omit to mention that Captain Ringland's company made a charge in support of Skelly, and that during the fight a charge was made upon a line of skirmishers in rear of the Union line of battle, who were commanded by Lieutenant Blake, by the enemy's cavalry, who were most successfully repulsed. The result of this feature of the reconnoissance was the undisputed possession of the bridge, and the capture of a lieutenant-colonel, six officers, and one hundred and thirty prisoners of war, who were sent down the river to-day. The bridge and block-house were burned, the track torn up, and several culverts destroyed. After this our forces fell back to Hanover Court-House, where Major Wetherell, of Colonel Spear's command, had been left to destroy the trains and culverts at the station, which he accomplished. It was here that Brigadier-General William H. Lee, (not General Fitz-Hugh Lee,) a nephew of the rebel Lee, Commander-in-Chief of the traitors, and who was wounded at Beverly Ford, was found recruiting at the farm-house of a widow. He was, however, in a condition admitting of removal, and was taken by order of Colonel Spear. Our forces continued moving down the river, crossing about six miles below Hanover Court-House, encamping for the night on a rebel farm. On the morning of the twenty-eighth the troops reached White House by way of King William Court-House. In addition to the results already stated, the troops captured forty good army wagons, and upward of four hundred mules and horses. Throughout the expedition our scouting parties were frequently fired on by the enemy hanging on our flanks, doing no other damage, however, than the capturing of one private.

Doc. 36.

THE SIEGE OF VICKSBURGH.

McPHERSON'S ATTACK, JUNE TWENTY-FIFTH.

HEADQUARTERS LOGAN'S DIVISION,
CENTRE CORPS ARMY BESIEGING VICKSBURGH,
Friday, June 26.

I APPEND below a few of the particulars of the most important operation of the siege since the mournful result of the twenty-second—the attempt of the central division to effect a lodgment in one of the enemy's most conspicuous forts. You are informed that the method of reducing the stronghold in front of us is, first, a complete investment of the garrison, cutting off all supplies and intercourse; second, a system of earthworks protecting batteries, by which the guns of the enemy are silenced, and a curtain of rifle-pits and galleries, by which he is intimidated from strengthening his position.

In the selection of the site for this chain of works, the rebels have of course seized all the advantages which the very remarkable ground afforded. The highest hills and steepest hollows have all been duly taken into their account, and whenever the finale shall permit, the few square miles between us and the river will show some of the most remarkable fortifications the engineering world has ever seen.

Running in a slanting line from the north side of the city of Vicksburgh, backward toward the railroad, runs a prominent ridge with a system of spurs or branches. Along the north side of this rests the rebel left, crossing the main ridge at the centre in the position assigned at present to the division of General Logan. On the crest of this backbone they have constructed, in the system of intrenchments, a salient fort, originally designed for a number of guns. The guns originally in this work have for three weeks been silent, and more recently been removed. Here as elsewhere our sappers have been at work crawling up to the side of the fort. On the outer side the fort overlooked a steep chasm. Here the ingenuity of sapping was at fault.

On Saturday last we had a general bombardment, and advantage was taken of it to send a couple of adventurous diggers across the ravine, who commenced an earnest excavation under the very walls of the fort, hewn as they are, in part, out of the natural sedimentary cliff. Since then the miners have been faithfully at work, the rebels have been kept silent by our ever-watchful sharp-shooters, and perhaps ignorant of the operations going on under their very feet. Indeed, nothing is more striking in this whole siege than the fact that the two lines are so close together that at points the muzzles of the rifles are not more than twenty feet apart, and those of the cannon not more than two hundred and fifty yards.

Here have we seen for days the forts blazing in lightning flashes and storming thunder crashes at less than half the usual distance, although all the protection is a rude wall of earth thrown up in front of gabions, which latter are planted under fire of the concealed riflemen of the enemy. In fact, the lines described by the works of Both parties may be indicated in outlines by conceiving two thirds of a circle. On the chord rests Vicksburgh; on the same side are heavy guns and rifle-pits, with which we have no present concern. On the circle commencing from the supposed centre is, first a line of heavy batteries of the enemy; at a distance of perhaps a mile to those quarters is a second line of abandoned forts from which the enemy has been driven by successive bombardment; between these is one ground chain of rifle-pits.

Beyond and still further from the centre, about two hundred yards, is a line of national rifle-pits with crooked branches extending toward, touching at points, the last mentioned line. Further out still is a line of abandoned rifle-pits, with their branching saps, and an irregular line of forts on every considerable crest of the series. Thus the lines present two sets of lines for each party; an interior double line for which we are contending, and which is at places blended and interplexed; on each side of it a line of batteries.

Our superiority in artillery has aided to force the rebels back from their original line. While we have more than a hundred guns of every desirable calibre and pattern along our line, the enemy is not supposed to have more than fifty movable pieces, and the same number of heavy pieces on the river-bank, where they silently grin at the equally silent navy's long-range cannon.

On yesterday afternoon, about three o'clock, the troops all along the line might have been seen in order of battle, the guns keeping up their usual din and the sharp-shooters more than usually brisk with their fire.

Several prominent officers might have been seen, glasses in hand, and their eyes turned in two directions; mainly, however, on the hump of land in the centre. Presently a movement might have been seen of the earth; upward it rose, as if some slumbering man of the mountain were shaking off the superfluous covering; in a moment more, through a gaping crater, a shaft of white smoke rushed through, and then a cloud of dust. An instant clatter of fire-arms then commenced, and raged with painful intensity for an hour, when, out of the confusion of smoke something might have been seen of two sets of combatants, almost, as you may say, at arm's length.

All this while, before and after the explosion, there was a terrific cannonade. Previously every gun along the line was in play, and the intervals of a few seconds not filled with the burst of shells, the crack of guns of all calibres, were closed up by the more awful crackle of the infantry along the whole line. It is true that no assault was being made along the line, but the whole circuit of muskets was firing, firing into the aimless air; nobody was to be seen; there were the bleak ridges as ever; there the silent forts; but the bullets were whizzing into their intrenchments in myraids of radial lines. We have come to learn and to realize how fatal all this shower of leaden hail may have been, if it had no ulterior purpose, though not a soul was to be seen. Its real purpose was, however, to prevent any concentration on the critical points, by feigning an attack at all. Besides the one on the centre, another was selected on Blair's front, which, as we learned afterward, proved abortive, there being an insufficiency of powder, or it being placed too loosely in the mine.

The way in which the fort on McPherson's front was exploded is, as we learn from some of the participants, as follows: After the diggers had cut across the middle of the fort, which was a prominent fort, and, by reason of our flanking it, has been so pierced as to be almost of the parallelogram or nearly an oblong shape, they deposited in it a ton of powder, and then sealed up the cavity as tightly as possible. A train of powder and slow match were only required to explode this immense mass and set free the enormous gaseous force, so soon as the disposition was made for the climacteric. The efficient superintendence of this operation is due to Captain Hickenlooper, of McPherson's staff.

After the explosion, which, by the way, was either noiseless, or at least not noticeable in the rear of heavy guns, our soldiers rushed for the breach, intending to occupy the whole of the work. The blast had opened up a rift right across the fort, extending from wall to wall. The rebels, as if they had knowledge of the design, or else by a marvellous coincidence, rushed simultaneously from the other end. The powder had left a couple of huge projecting lips, and between them a crater-like fissure, making the distance from furrow to furrow from ten to twenty feet. Thus, ranged behind these new-formed walls, our men found themselves face to face with their foes, and a dire and dreadful slaughter commenced from perhaps three hundred men on each side, within this arena of two hundred feet in length.

The contest was severe, and the fresh packs of rifles kept opening on all sides. The gunners loaded and fired away vigorously. The rebels crowded up with great spirit. Our men went in, a regiment at a time, with full cartridge-boxes, and in thirty minutes were relieved by others. The firing for about an hour was more terrific than any battle-field ever the gory field of war has witnessed. Had every shot touched its man there would have been half a million slain; as it was, by far the greater portion of them found lodgment in the solid clay.

The first regiment which rushed in was the scarred remnant of the Forty-fifth Illinois, whose members lie on a dozen illustrious fields, led by Colonel Maltby. Its loss was necessarily severe. It was seconded by the "Bloody Seventh" Missouri, who were soon recalled.

Next went in the Twentieth Illinois, who kept up a gallant resistance for a half-hour, when the Thirty-first Illinois, under Lieutenant-Colonel Reese, went in. Subsequently, during the evening and night, the Twenty-third Indiana, the Forty-sixth Illinois, and the Fifty-sixth Illinois, the latter under its beloved Colonel, Melancthon Smith. The list then commenced again, relieving in this same order.

The *mêlée* at first was terrible, although the losses were not proportionate at all to the noise. The men on both sides were engaged in throwing up temporary works with a view to getting a light field-piece in position. They had gotten a notched piece of timber rolled up to the top of the rough bank, when smash came a blast from a ten-pounder right in their faces, sending the stick of timber right amongst them, singeing their hair and blackening them with the discharge, killing two or three outright.

This blow struck Colonel Maltby with stun-

ning force. The rattle of musketry kept up until nightfall. Our batteries on Lightburn's and Giles Smith's front, as well as from Burbridge, kept firing on the rebels; but from the nearness of the combatants, the missiles either did not reach the thick of the rebel opposition, or came so close as to injure our own men. In a few hours, however, they had felt so much reconciled to their position as to commence a most dangerous and dreadful piece of warfare—casting lighted shells over into one end of the fort. Some grenades, it is said, were first thrown, and afterward twenty-twos and twenty-fours. Our forces seeing the dismay and destruction, still felt secure enough to commence the same game, heaving however, some very heavy shells to the rebel end of the work.

I may say here that our possession of this end of the fort is regarded as complete as that of the enemy to the rest. It is believed, also, by General McPherson and his engineers that, if not too much pressed, he can in a day or two establish a battery within the work. The contest still rages, and as both sides are throwing up earthworks, it seems as if we might find at the end of a few days our point gained and our lines advanced to a most commanding position.

Our losses, I grieve to say, include several very fine officers. The total up to noon to-day, in this particular division, will amount to about three hundred in killed and wounded—perhaps forty of the former. Major Leander Fink was killed by a ball through the forehead. Colonel Melancthon Smith, an excellent soldier and a model gentleman, is dangerously and we fear mortally wounded. Lieutenant-Colonel Reese, of the Thirty-first Illinois, is wounded in the arm. Lieutenant J. Clifford, of the Forty-fifth Illinois, is wounded severely. Captain Boyce and Adjutant Frohok, of the same regiment, are wounded also. There are some others, removed to the general hospital, whose names I cannot send at present.[*]

Doc. 37.

COLONEL WILDER'S EXPEDITION.

INDIANAPOLIS "JOURNAL" NARRATIVE.

WARTRACE, TENN., July 4, 1863.

FRIEND TERRELL: You have doubtless heard before this of the evacuation of the rebel stronghold, Tullahoma. As Wilder's command had "a hand" in it, I will write you some particulars. He started from Murfreesboro on the twenty-fourth of June. His brigade had the advance of the "centre" on the Manchester road. At nine o'clock A.M. he met the rebel pickets eight miles from Murfreesboro, and drove them and all their reserves on a run through Hoover's Gap, a long, narrow, winding hollow through a chain of hills dividing the waters of Stone and Duck Rivers, and about seventeen miles from Murfreesboro. Two thirds through the gap the rebels had forti-

[*] See Report of General Grant, page 142, Docs. *ante.*

fied a strong position, but his brigade was so close on their heels that they had not time to deploy into their works before it was inside also. They immediately "skedaddled," losing forty-two prisoners and the battle-flag of the First Kentucky cavalry, the one presented them at Elizabethtown, Ky., by the sister of General Ben. Hardin Helm, and worked by her hands. Colonel Wilder will send it to the State library to grace its walls. He drove them on a run four miles beyond the gap, and had halted the main part of his force at the mouth of the gap, when he heard the long-roll sounded in their infantry camps two miles down the Garrison fork of Duck River to his right. He immediately made the proper dispositions for a fight, being determined to hold the mouth of the gap until General Reynolds arrived with the balance of the division. The proper dispositions were hardly made before two brigades of infantry came up in line of battle, "double-quick," and apparently as confident as if they already had possession. As soon as they came within four hundred yards "Lilly" gave them a few rounds of double-shotted canister from his "Rodmans," and on their nearer approach Colonel Miller, Seventy-second Indiana, let loose his "travelling arsenal" on their right, which sent them "right-about" as fast as they could go, fully persuaded that charging a battery, supported by Spencer rifles in the hands of Hoosiers, was an up-hill business. On Wilder's right the old Seventeenth had opened their "horizontal shot-tower" (as the boys call their Spencer rifles) upon five regiments of rebels under General Bates, who outflanked them and were closing on their rear, charging and yelling like the bottomless pit broke loose. Wilder immediately sent the Ninety-eighth Illinois, Colonel Funkhouser, to their relief, who outflanked the rebel left, and then you ought to have heard the rattle. The rebels stood about five minutes, or rather lay that length of time, waiting for our men to stop and load, (our repeaters shoot seven times without loading, and are reloaded in less time than an ordinary musket;) finding that they were fast getting their "rights in the territories," and that they were emigrating to the realms of the first secessionist faster than the Irish are to America, they concluded that was not just the place for the "last ditch," and those who could, left as fast as their legs could carry them. Their officers tried to bring them up a second time, but after a few feeble attempts they concluded to fight it out on the Chinese principle, by making a great noise with two batteries at a safe distance; but "Lilly" made them change their position several times, until they took a position behind some hills, where they continued to belch away without harm until night.

Wilder's entire loss was sixty-one killed and wounded, the rebels admitting a loss of one hundred killed and five hundred wounded, and claiming that they had fought sixteen regiments, when only Wilder's four regiments were in it, the nearest infantry of ours being six miles in the rear, who did not get up until the fight was over. So

much for the first fight of these regiments as a brigade.

Two days afterward, when the wings of the army had caught up with them, the brigade started forward, Wilder's command making a flank movement around the rebel right, which made them fall back to Wartrace the next morning. Wilder moved to Manchester, where he found about forty rebels taking their breakfast. He kindly offered to transplant them to a cooler climate until swapped off for better men — they "dickered."

The twenty-eighth he started for Dixie, sure enough. He came to Elk River, and on trying to ford it, found water enough to have discouraged old Noah, and too swift to swim. He went up-stream six miles, and found a place still enough for his horses to swim across, by being washed down-stream thirty yards. He made a raft of an old saw-mill, and floated his mountain howitzer over, towing it by our picket-ropes. Every body was in a good humor, and had lots of fun over our "gunboat," as the boys called the raft. He had sent Colonel Munroe (One Hundred and Twenty-third Illinois) with his regiment to destroy the railroad bridge over Elk River in the rear of Tullahoma, but Withers's division of infantry got there three hundred yards ahead of him. He then returned to Hillsboro. Wilder's command moved on to Dechard that night, and after a sharp skirmish with the garrison of about eighty men in a stockade, drove them out—they escaped in the dark. He destroyed the telegraph-wire, capturing the instruments, and burning the depot, which was full of commissary goods; also the water-tanks and railroad bridge on the Winchester road, and tore up and destroyed three hundred yards of the Chattanooga railroad track. This could not be done very fast on account of the darkness. At twelve o'clock, midnight, six regiments of infantry came after his brigade, and he left, taking the road to Chattanooga, over the mountains, intending to strike the Cow Creek bridges, near Stevenson, but on attempting to get down the mountain single-file, at Tantalon, he found three trains loaded with infantry awaiting him, and by this time all their cavalry was after him. He then attempted to go to Anderson, ten miles further on, and destroy the bridge at that point, but also found a brigade of Buckner's troops at that point, which was inapproachable if defended, the only road down the mountain being a bridle-path over which but one man could go abreast, and the depot is but three hundred yards from the foot of the mountain. He could not reach the road, and now had to make his escape.

The whole of the rebel cavalry and Buckner's division of infantry were after him, and his men had been in their saddles and their horses under them for seven days. His men were out of rations and his horses starved, and the mountains without farms or inhabitants, and to leave them was certain capture.

He started the head of the column, after Colonel Munroe came up from Hillsboro, toward Chattanooga, and on the other slope of the mountains, during a terrible rain which washed out his trail, moved by his left flank two miles over the rocks into the woods, leaving a picket to watch for the rebels.

He had not been hid more than an hour before the rebel column came along and followed the road toward Chattanooga, without discovering him. As soon as they had passed he struck across the mountains without guides or a road, but luckily came out on the Tracy City road at the point aimed at, and came down the mountain on an old road to Pelham, in the night, rocky enough to have been the Caucasus to which Prometheus was chained. The troops slept a few nours at the foot of the mountain, their horses revelling in a wheat-field, and started early enough to just escape from Forrest, who, with ten regiments of cavalry, was waiting to intercept the force.

Wilder got back to Manchester at one o'clock P.M., and reported to General Rosecrans, who was just betting two thousand dollars with General Stanley that they would get back, which they did, without the loss of a single man ; having marched one hundred and twenty-six miles in two days and a half, swam four streams, tore up three railroads, and got back safely — the tiredest set of mortals you ever saw.

General Rosecrans seemed delighted with the trip, and ordered the brigade here to feed and rest their horses preparatory to more of the same sort.

If it had not been for the incessant rains and consequent high water, we would as certainly have had Bragg's whole army as that we have Tullahoma now. As it is, he will escape across the Tennessee River, with the loss of nearly all his Tennessee troops, who are deserting in squads, coming in and taking the oath of allegiance, swearing that they are tired of the war and will die before they go into service again.

Bragg has lost more by evacuation than he would have done by defeat.

Wilder's command is now here, resting and feeding their horses, preparatory to another trip to the territories of King Jeff. * *

Doc. 38.

CAPTURE OF PORT HUDSON.

OFFICIAL CORRESPONDENCE.

HEADQUARTERS OF THE NINETEENTH ARMY CORPS,
DEPARTMENT OF THE GULF,
PORT HUDSON, July 9.

GENERAL : I have the honor to inform you that Port Hudson surrendered yesterday morning without conditions. We took possession at seven o'clock this morning. The number of prisoners and guns is unknown as yet, but is estimated at five thousand prisoners and fifty pieces of artillery. Very respectfully,

Brigadier-General W. H. EMORY,
Commanding Defences of New-Orleans.

RICHARD B. IRWIN,
A. A. General.

To Major-General Banks, Commanding United States Forces near Port Hudson :

HEADQUARTERS PORT HUDSON, LA., July 7.

GENERAL : Having received information from your troops that Vicksburgh has been surrendered, I make this communication to ask you to give me the official assurance whether this is true or not, and if true I ask for a cessation of hostilities with a view to the consideration of terms for surrendering this position.

I am, General, very respectfully, your obedient servant,

FRANK GARDNER,
Major-General Commanding C. S. Forces.

HEADQUARTERS DEPARTMENT OF THE GULF,
BEFORE PORT HUDSON, July 8.

To Major-General Frank Gardner, Commanding C. S. Forces, Port Hudson :

GENERAL : In reply to your communication dated the seventh instant, by flag of truce received a few moments since, I have the honor to inform you that I received yesterday morning, July seventh, at forty-five minutes past ten o'clock, by the gunboat General Price, an official despatch from Major-General Ulysses S. Grant, U. S. army, whereof the following is a true extract :

HEADQUARTERS DEPARTMENT OF THE TENNESSEE,
NEAR VICKSBURGH, July 4.

To Major-General N. P. Banks, Commanding Department of the Gulf :

GENERAL : The garrison of Vicksburgh surrendered this morning. The number of prisoners, as given by the officers, is twenty-seven thousand ; field artillery, one hundred and twenty-eight pieces ; and a large number of siege-guns, probably not less than eighty.

Your obedient servant, U. S. GRANT,
Major-General.

I regret to say, that under present circumstances, I cannot, consistently with my duty, consent to a cessation of hostilities for the purpose you indicate.

Very respectfully, your obedient servant,

N. P. BANKS,
Major-General Commanding.

PORT HUDSON, July 8.

To Major-General Banks, Commanding U. S. Forces :

GENERAL : I have the honor to acknowledge the receipt of your communication of this date, giving a copy of an official communication from Major-General U. S. Grant, U. S. A., announcing the surrender of the garrison of Vicksburgh.

Having defended this position as long as I deem my duty requires, I am willing to surrender to you, and will appoint a commission of three officers to meet a similar commission appointed by yourself at nine o'clock this morning, for the purpose of agreeing upon and drawing up the terms of the surrender, and for that purpose I ask for a cessation of hostilities. Will you please designate a point outside of my breastworks where the meeting shall be held for this purpose?

I am, very respectfully, your obedient servant,

FRANK GARDNER, Commanding C. S. Forces.

HEADQUARTERS UNITED STATES FORCES, }
BEFORE PORT HUDSON, July 8. }

To Major-General Frank Gardner, Commanding C. S. Forces, Port Hudson:

GENERAL: I have the honor to acknowledge the receipt of your communication of this date, stating that you are willing to surrender the garrison under your command to the forces under my command, and that you will appoint a commission of three officers to meet a similar commission appointed by me, at nine o'clock this morning, for the purpose of agreeing upon and drawing up the terms of surrender.

In reply I have the honor to state that I have designated Brigadier-General Charles P. Stone, Colonel Henry W. Birge, and Lieutenant-Colonel Richard B. Irwin as the officers to meet the commission appointed by you. They will meet your officers at the hour designated at a point where the flag of truce was received this morning. I will direct that active hostilities shall entirely cease on my part until further notice, for the purpose stated.

Very respectfully, your most obedient servant,

N. P. BANKS,
Major-General Commanding.

The following were the articles of capitulation proposed between the commissioners on the part of the garrison of Port Hudson, La., and the forces of the United States before said place, July eighth, 1863:

ARTICLE 1. Major-General Frank Gardner surrendered to the United States forces under Major-General Banks, the place of Port Hudson and its dependencies, with its garrison, armament, munitions, public funds, material of war, in the condition as nearly as may be in which they were at the hour of cessation of hostilities, namely, six o'clock A.M., July eighth, 1863.

ARTICLE 2. The surrender stipulated in Article 1 is qualified by no condition, save that the officers and enlisted men composing the garrison shall receive the treatment due to prisoners of war, according to the usages of civilized warfare.

ARTICLE 3. All private property of officers and enlisted men shall be inspected and left to their respective owners.

ARTICLE 4. The position of Port Hudson shall be occupied to-morrow at seven o'clock A.M. by the forces of the United States, and its garrison received as prisoners of war by such general officers of the United States service as may be designated by Major-General Banks, with the ordinary formalities of rendition. The confederate troops will be drawn up in line, officers in their positions, the right of the line resting on the edge of the prairie south of the railroad depot, the left extending in the direction of the village of Port Hudson. The arms and colors will be piled conveniently, and will be received by the officers of the United States.

ARTICLE 5. The sick and wounded of the garrison will be cared for by the authorities of the United States, assisted, if desired, by either party of the medical officers of the garrison.

CHARLES P. STONE,
Brigadier-General.
W. N. MILES,
Colonel Commanding Right Wing of the Army.
WM. DWIGHT,
Brigadier-General.
G. W. STEEDMAN,
Colonel Commanding Left Wing of the Army.
MARSHAL J. SMITH,
Lieutenant-Colonel, Chief of Artillery.
HENRY W. BIRGE,
Colonel Commanding Fifth Brigade, Grover's Division.
N. P. BANKS,
Major-General.
FRANK GARDNER,
Major-General.

A NATIONAL ACCOUNT.

HEADQUARTERS PORT HUDSON, }
Thursday, July 9, 1863. }

Heaven be praised! Port Hudson is ours!

In my late letters I have informed you how, step by step, we were encroaching upon the enemy, until all resistance would be useless. Somewhere about midnight of the seventh, a Lieutenant of Holcomb's battery came to the tent of Major-General Augur's Assistant Adjutant-General, and said that the enemy were sounding a bugle, which foreboded he knew not what. Shortly afterward another came to say that they had sent out a flag of truce. Very soon after that an officer came galloping up, in the bright light of a waning moon, from General Banks's headquarters; and I heard the voice of Colonel Irwin eagerly inquiring for the tent of General Augur—the whole camp being in calm repose. The few who were awake wondered, of course, what all this could mean; and what it did the official correspondence will best explain.

At the earliest dawn of the—now ever memorable—ninth July, the whole camp was necessarily in the highest state of glee and commotion, and the "Star-Spangled Banner," "Yankee Doodle," and "Dixie" came borne upon the morning air—never sounding sweeter.

At seven o'clock, General Andrews, Chief of the Staff of General Banks, made his grand entrance into the rebel fortifications, with Colonel Birge leading his brave storming column, whose noble services have thus been, happily for their friends, dispensed with; but to whom the country is no less indebted—taking the will for the deed. These were followed by two picked regiments from each division, with Holcomb's and Rawle's battery of light artillery, and the gunners of the naval battery.

The rebels were drawn up in line, and an immense line they made, their officers in front of them on one side of the road, their backs to the river. General Gardner then advanced toward General Andrews, and, in a few accompanying words, offered to surrender his sword with Port Hudson; but General Andrews told him that, in appreciation of his bravery—however misdirected—he was at liberty to retain his sword.

Our men were then drawn up in two lines on the other side of the road, opposite to the rebels, and our officers placed themselves in front of their men. General Gardner then said to General Andrews: "General, I will now formally surrender my command to you, and for that purpose will give the orders to ground arms." The order was given and the arms were grounded.

After that General Andrews sent for the enemy's general officers, staff and field-officers. The line-officers were left with their companies and guard, composed of the Twenty-second Louisiana and Seventy-fifth New-York, placed over them. These formalities over, the glorious old flag of the Union was unfolded to the breeze from one of the highest bluffs facing the river, by the men of the Richmond—a battery thundered forth its salute, which rolled majestically up and down the broad surface of the Mississippi—and Port Hudson was ours!

WHAT WE OBTAINED WITH IT.

Five thousand prisoners, as stated by General Gardner himself.

Serviceable: Three forty-two pound barbette guns; two thirty-two pound barbette guns; one thirty-two pound barbette gun, (rifled;) one eight-inch barbette gun; two ten-inch barbette guns; one twenty-four pound barbette gun; four twenty-four pound barbette guns, (rifled;) one twelve-pound barbette gun.

Disabled: One twenty-four pound barbette gun; one eight-inch barbette gun; one thirty-two pound barbette gun; one twenty-four pound barbette gun; one thirty-pound barbette gun.

Recapitulation: Fifteen heavy guns, in good condition; five complete field-batteries, thirty-one guns in good condition, besides disabled guns; one thousand nine hundred and eleven shot and shell for heavy guns, various calibres; seven hundred and seventy-five cartridges; twelve thousand pounds of powder, made up in cartridges, for heavy guns, various calibres; thirty-two thousand pounds cannon powder; one hundred and fifty thousand cartridges, small arms; five thousand muskets.

It was with no little delight that I found myself riding at last over every portion of this long-forbidden ground, noting the havoc which our cannon made not only in the ramparts but over the whole internal surface. Not a square rood but bore some indisputable proof of the iron deluge that had fallen upon it, in earth ploughed up, trees with the bark almost completely torn off by rifle-shot, and some—twice the bulk of a man's body—fairly snapped in two by some solid ball, as easily as a walking-cane.

As to what they called the town of Port Hudson—a miserable little conglomeration of two or wooden buildings, and a nondescript church among them—the destruction is so complete that I cannot see how they escaped being utterly swept away. I went into the old church, looking out for any crazy timber that might fall from shattered roof or tumbling walls, with orifices made by cannon, larger than the windows, and found the whole floor strewed with beans, broken beams and laths, plaster, etc. If those were all

the beans they had left, I don't think the quantity of their food exceeded the quality; and beans were what they had left to most depend upon.

Their river fortifications were terribly effective, and might have resisted any amount of attack had they been impregnable elsewhere. Far down in the bowels of the lofty bluffs they had dug deep recesses, approached by steps cut out of the earth, and here their magazines were placed quite safe—owing to the enormous thickness of earth above—from any projectiles that could be sent against them. One or two "quaker guns" were found. On the fortifications to the land side, every thing told of the terrible efficiency of our artillery, which never did its work better. Foremost among these were Mack's, Holcomb's, and Rawle's batteries, the Indiana battery, and the naval battery of heavy guns, under the gallant Lieutenant Terry, of the Richmond, and his fine crew, who sent desolation along with every shot from their large pieces. The effect was, that soon after we began bombarding in earnest, every gun upon the front batteries was silenced; and they have so remained for weeks since; any one they replaced being knocked over as soon as we got the range of it. In speaking of how much we owe the artillery, we cannot speak too highly of the unsparing exertions and skilful dispositions of General Arnold, under whom the whole of this arm of the service was placed.

Collateral praise must necessarily fall upon those faithful underworkers who, although unseen at the surface, have nevertheless the most mighty results depending upon the accuracy and promptness of their observations—I mean the Topographical Engineers under Major Houston. Foremost among these were Lieutenant Ulfers, Mr. Oltmans, Mr. Robins, and the lamented Mr. Luce, who was killed a short time ago while in the act of taking an observation. The enormous amount of personal hardships and dangers these gentlemen have to undergo, after going far ahead of the army and little exploring expeditions of their own in the enemy's country—the coolness and self-possession which their services require of them in every emergency, are things of which few people probably think, but which, nevertheless, have the most momentous bearing upon the success or failure of a general's plan of attack. They are the real scouts and pioneers, who have first detected many a new move of the enemy, and who first espy every new earth-work thrown up silently over night—every new gun put in position.

As we rode along the earth-works inside, it was curious to mark the ingenious ways in which the enemy had burrowed holes to shelter themselves from shell and the intolerable rays of the sun. While at their work they must have looked like so many rabbits popping in and out of their warren. The breastworks, instead of being straight at the top, present a continuous succession of little hills and valleys, from the perpetual ploughing up of our artillery. As to the guns, there were many of them knocked clean away from their carriages, and looking as if some earthquake had heaved up the earth from under them. The amount of mortality and casualties from all this terrible and continuous cannonading fell amazingly short of what I should have imagined. The rebels assert that it did not exceed seven hundred and eighty.

Many opportunities were naturally afforded for feeling the pulse of the rebels after two such overwhelming discomfitures. They seemed to bear it with great composure, whether real or feigned, I know not, but I think they were quite as glad to see us enter as we were to come in. Our men were to be seen everywhere mingling and exchanging notes freely with them. They were certainly a much finer looking set of fellows than I expected to meet in starving men; for it is no longer denied that they were getting to the last extremity for food. Indeed a friend of mine had the curiosity to lunch off a piece of their *mule's tongue*, and he said the only difference he found was that it was a little poor, compared with ox-tongue.

While standing on a cliff, calmly and pleasantly contemplating the fleet of busy steamers already sending up their well-accustomed noise and smoke under our newly conquered territory, and admiring the beauty of the Union flag as its graceful form waved sharp and clear against the blue sky, a rebel captain, gaily dressed—(the officers were all arrayed as if for some grand parade)—came up to me and said, thoughtfully:

"It is a long time, sir, since we have seen so many vessels lying there."

"Yes, sir, and I am glad of it, for *your* sake as well as *ours*," I replied.

"How so?" he asked in a somewhat surprised tone.

"Because," said I, "it looks to me very much like the beginning of the end; and that is what we all wish to see."

"The *end* is very far off yet," he continued in a proud manner. "In the first place, I do not believe, even now, that Vicksburgh is lost to us; and you never yet knew a rebellion of such magnitude to fail in achieving its object."

"Nor did you ever know a rebellion so causeless and unnatural to succeed," was my reply. "If you were like Poles or Circassians, and we Russians, trying to crush out your existing nationality—if this were a war of religion or of races, I could imagine it lasting through many, many years. But it is not so. Instead of trying to crush out your nationality, we are merely fighing to prevent you from crushing out our mutual one; and every acre, every liberty we save from destruction is as much yours as ours. War for such a cause was never waged before, and therefore cannot last. When a few more decisive successes like the present shall have proved beyond all doubt to the Southern people that the cause of separation is utterly hopeless, I think we shall all be glad to meet again as citizens of a common country, greater for the very ordeal through which it has passed. The only difference will be that Slavery — the cause of all this trouble—will have died during the progress of the war."

"We shall see," said the captain, either unwilling or unable to maintain his position further. "I suppose you will allow we defended our position here well."

"Too well," I replied; "I think a great many good lives, on both sides, might have been saved by sooner surrendering a place which, it must have been evident, you could not possibly retain."

"We should have done so," he candidly avowed, "only we were all the while hoping for reënforcements."

After a few more polite remarks, I left him for another part of the field. He was a young officer from Maryland, and said he had not seen his home for three years. Surely, never were more splendid zeal and courage exhibited in a worse cause.

General Gardner is a man of about forty-five, apparently, tall and erect, with well-developed dark-brown beard and moustache, and of quite a martial bearing.

When the ceremonies of a formal surrender were over, he came, in company with General Stone, to make a call on General Augur, on his way to the headquarters of General Banks. He and his staff seemed to be quite at home, and nobody, in looking at them, could feel that they were the people who had just been causing all this terrible outpouring of Northern blood.

I suppose it is all very chivalrous, brave, and according to the regular military code of etiquette; but while seeing the attentions paid to these worthies, I could not help wondering if they were as polite to us. I could not help coming to a negative conclusion when an officer, of some rank in our army—in looking at the gay cavalcade, as General Banks and staff, with a full escort, accompanied by General Gardner and some of his officers, came up to General Augur's headquarters—whispered in my ear the following grave contrast:

"When I, an officer of the United States army, was confined in the Libby Prison, we were not even allowed to look out of a window under penalty of death. A brother officer—only a few feet from me—in innocently going to a window to hang something on a peg, was deliberately shot in the region of the heart by an infernal villain below, called a sentinel. At another time the sentinel, seeing a man looking out of a window in the second story of the same building, deliberately fired at him.

"The ball missed the intended victim; but, passing through the second floor into the story above, killed a poor fellow who was at the further end of the room doing nothing! These things I know to be so, for I was there and saw them!"

I am told that the rebels now treat our prisoners just as well as we treat theirs. The country will be glad to know that it is so, and that if they cannot afford champagne to their brave prisoners, they at least show them the same polite attentions and allow them the same latitude of visiting families in the neighborhood. It will be equally satisfactory to know that this lovely spirit of humanity and chivalry does not exist alone at Richmond, but among the chivalrous cut-throats of Missouri, Tennessee, and Texas. The rebels hung Colonel Montgomery in Texas recently, and Colonel Davis nearly escaped the same fate. If it be argued that these men were deserters, pray what is Gardner himself? We feast their officers with liberty and champagne. Which code of etiquette is the right one our military authorities must determine; but, in the name of common-sense, let the rule be uniform and reciprocal.

After the two attempts made to reduce Port Hudson by a land assault, or rather the reconnoissances in force to that effect, on the twenty-seventh May and fourteenth June, General Banks showed great judgment and humanity in not attempting it again until he had fully invested the place by a series of irresistible approaches.

His wisdom in this matter is proved not only by the very difficult nature of the ground we found within the fortification—full of deep and impenetrable ravines, where a very small force could oppose a large one—but by the testimony of Gardner himself. It is really pleasurable to look back now and see how much blood has been saved that might have been uselessly shed.

General Gardner says (and I give you this as no idle gossip, but I know to be so)—that Vicksburgh only made a difference to him of three days. That he had made up his mind to surrender at the expiration of that time, and that any serious demonstration would have brought out a flag at any moment. We learn from this, that the glory of Port Hudson is not to be hidden in the larger but fuller one of Vicksburgh; but must stand upon its own intrinsic individuality; a result of certain irresistible combination, and not the mere sequence of a previous disaster to the rebels.

General Gardner also says that the very day our lines closed in on him—May twenty-fourth—brought him, by a courier who came through safely, a positive order from General Johnston to evacuate the post. This shows the wonderful rapidity and dexterity with which General Banks wheeled his army round from Alexandria and Baton Rouge upon the unsuspecting rebel chief, and should never be lost sight of in forming a fair estimate of this very brilliant military movement.

Two grand things are taught us by both Vicksburgh and Port Hudson—(so like in their aim, details and results, that Colonel Smith, of General Grant's staff, while riding along our intrenchments, said he could not help "fancying he was at Vicksburgh")—and those are: First, that there is nothing like dash and determined, rapid aggressive movement against the enemy we are contending with; and second, that there is no hole now in which he can hide himself, from which we cannot—with time and proper appliances—dislodge him, as surely as a ferret upon the track of a rat.

Vol. VII.—Doc. 14.

THE FLEET.

This great arm of our service, which has hitherto reaped the far greater share of glory in positive successes, and which, on the first grand attack upon Port Hudson, had the honor all to itself, cannot on this last occasion claim but a secondary part. The army has really done the work; aided by the navy, of course, to some extent, but not materially.

Owing to the excessive fall in the river, which left Port Hudson perched high upon its impregnable cliffs, the cannonading from the fleet did little more than bother and harass them with perpetual noise; but causing—so they all declare—very little damage. It was the terrific potency of our land-batteries they dreaded; the horrible skirmishers and sharp-shooters who, night and day, were perpetually popping away at every head that showed itself at the breastworks during the entire week; and—worse than all—it was that entire cutting him off from all supplies and communication—literally walling them in by fire—which brought them to at last.

Still, we must not forget that in this work on land the sailors took a very important part. The marine battery, directed by Lieutenant Terry, of the Richmond—the same who so conspicuously distinguished himself in the grand attack upon Port Hudson—and the gallant crew under him, did their work so effectively, soon after they began, that they had no gun to stand against them.

At this juncture came out General Banks's call for a storming party of one thousand. Lieutenant Terry was among the foremost of the volunteers. Owing, however, to the assault being delayed, and Captain Alden, of the Richmond, having left on account of ill-health, Lieutenant Terry was commanded to return to his vessel. Though disappointed in his aim, his bravery was none the less conspicuous.

Nothing can be more amusing than the notion the rebels seem to have of their utter invincibility. I mentioned before how my quondam friend, the captain, said he did not believe, even then, that Vicksburgh had capitulated. Another amusing instance came to my knowledge. News having reached us on the seventh instant of the fall of Vicksburgh, Colonel Nelson, commanding the colored regiment on our right, received official intelligence of the same from his commander, General Grover.

It appears that Colonel Nelson's approaches upon the enemy had got so very close—only twenty feet apart—that, by mutual concession, they had stopped the murderous work of perpetually shooting at each other, and the officers and men used to come out from the opposite sides and have quite a pleasant confab. This had gone on for three days, hourly expecting the order for an assault.

When Nelson got his delightful information, happening to meet a rebel colonel, he told him the fact and showed him the document. "I'm not a betting man," said the colonel, "and don't know that you are, but I will bet you an even hundred that this is not so."

"Done," said Nelson; "I have not one hundred dollars with me, but here is my gold watch as a stake." The watch and the one hundred dollars were put into the hands of another rebel officer and taken into Port Hudson; and this before there were any symptoms of Gardner's surrender! Colonel Van Pettin, one of the storming party, happening to come up with a similar notice to Nelson's in his pocket, the rebel colonel seemed inclined to back out of his bet, but Colonel Nelson held him to it, and has, since the surrender of Port Hudson, received back his watch and the hundred dollars, in confederate notes—worth nothing to him, of course, but little pictorial mementoes of a curious event of the war. I have no doubt whatever that it was this little sporting transaction which first gave Gardner an inkling of his position, and led to the correspondence which terminated in a capitulation of the place.

One more point and I close my remarks about the capitulation of Port Hudson. I am sorry to say that rumors are afloat, borne out, unfortunately, too strongly by facts, that our colored soldiers who have fallen into the hands of the rebels have not received the treatment recognized by civilized nations. In other words, we could find no negro prisoners in Port Hudson, and there were none in the hospital. The simple question is, Where are they? I leave each one to draw his own conclusion, merely saying that I consider this a matter fully warranting the investigation of our authorities.* NEMO.

Doc. 39.

REBEL CONSCRIPTION.

PROCLAMATION BY JEFFERSON DAVIS.

WHEREAS, it is provided by an act of Congress, entitled, "An act to further provide for the public defence," approved on the sixteenth day of April, 1862, and by another act of Congress, approved on the twenty-seventh September, 1862, entitled, "An act to amend an act entitled an act to provide further for the public defence," approved sixteenth April, 1862, that the President be authorized to call out and place in the military service of the confederate States, for three years, unless the war shall have sooner ended, all white men who are residents of the confederate States between the ages of eighteen and forty-five years, at the time the call may be made, and who are not at such time legally exempted from military service, or such part thereof as in his judgment may be necessary to the public defence.

And whereas, in my judgment the necessities of the public defence require that every man capable of bearing arms, between the ages aforesaid, should now be called out to do his duty in the

defence of his country, and in driving back the invaders now within the limits of the Confederacy.

Now, therefore, I, Jefferson Davis, President of the confederate States of America, do by virtue of the powers vested in me as aforesaid, call out and place in the military service of the confederate States, all white men residents of said States between the ages of eighteen and forty-five years, not legally exempted from military service; and I do hereby order and direct that all persons subject to this call and not now in the military service, do, upon being enrolled, forthwith repair to the conscript camps established in the respective States of which they may be residents, under pain of being held and punished as deserters in the event of their failure to obey this call, as provided in said laws.

And I do further order and direct that the enrolling officers of the several States proceed at once to enroll all persons embraced within the terms of this proclamation, and not heretofore enrolled.

And I do further order that it shall be lawful for any person embraced within this call to volunteer for service before enrolment, and that persons so volunteering be allowed to select the arm of service and the company which they desire to join, provided such company be deficient in the full number of men allowed by law for its organization.

Given under my hand and the seal of the confederate States of America, at the city of Richmond, this fifteenth day of July, in the year of our Lord one thousand eight hundred and sixty-three. JEFFERSON DAVIS.

By the President.
J. P. BENJAMIN,
Secretary of State.

Doc. 40.

GOVERNOR BROWN'S PROCLAMATION.

AN APPEAL TO THE GEORGIANS.

THE late serious disasters to our arms at Vicksburgh and Port Hudson, together with General Bragg's retreat with his army to our very borders, while they are no cause of despair of ultimate success, if we are true to ourselves and place our trust in God, admonish us that, if we would protect our homes from the ravages of the enemy, it is time for every Georgian able to bear arms to unite himself without delay with a military organization, and hold himself in readiness at a moment's warning to strike for his home and the graves of his ancestors, with an unalterable determination to die free rather than live the slave of despotic power.

Tens of thousands of our fellow-citizens have volunteered for the war, and those of them who have not been slain or disabled are still risking every thing for our success in distant fields upon the borders of the Confederacy. On account of the near approach of the enemy to the interior the call is now upon those at home, who have made comparatively little sacrifice, to volunteer

* See "The Siege of Port Hudson."

to defend their own habitations and property, and the homes and families of their neighbors who are in the army, against the threatened attacks of the enemy.

Is there a Georgian able to bear arms so lost, not only to patriotism, but to all the nobler impulses of our nature, that he will in this emergency refuse to take up arms for the defence of his home and his family, when the enemy comes to his very door to destroy the one and insult and cruelly injure other ? If there be a Georgian possessed of so little courage or manliness, let his fellow-citizens mark and remember him. If he hides himself behind some legal exemption as a mere pretext to avoid duty, let him be exposed to the censure he deserves ; or if, in his anxiety to make money and become rich, he turns a deaf ear to the promptings of patriotism, and would sacrifice his liberties to his avarice, let him be exposed with indignant scorn to public contempt. The time has come for plain talk and prompt action. All that is dear to a people on earth is at stake. The best efforts of every patriot are required to save our cause from ruin and our children from bondage. We are determined to be a free people, cost what it may ; and we should permit no man to remain among us and enjoy the protection of the government who refuses to do his part to secure our independence.

If all our people at home will organize for home defence, and the Secretary of War will issue and enforce such orders as will compel the thousands of persons in confederate service who, on account of the wealth of parents or political influence, or other like causes, are now keeping out of the reach of danger—as passport agents, impressment agents, useless subalterns connected with the different departments, including other favorites of those in position, stragglers, etc., many of whom are suspected of riding over the country at public expense, engaged on private speculations, enrolling officers in counties where the officers exempt are almost as numerous as the conscripts now in the counties subject to enrolment, and the host of officers in uniform, and others, who are daily seen in every city, town, and village, and upon every railroad train, and in every hotel in the Confederacy—to return immediately to their respective commands in the field, we should soon have armies strong enough to roll back the dark cloud of war which hangs over us, and drive the invaders from our soil.

By reference to the General Order herewith published, it will be seen that a draft will be had on Tuesday, the fourth day of August next, in each county in this State which neglects or refuses to furnish the quota of men required of it.

Though some few of the counties have exhibited too little interest, I cannot believe that a single one will have its character stained by the necessity for a draft to defend their own homes.

To those counties which have nobly and promptly responded, and especially to those which have tendered much more than their quota, I return my sincere thanks.

While the militia officers of this State have generally responded promptly and willingly, I regret to learn that some of them, in contradiction of all the professions they have made, having remained at home for home defence, now refuse to volunteer. To all such I hereby give notice that if they fail to come out themselves as volunteers with the organizations now called for, and to enter the service as invited in my proclamation calling for eight thousand troops by the fourth of August next, the protection of the State against conscription will be withdrawn from them, and they will be turned over to the enrolling officers under the conscript act. If, however, any militia officer, when approached by the conscript officer, will make an affidavit that he has not heard of or seen this proclamation, or had notice of it, he shall have five days from that date within which to join one of the companies now called for as a volunteer.

This rule does not embrace any one connected with the staff of the Commander-in-Chief, as they are expected to hold themselves in readiness at all times to obey his orders, and are not expected to join these companies. All justices of the peace and constables are to be subject to the same rule as militia officers, as their offices are not now so important that they cannot be spared to do local and temporary service in the defence of the State.

In protecting State officers against conscription, I have acted upon what I consider an important principle. If any of them now refuse to aid in the defence of their homes, it will be proper that the State withdraw its protection from such in future.

Let no one despair of ultimate success. We should not expect to be victorious on every field. The splendid achievements of our arms in the past have made us an historical people, and have clearly foreshadowed the final triumph of our arms and the future glory and grandeur of the Confederacy. Such a people, inhabiting such a country, and having such mothers, wives, sisters, and daughters, need only be true to themselves, and humbly trust in Almighty power, to be invincible.

Given under my hand and seal of the Executive Department, this July seventeenth, 1863.

JOSEPH E. BROWN.

Doc. 41.

THE ATTACK ON FORT WAGNER.

NEW-YORK "TRIBUNE" ACCOUNT.

MORRIS ISLAND, S. C., July 19, 1863.

AGAIN Fort Wagner has been assaulted and again we have been repulsed, and with, I regret to say, a much more formidable loss in killed, wounded, and missing than in the first attempt.

The first assault failed, as I stated in my last letter, on account of the tardiness of the Seventy-sixth Pennsylvania and the Ninth Maine to properly support the successful assault of the Seventh Connecticut, who were left alone on the parapet and within the ditches of the Fort to battle with the whole rebel garrison.

In the assault of the eleventh instant, but one brigade, and that a very small one, under the command of General Strong, were engaged; in that of last evening a whole division, consisting of three full brigades, were drawn out in line to take part in the action, but on account of some misunderstanding of orders, but two actually participated in the fight.

Since the engagement of the eleventh, General Gillmore has strained every nerve to strengthen his position on Morris Island, and so far as human foresight can discern, has made his lines of defence impregnable before advancing to the attack.

Three fourths of the island is in our possession; five batteries have been erected, in all containing nine thirty-pound and four twenty-pound Parrotts, and ten ten-inch mortars on the left, with two thirty-pound Parrotts, ten ten-inch mortars, and three full batteries of light artillery on the right. The earth-works protecting these guns have all been erected by the New-York volunteer engineers, under the direction of Captain Brooks and Lieuts. Mirché and Suter of General Gillmore's staff. During the action of yesterday, Lieutenant-Colonel Jackson, Chief of Artillery on General Gillmore's staff, commanded on the left, and Captain Langdon, of the First U. S. artillery, company M, on the right. The extreme right rests on the ocean beach; the extreme left on the edge of a swamp, about five hundred yards from the small creek separating Morris Island from James Island. The whole line of batteries sweeps in the form of a semicircle, and is at all points about one thousand eight hundred yards from Fort Wagner. Nearly all the guns upon the left are about four thousand yards from Fort Sumter; but being of light calibre compared with the one on that formidable structure, were not brought to bear upon her at any time during the action.

General Gillmore designed to commence the bombardment of the Fort at daylight yesterday morning, but on account of a terrific thunderstorm, which commenced early in the evening and continued until morning, delaying the work of the engineers and dampening the ammunition, the action did not open until half-past twelve. At that hour Admiral Dahlgren signalled that he was ready, and in a few moments the Montauk, (his flag-ship,) the Ironsides, the Catskill, the Nantucket, the Weehawken, and the Patapsco moved into line in the order in which I have named them, and commenced hurling their heaviest shot and shell around, upon, and within the Fort, and, with intervals of but a very few minutes, continued this terrible fire until one hour after the sun had gone down. During all the afternoon the iron fleet lay about one mile off from the Fort, but just at the close of the engagement, and but a few moments before the first assault was made by General Strong, the Admiral ran the Montauk directly under the guns of Fort Wagner, and, within two hundred and eighty

yards, fired round after round from his fifteen-inch gun, sending, as every shot struck, vast clouds of sand, mud, and timber high up into the air, making one huge sand-heap of that portion of the Fort facing the sea, and dismounting two of the heaviest guns.

Deserters and prisoners tell us that Fort Wagner mounts thirteen rifled guns of heavy calibre, but during all this furious bombardment by land and sea, she condescended to reply with but two—one upon the whole fleet of iron-clads, and one upon the entire line of land-batteries. She may possibly have fired one shot to our one hundred, but I think even that number is a large estimate. There were no casualties on the monitors or Ironsides, and but one man killed and one slightly wounded within the batteries. The firing was almost entirely from our own side. With the most powerful glass, but very few men could be seen in the Fort. At half-past two, a shot from one of our guns on the left cut the halyards on the flag-staff and brought the rebel flag fluttering to the ground.

In a moment, almost before we had begun to ask ourselves whether they had really lowered their flag, and were upon the point of surrendering or not, the old red battle-flag, which the army of the Potomac has so often had defiantly shaken in its face, was run up about ten feet above the parapet, a little cluster of men rallied around it, cheered, waved their hats, and then disappeared, and were not again seen during the day. Fort Sumter, the moment the rebel flag came to the ground, sent a shot over our heads to assure us that it had been lowered by accident and not by design. In this shot she also desired us to distinctly understand that before Fort Wagner surrendered, she herself would have to be consulted. With the exception of this little episode, almost profound silence, so far as the rebel garrison themselves could maintain it, prevailed within the Fort. A heavy cloud of smoke and sand, occasioned by our constantly exploding shell, hung over the Fort all the afternoon, and it was only when the wind drifted it away that we were able to see the amount of damage we had done. In a few hours what had been the smooth, regular lines of the engineer, and the beautiful sodded embankments, became rugged and irregular heaps of sand with great gaps and chasms in all the sides of the Fort exposed to our fire. From my point of observation, a wooden look-out, fifty feet high, erected for General Gillmore and staff upon a sand-hill of about the same height, and situated a short distance back of the batteries, it seemed as if no human being could live beneath so terrible a fire whether protected by bomb-proofs or not, and in this opinion I was fully sustained by nearly every person around me. There seemed to be but one opinion, and that was that we had silenced nearly every gun, that the fifteen-inch shells had driven the rebels from the bomb-proofs, and that if there had been a strong infantry force in the rear of the Fort we had made it impossible for them to remain there and had slaughtered them by hundreds. But there were a few later developments that proved their opinion was the correct one, who said this profound silence on the rebel side was significant, not of defeat and disaster, but of ultimate success in repulsing our assault; that they were keeping themselves under cover until they could look into the eyes of our men, and send bullets through their heads, and would then swarm by thousands, with every conceivable deadly missile in their hands, and drive us in confusion and with terrible slaughter back to our intrenchments.

The afternoon passed, and the heavy roar of the big guns on land and sea gradually ceased. Slowly and sullenly the monitors, with the exception of the Montauk, moved back to the anchorage ground of the morning. The music of the sublime billows, forever hymning their sublime chants, was again heard along the shore; the sun went down, not in golden glory, but in clouds of blackness and darkness, and mutterings of thunder and flashes of lightning. In the slight interval between the cessation of the cannonade and the assault at the point of the bayonet, the artillery of heaven opened all along the western horizon, and in peal after peal demonstrated how insignificant is the power of man when compared with that of Him who holds the elements in the hollow of his hand.

For eight hours the monitors and the Ironsides have kept up a continuous fire, and Fort Wagner has not yet surrendered. For eight hours fifty-four guns from the land-batteries have hurled their shot and shell within her walls, and still she flaunts the red battle-flag in our face.

"Something must be done, and that, too, quickly, or in a few days we shall have the whole army in Virginia upon us," said an officer high in command. "We *must* storm the Fort to-night and carry it at the point of the bayonet!"

In a few moments signals are made from the top of the look-out, and soon generals and colonels commanding divisions and brigades were seen galloping to the headquarters of the Commanding General. A few words in consultation, and Generals Seymour, Strong, Stevenson, and Colonels Putnam and Montgomery are seen hastening back to their respective commands. Officers shout, bugles sound, the word of command is given, and soon the soldiers around, upon, and under the sand-hills of Morris Island spring from their hiding-places, fall into line, march to the beach, are organized into new brigades, and in solid column stand ready to move to the deadly assault.

Not in widely extended battle-line, with cavalry and artillery at supporting distances, but in solid regimental column, on the hard ocean beach, for half a mile before reaching the Fort, in plain sight of the enemy, did these three brigades move to their appointed work.

General Strong, who has so frequently since his arrival in this department braved death in its many forms of attack, was assigned to the command of the First brigade. Colonel Putnam of the Seventh New-Hampshire, who, although of the regular army, and considered one of the best officers in the department, had never led his men into battle nor been under fire, took command of the Second, and General Stevenson the Third, constituting the reserve. The Fifty-fourth Massachusetts, (colored regiment,) Colonel Shaw, was the advanced regiment in the First brigade, and the Second South-Carolina, (negro,) Colonel Montgomery, was the last regiment of the reserve. The selection of the Fifty-fourth Massachusetts to lead the charge was undoubtedly made on account of the good fighting qualities it had displayed a few days before on James Island, an account of which you have in my letter of the seventeenth.

These brigades, as I have remarked before, were formed for this express duty. Many of the regiments had never seen their brigade commanders before; some of them had never been under fire, and, with exception of three regiments in the First brigade, none of them had ever been engaged in this form of attack. All had fresh in their memories the severe repulse we had met on the morning of the eleventh instant. For two years the department of the South had been in existence, and until the storming of the batteries on the south end of Morris Island the army had won no victory fairly acknowledged by the enemy.

Just as darkness began to close in upon the scene of the afternoon and the evening, General Strong rode to the front and ordered his brigade, consisting of the Fifty-fourth Massachusetts, Colonel Shaw, (colored regiment,) the Sixth Connecticut, Colonel Chatfield, the Forty-eighth New-York, Colonel Barton, the Third New-Hampshire, Colonel Jackson, the Seventy-sixth Pennsylvania and the Ninth Maine, Colonel Emery, to advance to the assault. At the instant, the line was seen slowly advancing in the dusk toward the Fort, and before a double-quick had been ordered, a tremendous fire from the barbette guns on Fort Sumter, from the batteries on Cumming's Point, and from all the guns on Fort Wagner, opened upon it. The guns from Wagner swept the beach, and those from Sumter and Cumming's Point enfiladed it on the left. In the midst of this terrible shower of shot and shell they pushed their way, reached the Fort, portions of the Fifty-fourth Massachusetts, the Sixth Connecticut, and the Forty-eighth New-York dashed through the ditches, gained the parapet, and engaged in a hand-to-hand fight with the enemy, and for nearly half an hour held their ground, and did not fall back until nearly every commissioned officer was shot down. As on the morning of the assault of the eleventh instant, these brave men were exposed to a most galling fire of grape and canister, from howitzers, raking the ditches from the bastions of the Fort, from hand-grenades, and from almost every other modern implement of warfare. The rebels fought with the utmost desperation, and so did the larger portion of General Strong's brigade, as long as there was an officer to command it.

When the brigade made the assault General Strong gallantly rode at its head. When it fell back, broken, torn, and bleeding, Major Plimpton of the Third New-Hampshire was the highest commissioned officer to command it. General Strong, Colonel Shaw, Colonel Chatfield, Colonel Barton, Colonel Green, Colonel Jackson, all had fallen; and the list I send you will tell how many other brave officers fell with them. Stories are flying about that this regiment and that regiment broke and run; that but for the frightened Fifty-fourth Massachusetts (negro) we would have carried the Fort; that the Ninth Maine did not reflect much honor upon the gallant State she represents, and a thousand other reasons which I care not to enumerate. It is absurd to say these men did not fight and were not exposed to perhaps the most deadly fire of the war, when so many officers and so many of the rank and file were killed. It must be remembered, too, that this assault was made in the night—a very dark night—even the light of the stars was obscured by the blackness of a heavy thunder-storm, and the enemy could be distinguished from our own men only by the light of bursting shell and the flash of the howitzer and the musket. The Fifty-fourth Massachusetts, (negro,) whom copperhead officers would have called cowardly if they had stormed and carried the gates of hell, went boldly into battle, for the second time, commanded by their brave Colonel, but came out of it led by no higher officer than the boy, Lieutenant Higginson.

The First brigade, under the lead of General Strong, failed to take the Fort. It was now the turn of Colonel Putnam, commanding the Second brigade, composed of the Seventh New-Hampshire, the Sixty-second Ohio, Colonel Steele, the Sixty-seventh Ohio, Colonel Vorhees, and the One Hundredth New-York, Colonel Dandy, to make the attempt. But alas! the task was too much for him. Through the same terrible fire he led his men to, over, and into the Fort, and for an hour held one half of it, fighting every moment of that time with the utmost desperation, and, as with the First brigade, it was not until he himself fell killed, and nearly all his officers wounded, and no reënforcements arriving, that his men fell back, and the rebel shout and cheer of victory was heard above the roar of Sumter and the guns from Cumming's Point.

In this second assault by Colonel Putnam's brigade, Colonel Turner, of General Gillmore's staff, stood at the side of Colonel Putnam when he fell, and with his voice and sword urged on the thinned ranks to the final charge. But it was too late. The Third brigade, General Stevenson's, was not on hand. It was madness for the Second to remain longer under so deadly a fire, and the thought of surrendering in a body to the enemy could not for a moment be entertained. To fight their way back to the intrenchments was all that could be done, and in this retreat many a poor fellow fell, never to rise again.

Without a doubt, many of our men fell from our own fire. The darkness was so intense, the roar of artillery so loud, the flight of grape and canister shot so rapid and destructive, that it was absolutely impossible to preserve order in the ranks of individual companies, to say nothing of the regiments.

More than half the time we were in the Fort, the fight was simply a hand-to-hand one, as the wounds received by many clearly indicate. Some have sword-thrusts, some are hacked on the head, some are stabbed with bayonets, and a few were knocked down with the butt-end of muskets, but recovered in time to get away with swollen heads. There was terrible fighting to get into the Fort, and terrible fighting to get out of it. The cowardly stood no better chance for their lives than the fearless. Even if they surrendered, the shell of Sumter were thickly falling around them in the darkness, and, as prisoners, they could not be safe, until victory, decisive and unquestioned, rested with one or the other belligerent.

The battle is over; it is midnight; the ocean beach is crowded with the dead, the dying, and the wounded. It is with difficulty you can urge your horse through to Lighthouse Inlet. Faint lights are glimmering in the sand-holes and rifle-pits to the right, as you pass down the beach. In these holes many a poor wounded and bleeding soldier has lain down to his last sleep. Friends are bending over them to staunch their wounds, or bind up their shattered limbs, but the deathly glare from sunken eyes tells that their kind services are all in vain.

In this night assault, and from its commencement to its close, General Gillmore, his staff, and his volunteer aids, consisting of Colonel Littlefield, of the Fourth South-Carolina, and Majors Bannister and Stryker, of the Paymaster's Department, were constantly under fire and doing all in their power to sustain the courage of the troops and urge on reënforcements. All that human power could do to carry this formidable earth-work seems to have been done. No one would have imagined in the morning that so fierce a cannonade from both the navy and the batteries on shore could fail to destroy every bomb-proof the rebels had erected. But the moment our men touched the parapets of the Fort one thousand three hundred strong streamed from their safe hiding-place, where they had been concealed during the day, and fresh and strong, were prepared to drive us back. We then found to our sorrow that the fifteen-inch shot from the monitors, even when fired at a distance of but one thousand and eighty yards, had not injured them in the least. Only the parapets of the Fort had been knocked into sand heaps.

In their proper places I forgot to mention that the gunboats Wissahickon, Captain Davis, the Chippewa, Captain Harris, the Paul Jones, Captain Buger, and the Ottawa, were also engaged in the bombardment at long-range, and that during every day of the week, from the tenth to the seventeenth, had been more or less engaged with the work.

The amount of shell thrown at Fort Wagner would almost build another Ironsides. N. P.

LETTER OF EDWARD L. PIERCE.

The following letter from Edward L. Pierce, Esq., was addressed to Governor Andrew, of Massachusetts:

BEAUFORT, July 22, 1863.

MY DEAR SIR: You will probably receive an official report of the losses in the Fifty-fourth Massachusetts by the mail which leaves to-morrow, but perhaps a word from me may not be unwelcome. I saw the officers and men on James Island on the thirteenth instant, and on Saturday last saw them at Brigadier-General Strong's tent, as they passed on at six or half-past six in the evening to Fort Wagner, which is some two miles beyond. I had been the guest of General Strong, who commanded the advance, since Tuesday. Colonel Shaw had become attached to General Strong at St. Helena, where he was under him, and the regard was mutual. When the troops left St. Helena they were separated, the Fifty-fourth going to James Island. While it was there General Strong received a letter from Colonel Shaw, in which the desire was expressed for the transfer of the Fifty-fourth to General Strong's brigade. So when the troops were brought away from James Island General Strong took this regiment into his command. It left James Island on Thursday, July sixteenth, at nine P.M., and marched to Cole's Island, which they reached at four o'clock on Friday morning, marching all night, most of the way in single file, over swampy and muddy ground. There they remained during the day, with hard tack and coffee for their fare, and this only what was left in their haversacks; not a regular ration. From eleven o'clock of Friday evening until four o'clock of Saturday they were being put on the transport, the General Hunter, in a boat which took about fifty at a time. There they breakfasted on the same fare, and had no other food before entering into the assault on Fort Wagner in the evening.

The General Hunter left Coles's Island for Folly Island at six A.M., and the troops landed at the Pawnee Landing about half-past nine A.M., and thence marched to the point opposite Morris Island, reaching there about two o'clock in the afternoon. They were transported in a steamer across the inlet, and at five P.M. began their march for Fort Wagner. They reached Brigadier-General Strong's quarters about midway on the Island, about six or half-past six, where they halted for five minutes. I saw them here, and they looked worn and weary.

General Strong expressed a great desire to give them food and stimulants, but it was too late, as they were to lead the charge. They had been without tents during the pelting rains of Thursday and Friday nights. General Strong had been impressed with the high character of the regiment and its officers, and he wished to assign them the post where the most severe work was to be done, and the highest honor was to be won. I had been his guest for some days, and knew how he regarded them. The march across Folly and Morris Islands was over a very sandy road, and was very wearisome. The regiment went through the centre of the island, and not along the beach where the marching was easier. When they had come within about one thousand six hundred yards of Fort Wagner, they halted and formed in line of battle—the Colonel leading the right and the Lieutenant-Colonel the left wing. They then marched four hundred yards further on and halted again. There was little firing from the enemy at this point, one solid shot falling between the wings, and another falling to the right, but no musketry.

At this point the regiment, together with the next supporting regiments, the Sixth Connecticut, Ninth Maine, and others, remained half an hour. The regiment was addressed by General Strong and Colonel Shaw. Then at half-past seven or a quarter before eight o'clock the order for the charge was given. The regiment advanced at quick time, changed to double-quick when at some distance on. The intervening distance between the place where the line was formed and the Fort was run over in a few minutes. When within one or two hundred yards of the Fort, a terrific fire of grape and musketry was poured upon them along the entire line, and with deadly results. It tore the ranks to pieces and disconcerted some. They rallied again, went through the ditch, in which were some three feet of water, and then up the parapet. They raised the flag on the parapet, where it remained for a few minutes. Here they melted away before the enemy's fire, their bodies falling down the slope and into the ditch. Others will give a more detailed and accurate account of what occurred during the rest of the conflict.

Colonel Shaw reached the parapet, leading his men, and was probably killed. Adjutant James saw him fall. Private Thomas Burgess of company I told me that he was close to Colonel Shaw; that he waved his sword and cried out, "Onward, boys!" and, as he did so, fell. Burgess fell, wounded, at the same time. In a minute or two, as he rose to crawl away, he tried to pull Colonel Shaw along, taking hold of his feet, which were near his own head, but there appeared to be no life in him. There is a report, however, that Colonel Shaw is wounded and a prisoner, and that it was so stated to the officers who bore a flag of truce from us, but I cannot find it well authenticated. It is most likely that this noble youth has given his life to his country and to mankind. Brigadier-General Strong (himself a kindred spirit) said of him to-day, in a message to his parents: "I had but little opportunity to be with him, but I already loved him. No man ever went more gallantly into battle. None knew him but to love him." I parted with Colonel Shaw between six and seven Saturday evening, as he rode forward to his regiment, and he gave me the private letters and papers he had with him to be delivered to his father. Of the other officers, Lieutenant-Colonel Hallowell is severely wounded in the groin; Adjutant James has a wound from a grape-shot in his ankle, and a flesh-wound in his side from a glancing ball or a piece of shell. Captain Pope has had a musket-ball extracted from his shoulder. Captain Appleton is wounded in the thumb, and also has a contusion on his right breast from a hand-grenade. Captain Willard has a wound in the leg, and is doing well. Captain Jones was wounded in the right shoulder. The ball went through and he is doing well. Lieutenant Homans wounded by a ball from a smooth-bore musket entering the left side, which has been extracted from the back. He is doing well.

The above-named officers are at Beaufort, all but the last arriving there on Sunday evening, whither they were taken from Morris Island to Pawnee Landing, in the Alice Price, and thence to Beaufort in the Cosmopolitan, which is specially fitted up for hospital service and is provided with skilful surgeons under the direction of Dr. Bontecou. They are now tenderly cared for with an adequate corps of surgeons and nurses and provided with a plentiful supply of ice, beef and chicken broth and stimulants. Lieutenant Smith was left at the hospital tent on Morris Island. Captain Emilio and Lieutenants Grace, Appleton, Johnston, Reed, Howard, Dexter, Jennison, and Emerson, were not wounded and are doing duty. Lieutenants Jewett and Tucker were slightly wounded and are doing duty also. Lieut. Pratt was wounded and came in from the field on the following day. Captains Russell and Simpkins are missing. The Quartermaster and Surgeon are safe and are with the regiment.

Dr. Stone remained on the Alice Price during Saturday night, caring for the wounded until she left Morris Island, and then returned to look after those who were left behind. The Assistant Surgeon was at the camp on St. Helena Island, attending to duty there. Lieutenant Littlefield was also in charge of the camp at St. Helena. Lieutenant Higginson was on Folly Island with a detail of eighty men. Captain Bridge and Lieutenant Walton are sick and were at Beaufort or vicinity. Captain Partridge has returned from the North, but not in time to participate in the action.

Of the privates and non-commissioned officers I send you a list of one hundred and forty-four who are now in the Beaufort hospitals. A few others died on the boats or since their arrival here. There may be others at the Hilton Head hospital; and others are doubtless on Morris Island; but I have no names or statistics relative to them. Those in Beaufort are well attended to—just as well as the white soldiers, the attentions of the surgeons and nurses being supplemented by those of the colored people here, who have shown a great interest in them. The men of the regiment are very patient, and where their condition at all permits them, are cheerful. They expressed their readiness to meet the enemy again, and they keep asking if Wagner is yet taken. Could any one from the North see these brave fellows as they lie here, his prejudice against them, if he had any, would all pass

away. They grieve greatly at the loss of Colonel Shaw, who seems to have acquired a strong hold on their affections. They are attached to their other officers, and admire General Strong, whose courage was so conspicuous to all. I asked General Strong if he had any testimony in relation to the regiment to be communicated to you. These are his precise words, and I give them to you as I noted them at the time:

"The Fifty-fourth did well and nobly, only the fall of Colonel Shaw prevented them from entering the Fort They moved up as gallantly as any troops could, and with their enthusiasm they deserved a better fate." The regiment could not have been under a better officer than General Strong. He is one of the bravest and most genuine men. His soldiers loved him like a brother, and go where you would through the camps you would hear them speak of him with enthusiasm and affection. His wound is severe, and there are some apprehensions as to his being able to recover from it. Since I found him at the hospital tent on Morris Island, about half-past nine o'clock on Saturday, I have been all the time attending to him or the officers of the Fifty-fourth, both on the boats and here. Nobler spirits it has never been my fortune to be with. General Strong, as he lay on the stretcher in the tent, was grieving all the while for the poor fellows who lay uncared for on the battle-field, and the officers of the Fifty-fourth have had nothing to say of their own misfortunes, but have mourned constantly for the hero who led them to the charge from which he did not return. I remember well the beautiful day when the flags were presented at Readville, and you told the regiment that your reputation was to be identified with its fame. It was a day of festivity and cheer. I walk now in these hospitals and see mutilated forms with every variety of wound, and it seems all a dream. But well has the regiment sustained the hope which you indulged, and justified the identity of fame which you trusted to it.

I ought to add in relation to the fight on James Island, on July sixteenth, in which the regiment lost fifty men, driving back the rebels, and saving, as it is stated, three companies of the Tenth Connecticut, that General Terry, who was in command on that Island, said to Adjutant James:

"Tell your Colonel that I am exceedingly pleased with the conduct of your regiment. They have done all they could do."

Yours truly,   EDWARD L. PIERCE.

Doc. 42.

SPEECH OF ALEX. H. STEPHENS.

RICHMOND, July 25, 1863.

VICE-PRESIDENT Stephens, who is on his way to the South, stopped at Charlotte, N. C., on Friday night, and was serenaded by a large concourse of citizens. In reply he made them a speech about an hour in length. He commenced by alluding to the invasion of Maryland and

Pennsylvania by General Lee's army; said that it had whipped the enemy on their own soil, and obtained vast supplies for our own men, and was now ready to again meet the enemy on a new field. Whatever might be the movements and objects of General Lee, he had entire confidence in his ability to accomplish what he undertook, for in ability and intellect he was a head and shoulders above any man in the Yankee army. He commended General Lee for keeping his own secrets, and told the people not to be discouraged because they did not hear from Lee over his own signature. He would come out all right in the end.

Mr. Stephens next spoke of the surrender of Vicksburgh, and said that it was not an occurrence to cause discouragement or gloom; that the loss of Vicksburgh was not as severe a blow as the loss of Fort Pillow, Island Number Ten, or New-Orleans. The Confederacy had survived the loss of these points, and would survive the loss of Vicksburgh, Port Hudson, and other places. Suppose, said he, we were to lose Mobile, Charleston, and Richmond, it would not affect the *heart* of the Confederacy. We could and would survive such losses, and finally secure our independence. He was not at all discouraged at the prospect; he never had the "blues" himself, and had no respect or sympathy for "croakers." The enemy has already appropriated two billion seven hundred million dollars, and one million of men for our subjugation, and after two years' war had utterly failed, and if the war continued for two years longer, they would fail to accomplish our subjugation. So far they had not broken the shell of the Confederacy.

In the Revolutionary war the British at one time had possession of North-Carolina, South-Carolina, and other States; they took Philadelphia, and dispersed Congress, and for a long time held almost complete sway in the Colonies—yet they did not conquer our forefathers. In the war of 1812 the British captured the capital of the nation, Washington City, and burnt it, yet they did not conquer us; and if we are true to ourselves now, true to our birth-right, the Yankee nation will utterly fail to subjugate us. Subjugation would be utter ruin and eternal death to Southern people and all that they hold most dear. He exhorted the people to give the government a cordial support, to frown down all croakers and grumblers, and to remain united and fight to the bitter end for liberty and independence.

As for reconstruction, said Mr. Stephens, such a thing was impossible—such an idea must not be tolerated for an instant. Reconstruction would not end the war, but would produce a more horrible war than that in which we are now engaged. The only terms on which we can obtain permanent peace is final and complete separation from the North. Rather than submit to any thing short of that, let us all resolve to die like men worthy of freedom.

In regard to foreign intervention, Mr. Stephens advised his hearers to build no hopes on that yet awhile. He did not believe that the leading foreign powers ever intended that the North and South should be again united—they preferred that the separation should be permanent, but they considered both sides too strong now, and did not deem it good policy on their part to interfere and put a stop to the war. Foreign nations see that the result of the war will be to establish a despotism at the North, and are therefore willing to allow it to continue awhile longer.

The whole tone of Mr. Stephens's speech was very encouraging, and showed not the slightest sign of despondency. He concluded by expressing entire confidence in the ability of the Confederacy to maintain our cause and achieve independence.　　　　　—*Richmond Dispatch.*

Doc. 43.

THE BATTLE OF CHICKAMAUGA.

REPORT OF MAJOR-GENERAL ROSECRANS.

THE rebel army, after its expulsion from Middle Tennessee, crossed the Cumberland Mountains by way of the Tantallon and University roads, then moved down Battle Creek, and crossed the Tennessee River on bridges, it is said, near the mouth of Battle Creek, and at Kelly's Ferry, and on the railroad bridge at Bridgeport. They destroyed a part of the latter, after having passed over it, and retired to Chattanooga and Tyner Station, leaving guards along the river. On their arrival at Chattanooga, they commenced immediately to throw up some defensive field-works at that place, and also at each of the crossings of the Tennessee as far up as Blythe's Ferry.

Our troops, having pursued the rebels as far as supplies and the state of the roads rendered it practicable, took position from McMinnville to Winchester, with advances at Pelham and Stevenson. The latter soon after moved to Bridgeport in time to save from total destruction a saw-mill there, but not to prevent the destruction of the railroad bridge.

After the expulsion of Bragg's forces from Middle Tennessee, the next objective point of this army was Chattanooga. It commands the southern entrance into East-Tennessee, the most valuable, if not the chief sources of supplies of coal for the manufactories and machine-shops of the Southern States, and is one of the great gateways through the mountains to the champaign counties of Georgia and Alabama.

For the better understanding of the campaign, I submit a brief outline of the topography of the country, from the barrens of the north-western base of the Cumberland Range to Chattanooga and its vicinity.

The Cumberland-Range is a lofty mass of rocks separating the waters which flow into the Cumberland from those which flow into the Tennessee, and extending from beyond the Kentucky line, in a south-westerly direction, nearly to Athens, Alabama. Its north-western slopes are steep and rocky, and scalloped into coves, in which are the heads of numerous streams that water Middle Tennessee. Its top is undulating, or rough, covered with timber, soil comparatively barren, and in dry seasons scantily supplied with water. Its south-eastern slope, above Chattanooga, for many miles, is precipitous, rough, and difficult all the way up to Kingston. The valley between the foot of this slope and the river seldom exceeds four or five miles in width, and, with the exception of a narrow border along the banks, is undulating or hilly.

The Sequatchie Valley is along the river of that name, and is a canon, or deep cut, splitting the Cumberland Range parallel. It is only three or four miles in breadth and fifty in length. The sides of this valley are even more precipitous than the great eastern and western slopes of the Cumberland, which have just been described. To reach Chattanooga from McMinnville, or north of the Tennessee, it is necessary to turn the head of this valley by Pikeville and pass down the Valley of the Tennessee, or to cross it by Dunlap or Thurman.

That part of the Cumberland Range between Sequatchie and the Tennessee, called Walden's Ridge, abuts on the Tennessee, in high, rocky bluffs, having no practicable space sufficient for a good wagon-road along the river. The Nashville and Chattanooga Railroad crosses that branch of the Cumberland Range, west of the Sequatchie, through a low gap, by a tunnel, two miles east of Cowan, down the gorge of Big Crow Creek to Stevenson, at the foot of the mountain, on the Memphis and Charleston Railroad, three miles from the Tennessee and ten from Bridgeport.

Between Stevenson and Chattanooga, on the south of the Tennessee, are two ranges of mountains, the Tennessee River separating them from the Cumberland. Its channel, a great chasm cut through the mountain masses, which in those places abut directly on the river. These two ranges are separated by a narrow valley through which runs Lookout Creek.

The Sand Mountain is next the Tennessee, and its northern extremity is called Raccoon Mountain. Its sides are precipitous and its top barren oak ridges, nearly destitute of water. There are but few, and those very difficult, wagon-roads by which to ascend and descend the slopes of this mountain.

East of Lookout Valley is Lookout Mountain, a vast palisade of rocks rising two thousand four hundred feet above the level of the sea, in abrupt, rocky cliffs, from a steep, wooded base. Its eastern sides are no less precipitous. Its top varies from one to six or seven miles in breadth, is heavily timbered, sparsely settled, and poorly watered. It terminates abruptly upon the Tennessee, two miles below Chattanooga, and the only practical wagon-roads across it, are over the nose of the mountain, at this point, one at Johnson's Crook, twenty-six miles distant, and one at Winston's Gap, forty-two miles distant from Chattanooga.

Between the eastern base of this range, and the line of the Chattanooga and Atlanta or Georgia State Railroad are a series of narrow valleys, separated by smaller ranges of hills or low mountains, over which there are quite a number of practicable wagon-roads running eastward toward the railroad.

The first of these ranges is Missionary Ridge, separating the waters of Chickamauga from Chattanooga Creek.

A higher range with fewer gaps, on the southeast side of the Chickamauga, is Pigeon Mountain, branching from Lookout, near Dougherty's Gap, some forty miles south from Chattanooga. It extends in a northerly direction, bearing eastward, until it is lost in the general level of the country near the line of the Chattanooga and La Fayette road.

East of these two ranges and of the Chickamauga, starting from Ottowah and passing by Ringgold, to the west of Dalton, is Taylor's Ridge, a rough, rocky range, traversable by wagon-roads only, through gaps generally several miles apart.

Missionary Ridge passes about three miles east of Chattanooga, ending near the Tennessee at the mouth of the Chickamauga. Taylor's Ridge separates the East-Tennessee and Georgia Railroad from the Chattanooga and Atlanta Railroad.

The junction of these roads is at Dalton, in a valley east of Taylor's Ridge, and west of the rough mountain region, in which are the sources of the Cossa River. This valley, only about nine or ten miles wide, is the natural southern gateway into East-Tennessee, while the other valleys just mentioned terminate northwardly on the Tennessee to the west of it, and extend in a southwesterly direction toward the line of the Cossa, the general direction of which, from the crossing of the Atlanta road to Rome and thence to Gadsden, is south-west.

From the position of our army at McMinnville, Tullahoma, Decherd, and Winchester, to reach Chattanooga, crossing the Tennessee above it, it was necessary, either to pass north of the Sequatchie Valley, by Pikesville or Kingston, or to cross the main Cumberland and the Sequatchie Valley by Dunlap or Thurman and Walden's Ridge, by the routes passing through these places, a distance from sixty-five to seventy miles, over a country destitute of forage, poorly supplied with water, by narrow and difficult wagon-roads.

The main Cumberland Range could also have been passed, on an inferior road, by Pelham and Tracy City to Thurman.

The most southerly route on which to move troops and transportation to the Tennessee, above Chattanooga, was by Cown, University, Battle Creek, and Jasper, or by Tantallon, Anderson, Stevenson, Bridgeport, and the mouth of Battle Creek, to same point, and thence by Thurman, or Dunlap and Poe's Tavern, across Walden Ridge. The University Road, though difficult, was the best of these two, that by Cowan, Tantallon, and Stevenson being very rough between Cowan and Anderson, and much longer.

There were also three roads across the mountains to the Tennessee River below Stevenson, the best, but much the longest, by Fayetteville and Athens, a distance of seventy miles.

The next, a very rough wagon-road from Winchester by Salem, to Larkinsville, and an exceedingly rough road by the way of Mount Top, one branch leading thence to Bellefont and the other to Stevenson.

On these latter routes little or no forage was to be found, except at the extremities of the lines, and they were also scarce of water. The one by Athens has both forage and water in abundance.

It was evident from this description of the topography, that to reach Chattanooga, or penetrate the country south of it, on the railroad, by crossing the Tennessee below Chattanooga, was a difficult task. It was necessary to cross the Cumberland Mountains, with subsistence, ammunition, at least a limited supply of forage, and a bridge-train; to cross Sand or Raccoon Mountains into Lookout Valley, then Lookout Mountain, and finally the lesser ranges, Missionary Ridge, if we went directly to Chattanooga; or Missionary Ridge, Pigeon Mountain, and Taylor's Ridge, if we struck the railroad at Dalton, or south of it. The valley of the Tennessee River, though several miles in breadth between the bases of the mountains, below Bridgeport, is not a broad alluvial farming country, but full of barren oak ridges, sparsely settled, and but a small part of it under cultivation.

PRELIMINARY OPERATIONS OF THE ARMY.

The first step was to repair the Nashville and Chattanooga Railroad, to bring forward to Tullahoma, McMinnville, Dechard, and Winchester needful forage and subsistence, which it was impossible to transport from Murfreesboro to those points over the horrible roads which we encountered on our advance to Tullahoma. The next was to extend the repairs of the main stem to Stevenson and Bridgeport and the Tracy City Branch, so that we could place supplies in depot at those points, from which to draw after we had crossed the mountains.

Through the zeal and energy of Colonel Innis and his regiment of Michigan engineers, the main road was open to the Elk River bridge by the thirteenth of July, and the Elk River bridge and the main stem to Bridgeport by the twenty-fifth, and the branch to Tracy City by the thirteenth of August.

As soon as the main stem was finished to Stevenson, Sheridan's division was advanced, two brigades to Bridgeport and one to Stevenson, and commissary and quartermaster stores pushed forward to the latter place, with all practicable speed. These supplies began to be accumulated at this point in sufficient quantities by the eighth of August, and corps commanders were that day directed to supply their troops, as soon as possible, with rations and forage sufficient for a general movement.

The Tracy City Branch, built for bringing coal down the mountains, has such high grades and

sharp curves as to require a peculiar engine. The only one we had, answering the purpose, having been broken on its way from Nashville, was not repaired until about the twelfth of August. It was deemed best, therefore, to delay the movement of the troops until that road was completely available for transporting stores to Tracy City.

The movement over the Cumberland Mountains began on the morning of the sixteenth of August, as follows:

General Crittenden's corps in three columns, General Wood from Hillsboro by Pelham to Thurman, in Sequatchie Valley.

General Palmer from Manchester by the most practicable route to Dunlop.

General Van Cleve with two brigades from McMinnville, the third being left in garrison there, by the most practicable route to Pikeville, the head of Sequatchie Valley.

Colonel Minty's cavalry to move, on the left, by Sparta, to drive back Debrel's cavalry toward Kingston, where the enemy's mounted troops, under Forrest, were concentrated, and then, covering the left flank of Van Cleve's column, to proceed to Pikeville.

The Fourteenth army corps, Major-General George H. Thomas commanding, moved as follows:

General Reynolds from University by way of Battle Creek, to take post, concealed, near its mouth.

General Brannan to follow him.

General Negley to go by Tantallon and halt on Crow Creek, between Anderson and Stevenson.

General Baird to follow him, and camp near Anderson.

The Twentieth corps, Major-General A. McD. McCook commanding, moved as follows:

General Johnson by Salem and Larkin's Ford to Bellefont.

General Davis by Mount Top and Crow Creek to near Stevenson.

The three brigades of cavalry by Fayetteville and Athens, to cover the line of the Tennessee from Whitesbury up.

On his arrival in Sequatchie Valley, General Crittenden was to send a brigade of infantry to reconnoitre the Tennessee, near Harrison's Landing, and take post at Poe's Cross-Roads. Minty was to reconnoitre from Washington down, and take post at Smith's Cross-Roads, and Wilder's brigade of mounted infantry was to reconnoitre from Harrison's Landing to Chattanooga, and be supported by a brigade of infantry which General Crittenden was to send from Thurman to the foot of the eastern slope of Walden's Ridge, in front of Chattanooga.

These movements were completed by the evening of the twentieth of August. Hazen's brigade made the reconnoissance on Harrison's Landing, and reported the enemy throwing up works there, and took post at Poe's Cross-Roads on the twenty-first. Wagner with his brigade supported Wilder in his reconnoissance on Chattanooga, which they surprised and shelled from across the river, creating no little agitation.

Thus the army passed the first great barrier between it and the objective point, and arrived opposite the enemy on the banks of the Tennessee.

The crossing of the river required that the best points should be chosen, and means provided for the crossing. The river was reconnoitred, the pontoons and trains ordered forward as rapidly as possible, hidden from view in rear of Stevenson, and prepared for use. By the time they were ready, the places of crossing had been selected, and dispositions made to begin the operation.

It was very desirable to conceal to the last moment the points of crossing, but as the mountains on the south side of the Tennessee rise in precipitous rocky bluffs to the height of eight hundred or one thousand feet, completely overlooking the whole valley and its coves, this was next to impossible.

Not having pontoons for two bridges across the river, General Sheridan began trestle-work for parts of one at Bridgeport, while General Reynolds's division seizing Shellmount, captured some boats, and from these and material picked up, prepared the means of crossing at that point, and General Brannan prepared rafts for crossing his troops at the mouth of Battle Creek.

The laying of the pontoon-bridges at Caperton's Ferry was very handsomely done by the troops of General Davis, under the direction of General McCook, who crossed his advance in pontoons at daylight, driving the enemy's cavalry from the opposite side. The bridge was ready for crossing by eleven o'clock A.M. the same day, but in plain view from the rebel signal-stations opposite Bridgeport.

The bridge at Bridgeport was finished on the twenty-ninth of August, but an accident occurred which delayed its final completion till September second.

The movement across the river was commenced on the twenty-ninth, and completed on the fourth of September, leaving the regular brigade in charge of the railroad and depot at Stevenson until relieved by Major Granger, who was directed, as soon as practicable, to relieve it and take charge of the rear.

General Thomas's corps was to cross as follows: One division at Caperton's and one at Bridgeport, Reynolds at Shellmount in boats, and one division at Battle Creek on rafts. All were to use the bridge at Bridgeport for such portions of their trains as they might find necessary, and to concentrate near Trenton, and send an advance to seize Frick or Cooper's and Stevens's Gaps, on the Lookout Mountain, the only practicable routes leading down the mountains into the valley, called McLemore's Cove, which lies at its eastern base, and stretches north-westwardly toward Chattanooga.

General McCook's corps was to cross: Two divisions at Caperton's Ferry, move to Valley Head and seize Winston's Gap, while Sheridan was to cross at Bridgeport, as soon as the bridge was laid, and join the rest of his corps, near Winston's, by way of Trenton.

General Crittenden's corps was ordered down the Sequatchie, leaving the two advanced brigades, under Hazen and Warren, with Minty's cavalry and Wilder's mounted infantry, to watch and annoy the enemy. It was to cross the river, following Thomas's corps, at all three crossings, and to take post on the Murphy's Hollow road, push an advance brigade to reconnoitre the enemy at the foot of Lookout, and take part at Wauhatchie, communicating from his main body with Thomas, on the right, up the Trenton Valley, and threatening Chattanooga by the pass over the point of Lookout.

The cavalry, crossed at Caperton's and a ford near Island Creek, were to unite in Lookout Valley, take post at Rawlingsville, and reconnoitre boldly toward Rome and Alpine.

These movements were completed by McCook's and Crittenden's corps on the sixth, and by Thomas's corps on the eighth of September. The cavalry for some reason was not pushed with the vigor nor to the extent which orders and the necessities of the campaign required. Its continual movement since that period, and the absence of Major-General Stanley, the Chief of Cavalry, have prevented a report which may throw some light on the subject.

The first barrier south of the Tennessee being crossed, the enemy was found firmly holding the Point of Lookout Mountain with infantry and artillery, while our force on the north side of the river reported the movement of the rebel forces from East-Tennessee, and their concentration at Chattanooga. To dislodge him from that place, it was necessary to carry Lookout Mountain, or so to move as to compel him to quit his position, by endangering his line of communication. The latter plan was chosen.

The cavalry was ordered to advance on our extreme right to Summerville in Broomtown Valley, and General McCook was ordered to support the movement by a division of infantry thrown forward to the vicinity of Alpine, which was executed on the eighth and ninth of September.

General Thomas was ordered to cross his corps by Frick's or Cooper's and Stevens's Gaps, and occupy the head of McLemore's Cove.

General Crittenden was ordered to reconnoitre the front of Lookout Mountain, sending a brigade upon an almost impracticable path, called the Nickajack Trace, to Summertown, a hamlet on the summit of the mountain, overlooking Chattanooga, and holding the main body of his corps, either to support these reconnoissances, to prevent a sortie of the enemy over the nose of Lookout, or to enter Chattanooga in case the enemy should evacuate it or make but feeble resistance. Simultaneously with this movement, the cavalry was ordered to push, by way of Alpine and Broomtown Valley, and strike the enemy's railroad communication between Resaca Bridge and Dalton.

These movements were promptly begun on the eighth and ninth of September. The reconnoissance of General Crittenden on the ninth developed the fact that the enemy had evacuated Chattanooga the day and night previous, and his advance took peaceable possession at one o'clock P.M.

His whole corps with its train passed around the point of Lookout Mountain on the tenth, and encamped for the night at Rossville, five miles south of Chattanooga.

During these operations Gen. Thomas pushed his corps over the mountains at the designated points, each division consuming two days in the passage.

The weight of evidence, gathered from all sources, was that Bragg was moving on Rome, and that his movement commenced on the sixth of September. General Crittenden was, therefore, directed to hold Chattanooga with one brigade, calling all the forces on the north side of the Tennessee across, and to follow the enemy's retreat vigorously, anticipating that the main body had retired by Ringgold and Dalton.

Additional information, obtained during the afternoon and evening of the tenth of September, rendered it certain that his main body had retired by the La Fayette road, but, uncertain whether he had gone far, General Crittenden was ordered at one o'clock A.M., on the eleventh, to proceed to the front and report, directing his command to advance only as far as Ringgold, and order a reconnoissance to Gordon's Mill. His report and further evidence satisfied me that the main body of the rebel army was in the vicinity of La Fayette.

General Crittenden was, therefore, ordered to move his corps with all possible despatch from Ringgold to Gordon's Mill, and communicate with General Thomas, who had by that time reached the foot of Lookout Mountain. General Crittenden occupied Ringgold during the eleventh, pushing Wilder's mounted infantry as far as Tunnel Hill, skirmishing heavily with the enemy's cavalry. Hazen joined him near Ringgold on the eleventh, and the whole corps moved rapidly and successfully across to Gordon's Mill on the twelfth. Wilder, following and covering the movement, had a severe fight at Lett's tan-yard.

During the same day, the Fourth United States cavalry was ordered to move up the Dry Valley road, to discover if the enemy was in the proximity of that road on Crittenden's right, and open communication with Thomas's command, which, passing over the mountain, was debouching from Stevens's and Cooper's Gaps, and moving on La Fayette through Dry Gap of the Pigeon Mountain.

On the tenth, Negley's division advanced to within a mile of Dug Gap, which he found heavily obstructed, and Baird's division came up to his support on the morning of the eleventh. Negley became satisfied that the enemy was advancing upon him in heavy force, and perceiving that if he accepted battle in that position he would probably be cut off, he fell back, after a sharp skirmish in which General Baird's division

participated, skilfully covering and securing their trains, to a strong position in front of Stevens's Gap. On the twelfth, Reynolds and Brannan, under orders to move promptly, closed up to the support of these two advanced divisions.

During the same day General McCook had reached the vicinity of Alpine, and, with infantry and cavalry, had reconnoitred the Broomtown Valley to Summerville, and ascertained that the enemy had not retreated on Rome, but was concentrating at La Fayette.

Thus it was ascertained that the enemy was concentrating all his forces, both infantry and cavalry, behind the Pigeon Mountain, in the vicinity of La Fayette, while the corps of this army were at Gordon's Mill, Bailey's Cross-Roads, at the foot of Stevens's Gap, and at Alpine, a distance of forty miles from flank to flank, by the nearest practicable roads, and fifty-seven miles by the route subsequently taken by the Twentieth army corps. It had already been ascertained that the main body of Johnston's army had joined Bragg, and an accumulation of evidence showed that the troops from Virginia had reached Atlanta on the first of the month, and that reënforcements were expected soon to arrive from that quarter. It was, therefore, a matter of life and death to effect the

CONCENTRATION OF THE ARMY.

General McCook had already been directed to support General Thomas, but was now ordered to send two brigades to hold Dougherty's Gap, and to join General Thomas with the remainder of his command with the utmost celerity, directing his march over the road on the top of the mountain. He had, with great prudence, already moved his trains back to the rear of Little River on the mountain, but unfortunately, being ignorant of the mountain road, moved down the mountain at Winston's Gap, down Lookout Valley to Cooper's Gap, up the mountain and down again, closing up with General Thomas on the seventeenth, and having posted Davis at Brooks's, in front of Dug Gap, Johnson at Pond Spring, in front of Catlett's Gap, and Sheridan at the foot of Stevens's Gap.

As soon as General McCook's corps arrived General Thomas moved down the Chickamauga toward Gordon's Mill. Meanwhile to bring General Crittenden within reach of General Thomas, and beyond the danger of separation, he was withdrawn from Gordon's Mill on the fourteenth and ordered to take post on the southern spur of Missionary Ridge, his right communicating with General Thomas, where he remained until General McCook had effected a junction with General Thomas.

Minty with his cavalry reconnoitred the enemy on the fifteenth, and reported him in force at Dalton, Ringgold, Letts, and Rock Springs Church. The head of General McCook's column being reported near the same day, General Crittenden was ordered to return to his old position at Gordon's Mill, his line resting along the Chickamauga *via* Crawfish Springs.

Thus, on the evening of the seventeenth, the troops were substantially within supporting distance. Orders were given at once to move the whole line north-eastwardly down the Chickamauga, with a view to covering the La Fayette road toward Chattanooga, and facing the most practicable route to the enemy's front.

The position of our troops and the narrowness of the roads retarded our movements. During the day, while they were in progress, our cavalry under Colonel Minty was attacked on the left, in the vicinity of Reed's Bridge, and Wilder's mounted infantry were attacked by infantry and driven into the La Fayette road.

It became apparent that the enemy was massing heavily on our left, crossing Reed's and Alexander's Bridges in force, while he had threatened Gordon's Mill.

Orders were therefore promptly given to General Thomas to relieve General Crittenden's corps, posting one division near Crawfish Spring, and to move with the remainder of his corps by the Widow Glenn's house to the Rossville and La Fayette road, his left extending obliquely across it near Kelly's house.

General Crittenden was ordered to proceed with Van Cleve's and Palmer's divisions to drive the enemy from the Rossville road, and form on the left of General Woods then at Gordon's Mill.

General McCook's corps was to close up on General Thomas, occupy the position at Crawfish Springs and protect General Crittenden's right while holding his corps mainly in reserve.

The main cavalry force was ordered to close in on General McCook's right, watch the crossing of the Chickamauga, and act under his orders.

The movement for the concentration of the corps more compactly toward Crawfish Springs was begun on the morning of the eighteenth, under orders to conduct it very secretly, and was executed so slowly that McCook's corps only reached Pond Spring at dark, and bivouacked, resting on their arms during the night. Crittenden's corps reached its position on the Rossville road near midnight.

Evidence accumulated during the day of the eighteenth that the enemy was moving to our left. Minty's cavalry and Wilder's mounted brigade encountered the enemy's cavalry at Reed's and Alexander's bridges, and toward evening were driven to the Rossville road. At the same time the enemy had been demonstrating for three miles up the Chickamauga. Heavy clouds of dust had been observed three or four miles beyond the Chickamauga, sweeping to the northeast.

In view of all these facts the necessity became apparent that General Thomas must use all despatch in moving his corps to the position assigned it. He was therefore directed to proceed with all despatch, and General McCook to close up to Crawfish Springs as soon as Thomas's column was out of the way. Thomas pushed forward uninterruptedly during the night, and at daylight the head of his column had reached Kelly's house on the Lafayette road, where Baird's division was posted. Brannan followed and was posted on Baird's left, covering the roads leading to Reed's and Alexander's bridges.

At this point Colonel McCook, of General Granger's command, who had made a reconnoissance to the Chickamauga the evening before, and had burned Reed's bridge, met General Thomas and reported that an isolated brigade of the enemy was this side of the Chickamauga, and the bridge being destroyed, a rapid movement in that direction might result in the capture of the force thus isolated.

General Thomas ordered Brannan with two brigades to reconnoitre in that direction and attack any small force he should meet. The advance brigade, supported by the rest of the division, soon encountered a strong body of the enemy, attacked it vigorously, and drove it back more than half a mile, where a very strong column of the enemy was found, with the evident intention of turning our left and gaining possession of the La Fayette road between us and Chattanooga.

This vigorous movement disconcerted the plans of the enemy to move on our left, and opened the

BATTLE OF THE NINETEENTH SEPTEMBER.

The leading brigade became engaged about ten A.M. on the nineteenth, on our extreme left and extending to the right, where the enemy combined to move in heavy masses. Apprehending this movement, I had ordered General McCook to send Johnson's division to Thomas's assistance. He arrived opportunely.

General Crittenden, with great good sense, had already despatched Palmer's, reporting the fact to me and received my approval. The enemy returned our attack, and was driving back Baird's right in disorder when Johnson struck the attacking column in flank and drove it back more than half a mile, until his own right was overlapped and in imminent danger of being turned, when Palmer, coming in on Johnson's right, threw his division against the enemy and drove back his advance columns.

Palmer's right was soon overlapped, when Van Cleve's division came to his support, but was beaten back, when Reynolds's division came in and was in turn overpowered. Davis's division came into the fight then most opportunely, and drove the enemy, who soon, however, developed a superior force against his line, and pressed him so heavily that he was giving ground, when Wood's division came and turned the tide of battle the other way.

About three P.M. General McCook was ordered to send Sheridan's division to support our line near Wood and Davis, directing Lytle's brigade to hold Gordon's Mill, our extreme right. Sheridan also arrived opportunely to save Wood from disaster, and the rebel tide was thoroughly staid in that quarter.

Meanwhile the roar of musketry in our centre grew louder, and evidently approached headquarters at Widow Glenn's house, until musket-balls came near and shells burst about it. Our centre was being driven.

Orders were sent to General Negley to move his division from Crawfish Springs and above, where he had been holding the line of the Chickamauga, to Widow Glenn's, to be held in reserve to give succor wherever it might be required, at half-past four P.M. He reported with his division, and as the indications that our centre was being driven became clearer he was despatched in that direction, and soon found the enemy had dislodged Van Cleve from the line, and was forming there even while Thomas was driving his right. Orders were promptly given Negley to attack him, which he soon did, and drove him steadily until night closed the combat.

General Brannan, having repulsed the enemy on our extreme left, was sent by General Thomas to support the centre, and at night took a position on the right of Reynolds.

Colonel Wilder's brigade of mounted infantry occupied during the day a position on the La Fayette road, one mile north of Gordon's Mill, where he had taken position on the afternoon previous, when, contesting the ground step by step, he had been driven by the enemy's advance from Alexander's bridge.

Minty's cavalry had been ordered from the same position about noon of the nineteenth to report to Major-General Granger at Rossville, which he did at daylight on the twentieth, and was posted near Mission Mills, to hold in check the enemy's cavalry on their right from the direction of Ringgold and Greysville.

The reserve corps covered the approaches from the Chickamauga toward Rossville, and the extension of our left.

The roar of battle hushed in the darkness of night, and our troops, weary with a night of marching and a day of fighting, rested on their arms, having everywhere maintained their positions, developed the enemy, and gained thorough command of the Rossville and Dry Valley roads to Chattanooga, the great objects of the battle of the nineteenth of September.

The battle had secured us these objects. Our flanks covered the Dry Valley and Rossville roads, while our cavalry covered the Missionary Ridge and the valley of Chattanooga Creek, into which latter place our spare trains had been sent on Friday the eighteenth.

We also had indubitable evidence of the presence of Longstreet's corps, and Johnson's forces, by the capture of prisoners from each.

And the fact that at the close of the day, we had present but two brigades, which had not been opportunely and squarely in action, opposed to superior numbers of the enemy, assured us that we were greatly outnumbered, and that the battle the next day must be for the safety of the army and the possession of Chattanooga.

THE BATTLE OF THE TWENTIETH.

During the evening of the nineteenth, the corps commanders were assembled at headquarters at Widow Glenn's house, the reports of the positions and condition of their commands heard, and orders given for the disposition of the troops for the following day.

Thomas's corps, with the troops which had reënforced him, was to maintain substantially his present line, with Brannan in reserve.

McCook, maintaining his picket-line till it was driven in, was to close on Thomas, his right refused, and covering the position at Widow Glenn's house, and Crittenden to have two divisions in reserve near the junction of McCook's and Thomas's lines, to be able to succor either.

Plans having been explained, written orders given to each, and read in the presence of all, the wearied corps commanders returned about midnight to their commands.

No firing took place during the night. The troops had assumed position when day dawned. The sky was red and sultry. The atmosphere and all the woods enveloped in fog and smoke. As soon as it was sufficiently light, I proceeded, accompanied by General Garfield and some aids, to inspect the lines.

I found General McCook's right too far upon the crest, and General Davis in reserve on a wooded hill-side west of and parallel to the Dry Valley road. I mentioned these defects to the General, desiring Davis's division to be brought down at once, moved more to the left and placed in close column by division doubled in the centre in a sheltered position.

I found General Crittenden's two divisions massed at the foot of the same hill, in the valley, and called his attention to it, desiring them to be moved further to the left.

General Thomas's troops were in the position indicated, except Palmer's line was to be closed more compactly.

Satisfied that the enemy's first attempt would be on our left, orders were despatched to General Negley to join General Thomas, and to General McCook to relieve Negley. Returning to the right I found Negley had not moved, nor were McCook's troops coming in to relieve him. Negley was preparing to withdraw his two brigades from the line. He was ordered to send his reserve brigade immediately and follow it with the others, only when relieved on the line of battle. General Crittenden, whose troops were nearest, was ordered to fill General Negley's place at once, and General McCook was notified of this order, growing out of the necessity of promptly sending Negley to Thomas.

Proceeding to the extreme right, I felt the disadvantages of its position, mentioned them to General McCook, and, when I left him, enjoined on him that it was an indispensable necessity that we should keep closed to the left, and that we must do so at all hazards.

On my return to the position of General Negley, I found to my astonishment that General Crittenden had not relieved him, Wood's division having reached the position of Negley's reserves. Peremptory orders were given to repair this, and Wood's troops moved into position, but this delay subsequently proved of serious consequence. The battle began on the extreme left at half-past eight A.M., and it was forty-five minutes past nine o'clock when Negley was relieved.

An aid arriving from General Thomas requesting that Negley's remaining brigades be sent forward as speedily as possible to succor the left, General Crittenden was ordered to move Van Cleve with all possible despatch, to a position in the rear of Wood, who closed in on Brannan's right. General McCook was ordered to move up to close in on Wood, and fill an opening in the line.

On my return from an examination of the ground in the rear of our left centre, I found to my surprise that General Van Cleve was posted in line of battle on a high ridge, much too far to the rear to give immediate support to the main line of battle, and General Davis in line of battle in rear of the ridge occupied by General Negley's reserve in the morning. General Crittenden was ordered to move Van Cleve at once down the hill to a better position, and General Davis was also ordered to close up the support of the line near Wood's right.

The battle, in the mean while, roared with increasing fury and approach from the left to the centre. Two aids arrived successively within a few minutes from General Thomas, asking for reenforcements. The first was directed to say that General Negley had already gone and should be nearly at hand at that time, and that Brannan's reserve brigade was available. The other was directed to say that General Van Cleve would at once be sent to his assistance, which was accordingly done.

A message from General Thomas soon followed that he was heavily pressed, Captain Kellogg, A. D. C., the bearer, informing me at the same time that General Brannan was out of line, and General Reynolds's right was exposed. Orders were despatched to General Wood to close up on Reynolds, and word was sent to General Thomas that he should be supported, even if it took away the whole corps of Crittenden and McCook.

General Davis was ordered to close on General Wood, and General McCook was advised of the state of affairs, and ordered to close his whole command to the left with all despatch.

General Wood, overlooking the direction to "close up" on General Reynolds, supposed he was to support him by withdrawing from the line and passing to the rear of General Brannan, who, it appears, was not out of line, but was in echelon, and slightly in rear of Reynolds's right. By this unfortunate mistake a gap was opened in the line of battle, of which the enemy took instant advantage, and striking Davis in flank and rear, as well as in front, threw his whole division in confusion.

The same attack shattered the right brigade of Wood before it had cleared the space. The right of Brannan was thrown back, and two of his batteries, then in movement to a new division, were taken in flank and thrown back through two brigades of Van Cleve, then on the march to the left,

throwing his division into confusion, from which it never recovered until it reached Rossville.

While the enemy poured in through this breach, a long line, stretching beyond Sheridan's right, was advancing. Lerbold's brigade shared in the rout of Davis. Sheridan's other two brigades in movement toward the left, under orders to support Thomas, made a gallant charge against the enemy's advancing column, but were thrown into disorder by the enemy's line advancing on their flank, and were likewise compelled to fall back, rallying on the Dry Valley road, and repulsing the enemy, but they were again compelled to yield to superior numbers, and retired westward of the Dry Valley, and by a circuitous route reached Rossville, from which they advanced by the La Fayette road to support our left.

Thus Davis's two brigades, one of Van Cleve's, and Sheridan's entire division were driven from the field, and the remainder, consisting of the divisions of Baird, Johnson, Palmer, Reynolds, Brannan, and Wood, two of Negley's brigades, and one of Van Cleve's, were left to sustain the conflict against the whole power of the rebel army, which, desisting from pursuit on the right, concentrated their whole effort to destroy them.

At the moment of the repulse of Davis's division, I was standing in rear of his right, waiting the completion of the closing of McCook's corps to the left. Seeing confusion among Van Cleve's troops, and the distance Davis's men were falling back, and the tide of battle surging toward us, the urgency for Sheridan's troops to intervene became imminent, and I hastened, in person, to the extreme right, to direct Sheridan's movement on the flank of the advancing rebels. It was too late. The crowd of returning troops rolled back, and the enemy advanced. Giving the troops directions to rally behind the ridges west of the Dry Valley road, I passed down it, accompanied by General Garfield, Major McMichael, and Major Bond, of my staff, and a few of the escort, under a shower of grape, canister, and musketry for two or three hundred yards, and attempted to rejoin General Thomas and the troops sent to his support, by passing to the rear of the broken portion of our line, but found the routed troops far toward the left, and hearing the enemy's advancing musketry and cheers, I became doubtful whether the left had held its ground, and started for Rossville. On consultation and further reflection, however, I determined to send General Garfield there, while I went to Chattanooga, to give orders for the security of the pontoon-bridges at Battle Creek and Bridgeport, and to make preliminary disposition either to forward ammunition and supplies, should we hold our ground, or to withdraw the troops into good position.

General Garfield despatched me from Rossville, that the left and centre still held its ground. General Granger had gone to its support. General Sheridan had rallied his division, and was advancing toward the same point, and General Davis was going up the Dry Valley road to our right. General Garfield proceeded to the front, remained there until the close of the fight, and despatched me the triumphant defence our troops there made against the assaults of the enemy.

The fight on the left after two P.M., was that of the army. Never, in the history of this war at least, have troops fought with greater energy and determination. Bayonet-charges, often heard of, but seldom seen, were repeatedly made by brigades and regiments, in several of our divisions.

After the yielding and severance of the division of the right, the enemy bent all efforts to break the solid portion of our line. Under the pressure of the rebel onset, the flanks of the line were gradually retired until they occupied strong, advantageous ground, giving to the whole a flattened crescent shape.

From one to half-past three o'clock, the unequal contest was sustained throughout our line. Then the enemy, in overpowering numbers, flowed around our right, held by General Brannan, and occupied a low gap in the ridge of our defensive position, which commanded our rear. The moment was critical. Twenty minutes more and our right would have been turned, our position taken in reverse, and probably the army routed.

Fortunately, Major-General Granger, whose troops had been posted to cover our left and rear, with the instinct of a true soldier and a General, hearing the roar of battle on our left, and being beyond the reach of orders from the General Commanding, determined to move to its assistance. He advanced and soon encountered the enemy's skirmishers, whom he disregarded, well knowing that, at that stage of the conflict, the battle was not there. Posting Colonel Daniel McCook's brigade to take care of any thing in the vicinity and beyond the left of our line, he moved the remainder to the scene of action, reporting to General Thomas, who directed him to our suffering right.

Arrived in sight, General Granger discovered at once the peril, and the point of danger—the gap—and quick as thought he directed his advance brigade upon the enemy. General Steadman, taking a regimental color, led the column. Swift was the charge and terrible the conflict, but the enemy was broken. A thousand of our brave men, killed and wounded, paid for its possession, but we held the gap.

Two divisions of Longstreet's corps confronted the position. Determined to take it, they successively came to the assault. A battery of six guns, placed in the gorge, poured death and slaughter into them. They charged to within a few yards of the pieces, but our grape and canister and the leaden hail of our musketry, delivered in sparing but terrible volleys from cartridges taken, in many instances, from the boxes of their fallen companions, was too much even for Longstreet's men. About sunset they made their last charge, when our men, being out of ammunition, rushed on them with the bayonet, and they gave way to return no more.

The fury of the conflict was nearly as great on the fronts of Brannan and Wood, being less furious toward the left. But a column of the enemy

VOL. VII.—DOC. 15

had made its way to near our left and to the right of Colonel McCook's position. Apprised of this, General Thomas directed Reynolds to move his division from its position, and, pointing out the rebels, told him to go in there.

To save time, the troops of Reynolds were faced by the rear rank, and moved with the bayonet at a double-quick, and with a shout walked over the rebels, capturing some five hundred. This closed the battle of the twentieth. At nightfall the enemy had been repulsed along the whole line, and sunk into quietude, without attempting to renew the combat.

General Thomas, considering the excessive labors of the troops, the scarcity of ammunition, food, and water, and having orders from the General Commanding to use his discretion, determined to retire on Rossville, where they arrived in good order, took post before morning, receiving supplies from Chattanooga, and offering the enemy battle during all the next day, and repulsing his reconnoissance. On the night of twenty-first we withdrew from Rossville, took firm possession of the objective point of our campaign—Chattanooga—and prepared to hold it.

The operations of the cavalry during the battles on the nineteenth were very important. General Mitchell, with three brigades, covered our right flank along the line of the Chickamauga, above Crawfish Springs, against the combined efforts of the great body of the rebel cavalry, whose attempts to cross the stream they several times repulsed.

Wilder fought dismounted near the centre, intervening two or three times with mountain howitzers and Spencer rifles very opportunely.

On the twentieth, Minty covered our left and rear at Missionary Mills, and later in the day on the Ringgold road.

General Mitchell, with his three brigades, covered our extreme right, and with Wilder, after its repulse, extended over Missionary Ridge, held the whole country to the base of Lookout Mountain, and all our trains, artillery, caissons, and spare wagons, sent there for greater safety, retiring from the field. He was joined by Post's brigade of Davis's division, which had not closed on the army, and was not in action.

On the twenty-first the cavalry still covered our right as securely as before, fighting and holding at bay very superior numbers. The number of cavalry combats during the whole campaign have been numerous, and the successes as numerous, but the army could not have dispensed with those of the nineteenth, twentieth, and twenty-first.

OUR ARTILLERY

fired fewer shots than at Stone River, but with even greater effect. I cannot but congratulate the country on the rapid improvement evinced in this arm of the service. Our loss of pieces is in part attributable to the rough wooded ground in which we fought and the want of experience in posting artillery, and partly to the unequal nature of the contest, our infantry being heavily outnumbered.

For the details of these actions, the innumerable instances of distinguished bravery, skill, and gallantry displayed by officers of every rank, and above all for self-reliant, cool, and steady courage displayed by the soldiers of the army, in all arms, in many instances even shining above that of their officers, I must refer to the accompanying reports of the corps, division, brigade, regimental, and battery commanders. The reports of the cavalry command are not in, for the best of all reasons, that they have been out nearly ever since, writing with their sabres on the heads and backs of the enemy.

The signal corps has been growing into usefulness and favor daily for the last four months, and now bids fair to become one of the most esteemed of the staff services. It rendered very important service from the time we reached the valley of the Tennessee. For its operations I refer to the report of Captain Jesse Merrill, Chief Signal Officer.

Our medical corps proved very efficient during the whole campaign, and especially during and subsequent to the battle. A full share of praise is due to Dr. Glover Perin, Medical Director of the Department, ably assisted by Dr. Grose, Medical Director of the Fourteenth, Dr. Perkins, Twentieth, and Dr. Phelps, Twenty-first army corps.

A very great meed of praise is due Captain Horace Porter, of the ordnance, for the wise system of arming each regiment with arms of the same calibre, and having the ammunition-wagons properly marked, by which most of the difficulties in supplying ammunition where troops had exhausted it in battle were obviated. From this report will be seen that we expended two million six hundred and fifty thousand rounds of musket-cartridges, seven thousand three hundred and twenty-five rounds of cannon ammunition. We lost thirty-six pieces of artillery, twenty caissons, eight thousand four hundred and fifty stand of small arms, five thousand eight hundred and thirty-four infantry accoutrements, being twelve thousand six hundred and and seventy-five rounds less of artillery, and six hundred and fifty thousand rounds more of musketry than at Stone River.

From the report of Lieutenant-Colonel Wiles, Provost-Marshal General, it will be seen that we took two thousand and three prisoners. We have —— missing, of which some six hundred have escaped and come in, and probably seven hundred or eight hundred are among the killed and wounded. Of our wounded about two thousand five hundred fell into the hands of the enemy, swelling the balance of prisoners against us to about five thousand five hundred.

It is proper to observe that the battle of Chickamauga was absolutely necessary to secure our concentration and cover Chattanooga. It was fought in a country covered with woods and undergrowth, and wholly unknown to us. Every division came into action opportunely, and fought squarely on the nineteenth. We were largely outnumbered, yet we foiled the enemy's flank movement on our left, and secured our own position on the road to Chattanooga. The battle of the twentieth was fought with all the troops we had, and but for the extension and delay in closing in our right, we should probably have driven the enemy, whom we really beat on the field. I am fully satisfied that the enemy's loss largely exceeds ours.

It is my duty to notice the services of those faithful officers who have none but myself to mention them.

To Major-General Thomas, the true soldier, the prudent and undaunted commander, the modest and incorruptible patriot, the thanks and gratitude of the country are due for his conduct at the battle of Chickamauga.

Major-General Granger, by his promptitude, arrived and carried his troops into action in time to save the day. He deserves the highest praise.

Major-General McCook, for the care of his command, prompt and willing execution of orders, to the best of his ability, deserves this testimonial of my approbation.

I bear testimony, likewise, to the high-hearted, noble Major-General Crittenden. Prompt in the moving and reporting the position of his troops, always fearless in the field of battle, I return my thanks for the promptness and military good sense with which he sent his division toward the noise of battle on the nineteenth.

To Brigadier-General James A. Garfield, Chief of Staff, I am especially indebted for the clear and ready manner in which he seized the points of action and movement, and expressed in orders the ideas of the General Commanding.

Colonel J. C. McKibben, A. D. C., always efficient, gallant, and untiring, and fearless in battle.

Lieutenant-Colonel A. C. Ducat, brave, prompt, and energetic in action.

Major Frank S. Bond, Senior A. D. C.; Captain J. P. Drouillard, A. D. C.; Captain R. S. Thoms, A. D. C., deserve very honorable mention for the faithful and efficient discharge of their appropriate duties always, and especially during the battle.

Colonel James Barnett, Chief of Artillery; Lieutenant-Colonel S. Simmons, Chief Commissary; Lieutenant-Colonel H. C. Hodges, Chief Quartermaster; Dr. G. Perin, Medical Director; Captain Horace Porter, Chief of Ordnance; Captain William E. Merrill, Chief Topographical Engineer; Brigadier-General J. St. Clair Morton, were all in the battle and discharged their duties with ability and to my entire satisfaction.

Colonel William J. Palmer, Fifteenth Pennsylvania cavalry, and his command, have rendered very valuable services in keeping open communications and watching the movements of the enemy, which deserve my warmest thanks.

Lieutenant-Colonel W. M. Ward, with the Tenth Ohio, Provost and Headquarter Guard, rendered efficient and valuable services, especially on the twentieth, in covering the movement of retiring trains on the Dry Valley road, and stopping the stragglers from the fight. Captain Garner and the escort deserve mention for untiring energy in carrying orders.

Lieutenant-Colonel Goddard, A. A. G.; Lieutenant-Colonel William M. Wiles, Provost-Marshal General; Major William McMichael, A. A. G.; Surgeon H. H. Sexes, Medical Inspector; Captain D. G. Swaim, A. A. G., Chief of the Secret Service; Captain William Farear, A. D. C.; Captain J. H. Young, Chief Commissary of Musters; Captain A. S. Burt, Acting Assistant Inspector-General; Captain Hunter Brooke, Acting Judge-Advocate; Captain W. C. Margendant, Acting Topographical Engineer; Lieutenant George Burroughs, Topographical Engineer; Lieutenant William Porter, Acting A. D. C.; Lieutenant James Reynolds, Acting A. D. C.; Lieutenant M. J. Kelley, Chief of Couriers; Assistant Surgeon D. Bache, were on the field of battle, and there and elsewhere discharged their duties with zeal and ability.

I must not omit Colonel J. P. Sanderson of the regular infantry, who, having lately joined us, on those two days of battle acted as Aid-de-Camp, and carried orders to the hottest portions of the field.

Of those division and brigade commanders whose gallantry, skill, and services were prominent, individual special mentions accompany this report. A list of names of these, and others of every grade, whose conduct, according to the reports of their commanders, observes special praise, is also herewith sent.

W. S. ROSECRANS,
Major-General.

REPORT OF MAJOR-GENERAL THOMAS.

HEADQUARTERS FOURTEENTH ARMY CORPS,
CHATTANOOGA, TENN., Sept. 30, 1863.

GENERAL: I have the honor to report the operations of my corps from the first of September up to date, as follows, namely, General Brannan's (Third) division crossed the Tennessee River at Battle Creek; General Reynolds's (Fourth) division at Shellmound; General Baird ordered to cross his (First) division at Bridgeport, and to move to Taylor's Store; General Negley's (Second) division to cross the river at Culperton's Ferry, and to report at Taylor's Store also.

September 2.—General Baird's division moved to Widow's Creek. General Negley reports having arrived at Moore's Spring, one and a quarter miles from Taylor's Store, and two miles from Bridgeport. He was ordered to cross the mountain at that point, it being the most direct route to Trenton, in the vicinity of which the corps was ordered to concentrate.

September 3.—Headquarters of the Fourteenth army corps moved from Bolivar Springs at six A.M., *via* Culperton's Ferry to Moore's Spring, on the road from Bridgeport to Trenton. Baird's division reached Bridgeport but could not cross, in consequence of damage to the bridge. Negley's division marched to Warren Mill, on the top of Sand Mountain, on the road to Trenton. Brannan's division reached Graham's Store, on the road from Shellmound to Trenton. Reynolds's division marched six miles on the Trenton road from Shellmound.

September 4.—Negley's division camped at Brown's Spring, at the foot of Sand Mountain, in Lookout Valley; Brannan's division at Gordon's Mill, on Sand Mountain; Reynolds's division at foot of Sand Mountain, two miles from Trenton. Baird's division crossed the river at Bridgeport, and camped at that point.

September 5.—Corps headquarters at Moore's Spring. First division (Baird's) arrived at Moore's Spring. Negley's division still in camp at Brown's Spring. He reports having sent forward a reconnoissance of two regiments of infantry and a section of artillery to scour the country toward Chattanooga, and secure some captured stores near Macon Iron-Works. They captured some confederate army supplies. No report from Brannan's division. Reynolds's division in camp at Trenton; Brannan somewhere in the neighborhood. Corps headquarters at Warren's Mill.

September 6.—Baird's division encamped at Warren's Mill. Negley's division reached Johnson's Crook. Beatty's brigade was sent up the road to seize Stevens's Gap; met the enemy's pickets, and it being dark, did not proceed further. The Eighteenth Ohio, of Negley's division, went to the top of Lookout Mountain beyond Paine's Mills; met the enemy's pickets, and dispersed them. The head of Brannan's division reached Lookout Valley two miles below Trenton. Reynolds's division in camp at Trenton. Rumors of the enemy's design to evacuate Chattanooga. Corps headquarters at Brown's Spring.

September 7.—Baird's division closed up with Negley's in the mouth of Johnson's Crook. Negley gained possession of the top of the mountain, and secured the forks of the road. Brannan's division reached Trenton. Reynolds remained in camp at that place. Corps headquarters still at Brown's Spring.

September 8.—Baird's division remained in its camp of yesterday, at the junction of Hurricane and Lookout Creeks. Negley's division moved up to the top of Lookout Mountain, at the head of Johnson's Crook, one brigade occupying the pass; another brigade was sent forward and seized Cooper's Gap, sending one regiment to the foot of the Gap to occupy and hold it. One regiment was also sent forward to seize Stevens's Gap, which was heavily obstructed with fallen trees. Brannan's division occupied the same position as last night. Reynolds's division headquarters at Trenton, with one brigade at Paine's Mill, three miles south of Trenton. Headquarters of the corps still at Brown's Spring.

September 9.—Baird's division moved across Lookout Mountain to the support of Negley. Negley's division moved across the mountain and took up a position in McLemore's Cove, near Rogers's farm, throwing out his skirmishers as far as Bailey's Cross-Roads. Saw the enemy's cavalry in front, drawn up in line. Citizens reported a heavy force concentrated in his front at Dug Gap, consisting of infantry, cavalry, and artillery. Brannan's division in same camp as yesterday.

Reynolds's division camped as yesterday. The Ninety-second Illinois (mounted infantry) sent on a reconnoissance toward Chattanooga, along the ridge of Lookout Mountain. Corps headquarters moved from Brown's Spring to Easeley's Farm, on Trenton and Lebanon road.

September 10.—General Negley's division, in front of or one mile west of Dug Gap, which has been heavily obstructed by the enemy and occupied by a strong picket-line. General Baird ordered to move up to-night to Negley's support. General Reynolds to move at daylight to support Baird's left, and General Brannan to move at eight A.M. to-morrow morning to support Reynolds. Headquarters of General Reynolds's division camped for the night at foot of the mountain. Brannan's division at Easeley's.

September 11.—Baird's division closed up on Negley's at Widow Davis's house, about eight A.M. Soon afterward, Negley, being satisfied from his own observations and from the reports of officers sent out to reconnoitre, and also from loyal citizens, that the enemy was advancing on him in very superior force, and that his train was in imminent danger of being cut off if he accepted battle at Davis's Cross-Roads, determined to fall back to a strong position in front of Stevens's Gap. This movement he immediately proceeded to put into execution, and by his untiring energy and skill, and with the prompt coöperation of Baird, succeeded in gaining possession of the hills in front of Stevens's Gap, and securing his trains without losing a single wagon. For a detailed account of this movement see reports of Generals Negley and Baird, annexed, marked A and B. General Turchin, commanding Third brigade of Reynolds's division, was pushed forward, by way of Cooper's Gap, to Negley's support on the left, reaching his position about ten o'clock P.M. Orders were sent to General Brannan to close up as rapidly as possible. Corps headquarters at the top of Cooper's Gap.

September 12.—Brannan's division reached Negley's position by eight A.M., and took position next on the left, one brigade covering Cooper's Gap. Reports from citizens go to confirm the impression that a large force of the enemy is concentrated at La Fayette. A report from General McCook confirms that fact. A later despatch from the same source says, it is reported that Bragg's whole army, with Johnston's, is at La Fayette. Generals Brannan and Baird, with part of their commands, went out on a reconnoissance toward Dug Gap at one o'clock P.M. to-day. General Brannan reports they advanced two miles beyond Davis's Cross-Roads without finding any enemy, with the exception of a few mounted men. Corps headquarters encamped at top of Stevens's Gap.

September 13.—Negley's, Baird's and Brannan's divisions remained in their camps of yesterday, awaiting the arrival of McCook's corps, which had been ordered to close to the left. Reynolds concentrated his division on the road from Cooper's Gap to Catlett's Gap. Two deserters from the Eighteenth Tennessee state that they belong to Buckner's corps. Buckner's corps consist of eight brigades and two batteries of six guns each, and was in the fight with Negley. They saw a brigade of Forrest's cavalry, commanded by Forrest himself, pass toward the fight on the eleventh. Miles's and Buckner's corps were both engaged. Bragg's army is concentrated at La Fayette. Headquarters moved by way of Cooper's Gap to the foot of the mountain.

September 14.—General Reynolds took up a position at Pond Spring with his two infantry brigades, and was joined by Wilder at that place. Turchin, of Reynolds's division, made a reconnoissance to the mouth of Catlett's Gap, with the Ninety-second Illinois mounted infantry; was opposed by rebel mounted pickets from Chickamauga Creek to the mouth of Catlett's Gap, at which place he found their reserve drawn up, also a strong line of skirmishers to the right of the road; but, having received instructions to avoid bringing on an engagement, he retired to camp with the regiment. General Brannan advanced one brigade of his division to Chickamauga Creek, east of Lee's Mills, one mile to the right and south of Reynolds's position at Pond Spring. A mounted reconnoissance was also pushed forward to within a mile of Blue Bird Gap, without encountering any of the enemy. A negro, who had been taken before General Buckner, yesterday, and released again, reports that Buckner and his corps are in Catlett's Gap, preparing to defend that place. A negro woman, lately from the neighborhood of Dug Gap, reports a large force of rebels between Dug Gap and La Fayette.

September 16.—Corps headquarters, and First and Second divisions, remain camped as last reported at foot of Stevens's Gap. Turchin's brigade of Reynolds's division, made a reconnoissance toward Catlett's Gap. The enemy fell back as he advanced, until he came upon a force strongly posted, with two pieces of artillery, in the roads. He made a second reconnoisance at two P.M. that day, with but little further result, as he could advance but a short distance further, the enemy being in force in his front.

September 17.—First, Second, and Third divisions changed their position from their camp yesterday: First division, with its right resting at Gower's Ford, and extending along Chickamauga Creek to Bird's Mill; Second division, with its right at Bird's Mill and its left connecting with Van Cleve's division, at Owen's Ford; Third division, on the right of the First, covering four fords between Gower's Ford and Pond Spring. One brigade of the Fourth division, thrown out in front of Pond Spring, on the Catlett's Gap road, covering the pass through the mountain; Wilder's brigade detached and ordered to report to department headquarters. The left of McCook's corps closed in, connecting with our right, near Pond Spring.

September 18.—At four P.M. the whole corps moved to the left along Chickamauga Creek to Crawfish Springs. On arriving at that place, I received orders to march on the cross-road leading by the Widow Glenn's to the Chattanooga and La Fayette road, and take up a position near Kelley's farm, on the La Fayette road, connecting with Crittenden on my right at Gordon's Mill. The head of the column reached Kelley's farm about daylight on the nineteenth, Baird's division in front, and took up a position at the forks of the road, facing toward Reid's and Alexander's bridges over the Chickamauga. Colonel Wilder, having informed me that the enemy had crossed the Chickamauga at those two bridges in force the evening before, and driven his brigade across the State road to the heights on the east of the Widow Glenn's house, this position of Baird's threw my right into close proximity to Wilder's brigade. The interval I intended to fill with the two remaining brigades of Reynolds's division on their arrival. General Brannan, closely following Baird's division, was placed in position on his left, on the two roads leading from the State road to Reid's and Alexander's bridges.

Colonel Dan McCook, commanding a brigade of the reserve corps, met me at General Baird's headquarters, and reported that he had been stationed the previous night on the road leading to Reid's Bridge, and that he could discover no force of the enemy except one brigade, which had crossed to the west side of Chickamauga at Reid's Bridge the day before, and he believed it could be cut off, because he had destroyed the bridge after they had crossed. Upon this information I ordered General Brannan to post a brigade within supporting distance of Baird, on the road to Alexander's Bridge, and with his other two brigades to reconnoitre the road leading to Reid's Bridge, to see if he could locate the brigade reported by Dan McCook, and if a favorable opportunity occurred, to capture them. His dispositions were made according to instructions by nine A.M. Gen. Baird was directed to throw forward his right wing so as to get more nearly in line with Brannan, but to watch well on his right flank. Soon after this disposition of these two divisions, a portion of General Palmer's division of Crittenden's corps took position to the right of General Baird's division. About ten A.M. Croxton's brigade of Brannan's division became engaged with the enemy, and I rode forward to his position to ascertain the character of the attack. Colonel Croxton reported to me that he had driven the enemy nearly half a mile, but that he was then meeting with obstinate resistance. I then rode back to Baird's division and directed him to advance to Croxton's support, which he did with his whole division, Starkweather's brigade in reserve, and drove the enemy steadily before him for some distance, taking many prisoners.

Croxton's brigade, which had been heavily engaged over an hour with greatly superior numbers of the enemy, and being nearly exhausted of ammunition, was then moved to the rear to enable the men to fill their boxes, and Baird and Brannan having united their forces drove the enemy from their immediate front. General Baird then halted for the purpose of readjusting line, and learning from prisoners that the enemy were in heavy force on his immediate right, he threw back his right wing in order to be ready for an attack from that quarter. Before his disposition could be completed, the enemy in overwhelming numbers assaulted Scribner's and King's brigades and drove them in disorder. Fortunately, at this time, Johnson's division of McCook's corps, and Reynolds's division of my corps, arrived, and were immediately placed in position, Johnson's preceding Reynolds's, his left connecting with Baird's right, and Palmer's being immediately placed on Johnson's right. Reynolds was placed on the right of Palmer, with one brigade of his division in reserve. As soon as formed, they advanced upon the enemy, attacking him in flank and driving him in great confusion for a mile and a half, while Brannan's troops shot them in front as they were pursuing Baird's retiring brigades, driving the head of their columns back and retaking the artillery, which had been temporarily lost by Baird's brigades. The enemy at this time being hardly pressed by Johnson's, Palmer's, and Reynold's divisions in flank, fell back in confusion on his reserves, posted in a strong position on the west side of Chickamauga Creek, between Reid's and Alexander's bridges. Brannan and Baird were then ordered to reorganize their commands and take position on commanding ground on the road from McDaniel's house to Reid's Bridge and hold it to the last extremity, as I expected the next effort of the enemy would be to gain that road and our rear.

This was about four P.M. After a lull of about an hour a furious attack was made on Reynolds's right, and he having called upon me for reënforcements, I directed Brannan's division to move to his support, leaving King's brigade of Baird's division in the position at which Baird and Brannan had been posted, the balance of Baird's division closing up to the right on Johnson's division. It will be seen, by reference to Major-General Reynolds's report, that a portion of Brannan's division reached his right just in time to defeat the enemy's efforts to turn Reynolds's right and rear. About five P.M., my lines being at that time very much extended in pursuing the enemy, I determined to concentrate them on more commanding ground, as I felt confident that we should have a renewal of the battle the next morning. I rode forward to General Johnson's position and designated to him where to place his division; also to General Baird, who was present with General Johnson. I then rode back to the cross-roads to locate Palmer and Reynolds on the prolongation of Johnson's line, and on the crest of the ridge. Soon after Palmer and Reynolds got their positions, and while General Brannan was getting in his position on the ridge to the west of the State road, near Dyer's house, to the rear and right of Reynolds, where I had ordered him as a reserve, the enemy assaulted first Johnson and then Baird in a most furious manner, producing some confusion; but order was soon restored, and the enemy repulsed in fine style, after which these two divisions took up the positions assigned them for the night. Before adjusting the line satisfactorily, I received an order to report at headquarters, and was absent from my command until near midnight.

After my return, and about two A.M. on the twentieth, I received a report from General Baird that the left of his division did not rest at the Reid's bridge road, as I had expected. I immediately addressed a note to the General Commanding, requesting that General Negley be sent me to take position on General Baird's left and rear, and thus secure our left from assault. During the night the troops threw up temporary breastworks of logs, and prepared for the encounter which all anticipated would come off the next day.

Although informed by note from General Rosecrans that Negley's division would be sent immediately to take post on my left, it had not arrived at seven A.M. on the twentieth, and I sent Captain Willard of my staff to General Negley, to urge him forward as rapidly as possible, and to point out his position to him. General Negley, in his official report, mentions that he received this order through Captain Willard at eight A.M. on the twentieth, and that he immediately commenced withdrawing his division for that purpose, when the enemy was reported to be massing a heavy force in his front, sharply engaging his line of skirmishers, and that he was directed by General Rosecrans to hold his position until relieved by some other command. General Beatty's brigade, however, was sent under guidance of Captain Willard, who took it to its position, and it went into action immediately—the enemy at that time having commenced a furious assault on Baird's left, and partially succeeded in gaining his rear. Beatty, meeting with greatly superior numbers, was compelled to fall back until relieved by the fire of several regiments of Johnson's reserve, which were placed in position by General Baird, and which regiments, with the coöperation of Vandeveer's brigade of Brannan's division, and a portion of Stanley's brigade of Wood's division, drove the enemy entirely from Baird's left and rear.

To prevent a repetition of this attack on the part of the enemy, I directed Captain Gaw, my chief topographical officer, to go to the commanding officer of these troops and direct him to mass as much artillery on the slopes of Missionary Ridge, directly west of the State road, as he could conveniently spare from his lines, supported strongly by infantry, so as to sweep the ground to the left and rear of Baird's position. This order General Negley mentions in his report having received from Captain Gaw, but from his description of the position he assumed he must have misunderstood my order, and instead of massing the artillery near Baird's left, it was posted on the right of Brannan's division, nearly in the rear of Reynolds's right.

At the same time the assault just described was made on Baird, the enemy attacked Johnson and Palmer and Reynolds with equal fierceness, which was continued at least two hours, making assault after assault with fresh troops, which were met by my troops with a most determined coolness and deliberation. Having exhausted his utmost energies to dislodge us, he apparently fell back entirely from our front and we were not disturbed again until toward night, after the withdrawal of the troops to Rossville commenced.

Just before the repulse of the enemy on our left, General Beatty came to me in person and asked for fresh troops, stating that most of those I had sent to him had gone back to the rear and right, and he was anxious to get at least another brigade before they attacked him again. I immediately sent Captain Kellogg to hurry up General Sheridan, whose division I had been informed would be sent to me. He soon after returned, reporting that in attempting to hurry up the troops that were ordered to report to me, he had met a large force of the enemy in the open corn-field to the rear of Reynolds's position, advancing cautiously, with a strong line of skirmishers thrown out. He had met Colonel Harker, whose brigade was posted on a ridge a short distance to the rear of Reynolds's position, who also saw this force advancing upon him, but, with Captain Kellogg, was of the opinion that they were Sheridan's troops coming to our assistance. Hearing heavy firing to my right and rear through the woods, I rode to the slopes of the hill to ascertain its cause. Just as I left the woods, I met Colonel Harker and Captain Kellogg with the above information. I told Colonel Harker that I was expecting Sheridan's troops from that direction, but if these troops fired on him, seeing his flag, that he was to return their fire, and resist their further advance. He immediately ordered his men to commence firing, and skirmished with them from that point to the crest of the hill slightly in his rear, placing his right in connection with Brannan's division and portions of Beatty's and Stanley's brigades of Negley's division, which had retired from the extreme left to that point.

I rode toward the crest of the hill, when I saw a body of our troops assembled in line of battle. On the way I met General Wood, who confirmed me in the opinion that the troops advancing upon us were the enemy, although we were not then aware of the disaster to the centre and right of our army. I then directed him to place his division on the prolongation of Brannan's, who, I had ascertained from Wood, was on the top of the hill above referred to, and to resist the further advance of the enemy as long as possible. I sent my aid, Captain Kellogg, to notify General Reynolds that our right had been turned, and that the enemy was in his rear in force. General Wood barely had time to dispose his troops on the left of Brannan before another of those fierce assaults, similar to those made in the morning on my lines, was made on him and Brannan combined, and kept up by the enemy throwing in fresh troops as fast as those in their front were driven back, until near nightfall.

About the time that Wood took up his position, General Gordon Granger appeared on my left flank at the head of Steedman's division of his corps. I immediately despatched a staff-officer to him, with orders to push forward and take position on Brannan's right, which order was complied with with the greatest promptness and alacrity, Steedman moving his troops into position with almost as much precision as if on drill, and fighting his way to the crest of the hill on Brannan's right, moved forward his artillery, driving the enemy down the southern slope, inflicting on him a most terrible loss in killed and wounded. This opportune arrival of fresh troops revived the flagging spirits of our men on the right, and inspired them with more ardor for the contest. Every assault of the enemy from that time until nightfall was repulsed in the most gallant style by the whole line. By this time the ammunition in the boxes of the men was reduced on an average to two or three rounds per man, and my ammunition-trains having been unfortunately ordered to the rear by some unauthorized person, we should have been entirely without ammunition in a very short time had not a small supply come up with General Steedman's command. This being distributed among the troops, gave them about ten rounds per man.

General Garfield, Chief of Staff of General Rosecrans, reached this position about four P.M., in company with Colonel Houston, of McCook's staff, and Captains Gaw and Barker, of my staff, giving me the first reliable information that the centre and right of our army had been driven. Soon after I received General Rosecrans's despatch from Chattanooga, directing me to assume command of all the forces, and, with Crittenden and McCook, take a strong position and assume a threatening attitude at Rossville, sending the unorganized forces to Chattanooga for reörganization, stating that he would examine the ground at Chattanooga and make all necessary dispositions for defence and then join me; also that he had sent out rations and ammunition to meet me at Rossville. I determined to hold the position until nightfall, if possible — in the mean time sending Captains Barker and Kellogg to distribute the ammunition, Major Lawrence, my Chief of Artillery, having been previously sent to notify the different commanders that ammunition would be supplied to them shortly. As soon as they had reported the distribution of the ammunition, I directed Captain Willard to inform the division commanders on the left to withdraw their commands as soon as they received orders.

At half-past five P.M. Captain Barker, commanding my escort, was sent to notify General Reynolds to commence the movement, and I left the position behind General Wood's command to meet Reynolds and point out to him the position where I wished him to form line to cover the retirement of the other troops on the left. In passing through an open woods, bordering the State road, and between my last and Reynolds's position, I was cautioned by a couple of soldiers who had been to hunt water, that there was a large rebel force in these woods drawn up in line and advancing toward me. Just at this time I saw the head of Reynolds's column approaching, and calling to the General himself, directed him to change the head of his column to the left, and form line perpendicular to the State road, his right resting on that road, and to charge the enemy, who were then in his immediate front. This movement was made with the utmost promptitude, and facing to the right while on the march. Turchin threw his brigade upon the rebel force, routing them and driving them in utter confusion entirely beyond Baird's left. In this splendid advance more than two hundred prisoners were captured and sent to the rear. Colonel Robinson, commanding Second brigade, Reynolds's division, followed closely upon Turchin, and I posted him on the road leading through the ridge to hold the ground while the troops on our right and left passed by. In a few moments General Willich, commanding a brigade of Johnson's division, reported to me that his brigade was in position on a commanding piece of ground to the right of the ridge road. I directed him to report to General Reynolds and assist in recovering the retirement of our troops. Turchin's brigade, after driving the enemy a mile and a half, was reassembled and took its position on the ridge road with Robinson and Willich.

These dispositions being made, I sent orders to Generals Wood, Brannan, and Granger to withdraw from their positions. Johnson's and Baird's divisions were attacked at the moment of retiring, but by being prepared retired without confusion or any serious losses. I then proceeded to Rossville, accompanied by Generals Granger and Garfield, and immediately prepared to place the troops in position at that point. One brigade of Negley's division was posted in the Gap on the Ringgold road and two brigades on the top of the ridge to the right of the road, adjoining the brigades in the road; Reynolds's division on the right of Negley's, and reaching to the Dry Valley road; Brannan's division in the rear of Reynolds's right as a reserve; McCook's corps on the right of Dry Valley road and stretching to the west, his right reaching nearly to Chattanooga Creek. Crittenden's entire corps was posted on the heights to the left of the Ringgold road, with Steedman's division of Granger's corps as a reserve behind his left, Baird's division in reserve and in supporting distance of the brigade in the Gap. McCook's brigade of Granger's corps was also posted as a reserve to the brigades of Negley's on the ridge to the right of the road. Minty's brigade of cavalry was on the Ringgold road about one mile and a half in advance of the Gap.

About ten A.M. on the twenty-first, receiving a message from Minty that the enemy were advancing on him with a large force of infantry and cavalry, I directed him to retire through the Gap, and post his command on our left flank, and throw out strong reconnoitring parties across the ridge, to observe and report any movements of the enemy on our left front. From information received from citizens, I was convinced that the position was untenable in the face of such odds as we had opposed to us, as the enemy could easily concentrate on our right flank, which, if driven, would expose our centre or left to be cut entirely off from our communications. I therefore advised the General Commanding to concentrate the troops at Chattanooga. About the time I made the suggestion to withdraw, the enemy made a demonstration on the direct road, but were soon repulsed. In anticipation of this order to concentrate at Chattanooga, I sent for the corps commanders, and gave them such general instructions as would enable them to prepare their commands for making the movement without confusion. All wagons, ambulances and surplus artillery carriages were sent to the rear before night. The order for the withdrawal being received about six P.M. the movement commenced about nine P.M., in the following manner:

Strong skirmish lines, under the direction of judicious officers, were thrown out to the front of each division, to cover their movement, with direction to retire at daylight, deployed and in supporting distance, the whole to be supported by the First division, Fourteenth army corps, assisted by Minty's brigade of cavalry, which was to follow after the skirmishers. Crittenden's corps was to move from the hills to the left of the road at nine P.M., followed by Steedman's division; next Negley's division was to withdraw at ten P.M., then Reynolds's after. Reynolds's and McCook's corps, by division, left to right, moving within supporting distance, one after the other. Brannan's division was posted at six A.M. on the road about half-way between Rossville and Chattanooga, to cover the movement. The troops were withdrawn in a quiet orderly manner, without the loss of a single man, and by seven A.M. of the twenty-second, were in the position in front of Chattanooga, which had been assigned to them previous to their arrival, and which they now occupy, covered by strong intrenchments, thrown up on the day of our arrival, and strengthened from day to day until they were considered sufficiently strong for all defensive purposes. It affords me great pleasure to refer to the reports of the various division and brigade commanders for the names of those distinguished for bravery and good conduct.

Very respectfully, your obedient servant,
GEO. H. THOMAS,
Major-General U. S. A. Commanding.
Brig.-Gen. J. A. GARFIELD,
Chief of Staff Department of the Cumberland.

REPORT OF MAJOR-GENERAL McCOOK.

HEADQUARTERS TWENTIETH ARMY CORPS,
CHATTANOOGA, October 1, 1863.

Brigadier-General J. A. Garfield, Chief of Staff:

GENERAL: I have the honor to submit the following detailed account of the operations of the Twentieth army corps, from the date of constructing the pontoon-bridge over the Tennessee River, at Culperton's Ferry, on the twenty-seventh of August, 1863, until the occupation of Chattanooga by the army of the Cumberland:

At four A.M., August twenty-ninth, the pontoons were ready for the construction of the bridge. Keys's brigade of Davis's division of this corps was placed in the boats and crossed to the opposite bank to cover the construction, to drive away the enemy's pickets, and to seize the heights of Sand Mountain. This duty was well performed, and the bridges completed at fifteen minutes past nine P.M. Carlin's brigade, assisted by one hundred officers and men of the Pioneer corps, guarded the bridge.

August thirtieth, General Davis crossed his remaining brigades, concentrating them at the foot of Sand Mountain.

Johnson's division, stationed at Bellefonte, Alabama, marched to the ford at Crow Creek, and Davis's entire division encamped on the night of the thirtieth on the top of Sand Mountain.

Sheridan's division assisted in building a bridge at Bridgeport, to enable it to cross at that point. His line of march was to Trenton, Georgia, thence to Wills's Valley.

August 31.—Johnson's division crossed the river at Culperton's Ferry, and encamped at the foot of Sand Mountain.

September 1.—The headquarters of the corps were at Stevenson, Alabama.

On September second, Davis's division advanced and encamped at the foot of Sand Mountain in Wills's Valley; Johnson's division moved up the mountain, and encamped near the western summit, and Sheridan crossed at Bridgeport, and marched toward Trenton, Georgia.

On September third, Davis encamped in Wills's Valley, and Johnson marched to near the eastern summit of Sand Mountain. The headquarters of the corps were with this division. The First and Second divisions of cavalry passed this point at one P.M.

September 4.—Davis marched to Winston's, at the foot of Lookout Mountain, and seized the pass at that point. Johnson's division marched down Sand Mountain, and camped on the ground vacated by Davis.

Winston's is forty-two miles from Chattanooga, twenty-five from Culperton's Ferry, and forty-eight from Rome, Georgia.

September 5.—General Sheridan reported his command to be encamped a few miles south-west of Trenton, it having been delayed on its march by Negley's wagon-train.

September 6.—Sheridan encamped at Stearn's Mills, twelve miles distant from Winston's.

On September seventh, no movements.

September 8.—Johnson's division marched to Long's Springs, on the Trenton road, and two brigades of Davis's division were ordered into Broomtown Valley, to support Stanley's cavalry.

On September ninth, Carlin's brigade of Davis's division marched on Alpine, Ga., to support the cavalry. Heg's brigade, of the same division, marched toward Broomtown Valley by way of Wills's Gap.

At forty-five minutes past six P.M., on the same day, I received information from the Commanding General stating that the enemy had evacuated Chattanooga and was retreating southward, and ordering me to move rapidly upon Alpine and Summerville, Ga., in pursuit, to intercept his line of retreat, and attack him in flank.

On September tenth, Post's brigade of Davis's division, was ordered to remain at Winston to guard trains, etc., etc. Johnson marched at five P.M. from Long's Springs, and crossed Lookout Mountain, encamping at the base, near Henderson's. Sheridan's division marched at five A.M. from Stearn's Mills, and encamped at Little River, about two miles and a half from the western crest. Headquarters of the corps were moved to near Alpine, Ga.

On arriving at Alpine, I discovered that the enemy had not retreated very far from Chattanooga, and, not being able to communicate with General Thomas by way of the valley, I despatched couriers by way of Valley Head, and learned, to my surprise, that he had not reached La Fayette as ordered. His reasons for not having reached that place became more apparent as we progressed. Under the circumstances, I did not move upon Summerville as ordered. My corps was isolated at Alpine, and, had it moved upon Summerville, it would have been exposed to the entire rebel army, which reconnoissances soon convinced me was being concentrated at or near La Fayette, Georgia.

On September eleventh, at half-past nine P.M., I received a communication from General Thomas, reporting his difficulties on the march, and that he could not reach La Fayette until the thirteenth. Believing that no coöperation could take place between General Thomas and myself by way of Broomtown Valley, I ordered all my wagons and materials not necessary for the troops to be returned to the summit of Lookout Mountain, there to await the result of the cavalry reconnoissance sent by General Stanley to ascertain the whereabouts of the enemy. The General Commanding was apprised of my movements and dispositions.

September 12.—My command rested in position near Alpine.

September 13.—Orders were received from General Thomas at midnight, directing two divisions of my corps to be moved to his support and the other divisions to be left to guard the trains. This order was given by direction of General Rosecrans. It was my desire to join General Thomas by the Mountain road, *via* Stephens's Gap; but, not having any guide, and all the citizens concurring that no such road existed, and General Thomas also stating that the route by Valley Head was the only practicable one, I determined to join him by it.

A brigade from each division was detailed as a guard from my trains, and General Lytle placed in command. My corps was moved up the mountain at Alpine, Ga., on the night of the thirteenth, and on the night of the fourteenth it was again encamped in Lookout Valley, except the division guarding the trains, which was encamped at Little River, on the mountains.

Sheridan's division marched down Lookout Valley to Johnson's Creek, and encamped at the base of the mountain. Being informed that a good mountain road ran directly from Valley Head to Stevens's Gap, Generals Johnson and Davis were ordered to march on that road with the utmost expedition. By direction of the General Commanding, General Lytle was directed to move with two brigades toward McLemore's Cove to observe Dougherty's Gap.

On the seventeenth, my corps was concentrated in McLemore's Cove, Sheridan being posted at the foot of Stevens's Gap, Davis at Brooks's, in front of Dug Gap, and Johnson at Pond Spring, in front of Catlett's Gap, in Pigeon Mountains. My instructions were to concentrate my commands between Pond Springs and Gower's and Chickamauga Creek. It was impossible for me to comply with these orders, as General Thomas occupied the ground. My instructions were subsequently modified. On the eighteenth, General Lytle arrived with his two brigades, and on the night of the eighteenth my corps was closed up compactly on the Fourteenth corps, with the exception of Post's brigade, Davis's division, which was, by direction of the General Commanding, ordered to hold Stevens's Gap in Lookout Mountains, at all hazards. Subsequently, Colonel Post was ordered to report to General R. B. Mitchell, commanding the cavalry, and he did not report to General Davis until his arrival at Chattanooga on the morning of the twenty-second.

On September nineteenth, at fifteen minutes past twelve A.M., I was ordered to move down to Crawfish Springs as soon as General Thomas's troops were out of the way. In compliance with this order General Johnson's division marched at early dawn, followed by Davis's and Sheridan's. I arrived at Crawfish Springs at an early hour, and reported in person to the General Commanding, who directed me to mass my troops at that place and await further orders. This was done as my command arrived.

At fifteen minutes past ten A.M. I was ordered to take command of the right and the cavalry, including Negley's division of the Fourteenth corps then observing the fords of the Chickamauga near Crawfish Springs, one brigade of this division being then engaged with the enemy. The same order directed me to send General Johnson's division forward to Widow Glenn's house to report to General Thomas. Immediately afterward I received orders to send General Davis's division to the same point to report to General Thomas or the General Commanding. These orders were at once complied with.

By this time the advance of General Sheridan's division came up, and as soon as he was posted to support the right of Crittenden's corps at Gordon's Mills, General Negley's division was withdrawn from the fords of Chickamauga Creek, and by direction of the General Commanding, ordered to report to General Thomas, which it did.

This left me with but one division (Sheridan's) and the cavalry, (which had not yet been heard from,) to take care of the right.

Learning from an aid-de-camp of General Wood, that General Wood's troops had been withdrawn from Gordon's Mills, and appreciating the great importance of that point, General Sheridan's division was at once ordered to take position there, and arrived just in time to prevent the enemy from crossing. Subsequently an order reached me from the General Commanding, to hold the position at Gordon's Mills.

At three P.M., I received an order to send two brigades of Sheridan's division to the Widow Glenn's house, leaving the First brigade (General Lytle) at Gordon's Mills; also directing me, should the right be secure, to go forward in person and take command of the troops of the corps already engaged. General Mitchell reporting with his cavalry, I was enabled to obey this order at once, arriving upon the field at the close of the engagement of the nineteenth.

On the nineteenth General Johnson's division fought near the extreme left of the line. It fought gloriously, driving the enemy for more than a mile, capturing seven of the enemy's guns and a large number of prisoners.

General Davis's division fought on the right of Widow Glenn's house, against vastly superior numbers, maintaining the conflict gallantly until near nightfall, when it was relieved by Bradley's brigade of Sheridan's division, which was hastily thrown forward and gallantly drove the enemy from the open ground and across the Chattanooga and La Fayette road, after a sanguinary engagement, recapturing the Eighth Indiana battery, which had been previously taken by the enemy, and capturing also a large number of prisoners belonging to Hood's division of Longstreet's corps. Darkness coming on, the battle closed.

At midnight on the night of September nineteenth, I received the following order:

HEADQUARTERS DEPARTMENT OF THE CUMBERLAND, WIDOW GLENN'S, September 19, 11.45 A.M.

Major-General McCook, Commanding the Twentieth Army Corps:

The General Commanding directs you, as soon as practicable, after the receipt of this order, to post your command so as to form the right of the new battle-front, and hold the same. Leave your outposts and grand-guard where they now are till they are driven in by the enemy, when they will fall back upon the main body of your command, contesting the ground inch by inch.

Very respectfully, J. A. GARFIELD, Chief of Staff.

The date of this order should read forty-five minutes past eleven P.M.

This order was strictly complied with. Lytle's brigade, of Sheridan's division, was posted in the strong position in the rear of Glenn's house. Sheridan's other two brigades were posted on very strong ground to the right and rear of this position. Davis's division, consisting of two small brigades, was posted to the left and rear of this position, in reserve, his left resting on the right of Crittenden's corps. These movements were completed by daylight on the twentieth, when the General Commanding visited my position in person. Johnson's division was still retained near the extreme left of the line and not under my immediate orders.

At six A.M. Colonel Wilder, commanding a brigade of mounted infantry, reported in person to me, stating he had, with his troops, been ordered to join my command, and receive orders from me; also stating that he had two regiments, armed with the Spencer rifles, posted in the woods, on the right of Negley's position, which was to the left and front of General Lytle's. The remainder of Wilder's command, with his artillery, was posted on strong ground immediately to Sheridan's right.

At about seven A.M., the following was received:

HEADQUARTERS DEPARTMENT OF THE CUMBERLAND, September 20—6.35 A.M.

Major-General McCook, Commanding Twentieth Army Corps:

General Negley's division has been ordered to General Thomas's left. The General Commanding directs you to fill the space left vacant by his removal, if practicable. The enemy appears to be moving toward our left.

Very respectfully, J. A. GARFIELD, Chief of Staff.

Immediately on the receipt of this order, Major-General Sheridan and myself rode to the position evacuated by General Negley. We found nearly all this space already occupied by General Wood's division. He informed me that his left rested upon General Brannan's right, and that his orders were to close up on General Brannan.

Discovering that a portion of the rude barricades on Wood's right were not occupied by our troops, I ordered General Sheridan to bring forward one of his brigades to fill up the space between Wood's left and Wilder. On turning from this position I met General Davis's division marching toward and about one hundred yards from the vacant barricade on Wood's right; he informed me that he had been ordered there by General Rosecrans. Seeing his position, and knowing the advantage of occupying the barricades at once, I directed him to place one brigade there, holding the other in reserve. On the arrival of the brigade from Sheridan's division, it was posted in column on Davis's right and rear, as his support. Davis's instructions were to keep well closed up to the left. These dispositions being just completed, the following order was received:

HEADQUARTERS ARMY OF THE CUMBERLAND, IN THE FIELD, September 20—10.10 A.M.

Major-General McCook, Commanding Twentieth Army Corps:

General Thomas is being heavily pressed on the left. The General Commanding directs you to make immediate dispositions to withdraw the right, so as to spare as much force as possible to reënforce Thomas. The left must be held at all hazards, even if the right is withdrawn wholly back to the present left. Select a good position back this way, and be ready to start reënforcements to Thomas at a moment's warning.

J. A. GARFIELD,
Brigadier-General and Chief of Staff.

Within five minutes after the receipt of the above order and instructions given to carry it out, the following was received:

HEADQUARTERS DEPARTMENT OF CUMBERLAND, }
IN THE FIELD, }
September 20—10.30 A.M. }

Major-General McCook, Commanding Twentieth Army Corps:

The General Commanding directs you to send two brigades of General Sheridan's division at once, and with all possible despatch, to support General Thomas, and send the Third brigade as soon as the lines can be drawn sufficiently. March them as rapidly as you can without exhausting the men. Report in person to these headquarters as soon as your orders are given in regard to Sheridan's movement.

Have you any news from Colonel Post?

J. A. GARFIELD,
Brigadier-General and Chief of Staff.

This order was executed at once. Two brigades of Sheridan's division—Lytle's and Walworth's—were taken from the extreme right and moved, at the double-quick, to the support of General Thomas. Simultaneously with this movement, and much to my surprise, Wood's division left the position it had in line of battle, on Davis's left, marching by the left flank, leaving a wide gap in the line. An attempt was made by General Davis to fill up the space thus vacated. Buell's brigade of Wood's division had scarcely marched more than its length when a most furious and impetuous assault was made by the enemy, in overwhelming numbers, on this portion of the line, the enemy's line of battle extending from a point beyond Brannan's right to a point far to the right of the Widow Glenn's house, and in front of the strong position just abandoned by General Sheridan's two brigades. To resist this attack I had just two brigades of Davis's division, numbering about one thousand two hundred men, and Colonel Laibold's brigade of Sheridan's division as a support.

Finding the enemy pouring through the interval between Davis and Brannan, Lytle's and Walworth's brigades are deflected from their line of march, and ordered to assist in resisting the enemy. Colonels Wilder and Harrison closed in with their commands on Sheridan's right as speedily as possible, and did good service. General Davis's command being overwhelmed by numbers, was compelled to abandon its position in order to save itself from complete annihilation or capture. Laibold's troops coming up to Davis's support, met with a similar fate. The other two brigades of Sheridan's division were illy prepared to meet such an attack. They struggled nobly, and for a time checked the enemy in their immediate front. But the position being turned far to the left, they

were compelled to withdraw from the unequal contest.

It was thus that these five brigades of the Twentieth army corps were cut off and separated from the remainder of the army. No troops fought with more heroism, or suffered greater losses than these small five brigades; their loss being over forty per cent of the number engaged, in killed and wounded.

In regard to the numbers of the enemy that attacked on the right, I can make no estimate. General Sheridan captured prisoners from five different rebel divisions. The Fifty-first Illinois, of Walworth's brigade, captured the colors of the Twenty-fourth Alabama.

The troops of Generals Sheridan and Davis were rallied a short distance in the rear of the line of battle, and marched toward Rossville, to endeavor to form a junction with the troops of General Thomas. Their presence was reported to General Thomas by my Chief of Staff, Lieutenant-Colonel Thurston. They were placed in position by order of General Thomas, on the road leading from the battle-field to Rossville. During the night they withdrew to Rossville with the remainder of the army.

The Second division of the Twentieth corps, under General Johnson, fell back to Rossville with the Fourteenth corps, Willich's brigade forming the rear-guard. On the night of the twentieth, the Twentieth corps was in good order united at Rossville.

On the morning of the twenty-first, a short time after daylight, the corps was again put in line of battle, the left resting on Mission Ridge, covering the Crawfish Spring road, the right extending toward Chattanooga Creek and Lookout Mountain. The corps remained in this position until two A.M. of the twenty-second of September, when it was withdrawn to Chattanooga with the rest of the army.

Since arriving at Chattanooga, the corps has been engaged in heavy guard-duty, and erecting strong lines of intrenchments, which, in my opinion, can only be taken by regular approaches.

My thanks are due to Colonel Joseph E. McKibben, Captain A. S. Bart, Captain R. S. Thoms, and Lieutenant George Burroughs, of General Rosecrans's staff, for valuable assistance in rallying portions of Sheridan's and Davis's divisions which had been overwhelmed. Brigadier-General J. St. Clair Morton, Chief Engineer of the army, being separated from his staff, reported to me for duty.

After ascertaining that the centre of our line had been broken, my first object was to endeavor to find the General Commanding, to ascertain to what point he wished the rallied troops marched. Failing to find the General, and believing that an efficient stand could not be made by the army until it reached Chattanooga, the forces on the left retired toward Rossville. From statements of General Rosecrans's guides, and from observations made by General Morton, I was satisfied that the enemy was endeavoring to cut our army off from Rossville. At this juncture, Lieutenant-

Colonel Lyne Starling, of General Crittenden's staff, rode up and reported to me that his chief had gone to Chattanooga to report to General Rosecrans. I then decided to report to General Rosecrans at once for instructions, as my last orders from his headquarters required.

Finding the General Commanding at Chattanooga, he directed me to go out on the road to Rossville, collecting all the troops possible, and report to General Thomas. Leaving Chattanooga at midnight, I arrived at Rossville at about four A.M., on the morning of the twenty-first, when the line of battle above referred to was formed and strong barricades erected.

The conduct of the troops of the Twentieth corps was every thing that could be expected of men.

During the second day's battle, Johnson's division fought on the left, separated from the corps. All acknowledged the gallantry of this division. It never attacked that it was not successful, and the enemy never attacked it without being handsomely repulsed. I depend upon General Thomas and the official reports to do this gallant division justice.

The troops of Sheridan's and Davis's divisions behaved with great courage, never yielding, except to overwhelming numbers, when it would have been suicidal to have contested the ground longer.

To the families of the heroic dead the sympathies of the nation are due. Such names as Heg, Lytle, and Baldwin, Brigade Commanders, and Colonels Alexander, Gilmer, and McCreary, and many other distinguished field and line officers who fell upon this memorable battle-field, will make a radiant space in our history as a nation. These expressions should also extend to the many non-commissioned officers and privates who gave their lives in defence of their country and flag.

To Major-General Sheridan, commanding Third division; Brigadier-General Johnson, commanding Second division, and Brigadier-General Davis, commanding First division, of my corps, my thanks are due for their earnest coöperation and devotion to duty.

Major-General Sheridan is commended to his country, and Brigadier-Generals Johnson and Davis are commended to their country and recommended to my superiors for promotion.

Brigadier-General Aug. Willich, commanding First brigade, Second division, and Colonel W. W. Berry, Fifth Kentucky volunteers, commanding Third brigade, are strongly recommended by General Johnson for promotion.

Lieutenant-Colonel Bradley, Fifty-first Illinois volunteers, commanding Third brigade, Third division, and Colonel Laibold, Second Missouri volunteers, commanding Second brigade, Third division, are strongly recommended for promotion by General Sheridan.

It affords me great pleasure to add my testimony as to the gallantry of these distinguished soldiers, and commend them to my superiors for promotion.

The Twentieth corps, during the two days' bat-tle, lost five pieces of artillery, and captured seven from the enemy; also, retaking the Eighth Indiana battery, lost on Saturday. Two guns lost by Johnson's division were so disabled by shot, and the killing of the horses, that it was impossible to move them. Davis's division did not lose a gun or wagon during the conflict.

To my staff—Lieutenant-Colonel G. P. Thurston, A. A. G. and Chief of Staff; Major Caleb Bates, A. D. C.; Captain B. D. Williams, A. D. C.; Captain F. J. Jones, A. D. C.; Captain J. M. Fisher, volunteer A. D. C.; Lieutenant-Colonel H. A. Fisher, Assistant Inspector-General; Lieutenant-Colonel J. F. Boyd, Quartermaster; Lieutenant-Colonel G. W. Burton, Commissary of Subsistence; Major G. A. Hensel, Chief of Artillery; Captain A. C. McClurg, A. A. A. G. and Ordnance Officer; Surgeon J. Perkins, Medical Director; Captain A. T. Snodgrass, Provost-Marshal; Captain J. C. McElpatrick, Topographical Engineer; Lieutenant B. R. Wood, Signal Officer—my thanks are due for their devotion to duty, gallantry in action, and intelligence on the field.

For particular instances of individual bravery, I refer you to the inclosed reports of division and brigade commanders.

All of which is respectfully submitted.

A. McD. McCook,
Major-General Commanding Twentieth Army Corps.

BRIGADIER-GENERAL HAZEN'S REPORT.

HEADQUARTERS SECOND BRIGADE, SECOND DIVISION,
TWENTY-FIRST ARMY CORPS,
CHATTANOOGA, September 28, 1863.

Capt. D. W. Norton, A. A. A. General Second Division:

In obedience to instructions I have the honor to submit the following report of the part taken by the troops under my command, in the battles of the nineteenth and twentieth instant. The narrative commences with the crossing of the Tennessee River, September tenth, when the brigade consisted of the One Hundred and Twenty-fourth Ohio volunteers, Colonel O. H. Payne; Forty-first Ohio volunteers, Colonel Aquila Wiley; the Ninth Indiana volunteers, Colonel J. C. B. Suman; the Sixth Kentucky volunteers, Colonel George F. Shackelford; and battery F, First Ohio volunteer artillery, Lieutenant G. J. Cockerill; in all, an effective aggregate of one thousand five hundred and thirty-one officers and men.

My brigade moved to Graysville, and there joined its proper division on the eleventh. We reached Ringgold the same day, and the next day moved over to Gordon's Mills, skirmishing a portion of the way, losing two men and wounding and capturing three from the enemy. In the evening of this day the brigade made a reconnoissance about three miles in the direction of La Fayette, meeting the enemy and skirmishing briskly with him, when we returned to the Mills. The next day the division marched to Chattanooga Creek, and the day after, to Gowen's Ford on the West-Chickamauga, where we remained quietly until the morning of the seventeenth, when my pickets on the La Fayette road were vigorously attacked. They, however, repulsed the enemy with a loss to him of one captain and several men. On the evening of this day we marched to within two miles of Crawfish Springs, and in the night of the eighteenth to a position one mile north of Gordon's Mills, where we formed in line of battle on the left of General Cruft, and near the La Fayette and Rossville road. Here we remained with an occasional shot in our front until about eleven o'clock A.M. of the nineteenth, when I received orders to move in the direction of the firing, then growing severe, about one and a half miles to our left, in front of General Thomas's position.

On reaching McNamus's house, on the La Fayette and Rossville road, the brigades of the division were formed in two lines facing the east, the second line being doubled by regiments on the centre. My brigade was on the left of the division, General Cruft being on my immediate right. The line was then moved forward in *echelon* by brigades, my brigade commencing the movement. The enemy was struck after advancing about three quarters of a mile, when a terrific contest here was added to the already severe battle on our left. The enemy gave ground freely, and the left at this juncture, making an advance, all the ground desired on the left was carried, extending to the right as far as the *echelons* of the Second division had been placed.

I was at this time relieved by General Turchin and ordered back to the road to fill my boxes with ammunition, already twice exhausted, and take charge of some batteries left there without supports. This I had just accomplished when a vigorous attack appeared to be going on upon that part of our line immediately to the right of the ground fought over by the last *echelon* of our division. I at once moved my brigade to the right, and forming it so as to face the sound of battle, moved forward and placed it in position as a support to some troops of General Reynolds, my left resting on the La Fayette and Rossville road, near McNamus's house, the right thrown forward, forming an angle of about forty-five degrees with the road. The battle neared my position rapidly. At this moment I met General Van Cleve, whose division the enemy had engaged, and who told me his men had given way and that he could no longer control them. The enemy continued to advance steadily, and the line in my front gave way. My own men then advanced to the top of the crest and withstood the shock until they were completely flanked upon their left, then obliqued well to the right and took position upon a high elevation of ground, confronting the left flank of that portion of the enemy which had broken our centre. The advance of the enemy was now steady and northward, nearly in the direction of the La Fayette and Rossville road. I found myself the only general officer upon that part of the field, and to check the farther advance of the enemy was of the utmost importance. I hastily gathered and placed in position all the artillery then in reach, including a portion of Standart's, Cockerill's, Cushing's, and Russell's batteries; in all, about twenty pieces, and with the aid of all the mounted officers and soldiers I could find, succeeded in checking and rallying a sufficient number of straggling infantry to form a fair line in support of the artillery. My brigade could not be brought into position in time, there being but about two minutes to make these dispositions before the blow came, when the simultaneous opening of all the artillery with grape checked and put to rout the confronting columns of the enemy. It is due Lieutenants Baldwin, First Ohio volunteer artillery, commanding Standart's battery, Cockerill of the same regiment, commanding battery, Cushing and Russell, Fourth United States artillery, commanding batteries, to state that for accuracy in manœuvring and firing their guns in the immediate presence of the enemy on the occasion above referred to, the army and country are placed under lasting obligations.

Major-General Reynolds came to this position soon afterward and made further dispositions of troops, but the fight was closed for the day, except a fierce attack made at nightfall upon General Johnson. Soon after the above repulse, General Thomas came to this place, and took command of all the troops in this part of the field.

It would appear that all the troops, except General Johnson's division, had been withdrawn from the portion of the field he occupied, leaving him well advanced and entirely unsupported. When the attack was made upon him, my brigade was sent with the balance of the Second division to his support, but the firing ceased when we had marched some four hundred yards east of the La Fayette and Rossville road, opposite Kelley's house, and we were placed here in position for the fight of Sunday.

Although my losses this day had been great, including Colonels Payne and Shackelford severely wounded, and Lieutenant-Colonel Rockingham killed, besides the loss of four hundred and thirty-nine officers and men, the brigade, with the exception of the Sixth Kentucky, was in good condition with few absentees. The latter regiment from the great mortality among its officers, was very much broken, and its fragments attached to the other regiments of the brigade.

On the morning of the twentieth, the men were moved at three A.M. and directed to make coffee where they had water, and at daybreak a breastwork of logs and rails was commenced, which was taken up on my right and carried through one entire division and that of Reynolds on our right, and Baird and Johnson on our left. Wherever this work was done the line remained the entire day with firmness and little loss. At about eight o'clock the attack commenced upon the left of this line and swept along toward the right, arriving at my position about fifteen minutes afterward, passing on, but producing no effect until it had passed General Reynolds. This assault was kept up without interruption till about eleven o'clock A.M., with a fury never witnessed upon the field either of Shiloh or Stone River. The repulse was equally terrific and finally complete. A few light attacks on this front were made up to one o'clock P.M., after which every thing was comparatively quiet. The value of this simple breastwork will be understood, since my loss behind it this day was only about thirteen men, during a period of more stubborn fighting than at Shiloh or Stone River, when the same brigade at each place lost over four hundred men. Our left flank was twice turned and partially driven this day, but the enemy was easily checked and our lines speedily restored.

At about ten o'clock A.M. our couriers for ammunition, previously prompt to return, did not come back, and it soon came to be believed that our trains had been captured. I at once cautioned my colonels, who fired only by volleys, not to waste a single round of ammunition, and my battery was similarly cautioned.

During the quiet that afterward settled upon us, several officers were struck by sharp-shooters from distant trees. Ascertaining the proper direction, I caused volleys to be fired into the tops of the trees, and thus brought several of them from their hiding-places, checking for a time this species of warfare. Skirmishers sent out along this front reported the execution of our arms during the engagement to have been terrible, beyond any thing before seen in this war, as I believe the fight from eight to eleven o'clock to have been.

The stillness that now hung over the battle-field was ominous. We had four divisions in line that, although they had withstood one of the most terrific assaults on record, had hardly felt the breath of the battle. There were four more upon our right with General Thomas, as fresh as we were. But the feeling that our ammunition was gone, was like a leaden weight in the breast of many. The men, however, were confident of success. It afterward appeared that the breaking up of the troops on our right had swept away our ammunition and *much else* along with their fragments to Chattanooga.

No new dispositions of troops on our part of the line were made, except that General Reynolds's right was somewhat withdrawn, to cover that flank. General Wood, General Brannan, and two divisions of the reserve corps were found in a line at right angles with, and directly in rear of the position before described, the left of this line being about one half mile from, and opposite Reynolds's right. At about three o'clock P.M. a fearful onslaught was made upon this line. The battle raged for an hour with apparently varying fortunes, when several general officers at our position expressed a sense of the necessity for a brigade to move over and strike the deciding blow. No one appeared to have any ammunition. I found upon examination that I still had forty rounds per man, and immediately moved my men over at double-quick with a front of two regiments. Arriving near the scene of action, I caused a partial change of direction to the left, and was quickly pouring in volleys, my second line alternating with my first. The ac-

tion lasted but a few minutes, the enemy retiring.

There was no more fighting. At dusk I received orders from General Thomas to retire on Rossville, which I did quietly and in perfect order, the pickets of the enemy following mine closely as they were withdrawn, and confronting an officer, sent to see that it was thoroughly done.

There are several lessons to be learned from this fight, and to me, none more plainly than that the iron hand that strikes justly yet firmly, can alone make the soldier that can be relied upon in the hour of trial. The effect of firing by volleys upon the enemy has invariably been to check and break him. It further gives a careful colonel complete control of his fire. The effect of sending in fractions to battle with an entire army is to waste our own strength without perceptibly weakening the enemy.

My entire brigade has my warmest thanks for its services. Colonel O. H. Payne, One Hundred and Twenty-fourth Ohio volunteers, and Colonel George F. Shackelford, Sixth Kentucky volunteers, both of whom fell early in the fight of Saturday, carried in their commands bravely and at the opportune moment. The One Hundred and Twenty-fourth Ohio volunteers, although in its maiden engagement, bore itself gallantly and efficiently. Major Hampson, who commanded this regiment after the fall of its Colonel, bore his part with ability and success. Colonels Wiley, Forty-first Ohio volunteers, and Suman, Ninth Indiana volunteers, with their regiments, are veterans of so frequent trial that it would be mockery to praise them with words. The country cannot too highly cherish these men. Colonel Wiley had his horse shot from under him. The services of Lieutenant-Colonels Kimberly, Forty-first Ohio volunteers, and Lasselle, Ninth Indiana volunteers, were conspicuous and valuable. Lieutenant-Colonel Kimberly had two horses killed under him.

Of the noble dead there are Lieutenant-Colonel Rockingham, Captains McGraw, Johnson, Marker, Lieutenants Lockman and Ewbanks, all of the Sixth Kentucky; Lieutenants Crisswell, Nickeson, and Parks of the Ninth Indiana, with a long list of others, as brave and true, but bearing no title. Many tears are shed for them.

My staff were efficient, performing every duty assigned them with promptness and accuracy. Captain H. W. Johnson, Forty-first Ohio, Acting Quartermaster, was with me the entire day on Saturday, and at night brought upon the battle-field such portions of his train as were needed for the comfort of the command, taking them away before daylight the next morning. Captain John Crowell, Jr., Assistant Adjutant-General, and my Aids, Lieutenants Wm. M. Beebe and E. B. Atwood, Forty-first Ohio; my Inspector-General, Captain James McCleery, Forty-first Ohio; my Provost-Marshal, Captain L. A. Cole, Ninth Indiana; my Commissary of Subsistence, Lieutenant F. D. Cobb, Forty-first Ohio; and my Topographical officer, Lieutenant A. G. Bierce,

Ninth Indiana, were with me at all times doing valuable service. My Surgeon, M. G. Sherman, Ninth Indiana, was, as he always is, in his place.

Of my orderlies, Waffee, Brise, Morrison, and Sweeney deserve special mention. Shepard Scott was particularly distinguished for bravery and good service. He on two occasions brought brigades to my assistance when greatly needed. His horse was shot, and he killed or captured. Should he be restored, I recommend that he be appointed a Second Lieutenant. Quite a number of horses were killed and disabled in the service of my staff.

The entire casualties of the brigade were as follows:

Regiments, etc.	Killed. Officers.	Men.	Wounded. Officers.	Men.	Miss-ing.	Aggre-gate.
124th Ohio,	..	15	4	88	34	141
41st Ohio,	..	6	5	95	9	115
9th Indiana,	3	22	6	59	18	108
6th Kentucky,	5	9	5	88	11	118
Bat'ry F, 1st O. V. A.,	1	1	..	8	2	12
Total,	9	53	20	338	74	494

The commander of the brigade was twice struck, but not injured. Two or three members of my staff were also struck, but without effect. Attention is called to accompanying reports of regimental commanders.

I am, very respectfully,
Your obedient servant,
W. B. HAZEN,
Brigadier-General.

COLONEL WILEY'S REPORT.

CAMP OF FORTY-FIRST REGIMENT O. V. I., CHATTANOOGA, TENN., September 25, 1863.

Captain John Crowell, Jr., A. A. G.:

In compliance with your order I have the honor to submit the following report of the part taken by this regiment in the operations terminating in the general engagement on the Chickamauga River on the nineteenth and twentieth instant.

On the morning of September tenth, the regiment forded the Tennessee River at Friar's Island, at which place it had been on outpost duty for two days previous, and marched the same day to Tiner's Station, on the Knoxville and Chattanooga Railroad. On the eleventh it marched thence to Ringgold, *via* Graysville, at which place we joined the rest of the division. On the twelfth it marched from Ringgold to Gordon's Mills, acting as advance-guard of the division. During the day's march, a body of rebel cavalry attempted to cut off a portion of the advance-guard by charging on its flank, but the vigilance of Lieutenant-Colonel Kimberly, commanding it, frustrated their object, a volley from the skirmishers—killing one horse and wounding one man, who, with two others, fell into our hands — caused them to retreat precipitately. After going into bivouac the same day at Gordon's Mills, the enemy's cavalry exhibiting great audacity in approaching our position, the brigade was ordered on a reconnoissance, the regiment again forming the advance. Four companies deployed, under command of Lieutenant-Colonel

Kimberly, drove them easily, and without loss, a distance of two and a half miles, when we were ordered to return to camp. Remained in bivouac on the thirteenth at Gordon's Mills, marched thence to Chattanooga Valley on the fourteenth, thence on the fifteenth to a position on the Chickamauga River, about five miles from Gordon's Mills, and — miles from Lafayette; remained in bivouac here, receiving supplies of clothing, etc., until the evening of the seventeenth, when we went into position in line of battle about three miles further north on the same road. In the night of the eighteenth took up a new position about four miles further north on the same road; bivouacked here in line of battle, covering the front of the regiment with skirmishers. On the nineteenth the engagement began still further on the left. As the firing of musketry became brisk, the regiment, with the rest of the brigade, was again moved to the left. About one P.M. we advanced in line of battle to the attack, being on the right of the first line of the brigade, with two companies deployed as skirmishers. Passing through an open wood, our skirmishers soon became engaged with those of the enemy, and drove them. On emerging from the wood, we came to an open field about four hundred yards in width with another skirt of woods beyond. Through this wood the enemy started in line across the field to meet us. Near the middle of this field, and a little to our left, was a narrow strip of timber. The enemy had advanced but a short distance when he delivered his fire, and then sought to gain the cover of this strip of timber. We were too quick for them, gaining it first, and delivering our fire by battalion at short-range, sent them back to the woods from which they started. As soon as they began to retreat, a battery planted in the edge of the wood opened fire, inflicting considerable loss. As soon as the retreating forces gained the cover of the woods a heavy infantry fire was also opened on us. This position the regiment maintained till about four P.M., replying to the enemy's fire and repelling their attempt to dislodge us. In repelling their last assault we were supported and assisted by two companies of the One Hundred and Twenty-fourth O. V. I. The regiment was then relieved by the Sixth Kentucky and ordered to retire to procure ammunition and clean their arms. While replenishing our boxes, we were again ordered forward to the right to the support of a portion of Van Cleve's division. We had barely got into position in rear of the line when it began to fall back. The regiment remained in position until the troops to whose support we had gone had retired. Those on the left retiring toward the left created an interval through which the enemy advanced. We fired our volley by battalion and then retired slowly, halting, facing about, and firing by battalion as soon as the regiment had loaded, and effectually holding the enemy in check in our front. Finally the advance of the enemy on the left having been checked, and the troops to whose support we had been sent having been reënforced, on a ridge in our rear, the regiment again moved off to the left and joined the rest of the brigade. It was now sundown, and our part in the engagement for the day was ended. The regiment bivouacked for the night in the first line, on a ridge on the east side of the road, and maintained the same position on the twentieth till about three P.M. A small parapet of logs, hastily constructed on the morning of the twentieth, enabled us to repel two assaults on the position during the day, without loss to ourselves. About three P.M. it was moved to the right to the support of a portion of Harker's brigade, Wood's division, which was in position on the crest of a hill which the enemy was endeavoring to carry. The possession of the hill was maintained, the regiment losing about a dozen wounded in this part of the action. As soon as it became dark we withdrew from this position, marched to Rossville, where the regiment bivouacked, and on Monday morning again went into position in the first line on Missionary Ridge, throwing up a parapet of rails and covering our front with skirmishers. The enemy soon afterward engaged our skirmishers, and later in the day opened with artillery, evidently for the purpose of feeling our position; the main line, however, did not become engaged, and at night we were again withdrawn, and the next day took up the position in the present line, which we now occupy.

The following is the list of casualties:

Killed—Men, six. Wounded—Officers, five; men, ninety-five. Missing—Men, nine. Aggregate—Killed, six; wounded, one hundred; missing, nine. Number engaged—Officers, twenty-three; men, three hundred and thirty-seven; aggregate, three hundred and sixty.

Lieutenant-Colonel Kimberly had two horses and Major J. H. Williston one horse wounded and disabled in the engagement. My own horse was killed.

I cannot speak too highly of the gallantry and fortitude of both officers and men, nor of the enthusiasm, that two days' hard fighting and their thinned ranks failed to depress. My thanks are especially due Lieutenant-Colonel R. L. Kimberly and Major J. H. Williston, as well for their untiring vigilance and zeal as for their gallantry in action. Lieutenant Fisher, Acting Adjutant, deserves and has my thanks for promptness in communicating orders under severe fire. Late on the nineteenth he was severely and it is supposed mortally wounded while going to the rear to bring up ammunition. He is supposed to be in the hands of the enemy. Lieutenant J. N. Clark performed the duties of Adjutant during the remainder of the engagement and deserves mention for zeal and gallantry. Among company officers, while I can commend all for their cheerful and steady courage throughout the engagement, Lieutenant C. W. Hills deserves special mention for deliberation and coolness which attracted my attention in the heat of the engagement on Saturday, and for the obstinacy with which he held his ground on Monday while commanding a line

of skirmishers that was vigorously attacked by the enemy. Corporal Strock, of company E, also deserves notice for pursuing and bringing in two prisoners who took refuge in a house when the regiment repelled the last attack on their position on Saturday afternoon. They belonged to the Twelfth Tennessee, Colonel Watkins, Smith's brigade, Cheatham's division. Corporal Strock's name had previously been placed upon the roll of honor, and his conduct in this engagement shows that the confidence of his comrades has not been misplaced.

Of the nine men "missing," should any prove skulkers or cowards, I shall take the same interest in having them punished that I shall always take in securing to good soldiers the reward due gallant and noble conduct.

I have the honor to be your obedient servant,

AQUILA WILEY,
Colonel Commanding Forty-first O. V. I.

A NATIONAL ACCOUNT.

ON the ninth of September, it became definitely known that the movement of General Rosecrans against Chattanooga had been successful in compelling the enemy to evacuate the place without fighting, and orders were given for the advance of all forces not designed for garrison duty at the several points on the Tennessee River. The position of the army at the time was: the right corps, under McCook, at Winston's Springs, in Lookout Valley, forty-five miles south of Chattanooga, separated from the enemy's line of retreat by the Lookout Mountains; the centre corps, under Thomas, thirteen miles nearer Chattanooga, in the same valley; and the left corps, under Crittenden, in the lower part of the valley, the left resting upon the Tennessee River, not more than eight miles from Chattanooga. Two brigades of Crittenden's corps were yet west of the Tennessee; Wagner's at the crossing of Waldron's Ridge, on the Thurman Road, and Hazen's at Poe's Tavern, the former five miles from Chattanooga, the latter ten miles from there up the river. These brigades, with Wilder's mounted brigade, and Minty's brigade of cavalry, watched the various fords for thirty miles above Chattanooga, and made constant demonstrations at various points. Van Cleve's division (two brigades) had been at Piketon, thirty-two miles above Poe's, but was withdrawn a few days previous to the ninth. These forces crossed the Tennessee on the ninth and tenth, and on the eleventh, having met the enemy's cavalry in considerable force, Crittenden's corps reached Ringgold, Georgia, fifteen miles south-east from Chattanooga. The corps, except the brigades that had been watching the fords above Chattanooga, had marched southward on the Rossville road. At Rossville, Wood's division, leaving the main column to proceed to Ringgold, marched southward to Gordon's Mills, ten and a half miles south of Chattanooga. Arriving at Gordon's Mills on the evening of the eleventh, Wood came unexpectedly upon the ground where, the night before, the rebel General Polk's corps had bivouacked, and at once apprised General Crittenden of the close proximity of the formidable rebel force. The enemy had evacuated Chattanooga and its vicinity without destroying bridges or track on the railroads, and left large quantities of supplies in the country about. He had had abundant time and opportunity to remove these supplies, and if he was to transfer his line of defence to Dalton, it would certainly have been worth his while to render the railroads immediately unserviceable.

On the morning of the twelfth, Crittenden's divisions, at Ringgold, were put in march for Gordon's Mills, to join Wood, and diminish the distance isolating him from the rest of the army. Near Gordon's the enemy's cavalry was again encountered, and, although they gave ground readily before the infantry advance on the march and in a subsequent reconnoissance from Gordon's toward La Fayette, still their spirit of enterprise, while hovering constantly about, and boldly venturing between the infantry columns, indicated a confidence in substantial supports close at hand. Their cavalry was evidently performing its duty in a way little like its ordinary manner of covering a retreat. On the morning of the thirteenth, the corps crossed to the west side of the creek and took position.

A reconnoissance toward La Fayette met a stubborn resistance, at a distance of two miles from the Mills, the enemy using artillery. On the fourteenth, two divisions marched westward to the Chattanooga Valley, and in the afternoon found Thomas's corps some miles further up the valley; the left and centre were now together, but the right corps was far up the valley, and without supporting distance.

General Thomas had pushed Negley's division across Lookout Mountain, at Stephens's Gap, about sixteen miles from Gordon's. On the eighth and ninth, his whole corps crossed. On the tenth, Negley was sent forward to the passes of Pigeon Mountain, which closes Chattanooga Valley, a few miles south of Stephens's Gap.

Here Negley found the enemy strong and active, and was obliged to fall back upon the corps, the enemy manifesting much enterprise in attacking his trains during the movement. Development since the battle shows the isolation of Crittenden's corps during the tenth, eleventh, and twelfth to have been hazardous in the extreme; while it was at Gordon's Mills it was reported that the rebel General Polk, with a strong corps, was near Rock Spring, three miles from the Mills, meditating an offensive movement. Rebel officers, now prisoners, confirm this, and state that Hindman's division was ordered to seize Stephens's Gap, in Lookout Mountains, to prevent the junction of Crittenden with Thomas. Hindman failed to execute this order in proper time; the junction was made, General Polk's forces were withdrawn, and the concentration of Bragg's army, and the reënforcements sent him from Virginia and elsewhere, were made at La Fayette. For his failure here Hindman is said to be now in arrest. An attack by Polk at daylight on the thirteenth would have been disastrous to Crittenden, and without doubt

have left the road to Chattanooga, and the rear of the entire army with its lines of communication, unobstructed. Leaving Wood's division in position at Gordon's Mills, General Crittenden on the fifteenth, moved his corps to the left and front, taking position on Chickamauga River, to the left of Thomas, seven miles north of Gordon's. During the sixteenth and seventeenth, the position was not materially changed. On the night of the seventeenth, the line moved to Crawfish Springs. Developments since the battle are to the effect that the isolation of McCook was as dangerous as that of Crittenden. When ordered to join the army at Crawfish Springs, McCook recrossed the Lookout Mountains and came down Lookout Valley, crossing again into Chattanooga Valley at Stephens's Gap. Had he attempted to join by moving down the east side of Lookout, as was expected, he would, say prisoners whose rank entitles them to credit, have encountered a force sufficient to overpower him. During the eighteenth, heavy clouds of dust east of Chickamauga River, and demonstrations upon General Wood at Gordon's, indicated that the enemy was moving toward our left. Toward evening the movement of General Rosecrans's army to its left commenced, and early on the morning of September nineteenth, the disposition and the ground were as follows:

From Gordon's Mills to Chattanooga (ten miles) the road runs nearly north, for six miles nearly parallel to, and one to two miles from Missionary Ridge, which it crosses by a pass at Rossville.

At Gordon's Mills the Chickamauga River is close upon the road, and runs parallel to it for half a mile northward, where it makes a sudden bend to the right and gradually increases the distance between it and the road. The ridge is high, and in many places very steep and impracticable.

The river at Gordon's runs in a bed with rocky, precipitous banks, impassable for artillery, except at the established fords, north of the Mills; though not always impracticable, it is a good obstacle, and crossing is difficult if contested.

The country between the ridge and river is generally level but rolling, thickly wooded, with comparatively little cleared land. Too much wooded for artillery, the ground is yet open for manoeuvre.

Crittenden's corps, its left in the strong position at Gordon's, was in line parallel with the road and east of it. Thomas was on his left, at Owen's Ford, two miles south of the Mills. The line followed the road, not the river, though the left was considerably beyond the road, while the right was upon it. Two of McCook's divisions were yet on the march from Crawfish Springs. There was a ford at the river in front of the left, but it was unguarded, and there were other practicable points on the stream toward the Mills.

A division of the reserve corps, under General Granger, was at Rossville, four miles from the left of the line, and on Saturday morning a brigade from this force advanced on the Ringgold road, and burned the bridge at the Chickamauga River.

From Crawfish Springs it had been a race, both armies marching by the flank. The movement of Rosecrans's whole line on the night of the eighteenth, until the right rested where the left had been, was supposed to have put him again in front of the enemy, and for the present saved his line of operations. Of the several enterprises the enemy might undertake, the most probable was that he would concentrate as far to his right as possible, if he fought; for the Federal left was in a much weaker position than the right, and an attack here afforded the tempting prospect of securing Rosecrans's line. To allow the enemy to bring across the river a portion of his force to attack, and then, with the obstruction in their rear, preventing alike a good retreat and a prompt reënforcement, to fall violently upon and overwhelm them by striking on front and flank, was an operation of rich promise, but requiring great vigilance and correct judgment in determining the moment for assuming the offensive.

Of course it is not pretended that this plan was in view during the confused night march of the eighteenth, and the still more confused movements of the nineteenth.

Until late in the morning of the nineteenth, every thing was quiet on the rebel side. At length the brigade from General Thomas's left was sent forward to the ford mentioned as being in front of that point. This force encountered a rebel brigade, drove it from its position, and reached the river. Almost immediately, however, it was in turn attacked and driven back.

Whatever force the enemy may have crossed previous to this time, he now maintained the fight much in advance of the river, and brought his forces into action so rapidly that all attempts to drive him back upon the river were futile, and no advantage of ground lay with either side. Thomas's left divisions (Brannan's, Baird's, and Johnson's) were found insufficient to force the enemy, and Crittenden's left division (Palmer's) was' ordered to the ground to strike the enemy's left flank. Palmer went to the left of Thomas's right division, (Reynolds's — not then engaged,) but came full in the face of the enemy, not on his flank. Soon after Reynolds became engaged, but still the Federal right did not outflank the abundant foe. Van Cleve, commanding Crittenden's next division, was sent in, and his leading brigade (Beatty's) formed within half musket-shot of a rebel force preparing to flank the Federal right, ran over and captured, almost without fighting, a rebel battery, but was immediately hurled violently back. The last division at hand (Wood's, of Crittenden's corps, which formed the right of the line) was then thrown in to find the flank of that rebel line which had grown so alarmingly that it now covered the whole front of the Federal army. The fine position at the Mills, the cover of the right flank, was abandoned by this movement, but subsequently temporarily reöccupied by one of McCook's brigades, (Lytle's.) Wood sent in his brigades as ordered,

but almost upon the ground where they went into line, they were nearly enveloped on the instant by the swarming enemy, and could of course accomplish nothing. It was even necessary to send to this point, as they came up, McCook's two divisions, Davis's and Sheridan's. This force sufficed to hold the ground only, and the attempt to strike the enemy's left flank was of course at an end—the whole Federal force being now engaged with his front. The enemy had made his battle, suffering nothing from the disadvantage of having to cross the river almost within rifle-shot of the Federal lines, had maintained a superiority in force, and fought upon equal ground. Late in the afternoon, coming heavily upon Reynolds and Van Cleve, he drove them furiously back, and penetrated the line. Palmer's brigades, attempting to assist Reynolds, were sent back with him. Nearly the whole force was in confusion, and the enemy bearing strongly down upon the broken flank to his right, had like to have swept in reverse the entire Federal line left of the break, when twenty pieces of artillery, hastily posted by General Hazen, and rapidly served with canister, brought him to a stand, and he withdrew from the interval. After dusk an energetic attack, maintained with some promise of persistency, upon Johnson's division, but successfully resisted, closed the battle for the day. Had the enemy, after penetrating Reynolds's line, followed with proper force the movement stopped by the artillery, he would have had probably little to do on the twentieth, to make his victory decisive.

There had been gallant fighting on both sides, and both had suffered severely. Little artillery had been lost, but the Federals had made the gain, three guns. What advantage generally had been gained, however, was with the rebels. They had successfully overcome the obstacle of the river in their front on Sunday morning forcing the Federal line from it at every point, until it lay in a country almost destitute of water. Not enough could be had for the men's coffee, and what was obtained was from springs several miles distant. During the day Negley's division had been withdrawn from Owen's Ford, and in the afternoon Lytle's brigade, which had reöccupied Gordon's Mills after Wood was withdrawn, was recalled, so that the whole army was in the line. There was, indeed, little need of detachments now, for there was left nothing south of Rossville to hold, except the plain country, which the enemy shared. The force and position of both armies had, it was safe to assume, been well developed, and with this knowledge the night was before the hostile commanders for tactical dispositions, if it was decided to fight on the morrow. On the Federal side there was less reason for retreat than in the morning; all uncertainty as to the rebel position had vanished, and it only remained to look to his movements during the night. Gordon's Mills having been abandoned, there was but one great strategic point to claim attention — the pass at Rossville, on the Chattanooga road. With this in possession of the enemy, a retreat other than disastrous could hardly be hoped for. During the night of the nineteenth, the Federal force was thus disposed, commencing at the left and proceeding to the right. Baird's division of Thomas's corps was in line four hundred yards east of the Chattanooga road, the left of course refused; next Johnson's division of McCook's corps, then Palmer's, of Crittenden's corps, then Reynolds's, of Thomas's corps. As this part of the line subsequently became isolated, it is particularly described. The first line occupied a very slight crest in a forest which prevented a view in front of more than one hundred and fifty or two hundred yards. Along this line a slight breastwork of rails, logs, etc., commenced first in Hazen's brigade, had been carried shortly after daylight. It proved invaluable during the day. In rear of Johnson's, Palmer's, and part of the lines of the other divisions, was an open field, extending as far as the road, to which the line was parallel at a distance of about four hundred yards. The northern part of the open ground was a cornfield, much of the standing stalk having been consumed during the night; the southern part was a fallow field. Beyond the road looking to the rear were dense woods. Next on the right of Reynolds, was Brannan's division of Thomas's corps, which had been brought up from the extreme left on Saturday evening, at the time the enemy penetrated the centre; then Negley's division, Thomas's corps, its right making a crotchet to the rear; and the line across the Chattanooga road toward Missionary Ridge was completed by Sheridan's and Davis's divisions of McCook's corps. Wood's and Van Cleve's divisions of Crittenden's corps, were in reserve at a proper distance in rear of the angle in the line. It will be seen that the divisions of the three corps were much scattered, no corps being complete on the line. It was daylight before the divisions had all taken position, and when this was accomplished, there was begun the closing of the line to the left, the divisions moving successively, and apparently in obedience to orders not from a general on the ground, so tardily was it done.

While the closing up of the line was still in progress, the attack commenced upon the left, and gradually progressed toward the right. Baird maintained his ground for a time, but was finally forced backward. The reserves of the left divisions were, however, sufficient to recover the ground — Willich's brigade, of Johnson's division, being taken in with much effect. The attack travelling toward the right, fell furiously but vainly upon Palmer and Reynolds, whose breastworks served them well. While this was in progress, Negley's division, forming the crotchet in the line, was ordered to the extreme left by General Rosecrans, to support that portion of the line. Wood's division, from the reserve, was sent to occupy the ground left vacant by Negley. In the mean time the attack had reached Reynolds, and the process of closing up the line to the left had gone as far as Brannan, on Reynolds's right. At this time Wood received an order from General Rosecrans to close well up on Reynolds, and support him. Wood's skirmishers were already firing, and to withdraw, leaving an interval at that important point, seemed hazardous, but the order was positive. Wood marched to the rear, to pass to the left behind Brannan, who was between him and Reynolds, and almost instantly a heavy column of the enemy entered the interval. Van Cleve's, the other reserve division sent to support Brannan, was posted behind the latter, very close to him. The enemy, pressing briskly through the interval left by Wood, at once caught Sheridan and Davis in reverse and upon the flank, compelling a confused retreat.

Brannan was struck upon the flank, and with Van Cleve, his support, driven violently back. The latter division was not again formed on the field. Wood, taken on the march, resisted as he fell backward, and at length sending Harker's brigade at them at a charge, cleared his front, and after holding the ground a short time, fell back to a strong ridge, which he held. Here Brannan re-formed his division, being with Wood all that remained of the right of the army, if some fragments of regiments be excepted. Four or five batteries of reserve artillery, which were left in position when the reserve divisions were ordered up to the line, being directly in the enemy's course as he came through the interval above described, fared as might be expected. Almost without warning, a rebel line marched quietly upon the astonished gunners without receiving a shot, and seventeen pieces were captured. The rebels turned their pieces toward Wood, and their shells, flying high, burst in rear of the extreme left, killing the wounded in a hospital in rear of Palmer's division, and firing the building. A few words will end the story of the right.

Swarming through the woods in confused masses, the men of Sheridan's, Davis's, and Van Cleve's divisions, with some from Brannan's, passed backward. Headquarters, which had been in rear of the position of the reserve, was caught up by the multitude and carried back. To those in the crowd the disaster appeared irremediable; apparently the whole army was in confused flight. Even the Commanding General, after a vain effort to arrest the foremost of the crowd as they came up to his position, and the commanders of the Twentieth and Twenty-first corps, were carried away by the living tide, and cut off from the remainder of the army. There was no panic among the retreating mass; but they were not stopped, though unpursued, until they reached Rossville. Sheridan indeed rallied his men and essayed a stand, but could not hold his ground; with much dexterity, however, he avoided the enemy and brought his division, almost complete, to Rossville. Negley, who, it has been mentioned, was withdrawn from the right and ordered to the left, by some unexplained fatality was in the retreating mass with two brigades, his other brigade having been formed on the left of Baird's division.

The disaster had been terrible; the ammunition trains were gone, no one knew whither, and the troops that remained upon the field were rapidly exhausting their cartridges. Four divisions, complete, save one brigade, were effectually out of the fight.

While some of the events above narrated were yet in progress, the battle was critical upon the left. Baird's division, the extreme left, flanked and sorely pressed, was driven back until its line and that of Johnson's formed a right angle with the line of Palmer's and Reynolds's. The enemy pressed on as if determined to make his final effort to possess Rosecrans's line of retreat. Indeed he was already upon the Chattanooga road behind Baird's original position, when relief came. Brannan's reserve (Vandeveer's brigade) came down the road from the right, and quickly forming, dashed upon the victorious enemy at a charging pace. They could not be withstood, and Baird and Johnson, with one of Palmer's brigades, (Grose's,) promptly following the advantage, restored the line. In front of Palmer and Reynolds the enemy made furious attempts to force his columns upon the line, but the steady volleys from the breastworks dismayed his troops, and they went back with loss. These four divisions were now isolated, and there was no corps commander present. Reynolds was obliged to refuse his right flank, which had become exposed by the falling back of Brannan.

At about one o'clock of the day, it became known here that some grievous disaster had befallen the right. Staff-officers sent for ammunition reported none to be found, and that the line ended with Reynolds's division; if there were more troops beyond this, there was an interval too great for coöperation between the separated forces. The enemy failing to carry the breastworks, had filled the trees in front with sharp-shooters, and these now worked around Reynolds's right, until, from the woods in the very rear of the whole position, their balls came whizzing at the backs of the men. Several shells coming from the right and rear, had also taken Palmer's line full in reverse. Still there were here four good divisions, their organization intact, and when it was learned that Brannan's and Wood's divisions were in position a mile to the right, and that Steedman's division, from General Granger's reserve corps, had come up, the feeling of despondency passed away, and officers and men thought it was not in the fates that their gallant and successful struggles of two days should be wholly without reward. The fighting ceased, but evidently only to allow time for fresh dispositions of the enemy. Brannan's and Wood's position, upon which the next attack fell, was on the crest of a ridge half a mile behind Reynolds's right. General Thomas was also at this position. It was mostly wooded, and toward the right trended backward until it ran nearly at right angles with the line of Reynolds, Palmer, etc. Through the wooded interval between this line and that of Reynolds ran the Chattanooga road, which, looking di-

rectly to the rear from Thomas's position, came into view again beyond the left of Baird's division, which was the left of the entire army. General Thomas had here one brigade (Harker's) of Wood's division; Brannan much reduced in strength but with organization complete; and two brigades of Steedman's division, (Whittaker's and Mitchell's,) reserve corps, with whom came General Granger. Steedman arrived at ten minutes past two o'clock, and at once sent these brigades upon the enemy at a charge. The enemy was driven, but came back in great force, inflicting heavy losses. Several attacks had been repulsed by these forces, and the day was drawing to a close, when the enemy prepared for a final attempt. The sharp crack of the musketry, announcing the bursting of the new storm, was heard with apprehension at the position of the four left divisions, and the necessity of sending relief admitted. In the consultation to determine what portion of the line could best spare a part of its force, General Hazen offered to send his brigade (of Palmer's division) across the interval to General Thomas's support. The offer was accepted, and Hazen safely crossed and formed on the left of General Thomas's line. The enemy attacked with great vigor, but was unable to bring his men up to the crest under the rapid volleys that swept the slope, and finally he abandoned the contest.

Just before dark, the withdrawal of the four left divisions was commenced, Reynolds moved back first, and without molestation; then Palmer commenced his movement, then Johnson, and lastly Baird. Palmer, however, had not gained the road in his rear, when the enemy appeared at the breastworks just abandoned. The withdrawal of the two remaining divisions was necessarily hurried. Indeed, before Palmer was out of reach, the enemy had opened upon him with artillery. One of Baird's brigades, (King's,) the last to move, was caught by the oncoming foe, and lost some hundred prisoners. No sooner was it dark, than the entire army, moving quietly on an unfrequented road along Missionary Ridge, retreated in good order to Rossville. The enemy, though following the withdrawing skirmishers at one hundred yards, in his eagerness to occupy the abandoned ground, did not fire a shot at the troops that left Thomas's position, and did not follow the retreat.

At daylight of September twenty-first, a new line was formed on Missionary Ridge at Rossville, and after lying during the day without attack, the army that night continued its retreat to Chattanooga.

From the above facts it is just to draw conclusions. The first is, that the junction of Crittenden with Thomas, on the fourteenth, was due to a failure in the rebel plan, not to any adequate provision for such a contingency by the Federal commander. That McCook effected his junction successfully, is probably due to his own correct judgment in recrossing the mountain to Winston's Springs, even at the expense of a day's delay in the concentration of the army, instead of attempting to come down on the east side of Lookout.

The movement of the army from the Tennessee River seems to have proceeded upon the supposition that the enemy was unable to make a stand against a single corps, and without a suspicion that he was only retiring to meet his reenforcements, as proved to be the case. It was a matter of remark at the time, that the abundant supplies left at various points, and the neglect to destroy bridges or obstruct roads, indicated the enemy's confidence in his ability to repossess the country quickly.

When the battle commenced on Saturday, the nineteenth, there was probably no great disparity of numbers in the two armies. But one of Longstreet's divisions (Hood's) was present, and but three brigades of that. Statements of prisoners, and previous information of the rebel organization, fail to give more than thirty-four brigades; and this, at the fair allowance of one thousand five hundred to a brigade, would make the rebel strength between fifty thousand and fifty-five thousand, exclusive of cavalry. General Rosecrans had very nearly the same number of men in his army. This, it will be remembered, is the estimate for the Saturday's battle; the enemy had reenforcements on the march, including the Georgia militia, some part of Longstreet's corps, and others, which arrived before the close of Sunday's fight. Rosecrans got into that fight only the two brigades of Steedman's division, in addition to what he had on Saturday. Probably it will be found necessary to look farther than the assertion of "overwhelming numbers," for an explanation of the disaster to the Union arms. At all events, it is certain that seven divisions, after losing heavily on Saturday, were able, with all the disadvantages of a divided line and open position, and after the disastrous retreat of four divisions, with the loss of twenty pieces of artillery, ammunition, etc., to hold the battle-ground against the entire Southern army during Sunday afternoon, and then at night retreat, not at all as if they felt themselves whipped by the enemy. To indicate, in this connection, the spirit of the rebels, it may be stated that in an attempt to feel the Federal position on Missionary Ridge, on the afternoon of the twenty-first, although they vigorously engaged and drove back the skirmishers, they could not be made to follow far enough to discover the Federal line, despite the liberal curses of their officers within hearing of the Federals.

Finally, credit for saving the army from the most disastrous defeat, if not practical annihilation, is due to no corps alone, not to any General exclusively; but more than to any other cause to the sturdy fighting qualities of the army, which, properly controlled, was able to have whipped "the whole Southern Confederacy," if (as has been asserted) that was the force in front of it on September nineteenth and twentieth, 1863.

Since the battle, the General commanding the army, two corps commanders, McCook and Crittenden, and two division commanders, Negley and Van Cleve, have been relieved from their commands.

ADDENDA.

It has often been asserted, and the opinion is evidently gaining ground, that the advance from Chattanooga to the Chickamauga was necessary to the possession of the former place. In other words, that General Rosecrans, having compelled the evacuation of Chattanooga by throwing McCook's and Thomas's corps up Lookout Valley, was obliged to concentrate his army at Chickamauga to get it safely back to Chattanooga. This is said to relieve the responsible party of blame for not resting at Chattanooga until the reenforcements, etc., came up, and if it be true, it is of course conclusive on that point. The facts are these: As early as September sixth, indications of a purpose to evacuate Chattanooga were observed, and the event was confidently looked for every day thereafter. On the ninth, the order to advance beyond Chattanooga had reached the extreme detached command, thirty miles from Chattanooga by the ordinary means of couriers. It would appear then, that the enemy's movement from Chattanooga was known at headquarters at least as early as the night of the eighth, and it remains to note the position of the army at that date. Crittenden's corps was principally in Lookout Valley, and could march into Chattanooga in two hours. Thomas's corps was near Stephens's Gap, some twenty miles southward in Lookout Valley, and McCook in the same valley, a little more than twenty miles further south. Between the army thus situated and the enemy's line of retreat was Lookout Mountain, "a perpendicular wall of limestone over which no wheel could pass." It is very evident that on the ninth, while Crittenden marched into Chattanooga, and commenced the work of strengthening the place, Thomas could have marched back down Lookout Valley without molestation; but McCook would have been endangered, without some further provision. Thomas was on the ninth in Stephens's Gap, the only point at which the enemy could pass Lookout between McCook and Chattanooga to cut him off. A division would have been ample to secure this Gap until McCook, marching down the valley for Chattanooga, should have passed it. By night of the tenth, Crittenden's corps and at least two divisions of Thomas's would have been fortifying Chattanooga, while McCook's and Thomas's other divisions, separated and protected from the enemy by the "perpendicular wall" of Lookout Mountain, and holding its only pass, would have been marching with what speed was possible to join them.

Instead of this, Crittenden was sent south-easterly to Ringgold, a point further from Thomas than Chattanooga was, leaving the Chickamauga River, Missionary Ridge, and Lookout Mountain, between Crittenden and the rest of the army. To effect the concentration on the Chickamauga the left corps marched thirty miles, the centre corps sixteen miles, and the right corps twenty-seven miles, the two latter corps crossing a difficult mountain, and each of the three corps being during its movements completely isolated. To effect a concentration at Chattanooga by the Lookout Valley the left corps would have marched six miles, (or into Chattanooga;) the centre corps twenty miles, and the right corps forty miles ; but the two former would have effected a junction in twenty-four hours instead of five days, as at Chickamauga, and the right corps, marching down the valley instead of over the mountains, might have accomplished its forty miles in two days instead of eight. The several corps, too, pending their march down Lookout Valley, would have been safe from attack in detail, for the reason that neither could be attacked over Lookout Mountain.

GENERAL STEEDMAN'S DIVISION.
ITS OPERATIONS ON THE TWENTIETH.

In the Field, Opposite Chattanooga,
September 30, 1863.

Among the many divisions of the army of the Cumberland which acquitted themselves nobly in the battles of the nineteenth and twentieth, the First division of the reserve corps, commanded by Brigadier-General James B. Steedman, deserves some mention.

On the eighteenth the First brigade of the division, commanded by Brigadier-General W. C. Whittaker, was sent from Rossville to the Little Chickamauga, on the road to Ringgold. Here, after sundown, a brief skirmish was had with the enemy, in which neither party suffered any considerable loss.

On the afternoon of the nineteenth, the tide of battle, which had been running heavily on our right during the day, reached this brigade, and an engagement of some fierceness was had with the enemy. The position held by the brigade was on the extreme left of our lines, and the key to Rosecrans's line of retreat. The position was much coveted by the enemy, and they made repeated assaults to obtain it, but were handsomely repulsed, and suffered quite severely, especially from our artillery.

During the night of the nineteenth, the Second brigade, commanded by Colonel J. M. Mitchell, of the One Hundred and Thirteenth Ohio, was sent to the aid of Whittaker; also, Colonel Dan McCook's brigade, of the Second division of the reserve, and the Twenty-second Michigan and Eighty-ninth Ohio, which two regiments were attached to Whittaker's command.

During the forenoon of the twentieth, these forces, under the command of General Steedman, held their position, at that point, in line of battle, awaiting a more formidable effort, which it was supposed the enemy would make to turn our left. But no assault was made, for the enemy had withdrawn his troops from that point, to mass them against Thomas.

While waiting there, pursuant to orders from General Rosecrans, the troops listened with anxious impatience to the heavy cannonading and sharp musketry which resounded along the line on the right, and which, approaching nearer and nearer, begat fearful suspicions that it was not Rosecrans, but the enemy, who were driving the opposing forces. Our suspense was broken, and our fears confirmed when, about noon, urgent orders were received to hasten to the relief of Thomas, who was in great danger.

The troops did not then know in how critical a condition the army of the Cumberland was compelled to meet, unassisted, the flower of three large armies which the rebels had assembled, intending to overwhelm it. They did not then know that, while they were hastening to turn the tide of battle, if possible, portions of Crittenden's and McCook's corps were retiring from the field. But they did know the time had come when the reserve must be tested, and the question determined whether or no it were worthy of its honorable position in the great army of the Cumberland.

Steedman's division, followed by McCook's brigade, was speedily put in motion, and the columns moved forward at a rapid pace, sometimes breaking into a double-quick. The sun shone hot, and the dust in the narrow road rose in dense, suffocating clouds ; but all thought of heat and dust and fatigue was lost in the eager anxiety to relieve our brave comrades who were in peril. After thus marching some three miles, the head of the column reached a portion of the battle-field from which our forces had retired, and which the enemy occupied with his mounted infantry. Formed hastily in line of battle, Whittaker's brigade advanced upon them. They did not await our approach, but gave up the ground, retreating in a direction, which had we followed, would have diverted us from the main purpose. In passing over this portion of the field, the dead and dying of both armies were seen in considerable numbers, and some rebels, separated from their commands, were encountered on the right, and taken prisoners by the Ninety-sixth Illinois.

Soon a point was reached, directly opposite to, and about three fourths of a mile distant from General Thomas, and the whole division turned square to the right. Here they were formed into close columns by regiments, with division front ; and, with a line of skirmishers thrown forward, and along the left flank, the division resumed its march. It was through an extensive stretch of meadow land, overgrown with weeds almost breast high, that our course lay. Heavy batteries of the enemy's artillery were posted in the woods on our left, and as we advanced through the meadow, to form a junction with Thomas, they opened upon us a fearful fire. But few troops in the division had ever seen more of war than is encountered in brisk skirmishing, and none had ever been under such a fire. But Whittaker, with his staff, and Colonel Mitchell and staff, rode steadily in front of their brigades, and their troops, although the shells and shot fell fast and thick around and among them, wavered not in their march, but kept right on, leaving many of their comrades dead and wounded on the field. At that moment, the spectacle, to one not inured to all the pageantry of war, was intensely grand. The brigade and regimental colors floated gayly in the light of the mid-day sun. The far-stretching columns of troops, with glistening weapons, moved forward with uniform motion, presenting, at a distance, the appearance of one compact mass. On the left, dense masses of sulphurous smoke hung just above the trees, and in front and along the lines the shells were bursting in the air, while the solid shot, seemingly imbued with infernal energy, ploughed the ground, bounding and plunging over the field, leaving all over the meadow little clouds of dust to mark their course. That march, through that storm of shell and shot, was a fit introduction to the scenes upon which that division was about to enter.

But little time was occupied in reaching Thomas, where General Granger, commanding the reserve, and General Steedman, were already holding consultation with him. As we approached, General Whittaker, whose brigade was in the advance, was told that it was absolutely necessary that he should drive the enemy from the ridge on our right, where heavy forces had been massed, as if for the purpose of flanking Thomas. Indeed, the occupation of that ridge was so threatening, that, if the enemy continued to hold it, Thomas must have retired. Whittaker said he would take the ridge, and he did it.

This is the way it was done: The six regiments of the First brigade were formed in two lines—the first comprising the Ninety-sixth Illinois, Colonel Thomas E. Champion, on the right; One Hundred and Fifteenth Illinois, Colonel J. H. Moore, in the centre; and the Twenty-second Michigan, Colonel Le Fevre, on the left. Then came the order to advance. With a yell, the first line bounded forward on the double-quick. Up and down the little hills and through the narrow valleys which intervened, they pressed hastily forward, until they came within short range of the rebel musketry, which opened upon them furiously, while the grape and canister from the battery on the ridge swept cruelly through their ranks. Almost exhausted with their hurried march, and their long-continued double-quick, the troops recoiled for a moment under that withering fire; but ere the most timid could think of retreating, Colonel Champion promptly gave the command to halt, lie down, and fire, which was obeyed on the instant. There the line lay for five minutes, responding resolutely to the fire of the enemy. That five minutes was a terrible ordeal for our soldiers—for during that short period their ranks were more than decimated. Then came the order to fix bayonets, and charge upon the enemy. The ardor of the men overcame their fatigue, and, tired as they were, they resumed the double-quick march as they advanced up the ridge, right in the face of a galling fire. If a man fell—and many did—he was left to enrich the soil of Georgia with his life's blood, or if able, to creep, alone and unassisted, to the rear, for none who were able to march left the ranks, which were kept well closed up, and the line was firmly maintained.

By this time the Seventy-eighth Illinois and One Hundred and Twenty-first Ohio, of the Second brigade, had came up and were advancing on the right of the first, and a little to the rear. Never was support more opportune, for while Whittaker's men were charging up the ridge, the enemy received a well-directed fire from Colonel Mitchell's forces, and when the crest of the ridge was gained, the enemy was discovered retreating in confusion, and their battery had disappeared. With a loud huzza we followed them; but not far. Fresh troops were sent against us, and the fire became as scathing as ever. We halted in our advanced position, and held it, while the contending musketry, sharp and incessant, almost stunned the ear. The enemy constantly strengthened his lines, and their fire became hotter and quicker. The first line was ordered to fall back. The second line took its place, and held the position a short time, when the forces were ordered to retire to the crest of the ridge, from which the enemy had been driven.

That was the way the fight, on the part of Steedman's division, opened on that day: It had gained a great advantage, but it was not to maintain it without a severe contest. Bragg's reserves—the flower of the Potomac army—were sent to dislodge us from our newly gained position. But it availed them not. Battery M, First Illinois artillery, was planted far to the right, in a commanding position; and such was the conformation of the ground, that as the rebel line advanced to the assault, they came under the sure and effective range of our guns. Their battery had been planted in a new position, bearing upon ours, and the continued roar of artillery soon was mingled with the sound of musketry.

Our lines were extended to the right, so as to reach and support our battery, which the rebels were threatening to attack. A general assault was soon made upon our lines, but it proved disastrous to the rebels. Our grape and canister made great havoc in their ranks, while our soldiers took careful aim before pulling the triggers of their Enfield muskets. The rebels were badly repulsed, and as they retreated we followed, pursuing them a considerable distance. But while this move exposed us to the fire of their artillery, they were much less in danger from our battery. Other troops, in heavier force, took the place of those whom we had driven, and the battle waged fiercely again until we were ordered to retire.

Let the simple truth be told. That retreat, in fact that whole battle in which our division was engaged, was not conducted with precisely the same order observed on a dress parade. I have read of such things; I have heard of troops acting with Arctic coolness and impassibility under the most galling fire, minutely observing every direction of the tactics. It may be so, but it was not so with our division on that day. When the men were ordered to advance they kept their line pretty well, but there were many whose eagerness carried them ahead of it, and some whose timidity kept them in rear of it. In retreating, the men paid but little attention to keeping their lines well dressed, and had the appearance of a *mass* rather than a *line*. Nay, more; some of the troops on the left actually broke, and were thrown into some disorder. But it is also true that when the desired point was gained the troops were readily halted and rallied with but little difficulty. Once, the One Hundred and Fifteenth Illinois — which did exceedingly well that day—seemed unable to rally; but General Steedman was near at hand, and, seizing the colors from the standard-bearer, advanced toward the enemy, saying to the men: "Boys, I'll carry your flag if you'll defend it." They rallied around him and did noble deeds. There was not one instance of failure to rally the troops, though the leaden hail fell so thick and fast among them that nothing but their native heroism and the animating courage of their officers could have kept them up to the work. Let it not be forgotten that on that afternoon there was but little fighting, except upon Thomas's lines, whose right Steedman held, and on the right the fiercest fighting apparently was done. There was nothing to prevent the enemy from sending almost overwhelming forces against us, and we learn from prisoners, and we judge from the incidents and character of the contest, that they were fighting Steedman with the odds of at least three to one in their favor. Thomas was holding their whole army in check, saving from irretrievable disaster the army of the Cumberland; and there was nothing akin to a holiday parade in the terrible momentum of their assaults to break through that bulwark, or the heroic endurance with which our soldiers met and repulsed them. More depended upon the individuality of the soldier than upon the harmonious movements of regiments and brigades. This was felt by our officers and soldiers. There was little manœuvring, but there was a great deal of fighting. There was no waiting for commands in detail — no firing of volleys by platoons and companies. When we had gained a position in advance, and the line was halted in view of the enemy, the men fired at will, each intent only on doing his own duty well.

After that repulse another assault was made, and with the same result. The rebels advanced, were checked; we drove and followed them until fresh troops were arrayed against us, and we in turn were forced to retire. But this time we drove them further, and kept them at bay longer, than before. One of our regiments—the Ninety-sixth Illinois — pursued them nearly half a mile, and held that advanced position until it began to receive an enfilading fire from some of our own troops.

Thus the contest continued until dark, and all the time we held the ridge. Sometimes a regiment or more would fall back beyond the ridge, but enough always remained to hold it. At last General Thomas gave the order to retire; but it failed to reach a portion of the Ninety-sixth Illinois, and a remnant of the One Hundred and Twenty-first Ohio, who at the time occupied a position on the right, somewhat advanced beyond the line, and there for a considerable time they continued to fight with unabated vigor. The order to retire was at last given to this devoted band, who reluctantly left their position. That closed the fighting for the day. We retired from the field, not knowing that the enemy was at the same time also retreating, baffled and discouraged, in fact beaten.

So the bloody field was left unoccupied that night. No, not wholly unoccupied; for James T. Gruppy, a private of company D, Ninety-sixth Illinois, not knowing that our troops had fallen back, slept upon the battle-field, and next morning, as he awoke, found a rebel surgeon near him, looking for rebel dead, and who advised him, if he ever wished to see his regiment again, to hurry on to Chattanooga.

The fight was over, and while the Union army was sad, the rebels were not exultant. The fight was over, and Steedman's division had made its record. It had done more than that. Said General Thomas to General Steedman: "You have saved my corps!"

That was a deed worthy to be proud of; for from what disaster did not that corps save our army and our cause!

But there was little feeling of pride that night among the troops of the First division of the reserve. We were busy in reckoning up our losses, and they were appalling! The long list of killed and wounded is a sad proof of the trial by fire to which, that afternoon, our division was subjected.

Was ever such havoc made with a staff as that which General Whittaker's suffered? There were eight of them, including the General. Three were killed, three wounded, one captured or killed, and only one escaped. How often has it happened that a regiment, in one afternoon's engagement, has endured a greater loss in killed and wounded than the Ninety-sixth Illinois? It took into battle four hundred and fifteen men. It lost forty-two killed and one hundred twenty-one wounded—considerably more than one third. Of its twenty-three field, staff, and line-officers engaged, eleven were killed and wounded. It happened that that regiment, during the fight, was always in the front line, and was greatly exposed to the enemy's artillery; but, under the cool and able leadership of Colonel Champion, it maintained its place, and, with the One Hundred and Twenty-first Ohio, was the last to leave the field.

Whittaker's brigade of six regiments lost nearly one thousand men, killed and wounded, and Colonel Mitchell's brigade of four regiments lost nearly four hundred.

There were many noble men who fell on that hard-fought field—many who deserve special mention. I know but few of the many, yet let me speak of two or three.

Captain S. B. Espy, Assistant Commissary on General Whittaker's staff, was a very lion that day. He was advised to remain with his trains; but, too noble-spirited for that, he remained on the field, fearless of danger, doing wonders in cheering and rallying the men under the destructive fire of the enemy. He was one of Illinois's noble sons, and his loss is severely felt.

And there was a Quartermaster-Sergeant—William S. Bean—who, like Captain Espy, chose the field of danger rather than the post of safety. He might have remained in the rear, and the breath of censure could not have touched him ; but he was right where the bullets flew thickest and fastest, and did the work almost of a general in encouraging the bold and animating the timid. He was a genuine hero.

Captain Wells, of the One Hundred and Thirteenth Ohio, and Lieutenant-Colonel Kinman, of the One Hundred and Fifteenth Illinois, were two of the best men, and bravest soldiers, who yielded up their lives on the twentieth, on their country's altar.

And the scores of privates, corporals, and sergeants, men of families, who had left all—wife, children, home—for their country—from a pure sense of duty ; young men, who left college walls, and the merchant's desk, and the plough and the anvil, all because their country called them, to face death on a battle-field ; darling sons, the hope and stay of widowed mothers, whose early death will break more than one sorrowing heart—what of these ? Alas! too many such there are —as brave, as heroic, as truly martyrs as ever died in the cause of Humanity—to mention here by name. Would you know them ? Read the list of the killed !

We will not, in our sorrow for the heroes dead, forget the surviving brave. These, thanks to a merciful Providence, are even more numerous than the dead. Among the many who did well, General Steedman, and Major Smith and Captain Moe, of his staff, merit special praise. And General Whittaker and Colonel Mitchell, and their staff-officers, and the regimental commanders, are most highly honored by the soldiers, for they were brave and unflinching leaders.

Let me refer to two men in humbler positions. One is Lieutenant C. W. Earle, commanding the color company of the Ninety-sixth. He stood by the colors throughout the fight, and, though all but two of the color-guard were killed and wounded, and the colors were cut to pieces by the bullets and grape and canister that pierced its folds, he faltered not one instant. He is a Second Lieutenant, and but a boy ; yet few full-grown men, in much more exalted positions, excelled him in cool, cheerful courage.

The other is Captain Clason, of the One Hundred and Twenty-first Ohio, who, with the little remnant of the regiment, fought so stubbornly and unyieldingly to the very last, preserving their colors and keeping them afloat proudly in the face of the enemy, until the last shot was fired.

And Colonel Le Fevre, who led his Twenty-second Michigan on a bayonet-charge, after they had expended all their ammunition, should not be forgotten when the roll of honor is made out.

But time and space would fail to name every man who flinched not from his duty on that memorable day. The Eighty-fourth Indiana, the For-tieth, Ninety-eighth, and Eighty-ninth Ohio, and the Seventy-eighth Illinois—all of Steedman's division—has each its list of heroes.

Enough that, at that critical hour, the reserve failed not. And it could have done more had it been necessary, for Colonel McCook's brigade was not engaged. As to our division, it has confidence in its officers, while they are proud of their men ; and it is now ready to test its metal again with a rebel foe. It is with not a little of pride that I can write of such a division, and its fight on the twentieth, *parva pars fui.* MILES.

Doc. 44.

THE BATTLE OF TEBB'S BEND, KY.

LEBANON, KY., July 12, 1863.

A FEW of the particulars of the battle of Tebb's Bend, on the Green River, between General John Morgan, with his entire division, and Colonel O. H. Moore, Twenty-fifth Michigan infantry, with two hundred of his men, may be interesting.

The battalion of the Twenty-fifth Michigan infantry, stationed at or near Green River bridge, occupied a position of much importance—all forces in front were drawn off and no reënforcements within thirty-five miles.

For some days before the fight it was currently reported that Duke and Johnson, under the direction of Morgan, were crossing the Cumberland at Berksville and Creelsboro with a force of ten regiments of cavalry and several pieces of artillery. On the second instant, information was received that the enemy was advancing on our position ; Colonel Moore mounted his horse, and, riding over the surrounding country, chose his ground and planted his men for a fight, determined that the first opportunity of engaging the enemy should not go untried.

Men were that night set at work with spades and axes, and when the morning dawned a fine rifle-pit was to be seen, while in the rear a barricade of fallen trees was thrown to check all cavalry charges. Seventy-five men were kept in the trenches during the day, and in the evening, after the enemy's spies had visited our lines, found our exact position, and made their reports, we began a movement of our force, with all our stores and camp and garrison equipage. While we were thus engaged, the enemy was by no means neglectful—the sound of preparation on our front proclaimed that they were busy.

Our lines were visited at about one o'clock A.M., and all seemed in order. Companies D, E, F, and K occupied the earth-works, while company I was held as a reserve. The scene was exciting and beautiful—the men, wakeful with the thoughts of the coming struggle, were jovial and happy, the brightened barrels of the arms glittering in the moonlight rendered the view soul-inspiring. Thus all continued, and as the first bright rays of morning streamed up the eastern sky, our last wagon crossed the ford, and the sharp-shooters of the enemy opened the ball. Thus the engagement began and thus it continued for nearly an hour, when the enemy, having their artillery in position, sent a shell plunging into our earth-works, disabling two of our men. Before we had an opportunity of clearing the enemy away from their guns, Major Elliot, of Morgan's staff, approached with a flag of truce, with the following despatch:

HEADQUARTERS MORGAN'S DIVISION,
IN THE FIELD IN FRONT OF GREEN RIVER STOCKADE,
July 4, 1863.

To the Officer Commanding Federal Forces at Stockade near Green River Bridge:

SIR: In the name of the confederate States government I demand an immediate and unconditional surrender of the entire force under your command, together with the stockade.

I am, very respectfully,

JOHN H. MORGAN,
Commanding Div. Cavalry C. S. A.

Colonel Moore replied: "Present my compliments to General Morgan, and say to him that this being the Fourth of July, I cannot entertain the proposition." Shaking hands, the Colonel and Major parted, and the Colonel regaining our lines said: "Now, my men, rise up, take good aim, and pick those gunners." The words were sufficient; but ere the deadly fire was poured in upon them, the old Parrott gun of the enemy boomed forth again in its tones of thunder. The volley from our fortification did splendid execution, for not a man was left to tell the story. The enemy charged upon us, and we fell back to the timber. The fight now became terrible. The men fought with a desperation I never saw equalled. They seemed to feel that the enemy was yet to be organized that was to whip them. All possible chance of retreat was cut off, and no support within thirty-five miles. The enemy occupied one side of the tree-tops while we held the other. The case was indeed one that called forth the exertions of every member of the little band. 'Twas life or death, and all were determined rather to die nobly and manfully fighting than cowardly surrendering without a struggle; seven charges followed the first, but the advancing foe fell dead before us. The firing continued for nearly four hours, when the enemy retreated, leaving their dead on the field. Their loss in killed and wounded was very severe, being much greater than our entire numbers, and among the former many of Morgan's ablest officers. There cannot be too much said in praise of the men. In a fair field-fight they defeated John Morgan, the rebel raider, the terrifier of Kentucky. The officers were ever where needed, and deserve credit for their coolness and bravery. Colonel Moore's courage, coolness, daring, and will must call forth the admiration of all. His conduct on the field of battle cheered his men to strenuous efforts, for in every post of danger he was in their midst. He was ever where the bullets fell the thickest, and by his good generalship won the day. General Morgan admired his generalship so much that he promoted him to a Brigadier-General, but the Colonel says that the largest

brigade he wishes to command is the Twenty-fifth Michigan infantry.

Our loss was six killed and twenty-three wounded. I send inclosed the official report. The enemy acknowledged a loss of seventy-three killed, and over two hundred wounded.

About a mile in our rear was a dilapidated stockade which Morgan had on a previous raid endeavored to destroy; we, however, did not think enough of such pens to refit it, and accordingly engaged the enemy in a fair field-fight.

After the battle, as we paid our last honors to the brave men that had fallen, the Colonel issued the following order:

HEADQUARTERS TWENTY-FIFTH MICHIGAN INFANTRY,
BATTLE-FIELD OF TEBB'S BEND, GREEN RIVER,
July 4, 1863.

SPECIAL ORDERS No. 42.

My brave, my noble men! It is with pride and pleasure that I congratulate you upon the great victory won to-day. While you numbered but two hundred men, the enemy numbered thousands. Being advised of their strength, and of their advantage in having artillery bearing upon us, their demand for a surrender was answered with a response that echoed the feelings of the gallant little band of the Twenty-fifth Michigan infantry that was about to engage them.

The engagement was long and bloody; charge after charge was successfully repelled, and after three and a half hours' hard fighting, the enemy was defeated and victory crowned our efforts.

Our brave companions who fell, fell gallantly fighting for their country, and in defence of the starry flag; their names, deeply inscribed on the pages of memory, will be wreathed ever in bright laurels of fame, and though 'tis hard to part with our noble dead, we know 'tis sweet in the cause of our country to die. Although no marble slab have we placed o'er their heads to mark their last resting-place; although no monumental pile have we erected o'er their graves; yet, in the hearts of the people of our own Peninsula State will be erected a monument that will perpetuate their names to all eternity.

By order of Colonel O. H. MOORE.

ED. M. PRUTZMAN,
Lieutenant and Adjutant.

Thus the fourth day of July, made memorable ever in the annals of history, was to-day brought nearer and dearer to us by the gaining of a splendid victory over John Morgan's entire division.

E. M. P.

COLONEL MOORE'S REPORT.

HEADQUARTERS TWENTY-FIFTH MICHIGAN INFANTRY,
BATTLE-FIELD OF TEBB'S BEND, GREEN RIVER,
July 4, 1863.

COLONEL: I have the honor to report that I have had a fight with the rebel General, John Morgan.

I did not move my command from where it was encamped, on the north side of the river, until Morgan's advance had entered Columbia. I then moved forward to occupy the ground I had previously selected, and had the night before prepared for the fight, which was one and a half miles in advance, on the Columbia road, south side of the river. I did not at any time occupy the stockade, which was far in my rear, but gave battle on the narrows entering the bend.

I engaged the enemy's force this morning at half-past three o'clock; early in the engagement he opened on our breastworks with a battery, and after firing a shot, disabling two of my men, he sent a flag of truce with the following despatch:

HEADQUARTERS MORGAN'S DIVISION,
IN FIELD IN FRONT GREEN RIVER STOCKADE,
July 4, 1863.

To the Officer Commanding the Federal Forces at Stockade near Green River Bridge, Ky.:

SIR: In the name of the confederate States government, I demand an immediate and unconditional surrender of the entire force under your command, together with the stockade.

I am, very respectfully, sir,
JOHN H. MORGAN,
Commanding Division Cavalry C. S. A.

I sent a reply to General John Morgan that the Fourth day of July was no day for me to entertain such a proposition. After receiving the reply, he opened fire with his artillery and musketry. My force, which occupied the open field, were withdrawn to the woods where they engaged the enemy with a determination not to be defeated. The battle raged for three and a half (3½) hours, when the enemy retreated with a loss of over fifty (50) killed and two hundred (200) wounded. Among the killed were Colonel Chenault, Major Brent, another major, and five (5) captains, and six (6) lieutenants, as near as can be estimated.

The conflict was fierce and bloody. At times the enemy occupied one side of the fallen timber, while my men held the other, in almost a hand-to-hand fight. The enemy's force consisted of the greater part of Morgan's division. My force was a fraction of my regiment, consisting of two hundred (200) men, who fought gallantly. I cannot say too much in their praise.

Our loss was six (6) killed and twenty-three (23) wounded.

After the battle, I received, under a flag of truce, a despatch asking permission to bury their dead, which request I granted, proposing to deliver them in front of our lines.

The detachment of forty men, under command of Lieutenant M. A. Hogan, Eighth Michigan infantry, held the river at the ford, near the bridge, and repulsed a cavalry charge made by the enemy in a very creditable and gallant manner.

The gallantry of my officers and men in the action was such that I cannot individualize; they all did their duty nobly, and the wounded were treated with the greatest care and attention by Assistant Surgeon J. N. Greggs, of my regiment, whose fine abilities as a surgeon are highly appreciated.

I am, Colonel, very respectfully, your obedient servant, ORLANDO H. MOORE,
Colonel Twenty-fifth Mich. Inf.
Lieutenant-Col. Geo. B. DRAKE,
Assistant Adjutant-General, Lexington, Ky.

HEADQUARTERS TWENTY-THIRD ARMY CORPS,
LEXINGTON, July 17, 1863.

GENERAL ORDER No. 12.

The General commanding the corps hereby extends his thanks to the two hundred officers and soldiers of the Twenty-fifth Michigan regiment, under Colonel O. H. Moore, who so successfully resisted, by their gallant and heroic bravery, the attack of a vastly superior force of the enemy, under the rebel General, John Morgan, at Tebb's Bend, on Green River, on the fourth of July, 1863, in which they killed one fourth as many of the enemy as their own little band amounted to, and wounded a number equal to their own.

By command of Major-Gen. HARTSUFF.
Official. GEO. B. DRAKE, A. A. G.

Official Report of killed and wounded at the battle of Tebb's Bend, Green River, Ky., July fourth, 1863:

Company D, killed, Rosewell Beebe, Third Corporal, Morgan Wallace, Sixth Corporal, Southard Perrin, private; wounded, Harvey C. Lambert, First Sergeant, Simon Young, Corporal; privates Gillespie Parson, Samuel Steeker, Bruce Beebe, Henry Beebe, Jonathan Walbert. Company E, wounded, Joseph Gault, Sergeant; privates George W. Hicks, since died, Orin D. White, Richard W. Baxter, Thomas W. Preston. Company F, killed, Peter G. Cuddeback, Second Corporal; wounded, Arthur M. Twombly, Second Lieutenant, Irving Paddock, Second Sergeant, Henry Bond, Third Sergeant, Henry F. Garmon, First Corporal, Julius C. Webb, Seventh Corporal, George Bennet, Eighth Corporal; privates Marcus Tuttle, Thomas Wood, Arbutt M. Nott, Isaac Smith. Company I, killed, Peter Van Schure, private. Company K, killed, James L. Slater, Fourth Sergeant; wounded, Hiram H. Dunham, private.

Six (6) killed and twenty-three (23) wounded.

Doc. 45.

BRITISH CONSUL AT RICHMOND.*

CONFEDERATE STATES OF AMERICA,
DEPARTMENT OF STATE,
RICHMOND, June 6, 1863.

No. 24.

SIR: Herewith you will receive copies of the following papers:

A.—Letter of George Moore, Esq., Her Britannic Majesty's Consul in Richmond to this department, dated February sixteenth, 1863.

B.—Letter from the Secretary of State to Consul Moore, February twentieth, 1863.

C.—Letters patent by the President, revoking the exequatur of Consul Moore, June fifth, 1863.

D.—Letter inclosing to Consul Moore a copy of the letters patent revoking his exequatur.

It is deemed proper to inform you that this action of the President was influenced in no small degree by the communication to him of an unofficial letter of Consul Moore, to which I shall presently refer.

See Doc. 6, page 9, *ante.*

It appears that two persons, named Molony and Farrell, who were enrolled as conscripts in our service, claimed exemption on the ground that they were British subjects, and Consul Moore, in order to avoid the difficulty which prevented his corresponding with this department as set forth in the paper B, addressed himself directly to the Secretary of War, who was ignorant of the request made by this department for the production of the Consul's commission. The Secretary of War ordered an investigation of the facts, when it became apparent that the two men had exercised the right of suffrage in this State, thus debarring themselves of all pretext for denying their citizenship; that both had resided here for eight years, and had settled on and were cultivating farms owned by themselves. You will find annexed the report of Lieutenant-Colonel Edgar, marked E, and it is difficult to conceive a case presenting stronger proofs of the renunciation of native allegiance, and of the acquisition of *de facto* citizenship, than are found in that report. It is in relation to such a case that it has seemed proper to Consul Moore to denounce the government of the confederate States to one of its own citizens as being indifferent "to cases of the most atrocious cruelty." A copy of his letter to the counsel of the two men is annexed, marked F.

The earnest desire of this government is to entertain amicable relations with all nations, and with none do its interests invite the formation of closer ties than with Great Britain. Although feeling aggrieved that the government of her Majesty has pursued a policy which, according to the confessions of Earl Russell himself, has increased the disparity of strength which he considers to exist between the belligerents, and has conferred signal advantage on our enemies in a war in which Great Britain announces herself to be really and not nominally neutral, the President has not deemed it necessary to interpose any obstacle to the continued residence of British consuls within the Confederacy by virtue of exequaturs granted by the former government. His course has been consistently guided by the principles which underlie the whole structure of our government. The State of Virginia having delegated to the Government of the United States, by the Constitution of 1787, the power of controlling its foreign relations, became bound by the action of that Government in its grant of an exequatur to Consul Moore. When Virginia seceded, withdrew the powers delegated to the Government of the United States, and conferred them on this government, the exequatur granted to Consul Moore was not thereby invalidated. An act done by an agent while duly authorized continues to bind the principal after the revocation of the agent's authority. On these grounds the President has hitherto steadily resisted all influences which have been exerted to induce him to exact of foreign consuls that they should ask for an exequatur from this government as a condition of the continued exercise of their functions. It was not deemed compatible with the dignity of the government to extort, by enforcing the withdrawal of national protection from neutral residents, such inferential recognition of its independence as might be supposed to be implied in the request of an exequatur. The consuls of foreign nations, therefore, established within the Confederacy, who were in possession of an exequatur issued by the Government of the United States prior to the formation of the Confederacy, have been maintained and respected in the exercise of their legitimate functions, and the same protection and respect will be accorded to them in future, so long as they confine themselves to the sphere of their duties, and seek neither to evade or defy the legitimate authority of this government within its own jurisdiction.

There has grown up an abuse, however, the result of this tolerance on the part of the President, which is too serious to be longer allowed. Great Britain has deemed it for her interest to refuse acknowledging the patent fact of the existence of this Confederacy as an independent nation. It can scarcely be expected that we should, by our own conduct, imply assent to the justice or propriety of that refusal, now that the British Minister accredited to the government of our enemies assumes the power to issue instructions and exercise authority over the consuls of Great Britain residing within this country; nay, even of appointing agents to supervise British interest in the confederate States. This course of conduct plainly ignores the existence of this government, and implies the continuance of the relations between that Minister and the consuls of her Majesty resident within the Confederacy which existed prior to the withdrawal of these States from the Union. It is further the assertion of a right on the part of Lord Lyons, by virtue of his credentials as her Majesty's Minister at Washington, to exercise the power and authority of a minister accredited to Richmond, and officially received as such by the President. Under these circumstances, and because of similar action by other ministers, the President has felt it his duty to order that no direct communication be permitted between the consuls of neutral nations in the Confederacy and the functionaries of those nations residing within the enemy's country. All communications, therefore, between her Majesty's consuls or consular agents in the Confederacy and foreign countries, whether neutral or hostile, will hereafter be restricted to vessels arriving from or despatched for neutral points. The President has the less reluctance in imposing this restriction because of the ample facilities for correspondence which are now afforded by the fleets of confederate and neutral steamships engaged in regular trade between neutral countries and the confederate ports. This trade is daily increasing, in spite of the paper blockade, which is upheld by her Majesty's government in disregard, as the President conceives, of the rights of this Confederacy, of the dictates of public law, and of the duties of impartial neutrality.

You are instructed by the President to furnish

a copy of this despatch, with a copy of the papers appended, to her Majesty's Secretary of State for Foreign Affairs.

I am, very respectfully, your obedient servant,

J. P. BENJAMIN,
Secretary of State.

Hon. JAMES M. MASON,
Commissioner, etc. etc., London.

Doc. 46.

THE HISTORY OF SECESSION.

BY A SOUTHERN MAN.

MR. EDITOR: There is, so far as I remember, no war to be met with in history entirely analogous to the one now raging between the North and the South. That produced by an attempt on the part of three of the Swiss Cantons to separate themselves from the Confederation a few years since, in some respects resembles it most nearly. That attempt, it will be remembered, was arrested, and the rebellious Cantons speedily reduced to submission by the arms of the Confederacy. It is frequently compared to our revolutionary struggle with the mother country, but there is scarcely any analogy between the two cases. The thirteen Colonies were not like the Southern States, equal in political rights with the other States of the British Empire. They possessed no sovereign power whatever. They were not, as we were, entitled to representation in the common Parliament of the British Union, but were mere Colonies—mere dependencies upon the mother country. In an evil hour the administration of George Grenville, and afterward that of Lord North, attempted to impose an unjust tax upon the Colonies. This oppression was resisted, and the resistance was made the pretext for other oppression more unjust still. The Colonies continued their resistance in a constitutional way for near ten years, by representations, remonstrances, and petitions, for the redress of grievances; but all in vain. At length they took up arms, with the avowed object of enforcing such redress. They solemnly *disclaimed all* intention of separation from the parent State, for they were as loyal in their feelings of attachment to the British Constitution as were the inhabitants of Surrey or Cornwall. This resolute step they confidently expected would procure the desired redress; but the advice of all the ablest statesmen at that age—of Chatham, of Camden, of Burke, of Fox, of Rockingham and others, was thrown away on the narrow-minded monarch and the bigoted ministry which then swayed the destinies of the British Empire. Still in hope, they continued the struggle for one whole year. At length the British Parliament declared the Colonies out of the protection of the parent State. And then at last no other course was left them but to proclaim their independence, and defend it if need be with their life's blood. The battle of Lexington was fought on the nineteenth of April, 1775, and on the twelfth of April, 1776, the Provincial Congress of North-Carolina empowered their delegates in Congress to concur with the delegates of the other Colonies in "declaring independence and forming foreign alliances," and on the fifteenth of the following month Virginia, through her Convention, instructed her delegates in the Continental Congress "to propose to that body to declare the United Colonies free and independent States, absolved from all allegiance to, or dependence on, the Crown or Parliament of Great Britain," and on the fourth of July following the ever memorable Declaration was made.

But how different has been the course of the Secessionists. They seem to have resolved years ago that the Union *should* be destroyed, and then to have set themselves to work to *forge* such grievances as would seem to give them a decent pretext for the accomplishment of their premeditated schemes. The first effort was made in the days of nullification by the Secessionists of South-Carolina. The grievance then complained of was the tariff, although the State of South-Carolina, herself, had been from the foundation of the Government nearly up to that period, as strong an advocate of a high tariff as any State in New-England. That question was compromised—South-Carolina obtained all that she *ostensibly* demanded. A revenue tariff, with incidental protection, became the settled policy of the Government, and except for a short period under the tariff of 1842, was never departed from. But still they were not satisfied. Immediately after the passage of Mr. Clay's compromise bill, the newspaper organ of the Secessionists at Washington, declared "that *the South could never be united on the tariff question,* and that the *slave question* was the only one that could unite them." And Mr. Calhoun, if I mistake not, said the same thing in a speech at Abbeville, in South-Carolina, about the same time; and of course was followed by all lesser lights among his adherents. Then commenced that violent agitation of the Slavery question which had nearly culminated upon the admission of California in 1850. Again, by the efforts of those immortal statesmen of the last age, Messrs. Webster, Clay, and others, was the matter compromised. The whole country at first appeared to be satisfied with the settlement, but it soon appeared that there were a number of restless spirits among the extremists of the South, that would be satisfied with nothing short of a dissolution of the Union. Of this class of politicians, W. L. Yancey may be fitly selected as representative man. He immediately began to agitate the question again. He went to the Democratic National Convention at Baltimore, in 1852, as a delegate from the State of Alabama, and there proposed as the *ultimatum* on which he could continue to act with the Democratic party, and upon which, in his opinion, the Slave States could consent to remain in the Union, that the doctrine of non-intervention by Congress in regard to slavery in the territories should be incorporated into the Democratic platform. In this he failed, and therefore did not support the nominee of the Convention, Mr. Pierce. He could not, however, at that time, succeed in creating a great schism in the Democratic party, so great had been the calm which the compromise measures of 1850 had produced. In 1856 he again went as a delegate from the State of Alabama to the Cincinnati Convention, with his old *ultimatum* in his pocket. Contrary to his wishes and expectations, it was incorporated into the Cincinnati platform, and being thus left without an excuse, he supported Mr. Buchanan for the Presidency in the fall of that year. In the mean time, however, that fatal measure, the repeal of the Missouri compromise, had been consummated. It was brought about by the extremists of the South, aided by a few partisan Democrats of the North. The avowed object of its authors was to open to Slavery the territories north of the Missouri compromise line, notwithstanding the agreement of 1820 that said line should forever divide the territories between the slave and free States. It is said, however, that the compromise of 1820 was unconstitutional, but what is that to the purpose? It was a most solemn compact between the two sections of the country, made for the settlement of a most perplexing question, and without any reference to its constitutionality, should have been regarded as an organic law, and observed as sacredly as the Constitution itself.

The effect of this measure was great and rapid, and there can be but little doubt that it was such as a majority of its authors contemplated. The result was the formation of a great party at the North opposed to the further extension of Slavery, and which party very nearly succeeded in electing their candidate for the Presidency, Mr. Fremont, in 1856.

After the election, this party seemed to be on the wane, until the anti-Slavery spirit of the whole North was aroused to madness, by an attempt on the part of Mr. Buchanan's administration to force the Lecompton Constitution with Slavery upon the people of Kansas, in opposition to the known and expressed wish of three fourths of them. But for this most unjustifiable measure the Republican party would undoubtedly have dwindled down to moderate proportions; and even after this, it is doubtful if they could have succeeded in the Presidential election of 1860, if the Secessionists with Yancey at their head, had not determined that they should succeed. After Mr. Yancey and his party had, against their wishes, succeeded in getting their ultimatum of non-intervention incorporated into the Cincinnati platform, they went to work to conjure up another to present to the Charleston Convention. Abandoning their doctrine of non-intervention, they went to the opposite extreme and demanded that the intervention of Congress for the protection of slavery in the territories should constitute a part of the Charleston platform. This demand they well knew would not be complied with, nor did they desire that it should be. Their object was to procure the secession of the delegates of the Cotton States from the Convention, and thus by defeating the nomination of Mr. Douglas, and rending asunder the Democratic party, to insure the election of Mr. Lincoln, and thereby forge for themselves a grievance which would seem to justify them in the execution of their long meditated designs of destroying the Union. All of this they accomplished, and the election of Mr. Lincoln was perhaps hailed with greater joy at Charleston than at New-York. I will do them the justice to state that they also claimed to have some other grievances; among them, that some of the Northern States by their statutes obstructed the execution of the fugitive slave law, but the only States that could complain much on that score, were willing to remain in the Union, while South-Carolina, the State which set the ball in motion, perhaps never lost a slave. But it must be borne in mind that no act of the National Government constituted any part of their grievances. They did not pretend that any act of Congress infringed their rights, and the decisions of the Supreme Court were mainly such as they would themselves have made. Nay, even at the very time of Mr. Lincoln's inauguration, if the Cotton States had allowed their Senators and Representatives to remain, they would have had a decided majority in both Houses of Congress in favor of the extension of Slavery, and in opposition to the policy of the party which elected him.

The great cause of complaint was, that a man opposed to the extension of Slavery in the territories had been elected President of the United States according to the forms of the Constitution which he was sworn to defend and protect, and who disclaimed any other than constitutional means in the accomplishment of his objects. Under such circumstances it seems that if they had labored under any real grievance, their course was plain. They should have taken the course of our revolutionary fathers. When the States assembled in Convention, instead of proceeding at once to declare their independence—for the idea of Secession, *peaceable if right*, seems, as Publius says, to have exploded and given up the ghost—should clearly and concisely have stated what their grievances were, and demanded redress in respectful yet firm and decided terms. They should have exhausted every constitutional means of obtaining guarantees—if any were needed—by representation, by remonstrance, by petition; and failing in all these, they should have done as our revolutionary sires did, that is, fight in the Union for their rights until they were driven out of it. Such a course would have procured for us, as it did for our fathers, the respect, the sympathy, and the assistance of other nations. Instead of that, we have not a friend in Europe. But such was not the course which these—in their own estimation—wise statesmen chose to pursue. When such a course was suggested or recommended to them, they evaded it by a long list of magnificent promises which looked so splendid as almost to dazzle the mind with their brilliancy.

First and foremost, they promised that Secession should be peaceable.

Secondly, they promised that if perchance war should ensue, it would be a very *short* war, that it would not last *six* months; that the Yankees would *not* fight; that *one* Southerner could whip from *ten* to *one hundred* of them; that England and France would speedily recognize us and render us every assistance we might desire; that whatever might be their abstract opinions of the subject of slavery, their interests would impel them to promote its perpetuity in the Southern States; that if after *all* they should not be disposed to assist us, *Cotton was King*, and would soon bring *all* the crowned heads of Europe on their knees in supplication to *us;* would compel them to raise the blockade—should one be established—in thirty days, in sixty days, in ninety days, in one hundred and twenty days, in six months, in nine months, in *one year* at farthest.

Thirdly, they promised us that all the slave States except Delaware would join the Southern Confederacy — that slavery should not only be perpetuated in the States, but that it should be extended into all the Territories in which the negro could live; that all the grievances occasioned by the non-execution of the fugitive slave law should be speedily redressed; that slave property should be established upon a basis as safe as that of landed property.

Fourthly, they promised us that the new government should be a mere confederacy of States of absolute sovereignty and equal rights; that the States should be tyrannized over by no such "*central despotism*" as the old Government at Washington; that the glorious doctrine of States rights and nullification, as taught by Mr. Jefferson and Mr. Calhoun, should prevail in the new Confederacy; that the sovereignty of the States and their judicial decisions should be sacredly respected.

Fifthly, they promised us the early and permanent establishment of the wealthiest and best government on the earth, whose credit should be better than that of any other nation; whose prosperity and happiness should be the envy of the civilized world.

And lastly, they promised us that if a war should ensue, they would go to the battle-field and spill, if necessary, the last drop of their blood in the cause of their beloved South.

While such have been their promises, what have been their performances? Instead of secession being peaceable as they promised that it would, it has given rise to such a war as has never before desolated any country, since the barbarians of the North overran the Roman Empire.

So far from the war's ending in six months, as they said it would, should it ensue, it has already lasted more than two years, and if their policy is to be pursued, it will last more than two years longer; and notwithstanding their predictions, the Yankees have fought on many occasions with a spirit and determination worthy of their ancestors of the Revolution—worthy of the descendants of those austere old Puritans whose heroic spirit and religious zeal made Oliver Cromwell's army the terror of the civilized world; or of those French Huguenots, "who, thrice in the sixteenth century, contended with heroic spirit and various fortunes against all the genius of the house of Lorraine, and all the power of the house of Valois." England and France have not recognized us — have not raised the blockade — have not shown us any sympathy, nor is there any probability that they ever will, and that cotton is *not* king is now universally acknowledged. And Maryland has *not* joined the Confederacy, nor has Kentucky nor Missouri ever really been with us. Slavery has not only not been perpetuated in the States, nor extended into the Territories, but Missouri has passed an act of *emancipation*, and Maryland is ready to do so rather than give up her place in the Union, and the *last* hope of obtaining one foot of the Territories for the purpose of extending slavery has departed from the Confederacy *forever*. The grievances caused by the failure of some of the Northern States to execute the fugitive slave law have not only not been remedied, but more slaves have been lost to the South forever since secession was inaugurated, than would have escaped from their masters *in* the Union in five centuries. And how have they kept their promise that they would respect the sovereignty and rights of the States? Whatever the Government may be in *theory*, in *fact* we have a grand military *consolidation*, which almost entirely ignores the existence of the States, and disregards the decisions of their highest judicial tribunals. The great central despotism at Washington, as they were pleased to call it, was at any time, previous to the commencement of the secession movement, and even for some time after it had commenced, a most mild and beneficent Government compared with the *central despotism* at Richmond, under which we are now living.

Instead of an early and permanent establishment of the "wealthiest and best government in the world with unbounded credit," what have we got? In spite of all the victories which they profess to have obtained over the Yankees, they have lost the States of Missouri, Kentucky, Arkansas, Texas, Louisiana, Mississippi, and Tennessee, and in my humble opinion, have lost them forever; and, in all probability, Alabama will soon be added to the number. This will leave to the Confederacy but *five* States out of the original thirteen, and of these five the Yankees have possession of many of the most important points, and one third of their territory. So far the Yankees have never failed to hold every place of importance which they have taken, and present indications are that Charleston will soon be added to the number. The campaign of General Lee into Pennsylvania has undoubtedly proved a failure, and with it the last hope of conquering a peace by a successful invasion of the enemy's country. Our army has certainly been much weakened and dispirited by this failure and the fall of Vicksburgh, and how long even Richmond will be safe no one can tell. As the *Richmond Enquirer* said some time ago, " they are slowly but *surely* gaining upon us acre by acre, mile by mile," and, unless Providence interposes in our behalf—of which I see no indications—we will, at no great distance of time, be a subjugated people.

As to our unbounded credit based upon the security of King Cotton, it is unnecessary to speak. When we see one of the most influential States in the Confederacy discrediting a very large part of the confederate currency, and the confederate Government itself repudiating, to some extent, its most solemn obligations, we cannot but suppose that the confidence of other nations in the good faith and credit of this government is small indeed. As regards their promise, "to go to war and spill the last drop of their blood in the cause of their beloved South," I will say nothing. Every body knows how the secessionists of North-Carolina have kept their promise. Every body knows that the leaders, with few exceptions, will neither fight nor negotiate.

What a deplorable spectacle does the foregoing history present to our view! To what a desperate pass have they brought us, and for what? They say that they did it because the North would give us no guarantee in the slavery question. I have before stated that not one of the conventions of the seven Cotton States ever demanded any guarantee whatever. Nay, they even refused to accept of any if their friends of the Border States would procure them for them.

The Legislature of North-Carolina, at its regular session in January, 1861, adopted resolutions appointing commissioners to the Peace Congress at Washington City, and also to the Convention which assembled at Montgomery, Alabama, in February, 1861, for the purpose of adopting a constitution, and establishing a provisional government for the confederate States of America. On the motion of the writer of this, the resolution appointing commissioners to Montgomery was amended so as to instruct them "to act only as *mediators*, and use every effort possible to restore the Union upon the basis of the *Crittenden propositions as modified by the Legislature of Virginia.*" The commissioners under these instructions were the Hon. D. L. Swain, General M. W. Ransom, and John L. Bridgers, Esq., who, upon their return, submitted a report to his Excellency, Governor Ellis, which was by him laid before the Legislature, and was printed among the legislative documents of that year, where it may be consulted. In this report they say that they had the most ample opportunities of ascertaining public opinion in the Cotton States, and then add: "We regret to be constrained to state, as the result of our inquiries, made under such circumstances, that only a very *decided minority* of the community in these States are disposed, at present, to entertain favorably *any* proposition of adjustment which looks toward a reconstruction of our National Union. In this state of things we have not deemed it our duty to attend any of the secret sessions of the Congress. The resolutions of the General Assembly are upon the table of the Congress, and having submitted them as a peace-offering, we would poorly perform the duties assigned to us by entering into discussions which would serve only to enkindle strife."

But it will be said that these guarantees could not have been obtained from the North. This I admit to be true, and only produce this piece of history to prove that whatever might have been obtained, nothing would have been accepted. But the Congress of the United States did pass, by the constitutional majority of two thirds, the proposition reported by Mr. Corwin, from the Committee of Twenty-six, to so amend the Constitution as to perpetuate slavery in the States. What stronger guarantees could be given so far as the States were concerned, it would be difficult to conceive. What then would have been left to quarrel about? The Territories. During the session of Congress which closed on the fourth of March, 1861, acts were passed to provide temporary governments for the three remaining new Territories, to wit, Colorado, Nevada, and Dacotah. These acts contain no trace or indication of the Wilmot Proviso, nor any other prohibition against the introduction of slavery, but, on the other hand, expressly declare among other things, that "no law shall be passed impairing the rights of private property; nor shall any discrimination be made in taxing different kinds of property, but all property subject to taxation shall be in proportion to the value of the property taxed."

Now, when it is considered that all three of these Territories are north of thirty-six degrees thirty minutes, and that in the new territory now owned by the United States south of that line, slavery actually exists and is recognized by the territorial law, the question may well be asked: "What was there worth quarrelling, much less fighting about?" Here was a settlement of the question in the Territories made by a Republican Congress which gave the South all that, up to the time of the Charleston Convention, she had ever asked, and far more than she could hope to gain in any event, by secession. Indeed, I think it must now be apparent that secession, even if it could have been effected peaceably, would have been no remedy for the grievances of which they complained. Nay, so far as any grievances arising from a failure to obtain a return of our fugitive slaves was concerned, I think it must be apparent that it would have been an aggravation instead of a remedy for the evil. I think that all calm and dispassionate men everywhere, are now ready to admit that it would have been far better for us to have accepted the terms offered us and preserved peace and the Union, than to have plunged this once happy country into the horrors of this desolating war, which has spread a pall over the whole land—has brought mourning into every family—has rendered hundreds of thousands of hearthstones desolate—has filled the land with the maimed and disabled, with widows and orphans, and squalid poverty—has crowded our poor-houses and alms-houses—has sported away many hundreds of thousands of lives, and many hundreds of millions of treasure, only to find the institution for which they profess to have gone to war, in a thousand times greater jeopardy than ever before.

Such being the condition into which they have brought the country, the question presents itself: "Is there any remedy?" A full, complete, and adequate remedy, there is not; for what can restore the loved ones lost—repair at once the desolation, or remove immediately the mourning from our land? Yet there is a remedy which, with the helping hand of time, will accomplish much, very much indeed, and which, with the energy that usually follows desolating war, will, perhaps, remove most of its traces, in a half-century. This remedy is peace, speedy peace! But they say that we are so situated that no proposition for peace can be made by us; that having proclaimed our independence we must fight until it is voluntarily acknowledged by the United States, or until we are completely subjugated. On the meeting of the British Parliament, which took place on the thirteenth of December, 1792, the King in his speech to the Houses, intimated his intention of going to war with the French Republic. On moving the address in answer to the speech a memorable debate arose. On this occasion Charles James Fox delivered one of those powerful speeches which have made his name immortal — which have forever stamped him as the ablest of British debaters, and the first of British statesmen. In the course of that speech he said: "But we now disdain to negotiate. Why? Because we have no minister at Paris. Why have we no minister there? Because France is a Republic! And so we are to pay in the blood and treasure of the people for a *punctilio!* . . . The road of common-sense is simple, plain, and direct. That of *pride* and *punctilio* is as tangled as it is serpentine." In the impassioned language of Mr. Fox, I would ask, are we to pay in blood and treasure of the people for a *punctilio?* Shall we pursue the path of pride and punctilio, which is as tangled as it is serpentine; or shall we take the simple, plain and direct road of common-sense, which may lead to the happiest results? Four fifths of the people of that portion of North-Carolina bordering for many miles on the Yadkin River, and I believe of the whole State, are in favor of the latter course.

The one great demand of the *people* of this part of the State is *peace; peace* upon any terms that will not enslave and degrade us. They may prefer that the independence of the South should be acknowledged, but this they believe cannot now be obtained, nor in viewing the situation of affairs do they see much hope of it in the future. They naturally ask if, with no means of recruiting to any extent, we cannot hold our own against the armies which the Yankees now have in the field, how can we meet with their three hundred thousand new levies which will soon be in readiness, while they can keep their army recruited to a great extent, if not up to its maximum number from adventurers who are constantly arriving in their ports from every country in Europe? But if independence cannot

be obtained, then they are for any terms that are honorable, any terms that do not degrade us. They would be willing to compromise upon the amendment to the Constitution proposed by Mr. Corwin from the Committee of Twenty-six, perpetuating slavery in the States to which I have before alluded. But in what precise way overtures shall be made, or the movement inaugurated, I leave to wiser men and abler statesmen than myself to propose. I would, however, suggest to the people to elect members to the next Congress who are in favor of proposing an armistice of six months, and in the mean time, of submitting all matters in dispute to a Convention of delegates from all the States North and South, the delegates to be elected by the people themselves, in such manner as may be agreed upon by the two parties. Others there are who desire that the people of North-Carolina should be consulted in their sovereign capability through a Convention—that the Legislature should submit the question of "Convention or no Convention" to the people as was done in February, 1861. Such a Convention would undoubtedly speak the sentiments of the people of the State, citizens as well as soldiers, as all would be consulted. But I propose nothing definite, and only make these suggestions to bring the matter before the public. I would, however, most earnestly appeal to the friends of humanity throughout the State to use their utmost efforts to procure as speedily as possible an *honorable peace.* In the name of reason, of suffering humanity, and of the religion which we profess, would I appeal to the public men and statesmen of North-Carolina, and especially of that eminent statesman who possess in a greater degree than all others the confidence of the people of the State, and who has recently been elevated to a high place in the confederate government, to lend a helping hand and use his influence to bring about an *honorable peace.* And, lastly, I would appeal to ministers and professors of our holy religion to pray constantly — without dictation of terms — to Almighty God for an *honorable peace.*

Having but recently occupied a large space in your columns, I feel that I am intruding, and will, therefore, after expressing my obligations to you, close for the present. DAVIDSON.

CLEMONTSVILLE, N. C., July 16, 1863.
—*Raleigh Standard, July* 31.

Doc. 47.

MORGAN'S INVASION OF OHIO.

ACCOUNT BY AN EYE-WITNESS.

ON the twenty-seventh of June, 1863, the Second and Seventh Ohio cavalry and the Forty-fifth Ohio mounted infantry, together with Laws's howitzer battery, left Somerset, Ky., for Jamestown, for the purpose of watching Morgan, who, with his whole brigade, was encamped on the other side of the Cumberland River. We lay there from the twenty-ninth June to the third July, more or less skirmishing going on all the while—

when on that day Captain Carter of the First Kentucky cavalry, with detachments of the Second Ohio cavalry and Forty-fifth Ohio mounted infantry, went on a reconnoissance toward Columbia. There they had a fight with the advance of Morgan's division, which we then found had crossed the river on the second of July. About five o'clock on the afternoon of the third, Captain Carter was very seriously wounded, and the enemy pressed us so closely, that we were compelled to fall back. At six o'clock a detachment of the First Kentucky, Seventh Ohio cavalry, and Forty-fifth Ohio mounted infantry left Jamestown to reënforce Carter, and arrived at Columbia about eleven o'clock. They found Carter in a dying condition, and Morgan with three brigades in full possession of the town.

A short struggle ensued between us, for we had not then learned the strength of the enemy, and supposed it to be a force we might easily crush; but as the fight went on we found the forces with which we were contending were larger than we had supposed; when we fired musketry we were answered with grape and canister; when we fired a few rifle shots we were answered with whole volleys of musketry; and speedily beating a hasty retreat, we went as fast as our horses would carry us to Jamestown. We reached that place about five o'clock on the morning of the fourth, and a courier was instantly despatched by Colonel Wolford to General Carter, in command of the United States forces at Somerset, announcing that Morgan, with his whole force, had effected a crossing of the Cumberland River at Burkesville, and had advanced north to Columbia. From this date the pursuit of Morgan commenced.

At six o'clock P.M. there was an unusual amount of satisfaction expressed in the countenances of our boys, for orders had just been issued for all the mounted troops stationed in Jamestown to prepare to move at a moment's notice, and to provide themselves with six days' rations. It was a relief after the wearisome monotony incidental to the comparative inactivity of camp life, to be suddenly called into active service, and, if I must admit it—the pleasure was none the less, because the prospects were that the chase would not be too long to be pleasant. Our boys therefore set about making their preparations with a will, and in a few moments we were ready to start. It was well that there was so much alacrity displayed, for these first orders were barely issued before it was followed by another ordering us off at once, and a few moments more saw us fairly off in pursuit of the celebrated raider.

We could not have made a more propitious start. The night was fine, clear and cool. The moon, although occasionally obscured by light fleecy clouds, gave sufficient light to enable us to see well and clearly all around us, so that we were to some extent free from apprehensions of a sudden attack from any hidden foe. The weather was sufficiently cool to enable us to ride along without discomfort, and altogether the ride

from Jamestown to the banks of the Green River, on that splendid July night, was one of the pleasantest marches our boys have ever made. The future we cared little about; chatting and laughing and singing, we proceeded gayly enough on our journey, occasionally speculating among ourselves where we should meet with the man who had become the great object of our desires, and what we should do with him when we got him, for the possibility of his escaping from us was never entertained for a moment.

We reached the northern bank of the Green River about daylight on Sunday morning, the fifth instant, and after a hurried breakfast we again started in pursuit, marching all that day and camping on Sunday night, at eight o'clock, at Casey street, where we were joined by the Second Tennessee mounted infantry. The result of our observations convinced us that our commissary department had been neglected. We had been ordered to prepare ourselves with six days' rations, but many of our boys, having faith in Providence, had failed to provide themselves, and the consequence was, we found ourselves with a bare average of three days' rations for the whole number of troops. Consoling ourselves with vague speculations as to the prospects for foraging, we lay down to rest that night, and started again in pursuit at half-past six o'clock the next morning, the sixth instant, and drew rein again at Bradfordsville at ten o'clock. There we heard, for the first time since our departure, of any of the movements of Morgan. We were informed that he had captured our forces at Lebanon, and had then left that place for Bargetown. Leaving Bradfordsville within half an hour of our arrival, we took up our line of march for Lebanon, arriving there at three o'clock in the afternoon. At this place our forces had made some resistance, in which Tom Morgan, the brother of the guerrilla chieftain, was killed. In revenge the rebels burned some eighteen or twenty houses, robbed the post-office, cleaned out the stores, and plundered and robbed and destroyed all they could lay their hands on. An incident occurred here which may perhaps be worth relating. An old man living in Lebanon had two sons in Morgan's command, who had been with him ever since the commencement of his military career. During the absence of the young men, the old man's house and lot had been sold at sheriff's sale, and had been purchased by a strong Union man.

The rebels were informed of all these circumstances by the two sons, and proceeding to the house they burnt it to the ground, leaving its owner almost penniless to begin the world again. Another significant thing began to be evident here. John Morgan, who had heretofore been so popular with all Kentucky men, was beginning to lose a little of his popularity. Certain little murmurs of discontent reached our ears for the first time from some of those who are spoken of by the out-and-out traitors—as "good, strong Kentuckians." Morgan's men, in their passage through the central part of the State, had been blinded to some extent by the superior refulgence of "State rights." and had, in a great measure, lost sight of individual rights. And many were the complaints of those who once possessed property which was not forthcoming, and who refused to be comforted by the reflection that it was all for the good of the sunny South.

Leaving Lebanon at half-past three, we arrived at Springfield at six o'clock, and there we met many of those belonging to the Union forces which had been captured by the rebels at Lebanon.

These men presented a very sorry appearance when we arrived among them. The number of troops captured by the rebels at Lebanon was about three hundred. Immediately on surrendering, the rebels had made them fall in, and putting a guard around them had forced them to march on foot at a double-quick from Lebanon to Springfield — a distance of fully twelve miles. During the way many of them exhibited signs of giving out, but they were compelled to keep up by their merciless captors. At last one sergeant found it impossible to keep up with the ranks. The guards knocked him down with the butt-end of their muskets, and his brains were tramped out by the feet of the horses of the rebel rear-guard, and his body left lying in the road. On their arrival at Springfield they were paroled, the Southern chivalry first robbing them of every dollar they had.

We camped on the night of the sixth at eight o'clock, on the Bargetown Road, about six miles beyond Springfield, and left again the next morning at two o'clock, reaching Bargetown at six. Here we found that Morgan had left that place at noon on the day before, going north on the Shepherdsville road. We were joined at this place by General Hobson, with Shackleford's brigade, comprising the Third, Eighth, Ninth, and Twelfth Kentucky cavalry and two pieces of artillery. General Hobson now took command, and continuing our journey we encamped on the night of the seventh about four miles from Shepherdsville. It was at this point that Morgan captured the mail-train on the Louisville and Nashville Railroad, and had captured and paroled about twenty soldiers who were passengers on board the cars. They also robbed all the passengers of any valuables they might have about them, stole all the contents of the mail-bags and appropriated all the express packages that were on board. Here our horses began to give out. We had been in the saddle with hardly any rest since the evening of the fourth of July, and it was more than horse-flesh could endure, so to recruit our horses we went into camp at six o'clock in the evening. On the morning of the eighth we were again on our way at half-past four o'clock, General Shackleford's brigade in the advance, and crossed the railroad where the rebels had robbed the mail. They had taken all the letters with them to amuse themselves by reading as they went along, and for twenty-five or thirty miles the road was strewed with fragments of paper—the letters which the rebels had

thrown down in the way to become the sport of every breath of air that blew, or to be picked up by any passer-by who might chance to come along. As we followed along the road we curiously picked up many of the notes and letters which were scattered so profusely around, and attempted to decipher the writing, an undertaking attended with considerable difficulty, for the writing—not often too distinct—was rendered almost totally illegible by reason of dust and dirt and the trampling of horses' feet. The first we picked out of the mass of fluttering paper commenced with "My dear wife," and, after a few commonplace remarks, went on to speak of some crushing trial that had lately fallen upon them both in the death of a loved relative, while the writer attempts to impart comfort in the affliction, and to lighten the load of grief, which, he says, he fears is greater than she can bear. The next is altogether different in character. It is a business letter and says: "Inclosed please find one hundred and fifty dollars, which you will please place to my credit." A third is written in rather a clerical sort of handwriting—at least it appears so to us. It commences very formally with "Madame," and in it we find that it has become the painful duty of the writer to inform her for whom the letter is intended that her husband "is no more." That after lingering for many weeks in some hospital, he had quietly breathed his last, with his last breath sending a message to the only woman he loved on earth. The letter covers all the four sides of the paper, but a large part is torn off, and singularly enough we cannot find a single name to give us any clue either to the parties to whom it was addressed, or to the writer of the sad news. A fourth letter is full of hope and joy, and speaks of weddings and dances and balls in a strange sort of jumbled-up way; while another is very sad, and gives a long description of a death-bed scene or a funeral. So they go on, strangely like the ever-changing scenes of every-day life, one day dark and cloudy, the next light and cheerful, and so amusing ourselves with perusing the letters, and reflecting on their contents, the day's march is made. Quietly enough, for the letters seem to have set every one thinking what will be the result of the loss of news. Thinking of children waiting to hear from a parent away off in the armies of the Tennessee. Of a sister watching for news of a dear brother. Of the news of the death of a husband to a newly-made widow, and speculating as to whether the news will ever reach her. So we go on to Laurenceville, about one mile from which place we pass the night. A little tiny stream runs close by our encampment, and I stroll out in the night and throw myself down by its side, and gaze on the little ripples that seem to glide over its surface. It was flowing on so peacefully and calmly in the midst of our warlike movements, that I insensibly catch myself repeating part of Willis's description of the pursuit of King David by his son Absalom, and saying:

·   ·   ·   ·   ·   ·   ·

"How strikingly the course of nature tells,
    By its light heed of human suffering,
    That it was fashioned for a happier world."

But, as I get so far, I suddenly find I have company, and am joined by one of my comrades, who, having heard my involuntary soliloquy, accuses me of getting sentimental, and shaking off the spell that seemed to enthrall me, I return to camp, and throwing myself on the ground, I sleep soundly until morning breaks, and the bugle calls us once more to mount.

Here we are informed that Morgan left Elizabethtown on his right, and struck for Brandenburgh, commencing to cross the Ohio River on the Alice Dean and the J. T. McCoombs. On the morning of the ninth, we again started in pursuit, feeling a little elated to find that we have gained something on him in the journey. We captured three prisoners shortly after leaving Laurenceville, who told us that at the fight at Green River they lost one hundred and ten men in killed and wounded, including Colonel Chenault, one major and four captains. As we drew near to Brandenburgh we saw a thick smoke rising up from the river, and quickened our speed in hopes of arriving in time to prevent the destruction of property which we presumed was going on, but as we arrived in the town we could see down in the river the Alice Dean burning rapidly away on the other side of the stream, while far back on the opposite shore of the river, could be seen the rear-guard of Morgan's force rapidly disappearing in the distance. The complaints of the inhabitants were longer, and deeper, and louder than at any other point on our route. The accustomed chivalry of Morgan's men, which is a matter of so much pride and exultation among the secesh of Kentucky, is, it seems, excelled by their cupidity, and they could not withstand the temptation offered by the well-filled stores of Brandenburgh. Plundering all indiscriminately, there was hardly a house in the place which had not suffered more or less from their visit. One firm, that of Weatherspool and Joekel, they robbed of goods to the amount of three thousand five hundred dollars, and when they expostulated with them for taking such goods as could not possibly be of service to them, such as silks and muslins, they replied that they wanted them to present to their Yankee cousins in Indiana.

In the fight that took place at Brandenburgh, at the time of the crossing, between the Leavenworth home guards and Morgan's men, they killed two of the Indianians and took forty-five of them prisoners, capturing their twelve pounder gun, which they threw into the river after spiking it. In the onward march of the rebels they burnt Peter Locke's mill, which lies about three miles from the river. This was the first work of destruction they performed after they commenced to invade the free States.

Our forces commenced to cross the river at noon of the ninth of July, and went into camp on the hill opposite Brandenburgh until the whole force was across, in order to give our horses rest, that they might be fresh when they resumed the pursuit. At three o'clock on the morning of the tenth, all our forces were across, and breaking up our camp, we at once resumed the pursuit. About five miles on the road we captured Lieutenant Arnold, of Gano's regiment, who was thrown from his horse and sprained his ankle, thus being rendered unfit for duty. Arriving at Corydon at ten o'clock we found that the home guards had made a stand there under Colonel Timberley, and had fought them for four hours, killing two of Morgan's men, and wounding seven, while they themselves lost fifteen in killed and wounded. It was at this place that Mr. Glenn was shot down, and his house burnt for having fired on the rebels as they passed by his house. As we rode by the place, the dead body of Robinson, the rebel he had killed, was still laid out in the open air, waiting for its burial to take place. In Corydon we found that here, as everywhere else, they had cleaned out all the stores, and had plundered all they could lay their hands on. Three mills which are situated in this place they threatened to burn, unless they raised one thousand dollars each in fifteen minutes. The money was raised and the mills were saved.

They captured two hundred home guards and paroled them, and when they left, they took with them all the horses they could find. Dick Morgan's regiment taking the advance. Up to this time they had stolen altogether about two hundred and fifty horses and had torn up and destroyed all the American flags they could find.

Encamping that night about two and a half miles from Salem, we broke camp at five o'clock on the eleventh, and arrived there quite early in the morning. We met with quite a grand reception there, the inhabitants supplying us with all the eatables we required, and doing for us all they had in their power. Morgan had burnt the railroad bridge across the Blue River at this point, and had also levied his usual tax of one thousand dollars each on the three mills of the place; and finished up by robbing all the houses in the place. At one or two houses, the inhabitants had locked up and fled at their approach, but they broke in the doors and helped themselves to all they could find.

On Saturday, July eleventh, we encamped at Vienna, where the rebels had burnt the bridge, and we found that Morgan had struck for Lexington and thence north; so leaving camp again at five o'clock on the morning of the twelfth, we followed on to Paris, where the rebels had made but a short stay, being apprehensive that we were too close in their rear for their own comfort. At Vernon, Morgan sent in to Colonel Lowe, who commanded the one thousand two hundred militia who had assembled at that point, demanding a surrender. Colonel Lowe replied: "Come and take it." Morgan then notified him to remove all the women and children, which was done. He then surrounded the town, burnt the bridges, and did all the damage that lay in his power, and then went on to Dupont without troubling himself to fight, and there burnt the railroad bridge and two other bridges, and left for Versailles, where he robbed the county treasurer of five thousand dollars, all the money he had, and again took his departure, expressing his sincere regret that the county was so very poor.

We arrived at Versailles on the thirteenth, at five o'clock, and found that Morgan, after sacking the town, had sent on a force to Osgood, where they burnt a bridge and captured a telegraph operator, and kept on to Pierceville, burning all the bridges on the road, and starting thence to Milan. They then struck off on the Brookfield road, and after travelling eight miles, turned off toward Wisebergh, where they had a skirmish with the home guards. At New-Ulsas, a small German settlement, they captured a wagon-load of lager beer, which they carried with them to refresh themselves on their way. On the night of the thirteenth, we encamped at Harrison, our horses being thoroughly jaded and worn out, and men being in a condition not much more encouraging than their horses. On that night Morgan nearly surrounded Cincinnati. Starting at three A.M. on the fourteenth, we followed in the wake of Morgan's troops through Springdale and Sharon to Montgomery, where we found he had captured one hundred and fifty good horses. At Miamiville, after turning over the train on the Little Miami Railroad, he burnt fifty new Government wagons. There had been two hundred wagons, but we succeeded in saving one hundred and fifty, together with one thousand mules. We camped that night at nine o'clock at Camp Repose, and started at two A.M. on the fifteenth for Batavia. We were led out of our way by a Methodist preacher, who had undertaken to guide us, and so far succeeded in misleading us, that instead of going by the direct road, which was only six miles, he took us by a roundabout way of fifteen miles. Whether this was intentional or otherwise we did not know, but he seemed very anxious to make his escape, and if hard swearing on the part of our boys will injure any one but the swearer, then is that Methodist preacher cursed for all eternity. Morgan on this day burnt two bridges on White Oak River, and Dick Morgan separated from the main body of the rebels with his regiment four miles from Williamsburgh and went to Georgetown, plundering that town. We encamped that night at Sardinia at eleven o'clock.

On the sixteenth instant, we broke camp at four o'clock in the morning and arrived at Winchester at eight. The rebels had entered the town at two P.M. of the previous day, had robbed the mail, and stolen thirty-five thousand dollars' worth of property and fifty horses. From one firm in this place they stole eleven thousand dollars' worth of property, which was the largest single robbery they effected during the whole of the raid. They tore up all the flags they could find at this place, and amused themselves by tying the fragments to mules' tails and driving them through the streets. At Jacktown they burnt a bridge and went on to Wheat Ridge, where they

robbed an old man, who was hardly able to walk from old age and feebleness, of thirty dollars. Here their forces again separated, part going through Mount Olive. Six miles this side of Jackson the citizens blockaded the road, and detained Morgan two hours. With the exception of the fight by the home guards at Corydon, where the rebels were detained four hours, this was the best service rendered by citizens during the whole of the raid. At Jasper the rebels gave the proprietor twenty-five minutes to raise one thousand dollars, or they would burn his mill. He was unable to procure the money and the mill was burnt accordingly. We went into camp at Jasper at two A.M., on the seventeenth, and resumed our journey at eleven, having to swim our horses across the canal. One of our men, a member of company L, Second Ohio, named McGoron, accidentally killed himself with his revolver. Arriving at Piketon we found that the rebels had killed a Mr. McDougal who was busily blockading the road when they came up. The same day they shot a Dr. Burroughs, who had fired on them as they passed by his place. We arrived at Jackson at six o'clock, where we were met with the same story we had heard so often before—robbery, and theft, and pillage, and destruction on every hand. There was one thing we must give the rebels credit for, and that is, that in the matter of thieving they showed the strictest impartiality, robbing the man who "had always been opposed to the war" with the same coolness with which they robbed his more loyal brethren. Indeed, it was with a kind of vindictive pleasure that they stole from those who were so forward in informing them that they had always been "good butternuts." At this place they destroyed the Jackson *Standard* printing-office —the only paper that they injured during the whole of the march. The home guards having reason to think it was done at the instigation of a butternut resident of the place, cleaned out the Jackson *Express* office, a copperhead sheet of the same place.

From this place Morgan had sent up some forces to Berlin, at which place there were three thousand militia posted, under the command of Colonel Runkle. Morgan's men threw one shell in their midst, which acted like a charm on the militia, who instantly became—missing.

We camped that night at Jackson, and started again at three o'clock on the morning of the eighteenth, and followed on by way of Keystone Furnace. We found that they had burnt a bridge over Raccoon Creek, and had captured two boxes of army clothing. At the little town of Linesville, the home guards tore up the bridge and blockaded the road, detaining the rebels another two hours, and doing as good service as the citizens of Jasper. Part of the rebel force had gone down by way of Wilkesville, where they burnt two or three bridges; we went on to Chester, where they had burnt a bridge over Shade Creek, and encamped for the night.

On the nineteenth, the battle of Buffington Island took place, if so slight a skirmish is worthy of the name of a battle. We started out at one o'clock, and at five o'clock we opened fire on the rear of the rebels, who were just then opening fire on General Judah's forces. The battle, although it has been often described, is not altogether well understood, on account of most correspondents having written from the gunboats, and were of course unable to see much of the fight. The river-road runs along nearly close to the bank of the river. About two miles back of the river, on the north side, runs a long range of hills, down over which comes a road running to the river at the island. About three hundred yards above this pike road was a small private roadway leading north into some corn-fields, while a large wheat-field separated the two roads from each other. The rebels had encamped on Saturday night in the corn-fields at the end of the by-road or lane, and General Judah's men coming down on the pike road had come on them almost unawares, the density of the morning fog having obscured the rebels from their view. The rebels fired on the advancing column, throwing them into temporary disorder, and were preparing to make a charge, when the gunboats opened on them from the river, and at the same time the Second and Seventh Ohio, of General Hobson's force, opened on them in their rear, having just come in a little way above the pike road, by which General Judah's forces had come up from Portsmouth. This staggered them for the time, and Colonel Saunders coming up immediately afterward with two pieces of artillery, threw two shells in their midst. Fired at from all sides, what could they do? Separating in two columns, one part of their force pushed forward to the right only to find themselves completely surrounded, and they quietly submitted themselves prisoners of war. Colonel Dick Morgan surrendered his command to General Shackleford, while Colonel Duke and Colonel Smith were cut off in a ravine, where they surrendered themselves to their captors. At this time the prisoners numbered about eight hundred and fifty. About forty-five men had succeeded in crossing over into Kentucky before the fight commenced. A portion of the rebels who ran to the left, at the end of the fight, numbering two hundred, marched under Colonel Johnston to Reedsville, where they succeeded in crossing over, with the loss of about twenty-five men who were killed by the fire of the gunboats. Another portion went up to Long-green Bottom, stealing all that lay in their way, crossing over at Harrisonville, and turning right around, struck for the river again, about forty miles below Buffington, where Coleman of Colonel Cluke's command surrendered all his force to about fifty men. The balance of Morgan's band accompanied their leader to Columbiana County, where they were all captured by General Shackleford.

So ends the great Morgan raid. It has proved one of the most remarkable events of the war, and God grant it may never be repeated.

* * *

THE BATTLE OF BUFFINGTON ISLAND.

NATIONAL FLEET ON OHIO RIVER BELOW
BUFFINGTON ISLAND, Monday, July 20.

The uniform peace which sat brooding with dove-like wings over the State of the "Beautiful River" was broken for the first time during the threatened invasion under Bragg; but fate reserved for a rebel of far less military calibre and importance the remarkable event of bringing about and causing the first battle of the war in Ohio, and the first in her history as a State. But the sensation of the State is over, and the great Morgan raid is over forever.

The long, tedious, and perplexing pursuit of Morgan has ended at last in a victory such as will not only add lustre to our land and naval forces engaged, but render famous the scene of his defeat, which is, without doubt, the death-blow to the brilliant career of the notorious and wonderfully successful guerrilla chief. The local press of the State has chronicled from time to time the progress of the rebel force toward the point where it was met and defeated, and it only now remains to recount in a necessarily general manner.

Buffington Island lies in the Ohio River close to the Ohio shore, about thirty-five miles above Pomeroy, and was chosen by the rebels as a place of crossing into Virginia on account of the shoals between it and Blennerhasset's Island, twenty miles above. They had doubtless been well advised of the movements of our forces sent from all points, to either head them off or keep them confined to the only route eastward for them, until they reached the mountainous region and the eastern frontier. Without following, then, the progress of Morgan's march eastward, we will take a glance at his course previous to the morning of the battle. Yesterday, Sunday, the nineteenth, Morgan's right kept the main or shore-road, from Pomeroy, having sent out skirmishers to feel the strength of that town and Middleport. This was on Friday night, but if he had any intention to attempt to ford at Eight Mile Island, he abandoned it on account of a show of resistance made by a small body of home guards, with a piece of ordnance made of cast-iron, and used only to fire salutes. A skirmish took place, in which the rebels lost two men killed and two or three wounded, and the home guards had one man slightly wounded and lost their gun, which, however, the rebels contemptuously left behind, after they found its utter uselessness. The main body were advancing on the road from Vinton, and uniting with the right, the entire force took the old stage-road to Pomeroy, and pushed for Buffington Island, or rather the shore opposite, which it reached, it is supposed, at two o'clock on Sunday morning.

When General Judah started from Portsmouth on Thursday evening, the sixteenth, it was expected that an engagement would take place; for reliable information had been received at the headquarters of Colonel P. Kinney, commander of the post, during the afternoon, that the rebels were at Miamiville, about eleven miles out. Now it was not the design to either court or bring on an engagement, as it was shown that the rebels were scattered over fifty or sixty miles of country, and the necessary concentration which they must make was rather humored than otherwise, so that the result would culminate in the complete capture or destruction of the entire horde.

General Judah then kept as close as possible to the rebels, but between them and the river, where that was practicable, until Morgan reached Jackson. Judah then pushed for Centreville, thinking that the enemy would take that route for the river; but he avoided it, and took through Winchester and Vinton toward Pomeroy, and thence north of that to the scene of action.

Our gunboats, namely, Moose, (flag-boat,) Reindeer, Springfield, Naumkeag, and Victory, in command of Lieutenant Commander Le Roy Fitch, were patrolling the river from an accessible point below Ripley to Portsmouth; but as soon as it was definitely ascertained that Morgan was pushing eastward, the Moose, towed by the Imperial, started up-stream, followed at proper distances by the other boats. The Moose made the foot of Buffington Island on Saturday night, and remained until next morning, without changing position, on account of a dense fog.

The rebel force made the shore opposite and above the island, as before stated, at two o'clock, and took position, under cover of artillery, in an extensive corn and wheat-field, skirted by hills and woods on its north and east sides. The position was a good one, and might have been held to advantage for a much longer time than it was, but for the coöperation of the gunboat Moose, the only one of the fleet which arrived in time to participate in the fight.

The rebels had their artillery placed on the highest elevation on the east and completely commanded the Pomeroy road, over which General Judah's force, heretofore enumerated by your correspondent, came filing along unaware of the close proximity of the enemy. It should be noted here that the old stage-road to Pomeroy, over which Morgan came, and the lower road travelled by Judah, meet in an acute angle three quarters of a mile from the battle-field. Our column came along the lower road within range at six o'clock, having marched all night, having started from Pomeroy, and was not as fresh by five or six hours' rest as the enemy.

The rebels met us in solid column, and moved in battalions, and at the first fire repulsed our advance, which was too far ahead to be assisted by our artillery. This was the best opportunity they had to make a successful fight, but we fell back to bring forward our artillery, and the enemy did not seem to care to follow up the advantage. During this encounter Captain John J. Grafton, of General Judah's staff, became separated from the advance and narrowly escaped capture, by shooting, as he represents, the rebel cavalryman who seized him. He was dismounted, and being left on the ground made his way with considerable difficulty to the river, where

he hailed the Moose and got aboard. Meantime the fight progressed, but in a desultory manner, until our artillery got into position and our lines were drawn closely around the enemy. A furious onset was made on our side and the rebels were driven over the field eastward and sought the shelter of the woods beyond.

No more fortunate circumstance could have transpired for the Union force than the escape of Captain Grafton to the gunboat Moose, for he pointed out to Lieutenant Commander Fitch the exact position of the rebels, and enabled that officer to so direct his guns as to throw shell in their very midst. The Moose is armed with twenty-four pounder Dahlgren guns, the most accurate and effective gun in the service for operation against exposed bodies of men, and on this occasion the weapon did not belie its character. A dense fog, however, prevailed, which prevented Lieutenant Fitch doing as great execution in the rebel works as he desired, but his shots from the larboard and forward guns told, and an extensive scattering took place. The Moose opened at seven o'clock, and as the rebels were driven she kept steadily moving up-stream, throwing shell and shrapnel over the heads of our lads into the ranks of the enemy.

It now became evident that the rebels were being pressed in all directions, and that hard fighting would not save them from destruction.

A simultaneous rush was then made for the river, and throwing away arms and even clothing, a large body ran down to the shore, some with horses and some without, and plunged into the stream. The point chosen to effect the crossing was one mile and a half above the head of Buffington Island, and the movement would undoubtedly have been attended with considerable success but for the presence and performance of the gunboat. The crossing was covered by a twenty-pounder Parrott and a twelve-pound howitzer dragged into position by the rebels in their hasty retreat, but before the guns could be loaded and sighted, the bow guns of the Moose opened on the rebel guns and drove the gunners away, after which the pieces were captured. Some twenty or thirty men only succeeded in crossing into Virginia at this point. Several were killed in the water, and many returned to the shore. While this was transpiring on the river, the roar of battle was still raging on the shore and back into the country. Basil Duke, under whose generalship the fight was conducted, was evidently getting the worst of it, and his wearied gangs of horse-thieves, cut-throats, and nondescripts began to bethink them only of escape. Many threw down their arms, were taken prisoners and sent to the rear. Others sought the shelter of trees, or ran wildly from one point to another, and thus exposed themselves far more to the deadly chances of the field than if they had displayed courage and stood up to the fight.

A running fight next ensued, as the main force of the enemy retreated up-stream toward a point on the Ohio shore, opposite Belleville, Va. The retreat was made as rapidly as possible, but con siderable confusion was apparent. The gunboat kept almost ahead of the retreating column, and, when practicable, threw shell over the river-bank toward it. It is said that the retreat was headed by Morgan, for Basil Duke was taken prisoner in the early part of the fight, but it was as rapidly followed up as possible. The Moose reached Belleville in time to fire upon the first party that attempted to cross the river. The crew report eight or nine killed and several wounded in the water, but twenty rebels or more got safely ashore in Virginia. It should have been stated above that General Scammon, with reënforcements from the Kanawha, arrived at the first scene of action in time to participate, but instead of landing his men on the Ohio side he disembarked them on the Virginia shore. This precaution may have been well enough in the event of the enemy effecting a crossing, but when the Moose moved up General Scammon reëmbarked his troops, and went up with the gunboat to head off Morgan's retreat.

Foiled at Belleville, the rebels still kept pushing up along the shore, and again attempted to cross at Hawkinsport, fourteen miles above the island, but again their efforts proved abortive on account of the gunboat. Passing Hawkinsport, the Moose came to Lee's Creek, Va., where she was greeted by a sharp volley of rifles and musketry from an ambuscade on the shore. It was now the turn of the starboard gunners to try the temper of their metal, and a smashing broadside was poured into the sneaking rascals on the "sacred soil." It was sufficient, for not another shot was fired, and Lieutenant Fitch learned afterward that nine of the bushwhackers were killed and several wounded.

The transports containing General Scammon's forces were then run up to a point between Hawkinsport, Ohio, and Lee's Creek, Va., and landed on the Ohio shore, to intercept the rebel retreat. This is the last information we had on the river of that expedition, although it was reported in the evening that Scammon had captured the force or compelled it to surrender.

While the Moose was winning her laurels the other boats of the fleet were not failing to enact their regularly assigned part of the programme, which was to guard the fords below the island, and prevent any skulking squads of the rebels crossing to the much wished for Virginia shore. It is said that some of Morgan's men sang, "Oh! carry me back to ole Virginny," with a pathos and sincerity of tone quite suggestive, not to say touching, and it certainly cannot be denied that Captain Fitch "went for them" with a degree of alacrity which proved his entire willingness to assist them as far as he could. The only regret which now in any way disturbs the repose of this officer is, that the rebels did not make a larger draft on the Moose, which might have been used as a ferry-boat to carry them even farther on their *direct* road than they bargained for. As it was, she did all she could under the circumstances, and as the river was falling very fast, she, together with the others compris-

ing the fleet, was compelled to return downstream. The Alleghany Belle, a light draught boat was fitted up temporarily for the occasion and armed with a rifled gun protected with bales of cotton, to guard the fords between Belleville and Buffington Island.

The scene of the battle was one of the most composite, perhaps, in the panorama of the war. The rebels were dressed in every possible manner peculiar to civilized man, but, generally speaking, their attire was very good. They wore in many instances large slouch hats peculiar to the slave States, and had their pantaloons stuck in their boots. A dirty, gray-colored coat was the most prevalent, although white "dusters" were to be seen.

They were armed with carbines, Enfield rifles, sabres, and revolvers, were well mounted, and looked in good health although jaded and tired. The battle-field and the roads surrounding it were strewn with a thousand articles never seen perhaps on a battle-field before. One is accustomed to see broken swords, muskets, and bayonets, haversacks, cartridge-boxes, belts, pistols, gun-carriages, caissons, cannon, wagons upset, wounded, dead, and dying on the battle-field, but besides all these on the battle-field of Buffington Island, one could pick up almost any article in the dry goods, hardware, house-furnishing, or ladies' or gentlemen's furnishing line. Hats, boots, gloves, knives, forks, spoons, calico, ribbons, drinking-cups, buggies, carriages, market-wagons, circus-wagons, and an almost endless variety of articles useful and all more or less valuable. An inventory of Morgan's plunder would tax the patience of an auctioneer's clerk, and I question if one man's life would be long enough to minutely catalogue the articles picked up during his raid.

The carnage of the field was not remarkable, although little groups of rebels were found slain by the deadly fragments of shell.

The result, as far as heard from at this time is all that could be wished for by the country. The entire rebel force was met, engaged, defeated, routed, and partially captured. All the enemy's arms, guns, accoutrements, most of his horses and all his plunder, were taken or fell into our hands, but the "full particulars" of his defeat and capture must be made the subject of another communication.

Nearly one thousand seven hundred prisoners are now in our hands, under guard of the Eighth Michigan cavalry, and others are constantly arriving by our scouts and pursuing parties.

Prisoners admit a loss of two hundred killed and wounded on the field, while our loss will not exceed a fourth of that number. The rebel raid into the North is over. It has been destroyed, and the prestige of its notorious leader is gone.

The saddest incident of the fight is the wounding of Major McCook, father of the lamented Colonel McCook, murdered last summer by guerrillas in Kentucky. The old gentleman received a shot in the breast, which is represented as very serious, but it is to be hoped that it may not prove so. Major McCook is a patriotic, loyal, sturdy old gentleman, who clung to the service for his country's sake, and especially because he desired above all things to assist in ridding it of an armed tyranny and despotism under which such a mode of warfare prospers as left him to lament the untimely death of a brave and loyal son.

From papers found in the chests of the enemy's artillery, it would appear that Byrne's battery, Captain John McMurray, First Kentucky brigade, was the one used by Morgan, besides two twenty-pounder Parrotts, which, after all, he had the energy and foresight to drag over the country in his remarkable march. One of these Parrotts and a brass piece were captured by Lieutenant Commander Fitch; all the other guns, five or six in number, were captured by the army.

The home guard and militia companies in the immediate neighborhood of the battle-field, and, indeed, along the lines of march, contributed very largely to the result, and were mainly instrumental in preventing the rebels from striking at points where a great destruction of property would necessarily have followed.

At Middleport the militia captured several prisoners; at Syracuse, eighty-five were brought in; at Racine, seventy-eight. Skirmishes frequently occurred between the rebel scouts and small parties of armed citizens, and many a household will have reason to remember the Morgan raid. But more than a score of rebels "bit the dust" during the last two or three days of the raid, and were laid low by the unerring aim of the sturdy farmer of South-western Ohio, so suddenly called to the defence of his home and happy fireside.

The loyal women of Portsmouth, Pomeroy, and other towns and villages, were not wanting in thoughtfulness for our brave boys on their perplexing and hurried marches. They prepared food and had it ready at all times, day and night, and with ready hands and smiling faces supplied the wants of the "brave defenders of our country." Nothing so gladdens the heart of the soldier as the kindly attention of patriotic women, for with the memory of their goodness and sweetness in his heart he goes forth encouraged to continued deeds of valor, which shall make their common future more peaceful and secure.

One of the features of the pursuit and defeat of the rebels was the wonderful stories of John Morgan and his conduct through Ohio. Some had it that he was "a perfect gentleman"—that most vulgar of phrases to express one of the greatest rarities on the face of the earth; while others were ready to swear that he had committed all the crimes known to the code, prominent among which were murder, rape, arson, and highway robbery. It would prove a bootless task to sift these stories, and a mere imposition upon the credulity and time of the reader to recount them. They are in no way revelant to the purpose of the present writing, and, if for no other reason, are left untold.

The rebels took one of our guns at the first charge, and captured over twenty prisoners, but these they immediately paroled, and the gun they

never used, for it was soon recovered, with the capture of all their own.

In closing this general account of the last moments of the Morgan raid, which culminated in the battle of Buffington Island, a name I have given it because no other place of note lay near the scene, I have to express my regret at not being able to speak intelligently of the operation of General Hobson, and in fact of all the forces engaged, besides those of General Judah, General Scammon, and the gunboat Moose. Time was pressing and opportunities limited, but the best use was made of them.

The gratitude of the country is due our soldiers and sailors to whose efforts the successful result of the brief but perplexing campaign against Morgan is due, and I know I hazard nothing in bespeaking for them the lasting gratitude of the patriotic and loyal people of Ohio.　　E. B.

ANOTHER ACCOUNT.

CINCINNATI, July 23, 1863.

MR. EDITOR: Upon the invitation of General Judah I applied to General Cox for permission to accompany him on his late expedition after John Morgan and Co., as Vol. A. D. C., which was kindly granted. We left this city Wednesday, the fifteenth, with about one thousand two hundred cavalry and artillery, arriving at Portsmouth the following afternoon, immediately disembarking, and at nine o'clock in the evening started in pursuit toward Oak Hill or Portland. During the night the guide lost his way, which caused us to march several miles more than we liked. At early day we arrived at Webster and halted an hour, after which we started for Oak Hill, at which place we learned that the rapid wild rangers were at Jackson destroying property and were about going eastward. General Judah immediately started for Centreville, a point on the main road to Gallipolis, some six miles distant, to intercept the villains. General Manson was sent for from Portsmouth, who was awaiting orders with a good infantry force to coöperate when he might with advantage. Judah arrived, after a hasty march of less than two hours, and took possession of the town for the night, making such disposition of his forces that all were anxious to have Morgan come that way to the river and try his disposition for a fight, but he took the old road from Jackson to Pomeroy, through Vinton, while we started early next morning for the same place through Potter. We arrived at Pomeroy about four o'clock, a few hours after Morgan had been scared away by a slight fight with the home guards and the close proximity of the United States forces under General Scammon. The roads to Pomeroy had been by the people barricaded very effectually to prevent the murderers from entering without trouble their active and thriving little city.

After a few hours' rest the order was sounded at ten o'clock at night to advance, which was obeyed with eager desire to go ahead, for all felt that General Judah knew his business, although he was suffering from severe illness known only by his surgeons, Dr. Kimberly of his staff, and Hunt of Covington, a personal friend. Some wiseacres at Pomeroy attempted to induce the General to follow Morgan *via* Chester, which would have increased our distance to Buffington some ten miles, but he, Napoleon-like, heard all reasonable suggestions and then decided promptly to go through Racine, which was his own judgment, and not thought well of by some who assumed to "know it all." After a tiresome night-march, day dawned, and within a few miles of the river rumors reached us that the enemy had crossed during the night. We pressed on. A scouting party returned from the river saying all was clear on our road. A paroled home guard and an escaped negro corroborated each other in saying that Morgan was now over the river, as they had been with him a few hours before, and it was his intention then to "push right on." We were then only a mile from the bar, and the General urging up the rear with the artillery, pushed forward with the Michigan cavalry in advance, himself, staff, and escort following close behind. A dense fog covered all the bottom-lands so that we moved slowly forward. About half a mile from the river Captain W. H. Day and Dr. J. F. Kimberly saw upon the left the enemy in line of battle, not seventy yards from us. It was doubted at first, but in a moment the whistling minie, carbine and pistol-balls were sending loud and quick calls for us to halt. Our road being narrow, and we confined by strong fences, with ditches on either side of us, all that was left for us was to retreat as best we could a few rods. Here it was that the noble and brave old hero, Major Daniel McCook, received his two mortal wounds, of which he died on Tuesday, twenty-first, on the boat from Portland to Pomeroy. Upon our retreat Captains R. C. Kise, A. A. G., —— Grafton, Vol. A. D. C., and Henshaw, of said battery, were, with a number of others, taken prisoners, and one piece of artillery captured. Lieutenant F. G. Price, a gallant young officer of the staff, was also seriously wounded in the head, which disabled him for the rest of the day.

For a time our prospects were quite dark, the fog was over us, the enemy near, and we entire strangers as to their localities, but Providence was with those who were for the Republic. The fog suddenly lifted, and the General, with Captains Day and J. E. McGowan, and Lieutenant H. T. Bissell, were all gallantly and coolly giving orders and making ready for a good fight with the enemy, who now appeared from three to four thousand strong, immediately before us on the plains. Lieutenant O'Neil, of the Fifth Indiana cavalry, now appeared by another road with but fifty men, and charged two different regiments so desperately that they broke and left our captured gun, officers and men in our possession. The tide had turned. Our guns were soon in position, and in two hours the enemy had left the field in confusion, and were hastened in their movements by a gun of a Michigan battery on board the steamer Alleghany Belle, commanded by Captain Sebastian, and the gunboat Moose, commanded by Captain Fitch,

U. S. N. Morgan's forces in their retreat soon fell into the hands of the noble Hobson, who had so persistently chased him for over four weeks, and then the rivalry among our forces as to whom should gobble the most of the renegades commenced. General Shackleford and Colonel Woolford, with the Forty-fifth Ohio, all did good service, and helped to secure the prize, which could not have been done by either command alone. Immediately after a few hours' rest all the forces were sent in different directions by Generals Judah and Hobson to intercept the enemy. All the artillery Morgan had on the field, some five pieces, were taken by us. The spoils with which the trails of the runaways were littered would make an honest warrior blush to name, such as books, stationery, cutlery, dry goods of all descriptions, crockery, boots and shoes, hats and caps, women's wearing apparel of all names — some articles not to be mentioned—even old women's bonnets, to say nothing of carriages, harness, small arms of all kinds, and worn and jaded horses and mules by the hundred that are worth only the price of dead animals for the use of tallow-chandlers.

On the persons of most of the rebels could be found greenbacks in abundance. Their own trash, which Brownlow says "is not worth ten cents a bushel," was also profuse among them. Watches and all kinds of jewelry, to a great extent, were in their pockets, which were not with them when they entered the North. The inference is, that they are a band of robbers under the guise of an army.

General Judah, for a few days, will make Pomeroy his headquarters, as he is the ranking officer in that part of the country. It is thought that some of Hobson's and Judah's forces will yet trap John and his few retainers before they can reach Dixie.

A disgraceful coward, called Sontag, from Portsmouth, with nearly four hundred men, well armed, surrendered to Morgan on Tuesday last without firing a gun. Morgan was in his grasp, if he had fought. Shame on such mountebanks! May he live long enough for his name to be a stench to himself, as it is to all who know him now.

I must not forget to testify to the intense loyal feeling manifested all along the route our army took. Many said Vallandigham's admirers were not as numerous as in days past. The raid may do good toward opening the eyes of the careless. May we not hope so?

It is again seen that the enemy attacked us on Sunday, and we whipped them. I only notice the fact. Major McCook was wounded within a short time after the first repulse, recovered by Captain Day, and by him sent to the nearest house, where Dr. Kimberly gave him all the attention possible; but from the first, all hope of recovery was dispelled by the Major and the Doctor. His wounds were necessarily mortal. The enemy, while he was yet in their lines, robbed him of money, watch, and all loose articles on his person. The silvery locks of the patriot-hero were no protection against the "Kentucky gentlemen" of John Morgan's and Basil Duke's command. Captain Kise, and all of our men whom they held for a few minutes, were robbed of money and personal property. A pistol was placed at Captain Kise's head and his boots demanded, but an officer interfered, and the contemplated outrage was prevented. Pretty return for Grant's kindness, was it not!

Our loss is very light. All told, it will not exceed thirty killed and wounded—some five killed—at the outside. The enemy have thus far lost full two hundred killed and wounded, and not less than two thousand two hundred prisoners—among them about a hundred officers, including Colonels Basil Duke, Dick Morgan, Ward, Hoffman, and Smith. Considering how slight our loss was, it is the greatest victory of the war, and makes Judah and Hobson rightly entitled to two stars. Judah received his military education at West-Point, and is a soldier in every respect. While he is not an abolitionist, there is no one who hates rebels more than he, or who is more willing to use all means (including the negro) to crush the rebellion—yea, even to the extermination of every rebel in the South, so that the desired end be accomplished. Hobson is a lawyer and a good soldier, having entered the service because he hated rebels and loved the old flag. The people will ever sing praise to Judah and Hobson.

Cincinnati was well represented in the chase by the gallant Guthrie Grays, commanded by Captain Disney, who ascended the river on the steamer Magnolia, and at the battle of Buffington Bar, were on the steamer Alleghany Belle, panting for a chance to return the fire on shore, while they were compelled to receive it from the enemy. They did good and valuable service as guard to the prisoners brought from Pomeroy on the steamer Ingomar. Of this company the Queen City may feel proud. May all the new Seventh prove as ready and effective as this tenth part have already. Success to the Seventh!

Nat. Pepper, son of Captain Pepper, of the late steamer Alice Dean, was a volunteer private at the gun on the steamer Alleghany Belle, which the rebels say did the most execution of any of our artillery. He is an only son, about eighteen years of age, and is anxious to remain in the service. Would that many who are older had the same willingness to risk their lives for the Republic.

Captain Wood, of the Eighteenth regulars, while stationed at Marietta, as mustering officer, was induced to take command of two companies of volunteers and proceeded to Buffington Bar on Saturday. He found the steamer Starlight aground, with only two men aboard, and loaded with three thousand barrels of flour. He immediately unloaded the vessel, raised steam and manned the boat, from the captain to the deck-hand, with his men, and run her out of the range of Morgan's guns, which, before he could get away, had arrived on the bank. Before leaving with his little band of true gallants, he rolled his two

heavy pieces of artillery over into a ravine, so that the enemy could neither take nor use them. After the fight Captain Wood reported to General Judah for duty, with the boat, and was highly complimented by the General, and placed in charge of several hundred of the prisoners to bring to Cincinnati. Had the boat not been seized by Captain Wood when it was, Morgan would have had it, and crossed the river with it; for the gunboats did not arrive till Sunday morning, while Morgan was there the night before; so let Marietta be proud of her gentlemen soldiers, who were not too proud to carry coal or do any work which would hinder the enemies of the Union and help her defenders.

The South boasts that all of her people are in the fight — rich and poor, old and young — and that they can yet whip us. When all our rich and poor and old and young, who are at heart right, are engaged, we can whip the South, even if France and England do help them. Our people have not yet awakened out of sleep. Only a little more of this kind of work from Wood and Vallandigham's friends, and the honest people, who are for the Union without an if or but, will arise and overthrow all who oppose them, to the eternal shame of all traitors.   G. P. E.

Doc. 48.

OPERATIONS AT PORT HUDSON.

DIARY OF A REBEL SOLDIER.*

May 2, 1863.—Fair and pleasant; rumors of evacuation of P. H. Guns being buried, etc. One ship, one transport, and Essex below. Went up river.

May 4.—Fair and pleasant. Saw a great many dead horses pass down the river, and other signs of a fight above. Have been receiving no mails in several days.

May 5.—The Yanks have come down, and been shelling Captain Stubbs's men. All the infantry portion of the regiment have gone over.

May. 6—The fleet is still above. The troops are leaving very fast; —— all gone but Lieutenant-General Beale's brigade and the artillery.

May 7.—Upper fleet gone. Rumors of fighting in Virginia. Jackson and A. P. Hill seriously wounded; Generals Smith and Banks are said to have fought. Banks lost ten thousand men, and badly whipped.

May 8.—Several boats below. A transport is towing mortar-boats behind the point; —— five in number. One ship and one sloop below, and the Essex. They commenced a bombardment.

May 9.—False alarm last night. Yanks shelled some, and are shelling to-day occasionally. Five mortars are planted behind the point.

May 10.—Yanks bombarded the latter portion of the night. Had an artillery skirmish this

* John A. Kennedy, of company H, First Alabama regiment, who was captured near Port Hudson while conveying a cipher letter, addressed by General Frank Gardner, commander of Port Hudson, to "General J. E. Johnston, or Lieutenant-General Pemberton, Jackson or Vicksburgh, Miss."

morning. We had one lieutenant and two privates killed and several wounded.

May 11.—Morman found a dead Yankee floating down the river, and secured a gold watch and chain, also thirty-seven dollars in greenbacks.

May 12.—I was below last night on the river. Bombs flew thick. We had an election to-day for lieutenant; Sergeant Card was elected. We drew bear (*Sic*) on his expenses.

May 13.—Considerable excitement last night. Boys all left the Hermitage. I sent half of my crew. Yanks are said to be in force two miles from the breastworks. I went to the breastworks. The Yanks cut the telegraph wire and destroyed a bridge five miles from here.

May 14.—We had a pretty hot bombardment last night. We are again in camps. The long-ranged guns dropped a few shells into our camps this evening.

May 18.—The Yanks came over to the Hermitage, and drove off the beef cattle. Sent over the infantry portion of the regiment, Colonel Locke commanding, but the Yanks had left. They took Captain Pruett, Lieutenants Andrews and Crymes, and several privates prisoners.

May 19.—The Yankee fleet is above. Our company has gone over the river. The boys has had a hot time over the river. Whipped the Yanks, one hundred in number. Killed two. Captain Knowles captured a saddle, overcoat, etc. Doctor Madding captured a horse, saddle and bridle. The boys captured some coats, hats, etc., also a gun.

May 20.—We are yet over the river. No alarm. Confirmation of Grant's defeat. A detail was made to load the boat, but it failed to come.

May 21.—Have received orders to go back to camps. They are fighting outside the breastworks. They brought in several prisoners this evening. Heroic conduct of a negro. The artillery is still booming outside the breastworks. There has been a severe fight this evening.

May 23.—We had an alarm. Captain Knowles burned Doctor Bates's cotton last night. Went out to the breastworks. Very muddy. Lay on our arms all night. The Yanks did not make the attack. We have returned to camp.

Hark! the alarm gun has fired. We doubled quick to our position. We are waiting for the advance of the enemy. Company F is out as skirmishers. The Yanks have been driven back. We are leaving our position.

May 24.—There is heavy skirmishing all along the line. I think we will get a chance shortly. The Yanks are using their artillery in the woods. The lower fleet is firing. Our cavalry made a charge and killed several, also the commander.

May 25.—We were thrown out as skirmishers at two o'clock A.M., and slept on our arms. At daybreak we were deployed forward. Skirmishing commenced at nine o'clock. We have killed one and wounded two, which we captured; also, killed one and captured one horse, also three repeaters, two sabres and two saddles. We killed one.

The engagement began at one, and continued six hours. We had a hot time, sure. We repulsed the enemy, first with yells, then the artillery opened on them. They dusted. We fought a brigade with six or seven hundred men. We lost several men. Our company lost none, but had three wounded. Thank heaven, I came out unhurt. We had to fall back, being overpowered. The fight has ceased; it is dark. I have fasted all day, and have the headache very bad.

May 26.—We are preparing for the fight, throwing up rails, and digging ditches. We have finished our breastworks. I never saw so much work accomplished in the same length of time. We had a fight at Sandy Creek bridge, and killed fifteen or twenty, and captured also one captain. Fought at Plains Store, and slaughtered the Yanks. We have all lain down on the soldier's couch to rest, with the calm celestial heaven and the gentle moon. Company H brought on the engagement above. All seems to smile upon the rebels.

May 27.—Skirmishing all along the lines. It has grown warm. The Yanks attempted to charge our lower battery. They were repulsed with heavy loss. The fight has opened. Our skirmishers is giving it to them. The artillery is deafening; it is one continual roar. The muskets pop as fast as canes when the fire is in a cane-brake. Our skirmishers have been driven in. We are laying in our rifle-pit, awaiting the hated foe. All are cool and determined. The Yanks are laying under the hill, but if they come in sight they will catch it, shure as two and two makes four. The balls fly as thick as hail. Negroes are fighting us on the left. They attempt to charge our works, but were repulsed with slaughter. They say there was a regiment of Yanks behind to make them fight. [So far from this being the case, these blacks could not always get their white officers to keep with them. ED. R. R.] Our breastworks caught fire. We had a hot time putting it out. The Heshians have made five assaults upon our works, but were repulsed with great loss. Yankee tricks. We had two men wounded to-day. The fight opened at daybreak and closed after dark.

May 28.—The fight has opened. It opened at daybreak. I am very sleepy. The fight ceased at eleven o'clock. An armistice was agreed upon by both parties until two o'clock, and has been extended until six, for the Yanks to bury their dead. The Yanks attempted to storm our works a dozen times, and was repulsed with great loss. They carried planks to cross the ditches. The Yanks are burying their dead in a ditch. Their loss is heavy. The armistice has been extended until seven. The armistice is out; the fight has been resumed with redoubled fury.

May 29.—The fight continued until long after night yesterday evening. The fight has opened—it opened at daybreak. The Yanks played a trick; they built a battery under a flag of truce. The fight has been very warm to-day. I received a shot in the foot, but it is slight. The Yanks attempted to charge the works, but was repulsed. It has clouded up and is raining. We have a muddy time—a very wet time for sleeping.

May 30.—The fight opened at daylight. Our company has three wounded in the hospital. The Yanks have been sharp-shooting all day. We have lost but one man belonging to company B. The Yanks are building rifle-pits—they fire very close. I have been sharp-shooting some to-day. The boys are very lively.

May 31.—We had a very hot time last night. We have quit living like men and are living like hogs. The Yanks have built rifle-pits with port-holes. Our battery was silenced this morning. Five of company A was wounded. Our regiment has lost twenty-six killed and forty or fifty wounded. We have been relieved from our position by Miles's Legion. We will return to our position, I guess, to-morrow. The Yanks are shelling from the lower fleet. Ten of us are going at a time to camps to get clean clothes.

June 1.—I was on guard last night. The Yanks shelled us last night but did no damage. Sam Hagin and Bob Bailey was killed by a rifled cannon-shot this morning. The Yanks are still sharp-shooting, also using their artillery. They have dismounted all our guns. They are the best artillerists I ever saw. The lower fleet has pitched us a few shots from Long Tom.

June 2.—The lower fleet shelled us last night. I am a little unwell this morning. There has not been much fighting to-day. The artillery is booming occasionally, and the sharp-shooters are still popping away. The Yanks threw a few balls at one of our batteries near us to-day. It is reported that we have reënforcements between Clinton and Osica.

June 3.—The Yanks has been shooting all around us to-day. The Hessions seem to be rather afraid to attempt to storm our works again; but seem rather inclined to starve us out. I hope we will receive reënforcements in time to prevent it. Heaven help us!

June 4.—I am very unwell this morning. The lower fleet shelled us last night. The shells made the boys hunt a place of safety; such as ditches, rat-holes, trees, etc. We are going to our old position. I am sick at camp.

June 5.—We are still besieged by the Yanks. Another day has passed and no reënforcements. Sim Herring was wounded in the head to-day. The Yanks are still sharp-shooting, also using their artillery with but little effect. We hear a great many different reports.

June 6.—The river is falling very fast. It is very, very hot weather. Several shots from "Whistling Dick" came over our camp to-day. Sewell is shelling the Yanks. I expect to go to the breastworks in the morning. Several of the boys are at camp sick.

June 7.—Another day has dawned and no reënforcements. I shall go to the breastworks this morning. The Yanks are still popping away from their rifle-pits. One of company B was killed to-day while looking over the breastwork.

It is very, very hot, and we have lain in the ditch all day.

June 8.—The Yanks began to sharp-shoot at daybreak. We had two men killed yesterday. I am afraid some of our company will get shot next. Another day has dawned and no reënforcements, but I hope we will receive them soon. The Yanks have been shelling our breastworks, but no damage done. It is very disagreeable sitting in these dirty ditches—but this the confederate soldier expects and bears cheerfully; but another long hot day has passed and who knows what may be our situation at this time to-morrow evening?

June 9.—The Yanks attempted a charge last evening but was repulsed. Whistling Dick is at work to-day, it has played a full hand, too. Whistling Dick is tearing our camps all to pieces. Charlie Dixon and Berry Hagin was wounded by fragments of our cook shelter, which was shot down. Our sick has been removed to the ravine. It is difficult to get something to eat. The Yankee artillery is playing upon us all around. The Heshians burned our commissary with a shell to-day.

June 10.—Another day and night has passed, and this poor, worn-out garrison has received no assistance. We have lain in the ditches twenty days, and still there is no prospect of succor—but I truly hope we will soon receive reënforcements. The men is getting sick very fast. The Yankee artillery is keeping a dreadful noise. I and Mormon have been detailed for some extra duty. The Hessions gave us a few rounds as we were crossing the field. I received despatches from the General in person.

June 11.—The Yanks used their artillery at a tremendous rate last night. I went to or attempted to visit Colonel Steedman's headquarters. I had a gay time trying to find them; falling in ravines, etc. I was in a hot place, shure. We captured a Yankee captain and lieutenant last night. The Yanks seemed disposed to make a general assault last night.

At this point the journal suddenly stops; the author having been taken prisoner.

Doc. 49.

THE EAST-TENNESSEE CAMPAIGN.

LOUISVILLE JOURNAL ACCOUNT.

KNOXVILLE, TENN., November 25, 1863.

SINCE it was first known to the public that Major-General Burnside would attempt the accomplishment of an object, namely, the occupation of East-Tennessee, and which would give a prestige to the Union arms heretofore unattained, if successful, and would sever the connection between the two and only great remaining armies of the Southern Confederacy, thus giving the final blow to the treasonable attempt at the disruption of our Government, all eyes have been turned in this direction. And if we are to believe, and we cannot well doubt, the tone of the papers of the loyal States, the greatest uneasiness has been felt by the people for the safety of our army, and anxiety felt for the result of the expedition. Fear and anxiety were well founded upon the expressed opinion of some of our greatest Generals that a successful campaign into East-Tennessee was impossible. And at best, if it should by any oversight of the rebel authorities be successful in the beginning, and the Union army occupy this territory, to hold it would be impossible by reason of the inability of the Government to feed and clothe the necessary number of men to make sure the conquest, and its incapacity to furnish forage for the stock necessary for transportation, and for the cattle required to feed the men.

The army of General Burnside is here, and has been for three months. During that time it been well fed and clothed, and will compare favorably in general appearance with any body of men in the service. In point of health it will show a better record than any other army in the field, for the reason that the hardships of the campaign were on the march and culled the light timber from the ranks, and has left us as hardy a set of men as ever were under arms.

I am not a prophet, nor do I pretend to read the future — especially not to solve the mystery attached to military movements—but propose to give an account of the events of a few days past, which have settled the fate of East-Tennessee and the brave army that wrenched it from the rebels.

Our troops evacuated Loudon the latter part of October. The Second division, Twenty-third army corps, commanded by Brigadier-General Julius White, was stationed upon the opposite banks of the river from the town. The rebels occupied Loudon and the heights around, in what force we could not learn, nor was it of great importance, as the river was to be the future base of operations, and for this reason it was, as I have learned, that General Burnside ordered the evacuation of the town. A division of the Ninth army corps occupied Lenoirs, six miles above. With this support for General White, one brigade of the Second division, Twenty-third army corps, was ordered by General Burnside to Kingston, twenty miles below, leaving near one thousand five hundred men and two batteries, which was considered ample to watch and operate against the rebel force occupying Loudon. This programme was carried out to the very letter.

On the night of the thirteenth of November, at nine o'clock, General White received the first report of any considerable force of rebels near us. This was reported to him by Captain Sims, of the Twenty-fourth Indiana battery, and was immediately communicated to General Burnside, who was at Knoxville. General White ordered the field-officer of the day to visit his pickets, make observations, and learn from the pickets all he could giving reason to suppose the enemy near us. The officer reported about an hour after that the pickets had heard men on the other side of the river; the rolling of wagons or artillery, and the handling of lumber near Huff's Ferry. The lumber, it was supposed, would be used to throw a pontoon-bridge across the river at the ferry. Shortly after this, a cavalry picket reported he had heard drums beating and a band playing opposite Huff's Ferry. At the same time another picket reported the enemy building a pontoon-bridge at the ferry, and that a party had crossed in pontoon-boats. Upon receipt of this intelligence, General White sent his Adjutant-General, Captain Curtis, with a small body of cavalry to watch the enemy, and report to him by courier what occurred as fast as it transpired. This Captain Curtis did. As a prudential measure, General White ordered Colonel Chapin to send one regiment of infantry and a section of artillery to dispute the enemy's crossing. The Twenty-third Michigan and a section of Henshaw's battery started for the ferry about one o'clock A.M., November fourteenth. All the information received by General White was immediately telegraphed to General Burnside through the Lenoirs office, thus giving the commandant of that post, General Potter, all the information received at Loudon.

The artillery and infantry that started to the ferry were ordered back by General White upon receipt of a telegram from General Burnside to hold his command ready to march in the direction of Knoxville at a moment's notice. The order was received and the troops took up a line of march and arrived at Lenoirs about seven o'clock A.M., November fourteenth.

A description of the situation of Huff's Ferry would not be inappropriate here. It is on the Tennessee River, half a mile from Loudon, on the south bank of the river, but by a long bend in the river at that point, it is six miles by the road, on the north side. This road is the only one the troops could take to get to that point.

Shortly after the arrival of General White at Lenoirs, General Burnside arrived on a train from Knoxville to command in person the movement of the troops. A countermarch to Loudon was immediately ordered. A "reliable spy" had brought information that the rebels were constructing a pontoon at Loudon, and doing nothing at Huff's Ferry. This he knew—"had seen it with his own eyes." "Reliable spies" are infallible. The "Holy City" never had within its sacred precincts an Otho or Pius, whose high conceptions of morality taught them the invaluable worth of truth more surely than the ordeal through which they had to pass taught the loyal East-Tennesseeans, and they whose "names lead all the rest" are the "reliable spies" and "scouts." One thousand five hundred soldiers, who had carried water from the river opposite Loudon for three weeks, and up to the time "reliable spy" *had seen* the bridge, and a part of them from the very spot where the bridge touched the north side of the river, and who knew there was no bridge there, and our pickets and scouts who knew the bridge was being built where and at the time "reliable spy" knew it wasn't, were certainly mistaken.

They had been deceived and blinded by some mesmer-magnetic influence of some rebel wizard. But the divinity of the "reliable" confounded the work and trampled the wicked machinations of this latter-day evil spirit, and would, by his power, discover to the deliverers of East-Tennessee the operations of these wily traitors. The troops, therefore, marched back to Loudon, expecting to meet the enemy at that point. Arrived there, they found no bridge, no enemy, nothing. They immediately pushed on in the direction of Huff's Ferry, the Second brigade, Second division, Twenty-third army corps Colonel Chapin commanding, in the advance, the entire command under the personal supervision of the division commander, Brigadier-General White, General Ferrero's division, of the Ninth army corps, in the rear. When three miles from the ferry, General White met General Potter, staff, and escort returning, who stated that they had been fired on a short distance ahead by rebel pickets. At this juncture there was a "crisis" in the market for the sale of stock in "reliable spies." It was so sudden and so unexpected to the holders, and came with such a crash, that I doubt if a revulsion in nature and the upheaving of the contents of earth would cause it to emerge from its resting-place. Spies and scouts are necessary to the successful prosecution of a war in a country to which they are native, or at least in which they are acquainted with roads and modes of egress and ingress which it is impossible for the commander to know. But how careful should they be of trusting too fully to such information, and how well know the person whom they trust, and how summary and severe should be the punishment of him who violates this confidence and trust and renders insecure the safety of an army, especially one on which so much depends as on that of the army of East-Tennessee. This man either wilfully misrepresented or his coward nature would not allow him to ascertain the facts, and reported by guess, supposing the army would move on to Knoxville, and no harm being done, the facts would never be discovered.

When a short distance from where General Potter and staff had been fired upon, General White sent forward Lieutenant Lowrie, of his staff, with a small party to reconnoitre; who had advanced but a short distance when they were driven back by a strong rebel picket, a regiment being on duty. The rebels followed up the Lieutenant, and soon opened fire on Generals Potter, White, and Ferrero, their staffs and escorts. General White immediately ordered Colonel Chapin forward with his brigade, the One Hundred and Eleventh Ohio in the centre, One Hundred and Seventh Illinois on the right, and the Thirteenth Kentucky on the left, the Twenty-third Michigan supporting the artillery. Then begun the battle of Huff's Ferry. The troops moved forward at a double-quick, cheered to the work before them by their regimental commanders, and a moral influence being given to the charge by the presence of their brigade commander, Colonel Chapin, and an influence incalculable was added by the coolness in the hour of danger of their division commander, General White, who knew the odds against which his gallant brigade had to contend, and the necessity of the exposure which he made of his person upon the field, issuing his orders as the occasion demanded, frequently carrying and attending to the execution of them in person. It was such influence and such cool bravery on the part of their division commanders as I shall ever believe, that enabled this little brigade, all unused to the smell of the "villainous saltpetre," to drive back two miles a superior force of the veterans of Longstreet, over ground which a lesser number should have held.

The One Hundred and Seventh Illinois was ordered to drive the rebels from a position they had taken on a hill upon the right, while the One Hundred and Eleventh Ohio and Thirteenth Kentucky swung around to inclose the fields and woods through which the rebels must pass, and would expose them to the fire of these two regiments. The One Hundred and Seventh did its work gallantly. Divesting themselves of all superfluous weight, knapsacks, overcoats, etc., as they moved to the charge, they gained the top of the hill, and scattered the troops of Longstreet in an almost perfect rout. Once getting a taste of the fight (it being their first) and exultant with this victory, their battle-cry the balance of the day was: "Forward!" While the One Hundred and Seventh was driving the enemy in such confusion on the right, the Thirteenth Kentucky and One Hundred and Eleventh Ohio were doing their work nobly. Elated by the success of their comrades, it seemed as if they were trying to outdo their achievements. The rebels were thus beaten back two miles, when they formed on a high hill, where they were sheltered by woods, and which they supposed impregnable — aided now as they were by their artillery, which had taken position on the opposite side of the river and had opened on our men. The Second brigade was now in an open field, exposed to the rebel fire from both the positions they had taken.

To clear this hill was the next work. Defended by three regiments of the famous corps, it seemed impossible. But it was to be done. The order had been issued and the men knew their General's meaning when he spoke, and were cheerful in obedience to him who had exposed himself to every danger for their good. The task devolved upon the Thirteenth Kentucky, supported by the One Hundred and Seventh Illinois. Before the charge the General rode along the lines encouraging the men to their duty. The order to charge was given. The Thirteenth Kentucky, led by their gallant young Colonel, Wm. E. Hobson, who seemed to scorn danger and defy death in the presence of his command, moved to their mission. Fifteen minutes decided the day. The rebels were routed, but the path of the Thirteenth Kentucky was marked by their dead and wounded. In this short time sixty of that brave regiment lay dead or wounded upon the field of their glory. Night had now come on and the fighting ceased, except an occasional shell from the rebel battery continued till nine o'clock, when all was quiet. The enemy's loss in this fight could not be ascertained, as he carried off a number of his killed and wounded, and the extreme darkness of the night prevented an examination of the field. In this fight the Ninth army corps was held in reserve, and was not engaged.

At daylight the next morning the troops took up the line of march to Lenoirs. The duty of rear-guard was assigned to the Second brigade of General White's division. The One Hundred and Eleventh Ohio and one section of Henshaw's battery were detailed to the extreme rear to cover the advanced troops. The roads had been rendered almost impassable by rains the day before, and it was with difficulty the artillery could be got up the hill where the fight began. It was all got up except one caisson, when the enemy, who had advanced in considerable force under cover of the woods and the crest of the hill, attacked the One Hundred and Eleventh Ohio from three points. The position would not warrant a general engagement, and the caisson had to be abandoned. A smart skirmish ensued, however, as the One Hundred and Eleventh fought its way to the top of the hill, where it formed, and a few well-directed volleys from their guns, and a few rounds of canister from the section of artillery, soon checked the enemy, and the march was resumed toward Lenoirs, where we arrived early in the afternoon. In this skirmish the One Hundred and Eleventh lost twenty men killed and wounded.

About four o'clock P.M., after arriving at Lenoirs, it was discovered that the main if not the entire rebel force had advanced and taken position to give us battle, and our troops were formed to resist the attack if made. They made no demonstration that evening. Our troops remained in line till nearly daylight, when an order was received to march in the direction of Knoxville, which was immediately obeyed. On this retreat the Second division Twenty-third army corps lost its transportation and ammunition train, and all its property, public and private, which could not be hurriedly taken away. The officers, division, brigade, and regimental, lost all their private property. This was done by order of Major-General Burnside, that the draft animals might be used to move the artillery; the state of the roads being such that it was impossible to move it otherwise. The rebels received no benefit from this abandonment of property, as every thing was destroyed.

Marching in the direction of Knoxville, we were overtaken by the enemy at Campbell's Station at twelve o'clock M., November sixteenth, and the battle of Campbell's Station commenced. One brigade of the Ninth corps was in the advance, the Second brigade of the Twenty-third corps in the centre, and one brigade of the Ninth corps as rear-guard. The skirmishing was begun by the Ninth corps, the First brigade of the Ninth corps forming in the rear of General White's command, which formed in line to protect the stock, etc., as

it passed to the rear, and to cover the retreat of the Ninth corps, which was the rear-guard and was to file past it. Again was the Second brigade in position where it must receive the first shock of battle, and must win more or lose the honors already won. The arrangements for battle had hardly been completed before the cavalry came in from the front followed by the infantry of the Ninth corps, and two heavy lines of the enemy emerged from the woods three quarters of a mile in front. Each line consisted of a division, and were dressed almost wholly in the United States uniform, which at first deceived us. Their first line advanced to within eight hundred yards of General White's front before that officer gave the order to fire. Henshaw's and the Twenty-fourth Indiana batteries then opened on them with shell, but they moved steadily forward, closing up as their lines would be broken by this terrible fire, until within three hundred and fifty yards of our main line, when the batteries mentioned opened on them with canister, and four batteries in the rear, and right and left of General White, opened on their rear line with shell. This was more than they could stand. Their front line broke, and ran back some distance, where they re-formed and deployed right and left, and engaged the Thirteenth Kentucky and Twenty-third Michigan on the right, and the One Hundred and Eleventh Ohio and One Hundred and Seventh Illinois on the left, which were supported by General Ferrero's command of the Ninth corps. This unequal contest went on for an hour and a half. The only advantage over them, so far, was in artillery, they not having any in position yet. It seemed to be their object to crush the inferior force opposing them with their heavy force of infantry. The men were too stubborn. They would not yield an inch, but frequently drove the rebels from their position and held the ground. Finding they could not move them with the force already employed, the rebels moved forward another line of infantry, heavy as either of the first two, and placed in position three batteries. Their guns were heavier and of longer range than those of the Second brigade, and were situated to command General White's position, while his guns could not answer their fire. They got the range of these guns at once, and killed and wounded several gunners and disabled several horses, when General White ordered them back to the position occupied by those in the rear, the infantry holding their position covered by the artillery on the hill. An artillery fight then began, which continued nearly two hours, till it was growing dark, and the order was given for our troops to fall back to resume the march to Knoxville.

The management of the troops as they moved from the field of battle was a picture of skill and generalship. The Ninth corps moved off first, devolving the duty of protecting the rear upon the troops of General White. They were hotly pursued by the enemy, who hoped to break the retreat into a rout. But not a man quickened his pace, and their lines, dressed as when marching in review, gave evidence of the utter disregard of personal safety to save the honor of three days' fighting and toil. The enemy made use of every advantage he thought he could gain, but not a move did he make that escaped the quick glance of the division or brigade commander, who would face about or change his front as the occasion required, delivering a few volleys so well directed as to check and drive back the enemy utterly discomfited. For two miles this military game was played with such success by the Second brigade as to cause the rebel chief to draw off, virtually acknowledging himself checkmated at the game he begun and seemed anxious to play. This retreat over that field was a sight so grand and beautiful in its management that it attracted the attention of every officer and man who could leave his command to witness it. The heights in front and on the rear were filled with persons of high and low rank, almost grown boisterous with pleasurable excitement as each move of the troops of General White showed them the discomfited enemy falling back to assume a new offensive movement, and to meet the same fate as before. General Burnside, who witnessed its management, pronounced it a masterly effort against such numbers.

Night coming on and the enemy growing less troublesome, Colonel Chapin, commanding the brigade, who had been unwell for a number of days but had refused to leave the field while the enemy was in the front, was now suffering so that he was ordered to quit his post, and the command devolved upon Colonel W. E. Hobson, of the Thirteenth Kentucky, who led the men from the field and conducted the retreat to Knoxville.

To mention the names of the brave men, officers and privates, who did deeds deserving of record, would be to name every man engaged. Not one flinched from the work before him. The historian of the war will find a goodly part of the material for his work here, and do credit to this band of heroes. Having been a witness of all that occurred during the time of which I have written, I feel justified in mentioning a few names that came forth covered with a halo of glory. Of General Burnside I shall say nothing. The country knows him, and he is a subject too grand for my pen. Of the General commanding the Second division, Twenty-third army corps, Brigadier-General White, I cannot say enough to do him justice. He was everywhere present during the fights, scorning to refuse to share the danger his men were exposed to, and endured cheerfully the hardships of the entire march. The "watchful General" he may well be called. Not a minute did he quit his post or take his eye off the enemy, from the time he received the news of his being at Huff's Ferry until his arrival here; but watching every movement they made, acted as his good judgment suggested when thrown upon his own resources, and always with success. He communicated to his chief at Knoxville all the information he received, and obeyed implicitly every order he obtained from that quarter. Among the Generals here is one at least "*sans peur et sans re-*

proche." To the members of his staff the report of General White will, I presume, do justice. Their names only are necessary here: Captains Henry Curtis, Jr., F. G. Hentig, James A. Lee, Lieutenants Lowrie and Edmiston. They were with the General always except when upon duty. Of Colonel Chapin, commanding the Second brigade of Second division, Twenty-third army corps, I need not add to what I have said. His excellent management of the troops upon three fields, and his personal bravery, have attached him to his men as few commanders are attached. His staff, Captains Gallup and Sheldon and Lieutenant Pearson, are worthy followers of their brave leader. Colonel W. E. Hobson, of the Thirteenth Kentucky, upon whom the command of the brigade at times devolved, behaved always as became the hero of Huff's Ferry. Lieutenant-Colonel Lowry, of the One Hundred and Seventh Illinois; Major Sherwood, of the One Hundred and Eleventh Ohio; and Major Wheeler, of the Twenty-third Michigan, each commanding, all carried themselves nobly. I must mention the name of ex-Colonel Joseph J. Kelly, of the One Hundred and Seventh Illinois, whose resignation had just been accepted, and who intended to start for his home in Illinois the day of the fight at Huff's Ferry, but would not leave while the regiment he had so long commanded was in the face of the enemy. He was with them all the time, urging them to the performance of their duty and to victory, and still remains, as he says, to "see it through."

The Ninth army corps was engaged only in the battle of Campbell's Station, and there sustained the honor of their past history.

The troops arrived at Knoxville at daylight November seventeenth, from which time dates the siege of the place, of which

MORE ANON.

Doc. 50.

FIGHT NEAR ROCHEPORT, MO.

GLASGOW, June 3, 1863.

Editors Missouri Democrat:

HAVING seen a very incorrect statement of the result of Captain S. W. Steinmitz's scout through the lower part of this county and the upper part of Boone, I ask a small space in your paper to give the facts as they occurred.

Captain Steinmitz belongs to company C, First Prov. regiment, E. M. M., Colonel Douglas commanding. The Captain left Glasgow at two o'clock P.M., May thirtieth, at the head of fifteen men of his company. He travelled till twelve o'clock that night, and reached Mrs. Jackman's farm, (mother of the bushwhacking colonel,) and after a good and complete search — for Captain Sam never leaves a thing half-finished — he was satisfied that the game had flown. He found some ammunition, and learned that the Colonel had been there only five hours before. We concluded it was best to stay in the vicinity until light, which we did.

At eight o'clock A.M., thirty-first, we took the

road for Rocheport, thoroughly scouring the intermediate country. We arrived at Rocheport at one P.M., thirty-first. During our rest of one hour, we learned that Major Rucker had been in the place the evening before, and other information not necessary to give here. We moved out to Forbis's farm, where we had our second meal. We moved again at eight o'clock P.M., and rode three hours, capturing a gun and more ammunition. We halted where we had supper, and remained there till daylight, June first. Again we were in the saddle, and had not gone over a mile when we struck a fresh trail of a horse. This we followed a half-mile, when we found a broad trail where forty or fifty horsemen had gone along. The chase was now exciting; we had not far to go when the advance saw two men with guns in their hands, coming down the opposite slope—we were following a ravine; our advance commanded them to halt, which they failing to do, the boys fired on them. They immediately returned the fire, when forty or fifty armed men showed their heads above the bank and fired on us. We gave them two volleys, and our captain ordered us to fall back on the hill and form in line of battle. About half our men heard the command and obeyed it; the others saw them going, and thinking it a run, started in a different direction. Captain Steinmitz and party were hotly pursued to within three miles of Fayette by the infuriated villains, where the First Sergeant's horse gave out, and he was taken prisoner. The others escaped.

We found them about three miles north-west of Rockport, encamped on the farm of John L. Jones. Captain Steinmitz had one man killed dead on the spot; Sergeant William H. Hensley mortally wounded, (lived about five hours,) private John M. Rhyne severely wounded in three places. We afterward learned that we killed one man dead, and wounded several who were taken from the field.

Captain Steinmitz and party went into Fayette and got a reënforcement from the Ninth Missouri—company A, Captain Leonard—and overtook them near the old battle-ground. They charged on Captain Leonard, which company A received gallantly and repulsed them. It was their time now, and Captain Leonard led them nobly. The bushwhackers ran, and we captured a keg of powder, several pistols and guns. About this time detachments from company F and —, (I forget the other company's letter,) of the Ninth Missouri, stationed at Columbia, came on the field under the command of the intrepid Captain Cook. The rout now became a perfect "skedaddle," and so we left them, to attend to the mournful duties caring for the dead and dying.

Captain Leonard had a buck-shot in the right knee, and a ball passed through his hat, producing a painful contusion on the right side of his head.

The casualties on the rebel side were four killed, left on the field, and perhaps twice that number wounded. We have it from reliable authority that they they (the citizens) worked all night carrying off the dead and wounded. The rebels were behind a bank, which was a natural breastwork. Their advantages in the first fight were about ten to one, taking position, arms, and numbers into the account. They were all armed with double-barrelled shot-guns and navy pistols, loaded with fixed ammunition, and were under the command of Jackman, Rucker, Pulliam, and Todd.

They paroled Sergeant Vance, and the parole was signed　　　　　　　　S. D. JACKMAN,
　　　　　　　　　　　　　　　Colonel Commanding.
By J. DRURY PULLIAM, A. A. G.

Yours very respectfully, one of the
　　　　　　　　　　　　　PARTICIPANTS.

P. S.—While Captain Steinmitz and party were going into Fayette, they overtook a very estimable citizen, and while he was in company the bushwhackers fired a volley, killing the citizen. I write this because Jackman has circulated it over the country that Captain Steinmitz killed him.　　　　　　　　　　　　　　　　P.

Doc. 51.

THE YAZOO EXPEDITION.

LIEUTENANT COMMANDING J. G. WALKER'S REPORT.

UNITED STATES STEAMER BARON DE KALB, }
MOUTH OF YAZOO RIVER, June 1, 1863. }

SIR: I have the honor to report that I left this place on the morning of the twenty-fourth May, with the De Kalb, Forest Rose, Linden, Signal, and Petrel. I pushed up the Yazoo as speedily as possible, for the purpose of destroying the enemy's transports on that river, with the Forest Rose, Linden, and Petrel, to within about fifteen miles of Fort Pemberton, where I found the steamers John Walsh, R. J. Shankland, Golden Age, and Scotland, sunk on a bar, completely blocking it up. I remained at this point during the night, and next morning at daylight was attacked by a force of the enemy, but after a sharp fire of a few minutes they beat a hasty retreat. Our only loss was two men wounded. Returning down the Yazoo, I burned a large saw-mill, twenty-five miles above Yazoo City. At Yazoo City I landed and brought away a large quantity of bar, round, and flat iron from the navy-yard. At Indian Shoal, I sent volunteer Lieutenant Brown, of the Forest Rose, with boats, through to Rolling Fork. He found a quantity of corn belonging to the rebels, which he burned. At the mouth of Bayou Quiver, hearing of steamers, I sent Lieutenant Brown, with the boats of the Forest Rose and Linden, up after them. Ascending ten miles, he found the Dew Drop and Emma Bell. The Linden burned the Argo in a small bayou about seventy-five miles up the Sunflower. I also found the Cotton Plant sunk in Lake George, with nothing out of the water but the tops of her smoke-stacks. At Gaines's Landing, on the Sunflower, I found, and brought away, a cutter which was lost on the Deer Creek expedition. I have as prisoners two engineers and a

pilot in the service of the rebels, and several deserters and refugees, JOHN G. WALKER,
Lieutenant Commanding United States Navy.
To Acting Rear-Admiral D. D. PORTER,
Commanding Mississippi Squadron.

CINCINNATI COMMERCIAL ACCOUNT.

UNITED STATES GUNBOAT BARON DE KALB, }
MOUTH OF THE YAZOO RIVER, May 31, 1863. }

We have just returned from our expedition in pursuit of the enemy's transports, and have been highly successful.

Having received orders from Admiral Porter to ascend the Yazoo to the highest possible point, and destroy every rebel transport found, we left the mouth of this river on the evening of the twenty-fourth, and proceeded rapidly up-stream. Captain J. G. Walker, of our boat, having been made Flag-Officer, proceeded on board the mosquito boat Forest Rose, in order to push ahead as rapidly as possible and press the enemy hard.

We advanced rapidly into the enemy's country, stopping at every plantation and delivering to the planters Admiral Porter's orders, in reference to our being fired upon by guerrillas from their property, which was to burn and destroy every house around on the plantations from which we received the fire. We passed many thousand bales of cotton, and were anxious that some transports might be captured and preserved, so that, on our return, we might be enabled to carry away the valuable article as a prize.

At night, when we came to, a vigilant watch was kept aboard, and the vessel anchored as far away as possible from the shore. The object of this was to prevent being boarded, should the enemy be about. During the daytime, while under way, every man was kept under cover of the casemates, to escape any fire from the banks.

Arriving at the head of Honey Island, in Choula Lake, the De Kalb came to anchor to await further orders and the return of the boats which had preceded us.

We remained here for two days, receiving no news whatever of the expedition which had gone ahead until the evening of the second day, when the three boats rejoined us. We learned that they had ascended the river to within eighteen miles of Fort Pemberton, and were prevented from going further up on account of the enemy having sunk across the river some seven steamers and innumerable torpedoes. Finding it dangerous to attempt the removal of the latter, they burned the former (as much as remained out of water) and began to return. The fine cotton steamers Magnolia and Magenta had retreated up the river and found safety under the guns of the fort. Descending the river, after burning the boats, the vessels were considerably annoyed, being fired upon by sharp-shooters from the bank. A number of the men on board were wounded, but fortunately none of the wounds were serious. The cotton which we had passed on going up was found in flames on returning. Acting upon orders, the Flag-Officer directed the destruction of the property which lay around, consisting of cot-

ton-gins, saw-mills, etc. Arriving at Yazoo City we were handed an official document from the rebel medical department, asking for medicines for their sick and wounded, which, of course, was refused.

We descended the Yazoo to the mouth of Big Sunflower, which river we proceeded up for the purpose of destroying what transports we could find. A rebel prisoner, who had been captured some days previous, being acquainted with the stream, volunteered his services as a guide. The De Kalb, as usual, brought up the rear, while the other vessels proceeded rapidly on. Finding the river receding, we came to at the mouth of Lake George to await the return of the expedition.

After remaining three days above, the boats returned, having penetrated the Rolling Fork of Deer Creek, and ascending the Sunflower as far up as Dunbar's Ferry, a distance of one hundred and eighty miles from the mouth of the river, some five more transports were destroyed, with a large amount of rebel provisions. The boats experienced considerable difficulty in navigating the streams, owing to their narrowness.

Acting Volunteer Lieutenant Brown, of the Forest Rose, rendered efficient service during the expedition, as did Acting Masters Kendrick of the De Kalb, and Smith of the Petrel.

I cannot here give you the names of the steamers destroyed, not having been furnished with a list. They were all of a good class, and their destruction will be keenly felt by the rebels.

The whole country through which we passed presented the appearance of desolation; no sign of cultivation could be seen, and it appeared as if the people had deserted agricultural pursuits altogether.

The river above Yazoo City is bordered by many beautiful plantations, which, previous to the war, presented a thriving appearance, but now seem desolate. At every one which we passed, the negroes, who now remained possessors, (the planters having fled,) gathered upon the banks, and seemed anxious for us to take them on board and make them free, and when we refused, on account of not having transportation, they seemed very much depressed in spirits.

The country, which has been overflowed ever since the levee was cut on the Mississippi to enter the Yazoo Pass, now, as the river recedes, begins to "dry up," making it extremely sickly around. What few inhabitants we saw and conversed with seemed to be badly in need of the necessaries of life, and hope soon to be relieved by our becoming permanent possessors of the land. They are poorly clad, and informed us that the only channel through which they received clothing was Memphis, and that the prices were enormous.

Doc. 52.

GENERAL TRIMBLE'S ADDRESS
TO THE CITIZENS OF MARYLAND.

HEADQUARTERS VALLEY DISTRICT, }
June 3, 1863. }

MAJOR-GENERAL J. R. TRIMBLE, having been assigned to the Department of Northern Virginia, invites all citizens of Maryland, in and out of the army, to join the Maryland troops now serving in this district, with a view to increase the organization from that State to a body formidable by its number and gallantry.

Under this command every Marylander will have a field for the display of that devotion and bravery in the cause of the South which it is well known they possess, but which have heretofore been much obscured by their separation into almost every brigade of the army.

Marylanders should bear in mind that upon themselves must rest the honor and renown of bringing their State into the Southern Confederacy, and of avenging the wrongs inflicted upon her sons and daughters by the Goths and Vandals of the North, who, true to the instincts of their race, have done more outrage to the feelings of humanity, to Christian civilization, and to Christian freedom, than any nation of this enlightened age.

Let us hope the day is near when, as Marylanders, we may do our part to avenge these wrongs.

By Order: Major-General Trimble.

W. Carvel Hall,
    Assistant Adjutant-General.

Doc. 53.

THE DESTRUCTION OF SIMMSPORT, LA.

Headquarters M. M. Brigade,
Flag-Ship Autocrat, Lake's Landing,
Yazoo River, June 11, 1863.

In accordance with instructions from Captain Henry Walke, commanding detachment of Mississippi squadron, Lieutenant-Colonel John A. Ellet, commanding the ram fleet of the Mississippi Marine Brigade, left the mouth of Red River June third, on the United States steam-ram Switzerland, on a reconnoissance as far as Simmsport, on the Atchafalaya River.

The approach to the town was made slowly and cautiously, in order to insure a timely detection of any earth defences the enemy might have with which to dispute the passage of the river. It was ordered, however, that no gun should be fired until the fact of the existence of a hostile force in the place should be definitely ascertained. When within half a mile of the town the enemy opened with a battery of field-pieces and a regiment of infantry. The men on the ram replied with great vigor.

Behind the levee and some heavy embankments thrown up for the purpose, within less than one hundred yards of the river channel, the enemy's infantry was safely protected, and all the time pouring rapid volleys of musketry into the boat. The fire also of the artillery was very severe and accurate. The ram was struck seven times by shells, two of which set fire to the cotton and other combustible material on the boat for the protection of her machinery; two entered the hull just above the water-line, and another cut the escape-pipe, filling the engine-room with steam,

without injuring any of the crew, nor were the engineers driven from their post.

Fearing a conflagration, the ram was now obliged to desist from the engagement, and dropped down, repassing the enemy's works, and anchored out of range. During the entire engagement the ram's battery replied to the enemy's shots, but with what effect is not known, except that the fire slackened considerably before the termination of the action.

The national loss in the engagement was three men seriously wounded.

The conduct of the men was very commendable throughout the entire action.

On the following day, June fourth, having the day before returned to the rest of the fleet at the mouth of the river, the Colonel set out, in company with the iron-clads Lafayette and Pittsburgh, for the same place he visited the day before. Immediately upon arriving at the town the iron-clads opened with their one hundred pounder rifled guns at long-range, when the enemy fled without firing a gun. Our men then landed and fired the town. The flight of the enemy was so hasty that a large number of arms and accoutrements were left in the houses and were destroyed. A file of regimental papers was secured, from which an estimate of the enemy's force was made. The papers were headed "Third regiment Arizona brigade," (Texans.) By these papers their numbers were given as eight hundred and seventy-nine. They had also a battery of six pieces. During the action two guns were dismounted. The nationals suffered no loss in the action.

Doc. 54.

EXPEDITION TO BLUFFTON, S. C.

LIEUTENANT COMMANDING GEORGE BACON'S REPORT.

U. S. S. Commodore McDonough,
Port Royal, S. C., June 4, 1863.

Sir: . . . On account of being detained by the Mayflower, it was long after daylight before we reached the point where the troops were to disembark, which was about three miles this side of Bluffton; meeting with no opposition at that point, the troops were landed in safety, and both them and ourselves advanced to the attack, the Mayflower having joined us in the mean time. I anchored from half to three quarters of a mile from the town, bringing our batteries to bear upon it.

The land forces having without opposition occupied the town, I moved up with this vessel and the transports for the purpose of being better able to cover their movements, as well as to be ready to reëmbark the troops in case of necessity, as the enemy had mustered quite a large force in the rear of the town of infantry and cavalry. Soon after we had anchored abreast of the town, and but a few yards from it, sharp firing was heard in the rear between the rebels and our forces. The commanding officer of the land forces made signal that he wished us to shell the woods in their rear, as the rebels were mustering in quite a strong force. I immediately opened with all my guns, firing both shell and shrapnel with five-second fuses, which compelled the enemy to fall back. In the mean time the town was fired in several places, by order of the commander of the land forces, the church being the only building spared.

The enemy, under cover of the fire and smoke of the burning town, which raged so dense as to cause us to move our position a little, and almost obscured immediate objects, attempted another attack on our forces. They were met by steady volleys from our troops and the enfilading fire of our heavy guns, and were obliged to retire in disorder.

As we had succeeded in carrying out the object of our expedition, . . . the troops were ordered to embark. . . . The enemy seeing that all the troops were leaving, collected all their troops for the third and last charge upon the rear-guard, who were left on shore to cover the reembarkation of their comrades. The enemy advanced down the street leading to the wharf, through the town, expecting, no doubt, to sweep off in the general rush the few who were covering the reëmbarkation.

As they were in considerable force by that time, they charged with cheers to within a short distance of the steamers, when, from their repeated volleys, we got their position, . . . when we opened with shrapnel and shell in the direction of the enemy, and the effect was instantaneous, as I have since been assured by the commander of the land forces that our shrapnel and shell passed directly over the heads of our own men, exploding in front of the ranks of the enemy, causing them to break and retreat in disorder. The guns of the Mayflower, which was at that time lying at the wharf and commanding the streets, were served with great effect.

GEORGE BACON,
Lieutenant Commanding United States Navy.
To Rear-Admiral S. F. Du Pont.

CHARLESTON MERCURY ACCOUNT.

CHARLESTON, June 6, 1863.

The destruction of property on Bull's Island some days ago, and the recent raid on the Combahee, involving an immense loss of property, is followed by the burning of the beautiful town of Bluffton on May River. This last outrage took place on Thursday morning last, and resulted in the loss of about forty private residences and nearly one hundred outhouses, stores, etc. We have succeeded in obtaining a list of the property owners who have suffered by the burning of their beautiful houses and settlements:

General J. F. Drayton, Colonel J. J. Stoney, Dr. J. W. Kirk, George Allen, Dr. Paul Pritchard, M. J. Kirk, J. McKenzie, A. Crosby, G. Allen, Dr. A. G. Verdier, Estate H. Guerard, Jos. Baynard, Jas. Seabrook, G. W. Lawton, W. Pope, Dr. Mellichamp, Dr. F. H. Pope, R. R. Pope, J. J. Pope, A. G. Verdier, Henry Verdier, "Squire Popes," Mr. Strobhart, Mrs. Hardee, J. Chalmers, J. G. Bulichen, D. & J. Canter, D. Freeman, — Crosby, — Langballe, — Chalmers, W. Winn, J. Bulichen, Mrs. Pickney, Mrs. Winingham, B. Wiggins, Estate Norton, H. F. Train, — Martain, (f. p. c.)

The enemy approached in transports, and landed about one thousand strong at what is known as Hunting Island. Five gunboats covered their landing, which was successfully accomplished about half-past six o'clock on the fourth instant. Three companies of the force that had landed took up the line of march, following the course of the river until they reached Bluffton, their gunboats steaming along up the river abreast of the troops. The pickets noticed the movement at sunrise, and reported the fact to Lieutenant-Colonel Johnson, commanding the outposts, at about seven o'clock, and the cavalry force from the Third and Fourth regiments, South-Carolina cavalry, moved at once toward the threatened point. Strange to say, the couriers failed to report the advance of the enemy either to the picket headquarters in Bluffton or the garrison encamped near the town, consisting of the fine infantry force from the Eleventh South-Carolina regiment. The consequence was, the gunboats arrived in the river nearly opposite the camps before they could be seen by the camp-guard, who gave the alarm. The men were soon under arms, and deployed as skirmishers, going some distance to the front in the movement. The enemy soon came in sight, having obtained possession of the town unmolested, and exchanged shots with the line of skirmishers. Soon after the town was fired in the lower part, near Colonel Stoney's, and the blowing fresh soon sent the flames broadcast through the town.

The heavy growth of trees between Mr. Pope's house and the Episcopal church saved the latter structure. They fired the Methodist church under the very altar ; but it burnt so slowly that it was discovered, and put out. The cavalry had now arrived. Earle's light battery, after a drive of thirteen miles, had also reported for duty. The Abolitionists having effected their purpose now withdrew, embarked on their transports, and were conveyed out of sight.

But one casualty occurred on our side. Sergeant Mew, of company E, Eleventh South-Carolina infantry, was struck by a fragment of a shell (which, by the way, the Yankee gunboats used very freely) in the right side ; the wound is not dangerous, however. The invaders, who were principally a New-Hampshire regiment, are not known to have been punished in any way. As we said in reference to the affair on the Combahee, the success of a marauding expedition of this character is certainly a very mortifying circumstance.

Doc. 55.

DESTRUCTION OF ASHEPOO, S. C.

BEAUFORT, June 5, 1863.

WITH but two hundred and fifty negro soldiers, on board the gunboat John Adams, and the transports Harriet A. Weed and Sentinel, Colonel Montgomery left Beaufort on the evening of the first instant, and at half-past two on the following morning anchored his little fleet in the Combahee River, thirty miles distant from the point of his departure, twenty miles from Charleston, and fifteen from the village of Ashepoo, on the Charleston and Savannah Railroad. The Sentinel unfortunately got aground at the mouth of the Coosaw River, and was of no service to the expedition; the troops on board of her were transferred to the John Adams and the Harriet A. Weed.

The village of Ashepoo is approached from the Combahee by three different roads, one from Field's Point, where the rebels had constructed a battery, but had deserted it—one from Tar Bluff, two miles above Field's Point, and one from Combahee Ferry, six miles further up the river.

In accordance with the plan fully determined upon before his departure, Colonel Montgomery, almost at the same instant, took possession of the three approaches to Ashepoo, placing Captain T. N. Thompson, with one company in the earthworks at Field's Point; Captain Carver with company E in the rifle-pits at Tar Bluff, and then with the balance of his force proceeded to Combahee Ferry, and with the guns of the John Adams and two howitzers, under command of Captain Brayton, completely covered the road and the approaches to the bridge.

These points were all occupied without opposition. To deceive the enemy, and lead him to suppose that his force was much larger than it really was, he instructed the officer in command at this difficult point to retain but a few men in reserve and throw out nearly their entire strength as skirmishers.

At Ashepoo the rebels had three regiments of infantry, one battalion of cavalry, and a full battery of artillery. As Captain Thompson advanced up the road leading from Field's Point, cavalry came in sight, but a few well-directed volleys soon sent them galloping back in confusion to their stronghold at Ashepoo.

At half-past three P.M., a battery of six pieces arrived and opened a brisk fire. Not a man flinched, but, from such hiding-places as they could find, poured volley after volley upon the gunners, killing and wounding a number. In the midst of this little engagement, the Harriet A. Weed came up, and a well-directed shell from her guns, under the direction of Captain Holden, caused a retreat of the rebel artillery. The raid upon this road then commenced in earnest. The soldiers scattered in every direction, and burned and destroyed every thing of value they came across. Thirty-four large mansions known to belong to notorious rebels, with all their rich furniture and rare works of art, were burned to the ground. Nothing but smouldering ruins and parched and crisped skeletons of once magnificent old oak and palmetto groves now remain of these delightful country-seats.

After scattering the rebel artillery, the Harriet

A. Weed tied up opposite a large plantation, owned by Nicholas & Kirkland. Major Corwin, in command of companies B and C, soon effected a landing, without opposition. The white inhabitants, terrified at the sight of negro soldiers with loaded muskets in their hands, ran in every direction, while the slave population rushed to the boats with every demonstration of joy and gratitude. Three rice-houses, well filled with rice, a large amount in ricks in the yard, and four large mills of different kinds, were destroyed. Mansions, negro-quarters, and every thing inflammable, were consigned to the flames. Sluices were opened, plantations flooded, and broad ponds and lakes made where, but a few hours before, luxuriant crops of rice and corn were putting forth their leaves.

Captain Carver, with company C, landed at Tar Bluff. After a skilful disposition of his pickets, the enemy's cavalry appeared in sight, and threatened to overwhelm his little party, but upon throwing out his whole force he succeeded in repulsing every charge, and finally drove them entirely out of sight. Upon this road several large steam rice-mills, three cotton-gins, and a fine saw-mill were destroyed, together with an immense amount of other property.

Captain Hoyt, company A, landed at Combahee Ferry, at half-past seven A.M.—encountered cavalry pickets the moment he began to advance, but after a short engagement drove them back in disorder. The fine bridge across the Combahee River was then destroyed, together with all the adjacent property.

Captain Brayton, of the Third Rhode Island artillery, who was present with a section of his battery, took part in this engagement from the John Adams.

Having brought within his lines nearly eight hundred valuable slaves; having destroyed property to the amount of two millions, most of which belonged to notorious leaders in this rebellion; having demonstrated that negro soldiers will follow and fight wherever a brave and bold man dares to lead them, and that the slave population of South-Carolina are eager to embrace the opportunity to escape, Colonel Montgomery returned to Beaufort early on the morning of the third instant, without the loss of a man.

Doc. 56.

THE MATTAPONY EXPEDITION.

THE following is a communication from Admiral Lee to the Navy Department, dated June fifth, inclosing report of Lieutenant Commanding Gillis, giving the details of a joint expedition of the army and navy forces up the Mattapony River, Va.

The main object of this expedition was to destroy a foundery at a point on the Mattapony River, some ten miles above Walkerton, where it was said ordnance matter was manufactured for the enemy.

With this object in view, four hundred infantry, on the morning of June fourth, arrived at Yorktown, on board the United States steamer Commodore Morris, Lieutenant Commanding Gillis; United States steamer Commodore Jones, Lieutenant Commanding Mitchell; the army gunboat Smith Briggs, and the transport Winnissimmet.

The expedition proceeded to Walkerton, about twenty miles above West-Point, on the Mattapony River, where it arrived at two A.M. of the fifth. Here the troops were landed and marched to Aylett's, where the objects of the expedition were successfully accomplished, and the foundery, with all its machinery, together with mills, grain, etc., destroyed.

The land forces also destroyed grain at other places, and captured horses, mules, and cattle, and at half-past five P.M. reëmbarked.

The vigilant dispositions of Lieutenant Commanding Gillis kept the river below clear, and the rebels attempting demonstrations at several points on the banks were dispersed by the gunboats.

The navy had no casualties.

Admiral Lee thinks the entire success of the expedition owing in a great measure to our evacuation of West-Point only five days before, thus precluding the probability of any movement in that direction, and throwing the enemy off his guard.

The following is

LIEUT. COM. GILLIS'S REPORT.

U. S. GUNBOAT COMMODORE MORRIS,
OFF YORKTOWN, VA., June 6, 1863.

. . . At eight P.M [on the fourth] . . . we started up the York River, passing West-Point at forty-five minutes past ten, without noticing any thing that would indicate the presence of the enemy. . . . We arrived at Walkerton at two A.M. The troops were landed with all expedition, and reached their destination (Aylett's) at eight A.M. At that place they found the information they had previously received was correct in every particular, and the work of destruction was soon accomplished.

An immense amount of machinery of all kinds, and also a very large quantity of flour and grain, which was in a large flouring mill belonging to the rebel government, was soon rendered useless. Colonel Levis then started on his way back, stopping at different places to destroy grain, capture horses, mules, and cattle. . . . Having received information that the rebels were making preparations to obstruct the river at Mantapoke, I sent the Smith Briggs down at two P.M. to keep the river clear, and to remain at that place until my arrival.

Captain Lee, of that vessel, reports that when he came in sight of Mantapoke there were about sixty or seventy rebels collected on the bluff at Indiantown, but a few shell dispersed them. . . .

. . . I am happy to state that so far as the naval portion of the expedition was concerned, every thing passed off in the most admirable manner, and without a single casualty. . . .

The land forces were not so fortunate — one man being killed and two wounded, also one missing; but, in consideration of the fact that Longstreet's corps was at or near Newton, ten miles from Aylett's, and Pickett's division at the White House, twelve miles from where we landed, I think they were as fortunate as could be expected. . . . J. H. GILLIS,
Lieut. Com. and Sen. Officer, off Yorktown.
To A. R. Admiral LEE.

A NATIONAL ACCOUNT.

YORKTOWN, VA., June 6, 1863.

We have just returned from one of those interesting little expeditions through King William County, Va., that are now termed raids. The whole affair was a perfect success. It was carried out in a soldierly way, and one of the most satisfactory features of the affair was the absence of plundering and pilfering, which on too many former occasions have been permitted to a fearful extent.

While our forces were at West-Point, Major-General Keyes proposed the expedition, and the coast being clear for operations, an expedition was gotten up and put in execution during the past few days.

The following orders were issued to guide those in command:

HEADQUARTERS FOURTH ARMY CORPS,
FORT YORKTOWN, VA., June 4, 1863.

A combined expedition of land and naval forces will leave this place at six o'clock this P.M., for the purpose of destroying a foundery at a point on the Mattapony River, some ten miles above Walkerstown. The land forces will consist of four hundred infantry — one hundred each from the Fourth Delaware, One Hundred and Sixty-eighth New-York, and One Hundred and Sixty-ninth and One Hundred and Seventy-ninth Pennsylvania drafted militia — assisted by three gunboats and a transport under Lieutenant Commanding Gillis. The main purpose of the expedition is to destroy the foundery, where it is said that shot and shell and other instruments of rebellion are manufactured. In addition to that, all collections of supplies for the rebel army will be captured or destroyed. Horses and mules fit for the saddle and for draught, also sheep, cattle, and swine fit for slaughter, will be captured as far as practicable.

It is strictly forbidden, however, to take any thing or to destroy any thing not useful to troops in the field.

As the expedition is intended to penetrate far within the enemy's lines, the infantry are expected to set out with a determination to achieve success at any cost.

Volunteers will be called for to move at thirty minutes' notice, and the commanding officer will be designated at the moment of departure.

The men will carry nothing but their overcoats, canteens and cartridge-boxes, with at least fifty rounds per man. E. D. KEYES,
Major-General Commanding Fourth Army Corps.

Lieutenant-Colonel C. Carroll Tevis is the commander of the infantry, and will be obeyed accordingly.   E. D. KEYES,
Major-General.

The troops were all embarked according to orders, on the Gemsbok and transport, and started up the York River at seven o'clock on the evening of Thursday, the fourth of June. The gunboat Commodore Jones, Lieutenant Commander J. G. Mitchell, led the way, followed by the Commodore Morris and the Smith Briggs, Captain Lee. The latter is an army boat, mounting four guns — the boat that proved so serviceable in running the blockade on the Nansemond River. The flotilla reached West-Point about ten o'clock in the evening, and then proceeded to Walkerstown, via the Mattapony River, reaching the latter place about three o'clock in the morning.

About half-past four, the troops were put in motion for Aylett's warehouse, about ten miles from the point of landing, and forty-five miles from the mouth of the river. The shoal water prevented the boats from going further up the river. The Fourth Delaware and the One Hundred and Sixty-eighth New-York led the way. As the White House was but ten miles distant, and knowing there was a large force of rebels there, the three points of intersection of the Dunkirk and King William Court-House roads were left in charge of detachments of the One Hundred and Sixty-eighth New-York, in order to prevent the main body from being cut off.

Small skirmishing parties of rebel infantry and cavalry attacked our men in front and in the rear, but were repulsed, with some loss in wounded and prisoners. A large number sought shelter in the swamps and dense woods, whither it was of no special benefit for us to pursue them, for time was valuable, and the expedition rested mainly in accomplishing the destruction of certain property before the enemy could bring his larger forces against us.

At Aylett's the iron foundery, machine-shops, cotton-mills, lumber-yard, and four government warehouses, containing large quantities of corn and grain, were burned; also a large mill, owned by Colonel Aylett, of the rebel army, with six thousand bushels of grain. The Colonel made his escape, although in the vicinity. The surgeon of the Fourth Delaware, I understand, captured his horse, which was nicely saddled and bridled. A great number of barns, containing stores for the rebels, such as grain, corn, whisky, cotton goods, etc., were destroyed. The amount of loss to the enemy in this way, if estimated by dollars, cannot fall short of one hundred or one hundred and twenty thousand dollars. A large number of horned cattle and about one hundred and fifty horses and mules, collected for the Richmond market, were brought down to the boats, but our limited space prevented us from taking them all. Only a portion of the horses were brought away. The contrabands, women and children, proved an immense nuisance. They followed the column, and we had to find

transportation for them, to the exclusion of horses and cattle, that are really needed for the service.

General Picket's rebel division of eight thousand men was at Newton, ten miles from Aylette. He had also a strong outpost within three miles of that place; but the panic was so great in the country through which we passed that there was no serious attack on our forces. It was not credited that two hundred men would have ventured so far into the enemy's lines without any support.

Our own loss during the skirmishing was one killed and three wounded, one of the latter by the accidental discharge of his own piece, fracturing his left arm, which it may be necessary to amputate. His name is W. H. Dickerson, of the Fourth Delaware. I could not ascertain the name of the unfortunate killed. The two other wounded will get along very well, they having escaped very serious injury. Our men derived some satisfaction when they saw the effect their fire was producing. I allude to the number of secesh saddles that were emptied.

The negroes served as faithful guides, and furnished us with all the particulars we required of the male population. I omitted to mention that Captain L. H. Howard, of General Keyes's staff, accompanied us, and while ashore learned that an attempt was being made to blockade the river at a very narrow point, by felling trees about ten miles below where we were lying. The Smith Briggs immediately went down, but the report appears to have been unfounded.

During our return, we shelled the woods thoroughly. Certain portions of the banks were lined with sharp-shooters, but their spiteful, whistling shot fell harmlessly against the plating of our boats. The spattering caused more than ordinary amusement. One lone Boston Abolitionist appeared to be uneasy; but I believe scariness is a marked trait in the animal.

A prisoner in our hands, formerly of the Forty-second Virginia infantry, boasted that Stuart would be in Maryland and Pennsylvania before we had any idea, and that he would lay every thing waste. He was going prepared to fight and destroy—in fact, would spare nothing. He is very anxious to destroy the counties of Maryland bordering to the northward, which he is pleased to call "abolition-holes."

Doc. 57.

GUERRILLAS IN VIRGINIA.

BERRYVILLE, VA., June 9, 1863.

THIS county is still infested with bushwhackers. Formerly residents here, they, as a matter of course, belong to the *soi disant* chivalry. Among their *daring* deeds, I have to record the cold-blooded assassination of a corporal of company C, First New York cavalry.

On Friday, June fifth, Corporal Lewis, attended by a comrade, passing on a by-road, about two miles and a half from town, was fired upon and killed by six butternut-colored bushwhackers. His comrade was taken prisoner. The demons rifled the body of the dead man of watch, pocket-book, etc., and left him lying where he had fallen. On the way to their crossing-place on the Shenandoah they came upon a scouting-party of infantry from Winchester, but escaped by taking to a thicket on the Opequan Creek. Here the prisoner escaped and returned to camp. He states that one of the bushwhackers said he had registered an awful oath in the morning to kill a Yankee before the sun went down. What noble fellows the chivalry are!

On Saturday afternoon, June sixth, a party of rebel horsemen, estimated to number one hundred men, dashed upon a small wagon train on its way to this place with supplies from Winchester. The infantry guard of the train, composed, if I mistake not, of a detail from the Sixty-seventh Pennsylvania regiment, fought bravely against tremendous odds, and not until one of their number had been killed and several wounded, did they surrender. A teamster, with his revolver, blew the brains out of a rebel who stopped his team, and escaped on foot. An infantry man, standing in a wagon, ran a horseman through the body with his bayonet before the rebel could reach him with his sword. As the guerrillas carried off their killed and wounded, we are unable to estimate their loss. Our loss of government property amounts to only eighteen horses—all the horses from five wagons, except two killed in the skirmish.

To the honor of the intrepid boys guarding the train, be it said, their resolute and determined resistance in defence of it saved all but the five government wagons and horses, as stated above. With these the confederate thieves hurriedly decamped, abandoning the wagons when some distance from the turnpike, and mounting the prisoners upon the captured horses. They effected their escape with their prisoners and plunder, although closely pursued by detachments of the First New-York cavalry, from this place, and of the Thirteenth Pennsylvania from Winchester. They crossed the Shenandoah near Front Royal.

The attack upon the train was made near the Opequan, about three miles from Berryville. Citizens, residents of the neighborhood visited by the rebels, say they belonged to Colonel Harmon's regiment, of General Jones's command. Moseby, according to the statements of men of his since captured by us, had nothing to do with this affair. At the time of its occurrence he was in Warren County with his command.

Sunday, at ten o'clock P.M., Captains Boyd, of C, and Bailey, of K, with one hundred men of the First New-York cavalry, started on an expedition into Loudon and Fauquier counties. Crossing the Shenandoah opposite Schley's Gap, the detachment moved in the direction of Piedmont, on the Manassas Gap Railroad, en route to Piedmont Station. On what is known as the Crooked Creek road a number of prisoners were taken belonging to Moseby's command.

In this locality private Kellogg, of company K, was killed in a running fight with a rebel. He belonged to the "advance-guard," and, in the pursuit of the guerrilla, left his comrades far behind by the uncommon speed of his horse. When the "advance" reached the scene of the skirmish they found Kellogg mortally wounded—the Rebel had *skedaddled!*

At Piedmont Captain Boyd received information, through the agency of his valuable guides, indicating the whereabouts of a party of White's men—all lawless bushwhackers. An intricate by-road through underbrush and over hills brought us to the rendezvous. The game had gone. A farmer had warned them of the coming of our cavalry—the deep woods affording them every facility to successfully "vamoose the ranche," and continue to enjoy life, liberty, and the pursuit of happiness ; and it is assuredly happiness for them to be able to shoot pickets, assassin-like, at midnight, or plunder farmers in a style worthy the palmiest days of Dick Turpin.

We reached Salem about eight o'clock in the evening, picked up two or three of Moseby's men, and learned that Moseby had taken quarters in the neighborhood. This was decidedly refreshing news. The next question under discussion was how to find him. Captain Boyd in this succeeded admirably. He learned that Moseby's rendezvous and principal headquarters had been for a long time at the residence of Colonel Hathaway, about five miles from Salem and twenty from Front Royal.

It was an out-of-the-way place. We followed by-roads, travelled through woods, leaped ditches, and waded creeks, arriving at last at the imposing mansion wherein we hoped we might find the leader of Loudon guerrillas. In an instant we had surrounded the dwelling. An entrance being effected, every nook from basement to attic was explored; but Moseby had left a few minutes before we reached the place. His sergeant had seen us at Salem, and managed to warn him in sufficient time to make good his exit. We found Mrs. Moseby here with her two children—in no pleasant humor, because the slumbers of herself and husband had been broken by Yankee cavalry. Mrs. Moseby is decidedly handsome, and converses with more than ordinary intelligence. She is a sociable and good-natured woman naturally, but is very unkindly disposed toward "Northerners." She could not comprehend by what chance we had discovered her husband's whereabouts. As Moseby's departure had been somewhat hurried, he left three valuable horses behind. Besides those left by Moseby, we brought away with us several "U. S." horses found upon Hathaway's place.

Colonel Hathaway, or, more properly, Brigadier-General Hathaway, (he commanded the rebel militia,) accompanied Captain Boyd into headquarters as a prisoner. Dressed in citizen's clothing, he rode one of his own horses, and in the best possible humor reached Berryville. He admires Moseby. In his opinion, Moseby is the soul of honor, a model man, a high-toned, whole-souled gentleman, incapable of encouraging bushwhacking, etc. "A fellow feeling makes us wondrous kind." I look upon Moseby and Hathaway as *"par nobile fratrum"* and "birds of a feather."

Near this place Captain Boyd also captured a middle-aged man, who would now be in the rebel army were it not for a constitutional fear of "villainous gunpowder." Possessing no desire to snuff the smoke of battle, he remained at home, and, out of pure patriotism for the "C. S. A.," engages in the sanctified and Christian-like vocation of raising a company of bushwhackers. He had labored with zeal. His heart was in the business. It was a labor of love. Alas! that now, in Captain Boyd's grasp, his delightful "occupation's gone." Unfortunate fellow!

We left Hathaway's residence at six o'clock A.M. on Monday, passing through Middleburgh on the road campward. On the road leading to the latter place we took several mounted men. They belonged to Moseby's gang. Upon every road small squads might be seen getting out of the way with wonderful alacrity. A sergeant and five men, mistaking us for their own cavalry, rode into our presence in a friendly way, and were captured without difficulty.

We reached camp Monday afternoon *via* Snicker's Ferry, with fourteen prisoners and sixteen captured horses. Captain Boyd, commanding the detachment, is entitled to all credit due a successful enterprise. With one hundred men he penetrated Moseby's chosen haunts and has broken up his favorite rendezvous.

Not many weeks ago Captain Boyd marched to Fairfax Court-House with one hundred men. Moseby, with a choice battalion, watched his return, but had not the courage to assail him. However, he *boasted* of his intention to capture that detachment of the First New-York at that time. What will Moseby say now that he has lost another excellent opportunity? J. H. H.

Doc. 58.

BATTLE OF CHANCELLORSVILLE, VA.

BRIGADIER-GENERAL HOWE'S REPORT.[*]

HEADQUARTERS SECOND DIVISION, }
SIXTH CORPS, May 10, 1863. }

Lieutenant-Colonel McMahon, Assistant Adjutant-General Sixth Corps:

SIR: I have the honor to report the operations of the Second division, Sixth corps, from the time it crossed the Rappahannock on the evening of the second of May, until it recrossed on the night of the fourth and fifth of May.

The division crossed the river early in the evening of the second, and about twelve that night I received notice to march in rear of General Newton's division to Fredericksburgh. About three A.M., the rear of General Newton's division marched, and the head of my column reached Hazel Run some time after daylight, uninterrupted except by the troops in front. About eleven o'clock A.M. on the third, I received notice from the commanding officer of the Sixth

[*] See Volume VI. REBELLION RECORD.

corps that he was about to attack the enemy's position between Hazel Run and Fredericksburgh, and wished me to assist. I immediately formed three storming columns, the first column commanded by General Neill, composed of the Seventh Maine, Lieutenant-Colonel Conner, the Seventy-seventh New-York, Lieutenant-Colonel French, the Thirty-third New-York, Colonel Taylor, and a portion of the Twenty-first New-Jersey, Lieutenant-Colonel Mettler. The second column, under the command of Colonel Grant, Acting Brigadier-General, was composed of the Second Vermont, Colonel Woolbridge, the Sixth Vermont, Colonel Barney, and the Twenty-fifth New-Jersey, Colonel Morrison. The third column was composed of the Third Vermont, Colonel Seaver, the Fourth Vermont, Colonel Stoughton, and a portion of the Twenty-first New-Jersey, Colonel Van Hauten, led by Colonel Seaver, of the Third Vermont.

I also placed the division artillery in favorable range, and where they could have an effective fire upon the enemy's works, at the same time allowing the most practicable lines of advance for our assaulting columns, so that they would not interfere with the line of artillery fire.

As soon as the fire was heard on my right I opened my artillery fire with full force, and advanced the two columns under Neill and Grant with the bayonet on Cemetery Hill. This point was gallantly carried without any check to our columns.

From this point Neill's and Grant's columns were moved to assault, on our right, the main work on Marye Hill. I at once brought all the division artillery to bear upon the works on those heights, and advanced the column led by Colonel Seaver to make an assault, on our left, of the same work.

Neill's column charged and successfully carried the strong covered way leading from the first work on Marye Heights to Hazel Run, and then threw itself to the right and rear of the work. Grant's point of assault was on our right and front, while Seaver's was on our left.

The enemy kept up his artillery and infantry fire upon our columns, doing some execution, but wholly failing to check any one of them. Each of our columns gallantly dashed on and carried with the bayonet the first work and then successfully the three other works on the Heights, taking two stands of arms, all of the armament of the works, except one section of a field battery, some two hundred prisoners, and all the enemy's camp equipage.

Much credit is due to Captain Martin, commanding regular battery, and Captain Cowen, commanding the New-York battery, for the skill and efficiency with which they worked their batteries. The severe and well-directed fire which they poured upon the enemy's works very materially impaired the force of the enemy's fire upon our storming columns.

I desire specially to mention General Neill, Colonel Grant, and Colonel Seaver for the gallant and intrepid manner in which they led the storming columns to the assault. Nothing has been more handsomely or successfully done. My thanks are due to Major Mundee, Assistant Adjutant-General; Lieutenant Egerton, Aid-decamp; Lieutenant-Colonel Stone, Division Inspector; Lieutenant Hoag, Division Commissary; Lieutenant Cole, Provost-Marshal; and Lieutenant Matlock, Commissioner of Musters, for the able assistance they gave me in preparing and executing the attack.

Soon after the attack was completed, I received orders to move my division on the Chancellorsville road, and join the other divisions of the corps. I did so, and after marching some three miles from Fredericksburgh, the advance of the corps became engaged. I soon received orders to throw my division to the left to check a flank attack. I did so. No flank attack being made, and night coming on, I encamped my division on the road.

Early on the morning of the fourth, the enemy showed himself on my left and rear, on the Richmond and Fredericksburgh road. I then threw back my left, resting it on the river, between Fredericksburgh and Banks's Ford, my right resting on the Chancellorsville road, and connecting with the division on my right. My line was now some two miles in length, with less than six thousand men upon it. About eleven A.M. the enemy in force attacked my right centre. This attack was successfully repulsed by a portion of General Neill's brigade and Martin's battery, in which repulse three companies of the Nineteenth New-York and one of the Seventh Maine gallantly captured a stand of colors and between one and two hundred prisoners.

About one P.M., I received reliable information that the enemy was assembling a force largely outnumbering my division, immediately in rear of Fredericksburgh, for another attack.

After the repulse which the enemy had met with in the morning, I expected, if he made a second attack, it would be mainly directed on my left. I therefore carefully examined the ground, and made arrangements so that in case my left was unable to hold its position, it could fall back some little distance behind the left of a small covering of wood which was immediately in rear of the centre of my first line. In this covering of wood I held a portion of my reserve force ready, in case the enemy should force my left, to make a flank attack, should he attempt to advance.

My first line was held by General Mills's brigade, strengthened by two regiments of Colonel Grant's brigade. About five P.M. the enemy advanced with a strong line of battle, and attacked my left and centre, and followed this with a heavy column upon my left. The attack from the enemy's left was successfully broken, and my right advancing, we succeeding in taking a large number of prisoners, among them twenty-one officers and nearly all of the men of the Eighth Louisiana regiment. I then immediately withdrew a portion of my force to my right, and reënforced my left, and sent to the corps commanders for additional force. At this time our left was vigorously and stubbornly contending against large odds, and after contesting the ground as long as advantageous, our artillery and its support moved a short distance to the rear to the position before indicated.

At this time Lieutenant Butter's regular battery and two regiments reported to me, and were quickly thrown into position on our left. The enemy apparently thinking our left was giving way, rallied and confidently advanced until they brought their flank opposite the wood, in which was placed those sterling soldiers of the Vermont brigade at the favorable moment. This brigade opened its fire upon the flank of the enemy's columns, and immediately the batteries in front opened a direct fire. The effect of this flank and direct fire upon the enemy was most marked. In a short time not a hostile shot came into our lines. Darkness now came on, but soon the moon rose and again lighted up the field, and not a rebel could be seen between our lines and the heights of Fredericksburgh.

At half-past ten P.M., I was ordered to move the division back to Banks's Ford, and that night the division recrossed the Rappahannock. Great credit is again due our artillery for their services in repulsing the attack. In the action of Guest's farm the section under Lieutenant Simon, Fifth artillery, and Captain Rigsby's battery, were largely instrumental in breaking the attack of the enemy's left, and the artillery on our left, under Captain Martin, was used with great effect in checking the advance of the enemy on that point, and afterward in connection with Lieutenant Butler's battery, in wholly breaking the attack.

I would again make mention of the efficient services of Brigadier-General Neill and Colonel Grant, commanding brigades. The great extent of our line, and the large odds with which we were attacked, rendered it necessary during the action to make several important charges, all of which they successfully and skilfully executed. Brigadier-General Neill, although partially disabled by being fallen upon by his horse, which was shot under him, continued in command of his brigade until the action was over.

My thanks are again due to Major Mundee, Assistant Adjutant-General; Lieutenant-Colonel Stone, Division Inspector; Lieutenant Egerton, Aid-de-Camp; Lieutenant Cole, Provost-Marshal; Lieutenant Hoag, Division Commissary, and Lieutenant Matlock, Commissary of Musters, of the division staff, for the able and prompt assistance they gave me on the field, in the action of the fourth.

Much credit is due to Captain Hickman, Ordnance officer for the division, for the gallantry and energy displayed in supplying the division on the field with necessary ammunition in the actions of the third and fourth.

The list of casualties in the division on the third and fourth (amounting in the aggregate to one thousand five hundred and fifteen) has been previously forwarded.

The importance of the action fought by the

Second division on the fourth will be understood when it is known that it was attacked by three strong divisions of the enemy, (McLaws's, Anderson's, and Early's,) the attack directed by the senior General of the army, (General Lee,) and with a view to cut the communication of the Sixth corps with its river crossing, which attack, if successful, must have resulted either in the destruction or capture of the Sixth corps. Yet the Second division, almost unaided, successfully repulsed the attack, and without losing a gun or prisoner to the enemy.

I am, Colonel, very respectfully, your obedient servant, A. P. Howe,
Brigadier-General Commanding Division.

Doc. 59.

NEUTRALITY OF ENGLAND.

PETITION TO EARL RUSSELL.

To the Right Honorable the Earl Russell, Her Majesty's Principal Secretary of State for the Foreign Department:

The memorial of the undersigned ship-owners of Liverpool showeth:

That your memorialists, who are deeply interested in British shipping, view with dismay the probable future consequences of a state of affairs which permits a foreign belligerent to construct in and send to sea from British ports, vessels of war, in contravention of the provisions of the existing law.

That the immediate effect of placing at the disposal of that foreign belligerent a very small number of steam cruisers has been to paralyze the mercantile marine of a powerful maritime and naval nation, inflicting within a few months losses, direct and indirect, on its ship-owning and mercantile interests, which years of peace may prove inadequate to retrieve.

That your memorialists cannot shut their eyes to the probability that in any future war between England and a foreign power, however insignificant in naval strength, the example now set by subjects of Her Majesty, while England is neutral, may be followed by citizens of other countries neutral when England is belligerent; and that the attitude of helplessness in which Her Majesty's government have declared their inability to detect and punish breaches of the law, notoriously committed by certain of Her Majesty's subjects, may hereafter be successfully imitated by the governments of those other countries in answer to English remonstrances.

That the experience of late events has proved to the conviction of your memorialists that the possession by a belligerent of swift steam cruisers, under no necessity actual or conventional, to visit the possibly blockaded home-ports of that belligerent, but able to obtain all requisite supplies from neutrals, will become a weapon of offence against which no preponderance of naval strength can effectually guard, and the severity of which will be felt in the ratio of the shipping and mercantile wealth of the nation against whose mercantile marine the efforts of those steam cruisers may be directed.

That the effect of future war with any power thus enabled to purchase, prepare, and refit vessels of war in neutral ports, will inevitably be to transfer to neutral flags that portion of the sea-carrying trade of the world which is now enjoyed by your memorialists and by other British ship-owners.

That over and above the chances of pecuniary loss to themselves, your memorialists share in the regret with which a law-regarding community must naturally look on successful attempts to evade the provisions of an act of Parliament, passed for a single and simple purpose, but which has been found not to give the Executive all the powers needed for its effective execution.

That your memorialists would accordingly respectfully urge upon your Lordship the expedience of proposing to Parliament to sanction the introduction of such amendments into the Foreign Enlistment act as may have the effect of giving greater power to the Executive to prevent the construction in British ports of ships destined for the use of belligerents; and your memorialists would further suggest to your Lordship the importance of endeavoring to secure the assent of the Government of the United States of America, and of other foreign countries, to the adoption of similar regulations in those countries also.

All which your memorialists respectfully submit. Signed,

Thomas Chilton,
Jones, Palmer & Co.,
Farnworth & Jardine,
Thos. & Jas. Harrison,
L. H. Macintyre,
Potter Brothers,
Chas. Geo. Cowre & Co.,
M. J. Sealby,
R. Gervin & Co.,
J. Aikin,
Finlay, Campbell & Co.,
Cropper, Ferguson & Co.,
J. Campbell,
S. R. Graves,
Rankin, Gilmore & Co.,
Rathbone Bros. & Co.,
James Brown & Co.,
James Poole & Co.,
W. T. Jacob,
Henry Moore & Co.,
Imrie & Tomlinson,
Sampson & Holt,
James Barnes,
Richard Nicholson & Son,
W. B. Boadle,
J. Prowse & Co.,
Currie, Newton & Co.,
Nelson, Alexander & Co.,
Kendall Brothers,
C. T. Bowrin & Co.,
G. H. Fletcher & Co.,
Alfred Holt.

Liverpool, June 9, 1863.

Doc. 60.

FIGHT NEAR MONTICELLO, KY.

Somerset, Ky., June 10, 1863.

One of the most exciting and trying reconnoissances that I have ever seen I returned from this morning. Noticing a stir at headquarters about noon on Monday, I was soon convinced that something was on foot, and, learning that a considerable force was to take a tramp in some direction, I determined on accompanying it. About four o'clock, detachments of the Second Ohio cavalry, consisting of companies B, (Lieutenant Deming,) E, (Captain Stewart,) F, (Sergeant McBride,) H, (Lieutenant Case,) K, (Lieutenant Patrick,) L, (Captain Easton,) and M, (Captain Ulrey,) commanded by Majors Purington and Seward; also, of the Seventh Ohio cavalry, Colonel Garrard, divided into three divisions—the first, commanded by Captain Lindsey; second, Lieutenant Shaw; third, Captain Brownfield—all commanded by Colonel A. V. Kautz, of the Second Ohio, left here about half-past three o'clock, and proceeded direct to Waitsboro, a distance of seven miles, where we forded the river, the howitzers, (two sections,) ambulances, and ammunition-wagon being ferried at Stigall's. We made a distance of four miles, where we bivouacked for the night. Thus far we had not seen the semblance of an enemy. The next morning the camp-fires were brightly burning, and the camp astir as early as three o'clock. A hastily prepared breakfast fitted us for the beginning of a day of severe riding and hard work. At four o'clock we were in the saddle, and moving at a brisk walk in the direction of Monticello. We were regaled on our way by the perfume of the clover-fields and early flowers, and the sweet songs of the numerous birds that make their homes in these groves of Southern Kentucky. Our men seemed impressed with the idea that we were going on an important mission.

Upon reaching Captain West's, a distance of eight miles from Waitsboro, we met Lieutenant-Colonel Adams with a detachment of the Second East-Tennessee infantry, mounted, composed of company G, Lieutenant McDow; F, Captain Fry; D, Captain Honeycutt; and B, Captain Millsap. These had come up from Mill Springs, a little after daylight, and captured five pickets and six horses at Captain West's. Unfortunately, the greater part of Captain Brown's company (rebel) made good its escape. The whole force now moved south, and was not very long in reaching Steubenville, beyond which the rebels seemed inclined to make the first stand. A column of rebel cavalry, with the stars and bars floating, now made its appearance. Our advance, consisting of companies H and L, Second Ohio cavalry, followed closely by other troops, now made at them. Considerable firing followed, but the rebels soon broke and ran. Law's howitzer battery was brought to bear upon them, which served to accelerate their speed. The force consisted of the Tenth confederate cavalry, under Colonel Gorde. Colonel Morrison's regiment, which was encamped two miles out on the Robertsport road, having ascertained what was going on, could be seen to the right, flying as if pursued by millions. Away the enemy flew, under the command of General Pegram, hotly pursued by our enthusiastic troops. Two mountain howitzers belonging to them were hurried at an alarming rate through the village. Citizens said that the artillery horses were not more than half-harnessed, and this agrees with the fact that for half a mile beyond the town the road was literally strewn with pieces of harness, straps, etc. Three rifled guns were a mile below when the cannonading began. The horses for the same were quietly grazing in an adjacent field, and Pegram, up to the time of our arrival at Steubenville, considered the firing only a little trouble among the pickets. Our men pressed on vigorously till they reached Monticello, where they captured two boxes of small arms of all patterns and sizes, and ten boxes of artillery ammunition, consisting of one hundred and fifty rounds. The arms they were compelled to destroy, while such ammunition as could be used was loaded.

Colonel Garrard, with the Seventh Ohio cavalry, was sent out on the road to Albany to watch the approaches from that direction. A portion of the remaining force, under Majors Purington and Seward, with one section of howitzers, drove the enemy three miles below, on the Jamestown road.

It not being the object of Colonel Kautz to hold the position, he left companies H and K, Second Ohio cavalry, and A and F, Forty-fifth Ohio, all commanded by Major Seward, to hold the gorge for an hour or so, while the main portion retired. Colonel Garrard, with his regiment, was also to hold the Albany road for an hour, which he did in the face of a superior force, and fell back without loss.

At Monticello, the rear-guard was joined by a company of the Seventh Ohio cavalry, Captain Lindsey. The main force reached Captain West's, distant eleven miles, about five o'clock. As for us, we knew the rear-guard was coming along quietly. Soon, however, a courier came rushing in, saying that a large force were engaging them fiercely only a little way back. Looking off to the left, a cloud of dust was rising which shut out the combatants from view. But the rapid discharge of musketry told us that a severe conflict was going on not over a half-mile from where we were. In a few minutes Colonels Kautz and Carter gathered up a company of Second East-Tennessee, and parts of other companies that were just at hand, and galloped away in the direction of the enemy. Our men dismounted, and, meeting the rebel columns that filled the road, hurled such deadly volleys at them that they were driven back, from place to place, till they had retired a mile, leaving their unfortunate dead and wounded behind them. They now got behind a stone fence that was favorably situated, and fired severe volleys at our men, who were in the woods.

By this time parts of the Forty-fifth Ohio and Second Ohio cavalry had become warmly engaged, and the musketry firing was heavy. Our forces at this point were greatly inferior in numbers to the enemy, who, at this juncture, from the fact that there was an apparent or real wavering in our men, sprung out from their covert, and, leaping the wall, took possession of the thick woods to our left, and pressed down in the direction of the road with a wild shout and an audacity which they paid dearly for finally. The firing was severe. Balls rained down from the hill-side like hail. A little while before the Second East Tennessee, which had been dismounted and formed on our right, was ordered up, and, at this juncture, came in sight on the double-quick. It was a noble spectacle to see them rushing on to the extreme point of danger, with their colors flying, and hear their loud shouts mingling with the rattling of musketry. Parts of the Seventh Ohio cavalry had previously been dismounted and brought to bear against the increasing number of rebels, no doubt with considerable effect, still not dislodging them.

The Tennesseeans seemed wild to get at them, and rushing into the woods with the most audacious bravery, provoked a fire, which, if better directed by the enemy, must have inflicted sore loss upon us. The next was a volley from our own men, mingling its noise with the shouts of our own brave fellows, who were determined on driving back the impudent foe. The rattle of musketry for a little while was incessant. Each Tennesseean picked his man, and blazed away at him until the gray-back either fell or used his legs to get away.

One section of the howitzer battery was now ordered-up to the front, and soon mingled its roar with the incessant rattle of musketry and the shouts of the combatants. The contest was sharp, short, and decisive. It was no child's play, for the enemy, who had advanced upon us with so much audacity, was now compelled to leave the wood as rapidly as he came into it, and seek safer positions in the rear. It was now past sundown; night was rapidly drawing its curtain about the scene of strife. The firing had, with the exception of an occasional shot, ceased. The enemy, who came on with the consciousness of being able to gobble us up at one mouthful, had not found a savory meal, and had retired to safer positions in the direction of Monticello.

The wounded were brought to Captain West's, and laid down in his yard, while such attentions were given them as the circumstances would allow. The surgeons were particularly active. Wherever duty called they went, without regard to their own safety. Among those most active I noticed Surgeon Smith, of the Second Ohio cavalry, who was, much to our regret, left behind to take care of Lieutenant Case and one or two other wounded men, who, it was thought, could not be removed with safety. Of course we cannot regret that means were taken to relieve the wants of our wounded, and to see that they would be properly cared for, but that there was a seeming necessity of leaving any one behind. It was but one mile to Mill Springs, and to that place the very few that could not have been taken in ambulances might have been carried on litters, and crossed in canoes to the other side. That this was not done by those whose duty it was to look after such matters is highly unfortunate.

It was now about dark. Such of the wounded as could not ride on horseback were placed in ambulances, and the march for the river again taken up. We made four miles and bivouacked. This morning at two o'clock the column was again placed in motion, and reached Waitsboro a little after daylight.

The Seventh Ohio cavalry, under the command of Colonel Garrard, was our rear-guard from the time we left the battle-field till we reached the river. They had a responsible post, but the enemy had already been taught a sufficient lesson, and gave us no trouble whatever.

On arriving at the river the forces were halted, in accordance with the command of General Carter, hoping the enemy might come on and give us fight; but no rebel was to be seen, and our men finally crossed the Cumberland at their leisure, and marched to their camps to rest from as hard labor as they are usually called upon to endure.

I this evening tried to telegraph you a complete list of our losses, with some details of the fight, but the lightning interrupted, and up to the hour of writing it has not been sent.

Some persons, who do not understand the object of the expedition, are inclined to look upon our return as unfavorable, thinking that it was the intention to hold that country. Such could not be further from the truth. The object of those who projected it was obtained, and the reconnoissance was a complete success. It is true there was some hard fighting, and we sustained some losses; but the former the soldier came to do, and the latter is unavoidable in war, while the fact that we inflicted a greater loss upon the enemy is a matter of congratulation.

I cannot speak in too praiseworthy terms of the gallantry of our men. Wherever they had any thing like a chance they drove every thing before them. The East-Tennesseeans are deserving of special praise. It is simple justice to say that they threw themselves against the enemy with such bravery and enthusiasm that nothing could withstand them. Many a poor fellow fell a victim before their unerring aim.

Colonels Kautz and Carter were in the thickest of the fight, and were as cool, apparently, as if their troops were on parade. The forces of the enemy were the principal part of the command of General Pegram, who evidently commanded in person.

The losses inflicted upon them we cannot now ascertain. They lost ten killed during the day, that were seen; but the heaviest loss, no doubt, took place in the thick woods that our men had not time to examine. It would be safe, I think, to say they lost twenty killed, and a proportionate number wounded. Our losses will not vary much from the telegram, to wit, four killed, twenty-six wounded and six missing. We had wounded one captain and two lieutenants. We wounded and paroled two lieutenants and captured one. Lieutenant Case was badly wounded in the left breast. He fell while gallantly discharging his duty to his country.

The people of Monticello, supposing we were coming in force, expressed, in private, much gratification at the prospect of being relieved from the rebel army.

One negro that I saw exclaimed as he approached us, "Glory to God, I'se so happy now," clapping his hands with delight and thankfulness, and continuing: "It's been cloudy dis many a day, but its cleared away now, and I sees de sun shine again."   SIDNEY.

Doc. 61.

EXECUTION OF REBEL SPIES AT FRANKLIN, TENNESSEE.

MURFREESBORO, June 10, 1863.

I INFORMED you last evening, by telegraph, of the singular circumstances connected with the hanging of two spies at Franklin. I have this morning obtained a copy, from the Adjutant-General's office of this department, of the correspondence on the subject which passed between Colonel Baird, commanding at Franklin, and General Rosecrans.

The two men were in reality, first, Colonel Lawrence A. Williams, formerly Second United States cavalry; (according to the *Army Register*, he was First Lieutenant of the Tenth infantry, and was appointed by President Lincoln Major of the Sixth United States cavalry on September seventh, 1861. He must have deserted the United States service since September, 1862, as his name appears in the *Register* of that date. At one time he was on General Winfield Scott's staff, latterly on Bragg's staff;) and, secondly, a Lieutenant Dunlap, whose position in the rebel army I do not know. They represented themselves, on arriving at Colonel Baird's headquarters, as Colonel Auton, United States army, and his assistant, Major Dunlap. They were dressed in our uniform, and had horses with the equipments complete of a colonel and major. They represented their duty to be the inspection of the outposts of this army, and said they had come from Murfreesboro *via* Triune, and were in haste to reach Nashville. Conversation became quite free, and their language grew somewhat suspicious, so much so, that Colonel Watkins, commanding the cavalry, began to doubt the truth of their statements, and communicated his doubts to Colonel Baird. After further conversation with them, Colonel Baird sent the following despatch to General Rosecrans:

NO. 1.—TELEGRAM FROM COLONEL BAIRD TO GENERAL ROSECRANS.

FRANKLIN, June 8, 1863.

To Brigadier-General Garfield, Chief of Staff:

Is there any such Inspector-General as Lawrence Auton, Colonel United States army, and Assistant-Major Dunlap? If so, please describe their personal appearance, and answer immediately.
J. P. BAIRD,
Colonel Commanding Post.

NO. 2.—GENERAL GARFIELD TO COLONEL BAIRD.

HEADQUARTERS DEPARTMENT OF THE CUMBERLAND, }
June 8, 10.15 P.M. }

Colonel J. P. Baird, Franklin:

There are no such men as Inspector-General Lawrence Auton, Colonel United States army, and Assistant-Major Dunlap, in this army, nor in any army, so far as we know. Why do you ask?
J. A. GARFIELD,
Brigadier-General and Chief of Staff.

Upon the receipt of this despatch, Colonel Baird appears to have instituted a search of the

persons of the two men. He appears to have found nothing suspicious upon them, though their conduct was singular enough to create suspicion. The following is the second despatch of Colonel Baird, in answer to General Garfield's inquiry as to his reasons for asking:

NO. 3.—COLONEL BAIRD EXPLAINS THE CAUSE OF HIS SUSPICIONS.

FRANKLIN, June 8, 10.30 P.M.

To Brigadier-General Garfield, Chief of Staff:

Two men came into camp about dark, dressed in our uniforms, with horse equipments to correspond, saying that they were Colonel Auton, Inspector-General, and Major Dunlap, assistant, having an order from Adjutant-General Townsend, and your order to inspect outposts, but their conduct was so singular that we have arrested them. They insisted that it was important to go to Nashville to-night. The one representing himself as Colonel Auton is probably a regular officer of the old army, but Colonel Watkins, commanding cavalry here, in whom I have the utmost confidence, is of the opinion that they are spies, who have either forged or captured these orders. They can give no consistent account of their conduct. I want you to answer immediately my last despatch. It takes so long to get an answer from General Granger, at Triune, by signal, that I telegraphed General Robert Granger, at Nashville, for information. I also signalled General Gordon Granger. If these men are spies, it seems to me important that I should know it, because Forrest must be waiting their progress.

General, I am your obedient servant,
J. P. BAIRD,
Colonel Commanding Post.

The possession of the order said to have been given by General Rosecrans at once established the fact in General Rosecrans's mind that the men were spies, and he instructed his Chief of Staff to order a court-martial of them. The following is the order:

NO. 4.—HEADQUARTERS DEPARTMENT OF THE CUMBERLAND, }
MURFREESBORO, June 8, 12 P.M. }

Colonel J. P. Baird, Franklin:

The two men are no doubt spies. Call a drum-head court-martial to-night, and if they are found to be spies, hang them before morning, without fail. No such men have been accredited from these headquarters.
J. A. GARFIELD,
Brig.-Gen. and Chief of Staff.

THE REBELS CONFESS THEMSELVES SPIES.

On learning that they were to be court-martialed by order of General Rosecrans, the men owned up. It is supposed here that they imagined they would not meet with any regular officers at Franklin; a supposition in which they were entirely correct. Colonel Baird thus narrates what followed:

NO. 5.—HEADQUARTERS, FRANKLIN, June 8, 1863.

To General Garfield, Chief of Staff:

I had just sent you an explanation of my first despatch when I received your despatch. When

your despatch came, they owned up as being a rebel Colonel and Lieutenant in the rebel army. Colonel Auton by name, but in fact Williams, was once on General Scott's staff, and belonged to the Second cavalry of the regular army. Their ruse was nearly successful on me, as I did not know the handwriting of any commanding officer. I am much indebted to Colonel Watkins, Sixth Kentucky cavalry, for their detection, and to Lieutenant Wharton, of General Granger's staff, for the detection of the forgery of the papers. As these men don't deny their guilt, what shall I do with them? I communicate with you because I can get an answer sooner than by signal, but I will keep General Granger posted. I will telegraph you in a short time, as we are trying to find out, and believe there is an attack contemplated in the morning. If Watkins can get any thing out of Auton I will let you know. I am, General, your obedient servant, J. P. Baird,
Colonel Commanding.

Upon the receipt of this, General Garfield sent an order to Colonel Baird to take the confessions of the two men in writing and then to hang them forthwith.

No. 6.—Franklin, June 9, 3.25 A.M.

To General Garfield, Chief of Staff:

Colonel Watkins says that Colonel Williams is a first cousin of General Robert Lee, and he has been Chief of Artillery on Bragg's staff. We are consulting. Must I hang him? If you can direct me to send him to be hung somewhere else I would like it; but if not, or I do not hear from you, they will be executed. This despatch is written at the request of Colonel Watkins, who detained the prisoners. We are prepared for a fight. J. P. Baird,
Colonel Commanding.

The confession of the men having placed their guilt beyond doubt, this delay appears to have somewhat fretted General Rosecrans, who appears, from the date of his next despatch, to be losing sleep over the matter. General Garfield having also retired, the next despatch is signed by Major Bond, the senior Aid-de-Camp of General Rosecrans, a most discreet and careful gentleman. The despatch is as follows, and is an important one in the official history of this most important case. Does it not sound like the style of one Israel Putnam? It is certainly positive enough, even for Colonel Baird, who had no disposition to do the hanging:

No. 7.—Headquarters Department of the Cumberland, Murfreesboro, June 9, 4.40 A.M.

Colonel J. P. Baird, Franklin:

The General Commanding directs that the two spies, if found guilty, be hung at once, thus placing it beyond the possibility of Forrest's profiting by the information they have gained. Frank S. Bond,
Major and A. D. C.

Upon being informed that they were to be hung, the two men protested against it, asserting that they were not spies in the ordinary sense of the term. This was in despite of the fact that they were found in our lines, in our uniform, and bearing forged papers, purporting to be signed by Assistant Adjutant-General E. D. Townsend and Major-General Rosecrans. They did not explain upon what grounds they made the plea of not being spies under these circumstances. It is to be regretted that they did not, as it might have explained their reasons for coming into our lines. No such unimportant matter as a proposed attack on Franklin could have induced two officers of their rank and character to undertake so hazardous an enterprise.

Upon finding themselves about to be executed, Williams or Auton made the following request, which was transmitted by telegraph to General Rosecrans:

No. 8.—Franklin, June 9, 1863.

To Brigadier-General Garfield:

"Will you have any clemency for the son of Captain Williams, who fell at Monterey, Mexico? As my dying speech, I protest our innocence as spies." (What follows is rather inexplicable. The document appears to be signed "Lawrence W. Auton, formerly L. Auton Williams.")* Williams then adds: "I send this as a dying request." Colonel Baird concludes the despatch:

The men are condemned and we are preparing for their execution. They prefer to be shot. If you can answer before I get ready, do. J. P. Baird,
Colonel Commanding Post.

No. 9.—Franklin, June 9, 10.30 A.M.

To General Garfield, Chief of Staff:

The men have been tried, found guilty, and executed, in compliance with your order.

I am ever yours, J. P. Baird,
Colonel Commanding Post.

Doc. 62.

FIGHT AT BRANDY STATION, VA.

THE DOINGS OF THE FIRST MARYLAND CAVALRY.

Cavalry Camp, near Rappahannock Station, Va., June 10, 1863.

Yesterday introduced and ended the most terrific and desperate cavalry fight that ever occurred on this continent—a fight which commenced at sunrise and closed at the setting of the same.

We had learned that Stuart, with a heavy force of cavalry and artillery, was encamped at Brandy Station. It was determined to give him fight for two reasons: to find out the whereabouts of the enemy, and to disturb his plan of a contemplated raid into Pennsylvania. Our success was com-

* TO THE EDITOR OF THE NEW-YORK HERALD.
Tuesday, June 16, 1863.

I notice in the issue of the *Herald* of this date that the rebel spy "Williams," who was hanged, is stated to be Lawrence A. Williams by your Murfreesboro correspondent, the military history of L. A. W. being given editorially.

This is an error; and would it not be well to correct it? The spy was W. Orton Williams, formerly of the Second United States cavalry, who resigned his commission of first lieutenant on the tenth of June, 1861.

Lawrence A. Williams (a graduate of West-Point, which W. O. Williams was not) is now a resident of this city, and has not been South during the war, except as an officer of our army.

plete. We found out the whereabouts of the enemy emphatically. We interfered with his purposed raid, for we captured his plan and letters of instruction, which we have now at headquarters, Second brigade, Third cavalry division. General Buford was to cross Beverly Ford and attack the enemy in front, while General Gregg's and Colonel Duffie's divisions crossed at Kelly's Ford, and passing around his rear attacked him there.

Your correspondent was with General Gregg's division. At sunrise we heard the cannonading of Buford's command. At half-past seven A.M., we commenced to cross; at ten, we nabbed the enemy's picket; at half-past ten, the Second brigade, Third division, commanded by Colonel Wyndham, struck his main body, and the play began. A section of artillery, supported by the First Maryland cavalry, was instantly thrown to the front and placed in position. As soon as his regiment was formed Major Russell, First Maryland cavalry, led his second squadron to the charge. He routed the enemy's advance, sent it flying over fields and roads, captured an ambulance—which was afterward found to contain a major and all General Stuart's plans and letters of instruction from General Lee—drove the enemy before him down the Culpeper road, and, alas! charged too far. Before he could rally his men and bring them back, the enemy had brought up two regiments and cut him off, with fifteen of his command. The artillery now opened on both sides. Captain Buckley and Lieutenant Apple led the third squadron First Maryland cavalry into the charge to meet the advancing foe. The Captain was taken prisoner, then rescued by his boys. The Lieutenant was wounded; his men faltered and shivered before an overwhelming force. Lieutenant Erick rallied them and led them to the charge again. He, too, was wounded. Then brave, fearless Captain Creager led on his brave boys of company I. Three times they charged the foe. Twice they were driven back; but in the third charge Captain Creager fell from his horse, wounded in the left breast. Then Lieutenant Kinble took command of company I, rallied the men behind a hill and led them back to the charge. Eight times did that fearless officer and those brave boys charge with shrieks and yells against fearful odds. Lieutenant-Colonel Deems was conspicuous on the field, rallying and cheering on his men.

On our left stood a house around which a body of rebel cavalry had gathered. Lieutenant-Colonel Broderick led his brave New-Jersey boys in a charge by battalions against them. As they closed up, the rebels fell back, when the whole house full of infantry poured a murderous fire from the hundreds of loop-holes which pierced the walls of the house. The Lieutenant-Colonel and the Major were wounded, and the boys fell back.

The scene now became terrific, grand, and ludicrous. The choking dust was so thick that we could not tell "t'other from which." Horses, wild beyond the control of their riders, were charging away through the lines of the enemy and back again. Many of our men were captured, and escaped because their clothes were so covered with dust that they looked like graybacks. Captain Buckley was three times a prisoner, and finally escaped. Sergeant Embrey, of company I, was taken prisoner. He wore a brown blouse. He played secesh orderly to a secesh colonel for a while, and then escaped. Sergeant Hiteshem, same company, was captured, and escaped because he wore a gray pair of trowsers.

Our men fought well and lost heavily. But the enemy met every charge with overwhelming numbers. He had both wings supported by infantry; had three batteries against our three guns.

I was in the fight, and have only mentioned, therefore, what passed under my own eye, and in the dust one man could not see far.

I must not forget to mention that Major Russell, after he found that he was cut off, lost none of his usual coolness, courage, and sagacity. His wit sharpened with the emergency; he reached the rear of the enemy's army. He rallied his fifteen men, and set immediately to work. The enemy moved out of the woods and tried to turn our left flank. The Major had most of his men partly concealed, partly exposed. Every time the enemy moved out of the woods the Major would dash at them with three or four men, and when close upon them would turn upon his horse and call upon some imaginary officer to bring up those imaginary squadrons out of those woods. Then he would retire, always bringing some prisoners with him. When they (the enemy) moved out again he would repeat the joke. At one time he had between forty and fifty prisoners whom he had thus captured. He thus perplexed and checked them until our division had retired.

At length the rebels charged upon him and retook all the prisoners excepting fourteen. The Major turned, fired his pistol into their faces, and again called upon that imaginary officer to bring up those imaginary squadrons. The charging squadron of rebels halted to re-form for the charge, and while they were forming he slid his men and prisoners between two divisions of the rebel cavalry and rejoined his regiment.

Two things probably saved the Major. He lost his hat and took a secesh cap from a prisoner. He looked like a reb. When he returned through the two divisions of rebel cavalry he had so many prisoners and so few men that they doubtless mistook him and his party for their own men moving out to reconnoitre.

This may sound extravagant, but I have the word of the prisoners he brought in (fourteen) and of his own men for its fidelity, and the ambulance he captured, with General Stuart's trunk, papers, letters, and plans, are at headquarters.

The battle soon became a fight for Beverly Ford. We drove the enemy back, secured the ford, and recrossed about sundown.

We accomplished our great design, that is, found out that the enemy was there.

Our regiment has suffered severely, but I cannot yet give you the particulars.

DEVENPORT.

Doc. 63.

CAPTURE OF THE BOSTON.

JUNE 10, 1863.

MOBILE, June 11, 1863.

A PARTY of our daring marines started to get a steamboat; the party was under the command of Captain James Duke. After experiencing rather hard fare in the marshes of the Mississippi for some days, they discovered the Boston towing the ship Jenny Lind, loaded with ice, up to New-Orleans. This was some three miles from the Pass a l'Outre lighthouse. The brave fellows hailed the ship, and a line was thrown out to them—they were in an open boat. On getting aboard of the Boston the confederates made a very pretty display of revolvers, when the Captain of the ship remarked: "I told you they were —— rebels." It was too late; the fastenings were instantly cut, and our men were in possession of the steamer.

In coming round at sea, they met the bark Lennox, from New-York, loaded with an assorted cargo, principally stores, to which they helped themselves, and retaining the captain and mate as prisoners, sent the passengers and crew ashore. They then set fire to her, completely destroying the vessel. This took place yesterday, (Wednesday.) There were about forty on the Lennox.

About an hour afterward they came up with the bark Texana, also from New-York. They did not take any thing from her but the captain and mate—the balance they sent ashore. The Texana was then set afire, and was burning splendidly when she was left.

Among the prisoners is Captain Woolf, of the old bark Asa Fish, well known here.

There are about seventeen prisoners on board of the Boston, all of whom seem quite resigned to their fate.

The Boston arrived at Fort Morgan this morning about two o'clock, and at the wharf at eleven o'clock. She is a staunch tug—runs about twelve knots an hour, and is a propeller.

In the Mississippi River the confederates were for some time within speaking distance of the United States man-of-war Portsmouth, sixteen guns, and about half an hour previous to their capturing the Boston, a gunboat had passed up within gun-shot of our men.

This prize will prove very valuable to the captors—and shows what daring can accomplish in the way of a little private enterprise. What a howl will go up in New-York when they hear the news.

The Boston was cheered all along our front as she came in, the confederate flag over the gridiron. She now lies in at the slip back of Gage's icehouse.

Doc. 64.

THE SIEGE OF SUFFOLK, VA.

APRIL AND MAY, 1863.

THE siege of Suffolk was raised on the third of May, 1863, almost simultaneously with the mortifying disaster at Chancellorsville.

The latter event in its absorbing influence upon the public mind drew away all thought from the minor operations about Suffolk, and in the absence of any apparent important results, the stubborn and successful defence of that town has never received a tithe of the public recognition its merit warranted. Close examination of the facts, however, will reveal that in two points of view it presents one of the most interesting chapters of the war.

1st. In its bearing upon the general progress of our arms, and secondly, as presenting to the military student an example of the defence of a fortified place against an enormous investing force, in which the entire success of the garrison was unblemished by a single reverse. Its fortifications were hastily constructed by the troops with incredible labor, they were guarded with a sleepless vigilance and defended with unflinching bravery and tireless energy.

Longstreet designed to make a sudden descent in overwhelming force; to cross the Nansemond, a narrow and crooked stream, and overwhelm the garrison, or at least seize the roads to Norfolk and cut off the supplies. In either event there would have been no earthly obstacle to his marching unchecked into Norfolk and Portsmouth, as two small and raw regiments alone constituted the garrison of those places. His designs were brought to naught by the watchfulness and skill of the Federal commander, and the obstinate resistance of the Federal troops when conscious of their danger.

Longstreet's plans were laid with a completeness, forethought, and subtlety, that at once stamp him as the able leader he is known to be. Had General Peck permitted his army to be surprised, beaten or captured by his wily and daring foe, it would have only been in imitation of a precedent that has unfortunately been too often established by some of our officers, and his reputation as a soldier might have been blasted for ever, despite his previously long and honorable career. But in him the rebel general found an adversary whose watchfulness was more than a match for his own skill and daring. Justice to General Peck requires that even at this late day the true history of the Suffolk campaign should be made public.

Suffolk lies at the head of the Nansemond, twelve miles from its confluence with the James. Two railroads unite at this town, one from Norfolk to Petersburgh, the other from Portsmouth to Weldon, etc., N. C. By means of them General Peck's supplies were forwarded from Norfolk, a distance of twenty miles, and on the other hand the rebel stores and reënforcements were forwarded from the opposite extremities almost to the very lines of investment.

The objects of Longstreet's attack were important and manifold. By crossing the narrow Nansemond and occupying the railroads in rear, the city would fall an easy prey together with its thirteen thousand defenders, its vast commissary, quartermaster, medical, and ordnance stores, and sixty miles of railroad iron. Thence the occupation of Norfolk would be but a holiday march. It is also assumed that the *éclat* attaching to the name of a General who should accomplish these objects, may have had some influence on a mind notoriously eager for military renown.

To crown his undertaking with success three preliminary movements were carefully planned and put into execution.

1st. The Suffolk garrison must be weakened. To accomplish this, Hill was sent with a considerable force to attack Little Washington, N. C., whence he could in three or four days rejoin the main army in Virginia.

2d. Pontoon and siege trains were collected at proper points and held in readiness for an instant move.

3d. The troops were also conveniently stationed in such manner that they might be literally *precipitated* upon the doomed town, sixteen thousand being posted on the Blackwater, the remainder along the railway to Petersburgh. As was anticipated, Hill's movement resulted in an order directing General Peck to forward three thousand troops to General Foster. It will now be seen in what manner was sprung the trap thus skilfully prepared.

Longstreet's spies advised him promptly of the order removing the three thousand troops, and he instantly put his army in march, crossed the Blackwater on several bridges, with four divisions,* in all thirty thousand men, moving in three columns, and by a forced march arrived in a few hours before the Federal camps, surprising and capturing the cavalry pickets as they advanced.

The Federal General, from information given by spies, deserters, contrabands, and the contents of a captured rebel mail, fathomed the plans of the rebel commander, and was in readiness to receive him. Admiral Lee having been telegraphed, gunboats were sent up the Nansemond, in readiness to resist and delay, though it was impossible for them to prevent a crossing. Seeing this, Longstreet apparently made a sudden change of plan, and resolved to carry the place by storm. His columns advanced on our works, capturing pickets as above stated, just as the reenforcements for General Foster were leaving on the train. As a matter of course these troops were retained.

The enemy, upon coming within range of our works, found them firmly garrisoned and bristling with steel. An interchange of a few shots convinced them that the surprise was a total failure, and there remained only their numerical superiority as a guarantee for final success. Leaving a considerable force in front of the main

defences of the town, who from time to time engaged our troops to divert attention from his real designs, he then directed his attention to the Nansemond.

The first object to be attained was of course to destroy or expel the army and navy gunboats from the river. As the gunboats consisted only of a half-dozen armed tugs and ferry-boats, (of these the Smith Briggs and West End being army boats,) with machinery and magazines unprotected, almost unable to manoeuvre in the narrow, shallow, and crooked stream, this was apparently an easy task. In the silence of the night, battery after battery was constructed and powerful guns placed in position at points favorable to command the stream and protect a bridge. These batteries, as soon as unmasked, engaged the gunboats. Fortunately the river fleet was commanded by two officers, young in years, but of unconquerable bravery, skill, and pertinacity. And though the frail steamers were riddled with countless shot-holes, and a long list of casualties attested the severity of their trials, they were never driven from the river, and but for a few days from the close vicinity of the town. The army gunboats, under Captains Lee and Rowe, never left the Upper Nansemond.

To Brigadier-General Getty, commanding Third division Ninth army corps, was intrusted the defences of the Nansemond River. A more capable officer or more efficient troops could not have been selected for this arduous and responsible duty. The nature of the duty is comprehended in the statement that five thousand men were to hold a line eight miles long, and prevent forty thousand from crossing a stream too small to permit a large steamer from turning round. Moreover, the banks of the Nansemond were of such a character that troops could not, without making long marches around ravines, creeks, and swamps, pass as reenforcements from one point to another. To remedy this feature in the topography, General Getty instantly commenced the construction of a military road several miles long, including several bridges and long spaces of corduroy, following the general course of the river-bank. By means of the most unheard of exertions the troops completed this road in three days, making it passable for artillery.

As soon as the rebel batteries on the opposite bank were unmasked, General Getty's skill as an artillerist was brought into play with remarkable effect. In company with Colonel Dutton, commanding his Third brigade, (an officer of engineers,) he selected positions for rifle-pits and batteries. The ground was traced out at nightfall, and the next morning the astonished rebels would be saluted in their works by a storm of rifled shells, fired by invisible gunners. This system of warfare continued for several days, the rebels continually striving to gain a permanent foothold on some point of the shore, and being as continually baffled by the resistless gunnery of our land batteries and the gunboats.

On the eighteenth of April, however, it seemed that their object was finally accomplished. An

---

* Those of Hood, French, Pickett, and Anderson.

earth-work, mounting five heavy rifled guns, was established at Hill's Point, about six miles from Suffolk, and of such strong profile and skilful construction that our missiles could only bury themselves harmlessly in the parapet, while from their protected position they maintained a destructive fight with the gunboats. The Mount Washington, already disabled in an unequal contest with a battery higher up, grounded off Hill's Point, directly under the rebel guns. Her companions refused to leave her in this emergency, and then for six long hours raged one of the most desperate and unequal contests of the war. The gallant Lamson, on his crippled vessel, and the equally gallant Cushing, stood over their smoking guns and bleeding gunners till the rising tide at last floated them off in safety. The Commodore Barney showed one hundred and fifty-eight ball and bullet-holes in her hull and machinery; the Mount Washington was even worse riddled.

Admiral Lee having now ordered the gunboats out of the Upper Nansemond, matters wore a desperate aspect. At this crisis the fertile genius of Lieutenant Lamson devised a plan which was approved by General Peck, the conception of which was only less brilliant than its subsequent execution. He proposed to General Getty the capture of the Hill's Point battery. The following extract, from an eye-witness, describes this brilliant feat:

"Shortly before sunset, on the nineteenth of April, the gunboats on the river, and the four rifled guns at and near battery Stevens, opened a terrific fire upon the rebel battery. Meantime, detachments from the Eighty-ninth New-York volunteers, Lieutenant-Colonel England, and Eighth Connecticut, Colonel Ward, in all two hundred and eighty men, embarked on board the gunboat Stepping Stones, Lieutenant Lamson, at a point about a mile above the battery. Protected by the artillery fire, the gunboat boldly steamed down the river, and ran close to the shore about two hundred yards above the rebel works, the shore at that point being an abrupt bluff. Immediately the troops disembarked, wading to their waists in water, ascended the bluff, and with loud cheers charged on the rear of the fort. Meantime, the gunboat's crew had landed four boat howitzers, placed them in position, and opened on the fort. The enemy, taken completely by surprise, were able to discharge but two or three volleys of musketry, and one gun, when our troops entered the work and captured the entire party of seven officers and one hundred and thirty men, with five brass guns and a large supply of ammunition."

The capture of the Hill's Point battery alarmed the rebels to such an extent that they instantly turned their attention to securing their own position. Defensive lines of vast length and considerable strength protected their front for a distance of several miles, trees were felled and abattis planted in front, and every measure which the resources of skilful engineering could devise were adopted to resist the terrible artillery fire of our batteries, and to foil sorties should any be made.

General Peck, continually vigilant to observe any change in the location, strength, or plans of the enemy, repeatedly sent out columns of moderate strength to attack the enemy. A reconnoissance, made on the twenty-fourth, by General Corcoran on the Edenton, and another by Colonel Foster on the Somerton road resulted in lively skirmishes, in which the enemy's outposts were driven back to their main lines, before whose formidable strength our weak columns were in turn compelled to retire.

General Peck had divided his entire circle of defence (including the Nansemond) into sections of convenient length, to the direct responsibility of which he assigned his principal subordinates. That of General Getty, which was by far the longest and weakest, was subsequently subdivided into the line of the Jericho, under General Harland, and that of the Nansemond, under Colonel Dutton.

The vast labors performed by Getty's division during the three weeks of the siege, consisting of forts, rifle-pits, batteries, roads, bridges, and timber-cutting, must be seen to be appreciated. Nevertheless, these troops exhibited to the last no other feeling than that of the most praiseworthy patience, courage, and devotion to duty. Every able-bodied man in this division was employed every day, and not unfrequently at night either on picket or fatigue duty. Repeatedly also, the pickets themselves were compelled to handle the pick and shovel.

An amusing incident is related in this connection. A soldier in a New-Hampshire regiment, while wearily digging during the small hours of the morning, was heard to remark to his neighbor: "I say, Bill! I hope 'Old Peck' will die two weeks before I do."

"Why so?" queried his friend.

"Because he'll have hell so strongly fortified that I can't get in," was the irreverent reply.

An inspection of the defences of the Nansemond at the close of the siege, would have convinced an observer that if the river Styx is ever made equally difficult to cross, the soldier's remark was not void of reason.

On the twentieth of April, rebel reënforcements commenced arriving, fresh from the fruitless siege of Little Washington. Before the thirtieth, more than ten thousand troops under General D. H. Hill had joined Longstreet. Fortunately, however, reënforcements from Washington had commenced arriving at Suffolk, and the enemy having lost the golden moments afforded by its originally weak condition, it was now regarded as almost impregnable.

Longstreet manifestly entertained a similar opinion, but was loth to relinquish his attempt, and with his accustomed pertinacity made new but futile efforts for final success. New batteries were secretly constructed and unmasked only to be silenced by the deadly fire of our gunboats and the Parrotts from our own works. Meantime instances of individual daring and skill, on the part of both soldiers and sailors, were frequent, and prevented the siege from assuming a monotonous character. Many of these actions would adorn the pages of a romance, but the limited space of this sketch must exclude them.

By the second of May, the approaching terrible conflict between the armies of Hooker and Lee, compelled Longstreet to raise the siege. Continually on the alert, General Peck did not intend that his enemy should steal off secretly and unmolested, and no sooner had the retreat fairly commenced than he resolved to test its reality. On the third of May, therefore, a column about seven thousand strong, under Generals Getty and Harland, crossed the drawbridge and advanced up the Providence Church road. Simultaneously Colonel Dutton was directed to cross two small columns six or eight miles lower down, and attack the enemy in flank. General Getty encountered a powerful rear-guard of the enemy in a position of immense strength. From a cover of rifle-pits and abattis, and protected by impassable ground on either side, they poured a terrible fire of musketry and artillery across the plain over which our troops advanced. With undaunted bravery, however, they moved onward preceded by skirmishers and from noon till night maintained an unequal contest. The rebels were forced from all their advanced and some of their retired positions, but at nightfall still held their principal lines. During the night (which was excessively dark) they stole away while our weary troops rested on the field. Meantime Colonel Dutton had sent the Twenty-first Connecticut with a section of artillery and a dozen cavalrymen, in all less than four hundred men, across the Nansemond eight miles below. Advancing toward the village of Chuckatuck, they encountered the rebel cavalry about four hundred strong, who charged the column. Major Crosby commanding, instantly formed line and opened fire with musketry and artillery, promptly routing the enemy. Continuing his march, he was perpetually harassed by the enemy, who with skirmishers disputed his advance. But driving all before him, he arrived after a march of eight miles at the west branch of the Nansemond, which he had hoped to cross and feel the enemy's main force, but the bridge was burned, there was no means of crossing, and both banks of the stream were lined with the enemy. However, he advanced at double-quick, driving all those on his own side into the stream except eighteen whom he captured. Thus finding his further progress at an end, he marched down the West Branch to the Nansemond, where he bivouacked under cover of the gunboats.

Colonel Dutton with a small force crossed in row-boats at "Hill's Point." After advancing a short distance he found the enemy in largely superior numbers and strongly intrenched. Nevertheless, the attack commenced, and resulted of course in a repulse. The troops were then deployed as skirmishers and as such engaged the enemy the greater part of the day without important results. Colonel Dutton thus continued

the action with the expectation that he would soon be joined by General Getty's advancing column.

About midnight on the third, our troops under Corcoran, Dodge, and Foster started in pursuit of the retreating foe, but only succeeded in capturing a few hundred stragglers before the enemy crossed the Blackwater.

Thus ended the memorable siege of Suffolk, resulting to the rebels in a gain of nothing and a loss of one thousand five hundred men, five guns, and a considerable quantity of small arms and stores.

The writer cannot relinquish his theme without allusion to contemporary events. As late as the second of May, Lieutenant-General Hill confronted Suffolk with some thirty thousand men, Longstreet having gone by rail with one division, to aid Lee at Chancellorsville. Of this fact, the writer who has every facility for information, speaks without fear of truthful contradiction. On the same day Hooker and Lee fought their desperate engagement in the "Wilderness." Lee's army, thus depleted by Longstreet's diversion, numbered not far from fifty thousand, and Hooker knew that General Stoneman's operations would delay if not prevent reënforcements from Suffolk. The returns of the army of the Potomac for that date exhibit about one hundred and twenty-five thousand men present for duty, yet notwithstanding this disparity in numbers, our magnificent army, the boast of the North, was ignominiously defeated, despite the high-sounding proclamation that heralded its advance. This truth is mournful, yet it is no less a truth. Nor is it possible to review in connection the events of the last of April and first of May on the Rappahannock and on the Nansemond, without reflecting that had both Federal armies been commanded with equal ability, the united results might and could have been one of the most glorious triumphs to our arms that history has yet recorded.

The Richmond *Examiner* of the twenty-seventh November, 1863, has the following in its leading editorial upon Lieutenant-General Longstreet and his Knoxville and Suffolk campaigns, which are pronounced as parallel failures:

"Perhaps the result might have been different if Longstreet and his corps of the Virginia army had been in line. His operations in East-Tennessee afford little compensation for the reverse at Chattanooga, nor have the late bare and scanty news from that quarter sustained the high hope which the public justly based on the first intelligence briskly forwarded by General Bragg. His telegram declared that Longstreet's cavalry had pursued the enemy into Knoxville; that the infantry was 'close up,' and it was natural to suppose that the next news would be that of Knoxville's recapture. But the next news from Longstreet contained a mention of intrenching, which suggested disagreeable reminiscences of Suffolk. Since then, little or nothing has been heard from Longstreet, unless we are to receive the 'unofficial' story of the telegraph this morning to be trustworthy. Oh! that it may be so!

His pressure on Burnside has, undoubtedly, quickened Grant's attack on Bragg; while the absence of his whole corps from the confederate line at the time of Sherman's arrival in the Federal host has given the enemy a great opportunity. It was during the parallel campaign of Longstreet against Suffolk that Hooker made his coup at Chancellorsville; but he found there Jackson, while Grant had to do with Bragg alone."

Honor to whom honor is due!

Doc. 65.

CAPTURE OF THE CALYPSO.

United States Steamer Florida, stationed off Wilmington, N. C., at 7 P.M., 40 miles South of Cape Fear, June 11, 1863.

This afternoon we gained permission from the flag-ship Sacramento, to go off fishing a few miles outside the blockaders that lay huddled together some four miles off Fort Caswell and the mouth of the Cape Fear River. The result of which was some fine fishing and finer catching; for, by getting well out from the land, we were enabled to spy a rebel steamer which we saw as a faint speck on the distant horizon, where she lay waiting for nightfall to screen her as she ran in. We signalled to the fleet that we saw a suspicious sail, and immediately got under way and gave chase. For the first half-hour we gained upon her fast, but then she espied us making for her, a line of black smoke streamed up into the sky and she took to her heels; but our steamer is fast, and continued to gain upon her; the first hour of the chase is nearly over now, and we can distinguish a faint line almost as delicate as a hair standing up against the southern horizon—and we know it to be the smoke-stack of a steamer, for above it curls a hazy column of smoke which, too, is barely distinguishable; she must be some twelve miles off, and already we have gained some two or three upon her; but now there comes up a wild thunder gust—the rain pours down in sheets almost, and soon we can only see a few ship's lengths ahead, and we hardly know whether to keep straight on, or whether to take a more easterly course, in anticipation of her turning on her track under cover of the storm, and like a hunted hare seek to elude and baffle us. Our captain knows all this coast, has surveyed, and sounded, and measured it out, till he knows it like a book; he knows, too, there is a reef to the eastward of us, and fears this steamer will try to cut across it, and thus escape us, for we draw too much water to cross it, and most of the rebel steamers are light draught enough to do so; accordingly we head so as to cut her off from that resort, if possible, and still keep as directly toward her as we can. After half an hour's anxious waiting, the storm clears up, and the man at the masthead can see her hull. We are overhauling her fast. Another half-hour brings us within eight or nine miles of her—and we are fast overhauling her, when our western sky grows fairly black—with another thunder-storm that sweeps upon us like mad. The storm throws up against our bows long rolls of waves, and beats right against us, making us lose a number of knots. The tempest did not reach the blockade-runner, and when the clouds lifted she had left us far behind, and was almost out of sight. Only a few more hours and it would be dark. The wind that helped her on put us back dreadfully, and we began to despair of catching her; but we raised all the steam we could, used a little oil and wood to brighten up, and make a quick fire. Now we have a little wind and spread all the sail we can to advantage; hauled our guns from one side of the deck to the other, to keep the vessel in the best of trim; even spread hammock covers and table cloths to catch all the wind we could get. All these things told, and the staunch, good old Florida, catching the spirit of the chase, like some high-blood horse in a race, fairly flew through the water; every minute we gained upon the flying rebel, and in one short hour we regained all we had lost, and some good long miles besides, for her masts and hull and smoke-stack all show quite plainly; she is within six miles of us, and though she knows a stern chase is a long one, yet she sees it is useless for her to try to keep us at it longer, and as a last resource heads in for shore. We make for a point across her bows, and the race from that time on is one steady and rapid gain upon her, and the captain said she would hardly get on too shoal water for us to follow, ere we overhauled her. At seven P.M., we were within three or four miles of her, and Captain Bankhead orders the fifty-pound rifle to be fired to bring her to. It was done, but she paid no attention to it—he orders a solid shot to be fired across her bows. It was fired, and struck the water about a hundred yards ahead of her. Still she don't seem to heave to, and another shot is fired, which struck the water within twenty yards of her, so we have since been told. This brought her to, and she showed the white flag. A few minutes later brought us near enough to see her boats filled and shoving off from her, and a sickening fear came over us that they had scuttled her, or touched a slow match to her and we should lose her after all, and have nothing but her crew to take back. Captain B. threatened, as soon as she got within hail, to blow her out of the water, if they made a single further attempt to scuttle her, or blow her up, or even throw her cargo overboard. Thus warned, the few that seemed to be left on board to do that work hesitated. Meanwhile, our boat, with officers and men, pushed off to the steamer, when lo and behold! we saw some half-dozen women in one boat, being pulled toward us. They were a good deal frightened, but a few words from us, and our manners, convinced them they would be treated with the gentlemanly, chivalric courtesy that the American officer and sailor and patriot knows how to do better than any other class of men on the face of the globe. The men on the rebel steamer had indeed begun to scuttle her, but dared not run the risk of blowing her up after what the Captain had threatened, for they knew they would not deserve to be picked up by us, after our warning. Our First Lieutenant, engineer, carpenter, and a picked crew boarded her at once, found four feet of water in her, plugged the holes and leaks, put the pump in action, and the water in her hold lowered, and hopes were entertained that she might float and be saved.

The vessel is the iron steamer Calypso, of about six hundred or seven hundred tons. The steamer will probably bring sixty thousand dollars, and her cargo has been variously estimated at from forty thousand dollars to sixty thousand dollars. She has not yet, (while I write this,) however, been fully examined, and her cargo may be found to be worth more. Rum, molasses and medicines is what I have heard reported as being the principal part of what they have found so far. To-morrow (if the mail don't go before I have a chance) I will give more particulars about the matter. The Captain has just sent out to know if she is sinking, for our men on board of her are halloaing out to us, and we fear we shall lose her after all. Lieutenant Green answers back, but whether he says she'll sink or swim, I can't make out. Will hear by morning.

P. S.—*Later*—*June 12.*—Our prize steamer looms up splendidly this morning, all right ; and we have learned from the prisoners and list of cargo that she is even more valuable than was at first estimated. The English, I am told, sold the vessel alone (which is quite new) to her owners for forty-five thousand pounds—about two hundred and twenty-five thousand dollars in American currency ; and her cargo they say is worth one hundred thousand dollars—she is estimated by some of them to be worth at least two hundred thousand dollars.

Doc. 66.

THE INVASION OF GEORGIA.

COLONEL MONTGOMERY'S EXPEDITION.

HILTON HEAD, June 17, 1863.

EARLY on the morning of the eleventh instant, Colonel Montgomery left St. Simon's Island, where his brigade is now encamped, to present his compliments to the rebels of Georgia, having the week before sent them to those of South-Carolina.

This force consisted of five companies of the Second South-Carolina, eight companies of the Fifty-fourth Massachusetts, Colonel Shaw, all negro, and the Third Rhode Island battery, Captain Brayton. The gunboat John Adams, Captain Smith, and the transports Sentinel and Harriet A. Weed, constituted the fleet.

The expedition ready, the order was given to sail through Dubois Sound, and up the Altamaha River, the largest stream in Georgia, to the village of Darien, which is said to have contained before the war some two thousand inhabitants, most of whom were wedded to the rebel cause.

As the John Adams approached the village she poured a constant shower of shot and shell into the woods, along the shore, and into the town, as she came up to the wharf. The few "crackers" and paupers remaining in the place ran frightened and terror-stricken in every direction, and when Colonel Montgomery landed his troops, he found not a single armed inhabitant to dispute his right. Through the activity of some of the negro soldiers, a few of these poor "white trash" were caught, who told the story of there being a strong cavalry force within five miles of the place, which may or may not have been true. At any rate, Colonel Montgomery, from the information obtained from them, did not desist from his original purpose, but marched nearly his whole force into the town, posted his sentries and prepared to do his work. In a few hours all the valuable property he could find, of a movable character, was transferred to his boats. A large quantity of second-class furniture, considerable live stock, horses, cows, and sheep, and rice and corn, sufficient to feed his command for at least a month, was thus disposed of.

The inhabitants driven out and the town sacked, the next step in Colonel Montgomery's programme was to burn and destroy every thing he could not carry off with him. In a few moments the principal buildings were all in flames, and, a strong south-west wind prevailing at the time, the whole village was soon enshrouded in flame and smoke, and before the expedition returned, not a single tenantable habitation remained.

Darien destroyed, Major Corwin of the Second South-Carolina took the Harriet A. Weed and proceeded up the river in search of a rebel craft he had heard of through some negroes. When four miles up the stream he found the report to be correct, and overhauled and captured a copper-bottomed schooner, a large flat-boat, and eighty bales of long staple cotton, estimated to be worth thirty thousand dollars. Major Corwin was absent from Darien two hours, and when he returned with his prize, was received by the Massachusetts and South-Carolina negro soldiers with nine tremendous cheers.

These bold, rapid, and successful expeditions of Colonel Montgomery are spreading terror throughout the entire coast, and are compelling the rebels to abandon their rice and cotton fields and all the smaller villages which would be at all likely to be visited by him.

A NATIONAL ACCOUNT.

ST. SIMON'S ISLAND, GA., Tuesday, June 16, 1863.

When I last wrote we were just leaving Beaufort, on the eve of an expedition into Secessia. That expedition has been made, was eminently successful and bloodless, but how far creditable to us, and fruitful in results, I leave you to judge after you have heard the particulars. All Sunday afternoon of the seventh and until eleven o'clock at night, we were at work with ten teams and one hundred and twenty-five men, carrying our stores and luggage from the camp and stowing it on board the transport, from which it had only been removed two days before. The men worked like heroes, and by one o'clock the work was done, and we marched back to camp an "turned in" on the open ground. We had onl three hours' sleep, for we broke camp at four o'clock Monday morning, and took up our march to the wharf. It is a "big job" simply to march and stow away one thousand men on board a vessel. After several delays at last all was ready, and we swung off at nine o'clock, the men cheering and singing their "John Brown." At noon we reached Hilton Head, where the Colonel reported for orders. He got them, and to this effect: to proceed immediately to St. Simon's Island, and join Montgomery. By six P.M. we were off again, bound south-west, and on Tuesday morning at six o'clock, dropped anchor off the southern end of St. Simon's Island, in sight of the plantation of T. Butler King. Here several of us went ashore, the Colonel to ride across the Island to Montgomery's camp for further orders. I, with the Adjutant and Doctor, took the opportunity to look about the plantation. The house was occupied by a negro sergeant with a squad of men, but utterly deserted by its former owners. But it was a splendid place! It would make your eyes open to see things grow here, and to see what grows! Tamarinds and oranges were all about me, to say nothing of figs.

And then the whole catalogue of tropical plants and flowers, such as we only see at home in hot houses, are here so abundantly and luxuriantly spread before you, that you are lost in wonder and delight. But the live oaks are the most magnificent spectacle of all; they are large and symmetrical, and almost invariably, too, festooned with a peculiar, dark, parasitic vine which adds a strange weirdness to their sturdy grandeur. The Colonel returned with orders to land at a place further up, called Old Frederica.

The De Molay could not proceed, and we had to await a transport of lighter draught, which Montgomery was to send to us. It came alongside at noon, and proved to be the Sentinel, but looked like a New-York canal-boat built up a story. The Colonel, with eight companies, went on board and proceeded immediately to camp. Headquarters are established in a large two-story dwelling house close to the wharf; the line officers and men are in tents. Two companies (two hundred men) were set at work on the cargo, and I never saw men work so in my life. We all supposed we were going on an expedition the next day, and they had no idea of being left. We opened both hatchways, and put a hundred men at work on each. Consider, we were anchored in the stream, and the boat we were to transfer the cargo to, was off and would not be back for several hours. Of course we could hurry matters only by hoisting out the cargo and stowing it on deck. We fell to about three o'clock. At six the transport was alongside, and at ten we had every thing transferred to her decks! It was quick work,

but the men worked as if for their very lives. Waited on the tide till two o'clock in the morning, (Wednesday,) when we got under way, and reached camp at five o'clock. Took a fresh relay of two hundred men and ran the cargo ashore. We "confiscated" and seized upon an old barn close to headquarters, put twenty-five men to work on it, cleaned it out and rushed the stores in there as fast as they came ashore. It was very large, and now that it is well filled, looks like a large wholesale store. We had the cargo all out by the middle of the forenoon. In the afternoon we began to distribute and pitch tents. In the thick of this came an order from Montgomery to embark immediately on the Sentinel and report at his camp! The long-roll was sounded—and—I can give you no idea of what followed. We had heard the roll often enough, but never before the long-roll—the long-roll that means fight! The men rushed pell-mell to their quarters, seized their guns, filled their haversacks, and fell in by companies. Two companies were detailed to stay behind and guard the camp, and they formed a sad contrast to the others, I assure you. The rest were all aboard the transport in an hour from the time we received the order.

We proceeded down the river about five miles to Montgomery's camp. Here we joined the other vessels of the expedition, which made up as follows, all told: Flag-ship John Adams, (an old friend, to wit, East-Boston ferry-boat,) with part of the Second South-Carolina, numbering eight hundred, on board; the Harriet A. Weed, with the rest of the Second, (formerly a North River boat, I should say;) the Sentinel, with the Fifty-fourth Massachusetts volunteers; and the gunboat Paul Jones, carrying eight guns, two eleven-inch, three pivot, and three side. The John Adams also had four or five guns, including one large Parrott. It was truly quite a formidable expedition. All the vessels got under way, and proceeded down the river about sunset. The prominent idea of the expedition was to "run off" slaves, and also get what rebel stores we could. The plan was this: to sail with all speed up the Altamaha River to Fort Barrington, there disembark, send the boats below to Darien, and then march the regiment thither, sweeping all the slaves on before us. Thus we would sweep a district of some twenty or thirty miles in length. Could we have carried this out, no doubt we should have been richly repaid, but we met with so many delays that it became impracticable. We had gone but a little ways down the river when our boat ran aground, and the tide being on the ebb, there she staid till morning. This was unfortunate, for it necessitated making the whole trip by daylight, in place of by night. We grounded several times in going up the Altamaha, and altogether consumed so much time that the rebels had leisure to spread the news all over Georgia. They made their preparations accordingly, deserting all the plantations near the river, and, judging from the smoke, burning many a rice-mill and store-house further in the interior. We shelled the woods on both sides as we advanced, but failed to find an enemy. The country for miles on both banks of the river was flat and marshy, and of the most uninviting kind. The river itself was so muddy and red you could hardly persuade yourself there wasn't an immense brick-yard underneath. It was full of alligators of all sizes and degrees of ugliness. It was past noon when we reached Darien, and, of course, from the warning we had given, it was useless to proceed further—we should find the country deserted, go where we would. Not a soul was to be seen in Darien. We were ordered to disembark and form in line of battle in the public square. Pickets were sent out to the limits of the town. Orders were then given to search the town, take what could be found of value to the vessels, and then fire it. Officers then started off in every direction, with squads of men to assist. In a very short time every house in town was broken into and the work of pillage and selection was begun. The fire had begun, too, from the lower end of the town (caused by a shell thrown before we landed) and a high wind was driving it resistlessly up the main street.

Soon the men began to come in in twos, threes, and dozens, loaded with every species and all sorts and quantities of furniture, stores, trinkets, etc., etc., till one would be tired enumerating. We had sofas, tables, pianos, chairs, mirrors, carpets, beds, bedsteads, carpenters' tools, coopers' tools, books, law books, account books in unlimited supply, china sets, tin ware, earthen ware, confederate shinplasters, old letters, papers, etc., etc., etc. A private would come along with a slate, yardstick, and brace of chickens in one hand, a table on his head, and in the other hand a rope with a cow attached. (I here actually described Milo's state on his first return to the ship.) An immense pile of lumber lay on the wharf, and men were detailed to load it on the boats. Droves of sheep and cows were driven in and put aboard. Along the shore were large warehouses of rice and rosin—what rosin we could, we put aboard. While this was going on, the Harriet A. Weed steamed up the river and captured a schooner and flatboat with eighty-five bales of cotton. She was loudly cheered as she passed us on her way down. Darien contained from seventy-five to one hundred houses, not counting slave cabins, of which there were several to every house, the number varying evidently according to the wealth of the proprietor: one fine broad street along the river, the rest starting out from it. All of them were shaded on both sides, not with young saplings, but good sturdy oaks and mulberries, that told of a town of both age and respectability. It was a beautiful town, and never did it look so both grand and beautiful as in its destruction. As soon as a house was ransacked, the match was applied, and by six o'clock the whole town was in one sheet of flame. It was a magnificent spectacle, but still very few were found to gloat over it. Had we had a hard fight to gain the place, or had we taken a thousand slaves by its destruction, we would have had no

compunctions. And I suppose we should have none any way. The South must be conquered inch by inch, and what we can't put a force in to hold, ought to be destroyed. If we must burn the South out, so be it. The store-houses along the river were fired last, and the burning of them was the signal for departure. We hurried on board, and well it was for us—it was so hot then we could not stay on that side of the boat next the wharf. Had the wind shifted, no power on earth could have saved us—we barely escaped as it was. It was sundown as we dropped into the stream. A whole town on fire, from one end to the other! it isn't often one sees it, and it's seldom he wants to. But it is a spectacle grand in the extreme. When the rosin took fire a dense black smoke rolled up and almost shut out the light of the conflagration. As night came on, a terrific thunder-storm came up, and heaven's artillery finished the havoc that ours had begun. We anchored in the stream for the night. Thus began, continued and ended the first expedition or raid into Secessia, in which the Fifty-fourth Massachusetts bore a part. We have all only this comment to make—we pray God that the next town we burn we may first have to fight to get it.

We reached camp next day, Friday, about three P.M. The next morning the plunder was divided, and now it is scattered all over camp, but put to good use, the whole of it. Some of the quarters really look princely, with their sofas, divans, pianos, etc. In place of the customary privations of camp, we have almost the comforts of home, with not a few of its luxuries. Don't get the idea that the rebels had taken themselves away only. They took every thing they could carry off in the time they had. Many houses had absolutely nothing in them of value to any body.

St. Simon's Island is flat, but wonderfully productive and beautiful. It has never been my fortune before to see its equal. Our camp is close on to the old town of Frederica, which in its palmy days had some three thousand inhabitants. Now it has not one. The north end of the island forms Pierce Butler's plantation—Fanny Kemble's husband, and the man who had that immense auction sale of negroes several years ago. It is deserted now, save by some dozen or two darkies, once Butler's slaves. "Ole massa run away, de darkies stay at home." Truly the "Kingdom is coming" to these poor blacks.

The weather here is warm, and uniformly so. We have had nothing here yet hotter than our July's best at home. Thus far I have experienced no great inconvenience from the heat, and am in good health and good spirits day in and day out.

A REBEL ACCOUNT.

SAVANNAH, June 16, 1863.

Our readers have been informed that the city of Darien, one of the oldest towns in the State, the New-Inverness of Oglethorpe's time, has been totally destroyed by Yankee negro forces. We have been kindly permitted to make some extracts from private letters received by one of our citizens, which contain some facts in relation to this crowning act of wanton vandalism on Georgia soil which have not before been published. A citizen of Darien, writing from "Dunwoody's Plantation, near where Darien once stood," under date of June twelfth, says:

"What has been so long threatened has at length come to pass. Darien is now one plain of ashes and blackened chimneys. The accursed Yankee negro vandals came up yesterday with three gunboats and two transports, and laid the city in ruins. There are but three small houses left in the place. The Methodist church was set on fire, but it did not burn. All the other churches, the market-house, court-house, jail and clerk's office are all gone. The villains broke open all the houses and stores and took what they wanted, and then poured spirits of turpentine over the floors and applied the torch. It is a sad sight to see the smoking ruins now.

"The wretches shot the milch cows and calves down in the streets, took some of them on board their vessels, and left the rest lying in the streets, where they still lie. They carried off every negro that was in the place, except one old African woman named Nancy, who told them she was from Africa, and that she would not go again on the big water. After destroying the town, on their way to Dobb's they burned Mr. Morris's plantation buildings. For myself, I feel this calamity severely. You know I have lost heavily since the war commenced; but I had still a good home left. This is now also gone.

"The value in money I would not have thought so much of, as I am getting used to it; but there is something in the word home that puts money out of the question. And then to think it was burned in broad daylight by the cowardly Yankee negro thieves. But a truce to regrets. One of the boats started to come up Cathead Creek to this place, but the sneaking rascals changed their minds, and contented themselves with sending us a few compliments in the shape of shells. We of course had to leave here for a time, and, as there are more raids expected, I have concluded to remove a little way into the pine woods until I see whether I can harvest my crop or not.

"The town was destroyed by a negro regiment officered by white men. They left a book, which I found, and in which the following entry was made, and which I presume is a list of the regimental officers. The writing is in a large, coarse hand, and in pencil.

"Stewart W. Woods, June eleventh, 1863, Company I, Fifty-fourth Massachusetts volunteers; Penn Township, Cumberland County, Pennsylvania; Stewart W. Woods was born September twenty-first, 1824. Hidlers, Hidlersburgh, Adams County, Pennsylvana, Fifty-fourth Massachusetts volunteers, Fifty-fourth regiment Massachusetts volunteers of Colonel Shaw. Captain G. Pope; First Lieutenant Higginson; Second Lieutenant Tucker.

"Should these Yankee negro brigades ever fall into our hands the above record may be useful."

Doc. 67.

MILITARY ARRESTS.

CORRESPONDENCE IN RELATION TO THE PUBLIC MEETING AT ALBANY, N. Y.—LETTER OF THE COMMITTEE AND RESOLUTIONS.

ALBANY, May 19, 1863.

To His Excellency the President of the United States:

THE undersigned, officers of a public meeting held at the city of Albany on the sixteenth day of May, instant, herewith transmit to your Excellency a copy of the resolutions adopted at the said meeting, and respectfully request your earnest consideration of them. They deem it proper on their personal responsibility to state that the meeting was one of the most respectable as to numbers and character, and one of the most earnest in the support of the Union ever held in this city.　　Yours, with great regard,

ERASTUS CORNING, President.
ELI PERRY, Vice-President.
PETER GANSEVOORT, Vice-President.
PETER MONTEATH, Vice-President.
SAMUEL W. GIBBS, Vice-President.
JOHN NIBLACK, Vice-President.
H. W. McCLELLAN, Vice-President.
LEMUEL W. RODGERS, Vice-President.
WILLIAM SEYMOUR, Vice-President.
JEREMIAH OSBORN, Vice-President.
WILLIAM S. PADOCK, Vice-President.
J. B. SANDERS, Vice-President.
EDWARD MULCAHY, Vice-President.
D. V. N. RADCLIFFE, Vice-President.
WILLIAM A. RICE, Secretary.
EDWARD NEWCOMB, Secretary.
R. W. PECKHAM, JR., Secretary.
M. A. NOLAN, Secretary.
JOHN R. NESSEL, Secretary.
C. W. WEEKS, Secretary.

RESOLUTIONS ADOPTED AT THE MEETING HELD IN ALBANY, N. Y., ON THE 16TH OF MAY, 1863.

Resolved, That the Democrats of New-York point to their uniform course of action during the two years of civil war through which we have passed, to the alacrity which they have evinced in filling the ranks of the army, to their contributions and sacrifices, as the evidence of their patriotism and devotion to the cause of our imperilled country. Never in the history of civil wars has a government been sustained with such ample resources of means and men as the people have voluntarily placed in the hands of the Administration.

Resolved, That as Democrats we are determined to maintain this patriotic attitude, and, despite of adverse and disheartening circumstances, to devote all our energies to sustain the cause of the Union, to secure peace through victory, and to bring back the restoration of all the States under the safeguards of the Constitution.

Resolved, That while we will not consent to be misapprehended upon these points, we are determined not to be misunderstood in regard to others not less essential. We demand that the Administration shall be true to the Constitution;

shall recognize and maintain the rights of the States and the liberties of the citizen; shall everywhere, outside of the lines of necessary military occupation and the scenes of insurrection, exert all its powers to maintain the supremacy of the civil over military law.

Resolved, That in view of these principles we denounce the recent assumption of a military commander to seize and try a citizen of Ohio, Clement L. Vallandigham, for no other reason than words addressed to a public meeting, in criticism of the course of the Administration, and in condemnation of the military orders of that General.

Resolved, That this assumption of power by a military tribunal, if successfully asserted, not only abrogates the right of the people to assemble and discuss the affairs of government, the liberty of speech and of the press, the right of trial by jury, the law of evidence, and the privilege of habeas corpus, but it strikes a fatal blow at the supremacy of law, and the authority of the State and federal constitutions.

Resolved, That the Constitution of the United States—the supreme law of the land—has defined the crime of treason against the United States to consist "only in levying war against them, or adhering to their enemies, giving them aid and comfort;" and has provided that "no person shall be convicted of treason, unless on the testimony of two witnesses to the same overt act, or on confession in open court." And it further provides that "no person shall be held to answer for a capital or otherwise infamous crime, unless on a presentment or indictment of a grand jury, except in cases arising in the land and naval forces, or in the militia, when in actual service in time of war or public danger;" and further, that "in all criminal prosecutions, the accused shall enjoy the right of a speedy and public trial by an impartial jury of the State and district wherein the crime was committed."

Resolved, That these safeguards of the rights of the citizen against the pretensions of arbitrary power were intended more especially for his protection in times of civil commotion. They were secured substantially to the English people, after years of protracted civil war, and were adopted into our Constitution at the close of the revolution. They have stood the test of seventy-six years of trial, under our republican system, under circumstances which show that, while they constitute the foundation of all free government, they are the elements of the enduring stability of the republic.

. *Resolved,* That, in adopting the language of Daniel Webster, we declare, "it is the ancient and undoubted prerogative of this people to canvass public measures and the merits of public men." It is a "home-bred right," a fireside privilege. It has been enjoyed in every house, cottage, and cabin in the nation. It is as undoubted as the right of breathing the air or walking on the earth. Belonging to private life as a right, it belongs to public life as a duty, and it is the last duty which those whose representatives we

are shall find us to abandon. Aiming at all times to be courteous and temperate in its use, except when the right itself is questioned, we shall place ourselves on the extreme boundary of our own right, and bid defiance to any arm that would move us from our ground. "This high constitutional privilege we shall defend and exercise in all places—in time of peace, in time of war, and at all times. Living, we shall assert it; and should we leave no other inheritance to our children, by the blessing of God we will leave them the inheritance of free principles and the example of a manly, independent, and constitutional defence of them."

Resolved, That in the election of Governor Seymour, the people of this State, by an emphatic majority, declared their condemnation of the system of arbitrary arrests and their determination to stand by the Constitution. That the revival of this lawless system can have but one result—to divide and distract the North, and destroy its confidence in the purposes of the Administration. That we deprecate it as an element of confusion at home, of weakness to our armies in the field, and as calculated to lower the estimate of American character and magnify the apparent peril of our cause abroad. And that, regarding the blow struck at a citizen of Ohio as aimed at the rights of every citizen of the North, we denounce it as against the spirit of our laws and Constitution, and most earnestly call upon the President of the United States to reverse the action of the military tribunal which has passed a "cruel and unusual punishment" upon the party arrested, prohibited in terms by the Constitution, and to restore him to the liberty of which he has been deprived.

Resolved, That the President, Vice-Presidents, and Secretary of this meeting be requested to transmit a copy of these resolutions to his Excellency the President of the United States, with the assurance of this meeting of their hearty and earnest desire to support the Government in every constitutional and lawful measure to suppress the existing rebellion.

PRESIDENT LINCOLN'S REPLY.

Executive Mansion, Washington, June 12, 1863.

Hon. Erastus Corning and others:

Gentlemen: Your letter of May nineteenth, inclosing the resolutions of a public meeting held at Albany, New-York, on the sixteenth of the same month, was received several days ago.

The resolutions, as I understand them, are resolvable into two propositions—first, the expression of a purpose to sustain the cause of the Union, to secure peace through victory, and to support the Administration in every constitutional and lawful measure to suppress the rebellion; and secondly, a declaration of censure upon the Administration for supposed unconstitutional action, such as the making of military arrests. And from the two propositions a third is deduced, which is, that the gentlemen composing the meeting are resolved on doing their part to maintain our common Government and country, despite the folly or wickedness, as they may conceive, of any Administration. This position is eminently patriotic, and as such, I thank the meeting and congratulate the nation for it. My own purpose is the same; so that the meeting and myself have a common object and can have no difference, except in the choice of means or measures for effecting that object.

And here I ought to close this paper, and would close it, if there were no apprehension that more injurious consequences than any merely personal to myself might follow the censures systematically cast upon me for doing what, in my view of duty, I could not forbear. The resolutions promise to support me in every constitutional and lawful measure to suppress the rebellion; and I have not knowingly employed, nor shall knowingly employ, any other. But the meeting, by their resolutions, assert and argue that certain military arrests, and proceedings following them, for which I am ultimately responsible, are unconstitutional. I think they are not. The resolutions quote from the Constitution the definition of treason, and also the limiting safeguards and guarantees therein provided for the citizen on trial for treason, and on his being held to answer for capital or otherwise infamous crimes, and, in criminal prosecutions, his right to a speedy and public trial by an impartial jury. They proceed to resolve "that these safeguards of the rights of the citizens against the pretensions of arbitrary power were intended more *especially* for his protection in times of civil commotion." And, apparently to demonstrate the proposition, the resolutions proceed: "They were secured substantially to the English people *after* years of protracted civil war, and were adopted into our Constitution at the close of the Revolution." Would not the demonstration have been better, if it could have been truly said that these safeguards had been adopted and applied during the civil wars and during our Revolution, instead of after the one and at the close of the other? I, too, am devotedly for them after civil war, and before civil war, and at all times, "except when, in cases of rebellion or invasion, the public safety may require" their suspension. The resolutions proceed to tell us that these safeguards "have stood the test of seventy-six years of trial, under our republican system, under circumstances which show that while they constitute the foundation of all free government, they are the elements of the enduring stability of the republic." No one denies that they have so stood the test up to the beginning of the present rebellion, if we except a certain occurrence at New-Orleans; nor does any one question that they will stand the same test much longer after the rebellion closes. But these provisions of the Constitution have no application to the case we have in hand, because the arrests complained of were not made for treason—that is, not for the treason defined in the Constitution, and upon the conviction of which the punishment is death; nor yet were they made to hold persons to answer for any capital or otherwise infamous crimes; nor

were the proceedings following, in any constitutional or legal sense, "criminal prosecutions." The arrests were made on totally different grounds, and the proceedings following accorded with the grounds of the arrests. Let us consider the real case with which we are dealing, and apply to it the parts of the Constitution plainly made for such cases.

Prior to my installation here it had been inculcated that any State had a lawful right to secede from the national Union, and that it would be expedient to exercise the right whenever the devotees of the doctrine should fail to elect a President to their own liking. I was elected contrary to their liking; and accordingly, so far as it was legally possible, they had taken seven States out of the Union, had seized many of the United States forts, and had fired upon the United States flag, all before I was inaugurated, and, of course, before I had done any official act whatever. The rebellion thus begun soon ran into the present civil war; and, in certain respects, it began on very unequal terms between the parties. The insurgents had been preparing for it more than thirty years, while the Government had taken no steps to resist them. The former had carefully considered all the means which could be turned to their account. It undoubtedly was a well-pondered reliance with them that in their own unrestricted efforts to destroy Union, Constitution, and law, all together, the Government would, in great degree, be restrained by the same Constitution and law from arresting their progress. Their sympathizers pervaded all departments of the Government and nearly all communities of the people. From this material, under cover of "liberty of speech," "liberty of the press," and *habeas corpus*, they hoped to keep on foot amongst us a most efficient corps of spies, informers, suppliers, and aiders and abettors of their cause in a thousand ways. They knew that in times such as they were inaugurating, by the Constitution itself, the *habeas corpus* might be suspended; but they also knew they had friends who would make a question as to who was to suspend it; meanwhile their spies and others might remain at large to help on their cause. Or if, as has happened, the executive should suspend the writ, without ruinous waste of time, instances of arresting innocent persons might occur, as are always likely to occur in such cases; and then a clamor could be raised in regard to this, which might be, at least, of some service to the insurgent cause. It needed no very keen perception to discover this part of the enemy's programme so soon as by open hostilities their machinery was fairly put in motion. Yet, thoroughly imbued with a reverence for the guaranteed rights of individuals, I was slow to adopt the strong measures which by degrees I have been forced to regard as being within the exceptions of the Constitution and as indispensable to the public safety. Nothing is better known to history than that courts of justice are utterly incompetent to such cases. Civil courts are organized chiefly for trials of individuals, or, at most, a few individuals acting in concert; and this in quiet times, and on charges of crimes well defined in the law. Even in times of peace, bands of horse-thieves and robbers frequently grow too numerous and powerful for the ordinary courts of justice. But what comparison in numbers have such bands ever borne to the insurgent sympathizers even in many of the loyal States? Again, a jury too frequently has at least one member more ready to hang the panel than to hang the traitor. And yet, again, he who dissuades one man from volunteering, or induces one soldier to desert, weakens the Union cause as as much as he who kills a Union soldier in battle. Yet this dissuasion or inducement may be so conducted as to be no defined crime of which any civil court would take cognizance.

Ours is a case of rebellion—so called by the resolutions before me—in fact, a clear, flagrant, and gigantic case of rebellion; and the provision of the Constitution that "the privilege of the writ of *habeas corpus* shall not be suspended unless when, in cases of rebellion or invasion, the public safety may require it," is the provision which specially applies to our present case. This provision plainly attests the understanding of those who made the Constitution, that ordinary courts of justice are inadequate to "cases of rebellion"—attests their purpose that, in such cases, men may be held in custody whom the courts, acting on ordinary rules, would discharge. *Habeas corpus* does not discharge men who are proved to be guilty of defined crime; and its suspension is allowed by the Constitution on purpose that men may be arrested and held who cannot be proved to be guilty of defined crime, "when, in cases of rebellion or invasion, the public safety may require it." This is precisely our present case—a case of rebellion, wherein the public safety does require the suspension. Indeed, arrests by process of courts, and arrests in cases of rebellion, do not proceed together altogether upon the same basis. The former is directed at the small percentage of ordinary and continuous perpetration of crime, while the latter is directed at sudden and extensive uprisings against the government, which, at most, will succeed or fail in no great length of time. In the latter case, arrests are made, not so much for what has been done as for what probably would be done. The latter is more for the preventive and less for the vindictive than the former. In such cases the purposes of men are much more easily understood than in cases of ordinary crime. The man who stands by and says nothing when the peril of his government is discussed cannot be misunderstood. If not hindered, he is sure to help the enemy; much more, if he talks ambiguously—talks for his country with "buts," and "ifs," and "ands." Of how little value the constitutional provisions I have quoted will be rendered, if arrests shall never be made until defined crimes shall have been committed, may be illustrated by a few notable examples. General John C. Breckinridge, General Robert E. Lee, General Joseph E. Johnston, General John B.

Magruder, General William B. Preston, General Simon B. Buckner, and Commodore Franklin Buchanan, now occupying the very highest places in the rebel war service, were all within the power of the government since the rebellion began, and were nearly as well known to be traitors then as now. Unquestionably, if we had seized and held them the insurgent cause would be much weaker. But no one of them had then committed any crime defined in the law. Every one of them, if arrested, would have been discharged on *habeas corpus* were the writ allowed to operate. In view of these and similar cases, I think the time not unlikely to come when I shall be blamed for having made too few arrests rather than too many.

By the third resolution, the meeting indicate their opinion that military arrests may be constitutional in localities where rebellion actually exists, but that such arrests are unconstitutional in localities where rebellion or insurrection does not actually exist. They insist that such arrests shall not be made "outside of the lines of necessary military occupation and the scenes of insurrection." Inasmuch, however, as the Constitution itself makes no such distinction, I am unable to believe that there is any such constitutional distinction. I concede that the class of arrests complained of can be constitutional only when, in cases of rebellion or invasion, the public safety may require them; and I insist that in such cases they are constitutional wherever the public safety does require them, as well in places to which they may prevent the rebellion extending as in those where it may be already prevailing; as well where they may restrain mischievous interference with the raising and supplying of armies to suppress the rebellion, as where the rebellion may actually be; as well where they may restrain the enticing men out of the army, as where they would prevent mutiny in the army; equally constitutional at all places where they will conduce to the public safety, as against the dangers of rebellion or invasion. Take the particular case mentioned by the meeting. It is asserted, in substance, that Mr. Vallandigham was, by a military commander, seized and tried "for no other reason than words addressed to a public meeting, in criticism of the course of the Administration, and in condemnation of the military orders of the general." Now, if there be no mistake about this—if this assertion is the truth and the whole truth—if there was no other reason for the arrest, then I concede that the arrest was wrong. But the arrest, as I understand, was made for a very different reason. Mr. Vallandigham avows his hostility to the war on the part of the Union; and his arrest was made because he was laboring, with some effect, to prevent the raising of troops, to encourage desertions from the army, and to leave the rebellion without an adequate military force to suppress it. He was not arrested because he was damaging the political prospects of the Administration, or the personal interests of the commanding general, but because he was damaging the army, upon the existence and vigor of which the life of the nation depends. He was warring upon the military, and this gave the military constitutional jurisdiction to lay hands upon him. If Mr. Vallandigham was not damaging the military power of the country, then his arrest was made on mistake of fact, which I would be glad to correct on reasonably satisfactory evidence.

I understand the meeting, whose resolutions I am considering, to be in favor of supressing the rebellion by military force—by armies. Long experience has shown that armies cannot be maintained unless desertion shall be punished by the severe penalty of death. The case requires, and the law and the Constitution sanction, this punishment. Must I shoot a simple-minded soldier boy who deserts, while I must not touch a hair of a wily agitator who induces him to desert? This is none the less injurious when effected by getting a father or brother or friend into a public meeting, and there working upon his feelings till he is persuaded to write the soldier boy that he is fighting in a bad cause, for a wicked administration of a contemptible government, too weak to arrest and punish him if he shall desert. I think that in such a case to silence the agitator and save the boy is not only constitutional, but withal a great mercy.

If I be wrong on this question of constitutional power, my error lies in believing that certain proceedings are constitutional when, in cases of rebellion or invasion, the public safety requires them, which would not be constitutional when, in absence of rebellion or invasion, the public safety does not require them. In other words, that the Constitution is not in its application in all respects the same, in cases of rebellion or invasion involving the public safety, as it is in times of profound peace and public security. The Constitution itself makes the distinction; and I can no more be persuaded that the government can constitutionally take no strong measures in time of rebellion, because it can be shown that the same could not be lawfully taken in time of peace, than I can be persuaded that a particular drug is not good medicine for a sick man, because it can be shown to not be good food for a well one. Nor am I able to appreciate the danger apprehended by the meeting that the American people will, by means of military arrests during the rebellion, lose the right of public discussion, the liberty of speech and the press, law of evidence, trial by jury and *habeas corpus*, throughout the indefinite peaceful future, which I trust lies before them, any more than I am able to believe that a man could contract so strong an appetite for emetics during temporary illness as to persist in feeding upon them during the remainder of his healthful life.

In giving the resolutions that earnest consideration which you request of me, I cannot overlook the fact that the meeting speak as "democrats." Nor can I, with full respect for their known intelligence, and the fairly presumed deliberation with which they prepared their resolutions, be permitted to suppose that this occurred by accident, or in any way other than that they preferred to designate themselves "democrats"

rather than "American citizens." In this time of national peril I would have preferred to meet you upon a level one step higher than any party platform, because I am sure that, from such more elevated position, we could do better battle for the country we all love than we possibly can from those lower ones where, from the force of habit, the prejudices of the past and selfish hopes of the future, we are sure to expend much of our ingenuity and strength in finding fault with and aiming blows at each other. But since you have denied me this, I will yet be thankful, for the country's sake, that not all democrats have done so. He on whose discretionary judgment Mr. Vallandigham was arrested and tried is a democrat, having no old party affinity with me; and the judge who rejected the constitutional view expressed in these resolutions, by refusing to discharge Mr. Vallandigham on *habeas corpus*, is a democrat of better days than these, having received his judicial mantle at the hands of President Jackson. And still more, of all those democrats who are nobly exposing their lives and shedding their blood on the battle-field, I have learned that many approve the course taken with Mr. Vallandigham, while I have not heard of a single one condemning it. I cannot assert that there are none such. And the name of President Jackson recalls an instance of pertinent history. After the battle of New-Orleans, and while the fact that the treaty of peace had been concluded was well known in the city, but before official knowledge of it had arrived, General Jackson still maintained martial or military law. Now, that it could be said the war was over, the clamor against martial law, which had existed from the first, grew more furious. Among other things a Mr. Louaillier published a denunciatory newspaper article. General Jackson arrested him. A lawyer by the name of Morel procured the United States Judge Hall to order a writ of *habeas corpus* to relieve Mr. Louaillier. General Jackson arrested both the lawyer and the judge. A Mr. Hollander ventured to say of some part of the matter that "it was a dirty trick." General Jackson arrested him. When the officer undertook to serve the writ of *habeas corpus* General Jackson took it from him, and sent him away with a copy. Holding the judge in custody a few days, the General sent him beyond the limits of his encampment, and set him at liberty, with an order to remain till the ratification of peace should be regularly announced, or until the British should have left the Southern coast. A day or two more elapsed, the ratification of the treaty of peace was regularly announced, and the judge and others were fully liberated. A few days more, and the judge called General Jackson into court and fined him a thousand dollars for having arrested him and the others named. The General paid the fine, and there the matter rested for nearly thirty years, when Congress refunded principal and interest. The late Senator Douglas, then in the House of Representatives, took a leading part in the debates, in which the constitutional question was much discussed. I am not prepared to say whom the journals would show to have voted for the measure.

It may be remarked, first, that we had the same Constitution then as now; secondly, that we then had a case of invasion, and now we have a case of rebellion; and thirdly, that the permanent right of the people to public discussion, the liberty of speech and of the press, the trial by jury, the law of evidence, and the *habeas corpus*, suffered no detriment whatever by that conduct of General Jackson, or its subsequent approval by the American Congress.

And yet, let me say that, in my own discretion, I do not know whether I would have ordered the arrest of Mr. Vallandigham. While I cannot shift the responsibility from myself, I hold that, as a general rule, the commander in the field is the better judge of the necessity in any particular case. Of course, I must practise a general directory and revisory power in the matter.

One of the resolutions expresses the opinion of the meeting that arbitrary arrests will have the effect to divide and distract those who should be united in suppressing the rebellion, and I am specifically called on to discharge Mr. Vallandigham. I regard this as, at least, a fair appeal to me on the expediency of exercising a constitutional power which I think exists. In response to such appeal I have to say, it gave me pain when I learned that Mr. Vallandigham had been arrested—that is, I was pained that there should have seemed to be a necessity for arresting him—and that it will afford me great pleasure to discharge him so soon as I can, by any means, believe the public safety will not suffer by it. I further say that, as the war progresses, it appears to me, opinion and action, which were in great confusion at first, take shape and fall into more regular channels, so that the necessity for strong dealing with them gradually decreases. I have every reason to desire that it should cease altogether, and far from the least is my regard for the opinions and wishes of those who, like the meeting at Albany, declare their purpose to sustain the Government in every constitutional and lawful measure to suppress the rebellion. Still I must continue to so much as may seem to be required by the public safety. A. LINCOLN.

REPLY OF THE ALBANY DEMOCRACY.

STATEMENT.

At a public meeting held at the Capitol, in the city of Albany, on the sixteenth day of May, 1863, to consider the arbitrary arrest of Mr. Vallandigham, certain resolutions were adopted, copies of which were, by the direction of the meeting, transmitted by its officers to President Lincoln, who, in a communication dated the twelfth of June, 1863, addressed to the gentlemen referred to, which has appeared very generally in the public prints, discussed the resolutions and controverted certain positions which they maintained in regard to personal rights and constitutional obligations.

On the receipt of this communication the Hon.

Erastus Corning, chairman of the meeting referred to, addressed the President, informing him in substance that the special duty assigned to the officers of the meeting had been fulfilled by sending the resolutions to his Excellency, but adding that in view of the importance of the principles involved, and the public interest which the matter had assumed, he had deemed it proper to submit the President's letter to the committee who reported the resolutions, for such action as in their judgment it might demand.

The committee having considered the subject, and viewing the questions at issue as of the gravest importance, replied to the President's communication, which reply is now laid before the public. At the request of the committee it was sent to the President by the officers of the meeting, in a letter under their signatures, of which the following is a copy:

To His Excellency the President of the United States:

SIR: The undersigned, officers of the public meeting held in this city on the sixteenth day of May last, to whom your communication of the twelfth of this month, commenting on the resolutions adopted at that meeting, was addressed, have the honor to send to your Excellency a reply to that communication by the committee who reported the resolutions. The great importance to the people of this country of the questions discussed must be our apology, if any be needed, for saying that we fully concur in this reply, and believe it to be in entire harmony with the views and sentiments of the meeting referred to.

We are, with great respect, very truly yours,

ALBANY, June 30, 1863.

ERASTUS CORNING,
President.

ELI PERRY,	JEREMIAH OSBORN,
JOHN TAYLER COOPER,	D. V. N. RADCLIFFE,
PETER MONTEATH,	MOSES PATTEN,
PETER GANSEVOORT,	FRANCIS KEARNEY,
WM. S. PADDOCK,	SAMUEL W. GIBBS,
JAMES B. SANDERS,	TIMOTHY SEYMOUR,
H. W. McCLELLAN,	L. D. HOLSTEIN,
L. M. RODGERS,	JOSEPH SPORBORG,
ALANSON SUMNER	PETER P. STAATS,
JOHN NIBLOCK,	RICHARD PARR,
JOHN I. BURTON,	JOHN McELROY,
B. P. STAATS,	E. MULCAHY,
JAMES D. WASSON,	SIGMUND ADLER,
STEPHEN CLARK,	WM. SEYMOUR,
BERNARD REYNOLDS,	JAMES QUINN,
JOHN P. NESSLE,	JOS. T. RICE,
JOHN KENNEDY, Jr.,	JOHN MORGAN,
DAVID ORR,	JOS. KRESSER,
JOHN STEWART,	Vice-Presidents
WILLIAM A. RICE,	HALE KINGSLEY,
R. L. BANKS,	JAMES McQUADE,
I. McB. DAVIDSON,	J. H. BULLOCK,
PHILIP O'BRIEN,	R. W. PECKHAM, Jr.,

M. A. NOLAN,
Secretaries.

To His Excellency Abraham Lincoln, President of the United States:

SIR: Your answer, which has appeared in the

public prints, to the resolutions adopted at a recent meeting in the city of Albany affirming the personal rights and liberties of the citizens of this country, has been referred to the undersigned, the committee who prepared and reported those resolutions. The subject will now receive from us some further attention, which your answer seems to justify, if not to invite. We hope not to appear wanting in the respect due to your high position if we reply with a freedom and earnestness suggested by the infinite gravity and importance of the questions upon which you have thought proper to take issue at the bar of public opinion.

You seem to be aware that the Constitution of the United States, which you have sworn to protect and defend, contains the following guarantees, to which we again ask your attention: First. Congress shall make no law abridging the freedom of speech or of the press. Second. The right of the people to be secure in their persons against unreasonable seizures shall not be violated, and no warrant shall issue but upon probable cause supported by oath. Third. No person, except soldiers and mariners in the service of the Government, shall be held to answer for a capital or infamous crime, unless on presentment or indictment of a grand jury, nor shall any person be deprived of life, liberty, or property without due process of law. Fourth. In all criminal prosecutions the accused shall enjoy the right of a speedy and public trial by an impartial jury of the State or district in which the crime shall have been committed, and to be confronted with the witnesses against him.

You are also no doubt aware that on the adoption of the Constitution these invaluable provisions were proposed by the jealous caution of the States, and were inserted as amendments for a perpetual assurance of liberty against the encroachments of power. From your earliest reading of history, you also know that the great principles of liberty and law which underlie these provisions were derived to us from the British Constitution. In that country they were secured by *magna charta* more than six hundred years ago, and they have been confirmed by many and repeated statutes of the realm. A single palpable violation of them in England would not only arouse the public indignation, but would endanger the throne itself. For a persistent disregard of them, Charles the First was dethroned and beheaded by his rebellious subjects.

The fact has already passed into history that the sacred rights and immunities which were designed to be protected by these constitutional guarantees have not been preserved to the people during your administration. In violation of the first of them, the freedom of the press has been denied. In repeated instances newspapers have been suppressed in the loyal States because they criticised, as constitutionally they might, those fatal errors of policy which have characterized the conduct of public affairs since your advent to power. In violation of the second of them, hundreds, and we believe thousands, of men have been seized and immured in prisons and bastiles, not only without warrant upon probable cause, but without any warrant, and for no other cause than a constitutional exercise of the freedom of speech. In violation of all these guarantees, a distinguished citizen of a peaceful and loyal State has been torn from his home at midnight by a band of soldiers, acting under the order of one of your generals, tried before a military commission, without judge or jury, convicted and sentenced without even the suggestion of any offence known to the Constitution or laws of this country. For all these acts you avow yourself ultimately responsible. In the special case of Mr. Vallandigham, the injustice commenced by your subordinate was consummated by a sentence of exile from his home pronounced by you. That great wrong, more than any other which preceded it, asserts the principles of a supreme despotism.

These repeated and continued invasions of constitutional liberty and private right have occasioned profound anxiety in the public mind. The apprehension and alarm which they are calculated to produce have been greatly enhanced by your attempt to justify them. Because in that attempt you assume to yourself a rightful authority possessed by no constitutional monarch on earth. We accept the declaration that you prefer to exercise this authority with a moderation not hitherto exhibited. But, believing as we do, that your forbearance is not the tenure by which liberty is enjoyed in this country, we propose to challenge the grounds on which your claims of supreme power is based. While yielding to you as a constitutional magistrate the deference to which you are entitled, we cannot accord to you the despotic power you claim, however indulgent and gracious you may promise to be in wielding it.

We have carefully considered the grounds on which your pretensions to more than legal authority are claimed to rest; and if we do not misinterpret the misty and clouded forms of expression in which those pretensions are set forth, your meaning is, that while the rights of the citizen are protected by the Constitution in time of peace, they are suspended or lost in time of war, when invasion or rebellion exists. You do not, like many others in whose minds reason and the love of regulated liberty seem to be overthrown by the excitements of the hour, attempt to base this conclusion upon a supposed military necessity existing outside of and transcending the Constitution, a military necessity behind which the Constitution itself disappears in a total eclipse. We do not find this gigantic and monstrous heresy put forth in your plea for absolute power, but we do find another equally subversive of liberty and law, and quite as certainly tending to the establishment of despotism. You claim to have found, not outside but within the Constitution, a principle or germ of arbitrary power, which in time of war expands at once into an absolute sovereignty, wielded by one man, so that liberty perishes, or is dependent on his will, his discretion, or his caprice. This extraordinary doctrine you claim to derive wholly from that clause of the Constitution which, in case of invasion or rebellion, permits the writ of *habeas corpus* to be suspended. Upon this ground your whole argument is based.

You must permit us to say to you, with all due respect, but with the earnestness demanded by the occasion, that the American people will never acquiesce in this doctrine. In their opinion the guarantees of the Constitution which secure to them freedom of speech and of the press, immunity from arrest for offences unknown to the laws of the land, and the right of trial by jury before the tribunals provided by those laws, instead of military commissions and drum-head courts-martial, are living and vital principles in peace and in war, at all times and under all circumstances. No sophistry or argument can shake this conviction, nor will the people require its confirmation by logical sequences and deductions. It is a conviction deeply interwoven with the instincts, the habits, and the education of our countrymen. The right to form opinions upon public measures and men, and to declare those opinions by speech or writing, with the utmost latitude of expression, the right of personal liberty unless forfeited according to established laws, and for offences previously defined by law, the right when accused of crime to be tried where law is administered, and punishment is pronounced only when the crime is legally ascertained; all these are rights instantly perceived without argument or proof. No refinement of logic can unsettle them in the minds of freemen; no power can annihilate them; and no force at the command of any chief magistrate can compel their surrender.

So far as it is possible for us to understand, from your language, the mental process which has led you to the alarming conclusions indicated by your communication, it is this: The *habeas corpus* is a remedial writ, issued by courts and magistrates to inquire into the cause of any imprisonment or restraint of liberty, on the return of which and upon due examination the person imprisoned is discharged, if the restraint is unlawful, or admitted to bail if he appears to have been lawfully arrested, and is held to answer a criminal accusation. Inasmuch as this process may be suspended in time of war, you seem to think that every remedy for a false and unlawful imprisonment is abrogated; and from this postulate you reach, at a single bound, the conclusion that there is no liberty under the Constitution which does not depend on the gracious indulgence of the Executive only. This great heresy once established, and by this mode of induction there springs at once into existence a brood of crimes or offences undefined by any rule, and hitherto unknown to the laws of this country; and this is followed by indiscriminate arrests, midnight seizures, military commissions, unheard-of modes of trial and punishment, and all the machinery of terror and despotism. Your language does not permit us to doubt as to your essential meaning, for you tell us, that "arrests

are made not so much for what has been done, as for what probably would be done." And, again: "The man who stands by and says nothing when the peril of his government is discussed, cannot be misunderstood. If not hindered (of course by arrest) he is sure to help the enemy, and much more if he talks ambiguously, talks for his country with 'buts' and 'ifs' and 'ands.'" You also tell us that the arrests complained of have not been made "for the treason defined in the Constitution," nor "for any capital or otherwise infamous crimes, nor were the proceedings following in any constitutional or legal sense criminal prosecutions." The very ground, then, of your justification is, that the victims of arbitrary arrest were obedient to every law, were guiltless of any known and defined offence, and therefore were without the protection of the Constitution. The suspension of the writ of *habeas corpus* instead of being intended to prevent the enlargement of arrested criminals until a legal trial and conviction can be had, is designed, according to your doctrine, to subject innocent men to your supreme will and pleasure. Silence itself is punishable, according to this extraordinary theory, and still more so the expression of opinions, however loyal, if attended with criticism upon the policy of the government. We must respectfully refuse our assent to this theory of constitutional law. We think that men may be rightfully silent if they so choose, while clamorous and needy patriots proclaim the praises of those who wield power; and as to the "buts," the "ifs," and the "ands," these are Saxon words and belong to the vocabulary of freemen.

We have already said that the intuition of a free people instantly rejects these dangerous and unheard-of doctrines. It is not our purpose to enter upon an elaborate and extended refutation of them. We submit to you, however, one or two considerations, in the hope that you will review the subject with the earnest attention which its supreme importance demands. We say, then, we are not aware that the writ of *habeas corpus* is now suspended in any of the peaceful and loyal States of the Union. An act of Congress approved by you on the third of March, 1863, authorized the President to suspend it during the present rebellion. That the suspension is a legislative, and not an executive act, has been held in every judicial decision ever made in this country, and we think it cannot be delegated to any other branch of the government. But passing over that consideration, you have not exercised the power which Congress attempted to confer upon you, and the writ is not suspended in any part of the country where the civil laws are in force. Now, inasmuch as your doctrine of the arbitrary arrest and imprisonment of innocent men, in admitted violation of express constitutional guarantees, is wholly derived from a suspension of the *habeas corpus*, the first step to be taken in the ascent to absolute power, ought to be to make it known to the people that the writ is in fact suspended, to the end that they may know what is their condition. You have not yet exercised this power, and therefore, according to your own constitutional thesis, your conclusion falls to the ground. It is one of the provisions of the Constitution, and of the very highest value, that no *ex post facto* law shall be passed, the meaning of which is, that no act which is not against the law when committed can be made criminal by subsequent legislation. But your claim is, that when the writ of *habeas corpus* is suspended, you may lawfully imprison and punish for the crimes of silence, of speech, and opinion. But as these are not offences against the known and established law of the land, the constitutional principle to which we now refer plainly requires that you should, before taking cognizance of such offences, make known the rule of action, in order that the people may be advised in due season, so as not to become liable to its penalties. Let us turn your attention to the most glaring and indefensible of all the assaults upon constitutional liberty, which have marked the history of your administration. No one has ever pretended that the writ of *habeas corpus* was suspended in the State of Ohio, where the arrest of a citizen at midnight, already referred to, was made, and he placed before a court-martial for trial and sentence, upon charges and specifications which admitted his innocence according to the existing laws of this country. Upon your own doctrine, then, can you hesitate to redress that monstrous wrong?

But, sir, we cannot acquiesce in your dogmas that arrests and imprisonment, without warrant or criminal accusation, in their nature lawless and arbitrary, opposed to the very letter of constitutional guarantees, can become in any sense rightful, by reason of a suspension of the writ of *habeas corpus*. We deny that the suspension of a single and peculiar remedy for such wrongs brings into existence new and unknown classes of offences, or new causes for depriving men of their liberty. It is one of the most material purposes of that writ to enlarge upon bail persons who, upon probable cause, are duly and illegally charged with some known crime, and a suspension of the writ was never asked for in England or in this country, except to prevent such enlargement when the supposed offence was against the safety of the government. In the year 1807, at the time of Burr's alleged conspiracy, a bill was passed in the Senate of the United States, suspending the writ of *habeas corpus* for a limited time in all cases where persons were charged on oath with treason, or other high crime or misdemeanor, endangering the peace or safety of the government. But your doctrine undisguisedly is, that a suspension of this writ justifies arrests without warrant, without oath, and even without suspicion of treason or other crime. Your doctrine denies the freedom of speech and of the press. It invades the sacred domain of opinion and discussion. It denounces the "ifs" and the "buts" of the English language, and even the refuge of silence is insecure.

We repeat, a suspense on the writ of *habeas corpus* merely dispenses with a single and peculiar remedy against an unlawful imprisonment; but if that remedy had never existed, the right to liberty would be the same, and every invasion of that right would be condemned not only by the Constitution, but by principles of far greater antiquity than the writ itself. Our common law is not at all indebted to this writ for its action of false imprisonment, and the action would remain to the citizen, if the writ were abolished for ever. Again, every man, when his life or liberty is threatened without the warrant of law, may lawfully resist, and if necessary in self-defence, may take the life of the aggressor. Moreover, the people of this country may demand the impeachment of the President himself for the exercise of arbitrary power. And when all these remedies shall prove inadequate for the protection of free institutions, there remains, in the last resort, the supreme right of revolution. You once announced this right with a latitude of expression which may well be considered dangerous in the present crisis of our national history. You said: "Any people, anywhere, being inclined and having the power, have the right to rise up and shake off the existing government, and form a new one that suits them better. Nor is this right confined to cases where the people of an existing government may choose to exercise it. Any portion of such people that can may revolutionize and make their own of so much of their territory as they inhabit. More than this, a majority of any portion of such people may revolutionize, putting down a minority intermingled with or near about them, who may oppose their movements." (Vol. 19, *Congressional Globe*, p. 94.) Such were your opinions, and you had a constitutional right to declare them. If a citizen now should utter sentiments far less dangerous in their tendency, your nearest military commander would consign him to a dungeon or to the tender mercies of a court-martial, and you would approve the proceeding.

In our deliberate judgment the Constitution is not open to the new interpretation suggested by your communication now before us. We think every part of that instrument is harmonious and consistent. The possible suspension of the writ of *habeas corpus* is consistent with freedom of speech and of the press. The suspension of that remedial process may prevent the enlargement of the accused traitor or conspirator until he shall be legally tried and convicted or acquitted; but in this we find no justification for arrest and imprisonment without warrant, without cause, without the accusation or suspicion of crime. It seems to us, moreover, too plain for argument that the sacred right of trial by jury, and in courts where the law of the land is the rule of decision, is a right which is never dormant, never suspended, in peaceful and loyal communities and States. Will you, Mr. President, maintain, that because the writ of *habeas corpus* may be in suspense, you can substitute soldiers and bayonets for the peaceful operation of the laws, military commissions, and inquisitorial modes of trial for the courts and juries prescribed by the Constitution itself? And if you cannot maintain this, then let us ask where is the justification for the monstrous proceeding in the case of a citizen of Ohio, to which we have called your attention? We know that a recreant judge, whose name has already descended to merited contempt, found the apology on the outside of the supreme and fundamental law of the Constitution. But this is not the foundation on which your superstructure of power is built. We have mentioned the act of the last Congress professing to authorize a suspension of the writ of *habeas corpus.* This act now demands your special attention, because if we are not greatly in error, its terms and plain intention are directly opposed to all the arguments and conclusions of your communication. That act, besides providing that the *habeas corpus* may be suspended, expressly commands that the names of all persons theretofore or thereafter arrested by authority of the President, or his cabinet ministers, being citizens of States in which the administration of the laws has continued unimpaired, shall be returned to the courts of the United States for the districts in which such persons reside, or in which their supposed offences were committed; and such return being made, if the next grand jury attending the courts does not indict the alleged offenders, then the judges are commanded to issue an order for their immediate discharge from imprisonment. Now, we cannot help asking whether you have overlooked this law, which most assuredly you are bound to observe, or whether it be your intention to disregard it? Its meaning certainly cannot be mistaken. By it the national Legislature has said that the President may suspend the accustomed writ of *habeas corpus,* but at the same time it has commanded that all arrests under his authority shall be promptly made known to the courts of justice, and that the accused parties shall be liberated, unless presented by a grand jury according to the Constitution, and tried by a jury in the ancient and accustomed mode. The President may possibly, so far as Congress can give the right, arrest without legal cause or warrant. We certainly deny that Congress can confer this right, because it is forbidden by the higher law of the Constitution. But, waiving that consideration, this statute, by its very terms, promptly removes the proceeding in every case into the courts where the safeguards of liberty are observed, and where the persons detained are to be discharged, unless indicted for criminal offences against the established and ascertained laws of the country.

Upon what foundation, then, permit us to ask, do you rest the pretension that men who are not accused of crime may be seized and imprisoned, or banished at the will and pleasure of the President or any of his subordinates in civil and military positions? Where is the warrant for invading the freedom of speech and of the press? Where the justification for placing the citizen on trial without the presentment of a grand jury and before military commissions? There is no power in this country which can dispense with its laws. The President is as much bound by them as the humblest individual. We pray you to bear in mind, in order that you may duly estimate the feeling of the people on this subject, that for the crime of dispensing with the laws and statutes of Great Britain, our ancestors brought one monarch to the scaffold, and expelled another from his throne.

This power which you have erected in theory is of vast and illimitable proportions. If we may trust you to exercise it mercifully and leniently, your successor, whether immediate or more remote, may wield it with the energy of a Cæsar or Napoleon, and with the will of a despot and a tyrant. It is a power without boundary or limit, because it proceeds upon a total suspension of all the constitutional and legal safeguards which protect the rights of a citizen. It is a power not inaptly described in the language of one of your secretaries. Said Mr. Seward to the British minister in Washington: "I can touch a bell on my right hand and order the arrest of a citizen of Ohio. I can touch the bell again and order the imprisonment of a citizen of New-York, and no power on earth but that of the President can release them. Can the Queen of England, in her dominions, do as much?" This is the very language of a perfect despotism, and we learn from you with profound emotion that this is no idle boast. It is a despotism unlimited in principle, because the same arbitrary and unrestrained will or discretion which can place men under illegal restraint, or banish them, can apply the rack or the thumbscrew, can put to torture or to death. Not thus have the people of this country hitherto understood their Constitution. No argument can commend to their judgment such interpretations of the great charter of their liberties. Quick as the lightning's flash, the intuitive sense of freemen perceives the sophistry and rejects the conclusion.

Some other matters which your Excellency has presented demand our notice.

In justification of your course as to Mr. Vallandigham, you have referred to the arrest of Judge Hall at New-Orleans, by order of General Jackson; but that case differs widely from the case of Mr. Vallandigham. New-Orleans was then, as you truly state, under "martial or military law." This was not so in Ohio, where Mr. Vallandigham was arrested. The administration of the civil law had not been disturbed in that commonwealth. The courts were open, and justice was dispensed with its accustomed promptitude. In the case of Judge Hall, General Jackson in a few days sent him outside the line of his encampments, and set him at liberty; but you have undertaken to banish Mr. Vallandigham from his home. You seem also to have forgotten that General Jackson submitted implicitly to the judgment of the court which imposed the fine upon him; that he promptly paid it; that he enjoined his friends to assent, "as he most freely did, to the decision which had just been pronounced against him."

More than this, you overlook the fact that the then administration (in the language of a well-known author) "mildly but decidedly rebuked the proceedings of General Jackson," and that the President viewed the subject with "surprise and solicitude." Unlike President Madison, you in a case much more unwarranted, approve the proceedings of your subordinate officer, and in addition justify your course by a carefully considered argument in its support.

It is true that after some thirty years, Congress, in consideration of the devoted and patriotic services of General Jackson, refunded the amount of the fine he had paid! But the long delay in doing this, proved how reluctant the American people were to do any thing which could be considered as in any way approving the disregard shown to the majesty of the law, even by one who so eminently enjoyed their confidence and regard.

One subject more, and we shall conclude. You express your regret that our meeting spoke "as Democrats;" and you say that "in this time of national peril you would have preferred to meet us upon a level, one step higher than any party platform." You thus compel us to allude to matters which we should have preferred to pass by. But we cannot omit to notice your criticism, as it casts, at least, an implied reproach upon our motives and our proceedings. We beg to remind you that when the hour of our country's peril had come, when it was evident that a most gigantic effort was to be made to subvert our institutions and to overthrow the government, when it was vitally important that party feelings should be laid aside, and that all should be called upon to unite most cordially and vigorously to maintain the Union; at the time you were sworn into office as President of the United States, when you should have urged your fellow-citizens in the most emphatic manner to overlook all past differences and to rally in defence of their country and its institutions, when you should have enjoined respect for the laws and the Constitution, so clearly disregarded by the South, you chose, for the first time, under like circumstances in the history of our country, to set up a party platform, called the "Chicago platform," as your creed; to advance it beyond the Constitution and to speak disparagingly of that great conservative tribunal of our country, so highly respected by all thinking men who have inquired into our institutions—THE SUPREME COURT OF THE UNITED STATES.

Your administration has been true to the principles you then laid down. Notwithstanding the fact that several hundred thousand Democrats in the loyal States cheerfully responded to the call of their country, filled the ranks of its armies, and by "their strong hands and willing arms" aided to maintain your Excellency and the officers of government in the possession of our national capital; notwithstanding the fact that the great body of the Democrats of the country have in the most patriotic spirit given their best efforts, their treasure, their brothers and their sons, to sustain the government and to put down the rebellion, you, choosing to overlook all this, have made your appointments to civil office, from your cabinet officers and foreign ministers down to the persons of lowest official grade among the tens of thousands engaged in collecting the revenues of the country, exclusively from your political associates.

Under such circumstances, virtually proscribed by your administration, and while most of the leading journals which supported it approved the sentence pronounced against Mr. Vallandigham, it was our true course—our honest course to meet as "Democrats," that neither your Excellency nor the country might mistake our antecedents or our position.

In closing this communication, we desire to reaffirm our determination, and we doubt not that of every one who attended the meeting which adopted the resolutions we have discussed, expressed in one of those resolutions, to devote "all our energies to sustain the cause of the Union."

Permit us, then, in this spirit, to ask your Excellency to reëxamine the grave subjects we have considered, to the end that on your retirement from the high position you occupy, you may leave behind you no doctrines and no further precedents of despotic power to prevent you and your posterity from enjoying that constitutional liberty which is the inheritance of us all, and to the end, also, that history may speak of your administration with indulgence, if it cannot with approval.

We are, sir, with great respect, yours very truly,   JOHN V. L. PRUYN,
              Chairman of Committees.

JAMES KIDD,	GEORGE H. THACHER,
GILBER C. DAVIDSON,	C. W. ARMSTRONG,
J. V. P. QUACKENBUSH,	WILLIAM DOYLE,
WM. A. FASSETT,	FRANKLIN TOWNSEND,
O. M. HUNGERFORD,	WM. APPLETON,
JOHN HOGAN,	B. R. SPILMAN,
HENRY LANSING,	JAMES McKOWN,
S. HAND,	A. H. TREMAIN,
M. K. COHEN,	DANIEL SHAW,
JOHN CUTLER,	W. SIMON,
C. VAN BENTHUYSEN,	A. E. STIMSON,

ISAAC LEDERER.

ALBANY, June 30, 1863.

Doc. 68.

CAPTURE OF THE REDGAUNTLET.

CAPTAIN LUCAS'S LETTER.

June 20, 1863.

DEAR SIR: I regret to write to you that the Redgauntlet was captured by the confederate steamer Florida (otherwise the British steamer Oreto) on the fourteenth of June, when twenty-three days out, in latitude eight degrees thirty minutes north, longitude thirty-four degrees fifty minutes west. We first discovered her at half-past five in the morning, about seven miles off, two points on the lee bow, and standing toward us; escape was impossible on account of the scant wind and our position; they had the British flag set, came up with us under canvas and steam, passed us, then tacked ship, furled sails, fired a shot across our bow, spoke us, and sent a boat on board.

The moment the officer stepped on deck the confederate flag was set and the British flag hauled down. He demanded the ship's papers, examined them, and said that the ship was a prize. I told him our cargo was principally British, and called his attention to the consular certificate. He said that made no difference, the ship was a prize, and I must get my wardrobe ready and go on board the steamer, adding at the same time that the boat was ready, and in five minutes from the time we were boarded all hands were transferred to the steamer. As soon as I was aboard the Florida I went to Captain Maffit and told him that our cargo was principally British, and asked him to bond the ship and let us proceed; but he refused decidedly, saying that "since Lincoln had decided that the bonds of the Ariel were null and void, he had determined to bond no more ships; that he should destroy them all, and if British merchants shipped goods in American ships they must run the risk of losing them."

I asked him what he would do if he should come across an American ship under British colors with a register from a British consul? He said that he should take her as a prize unless she had a British register in due form from a British custom-house. They commenced plundering the Redgauntlet at the moment of capture, and in smooth water plundered her from day to day. On the eighteenth of June, I, with ten others, were put on board the Italian brig Duo Fratelli, from Montevideo for Antwerp. We saw the Florida and Redgauntlet last on Friday, June nineteenth, in latitude fifteen degrees forty minutes north, longitude forty degrees west, both standing to the northward. They were only waiting for a smooth day to finish plundering the Redgauntlet before destroying her. She was pretty well plundered before I left the Florida. The provisions put on board for us were two barrels of beef, thirty tins of crackers, ten pounds of coffee, one half bushel of beans, and twenty pounds of sugar.

We have been aboard twenty-five days, and the prospect is, that we may reach port in ten more, and we are now short of provisions. No water was put aboard, the captain of the brig being told that if he wanted any he must send his casks for it; he was also told that they would compel him to take us whether he was willing or not. They took my chronometer and nautical instruments, books and charts, and a variety of articles, amounting in value to nine hundred dollars. I saved nothing except what was already in my trunks, as I was hurried off so quick. I trust that you had a war risk on the ship, and was not deceived as I was by the idea that a British consul's certificate would prevent the destruction of the ship. As others had been bonded, it was reasonable to suppose that they would bond the Redgauntlet.

We left on board as prisoners nineteen from the Redgauntlet, twenty-three from the B. F. Hoxie, and seventeen from the Southern Cross. They were all handcuffed, and kept on deck day and night, rain or shine. Five of the Redgauntlet's men shipped on board the Florida two days after their capture.

The discipline on board the Florida is bad, but probably as good as can be enforced under the circumstances. The officers, with the exception of the first lieutenant, are an inexperienced set of men; the chief engineer is a very efficient man, and every thing appears to be well conducted in his department. Her armament consists of six sixty-eights and two one hundred and twenties, all rifled and of British manufacture. I think they trust more to running away than they do to fighting with their undisciplined crew. With the exception of being plundered, I was treated with courtesy by Captain Maffit and his officers. All hands except the mate and myself were put in irons, but after the first day were let out at times, until the B. F. Hoxie was captured.

Doc. 69.

PROCLAMATION OF PRESIDENT LINCOLN.

By the President of the United States of America.

A PROCLAMATION.

WHEREAS, the armed insurrectionary combinations now existing in several of the States are threatening to make inroads into the States of Maryland, Western Virginia, Pennsylvania, and Ohio, requiring immediately an additional military force for the service of the United States.

Now, therefore, I, Abraham Lincoln, President of the United States, and Commander of the army and navy thereof, and of the militia of the several States when called into the actual service, do hereby call into the service of the United States one hundred thousand militia from the States following, namely:

From the State of Maryland, ten thousand.

From the State of Pennsylvania, fifty thousand.

From the State of Ohio, thirty thousand.

From the State of West-Virginia, ten thousand.

To be mustered into the service of the United States forthwith, and to serve for the period of six months from the date of such muster into said service, unless sooner discharged, to be mustered in as infantry, artillery, and cavalry, in proportions which will be made known through the War Department, which department will also designate the several places of rendezvous.

These militia are to be organized according to the rules and regulations of the volunteer service, and such orders as may hereafter be issued.

The States aforesaid will be respectively credited under the enrolment act for the militia service rendered under this proclamation.

In testimony whereof, I have hereunto set my hand and caused the seal of the United States to be affixed.

Done at the city of Washington, this fifteenth day of June, in the year of our Lord, 1863, and of the independence of the United States the eighty seventh.   ABRAHAM LINCOLN.

By the President:
WM. H. SEWARD,
              Secretary of State.

Doc. 70.

GOVERNOR TOD'S PROCLAMATION.

COLUMBUS, Monday, June 15.

LEE'S rebel army is advancing in force upon Pennsylvania, Western Virginia, and the eastern portion of our own State. To meet this horde of rebels, the President of the United States has, by proclamation, called out one hundred thousand militia for the period of six months, unless sooner discharged. Of this force, thirty thousand are called from Ohio.

And now, gallant men of Ohio, will you promptly respond to this necessary call without hesitancy? I have assured the President that you would do so. Remember that our own sacred homes are threatened with pillage and destruction, and our wives and daughters with insult.

To the rescue, then, at once, and thus save all that is dear to man. As we have but few, if any, regularly organized companies of volunteer militia, I can but invite and implore you to duty. The few companies which have been recently organized are requested to repair at once, with their entire force, to the camps hereinafter indicated. All others will go forward in squads, and be organized into companies after their arrival in camp, for which purpose efficient officers will be designated.

Railroad transportation has been duly provided, and every provision necessary for the comfort of the men after their arrival in camp. A reasonable allowance will be made to every volunteer for his subsistence when *en route* to the camp; the pay and allowance for clothing will be the same as that of the volunteer service. Should more respond than the Government requires, the surplus men will be returned to their homes free of all expenses to themselves, with the regular pay for the period necessarily absent.

I have now but to designate the camps of rendezvous for the several counties, to wit: Camp Dennison, for all who may respond from the Counties of Hamilton, Butler, Preble, Darke, Miami, Montgomery, Warren, Greene, Clinton, Clermont, Brown, Adams, Highland, Ross, Scioto, and Pike. At Camp Marietta—Lawrence, Gallia, Jackson, Meigs, Vinton, Monroe, Noble, Morgan, and Hocking. At Camp Chase—Franklin, Pickaway, Fairfield, Fayette, Madison, Clark, Perry, Muskingum, Guernsey, Coshocton, Licking, Knox, Delaware, Union, Champaigne, Logan, Shelby, Morrow, Carroll, Harrison, Tuscarawas, Vanwert,

Paulding, Defiance, Williams, Marion, Mercer Auglaize. For Camp Cleveland — Cuyahoga, Medina, Lorain, Ashland, Wayne, Holmes, Richland, Crawford, Wyandotte, Hardin, Hancock, Putnam, Henry, Wood, Lucas, Ottowa, Sandusky, Seneca, Erie, Huron, Lake, Ashtabula, Geauga, Trumbull, Mahoning, Portage, Summit, and Stark. At Camp Pittsburgh, in the city of Pittsburgh— Columbiana, Jefferson, and Belmont. The military commissioners of the several counties are especially requested to exert themselves in securing a prompt response to this call.

The troops will all be organized into regiments and well armed before being ordered into service; and now, fellow-citizens of the State, in the name and behalf of the best government on earth, let me implore you to lay aside all other duties and obligations, and come forward promptly and cheerfully for the preservation of all that is dear to us. You will thus secure the gratitude of your children's children, and the smiles and blessings of heaven.   DAVID TOD,
                                            Governor.

Doc. 71.

PROCLAMATION OF GOVERNOR CURTIN.

IN the name and by the authority of the Commonwealth of Pennsylvania and Andrew G. Curtin, Governor of the said Commonwealth,

A PROCLAMATION.

The State of Pennsylvania is again threatened with invasion, and an army of rebels is approaching our borders. The President of the United States has issued his Proclamation calling upon the State for fifty thousand men. I now appeal to all the citizens of Pennsylvania who love liberty and are mindful of the history and traditions of their revolutionary fathers, and who feel that it is a sacred duty to guard and maintain the free institutions of our country, who hate treason and its abettors, and who are willing to defend their homes and firesides, and do invoke them to rise in their might and rush to the rescue in this hour of imminent peril. The issue is one of preservation or destruction. It involves considerations paramount to all matters of mere expediency and all questions of local interest. All ties, social and political, all ties of a personal and partisan character, sink by comparison into insignificance. It is now to be determined by deeds, and not by words alone, who are for us, and who are against us. That it is the purpose of the enemy to invade our borders with all the strength he can command, is now apparent. Our only defence rests upon the determined action of the citizens of our free commonwealth.

I therefore call on the people of Pennsylvania capable of bearing arms, to enrol themselves in military organizations, and to encourage all others to give aid and assistance to the efforts which will be put forth for the protection of the State and the salvation of our common country.

Doc. 72.

DESTRUCTION OF REBEL SALT WORKS

IN PRINCESS ANN COUNTY, VA.

NORFOLK, VA., June 20, 1863.

ON Tuesday morning Major Murray, of the One Hundred and Forty-eighth New-York, with one hundred men of his regiment, started from Portsmouth upon a raiding expedition into Princess Ann County. As he journeyed along he picked up all the horses and mules that he found upon the route, and mounted his men. He made his way direct to the coast, and when at Land Bridge, which is about fifteen miles below Cape Henry, he destroyed seven rebel salt works. Proceeding five miles below on the coast, he destroyed another. Ten miles further south ten more salt works were levelled to the ground, and over one thousand bushels of salt destroyed. A sloop lying near by, containing four hundred bushels, was destroyed.

After all this had been accomplished, the expedition visited Wales Neck, and there found a large lot of pans and lumber, intended to be used in the construction of other salt works. The lumber was burned, as were some additional five hundred cords of fire-wood that were intended for fuel. The pans were rendered useless. Currituck Sound was then struck, where the expedition halted all night on Wednesday, having marched nearly forty miles a day up to that time.

The Major and his men wended their way slowly back, reaching Portsmouth yesterday afternoon. This morning the horses and mules, numbering about a hundred, were brought across the river, and taken to the Custom-House yard, to be delivered over to the military authorities. Many of the animals were of an indifferent character, but there were a number of valuable beasts among the lot. Several were valued at about five hundred dollars each. These were blooded stock, and belonged to a horse-jockey who has been engaged in buying up horses for the rebel government. The finer horses he disposed of privately to officers in the secesh army. He narrowly escaped being captured.

Two prisoners were brought in. Besides the captures, Major Murray gained some important and interesting information relative to the prisoners who made their escape from the steamer Maple Leaf, last week. After leaving the coast below Cape Henry Light-House, where they landed, they went to the house of a Mr. Borroughs, (late a Major in the rebel army,) at Long Island, which was some twenty miles distant. He entertained them handsomely, and then piloted them through a portion of North-Carolina, after which he reëntered this State, and took them safely to Richmond, where he now is.

This Major Borroughs four months ago resigned his commission in the rebel army, and was paroled by us not to aid the confederates in any way. He broke his parole, and from letters found in his house, it appears that he stated the fact to the rebel Secretary of War, informing him that he desired to be reïnstated, and asking his opinion what would be done with him by us if captured, for breaking his parole. If he were to be caught, our Government would not be slow in determining what punishment he merits.

A letter which was being written by one of his daughters (and yet unfinished) to her cousin, stated that Captain Semmes, son of the famous rebel pirate, said the compliments of the escaped party were due General Dix, and when again seventy-five rebel prisoners are to be transported a guard of three hundred armed Yankees will have to be put over them. This was nothing more than Southern braggadocio, and Captain Semmes may rest easy that no more rebel prisoners will escape from a steamer, no matter what may be their number.

The whole expedition was attended with much success, and reflects favorably upon the skill and courage of the officer in charge, together with his men, not one of whom was lost. Some of the salt was brought in here, and is of a very fair quality. The destruction of so many works will greatly limit the rebels in the use of this luxury, which they were so short of directly after the war broke out.

Princess Ann County was pretty well scoured, and a few more raids like the above will clean it out of every thing which it possesses, that is of any value to the enemy.

Doc. 73.

PROCLAMATION OF GOVERNOR PARKER.

EXECUTIVE CHAMBER, TRENTON, N. J., June 16, 1863.

A PROCLAMATION

JERSEYMEN: The State of Pennsylvania is invaded. A hostile army is now occupying and despoiling the towns of our sister State. She appeals to New-Jersey, through her Governor, to aid in driving back the invading army. Let us respond to the call upon our patriotic State with unprecedented zeal.

I therefore call upon the citizens of this State to meet and organize into companies, and report to the Adjutant-General of the State, as soon as possible to be organized into regiments as the militia of New-Jersey, and press forward to the assistance of Pennsylvania in this emergency. The organization of these troops will be given in General Orders as soon as practicable.

JOEL PARKER.

Attest: S. M. DICKINSON,
Private Secretary.

Doc. 74.

THE FIGHT AT ALDIE, VA.

ALDIE, Wednesday, June 17, 1863.

THE advance of General Gregg's cavalry command reached this place at about two o'clock this afternoon, where two brigades of the enemy, commanded by General Stuart in person, were found in possession. After three hours' hard fighting they were forced to retire. The fight, while it lasted, was one of the sharpest that has occurred during the war, and, as a consequence, the loss of officers and men on both sides is very heavy.

The enemy's pickets were first encountered a little east of the village by companies H and M, of the Second New-York (Harris Light) cavalry, under the command of Lieutenant Dan Whitaker, and were by them driven through the town back to a ridge of hills half a mile to the west, extending across from the Middleburgh and Snicker's Gap road, where the rebel force was in position ready for action. The advance brigade under General Kilpatrick, immediately moved through to the westerly edge of the town. The First Maine, Colonel Douty, was sent off to a point half a mile to the left, and the Fourth New-York, Colonel Cesnola, to the right, to support a section of Andrews's battery placed on a rise of ground north of the Snicker's Gap road. The enemy at this time occupied the hill, as before stated, where they had four guns in position; a line of their skirmishers occupied a fence on the eastern slope, and a long ditch, just in front of which were half a dozen stacks of hay, thus commanding both Middleburgh and Snicker's Gap roads. A stronger position could not well have been selected.

When the exact position of the enemy had been ascertained by drawing their fire, General Kilpatrick rode up to the Second New-York, (Harris Light,) and said then was the time for them to wipe out the reflection cast upon them for their alleged misconduct in the fight of last week, at Brandy Station. He ordered them to charge into the valley and secure the haystacks; the ditch or ravine at the rear of the position had not then been discovered. Companies H and M, accompanied by Lieutenants Whitaker, Raymond, Martinson, Homan, and Stuart, moved off down the Middleburgh road, the fence to the right was quickly thrown down, and, with a dash, this forlorn hope rushed up to the hay-stacks. For the first time their fire was opened from the ditch a little to the rear of the hay-stacks. This was filled with rebel cavalry—many of them armed with rifles. Captain Grintar, with Lieutenants Mattison and Shafer, and company K, dashed up immediately to the support of these companies, F, I, D, and G, went to the right up the Snicker's Gap road a piece, turned to the left, crossed the field, and reached the scene of conflict in time to take an active part.

The contest for twenty minutes at this point was about as spirited a scene as is often witnessed on a battle-field. The Sixth Ohio, Major Steadman, was sent up the road to the left to support the Harris Light, when the whole command, with the Major at its head, dashed into the fight just in time to decide the unequal contest. The rebels were forced to abandon their position, and all who were not killed or captured, fled precipitately up the hill. They made a short stand behind the fence, when a dash from a battalion of the Fourth New-York, called in from its position behind the battery, together with the other regiments already named, drove them pell mell over the hill. The First Maine, at about this time, was called in from the left, and, with the First Massachusetts, stationed on the Snicker's Gap road, to a position held by the second battalion of the Fourth New-York.

The rebels, at this time, charged down the same road, and drove before them a squadron, when General Kilpatrick ordered the First Maine, Colonel Douty, First Massachusetts, Lieutenant-Colonel Curtis, and a battalion of the Fourth New-York, under Colonel Cesnola, to charge up the road. There was a little hesitancy at first, when General Kilpatrick, accompanied by Colonel Douty, of the First Maine, and Captain Costar, of General Pleasanton's staff, went to the front, and called upon the troops to follow. There was no hesitancy then. The Maine boys gave three cheers for General Kilpatrick, and the whole column made a dash up the road in the face of a terrible fire from carbines, rifles, and cannon, sweeping every thing before them. This virtually ended the fight. The rebels, after a little more skirmishing, fell back, and our forces to-night occupy their position.

Colonel Cesnola was under arrest at the commencement of the action, but set such a gallant example to his men, by leading the first charge without his sword, that, upon returning to the road, General Kilpatrick released him from arrest, and placed upon him his own sword. He immediately after participated in the charge with the First Maine, First Massachusetts, and Fourth New-York, and has not been seen since. A sergeant of the regiment asserts that he saw the Colonel fall, and is sure that he was killed, and some of the rebel prisoners confirm this report. But the report of his death is not generally believed. In this charge General Kilpatrick had a horse shot under him, and Colonel Douty, of the First Maine, was killed. When returning from the charge, the body was found by Captain Vaughn, who had it properly cared for. Two shots struck him, probably at about the same time. The First Massachusetts captured the battle-flag of the Fourth Virginia cavalry.

More than one hundred prisoners were captured, members, principally, of the First, Third, Fourth, and Fifth Virginia cavalry. They say they were under the command of General Stuart. Among the prisoners is one colonel, three majors, and a lot of line officers. The major and sixty men, who were stationed behind the haystacks, were nearly all captured. The major considered his position impregnable, not believing that any cavalry would dare make a charge upon the place, swept as the whole field was by three lines of guns.

The meeting of General Gregg's command was entirely unexpected by the rebels. Stuart had arrived thus far on a forced march into Maryland, having marched twenty-five miles this morning, and expecting to be on the road again in the evening. Two regiments had entered the town, and had pressed into their service all the blacksmith tools to be found; and when our advance-guard approached they were busily engaged shoeing horses.

To-day the command of Colonel Duffie passed through Thoroughfare Gap, after a brief fight, and to-night occupies Middleburgh, five miles from Aldie, and in the rear of Stuart's army. Stuart will have to fight to-morrow at a disadvantage, or, what is more probable, sneak off to-night. Captain Allen, of the Fourth New-York cavalry, came through the rebel lines with this news.

During the engagement to-day General Gregg managed affairs in a manner reflecting the highest credit upon his profession. He was fortunate not only in having an efficient staff, but able commanders under him to execute all orders received.

COLONEL DUFFIE'S REPORT.

HEADQUARTERS FIRST RHODE ISLAND CAVALRY, NEAR CENTREVILLE, June 18, 1863.

SIR: I have the honor to report that on the morning of the seventeenth instant I received from the headquarters of the Second brigade, Second cavalry division the following order.

Colonel A. N. Duffie, First Rhode Island Cavalry:

You will proceed with your regiment from Manassas Junction, by way of Thoroughfare Gap, to Middleburgh, there you will camp for the night and communicate with the headquarters of the Second cavalry brigade.

From Middleburgh you will proceed to Union, thence to Snickersville; from Snickersville to Percyville, thence to Wheatland, and passing through Waterford to Nolan's Ferry, where you will join your brigade.

In accordance with this order I left camp on the morning of the seventeenth instant with my regiment, two hundred and eighty strong, and proceeded to Thoroughfare Gap. At this place the enemy was met in force, and being much stronger than my command, I was obliged, in order to pass my regiment on to the Middleburgh road unseen, to make a demonstration on my left flank. This manœuvre was successful; the enemy retired and I was enabled to gain the Middleburgh road. Nevertheless, they followed in my rear, but at a considerable distance, causing me no uneasiness. It was then half-past nine o'clock A.M.

At eleven o'clock, their skirmishers disappeared, and I proceeded unmolested until four o'clock P.M., when, approaching Middleburgh, my skirmishers again met and engaged the enemy, capturing his first picket in the road. I ordered Captain Allen, commanding the advanced squadron, to charge through the town. By this movement the rear-guard of General Stuart was cut off, and then a brisk cavalry fight ensued between his rear and my advance-guard. This engagement lasted half an hour, when the enemy was completely routed, and forced to retreat in the greatest disorder and confusion, scattering in every direction.

Learning that Stuart with two thousand cavalry and four pieces of artillery had left town but half an hour before my arrival, and proceeded

toward Aldie, I ordered that the different roads leading into the town be barricaded and strongly picketed, and instructed the officer commanding the outposts to hold the place at all hazards, hoping that after effecting communication with the brigade, which I supposed to be at Aldie, I should receive reënforcements.

Captain Allen was selected to carry a despatch to General Kilpatrick, and directed to avoid as much as possible all main roads.

The town was held by my command from half-past four to seven o'clock P.M., during which time the skirmishers had been constantly engaged. At seven, I learned that the enemy was approaching in force from Union, Aldie, and Upperville. Determined to hold the place, if possible, I dismounted one half of the regiment, placing them behind stone walls and the barricades. The enemy surrounded the town and stormed the barricades, but were gallantly repulsed by my men with great slaughter. They did not desist, but, confident of success, again advanced to the attack, and made three successive charges. I was compelled to retire on the road by which I came, that being the only one open to retreat, and with all that was left of my command I crossed Little River, north-east of Middleburgh, and bivouacked for the night, establishing strong pickets on the river.

At ten P.M., having heard nothing from the despatch sent to General Kilpatrick at Aldie, I sent twenty men under an officer to carry a second despatch. I have since learned that Captain Allen succeeded in making his way through the enemy's lines to Aldie. The party bearing the second despatch was probably captured.

At half-past three o'clock the next morning, eighteenth instant, I was informed by scouts, whom I had previously sent out, that the roads in every direction were full of the enemy's cavalry, and that the road to Aldie was held by a brigade with four pieces of artillery. Under these circumstances I abandoned the project of going to Union, but made up my mind not to surrender in any event. I directed the head of my column on the road to Aldie, when an engagement commenced at once, the enemy opening on both flanks with heavy volleys, yelling to us to surrender. I at once directed Captain Bixby, the officer commanding the advance-guard, to charge any force in his front, and follow the Aldie road to that point where it connects with the road to White Plains.

This order was executed most admirably. Captain Bixby's horse was shot and he himself wounded. We were then in an extremely hazardous position, the enemy being in front, rear and on both flanks, and were intermixed with us for more than an hour, till we reached the road leading to Hopeville Gap.

I must freely praise the gallant conduct of the brave officers and men who were fighting side by side with overwhelming numbers of the enemy with the most determined valor, preferring rather to die than to surrender.

I returned here exhausted at half-past one P.M.

to-day with the gallant debris of my much-loved regiment—four officers and twenty-seven men.

My colors did not fall into the hands of the enemy, but were destroyed when they could not be saved, the color-bearer being captured.

I can praise no one more than another, but I desire to call your attention to the gallant conduct of all the officers and men of the First Rhode Island cavalry.

I am, sir, very respectfully, your obedient servant,

A. N. DUFFIE,
Colonel Cavalry Regiment.

CAPTAIN ALLEN'S REPORT.

CAMP FIRST RHODE ISLAND CAVALRY,
ALEXANDRIA, VA., June 22, 1863.

Colonel A. N. Duffie:

SIR : I have the honor to report that about five o'clock P.M., on the evening of the seventeenth instant, I was sent from Middleburgh, where the regiment was then engaged with the enemy, to carry a despatch to General Kilpatrick at Aldie, accompanied by two men. I first attempted to proceed by the main road, but was halted and fired upon by a body of the enemy, who said they were the Fourth Virginia cavalry. I then returned toward Middleburgh, and leaving the road, attempted to make my way across the the country. I found the fields and woods in every direction full of bodies of the enemy ; by exercising the greatest care I succeeded in making my way through them to Little River; here I encountered five of the enemy, and forced them to give me passage. Following the river down, I struck the main road about one mile from Aldie, and by inquiry, I learned that our pickets were on that road. I reached Aldie and delivered my despatch to General Kilpatrick at nine P.M.

General Kilpatrick informed me that his brigade was so worn out that *he* could not send any reënforcements to Middleburgh, but that he would report the situation of our regiment to General Gregg. Returning, he said that General Gregg had gone to state the facts to General Pleasanton, and directed me to remain at Aldie until he heard from General Pleasanton. I remained, but received no further orders.

Respectfully submitted. FRANK ALLEN,
Captain First Rhode Island Cavalry.

A NATIONAL ACCOUNT.

The fight at Aldie, on Wednesday, which was noticed briefly yesterday, was far more desperate than was at first supposed here. The cavalry engaged on our side were the Second New-York, Sixth Ohio, First Massachusetts, and Fourth New-York, under command of Colonel Kilpatrick, and the First Maine, of Colonel J. J. Gregg's brigade ; and a portion of General Fitz-Hugh Lee's brigade, under command of Colonel Rousseau, on the part of the confederates. Colonel Kilpatrick's command was leading the advance of our cavalry corps, moving from Fairfax Court-House to Aldie.

The rebel force (cavalry and mounted infantry) had come from the direction of Snicker's Gap, arriving at Aldie some two hours before our force reached that point ; and the rebels getting warn-

ing of the approach of Kilpatrick, posted themselves in commanding positions, and with their mounted sharp-shooters placed behind stone walls ready to pour a murderous fire upon our advancing column. Kilpatrick charged upon the rebel advance, and drove them furiously through the town, the rebels making a stand on the other side, where was posted a rebel battery of four guns on the road to Ashby's Gap ; and the rebel cavalry posted themselves along the wooded hills and stone walls toward Snicker's Gap.

Here desperate charges were made by our own and the rebel cavalry alternately, and after a fight of over three hours, and with varying success, the rebel force seemed to be gaining some advantage, when the First Maine regiment, Colonel C. S. Douty, which had been detached from Colonel J. J. Gregg's brigade for that purpose, came up to the contest, and by a desperate charge against the rebel battery of four guns and a regiment of mounted Mississippi infantry, the tide was turned in our favor, and the rebels were routed with loss—the horses galloping over the field riderless, and all of the foe that had not been killed being captured.

But the victory was dearly bought by the loss of the gallant Colonel Douty, who fell mortally wounded. The fight lasted four hours, and some officers who participated and who have been in other fights say it was most desperate, such cutting and slashing with sabres not having occurred before in our encounters with rebel cavalry. As soon as the rebels wavered they were driven in the direction of Ashby's Gap, and as they were going toward the latter, the First Rhode Island cavalry, Colonel Duffie, which had advanced through Thoroughfare Gap, intercepted the retreating rebels at Middleburgh, five miles from Aldie, and made a charge upon their rear, compelling the rebels to move yet faster toward Ashby's Gap, the Rhode Island boys following them up.

Colonel Kilpatrick heard from the latter that they were still fighting at seven o'clock P.M., but no subsequent information as to the result of the contest at that point has yet been received.

The force thus engaged was the advance of the rebel General Stuart's cavalry, who, it is alleged by prisoners, was advancing thus through Aldie with the expectation of making a new raid.

Our loss is estimated at two hundred in killed, wounded, and missing. We captured over one hundred prisoners and a battle-flag belonging to the Fifth Virginia cavalry.

Among the killed, besides Colonel Douty, were Captain G. J. Summatt, of the First Maine, and Lieutenants D. Whittaker and Martinson, of the Second New-York. The remains of the above were brought to this city in charge of Lieutenant E. W. Whittaker, (brother of Lieutenant W., killed,) aid to Colonel Kilpatrick, and Adjutant A. P. Russell, of the First Maine.

The bodies will be embalmed by Drs. Brown and Alexander, preparatory to being conveyed to their late homes in Maine and Connecticut.

The fact that the fight was so desperate is explained by the importance of the position to be gained, that is, the commanding Gap at Aldie in the Bull Run and Catoctin ridge.

General Pleasanton was pushing on at last accounts in the direction of Snicker's Gap.

The names of the prisoners we captured are as follows: Captain R. P. Boston, Fifth Virginia cavalry; Major Carrington, Third Virginia; Captain F. R. Winser, after a desperate resistance; Captain L. B. White, Fifth Virginia, wounded; Captain Jones, Third Virginia; Lieutenant Boston, Fifth Virginia; Lieutenant Turnell, Fifth Virginia; Lieutenant Douglass, Fifth Virginia, and seventy-seven privates, principally from the Third and Fifth Virginia cavalry.

Lieutenant Howard and Lieutenant Bagsdale, of the Fifth Virginia, were left on the field, supposed to be mortally wounded. A number of the privates of the rebels are known to be killed and wounded.

Doc. 75.
RE-ADMISSION OF LOUISIANA.
LETTER FROM PRESIDENT LINCOLN.

EXECUTIVE MANSION, WASHINGTON, June 19, 1863.

Messrs. E. E. Mathiot, Bradish Johnston, and Thomas Cottman:

GENTLEMEN: Your letter, which follows, has been received and considered:

To his Excellency Abraham Lincoln, President of the United States:

The undersigned, a committee appointed by the planters of the State of Louisiana, respectfully represent that they have been delegated to seek of the General Government a full recognition of all the rights of the State as they existed previous to the passage of an act of secession, upon the principle of the existence of the State Constitution unimpaired, and no legal act having transpired that could in any way deprive them of the advantages conferred by the Constitution.

Under this Constitution the State wishes to return to its full allegiance, in the enjoyment of all rights and privileges exercised by the other States under the Federal Constitution. With the view of accomplishing the desired object, we further request that your Excellency will, as Commander-in-Chief of the army of the United States, direct the Military Governor of Louisiana to order an election, in conformity with the Constitution and laws of the State, on the first Monday of November next, for all State and Federal officers.

With high consideration and respect, we have the honor to subscribe ourselves your obedient servants, E. E. MATHIOT,
BRADISH JOHNSTON,
THOMAS COTTMAN.

Since receiving the letter reliable information has reached me that a respectable portion of the Louisiana people desire to amend their State Constitution, and contemplate holding a Convention for that object. This fact alone, as it seems to me, is a sufficient reason why the general Government should not give the committee the authority you seek, to act under the existing State Constitution. I may add, that while I do not perceive how such a committal could facilitate our military operations in Louisiana, I really apprehend it might be so used as to embarrass them.

As to an election to be held next November, there is abundant time without any order or proclamation from me just now. The people of Louisiana shall not lack an opportunity for a fair election for both Federal and State officers by want of any thing within my power to give them.

Your obedient servant, A. LINCOLN.

Doc. 76.
GOVERNOR BRADFORD'S APPEAL.

BALTIMORE, MD., June 21, 1863.

To the People of the State and City:

THE proclamation which I issued on the seventeenth instant, calling upon you to furnish six months' volunteers for the quota of militia required of us by the Government has not met with that prompt and practical response which I thought I had the right to expect. Whilst some, with a cheerful alacrity worthy of all praise, have offered themselves for the service, the number, I regret to say, has fallen far short of what is required.

Some, assuming to be ready for any emergency which the defence of the State may require, hesitate to enlist in Government service lest they may be ordered elsewhere; but the very proclamation of the President which makes this call upon us assumes as the true reason for it the threatened invasion of our State, and would seem to be an implied assurance that such force is only required within the borders. But suppose it were otherwise, and that it could be made available elsewhere, are we willing so to qualify and cramp the service that may be asked of us as to say that it shall be rendered within the confines of our State, but nowhere else? It may well be that the very best stand-points for State defences are to be found on the other side of the Potomac.

Who are the men here in our midst to-day ready to meet the approaching foe? They come from the North, and the East, and the West. Volunteers representing six States now man the works upon Maryland Heights, and the citizens of the State, sheltered as they are under the very shadow of the capital, should be the last in the Union to hesitate over any service of a national character that may be required of them.

The Commanding General authorizes me to say that whilst he has accepted for special duty in the neighborhood of the barricades the proffered service of some of our patriotic citizens, such service will be no obstacle to the enlistment of those who would volunteer for six months, and who, while in discharge of this special duty, will be still accepted and mustered into the six months' service.

Some, as I am told, decline to volunteer, preferring a draft, because, as they say, only the loyal will volunteer, while the draft compels the rebel sympathizer to discharge his just share of the public duty. The duty to which we are now summoned is emphatically a patriotic one — one which we should be unwilling to share with any whose whole heart is not devoted to his country. Do you expect a heart service of this kind from secessionists? Are you willing to leave the metropolis of the State undefended because they may fold their arms and offer no assistance? God forbid.

The patriots of the Revolution recognized no such reasoning. No whig failed to respond in those days because the tories stood aloof; but, when struggling for the liberties which it is now your duty defend, they mustered to a man, and sought no aid from the traitors in their midst, and left the very name of tory a term of contumely and scorn for all time to come.

Let me, then, once more appeal to you, my fellow-citizens, and remind you that the foot of the invader is once more upon the soil of Maryland. In other days her citizens did not require to be twice told of such an event. And you, I trust, will show the world that the blood of the old defenders still courses through your veins. Come, then, at once. Come with a will, and come in crowds; and, as our fathers did fifty years ago, meet the invader before his tread shall desecrate the threshold of our homes.

The General commanding this department informs me that, beside the work upon the intrenchments now being done by a force of colored laborers impressed for the purpose, he will have occasion to-morrow (Monday) morning for one or two thousand patriotic citizens to be employed in different fortifications at other points. To wield a pick or a spade for such a purpose is fully as honorable, and just now quite as essential, as to shoulder a musket or unsheathe a sword.

All citizens who will volunteer for this work are invited to present themselves at Monument Square, in front of the General's headquarters, at nine o'clock Monday morning.

A. W. BRADFORD.

Doc. 77

CAVALRY FIGHT NEAR ALDIE, VA.

GENERAL PLEASANTON'S DESPATCH.

HEADQUARTERS CAVALRY CORPS,
CAMP NEAR UPPERVILLE, 5.30 P.M., June 21, 1863.

Brigadier-General S. Williams:

GENERAL: I moved with my command this morning to Middleburgh and attacked the cavalry force of the rebels under Stuart, and steadily drove him all day, inflicting a heavy loss at every step.

We took two pieces of artillery, one being a Blakely gun, together with three caissons, beside blowing one up. We also captured upward of sixty prisoners, and more are coming in, including a lieutenant-colonel, major, and five other officers, beside a wounded colonel, and a large number of wounded rebels left in the town of Upperville.

They left their dead and wounded upon the field. Of the former I saw upward of twenty. We also took a large number of carbines, pistols, and sabres. In fact, it was a most disastrous day to the rebel cavalry.

Our loss has been very small both in men and horses. I never saw the troops behave better, or under more difficult circumstances. Very heavy charges were made, and the sabre was used freely, but always with great advantage to us.   A. PLEASANTON,
                              Brigadier-General.

E. A. PAUL'S NARRATIVE.

UPPERVILLE, VA., Sunday, June 21—5 P.M.

This has been truly a glorious day for that portion of the army commanded by General Pleasanton.

On Saturday but little advance was made, our forces in front bivouacking at night in a piece of woods but a short distance west of Middleburgh. At eight o'clock this morning active hostilities were resumed, and there has been a running fight up to several miles west of this town. The contest, as well as the result, must be particularly gratifying to the commanding general, for he has met the famous General Stuart in pitched combat, half a dozen times, and in all cases defeated him, and caused his forces to fall back precipitately.

Stuart, all along the road between Paris and Middleburgh, told the inhabitants that he would certainly drive our forces back to Manassas, and there whip them. *Per contra*, he has himself been driven back to the Blue Ridge, and from the stone where I am seated penning these lines, I can see the smoke of his guns fired in the defence of Ashby's Gap. So hard pressed was he, and so fearful that his defeat might result in an entire rout, that at Common or Hatch's Run, three miles west of Middleburgh, he sent an express messenger, ordering up a brigade of infantry to meet him at Rector's Cross-Roads. The wished-for assistance came, but it availed him little. Our men nerved themselves to the task, and drove every thing before them—the enemy, in their haste, throwing away their accoutrements, provisions, clothing, wagons, cannon, and camp equipage. Three cannon have been captured, a number of horses, and more than one hundred prisoners, representing nearly every State in the Confederacy.

Moving out of Middleburgh this morning, the troops under General Buford took a road to the right, leading to Unionville, while General Gregg moved up the main road direct toward Ashby's Gap, passing through Rector's Cross-Roads. Colonel Vincent, with the Eighty-third Pennsylvania, Sixteenth Michigan, Forty-fourth New-York, and Twentieth Maine infantry, also moved up this road in advance, two companies in advance of each regiment deployed as skirmishers, while other companies acted as supports. Fuller's regular battery was placed in the first favorable position west of the town, and fired several shots before receiving any response. The enemy finally opened fire with two guns, and a brisk cannonading was kept up for half an hour, when the caisson of one of the enemy's guns was exploded by a shell thrown from a section of Fuller's battery, commanded by Lieutenant Kelly, and another shell broke the limber of another piece. Both guns were captured by the cavalry. The rebels at another point abandoned a brass howitzer and caisson.

They fell back from one position to another until they reached their present one on the mountain. The strongest resistance was made at Comell's River, Goose Creek, and just above the Upperville bridge, over Goose Creek. The enemy had made every arrangement to destroy the bridge, but General Kilpatrick, whose brigade was in the advance—in fact, it was during the whole day, pursuing the retreating forces—ordering a charge to be made as he reached the bridge, completely frustrated the design. Captain Coons, of the Harris Light cavalry, led this charge, while the Fourth New-York advanced as dismounted carbineers, enfilading the bridge.

Arriving at Upperville, two squadrons of the First Maine were ordered to charge through the town, which they did in the most gallant manner. The rest of the First Maine and the Fourth New-York acted as supports. Just beyond the town considerable force of the enemy was massed. The First Maine, Sixth Ohio, Tenth New-York, Second New-York, and Fourth Pennsylvania charged upon them furiously. The resistance was greater here than at any other point. Two of our regiments were in the road, and one on each side. They charged and were repulsed; the enemy charged and were likewise repulsed. Several charges were made with like results, untill the two forces became jammed in together, and a regular hand-to-hand conflict took place, lasting more than twenty minutes. In the first charge the enemy placed sharp-shooters along the stone walls at the side of the road, and our troops suffered from their fire. General Kilpatrick also arranged a similar reception for the enemy, and thus the two forces swayed to and fro under a galling cross-fire. The officers and men on both sides fought like fiends, and in the excitement many of the enemy were killed who might have been taken prisoners. General Kilpatrick nearly lost his own life in attempting to save the life of the colonel of a North-Carolina regiment. Finally the enemy yielded, and fell back, hotly pursued by General Kilpatrick's bloody brigade, until the concentrated fire from a battery warned General Gregg that it was time to withdraw his men. The brigade of regulars which had been sent up as a support, much to the amusement of all about, wheeled and hurried out of range. The Harris Light and First Maine marched out of range as slowly and deliberately as if going upon parade. No troops in the world ever stood such a terrible fire more unflinchingly.

From Rector's Cross-Roads to Upperville was almost a rout. The enemy turned at bay near Upperville. The Fourth New-York charged, with General Kilpatrick at their head, and, breaking, retired, leaving General Kilpatrick a prisoner. The Fourth, however, promply rallied, charged again, and the General was rescued. The troops, with the single exception noted, all behaved well, as did most of the officers. General Kilpatrick, commanding the centre, was always in the right place, and inspiring the men under him by his dashing example. He led several charges in person, the most dashing of all being the onset west of Upperville. Colonel Gregg, commanding the left, discharged his duties promptly and like a brave man. General Gregg, commanding this division, and General Pleasanton, were near the front all day, carefully watching every movement. The former had a horse killed under him by a round shot. The conduct of Colonel Vincent, commanding the infantry, is everywhere spoken of in the highest terms. Captain Armstrong and Lieutenant Estes, of General Kilpatrick's staff, on two occasions, after delivering an order, led a column against the enemy under a most terrific fire, and excited the admiration of all for their gallant conduct and excellent example.

While the centre and left were engaged with General Stuart in person, General Buford, with varying success, was fighting "Alphabet" Lee on the right. At this hour he has the enemy in front forced back to the mountains.

The rebels along the line of march are completely chopfallen at the ill success of their favorite General Stuart, and they predict that he will yet pay us off.

Strange as it may appear, while our loss is comparatively trifling, that of the enemy is very heavy. We have already as many dead rebels in our possession as our entire loss in killed. Besides, it is known that they carried off several ambulances loaded with their own dead. Our loss is about ten killed and one hundred wounded. Among the enemy's killed is Colonel Wilcox, of the Ninth Virginia cavalry. The colonel of a South-Carolina regiment is a prisoner, and the colonel of the Fifty-ninth North-Carolina is seriously wounded and a prisoner.

E. A. PAUL.

INDIANAPOLIS JOURNAL ACCOUNT.

ALDIE, June 23, 1863.

EDITOR JOURNAL: Pleasanton's cavalry has won new laurels, additional lustre attaches to our name, and we are far removed from that derisive contempt in which our arm of the service has been held for many months. On the morning of the twenty-first, we attacked Stuart's force at Middleburgh, and, after an hour's stubborn resistance, they were in motion toward Ashby's Gap, no doubt impressed with the idea that there was more safety than gallantry in such a movement. General Buford, commanding the First division, followed up closely on the right, and Gregg, with his Second division, was close at their heels on the left. It was a running fight, and continued from "early morn till dewy eve." Eight miles, the distance from Middleburgh to Ashby's Gap, were passed over by the contending forces, the rebels in their retreat posting batteries on every commanding hill by which our progress was stayed until the superiority of our guns or a flank charge compelled a further retrograde on the part of the enemy. General Kilpatrick led many brilliant charges on the left; but on the right of Upperville, Gamble's brigade, comprising the Eighth and Twelfth Illinois and Third Indiana, made one charge and repulsed three, that confirmed the very few incredulous in the belief of the genuine pluck of this brigade. They drove three rebel brigades to the rear of the town; and when the rebels, stung with chagrin at the idea of being compelled to fall back before one third their number, re-charged furiously, our line continued unbroken, and the enemy recoiled in dismay before a stormy greeting of cold iron. Here the most desperate fighting and bloody work of the day occurred. Some half-dozen charges were made by our forces and equally as many by the rebels for the possession of the place, but Stuart was forced to sullenly retire to his stronghold, the Gap, as night closed upon the bloody scene. Pickets were thereupon established along our entire line, while the main force retired to the vicinity of Middleburgh and passed the night.

General Pleasanton's "official report" correctly says it was a disastrous day for the rebel cavalry. Our loss was insignificant in comparison with the enemy's. Some of their dead were left on the field, while we captured most of their wounded, besides capturing and recapturing fifty Federals and rebels; the wounded inmates of a hospital at Upperville. The latter were taken to Upperville after the fight of the sixteenth at this place. None of our captured had been paroled.

Our loss is not yet definitely ascertained, but will not amount to over seventy-five killed and wounded.

The casualties of the Third cavalry are as follows: Orderly Sergeant Charles Johnson, company C, shot through right knee, making amputation necessary; Sergeant Peters, company C, wounded in the shoulder severely; private Balser Noah, in the face, slightly; Sergeant W. H. Hyden, company F, in the foot, slightly. The Third Illinois lost four killed and fifteen wounded. The Twelfth Illinois lost twelve wounded.

The loss in rebel officers at this fight was much more serious than usual. Several captains, lieutenants, and majors, with Colonel Meriwether Lewis, of the Ninth Virginia cavalry, were left on the field; the latter mortally wounded, was found in a ravine by members of the Third cavalry, and conveyed to a neighboring farm, where in his dying agony he groaned out his remorse at the folly of his cause. He was a man of more than ordinary intelligence. His death-struggle at sunset brought tears to the eyes of those beholding the scene. It was then he uttered the honest sentiments of his heart—his supreme love for the Union over the cause of secession.

Yesterday our cavalry returned to Aldie, and moved out on the Leesburgh pike to Dover, where they are now encamped with the expectation of resting and recruiting the men and horses for at least a day or two. But alas! the uncertainty in the tide of events decreed otherwise. Two hours of repose was all they had until the rebels were reported driving in our pickets. Throughout the corps bugles sounded the "saddle-call," and the Second brigade, First division, Colonel Diven, was sent forward to find out the intentions of the advancing foe. Skirmishing on the Leesburgh and Middleburgh pike ensued, and two or three charges by squadrons were made by our men and the rebels, respectively.

The rebels proved not to be in force, but as their main body was momentarily expected to appear in sight, we were kept in constant readiness to resist any attack, and consequently little rest was obtained yesterday by the wearied cavalrymen.

Last night Pleasanton's artillery was posted to command all the approaches to Aldie, and as the rebels appeared on our front this morning, the cavalry was again drawn out in line of battle, where it remains at this writing.

Away off on the hills and down the ravines we now and then see a quick flash and a column of blue smoke curling upward, telling us that our skirmishers are vigilant and doing their duty.

Half a dozen different bands are discoursing sweet music along the lines this evening, and I verily believe, should Stuart with all his cavalry appear in solid column on the front, our fellows would go down on them with a rush that could forebode nothing but destruction to the rebels.

Our men are in the best of spirits. The victories of the past week have convinced the men of their ability to accomplish great and daring deeds, and established mutual confidence between men and officers. All have faith in the present management of the cavalry.

Another fight may occur at any time in this vicinity, but, should such be the case, the rebels will be the attacking party, for we are disposed to rest.

The disposition of Hooker's infantry is a little different from what it was three days ago, while the rebels are doubtless sending a considerable force through Thoroughfare Gap. Should Lee attempt to reach the Potomac by way of Leesburgh, he will be seriously opposed, for, at an hour's notice, Hooker can throw a formidable force of veterans on his front.

The weather continues most favorable for all our operations, the atmosphere of these mountains being a comfortable medium between heat and cold.

Fairfax Station is our base of supplies, and the many fine farms in this vicinity afford luxurious grazing for our horses.

Loudon County has been reported all right for the Union, but the loyal element is not found here, and I deem it just that we should appropriate what we cannot well do without.

John Hood, Commissioner for the District Court of Eastern Virginia, amidst persecution

has-stood faithfully by the Union, and he is the only loyal man now known in all this vicinity. He welcomed the arrival of our army, and will mourn its departure should such a thing occur.
PHI.

Doc. 78.
THE INVASION OF MARYLAND.
ORDERS OF GENERAL LEE.
HEADQUARTERS ARMY NORTHERN VIRGINIA, June 21, 1863.

WHILE in the enemy's country the following regulations for procuring supplies will be strictly observed, and any violation of them promptly and rigorously punished:

1. No private property shall be injured or destroyed by any person belonging to or connected with the army, or taken, except by the officers hereinafter designated.

2. The chiefs of the commissary, quartermaster, ordnance, and medical departments of the army will make requisitions upon the local authorities or inhabitants for the necessary supplies for their respective departments, designating the places and times of delivery. All persons complying with such requisitions shall be paid the market price for the articles furnished, if they so desire; and the officer making such payments shall take duplicate receipts for the same, specifying the name of the person paid, and the quantity, kind, and price of the property; one of which receipts shall be at once forwarded to the chief of the department to which such officer is attached.

3. Should the authorities or inhabitants neglect or refuse to comply to such requisitions, the supplies required will be taken from the nearest inhabitants so refusing, by the order and under the directions of the respective chiefs of the departments named.

4. When any command is detached from the main body the chiefs of the several departments of such command will procure supplies for the same, and such other stores as they may be ordered to provide, in the manner and subject to the provisions herein prescribed, reporting their action to the heads of their respective departments, to which they will forward duplicates of all vouchers given or received.

5. All persons who shall decline to receive payment for property furnished on requisitions, and all from whom it shall be necessary to take stores or supplies, shall be furnished by the officer receiving or taking the same with a receipt specifying the kind and quantity of the property received or taken, as the case may be, the name of the person from whom it was received or taken, the command for the use of which it was intended, and the market price. A duplicate of said receipt shall be at once forwarded to the chief of the department to which the officer by whom it is executed is attached.

6. If any person shall remove or conceal property necessary for the use of the army, or attempt to do so, the officers hereinbefore mentioned will cause such property and all other property belonging to such person that may be required by the army, to be seized, and the officer seizing the same will forthwith report to the chief of this department the kind, quantity, and market price of the property so seized, and the name of the owner. By command of
General R. E. LEE.
R. H. CHILTON, A. A. and I. G.
Lieutenant-General R. S. EWELL,
Commanding Second Army Corps.

Doc. 79
INVASION OF PENNSYLVANIA.
PROCLAMATION OF GOVERNOR CURTIN.

IN the name and by the authority of the Commonwealth of Pennsylvania, Andrew Curtin, Governor of said Commonwealth.

A PROCLAMATION.

Pennsylvanians: The enemy is advancing in force into Pennsylvania. He has a strong column within twenty-three miles of Harrisburgh, and other columns are moving by Fulton and Adams counties, and it can no longer be doubted that a formidable invasion of our State is in actual progress. The calls already made for volunteer militia have not been met as fully as the crisis requires. I therefore now issue this my proclamation, calling for sixty thousand men to come promptly forward to defend the State. They will be mustered into the service of the State for a period of ninety days, but will be required to serve only so much of the period of muster as the safety of our people and honor of our State may require. They will rendezvous at points to be designated in the general order to be issued this day by the Adjutant-General of Pennsylvania, which order will also set forth the details of the arrangements for organization, clothing, subsistence, equipments, and supplies.

I will not insult you by inflammatory appeals. A people who want the heart to defend their soil, their families, and their firesides, are not worthy to be accounted men. Heed not the councils of evil-disposed persons, if such there be in your midst. Show yourselves what you are—a free, loyal, spirited, brave, vigorous race. Do not undergo the disgrace of leaving your defence mainly to the citizens of other States. In defending the soil of Pennsylvania we are contributing to the support of our national government, and vindicating our fidelity to the national cause. Pennsylvania has always heretofore responded promptly to all the calls made by the Federal Government, and I appeal to you now not to be unmindful that the foe that strikes at our State strikes through our desolation at the life of the republic, and our people are plundered and driven from their homes solely because of their loyalty and fidelity to our free institutions.

People of Pennsylvania! I owe to you all my faculties, my labors, my life. You owe to your country your prompt and zealous services and efforts. The time has now come when we must all stand or fall together in defence of our State and in support of our government. Let us so discharge our duty that posterity shall not blush for us. Come heartily and cheerfully to the rescue of our noble Commonwealth. Maintain now your honor and freedom!

Given under my hand and the great seal of the State, at Harrisburgh, this twenty-sixth day of June, in the year of our Lord one thousand eight hundred and sixty-three, and of the Commonwealth the eighty-seventh.

By the Governor.　　　　　A. G. CURTIN.

ELI SLIFER,
　　Secretary of the Commonwealth.

Doc. 80.

THE OPERATIONS IN LOUISIANA.

REAR-ADMIRAL FARRAGUT'S REPORTS.

FLAG-SHIP PENSACOLA,
NEW-ORLEANS, June 29, 1863.

SIR: I have to inform the Department that while I was at Port Hudson, I received a despatch stating that the rebels were in force on the west bank of the river threatening Plaquemine and Donaldsonville. I started immediately for the first-named place, but on my arrival at Baton Rouge, found a despatch from Lieutenant Commander Weaver, to the effect that the rebels, about one hundred and fifty Texans, had made a raid into Plaquemine, some three hours previous to his arrival, and had burnt two steamers that were lying there. Lieutenant Commander Weaver shelled the place, driving the enemy out of the town, and followed them down the river to Donaldsonville, which place he reached in advance of them; by dark, I was also there and found that the Kineo had also been sent up by Commander Morris. The enemy finding us in such strong force of gunboats gave out that they would not attack Donaldsonville, but would go by railroad to Brashear City. I therefore ordered the Winona, Lieutenant Commanding Weaver, to cruise up and down the river, and he seeing the enemy on two occasions, shelled them.

As I had much to attend to in New-Orleans, I dropped down, placing the gunboats to the best advantage, above and below; Lieutenant Commander Walters volunteered to assist the volunteer officer commanding the fort, in the drilling of his men at great guns. I paid them a visit and gave them my advice in case of an attack, which I looked for sooner or later. I left Commander Woolsey in the Princess Royal, in command at Donaldsonville, ordered the Winona to Plaquemine and stationed the Kineo at a place below where the railroad ran near the river, distance about twenty-three miles from New-Orleans. On the seventeenth instant, the enemy reached the Lafourche, crossing and attacking our pickets, who repulsed them, causing them a heavy loss. On the eighteenth they had a second fight and were again repulsed.

On the twenty-sixth, the enemy, under Generals Green and Mouton, attacked and captured Brashear City. Our force there was very small. I had only a small steamer, mounting two twelve-pound howitzers, which I purchased as a tug, but I regret to say that her commander is not represented as having been any more vigilant than the rest and backed down the bay. Mr. Ryder says, however, that he could not fire into the enemy without firing into our own people, so he withdrew and retired to New-Orleans, leaving Brashear City in possession of the enemy.

On the twenty-seventh, Commander Woolsey informed me by telegraph, and Brigadier-General Emory personally, that General Green, of Texas, had notified the women and children to leave Donaldsonville, as he intended to make an attack. I immediately ordered the Kineo up to the assistance of the Princess Royal, and Lieutenant Commander Weaver, in the Winona, being on the alert, was also at Donaldsonville in time to take part in the repulsing of the enemy. I inclose herewith Commander Woolsey's report of the affair.

At twenty minutes past one, A.M., of the twenty-eighth, the enemy made the attack, and their storming party got into the fort; but the gunboats opened a flanking fire above and below the fort, hurling destruction into the rebel ranks and driving back the supporting party, so that they broke and fled, and the twenty who entered the fort were captured. At ten minutes to five A.M., the rebels (Texans) fell back in great rage, vowing vengeance. I had in the mean time ordered up the Monongahela, Commander Read, and General Emory first, and then General Banks sent forward reënforcements. General Stone is now in command there, and the place is perfectly secure.

The prisoners arrived from Donaldsonville number one hundred and twenty-four—among which are one lieutenant-colonel, two majors, two captains, and five lieutenants. Our forces have buried sixty-nine rebel dead, and are still employed, calculating there are about one hundred. Colonel Phillips is among the number of the rebel dead.

All of which is respectfully submitted by your obedient servant,　　　　　D. G. FARRAGUT,
　　　　　　　　　　　　　　　Rear-Admiral.

Hon. GIDEON WELLES,
　　Secretary of the Navy.

NEW-ORLEANS, June 30.

SIR: The following is a list of the killed and wounded on board the United States steamer Princess Royal, during an action at Donaldsonville, Louisiana, on the morning of the twenty-eighth instant, namely:

Killed—Isaac Foster, landsman, killed instantly by rifle-ball.

Wounded—Charles Preston, seamen, left ankle and right leg, rifle-ball; Alexander Gordon, captain forecastle, wrist.

Total—One killed, two wounded.

T. K. CHANDLER,
Surgeon Princess Royal.

I am, very respectfully, your obedient servant,
J. M. FOLTZ,
Fleet Surgeon.

Rear-Admiral D. G. FARRAGUT,
　Commanding W. G. B. Squadron.

Doc. 81.

THE OCCUPATION OF YORK, PA.

YORK GAZETTE ACCOUNT.

YORK, June 29, 1863.

NEWS of the advance of the forces of the enemy upon York reached this place on Friday last, and although it was believed to be only a cavalry raid, on Saturday it was discovered by a Union scout that the force was large, numbering some ten thousand. Mr. Arthur Farquhar, a citizen of this place, entered their lines some distance from town, and obtained permission to inform the citizens of York of their approach, on the condition that he should return to their command and inform them whether or not our forces would make any resistance to the occupation of this place. A meeting of the Safety Committee was called, and it was then determined, on account of the strong force of the enemy, to make no resistance, and Chief Burgess Small and George Hay, Thomas White and W. Latimer Small, members of the committee, accompanied by Mr. Farquhar, went out to meet the advance, to inform them of the decision of the committee, and ask the protection of the private property and unarmed citizens.

They met General Gordon, of Early's division, and informed him that, having no sufficient force to resist their advance, they were authorized to ask that no injury be done the citizens in their persons or private property. General Gordon heard their request, and assured them that no injury should be done to either.

On Sunday morning, about ten o'clock, the vanguard of the enemy approached in three columns, the centre through Main street. Gordon's brigade passed through town and encamped on the turnpike about two miles east of town. General Early next arrived with another brigade of his division, and, after an interview with the Chief Burgess, took possession of the Fair Ground and Government Hospital. Thither the forces were stationed with their artillery, consisting of some fourteen pieces, together with their infantry, mounted riflemen, cavalry, etc. Headquarters were established in the court-house, General Early occupying the sheriff's office, the provost-marsal the register's office, and other members of the staff of the general commanding other offices.

The following requisitions were made upon the citizens by General Early :

REQUIRED FOR THE USE OF EARLY'S DIVISION.

One hundred and sixty-five barrels flour, or twenty-eight thousand pounds baked bread. Three thousand five hundred pounds sugar. One thousand six hundred and fifty pounds coffee. Three hundred gallons molasses. One thousand two hundred pounds salt. Thirty-two thousand pounds fresh beef, or twenty-one thousand pounds bacon or pork.

The above articles to be delivered at the market-house on Main street, at four o'clock P.M.

WM. W. THORNTON,
Captain and A. C. S.

REQUIRED FOR THE USE OF MAJOR-GENERAL EARLY'S COMMAND.

Two thousand pairs shoes or boots. One thousand pairs socks. One thousand felt hats. One hundred thousand dollars in money.

C. E. SNODGRASS,
Major and Chief Q. M. Early's Division.
June 28, 1863.

Approved, and the authorities of the town of York will furnish the above articles and the money required, for which certificates will be given.

J. A. EARLY,
Major-General Commanding.

A meeting of the citizens was called, and every effort was made to fill the requisition. Upon the representation of the committee appointed to see to the obtaining of the required articles, that they had done the best in their power to do, General Early signified his satisfaction, and agreed to accept their offer.

On Sunday afternoon, Gordon's brigade reached Wrightsville, and after a slight skirmish, in which two of Bell's Adams County cavalry are supposed to have been taken prisoners, our forces, consisting of several regiments of New-York and Pennsylvania militia, fell back across the Susquehanna, destroying the bridge in their rear by fire. The fire was distinctly seen from town. No property was burnt at Wrightsville, except Moore's foundery and some frame buildings attached, which took fire from the burning bridge. No property was burned at Columbia. The rebel cavalry dismounted and used their muskets and rifles.

On Sunday, the bridges on the Northern Central Railway, north to near Harrisburgh, and south to below Hanover Junction, were burned by the enemy's forces. We are also informed that some bridges on the Wrightsville Railroad were burned, and the large bridge over the Conewago, on the Harrisburgh turnpike.

Last evening General Early visited the railroad property and machine-shops in this borough, in company with the Chief Burgess and other citizens, to see what should be destroyed, but, upon their urgent request, abstained from burning them, because their destruction would have endangered the safety of the town.

Beyond the destruction of the switches, portions of the track and of the telegraph, and some company cars yet remaining here, no public property, as far as we are informed, was destroyed. Several cars, the property of citizens, were not destroyed. Last evening Gordon's brigade returned through town and encamped several miles from the borough on the Carlisle road. This morning the other brigades followed westward, with their artillery and munitions. The town is now no longer occupied by the enemy in force, but a few pickets and scouts are passing through town as we write, and they are no doubt yet in the surrounding country. Let us hope that they are on the retreat, and that the invasion of our fair State by the enemy may soon be at an end, and never again be repeated.

We have no news from the outside world, being completely cut off from all sources of intelligence.

There are rumors, which we shall not now repeat for the want of reliability.

While the enemy was in occupation of the town the citizens were left free to pass through the streets from place to place, though passes were required to get out of town. Many horses and cattle were taken, and the losses of our farmers are heavy, though during the whole of the latter part of last week large droves with wagons were passing through across the river. In several cases the horses were returned on identification and demand of the owners. Guards were placed at the hotels, stores, etc., and the town was kept comparatively quiet, the soldiers being under very strict discipline. Places of business were generally closed, though in many cases were on request opened and articles were purchased, the soldiers and officers paying for them in confederate money. So far as we are informed, their promise to respect the rights of persons and property was kept.

The time the enemy remained here in force was nearly two days, and long weary days they were, rendered more dark by the gloomy weather which prevailed. The apprehension, excitement, and humiliation at the presence of the enemy, together with the total suppression of business, cast an universal gloom over the place, which we pray we may be spared from ever beholding again. But the people submitted with becoming resignation to imperious necessity. What shall yet be our fate or the fate of our beloved country must be developed by the future. God grant us a happy deliverance!

The rebel force in and around the borough of York, consisted of Early's division, made up of Gordon's, Hoke's, Hayes's, and Smith's ("Extra Billy," recently elected Governor of Virginia) brigades, and numbered about ten thousand men in cavalry, artillery, and infantry. Their cannon were part of those captured from Milroy at Winchester, and consisted of heavy brass pieces and five-inch Parrott rifled guns. Some of these were planted on the hills commanding the borough early on Sunday morning.

The amount of money received by the rebels in York, on their requisition or demand for one hundred thousand dollars, was about twenty-eight thousand dollars. The compliance, in part, of their demand, beyond all doubt saved the burning of all the shops and buildings of the railway company and machine-shops where government work is done, the burning of which would have involved the destruction of an immense amount of private property in the immediate neighborhood of these shops.

FIGHT AT WRIGHTSVILLE.

COLUMBIA, PA., June 29, 5 A.M.

The conflict near Wrightsville, Pa., commenced about half-past six o'clock on Sunday evening last. Colonel Frick, with a regiment composed of men from the interior counties of Pennsylvania, principally those of Schuylkill, Lehigh, Berks, and Northampton, with three companies of Colonel Thomas's (Twentieth) regiment, the City Troop of Philadelphia, Captain Bell's independent company of cavalry from Gettysburgh, and several hundred men unattached to any particular command, aided by about two companies of volunteer negroes, held the enemy, supposed to consist of eight thousand men, at bay for at least forty-five minutes, retreating in good order and burning the bridge over the Susquehanna to prevent the crossing of the rebel cavalry.

The intrenchments of Colonel Frick were thrown up across the centre of the valley leading from Wrightsville, opposite Columbia, to York. They were simply trenches constructed by negroes, and commanded the turnpike approach to the Susquehanna. Had they been supported on each adjacent hill by other works, the position would have been tenable, but Colonel Frick had not a sufficient number of men to protect himself from a flank movement. The rebels came not only in his front, but sent flanking parties along roads leading to the river, which skirted his position on either side. After the contest commenced, it soon became apparent that a retreat was necessary.

The rebel batteries throwing shell into the intrenchments were stationed at various points. That the range of their guns was great, was evident from the fact that some of the shell passed over our troops, and either fell into the river beyond Wrightsville or into the town itself, doing an execution among the peaceable inhabitants, the extent of which is as yet unknown. As we stated yesterday, nearly all of the women and children had remained at Wrightsville.

In order to insure the safety of the command, should a retreat become necessary, a train of coal-cars was drawn across the entrance to the bridge, on the Wrightsville side of the River, leaving between them only an opening sufficient for the passage of our men. These cars protected the retreat during the time that a party of workmen, with torpedoes and axes, were preparing the structure for demolishment. After our men had all retired, closely followed by the rebel cavalry, the torch was applied to the fourth span from Wrightsville, and before the flames could be checked by the enemy they had enveloped the entire span and were making rapid headway toward the two ends, which they reached. The remains of the bridge, on Monday morning, consisted only of the piers, which stretched themselves across the river—more than a mile wide—like giant's stepping-stones.

It was almost eight o'clock in the evening of Sunday when the fire first gained headway, and the scene was magnificent. Some of the arches remained stationary even when the timbers were all in flames, seeming like a fiery skeleton bridge whose reflection was pictured in the water beneath. The moon was bright, and the blue clouds afforded the best contrast possible to the red glare of the conflagration. The light in the heavens must have been seen for many miles. Some of the timbers as they fell into the stream seemed to form themselves into rafts, which floated down like infernal ferry-boats of the region pictured by Dante.

The heavy fog this (Monday) morning, at the hour this is written, prevents any object over the river from being distinctly seen. The flames do not appear, however, to have extended to any dwelling in Wrightsville, although two or three board-yards above the town were destroyed. Another yard below the town still contains sufficient lumber for the enemy to construct as many rafts as may seem desirable, but it is impossible to see whether the rebel guns are planted in its vicinity, or on the hills which come out naked and abrupt, with fields upon their tops, to the very edge of the river. One fact is certain, and the truth may as well be told, Columbia is completely at the mercy of the enemy, who, from the opposite hills just mentioned, can shell every building in the town. Nothing of importance was captured at the intrenchments except about five hundred rations, which have since been replaced.

At the intrenchments the rebel fire was returned by our men to the best of their ability. The adjacent fields, however, were covered with long grain, in which the enemy could hide and fire at leisure. For this purpose some of their cavalry dismounted. During the whole affair the coolness and intrepidity of Colonel Frick were displayed, and to other officers the official report will do full justice.

The three companies of Colonel Thomas's regiment were on the right. The City Troop and Bell's cavalry acted as scouts, aids, and orderlies. The colored volunteers behaved well. After the retreat the troops encamped on a hill back of Columbia, a portion of them, however, being detailed to guard a ford. One negro was killed in the intrenchments, and as many members of the white companies are still missing, it is not possible to give the exact loss. It will not exceed twenty, however; a small number, comparatively, but it must be recollected that the engagement derives its importance more from the fact of its proximity to Philadelphia, and the danger which threatens to the State, than from the mere loss in killed, wounded, and missing. The City Troop and Colonel Thomas's companies suffered no loss.

Doc. 82.

ADVANCE INTO PENNSYLVANIA.

GENERAL LEE'S ADDRESS TO HIS SOLDIERS.

HEADQUARTERS ARMY OF NORTHERN VIRGINIA, }
CHAMBERSBURGH, PA., June 27. }

THE Commanding General has observed with marked satisfaction the conduct of the troops on the march, and confidently anticipates results commensurate with the high spirit they have manifested. No troops could have displayed greater fortitude or better performed the arduous marches of the past ten days. Their conduct in other respects has, with few exceptions, been in keeping with their character as soldiers, and entitles them to approbation and praise.

There have, however, been instances of forget-fulness on the part of some that they have in keeping the yet unsullied reputation of the army, and that the duties exacted of us by civilization and Christianity are not less obligatory in the country of the enemy than in our own. The Commanding General considers that no greater disgrace could befall the army, and through it our whole people, than the perpetration of the barbarous outrages upon the innocent and defenceless, and the wanton destruction of private property, that have marked the course of the enemy in our own country. Such proceedings not only disgrace the perpetrators and all connected with them, but are subversive of the discipline and efficiency of the army, and destructive of the ends of our present movement. It must be remembered that we make war only upon armed men, and that we cannot take vengeance for the wrongs our people have suffered without lowering ourselves in the eyes of all whose abhorrence has been excited by the atrocities of our enemy, and offending against Him to whom vengeance belongeth, and without whose favor and support our efforts must all prove in vain.

The Commanding General therefore earnestly exhorts the troops to abstain with most scrupulous care from unnecessary or wanton injury to private property; and he enjoins upon all officers to arrest and bring to summary punishment all who shall in any way offend against the orders on this subject. R. E. LEE,
General.

RICHMOND SENTINEL ACCOUNT.

CAMP ALEXANDER'S BATTERY LIGHT ARTILLERY, }
CHAMBERSBURGH, PA., June 28. }

Up to the battle of Chancellorsville, I had hardly conversed with a man who was in Maryland last year, (except Marylanders,) who was not opposed to another trip across the Potomac. But since then, matters have changed. It seems to be felt that the only obstacle to a successful invasion of Maryland or Pennsylvania, is to be made by Hooker or his army, and this army is willing any day to make a trial of strength.

This last march was badly managed. The whole corps moved at once, and the consequence was, that the road was half the time "blocked."

You have had full description of things about Winchester. We had heard that the Union feeling was strong at Martinsburgh; but on our arrival, I was greatly relieved by seeing a half-dozen girls run into the middle of the street, seize our flag and kiss it devoutly. I was near by when this occurred, and could but resolve, as the blood rushed to my face, that, by God's help, when the time came, I would remember this happy baptism of virgin lips. One woman in this town was thorough Union. She faced a crowd of men in the street and talked with much spirit; had a husband in Bragg's army, she said, and argued the question of the war very glibly, but not logically. I was glad to find, on inquiry, that she was from Massachusetts. Her tongue, I fancy, drove her husband so far from her. With some of the poorer classes the Yankees have, during Milroy's reign, become very familiar, and one of my sergeants found a Yankee concealed in one of their houses.

The country between Martinsburgh and Winchester is much desolated; little grain raised; the lands not good. On Thursday evening we crossed the Potomac at Williamsport. The river is one hundred and fifty yards wide here, but not more than two and a half feet deep. The day was cool and rainy, but the boys waded in cheerfully, and the air was rent with shouts of laughter as now and then some clumsy fellow stumbled and went under, head and ears. There are bluffs on the opposite shore, and here the towns-people collected to witness this singular spectacle. As we passed through the streets, the women and men in great numbers looked on in silence, as they did in Frederick City last year. These people seem to be neither "fish nor fowl." I saw great numbers of young men of conscript age here, and also in Hagerstown next day. I understand that upward of two hundred of those in Hagerstown joined our army. On entering that pretty town of five thousand inhabitants, Friday afternoon, I was glad to see some very decided demonstrations of white handkerchiefs, and that, too, from dwellings indicating intelligence and refinement. Our boys recognized this greeting of the fair in repeated and hearty cheers. There was really a crowd in the streets. As we halted but a short time, no opportunity was given to converse with the people. The only man I spoke to turned out to be a secessionist.

The crops of wheat all along the road in Maryland, and up to this point in Pennsylvania, are remarkably fine. Considerable corn has been planted, but wheat seems to be the grain best adapted to the soil. You see no such fields, in extent, as we have in Virginia. A lot rarely exceeds fifty acres.

Middleburgh, five miles from Hagerstown, is on the dividing line between Maryland and the Keystone State. About half of it is in the former, and in this part of the town I was glad to witness one or two secession demonstrations. From this point to Greencastle, where we encamped on Friday night, distant nine miles, we passed a succession of Dutch farms, all small, but highly improved, with grain nearly ready for the sickle. The North and South-Mountain, a continuation of the Virginian mountains, causes this country to resemble the Virginia Valley very much. The lands are no better than ours.

The people are exceedingly ignorant. I saw no houses indicating refinement. Were I to tell you how profoundly ignorant some of these Dutch are, you would hardly believe me. Our Virginia negroes are vastly better informed about military matters. Some think that Governor Curtin has a wand by which he can collect a body of militia, who will whip us out of our boots; and in the redundancy of their affections, they even express some little sympathy for us in the event we shall await the shock of this militia host. They think our confederate money is worth no more than brown paper, and one man sold one hundred and fifty dollars of it for a twenty shilling gold piece. Most refuse to take it, and prefer that you take what you wish without compensation in this form.

By the way, Order No. 72 of General Lee is being pretty generally carried out. To enforce it strictly, is impossible. The doctrine of not using or destroying some of the private property of an enemy while in his country, is a pure abstraction. You cannot possibly introduce an army for one hour into an enemy's country without damaging private property, and in a way often in which compensation cannot be made. I am entirely opposed to a wanton destruction of the private property of an enemy, but to use it even without compensation, for the men and animals of our army, is, I think, proper. Yet if a man takes an onion, or climbs a cherry tree, he is, by this order, to be punished. Hundreds of men die annually, yea, thousands, for want of a mixture of vegetable and animal food. A soldier who has been living on dry bread and salt meat for months, feels a longing, especially in summer, which no other man can understand, for succulent fruits or vegetables; and that they should not be permitted occasionally (for it is only occasionally they have the opportunity) to eat this common and every-day diet of an enemy, is singular indeed. If we take all his vegetables, he has some substitute in acids, but the soldier has none. It is wanton and wicked for me to turn my horses into an enemy's wheat-field, when a clover-field, just as good for the animals, is on the other side of the fence. When I am hungry, I have a right to eat at an enemy's table, but I have no right afterward to turn round and break up his crockery. The distinction is too manifest to need further illustration; though, simple as it is, it seems not to be comprehended by some of our authorities. I have no idea that General Lee's late Order No. 72 should be construed in that literal sense that some imagine. It is generally and eagerly discussed. According to the literal construction, the corps quartermaster and commissaries are the only persons who can impress; but it must be manifest that they have a right to delegate their authority—otherwise nothing worth mentioning can be done by *these* men. I have been informed from good authority that no such idea was entertained by General Lee.

But I must hasten to close this lengthy communication. The roads here are not so good as in Maryland. Yesterday we travelled a mud pike resembling a bad Virginia road. From this point the roads promise to be better. We are about seventeen miles in Pennsylvania. General Ewell left this place, I understand, for Harrisburgh, Friday morning. I presume his force is sufficient to take the capital. If not, we will help him. I know nothing of the future movements of this army, but I think the bulk of it will remain in this vicinity until some large Yankee force is brought out to meet us. One division, I imagine, will suffice to disperse any militia that may be collected.

Chambersburgh is a beautiful town of about

eight or ten thousand inhabitants. The houses here, and in most of the towns, are built with much taste. Some are elegant. In the country, as before intimated, the Dutchman expends all his taste and money on his cows, horses, or barns. Great consternation prevails among the country people — the women are terribly frightened. Many, and indeed most of the girls are barefooted, and can get a dinner or breakfast for you in "no time." Poor creatures! They think that we are as mean and as vile as their own soldiers. A man in town said to-day that the State militia did them worse than our own men. There is much excitement among the artillery in impressing horses. The farmers only ask one hundred and fifty dollars for the finest horses. Every one I have spoken to is in favor of peace. A hot Black Republican and a Democrat both agree on this question. They say they have heretofore felt none of the effects of the war worth speaking of, and from the number of new houses and barns, it seems they speak the truth. But I must close.

A REBEL LETTER.

The following letter was picked up on the battle-field of Gettysburgh, by a member of one of the Philadelphia regiments:

CAMP NEAR GREENWOOD, PA., June 28, 1863.

MY OWN DARLING WIFE: I have written two letters to you since I left the trenches at Fredericksburgh. I received a letter from you, dated the fourteenth instant. You may be sure I devoured its contents with great eagerness, but oh! how I was pained to hear that you were so unwell! It makes me miserable to think of you as suffering bodily afflictions, with all the great troubles you now have to contend with, and I not there to help you.

You can see by the date of this, that we are now in Pennsylvania. We crossed the line day before yesterday, and are resting to-day near a little one-horse town on the road to Gettysburgh, which we will reach to-morrow. We are paying back these people for some of the damage they have done us, though we are not doing them half as bad as they done us. We are getting up all the horses, etc., and feeding our army with their beef and flour, etc., but there are strict orders about the interruption of any private property by individual soldiers.

Though with these orders, fowls and pigs and eatables don't stand much chance. I felt when I first came here, that I would like to revenge myself upon these people for the desolation they have brought upon our own beautiful home; that home where we could have lived so happy, and that we loved so much, from which their vandalism has driven you and my helpless little ones. But though I had such severe wrongs and grievances to redress, and such great cause for revenge, yet when I got among these people I could not find it in my heart to molest them. They looked so dreadfully scared and talked so humble, that I have invariably endeavored to protect their property, and have prevented soldiers from taking chickens, even in the main road; yet there is a good deal of plundering going on, confined principally to the taking of provisions. No houses were searched and robbed, like our houses were done, by the Yankees. Pigs, chickens, geese, etc., are finding their way into our camp; it can't be prevented, and I can't think it ought to be. We must show them something of war. I have sent out to-day to get a good horse; I have no scruples about that, as they have taken mine. We took a lot of negroes yesterday. I was offered my choice, but as I could not get them back home I would not take them. In fact, my humanity revolted at taking the poor devils away from their homes.

They were so scared that I turned them all loose. I dined yesterday with two old maids. They treated me very well, and seemed greatly in favor of peace. I have had a great deal of fun since I have been here. The country that we have passed through is beautiful, and every thing in the greatest abundance. You never saw such a land of plenty. We could live here mighty well for the next twelve months, but I suppose old Hooker will try to put a stop to us pretty soon. Of course we will have to fight here, and when it comes it will be the biggest on record. Our men feel that there is to be no back-out. A defeat here would be ruinous. This army has never done such fighting as it will do now, and if we can whip the armies that are now gathering to oppose us, we will have every thing in our own hands. We must conquer a peace. If we can come out of this country triumphant and victorious, having established a peace, we will bring back to our own land the greatest joy that ever crowned a people. We will show the Yankees this time how we can fight.

Be of good cheer, and write often to your fondly attached husband,   WM. S. CHRISTIAN.

Doc. 83.

REBEL ATTACK NEAR ROCKVILLE, MD.

WASHINGTON, D. C., June 29, 1863.

YESTERDAY morning, at about half-past nine o'clock, I started from Washington in company with three officers of the topographical engineers. It was our intention to ride through to Frederick, stopping at Rockville for the purpose of taking dinner, but we all knew the liability of well-laid schemes, whether bi or quadrupedal, to go wrong. By the time we reached our first post of cavalry pickets we came up with the rear of a long wagon train, comprising one hundred and fifty vehicles, each drawn by six mules, driven by a very black and picturesque negro. This train must have been at least two miles long, for by the time we had reached the other end, riding leisurely, we were within a mile or two of Rockville. Here, just as we had passed the last wagon, an excited horseman, coming from the direction of Rockville, halted our party, and in a somewhat confused voice gave us the pleasing intelligence that about four hundred rebel cavalry were close at his heels. A short consultation of war resulted in our making up our minds to retreat. This conclusion was scarcely arrived at when two more men came full tilt past us, shouting that the rebels had fired on them and were close behind. Then came a cavalry soldier, one of the six who formed our paltry guard, leading a riderless horse, whose master (another of our guard) had just been shot. Then came thundering along a second trooper, much excited, and evidently charged with some important mission. He immediately halted all the mule teams, ordering them to turn back. And now commenced a scene of excitement and confusion which none but a maniac could properly describe. Wagons upset by their drivers in abortive attempts to turn them round, others locked together, mule teams inextricably snarled up, and through this jam and mess some twenty or thirty horsemen (your correspondent among the number) galloping like mad. Had the devil been behind us, it would have been impossible to go faster; as fast as the frightened horses could lay their legs to the ground they went, kicking up stones and earth with their heels in the most exciting manner. Two scared farmers led the retreat on powerful horses, and so long as they galloped it was impossible to stop any of the other horses. At last we got sufficiently far from the train to deem ourselves safe, and as the farmers had got out of reach, we pulled up and reconnoitred. Away far back on the road we could distinguish smoke from the burning teams. They were doubtless all destroyed. All the mules were captured, and two ambulances containing officers were likewise gobbled up.

At about four o'clock we, the fortunate ones, reached the city, after a six hours' ride of nearly thirty miles, very sore and very tired.

This bold dash of the enemy caused considerable excitement in the city directly we arrived. Colonel Wyndham was immediately put in command of all the cavalry in and around Washington, with authority to mount and organize all the horseless troopers he could lay his hands on, and to mount a Maine regiment whose time is just up, to act as mounted infantry, provided they would consent to serve in that capacity for a few weeks. The Scott's Nine Hundred (cavalry) marched through town at two o'clock this morning, and the Sixteenth New-York leave for Frederick at three P.M. It is Colonel Wyndham's intention to see if he cannot fall foul of these rebel gentlemen and recover our mules, and take a few hundred prisoners at the same time. The appointment of Colonel Wyndham gives great satisfaction. No officer in the army has a higher reputation for energy, activity, and soldierly knowledge.

Doc. 84.

AFFAIR AT SHELBYVILLE, TENNESSEE.

MANCHESTER, TENN., July 1, 1863.

HEADQUARTERS still remain here, and the efforts of the General for the past three days have been confined to get his troops and trains all concentrated at this point. The corps of General Thomas was yesterday thrown forward, and his advance is within four miles of the enemy. We shall probably advance to-day; and if so, the chances are in favor of a great battle to-morrow. It seems likely that Bragg intends to make a stand at Tullahoma. Tullahoma is a strong position naturally; its artificial defences are respectable, and the troops are laboring day and night strengthening them.

While sitting to-day with General Rosecrans and a number of the members of his staff, under the General's marquée, General Stanley, Chief of Cavalry, with General Mitchell and his division of horse, reached headquarters—being just back from his brilliant expedition to Shelbyville, the headquarters of the rebel army. I have already sent by telegraph the leading points of the affair; but, in the course of an afternoon's gossip, there are many details which may be of interest.

Our force, all of which was under command of General Gordon Granger, first met the enemy at Guy's Gap, where he occupied a strong position. It was determined to take it by direct assault. The head of our column deployed as skirmishers, and advanced in échelon up the hill, the enemy meanwhile falling back, their rearguard resisting our progress up the hill. On reaching the top, however, we found the rebel force on the full run down the pike for Shelbyville. They were, however, closely pursued by the First Middle Tennessee cavalry, (Colonel Galbraith,) supported by the Fourth regulars, (Captain McIntyre,) and forty or fifty of them were ridden down and captured. Minty's entire brigade followed the fleeing foe until they reached their intrenchments at Shelbyville, where, under cover of their breastworks and two pieces of artillery, they made a stand. Colonel Minty accordingly dismounted the Fourth Michigan and Third Indiana, and sent them to right and left in the woods, as skirmishers. On the advance of the skirmishers, the rebels limbered up their guns, when one hundred and fifty men of the Seventh Pennsylvania and two companies of the Fourth regulars pursued the battery to within a mile of Shelbyville, at which point two more guns were opened on our column, causing it to halt. A section of our artillery was presently brought up, which fired two rounds, after which the detachments already mentioned—being in their saddles on the road in rear of the guns—immediately charged forward, chasing the enemy into the town. The rebels here took up a strong position on the public square, with three guns commanding the pike by which we had to approach. A charge was forthwith sounded—the Seventh and Ninth Pennsylvania, under command of Major Davis, being selected for the work. It was made with sabre drawn—first rank, tierce point, second, right cut. The column rushed forward into the teeth of the guns, but with such rapidity that before the artillerymen could serve the pieces a second time, they were captured, with the rammer half-way out of the muzzle. We now engaged the enemy's cavalry hand to hand, and from all that I can learn, the public square and streets of Shelbyville must have been witnesses to some of the most exciting hand-to-hand encounters that have occurred during the war. The enemy was completely routed, and while they were still running, Colonel Campbell, with his command, reached their flank near the upper bridge of Duck River, into which they were driven, and a hundred of them killed and drowned. The rebel General Wheeler's horse was killed, and he escaped on foot, without coat or hat. Our captures foot up sixty or seventy officers and nearly seven hundred men. Our loss six killed and between thirty and forty wounded.

The joy of the loyal people of this thoroughly Union town of Tennessee, is said to have been beyond all expression. The Stars and Stripes were displayed from the house-tops and windows, and the ladies, after waving their handkerchiefs, threw them away with joy and waved their skirts.

The fortifications of Shelbyville—the result of five months' assiduous labor on the part of an enemy who has vast faith in digging—prove to have been of the most formidable character, and could not have been taken by direct assault without enormous loss of life. They covered Shelbyville three miles and a half north of the town, and for nine miles across—rifle-pits, abattis, and enfilading works for heavy artillery. The strategic manoeuvre on the rebel flank made these utterly useless to the enemy, and caused them to be voluntarily evacuated.

Doc. 85.

INVASION OF PENNSYLVANIA.

PROCLAMATION OF MAYOR HENRY.

MAYOR'S OFFICE, PHILADELPHIA, June 29, 1863.

Citizens of Philadelphia:

ONE more appeal is made to you in the name of duty and of manhood. You can close your eyes no longer to the startling danger and disgrace which hang over your State and city. The foot of the rebel is already at the gates of your capital, and unless you arouse to instant action it may in a few days hence cross your own thresholds. There is yet time to prepare for defence. You number more than fifty thousand able-bodied men; the means to arm and equip yourselves are at hand. Close your manufactories, work-shops, and stores before the stern necessity for common safety makes it obligatory. Assemble yourselves forthwith for organization and drill. Come ready to devote yourselves to the protection of your homes until your services shall be no longer needed.

Spurn from you those who would delude you to inactivity or disaffection. Their tongues and hearts are more false and hateful than even the invaders of your soil. Let no one refuse to arm who will not be able to justify himself before man and God in sight of a desolated hearth or of a dishonored family.

ALEXANDER HENRY,
Mayor of Philadelphia.

EXPLOIT AT McCONNELLSBURGH

McCONNELLSBURGH, June 30, 1863.

I take advantage of to-day's mail (the first that has gone north for many days, and perhaps the last that will go for many more) to inform you of the particulars of the brilliant affair that came off in our streets yesterday. Captain Jones, at the head of a detachment of the First New-York cavalry, entered this place, at nine yesterday morning, on a reconnoissance. Scarcely had he dismounted his men and established his pickets, when one of the latter came rushing into town and reported the rebels but a short distance up the Mercersburgh road, and advancing. The bustle and excitement usually incident upon the receipt of such intelligence was not exhibited by the New Yorkers. Captain Jones asked their number. A hundred was the reply; and, although his force did not amount to half that number, he coolly answered: "I'll fight them; men, take your places!" By this time the rebel advance was entering town. Our men had mounted, and were proceeding leisurely down street; the enemy, supposing them on a retreat, followed cautiously. Suddenly the New-Yorkers wheeled, the rebs halted. The distance between the parties was but two hundred yards; for a moment they gazed on each other, and oh! the anxiety of that moment! but it was soon dispelled. The rebel officers, standing far in the rear of their men, cried to them to "Charge, charge the —— Yankees, charge them!" But it was no use, the men wouldn't move. But when the clear voice of Captain Jones rang out, "Charge!" the order had not to be repeated; led by that gallant officer, his men, with one wild whoop, that sent terror into the hearts of their cowardly foe, sabre in hand, sprang forward to the work. Had the rebel lines been braced with iron, they never could have stood that shock; they broke and fled, and, amid the waving of handkerchiefs and the cheers of the citizens, the New-Yorkers dashed after their flying foe. The sharp ring of the carbine, the clang of the sabres, and the shouts of the pursuers, created a scene at once so wild, so exciting, and so full of interest, that I doubt whether it has been equalled during the war. The rebels were overtaken at the edge of the town; our cavalry dashed in amongst them, and a regular hand-to-hand fight ensued; for a few moments the crack of the revolvers and the rattle of the sabres was incessant. The result, however, was soon decided in our favor; three only of the rebels escaped, and the New-York boys returned to town driving before them more prisoners than their own number. Cheer after cheer rent the air as they marched down the street, and such an amount of good feeling was never before exhibited by our citizens. Two of the rebels were killed and a number wounded; several dangerously. Captain Jones had one man slightly wounded.

The rebels, in their flight, threw away every thing that impeded them. Guns, sabres, and haversacks were distributed all along the route. The whole was a perfect success, and too much credit cannot be awarded to Captain Jones and his men for their gallantry in this affair, and our citizens will always remember with gratitude the brave boys of the First New-York.

In the evening, the rebels returned, expecting to capture our men and rescue the prisoners. They surrounded the town and moved in on all sides, but the bird had flown. So confident were they of their prey, that they supposed the Yankees were concealed in the houses, and ordered them all to be searched; but, finding themselves mistaken, they returned to their camp, feeling very little better than they had in the morning.

W.

GENERAL EARLY'S ADDRESS.

York, Pa., June 30, 1863.

To the Citizens of York:

I have abstained from burning the railroad buildings and car-shops in your town, because after examination I am satisfied that the safety of the town would be endangered, and, acting in the spirit of humanity which has ever characterized my government and its military authorities, I do not desire to involve the innocent with the same punishment of the guilty. Had I applied the torch without regard to consequences, I would have pursued a course that would have been fully vindicated as an act of just retaliation for the unparalleled acts of brutality perpetrated by your own army on our soil. But we do not war upon women and children, and I trust the treatment you have met with at the hands of my soldiers will open your eyes to the odious tyranny under which it is apparent to all you are groaning.   J. A. EARLY,

Major-General C. S.

Doc. 86.

MARTIAL LAW IN BALTIMORE.

GENERAL SCHENCK'S PROCLAMATION.

Headquarters Middle Department,
Eighth Army Corps, Baltimore, June 30, 1863.

THE immediate presence of a rebel army within this Department and in the State of Maryland requires, as a military necessity, a resort to all the proper and usual means of defence and security. This security is to be provided against known hostilities, and opposition to the lawful and National Government, from every quarter and in every form. Traitors and disaffected persons within must be restrained, and made to contribute to the common safety; while the enemy in front is to be met and punished for this bold invasion.

Martial law is therefore declared and hereby established in the city and county of Baltimore, and in all the counties of the western shore of Maryland.

The Commanding General gives assurance that this suspension of the civil government within the limits defined shall not extend beyond the necessities of the occasion. All the civil courts, tribunals, and political functionaries of State, county, or city authority, are to continue in the discharge of their duties, as in time of peace, only in no way interfering with the exercise of the predominant power assumed and asserted by the military authority.

All peaceful citizens are requested to remain quietly at their homes and in the pursuit of their ordinary avocations, except as they may be possibly subject to calls for personal services, or other necessary requisitions for military purposes or uses hereafter.

All seditious language or mischievous practices tending to the encouragement of rebellion are especially prohibited, and will promptly be made the subject of observation and treatment. Traitorous and dangerous persons must expect to be dealt with as the public safety may seem to require.

To save the country is paramount to all other considerations. When the occasion for this proclamation passes by, no one will be more rejoiced than the Commanding General that he can revoke his order and return to the normal condition of a country at peace, and a Government sustained by a united and loyal people.

ROBERT C. SCHENCK,

Major-General Commanding.

ORDERS UNDER MARTIAL LAW.

Headquarters Middle Department,
Eighth Army Corps,
Baltimore, Md., June 30, 1863.

Orders.—Until further orders, no arms or ammunition shall be sold by any dealer or other person within the city and county of Baltimore without a permit from the General commanding the Military Deparment, or from such officer as shall be duly authorized to grant the same. Any violation of this order shall subject the party offending to arrest and punishment.

Until further orders, no person will be permitted to leave the city of Baltimore without a pass properly signed by the Provost-Marshal, and any one attempting to violate this order shall be promptly arrested and brought before the Provost-Marshal for examination.

Until further orders, no one will be permitted to pass the barricades or into or out of the city, between the hours of ten P.M. and four o'clock A.M., without giving the proper countersign to the guard in charge.

Until further orders no club-house or other place of like resort shall remain open, without a permission given by the General Commanding. Any attempt to violate this order will subject the club-house and property to seizure and occupation by the military, and the frequenters who engage in or encourage such violation, to arrest.

Until further orders, all bars, coffee-houses, drinking-saloons, and others places of like resort shall be closed between the hours of eight P.M. and eight A.M. Any liquor-dealer or keeper of a drinking-saloon or other person selling intoxicating drinks who violates this order shall be put under arrest, his premises seized and his liquors confiscated for the benefit of the hospitals.

Until further orders, the General Commanding directs that the stores, shop, manufactories and other places of business other than apothecary shops and printing-offices of daily journals be closed at five o'clock P.M., for the purpose of giving patriotic citizens an opportunity to drill and make themselves expert in the use of arms.

By order   Major-General SCHENCK.
DONN PIATT,
Lieutenant-Colonel and Chief of Staff.

Doc. 87.

OPERATIONS IN VIRGINIA.

GENERAL DIX'S EXPEDITION.

HEADQUARTERS FOURTH ARMY CORPS, }
IN THE FIELD, July 2, 1863. }

THE object of the reöccupation of the Peninsula ground, rendered ever memorable by the battles of last year, is being now rapidly developed by the fresh events transpiring here. If not of so much passing interest and national importance to the casual observer as were those which culminated from time to time during the previous campaign, yet they may be fraught with advantages to the nation equal to those so ardently hoped for and confidently anticipated from General McClellan's operations against Richmond in 1862. The best efforts, the most single devotedness of purpose, with the practical experience of a patriot soldier, are strained to the accomplishment of the important duties intrusted to the general commanding the operations of this department in the field.

The reöccupation of the Peninsula by General Keyes was determined on by the Government several week ago, and communicated to Maj.-General Dix, commanding the Department of Virginia. The Government at the same time selected Major-General E. D. Keyes to command the forces which it was intended to concentrate there, and to carry out those plans which are now being demonstrated to the country. No more prudent and judicious selection could have been made in view of the duty to be performed—operating in an enemy's country—for General Keyes commanded a corps under General McClellan from that able chief's first occupation of the Peninsula till our evacuation of it. He participated in every action, and conspicuously distinguished himself at the battles of Fair Oaks and Seven Pines.

On being informed of the views of the Government, and his appointment to the command of the forces on the Peninsula, General Keyes set to work to concentrate the forces intended for him, and to a great extent superintended many of the details of disembarkation and location in camp of the various regiments as they arrived. A large number of troops having been concentrated at Yorktown, and supplies collected on the river, Colonel Spear, with the Eleventh Pennsylvania cavalry and some New-York and Massachusetts cavalry, made a sudden dash on the White House, and drove off the rebels who had been up to that time holding it. The troops collected at Yorktown were then hurried to the White House, and General Keyes then submitted the plan of operations to General Dix, which he is now carrying out, and which that General approved.

General Keyes, after due deliberation and much study of the subject, the chances for or against success, and after ascertaining as nearly as possible the strength reserved for the defences of Richmond and its approaches, determined to make a reconnoissance in force by two routes as near to the rebel capital as might be. For this purpose two separate forces were necessary at the outset only. For, according to the design of the General commanding, it was expected that both, acting on preärranged plans, would be able to join their forces at the point fixed for each as the limit of the march, on continuing the march forward or on returning to their encampments at White House, as might at the time be deemed most desirable, both forces at this time being supposed to have accomplished their separate undertakings. A mere outline of what they were will be enough at this point, especially as regards the expedition under General Getty, second in command. Your correspondent accompanying the expedition will give you full information on that head, and I will but refer to General Getty's instructions, in so far as it is necessary to explain General Keyes's movements.

General Getty, with a force consisting of infantry, cavalry, and artillery, probably to the amount of seven or eight thousand men, started from White House under instructions to proceed as far as Hanover Junction, and there, as completely as possible, destroy South and North-Anna bridges, and as much of the railway track as time and his strength would enable him to accomplish. This done, the rebels north of Richmond would be completely cut off from all railway communication with that capital—an imperative necessity to carrying into execution a more important project of General Keyes. In carrying out this preliminary plan the Commanding General selected himself what he expected and desired to be the fighting part of the programme. This was to start from White House with a force of some five thousand men, composed of the three arms, in military proportion, to demonstrate against whatever force might be found guarding the Chickahominy, if possible to bring them out, lure them for some little distance from their central position on Bottom Bridge, secure for General Getty clear and unobstructed roads, and, when an advantageous position offered, form in line of battle and attack whatever rebel foe might be opposed to him.

This latter alternative, however, to be adopted only in two contingencies—one in the event of the rebels attacking us; the other, should it be found desirable to offer them battle even on their own ground, with a fair prospect of success, and in the event of General Getty's operations being in any way dependent on such action. This, briefly, was the plan laid down by General Keyes, and the object sought to be attained by the expedition which I accompanied.

Pursuant to general orders, the commanders of brigades, batteries, and detachments reported at corps headquarters, Tuesday evening, for special instructions for the order of march. On the following morning (Wednesday) the encampment was alive and busy with the hum and motion of preparation. A little before daylight the advance troops of General Getty's command were on the march, and the rear-guard was yet hurrying forward when trumpet and drum called the troops composing General Keyes's expedition into line. At the appointed hour, almost to the minute, the advance cavalry videttes took the road to Baltimore Cross-Roads, followed immediately by the head of the advanced column. The troops carried but two days' rations and one hundred rounds of ammunition per man, the march, as much as possible, being unencumbered by baggage-wagons and trains, rapid movements and long marches being anticipated. Only one wagon was allowed to each brigade headquarters, one to each regimental battery, one to the New-York cavalry, and two to the Pennsylvania cavalry. A proper allowance of ambulances—so read the orders—were allowed to each column.

Scarcely had the head of the first column begun to move on the outskirts of the encampment when General Keyes and staff rode from headquarters toward the front. The General's staff on the occasion was composed of the following officers: Medical Director Mulford, Major Whitehead, Major Jackson, Captain Howard, and Captain Rice.

Though the kindness of Captain Howard, I was mounted on a captured secesh horse, which kept me well up with the staff during the march and the many inspections personally made by the General during the two days of our operations. The usual line and order of march were observed during the expedition.

In this order the expedition took up the march for Baltimore Cross-Roads—the first designated halting-place on the route to Bottom Bridge. The morning, like many succeeding ones, was cloudy and threatening rain, and for the first mile the route lay through an opening in the woods, the road being in many places flooded, and in others very badly rutted and cut up. At eight o'clock the sun came out warmly, which seemed to increase the hilarity and good humor of the men, as they sang, joked, and laughed along the road. The first point of interest reached was St. Peter's Church, where General Washington was married. The memories attached to the sacred edifice from this circumstance appeared to be known to many in the ranks—men who served in the Peninsula campaign—and, from time to time, as the church came in view, the veterans pointed it out to their younger companions, with an explanation of the interest attached to it. Once or twice the columns had to be halted from the impediments on the broken roads; but these halts were of short duration, General Keyes not permitting the slightest relaxation of energy at any point or under any circumstances. When about half the distance between White House and Baltimore Cross-Roads had been gained, Brigadier-General Terry joined in with his staff, and the two generals rode on together, chatting on military matters. Precisely at twelve o'clock the head of the advancing column reached Baltimore Cross-Roads.

The whole force was then halted for dinner. and General Keyes, with his staff, rode to the front. Once on the road, inquiry was made as to the appearance of rebels, when the General was informed that rebel pickets had been seen within three or four miles of White House every day for several days, and that they had fallen back before our videttes that same morning. General Keyes, having gone to the extreme front, was informed by Colonel West that he had been chasing the bushwhackers from the woods around Baltimore Cross-Roads, and that he thought the enemy was in some force right in front of his line of videttes. Skirmishers were sent out to support the cavalry, with orders not to press the rebels till further orders. So matters stood while the troops rested.

A quartermaster of one of our regiments was seized by rebel scouts or guerrillas at Baltimore Store in less than fifteen minutes after the troops marched past. Straggling was by special orders strictly prohibited, invalids and bad marchers being enjoined to remain in camp. It was impossible, however, to prevent a few from dropping to the rear; but none, so far as I can learn, had been captured but the quartermaster, for whose disobedience of orders there can be no palliation. On learning the fact Lieutenant Duryea and a detail of men were sent off in pursuit; but some time after he returned unsuccessful, reporting that, from a curve of the road branching from the store to the Chickahominy, his party had been fired at, a soldier beside him at the time being hit with a slug shot, but fortunately not hurt.

General Keyes determined on making his headquarters at Baltimore Cross-Roads, for a few hours, it might be, or for the night, according to circumstances. For a couple of hours, therefore, he was engaged in disposing of his troops as they came up, selecting the regiments according to their experience in the field or his own knowledge of their reliability in any emergency. Mounted videttes were again sent out to picket the numerous roads that branch off in every direction toward the Chickahominy. The encampment was made to present to the eye ground prepared for a terrible resistance to an anticipated attack, rather than the halting-place for a few thousand men. Artillery, cavalry, and infantry were disposed as in line of battle. Artillery in front on the ascents; infantry behind in line, with stacked arms, while in a little plain on the right of the ground were placed the cavalry, horses saddled and bridled, and the men ready to mount at the first trumpet-note. The horses of the caissons were kept harnessed and in their traces, and all betokened a fight on the ground thus selected and so strongly guarded, or else a move in order of battle. As I looked upon the array and pondered, I asked myself, What can the General mean by a halt of this kind—intended for rest, and yet every thing betokening preparations for battle? The strategy of the great Theban general suggested itself to my memory—a strategy by which Leuctra and other famous battles were won, and which was unknown before his day—that was of always marching his army in the order in which he intended to fight it.

Scarcely had the General made, as all supposed, his final dispositions for the evening, when Colonel West, whose brigade—he acting as brigadier-general—held still the front, was ordered to advance on the direct road to Bottom Bridge. Instantly the brigade was in motion. But a moment before it occupied a slight elevation over a plain which stretched away to the south for a mile and a half, a small opening in the woods in front, and which the eye, without the aid of a glass, could not discern, giving the only opening to the road. The artillery are moving down the plain, the cavalry are skirting the woods on West's left flank, a dark line of single skirmishers are seen cautiously approaching the woods in front. At that wood, from the copse on the extreme left and front, is seen a party of the enemy. They dash on almost as quickly as the exclamation broke from the lips of several near me: "There they go!" The skirmishers fire, and right before them, yet some distance off, appears a line of rebel skirmishers. Stray pops of musketry tell that the skirmishers are engaged. Our boys keep going ahead; the others fall back into the gloom of the woods and disappear. Our skirmishers are called in, and take their places behind the line of battle, which was now formed. In front was Minks's battery, First New-York artillery, supported by the One Hundred and Seventy-eighth Pennsylvania, with cavalry a little to the rear and rather to the right of the line. The rebel fire on our left, from the woods, was at one time pretty brisk, when it would suddenly die away, to be renewed on our front.

The fire of the skirmishers drew General Keyes rapidly to the scene. Apparently a glance told him what was likely to come, and back he galloped to the ground occupied by the main body of his forces. Orders were despatched with surprising readiness and coolness, and order of battle was again formed. This was done by merely ordering the supporting forces to positions on readier supporting distance of the advance line than some of them previously occupied.

The ground here represented a greater inequality of surface than that where the front line was formed. On the rising ground, some six or seven hundred yards to the rear of these regiments, was posted McKnight's battery, supported by the gallant Fourth Delaware, Colonel Grimshaw, ready and eager for a grapple with the foe. Still on to the left of these, where the woods offered a splendid chance to the rebels for a flank movement, were posted, in the same order, other troops. These dispositions were made with wonderful celerity, and almost in as short a time as is taken to explain them here, they were concluded, and General Keyes again appeared on the scene of conflict.

The rebels still sustained their fire, but not in such volume, or with the rapidity they did at first. Up to this time only one of our men had fallen. This was one of the cavalry videttes, watching the woods on the left of the line. He was shot in the head, the ball striking him in the left eye. He fell dead from his horse. Six others of the cavalry were wounded, but none seriously. The poor fellow fell in the discharge of his duty, in the presence of all in the field.

General Keyes having now returned, rode to the front, attended by his staff. He passed first to the right of the line, and having surveyed the ground, rode quietly along to the extreme left, where the fire from the first was the warmest. Our guns now threw shot at longer intervals, the enemy's replies dying gradually away. For nearly an hour longer the line was preserved, when it opened from the centre and the cavalry advanced. The rebels, seeing themselves foiled in enticing our troops into the treacherous woods, evidently gave the hope up; and as they ceased to show themselves the troops were ordered back to the position first occupied by them as the advance. This was the rising ground overlooking the plain where the skirmishers first encountered The remainder of the forces also retired to their previous positions, and the excitement which the prospect of an imminent engagement always creates gradually subsided. In an hour afterward General Keyes and staff for the first time that day sat down on the grass and partook of some refreshment.

Toward the close of the skirmishing in front Adjutant Frank Robinson, of the Fifth Pennsylvania, while executing some order of General Keyes, visited the extreme point of ground occupied by our videttes, members of his own regiment. While here he observed a rebel come out of the woods, having his musket at the aim and ready to fire. With a shout Robinson and his orderly made a dash at him, the former revolver in hand. The word was surrender or die, and the frightened rebel chose the former, gave up his gun, and was escorted within our lines. When brought before General Keyes he said that he belonged to one of the North-Carolina regiments that had been brought from the Blackwater to the defence of Richmond. He belonged to Hampton's Legion. He stated that there was a large force in our front, who were continually shifting their position on the Chickahominy. The bridges, he said, had been all repaired, and bodies of troops frequently crossed and recrossed them.

They were almost daily moved from place to place, evidently with the view of getting a knowledge of the country. The prisoner was a very intelligent young fellow, a corporal, who had served some considerable time in the rebel service. His uniform was quite new, a bright blue loose jacket and blue pants, with gaiters *chasseur de pied* fashion. After a brief examination of him, General Keyes had him and another prisoner found on the march, and who also had the rebel uniform on him, sent down to White House.

At an early hour the succeeding morning the troops were all in motion. General Keyes determined, from the information he received of the strength of the enemy in his front, and from the fact that during the night the rumbling of artillery on the march was heard on our right, to get his command clear of the network of roads branching from the Chickahominy, and which, within a mile or two of one point, converged on his position. He therefore fell back, and after a short march a favorable position was chosen for his purpose, and here the forces were halted and disposed of somewhat similar to the day before. The General's headquarters are at present at a place known as Tallowsville, four miles south of the White House, and within a mile and a half perhaps of Baltimore Store. Our pickets, however, extended as far in the front as the ground occupied by us in the morning.

Baltimore Store, the grand debouching point from Bottom Bridge, and the key to his position, if he has left an entering wedge at all, is held by the brave Delawares, the Fourth, under their gallant leader, Colonel Grimshaw. This may be considered the post of honor and of danger, and no men in the army are more deserving of the honorable recognition of a commander for bravery and zeal in the cause for which they fight than the Delaware Fourth.

Our future movements will be altogether determined by circumstances. I may say, so far as I have had opportunity of ascertaining, that General Keyes has no desire to bring on a general engagement with the strong force that is evidently close before him, with the advantage all on their side, and all the disadvantage on his. Brave, skilful, and calculating, he is performing the main object of the expedition in holding a strong force in his front, and thus weakening the enemy at the point to be struck by General Getty; but while holding back his force, and declining to follow the enemy into unknown ambuscades, he is anxious to draw them out and give them a taste of his mettle.

General Keyes's headquarters are at Mrs. Green's farm-house, about a mile and a half from the advance under Colonel West. The locality is known as Tallowsville. The position is a very central one, in the midst of his forces. Since selecting it he has not been a moment out of the saddle, as he imposes upon himself the duty of visiting every post, and assuring himself against surprise by the watchful foe that swarm in the woods around him. It was not till near two o'clock this afternoon the General returned to or rather took possession of his new headquarters.

About six o'clock this evening, the fire of musketry, quickly followed by the loud report of artillery, called the General and staff to their saddles. Leaving orders with colonels of regiments as he passed along, he dashed to the front and on to the field of the previous day's encounter. On the road we met some of our forces falling hastily back; but without inquiry the General rode on till he joined Colonel West, commanding the advance. From him he ascertained the following particulars: It was deemed proper before night came on, to scout the woods commanding our position, and Colonel West sent out skirmishers for that purpose. One hundred men of the One Hundred and Thirty-ninth New-York were selected for the duty, to whom were added some forty volunteers. A section of Minks's battery took up the same position it occupied on the previous day, supported by the remainder of the One Hundred and Thirty-ninth regiment. The skirmishers passed down the road past the woods on the left, some cavalry skirmishers guarding the road. They were thus between two woods, with but a small open space on their right. They had proceeded some two hundred yards when they received the enemy's fire. After some exchanges our men were withdrawn and a new line formed, the reserves and supporting bodies moving up. Again the skirmishers advanced, but had not got more than a hundred yards, screening themselves along the wood, when the enemy opened upon our two guns and line of battle from a masked battery. Minks gallantly returned the fire, maintaining his position for about half an hour, when the weight of the enemy's fire compelled him to fall back. The enemy continued shelling us for some time longer, preventing the doctor attending to the wounded on the field.

Our losses were eight skirmishers—one killed in the woods and six wounded, two seriously, four but slightly. The casualties to the battery and supporting forces I could not ascertain, for it was now dark and the continuation of the fight or the renewal of it on our side had to be put off till to-morrow.

The following are the names of the wounded skirmishers: John Geerer, company K, neck, badly; Jacob Van Wickley, company F, leg; S. B. Howell, company H, scalp wound; Oscar Lockwood, company I, lower jaw and neck, badly; Corporal Louis A. Le Blanc, company D, leg; Denis McCabe, company I, mouth — all of the One Hundred and Thirty-ninth New-York.

To-morrow I expect a severe engagement on the same ground. General Keyes must fight and dislodge the enemy from their position in front, or himself fall back to White House.

HEADQUARTERS FOURTH ARMY CORPS, }
BALTIMORE CROSS-ROADS, July 3, 1863. }

In my previous correspondence from this point I had but time to state the fact that the gallantry of Colonel West, commanding the advance, had, on Thursday last, the second day of our occupation of this place, drawn upon us an attack from the enemy in force, which unmistakably developed their strength to be considerable. In that letter I could not report particulars, as the last chance for the night from here to the White House was going down. I must again briefly state that the whole of Thursday, up to about half-past four o'clock, passed very quietly, little disturbing the monotony that reigned supreme around the encampment, beyond the visits of General Keyes, who rode from one headquarters to another several times during the day, closing with an afternoon visit to all the picket-stations encircling the ground he has guarded like a citadel. I had endeavored to make myself thoroughly acquainted with the position, and to glean from personal observation, if possible, the design and object of a halt which seemed to me premature, considering the avowed original purpose of the expedition—to aid and abet General Getty in his attempt upon the upper bridges of the Pamunkey, the North and South-Anna bridges, and the railroads which connect Richmond with the North. Indeed, I had deemed the demonstration of the rebels on the previous day but so much of an incentive to advance brave troops as a general might desire. The blood of the men was set coursing, the dispositions were admirable, and the coolness of the General, his officers and attendant aids-de-camp, such as to inspire confidence in the men. There was nothing which should deter the faintest heart from daring an advance.

But what at first seemed a questionable Fabian policy proved to be the result of an astute understanding and a perfect comprehension of what even a few hostile troops could do in a country checkered with woods and small open fields—too small for opposing troops to operate in, but large enough, if tempted or commanded to enter them, to make their deadly marks upon ambushed enemies and masked batteries against treble their number. This I at once saw and admitted, after a couple of hours' ride, taken alone within the lines, and with the view of forming a judgment upon a doubt which exercised me a good deal.

While on this particular subject, I may say, and as briefly as possible, that, unless against incontestably overwhelming numbers, the real defence of Richmond lies in the innumerable roads which permeate and intersect this portion of the peninsula, all debouching at numerous external points and converging at the very entrance to the city. With these preliminary remarks, dictated by a conviction of their necessity to enable the distant reader to thoroughly understand the present movement, I proceed to give you the details of the night attack upon our lines.

As I said, Colonel West, not "blue moulding for want of a beating," but anxious for a bit of a fight, after a pleasant conference with a brother officer, Major Candless, on the subject, moved to feel the enemy in front. Colonel West thought he would exercise some men in skirmishing, and Major Candless that he would throw out a foraging party. Some one hundred and forty infantry of the One Hundred and Thirty-ninth, and a few cavalry, were almost immediately deployed as skirmishers on the plain which was the scene of the previous day's fight. The One Hundred and Thirty-ninth steadily advanced to the fringe of the woods without being once confronted; but scarcely had they done so when they were encountered by an opposing line of sharp-shooters, three deep, before whom our boys, after a second discharge of their muskets, fell back only in time, indeed, to save themselves from being surrounded. When the rebel skirmishers appeared on the plain in pursuit, they showed themselves to be at least one thousand strong. Colonel West, judging from the fire that we were strongly opposed, drew out his brigade in line of battle, Captain Fagan instantly advancing his section of artillery in front of the line. The skirmishers, being reenforced, again advanced, but before shots were exchanged a battery of heavy guns opened upon our line from the crest of the wooded knoll on our left. Captain Fagan, with his couple of six-pounders, blazed away in response, but his ineffectual fire paled before the thundering of eight heavy field-pieces, throwing shot and shell into the midst of the line. One great advantage the rebel skirmishers had over us was that, while they were armed with rifles, the One Hundred and Thirty-ninth had only smooth-bores, and thus, while our shot would not reach the rebels, they took down our men standing in line of battle hundreds of yards beyond the line of skirmishers. I saw the dogma thoroughly established: "Observe the first duty of a soldier." The One Hundred and Thirty-ninth, last evening, knowing the disadvantage they were to labor under as to arms, and that the rebel skirmishers were thirty to one of them, advanced to the fight with surprising readiness and coolness. The loss was eighteen left on the field, besides those taken away by the Medical Director, Dr. O'Reilly, whom no shelling deterred from his humane and noble duty.

The medical director testifies to their bravery. Dr. O'Reilly, on the first intimation that ambulances were required, took that especial duty into his own hands, without any circumlocution whatever. "General," he said, "Colonel West is engaged; let me have those ambulances of yours to take to the front." "Take them off, doctor, at once," was the reply. And I must say that this promptitude saved eight men from imprisonment and some others from death, for under the kind care of their nurses the more seriously wounded are now out of danger.

Colonel West and Captain Fagan made the best fight they could against the forces opposed to them, but were eventually compelled to fall back upon our next line.

Here the brave Grimshaw and the Fourth Delaware were stationed; but before their services were required Colonel Porter had pushed forward to the support with two regiments, and Colonel West, after two days' fatiguing marches in the front, and two skirmishes against greatly superior numbers, retired within our main lines. Colonel

Porter's orders were: "Fight them to the last extremity. Don't fall back till ordered." Two miles now intervened between the ground where the skirmish opened and where Colonel Porter stood ready to receive them, yet the rear of our column had scarcely reached Baltimore Store when the rebels, by another road, dashed upon Colonel Porter's command, hoping to cut it off; but the gallant Colonel had received his orders and knew his duty. The attack was repulsed, and, true to their system, the rebels, instead of musket and bayonet, again plied us with shot and shell, while their perfect knowledge of the country enables them to move from one point to another with almost magical celerity.

General Keyes now rode to the front, and Colonel Porter and Colonel Grimshaw were withdrawn from their positions. Their line of retreat was a divergence from the line of battle conceived for the occasion. Our troops fell back in the direction of the New-Kent road, and were most persistently and hotly followed up by the rebels, who shelled them every yard of the road. The design was to draw them after our retreating forces until they came in front of our line of battle, now drawn up in a most advantageous position upon the very ground occupied as headquarters. Our right was toward the woods, and the line of retreat and pursuit, while facing the woods, was a strong place, which the falling night completely shut out from the view of the rebels. The latter force had most positive orders not to fire a shot or in any way to expose our position. In the mean time Grimshaw and Porter skirted the large field on which our line was formed, Captain Fagan, of the artillery, and a squadron of cavalry, under Major Candless, protecting their rear, Captain Fagan sending a random shot occasionally into the woods.

The General's plan was working admirably; the retreating forces were now traversing the road in our front, the enemy's shell tore through the woods on their right or passed over their heads, and in a few moments more we hoped to have them before us. Captain McKnight's battery was on the right of our line, ready to fire upon them; a strong force, directed to cut off their retreat by throwing itself into the woods, was on the spring, when, strangely and perversely enough, the rebels ceased the pursuit just at the very point or turn of the road, their occupation of which would have left them at our mercy. The most exciting few moments of my life passed here, while I looked upon the deadly disposition of our forces, and hoped, with a savage hope, for the accomplishment of our purposes. But no; the rebels suddenly ceased firing and halted in their pursuit. In vain was our net set for their catching, even at the moment we deemed their entanglement most certain. General Keyes was at first delighted, thinking that perhaps they were closing up for a dash upon the road. My own and the feeling of those near me favored the same idea. Whispered orders for the strictest silence passed down the line, and all was profound quiet, save the chirping of myriads of in-

sects, before almost unheard, but which now burst painfully and spell-like upon the ear. After a few anxious minutes, the silence was first broken by General Keyes himself, who remarked: "There is a regularly trained soldier opposed to me there, whoever he is." Whoever he was, he halted at the right time, and we heard no more of the rebels for that night. We unfortunately left some eighteen dead and wounded men in their hands, Dr. O'Reilly having just carried off eight wounded men, who are all doing well.

AN ANXIOUS NIGHT.

Very little sleep was enjoyed at headquarters that night; and although General Keyes had but an hour or two previous to the firing in front made his headquarters at Dr. Tyler's house — a relative of ex-President Tyler — he preferred to remain on the field till morning. Colonel Porter, who commanded a brigade, occupied Dr. Tyler's abandoned house as headquarters — Colonel Grimshaw holding the advance and protecting our front.

Before dawn this morning (Friday) Captain Howard, with a strong body of pioneers from various regiments, visited the outposts and barricaded all the roads debouching upon or contiguous to our lines, strengthening our position very much. Colonel Suydam, Adjutant-General of the corps, arrived in camp last night.

THE CAPTURED QUARTERMASTER.

The name of the quartermaster captured by the rebels on the march is Morgan Kupp, of the One Hundred and Sixty-seventh Pennsylvania regiment. He was detained on duty at our rear and had not yet joined us, but was hurrying forward when seized. He is very highly spoken of indeed, and his loss is much regretted by his brother officers.

Sergeant John Jones, company H, Sixth New-York cavalry, who was fired at by a bushwhacker when in pursuit of Mr. Kupp and struck in the belt, received no injury from the shot. He, of course, feels happy at his luck, as who would not, and retains the slug, which remained in his belt, as a memento of his escape.

RICHMOND DISPATCH ACCOUNT.

RICHMOND, June 29, 1863.

For a city besieged, Richmond presented a very quiet and composed appearance yesterday. The sky was overcast, and the day was not a very cheerful one; but nothing seems to dampen the spirits of our citizens. The men generally seem to have become possessed with the idea that they are regular troops, and have been in the army since the war commenced. They obey the summons to the militia with the promptness, coolness, and that imperturbable stolidity which characterizes old soldiers. The ladies, too, deserve as much credit as the men. They are the commissaries of the militia, and prepare the inevitable rolls with legs of fine chickens inserted, and the sliced ham, with which the married men particularly are well supplied. The single men are, of course, not so well supplied, being forced, as a general thing, to raid on their boarding-house tables and take the chances, while the proprietor is looking the other way, of surreptitiously putting their two days' rations into their haversacks. Saturday afternoon the following notice was posted in the city:

To THE CITIZENS OF RICHMOND: The President and the Governor of Virginia, deeply impressed with the necessity of a speedy organization of all able-bodied and patriotic citizens for local defence in and around the city of Richmond and throughout the State, urgently appeal to their fellow-citizens to come forth in their militia organization and to commence and perfect at once other organizations by companies, battalions, and regiments. An imperious necessity for instant action exists, and they trust that this appeal will be all that is necessary to accomplish the result. No time is to be lost—danger threatens the city.

Therefore, with a view to secure the individual attention of all classes of the citizens of Richmond, and to impress upon them the full importance of the crisis, it is hereby ordered that all stores and places of business in this city be closed to-day at three o'clock P.M., and daily thereafter until further order, and the people be invited to meet and form organizations for local defence. They will be armed and equipped as fast as the companies are formed. By command of the Secretary of War.   S. COOPER,
                    Adjutant and Inspector-General.
By order of the Governor of Virginia
    JOHN G. MOSBY, JR., A. A. A. General.

A great many rumors had prevailed throughout the city during the day, all placing the Federal force at about three times its actual strength. The city troops, as we may call the militia, rapidly armed, and in an incredibly short time regiments were assembled on the public square. While this gathering was going on another notice was posted, of which the following is a copy:

MY FELLOW-CITIZENS, TO ARMS.—I have just received a message direct from the highest authority in the Confederacy, to call upon the militia organizations to come forth, and upon all other citizens to organize companies for the defence of this city against immediate attack of the enemy. They are approaching, and you may have to meet them before Monday morning. I can do no more than give you this warning of their near approach. Remember New-Orleans. Richmond is now in your hands. Let it not fall under the rule of another Butler. Rally, then, to your officers to-morrow morning, at ten o'clock, on Broad street, in front of the City Hall.   Jos. MAYO,
                            Mayor of Richmond.

Saturday Afternoon, June 27, 1863.

The regiments which assembled in the square were notified to be in readiness at the same place yesterday morning at ten o'clock, and assembled at the time appointed, with ranks very much increased. It was the general impression on the part of those who witnessed the parade that the city troops of Richmond were numerous enough, and well drilled enough, to defend the city without the aid of the very large body of regulars who are in and around the place. While there was no need for them yesterday, yet we have the satisfaction of knowing that an organization has been effected which will, with the addition of a little drilling, render Richmond perfectly secure against any raids or even regularly planned attacks of the enemy.

Our scouts were busy during the day in the country below the city, but did not gather much information that we have had access to. At one time the report was that the enemy were at Diascund bridge and numbered twenty-three thousand. The report, it was said, might be relied upon. We conversed with an intelligent gentleman, who was a prisoner within the enemy's lines on Friday, but, after being paroled, made his escape and walked to Richmond. He was captured Friday morning while within a short distance of the Pamunkey River, near Cumberland. The Dutch Yankees who arrested him carried him to the headquarters of Keyes, who was in command of the division which landed at the White House. The division was drawn up in line of battle. He reached the headquarters near New-Kent Court-House, and upon being carried before the Commanding General was closely questioned. During the examination General Keyes spoke several times in a very boastful manner of the ease which he would enter Richmond. He said that Wise was "a damned old coward;" that Wise had challenged him for a fight anywhere between Williamsburgh and Richmond, and that now he had come, Wise had run away. The officers at headquarters participated in the confidence of their braggart chief, with the addition of the lie that they had fifty thousand men. Our informant, who is a soldier himself, says he thinks they had about fifteen thousand men—cavalry, artillery, and infantry. He counted sixteen pieces of artillery. They claimed to have a brigade of cavalry, but he only saw two regiments. The infantry was composed chiefly of foreigners, the Dutch predominating. After being paroled, the prisoner was allowed to go at large, and escaped by way of Charles City County, arriving in this city yesterday morning.

By the evening train on the York River road, we have the latest intelligence of the movements of the enemy. Saturday evening the force from Diascund bridge, in James City County, arrived at the White House, after a march of fifteen miles. That evening a lieutenant-colonel, who was with McClellan while he occupied that point, made a visit to the farm of a lady near by, and stated in conversation that the Federal force on the peninsula numbered about eleven thousand, and was under the command of General Keyes and Gordon, the former being chief. Persons who saw them at the White House do not think they were over eleven thousand. A scout of ours who had been to Diascund bridge reported that there are none of the enemy now at the bridge. Since their arrival at the White House they have not advanced at all, and their pickets are not thrown out even as far as Tunstall's Station, four miles off. There were gunboats in the river, and the move is probably made with the view of embarking again for Yorktown.

The Yankees have committed very few depredations in New-Kent, but on Friday a raid was made by them across the Pamunkey into King William, during which they destroyed a good deal of property and carried off a large number of negroes. The soldiers making this incursion into the country were carried over from the White House in gunboats, and returned with their plunder by the same conveyance.

A report was in circulation here on Saturday that a body of Federals had been seen on the Mechanicsville road, nine miles from Mechanicsville.

From all the facts, we conclude that Keyes, with about five thousand men, came up the Pamunkey, landed at the White House, and proceeded to the vicinity of New-Kent Court-House, from whence his cavalry raid on the Central Railroad at Hanover Court-House was made. Gordon marched from Yorktown and took up his position at Diascund bridge, with about the same number of men, and on Friday advanced and formed a junction with Keyes's division, after which, on Saturday, both divisions marched to the White House. What will be their next move it is of course impossible to know; but the general opinion of those who came up on the York River train yesterday evening was that they intended to embark for Yorktown.

A report "got loose" yesterday morning that a fight had occurred below Chaffin's Bluff, between the confederates and Yankees, in which the latter were defeated. No such fight had occurred, and the rumor died out with the setting of the sun.

When the bridge over South-Anna River, on the Central Railroad, Friday, was burned, the position was defended by Lieutenant Rice and fifty-one men of company A, Forty-fourth North-Carolina troops, under the command of Lieutenant-Colonel Hargrove, of that regiment. The defence was most gallant and obstinate, though against such odds as to be unsuccessful. They were attacked from all directions by one thousand cavalry, two hundred dismounted men, and two pieces of artillery. We give the list of killed and wounded. Killed—Privates John W. Newman, Joseph Cash, and Burton Nevis. Wounded—Sergeant John Buchanan, mortally; private John Pitland, mortally, (both since dead;) Sergeant Alexander Pearce, J. G. Hays, and William Strum; privates Stephen Knott, William Sherron, James Ladd, James Sanford, Dennis O'Brien, J. Satterwhite, Thomas Clopton, William Morgan, D. Buck, James Emory, and Isaac Jinkins. Lieutenant-Colonel Hargrove received a sabre-cut. The desperate courage of the defenders of this bridge against such odds may be understood when it is stated that out of fifty-three men, twenty-two—nearly half—were killed or wounded before it was captured.

Doc. 88.

GENERAL WILLCOX'S ORDER AGAINST SECRET SOCIETIES.

HEADQUARTERS DISTRICT OF INDIANA AND MICHIGAN,
DEPARTMENT OF THE OHIO,
INDIANAPOLIS, June 30, 1863.

THE peace of Indiana has lately been disturbed by violence, murder, and other acts contrary to law, and having their origin in certain secret political societies, clubs, or leagues. The common safety now demands that all such associations should be discontinued, no matter to what political party they may belong. They are a constant source of dread and mistrust—they divide and provoke hostility between neighbors, weaken the dignity and power of courts of justice, expose the country to martial law, and discourage the people from enlisting in defence of the nation.

No matter how honest or worthy may have been the reason for such societies in the beginning, their very secrecy and the oaths they impose do enable wicked men to use them unto unlawful ends, and pervert them into public nuisances.

All good objects can be accomplished openly, and none but the enemies of their country ever need disguises.

It is perfectly plain that such secret organizations are both dangerous and beyond the ordinary grasp of the law; they are therefore declared to be hostile, and will be put down by all the military power of the district, if need be.

I invoke against such secret societies the good influence and active aid of all men who are friendly to the Union—to discontinue and peaceably break up such organizations within the limits of this district; and call upon the members thereof speedily to withdraw from their dark meetings, and openly show that their intentions and acts are such as may well become the true and loyal citizens of a country whose freedom and integrity they will maintain against all enemies whatsoever, and before the eyes of all the world. O. B. WILLCOX,
Brigadier-General Commanding.

Official.
ROBERT A. HUTCHINS,
Captain and A. A. G.

All papers in Indiana and Michigan please publish.

Doc. 89.

SIEGE OF PORT HUDSON.

A REBEL NARRATIVE.

MOBILE, July 20, 1863.

WE have conversed with an officer who succeeded in passing out from Port Hudson while the surrender was taking place on Thursday, the ninth instant, from whom we have been furnished with details of the siege which will not fail to prove interesting to our readers.

The initiatory steps of the siege may be reckoned from the twentieth of May, when General Augur advanced from Baton Rouge. His approach being reported by our cavalry, on the twenty-first, General Gardner sent out Colonel Miles, with four hundred cavalry and a battery, under orders to proceed to the Plain Store, six or seven miles from Port Hudson, and reconnoitre. About four miles from Port Hudson he encountered the enemy, and a severe action ensued of two and a half hours' duration, with a loss of thirty killed and forty wounded on our side. At night, in pursuance of an order of recall from General Gardner, our forces fell back within the fortifications.

At the same time Colonel Powers's cavalry, some three hundred strong, were engaged on the Baton Rouge and Bayou Sara road, a mile and a half or two miles from Colonel Miles. No communication has been had with them since, and their loss is unknown.

On the morning of the twenty-second, the enemy pushed his infantry forward within a mile of our breastworks, and at the same time it was reported by the cavalry scouts that General Banks, who had recently completed his Teche campaign, was landing troops at Bayou Sara, (twelve miles above,) and moving in the direction of Port Hudson. From Saturday the twenty-third, to Tuesday the twenty-sixth, inclusive, the enemy was engaged in taking his position for the investment of our works. This being completed, on the morning of the twenty-seventh he advanced with his whole force against the breastworks, directing his main attack against the left, commanded by Colonel Steadman. Vigorous assaults were also made against the extreme left of Colonel Miles and General Beale, the former of whom commanded in the centre, the latter on the right.

On the left, the attack was made by a brigade of negroes, comprising about three regiments, together with the same force of white Yankees, across a bridge which had been built over Sandy Creek on the night of the twenty-fifth. This force was thrown against the Thirty-ninth Mississippi regiment, commanded by Colonel Shelby. About five hundred negroes in front advanced at double-quick, within one hundred and fifty yards of the works, when the artillery on the river bluff and two light pieces on Colonel Shelby's left opened upon them, and at the same time they were received with volleys of musketry from five companies of the Thirty-ninth. The negroes fled every way in perfect confusion, without firing a gun, probably carrying with them, in their panic flight, their sable comrades further in the rear, for the enemy themselves report that six hundred of them perished. If this be so, they must have been shot down by the Yankees in the rear, for the execution we did upon them did not exceed two hundred and fifty; and, indeed, volleys of musketry were heard in the direction of their flight. Among the slain were found the bodies of two negro captains with commissions in their pockets.

The First Alabama, Lieutenant-Colonel Locke, and the Tenth Arkansas, Colonel Witt, engaged the enemy outside the works, in the thick woods, and fought most gallantly, but were compelled by the heavy odds brought against them to fall back across the creek, and within the works. In this action Colonel Witt was captured, but was not fated to remain long a prisoner, being one of the daring band who effected their escape from the Maple Leaf, while on their way to a Yankee prison.

Colonel Johnson, with the Fifteenth Arkansas regiment, numbering about three hundred men, occupied a hill across Sandy Creek, which he had been fortifying for the previous week. About five thousand of the enemy came against this position, moving down a very narrow road, and many of them succeeded in gaining the breastworks, but they were repulsed and compelled to fall back into the woods, leaving eighty or ninety dead in front of the works.

On General Beale's left, consisting of the First Mississippi and the Forty-ninth Alabama, the enemy advanced in strong force, and were driven back with great slaughter. The repulse on Miles's left was decisive.

About three o'clock the Yankees, true to their knavish national instinct, raised the white flag, and under it attempted to make a rush with their infantry. This being reported to General Gardner, he sent orders to the different commanders not to recognize any white flag unless sent by the Federal commander himself. At sunset, the firing ceased, after a hotly contested engagement of twelve hours, during the whole of which our men had behaved with unflinching gallantry, and had completely repulsed the enemy at every point. Every man along the entire line had done his duty nobly. While this assault was going on, all the gun and mortar-boats kept up an incessant firing upon the lower batteries, but without inflicting any damage.

On the twenty-eighth, General Banks sent a flag proposing a cessation of hostilities, for the purpose of burying the dead, which was granted. About three o'clock P.M., the truce ceased, and the enemy, in heavy force, made a furious attack upon the First Alabama, which was gallantly repulsed.

From this time till June thirteenth, heavy skirmishing was constantly kept up, the men were behind the breastworks night and day, and one could scarcely show his head an instant without being made the mark of a sharp-shooter. Many were sick from exposure to the sun and other causes. The enemy were, meanwhile, engaged in digging ditches, erecting batteries, and advancing their parallels. The gun and mortar-boats kept up a continual fire by night and day, more, it would seem, for the purpose of exhausting the garrison by wakefulness than from any hope of direct advantage.

Saturday, the thirteenth of June, a communication was received from General Banks, demanding the unconditional surrender of the post. He complimented the garrison and its commander in high terms. Their courage, he said, amounted almost to heroism, but it was folly for them to attempt to hold the place any longer, as it was at his will, and he demanded the surrender in the name of humanity, to prevent the sacrifice of lives, as it would be impossible for his commanders to save the garrison from being put to the sword when the works should be carried by assault. His artillery, he said, was equal to any in extent and efficiency, and his men outnumbered ours five to one. He knew to what a condition they were reduced, as he had captured General Gardner's courier sent out with despatches to General Johnson. As these despatches were in cipher, it is probable that Banks exaggerated the amount of information he had derived from them.

General Gardner replied that his duty required him to defend the post, and he must refuse to entertain any such proposition.

On the morning of the fourteenth, just before day, the fleet and all the land batteries which the enemy had succeeded in erecting at one hundred to three hundred yards from our breastworks, opened fire at the same time. About daylight, under cover of the smoke, the enemy advanced along the whole line, and in many places approached within ten feet of our works. Our brave fellows were wide awake, and opening upon them with "buck and ball," drove them back in confusion, a great number of them being left dead in the ditches. One entire division and a brigade were ordered to charge the position of the First Mississippi and the Forty-ninth Alabama, and by the mere physical pressure of numbers some of them got within the works, but all those were immediately killed. Every regiment did its duty nobly, but this was the main attack. After a sharp contest of two hours, the enemy were everywhere repulsed, and withdrew to their old line, but heavy skirmishing was kept up most of the day.

After this repulse, General Banks sent no flag of truce to bury his dead, which remained exposed between the lines for three days. At the end of that time General Gardner sent a flag to Banks, requesting that he would remove them. Banks replied that he had no dead there. General Gardner then directed General Beale to send a flag to General Augur, and request him to bury the dead of his division, which lay in front of the First and Forty-ninth. Augur replied that he did not think he had any dead there, but he would grant a cessation of hostilities to ascertain. Accordingly parties were detailed to pass the dead bodies over to the Yankees, and two hundred and sixty odd were removed from this portion of the works, and with them one wounded man, who had been lying there three days without water, and was fly-blown from head to foot. It was surmised that Banks was unwilling that his men should witness the carnage which had been committed; but if that were the case, he only made matters worse by this delay, for much exasperation was manifested at the sight of the wounded man, and a great many were heard to say that, if that was the way the wounded were to be treated, they wanted to be out of the army. A great many of the dead must have perished during the three days' interval. In front of Johnson, Steadman, and elsewhere, none were buried, and the bodies of the slain could be seen from the breastworks on the day of the surrender, twenty-six days after the fight.

During the rest of the month there was heavy skirmishing daily, with constant firing night and day from the gun and mortar-boats, and the works were generally drawn close to our line, which, it may here be remarked, was about three miles in extent, and in the centre some three fourths of a mile from the river. Batteries of Parrott guns had been erected across the river, which were well served by the United States regulars, and maintained a continuous and very effective fire upon our river batteries, disabling many of the guns. On the land side a formidable battery of seventeen eight, nine, and ten-inch columbiads was established one hundred and fifty paces from our extreme right, one of seven guns in front of General Beale's centre; one of six guns in front of the First Mississippi, on the Jackson road; and seven guns and mortars were planted in front of Colonel Steadman. From these a fire was maintained day and night, doing but little damage to our men; but, as the siege continued, most of our artillery was disabled, only about fifteen pieces remaining uninjured at the time of the surrender.

During the siege of six weeks, from May twenty-seventh to July seventh, inclusive, the enemy must have fired from fifty to seventy-five thousand shot and shell, yet not more than twenty-five men were killed by these projectiles. They had worse dangers than these to contend against, but against them all they fought like heroes, and did their duty cheerfully. Several buildings were burned by the enemy's shells, among which was the mill, entailing a loss of two or three thousand bushels of corn.

About the twenty-ninth or thirtieth of June the garrison's supply of meat gave out, when General Gardner ordered the mules to be butchered, after ascertaining that the men were willing to eat them. Far from shrinking from this hardship, the men received their unusual rations cheerfully, and declared that they were proud to be able to say that they had been reduced to this extremity. Many of them, as if in mockery of famine, caught rats and ate them, declaring that they were better than squirrels.

At the same time the supply of ammunition was becoming exhausted, and at the time of the surrender there were only twenty rounds of cartridges left, with a small supply for artillery.

The hardships, privations, and dangers of the situation were diversified by many exciting incidents. One day our men were rolling ten-inch shells over the ramparts to explode against the enemy's works, which were not more than fifteen feet off, when a rush was made at our breastworks by about two hundred of the enemy. Two companies were hurried to the spot, and they were driven back. Of some sixteen who had gained the interior of our works every one was killed.

Mining was resorted to by the enemy; and after the surrender they said that they had a charge of three thousand pounds of powder already laid under the lower river battery. This, in fact, consisting of a single pivot gun, was the key to the whole position, as it commanded both the river and the land approaches, and against this the heaviest guns of the enemy, and their most vigorous efforts by land and water, were directed. Their story, however, is somewhat doubted.

But if the enemy mined, the garrison countermined and succeeded in blowing up the works in front of the First Mississippi.

Some time between the twentieth and thirtieth of June, a singular circumstance occurred one night about eleven o'clock, after a heavy fire. The water commenced running up-stream, and in half an hour rose six feet. In one place about twenty feet of the bluff disappeared, carrying away one of our river batteries. The roar of the water could be heard like distant thunder. If this were an earthquake—and it is difficult to give any other explanation—it must have "rolled unheededly away," so far as the enemy was concerned, for no notice of it has appeared in any of the Yankee papers.

We are obliged to omit incidents generally, including the brilliant sortie and spiking of the enemy's guns, but merely remark that the story about Banks's capturing fifteen prisoners on that occasion, and sending them back, for whom Gardner liberated a like number of Yankee prisoners, is merely a Yankee romance—in short, a lie.

On Tuesday, July seventh, salutes were fired from the enemy's batteries and gunboats, and loud cheering was heard along the entire line, and Yankees who were within conversing distance of our men, told them that Vicksburgh had fallen. That night, about ten o'clock, General Gardner summoned a council of war, consisting of General Beale, Colonels Steadman, Miles, Lyle, and Shelby, and Lieutenant-Colonel Marshal J. Smith, who, without exception, decided that it was impossible to hold out longer, considering that the provisions of the garrison were exhausted, the ammunition almost entirely expended, and a large proportion of the men sick, or, from exhaustion, unfit for duty. A communication was sent to General Banks, stating what had been heard from the men, asking for official information as to the truth of the news, and stating if it were, that General Gardner was ready to negotiate terms of surrender. General Banks's reply was received just before day, inclosing a letter from General Grant, announcing the fall of Vicksburgh. General Banks asked General Gardner to appoint commissioners to arrange with those on his part the terms of surrender, and Colonels Miles and Steadman, and Lieutenant-Colonel Smith were appointed.

General Banks demanded an unconditional surrender, as in the first instance, but finally agreed that officers and soldiers should retain their private property (in which negroes were not included.) A demand for a parole of the garrison was refused. General Banks said he would grant such terms with the greatest pleasure, but the orders of the Secretary of War forbid it.

The surrender was fixed to take place at seven o'clock on the morning of the ninth. At six o'clock the garrison were drawn up in line, and two officers of General Gardner's staff were sent to conduct the Federal officer deputed to receive the surrender. This was General Andrews, who entered the lines shortly after seven o'clock, on the Clinton road. General Gardner met him at the right of our line and delivered up his sword, observing that he surrendered his sword and his garrison since his provisions were exhausted. General Andrews replied that he received General Gardner's sword, but returned it to him for having maintained his defence so gallantly.

Meantime the enemy's infantry moved down in front of our line, both wings resting on the river, and completely encircling the little garrison, as if to cut off any attempt to escape. About that time our informant succeeded in passing through the lines, and evading the enemy's outposts. A great many of the garrison—probably several hundred—had made an attempt to escape the previous night, but the guard of the enemy was so strict that they could not pass out.

The number of the garrison which surrendered was between five thousand and six thousand, of whom there were not more than two thousand effective men for duty. During the siege about two hundred had been killed and three hundred wounded, besides several deaths from sickness. Among the officers killed were Colonel Pixley, of Arkansas, Captain Boone, of Louisiana, and Lieutenant Simonton, of the First Mississippi, besides a few others with whose names our informant was not familiar.

The universal feeling in the garrison is, that General Gardner did every thing in his power to foil the enemy and protract the siege, and only succumbed to the direst necessity. The garrison, too, have made a noble record. Even the enemy's accounts, upon which we have been entirely dependent for nearly two months, bear testimony to heroism unsurpassed during the war; but much yet remains to be told, and not a word of it but will reflect the greatest honor upon those devoted men.

Doc. 90.

EMANCIPATION IN MISSOURI.

JEFFERSON CITY, Mo., Wednesday, July 1.

THE following ordinance of emancipation was passed by the Convention this morning, by a vote of 84 ayes against 30 noes:

SECTION 1. The first and second clauses of the twenty-sixth section of the third article of the Constitution is hereby abrogated.

SEC. 2. That slavery, or involuntary servitude, except in punishment of crime, shall cease to exist in Missouri on the fourth of July, 1870, and all slaves within the State on that day are hereby declared to be free. Provided, however, that all persons emancipated by this ordinance shall remain under the control and be subject to their late owners, or their legal representatives, as servants during the following period, to wit: Those over twenty years of age, for and during their lives; those under twelve, until they arrive at the age of twenty three; and those of all other ages, until the fourth of July, 1876. The persons, or their legal representatives, who, up to the moment of emancipation, were owners of slaves hereby freed, shall, during the period for which the services of such freedmen are reserved to them, have the same authority and control over the said freedmen for the purpose of receiving the possessions and services of the same that are now held by the master in respect of his slaves: provided, however, that after the said fourth of July, 1870, no person so held to service shall be sold to non-residents, or removed from the State by authority of his late owner, or his legal representative.

Sec. 3. All slaves hereafter brought into the State, and not now belonging to citizens of the State, shall thereupon be free.

Sec. 4. All slaves removed by consent of their owners to any seceded State after the passage by such State of an act or ordinance of secession, and thereafter brought into this State by their owners, shall thereupon be free.

Sec. 5. The General Assembly shall have no power to pass laws to emancipate slaves without the consent of their owners.

Sec. 6. After the passage of this ordinance, no slave in this State shall be subject to State, county, or municipal taxes.

Doc. 91.

RANK OF MAJOR-GENERALS.

War Department, Adjutant-General's Office,
Washington, July 1, 1863.

General Order, No. 203.—The Board of Officers constituted by special orders No. 262 of the War Department, to investigate the subject of the precedence in rank claimed by Major-General B. F. Butler, U. S. volunteers, over the following officers, or any one of them, namely, Major-General Geo. B. McClellan, U. S. Army; Major-General J. C. Fremont, U. S. Army; Major-General J. A. Dix, U. S. volunteers, Major-General N. P. Banks, U. S. volunteers, have reported that in compliance with said orders they have examined the law and facts involved in the question referred to them, and the arguments submitted thereupon, and find as follows:

The Board, after careful examination of the law and facts involved in the question referred to them, and the arguments submitted therefrom, unanimously find, the question having been separately submitted as to the precedence in point of rank of each of them, that Major-Generals Geo. B. McClellan and J. C. Fremont, U. S. A., and Major-Generals J. A. Dix and N. P. Banks,

U. S. V., have precedence respectively in point of rank over Major-General B. F. Butler, U. S. V.

Jos. G. Totten,
Brigadier-General and Chief of Engineers.
J. H. Martindale,
Brigadier-General and Military Governor, D. C.
E. D. Townsend,
Assistant Adjutant-General.
J. Holt.

Approved.

Edwin M. Stanton,
Secretary of War.
By order of the Secretary of War.
E. D. Townsend,
Assistant Adjutant-General.

Doc. 92.

CAPTURED BATTLE-FLAGS.

GENERAL MEADE'S REPORT.

Headquarters Army of the Potomac,
July 18, 1863.

General: I have the honor herewith to transmit thirty-one battle-flags, captured from the enemy in the recent battle at Gettysburgh. Several other flags were captured on that occasion, but those sent embrace all thus far sent in by corps commanders.

Very respectfully your obedient servant,
George G. Meade,
Major-General Commanding.
Brigadier-General L. Thomas,
Adjutant-General, Washington.

General Barksdale's sword was given in my charge to bring with the above flags.

Ed. Schriver,
Inspector-General.

War Department, Adjutant-General's Office,
Washington, July 10, 1863.

General: By direction of the Secretary of War, I have the honor to acknowledge the receipt, at the hands of Colonel Schriver, Inspector-General, of thirty-one flags and one officer's sword, a part of the trophies won by your army at the battle of Gettysburgh.

These proofs of the heroic bravery and good conduct through which such brilliant and substantial results have been won to the country, will be carefully preserved as objects of the highest interest.

A list is herewith inclosed.

I have the honor to be, General, very respectfully, your obedient servant,
E. D. Townsend,
Assistant Adjutant-General.
Major-General Geo. G. Meade,
U. S. Vols., Commanding Army Potomac.

BATTLE-FLAGS CAPTURED AT GETTYSBURGH, JULY 3, 1863.

First Virginia infantry—captured by Eighty-second New-York volunteers.

Third Virginia infantry—no statement of capture.

Seventh Virginia infantry—captured by Eighty-second New-York volunteers.

Eighth Virginia infantry—captured by private Piam Haines, Co. E, Sixteenth Vermont volunteers.

Ninth Virginia infantry—statement of capture not legible.

Fourteenth Virginia infantry—statement of capture not legible.

Eighteenth Virginia infantry—no statement of capture.

Twenty-eighth Virginia infantry—no statement of capture.

Thirty-eighth Virginia infantry—captured by Co. G, Eighth Ohio volunteers, First brigade, Third division, Second corps.

Fifty-third Virginia infantry—no statement of capture.

Fifty-sixth Virginia infantry—no statement of capture.

Fifty-seventh Virginia infantry—statement of capture not legible.

Battle-flag, Virginia infantry—no statement of capture.

Seventh North-Carolina—no statement of capture.

Twenty-second North-Carolina—captured by Forty-second —— volunteers, Second division, Second corps.

Twenty-third North-Carolina — captured by Second division, First corps.

Thirty-fourth North-Carolina—captured by Co. G, Eighth Ohio volunteers, First brigade, Third division, Second army corps.

Fifteenth Georgia—captured by Sergeant J. B. Thompson, Co. G, First rifles, Pennsylvania Reserve corps.

. Forty-eighth Georgia—no statement of capture.

Thirteenth Alabama—captured by Co. C, First Delaware volunteers.

Second Florida regiment—captured by Sergeant Charles D. Brink, color-bearer, Co. K, Sixteenth Vermont volunteers.

Second Mississippi regiment—captured, with the entire regiment, by the Sixth Wisconsin, kept for two days by Sergeant Evans, while a prisoner in the hands of the enemy.

Battle-flag, (State number not given) — captured by Corporal Naveris, Thirty-ninth regiment New-York volunteers.

Battle-flag, (State number not given) — captured by —— Dore, Co. D.

Battle-flag, (State number not given) — captured by Twelfth New-Jersey volunteers.

Battle-flag, (State number not given)—on blue field the words, " *Dulce et decorum est pro patria mori ;*" reverse side, a female, with wreath, and the words, " A crown for the brave." Captured by Sixtieth regiment New-York volunteers, Colonel Abel Goddard, Third brigade, Second division, Twelfth army corps.

Battle-flag, (State number not given) — captured by First Sergeant Maggi, Thirty-eighth New-York volunteers.

Battle-flag, (State number not given) — captured by Captain M. Brown, Jr., Co. A, One Hundred and Twenty-sixth New-York volunteers.

Battle-flag, (State number not given) — captured by Sixtieth New-York volunteers.

Battle-flag, (State number not given) — captured by Twelfth New-Jersey volunteers.

CAPTURED AT HANOVER.

Brigadier-General Kilpatrick—Battle-flag.

Doc. 93.

FREEDMEN IN VIRGINIA.

OFFICIAL REPORT.

FREEDMEN'S DEPARTMENT, }
SOUTH-POTOMAC, July 10, 1863. }

Chief Quartermaster for the Department of Washington :

SIR : In accordance with orders issued from headquarters, I herewith submit my report of the numbers and condition and health of the freedmen established, by an order of the Secretary of War, upon the abandoned farms of rebels in Virginia.

We landed on our camping ground on the Arlington estate, naming it Camp Springdale, Monday afternoon, May eighteenth, and pitched our tents for the night, and thus began our improvements.

At the beginning, there were about ninety persons in all. The work commenced the second day on the farm.

May thirtieth we established a camp on Major Nutt's farm, near Falls Church, Virginia, calling it Camp Rucker. The people at this place had to be sheltered in tents, there being no houses in the vicinity belonging to rebel owners.

On the same day, May thirtieth, we commenced an encampment on rebel Cooke's farm, near Langley, on the Leesburgh turnpike. This encampment we called Camp Wadsworth. A branch of this camp was shortly after formed on a farm of rebel Means near by. A week later we organized the two encampments—Camp Todd, where General Casey had his encampment formerly, near by Fort Albany, and Camp Beckwith on McVay's and Jackson's farms, near Lewinsville. The number of the several encampments on June thirtieth is as follows: Camp Springdale, three hundred; Camp Todd, two hundred and thirty ; Camp Rucker, one hundred and five ; Camp Wadsworth, one hundred and seventy-eight ; Camp Beckwith, seventy-two—total, eight hundred and eighty-five.

The people in my charge have subsisted on Government rations as follows : Every man or woman above the ages of sixteen and fourteen years has drawn daily one ration; every boy from one year to sixteen years, and every girl from one to fourteen years, has drawn one half rations; all below one year have drawn nothing.

There has been a manifest improvement in the tone of health since we came over this side of the Potomac.

We have had fresh air and pure water, and work on the soil to employ the people. This has contributed to the health of the people. Though several contagious diseases appeared among the people, yet they have easily yielded to the treatment, or have been removed to the Pest-House in Washington.

Twenty persons have died during the month of June, fifteen of whom were children, and five of the fifteen were only twelve months old, or under.

At Camps Springdale and Rucker we have sheltered the people in tents, there being no houses near the grounds to be cultivated to be occupied. At Camp Todd we have used the log huts put up for the accommodation of General Casey's encampment. These houses have capacity of holding not less than one thousand people, and are in a good degree of preservation. At Camps Wadsworth and Beckwith the people occupy two of the farms abandoned by the rebel owners.

We have constructed quarters for the Superintendent of Freedmen and an office for the same, a store-room for Commissary Department, and another for agricultural implements, and a forage house and quarters and an office for the Surgeon. Also, we have hauled down a large supply of poles from abandoned camps on Minor's Hill and vicinity, which we purpose for quarters for freedmen at an early day.

This work has been well done, and has a respectable show as regards amount, and the promise of ample remuneration is cheering.

I would suggest that the good of these people could be best secured by having the women and children remain at Camps Springdale and Todd, the last being just under the fortifications of Fort Albany, or at least the outside of defence of that fort, while the former is inside the fortifications, and send only a sufficient force of men to the outposts with a proper guard, and return each Saturday night, and go back to their work on Monday morning. This plan would be well for several considerations; mainly it would place them in a greater degree of security, and then it would place them more immediately under the eye of the Superintendent of them, and thus take away the necessity of having any assistant on each of these farms, except that of the farmer.

Second. I would request that a military order be obtained from General Heintzelman, giving Superintendent of Freedmen the power to perform the marriage ceremony among them. A similar order has been passed in the Department of South-Carolina. Also a military commission (or a commission) be appointed, consisting of the military commander of the post and the Superintendent of the Freedmen and the Surgeon in charge, who shall hear causes of complaint made by them in relation to want of fidelity of parties to the marriage contract, and determine the facts and the penalty of every violation of the same. There has been a similar order for the Department of South-Carolina.

All of which is respectfully submitted.

D. B. NICHOLS,
Superintendent of Freedmen.

Doc. 94.

THE NAVY ON THE MISSISSIPPI.

OFFICIAL DESPATCHES.

UNITED STATES MISSISSIPPI SQUADRON,
FLAG-SHIP BLACK HAWK,
OFF VICKSBURGH, July 13, 1863.

SIR: I have made reports to the Department of the different actions that have occurred on this river since the investment of Vicksburgh; and it now remains for me to give credit to the different officers who have participated in the events transpiring here.

When I took command of this squadron, this river was virtually closed against our steamers from Helena to Vicksburgh. It was only necessary to impress the officers and men with the importance of opening communication with New-Orleans, and every one, with few exceptions, have embarked in the enterprise with a zeal that is highly creditable to them, and with a determination that the river should be opened if their aid could effect it.

With such officers and the able General who commanded the army, I have not feared for the result, though it has been postponed longer than I thought it would be.

First and foremost, allow me to speak of Captain Pennock, Fleet Captain and Commandant of Station at Cairo. To him I am much indebted for the promptness with which he has kept the squadron supplied with all that was required or could be procured. His duty has been no sinecure, and he has performed it with an ability that could not have been surpassed by any officer of the navy. He has materially assisted me in the management of the Tennessee and Cumberland squadrons, keeping me promptly informed of all the movements of the enemy, and enabling me to make the proper dispositions to check him, exercising a most discreet judgment in moving the vessels to meet the rebels when there was no time to hear from me.

The war on the banks of the Tennessee and Cumberland has been carried on most actively. There has been incessant skirmishing between the guerrillas and gunboats, in which the rebels have been defeated in every instance. So constant are these attacks that we cease to think of them as of any importance, though there has been much gallantry displayed on many occasions.

Lieutenant Commanders Phelps and Fitch have each had command of these rivers, and have shown themselves to be most able officers. I feel no apprehension at any time with regard to movements in that quarter. Had it not been for the activity and energy displayed by Lieutenant Commander Fitch, Captain Pennock, and Lieutenant Commander Phelps, General Rosecrans would have been left without provisions.

To Captain Walke, Commander Woodworth, Lieutenant Commanders Breese, Greer, Shirk, Owen, Wilson, Walker, Bache, Murphy, Selfridge, Prichett, Ramsay, and acting volunteer Lieutenant Hoel I feel much indebted for their active and energetic attention to all my orders, and their ready coöperation with the army corps commanders at all times, which enabled them to carry out their plans successfully.

The Benton, Lieutenant Commander Greer, Mound City, Lieutenant Commander Byron Wilson, Tuscumbia, Lieutenant Commander Shirk, Carondelet, Acting Lieutenant Murphy, and the Sterling Price, Commander Woodworth, have been almost constantly under fire of the batteries at Vicksburgh since the forty-five days' siege commenced.

The attack of the twenty-second of May by the Benton, Mound City, Carondelet, and Tuscumbia on all the water batteries, in which three were silenced, and four guns injured or dismounted, was one of the best contested engagements of the kind during the war.

On the next attack of the same gunboats, when General Grant opened all his batteries for six hours, the river batteries were all deserted, and the gunboats moved up and down without having a shot fired at them, showing the moral effect the first attack had.

The attack of the Cincinnati, Lieutenant Commander Bache, on the water-battery will long be ranked among the most gallant events of this war; and though Lieutenant Bache had the misfortune to have his vessel sunk under him, he well deserves the handsome commendations bestowed upon him by the Department.

To Lieutenant Commander Ramsay, of the Choctaw, was assigned the management of three heavy guns placed on scows, and anchored in a position that commanded the town and water-batteries. Every gun the enemy could bring to bear on these boats was fired incessantly at them, but without one moment's cessation of fire on the part of our seamen, though the enemy's shot and shell fell like hail among them. This battery completely enfiladed the batteries and rifle-pits in front of General Sherman, and made them untenable.

The mortar-boats were under charge of Gunner Eugene Mack, who for thirty days stood at his post, the firing continuing night and day. He performed his duty well and merits approval. The labor was extremely hard, and every man at the mortars was laid up with sickness, owing to excessive labor. After Mr. Mack was taken ill, Ensign Miller took charge and conducted the firing with marked ability. We know that nothing conduced more to the end of the siege than the mortar-firing, which demoralized the rebels, killed and wounded a number of persons, killed the cattle, destroyed property of all kinds, and set the city on fire. On the last two days we were enabled to reach the outer works of the enemy by firing heavy charges of twenty-six pounds of powder; the distance was three miles, and the falling of shells was very annoying to the rebels—to use the words of a rebel officer, "our shells intruded everywhere."

Lieutenant Commander Breese has been very efficient in relieving me of a vast amount of duty, superintending personally all the requirements made on the navy, and facilitating the operations of the army in every way that lay in his power. In every instance where it was at all possible to bring the Black Hawk into action against the enemy's batteries he has not hesitated to do so, though she is not fortified exactly for such a purpose. His long-range guns have done most excellent service at different times.

I beg leave to mention the different commanders of the light-draughts, who have carried out my orders promptly, aided in keeping guerrillas from the river, convoyed transports safely, and kept their vessels in good condition for service, namely, Acting Volunteer Lieutenant George W. Brown, commanding Forest Rose; Acting Volunteer Lieutenant C. Downing, commanding Signal; Acting Volunteer Lieutenant J. S. Hurd, commanding Covington; Ensign Wm. C. Handford, commanding Robb; Acting Master J. C. Bunner, commanding New Era; Acting Volunteer Lieutenant J. V. Johnstone, commanding Romeo; Acting Volunteer Lieutenant John Pierce, commanding Petrel; Acting Master W. E. Fentress, commanding Rattler; Acting Volunteer Lieutenant T. E. Smith, commanding Linden; Acting Volunteer Lieutenant E. C. Brennand, commanding Prairie Bird; Acting Volunteer Lieutenant J. Gandy, commanding Queen City. There are others who deserve commendation, but these seem to me the most prominent.

The action of the fourth of July, at Helena, wherein the Tyler participated so largely, has already been reported to the Department. There is no doubt left in the minds of any but that the Tyler saved Helena, for though General Prentiss fought with a skill and daring not excelled in this war, his little force of three thousand five hundred men were fast being overpowered by the enemy with eighteen thousand men, when the Tyler took a position and changed the fortunes of the day.

I must not omit to mention Acting Volunteer Lieutenants Hamilton and Richardson, of the powder vessels Great Western and Judge Torrence. They were unremitting in their attention to their duties during the siege, supplying without delay every requisition made on them by army and navy, and volunteering for any service.

When the army called on the navy for siege-guns, I detailed what officers and men I could spare to man and work the batteries. Lieutenant Commander Selfridge had command of the naval battery on the right wing, General Sherman's corps. This battery was worked with marked ability, and elicited the warmest praises from the Commanding General. One thousand shells were fired into the enemy's works from Lieutenant Commander Selfridge's guns. His services being required up the river, I relieved him a few days before the surrender, and Lieutenant Commander Walker supplied his place, and conducted the firing with the same ability.

Acting Master Charles B. Dahlgren was ordered to report to General McPherson for duty, and was assigned the management of two nine-inch guns, which were admirably served.

Acting Master Reed, of the Benton, had charge of the batteries at Fort Benton, so named by General Herron in honor of the occasion. General Herron generously acknowledged the services of those I sent him, which communication I inclose with this report.

I have endeavored to do justice to all who were immediately engaged in the struggle for the mastery of the Mississippi. To the army do we owe immediate thanks for the capture of Vicksburgh; but the army was much facilitated by the navy, which was ready at all times to coöperate. This has been no small undertaking. The late investment and capture of Vicksburgh will be characterized as one of the greatest military achievements ever known. The conception of the idea originated solely with General Grant, who adopted a course in which great labor was performed, great battles were fought, and great risks were run. A single mistake would have involved us in difficulty; but so well were all the plans matured, so well were all the movements timed, and so rapid were the evolutions performed, that not a mistake has occurred from the passage of the fleet by Vicksburgh and the passage of the army across the river, up to the present time. So confident was I of the ability of General Grant to carry out his plans when he explained them to me, that I never hesitated to change my position from above to below Vicksburgh. The work was hard, the fighting severe, but the blows struck were constant.

In forty-five days after our army was landed, a rebel army of sixty thousand men had been captured, killed, and wounded, or scattered to their homes, perfectly demoralized, while our loss has been only about five thousand killed, wounded, and prisoners, and the temporary loss of one gunboat.

The fortifications and defences of the city exceed any thing that has been built in modern times, and are doubly unassailable from their immense height above the bed of the river.

The fall of Vicksburgh insured the fall of Port Hudson and the opening of the Mississippi River, which I am happy to say can be traversed from its source to its mouth without apparent impediment, the first time during the war.

I take this opportunity to give to Mr. Fendal and Mr. Strausz, assistants in the coast survey, the full credit they deserve for their indefatigable industry. Since they have been attached to the squadron they have been connected with almost every expedition that has been undertaken; they have kept both army and navy supplied with charts when they could not otherwise be obtained; they were found ready at all times to go anywhere or do any thing required of them, whether it was on a gunboat expedition or in the trenches before Vicksburgh engineering, when the General Commanding called for volunteers from the navy. They have added to our collection of maps many geographical corrections which are valuable, and they have proved to me that no squadron can operate effectively without a good corps of surveyors.

I have the honor to be, very respectfully, your obedient servant, DAVID D. PORTER,
Acting Rear-Admiral Com'g Miss. Squadron.
Hon. GIDEON WELLES,
Secretary of the Navy, Washington.

HEADQUARTERS LEFT DIVISION INVESTING FORCES, }
VICKSBURGH, July 5, 1863. }

ADMIRAL: While congratulating you on the success of the army and navy in reducing this Sebastopol of rebeldom, I must at the same time thank you for the aid my division has had from yourself and your ships.

The guns received from the Benton, under charge of Acting Master Reed, a gallant and efficient officer, have formed the most effective battery I had, and I am glad to say that the officer in charge has well sustained the reputation of your squadron. For the efforts you have made to coöperate with me in my position on the left I am under many obligations.

Very respectfully your obedient servant,
F. J. HERRON,
Major-General.
Admiral D. D. PORTER,
Commanding Mississippi Squadron.

HEADQUARTERS LEFT DIVISION INVESTING FORCES, }
VICKSBURGH, July 5, 1863. }

CAPTAIN: Having had from your ship, since the first of our siege operations on the left of the investing line, four of your heavy guns, under charge of Acting Master J. Frank Reed, I must, before their return to the ship, express to you my thanks for the good service they have rendered, and the admirable and officer-like manner in which they were handled by Acting Master Reed. His battery (which I have named after your ship, Battery Benton) has been our main support in advancing, and I learn has been a terror to the rebels in our immediate front.

The management and conduct of Acting Master Reed and his subordinates, Wm. Moore and W. P. Brownell, cannot be too highly spoken of, and I can assure you they have nobly sustained the reputation of your ship and the Mississippi Squadron.

Acting Master Reed is well worthy of promotion.

Congratulating you, Captain, on the combined success of the army and navy in reducing this Sebastopol of the rebels, I remain, very truly, yours, F. J. HERRON,
Major-General.
To Captain J. H. GREER,
Commanding Benton.

UNITED STATES STEAMER CONESTOGA, }
MISSISSIPPI RIVER, July 8, 1863. }

SIR: I have the honor to present the following report of the naval battery, consisting of two eight-inch columbiads, whilst under my command.

Acting under your orders of June first, I reported to General Sherman, who located the battery nearly on the extreme right, not far from the river. After many delays I succeeded in getting one gun in position the night of June fourth. Fire was opened from it the next morning, and the next night the other was got in position. Opposed to us was an eight-inch columbiad, six hundred yards distant, and a thirty-two pounder, one thousand yards distant.

The columbiad was disabled by our fire the second day, and no further use made of it; the thirty-two pounder was also effectually silenced. There was nothing left at which to direct our fire, but rifle-pits. Upon these I kept up a slow and steady fire at different intervals during the day. Operating upon earth-works, it was impossible to know the damage inflicted. Deserters report, however, that our fire was so accurate as to cause the battery to be greatly feared, and that it had done them much harm. On June twenty-fifth, agreeably to your orders, I turned my command over to Captain Walker.

It gives me pleasure to bear testimony to the good conduct of my officers and men. The labor imposed upon them was very arduous—working their guns under a hot sun, and frequently employed half the night repairing the damage inflicted during the day.

Very respectfully, your obedient servant,
THOS. J. SELFRIDGE,
Lieutenant Commander.

Acting Rear-Admiral DAVID D. PORTER,
Commanding Mississippi Squadron.

HEADQUARTERS EXPEDITIONARY ARMY, }
BLACK RIVER, July 4, 1863. }

Admiral D. D. Porter, Commanding Fleet.

DEAR ADMIRAL: No event in my life could have given me more personal pride or pleasure than to have met you to-day on the wharf at Vicksburgh—a Fourth of July so eloquent in events as to need no words or stimulants to elevate its importance.

I can appreciate the intense satisfaction you must feel at lying before the very monster that has defied us with such deep and malignant hate, and seeing your once disunited fleet again a unit, and better still, the chain that made an inclosed sea of a link in the great river broken for ever. In so magnificent a result I stop not to count who did it. It is done, and the day of our nation's birth is consecrated and baptized anew in a victory won by the united Navy and Army of our country. God grant that the harmony and mutual respect that exists between our respective Commanders and shared by all the true men of the joint service may continue for ever and serve to elevate our national character, threatened with shipwreck. Thus I muse as I sit in my solitary camp out in the wood far from the point for which we have justly striven so long and so well, and though personal curiosity would tempt me to go and see the frowning batteries and sunken pits that have defied us so long, and sent to their silent graves so many of our early comrades in the enterprise, I feel that other tasks lie before me, and time must not be lost. Without casting anchor, and despite the heat and the dust and the drought, I must again into the bowels of the land to make the conquest of Vicksburgh fulfil all the conditions it should in the progress of this war. Whether success attend my efforts or not, I know that Admiral Porter will ever accord to me the exhibition of a pure and unselfish zeal in the service of our country.

It does seem to me that Port Hudson, without facilities for supplies or interior communication, must soon follow the fate of Vicksburgh and leave the river free, and to you the task of preventing any more Vicksburghs or Port Hudsons on the bank of the great inland sea.

Though farther apart, the navy and army will still act in concert, and I assure you I shall never reach the banks of the river or see a gunboat but I will think of Admiral Porter, Captain Breese, and the many elegant and accomplished gentlemen it has been my good fortune to meet on armed or unarmed decks of the Mississippi Squadron. Congratulating you and the officers and men of your command at the great result in which you have borne so conspicuous a part,

I remain, as ever, your friend and servant,
W. T. SHERMAN,
Major-General.

Doc. 95.

THE ESCAPE OF LEE'S ARMY.

L. L. CROUNSE'S ACCOUNT.

FREDERICK, Thursday, July 16, 1862.

THE campaign north of the Potomac is ended. The enemy has made an inglorious and hazardous escape across a river which we had fondly hoped was the great barrier to his retreat. The particulars of the retreat you have had in full. There remains, however, a brief history of the movements of both armies for the past ten days yet untold. The material portions of it I will give, as nearly as possible, and the public may draw its own conclusions. My *rôle* is fact, not comment.

The rebel army under General Lee, repulsed with sanguinary loss, but not literally defeated, began its retirement from the field of Gettysburgh on Friday night, July third. His left wing, which had fiercely assailed our right on that day, and had, in addition, occupied the village of Gettysburgh, was found to be withdrawn early on Saturday morning, when our forces, under General Howard, advanced and occupied the place. His right wing and centre fell back a short distance on Saturday night, and on Sunday morning the rebel rear was found by a small reconnoissance to rest in the vicinity of Fairfield, eight miles from our front.

General Howard reconnoitred the enemy's rear in person, and came suddenly upon their skirmishers, who fired, wounding severely his valuable Aid, Captain James J. Griffiths, who, I regret to learn, died in Philadelphia on the fourteenth instant.

On Sunday morning the Sixth corps, under General Sedgwick, was ordered to make a reconnoissance in force, ascertain the position of the enemy, and, as nearly as possible, his line of retreat. At some time during the day General Sedgwick brought up with the enemy in force, near Fairfield. A severe skirmish followed, but General Sedgwick refrained from bringing on a general engagement.

During Sunday, between the hours of ten o'clock A.M. and six P.M., after the details for burying the dead had been made, all the corps were ordered to move in three columns, as nearly as possible upon the heels of the enemy. Headquarters, itself, was ordered to move to Creagerstown that evening, twenty-two miles distant. This, I think, was before the result of General Sedgwick's reconnoissance had become known.

Subsequently all the orders for moving were countermanded, and the various corps halted from Sunday night until Tuesday morning. Headquarters remained at a point ten miles south-east of Gettysburgh until that time.

In the mean time our cavalry were rapidly developing the line of the enemy's retreat. Instead of moving toward Chambersburgh, which is almost south-west of Gettysburgh, Lee took a shorter line of retreat, and at once seized the two upper gaps in the South-Mountain, namely, the gap leading from Fairfield through Jack's Mountain to Waynesboro, known as Fountaindale Gap, and the gap through which passes the road from Emmittsburgh to Waynesboro and Greencastle, known as Monterey Gap. Then by the country roads, in a south-westerly direction, toward Hagerstown.

There were then left to General Meade two routes to pursue—one to follow directly on the heels of the enemy, and fight him in these gaps, or march at once for Harmon's, Braddock's, Turner's, and Crampton's Gaps, in South-Mountain range—all below those occupied by the enemy.

The latter route was adopted, involving an average of march of from fifteen to twenty miles further than the enemy had to go, and on Tuesday morning, two days after Lee had fully abandoned his position, the army was put upon forced marches for the western slope of the South-Mountain. The general rendezvous of the corps was Middletown, in the valley, between the Catoctin and South-Mountain ranges. Four or five of the army corps entered this valley by a road six or eight miles north of Frederick, while two or three of them moved around by the angle of Frederick, and thence west into the Middletown Valley.

The concentration of the different corps at Middletown was made substantially on Wednesday night—some being in advance, some at, and some just in the rear of Middletown. Headquarters, which made a single leap of thirty-five miles from Gettysburgh to Frederick on Tuesday, moved to Middletown on Wednesday.

On Thursday, July ninth, the march was resumed, the Second and Twelfth corps passing down the Middletown Valley to Crampton's Gap, eight miles below Turner's Gap, through which the balance of the army passed. Thursday night's headquarters were moved to the Mountain House in the Gap, four miles west of Middletown.

On Friday, the army was all well over the mountain, well in hand for attack or defence—more so by far than when the enemy made the attack at Gettysburgh, for the corps were then twenty miles away. Thursday night, the Sixth corps, which was in advance, had pushed out four miles beyond Boonsboro, or within three miles of Funkstown, Buford's cavalry having gallantly cleared the road after two days' severe fighting with Stuart.

On Friday, the headquarters of General Meade were established near Antietam Bridge, on the Williamsport road, three miles west of Boonsboro, and seven miles south of Hagerstown, they remaining there until Tuesday night.

From Friday until Tuesday morning, our average advance against the enemy was about three miles. During this time our line was formed on the west side of the Antietam, and we approached the enemy to within a distance ranging from half a mile to a mile and a half. Here we fell to throwing up works of defence.

The lines of the two armies were from six to eight miles long, that of the enemy being the longest. Of course, thus extended, both were very weak, and the advantage rested with the party who made a vigorous and sudden attack. I believe I am correct in saying that we never fully compelled the enemy to develop his line. We knew he had one, but its exact location, character, and strength was not, as far as I am able to learn, fully ascertained. There is good evidence, however, for the belief that the chief portion of the enemy's works were thrown up between Thursday and Monday. What little information we got of their doings tended to show this. In addition, they kept up an exceedingly stubborn front, with their pickets and skirmishers, and acted in every way just as we know they always do, when they wish to conceal some important movement—just as we do when we desire to do the same thing.

On Sunday evening a council of the corps commanders, also attended by the Chief Engineer, the Chief of Cavalry, and the Chief of Staff, was held. The question of attacking the enemy was discussed. Of the seven infantry corps commanders, five opposed an attack and two favored it—Generals Howard and Wadsworth. In addition, General Warren, Chief Engineer, and General Pleasanton, commanding the Cavalry corps, earnestly favored a forward movement, as they had not failed to do from the first. A council was said to be necessary, because it was the only way, in view of the active nature of the campaign thus far, by which a correct idea of the efficiency of each corps could be ascertained. It is worthy of note that Generals Howard and Wadsworth, who advised an attack, were the weakest in numbers.

What General Meade's own inclination was I am not positively informed, but I think he desired to push ahead, but finally deferred to the opinion of the majority of his subordinates. A consideration which, doubtless, had some influence in delaying a movement, was the fact that reënforcements were slowly arriving, and we were growing stronger. Another idea prevailed very strongly with some of the corps commanders, namely, that Lee would be compelled to attack us, because of the continued high stage of the Potomac, and that he could not, so long as it lasted, obtain any reliable means of crossing; and the belief also existed that, as a matter of pride, he would not retreat, but would arbitrate again on the bloody field of another battle. I may add here that our information concerning the condition of the river and the operations of the enemy in its vicinity was exceeding scanty, and generally considered unreliable. One or two reports of scouts, however, which were at first discredited, afterward proved to have been well founded, namely, that Lee had obtained a number of pontoons from Winchester, and that he was building flat-boats at Williamsport.

On Sunday night, July twelfth, some of the corps commanders began, on their own responsibility, to throw up earthworks for a line of defence. This was continued through Monday and Monday night, even up to the very moment of the departure of the enemy's rear-guard. It is due to General Warren, Chief Engineer, to say that this was entirely without his orders, and he strongly disapproved the proceeding, as well as condemned the position of much of the line.

The escape of Lee was reported at daylight on Tuesday morning, by a negro who came in from Williamsport. His statement was not credited, General Meade believing that the enemy was merely concentrating his forces at some point on his long line to resist an attack. But by nine A.M. every body was convinced. The manner and means by which he escaped you have already had in full.

Three or four facts grouped together tell the whole story. The national army took up its line on Friday and remained nearly in the same position until Tuesday; the troops were in superb spirits, and their confidence that they could whip the rebels was stronger than I have ever yet seen it, and was fully exemplified in the few sharp skirmishes that took place—all, both cavalry and infantry, resulting uniformly in our favor. The enemy had a strong line, but not one-third so formidable as ours at Gettysburgh—dangerously weak because of its length, and weaker by far on Friday, July tenth, than on Monday, July thirteenth. The enemy's means of crossing on Friday were incomplete, on Monday they were complete enough to carry him away; and yet on Monday his army was divided by the river, and in a state of trepidation for fear their hazardous movement should be discovered. We were growing stronger, by additions of troops, while we lay still, and the enemy was improving the same time in recovering from the disheartenment of his defeat, and the aggregation of supplies and ammunition from Winchester. In short, delay proved of far more advantage to the enemy than to us. Add to this the fact, of which I am personally cognizant, that the soldiers received the news of Lee's escape with feelings of bitter disappointment, and that they would rather have fought him two to one than to chase all over Virginia again after him, and the policy of "a vigorous prosecution of the war" at all times and under all circumstances is vindicated with greater emphasis than ever heretofore.

A *resumé* of the campaign since the army left Fredericksburgh, I will give in my next.

Doc. 96.

THE BATTLE OF WAUHATCHEE.

OFFICIAL REPORT OF GENERAL THOMAS.

HEADQUARTERS DEPARTMENT OF THE CUMBERLAND,
CHATTANOOGA, Nov. 7, 1863.

GENERAL: I have the honor to forward herewith the official reports of Major-General Hooker, (commanding the Eleventh and Twelfth corps,) and of Brigadier-General W. F. Smith, Chief Engineer Department of the Cumberland, (commanding the expedition, composed of Turchin's brigade, Baird's division, Fourteenth army corps, and of Hazen's brigade, Wood's division, Fourth army corps, and detachments of the Eighteenth Ohio infantry, under command of Colonel T. R. Stanley, and of the First Michigan engineers, under command of Captain B. D. Fox,) of the operations of their respective commands between the twenty-sixth and twenty-eighth ultimo, to gain possession of the south bank of the Tennessee River, and to open the road for a dépôt of supplies at Bridgeport.

Preliminary steps had already been taken to execute this vitally important movement before the command of the department devolved on me. The bridge, which it was necessary to throw across the river at Brown's Ferry, to gain possession of the northern end of Lookout Valley, and open communication with Bridgeport by road and river, was nearly complete. On the twenty-third, orders were sent to General Hooker to concentrate the Eleventh corps and one division of the Twelfth corps at Bridgeport, informing him at the same time what his force was expected to accomplish, and that a force from this place would coöperate with his, by establishing a bridge across the river at Brown's Ferry, and seize the heights on the south or Lookout Valley side, thus giving him an open road to Chattanooga, when his forces should arrive in Lookout Valley. The force to throw the bridge was organized by Saturday, the twenty-fourth, and the bridge completed, giving General Smith two days to examine the ground with the two brigade commanders, and to give all the necessary detailed instructions to insure success.

General Hooker reported on the twenty-sixth that he would be ready to move on the twenty-seventh at daylight. He was instructed to move at the appointed time with full directions how to provide for the defence of his flank, and to cover the approaches to the road from the direction of Trenton. The bridge was successfully thrown across the rivers on the night of the twenty-sixth, and General Hooker reached Lookout

Valley, and communicated with this place on the twenty-eighth. The enemy attempted to surprise him the night after he reached his position in Lookout Valley, and after an obstinate contest of two hours' duration was completely repulsed, with a loss of upward of one thousand five hundred killed and wounded, over one hundred prisoners, and several hundred stand of arms. I refer you to the reports of Generals Hooker and Smith for the details of the operations of their commands, commending to favorable consideration the names of those officers especially mentioned by them for gallant and meritorious conduct.

The skilful execution by General Smith of the work assigned him, and the promptness with which General Hooker with his troops met and repulsed the enemy on the night of the twenty-eighth, reflects the greatest credit on both of these officers and their entire commands. I herewith annex consolidated returns of casualties.

I am, General, very respectfully, your obedient servant, GEORGE H. THOMAS, Major-General U. S. V., Commanding.
Brigadier-General L. THOMAS, Adjutant-General U. S. A., Washington.

MAJOR-GENERAL HOOKER'S COMMAND.

	Killed.	Wounded.	Missing.	Total.
Eleventh Corps,	38	148	14	200
Second Division, 12th Corps,	34	174	8	216
Brig.-Gen. Smith's command,	4	17	—	21
Total,				437

REPORT OF BRIGADIER-GENERAL W. F. SMITH.

HEADQUARTERS DEPARTMENT OF THE CUMBERLAND, OFFICE CHIEF ENGINEER, CHATTANOOGA, Nov. 4, 1863.

GENERAL: I have the honor to submit the following report of the operations for making a lodgment on the south side of the Tennessee River, at Brown's Ferry.

On the nineteenth of October, I was instructed by General Rosecrans to reconnoitre the river in the vicinity of Williams Island, with a view of making the island a cover for a steamboat landing and storehouses, and began the examination near the lower end of the island. Following the river up, I found on the opposite bank, above the head of the island, a sharp range of hills whose base was washed by the river. This range extended up the river nearly to Lookout Creek, and was broken at Brown's Ferry by a narrow gorge, through which ran the road to the old ferry, and flowed a small creek. The valley between the ridge of hills and Raccoon Mountains was narrow, and a lodgment effected there would give us the command of the Kelly's Ferry road, and seriously interrupt the communications of the enemy up Lookout Valley, and down to the river on Raccoon Mountain. The ridge seemed thinly picketed, and the evidences were against the occupation of that part of the valley by a large force of the enemy, and it seemed quite possible to take by surprise what could not have been carried by assault, if heavily occupied by an opposing force.

The Major-General commanding the Geographical division and the Major-General commanding the department visited with me the ferry, a few days after this reconnoissance, and both agreed as to the importance of the position by itself, and especially in connection with the movements to be made from Bridgeport to open the river, and I was directed to make the necessary arrangements for the expedition to effect a lodgment. To do this fifty pontoons with oars to carry a crew and twenty-five armed men were prepared, and also two flat-boats carrying forty and seventy men. The force detailed for the expedition consisted of the brigades of Brigadier-General Turchin and Brigadier-General Hazen, with three batteries, to be posted under the direction of Major Mendenhall, Assistant Chief of Artillery. Sunday, the twenty-fifth of October, I was assigned to the command of the expedition, and the troops were distributed as follows:

One thousand five hundred men, under Brigadier-General Hazen, were to embark in the boats and pass down the river, a distance of about nine miles, seven of which would be under the fire of the pickets of the enemy. It was deemed better to take this risk than to attempt to launch the boats near the ferry, because they would move more rapidly than intelligence could be taken by infantry pickets, and, in addition, though the enemy might be alarmed, he would not know where the landing was to be attempted, and therefore could not concentrate with certainty against us. The boats were called off in sections, and the points at which each section was to land were carefully selected and pointed out to the officers in command, and range-fires kept burning, lest in the night the upper points should be mistaken.

The remainder of Generals Turchin's and Hazen's brigades were marched across and encamped in the woods out of sight, near the ferry, ready to move down, and cover the landing of the boats, and also ready to embark so soon as the boats had landed the river force, and crossed to the north side. The artillery was also halted in the woods during the night, and was to move down and go into position so soon as the boats had landed, to cover the retirement of our troops in case of disaster. The equipage for the pontoon-bridge was also ready to be moved down to the river so soon as the troops were across. Axes were distributed to the troops, to be used in cutting abattis for defence so soon as the ridge was gained. General Hazen was to take the gorge and hills to the left, while General Turchin was to extend from the gorge down the river. The boats moved from Chattanooga at three A.M., on the twenty-seventh, and, thanks to a slight fog and the silence observed, they were not discovered until about five A.M., when the first section had landed at the upper point, and the second section had arrived abreast of the picket stationed at the gorge.

Here a portion of the second section of the flotilla failed to land at the proper place, and alarming the pickets, received a volley. Some time was lost in effecting a landing below the gorge, and the troops had hardly carried it be fore the enemy began the attack. The boats by this time had recrossed the river, and Lieutenant-Colonel Langdon, First Ohio volunteers, in command of the remnant of the brigade of General Hazen, was rapidly ferried across, and, forming his men, quickly pushed forward to the assistance of the troops under Lieutenant-Colonel Fay, Twenty-third Kentucky volunteers, already hard pressed. The skirmish was soon over, and General Turchin, who followed Lieutenant-Colonel Langdon, quietly took possession of the hills assigned him. So soon as the skirmishers were thrown out from each command, the axes were set at work felling an abattis, and in two hours the command was sufficiently protected to withstand any attack which was likely to be made.

So soon as the last of the troops were across, the bridge was commenced, and continued under some shelling for an hour or so, and was completed at half-past four P.M., under the vigorous and skilful superintendence of Captain P. V. Fox, First Michigan engineers, and Captain George W. Dresser, Fourth artillery. Six prisoners were taken and six rebels buried by our command, and several wounded reported by citizens, and among the wounded the Colonel of the Fifteenth Alabama. Twenty beeves, six pontoons, a barge, and about two thousand bushels of corn, fell into our possession. Our loss was six killed, twenty-three wounded, and nine missing.

The artillery placed in position was not used, but credit is due Major Mendenhall for his promptitude in placing his guns. To Brigadier-General Turchin, Brigadier-General Hazen, Colonel Stanley, Eighteenth Ohio volunteers, who had the superintendence of the boats, and was zealous in his duty, and to Captain Fox, First Michigan engineers, all credit is due for their zeal, coolness, and intelligence. Captain Dresser, Fourth artillery, and Captain P. E. F. West, U. S. Coast Survey, rendered every service on my staff. Lieutenants Klokke, Fuller, Hopkins, and Bent of the Signal corps, were zealous in the discharge of their duties, and soon succeeded in establishing a line of communication from the south side of the river. I inclose the reports of the various commanders.

Respectfully submitted. W. F. SMITH,
Brigadier-General C. E., Commanding Expedition.

Doc. 97.

GENERALS MEADE AND LEE.

GENERAL LEE'S DESPATCH.

HEADQUARTERS ARMY NORTHERN VA., }
July 21, 1863. }

General S. Cooper, Adjutant and Inspector-General, C. S. A., Richmond, Va.:

GENERAL: I have seen in Northern papers what purported to be an official despatch from Gen. Meade, stating that he had captured a brigade of infantry, two pieces of artillery, two caissons, and a large number of small arms, as this army retired to the south bank of the Potomac, on the thirteenth and fourteenth instants.

This despatch has been copied into the Richmond papers, and as its official character may cause it to be believed, I desire to state that it is incorrect. The enemy did not capture any organized body of men on that occasion, but only stragglers and such as were left asleep on the road, exhausted by the fatigue and exposure of one of the most inclement nights I have ever known at this season of the year. It rained without cessation, rendering the road by which our troops marched to the bridge at Falling Waters very difficult to pass, and causing so much delay that the last of the troops did not cross the river at the bridge until one P.M. on the fourteenth. While the column was thus detained on the road a number of men, worn down with fatigue, lay down in barns and by the roadside, and though officers were sent back to arouse them, as the troops moved on, the darkness and rain prevented them from finding all, and many were in this way left behind. Two guns were left in the road. The horses that drew them became exhausted, and the officers went forward to procure others. When they returned the rear of the column had passed the guns so far that it was deemed unsafe to send back for them, and they were thus lost. No arms, cannon, or prisoners were taken by the enemy in battle, but only such as were left behind under the circumstances I have described. The number of stragglers thus lost I am unable to state with accuracy, but it is greatly exaggerated in the despatch referred to.

I am, with great respect,
Your obedient servant,
R. E. LEE,
General.

GENERAL MEADE'S DESPATCH.

HEADQUARTERS OF THE ARMY OF THE POTOMAC, }
August 9, 1863. }

Major-General H. W. Halleck, General-in-Chief:

GENERAL: My attention has been called to what purports to be an official despatch of General R. E. Lee, Commander of the confederate army, to General S. Cooper, Adjutant and Inspector General, denying the accuracy of my telegram to you of July fourteenth, announcing the result of the cavalry affair at Falling Waters.

I have delayed taking any notice of General Lee's report until the return of Brigadier-General Kilpatrick, absent on leave, who commanded the cavalry engaged on the occasion referred to, and on whose report from the field my telegram was based.

I now inclose the official report of Brigadier-General Kilpatrick, made after his attention had been called to General Lee's report. You will see that he reiterates and confirms all that my despatch averred, and proves most conclusively that General Lee has been deceived by his subordinates, or he would never, in the face of the facts now alleged, have made the assertions his report contains.

It appears that I was in error in stating that

the body of General Pettigrew was left in our hands, although I would not communicate that fact until an officer from the field reported to me that he had seen the body.

It is now ascertained from the Richmond papers that General Pettigrew, though mortally wounded in the affair, was taken to Winchester, where he subsequently died. The three battle-flags captured on this occasion and sent to Washington belonged to the Forty-fifth, Forty-seventh, and Fifty-fifth Virginia regiments of infantry. General Lee will surely acknowledge that these were not left in the hands of "stragglers asleep in barns." Respectfully yours,

GEORGE G. MEADE,
Major-General Commanding.

GENERAL KILPATRICK'S REPORT.

HEADQUARTERS THIRD DIVISION CAVALRY CORPS,
WARRENTON JUNCTION, VA., August 7, 1863.

To Col. A. J. Alexander, Chief of Staff, Cavalry Corps:

COLONEL: In compliance with a letter just received from the headquarters of the cavalry corps of the army of the Potomac, directing me to give the facts connected with my fight at Falling Waters, I have the honor to state that at three o'clock, on the morning of the fourteenth ultimo, I learned that the enemy's pickets were retiring in my front.

Having been previously ordered to attack at seven A.M., I was ready to move at once. At daylight I had reached the crest of hills occupied by the enemy an hour before, and at a few moments before six o'clock General Custer drove the rear-guard of the enemy into the river at Williamsport.

Learning from citizens that a portion of the enemy had retreated in the direction of Falling Waters, I at once moved rapidly for that point, and came up with the rear-guard of the enemy at half-past seven A.M., at a point two miles distant from Falling Waters.

We pressed on, driving the enemy before us, capturing many prisoners and one gun. When within a mile and a half from Falling Waters the enemy was found in large force, drawn up in line of battle on the crest of a hill, commanding the road on which I was advancing. His left was protected by earthworks, and his right extended to the woods far on my left.

The enemy was, when first seen, in two lines of battle, with arms stacked. Within less than one thousand yards of this large force a second piece of artillery, with its support, consisting of infantry, was captured while attempting to get into position. The gun was taken to the rear.

A portion of the Sixth Michigan cavalry, seeing only that portion of the enemy behind the earthworks, charged. This charge, led by Major Weber, was the most gallant ever made. At a trot he pressed up the hill, received the fire from the whole line, and the next moment rode through and over the earthworks, passed to the right, sabring the rebels along the entire line, and returned with a loss of thirty killed, wounded, and missing, including the gallant Major Weber killed.

I directed General Custer to send forward one regiment as skirmishers. They were repulsed before support could be sent them, and driven back, closely followed by the rebels, until checked by the First Michigan and a squadron of the Eighth New-York.

The Second brigade having come up, it was quickly thrown into position, and after a fight of two hours and thirty minutes, we routed the enemy at all points, and drove him toward the river.

When within a short distance of the bridge General Buford's command came up and took the advance. We lost twenty-nine killed, thirty-six wounded, and forty missing.

We found upon the field one hundred and twenty-five dead rebels, and brought away afterward fifty wounded. A large number of the enemy's wounded were left upon the field in charge of their own surgeons.

We captured two guns, three battle-flags, and upward of one thousand five hundred prisoners.

To General Custer and his brigade, Lieutenant Pennington and his battery, and one squadron of the Eighth New-York cavalry, of General Buford's command, all praise is due.

Very respectfully, your obedient servant,

J. KILPATRICK,
Brigadier-General Volunteers, Commanding the Division.

Doc. 98.

THE CAPTURE OF JACKSON.

JACKSON, MISS., July 17, 1863.

THE siege of Jackson, if such any may term it, was brought to a sudden termination about daylight this morning, by the discovery by our advance skirmishers that the batteries which frowned from the enemy's works the evening before had been removed. A reconnoissance revealed the fact that, under cover of the night, General Johnston had evacuated the place, taking with him his sick and wounded, his artillery, and almost every thing else of value. The work of evacuation was commenced about dark on the evening of the sixteenth, and conducted noiselessly and rapidly until about three o'clock this morning, when Johnston's rear-guard withdrew across the river, and set the three floating bridges on fire.

The stand of Johnston at this place was probably made to give time for the removal of large quantities of government stores. Ever since our army commenced moving eastward from Vicksburgh, every train has been loaded to its utmost capacity. Johnston was probably informed of the arrival of Sherman's ammunition train last night, and consigned the remainder of the government stores to the flames. The large brick block almost west of the State House, and adjoining to the north the block destroyed by our forces at the previous occupation of the city, was filled with stores of the confederate army. As the rear-guard left the city it fired this block of buildings in two or three different places. The burning buildings made it as light as day in our camp. Nearly every one surmised that Johnston was evacuating, and the opinion prevailed that he was destroying the whole city.

As soon as it was rendered certain that the place was evacuated, crowds of soldiers marched into the city, despite orders against straggling, and commenced plundering the houses and stores of citizens. Most of the officers endeavored to prevent this indiscriminate plundering, and soon succeeded in comparatively putting an end to it.

The only pieces of artillery left by Johnston in his retreat were two sixty-four pound rifled siege-guns. One of them was uninjured, but the other had been dismounted by our batteries, and a trunnion knocked off. It had been propped up, however, in the capacity of a "quaker," in its old position. But the "religious silence" it maintained, however, for some days, led our boys to suspect that something was wrong with it.

Some forty or fifty railroad-cars and a small quantity of cotton were left in the city, and fell into the hands of our forces.

The rebels had been busily at work in the construction of a temporary bridge across the Pearl River. The timbers for the purpose had all been framed, and half of the structure already put up. The piers of the old bridge were being used in the construction of the new one. The work was left just as the mechanics had discontinued it.

. All the railroad track inside the city limits, which had been torn up by our troops on the occasion of their visit in May last, had been relaid.

The rebel works for the defence of Jackson consisted of a very formidable line of rifle-pits around three sides of the city, and at about a mile's distance from it. At intervals along this line, splendid turf-works had been constructed, which were pronounced models of engineering. These forts were embrasured for a large number of field-pieces, and two or three contained, *en barbette*, large sixty-four pound rifled siege-guns. One of these was located in the works on the north of the city, and the other on the west, commanding the regular Vicksburgh road. It was the latter gun which was dismounted and permanently injured, in the loss of a trunnion, by our batteries. The line of rifle-pits was constructed in that zig-zag course which brings the approaches to almost every part of the line under an enfilading fire from those parts not assailed. The timber and undergrowth had been removed for several hundred yards in front of the rebel lines, in order to give them a sweeping fire for a long distance. These trees were left lying where they fell, presenting an obstruction which would have rendered the approach of an assaulting party quite slow, and crowded the men much together. The ground was greatly undulating, as I wrote you before. But, although not steep, the ascent could not have been carried without a terrible loss of life. They were so near level as

to obviate all danger of over-shooting, and the peculiar hardness and formation of the ground were particularly favorable to *ricochet* shots. The batteries and long lines of rifle-pits could have enfiladed and swept the wide, open space in front with a murderous fire. It is well that an assault was not ordered.

Johnston, in retreating, took the road to Meridian, the junction of the Mobile and Ohio with the railroad running east from Jackson. Here a stand can be made, or he can fall back on Mobile or Montgomery. Meridian is six miles south of Marion, which you will find laid down on all the old maps; it is about one hundred miles east of Jackson, and twenty from the Alabama line. This is a virtual surrender of Mississippi to our forces, even if Johnston withdraws no further than Meridian.

There have been several fires in Jackson already, since our brief possession of the place. Almost a whole block of stores was destroyed this morning, and one fine dwelling-house, just outside the rebel line of defence. This evening, as I write, the skies are illuminated by a fire in the northern portion of the city. How extensive it is, I am unable to say. By the time our army has captured, evacuated, and again captured Jackson, there will be nothing left of it. Nothing is safe or respected here, but every thing destructible seems doomed to destruction. Such is war.

During a portion of the day the rebels held the extreme upper and lower fords, but were finally dislodged by our troops crossing at the central ford, between the floating bridges, a few hundred yards above the old railroad bridge. Their object was to delay the crossing of our cavalry until the rear of Johnston's column had reached a safe distance. One of our cavalrymen, crossing at the central ford, captured a confederate prisoner about half a mile from the river, and was proceeding to bring him back into the city. When within a few hundred yards of the ford, with his prisoner walking beside him, his horse stepped upon and exploded a torpedo, planted in the ground and concealed in the dust. The horse was literally split wide open by the explosion, and the rider almost instantly killed. A fragment struck the prisoner a short distance below the thigh, completely shattering the leg to the knee. His life is despaired of. It is not known whether there are any more of these torpedoes planted in the roads or not, but it is presumed they are, and great caution is exercised by our soldiers in consequence.

The Deaf and Dumb Asylum was between the two lines, and consequently in the line of fire from both sides. It is riddled with shot, and is now but a mere wreck. It never was a first-class building, and the loss cannot be very great. The Insane Asylum was within our lines from the first, and has been under the protection of a guard detailed by General Parks. The only injury it sustained was from a thirty-two pound solid shot from the enemy's guns, which passed through it. An insane woman was slightly wounded by a splinter, but otherwise no injury was inflicted upon the inmates.

Colonel Wood, of Thayer's division, Steele's army corps, with a brigade of infantry, left for Canton last evening. They will destroy the railroad in that neighborhood, and also the large railroad machine-shops at that place. It has been determined upon to destroy all the railroads within our reach, inflicting damages of such a permanent character that they will never be re-built, except after a return of peace. Work will be commenced upon the roads here to-morrow, and the hurried injuries of the previous occupation will become permanent. With Johnston's army withdrawn to the eastern limits of the State, and all the railroads torn up, the rebels will never resume control of the Mississippi. There are said to be ninety locomotives belonging to the Mississippi Central and other roads north of Jackson. If this report is true, they will probably be destroyed, unless some means presents itself of getting them to Corinth or Memphis.

Johnston had removed his hospitals some two miles east of the Pearl River, where a very few of his own sick, and our wounded in the affair of the twelfth, are said to have been left.

From the first investment of the place, General Sherman was short of ammunition. Only a limited number of guns were at first placed in position, and all pieces were limited to one shot every five minutes. The ammunition train was expected on the sixteenth, and on the night of the fifteenth our lines were moved about a half a mile nearer the front, and almost double the number of guns were placed in position. In anticipation of the arrival of the train, a vigorous bombardment was to have commenced on last evening. The train did not arrive, however, until near midnight, when orders were issued for each piece to fire two hundred rounds as rapidly as possible this morning. Johnston was of course aware of our being short of ammunition, or he would not have remained so long. His cavalry scouts must also have notified him of the progress of our ammunition train, and thus enabled him to leave just in time to avoid the severe fire which would have followed its arrival.

There are many reports in circulation to the effect that some of our men have been poisoned by drinking liquor left by the rebels. The reasonable conclusion would be this: A drug-store, being endangered by the fire last night, the stock was removed into the street, and this morning scattered in all directions, and trampled in the dust by our soldiers. Several kegs of liquor were found among the stock of this drug-store, and it is not at all improbable that the soldiers, ignorant of its nature, partook of anti-monial wine.

The operations of the siege, aside from the terrible blunder of General Lauman on the twelfth instant, were conducted with the loss of but few lives, as was also the skirmishing in advancing from Vicksburgh.

This morning I rode over the ground upon which General Lauman operated his division in the affair of the twelfth instant, concerning which I wrote you from Black River bridge on Tuesday last. A view of the ground enables one to form a correct idea of the manner in which the blundering movement was made, which terminated so disastrously.

General Lauman's division was attached to General Ord's army corps, being the extreme right. On the morning of the twelfth, General Hovey, whose division was next to the left, advanced his line about half a mile, and General Lauman was ordered to advance his line until his left rested upon General Hovey's right. Lauman's right did not extend to Pearl River, as was reported, but simply extended the length of one brigade on the east side of the railroad.

The line of the enemy's works, after reaching far enough south to protect the approaches to the west of the city, make a curve around to the east and cover the approaches to the south. This last line, when it reaches the railroad south of the city, is running almost north-west and south-east. When it crosses the railroad it bears from north-east to south-west for some distance, and then again changes from north-west to south-east, running to the river.

Colonel Isaac L. Pugh, of the Forty-first Illinois, commanded the brigade upon the extreme right of General Lauman's division. The brigade consisted of the Forty-first, Fifty-third, and Twenty-eighth Illinois, Third Iowa and Fifth Ohio battery. The left of the brigade rested on the railroad, it being upon the east side of it. Although he could not see the rebel lines on the east side of the railroad, General Lauman could see enough to know that they did not run parallel with those on the west side of the railroad, and, presuming that, after crossing the railroad, their course was about east to the river, he swung the right of General Pugh's brigade around until the line was formed almost due east and west. The brigade on the left of Pugh's had been dropped from the line, leaving a gap. In this position the division advanced. Presently Colonel Pugh came to a corn-field, where the corn had all been carefully removed except in one place, and the timber upon his left all cut down. His skirmishers, about the same time, were driven in by sharp-shooters. Colonel Pugh determined not to advance any further, and sent for General Lauman, to whom he communicated that his skirmishers had been driven in, and he feared that the enemy were in force in front of him. General Lauman gave the order to the brigade to move on, and left it. After crossing the corn-field it came into a piece of open woods, from which the undergrowth had been removed. Here it was opened upon by a galling fire from the enemy's artillery, sharp-shooters, and twelve cannon with grape and canister, at one hundred and fifty yards, those upon the right enfilading the line. It was the most murderous fire to which any considerable body of infantry has been exposed during the war, and it beat a hasty retreat, but not until over one half of the men had been killed or wounded.

Doc. 99.

PRESIDENT LINCOLN'S PROCLAMATION.

JULY 15, 1863.

By the President of the United States of America.

A PROCLAMATION.

It has pleased Almighty God to hearken to the supplications and prayers of an afflicted people, and to vouchsafe to the army and the navy of the United States, on the land and on the sea, so signal and so effective victories as to furnish reasonable grounds for augmented confidence that the Union of these States will be maintained, their Constitution preserved, and their peace and prosperity permanently preserved; but these victories have been accorded not without sacrifice of life, limb, and liberty, incurred by brave, patriotic, and loyal citizens. Domestic affliction in every part of the country follows in the train of these fearful bereavements. It is meet and right to recognize and confess the presence of the Almighty Father, and the power of his hand equally in these triumphs and these sorrows.

Now, therefore, be it known that I do set apart Thursday, the sixth day of August next, to be observed as a day for National Thanksgiving, praise, and prayer, and I invite the people of the United States to assemble on that occasion in their customary places of worship, and in the from approved by their own conscience, render the homage due to the Divine Majesty for the wonderful things he has done in the Nation's behalf, and invoke the influence of his Holy Spirit, to subdue the anger which has produced and so long sustained a needless and cruel rebellion; to change the hearts of the insurgents; to guide the counsels of the Government with wisdom adequate to so great a National emergency, and to visit with tender care and consolation throughout the length and breadth of our land, all those who, through the vicissitudes of marches, voyages, battles, and sieges, have been brought to suffer in mind, body, or estate, and finally to lead the whole nation through paths of repentance and submission to the Divine will, back to the perfect enjoyment of union and fraternal peace.

In witness whereof, I have hereunto set my hand and caused the seal of the United States to be affixed.

Done at the city of Washington this fifteenth day of July in the year of our Lord one thousand eight hundred and sixty-three, and of the Independence of the United States of America the eighty-eighth.

By the President,   ABRAHAM LINCOLN.

WILLIAM H. SEWARD,
       Secretary of State.

VOL. VII.—DOC. 23.

Doc. 100.

BATTLE OF ELK CREEK, KANSAS.

LETTER OF GENERAL JAMES G. BLUNT.*

HEADQUARTERS DISTRICT OF THE FRONTIER,
IN THE FIELD, FORT BLUNT, CREEK NATION,
July 20, 1863.

DEAR SIR: Yours of the twenty-eighth of June came to hand by expressman, late on the eve of the sixteenth instant, while on the march to the battle-field of Honey Springs, Creek Nation, which took place the following morning. On learning that this place, which had been beleaguered for months by an overwhelming force, was in imminent danger, and being unable to get any reënforcements to send to their relief, I determined to play a bold game. On the night of the fifth instant, with a portion of my staff and a small escort, I left Fort Scott and made this place in five days, (one hundred and seventy-five miles,) without any transportation, and only the baggage we could carry on our backs and on our horses. On arriving here I found the Arkansas River too high to ford, and commenced the construction of ferry-boats. The rebels had all the fords on the other side of the river for forty miles guarded by rifle-pits. On the fifteenth instant I learned that General Cooper's headquarters were at Honey Springs, on Elk Creek, twenty-five miles south from this post, on the Texas road; that his force was six thousand strong; and that he expected a reënforcement of three Texas regiments on the seventeenth, when he intended to make a demonstration upon this place.

At midnight, on the fifteenth, I took two hundred and fifty cavalry and two six-pound guns, and proceeded thirteen miles up the river to a point that was fordable, drove their pickets from the opposite side, crossed over, came down on the south side to the ford at the mouth of Grand River, near which this fort is located, drove their outpost from there, and commenced crossing all my available force, which was less than three thousand men and twelve pieces of light artillery. At ten o'clock P.M. the little column commenced moving. At daylight we came upon the enemy's advance, which fell back, as we pressed them, upon their main line, which was on Elk Creek, five miles beyond. Their line was formed in the edge of the timber, (which was very bushy,) on the north side, in a semicircular form, one and a half miles in length, the main road running through the centre. I directed the command halted as it came up behind a little rise of ground half a mile in front of their line, while I went forward with a small party of mounted men to reconnoitre their position. I soon discovered their entire force crouched in the bushes waiting for their prey. The locality of their artillery I could not learn, as it was masked. I gave time for the stragglers all to come up, and the men to rest a short time and eat a lunch from their haversacks. At ten o'clock A.M. I formed the command in two columns, by companies closed in mass, and marched with one column on either side of the road until

* This letter was addressed to Mr. Frank J. Bramhall.

within a quarter of a mile of their line, when I quickly deployed one column to the right and the other to the left, with such rapidity that in five minutes my line covered their entire front. They now opened upon us from their batteries, which revealed the location. In a moment the engagement became general and desperate. My cavalry force, which was upon either flank, and armed with carbines, were dismounted and sent into the timber as infantry. The Texans fought gallantly and maintained their line for nearly two hours, but at last gave way. Then commenced a running fight, which lasted between two and three hours, the enemy making a stand at every available point, and being as often routed. Three miles through the timber of Elk Creek brought us again to the prairie, where they made a vigorous stand to enable them to destroy their commissary supplies by setting fire to the buildings. I soon shelled them from this position, and they fled in confusion. My cavalry horses were now tired out, infantry exhausted, artillery horses unable to draw the guns farther, and the pursuit had to be abandoned.

In about two hours General Cooper was reënforced by three Texas regiments, and I supposed he would make a stand. Consequently I bivouacked on the field until morning, when I found he had retreated twenty-five miles during the night, and is still on the skedaddle. My loss was seventeen killed and thirty-six wounded. We buried one hundred and eighty of the rebel dead, have sixty prisoners, (among them several officers,) captured one stand of colors, two hundred stand of small arms, one piece of artillery, (which we dismounted early in the fight,) and have forty of their wounded, most of whom will die. All of their wounded that could be carried away on a horse were removed by them to the rear, as they fell, and thus escaped.

I have merely noted these facts for your perusal, thinking it might instruct a New-Yorker to know how we do up matters in the West. You must excuse the bad scribbling, as I am sitting up in a sick-bed, and it is the first time I have attempted to write for some days. I was taken with a bilious fever the day after I started after Cooper, and forty-eight hours in the saddle, without rest or sleep, or a mouthful to eat, and all the time with a burning fever, did not improve my health much. When the excitement of the battle was over, my powers of endurance were completely exhausted, and I had to come down. Have not been able to sit up since, but am improving, and hope to be all right again soon.

Yours truly,
JAMES G. BLUNT.

F. J. BRAMHALL,
New-York City.

Doc. 101.

GENERAL POTTER'S EXPEDITION

THROUGH NORTH-CAROLINA, JULY, 1863.

NEWBERN, N. C., July 23, 1863.

THE present expedition being on a grander and more responsible scale than any that had preceded it, Major-General Foster concluded to confide its chief direction to an officer of higher rank than Lieutenant-Colonel Lewis, and selected his Chief of Staff, General Potter, for that purpose. Colonel Lewis retained the immediate command of the cavalry force. General Potter was accompanied by Captain Gouraud, Lieutenant Farquhar, and Lieutenant Myers, Chief of Ordnance of Major-General Foster's staff, all of whom have seen active service in North-Carolina.

Early on Saturday morning, the eighteenth instant, orders were received for the cavalry to get in readiness to start on the expedition. Every man leaped into his saddle with alacrity, and the column went across the Neuse to Fort Anderson without incident. The cavalry and artillery at this time consisted of the following:

Twelve companies of the Third New-York cavalry, under command of Lieutenant-Colonel Lewis, Lieutenant Nourse Acting Adjutant.

One company (L) North-Carolina Union cavalry, Lieutenant Graham commanding.

Three companies (A, B, and F) Twelfth New-York cavalry, Major Clarkson commanding.

Two companies (A and B) of what is called Mix's new New-York regiment.

Four mountain howitzers, commanded by Lieutenants Allis and Clark.

The cavalry force was divided into three detachments. The first detachment was under the command of Major Cole, of the Third; the second under Major Clarkson, of the Twelfth; and the third under Major Jacobs, of the Third—the whole under Lieutenant-Colonel Lewis, with General Potter as chief.

About half-past eleven o'clock on the morning of the eighteenth, the cavalry moved forward in splendid order in the direction of Swift Creek. The enemy's pickets were not near the creek; but they took to their boats and hurried across, giving our men a volley from their muskets as they left, but doing no injury. Reaching the creek, without further molestation, although it was known that a force of at least four hundred rebels were encamped in the vicinity but a short time before, our men bivouacked for the night, videttes being thrown out to guard against surprise.

On Sunday morning, the nineteenth, at daybreak, orders were received from General Potter, to prepare to move, and in a brief time the men commenced moving with their usual alacrity. They had proceeded as far as a place which was known as "The Chapel," when they encountered, or rather surprised, a rebel picket-guard, consisting of one company of Whitford's men, under Captain White. Upon the approach of our men, the rebels stood gaping with wonder, apparently not knowing whether we were friends or enemies; but a peremptory demand to "surrender" brought them to their senses, and off they attempted to scamper. About fifteen were captured, and one man who was making hasty tracks through the woods, refusing to obey the command to halt and surrender, was brought down by one of our carbineers, who put a bullet through his thigh. We not wishing to be encumbered with any prisoners at this stage of the expedition, General Potter ordered the captives to be paroled, which was accordingly done.

This over, General Potter proceeded at once toward the town of Greenville, a place noted as of much consequence as a rebel stronghold during the protracted siege of Washington, and, taking the Kinston fork of the cross-roads between Washington and Greenville, he reached Greenville about three o'clock in the afternoon.

No one having apparently warned the people or the guard, if any, of our approach, no preparations were found to be made for our reception. The place was strongly fortified; but the defences had been abandoned by all save a few cavalrymen, who appeared to be detained to act more as messengers or couriers than as scouts or videttes.

Finding the intrenchments and breastworks undefended, General Potter dashed at once into the town, and took possession of the post-office and other public buildings, seizing the mails, and destroying such government matter as could not be conveniently carried away. A few prisoners were made and paroled. Some large guns, intended for use in the defences of the place, were spiked, a number of small arms thrown into the river, and some damage done to the enemy's works. The day being a quiet Sabbath, and the rebel troops having been all withdrawn, the amazement of the inhabitants of this pretty village at the sudden advent of so formidable a cavalry host as ours may be imagined. They threw no obstructions in the way of the officers executing the orders of General Potter; on the contrary, they either pretended to lend assistance or acted as if stupefied.

Having done every thing to cripple the enemy that the usages of war allowed, and refrained as much as possible from disturbing private property, or alarming peaceably disposed inhabitants, General Potter, about five o'clock in the afternoon, issued orders to start forward on the line of march, which proved to be on the road leading to the little village of Sparta, which lay in a northerly direction, about eighteen miles from Greenville, and some eight or ten miles south of Tarboro. This place was reached in the night, and here General Potter bivouacked.

About this time it is presumed the enemy had obtained some information of our advance, and that our intentions were to at once visit Tarboro, being in such close proximity to that place. But instead of proceeding directly to Tarboro, General Potter ordered Lieutenant-Colonel Lewis to detail a detachment of his cavalry to take another road and pounce upon Rocky Mount—a most important point on the Wilmington and Weldon Railroad—before the enemy there had any expectation of our approach. Major Jacobs's detachment of the Third was detailed for this important service, upon the result of which depended the success or defeat of the great objects of the expedition. Proud of having so fair an opportunity to distinguish himself, this young and judicious officer proceeded with his detachment, by a new and hitherto untried route, across ditches, through swamps, and through creeks and larger streams, and over bridges none the better for age and rottenness, until he came in sight of the desired place of destination, the main force meanwhile remaining for a time near Sparta, and keeping within eyesight distance of any movement of the enemy in the direction of Tarboro, but soon after advancing on the town with such effect as shall presently be seen.

Major Jacobs's only artillery force was one howitzer, under Allis, and yet with that and his heroic detachment of troops he committed a greater amount of destruction, and such as will be regarded by the rebels themselves as more deplorable and ruinous to them, than any that has been inflicted upon them in the State of North-Carolina during the war.

With a dash and daring uneclipsed by any cavalry raid directed for similar purpose against the enemy during the war, Major Jacobs destroyed and laid in ruins the costly structure known as the Rocky Mount railroad bridge over Tar River, on the line of the Wilmington and Weldon Railroad, and the connecting link, by this route, of Richmond with Wilmington and the far South. The bridge was the most expensive to construct in the State, and was over four hundred feet long. It will take weeks, perhaps months, to reconstruct and to rebuild the trestle-work also destroyed. The demolition of this bridge has long been an object kept in view by the general commanding the department, and now it has been accomplished, a much-coveted desideratum has been reached.

Major Jacobs destroyed the finest cotton-mill in the State—one used for the manufacture of rebel army cloth, and employing some two hundred hands, mostly girls. About five hundred bales of cotton were also destroyed.

He destroyed a rebel quartermaster's train, containing a large amount of stores for the rebel army. When Major Jacobs destroyed the cotton factory he said to the girls who had been employed in it, "Girls, I am sorry to throw you out of work; but," he continued, pointing to a rich store of rebel provisions, "go there and help yourselves." The suggestion was immediately improved by many. Major Jacobs destroyed a railroad train of thirty cars, all loaded with ammunition, etc. The train had just been sent up from Tarboro for safety, and was in motion, backing out, when Jacobs ordered its capture. Private White, of company A, Third New-York cavalry, deserves credit for its capture. Riding up to the locomotive, he discharged his pistol at the engineer, who instantly dropped. The train was then backing at the rate of about five miles an hour, having not yet got under full head or back way. White immediately dismounted, sprang upon the locomotive, reversed the engine and brought the train to a point where it and its freight—except some rebel officers who were on board—could be destroyed. The ammunition was effectually destroyed and the locomotive essentially smashed. They also captured a rebel paymaster, with all his funds, some $50,000 in North-Carolina and South-Carolina notes.

The quartermaster's train captured consisted of eighteen six-mule teams, well loaded with stores and stuff, which, with the teams, were destroyed. The mules were taken, and negroes, who were ready and willing, standing by grinning, were given a chance for a free ride. The paymaster referred to was captured in the road, while on a tour distributing to families the allotment money appropriated by the State for their support. The money was placed in the hands of Lieutenant Gardner, of the Third cavalry, who acted as provost-marshal of the expedition.

After accomplishing all this destruction, and I do not know how much more, Major Jacobs returned to the main column, having made a march of ninety miles, and executed his important orders to the letter, within the brief space of twenty-four hours. Truly a magnificent day's work.

After Major Jacobs had started with his detachment to Rocky Mount, the main column (about five A.M.) commenced its march for Tarboro, where, report alleged, a large amount of rebel government stores was housed, some steamboats built, and some rams and other rebel deviltries under way. The town is an important one, and once the seat of considerable traffic and commerce. It is situated on Tar, or Tarr, River, ("River of Health" in the Indian tongue,) and is the terminus of a branch of the Weldon and Wilmington Railroad, running from the town of Wilson.

Our advance, Major Clarkson's detachment, reached Tarboro about nine A.M.; and, without waiting for any ceremony, Major C. dashed into the town, and drove the enemy's pickets (cavalry) across the bridge on a full run. The flying troopers were pursued until the danger of falling into an ambuscade was to be apprehended. Indeed, such was the report at one time, accompanied by a rumor that Major Clarkson had lost severely, and had made a very narrow escape with his command. It afterward appeared, however, that the report was much exaggerated, and it is believed at headquarters had no foundation, in fact, so far as the ambuscade was concerned. Major Clarkson's loss during the entire expedition was but three officers (Captain Cyrus Church and his two lieutenants) and some fifteen or twenty men—all missing.

Without proceeding to give in detail the mode and manner by which the rebel property in Tarboro was destroyed, it may suffice to say that the amount was immense and consisted of—

1. Two steamboats, one a very fine one.

2. The framework of an iron-clad which has been in the course of construction for several months.

3. A number of iron rams or rebel devils.

4. Four cannon, with caissons and ammunition, which were thrown into the river.

5. A large building, two stories high and one hundred and fifty feet long, filled with commissary stores, such as bacon, flour, rice, sugar, etc., etc.

6. Another building, of similar dimensions, containing quartermaster's stores, such as camp equipage, wagons, harness, etc.

7. The railroad dépôt, consisting of two large brick buildings.

8. About six hundred bales of cotton.

9. The extensive bridge over the Tar River, the destruction of which was attended with probably more inconvenience and distress than any other event during the expedition.

The work of demolition in Tarboro was accomplished without much resistance, so sudden was our arrival, and so alert our movements. Major Cole's command did good work. A few inhabitants fired upon our men from windows; but that work stopped soon after a few summary examples were made. The enemy attempted to shell us from the other side of the river, but desisted as soon as they found they were doing more damage to their own property than they were to us, and also, probably, from the effects of the shells from Clark's howitzers.

Some infantry and cavalry also showed themselves, and, the appearance gradually becoming more and more formidable, General Potter, as soon as Major Jacobs's command had rejoined the main column from its successful raid at Rocky Mount, ordered the line of march to be taken up on the return of the expedition, via Sparta.

The order to apply the torch to Tarboro bridge, so as to prevent the advance of the enemy from the opposite side upon our rear, was executed a little too soon. A large number of contrabands had just got over, many were still on the bridge, and many were yet on the other side, all eager to join our column and flee from their masters in Dixie to their worshippers among the Yankees. Some of our own men were also on the other side; but, with a few exceptions, they contrived to make their escape. When the burning bridge fell, it is feared it carried into the stream below, or consumed in the vain effort to extricate themselves, between five and six hundred poor frantic negroes.

No sooner had the enemy ascertained that we were retreating than they began to make a movement to cut us off, having been foiled in the rapid execution of their plan of advancing on our rear by the destruction of the bridge.

The rebels who had by this time been largely reënforced with cavalry, infantry, and artillery, having six pieces of the latter, followed our retreating column closely. Their force is understood to have been composed of Martin's brigade, consisting of the Seventeenth, Forty-second, Fiftieth, and Sixty-third North-Carolina infantry; Whitford's battalion of rangers, and a part of

Nethercutt's battalion of rangers. The name of their artillery was not known; but it is certain it was handsomely handled, giving our four little pieces all the work they could conveniently do. Their object being to head us off, it was accomplished by nightfall at a point called Tyson's Creek. Here we found that the enemy had destroyed a bridge which we were obliged to cross if we kept on our present line of retreat, and had also planted artillery on the opposite bank, apparently determined to make a most obstinate resistance to our further progress. Taking advantage of the darkness, General Potter moved his column down the creek, and instead of going through Greenville, as the enemy might have supposed, took the Snowhill road, one that runs in a different direction. This adroit movement seemed to perplex the enemy for a little while; but in a short time, amid all the darkness, he was heard to approach, and the firing of his cannon told us that we had been betrayed by guides, who had proclaimed their loyalty to the Union and said they were ready to seal it with their lives.

The enemy kept on harassing our rear, occasionally doing a little execution, wounding a few men and killing a few horses, until we reached Street's Ferry, on the Neuse, with transports ready to carry our weary and worn-out bodies to Newbern. The expedition having been attended with such brilliant success, neither officers nor men uttered a word of complaint, almost dead as they were with fatigue and want of rest. The expedition had been absent about six days, and many of the officers and troopers avow that they have not slept five hours in all that time. It was hard, very hard work, and those brave hearts engaged in it are deserving the unqualified approbation of their countrymen.

Throwing aside the negro catastrophe, if it should even prove true, our losses have been meagre, considering the magnitude of the work accomplished. The Twelfth probably lost some twenty men missing and wounded, the Third nearly the same number. The losses of Graham's North-Carolinians, who behaved gallantly under their intrepid leader, and Mix's new regiment, as well as those of the artillery, which was on all occasions handsomely served, are inconsiderable, except those resulting from extreme fatigue and exposure to the blazing sun. The enemy's losses in men undoubtedly treble ours, although they had the advantage of selecting their positions in harassing our retreat. So confidently was it reported in Newbern that we were badly cut up that reënforcements were at one time ordered to hurry up to our relief. Colonel Jourdan's brigade of infantry approached as far as Swift Creek on the first day's march of the cavalry, as a support, but had returned to Newbern some time before the cavalry came back.

The aggregate amount of rebel property destroyed on the expedition cannot be less than five millions of dollars, while the value of mischief done to their facilities for railroad transportation on the Wilmington and Weldon road is incalculable. A pretty good week's work for the little but noble band of heroes who are serving their country *en cheval* in North-Carolina.

Doc. 102.

EXPEDITION UP RED RIVER.

REPORT OF ADMIRAL PORTER.

UNITED STATES MISSISSIPPI SQUADRON, FLAG-SHIP BLACK HAWK, OFF VICKSBURGH, July 18, 1863.

SIR: I have the honor to inform you that the expedition I sent into the Red River region proved very successful. Ascending the Black and Tensas Rivers, (running parallel with the Mississippi,) Lieutenant Commanding Selfridge made the head of navigation—Tensas Lake and Bayou Macon, thirty miles above Vicksburgh, and within five or six miles of the Mississippi River.

The enemy were taken completely by surprise, not expecting such a force in such a quarter. The rebels that have ascended to that region will be obliged to move further back from the river, if not to go away altogether. Lieutenant Commanding Selfridge divided his force on finding that the transports, which had been carrying stores to Walker's army, had escaped up some of the narrow streams. He sent the Mainton and Rattler up the Little Red River, (a small tributary of the Black,) and the Forest Rose and Petrel up the Tensas. The night was dark, and it was raining very hard, and the Mainton and Rattler succeeded in capturing the rebel steamer Louisville, one of the largest and perhaps the best steamer now in the Western waters. Up the Tensas, or one of its tributaries, the Forest Rose and Petrel captured the steamer Elmira, loaded with stores, sugar, and rum for the rebel army.

Finding that the steamers which had conveyed General Walker's army had returned up the Washita, the expedition started up that river, and came suddenly upon two rebel steamers; but the rebels set them on fire, and they were consumed so rapidly that their names could not be ascertained. One steamer, loaded with ammunition, escaped above the fort at Harrisonburgh, which is a very strong work, and unassailable with wooden gunboats. It is on an elevation over one hundred feet high, which elevation covers what water-batteries of heavy guns there are.

Lieutenant Commander Selfridge was fortunate enough, however, to hear of a large quantity of ammunition that had lately been hauled from Natchez, and deposited near Trinity, (nearly due west of Natchez,) and from whence stores, provisions, cattle, guns, and ammunition are transported. He captured fifteen thousand rounds of smooth-bore ammunition, one thousand rounds of Enfield rifle, and two hundred rounds of fixed ammunition for guns, a rifle thirty-pounder Parrott gun-carriage, fifty-two hogsheads of sugar, ten puncheons of rum, nine barrels flour, fifty barrels salt, all belonging to the confederate government.

At the same time he heard of a large amount of ammunition that had started from Natchez for Trinity, and was lying in wagons on the road half way across. He despatched a boat around to inform me of it, but General Ransom, who had landed a few days before at Natchez, hearing of it, also sent a detachment of cavalry and captured the whole. Thus Walker's army is left almost without ammunition.

The officers and men have shown great energy on this expedition, and have met with no mishaps. They procured a good deal of information by which future movements will be regulated.

The people in the whole of that section are very hostile to the Government—rank rebels.

I have the honor to be, etc.,

DAVID D. PORTER,
R. A. Commanding Mississippi Squadron.

Hon. GIDEON WELLES,
Secretary of the Navy.

Doc. 103.

MORGAN'S RAID THROUGH KENTUCKY.

JOURNAL OF LIEUTENANT-COLONEL ALSTON.

THE following is the journal of Lieutenant-Colonel Alston, Morgan's Chief of Staff, who was captured by the national pickets on the fifth of July. The journal is complete from the morning of the first to noon of the eighth, at which time he was sent to Camp Chase, Ohio.

July 1st, 1863.—On the banks of the Cumberland. The river very high. No boats. General M. obliged to build a number of boats, which he accomplished with very little delay, and commenced crossing at sundown.

July 2d.—Bucksville. He had great difficulty in making the horses swim, but by united and systematic exertion succeeded in getting the entire command of —— regiments over by ten A.M., though the command was very much scattered. At eleven o'clock, scouts came into Bucksville and reported the enemy advancing, and within four miles of the town. It was supposed to be only a scouting party, and a portion of Dick Morgan's command was sent out to make a reconnoissance. The report of the scouts of the enemy advancing proved to be correct, and a message was received from Colonel Ward that he was attacked. Colonel Grigsby was sent to reenforce him, and succeeded in driving the Yankees back in great confusion upon their reenforcements. My regiment lost two mortally wounded and two others slightly. Five of the Yankees were known to be killed and a number wounded, with about fifteen prisoners. No tidings heard of the Second brigade until dark, when they arrived and reported that Colonel Johnson, commanding, had experienced great difficulty in crossing, and that in addition to the precipitous banks and absence of all boats or other means of transportation, the enemy were hovering on the river and harassing him as far as they could. He was, however, quite successful in driving them back. Yesterday a young man, calling himself Charles Rogers, dressed in full confederate uniform, came into our lines and expressed a desire to join our command. I suspicioned him, and, after a few questions, I was convinced that he was a spy. I threatened to shoot him, when he confessed that he had been lying, and that his name was Simon Blitz—in fact he convicted himself of being a spy. I hated to shoot him, although he deserved it.

July 3d.—My regiment behaved very gallantly in yesterday's fight with the enemy, frequently having hand-to-hand encounters. To-day (third) we experienced the same difficulty in getting the artillery on, and had to press a number of oxen for the purpose. After two halts for the column to close up, our advance proceeded to Columbia. They were met by detachments from three regiments (Forty-fifth Ohio, Second Ohio, and First Kentucky) said to be under command of Colonel Wolford. A brief engagement followed, in which we drove the enemy in great haste through the town, capturing six prisoners, killing two, among them Captain Carter, and wounding three. Our loss was two killed and two wounded, among them Captain Cassel, a most dashing and daring officer, wounded in the thigh. Our men behaved badly at Columbia, breaking open a store and plundering it. I ordered the men to return the goods, and made all the reparation in my power. These outrages are very disgraceful, and are usually perpetrated by men accompanying the army simply for plunder. They are not worth a ——, and are a disgrace to both armies. Passed through Columbia, and camped six miles from Green River Bridge.

July 4th.—New-Market, Ky. A day of gloom, deep gloom, to our entire command. How many who rose this morning full of enthusiasm and hope now "sleep the sleep that knows no waking." The sun rose bright and beautiful, the air was cool and balmy, all nature wore the appearance of peace and harmony. While riding along, affected by the stillness of all around, Captain Magennis, the Adjutant-General, rode up and remarked how dreadful to reflect that we were marching on to engage in deadly strife, and how many poor fellows would pass into eternity before the setting of yonder sun. I have no doubt the poor fellow was moved to these reflections by one of those unaccountable presentiments which are so often the harbingers of evil. (Before dark he was a corpse.) About sunrise we drove in the enemy's pickets and were soon near their fortifications, which had been erected to prevent our crossing. General Morgan sent in a flag of truce and demanded the surrender, but the Colonel quietly remarked: "If it was any other day he might consider the demand, but the Fourth of July was a bad day to talk about surrender, and he must therefore decline." This Colonel is a gallant man, and the entire arrangement of his defence entitles him to the highest credit for military skill. We would mark such a man in our army for promotion.

We attacked the place with two regiments,

sending the remainder of our force across at another ford. The place was judiciously chosen and skilfully defended, and the result was that we were repulsed with severe loss—about twenty-five killed and twenty wounded. Among the killed, as usual, were our best men and officers, including Colonel Chenault, Major Brent, Captain Tribble, Lieutenants Cowan, Ferguson, and another lieutenant whose name I do not remember. Our march thus far has been very fatiguing—bad roads, little rest or sleep, little to eat, and a fight every day. Yet our men are cheerful, even buoyant, and to see them pressing along barefooted, hurrahing and singing, would cause one to appreciate what those who are fighting in a just and holy cause will endure. About three o'clock, as I rode on about forty yards in advance, I heard the General exclaim something in a very excited tone, which I could not understand, and heard at the same time the report of a pistol. I turned, and, great God! to my horror I saw Captain Magennis falling from his horse, with the blood gushing out of his mouth and breast. His only remark was: "Let me down easy." In another moment his spirit had fled. He was killed by Captain Murphy because Magennis, by the direction of General Morgan, had ordered Murphy to restore a watch taken from a prisoner. Thus was the poor fellow's language of the morning dreadfully realized. I was terrible affected. I had seen blood flow freely on many a battlefield—my friends had been killed in the morning—but this caused a deeper impression and shock than any occurrence I ever witnessed. Truly this has been a sad day. General Morgan looks haggard and weary, but he never despairs. May to-morrow dawn more bright than to-day closes.

July 5th.—Another day of gloom, fatigue, and death. Moved on Lebanon at sunrise—placed our men in line. Sent around Colonel J—— with his brigade to the Danville road to cut off reënforcements, which we knew were expected from Danville. I went in with a flag of truce. It was fired on five times. Officer apologized, saying he thought it was a man with a white coat on. Very dangerous mistake, at least for me. Demanded unconditional surrender. Told Colonel Hanson we had his reënforcements cut off, and resistance was useless. He refused to surrender, and I then ordered him to send out the noncombatants, as we would be compelled to shell the town. He posted his regiment in the dépôt and in various houses, by which he was enabled to make a desperate resistance. After a fight of seven hours, General Morgan, finding the town could be taken in no other way, ordered a charge to be made. This ought to have been done at first, but General Morgan said, when it was urged on him, that he wished to avoid the destruction of private property as much as possible, and he would only permit it as a last and final resort. Colonel Hanson still held out in hopes of receiving reënforcements, and only surrendered after we had fired the buildings in which he was posted. His force consisted of the Twentieth

Kentucky, about three hundred and seventy men, and twenty or twenty-five stragglers from other commands.

By this surrender we obtained a sufficient quantity of guns to arm all our men who were without them; also a quantity of ammunition, of which we stood sorely in need. At the order to charge, Duke's regiment rushed forward, and poor Tommy Morgan, who was always in the lead, ran forward and cheered the men with all the enthusiasm of his bright nature. Almost at the first volley he fell back, pierced through the heart. His only words were: "Brother Cally, they have killed me." Noble youth! how deeply lamented by all who knew you! This was a crushing blow to General Morgan, as his affection for his brother exceeded the love of Jonathan to David. It caused a terrible excitement, and the men were in a state of frenzy. It required the utmost energy and promptitude on the part of the officers to prevent a scene of slaughter, which all would deeply have lamented. Our men behaved badly here, breaking open stores and plundering indiscriminately. All that officers could do was done to prevent, but in vain. These occurrences are very disgraceful, and I am truly glad that they form exceptions to the general conduct.

While I was paroling the prisoners, a courier arrived, informing me that the enemy were approaching with two regiments of cavalry and a battery of artillery, and that skirmishing was then going on with our pickets. I was therefore obliged to order the prisoners to Springfield on the double-quick. Soon after we left Lebanon, the hardest rain I ever experienced commenced to fall, and continued till nine o'clock. Arrived at Springfield at dark, when I halted the prisoners in order to parole those who were not paroled at Lebanon, and formally dismissed them. This detained me at Springfield two hours after the command had passed. Wet and chilly, worn out, horse tired and hungry. Stopped to feed her. Falling asleep, was aroused by one of the men. Started on to the command. When I reached the point on the Bardstown road where I had expected the Second brigade to encamp, was halted by a party of cavalry. Supposing them to be our own pickets, I rode up promptly to correct them for standing in full view of any one approaching, when lo! to my mortification, I found myself a prisoner. My God! how I hated it, no one can understand. The first thought, after my wife and children, was my fine mare, Fannie Johnson, named after a pretty little cousin, of Richmond, Va. I said: "Poor Fannie, who will treat you as kindly as I have?" I turned her over to the captain and begged him to take good care of her, which he promised to do.

July 6th.—Travelled all day. Treated very kindly by Captain Smith. Sick, worn out, completely wearied out. Spirits cheerful. Met Captain Walcott on the road from Springfield. He got Captain Smith to parole me. Captain Smith anxious to do so, as he had more prisoners than he could well take care of. Accompanied Captain Walcott to Danville. Staid all night there.

July 7th.—Arrived at Nicholasville. Ordered before the Provost-Marshal. Sent on to Lexington. Arrived in the afternoon, and immediately ordered to prison. Visited by some sweet, pretty, and kind ladies. God bless them! I know he will.

July 8th.—Great rejoicing in Lexington over the fall of Vicksburgh. (I do not believe it.) It is a great disaster, one among the very worst that could befall us. But even if it is so, and even should Lee's army be destroyed and every town in the South burned, the rebellion would be unsubdued. There are a hundred thousand men in the South who feel as I do, that they would rather an earthquake should swallow the whole country than yield to our oppressors—men who will retire to the mountains and live on acorns, and crawl on their bellies to shoot an invader wherever they can see one.

Doc. 104.

BATTLE OF WAPPING HEIGHTS, VA.

NATIONAL ACCOUNT.

ARMY OF THE POTOMAC, July 28, 1863.

LEE, with his army, having pushed into the Shenandoah Valley, no sooner found that Meade was at his heels than he made a feint as if he would turn and recross the Potomac. So soon, however, as Meade ascertained to his own satisfaction that Lee had not turned back in force, but only as a feint, he again put his columns in motion, and by the most rapid and fatiguing marches got possession of all the passes in the Blue Ridge Mountains down to Manassas Gap, thus hemming the enemy into the Shenandoah Valley. On the second instant his scouts reported to him that one corps of the enemy was at or below Front Royal, just through Manassas Gap, and that the other two corps were behind and rapidly approaching that point.

Buford's division of cavalry were alone in occupation of this important mountain-pass, through which it seemed probable the enemy intended to force his way, and they were calling loudly for reënforcements, representing that the entire rebel army was menacing them. In this emergency the Third army corps, then guarding Ashby's Gap, was ordered down to Manassas Gap. The order was received late in the day, and by four o'clock the corps was in motion. By an almost unprecedented march they reached Piedmont before dark, when, without halting, the First division, (Birney's command,) temporarily commanded by General Ward, was thrown forward to support General Buford, who was found to be ten miles in advance up the gap. Thus it was nearly midnight when this division reached its camping ground, in the vicinity of Linden, a little town close in among the mountains. Early on the following morning General French moved the rest of the corps up to support the First division, and

despatched his chief of staff, Colonel Hayden, to ascertain the position of the enemy.

Colonel Hayden, in obedience to his instructions, pushed ahead and got a position upon the summit of a lofty mountain, whence he had a splendid view of the Shenandoah Valley for miles in all directions. At his very feet rolled the murky waters of the Shenandoah; just in front lay the pretty town of Front Royal; beyond and stretching as far as the eye could reach, south, west, and north, were broad fields, rich with their abundant crops. The scene was a beautiful one, well calculated to rivet the attention and awaken the admiration of the beholder.

But other scenes, of greater interest to the veteran soldier, met the gaze of the observing staff-officer. Upon an ordinary country road, approaching the Shenandoah River almost at the base of the mountain on which he stood, and crossing the stream at that point by a ford, thence losing itself in the system of ravines and hills leading to Chester's Gap, a large body of rebel infantry were moving in close column and most perfect order. Several thousand of these infantry were seen, followed by a large body of mounted men, subsequently shown to be sick and disabled soldiers mounted on horses stolen in Pennsylvania. The rear of the line was covered by a large body of cavalry.

On the turnpike beyond, running nearly parallel with the country road above described, leading directly to Front Royal, were the long wagon trains of the enemy, pushing southward as rapidly as possible, and extending as far as could be seen.

No reconnoissance could be more perfect and satisfactory than this. Taken in connection with the information that had been brought in by scouts on the previous day, it seemed clear that this must be a portion—perhaps the advance—of the rebels' second corps. Their first corps had already passed down the valley; the third must be yet in the rear. The situation was eminently favorable. This was precisely the time to attack. We could now cut the rebel column in two. This was the natural and common supposition, and there was no dissent from it.

So soon as Colonel Hayden returned and reported his observations, Wood's old brigade of the First division, temporarily commanded by Colonel Berdan, was deployed as skirmishers and ordered forward. Besides the celebrated Berdan Sharp-shooters, there are in this brigade the well-known Twentieth Indiana, which did such splendid service as skirmishers at Chancellorsville, the Sixty-third Pennsylvania, and the Third and Fourth Maine—all regiments of the highest reputation, and together forming a skirmishing line of unusual strength and excellence. They were immediately supported by the Ninety-ninth Pennsylvania, and the Eighty-sixth and One Hundred and Twenty-fourth New-York.

The line was formed just beyond the little village of Linden, where the pass is very narrow and would admit of no extended line. There was but a single, and that a very narrow, road leading through the gap by which to move up the main body of the corps; but, in the face of these obstacles, General French kept his command well closed up and ready for immediate use.

But the enemy appeared to have no great force in the gap, having been content with occupying its western end with a picket force of a few hundred men. They fell back as our skirmishers advanced, until they came upon a supporting force strongly posted on a lofty hill, facing directly up the gap, and around which the road leading through the gap passed by a debouch to the right. On this hill the enemy made a stand, and seemed disposed to resist our further advances.

General Ward then detached two regiments from his skirmish line—the Third and Fourth Maine, veterans of Kearny's old division—and directed them to clear this hill by assault. Our sharp-shooters held the attention of the enemy while the Maine men crept silently and all unobserved up the face of the hill. On gaining the summit they sprang to their feet, delivered a volley, and with a most determined charge cleared the hill, gaining a number of prisoners and spreading the ground with killed and wounded rebels. The charge was a right gallant one, such as soldiers may well feel proud of having participated in, and will ever be a bright credit mark for these fine regiments.

. But, when this hill was gained, it was discovered that the enemy were more strongly posted on a system of hills beyond and in front, commanding the main road through the gap, and to some extent fortified there, having a stone wall, a sunken road, and some hastily constructed breastworks of brush and logs to cover them.

General French was determined to sustain the reputation of the old Third corps, and was not willing that any obstacles should retard its advance when it had received orders to move forward. He directed General Prince, commanding the Second division, to detail a brigade to charge this system of hills, commanding the debouch of the road, and dislodge the enemy.

The famous Excelsior brigade was selected for this bold enterprise. The men were formed in line, and their new commander, General Spinola, addressed them a single word of encouragement, when the gallant fellows gave one of their peculiar cheers, so full of determination and confidence, and started forward. Room was made for them to pass through the line of skirmishers, and in a few minutes they were at the base of the hill.

The eastern slope of the hill was very rocky and precipitous, at some places being so nearly perpendicular that the men were obliged to scramble up on their hands and knees. The enemy, posted on the summit of the hill, were pouring down upon them a murderous fire of musketry; yet the men never flinched nor hesitated, but pushed forward and upward—now hanging by the bushes and scrambling on all fours, again panting and puffing at a doublequick, fearless of danger and intent only on dislodging the enemy. The elevation is estimated at three or four hundred feet.

Up this steep and rough mountain-side this glorious old brigade forced its way, and on reaching the summit fired and received one volley from the enemy, and then, fixing bayonets, gave another shout and rushed upon the rebels.

This charge was too much for flesh and blood to withstand. The enemy quailed before it and fled in confusion, closely and hotly pursued by our victorious troops.

The flight of the enemy from their first position disclosed a second ridge or crest back of the first that had been so gallantly carried, to which the rebels betook themselves and prepared to make another stand.

General Spinola was twice wounded in the assault of the first hill, and was obliged to leave the field he had so nobly won. Colonel Farnum, of the First Excelsior regiment, succeeded to the command of the brigade. The ferocity of the assault had disarranged the line somewhat, and Colonel Farnum, as commander, halted them for a moment to re-form, and then gave the order to advance again, placing himself in front of the line. Not a man hesitated or faltered at the renewal of the fight. Another cheer was given, and with a rush the entire brigade passed over the crest, into and across the ravine, and were quickly seen ascending the slope of the second hill. Here the resistance of the enemy was equally as desperate as on the first hill. But the assailants were flushed with victory, and could not have been checked had the whole rebel army stood in front of them.

All breathless and exhausted with fatigue they gained the summit of the second crest, the line broken and disordered, but only disordered as one and another strove more successfully with their companions for the honor of being first at the top. It was an exciting race, in which the danger was forgotten in the noble strife to be ahead. And as they came up the hill, singly and in squads of five, a dozen, twenty, fifty, and so on, each man rushed forward on his own account to secure prisoners.

Like demons they charged upon the bewildered foe, each man catching his prisoner by the hair, an arm, or perhaps a coat-tail, with the usual exclamation: "Here, you —— son of a ——, you're my prisoner!" And thus the second crest was carried as quickly as the first, and the Excelsior brigade were unanimously accredited with having made the most desperate and brilliant charge of the war. Their heroic deeds had been watched from the lofty summits in the rear by General Meade and staff, General French and his staff, and by the officers and many men of other corps; and as their success was made certain hill-top echoed to hill-top in a prolonged shout of admiration and praise. The accompanying list of casualties, sustained mainly by this brigade in making this almost unexampled charge, will attest the character of the affair more fully than any words I can give. A parley was now sounded. We had gained a second crest to discover lying yet between it and the valley a third lofty elevation, to which the enemy had fled.

Word was also received by General Meade that the rebel corps that had moved down the valley was returning, leaving the impression that it was their intention to make the desperate stand and give us the decisive battle at that point. Acting upon this information General Meade directed General French to suspend his main operations for the present and mass his troops in rear of the points already gained, and ordered up the bulk of his army, in anticipation of a battle on the following morning. The narrow gap was crowded all night with bodies of troops, packed in dense masses so thick as scarcely to be able to lie down. What sleeping was done was done under arms and in battle array.

The dispositions for battle were all made as the troops arrived during the evening, and at early daylight we had a line of battle which, if it was not very extensive, was certainly most formidable. It stretched, however, from mountain to mountain across the mouth of the pass, and would have defied assault. But no assault came. When daylight appeared the fact was revealed that the enemy had wholly disappeared.

From prisoners captured during the morning more exact information of the enemy's movements was obtained. It appeared then that the information brought in by our scouts was entirely erroneous; that the column of troops seen by Colonel Hayden was the rear of their whole line, and was a portion of Rhodes's division; that the forces met in the gap were some of Ewell's corps, who merely wished to hold the gap long enough to allow their column to cross the Shenandoah and move by on its way down the valley.

A detachment from the Third corps was ordered forward early in the morning, and passed unopposed into Front Royal, arriving there only in time to see the dust of the rear of the enemy's column moving away southward. The returning force of the rebels that our scouts had reported, and on which information General Meade had based his calculations for a great battle, proved to be simply a battery sent back by Longstreet to aid in holding the mouth of the gap during the night.

Thus it is seen on how small a circumstance a whole campaign may turn. General Meade, by moving into Manassas Gap and preparing for battle there—for which he certainly was justifiable, having such positive information to guide him—lost two days and a half of time in his southerly march, thus fully enabling Lee to reach the south of the Rappahannock before General Meade could possibly do so.

The brilliant affair in the Manassas Gap receives the title of the battle of Wapping Heights from the name of the system of hills upon which it occurred. There were a number of interesting incidents that occurred during the engagement, of which I have time to give but a few.

The old Excelsior brigade never behaved with greater credit to itself and the army than on this occasion. Officers and men vied with each other in deeds of heroism.

Color-Sergeant Dodds, of the Fifth regiment, carried his colors in front of the regiment until exhausted with fatigue, the enemy's bullets perforating the old flag at every step, and flying about the gallant color-bearer like hail. When too much exhausted to lead the regiment, Colonel Hall took the flag himself and bore it before the command on horseback, making himself a target for the enemy's shots. Color-Sergeant Smith, of the First, was wounded in the arm while bearing the flag of his regiment in front of the line. Although severely wounded, he simply changed hands and continued to bear the national emblem, waving it before the men to encourage them to press forward.

Colonel Farnum, of the First, was shot in his foot, and his horse was badly wounded; but he refused to leave the field.

Major Mehan, of the First, and Major Burns, of the Fourth, both had horses shot from under them, the former also suffering a severe contusion by his fall.

Captain Price, of the First, who was killed, was the author of the famous Homestead bill, and has a wide reputation in the country as the champion of homestead exemptions. He was a brave and gallant soldier, much beloved by his command.

Lieutenant Preston, of the Fifth, who was also killed, was wounded at Chancellorsville. He had just returned to his command, his former wounds having but recently healed.

General Prince, commanding the Second division, accompanied the Excelsior brigade in its charge, assuming the general direction of its movements. He would have pressed the noble brigade forward into Front Royal had he not been overtaken by a staff-officer, with orders to him to halt in his pursuit. He showed himself a most gallant and brave soldier, as he has done on former occasions.

General French handled his corps most efficiently, winning the highest encomiums from his superiors and from the commanders of corps in his rear, who were watching his movements. He fully demonstrated that, in his hands, the old Third corps would lose none of its ancient renown.

Doc. 105.

BATTLE OF CHICKAMAUGA, GA.

BY S. C. REID, ("ORA,")[*]

I HAVE already sent you an outline of the great battle of Chickamauga, and now undertake to give you a detailed account of its prominent features, without going into minute particulars, which would fill a volume. It has taken me some time to gather the information, and which has been attended with no slight obstacles. Besides this, the inconveniences in camp afford one but a poor opportunity to write with any satisfaction to one's self.

After a year of sad and disheartening reverses in the West, our arms have achieved a great and glorious victory. From the time General Johnston fell back from Bowling Green, Kentucky, a

[*]Correspondent of the *Mobile Tribune.*

dark and bloody struggle has ensued, in which, on every occasion, we have fought against superior numbers, victory wavering first on one side and then on the other. Notwithstanding the disasters of the Kentucky campaign, we retrieved a portion of Middle Tennessee and North-Alabama. The battle of Murfreesboro, in which we won a brilliant victory on the thirty-first of December last, afterward proved but a drawn battle, and on the night of second January following, we retreated to Tullahoma. Several months elapsed after this terrible conflict. We advanced to Wartrace and Shelbyville, were again ready to give the enemy battle, when a large portion of General Bragg's forces were withdrawn to Mississippi for the rescue of Vicksburgh. Nothing was accomplished by the move. General Bragg was left in a critical position as a mere army of observation, opposed to an overwhelming army in his front, which for months he held at bay. The enemy at last succeeded in surprising our forces at Liberty and Hoover's Gaps by a flank movement, and General Bragg, most prudently, to save his army, fell back, on the twenty-seventh of June last, to Chattanooga. The enemy followed at leisure to the banks of the Tennessee.

About the first of September, it was known that Burnside's forces were approaching Knoxville, threatening our right, when it was deemed expedient to evacuate that point, and concentrate General Buckner's forces with those of General Bragg. This movement was being effected, when it became apparent that Rosecrans was crossing his army at Bridgeport, having previously shelled Chattanooga by a small force in front. The threatening position of the enemy on our left now made it beyond doubt that he intended a flank-movement toward Rome, and no time was to be lost in cutting him off. To save the State of Georgia, Chattanooga had to be abandoned, and, knowing the superiority of the enemy's numbers, General Bragg could not afford to leave behind a sufficient garrison to defend the place. At this time, it must be understood, General Bragg had no knowledge that General Longstreet's corps was on its way from Virginia to reënforce him. Our troops evacuated Chattanooga on the seventh of September, and after a severe march through the dust, which was ankle deep, and exposed to the burning rays of the sun, they reached the vicinity of Lafayette, Georgia, on the ninth. The enemy's cavalry, under General Wilder, had already reached Alpine, and driven back Pegram's cavalry, and it was reported that a large body of the enemy was in the direction of McLemore's Cove.

Breckinridge's division, composed of Adams's, Helm's, and Stovall's brigades, guarded the various roads leading into Lafayette from the southward. On the morning of the thirteenth, our scouts reported a large force of the enemy advancing on our position from the direction of Alpine, twenty-five miles south-west of Lafayette. Adams's brigade was immediately thrown across the road to oppose the threatened advance, Stovall forming on the left of Adams, with his artillery, commanding a wide extent of open ground in our front. At mid-day, a squadron of our cavalry came dashing through our lines of skirmishers, followed by the "Lightning brigade" of Wilder. Our infantry and artillery immediately opened with buck, ball, and canister, and sent them to the right about with many an empty saddle.

In the mean time a large force of Thomas's corps was moving up McLemore's Cove, supposed to be Negley's and another division. Cheatham's division was moved rapidly forward to Lafayette in front, a portion of Hill's corps occupied Catlett's Gap, in Pigeon Mountain, (which is a spur of Lookout, about fifteen miles from Chattanooga,) flanking the enemy on his right, while General Hindman was ordered to attack the enemy immediately in the Cove. For some reason, attributed to the nature of the ground, the attack was not made, and the enemy escaped.

To understand the advance of Rosecrans's army, it would seem that Thomas's and McCook's corps, with Stanley's division of cavalry, commanded by Mitchell, crossed the Tennessee at Bridgeport, marching over Sand Mountain into Will's Valley, and from thence down McLemore's Cove in the direction of Lafayette. Crittenden's corps had crossed above Chattanooga at Harrison's, and was moved in the direction of Ringgold. A portion of Park's corps, of Burnside's army, and a brigade of his cavalry, came down from Knoxville to Loudon and Cleveland.

On the morning of the fourteenth, it was reported that the enemy had abandoned his position in the vicinity of Alpine, and that he was moving up McLemore's Cove in the direction of Chattanooga. General Cheatham's division was ordered to proceed toward Crawfish Springs, about half-way between Lafayette and Chattanooga, to reconnoitre the enemy, which he did, and returned on Tuesday, the fifteenth.

A council of war was then held at Lafayette, Georgia, on that day, and it was resolved to advance toward Chattanooga and attack the enemy wherever he could be found. On the sixteenth, General Bragg issued a spirited address to his troops, and preliminary orders directing the troops to be held in readiness to march that night. These orders were subsequently countermanded, and renewed at seven A.M. on the seventeenth, and Buckner's corps accordingly marched north from Lafayette at nine A.M. on that day, and encamped on Pea Vine Creek, ten miles from Lafayette; Walker camping a mile further on, and Polk's corps camping at Rock Spring. General Bragg made his headquarters at Leet's Tanyard, near Walker County, on Pea Vine Creek. The following order defined the movement:

HEADQUARTERS ARMY OF TENNESSEE, LEET'S TANYARD, September 18, 1863.

CIRCULAR.

I. Major-General W. H. T. Walker's division will move to Alexander's Bridge, or Byram's Ford, and there cross the Chickamauga.

II. Major-General Buckner will move on Tedford's Ford, and there cross the river. Both these columns will be put in motion at six A.M. this day. None but ambulances and artillery wagons will move with these columns.

III. Lieutenant-General Polk will move at the same hour, and by pressing, engage the attention of the enemy at Gordon's Mills, and be prepared to move by his right flank to cross the river by the nearest ford.

IV. The cavalry of General Pegram will cover the front of Buckner and Walker, and that of General Armstrong the front of General Polk.

By command of General BRAGG.

G. W. BRENT, A.A.G.

Buckner's corps was accordingly early upon the road, and, passing by Pea Vine Church, started for Tedford's Ford by the best and nearest road. His movement was unexpectedly checked, however, by encountering Walker's column, and when relieved by its passage, that of General Cheatham. At eleven o'clock, and while matters were brought to a halt by this collision, the following circular, of same tenor with the previous one, but more ample, was received:

HEADQUARTERS ARMY OF TENNESSEE,
IN THE FIELD, LEET'S TANYARD, September 18, 1863.

CIRCULAR.

I. Johnson's column, (Hood's,) on crossing at or near Reid's Bridge, will turn to the left by the most practicable route, and sweep up the Chickamauga toward Lee and Gordon's Mills.

II. Walker, crossing at Alexander's Bridge, will unite in this move and push vigorously on the enemy's flank and rear in the same direction.

III. Buckner, crossing at Tedford's Ford, will join in the movement to the left, and press the enemy up the stream from Polk's front at Lee and Gordon's Mills.

IV. Polk will press his forces to the front of Lee and Gordon's Mills, and if met by too much resistance to cross, will bear to the right and cross at Dalton's Ford, or Tedford's, as may be necessary, and join in the attack wherever the enemy may be.

V. Hill will cover our left flank from any advance of the enemy from the Cove, and by pressing the cavalry in his front ascertain if the enemy is reënforcing at Lee and Gordon's, in which event he will attack them in flank.

VI. Wheeler's cavalry will hold the gaps in Pigeon Mountain, and cover our rear and left, and bring up stragglers.

VII. All teams, etc., not with troops, should go toward Ringgold and Dalton, beyond Taylor's Ridge. All cooking should be done at the trains. Rations, when cooked, will be forwarded to the troops.

VIII. The above movements will be executed with the utmost promptness, vigor, and persistence.

By command of General BRAGG.

G. W. BRENT, A.A.G.

It must be borne in mind that the Chickamauga runs in a course nearly north; that Lee and Gordon's Mills are at the crossing of the Chattanooga and Lafayette road, and that Dalton's, Tedford's, Alexander's, and Reid's are respectively in their order further down the river (north) from Lee and Gordon's Mills. The crossing of the Chickamauga was to begin at the lowest ford and to be effected successively.

Breckinridge's division marched by the way of Catlett's Gap and the Crawfish Spring road to the main Chattanooga road. On the seventeenth, Adams's brigade occupied this gap, and from a lofty eminence near, could be seen the enemy's long wagon trains, solid columns of infantry, squadrons of horse, and batteries of artillery, passing all day long, and which seemed interminable. The enemy was evidently making his way across the slope, or south-west point of Lookout, to the Chickamauga, with a view of advancing on the line toward Ringgold and Dalton. Our chances of success against this immense and splendidly equipped army seemed small indeed, but instead of disheartening, it only seemed to nerve our boys and add impetuosity to their eagerness for the fray. At twilight the flood of their tens of thousands rolled on. As the veil of night covered the plain below, it became spangled with the thousands of lights of the enemy's bivouacs, revealing their immense encampment.

On Friday morning, the eighteenth, the enemy was found to occupy the opposite side of the west fork of the Chickamauga, which runs east of north, emptying into the Tennessee above Chattanooga. Our army had now advanced to the Chickamauga, General Forrest's cavalry being in front, on our right, reconnoitring and skirmishing with the enemy. General Law's Alabama brigade, Benning's Georgia brigade, and Robertson's Texas brigade, of Longstreet's corps, under command of General Hood, with Johnson's division, came up that morning from Dalton. It was now determined to force the passage of the Chickamauga, the enemy holding Alexander's Bridge in force, as well as the other. General Walker, commanding a sub-corps, composed of Liddell's and Walthall's brigades, under General Liddell, and Ector's, and another, commanded by Colonel Wilson, of Georgia, under General Gist, were ordered to carry this bridge. It was now three P.M., and Walthall's brigade, supported by Liddell's, in command of Colonel D. C. Govan, gallantly advanced for this purpose. A severe fight ensued, the enemy resolutely disputing the passage, but Walthall's men were irresistible, and after a bloody struggle, in which Walthall lost one hundred and two of his men killed and wounded, the point was carried, but the enemy burned the bridge in their retreat. Walker's corps then marched a mile below to Bryam's Ford, and crossed crotch deep. They bivouacked that night in front of Alexander's Bridge, occupying the position held by the enemy that day.

At the same time, while Walker was engaging the enemy, Stewart's division of Buckner's corps, composed of Clayton's, Brown's, and Bate's brigades, were moving on Tedford's and

Dalton's Fords. Bate's brigade was being thrown forward to a commanding position, supported by Clayton and Brown, but before getting into line the enemy opened a severe fire with musketry and artillery. General Bate soon formed his brigade in a skirt of woods immediately in front and opened fire, the Eufaula battery at the same time unlimbering and playing with such admirable effect on the enemy's guns, that he was soon induced to retire from his position, near Mr. Alexander's house, which was set on fire by our shells and destroyed. Stewart's division then camped near the ford which was held by Pegram's cavalry during the night, while Preston's division effected an unobstructed passage at Hunt's Ford, a mile higher up. Thus was secured the crossing of the Chickamauga by our army, to the astonishment of the enemy, who was surprised to find that we had really advanced upon him in force. That night Adams's brigade, of Breckinridge's division, guarded Childress Bridge, on the extreme left of our army, and Ector's brigade was in front of Reid's Bridge on our right.

While our army was thus advancing toward Lafayette to check the main body of Rosecrans's army, Crittenden's corps was vainly dreaming of a triumphant march toward Atlanta. The enemy's cavalry had advanced as far as Tunnel Hill, from where they were driven back, on the eleventh of September, by Forrest's and Scott's cavalry, General Bushrod Johnson's forces occupying the ridge back of the railroad tunnel. To show that Rosecrans had no idea of being attacked by Bragg, on the eighteenth, while he was securing the bridges and fords across the Chickamauga, the enemy's cavalry made a dash on Ringgold, shelling the town, but were driven back by our cavalry with considerable loss. It is stated that at this time, some of our people informed Crittenden that we had received large reënforcements from Virginia, which caused him to make a precipitate retreat. On the same day, Brigadier-General Hodge's Kentucky cavalry, which had been serving in Virginia, drove the enemy out of Cleveland, after a severe skirmish, in which some sixty of the enemy were killed and wounded, and thirty of a Michigan regiment taken prisoners.

Early on Saturday morning, the nineteenth, General Bragg came up to Tedford's Ford, and the commands of Hood and Johnson and Walker and Buckner were advanced for formation into line.

All our forces, but a portion of Hill's and Longstreet's, were across the river, being on the west side of the west fork of the Chickamauga, which is a very tortuous stream, its general direction running north by east. Our position was in the extreme north-west corner of Georgia, about eight miles west of Ringgold, and seven miles south of Chattanooga. The battle-ground extended from the right, four miles from the Tennessee State line, and across the boundary line of the counties of Catoosa and Walker, in Georgia, to about six miles, near Lee and Gordon's

Mills on our left. The nature of the ground is undulating and heavily timbered with oak and a thick undergrowth. Toward the west, approaching Missionary Ridge, the ground becomes broken into hills and valleys. Our line of battle rested on the bends of the river, forming an obtuse angle, and was formed that morning without much regard to corps organization as follows: General Walker's corps, composed of Liddell's and Gist's divisions, the former commanding his own brigade, under Colonel D. C. Govan, and Walthall's brigade; and Gist commanding Ector's brigade, and another, under Colonel Wilson, took position on our right, with Cheatham's division in reserve. Stewart's division, composed of Clayton's, Bate's and Brown's brigades of Buckner's corps, formed the centre; and Bushrod Johnson's division, composed of his own brigade, under Colonel Fulton, and McNair's and Gregg's, with Hood's division, commanded by General Law, and Preston's and Breckinridge's division, formed on our left wing, under command of General Hood, General Longstreet not having come up. Our right wing was commanded by General Polk.

It was contemplated by General Bragg to make a flank movement and turn the enemy's left, so as to get our forces between him and Chattanooga, and thus cut off his retreat, believing that the main force of the enemy was at Lee and Gordon's Mills, and upon which he had intended to move. But, unfortunately, General Thomas, who commanded the left of the Abolition army, had that very morning, at nine o'clock, sent a despatch to General Palmer, commanding the Abolition centre, ordering him to attack our front immediately, while Thomas proceeded to flank us on the right. Thus, before we were prepared, the enemy commenced a counter attack, while General Walker at the time was awaiting orders to move into position. General Forrest, who was on our right flank, in front, annoying the enemy and retarding his movements, was now being sorely pressed by Thomas, and requested Ector's brigade to support him, Colonel Wilson's brigade at the same time moving forward. After a gallant fight, against tremendous odds, these two brigades were driven back. At this time General Walker was ordered by General Bragg to ascertain the cause of such heavy firing. Walker and Liddell, after a reconnoissance, then ascertained that a corps of the enemy, under Thomas, was moving to turn our right wing, and Liddell's division was immediately advanced to support Ector and Wilson, who had been badly repulsed. It was now about noon when Walthall's and Govan's brigades, under Liddell, gallantly met the enemy, and such was the impetuous charge made by these troops that they broke through two lines, driving back the Fourteenth, Sixteenth, and Eighteenth United States regulars, and capturing two batteries; Walthall's brigade capturing the whole of the Fifth United States infantry, four hundred and eleven officers and men; and Govan's, one hundred prisoners, and the celebrated Loomis battery, a captain of which refused to leave his gun and was captured with it. By this time the enemy's centre being broken, their extended lines flanked Liddell on both sides, compelling him to retire with his prisoners, and was only enabled to bring off three of the guns.

At the same time Stewart's division had advanced to meet the foe, Clayton's brigade becoming engaged at noon, and was exposed to a most destructive fire, Brown's brigade then advanced and relieved Clayton, but such became the fury of the enemy's fire that they were compelled, after a determined stand, to fall back. Bate's brigade was then ordered forward and staggered for a moment, but breasting the storm they delivered a constant fire into the enemy's ranks with good effect, and then rushing forward, charged a battery and drove the enemy from their guns, three of which were brought off the field. The Abolitionists fell back to a second battery, which opened with grape and canister so severely, that in making a charge the brigade became divided and the effect was lost, enabling the enemy to recover their guns by throwing forward their infantry. Bate soon rallied his brigade, which formed in line again, confronting the enemy with such daring that it drew forth general admiration and the praise of officers high in rank. It was at this time the brave, chivalrous Colonel A. F. Rudler, of the Thirty-seventh Georgia, received a slight wound, and his gallant color-bearer, John C. Clemence, fell mortally wounded while bearing forward the regimental flag. The enemy's artillery was capably and continuously served, and with terrible effect. Our troops moved through a tempest of grape and canister. The woods had been fired by the burning missile of the enemy which was calculated to appall the stoutest heart; but still our men pressed forward undaunted, and made the burning forest vocal with their yells, while the terrified enemy gave away before them.

It was now about two P.M. The enemy was being largely reënforced, and hurrying forward his multiplied numbers to recover his lost ground, when the chafing Cheatham moved forward his veterans of J. K. Jackson's, Maney's, Strahl's, Wright's, and Preston Smith's brigades, relieving Liddell's command, and met the shock of battle as the enemy's forces came rolling down toward them. The artillery, under Major Melancthon Smith, opened on them a sweeping fire which made their columns shake. Then again our lines wavered before the desperate struggle of the enemy, and the fight was kept up with varied success until five P.M., we having sustained a slight repulse. It was here fell the brave Preston Smith. At the same time Stewart had been again pushing them in the centre, and had also failed to dislodge the enemy. General Liddell was now ordered still further to the right, and again engaged the enemy. Govan's brigade charged and took another battery, and while engaged with the enemy one of our batteries in the rear opened on his men, causing them to fall back. Walthall held his own against fearful odds, but was finally compelled to retire under the fire

of the enemy, whose position was now very strong, they occupying the crest of a slight eminence which they had fortified with fallen timber, and by this great advantage had maintained their ground against two desperate assaults.

The sun was setting when the Stonewall of Bragg's army, Cleburn, of Hill's corps, came up with his braves under Deshler, Polk, and Wood, relieving Walker, and passing to the front over the bloody ground that had been so stubbornly contested by Cheatham, charging the enemy up to their very breastworks. A crashing fire of musketry from the enemy made Cleburn's men reel, when forward dashed the batteries of the gallant Semple and Lieutenant Key, who opened a terrific fire on the enemy's works, while the division charged with such impetuosity that the enemy recoiled and were driven half a mile from their line of battle.

That night our troops slept on the field, surrounded by the dead. No cheerful fire dispelled the gloom, and profound silence brooded over the field of carnage.

We must now go back to bring up the movements of our left wing, which occurred on the nineteenth. General Hood was in command of two divisions, his own, under General Law, Colonel Sheffield commanding Law's brigade, and Bushrod Johnson's, which formed on the left of Stewart's. Preston's division of Buckner's corps, consisting of Gracie's, Trigg's, and Kelley's brigades, formed on the left of Hood's, holding an important hill and bluff, upon which were placed two batteries. Adams's brigade of Breckinridge's division formed into line near Glass's Mill, on the Chickamauga, and was the extreme left of our army. None of the infantry on our extreme left was engaged that day, but in the morning Slocomb's battery of the Washington artillery had a bloody duel with the enemy, and suffered severely in men and horses, and the gallant Lieutenant Blair was killed. The enemy's battery did not escape, however, without being completely riddled. About three o'clock, when Stewart was hotly engaged, Hood's command attacked the enemy, driving them back across the Chattanooga road, which fronted our whole line of battle, capturing a battery and taking off three guns. It was late in the afternoon when Hood's division was being sorely pressed, that Trigg's brigade of Preston's division, was detached, rendering timely aid, and driving the enemy from the desired position. At dark, Hood's command fell back three hundred yards across the Chattanooga road, and formed line of battle on a ridge. It should have been stated that in the morning of this day Colonel Johnson, commanding Morgan's cavalry, as well as Pegram's cavalry, took a gallant part in the fight on our right, and that Scott's Louisiana cavalry with three companies held at bay seven regiments of infantry.

The battle of Saturday had closed without our having gained any decided advantage, and from the stubborn resistance made by the enemy, our lines were but little advanced. All night long the enemy's axes were heard cutting timber to make breastworks, and they actually piled up their own dead for this purpose. The position on which Buckner's left rested (Preston's division) had been selected as the *point d'appui*, and the pivot upon which the army was to swing in the movement which had failed by reason of the attack on our right. It was now understood that the battle would commence at daylight Sunday, and that the same movement would be attempted. For this purpose Breckinridge's division, of Hill's corps, was moved that night on our extreme right, to strengthen that wing. Preston was ordered to a position further to the left. Hindman's division, of Manigault's, Deas's, and Anderson's brigades, came up and took position between Hood and Preston. General Longstreet came up at midnight and took command of the right wing. McLaws's division had also come up, Kershaw's and Humphrey's brigades, and formed in reserve half a mile in the rear of Hood. All was now ready for the grand attack of the coming Sabbath.

Sunday, twentieth of September, the sun rose clear and bright, but an impenetrable mist covered the field between the two belligerent armies. Our troops were all in line waiting but for the word to "forward." General Polk had the night previous received orders to commence the attack with Hill's corps at daylight, and had despatched two couriers that night to the headquarters of General Hill, but they failed to find him, he being in the rear at Tedford's Ford, and the order consequently did not reach General Hill until late Sunday morning, General Polk having despatched one of his aids to look for him. This delay unfortunately lost us at least three hours of daylight, which, as the sequel will show, proved very lucky for Rosecrans's army. The enemy had worked like beavers during the night, and had made three lines of intrenchments, besides having the advantage of position on a rising ridge, and were still at work during the early part of the morning. Skirmishing had commenced in front of our lines, but the battle did not open on our right wing until ten o'clock, when the command "forward" ran down our ranks. It was a splendid sight to see that martial array of glorious heroes as our long lines advanced to the bloody contest with the abolition infidel foe. Major Austin's Louisiana battalion, on the extreme right of Hill's corps, moved boldly forward, deployed as skirmishers, and engaged the enemy eight hundred yards in front. That intrepid warrior Breckinridge moved forward his division in as perfect order as if on dress parade, followed closely in the rear by his splendid battery of artillery. Soon the sharp rattle of volleys of musketry were heard, and the roar of battle thundered through the forest. Having driven in two lines of skirmishers, and exposed to a severe cannonading, the division met and drove the enemy from a dense thicket, Adams's brigade capturing a battery, one of the guns being secured by Colonel R. L. Gibson's regiment, and two more by Major Austin's battalion. Breckinridge's division had now crossed the Chattanooga road, having been advancing parallel with it, when by a flank movement to the left, the division formed its line of battle at a right angle with the road, Adams being on the right, Stovall in the centre, and Helm on the left. Advancing for about eight hundred yards through open fields and dense thickets, subject to a constant artillery fire, the division encountered at one hundred yards a division of regulars intrenched in a strong position. Helm, encountering a deadly fire from the intrenchments, was held in check, while Adams and Stovall passed on exposed to a terrible fire of grape and shot from the enemy's front, at the same time a galling fire enfilading them from the left. Notwithstanding, Breckinridge's line stood firm and steadfast, and delivering a volley and charging the enemy with a shout, dispersed their first line in gallant style. At this moment a second line came up on our right flank, sustained by a heavy battery, and delivered an unbroken volley which staggered our whole line and forced it to retire. It was at this time General Adams received a severe wound in his shoulder, making the fifth time that this veteran soldier had suffered for his country. Such was the proximity of our troops at the time, that Adams was taken prisoner; the heroic Helm was killed, and Major Graves, chief of artillery, mortally wounded. The command fell back some three hundred yards to a commanding height, from which Slocomb with his Napoleon guns checked the hosts of the advancing enemy, Adams's brigade having been successfully rallied by the gallant Gibson, who, colors in hand, again fronted the foe. Had the reserve ordered forward to Breckinridge's support come up in time, the enemy's position might have been carried, and prevented the conflict of the afternoon. As it was, notwithstanding our partial repulse, several pieces of artillery were captured and a large number of prisoners.

At the same time each succeeding division to the left gradually became engaged with the enemy, extending to Longstreet's wing. Walker's division now advanced to the relief of Breckinridge, and after an engagement of half an hour, was also compelled to retire under the severe fire of the enemy. The gallant champions of Tennessee, under Cheatham, then advanced to the relief of Walker, but even they wavered and fell back under the terrible fires of the enemy. Cleburn's division, which had several times gallantly charged the enemy, had also been checked, and Stuart's division, occupying the centre and left of our wing, detached from Buckner's corps, had recoiled before the enemy, but not without slaying their battalions in heaps, charging across an open wood and field under a tornado of grape and canister.

Up to noon the struggle had been most desperate on our right, and resistance made on both sides with unparalleled stubbornness, our right wing having been repulsed by the enemy's superior numbers, thus for a second time thwarting the intended swinging movement. The meridian sun, which had witnessed the terrible carnage of the conflict, now commenced its westward course, as if declining further to side with the abolition banners of the east. A reconnoissance made in our front showed that the enemy had fallen back from that portion of the field.

At this critical juncture, it being now about one P.M., the lion-hearted Longstreet ordered General Buckner to advance, which he did as a second line to McLaws's and Hood's divisions. This movement, effected by Longstreet, was in the nature of a left wheel upon his right, Hood's division being as a centre. By this manœuvre he advanced one mile and a half, and formed at right angles with the Chattanooga road, the movement at the same time uniting Buckner's corps, by bringing Preston's division within a short interval on Stewart's left. Longstreet's corps proper, Hindman's and Bushrod Johnson's divisions now advanced like tigers on the foe. The second line of the enemy, who had taken up a position on a ridge or range of hills, with temporary breastworks formed of rails and fallen timber, had been driven back with great slaughter, Hood's corps having captured thirteen pieces of artillery and a large number of prisoners. The North-Carolinians of McNair's gallant brigade on this occasion made their mark. Lieutenant-Colonel Frank A. Reynolds, of the Thirty-ninth North-Carolina, capturing ten pieces of cannon, seven of which were brought off the field, with two standards of colors, the regiment losing one hundred men out of two hundred and thirty-eight. The glorious Hood himself was seriously wounded, having his leg amputated on the field. Longstreet now took command of Hood's corps in person with other troops, when charge after charge was made, pressing back the enemy's right, until their line was doubled on their centre, for a distance of three miles. Kershaw's South-Carolinians and Humphrey's Mississippians now advanced to the assault of the ridge, and soon became engaged in a desperate struggle, the tide of victory vacillating, when the peerless Preston was ordered to advance his division of united troops, Gracie's, Kelley's, and Trigg's brigades, who had never before been in action, to their aid. They moved forward through a deadly fire with the firmness and courage of veterans, exciting the highest admiration, when a simultaneous assault was made, and the enemy driven from and over the crest of the ridge with great slaughter, thus wresting from him his supposed impregnable position. General Longstreet, in passing over the scene afterward, remarked that the troops who could take such a stronghold could carry any works the enemy could construct.

It was now about five o'clock when the enemy's right wing had been driven back in dismay, and Rosecrans, to check our further advance and save his army, attempted to reënforce his right by throwing over a heavy body of troops from his left. The movement was at once perceived by the eagle eyes of Longstreet and Buckner, who had reconnoitred the ground, and it being suggested by General Law, commanding Hood's division, that we could enfilade the enemy as he approached by placing artillery near the Chattanooga road, and opposite the angle formed by the enemy's

lines, Major Williams, commanding a battery of artillery, of Buckner's corps, was ordered to concentrate his batteries at the point it was supposed the enemy would cross. Soon after, as was expected, the heavy columns of the enemy made their appearance and were about wheeling into line, when Williams opened on them a terrific fire with grape, canister, and shrapnel, mowing down the abolition foe, and shivering the woods behind which they attempted to take shelter. At the same time, Stewart's division, which had been ordered forward by General Longstreet, fell furiously upon the flank of the column, on the right of the road, while Law opened a most unmerciful fire on the left. The enemy's right and centre gave way before the mighty shock, and broke with frantic confusion; over twenty pieces of artillery were captured, and several thousand made prisoners.

General Bragg, upon whom rested the mighty responsibility of the immense stake at hazard, and who, upon every part of the battle-field, watched with intense anxiety the fate of the day—as he directed the storm of death—then felt that the God of battles would award to him the victory.

The western horizon, crimsoned with vermilion hues, now shed its ruddy light on the hill-top and forest-plain, painting the bloody battle-field still reeking with human gore—but the battle strife had not yet ceased. Driven to desperation, and determined at all hazards to hold their position on their left wing, the enemy with a resolute ferocity hurled his battalions upon our right, at the same time opening his batteries with a storm of shell and grape. Liddell and Gist, of Walker's corps, who had been again ordered forward, being their fifth engagement with the enemy, were met by a most destructive fire, which enfiladed them on both flanks and drove them back. Our line of battle on the right was now about half a mile from the Chattanooga road. The enemy was sorely pressing our wavering lines. General Polk, who had borne the brunt of the battle during the day, and fought his wing against the concentrated masses of the enemy with unequalled bravery and endurance, had now marshaled his forces for a last desperate charge, on which depended the fate of the day. His flashing eye at this moment discovered that Granger's reserve corps of abolition troops was moving down upon us, and not a moment was to be lost. At the same time it was reported that Longstreet was driving the enemy's right flank, which added fresh nerve and vigor to our already exhausted men. The signal being given, the whole line advanced, Breckinridge leading off on the extreme right, the division making a left half wheel, which brought it parallel to the enemy's lines, whose artillery belched forth a blasting fire. Forward pressed Stovall, Gibson, and Helm, in perfect order, cheered by other lines of troops as they advanced, and passing through the "unterrified" of Walker's line, who was then engaging the enemy, without halting, and reserving their fire until within a few yards of the foe, when they sprang forward with a wild yell to the charge, receiving a volley from the enemy without effect. A second volley from the barricades of trees and stones checked Breckinridge for a moment, and many a brave, with the noble Helm, fell, but the officers rushed forward, mounting the barricades, followed by their men, dealing destruction to the panic-stricken hordes, who fled on every side, a brigade of U. S. regulars, under General King, being perfectly routed by Gibson. Still onward pressed the division of Breckinridge, driving the enemy for three quarters of a mile, capturing nine pieces of cannon and hundreds of prisoners, until entering the woods about seventy yards west of the Chattanooga road, the enemy's killed and wounded making its bloody track in the pursuit.

At the same time on came the chivalrous Cleburn, with the brave Deshler, Wood, and Polk, who soon came in conflict with Granger's corps, sweeping them before their ranks like leaves, and facing the murderous fire of their barricades. The heroic and dashing Deshler went down, but still the men pressed forward; Wood, with Lucius Polk's brigade, storming breastwork after breastwork, until the third work was carried—Polk capturing three pieces of cannon, the standards of the Second Ohio, Seventy-seventh Pennsylvania, Seventy-ninth Illinois, and five hundred prisoners. Like the ocean's wave, rolled onward the brigades of the warrior Cheatham toward the centre of the enemy's works, which were carried with an irresistible impetuosity. Maney's brigade adding new laurels to its fame, as well as Strahl's, Wright's, Jackson's, and the lamented Preston Smith's capturing several pieces of artillery, and a large number of prisoners. This sealed our victory. The enemy was totally routed from right, left, and centre, and was in full retreat to Chattanooga, night alone preventing their further pursuit. Then arose along our lines, from wing to wing for miles, one wild, tumultuous yell, and cheers which made the hills and forest shake again. The day was ours; while the croaking raven of the night perched on the ill-starred banner of the vain, boasting Rosecrans, now crestfallen, defeated, and humiliated. Polk's wing captured twenty-eight pieces of artillery, and Longstreet's twenty-one, making forty-nine pieces of cannon, both wings taking nearly an equal number of prisoners, amounting to over eight thousand, with thirty thousand stand of arms, and forty stands of regimental colors. The enemy's loss in killed, wounded, and prisoners, by their own account, is not less than thirty thousand. Ours is computed at twelve thousand, our wounded being unusually large compared to the killed. The enemy is known to have had all his available force on the field, including his reserve, with a portion of Burnside's corps, numbering not less than eighty thousand, while our whole force did not exceed fifty thousand. Nothing was more brilliant in all Bonaparte's Italian campaigns; it was equally as desperate as the battle of Arcola, and far more decisive in its results. So far it exceeds all previous battles of our revolution, and nothing could surpass the irresistible courage and heroic intrepidity of our officers and soldiers.

It is impossible to crowd into this limited space

the numerous personal heroic deeds, or the valorous and chivalrous incidents, recalling the exploits of the knights of romance, which occurred on the ever-memorable field of Chickamauga, even were they known to the writer, while it is a source of regret that I cannot do full justice to companies and regiments by recording here the noble and heroic part which they bore on this bloody battlefield, where all were alike distinguished for heroism and bravery.

It is but justice to General Longstreet to accord to him the turning of the tide of victory by his masterly manœuvre, which was followed up and completed by General Polk, while it must be conceded that the resolute decision of General Bragg in checking the enemy's advance into Georgia, striking him at a disadvantage, with great odds against us, and driving him from the State, defeated and routed, deserves the gratitude of our countrymen.

Too much praise cannot be given to the gallant Georgians. In Hood's division thirteen pieces of artillery were captured, to secure which our boys forced the abolition prisoners to haul them off the field. It was a novel sight to see two confederate soldiers mounted on a gun-carriage, with their rifles in hand, driving a team of "abolish," which had been harnessed up for the occasion. The able manner in which Hood's division was handled by the accomplished Brigadier-General E. M. Law, called forth the high praise and congratulations of General Longstreet. The most eminent service had been rendered by our bold dragoons under the daring chieftains Forrest, Wheeler, Wharton, and Scott, who drove back and checked the enemy's advances, and during the fight greatly annoyed their flanks, capturing a large number of prisoners.

Not since the battle of Cressy, 1346, when cannon were first used, was the artillery arm of the service more effective on both sides, or more chivalry shown. During the evening of the twentieth, when Liddell's brigades were in desperate conflict with the enemy, Captain Sweet's battery silenced a battery of the enemy, which was afterward captured. The officer in command, on being taken prisoner, inquired the name of the confederate officer who served the guns, as he desired to present him with his sword and glass, for his gallantry and great skill. The officer referred to was the brave Lieutenant Shannon, and the glass and sword were left with Major M. Smith for the heroic artillerist. The batteries commanded by Captains Cobb, Carns, Lumsden, Fowler, and indeed all our artillery officers, rendered distinguished service, and none more so than the lamented Major E. E. Graves, chief of artillery of Breckinridge's division, who was killed on the field. Major J. K. Porter, Chief of Artillery of Buckner's corps, Lieutenant-Colonel James H. Hallonquist, Chief of Artillery of General Bragg's staff, and Major Palmer also rendered distinguished service.

An idea of the desperation of the fight may be had from the casualties in Govan's and Walthall's brigades, which suffered the largest loss of any two brigades in the army. But one colonel was left in command in Govan's brigade. Colonel Featherston, of the Fifth Arkansas, fell in the first engagement while gallantly taking a battery; Lieutenant-Colonel Baucum, of the Eighth Arkansas, and Colonel Gillespie, of the Seventh, were both wounded. Ten company officers out of twelve, in the First Louisiana and Eighth Arkansas, consolidated, were killed and wounded. In the two brigades one thousand and six hundred men and officers were killed and wounded in five desperate engagements. Eight field officers out of ten were killed and wounded in Walthall's brigade, and Colonel J. J. Scales, of the Thirtieth Mississippi, captured. In the Twenty-fourth Mississippi, Lieutenant-Colonel R. P. Mackelvaine and Major W. C. Staples were wounded; also, Lieutenant-Colonel A. J. Jones, of the Twenty-seventh; Lieutenant-Colonel L. B. Morgan, of the Twenty-ninth; Major J. M. Johnson, of the Thirtieth; Major W. G. Pegram, and Captain Fowler, afterward commanding Thirty-fourth Mississippi. Lieutenant-Colonel H. A. Reynolds, Thirty-fourth Mississippi, was killed. Colonel Brantley, of Twenty-ninth, and Colonel Campbell, Twenty-seventh, were the only officers uninjured. Whole loss, seven hundred and eighty-one killed, wounded, and missing.

The Louisiana, Kentucky, and Alabama troops were also conspicuous for their gallantry. Sergeant J. C. McDevitt, the color-bearer of Gibson's regiment, Adams's brigade, was mortally wounded in both legs with canister. The brave Major Loudon Butler, of the Nineteenth Louisiana, was killed at the head of his regiment, and Lieutenant-Colonel R. W. Turner, of same regiment, was wounded, also Captain E. P. Guilliet, of General Adams's staff. Colonel Daniel Gober and Major C. H. Moore, of Sixteenth and Twenty-fifth Louisiana; Colonel L. Von Zinken and Captain E. M. Dubroca, of Thirteenth and Twentieth Louisiana; Captain John W. Labouisse, A. I. G.; Major J. C. Kimball, Thirty-second Alabama, and Lieutenants S. L. Ware and Scott Yerger, were distinguished for their gallantry and bravery. Major James Wilson, A. A. G.; Captains Cabell, Breckinridge, Clay, Coleman, and Maston, of General Breckinridge's staff, also won additional distinction. The brave and chivalrous Colonel Hewitt, of the Second Kentucky, and Lieutenant-Colonel Inge, of the Eighteenth Alabama, were killed.

Bate's brigade, of Stewart's division, retook a gun and confederate flag which had been captured by the enemy the evening before. General Bate had two horses shot under him, suffering considerably from the fall of the last. General Brown was struck in the breast by a spent ball, which shocked him severely, and General Clayton was struck with a fragment of shell on the side. Bate's brigade lost six hundred and eight, out of one thousand and eighty-five, including sixty-seven officers. Every staff-officer had his horse shot under him. Colonel R. C. Tyler, of the Fifteenth and Thirty-seventh Tennessee, lost one hundred and twenty out of two hundred and two men. All the field-officers were wounded, six company officers were killed, and two color-bearers were shot down. During the evening of the twentieth, this gallant regiment became disconnected from Bate's brigade, and fought independently, capturing, with a portion of the Fourth Alabama, a fine battery, the men of the regiment managing the guns and carrying them to the rear, the horses being all killed. During the night after the battle, Preston's division captured two regiments, being part of a small force which held its position on our left. Major J. Stoddard Johnson, A. A. G.; Major T. H. Clay, Inspector-General; Major A. C. Gibson, Chief of Ordnance, and Major T. K. Porter, Chief of Artillery, of General Buckner's staff, were distinguished for the gallant service which they rendered on the field.

On Monday, twenty-first, Forrest and Wheeler pursued the enemy, who did not stop until they reached Chattanooga, the former keeping up a running fire and capturing a number of prisoners. Wheeler also destroyed a wagon train and captured one hundred prisoners. Major John Taylor, of the First Louisiana cavalry, went within five miles of Chattanooga, and captured the splendid colors of the Thirtieth Indiana, with one hundred prisoners. Our whole army moved forward on Tuesday, and formed in front of Missionary Ridge, taking possession of Lookout Mountain, and securing the river road toward Bridgeport. It is stated that the enemy had already crossed a portion of his army over the river, but finding he was not pursued, returned. There is hardly a doubt, however, that if our troops could have pursued him that night, we would have at least occupied Chattanooga, as the enemy was most precipitous in his flight, leaving his hospitals, wounded and dead alike, abandoned, on the banks of the "River of Death!"

Doc. 106.
PROCLAMATION OF JEFFERSON DAVIS.
JULY 25TH, 1863.

AGAIN do I call upon the people of the Confederacy—a people who believe that the Lord reigneth and that his overruling providence ordereth all things—to unite in prayer and humble submission under his chastening hand, and to beseech his favor on our suffering country.

It is meet that when trials and reverses befall us we should seek to take home to our hearts and consciences the lessons which they teach, and profit by the self-examination for which they prepare us. Had not our successes on land and sea made us self-confident and forgetful of our reliance on him; had not love of lucre eaten like a gangrene into the very heart of the land, converting too many among us into worshippers of gain and rendering them unmindful of their duty to their country, to their fellow-men, and to their God—who then will presume to complain that we have been chastened or to despair of our just cause and the protection of our heavenly Father?

Let us rather receive in humble thankfulness the lesson which he has taught in our recent reverses, devoutly acknowledging that to him, and not to our own feeble arms, are due the honor and the glory of victory; that from him, in his paternal providence, come the anguish and sufferings of defeat, and that, whether in victory or defeat, our humble supplications are due at his footstool.

Now, therefore, I, Jefferson Davis, President of these confederate States, do issue this, my proclamation, setting apart Friday, the twenty-first day of August ensuing, as a day of fasting, humiliation, and prayer; and I do hereby invite the people of the confederate States to repair on that day to their respective places of public worship, and to unite in supplication for the favor and protection of that God who has hitherto conducted us safely through all the dangers that environed us.

In faith whereof, I have hereunto set my hand and the seal of the confederate SEAL. States, at Richmond, this twenty-fifth day of July, in the year of our Lord one thousand eight hundred and sixty-three.

By the President: JEFFERSON DAVIS.
　J. P. BENJAMIN,
　　Secretary of State.

Doc. 107.

MILITARY ARRESTS.

THE following is a correct copy of the correspondence between President Lincoln and the committee appointed by the Ohio Democratic State Convention to ask for permission for Hon. C. L. Vallandigham to return to Ohio:*

THE LETTER TO THE PRESIDENT.

WASHINGTON CITY, June 26, 1863.

To His Excellency the President of the United States :

The undersigned, having been appointed a committee, under the authority of the resolutions of the State Convention, held at the city of Columbus, Ohio, on the eleventh instant, to communicate with you on the subject of the arrest and banishment of Clement L. Vallandigham, most respectfully submit the following as the resolutions of that Convention, bearing upon the subject of this communication, and ask of your Excellency their earnest consideration. And they deem it proper to state that the Convention was one in which all parts of the State were represented, and one of the most respectable as to character and numbers, and one of the most earnest and sincere in support of the Constitution and Union ever held in that State.

Resolved, 1. That the will of the people is the foundation of all free government; that to give effect to this will, free thought, free speech, and a free press are absolutely indispensable. Without free discussion there is no certainty of sound judg-

* See Doc. 67, page 298, *ante.*

ment; without sound judgment there can be no wise government.

2. That it is an inherent and constitutional right of the people to discuss all measures of their government, and to approve or disapprove, as to their best judgment seems right. That they have a like right to propose and advocate that policy which in their judgment is best, and to argue and vote against whatever policy seems to them to violate the Constitution, to impair their liberties, or to be detrimental to their welfare.

3. That these and all other rights guaranteed to them by their constitutions are their rights in time of war as well as in time of peace, and of far more value and necessity in war than in peace, for in peace, liberty, security, and property are seldom endangered; in war they are ever in peril.

4. That we now say to all whom it may concern, not by way of threat, but calmly and firmly, that we will not surrender these rights nor submit to their forcible violation. We will obey the laws ourselves, and all others must obey them.

11. That Ohio will adhere to the Constitution and the Union as the best, it may be the last, hope of popular freedom, and for all wrongs which may have been committed or evils which may exist will seek redress, under the Constitution and within the Union, by the peaceful but powerful agency of the suffrages of a free people.

14. That we will earnestly support every constitutional measure tending to preserve the Union of the States. No men have a greater interest in its preservation than we have—none desire it more; there are none who will make greater sacrifices or endure more than we will to accomplish that end. We are, as we ever have been, the devoted friends of the Constitution and the Union, and we have no sympathy with the enemies of either.

15. That the arrest, imprisonment, pretended trial, and actual banishment of Clement L. Vallandigham, a citizen of the State of Ohio, not belonging to the land or naval forces of the United States, nor to the militia in actual service, by alleged military authority, for no other pretended crime than that of uttering words of legitimate criticism upon the conduct of the Administration in power, and of appealing to the ballot-box for a change of policy—said arrest and military trial taking place where the courts of law are open and unobstructed, and for no act done within the sphere of active military operations in carrying on the war—we regard as a palpable violation of the following provisions of the Constitution of the United States:

1. "Congress shall make no law . . . . abridging the freedom of speech or of the press, or the right of the people peaceably to assemble, and to petition the Government for a redress of grievances."

2. "The right of the people to be secure in their persons, houses, papers, and effects, against unreasonable searches and seizures, shall not be violated; and no warrants shall issue, but upon

probable cause, supported by oath or affirmation, and particularly describing the place to be searched and the persons or things to be seized."

3. "No person shall be held to answer for a capital or otherwise infamous crime unless on a presentment or indictment of a grand jury, except in cases arising in the land or naval forces, or in the militia, when in actual service in time of war or public danger."

4. "In all criminal prosecutions, the accused shall enjoy the right to a speedy and public trial, by an impartial jury of the State and district wherein the crime shall have been committed, which district shall have been previously ascertained by law."

And we furthermore denounce said arrest, trial, and banishment, as a direct insult offered to the sovereignty of the people of Ohio, by whose organic law it is declared that no person shall be transported out of the State for any offence committed within the same.

16. That Clement L. Vallandigham was, at the time of his arrest, a prominent candidate for nomination by the Democratic party of Ohio, for the office of Governor of the State ; that the Democratic party was fully competent to decide whether he is a fit man for that nomination, and that the attempt to deprive them of that right, by his arrest and banishment, was an unmerited imputation upon their intelligence and loyalty, as well as a violation of the Constitution.

17. That we respectfully, but most earnestly, call upon the President of the United States to restore Clement L. Vallandigham to his home in Ohio, and that a committee of one from each Congressional district of the State, to be selected by the presiding officer of this Convention, is hereby appointed to present this application to the President.

The undersigned, in the discharge of the duty assigned them, do not think it necessary to reiterate the facts connected with the arrest, trial, and banishment of Mr. Vallandigham—they are well known to the President, and are of public history—nor to enlarge upon the positions taken by the Convention, nor to recapitulate the constitutional provisions which it is believed have been contravened ; they have been stated at length, and with clearness in the resolutions which have been recited. The undersigned content themselves with brief reference to other suggestions pertinent to the subject.

They do not call upon your Excellency as suppliants, praying the revocation of the order banishing Mr. Vallandigham, as *a favor* ; but, by the authority of a convention representing a majority of the citizens of the State of Ohio, they respectfully ask it as *a right* due to an American citizen, in whose personal injury the sovereignty and dignity of the people of Ohio, as a free State, have been offended. And this duty they perform the more cordially from the consideration that, at a time of great national emergency, pregnant with danger to our Federal Union, it is all-important that the true friends of the Constitution and the Union, however they may differ as to *the mode*

of administering the Government, and *the measures* most likely to be successful in the maintenance of the Constitution and the restoration of the Union, should not be thrown into hostile conflict with each other.

The arrest, unusual trial and banishment of Mr. Vallandigham have created widespread and alarming disaffection among the people of the State, not only endangering the harmony of the friends of the Constitution and the Union, and tending to disturb the peace and tranquillity of the State, but also impairing that confidence in the fidelity of your administration to the great landmarks of free government, essential to a peaceful and successful enforcement of the laws in Ohio.

You are reported to have used, in a public communication on this subject, the following language :

"It gave me pain when I learned that Mr. Vallandigham had been arrested—that is, I was pained that there should have seemed to be a necessity for arresting him ; and that it will afford me great pleasure to discharge him, so soon as I can by any means believe the public safety will not suffer by it."

The undersigned assure your Excellency, from our personal knowledge of the feelings of the people of Ohio, that the public safety will be far more endangered by continuing Mr. Vallandigham in exile than by releasing him. It may be true, that persons differing from him in political views may be found in Ohio and elsewhere, who will express a different opinion. But they are certainly mistaken.

Mr. Vallandigham may differ with the President, and even with some of his own political party, as to the true and most effectual means of maintaining the Constitution and restoring the Union ; but this difference of opinion does not prove him to be unfaithful to his duties as an American citizen. If a man devotedly attached to the Constitution and the Union conscientiously believes that from the inherent nature of the Federal compact the war, in the present condition of things in this country, cannot be used as a means of restoring the Union ; or that a war to subjugate a part of the States, or a war to revolutionize the social system in a part of the States, could not restore, but would inevitably result in the final destruction of both the Constitution and the Union, is he not to be allowed the right of an American citizen to appeal to the judgment of the people for a change of policy by the constitutional remedy of the ballot-box ?

During the war with Mexico many of the political opponents of the administration then in power thought it their duty to oppose and denounce the war, and to urge before the people of the country that it was unjust, and prosecuted for unholy purposes. With equal reason it might have been said of them that their discussions before the people were calculated to discourage enlistments, "to prevent the raising of troops," and to induce desertions from the army and leave the Government without an adequate military force to carry on the war. If the freedom of speech and of the press are to be suspended in time of war, then the essential element of popular government to effect a change of policy in the constitutional mode is at an end. The freedom of speech and of the press is indispensable and necessarily incident to the nature of popular government itself. If any inconvenience or evils arise from its exercise, they are unavoidable.

On this subject you are reported to have said further:

"It is asserted, in substance, that Mr. Vallandigham was, by a military commander, seized and tried 'for no other reason than words addressed to a public meeting in criticism of the course of the administration, and in condemnation of the military order of the general.' Now, if there be no mistake about this, if there was no other reason for the arrest, then I concede that the arrest was wrong. But the arrest, I understand, was made for a very different reason. Mr. Vallandigham avows his hostility to the war on the part of the Union, and his arrest was made because he was laboring, with some effect, to prevent the raising of troops, to encourage desertions from the army, and to leave the rebellion without an adequate military force to suppress it. He was not arrested because he was damaging the political prospects of the Administration or the personal interest of the commanding general, but because he was damaging the army, upon the existence and vigor of which the life of the nation depends. He was warring upon the military, and this gave the military constitutional jurisdiction to lay hands upon him. If Mr. Vallandigham was not damaging the military power of the country, then his arrest was made on mistake of facts, which I would be glad to correct on reasonable satisfactory evidence."

In answer to this, permit the undersigned to say, first, that neither the charge, nor the specifications in support of the charge on which Mr. Vallandigham was tried, impute to him the act of laboring either to prevent the raising of troops or to encourage desertions from the army; secondly, that no evidence on the trial was offered with a view to support, or even tended to support any such charge. In what instance, and by what act did he either discourage enlistments or encourage desertions in the army? Who is the man who was discouraged from enlisting, and who encouraged to desert by any act of Mr. Vallandigham? If it be assumed that perchance some person might have been discouraged from enlisting, or that some person might have been encouraged to desert on account of hearing Mr. Vallandigham's views as to the policy of the war as a means of restoring the Union, would that have laid the foundation for his conviction and banishment? If so, upon the same grounds every political opponent of the Mexican war might have been convicted and banished from the country. When gentlemen of high standing and extensive influence, including your Excellency, opposed, in the discussions before the people, the policy of the Mexican war, were they "warring upon the military," and did this "give the military constitutional jurisdic-

tion to lay hands upon" them? And, finally, the charge in the specifications upon which Mr. Vallandigham was tried, entitled him to a trial before the civil tribunals according to the express provisions of the late acts of Congress, approved by yourself, July seventeenth, 1862, and March third, 1863, which were manifestly designed to supersede all necessity or pretext for arbitrary military arrests.

The undersigned are unable to agree with you in the opinion you have expressed, that the Constitution is different in time of insurrection or invasion from what it is in time of peace and public security. The Constitution provides for no limitation upon, or exceptions to, the guarantees of personal liberty, except as to the writ of *habeas corpus*. Has the President, at the time of invasion or insurrection, the right to engraft limitations or exceptions upon these constitutional guarantees, whenever, in his judgment, the public safety requires it?

True it is, the article of the Constitution which defines the various powers delegated to Congress, declares that "the privilege of the writ of *habeas corpus* shall not be suspended unless where, in cases of rebellion or invasion, the public safety may require it." But this qualification or limitation upon this restriction upon the powers of Congress has no reference to or connection with the other constitutional guarantees of personal liberty. Expunge from the Constitution this limitation upon the power of Congress to suspend the writ of *habeas corpus*, and yet the other guarantees of personal liberty would remain unchanged. Although a man might not have a constitutional right to have an immediate investigation made as to the legality of his arrest upon *habeas corpus*, yet his "right to a speedy and public trial by an impartial jury of the State and district wherein the crime shall have been committed," will not be altered; neither will his right to the exemption from "cruel and unusual punishments;" nor his right to be secure in his person, houses, papers, and effects, against unreasonable seizures and searches; nor his right not to be deprived of life, liberty, or property, without due process of law; nor his right not to be held to answer for a capital or otherwise infamous offence, unless on presentment or indictment of a grand-jury, be in any wise changed. And certainly the restriction upon the power of Congress to suspend the writ of *habeas corpus*, in time of insurrection or invasion, could not affect the guarantee that the freedom of speech and of the press shall not be abridged. It is sometimes urged that the proceedings in the civil tribunals are too tardy and ineffective for cases arising in times of insurrection or invasion. It is a full reply to this to say that arrests by civil process may be equally as expeditious and effective as arrests by military orders. True, a summary trial and punishment are not allowed in the civil courts. But if the offender be under arrest and imprisoned, and not entitled to a discharge on a writ of *habeas corpus* before trial, what more can be required for the purposes of the Government? The idea that all the constitutional guarantees of personal liberty are suspended throughout the country at a time of insurrection or invasion in any part of·it, places us upon a sea of uncertainty, and subjects the life, liberty, and property of every citizen to the mere will of a military commander, or what he *may say* that he *considers* the public safety requires. Does your Excellency wish to have it understood that you hold that the rights of every man throughout this vast country, in time of invasion or insurrection, *are subject to be annulled whenever you may say that you consider the public safety requires it?*

You are further reported as having said that the constitutional guarantees of personal liberty have "no application to the present case we have in hand, because the arrests complained of were not made for treason—that is, not for the treason defined in the Constitution, and upon the conviction of which the punishment is death—nor yet were they made to hold persons to answer for capital or otherwise infamous crime; nor were.the proceedings following in any constitutional or legal sense 'criminal prosecutions.' The arrests were made on totally ' different grounds, and the proceedings following accorded with the grounds of the arrests," etc.

The conclusion to be drawn from this position of your Excellency is, that where a man is liable to a "criminal prosecution," or is charged with a crime known to the laws of the land, he is clothed with all the constitutional guarantees for his safety and security from wrong and injustice; but that, where he is not liable to a "criminal prosecution," or charged with any crime known to the laws, if the President or any military commander shall say that he considers that the public safety requires it, this man may be put outside of the pale of the constitutional guarantees, and arrested without charge of crime, imprisoned without knowing what for, and any length of time, or be tried before a court-martial and sentenced to any kind of punishment, unknown to the laws of the land, which the President or the military commander may see proper to impose. Did the Constitution intend to throw the shield of its securities around the man liable to be charged with treason as defined by it, and yet leave the man, not liable to any such charge, unprotected by the safeguards of personal liberty and personal security? Can a man not in the military or naval service, nor within the field of the operations of the army, be arrested and imprisoned without any law of the land to authorize it? Can a man thus, in civil life, be punished without any law defining the offence and prescribing the punishment? If the President or a court-martial may prescribe one kind of punishment unauthorized by law, why not any other kind? Banishment is an unusual punishment and unknown to our laws. If the President has a right to prescribe the punishment of banishment, why not that of death and confiscation of property? If the President has the right to change the punishment prescribed by the court-martial, from imprisonment to ban-ishment, why not from imprisonment to torture upon the rack, or execution upon the gibbet?

If an indefinable kind of constructive treason is to be introduced and engrafted upon the Constitution, unknown to the laws of the land, and subject to the will of the President whenever an insurrection or invasion shall occur in any part of this vast country, what safety or security will be left for the liberties of the people? The constructive treasons that gave the friends of freedom so many years of toil and trouble in England, were inconsiderable compared to this. The precedents which you make will become a part of the Constitution for your successors, if sanctioned and acquiesced in by the people now.

The people of Ohio are willing to coöperate zealously with you in every effort, warranted by the Constitution, to restore the Union of the States; but they cannot consent to abandon those fundamental principles of civil liberty which are essential to their existence as a free people.

In their name, we ask that, by a revocation of the order of his banishment, Mr. Vallandigham may be restored to the enjoyment of those rights of which they believe he has been unconstitutionally deprived.

We have the honor to be, respectfully yours, etc.,

M. BIRCHARD, Chairman, Nineteenth District.
DAVID A. HOUK, Secretary, Third District.
GEORGE BLISS, Fourteenth District.
T. W. BARTLEY, Eighth District.
W. J. GORDON, Eighteenth District.
JOHN O'NEILL, Thirteenth District.
C. A. WHITE, Sixth District.
W. E. FINCK, Twelfth District.
ALEXANDER LONG, Second District.
J. W. WHITE, Sixteenth District.
JAMES R. MORRIS, Fifteenth District.
GEORGE S. CONVERSE, Seventh District.
WARREN P. NOBLE, Ninth District.
GEORGE H. PENDLETON, First District.
W. A. HUTCHINS, Eleventh District.
ABNER L. BACKUS, Tenth District.
J. F. McKINNEY, Fourth District.
F. C. LE BLOND, Fifth District.
LOUIS SCHAFFER, Seventeenth District.

THE REPLY.

WASHINGTON, D. C., June 29, 1863.

Messrs. M. Birchard, David A. Houck, George Bliss, T. W. Bartley, W. J. Gordon, John O'Neill, C. A. White, W. E. Finck, Alexander Long, J. W. White, George H. Pendleton, George L. Converse, Warren P. Noble, James R. Morris, W. A. Hutchins, Abner L. Backus, J. F. McKinney, P. C. Le Blond, Louis Schaffer.

GENTLEMEN: The resolutions of the Ohio Democratic State Convention, which you present me, together with your introductory and closing remarks, being in position and argument mainly the same as the resolutions of the Democratic meeting at Albany, New-York, I refer you to my response to the latter as meeting most 'of the points in the former. This response you evidently used in preparing your remarks, and I desire no more than that it be used with accuracy. In a single reading of your remarks, I only discovered one inaccuracy in matter, which I suppose you took from that paper. It is where you say: "The undersigned are unable to agree with you in the opinion you have expressed that the Constitution is different in time of insurrection or invasion from what it is in time of peace and public security." A recurrence to the paper will show you that I have not expressed the opinion you suppose. I expressed the opinion that the Constitution is different *in its application* in cases of rebellion or invasion, involving the public safety, from what it is in times of profound peace and public security; and this opinion I adhere to, simply because by the Constitution itself things may be done in the one case which may not be done in the other.

I dislike to waste a word on a merely personal point, but I must respectfully assure you that you will find yourselves at fault should you ever seek for evidence to prove your assumption that I "opposed in discussions before the people the policy of the Mexican war.'

You say: "Expunge from the Constitution this limitation upon the power of Congress to suspend the writ of *habeas corpus*, and yet the other guarantees of personal liberty would remain unchanged." Doubtless if this clause of the Constitution, improperly called, as I think, a limitation upon the power of Congress, were expunged the other guarantees would remain the same; but the question is, not how those guarantees would stand, with that clause *out* of the Constitution, but how they stand with that clause remaining in it, in cases of rebellion or invasion, involving the public safety. If the liberty could be indulged of expunging that clause, letter and spirit, I really think the constitutional argument would be with you. My general view on this question was stated in the Albany response, and hence I do not state it now. I only add that, as seems to me, the benefit of the writ of *habeas corpus* is the great means through which the guarantees of personal liberty are conserved and made available in the last resort; and corroborative of this view, is the fact, that Mr. Vallandigham, in the very case in question, under the advice of able lawyers, saw not where else to go but to the *habeas corpus.* But by the Constitution the benefit of the writ of *habeas corpus* itself may be suspended when in cases of rebellion or invasion the public safety may require it.

You ask in substance, whether I really claim that I may override all the guaranteed rights of individuals, on the plea of conserving the public safety—when I may choose to say the public safety requires it. This question, divested of the phraseology, calculated to represent me as struggling for an arbitrary personal prerogative, is either simply a question *who* shall decide, or an affirmation that *nobody* shall decide, what the public safety does require in cases of rebel-

lion or invasion. The Constitution contemplates the question as likely to occur for decision, but it does not expressly declare who is to decide it. By necessary implication, when rebellion or invasion comes, the decision is to be made, from time to time; and I think the man whom, for the time, the people have, under the Constitution, made the commander-in-chief of their army and navy, is the man who holds the power and bears the responsibility of making it. If he uses the power justly, the same people will probably justify him; if he abuses it, he is in their hands, to be dealt with by all the modes they have reserved to themselves in the Constitution.

The earnestness with which you insist that persons can only in times of rebellion be lawfully dealt with, in accordance with the rules for criminal trials and punishments in times of peace, induces me to add a word to what I said on that point in the Albany response. You claim that men may, if they choose, embarrass those whose duty it is to combat a giant rebellion, and then be dealt with only in turn, as if there were no rebellion. The Constitution itself rejects this view. The military arrests and detentions which have been made, including those of Mr. Vallandigham, which are not different in principle from the other, have been for *prevention* and not for *punishment*—as injunctions to stay injury—as proceedings to keep the peace—and hence, like proceedings in such cases, and for like reasons, they have not been accompanied with indictments, or trials by juries, nor, in a single case, by any punishment whatever, beyond what is purely incidental to the prevention. The original sentence of imprisonment in Mr. Vallandigham's case was to prevent injury to the military service only, and the modification of it was made as a less disagreeable mode to him of securing the same prevention.

I am unable to perceive an insult to Ohio in the case of Mr. Vallandigham. Quite surely, nothing of the sort was or is intended. I was wholly unaware that Mr. Vallandigham was, at the time of his arrest, a candidate for the Democratic nomination for Governor, until so informed by your reading to me resolutions of the Convention. I am grateful to the State of Ohio for many things, especially for the brave soldiers and officers she has given, in the present national trial, to the armies of the Union.

You claim, as I understand, that, according to my own position in the Albany response, Mr. Vallandigham should be released; and this because, as you claim, he has not damaged the military service by discouraging enlistments, encouraging desertions, or otherwise; and that if he had, he should have been turned over to the civil authorities, under recent acts of Congress. I certainly do not *know* that Mr. Vallandigham has specifically, and by direct language, advised against enlistments, and in favor of desertion and resistance to drafting. We all know that combinations, armed, in some instances, to resist the arrest of deserters, began several months ago; that more recently the like has appeared in resistance to the enrolment, preparatory to a draft; and that quite a number of assassinations have occurred from the same animus. These had to be met by military force, and this again has led to bloodshed and death. And now, under a sense of responsibility more weighty and enduring than any which is merely official, I solemnly declare my belief that this hindrance of the military, including maiming and murder, is due to the course in which Mr. Vallandigham has been engaged, in a greater degree than to any other cause; and is due to him personally in a greater degree than to any other one man. These things have been notorious, known to all, and of course known to Mr. Vallandigham. Perhaps I would not be wrong to say they originated with his especial friends and adherents. With perfect knowledge of them, he has frequently, if not constantly, made speeches in Congress and before popular assemblies; and if it can be shown that with these things staring him in the face he has ever uttered a word of rebuke or counsel against them, it will be a fact greatly in his favor with me, and one of which, as yet, I am totally ignorant. When it is known that the whole burden of his speeches has been to stir up men against the prosecution of the war, and that in the midst of resistance to it he has not been known in any instance to counsel against such resistance, it is next to impossible to repel the inference that he has counselled directly in favor of it. With all this before their eyes, the Convention you represent have nominated Mr. Vallandigham for Governor of Ohio; and both they and you have declared the purpose to sustain the national Union by all constitutional means. But of course they and you, in common, reserve to yourselves to decide what are constitutional means, and, unlike the Albany meeting, you omit to state or intimate that in your opinion an army is a constitutional means of saving the Union against a rebellion, or even to intimate that you are conscious of an existing rebellion being in progress, with the avowed object of destroying that very Union. At the same time your nominee for Governor, in whose behalf you appeal, is known to you and to the world to declare against the use of an army to suppress the rebellion. Your own attitude, therefore, encourages desertion, resistance to the draft and the like, because it teaches those who incline to desert and to escape the draft to believe it is your purpose to protect them, and to hope that you will become strong enough to do so. After a short personal intercourse with you, gentlemen of the committee, I cannot say I think you desire this effect to follow your attitude; but I assure you that both friends and enemies of the Union look upon it in this light. It is a substantial hope, and by consequence a real strength to the enemy. It is a false hope, and one which you would willingly dispel. I will make the way exceedingly easy. I send you duplicates of this letter, in order that you or a majority of you may, if you choose, indorse your names upon one of them, and return it thus indorsed to me, with the understanding that those signing are thereby committed to the following propositions, and to nothing else:

1. That there is a rebellion now in the United States, the object and tendency of which is to destroy the national Union, and that, in your opinion, an army and navy are constitutional means for suppressing that rebellion.

2. That no one of you will do any thing which, in his own judgment, will tend to hinder the increase or favor the decrease, or lessen the efficiency of the army or navy, while engaged in the effort to suppress that rebellion; and

3. That each of you will, in his sphere, do all he can to have the officers, soldiers, and seamen of the army and navy, while engaged in the effort to suppress the rebellion, paid, fed, clad, and otherwise well provided and supported.

And with the further understanding that, upon receiving the letter and names thus indorsed, I will cause them to be published, which publication shall be, within itself, a revocation of the order in relation to Mr. Vallandigham.

It will not escape observation that I consent to the release of Mr. Vallandigham upon terms not embracing any pledge from him or from others, as to what he will or will not do. I do this because he is not present to speak for himself, or to authorize others to speak for him; and hence I shall expect that on returning he would not put himself practically in antagonism with the position of his friends. But I do it chiefly because I thereby prevail on other influential gentlemen of Ohio to so define their position as to be of immense value to the army, thus more than compensating for the consequences of any mistake in allowing Mr. Vallandigham to return, so that on the whole the public safety will not have suffered by it. Still, in regard to Mr. Vallandigham and all others, I must hereafter, as heretofore, do so much as the public safety may seem to require. I have the honor to be respectfully yours, etc.

A. LINCOLN.

THE REJOINDER.

NEW-YORK CITY, July 1, 1863.

To His Excellency the President of the United States:

SIR: Your answer to the application of the undersigned for a revocation of the order of banishment of Clement L. Vallandigham requires a reply, which they proceed, with as little delay as practicable, to make.

They are not able to appreciate the force of the distinction you make between the *Constitution* and *the application* of the Constitution, whereby you assume that powers are delegated to the President at the time of invasion or insurrection in derogation of the plain language of the Constitution. The inherent provisions of the Constitution remaining the same in time of insurrection or invasion as in time of peace, the President can have no more right to disregard their positive and imperative requirements at the former time than at the latter. Because some things may be done by the terms of the Constitution at the time of invasion or insurrection which would not be required by the occasion in time of peace, you assume that *any thing whatever*, even though not expressed by the Constitution, may be done on the occasion of insurrection or invasion which the President may choose to say is required by the public safety. In plainer terms, because the writ of *habeas corpus* may be suspended at the time of invasion or insurrection, you infer that all other provisions of the Constitution having in view the protection of the life, liberty, and property of the citizen may be in like manner suspended. The provision relating to the writ of *habeas corpus*, being contained in the first article of the Constitution, the purpose of which is to define the powers delegated to Congress, has no connection in language with the declaration of rights as guarantees of personal liberty, contained in the additional and amendatory articles. And inasmuch as the provision relating to *habeas corpus* expressly provides for its suspension, and the other provisions alluded to do not provide for any such thing, the legal conclusion is, that the suspension of the latter is unauthorized. The provision for the writ of *habeas corpus* is merely intended to furnish *a summary* remedy, and not the means whereby personal security is conserved, in the final resort; while the other provisions are guarantees of personal rights, the suspension of which puts an end to all pretence of free government. It is true Mr. Vallandigham applied for a writ of *habeas corpus* as a summary remedy against oppression. But the denial of this did not take away his right to a speedy public trial by an impartial jury, or deprive him of his other rights as an American citizen. Your assumption of the right to suspend all the constitutional guarantees of personal liberty, and even of the freedom of speech and of the press, because the summary remedy of *habeas corpus* may be suspended, is at once startling and alarming to all persons desirous of preserving free government in this country.

The inquiry of the undersigned, whether "you hold that the rights of every man throughout this vast country, in time of invasion or insurrection, are subject to be *annulled*, whenever *you may say* that *you* consider the public safety requires it," was a plain question, undisguised by circumlocution, and intended simply to elicit information. Your affirmative answer to this question throws a shade upon the fondest anticipations of the framers of the Constitution, who flattered themselves that they had provided safeguards against the dangers which have ever beset and overthrown free government in other ages and countries. Your answer is not to be disguised by the phraseology that the question "is simply a question *who* shall decide, or an affirmation that *nobody* shall decide what the public safety does require in cases of rebellion or invasion." Our government was designed to be a government of *law, settled* and *defined*, and not of the arbitrary will of a single man. As a safeguard, the powers granted were divided, and delegated to the legislative, executive, and judicial branches of the government, and each made coördinate with the others, and supreme within its sphere, and thus a mutual check upon each other, in case of abuse of power. It has been the boast of the American people that they had a *written Constitution*, not only expressly *defining*, but also *limiting* the powers of the Government, and providing effectual safeguards for personal liberty, security, and property. And to make the matter more positive and explicit, it was provided by the amendatory articles, nine and ten, that "the *enumeration* in the Constitution of *certain rights* shall not be construed to *deny* or *disparage* others retained by the people," and that "the powers not delegated to the United States by the Constitution, nor prohibited by it to the States, are reserved to the States respectively or to the people." With this care and precaution on the part of our forefathers, who framed our institutions, it was not to be expected that, at so early a day as this, a claim of the President to arbitrary power, limited only by his conception of the requirements of the public safety, would have been asserted. In derogation of the constitutional provisions making the President strictly an executive officer, and vesting all the delegated legislative power in Congress, your position, as we understand it, would make *your will the rule of action*, and your declarations of the requirements of the public safety the law of the land. Our inquiry was not, therefore, "simply a question *who* shall decide, or the affirmation that *nobody* shall decide what the public safety requires." Our government is a government of *law*, and it is the *law-making power* which ascertains what the public safety requires, and prescribes the rule of action; and the duty of the President is simply to execute the laws thus enacted, and not *to make or annul laws*. If any exigency shall arise, the President has the power to convene Congress at any time, to provide for it; so that the plea of necessity furnishes no reasonable pretext for any assumption of legislative power.

For a moment contemplate the consequences of such a claim to power. Not only would the dominion of the President be absolute over the rights of individuals, but equally so over the other departments of the government. If he should claim that the public safety required it, he could arrest and imprison a judge for the conscientious discharge of his duties, paralyze the judicial power, or supersede it, by the substitution of courts-martial, subject to *his own will*, throughout the whole country. If any one of the States, even far removed from the rebellion, should not sustain his plan for prosecuting the war, he could, on this plea of the public safety, annul and set at defiance the State laws and authorities, arrest and imprison the Governor of the State, or the members of the Legislature, while in the faithful discharge of their duties, or he could absolutely control the action, either of Congress or of the Supreme Court, by arresting and imprisoning its members; and, upon the same ground, he could suspend the elective franchise, postpone the elections, and declare the perpetuity of his high prerogative. And neither the power of impeachment, nor the elections of the people, could be made available against such concentration of power.

Surely it is not necessary to subvert free government in this country in order to put down the rebellion; and it *cannot be done*, under *the pretence* of putting down the rebellion. Indeed, it is plain that your Administration has been weakened, greatly weakened, by the assumption of power not delegated in the Constitution.

In your answer you say to us: "You claim that men may, if they choose, embarrass those whose duty it is to combat a giant rebellion, and then be dealt with in turn only as if there were no rebellion." You will find yourself at fault if you will search our communication to you, for any such idea. The undersigned believe that the Constitution and laws of the land, properly administered, furnish ample power to put down an insurrection, without the assumption of powers not granted. And if existing legislation be inadequate, it is the duty of Congress to consider what further legislation is necessary, and to make suitable provision by law.

You claim that the military arrests made by your Administration are merely *preventive remedies* "as injunctions to stay injury, or proceedings to keep the peace, and *not for punishment*." The *ordinary* preventive remedies alluded to are authorized by established law, but the preventive proceedings you institute have their authority merely in the will of the Executive or that of officers subordinate to his authority. And in this proceeding, a discretion seems to be exercised as to whether the prisoner shall be allowed a trial; or even be permitted to know the nature of the complaint alleged against him, or the name of his accuser. If the proceeding be merely preventive, why not allow the prisoner the benefit of a bond to keep the peace? But if no offence has been committed, why was Mr. Vallandigham tried, convicted, and sentenced by a court-martial? And why the actual punishment, by imprisonment or banishment, without the opportunity of obtaining his liberty in the mode usual in preventive remedies, and yet say, it is not for punishment?

You still place Mr. Vallandigham's conviction and banishment upon the ground that he had damaged the military service by discouraging enlistments and encouraging desertions, etc.; and yet you have not even pretended to controvert our position, that he was not charged with, tried or convicted for *any such offence* before the court-martial.

In answer to our position that Mr. Vallandigham was entitled to a trial in the civil tribunals, by virtue of the late acts of Congress, you say: "*I certainly do not know that Mr. Vallandigham has specifically and by direct language advised against enlistments and in favor of desertions and resistance to drafting*," etc.; and yet, in a subsequent part of your answer, after speaking of certain disturbances which are alleged to have occurred in resistance of the arrest of deserters, and of the enrolment preparatory to the draft, and which you attribute mainly to the course Mr. Vallandigham has pursued; you say that he has made speeches against the war in the midst of resistance to it; and that "he has never been known, in any instance, to counsel against such resistance," and that "*it is next to impossible to repel the inference that he has counselled directly in favor of it*." Permit the undersigned to say that your information is most grievously at fault. The undersigned have been in the habit of hearing Mr. Vallandigham speak before popular assemblages, and they appeal with confidence to every truthful person who has ever heard him, for the accuracy of the declaration that he has never made a speech before the people of Ohio in which he has not counselled submission and obedience to the laws and the Constitution, and advised the peaceful remedies of the judicial tribunals and of the ballot-box for the redress of grievances, and for the evils which afflict our bleeding and suffering country. And, were it not foreign to the purposes of this communication, we would undertake to establish, to the satisfaction of any candid person, that the disturbances among the people, to which you allude, in opposition to the arrest of deserters and the draft, have been occasioned mainly by the measures, policy, and conduct of your Administration, and the course of its political friends. But if the circumstantial evidence exists, to which you allude, which makes "it next to impossible to repel the inference that Mr. Vallandigham has counselled directly in favor" of this resistance, and that the same has been mainly attributable to his conduct, why was he not turned over to the civil authorities to be tried under the late acts of Congress? If there be any foundation in fact for your statements implicating him in resistance to the constituted authorities, he is liable to such prosecution. And we now demand, as a mere act of justice to him, an investigation of this matter before a jury of his country; and respectfully insist that fairness requires, either that you retract these charges which you make against him, or that you revoke your order of banishment and allow him the opportunity of an investigation before an impartial jury.

The committee do not deem it necessary to repel at length the imputation that the attitude of themselves or of the Democratic party in Ohio "encourages desertions, resistance to the draft, and the like," or tends to the breach of any law of the land. Suggestions of that kind are not unusual weapons in our ordinary political contests. They rise readily in the minds of politicians heated with the excitement of partisan strife. During the two years in which the Democratic party of Ohio has been constrained to oppose the policy of the Administration and to stand up in defence of the Constitution and of personal rights, this charge has been repeatedly made. It has fallen harmless, however, at the feet of those whom it was intended to injure. The committee believe it will do so again. If it were proper to do so in this paper, they might suggest that the measures of the Administration and its changes of policy in the prosecution of the war have been the fruitful sources of discouraging enlistments and inducing desertions, and furnish a reason for the undeniable fact that the first call for volunteers was answered by very many more than were demanded, and that the next call for soldiers will probably be responded to by drafted men alone. The observation of the President in this connection that neither the Convention in its resolutions, nor the committee in its communication, intimate that they "are conscious of an existing rebellion being in progress with the avowed object of destroying the Union," needs, perhaps, no reply. The Democratic party of Ohio has felt so keenly the condition of the country, and been so stricken to the heart by the misfortunes and sorrows which have befallen it, that they hardly deemed it necessary by solemn resolution, when their very State exhibited everywhere the sad evidences of war, to remind the President that they were aware of its existence.

In the conclusion of your communication, you propose that, if a majority of the committee shall affix their signatures to a duplicate copy of it, which you have furnished, they shall stand committed to three propositions therein at length set forth; that you will publish the names thus signed, and that this publication shall operate as a revocation of the order of banishment. The committee cannot refrain from the expression of their surprise that the President should make the fate of Mr. Vallandigham depend upon the opinion of this committee upon these propositions. If the arrest and banishment were legal, and were deserved; if the President exercised a power clearly delegated, under circumstances which warranted its exercise, the order ought not to be revoked, merely because the committee hold, or express, opinions accordant with those of the President. If the arrest and banishment were not legal, or were not deserved by Mr. Vallandigham, then surely he is entitled to an immediate and unconditional discharge.

The people of Ohio were not so deeply moved by the action of the President, merely because they were concerned for the personal safety or convenience of Mr. Vallandigham, but because they saw in his arrest and banishment an attack upon their own personal rights; and they attach value to his discharge chiefly, as it will indicate an abandonment of the claim to the power of such arrest and banishment. However just the undersigned might regard the principles contained in the several propositions submitted by the President, or how much soever they might, under other circumstances, feel inclined to indorse the sentiments contained therein, yet they assure him that they have not been authorized to enter into any bargains, terms, contracts, or conditions with the President of the United States to procure the release of Mr. Vallandigham. The opinions of the undersigned, touching the questions involved in these propositions, are well known, have been

many times publicly expressed, and are sufficiently manifested in the resolutions of the Convention which they represent, and they cannot suppose that the President expects that they will seek the discharge of Mr. Vallandigham by a pledge, implying not only an imputation upon their own *sincerity* and *fidelity* as citizens of the United States, but also carrying with it by implication a concession of *the legality* of his arrest, trial, and banishment, against which they, and the Convention they represent, have solemnly protested. And while they have asked the revocation of the order of banishment not as a *favor*, but as a *right*, due to the people of Ohio, and with a view to avoid the possibility of conflict or disturbance of the public tranquillity, they do not do this, nor does Mr. Vallandigham desire it, at any sacrifice of their dignity and self-respect.

The idea that such a pledge as that asked from the undersigned would secure the public safety sufficiently to compensate for any mistake of the President in discharging Mr. Vallandigham is, in their opinion, a mere evasion of the grave questions involved in this discussion, and of a direct answer to their demand. And this is made especially apparent by the fact that this pledge is asked in a communication which concludes with an intimation of a disposition on the part of the President to repeat the acts complained of.

The undersigned, therefore, having fully discharged the duty enjoined upon them, leave the responsibility with the President.

M. BIRCHARD, Nineteenth District, Chairman.
DAVID HOUK, Secretary, Third District.
GEO. BLISS, Fourteenth District.
T. W. BARTLEY, Eighth District.
W. J. GORDON, Eighteenth District.
JNO. O'NEILL, Thirteenth District.
C. A. WHITE, Sixth District.
W. E. FINCK, Twelfth District.
ALEXANDER LONG, Second District.
JAS. R. MORRIS, Fifteenth District.
GEO. S. CONVERSE, Seventh District.
GEO. H. PENDLETON, First District.
W. A. HUTCHINS, Eleventh District.
A. L. BACKUS, Tenth District.
J. F. McKINNEY, Fourth District.
J. W. WHITE, Sixteenth District.
F. C. LE BLOND, Fifth District.
LOUIS SCHAFFER, Seventeenth District.
WARREN P. NOBLE, Ninth District.

Doc. 108.

GEN. LEE'S ADDRESS TO HIS ARMY.

FREDERICK, July 12, 1863.

THE following general order of General R. E. Lee to the rebel army, issued from Hagerstown, on Saturday, was found when General Kilpatrick entered the town on Sunday morning:

GENERAL ORDERS, No. 16.

HEADQUARTERS ARMY OF NORTHERN VIRGINIA,
July 11, 1863.

After the long and trying marches, endured with the fortitude that has ever characterized the soldiers of the army of Northern Virginia, you have penetrated to the country of our enemies, and recalled to the defence of their own soil those who were engaged in the invasion of ours. You have fought a fierce and sanguinary battle, which, if not attended with the success that has hitherto crowned your efforts, was marked by the same heroic spirit that has commanded the respect of your enemies, the gratitude of your country, and the admiration of mankind.

Once more you are called upon to meet the enemy from whom you have torn so many fields, the names of which will never die. Once more the eyes of your countrymen are turned upon you, and again do wives and sisters, fathers and mothers, and helpless children, lean for defence on your strong arms and brave hearts. Let every soldier remember that on his courage and fidelity depends all that makes life worth having, the freedom of his country, the honor of his people, and the security of his home. Let each heart grow strong in the remembrance of our glorious past, and in the thought of the inestimable blessings for which we contend ; and, invoking the assistance of that benign Power which has signally blessed our former efforts, let us go forth in confidence to secure the peace and safety of our country. Soldiers, your old enemy is before you. Win from him honor worthy of your right cause, worthy of your comrades dead on so many illustrious fields.   R. E. LEE.
                                        General Commanding.

Doc. 109.

BATTLE OF HONEY SPRINGS.

LETTER FROM GENERAL BLUNT.*

HEADQUARTERS DISTRICT OF THE FRONTIER, IN THE FIELD, FORT BLUNT, C. N., July 25, 1863.

DEAR FRIEND: The boys have probably written you concerning our trip down here, and of the battle of the seventeenth. I have been pressed with official business, besides being sick. This is the reason I have not written before. My health is quite good again now, although the "fat boy" has lost about thirty pounds since leaving Fort Scott. I was taken sick on the fourteenth, and on the fifteenth, at midnight, I got out of a sick-bed with a burning fever, and, taking three of my staff, ferried over Grand River, got two hundred cavalry and two howitzers and twenty-six-pound guns, marched thirteen miles up the Arkansas, forded the river in the face of the enemy's pickets, passed down on the south side of the crossing at the mouth of Grand River, opposite Fort Blunt, expecting to come in the rear and capture the enemy's outpost, but they had got the scent and had "skedaddled." I had learned that Cooper was on Elk Creek, twenty-five miles south of the Arkansas with six thousand men, and was to be reenforced the next day, the seventeenth, by three thousand men from Fort Smith, when they ex-

* See page 358 Docs. ante.

pected to move upon this place. I immediately commenced crossing my forces at the mouth of Grand River, ferrying the infantry on boats I had built when I arrived here and found the river high.

The column moved from the south bank about ten o'clock P.M., less than three thousand strong, and twelve pieces of artillery, the latter of very poor quality.

At daylight I came up with their advance, five miles this side of Elk Creek, and drove them in. I kept all the time with the advance-guard and watched and superintended every movement, as I was playing a desperate game and did not dare trust any one but myself. With a small party I went forward and reconnoitred their position with a glass. They were formed on the north side of the timber of Elk Creek, which formed a partial semicircle, the road running through the centre. The timber here was quite brushy, and formed a complete cover for them, but I had watched them take their position, and knew the "game" was there, and, as the prisoners have since told me, they thought they had a very "soft snap" when they saw us approaching, and intended to "gobble" us up certain. I could not tell where their artillery was posted, as it was masked in the timber, but I soon found out by the "bark," as my little wearied column closed up. I had then halted behind a little rise of ground to rest and take a lunch from their haversacks. After they had rested I went back among the officers and men of the different commands, and told them what I expected of them. They were now about one half-mile from the rebel line.

About ten o'clock in the morning I formed them in two columns, one under Colonel Judson on the right of the road, and the other under Colonel Phillips on the left. The columns were closed in mass infantry by companies, cavalry by platoons, and artillery by sections, with the cavalry in the front. I moved up this way to within four hundred yards of their guns, when I suddenly deployed the column into line on his right and left, and in five minutes my entire force was in line of battle, covering the whole rebel front. Without halting a moment, I moved up in line, going myself in the advance to encourage the men, and soon my skirmishing drew their fire, and now the fun commenced. The cavalry who were on the flanks I dismounted, and fought them on foot with their carbines. The attack was one of the prettiest affairs I ever witnessed. They all moved up to the rebel lines as cool and steady as if going on dress-parade. I encouraged them to push into the timber and engage them at close quarters, which they did with a will for two hours. The rattle of musketry and artillery was incessant, until at last their line gave way and became a rout.

They made quite a formidable stand at the bridge on the creek, but were repulsed. Honey Springs, the headquarters of General Cooper, was two miles south of where the battle commenced, on the south side of the timber, and when they commenced their retreat they set fire to all their commissary buildings and destroyed all their supplies. I followed them up until my artillery horses could draw the guns no further, and infantry and cavalry were all "played out" with fatigue. Their cavalry still hovered on the prairie in my front, and about four o'clock P.M., Cabell came up with his three thousand reënforcements. My ammunition was nearly exhausted, but I bivouacked upon the field all night, determined to give them the best turn I had in the morning if they were not yet satisfied; but daylight revealed the fact that they had all "skedaddled."

Their loss killed upon the field, which we buried, was one hundred and fifty, and fifteen or twenty have since died of their wounds. Parties who have come in with a flag of truce say their wounded is between three hundred and four hundred, and they all acknowledge that they were badly thrashed. They had no knowledge that I was in the country, until they learned it in the fight. Some of the rebel officers, when taken prisoners, asked who was in command, and when told, replied, "that they thought that either Blunt or the devil was there." I have about fifty prisoners, all Texans, among them several commissioned officers. They are much surprised at the treatment they receive, as they all expected to be murdered if taken prisoners. Cooper sent me a very warm letter of thanks for the care I had taken of his wounded and the burial of his dead. They continually overshot my men, which explains the comparatively small loss of our side. One Texas regiment went in with three hundred men, and came out with only sixty. This regiment was opposed to the First colored, and the negroes were too much for them; and let me say here, that I never saw such fighting done as was done by the negro regiment at the battle of Honey Springs. They fought like veterans, with a coolness and valor that is unsurpassed. They preserved their line perfect throughout the whole engagement, and although in the hottest of the fight, they never once faltered. Too much praise cannot be awarded them for their gallantry. The question that negroes will fight is settled; besides, they make better soldiers in every respect than any troops I have ever had under my command. Among the trophies, I have one piece of artillery, two hundred stand of arms, mostly English Enfield rifles, and a stand of rebel colors. But I did not intend to scribble at this length. I commenced to tell you how I got along, being sick as I was, and have got entirely off the track. The excitement kept me up until after the battle, when my powers of endurance gave way, and I had to come down in the bottom of an ambulance, from which I issued my orders until I got back here on the nineteenth, then I was confined to my bed for several days. I had been, when the battle closed, forty hours in the saddle, with a burning fever all the time — had eaten nothing for several days, and drank gallons of dirty, warm water. But such is a soldier's life, and if they don't like it they should not go to war.

I know not what I am to do in future. I have given up all idea of getting troops, and shall make no more applications. The weather is very warm here now, and much sickness prevails. I shall do every thing I can to preserve their health by scattering them around where they can get good water. My cavalry are on the south side of the Arkansas. I cannot raise over three thousand effective men for a fight. Cooper has since been reënforced. His morning report of the seventeenth, which I captured, showed five thousand seven hundred enlisted men present for duty that day. Unless he gets additional force, I can maintain my line to the Arkansas River; but if Price and Holmes, with what they had left after the Helena fight, should swing around this way, it will put me to my trumps. However, the "old man" will do the best he can. It is better after all and under all the circumstances, than being a *police officer* in Kansas. Yours truly,

JAMES G. BLUNT.

Doc. 110.

BATTLE OF BIG MOUND, DAKOTAH.

REPORT OF LIEUTENANT-COLONEL WILLIAM R. MARSHALL.

HEADQUARTERS SEVENTH REGIMENT M. V.,
CAMP SIBLEY, ON MISSOURI COTEAU,
July 25, 1863.

Captain R. C. Olin, Assist. Adjutant-General:

CAPTAIN: I respectfully submit the following report of the part taken by the Seventh regiment—eight companies—in the engagement with the Indians yesterday:

Immediately after news was received of the presence of the Indians, the regiment was formed in order of battle in the line designated by you for the protection of the corral—subsequently the camp—then being formed. A detail of ten men from each company was set to digging trenches in front of our line, which fronted a little south of east—the Big Mound being directly east. The men remained upon the color-line until the firing commenced on the foot-hill directly in front, where Dr. Weiser was killed. I was then ordered to deploy Captain Banks's company—armed with Colt's rifles—along the foot-hill to the left of the ravine, that opened toward the Big Mound. This done, Major Bradley was ordered with two companies—Captains Gilfillan's and Stevens's—to advance to the support of the first battalion of cavalry, then out on the right of the ravine, where Dr. Weiser was shot.

Major Bradley's detachment became engaged along with the cavalry as soon as he reached the top of the first range of hills. I asked to advance to their support with the other five companies, and received your order to do so. With Captains Kennedy's, Williston's, Hall's, Carter's, and Arnold's companies, leaving Captain Carter in charge of the detail to finish the trenches and protect the camp, I advanced at double-quick up the ravine toward Big Mound. When opposite the six-pounder on the left of the ravine, where the General then was, I deployed the five companies at three paces intervals, without any reserve. The line extended from hill to hill across the ravine, which was here irregular or closed. Advancing as rapidly as possible, the line first came under fire when it reached the crest of the first range of hills, below the summit peak. The Indians then occupied the summit range, giving way from the highest peak or Big Mound, driven by the fire of the six-pounder, but in great numbers along the ridge southward. Captain Eugene Wilson's company of cavalry—dismounted—passed to my left and occupied the Big Mound, while I charged across the little valley and up to the summit, south of the Mound. We advanced firing, the Indians giving way as we advanced. I crossed the ridge and pursued the Indians out on the comparatively open ground east of the peaks. Their main body, however, was to our right, ready to dispute possession of the rocky ridges and ravines, into which the summit range is broken in its continuation southward. I had flanked them turning their right, and now gradually wheeled my line to the right until it was perpendicular to the range, my left being well out in the open ground over which the enemy's extreme right was retreating. I thus swept southward, and as the open ground was cleared—the Indians in that direction making for the hills, two miles southeast, just beyond which was their camp, as we afterward discovered. I wheeled still more to the right, directing my attention to the summit range again, where the Indians were the thickest. Advancing rapidly, and firing, they soon broke, and as I reached and recrossed the ridge, they were flying precipitately and in great numbers from the ravines, which partly covered them, down toward the great plain at the southern termination of the range of hills.

Colonel McPhail, who, with a part of the cavalry, had crossed to the east side of the range, and kept in line in my rear, ready to charge upon the Indians when they should be dislodged from the broken ground, now passed my line and pursued the enemy out on the open plain.

After I recrossed the range I met Major Bradley, and united the seven companies. He, in conjunction with Captains Taylor's and Anderson's companies of the cavalry—dismounted—had performed much the same service on the west slope of the range of hills, that I had done on the east and summit, driving the enemy from hill to hill southward, a distance of four or five miles from camp to the termination of the range.

Happily no casualties happened in my command. Indeed, the Indians from the first encounter gave way, seeming to realize the superior range of our guns—yielding ridge after ridge and ravine after ravine, as we occupied successive ridges from which our fire reached them. The hat of one soldier, the musket-stock of another, gave proof of shots received; other like evidences, and their balls occasionally kicking the dirt up about us, and more rarely whistling past us, were the most sensible evidences of our being under fire.

The Indians were in far greater numbers than I had seen them before, certainly three times the number encountered at the relief of Birch Coolie, afterward ascertained to be three hundred and fifty, and more than double the number seen at Wood Lake. I judge there were from one thousand to one thousand five hundred. Their numbers were more apparent when we had combed them out of the hills into the plain below.

After uniting the battalion at the southern termination of the great hill, I received orders to follow on in support of the cavalry and artillery. The men were suffering greatly for water, and I marched them to a lake off to the right, which proved to be salty. I then followed on after the cavalry. We passed one or more lakes that were alkaline. It was the experience of the ancient mariner—

> " Water, water everywhere,
> But not a drop to drink."

We continued the march until nine o'clock at night, reaching a point twelve or fifteen miles from camp. The men had been on their feet since four o'clock in the morning—had double-quicked it five miles during the engagement—had been without food since morning and without water since noon. They were completely exhausted, and I ordered a bivouac.

The trail was strewed with buffalo-skins, dried meat, and other effects abandoned by the Indians in their wild flight. The men gathered the meat and eat it for supper, and the skins for beds and covering. At this point Captain Edgerton's company of the Tenth regiment joined us and shared the night's hardships. We had posted guard and lain an hour when Colonel McPhail returned from pursuing the Indians. He urged that I should return with him to camp. The men were somewhat rested, and their thirst stimulated them to the effort. We joined him and returned to camp. About midnight we got a little dirty water from the marshy lake where the Indians had been encamped. We reached camp at daylight, having marched nearly thirty-four hours, and over a distance estimated at from forty to forty-five miles.

My thanks are due to Major Bradley and the line-officers for steady coolness and the faithful discharge of every duty, and to every man of the rank and file for good conduct throughout. The patient endurance of the long privation of water, and the fatigue of the weary night's march in returning to camp after such a day, abundantly prove them to be such stuff as true soldiers are made of.

Very respectfully, your obedient servant,
WILLIAM R. MARSHALL,
Lieutenant-Colonel Commanding Seventh Regiment M. V.

SUPPLEMENTARY REPORT OF LIEUT.-COL. MARSHALL.

HEADQUARTERS SEVENTH REGIMENT MINN. VOLS.,
CAMP WILLISTON, ON MISSOURI COTEAU,
August 5, 1863.

Captain R. C. Olin, Assist. Adjutant-General:

CAPTAIN: I respectfully submit the following report of the part taken by the Seventh regiment in the pursuit of and engagements with the Indians subsequent to the battle of Big Mound, on the twenty-fourth ultimo. In my report of the twenty-fourth of July, I detailed the movements of this regiment in that engagement. On Sunday, the twenty-sixth of July, when the column was halted at the Dead Buffalo Lake, and the Indians made a demonstration in front, I was with the right wing of my regiment on the right flank of the train. Major Bradley was with the left wing on the left, the regiment being in the middle in the order of march. Leaving Major Bradley to protect the left flank, I deployed company B, Captain Stevens, obliquely forward to the right. He advanced further than I intended, and did not halt until on the right of and even with the line of skirmishers of the Sixth regiment then in the extreme advance. Thinking it better not to recall him, I advanced the three other companies of the right wing, Captains Gilfillan's, Kennedy's, and Carter's, near enough to support company B, and at the same time protect the right of the train, which was then well closed up on the site of our camp. I remained in this position without the Indians approaching in range until orders were given to go into camp. I had but just dismissed the battalion from the color-line to pitch tents, when the bold attack of the mounted Indians was made on the teams and animals in the meadow on the north side of the camp. My line was on the south side of the camp. I assembled and re-formed the line, awaiting an attack from the south, but the Indians that appeared on that side quickly withdrew after they saw the repulse on the north side, not coming within gun-shot range. I cannot withhold an expression of my admiration of the gallant style in which the companies of cavalry—I believe Captain Wilson's and Davy's, the latter under Lieutenant Kidder—dashed out to meet the Indians that were very nearly successful in the dash upon the teams and loose animals. The rangers, putting their horses on the run, were but a few seconds in reaching the Indians, whose quick right-about did not save them from carbine and pistol-shot and sabre-stroke that told so well. I also saw and admired the promptitude with which Major McLaren, with part of the Sixth regiment, moved from his color-line on that side of the camp to the support of the cavalry.

On the morning of the twenty-eighth of July, at Stony Lake, the Seventh regiment in the order of march was in the rear. The rear of the wagon-train was just filing out of camp, going around the south end of the lake; a part still within the camp-ground, which extended almost to the end of the lake. My regiment was in line waiting for the train to get out, when the alarm was given. Quickly the Indians appeared south of the lake and circled around to the rear. I promptly advanced the right wing on the flank of the train south of the lake, deploying Captain Gilfillan's and Stevens's companies as skirmishers. With these and Captain Kennedy's and Carter's companies in reserve, I immediately occupied the broken, rocky ground south of the lake. But not any too soon, for the Indians had entered it at the outer edge, not over five hundred yards from the train. Lieutenant Western, of the battery, was in the rear, and promptly reported to me. I placed his section of the battery—two mountain howitzers—on the first elevation of the broken ground outside the train. The fire of my line of skirmishers, then somewhat advanced on the right of the howitzers, and a few well-directed shots from Lieutenant Western's guns, discouraged the Indians from attempting to avail themselves of the cover of the small hills near us, dislodged the few that had got in, and drove the whole of them in that quarter to a very respectful distance, quite out of range. One shot from the Indians struck the ground near my feet, while I was locating a howitzer.

While I was thus occupied, Major Bradley, with the left wing, Captains Banks's and Williston's, Hall's and Arnold's companies advanced out upon my left so as to cover the portion of the train still in camp from the threatened attack from the rear. There was a battalion of cavalry, also protecting the rear to the left of Major Bradley. We thus formed a line from the left flank of the train around to the rear that effectually protected it. The Indians galloped back and forth just out of range of the howitzers, and our rifles, almost of equal range, until the order came to close up the train and continue the march. As the rear of the train passed the lake, I took the right wing to the right flank of the train near the rear, marched left in front, and so deployed as to well cover that portion of the train. Major Bradley, with the left wing, did similarly on left flank. As the column moved forward the Indians withdrew out of sight.

On the twenty-ninth instant, when the column arrived at Missouri River, the Seventh regiment was the second in order of march, and was held on the flanks of the train, while the Sixth regiment, which was in the advance, penetrated the woods to the river. By order of the General, companies B and H were advanced as skirmishers obliquely to the right of the train to explore for water. They had entered the woods but a little way when recalled by an aid of the General.

On the thirtieth instant, companies A, B, and H, Captains Arnold, Stevens, and Gilfillan, were detailed under Major Bradley to form part of the force under Colonel Crooks to again penetrate to the river, destroy the wagons and other property of the Indians on the bank, and to search for the bodies of Lieutenant Beever and private Miller of the Sixth regiment. Major Bradley, with the companies named, participated in the successful execution of the duty assigned Colonel Crooks.

On the night of the thirty-first of July I received instructions to place the entire regiment along the front and flank of our part of the camp. This was done. About two o'clock the Indians fired a volley into the north side of camp—that occupied by the Tenth regiment. The volley was evidently aimed too high for effect on the men in the trenches. That side of the corral was open, for passing the animals in and out, and some of the shots must have struck the cattle, in addition to the horses and mules killed. The cattle dashed out of the corral utterly wild with fright, and making the ground tremble with their tread. They were turned back and to the right by part of the line of the Tenth regiment. They then came plunging toward the left companies of the Seventh. These rose up and succeeded in turning them back into the corral. But for the living wall that confronted them, the animals would have escaped, or stampeded the mules and horses, with great destruction of life in the camp. The prompt return of the fire, by the companies of the Tenth on my left, discouraged any further attempt on the camp.

The next morning we resumed the march homeward. Since then no Indians have appeared, and nothing relating to this regiment occurred to add to the above.

In concluding this report, supplementary to that made on the twenty-fifth ultimo, I beg leave to add a few things, of a more general nature, relating to the regiment I have the honor to command. The health of the regiment, during the long march from Camp Pope, has been remarkably good. There have been but two cases of serious illness, both convalescent.

Surgeon Smith and Assistant-Surgeon Ames have been assiduous and skilful in their attention to the medical wants and the general sanitary condition of the regiment. Adjutant Trader and Quartermaster Cutter have been laborious in their duties. During the first three weeks of the march Lieutenant F. H. Pratt was acting Quartermaster, and gave the fullest satisfaction in that position.

Captain Light, who remained at Camp Atchinson, has been faithful in his ministrations.

The non-commissioned staff has been every way effective.

The good order and discipline of the regiment has been perfect. But two or three arrests have been made, and those for trivial offences.

I feel it due to Major Bradley to again refer to him in acknowledgment of the assistance he has constantly rendered me. Soon after the march began, I became so affected with irritation of the throat, from dust, that the Surgeon forbade my giving commands to the battalion on the march. Major Bradley has relieved me almost entirely in this respect, and has otherwise shared with me fully the responsibilities of the command.

Your obedient servant,
WILLIAM R. MARSHALL,
Lieut.-Col. Commanding Seventh Regiment Minnesota Vols.

REPORT OF COLONEL SAMUEL McPHAIL.

HEADQUARTERS FIRST REGIMENT MINNESOTA M. R.,
IN CAMP ON THE PLAINS, August 5, 1863.

Brigadier-General H. H. Sibley, Commanding Expeditionary Forces:

GENERAL: On the twenty-first of July, 1863, pursuant to your order to recover the body of Dr. J. S. Weiser, Surgeon of the First Minnesota Mounted Rangers, murdered by the Indians, I proceeded to the hills in the rear of Camp Sibley, with companies A and D of my regiment. When some five hundred yards from camp, we were fired upon by the Indians, occupying the summit of the hill. I immediately ordered company A, under Captain E. M. Wilson, to advance and fire upon the enemy, which was done in good style. The ground being rocky and broken, companies A, D, and G were ordered to dismount and skirmish the hill. Companies B and F, under Major Hays, and company L, under Captain Davy, were to support them. The first battalion, under Major Parker, cleared the hill, and drove the Indians some two miles, followed by companies B and F mounted. Here I met Lieutenant-Colonel W. R. Marshall, of the Seventh Minnesota volunteers, and requested him to protect my right flank, which he did in gallant style. Major Parker was then ordered to rally the companies of his battalion, and prepare to engage the enemy mounted. I then moved forward of the skirmishers, with companies B and F, and ordered a charge upon the enemy posted on the highest peak of the range known as Big Hills. This order was promptly obeyed; the Indians were dislodged from their position and driven toward the plains west of the hills. While descending the hill I ordered another charge, by company B, under Captain Austin. While in the act of carrying out this order, one man was instantly killed by lightning, and others seriously injured.

This occasioned a momentary confusion. Order was, however, soon restored, and we pushed the enemy from their positions on the hills, and in the ravines on our front, to the plains below. I then ordered a rally. Companies A, B, F, and L assembled, and we pushed forward upon the Indians, who had taken refuge behind a few rude and hastily constructed intrenchments in their encampment, from which they were quickly dislodged, and a running fight commenced. At this juncture Lieutenant John Whipple, of the Third Minnesota battery, reached us with one six-pounder, his horses entirely given out, in consequence of which he could only give the flying enemy two shots, which apparently threw them into still greater confusion. I then again ordered a charge, which was kept up until we had reached at least fifteen miles from the first point of attack, and during which we drove them from their concealment in the rushes and wild rice of Dead Buffalo Lake by a well-directed volley from the deadly carbines, and ran into their lines five times, continuing the fight until nearly dark, when companies H, D, and G arrived, and I received your order to return to Camp Sibley, at the Big Hills. Some time having been consumed in collecting our wounded and providing transportation for them, we attempted to return, and only succeeded in reaching camp at five A.M., on the morning of the twenty-fifth, having in the darkness been unable to preserve our course, and having been in the saddle twenty-four hours, without guide, provisions, or water. The number of Indians engaged could not have been less than one thousand, and would doubtless reach one thousand five hundred warriors. The losses of my regiment, including a skirmish on Sunday evening the twenty-sixth, at Dead Buffalo Lake, are as follows:

Killed—Private Gustaff A. Starke, of company B; private John Murphy, of company B; and (at Buffalo Lake) Corporal John Platt, of company L.

Wounded—Private Andrew Moore, of company B, mortally; Corporal William B. Hazlep, of company B, in shoulder, doing well; Sergeant James Grady, of company L, in leg slightly; private Henry Stntz, of company B, slightly.

Murdered by the Indians—Doctor J. S. Weiser, Surgeon, and Lieutenant A. Freeman, of company D.

The number of Indians known to have been killed by the Mounted Rangers is thirty-one, all found with the peculiar mark of cavalry upon them. Doubtless many more were killed by the Rangers, as the wounded concealed themselves in the marshes, where it was impossible to follow them with cavalry.

In this report I esteem it a duty, and it affords me great pleasure, to say of the officers and men under my command, who were engaged in this series of fights and hand-to-hand encounters, that without exception the utmost coolness and bravery were displayed, the only difficulty I encountered being that of restraining the wild enthusiasm of the troops during the succession of cavalry charges; and I can only say of them further, that they have won for themselves a reputation of which veteran troops might well be proud.

It is also a duty and a gratification to mention favorably the name of First Lieutenant E. A. Goodell, Acting Adjutant, whose aid, in the hottest of the fight, rendered me great service; also the name of John Martin, of company F, who bore despatches with "certainty, celerity, and security."

I am, General, very respectfully, your obedient servant, SAMUEL M. McPHAIL,
Colonel Commanding Mounted Rangers.

Doc. 111.

THE BATTLE OF HELENA.*

REPORT OF LIEUTENANT-COLONEL HEATH.

HEADQUARTERS THIRTY-THIRD MISSOURI VOLUNTEERS, }
HELENA, ARK., July 6, 1863. }

COLONEL: I have the honor to submit the following report of the part taken by the Thirty-

* See Docs. page 135, ante.

third Missouri volunteers in the action of the fourth inst. Companies D and F manned the heavy guns in Fort Curtis; company A the guns in battery A; company C the guns in battery B; company E the guns in battery C, supported by company H, acting as sharp-shooters; company B the guns in battery D, supported by companies G, I, and K, acting as sharp-shooters.

The first assault of the enemy in force was made at four o'clock A.M. upon batteries A, C, and D simultaneously. In front of batteries A and D they were handsomely checked before any advantage had been gained, but the entire Missouri brigade of Parsons (said to have been personally directed by Major-General Sterling Price) charging furiously upon battery C, drove the infantry support (four companies of the Thirty-third Iowa) out of the rifle-pits in great confusion, and after killing, wounding, and capturing thirty men of the two companies on duty at the guns, succeeded in driving them from the battery, but not before they had spiked one of the guns and brought away all the friction-primers and priming wires, thus rendering the pieces useless to the enemy. The companies in Fort Curtis, with the siege-guns, supported by the remnants of companies E and H with numerous stragglers from other commands acting as sharp-shooters, succeeded in checking the enemy's further advance, and finally drove his main force back from battery C, compelling him by their steady and increasing fire to leave the guns of the battery uninjured and beat a hasty and disastrous retreat, leaving over three hundred and fifty prisoners, with their officers and colors, and his dead and wounded in our hands. The prisoners were mainly of the Seventh and Tenth Missouri regiments, and had taken refuge from the fire of our artillery in a deep ravine opening toward the river, but protected by a ridge from the direct fire of Fort Curtis. Immediately the Thirty-fifth Missouri was drawn up across the mouth of this ravine, part of the Thirty-third Iowa moving to attack the enemy's flank, and the siege-guns playing shell, grape, and canister upon the ridge above them, preventing retreat. They were surrendered by hoisting a white flag, their own sharp-shooters upon the ridge at their rear firing from cover upon and cursing them as they marched out prisoners of war.

At about nine o'clock A.M., a second attack was made upon battery D by Fagan's brigade of Arkansas troops, three regiments strong, and said, by prisoners, to have acted under the personal direction of Lieutenant-General Holmes. The battery was bravely supported by detachments from the Forty-third Indiana, under Major Norris, and the Thirty-third Iowa, under Major Gibson. In spite, however, of the most determined resistance, Bell's regiment, with small portions of Hawthorn's and Brooks's, succeeded in penetrating our outer line of rifle-pits, and securing a position in a deep ravine to the left of the battery and below the range of its guns. The remainder of the brigade was broken and scattered by the terrific fire of our artillery in the works, and compelled to seek shelter in the woods out of range. Immediately upon their retreating, our riflemen from all three regiments in the pits closed in upon those of the enemy who were in the ravine, from all sides, cutting off retreat. The reserve of the Forty-third Indiana formed across the mouth of the ravine, and two Parrott guns of the First Missouri battery, under Lieutenant O'Connell, were also brought to rake the enemy's position. Captain John G. Hudson of the Thirty-third Missouri, commanding battery D, then demanded the surrender of the entire force. The men at once threw down their arms, and Lieutenant-Colonel Johnson of Bell's regiment, made a formal surrender of his command, mustering twenty-one officers and between three and four hundred men, with all their arms and one stand of colors. At about half-past ten o'clock A.M., the main body of the enemy had entirely drawn off from in front of our batteries, and the firing ceased.

Companies E and H returned to battery C, capturing some fifty of the enemy, and finding both guns of the battery turned upon Fort Curtis and loaded with shell, but not discharged for want of friction-primers. The rout of the enemy was materially assisted by flank fires from batteries A, B, and D, and ten-inch shell from the gunboat Tyler.

Upward of three hundred killed and wounded were left by the enemy in the vicinity of this battery, seventy of these being killed outright and a great number so wounded they cannot survive. Nearly the same number were found in front and on the left flank of battery D.

The immense power of the batteries supporting each other, and with the guns of the Fort affording the most perfect concentration upon any given point, entirely demoralized the enemy, who broke at the first few rounds, and could only be coaxed and forced forward after that in a shapeless and disorganized mob. Considering that the gunners in Fort Curtis had had no target practice, the firing from the Fort as well as the batteries was in the main remarkably good, and our riflemen and the infantry supports sent to the batteries behaved with rare courage and steadiness, being in position from two o'clock A.M. until eleven o'clock A.M. without food, and fighting steadily for six and a half hours of that time.

I desire especially to mention Majors Norris and Gibson, Captains Schenck and Tracy, and Lieutenant Reid for gallantry for leading their men, upon the suggestion of Captain Hudson, against Bell's regiment. Of the men of the Thirty-third Missouri who distinguished themselves by coolness, activity, and determination, may be mentioned Major George W. Vanbeak, superintending batteries A and B; Captains William J. McKee, commanding Fort Curtis; Daniel D. Carr, three siege-guns; William M. Blake, battery A; Alexander J. Campbell, battery B; Thomas M. Gibson, battery C; John S. Hudson, battery G; Stuart Carkner, company G, (wounded;) George H. Tracy, company I; Elias S. Schenck, company K; Lieutenants Henry Cochran, commanding company H; Stephen J. Burnett, (wounded;) Adam B. Smith, (killed at his post;) Luther P. Eldridge, Isaac S. Coe, Charles L. Draper, —— Lombar, Joseph W. Brooks, (killed while gallantly leading a charge,) Moses Reed, Robert M. Reed, Edgar L. Allen, Henry H. Knowlton, and James M. Conner, and gunners. Sergeant E. Bates, J. W. Welles, L. D. Alden, company F; Sergeant Henry S. Carroll, Corporal James K. Frier, private J. S. Martin, company D; private John Driscoll, Kansas cavalry, all in Fort Curtis. Battery A—Sergeants D. R. McClammer and George B. Maher. Battery B—Corporal George W. Coleman. Battery C—Sergeant James M. Freeman; privates Thomas W. Wheeler and Joseph W. Phillips. Battery D—Corporal Robert McPhate (Dubuque battery) and Luke P. Maxen. Nathaniel Leavitt, commissary sergeant, killed at his post. Color-Sergeant Patrick Collins, a regular soldier of twenty-six years' standing, wounded in the face while bravely fighting over the parapet of battery D.

There were others who did as well as those named, but whose names have not been handed me. The entire regiment, officers and men, behaved with steadiness and judgment.

Very respectfully,

WILLIAM H. HEATH,
Lieutenant-Colonel Commanding Regiment.

To Colonel S. A. RICE,
Commanding Second Brigade, Third Division, Thirteenth Army Corps.

Doc. 112.

THE FIGHT AT SHELBYVILLE, TENN.

COLONEL MINTY'S REPORT.

HEADQUARTERS FIRST BRIGADE,
SECOND CAVALRY DIVISION,
CAMP NEAR SALEM, TENN., July 8, 1863.

Captain Curtis, A. A. G., Second Cavalry Division:

SIR: At half-past six A.M., on the twenty-fourth of June, I marched from Murfreesboro to Cripple Creek, on the Woodbury pike, with my brigade, consisting of two thousand five hundred and twenty-two officers and men. At one o'clock I was ordered to countermarch to Murfreesboro and report to Major-General Stanley at that place. General Stanley directed me to move out on the Salem pike and get within supporting distance of General Mitchell, who, with the First cavalry division, was supposed to be hard pressed somewhere near Middleton. I encamped within two miles of General Mitchell that night.

June 25.—Crossed the country to Shelbyville pike and camped at Christiana. Pickets of the Fourth United States cavalry on Shelbyville pike were driven in by rebel cavalry. Fifth Iowa and Fourth Michigan went out and drove the enemy through Fosterville to Guy's Gap.

June 26.—Remained in camp at Christiana, with heavy pickets on front and right.

June 27.—At eight A.M. the entire cavalry force was ordered to move on Guy's Gap, the First division in advance, my brigade, with the exception of the Fifth Iowa, (which was left at Christiana to guard baggage-trains,) following. On nearing the Gap, General Stanley ordered me to the front. I found the enemy in position at the Gap, with a strong force of skirmishers behind the fences on the face of the mountain, and a column moving through the woods threatening our right flank. I deployed the Fourth regulars to the front, and General Stanley took the Fourth Michigan, Seventh Pennsylvania, and Third Indidna to the right, and drove the enemy from there. I now received permission to advance on the Gap. The Fourth United States cavalry advanced in line. I moved up the road with the First Middle Tennessee, and ordered in the other regiments from the right.

Lieutenant-Colonel Galbraith, with a dozen men, dashed forward and removed a barricade which the rebels had built across the road at the top of the hill, and then with his regiment charged the rebels, who were now rapidly falling back. I followed to his support with the Fourth regulars for about two miles, when finding that his men were very much scattered, picking up prisoners, I formed line and waited their return. In about twenty minutes a messenger came in from Colonel Galbraith, who stated that the enemy had rallied and was showing fight. I immediately pushed forward with the Seventh Pennsylvania, Fourth Michigan, and Third Indiana, (who had just come up,) and found the enemy behind their intrenchments, about three miles from Shelbyville with an abattis and an open space, about a mile in width, between them and us. Captain Davis, Seventh Pennsylvania, took his battalion, dismounted the front, deployed as skirmishers, and engaged the enemy, who immediately opened on us with artillery. I ordered Major Mix to take the Fourth Michigan to the right, about three quarters of a mile, push across the intrenchments, and take the enemy in flank. Lieutenant-Colonel Klein, with the Third Indiana, I sent to the left, with the same directions. I at the same time despatched a messenger to Captain McIntyre to move forward with the Fourth regulars, to General Mitchell, asking him to send me a couple of pieces of artillery, and to General Stanley, notifying him of the position of affairs.

Immediately after the arrival of the Fourth regulars on the ground, I heard the Michigan rifles speaking on the right, and at once moved forward the Seventh Pennsylvania on the right of the road and the Fourth regulars on the left. Captain Davis at the same time pushed forward with his skirmishers and relaid the planks which had been torn off a small bridge on the road. Finding that the enemy was now giving way, I brought the Seventh Pennsylvania into the road in columns of fours, and ordered them to charge, which they did most gallantly, led by Lieutenant Thompson (who was honorably mentioned for his conduct at McMinnville, April twenty-first,) and well supported by the Fourth regulars.

At this point we made about three hundred prisoners; the Fourth Michigan had one officer

and seven men wounded and twenty-one horses killed and wounded, while charging the breast works, and Lieutenant O'Connell of the Fourth regulars, (who distinguished himself so nobly at Middleton,) was thrown from his horse and had his shoulder broken.

When within a quarter of a mile of Shelbyville, the rebels opened on us with four pieces of artillery, well posted in the town. I again sent back to General Mitchell, requesting him to hurry forward a couple of guns, but finding that the enemy was getting our range, I was forming for a charge, when Captain Ayleshire (Eighteenth Ohio) reported to me with four pieces from his battery. I ordered two to the front, placed one each side of the road at less than a quarter of a mile from the rebel battery, and directed Captain Ayleshire to throw one shell from each gun; the moment they were fired, the Seventh Pennsylvania, in columns of fours, passed between them, and, with a yell, rushed upon the enemy.

I had, before ordering the charge, sent Lieutenant Lawton, Fourth Michigan, to Captain McIntyre, directing him to take his regiment (Fourth regulars) through the woods to the left, and turn the enemy's right flank. This would effectually have cut off their retreat by Newsomes or Scull Camp Bridge. General Mitchell came up at the moment that Captain McIntyre received my order, and told him not to go, but that he would send a fresh regiment in that direction. The regiment sent by him was without a guide, mistook the direction, and got on the ground about one minute too late, and thus Generals Wheeler and Martin escaped capture.

The Seventh Pennsylvania were followed by one platoon of the Fourth regulars under Lieutenant McCafferty, of the First Middle Tennessee under Lieutenant-Colonel Galbraith, and the Fourth regulars, under Captain McIntyre. There was one discharge from the rebel artillery, as we charged down the narrow road, but being badly aimed, killed only one man and two horses.

At the railroad station, a party in ambush poured a volley into the head of the column of the Seventh Pennsylvania, killing Lieutenants Rhodes and Reed and two men.

On the hill directly in rear of the railroad buildings, the First confederates (regulars) attempted to rally, but in doing so they lost their colonel, lieutenant-colonel, major, and nearly half the regiment taken prisoners.

As the Seventh Pennsylvania arrived at Scull Camp Bridge, the Third Indiana, who had kept well to the left after crossing the intrenchments, swept down the north bank of the river, driving a crowd of refugees before them. The bridge being completely blocked, these men were driven into the river, where they perished by scores.

Major Sinclair kindly sent an orderly to General Stanley, informing him of our success, and that we had captured three pieces of artillery and many prisoners.

General Mitchell came up with his division shortly after. I rode forward a short distance with him, and got my brigade together once more, and found that I had lost two officers and eighteen men wounded; but I had captured three pieces of artillery and five hundred and ninety-nine men and thirty commissioned officers. Their killed and wounded must have been at least two hundred, including those drowned in the river.

Generals Wheeler and Martin had to take to the water with the other fugitives. The Adjutant of the Eighth confederates reined in his horse to allow the two generals to take their dip before him, but his doing so threw him into the hands of the Third Indiana. I bivouacked near the railroad station.

June 28.—Returned to within two miles of Guy's Gap.

June 29.—Reveille at one o'clock A.M. Marched to Fairfield *via* Shelbyville. The Fifth Iowa and Third Indiana were detached and left with General Granger at Guy's Gap.

June 30.—Marched to within four miles of Manchester.

July 1.—Returned to Walker's Mills, within three miles of Manchester.

July 2.—Reveille at one A.M. Waited four hours for the First division to move. Marched to Elk River, where I rejoined the Second division. The enemy showed himself in force, the Seventh Pennsylvania skirmished with him a short time. Camped one mile south of the river, the Fourth Michigan remaining on the north side to guard Stokes's battery.

July 3.—Marched to Decherd, the Fourth Michigan making a dash into that place, but finding that the rebs had removed, camped a mile and a half from Decherd.

July 4.—In camp, Fourth Michigan sent to Tullahoma for rations.

July 5.—In camp, rejoined by Third Indiana.

July 6.—Marched to within five miles of Salem and went into camp.

July 7.—In camp.

I am, respectfully, your obedient servant,
ROBT. H. G. MINTY,
Colonel Commanding.

General Wheeler received a severe wound (shot through the body a little above the left groin) while crossing the river.

One hundred and eighteen dead rebels have been taken out of the river. Fifteen were buried on the field, and in every house was left from one to four too badly wounded to be moved.

Doc. 113.

JEFFERSON DAVIS'S ADDRESS.

To the Soldiers of the Confederate States:

AFTER more than two years of a warfare scarcely equalled in the number, magnitude, and fearful carnage of its battles—a warfare in which your courage and fortitude have illustrated your country, and attracted not only gratitude at home, but admiration abroad—your enemies continue a struggle in which our final triumph must be inevitable. Unduly elated with their recent successes, they imagine that temporary reverses can quell your spirit or shake your determination, and they are now gathering heavy masses for a general invasion, in the vain hope that by a desperate effort success may at length be reached.

You know too well, my countrymen, what they mean by success. Their malignant rage aims at nothing less than the extermination of yourselves, your wives and children. They seek to destroy what they cannot plunder. They propose as the spoils of victory that your homes shall be partitioned among the wretches whose atrocious cruelties have stamped infamy on their government. They design to incite servile insurrection, and light the fires of incendiarism whenever they can reach your homes, and they debauch the inferior race, hitherto docile and contented, by promising indulgence of the vilest passions as the price of treachery. Conscious of their inability to prevail by legitimate warfare, not daring to make peace lest they should be hurled from their seats of power, the men who now rule in Washington refuse even to confer on the subject of putting an end to outrages which disgrace our age, or to listen to a suggestion for conducting the war according to the usages of civilization.

Fellow-citizens, no alternative is left you but victory, or subjugation, slavery and the utter ruin of yourselves, your families and your country. The victory is within your reach. You need but stretch forth your hands to grasp it. For this and all that is necessary is that those who are called to the field by every motive that can move the human heart, should promptly repair to the post of duty, should stand by their comrades now in front of the foe, and thus so strengthen the armies of the Confederacy as to insure success. The men now absent from their posts would if present in the field suffice to create numerical equality between our force and that of the invaders—and when with any approach to such equality have we failed to be victorious? I believe that but few of those absent are actuated by unwillingness to serve their country; but that many have found it difficult to resist the temptation of a visit to their homes, and the loved ones from whom they have been so long separated; that others have left for temporary attention to their affairs, with the intention of returning, and then have shrunk from the consequences of their violation of duty; that others again have left their posts from mere restlessness and desire of change, each quieting the upbraidings of his conscience by persuading himself that his individual services could have no influence on the general result.

These and other causes (although far less disgraceful than the desire to avoid danger, or to escape from the sacrifices required by patriotism) are, nevertheless, grievous faults, and place the cause of our beloved country, and of every thing we hold dear, in imminent peril. I repeat that the men who now owe duty to their country, who have been called out and have not yet reported for duty, or who have absented themselves from their posts, are sufficient in number to secure us victory in the struggle now impending.

I call on you, then, my countrymen, to hasten to your camps, in obedience to the dictates of honor and of duty, and summon those who have absented themselves without leave, who have remained absent beyond the period allowed by their furloughs, to repair without delay to their respective commands; and I do hereby declare that I grant a general pardon and amnesty to all officers and men within the Confederacy, now absent without leave, who shall, with the least possible delay, return to their proper posts of duty, but no excuse will be received for any delay beyond twenty days after the first publication of this proclamation in the State in which the absentee may be at the date of the publication. This amnesty and pardon shall extend to all who have been accused, or who have been convicted and are undergoing sentence for absence without leave or desertion, excepting only those who have been twice convicted of desertion.

Finally, I conjure my countrywomen, the wives, mothers, sisters and daughters of the Confederacy —to use their all-powerful influence in aid of this call, to add one crowning sacrifice to those which their patriotism has so freely and constantly afforded on their country's altar, and to take care that none who owe service in the field shall be sheltered at home from the disgrace of having deserted their duty to their families, to their country, and to their God.

Given under my hand, and the Seal of the Confederate States, at Richmond, this [SEAL.] first day of August, in the year of our Lord one thousand eight hundred and sixty-three.
JEFFERSON DAVIS.

By the President:
J. P. BENJAMIN,
Secretary of State.

The papers throughout the confederate States are requested to copy this proclamation at the earliest moment, and for twenty days thereafter, and send their bills to the Private Secretary of the President.

Doc. 114.

THE CAPTURE OF JOHN MORGAN.

GENERAL SHACKLEFORD'S REPORT.*

HEADQUARTERS U. S. FORCES, IN FIELD,
GREGG'S CREEK, July 20, P.M.

To Lieutenant-Colonel Richmond, A. A. G.:

WE chased John Morgan and his command over fifty miles to-day.

After heavy skirmishing for six or seven miles between the Forty-fifth Ohio and Colonel Wolford's brigade, which was in advance of the enemy, we succeeded in bringing the enemy to a stand about three o'clock this P.M., when a fight ensued which lasted an hour, when the rebels fled, taking refuge upon a very high bluff.

* See Doc. 47, page 257, ante.

I sent a flag of truce demanding the immediate unconditional surrender of Morgan and his command. The flag was received by Colonel Coleman and other officers, who came down and asked a personal interview. They asked an hour for consultation, and I granted forty minutes; in which time the command, excepting Morgan, who deserted his command, taking with him a very small squad, surrendered.

It was my understanding that Morgan himself had surrendered, and found it was the understanding of Morgan's officers and men that the number of killed and wounded is inconsiderable. The number of prisoners is from one thousand to one thousand five hundred, including a large number of colonels, majors, and line-officers.

I captured between six hundred and seven hundred prisoners yesterday.

I will capture Morgan himself to-morrow.
SHACKLEFORD,
Brigadier-General.

REPORT OF LIEUT.-COLONEL WARNER.

HEADQUARTERS EIGHTH MICHIGAN CAVALRY,
IN THE FIELD, July 20, 1863.

John Stockton, Colonel Eighth Michigan Cavalry, Commanding Post Hickman Bridge, Ky.:

COLONEL: I have the honor to submit the following report of the marches, etc., of the Eighth Michigan cavalry, under my command, since leaving Hickman Bridge, Ky., July fourth, 1863, to this time:

Receiving orders on the evening of July fourth to make a forced march with my command to Lebanon, Ky., and there support the garrison threatened by John Morgan, I broke camp at nine o'clock pursuant to said orders. I ordered all tents and baggage left behind, and but two days' rations in the men's haversacks.

At two o'clock A.M. of the fifth I halted my command for two hours, four miles beyond Danville, having marched twenty-four miles. At this place I fell in with the Eleventh Michigan battery and Ninth Michigan cavalry, in command of Colonel James I. David, and he being the senior officer, I came under his orders.

At Parksville I halted for wood and water, and was here ordered to follow the Ninth cavalry and Eleventh battery, which I did.

We reached Lebanon at two o'clock P.M., when the Eleventh battery immediately opened upon the rear-guard of the enemy, then leaving town on the Lexington Pike. My desire to charge into the town, or cut off the enemy by a cross-road, not being concurred in by Colonel David, they were permitted to escape without molestation, much to the disappointment of my whole command.

The Twentieth Kentucky infantry, Colonel Hanson, had surrendered an hour before our arrival, after a most gallant fight against vastly superior numbers.

The enemy had burnt the railroad dépôt and station-house, with several private dwellings, and pillaged the principal stores in the town.

At eight o'clock, the same day, I was ordered

to countermarch with the Ninth cavalry and the Eleventh battery to Danville, which place we reached at four o'clock P.M. of the sixth, making the march without halt, except for wood and water.

At Danville, Colonel W. P. Saunders, Fifth Kentucky cavalry, took command of the whole force, constituting the Eighth and Ninth Michigan cavalry brigade.

At half-past twelve o'clock A.M. of the seventh we took up our line of march for Lawrenceburgh, Ky., forty-three miles distant from Danville. Halting at Harrodsburgh for breakfast, feed, and water, we pushed on, reaching Lawrenceburgh at four o'clock P.M.

From Lawrenceburgh I sent out Lieutenant J. E. Babbitt, with fifty men, to scout between the Kentucky and Salt Rivers. On the Salt River, near Salvisa, Lieutenant Babbitt came upon Captain Alexander's company, of Morgan's division, and captured thirty, killing fourteen.

The command remained at Lawrenceburgh awaiting orders until nine o'clock P.M. on the eleventh instant, when we took up our line of march for Westport *via* Eminence and Lagrange, reaching Westport at twelve o'clock at midnight, having marched seventy-three miles over a very rough and hilly road, with but four hours' halt at Eminence for rest, feed, and water.

At Westport, Charles Laturner, private, company G, was accidentally shot through the body, and was left at that place under proper care.

Morgan having crossed the Ohio River into Indiana, we took transports on Sunday morning, the twelfth instant, for Madison, Indiana, in order to cut him off, leaving behind company I, of my command, a portion of the Ninth, with all our extra baggage, wagons, etc., in command of Colonel David, not having transportation sufficient for the entire command. At Madison we found Morgan had got ahead of us, so we moved on to Lawrenceburgh, Indiana, where Major Mix was sent out to reconnoitre the enemy, learn his force, etc. He proceeded to Guilford, ten miles, and reported again in three hours to the entire satisfaction of General Manson, commanding forces on transports. From Lawrenceburgh we moved on to Cincinnati, reaching that city at half-past five o'clock P.M., on the thirteenth instant.

At Cincinnati, Major Edgerly was sent out with his battalion by Colonel Saunders, on a scout, joining us again at Batavia, Ohio, on the fifteenth, having accomplished his mission with success. Lieutenant Babbitt was also sent out two miles from the city to guard a bridge. I have not heard from him since that time.

At four o'clock P.M., the fourteenth, Colonel Saunders, with the balance of his command, moved out to Evandale, three miles from the city, remaining there until half-past three o'clock P.M. of the same day, when he received orders to join Brigadier-General Hobson's command in pursuit of Morgan, which command we reached sixteen miles north of Cincinnati. From this time we continued the pursuit with but short halts for feed and rest for our horses, until Sunday morning, the

nineteenth instant. After marching all the previous night, we came upon the enemy at Buffington Island Ford, near Portland, Ohio, some two hundred and fifty miles east of Cincinnati. On coming upon the enemy, the Second and Seventh Ohio cavalry being in our front, were dismounted and deployed as skirmishers. Our brigade then came up, when Colonel Saunders ordered the Eleventh Michigan battery to open upon the rebels, and the Eighth and Ninth to charge. This was done with alacrity and spirit, when the enemy, already slowly retiring, took to flight in great disorder, strewing the ground over which they fled with the plunder which they had accumulated all along their line of march. On reaching the woods, I deployed Major Edgerly, with his battalion, to the right, and Major Mix to the left. The pursuit was continued until the horses were worn down, when we returned to Buffington. Major Edgerly's command took one hundred and forty-seven prisoners, Major Mix seventy, making two hundred and seventeen prisoners, with their horses and equipments. Not any of my command were killed, and but two wounded, namely, E. A. Kesler, Sergeant company A, and Jas. Reed, Corporal company A. First Sergeant G. Warner, company A, received a severe wound in the leg, by the accidental discharge of his pistol, while on the march.

I cannot speak in terms of too strong praise of my command since breaking camp at Hickman. During the long, tedious march of five hundred and seventy-three miles, which took sixteen days, much of the time night and day, and that with short rations, they have endured it as Michigan soldiers through this ungodly war have done, without complaint. With cheerfulness and alacrity have my orders been responded to by both officers and men. I was obliged to leave several along the line of march, either sick or worn out, some on account of their horses giving out, with no fresh ones to be procured at the time.

Our arms—the Spencer rifle—proved, as before, a terror to the rebels. They thought us in much stronger force than we were, when each man could pour seven shots into them so rapidly. This is the first instance during the war, I think, where the proportion of killed was greater than the wounded. As far as reports have come in, it is, at least, three killed to one wounded, and this fact is owing to the terrible execution of our rifles.

We remain here a short time to gather up captured property, arms, etc., and then expect to be ordered back to Hickman.

Captain S. Wells, Lieutenant Tubbs, and Lieutenant W. B. Smith represent my command on Colonel Saunders's staff.

With much respect,

G. S. WARNER,
Lieut.-Colonel Commanding Eighth Michigan Cavalry.

OFFICIAL REPORT OF COLONEL HILL.

HEADQUARTERS SECOND BRIGADE OHIO MILITIA,
ZANESVILLE, OHIO, July 24, 1863.

To His Excellency David Tod, Governor of Ohio:

By order of Colonel Benjamin B. Runkle, commanding division Ohio militia, I left Scott's Landing on the morning of the twenty-second instant, with a portion of my brigade, for the purpose of intercepting Morgan's forces on the Muskingum River, at any point where he might attempt to cross. His movements during the day, as indicated by my scouts, led me to suspect he would attempt to cross at Beverly, or at some other point between that place and McConnellsville—most probably at Windsor. Placing guards at the fords, and covering my entire front with scouts, I landed my main force at Windsor for the night. At an early hour the next morning a courier from McConnellsville brought intelligence that Morgan was within five miles, on the opposite side of the river, and approaching that place. I moved my command promptly, but upon reaching McConnellsville I ascertained that the enemy was crossing at Eagleport ferry, seven miles above. Before I could accomplish this march he had crossed the river. By taking an unfrequented route over the hills from the river, I succeeded in flanking him, and opening upon him with my artillery. His entire force was thrown into confusion, throwing away their arms, clothing, etc., along the route of his retreat. I followed with infantry and artillery, opening upon him from every available point, until about four o'clock P.M., when General Shackleford's cavalry came in, moving upon Morgan's rear from the left. My forces being completely exhausted, I drew them off, and moved back to the river.

I have the honor to be, Governor, respectfully your obedient servant,

JOSEPH HILL,
Colonel Commanding Second Brigade, Runkle's Division, O. M.

COMMANDER FITCH'S REPORT.

UNITED STATES STEAMER MOOSE,
ABOVE BUFFINGTON ISLAND, OHIO RIVER, July 19.

To Hon. Gideon Welles, Secretary of the Navy :

After chasing Morgan nearly five hundred miles, I at last met him at this point, and engaged and drove him back, capturing two pieces of his artillery, and abandoned the rest to General Judah.

The enemy broke in confusion from the banks, and left his wagon trains, many horses, and small arms in my possession.

Since writing the above, I followed further up the river, and met another portion of Morgan's force fording fourteen miles above ; shelled and drove most of them back. Several were killed, fifteen or thirty wounded, and twenty horses captured. I have but two men wounded slightly.

Our shell and shrapnel created great confusion in the rebel ranks, killing and wounding many.

LEROY FITCH,
Lieutenant Commanding.

CAPTAIN OAKES'S LETTER.

STEAMBOAT IMPERIAL, July 21.

Captain Bowen:

DEAR SIR: We left here on Tuesday last, in the capacity of despatch-boat to the gunboat fleet under command of Commodore Fitch, in pursuit of John Morgan. I think that the credit of the rout and damage of Morgan and his band belongs to the gunboats. The gunboats were on hand at all fording points all along the river, and kept him from crossing, and so checked him until the arrival of our troops completed the work. Morgan came in and camped there during Saturday night, and our forces came up and attacked him during Sunday morning. The gunboat Moose, under command of Commodore Fitch, was anchored at the foot of Buffington, having arrived there on Saturday evening, and, as you are aware, the river is low, and there is but little water in Buffington chute. The night being dark, Commodore Fitch kept his boat at the foot until daylight, when he started up through the chute. Morgan's men made an attempt to plant a cannon on the bank opposite the chute, when Commodore Fitch gave them a shell or two, and they left. Commodore Fitch then went on through the chute, and took his position at the head of the island, and shelled them during the battle, throwing them into confusion and disorder. They then started at full speed up the river road. Commodore Fitch met them at a narrow place in the road, and gave them some more shell, when Morgan abandoned all his guns, wagons, buggies, surplus horses, dry goods, boots, shoes, hardware, etc., of which he had a good supply, and made his escape with what men he had left, and they kept on up the river at such a distance that the gunboat could not reach them. A part of them came in at the head of Belleville Island, numbering one hundred to one hundred and twenty-five men. We had the gunboat Moose in tow, and were at the foot of the island, coming up as fast as we could. Commodore Fitch shelled them while they were in the river fording. We saw three empty saddles, and got the horses. The balance of this party made their escape into Virginia. We came on up, and at the foot of Belleville bar, saw fourteen more cross, but they were at too great a distance to reach them, and they got over to the Virginia shore, and as we came by, fired at us in ambush ; so Commodore Fitch shelled the woods. We went on to the foot of Mustapha, and as we were ahead of them, they having gone back into the hills, he thought best to return, and landed at Reed's Landing, opposite Belleville, and took on board some rebel horses. These two parties of men are all we saw cross the river. From Reed's we came to head of Buffington, and took on what captured cannon, wagons, horses, etc., we could, and got down the chute. We followed the Moose through the chute, and tied up to her at the foot of Buffington Sunday night. On Monday morning, Commodore Fitch ordered us to Cincinnati, at which point we arrived this morning, at one A.M. The other gunboats were at other points all along the river, as Commodore Fitch thought best to station them to guard the ford. I think the credit of this defeat of Morgan is due entirely to the gunboats. I could say a great deal more, but have not time. Yours respectfully,

T. J. OAKES.*

CLEVELAND "HERALD" ACCOUNT.

CLEVELAND, July 27, 1863.

We have already mentioned the fight that took place at Springfield, between Steubenville and Salineville, on Saturday evening. That fight was in reality a blundering attack of one portion of our forces upon another portion of the same. A plan had been laid for the capture of Morgan's entire band. The militia were stationed on a hill overlooking a road which Morgan was expected to traverse, and the cavalry and other regular forces were to occupy positions, that would have enabled them to surprise and "bag" the entire rebel command. As the Ninth Michigan cavalry, under Major Way, were moving along the road to take up the position assigned to them, they were mistaken by the militia for the rebels, and were fired into. This of course compelled the cavalry to fall back, and before the error could be retrieved, Morgan and his forces had escaped.

General Brooks, commanding the department, had gone to Wellsville and established his headquarters in the Cleveland and Pittsburgh dépôt, where he was assisted by the managing officers of the road, who had placed the transportation and telegraphic resources of the road at his disposal. Finding that there was a probability that Morgan would cross the road in the vicinity of Salineville, a train of cars was sent up the road about six o'clock Sunday morning with a regiment of six months' Pennsylvania infantry, under command of Colonel Gallagher. These were disembarked at Salineville and marched to a point about two miles distant, where the rebels were expected to cross. The infantry were posted on some rising ground commanding the road, with orders to prevent Morgan's passage.

At this time the utmost alarm existed among the people of Salineville. The houses were closed, doors and windows locked and barred, and women and children stampeding into the country with whatever portable property could be carried along. The men who had weapons and courage turned out to resist the progress of the dreaded rebel, while all the others fled with the women and children.

In a short time the expected rebels made their appearance, coming around a bend in the road. On catching sight of the infantry they halted, and turned their horses' heads in another direction. Before they could get out of the trap they found themselves in, Major Way, with two hundred and fifty men of the Ninth Michigan cavalry, dashed among them and commenced cutting right and left. The rebels made but a brief resistance. A few shots were fired by them, and then the whole party broke in utter confusion. The scene that followed was almost ludicrous, and could only be matched by the previous

* Captain Oakes commanded the steamer Imperial during the Morgan raid.

stampede at Buffington Island. Men dismounted, threw down their arms and begged for quarter, whilst others galloped around wildly in search of a place of escape, and were "brought to time" by a pistol-shot or sabre-stroke.

Morgan himself was riding in a carriage drawn by two white horses. Major Way saw him, and galloping up, reached for him. Morgan jumped out at the other side of the carriage, leaped over a fence, seized a horse, and galloped off as fast as horse-flesh, spurred by frightened heels, could carry him. About a couple of hundred of his men succeeded in breaking away, and following their fugitive leader. In the buggy thus hastily "evacuated" by Morgan were found his "rations," consisting of a loaf of bread, some hard-boiled eggs, and a bottle of whisky.

The number of killed in this fight was much less than at first reported. The number of killed rebels was set down as from twenty to thirty, but this must be overrated, as we cannot learn of more than five or six dead bodies having been found. There was a considerable number of wounded, and about two hundred prisoners taken, together with horses and arms. A special train was sent to Wellsville in the afternoon with about two hundred and fifty prisoners, captured in the fight or picked up in the neighborhood afterward.

A few of our cavalry were wounded, two or three seriously. Lieutenant Fiske was shot through the breast. His wound is dangerous, and he has telegraphed for his wife to come from Michigan.

Morgan and the remainder of his scattered forces pressed three citizens of Salineville into their service as guides, and continued their flight on the New-Lisbon road. One of the impressed guides made his escape and rode back, conveying intelligence of the route taken, which it was believed was with the ultimate design of reaching the Ohio River higher up. Forces were immediately despatched from Wellsville to head him off, whilst another force followed hotly in his rear, and a strong militia force from New-Lisbon came down to meet him.

About two o'clock in the afternoon these various detachments closed in around Morgan in the vicinity of West-Point, about midway between New-Lisbon and Wellsville. The rebels were driven to a bluff, from which there was no escape except by fighting their way through or leaping from a lofty and almost perpendicular precipice. Finding themselves thus cooped, Morgan concluded that "discretion was the better part of valor," and "came down" as gracefully as the coon did to Davy Crockett. He, with the remainder of his gang, surrendered to Colonel Shackleford, who was well acquainted with the redoubtable "John," and is said to be a distant relative.

The prisoners were brought back to Wellsville, where their arrival caused great excitement. Morgan retained his side-arms, and moved about freely, although always accompanied by Colonel Shackleford. Last night (Sunday) Morgan and his staff slept at the Whittaker House, in Wellsville, and at two o'clock this morning they, accompanied by Colonel Shackleford and his staff, left on the regular train for Columbus. Later in the morning a special train was to be sent to Columbus with the remainder of the prisoners and their guards.

The militia are constantly bringing into the line of road stray prisoners, picked up in the country. The hills are swarming with armed men hunting for fugitive rebels. Nine of Morgan's party were brought to Bayard Station this morning, who were captured in the neighborhood by the provost-marshal's force. They were taken to Alliance, to be sent from that place to Columbus.

Morgan's men were poorly dressed, ragged, dirty, and very badly used up. Some of them wore remnants of gray uniform, but most of them were attired in spoils gathered during their raid. They were very much discouraged at the result of their raid, and the prospect of affairs generally.

Morgan himself appeared in good spirits, and quite unconcerned at his ill-luck. He is a well-built man, of fresh complexion, and sandy hair and beard. He last night enjoyed for the first time in a long while the comforts of a sound sleep in a good bed, which was some compensation for his otherwise bad luck.

Five companies of Pennsylvania cavalry had been loaded up on the cars of the Cleveland and Pittsburgh road at Pittsburgh on Sunday afternoon, to take part in the chase, but the news of the capture of the entire rebel force rendered their departure unnecessary.

LOSSES CAUSED BY MORGAN'S RAID.

JACKSON C. H., OHIO, August 8, 1863.

The Military Committee of this county were engaged seven days in taking testimony as to the losses caused by Morgan's raid. This was done by order of Governor Tod:

The whole number of horses taken by Morgan's men was	290
Taken by the Union forces in pursuit,	46
Total,	330
Average value,	$90 00
Total,	29,700 00
Merchandise, cash, buggies, etc.,	16,000 00
Total,	$45,700 00

The damage to the Portsmouth and Newark Railroad, and some other items, have not been presented. The entire loss will be nearly fifty thousand dollars. D. MACKLEY.

Doc. 115.

THE PURSUIT OF BRAGG.

CAPTAIN CHURCH'S OFFICIAL REPORT.

HEADQUARTERS FOURTH MICHIGAN BATTERY, }
CAMP WINFORD, TENN., July 15, 1863. }

Lieutenant A. J. Davis, Acting Assistant Adjutant-General First Brigade, Third Division, Fourteenth Army Corps:

LIEUTENANT: In compliance with orders from brigade headquarters, I have the honor to submit the following report:

We marched from Triune, Tennessee, at twelve o'clock M., on the twenty-third of June, 1863; marched eight miles toward Salem, Tenn., and bivouacked by the side of the road.

June 24.—Commenced the march again at six o'clock A.M., and arrived at Salem at noon, where we remained one hour, when we were ordered forward. Crossed the Shelbyville Pike at seven P.M., and encamped one mile south of Christiana Station, which is on the Nashville and Chattanooga Railroad.

June 25.—Marched from camp at seven o'clock A.M., and arrived at Hoover's Gap at twelve o'clock, noon, where we encamped for the night.

June 26.—Ready to march at three o'clock A.M. Left camp at seven and marched to within one mile of Beech Grove. Were soon ordered to a position on the right, with the First brigade in front of the enemy. After ascertaining their position I opened with one piece upon a body of cavalry to our right and front, about eight hundred yards distant, and with the second piece on a battery about six hundred yards in our front. After dislodging them I opened with the section of Parrotts, commanded by Lieutenant Corbin, on a battery which was on a hill about one thousand two hundred yards to our front, and a little to our left. Lieutenant Corbin soon drove them from their position. I then received orders from General Brannan to remain at this point until further orders, which I soon received, to join the First brigade. I did so by crossing a low piece of ground and a creek, to my right, and went into battery on the top of a hill near an orchard, where we exchanged a few shots with the enemy and drove them from their position.

I was then ordered by Colonel Walker, commanding First brigade, to a wheat-field about two hundred yards to front and right, from which point I opened fire upon a body of cavalry and infantry in the edge of the woods, and about some old buildings, to our front and right some nine hundred yards. The next that attracted our fire was a battery to our left and front about one thousand two hundred yards, in the edge of the woods and partially covered by some negro huts. This battery we soon silenced, when I noticed a signal flag of the enemy, some two miles distant, delivering a message. To this I ordered Lieutenant Corbin and Lieutenant Sawyer to pay their compliments, which they did, giving their pieces full elevation. The second round from their pieces drove the signal corps from their position. I then shelled the woods from front to right, entirely clearing it of the enemy. I then moved to the right of the field, into the edge of the woods, and then forward to the position which I had been shelling, where I formed the battery, but did no firing here.

I soon moved forward again and went into position in the opposite edge of the skirt of woods. Here we were warmly met by a force of infantry and a battery, the latter being across a field about eight hundred yards, and partially obscured by the woods, the infantry occupying positions both in front and rear of their battery. Here we were hotly engaged, at intervals until dark. At one time a body of infantry was seen forming to charge upon our left. I immediately ordered Lieutenant Wheat, with his howitzers, to a position on our left, where he could get a more perfect range. He at once moved to his new position and opened on them with a deadly fire, firing low and directly into their ranks, which broke them up and forced them to retire. I then sent Lieutenant Fuller to the rear with one caisson from each section, for ammunition.

During the fight here, I lost one man killed, (Samuel Fowler,) a private, also two horses, all from the effect of the enemy's shell, which was all the loss I sustained during the day.

It becomes my duty, as well as a pleasure, to say that my men behaved, without an exception, like veterans, calm, and determined to conquer or die upon the field. I am also pleased to mention the handsome manner in which my battery was in every case supported, during this day's fighting, as well as on former occasions, by the First brigade, commanded by Colonel M. B. Walker.

June 27.—At daylight we were ready for another contest, with which, however, we were not favored. It was soon ascertained by our skirmishers that the enemy had retired from their position of last night, and at about eight A.M. I received orders to take a position on the right of the brigade, and to move to the front with them. When we arrived in the woods, which were occupied by the rebels the previous night, we came to a halt of about ten minutes, during which time I was able to learn, to some extent, the effect of our previous day's work. The ground was profusely covered with blood, mutilated clothing, and pieces of wheels and ammunition-chests. A short distance from here were nineteen dead rebels. I afterward learned from a prisoner that one of our shells burst, killing two and wounding eighteen of their infantry. He also stated that they had one piece and one caisson disabled. I then moved forward with the brigade, to Fairfield, Tenn., where we halted about an hour, and then moved forward about six miles in the direction of Manchester, Tenn., where we halted for supper. We had just fed our horses and got some coffee over the fire, when orders came to "get ready to move at once"—over went the kettles of coffee, and every man was at his post, and in ten minutes we were ready to march. Proceeding toward Manchester, we forded Duck River, and about two o'clock on the morning of the twenty-eighth, we encamped in the southern outskirts of the town.

June 28.—We marched about seven miles, toward Tullahoma, Tenn., and encamped for the night.

June 29.—Remained in camp all day. Lieutenant Corbin was sent to the front with one section of the battery for picket. Left camp at six P.M.

June 30.—Lieutenant Corbin returned to camp with the section at seven A.M.

July 1.—Marched to Tullahoma. The enemy were gone, evidently having left in great haste. We encamped one mile south of the town.

July 2.—Marched from Tullahoma in the direction of Decherd, Tennessee. Arrived at Stearns's Mill at ten o'clock A.M., where we halted to await orders. General Negley soon ordered me to the front on "double-quick." Arriving at the front, I found that the position which I was to occupy was filled by two batteries from his own division. In compliance with General Beattey's order I remained in the road, directly in their rear, until General Thomas ordered me to rejoin the First brigade, which I did, and with it moved to the upper ford on Elk River, where we encamped for the night.

July 3.—Left camp at three o'clock P.M. Crossed the river and moved forward to Marsh's Ford, where we arrived at eight o'clock P.M., and went into camp.

July 8.—Moved from Marsh's Ford to "Camp Winford, Tennessee."

I am, Lieutenant, very respectfully, your obedient servant,   J. W. CHURCH,
Captain Commanding Fourth Michigan Battery.
Lieutenant A. J. DAVIS,
Acting Assistant Adjutant-General, First Brigade, Third Division, Fourteenth Army Corps.

Doc. 116.

SLAVES IN BALTIMORE, MD.

COLONEL BIRNEY'S OFFICIAL REPORT.

BALTIMORE, July 24.

To Lieutenant-Colonel Wm. H. Cheesebrough, Assistant Adjutant-General:

SIR: I have the honor to report that immediately on the receipt of Special Order No. 202, of this date, I proceeded to Camlin's slave-pen, in Pratt street, accompanied by Lieutenant Sykes and Sergeant Southworth. I considered any guard unnecessary. The part of the prison in which slaves are confined incloses a brick paved yard, twenty-five feet in width by forty in length. The front wall is a high brick one; the other sides are occupied by the cells of prisons. In this yard no tree or shrub grows—no flower or blade of grass can be seen. Here the mid-day sun pours down its scorching rays, and no breeze comes to temper the summer heat. A few benches, a hydrant, numerous wash-tubs and clothes-lines, covered with drying clothes, were all it contained.

In this place I found twenty-six men, one boy, twenty-nine woman, and three infants. Sixteen of the men were shackled together by couples, at the ankles, by heavy irons, and one had his legs chained together by ingeniously contrived locks connected by chains suspended to his waist. I sent for a blacksmith and had the shackles and chains removed.

[The report then gives the names of the male prisoners, which we omit.]

These all expressed their desire to enlist in the service of the United States, and were conducted to the recruiting office on Camden street, to be examined by the surgeons. The women are in number thirty-three.

These unfortunates were all liberated in accordance with your orders. It appears from their statements that this slave-pen has been used chiefly for the purpose of holding persons, in evasion of the law of Congress, entitled to their freedom in the District of Columbia, and persons claimed as slaves by rebels or rebel sympathizers.

Respectfully submitted. WM. BIRNEY,
Colonel Second United States Colored Troops, Inspector and Mustering Officer.

Doc. 117.

COLONEL LAKEMAN'S REPORT

OF THE OPERATIONS OF THE THIRD MAINE REGIMENT.

HEADQUARTERS THIRD MAINE REGIMENT,
IN THE FIELD, UPPERVILLE, VA.,
July 21, 1863.

Adjutant-General State of Maine:

SIR: I have the honor to submit the following report of the movements of my regiment, with its respective brigade and division of the Third army corps, since leaving Potomac Creek, Va.:

On Thursday, June eleventh, my regiment was relieved from picket-duty on the Rappahannock River at twelve M., and at two P.M. took their position in line, and with the brigade marched to Rappahannock Station, from thence to Bealton Station, Catlet's Station, Manassas, Bull Run, Centreville, Gum Springs, and from thence to Monocacy, Md., where we arrived on the night of the twenty-fifth, performing a forced and very tedious march of twenty-seven miles that day, the rain having fallen heavily during the entire afternoon and evening. At Gum Springs, Va., four of my officers were captured by guerrillas, while breakfasting at a farm-house about one mile from the camp, Lieutenants John R. Day, and Geo. F. Blake, company H, Lieutenant H. M. Anderson, company I, and Lieutenant S. L. Gilman, company F.

The regiment marched from Monocacy to Point of Rocks, on the twenty-sixth, and from thence through Middleton, Frederick City, Walkersville, Woodborough, and Taneytown, where we arrived on the thirtieth and mustered the regiment for pay. Immediately after taking up the line of march for Emmittsburgh, where a temporary halt was made, when the entire corps were ordered on a forced march to Gettysburgh, Pa., at which place, or in its immediate vicinity, we arrived at ten o'clock on the night of the first instant, and at daylight on the following morning took position in line of battle and momentarily expected to meet the enemy. At nine o'clock A.M., the attack by the enemy on the extreme right of our line was commenced and carried on in a spirited manner, while the *left*, and in our front, was ominously still. General Sickles or-

dered a reconnoissance of the position, and chose from the corps my regiment, and one hundred sharp-shooters to "feel for and find the enemy at all hazards." At this time my regiment numbered one hundred and ninety-six rifles, and fourteen officers, but they are all heroes, as their conduct that day proved. The duty thus assigned me, with so small a command, was an arduous one; but on looking at my little line of well-tried men, I had no fear of the result. At the words, "Column forward," they advanced with measured steps and defiant bearing, and for half a mile outside our lines pierced the enemy's territory, when a dense wood obstructed my front. Here, I found a line of battle, the skirmishers covering my front. As this was the most likely spot to find the enemy, we advanced some half a mile through the wood, when the skirmishers became hotly engaged, and drove the enemy's pickets and skirmishers before them. I then advanced my regiment, and found the enemy concentrating his forces in mass on our left, with the evident intention of turning that flank. I engaged him, and for half an hour, or near, held them in check, though they came forward upon me in thousands, my gallant men, notwithstanding the disparity of force, refusing to yield one inch of ground. The brigade commander complimented me highly on the conduct of my officers and men. Said he: "Colonel, I had to send three times to you before I could get your regiment to retire. I believe you intended to stop there all day; they did nobly, sir, and your officers and men are deserving unbounded praise." For myself, I can only say that I am truly gratified with, and proud of the manner in which my officers executed my commands, and for the masterly manner they handled their companies in that trying position. In this engagement I lost forty-eight men in killed and wounded, but I have the satisfaction of knowing that *five* times that number will not cover the enemy's loss at this time, for, with every volley from the rifles of my gallant men, their ranks were fearfully thinned. Indeed, it is a matter of surprise to me, severe as was my loss, why I was not annihilated; but the fact of the enemy's random firing, while mine was measured and by command, must account for it.

My regiment retired in splendid line, giving volley after volley, long after the bugle had sounded to cease firing; but so impetuous were they to engage the enemy, that they did not seem to know or acknowledge a superior force. I then joined the brigade, and was again sent forward to hold a position in the extreme front, on the Emmittsburgh road, and placing my skeleton regiment in position in a peach orchard, which promised to be the most advantageous position I could select, and throughout the day, so harassed the enemy, that their skirmishers could not obtain a footing in our front; they charged us several times during the day, but were handsomely repulsed with great slaughter—my men obstinately refusing to relinquish the position.

In the afternoon, our position here was critical in the extreme, as we lay midway between our own and the enemy's batteries; and many of our shells, in addition to theirs, burst among us, wounding a number of my men. During the latter part of the day, we did splendid execution on the enemy's flanks as they advanced in mass, for their sole object now would seem to be in turning our flank at any cost. The slaughter was terrible, and of the conduct of my officers and men in every instance during that terrible day, I cannot speak in terms of praise sufficient. There were no stragglers reported from my regiment, but each little squad of fifteen or twenty men, which composed the fighting strength of the companies, were a host in themselves! At five P.M. the battle raged in a most terrific manner, and our gallant heroes fell thick and fast all around us, but still, those unhurt stood up to their work with coolness and confidence surprising. The enemy having concentrated his heavy masses on us, pushed them forward with perfect maniac strength and ferocity, but for nearly two hours we held them back with frightful loss to them, the entire plain in our front being strewn thickly with his dead and struggling troops. Our left flank being found weak, the brigade fell back to let the batteries open on the enemy, and my regiment, still holding its position, fell back at twilight with the First brigade, and immediately joined our own; the men being weary from hard marching, hard but glorious fighting, and scarcity of rations, were soon wrapped in slumber. The enemy were defeated along the entire line.

My entire loss throughout the day was very severe, in proportion to the strength of my regiment. My color-guard were all either killed or wounded. Captain Keene, of the color company, fell pierced by four bullets, and so severe was the engagement from four o'clock till dark, that scarcely a single officer or man in my regiment escaped without a shot through some portion of his clothing or equipments. Indeed, General Sickles did us the honor to say, that: "The little Third Maine saved the army to-day!"

On the morning of the third, I was placed in command of the brigade, and Captain Wm. C. Morgan in command of the regiment. I moved to the centre at about ten o'clock A.M., by order, to the support of General Hancock, of the Second corps, who was reported to have been heavily pressed by the concentrated columns of the enemy. I moved forward with my own gallant little regiment occupying the right and front, (with the Fourth Maine, Twentieth Indiana, and Ninety-ninth Pennsylvania,) a post of honor none will dispute with them; and although my movements were of the most hurried nature, we only arrived in time to witness the total rout of the enemy, the capture of some four thousand prisoners, and the entire field of forty acres a mass of struggling humanity; the sight was sickening, and the repulse of the enemy complete.

In this position, my regiment supported the batteries, while they shelled the mob of the enemy's troops, now rushing headlong to the cover of their earthworks, after which we moved to the extreme front and relieved the line of skirmish-

ers, and occupied the first line of defence, supported by, instead of supporting the Second corps, till the morning of the fifth, when, finding the enemy had disappeared from our front, and on being relieved, I marched my brigade to the ground occupied by the division, afterward sending forward several squads of men to gather and bring in their deceased comrades, which was done with all the solemnity possible under the circumstances.

I regret to say, that on account of not being able to visit those portions of the field where my loss was greatest, from Thursday till Sunday, the dead were, in many cases, so disfigured as to defy identification, these persons having been robbed (as usual) by the enemy (who occupied the ground on the night of the second after we had retired) of every thing portable.

On the morning of the seventh, with the brigade, division, and corps, started in pursuit of the retreating forces of the enemy.

The following is a complete revised list of the casualties up to the present date:

Field and Staff.—Major S. P. Lee, arm amputated at shoulder; Sergeant-Major Henry S. Small, killed.

Company A.—Corporal John L. Little, killed; Sergeant William Parris, wounded slightly, leg; Sergeant Charles N. Osgood, leg, severe; privates, Augustus Emery, side, severely; Ed. S. Ramsey, hand, slightly; Corporal Jona Newcomb, wounded and prisoner; privates, Wm. Hughes, prisoner; Wm. F. Crocker, missing; Phineas Small, missing; Oliver Webber, missing; Edgar W. Preble, missing.

Company B.—Sergeant Asa C. Rowe, killed; privates, John Jones killed; Nathan Call, leg amputated: First Sergeant Hannibal Johnson, prisoner; privates, Joseph Winslow, missing; Enoch Barker, missing; Charles Gannett, prisoner.

Company C.—Private Horace Dale, killed; First Sergeant Parlin Crawford, wounded in arm; Corporal Danforth M. Maxcy, leg amputated; privates, Daniel M. Moody, leg amputated; Charles M. Landers, head, slightly; John S. Lewis, hip, slightly; Charles H. Foye, foot severely; Orren Heath, hand, severely; Lyman C. Heald, leg, slightly; William H. Sturtevant, leg, slightly; Sergeant George F. Spear, missing; Corporal Charles F. Martin, missing.

Company D.—First Sergeant Eben S. Allen, leg amputated; Sergeant Shaw, wounded slightly; Corporal George Farnham, heel, severely; privates, Joseph Roach, leg amputated; Jerry Wakefield, leg, slightly; James Fletcher, missing; Patrick T. Hartnett, missing.

Company E.—Sergeant George S. Chamberlain, shoulder, severely; privates, A. H. Sprague, leg amputated; Sherburn E. George, slightly; Silas F. Leighton, slightly; Charles W. Bancroft, leg, severely; George W. Bailey, leg, severely; Alden F. Murch, leg, severely; Charles B. Rogers, leg, severely; Seth Sweatland, prisoner; Stephen M. Symons, missing.

Company F.—Corporals, Henry B. Swan, (color-guard,) killed; Amos H. Cole, killed; privates,

Asbury Luce, killed; Thomas Currier, killed; Sergeant J. P. Durgin, leg, slightly; Corporal Henry H. Chase, arm, severely; privates, William J. Rackliff, leg, severely; Charles L. Towle, thigh, severely; George E. Dorothy, leg, slightly; John H. Stevens, arm, severely; Sergeant Ora M. Nason, prisoner; privates, Frank Swan, prisoner; Luke T. Shattuck, prisoner; William H. Maxim, missing.

Company G.—Sergeants, William Brown, thigh, severely; George W. Davis, arm, slightly; privates, H. C. Webber, arm, severely; John E. Fossett, arm, severely; James Perry, leg, severely; Charles H. Arnold, prisoner; Charles C. Grover, prisoner; Henry Derocher, prisoner; Corporals Orren Austin, missing; A. P. Herrick, missing; Private, Samuel E. Frost, missing.

Company H.—Corporal Eben Farrington, killed; private, Albert Corson, killed; Color-Sergeant William Livermore, side, slightly; Corporals John Bacon, leg and arm, severely; J. F. Stanley, arm, slightly; privates, George Dickson, leg, slightly; William T. Preble, leg, slightly; C. Major, missing; P. F. Rowe, missing.

Company I.—Sergeants N. W. Jones, killed; Henry H. Lyon, killed; Corporal George L. Fellows, killed; private, Calvin Burdin, killed; Corporal H. W. Cooper, wounded; privates, Charles Bachelder, side, slightly; A. J. Bailey, hand, severely; H. W. Neal, foot, severely; A. J. Lewis, arm, slightly; Alexander Lewis, prisoner; William B. Palmer, missing.

Company K.—Captain John C. Keene, killed; privates, Albert Frost, killed; William Burgess, killed; First Lieutenant Henry Penniman, leg, severely; Sergeant Edward K. Thomas, eye, severely; Corporal A. G. H. Wood, leg and arm, severely; privates, Charles Smart, hand, severely; Henry Stearns, ankle, severely; Samuel G. Chandler, leg, severely; William Raymond, both legs, severely; William Heald, arm, severely; Henry Turner, shoulder, severely; George Perkins, knee, severely; James Ricker, prisoner; Elias Wood, prisoner; Hiram Cochran, prisoner; R. S. Key, prisoner; William Wilson, missing; George A. Butler, missing.

Making a total of one hundred and thirteen, namely, one field-officer wounded; one non-commissioned staff killed; one line-officer killed; one line-officer wounded; sixteen enlisted men killed; fifty-six enlisted men wounded; seventeen enlisted men taken prisoners; and twenty enlisted men missing.

The prisoners having all been heard from, I fear we shall ultimately be compelled to reckon the missing amongst the killed.

All of which is respectfully submitted.

M. B. LAKEMAN,
Colonel Commanding Third Maine Regiment.
JOHN L. HODSDON,
Adjutant-General State of Maine.

Doc. 118.

BATTLE OF GETTYSBURGH, PA.

OFFICIAL REPORT OF GENERAL CUSTER.

HEADQUARTERS SECOND BRIGADE, THIRD DIVISION, CAVALRY CORPS, ARMY OF THE POTOMAC, BEREA CHURCH, August 22, 1863.

Captain Estes, A.A.G., Third Division, Cavalry Corps, Army of the Potomac:

IN compliance with instructions received from the headquarters of the Third division, I have the honor to submit the following report of the part taken by my command in the engagements near Gettysburgh, July third, 1863.

At an early hour on the morning of the third, I received an order through a staff-officer of the Brigadier-General commanding the division, to move at once my command, and follow the First brigade on the road leading from Two Taverns to Gettysburgh.

Agreeably to the above instructions, my column was formed and moved out on the road designated, when a staff-officer of Brigadier-General Gregg, commanding Second division, ordered me to take my command and place it in position on the pike leading from York to Gettysburgh, which position formed the extreme right of our line of battle on that day. Upon arriving at the point designated, I immediately placed my command in position, facing toward Gettysburgh. At the same time I caused reconnoissances to be made on my front, right, and rear, but failed to discover any considerable force of the enemy. Every thing remained quiet till ten A.M., when the enemy appeared on my right flank and opened upon me with a battery of six guns, leaving two guns and a regiment to hold my first position and cover the road leading to Gettysburgh. I shifted the remaining portion of my command, forming a new line of battle at right angles to my former line. The enemy had obtained correct range of my new position and were pouring solid shot and shell into my command with great accuracy. Placing two sections of battery M, Second regular artillery, in position, I ordered them to silence the enemy's battery, which order, notwithstanding the superiority of the enemy's position, was successfully accomplished in a very short space of time. My line, as it then existed, was shaped like the letter L, the shorter branch formed of one section of battery M, supported by four squadrons of the Sixth Michigan cavalry faced toward Gettysburgh, covering the Gettysburgh pike; the long branch composed of the remaining two sections of battery N, Second artillery, supported by a portion of the Sixth Michigan cavalry on the left, and the First Michigan cavalry on the right, with the Seventh Michigan cavalry still further to the right and in advance, was held in readiness to repel any attack the enemy might make coming on the Oxford road. The Fifth Michigan cavalry was dismounted and ordered to take position in front of my centre and left. The First Michigan cavalry was held in a column of squadrons, to observe the movements of the enemy. I ordered fifty men to be sent one mile and a half on the Oxford road, while a detachment of equal size was sent one mile and a half on the road leading from Gettysburgh to York, both detachments being under the command of the gallant Major Webber, who from time to time kept me so well informed of the movements of the enemy that I was enabled to make my dispositions with complete success. At twelve o'clock an order was transmitted to me from the Brigadier-General commanding the division by one of his aids, directing me, upon being relieved by a brigade from the Second division, to move with my command and form a junction with the First brigade on the extreme left. On the arrival of the brigade of the Second division, commanded by Colonel McIntosh, I prepared to execute the order. Before I had left my position, Brigadier-General Gregg, commanding the Second division, arrived with his entire command. Learning the true condition of affairs on my front, and rightly conjecturing that the enemy was making his dispositions for vigorously attacking our position, Brigadier-General Gregg ordered me to remain in the position I then occupied. The enemy was soon after reported to be advancing on my front. The detachment of fifty men sent on the Oxford road were driven in, and at the same time the enemy's line of skirmishers, consisting of dismounted cavalry, appeared on the crest of the ridge of hills on my front. The line extended beyond my left. To repel their advance, I ordered the Fifth cavalry to a more advanced position, with instructions to maintain their ground at all hazards. Colonel Alger, commanding the Fifth, assisted by Majors Trowbridge and Ferry, of the same regiment, made such admirable disposition of their men behind fences and other defences, as enabled them to successfully repel the repeated advance of a greatly superior force. I attributed their success in a great measure to the fact that this regiment is armed with the Spencer repeating rifle, which, in the hands of brave, determined men, like those composing the Fifth Michigan cavalry, is, in my estimation, the most effective fire-arm that our cavalry can adopt. Colonel Alger held his ground until his men had exhausted their ammunition, when he was compelled to fall back on the main body. The beginning of this movement was the signal for the enemy to charge, which they did with two regiments, mounted and dismounted. I at once ordered the Seventh Michigan cavalry, Colonel Mann, to charge the advancing column of the enemy. The ground over which we had to pass was very unfavorable for the manœuvring of cavalry, but despite all obstacles this regiment advanced boldly to the assault, which was executed in splendid style, the enemy being driven from field to field until our advance reached a high and unbroken fence, behind which the enemy were strongly posted. Nothing daunted, Colonel Mann, followed by the main body of his regiment, bravely rode up to the fence and discharged their revolvers in the very face of the foe. No troops could have maintained this position; the Seventh was, therefore, compelled to retire, followed by twice the number of the enemy. By this time, Colonel Alger, of the Fifth Michigan cavalry, had succeeded in mounting a considerable portion of his regiment, and gallantly advanced to the assistance of the Seventh, whose further pursuit by the enemy he checked. At the same time an entire brigade of the enemy's cavalry, consisting of four regiments, appeared just over the crest in our front. They were formed in column of regiments. To meet this overwhelming force I had but one available regiment, the First Michigan cavalry, and the fire of battery M, Second regular artillery. I at once ordered the First to charge, but learned at the same moment that similar orders had been given by Brigadier-General Gregg. As before stated, the First was formed in column of battalions. Upon receiving the order to charge, Colonel Town, placing himself at the head of his command, ordered the "trot" and sabres to be drawn. In this manner this gallant body of men advanced to the attack of a force outnumbering them five to one. In addition to this numerical superiority, the enemy had the advantage of position, and were exultant over the repulse of the Seventh Michigan cavalry. All these facts considered, would seem to render success on the part of the First impossible. Not so, however. Arriving within a few yards of the enemy's column, the charge was ordered, and with a yell that spread terror before them, the First Michigan cavalry, led by Colonel Town, rode upon the front rank of the enemy, sabring all who came within reach. For a moment, but only a moment, that long, heavy column stood its ground, then unable to withstand the impetuosity of our attack, it gave way into a disorderly rout, leaving vast numbers of their dead and wounded in our possession, while the First, being masters of the field, had the proud satisfaction of seeing the much vaunted "chivalry," led by their favorite commander, seek safety in headlong flight. I cannot find language to express my high appreciation of the gallantry and daring displayed by the officers and men of the First Michigan cavalry. They advanced to the charge of a vastly superior force with as much order and precision as if going upon parade; and I challenge the annals of warfare to produce a more brilliant or successful charge of cavalry than the one just recounted. Nor must I forget to acknowledge the invaluable assistance rendered by battery M, Second regiment of artillery, in this charge. Our success in driving the enemy from the field is due, in a great measure, to the highly efficient manner in which the battery was handled by Lieutenant A. C. M. Pennington, assisted by Lieutenants Clark, Woodruff, and Hamilton. The enemy made but slight demonstration against us during the remainder of the day, except in one instance he attempted to turn my left flank, which attempt was most gallantly met and successfully frustrated by Second Lieutenant J. H. Kellogg, with company H, Sixth Michigan cavalry. We held possession of the field until dark, during which time we collected our dead and wounded. At dark I returned with my command to Two Taverns, where I encamped for the night. In this engagement my command lost as follows:

	Officers.	Men.
Killed......	9	69
Wounded.....................	25	207
Missing	7	225

making a total of five hundred and forty-two. Among the killed I regret to record the name of Major N. H. Ferry, of the Fifth Michigan cavalry, who fell while heroically cheering on his men. It would be impossible for me to particularize in those instances deserving especial mention; all, both men and officers, did their duty. There were many cases of personal heroism, but a list of their names would make my report too extended. To Colonel Town, commanding the First Michigan cavalry, and to the officers and men of his regiment for the gallant manner in which they drove the enemy from the field, great praise is due. Colonel Mann, of the Seventh Michigan cavalry, and Colonel Alger, of the Fifth Michigan cavalry, as well as the officers and men of their commands, are entitled to much credit for their united efforts in repelling the advance of the enemy. The Sixth Michigan cavalry rendered very good service by guarding both my right and left flank; also by supporting battery M under a very hot fire from the enemy's battery. Colonel Gray, commanding the regiment, was constantly seen wherever his presence was most needed, and is deserving of special mention. I desire to commend to your favorable notice Lieutenants Pennington, Clark, Woodruff, and Hamilton, of battery M, Second artillery, for the zeal and ability displayed by each on this occasion. My thanks are personally due to the following named members of my staff, who on many occasions exhibited remarkable gallantry in transmitting and executing my orders on the field:

Captain G. A. Drew, Sixth Michigan cavalry, Assistant Inspector-General.

First Lieutenant R. Baylis, Fifth Michigan cavalry, Acting Assistant Adjutant-General.

First Lieutenant William H. Wheeler, First Michigan cavalry, A. D. C.

First Lieutenant William Colerick, First Michigan cavalry, A. D. C.

I desire also to mention two of my buglers, Joseph Fought, company D, Fifth U. S. cavalry, and Peter Boehn, company B, Fifth U. S. cavalry; also, Orderlies Norval Churchill, company L, First Michigan cavalry, George L. Foster, company C, First Michigan cavalry, and Benjamin H. Butler, company M, First Michigan cavalry. Respectfully submitted,

G. A. CUSTER,
Brigadier-General Commanding Second Brigade.

JACOB L. GREENE,
Assistant Adjutant-General.

Doc. 119.

THE MASSACRE AT LAWRENCE, KANSAS.

STATEMENT OF WILLIAM KEMPF.*

YESTERDAY, the twenty-first of August, about half-past four o'clock, the citizens of Lawrence were surprised to hear a body of cavalry ride rapidly toward the Kansas River. As soon as the first of these men reached the river by Massachusetts street and the streets east and west of it, they raised a shout, which was repeated down the streets as far as it was possible to hear. The citizens, startled by the noise, rushed into the streets to ascertain the cause. Many of the citizens were then shot down. With the quickness of lightning, the news spread over town that the accursed Quantrell, with his bushwhackers, was in town. The surprise was so complete that it was utterly impossible for the citizens to undertake any thing whatever for their defence. The few who heroically run out with their guns were quickly murdered, as were, in fact, all who showed themselves during the first half-hour. The hills above and the woods below the town were well guarded by guerrillas, so that it was impossible for persons living on the outskirts of town to make their escape. Every thing was done by command, or well understood beforehand by these murderers. After they had spread over town, they commenced to plunder in the most deliberate manner conceivable. Every store was broken open by a few men, guarded against surprise from the inside. The first thing they looked after was the safe; then every thing else of value. Every safe was bursted open when they could not get the key; but they were so well informed about every thing, that they sent, in several instances, to the private residences of persons, demanding the keys for the safes in the stores. Well-informed citizens think they took three hundred thousand dollars in cash along with them. It would seem they took more. They had been in town some time before they commenced burning the buildings.

The inmates of the Eldridge House were roused by somebody violently beating the gong. Most of them soon assembled in the hall, and it was found that not an arm was in the house. Captain Banks told them the best thing they could do was to surrender, and this being agreed upon, Captain Banks took a white sheet, and waved it from the balcony. This was greeted by a universal shout from the guerrillas. The commander of the bushwhackers around the house asked Banks: "Do you surrender this house?" "We do, and hope that you will treat our women and children with decency." To this the rebels agreed, and Banks asked for Colonel Quantrell. Quantrell was sent for, and soon came. He asked Banks whether he was a Federal officer, and being answered in the affirmative, assured Banks that they would all be treated as prisoners,

* Mr. Kempf was an attaché of the Provost-Marshal's office at Lawrence.

and should not be molested. They were all searched, and every thing valuable taken away from them—even the finger-rings of men and women. The whole house was then ransacked, and every thing of value taken out by the guerrillas. The prisoners were marched over to the Whitney House, and there guarded.

By this time most of the plunder had been secured on horses driven together from all parts of the town. The safes had all been broken, some blown up by powder, others deliberately chiselled open. They picked out the horses, only retaining the best, and driving the poorer ones off.

At about seven o'clock they set fire to the court-house. We heard several explosions, which at a distance would have been taken for cannon-shots. We heard some person riding down the street, commanding their friends to burn the stores; and we soon heard the crackling of the fire, and saw most of the buildings east and west of us wrapped in flames. To the south we could not see from the houses we were in.

During all this time citizens were being murdered everywhere. Germans and negroes, when caught, were shot immediately. Many persons were shot down after they had been taken prisoners, and had been assured that they would not be hurt if they would surrender. Messrs. Trask and Baker, and two other citizens, were so taken, and while being marched toward the river as prisoners, after being assured that they would not be harmed, some guerrillas asked their names. Mr. Trask gave the names, when they were immediately fired upon, and all four killed on the spot, except Mr. Baker, who is not expected to live, however. Mr. Dix had been taken prisoner and his house set on fire, when one of the fiends told him, if he would give them his money, he would not be killed; otherwise he would. Mr. Dix went into the burning house, and got a thousand dollars, and handed it over. He was told to march toward the river, and had not proceeded twenty steps when he was shot dead from behind. Mr. Hampson, clerk of the Provost-Marshal, had a revolver, and tried to defend the few things he had saved from the Johnson House. His wife interfered, and they told him if he would surrender he should be treated as a prisoner, and be safe from harm. He surrendered, and was immediately shot from behind, the ball entering near the spine, and coming out below the kidneys in front. The wound is not considered fatal.

In one instance, the wife and a daughter of a man threw themselves over his body, begging for his life; but one of the murderers deliberately thrust his revolver down between the two women, and killed the man.

Before ten o'clock the body of the guerrillas left with their plunder, leaving a guard over the prisoners in town, and a few stragglers. The few persons wounded were wounded at this time by the passing fiends. In the earlier part of the day most persons were fired at from very near, and killed instantly.

One of the first persons out was Colonel Deitzler. Mr. Williamson and myself helped him carry off the dead. The sight that met us when coming out, I cannot describe. I have read of outrages committed in the so-called dark ages, and horrible as they appeared to me, they sank into insignificance in comparison with what I was then compelled to witness. Well-known citizens were lying in front of the spot where their stores or residences had been, completely roasted. The bodies were crisp and nearly black. We thought, at first, that they were all negroes, till we recognized some of them. In handling the dead bodies, pieces of roasted flesh would remain in our hands. Soon our strength failed us in this horrible and sickening work. Many could not help crying like children. Women and little children were all over town, hunting for their husbands and fathers, and sad indeed was the scene when they did finally find them among the corpses laid out for recognition. I cannot describe the horrors; language fails me, and the recollection of the scenes I witnessed makes me sick when I am compelled to repeat them.

The town is a complete ruin. The whole of the business part, and all good private residences are burned down. Every thing of value was taken along by the fiends. No store is left, and it is necessary that the good people of Leavenworth send provisions immediately. Persons who were rich yesterday are now utterly destitute.

One of the first places surrounded was the Eldridge House. It seems the guerrillas demanded a surrender before firing into it. After a short consultation the occupants concluded to surrender, and a white flag (sheet) appeared from the balcony, which was greeted with cheers. Quantrell was sent for, and made his appearance. On being asked what were his intentions, he replied, "Plunder;" he finally agreed that they should be protected, and gave them an escort to a place of safety. The last-named place not being found safe on account of indiscriminate shooting by the men, Quantrell allowed them to go to the Whitney House, kept by Mr. Stone. Quantrell said Mr. Stone once saved his life, and he was not the man to forget past favors. As soon as the Eldridge was surrendered, the house was searched. The inmates of the rooms were aroused from their beds, and their money, jewelry, and other valuables demanded of them. Some gentlemen from Ohio who occupied one room were not as expeditious as the guerrillas thought, and they commenced firing through the door. One ball took effect in the calf of the leg of one of them. This same man was again shot through the shoulder, but is now doing well at the Merchants', in this city. Soon after, the building was destroyed; whether it was fired or caught from the adjoining buildings, we have not heard. It is supposed that a gentleman who has been connected with L. Levenson & Co., who had a store underneath, was burned.

After the second move, the Eldridge House

party, which numbered about sixty, were safely, as they supposed, located in the Whitney House. Quantrell had chosen this place for his headquarters, and swore he would shoot any of his men who attempted to molest any of them. Many people, knowing this, slipped in and were saved. One brute came in upon his horse while the party were going from one place to the other, and was told by one of Quantrell's head men, named Porter, that he would kill him if he did not dry up. Every thing went on very well while Quantrell was there; he promised that he would be the last man to leave the town, and none of his men should return. He took a lunch, and finally ordered the command to move out of the city, which they did. After mounting his horse, he lifted his hat to the ladies, and bowing politely, said: "Ladies, I now bid you good morning. I hope when we meet again, it will be under more favorable circumstances." Putting spurs to his horse, he was soon out of sight. He was dressed in a dark-colored shirt, blue blouse, and had on a black hat. After Quantrell left, four of his men came back and said they were determined to kill some one out of the crowd—didn't much care who; that they had been promised the privilege of killing all they pleased, and through some reason, Quantrell had been humbugged. One of the party said that he had a sister killed in the prison at Kansas City, and another said that he had a sister shot by Union men; the third said he wanted to kill Miss Lydia Stone, the landlord's daughter; the fourth was a sober man, and seemed anxious to help save the lives of those in the house. It seems that one of the party had forcibly taken possession of a gold ring from Miss Stone, and she informed Quantrell of the fact, who told the fellow if he did not hand it over he would shoot him. But Miss Stone escaped. They wanted also to kill Mr. R. S. Stevens and another man, but they made their escape through a back-door to the bank of the river, where they could be protected by the few soldiers across the river. The men prowled through the house, but did not find what they wanted. Finally they ordered all in the house to form a line outside. This was done. One gentleman answered, Central Ohio. The fellow said that was as bad as Kansas, and shot him, but the wound did not prove fatal. Others were shot. Mr. Stone remonstrated with them, when one of them shot him through the head, killing him almost instantly. The party then left. It is reported that three of them were killed before getting out of town.

The banks were robbed, as well as the safes of the stores and offices. One man gave up all he had, and was then shot down. It is supposed they carried away in greenbacks some ten thousand dollars. The other property—except horses—they took away, was not much. The loss is estimated at between one and two millions.

Among the houses saved was that of ex-Governor Robinson, which, fortunately, is situated on the bank of the river. The guerrillas came and ordered the family (Mr. Robinson not being at home) to take out what they wanted, as they were going to burn it. They then left for town. When they returned, they were greeted with a volley from a small party of the Twelfth Kansas, on the opposite side, and three killed. Thinking the game would not pay, the scamps left.

General Lane had a miraculous escape. He heard the firing, and saw Willis's stable burning, and made tracks through a large corn-field near his house. Inquiries were made by the gang for Lane's house, and a Mr. Spicer was detailed by them to show his house. Placing a pistol to his head they compelled him to pilot them to Lane's house. They could not catch the General, but burnt his house. The General soon after made his appearance, and is now after the murderers.

Eighteen soldiers out of twenty-two, of the Kansas Fourteenth, at their recruiting rendezvous, near Lawrence, were shot; also a number of negroes of the Second colored regiment, were killed.

There were many heroic deeds performed by the ladies. In many instances they placed themselves between their husbands and fathers and danger when the drunken fiends held cocked pistols at them. One lady we hear spoken of and deserves particular mention; her name is Miss Lydia Stone, daughter of the landlord of the Whitney House. She moved round through the crowd doing all she could to alleviate the suffering. The dead body of one person was on fire, and she at once procured water and put it out. When the scoundrels came back a second time, saying they would kill some one, she replied, that: "They might as well kill me as any body." Heroic deeds were performed by other ladies whose names have escaped us.

One of the most cowardly acts was the shooting at men, women, and children as they passed down under the bank toward the river.

There is no doubt but that Quantrell had spies at Lawrence. One man at the Eldridge House acted as a guide, and pointed out prominent men and things.

One fellow got Captain Banks's uniform and made quite a display with it.

A riding party of two ladies and gentlemen were met just outside the city, and compelled to go back. Quantrell invited the ladies to ride beside him into town, and they did so.

General Collamore was suffocated to death by damps in his well. When he first discovered the guerrillas in town, he went into the well, and his hired man, named Keith, covered it up. After the trouble was over, the man went to the well and found the General at the bottom. He went down after him, and unfortunately met the same fate. A neighbor, named Lowe, passing along, went down to rescue both of them, and was also suffocated.

It was peculiarly noticeable that the fury of the incarnate fiends was particularly directed against the Germans and the few unfortunate negroes who were in the doomed city.

Doc. 120.

OPERATIONS IN MIDDLE TENNESSEE.

GENERAL ROSECRANS'S REPORT.

HEADQUARTERS DEPARTMENT OF THE CUMBERLAND,
WINCHESTER, TENN., July 24, 1863.

GENERAL: For the information of the General-in-Chief and the War Department, I respectfully submit the following report of the preliminaries and operations which resulted in driving the rebels out of Middle Tennessee, from the occupation of Murfreesboro, a point two hundred and twelve miles from the nearest point of supplies.

To enable this army to operate successfully in advance of this position, it was necessary—

1. To establish and secure a dépôt of supplies at this point.

2. To organize an adequate cavalry force to combat that of the enemy, protect our own line of communication, and take advantage of the enemy should he be beaten or retreat.

The dépôt was established and in a defensible condition by the first of May, as has been reported, but the inferior numbers of our cavalry and the scarcity of long forage wore out our cavalry horses faster than we could replace them, and it was not before the fifteenth of June that we had brought what we had into available condition.

The General-in-Chief has been informed of the reasons why an advance was not deemed advisable until all things were prepared.

THE POSITION OF THE REBELS.

Their main base of supplies was at Chattanooga, but a vastly superior cavalry force had enabled them to command all the resources of the Duck River Valley and the country southward. Tullahoma, a large intrenched camp, situated on the "barrens" at the intersection of the Nashville and Chattanooga Railroad with the McMinnville branch, was their main dépôt. Its front was covered by the defiles of Duck River, a deep narrow stream, with but few fords or bridges, and a rough, rocky range of hills which divides the "barrens" from the lower level of Middle Tennessee.

Bragg's main army occupied a strong position north of Duck River, the infantry extending from Shelbyville to Wartrace, and their cavalry on their right to McMinnville, and on their left to Columbia and Spring Hill, where Forrest was concentrated and threatening Franklin.

The position of Bragg's infantry was covered by a range of high, rough, rocky hills, the principal routes passing southward from Murfreesboro toward Tullahoma and line of the enemy's communications.

1. By McMinnville it is seventy-five miles to Tullahoma. Its length precludes it, while the intermediate by-roads between that and Manchester were so difficult as to be regarded as unsuited for the movement of an army; and

2. The Manchester Pike passing these hills through Hoover's Gap and ascending to the "barrens" through a long, difficult cañon, called Matt's Hollow.

3. The Wartrace road through Liberty Gap, which passes into the one along the railroad by Bellbuckle Gap.

4. The Shelbyville turnpike running through Guy's Gap.

5. The Middleton dirt road.

6. The road by Versailles, into the Shelbyville and Triune roads, both of which avoid passes and have few defiles.

The enemy held all these passes, and his main position in front of Shelbyville was strengthened by a redan line extending from Horse Mountain on the east, to Duck River on the west, covered by a line of abattis.

Polk's corps was at Shelbyville. Hardee's headquarters was at Wartrace, and his troops held Hoover's, Liberty, and Bellbuckle Gaps. Polk's corps was generally estimated by intelligent rebels and Union men at about eighteen thousand, infantry and artillery; Hardee's, at twelve thousand, infantry and artillery—making a total of thirty thousand of these arms, and probably eight thousand effective cavalry.

Positive information from various sources concurred to show the enemy intended to fight us in his intrenchments at Shelbyville, should we advance by that route, and that he would be in good position to retreat if beaten, and so retard our pursuit through the narrow winding roads from that place which lead up to the "barrens," and thus inflict severe loss without danger to their own line of retreat to the mountains toward the base. I was determined to render useless their intrenchments, and, if possible, secure their line of retreat by turning their right and moving on the railroad bridge across Elk River. This would compel a battle on our own ground, or drive them on a disadvantageous line of retreat. To accomplish this, it was necessary to make Bragg believe we could advance on him by the Shelbyville route, and to keep up the impression, if possible, until we had reached Manchester with the main body of the army, as this point must be reached over a single practicable road passing through Hoover's Gap, a narrow way three miles in length, between high hills, and then through Matt's Hollow, a gorge two miles long, with scarce room anywhere for wagons to pass each other. These passes were occupied by the enemy, but eight miles from Hardee's headquarters, not more than sixteen miles from their left at Shelbyville.

The plan was, therefore, to move General Granger's command to Triune, and thus create the impression of our intention to advance on them by the Shelbyville and Triune pikes, while cavalry movements and an infantry advance toward Woodbury would seem to be feints designed by us to deceive Bragg, and conceal our supposed real designs on their left when the topography and the roads presented comparatively slight obstacles and afforded great facilities for moving in force.

Events proved that this had the desired effect; and accordingly Bragg called forward Buckner and all the spare troops at his command from East-Tennessee and the lines of the railroads, the last of them arriving on the very evening they began their retreat from their position in front of Duck River. The operations which followed these successful preliminaries were as follows:

On the twenty-third of June, Major-General Granger, under orders, sent General Mitchell, with his cavalry division, on the Eagleville and Shelbyville pike, to make a furious attack on the enemy's cavalry and drive in their infantry guards on their main line, while General Granger, with his own troops and Brannan's division, moved, with ten days' rations, to Salem, sending his sick and baggage to the camps at Murfreesboro. On the same day Palmer's division and a brigade of cavalry were ordered to move, *via* Cripple Creek and Readyville, to the vicinity of Bradyville; his advance to seize the head of the defile leading up to the "barrens" by an obscure road leading them to Manchester by Lumley's Station. All the other troops were ordered to be in readiness to march with twelve days' rations of bread, coffee, sugar, and salt; six days' meat on hoof, and six days' pork or bacon. General Mitchell accomplished his work after a sharp and gallant fight, for the details of which I must refer you to his own report. General Granger arrived and took position at Salem, in pursuance of orders.

The corps commanders met at headquarters in the evening, when the plan of the movement was explained to them, and each received written orders for his part, as follows:

Major-General McCook's corps was to advance on the Shelbyville road, turn to the left, move two divisions by Millersburgh, and, advancing on the Wartrace road, seize and hold Liberty Gap. The third division was to advance on Fosterville, and cover the crossing of General Granger's command from the Middleton road, and then move by Christiana to join the rest of the corps.

General G. Granger was to advance on the Middleton road, threatening that place, and cover the passing of General Brannan's division of the Fourteenth corps, which was to pass by Christiana and bivouac with the rear division of the Twentieth corps.

The Fourteenth corps, Major-General Thomas, was to advance on the Manchester pike, seize and hold with its advance, if practicable, Hoover's Gap, and bivouac so as to command and cover that and the Millersburgh road, so that McCook and himself could be within supporting distance of each other.

Major-General Crittenden was to leave Van Cleve's division of the Twenty-first army corps at Murfreesboro, concentrate at Bradyville with the other two, and await orders.

The cavalry, one brigade under General Turchin, was sent with the Twenty-first army corps to look out toward McMinnville. All the remainder under Major-General Stanley, were to meet General Mitchell coming in from Versailles, and attack the rebel cavalry at Middleton.

The headquarters of the army was to be established at Mrs. McGill's, at Big Spring branch.

All these movements were executed with commendable promptitude and success in the midst of a continuous and drenching rain, which so softened the ground on all the dirt roads as to render them next to impassable.

General McCook's taking of Liberty Gap was very gallant and creditable to the troops of Johnson's division, Willich's brigade leading, supported by Carlin's brigade of Davis's division on the right.

General Reynolds had the advance in the Fourteenth corps, Wilder's mounted brigade leading. He surprised and carried Hoover's Gap, a defile three miles in length, before the main infantry support of the rebels (two brigades) could come up, and when they did arrive, fought them and held the position until the remainder of Reynolds's division arrived. The enemy kept at artillery distance from them, and left us to hold the bridge across the Garrison fork and the debouch of the Fairfield road. For the details of this fight, I refer to the reports of the immediate commanders of the troops.

As it was not yet certain whether the enemy would advance to test our strength on McCook's front or mass on the flank of the Fourteenth corps, near Fairfield, the orders for June twenty-fifth were as follows:

Major-General Crittenden to advance to Lannon's Stand, six miles east of Beech Grove, and open communication with General Thomas.

General Thomas to attack the rebels on the flank of his advance position at the forks of the road, and drive the rebels toward Fairfield.

General McCook to feign and advance, as if in force, on the Wartrace road, by the Liberty Gap passes.

General Stanley with his cavalry to occupy their attention at Fosterville, and General Granger to support him with his infantry at Christiana.

Should Thomas succeed, and find the enemy retreating toward Wartrace, he was to cover that road with a division, and move with the remainder of troops rapidly on Manchester, McCook to move in and taking his place at Beech Grove, holding Liberty Gap with a division, and finally withdrawing that and following Thomas to Manchester. The incessant rain delayed the arrival of General Brannan to join the Fourteenth corps on the Manchester pike; but every thing was finally in position, and General Reynolds's division had advanced on the heights toward Fairfield, but did not attack the enemy, who appeared to show a disposition to contest our advance by that route. At Liberty Gap the enemy tried to regain possession, but finally retreated, leaving our pickets in position.

On the twenty-sixth, most of the movements ordered for the twenty-fifth were completed, amid continuous rains. Generals Rousseau, Reynolds, and Brannan's divisions coöperated in a gallant advance on the enemy, who after a short resistance fled toward Fairfield, near to which place our pickets were advanced, while Reynolds's division and the baggage moved forward during the night toward Manchester, Wilder's brigade having seized Matt's Hollow early in the afternoon, and thus secured the passage.

June twenty-seventh, headquarters reached Manchester, where General Reynolds's and part of Negley's division had already arrived. The remainder of Thomas's corps came in during the night. It was now manifest that the enemy must leave his intrenched position at Shelbyville, and that we must expect him at Tullahoma, only twelve miles distant. It was therefore necessary to close up our column on Manchester, distribute our rations, and prepare for the contest.

While this was progressing, I determined to cut, if possible, the railroad in Bragg's rear. Wilder's brigade was sent to burn Elk River bridge and destroy the railroad between Decherd and Cowan, and Brigadier-General John Beatty, with a brigade of infantry, to Hillsboro, to cover and support his movements.

General Sheridan's division came in June twenty-eighth, and all McCook's corps arrived before the night of the twenty-ninth, troops and animals much jaded.

The terrible rains and desperate roads so delayed Crittenden, who on the twenty-sixth got orders to march to Manchester with all speed, that it was not until the twenty-ninth that his last division arrived, badly worn. The column being now closed up, and having divisions of the Fourteenth and Twentieth corps at Crumpton's Creek, orders were given for the Fourteenth corps to occupy the centre at Concord Church and Bobo Cross-Roads, with a division in reserve.

The Twentieth corps to take the right on Crumpton's Creek, two divisions in echelon retired, one in reserve. The Twenty-first corps to come up on the left, near Hall's Chapel, one division front and one division in reserve.

It rained almost incessantly during the thirtieth, but the troops, by dint of labor and perseverance, had dragged their artillery and themselves through the mud into position. It is a singular characteristic of the soil on the "barrens," that it becomes so soft and spongy that wagons cut into it as if it were a swamp, and even horses cannot pass over it without similar results. The terrible effect of the rains on the passage of our troops may be inferred from the single fact that General Crittenden required four days of incessant labor to advance the distance of twenty-one miles.

While the troops were thus moving into position, General Thomas sent Steadman's brigade of Brannan's division, two regiments of Reynolds's division, and two regiments of Negley's division, on separate roads, to reconnoitre the enemy's position, while General Sheridan sent Bradley's brigade of his own division on another for the same purpose. These reconnoissances all returned and reported having found the enemy in force on all roads except the one leading to Estill

Springs. Scouts all confirmed this, with the fact that it was the general belief that Bragg would fight us in his intrenchments at Tullahoma.

Wilder returned from his expedition, reporting that he found the enemy at Elk Bridge, with a brigade of infantry and a battery, which prevented him from destroying that bridge; but he had damaged the road considerably at Decherd, where his appearance with his mountain howitzers created great consternation, and within three hours brought down some heavy trains of infantry.

Meanwhile we had information that Stanley's cavalry, supported by Major-General Granger's infantry, and acting under his general directions, had attacked the enemy's cavalry and artillery at Guy's Gap, on the Murfreesboro and Shelbyville pike, and driven them from stand to stand, killing, wounding, and capturing as they went, until the enemy reached their intrenchments, from which they were soon driven by flanking and a direct charge, wherein the cavalry captured three pieces of artillery, some with loads in, but not rammed down.

From their intrenchments the rebels fled to town, when they made another stand, but in vain. Our cavalry came down with resistless sweep, and drove them in confusion into the river. Many were killed and drowned, and Shelbyville, with a large number of prisoners, a quantity of arms and commissary stores, were the crowning results of the cavalry operations that day. It was worthy of note that the waving of flags and cheers of welcome from the inhabitants of this unconquerable stronghold of loyalty, doubtless added vigor and energy to the advance of our troops. The reports from this cavalry battle showed also the enemy's withdrawal on Tullahoma, and the general expectation that he would fight there.

June thirtieth, orders having been given to General Morton to ascertain the practicability of moving by column in mass in line of battle from our position, to gain the rear of the rebel position at Tullahoma, and who reported favorably thereon, preparations were completed, and Crittenden's Second division was moved into position.

July first, I received a despatch from General Thomas that the enemy had retreated from Tullahoma during the night.

Brannan's, Negley's, and Sheridan's divisions entered Tullahoma, where the infantry arrived about noon. Negley's and Rousseau's divisions pushed on by Spring Creek, and overtook the rear-guard of the enemy late in the afternoon, at Bethpage Bridge, two miles above the railroad crossing, where they had a sharp skirmish with the rebels occupying the heights, south side the river, and commanding the bridge by artillery, which they had placed behind epaulements.

July second, having brought forward the ammunition, McCook with two divisions pursued on the roads west of the railroad. Arriving at Rock Creek ford, General Sheridan found Elk so swollen as to be barely fordable for cavalry, and the rebel cavalry on the south bank to resist a crossing, but he soon drove them away and occupied the ford. General Thomas found equal difficulties in crossing, for the enemy during the night burned the bridge and retired before morning. General Turchin, with a small brigade of cavalry, had pushed forward from Hillsboro, on the Decherd road, and found the enemy's cavalry at the fords of Elk, near Morris Ferry; engaged them coming up, and, reënforced by the arrival of General Mitchell, they forced the passage of the river after a sharp conflict. Night closed the pursuit.

July third, General Sheridan succeeded in crossing Elk River, and, supported by General J. C. Davis's division, pursued the enemy to Cowan, where he learned the enemy had crossed the mountains with his artillery and infantry by University and Sweden's Cove, and that the cavalry only would be found covering their rear. General Thomas got over his troops the same day, Negley's division moving on the Brakefield Point road toward the University. Sheridan sent some cavalry from his position, and Stanley some from the main column, now in pursuit, but they only developed the fact that the enemy was gone, and as our troops were out of provisions, and the roads worn well-nigh impracticable from rain and travel, they were obliged to halt till their supplies could be brought forward from Murfreesboro, to which point the wagons had been sent for that purpose.

Thus ended a nine days' campaign, which drove the enemy from two fortified positions, and gave us possession of Middle Tennessee, conducted in one of the most extraordinary rains ever known in Tennessee at that period of the year, over a soil that becomes almost a quicksand. Our operations were retarded thirty-six hours at Hoover's Gap, and sixty hours at and in front of Manchester, which alone prevented us from getting possession of his communications, and forcing the enemy to a very disastrous battle. These results were far more successful than was anticipated, and could only have been obtained by a surprise as to the direction and force of our movement.

For the details of the action at Liberty Gap, Hoover's Gap, Shelbyville, and Rover, I beg to refer to the reports of Major-Generals Thomas, McCook, and Stanley, and the accompanying sub-reports.*

Bearing testimony to the spirit and gallantry of all, both officers and men, I must refer to the reports of the several commanders for the details thereof. I am especially proud of and gratified for the loyal support and soldierly devotion of the corps and division commanders, all the more touching to me as the movement was one which they regarded with some doubt, if not distrust. It affords me pleasure to return my thanks to Major-General Granger and Major-General Stanley, commanding the cavalry, for their operations on our right, resulting in the capture of

* For these Reports see Supplement.

Shelbyville; and to General Granger for subsequently despatching our supplies when they were so pressingly needed.

Colonel Wilder and his brigade deserve a special mention for long-continued exertions, enterprise, and efficiency in these operations. Colonel Wilder ought to be made a brigadier-general. Colonel Minty, who commanded the advance on Shelbyville, for gallantry on that and many other occasions, merits the like promotion.

The management of the medical department was worthy of all praise. I cannot forbear to make special mention of the energy, ability, foresight, and devotion to duty of Dr. Perin. His superior in these qualities has not fallen under my observation.

All my staff merited my warm approbation for ability, zeal, and devotion to duty, but I am sure they will not consider it invidious if I especially mention Brigadier-General Garfield, ever active, prudent, and sagacious. I feel much indebted to him for both counsel and assistance in the administration of this army. He possesses the instincts and energy of a great commander.

The reports of the corps commanders herewith show our total loss during these operations was:

	Killed.	Wounded.	Missing.
Officers,	14	26	..
Non-Commissioned officers and privates,	71	436	13
Total,	85	462	13

We captured —— stand small arms, eight field-pieces, six caissons, three limbers, three rifled siege-pieces without carriages, besides arms destroyed by the cavalry. Quartermasters' stores: eighty-nine tents, eighty-nine flies, three thousand five hundred sacks corn and corn-meal.

The total number of prisoners taken, as will be seen by the accompanying report of the Provost-Marshal General, Major Wiles, is fifty-nine commissioned officers, and one thousand five hundred and seventy-five non-commissioned officers and privates.

Before closing this report, I call the attention of the General-in-Chief and the War Department to the merits and ability of Captain W. E. Merrill, the engineer, whose successful collection and embodiment of topographical information, rapidly printed by Captain Morgadanti's quick process, and distributed to corps and division commanders, has already contributed very greatly to the ease and success of our movements over a country of difficult and hitherto unknown topography. I sincerely trust the War Department will show its appreciation of the merits and services of this promising young officer, who fortified the frontiers of Western Virginia, lingered in a rebel prison for six months, was wounded at Yorktown, and who put in order and a state of defence the Kentucky Railroad, injured by Bragg and Kirby Smith.

W. S. ROSECRANS,
Major-General.

Brigadier-General L. THOMAS,
Adjutant-General, Washington, D. C.

Doc. 121.

ADDRESS OF THE REBEL GOVERNORS.

AUGUST 13TH, 1863.

To the People of Texas, Louisiana, Arkansas, and Missouri, and the Allied Indian Nations:

AT the invitation of the Lieutenant-General commanding the Trans-Mississippi Department, we assembled at this place, with several of your Judges, confederate Senators, and other distinguished citizens, to confer with him on the measures to be taken for the defence of our common cause. Those measures we do not particularize, as they had best be disclosed by the execution of them, and by the benefits they must produce. Coming to a thorough understanding with him, the members of the conference unanimously sustain the vigorous and decided policy he proposes to pursue.

We will not attempt to disguise the change in our position by the fall of our stronghold on the Mississippi River. Interrupting communication between the two sections of the Confederacy, it throws each mainly on its own resources. But the apprehensions of evil from this interruption have been greatly exaggerated. The warning given by the fall of New-Orleans has not been unheeded, and the interval since that event has been used to develop the great resources of this department. We now are self-dependent, but also self-sustaining.

With our own manufactories of cannon, arms, powder, and other munitions of war, with mines opened and factories established, with cotton as a basis for financial measures, and with abundance of food, we are able to conduct a vigorous defence, and seize occasions for offensive operations against the enemy. The immense extent of our territory, the uncertainty of navigating our rivers, the unwholesomeness of the regions through which our interior is approached, the difficulties of transportation on our roads, present immense obstacles to the advance of large armies of the enemy, with their cumbrous trains of luxurious supplies; small bodies will ignominiously fall in the attempt at our subjugation. To crush even his largest armies, we rely on the energy and skill of our military commanders, the zeal and activity of our civil authorities, the discipline and courage of our armies, and the vigorous, self-sacrificing patriotism of our whole people. There is every thing to incite us to renewed efforts, nothing to justify despondency.

We are fortunate in the military chief of this department. In the prime of life, large experience, active, intelligent, and with the prestige of uniform success in his undertakings, he is guided by a profound respect for law and the constitutional rights of the citizens. Reposing full trust in him, we cordially commend him to your entire confidence and support. In view of the existing state of our affairs, he has been clothed with more than usual powers by the President, to be exercised within the bounds of the Constitution and the law. These just and legal powers he may have to exert, promptly and boldly, to their fullest extent, for the common good; in so doing he will receive the zealous support of every patriot. The entire military force and means in this department should be liberally used for our protection when necessary. Some measures may inconvenience particular individuals, but we rely on their patriotism and good sense to produce a cheerful endurance of the hardships to be expected in a war for our very existence as a nation.

To organize and combine without delay the individual efforts of our citizens to sustain our cause, we have formed, unofficially, a Committee of Public Safety, to be composed of the Executives, for the time being, of the States in this department, and have selected the Governor of Missouri as present Chairman thereof. By committees of correspondence and voluntary associations in every parish and county, we hope to unite all our patriotic citizens in a vigorous support of the confederate and State authorities in defence of our families and homes. Let every one rally to the call and promptly perfect an organization which will fill the Southern heart with renewed enthusiasm throughout the whole department. Let a patriotic press and clergy stimulate exertion. Under the searching eye of a whole people aroused to ceaseless vigilance, the plots of secret foes will wither in the bud. By the wholesome influence, gentle and peaceful, but imposing, of an organized, all-pervading patriotic public opinion, the despondent will be inspired with fresh hope, the steadfast be nerved to heroic energy, the rapacious extortioner learn liberality, the selfish trimmer abandon his neutrality, and the vile traitor be cowed into the inaction of despair.

We address you in the true language of firm confidence in the final triumph of our cause, concealing nothing of our perils, exaggerating nothing of our hopes. Our powerful and haughty foes propose not only to coerce us into submission, but to despoil us of our whole property, and subject us to every species of ignominy. Base is he who would not continue to contend for our rights even when all shall be lost but honor. The capitalist must be liberal of his means, the speculator forego his gain, the straggler hasten to his regiment, every able-bodied man hold himself in readiness for military service; our women, the glory of our race, tend the loom and even follow the plough; our boys guard the homes their fathers are defending on the frontier, and Western skill and valor will prepare a San Jacinto defeat for every invading army that pollutes the soil of this department. Unsurpassed in courage, intelligence, and energy, you have only to arise in your might and the enemy will be speedily driven back. Be true to yourselves, your past history, to your hopes of the future, and a baffled foe will gladly seek the peace which we war to obtain.

The enemy may dismiss all hopes that the Western section of the Confederacy will seek any destiny separate from that of our sisters east of the Mississippi. Attached to the Confederacy by community of race, institutions, and interests, baptized in the blood we and they have poured out together, we desire no new political connection. Let our eastern confederates do their duty; these States and our Indian allies will do theirs, and when our joint efforts shall have secured our common safety, the remembrance of the danger from a temporary cessation of intercourse will only strengthen the ties which bind us together. In the darkest hours of our history, the protection extended to us by Almighty God has been so manifest, as even to be acknowledged by candid foes. Their victories have been to them as fruit turning to ashes on their lips; our defeats have been chastenings to improve us and arouse our energies. On His help and our own right arms we steadfastly rely; counting on aid neither from the policy of neutral nations, nor from the distractions in the midst of our enemies, we look confidently forward to the day when thirteen confederate States will in peace and safety occupy their rightful position among the great powers of the earth.

THOMAS O. MOORE,
Governor of the State of Louisiana.
F. R. LUBBOCK,
Governor of the State of Texas.
HARRIS FLANNAGAN,
Governor of the State of Arkansas.
THOMAS C. REYNOLDS,
Governor of the State of Missouri.

MARSHALL, TEXAS, August 18, 1863.

Doc. 122.

THE EAST-TENNESSEE CAMPAIGN.

OPERATIONS OF GENERAL BURNSIDE.

MAJOR W. H. CHURCH'S ACCOUNT.

GENERAL BURNSIDE left Camp Nelson on the sixteenth of August for East-Tennessee. He left Crab Orchard on the twenty-fourth, having completed his preparations, his columns having been in motion for several days. He reached Mount Vernon, twenty miles distant, on the same day. He left Mount Vernon on the twenty-third, and reached London, twenty-five miles. On the twenty-fourth he reached Williamsburgh, thirty miles from London. On the twenty-fifth he reached Chitwood, Tennessee, twenty-eight miles southwest of Williamsburgh, where he came up with Major-General Hartsuff, commanding the Twenty-third army corps. Major Emory here made a cavalry reconnoissance toward Jacksboro, encountered two regiments of rebel cavalry, and routed them, taking forty-five prisoners. General Burnside, with the main body of his army, left Chitwood on the twenty-eighth and reached Montgomery, the county-seat of Morgan County, Tennessee, forty-two miles from Chitwood, on the thirtieth. Here another column of infantry, under Colonel Julius White, came in, having marched from Central Kentucky, by way of Albany, Monticello, and Jamestown. Colonel Burt, commanding the cavalry advance, sent word that the rebel General Pegram was holding the gap in the mountains, near the Emery Iron-Works, with

two thousand men. The position was a very strong one, and the gap was the gate to the Clinch River Valley. A battle was expected, as there was not a better place in the country to check our forces. But on the morning of the thirty-first it was discovered that the enemy had fled in the night.

Emery River, nine miles east of Montgomery, General Burnside ordered Colonel Foster to march directly on Knoxville, where he arrived and took the town without opposition on the first of September. General Burnside proceeded to Kingston, where his scouts encountered the cavalry pickets of General Rosecrans, and communicated with a splendid body of cavalry of the army of the Cumberland, under Colonel Minty. Burnside's object in moving to Kingston was to make a push for the great Loudon bridge over the Holston River. This was twenty miles from Kingston. General Shackleford was sent to London. On his approach the rebels retreated across the bridge, which they had barricaded, and fired it. Turpentine had been poured on the planks, and it was soon a mass of flames. Our troops fired across the river with artillery and musketry, and the people in the neighborhood said several rebels were killed and wounded. General Burnside left Kingston on the second and entered Knoxville on the third. The reception of our troops at this place was most gratifying. General Buckner with his rear-guard had left the day before Colonel Foster's arrival, for Chattanooga. There is reason to believe Rosecrans had in front of him, at Chattanooga, the whole force of Buckner, Bragg, and Johnston. The people about Knoxville say the flight of the rebels, when Burnside's approach was announced, was something wonderful. Their panic was immense. They had a report among them that Burnside had an army of from sixty to one hundred and twenty thousand men, and were of the opinion that their safety depended upon their speed. They left behind a considerable quantity of quartermaster's stores in pretty good order, and they had several valuable shops which they did not dismantle. Two million rations of salt were among the spoils. The secesh had a story that Longstreet was coming from Virginia with twenty thousand men, but it was one of their vain imaginings.

The East-Tennessee troops, of whom General Burnside had a considerable number, were kept constantly in the advance, and were received with expressions of the profoundest gratitude by the people, who are described as the most heartily and generally loyal people in the United States. There were many thrilling scenes of the meeting of our East-Tennessee soldiers with their families, from whom they had been so long separated.

The East-Tennesseeans were so glad to see our soldiers that they cooked every thing they had and gave it to them freely, not asking pay, and apparently not thinking of it. Women stood by the roadside with pails of water, and displayed Union flags. The wonder was, where all the stars and stripes came from. Knoxville was radiant with flags. At a point on the road, from Kingston to Knoxville, sixty women and girls stood by the roadside waving Union flags and shouting: "Hurrah for the Union." Old ladies rushed out of their houses and wanted to see General Burnside and shake hands with him, and cried: "Welcome, welcome, General Burnside, welcome to East-Tennessee!"

A meeting of the Union citizens of Knoxville was held and addressed by General Burnside and General Carter. It was attended by about five hundred men, and a large number of women and children. The demonstrations were not boisterous, but there was intense, quiet rejoicing. Men who had been hidden for months, came in, full of gratitude for their deliverance.

The people of Knoxville made many inquiries for Parson Brownlow, who has their confidence as no other man has. They thought the old flag, supported by United States bayonets, meant Brownlow, and will look for him daily until he comes. The people of East-Tennessee generally want to see Andy Johnson, whom they look upon as a sort of political high-priest. The reception that awaits Johnson and Brownlow will be a remarkable exhibition of the enthusiastic devotion of people who have suffered to those who have been true to their cause.

About Knoxville the people were pointing out the hiding places of rebel stores, and were zealous in so doing. The prominent secessionists at Knoxville fled with Buckner. There are a few left who have assisted the secession blood-hounds, and the popular expression was: "They must leave here or they must die. They can't live here."

Intelligence was received that the rebels were prepared to make a stand at Cumberland Gap. Burnside was not afraid of their standing, but of their running, and on the fifth, despatched General Shackleford from Knoxville to cut off all means of escape. On the seventh General Burnside left Knoxville with a force of cavalry and artillery, and arrived at Shackleford's headquarters early on the morning of the ninth. General De Courcey, who had advanced upon the Gap, direct from London, Kentucky, was hemming the rebels in on the north side. The rebel force was commanded by General Frazer, of Mississippi. He had, when rumors of Burnside's movements reached Buckner, been ordered by that General to fall back to Knoxville, but the order was countermanded by Johnston, and Frazer's instructions were to hold the Gap to the last extremity. When Burnside arrived, Frazer had been summoned to surrender by both De Courcey and Shackleford, and had returned a firm refusal. Burnside sent an officer with a flag of truce, demanding an unconditional surrender, instructing the officer to wait for an answer at the picket-line only one hour. At the expiration of the hour, no answer having been given, the officer withdrew. Preparations for an immediate attack were made, but in fifteen minutes General Frazer sent a flag of truce, offering to surrender the position, provided he and his men were paroled on the spot. General Burnside responded that

under the cartel of the United States Government and the confederates for the exchange of prisoners, Frazer had no right to stipulate for a parole on the spot, and that he must insist upon the surrender being unconditional.

Pretty soon General Frazer sent a very politely worded letter, saying he was convinced that he could not resist the force brought against him, and he would yield to the fortunes of war. His brigade consisted of two North-Carolina, one Virginia, and one Georgia regiment, and some artillery companies, with fourteen guns. The Georgia regiment was the Fifty-fifth, and was eight hundred strong. The effective force was above two thousand men. The prisoners are on their way to this place, and will arrive here some time this week. The North-Carolina and Virginia regiments were small, owing to desertions. They were bitterly dissatisfied with the war. A vote was taken a few days before the surrender, by the North-Carolina regiments, (that is, the regiments were polled to ascertain the sentiments of the soldiers,) and there was a considerable majority in favor of giving up the Southern Confederacy and restoring the Union! The Georgians, however, were fighting men, and the regiment composed of them was the only reliable one General Frazer had.

On the seventh, two days before the surrender, two companies of Shackleford's men penetrated the rebel lines, and burned the mill upon which the garrison at the Gap depended for their supply of flour. It was a hazardous and brilliant affair.

When Shackleford's advance was at Tazewell, they were fired upon by a rebel company of home guards, and one man was killed. This was the only casualty of the campaign! General Burnside expected to leave the Gap on Thursday, (tenth,) to return to Knoxville.

The information given of the outrages committed by the secessionists, confirm and more than confirm all that Brownlow has had to say of them. There is hardly a neighborhood in which Union men have not been murdered, and hundreds of them have been hidden for months in caves in the mountains, and supplied with food by the women. The able-bodied males were all absent in the army or wandering in exile. The roads in South-Eastern Kentucky now swarm with them, returning to their long deserted homes. The women and old men and children have done a wonderful work raising crops. The wheat crop was very large and heavy, and supplies collected by the rebels fell into our hands at Knoxville and elsewhere. The country is full of corn, mostly raised by women, and there will be no difficulty in supplying the army from the territory it occupies. Guerrilla warfare is not feared, as the loyalty of the inhabitants will prevent it. Kentucky also is becoming settled. There is not a symptom of bushwhackers from Covington to Cumberland Gap. A traveller could ride from here to Knoxville undisturbed.

The people of East-Tennessee care little about the "policy of the Administration." All they want is that the rebels shall be whipped and the Union restored. They have no fears after that. They associate, as well they may, liberty, justice, and peace with the Union; and they know they have had oppression, anarchy, and bloodshed in the Southern Confederacy. It is a common expression among them: "We were born under the old flag and the Constitution. They are good enough for us, and we intend to die under them."

General Carter, an East-Tennessean, has been appointed Provost-Marshal General of East-Tennessee. He is well known to, and highly esteemed by the inhabitants, and is the right man in the right place.

Our forces have occupied the East-Tennessee Railroad as far east as Morristown, and the indications were that they might extend their lines at pleasure. A considerable force had proceeded down the road toward Chattanooga. The universal report was, that the rebels were disheartened and demoralized so that there was no fight in them. They fled like sheep from Emery's Gap, and showed all the signs of being a worthless rabble.

Our troops, on the contrary, were in splendid spirits—perfectly happy and in high condition. The infantry marched with surprising alacrity and rapidity. They thought nothing of moving twenty-five miles per day, and would go into camp, after such a march, merry as school-boys. They were delighted to be the liberators of East-Tennessee, and feel that they were not in an enemy's country.

Doc. 123.

BATTLE OF CHICKAMAUGA.

A NATIONAL ACCOUNT.*

HEADQUARTERS ARMY OF THE CUMBERLAND,
Monday, Sept. 21, 1863.

THE rebel army, after evacuating Chattanooga, retired to La Fayette, twenty-eight miles to the southward, concentrated his troops at that point, restored their courage and hopes by the promise of reënforcements, and awaited the arrival of the same. Meantime he took possession of the gaps in Pigeon Mountain, (which General Rosecrans must cross in order to reach the Georgia State road and the great railroad which formed Bragg's line of communication with Atlanta,) and carefully fortified them. This obstruction delayed for some hours the advance of our forces, which had already crossed the Raccoon and Lookout Mountains, and gave the enemy time not only to recover their spirits, but to receive a portion of their reënforcements.

Hitherto our army had been marching in three great columns—Crittenden, followed by Granger, by way of Chattanooga; Thomas, by way of Trenton; and McCook, with Stanley's cavalry, still further to the southward. The daily increasing numbers and boldness of the enemy compelled a concentration of our forces as rapid-

* See Docs. pages 217 and 363, *ante.*

ly as the nature of the case would admit, and by evening of the tenth inst., the whole army was in line along the West-Chickamauga, between the Lookout and Pigeon Mountains, and just to the east of that low chain of wooded hills called Mission Ridge.

On Thursday, the seventeenth, the army shifted toward the north, contracted its lines, and, as the enemy's demonstrations became each hour more threatening, prepared for battle.

On Friday morning the extreme left of the army rested upon the Chickamauga, at Gordon's Mill, the point where the La Fayette road crosses the Chickamauga, about twelve miles south-west of Chattanooga. The right could only be loosely defined, and was in a constant state of preparation to shift northward, in order to baffle the rebels, who seemed bent on turning our left and getting between us and Chattanooga.

About eleven A.M., hearing some cannonading to the northward, I started from near the centre of our lines, and, riding past Palmer's and Van Cleve's divisions, came upon General Wood's troops at Gordon's Mill. Here had this dauntless commander been stationed for a week, liable at any moment to be attacked from La Fayette by the whole army of the enemy, and cut to pieces before assistance could reach him. But it was a matter of the first importance that, while Crittenden's main body was moving to form a junction with Thomas, the rebels should not be allowed to get in the rear of the former and take Chattanooga. Consequently, Wood was ordered to hold this important point at all hazards, and as long as possible, and if overpowered, to fall back to Rossville, renew the fight there, and *then,* if he could not sustain himself, to retreat to the foot of Lookout Mountains, and at the narrow passage between it and the river to fight while a man remained. To execute his difficult and perilous task General Wood had but two brigades, Harker's and Buell's, General Wagner's command, of his division, having been left in Chattanooga.

On Thursday night the concentration of our forces in the vicinity of the mill promised these faithful guardians relief; but on Friday morning, at the hour I have mentioned, General Wood found that his two brigades, still in position, constituted the extreme left division of the army in line, only Wilder's mounted infantry and Minty's cavalry being any further down the Chickamauga.

A stronger position naturally than that which General Wood occupied can scarcely be imagined. The creek at Gordon's Mill bends round in the form of a semicircle, the convexity being toward the south, whence the enemy would have advanced toward General Wood. An eminence, forming what would be a diameter of the circle if completed, runs from east to west, uniting the extremities of the bend. Upon this, General Wood had placed his artillery. The creek itself, of considerable depth, and with a bank several feet high upon our side of it, constituted a splendid ditch, and all along its bank lay Wood's men, behind a rude but efficient breastwork of logs and rails.

I am particular in describing this position, because the enemy's movements made for the purpose of avoiding it were the immediate cause of bringing on the battle of Saturday.

This state of things continued until one o'clock, when Van Cleve moved from his place in line, and took position upon Wood's left, while Palmer, marching by the left flank, came into communication with Wood's right. This made an immense opening between General Crittenden's corps and the left wing of General Thomas, which was eventually filled by another general shifting from south to north.

Meantime the sound of a brisk cannonade in the direction of Ringgold indicated either that our mounted troops or General Granger's corps were engaged with the enemy. From half-past one to three, couriers came dashing past, now from Minty and now from Wilder, bearing despatches to Wood, or Crittenden, or Rosecrans, the general tenor of which was, that they were fighting the enemy briskly, and, although meeting with some losses, were firmly holding their ground.

In fact, there were to-day three separate affairs, each one of which is of sufficient importance to engage for a moment the attention of the historian.

By marching on the east side of the Tennessee, from Bridgeport immediately to the rear and left of General Crittenden, General Gordon Granger, with the reserve corps, had reached a position a few miles south of Chattanooga. On Friday morning he sent General Steadman with two of his brigades, Colonel Dan McCook's and Colonel John G. Mitchell's, to beat up the enemy's quarters in the vicinity of Reid's Bridge over the Chickamauga, and discover his intentions in that direction. The movement was successful. Colonel McCook claims to have first encountered Longstreet's men; and the fact that he brought in some twenty-five prisoners from McNary's brigade of Hood's division, is pretty solid evidence that his claim is well founded. Advancing toward Ringgold, the two brigades, after some skirmishing, were about to engage a much larger force of rebels, when a peremptory order arrived for them to fall back immediately to their old position.

On Thursday, Minty and Wilder were at Reid's Bridge, but on Friday morning Wilder moved to Anderson's Bridge, higher up the creek. During the day the latter closely watched the enemy's movements, and observed a troop of rebel cavalry come through Napier's Gap, in Pigeon Mountain, and move toward General Wood's position at Gordon's Mill.

At the same time a strong column came over, directly in front of Wilder, and another column, boldly advancing on the Ringgold road, threatened Minty. Both attacked simultaneously. Wilder succeeded in repulsing his opponents, but Minty's flank being turned by the rebels, he was considerably distressed, until the more fortunate Wilder sent two regiments and a section of artillery to his assistance. With the help of these he maintained his ground; but the same movement by which the rebels had succeeded in turning Minty's right flank enabled them to get upon Wilder's left and in his rear. Under these disadvantageous circumstances, the latter was compelled to renew the fight; but, although severely pressed, he succeeded in holding the bridge until near dark. Then fresh forces of the enemy coming up and his own men being entirely exhausted, Wilder began to fall back. The rebels perceiving this, made a determined effort to cut him off. He slowly retired, resisting at every step, until he arrived to within a mile and a half of Gordon's Mill, where the Forty-fourth Indiana and Fifty-ninth Ohio coming to his assistance, he was enabled to check the rebels and encamp for the night. During the night, his own pickets and those of the enemy actually grasped each other's guns in the darkness, and several times engaged in fierce struggles for their possession!

Before daylight Wilder was ordered to move to the La Fayette road, and take position there, which he did, throwing up for his protection a breastwork of rails.

All night long on Friday night the movement of Thomas's corps continued. Crittenden's was already in the position it was intended to hold the next day, so that Thomas passed it by and placed his divisions upon the left of the line. General Negley being in position at Owens's Ford, higher up the valley, for the purpose of preventing the enemy from coming into the breach which Thomas's movements would leave in our line, General Johnson's division, of McCook's corps, reported to General Thomas, and marched with him to take position upon the left of Crittenden. Generals Davis and Sheridan were in the mean time moving as rapidly as possible toward the left, so as to connect with the right of Crittenden, and thus complete the line, which would be much shorter than it was the day before.

For the first half of the night during which the march I am referring to took place, every thing was comfortable enough, but near midnight it turned freezingly cold, and as it was necessary, after passing General Crittenden, for us to feel our way with caution, long wearisome halts took place, during which skirmishers scoured the woods immediately upon our front and right flank. The boys who were not skirmishing becoming very cold during these halts, began to kindle fires at every stopping-place to warm themselves. At first they made these fires of logs of wood and rails taken from the neighboring fences, but afterward they ceased to trouble themselves about removing the rails, and set fire to the fences themselves wherever they chanced to stop. In the course of an hour a line of fires stretching all along the La Fayette road illuminated the clouds above, and showed the silent columns of General Thomas gliding by like an army of spectres!

At last the weary march came to an end; the

artillery was wheeled into position, and the marching columns facing to the right stood in order of battle looking toward the east.

An hour or two longer and the sun rose in glory, thawed the crisp white frost which had collected upon the grass, dispersed the mists that had gathered around the tops of the mountains, and sending a golden light into the valley of the Chickamauga, showed at least two thirds of the Union army drawn up in battle array. Not that any individual, save old Sol, could see them all; for the peculiar nature of the ground, covered almost everywhere with thick woods, rendered it impossible in many places to see even the whole of a single regiment.

As soon as the sun was fairly risen, I mounted my horse, intending to ride to the extreme left of our line, and thence to proceed from left to right, so as to get as accurate an idea of it as possible before the real work of the day should commence. Riding about a mile I saw troops coming into the road from the woods to the east of it, and had I not perceived through my glass that they were habited in blue, I should have judged, from the direction whence they came, that they were a portion of the rebel army. Suddenly I saw a courier shoot out from the crowd and coming toward me hatless and with frantic speed.

As he came, a dozen rifle-cracks from the woods skirting a corn-field along which he was passing, informed me that hostile demonstrations of some kind were being made in our immediate vicinity. I halted until the courier came up. He delivered his despatches to another horseman, who immediately started with them toward the headquarters of General Thomas. I then asked the hatless courier what troops those were ahead. He informed me that they were the two brigades (Colonel Mitchell's and Colonel McCook's) of General Gordon's corps, who had been skirmishing the day before in the neighborhood of Reid's Bridge and of Ringgold, as I have already described. They had come to form a junction with the main army, had halted and were waiting for orders.

Soon after this, an order from General Rosecrans, which had reached General Granger by another route, directed the two brigades to fall back at once to Rossville, get a supply of rations for three days, and hold themselves in readiness to march at a moment's notice. As the close proximity of the rebels rendered it somewhat difficult just then to reach General Baird's men, who were nearest to me on the right, I "fell back" with General Granger's troops, and remained in the vicinity of Rossville until the sounds of battle in the direction whence I had come attracted my attention. A wild gallop back to the left immediately ensued.

A few miles' riding brought us so far on the way that we began to get glimpses of that stream of wreck, debris, mingled life and mangled humanity which always flows from a battle-field. For a time we asked the news of each one we came to, and the replies filled us alternately with sorrow, with indignation, with keen apprehension, and with hopes.

One said the battle had been going on several hours, and our arms had met with disaster along the whole line.

Another declared that although unsuccessful at first, our troops at length recovered their ground, and were now driving the enemy.

Here comes a single soldier, covered with dust and sweat. Let us question him. "Where do you belong?" "To the regular brigade." "Has it been engaged this morning?" "I should think it had." "With what result?" "It is nearly all cut to pieces." "Which regiment is yours?" "The Sixteenth United infantry." "Did it suffer much?" "Only thirty or forty of its members are left."

Here is a man with an arm roughly bandaged and very bloody. The blood has dried upon it and hangs to it in great black clots. "Who are you?" "Private ——, of the Thirty-eighth Indiana." "What news have you?" "Bad enough." "Has your regiment been in the fight?" "If it has not no one has." "With what result?" "One third of its members are killed and wounded." "Were you whipped?" "Our brigade was left unsupported, overpowered by numbers, and compelled for a time to give way." "Is Colonel Scribner safe?" "So far as I know, he is."

Another with a ghastly wound in the head has upon his jacket the red stripes which show him to be an artilleryman. "Whose battery do you belong to?" "Guenther's." "Why, that is the regular battery belonging to General King's brigade; what has it been doing?" "It has all been taken by the enemy." "Can that be possible?" "It is, but I have heard since that it was retaken." "How came it to be lost?" "The infantry supports gave way, and the horses being nearly all killed, of course the guns were captured."

The stream grew stronger and stronger. Stragglers were run over by wagons dashing back toward the rear. Ambulances, filled with wounded, came in long procession from toward where the battle was raging. Men with wounds of every imaginable description not affecting their locomotion, came staggering by on foot, and scores even of those who had been shot in their lower limbs, hobbled slowly on through blinding masses of dust, which at times concealed every thing from view.

At length we reached the hospital for General Brannan's division. The house had already been filled. The outhouses had been brought into requisition, and large numbers of sufferers were lying on the ground in the yard. In one corner was an operating table, beneath which lay the usual quantity of legs, arms, hands, feet, fingers, and toes. Here and there among the wounded were some cold and stiff, the seal of death upon their countenances. These had died after being carried to the yard.

During all this time the roar of battle in front of us never ceased for a moment, and now we began to get authentic intelligence of the progress and incidents of the fight.

The flame of battle had first broken out upon the extreme left, where General Brannan's division was posted. The troops composing it behaved most gallantly; some of the regiments had covered themselves with glory, but they were compelled to retire at length, leaving uncovered the left flank of General Baird, upon which the enemy at once threw himself with great force.

The brigade commanded by Colonel B. F. Scribner, Thirty-eighth Indiana, one of the very first in the army, was left particularly exposed, as its right flank had been somewhat too far advanced where it had taken position in the morning.

Almost before its pickets were driven in, it found itself literally surrounded by thrice its numbers, who came on with their infernal yells, pouring volley after volley of deadly bullets into the very bosom of this gallant brigade. For a moment it was thrown into confusion, and that moment sufficed to place the rebels upon its front, flanks, and rear. The Second, Thirty-third, and Ninety-fourth Ohio, the Thirty-eighth Indiana, the Tenth Wisconsin, and Loomis's battery are composed of the best material in their respective States, and their commander, Scribner, succeeded in infusing into them his own magnanimous and gallant spirit. Gathering together their broken ranks under the infernal fire which every instant mowed them down, and following their heroic leader, they charged the dense legions surrounding them, and like a whirlwind in a forest, tore their way through.

But, alas! the guns of the immortal First Michigan battery were left behind—those black, stern-looking, rifled cannon, each one of whom I had come to regard with a feeling of almost reverential awe, because upon a dozen battle-fields I had seen them flinging destruction into the ranks of traitors, and never knew them once turned against a legion of my country's enemies which they did not scatter like leaves before the blast. Even in the opinion of the rebels themselves, Loomis had made these guns invincible. They were commanded now by a young man who, possessing naturally the noblest qualities, had thoroughly learned the lessons of his teacher, and promised to prove a most worthy successor, even to Loomis himself—Lieutenant Van Pelt. Van Pelt loved his pieces with the same unselfish devotion which he manifested for his wife. In the desperate conflict which broke around Scribner's brigade he managed the battery with much dexterity and coolness, and for some moments rocked the very trees over the heads of the rebels by the fiery blasts from his guns. But his horses were shot down. Many of his artillerists were killed or wounded. The infantry supporting him had been compelled to turn and cut their way through the enemy, and a horde of traitors rushed up to the muzzles of the now harmless pieces. Van Pelt, almost alone, stationed himself in front of them and drew his sword. "Scoundrels," said he, "dare not to touch these guns!" The miserable barbarians, unable to appreciate true hero-

ism, brutally murdered him where he stood. The history of the war furnishes not an incident more touching or more sublime than the death of Lieutenant Van Pelt.

All the guns of the battery save one fell into the enemy's hands.

Along the entire line of the left and centre there were similar instances of heroism, only two or three of which I have time to mention.

At one time the guns of the Forty-fourth Indiana battery (Captain Bush) were all in the hands of the enemy, but were retaken subsequently by a simultaneous charge of the infantry and artillerymen. This battery is attached to General Starkweather's brigade.

During the fierce assault upon the First division, the Second Ohio, being in confusion, was rallied by General Baird in person, and led back to a most effective charge.

Major-General J. J. Reynolds, who combines the chivalrous courage of an olden knight with the cool, calm ability of a Turenne, had time, not only to keep his own division in effective order, but to give his generous assistance to the forces around him. A tremendous onslaught of the enemy broke General Palmer's lines, and scattered several of his regiments in wild dismay toward the rear. Amongst these was the Sixth Ohio, which, in charge of the fine-spirited Anderson, had, up to this moment, nobly maintained its ground. General Reynolds perceiving the danger, quick as lightning threw himself amongst the brave but broken Guthries.

"Boys!" he shouted, "are you the soldiers of the Sixth Ohio, who fought with me at Cheat Mountain? You never turned your backs upon traitors in Virginia. Will you do it here?"

"No! no!" they screamed almost frantically. "Lead us back! lead us back!!"

From every quarter came rushing up the scattered fragments of the regiment; with magic swiftness they re-formed the ranks; with General Reynolds at their head, they charged the insolent enemy, and, after a moment's struggle, every rebel in front of them not killed or wounded was in confused retreat.

The example of the Sixth Ohio was communicated to the flying fragments of other regiments, and it is a fact which will long be memorable in the history of this battle, that these rallied stragglers, principally from Palmer's division, reformed ranks almost of their own accord, and drove back the enemy who had been victoriously pressing on.

But I cannot linger to gather up these scattering facts. Let me endeavor to give a brief and succinct view of the course of events on Saturday, and then pass on to the great drama of the succeeding day.

The shifting of Thomas's corps during the night of Friday placed it on the left of the line, in the following order: Brannan on the extreme left, Baird next, and Reynolds next. Negley was assisting Wood to hold the passage of Owen's Ford and the position of Gordon's Mill, which had now become our extreme right. One division of McCook's corps, (Johnson's,) having come up to the new line sooner than the rest, reported to Thomas for orders, and was assigned to a position upon the left, between Baird and Reynolds. Two divisions of Crittenden's corps held the centre of the line, Palmer on the right of Reynolds, and Van Cleve next to Palmer. When the battle began, Davis and Sheridan, of McCook's corps, were rapidly marching toward the left, to complete the line and take possession on the right of Van Cleve. Generally, the line took the direction of the Chickamauga, withdrawn upon the left so as to follow for a considerable distance the course of the La Fayette road, which runs directly north and south.

It was between ten and eleven when Cronton's brigade, of Brannan's division, going down to a ford over the creek, just opposite their position, encountered the enemy, who was advancing in force, and, after a gallant combat, was driven back. Reënforcements immediately coming from the remainder of Brannan's division, the rebels in turn were driven pell-mell toward the ford. Another terrible charge by a largely increased force of the enemy pushed back the whole of Brannan's division, involving General Baird, who at once became fiercely engaged. The regulars, outflanked after the withdrawal of Brannan's men, fought like tigers, but were rolled back and over Scribner's brigade — the right of which being rather too far advanced, was crumpled up, and the brigade literally surrounded, until, by unparalleled gallantry, it cut its way through. The storm, rolling from left to right, fell next upon Johnson, and almost simultaneously upon Reynolds, who both fought with desperate valor, wavering at times, but again regaining their firmness, giving back a little, but again advancing, until the troops of Brannan and Baird, rallied by their able leaders, and by the personal exertions of Thomas himself, whose courage was as conspicuous as his coolness, came up once more to the work.

Then the order was issued for the entire line to advance, and nothing in history exceeds in grandeur the charge of that powerful corps. Longstreet's men from Virginia were directly opposed to the troops of Thomas, and although they fought with stubborn determination, they could not for an instant check the slow and stately march of our battalions. In vain they rallied and re-rallied; in vain they formed double lines, which fired simultaneously; in vain they wheeled their cannon into a score of new positions. Thomas moved resistlessly on. Much of our artillery lost in the morning was re-captured. Seven pieces were taken from the enemy. They had been pushed already three quarters of a mile, and Longstreet was threatened with actual annihilation, when a new danger caused Thomas to halt.

While our left was so remorselessly driving the rebels, Polk and Hill, collecting their chosen legions, threw them with great impetuosity upon Palmer and Van Cleve, in order to effect a diversion in favor of Longstreet. An obstinate contest ensued, but the overpowering numbers of the enemy speedily broke to pieces large portions of our two divisions, especially Van Cleve's. In fact, the rout of this part of our line was becoming as complete as that of the enemy's right, when Davis, who had been marching up as rapidly as possible to intersect with Van Cleve's left, arrived upon the ground, went in most gallantly, and for a time restored in that locality the fortunes of the day. But the enemy knowing that all depended upon his effecting a diversion in favor of the defeated Longstreet, massed nearly the whole of his available force, hurled it upon Van Cleve and Davis, drove the former to the left and the latter to the right, and entered boldly the opening thus made. It was just at this juncture that Thomas's troops, whose attention had been called to the extreme danger of our centre, began to return. Reynolds immediately sent the heroic Wilder to the assistance of Davis, and the celebrated brigade of mounted infantry at first scattered the enemy in terror before them. But the persevering rebels rallying again, and charging in fresh numbers, even Wilder began to fall slowly back. General Sheridan, who had been following after Davis, now came up, and led Colonel Bradley's brigade into the fight. It held its own nobly, until the rebels, in large force, getting possession of a piece of timber near its flank, opened upon it an enfilading fire, which compelled it to give way.

But now new actors appear upon the scene. Wood and Negley, who had gallantly repelled the assaults of the enemy at Owen's Ford, (assaults intended as a feint to conceal the design of the enemy upon our left,) came up to the rescue. Their troops went to work with a will. The progress of the enemy against Davis, Van Cleve, and Sheridan was speedily checked. Reynolds, returning from the pursuit of Longstreet, assisted in rallying the broken battalions of Palmer. Thousands of our scattered troops reörganized almost of their own accord. Baird, Brannan, and Johnson resumed their places. A consuming fire swept all along our front. The rebels retired everywhere before it, and before sunset our line was in battle array upon almost precisely the ground held that morning.

Just before dusk, the enemy, as if in spite of his unsuccessful efforts, opened a heavy fire of artillery and musketry upon the same troops, and continued it until after nightfall. But it was so promptly returned that he sustained certainly as much injury as he inflicted, and about six o'clock he drew off entirely, leaving the day clearly our own.

During the night of Saturday some change was made in the disposition of our forces, and the line was so far withdrawn that it rested along a cross-road running north-east and south-west, and connecting the Rossville with the La Fayette road. By this arrangement our extreme right was made to rest on Mission Ridge, as it should probably have done in the first place. The new line that was formed was a mile shorter than that of the day before.

The changes in the order of the different divisions made the new line stand thus: One brigade of Negley's division was on the extreme right; then came Johnson, then Baird, then Palmer, then Reynolds, then Brannan, then Negley's other brigades, then Van Cleve, then Wood, and then Sheridan. Wilder and Minty, with their mounted force, held the extreme right. I have given only the general order of our line; Brannan and Van Cleve were really held somewhat in reserve. That was indeed a night of awful suspense which settled around us after the last gun had been fired on Saturday.

The morrow came. No sound of cracking musketry, or roaring of cannon, or bursting shell disturbed the peacefulness of that Sabbath morning. The first hour after sunrise passed. "Surely," said our officers and soldiers, "there will be no fight; for if the enemy had intended to attack us he would, following his usual tactics, have fallen upon us at daybreak."

Two hours more had gone by, and some dropping musketry began to be heard along the various parts of our line. Finally, at about ten o'clock, there were several fierce volleys, and the loud booming of half a dozen pieces of artillery announced that the enemy had again, as on the day before, assaulted our left.

And now that the battle has begun, let us glance one moment at the contending forces. On one side is our old army which fought at Stone River, reënforced by two divisions (Brannan's and Reynolds's) of Thomas's corps, and Starkweather's brigade, of Baird's division. But counterbalancing these to some extent, Post's brigade of Davis's division and Wagner's of Wood's were both absent. We might or might not also rely for assistance upon Steadman's division of General Granger's corps.

Opposed to these was the old army of the Tennessee, which Bragg has so long commanded; Longstreet's formidable corps from Virginia, one half of Johnston's army from Mississippi; Buckner's division from East-Tennessee; Dabney Maury's division from Mobile; Brigadier-General Lee's command from Atlanta, and from twelve to fifteen thousand fresh troops in the service of the State of Georgia—in all, amounting to at least seventy-five thousand men. The Union army confronting them was certainly not more than fifty-five thousand strong.

The firing which had begun on our left swelled almost immediately into a dreadful roar, which filled even the souls of the bravest with awe. Nothing that I have yet listened to since the breaking out of the war exceeded it in continuity and volume of sound. It was not a tumult which now rages and now subsides, but one which for two long hours rolled incessantly all along the lines of Thomas's seemingly devoted corps. So loud was the crash of musketry that the repeated discharges of cannon, following each other in quick succession, could with difficulty be distinguished, and seemed only like more emphatic passages in the grand diapason of thunderous harmony which burst from the vast clouds of smoke and dust enveloping the contending hosts.

The fight upon the extreme left commenced by a desperate assault of the enemy upon General John Beatty's brigade of Negley's division. The brigade, as well as its famous leader, stood their ground nobly; but being somewhat isolated from the remainder of the line, finally retired. It will be remembered that the other brigades of Negley's division were posted much further to the right. A desire to reünite the two portions of his command induced General Rosecrans to send General Wood to take General Negley's place in the line until the latter should effect the reünion of his brigades. Wood proceeded immediately to execute the order, filling up the gap as Negley retired. The rebels, understanding this movement of Negley's to be a retreat, immediately advanced their skirmishers, not only here, but all along the left, and the fighting at once became terrific, as I have described. The rebels, however, soon ceased to attack General Wood's front, and for a time appeared to devote their entire attention to General Thomas. I went down to the extreme left of General Wood's position about this time, and looking thence into some corn-fields, could see the desperate efforts of the enemy to break the lines of Brannan and Reynolds. The soldiers of these two noble divisions were lying behind rude breastworks of logs and rails constructed the night before; their artillery in the rear fired over their heads, and it really seemed as if that long line of defences was some immense serpent, instinct with hideous life, and breathing continually from its huge tough sides volumes of smoke and flame.

Again and again the rebel lines advancing from the cover of the woods into the open corn-fields, charged with impetuous fury and terrific yells toward the breastworks of logs and rails, but each time the fiery blasts from our batteries and battalions swept over and around them, and their ranks were crumbled and swept away as a bank of loose clay washed by a rushing flood. But as fast as one line fell off another appeared, rushing sternly on over the dead and bleeding bodies of their fallen comrades. Longstreet's corps was seeking to regain its lost laurels of yesterday. D. H. Hill, at the head of Hardee's old corps, was lending them the assistance of a division, and Buckner's troops were throwing their weight into the scale. Thomas fought only with his forces of Saturday weakened by Saturday's heavy losses. It was an unequal contest, and a pang of agony shot through my heart as I saw our exhausted veterans begin to waver. To waver in the face of the charging, shouting, thundering host which confronted them, was to lose all, and the next moment wave after wave of the rebel sea came surging down toward the breastworks, dashing madly against and over the barrier, and greedily swallowing up its defenders, with all their ammunition and *materiel*. Never was resistance more stubborn and determined, but never was attack prosecuted with more devilish pertinacity.

Meantime, as General Reynolds was so sorely pressed, General Wood was ordered to march instantly by the left flank, pass Brannan, and go to his relief. Davis and Sheridan were to shift over to the left, and thus close up the line. As the occasion was urgent, General Wood drew in his skirmishers with considerable haste, and the rebels for the second time mistaking a withdrawal for a flight, pressed forward like a torrent and poured into the flanks of General Wood a storm of musket-balls, canister, and grape. Moving upon the double-quick, the men endeavored for a time to keep their files in order, but as that pitiless storm of lead and iron continued to be hurled against them, the regiments began to spread out like a fan, wider and wider, until they were finally torn to flinders. This was especially the case with the brigade commanded by Colonel Buell. The undaunted Wood, with Harker's brigade comparatively intact, passed on to his destination.

Here was the great turning-point in the battle. Here, indeed, the battle was lost.

Davis coming up to fill the vacancy occasioned by Wood's withdrawal, was caught upon the left flank by the fiery rebel torrent now pouring through the opening, and pushed off toward the right in utter disorder, like a door swung back upon the hinges and shattered by the same blow. Van Cleve, and what remained of Palmer, were struck upon the other side, and shivered as a sapling by a thunderbolt. Even the personal exertions of Rosecrans himself, who, with drawn sword and at the head of his devoted staff, endeavored to check the rout, was ineffectual.

After that fatal break our line of battle was not again re-formed during the day. The army was in fact cut in two; McCook, with Davis, Sheridan, and Wilder, being thrown off to the right, (Crittenden — except one brigade of Wood's — being broken in pieces,) and Thomas, with his indomitable corps, and Johnson's division of McCook's, remaining alone upon the left. In the fierce tornado which had swept over his log breastworks, Thomas had been much shaken, all his divisions fighting desperately, all rallying at the earliest practicable moment, but only General Reynolds retiring from the works toward the hills in any thing like tolerable order.

As soon, however, as the corps had reached the foot of Mission Ridge, it formed anew its broken ranks with an alacrity and rapidity less remarkable than the obstinacy with which it so long endured the assault of the enemy upon the level ground below. The great leader himself, General Thomas, assisted by Baird, Reynolds, Brannan, Scribner, Harker, Negley, John Beatty, Wood, and Turchin, reörganized the brigades with wonderful celerity, and immediately began making head against the enemy.

From this, McCook disappeared from the general history of the battle, as, indeed, extricating himself from his demoralized and routed corps, he headed toward Chattanooga, and at about one o'clock disappeared entirely from the field. His two divisions, Davis's and Sheridan's, forced off

toward the right, far behind their original position, were assailed by immense squadrons of the enemy, and fearfully battered. Each had but a handful left as it retired, toward nightfall, upon the Rossville road, but the men must have done gallant fighting or they would not have come off as well as they did. In fact, wherever Sheridan is, whether isolated or in company, and whether the odds against him be one or many, there is certain to be a fight.

It was about half-past twelve when, hearing a heavy cannonade upon the right, I galloped over in that direction to see what it might mean. A longitudinal gap in Mission Ridge admits the Rossville road into Chattanooga Valley, and skirts along a large corn-field at the mouth of the gap. Looking across the corn-field from the gap you see thick woods upon the other side. The corn-field itself is a sort of "cove" in the ridge, and here were numbers of all sorts of army vehicles mingled with the debris of dismantled and discomfited batteries. Fragments of Davis's flying squadrons had also lodged in this field.

While I stood gazing upon this scene from the summit of the ridge, some rebel skirmishers appeared in the skirts of the woods opposite the gap I have mentioned, and flung perhaps a dozen musket-balls into the field. Instantly men, animals, vehicles became a mass of struggling, cursing, shouting, frightened life. Every thing and every body appeared to dash headlong from the narrow gap, and men, horses, mules, ambulances, baggage-wagons, ammunition-wagons, artillery-carriages and chissons were rolled and tumbled together in a confused, inextricable, and finally motionless mass, completely blocking up the mouth of the gaps. Nearly all this booty subsequently fell into the hands of the enemy. Sickened and disgusted by the spectacle, I turned away to watch the operations of General Thomas's corps, upon which alone depended the safety of the army.

General Thomas had withdrawn his men almost entirely from the valley, and taken up a position on the side of Mission Ridge. His left still rested on the La Fayette road, and his right upon the ridge near the gap I have already spoken of. Here were collected the shattered remnants of the powerful corps which had so long breasted the fierce assaults of the enemy in the forenoon. Here was Johnson, who seems to have done better work to-day and yesterday than ever before. Here was the unconquerable Wood, with Harker's brigade, and here were also such fragments of Crittenden's corps as could be induced to venture upon another stand. The whole were drawn up in a line forming a circular curve, facing the southeast. A hill near the middle of the curve was the key of the position, and Harker's brigade was appointed to defend the same. Soon after the hill was occupied, a house upon its summit was set on fire by the enemy's shells, and continued to burn for a long time with great fury.

Not long was the new line of battle permitted to remain idle. Cannon bellowed against it missiles of every kind were hurled into it; shells burst above it; rifle-balls went tearing through it; but still it remained firm.

It was certain, however, as truth itself, that unless assistance should reach it from some quarter, and that right speedily, it must at length succumb, for the rebel leaders, emboldened by the rout of McCook and Crittenden, were gathering their hosts to hurl them in a last mighty effort against the feeble band that confronted them. Whence should that succor come?

Suddenly a vast cloud of dust was seen to rise above the trees, away to the left, and a few minutes afterward long lines of men emerged from the woods, crossed the La Fayette road, and began advancing toward us over the fields. Their discipline seemed very perfect, and it was an imposing pageant when, as they came on, their banners fluttered above their heads, and their glittering arms flashed back the sunlight through the thick black clouds of dust.

Captain Johnson, of General Negley's staff, who, on being severed from his own division, had immediately reported to General Thomas for duty, had already, at great personal risk, ascertained that the advancing battalions were infantry, and now the question arose, was it our own or the enemy's. Hope and fear alternately agitated our bosoms, until at last, looking through our glasses, we could clearly distinguish the red and blue, with the white crescent! It was the battle-flag of General Granger, and the troops we saw were two brigades, Mitchell's and Whitaker's, of Steadman's strong division. These were comparatively fresh troops. True they had marched some weary miles over roads ankle-deep with dust. True, they had hurried along rapidly to succor their comrades, and participate in the fight. But they had not as yet been engaged that day, and hence they could indeed be considered help to the battle-scarred veterans who held the hill.

As soon as General Granger had reported to General Thomas for duty, he was sent by the latter to bring over an ammunition-train from the Rossville road. The train had fallen into the hands of the enemy, but the march in search of it brought Steadman at once into contact with the rebels, and a desperate conflict immediately ensued. It was now that the brilliant courage of Colonel John G. Mitchell, commanding one of General Steadman's brigades, became conspicuous. Now General Whitaker had an opportunity of baptizing in glory the star recently placed upon his shoulder; and now the troops of the reserve corps, comparatively unused to battle, had an opportunity of testing their mettle. Nobly did all pass through the ordeal, and although once thrown into confusion by the concentrated fire from a score of rebel regiments, and half as many batteries, they rallied under the fire, and drove the enemy from a hill almost as formidable as that which formed the key of General Thomas's position. The rebels made one desperate endeavor to retake this position, but were blood-

ily repulsed, and almost for the first time since the fight began there was a lull in the fearful storm.

An hour passed by, and it became evident that Bragg would not be foiled in his attempt to annihilate our gallant army without another effort. Polk's corps, assisted by the Georgia State troops, by Dabney Maury's division, and by various detached fragments of the rebel army, were to try their hands upon the heroic band who, as the forlorn hope of the army, still held the hill. Our feeble ranks were gathered up. The thinned battalions were brought closer together. The dozen pieces of artillery were planted to sweep all approaches to the hill; and each man, looking at his neighbor, vowed, some mentally, and others audibly, to die right there, if it were necessary, for their country, for freedom, and for mankind!

All along the woods skirting the cleared fields, at the south-eastern foot of the hill, in the hollows and ravines to the right, and away to the left, upon and beyond the La Fayette road, the rebel legions were seen gathering for the onset.

Just before the storm broke, the brave and high-souled Garfield was perceived making his way to the headquarters of General Thomas. He had come to be present at the final contest, and in order to do so had ridden all the way from Chattanooga, passing through a fiery ordeal upon the road. His horse was shot under him, and his orderly was killed by his side. Still he had come through, he scarce knew how, and here he was to inspire fresh courage in the hearts of the brave soldiers who were holding the enemy at bay, to bring them words of greeting from General Rosecrans, and to inform them that the latter was reörganizing the scattered troops, and, as fast as possible, would hurry them forward to their relief.

At last a shell came hurtling through the air, and burst with a loud explosion over the hill. This was the signal for rebel attack, and at once the bullets flew thick and fast amongst us.

The fight around the hill now raged with terror inexperienced before, even upon this terrible day. Our soldiers were formed in two lines, and, as each marched up to the crest, and fired a deadly volley at the advancing foe, it fell back a little ways; the men lay down upon the ground to load their guns, and the second line advanced to take their place! They, too, in their turn retired, and thus the lines kept marching back and forth, delivering their withering volleys till the very brain grew dizzy as it watched them. And all the time not a man wavered. Every motion was executed with as much precision as though the troops were on a holiday parade, notwithstanding the flower of the rebel army were swarming round the foot of the hill, and a score of cannon thundering from three sides upon it. Every attempt of the enemy to scale it was repulsed, and the gallant Harker looked with pride upon his lines, standing or lying just where they were when the fight began.

But our troops are no longer satisfied with the

defensive. General Turchin, at the head of his brigade, charged into the rebel lines, and cut his way out again, bringing with him three hundred prisoners. Other portions of this brave band followed Turchin's example, until the legions of the enemy were fairly driven back to the ground they occupied previous to commencing the last fight. Thus did twelve or fifteen thousand men, animated by heroic impulses and inspired by worthy leaders, save from destruction the army of the Cumberland.

At night General Thomas fell back to Rossville, four miles from Chattanooga, around and in which city the army lies to-night.

Our losses have been most severe, and can scarcely fall short of one thousand seven hundred killed and eight thousand wounded. Colonel Barnett tells me that our loss in artillery will not fall short of fifty pieces. Our deficiency in transportation and baggage cannot now be estimated.

But the enemy has suffered as severely as we in that which he can least afford—human life and limb. He intended by massing all his available forces together, to annihilate the army of the Cumberland. He has failed to do so, and although it would be childish to deny or conceal our own fearful losses, yet we may console ourselves by the assurance that in his circumstances his failure to destroy us is for us a signal victory, and for him an irreparable defeat.

—*Cincinnati Gazette.*

REBEL DESPATCHES.

TEN MILES SOUTH OF CHATTANOOGA,
via RINGGOLD, Sept. 21, 1863.

To General S. Cooper:

The enemy retreated on Chattanooga last night, leaving his dead and wounded in our hands. His loss is very large in men, artillery, small arms, and colors. Ours is heavy, but not yet ascertained. The victory is complete, and our cavalry is pursuing.

With the blessing of God, our troops have accomplished great results against largely superior numbers. We have to mourn the loss of many gallant men and officers. Brigadier-Generals Preston Smith, Helm, and Deshler are killed. Major-General Hood and Brigadier-Generals Adams, Gregg, and Bunn, are wounded.

BRAXTON BRAGG,
General.

ORDER FROM GENERAL BRAGG.

HEADQUARTERS ARMY OF TENNESSEE, IN THE
FIELD, LA FAYETTE, GA., Sept. 10.

General Orders No. 180 :

The troops will be held ready for an immediate move against the enemy. His demonstrations on our flanks have been thwarted ; and twice he has retired before us when offered battle. We must now force him to the issue. Soldiers, you are largely reënforced—you must now seek the contest. In doing so, I know you will be content to suffer privations and encounter hardships. Heretofore you have never failed to respond to your

General, when he has asked a sacrifice at your hands. Relying upon your gallantry and patriotism, he asks you to add a crowning glory to the wreaths you wear. Our credit is in your keeping. Your enemy boasts that you are demoralized, and retreating before him. Having accomplished our object in driving back his flank movement, let us now turn on his main force and crush it in its fancied security. Your General will lead you. You have but to respond to assure us of a glorious triumph over an insolent foe. I know what your response will be. Trusting in God and the justice of our cause, and nerved by the love of the dear ones at home, failure is impossible, and victory must be ours.

BRAXTON BRAGG,
General Commanding.

Doc. 124.

BATTLE NEAR LITTLE ROCK, ARKANSAS.

A NATIONAL ACCOUNT.

LITTLE ROCK, ARKANSAS, September 13.

THIS city was captured by General Steele's forces on the evening of the tenth, and I avail myself of the departure of the first courier to send you the particulars. In order to properly appreciate the movement and the value of our success, it will be necessary to consider some of the difficulties under which our forces labored. When General Steele concentrated his army at Brownsville, on the first of September, he ascertained definitely that General Price, with a force largely superior in numbers, had taken up a strong position four miles from Little Rock, and was awaiting his advance behind intrenchments of the most formidable character, protected upon one flank by the Arkansas River, and upon the other by an impassable cypress swamp. The roads leading to the rebel position from the front pursued a devious course through swamps crossed by narrow causeways, which had been obstructed by tearing up the corduroy foundation at the impassable places, and by felling the timber on both sides across it. Ample cover was afforded by the canebrakes and thickets for the enemy's sharp-shooters to annoy both flanks of an advancing column. To advance along such a road to the assault of the skilfully constructed defences of the enemy, was to subject his army to a loss and labor which was not to be thought of.

Some kind of a flank movement was accordingly determined upon, though its exact character was necessarily left for circumstances to determine. The existence of a ford across the Arkansas, eight miles above Little Rock, had become known to General Steele, and on the evening of September second he sent General Davidson, with two of the three brigades of his cavalry division, to reconnoitre the country in that direction, and gather information touching the feasibility of making a crossing at that point. General Davidson ascertained that, by the détour our forces would be required to make, the Arkansas

River was at least fifty miles from Brownsville, and that our line of march would cross the Searcy and Batesville roads, along either of which a section of six-pounders could be galloped abreast, our column cut in two, and, in case of disaster, a superior force thrown directly in our rear, intercepting at once support and supplies. A flank movement upon the enemy's left was not deemed practicable after this reconnoissance.

Upon the enemy's right the Arkansas River inclined toward us, and could not be over eighteen miles distant, with no roads of consequence opening our rear to the enemy, in case of an advance in that direction. The most feasible plan, then, presenting itself was to avoid the road the enemy had so carefully obstructed, and was so well prepared to defend, and by a detour to the left reach the Arkansas River below Little Rock, and, moving up, assault the enemy's works upon their extreme right, where they were known to be weaker than at the point or intersection with the Brownsville road.

Accordingly General Steele placed his whole column in motion on the morning of the seventh, with the exception of one brigade of infantry and two of cavalry, which followed on the eighth. Bayou Metaire was reached and crossed the same day with much difficulty, and consequent delay, at Shallow Ford, some eight or ten miles to the left of the usual crossing at the bridge. On the following morning General Davidson, with a single brigade of his cavalry, was assigned the advance, and pushed on, through by-paths and obscure roads, through the canebrakes and jungles of bushes and vines, in the direction of Terry's Ferry, on the Arkansas, eight miles in a direct line below Little Rock. The enemy was not seen until within three miles of the river, where a brigade of cavalry was encountered in a strong position behind Ashley's Bayou. Dismounting "Merrill's Horse," and deploying them in the woods, the rebels were driven back toward their works, and in the mean time General Davidson, with the remainder of the brigade and a section of Stange's howitzers and Hadley's battery of rifled guns, dashed down a road upon the east side of the bayou, which was crossed lower down, and reached the river a short distance below the point desired. A rebel picket was surprised upon the river-bank, part of it captured, and the remainder, to General Davidson's great surprise—for he had been led to believe it quite deep—forded the river.

Had his entire division been with him, he would have crossed the river and dashed immediately upon Little Rock. But with only two regiments, and in ignorance of the force he would encounter upon the opposite bank, the crossing could not be attempted. General Steele arrived the same evening, with General Rice's and Colonel Engleman's infantry divisions. An examination of the ford led Generals Davidson and Steele to hesitate about trusting their batteries in the treacherous quicksands of the Arkansas, and demonstrated that artillery could only be crossed by a pontoon-bridge. The advance of the trains was very slow and tedious, notwithstanding General Rice's pioneers had widened the road, and in many places constructed an entirely new one. The wheels sank to the hub at every revolution for miles, and the pontoon train did not arrive until the afternoon of the day following, being the ninth. In the mean time the enemy had brought down a battery and two or three regiments to dispute our crossing.

The possibility of crossing the Arkansas, which would enable us to effectually turn Price's position, opened a new field to General Steele, of which he at once determined to take advantage. It was at first suggested to cross the entire army to the south bank of the river, and move with the whole force upon Little Rock at once. This plan was open to the very serious objections of exposing to inevitable interruption our communication with our base of supplies at Duvall's Bluffs, on White River, perhaps involving the capture of Duvall's Bluffs, with all its supplies of ammunition, quartermaster and commissary stores.

We were, besides, with short supplies, the whole army being on half-rations. And, had General Steele crossed his entire force to the south bank of the Arkansas, and left Price upon the north bank, with five or ten days' supplies, he would not only have exposed his communications to interruption, but he would have subjected himself to the necessity of recrossing the river in the face of Price's army, and cutting his way back to Duvall's Bluffs, or retreat upon Napoleon! The former, under the circumstances, would be hazardous in the extreme, as it would dishearten our troops, and lend to the superior forces of Price an enthusiasm which would prove but the forerunner of victory. The retreat upon Napoleon would have given Price an open road to Missouri, where we have no adequate force to meet him. In short, the plan was not feasible, and there remained to be done but the one thing, which was done.

A reconnoissance revealed the fact that, in advancing along the river to the assault of the rebel works on the north bank, we would be subjected for eight miles, as well as in the attack itself, to an enfilading fire from rebel batteries, along the south bank of the Arkansas. This new obstacle would probably make our advance along the north bank, unsupported by a column upon the south bank, and an assault upon the enemy's works, a failure, or, in the event of success, subject us to a heavy loss.

It was then determined that General Davidson should cross the Arkansas with his whole division, and, taking with him Hadley's and Clarkson's batteries, and Stange's and Lovejoy's howitzers, follow up the south bank of the stream, while General Steele, with the infantry and the remaining batteries, advanced along the opposite bank to the assault of the rebel works on the north side. Dividing the army by placing an impassable river between its two wings, gave Price the opportunity of concentrating his whole force upon either one, and fighting one part of our army under circumstances preventing all support from the other. The plan was a bold one—a desperate one—such as only the peculiar necessities of General Steele's position would have permitted. But it was the only one promising success, and General Davidson readily accepted the part assigned him, although sensible of the probability of meeting the whole of Price's army in his front, with the necessity of giving battle with cavalry in a dense forest, instead of an open plain, where alone it had heretofore been considered effective, while an impassable river destroyed the most remote possibility of receiving the support of infantry, even in the most desperate emergency.

There may be those who cannot see why Steele, instead of moving to an assault of the rebel position with an inferior force, under such marked disadvantages, did not remain in his position at Brownsville until properly reënforced. To such I would say, that when General Steele left Helena on the fifteenth of August, he did not have in his command a single sick man. When he left Duvall's Bluffs on the first of September, he left one thousand four hundred sick behind him, and a week later he left seven hundred more behind him, in advancing from Brownsville, besides a large number taken in moving by Davidson's cavalry. At this rate General Steele would soon have no army at all, and been driven ingloriously from the State by the foe he came to vanquish. Steele had loudly called for reënforcements, but some one had seen proper not to provide him with an army adequate to the accomplishment, under ordinary circumstances, of the enterprise confided to him. The instinct of self-preservation demanded that Steele should at least offer battle, and quickly, and in doing so he selected the only plan promising success in any event.

The plan was determined upon on the afternoon of the ninth, and the morning of the tenth selected as the time when it should be carried into execution. Generals Steele and Davidson reconnoitred the ground in person, and selected the point for the pontoon-bridge, and Captain Gerster, Chief-Engineer on General Davidson's staff, was instructed to construct it in time for the forces to cross at six o'clock on the following morning. Work was commenced immediately in cutting a road through the timber, but, through the imprudence of some of the working party in exposing themselves to the view of the enemy, it became necessary to select another point, in order to enable our men to dig down a bank thirty feet high during the night. This new point was some distance above the other one. The pontoon was to be thrown across in a bend of the river.

At this point there is a sand-bar varying in width from eight hundred to one thousand yards, across which the enemy's sharp-shooters could not advance to pick off the workmen, without exposing themselves to a murderous fire from our infantry. Beyond this sand-bar are the woods, with which this whole region is overgrown. Around this bend were stationed batteries, from which twenty-four guns, placed in position during the night, and concealed from the enemy, could pour a cross and enfilading fire into all parts of the timber opposite the bridge. The plan was for General Davidson, with Glover's and Merrill's brigades, Hadley's battery, and Stange's and Lovejoy's howitzers, to cross at the bridge, Colonel Ritter, with his brigade, and Clarkson's battery, to make a feint, at the same time, at the fort two miles below, and, if found practicable, to cross, and bring the forces of the enemy, known to be between the two points, between Davidson and Ritter, where their escape would be impossible. In the event of his crossing being seriously resisted, Ritter and his batteries were to hurry to the bridge, and, crossing behind the brigades of Merrill and Glover, take position in their rear as a reserve.

As soon as it was dark, on the night of the ninth, Captain Gerster, with a strong working party, commenced digging down the bank, in order to enable the artillery and cavalry to reach the level of the bridge. The enemy's pickets could approach within three hundred feet of the party, and strict silence was enjoined upon them. All commands were given in a whisper, and cigars and pipes, as well as camp-fires, tabooed.

Daylight did not see the work of digging down the bank completed, although as many men as could work to advantage had been busily engaged all night, with reliefs every half an hour. The work had progressed so far, however, as to enable Captain Gerster to get his pontoons down with considerable difficulty, and the work of constructing the bridge was soon after commenced. The rebels, in constantly increasing numbers, were soon visible in the woods opposite the bridge, and officers came boldly out upon the bank and examined our operations with their glasses. No interruption was made until about half-past eight o'clock, when a battery of four guns, posted a short distance back in the timber, suddenly opened with solid shot upon the bridge, and the troops massed behind it; and at the same moment a large body of sharp-shooters manifested an intention of occupying a line of drift-wood running diagonally across the bar, midway between the bridge and the timber. Our twenty-four guns, masked for this very purpose, at once opened upon the timber, filling every part of it with bursting shells, the fragments of which were flying in all directions, and soon rendering the position untenable for the enemy, who wisely abandoned it. An occasional shell was thrown in the same direction by our guns, in order to satisfy the rebels that they were still in position. About nine o'clock Clarkson's battery, occupying a position with Ritter's brigade, two miles below the bridge, opened upon the woods opposite the lower ford, with a view of ascertaining what opposition our cavalry would meet with in crossing. Clarkson was replied to vigorously from a rebel battery planted inside of a fort made of cotton bales. The enemy's battery was served with great accuracy, and a half-hour's brisk firing demonstrated that it could not be silenced, although

Clarkson had succeeded in setting the cotton-bales on fire on two different occasions. Clarkson's battery was stationed in a corn-field where there was not a breath of air stirring, and when General Davidson sent an order for it and Ritter's brigade to move up the bridge, it found almost every one in this battery utterly exhausted from over-exertion and the heat.

About this time a slight smoke was seen rising from two steamboats — the Arkansas and Thalequah—which were lying upon the opposite shore about two miles above us. At first it was supposed that they were getting up steam to move further up the river, but the increasing density of the smoke, through which the flames were soon visible, showed that they had been fired by the rebels. It was a grand sight, even in the bright clear sunlight, though night would have rendered it more magnificent, to see the flames curling and mounting upward through a black column of smoke which towered far above the tallest trees of the forest. It was an omen of good fortune to us, showing the rebels had abandoned all hopes of preventing our crossing, and deploying upon the Little Rock road beyond the woods.

As soon as Colonel Ritter moved off with his brigade and battery from the lower ford, and taking the road toward the bridge, the rebel battery and a regiment of cavalry which had been dismounted and acting as sharp-shooters, abandoned their position and galloped up the road toward Little Rock. They were in danger of being cut off by Davidson, of whose intended crossing they had been apprised, and they lost no time in getting beyond the point at which his advance would reach the road. The precipitancy of their flight was shown by the handspikes, buckets, and other articles belonging to the guns, and the hats of the men left behind them on the road. When they came abreast of the burning steamboats, where the road approaches close to the river, the cloud of dust rising from the road revealed their locality. Our long-range guns in Engleman's batteries opened upon them with shell, and kept up a vigorous fire as long as they were in range. The firing at that time appeared to be very accurate, as many of the shells were seen to explode in the midst of the dust. Afterward, when our forces came into possession of the road along which this body of the enemy had passed, two of our shells, which did not explode, were found on the road, and the fences and trees were much torn by fragments. Blood was found in several places upon the grass at the edge of the road, and marching in close column the rebels must have suffered a severe loss in running the gauntlet of our batteries. Some of them could not endure the fire and turned back, as was shown by the tracks in the road, and went up by an almost impassable road running through a swamp.

At ten o'clock the bridge was completed and in readiness for crossing. Captain Gerster, the engineer who had worked so faithfully in its construction, had become literally exhausted by his labors, and, pronouncing his work finished, sank to the ground with a sun-stroke induced by over-exertion. He was borne to the shade, and proper restoratives immediately applied. He is now almost entirely recovered. To his promptness and skill is largely due the success of General Davidson's movements.

Crossing a river under fire is a difficult undertaking, and none but men of undoubted bravery will attempt it. Ready to cross, General Davidson signaled the batteries, and every gun again opened with shell upon the woods, which were believed to contain a large number of sharp-shooters. After a few minutes' brisk firing, the Fortieth Iowa and Twenty-seventh Wisconsin, of Colonel Wood's brigade, Engleman's infantry division, rushed across the bridge, formed in line of battle upon the sand-bar, and swept forward upon the double-quick to the woods, which were reached and occupied without opposition. Stange's and Lovejoy's howitzers followed on the gallop, and took position in the rear, ready for action in case their services were found necessary. Under cover of this advance, Glover's brigade of cavalry were crossed, and then Merrill's, and then Ritter's, the batteries of each brigade keeping their proper place in column. Part of the cavalry crossed at a few hundred yards above the bridge. Steele was already upon the move, and Davidson, pushing past the infantry, which was immediately recrossed to its proper division, galloped through the woods to the main road, no enemy being found. There the column was properly formed, and skirmishers deployed to the right and left, and pushed forward to discover the positions of the enemy.

The head of the column having reached a point on the road opposite the burning steamboats, the Tenth Illinois, with Stange's and Lovejoy's howitzers, was sent forward upon the gallop to the mouth of Fourche Bayou, some two miles ahead. This bayou had been turned from its original course into a swamp by a levee, over which the road crossed a mile and a half from its mouth. This levee was supposed to be immediately at the mouth, and General Davidson was fearful that it might be cut by the rebels and the crossing rendered difficult. When near the mouth of the bayou the rebels were encountered posted in thick woods, and opened a heavy fire of artillery and musketry. Hadley's battery was brought up from the rear of Merrill's brigade to the front, and the whole column placed in rapid motion for the point at which Stange's howitzers were at work. By the time the column came in sight the rebels had been driven from their position, and the firing altogether subsided. The mouth of the bayou was found perfectly dry, though a few yards above a deep, impassable pool commenced, which continued the entire distance to the levee. The road at this point turned to the left, following near the bank of the bayou to the levee. Opposite the mouth was a sand-bar seven or eight hundred yards in width, which stretched two miles above and about half that distance below. The Sixteenth Illinois, leaving the road at this point, debouched upon this bar, following it up, close under the bank, which was covered with a dense forest. Companies B and H were in the advance, fifty yards behind them followed Stange's and Lovejoy's howitzers, the other ten companies of the Fourth Illinois immediately following, and the remainder of Glover's brigade coming after. About three hundred yards from the mouth of the bayou the timber bore off to the left, and nearly half a mile beyond this made still another turn in the same direction, forming two points beyond which the bar was not visible. The Tenth Illinois had turned the first point, still keeping near the bank, entirely out of sight of the remainder of the column, and very imprudently pushed on full half a mile in advance of the skirmishers in the woods upon the left, who were advancing with proper caution. The two companies in advance were not dismounted as they should have been in their advanced position, and had almost reached the second point of timber, followed by the howitzers and the remainder of the regiment, marching in column. Not a dismounted man, keeping pace with the advance, was thrown out to feel the enemy in the woods. Suddenly, from the woods on the left a deadly fire of musketry was opened upon the whole regiment. Three or four volleys were fired in rapid succession, when, with a yell which made the whole forest ring, the rebels broke from their cover, and swarming down the steep bank, made a grand rush for the howitzers. The suddenness of the attack threw the entire regiment of cavalry into the wildest confusion. Saddles were emptied by scores. Horses, goaded to desperation by the shower of bullets sweeping among them, became unmanageable. The companies in front came tumbling back over the battery which was just getting to work, and increased the disorder into which the galling flank fire had thrown the remainder of the regiment. The angry roar of the musketry, quickly followed by the deep-toned sound of the howitzers, the savage shouts of the rebels as they rushed from their cover, fairly drowning the loud explosion of the shells with which they were greeted, were distinctly heard at the mouth of the bayou at which General Davidson, bringing up the remainder of the column, had just arrived. "An ambuscade!" "An ambuscade!" broke from hundreds of lips, and in a moment more the entire regiment, bearing off toward the river in its flight, came pouring from behind the point of woods which heretofore had concealed it from view. A single glance was sufficient to show that it was completely disordered, and it was feared that the remainder of Glover's brigade, not knowing what was ahead of them, would share in the panic. Giving a hasty order to Colonel Merrill to form a line of battle upon the bar with all possible rapidity, General Davidson dashed among the fugitives with his drawn sabre, the rebel bullets from the woods flying in a perfect shower around him, and rallied the regiment once more into line, and brought

it again into the advance just behind the first point of woods.

With the first volley of musketry, Captain Stange and Lieutenant Lovejoy quickly placed their light mountain howitzers in position, and with the whole eight pieces opened a deadly fire of shell and spherical case upon the rebels swarming from the woods. Nothing but the most desperate courage could have enabled any soldiery in the world to have faced a fire so deadly, and yet, without even stopping to form in line, the rebels rushed *en masse* upon the guns, and, after receiving over a dozen rounds, were literally crowding over their muzzles. Deprived of all support, and far in advance of the head of the column, it was impossible to keep the enemy at bay, and an attempt was accordingly made to bring the guns from the field. A portion of them were limbered up and galloped off after the cavalry, and others were withdrawn by hand. The section of two guns nearest the woods in Lovejoy's battery, with one of the caissons, was captured. Lieutenant Lovejoy remained with them to the last. R. A. Ficklin and George Kibbel, two as noble, brave-hearted fellows as ever wore a uniform, were pulling one of the guns off with a prolongue. Behind it, keeping the enemy at bay with his sabre, was the gallant Lovejoy. A musket-ball, fired at such close range that the powder burned his clothes, passed entirely through the body of Ficklin. Another passed through the kidneys of Kibbel, and both went down mortally wounded. At the same instant Lovejoy fell with a ball in his leg. Dropping his sabre, he drew his pistol, and was seen to shoot the man who had wounded him. The two guns, with one of the caissons, were immediately rushed into the woods. The other guns, being run off by hand, were hotly contested for by the rebels, and gallantly defended by the cannoneers. They would have been overpowered by numbers, however, but for the timely rallying of the Tenth Illinois by General Davidson, under cover of which they were withdrawn, and the rebels driven away from the other caisson left upon the field.

Every man belonging to the two captured guns were either killed or wounded. One of them—John Rath—was found shot through the heart, with a shell in his hand, which he was in the act of placing in the gun. No blame can be attached to the Tenth Illinois for its conduct. Its advance was very unfortunate, but was the result of a belief that the skirmishers in the woods were advancing parallel with it. No regiment of cavalry marching in column could receive such a murderous fire in flank without being thrown into disorder. Lieutenant-Colonel Stuart received a musket-ball through the cap, which stunned him and brought him to the ground. Had he not fallen, the disorder of his regiment would not have been so great.

Hadley's battery, fortunately placed by General Davidson at the head of Merrill's brigade, took position on the sand-bar near enough the river to give a fair view of the second point of timber, and opened a rapid fire of shells upon the woods in which the rebels were lying. The remaining six howitzers took up a position in front of them, and participated in the cannonade. Colonel Glover's entire brigade was immediately brought under shelter of the bank, two squadrons of the First Iowa mounted and two dismounted being detailed to support the howitzers. Hadley's battery and a section of howitzers were withdrawn, and, with Merrill's brigade, sent back to the mouth of the bayou to follow up the road. In a few moments they were heard vigorously at work. Glover advanced the left of his brigade cautiously, keeping Merrill's left flank well covered, and by the time Merrill's line was abreast of Glover's right, Glover was occupying a parallel position, completing the line to the river.

At this time the reserves, all the horses, and the ammunition trains were upon this open sand-bar to the rear and right of the line of battle, and, with our right flank, were exposed to an enfilading fire from the opposite side of the river, in case Price should bring down a battery and plant it upon the bank. A cloud of dust undoubtedly caused by troops in rapid motion was plainly visible upon the other side of the river, but it was impossible to determine in what direction the troops were travelling. Nothing had been heard from Steele, and it seemed scarcely credible that he could have pushed the head of his column far enough to lend us any assistance. The most intense anxiety for our position took possession of men and officers.

Under these circumstances of peril, the line was ordered to advance. In a few minutes an angry roar of musketry closely mingling with the thunders of cannon arose from the woods in our front, and shell and balls came pouring upon our line in a perfect shower. The echo of the first discharge had scarcely died away in the thunders of the second, when some distance above us on the opposite side of the river a puff of blue smoke arose from the bushes; a second later the sound of a cannon came booming over the water. Price or Steele was there, and in anxious suspense the whole line paused to see where the shell would strike, in order that from the line of fire, it could be ascertained whether the other side of the river was held by friends or foes. The shell fell directly among the rebels in our front. It was quickly followed by one after another, as all of Steele's batteries wheeled into action. Steele had heard the roar of our own and the enemy's artillery, and, understanding our peril, had pushed forward to our assistance. With a wild shout our boys advanced through the roads, driving the enemy rapidly before them. A guidon was placed upon the sand-bar to keep pace with our advance, in order that Steele might know the position of our line in the woods. The line was very short and the roar of battle terrific. Hadley's battery and Lovejoy's howitzers upon the left were perfectly ablaze,

pouring shell into the rebel batteries, responding with three guns to their one, Stange's howitzers upon our right, Steele's batteries upon the opposite side of the Arkansas, and a grim old sixty-four near Little Rock 'thundering in response, shells shrieking through the air and bursting everywhere among the trees, the sharp rattle of musketry and the wild shouts of Glover's and Merrill's brigades, as they pushed the enemy from one position to another, filled the air with a din rarely equalled.

The resistance of the enemy was of the most desperate character, not a single foot of tenable ground being surrendered until they were driven from it. At five o'clock we had fought closely over four hours, and were still two miles from the city. General Steele sent a message that Price had evacuated the works in his front, the rear-guard being at that time crossing the bridges. General Davidson had been opposed by a superior force during the whole afternoon, and he was now called upon, as a prudent commander, to guard against an attack from Price's whole army. There were innumerable roads, which he was too weak to guard, leading directly into Davidson's rear, by which Price could precipitate a large force where it would be most effective. The position of General Davidson now became one of imminent peril. Assuming the policy which has governed him in his whole campaign, he determined to conceal his own weakness and confuse the plans of the enemy by a bold push ahead.

Keeping the road immediately upon his left, by the general course of the river, Glover's line became very much shorter than when first formed. At five o'clock it was re-formed in three lines, and, by a gallant charge across an open field, obliqueing to the left as it advanced, forced the enemy from a strong position in the woods across the road, and into a corn-field directly in Merrill's front. Coming to the river-bank at this point, Glover's brigade was called off, utterly exhausted.

Time was every thing in entering the city, and General Davidson called up Colonel Ritter's brigade, which, up to this time, had been in reserve. The First Missouri, by a gallant sabre-charge, cleared the corn-field in Merrill's front, and then, dismounting, deployed as skirmishers to the relief of his brigade. The Third Iowa and Thirteenth Illinois, accompanied by Lieutenant-Colonel Caldwell, General Davidson's Chief of Staff, were ordered to charge into the city with drawn sabres. The river was immediately upon the right flank of the advancing column, but the left presented a continuous shelter, from which the rebels saluted it with a galling fire of musketry as it passed. Disregarding it altogether, the column pushed forward at a sweeping gallop, driving the rebel gunners away from a sixty-four pounder which was annoying Steele very much, before they could even complete the hasty preparations they were making to blow up the magazine. The suburbs were soon reached, and disregarding the sharp-shooters in the houses, who emptied several saddles, the column pressed on into the city amid the wildest shouts. A superior force of rebel cavalry was encountered, but not relishing the appearance of the drawn sabres, which gleamed everywhere from the cloud of dust in which our column was enveloped, they turned and fled in the greatest disorder from the city.

Nothing could equal the panic and confusion into which our sudden appearance precipitated Little Rock. The streets were filled with women and children, and knots of citizens, listening to the sound of cannon constantly growing nearer and nearer, and the shell from Steele's batteries, which had now been planted almost opposite the city, shrieking over their heads and bursting in the woods beyond them, were anxiously discussing the question of their own safety. Rebel officers, thinking themselves secure, were eating their suppers in the houses. The rapid rush of flying horsemen, the clouds of dust, the glad hurrahs and gleaming sabres of others dashing through the dusty streets in hot pursuit, was the first intimation of our near approach. Women and children ran shrieking to their homes, the crowds of citizens quickly dispersed, and rebel officers, mounting their horses, were captured while endeavoring to escape. A second later, windows were thrown up and handkerchiefs waved, and the curious throngs gathered in the door-yards, closely scrutinizing each squadron as it passed.

As we entered the city upon the east side, General Cabbell, with four thousand five hundred cavalry and mounted infantry and two full batteries of artillery, hurrying down from the Fort Smith region, entered the city upon the west. Prisoners state that he had been assigned a position upon the extreme left of the rebel line, and that that portion of the line had been much weakened in anticipation of his arrival, when we made the sabre-charge which gave us possession of the city. Cabbell's Adjutant was riding with an orderly some distance in advance of the column, and, encountering our cavalry, was enabled to give notice in time to Cabbell, who immediately reversed his column upon the road it was marching. He will be compelled to make a wide detour in order to effect a junction with Price.

The entry of our troops into the city turned the rebel left, and they retreated through the woods to the Arkadelphia road, leading south.

General Steele's advance had been so rapid that he was not only enabled to lend General Davidson the most invaluable assistance from the beginning, but in a measure covered the gallant charge which terminated the labors of the day. He possessed himself of the bridges across the river, which Price had fired, before the damage sustained by them was serious, and was crossing his infantry upon them at daylight next morning. He also saved seven platform and box-cars and two locomotives on the Memphis and Little Rock Railroad from serious injury.

The forces encountered by General Davidson were Marmaduke's, Dobbins's, and Shelby's cavalry, dismounted, and Tappan's infantry. Price was made aware of our crossing the moment it commenced by means of the Pine Bluff telegraph, and immediately commenced the evacuation of his works on the north bank of the stream. He was evidently fearful that Steele had another pontoon, and would cross the river with the remainder of the forces as soon as he evacuated his works, relieve Davidson upon the river, and send him around to the Arkadelphia road to a point where Price had six hundred wagons parked. To guard against this, McCrea's, Frost's, and Fagan's infantry were pushed out on the Arkadelphia road as soon as they crossed the river. Price with Holmes, who came to give unofficial counsel, and Governor Flanigan remained until four o'clock, when the command was turned over to Marmaduke. Price by this time had discovered that there was no movement against his trains, and Marmaduke had promised, with Cabbell's assistance, to hold us in check until night. Next morning Price was to have the remainder of the infantry countermarched. Our sudden success in entering the city of course changed Price's plans and necessitated a retreat.

A squadron of cavalry dashed up to the United States arsenal as soon as our forces entered the city, and arrived just in time to prevent its being blown up by the rebels. There was over a ton of powder in the magazine, and two or three thousand rounds of fixed ammunition in the various buildings. Every thing is uninjured, if I except alone the machine-shops, from which the machinery was removed some months ago to Arkadelphia.

The public records were all removed some months ago to Washington, and, aside from the bare State-House and the law library, we found nothing of the State Government. The penitentiary was not touched. The prisoners were marched out, leaving their suppers upon the tables, and all their clothes and bedding in their cells.

The two howitzers taken from us were spiked by the rebels before they effected the capture, and were immediately started for the trains. They were of the smallest pattern of mountain howitzers, and are worth little in comparison with the two sixty-fours, one twenty-four, and three twelve-pounders we captured from the enemy.

The rebel force, not including that of Cabbell, was about fifteen thousand, with thirty-six pieces of artillery.

MAYOR'S OFFICE, LITTLE ROCK, Sept. 10, 1863.

To the Officer Commanding Federal Army:

The army of General Price has retreated and abandoned the defence of this city. We are now powerless and ask your mercy. The city is now occupied alone by women and children and non-combatants, with, perhaps, a few stragglers from the confederate forces. May I ask of you protection for persons and property? I have been ill for some days and am unable to visit you in person. Very respectfully,

C. P. BERTRAND,
Mayor.

General Davidson caused guards to be placed upon every street-corner of the city, and, to the everlasting credit of his division, let it be said, that although they beheld their comrades shot from their saddles from houses in the suburbs, and entered the city amid the gathering shades of night, which would have concealed all manner of crimes, not a single act of violence or injustice was done the citizens of the place, or a single article of private property disturbed. Such a record is seldom made in these days.

General Steele and staff, crossing the Arkansas in a skiff, for the bridges were not yet passable, entered Little Rock soon after General Davidson. The greeting of the two Generals and the officers surrounding them was a cordial one—such as can only be seen under similar circumstances. As a mark of his appreciation of General Davidson's gallant conduct during the day, General Steele directed the following order to be issued, making General Davidson "Military Commander" of the capital and vicinity:

HEADQUARTERS ARMY OF ARKANSAS EXPEDITION,
LITTLE ROCK, September 10, 1863.

General Orders No. 22 :

I. The rebels under command of Sterling Price having been driven from the town of Little Rock, and it having been duly surrendered by the civil authorities to the Federal forces, Brigadier-General Davidson is hereby invested with the command of the town and its vicinity, which shall be occupied by the troops.

II. Upon assuming the command, General Davidson will immediately organize such police and provost guard as may be sufficient to insure the good conduct of the troops and proper police of the city, instituting therefor such rules and regulations as shall be needful for good government of and protection to the city and its inhabitants ; and for that purpose he will, on application to these headquarters, have such details of infantry as may be by him deemed necessary.

III. Captain S. S. McNaughton, Provost-Marshal, will report to Brigadier-General Davidson for duty.

By order of Major-General F. STEELE.
F. H. MANTER,
Colonel and Chief of Staff.

General Davidson, in assuming command, appointed Colonel Andrews, Third Minnesota infantry, commander of the post; detailed the Forty-third Illinois infantry, Major Stefauney, as garrison at the United States Arsenal; appointed Lieutenant-Colonel Chandler, Seventh Missouri, Provost-Marshal General, with Captain S. S. McNaughton, Seventy-seventh Ohio, as his assistant; created a Board of Health, consisting of E. P. Smith, Medical Director of the cavalry division; E. A. Clark, Surgeon of the Eighth Missouri cavalry; and Assistant Surgeon A. C. Wedge, Third Minnesota infantry.

Among the regulations adopted is one allowing the municipal authorities of the city to temporarily continue the exercise of their functions. Another invites citizens of the surrounding country to bring in their produce for sale to the inhabitants and the troops. Another prohibits all officers and soldiers, other than those on provost-guard duty, or belonging to the staffs or escorts of Generals, from being in the city without a pass ; "officers and soldiers are expected to remain constantly with their commands, unless absent from duty." Another regulation provides that no house will be occupied by any officer or soldier without the order of the General commanding the city.

The day's work had been so arduous that it was impossible to start immediately in pursuit of Price's retreating army. A strong force was organized and sent out under command of Colonel Merrill, on the following morning, however. It has not yet returned.

General Davidson issued the following congratulatory order this morning, addressed to the soldiers of his division :

HEADQUARTERS CAVALRY DIVISION,
DEPARTMENT OF THE MISSOURI,
LITTLE ROCK, ARK., Sept. 13, 1863.

General Orders No. 62 :

Soldiers of the cavalry division ! I congratulate you, that your long and weary march is at length terminated by victory. Little Rock, the capital of the State of Arkansas, the key of the Trans-Mississippi department, is in our hands. The United States Arsenal, uninjured, is "repossessed." The feet of the rebel army—who, but a day or two ago, filed with downcast heads through the streets of the city—will tread the sands of the Arkansas no more.

But, comrades, you have gained two victories on the same day. Though flushed with success, though entering the city when the darkness of night would have covered up misdeeds, though your passions were stirred that our soldiers were shot from their saddles within the suburbs of the city, no outrage upon its defenceless inhabitants has stained your hands. I thank you from the bottom of my heart. Your conduct has more than repaid me for many an anxious day and sleepless night. For you may there be continued success wherever it may be our lot to go. For me, I have no higher aim, and ask no greater honor, than to lead such men.

J. W. DAVIDSON,
Brigadier-General Commanding.

Little Rock has been long considered as a Union city, and, but for the sudden manner in which our forces entered it, the confederates would have carried into execution the threats they have so often made, to burn it for its "Yankee preferences." An army was never more astonished upon entering a city than was ours upon its entry of Little Rock. Instead of a warm, cordial welcome from the citizens, we were greeted, at best, with cold, frigid politeness. Handkerchiefs were waved from the windows when first we entered, with a view of propitiating our friendship, doubtless with the idea of preventing the destruction of property. When, however, it was seen that our troops molested nothing, this poor, false profession of sympathy was withdrawn. A cold, haughty stare met your gaze on every side, and no smile of genuine welcome was visible anywhere.

The rebels endeavored to make a clean sweep of the steamboats here. The General Ashley, the Thalequah, the Pine Bluff, the Julia Roan, the St. Francis, the Leon, and the Arkansas, were all destroyed. The Alma, the Stonewall, the Ben Corson, and a ferry-boat were saved. The Ben Corson had been sent to Pine Bluff for a load of corn a few days before our arrival upon the banks of the river, and its owners ran it ashore where the rebels could not destroy it. The Stonewall, a new steamboat named after Stonewall Jackson, was run out into the centre of the stream, a few days before our arrival, and "accidentally snagged," where she could not be easily destroyed, and could be easily raised. There are said to be a number of boats above here on the river.

The rebels destroyed their famous gunboat Ponchartrain, formerly the Lizzie Simmonds, one of the largest and strongest boats on the lower waters. This boat was out on the banks receiving a plating of railroad iron. Her boilers and machinery were already properly protected, and work was being pushed forward with great vigor. It was intended that she should be in readiness for operations in November, when the river raises with the rains upon the Plains.

The railroad track from here to Duvall's Bluffs is comparatively uninjured, and the train will be running in a few days.

Doc. 125.

GENERAL FRANKLIN'S EXPEDITION.

OFFICIAL NAVAL REPORTS.

UNITED STATES SLOOP PENSACOLA,
NEW-ORLEANS, September 4.

SIR: I have the honor to inform the Department that Major-General Banks, having organized a force of four thousand men under Major-General Franklin, to effect a landing at Sabine Pass, for military occupation, and requested the coöperation of the navy, which I most gladly acceded to, I assigned the command of the naval force to acting volunteer Lieutenant Frederick Crocker, commanding United States steamer Clifton, accompanied by the steamer Sachem, acting volunteer Lieutenant Amos Johnson; United States steamer Arizona, Acting Master Howard Tibbetts, and United States steamer Granite City, Acting Master C. W. Lamson, those being the only available vessels of sufficiently light draught at my disposal for that service, and as they have good pilots, I have no doubt the force is quite sufficient for the object.

The defences ashore and afloat are believed to consist of two thirty-four pounders, en barbette, a battery of field-pieces, and two bay-boats, converted into rams. It was concerted with General Franklin that the squadron of four gunboats, under Lieutenant Crocker, should make the attack alone, assisted by about one hundred and eighty sharp-shooters from the army, divided among his vessels, and having driven the enemy from his defences, or having driven off the rams, the transports are then to advance and land their troops. I regret exceedingly that the officers and crews who have been on blockade there, cannot participate in the attack in consequence of the extensive draught of water drawn by their vessels. The New-London, drawing nine and a half feet, is the lightest draught of all the blockaders, and has made repeated attempts to go in alone without success.

I have the honor to be,
Your obedient servant,
H. H. BELL,
Commanding W. G. Squadron, pro tem.
To Hon. GIDEON WELLES.

STEAMER PENSACOLA, NEW-ORLEANS, September 13.

SIR: My despatch number forty-one informed you of the repulse of the expedition to Sabine Pass, and the capture of the Clifton, acting volunteer Lieutenant Crocker, and the Sachem, by the rebels, and the safe return of the troops and transports to the river without loss. Lieutenants Crocker and Johnson are reported to have fought their vessels gallantly, and are unhurt. The rebel steamers took the Clifton and Sachem in tow within twenty minutes after their surrender. The extent of their damage is unknown. The arrival of the Owasco, this morning, has given me the only reports from the naval officers concerned that I have yet received. The attack, which was to have been a surprise, and made at early dawn on the seventh, was not made until three P.M., on the eighth, after the entire expedition had appeared off Sabine for twenty-eight hours, and a reconnoissance had been made on the morning of the eighth by Generals Franklin and Weitzel, and Lieutenant Commanding Crocker, when they decided on a form of attack different from that recommended by myself. I have the honor to be,
Your obedient servant, H. H. BELL.
To Hon. GIDEON WELLES,
Secretary Navy.

UNITED STATES STEAMSHIP ARIZONA,
SABINE BAR, September 10, 1863.

SIR: At six A.M., on the eighth, the Clifton stood in the bay, and opened fire on the fort, to which no reply was made. At nine A.M., the Arizona, Sachem, and Granite City, followed by the transports, stood over the bay, and with much difficulty, owing to the shallowness of the water, reached anchorage, but miles from the fort, at eleven A.M., the gunboats covering the transports. At half-past three P.M., the Sachem, followed by the Arizona, advanced up the eastern channel to draw the fire of the forts, while the Clifton advanced up the western channel, followed by the Granite City, to cover the landing of a division of troops under General Weitzel. No reply to the fire of the gunboats was made until we were abreast of the forts, when they opened with eight guns, three of which were rifled, almost at the same moment. The Clifton and Sachem were struck in their boilers, enveloping them in steam. There not being room to pass the Sachem, this vessel was backed down the channel, and a boat sent to the Sachem, which returned with the engineer and fireman, badly scalded—since dead. The Arizona had now grounded by the stern, the ebb-tide caught her bow and swung her across the channel. She was with much difficulty extricated from this position, owing to her engine becoming disabled. The flags of the Clifton and Sachem were run down, and white flags were flying at the fore. As all the transports were now moving out of the bay, this vessel remained, covering their movements, until she grounded. She remained until midnight, when she was kedged off, as no assistance could be had from any of the tugs of the expedition. Very respectfully,

Your obedient servant,   H. TIBBETTS,
                    Acting Master, Commanding the Arizona.
To Commodore H. H. BELL, New-Orleans.

A NATIONAL ACCOUNT.

HEADQUARTERS GENERAL WEITZEL'S DIVISION,
NINETEENTH ARMY CORPS, STEAMER BELVIDERE,
MISSISSIPPI RIVER, September 11.

The expedition of the Nineteenth army corps, Major-General Franklin commanding, which left New-Orleans on the fourth inst., has returned without accomplishing the object for which it was despatched. All the preliminary arrangements were made in the most expeditious and secret manner, and the promise of success was most flattering up to the very last moment, when a combination of those unfortunate accidents which no human foresight or determination can prevent or overcome, turned victory into defeat, and rendered nugatory all the efforts of the gallant officers and men composing the expedition, compelling them to relinquish for the present the attempt, and return to the base of operations at this place.

The aim of the expedition was the occupation of Sabine City, situated on the right bank, at the mouth of the Sabine River, the dividing line of Louisiana and Texas, a point of great strategic importance as a base of operations against either Western Louisiana or Eastern and Central Texas. The city is only forty to forty-five miles from Galveston by land, and about sixty miles by sea; from Houston, the capital of Texas, it is distant about sixty miles, and is connected with a branch railroad from Beaumont. This railroad is not in operation at present, a portion of the track being torn up. The distance from the mouth of the Mississippi is two hundred and eighty miles. The strategic importance of the place can thus be comprehended at a glance, and its occupation was doubtless intended as the first step in a campaign the results of which promised to be of the most brilliant and lasting character.

Accompanying the land force was a naval force of four light draught gunboats, consisting of the Clifton, Arizona, Granite City, and Sachem, and the plan was for these to silence the batteries, drive back the enemy, and cover the landing of the troops. How gallantly and nobly they strove to carry out successfully their part of the programme, and how they failed, and how the many brave hearts within sight and hearing of the conflict witnessed that failure with bitter feelings of anger and regret that they could not be relieved, may never become portions of our history, but will remain indelibly recorded on the hearts of all who were present, and nerve them to still greater exertions in the glorious cause of redeeming their country.

At the last place of rendezvous, off Berwick Bay, it was determined that the entire fleet should endeavor to reach the point of destination by midnight of the seventh, and the attack was to take place at three or four o'clock on the morning of the ninth. With this understanding, the long line of vessels moved on their way, piloted by the gunboat Arizona, Captain Tibbetts, which was followed by the transport Belvidere, Captain Fletcher, having on board the veteran Brigadier-General Godfrey Weitzel, commanding the First division of the corps, and the gallant members of his staff, the General being assigned to that post of honor and of danger which he not only willingly accepts, but modestly requests the command of the advance. The blockading vessel stationed off Sabine Pass was now the object, and the fleet steamed swiftly on, while a bright lookout was constantly kept to discover the vessel. Hour after hour passed, and no vessel appearing up to three o'clock on the morning of the eighth, the fleet was hove to, and upon examination it became apparent that the fleet had run by the designated point quite a distance, in consequence of the absence of the blockader. It was, of course, too late in the day to carry out the original plan, and the consequence was a delay of an entire day was necessitated, thus giving the enemy, if advised of the expedition, an opportunity of receiving reënforcements and making all necessary preparations either for evacuation or a more vigorous defence. I would add in this connection that the blockader was absent on a cruise, from which she returned before the battle.

During Monday night, therefore, the entire fleet were collected in the neighborhood of Sabine. The gunboats and lightest draught vessels of the transport fleet crossed the bar, and immediate preparations were made for the attack; the unavoidable delay necessitating some changes in the mode. Captain Crocker, of the Clifton, as gallant a sailor as ever fought a ship, was to inaugurate the action by feeling and uncovering the enemy's batteries, ascertaining the number and disposition of the opposing force, and drawing their fire, while Generals Franklin and Weitzel personally examined the shore of the pass and ascertained the most eligible point for disembarking the land forces. Accordingly the Clifton steamed up the pass, throwing a shell now and then from her huge rifled guns at the only work visible, (an earthwork containing six heavy guns,) and making a careful reconnoissance of the surrounding locality. She received no response to her numerous shots, and with daring bravery steamed within easy range of the fort, turned about, and leisurely returned to her former position. The face of the enemy's work was from one hundred to one hundred and fifty yards in length, and was supposed to be open at the rear.

On the return of the Clifton the order of battle was immediately arranged and rapidly perfected. The gunboats Clifton, Arizona, and Sachem were to engage the enemy's work, while the Granite City, which carried only a broadside of small brass guns, was to cover the landing of an advance force of five hundred men of General Weitzel's division, selected from the heroes of Port Hudson, and composed of two companies of the One Hundred and Sixty-sixth New-York, four companies of the One Hundred and Sixty-first New-York, and a detachment from the Seventy-fifth New-York regiments, under command of Captain Fitch, of the last-named regiment. The General himself came on board at the last moment to superintend personally the operation of disembarking his troops.

"All ready" was the signal, and about four o'clock P.M. the gunboats steamed slowly forward, the Clifton advancing directly toward the fort, followed by the Granite City, and she in turn by the transport General Banks, having on board the advance of the army. The Sachem and the Arizona steamed off to the right and ran up nearly opposite the battery. The Clifton opened the ball with a shell from one of her nine-inch pivot guns, which exploded inside the rebel works, throwing up a perfect shower of debris, and instantly followed it with a second shot of the same kind. Soon the little Sachem, commanded by Captain Johnson, opened her broadside thirty-two pounder guns on the work, and the next moment the Arizona also paid her compliments to the foe. The gunnery was magnificent, a few of the shells only exploding prematurely, and the pieces dropping in the water. Up to this time, and until from thirty to forty shell had exploded in the works, not a shot had been returned by the enemy. An ominous silence pervaded the fort, and many were of opinion that the works had been abandoned. Neither soldiers nor inhabitants made their appearance, and the only signs of life apparent were the movements of a small steamer in the river, which had run up above the city and down as far as the fort once or twice during the forenoon, and which was joined by a second steamer about the time the action commenced.

The action of the enemy, however, was the deceptive calm which often precedes the storm, and the sudden flash of flame which was plainly visible from the deck of the General Banks with the naked eye, and the cloud of white smoke which floated lazily up from the parapet of the enemy, were instantly followed by a heavy shot thrown at the Arizona, the largest boat of the fleet, and which passed directly over her, striking in the edge of the water beyond. This was followed in quick succession by a shot at the Sachem and another at the Clifton, neither of which, however, took effect. The engagement now became general and very warm, the Clifton and Arizona moving very slowly forward and back, while the brave little Sachem, under a heavy fire, kept pushing steadily forward, endeavoring to pass the battery and engage it in the rear, which was supposed to be unprotected. This movement the enemy divined, and redoubled their fire at her, answered shot for shot by the three boats, the huge shells every instant bursting in their midst, carrying destruction in their wake and knocking great holes in the parapet, which appeared of sufficient size to admit the passage of a carriage and horses. The enemy acted with great bravery, however, and, if their fire slackened an instant after one of those terrific explosions, which seemed to shake the very earth around them, it was instantly resumed with increased, rather than diminished determination. Steadily but surely the little Sachem was gaining her desired position. A moment more and she would pass out of range, and the day would be won. All eyes were bent upon the noble little craft, when suddenly a shot was seen to strike her amidships, crushing in her sides and tearing their iron plating for the protection of sharp-shooters as a piece of paper, causing her to career and tremble from stern to stern. An instant more and she was enveloped in the scalding vapor of escaping steam, and lay a helpless wreck, at the mercy of the enemy. The flag was lowered, and the enemy, ceasing their fire on her, now turned their entire attention to the Clifton, probably aware of the fact that the draught of the Arizona would not permit her to advance near enough to become a very formidable antagonist. The disabling of the Sachem at the instant when victory was within her grasp was the second of those unfortunate accidents referred to, and was, of course, of so serious a character as to imperil the success of the entire affair. The Clifton was now the only effective boat engaged. She was called upon to do double duty, and not for one breath did her gallant commander and brave crew hesitate, but, with three rousing cheers, which were heard above the din of battle, they poured in their fire, running in closer and closer to the batteries, in the face of the concentrated fire of the entire rebel fortification.

Putting on a full head of steam, the Clifton ran swiftly down directly toward the battery, with the intention, doubtless, of delivering her broadside, giving her sharp-shooters an opportunity to pick off the enemy's gunners and thus silencing the works. At the same time the Granite City and the General Banks gradually followed in her wake for the purpose of reaching the point of debarkation as soon as the Clifton had effected her object, although the heavy solid shot and hissing shell which were intended for the Clifton, but which passed her, came ricochetting along on the water, almost reaching them. Just as the Clifton gained the point she aimed at reaching, and as her bow was thrown round slightly, in the act of turning, she struck, the velocity with which she was running driving her a long distance into the thin mud at the bottom of the pass. At the same time a hitherto undiscovered battery to the left of the main work, and in easy range, opened upon her as she lay, her broadside offering a target of which the enemy took every advantage. The gallant Crocker still kept up a constant fire from both bow and broadside guns, the quick rifles, loaded with double charges of grape, being poured into the main work, sweeping the parapet clean at every discharge, and killing the enemy by scores, while with his broadside guns he administered dose after dose of shell and solid shot to the battery on the left. Lying as he did, he would probably have succeeded in silencing the main work, thus enabling the troops to land, had it not been for the broadside work; for it was from that his boat was disabled. Up to this time she has sustained no material damage. The shots which had struck her had been harmless to the ship, and but very few of his crew were injured. But fate was against him, and he was obliged to succumb. A shot from the small battery struck his boat about the centre, passing through her side and entirely through the boiler, leaving her a stranded wreck at the enemy's mercy. The flag was instantly lowered; but the firing still continued, both from the boat and the batteries. It must have been lowered without the Captain's knowledge, or he may have been killed and the crew left without a leader. An instant more, and just after a shower of grape was poured into the noble little craft, the white flag was run up and the firing ceased. The engagement was concluded. Brave hearts and manly forms had been sacrificed upon the altar of their country, but without success. There was but one available gunboat left uninjured, the Arizona, and she was incapable of offensive operations against works of such strength. She was immediately withdrawn from the unequal contest, and the order reluctantly issued to the fleet to withdraw.

Considering the number of the forces engaged, it is doubtful if any affair of the whole war can compare with the battle of Sabine Pass in obstinacy of fighting, loss of life, and the amount of interest involved. To the enemy it was a matter of life and death, and to the Union forces it was the opening battle of a most brilliant campaign. The enemy retained their prize; but their loss has been undoubtedly without precedent in the annals of the war, and they will, in the midst of their rejoicing, tremble at the thought of a repetition of the attack. There were on board the Clifton, beside her crew, a party of seventy-five sharp-shooters and three of the signal corps, and on the Sachem a detachment of thirty sharp-shooters. Of the crew of the Clifton, five soldiers, one sailor, and one signal man escaped down the beach, and were taken off by a boat from the fleet. The number of killed and wounded must have been large, particularly on the Clifton, as she was not only exposed to a cross fire, but was raked from stern to stern by grape. As to the killed and wounded on the Sachem nothing is known; but the loss is supposed to be light, and mostly from the escaping steam, as but the one shot was known to have struck her. The loss of the enemy was undoubtedly enormous, as the huge nine-inch shell apparently searched every

nook and corner of the earthwork; and when the Clifton was aground the same guns poured in a murderous fire of grape, sweeping the parapet from end to end. Their loss, however, will probably never be known.

Where the blame is to rest in this affair it is difficult to determine, as the arrangement appeared to be of the most perfect character throughout, and the action of all engaged unsurpassed in determination. There appeared to be a failure in some respects in the quartermaster's department; but the result of the entire affair will probably, and with justice, be ascribed to those accidents which so often determine the fate of armies as well as nations.

ANOTHER ACCOUNT.

NEW-ORLEANS, September 12, 1863.

On arriving at the spot on which our troops were destined to land, it was soon found to be impossible to attempt any thing of the kind, owing to the marshy nature of the ground and the excessively shallow water. It soon, therefore, became evident that upon our gunboats would devolve the whole task of attacking; and gallantly did some of them go into an engagement that is pronounced by all who saw it one of the most desperately contested of the whole war.

The attack was commenced about half-past three o'clock on the afternoon of the eighth, by the gunboat Clifton, Captain Crocker commanding, carrying nine heavy guns, two of which—one at the bow and the other at the stern—were nine-inch pivots.

Captain Crocker opened fire at a distance of about two miles from his bow pivot, and after an experimental shot or two, acquired the range, pouring in upon the enemy a continuous stream of fire.

The Sachem, Captain Johnson commanding, in the mean time took up a position where she could pour a raking cross-fire, and also opened with her broadside of rifled pieces, which were served with equal precision and effect.

About the same time the powerful battery of the Arizona, Captain Tibbetts, from a position at the stern of the Sachem, also opened upon the enemy with screaming shell and hissing round shot—every one of which could be plainly seen plowing up the interior of the fort and crashing through the breastworks.

This continued for some time before the enemy replied, the ships gradually nearing the fort and increasing the rapidity of their fire until they were within point-blank range, and the Sachem had nearly passed by the works—on the right hand side of the oyster reefs fronting them—when the enemy suddenly opened a terrific fire from his entire battery.

The firing now continued hot and fierce, the enemy's shot being generally aimed too high, passing over the tops of the vessels, and striking in the water beyond them; while on the other hand nearly all the shots from the vessels were effective, searching every portion of the larger work, and, at times, with such effect that every man was driven from the guns.

But just at this moment, when every thing appeared most favorable, and the fortunes of war seemed about to assign the meed of victory to the gallant little vessels, the Sachem unfortunately grounded, broadside on, exposing her most vulnerable part to the concentrated fire of the enemy's largest work, the steamers, and the sailing craft.

This was speedily taken advantage of by them, and a perfect storm of shot and shell fell upon, over, and around her, making the water hiss and foam like a boiling cauldron. Soon a heavy rifled shot struck her fair in the side, crushing in the iron plating and wood-work, and striking her machinery, exploded her steam-chest, filling the vessel with the scalding vapor, and leaving her a helpless wreck, with no hope of getting off the shore.

The enemy now ceased their fire on the Sachem and turned their attention to the remaining two boats; the crews of which, realizing the position of their brave comrades, redoubled their exertions.

The Arizona, unfortunately, drew too much water to get to close quarters, and it devolved upon the Clifton alone to undertake the perilous task of silencing the works.

Putting on a full head of steam, the devoted little craft ran down directly toward the largest fort, keeping up a hot fire all the time from her pivot-guns, and as she neared the works loading with double charges of grape, sweeping the parapet at every discharge.

The Clifton had now approached to within about five hundred yards, and after giving the enemy a last discharge of grape from her pivot, attempted to throw her bow around, and take up a broadside position. But she had gone a few yards too near, and as she slightly swung around her bow struck—the velocity with which she was running driving her far upon the shore. She instantly commenced backing, keeping up a constant fire from her bow and port broadside guns, the former keeping the main parapet entirely clear of the enemy, while the latter played on the second battery.

This continued for some time, and faint hopes were entertained that the gallant captain would succeed in extricating the boat from her terrible position. But this was not to be; for, at last, a shot from the battery at the left penetrated her boiler, in an instant reducing her to the same condition as the Sachem.

The battle was now, to all intents and purposes, ended. Further resistance seemed utterly hopeless, but still the brave Crocker could not endure the idea of giving up his vessel, and ordered his men to fight on. Without his knowledge, however, some party struck the white flag, and the enemy instantly ceased firing.

When informed of this, the captain ordered the deck to be cleared, and loading the after pivot-gun with a nine-inch solid shot, he fired it through the centre of the ship, from stem to stern, tearing the machinery to pieces, and rendering it utterly worthless to the enemy. After doing this, and spiking all the guns, the Clifton surrendered.

The remaining gunboat, the Arizona, quite unable to cope with the enemy single-handed, and drawing too much water to engage them in close quarters, reluctantly withdrew from the unequal contest, firing a farewell shot of defiance as she steamed slowly down the bay, the enemy not replying to her challenge.

The Clifton had on board, beside her regular crew of one hundred and ten men, seventy-five sharp-shooters—all of whom were captured, with the exception of seven men, who swam ashore, ran down the beach, and were taken off by a small boat.

The loss of the armament of the Clifton is unquestionably a serious one; her powerful battery of rifled guns being one of the most powerful in the service. The boats, however, are so much damaged that the guns, to be of any service to the enemy, will have to be removed from them, and remounted, and consequently it will be a long time before they can be made available.

Doc. 126.

THE INDIAN CAMPAIGN.

OFFICIAL REPORT OF COLONEL WILLIAM CROOKS.

HEADQUARTERS SIXTH MINNESOTA INFANTRY, CAMP WILLISTON, D. T., August 5, 1863.

Captain R. C. Olin, Assist. Adjutant-General:

SIR: Pursuant to order of Brigadier-General H. H. Sibley, this regiment reported at Camp Pope, Minnesota, for services in the expedition directed against the Sioux Indians.

The march was taken up early on the morning of the sixteenth, and on the twenty-sixth day of June, the forces encamped at the foot of Lake Traverse, a distance of one hundred and nineteen miles from Camp Pope.

From this point a train was despatched to Fort Abercrombie for supplies; the guard consisting of three companies of infantry, including company H of the Sixth regiment, Captain Tattersall commanding one battalion of cavalry, Major Parker commanding, and one section of artillery, the whole under command of Lieutenant-Colonel Averill, of this regiment. The brigade left Lake Traverse on the thirtieth of June, and reached the first crossing of the Sheyenne River on the evening of the fourth of July, distant from the foot of Lake Traverse seventy-four miles.

At this point, called Camp Hayes, the command lay over six days awaiting the arrival of the supply train from Fort Abercrombie. The train arrived on the ninth of July, and the expedition resumed the line of march on the morning of the eleventh. From this point to the second crossing of the Sheyenne, where we arrived on the seventeenth, the distance was eighty-three miles. On the morning of the eighteenth, we resumed the march and reached Camp Atcheson, on Lake Emily, the day's march being twelve miles.

At this point I was directed to lay out an intrenched camp, and a force was selected from the several regiments to hold the same, with a view to disembarrassing the active force of all men unable to march; and of all supplies not actually necessary in a more rapid pursuit of the enemy. Companies G and C of my regiment were designated by me as part of the garrison, together with invalids from all other companies.

Having put the command in light marching order, on the morning of the twentieth of July, with twenty-five days' rations, the command again commenced with renewed energy the pursuit of the Sioux, and at noon, on the twenty-fourth, at a distance of seventy-eight miles from Camp Atcheson, a shout from the advance told that our pursuit had not been in vain. The savages lined the crest of the surrounding hills, covering their camp some five miles to the southwest. By direction of the General, the Sixth regiment, together with company M of the Mounted Rangers, under command of Lieutenant Johnson, and a section of artillery, under command of Lieutenant Weston, occupied the east front, and threw up earthworks supporting the guns.

About this time Surgeon Weiser, of the Mounted Rangers, in company with others, rode up the heights and engaged in conversation with the Indians, who, true to their proverbial treachery, pierced his manly heart at the moment he offered them bread. Observing this act, I at once deployed companies E, I, and K well to the front, and with company E, under command of Captain Schoennemann, together with Captain Chase's company A, of the Ninth regiment, on Schoennemann's left, supported by Captains Slaughter and Braden, drove the savages for three miles, and prevented their turning our left.

Lieutenant-Colonel Averill was directed by me to advance three companies to support the extreme left, where a strong demonstration was being made; Major McLaren remaining in command of the reserve and camp.

The movements were well and regularly made, the officers and men displaying those traits of most consequence to soldiers.

My advance was checked by an order to draw in my lines to the lines of the skirmishers of the other regiments to my right, and to report in person to the Brigadier-General commanding. Having turned the command over to Lieutenant-Colonel Averill, with instructions to draw in his men, I reported to General Sibley, and in conformity with his orders, I despatched a messenger to Major McLaren to come forward with all haste with five companies, to the support of the Mounted Rangers, who were driving the Indians on toward their camp, at the moment supported by the Seventh infantry and Captain A. J. Edgerton's company of the Tenth. The Major came forward at a double-quick, with companies A, B, D, I, and K, and reported to me some four miles in the advance, where General Sibley was awaiting the arrival of reënforcements. I immediately reported to the General the arrival of my

men, and soon thereafter was ordered to return to camp.

The next day the camp was moved some four miles in order to recruit the animals, and the command rested until Sunday morning, the twenty-sixth of July, when the march was resumed, and having marched fourteen miles, the Sixth regiment leading, the Indians again assembled for battle. The regiment at once deployed skirmishers and advanced steadily, driving the Indians; Lieutenant-Colonel Averill, with marked coolness and judgment, commanding the extended line of skirmishers, while the reserve, under Major McLaren, was but too eager to engage. At two o'clock P.M., General Sibley, coming to the extreme front and observing the state of affairs, pushed cavalry to our right, with a view to massing the Indians in front, also ordering Captain Jones forward with his field-pieces. Major McLaren was now ordered to take the reserve to camp, a mile and a half to the rear, the front being held by three companies of the Sixth, and company A of the Ninth; the whole supporting Lieutenant Whipple, with his section of the battery.

The Indians observing McLaren's movement, having made a feint to the left, made a desperate attack on the north front, with a view to destroying our transportation; but the Major had his men well in hand, and throwing them rapidly upon the enemy, completely foiled this, their last move, and the savages giving a parting volley, typical of their rage and disappointment, left a field where heavy loss and defeat but retold their doom.

Too much praise cannot be awarded Captain Oscar Taylor, of the Mounted Rangers, who chafed for an order to advance, and who bore his part nobly when that order was finally given. His horses being exhausted, this officer dismounted his men, and as skirmishers, added their strength to that of company A, Sixth regiment, where, under the immediate eye of Colonel Averill, they did splendid service. Lieutenant Whipple, in direct charge of the guns, was as usual cool and efficient; and Captain Jones had but another opportunity of congratulating himself upon the efficiency of his battery.

The march was resumed on the morning of the twenty-seventh, and in the afternoon we camped on Stony Lake, having marched eighteen miles. No demonstrations were made by the Indians during the night, but as the column was forming on the morning of the twenty-eighth, and the transportation was somewhat scattered, the wily foe saw his opportunity, and to the number of two thousand mounted men at least, made a most daring charge upon us. The Sixth regiment holding the centre of the column, and being upon the north side of the lake, Lieutenant-Colonel Averill commenced deploying the right wing, and having deployed strongly from my left, so as to hold the lake, the advance was ordered. The men went boldly forward and worked splendidly, Lieutenant-Colonel Averill displaying much judgment in an oblique formation to cover a threatened movement on my right by the Indians in great force, who, whooping and yelling, charged our lines. The consequences must have been destructive in the extreme had the lake and flank not been stiffly held. The savages were driven back reeling under their repulse, and the General commanding coolly and determinately formed his column of march in the face of the attack, the object of which was manifold: first, to destroy our transportation, and second, to delay our advance, allowing their families more time to escape.

No time was lost, the column moved on, and by nine A.M. our advance saw the masses of the retreating foe. The pursuit was continued until late, when we encamped on Apple River. Men and horses were not in a condition to pursue that night, but early on the morning of the twenty-ninth, with the regiment in the advance, pursuit was commenced, and after marching six miles and overcoming a rise of ground, our eyes first beheld the timber on the Missouri River, distant nine miles.

General Sibley had, with much forethought, early that morning, despatched Colonel McPhaill and his regiment, with Captain Jones and his field-pieces, to the front, with the view to intercepting the savages ere they crossed the river. Rapidly McPhaill pushed forward, but the Indian rear was covered by a dense forest, and a tangle of prickly ash and thorn bushes almost impenetrable. Our advance was soon up, and by order of the General the Sixth regiment was ordered to scour the woods to the river, and ascertain the exact position of the enemy. I deployed companies D, I, and K, commanded by Captains Whitney, Slaughter, and Braden, as skirmishers under the command of Major McLaren, while the five other companies under Colonel Averill were held as reserve. Captain Jones accompanied me with Whipple's and Western's sections of his battery. We advanced slowly but surely, shelling the woods in my advance, and we reached the river to find the enemy just crossed, after abandoning all their transportation and losing many of their women and children drowned in their hasty flight. Lieutenant-Colonel Averill with the reserve, received the fire of an enemy in large numbers concealed in the tall rushes across the river, and returned it with spirit; but an order having reached me to return, a retrograde movement was ordered.

Just prior to the fire of Colonel Averill's reserve, Lieutenant F. J. H. Beever, an English gentleman of qualities worthy of the best, a fellow of Oxford University, and a volunteer aid to the General, rode up alone and delivered the order to return. I wrote a short despatch and directed him to return at once, as my communication might prove of much value to the General.

All being accomplished that was desired, the regiment returned and joined the camp near the mouth of Apple River, with the loss of private N. Miller, of company K. On my return to camp I learned that Beever had never reported, and we had just grounds to believe him lost.

Guns were fired and rockets sent up, but our friend did not return.

At noon on the thirtieth of July, a detachment consisting of companies A, I, and K, of the Sixth regiment, commanded by Captains Grant, Slaughter, and Braden; A, B, and H of the Seventh, commanded by Captains Arnold, Gillfillan, and Stevens, and B, F, and K of the Tenth infantry, commanded by Captains Edgerton, White, and O'Connor, and companies L and M of the cavalry, commanded by Captain Davy and Lieutenant Johnson; Lieutenant Whipple's and Lieutenant Dwelle's sections of the battery, together with a detachment of company A, Ninth regiment infantry as pioneers, under Lieutenant Jones; the whole under my command, was ordered to proceed to the place where I had been the day before, with directions to destroy the transportation left by the Indians, and to find the body of Lieutenant Beever and that of private Miller, if dead, and engage the savages if the opportunity presented. Lieutenant-Colonel Jennison of the Tenth infantry, Major McLaren of the Sixth, and Major Bradley of the Seventh, commanded the detachments of the respective regiments. All the objects contemplated were fully accomplished.

It was apparent that Lieutenant Beever, on his way back with my despatch, became embarrassed by the many trails left by an alarmed and conquered enemy, lost his way, and after bravely confronting a large party of savages and dealing death into their ranks, had fallen pierced by arrows and bullets, his favorite horse lying dead near him. He was buried in the trenches with the honors due his rank, and every heart beat in sympathy with the family of this brave stranger, as we retraced our steps toward the boundary of our own State.

I take pleasure in mentioning the services of Surgeon and Acting Medical Director Wharton, of Assistant Surgeons Daniels and Potter, for duties performed wherever they were needed, in and out of the regiment, also to Lieutenants Carver and Snow for assistance fearlessly rendered in the field. Lieutenant-Colonel Averill and Major McLaren have proven themselves worthy of the regiment.

For the officers of the line and men I proudly say that they did all that they were ordered to do with an alacrity and a spirit which promise well for the future.

I made the distance from Fort Snelling to the Missouri by our line of march, five hundred and eighty-five miles.

I have the honor to remain, Captain,
    Very respectfully,
        Your obedient servant,
            WILLIAM CROOKS,
     Colonel Commanding Sixth Minnesota Infantry.

REPORT OF COLONEL JAMES H. BAKER.

HEADQUARTERS TENTH REGIMENT MINNESOTA INFANTRY,
    CAMP WILLISTON, August 5, 1863.

Captain R. C. Olin, Assist. Adjutant-General:

I have the honor herewith to submit a report of such part as was borne by my regiment, or any portion of it, in the several actions from July twenty-fourth, at Big Mound to the Missouri River.

About half-past three o'clock on Friday, the twenty-fourth of July, while on the march, doing escort duty in the centre, I received information from the General commanding that a large force of Indians were immediately in our front, accompanied by an order communicated by Lieutenant Beever to prepare my regiment for action, which order was immediately executed. Meantime the train was being corraled on the side of the lake, after which I received orders to form my regiment on the color line indicated for it, immediately in front of the corral and fronting outward from the lake, and to throw up intrenchments along this line, which was speedily done. The action of this day began on my right, more immediately in front of the Seventh, (which regiment, being in advance during the day's march, was entitled to the forward position,) by the artillery, under Captain Jones, when at half-past four P.M. I received an order by Captain Olin to deploy a company to support this battery. I immediately deployed company B, Captain Edgerton, and that company, though fatigued already with an ordinary day's march, continued with the battery, (marching for many miles on the double-quick,) during the entire pursuit of the enemy for fifteen miles, and throughout the night, till sunrise the next morning, when they returned from the pursuit to the camp, having made, during the day and night, the almost unparalleled march of quite fifty miles.

At about five o'clock I received an order by Captain Pope to send Lieutenant-Colonel Jennison, with four companies, to be deployed, and to follow in the direction of the retreating enemy, as a support for the cavalry and artillery. Colonel Jennison moved forward with companies A, F, C, and K, five miles, more than half of it on the double-quick, and reported his command to the General commanding, at that time in the front. After resting about one hour, by the order of the General commanding, Colonel Jennison was directed to return with his force to camp, and arrived a little after nine o'clock P.M.

At the same time that the first order above alluded to was given, I was directed to assume command of the camp, and make the proper dispositions for its defence, which I did by completing all the intrenchments, and organizing and posting such forces as were yet left in camp, not anticipating the return of our forces that night.

The action of the twenty-sixth of July took place on the side of the camp opposite from my regiment, and consequently we did not participate in it. We were, however, constantly under arms, ready at any moment for orders or an opportunity.

On Tuesday, the twenty-eighth of July, my regiment being in the advance for the day's march, we started out of Camp Ambler at five o'clock in the morning. The General commanding, some of the scouts, and a few of the head-quarters wagons had preceded my regiment out of camp, and were ascending the long sloping hill which gradually rose from Stony Lake. I had just received directly from the General commanding, orders for the disposition of my regiment during the day's march, when the scouts came from over the hill on a full run, shouting, "They are coming! they are coming!" when immediately a large body of mounted Indians began to make their appearance over the brow of the hill, and directly in the front of my advancing column. I instantly gave the necessary orders for the deployment of the regiment to the right and left, which, with the assistance of Lieutenant-Colonel Jennison, and the great alacrity of the commandants of companies, were executed with the utmost rapidity, though a portion of my line was thrown into momentary confusion by the hasty passage through it of the returning scouts and advance wagons. At this moment an Indian on the brow of the hill shouted: "We are too late; they are ready for us!" Another one replied: "But remember our children and families; we must not let them get them." Immediately the Indians, all well mounted, filed off to the right and left along the hill in my front with the utmost rapidity. My whole regiment was deployed, but the Indians covered my entire front, and soon far outflanked on both sides, appearing in numbers that seemed almost incredible, and most seriously threatening the train to the right and left of my widely-extended line. The position of the train was at this moment eminently critical. It had begun to pass out of the corral around both ends of the small lake to mass itself in the rear of my regiment, in the usual order of march. The other regiments were not yet in position, as the time to take their respective places in the order of march had not yet arrived. Fortunately, however, Captain Jones had early moved out of camp with one section of artillery, and was in the centre of my left wing, and Lieutenant Whipple, with another near the centre of my right, which was acting under Colonel Jennison.

Simultaneously with the deployment of the regiment, we began a steady advance of the whole line up the hill upon the foe, trusting to the speedy deployment of the other infantry regiments, and the cavalry for the protection of the train, so threatened on either flank at the ends of the lake. My whole line was advancing splendidly up the hill directly upon the enemy, the artillery doing fine work, and the musketry beginning to do execution, when I received a peremptory order to halt the entire line, as a further advance would imperil the train. So ardent were both officers and men for the advance, that it was with some considerable difficulty that I could effect a halt. Believing fully that the great engagement of the expedition was now begun, and seeing in my front, and reaching far beyond either flank, more than double the number of Indians that had hitherto made their appearance, I took advantage of the halt to make every preparation for a prolonged and determined action. Meantime long-range firing continued throughout the entire line, and frequently the balls of the enemy would reach to, and even pass over my men, though it was evident that the range of the Indian guns bore no comparison to ours. About this time I twice received the order to cause the firing to cease, which order I found difficult to execute, owing to the wide extent of my line, and the intense eagerness of the men.

I then received orders that, as the train was closed up, I should form my regiment in order of battle, deployed as skirmishers, holding two companies in reserve, and that, thus advancing, our order of march would be resumed in the face of the enemy. In a few minutes the dispositions being made, all was ready, and in the order of battle indicated we passed the hill, and found that the enemy had fled. We saw them but once again for a moment on a distant hill in great numbers, when they entirely disappeared. My regiment marched in deployed order of battle in echelon at the head of the column for eighteen miles, expecting and ready at any moment to meet the enemy.

The number of Indians so suddenly charging upon us was estimated at not less than from one thousand five hundred to two thousand. They were well mounted and moved about with the utmost rapidity and with their characteristic hideous yells. The artillery, under Captain Jones and Lieutenant Whipple, did great execution, as I could well observe, and the fire of my men did effective service, and enabled us to hold the enemy at bay till the train was closed up and the regular dispositions for its defence made. At least three of the enemy were seen to fall by the fire from my line, their bodies being thrown on ponies and rapidly carried away. The artillery must have killed and wounded a considerable number. Nothing could exceed the eagerness, firmness, and gallant bearing of all the officers and men of my command during this unexpected, and by far numerically, the greatest effort the Indians had yet made upon the forces of the expedition. In their courage and earnest desire to clear the enemy from the hill by a double-quick charge, my officers and men were a unit. Nothing but the imminent peril of the train could induce them to cease the advance they had so gallantly begun.

On the thirtieth of July, while at Camp Slaughter, on the Missouri, I received an order to send three companies of my regiment, under Lieutenant-Colonel Jennison, to join an expedition under Colonel Crooks, the object of which was to skirmish through the timber and heavy underbrush to the river, and destroy the property of the Indians known to be upon its banks. This most laborious task was assigned to companies B, F, and K, and a portion of company C. A report of their operations will, of course, be given you by the officer commanding the expedition.

I desire, Captain, to avail myself of this opportunity to express my sincere gratification at the good order, faithful devotion to every duty, most determined perseverance in the long and weary marches, uncomplaining in the severe guard and trenching labors, submitting unmurmuringly to

every fatigue which has characterized the officers and men of my regiment during the tedious and arduous march we have made to the distant shores of the Missouri River. It is with justifiable pride that I here note how nobly they have performed all that has been required at their hands.

I have the honor to be, Captain,
Very respectfully,
Your obedient servant,
J. H. BAKER,
Colonel Tenth Regiment Minnesota Infantry.
Captain R. C. OLIN,
A. A. General, Dist. Minnesota.

Doc. 127.

ARMING THE NEGROES.

A REBEL PROTEST.

RICHMOND, VIRGINIA, July 16, 1863.
To the Editor of the New-York Tribune:

SIR: In the almost vain hope of helping to avert new horrors of war from which the soul of every Christian citizen must shrink—with the prayerful wish, rather than with the expectation, of saving your people and mine, your Government and mine, your cause and mine, from crimes political and military too terrible to contemplate without a shudder, I ask you to lay before your countrymen certain most grave facts, affecting at once their character and their existence as a nation, and coming home with a most kindly warning to "the business and the bosom" of every man among you who has interest to appeal to, a conscience to rouse, or a heart to touch. And I ask the *New-York Tribune* thus to speak for the humane among us to the humane among you, for two reasons; first, because that journal is the exponent of the doctrines of the Federal Administration, of the dominant party in the United States; and then, because abominable as those doctrines must ever be to us—cruel as are your counsels, impracticable as is your language—the *Tribune* has at least been from the beginning a consistent and courageous partisan, a fair and open foe—neither asking nor giving favors, playing no fantastic political tricks, nor bidding for all applause at once.

How I came by the knowledge of the facts which, in the very eagerness of a patriotic fear, I take this extraordinary means of imparting to your party, your rulers, and your people is "neither here nor there." Let it suffice to assure you, and I know you will believe me, that my opportunities have been as sure as the use I make of them is pure.

Let me comfort you with the assurance that I shall serve these facts to you in a form as compact as possible; for, indeed, I have but little to hope from the chances of this letter's ever reaching you. As to the peril to myself—that is nothing.

On the third day of July, 1863, the Honorable Alexander H. Stephens, Vice-President of the confederate States of America, ran down from

Richmond in a confederate steamer, under a flag of truce, to the mouth of the James River, where he had conference with Acting Rear-Admiral S. P. Lee, commanding your blockading squadron, as to certain matters of state.

I need not occupy your space (or at least your time, sir) with formal dilations. You know there was brief correspondence between our Vice-President and your Government. Mr. Stephens desired audience for the purpose of presenting to the consideration of Mr. Lincoln certain propositions bearing upon the spirit and conduct of the war. Mr. Lincoln declined to confer with Mr. Stephens, and Mr. Stephens returned to Richmond. Not to waste words in controversy, that, Mr. *Tribune*, was, I believe, the end of the expedition.

But not the end of speculations as to its real object. The guesses of your journals have been far more numerous than the possibilities. I propose to disenchant you. Therefore this letter.

The Vice-President of the confederate States was sent to ask the President of the United States to coöperate with the former government in measures conducive to the cause of humanity, to the cultivation of the most Christian shapes of warfare—such measures, in the first place, as might be agreed upon between them to lighten the troubles of prisoners, and alleviate the pains of the wounded. And had Mr. Stephens been so fortunate as to procure the audience he so frankly and simply sought, I, for one, believe that the mercy of his errand would have met with proper recognition. This, however, secondarily.

The primary object of the Vice-President's mission was to protest, in the name of his government and people, against the mustering and arming of the blacks, which now constitutes almost the only clear feature of your policy. He came to implore you, in the name of a people whose resources must have surprised you, of a government whose ability you have frankly acknowledged, of soldiers whose courage and devotion and endurance you have felt, to this consummation not to come at last. He came to assure you, on the good faith of his government, on the simple truth of his fellow-countrymen, that not one single regiment or corps of negroes has ever been brought into the confederate service, to be turned armed against you.

He came to remind you that such negroes as have, from time to time, been found on breastworks and in trenches, have been caught with spades only or picks in their hands; that, such as have been found in regiments, an insignificant number, have been, in all cases, body-servants, sometimes of officers, sometimes of privates, who of their own will, out of the love which you know they bear us, have chosen to follow their masters to the death. And these you have found among your prisoners. He could have told you, if diplomacy permitted sentiment, (God save the mark!) of many such "chattels," some of them white-haired, begging, stealing, fighting their way home again, to the "ole missus" and the old

place, with all that was left of the "young massa"—a lock of hair or a trinket.

But no matter for that. He came to talk to you of self-preservation, of retaliation, and all that's shocking in the meaning of that word. He came to tell you of the native devil that has slept so long, to be awoke at last, in the bosoms of a simple, dependent, affectionate race. He came to implore you in the name of God not to do this abominable thing.

Else he would have to fall back upon statistics and the grim phraseologies of war, and remind you that the four millions of negroes that appear in the tablets of your census for 1860 are the working hands of both sexes only. That number does not include the superannuated or the infants. Out of these four millions, at least seven hundred and fifty thousand able-bodied fellows, loving, and trusting their masters, and ready to follow them up to the mouths of your cannon, (ah! do not continue to befool yourself on that question of ties,) can be enrolled, armed, drilled in three months.

They can be officered in every grade by their own masters, those who have seen most service and won most honor. They can be segregated, regiment by regiment, with the white troops. In all the departments, the quartermasters, the commissariat, and the medical, white officers can administer for them. Superior commands in the black regiments can be made the meed of gallant service in the white. In fine, the entire system, as it operates in the Sepoy service in India, and as it has been modified by distinguished British officers at the request of our government to meet the peculiarities of our people—peculiarities which constitute incalculable advantages, presenting as they do, love and confidence in place of hate and jealousy and suspicion—can be put in working order at once.

This is what I tell you can be done. This is what the Vice-President of the confederate States came to tell you will certainly be done forthwith. Will you tell your people this?

It is not for me to speculate upon the consequences of these new and dreadful elements, whirled into new forms of conflict and complication, to prolong and intensify the war. My mind, in striving to grasp the subject, lets go its hold, and shrinks as from something at once terrible and loathsome. I cannot speak of things which seem to cry aloud out of the future with the tongues of women and of babes, with the contention of angels of friends, mixed of pity and fury.

But I do see in all this a hidden mine of power in the South which your policy may in one fatal moment spring upon the country, to bury all we once loved and were proud of in an undistinguishable monstrosity of disgust and death.

RANDOLPH.*

* See the Mission of Alexander H. Stephens, *t* pages 135 and 199 Documents, *ante.*

Doc. 128.

THE DRAFT RIOT IN BOSTON.

BOSTON "POST" NARRATIVE.

Boston, July 15, 1863.

THERE was no little excitement in the city yesterday afternoon and last evening, growing out of the preliminary enforcement of the conscription act. It appears that Mr. David Howe and Mr. Wesley Hill, connected with enrolling office, District Four, were engaged yesterday noon in serving notices to those who had been drafted. While in the prosecution of this work they were interrupted, and somewhat severely treated, as will be seen further on. Mr. Howe was in the act of leaving a notice at No. 146 Prince street, when he and Mr. Hill were set upon with violence by a small crowd which had been following them. Mr. Hill immediately escaped and proceeded as quickly as possible to the provost-marshal's office, No. 106 Sudbury street, to inform Captain Howe of what was taking place. Mr. Howe was pushed and hustled, and finally struck upon the head. At this point Officer Wilkins, of Station One, arrived and rendered assistance to the imperilled man. Mr. Wilkins succeeded in getting Mr. Howe away from the crowd, and entered the store of Mr. Stearns, on the corner of Prince and Commercial streets, where the blood was washed from his face. The officer then started to walk with Mr. Howe to his lodgings—the Merrimac House—but as soon as they reached the street, the crowd, which had by this time greatly increased in numbers, again set upon Mr. Howe. This time he was thrown down and badly beaten. He was subsequently taken into a house on Causeway street, where Dr. A. B. Hall attended him. He had five or six cuts about his head, which bled freely, and an equal number about his face. Both eyes were cut, and so swelled that the sight was temporarily lost. There were several severe bruises on his side, but no bones were broken. He was removed to his lodgings at night.

While these acts of violence and disorder were progressing, a corps of policemen was detailed to quell the same. Officer Trask, of Station Two, was severely wounded about the head and neck, mostly by bricks and other missiles thrown at him. Officer Winship, of Station One, was severely used after the same style. Officers Ostrando and Wasgatt, of the same station, were more or less bruised; but on no occasion did either of the officers give way to the rioters, or allow themselves to be intimidated in the least degree. The above are all the acts of violence we could learn. The crowds that assembled were evidently overawed. They proceeded without further demonstrations to the vicinity of Station One, Hanover street. Squads also gathered in Commercial and North streets, Haymarket Square, and other localities at the North End. The same was the case last evening.

In the mean time the city authorities instituted measures of the most efficient nature to quell any riotous demonstrations that might have been made, and to which the State authorities lent a willing hand. Captain E. J. Jones, of the Eleventh battery, was ordered to proceed to the armory, Cooper street, and be in readiness for any emergency which might arise. During the afternoon extra cannon and other material of a like nature were brought in from Readville. An order was also issued to the Metropolitan horse railroad to furnish thirty horses for the battery, which was at once complied with. At five o'clock a company of one hundred men from the Third artillery regiment at Fort Independence reached the city, and marched up State, Washington, and Court streets, in which thoroughfares they were cheered lustily. The company was fully prepared for immediate service, had such been required. Their presence in the city was quite generally welcomed. The First battalion of dragoons, Major Wilder, were notified to be in immediate readiness, in case their services were required. Governor Andrew issued an order for the Forty-fourth regiment to assemble at their armory, Boylston Hall, forthwith, and await orders. They assembled with alacrity, and were ready for service during the afternoon, evening, and night. The Forty-fifth regiment were ordered to assemble this morning at Readville at sunrise, or as soon afterward as possible.

Since the above was in type, matters have assumed a much more serious aspect, involving the loss of life of several persons. At half-past eight o'clock the telegraph fire alarm was sounded. This had previously been agreed upon as the signal of danger. A crowd had assembled in Dock Square, numbering some five hundred persons, evidently premeditating a demonstration of some sort. This was soon developed. The hardware store of Thomas P. Barnes, No. 28 Dock Square, was broken open by the mob, and in a very short time rifled of guns, pistols, bowie-knives, and other similar goods. About one hundred guns, seventy-five pistols, four dozen bowie-knives, and a quantity of superior cutlery were stolen, valued at about four thousand dollars. From the fact that these articles were selected, and no other goods harmed, it is supposed that the rioters were aware of their location in the store. The mob next attempted to enter the gun-store of John P. Lovell, over the store of Mr. Barnes. But in this they did not appear to have succeeded. They next went to the well-known store of Mr. Reed, Faneuil Hall Square, and were about to obtain a forcible entrance, when they were met by the police, under command of Mr. Dunn, of the detective force, who at once made an assault upon the invaders. In the *mélée* a man named James Campbell, the ringleader, was shot in the head and one arm. He was arrested and taken to Station Two, where his wounds were attended to by Dr. Palmer. They are not dangerous. He is in the employ of Michael Doherty, a well-known liquor-dealer in North street. An attempt was made to bail him out, but this was unsuccessful. He endeavored to shoot Officer Dunn, who appeared to be too quick for him. As soon as the police fired upon the mob they dispersed in great haste, evidently thinking danger was at hand.

Shortly after the scene just described had occurred, a large force of police arrived, and immediately following was the company from Fort Independence. The light dragoons completed the column. The arrival of this formidable force was greeted by the enthusiastic applause of the assembled multitude. Their advent completely squelched any demonstration on the part of the mob. The police shortly afterward began to clear the square and the vicinity of Faneuil Hall. Military were placed at each avenue. In Faneuil Hall Square two cannon, well charged, were made ready for service in case of necessity. We are glad to state that this extremity did not occur. About eleven o'clock a rain set in, and most of the crowd dispersed.

While these things were progressing, a much more serious affair took place at and in the vicinity of the armory in Cooper street, the headquarters of Jones's battery. About half-past eight o'clock the armory was surrounded by a crowd which was unmistakably bent on mischief. It commenced by the throwing of stones, bricks, and other missiles. This was followed by a forcible entrance into the armory. The company were driven back from the doors. Lieutenant Sawin was seized, taken out, thrown down, and frightfully beaten. Captain Jones, finding matters had reached a crisis, and all warnings having failed, and finding, moreover, that the mob was likely to prevail, ordered one of his field-pieces, loaded with canister, to be discharged. This was followed, as might be naturally supposed, with fatal results. At least three persons were killed outright, and some estimate as many as ten, though of the latter number we have no definite information. A man whose name is not known, about thirty years old, was shot in eleven places. The body presented a frightful appearance. One arm was nearly shot away. His head and body were perforated in every direction. The body was taken to Police Station No. One. An elderly man named William Currier, seventy-two years old, father of Officer Currier of Station One, was shot dead in the armory by one of the mob. He was in the armory looking after his son. A boy named John Norton, ten years old, living at No. 166 Endicott street, was shot through the heart, and died immediately. Michael Geffey, a lad of about the same age, was shot in the bowels. His wounds are of a hopeless nature, and he was not expected to survive the night. A boy named Patrick Reynolds, living in Bolton Place, leading from Hanover street, was shot in the hip, the large bones of which were fractured. He was taken to the hospital, and is not expected to live. A woman was shot in the breast, and was carried off among the crowd; as were also some half-dozen others. The precise extent of the injuries could not be ascertained amid the confusion and terror of the hour. After this terrible but just punishment, the mob dispersed. No further acts of violence were perpetrated during the evening.

A large crowd assembled in Kingston street, about eight o'clock, but we do not hear that any special riotous acts were committed. The alarm by telegraph appeared to attract them downtown. The entire police force of the city was on duty—each man being armed, besides the usual equipments, with a six-barrelled revolver. The South-Boston police reported itself ready for duty in Court square, in twenty-eight minutes after the alarm was given. The management of the police throughout was very efficient.

Besides the regulars from Fort Warren, Companies B, C, and D, from Fort Warren, came up to the city, and were put on duty during the evening. A company of heavy artillery from Readville also reached the city at ten o'clock. All these companies were on duty during the night, well posted for active service. The dragoons patrolled the city all night, visiting such portions as might be supposed to harbor disorderly characters.

BOSTON "COURIER" ACCOUNT.

BOSTON, July 15, 1863.

A riot took place in this city last night which, but for the promptness of the measures taken to suppress it, would have probably proved as disastrous as that in New-York. The outbreak was apparently sudden, and with the fatal consequences, it is not unreasonable to believe that a repetition of it will not be made.

Wesley Hill and David Howe were engaged in distributing notifications to drafted men about noon. A notice had been left at a shop in Prince street, for a man who was not present, and Mr. Howe, stopping to talk with a woman in relation to the matter, was struck by her. An attempt was made to arrest the woman, when a gathering crowd hearing who the officers were, made an assault upon Howe, beating him severely. He was rescued from the mob by officer Wilkins, and carried into a store, corner of Prince and Causeway streets. When it was supposed the crowd had dispersed, they proceeded toward the Merrimac House, where Howe boarded, when they were again assailed, and Howe was separated from the officer and further beaten. Dr. Hall was called to dress the wounds of Howe, and found five or six cuts about his head, his eyes swelled, and face severely bruised. Meanwhile Mr. Hill, escaping from the mob, reported the difficulty at the office of the Provost-Marshal.

A force of police officers was sent to the scene of the disturbance, and in the attempt to quell it Officer Ostrander was severely injured in the head. Curtis Trask, of the Second Station, was cut with a knife immediately under one of his eyes, cut through his clothes on his right side, and was severely bruised in his back. For a time there were fears that other riotous acts would be committed, but nothing further occurred beyond the gathering of crowds of people in and near the First station-house. These crowds increased as a knowledge of the disturbances was made known, and during the afternoon many were looking on through curiosity, while others talked over the matter of the draft with considerable feeling.

These serious indications of difficulty caused measures to be taken to increase the police force in suitable locations, and orders were issued to notify the Lancers, the Eleventh battery, Captain Jones, and the Forty-fourth regiment, to be ready for immediate service. An order was also sent to Fort Warren for troops, and three companies ware sent up, which, after being marched through several of the principal streets, were quartered at the barracks in Beach street. A company of regulars was also sent up from Fort Independence, and nearly a company of the Second cavalry, from Readville. These precautions, it was believed, would be sufficient to prevent any difficulty during the night.

As night approached, many young men, in squads of from six to twelve or more, from various parts of the city, were seen moving toward the North End, some of them with sticks or clubs, but even then it was not clear that any mischief was designed. At about half-past eight o'clock, a crowd of from five hundred to one thousand gathered in front of the armory of the Eleventh battery, in Cooper street, with riotous demonstrations. Captain Jones warned the crowd of the dangers of a riot, but this did not avail, and an assault was made upon the building. Stones and bricks were freely thrown, the windows were broken, and the door forced, when some of the rioters entered the building, and several of the members of the battery were injured. It was then manifest that some more effectual measures must be taken, or the guns in possession of the battery would be captured. A gun had been loaded with canister-shot, and when the mob were about to triumph, it was fired with fatal effect, killing several and wounding many more.

This shot caused the mob to waver, but they did not give way entirely until a bayonet-charge was made upon them. The statements during the evening were very conflicting as to the result of the firing, but as near as could be ascertained at a late hour, the killed and wounded were as follows: A man about thirty-five years of age, name not known, was killed, eleven shot taking effect in his head and body, and his right arm was nearly shot off. The body was taken to the First station-house. William Currier, a man of seventy-one years, father of Officer William W. Currier, who lived near the Armory, was killed, it is supposed, by the mob. He belonged in Bow, New-Hampshire, and had been living in this city about six months. John Norton, a boy ten or twelve years of age, living at No. 166 Endicott street, shot through the heart, and died instantly. Michael Gaffy, fourteen years old, living at No. 31 Cross street, was shot in the bowels, and probably did not survive the night; his hand was also shot off. P. Reynolds, a boy of twelve years, living in Boston Place, was shot

in the hip, the bone being badly shattered, and his arm broken. He was sent to the hospital, and may survive.

The boys were all taken to the office of Dr. Walsh, in North square, and such measures were taken for the relief of the living as were found to be necessary. There were reports that the body of a woman was seen carried through the streets on a bier, but it could not be learned who she was. Reports of other persons being killed and wounded it was difficult to verify.

About the same time with the attack on the Armory, a mob of several hundred persons made a rush into Dock Square, to procure arms. The store of Thomas P. Barnes, No. 28, was broken open, the door and window being demolished, when the best arms in the store were immediately seized upon and carried away. Not less than one hundred guns, nearly as many pistols, and three or four dozen bowie-knives, valued at some three thousand dollars, were stolen. From appearances in the choice of the articles, and the position from which some of them were taken, it is believed that the leaders must have had knowledge of their location. The door of the entry adjoining was broken open, and the mob rushed up-stairs to the shop of John P. Lovell, gunsmith, but it did not appear that the shop was entered.

The next rush was made for the store of William Read & Son, Faneuil Hall Square. A guard of several officers has been stationed in this store, known to have a larger and more choice stock of fire-arms than any other in the city. When the mob entered Dock Square, John M. Dunn, detective officer, who was at Mr. Read's store, hurried to the Second station-house, filled a carriage with officers well armed, and driving rapidly reached the store just as the mob was breaking in. One man who struck a blow upon the window was shot in the head, and the mob received a check. This man was James Campbell, very stout and muscular, and although the shot took effect above his eye, causing much blood to flow, it did not appear that he was seriously injured. He was carried to the station-house, and locked up. Some efforts were made to effect his release on bail, which, however, proved ineffectual.

As soon as the riotous demonstrations became known, an alarm was given to turn out the military, as well as the police force. It was but a short time before nearly the entire day police force in the city proper reported for duty at the Second station, with a delegation of some thirty from South-Boston. This force was sent to Dock Square as fast as assembled, but the mob had separated, departing in different directions. The Mayor, Chief of Police, and Deputy Chief, were early at the scene of the riot, promptly and efficiently directing the movements of the police, and giving directions for the posting of the military.

The Light Dragoons were early on duty, and were placed as a patrol force in the neighborhood of the Cooper street Armory, in Haymarket

Square, at Faneuil Hall, and other points where there were any gatherings or probability of a riot. The force from the forts was placed in and around Faneuil Hall, to be used as required, with two field-pieces loaded in the square. The cavalry from Readville was posted as a support to these guns. The lancers were at their Armory in Sudbury street, ready at any moment on call.

When the rumor of the acts of the mob became known, the streets in the vicinity of Dock Square, Faneuil Hall and Haymarket Square, were soon thronged with people, to see or hear what was going on. The police force immediately cleared the squares, and the people were directed to go to their homes. At a late hour the police occupied Dock Square, allowing no one to pass except to go to their homes, when the entrance to Faneuil Hall Square was rigidly held under military rule.

The alarm of fire soon after one o'clock this morning was caused by an attempt to set fire to the Armory in Cooper street, during the absence of the guard. The fire was extinguished with but little injury.

PROCLAMATION BY MAYOR LINCOLN.

To the Citizens of Boston:

The peace and good order of this city have been violated by an assembly of rioters and evil-disposed persons, and still further violence is threatened. I therefore deem it my duty to ask the aid of all good citizens in suppressing any tumultuous assemblages that may be gathered, and in bringing to condign punishment all violators of law and good order; and I also deem it my duty to notify and warn all persons who have been or shall be engaged in making depredations upon property, in assaulting individuals, or in any way disturbing the public peace, that full preparation has been made for any exigency their conduct shall create.

The good order and quiet of the city shall be preserved at all hazards, and those who riotously attempt them shall be brought to punishment, whatever vigor may be necessary to these ends. That innocent parties may not suffer with the guilty, all persons whose duty does not call them into proximity are requested to keep away from them; and all parents and guardians are earnestly desired to see that the minors under their control are not in the streets after sunset.

F. W. LINCOLN, JR.,
Mayor.

CITY HALL, BOSTON, July 15.

Doc. 129.

VALLANDIGHAM'S ADDRESS

TO THE PEOPLE OF OHIO.

NIAGARA FALLS, Canada West, July 15, 1863.

ARRESTED and confined for three weeks in the United States, a prisoner of state; banished thence to the Confederate States, and there held as an alien enemy and prisoner of war, though on parole, fairly and honorably dealt with and

given leave to depart—an act possible only by running the blockade, at the hazard of being fired upon by ships flying the flag of my own country, I found myself first a freeman when on British soil. And to-day, under protection of the British flag, I am here to enjoy and in part to exercise the privileges and rights which usurpers insolently deny me at home.

The shallow contrivance of the weak despots at Washington and their advisers has been defeated. Nay, it has been turned against them; and I, who was maligned as in secret league with the confederates, having refused when in their midst, under circumstances the most favorable, either to identify myself with their cause, or even so much as to remain, preferring rather exile in a foreign land, return now with allegiance to my own State and government, unbroken in a word, thought, or deed, and with every declaration and pledge to you while at home, and before I was stolen away, made good in spirit and to the very letter.

Six weeks ago, when just going into banishment because an audacious but most cowardly despotism caused it, I addressed you as a fellow-citizen. To-day, and from the very place then selected by me, but after wearisome and most perilous journeyings for more than four thousand miles by land and upon sea; still in exile, though almost within sight of my native State, I greet you as your representative. Grateful certainly I am for the confidence in my integrity and patriotism, implied by the unanimous nomination as candidate for Governor of Ohio, which you gave me while I was yet in the confederate States. It was not misplaced; it shall never be abused. But this is the last of all considerations in times like these. I ask no personal sympathy for the personal wrong. No; it is the cause of constitutional liberty and private right, cruelly outraged beyond example in a free country by the President and his servants, which gives public significancy to the action of your Convention. Yours was, indeed, an act of justice to a citizen who for his devotion to the rights of the States and the liberty of the people had been marked for destruction by the hand of arbitrary power. But it was much more. It was an example of courage worthy of the heroic ages of the world; and it was a spectacle and a rebuke to the usurping tyrants, who, having broken up the Union, would now strike down the Constitution, subvert your present government, and establish a formal and proclaimed despotism in its stead. You are the restorers and defenders of constitutional liberty, and by that proud title history will salute you.

I congratulate you upon your nominations. They whom you have placed upon the ticket with me are gentlemen of character, ability, integrity, and tried fidelity to the Constitution, the Union, and to liberty. Their moral and political courage—a quality always rare, and now the most valuable of public virtues—is beyond question. Every way, all these were nominations fit to be made. And even jealousy, I am sure, will now be hushed if I especially rejoice with you in the nomination of Mr. Pugh as your candidate for Lieutenant-Governor and President of the Senate. A scholar and a gentleman, a soldier in a foreign war, and always a patriot; eminent as a lawyer and distinguished as an orator and a statesman, I hail his acceptance as an omen of the return of the better and more virtuous days of the republic.

I indorse your noble platform—elegant in style, admirable in sentiment. You present the true issue and commit yourselves to the great mission just now of the Democratic party—to restore and make sure, first, the rights and liberties declared yours by your constitutions. It is vain to invite the States and people of the South to return to a Union without a constitution, and dishonored and polluted by repeated and most aggravated exactions of tyrannic power. It is base in yourselves and treasonable to your posterity to surrender these liberties and rights to the creatures whom your own breath created and can destroy.

Shall there be free speech, a free press, peaceable assemblages of the people, and a free ballot any longer in Ohio? Shall the people hereafter, as hitherto, have the right to discuss and contemn the principles and policy of the party—the ministry—the men who, for the time, conduct the government—to demand of their public servants a reckoning of their stewardship, and to place other men and another party in power at their supreme will and pleasure? Shall Order Thirty-eight or the Constitution be the supreme law of the land? And shall the citizen any more be arrested by an armed soldiery at midnight, dragged from wife and child and home to a military prison, thence to a mock military trial, thence condemned, and then banished as a felon for the exercise of his rights?

This is the issue, and nobly you have met it. It is the very question of free, popular government itself. It is the whole question—upon the one side liberty, on the other despotism. The President, as the recognized head of his party, accepts the issue. Whatever he wills, that is law. Constitutions, State and federal, are nothing; acts of legislation nothing; the judiciary less than nothing. In time of war there is but one will supreme—his will; but one law—military necessity, and he the sole judge.

Military orders supersede the Constitution, and military commissions usurp the place of the ordinary courts of justice in the land. Nor are these mere idle claims. For two years and more, by arms, they have been enforced. It was the mission of the weak but presumptuous Burnside—a name infamous forever in the ears of all lovers of constitutional liberty—to try the experiment in Ohio, aided by a judge whom I name not, because he has brought foul dishonor upon the judiciary of my country.

In your hands now, men of Ohio, is the final issue of the experiment. The party of the Administration have accepted it. By pledging support to the President, they have justified his outrages upon liberty and the Constitution, and whoever gives his vote to the candidates of that party commits himself to every act of violence and wrong on the part of the Administration which he upholds; and thus, by the law of retaliation, which is the law of might, would forfeit his own right to liberty, personal and political, whensoever other men and another party shall hold the power. Much more do the candidates themselves. Suffer them not, I entreat you, to evade the issue; and by the judgment of the people we will abide.

And now, finally, let me ask, what is the pretext for all the monstrous acts and claims of arbitrary power which you have so nobly denounced? "Military necessity." But if indeed all these be demanded by military necessity, then, believe me, your liberties are gone and tyranny is perpetual. For if this civil war is to terminate only by the subjugation or submission of the Southern force and arms, the infant of to-day will not see the end of it. No, in another way only can it be brought to a close. Travelling a thousand miles or more, through nearly one half of the confederate States, and sojourning for a time at widely different points, I met not one man, woman, or child who was not resolved to perish rather than yield to the pressure of arms even in the most desperate extremity.

And whatever may and must be the varying fortune of the war—in all which I recognize the hand of Providence pointing visibly to the ultimate issue of the great trial of the States and people of America—they are better prepared now every way to make good their inexorable purpose than at any period since the beginning of the struggle. These may indeed be unwelcome truths, but they are addressed only to candid and honest men. Neither, however, let me add, did I meet any one, whatever his opinions or his station, political or private, who did not declare his readiness, when the war shall have ceased and invading armies been withdrawn, to consider and discuss the question of reünion. And who shall doubt the issue of the argument?

I return, therefore, with my opinions and convictions as to war or peace, and my faith as to final results from sound policy and wise statesmanship, not only unchanged but confirmed and strengthened. And may the God of heaven and earth so rule the hearts and minds of Americans everywhere, that with a Constitution maintained, a Union restored, and liberty henceforth made secure, a grander and nobler destiny shall yet be ours than that even which blessed our fathers in the first two ages of the republic.

C. L. VALLANDIGHAM.

Doc. 130.

SECRETARY SEWARD'S CIRCULAR.

CIRCULAR No. 39.

DEPARTMENT OF STATE, WASHINGTON, August 12.

SIR: Whenever the United States have complained of the premature decrees of Great Britain and France, which accorded the character of a belligerent to the insurgents, the statesmen of those countries have answered, that from the first they agreed in opinion that the efforts of the Government to maintain the Union, and preserve the integrity of the Republic, could not be successful. With a view to correct this prejudgment of so vital a question, I addressed a circular letter to the representatives of the United States in foreign countries on the fourteenth day of April, 1862, in which I reviewed the operations of the war on sea and land, and presented the results which had attended it down to that period. The prejudice, which I then attempted to remove, still remains, and it constitutes the basis of all that is designedly or undesignedly injurious to this country in the policy of foreign nations. The insurgents have been enabled to protract their resistance by means of sympathy and aid they have received from abroad, and the expectation of further and more effective foreign assistance is now their chief resource. A new effort, therefore, to correct that prejudice is demanded equally by a prudent concern for our foreign relations, and by the paramount interests of peace and humanity at home.

In the battles of August, 1862, the Union forces suffered some severe and appalling reverses. But they resulted in the reünion of the army which had been called in from the Peninsula, below Richmond, with the army which had its position between that strongly fortified seat of the insurrection and this capital. The wisdom of this reünion was soon to be vindicated. The insurgent army, flushed with its recent successes, and expecting that a sympathetic interest of slavery would produce an uprising of the people of Maryland in its favor, for the first time crossed the Potomac River. Harper's Ferry, with many prisoners, fell into its hands, rather through accidents in preparing its defence, than because it was indefensible. Nevertheless, the expectation of recruits signally failed. General McClellan, commanding the now consolidated forces of the Army of the Potomac, was reënforced by fresh levies from Pennsylvania, and by detachments called in from neighboring forts. He drove the insurgents from their positions at South-Mountain and Crampton's Gap. About the middle of September the two opposing armies confronted each other at Sharpsburgh, and a pitched battle was fought on the banks of the Antietam and Potomac. It was well sustained on both sides. Men of one race and training directed the armies whose rank and file were substantially of one blood, and even nearly equal in numbers. The arrogant assumption of superior valor and heroism which the insurgents had brought into the contest, and had cherished throughout its early stages, perished on that sanguinary field. The insurgent army, shattered in the conflict, abandoned the invasion of Maryland, and sought refuge and opportunity to recover its wasted strength in Virginia, behind its accustomed barrier—the Potomac.

While Lee was thus attempting Maryland, the equally bold and alarming enterprise of carrying the war through Kentucky into Ohio, was as-

signed to Bragg, who was in command of the insurgent army on the southern border of Tennessee. He, with great rapidity, moved from Chattanooga, turning the left flank of General Buell, and, appealing for reënforcements to the slavery-inspired sentiments which existed in Kentucky and Tennessee, directed his forces against Louisville and Cincinnati. An uprising of the farmers of Ohio confronted and turned away the devastation from the latter city. General Buell followed the main column of invasion, outmarched it on the way to Louisville, and obliged it to take a direction eastward. The two insurgent columns being united at Perryville, were attacked by General Buell. The battle, like all of our contests, was obstinate and bloody. Bragg, after severe losses, retreated through a comparatively barren region, and Buell was obliged to abandon the pursuit, by the complete exhaustion of all sources of supply. The insurgent commander crossed the Cumberland Mountains, and then, marching westward, took up a position at Murfreesboro, fortified them, and proceeded to recruit his wasted forces.

Van Dorn and Price were at the same period in command of very considerable forces in Mississippi and Alabama, and to them was assigned the third part in the grand invasion of the loyal States, which the cabal at Richmond had decreed. This was an attempt, as they called it, to deliver, but in fact to subjugate Western Tennessee and Kentucky. General Rosecrans received the assault of those portions of the insurgent forces at Corinth, defeated them with great slaughter, and drove them backward, so that they neither reached nor approached the region which they were appointed to invade. General Rosecrans, called to succeed General Buell in command of the army of the Cumberland, then entered Nashville, which the insurgents had before invested, in carrying out their general scheme of invasion. He raised the siege, and prepared for offensive action. In the last days of the year he issued from Nashville and delivered a sanguinary battle at Stone River, which gave him possession of Murfreesboro. Bragg retreated to Shelbyville and Tullahoma, and there again rested and intrenched. A long period of needed rest was now employed by the respective parties in increasing the strength and efficiency of their armies; but this repose was broken by frequent skirmishes, and by cavalry expeditions, which penetrated hostile regions, sometimes hundreds of miles, and effected breaches of military connections and a destruction of military stores upon an extensive scale, while they kept up the spirit of the troops, and hardened them for more general and severe conflicts.

Vicksburgh then remained in the hands of the insurgents, the principal key to the navigation of the Mississippi River, a navigation which was confessed on all sides to be absolutely essential to the United States, and, when reöpened by them, fatal to the insurrection. The duty of wresting that key from the insurgents had been devolved on the navy, with the aid of a considerable land force then encamped on the west bank of the Mississippi River. But new and unforeseen difficulties continually baffled the enterprise, and seemed to render it impossible. General Grant, who was at the head of the department and of the army of the Tennessee, at length assumed the active command of the troops investing the stronghold, and these were adequately reënforced. The naval squadron on the Mississippi, under command of Rear-Admiral Porter, was also steadily increased until more than one hundred armed vessels were employed upon the river, including many iron-clad gunboats of great power. Part of the Gulf Squadron, under Admiral Farragut, gallantly running the batteries of Port Hudson, under a fierce fight, coöperated with the river fleets. Laborious and persevering attempts were made to open an artificial channel for the river opposite Vicksburgh, as had been done with such signal success at Island No. 10. But the various canals, projected and executed, failed, and only a few small steamers, of no considerable power, were thus enabled to pass the city. Combined land and naval expeditions were also sent forth, which, with infinite pains and endurance, attempted to turn the enemy's works by navigating the various bayous and sluggish rivers, whose intricate network forms so singular a feature of the military topography of the banks of the Mississippi. All these attempts having failed from physical obstacles found to be insurmountable, General Grant and Admiral Porter at last put afloat armed steamers and steam-transports, which ran through the fires of the long line of shore batteries which the insurgents had erected at Vicksburgh, and its chief supports, Warrenton and Grand Gulf. At the same time the land forces moved down the right bank of the river to a point below Grand Gulf, where they crossed in the steamers which had effected so dangerous a passage. The batteries of Grand Gulf for several hours resisted a bombardment by the gunboats at short-range, but they fell into the hands of the Admiral as soon as General Grant's forces appeared behind them. General Grant, through a series of brilliant manœuvres, with marches interrupted by desperate battles day by day, succeeded in dividing and separating the insurgent forces. He then attacked the chief auxiliary column under Johnston, and drove it out of Jackson, the capital of Mississippi. Having destroyed the railroad bridges and military stores there, General Grant turned at once to the west. Numerous combats ensued, in all of which the loyal arms were successful. Loring, with a considerable insurgent force, was driven off toward the south-east, while Pemberton, after a loss of sixty pieces of artillery and many prisoners, regained his shelter within the fortified lines of Vicksburgh, with an army now reduced to between thirty thousand and forty thousand men. During these movements the heavy batteries of the insurgents which were established near the mouth of the Yazoo River, and which constituted an important part of the defensive system of Vicksburgh, were taken and raised by Rear-Admiral Porter, who thereupon sent a detachment of his fleet up that important tributary of the Mississippi, and effectually destroyed the numerous vessels and stores which were found within and upon its banks. General Grant, during these brilliant operations, had necessarily operated by a movable column. He now reëstablished his communications with the river fleets above as well as below Vicksburgh, invested the town, and, ignorant of the numbers inclosed within its defences, attempted an assault. Though bravely and vigorously made, it was nevertheless unsuccessful. He thereupon sat down before the fortifications, to reduce them by the less bloody but sure methods of siege. Pemberton made a gallant defence, hoping for relief from Johnston. Strenuous efforts were made by the chiefs at Richmond to enable Johnston to render that assistance. They detached and sent to him troops from Bragg's army on the frontier of Alabama, and from Beauregard's command in South-Carolina, and in doing this they endangered both those armies. All the capable free men of Mississippi were called to the rescue of the capital of their State, and to save the stronghold of the treasonable Confederacy which was besieged within their limits. Moreover, the besieged post was in the very centre of the slave population of that Confederacy, and the President's proclamation of freedom would be sounded in their hearing if the stronghold should fall. But the effort required was too great for the demoralized and exhausted condition of the insurgents. Johnston did not arrive to raise the siege, nor did success attend any of the attempts from within to break the skilfully drawn lines of General Grant. On the fourth of July, General Pemberton laid down his arms and surrendered the post, with thirty thousand men, two hundred pieces of artillery, seventy thousand small arms, and ammunition sufficient for a six years' defence. This capture was as remarkable as the famous one made by Napoleon at Ulm.

On the same day an insurgent attack upon General Prentiss, at Helena, situated on the west bank of the Mississippi, in the State of Arkansas, was repulsed with the loss of many prisoners on the part of the assailants. As if the anniversary so identified with the nation's hopes was appointed to be peculiarly eventful, Lee, who had again entered Maryland, and, passing through that State, had approached the Susquehanna, threatening Harrisburgh, Pittsburgh, Philadelphia, and Baltimore, fell back, after pitched battles continued for three days at Gettysburgh, and resumed his retreat, with an army even worse shattered than before, to his accustomed position on the Rappahannock.

On the eighth of July, the insurgent garrison at Port Hudson, six thousand strong, after enduring a long siege with the utmost courage, surrendered unconditionally to General Banks; and thus the United States recovered from the insurgents the last of the numerous posts by which, for more than two years, they had effectually destroyed the navigation of the Mississippi.

This great river, which in time of peace contributes relatively as much toward a supply of the increased wants of mankind as the Nile did to those wants in the time of the Roman Empire, is now again opened to the inland commerce of the country. Steamers descend the river and its tributaries from the navigable floods to the Gulf of Mexico. It is not to be doubted that the insurgent losses in these operations upon the Mississippi amount to fifty thousand men and three hundred pieces of artillery, a large portion of which were of heavy calibre. Johnston's army, which, at the time of the surrender, was advancing to threaten the besiegers, at once fell back to Jackson, and it was again driven from that capital by a detachment which General Grant had committed to the command of General Sherman. In retiring, Johnston fired many buildings filled with munitions of war, and abandoned a large quantity of railroad locomotives and cars, which had been detained at that place by reason of the railroads north, south, east, and west of Jackson having been previously cut by the Government forces.

General Sherman now desisted from the pursuit of Johnston and returned to Vicksburgh, where a portion of the army is enjoying repose, not more necessary than well earned, while others are engaged in expelling from the vicinity of the Mississippi roving bands of the insurgents, who infest its banks and fire from thence upon passing steamers. It is reported that Johnston, with the troops at his command, now said to be twenty-five thousand, has fallen back to Meridian, on the eastern border of the Mississippi, a hundred and twenty miles east of Vicksburgh, so that the State, whose misguided people were among the earliest and most intemperate abettors of the insurrection, is virtually abandoned by its military agents.

In Louisiana, General Banks succeeded General Butler. After spending some months in organizing the department and disciplining the new levies which constituted its force, General Banks made a rapid and successful series of marches and contests, in which he drove the insurgent troops out of the Attakapas and Teche regions, well known as the richest portions of that very productive State, captured Alexandria and Donaldsonville, the seats of its fugitive seditious executive and legislative authorities, crossed the Mississippi at Bayou Sara, and there receiving an additional column which was ascending from Baton Rouge, invested Port Hudson, which, excluding Vicksburgh, was the only remaining stronghold of the insurrection on the great river.

It will be remembered that on the twenty-second day of September, 1862, the President issued a proclamation requiring the insurgents to lay down their arms and return to their allegiance, under the penalty that in all the districts where the insurrection should be still maintained with the support of the people, he would on the first of January then next proclaim, as a military measure, the freedom of the slaves. The warning was generally rejected and defied, but the proclamation which it heralded was duly issued. As the National armies advanced into the insurrectionary territories, slaves in considerable numbers accepted their freedom and came under the protection of the National flag. Amidst the great prejudice and many embarrassments which attended a measure so new and so divergent from the political habits of the country, freedmen with commendable alacrity enlisted in the Federal army. There was in some quarters a painful inquiry about their moral capacity for service. That uncertainty was brought to a sudden end in the siege of Port Hudson. The newly raised negro regiments exhibited all necessary valor and devotion in the military assaults which were made, with desperate courage, and not without fearful loss, by General Banks. This protracted operation engaged nearly all General Banks's available forces. While it was going on, insurgent troops which were called up from Texas reöccupied much of the south-western portion of Louisiana, which he had before reclaimed. The surrender of Port Hudson, however, set his army at liberty, and he has already made considerable progress in restoring the national authority thus temporarily displaced.

The complete occupation of the Mississippi by the national forces has effectually divided the insurrectionary region into two parts, and among the important features of this division, one which is of the highest practical significance is, that the field of military operations of the insurrection is chiefly on the eastern side of the river, while its supplies have been mainly drawn from the prairies of Arkansas and Texas, which stretch away from the western shore. These prairies can no longer supply the insurgents with cattle for sustenance and use in the field, and, on the other hand, arms, ordnance, and ammunition can no longer be sent from the eastern manufactories and deposits to forces employed or in garrison in the West. The value of the acquisition of the Mississippi in this respect was illustrated only a few days since in the capture by General Grant, near Natchez, of five thousand beeves and two thousand mules, which had crossed to the eastern bank, and at the same time many hundred thousands of cartridges and other stores which had just been landed at the western end of the same ferry.

A vigorous blockade has been maintained at Charleston, and although fast steamers, of light draught and painted with obscure colors, occasionally succeed in slipping through the blockading squadron in the morning and evening twilight, many are destroyed and more are captured. An attack by the fleet, made on the seventh day of April last, upon the forts and batteries which defend the harbor, failed because the rope obstructions in the channel fouled the screws of the iron-clads and compelled them to retire after passing through the fire of the batteries. Those vessels bore the fire of the forts, although some defects of construction were revealed by the injuries they received. The crews passed through an unexampled cannonade with singular impunity. Not one life was lost on board of a Monitor. The defects disclosed have been remedied, and an attack is now in progress, with good prospects of ultimate success, having for its object the reduction of the forts in the harbor by combined sea and land forces. We occupy more than one half of Morris Island with land forces, which, aided by batteries afloat and batteries ashore, are pushing siege-works up to Fort Wagner, a strong earthwork which has been twice assaulted with great gallantry, but without success. On the seventeenth of June, the Atlanta, which was regarded by the insurgents as their most formidable iron-clad vessel, left Savannah, and came down the Wilmington River. The national iron-clads Weehawken, Captain John Rogers, and Nahant, Commander John Downs, were in readiness to meet her. At four o'clock fifty-four minutes the Atlanta fired a rifle-shot across the stern of the Weehawken, which struck near the Nahant. At quarter-past five the Weehawken, at a range of three hundred yards, opened upon the Atlanta, which had then grounded. The Weehawken fired five shots, four of which took effect on the Atlanta. She surrendered at half-past five.

Our lines have not changed in North-Carolina. All attempts of the insurgents to recapture the towns from which they had been expelled have been repulsed. Much damage has been inflicted upon their communications, and valuable military stores have been destroyed by expeditions into the interior. North-Carolina shows some symptoms of disaffection toward the insurgent league. Similar indications are exhibited in Mississippi, Alabama, Arkansas, and Texas.

The situation on the York and James Rivers has remained unchanged since the withdrawal of the army of General McClellan from the Peninsula a year ago. Attempts by the insurgents to retake Williamsburgh and Suffolk have been defeated, but the garrison at the latter place has been withdrawn for purely military reasons to a more defensible line.

I now return to the army of the Potomac, which was left resting and refitting after putting an end to the first insurgent invasion of Maryland. General McClellan recrossed the Potomac and entered Virginia in November, and obliged the invading forces under Lee to fall-backward to Gordonsville, south of the Rappahannock. When the army of the Potomac reached Warrenton it was placed under command of General Burnside. He marched to Falmouth, hoping to cross the Rappahannock at Fredericksburgh, and to move at once upon Richmond. Delays, resulting from various causes, without fault of the General, permitted the insurgents to occupy the heights of Fredericksburgh, and when, at length, in December, General Burnside crossed the Rappahannock, his assault upon Lee's well-fortified position failed. He skilfully recrossed the river without loss. General Hooker succeeded to the command, and it was not until the beginning

of May that the condition of the roads permitted a renewal of offensive operations. The General crossed the Rappahannock and accepted a battle, which proved equally sanguinary to both parties, and unsuccessful to the army of the Potomac. The heights of Fredericksburgh were captured by General Sedgwick's corps, but the whole army was compelled to return to the north bank of the river. After this battle, Lee, in the latter part of May and in June, withdrew his army from General Hooker's front, and ascending the south bank of the Rapidan, toward the sources of the Rappahannock, entered the Shenandoah Valley, and once more tempted the fortunes of war by invading the loyal States. A severe cavalry engagement at Beverly Ford unmasked this movement. The army of the Potomac broke up its camps and marched to the encounter. The militia of Maryland, Pennsylvania, and New-York flew to arms, and occupied Baltimore, Harrisburgh, and the line of the Susquehanna. The two armies met at Gettysburgh, in Pennsylvania, and after a fierce contest of three days' duration, and terrible slaughter on both sides, the insurgents recoiled from the position held by General Meade, who had been then only four days in command of the army of the Potomac. On the fourth of July, the day of the surrender of Vicksburgh, Lee retreated, passing through Chambersburgh and Hagerstown to Williamsport, where the proper disposition to attack him was made by General Meade. Deceived concerning the state of the river, supposed to be unfordable, General Meade, hourly expecting reënforcements, delayed the attack a day too long, and the insurgents, partly by fording and partly by floating bridges, succeeded in withdrawing across the river by night, with their artillery and a great part of their baggage. Much of this baggage, as well as of the plunder which Lee had collected, was destroyed by cavalry, or thrown out of the wagons to make room for the wounded whom Lee carried off from the battlefield. He had buried most of his dead of the first day's conflict at Gettysburgh. The remainder, together with those who fell on the second and third days of the battle, in all four thousand five hundred, were buried by the victorious army. Many thousand insurgents, wounded and captives, fell into the hands of General Meade. It is not doubted that this second unsuccessful invasion cost the insurgents forty thousand men. Our own loss was severe, for the strife was obstinate and deadly. General Meade crossed the Potomac. Lee retired again to Gordonsville, where he is now understood to be in front of our forces.

While the stirring events which have been related were occurring in the East and in the West, General Rosecrans advanced upon Bragg, who, with little fighting, hastily abandoned his fortified positions of Shelbyville and Tullahoma, in Southern Tennessee. General Rosecrans took, and he yet holds them, while Bragg, with severe loss in a hurried retreat, has fallen back to Chattanooga. It is understood that his army had been already much weakened by detachments sent from it to reënforce Johnston, with a view to a raising of the siege of Vicksburgh.

I must not overlook the operations of cavalry. General Stoneman, in connection with the movement upon Chancellorsville, made a rapid and effective passage through the insurgent country, from the Rappahannock to the York River, which will be remembered among the striking achievements of the war. While our forces were operating against Vicksburgh and Port Hudson, Colonel Grierson, with a force of one thousand five hundred men, left Corinth, on the northern border of the State of Mississippi, and made an expedition, in which he broke military communications, destroyed stores, and effected captures through the length and breadth of the State, and, finally, without serious loss, joined the army of General Banks, then engaged in the siege of Port Hudson.

John Morgan, hitherto the most successful of the insurgent partisans, recently passed around the lines of General Burnside, crossed the States of Tennessee and Kentucky, moving northward, and avoiding all large bodies of our troops, he reached the Ohio River at Brandenburgh, below Louisville, and seized two steamboats, with which he crossed into Indiana. Thence proceeding rapidly westward, subsisting on the country and impressing horses as his own gave out, he traversed a portion of Indiana and nearly the whole breadth of Ohio, destroying railroad stations and bridges, and plundering the defenceless villages. The people rallied to arms under the calls of their Governors. Some of them occupied the most important points, while others barricaded the roads or hung upon the rear of the intruders. Morgan found no disaffected citizens to recruit his wasted ranks, and when he reached the Ohio his force was prevented from crossing by the gunboats and driven backward with great slaughter. His force was between two thousand five hundred and four thousand horse, with several pieces of artillery. Only some three hundred succeeded in recrossing the Ohio and escaping into the wilds of Western Virginia. Many perished in battles and skirmishes, and the remainder, including Morgan himself, his principal officers, and all his artillery, were finally captured by the national forces. An attempt has just been made by the insurgents to invade Eastern Kentucky, which probably was begun with a view to make a diversion in favor of Morgan's escape, but the forces, after penetrating as far as Lexington, have been routed by detachments from General Burnside's army, and pursued, with the capture of many prisoners and of all their artillery.

This review of the campaign shows that no great progress has been made by our arms in the East. The opposing forces there have been too equally matched to allow great advantages to accrue to either party, while the necessity of covering the national capital in all contingencies has constantly restrained our generals and forbidden such bold and dangerous movements as usually conduct to brilliant military success. In the West, however, the results have been more gratifying. Fifty thousand square miles have been reclaimed from the possession of the insurgents. On referring to the annexed map it will be seen that since the breaking out of the insurrection, the Government has extended its former sway over and through a region of two hundred thousand square miles, an area as large as Austria or France, or the Peninsula of Spain and Portugal. The insurgents lost in the various field and siege operations of the month of July which I have described, one third of their whole forces.

Jefferson Davis, the leader of the sedition, has since proclaimed a levy of all the able-bodied men within his military lines. This, if carried into effect, will exhaust the whole material of which soldiers can be made. The insurgents estimate the total number of conscripts thus to be gained at from seventy thousand to ninety-five thousand. Our armies now confront the insurgents at all points with superior numbers. A draft for three hundred thousand more is in progress to replace those whose terms of service have expired, and to fill up the wasted ranks of our veteran regiments, and the people, just so fast as the evidence of the necessity for that measure is received and digested, submit with cheerfulness to the ascertained demands. Our armies everywhere are well equipped, abundantly fed, and supplied with all the means of transportation. The soldiers of two years' service bear themselves as veterans, and show greater steadiness in every conflict. The men, accustomed to the camp, and hardened by exercise and experience, make marches which would have been impossible in the beginning of the contest. The nation is becoming familiar with arms, and easily takes on the habits of war. Large voluntary enlistments continually augment our military force. All supplies are abundantly and cheaply purchased within our lines. The country shows no signs of exhaustion of money, material, or men. A requisition for six thousand two hundred remount horses was filled and the animals despatched from Washington all in four days. Our loan is purchased at par by our own citizens, at the average rate of one million two hundred thousand dollars daily. Gold sells in our market at one hundred twenty-three to one hundred eighteen, while in the insurrectionary region it commands one thousand two hundred per cent premium.

Every insurgent port is either blockaded, besieged, or occupied by the national forces. The field of the projected Confederacy is divided by the Mississippi. All the fortifications on its banks are in our hands, and its flood is patrolled by the national fleet.

Missouri, Kentucky, Delaware, Maryland—all slave States—support the Federal Government. Missouri has already in convention ordained the gradual abolition of slavery, to take effect at the expiration of seven years. Four fifths of Tennessee, two thirds of Virginia, the coasts and sounds of North-Carolina, half of Mississippi and half of Louisiana, with all their large cities, part of Alabama, and the whole sea-coast of Georgia and South-Carolina, and no inconsiderable part of the coast of Florida, are held by the United States. The insurgents, with the slaves whom they yet hold in defiance of the President's proclamation, are now crowded into the central and southern portions of Virginia, North-Carolina, South-Carolina, Georgia, and Alabama, while the pioneer slaveholding insurgents beyond the Mississippi are cut off from the main force. On the other hand, although it is less than six months since the laws or customs of the United States would allow a man of African descent to bear arms in defence of his country, there are now in the field twenty-two thousand regularly enlisted, armed, and equipped soldiers of that class, while fifty regiments of two thousand each are in process of organization, and sixty-two thousand eight hundred persons of the same class are employed as teamsters, laborers, and camp followers. These facts show that, as the insurrection continues, the unfortunate servile population, which was at the beginning an element of its strength, is being transferred to the support of the Union.

You will use the facts presented in this paper in such a way as may be most effective to convince those who seek a renewal of commercial prosperity through the restoration of peace in America, that the quickest and shortest way to gain that desirable end is to withdraw support and favor from the insurgents, and to leave the adjustment of our domestic controversies exclusively with the people of the United States.

I am, sir, your obedient servant,
WILLIAM H. SEWARD.

Doc. 131.

EXPEDITION TO MONROE COUNTY, KY.

CAPTAIN STONE'S OFFICIAL REPORT.

GLASGOW, KENTUCKY, September 7, 1863.

Major Samuel Martin:

SIR: I have the honor of reporting to you the result of my expedition into Monroe County, Kentucky, having received orders from yourself, on the third instant, to take all the men who had serviceable horses, of your battalion, and proceed to Monroe County, Kentucky, for the purpose of bringing into Glasgow for safety some Government property, said to be deposited on Peters Creek, in Monroe County, Kentucky. I started on the evening of the third instant from Glasgow, Kentucky, with eleven men beside myself. We travelled fourteen miles that evening and camped for the night. On the morning of the fourth instant we rode into Tompkinsville, where we had some horses shod; then riding out of town two miles, we camped for the night.

On the morning of the fifth instant we went to Bethlehem meeting-house; then went to the Widow Lane's, and stopped to rest and feed our horses— this in Monroe County, Kentucky. The boys being very tired, lay down to sleep awhile and rest. I stepped out of the house when the boys were sleeping to see that all was right, and I soon heard distinctly the sound of horses' feet approaching us, which seemed to be about seven hundred yards distant, though coming rapidly. I returned to arouse the boys, and did so with considerable difficulty. Every man soon had his gun, and was ready for any emergency. We went to where our horses were tied, and succeeded in moving them all to the rear of the house save two. The rebels were then upon us. The night was dark, but they numbered between two hundred and fifty and three hundred. The advanced-guard, consisting of about seventy-five men, passed the house far enough so as to let the centre of the column rest opposite the house. Seeing our two horses, they halted their column, and commenced an examination of the horses. The information they received was from our twelve carbines, which told them that Yankees were about. The sudden fire confused the rebels, though they returned our fire; but their column was cut in the centre, both ends falling back on the road to our right and left.

We were soon ready for another exchange of shots, and bouncing over the fence into the road —changing our base of operations right and left, facing six each way—we let them have twelve more shots, which were returned by about seventy-five rounds from the enemy, who were still falling back. Seizing this favorable opportunity, we took off on double-quick to a grove of timber about two hundred yards off. We had hardly reached the timber before the house we had left was surrounded by the whole of the rebel command, hallooing out: "Where are these d—n Yankees?" They were soon informed by the reply of our twelve carbines, which told the rebels well of our whereabouts. We then fell further back into the woods to avoid pursuit, knowing we were fighting twenty times our number. We were now dismounted, our horses all having broke loose on the first round of firing. We lay in the woods until sun-up, hoping to recover our horses; but to our regret, when the sun rose it showed the enemy in possession of our battle-field, and they were picking up our horses. We were at this time almost helpless, and observing the old adage, "that small boats should keep near the shore," we struck up our march for Glasgow, which place was reached on the morning of the seventh instant. Our losses were twelve horses and twelve equipments, and one gun. The boys had several holes shot through their clothes, but no flesh wounds. The rebels report their loss as follows: Four men killed, one horse killed and three wounded.

Yours respectfully,

GEORGE P. STONE,
Captain Commanding Squad Thirty-seventh Kentucky M. I.

Doc. 132.

THE WYTHEVILLE EXPEDITION.

GENERAL SCAMMON'S DESPATCH.

CHARLESTOWN, July 24.

GENERAL KELLY: Colonel Toland, with the Second Virginia cavalry and the Thirty-fourth

Ohio mounted infantry, cut the railroad at Wytheville, Virginia, and destroyed two pieces of artillery, seven hundred muskets, and a large amount of ammunition and stores, and had a sharp fight in Wytheville. Captured one hundred and twenty-five prisoners, who were paroled. Killed, seventy-five. Wounded, not known. Our loss is seventy-eight killed, wounded, and missing. Seventeen were killed, including Colonel Toland and Captain Delaney. Colonel Powell is very dangerously wounded, and is a prisoner. We were fired upon from houses, public and private, by the citizens, even by the women. My men totally destroyed the town, and reached Fayette yesterday, after a march of about three hundred miles.   E. P. SCAMMON.
                                  Brigadier-General.

A NATIONAL ACCOUNT.

CAMP PIATT, VIRGINIA, July 26, 1863.

On the afternoon of the thirteenth instant, the Second Virginia volunteer cavalry, and the Thirty-fourth Ohio volunteer infantry, mounted, left Browntown, Virginia, under command of Colonel John Toland, and proceeded up Lens Creek to Lens Mountain. Crossing this, we reached Coal River, a small river which empties into the Kanawha. As the time allotted for our special duty was passing away, we travelled through the night, resting a few minutes at daylight to arrange our affairs for continuing our march. Moving along the river toward Raleigh Court-House, which place we passed to our left, we struck the Shady Spring road, and at eight P.M., encountered the enemy's pickets, of about one hundred men, who immediately fired upon our advance, killing two and wounding three others of the Second Virginia cavalry. The pickets immediately gave the news of our approach, and the rebels, though fortified, began to prepare for a backward movement, and fearing an ambush, we awaited the approach of day before renewing the attack. The night was intensely dark, and our command became divided, one taking the road to Raleigh, the other to Wyoming. However, the mistake was soon rectified, and on Wednesday morning, tired and hungry, the column again moved on the Wyoming road. The country is barren of grain and produce. No males remain at home, having either entered one or the other armies, or removed to places more secure. After travelling hard all day we reached Trumps's Farm, the owner being in the rebel army. Little or no attention was paid to our troops by the citizens, and they received little in return at this place. General Scammon had ordered a train of forage and rations, and orders were received to take six days' rations for men, two for horses, and after a short sleep we arose from our grassy beds and prepared to continue our march toward Dixie. At three A.M., Thursday, we took the Marsh Fork road of Coal River, and struck the Guyan Mountain. The ascent of this mountain was tedious, as the road has not been travelled for a long time; consequently our

way had to be cleared of obstructions that impeded our march. The summit at last reached, we began to descend, and enter a valley destitute of name or people. What few inhabitants live (?) here obtain a livelihood by digging ginseng and other roots, and are satisfied with that scanty allowance. The country is destitute of improvements. The grist-mills, if I may be allowed to call them such, are erected by joint-stock companies, with a capital of about seventy-five cents and a few hours' labor, and this does the work of two or more families. They live in huts that the Esquimaux would scorn to be invited into. Long, dirty, tobacco-dried, sallow-complexioned women stare at you as you pass. Ask them a question, they answer you, giving what information they possess, but it is so little as to render you no assistance. Continuing through the valley, we reached Wyoming Court-House, a place of no importance. It contains a few dilapidated buildings, and points again to the native genius and industry of the people, who eke out a miserable existence in this God-forsaken country. Here a small dirty tavern stands, with two or three half-starved old men gazing upon the Yankees as they march along, eyeing them, expecting that they will destroy all property, and insult women and murder the children. We passed through this place about noon, and struck the Indian Creek road. Proceeding through a most miserable country, we camped for the night about thirty miles south-east of Wyoming Court-House, and grounded ourselves for the night. At two A.M., Friday, the seventeenth, "boot and saddle sounded," and at three A.M. our column was in motion. We crossed the Tug range of mountains and met the Tug Fork of Big Sandy, continued down the creek to near Abb's Valley, where we learned the rebel Colonel Beckley was organizing a battalion at Camp Pemberton, under Captain Stoting. The rain came down in torrents, drenching all to the skin. No one, except they that have travelled through the mountains of Virginia, can conceive how it rains on the mountains. Arriving within four miles of this camp, our advance started on a trot, and about three o'clock P.M. the rebel pickets and entire camp were captured, consisting of one captain and thirty-five men; but one escaped, who was then on horse.

We went ahead, and began to move more rapidly until within five miles of Jeffersonville, the county-seat of Tazewell County, where we encamped for the night. Through Abb's Valley the scenery beggars description for beauty. As far as the eye can reach stretch, in every direction, hills and vales. The country is rich, owned principally by wealthy citizens, who were very influential in bringing about the rebellion, living in luxury and ease. They little dreamed that they, living in so remote a place, should be made to feel the weight of the hand of war. On Saturday morning, at two o'clock, we left our camping ground, without feed for horses, and our men, having got all their rations wet while crossing rivers, began to feel the want of food. We left

Jeffersonville to our right, and struck Clinch River. The country is beautiful; good farms, poorly attended. We then crossed Rich Mountain. From this mountain the scenery is grand, and nothing can be traced to lead one to believe that desolating war has ever paid them his visits. The people had heard much and seen little of Yankee soldiers; none, save prisoners, had ever passed through this part of Dixie, and the white population looked upon us with fear, ready to give all when asked. On the other hand, the negroes assembled in groups, threw themselves in every conceivable form; jumping, singing, dancing, yelling, and giving signs that "the year of jubilee had come." The white men fled, as we approached, leaving their homes at our mercy, which were not molested, except used in some way to benefit the rebel army; in such cases, they were always destroyed. We now struck Beartown Mountain, and then entered Buck Garden, a place of resort, owned principally by Erl Perry, a man of considerable influence among the ignorant. At this place a store was owned by the rebel Colonel Callahan, and in his charge the brother of the thief J. B. Floyd had placed a splendid medical library; the buildings were destroyed, as well as a flour-mill in the same vicinity. Passing through this rich strip to Garden Mountain, Bland County, Virginia, which is well worth a visit in peaceable times, and crossing this, we enter Rich Valley and continue to Walker's Mountain; crossing this, we strike Strong Fork road toward Wytheville, Wythe County, Virginia, (a place of one thousand eight hundred inhabitants, on the Virginia and Tennessee Railroad;) after proceeding a few miles, we came in sight of the enemy's pickets; skirmishing immediately commenced, and when we were within four miles from the town the charge was sounded and the cavalry put in motion. The charge was led by Captain Delany, of the First Virginia cavalry. About four o'clock P.M., we came in sight of the town of Wytheville. The charge began in earnest. The cavalry, under command of Colonel Powell, all expected to find the enemy in line of battle; but, instead of this, they assembled in various buildings commanding the principal streets, and opened a deadly volley upon our advancing column. The town was entered, and scarce had the first company passed ere the citizens and soldiers opened from every house a terrible fire; one volley killed Captain Delany and his First Lieutenant, and severely wounded his Second Lieutenant; but three companies entered the town on the charge, two companies, the First Virginia cavalry, and company I, Second Virginia cavalry, the remainder having been thrown in disorder by the dead horses and men that strewed the narrow street. These three companies now in town began to work in earnest, dashing from one end of the town to the other; they discovered two pieces of artillery being placed in position; one grand dash and the pieces changed hands, with the commander and four men. Word was now sent to Colonel Toland for reënforcements; the Thirty-fourth dismounted and came double-quick to our relief.

Charging on the buildings, they soon began to dislodge the rebels; the town was ordered to be burned, to drive them from their fortified places. Colonel Toland rode from the rear, and took his position in the centre of the street; sharp-shooters immediately began to play destruction among the officers, and ere he had been there ten minutes a fatal shot struck him in the breast, producing instant death. Colonel Powell, who had just received a wound in the right shoulder, was carried from the field; thus in an instant both commands lost their leaders, and all deeply felt the loss. Reënforcements were sent to the rebels from Dullin's Depot and other places, and the town of Wytheville, from this moment, was erased from existence; the small bridge near the town, was burned, and we fell back, not being able to procure our dead for burial. All our wounded having been left in the enemy's hands, we fell back about two miles, and awaited the approach of day. At this time we learned our rear-guards were attacked; they having all prisoners captured up to this time in their possession, were compelled to divide their force, but the rebel numbers being four to one, soon captured the prisoners, killing two of their own, and two of the Thirty-fourth Ohio regiment, and taking thirteen prisoners; they made good their escape. Upon the approach of daylight on Sunday, the nineteenth, the question was what was best to be done. Lieutenant-Colonel Franklin, of the Thirty-fourth Ohio, assumed command. It appears that the orders given Colonel Toland were in cipher, and understood by no others than the General and himself. To return by the road we came all knew would be attended with difficulty, and loss of life and property; however, the course was adopted, and we began the backward movement. A few miles from this place we found two dead Zouaves lying on the road; one had been stripped of his boots and pants by his murderer, and left thus to be devoured by the starving swine, or lie thus exposed to the scorching sun, an idea too horrible to dwell upon. I thought, certainly, we would have taken time to perform the last and sacred rite, but through no apprehension and fear of further trouble in front and rear, they were left to be disposed of as kind Providence should dictate. On we journeyed, until we reached East River mountain, and learned that the road had been blockaded to prevent our escape, and trouble us, till a sufficient force could be had to capture us. We had already been forty-eight hours without food for ourselves and horses. The latter began to show signs of exhaustion. Proceeding on, toward evening, the column was halted, and the rebel cavalry announced in front.

We at once drew up in line of battle, awaiting their approach. After a skirmish of three quarters of an hour, they withdrew. We at once ascended Blue Stone Mountain by file. The road was very steep, and ere we reached the top twenty-three horses lay stretched across the road, having fallen from exhaustion; we now had to go afoot, one hundred and eighty miles from camp. The summit being reached, it was now dark. "Why don't we rest?" was the anxious inquiry of the weary soldier, who thought capture nothing compared with starvation. The descent was terrible; cliffs of ten to thirty-one feet, down which the smooth-footed horse would slide, with scarce life enough to arrest his progress, except it be stopped by contact with a tree or some other obstacle. Many horses left alone staggered over the cliffs and were for ever lost. It was not until midnight we reached Blue Stone Creek, and all threw themselves upon the ground, hungry and tired. On Monday, the twentieth, we left our camping ground at three A.M., the third day, without food and no prospect of any; we pass along Blue Stone Creek, until we strike Tug Fork, Big Sandy. This day was extremely hot, and taking the Wyoming road, we camped for the night. This ended four days without food. Here cattle were killed, and we soon ate what little could be had, and by daylight, the twenty-first, every thing was ready. We travelled along the ridge until we struck the Guyan Mountain. The weather was warm and sultry, and our horses began to tire out and show signs of giving out. This was about thirty-five miles from Raleigh, in the mountains. No one knew the road. Here we procured a guide, who manœuvred with us all day, and after we camped at night, we ascertained we were still thirty-five miles away. The guide had deceived us. Upon inquiring for him, we learned he had escaped to parts unknown, taking a horse and revolver. Had he been found, death would have been his fortune. We procured another guide. On the following day we started at daylight in search of Raleigh, hungry and tired. Messengers had been sent ahead to procure food for horses and men, when finding our forces had fallen back to Fayetteville, we camped for the night. At daylight the train from Fayetteville, with rations and feed, arrived. Three good, hearty huzzas rent the air for crackers and coffee, and in a few hours we reached Fayetteville, where we remained, rested our horses, and left on Friday morning, the twenty-fourth, for camp. All were tired and worn out, having been eleven days, part of the time (about five days) without food, and six nights without sleep, having been bushwhackers during the entire time, both annoyed by front and rear. We drew a large force after us, and proved that cavalry could go wherever it wanted, regardless of roads or expense.

We travelled over five hundred miles, over mountains of the worst character, and the most desolated country known to civilized men. Our loss in driving the troops was about eighty-five men and officers, killed, wounded, and prisoners. About three hundred horses were left on account of not being able to travel. While the loss is great to the Government, it is a success beyond a doubt. Some five thousand troops had been sent to intercept us on our backward movement, but we reached camp, tired out.

DUBLIN, July 19.

To General S. Cooper:

The enemy, one regiment of cavalry and parts of two regiments of infantry, about one thousand strong, rode into Wytheville a little before sunset yesterday. Almost at the same instant two newly organized companies and the employés of this place, in all about one hundred and thirty men, with two field-pieces, whom I had despatched under Major T. M. Bowyer by the passenger train, arrived. A sharp skirmish immediately commenced in the street and continued about three quarters of an hour, when Major Bowyer retired with a part of his men and brought them off in the train. Captain Oliver and two citizens were killed and Lieutenant Rosany badly wounded.

The enemy lost Colonel Toland, commanding the brigade, one other colonel, one major, and seven privates killed; one lieutenant-colonel and about twenty-five men wounded, and in our hands. The Lieutenant-Colonel, Powell, is reported mortally wounded. I am informed they lost every one of their field-officers. The command left Wytheville about ten o'clock last night, retreating toward Tazewell Court-House. It is now reported they are coming down Walker's Creek to this place. If they retreat by the way they came they will probably be intercepted and cut up. They paroled on their retreat seventy-five or eighty of our men, whom, I suppose, they found it inconvenient to carry off. Of course the parole under such circumstances is worthless under their own order. The damage to the railroad can be repaired in an hour or so. The jail, commissary, and quartermaster storehouses and several private houses were burned.

SAMUEL JONES,
Major-General.

Doc. 133.

THE DRAFT RIOT IN NEW-YORK.

ADDRESS BY BISHOP TIMON, OF BUFFALO.

JOHN, BY THE GRACE OF GOD AND THE AUTHORITY OF THE HOLY SEE, BISHOP OF BUFFALO.

To the Dearly Beloved, Faithful Laity of the Diocese, Health and Benediction:

DEARLY BELOVED: In the name of the God of charity, and through that charity which he, who called us to be your bishop, has given us for you; through that charity of Christ in us, however unworthy, through which we would cheerfully give our life, if necessary, for each and every one of you; we beg of you, for Christ's sake, and for the sake of all that you love in heaven and on earth, to abstain from all resistance to the law, from all riot, from all tumultuous gatherings, from all violence.

In New-York, many misguided men, yet very few, we believe, of practical Catholics, have shed blood in the late riot; and "the voice of their brother's blood cried to the Lord from the earth." Some of the rioters have fallen; many more will, we fear, suffer much; many will, perhaps, be ruined; all will feel the painful sting of a guilty conscience, during the rest of life, and, on their death-bed, (if, indeed, rioters who aid in murder could die otherwise than is written: "He that shall kill by the sword, must be killed by the sword," Apoc. 13 : 10,) they will, either through God's mercy, sincerely repent for their participation in the riots, or be lost for ever! Dearly beloved, listen to the advice of a father who dearly loves you; submit to law, and God will protect you. Should there be a draft, fewer will be drafted than would, probably, be killed in an unholy struggle against law. And if any of you be drafted, we will try to protect and aid; friends will protect and aid; God will protect, aid, and bless, in more ways than we know or dare name. Withdraw yourselves, then, we beg and exhort, from all who would excite to associations against the law of the land, or to violence and mob-law. For God's sake—for the sake of your dear families—for the sake of your fathers and mothers, whether still pilgrims on earth or mingling with the "blessed crowd of witnesses" who from heaven watch over your conduct on earth—we exhort you to trust in God, and not to lend yourselves to any exciter of mob violence, which leads so often to murder. If you follow this advice of your Father in Christ, we confidently assure you that "Whosoever shall follow this rule, peace will be upon him, and mercy, and upon the Israel of God." (Gal. 6.)

We require that this letter be read in every church on the Sunday after its reception.

Given at St. Joseph's Cathedral, Buffalo, on the Feast of Our Lady of Mount Carmel, A.D. 1863. † JOHN,
Bishop of Buffalo.

LETTER FROM JAMES T. BRADY.

NEW-YORK, July 19, 1863.

While I was in Washington, detained there by the interruption of travel between that city and Baltimore, the recent riot broke out.

Certain individuals, who spoke rather what they wished than what they knew, suggested that the crowd would assail my residence.

I do not believe that any rioters of this city ever contemplated any such movement; but if they had made an attempt of the kind, they would have regretted the measure, I assure you.

I know very well to whose ingenious suggestions I am indebted for this expression of a threat, and address you merely for the purpose of saying to the mob, and to all men who feel inclined to take part in a mob, two things:

First. There is no instance in the history of mankind in which a mob or riot did not fail to win any permanent advantage.

Second. In most mobs of any consequence the exhibitions of courage have been by those whom concealed agitations moved. The agitators themselves have, as in the recent instances, remained in secure secrecy.

I have heard with regret of the expressions made by men claiming to be gentlemen, having property and influence, who have privately chuck-

VOL. VII.—DOC. 29

led over the merciless massacres of unoffending negroes.

Not one of these men would dare to expose his precious person in any of the murderous exploits he praises.

And now let me say to the men who have been or mean to be engaged in a riot: Why should you expose yourselves to all the danger, and the men who set you on keep out of it? I tell you, my deluded fellow-citizens, that not one of the scheming demagogues who urge you to the peril they never intend to encounter—not one of them will ever consent to act with you or to lead you.

Try it! Go to any of the men who applaud your course or pretend to be your friends, and you will find that they don't dare to fight for your opinions as you do.

I detest murderers, house-burners, and thieves. I regard neither with honor, but I have more respect for the misguided man who opposes by violence a law which he deems unjust and oppressive, than for the miserable sneaks who, to carry out their opinions or to promote their views, skulk in the rear while they expose their foolish but courageous dupes in the front.

The people of New-York will find out that the way to avoid injustice is not to court or follow the directions of political "rings" or cliques, but to rely upon the assistance of those who, like myself, mean that our country shall continue to exist and no injustice be done to any of her citizens.

I do not admire the provision in the conscript law generally called the three hundred dollar clause; but I will obey the law. I will pay this amount for any four men of family whose courage being good are yet so placed that they cannot leave their families. If I were richer I would do more. I will also do all in my power to have the right to draft tested before the judiciary as a constitutional question. But I beg and implore the brave but misled men who are willing to fight for their principles, not to let themselves be used by political sneaks, who don't care how many houses are burned or lives are sacrificed, if their own schemes can be promoted consistently with their personal safety. JAMES T. BRADY.

Doc. 134.

GENERAL BOYLE'S ORDER.

HEADQUARTERS DISTRICT OF KENTUCKY,
LOUISVILLE, July 25, 1863.

By authority of the General Commanding the Department, the following General Order is made:

1. It is ordered that no forage or other property belonging to loyal citizens in the State of Kentucky be seized or impressed except in cases of absolute necessity, and then only on written authority from the headquarters of the Twenty-third army corps, or from these headquarters.

2. Whenever it becomes necessary to seize or impress private property for military purposes, the property of sympathizers with the rebellion

and of those opposed to furnishing any more men or any more money to maintain the Federal Government and suppress the rebellion will be first seized and impressed.

3. The negroes of loyal citizens will not be impressed on the public works and military roads unless absolutely necessary. The negroes of citizens who are for no more men and no more money to suppress the rebellion, and the supporters, aiders, and abettors of such, will be first impressed, and officers detailed for the purpose are required strictly to observe this order in the execution of their duties.

4. All horses of the enemy captured or subject to capture will be taken possession of by Quartermasters, and reported to Captain Jenkins, Chief-Quartermaster, Louisville, who is ordered to allow loyal citizens to retain horses to supply the places of those taken by the enemy; but disloyal persons mentioned in paragraphs two and three, who encourage raids by the enemy, will not in any case be allowed to retain captured horses or horses justly subject to capture.

5. For all property seized or impressed, proper and regular vouchers will be given, with indorsement as to the loyalty or disloyalty of the owners of the property. By order of
Brigadier-General BOYLE.
A. C. SEMPLE, A. A. G.

Doc. 135.

THE CAPTURE OF RUCKER.

GENERAL CRAWFORD'S REPORT.

JEFFERSON CITY, Mo., September 10, 1863.

COLONEL: I have the honor to report the wounding and capture of the notorious bushwhacker, John F. Rucker, under the following circumstances: He was travelling up the river on the steamer Calypso, and on Monday evening joined a party of fishermen, who had fastened their skiff to the boat's yawl, while at St. Aubert's Station, and were towed up the river some four or five miles. As the skiff was let loose he was seen to enter it with the other parties, and was recognized by some one of the passengers on board. The captain of the boat and passengers reported the circumstances to me as they passed up; whereupon I despatched Captain Williams, company A, Ninth Provisional regiment, at twelve o'clock at night, on an extra train, with detachments from his company and company E, instructing him to make diligent search for and capture or kill the scoundrel, if possible.

On arriving at St. Aubert's, Captain Williams learned that the party of fishermen belonged on the opposite (north) side, and had landed there on their return from the fishing excursion. Captain Williams immediately procured a boat and crossed his men to the town of St. Aubert, where he learned that a man answering the description had been seen about dark, some three or four miles in the country, at or near the house of one Bagby.

He then marched as rapidly as the darkness and woods would permit to Bagby's house, arriving there just at daylight. His men surrounded the house, and approaching the front, saw Rucker issuing from the front-door. Having just arisen, and totally unsuspicious of danger, he was proceeding leisurely to perform his morning ablutions. Seeing the party of soldiers, he "bolted," attempting to escape by the rear of the house. Here, however, he met with some difficulty, and, refusing to halt, was fired at several times, two of the shots taking effect, one shattering his left wrist, the other entering and passing through his hip and abdomen. The latter, it is thought, is mortal. I have sent down for him, and if he can be moved will have him brought here.

Very respectfully, T. L. CRAWFORD,
Brigadier-General Commanding.
To Colonel JOHN B. GRAY,
Adjutant-General, Mo.

Doc. 136.

ROSECRANS'S CONGRATULATORY ORDER.

July 28, 1863.

ARMY OF THE CUMBERLAND: By the favor of God, you have expelled the insurgents from Middle Tennessee. You are now called upon to aid your unfortunate fellow-citizens of this section of the State in restoring law and securing protection to persons and property—the right of every free people. Without prompt and united efforts to prevent it, this beautiful region will be plundered and desolated by robbers and guerrillas; its industry will be suspended or destroyed, and a large part of the population be left without sufficient food for the coming winter. It is true many of the people have favored the rebellion, but many were dragged unwillingly into it by a current of mad passion they could not or dared not resist. The conspirators and traitors, bankrupts in fortunes and in reputations; political swindlers, who forced us from our homes to defend the government of our fathers, have forced the inhabitants of Middle Tennessee into this unnatural attempt to ruin and destroy it. Remember we fight for common rights; what we ask for ourselves we willingly accord to others—freedom under the Constitution and laws of our country—the country of Washington and Jackson. Assure Tennesseans of this. Assure them that, foreseeing the waste and suffering that must arise from a state of anarchy, you stand ready to aid them in reëstablishing and maintaining civil order. Tell them to assert their former rights against an arbitrary and cruel revolutionary party that has ruined their State, impoverished their families, rendered their slave property insecure, if not altogether valueless, dragged their sons, fathers, and brothers from home, and caused their blood to be shed for an insane project, the success of which would be the proclamation of interminable war and the death-knell of State rights as well as individual freedom. And if they are willing to help themselves, give them every assistance, and protection in persons and property consistent with your military duties.

1. Officers and soldiers of the army of the Cumberland, some grave outrages and wrongs have been perpetrated on loyal citizens and helpless women by lawless and unprincipled men wearing our uniform and calling themselves soldiers. Such violation of orders disgrace our country and cause. I appeal to you by your honor, your love of country, and the noble cause in which you serve, to denounce and bring to punishment all such offenders. Let not the slightest stain tarnish your brilliant record. Let no thief, pillager, or invader of the rights of person or property go unpunished. Remember that the truly brave and noble are always just and merciful, and that, by a strict observance of orders, you will crown your noble work and establish your claims to the respect and gratitude of our country.

2. Stragglers and marauders separated from their commands without authority, who go thieving and pillaging around the country, are not entitled to the privileges of soldiers and prisoners of war. They are to be regarded as brigands—enemies of mankind, and are to be treated accordingly.

3. Deserters, conscript agents, and prisoners of war desirous of abandoning the rebellion and becoming peaceable citizens, will be paroled as prisoners of war, and permitted to return to their homes, on giving bonds and security, or satisfactory assurance for the faithful observance of their paroles, and will not be exchanged unless they violate their promises.

4. All citizens are invited to unite in restoring law and order, and in suppressing marauders and guerrillas. All privileges and protection compatible with the interests of the service will be accorded to those who are willing and give assurance by their parole, oath, and bond, or other satisfactory voucher, that they will conduct themselves peaceably, and do no injury to the Government.

5. Those claiming allegiance to the rebellion, or who cannot or will not give satisfactory assurance that they will conduct themselves peaceably, are, on their own theory, by the law of nations, bound to leave the country. This rule will hereafter be observed in such districts as come within our control, at the discretion of the commanding officer of troops in the district.

6. Persons desiring to vote, or to exercise any other right of citizenship, will be permitted to take the oath of allegiance, unless the commanding officer has reason to suppose a fraudulent intent on the part of such person.

7. Provost-marshals are authorized to parole prisoners of war, to administer the parole to noncombatants, and oath of allegiance to citizens, in accordance to the provisions of this order, under such instructions and limitations as may be prescribed by the Provost-Marshal General, on the provost-marshals of corps or divisions, detached or acting at inconvenient distances from their corps headquarters, reporting promptly a list of the names and descriptions of all persons so paroled by them, with their bonds, if any have been given, to the Provost-Marshal General of the army, at the headquarters of the department for record.   By command of

Major-General ROSECRANS.

J. BATES DICKSON, A.A.G.

Doc. 137.

PRESIDENT LINCOLN'S ORDER.

WAR DEPARTMENT, ADJUTANT-GENERAL'S OFFICE, WASHINGTON, July 31.

GENERAL ORDER No. 252.

THE following order of the President is published for the information and government of all concerned:

EXECUTIVE MANSION, WASHINGTON, July 30.

It is the duty of every government to give protection to its citizens of whatever class, color, or condition, especially those who are duly organized as soldiers in the public service. The law of nations and the usages and customs of war, as carried on by civilized powers, permit no distinction as to color in the treatment of prisoners of war as public enemies. To sell or enslave any captured person on account of his color, and for no offence against the laws of war, is a relapse into barbarism and a crime against the civilization of the age. The Government of the United States will give the same protection to all its soldiers, and if the enemy shall sell or enslave any one because of his color, the offence shall be punished by retaliation upon the enemy's prisoners in our possession. It is therefore ordered that for every soldier of the United States killed in violation of the laws of war, a rebel soldier shall be executed, and for every one enslaved by the enemy or sold into slavery, a rebel soldier shall be placed at hard labor on the public works, and continued at such labor until the other shall be released and receive the treatment due to a prisoner of war.

ABRAHAM LINCOLN.

By order of the Secretary of War.

E. D. TOWNSEND,
Adjutant-General.

Doc. 138.

COLONEL BUSSY'S EXPEDITION.

JACKSON, MISS., July 20, 1863.

ON the sixteenth instant, Colonel Bussy, Chief of Cavalry of General Sherman's army, with one thousand of his cavalry, and Wood's brigade of Steele's division, started for Canton, Miss. It was known that Jackson's cavalry division, numbering about four thousand men, had crossed the river, and was supposed to be in the neighborhood of Canton.

Our forces reached Grant's Mill, ten miles north of Jackson, at nine o'clock A.M., where the enemy made his appearance and fired on our advance.

Colonel Wood sent forward a party of infantry, drove the enemy from their position on the bank of the river, and destroyed the ferry-boat. Our forces proceeded on to Calhoun Station, on the New-Orleans and Jackson Railroad, where Colonel Bussy burned two locomotives, twenty-five cars, the depot building, and a large quantity of cotton, while Colonel Wood's forces tore up and burned two miles of the railroad track. This is done by marching a regiment in line along the road, and with crowbars and handspikes raise the ties and iron on one side, throwing it over, which breaks the ties loose from the rails. The ties are then piled up, the iron laid across, and the whole fired ; the ties burn up, heating the iron bars in the centre, the ends fall down and the rail is effectually destroyed. Here the expedition camped.

The next day at an early hour the troops were in motion, and when within two miles of Canton, Jackson's forces were discovered in position ready to meet an attack. He occupied the west side of Bear Creek, and his line extended from the creek along the road, and circling round to the woods on our left. Colonel Stephens, with the Second Wisconsin cavalry, was deployed to the right of the road in the open field, while a regiment of infantry of Colonel Wood's brigade was moved to the front as skirmishers. Two pieces of artillery were ordered forward and preparations made for attacking the enemy. Our forces took with them a large wagon train, numbering seventy-five wagons that were not yet parked. As they were in plain view from the enemy a movement was soon made by him to get possession of the train. While they made a demonstration front a large force was seen moving around our left flank toward the train. Colonel Bussy discovering the intention of the enemy, ordered one piece of artillery to the point threatened, and sent forward a battalion of the Fifth Illinois cavalry, under command of Major Farnan, who encountered the enemy within four hundred yards of the train. The Major moved into the field and opened fire on the enemy at short-range, while our artillery sent a few shells into his ranks, which caused them to fall back. Our gun was now sent forward into the field to a better position, supported by the Seventy-sixth Ohio and Twenty-fifth Iowa infantry, and the Fourth Iowa cavalry, Colonel Winslow, and the Third Iowa cavalry, Major Scott, were formed in line on the left, the Fifth Illinois cavalry, Major Seley, on the right of the infantry. This disposition had hardly been made before the enemy came pouring out of the woods with the evident intention of charging the train. Our artillery opened a fire while the skirmishers from the Seventy-sixth Ohio pushed forward, causing the enemy to fall back in great disorder. It was impossible to pursue, as the fences are heavy hedges of Osage orange, which makes it difficult to get man or beast through them.

While these operations were going on under the immediate direction of Colonel Bussy, Colonel Woods, with the Third, Thirteenth, and Seventeenth Missouri and Thirty-first Iowa, were gaining ground to the front. The enemy now fell back along the whole line, and disappeared behind the thick brush on Bear Creek. Colonel Woods moved his forces into the thick brush, where the enemy, from his cover, opened a severe fire, which was returned by our skirmishers. The enemy's position was very strong. He posted his artillery—one six-pound and one twelve-pound gun—in position, raking the road, and being covered by the dense underbrush, it was impossible to discover his position. He kept up a vigorous shelling, which, however, did no injury. Colonel Wood finally dislodged the enemy, reached the bridge over Bear Creek, which the enemy had destroyed, and soon erected a crossing sufficient to cross our forces, when it was discovered the enemy were in full retreat. His loss is known to have been severe ; his ambulances were seen moving about on the field collecting the wounded. The expedition camped here for the night.

At five o'clock next morning the forces moved into the town, which is one of the most beautiful places in the South—a town of about one thousand five hundred inhabitants. The junction of the Mississippi Central with the New-Orleans and Jackson Railroad makes it a place of considerable importance. At this place were located the "Dixie Works," containing twenty-four forges and machinery for the construction of gun-carriages and materials of war. This establishment has been in successful operation for the confederate government. It was completely destroyed by our forces. They tore up and burned six miles of railroad track in the vicinity of Canton. They also burned thirteen large machine-shops and railroad buildings, with all their contents, five locomotives, fifty cars, and one hundred thousand feet of lumber belonging to the Confederacy. Jackson burned the railroad depot and six hundred bales of cotton as he was leaving the town. Not a dollar's worth of public property was left in Canton.

Colonel Bussy also sent a force of cavalry and destroyed a pontoon-bridge over Pearl River. He also burned the railroad bridge over Big Black, twenty miles north of Canton, with one mile of trestle work, and the depot at Ways Bluff. The expedition returned to Jackson last night, having lost about twenty men. They captured seventy-two prisoners, and lost none. Our whole force did not exceed two thousand men. Several regiments were represented, but they were very small ones, the Fifty-first Iowa numbering less than sixty men. The enemy's force consisted of two brigades, and two regiments of another brigade. They claimed to have four to five thousand men, with two pieces of artillery. General Jackson commanded, with General Whitfield, of Kansas notoriety, commanding one brigade, General Crosby and General Adams the others. The whole expedition was a most brilliant success. The railroad has been completely destroyed for forty miles. It cannot be repaired while the war lasts, and therefore cannot be used to transport supplies to support an army within striking distance of the Mississippi River.

The expedition is an important one connected with the war in the South, and reflects great credit upon Colonel Bussy and Colonel Wood for their successful management. Johnston's army, when last heard from, was in full retreat toward Meridian. His troops were scattered through the country, swearing they would never bear arms again.

The proud and haughty State of Mississippi has been humbled, and is now bowing under the Stars and Stripes, pleading for mercy. The people everywhere feel that the Confederacy is a failure, that Mississippi is out of the contest, and they are ready for any thing that will relieve them from the iron rule of the tyrannical leaders at Richmond. Hundreds and thousands of citizens want to go North, and all are going who can procure transportation for their families. Many of the slaveholders throughout the country have sacrificed every thing on their plantations, and gone with their negroes to Alabama. They sacrifice every thing but their negroes. They left in such haste that in many instances the wearing apparel of the family has been much of it left behind. Stock, crops, and every comfort of home has been sacrificed. The wife and family are made to suffer all these privations for the bare chance of saving the nigger.

General Steele has not yet returned from the pursuit of the enemy. Our whole army will, no doubt, return to Vicksburgh immediately on his return. This army has been eighty days in constant fighting with some portion of its force. It has achieved the most brilliant success of the war, and deserves the gratitude of every loyal heart.

Doc. 139.

MORGAN'S INVASION OF INDIANA.

A REBEL OFFICIAL NARRATIVE.

RICHMOND, VA., Friday, July 31, 1863.

To the Editors of the Enquirer:

MESSRS. EDITORS: As much interest has been manifested in reference to the recent raid of General Morgan, I have thought it but right to add my "mite" to assist in appeasing the appetite of the public who are eagerly devouring every morsel or crumb of news coming from General Morgan's command. Sincerely sorry that the Federal gunboats cut off the finishing of the account, I shall at once commence.

The command of General J. H. Morgan, consisting of detachments from two brigades, numbering two thousand and twenty-eight effective men, with four pieces of artillery—two Parrotts and two howitzers—left Sparta, Tenn., on the twenty-seventh of June, crossed the Cumberland near Burkesville on the second of July, finished crossing at daylight on the third. Means of transportation—canoes and dug-outs, improvised for the occasion. Were met by Colonel Hobson's cavalry, estimated at six thousand, drove them back toward Jamestown, Ky., and our column marched on through Columbia, at which point found the advance of Wolford's celebrated Kentucky cavalry, numbering two hundred and fifty men, dispersed it, killing seven and wounding fifteen men. Our loss, two killed and two wounded. Marched on to stockade, at Green River, on the fourth. Colonel Johnson, commanding the Second brigade, attacking stockade rifle-pits and abattis of timber. After heavy slaughter on both sides, our forces withdrew—loss about sixty killed and wounded on each side. Of Morgan's command, the gallant Colonel Chenault fell pierced through the head by a Minie ball, as he led his men in a charge upon the rifle-pits. The lion-hearted Major Brent also poured out his life-blood upon the field. Indeed, this was the darkest day that ever shone upon our command — eleven commissioned officers were killed and nine wounded. Moving on to Lebanon on the fifth, we attacked the town, (fortified,) and after five hours' hard fighting, captured the place, with a vast amount of stores, four hundred and eighty-three prisoners, one twenty-four pounder, and many fine horses. The commandant of the post was Colonel Charles Hanson, brother to the lamented Brigadier-General Roger Hanson, who fell at Murfreesboro. His command, raised in the heart of the Blue Grass regions, contained brothers and other near relatives to many of our brave boys; notwithstanding which, when the gallant patriot, young Lieutenant Tom Morgan, a brother to our General, and the idol of the command, fell, loud and deep were the maledictions that ascended against the cowardly cravens for seeking shelter in dwelling-houses, and the question was raised as to their right to receive quarter. The enemy lost nine killed and fifteen wounded; our loss, three killed and six wounded. Rapid marches brought us to Bradensburgh on the seventh, where Captain Sam Taylor, of the old Rough and Ready family, had succeeded in capturing two fine steamers. From eight A.M., on the eighth, until seven A.M., on the ninth, was consumed in fighting back the Federal gunboats, whipping out three hundred home-guards, with artillery, on the Indiana shore, and crossing the command. The first was accomplished by Captain Byrne with his battery, two Parrotts, and two twelve-pound howitzers; the second, by an advance regiment, capturing the guards, and securing a splendid Parrott gun, elegantly rigged. Ninth.—Marched on to Corydon, fighting near there four thousand five hundred State militia, and capturing three thousand four hundred of them, and dispersing the remainder; then moving without a halt through Salisbury and Palmyra to Salem, at which point, telegraphing with our operator, we first learned the station and numbers of the enemy aroused for the hunt — discovered that Indianapolis was running over with them—that New-Albany contained ten thousand — that three thousand had just arrived at Mitchell—and, in fact, twenty-five thousand men were armed, and ready to meet the "bloody invader." Remaining at Salem only long enough to destroy the railroad bridge and track, we sent a scout to the Ohio and Mississippi road, near Seymour, to burn two bridges, a depot, and destroy the track for two miles, which was effected in an incredibly short time. Then taking the road to Lexington, after riding all night, reached that point at daylight, capturing a number of supplies, and destroying during the night the depot and track at Vienna, on the Jeffersonville and Indianapolis Railroad. Leaving Lexington, passed on north to the Ohio and Mississippi Railroad, near Vernon, where, finding General Manson with a heavy force of infantry, we skirmished with him two hours as a feint, while the main command moved round the town to Dupont, where squads were sent out to cut the roads between Vernon and Seymour on the west, Vernon and Laurenceburgh on the east, Vernon and Madison on the south, and Vernon and Columbus on the north. Not much brighter were the bonfires and illuminations in celebration of the Vicksburgh victory by the Yankees than our counter illuminations around Vernon. Many old ladies were aroused from their slumbers to rejoice over the brilliant victories recently achieved. Surmises were various and many. One old lady knew that the city of Richmond was on fire; another that Jeff Davis had been killed; a third that the army of Virginia was used up. Not one knew that General John H. was within two hundred miles of them. Daylight brought the news, and then for miles houses were found vacant. Loaves of bread and buckets of pure, fresh water, with an occasional sprinkle of wines, liquors, and sweetmeats, were thrust upon us. Terror was depicted upon every countenance, until a brief conversation assured them that we were not warring upon women and children. Then their natural effrontery would return, and their vials of uncorked wrath would pour upon us streams as muddy as if emanating from old Abe's brain. From Vernon we proceeded to Versailles, capturing five hundred militia there and gathering on the road. Near this point, Captain P——, a Presbyterian chaplain and former line officer in one of our regiments, actuated by a laudable desire to change steeds, moved ahead, flanking the advance, and running upon a full company of State militia. Imitating his commander's demeanor, he boldly rode up to the company and inquired for the captain. Being informed that there was a dispute as to who should lead them, he volunteered his services, expatiating largely upon the part he had played as an Indiana captain at Shiloh, and was soon elected to lead the valiant hoosiers against the "invading 'rebs." Twenty minutes spent in drilling inspired complete confidence; and when the advance-guard of Morgan's command had passed without Captain P—— permitting the hoosiers to fire, he ordered them into the road, and surrendered them to our command. Crestfallen, indeed, were the Yanks; but General Morgan, treating them kindly, returning to them their guns, advised them to go home and not come hunting such game again, as they had every thing to lose and nothing to gain by it.

From Versailles we moved without interrup-tion across to Harrison, Ohio, destroying the track and burning small bridges on the Lawrenceburgh and Indianapolis Railroad. At Harrison we burned a fine bridge. Leaving Harrison at dusk with noiseless tread, we moved around Cincinnati, passing between that city and Hamilton, destroying the railroad, and a scout running the Federal pickets into the city, the whole command marched within seven miles of it. Daylight of the fourteenth found us eighteen miles east of Cincinnati. Sunset had left us twenty-two miles west, but the circuitous route we travelled was not less than one hundred miles. During this night's march many of our men, from excessive fatigue, were riding along fast asleep. Indeed, hundreds would have been left asleep on the road, had it not been for the untiring vigilance of our gallant General. Up and down the line he rode, laughing with this one, joking with that, assuming a fierce demeanor with another, and so on. None were left, and when we reached the railroad near Camp Dennison, few persons would have guessed the fatigue the men had undergone from their fresh and rosy appearance. A fight was imminent. Madame Rumor had been whispering that old Granny Burnside would pay us a visit that morning, but instead of arriving he sent us a train of cars with several of his officers, who were kindly received, and in honor of their arrival a grand fire was made of the cars, etc. Nothing of special importance occurred after passing Dennison, except at Camp Shady the destruction of seventy-five army-wagons, and a vast amount of forage, until the morning of the nineteenth our command had heavy marches over bad roads. Making detours, threatening both Chillicothe and Hillsboro, on the north, and Gallipolis on the south. Daily were we delayed by the annoying cry of "Axes to the front," a cry that warned us of bushwhackers, ambuscades, and blockaded roads. From the fourteenth to the nineteenth every hillside contained an enemy, and every ravine a blockade. Dispirited and worn down, we reached the river at three A.M., on the nineteenth, at a ford above Pomroy, I think, called Portland. At four, two companies were thrown across the river, and were instantly opened upon by the enemy; a scout of three hundred men were sent down the river a half-mile, who reported back that they had found a small force behind rifle-pits, and asked permission of General Meade to charge. He assented, and by five he was notified that Colonel Smith had successfully charged the pits, capturing one hundred and fifty prisoners. Another courier arriving about the same time reported that a gunboat had approached near our battery, and on being fired upon had retired precipitately.

General Morgan finding both of these reports correct, and believing that he had sufficient time to cross the command, was using every exertion to accomplish the task, when simultaneously could be heard the discharge of artillery from down the river—a heavy, drumming sound of small arms in the rear and right, from the banks of the river, came up three black columns of infantry, firing upon our men, who were in close column, preparing to cross. Seeing that the enemy had every advantage of position, an overwhelming force of infantry and cavalry, and that we were becoming completely environed in the meshes of the net set for us, the command was ordered to move up the river double-quick. The gallant field staff and line-officers acted with decision and promptitude, and the command was moved rapidly off the field, leaving three companies of dismounted men, and perhaps two hundred sick and wounded men in the enemy's possession. Our artillery was doubtless captured at the river, as two horses had been killed in one piece, and one in each of two others; and the mountain path, from which we made our exit, was too precipitous to convey them over. Two lieutenants and five privates were known to have been killed on our side. After leaving the river, at Portland, the command was marched to Belleville, some fourteen miles, and commenced fording, or rather swimming, at that point. Three hundred and thirty men had effected a crossing, when again the enemy's gunboats were upon us —one iron-clad and two transports. Again we moved up the river. The Second brigade, commanded by Colonel Adam R. Johnson, was ordered to cross, guides having represented the stream as fordable, In dashed the Colonel, closely followed by Lieutenant Woodson; Captain Helm, of Texas; young Rogers, of Texas; Captain McClain, A. C. S., Second brigade, and myself. The Colonel's noble mare falters, strikes out again, and boldly makes the shore. Woodson follows. My poor mare being too weak to carry me, turned over and commenced going down; encumbered by clothing, sabre, and pistols, I made but poor progress in the turbid stream, but the recollections of home, of a bright-eyed maiden in the sunny South, the pressing need of soldiers, and an inherent love of life, actuated me to continue swimming. Behind me I heard the piercing call of young Rogers for help; on my right, Captain Helm was appealing to me for aid; and in the rear my friend, Captain McClain, was sinking. Gradually the gunboat was nearing me. Should I be able to hold up until it came; and would I then be saved to again undergo the horrors of a Federal bastile? But I hear something behind me snorting! I feel it passing! Thank God! I am saved! A riderless horse dashes by; I grasp his tail; onward he bears me, and the shore is reached. Colonel Johnson, on reaching the shore, seizes upon a ten-inch piece of board, jumps into a leaky skiff, and starts back to aid the drowning. He reaches Captain Helm, but Captain McClain and young Rogers are gone. Yes, Captain McClain, the true gentleman, faithful soldier, and pleasant companion, has been buried in the depths of the Ohio. We sadly miss him at quarters and in the field. His genial smile and merry laughter will no longer ring upon our ear. But from his manly piety and goodness of heart the angels of heaven will never mark him as an absentee.

May the memory of his many virtues serve as a beacon-light to guide us all to the same heavenly abode, where he is now stationed!

Two men were drowned in the crossing. The gunboats and transports cutting us off again, General Morgan fell back again, and just as daylight was disappearing, the rear of his command was leaving the river. Sad and dispirited, we impressed guides, collected together three hundred and sixty men who had crossed—many without arms, having lost them in the river—and marched out toward Claysville. But before leaving the river, I will briefly recapitulate and sum up in short order the damage to the enemy in this raid, and the sufferings through which General Morgan's command passed. On first crossing the Cumberland, we detached two companies—one to operate on the Louisville and Nashville Railroad, the other to operate between Crab Orchard and Somerset, Ky. The first captured two trains, and returned to Tennessee. The second captured thirty-five wagons, and also returned. We then detached a hundred men at Springfield, who marched to Frankfort, and destroyed a train and the railroad near that point. We also captured a train, with a number of officers, on the Louisville and Nashville Railroad, near Shepherdsville, sent a detachment around Louisville, who captured a number of army supplies, and effected a crossing by capturing a steamer between Louisville and Cincinnati, at Carrolton, and rejoined us in Indiana. We paroled, up to the nineteenth, near six thousand Federals; they obligating themselves not to take up arms during the war. We destroyed thirty-four important bridges, destroying the track in sixty places. Our loss was by no means slight; twenty-eight commissioned officers killed, thirty-five wounded, and two hundred and fifty men killed, wounded, and captured. By the Federal accounts, we killed more than two hundred, wounded at least three hundred and fifty, and captured, as before stated, near six thousand. The damage to railroads, steamboats, and bridges, added to the destruction of public stores and dépôts, cannot fall far short of ten million dollars. We captured three pieces of artillery, and one twenty-four pounder, at Lebanon, which we destroyed; one, a Parrott three-inch gun at Brandenburgh, and a twelve-pounder at Portland. These guns may have fallen into the enemy's hands again; I do not know it to be so, but fear they have. After crossing into Indiana, the inhabitants fled in every direction, women and children begging us to spare their lives, and amazingly surprised to find we were humans. The Copperheads and Butternuts were always in the front opposing us. Occasionally we would meet with a pure Southron, generally persons banished from the Border States. In Indiana one recruit was obtained, a boy fourteen years old, who came as an orderly. Our command was bountifully fed, and I think the people of Indiana and Ohio are anxious for peace; and could the idea of their ability to conquer us once be gotten rid of, they would clamor for an immediate recognition.

Every town was illuminated, and the people everywhere rejoicing over the downfall of Vicksburgh.

Crops of wheat and oats are very good, but corn very poor indeed.

After leaving the Ohio at Belleville, on the night of the nineteenth, we marched to near Elizabethtown, in Wirt County, from there to Steer Creek, and across the mountains to Sutton; from Sutton on the Gauley Bridge road to Birch Creek, crossing Gauley at mouth of Cranberry, and thence into the Greenbrier County, crossing Cold Mountain, passing over a heavy blockaded road, tired steeds preventing rapid marches, and six days were consumed ere we reached Lewisburgh, near which we left Colonel Grigsby, with a detachment, which then numbered about four hundred and seventy-five men. From the crossing of the Ohio to our entrance into Greenbrier, our men lived on beef alone, without salt, and no bread. Yet their only wish seemed to be for the safety of General Morgan and the command.

To the kind officers, soldiers, and citizens that we have met upon our journey since reaching the Old Dominion, in behalf of our command, we tender them our undying regard, and assure them if unbounded success has not fallen to our lot this time, that we are more fully determined to strive for our country and cause than ever.

I have the honor to be your obedient servant,

S. P. CUNNINGHAM,
A. A. A. General Morgan's Cavalry Division.

Doc. 140.

EXPEDITION TO HUNTSVILLE, ALA.

WINCHESTER, TENN., July 23.

ON the twenty-third, Major-General Stanley, commanding the cavalry, returned from his expedition to Huntsville, Alabama. The object of the raid was to collect as many negroes as possible for service in the colored command, and all the horses and mules yet in the country, for the use of the army.

The expedition, consisting of the cavalry divisions of Generals Mitchell and Turchin, started from Salem on the thirteenth instant. Colonel Long, with his brigade, took the advance on the twelfth, while Colonel Galbraith, on the same day, with the First Middle Tennessee and Third Ohio, took the road leading to Pulaski, by way of Fayetteville.

The main column proceeded as far as New-Market, where a halt was ordered, and foraging parties were sent through the country to collect supplies—the command having started with the intention of subsisting off of the country.

Irregularities and insufferable outrages in the way of foraging having been practised by soldiers on former expeditions, the General issued the following order before leaving camp:

HEADQUARTERS CHIEF OF CAVALRY,
DEPARTMENT OF THE CUMBERLAND, BURK'S HOUSE,
FIVE MILES FROM WINCHESTER, July 9, 1863.

GENERAL ORDERS, No. 63.

Hereafter no soldier will be allowed to enter the house of any citizen in the country through which the command passes. Any soldier violating this order will be arrested at once and summarily dealt with.

The manner of pressing mules and horses for the use of the United States has been repeatedly explained to this command. It is now repeated, that the taking of any horse or mule, or other property, without the receipt of a commissioned officer, is theft; and any soldier found in possession of a horse or mule not properly receipted for, will be guilty of horse-stealing, and, upon conviction, such soldier will be whipped, his uniform stripped from him, and be drummed out of camp.

By command of Major-General D. S. STANLEY.

WILLIAM H. SINCLAIR,
Assistant Adjutant-General.

On the night of the thirteenth, heavy rains so increased the volume of the streams that the march on the following day was seriously impeded and delayed.

After an arduous march the column on the evening following entered Huntsville, leaving General Turchin's division to guard the train at Beaver Dam Creek, eight miles in the rear.

The town, perhaps the most pleasant one in the South, delightfully located and handsomely improved, was found almost deserted.

The railroad machinery in the round houses have all been removed southward, and the citizens, frightened by the reports, heralded by the retreating rebels, that the "Yankees" were burning houses and devastating the country along their line of march, had quitted quiet homes and elegantly furnished dwellings, and fled farther southward. The panic throughout the country, causelessly excited, was intense. Jewelry and valuables of every description were secreted in the fields and covert places among the hills.

Colonel Long, holding the advance, proclaimed to the citizens, on entering Huntsville, that the command had no provisions, and that to all those who would voluntarily contribute and bring to the village a certain portion of their provender, he would give protection papers, which should insure them against further seizure of property. On the following day, the fifteenth, large numbers of wagons were early wending their way to camp, with contributions of meat, corn, meal, flour, potatoes, and such other articles of food as could be spared. The opportunity seemed a favorable one to secure that protection which their principles would never procure, and wealthy planters, with overflowing granaries and groaning larders, imitating a poverty that they loathed in others, were seen drawing along to camp a mere handful of forage and provisions, which they would stoutly aver was all that the necessities of the family could permit a sacrifice of. Impostors of this character were invariably worsted, and their property levied on more heavily than if honesty, rather than deception, had been their chosen policy.

Colonel Galbraith passed without molestation through Fayetteville and the country intervening between that place and Pulaski, until his advance-guard had entered the limits of the latter village. Three hundred rebel cavalry entered the opposite side of the town just as Colonel Galbraith's command entered on the main road leading to Athens. A fight ensued, which resulted in the killing of three of the enemy, the taking of fifty prisoners, and the precipitate retreat of the remainder. Among the prisoners taken is General Cheatham's quartermaster, who, detained by the charms of a bewitching young wife, to whom he had been married but a few short days, was spending a blissful honeymoon, besides collecting, for the use of the rebel army, all the horses and mules in the neighborhood. The fruits of his labors in the way of collecting animals were turned to good account. He was mercilessly torn from the arms of a loving wife, and, together with his booty, turned into Uncle Sam.

Colonel Galbraith reached Huntsville by way of Athens, with two hundred horses and mules, and nearly two hundred negroes.

There are numerous Union families at Huntsville, who were overjoyed at the coming of our troops, and who were untiring in their efforts to conduce to their comfort. Ripe fruits, green corn and vegetables, were found in abundance through the country contiguous to Huntsville, and on this most acceptable species of food the men fairly gormandized.

On the sixteenth, Colonel Long, with his brigade, was sent to Athens, to scour the country in search of bushwhackers, who had been reported as lurking through that region, and, if any advantages offered, to continue his researches and captures until prudence dictated a return.

On the seventeenth, Major Godley, with detachments of the Second and Fourth Michigan, was sent to the mountains near New-Market to rout out a guerrilla band supposed to be in that section of country. No enemy was found, and the force returned to camp with sixty horses and forty negroes.

During these few days and the thirteenth, the General's quarters at Huntsville fairly swarmed with applicants for protection, and citizens seeking the return of some favorite servant or captured property.

It was a thorough and trying test of the administrative capacity of the General and his faithful coadjutor, Major Sinclair. Many were the perplexing dilemmas from which it became necessary to escape without sacrificing the requirements of duty to those of a philanthropy that could not be fully subserved without disregarding in a measure the good of the service.

On Sunday, the nineteenth, the negroes were permitted to assemble in their churches as usual. The presence of the Federals gave an impetus to the influx of pious contrabands, and the churches were filled to overflowing. The object of the expedition appeared to the authorities a justification for the procedure, and, impelled by the prudential policy that possessed the Romans in their seizure of the Sabine women, it was decided to gobble this collection of male piety for the good of the service. Guards were placed around the buildings, and when the service closed, the "bucks" found themselves prisoners in the house of God. The *furore* that this action created among the citizens was even greater than that which followed among the negroes. Women, with faces ruddy with oppressive excitement, were lying about, regardless of calico, and accosting every officer they met for assistance. The excitement was growing in intensity, and business accumulating in an equal ratio. It was concluded best, by the General, to avoid trouble and perplexity, to return to camp, and orders were issued for a departure on the following morning.

On the twentieth, the whole command moved out as far as Bell Factory.

On the following day, General Mitchell came to Fayetteville; Colonel Galbraith, with the First Middle Tennessee, was sent to Shelbyville to rid the country of bushwhackers, and to recruit; while the balance of the command moved on to Salem.

The expedition brought into camp, on the twenty-second, between five and six hundred negroes, and one thousand horses and mules.

It is common to represent that expeditions prove entire successes; but this brought along the evidence, and it is so patent that it is unnecessary to mention that flattering success attended it.

Doc. 141.

SURPRISE AT MOOREFIELD, VIRGINIA.

WHEELING INTELLIGENCER ACCOUNT.

CAMP NEAR PETERSBURGH, }
September 12, 1863. }

ON the morning of Friday, the fifth, at about reveille—say half-past four o'clock in the morning—that portion of the First West-Virginia volunteer infantry in command of Major E. W. Stephens—five companies—were surrounded by the combined forces of Imboden and Jones, some one thousand six hundred strong. By the judicious disposition of our small division—some two hundred and fifty men—by our gallant young Major, and the determined front displayed to the enemy, they were deterred from making an attack "from early morn till dewy eve." Thus the cool courage and dauntless bravery of a comparatively young man and commander, saved our heroic band from the impending danger that menaced them from the vastly superior numbers of the insolent foe.

Friday night the enemy retired into their mountain fastnesses, and our Major led us to the junction, the union of the Moorefield and Franklin pikes, a distance of twelve miles. We encamped at the junction from Saturday morning, the fourth instant, until the morning of the eleventh, when, according to the orders of Colonel Mulligan, we returned to Moorefield, where, barely arrived, our indefatigable young Major, thinking our camping ground unsafe in the extreme, from its exposed position and the numerous roads and by-paths converging there, at once crossed the river, and selected a spot, less exposed, and in every way more suitable for the camp of our small detachment. Returning from his exploration, he ordered the men to be ready to start at an early hour, for the purpose of clearing a road to the selected spot; pickets were thrown out, an alarm-guard stationed, and the command retired to their repose.

By some unaccountable remissness, or some combination of fortunate circumstances for the enemy, at daylight, or rather before, on Friday morning last, a large detachment of Imboden's cavalry, under the immediate command of Captain McNiel, got within our camp, and fired volley after volley into the tents of our sleeping comrades. The Major being awake, rushed down to the door of his markee, and loudly called upon the men "to form into line," "to rally at the foot of the hill," as our camp was completely in the hands of the enemy. It was too late to rally. We were surrounded; and as "discretion is the better part of valor," we yielded to the successful foe; and by the flashing eyes, grinding of teeth, the compressed lips, lowering brows, and the curses loud and deep of the men of 'the First Virginia, we saw that the iron tooth of chagrin and the resolve of future revenge, dire and deep, had entered into the soul of the whole detachment. Several of our boys were shot while trying to make their escape; others were more successful, among whom, I am happy to state, was our worthy Major, who immediately hastened to bring reënforcements from the detachment at Petersburgh. These last, led by Colonel Thoburn, arrived too late. Our detachment were already upon their way to Richmond. Among the many valuable officers lost to the service by this surprise, may be mentioned Captains Craig, White, and Reed; Lieutenants Hall, Helms, McKee, and Baird. Captains Daugherty and McElvoy and Lieutenant Apple have already made their escape, and returned safely to the camp at Petersburgh. I am happy to state many of the men have also made good their escape. Foot-sore and weary from their wanderings upon "the dark and weary mountains," they are greatly rejoiced to arrive, even to the shelter and protection that an exposed camp can afford.

The sutler of the regiment, D. J. Smith, Esq., of your city, as I am informed, lost all the goods he had in camp, his company-books, team, and wagon. The loss falls heavily upon a worthy man.

I had forgotten to state that, upon our return to Moorefield, no immediate cause of an apprehended attack was apparent, as all the information elicited from all sorts of men—spies, scouts, and citizens—went to prove that no enemy was in the vicinity of the village, except Captain Imboden and forty men. But we were deceived, and the result, as far as has transpired, is before you.

I dare not trust myself to attempt to give a list of the killed and wounded. The camp is full of contradictory rumors, each worse than

the other, and each diametrically opposing the other. When a close approximation of the truth can be arrived at, you may hear from me again.

J. F. S.

Doc. 142.

CRUISE OF THE FLORIDA.

OFFICIAL REBEL ACCOUNT.

C. S. STEAMER FLORIDA,
ST. GEORGE'S, BERMUDA, July 21, 1863.

To the Editors of The Daily Journal, Wilmington, N. C.:

You and your readers are doubtless well aware that this steamer ran out of the harbor of Mobile on the sixteenth day of January, 1863, so I will say nothing on that head, but endeavor to give you a full account of what we have done since. Our first work was the hermaphrodite brig Estelle, of Boston, on her first voyage and homeward bound from Santa Cruz, with a full cargo of sugar and honey for the good people of Boston. But we consigned her to "Old Father Neptune." She was valued at one hundred and thirty-eight thousand dollars.

In Havana we received our coal, stores, etc. At daylight on the morning of the twenty-second of January we catted our anchor and ran along the coast eastward, and at eleven A.M. captured and burned the hermaphrodite brig Windward, from Matanzas, bound to Portland, and just at sunset we sent the hermaphrodite brig Corris Annie, of Philadelphia, on the same (fiery) road. She was within two hours' sail of her destination, which was Cardenas. We left the Cuban coast for the Banks, and on the twenty-sixth dropped our anchor in the harbor of Nassau. Here we also took in our coal, and our hull looking any thing but Christian-like, we went to Green Keys to "paint ship."

On the twenty-eighth January, came to an anchor, and for two or three days all hands were busy as bees, scrubbing the whitewash from our sides, and on the first day of February we started on a cruise. But a sail being reported, and proving to be the Yankee gunboat Sonoma, and being of heavier metal than us, we showed our heels; but for forty-eight hours she chased us, but got nothing for her pains, for on the third morning she could hardly be seen from the mast-head. From the time of eluding the Sonoma till the twelfth of February we saw no Yankee vessels, and all the boys were getting impatient for a prize, or even a sail, when we heard the mast-head lookout sing out: "Sail, ho!"

Steam was raised and our propeller lowered, and at four P.M. we boarded her and found that she was indeed a prize. Her name was the Jacob Bell, from Foo-Chow, bound to New-York, with a valuable cargo of teas, silks, etc. We burned her and then went to Barbadoes.

Our next prize was the Star of Peace, which we captured on the twelfth of March; she was from Calcutta, bound to Boston, with saltpetre! The schooner Aldebaran was the next victim of the pirate Florida. For fifteen days did we look for another, and she brought us the most needful article, and that was coal. The Lapwing was captured on the twenty-eighth, and sent a cruising against Yanks, and captured the ship Kate Dyer, and bonded her for forty thousand dollars. On the thirtieth March fell in with the bark M. J. Colcard, from New-York, bound to Cape Town, and she was burned.

On the line we met the Oreto, (Lapwing,) coaled, and then took a cruise along the line, and on the seventeenth April burned ship Commonwealth, from New-York for San Francisco. On the twenty-third April, burned the bark Henrietta, from Baltimore for Rio Janeiro. The next day (twenty-fourth) burned the ship Oneida, from Shanghae, for New-York, with tea. May sixth, took hermaphrodite brig Clarence, put one twelve-pounder howitzer, twenty men, and two officers on board, and sent her on a cruise. What execution Lieutenant Reed did, I refer you to the papers about. The Tacony was one of her prizes.

On the tenth of May we were in Pernambuco; sailed on the twelfth. Next day (May thirteenth) burnt ship Crown Point, another San Francisco packet from New-York. We then went to Seara, where we again coaled, and started for the Northern coast; and on the sixth June burnt ship Southern Cross, from San Francisco, bound to New-York. On the fourteenth June, burnt the ship Red Gauntlet, from Boston to Hong-Kong. From her we also got coals, but they were not good, as we afterward found out. On the sixteenth, took ship B. F. Hoxie, bound from California to England. From her we got about one hundred and twenty-five thousand dollars' worth of silver, and burnt in her over fifty tons of silver ore.

On the twenty-seventh June, captured schooner V. H. Hill, and bonded her for ten thousand dollars, on condition that she would carry our prisoners, some fifty or more, to Bermuda. Our next prize was the ship Sunrise, eight days from New-York to Liverpool, having a neutral cargo, bonded her for sixty thousand nine hundred dollars; this was on the seventh July. We were now close to New-York; the eighth July we were not more than fifty or sixty miles from that city. About twelve m. this day (eighth) we exchanged signals with an English brig—another sail being reported, started in pursuit, and as the fog cleared up, saw a large steamer lying by her and had sent her boat alongside. We ran down until we saw the Yankee colors flying from her peak. "All hands" were then called to quarters.

After manœuvring about half an hour, she finally ran down to us. As soon as she was near enough we hauled down the English colors, (which were flying at the time,) and showed to their view the "stars and bars," and at the same time gave her a broadside. Her men ran from their after pivot and sought protection behind the ship's bulwarks. But the weather was in their favor, for just then the fog came down so dense that the Ericsson could not be seen, so all we could do was to wait till it cleared up. But

judge our astonishment when it did clear up, to see the Yankee about five or six miles ahead of us, and travelling for Sandy Hook. Now it was we felt the need of good coal.

Our brave Captain Maffit offered one thousand five hundred dollars for fifteen pounds of steam, but we could not get but eight and ten pounds, although we used pitch and rosin. All hands were anxious to catch her, for she had been sent out to catch "rebel cruisers," but she caught a tartar this time. But we had the pleasure of burning two vessels under her nose — the brig N. B. Nash, from New-York, and the whaling schooner Rienzi, from Provincetown; but the crew, however, had left when they saw us burn the brig. We showed the crew of the Nash the steamer Ericsson making tracks for New-York.

With a sad heart we left the Ericsson and steered for Bermuda, at which place we arrived on the sixteenth instant, and as soon as we coal we leave this place for a cruise, and you and your readers may be assured that the Florida will sustain her reputation, and do all she can to annoy the Yankees. Hoping this will meet your approbation, I close. Respectfully, etc.

The following is a list of the deaths on board the Florida, since she commenced her cruise:

Seaman John Johnson, liver complaint; seaman Isaac White, lost overboard; seaman John Lohman, consumption; Surgeon Grafton, drowned near the line; James Sudley, steward; Paymaster Lynch, died at sea, of hemorrhage of the lungs.

Doc. 143.

PRESIDENT LINCOLN'S LETTER.

EXECUTIVE MANSION, WASHINGTON,
August, 16, 1863.

Hon. James C. Conkling:

MY DEAR SIR: Your letter inviting me to attend a mass meeting of unconditional Union men, to be held at the capital of Illinois on the third of September, has been received. It would be very agreeable to me thus to meet my old friends at my own home, but I cannot just now be absent from this city so long as a visit there would require.

The meeting is to be composed of all those who maintain unconditional devotion to the Union; and I am sure that my old political friends will thank me for tendering, as I do, the nation's gratitude to those other noble men whom no partisan malice or partisan hope can make false to the nation's life.

There are those who are dissatisfied with me. To such I would say, you desire peace, and you blame me that we do not have it. But how can we obtain it? There are but three conceivable ways. First, to suppress the rebellion by force of arms. This I am trying to do. Are you for it? If you are so, we are agreed. If you are not for it, a second way is to give up the Union. I am against this. If you are you should say so plainly. If you are not for force, nor yet for dissolution, there only remains some imaginary compromise.

I do not believe that any compromise embracing the maintenance of the Union is now possible. All that I learn leads to a directly opposite belief. The strength of the rebellion is its military, its army. That army dominates all the country and all the people within its range.

Any offer of terms made by any man or men within that range in opposition to that army, is simply nothing for the present; because such man or men have no power whatever to enforce their side of a compromise, if one were made with them.

To illustrate: Suppose refugees from the South and peace men of the North get together in convention and frame and proclaim a compromise embracing a restoration of the Union. In what way can that compromise be used to keep General Lee's army out of Pennsylvania?

General Meade's army can keep Lee's army out of Pennsylvania; and I think can ultimately drive it out of existence. But no paper compromise to which the controllers of General Lee's army are not agreed can at all affect that army. In an effort at such compromise we would waste time, which the enemy would improve to our disadvantage, and that would be all.

A compromise, to be effective, must be made either with those who control the rebel army, or with the people first liberated from the domination of that army by the success of our army. Now, allow me to assure you that no word or intimation from the rebel army, or from any of the men controlling it, in relation to any peace compromise, has ever come to my knowledge or belief. All charges or intimations to the contrary are deceptive and groundless. And I promise you that if any such proposition shall hereafter come it shall not be rejected and kept secret from you. I freely acknowledge myself to be the servant of the people, according to the bond of service, the United States Constitution; and that, as such, I am responsible to them.

But to be plain. You are dissatisfied with me about the negro. Quite likely there is a difference of opinion between you and myself upon that subject. I certainly wish that all men could be free, while you, I suppose, do not. Yet I have neither adopted nor proposed any measure which is not consistent with even your views, provided that you are for the Union.

I suggested compensated emancipation, to which you replied that you wished not to be taxed to buy negroes. But I had not asked you to be taxed to buy negroes, except in such way as to save you from greater taxation to save the Union exclusively by other means.

You dislike the Emancipation Proclamation, and perhaps would have it retracted. You say it is unconstitutional. I think differently. I think the Constitution invests its Commander-in-Chief with the law of war in time of war. The most that can be said, if so much, is that slaves are property. Is there, has there ever been, any question that by the law of war, property, both

of enemies and friends, may be taken when needed?

And is it not needed whenever taking it helps us or hurts the enemy?

Armies the world over destroy enemy's property when they cannot use it; and even destroy their own to keep it from the enemy. Civilized belligerents do all in their power to help themselves and hurt the enemy, except a few things regarded as barbarous or cruel. Among the exceptions are the massacre of vanquished foes and non-combatants, male and female.

But the Proclamation, as law, is valid or is not valid. If it is valid, it cannot be retracted, any more than the dead can be brought to life. Some of you profess to think that its retraction would operate favorably for the Union. Why better after the retraction than before the issue?

There was more than a year and a half of trial to suppress the rebellion before the Proclamation was issued, the last one hundred days of which passed under an explicit notice that it was coming, unless averted by those in revolt returning to their allegiance. The war has certainly progressed as favorably for us since the issue of the Proclamation as before.

I know, as fully as one can know the opinions of others, that some of the commanders of our armies in the field, who have given us our most important victories, believe the emancipation policy and the aid of colored troops constitute the heaviest blows yet dealt to the rebellion, and that at least one of those important successes could not have been achieved when it was, but for the aid of black soldiers.

Among the commanders holding these views are some who never had any affinity with what is called Abolitionists, or with "Republican party politics;" but who hold them purely as military opinions. I submit their opinions as being entitled to some weight against the objections often urged, that emancipation and arming the blacks are unwise as military measures, and were not adopted as such in good faith.

You say that you will not fight to free negroes. Some of them seem to be willing to fight for you. But no matter. Fight you, then, exclusively to serve the Union. I issued the Proclamation on purpose to aid you in saving the Union.

Whenever you shall have conquered all resistance to the Union, if I shall urge you to continue fighting, it will be an apt time then for you to declare that you will not fight to free negroes.

I thought that in your struggle for the Union, to whatever extent the negroes should cease helping the enemy, to that extent it weakened the enemy in his resistance to you. Do you think differently? I thought that whatever negroes can be got to do as soldiers, leaves just so much less for white soldiers to do in saving the Union? Does it appear otherwise to you? But negroes, like other people, act upon motives. Why should they do any thing for us if we will do nothing for them? If they stake their lives for us they must be prompted by the strongest motive, even the promise of their freedom. And the promise, being made, must be kept.

The signs look better. The Father of Waters again goes unvexed to the sea. Thanks to the great North-West for it. Nor yet wholly to them. Three hundred miles up they met New-England, Empire, Keystone, and Jersey, hewing their way right and left. The sunny South, too, in more colors than one, also lent a hand. On the spot their part of the history was jotted down in black and white. The job was a great national one, and let none be banned who bore an honorable part in it. And while those who have cleared the great river may well be proud, even that is not all. It is hard to say that any thing has been more bravely and better done than at Antietam, Murfreesboro, Gettysburgh, and on many fields of lesser note.

Nor must Uncle Sam's web-feet be forgotten. At all the waters' margins they have been present, not only on the deep sea, the broad bay, and the rapid river, but also up the narrow, muddy bayou, and wherever the ground was a little damp, they have been and made their tracks.

Thanks to all. For the great Republic — for the principles by which it lives and keeps alive for man's vast future —thanks to all.

Peace does not appear so distant as it did. I hope it will soon come, and come to stay; and so come as to be worth keeping in all future time. It will then have been proved that, among freemen, there can be no successful appeal from the ballot to the bullet, and that they who take such appeal are sure to lose their case, and pay the cost.

And then there will be some black men who can remember that, with silent tongue, and clenched teeth, and steady eye, and well-poised bayonet, they have helped mankind on to this great consummation, while I fear there will be some white men unable to forget that, with malignant heart and deceitful speech, they have striven to hinder it.

Still, let us not be over-sanguine of a speedy final triumph. Let us be quite sober. Let us diligently apply the means, never doubting that a just God, in his own good time, will give us the rightful result.

Yours very truly,　　　A. Lincoln.

Doc. 144.

COLONEL GRIERSON'S EXPEDITION

from la grange, tenn., to baton rouge, la.

Headquarters First Cavalry Brigade,
Baton Rouge, La., May 5, 1863.

Colonel : In accordance with instructions from Major-General S. A. Hurlbut, received through Brigadier-General W. S. Smith, at La Grange, Tenn., I left that place at daylight on the morning of the seventeenth of April, with the effective force of my command, one thousand seven hundred strong. We moved southward without material interruption, crossing the Tallahatchie River on the afternoon of the eighteenth at three

different points. One battalion of the Seventh Illinois, under Major Graham, crossing at New-Albany, found the bridge partially torn up, and an attempt was made to fire it. As they approached the bridge they were fired upon, but drove the enemy from their position, repaired the bridge, and crossed. The balance of the Seventh Illinois and the whole of the Sixth crossed at a ford two miles above, and the Second Iowa crossed about four miles still further up. After crossing, the Sixth and Seventh Illinois moved south on the Pontotoc road, and encamped for the night on the plantation of Mr. Sloan ; the Second Iowa also moved south from their point of crossing, and encamped about four miles south of the river. The rain fell in torrents all night. The next morning, April nineteenth, I sent a detachment eastward to communicate with Colonel Hatch, and make a demonstration toward Chesterville, where a regiment of cavalry was organizing. I also sent an expedition to New-Albany, and another north-west toward King's Bridge, to attack and destroy a portion of a regiment of cavalry organizing there, under Major Chalmers. I thus sought to create the impression that the object of our advance was to break up these parties. The expedition eastward communicated with Colonel Hatch, who was still moving south parallel to us. The one to New-Albany came upon two hundred rebels near the town and engaged them, killing and wounding several. The one north-west found that Major Chalmers's command, hearing of our close proximity, had suddenly left in the night, going west. After the return of these expeditions, I moved with the whole force to Pontotoc. Colonel Hatch joined us about noon, reporting having skirmished with about two hundred rebels the afternoon before and that morning, killing, wounding, and capturing a number. We reached Pontotoc about five o'clock p.m. The advance dashed into the town, came upon some guerrillas, killed one, and wounded and captured several more. Here we also captured a large mail, about four hundred bushels of salt, and the camp-equipage, books, papers, etc., of Captain Weatherall's command, all of which were destroyed. After slight delay, we moved out and encamped for the night on the plantation of Mr. Daggett, five miles south of Pontotoc, on the road toward Houston.

At three o'clock the next morning, April twentieth, I detached one hundred and seventy-five of the least effective portion of the command, with one gun of the battery, and all the prisoners, led horses, and captured property, under the command of Major Love, of the Second Iowa, to proceed back to La Grange, marching in column of fours, before daylight, through Pontotoc, and thus leaving the impression that the whole command had returned. Major Love had orders also to send off a single scout to cut the telegraph wires south of Oxford. At five o'clock a.m. I proceeded southward with the main force, on the Houston road, passing around Houston about four o'clock p.m., and halting at dark on the plantation of Benjamin Kilgore, eleven and a half miles south-east of the latter place, on the road toward Starkville. The following morning, at six o'clock, I resumed the march southward, and about eight o'clock came to the road leading south-east to Columbus, Miss. Here I detached Colonel Hatch, with the Second Iowa cavalry and one gun of the battery, with orders to proceed to the Ohio and Mobile Railroad in the vicinity of West-Point, destroy the road and wires, thence move south, destroying the railroad and all public property as far south, if possible, as Macon; thence cross the railroad, making a circuit northward, if practicable take Columbus and destroy all government works in that place, and again strike Okalona, and destroying it, return to La Grange by the most practicable route. Of this expedition and the one previously sent back I have since heard nothing except vague and uncertain rumors through secession sources. These detachments were intended as diversions, and even should the commanders not have been able to carry out their instructions, yet, by attracting the attention of the enemy in other directions, they assisted us much in the accomplishment of the main object of the expedition.

After having started Colonel Hatch on his way, with the remaining portion of the command, consisting of the Sixth and Seventh Illinois cavalry, about nine hundred and fifty strong, I continued on my journey southward, still keeping the Starkville road, arriving at Starkville about four o'clock P.M.; we captured a mail and a quantity of government property, which was destroyed. From this point we took the direct road to Louisville. We moved out on this road about four miles, through a dismal swamp near belly-deep in mud, and sometimes swimming our horses to cross streams, when we encamped for the night in the midst of a violent rain. From this point I detached a battalion of the Seventh Illinois cavalry, under ——, to proceed about four miles, and destroy a large tannery and shoe manufactory in the service of the rebels. They returned safely, having accomplished the work most effectually. They destroyed a large number of boots and shoes, and a large quantity of leather and machinery, in all amounting probably to fifty thousand dollars, and captured a rebel quartermaster from Port Hudson, who was there laying in a supply for his command. We now immediately resumed the march toward Louisville—distance twenty-eight miles—mostly through a dense swamp — the Noxubee River bottom. This was for miles belly-deep in water, so that no road was discernible. The inhabitants through this part of the country, generally, did not know of our coming, and would not believe us to be any thing but confederates. We arrived at Louisville soon after dark. I sent a battalion of the Sixth Illinois, under Major Starr, in advance, to picket the town and remain until the column had passed, when they were relieved by a battalion of the Seventh Illinois, under Major Graham, who was ordered to remain until we should have been gone an hour, to prevent persons leaving with information of the course we were taking, to drive out stragglers, preserve order, and quiet the fears of the people. They had heard of our coming a short time before we arrived, and many had left, taking only what they could hurriedly move. The column moved quietly through the town without halting, and not a thing was disturbed. Those who remained at home acknowledged that they were surprised. They had expected to be robbed, outraged, and have their houses burned. On the contrary, they were protected in their persons and property. After leaving the town we struck another swamp, in which, crossing it, as we were obliged to, in the dark, we lost several animals drowned and the men narrowly escaped the same fate. Marching until midnight, we halted until daylight at the plantation of Mr. Estus, about ten miles south of Louisville.

The next morning, April twenty-third, at daylight, we took the road for Philadelphia, crossing Pearl River at a bridge about six miles north of the town. This bridge we were fearful would be destroyed by the citizens to prevent our crossing, and upon arriving at Philadelphia, we found that they had met and organized for that purpose, but hearing of our near approach, their hearts failed, and they fled to the woods. We moved through Philadelphia about three P.M., without interruption, and halted to feed about five miles south-east on the Enterprise road. Here we rested until ten o'clock at night, when I sent two battalions of the Seventh Illinois cavalry, under Lieutenant-Colonel Blackburn, to proceed immediately to Decatur, thence to the railroad at Newton Station. With the main force I followed about an hour later. The advance passed through Decatur about daylight, and struck the railroad about six o'clock A.M. I arrived about an hour afterward with the column. Lieutenant-Colonel Blackburn dashed into the town, took possession of the railroad and telegraph, and succeeded in capturing two trains in less than half an hour after his arrival. One of these, twenty-five cars, was loaded with ties and machinery, and the other thirteen cars were loaded with commissary stores and ammunition, among the latter several thousand loaded shells. These, together with a large quantity of commissary and quartermaster's stores, and about five hundred stand of arms stored in the town, were destroyed. Seventy-five prisoners captured at this point were paroled. The locomotives were exploded and otherwise rendered completely unserviceable. Here the track was torn up, and a bridge half a mile west of the station destroyed. I detached a battalion of the Sixth Illinois cavalry, under Major Starr, to proceed eastward, and destroy such bridges, etc., as he might find over Chunkey River. Having damaged as much as possible the railroad and telegraph, and destroyed all government property in the vicinity of Newton, I moved about four miles south of the road and fed men and horses. The forced marches which I was compelled to make in order to reach this point successfully necessarily very much fatigued and exhausted my command, and rest and food were absolutely necessary for its safety.

From captured mails and information obtained by my scouts, I knew that large forces had been sent out to intercept our return, and having instructions from Major-General Hurlbut and Brigadier-General Smith to move in any direction from this point which, in my judgment, would be best for the safety of my command and the success of the expedition, I at once decided to move south, in order to secure the necessary rest and food for men and horses, and then return to La Grange through Alabama, or make for Baton Rouge, as I might hereafter deem best. Major Starr in the mean time rejoined us, having destroyed most effectually three bridges and several hundred feet of trestle-work, and the telegraph, from eight to ten miles east of Newton Station. After resting about three hours, we moved south to Garlandsville. At this point we found the citizens, many of them venerable with age, armed with shotguns, and organized to resist our approach. As the advance entered the town, these citizens fired upon them, and wounded one of our men. We charged upon them, and captured several. After disarming them we showed them the folly of their actions, and released them. Without an exception they acknowledged their mistake, and declared that they had been grossly deceived as to our real character. One volunteered his services as guide, and upon leaving us declared that hereafter his prayers should be for the Union army. I mention this as a sample of the feeling which exists, and of the good effect which our presence produced among the people in the country through which we passed. Hundreds who are skulking and hiding out to avoid conscription, only await the presence of our arms to sustain them, when they will rise up and declare their principles; and thousands who have been deceived, upon the vindication of our cause, would immediately return to loyalty. After slight delay at Garlandsville, we moved south-west about ten miles, and camped at night on the plantation of Mr. Bender, two miles west of Montrose. Our men and horses having become gradually exhausted, I determined on making a very easy march the next day, and looking more to the recruiting of my weary little command than to the accomplishment of any important object; consequently I marched at eight o'clock the next morning, taking a west and varying slightly to a north-west course. We marched about five miles, and halted to feed on the plantation of Mr. Nichols. After resting until about two o'clock P.M., during which time I sent detachments north to threaten the line of the railroad at Lake Station and other points, we moved south-west toward Raleigh, making about twelve miles during the afternoon, and halting at dark on the plantation of Dr. Mackadora. From this point I sent a single scout, disguised as a citizen, to proceed northward to the line of the Southern Railroad, cut the telegraph, and, if possible, fire a bridge or trestle-work. He started on his journey about midnight, and when within seven miles of the railroad he came upon a regiment of Southern cavalry from Brandon, Miss., in search of us. He succeeded in misdirecting them as to the place where he had last seen us, and having seen them well on the wrong road, he immediately retraced his steps to the camp with the news. When he first met them they were on the direct road to our camp, and had they not been turned from their course would have come up with us before daylight. From information received through my scouts and other sources, I found that Jackson and the stations east, as far as Lake Station, had been reënforced by infantry and artillery, and hearing that a fight was momentarily expected at Grand Gulf, I decided to make a rapid march, cross Pearl River, and strike the New-Orleans, Jackson, and Great Northern Railroad at Hazlehurst, and after destroying as much of the road as possible, endeavor to get upon the flank of the enemy, and coöperate with our forces, should they be successful in the attack upon Grand Gulf and Port Gibson. Having obtained, during this day, plenty of forage and provisions, and having had one good night's rest, we now again left, ready for any emergency. Accordingly, at six o'clock on the morning of the twenty-sixth, we crossed Leaf River, burning the bridge behind us, to prevent any enemy who might be in pursuit from following; thence through Raleigh, capturing the sheriff of that county with about three thousand dollars in Government funds; thence to Westville, reaching this place soon after dark. Passing on about two miles we halted to feed, in the midst of a heavy rain, on the plantation of Mr. Williams. After feeding, Colonel Prince, of the Seventh Illinois cavalry, with two battalions, was sent immediately forward to Pearl River to secure the ferry and landing. He arrived in time to capture a courier, who had come to bring intelligence of the approach of the Yankees, and orders for the destruction of the ferry. With the main column I followed in about two hours. We ferried and swam our horses, and succeeded in crossing the whole command by two o'clock P.M. As soon as Colonel Prince had crossed his two battalions, he was ordered to proceed immediately to the New-Orleans, Jackson, and Great Northern Railroad, striking it at Hazlehurst. Here he found a number of cars containing about six hundred loaded shells and a large quantity of commissary and quartermaster's stores, intended for Grand Gulf and Port Gibson. These were destroyed, and as much of the railroad and telegraph as possible. Here, again, we found the citizens armed to resist us, but they fled precipitately upon our approach.

From this point we took a north-west course to Gallatin, four miles, thence south-west three and a half miles to the plantation of Mr. Thompson, where we halted until the next morning. Directly after leaving Gallatin we captured a sixty-four pound gun and a heavy wagon-load of ammunition, and machinery for mounting the gun, on the road to Port Gibson. The gun was spiked and the carriages and ammunition destroyed. During the afternoon it rained in torrents, and the men were completely drenched. At six o'clock the next morning, April twenty-eighth, we moved westward; after proceeding a short distance, I detached a battalion of the Seventh Illinois cavalry, under Captain Trafton, to proceed back to the railroad at Bahala, and destroy the road, telegraph, and all government property he might find. With the rest of the command, I moved south-west toward Union Church. We halted to feed at two o'clock P.M., on the plantation of Mr. Snyder, about two miles north-east of the church. While feeding, our pickets were fired upon by a considerable force. I immediately moved out upon them, skirmished with and drove them through the town, wounding and capturing a number. It proved to be a part of Wirt Adams's Alabama cavalry. After driving them off we held the town, and bivouacked for the night. After accomplishing the object of his expedition, Captain Trafton returned to us about three o'clock in the morning, of the twenty-ninth, having come upon the rear of the main body of Adams's command. The enemy having a battery of artillery, it was his intention to attack us in front and rear at Union Church, about daylight in the morning, but the appearance of Captain Trafton with a force in his rear, changed his purpose, and turning to the right he took the direct road toward Port Gibson. From this point I made a strong demonstration toward Fayette, with a view of creating the impression that we were going toward Port Gibson or Natchez, while I quietly took the opposite direction, taking the road leading south-east to Brookhaven, on the railroad. Before arriving at this place, we ascertained that about five hundred citizens and conscripts were organized to resist us. We charged into the town, when they fled, making but little resistance. We captured over two hundred prisoners, a large and beautiful camp of instruction, comprising several hundred tents and a large quantity of quartermaster's and commissary stores, arms, ammunition, etc. After paroling the prisoners and destroying the railroad, telegraph, and all government property, about dark we moved southward, and encamped at Mr. Gill's plantation, about eight miles south of Brookhaven.

The following morning we moved directly south along the railroad, destroying all bridges and trestle-work to Bogue Chitto Station, where we burned the depot and fifteen freight-cars, and captured a very large secession flag. From thence we still moved along the railroad, destroying every bridge, water-tank, etc., as we passed, to Summit, which place we reached soon after noon. Here we destroyed twenty-five freight-cars and a large quantity of government sugar. We found much Union sentiment in this town, and were kindly welcomed and fed by many of the citizens. Hearing nothing more of our forces at Grand Gulf, I concluded to make for Baton Rouge, to recruit my command, after which I could return to La Grange through Southern Mississippi and West-Alabama; or, crossing the Mississippi River, move through Louisiana and Arkansas. Accordingly, after

resting about two hours, we started south-west on the Liberty road, marched about fifteen miles, and halted until daylight on the plantation of Dr. Spurlark. The next morning we left the road and threatened Magnolia and Osyka, where large forces were concentrated to meet us; but instead of attacking those points, took a course due south, marching through woods, lanes, and by-roads, and striking the road leading from Clinton to Osyka. Scarcely had we touched this road when we came upon the Ninth Tennessee cavalry, posted in a strong defile, guarding the bridges over Tickfaw River. We captured their pickets, and attacking, drove them before us, killing, wounding, and capturing a number. Our loss in this engagement was one man killed, and Lieutenant-Colonel William D. Blackburn and four men wounded. I cannot speak too highly of the bravery of the men upon this occasion, and particularly of Lieutenant-Colonel Blackburn, who, at the head of his men, charged upon the bridge, dashed over, and by undaunted courage dislodged the enemy from his strong position. After disposing of the dead and wounded, we immediately moved south on the Greensburgh road, recrossing the Tickfaw River at Edward's bridge. At this point, we met Garland's rebel cavalry, and with one battalion of the Sixth Illinois and two guns of the battery, engaged and drove them off without halting the column.

The enemy were now on our track in earnest. We were in the vicinity of their strongholds, and from couriers and dispatches which we captured, it was evident they were sending forces in all directions to intercept us. The Amite River — a wide and rapid stream—was to be crossed, and there was but one bridge by which it could be crossed, and this was in exceeding close proximity to Port Hudson. This I determined upon securing before I halted. We crossed it at midnight, about two hours in advance of a heavy column of infantry and artillery, which had been sent there to intercept us. I moved on to Sandy Creek, where Hughes's cavalry, under Lieutenant-Colonel Wilburn, were encamped, and where there was another main road leading to Port Hudson.

We reached this point at first dawn of day, completely surprised and captured the camp with a number of prisoners. Having destroyed the camp, consisting of about one hundred and fifty tents, a large quantity of ammunition, guns, public and private stores, books, papers, and public documents, I immediately took the road from Baton Rouge. Arriving at the Commite River, we utterly surprised Stuart's cavalry, who were picketing at this point, capturing forty of them, with their horses, arms, and entire camp. Fording the river, we halted to feed within four miles of the town. Major-General Augur, in command at Baton Rouge, having now, for the first, heard of our approach, sent two companies of cavalry, under Captain Godfrey, to meet us. We marched into the town about three o'clock P.M., and were most heartily welcomed by the United States forces at this point.

Before our arrival in Louisville, company B, of the Seventh Illinois cavalry, under Captain Forbes, was detached to proceed to Macon, on the Mobile and Ohio Railroad, if possible to take the town, destroy the railroad and telegraph, and rejoin us. Upon approaching the place, he found it had been reënforced, and the bridge over the Oka Noxubee River destroyed, so that the railroad and telegraph could not be reached. He came back to our trail, crossed the Southern Railroad at Newton, took a south-east course to Enterprise, where, although his force numbered only thirty-five men, he entered with a flag of truce, and demanded the surrender of the place. The commanding officer at that point asked an hour to consider the matter, which Captain Forbes (having ascertained that a large force occupied the place) granted and improved in getting away. He immediately followed us, and succeeded in joining the column while it was crossing Pearl River at Georgetown. In order to catch us, he was obliged to march sixty miles per day for several consecutive days. Much honor is due to Captain Forbes for the manner in which he conducted this expedition.

At Louisville I sent Captain Lynch, of company E, Sixth Illinois cavalry, and one man of his company, disguised as citizens, who had gallantly volunteered to proceed to the Mobile and Ohio Railroad, and cut the wings, which it was necessary should be done to prevent the information of our presence from flying along the railroad from Jackson and other points. Captain Lynch and his comrade proceeded toward Macon, but meeting with the same barrier which had stopped Captain Forbes, could not reach the road. He went to the pickets at the edge of the town, ascertained the whole disposition of their forces and much other valuable information, and returning joined us above Decatur, having ridden without interruption for two days and nights without a moment's rest. All honor to the gallant Captain, whose intrepid coolness and daring characterize him on every occasion.

During the expedition we killed and wounded about one hundred of the enemy, captured and paroled over five hundred prisoners, many of them officers, destroyed between fifty and sixty miles of railroad and telegraph, captured and destroyed over three thousand stand of arms, and other army stores and Government property to an immense amount; we also captured one thousand horses and mules.

Our loss during the entire journey was three killed, seven wounded, five left on the route sick, the Sergeant, Major, and Surgeon of the Seventh Illinois left, with Lieutenant-Colonel Blackburn, and nine men missing, supposed to have straggled. We marched over six hundred miles in less than sixteen days. The last twenty-eight hours we marched seventy-six miles, had four engagements with the enemy, and forded the Comite River, which was deep enough to swim many of the horses. During this time the men and horses were without food or rest.

Much of the country through which we passed

was almost entirely destitute of forage and provisions, and it was but seldom that we obtained over one meal per day. Many of the inhabitants must undoubtedly suffer for want of the necessaries of life, which have reached most fabulous prices.

Two thousand cavalry and mounted infantry were sent from the vicinity of Greenwood and Grenada north-east to intercept us; one thousand three hundred cavalry and several regiments of infantry with artillery were sent from Mobile to Macon, Meridian, and other points on the Mobile and Ohio Road. A force was sent from Canton north-east to prevent our crossing Pearl River, and another force of infantry and cavalry was sent from Brookhaven to Monticello, thinking we would cross Pearl River at that point instead of Georgetown. Expeditions were also sent from Vicksburgh, Port Gibson, and Port Hudson, to intercept us. Many detachments were sent out from my command at various places to mislead the enemy, all of which rejoined us in safety. Colton's pocket map of the Mississippi, which, though small, is very correct, was all I had to guide me, but by the capture of their couriers, despatches, and mails, and the invaluable aid of my scouts, we were always able by rapid marches to evade the enemy when they were too strong, and whip them when not too large.

Colonel Prince, commanding the Seventh Illinois, and Lieutenant-Colonel Loomis, commanding the Sixth Illinois, were untiring in their efforts to further the success of the expedition, and I cannot speak too highly of the coolness, bravery, and above all of the untiring perseverance of the officers and men of the command during the entire journey. Without their hearty coöperation, which was freely given under the most trying circumstances, we could not have accomplished so much with such signal success.

Respectfully, your obedient servant,

B. H. GRIERSON,*
Colonel Commanding Brigade.

Lieut.-Col. JOHN A. RAWLINGS,
Assistant Adjutant-General.

Doc. 145.

CAPTURE OF LITTLE ROCK, ARKANSAS.

GENERAL STEELE'S OFFICIAL REPORT.†

HEADQUARTERS ARMY OF ARKANSAS,
DEPARTMENT OF THE MISSOURI,
LITTLE ROCK, ARK., Sept. 12, 1863.

GENERAL: I have the honor to submit the following as a summary of the operations which led to the occupation of the capital of Arkansas by the expeditionary army under my command:

On the twenty-first of July I arrived at Helena, and pursuant to instructions from Major-General Grant, reported by letter to the commander of the Sixteenth army corps for the instructions relative to the fitting out of an expedition against Little

* See page 548 Docs. REBELLION RECORD, Vol. VI.
† See Doc. 124, page 417 ante.

Rock. General Hurlbut placed under my command all the troops at Helena, and the cavalry division under Brigadier-General Davidson, then operating in Arkansas. The garrison at Helena had been reënforced by two brigades of Kimball's division, which had just arrived from Snyder's Bluff, and were suffering severely from the influences of the Yazoo country.

The proportion of sick and wounded Helena troops was also very large. Three regiments were designated to remain at Helena, and these, with the sick and convalescent, were to constitute the garrison of that place. The troops designated for the expedition amounted to about six thousand, of all arms. There were three six-gun batteries and one four-gun battery, including six ten-pound Parrotts. The cavalry—First Indiana and Fifth Kansas—amounted to less than five hundred for duty. The First Indiana had three small rifled guns. Davidson reported some less than six thousand present for duty in his cavalry division and eighteen pieces of artillery—showing an aggregate of about twelve thousand fit for duty. Brigadier-Generals Kimball and Salomon obtained leaves of absence, and the resignation of General Ross was accepted, which left me with but one general officer—Davidson.

The resignation of my Assistant Adjutant-General was accepted just at this time, and there were no officers of the Quartermaster's and Subsistence Department at Helena, except Captain Allen, A. C. S., and Captain Noble, A. Q. M., who were in charge of the stores in the depot. I ordered the establishment of camps for the sick and convalescents, and organized the command in the best manner possible. Davidson pushed on to Clarendon, and established a ferry for crossing the troops; corduroying two miles of bottom, and laying down the pontoon-bridge across Rock Roe Bayou. On the nineteenth of August, the Helena troops organized into a division, Colonel now Brigadier-General S. A. Rice marched toward Clarendon, with orders to reconstruct the bridges which had been destroyed by the rebels, and to make all necessary repairs on the road, which was in bad condition. Kimball's division, under Colonel William E. McClean, followed next day.

The whole command was at Clarendon and commenced crossing the river on the seventeenth of August. Before the crossing was effected I found my operations encumbered by over a thousand sick. To have established a hospital and depot at this point would have involved the necessity of occupying both sides of the river. Duvall's Bluff was a more healthy location, and the route to Little Rock possessed many advantages over the other as a line of operations. I therefore ordered all the stores and sick to be sent to Duvall's Bluff by water. The enemy had constructed rifle-pits in a commanding position, fronting the crossing on Rock Roe Bayou, but on the approach of Davidson's division had fallen back, leaving only a picket. This position could easily have been turned by the road leading up from Harris's Ferry.

On the twenty-third, Davidson was directed to move with his division to Deadman's Lake, and reconnoitre the enemy's position at Brownsville.

On the twenty-third, the rest of the command moved to Duvall's Bluff, the transports carrying the sick and stores, under convoy of the gunboats. An advantageous site was selected on the bluff for a hospital and depot, and details immediately ordered to throw up intrenchments, cut away the timber on the flanks to give the gunboats clear range, and to erect sheds, etc. On the twenty-fourth, Davidson advanced to Prairie Bayou, and, on the twenty-fifth, continued the march, skirmishing with Marmaduke's cavalry up to Brownsville, dislodging him at that place, and driving him into his intrenchments at Bayou Metou, on the twenty-sixth.

The attack was renewed on the twenty-seventh, and the enemy, driven from his works on the bayou, fired the bridges as he retreated. Davidson was unable to save the bridge, every thing having been prepared for its destruction beforehand. The bayou was deep and miry, and his pursuit of the rebels being thus checked, he withdrew to his camp at Brownsville, leaving pickets at the crossing on the bayou.

I received information that "True's" brigade from Memphis would arrive at Clarendon on the thirtieth, and immediately sent a party to construct a bridge across Rock Roe Bayou, and a ferry-boat to cross the troops over White River. True crossed on the thirty-first, and on the first of September moved up to Deadman's Lake. The advance from Duvall's Bluff also commenced on the first, the place having been put in such a state of defence that the convalescents, and a small detail left there, were deemed sufficient to hold it against any force the enemy would be likely to send in that direction.

On the second instant all my available force was concentrated at Brownsville. It had been ascertained that the military road on the south side of Bayou Metou passed through a section impracticable for any military operations—swamp, timber, and entanglement of vines and undergrowth—and was commanded by the enemy's works. I therefore directed Davidson to make a reconnoissance in force around to the enemy's left, by way of Austin, and, if practicable, to penetrate his lines and ascertain both his strength and position. Rice's division was ordered forward to make a diversion in Davidson's favor on the Bayou Metou. Rice drove in the enemy's pickets, shelled the woods on the south side of the bayou for several hours, and encamped for the night.

In the mean time Davidson pushed his reconnoissance until the numerous roads on his flanks and rear rendered it dangerous for him to proceed any further. The great length to which it would increase our line of communication with our base, rendered it impracticable for us to attack the enemy on his left flank. This reconnoissance occupied two days. By this time I had collected information in regard to the road leading by "Shallow Ford," and Ashley's Mills to the Arkansas, on the right of the enemy's works, which determined me to take that route. The march to the front was resumed on the sixth. Here we found ourselves encumbered with a large number of sick—near seven hundred. True's brigade and Ritter's brigade of cavalry were left to guard the supply train and the sick. On the seventh, we reached the Arkansas River, near Ashley's Mills. At this point Davidson's cavalry, in advance, had a sharp skirmish, with a loss of five or six wounded on each side, and one rebel captain prisoner. The eighth and ninth were employed in reconnoissance, in repairing the road back to Bayou Metou, and in bringing up the sick and the supply trains with the two brigades left at Brownsville. I had now definitely determined upon a plan of attack.

Davidson was directed to lay his pontoonbridge at an eligible point, throw his division across the Arkansas, and move directly on Little Rock, threatening the enemy's right flank and rear, while I moved with the rest of the force on the north bank of the river, and assailed the right of his works. During the night of the ninth he made his dispositions for crossing the Arkansas, and on the morning of the tenth had the pontoon-bridge laid. The Second division was ordered to report to him at daylight, to assist in covering his crossing. The bridge was placed in a bend of the river, and the ground on the south side was so completely swept by the artillery that the enemy could not plant a battery in any position from which he could interrupt the crossing.

Two regiments of infantry passed over the river to drive the enemy's skirmishers out of the woods, and the cavalry division passed on without serious interruption until they reached Bayou Fourche, where the enemy were drawn up in line to receive them, consisting of the brigades of Fagan and Tappan, and the cavalry division, under Marmaduke.

The rebels held their position obstinately until our artillery on the opposite side of the river was opened upon their flank and rear, when they gave way and were steadily pushed back by Davidson, the artillery constantly playing upon them from the other side of the river. Our two columns marched nearly abreast on either side of the Arkansas. Volumes of smoke in the direction of Little Rock indicated to us that the rebels had evacuated their works on the north side of the river, and were burning their pontoon-bridges. Heavy clouds of dust moving down toward Davidson, on the other side of the river, made me apprehensive that the enemy contemplated falling upon him with his entire force. He was instructed, in such event, to form on the beach, where his flank could be protected by our artillery on the other side, and where aid might be sent him by a ford. But they were in full retreat. Marmaduke's cavalry only were disputing Davidson's entry of the city. The rebels had fired three pontoon-bridges, laid across the Arkansas at the city. Two locomotives were also on fire, but were saved by us. Part of the pontoons were also saved. Six steamboats and one

gunboat were entirely destroyed by fire. We are informed that Price intended to have blown up the arsenal, but was pressed so close that he failed in this.

Our cavalry was too much exhausted to pursue the enemy's retreating columns far on the evening of the tenth. Next morning Merrill's and Clayton's brigades renewed the chase, and followed them twenty miles, taking a number of prisoners and causing the enemy to destroy part of his train.

Little Rock was formally surrendered by the municipal authorities on the evening of the tenth. Price had undoubtedly intended to give us battle in his intrenchments, but was completely surprised by our movement across the Arkansas, and did not suspect it until after the pontoonbridge was laid. When it was reported to him that our infantry was crossing, he took it for granted that our whole force was moving to cut off his retreat to Arkadelphia.

I have been assured by citizens that General Cabell with about four thousand (4000) troops, from Fort Smith, had joined Price on his retreat, he having failed to reach here in time to assist in defence of the place.

I marched from Ashley's Mills on the morning of the tenth with not more than seven thousand (7000) troops, having parked the trains and left a strong guard to defend them and the sick.

The operations of this army from the time that I commenced organizing it at Helena, have occupied exactly forty days.

Our entire loss in killed, wounded, and prisoners, will not exceed one hundred, (100.) The enemy's is much greater, especially in prisoners —at least one thousand, (1000.)

I shall reserve the list of casualties and my special recommendations for a future communication. However, I will say that Davidson with his cavalry division deserve the highest commendation. Very respectfully, General,

Your obedient servant,
Fred. Steele,
Major-General.

Major-General J. M. Schofield,
Commanding Department of the Missouri.

GENERAL DAVIDSON'S OFFICIAL REPORT.

Headquarters Cavalry Division,
Department of the Missouri,
Little Rock, Ark., September 12, 1863.

Colonel F. H. Manter, Chief of Staff:

Colonel: I have the honor to report the operations of my division on the tenth instant— the day of the capture of Little Rock.

The plan agreed upon by Major-General Steele, the preceding day, was, that he, with the whole infantry force, should move up the north bank of the Arkansas, directly upon the enemy's works, while my cavalry division forced the passage of the river, and moved up the south bank, turning the enemy's right, and assaulting the city in the rear. All necessary orders were given by me that night. Lieutenant-Colonel Caldwell, Captain Hadley, and Captain Gerster of my staff, worked all night at the cutting of the bluff bank of the river, the location of the batteries, and the laying of the pontoon-bridge.

A division of infantry, Colonel Ingelmann commanding, was placed temporarily at my disposition, and was in position at daylight. So also, Hadley's and Stange's and Lovejoy's batteries, and those of the Fifth and Eleventh Ohio. Merrill's and Glover's brigades were massed behind the crossing at eight A.M. of the tenth, and the laying of the bridge was completed at that hour. Ritter's brigade, with Clarkson's battery, was ordered to make a demonstration four miles below, at Banks's Ford, then held by the enemy. The passage of the river was effected by seven A.M.—all three brigades crossing at the same point—Ritter being ordered up to the bridge, the opposition of the enemy not lasting fifteen minutes under the concentrated fire of our batteries.

No further opposition was met by my division until we reached Fourche Bayou, five miles from Little Rock. Here we found the enemy, consisting of Marmaduke's cavalry, dismounted, and Tappan's and Fagan's brigades of infantry, with two batteries, strongly posted. A sharp fight of two hours' duration, of Glover's brigade on one road and Merrill's on another, leading into the main one, during which the Second brigade lost two mountain howitzers, unavoidably, and captured a caisson, drove them from the position toward the city. Every advantageous foot of ground from this point on was warmly contested by the enemy, my cavalry dismounting and taking it afoot through the timber and corn-fields. I had previously sent an officer of my escort, Lieutenant Armstrong, with a guidon to follow along the bank of the river, to mark the progress of my advance to General Steele. The fire of his batteries from the opposite bank, progressively, was of great service to us.

My advance was here made slow by the fact that the enemy, finding themselves threatened in rear, evacuated their works in front of General Steele, and I did not know but that at any moment their whole force would be thrown upon me. I received a message from General Steele, in the event of such contingency, to withdraw my horses from below the bluff bank of the river, and his batteries would cover my flanks.

Finding, however, that the opposition of the enemy was not stubborn enough to warrant the belief that they were all in front of me, I ordered a vigorous advance of Glover's brigade, and when they became exhausted, within two miles of the city, threw Ritter's brigade, sabre in hand, and Stange's howitzers, supported by two squadrons of the First Iowa cavalry, under Captain Jenks, into the city, and on the heels of the now flying enemy. At seven P.M., the capital of Arkansas was formally surrendered by its civil authorities, and the arsenal of the United States, uninjured, with what stores remained in it, was "repossessed."

Later in the evening General Steele, whose forces had entered the works on the opposite side, came over the river, the enemy being pushed too closely to destroy the bridges.

A column, consisting of Merrill's Horse, the Seventh and Eighth Missouri cavalry, the Tenth and Thirteenth Illinois cavalry, and the First Indiana cavalry, with Clarkson's and Stange's batteries, the whole under Colonels Merrill and Clayton, was organized to pursue vigorously the next morning.

My losses do not exceed seventy killed and wounded. That of the enemy is not yet known. Among their killed is Colonel Corley, commanding General Dodbins's former regiment.

My whole staff—Lieutenant-Colonel Caldwell, Captains Hadley, Gerster, Lieutenants Montgomery, McGunnegle, Gray, Sprague, and Surgeon Smith, Quartermaster Johnson, and Captain Thompson, Commissary Subsistence—served me faithfully throughout the day.

The brigade commanders, especially Colonel Glover, of the Second brigade, and Ritter, of the reserve brigade, deserve honorable mention. Colonel Glover deserves, for his services throughout this campaign, promotion to the rank of a general officer. Lieutenant-Colonel Caldwell, whose untiring devotion and energy never flagged during the night or day, deserves for his varied accomplishments as a cavalry officer, promotion to the rank of a general officer.

Beyond these, I must refer to the reports of brigade commanders, herewith inclosed, for the many cases of individual good judgment and gallantry displayed.

I am, sir, your obedient servant,
                    J. W. DAVIDSON,
                            Brigadier-General.

Doc. 145½.

BATTLE NEAR SHEPHERDSTOWN, VA.

CAMP SIXTEENTH PENNSYLVANIA CAVALRY,
BOLIVAR HEIGHTS, VA., July 17, 1863.

ON Wednesday, the fifteenth instant, the Third brigade, Second cavalry division, commanded by Colonel J. Irwin Gregg, left Bolivar Heights, taking the Winchester Pike. At Hall's Mills we turned to the right, on the road to Shepherdstown; the Sixteenth Pennsylvania in advance, commanded by Lieutenant-Colonel John K. Robison, a reliable and excellent officer. The advance-guard was composed of the squadrons of Captains Fisher and Swan, under Major W. H. Fry. After proceeding a couple of miles, we captured a mounted vidette of the enemy, and from that time until we reached Shepherdstown, kept up a continual skirmish with them, capturing seventeen, with their horses and equipments, with a loss to us of one killed and two wounded. At Shepherdstown Major Fry, with his command, charged through the streets, driving out over fifty of the enemy's cavalry, and scattering them in all directions, capturing eight prisoners, of whom one was a Major (Morgan, of the Sixth Virginia cavalry) and two lieutenants, two ambulances, and finding there over one hundred of the enemy's sick. The Sixteenth continued the advance through the town on the Martinsburgh road to within six miles of that place, being engaged with and driving the enemy's skirmishers all the way. At this point we were so near the enemy's lines that we could hear distinctly their bands playing on our right and left. We obtained valuable information of their movements and location from parties who had left Martinsburgh that day. The object of the reconnoissance having been accomplished, we returned to within a mile of Shepherdstown, where we remained on picket. A little before dark our videttes were driven in, but we speedily charged and repulsed the attack. The other regiments of the brigade had camped near Shepherdstown, with the roads around well picketed.

The next day, the sixteenth instant, as the First Maine regiment was going out on the Winchester road for forage, they met our pickets (from the Tenth New-York) running in, pursued by two squadrons of the enemy's cavalry. This truly noble little regiment instantly formed and charged the assailants, driving them back beyond the abandoned picket-line. The enemy now appeared in force, bringing up their artillery rapidly, and opening fire on our line. The Maine held their ground, deploying skirmishers, and made a desperate fight. Our artillery was then advanced, and posted in an advantageous position on the right and left of the road, supported by the Forty-seventh and Sixteenth Pennsylvania regiments. The Fourth was soon sent out to the right front, dismounted, and thrown forward as skirmishers. Shortly after, the Sixteenth regiment was sent to relieve the First Maine, which had been engaged about two hours, and had expended all its ammunition. As we moved along the road they got our range very fairly, sending their shells in very disagreeable proximity to us. The tall figure of Colonel Gregg, as he and his aid, Lieutenant Martin, and his escort rode along with us, attracted their attention, and wherever he moved thereafter, very leisurely over the field, their shell followed him, the fragments scattering all around; but he appeared to bear a charmed life and escaped unhurt. Three squadrons of the Sixteenth were dismounted and sent forward; Fisher's and McDowell's, under Major Fry, on the right, each officer dismounted, with carbine in hand; and the third, under Captains Swan and Day, on the left; the fourth and last, under Captain Alexander, in reserve.

The country in which we were fighting is illy fitted for cavalry movements—the ground very rocky and broken, cut up into small fields, with high stone and rail-fence, and frequent small patches of timber. This will account for the strange event of a fight between cavalrymen, where all the fighting was on foot, aided by artillery. Our artillery consisted of four pieces. Soon after the Sixteenth was thrown forward; two of these were sent to secure an important position on our left, and were not brought into play during the fight; so we fought with two pieces of artillery, and these not as effective as they should have been, on account of bad am-

munition; two of the shells which should have gone over our heads into the enemy's line, striking the ground between our reserve and the dismounted men. The rebels had eight guns in position firing at one time, and far better served than usual for them, in the cavalry fights I have noticed, whether Kelly's Ford, Aldie, Middleburgh, or Upperville. At times their firing was terrific to be concentrated on so small a line as ours; their shot, shell, grape, and canister coming all around and among us, lopping the branches from the trees, and splintering huge fragments from the rocks they came in contact with. Nothing but the uneven character of the ground preserved our little brigade from annihilation.

The Sixteenth took up the fighting for the Maine, which retired; but seeing us pushed at one time, they came out gallantly, without being asked, and we made "Johnny" travel. As our men's passions became excited in the contest, having repulsed an attack on the right, they forgot the order of Colonel Gregg, "to hold the line, but not to advance," and with a cheer sprang forward after the foe, driving them to their guns, where they, having a fair sweep, open all their pieces on us at once, with grape and canister. We were driven back. They charged us with exulting shouts, while their artillery hurled shell without cessation. We were driven back a quarter of a mile from our old line—all we were driven that day. In this charge the noble Captain Fisher was mortally wounded, one ball passing through his thigh, another through his breast. Colonel Gregg looked anxious, and appeared irritated that his order was not obeyed. On the left, Captain Swan had advanced in imitation of the right, and had fared the same fate, having his horse shot from under him and losing some of his best men. A new line is soon formed, strengthened by Alexander's squadron, a couple of squadrons of the First Pennsylvania regiment, from McIntosh's brigade having come up to support us. The fight goes on as wickedly as ever. The rebel battle-flag is shot down three times in a few minutes, and the last color-bearer compelled to crouch behind a wall and hold up the flag from his lurking-place. As night came on the enemy made several desperate attempts, all of which were steadily repulsed; after the last, our men, mounting the stone wall behind which the last line was formed, cheering and waving their hats, and challenging their opponents to come on, although their ammunition was exhausted.

Night put an end to the contest. At about nine o'clock the First Maine and First and Fourth Pennsylvania were ordered to fall back, leaving the Sixteenth to hold the battle-field. At about midnight Assistant Adjutant-General Maitland came and announced to Lieutenant-Colonel Robison that our wounded and all the other regiments had left, and that we were to bring up the rear, but to remain until two o'clock. At that hour we noiselessly marched through the fields for a couple of miles, until we struck the road to

Harper's Ferry, when we soon rejoined the brigade, and by five A.M. formed squadron on Bolivar Heights.

Thus ended one of the most desperate cavalry fights of the war, considering the number actually engaged; our brigade not numbering over eight hundred men, having become reduced by detachments sent to different points, and men left in the rear dismounted, their animals having become used up by the hard work of the past two months. At different times our fire ceased entirely, from want of ammunition. A remarkable circumstance is, that, to our knowledge, not one prisoner was taken on either side, except those of ours so badly wounded that they could not move, and were left behind when we were driven back. General Gregg accompanied us to Shepherdstown, and McIntosh's brigade was posted on our left, toward Harper's Ferry, but, with the exception of that portion of the First Pennsylvania referred to, did not participate. Captain Fisher, to whom I have referred, is well known to Philadelphia merchants as an old merchant of Uniontown, Pennsylvania. A gallant soldier, a gentleman, and a pleasant companion, his loss will be deeply regretted.

RICHMOND DESPATCH ACCOUNT.

ARMY NORTHERN VIRGINIA,
July 18, 1863.

The heavy cannonading heard in the direction of Shepherdstown Thursday originated from a severe cavalry fight, of which you have been advised by telegraph. I will now furnish you the particulars as they have been ascertained.

After the return of General Lee's army to Virginia, the enemy, evidently too much crippled for immediate pursuit, and desirous of ascertaining our movements, and feeling our position, despatched a large body of cavalry down the river to accomplish this object, if possible. They crossed at Harper's Ferry, where pontoon-bridges were thrown across for the purpose, and proceeded up the river as far as Shepherdstown, where they arrived on Wednesday; then coming down the Leetown and Winchester road to the distance of about five miles, halted. Meantime, Fitzhugh Lee, who was in the vicinity, and hearing of their whereabouts, proceeded up the Shepherdstown road for the purpose of checking the enemy's advance. He arrived in sight of the Yankees Thursday morning, which brought on desultory skirmishing and cannonading, which continued throughout the day until about four o'clock P.M. Then dismounting his men and advancing, the fight became general along both lines, the enemy having also dismounted.

A charge was ordered, and our men rushed upon the enemy, who were driven back two or three miles, where they sought the protection of a stone wall extending to the right and left of the road, their right and left flank stretching some distance either extremity of the wall. Here the fight raged for some time, our men frequently charging up to the enemy's front, and delivering their fire with telling effect, but exposed to an incessant fire of shot, shell, and small arms from the enemy, who had availed themselves of the protection of the stone wall, and every rock, tree, and stump that afforded the least shelter. While our men were in dangerous proximity, without the slightest shelter to cover their movements, bodies of the enemy's cavalry would frequently charge up to the stone wall, file to the right and left, rapidly deliver their fire, and gallop into a wood that skirted the wall on either side. Later in the afternoon, when the fight had progressed some time, the Fourteenth, Sixteenth, Seventeenth, and Thirty-sixth battalion, of Jenkins's brigade, came up from near Martinsburgh, and reënforced General Lee, taking a position on the left of the road toward Shepherdstown. During the remainder of the day they rendered gallant and efficient service with their long-range guns, and participated with their comrades, previously on the field, in the subsequent charges on the enemy's position. The enemy was repulsed and driven back on the right and left, but so effectual was their protection behind the wall, they were enabled to hold that position until night. Our line of battle extended about the distance of a mile and a half to the right and left of the road, the enemy's about the same distance, with reserves in supporting distance.

We had three pieces of artillery, and the enemy it is believed about the same number, planted in an admirable position on the right of the stone wall and in front of the woods, commanding the whole field in front. During the entire engagement our officers and men displayed the utmost gallantry. General Jenkins being absent by reason of a wound in the head received at Gettysburgh, his men were led by Colonel Ferguson, the whole under command of Fitzhugh Lee. Our loss, not yet definitely known, is unofficially reported at from seventy-five to one hundred from all causes. We lost no prisoners. The loss of the enemy is estimated at from one hundred and fifty to two hundred. Night having drawn her sable curtain over the scene, the enemy fell back from this position behind the stone wall, leaving their dead and wounded in our hands, and our men in possession of the field. They retreated down the river road toward Harper's Ferry, and it is reported have since gone to the other side of the river.

The casualties, as usual latterly, were considerable among the officers, who greatly exposed themselves leading and encouraging the men, and forming conspicuous marks for the enemy's sharp-shooters. Colonel Drake, First Virginia, and Adjutant Barbour, Seventeenth Virginia, are reported killed; the latter while cheering the men to a charge. Colonel Gregg, of Lee's brigade, reported mortally wounded, and Major Jos. H. Newman, of the Sixteenth, wounded in the head.

Prisoners taken report that the enemy was commanded by General Gregg.

I should mention that the enemy, on their entrance into Shepherdstown, found fifty or sixty of our sick and wounded, who were told they would be paroled, and those physically able carried off; but the issue of the fight was so unexpected to them they were compelled to leave the intended prisoners behind.

"All is quiet" in and along the lines, and this is all I am at liberty to report at this writing. The movements of the army since the great battle of Gettysburgh, which are as well known to the enemy as ourselves, may be briefly summed up as follows: Withdrawing from our position at Gettysburgh almost simultaneously with the enemy, our army formed line of battle, our right resting near Hagerstown, our left on the river, near Williamsport. Here we lay two tedious days and nights, offering fight, which the enemy declined, when it was determined to recross the river, which was most successfully accomplished. Of our movements since, or present position, I cannot speak, though it would appease a prurient curiosity, which seeks gratification even at the expense of the public interests and safety. I will always promptly advise you of facts accomplished, and events that may be given to the public without detriment.

No considerable body of the enemy are yet reported to be on the south side of the river. A small body of cavalry advanced from the direction of Williamsport to-day, and captured three of our wagons and as many men, who had been foraging in the vicinity of the mountain, about seven miles from Martinsburgh. The remainder of the party escaped.

General Pettigrew, of North-Carolina, died of his wound at half-past six yesterday morning, at the residence of Mr. Boyd, Bunker Hill, from the effect of his wound received in repelling a cavalry charge into his brigade just before recrossing the Potomac, Wednesday last. His confinement was soothed by every attention his condition required, and his faithful body-servant attended him to the last. His noble features, calm and placid in death, and his body arrayed in full uniform, with his limbs composed, he appeared, instead of death, more like one who "wraps the drapery of his couch about him, and lies down to pleasant dreams." It being impossible to procure a metallic coffin to convey his remains home, they were interred temporarily at Bunker Hill.   **

Doc. 146.

REPORT OF GENERAL JOSEPH E. JOHNSTON.

REBEL OPERATIONS IN MISSISSIPPI AND LOUISIANA.

MERIDIAN, MISS., Nov. 1, 1863.

General S. Cooper, Adjutant and Inspector-General:

SIR: The following report of my operations in the Department of Mississippi and East-Louisiana is respectfully offered as a substitute for the imperfect one forwarded by me from Jackson on May twenty-seventh, 1863.

While on my way to Mississippi, where I thought my presence had become necessary, I received, in Mobile, on March twelfth, the following telegram from the Secretary of War, dated March ninth:

Order General Bragg to report to the War Department for conference. Assume yourself direct charge of the Army of Middle Tennessee.

In obedience to this order I at once proceeded to Tullahoma. On my arrival I informed the Secretary of War, by a telegram of March nineteenth, that General Bragg could not then be sent to Richmond, as he has ordered, on account of the critical condition of his family.

On the tenth of April, I repeated this to the President, and added: "Being unwell then, I afterward became sick, and am not now able to serve in the field. General Bragg is, therefore, necessary here." On the twenty-eighth, my unfitness for service in the field was reported to the Secretary of War.

On the ninth of May I received, at Tullahoma, the following despatch of the same date from the Secretary of War:

Proceed at once to Mississippi and take chief command of the forces there, giving to those in the field, as far as practicable, the encouragement and benefit of your personal direction.

It is thus seen that neither my orders nor my health permitted me to visit Mississippi after the twelfth of March, until the time when I took direct charge of that department.

From the time of my arrival at Tullahoma until the fourteenth of April, General Pemberton's reports, all by telegraph, indicated that the efforts of the enemy would be against General Bragg rather than himself, and looked to the abandonment of his attempts on Vicksburgh. In that of April thirteenth he says:

I am satisfied Rosecrans will be reënforced from Grant's army. Shall I order troops to Tullahoma?

On the seventeenth of April General Pemberton telegraphed the return of Grant and the resumption of the operations against Vicksburgh.

On the twenty-ninth of April he telegraphed:

The enemy is at Hard Times, in large force, with barges and transports, indicating a purpose to attack Grand Gulf, with a view to Vicksburgh. He also reported heavy firing at Grand Gulf. The enemy shelling our batteries both above and below.

On the first of May he telegraphed:

A furious battle has been going on since daylight just below Port Gibson. . . . Enemy can cross all his army from Hard Times to Bruinsburgh. I should have large reënforcements. Enemy's movements threaten Jackson, and if successful cut off Vicksburgh and Port Hudson.

I at once urged him to concentrate and to attack Grant immediately on his landing; and on the next day I sent the following despatch to him:

If Grant crosses, unite all your troops to beat him. Success will give back what was abandoned to win it.

I telegraphed to you on the first:

General Pemberton calls for large reënforcements. They cannot be sent from here without giving up Tennessee. Can one or two brigades be sent from the East?

On the seventh I again asked for reënforcements for the Mississippi.

I received no further report of the battle of Port Gibson, and on the fifth asked General Pemberton: "What is the result, and where is Grant's army?" I received no answer, and gained no additional information in relation to either subject, until I reached the Department of Mississippi, in obedience to my orders of May ninth.

Then, on May thirteenth, I received a despatch from General Pemberton, dated Vicksburgh, May twelfth, asking for reënforcements, as the enemy, in large force, was moving from the Mississippi, south of the Big Black, apparently toward Edwards's Depot, "which will be the battle-field, if I can forward sufficient force, leaving troops enough to secure the safety of this place."

Before my arrival at Jackson, Grant had beaten General Bowen at Port Gibson, made good the landing of his army, occupied Grand Gulf, and was marching upon the Jackson and Vicksburgh Railroad.

On reaching Jackson, on the night of the thirteenth of May, I found there the brigades of Gregg and Walker, reported at six thousand; learned from General Gregg that Maxey's brigade was expected to arrive from Port Hudson the next day; that General Pemberton's forces, except the garrison of Port Hudson (five thousand) and of Vicksburgh, were at Edwards's Depot—the General's headquarters at Bovina; that four divisions of the enemy, under Sherman, occupied Clinton, ten miles west of Jackson, between Edwards's Depot and ourselves. I was aware that reënforcements were on their way from the East, and that the advance of those under General Gist would probably arrive the next day, and with Maxey's brigade, swell my force to about eleven thousand.

Upon this information I sent to General Pemberton on the same night (thirteenth) a despatch informing him of my arrival, and of the occupation of Clinton by a portion of Grant's army, urging the importance of reëstablishing communications, and ordering him to come up, if practicable, on Sherman's rear at once, and adding: "To beat such a detachment would be of immense value. The troops here could coöperate. All the strength you can quickly assemble should be brought. Time is all-important."

On Thursday, May fourteenth, the enemy advanced by the Raymond and Clinton roads upon Jackson. The resistance made by the brigades of Gregg and Walker gave sufficient time for the removal of the public stores; and at two P.M. we retreated by the Canton road, from which alone we could form a junction with General Pemberton. After marching six miles the troops encamped.

From this point I sent to General Pemberton the despatch of May fourteenth, of which the following is a copy:

GENERAL: The body of troops mentioned in my note of last night compelled Brigadier-General Gregg and his command to evacuate Jackson about noon to-day. The necessity of taking the Canton road, at right angles to that upon which the enemy approached, prevented an obstinate defence. A body of troops, reported this morning to have reached Raymond last night, advanced at the same time from that direction. Prisoners say that it was McPherson's corps (four divisions) which marched from Clinton. I have no certain information of the other: both skirmished very cautiously. Telegrams were despatched when the enemy was near, directing General Gist to assemble the approaching troops at a point forty or fifty miles from Jackson, and General Maxey to return to his wagons, and provide for the security of his brigade—for instance, by joining General Gist. That body of troops will be able, I hope, to prevent the enemy in Jackson from drawing provisions from the East, and this one may be able to keep him from the country toward Panola. Can he supply himself from the Mississippi? Can you not cut him off from it? And, above all, should he be compelled to fall back for want of supplies, beat him. As soon as the reënforcements are all up, they must be united to the rest of the army. I am anxious to see a force assembled that may be able to inflict a heavy blow upon the enemy.

Would it not be better to place the forces to support Vicksburgh between General Loring and that place, and merely observe the ferries, so that you might unite, if opportunity to fight presented itself?

General Gregg will move toward Canton to-morrow. If prisoners tell the truth, the forces at Jackson must be half of Grant's army. It would decide the campaign to beat it, which can be done only by concentrating, especially when the remainder of the Eastern troops arrive; they are to be twelve thousand or thirteen thousand.

This despatch was not answered. General Pemberton stated, in his official report, that it was received at six P.M. on the sixteenth, "whilst on the retreat" from the battle-field of Baker's Creek.

On the next day, May seventeenth, (Friday,) the troops under me marched ten and a half miles further, to Calhoun Station. On the morning of that day I received a letter from General Pemberton, dated Edwards's Depot, May fourteenth, (Thursday,) five forty P.M.:

I shall move as early to-morrow morning as practicable a column of seventeen thousand on Dillon's. The object is to cut off the enemy's communications and force him to attack me, as I do not consider my force sufficient to justify an attack on the enemy in position or to attempt to cut my way to Jackson.

This was the first communication received from General Pemberton after my arrival at Jackson, and from it I learned that he had not moved toward Clinton ten hours after the receipt of my order to do so, and that the junction of the forces, which could have been effected by the fifteenth, was deferred, and that, in disobedience of my orders, and in opposition to the views of a majority of the council of war, composed of all his generals present, before whom he placed the subject, he had decided to make a movement by which the union would be impossible. General Pemberton was immediately instructed that there was but one mode by which we could unite, namely, by his moving directly to Clinton. The brigadier-generals representing that their troops required rest, after the fatigue they had undergone in the skirmishes and marches preceding the retreat from Jackson, and having yet no certain intelligence of General Pemberton's route, or General Gist's position, I did not move on Saturday. In the evening I received a reply to my last despatch, dated four miles south of Edwards's Depot, May sixteenth, stating it had reached him at thirty minutes past six that morning; that "it found the army on the middle road to Raymond. The order of countermarch has been issued. Owing to the destruction of a bridge on Baker's Creek, which runs, for some distance, parallel with the railroad, and south of it, our march will be on the road leading from Edwards's Depot, in the direction of Brownsville. This road runs nearly parallel with the railroad. In going to Clinton we shall leave Bolton's Depot four miles to the right. I am thus particular, so that you may be able to make a junction with this army." In a postscript, he reported "heavy skirmishing now going on in my front."

On the afternoon of the same day I received General Pemberton's first reply to the order sent him from Jackson to attack Sherman, dated Bovina, May fourteenth, nine o'clock and ten minutes A.M., as follows:

I move at once with my whole available force from Edwards' Depot. In directing this move I do not think you fully comprehend the condition Vicksburgh will be left in; but I comply at once with your orders.

On May seventeenth, (Sunday,) I marched fifteen miles in the direction indicated in General Pemberton's note, received the previous evening. In the afternoon a letter was brought from him dated Bovina, May seventeenth, a copy of which has been forwarded to the War Department. In this, referring to my despatch of May thirteenth from Jackson, General Pemberton wrote:

I notified you on the morning of the fourteenth of the receipt of your instructions to move and attack the enemy toward Clinton. I deemed the movement very hazardous, preferring to remain in position behind the Big Black and near to Vicksburgh. I called a council of war, composed of all the general officers. . . . .
A majority of the officers expressed themselves favorable to the movement indicated by you. The others, including Major-Generals Loring and Stevenson, preferred a movement by which this army might endeavor to cut off the enemy's supplies from the Mississippi. My own views were

expressed as unfavorable to any movement which would remove me from my base, which was, and is, Vicksburgh. I did not, however, see fit to place my own judgment and opinions so far in opposition as to prevent the movement altogether; but, believing the only possibility of success to be in the plan proposed, of cutting off the enemy's supplies, I directed all my disposable force—say seventeen thousand five hundred—toward Raymond or Dillon's.

It also contained intelligence of his engagement with the enemy on the sixteenth, near Baker's Creek, three or four miles from Edwards's Depot, and of his having been compelled to withdraw, with heavy loss, to Big Black Bridge. He further expressed the apprehension that he would be compelled to fall back from this point, and represented that, if so, his position at Snyder's Mills would be untenable, and said: "I have about sixty days' provisions at Vicksburgh and Snyder's. I respectfully await your instructions."

I immediately replied, May seventeenth: "If Haynes's Bluff be untenable, Vicksburgh is of no value and cannot be held. If, therefore, you are invested in Vicksburgh, you must ultimately surrender. Under such circumstances, instead of losing both troops and place, you must, if possible, save the troops. If it is not too late, evacuate Vicksburgh and its dependencies, and march to the north-east." That night I was informed that General Pemberton had fallen back to Vicksburgh.

On Monday, May eighteenth, General Pemberton informed me, by letter, dated Vicksburgh, May seventeenth, that he had retired within the line of intrenchments around Vicksburgh, having been attacked and forced back from Big Black Bridge, and that he had ordered Haynes's Bluff to be abandoned. His letter concluded with the following remark: "I greatly regret that I felt compelled to make the advance beyond Big Black, which has proved so disastrous in its results." It will be remembered that General Pemberton expected that Edwards's Depot would be the battle-field before I reached Jackson, (see his despatch of the twelfth, already quoted,) and that his army, before he received any orders from me, was seven or eight miles east of the Big Black, near Edwards's Depot.

On May nineteenth, General Pemberton's reply (dated Vicksburgh, May eighteenth) to my communication of the seventeenth, was brought me, near Vernon, where I had gone with the troops under my command, for the purpose of effecting a junction with him in case he evacuated Vicksburgh, as I had ordered, in which he advised me that he had "assembled a council of war of the general officers of this command, and having laid your instructions before them, asked the free expression of their opinions as to the practicability of carrying them out. The opinion was unanimously expressed that it was impossible to withdraw the army from this position with such *morale* and material as to be of further service to the Confederacy." On receiving this information, I replied: "I am trying to gather a force which may attempt to relieve you. Hold out." The same day I sent orders to Major-General Gardner to evacuate Port Hudson.

I then determined, by easy marches, to reëstablish my line between Jackson and Canton, as the junction of the two commands had become impossible.

On the twentieth and twenty-first of May I was joined by the brigades of Generals Gist, Ector, and McNair. The division of General Loring, cut off from General Pemberton in the battle of Baker's Creek, reached Jackson on the twentieth, and General Maxey, with his brigade, on the twenty-third. By the fourth of June the army had, in addition to these, been reënforced by the brigade of General Evans, the division of General Breckinridge, and the division of cavalry, numbering two thousand eight hundred, commanded by Brigadier-General W. H. Jackson. Small as was this force, about twenty-four thousand, infantry and artillery, not one third of that of the enemy, it was deficient in artillery, in ammunition for all arms and field transportation, and could not be moved upon that enemy, already intrenching his large force, with any hope of success.

The draft upon the country had so far reduced the number of horses and mules that it was not until late in June that draught animals could be procured, from distant points, for the artillery and trains.

There was no want of commissary supplies in the department; but the limited transportation caused a deficiency for a moving army.

On the twenty-third of May I received a despatch from Major-General Gardner, dated Port Hudson, May twenty-first, informing me that the enemy was about to cross at Bayou Sara; that the whole force from Baton Rouge was in his front, and asking to be reënforced. On this, my orders for the evacuation of Port Hudson were repeated, and he was informed:

You cannot be reënforced. Do not allow yourself to be invested. At every risk save the troops, and if practicable move in this direction.

This despatch did not reach General Gardner, Port Hudson being then invested.

About the twenty-fourth of May the enemy made such demonstrations above the Big Black and toward Yazoo City, that I sent Walker's division to Yazoo City, with orders to fortify it; and the demonstrations being renewed, placed Loring's division within supporting distance of Walker's, and in person took post at Canton.

Despatches arrived from General Pemberton, dated Vicksburgh, May twentieth and twenty-first. In that of the twentieth he stated that the enemy had assaulted his intrenched lines the day before, and were repulsed with heavy loss. He estimated their force at not less than sixty thousand, and asked that musket-caps be sent, they being his main necessity. He concluded:

An army will be necessary to save Vicksburgh, and that quickly. Will it be sent?

On the twenty-first he wrote:

The men credit, and are encouraged by a re-port, that you are near with a large force. They are fighting in good spirits, and their organization is complete.

Caps were sent as fast as they arrived. On May twenty-ninth I sent a despatch to General Pemberton, to the following effect:

I am too weak to save Vicksburgh. Can do no more than attempt to save you and your garrison. It will be impossible to extricate you, unless you coöperate, and we make mutually supporting movements. Communicate your plans and suggestions, if possible.

The receipt of this was acknowledged in a communication, dated Vicksburgh, June third, in which General Pemberton says:

We can get no information from outside as to your position or strength, and very little in regard to the enemy.

In a despatch, dated June tenth, from General Gardner, the first received since his investment, he reported having repulsed the enemy in several severe attacks, but that he was getting short of provisions and ammunition. To which I replied, June fifteenth, informing him that I had no means of relieving him, adding:

General Taylor will do what he can on the opposite side of the river. Hold the place as long as you can, and, if possible, withdraw in any direction, or cut your way out. It is very important to keep Banks and his forces occupied.

In a despatch, dated June twentieth, I sent him word that General Taylor had intended to attack the enemy opposite Port Hudson on the night of the fifteenth, and attempt to send cattle across the river.

The want of field transportation rendered any movement for the relief of Port Hudson impossible had a march in that direction been advisable, but such a march would have enabled Grant (who had now completed his strong lines around Vicksburgh) to have cut my line of communication, and destroyed my army; and from the moment that I put my troops in march in that direction the whole of Middle and North Mississippi would have been open to the enemy.

On June seventh I repeated the substance of my despatch of May twenty-ninth to General Pemberton.

On the fourth of June I told the Secretary of War, in answer to his call for my plans, that my only plan was to relieve Vicksburgh, and my force was far too small for the purpose.

On June tenth I told him I had not at my disposal half the troops necessary.

On the twelfth I said to him: "To take from Bragg a force which would make this army fit to oppose Grant, would involve yielding Tennessee. It is for the government to decide between this State and Tennessee."

On the fourteenth I sent General Pemberton the following:

All that we can attempt to do is to save you and your garrison. To do this exact coöperation is indispensable; by fighting the enemy simultaneously at the same points of his line you may be extricated. Our joint forces cannot raise the siege of Vicksburgh. My communication with the rear can best be preserved by operating north of railroad. Inform me as soon as possible what points will suit you best. Your despatches of the twelfth received. General Taylor, with eight thousand men, will endeavor to open communications with you from Richmond."

To this communication General Pemberton replied, June twenty-first, recommending me to move north of the railroad toward Vicksburgh, to keep the enemy attracted to that side, and stating that he would himself move at the proper time, by the Warrenton road, crossing the Big Black at Hankinson's Ferry; that "the other roads are too strongly intrenched, and the enemy in too heavy force, for a reasonable prospect of success," unless I could compel him to abandon his communications by Snyder's.

On the fifteenth I expressed to the department the opinion that, without some great blunder of the enemy, we could not hold both, (Mississippi and Tennessee,) and that I considered saving Vicksburgh hopeless.

On the eighteenth I said Grant's position, naturally very strong, is intrenched and protected by powerful artillery, and the roads obstructed. His reënforcements have been at least equal to my whole force. The Big Black covers him from attack, and would cut of our retreat if defeated.

On June twenty-second, in reply to a despatch from General Pemberton of the fifteenth, in which he said that, though living on greatly reduced rations, he had sufficient for twenty days, I informed him that General Taylor had been sent by General E. K. Smith to coöperate with him from the west bank of the Mississippi, and that in a day or two I would try to make a diversion in his favor, and if possible open communications, adding:

Though I fear my force is too small to effect the latter. I have only two thirds of the force you told messenger Saunders to state to me as the least with which I ought to make an attempt. Scouts report the enemy fortifying toward us, and the roads blocked.

A day or two after this a despatch was brought me from General Pemberton, dated June twenty-second, suggesting that I should make to Grant "propositions to pass this army out, with all its arms and equipages;" renewing his hope of my being able, by force of arms, to act with him, and expressing the opinion that he could hold out for fifteen days longer. To this despatch I replied, June twenty-seventh, informing him that General E. K. Smith's troops had fallen back to Delhi, and that I had urged him to assume the direct command, and continued:

The determined spirit you manifest, and his expected coöperation, encourage me to hope that something may yet be done to save Vicksburgh, and to postpone both of the modes suggested of merely extricating the garrison. Negotiations with Grant for the relief of the garrison, should they become necessary, must be made by you. It would be a confession of weakness on my part, which I ought not to make, to propose them. When it becomes necessary to make terms, they may be considered as made under my authority.

On the twenty-ninth of June, field transportation and other supplies having been obtained, the army marched toward the Big Black, and on the evening of July first encamped between Brownsville and the river.

Reconnoissances, which occupied the second and third, convinced me that the attack north of the railroad was impracticable. I determined, therefore, to make the examinations necessary for the attempt south of the railroad—thinking, from what was already known, that the chance for success was much better there, although the consequences of defeat might be more disastrous.

On the night of the third a messenger was sent to General Pemberton with information that an attempt to create a diversion would be made to enable him to cut his way out, and that I hoped to attack the enemy about the seventh.

On the fifth, however, we learned the fall of Vicksburgh, and therefore fell back to Jackson.

The army reached Jackson the evening of the seventh, and on the morning of the ninth the enemy appeared in heavy force in front of the works thrown up for the defence of the place. These, consisting of a line of rifle-pits, prepared at intervals for artillery, extended from a point north of the town, a little east of the Canton road, to a point south of the town, within a short distance of Pearl River, and covered most of the approaches west of the river, but were badly located and constructed, presenting but a slight obstacle to a vigorous assault.

The troops promptly took their positions in the intrenchments on the appearance of the enemy, in expectation of an immediate assault. Major-General Loring occupying the right, Major-General Walker the right of the centre, Major-General French the left of the centre, and Major-General Breckinridge the left. The cavalry, under Brigadier-General Jackson, was ordered to observe and guard the fords of Pearl River above and below the town.

The reports that had at various times been made to me by the commanding officers of the troops encamped near Jackson of the scarcity of water, led me to believe that Sherman, who advanced in heavy order of battle from Clinton, could not besiege, but would be compelled to make an immediate assault. His force was represented to consist of his own and Ord's army corps, and three divisions in addition. The spirit and confidence manifested by the whole army under my command were such that, notwithstanding this vast superiority of numbers, I felt assured, with the advantage given by the intrenchments, weak as they were, an assault by him would result in his discomfiture.

Instead of attacking, the enemy, as soon as they arrived, commenced intrenching and constructing batteries. On the tenth there was spirited skirmishing, with slight cannonading, continuing throughout the day. This was kept up, with varying intensity and but little interruption, until the period of our evacuation. Hills, commanding and encircling the town within easy cannon range, offered favorable sites for batteries. A cross fire of shot and shell reached all parts of the town, showing the position to be entirely untenable against a powerful artillery.

On the eleventh I telegraphed the President:

If the position and works were not bad, want of stores, which could not be collected, would make it impossible to stand a siege. If the enemy will not attack, we must, or at the last moment withdraw. We cannot attack seriously without risking the army.

On the twelfth, besides the usual skirmishing, there was a heavy cannonade from the batteries near the Canton and south of the Clinton roads. The missiles reached all parts of the town. An assault, though not a vigorous one, was also made on General Breckinridge's line. It was quickly repelled, however, principally by the direct fire of Cobb's and Slocum's batteries, and flank attack of the skirmishers of the First, Third, and Fourth Florida, and Forty-seventh Georgia regiments. The enemy's loss was two hundred prisoners, nearly the same number killed, many wounded, and the colors of the Twenty-eighth, Forty-first, and Fifty-third Illinois regiments.

By the thirteenth, the enemy had extended his lines, until both his flanks rested on Pearl River.

I telegraphed the President on the fourteenth, that a large force lately left Vicksburgh to turn us on the north. This will compel us to abandon Jackson. The troops before us have been intrenching and constructing batteries since their arrival.

On the fifteenth I telegraphed the President:

The enemy is evidently making a siege which we cannot resist. It would be madness to attack him. The remainder of the army, under Grant, at Vicksburgh, is, beyond doubt, on its way to this place.

On the sixteenth of July information was received that a large train from Vicksburgh, loaded with ammunition, was near the enemy's camp. This, and the condition of their batteries, made it probable that Sherman would, on the next day, concentrate upon us the fire of near by two hundred guns. It was also reported that the enemy had crossed Pearl River in the rear of their left flank. The evacuation of Jackson that night was, therefore, determined on.

Our withdrawal was effected on the night of the sixteenth. All public property, and the sick and wounded, except a few not in a condition to be moved, had been previously carried to the rear. The right wing retired toward Brandon by the new Brandon road, and the left wing by the old Brandon road. The cavalry remained to destroy the bridges over Pearl River, and observe the enemy. The evacuation was not discovered by the enemy until the next day.

Our loss during the siege was estimated at seventy-one killed, five hundred and four wounded, and about twenty-five missing. The army retired by easy marches to Morton, distant about thirty-five miles from Jackson. Desertions during the siege and on the march were, I regret to say, frequent. Two divisions of the enemy, with cavalry, drove our cavalry through Brandon on the nineteenth, returning to Jackson the next day. Their object seemed to be to destroy the railroad bridges and depots.

Colonel J. L. Logan, commanding a mounted force around Port Hudson, reported three successful engagements with detachments of the enemy.

On the twelfth of July I received information from Colonel Logan of the surrender of Port Hudson on the ninth. Subsequently the report of Major Jackson, Assistant Adjutant-General, was received, informing me of the surrender. That officer stated that provisions were exhausted, and that the position of the enemy rendered it impossible for the garrison to cut its way out. But two thousand five hundred of the garrison were fit for duty at the time of surrender.

The enemy advanced against Yazoo City, both by land and water, on the thirteenth. The attack by the gunboats was handsomely repulsed by our heavy battery, under the command of Commander Isaac N. Brown, of the navy. The De Kalb, the flag-ship of the hostile squadron, an iron-clad, mounting thirteen guns, was sunk by a torpedo. To the force advancing by land no resistance was made by the garrison, commanded by Colonel Greasman, of the Twenty-ninth North-Carolina regiment.

[Here follows a review of some minor points in the orders, and General Johnston then proceeds.]

The time to strike the enemy, with the best hope of saving Vicksburgh, was when he was landing near Bruinsburgh. To do this with any prospect of success, a rapid concentration of all the forces should have been made and an attack. Under this conviction I telegraphed to General Pemberton, on May first, from Tullahoma: "If Grant's army lands on this side of the river, the safety of Mississippi depends on beating him. For that object you should unite your whole force." And again, on May second: "If Grant crosses, unite the whole force to beat him; success will give back what was abandoned to win it."

These instructions were neglected, and time was given to Grant to gain a foothold in the State. At Ports Gibson and Raymond detachments of our troops were defeated and driven back by overwhelming numbers of the enemy.

On the thirteenth, when I learned that there were four divisions of the enemy at Clinton, distant twenty miles from the main body of General Pemberton's forces, I gave him orders to attack them, and notified him that we could coöperate. This order General Pemberton disobeyed, and so reported to me in his letter of the seventeenth. It directed him to move twenty miles to the east, to coöperate with me in attacking Sherman. He moved to the south, and made our coöperation and junction impossible. He claims that this order compelled him to make the advance beyond the Big Black, which proved so "disastrous." Before I had reached Jackson, and before the order was given, General Pemberton made his first advance beyond (east of) the Big Black, to Edwards's Depot. After the receipt of the order, in violation of it, he made his second and last advance from that point to the field of Baker's Creek. He further claims that this order caused the subversion of his "matured plans." I do not know what those plans were, but am startled to find matured plans given up for a movement in violation of my orders, rejected by the majority of his council of war, and disapproved (as he states) by himself. On the twelfth, he wrote to me that if he could collect force enough, Edwards's Depot would be the battle-field. The battle of Baker's Creek was fought three or four miles from Edwards's Depot. The presence of the enemy was reported to him the night before. There was no apparent obstacle to prevent his resuming his original position, and carrying out his "matured plans."

It is a new military principle, that when an officer disobeys a positive order from his superior, that superior becomes responsible for any measure his subordinate may choose to substitute for that ordered.

But had the battle of Baker's Creek not been fought, General Pemberton's belief that Vicksburgh was his base, rendered his ruin inevitable. He would still have been besieged, and therefore captured. The larger force he would have carried into the lines would have added to and hastened the catastrophe. His disasters were due, not merely to his entangling himself with the advancing columns of a superior and unobserved enemy, but to his evident determination to be besieged in Vicksburgh, instead of manœuvring to prevent a siege.

Convinced of the impossibility of collecting a sufficient force to break the investment of Vicksburgh, should it be completed—appreciating the difficulty of extricating the garrison, and convinced that Vicksburgh and Port Hudson had lost most of their value by the repeated passage of armed vessels and transports, I ordered the evacuation of both places. General Gordon did not receive this order before the investment of Port Hudson, if at all. General Pemberton set aside this order, under the advice of a council of war; and though he had in Vicksburgh eight thousand fresh troops, not demoralized by defeat, decided that it "was impossible to withdraw the army from this position with such morale and material as' to be of further service to the Confederacy;" but "to hold Vicksburgh as long as possible, with the firm hope that the government may yet be able to assist me in keeping this obstruction to the enemy's free navigation of the Mississippi River." Vicksburgh was greatly imperilled when my instructions from Tullahoma to concentrate were neglected. It was lost when my orders of the thirteenth and fifteenth of May were disobeyed. To this loss were added the labor, privations, and certain capture of a gallant army, when my orders for its evacuation were set aside.

In this report I have been compelled to enter into many details, and to make some animadversions upon the conduct of General Pemberton. The one was no pleasant task—the other a most painful duty; both have been forced upon me by the official report of General Pemberton, made to the War Department instead of to me, to whom it was due.

General Pemberton, by direct assertion and by implication, puts upon me the responsibility of the movement which led his army to defeat at Baker's Creek and Big Black Bridge—defeats which produced the loss of Vicksburgh and its army.

This statement has been circulated by the press, in more or less detail, and with more or less marks of an official character, until my silence would be almost an acknowledgment of the justice of the charge.

A proper regard for the good opinion of my government has compelled me, therefore, to throw aside that delicacy which I would gladly have observed toward a brother officer, suffering much undeserved obloquy, and to show that in his short campaign General Pemberton made not a single movement in obedience to my orders, and regarded none of my instructions; and, finally, did not embrace the only opportunity to save his army, that given by my order to abandon Vicksburgh. Most respectfully, your obedient servant, J. E. JOHNSTON,
General.

Doc. 147.

OPERATIONS AGAINST CHARLESTON.

CAPTAIN H. S. GRAY'S* REPORT.

JULY 20, 1863.

EARLY on the ninth we received orders to be ready by sundown for a fresh start. To prevent any mistake in the night, each officer and man had on his left arm a white badge three inches wide. General Strong was to embark two thousand men in boats, and take them up Folly River in the Lighthouse Inlet; and at sunrise the batteries that had been erected (there were over forty guns and mortars in position) were to open, and the gunboats to engage the batteries on the opposite side of the island. The boats arrived with the troops in good time, preceded by eight boat-howitzers from the gunboats; the first boat contained General Strong and staff, and then came the battalion of the Seventh Connecticut volunteers.

General Gilmore told Colonel Rodman that the General had concluded that our battalion was the most reliable and could be trusted, and was selected for that reason. The batteries opened at daylight, and in a short time the enemy discovered the boats, and threw shell and solid shot,

* Commanded two companies of the Seventh Connecticut regiment, in the action.

trying to sink them. The shot and shell struck and burst all around us, but only one boat was struck, containing some of the Sixth Connecticut volunteers, killing one and wounding two or three.

The General's boat had got two discharges of grape. Just at this moment Lieutenant-Colonel Rodman said to the General: "Let me land my command and take that battery." The General hesitated at first, and then said: "Go!" Colonel Rodman stood up in the stern of his boat, and gave the command, as the boats were all in line and in good order: "Seventh Connecticut! man your oars and follow me." We had previously detailed fifty men as oarsmen, leaving us about one hundred and seventy-five effective men and officers. At the order we all headed for the shore, and, as the boats struck, every man sprang as if by instinct, and in an instant the men were in line.

We advanced rapidly to the first line of rifle-works; our skirmishers cleared it with a bound, and advanced to the second line. Our main forces moved to the first line—the foe retired, firing. Lieutenant-Colonel Rodman now sent word back for the General to land his whole force, as we could hold the line we occupied. After exchanging a few shots, and the brigade being landed and ready to advance, the enemy began to give way. Lieutenant Jordan, with a detachment of company I, pushed right up into their batteries on our right, and not finding the first gun in working order—it having been disabled by a shot—he pushed forward to what is now called Battery Rodman, in which there was an eight-inch sea-coast howitzer, and turned it on the retreating foe, bursting several shells over their heads before they reached Fort Wagner.

Our forces captured eight single gun batteries and three mortars, and not far from two hundred prisoners.

We bivouacked for the night under easy range of Fort Wagner. About half-past two A.M. General Strong came and called the Lieutenant-Colonel out. He soon returned and said: "Turn out! we have got a job on hand." The men were soon out and into line, but rather slow to time, as they were tired with the work the day before.

The programme was to try to take Fort Wagner by assault; we were to take the lead, and to be supported by the Seventy-sixth Pennsylvania and Ninth Maine. Silently we moved up to the advance line of our pickets, our guns loaded and aimed, and bayonets fixed. We were then deployed into line of battle, (we had one hundred and ninety-one men and officers, all told,) reached and crossed the neck of land that approached the fort, our right resting on the beach. We were deployed and ready for the start. Our orders were to move steadily forward until the pickets fired, then follow them close and rush for the works, and we were promised ready support. General Strong gave the order: "Aim low, and put your trust in God. Forward the Seventh!" And forward we went, being not over

five hundred yards from the fort when we started.

We had not gone far before the picket fired, and then we took the double-quick, and with a cheer rushed for the works. Before we reached the outer works, we got a murderous fire from the riflemen behind the works. A few fell—a check in the line. An encouraging word from the officers, and right gallantly we reached the outer works; over them with a will we went, down the opposite side, across the moat—there being about one foot of water in it—right up to the crest of the parapet; and there we lay, anxiously waiting for our support to come up so far as to make it a sure thing for us to rise up and go over with a bound, our men in the mean time busying themselves by picking off the sharp-shooters and gunners. We laid so near the top that one had to put his head up and point across the parapet to kill his man.

As near as I can ascertain, we were in this position from ten to twenty minutes, when both of the regiments that were to support us broke and fled, leaving us to take care of ourselves as best we might. As soon as the regiment in front broke and ran, they paid particular attention to our case. They threw hand-grenades over the parapet, and soon sent men into the flank of a bastion, which commanded the front upon which we lay. They had us there to a great disadvantage. The question was whether we should surrender as prisoners, attempt to carry the works, and to be entirely annihilated, (as they greatly outnumbered us,) or take the back track and run the gauntlet for our lives.

Upon consulting the Lieutenant-Colonel, he reluctantly gave the order to retreat. Lieutenant-Phillips exclaimed: "For God's sake, don't let us retreat." As if by magic, the order was recalled, although some had started; but the order had to be repeated, and down in and across the moat we went over the works. They had a perfect enfilading fire of small arms for a thousand yards, besides their pieces were giving us grape and canister. They fell on all sides of me, and I alone of four captains was spared; and out of one hundred and ninety-one officers and men that marched out to attack the foe, only eighty-eight returned safe to camp; and ever let it be said, to the credit of the Seventh Connecticut volunteers, that not one straggler could be discovered. Fifteen minutes after we got in camp the roll was called, and but one man came in afterward, and he was delayed in assisting a wounded comrade.

Met General Strong coming off, and with tears in his eyes he said we had done our whole duty, and covered ourselves all over with glory, and if the support had come to time, that we should have taken the works, and without a doubt we should have done so. But our loss is great. We had eleven officers in our mess. Now we have but four. It is hard, but such is the fate of war.

Our attack on the tenth July was a fearful surprise to them. They had but few troops on this island. Had they five thousand infantry here, the natural defences are of such a character that we never could have taken it.

Doc. 148.

EMPLOYMENT OF SLAVES.

GENERAL MERCER'S ORDER.

C. S. ENGINEER'S OFFICE, }
SAVANNAH, GA., Aug. 1, 1863. }

THE Brigadier-General Commanding desires to inform the slaveholders of Georgia that he has received authority from the Secretary of War to impress a number of negroes sufficient to construct such additional fortifications as are necessary for the defence of Savannah.

He desires, if possible, to avoid the necessity of impressment, and therefore urges the owners of slave property to volunteer the services of their negroes. He believes that, while the planters of South-Carolina are sending their slaves by thousands to aid the defence of Charleston, the slaveholders of Georgia will not be backward in contributing in the same patriotic manner to the defence of their own seaport, which has so far resisted successfully all the attacks of the enemy at Fort McAllister and other points.

Remember, citizens of Georgia, that on the successful defence of Savannah depends the security of the interior of your State, where so much of value both to yourselves and to the Confederacy at large is concentrated. It is best to meet the enemy at the threshold, and to hurl back the first wave of invasion. Once the breach is made, all the horrors of war must desolate your now peaceful and quiet homes. Let no man deceive himself. If Savannah falls the fault will be yours, and your own neglect will have brought the sword to your hearthstones.

The Brigadier General Commanding, therefore, calls on all the slaveholders of Eastern, Southern, and South-Western Georgia, but especially those in the neighborhood of Savannah, to send him immediately one fifth of their able-bodied male slaves, for whom transportation will be furnished and wages paid at the rate of twenty-five dollars per month, the Government to be responsible for the value of such negroes as may be killed by the enemy, or may in any manner fall into his hands. By order of

Brig.-Gen. MERCER, Commanding.

JOHN McCRADY,
Captain and Chief Engineer, State of Georgia.

GENERAL GRANT'S ORDER.

HEADQUARTERS DEPARTMENT OF THE TENNESSEE, }
VICKSBURGH, MISS., August 1, 1863. }

GENERAL ORDERS No. 50.—1. All regularly organized bodies of the enemy having been driven from those parts of Kentucky and Tennessee west of the Tennessee River, and from all of Mississippi west of the Mississippi Central Railroad; and it being to the interest of those districts not to invite the presence of armed bodies of men among them, it is announced that the most rigorous penalties will hereafter be inflicted upon the following class of prisoners, to wit: All irregular bodies of cavalry not mustered and paid by the confederate authorities; all persons engaged in conscription, or in apprehending deserters, whether regular or irregular; all citizens encouraging or aiding the same; and all persons detected in firing upon unarmed transports.

It is not contemplated that this order shall affect the treatment due to prisoners of war, captured within the districts named, when they are members of legally organized companies, and when their acts are in accordance with the usages of civilized warfare.

2. The citizens of Mississippi, within the limits above described, are called upon to pursue their peaceful avocations, in obedience to the laws of the United States. Whilst doing so in good faith, all United States forces are prohibited from molesting them in any way. It is earnestly recommended that the freedom of negroes be acknowledged, and that, instead of compulsory labor, contracts upon fair terms be entered into between the former master and servants, or between the latter and such other persons as may be willing to give them employment. Such a system as this, honestly followed, will result in substantial advantages to all parties.

All private property will be respected, except when the use of it is necessary for the Government, in which case it must be taken under the direction of a corps commander, and by a proper detail under charge of a commissioned officer, with specific instructions to seize certain property and no other. A staff officer of the Quartermaster or Subsistence Department will in each instance be designated to receipt for such property as may be seized, the property to be paid for at the end of the war, on proof of loyalty, or on proper adjustment of the claim, under such regulations or laws as may hereafter be established. All property seized under this order must be taken up on returns by the officer giving receipts, and disposed of in accordance with existing regulations.

3. Persons having cotton or other produce not required by the army, will be allowed to bring the same to any military post within the State of Mississippi, and abandon it to the agent of the Treasury Department at said post, to be disposed of in accordance with such regulations as the Secretary of the Treasury may establish. At posts where there is no such agent, the Post-Quartermaster will receive all such property, and, at the option of the owner, hold it till the arrival of the agent, or send it to Memphis, directed to Captain A. R. Eddy, A. Q. M., who will turn it over to the properly authorized agent at that place.

4. Within the county of Warren, laid waste by the long presence of contending armies, the following rules to prevent suffering will be observed:

Major-General Sherman, commanding the Fifteenth army corps, and Major-General McPherson, commanding the Seventeenth army corps, will each designate a commissary of subsistence, who will issue articles of prime necessity to all destitute families calling for them, under such restrictions for the protection of the Government as they deem necessary. Families who are able to pay for the provisions drawn will in all cases be required to do so.

5. Conduct disgraceful to the American name has been frequently reported to the Major-General commanding, particularly on the part of portions of the cavalry. Hereafter, if the guilty parties cannot be reached, the commanders of regiments and detachments will be held responsible, and those who prove themselves unequal to the task of preserving discipline in their commands, will be promptly reported to the War Department for "mustering out." Summary punishment must be inflicted upon all officers and soldiers apprehended in acts of violence or lawlessness.

By order of Major-General U. S. GRANT.

T. S. BOWERS, A. A. A. G.

GENERAL THOMAS'S ORDER.

VICKSBURGH, MISS., August 18, 1863.

SPECIAL ORDERS No. 45.—Under instructions from the Secretary of War, the undersigned hereby announces his return to this region of the country for the purpose of continuing the organization into the military service of the United States of all able-bodied male persons of African descent, who may come within our lines, or who may be brought in by our troops, or who may already have placed themselves under the protection of the Federal Government; also to take such measures as may prove most beneficial for the welfare of all women, children, aged and infirm persons of African descent who may have sought refuge within our lines, or who may hereafter do so.

In future all able-bodied male negroes of the above class will at once be organized by such officers as may be detailed for that duty, into the military service of the United States, when they will be assigned to regiments composed of persons of African descent now in process of formation or to be formed hereafter.

It has become apparent that the system of receiving all negroes who may have sought the protection of our Government, and allowing them, in many instances, to remain in a state of almost inactivity, has become at times not only injurious to the interests of the service, but to the welfare of the negroes themselves, resulting in habits of idleness, sickness, and disease.

It is further considered expedient that all children and families of negro descent who may hereafter be desirous of seeking refuge within the lines of the United States troops, be advised to remain on the plantations or elsewhere where they have heretofore been in a state of servitude, provided such place be under the control of the National troops. All such negroes will receive the protection of this Government while they remain in the locations that may be designated, and all such persons as may be authorized to occupy plantations or other places will be permitted to employ these families and children in any capacity most suited to their ability.

All male negroes who are incapacitated by old age, ill health, or in any other respect, from serving in regiments of African descent, will be duly cared for and assigned as heretofore to the nearest camp for such persons.

By order of the Secretary of War,

L. THOMAS,
Adjutant-General.

JOSEPH A. WARE.

GENERAL BANKS'S ORDER.

HEADQUARTERS DEPARTMENT OF THE GULF,
NEW-ORLEANS, August 21, 1863.

GENERAL ORDER.—I. Colonel John S. Clark, Major B. Rush Plumley, and Colonel George H. Hanks are hereby appointed a commission to regulate the enrolment, recruiting, employment, and education of persons of color. All questions concerning the enlistment of troops for the Corps d'Afrique, the regulation of labor, or the government and education of negroes, will be referred to the decision of this commission, subject to the approval of the commanding general of the department.

II. No enlistments for the Corps d'Afrique will be authorized or permitted, except under regulations approved by this commission.

III. The Provost-Marshal General will cause to be enrolled all able-bodied men of color, in accordance with the law of conscription, and such number as may be required for the military defence of the department, equally apportioned to the different parishes, will be enlisted for military service under such regulations as the Commission may adopt. Certificates of exemption will be furnished to those not enlisted, protecting them from arrest or other interference, except for crime.

IV. Soldiers of the Corps d'Afrique will not be allowed to leave their camps, or wander through the parishes, except upon written permission, or in the company of their officers.

V. Unemployed persons of color, vagrants, and camp-loafers, will be arrested and employed upon the public works by the Provost-Marshal's department, without other pay than their rations and clothing.

VI. Arrests of persons and seizures of property will not be made by colored soldiers, nor will they be charged with the custody of persons or property, except when under the command and accompanied by duly authorized officers.

VII. Any injury or wrong done to the family of any soldier, on account of his being engaged in military service, will be summarily punished.

VIII. As far as practicable, the labor of persons not adapted to military service will be provided in substitution for that of enlisted men.

IX. All regulations hitherto established for the government of negroes, not inconsistent herewith, will be enforced by the Provost-Marshals of the different parishes, under direction of the Provost-Marshal General.

By command of Major-General BANKS.

RICHARD A. IRWIN,
A. A. General.

Doc. 149.

RECONNOISSANCE FROM LAGRANGE.

LIEUTENANT SMITH'S REPORT.

LAGRANGE, TENN., August 9.

Colonel Hurst:

I beg leave to make the following report of a scout of which I had command, by order of Colonel Hatch:

On the second instant Colonel Hatch ordered me, with sixteen men, to take a despatch to General Dodge at Corinth. Leaving Colonel Hatch at Lexington, I started to Corinth, and on the morning of the third I met the First Alabama (Federal) cavalry on the waters of White Oak Creek, when the Major commanding requested me to let him send the message to General Dodge, and that I would go with him as a guide; to which I assented, being well acquainted with that portion of country. We then proceeded in the direction of Swallow Bluff, on the Tennessee River, meeting with no opposition. Near Swallow Bluff we separated, the Alabama cavalry moving up the river. After we parted I had a fight with some of Colonel Biffle's men across the river, but do not know the amount of damage done. We saw some of the rebels fall from their horses—three, if no more—but do not know whether they were shot dead or not. The rebels soon left the bank—yea, fled incontinently. I then turned north-west, and after marching about ten miles I met a squad of rebels and exchanged several shots with them, when, as usual, the rebels fled. We received no damage, and we presumed that we had done them but little. I then continued my course about four miles, and bivouacked for the night. On the morning of the fourth we mounted, and scouted the country in all directions until evening, when I started for Smith's Mill, on White Oak Creek, where we spent the night. On the morning of the fifth we again mounted, and went about seven miles in a north-western direction, when we met a portion of Captain Stinnett's guerrillas and had a right sharp fight, capturing his first lieutenant, first sergeant, and fifteen men. We had the fight on the north fork of White Oak Creek, about eight miles south-east of Jack's Creek. I then concluded to make my way back to Lagrange, which I did, arriving in camp on the seventh with my seventeen prisoners, neither myself nor any of my little squad having received a scratch.

I respectfully submit the above report, and also the seventeen "greybacks," to your paternal care. Respectfully,

WM. J. SMITH,
First Lieutenant Co. C. Commanding Squad.

Doc. 150.

GUERRILLA WARFARE.

GENERAL ROSECRANS'S ORDER.

HEADQUARTERS DEPARTMENT OF THE CUMBERLAND,
WINCHESTER, TENN., August 15, 1863.

GENERAL ORDER No. 199.— I. It is the earnest desire of the General Commanding that all peace-ful as well as loyal citizens of Tennessee should receive all possible protection to persons and property; that they should resume the exercises of their political and civil rights, under the Constitution of Tennessee and of the United States.

II. Since the rebel power has been driven from Middle Tennessee, numbers of men have left their army; they and others scattered through the country are in danger of being assembled into lawless bands for theft, pillage, and violence, under the name of guerrilla warfare.

To prevent this, which would destroy the whole country, the General Commanding earnestly warns all such persons not to engage in such a criminal course. If they wish to oppose the Government of the United States, they must take upon themselves the uniform, and subject themselves to the duties and restrictions of regularly organized rebel soldiers. If taken within the country subject to our control, in disguise, roaming as individuals or banding with other brigands, and living by stealing and plundering, they will be treated as spies or robbers, enemies of the human race, against whom it is the duty of all, both military and civilians, to wage a war of extermination.

III. Since it is for the salvation of civil society, no person within the limits of this command will be exempted from the duty of using their utmost efforts to put a stop to any attempt to inaugurate a state of plunder, rapine, and murder, under the name of guerrilla warfare. In enforcing this duty, the General Commanding will follow the old rule of common law, and hold the inhabitants of each locality responsible for the guerrilla warfare practised in their midst, and unless satisfied that they have done their full duty and used their utmost efforts to stop it, will lay waste their country and render it untenable for robbers.

IV. Peaceful inhabitants, without regard to political sympathies, being equally interested in preventing the ruin of their country, are counselled and enjoined to unite in putting a final end to all lawless and individual warfare, robbing and plundering under the name of partisans and guerrillas.

To this end they must use all the moral influence they can bring to bear, warning those who threaten, publicly denouncing the practice, and giving information which will lead to the prevention of the crimes, or the capture or punishment of the offenders.

They will further be permitted to resume the freeman's right of bearing arms in self-defence, whenever and wherever the Military Governor of the State and the Department Commander deems it practicable, without involving the risk of their being captured and used against the Government.

V. All persons heretofore acting with the rebellion, and desirous of becoming peaceable citizens, are referred to General Orders No. 175 for the terms upon which it will be allowed.

By command of Major-General ROSECRANS.

Doc. 151.

LETTER OF M. F. MAURY.

To the Editor of the London Times:

Sir: So far from the prospects of the South looking "blue," they were never more brighter. I think you also will so consider them if you will for a moment occupy with me the only standpoint from which a correct view may be had of the American struggle.

In the first place, what, let us inquire, is the object of the belligerents in this war? The North is fighting for conquest, and makes the attack. The South is fighting to be let alone, and it acts on the defensive. The South, therefore, cannot stop the war, but the North can.

It is generally conceded by military men, and admitted by most persons who are familiar with transatlantic affairs, that the North cannot overcome and subdue the South. All the world knows that it is no part of the programme of the South to attempt to subjugate the North. This it neither would, should, nor can do.

Again, almost all the statesmen, either of England or of the continent, who have watched the progress of events since the war began, admit that the Union, the bond of which was voluntary fraternization, cannot be restored by force of arms.

Since, then, the Union is gone, and neither party can subjugate the other, it follows that the war is not to be ended by the sword.

Other agents have to be called into play. What are they? Let us inquire. They are, divisions in the camp of the enemy, dissensions among the people of the North. There is already a peace party there. All the embarrassments with which that party can surround Mr. Lincoln, and all the difficulties that it can throw in the way of the war party in the North, operate directly as so much aid and comfort to the South.

As an offset, then, against the tide of military reverses which in the first weeks of July ran so strong against the South, and from which our friends in England seem not to have recovered, let us look to those agencies that are to end the war, and inquire what progress has been made on the road to peace, and, consequently, in our favor, notwithstanding these military reverses.

Notwithstanding these the war is becoming more and more unpopular in the North. In proof of this, I point to the conduct of the Pennsylvanians during Lee's invasion of that State, to the riots in New-York, to the organized resistance to the war in Ohio, and to other circumstances with which the English public has been made acquainted by the newspaper press.

New-York is threatening armed resistance to the Federal Government. New-York is becoming the champion of States' rights in the North, and to that extent is taking Southern ground. Mr. Lincoln has not only judged it expedient to unmuzzle the press in New-York, and deemed it prudent to give vent to free speech there, but he is evidently afraid to enforce the conscription in the Empire State. The conscription act itself, moreover, seems to be so abortive throughout Yankee land generally that he cannot now muster forces enough to follow up his July successes. Grant has become afraid of Johnston's decoy, which aimed to entice him off to the swamps and canebrakes of the Mississippi. He has, therefore, given up the so-called pursuit and taken to his darling gunboats.

Banks has left Port Hudson, to be routed, it is said, beyond the Mississippi, by Taylor, with severe loss.

Rosecrans has not sufficiently recovered from the blow that Bragg gave him last Christmas in Murfreesboro to follow up that retiring confederate, while Bragg has forces in the Federal General's rear.

In the attack upon Charleston the enemy is losing ground. He is evidently giving way. He has been driven from James's Island, and we are planting batteries there which will sweep Morris Island, which is nothing but a sand-beach. So Charleston may be considered safe.

As for Meade, he simply stands at bay behind Lee.

Thus the military tide which set in with so much Federal promise on the young flood in July, and which has so damped the spirits of our English friends and depressed Southern securities, appears suddenly to have slackened, and to be on the point of again turning in our favor, and that, too, under auspices which seem more propitious than ever.

Vallandigham waits and watches over the border, pledged—if elected Governor of the State of Ohio—to array it against Lincoln and the war, and to go for peace. What the result of the election there will be I cannot tell; but the canvass is going on, and we know that opposition to Lincoln and his war party is growing more and more popular every day, and throughout the whole North. Witness Burnside's decree, putting, in violation of all legal right and constitutional power, the State of Kentucky under martial law, and that, too, just as the elections are coming off in that State. He orders the Commissioners of Elections to let none vote but friends of Lincoln and the Union; and the last steamer brings the announcement, in the jubilant rhetoric of the Yankee press: "The Union ticket has been elected in Kentucky by a large majority." Well it might. There was no other ticket allowed.

Why, but for this growing hostility to Lincoln and the war, put Kentucky under martial law at this late day at all? Simply because of the growing activity and increasing energy of those influences which are at work in the cause of peace, and therefore on the side of the sword of the South. These influences are doing more toward bringing the war to an end than all the battles that have been fought since the war began have done.

Indeed, so straitened is Mr. Lincoln at this moment that his partisans are resorting to a desperate game. They are endeavoring to raise the war-cry against France and England, hoping thereby to rally the people to arms, and intending, if successful, to send the dupes to fight their brethren in the South.

Nay, more; there are rumors of a Peace Party in his Cabinet, and of a proposition there to revoke the Emancipation Proclamation and propose terms to the South. The leading newspapers of the North mention this, and not with disapprobation.

Nor are these all the agencies that time and events are bringing into play on the side of peace and the South.

The fall of Vicksburgh and Port Hudson was, according to those who are stirring the Northwestern people up to war, to open the way to market for them. Every English house in the American trade knows that the breadstuffs of Ohio and the North-west had, for years before the war, nearly ceased to pass by New-Orleans on the way to markets abroad. They went up to the Lakes, and so, *via* canal and rail, to Boston and New-York, for exportation to foreign countries. Can any one in the trade pretend that England would have taken a shipload more of American flour had the Mississippi been open all the war? Chicago, and not New-Orleans, has been the grand grain market of the West, and except London, it is the greatest in the world.

There was on the lower Mississippi a large trade in breadstuffs and provisions from the States above. This trade was chiefly with the planters of the South. But they have been despoiled, their plantations laid waste, their stock taken away, their houses burned, and they themselves banished. In short, those fighting farmers of the Upper Mississippi are likely soon to find out that it is Lincoln and his lieutenants, and nobody else, who has killed their goose of the golden eggs. Those 'cute "Buckeyes," "Suckers," and "Hoosiers," as the denizens of Ohio and her sister States are called, are bound before long to discover this. And will the discovery be more likely to incline their hearts to peace, or to revive in them the war fervor? Not the latter certainly.

This disappointment will come upon these farmers with redoubled force by reason of the financial bearings there of the abundant harvest here. This is a point of view upon which I wish you would dwell with me for a moment.

Before this war the South sent annually to England some twelve or fifteen thousand shiploads of stuff, consisting chiefly, as is well known, of cotton, rice, tobacco, naval stores and the like. The war put a stop to all this. But since the war the crops have been short until now, so short as to give employment to nearly the whole fleet of ships in bringing meat and bread to your people from the Northern States. Notwithstanding the withdrawal from its regular business of the immense amount of shipping which was required annually to get the Southern crops to market, and notwithstanding the loss to commerce of that trade, neither the Custom-house receipts of the nation, nor its shipping interests, nor its dock revenues, show any corresponding falling off in its great business of fetching and carrying by sea. The receipts from the Liverpool docks, from the Bristol docks, and from all the docks on the island, show larger figures this year than ever before, and that in despite of the very considerable reduction in the rate of charges.

Now, this shows plainly enough that while the trade of the South has disappeared, it has been made up from other quarters, and that more ships have been docked in Liverpool and other British ports, since they lost the Southern trade, than ever before. And it is accounted for in this way. By a rather singular coincidence, it so happened that as the markets of all the South were shut off from the world, the harvests of France and England fell short, and the cotton ships were required to fetch bread from the North. As a cotton freighter from the South, the same vessel could not carry more than two cargoes a year, but as a provision ship from the North, she could make five or six trips. Thus dock receipts were increased. Moreover, ham and eggs, butter and cheese, meat and bread, paid more duties than cotton, and thus Custom-house receipts were also enlarged. Thus, notwithstanding the shutting up of the Mississippi, which the North-western farmer did not use for sending his grain to sea, your short crops opened a market for him in which he did get something for his grain, and by reason of which the North had wherewithal to pay for importations. Hence the Yankees, profiting by scarcity here, have not felt the war as grievously as they are about to do.

The full harvest here, in Ireland, and in France, and the like of which has not been known for many years, will mightily reduce this corn trade of the North. It is already a losing business, and the grain which is to come will be in the category of coals to Newcastle.

Hence I infer that, notwithstanding the opening of the Mississippi, the North-western people will find a poorer market than ever for their corn. With the falling off of this trade, the New-York merchants will be no longer able to pay off their British creditors in grain; they will, therefore, have to part with their gold; it will go up, and "greenbacks" will come down, and so raise a voice from the lower levels of society that will be trumpet-tongued for peace. To smother that voice, even now Mr. Lincoln has to keep an armed force not only in New-York and Kentucky, but in Ohio, Indiana, and other States. He is even now marching one up into Iowa, to put down there a cry for peace. He is likely to have occupation for all the recruits his conscription will give in keeping down his own people.

Never were the chances of the South brighter. All that we have to do is to maintain the defensive, watch our chances, and strike whenever there is an opportunity for a good stroke, either with the sword or with the pen.

I am, sir, yours truly,
M. F. MAURY.

BOWDEN, Cheshire, August 17, 1863.

Doc. 152.

CAPTURE OF MAJOR McCANN.

REPORT OF CAPTAIN CLIFFORD.

NASHVILLE, TENN., August 23, 1863.

Captain Wm. O. Russell, A. A. General:

CAPTAIN: I have the honor to submit the following report of the expedition to Weems's Springs, Tennessee. In compliance with your instructions from Headquarters, District of the Cumberland, I left camp at Nashville, Tennessee, with my company, F, First Missouri cavalry, Major-General G. Granger's escort, at daybreak on the morning of the eighteenth instant, and proceeded to Hillsboro, where I arrived at one o'clock P.M. Here, in accordance with your instructions, I was joined by company C, Fourteenth Michigan infantry, (mounted,) under command of Captain Mackey. I left there at nine o'clock P.M., travelling all night, and arriving within half a mile of Weems's Springs at eight o'clock, on the morning of the nineteenth instant. Here I halted, and gave directions to Captain Mackey how he should manœuvre his company. Dividing both into four platoons, each under command of a commissioned officer, and every man being in readiness, I ordered the charge, which resulted in the capture of Major Dick McCann and fourteen others, together with twenty-seven horses, their arms and equipments. The notorious guerrilla chief was captured by private Martin W. Culp, of my company, and first recognized as the same by Lieutenant William Davis, who immediately introduced the gentleman to me. I of course had him well cared for, with the others of his command who fell into my hands as prisoners. I fed my horses and rested at Weems's Springs until noon, when I started for Franklin, Tennessee, where I arrived with my command soon after dark on the nineteenth instant. Here I turned Major Dick McCann and prisoners over to the Provost-Marshal, and rested my men and horses until the afternoon of the twenty-second instant, when I, with my company, departed for Nashville, arriving there about eight o'clock P.M., without the loss of a single man or horse.

Too much praise cannot be bestowed on Captain Mackey, and the officers and men of his company, also to First Lieutenant William Davis, and men of my company, for their gallant behavior throughout the entire expedition, having travelled one hundred and five miles in less than twenty-four hours.

I have the honor to be, Captain,

Very respectfully,

Your obedient servant,

JAMES CLIFFORD,

Captain Company F, First Missouri Cavalry, Major-General G. Granger's Escort, Commanding Expedition.

Doc. 153.

DESTRUCTION OF THE ALEXANDER COOPER.

REPORT OF LIEUTENANT CUSHING.

UNITED STATES STEAMER SHOCKOKON, OFF WILMINGTON, N. C., August 26, 1863.

SIR: I have the honor to report that we have destroyed the blockade-running schooner Alexander Cooper, under the following circumstances: On the twelfth I made a reconnissance with boats in New-Topsail Inlet, and was driven out by four pieces of artillery stationed opposite the mouth, but not before I had discovered a schooner at a wharf some six miles up the sound. This schooner I determined to destroy, and as it was so well guarded, I concluded to use strategy.

On the evening of the twenty-second the Shockokon anchored close into the sea-beach, about five miles from the inlet, and I sent ashore two boats' crews, who shouldered the dingui, and carried it across the neck of land that divides the sea from the sound. This was about half a mile in width, and covered with a dense thicket. The crossing placed my men some miles in rear of the artillery force guarding the entrance.

The dingui being launched on the inside waters, six men under my Executive Officer, Acting Ensign Joseph S. Cony, started with orders to destroy or capture any thing that could be of use to the enemy.

Now, it seems that a twelve-pounder howitzer was stationed at the point for which we were aiming, and the smoke-stack of my steamer having been seen over the trees, the commandant of the post, Captain Adams, had come down from the main camp to insure a bright lookout.

While the rebels at the schooner's mast-heads were straining their eyes looking to the south, my boat was approaching in the other direction, and the men succeeded in landing about sixty yards from the wharf without being discovered. The Master-at-Arms, Robert Clifford, crept into the rebel camp and counted the men, and having returned to his shipmates, a charge was ordered, and our seven men bore down on them with a shout.

In a moment the enemy (who outnumbered us three to one) were routed, leaving in Mr. Cony's possession ten prisoners, including Captain Adams and Lieutenant Leatham, one twelve-pounder army howitzer, eighteen horses, one schooner, and some extensive salt-works.

Mr. Cony then threw out two pickets, detached two men to guard the prisoners, and with the remaining two fired the vessel and salt-works. These were thoroughly consumed.

The object of the expedition being accomplished, my men returned to the vessel without loss, bringing with them three of the prisoners—all that the boat would contain. The rebel officers and privates dress alike, and Mr. Cony was at a loss to know what three to retain. He settled the matter, however, by picking out the three best-looking ones, who all turned out to be privates.

So the officers owed their safety to their lack of physique—a new feature in military strategy.

While this was going on at the mainland, my pickets on the beach side, under Acting Master's Mate Proudfit, engaged and repulsed the rebel picket force in that quarter without loss on our side.

This schooner cleared from New-York for Port Royal, S. C., with an assorted cargo, and was towed once outside the line of the blockade by a gunboat.

I shall try to learn the names of the patriotic citizens of my State who entered into this little speculation. W. B. CUSHING,
Lieutenant Commanding.
To Acting Rear-Admiral S. P. LEE,
Commanding N. A. B. Squadron.

Doc. 154.

CAPTURE OF GENERAL JEFF THOMPSON.

COLONEL WOODSON'S OFFICIAL REPORT.

PILOT KNOB, Mo., August 27, 1863.

General C. B. Fisk, Commanding District of South-east Missouri:

SIR: In obedience to orders from Colonel R. R. Livingston, of the seventeenth instant, (he then commanding the post of Pilot Knob,) I moved with a detachment of my regiment from this point on the eighteenth instant, from Greenville, to form a junction with a battalion from Cape Girardeau. I arrived at Greenville at noon on the twentieth instant, and had to remain there till the evening of the twenty-first, for the troops from the Cape. When they joined me on the morning of Thursday, the twenty-second, I moved with the whole force, about six hundred strong, for Pocahontas, Arkansas, by as rapid marches as the extreme heat of the weather and the condition of my stock would permit, and arrived at Pocahontas, Arkansas, on Saturday evening, the twenty-fourth instant.

When I was in four miles of Pocahontas, I ascertained that Brigadier-General Jeff Thompson was there with little or no force. My column was then scattered over several miles, from the extreme rapidity of my march. Being very desirous of capturing him, and knowing that I had to act with promptness or fail in that object, I ordered Captain Gentry, of the Second cavalry M. S. M., to move forward with all possible despatch, with the advance, and surprise and capture the General, and that I would support him as soon as I could get the column up.

So thoroughly and efficiently did Captain Gentry obey this order, that General Thompson, sitting quietly in his office, and tracing a map of South-east Missouri, as he thought in absolute security, had no idea of any Federal force in one hundred miles of him, until Captain Gentry, having occupied all the passes out of town, rode up to the window of the office, and demanded General Thompson.

Captain Gentry deserves the highest credit for this capture, it depending mainly, if not entirely, upon his promptness and efficiency in obeying my order to move forward the column and surprise him. I remained in Pocahontas about six hours, and being a good deal encumbered with prisoners, and fearful of their escape, camping in the brush, I determined to move back to this point with all possible despatch, and arrived here on the evening of the twenty-fourth instant, having sent the battalion from Cape Girardeau back there by Greenville. In ten days I have marched above two hundred and fifty miles, and laid still one day and a half of the time. I had no fight, but fired on several parties of guerrillas, and killed four of them, and wounded three that I know of. I captured and brought in Brigadier-General Jeff Thompson, his Adjutant-General, Captain Kay, his Medical Director, Dr. France, a Captain of artillery, a Lieutenant of cavalry, and a Captain of ordinance, and about fifty other prisoners, mostly deserters, discharged soldiers, and stragglers from the confederate army; also about thirty horses, the most of them taken to Cape Girardeau by the other battalion.

I regret exceedingly to have to report several cases of highway robbery, plunder, and theft, by the detachment of the First Missouri volunteers. I am satisfied that some of that detachment stole horses, watches, money—any thing they could lay their hands on—from citizens and prisoners.

I am, sir, respectfully your obedient servant,
R. G. WOODSON,
Colonel Third Cavalry M. S. M.,
Commanding Battalion, Expedition to Pocahontas.

FIRST MISSOURI CAVALRY.

PILOT KNOB, Mo., September 20, 1863.

Editors Missouri Democrat:

GENTLEMEN: We to-day, for the first time, had the privilege of reading Colonel Woodson's official report of the Pocahontas expedition, and the capture of the rebel General Jeff Thompson. We regret exceedingly to be called upon by the false and slanderous character of that report, to state that it is a document unbecoming any gentleman; a cowardly attempt on the part of Colonel Woodson to screen himself, and heap the onus and filth of the expedition on the First Missouri cavalry volunteers, when, in fact, his men committed nearly all of the outrages that were perpetrated on the scout; and he himself has been seen wearing the watch taken from Dr. Frame within the last two weeks. He also states that nearly all the horses taken, on the scout were carried off to Cape Girardeau. That is false. He brought over thirty horses to this place with him, and, so far as watches and money are concerned in the matter, we think Colonel Woodson pocketed as much, if not a little more, than any other man on the expedition. He talks very coolly about the capture of Jeff Thompson, about ordering Captain Gentry forward with all possible haste. The fact is just simply this, that Captain Gentry had a conversation with the officers of the First Missouri cavalry, they being in the advance that day, about the chance of taking Jeff in, by making a dash into Pocahontas and surprising him. We concluded it could be done, and sent back to the Captain for permission to do so. The Captain did not ride at the advance of his column that day, as he should have done. He said if we wanted to try it, we could do so. We wanted to try it, did try it, and did capture Jeff Thompson, as well as every other prisoner that was taken on the scout, and all the horses, all the arms, did all the shooting, all the killing, and in fact every thing else that was done, excepting the straggling and stealing. Colonel Woodson rode along at his ease some four or five miles in the rear, and did not reach Pocahontas with his command for nearly one hour and a half after the First Missouri entered the place and captured Jeff Thompson and his staff, and when he did come up and was introduced to Jeff, we think, from the position he took during the ceremony, that he was in the same predicament that Sterling Price was at Boonville, Missouri. We turned over eighteen contraband horses to the Quartermaster at Cape Girardeau, but we have never heard of any property being turned over by the M. S. M. or any other copperheads since we entered the department.

The reputation of our regiment for honesty, bravery, and efficiency, is too well know in this department to be injured by any attempt to screen the rascality of the M. S. M. by false reports. We will close by making this proposition to Captain Woodson, that if he will do the clean thing, come out like a man, and trade on the square, we will give him five hundred dollars for his net proceeds from the scout.

We, the undersigned, officers of the First Missouri, hold ourselves personally and officially responsible for the above statements.

Yours respectfully,

VALENTINE PREWITT,
Captain Co. M., Com'dg Detachment.
HOMES QUICK,
Captain Co. K., First Missouri Cavalry.
JAMES H. BURNETT,
First Lieut., Com'dg Co. G., First Mo. Cav.
O. P. STEELE,
Second Lieutenant, Co. K., First Mo. Cav.
THOMAS RALPH,
Second Lieutenant, Co. M., First Mo. Cav.

Doc. 155.

GENERAL SCHOFIELD'S ORDER.

HEADQUARTERS DEPARTMENT OF MISSOURI,
ST. LOUIS, August 25, 1863.

LARGE numbers of men are leaving the broken rebel armies in the Mississippi valley, and returning to Missouri. Many of them doubtless come back with the purpose of following a career of plunder and murder, under the form of guerrilla warfare, while others would gladly return to their homes as peaceable citizens, if permitted to do so, and protected from violence.

The State is in danger of a repetition of the scenes of violence and bloodshed which characterized the months of July and August, 1862. The united efforts of all loyal and peaceably-disposed citizens, as well as of the troops of this department, will be required to avert this evil. It is the desire of the Commanding General that all those who voluntarily abandon the rebel cause, and desire to return to their allegiance to the United States, shall be permitted to do so under such restrictions as the public peace shall require.

All such persons may surrender themselves and their arms at the nearest military post, and will be released upon taking the oath of allegiance and giving bonds for their future good conduct. They will be required to reside in such portion of Missouri or other State as the Provost-Marshal who releases them shall direct. All who shall fail to comply with these conditions, and shall remain within our lines without renewing their allegiance, will be treated as criminals, according to the laws of war.

Those who shall engage in robbery, murder, or other similar crimes, will be exterminated without mercy. Humanity demands of every citizen active and earnest coöperation with the military authorities in putting down these common enemies of mankind.

The Commanding General demands of every citizen the full discharge of his duty in this regard. Those who neglect it will be held responsible, in their persons and property, for the damage that may result from their neglect, and will be punished at the discretion of a military commission. If milder means shall fail, the Commanding General will order the destruction or seizure of all houses, barns, provisions, and other property belonging to disloyal persons in those portions of the State which are made the haunts of guerrillas. To enable them to protect themselves from violence, and to aid the troops when necessary, all loyal and peaceable citizens in Missouri will be permitted to bear arms. As far as practicable, arms which have heretofore been taken from such citizens will be returned to them.

By command of Maj.-Gen. SCHOFIELD.

Doc. 156.

BATTLE OF BAYOU METEA, ARK.

REPORT OF COLONEL GLOVER.

HEADQUARTERS SECOND BRIGADE, CAVALRY DIVISION,
Camp near BROWNSVILLE, ARK., Aug. 28.

LIEUTENANT: I have the honor to report that on the twenty-sixth August, 1863, two regiments of my brigade, the First Iowa and Third Missouri cavalry volunteers, and one section each of Lovejoy's and Clarkson's batteries, were ordered on a reconnoissance, and to "push the enemy as far as possible toward the Bayou Metea without bringing on a general engagement." The First Iowa cavalry being in advance, a heavy line of skirmishers, in command of Captain Jenks, was thrown to the front. Some six miles from Brownsville struck his pickets and drove them about four miles back to their main body; some two miles east of the bayou, killing one rebel captain, (Powell, of Platte City, Mo.,) two privates, and capturing one prisoner. Here the enemy opened artillery upon us, to which ours soon replied. After a considerable artillery duel, I ordered Lieutenant Lovejoy to advance his section, in the doing of which he had one cannonier pierced through with a solid shot, and killed instantly, so well did the enemy have the range of the road. I then advanced in person, reconnoitred hastily the enemy's position, and determined to feel him further, and so ordered up Lovejoy's section, well supported with cavalry. In this position we stood face to face. After a more thorough review of the enemy's position and my own, perceiving his great advantage in this respect, and knowing his great superiority in numerical strength, and being satisfied a further offensive demonstration would result in a general engagement, in which all the advantages were against me, I deployed quite an amount of cavalry in front of my artillery, masking the same while it was rapidly taken from the field, and retired with my command to a safe distance. This done, I called off the force covering my rear, and withdrew the whole in good order and without further loss to my former encampment, near Brownsville.

On the morning of the twenty-seventh, at sunrise, the division moved out upon the road leading to the Bayou Metea Bridge, my brigade taking the advance, protected by a battalion of the Tenth Illinois, deployed as skirmishers, supported by two other squadrons, all in the immediate command of Lieutenant-Colonel Stewart. At some five miles from the bridge our advance skirmishers met those of the enemy. A brisk fire ensued, the enemy falling back. At some three miles from the bayou he made another stand, when he was again sharply encountered by the Tenth Illinois. At this place Lieutenant Kavanaugh was killed. Here the Commanding General ordered my whole brigade forward for action, in obedience to which I made the following dispositions, namely: Placed two battalions Third Missouri cavalry volunteers, dismounted, to fight on foot on the right of the road in order of battle. On the left of the road placed in order of battle one battalion of the Thirty-second Iowa infantry, as it was ordered to report to me during the day. On the left of this placed the Third battalion of the Third Missouri, dismounted, the artillery being in the centre. As a reserve, the First Iowa cavalry and four squadrons of the Eighteenth Illinois cavalry, mounted, were formed in the rear. Six squadrons of the Tenth Illinois were placed on the right flank. In this order, with a heavy line of skirmishers covering my whole front, the brigade moved forward. It soon met opposition from the enemy's small arms and artillery, but he was steadily driven from ridge to ridge through the thick brush on either side of the road by the firm and resolute advance of my brigade, assisted by the timely use of the artillery, back to a very strong and elevated position covered by extended "rifle-pits" on the left, where he made a more obstinate stand, holding my command in check for a brief period,

when the Third Illinois cavalry on the right charged and drove back the enemy in their front, thus flanking his rifle-pits on the left, and compelling him to abandon them under a simultaneous charge on the left of the line, when the whole force of the enemy gave way and fled in the greatest disorder and confusion toward the Bayou Metea.

The artillery was now ordered up and poured a heavy bombardment with their fleeing columns for twenty-five or thirty minutes, when the bridge was seen to be on fire. The General Commanding then directed that the Iowa First cavalry should charge and save the bridge if possible. Lieutenant-Colonel Anderson, at the head of his regiment, led a gallant charge in the face of a terrible fire of artillery and small arms, having his own horse shot under him, his command suffering considerably. From the intensity of the fire in the direction of the First Iowa cavalry, it was evident they needed support. I suggested that a new position be selected for our batteries to cover and relieve the First Iowa cavalry, now dismounted and sharply engaged with the enemy. Receiving permission, I hastened to the front amidst a heavy fire of the enemy's artillery, reconnoitred and selected an excellent position overlooking and commanding his. Our artillery was instantly ordered up with supports, and placed in position under a continued fire from that of the enemy. Our batteries, in position, opened a tremendous fire, soon silencing the enemy's guns and driving them from their position. The Third Missouri cavalry and Thirty-second Iowa infantry had now boldly forced their way to the bank of the bayou on the left, pushing the enemy across it—it now being evident that there was a strong force of the enemy on this side the bayou on the right of our line. After taking proper precaution for the safety of my right flank, I ordered Lieutenant-Colonel Stewart, of the Tenth Illinois, with a portion of his regiment, to drive them back, which this excellent officer promptly executed, putting them across the bayou after a very hot contest. The purpose of the Commanding General now having been consummated, and the evening far advanced, I was ordered to retire with my brigade to my former camp near Brownsville, as there were no comforts for man or beast short of that point.

I now desire to speak in the highest terms of Lieutenant-Colonel Black, of the Third Missouri, Stewart, of the Tenth Illinois, and Anderson, of the First Iowa, my regimental commanders, for coolness, daring, and good judgment, cheerful and prompt in obedience to orders. The efficiency of our dismounted cavalry was to-day thoroughly tested. Of the Third Missouri and Tenth Illinois I must say they fought with the confidence of veteran infantry. I desire to bear testimony to the universal good conduct of officers and men. It is due to Major Eberhardt and his battalion of the Thirty-second Iowa infantry to say, they gave a hearty and efficient coöperation. Although the artillery was not formally under my command, yet circumstances sometimes placed it there. I am gratified to acknowledge the cheerful obedience to orders, and the fearless conduct of the officers in charge; especially in the case of Lieutenant Clarkson, whose battery was in the advance during the day. The earnest but honorable competition between the three regiments of my brigade resulted, as it is likely to do in the future, in the complete rout and defeat of the foe.

I must express my admiration for the coolness, bravery, and efficiency of my staff officers. Captains Freeman, Snelling, Lieutenants Haine and Johnson, who were exposed to the hottest of the fire and thickest of the danger, have my sincere thanks for their cordial support. Casualties, forty-three killed and wounded in my brigade proper. I have the honor to be,

Respectfully your ob't servant,
J. M. GLOVER,
Colonel Commanding Second Brigade, Cavalry Division.
ROBERT L. FREEMAN,
Captain and A. A. A. Gen. Second Brigade, Cavalry Division.

Doc. 157.

BATTLE AT WHITE SULPHUR SPRINGS, VIRGINIA.

REPORT OF GENERAL AVERILL.

HUTTONSVILLE, VA., Aug. 30, 1863.

GENERAL: I have the honor to report the safe return of my command to this place, after an expedition through the counties of Hardy, Pendleton, Highland, Bath, Greenbrier, and Pocahontas. We drove General Jackson out of Pocahontas and over the Warm Spring Mountain, in a series of skirmishes, destroyed their saltpetre works, burned Camp Northwest and a large amount of arms, equipments, and stores. We fought a severe engagement with a superior force, under command of Major-General Sam Jones and Colonel Patten, at Rocky Gap, near the White Sulphur Springs. The battle lasted during two days. We drove the enemy from his first position, but want of ammunition, and the arrival, on the second day, of three regiments to reënforce the enemy, from the direction whence the coöperation of General Scammon had been promised, decided me to withdraw. My command was withdrawn in good order, with the loss of only two men during the operation. Our loss in the battle is probably over one hundred officers and men killed and wounded, among whom are Captain Paul and Baron Von Koenig, Aid-de-Camp, killed while leading an assault upon the enemy's right; and Major McNally, of the Second Virginia, and Captain Ewing, of the artillery, dangerously wounded. I have reason to believe the enemy's loss greater than our own. One Parrott gun burst the first day, and becoming useless was abandoned. Great efforts, up to noon, to-day, have been made by the combined forces of Imboden and Jackson to prevent our return, but without success. We have brought in over thirty prisoners, including a Major and two or three Lieutenants; also a large number of cattle, horses, etc. Your Aid-de-Camp, Lieutenant J. R. Meigs, who accompanied me, is safe.

I am, General, very respectfully, your obedient servant, WM. W. AVERILL,
Brigadier-General.

WHEELING INTELLIGENCER ACCOUNT.

August 26, 1863.

Expect to visit the White Sulphur Springs, and camp near Lewisburgh at night. The writer pushed on to the front of the regiment for time to view the celebrated place; but to our great discomfiture, at eleven o'clock A.M., two miles this side of the Springs, on Antee Creek, the enemy opened their artillery upon us, calling us to a sudden halt. Our forces moved up in great haste, and planted their artillery. The fight soon became general and terrific—balls, shells, grape, and shot flying with fearful havoc in all directions, doing their work of death. The whole atmosphere resounds with the roar of artillery and musketry. Surgeons soon establish a hospital at two private houses. The dead and wounded are brought in as fast as men and horses can bring them. For four or five hours I believe there was not an intermission of firing of more than two minutes at any one time—almost an incessant fire.

As near as we can learn, the rebel force consisted of the Twenty-second, Forty-fifth, Fifty-fourth, and Sixty-second Virginia regiments; Edgar's battalion of cavalry, and Chapman's battery, of four guns—all commanded by Colonel Patten, in the absence of General Eckle. As to position, the enemy had the decided advantage. They selected a position where the road passed through a deep gorge of rocks, with mountains on either side and fearful precipices. The enemy was concealed behind rocks, trees, logs, and fences, a great part of the time lying on their faces. Their artillery was planted in front some four hundred yards from ours. The Third and Eighth Virginia M. I. occupied the left wing. The Second Virginia and Fourteenth Pennsylvania cavalry, Gibson's battalion, with three companies of the Third Virginia, on the right. Our artillery, well drilled and of good pluck, held a favorable position on the main road. General Averill remained near the batteries during the battle, directing the movement of the troops. Thus formed, the Federal soldiers sent the messengers of death among the rebels like hailstones and fire. At one time, the rebels made their appearance in open ground, when our guns mowed them down at a fearful rate. Under the heavy fire they fell back, until our guns were planted on the ground before occupied by the enemy. Lieutenant-Colonel Thompson, commanding the Third Virginia regiment, stood in the hottest of the fire, leading his brave men not less than seven times on a desperate charge upon the enemy. They lying in ambush, our men would move upon them under every disadvantage, though thus to move was almost certain destruction. Yet, as one order would come after another from the General, to charge on the enemy, the Colonel, cool and brave, would again and again renew the charge. Here more men were killed among the different regiments than anywhere else on the field. It is generally conceded that all the regiments fought desperately; officers and soldiers showed an unyielding purpose to fight until the enemy was routed. The night passed. Oh! how solemn silence reigns! We waited for the order. Morning came, but not to all our fellow-soldiers. Some we had laid in the grave, others were on the field, sleeping the sleep of death. The fight is renewed, and continued until all the ammunition was about spent. At ten o'clock a despatch comes from Lieutenant-Colonel Polsley, stating that the enemy was moving to flank our rear. The order came to fall back. This was done in good order, and well conducted. We removed all that were in a condition to be removed of the wounded. Others were left in the care of Assistant-Surgeon Worthington, of the Fourteenth Pennsylvania cavalry. We marched day and night until we reached this place. The enemy pursued us for some time. We were not whipped, but held our ground until a lack of shooting material compelled us to retreat. If we had been supplied with ammunition, the victory would surely have been ours. The fault lies at some man's door, not with the brave soldiers who were in the fight. I am much gratified to say that every officer of our regiment remained duly sober during the entire battle. We speak this to their praise. No soldier wants to risk his life under a drunken officer. The Second Virginia lost in killed, wounded, and missing, thirty-one; Third Virginia, forty-three; Eighth Virginia, twenty; Fourteenth Pennsylvania cavalry, ninety-five; batteries, twenty-one. In all, over two hundred. Our men say this was the severest and hottest battle they have been in during the war.

REBEL OFFICIAL DESPATCH.

WHITE SULPHUR SPRINGS, Aug. 27,
Via DUBLIN, Aug. 28.

To General S. Cooper:

We met the enemy yesterday morning about a mile and a half from this place, on the road leading to the Warm Springs. We fought him from nine A.M. to seven P.M. Every attack made by the enemy was repulsed. At night each side occupied the same position they had in the morning. This morning the enemy made two other attacks, which were handsomely repulsed, when he abandoned his position and retreated toward Warm Springs, pursued by cavalry and artillery. The troops engaged were the First brigade of this army, Colonel Geo. S. Patten commanding. The enemy were about three thousand strong, with six pieces of artillery, under Brigadier-General Averill. Our loss is about two hundred killed and wounded. The enemy's loss is not known. We have taken about one hundred and fifty prisoners and a piece of artillery.

SAMUEL JONES,
Major-General.

Doc. 158.

LIEUTENANT-GENERAL HARDEE'S ORDER.

THE following official order was issued by Lieutenant-General Hardee upon assuming command of the troops which had been defending Vicksburgh:

ENTERPRISE, MISS., August 23.

By direction of the President of the Confederate States, I assume command of the paroled prisoners of Mississippi, Arkansas, Missouri, Texas, and Louisiana, recently forming part of the garrisons of Vicksburgh and Port Hudson. I could desire no greater honor than the command of troops whose sufferings and achievements have added to the renown of their country, and compelled the admiration even of their enemies. The place of rendezvous of all paroled prisoners from the above-named States is changed from Demopolis, Ala., to Enterprise, Miss. In anticipation of an early exchange, the work of reörganization will proceed with energy. The troops must be organized and prepared to take the field when the exchange is effected. All officers and men must be at their posts. They should be there now. To those present at the roll-calls no word is needed. Their daily answers are uttered in the manly tones of duty and honor. Many are absent. They must repair at once to the post of duty. The appeals that meet us on every side are the strongest that in any age have stirred the human heart.

Soldiers! look at your country—the earth ravaged—property carried away, or disappearing in flame and ashes—the people murdered—the negroes arrayed in arms against the whites—cruel indignities inflicted upon women and children. Destruction marks the path of our invaders. Their motto is: "Woe to the conquered." He who falters in this hour of his country's peril is a wretch who would compound for the mere boon of life, robbed of all that makes life tolerable. Fellow-soldiers! there is but one path to follow. It leads to the camp. Come to your colors and stand beside your comrades, who, with heroic constancy, are confronting the enemy. Choose, now, between the glory of successfully defending all that entitles you to the name of men and the infamy of creeping abjectly to the feet of a foe, who will spurn your submission and despise your cowardice.

W. J. HARDEE,
Lieutenant-General.

Doc. 159.

GENERAL ONDERDONK'S EXPEDITION.

GLOUCESTER POINT, VA., Sept. 3, 1863.

ACTING Brigadier-General B. F. Onderdonk has just returned to this point from an extended and most successful raid up to the very gates of Richmond.

The start of this expedition was made at one o'clock P.M., on the twenty-sixth of August, from

Williamsburgh. After a quiet march, of little interest to the general reader, we halted and encamped at Twelve Mile Ordinary. On the morning of the twenty-seventh we moved forward without molestation; but at Slatersville we met a strong picket, whose insolent and defiant action would lead one to suppose that the enemy was in their rear in large supporting force. Colonel Onderdonk accordingly ordered a charge to be made on the force in our front, whatever it might be, and the result was, that they were chased in the most gallant style by our men a distance of two miles. One man of the rebels was killed, and two more captured, the rest escaping by reason of their fresh horses, which of course could distance our jaded animals. Proceeding further, when we arrived at New-Kent Court-House we were opposed by another picket. Two of these were captured, but we failed, for the former reason, to come up with the rest, although the most strenuous efforts were made to that effect by our forces, which consisted of the First New-York Mounted rifles and the Fifth Pennsylvania cavalry, the whole under command of Colonel Onderdonk, of the rifles, who, in his capacity of acting Brigadier, had full powers delegated him to act in the premises as he pleased, although the orders were explicit in writing not to go further than New-Kent Court-House. Verbal orders were, however, obtained, at the solicitation of Colonel Onderdonk, to the effect that we might move forward in the enemy's country as far as might be deemed prudent and safe in the mind of the commanding officer. Accordingly, with his customary dash, the Colonel commanding placed his own gallant regiment in the advance, and moved on to Baltimore Store, where one rebel picket was captured, and the rest retired in accelerated time. There was no delay; so on we dashed without a pause to Crump's Cross-Roads, where we met the enemy in force of about some thirty well mounted troopers. Of course a charge was in order, and our men, inflated with success, went plunging after the rebels, who quickly fled in the direction of Bottom's Bridge, up to which point we pursued them, making in all a continued chase of three miles.

The rifle-pits and earthworks of the enemy on the other side of the bridge were found to be quite formidable, and opened heavily on us the moment we appeared. In this furious affair the impetuosity of our troops was highly praised by all observers. Indeed the scene was splendid. Imagine a thousand troopers, brave, bold, and well trained, with staring eyes, determined looks, and flashing sabres, dashing down, with screams and yells, upon the foe. This was indeed one worthy of the pen and brain of Longfellow.

The loss of the enemy in this affair, we learned from authentic sources, was thirty killed and wounded. The Mounted rifles, who took the most active part in this fight, by their conduct exemplified to me what I never in my experience in the army could understand before—namely, a total unconsciousness of danger, and an apparent contempt for death.

McClellan's earthworks on the Richmond side of Bottom's Bridge had, it seems, been so altered by the rebels that they could most effectually resist our advance. These works are upward of six feet high, very strong, and defended by five hundred infantry and a squadron of cavalry. General Wise, with a force of four thousand men, was reported by contrabands to be lying in wait for us two miles further on toward Richmond, beyond the bridge; so Colonel Onderdonk thought it prudent, considering his explicit written orders, to retire, having done much more than was required of him by his commanding officer.

The return was at once made to Baltimore Store, where we encamped. Our position here was very strong indeed, and was selected with the view of repulsing any movement the enemy might make against us in the night. General Wise, it was ascertained, did actually cross to attack us, but, finding us in strong position, recrossed again before morning.

A pursuit was begun on the twenty-eighth by the enemy, who attempted to cut us off at New-Kent Court-House or Slatersville, but all in vain. At noon on this day we halted at Slatersville to feed our horses and refresh ourselves. There the enemy charged suddenly on the Fifth Pennsylvania cavalry, creating quite a panic on our surprised men; but the Mounted rifles came to the rescue in most gallant style, and charging with irresistible fury upon the presumptuous foe, drove him in confusion a distance of four miles, inflicting severe punishment on him meantime.

The enemy's force was, in all, five hundred effective men, consisting of Holcomb's Legion of South-Carolina troops, and the Fifth Virginia. In this splendid counter-charge of our troops we killed a major, an orderly sergeant, and two privates, and wounded fifteen men. On the twenty-ninth we returned to Williamsburgh, and were sent immediately to this point.

The national loss was very slight, we having only one killed and two wounded, whose names are as follows:

Killed.—John Noetting, Fifth Pennsylvania cavalry, troop A.

Wounded.—— —— Riley, Fifth cavalry, troop I; Corporal Fitzpatrick, Fifth cavalry, troop I.

The captures were not immense, but important. At New-Kent Court-House a civilian named O. M. Chandler was taken into custody by Colonel Onderdonk, and sent to Fortress Monroe. When the rebel pickets fled before us this man misled our officers, by wilfully stating that they took the road to the left, when he knew that they were on that to the right. By this means the greater portion escaped, and for this falsehood Chandler lost his liberty. Another arrest of a citizen was made by the Colonel at Baltimore Store, where Mr. Elmore, an employé of the rebel government, was seized and carried off.

The plunder in the shape of horses, equipments, etc., was not as large as usual; but the poverty of the country accounts for this. We captured a set of telegraph instruments, however, and a good quantity of horses, besides destroying a rebel army wagon, direct from Richmond, loaded with rifles. Of course their destruction was made complete, inasmuch as we could not carry them off with us.

The result of this affair is most satisfactory, and Colonel Onderdonk has received the encomiums of his commanding officers and all qualified for gallant actions. The conduct of the Mounted rifles was splendid, and well sustained their old reputation. All the troops, in fact, engaged in this raid acted with unsurpassed gallantry.

Doc. 160.

OPENING OF THE MISSISSIPPI.

MAJOR-GENERAL BANKS'S ORDER.

HEADQUARTERS DEPARTMENT OF THE GULF, }
NEW-ORLEANS, Sept. 3, 1863. }

GENERAL ORDERS No. 66.

1. The trade of the city of New-Orleans with Cairo, St. Louis, and the cities and towns of the Upper Mississippi, Missouri, and Ohio Rivers, is hereby declared free from any military restrictions whatever. The trade of the Mississippi at intermediate points within the Department of the Gulf is held subject only to such limitations as may be necessary to prevent a supply of provisions and munitions of war reaching the enemies of the country.

2. The products of the country intended for general market may be brought into military posts on the line of the Mississippi within the Department of the Gulf, without restraint, namely, at New-Orleans, Carrolton, Donaldsonville, Baton Rouge, and Port Hudson.

3. Officers or soldiers of the army are hereby directed to transfer to Hon. B. B. Sanders, Agent of the Treasury Department, or his deputies, taking receipts therefor, all captured, abandoned, or sequestrated property not required for military purposes, in accordance with General Orders No. 88.

4. The Military Court of this Department is hereby invested with exclusive jurisdiction in all cases of extortion, excessive or unreasonable charges, or unjust treatment of officers and soldiers of the United States, by proprietors or agents of steamboats, or other vessels in the navigation of the Mississippi or Gulf, and upon conviction of any offences herein described, offenders shall be liable to fine, imprisonment, or confiscation of property.

By command of Major-General BANKS.

G. N. LIEBER, A. A. G.

Doc. 161.

BATTLE OF WHITE STONE HILL, D. T.

GENERAL SULLY'S REPORT.

HEADQUARTERS INDIAN EXPEDITION, CAMP AT }
MOUTH OF LITTLE SHEYENNE RIVER, }
Sept. 11, 1863. }

MAJOR: The last report I had the honor to send you was from the mouth of this Little Sheyenne River, bearing date August sixteenth, 1863; since which time my movements have been too rapid and the danger of sending any communication such that it has been impossible for me to do so. I therefore have the honor to report my movements from last report up to date.

On the morning of the nineteenth the steamer I was waiting for with supplies finally arrived. She was immediately unloaded, and all the baggage of the officers and men of the command was sent down by her to the depot at Fort Pierre, together with every man who was in the least sick or not well mounted. By this I reduced my force considerably, and was enabled to transport with the wretched mules that had been furnished me about twenty-three days' rations and forage enough to keep these transportation animals alive, depending on grass I might find to feed the cavalry and artillery horses. Luckily for me, I found the grazing north much better than I had dared to hope for.

On the twentieth were visited by one of the most terrific rain and hail storms I have seen. This stampeded some of my animals and a few were lost—they swam across the Missouri—and it also destroyed a quantity of my rations in the wagons, thereby causing some delay in the march; but I succeeded in getting off the afternoon of the twenty-first, and marched up the Little Sheyenne about eleven miles, the road being very heavy. The next day we marched only seven miles, camping on a slough on the prairie without wood. The next day we marched in a north-westerly direction to the outlet of Swan Lake. On the twenty-fourth we marched due north eighteen miles, and encamped on a small creek called Bois Cache. Here we came into the buffalo country, and I formed a hunting party for the command, which I had soon to disband, as they disabled more horses than buffalo. We continued our march north about twenty-two miles, and reached a small stream called Bird Arche Creek. This day the hunters succeeded in killing many buffalo, and reported that they saw Indians near the Missouri.

Early on the morning of the twenty-sixth, I sent out a small scouting party, who captured two squaws and some children, and brought them into me. These Indians reported that General Sibley had had a fight near the head of Long Lake, and that they were on their way to the agency at Crow Creek, but were lost, and were alone; but the scouts found tracks of lodges going up the Missouri. I therefore immediately detailed companies F and K of the Second Nebraska cavalry, under command of Captain La Boo, ordering them to go to the Missouri, and follow up the trail, with orders to capture some Indians if possible, and bring them in, so that I might get information; if they could not do that, to kill them and destroy the camps. I continued the march with the rest of the command that day, passing through large herds of buffalo, and was obliged to make a march of thirty-five miles before I could reach water. The weather was very hot, and it was night before we reached camp on the Beaver River.

On the twenty-seventh, I started late, having had some difficulty in crossing the river, making a march of five miles still in a northerly direction, and encamped on another branch of the same river. Company K of the Second Nebraska joined me this day, having been separated from the other company. The next day we had to make some deviations to the west on account of hills and sloughs, and made the outlet of Long Lake, a march of about twenty miles. On the way we saw numerous signs of Indians in large numbers having been recently there, and found an old lame Indian concealed in the bushes, who was well known by many of the men of the command as having for some years resided near Sioux City. He had the reputation of being what is called a "good Indian." He stated that "his horse had been taken away from him and that he had been left there." He looked almost starved to death. He gave me the following details, which have since mostly turned out to be correct; he stated "General Sibley had fought the Indians at the head of Long Lake, fifty miles north-east from me, some weeks ago; that he followed them down to the mouth of Apple Creek; that the Indians attacked him on the way, and that there was some skirmishing.

"At Apple Creek, Sibley had another fight, and that in all the fights about fifty-eight Indians were killed; that General Sibley fortified his camp at Apple Creek, and after a while returned to James River; that a few days after General Sibley left, the Indians, who had their scouts out watching, recrossed the Missouri, and while doing so, discovered a Mackinaw boat on its way down. They attacked the boat, fought the entire day until sundown, sunk her, and killed all on board—twenty-one men, three women, and some children; that before she was sunk the fire from the boat killed ninety-one Indians and wounded many more; that a small war party followed Sibley some days, returned with the report that he had crossed the James River; then some of the Indians went north; the larger portion, however, went toward the head of Long Lake; and that he thought a portion of them were encamped on the Missouri River west of me."

The report was so much in keeping with the Indian mode of warfare, that, though it came from an Indian, I was led to give it some consideration, particularly the part that stated the Indians, after watching Sibley's return, recrossed when all danger was over, and went back to their old hunting-grounds. Besides, the guides who were acquainted with the country, stated that "a large body of Indians could not live on the other side long, without going a great distance west; that always at this season of the year the Indians camped on the Ooteau, near the tributaries of the James, where the numerous lakes or springs kept the grass fresh; here the buffalo were plenty, and the lakes and streams full of fish; and that here they prepared their meat for the winter, moving to the Missouri where the fuel was plenty to winter." I therefore determined to change my course toward the east, to move

rapidly, and go as far as my rations would allow.

I felt serious alarm for the safety of Captain La Boo, who had but fifty men with him, and who had already been out over two days without rations. I encamped here for the next day, and sent out four companies of the Second Nebraska and of the Sixth Iowa, under command of Major Pearman, Second Nebraska, to hunt him up, and see if there were any Indians on the Missouri. The next day, however, Captain La Boo's company returned, having made a march of one hundred and eighty-seven miles, living upon what buffalo and game they could kill, scouring the country to my left, overtaking the camp of ten lodges he was sent after, destroying them, but seeing no Indians.

This same day (twenty-ninth) I sent two companies of the Sixth Iowa to the mouth of Apple Creek. They reported on their return that they found the fortified camp of General Sibley, his trail, and his return trail toward the east; that they could see no signs of there having been any fight there, nor could they see the Mackinaw boat reported by the old Indian. This detachment was under command of Captain Cram, Sixth Iowa. The battalion of Major Pearman joined me before starting, having seen nothing, and, after a march of above ninety miles, through a country with no wood whatever, but with good grass and plenty of lakes of the most abominable water, on the third of September we reached a lake, where, on the plains near by, were the remains of a very large number of buffalo killed, some quite recently. Here I encamped to wait the reports of the commands I had out during the march, who every day discovered fresh signs of Indians, their lodge trails spread over the country, but all moving toward a point known to be a favorite haunt of the Indians. I had this day detailed one battalion of the Sixth Iowa, Major House commanding, and Mr. F. La Framboise as guide, to keep ahead of me five miles, and in case they saw a small band of Indians, to attack them, or take them prisoners. If they should find a large band, too large to successfully cope with, to watch the camp at a distance, and send back word to me, my intention being to leave my train under charge of a heavy guard, move up in the night-time so as to surround them, and attack them at daybreak. But, for some reason satisfactory to the guide, he bore off much to my left, and came upon the Indians in an encampment of over four hundred lodges, some say six hundred, in ravines, where they felt perfectly secure, being full persuaded that I was still on my way up the Missouri. This is what the Indian prisoners say. They also state that a war party followed me on my way up in hopes of stampeding me; but this they could not do. I marched with great care, with an advance-guard and flankers; the train in two lines sixty paces apart; the troops on each side; in front and centre myself, with one company and the battery; all the loose stock was kept between the lines of wagons. In this way I lost no animals on the campaign, except some few, about a dozen, that got out of camp at night. Nor did the Indians, during all the trip, ever attack me or try to stampede me.

Major House, according to my instructions, endeavored to surround and keep in the Indians until word could be sent me; but this was an impossibility with his three hundred men, as the encampment was very large, mustering at least one thousand two hundred warriors. This is what the Indians say they had; but I, as well as every body in the command, say over one thousand five hundred. These Indians were partly Santees from Minnesota, Cutheads from the Coteau, Yanktonais and Blackfeet who belong on the other side of the Missouri; and, as I have since learned, Unkapapas, the same party who fought General Sibley, and destroyed the Mackinaw boat. Of this I have unmistakable proof from letters and papers found in camp and on the persons of some of the Indians, besides relics of the late Minnesota massacre; also from the fact that they told Mr. La Framboise, the guide, when he was surrounded by about two hundred of them, that "they had fought General Sibley, and they did not see why the whites wanted to come and fight them, unless they were tired of living and wanted to die." Mr. La Framboise succeeded in getting away from them after some difficulty, and ran his horse a distance of more than ten miles to give me information—Major House, with his command, still remaining there. He reached me a little after four o'clock. I immediately turned out my command. The horses at the time were out grazing. At the sound of the bugle the men rushed with a cheer, and in a very few minutes saddled up and were in line. I left four companies and all the men who were poorly mounted in the camp, with orders to strike the tents and corral the wagons, and, starting off with the Second Nebraska on the right, the Sixth Iowa on the left, one company of the Seventh Iowa and the battery in the centre, at a full gallop, we made the distance of over ten miles in much less than an hour.

On reaching near the ground, I found that the enemy were leaving and carrying off what plunder they could. Many lodges, however, were still standing. I ordered Colonel Furnas, Second Nebraska, to push his horses to the utmost, so as to reach the camp and assist Major House in keeping the Indians corraled. This order was obeyed with great alacrity, the regiment going over the plains at a full run. I was close upon the rear of the regiment with the Sixth Iowa. The Second Nebraska took the right of the camp, and was soon lost in a cloud of dust over the hills. I ordered Colonel Wilson, Sixth Iowa, to take the left, while I with the battery, one company of the Seventh Iowa, Captain Millard, and two companies of the Sixth Iowa, Major Ten Broeck commanding, charged through the centre of the encampment. I here found an Indian chief by the name of Little Solder with some few of his people. This Indian has always had the reputation of being a "good Indian" and friendly. I placed them under guard and moved on. Short-

ly after I met with the notorious chief Big Head and some of his men. They were dressed for a fight, but my men cut them off. These Indians, together with some of their warriors, mustering about thirty, together with squaws, children, ponies and dogs, gave themselves up, numbering over one hundred and twenty human beings. About the same time firing began about half a mile from me ahead, and was kept up, becoming more and more brisk, until it was quite a respectable engagement. A report was brought to me (which proved to be false) that the Indians were driving back some of my command. I immediately took possession of the hillocks near by, forming line and placing the battery in the centre on a high knoll. At this time night had about set in, but still the engagement was briskly kept up, and in the melee it was hard to distinguish my line from that of the enemy. The Indians made a very desperate resistance, but finally broke and fled, pursued in every direction by bodies of my troops. I would here state that the troops though mounted were armed with rifles, and, according to my orders, most of them dismounted and fought afoot, until the enemy broke, when they remounted and went in pursuit. It is to be regretted that I could not have had an hour or two more of daylight, for I feel sure if I had, I could have annihilated the enemy. As it was, I believe I can safely say I gave them one of the most severe punishments that the Indians have ever received. After night set in the engagement was of such a promiscuous nature that it was hard to tell what results would happen; I therefore ordered all the buglers to sound the "rally," and building large fires, remained under arms during night collecting together my troops.

The next morning early (the fourth) I established my camp on the battle-field, the wagon-train, under charge of Major Pearman, Second Nebraska, having in the night been ordered to join me, and sent out strong scouting parties in different directions to scour the country, to overtake what Indians they could; but in this they were not very successful, though some of them had some little skirmishes. They found the dead and wounded in all directions, some of them miles from the battle-field; also immense quantities of provisions, baggage, etc., where they had apparently cut loose their ponies from "travailles" and got off on them; also numbers of ponies and dogs harnessed to "travailles" running all over the prairie. One party that I sent out went near to the James River, and found there eleven dead Indians. The deserted camp of the Indians, together with the country all round, was covered with their plunder. I devoted this day, together with the following, (the fifth,) to destroying all this property, still scouring the country. I do not think I exaggerate in the least when I say that I burned up four or five hundred thousand pounds of dried buffalo meat as one item, besides three hundred lodges, and a very large quantity of property of great value to the Indians. A very large number of ponies were found dead and wounded on the field; besides a large number were captured. The prisoners (some one hundred and thirty) I take with me below, and shall report to you more specially in regard to them.

The Surgeon of the Second Nebraska regiment, Dr. Bowen, who has shown a great energy and desire to attend to his duties during the campaign, started out during the night of the engagement with a party of fifteen men to go back to the old camp to procure ambulances. But as they did not return on the morning of the second day, I knew he was either lost or captured. (He returned about noon of the second day.) I therefore sent out small scouting parties in every direction to hunt them up. One of these fell into an ambuscade, by which four of the party were killed and the rest driven in. I immediately sent out five companies of the Second Nebraska regiment, Colonel Furnas in command, who, after a long march, found the Indians had fled. They succeeded, however, in overtaking three concealed in some tall grass, whom they killed. The fight has been so scattered, the dead Indians have been found in so many different places, that it is impossible for me to give an accurate report of the number killed of the enemy. I, however, think I am safe in reporting it at one hundred. (I report those that were left on the field and that my scouting parties found.)

During the engagement, for some time, the Second Nebraska, afoot and armed with rifles—and there are among them probably some of the best shots in the world—were engaged with the enemy at a distance not over sixty paces, pouring on them a murderous fire in a ravine where the enemy were posted. The slaughter, therefore, was immense. My officers and the guides I have with me think one hundred and fifty will not cover their loss. The Indian reports make it two hundred. That the General may know the exact locality of the battle-field, I would state that it was, as near as I could judge, fifteen miles west of James River, and about half way between the latitudes of Bonehute and headwaters of Elm River, as laid down on the Government map. The fight took place near a hill called by the Indians White Stone Hill.

In conclusion, I would state that the troops of my command conducted themselves well; and though it was the first fight that nearly all of them had ever been in, they showed that they are of the right material, and that in time, with discipline, they will make worthy soldiers. It is to be regretted that we lost so many valuable lives as we did, but this could not be helped; the Indians had formed a line of battle with good judgment, from which they could only be dislodged by a charge. I could not use my artillery without greatly endangering the lives of my own men; if I could, I could have slaughtered them.

I send you, accompanying, the reports of Colonel Wilson, Sixth Iowa, and Colonel Furnas, Second Nebraska, also official reports of killed and wounded, and take this occasion to thank both those officers for their good conduct and the cheerfulness with which they obeyed my orders on the occasion. Both of them had their horses shot in the action. I would also request permission to state that the several members of my staff rendered me every possible assistance.

On the morning of the sixth I took my up line of march for Fort Pierre. If I could have remained in that section of country some two or three weeks, I might have accomplished more; but I was satisfied by the reports of my scouts that the Indians had scattered in all directions; some toward the James River; some, probably the Blackfeet, to recross the Missouri, and a part of them went north, where they say they have friends among the half-breeds of the north. My rations were barely sufficient, with rapid marches, to enable me to reach Fort Pierre. The animals, not only the teams I have already reported to you as worthless, but also the cavalry horses, showed the effect of rapid marching and being entirely without grain.

I brought with me all the prisoners I had, and tried to question them to gain some information. The men refused to say much, except that they are all "good Indians," and the other bad ones joined their camp without their will.

Their squaws, however, corroborate the report I have already given you in regard to the destruction of the people on board the Mackinaw boat and the fights with General Sibley, in which these Indians had a part. They also state that the Indians, after recrossing to this side of the Missouri, sent a party to follow Sibley until he went to the James River, then returned to their camp on Long Lake, to procure a large quantity of provisions and other articles they had "catched" there, and then came to the camp where I met them.

After marching about one hundred and thirty miles, we reached the mouth of the Little Sheyenne on the eleventh, where I found the steamboat I had ordered to be there on the eighth instant. It was lucky she was there, for without the grain she brought up I could not have brought my empty wagons back. For some miles north of Sheyenne and Pierre the grass now is about all gone. I placed my wounded on the boat, and as many empty wagons as she could carry. I am afraid the loss of horses and mules will be considered very great, but it could not be helped. When I found it impossible for the rear guard to get an animal along, I had it killed to prevent its falling into the hands of the enemy.

Very respectfully, your obedient servant,
ALFRED SULLY,
Brigadier-General Commanding.

P. S.—By actual count, the number of my prisoners is one hundred and fifty-six—men thirty-two; women and children, one hundred and twenty-four. I would also beg leave to say that in the action I had of my command between six hundred and seven hundred men actually engaged.

My killed numbered, as far as ascertained, twenty; wounded, thirty-eight.

Very respectfully, your obedient servant,
ALFRED SULLY,
Brigadier-General Commanding.

MAJOR HOUSE'S REPORT.

IN CAMP ON BATTLE-FIELD OF }
"WHITE STONE HILL." }

Colonel D. S. Wilson:

DEAR SIR: On the third day of September, 1863, in obedience to your orders and under instructions from Brigadier-General Sully, I took the line of march from our camp of the previous night (which was about thirty miles from "White Stone Hill") at half-past five A.M., having under my command companies C, I, F, and H, of the Sixth Iowa cavalry, and proceeded in a southerly direction, halting every hour, dismounting the men, and allowing the horses to graze ten minutes at a time. At about three P.M., our guide informed me that a camp of Indians was about three miles distant. I ordered the men to load their carbines and pistols, and started on a gallop for the Indian camp. When within a mile of the camp we halted and formed in line of battle, with I in line, H and F as flankers, and C as a reserve. In this order we proceeded and took a position behind a ridge about fifty rods from the enemy, where we had then an easy range and where we were protected from their fire. Captain Marsh of company H, and Lieutenant Dayton of company C, were then sent forward to reconnoitre; they returned and reported that there were four hundred lodges of the enemy. Upon gaining this information our guide, with two picked men from company C, were started back to your camp, to give you information of our whereabouts, and that reinforcements might be sent if they were necessary. As the ground was very uneven, and it was difficult to ascertain what defences the enemy had, it was determined to make a reconnoissance in force. For this purpose company C was sent to the left, in command of Captain Ainsworth, who with great personal bravery pushed forward with vigor and rapidity in the face of the enemy, outnumbering his force ten to one. Captain Marsh with company H also pushed forward in the same direction, with a courage which would have done honor to a veteran of a hundred battles. As soon as these companies had returned and reported, Captain Shattuck with company F was sent out to the right to ascertain the position of the enemy in that direction. While these things were being done, the chiefs came in under a flag of truce and attempted a negotiation. They offered to surrender some of their chiefs, but as the Commandant did not know who was entitled to speak by authority, he demanded the unconditional surrender of all. This the Indians refused to do, and having sent away their squaws and pappooses, together with their stock of provisions, they placed themselves in battle array. Our command moved forward, and the enemy retreated precipitately, abandoning every thing except their ponies.

While we were thus following and scattering the enemy, the Second Nebraska regiment appeared on the hill, under the command of Colonel Furnas, who immediately informed the commander of the forces of the Sixth Iowa that he would take the right of the flying enemy and drive them in; whereupon we formed our forces in column, and took the left, first upon a trot, then a gallop, and finally at a full charge. The enemy having abandoned every thing in their flight, and finding that we were fast gaining upon them, collected together in a ravine and prepared for battle. We again formed in line of battle, and were advancing upon the enemy, when we discovered the Second Nebraska upon our left flank; they were dismounting and preparing to fight on foot. At the same time we saw that part of the Iowa Sixth which had been left behind formed in line parallel to the Nebraska Second. We at once advanced our lines within twenty rods of the enemy, and were fired upon by them. We returned the fire from our whole line with terrible effect, covering the ground with dead men and horses. The horses then became so restive as to be unmanageable under the fire even of our own men from their backs. The command was then taken back twenty-five rods in the rear, and were preparing to fight on foot, when darkness setting in, the command was formed in a hollow square, the men in front of their horses, and slept on their arms. We placed a picket-guard around our camp, under the charge of Sergeant-Major Fogg and Lieutenant Dayton, who promptly performed the duties assigned them; they went to the battle-field after dark to look after wounded, and for this I recommend them to your favorable consideration. I also recommend Dr. Camburn, who came promptly to the relief of the wounded, and did all he could in the darkness. Among those who distinguished themselves for personal bravery, I wish to mention Captain R. L. Wolf, who stood in front of his company and killed an Indian every shot he made. The whole command did well, and I must not mention individual instance for fear of making this report too long. About one hundred of the enemy were killed; we took a large number of prisoners and destroyed all the winter stores of the enemy, among which was four hundred tons of dried meat.

I am respectfully yours,
A. E. HOUSE,
Major Commanding.

Doc. 162.

SURPRISE OF QUANTRELL.

PLEASANT HILL, }
September 15, 1863—9 P.M. }

Brigadier-General Ewing, Commanding the District of the Border:

SIR: After a week spent in bushwhacking in search of Quantrell's guerrillas, I became convinced that some of his bands continued to secrete themselves upon the waters of the Sinabar and Blue Creeks, in Jackson county, Missouri.

This morning I made another night march with a view to surprise him if possible. I crossed the intervening prairie, and entered the timbers of the Sinabar without being observed. At daylight, the command being divided into four detachments, we commenced a thorough scouring of the Sinabar hills. The country is very rugged and filled with almost impenetrable thickets. Half of the different detachments were dismounted and penetrated the woods, deployed as skirmishers—the horses being led in the rear.

By three of the detachments nothing particular was discovered, except evidences that the guerrillas inhabited these woods. Captain Coleman, of the Ninth Kansas, who commanded on the extreme left, in the course of the day fell upon a trail, by following which he soon came upon Quantrell's own camp. He promptly attacked it, killed two of the guerrillas, captured some forty horses, destroyed all their subsistence stores, all their bedding, clothing, ammunition, and some arms. The enemy fired but one volley, and at once disappeared in the thick underwood, where pursuit was impossible.

Too much credit cannot be given to Captain Coleman for the ingenuity, courage, and energy with which he conducted this as well as other attacks upon guerrillas, or to the zeal and bravery of the men of his command in seconding the labors of their chief.

The effect of this surprise and capture is most damaging to the designs of Quantrell in making another raid upon Kansas. The loss of horses and clothing is to him worse than the loss of men, as the country is denuded of both.

The bushwhackers have within a day or two burned a splendid flouring mill at Lone Jack.

To-morrow morning I shall start an expedition to endeavor the capture of another camp of the guerrillas.

Respectfully, your obedient servant,
WILLIAM WEER,
Colonel, etc.

Doc. 163.

BATTLE OF LIMESTONE STATION.

RICHMOND ENQUIRER ACCOUNT.

JONESBORO, TENN., September 10, 1863.

BEFORE giving an account of the flight of the Ninth, I will give some light as to the state of affairs in Upper East-Tennessee. It is well known to you that about the twenty-seventh of August, General Buckner, with his entire force, withdrew from Knoxville, leaving the country east along the line of the East-Tennessee and Virginia Railroad to Bristol to be guarded and defended by General A. E. Jackson's brigade. Notwithstanding the evacuation of Knoxville and the abandonment of the country, except by the small force above alluded to, the Directors of the road (the Presidents, Colonel John Branner, being then at Knoxville) continued to run their trains into Knoxville for three days, although a large force of the enemy was known to be within fifteen or twenty miles of the city; and, marvellous to say, it is the common report of the country that the President and Directors resolved to run the road, declaring they were only common carriers, evidently indifferent whether the rolling stock fell into the hands of the enemy. This they must have known would have been the case. So, sure enough, on Tuesday they dashed into Knoxville and captured their best passenger train and three locomotives. On the same day our little force at the Plains was withdrawn by railroad to Bristol. On the morning of the fourth the enemy pushed up to Mossy Creek, captured a train, and then run into Jonesboro, one hundred miles distant from Knoxville, with four hundred men, and there took another.

A small company of cavalry, under Captain Jones, at this latter place, after firing a volley into the enemy, made their escape. Two females were wounded by the Yankees in the encounter.

The enemy then pushed on to Carter's bridge, where was stationed a small force of infantry and one section of artillery, under the accomplished Captain McClung, and demanded its surrender; when, upon refusal, they retreated toward Knoxville.

Having learned the above facts, General Jackson, who was at Bristol with the principal body of his forces, with a regiment of Kentucky cavalry and some other forces that had recently joined him, made a forced march for Jonesboro, at which place he arrived on the morning of the seventh. Here he learned that the enemy was returning in full force by railway, so he promptly threw forward a battalion of cavalry, (Colonel Giltner's regiment,) a section of artillery, and a detachment of infantry. A few miles below Jonesboro they found five or six hundred of the enemy, and a train of cars, unable to proceed on account of the destruction of a small bridge, effected by our scouts the day before. An attack was at once made upon them, Colonel Giltner commanding the cavalry, and Lieutenant J. E. Graham the artillery. They were driven back near a half a mile, but the enemy gaining a shelter, our forces were compelled to fall back to their first position, having, at the risk of losing our cannon, incautiously advanced too far.

Seizing this moment of temporary advantage, the enemy gained the railroad and got away with their train. Having previously sent a squad of cavalry to destroy the railroad in their rear, our forces, now joined by Lieutenant J. W. Blackwell, with a three-inch rifle gun, pursued with vigor, expecting momentarily to capture the train and forces; but our scouts had so ineffectually done their work that the enemy passed down to Limestone Bridge, seizing the heights and woods around the block house at the bridge, and sending their train toward Knoxville for reënforcements. Having now possession of the block house and the thick woods around it, the enemy resolved to make a bold stand.

General Jackson at once ordered Colonel Giltner's cavalry to cross Limestone Creek to cut off the retreat of the enemy, while our artillery—one rifle gun and one small one-pound mountain gun—opened fire upon the depot, block house, and other buildings occupied by the enemy, while Major McCauley's detachment of Thomas's legion was posted in rear of the battery.

Just at this time Lieutenant-Colonel M. A. Haynes, of the artillery, and Lieutenant-Colonel Walker, with a detachment of Thomas's legion, were ordered from Jonesboro to reënforce General Jackson. After this fire had been opened some forty minutes, Colonel Haynes brought gallantly forward at a gallop Lieutenant Graham's section of artillery, (Burrough's battery,) which also opened briskly. The enemy's sharp-shooters in the woods, meanwhile, kept up an incessant fire on the batteries. By this time Colonel Haynes had taken possession of the south side of the bridge, dismounted and deployed his men as skirmishers, and, after a spirited engagement, drove the enemy across the creek, and held the railroad and south end of the bridge. In this latter engagement, and up to the time of the capture of the enemy, Colonel Giltner had the valuable services of Lieutenant-Colonel J. L. Bottles, of the Twenty-sixth Tennessee regiment, who, being absent from his command at Chattanooga, volunteered his services for the occasion.

Just as this feat was accomplished by Colonel Giltner, Lieutenant-Colonel Walker's battalion, of Thomas's legion, was thrown out to the left, through a skirt of timber on the left of the enemy's sharp-shooters, and the artillery, led by Colonel Haynes in person, advanced to within two hundred yards of the roads occupied by the enemy, and opened a rapid fire of shell and canister upon the sharp-shooters. At the same time the infantry, upon the left of the artillery, drove in the enemy at a double-quick, where they took refuge in the block house and other buildings, from which they kept up a rapid fire.

Advancing at a trot, Colonel Haynes threw the guns into battery in the midst of a shower of balls, upon a height, not more than two hundred yards, and promptly fired several rounds of shell into the block house.

At this moment the enemy raised a white flag, and Colonel Haynes galloped forward and received the flag and sword of their commander, Lieutenant-Colonel Haynes, One Hundred and Fifth Ohio volunteers, and the surrender of near three hundred of the enemy, rank and file. Captain B. W. Jenkins, formerly of General Marshal's staff, volunteered for the occasion, and Lieutenant-Colonel J. L. Bottles was in at the death.

The enemy's loss was twelve killed and twenty wounded; our loss is six killed and ten wounded.

The officers and soldiers throughout behaved with gallantry. The artillery, first under Lieutenant Graham at Telford's, then Lieutenant Blackwell, and finally under Colonel Haynes, at Limestone, acted with coolness and intrepidity throughout. More anon.

Doc. 164.

PROCLAMATION OF GOVERNOR VANCE.

WHEREAS, a number of public meetings have recently been held in various portions of the State, in some of them threats have been made of combined resistance to the execution of the laws of Congress in regard to conscription and the collection of taxes, thereby endangering the public peace and tranquillity, as well as the common cause of independence, which we have so solemnly engaged to defend; and, whereas, it is my sworn duty to see all the laws in the land faithfully executed, and quiet and order maintained within our borders:

Now, therefore, I, Zebulon B. Vance, Governor of the State of North-Carolina, do issue this, my proclamation, commanding all such persons to renounce such evil intentions, and warning them to beware of the criminal and fatal consequences of carrying such threats into execution. The inalienable and invaluable right of the people to assemble together and consult for the common good, together with its necessary concomitants—the freedom of speech and the press—are secured to you, my countrymen, by the most sacred compacts. They shall never find a disturber in me. Yet you will remember that the same instruments which guarantee these great rights also limit you to the exercise of them within the bounds of law, and impose upon me the solemn duty of seeing that these bounds be not transgressed. The Constitution of the Confederate States, and all laws passed in pursuance thereof, are the supreme law of the land. Resistance to them by combination is treason, and, without combination, is a high crime against the laws of your country. Let no one be deceived.

So long as these laws remain upon the statute-book they shall be executed. Surely, my countrymen, you would not seek to cure the evils of one revolution by plunging the country into another. You will not knowingly, to the present desolating war with the common enemy, and the horrors of eternal strife and entire subversion of law and civil authority! You must not forget the enviable character which you have always maintained as a sober, conservative, and law-abiding people; nor would I have you to forget the plain, easy, and constitutional method of redressing your grievances. Meet and denounce any existing laws if you think proper—you have that right—and instruct your representatives in the Congress or the State Legislature, as the case may be, to repeal them. Your own chosen servants made these obnoxious laws—they can report them, if such are your instructions. If you regard them as unconstitutional, our Supreme Court sits ready to decide upon all cases properly brought before it. Its decisions are final in the State of North-Carolina, and shall be executed while the power remains in our Executive to enforce any law. There is no grievance to redress and no proposition to be made, but can be most beneficially effected in the way our fathers marked out by the ballot-box and the other constitutionally appointed means. In time of great public sensibility like the present, any departure from this legal channel is revolutionary and dangerous, and tends to the division and destruction of our people.

It is my great desire, and, I hope, that of all good citizens, that our people should remain united, befall us what may. Should we triumph in the great struggle for independence, let no feelings of revenge, no bitterness mar the rejoicing of that glorious day; should we fail, and come short of that great object for which we have struggled so long and bled so freely, let not our strifes and domestic feuds add to the bitterness of defeat. Attempts suddenly to change the existing order of things would only result in bloodshed and ruin. I therefore implore you, my countrymen, of all shades of political opinion, to abstain from assembling together for the purpose of denouncing each other, whether at home or in the army, and to avoid seeking any remedy for the evils of the times by other than legal means, and through the properly constituted authorities. We are embarked in the holiest of all causes which can stir the hearts of patriots—the cause of liberty and independence. We are committed to it by every tie that can bind an honorable people. Multitudes of our bravest and best have already sealed it with their blood, whilst others, giving up all earthly possessions, are either languishing in dungeons or are homeless wanderers through the land, and all have felt in a greater or less degree the iron hand of war. A great and glorious nation is struggling to be born, and wondering kingdoms and distant empires are stilled with listening hope and admiration, watching this greatest of human events. Let them not, I pray you, be shocked with the spectacle of domestic strife and petty, malignant feuds. Let not our enemy be rejoiced to behold our strong arms and stronger devotion, which have often made them tremble, turned against ourselves. Let us rather show that the God of liberty is in his holy temple—the hearts of freemen—and bid all the petty bickerings of earth keep silence before him.

Instead of engaging in this unholy and unpatriotic strife, and threatening to resist the laws of the land and endangering the peace of society, let us prepare diligently, and with hopeful hearts, for the hardships and sufferings of the coming winter. Heaven has blessed us with abundant crops, but thousands of the poor are unable to purchase. Let us begin in time, and use every effort to provide for them, and secure them against suffering. And let us exert ourselves to the utmost to return to duty the many brave but misguided men who have left their country's flag in the hour of danger, and God will yet bless us and our children, and our children's children will thank us for not despairing of the Republic in its darkest hours of disaster, and, still more, for adhering to and preserving, amid the fiery trials of war, conservative sentiments and the rights and civil liberties of the young confederacy.

In witness whereof, Zebulon B. Vance, our

[L. S.] Governor, Captain-General, and Commander-in-Chief, hath signed these presents, and caused the great seal of the State to be affixed.

Done at the city of Raleigh, this seventh day of September, A.D. 1863, and in the year of American independence the eighty-eighth.

Z. B. VANCE.

Doc. 165.

THE SABINE PASS EXPEDITION.

CONGRATULATORY ORDER FROM GEN. MAGRUDER.*

HEADQUARTERS DISTRICT OF TEXAS, NEW-MEXICO, AND ARIZONA, HOUSTON, TEX., Sept. 9, 1863.

GENERAL ORDERS, No.—:

I. The Major-General Commanding has the satisfaction of announcing to the army a brilliant victory, won by the little garrison of Sabine Pass against the fleet of the enemy. Attacked by five gunboats, the fort, mounting but three guns of small calibre, and manned by the Davis Guards, Lieutenant R. M. Dowling, assisted by Lieutenant Smith, of the engineers, supported by about two hundred men—the whole under command of Captain F. H. Odium—steadily resisted their fire, and at last forced the surrender of the two gunboats Clifton and Sachem, badly crippling another, which, with the others, escaped over the bar. The result of this gallant achievement is the capture of two fine gunboats, fifteen heavy guns, over two hundred prisoners, among them the Commodore of the fleet, and over fifty of the enemy killed and wounded, while not a man was lost on our side or a gun injured.

II. The enemy's fleet, with his land forces, is still off the coast, no doubt intending a landing at the first favorable moment. He may endeavor to retrieve his losses at Sabine by an attack upon the works at other points on the coast. Should this be the case, the Major-General Commanding confidently expects to receive from his troops at those points as cheering a report as that which he now communicates to the army from the defenders of Sabine.

III. The result of the engagement had with the enemy's fleet on the coast of Texas proves that true pluck and resolution are qualities which make up for disparity of metal and numbers; and that no position, defended with determination, can be carried by the enemy's gunboats alone. Should any of the forts on the coast, or the forces on land, be attacked, the troops need but remember the success of their comrades at Sabine, emulate their courage and skill, and victory will be the result.

By command of

Major-General J. BANKHEAD MAGRUDER.

EDMUND B. TURNER,
A. A. General.

Official: H. A. PRATT,
A. A. General.

Headquarters Department Trans-Mississippi, Shreveport, La., Sept. 13, 1863.

* See Doc. 125, page 425, ante.

Doc. 166.

MILITARY RIOTS AT RALEIGH, N. C.

OFFICIAL CORRESPONDENCE.

RALEIGH, September 10, 1863.

President Davis, Richmond :

A Georgia regiment, of Benning's brigade, entered this city last night at ten o'clock, and destroyed the office of the *Standard* newspaper. This morning a mob of citizens destroyed the office of the *State Journal* in retaliation. Please order immediately that troops passing through here shall not enter the city. If this is not done, the most frightful consequences may ensue.

Respectfully,   Z. B. VANCE.

RICHMOND, September 10, 1863.

Governor Z. B. Vance :

Your despatch of this date received. I deeply regret the occurrence you announce, and have sent by telegraph the following order to Major W. W. Pierce, Quartermaster: "You will not allow the troops in transit to be detained at Raleigh, and will communicate to the commanding officer of each detachment passing there that he is instructed not to permit his men to enter the city, but if transportation is not furnished to enable the detachment to proceed by railroad, will march, without halting, to an encampment at a safe distance from Raleigh."

JEFFERSON DAVIS.

STATE OF NORTH-CAROLINA, EXECUTIVE DEPARTMENT, RALEIGH, September 11, 1863.

His Excellency Jefferson Davis, Richmond, Va.:

MY DEAR SIR: You have received by telegraph before this information of the riots occurring in this city. . . I am now anxious about the effects upon the country, though I am greatly in hopes that the mob of citizens which destroyed the office of the *State Journal* will act as a counter-irritant, and help to allay excitement, the damage being equal to both parties. . . . The soldiers who originated the mob belonged to Benning's brigade, and were apparently led by their officers, several of whom I saw in the crowd; but I heard none of their names, except a Major Shepherd. I have also reason for believing that it was done with the knowledge and consent of General Benning, as he remarked to a gentleman an hour or two previous that his men had threatened it. During its continuance he could not be found.

A messenger sent by me to his supposed quarters at the depot was refused admission to him; and, although he had ample opportunity after the occurrence to have seen or written to me, disclaiming the outrage upon the honor and peace of North-Carolina, he did not do so. As it is my intention to enforce the laws rigidly against all citizens who participated in the second mob, so I feel it my duty to demand that punishment may be inflicted on the officers who assisted or countenanced the first. Should this not be done, I shall feel it my duty to demand the persons of these officers of the State of Georgia to answer the demands of justice. I feel very sad in the contemplation of these outrages. The distance is quite short to either anarchy or despotism when armed soldiers, led by their officers, can, with impunity, outrage the laws of a State. . . . I pray you to see that it does not occur again. Should any newspaper in the State commit treason, I would have its editor arrested and tried by laws, which many of us yet respect. I thank you for your prompt orders telegraphed to Major Pierce concerning the passage of troops through this city. They are now being enforced, and peace can be preserved if they are rigidly obeyed.

Very respectfully, your obedient servant,

Z. B. VANCE.

A second letter, dated September eleventh, from Governor Vance to President Davis, is omitted by the *Standard* for the present.

CONFEDERATE STATES OF AMERICA, EXECUTIVE DEPARTMENT, RICHMOND, VA., September 15, 1863.

Governor Z. B. Vance, Raleigh, N. C. :

MY DEAR SIR: Your two communications of the eleventh instant have been received. Upon the receipt of your telegram, informing me that measures, taken to put an end to the disturbances in Raleigh, had not proved effective, orders were issued, which, it is hoped, will be sufficient to prevent further disorders. I have referred to the Secretary of War your statement respecting particular officers alleged to have been concerned in the riot, and the matter will receive proper inquiry.

Very respectfully and truly yours,

JEFFERSON DAVIS.

General Benning, being written to by General Cooper, A. G., replied, showing that he had not been absent from the depot while his troops were going through, and asserting that he was utterly ignorant of any intention on the part of his men to mob the printing-office. He adds:

The true explanation of the affair I take to be this: When my brigade arrived at Weldon we found there a party of North-Carolinians, commanded by a lieutenant, who informed me that he was ordered to the vicinity of Salisbury, I think, to arrest some deserters, and urged me to let his party go along with my brigade for the sake of despatch. I said yes, if he could find room in the train for his party. He replied that he could take the tops of the cars. I told him then that he might do so. Accordingly, he and his party took the tops of the cars and went with my brigade through Raleigh. After we left Raleigh, this party freely avowed themselves the authors of the deed, and claimed credit for it. They said they led some of my men into it with them, and I have no doubt they did, but, I think, not many, and these merely unorganized individuals, each acting for and by himself. These things I learned from officers and men who heard the talk of the North-Carolinians on the train, after it left Raleigh. I learned them first at Charlotte, when the train stopped there; but the North-Carolinians were then off the cars, so that I had no opportunity to question them myself. Thus, sir, you have such an account of this affair as it is in my power to give you. I am, sir, very respectfully,

Your obedient servant,
HENRY L. BENNING,
Brigadier-General.

To S. Cooper, Adjutant and Inspector-General, Richmond, Va.:

Lieutenant-Colonel Shepherd, who was mentioned in Governor Vance's letter as Major Shepherd, writes a letter to the Adjutant-General, in which the following statement is made:

"My first knowledge of the disturbance was derived from Governor Vance calling upon me for this purpose at the hotel, inquiring first for General Benning, and, in his absence, for the commander of the Second Georgia regiment. Accompanying Governor Vance, I proceeded promptly to the *Standard* office, where a number of soldiers were engaged in the disturbance—some within the building and others without—many of whom I recognized as belonging to different regiments of Benning's brigade. It is to be marked that not one officer was seen by me in the midst of this outbreak. I experienced no difficulty whatever in restoring order; immediately after which Governor Vance addressed the crowd, who listened with respectful attention, and dispersed in a body. Allow me only to add than Governor Vance publicly thanked me for my timely interposition, and that many of the officers and men of the brigade were invited to share the hospitalities of the executive mansion. I have this day written to Governor Vance, requesting him to write to the department in my further vindication.

I have the honor to be yours, very respectfully,
W. S. SHEPHERD,
Lieut.-Col. Second Georgia Regiment, Benning's Brigade.

Doc. 167.

VIRGINIA PEACE RESOLUTIONS.

IN the Senate of Virginia, September ninth, 1863, Mr. Collier, of Petersburgh, submitted the following preamble and joint resolutions:

Whereas, the Constitution of the Federal Union of the late United States was established by the sovereign, separate action of the nine States by which it was first formed, and the number of the United States was afterward, from time to time, enlarged by the admission of other States separately; and, whereas, that Constitution failed to incorporate or indicate any method by which any one or more of the States might peaceably retire from the obligations of Federal duty imposed by it on each and every other State in the Union; and, whereas, it is consistent with the republican creed, on which the whole complex system is founded, that a majority of the States might peacefully disannul the compact as to any party to it; and, whereas, a conjunction in the Federal relations of the United States did arise in 1861, then culminated in a crisis, in which certain of the slaveholding States, by conventional action of their several sovereign people, in solemn form, declared and promulgated their desire and determination no longer to yield obedience to the Constitution and laws of that Federal Union, as authoritative over them, in that specific form; and, whereas, the executive branch of that Government, with the occasional sanction of the Federal Legislature, in the progress of belligerent events, has proceeded by force of arms to attempt to execute its laws within the disaffected States, without applying to the States remaining in the Union to ascertain whether they would agree that the disaffected States might depart in peace; and, whereas, these disaffected States were not, nor ever were, under any obligation to that General Government, except such as were self-imposed and explicitly defined in concert and comity with the other States, each being a contracting party with every other, in a compact to which there was and is no other party; and, whereas, the war waged on these States by that General Government, which is the creature of the States who armed it with power, deemed adequate to the common protection of them all, no less in their reserved rights than in their foreign relations—a war into which these States were thus precipitated—is yet being prosecuted with aspiring preëminence of craft and crime, although some of them, by large and earnest expressions of public or party opinion within their borders, have shown that they are constrained to contribute to its prosecution very much against their will, and to their own great detriment; and, whereas, any appropriate means, the timely use of which was omitted in the outset to prevent the war, is not only a proper resort in its progress, but is dictated and constrained to by all the sanctions of Christian civilization:

1. *Resolved*, therefore, by the General Assembly of Virginia, That three Commissioners from this State to each of the States remaining in the Union be appointed by the joint vote of the two Houses of the General Assembly, whose duty it shall be, under instructions to be prepared by the Governor of the State, and approved by the concurrent vote of each House of the General Assembly, to repair forthwith to the capital of each of the States that remains in that Union, and make known to the Governor of each, that the State of Virginia, appealing from the usurped power of the men who are charged with administering the government of that Union, exercised in the conduct of this war, demands of those States with whom she contracted, that they severally will, by the ballot-box, as the Union was formed and enlarged, decide, as solemnly and formally as they did in that transaction, whether they will consent that she will be allowed thenceforth to be separated from them in peace; provided, however, that this State, having joined other States in forming a confederacy, and with a view to regard scrupulously the obligations contracted with her confederates, shall not pro-

ceed to carry this proceeding into full execution until a majority of them shall agree to coäct in instituting a like commission; and to this end the Governor is authorized to communicate this proceeding to the Governor of each of the Confederate States, inviting their several concurrence and coäction in this proposed mission to the late co-States, but not to the Government of that Union, because it was and is the creature of the States, and should be their servant to do their will when certainly ascertained.

2. *Resolved,* As the opinion of this General Assembly, the undertaking to speak and to act for the sovereign people of Virginia, although we are but the ordinary Legislature thereof, that in case the men who are charged with administering the Government of the United States shall refuse our Commissioners transit and sojourn into and in those States for the exclusive purposes of this mission, which are avowed, such failure of our effort will but demonstrate to them the fearful extent of absolute rule over them by those men, and make our effort a more memorable instance of patriotic exertion and peaceful magnanimity, displayed in a well-meant attempt to cultivate peace on earth and good-will among men.

3. *Resolved,* That in initiating this mission for peace this General Assembly doth unequivocally disavow any desire, or design, or willingness, that the Confederate Administration shall relax its exertions, or the people theirs, to advance and establish the cause to which we are pledged in our fortunes, and by our victories, to the utmost of our talents, to use them in support of the separate independence of the States.

The offer of the resolution excited some debate. The question on the adoption was laid over.

A resolution was offered by Mr. James, of Botetourt and Craig, for confiscating or sequestrating the property of deserters from the confederate army.

Mr. Hall, of Wetzell, said the Constitution would not allow confiscation beyond the term of life. But the remedy for desertion did not lie in that direction. The evil was caused by the shameful conduct of those who have the oversight of the soldiers, and particularly the officers in Richmond. He proceeded to speak with much severity and bitterness of General Winder's department, and also that of the Surgeon-General. He hoped, too, that the Legislature would rebuke Jeff Davis before it adjourned.

Doc. 168.

OCCUPATION OF EAST-TENNESSEE.

GENERAL BURNSIDE'S REPORT.*

HEADQUARTERS DEPARTMENT OF THE OHIO, }
  NEAR LOUDON BRIDGE, TENN., September 9. }

Major-General H. W. Halleck, General-in-Chief:

I have the honor to inform you that our forces now occupy Knoxville, Kingston, and other im-

* See Doc. 122, page 407, *ante.*

portant points. General Hartsuff's corps, after the concentration, of which I notified you, moved forward. General Carter's cavalry division of that corps preceded the corps in three columns —one under command of General Shackelford, on Loudon Bridge; one under Colonel Bird, on Kingston; and one under Colonel Foster, on Knoxville. The last-named places were taken without material opposition; but at Loudon the enemy was strongly posted. After a brisk skirmish they were driven back by Shackelford's command. They fired the bridge before they retreated, and it is now in ruins. Colonel Bird captured at Kingston a steamboat in process of construction, but nearly finished. Colonel Foster captured at Knoxville two locomotives and a number of cars. And a very considerable amount of army stores was captured by different brigades of Carter's division.

Great praise is due to the troops of the command for their patience, endurance, and courage during the movement.

Hartsuff's corps, which has been in advance, has proved itself to be one of the best in the service.

I am thankful to report that we suffered no loss from the hands of the enemy, except a few wounded.

I have the honor to be, General, very respectfully, your obedient servant,

A. E. BURNSIDE,
Major-General.

Doc. 169.

FIGHT AT CULPEPER COURT-HOUSE, VA.

REPORT OF MAJOR WILLIAM WELLS.

HEADQUARTERS FIRST VERMONT CAVALRY, }
  GROVE CHURCH, VA., September 20, 1863. }

P. T. Washburn, Adjutant and Inspector-General of Vermont:

SIR: I beg leave to submit the following brief report of the part taken by this regiment (the first and second battalions) in the recent operations by our cavalry against the enemy.

We left our camp near Falmouth, Va., at one o'clock P.M., on Saturday, September twelfth, 1863, and proceeded with the division to which we are attached to Kelly's Ford. Crossed the Rappahannock River early the next morning, Sunday, thirteenth instant, and arrived in the vicinity of Culpeper Court-House at about twelve o'clock M., where our calvary were briskly engaged in skirmishing with the enemy's cavalry and artillery, driving them toward the town.

The regiment was immediately directed by General Kilpatrick, commanding division, to move to the left of the town, and endeavor to cut off a portion of the enemy's force stationed in that direction; but a stream of water, running along the border of the village, had become so much swollen by the rain of the day before, as to render it unfordable, and thus prevent these instructions from being carried out. We then received orders to charge into town, which we did, passing through, capturing eight prisoners, and one gun, with carriage, horses, etc., complete, and occupied a knoll on the south side of the village, where the regiment was subjected to a very severe artillery fire from the enemy's guns, stationed at our front and left. We were here directed by General Custer, commanding brigade, to attack the force occupying the woods to the left of the town, and holding the road leading in the direction of Orange Court-House. Companies E and I of the first battalion were sent to the right, dismounted, and engaged the skirmishers of the enemy's left. The second battalion, (companies B, C, H, and G,) under Captain Adams, being sent forward, charged the enemy, driving them from the road, and through the woods back under the protection of their artillery, capturing twenty-six prisoners. The fight at this place continued for a considerable length of time, three separate charges having been made by our men. The force in front of the second battalion largely outnumbering their opponents, and being strongly supported, rallied and gained a temporary advantage, during which time they succeeded in removing their artillery stationed in our front. A movement on our flanks was at one time attempted, but it failed in its purpose, the enemy being compelled to retire. The repulse of the enemy along the whole line being at this time—four o'clock P.M.—complete, they retreated in the direction of the Rapidan River. The pursuit was continued until dark, but their forces did not make a stand before crossing.

The commanding officer being temporarily disabled during the engagement by the bursting of a shell, the command was turned over for a short time to Captain Adams.

The engagement lasted nearly four hours, during which time the regiment was continually under fire. We captured about forty prisoners during the day, the enemy leaving several killed and wounded on the field.

All the officers and men did their whole duty, and are entitled to great praise for their bravery and good conduct.

Accompanying this is a list of the casualties.

I have the honor to be, very respectfully, your obedient servant, WILLIAM WELLS,
Major Commanding First Vermont Calvary.

LIST OF CASUALTIES OCCURRING IN FIRST REGIMENT OF VERMONT CAVALRY, SEPTEMBER THIRTEENTH, 1863.

Major William Wells, wounded slightly in the shoulder.
Adjutant C. D. Gates, missing.
Private John Henry, company B, killed.
Sergeant L. V. H. Haskell, company G, wounded in the left arm.
Private Monroe Lyford, company C, wounded in the shoulder.
Private F. A. Russell, company I, wounded in the side.
Sergeant B. G. Chapman, company B, missing.
Private B. J. Merrill, company B, missing.

Sergeant H. P. Aldrich, company C, missing.
Bugler A. F. Hacket, company M, missing.
WILLIAM WELLS,
Major Commanding First Vermont Cavalry.

A NATIONAL ACCOUNT

CULPEPER COURT-HOUSE, VA.,
Tuesday, Sept. 15, 1863.

On the morning of the thirteenth the cavalry division of General Kilpatrick crossed the Rappahannock at Kelly's Ford, and marched in the direction of Culpeper by Brandy Station. No rebels in force were encountered until reaching Brandy Station, where the advance, consisting of the Harris Light, or Second New-York, met them in some force. A brisk skirmish ensued, the rebels, however, immediately falling back toward Culpeper. At this place the division of Kilpatrick formed a junction with the divisions of Buford and Gregg, the whole under command of General Pleasanton. The whole corps advanced up the railroad toward Culpeper. General Kilpatrick had the left, resting on the left of the railroad; General Buford the centre, and General Gregg the right—the skirmishing and cannonading becoming quite sharp as we advanced. As the cavalry moved across the plain in perfect order, some of the regiments in line, some in column, and a long line of skirmishers in front, with the batteries a little to the rear, the respective division and brigade commanders moving up with their staffs, it presented one of the most brilliant spectacles of the war. The rebels did not make much resistance until we reached a point about one mile this side of Culpeper, where they opened three batteries upon Kilpatrick's division, but not checking the advance in the least. On approaching near the town, the rebels seemed disposed to dispute our further advance. A long line of dismounted infantry could be seen along a fence just across a deep creek, with two batteries in support. General Kilpatrick ordered General Custer to dislodge them, which he soon accomplished. The Sixth Michigan dismounted, and engaged the rebel skirmishers, and soon routed them in good style. The Harris Light charged the battery on the edge of the town, capturing two guns. This brought the division of Kilpatrick to the edge of the town. Buford and Gregg were driving the enemy on the right, and General Kilpatrick, with characteristic boldness, was about to charge the whole rebel force upon our left, and capture the train of cars that was moving off toward Orange, but was prevented by the unexpected discovery of a deep creek, which was only passable at one place in his front. This enabled the train to escape, affording time to the rebel cavalry to take up a strong position, a little to the rear of the town, in the woods on the Cedar Mountain road. In the mean time, General Custer, at the head of the First battalion of the First Vermont, commanded by Major Wells, dashed into town, driving the rebels out and capturing one piece of artillery to the right of the town. The rebels had two other pieces in the woods to the rear of the town, strongly supported by a strong force of cavalry. The Harris Light gallantly charged up into the woods where the rebels were posted, but were driven back by superior numbers. The First Vermont, consisting of two battalions, numbering about one hundred and fifty men, under command of Major Wells, now gallantly advanced to charge under a heavy fire from the enemy's battery. The Harris Light promptly rallied, and both regiments charged into the woods and drove the rebels further toward the Cedar Mountain road. Our loss here was the heaviest of any during the day. General Custer, while leading the First Vermont, was wounded in the leg by the bursting of a shell, which also killed his horse, and the Harris Light sustained some loss, the extent of which I have been unable to learn. The rebels now formed just beyond the woods, where they had a battery in position. The Fifth New-York and one battalion of the First Vermont charged upon the battery, but were repulsed, the rebels returning to the woods in great force, but were driven out the second time, whereupon they retreated for the Rapidan, closely pursued for four miles by General Buford, when operations for the day ceased.

Our casualties on this day were three killed and forty wounded. On the fourteenth the cavalry advanced to the Rapidan, and found the enemy strongly posted at the respective fords on the other side of the river. In the fight the day previous the rebels were commanded by General Stuart—his force consisted of Fitzhugh Lee's and Wade Hampton's divisions of cavalry and five batteries. TROOPER.

ANOTHER ACCOUNT.

The following private letter from one who accompanied the Second New-York cavalry in the advance upon Culpeper, gives the following particulars of the skirmishing:

NEAR RAPIDAN RIVER, VA., Monday, Sept. 14, 1863.

Kilpatrick's division moved Saturday morning. We arrived at Kelly's Ford in the evening, and lay by our horses in marching order during the night. Between three and four there came up one of the most drenching showers I ever experienced. The rain fell in torrents, and we were soon standing in pools of water. At daylight we crossed, capturing the enemy's picket. Our advance was rather slow and cautious till we reached the forest bordering on the old Brandy-Station battle-field. Here we first struck the enemy in some force. A rapid charge ensued. The First brigade, under Colonel H. E. Davies, which had the advance, kept it throughout the day, led the charge at a gallop. We soon emerged on the old Brandy Station battle-field. Here the sight was grand in the extreme. The Second New-York cavalry (Harris Light) had the advance of the brigade, and were charging over the plain, supported by the other regiments, Colonel Davies leading every thing. Off in the distance we could see Generals Gregg and Buford bringing up their columns at a gallop. In the far advance charges were being made, and skirmishers were circling over the hills like the advancing waves of a flood-tide. Prisoners and wounded began to come in. The plain was soon cleared of the enemy, and soon our force disappeared in pursuit. Now commenced a running fight, till we reached the vicinity of Culpeper—the Harris Light still keeping the advance, and giving the enemy not a moment's rest. Whenever they made the slightest pause, an impetuous charge from this regiment would start them again. For two miles before reaching Culpeper, the Harris Light was exposed to a very severe artillery fire, as great trees broken off and shattered clearly proved. The enemy finally planted their guns up a high hill, at the entrance of the town. It was a very commanding position. The enemy must be dislodged, and that right speedily, too. The Harris Light were ordered by General Davies to do the work. Major McIrwin led the charge, accompanied by Captains Downing and Mitchel, and Lieutenant Jones, and supported by two batteries. General Custer, whose irrepressible gallantry led him far ahead of his command, came up and went with them. Down the hill they went at a gallop—a perfect avalanche of shot and shell crashing above them, and ploughing the ground around them. Dressing the line for a moment at the foot of the hill on which the battery was, they charged up with such impetuosity that every thing gave way before them. With great rapidity they dashed around in the rear of the guns, and in a moment they were ours. After the guns were captured, General Custer came up, armed only with his riding whip, compelling many a man to surrender at discretion. Captain Mitchel ordered a rebel to help limber up the guns. He replied with perfect coolness that he was not going to help the Yankees capture their guns. He again received the order and again refused. Mitchel then drew his sabre and said : "Now do as you are ordered." This final pointed argument prevailed, and the rebel said : "Well, if I must, I suppose I must."

Perhaps the incident contains a moral. Captain Mitchel then rallied the men and charged through the town, which in a few minutes was ours also. We would have captured a train of cars loaded mainly with contrabands, but General Custer's flank movement was delayed by a deep and almost impassable ravine. At one point Captains Hasty and Mitchel fought the enemy, they having five to our one. After taking Culpeper, we drove the enemy till night—Kilpatrick's division encamped on Stony Mountain, on the extreme left. We had a hospital at Brandy Station and Culpeper. While at the latter place, Doctor Hackley, the Division Surgeon, requested him to find some bed-ticking, if possible, for the wounded. I was fortunate enough to discover within twenty yards of the hospital a lot of stuffed mattresses and ticking, and abundant provisions for the hospital. It was a rebel storehouse, a sort of sanitary commission. A young lady in town had her leg taken off by a shell. I saw two ladies on the porch of one house that had four or five shells through it. In one house off to the left both father and son were killed by a shell. Kilpatrick said our regiment never did so well before, which is saying a great deal. Colonel Karhouse, who commands the regiment, manœuvred it ably. Colonel Davies handled his brigade splendidly, as all remarked, and as the result proved.

We encamped at night on Stony Mountain, in a drenching shower of rain, and slept soundly on the wet ground. Doctor Kingston, our surgeon, showed himself a brave and skilful man, and our wounded got the best of attention.

A REBEL NARRATIVE.

RICHMOND, Sept. 14, 1863.

The following is an accurate statement of what transpired in Culpeper. About three o'clock on Sunday morning information was conveyed to the cavalry that the enemy were preparing to cross at Stark's Ford, some eight miles above our forces, and at Kelly's some five miles below them; and that they would no doubt be coöperated with by the corps of the enemy, which for some time past has been encamped on this side of the Rappahannock River, at the railroad bridge. The wagons were at once packed and sent to the rear, and the horses were ordered to be saddled, and the men were bidden to prepare for any emergency. At daybreak, Brigadier-General Lomax, in command of Jones's old brigade, now his own, and W. H. F. Lee's, under Colonel Beale, of the Ninth Virginia cavalry, moved at once to the front and found all quiet. Some hours later, couriers brought information that the enemy were crossing at Stark's Ford, with six hundred cavalry and artillery, and were advancing on Culpeper Court-House, by the Ridgeville road, and were driving in the pickets there stationed. The Seventh and Twelfth regiments Virginia cavalry were immediately sent forward to strengthen the picket on this road. Major Flournoy at this time held the front with the Sixth regiment and a squadron of sharp-shooters from the Ninth Virginia cavalry. About ten o'clock, Major Flournoy fell back to Brandy Station, and shortly thereafter Captain Moorman's artillery opened fire on the enemy from this point. Just then General Lomax received information that the enemy had crossed at Kelly's a large force of cavalry, artillery, and infantry, and were advancing on the Stevensburgh and Brandy roads. A very short time after this a sharp carbine fire announced their arrival at Brandy. Major Flournoy fell back rapidly, contesting every hill, and only giving way when in danger of being outflanked. The Thirteenth Virginia cavalry, supported by squadrons of the Ninth, was now thrown forward to the left of the railroad in Botts's (formerly J. A. Beckham's) woods. The Fifteenth Virginia cavalry was thrown forward to the right of the railroad in same woods. Six regiments of the enemy were now deployed in a field near Brandy, with two batteries of artillery. The infantry of the enemy were massed behind the cavalry and the timber. Of course our men were compelled to again give back. Another stand was made by our forces on the ground where the infantry first became engaged during Hampton's fight on the first of August, and here a severe fight took place, in which artillery, musketry, and carbines were freely used. At this time it was discovered that a column of at least two brigades of cavalry were moving on our right flank by way of Stevensburgh toward Culpeper Court-House. While the artillery on the left showed that the enemy, who were moving on the Rixeyville road, were nearly at the Court-House, our forces, of course, were compelled again to give back, and this time the Court-House fell into the hands of the enemy. In the fight made at this point, Colonel Beale, Ninth Virginia, was wounded slightly in the leg. At this time a train of cars was at the Court-House bringing off the plunder of our people. This was fired upon some three or four times, and though the shells exploded just above the cars, scattering the fragments over them, yet no damage was done. One shell passed into the house of Mr. Thomas Hill and exploded, but did no damage. I am told that nearly every thing was removed from the depot at Culpeper Court-House, though I hear that we lost some four or five boxes of saddles, eight boxes of ammunition, and forty sacks of corn. The excitement and confusion at Culpeper Court-House is said to have been very great and very striking. Women were shrieking, soldiers were groaning with their wounds, and children were crying from fright, and the death-shots hissing from afar were howling and screeching over the town. At last accounts the enemy had not advanced more than two miles out from Culpeper Court-House. The roar of artillery continued, however, until four o'clock, when it ceased.

I can get nothing definite as to our losses, save that we lost three pieces of Stuart's horse artillery yesterday evening.

LATER.—After the enemy obtained possession of Culpeper Court-House, on Sunday, our forces made a stand about one and a half miles this side. Whilst engaged at this point, the Ninth Virginia cavalry made a bold and dashing charge, going right up to the Court-House. In this charge they captured some twenty-one prisoners. The aim of the enemy was a surprise, and, by inclosing us, to capture our forces. In this they were most signally disappointed. The artillery (three pieces) which we lost were captured as we were retiring through the Court-House. The fifteenth Virginia made three gallant charges in the fight which occurred after leaving the Court-House, and which was decidedly the hottest of the day. In this fight, Colonel Beale having been wounded, Major Waller, of the Ninth, commanded W. H. F. Lee's brigade, and handled it with great ability. Our men were finally compelled to give back before superior numbers, and retired upon Cedar Run, fighting as they receded. The enemy advanced during the night as far as Rapidan bridge, on the railroad, and threw a column down as low as Raccoon Ford. Yesterday

(Monday) morning picket fighting began early, and was continued by the dismounted cavalry acting as sharp-shooters. In the evening there was a sharp artillery duel at Sommerville Ford, between a battery of the enemy and one of Colonel Carter's battalion of artillery, in which our loss was three killed and ten or fifteen wounded. Our fire is believed to have been very destructive to the enemy. At Rapidan bridge, about four o'clock, Beckham's horse artillery opened upon the enemy, doing good execution on their squadrons, which were carefully massed behind the declivity of a hill. Toward night, Major Flournoy, with the Sixth Virginia cavalry, was ordered to make a demonstration on the enemy, but no orders were given him to fight them. Major Flournoy formed his regiment and darted off. In a short time he had charged them three times most gallantly, driving before him a whole brigade of the enemy and capturing five prisoners, and but for the hour being late and near dark, and our own artillery playing upon our men by mistake as they advanced, a large number of prisoners would have been secured. I am satisfied that our cavalry fought well in this last fight, but they could do nothing, because of the vastly superior force which they had to confront. We must have lost at least seventy-five prisoners, from all accounts, and not over fifty in killed and wounded.

Doc. 170.

SKIRMISH NEAR SMITHFIELD, VA.

A NATIONAL ACCOUNT.

MARTINSBURGH, VA., Sept. 15, 1863.

LAST night at nine o'clock, a detachment of fifty men from the First New-York, and another of the same number from the Twelfth Pennsylvania cavalry, commanded by Lieutenant D. A. Irwin, were ordered out on scout, the whole under command of Captain Jones, First New-York. They proceeded to Charlestown and bivouacked for the night. At seven o'clock next morning marched to Summit's Point, and hearing of a force of the enemy in the vicinity of Smithfield, advanced on that place.

When within three miles of the town they overtook one of the enemy's scouting parties, and at once gave chase. They pursued them to the town, where the retreating "rebs" were reënforced by a detachment of the Twelfth Virginia rebel cavalry, who made a desperate charge upon a portion of our forces, when a sharp skirmish ensued, in which Captain Jones, commanding, was wounded in the hand and taken prisoner; also, a number of prisoners were captured by us. After the first charge the "rebs" rallied and attempted to come in upon four sides, but were handsomely met and repulsed at all points by detachments under Captain Bailey, Lieutenants Poindexter and Vermilyea, First Michigan, and Lieutenant D. A. Irwin, of the Twelfth Pennsylvania.

The fight, which lasted about two hours, was a complete succession of charges, and of captures and recaptures by both parties, one of the most important of which was the recapture of the gallant Captain Jones, together with the four men who were his captors, by Sergeant Thompson, First New-York, Corporal Casley, and private Amos Parks, Twelfth Pennsylvania, allowing the Captain an interview of not more than ten minutes with the chivalry, scarcely time enough to receive from them the congratulations due an officer of his rank upon so auspicious an occasion. After repulsing the enemy a number of times they were driven out of the town, and beat a hasty retreat toward Winchester, hotly pursued by our forces to within a few miles of that place.

Lieutenant D. A. Irwin, Twelfth Pennsylvania cavalry, is spoken of in the most flattering terms by Captain Jones for his gallantry and coolness, and the skill displayed in handling his men during the engagement. Both Captains Jones, Bailey, and Lieutenant Irwin are universally acknowledged to be a noble trio. No more gallant and efficient officers ever wielded a sabre in their country's defence than they.

Our casualties were two men wounded. Logonrock, company B, Twelfth Pennsylvania, dangerously, and one man of the First New-York, in leg, slightly. The enemy's loss in killed and wounded unknown. We captured ten prisoners, including two officers.

Doc. 171.

PRESIDENT LINCOLN'S PROCLAMATION.

SUSPENSION OF THE HABEAS CORPUS IN CERTAIN CASES.

By the President of the United States.

A PROCLAMATION.

WHEREAS, The Constitution of the United States has ordained that "The privilege of the writ of *habeas corpus* shall not be suspended, unless, when in cases of rebellion or invasion, the public safety may require it; and, whereas, a rebellion was existing on the third day of March, 1863, which rebellion is still existing; and, whereas, by a statute which was approved on that day, it was enacted by the Senate and House of Representatives of the United States, in Congress assembled, that during the present insurrection the President of the United States, whenever, in his judgment, the public safety may require, is authorized to suspend the privilege of the writ of *habeas corpus* in any case throughout the United States or any part thereof; and, whereas, in the judgment of the President the public safety does require that the privilege of the said writ shall now be suspended throughout the United States in cases where, by the authority of the President of the United States, military, naval, and civil officers of the United States, or any of them, hold persons under their command or in their custody, either as prisoners of war, spies or aiders or abettors of the enemy, or officers, soldiers, or seamen enrolled, drafted, or mustered or enlisted in or belonging to the land or naval forces of the United States, or as deserters therefrom, or otherwise amenable to military law, or to the rules and articles of war, or the rules and regulations prescribed for the military or naval services by the authority of the President of the United States, or for resisting a draft, or for any other offence against the military or naval service; now, therefore, I, Abraham Lincoln, President of the United States, do hereby proclaim and make known to all whom it may concern, that the privilege of the writ of *habeas corpus* is suspended throughout the United States, in the several cases before mentioned, and that this suspension will continue throughout the duration of the said rebellion, or until this Proclamation shall, by a subsequent one, to be issued by the President of the United States, be modified and revoked. And I do hereby require all magistrates, attorneys, and other civil officers within the United States, and all officers and others in the military and naval services of the United States, to take distinct notice of this suspension and give it full effect, and all citizens of the United States to conduct and govern themselves accordingly, and in conformity with the Constitution of the United States, and the laws of Congress in such cases made and provided.

In testimony whereof, I have hereunto set my hand and caused the seal of the United States to be affixed, this fifteenth day of September, in the year of our Lord one thousand eight hundred and sixty-three, and of the independence of the United States of America the eighty-eighth.   ABRAHAM LINCOLN.

By the President:
    WM. H. SEWARD, Secretary of State.

MARTIAL LAW IN MISSOURI.

HEADQUARTERS DEPARTMENT OF THE MISSOURI,
ST. LOUIS, Mo., September 17, 1863.

The Proclamation of the President, dated Washington, September fifteenth, 1863, suspending the privilege of the writ of *habeas corpus* in cases of persons belonging to the land and naval forces of the United States, and other persons therein described, will be held to apply to all Missouri militia called into active service under the orders of the department commander.

Hereafter martial law will be rigidly enforced throughout this department against all persons who shall in any manner encourage mutiny, insubordination, or disorderly conduct, or endeavor to create disaffection among troops, and against all persons who shall publish, or utter publicly, words calculated to excite insurrection or lawless acts among the people, or who shall publish falsehoods or misrepresentations of facts calculated to embarrass or weaken the military authorities, or in any manner to interfere with them in the discharge of their duties.

Any person guilty of either of the offences above mentioned shall be punished by fine and imprisonment, at the discretion of a military commission, and any newspaper which shall contain publications in violation of this order will be suppressed.

Special attention is called to paragraph two hundred and twenty, Revised Army Regulations, which will hereafter be strictly enforced.

By command of Major-General SCHOFIELD.
    J. A. CAMPBELL,
        Assistant Adjutant-General.

Doc. 172.

MESSAGE OF GOVERNOR BONHAM.

EXECUTIVE DEPARTMENT, COLUMBIA, S. C., Sept. 21, 1863.

Gentlemen of the Senate and House of Representatives:

THE day of your annual meeting is so near at hand that I should not have convoked you again in extra session but for what I deem a pressing emergency, admitting of no delay. The progress of the war for the last few months has not been favorable to our arms. The brilliant repulse of the enemy's iron-clad fleet, on the seventh of April last, in Charleston Harbor, has been succeeded by the fall of Vicksburgh and Port Hudson, our retirement from Pennsylvania, Maryland, and Tennessee, and also by our evacuation of Morris's Island, but not without a stubborn resistance by the brave garrisons of Wagner and Gregg, under a fire from naval and land batteries such as no works have ever before withstood. Fort Sumter still holds out with an infantry garrison, which has recently achieved a brilliant success. Her noble ruins afford the best proofs of the indomitable courage of the officers and men of the First South-Carolina artillery. Our malignant foe is now erecting on Morris's Island powerful batteries of Parrott guns, and repairing his damaged fleet, preparatory to another and more determined attack upon our harbor outposts, whilst his land forces are being increased with the hope, possibly, of carrying Charleston in a combined attack by land and sea. The call of the President for five thousand troops for six months' service within the State, beginning the first of August last, has been promptly responded to, with the exception of five companies, now in process of organization. This requisition and the enforcement of the Conscription Act to forty-five, embracing almost the entire population between the ages of forty and fifty, so impairs the efficiency of our militia organization that I find it impracticable to obtain readily a force adequate to such emergencies as seem likely now soon to be upon us. To meet those emergencies I have endeavored, under your late act and the act of 1841, to raise a volunteer force of one mounted regiment, two companies of cavalry, and one battery of artillery, for service wherever in the State they may be needed. This force has not been so promptly raised as the occasion requires, and I have therefore felt it my duty to again convene your bodies, and to recommend to you that you devise such a plan as in your wisdom may seem expedient for furnishing, for immediate service, a military force of at least two regiments of infantry, one of which should be mounted, and a proportionate force of cavalry and artillery. Also, that the law be so amended as to place in some military organization for the defence of the State every able-bodied citizen between the ages of sixteen and sixty not in the confederate service or otherwise legally exempted. The immediate danger to be apprehended arises from raiding parties of the enemy, who may dash suddenly into the State from Tennessee, through Upper Georgia or the passes of the mountains of North and South-Carolina. Should the enemy in large force attempt invasion from these sections, the confederate government will, no doubt, afford adequate protection. But to repel raids and protect our firesides, the State herself should make preparation. The persons to compose the organizations should be the able-bodied citizens between sixteen and sixty years of age not in the confederate service or otherwise legally exempted, and in this class should be embraced all persons who have procured exemptions by furnishing substitutes. No one should be relieved from the duty of defending his home because of having furnished a substitute for the war for confederate service. Aliens who have declared their purpose to become citizens, as also such as are domiciled among us enjoying our laws, should be included. I recommend also that the class of those whose service is limited to the district or regiment in which they reside be reduced to the lowest practicable point consistent with the safe policy of the State. I call your attention to the report of the Adjutant and Inspector-General upon that subject, herewith transmitted.

In connection with the subject of exemptions, I call your attention to my correspondence with the Commandant of conscripts for South-Carolina, Major C. D. Melton, who is the successor of Colonel John S. Preston, with whom, previous to your last extra session, I had a correspondence, a copy of which was then transmitted to you. Another copy, as also a copy of that with Major Melton, is now transmitted. This subject calls for legislation, so as to reconcile, as far as possible, the difference between the laws of the two governments. It is an important question, involving the jurisdiction of the two governments, and needs to be delicately handled. I am satisfied our true policy is as far as is compatible with the constitutional rights of the State, to conform to the law of Congress on this subject. I have not felt at liberty to make any distinction between the classes exempted by our law when the cases have been made, but have claimed the exemption of all alike. The action of the Executive Council, on the same subject, and the action of your two Houses, at your last session, (the House approving and the Senate by its silence acquiescing in my action,) made it proper that I should reply to Major Melton as I had done to Colonel Preston.

Additional legislation is needed to enable the Executive, through civil or military authority, or both, more effectually to aid the confederate government in arresting deserters from the army. In most cases the absentees have probably not left their commands with the intent to desert their colors; but the result of their absence is the same, so far as the good of the service and protection of the country are concerned. I have endeavored, so far as I was authorized, to afford assistance; but the law is inadequate to such efficient aid as is needed. Many construe your late act on this subject to mean that the sheriffs are not to render aid to the enrolling-officer till resistance has been made. In all such cases the deserter, of course, makes his escape. Such law as you may think proper to pass should embrace deserters from State service, and should also punish aiding and abetting deserters in escaping from the army and in resisting and avoiding arrest.

I invite your attention to the operation of the system of impressment adopted by the confederate government. I am informed that in some sections where the people have little more than is absolutely necessary for their own use, it is apprehended that destitution will be brought about by its unequal operation. Coming, as you do, from every section of the State, you are doubtless better informed upon this subject than myself, and better prepared to adopt a judicious policy than I am now to suggest it. I have called the attention of the confederate government to the subject, and suggested to them the probability that the collection of the tax in kind, which operates more equally on all, would obviate the necessity for the impressment of provisions.

The system adopted for furnishing labor for the coast defences has failed to accomplish its purpose. Large numbers have availed themselves of the provisions of the law, and paid one dollar and fifty cents instead of furnishing the labor; and others, with the hope of impunity, have neither furnished the labor nor paid the fine. With the money collected by the agent he has been unable to hire any labor. I recommend an amendment of the acts on this subject, so as to abolish the fine, and so as to authorize the Governor, through the Commissioners of Roads, (who in the main are true to their trusts,) to impress the labor requisite to enable him to respond to the calls of the Commanding General, giving credit for all labor previously furnished, and that the time of service be extended to two months. The free negroes should be included. I doubt not that there has been cause for the complaint heretofore made as to the treatment and detention of the negroes; but it is believed that, through the instrumentality of the energetic State Agent, (whose report is herewith transmitted,) many of the evils have been remedied.

M. L. BONHAM.

Doc. 173.

BATTLE AT BLOUNTVILLE, TENN.

CINCINNATI COMMERCIAL ACCOUNT.

CARTER'S STATION, TENN., Sept. 25, 1863.

THIS army has been continually on the move, and thus far have driven the rebel hordes out of East-Tennessee. The last remnant, under Gen eral Sam Jones—Mudwall Jackson, who wears not the mantle of Stonewall—and Cerro Gordo Williams, fortified Zollicoffer and Carter's, in order, as they said, to make a stand, and drive the Yankee horde back. But, alas for poor rebs! they knew not the metal they were contending with.

On the twelfth instant, Colonel Foster, Sixty-fifth Indiana Mounted infantry, commanding Second brigade of Shackelford's division, moved up toward Bristol, and got in the rear of the rebels, and burned two railroad bridges. The rebels moved out to meet him, but our forces drove them back and held possession of the town. Night coming on, the rebels retired within their works. Our loss in this engagement amounted to two killed, one mortally wounded, and four slightly wounded, while the rebels lost twenty killed and thirty-five wounded.

On the fourteenth the Third brigade, Colonel Carter commanding, was ordered to the front, and proceeded as far as Jonesboro, where he learned that the rebels intended to make a stand. More or less skirmishing ensued for the two or three days following.

General Shackelford arrived at Haynesville, (the residence of the rebel senator from this State, who, like all the chivalry, took to his heels,) on Monday morning at daylight, and took command of all the troops in the field. The rebels opened on our advance with their artillery, doing but little damage, our loss amounting to one man killed and one wounded. The rebels left four dead in our lines and two wounded, one of them a Captain. We captured about thirty prisoners. On the morning of the twenty-second, Tuesday, General Burnside arrived, and demanded the surrender of Carter. They refused. In the mean time Colonel Foster, who was still in the rear of the rebels, was ordered to attack them that afternoon. He did so. The rebels took their position in the town of Blountville. Colonel Foster sent a flag of truce, asking them to retire from the town, as he did not wish to destroy it. The citizens also remonstrated with their rebel friends, but without avail. They had sent the flower of their army to meet the fighting men of the fighting division—Georgia's gallant sons, who never ran.

Colonel Foster opened fire at one o'clock, and the fight lasted until dusk, when Georgia's sons, who never ran, broke and retreated like a quarter-horse, leaving one piece of artillery, twenty-four pounder, and sixty-nine prisoners, in the hands of our boys.

The rebel General Jones had picked the fresh troops, (he had Georgians,) for the purpose of driving back Foster's brigade, but met with a sad and sure defeat.

Our loss was five killed and twelve wounded, while the rebel loss was thirty killed and fifty-six wounded.

Colonel Carter's Third brigade was closely pushing the rebels on the west of Carter's Station, and succeeded in driving them into their works at Carter's, which, under cover of the

night, they evacuated, taking off their artillery, and leaving the gun-carriages and caissons in the fortifications. Most of the North-Carolina troops took to the mountains, while others returned to their homes, perfectly satisfied that they have been grossly humbugged and have at last found their rights!

General Shackelford's division has been constantly on the move since their arrival in East-Tennessee, the Second and Third brigades being on the east end of the road, (East-Tennessee and Virginia Railroad;) Colonel Bird, with the First brigade, was on the west end supporting General Rosecrans. The men are subjected to a great deal of hard work, but do it most cheerfully. General Burnside is daily gaining popularity with the people of East-Tennessee, as well as endearing himself to the soldiers. While he says but little, he knows who does the work.

General Shackelford, one of the best officers in the service, always at his post late and early, is universally liked by both officers and men. I predict for the General ere long another star.

Movements are now going on, and you will hear from this army ere long.   DELTA.

INDIANAPOLIS JOURNAL ACCOUNT.

IN CAMP NEAR KNOXVILLE, TENN., }
September 29, 1863.   }

Last Tuesday, the day of the battle, was clear and pleasant. The Second brigade, commanded by Colonel Foster, left camp early in the morning, to march fifteen miles and attack the enemy, who, it was reported, had made a stand at Blountville, Tennessee. All ready and eager to hear the roaring of the cannon, the brigade gayly wound its way through the woods and over the rough and dusty roads of East-Tennessee. Near the middle of the forenoon, we came upon the enemy's pickets. These gentlemen, thinking prudence the better part of valor, took to their heels and made their escape. A little further on a small portion of the chivalrous Southern soldiers, like a set of barbarous savages, had concealed themselves behind logs and trees to dispute our way. The Fifth Indiana cavalry, ever ready to take the front if called upon, entered the timber on the right and left to hunt these brave soldiers and drive them from their dens. Bushwhacking seemed to be the order of the day. For ten miles we made our way through the corn-fields and woods, with a flanking party on each side to prevent surprise, expecting every moment to come upon the secreted foe in force. As fast as our brigade advanced the bushwhackers retreated, covering their retreat by firing upon the "Yankees" from behind every hill and wood.

At two o'clock in the afternoon we came in sight of the town. Lieutenant Dumont, in command of the artillery, was ordered to the front. He took a position and opened upon the enemy with shells. The hills and woods echoed and re-echoed with the sound of the roaring cannon, until the last shell in the caisson was shot. At four o'clock the Sixty-fifth Indiana was sent out on the right to act as sharp-shooters, and flank the enemy. In half an hour the quick and continuous firing of their heavy rifles told plainly that they were hotly engaged. Lieutenant Colvin was then ordered forward with his battery, and did good execution. Company C, Captain Smith, and company I, Captain Morse, Fifth Indiana, were ordered by Colonel Foster to charge on a detachment of the enemy who were supporting their battery. The frightened rebs, seeing three columns moving upon them—the Sixty-fifth on the right, Colonel Butler leading the Fifth cavalry in the centre, the Eighth Tennessee on the left—gave up in despair, and, panic-stricken, left in hurried confusion. Our brave boys, seeing the enemy give way, raised a shout, put spurs to their horses and made chase. Colonel Butler charged on after them, capturing one twenty-four pound gun and one wagon. The gun was taken by Orderly St. John, company H, with a small squad of men. The charge through the town was perhaps the most exciting part of the battle. The sun had set far in the west, behind the column. The town in front was already on fire, and mostly consumed, from the rebel shells. The Sixty-fifth Indiana, on the right, was sharply engaging the enemy. Companies C and D, on the left, were driving the rebels out of the corn-field back to their guns, when our men dashed on through the smoky streets, with burning timbers and columns of blaze on both sides. The shout of victory was soon raised, and our never-flinching soldiers, who had been exposed from nine o'clock in the morning to the firing of a secreted enemy, now felt that they were reaping a full harvest in seeing the enemy completely whipped and themselves the victorious party. Great praise is due to each commander of the three regiments and two batteries engaged in the battle, and the men have the real Spartan metal in them.

The result of the battle is as follows: Rebel loss fifteen killed, fifty wounded, and one hundred taken prisoners. Our loss was five killed and twenty-two wounded. Only one killed in the Fifth Indiana cavalry—John W. Johnson, saddler in company C. We camped on the ground occupied by the enemy that night and the next day, when we took up our line of march for this place.

Since entering Knoxville, on the first of September, our regiment has been to Sevierville, nearly to the top of Smoky Mountains, N. C., to Greenville, to Bristol, Va., to Zollicoffer, where we had a sharp fight, killing fifty and wounding one hundred. We had a short skirmish also at Bristol, where we had five men wounded and none killed.

We are now at Knoxville, waiting further orders. Our horses are jaded and our men tired, but at the sound of the bugle will all jump, give one whoop and start off to win new laurels, and hasten the time when we can all return to our homes again. FIFTH CAVALRY.

Doc. 174.

JEFFERSON DAVIS AND POPE PIUS IX.

RICHMOND, September 23, 1863.

VERY VENERABLE SOVEREIGN PONTIFF: The letters which you have written to the clergy of New-Orleans and New-York have been communicated to me, and I have read with emotion the deep grief therein expressed for the ruin and devastation caused by the war which is now being waged by the United States against the States and people which have selected me as their President, and your orders to your clergy to exhort the people to peace and charity. I am deeply sensible of the Christian charity which has impelled you to this reiterated appeal to the clergy. It is for this reason that I feel it my duty to express personally, and in the name of the Confederate States, our gratitude for such sentiments of Christian good feeling and love, and to assure your Holiness that the people, threatened even on their own hearths with the most cruel oppression and terrible carnage, are desirous now, as they have always been, to see the end of this impious war; that we have addressed prayers to heaven for that issue which your Holiness now desires; that we desire none of our enemy's possessions, but that we fight merely to resist the devastation of our country and the shedding of our best blood, and to force them to let us live in peace under the protection of our own institutions and under our laws, which not only insure to every one the enjoyment of his temporal rights, but also the free exercise of his religion. I pray your Holiness to accept, on the part of myself and the people of the Confederate States, our sincere thanks for your efforts in favor of peace. May the Lord preserve the days of your Holiness and keep you under his divine protection.

JEFFERSON DAVIS.

REPLY OF THE POPE.

ILLUSTRIOUS AND HONORABLE PRESIDENT: Salutation. We have just received, with all suitable welcome, the persons sent by you to place in our hands your letter, dated twenty-third of September last. Not slight was the pleasure we experienced when we learned, from these persons and the letter, with what feelings of joy and gratitude you were animated, illustrious and honorable President, as soon as you were informed of our letters to our venerable brothers, John, Archbishop of New-York, and John, Archbishop of New-Orleans, dated the eighteenth of October of last year, and in which we have, with all our strength, excited and exhorted these venerable brothers that in their episcopal piety and solicitude they should endeavor, with the most ardent zeal, and in our name, to bring about the end of the fatal civil war which has broken out in those countries, in order that the American people may obtain peace and concord, and dwell charitably together. It is particularly agreeable to us to see that you, illustrious and honorable President, and your people, are animated with the same desires of peace and tranquillity which we have in our letters inculcated upon our venerable brothers. May it please God at the same time to make the other peoples of America and their rulers, reflecting seriously how terrible is civil war, and what calamities it engenders, listen to the inspirations of a calmer spirit, and adopt resolutely the part of peace. As for us, we shall not cease to offer up the most fervent prayers to God Almighty that he may pour out upon all the peoples of America the spirit of peace and charity, and that he will stop the great evils which afflict them. We, at the same time, beseech the God of mercy and pity to shed abroad upon you the light of his grace, and attach you to us by a perfect friendship.

Given at Rome, at St. Peter's, the third of December, in the year of our Lord 1863, of our Pontificate 18. PIUS IX.

Doc. 175.

PROCLAMATION OF PRESIDENT LINCOLN.

RAISING OF THE BLOCKADE OF THE PORT OF ALEXANDRIA, VIRGINIA.

By the President of the United States.

A PROCLAMATION.

WHEREAS, in my Proclamation of the twenty-seventh of April, 1861, the ports of the States of Virginia and North-Carolina were for reasons therein set forth, placed under blockade; and, whereas, the port of Alexandria, Virginia, has since been blockaded, but as the blockade of that port may now be safely relaxed, with advantage to the interests of commerce; now, therefore, be it known that I, Abraham Lincoln, President of the United States, pursuant to the authority in me vested by the fifth section of the Act of Congress, approved on the thirteenth of July, 1861, entitled "An Act further to provide for the collection of duties on imports, and for other purposes," do hereby declare that the blockade of the said port of Alexandria shall so far cease and determine from and after this date; that commercial intercourse with the said port, except as to persons, things, and information, contraband of war, may from this date be carried on, subject to the laws of the United States, and to the limitations, and in pursuance of the regulations which are prescribed by the Secretary of the Treasury, in his order, which is appended to my proclamation of the tenth of May, 1862.

In witness whereof, I have hereunto set my hand and caused the seal of the United States to be affixed. Done at the city of Washington, this twenty-fourth day of September, in the year of our Lord 1862, and of the independence of the United States the eighty-third.

ABRAHAM LINCOLN.

By the President:
WILLIAM H. SEWARD,
Secretary of State.

Doc. 176.

GENERAL BANKS'S ORDER.

HEADQUARTERS DEPARTMENT OF THE GULF,
NEW-ORLEANS, September 28, 1863.

GENERAL ORDERS, No. 70:

I. The heroic efforts of the army of the United States have reëstablished the free navigation of the Mississippi and its tributaries. The vindication of the freedom of these waters by the iron hand of war against a confederation of rebel States is an event of equal import with their discovery and settlement, and makes the Union a nation. It is a baptism of blood. In a brief period of time this vast and fertile valley will be opened to the peaceful commerce of the world.

Notwithstanding the ravages of war, the destruction of property, the dispersion of laborers, and the decimation of population, the inhabitable globe does not offer a nobler theatre for intelligent enterprise than the valley of the Mississippi. The cultivation of new products, the application of new elements and different systems of labor, the immediate reörganization of local governments, and the resistless energy of many millions of freemen, will create individual and national wealth, such as the world has never seen. Never was a country better worth fighting for, better worth defending.

The highest duty of the people is to maintain and defend the freedom of the Mississippi, upon which depends the support of the present and the hope of the future. The Government is entitled to the armed assistance of all those who claim the right of citizens or seek to share their privileges. Those who covet the profits of trade, disclaiming citizenship and acknowledging allegiance to foreign nations only, remain here by permission and favor, and not of right.

In the performance of this duty, and to assist in maintaining the important advantages secured by a free communication between the valley of the Mississippi and the markets of the world, the citizens of the First and Second Congressional Districts of Louisiana, liable to military duty, have been enrolled for general military service, in accordance with the provisions of the law of conscription, passed by Congress, so far as it may be applicable to this Department. Proper publication will be hereafter made of the number of troops required for this purpose, and the time and manner of their selection. The conscription will not be held to embrace those well-disposed persons who, in the event of capture by the enemy, would not be entitled to the full immunity of soldiers of the United States.

II. The organization of one or more volunteer regiments, to be designated "The Louisiana Volunteers," whose services will be limited by the term of enlistment, to the protection and defence of New-Orleans, is hereby authorized. Volunteers for this service will receive a bounty of one hundred dollars, twenty-five dollars of which and one month's pay will be advanced when the volunteer is mustered into service for the war. Captain C. W. Killborn, Provost-Marshal of the city of New-Orleans, is charged with the immediate organization and command of the first regiment; Captain R. B. Brown, Provost-Marshal of the parish of Jefferson, is authorized to organize and command the second regiment. The first regiment will be recruited and organized in the city of New-Orleans, excepting the Fourth District, and the second within the limits of the parish of Jefferson, and the Fourth District of New-Orleans.

III. Able-bodied men of color between the ages of twenty and thirty years, employed upon Government or on private plantations, will be detailed for military service in the Corps d'Afrique, upon order of the Commission of Enrolment. No officer or other person is allowed to recruit men for any special regiment of that corps; and every officer recruiting for this corps under this order will be furnished with, and required to exhibit, authority for his acts, signed by the Superintendent of Recruiting, and approved by the Commission of Enrolments. Substitutes will be received in cases where the labor of the recruit is specially required, and exemptions allowed in cases of necessity, upon application to the Commission of Enrolment, but by no other person or authority. Arrangements will be made to secure the crops of the season, and laborers will be furnished as far as practicable to supply the vacancies occasioned by the execution of this order. The first duty of those engaged in the cultivation of the soil is to protect it from invasion, and those whose interests are inconsistent with a vigorous defence of the Department, or who are indifferent to the invasions of a public enemy, can have no rights which the Government is bound to respect.

By command of Major-General BANKS.

G. NORMAN LIEBER,

A. A. A. General.

Doc. 177.

FIGHT AT MORGANZIA, LA.

HEADQUARTERS SECOND DIVISION, THIRTEENTH
ARMY CORPS, MORGANZIA, LA., Sept. 30, 1863.

SINCE the occupation of Morganzia by our forces, an outpost, consisting of the Twenty-sixth Indiana, Nineteenth Iowa, and about one hundred and fifty cavalry, under Major Montgomery, has been established some nine or ten miles from this place, in the direction of the Atchafalaya, under the command of Colonel Leake. The cavalry had been posted about two miles in advance of the infantry, with instructions to advance daily and skirmish with the rebels across the Atchafalaya. The object of this post was simply to hold the rebels in check.

Yesterday about four thousand five hundred of the enemy, commanded by General Green in person, crossed the Atchafalaya. They then divided into three detachments, and advanced on both flanks of Colonel Leake and the front of Major Montgomery. After skirmishing some time with the Major, they brought a piece of ar-

tillery against him and compelled him to fall back. He attempted to join Colonel Leake, but was unable. After considerable skirmishing, he succeeded in cutting his way out, with a loss of five men. About the same time that Major Montgomery was attacked the enemy engaged both flanks of Colonel Leake. The forces under Colonel Leake were taken completely by surprise, the enemy having advanced within one hundred yards and opened upon them before they were aware of their presence. Both regiments immediately formed into line of battle, and the engagement soon became general. Against overwhelming odds this little detachment obstinately contested every foot of ground. The enemy, for some unknown reason, did not use any of their artillery against our infantry; but not so with us; for, charged as heavily as they were with grape and canister, they did frightful execution. After two gallant charges, in which many of our bravest men fell, our forces fell back behind a levee near by. Here the enemy pressed us so closely that our line became broken, and every man fought for himself.

Just as our men were beginning to recover themselves, the third detachment, which had engaged Major Montgomery, appeared in our rear, and the whole of the enemy closed upon our force, thus completely surrounding them. It was impossible for our men to stand the galling fire which was poured into them from every side, and rather than surrender, the order was given for every man to save himself as best he could. They were not slow in taking the hint, and broke for the bushes. A portion of them succeeded in escaping; but the majority were taken prisoners. Among the latter were Colonel Leake, reported wounded, and Lieutenant-Colonel Rose.

This short but furious engagement lasted about two hours, and for the fierceness with which it raged, in proportion with the forces engaged, has never been equalled. From the obstinacy which the superior force of the enemy encountered, they estimated our force to be at least two thousand, when in reality it was but a little over five hundred. This report is corroborated by a number of persons who participated in the engagement, but were afterward captured. Our whole loss will not fall short of four hundred in killed, wounded, and taken prisoners, and two pieces of artillery.

ANOTHER ACCOUNT.

MORGANZIA'S LANDING, September 30.

We are still "snooping around" here, as Captain Gray says, with no immediate prospect of getting away, and no great present chance of doing any good. I will tell you why we came here. Nearly a month ago a transport was fired into near this place, which is very favorably located for enterprises of that description, the river being unusually narrow right here. The perpetration of the outrage having been reported to headquarters in New-Orleans, General Herron was forthwith ordered to proceed here with his division; and I suppose he was to stay here and keep the rebels back from the river, as he has done but very little else. On arriving at this place, which is twenty-five miles above Port Hudson, and thirty miles below the mouth of the Red River, we landed on the west side, and sent out the Second brigade, (ours is the First,) to feel of the rebels. The brigade started in the morning, taking a road that ran directly back from the river, and soon came upon a small rebel force, which commenced skirmishing and falling back. About ten miles out they turned off on a road that leads to the Atchafalaya (Shafalar) River, and soon entered the timber, which is very dense and effectually conceals every thing twenty rods distant. Here they began to contest our advance more earnestly, and at about nine o'clock our troops found themselves in the midst of darkness, on the bank of the Atchafalaya, in front of a fort of considerable size, and mounting several pieces of artillery—how many they could not tell; so they fell back for the night, and sent back for reenforcements.

The next day we went out, got in sight of the fort, staid over night, and marched back in the morning. It was understood that a rebel force, numbering from seven thousand to twelve thousand, were strongly intrenched on the other side of the Atchafalaya, which is about nine hundred feet wide at that point, with steep banks and very muddy near the water. We had no means of crossing, and they were too strong for us if we had; so General Herron contented himself with sending out a force of about six hundred men, under Lieutenant-Colonel Leake, to act as an army of observation. They were encamped about three miles distant, and were daily employed in skirmishing with rebs, who crossed the river on a small flat-boat. Colonel Leake has been out there about three weeks. Day before yesterday it began to rain a little, and the night following was dark and drizzly.

Under the cover of darkness the rebels crossed over seven regiments of infantry and some cavalry, and marching in a large circle, surrounded our little force, which, after a sharp fight, was captured. Very little is known about the matter, for a certainty, at the present time. I hear that Lieutenant-Colonel Leake is slightly wounded by a ball which killed his horse; but there is no telling as yet, except that it is certain he is wounded and a prisoner, as also is Lieutenant-Colonel Rose, of the Twenty-sixth Indiana.

There was only one man from any company in our regiment out on that duty, the force being mainly composed of the Nineteenth Iowa and Twenty-sixth Indiana, two pieces of artillery, and some cavalry. When the troops were ordered into line, the Thirty-seventh Illinois was ordered out to see what was going on, and the gunboats fairly swarmed here; but the rebels only came over to take Lieutenant-Colonel Leake's command, and having accomplished that, scampered back as fast as possible.

As far as is now known, we sustained a loss of fourteen killed and about forty wounded. No blame can be attached to Lieutenant-Colonel Leake for having been thus surprised. The

place is peculiarly favorable to the performance of such a feat. The camp was surrounded by cane-fields and weeds, which were so thick that a hundred thousand men might be concealed within a mile distance, and you not suspect the presence of a single man. Besides, the Colonel's force was entirely inadequate to guard against a surprise so easy of accomplishment. It is a result that every body here has foretold since he has been out there.

General Herron was relieved by General Dana, and left us just in time to be able to say: "I was not in command at the time." THOMAS.

Doc. 178.

GOVERNMENT OF THE FREEDMEN.

VICKSBURGH, MISS., September 29, 1863.

SPECIAL ORDERS, No. 63:

I. The following regulations for the government of freedmen are announced for the information and government of all concerned.

II. All male negroes, who after examination shall be found capable of bearing arms, will be organized into companies and regiments. All others, including men incapable of bearing arms, women and children, instead of being permitted to remain in camps in idleness, will be required to perform such labor as may be suited to their several conditions, in the several staff departments of the army, on plantations, leased or otherwise, within our lines, as wood-choppers, or in any way that their labor can be made available. For the carrying out these regulations, there will be established a system of general and local supervision.

III. The Quartermaster's Commissary and Medical Department will issue supplies necessary for the care and employment of these people, on the requisition of the properly authorized officers.

IV. All freed people, by whomsoever employed, will be paid for their labor as already ordered, or as hereafter may be determined by the Commanding General of the Department.

V. A tax of ten per cent on all labor rated at six dollars per month, or above, will be deducted from monthly payments and paid to Superintendents by all officers and private individuals employing or having in charge colored laborers, to be expended according to order for providing for the sick and otherwise dependent.

VI. Transportation will be furnished for persons and goods, for the benefit of these people, on Government transports and military railroads within the Department, on the order of the General Superintendent.

VII. Citizens voluntarily laboring for the benefit of these people, saving as they do to the Government cost of labor in providing for their care, will, when properly accredited by the General Superintendent, be entitled to rations, quarters, and transportation on Government transports and military railroads within the Department.

By order of the Secretary of War.

L. THOMAS,
Adjutant-General.

Doc. 179.

OCCUPATION OF FORT SMITH, ARK.

FORT SMITH, ARKANSAS, September 10, 1863.

ONCE more, by the favor of heaven upon the valor of our arms, the Federal authority holds sway at Fort Smith, in Arkansas. The brigade of the Army of the Frontier under Colonel Cloud is in complete possession of this ancient Federal post. General Blunt, with his body-guard and several of his daring scouts, was the first to enter the town and barracks, on Tuesday, September first. At noon, of the same day, the First infantry regiment of Arkansian volunteers, under Colonel J. M. Johnson, filed into the streets and Government inclosure, to the lively music of the regimental band of drums and fifes. It was a glad hour for the Union citizens and our tired and dusty braves who had been on the march for twenty days, making an average during that time of nearly twenty miles per day. We had pursued the rebel hordes under Cooper and Steel for several days, and finally yielded the palm of swift running to the fleeing rebels at Perryville, in the Choctaw nation. Returning thence, we came upon the trail of the rebel chieftain Cabbal and his crew. Within fighting range of this gang, (said to number two thousand five hundred,) we encamped on the night of the thirty-first ult. The enemy's position was a natural fortress on the left bank of Poteau Creek. Here, only three miles from our camp, we expected an encounter the next morning. His camp being on our direct route to Fort Smith, now only ten miles distant, what else could we expect but fierce resistance? But on we went, General Blunt with a portion of his dauntless cavalry leading the way, and lo! no enemy was there. The report is that Cabbal is always braver when drunk than when sober: perhaps on this occasion he was too drunk even to be brave. He, however, left a few sneaking bushwhackers along the road, who fired on our advancing column, and wounded one of our men.

Within a few miles of our destination, Colonel Cloud, with a part of the cavalry and a few pieces of artillery, turned aside in search of the fleeing foe. An encounter ensued on the rugged hill called the Back Bone, in which Colonel Cloud's advanced guard was ambushed, four of his men killed, and seven or eight wounded, with the loss of half a dozen horses. But his men took quick revenge by slaying and wounding some thirty or more of the enemy, and putting the whole cavalcade to a hastier flight than had ever quickened their speed before.

For two years and a half Fort Smith has been a general headquarters of rebellion and treason. Its garrison under Captain Sturgis had been driven away in the spring of 1861. The citizens of the town and of all the surrounding country had been dragooned into subserviency to the hateful confederacy of traitors, headed in Arkansas by such dastards as Rector, Hindman and Company. Few places, perhaps, within the scope of rebellion exhibit more vividly the desolation

VOL. VII.—DOC. 33.

of the secession mania. The town of Fort Smith once flourished, and was growing rapidly in business and wealth. Its present stagnation in industry, and the dilapidations everywhere visible along its streets—the stoppage of the Overland Mail, the destruction of the telegraph, and the utter and total emptiness of its warehouses and storerooms, are the legitimate products of a senseless and fanatic rebellion that has held dominion here ever since the madcaps in convention at Little Rock wrested Arkansas from the beneficent fraternity of the Federal Union. No Federal force had ever been here since the withdrawal of Captain Sturgis, until the entrance of the Army of the Frontier on the first of the present month. No part, therefore, of the destruction of property and business, and destitution and misery of the people, can be charged to the presence of the Federal army. The rebs had it all their own way; and a sorry way it was indeed—calico per yard, five dollars; a pair of coarse shoes, forty dollars; a pair of jean pants, thirty dollars; a pair of boots, one hundred dollars; box of blacking, two dollars and fifty cents; and all other things at the same starvation rates. Such was the reign in Fort Smith of the so-called Confederate States of America.

On our arrival here, Colonel Cloud was placed in command of the post. The Colonel, however, is restive under confinement. He evidently prefers to be on an adventurous dash at the head of his brave Kansians, (Second Kansas cavalry.) He is now out on an important scout.

Colonel J. M. Johnson, of the First Arkansas infantry, is Commander of the post, and his Lieutenant-Colonel, E. J. Searl, is Provost-Marshal. Matters are progressing finely. Hundreds of people have already come in and sworn allegiance to the Government of the United States. Large numbers have volunteered to enter our army. Of these volunteers the First Arkansas infantry regiment is receiving large accessions, because, doubtless, Arkansians prefer to join with the citizens of their own State.   THRIFTON.

Doc. 180.

PURSUIT OF THE GUERRILLAS.

GENERAL EWING'S REPORT.[*]

HEADQUARTERS DISTRICT OF THE BORDER,
KANSAS CITY, MISSOURI, Aug. 31, 1863.

Lieutenant-Colonel C. W. March, A. A. G., Department of the Missouri, St. Louis, Missouri:

SIR: Some commanders of detachments engaged in the pursuit of Quantrell are still out after his scattered forces. In advance of their return, I submit a report of the raid, which in some respects may be deficient, for want of official information from them.

Three or four times this summer the guerrillas have assembled to the number of several hundred, within twenty or thirty miles of the Kansas border. They have threatened alternately

* See Doc. 162, page 495, ante.

Lexington, Independence, Warrensburgh, and Harrisonville; and frequent reports have reached me from scouts and spies that they meant to sack and destroy Shawnee, Olathe, Paola, Mound City, and other towns in Kansas near the eastern border. I placed garrisons in all these Kansas towns, and issued arms and rations to volunteer militia companies there. From trustworthy sources I learned, toward the last of July, that they were threatening a raid on Lawrence; and soon after they commenced assembling on the Sinabar, in the western part of Lafayette county. I at once ordered a company of infantry, which was then coming down from Fort Ripley, to stop at Lawrence, which they did for more than a week, and until after the guerrilla force had been dispersed by a force I sent against them. From this time, though constantly receiving information as to their movements and plans, I could learn nothing of a purpose to make a raid into Kansas. Their forces were again scattered in small predatory bands, and I had all available forces in like manner scattered throughout the Missouri portion of this district, and especially the border counties, besetting their haunts and paths.

Quantrell's whole force was about three hundred men, composed of selected bands from this part of Missouri. About two hundred and fifty were assembled on Blackwater, near the eastern border of this district, at least fifty miles from the Kansas line, on the seventeenth and eighteenth. I am informed by Major Ross, M. S. M., who has been scouting in the south-west part of Saline county, that the rendezvous was there. Lieutenant-Colonel Lazear, commanding two companies of the First Missouri, at Warrensburgh, heard on the morning of the twentieth that this force had passed the day before twelve miles north of him, going west, and moved promptly after them, sending orders to Major Mullins, commanding two companies of the same regiment at Pleasant Hill, to move on them from that point. On the night of the nineteenth, however, Quantrell passed through Chapel Hill to the head of the middle fork of Grand River, eight miles north-west of Harrisonville, and fifteen miles south-east of Aubrey, the nearest station in Kansas. There he was joined on the morning of the twentieth by about fifty men from Grand River and the Osage, and at noon set out for Kansas, passing five miles south of Aubrey at six P.M., going west. Aubrey is thirty-five miles south of Kansas City, and about forty-five miles south-east of Lawrence. Kansas City is somewhat further from Lawrence.

Captain Pike, commanding two companies at Aubrey, received information of the presence of Quantrell on Grand River at half-past five o'clock P.M., of the twentieth. He promptly forwarded the information up and down the line, and to my headquarters; and called in his scouting parties to march upon them. One hour and a half later, he received information that Quantrell had just passed into Kansas. Unhappily, however, instead of setting out at once in pursuit, he remain-

ed at the station, and merely sent information of Quantrell's movements to my headquarters and Captain Coleman, commanding two companies at Little Santa Fé, twelve miles north of the line. Captain Coleman, with near one hundred men, marched at once to Aubrey, and the available force of the two stations, numbering about two hundred men, set out at midnight in pursuit. But Quantrell's path was over the open prairie, and difficult to follow at night, so that our forces gained but little on him. By Captain Pike's error of judgment in failing to follow promptly and closely, the surest means of arresting the terrible blow was thrown away—for Quantrell never would have gone as far as Lawrence, or attacked it, with a hundred men close on his rear.

The first despatch of Captain Pike reached here, thirty-five miles north of Aubrey, at half-past eleven P.M., the second an hour later. Before one o'clock, Major Plumb, my Chief of Staff, at the head of about fifty men, (which was all that could be got here and at Westport,) started southward, and at daylight heard, at Olathe, twenty-five miles from here, that the enemy had passed at midnight through Gardner, eighteen miles from Lawrence, going toward that town. Pushing on, Major Plumb overtook Captains Coleman and Pike, six miles south-east of Lawrence, at half-past ten o'clock, Friday, the twenty-first instant, and by the light of the blazing farm-houses saw that the enemy had got six miles south of Lawrence, on their way out of the State. The enemy were overtaken near Palmyra by Major Plumb's command, to which were there added from fifty to one hundred citizens, who had been hastily assembled, and led in pursuit by General Lane.

By this time the horses of our detachments were almost exhausted. Nearly all were young horses, just issued to the companies, and had marched more than sixty-five miles without rest and without food from the morning of the twentieth. Quantrell had his men mounted on the best horses of the border, and had collected fresh ones going to and at Lawrence, almost enough to remount his command. He skilfully kept over a hundred of his best-mounted and best-trained men in the rear, and often formed line of battle to delay pursuit, and give time and rest to the most wearied of his forces. By the time our scattered soldiers and citizens could get up and form line, the guerrillas' rear-guard would, after a volley, break into column, and move off at a speed which defied pursuit. Thus the chase dragged through the afternoon, over the prairie, generally following no roads or paths, until eight, when Quantrell's rear-guard formed line of battle three miles north of Paola, and twenty miles from where they entered the State. A skirmish ensued, the guerrillas breaking and scattering, so that our forces in the darkness lost the trail, and went into Paola for food and rest, while search was being made for it.

Lieutenant-Colonel Clark, Ninth Kansas volunteers, with headquarters at Coldwater Grove, was in command of the troops on the border south of Little Santa Fé, including the stations at Aubrey, Coldwater Grove, (thirteen miles south of Aubrey,) Rockville, (thirteen miles south of Coldwater Grove,) Choteau's Trading Post, (fifteen miles south of Rockville,) and Harrisonville. There were two companies at each station, but the force out patrolling rarely left fifty men in camp at each post. He received Captain Pike's message as to the gathering of Quantrell's forces on Grand River on the night of the twentieth, and at once sent for the spare troops at Rockville and Trading Post to march up to Coldwater Grove. At three o'clock on the morning of the twenty-first, he received a despatch from Captain Coleman, at Aubrey, saying that Quantrell had crossed into Kansas; and he set out with thirty men, following Quantrell's trail nearly to Gardner, and thence going south to Paola, reaching there at five P.M. With this command, and a force of perhaps fifty citizens, and a part of Captain Beuter's company of the Thirteenth Kansas infantry, which had been garrisoning Paola, he prepared to attack Quantrell at the ford of Bull Creek, three miles south of Paola, toward which he was then retreating. But Quantrell, on coming within four or five miles of that crossing, soon after dark, formed line of battle, as I stated above, broke trail, turned sharp to the north, and dodged and bewildered the force in waiting for him, as well as that in pursuit. These troops at the ford returned to Paola about the time the command which had followed Quantrell reached there. One of the parties in search of the trail found it five miles north of Paola, and reported the fact to Lieutenant-Colonel Clark, who was then ranking officer there, at between one and two o'clock. He was slow in ordering pursuit, which was not renewed until daybreak. He at that time sent Captain Coleman forward, with thirty men of the Ninth Kansas, which he himself had brought to Paola, and forty of the same regiment, which had got there from the Trading Post at about two o'clock that morning, and about seventy militia, chiefly of Linn county. He marched soon after himself with the troops which had followed Quantrell the day before.

Half an hour before Major Plumb started from Kansas City on the night of the twenty-first, Captain Palmer, eleventh Kansas, was sent by him from Westport, with fifty men of his company, down the line to near Aubrey, where he met a messenger from Captain Coleman, directing reënforcements to Spring Hill, at which point he struck Quantrell's trail and followed it to within seven miles of Lawrence. Thence learning that Quantrell had gone south, he turned south-east; and at Lanesfield (Uniontown) was joined by a force about eighty strong, under Major Phillips, composed of detachments of Captain Smith's Company, E. M. M., Captain Killen's Ninth Kansas, and a squad of the Fifth Kansas. This latter force had been collected by Major Thacher at Westport, and despatched from there at noon on Friday the twenty-first, via Lexington, Kansas. The command of Major Phillips, thus increased to one hundred and thirty, pushed south-east from Lanesfield, and struck Quantrell's trail about sunrise, five miles north of Paola, and but a little behind the commands of Coleman and Clark.

Major Thacher, commanding at Westport, when news arrived that Quantrell was returning by way of the Osage Valley, took the rest of the mounted troops on the upper border, (company A, Ninth, and E, Eleventh Kansas, numbering one hundred and twenty men,) and moved down the line. He struck Quantrell's trail below Aubrey, immediately in the rear of Lieutenant-Colonel Clark's command.

Quantrell, when after dark he had baffled his pursuers, stopped to rest five miles north-east of Paoli, and there, after midnight, a squad of Linn county militia, under Captain Pardee, alarmed the camp. He at once moved on, and between that point and the Kansas line his column came within gunshot of the advance of about one hundred and fifty of the Fourth M. S. M., under Lieutenant-Colonel King, which had been ordered from the country of the Little Blue, in Jackson county, down the line to interrupt him. The advance apprised Lieutenant-Colonel King of the approach of another force. Skirmishers were thrown out, but Quantrell, aided by the darkness and the broken character of the prairie, eluded the force and passed on. Lieutenant-Colonel King was unable to find his trail that night.

The pursuing forces thus thrown behind, Quantrell passed out of Kansas and got to the timber of the middle fork of Grand River in Missouri, near his last rendezvous, before starting, about noon of the twenty-second, an hour in advance of the head of the pursuing column. There his force scattered. Many dismounted, or, worn out through fatigue or wounds, sought concealment and safety in the fastnesses of that region. About one hundred moved down Grand River, while the chief part of the force passed north-east toward Chapel Hill. Our forces divided in like manner at that point, Major Plumb and Major Thacher following the main body.

On the twentieth of August I went to Leavenworth on official business. The despatches of Captain Pike were not sent to Leavenworth until eight A.M. on the morning of the twenty-first, because the telegraph offices at Leavenworth City and Fort Leavenworth close at eleven P.M. for want of relief of operators. I received those despatches and the one announcing that Quantrell had passed through Gardner going toward Lawrence, not until quarter to eleven A.M. on the twenty-first. There was no cavalry stationed at Fort Leavenworth, though five companies of the Eleventh Ohio were outfitting for Fort Laramie, but without arms.

There was one company at Leavenworth City just receiving horse equipments. Arms and horse equipments were issued at once, and at one P.M. I started from Fort Leavenworth with near three hundred men of these companies. News reached me at Leavenworth City of the burning of Lawrence, and of the avowed purpose of the rebels to go thence to Topeka. I thought it best to go to De Soto, and thence, after an unavoidable delay of five hours in crossing the Kansas River, to Lanesfield. Finding there, at daybreak, that Quantrell had passed east, I left the command to follow as rapidly as possible, and pushed on, reaching, soon after dark, the point on Grand River where Quantrell's force had scattered.

Lieutenant-Colonel Lazear, with the detachments of the First Missouri, from Warrensburgh and Pleasant Hill, numbering about two hundred men, after failing to find Quantrell on Blackwater on the twenty-second, encountered him at noon on the twenty-third, on Big Creek, broke up his force, and has since had five very successful engagements with different parties of his band.

The pursuit of Quantrell, after our forces had caught up with him at Brooklyn, was so close, that he was unable to commit any further damage to property on his route, but was compelled to abandon almost all his horses, and much of the plunder from the Lawrence stores; and since he reached Missouri a large part of his men have abandoned their horses, and taken to the brush afoot. The number of equipments so far captured exceeds one hundred, and the number of participants in the massacre already killed is fully as great. The most unremitting efforts are being made to hunt down the remainder of the band, before they recover from the pursuit.

Familiar as many of Quantrell's men were with our prairies—unobstructed as to course by any roads or fords—with a rolling country to traverse, as open as the sea—to head off his well-mounted, compact, and well-disciplined force, was extremely difficult. The troops which followed and overtook him south of Lawrence, without a coöperating force to stop him, were practically useless from exhaustion; and the forces which did not follow, but undertook to head him, failed, though they nearly all exerted themselves to the utmost to accomplish it. There were few of the troops which did not travel one hundred miles in the first twenty-four hours of the pursuit. Many horses were killed. Four men of the Eleventh Ohio were sun-stricken; among them Lieutenant Dick, who accompanied me, fell dead on dismounting to rest. The citizens engaged in pursuit, though they were able generally to keep close upon the enemy between Brooklyn and Paoli, killing and wounding many stragglers and men in the rear-guard, were without the requisite arms, organization, or numbers, to successfully encounter the enemy.

Although Quantrell was nearly eleven hours in Kansas before reaching Lawrence, no information of his approach was conveyed to the people of that town. Captain Pike, at Aubrey, sent no messenger either to Paola, Olathe, or Lawrence, one or the other of which towns, it was plain, was to be attacked. Captain Coleman, on getting the news at Little Santa Fé, at once despatched a messenger to Olathe, asking the commanding officer there to speed it westward,

That officer, not knowing in what direction the guerrillas were moving, sent a messenger out on the Santa Fé road, who, when nearly at Gardner, hearing that Quantrell had just passed through there, returned to Olathe.

With one exception, citizens along the route who could well have given the alarm, did not even attempt it. One man excused himself for his neglect on the plea that his horses had been working hard the day before. A boy living ten or twelve miles from Lawrence begged his father to let him mount his pony, and going a by-road alarm the town. But he was not allowed to go. Mr. J. Reed, living in the "Hesper neighborhood," near Eudora, started ahead of Quantrell from that place to carry the warning to Lawrence, but while riding at full speed, his horse fell and was killed, and he himself so injured that he died next day.

Thus surprised, the people of Lawrence were powerless. They had never, except on the occasion referred to above, thought an attack probable, and feeling strong in their own preparations, never, even then, asked for troops to garrison the town. They had an ambulance of arms in their city arsenal, and could have met Quantrell on half an hour's notice with five hundred men. The guerrillas, reaching the town at sunrise, caught most of the inhabitants asleep, and scattered to the various houses so promptly as to prevent the concentration of any considerable number of the men. They robbed the most of the stores and banks, and burned one hundred and eighty-five buildings, including one fourth of the private residences, and nearly all the business houses of the town, and, with circumstances of the most fiendish atrocity, murdered one hundred and forty unarmed men, among them fourteen recruits of the Fourteenth regiment, and twenty of the Second Kansas colored volunteers. About twenty-four persons were wounded.

Since the fall of Vicksburgh, and the breaking up of large parts of Price's and Marmaduke's armies, great numbers of rebel soldiers, whose families live in Western Missouri, have returned, and being unable or unwilling to live at home, have joined the bands of guerrillas infesting the border. Companies, which before this summer mustered but twenty or thirty, have now grown to fifty or one hundred. All the people of the country, through fear or favor, feed them, and rarely any give information as to their movements. Having all the inhabitants, by good will or compulsion, thus practically their friends, and being familiar with the fastnesses of a country wonderfully adapted by nature to guerrilla warfare, they have been generally able to elude the most energetic pursuit. When assembled in a body of several hundred, they scatter before an inferior force, and when our troops scatter in pursuit, they reassemble to fall on an exposed squad, or a weakened post, or a defenceless strip of the border. I have had seven stations on the line from which patrols have each night and each day traversed every foot of the border for ninety miles. The troops you have been able to spare me out of the small forces withheld by you from the armies of Generals Grant, Steel, and Blunt, numbering less than three thousand officers and men for duty, and having over twenty-five separate stations or fields of operations throughout the district, have worked hard, and (until this raid) successfully in hunting down the guerrillas, and protecting the stations and the border. They have killed more than a hundred of them in petty skirmishes and engagements between the eighteenth of June and the twentieth instant.

On the twenty-fifth instant I issued an order requiring all residents of the counties of Jackson, Cass, Bates, and that part of Vernon included in this district, except those within a mile of the limits of the military stations and the garrisoned towns, and those north of Bush Creek and west of Big Blue, to remove from their present places of residence within fifteen days from that date—those who proved their loyalty to be allowed to move out of the district or to any military station in it, or to any part of Kansas west of the border counties—all others to remove out of the district.

When the war broke out, the district to which this order applies was peopled by a community three fourths of whom were intensely disloyal. The avowed loyalists have been driven from their farms long since, and their houses and improvements generally destroyed. They are living in Kansas, and at military stations in Missouri, unable to return to their homes. None remain on their farms but rebel and neutral families, and practically the condition of their tenure is that they shall feed, clothe, and shelter the guerrillas, furnish them information, and deceive or withhold information from us. The exceptions are few—perhaps twenty families in those parts of the counties to which the order applies. Two thirds of those who left their families on the border and went to the rebel armies have returned. They dare not stay at home, and no matter what terms of amnesty may be granted, they can never live in the country except as brigands ; and so long as their families and associates remain, they will stay until the last man is killed, to ravage every neighborhood of the border. With your approval, I was about adopting before this raid measures for the removal of the families of the guerrillas and of known rebels, under which two thirds of the families affected by this order would have been compelled to go. That order would have been most difficult of execution, and not half so effectual as this. Though this measure may seem too severe, I believe it will prove not inhumane, but merciful to the non-combatants affected by it. Those who prove their loyalty will find houses enough at the stations, and will not be allowed to suffer for want of food. Among them there are but few dissatisfied with the order, notwithstanding the present hardship it imposes. Among the Union refugees it is regarded as the best assurance they have ever had of a return to their homes, and permanent peace there.

To obtain the full military advantages of this removal of the people, I have ordered the destruction of all grain and hay, in shed or in the field, not near enough to military stations for removal there. I have also ordered from the towns occupied as military stations, a large number of persons either openly or secretly disloyal, to prevent the guerrillas getting information of the townspeople, which they will no longer be able to get of the farmers. The execution of these orders will possibly lead to a still fiercer and more active struggle, requiring the best use of the additional troops the General Commanding has sent me, but will soon result, though with much unmerited loss and suffering, in putting an end to this savage border war.

I am, Colonel, very respectfully, your obedient servant,   THOMAS EWING, Jr.,
Brigadier-General.

Doc. 181.

WHEELER'S RAID IN TENNESSEE.

A NATIONAL ACCOUNT.

MAYSVILLE, ALA., October 19, 1863.

GENERAL CROOK, commanding Second cavalry division, after participating in the battle of Chickamauga, was ordered to take the Second brigade, Colonel Eli Long commanding, with five days' rations, up the north side of Tennessee River, to guard the fords. There were no rations to be had, excepting three days of hard bread, and he started on this duty. September twenty-sixth arrived at his destination, and all was quiet till the morning of the thirtieth. The fords nearest to Chattanooga were guarded by Wilder's brigade, Colonel Miller commanding. After him the First brigade, Colonel Minty commanding, on same duty, and Colonel Long's brigade was posted above Minty, in the neighborhood of Washington, Tennessee.

I desire to say nothing about why the rebels were permitted to cross, as the officer in command at the ford where the crossing was effected will have to answer for that hereafter, probably before a military tribunal.

On the morning of the thirtieth, the enemy crossed in force of four divisions — Wharton's, Martin's, Davidson's, and Armstrong's — the whole under command of Wheeler.

When General Crook learned they were across, notwithstanding his precautions, he immediately ordered the regiments on duty above to move down the river and rejoin him, which they did, finding the General four miles below Smith's cross-roads, and about twelve below Washington.

Next morning, October first, a reconnoissance to the cross-roads, by the Fourth Michigan, discovered the enemy ascending Waldron's Ridge. At two o'clock P.M., the Second brigade was ordered upon the ridge, on a parallel road. The brigade then consisted of the First Ohio, Second Kentucky, and the Chicago Board of Trade battery. The brigade camped that night on the ridge.

The following morning, October second, the

march was resumed, when the Second brigade was reënforced by the First, and Wilder's mounted infantry, as I said, commanded by Colonel Miller, and it was whispered that General Crook had received orders to "pursue, overtake, and annihilate," which sounded very grand. In descending the ridge into Sequatchie Valley, the advance ran on a rebel picket, which fired a volley and disappeared.

I learned from citizens in the valley that the rebel column had divided four miles above where we were, (Pitt's Cross-roads,) a portion going down the main valley road, and the main column through Piketown, and on the mountain toward McMinnville. While feeding our horses at the cross-roads, we heard what we thought was artillery, and hoped that General Mitchell with the First division had met and attacked the column below. Unfortunately, the First division arrived only in time to see the dying embers of a large supply and ammunition train, which the enemy had captured and burned. The explosion of shells in the burning train sounded like artillery. We camped that night on the mountain—a spur of the Cumberland—on a road running parallel with and between two roads, on which the divided column of the enemy was moving. Our advance camp, the Second brigade, was within two and a half miles of the main rebel camp, yet there was no collision—even of pickets.

A march of twenty miles next day, October third, without once halting, during which a battalion of the Fourth Ohio rejoined the brigade, brought the advance to the Gap in the western slope, where they met with stubborn resistance; but the First brigade forced a passage down the mountain. The rear of the column descended after night, and the fires of a large rebel camp were visible. Once down, Minty had to fight for forage and water. We were in a small space without either. This could not long remain so; the command must have water, and the animals forage. Wilder's invincible brigade went to Minty's assistance, and after half an hour's sharp musketry firing, we got what we wanted. I never heard the losses in this fight, but I saw, perhaps, half a dozen dead rebels in the road, and suppose their wounded were in proportion.

Citizens reported that the two columns had concentrated that day; that they were going to Murfreesboro with ten thousand men, and twenty-four pieces of artillery, occupy our fortifications, and effectually cut the communications of our army. Magnificent programme!

On the morning of October fourth, Colonel Miller moved out in advance toward McMinnville, twelve miles distant. As we approached the town, citizens told us that the garrison had surrendered on demand, been paroled, and were free again. Ascending the hill near the town, the column started into a gallop, and we pursued through the town at that gait. The streets were alive with citizens, and the square full of men in the Federal uniform—officers and privates. Ladies waved their handkerchiefs as we passed, but I presume they were officers' wives from the North, as in our former occupation of that town no lady lived there but carried in her heart the festering canker of secession. Arrived at the far side of the town, on the Murfreesboro road, Lieutenant Patton, A. A. G., rode back to Colonel Long, with orders for him to move immediately to the front, passing Wilder's brigade. The Second Kentucky cavalry was the advance regiment of the brigade, and Long ordered Colonel Nicholas to follow.

I heard General Crook give the order: "Colonel Long," said he, "I desire you to take a good regiment and charge with the sabre; there are only about forty of the rear-guard in front." The regiment moved slowly forward. Long and Nicholas at the head, till having crossed a deep ravine they halted, permitting the regiment to close up in column of fours, commanded—"Draw sabre, forward, gallop!" On they went for a mile, when a single shot fired by a rebel vidette warned them that the enemy was near, and the command "Charge!" was given.

The loud yelling of the troopers, rattling of scabbards, and tramp of charging horses together, give an insight into the unearthly sounds of Pandemonium. In a hundred yards or so, a rebel battalion, commanded by Captain White, Eighth Texas Rangers, is drawn up in line, fire a volley, and break in confusion. They would deserve credit never yet earned if they could stand. Once their backs are turned, it is impossible to rally them. One after another they are captured, excepting a few of them who rush excitably back to their regiment, a mile away, and communicate their panic as they go. The Second dash onward; the regiment of rangers are ready; but with the regiment, as with the battalion, they cannot withstand the approaching cloud of demons, yelling and flourishing their sabres. They fire, break, are terror-stricken, and think only of safety from the tornado, and that safety is in flight. For five miles the charge continued, and knowing that the main body of the enemy could be only a short distance away, a halt and the rally were ordered.

Lieutenant Hosmer, company A, wounded in two places, and is thought fatally. His horse was shot in four places. Sergeant W. E. Harris, same company, had his thigh broken. Five or six others of the Second were slightly wounded. Colonel Long's horse was killed under him.

This did not end the day's fighting, however. Colonel Miller again moved his command forward. A mile further on, Harrison's rebel brigade was in readiness in a woods, with a large field between Miller and him. Miller's brigade dismounted, formed in line in the field, his battery on a knoll in the centre, and moved forward to the wood. The battery opened, and when the line reached the wood heavy firing began. Long formed his brigade on Miller's left, but did not get under fire. The line steadily advanced, till the firing ceased two miles beyond. The enemy had retreated, and night set in. We went into camp along the road, and the wounded were brought back to town.

Here, for the first time, our brave fellows got

rations since the three days' rations of hard bread issued the day before leaving Chattanooga. No matter—this was sufficient. Minds in doubt and suspense as to the fate of Murfreesboro, and, perhaps, the army itself, prevented hunger among fasting men. Day dawned October fifth, and a spirit of hopeful cheerfulness pervaded every one. The march was resumed, and during that day's march of thirty-four miles, only one halt was ordered—that at Readyville, twelve miles from Murfreesboro. The enemy, undoubtedly, occupied the main road, and would, perhaps, delay our entrance into Murfreesboro—if we got there at all—so the General tried strategy, and succeeded. By taking an old road across the country, he struck the Liberty Pike, and approached Murfreesboro by that route. We listened for picket skirmishing with our advance, but were disappointed; the road was clear. The rebels had not even occupied the town, much less the forts.

Just in the suburbs of the town a solitary vidette sat, watchful, with expectation on the *qui vive*, for the rebel advance, little thinking that succor was near. The rebels had driven in pickets, and burned the small railroad bridge near town; beyond this nothing was known. Even then they were within two miles, on the Shelbyville pike, threatening the town. A gallop to that pike, in order to be ready should they advance, and we took a breathing spell. Showing no intention of advancing, and night being close at hand, we went into camp.

Never were men more welcome than was our column at this time. The greatest delight that could be manifested greeted us from every quarter. The cry, "We're saved," came from many a loyal heart that evening. All the quartermasters', commissaries', ordnance, and other departments had been hurriedly transferred to the forts; sutlers had packed and gone; citizens, men, women, and children had all gone to the same place. The small garrison were undaunted, and would have held out to the last; but still they cried with heartiness: "We're saved!"

That night, rations, quartermaster's stores and horse-shoes were drawn, and next morning, October sixth, we were again in motion. We marched on the Shelbyville pike, and having started late, it was dark when we arrived at Guy's Gap and went into camp, without having come up with the enemy. Here we heard very indefinitely that the First division was coming up behind. It was small gratification if they could not, even for one day, give us relief and rest.

Again *en route* next day, the seventh, and arriving at Shelbyville early, we halted a few moments. A portion of the rebel column had passed through there, and robbed and pillaged every store. Passing through town, we took the Lewisburgh pike, mounted infantry in advance, Long's brigade next, and the First brigade supposed to be following. Of the Second brigade, the Third Ohio, which had rejoined the brigade near McMinnville, had the advance; next the

Second Kentucky, the Fourth Ohio, and the First Ohio in the rear. Three miles out from town, sharp skirmish firing opened in front and to the right. The Second brigade started in a gallop, and soon arrived where the column had turned to the right, through a very rough lane. A part of the mounted infantry were engaged with a brigade of rebels, and we were to charge them. We passed Miller's brigade as they advanced in line. A moment only allowed for observation, and our column continued the gallop. It was the McMinnville charge repeated, with this difference—there a regiment charged, here a brigade. Heavy firing at the head of the column was now heard, and the furies again raised their yell. A continuous stream of prisoners was being guarded to the rear on the double-quick. The roads were strewn with dead and wounded men and horses, and other paraphernalia of the battlefield. The sabre is doing its work. We pass Colonel Long, who is slightly wounded, and his horse dead on the road. He got a remount, and was again at his post. Many of the prisoners are dressed in our uniform; some of them are killed on the spot, and the others forced to undress and go back *sans culottes*.

The charge continued for six miles. First a regiment was put to flight, then a brigade destroyed—all of them killed, wounded, captured, or dispersed. The halt and rally sounded. The long charge through the cedar glade, over a rough road, had lengthened and almost disorganized the brigade. We were close upon Wharton's division, and when he saw that we had halted, he immediately began an advance on our broken regiments. A line hurriedly formed, was formed none too soon; their advance was in force enough to crush us, but, notwithstanding, our fellows opened fire. Just when he was needed more than any other man, Captain Stokes galloped up with his battery, opened fire rapidly, and drove the enemy again on retreat. A further charge now was impracticable; the nature of the road made it so; besides, it was impossible, the horses were worn and jaded to such an extent. Minty's brigade could have been used advantageously just then, but on sending back for him, the orderly reported him not to be found. Miller's command advanced with a strong line of skirmishers, which became warmly engaged, and, having gone two miles, during which we got again on the Lewisburgh pike, had every prospect of stubborn resistance on the part of the rebels, who opened with his artillery. Stokes once more in position, and after half an hour firing ceased, the enemy once more *en retreat*. Here great preparations had been made for battle; fences laid down over a wide extent of country, but Miller and Stokes had not given them time to complete arrangements.

Half a mile from Farmington, which is about three miles from where the last stand had been made, the advance commenced firing on a rebel line of skirmishers. Long's brigade was ordered to the front, and halted on arriving there. Directly before us, the pike formed a straight cut through a very dense cedar glade. On the right and left, cedars large and small filled every space, and it was impossible for a horse to go through. The enemy opened with his artillery, the battery being in position in the main street of the town, which was nothing more than the pike. To our right and rear there was an old field of four acres, the cedars forming an impervious hedge around it. Stokes's battery was placed in position on the pike at one corner of the field, and the Second brigade, in column of battalions, within the field. The Third Ohio had been ordered off to the right, to guard that flank. Meantime, Miller's command had dismounted, deployed in line on the right and left of the road, and advanced into the cedars. We were not long kept in suspense. A terrible fire opened all along the line. Miller had become engaged, and Stokes gave shot for shot with his battery. The enemy used grape and canister on our advancing line, and Stokes replied with shell and solid shot against the rebel battery. The crashing of grape through the cedars made a peculiar and terrible noise; but those same cedars saved the lives of many soldiers. The firing of volley after volley, together with all the noises of battle, continued—increased. A portion of the rebel battery turned on Stokes, and he soon had to send a piece to the rear, with a wheel shattered. While at its height, and the battle had a doubtful aspect, General Crook cast many an anxious look back on the road, hoping, evidently, to see Minty's brigade approaching, but no Minty came. Presently the firing began to recede, and from that time it steadily got further away. The General, with the peculiar light of victory in his eye, ordered the Second brigade to advance in column down the road, at a gallop. On entering the town a scene of indescribable confusion presented itself: dead and wounded lay thick together—women and children screaming at the highest pitch of their lungs, as usual, after all danger to themselves had passed. One woman flourished a navy pistol, and uttered loud screams of vengeance against the rebels, who two hours before had told her to wait and see the Yankees run. Three pieces of the enemy's artillery stood in the street, one with caisson exploded. The Board of Trade battery had disabled, and the Seventeenth Indiana and two companies of the One Hundred and Twenty-third Illinois, had driven the rebels away from them. The victory was ours, but it must be made complete. Had the First brigade been there, two divisions of the enemy, which were disorganized and routed, might have been utterly destroyed. The Second brigade, with the Second Kentucky in advance, began a charge. They came upon the flying column, but an unexpected obstacle presented itself. The road was doubly barricaded, and in the check impossible to be prevented. Darkness following daylight, a halt was ordered, and our fatigued and hard-worked men went into camp.

As near as I can learn, the result of the day's fighting was as follows:

LEFT ON THE FIELD BY THE ENEMY.

Killed,	110
Wounded,	160
Prisoners,	340
Total,	610

OUR LOSS.

Killed,	15
Wounded,	60
Total,	75

The gallant Colonel Monroe, of the One Hundred and Twenty-third Illinois, and formerly from Kentucky, was killed. Colonel Clay (rebel Kentucky regiment) was killed.

The prisoners represented twenty-seven regiments—the two divisions of Wharton and Martin having been engaged. General Wheeler had command in person. Among the prisoners were majors, captains, and lieutenants. The First Kentucky Mounted Rifles (rebel) out of eight captains lost six killed. Among the latter was captain William Bowan, of Bardstown. I did not see him, but was informed so by a prisoner of his regiment, named Thomas, a son of Mr. Grisby Thomas, of Nelson County, Kentucky.

The First brigade arrived during the night. It was past noon when they left their camp. The march next day (October eighth) to Pulaski, thirty-five miles, was completed with a solitary halt of half an hour at Lewisburgh. During the night we had been reënforced by the Third brigade, Colonel Low commanding.

From the hill overlooking the town of Pulaski, the rear of the rebel column was seen passing out the far side, on the Lamb's Ferry road. The sun had set: a long and fatiguing march had been made during the day, and rest for man and horse was necessary, and the command went into camp on Richland Creek.

Colonel Low's command had the advance next day, October ninth, and the Second brigade the rear; consequently, I can write very little of the day's march. A brigade of the enemy had been strongly posted behind a double barricade near Sugar Creek, about twenty miles from Pulaski, and some distance from the Tennessee River. Colonel Low's command gallantly carried the barricades, taking a large number of prisoners, and killing and wounding several, with the loss of two men wounded. I believe from there the road to the ferry was clear. Arriving at Rogerville, four miles from the river, I heard that the enemy recrossed, and was then safe on the other side of the river. So the chase ended. It was night, and with a breath of relief the command slept.

From Murfreesboro till the Tennessee River had been placed between him and General Crook's command, no part of Wheeler's army was out of the saddle for more time than to cook their meals and feed their horses. His loss is estimated, including all those who were scattered and driven to the woods, at one thousand to fifteen hundred men, while by the activity of General Crook, the damage he did to the railroad is small and trifling.

In this chase General Crook and Colonel Long have shown all the noble qualities characteristic of the soldier, and the men under the command have seen and recognized the fact.

For vigilance, activity, and untiring energy, the army cannot show two better men. Although we of the Second brigade think ours the best in the cavalry command, yet it may be that any other would do as well, if such men as Colonel Long had command of them. Always at the head of his command, never tiring, and fearless under the most trying circumstances, he has won the respect and admiration of his men.

The day after our arrival at Rogerville, we lay in camp, and the quiet of the Sabbath in a country town settled upon us. The zeal of pursuit was gone.   * * *

COLONEL MILLER'S REPORT.

HEADQUARTERS FIRST BRIGADE, FOURTH DIVISION,
FOURTEENTH ARMY CORPS, DEPARTMENT OF CUMBERLAND,
BROWNSBOROUGH, FLA., Oct. 21, 1863.

Lieutenant Moore, A. D. C. and A. A. A. G.:

In pursuance of orders, I have the honor to submit the following report of the part taken by my command in the pursuit of the rebel forces under the command of Major-General Wheeler, in his recent raid through Tennessee and Northern Alabama.

In compliance with orders received September twenty-ninth, I reported my command; the Seventy-second Indiana, Lieutenant-Colonel S. C. Kirkpatrick commanding; the Seventeenth Indiana, Major Wm. Jones commanding; the Ninety-eighth Illinois, Lieutenant-Colonel Kitchell commanding; the One Hundred and Twenty-third Illinois, Colonel James Monroe commanding; the Eighteenth Indiana battery, Captain Eli Lilly commanding; a battery of four mountain howitzers, Sergeant Edward commanding; and a detachment of pioneers, Captain Kilborn commanding, in the vicinity of Blythe's Ferry, on the Tennessee River, September thirtieth. Here I received orders to leave my train, lead horses, three pieces of the Eighteenth Indiana battery, and three howitzers, and proceed with the remainder of the command to cross Waldon's Ridge into the Sequatchee Valley, which I did, reaching the valley, crossing it, and encamped on the Cumberland range on the night of the second of October. On the third I crossed the Cumberland Mountains in rear of Colonel Minty's cavalry brigade, who skirmished with the enemy through the day. Late in the afternoon I was ordered to pass my command down the mountain to the front, and dislodge the enemy who were in possession of the main road from McMinnville to Chattanooga, and which they were stubbornly holding, skirmishing briskly with Colonel Minty's cavalry. On reaching the foot of the mountain, the command was dismounted, and the Ninety-eighth Illinois and Seventeenth Indiana formed in line of battle and ordered to advance, the Seventy-second Indiana and One Hundred and Twenty-third Illinois being

held in reserve. Soon a brisk engagement ensued, which resulted in our getting possession of the road. Night being now upon us, the Seventy-second Indiana and One Hundred and Twenty-third Illinois were ordered up, when I advanced and took possession of the Gap through which the road passed leading to McMinnville. Being now in possession of the road, the Gap, and a good stream of water, orders were received from General Crook for the command to lay on arms in line of battle until morning. On the approach of day the enemy withdrew, leaving six dead on the field and a number of stand of arms. My loss was several wounded. The Seventeenth Indiana here captured a stand of national colors belonging to the Fourth Alabama cavalry. My brigade now having the advance, I skirmished with the enemy on the road to McMinnville, driving his rear through the town, which he had sacked, burning the government stores he could not carry away. A short distance from the town, on the Murfreesboro road, he made a stand, but was soon dislodged, when the Second Kentucky cavalry made a brilliant charge, killing some and bringing off a number of prisoners. Seven miles from McMinnville he again made a stand and offered battle. I at once dismounted my command, ordered the artillery into position, and advanced on him, across open fields on his position in the woods. Captain Lilly now opened on him with the artillery, at one time killing one man and four horses at one shot. Here again I dislodged him and drove him two miles, when night coming on I went into camp by order of General Crook. During the engagement the enemy came to me with a flag of truce, which I did not receive, but ordered the bearer back, and my men not to fire on him while between my lines and those of the enemy. The Seventeenth and Seventy-second Indiana lost several wounded—the former, one killed. On the fifth I proceeded to Murfreesboro and drew three days' rations for my command. On the night of the sixth I encamped several miles from Shelbyville. On the fourth, my brigade having the advance, I moved through Shelbyville, and passed out on the Farmington pike; after advancing some distance I learned that a division of the enemy were encamped at or near the Widow Sims, to my right, some distance from the main road. In compliance with orders from General Crook, I at once left the main road and proceeded in the direction the enemy were said to be, and soon came upon his pickets, which I drove in and charged the division, in line of battle, the Fourteenth Indiana, four companies of the Ninety-eighth Illinois on horseback, going in with the pickets. The enemy opened on me, killing and wounding some of my men, and killing twenty-five horses. I now dismounted the men, formed a line of battle under heavy fire, and charged the enemy, across open fields, who for a while offered a determined resistance, but soon fled, betaking themselves to their horses, when they were thrown into the utmost confusion and completely routed, closely followed by the Seventeenth Indiana, who, while they were mounting and pressing through a narrow lane, closely massed, poured into them a most deadly and destructive fire. The Seventy-second Indiana were arriving on that part of the field, participated in the work of death and slaughter. The enemy left the field thoroughly demoralized, and everywhere strewn with stolen goods, abandoned arms, and government clothing. The Ninety-eighth Illinois operating in another part of the field, captured an entire company. The enemy having left the field in my possession, I ordered the Ninety-eighth Illinois to mount their horses, and with the Seventeenth Indiana on one side and the Seventy-second Indiana on the other side of the road, I advanced in line of battle in the direction of Farmington, until coming to a point where the road on which I was moving intersected the Farmington pike, I found the enemy in line of battle, with artillery in position, and who opened fire on me as soon as I came in range. At this moment, Captain Stokes was ordered into position; and replied with great effect to the enemy's guns. Meanwhile my two regiments steadily advancing, the enemy soon fell back and offered no further resistance until I came to Farmington. Here the enemy made a bolder and more determined stand than ever. His position was well chosen, being covered on the front and both flanks by a dense growth of cedar, which, together with the natural inequalities and rocky surface of the country just at that place, strengthened by a temporary breastwork of rails and logs, gave him a secure position where he could await my advance. In this position, with all the natural advantages in his favor, he had three divisions dismounted and drawn up in four successive lines of battle, with a battery in position commanding the only road by which I could advance. I was now ordered by General Crook to move forward, which I did, sending the One Hundred and Twenty-third Illinois in on the left of the road and the Ninety-eighth Illinois on the right. They had not advanced far, however, when the heavy volleys of the enemy and the deadly fire of his artillery disclosed the hitherto unknown fact that the enemy greatly outnumbered me, and that support must be given to the two regiments engaged, as the enemy's lines extended far beyond both my right and left. I accordingly sent the Seventeenth and Seventy-second Indiana to advance, the former on the left and the latter on the right of the road, to support the Ninety-eighth and One Hundred and Twenty-third Illinois. Soon they were in position, and the whole line advancing, the engagement became general.

Here the gallant officer and soldier, Colonel Monroe, of the One Hundred and Twenty-third Illinois, fell mortally wounded, and many were sent wounded and bleeding to the rear, the enemy raking my lines with grape and canister at a range not exceeding three hundred yards, the shell exploding in all directions in the thick cedar above our heads and at our feet.

While thus closely engaged, the enemy with terrible energy and loud hurras charged my lines, but without effect. At this time Captain Stokes opened fire, which particularly drew the attention of the enemy's artillery, and seeing the critical condition of affairs, and believing victory could only be obtained by a successful charge, I at once ordered it, which was promptly executed, the whole line impetuously advancing with a shout, driving back the successive lines of the enemy and resulting in his complete route, the captures of three pieces of artillery, and the occupancy of the town, where orders were received from General Crook to halt and await the arrival of the cavalry. The cavalry arriving, were sent in pursuit of the retreating enemy. After remaining some time in position, orders were received to go into camp. The severity of this day's operations on the enemy will be better understood when we remember that eighty-six of his men lay dead on the field, and two hundred and seventy were taken prisoners. Of the number of his wounded I cannot speak, not being advised. My loss in killed and wounded was near one hundred. The part taken by my command in the two days' further pursuit of the enemy was unimportant. I can only say that I joined in the general pursuit, and occasionally picked up prisoners here and there on our passage over the country.

To the members of my staff—Captain Rice, A. A. G., Captain Newell, Topographical Engineer, Captain Hunt, A. D. C., Lieutenant C. I. Ward, Acting Inspector, Lieutenant Harding, Provost-Marshal, and Lieutenant Mayer, Acting Orderly, and the gallant officers and men of my command, who, marching over four hundred miles, through a country where subsistence was not furnished by the wayside, as was the case in the pursuit of the notorious Morgan—subsisting twenty-two days on five days' rations, and such supplies as could be gathered on our rapid march, fighting the enemy by day and by night, whenever and wherever he could be found, and bearing all without a murmur or complaint—my heartfelt thanks and the country's gratitude are due.

In closing this report, I refer with grief to the loss sustained by the brigade in the death of Colonel James Monroe, of the One Hundred and Twenty-third Illinois, the brave soldier, the true man, and the gallant officer. At the head of his regiment, in the thickest of the fight, where the death-storm raged the fiercest, he fell, as the soldier covets to die, in the defence of his country's honor and nation's life.

His death devolved the command of the regiment upon Lieutenant-Colonel Biggs, who is deserving of all praise for his courage, promptness, and efficiency in the new position he occupies.

Lieutenant-Colonel S. D. Kirkpatrick, commanding the Seventy-second Indiana, is deserving of special mention for his gallant conduct, his energy and promptness in the execution of all orders.

Lieutenant-Colonel Kitchell, commanding the Ninety-eighth Illinois, challenges admiration for his gallant conduct and soldierly bearing on all occasions.

Major Jones, commanding the Seventeenth Indiana, the oldest regiment in the volunteer service, won laurels whenever and wherever sent.

Captain Lilly, commanding Eighteenth Indiana battery, for his energy in keeping up with the command at all times, and for the handsome manner in which he paid his respects to the enemy whenever called on, deserves especial mention here.

The total loss in killed and wounded in my command is ninety-six.

I am, Lieutenant, very respectfully,

A. O. MILLER,
Colonel Seventy-Second Regiment Indiana Volunteers, Commanding Mounted Infantry.

Doc. 182.

PRESIDENT LINCOLN'S PROCLAMATION.

By the President of the United States :

THE year that is drawing toward its close has been filled with the blessings of fruitful fields and healthful skies. To these bounties, which are so constantly enjoyed that we are prone to forget the source from which they come, others have been added, which are of so extraordinary a nature that they cannot fail to penetrate and soften even the heart which is habitually insensible to the ever-watchful Providence of Almighty God. In the midst of a civil war of unequalled magnitude and severity, which has sometimes seemed to invite and provoke the aggression of foreign States, peace has been preserved with all nations, order has been maintained, the laws have been respected and obeyed, and harmony has prevailed everywhere, except in the theatre of military conflict, while that theatre has been greatly contracted by the advancing armies and navies of the Union.

The needful diversion of wealth and strength from the fields of peaceful industry to the national defence have not arrested the plough, the shuttle, or the ship. The axe has enlarged the borders of our settlements, and the mines, as well of iron and coal as of the precious metals, have yielded even more abundantly than heretofore. Population has steadily increased, notwithstanding the waste that has been made by the camp, the siege, and the battle-field, and the country, rejoicing in the consciousness of augmented strength and vigor, is permitted to expect continuance of years with large increase of freedom.

No human council hath devised, nor hath any mortal hand worked out these great things. They are the gracious gifts of the Most High God, who, while dealing with us in anger for our sins, hath nevertheless remembered mercy. It has seemed to me fit and proper that they should be solemnly, reverentially, and gratefully acknowledged as with one heart and voice, by the whole American people.

I do therefore invite my fellow-citizens in every part of the United States, and also those who are at sea and those who are sojourning in foreign lands, to set apart the last Thursday of November next as a day of thanksgiving and prayer to our beneficent Father, who dwelleth in the heavens, and I recommend too that while offering up the ascriptions justly due to him for such singular deliverances and blessings, they do also, with humble penitence for our national perverseness and disobedience, commend to his tender care all those who have become widows, orphans, mourners, or sufferers in the lamentable civil strife in which we are unavoidably engaged, and fervently implore the interposition of the Almighty hand to heal the wounds of the nation, and to restore it, as soon as may be consistent with divine purposes, to the full enjoyment of peace, harmony, tranquillity, and union.

In testimony whereof, I have hereunto set my hand and caused the seal of the United States to be affixed. Done at the city of Washington, this third day of October, in the year of our Lord one thousand eight hundred and sixty-three, and of the Independence of the United States the eighty-eighth.   ABRAHAM LINCOLN.

By the President.

W. H. SEWARD,
Secretary of State.

Doc. 183.

GENERAL ROSECRANS'S ORDER.

HEADQUARTERS DEPARTMENT OF THE CUMBERLAND,
CHATTANOOGA, Oct. 2, 1863.

ORDERS No. 3:

ARMY OF THE CUMBERLAND: You have made a grand and successful campaign; you have driven the rebels from Middle Tennessee. You crossed a great mountain range, placed yourselves on the banks of a broad river, crossed it in the face of a powerful opposing army, and crossed two other great mountain ranges at the only practicable passes, some forty miles between extremes. You concentrated in the face of superior numbers; fought the combined armies of Bragg, which you drove from Shelbyville to Tullahoma, of Johnston's army from Mississippi, and the tried veterans of Longstreet's corps, and for two days held them at bay, giving them blow for blow, with heavy interest. When the day closed, you held the field, from which you withdrew in the face of overpowering numbers, to occupy the point for which you set out—Chattanooga.

You have accomplished the great work of the campaign; you hold the key of East-Tennessee, of Northern Georgia, and of the enemy's mines of coal and nitre.

Let these achievements console you for the regret you experience that arrivals of fresh hostile troops forbade you remaining on the field to renew the battle; for the right of burying your gallant dead, and caring for your brave companions who lay wounded on the field. The losses you have sustained, though heavy, are slight, considering the odds against you, and the stake you have won.

You hold in your hands the substantial fruits of a victory, and deserve, and will receive the honors and plaudits of a grateful nation, which asks nothing of even those who have been fighting us but obedience to the Constitution and laws established for our own common benefit.

The General Commanding earnestly begs every officer and soldier of this army to unite with him in thanking Almighty God for his favors to us. He presents his hearty thanks and congratulations to all the officers and soldiers of this command for their energy, patience, and perseverance and the undaunted courage displayed by those who fought with such unflinching resolution.

Neither the history of this war, nor probably the annals of any battle, furnish a loftier example of obstinate bravery and enduring resistance to superior numbers—when troops, having exhausted their ammunition, resorted to the bayonet, many times, to hold their positions, against such odds—as did our left and centre, comprising troops from all the corps, on the afternoon of the twentieth of September, at the battle of Chickamauga.

W. S. ROSECRANS,
Major-General Commanding.

Doc. 184.

BATTLE OF CHICKAMAUGA.*

REPORT OF MAJOR-GENERAL CRITTENDEN

HEADQUARTERS TWENTY-FIRST ARMY CORPS,
CHATTANOOGA, October 1, 1863.

SIR: In obedience to directions from Department Headquarters, dated twenty-fifth ultimo, requiring me to forward as soon as practicable a report of the operations of my command during the late engagements, including a brief history of its movements from the time of crossing the Tennessee River up to the beginning of the battle, I have the honor to report:

1. The movements of the Twenty-first army corps, from the time of its crossing the Tennessee River, terminating on the nineteenth ultimo, when the battle of Chickamauga opened.

August 31.—My command, stationed in Sequatchie Valley, at Pikeville, Dunlap's, Thurman, respectively, excepting General Wagner's brigade, First division, opposite Chattanooga, and General Hazen at Hoe's Tavern, the latter fifteen miles north of Wagner, and both in Tennessee Valley. My command has been thus stationed since the nineteenth of August, having left Manchester, Tennessee, on the sixteenth of August, crossing the mountains at three different points, in obedience to orders from Department Headquarters, at half-past twelve A.M. of the sixteenth. At a quarter-past two P.M. I received your orders of the thirtieth, dated thirty minutes past twelve P.M., to move my entire command, except the brigades of Generals Hazen and Wagner, as soon as practicable, down the Sequatchie Valley, and to supply myself with every thing necessary for an active campaign. The orders further directed me to cross my trains at Bridgeport, and my troops at

* See Docs. pp. 217, 362, and 409, ante.

Bridgeport, Shellmound, and Battle Creek. Should Chattanooga be evacuated, Hazen and Wagner were to cross the river and occupy the place, and close down upon our left. Colonel Minty, with his brigade of cavalry, and Colonel Wilder, with his brigade of mounted infantry, were to coöperate with Hazen and Wagner.

September 1.—My command all in motion. General Wood and his command arrived at Jasper, General Palmer within three miles of Jasper, and General Van Cleve within five miles of Dunlap.

September 20.—Received orders to cross the river with one brigade at Jasper Crossing, and one at Battle Creek; other part of the command to follow as soon as the way is opened.

Colonel Buell's brigade.—One division marched at dark to Shellmound, where he crossed the river in flats during the night.

September 3.—General Wood with his other brigade (Hooker's) moved down early this morning to Shellmound, and was across the river by eight P.M., having been delayed till two P.M. by General Reynolds's train.

Colonel Grove and his brigade (Palmer's division) moved down early this morning to Battle Creek, but were unable to secure the ferry, being used all day by General Brannan's division. General Graft and his brigade, Palmer's division, was therefore ordered to Shellmound, and he following close on General Wood, succeeded in crossing his command by four A.M. on Monday. General Van Cleve, with his two brigades, arrived at Jasper, and went into camp to await the crossing.

Received from the General Commanding orders for my movements and position after crossing the river, namely:

To move up the valley of Running Water Creek and Whiteside, where I was to post one regiment and send one division along the Nashville and Chattanooga Railroad to the Trenton road, and to push forward as near to Chattanooga as practicable, and threaten the enemy in that direction. The remainder of the command to occupy a position near the junction of the Murphy Valley road, the road marked on the map as good wagon road to Taylor's. The movement to be completed on the evening of the fourth.

September 4.—At twenty minutes past three A.M., received word from General Graft that his brigade was all over. Moved General Van Cleve at once, and at one P.M. moved headquarters to Shellmound, which crossed before night. General Palmer succeeded in crossing with his own brigade at Battle Creek to-day. Thus the whole command was over the river.

September 5.—At thirty minutes past two P.M., after having the command organized and in position, and with all of the ammunition and most of the transportation up, troops all moved out light to Whiteside. General Wood in the advance, General Palmer centre, and General Van Cleve rear, taking with them their ammunition trains. Regimental and supply trains to move up at five P.M. to-morrow.

September 6.—Road up Running Water Creek rough but passable. At thirty minutes past nine A.M. arrived at junction of Murphy Valley and Nicajack road, and encamped there as ordered. Generals Palmer and Van Cleve and their divisions following us, and General Wood and his division pursuing road up Running Water Creek, and encamping seven miles from Chattanooga, reporting that the enemy was close before him in force.

September 7.—Colonel Harker, with his brigade, made a very satisfactory reconnoissance to spur of Lookout Mountain, drove the enemy's pickets and light advance two miles, and returned by dark, believing the enemy in force in his front.

September 8.—Gave orders to make two reconnoissances to-morrow morning, the one up Lookout Mountain, via Nicajack Trace, and for which General Beatty and his brigade was detailed; the other up same mountain to Summertown, for which Colonel Gross and three regiments was detailed, both to unite, if practicable, on top of the mountain, and to start on or before day to-morrow.

September 9.—At twenty minutes past two A.M., received despatch from the General commanding the army, approving the two reconnoissances ordered, and directing that the whole command be held in readiness to move round the point of Lookout Mountain, to seize and occupy Chattanooga, in the event of its being evacuated. To move with caution, and not to throw my artillery around the point of Lookout Mountain till I am satisfied that the evacuation is not a ruse. Should I occupy Chattanooga, I am to order General Wagner and all his force across to join me. At forty-five minutes past five A.M., further despatches from Department Headquarters apprising me of the evacuation of Chattanooga, and ordering that the whole command be pushed forward at once with five days' rations, and to make a vigorous pursuit. This later despatch was too late to stop the reconnoissances ordered; but I lost no time in putting the balance of the command in motion, and arrived in Chattanooga with General Wood's division at thirty minutes past twelve P.M., having taken peaceable possession of same. It was nightfall, however, before the troops were well up, owing to the great delay in getting the artillery and ammunition train up this very rough and precipitous hill. It was thus impossible to make any pursuit to-day. I, however, ordered Generals Palmer and Van Cleve to turn off south after having passed the spur of Lookout Mountain, and encamp at Rossville, distant five miles from Chattanooga. General Wood I placed in command of the town.

At fifteen minutes past two P.M., I received further instructions from Department Headquarters, ordering me to leave a light brigade to hold Chattanooga, and with the balance of my command to pursue the enemy with the utmost vigor. The line of march would probably lead me near Ringgold, and from thence in the vicinity of Dalton.

September 10. — Generals Palmer and Van Cleve with their division ordered to make vigorous pursuit early this morning, marching on the road from Rossville to Ringgold, thence to Dalton. General Wood, after leaving one brigade at Chattanooga, to follow with his two brigades in the same direct line. General Wagner, with his brigade, having crossed during the night, was left as post commander. At four P.M., received report from General Palmer, that owing to want of supplies, troops only marched six miles, the advance encamping at Chickamauga Creek, five miles from Ringgold—the rear, General Wood, on Pea Vine Creek, two miles to the rear of advance. Also, that the enemy's cavalry was in his front, and that a portion of it had charged his advance, rode over four companies of the First Kentucky infantry, and captured fifty men and two officers, without any one on either side being hurt. At night received from the front several reports, going to show that the enemy was in force this side of Lafayette, and threatening to retake Chattanooga.

September 11, at 1 A.M.—The General Commanding feeling uncertain about the position and strength of the enemy in our front, ordered me to proceed to the front at once. Was misled by the guide and did not reach my command until six A.M.; and two of my orderlies on duty with Captain McCook in search of me, thinking I had taken the wrong road, were captured, he narrowly escaping. Early in the morning, Colonel Harker, with his brigade, was moved back to Rossville, and by night made a reconnoissance up the Rossville road as far as Gordon's Mills, driving squads of the enemy before him. At half-past two P.M. gave General Wood his orders through one of my staff, who received them in person from Department Headquarters to move his other brigade at once to Gordon's Mills to support Colonel Harker, and at five P.M. my staff-officer reported to me at Ringgold. My entire second and third divisions were then at Ringgold. General Hazen, with his brigade, having crossed the river yesterday, rejoined his division (Palmer's) to-day. Colonel Deck, with second brigade, Van Cleve's division, (left at McMinnville to guard stores,) rejoined his command on the ninth. Your instructions received at this time, and dated a quarter-past nine A.M., were to move with the balance of my corps on the Chickamauga and Pea Vine Valley roads, keeping in view two objects: first to support General Thomas, in case the enemy is in force in the vicinity of Lafayette; or second, to move eastward and southward toward Rome, in case he has continued his retreat. Other verbal instructions received by my staff-officer urged upon me the importance of keeping my separate divisions in supporting distance of one another. At half-past eight A.M. I received your despatch of half-past three P.M., informing me that the enemy was in heavy force in the valley of Chattanooga, and instructing me to move my whole force across by the most available route, and as quickly as possible, to the Rossville and Lafayette road, to some defensible point between Gordon's Mills and

Shield's House, and to close Wood up with me or myself to him. I at once called my general officers together, and after a long consultation and diligent inquiry of citizens as to the nature of the roads and country, gave orders to move the command in the direction ordered at five in the morning.

September 12.—Sent word early this morning to Colonel Wilder, who was in the advance and near Tunnel Hill, to return to Ringgold with his command, and to follow on my line of march, covering my left flank. He moved promptly and met me at Ringgold, and reported that the enemy was in force in his front last night, and that he learned from deserters that Forrest was to leave to-day to flank and cut off this command, and Warton in an opposite direction to the same purpose. General Van Cleve, with the train, moved to Peeler's, and met no enemy; General Palmer to Gilbert's, where he met some squads of the enemy, and skirmished with him. After opening communicaton with General Van Cleve and General Wood, moved the whole command to Gordon's Mills, Colonel Wilder also coming in after night, having had a severe skirmish during the day near Leet's tan-yard, and losing thirty men killed and wounded.

September 13.—In the morning, the Fourth United States cavalry, six hundred and fifty strong, reported to me for duty. The three divisions were put into position for defence. General Graft and Colonel Wilder sent out to reconnoitre on the left, the Fourth cavalry on the right, to McLemore's Cove, and General Van Cleve to the front and centre on Lafayette road. The latter only found the enemy, (cavalry with artillery,) who retired skirmishing a distance of three miles, when the brigade was halted, and soon after returned to camp. In this skirmish Captain Drury, Chief of artillery, Third division, was severely wounded. At half-past two P.M. received your despatches of twenty minutes past twelve and twenty-five minutes past two P.M., respectively, the former ordering me to post General Wood in a strong, defensible position at Gordon's Mills, for him to resist stoutly the enemy's advance, and in case of extremity, if Granger's forces (a division of infantry) has not arrived at Chattanooga, so as to support Wood at Rossville, and he (Wood) should be compelled to fall back further, he must take his position at a point guarding the road to Chattanooga and around the point of Lookout Mountain, and hold them at all hazards. To move the balance of my command during the evening and night to a position on Missionary Ridge, so as to cover the road along the valley of Chattanooga Creek, and to send Wilder with his command up Chattanooga Creek, and also that running up the valley of West Chickamauga Creek, to feel his way carefully, and who is to join General Thomas as soon as possible, the latter ordering me to hold myself in readiness to execute to-night the orders sent to me at twenty minutes past twelve to-day.

September 30, at half-past six A.M.—Received despatch from Colonel Goddard, stating that

it was the instruction of the General Commanding, that I should move before daylight to Mission Ridge, and that it was perhaps his unfortunate wording that prevented it. I at once commenced the movement. In the night Colonel Minty, with the balance of his cavalry brigade, reported for duty. I sent him in the rear of my two divisions. Wilder with his command I sent to join General Thomas, then in Chattanooga Valley. Arrived at the position soon after nine A.M., and staid there all day, being unable to have communication with Department Headquarters. Saw nothing of the enemy. At forty minutes past seven P.M., received orders to return with the command, placing it at Crawfish Spring or along the Chickamauga Valley, near Gowan's. Too late to make the movement to-day.

September 15.—The two divisions moved as directed last night; the left, Van Cleve's division, at Crawfish Springs; right—Palmer's, near Gowan's, and supported on its right by the Ninth Pennsylvania cavalry. Balance of the command under Minty sent to reconnoitre the whole front and left. At half-past eleven P.M., Colonel Minty reported that the enemy was in force at Dalton, Ringgold, Leet's, and Rockspring Church.

September 16.—Nothing occurred of peculiar interest this day, except that Department Headquarters were established at Crawfish Spring. At half-past nine P.M., received orders to issue to the men three days' rations in haversacks, and twenty rounds of ammunition in the pockets of each man, in addition to having the cartridge-box full. There are indications that the enemy is massing for another attack on our left.

September 17. — General Thomas with his corps arrived on our lines to-day. In the afternoon moved General Palmer's division further to the left, in order to make room for General Thomas's troops and to concentrate my own. Toward dark, in obedience to orders, moved Corps Headquarters in vicinity of Department Headquarters.

September 18. — At half-past ten A.M., General Wood, holding position on Chickamauga at Gordon's Mills, sent in word that a strong force of skirmishers was advancing on his left. Soon after another of the staff rode up, reporting his line very thin and asking for a brigade. At eleven A.M. a third staff-officer rode up, reporting the enemy advancing on his right and on Van Cleve's left. At forty-five minutes past eleven an orderly came, reporting that the enemy, infantry, cavalry, and artillery, were advancing on the Lafayette road; at the same moment General Van Cleve was moving up to General Wood's left, and General Palmer was ordered to take Van Cleve's position on Wood's right. At forty-five minutes past three P.M., Colonel Wilder sent word that Colonel Minty with his cavalry, after being reënforced with two regiments of his, is falling back; that the enemy is getting in his (Wilder's) rear, and that he is also falling back on Wood. No firing to be heard. In the afternoon Palmer was ordered up to form on the left of Van Cleve's new position, on the line of the

Chickamauga River, which from Gordon's Mills runs in an easterly direction, while the road to Chattanooga via Rossville is nearly north or south. We hold the river at Gordon's Mills, but on our left the enemy's pickets were reported to be between the road and the river. I was informed by the General Commanding that we also occupied the bridge across the Chickamauga at Reid's Mills with one brigade of infantry, situated north-west of Gordon's Mills, and distant about three and a half miles; and thus the space between the two mills was in a great measure open to the enemy.

REPORT OF THE OPERATIONS OF THE TWENTY-FIRST ARMY CORPS DURING THE ENGAGEMENTS OF THE NINETEENTH AND TWENTIETH SEPTEMBER, ON CHICKAMAUGA RIVER, GEORGIA.

For continuation of my report of the movements of the Twenty-first army corps since crossing the Tennessee River, and ending the eighteenth ultimo, the day preceding the battle, I have now the honor to report the operations of my command during the last engagements. It was four o'clock in the morning of the nineteenth before the last brigade of Major-General Palmer's division arrived at its position on the left of Brigadier-General Van Cleve. During the evening and night of the eighteenth, my command was placed in position as directed by the General commanding the Department, the right resting at Gordon's or Lee's Mills, and the left running north-easterly along the Chickamauga and the road to Rossville. On the morning of the nineteenth I rode to the extreme left of my line, and there being no appearance of the enemy in my front, at forty minutes past seven A.M. I ordered Colonel Gross, Major-General Palmer's division, with his brigade, then in reserve, to make a reconnoissance down the road, and in the direction of Reed's Mills, on the Chickamauga, to ascertain if the main road from Gordon's Mills to Rossville was clear, and if practicable to ascertain if Colonel McCook with his brigade held the bridge at Reed's Mills, from which direction I had just heard the report of four or five cannon. On arriving at this position I found all quiet. Colonel Wilder, with his command, supported by two regiments of Brigadier-General Van Cleve's division, being on the extreme left. I found Colonel Wilder in the edge of the woods, some one hundred and fifty yards west of the road leading to Rossville, his men dismounted and behind a breastwork of rails. It was here reported to me that the command of General Thomas had been heard passing in our rear toward Chattanooga. I immediately directed an officer to go to the rear until he came to the road on which these troops were passing, and to report at once the character of the country which intervened, the distance, etc. I remained until the officer returned, and reported all still being quiet. I rode rapidly to Department Headquarters with this information, which I thought important, and which I believed would be gladly heard by the Commanding General. I promptly returned, and on my arrival at

the left of my lines, about eleven A.M., I heard heavy cannonading about one and a half or two miles to my left. Musketry firing began, and soon became so heavy that I was satisfied the battle had commenced. For a moment I felt embarrassed. The General commanding the department had inquired of me several times if I could hold my position, and I knew the importance to the movements of the army then going on of my ability so to do. I was on the left and thrown forward, covering a movement by which the entire army was to pass in my rear, leaving me on the right, should the movement take place without interruption. I hesitated but for a moment as to whether I should weaken myself by sending aid to Major-General Thomas, who, having passed to my rear, was already engaged on my left. All being quiet on my front, I ordered Major-General Palmer to the support of Major-General Thomas. I at once informed the General commanding the army of this movement, who approved of it in his note of twenty minutes past twelve P.M., when he informed me that from present appearance General Thomas will move in echelon, his left advanced, threatening the enemy's right. At twenty minutes past eleven I received a note from Captain Willard, Aid-de-Camp to Major-General Thomas, dated Mrs. Daniels's house, September fifteenth, (intended for nineteenth,) forty-five minutes past ten, stating that if another division can be spared it would be well to send it up without any delay. At the time of the receipt of this note I heard very heavy musketry in the direction of General Palmer, then advancing to the fight, and I at once sent Major Mendenhall, my Chief of artillery, and Colonel McKibbin, of General Rosecrans's staff, to see General Palmer, and learn particulars. They returned quickly without seeing him, having been halted and shot at by the enemy, which led me to believe that General Palmer was not only fighting in his front, but was also attacked in his rear, and perhaps surrounded. I at once despatched Lieutenant-Colonel Loder, my Inspector-General, and Colonel McKibbin to Department Headquarters, (which at this time had been moved to the Widow Glenn's, distant about a mile from my position,) to report facts, and ask permission to bring up General Van Cleve to support Major-General Palmer, as I was then well satisfied that the enemy was crossing the Chickamauga at several points, and at one near my position. During their absence I sent to General Van Cleve to move up where I then was stationed, and just at the time of his arrival Lieutenant-Colonel Loder returned with permission to send General Van Cleve in, which I immediately did. He brought with him but two brigades, leaving his Third brigade, Colonel Barnes, in position on the left of General Wood. At twelve M. I received your note of ten minutes past eleven A.M., ordering me to send Colonel Minty, with his cavalry brigade, to Chattanooga, and to report for orders at Widow Glenn's, which I at once complied with. I was then stationed in the woods in reserve.

At fifty minutes past twelve P.M. I received a note from General Palmer, dated thirty-five minutes past twelve P.M., stating that his division was just going in; enemy said to be in heavy force; fight is raging, but principally on his left flank. At fifteen minutes past one P.M. I wrote to General Wood, reporting the heavy fight, that Van Cleve and Palmer were hotly in, and that we must look out for his left. I then sent Colonel Starling, my Chief of Staff, to Department Headquarters, reporting General Van Cleve heavy in the fight, and asking that I might move also General Wood to assist. He shortly returned with the request granted, and I despatched Major Mendenhall to bring him up. The enemy appeared to have troops enough to fight us everywhere, and to fill up every interval as soon as my divisions passed. At two P.M. I received your despatch of forty-five minutes past one P.M., advising me that he had ordered General McCook to relieve me—to take command of my corps—and to take the best positions possible; also, that General Sheridan would come in if necessary on my right, and to take care of my right. On receipt of this note, the firing having ceased for a time, I immediately rode rapidly to headquarters, hoping to get final instructions before General Wood's command arrived, and returned just as General Wood, with his two brigades, came up to a position, that General Davis, of Major-General McCook's corps, was fighting over on the right of General Van Cleve. Colonel Barnes's brigade, Van Cleve's division, had been left back with General Wood, came up just in advance of Wood's two brigades, and had gone into position through the woods to the right of General Davis.

I rode forward to a battery, which I understood belonged to General Davis, when I was told that I would find both he and General Wood. Neither of them was there, and I rode back in search of General Wood. I had instructed Lieutenant-Colonel Starling to say to General Wood that in coming to the field he might have an opportunity, by leaving the road before he reached our position and moving to his right, to strike the enemy on the flank. I should regret that I had not sent an order instead of a mere suggestion, but that the Commanding General condemned the movement when I informed him that I had suggested it to General Wood. Colonel Barnes moved in the direction, and Colonel Harker, of Wood's division, was going into position on the right of Colonel Barnes, when Lieutenant-Colonel Starling, at the solicitation of General Davis, who was then being pressed by the enemy, recalled Colonel Harker, and in this way he was brought down the road beyond the position that Colonel Barnes had taken in the woods on Davis's right, and Colonel Buell with his brigade followed after Colonel Harker.

General Wood reached the field but a short time before the enemy attacked our right on Saturday evening, and had General Wood been in the position I suggested, he would have been

on the flank of the enemy, and I think would have punished him severely.

Colonel Buck went into position first off the road on the right, and to the rear of General Davis's battery, which was firing over an open field at the enemy in the woods, who could be seen plainly by their bayonets glistening. In the mean time General Wood with Harker's brigade had passed still further down the road, and went into position on Colonel Buell's left, striking the woods as he left the road. In Colonel Buell's front there was a large gap in the woods recently a corn-field.

The enemy in front of Colonel Buell came out at this time, and he with his men, lying down supporting Davis's battery, fell back in some confusion. All crossed the road through another open field, in which I and my staff were on a high point, when they came into the woods again, along the edge of which Colonel Wilder, with his brigade, was lying. His men soon opened fire, and when I ordered the artillery that was at hand to be put in position along the edge of the woods, under the superintendence of Major Mendenhall, he opened fire rapidly from twenty-six guns, and soon checked and drove the enemy to the cover of his own woods.

Our loss in this brief conflict was quite severe. General Wood and Colonel Buell were present, and were very active in rallying the men and restoring them to order. Soon after accomplishing this, Colonel Buell's brigade again advanced, General Carlin and his command coöperating, and reöccupied their former position. About this time General Sheridan came up through the woods I was in, and promptly sent in a brigade to support these troops. Soon after this, I received your note of three forty-five P.M. and four thirty-five P.M., stating that Davis was heavily pressed, and ordering me to assist him, if I could, with some of my command. At four forty-five P.M., I received your note of three-ten P.M., stating that Johnson was driving the rebels handsomely in the centre; that he had taken many prisoners, and expected to drive the enemy across Chickamauga to-night. Colonel Barnes, with his brigade, I had heard from as being in a commanding position and in good order. Generals Palmer and Van Cleve I had not heard from since they went in. Night was coming on, and I left for Department Headquarters, where, after sitting in council with the Commanding General, other corps commanders, and some general officers, I received, at midnight, the following order:

HEADQUARTERS DEPARTMENT OF THE CUMBERLAND, WIDOW GLENN'S HOUSE, Sept. 19, 1863—10.20 P.M.

GENERAL: The General Commanding directs me to inform you that General McCook has been ordered to hold this Gap to-morrow, covering the Dry Valley road, his right resting near this place, his left connecting with General Thomas's right. The General places your corps in reserve to-morrow, and directs you to post it on the eastern slope of Missionary Ridge, to support McCook or Thomas. Leave the grand guard from your command out, with instructions to hold their ground until driven in, and then to retire slowly, contesting the ground stubbornly.

I proceeded at once to remove General Wood back to the reserve position, leaving the grand guards as directed, and by daylight, September twentieth, I found General Van Cleve in the valley very near his new position. General Palmer (with my strongest division) having been sent to General Thomas the day before, was to remain with him. About eight or nine o'clock on the morning of the twentieth, I was ordered to move General Wood's division up to a position in front which had been occupied by General Negley, and to keep General Van Cleve in reserve and in supporting distance of Wood. This order had been executed but a short time, when I was ordered to move General Van Cleve with two brigades (his other brigade having been sent with General Wood, who otherwise could not have filled the place General Negley occupied) several hundred yards to the left and some two hundred yards to the front. His guns were placed in position on the crest of the ridge, and his command placed near the foot of the slope, formed in column, doubled on the centre and halted.

The General Commanding the department was at this time in the field near by. I was soon ordered to move Van Cleve directly to the front, to take part in the battle now raging in that direction. The order was immediately given, and I said to the Commanding General, as this was the last of my corps not already disposed of, I should accompany it. I rode immediately after General Van Cleve, whose troops were already in motion. On reaching the woods I was surprised to find Van Cleve's command halted. On inquiry, I was informed Van Cleve had run upon Wood's command. I directed him to take ground to the left, to pass through the first interval he could find, and engage the enemy. At this moment an officer rode to me from General Thomas, saying that the General still wanted support on his left. I directed this officer to General Rosecrans's position, then not far distant, and did not stop the movement of General Van Cleve, as he was going in the right direction, if the General Commanding the department should change my orders, and send him to General Thomas's left. In a few moments I received orders to move General Van Cleve's division with the utmost despatch, not exhausting the troops, to the support of General Thomas's left. I gave the order immediately to General Van Cleve, and its execution was at once begun. At this moment I received a message from General Wood that it was useless to bring artillery into the woods. The Chief of Artillery to this corps was ordered to put the batteries back on the ridge in a commanding position, with several hundred yards of open country in front, when I hoped, in the event of any reverse, these guns would cover our retiring troops. I now received a message from General Wood, informing me that he had received an order direct from headquarters

of the department to move at once to the support of General Reynolds. Looking at the artillery which Major Mendenhall had just put in position, and not knowing exactly what to do with it under my last order, my difficulty was suddenly removed by the enemy. While we had been steadily from the beginning of the battle, and very properly, in my judgment, weakening our right and strengthening our left, the object of the enemy being clearly to throw himself between us and Chattanooga, the enemy had been receiving accessions of fresh troops, and now made a sudden attack on our right and right centre, driving these attenuated lines from the field.

Upon turning from the batteries and looking at the troops, I was astounded to see them suddenly and unaccountably thrown into great confusion. There was but little firing at this moment near the troops, and I was unable, until some time afterward, to account for this confusion. In a moment, however, the enemy had driven all before them, and I was cut off from my command, though not a hundred yards in rear and in full view. The enemy had attacked and run over our extreme right at the same time. I was now cut off entirely, both on the right and left, from all our troops. The way, however, was open to the batteries, and I rode immediately there, hoping that stragglers enough, both from right and left, would rally there to hold the position, or at least enable me to carry off the guns. Upon reaching the batteries, I found them without the support of a single company of infantry. It was a time of painful anxiety; I still hoped that support would come from somewhere or be driven to me. But the signs grew rapidly worse. Lieutenant Cushing, commanding battery H, Fourth United States artillery, rode up to me at this moment, and said he thought the enemy's cavalry had got in our rear. Upon asking him for his reason, he answered that a shell had just been thrown from our rear. I started to look if this could possibly be so, stating to Lieutenant Cushing that I did not think it possible. He asked me, in case he was driven, which way he should go. I replied he must not be driven, still hoping for support. He said he would like to know what road to take in case he should be driven, and I pointed out the direction.

A short distance in rear of the guns, just at this moment, I met about sixty or seventy men, apparently rallied and led up to the batteries by a young officer whom I did not recognize, but who were nobly rallied and brought up by that pure-hearted and brave officer, Brigadier-General Van Cleve.

It will be best here to explain the cause of the confusion and consequent disaster which but a little while before had befallen two brigades of his division. While in the act of passing to the support of General Thomas, troops in his front—I do not know of what division—ran in great confusion, and a battery at great speed was driven through the ranks of his men, wounding several seriously. This, of course, threw his command into great confusion, and before he could possibly restore order the enemy was upon him. This accident for which the troops who suffered by it were not responsible, and which scarcely could have been avoided by any precaution, is deeply deplored by the officers and men of that gallant division, whose steady courage and discipline have been too often and well tried to be doubted now. Notwithstanding this disaster, three regiments of the right, composing these two brigades, namely, Forty-fourth Indiana volunteers, commanded by Lieutenant-Colonel Aldrich; Ninth Kentucky, commanded by Colonel Cram, and Seventeenth Kentucky, commanded by Colonel Stout, rallied and formed on the right of our main line, and, fighting all day, only left the field when ordered.

The little force brought by General Van Cleve to the support of the battery was insufficient. I rode rapidly toward the next ridge, hoping to find some general officer, and to obtain support for my battery. I had ridden but a few yards down the hill when I heard the batteries moving quickly away. Nothing but the greatest energy enabled their officers to save any of their guns.

The enemy had come close up to the batteries on the left while pouring in a severe fire from sharp-shooters from the front. All the horses attached to one of the guns of Lieutenant Cushing were shot almost at the same moment, yet he succeeded in bringing away three guns, losing but one. For the good conduct of artillery officers in this and other positions during the day, I refer you to the report of Major Mendenhall, Chief of Artillery, and to the reports of their division commanders.

On reaching the crest of the next hill I found only a small number of men — less than a hundred — who had been rallied by a captain of the Eighteenth regulars, as he told me, and whom he kept in line with great difficulty. I remained here for some time, probably a half hour, expecting to meet some officers of the commands which had been posted to my right. After this lapse of time Major Mendenhall informed me that the enemy had turned our own guns upon us from the hill we had just left. I then determined to go immediately to Rossville and Chattanooga, if it was practicable. I could hear nothing of General Rosecrans, nor of Generals McCook, Sheridan, and Davis, and I greatly feared that all had fallen into the hands of the enemy. I should have ridden rapidly to Rossville or Chattanooga, to apprise whoever was in command of the actual state of things on our right, but that I feared to add a panic to the great confusion. The road was filled with soldiers, wagons, cannon, and caissons all the way to Rossville. All were moving without organization, but without undue haste or panic. After leaving the hill and riding slowly about a mile and a half, I met Colonel Parkhurst with his regiment, and with men enough whom he had stopped to make another regiment of ordinary size, and who seemed to be well organized. The Colonel rode up to me, and asked if I would take command. I told

him no, that he was doing good service, and directed him to hold his position, and let the artillery-wagons, etc., pass, and then follow on, covering the rear.

About this time, I learned the General Commanding had not been captured, but that he had gone to Chattanooga. I rode to Rossville, where I expected to find some troops and to learn something of the locality of the main army and its condition, but finding no one who could give me any information, I rode to Chattanooga, where I found the General commanding the department, and reported briefly to him.

The General Commanding, having ordered the army to withdraw to Rossville, directed me to report to Major-General Thomas at that place for orders. I rode that night to Rossville, reported to General Thomas, and early in the morning of the twenty-first placed the two divisions of my command, which were at this place, (Wood's and Palmer's,) in the position assigned them. General Van Cleve, having collected about one thousand two hundred of his men, sent me word that he was encamped a few miles distant on the road leading from Chattanooga to Bridgeport, and that he had received orders from the General commanding the army. The enemy made some demonstrations during this day on my front, which covered the road leading from Ringgold to Rossville, but was easily made to keep a respectful distance, and after night, in obedience to orders, my command withdrew so quietly to Chattanooga that our own pickets were not aware of the movement. General W. C. Whitaker had reported to me on this day with two brigades and occupied the extreme left of my line. His were the last troops to withdraw, and I remained until he moved away with his command. On reaching Chattanooga, I was assigned to the position I now hold.

It is a source of much regret to me that circumstances made it impossible, with any regard to the interests of the service, for my corps to act as a unit in these battles. The pride of the corps was such that I think its attack would have been irresistible, and an attack upon it fatal to the enemy. But the great object of the battle was obtained. We foiled the enemy in his attempt to reöccupy Chattanooga; we hold the prize for which the campaign was made ; and if nothing has been added to the fame of the corps, it is only because its noble blood has been shed in detachments on every part of the field where an enemy was to be encountered, instead of flowing together, as at Stone River. The people will look with hissing and scorn upon the traducers of this corps, when they learn with what stubborn bravery it poured out its blood in their cause.

The army of the Cumberland matched itself against one army, and for two days disputed the field with three veteran armies, and then unmolested by them we moved to the coveted place, which we now hold, and where they have not ventured to assail us.

The conduct of the various detachments from

the Twenty-first army corps fully sustain their reputation. With pride I point to the services of Major-General Palmer, and his splendid division. Starting from Gordon's or Lee's Mills, they fought their way to General Thomas, and participated in all of the terrible struggles in that part of the field, and when ordered to withdraw, came off with music and banners flying. Such was the conduct of this part of my command, all of which has been published to the country as "having disgracefully fled from the field." With pride I call attention to the distinguished services of Brigadier-Generals Craft, and Hazen, and Colonel Grose, commanding the brigades of this division.

With pride I point to the services of Brigadier-General Van Cleve and his gallant division, which followed General Palmer into the fight. With daring courage they attacked the enemy on Saturday, capturing a battery, from which, however, they were driven by overwhelming numbers; but rallying, they maintained themselves, and, soon again advancing, captured another battery, which they brought off. With pride I mention the name of Brigadier-General Sam Beatty for his conduct on this occasion. On this day, and indeed whenever he was engaged, General Van Cleve's command was but two small brigades, his largest brigade, Colonel Barnes commanding, being detached. The accidental and unavoidable disaster of Sunday, which threw out of the fight altogether five regiments, cannot tarnish the fame of this division. Such was the conduct of this part of my command, which has been published as having "disgracefully fled from the field."

With pride I point to the services of Brigadier-General Wood and his gallant command. The last of my corps ordered to the scene of the conflict, they became engaged almost the very moment of their arrival.

Unexpectedly ran over by a portion of our troops who were driven back upon them, the brigade of Colonel Buell was thrown into confusion, and borne along with the flying for a short distance, but were soon and easily rallied by General Wood and Colonel Buell, and though the loss had been very heavy for so short a conflict, these brave men were led back by their division and brigade commanders to the ground from which they had been forced. On Sunday when our lines were broken, Brigadier-General Wood, with the brigades of Colonel Harker and Barnes, and that part of Colonel Buell's brigade not cut off by the enemy, reached Major-General Thomas, as ordered, and participated in the battle of the day with honors to themselves. Such was the conduct of this, the last part of my command, all of which has been published to the country as having "disgracefully fled from the field."

With pride I most respectfully call attention to the brilliant conduct of Colonel C. G. Harker, commanding Third brigade of Wood's division. On Saturday evening he skilfully avoided being thrown into disorder, and with good judgment

pressed the enemy, captured near two hundred prisoners, and withdrew his command in good order. On Sunday he equally distinguished himself by the skill with which he managed his command, and more than all by the gallantry with which he fought.

It is proper that I should mention the conduct of Colonel Barnes, commanding Third brigade of Van Cleve's division on Saturday morning. He was this time separated from his division, and in the fight of Saturday evening posted on our right. He had a very severe engagement with a superior force, and, in my judgment, prevented the enemy from attempting to turn our right by the firmness with which he fought. He suffered a severe loss, but withdrew his command in good order before night.

The names of the corps who particularly distinguished themselves have been mentioned by their respective commanders, and I most earnestly commend them to the consideration of the Commanding General and the Government.

With deep sorrow, yet not unmixed with pride, I call attention to the terrible list of casualties, amounting to nearly twenty-eight per cent of my entire command. The tabular statement herewith inclosed will show how small a portion of this percentage is missing or unaccounted for.

For a more detailed account of the operations of my command in this campaign, I refer you to the able reports of division, brigade, and regimental commanders. I also inclose the report of Major Mendenhall, of the operations of the artillery of his corps.

Captain Bradley, Sixth Ohio battery, acted with great energy and effect in repelling the advance of the enemy on Saturday, and Captain Swallow, with his battery, and Lieutenant Cushing, with his, acted with great coolness and decision, saving nearly all their pieces on the ridge Sunday, while the enemy was among them. Of the artillery commanders in the Second division, Captains Standart and Cockerill, Lieutenant Russell and Lieutenant Cushing, I refer to Major-General Palmer's very honorable mention of their conduct throughout both days' fight. My warmest thanks are due to my staff—to Lieutenant-Colonel Lyne Starling, Chief of Staff, as always on the battle-field, was courageous and active. Captain P. P. Oldershaw, A. A. G., discharged his duties with promptness and ability, displaying both coolness and bravery. He has earned and deserves promotion. Of Lieutenant-Colonel Lodor, Inspector-General of the corps, I can say no more than that he was as brave, active, and useful as at Stone River. Major Mendenhall, Chief of Artillery to my corps, has fairly earned and I hope will receive promotion. My Aids-de-Camp, Major L. M. Buford, Captain George G. Knox, and Captain John J. McCook, were active and attentive to their duties, freely exposing themselves throughout the battles.

I call particular attention to the efficiency and good judgment of the medical director of the corps, Surgeon A. J. Phelps. By his judicious arrangements nothing that could be done for our wounded was neglected. Assistant-Surgeon B. H. Cheney, medical surveyor of the corps, managed his department creditably.

Lieutenant-Colonel Sympson, Quartermaster, and Lieutenant-Colonel Knefflin, Commissary of Subsistence, were not on the field, but where I ordered them, performing these duties effectively in their respective departments.

Captain Henry Haldenbaugh, my own efficient Provost-Marshal, aided me materially in facilitating the movements of ambulances during the battles, and in the removal of the wounded from the field. I have rarely seen an officer of the department so thoroughly efficient as he has proved himself in camp and on the battle field.

Captain William Leonard, Lieutenants Foreaker and Messenger, of the Signal corps, were with me frequently during the battles, and made themselves useful.

It gives me much pleasure to call attention to Captain Sherer, Lieutenant Harvey, and the company they command, as my escort; to habitual good conduct in camp, they have added good conduct on the field of battle. Also to John Atkins, company D, Second regiment Kentucky volunteers, senior Clerk in the A. A. G. office, who remained on the field with my staff, both days, and aided me as much as any one in rallying the men. He is a good clerk, well-educated, and in every thing competent to command, and is deserving of a commission. The same may be said of George C. James, private, company A, clerk to my Chief of Artillery and Topographical Engineers, who, when detailed as a clerk, stipulated to join his regiment, when on the march, with the prospect of an engagement. On the march from Murfreesboro to Manchester, he joined his regiment, and also from the time of crossing the Tennessee River until the termination of the late engagements, in both of which he participated. If promotion cannot be had in their regiments, some distinguished mark of honor should be bestowed on both.

I am, sir, very respectfully, your obedient servant, T. L. CRITTENDEN,
Major-General Commanding.

Lieutenant-Colonel C. GODDARD, A. A. G.,
Department of the Cumberland.

REPORT OF MAJOR-GENERAL GRANGER.

HEADQUARTERS RESERVE CORPS, ARMY OF THE CUMBER-
LAND, CHATTANOOGA, Sept. 30, 1863.

COLONEL: I have the honor to submit the following report of the recent operations of a part of the Reserve corps.

On the sixth instant, I received orders from the General commanding the Army of the Cumberland to concentrate at Bridgeport, Ala., as much of my corps as could be spared from the duty of guarding the railroad depots, exposed points north of the Tennessee River, etc., and from that point to move them to the support of the main body of the army.

McCook's brigade, which was relieved by Colonel Mizner, was ordered from Columbia to Bridgeport, where it arrived on the tenth instant.

Two brigades of General Steedman's division, which were relieved from duty along the lines of railroad from Murfreesboro to Cowan, and from Wartrace to Shelbyville, by other troops from the rear, arrived at Bridgeport on the eleventh instant. The Twenty-second regiment Michigan infantry, under command of Colonel Le Favour, was sent direct to Bridgeport by railroad from Nashville, and was there attached to General Steedman's command.

The Eighty-ninth regiment Ohio infantry was also attached to the same command, having been sent to Bridgeport from Tracy City.

The difficulties to be overcome in forwarding and in concentrating these troops, and in bringing forward others to partially supply their place in so short a period, can only be appreciated when the large space of country over which they were scattered, the great distance from which relief had to come, and the necessity of leaving no point of communication exposed, is fully known.

On the twelfth instant, McCook's brigade, with Barnett's battery, was pushed to Shellmound.

At seven o'clock on the morning of the thirteenth instant, I started the following-mentioned forces, under the immediate command of Brigadier-General James B. Steedman, on a forced march from Bridgeport, Ala., for Rossville, Ga., namely, the First brigade First division Reserve corps, commanded by Brigadier-General Whitaker; Second brigade First division Reserve corps, commanded by Colonel J. G. Mitchell; the Twenty-second regiment Michigan infantry, Eighty-ninth regiment Ohio infantry, Eighteenth Ohio battery, and company M, First Illinois artillery. At the same time I started Colonel McCook's command from Shellmound for the same place. These forces arrived at Rossville, a distance of thirty-five miles from the place of starting, the next day at ten o'clock A.M., having marched the whole distance through a suffocating dust, and over a very rocky and mountainous road, on which it was exceedingly difficult for troops to travel.

I established my headquarters at Rossville, and there remained awaiting orders from the General commanding the Army of the Cumberland.

At three o'clock on the morning of the seventeenth instant, in accordance with orders that I had given, General Steedman started from his camp at Rossville with six regiments of infantry and a battery of artillery, for the purpose of making a reconnoissance in the direction of Ringgold. In this undertaking he met with no resistance from the enemy until within two miles from that place. Here he encountered the enemy's pickets, whom he drove rapidly across the East-Chickamauga, following them a mile and a quarter. He then halted and planted a section of artillery, by the fire of which he soon drove the enemy, who appeared to be in force, out of and beyond the town. Having accomplished the object of the reconnoissance, and discovering large clouds of dust arising from the Tunnel Hill and Lafayette roads, and which were approaching his position, he deemed it prudent to return to Rossville, and at once marched back to within eight miles of that place, where he halted for the night. The enemy advanced and shelled his camp before midnight, but they fell back and disappeared before morning. At daylight he broke up camp, started back to Rossville, and arrived there at one o'clock P.M. of the same day.

At four o'clock P.M., on the eighteenth instant, I ordered Brigadier-General Whittaker to move at once with his brigade and take possession of the crossing of the Chickamauga at Red House Bridge; and at the same time Colonel Daniel McCook was ordered to march to the support of Colonel Minty, who was disputing the crossing of the Chickamauga at Reed's Bridge with the enemy. Colonel McCook arrived within one mile of the bridge at dark, where he encountered the enemy, and with whom he had a slight skirmish, taking twenty-two prisoners. At five o'clock P. M. of the same day I sent Colonel Mitchell with his brigade to strengthen and support Colonel McCook, and he joined him during the night. General Whittaker was prevented from reaching the Red House Bridge by coming in contact with a superior force of the enemy on the road leading thereto. He had a severe skirmish, losing sixty men killed and wounded; but he held his ground until the next morning, when he received reënforcements. The enemy, however, withdrew from his immediate front before daylight.

The enemy obtained possession of Reed's Bridge on the afternoon of the eighteenth. At daylight on the morning of the nineteenth, Colonel McCook sent Lieutenant-Colonel Brigham with the Sixty-ninth Ohio Infantry, to surprise the enemy, and gain possession of it. He gallantly charged across the bridge, driving the enemy from it, and, in accordance with instructions received from General Steedman, destroyed it by fire. As the enemy were gathering in force around Colonel McCook, I sent him an order at six o'clock on the morning of the nineteenth instant, to withdraw from that position. This order was executed by seven o'clock A.M.

I now posted Colonel McCook's brigade at the junction of the Cleveland and Ringgold roads, covering the approaches to the rear and left flank of that part of my forces which were then on the road leading to the Red House Bridge, while Colonel Mitchell's brigade was led by General Steedman to the assistance of General Whittaker. Nothing further than slight skirmishing occurred in our front during the remaining part of the day. Yet all indications led us to believe that a large force of the enemy confronted us.

The position of my forces on the morning of the twentieth, and up to the hour of battle, was as follows: Colonel McCook's brigade was moved to a point near the McAfee Church, and was placed in such a position as to cover the Ringgold road; General Whittaker's brigade, together with Colonel Mitchell's, retained the same position that they had the evening before, and Colonel Minty, who reported to me at daylight on the morning of the twentieth with a brigade of cavalry, was posted at Missionary Mills, which positions completely covered our extreme left flank.

The enemy did not make his appearance in our immediate front during the morning, but large clouds of dust could be seen beyond our position arising from the Lafayette and Harrison roads, moving in the direction of the sound of battle. At ten thirty A.M. I heard very heavy firing, which was momentarily increasing in volume and intensity, on our right, in the direction of General Thomas's position. Soon afterward, being well convinced, judging from the sound of battle, that the enemy were pushing him hard, and fearing that he would not be able to resist their combined attack, I determined to go to his assistance at once. It was now about eleven o'clock A.M. I started with General Whittaker's and Colonel Mitchell's brigades, under the immediate command of General Steedman, and left Colonel McCook's brigade at the McAfee Church, in position to cover the Ringgold road. General Thomas was at this time engaging the enemy at a point between the Lafayette and Dry Valley roads, in the vicinity of —— house, about three and a half miles from our place of starting. We had not proceeded more than two miles when the enemy made his appearance in the woods to the left of our advancing column, about three fourths of a mile from the road. They opened upon us quite briskly with their skirmishers and a section of artillery. I then made a short halt to feel them, and becoming convinced that they constituted only a party of observation, I again rapidly pushed forward my troops. At this juncture I sent back and ordered up Colonel McCook's brigade to watch the movements of the enemy at this point, to keep open the Lafayette road, and cover the open field on the right of the road, and those that intervened between this point and the position held by General Thomas. As rapidly as possible, Colonel McCook brought up his brigade, took the position assigned to him, and held it until he marched to Rossville from the field of battle, at ten o'clock P.M. At six o'clock P.M. the enemy opened an artillery fire upon Colonel McCook, but he soon silenced their battery, which had done little or no damage to his troops.

At about one o'clock P.M. I reported to General Thomas. His forces were at that time stationed upon the brow of and holding a "horse-shoe ridge." The enemy were pressing him hard in front, and endeavoring to turn both of his flanks. To the right of this position was a ridge running east and west, and nearly at right angles therewith. Upon this the enemy were just forming. They also had possession of a gorge in the same, through which they were rapidly moving in large masses, with the design of falling upon the right flank and rear of the forces upon the "horse-shoe ridge."

General Thomas had not the troops to oppose this movement of the enemy, and in fifteen minutes from the time when we appeared on the field, had it not been for our fortunate arrival, his forces would have been terribly cut up and captured. As rapidly as possible I formed General Whittaker's and Colonel Mitchell's brigades, to hurl them against this threatening force of the enemy; which afterward proved to be General Hindman's division. The gallant Steedman, seizing the colors of a regiment, led his men to the attack. With loud cheers they rushed upon the enemy, and after a terrific conflict, lasting but twenty minutes, drove 'them from their ground, and occupied the ridge and gorge. The slaughter of both friend and foe was frightful. General Whittaker, while rushing forward at the head of his brigade, was knocked from his horse by a musket-ball, and was, for a short time, rendered unfit for duty; while two of his staff officers were killed, and two mortally wounded. General Steedman's horse was killed, and he was severely bruised, yet he was able to remain on duty during the day. This attack was made by our troops—very few of whom had ever been in an action before—against a division of old soldiers who largely outnumbered them. Yet with resolution and energy they drove the enemy from this position, occupied it themselves, and afterward held the ground they had gained with such terrible losses. The victory was dearly won, but to this army it was a priceless one.

There was now a lull in the battle; it was of short duration, however, for within thirty minutes after we had gained possession of the ridge, we were vigorously attacked by two divisions of Longstreet's veterans. Again the enemy was driven back, and from this time until dark the battle between these two opposing forces raged furiously.

Our whole line was continually enveloped in smoke and fire. The assaults of the enemy were now made with that energy which was inspired by the bright prospect of a speedy victory, and by a consciousness that it was only necessary to carry this position and crush our forces, to enable them to overthrow our army, and drive it across the Tennessee River. Their forces were massed and hurled upon us for the purpose of terminating at once this great and bloody battle. But the stout hearts of the handful of men who stood before them quailed not. They understood our perilous position, and held their ground, determined to perish rather than yield it. Never had a commander such just cause for congratulation over the action of his troops.

The ammunition which was brought in our train to this part of the field was divided with General Brannan's and Wood's divisions early in the afternoon, and we soon exhausted the remainder. All that we could then procure was taken from the cartridge-boxes of our own and the enemy's dead and wounded. Even this supply was exhausted before the battle was over, and while the enemy was still in our front, hurling fresh troops against us. It was almost dark; the enemy had been driven back, but we had not a round of ammunition left. All now seemed to be lost if he should return to the contest. Anticipating another attack, I ordered the command to be given to the men to stand firm, and to use the cold steel. After an ominous silence of a few minutes, the enemy came rushing upon us again. With fixed bayonets our troops gallantly charged them and drove them back in confusion. Twice more were these charges repeated, and the enemy driven back, before darkness brought an end to the battle. Night came, and the enemy fell back, whipped and discomfited. At three o'clock P.M. Brigadier-General Garfield, Chief of Staff, appeared upon that part of the field where my troops were then hotly engaged with the enemy. He remained with us until dark, animating and cheering both officers and men.

Although they were not under my command, I cannot refrain from herein noticing the troops that held the "horse-shoe ridge," and from testifying to their heroic bravery and unflinching steadiness under the heaviest fire. Their commanders, Generals Brannan and Wood and Colonel Harker, behaved with unqualified bravery and gallantry.

At seven o'clock P.M. I received instructions from Major-General Thomas to withdraw my troops from the position they held at dark, to march back to Rossville, and to cover the rear of the forces falling back upon that place with McCook's brigade. These instructions were promptly carried out, and I went into camp that night in accordance therewith.

My two brigades numbered two hundred and sixteen commissioned officers, and three thousand six hundred and ninety-seven men, when they went into the action. Between the hours of one P.M. and dark, there were killed, wounded, and missing one hundred and nine commissioned officers, and one thousand six hundred and twenty-three men—a total of one thousand seven hundred and thirty-two.

These losses are subdivided as follows: killed, two hundred and thirty-four; wounded, nine hundred and thirty-six; missing—all of whom, with the exception of a very small fraction, were taken prisoners—four hundred and sixty-one.

Among the gallant dead who fell upon the field of battle, was Captain William C. Russell, my Assistant Adjutant-General. He fell with his face to the enemy, in the thickest of the battle, while discharging an important duty. His loss is severely felt. Through his sterling qualities of heart and head, he became the idol of his corps. All who knew him now lament the loss of an accomplished soldier and sincere gentleman.

It is with pleasure that I call the attention of the Commanding General to the bravery and gallantry displayed during the battle by Brigadier-General James B. Steedman. He fearlessly rushed into the midst of danger, and was ever present with his troops, handling them with ease and confidence, rallying and encouraging them, and establishing order and confidence.

General Whittaker and Colonel Mitchell, commanding brigades, were also conspicuous for their bravery and activity. They managed their troops well, and contributed much to our success during the day

Colonel Daniel C. McCook, commanding Second brigade, Second division, properly and promptly carried out all orders and instructions I gave him. Although his brigade was not engaged in the battle, it held a very important position, protecting the rear of those who were fighting.

The aid and assistance rendered me by Colonel James Thompson, my Chief of Artillery, were timely and of great importance. His well-known ability and former experience rendered him a most efficient officer on the field.

The commanding officers of all my regiments, with but one exception, and of all my batteries, behaved nobly. Below I give a list of those most conspicuous for efficiency and bravery, and deserving special mention:

Colonel Champion, Ninety-sixth Illinois; Colonel Moon, One Hundred and Fifteenth Illinois; Colonel La Favour, Twenty-second Michigan; Colonel Carlton, Eighty-ninth Ohio; Lieutenant-Colonel Banning, One Hundred and Twenty-first Ohio; Lieutenant-Colonel Carter Van Vleck, Seventy-eighth Illinois; Lieutenant-Colonel Warner, One Hundred and Thirteenth Ohio; Major Brodies, (killed,) Ninety-sixth Illinois; Major Yeager, One Hundred and Twelfth Ohio; Lieutenant-Colonel Sanburn, (wounded,) Twenty-second Michigan; Captain Urquhart, commanding Ninety-eighth Ohio, (wounded;) Captain Thomas, who succeeded him in command, and was killed; Captain Espy, Commissary of Subsistence, (killed;) Captain Hicks, Ninety-sixth Illinois; Adjutant Hamilton, One Hundred and Thirteenth Ohio, and Captain Moe, A. A. G.; Major Smith, Lieutenant Blandin, and Captain Hays, all of General Steedman's staff. All of General Whittaker's staff officers were killed or wounded in the commencement of the battle. Their names have not been given to me.

I desire to return my thanks to the following members of my staff who were with me and rendered me efficient aid and service during the two days of battle:

Major J. S. Fullerton, Captain J. Gordon Taylor, Captain William L. Avery, and Lieutenant T. G. Braham.

Respectfully submitted, G. GRANGER,
Major-General.

COLONEL VAN DERVEER'S REPORT.

HEADQUARTERS THIRD DIVISION, FOURTEENTH ARMY
CORPS, CHATTANOOGA, TENN., Sept. 25, 1863.

Captain Lewis J. Lambett, A. A. G.:

CAPTAIN: I have the honor to report the part taken by the Third brigade in the actions of the nineteenth and twentieth instant, near the Chickamauga. My command consisted of the Second Minnesota, Colonel George; the Ninth Ohio, Colonel Kemmerling; the Thirty-fifth Ohio, Lieutenant-Colonel Boynton; the Eighty-seventh Indiana, Colonel Gleason; and Battery I, Fourth artillery, First Lieutenant F. G. Smith. Our effective strength on the morning of the nineteenth instant was one thousand seven hundred and eighty-eight officers and men.

After a fatiguing march during the night of the eighteenth, and without any sleep or rest, while halting near Kelly's house, on the Rossville and Lafayette road, I received an order from Brigadier-General Brannan, commanding the Second division, to move with haste along the road to Reed's Bridge over the Chickamauga, take possession of a ford near that point, and hold it. I immediately moved northward to McDaniel's house, and thence at right angles eastward toward the bridge, a short distance from McDaniel's. I formed the brigade in two lines, sent skirmishers to the front, and advanced cautiously, though without losing time, one and one half miles. In the mean time brisk firing was progressing upon my right, understood to be maintained by the First and Second brigades of this division. Being without a guide, and entirely unacquainted with the country, I am unable to state how near I went to Reed's Bridge, but perceiving from the fire upon my right that I was passing the enemy's flank, I wheeled the line in that direction, and began feeling his position with my skirmishers. About this time I received an order, stating that the Second brigade was gradually giving back, and that it was necessary I should at once make an attack. This we did with a will, the first line composed of the Thirty-fifth Ohio on the right and the Second Minnesota on the left, moving down a gentle slope, leaving the Eighty-seventh Indiana in reserve on the crest of the hill. At this time the Ninth Ohio, which had charge of the ammunition train of the division, had not arrived. Smith's battery, composed of four twelve-pound Napoleons, were placed in position in the centre and on the right of the line. The enemy, having discovered our location, opened a furious fire of artillery and musketry with considerable effect, but in half an hour the enemy slackened his fire, and his advanced line was compelled to fall back. I took advantage of this moment to bring forward the Eighty-seventh Indiana, and by a passage of lines to the front carried them to the relief of the Thirty-fifth Ohio, which had already suffered severely in the engagement. This movement was executed with as much coolness and accuracy as if on drill. Scarcely was the Eighty-seventh Indiana in line, before fresh forces of the enemy were brought up in time to receive from us a terrible volley, which made his ranks stagger, and held him for some time at bay. The Ninth Ohio, which I had previously sent for, arriving at this moment, I placed it on the right of my line. Still further to the right a section of Church's battery and the Seventeenth Ohio, which had been ordered to report to me, were in position.

As the enemy slackened his fire, Colonel Kemmerling, chafing like a wounded tiger, that he had been behind at the opening, ordered his men to charge, and away they went, closely followed by the Eighty-seventh Indiana and the Seventeenth Ohio, the enemy falling back precipitately. The Ninth, in the charge, recaptured the guns of Guenther's battery, Fifth artillery, and held them. In the mean time the enemy, massing his forces, suddenly appeared upon my left and rear; he came forward, several lines deep, at a double-quick, and opened a brisk fire, but not before I had changed my front to receive him. My new line consisted of the Second Minnesota on the right, next one section of Smith's battery, commanded by Lieutenant Rodney, then the Eighty-seventh Indiana, flanked by Church's and other sections of Smith's battery, and on the extreme left the Thirty-fifth Ohio. The two extremities of the line formed an obtuse angle, the vortex on the left of the Eighty-seventh Indiana, and the opening toward the enemy.

The Second Minnesota and Eighty-seventh Indiana lay on the ground, and were apparently unobserved by the enemy, who moved upon the left of my line, delivering and receiving a direct fire, Church opening with all his guns, and Smith with one section. He advanced rapidly, my left giving way slowly, until his flank was brought opposite my right wing, when a murdering and enfilading fire was poured into his ranks by the infantry, and by Rodney's section, shotted with canister. Notwithstanding this, he moved up his second and third lines. Having observed his great force as well as the persistency of his attack, I had sent messenger after messenger to bring up the Ninth Ohio, which had not yet returned from its charge made from my original right. At last, however, and when it seemed impossible for my brave men longer to withstand the impetuous advance of the enemy, the Ninth came gallantly up, in time to take part in the final struggle, which resulted in his sullen withdrawal. In this last attack his loss must have been very severe. In addition to the heavy fire of the infantry, our guns were pouring double charges of canister in front and on his flank, at one time delivered at a distance not exceeding forty yards. During the latter part of the contest reënforcements had arrived, and were, by General Brannan, then present, formed in line for the purpose of supporting my brigade, but they were not actually engaged at this time. Our dead and wounded were gathered up, and a new line, under the superintendence of General Brannan, was formed. The enemy, however, made no further demonstration and quietly withdrew.

A small number of prisoners were taken, who reported that the force opposed to us was two divisions of Longstreet's corps, one commanded by General Hood. They fought with great obstinacy and determination, only retreating when fairly swept away by our overwhelming fire.

After resting my command for an hour or more, I was ordered to report to Major-General Reynolds. Immediately moving toward his position we arrived near Kelly's house just before sundown, and then, by direction of General Brannan, went into bivouac.

At eight o'clock the next morning, Sunday, the twentieth of September, 1863, my brigade was posted as a reserve in the rear of the First and Second brigades of the division formed in two lines of columns closed in mass, where we remained for about an hour. Slowly moving over toward the left, for the purpose of occupying the space between the Third and Reynolds's division, I received an order to move quickly on the left and support General Baird, who, it was said, was being hard pressed by the enemy. I wheeled my battalions to the left, deployed both lines, and moved through the woods parallel to the Chattanooga road, gradually swinging round my left until when, in rear of Reynolds's position, I struck the road perpendicularly at a point just north of Kelly's house, near and back of his lines. On approaching the road, riding in advance of the brigade, my attention was called to a large force of the enemy moving southward in four lines, just then emerging from the woods at a run, evidently intending to attack Reynolds and Baird, who were both hotly engaged in the rear, and apparently unseen by these officers. I immediately wheeled my lines to the left, facing the approaching force, and ordered them to lie down. This movement was not executed until we received a galling fire delivered from a distance of two hundred yards; at the same time a rebel battery, placed in the road about five or six hundred yards to our front, opened on us with two guns. My command continued to lie down until the enemy approached within seventy-five yards, when the whole arose to their feet, and the front line, composed of the Second Minnesota and Eighty-seventh Indiana, delivered a murderous fire almost in their faces, and the Thirty-fifth and Ninth Ohio passing lines quickly to the front, the whole brigade charged and drove the enemy at a full run, over the open ground, for over a quarter of a mile, and several hundred yards into the woods, my men keeping in good order, and delivering their fire as they advanced.

The rebels fled hastily to cover, leaving the ground strewn with their dead and wounded. We took a position in the woods, and maintained a determined combat for more than an hour. At this time I greatly needed my battery, which had been taken from the brigade early in the day, by command of Major-General Negley. Finding a force moving on my right to support us, and the enemy being almost silenced, I ordered it to return to the open ground south of the woods. This movement was executed by passing lines to the rear, each line firing as it retired.

I learned from prisoners that the force we fought and put to flight this day was the division of the rebel General Breckinridge. That we punished them severely was proven by their many dead and wounded, among the former of which were several field officers, and among the latter one general officer of high rank. I thence moved to a position on the road, and the house near General Reynolds, and there remained, resting my men and caring for my wounded, for an hour or more.

Although I had not reported to either Generals Reynolds or Baird, as ordered in the morning, I believe I rendered them very substantial assistance, and at a time when it was greatly needed.

About two o'clock, hearing heavy firing on the right of the line, and learning that the high ground in that direction was being held by General Brannan with a part of our division, I moved cautiously through the woods, and at half-past two P.M. reported my brigade to him for duty. We were immediately placed in the front, relieving his troops, when almost exhausted. The position was well selected, and one capable of being defended against a heavy force, the line being the crest of a hill, for the possession of which the enemy made desperate and renewed efforts. From this time until dark we were hotly engaged. The ammunition failing, and no supply at hand, except a small quantity furnished by Major-General Gordon Granger, our men gathered their cartridges from the boxes of the dead, wounded, and prisoners, and finally fixed bayonets, determined to hold the position. Here, again, the Ninth Ohio made a gallant charge down the hill into the midst of the enemy, scattering them like chaff, and then returned to their position on the hill.

For an hour and a half before dusk the attack was one of unexampled fury—line after line of fresh troops being hurled against our position with a heroism and persistency which almost dignified their cause.

At length night ended the struggle, and the enemy, having suffered a terrible loss, retired from our immediate front. During the latter part of the day the position directly on our right had been held by the division of Brigadier-General Steedman, but which, early in the evening, had been withdrawn without our knowledge, thus leaving our flank exposed. From the silence at that point, Brigadier-General Brannan suspected all might not be right, and ordered me to place the Thirty-fifth Ohio across that flank, to prevent a surprise. This had scarcely been done before a rebel force appeared in the gloom, directly in their front. A mounted officer rode to within a few paces of the Thirty-fifth and asked: "What regiment is that?" To this some one replied: "The Thirty-fifth Ohio." The officer turned suddenly and attempted to run away, but our regiment delivered a volley that brought horse and rider to the ground, and put the force to flight. Prisoners said this officer was the rebel General Gregg.

At seven o'clock P.M. an order came from Major-General Thomas that the forces under General Brannan should move quietly to Rossville. This was carried into execution under the direction of Captain Cilley, of my staff, in excellent order.

During the whole of the two days' fighting, my brigade kept well together, at all times obeying orders promptly, and moving with almost as much regularity and precision as if on drill. They were subject to a very severe test on the nineteenth, when, being actively engaged with the enemy, another brigade (not of our division) ran, panic-stricken, through and over us, some of the officers of which shouted to our men to retreat, or they certainly would be overwhelmed;

but not a man left the ranks, and the approaching enemy found before him a wall of steel. Private Savage, of Smith's battery, struck one of the retreating officers with his sponge, and damned him for running against his gun.

Our loss in the engagement of both days amounts to thirteen officers and one hundred and thirty-two men killed, and twenty-five officers and five hundred and eighty-one men wounded, and fifty-one missing—the total loss being eight hundred and two men and officers. Doubtless many of those enumerated among the missing will be found either wounded or killed. There was no straggling, and I have little doubt those not wounded or killed will be found prisoners in the hands of the enemy. It is a noticeable fact that the Second Minnesota had not a single man among the missing, or a straggler, during the two days' engagement.

I cannot speak too highly of the conduct of my officers and men. Without exception they performed all that was required — much more than should have been expected.

When all did so well, it seems almost unjust to make distinctions; more gallantry and indomitable courage were never displayed upon the field of battle.

The attention of the General commanding the division is particularly called to the conduct of Colonel James George, commanding Second Minnesota; Colonel Gustavus Kemmerling, Ninth Ohio; Colonel N. Gleason, Eighty-seventh Indiana; Lieutenant-Colonel H. V. N. Boynton, commanding Thirty-fifth Ohio, and Lieutenant F. G. Smith, commanding battery I, Fourth artillery. These officers performed every duty required of them, with coolness and promptness, and by their energy and gallantry, contributed much to the favorable result which attended every collision with the enemy. Such officers are a credit to the service and our country. Smith's battery rendered great help in the action of the nineteenth, and was ably and gallantly served, Lieutenant Rodney being conspicuous in the management of his section.

Captain Church, of the First brigade, with one section of his battery, fought well, and is entitled to credit for the assistance he rendered me on the nineteenth.

I cannot refrain from alluding to the reckless courage and dash of Adjutant Harris, Ninth Ohio.

My staff upon the field consisted of Captain J. R. Beatty, Second Minnesota, Acting Assistant Adjutant-General; Captains Oliver H. Paschall, of the Thirty-fifth Ohio, and B. E. Throsseau, Ninth Ohio, Acting Aids; Captain C. A. Cilley, Second Minnesota, Brigade Topographical Engineer, and First Lieutenant A. E. Alden, Second Minnesota, Brigade Inspector. For efficiency, personal courage, and energy, their conduct deserves more than praise. They exposed themselves, upon all occasions, watching the movements of the enemy, carrying orders, rallying the men, and by every means in their power contributing to the success of the brigade. Captain Paschall was killed early in the action of the first day. He was a brave, noble soldier, an upright gentleman, and carries with him to the grave the love and respect of many friends.

Captain Throsseau was missing the evening of the same day, and I believe was captured. Captains Beatty and Cilley had each two horses shot under them.

There are many names particularly commended for courage and good behavior, for which I respectfully refer to the reports of the regiments and the battery.

We have lost many gallant officers and men, a list of whom is herewith furnished you.

In the charge made by the Ninth Ohio, on the nineteenth, which recaptured the battery of the regular brigade, their loss in killed and wounded was over fifty.

I am, Captain, very respectfully, your obedient servant,   F. VAN DERVEER,
Colonel Commanding Third Brigade.

Doc. 185.

OPERATIONS IN TENNESSEE VALLEY.

GENERAL HAZEN'S REPORT.

HEADQUARTERS SECOND BRIGADE, SECOND DIVISION,
TWENTY-FIRST ARMY CORPS, CHATTANOOGA,
October 8, 1863.

Lieutenant-Colonel C. Goddard, A. A. G., Headquarters Department Cumberland :

In obedience to orders received at Poe's Tavern, September third, 1863, from headquarters of the department, I assumed command of all the troops in the Tennessee Valley, embracing Wagner's and my own brigade of infantry, Minty's brigade of cavalry, and Wilder's brigade of mounted infantry, in all between six and seven thousand men, with orders to keep these forces well in hand, to closely watch the movements of the enemy at all the crossings of the Tennessee River, make such dispositions of the force as should lead the enemy to believe that the valley was occupied by a large force, and to cross ourselves and occupy Chattanooga at the earliest opportunity.

The forces were scattered from Kingston to Williams's Island, a distance of seventy miles, watching the entire line of the river for this distance, and guarding at least twenty ferries and fords.

I at once visited in person the entire length of the line, making such dispositions as I thought best for carrying out the design of the command, withdrawing as much as possible the left of the line, and giving orders for the construction of boats in the North-Chickamauga to be floated down and used for crossing when needed at the mouth of that stream.

Troops were made to appear simultaneously at three or four different crossings, and by ingeniously arranging their camp-fires and beating their calls, and the dexterous use of artillery, were made to represent a division of troops at such place.

The object desired was fully obtained.

I also placed all heavy stores on Waldon's Ridge, and as the enemy threatened to cross his cavalry in heavy force, made preparations to receive him, and failing to destroy him, to drive him up the valley beyond Pikeville, where he could be met by General Burnside.

A battery and two regiments of infantry were placed opposite Chattanooga, and the enemy at that point annoyed, and two of his boats disabled. I also established communication by signal between all the crossings near me and my headquarters.

On the second the enemy burned the Loudon Bridge, and Buckner's corps commenced moving slowly down the river, making strong demonstration upon its banks as if to cross at several places. They moved on Tyner's Station, reaching that point on the sixth and seventh, followed by a heavy cavalry force, that took the place of the infantry on the river as they were relieved, and from their numbers, Colonel Minty reported that indication made it pretty certain that a crossing was about to be attempted.

At the same time the pontoon-bridge of the enemy was moved at Chattanooga, as if to cross over troops at that point.

All the crossings were closely watched and the troops held in readiness for any movement. On the eighth the river was cleared of all rebel troops above Chickamauga, and I directed Minty to cross over at the mouth of Sale Creek, reconnoitring the country well in his front, and move cautiously down to Harrison, always controlling one of the fords near him, so as to cross back if it should be found necessary.

Before the order could be obeyed, a heavy cavalry force confronted him on the opposite side of the river, and the crossing was not attempted. On that night, however, they all retired from above Friar's Island, and at eleven A.M. on the ninth, from their works opposite that island.

The city of Chattanooga was also evacuated the same morning, and the troops of General Wagner crossed over and occupied the city, a portion of Wilder's force crossing at Friar's Island, reconnoitring thoroughly the country opposite and toward Chattanooga.

Colonel Minty was at once ordered down to cross and report to Colonel Wilder, while all the troops, not already over, were on the night of the ninth concentrated at Friar's Island, and on the morning of the tenth crossed by fording, which was accomplished within the space of six hours without loss of life or material.

The boats, although completed, were not required. I found in the Tennessee Valley an abundance of subsistence for my troops, and brought out of it seventy beeves for the army.

The casualties in all these operations were two killed, one drowned, and five or six wounded. Several hundred prisoners and deserters were sent to the rear.

I have earnestly to commend to the attention of the Government the services of Colonels Wilder and Minty, commanding cavalry brigades.

I am, very respectfully, your obedient servant,
W. B. HAZEN,
Brigadier-General.

Doc. 186.

AN APPEAL TO SOUTHERN MATRONS.

ASSISTANT QUARTERMASTER'S OFFICE, CLOTHING, CAMP, AND GARRISON DEPOT, SELMA, October 8, 1863.

I WANT all the blankets and carpets that can possibly be spared. I want them, ladies of Alabama, to shield your noble defenders against an enemy more to be dreaded than the Northern foe with musket in hand—the snows of coming winter. Do you know that thousands of our heroic soldiers of the West sleep on the cold, damp ground, without tents? Perhaps not. You enjoy warm houses and comfortable beds.

If the immortal matrons and maidens of heathen Rome could shear off and twist into bow strings the hair of their heads to arm their husbands and brothers in repelling the invader, will not the Christian women of the Confederacy give the carpets off their floors to protect against the chilly blasts of winter those who are fighting, with more than Roman heroism, for their lives, liberty, and more, their honor? Sufficient blankets cannot be had in time. Food and clothing failing the army, you and your children will belong to Lincoln. To get your daily bread, you will then be permitted to hire yourselves to your heartless enemies as servants, or perchance to your own slaves. Think of that! Think of your brothers, fathers, and sons drenched with the freezing rains of winter, and send in at once every blanket and carpet, old or new, you can spare. They will be held as a sacred trust. As soon as they can be gotten ready for issue, they will be sent to the Quartermaster-in-Chief of General Johnston's army for distribution.

As a guarantee that a proper disposition shall be made of such as may be donated, H. H. Ware, Esq., will receive and receipt for the same at Selma. Honorable and well-known names will be announced to receive and receipt for the same at Montgomery, Tuscaloosa, Demopolis, Marion, and elsewhere.

We will pay a liberal price for all that may be delivered at this place, or to any bonded quartermaster in this State, upon the presentation of his certified account upon form No. 12.

Honorable boards of mayor and aldermen of incorporated towns will please take such action in this regard as to them may be deemed best calculated to aid us in the premises.

Ministers of the Gospel also are urgently requested to call the attention of their congregations to this matter. Every one, male or female, who can furnish a blanket may save a man to the army.

Having been assigned to the duty of providing clothing and camp and garrison equipage for the army of the West, I make this appeal to the people in confidence.

Your obedient servant,
W. M. GILLASPIE,
Captain and A. Q. M.

Doc. 187.

FIGHT NEAR VERMILIONVILLE, LA.

HEADQUARTERS FIRST DIVISION NINETEENTH ARMY CORPS, VERMILIONVILLE, Oct. 10.

AFTER the slight skirmish with the rebels on Sunday evening, the fourth instant, and the rapid retreat of the enemy for some four miles, they again, as soon as our advance halted, assumed their air of defiance, sending their scouts within a short distance of our lines, and making a show of strength which they were not supposed to be possessed of. Accordingly, on Tuesday, Colonel Davis was ordered forward to furnish them an opportunity for a fight or foot-race, at their own option. Their determination was quickly taken at the appearance of our force, and the gallant Colonel gave them a hot chase for several miles, accelerating their unreluctant movement by a brisk application of musketry and shells from Captain Nim's battery. One horse was killed, and report says a few of the enemy were wounded.

The ground thus gained it was desirable to hold, and accordingly the First brigade of this division, Acting Brigadier-General Love commanding, was ordered forward to the support of the cavalry. They were not interfered with, the enemy preserving their distance, reconnoitring closely, and well in hand for a race upon our advancing. The morning of Thursday, the ninth instant, the Nineteenth corps was ordered to advance, the rear of the entire column, consisting of the Thirteenth army corps, Major-General Ord commanding, having closed up, and the entire command being well in hand, advancing cautiously, but surely, ready for service in a moment should occasion require. There was no occasion, however, for the troops to test the fighting qualities of the rebels, for they kept well out of range, retreating before the cavalry without firing a shot. At night the encampment was pitched on the open prairie, about seven miles from Vermilion Bayou, at which point the enemy were reported in force at from two to eight thousand men, with some heavy siege guns, two field batteries of artillery, quite a force of cavalry, and several regiments of infantry. Our cavalry were sent well to the front, and exchanged shots with the enemy's pickets, who were posted on the east side of the bayou. The position of the enemy was apparently a powerful one, and, if they mustered as strong as reported, every thing looked fair for a severe engagement. During our stay at this camp, Colonel Paine, of the Second Louisiana regiment, ranking officer of the First brigade, arrived and assumed command, relieving Colonel Love, who assumed command of his old regiment, the One Hundred and Sixteenth New-York volunteers.

Next morning, at eight o'clock, the advance was resumed, and about eleven o'clock reached a favorable position for forming line of battle, in the neighborhood of which Major-General Franklin, who had preceded the army a short distance, had established his headquarters. Colonel Davis, from a point about a quarter of a mile to the right, opened the fight with a brisk skirmish, driving the enemy across the bayou, and followed up the advantage with a hot fire from the section of Nim's rifled battery with his command. In a very short time a battery of the First Regular United States artillery, (Elaian's,) under command of Lieutenant Frank Taylor, was in position in the centre, immediately opened fire, sending shells some two or three miles across the bayou, stirring up the enemy in lively style. Taylor was followed by the First Indiana battery, Major Ray commanding, which was stationed on the extreme left, and opened with the twenty and thirty-pounder rifled pieces, shelling the woods on the shore of the bayou, up and down. The two last-named batteries were assisted by the One Hundred and Sixteenth New-York volunteers, Colonel Love, (of the First brigade, Colonel Paine, First division, General Weitzel,) who were deployed as skirmishers, supported by the One Hundred and Fifteenth New-York volunteers, Colonel Kinsy, of the same brigade. For about an hour the firing was very warm, the booming of the cannon being interspersed with the sharp reports of the muskets, the enemy replying but feebly, mostly from the left of their line, and soon ceasing altogether. A reconnoissance revealed the fact that they had fled, in their haste leaving behind them in their camp, dinner already cooked, some arms, camp furniture, and in one spot three of their hats. A force was immediately thrown across the cavalry fording, close to the remains of a destroyed bridge on our right, and the infantry by means of an improvised pontoon bridge laid on the half-burnt stringers of a bridge on the left.

There was some little skirmishing after crossing, the enemy firing on our cavalry as they retreated. That they met with severe loss is perfectly evident, as new-made graves were discovered this morning a short distance from the town, and the inhabitants report at quite a number of wounded rebels were carried through the place during the progress of the fight.

The army is now consolidated, and Major-General Banks arrived just after the fight of yesterday, assuming command of the entire force, consisting of the Thirteenth and Nineteenth army corps, under the command of Generals Ord and Franklin.

Our loss was none killed, and Major Cowan, of the Second Louisiana cavalry, and four privates wounded. The Major's wound is reported as very slight, and he will be on duty again in a very short time.

The conduct of all concerned in this affair was excellent, and the most conspicuous of all was the gallant General Weitzel on his war-horse, riding boldly to the front, whither he had forbidden any other going on horseback. His appearance inspired his troops with the wildest enthusiasm, and the firing, which was warm and rapid before, seemed to redouble as he rode along the line.

Doc. 188.

OPERATIONS IN VIRGINIA.

GENERAL ROBERT E. LEE'S REPORT.

HEADQUARTERS ARMY OF NORTHERN VIRGINIA, } October 23, 1863. }

General S. Cooper, Adjutant and Inspector-General:

GENERAL: In advance of a detailed report, I have the honor to submit, for the information of the department, the following outline of the recent operations of this army:

With the design of bringing on an engagement with the Federal army, which was encamped around Culpeper Court-House, extending thence to the Rapidan, this army crossed the river on the ninth instant, and advanced by way of Madison Court-House. Our progress was necessarily slow, as the march was by circuitous and concealed roads, in order to avoid the observation of the enemy.

General Fitz Lee, with his cavalry division and a detachment of infantry, remained to hold our lines south of the Rapidan ; General Stuart, with Hampton's division, moved on the right of the column. With a portion of his command he attacked the advance of the enemy near James City on the tenth, and drove them back toward Culpeper. Our main body arrived near that place on the eleventh instant, and discovered that the enemy had retreated toward the Rappahannock, ruining or destroying his stores.

We were compelled to halt during the rest of the day to provision the troops, but the cavalry, under General Stuart, continued to press the enemy's rear guard toward the Rappahannock. A large force of Federal cavalry, in the mean time, had crossed the Rapidan, after our movement began, but was repulsed by General Fitz Lee, and pursued toward Brandy Station.

Near that place the commands of Stuart and Lee united, on the afternoon of the eleventh, and after a severe engagement, drove the enemy's cavalry across the Rappahannock with heavy loss.

On the morning of the twelfth the army marched in two columns, with the design of reaching the Orange and Alexandria railroad north of the river, and interrupting the retreat of the enemy.

After a skirmish with some of the Federal cavalry, at Jeffersonton, we reached the Rappahannock at Warrenton Springs in the afternoon, where the passage of the river was disputed by cavalry and artillery. The enemy was quickly driven off by a detachment of our cavalry, aided by a small force of infantry and a battery. Early next morning (fifteenth) the march was resumed, and the two columns reünited at Warrenton, in the afternoon, when another halt was made to supply the troops with provisions.

The enemy fell back rapidly along the line of the railroad, and early on the fourteenth the pursuit was continued, a portion of the army moving by way of New-Baltimore toward Bristoe Station, and the rest, accompanied by the main body of the cavalry, proceeding to the same point by Auburn Mills and Greenwich. Near the former place a skirmish took place between General Ewell's advance and the rear guard of the enemy, which was forced back and rapidly pursued.

The retreat of the enemy was conducted by several direct parallel roads, while our troops were compelled to march by difficult and circuitous routes. We were consequently unable to intercept him. General Hill arrived first at Bristoe Station, where his advance, consisting of two brigades, became engaged with a force largely superior in numbers, posted behind the railroad embankment.

The particulars of the action have not been officially reported, but the brigades were repulsed with some loss, and five pieces of artillery, with a number of prisoners, captured. Before the rest of the troops could be brought up, and the position of the enemy ascertained, he retreated across Broad Run. The next morning he was reported to be fortifying beyond Bull Run, extending his line toward the Little River Turnpike.

The vicinity of the intrenchments around Washington and Alexandria rendered it useless to turn his new position, as it was apparent that he could readily retire to them, and would decline an engagement unless attacked in his fortifications. A further advance was therefore deemed unnecessary, and after destroying the railroad from Cub Run southwardly to the Rappahannock, the army returned on the eighteenth to the line of that river, leaving the cavalry in the enemy's front.

The cavalry of the latter advanced on the following day, and some skirmishing occurred at Buckland. General Stuart, with Hampton's division, retired slowly toward Warrenton, in order to draw the enemy in that direction, thus exposing his flank and rear to General Lee, who moved from Auburn, and attacked him near Buckland. As soon as General Stuart heard the sound of Lee's guns he turned upon the enemy, who, after a stubborn resistance, broke, and fled in confusion, pursued by General Stuart nearly to Haymarket, and by General Lee to Gainesville.

Here the Federal infantry was encountered, and after capturing a number of them during the night, the cavalry slowly retired before their advance on the following day. When the movement of the army from the Rapidan commenced, General Imboden was instructed to advance down the valley, and guard the gaps of the mountains on our left. This duty was well performed by that officer, and on the eighteenth instant he marched upon Charlestown, and succeeded, by a well-concerted plan, in surrounding the place, and capturing nearly the whole force stationed there, with all their stores and transportation; only a few escaped to Harper's Ferry. The enemy advanced from that place, in superior numbers, to attack General Imboden, who retired, bringing off his prisoners and captured property, his command suffering very little loss, and inflicting some damage upon the pursuing column. In the course of these operations, two thousand four hundred and thirty-six prisoners were captured, including forty-one commissioned officers. Of the above number, four hundred and thirty-four were taken by General Imboden.

A more complete account, with a statement of our killed, wounded, and prisoners, will be forwarded as soon as the necessary official reports have been received.

Very respectfully, your obedient servant,
R. E. LEE,
General.

Official: JOHN WITHERS, A. A. G.

GENERAL STUART'S REPORT.

BUCKLAND, VA., Oct 20, 1863.

GENERAL: After offering some considerable resistance to the advance of the enemy at this point yesterday, in accordance with the suggestions of Major-General Lee, I retired with Hampton's division slowly before the enemy, until within two miles and a half of Warrenton, in order that Major-General Lee, coming from Auburn, might have an opportunity to attack the enemy in flank and rear. The plan proved successful. The enemy followed slowly and cautiously after Hampton's division, when, on hearing Major-General Lee's guns on their flank, I pressed upon them vigorously in front. They at first resisted my attack stubbornly, but once broken, the rout was complete. I pursued them from within three miles of Warrenton to Buckland, the horses at full speed the whole distance, the enemy retreating in great confusion.

Major-General Lee had attacked them in flank just below Buckland. We captured about two hundred prisoners, eight wagons and ambulances, arms, horses, and equipments. The rout was the most complete that any cavalry has ever suffered during this war.

Crossing at Buckland, General Fitz Lee pushed down the pike toward Gainesville, while I with the few men of Gordon's and Rosser's brigades, who could be collected after our unusually long chase, moved around to our left, and pressed down toward Haymarket. Here I encountered, besides a large cavalry force, the First army corps, who retired a short distance beyond Haymarket, on the Carolina road. I attacked their infantry pickets by moonlight, and scattered them over the fields, capturing many. General Lee pressed down to within a short distance of Gainesville, when he encountered their infantry, and captured prisoners from the First army corps on that road also. The pursuit was continued until after dark. The cavalry force was commanded by Kilpatrick, and composed of ten regiments. Most respectfully,

(Signed) J. E. B. STUART,
Major-General.

Official: JOHN WITHERS, A. A. G.

See "Fights along the Rapidan."

GENERAL IMBODEN'S REPORT.

HEADQUARTERS VALLEY DISTRICT, IN THE FORK
OF THE SHENANDOAH, NEAR
FRONT ROYAL, Oct. 19, 1863.

Colonel R. H. Chilton, Chief of Staff, A. N. V:

COLONEL: Yesterday (Sunday) morning, at two o'clock, I moved from Berryville to surprise and capture the garrison at Charlestown. The surprise was complete, the enemy having no suspicion of our approach until I had the town entirely surrounded. I found the enemy occupying the court-house, jail, and some contiguous buildings in the heart of the town, all loop-holed for musketry, and the court-house yard inclosed by a heavy wall of oak timber. To my demand for a surrender, Colonel Simpson requested an hour for consideration. I offered him five minutes, to which he replied: "Take me, if you can." I immediately opened on the building with artillery, at less than two hundred yards, and with half a dozen shells drove out the enemy into the streets, where he formed and fled toward Harper's Ferry. At the edge of the town he was met by the Eighteenth cavalry, Colonel Imboden's and Gilmore's battalions.

One volley was exchanged, when the enemy threw down his arms and surrendered unconditionally. The Colonel, Lieutenant-Colonel, and five others, who were mounted, fled at the first fire, and ran the gauntlet, and escaped toward Harper's Ferry. The force I captured was the Ninth Maryland regiment, and three companies of cavalry, numbering between four and five hundred men and officers. I have not had time to have them counted. In wagons, horses, and mules, arms, ammunition, medicine, and clothing, were considerable, all of which I have saved, and will have properly accounted for. As I expected, the Harper's Ferry forces, infantry, artillery, and cavalry, appeared at Charlestown in less than two hours after I fired the first gun. Having promptly sent off the prisoners and property, I was prepared for them. I retired from the town and fell back slowly toward Berryville, fighting the enemy all the way, from ten o'clock till near sunset. My loss, as far as ascertained, is very small—five killed and fifteen or twenty wounded, more or less, three or four mortally. Captain Coleman will lose an arm, and Captain Cummel was badly shot in the hip. I think a few—ten or fifteen broken-down men—who straggled behind, were captured. We killed and wounded dreadfully several of the enemy in the court-house, including the Adjutant of the Ninth Maryland; and, in the fight along the road, the enemy's loss was considerable, as we ambuscaded them several times with good effect. I marched nearly all night, and reached the river here at daybreak. It was quite full, but I have effected a safe crossing of the north branch.

Very respectfully,

Your obedient servant,

J. D. IMBODEN,
Brigadier-General.

Official:

JOHN WITHERS, A. A. G.

NATIONAL ACCOUNTS.

HEADQUARTERS ARMY OF THE
POTOMAC, Oct. 15, 1863.

After the cavalry engagement on Sunday, it was rumored that the rebel infantry was in force, supporting their cavalry. This induced General Meade to countermarch the troops, with the intention of making the line of the Rappahannock his base of operations in case of an attack. He also intrenched his reserve artillery in the forts near the river. Their desperate attack on Gregg's cavalry on Monday evening seemed to open our eyes to their real intentions; so an order came for the troops to march in the dead of night.

On Tuesday morning, as our infantry were returning toward Auburn, on nearing the ford, which is in a dry ravine, with close trees and underwood, the enemy's dismounted cavalry opened a brisk fire on the front of the column from their sheltered position. The front line was composed of Graham's brigade, the Sixty-third Pennsylvania being in advance—a regiment chiefly of conscripts, and commanded by Colonel Danks. General Birney seeing them wavering, rode up, and cried out, "Come on, boys! go into them," and charged. The regiment at once rallied and forced back the enemy. The First division of the Third corps lost in this short but stubborn encounter, eleven men killed and forty-two wounded. Lieutenant Miller and Captain Consert were both wounded severely. The rebels retired, leaving eight killed and a large number of wounded, besides a lot of arms and accoutrements, behind them. Among the wounded were the bugler and two orderlies on the General's escort. The corps then moved on and encamped for the night at Greenwich. The Second corps bivouacked in the woods, beyond the ford.

About six o'clock we resumed our march, and soon crossed the ford at Auburn. The First division, commanded by General Caldwell, fell into line of battle on the heights beyond. So secure did we feel that the men were ordered to stack their arms and cook breakfast. We heard some firing on our left, and when the dark haze that obscured the morning cleared away, we could see the lines of cavalry within half a mile of us. Corn was stacked in the field; so we left our tired and hungry steeds to feed on it, and advanced to the top of the hill to witness the conflict going on in the plain beneath. We saw our cavalry (Gregg's) charging into the wood; but after a fierce shelling and musketry fight, we saw them break back, followed pell-mell by the enemy. They were now rushing toward our lines.

Our men were cooking their coffee, speculating on the chances of the conflict. It was to be many a poor fellow's last breakfast. On our right were a couple of high knolls, thickly wooded. From these all of a sudden masked batteries opened on our lines, shot and shell came shrieking through the air, and so accurate was their range, that nearly every one of them came ploughing through us. The men jumped to their arms, the officers rushed to their commands.

The very hill reeled beneath us like a drunken man. As I darted through the men fell on both sides of me. The Fifty-second New-York volunteers, a conscript regiment, chanced from our position to be in front. They wavered, and were falling back on the old regiments, when Colonel Frank, who commanded the Third brigade, rode in their front and rallied them, crying: "Stand boys! follow me." Behind them was the Second brigade—or Irish brigade—who coolly stood to their guns. Colonel Myles, too, rallied the lines. In a moment the panic subsided, and the men stood coolly in their lines, though the shot and shell of the enemy were knocking them over pretty fast.

The lines now fell back behind the crest of the hill, and Rickett's battery, having taken position, returned the enemy's killing compliments with interest, shelling the woods and ravine in which they were concealed.

All this time the rebels were shouting their demoniacal yell all round, and the sharp metallic sound of musketry ran along our picket and skirmish lines. The enemy's battery soon became silent; but the firing increased along our skirmishing lines.

The corps now wheeled round its head in the direction of Catlett's Station. It was evident that the enemy meant to contest every inch of ground, and to cut us off from forming a junction with the other corps. The troops had to move in fighting order, every now and then taking up lines of defence.

As there was little intermission from fighting all day, I could not ascertain ours or the rebel loss. I saw one rebel colonel mortally wounded. Gregg's cavalry suffered heavily, chiefly the Tenth New-York, which is severely cut up.

The Second corps nobly covered the retreat of the army, being successively engaged with the enemy at several different points throughout the day, and most desperately throughout the afternoon and evening. They stood like a wall of iron against the repeated and thundering assaults of the enemy, until our whole army, with all its transportation, was secure, and in a position to meet every attack.

THE BATTLE OF BRISTOE STATION.

The entire army left the line of the Rapidan, on its retrograde movement on Saturday night, marching along the line of railroad until Wednesday morning, encountering the enemy at times, and skirmishing occasionally, avoiding a general engagement. A general action might have been brought on at any time between the Rappahannock and our present position; but it was reserved for Wednesday to witness a renewed trial of the capabilities of our brave men in the field.

The Second corps had been assigned the arduous duty of guarding the rear of the army, and on the morning of Wednesday, at daylight, took up its line of march in the following order: General Hayes's Third division leading, followed by the First division, General Caldwell, the rear

being brought up by General Webb's Second division.

On reaching a point near the railroad, some three miles west of Bristoe, the Second division took the lead, followed by the Third, leaving the first at the rear. In this order they marched to Bristoe, on the south side of the track of the Orange and Alexandria railroad, with flankers well out on both sides and skirmishers deployed.

In order to understand fully the character of the fight, it is necessary to give the topography of the country in the vicinity of Bristoe. The Orange and Alexandria railroad here runs in a north-easterly and south-westerly direction over a broken and woody country: The town of Bristoe is *non est*. But a few old chimneys point out the place where the village once was, just at the west of Broad Run, about three miles west of Manassas Junction, and half a mile west of the station. There is a skirt of dense woods, undergrown with thick brush, through which, on either side of the railroad track, a tolerable road has been cut, both of which were used by our army on its march. On the west side of Broad Run the country is hilly up to the woods, and somewhat overgrown with brush. The run crosses the railroad at right angles under a high bridge, at the eastern end of which a dilapidated windmill stands, formerly used for pumping water for the use of the road.

About three fourths of a mile west of Bristoe is Cedar Run, a small stream; but, from its depth of mud and water, difficult to ford. On the north side of the track, about thirty rods west of the bridge, is a solitary house, or rather shanty, which, though insignificant of itself, figures somewhat extensively in the fight. There are here, also, just back of the shanty, three quite prominent hillocks or humps, upon which the rebels had planted batteries. Also there were several like elevations on the south side of the track, upon which the batteries of our own forces were located. West of Broad Run, extending for a few rods, is low ground, rocky and brushy, affording excellent opportunities for sharp-shooters. On the east side of Broad Run, for a hundred rods, is an open plain, with a little point of timber jutting out perhaps twenty rods, and having its north border about eight rods south of the railroad. The roads from the west run across Broad Run as follows: The one on the north side of the track branches about forty rods west of the run, one fork crossing the run about a hundred rods north of the bridge, and goes to Centreville; the other fork crossing the track about twenty rods west of the bridge, and leading to the fork on the south side of the bridge. The road on the south side of the track runs parallel with the railroad; but a branch makes off to the right at Cedar Run, and crosses Broad Run about thirty rods south of the bridge. East of Broad Run, about a hundred rods distant, is a belt of timber perhaps a quarter of a mile wide, east of which the country on the south side of the track is open to Manassas.

About half-past twelve o'clock the advance of

the Second corps (General Webb's division) reached the eastern edge of the wood looking out toward Broad Run. The rear of the Fifth corps was just crossing Broad Run by the northmost road, when, as suddenly as lightning and as astonishingly as a thunderbolt from a clear sky, boom, boom, boom, came a half dozen discharges of artillery, not a hundred yards away. It was the enemy emerging from the woods north of the railroad by an obscure road, and firing upon the rear of the Fifth corps. A few shells from the rebel battery killed four of the Pennsylvania reserves, and wounded eight others before they could be got over the run to a place of safety on the eastern side. Then a line of rebel skirmishers appeared, cresting the hill on the north of the track, and running obliquely from the road to the upper crossing of Broad Run.

General Warren immediately formed his plans, and right beautifully were they carried out. General Webb's division was thrown forward along the line of the south side of the railroad, with its right resting on Broad Run and its left at the wagon road. General Hayes's division was marched by the right flank, and took position to the left of Webb, while Caldwell faced the railroad and awaited action.

A section of Brown's battery, company A, First Rhode Island artillery, was thrown across Broad Run and put in position in the open field, where it could face the enemy and enfilade his skirmishers, the remainder being placed on the hill just west of the run and bearing directly upon the massing enemy. On the hill to the north-west of Brown was Arnold's famous battery — the same which at Gettysburgh did such terrible execution among the rebel infantry. Then there were other batteries not behind their compeers in the bloody fray.

As soon as the rebels discovered that the rear of the Fifth corps had crossed to the east of Broad Run, and that Warren was preparing for a fight, they developed two batteries in the edge of the wood, and commenced to send their respects to the Second corps. They were close by, their most distant guns being not over nine hundred yards from the line of the Union infantry. They had the advantage of us at first; for they, knowing our position and having their batteries ready planted, were able to open upon us before our line could be formed or our batteries planted, and they knew and appreciated their advantage, and right heartily did they improve it.

For full ten minutes they rained their bullets and hailed their shells with demoniac fury; but not a man of the gallant old Second quailed, not a gun was dropped, not a color dipped; but like Spartans they faced their foe, as if each man felt that upon himself rested the responsibility of crushing the rebellion.

But the rebels did not long maintain their advantage, for Brown and Arnold lost no time in getting their batteries placed, which, when accomplished, made short work of all opposition. Rebel lines of infantry skirmishers melted away like wax over a hot fire, and the rebel batteries

died out like camp-fires in a heavy rain. Simultaneously with the ripping, tearing, death-dealing artillery, the Union infantry stood hiding their forms behind a bank of flame and a fog of smoke, cheering as they discharged their pieces, and vainly begging to be permitted to rush over the track to the immediate locality of their adversaries.

Then came a lull in the awful music; for the enemy, unable to stand against the terrible storm, had fled to the woods for safety, leaving six of their guns upon the field, one too badly crippled to be brought away. When the enemy ceased playing upon us, and the smoke had lifted so as to exhibit the field, and it was known that the enemy had retired, a detail of ten men from each regiment was made to bring away the deserted pieces. With a cheer that could be heard for miles, the men bounded across the track and climbed the opposite hill, seized the pieces as best they could, wheeled them into position, turned them toward the retreating demons, and fired a parting salvo with the ammunition which had been designed for the Yankees. Then the boys dragged five of them away, shouting as they came to the south side of the track, and placed them in battery, the infantry acting as artillerists and doing wondrous works of carnage.

Shortly after the Second corps had got into position, the rebels tried their old tactics of massing and charging. A dense gray body of men were seen forming between the east of the woods and the run on the slope of the hill, north of the railroad, upon which the artillery and infantry opened at once, driving the throng back into the woods at a double-quick. After this manœuvre a second line of skirmishers was thrown forward to the brow of the hill skirting the river, and two regiments of North-Carolina troops—the Twenty-sixth and Twenty-eighth—came charging on our extreme right, over the railroad near the bridge.

This post was held by Colonel Heath, commanding the brigade, which was the first of the Second division, and consisted of the Nineteenth Maine, Fifteenth Massachusetts, First Minnesota, and Eighty-second New-York. Our boys waited for their "erring Southern brethren," who came on with a yell until they reached the track of the railroad, when a volley, and another, and another, sent them homeward at a pace which defies illustration.

The brigade of Carolinians, which was commanded by Brigadier-General Heth, broke and fled, hiding themselves behind the rocks and bushes along the stream. This brigade of North-Carolinians was Pettigrew's old brigade, and the men prided themselves on their prowess. But the men opposed to them were too well versed in fighting to be intimidated, and they gave the lauded heroes the best turn in the shop. It was laughable to see them extricate themselves from their dilemma.

They did not dare to rise from behind their cover when once hid; for no sooner would a head appear from behind a log, or rock, or bush, then a Minié would whistle it back to death.

Run they dared not, fight they could not, and the only alternative left them was to surrender at discretion, which they did by creeping out upon all fours without their guns, and piteously asking our boys, like Crockett's coon, "not to fire, as they would come in." The captured of this brigade numbered about five hundred, and General Heth will have to recruit before taking it into action again.

When the enemy found that the Second corps was ready and able to hold its ground, and had no notion of leaving, a fact they discovered after about five hours' hard fighting, they withdrew to the cover of the dense wood in their rear, only firing with their artillery when they could work themselves up to the fighting point sufficiently to enable them to thrust a gun out of the edge of the wood. Then they would fire, and the flame and smoke would act as a target for our gunners; so the firing would be irregular and inconstant; now chiming in, peal on peal, like the reverberations of a thunder-clap, then only a shot or two for several minutes.

The brunt of the fighting was done by General Webb's and General Hayes's division, with the artillery; but it was only so because General Caldwell, who was on the left, was employed in watching a heavy force of rebels which was massed in the woods across the railroad immediately in his front. At dark the fighting ceased, and darkness found us in full possession of the field, the rebels having fallen back to and beyond the woods, having suffered the loss of six pieces of artillery, two battle-flags, two colonels killed and one taken prisoner; probably five hundred killed and wounded, whom they left upon the field, and about seven hundred and fifty prisoners.

Among the rebel slain and left were Colonel Ruffin of the First, and Colonel Thompson of the Fifth North-Carolina cavalry. The battle-flags captured were that of the Twenty-sixth North-Carolina infantry, captured by the Nineteenth Maine, and that of the Twenty-eighth North-Carolina, taken by the Eighty-second New-York. The battery captured consisted of one large Whitworth gun, two fine Rodmans, and three brass field-pieces. One of these, however, was so badly broken up as to be worthless, and was left upon the field. The others were brought away, and to-day have been sent to Washington.

I ought not to pass over the capture of these guns without mentioning an incident which illustrates the valor of our men to a remarkable degree. After the enemy had been driven from their guns by the artillery and infantry combined, General Warren ordered a detail to be made of ten men from each regiment of the corps to bring off the pieces. This was done in order to debar any one regiment, brigade, or division from arrogating to itself the particular honor of their capture. The work to be done was a hazardous one; but the boys shouted as they started at a double-quick. The woods in the rear of the battery were full of graybacks, who, in all probability, would attempt to prevent their pets

from falling into the hands of the Yankee mudsills. Our infantry and artillery would be powerless to help, as a shot from either would be as likely to kill one of our own as one of the rebel troops. But the selected men went off in the direction of the prizes, reached them, seized them, turned them toward the foe, fired a parting salute, from such as the enemy, in his haste, had left loaded, then commenced dragging them away by hand.

They had not gone far, however, when the rebels flocked out of the woods, and came down at a charge toward them, seeing which the boys dropped the artillery, grasped their smaller arms and drove the Butternuts back to the pines. They then came back and dragged off their captures in safety.

I have heard some cheering on election nights, but I never heard such a yell of exultation as rent the air when the rebels' guns, caissons, and equipments were brought across the railroad track to the line of our infantry.

During the afternoon, while the heavy cannonading was going on, General Meade sent the Fifth corps, under General Sykes, to reënforce the Second, but they did not reach the field before dark, and then the fortunes of the day were closed and they could be of no service. General Warren had won his victory and vindicated the wisdom of the power which made him a Major-General. The victory was signal and complete.

I am reliably informed that the rebel Colonel Thompson stated that General Lee's object was to head us off before reaching Centreville, and supposed that when he made the attack upon Warren he was at the head of the entire army with his corps. Consequently he only threw forward one portion of A. P. Hill's corps, numbering in all about twelve thousand men, with four batteries of artillery, in order to hold us in check until the other corps of Ewell, together with the two remaining divisions of Longstreet's corps, could come up. I presume the story is true; but they have found out their mistake.

After the fight had closed, we buried all our dead, brought off all our wounded, and came over Broad Run in perfect order and safety.

We have not lost a dollar's worth of property by capture. Our forces are now safely and securely posted; our trains all parked in convenient and safe retreats, and the army is in excellent spirits.

Among the casualties in the above described battles were the following on the Union side.

In battery B, Second Rhode Island artillery, Chester Hunt, killed; Martin V. B. Eaton, leg shot off; John Kelley, wounded slight; Lieutenant Perrin, slight; Edward Howard, slight.

Captain Ball of the Third Minnesota was wounded in three places and under the most aggravating circumstances. When the enemy charged up the railroad, finding themselves in a dangerous place, they waved their hands in token of surrender. At this instant Captain Ball sprang to the top of the embankment, and a volley was fired at him, three shots taking effect. The Minnesotians returned the fire, and many a rebel suffered in retaliation for this act of treachery.

The First Maine cavalry, which was cut off Monday night near Jefferson, reached Bristoe Station Tuesday night. They lost twenty men, who were sent to communicate with General Gregg. Our men behaved handsomely. The following is a list of the casualties:

Killed—Colonel James E. Mallon, Forty-second New-York, commanding Third brigade, Second division, Second corps.

Wounded—Captain S. M. Smith, Seventh Michigan infantry, Inspector-General of General Webb's staff; four captains of Forth-second New-York; Lieutenant William B. Driver, Nineteenth Massachusetts, slight; Lieutenant J. I. Ferris, Nineteenth Massachusetts, slight; Captain Frank Wessels, Judge Advocate, Second division, Second corps; Captain Thomas Sinclair, First Minnesota, slight; Lieutenant J. D. Gray, First Minnesota, slight; Lieutenant Stevens, Fifteenth Massachusetts, slight. The Fifteenth Massachusetts lost two killed and eight wounded; Nineteenth Maine, one killed and twelve wounded; First Maine, one killed, twenty wounded, and one missing; Eighty-second New-York, seven killed and eighteen wounded. The above were in First brigade, Second division.

The casualties in the Third brigade, Third division, were four killed, eighty-five wounded, and twenty-five missing. In the Fourth brigade Third division, the loss was fourteen, in killed, wounded, and missing.

General Tile, of the Tenth Pennsylvania reserves, was wounded in head and foot.

Among the rebels slain were Colonel Ruffin, of the First, and Colonel Thompson, of the Fifth North-Carolina cavalry. The battle-flags captured belonged to the Twenty-eighth and Twenty-sixth North-Carolina infantry. The battery captured consisted of one large Whitworth gun, two fine Rodmans, and three brass field pieces; one of these, however, was so badly broken up as to be worthless, and was left upon the field.

Besides the rebels killed, whom I have mentioned, there was Brigadier-General Cooke, a son of General Philip St. George Cooke, of the Union army. His body was left on the field.

After the fight had closed, we buried all our dead, brought off all our wounded, and came over Broad Run in perfect order and safety.

We have not lost a dollar's worth of property by capture. Our forces are now safely and securely posted, our trains all parked, and the army in excellent spirits.

The rebel Colonel Thompson states that it was General Lee's object to head us off before reaching Centreville, and supposed when he made the attack upon General Warren he was at the head of the entire army with his corps; consequently he only threw forward one portion of D. P. Hill's corps, numbering in all about twelve thousand men, with four batteries of artillery, in order to hold us in check until the other corps of Ewell, together with the two remaining divisions of Longstreet's corps, could come up.

Probably our entire loss in killed and wounded will not reach two hundred, while that of the enemy will not fall short of five hundred, besides the prisoners captured. We lost none in battle except the killed and wounded, though it is probable a few stragglers fell into the hands of the rebels, between Warrenton Junction and Bristoe.

GENERAL MEADE'S ORDER.

HEADQUARTERS ARMY OF THE POTOMAC, }
October 15. }

The Major-General Commanding announces to the army that the rear guard, consisting of the Second corps, was attacked yesterday while marching by the flank. The enemy, after a spirited contest, was repulsed, losing a battery of five guns, two colors, and four hundred and fifty prisoners. The skill and promptitude of Major-General Warren, and the gallantry and bearing of the officers and soldiers of the Second corps, are entitled to high commendation.

By command of Major-General MEADE.

(Signed) S. WILLIAMS.

RICHMOND EXAMINER ACCOUNT.

RICHMOND, Oct. 26, 1863.

No connected account has yet been published of the movements of our army during the recent campaign in Northern Virginia. From the information in our reach, we make up a hasty and imperfect narrative.

It would appear to have been General Lee's plan to send A. P. Hill's corps by a route west of the Orange and Alexandria Railroad to Manassas Junction, there to cut off Meade's retreat, whilst Ewell's corps followed on the right flank of the retreating enemy, and would be ready to fall upon his rear when he should be brought to a stand. In furtherance of this plan, Hill left Madison county on or about the eighth instant, and moved toward Sperryville. On the same day Ewell crossed the Rapidan at Raccoon Ford. At this place occurred the first cavalry fight, in which we drove the enemy back, but not without sustaining considerable loss. Here Newton and other gallant officers fell.

Meade having apparently seen through the designs of General Lee, began his retreat simultaneously with our advance, and, having the benefit of the railroad, and moving on a direct line, it is no matter of surprise that he managed to frustrate them.

On Sunday, Hampton's cavalry, under the immediate command of Stuart, moving in advance of Ewell's corps, reached Culpeper Court-House, and, moving along the railroad, encountered the enemy at Brandy Station. The battle took place on the farm of John Minor Botts, one of the charges of our cavalry being made through his front yard. We may here remark that the property on the farm of this extraordinary individual, of whom the government of the Confederate States stand in such fear, had been religiously respected by the Yankees: whereas the country around was little better than a wilderness, his fences and crops were untouched. But that

Sunday night wrought a change in its condition. Three thousand confederate cavalry bivouacked there after the battle, and fed their horses in his corn-field. The next morning there were very few fence-rails and very little corn left. The men could be heard to say while building high their fires: "Pile on, boys, they are nothing but d—d old Union rails." Botts came down Monday morning and said he would like to get a certificate of the quantity of corn used and rails burnt. He was dismissed very cavalierly, and told that we had no time to attend to such matters.

Monday our cavalry came up with the enemy at Jefferson, on the road from Culpeper Court-House to Warrenton. There an obstinate fight took place, which resulted in the enemy being driven across Hedgeman's River to Warrenton Springs, from which place the enemy were also driven after a battle. In each of these battles we took several hundred prisoners. Ewell's corps, having changed its line of march, reached Warrenton on Tuesday morning. Meade's army was at this time across the Rappahannock, and believed to have halted at Warrenton Junction, and between that point and Catlett's Station. Two thousand cavalry were sent down from Warrenton to reconnoitre in the direction of Catlett's. On arriving near the latter place, Tuesday evening, they found the enemy were moving heavy columns of infantry along the railroad toward Manassas; and they thereupon immediately turned to retrace their steps toward Warrenton; but on reaching a road which crossed their route, leading from Warrenton Junction to Manassas, they found that the enemy were also moving infantry in large masses along this road. They were thus completely hemmed in. Night came on as they reached this road. The heavy tramp of the enemy's infantry and the rumble of their artillery sounded right in front of them. General Stuart withdrew his little force into a thicket of old field pines, hoping that the enemy would pass him by unnoticed, and leave his road to Warrenton clear. The enemy were moving so near our position that every word of command, and even ordinary conversation, could be distinctly heard by us. Our situation was extremely critical; any accident, the accidental discharge of a pistol, would have disclosed our position, and then, in view of the overwhelming force of the enemy, nothing awaited us but destruction or surrender. Stuart gave his officers and men to understand that surrender was not to be thought of, but that the enemy was to be fought to the last. A council of war having been called, it was resolved, as the best thing that could be done under the circumstances, to desert the nine pieces of horse artillery, and for the cavalry in six columns to endeavor to cut their way through the enemy. But after some reflection, Stuart resolved not to abandon his artillery, and struck upon a device for informing General Lee, who was at Warrenton, of his situation. He called for three volunteers to undertake a desperate enterprise. Crockett Eddins, of this city, and two other young men, immediately stepped forth to undertake any thing their General might order. Stuart ordered them to put on infantry knapsacks, and, shouldering muskets, to advance in the darkness to the road, fall into the enemy's column, and crossing it, to make their way to Warrenton, and say to General Lee that he was surrounded, and he "must send some of his people to help him out." Eddins and his two gallant comrades obeyed orders, and reached Warrenton in safety.

The last division of the enemy halted and bivouacked opposite Stuart and within one hundred and fifty yards of his positon—so close that we could hear the Yankees pouring out oats to feed their horses. During the night two of Meade's staff straggled into our lines and were taken prisoners. One of them, a gay young fellow, said to Stuart, "All right, General, we sup with you to-night, you dine with us to-morrow," intimating that Stuart would, by that time, be a prisoner.

At daylight Wednesday morning, Stuart was informed, by the cracking of our skirmishers' muskets, that Lee had received his message, and was sending "some of the people" to help him. As Lee's advancing columns attracted the enemy's attention, Stuart, from the rear, opened on them with grape and canister. The enemy were much disordered by the cannonade from so unexpected a quarter, and, taking advantage of the confusion, Stuart limbered up his guns, and, with with cavalry and artillery, dashed through the hostile ranks and rejoined General Lee. The enemy suffered a loss of one hundred and eighty killed in this affair.

That evening Hill's corps reached Bristoe Station just after Meade's army had passed that point. What appeared to be a small portion of the enemy was discovered behind a long embankment of the railroad, and two brigades of Heth's corps were ordered to dislodge them. Then followed the battle of Bristoe, which has already been mentioned in these columns. What appeared to be a trifling force of the enemy turned out to be two full army corps, lying in ambush to gobble up any inconsiderate brigades that might attempt to dislodge them. An hour's experiment convinced our men that a formidable force was in their front, and they withdrew. We had three or four hundred men killed and wounded in the fight. The enemy admit a severe loss, but they left but few dead upon the field. Before the main body of our army could get up, the battle was over. That night our men were drawn up in line of battle, but when the day broke on Thursday morning, the enemy was gone. Our forces followed them as far as Manassas Junction, and resting here a day, began a retrograde movement toward the Rappahannock. Our cavalry on Thursday crossed Bull Creek, near the foot of Bull Run Mountain, and made a reconnoissance as far as Centreville, where they were driven back by the enemy's infantry.

Thus ended this famous retreat and pursuit. Our army returned to the Rappahannock, having lost in the campaign about one thousand men, killed, wounded, and prisoners, and having taken near two thousand prisoners. Of the enemy's loss in killed and wounded we have no means of making an estimate. During the pursuit our troops never made over twelve miles a day. The results of the campaign are important. We took a large number of prisoners and horses, ascertained Meade's army to consist of not more than fifty thousand infantry, destroyed the railroad from Manassas to Rappahannock Station, and removed Meade's headquarters from the Rapidan to the Rappahannock.

During the campaign our cavalry did splendid service. They performed all the successful fighting, and took nine tenths of the prisoners.

As belonging rather to the period of our retreat than of Meade's, we have made no mention of the cavalry victory gained by Stuart over Kilpatrick on the nineteenth instant.

RICHMOND SENTINEL ACCOUNT.

CAMP —— CAVALRY, A. N. V., }
November 6, 1863. {

The late campaign is interesting from a cavalry point of view. We had the Yankees on what is called "a big drive." Some of the incidents of the campaign may be interesting.

One division of the cavalry corps, under General Fitz Lee, was left on the Rapidan, to watch the enemy below, while General Stuart advanced with Hampton's division to protect the flank of the army, then moving toward Madison Court-House, from observation. This division consisted of the brigades of Gordon, Young, and Jones; Colonel Funsten commanding the latter.

At Thoroughfare Mountain, General Gordon, whose brigade led the advance, encountered a regiment of infantry, and attacked with his habitual gallantry and skill. A brisk action ensued between the opposing sharp-shooters, the enemy giving way from the first. Just as they were breaking, Young's brigade, which General Stuart had taken round to the left, came down in a thundering charge on the flank of the Federals, and dispersed, killed, or captured nearly the entire party of about four hundred infantry and three hundred cavalry. The two brigades then pushed on, drove the enemy from the little town of James City, and our artillery opened on the Yankee batteries and cavalry, keeping up a brisk cannonade. The sharp-shooters were also hotly engaged, the enemy's whole force of cavalry, with French's division of infantry, remaining in our front, drawn up in heavy line of battle on a rising ground. It was no part of our plan to bring on an engagement, as General Stuart's design was to keep the enemy's cavalry off our flank; and no advance was made. On the following morning, the Federals had fallen back, and we pursued them, coming up with their cavalry below Griffinsburgh. Here we flanked an infantry regiment, which double-quicked to escape, and received, in so doing, the full benefit of our sharp-shooters' fire. At the same moment, Lieutenant Baylor, with a single company of cavalry, charged and broke them. A deep ditch alone prevented the cavalry from dashing in and sabring them. They were not thirty yards off; and, with one more volley into the cavalry, (which, strange to say, did not hurt man or horse,) took to their heels and escaped; for the most part in the woods. This was the second time, in two days, that the cavalry had charged and broken infantry.

Passing the large, abandoned camps, where the enemy had evidently intended to go into winter quarters, to judge from the elaborate board cabins and every arrangement for permanent comfort, we pushed on to Culpeper Court-House after the flying enemy. They posted a battery at Mr. George's, below the town, but a flank movement to the left made them quickly withdraw it; and then *sauve qui peut* was the order of the day with them. General Stuart pushed after them, riding ahead of his command; and was heard to say: "Oh! if Fitz Lee was only up!" Almost as he spoke the boom of artillery was heard from the direction of Stevensburgh, and Fitz Lee, who has a faculty of always "turning up" at the right moment, attacked the retreating enemy's flank. He had driven Buford's command from the neighborhood of Rapidan Station, on the Rapidan, on, on, before him; and now came up, flushed with victory, just in time to report to General Stuart, and make the rout of the enemy complete. A hard and desperate fight ensued—one of the most fiercely contested combats of the war. The enemy had two brigades of infantry to back their heavy force of cavalry; but our infantry was far away, making the flank movement to intercept Meade. The confederate cavalry, therefore, had every thing their own way, and they finished "the big drive" all by themselves. At nightfall the Federals were driven with heavy loss back to and then beyond the river, and our weary but triumphant boys desisted from the long pursuit.

On the next day—Monday—General Stuart flanked up to Jeffersonton, where the enemy made a brief but hot fight, taking refuge in the church and stone houses. They were speedily driven out, however, and our troops pushed on to Warrenton Springs. Here another fight occurred—cavalry and infantry, sharp-shooters of our army attacking. A gallant charge was made toward the bridge by the cavalry, but finding that some of the planks were torn up, they wheeled and dashed through the ford, driving the enemy before them. This little affair was witnessed by the infantry, and I hear that they were enthusiastic about the cavalry. The fact is, however, not that the cavalry did any harder fighting here than on a thousand other occasions, but that the infantry happened to see them at it. It is fortunate for the service, nevertheless, that this little affair was witnessed. It has tended to remove the groundless and absurd prejudice of the infantry against the cavalry arm of the service.

That night, General Stuart pushed on to Warrenton. He had guarded the flank of the army, driven off the enemy's forces everywhere, and performed invaluable service. On the next day the army pushed on, the cavalry now in advance.

In the afternoon, General Stuart took two brigades and several batteries and set out for Catlett's Station, to harass the enemy's flank and rear. Having passed Auburn, he at once discovered that he was between the advancing columns of the enemy. Enormous lines of infantry, cavalry, artillery, and baggage wagons were passing on both sides of him, and to have attacked them would have resulted in heavy loss. Nothing was left but to "lay low," in camp parlance; and orders were accordingly issued that no sound should be uttered throughout the command. This novel incident in the career of the gallant Stuart has been so repeatedly described in the papers, that I will not further dwell upon it. Suffice it to say, that in spite of the sounds issuing from the throats of indecent donkeys, in spite of rattling artillery chains and neighing horses, the band of Southern cavaliers was not discovered; and at daybreak the rear-guard of the enemy were seen in camp cooking their breakfasts, not a quarter of a mile distant. General Stuart had sent several scouts on foot through the enemy's lines to announce his situation to General Lee, and urge the good results which would attend an attack on the enemy's left flank, while he attacked on the right. The scouts, disguising themselves as Federal infantry, got through the line and reported the "situation," and at dawn General Rodes opened on the enemy, as suggested. At the same moment, General Stuart, who had gotten his artillery into position, hurled his thunders on them from an opposite direction, and the ball was opened in the liveliest way imaginable. The enemy formed and for a time resisted, but soon fell back, and our cavalry pushed on in pursuit, General Ewell following with his infantry.

General Fitz Lee's division of cavalry had gone round by New-Baltimore and Buckland's, and reached Bristoe on the evening of the fight there, just as it was over. General Stuart came up at the same time, and taking command of the corps, advanced on the next morning to Manassas. Fitz Lee attacked the enemy at Blackburn's Ford—the scene of the battle of July eighteenth, 1861—and drove them off, after an artillery and sharp-shooters' fight of an hour or two. General Stuart, with the other division, then proceeded toward Yates's Ford below to cut off their wagon train, and coming up with the enemy, had a brief but severe fight with them, which terminated in their retreat across Bull Run. They had hurried off their trains, however, and no part of Meade's baggage fell into our hands.

The entire command bivouacked that night in the waste and desolate country around Manassas, where there is neither sustenance for man nor beast. On the next morning, leaving General Fitz Lee at Manassas to watch the movements of the enemy in front, General Stuart, with Hampton's division, set out to make an expedition to their rear. At Groveton he encountered a heavy picket, which was driven away after some sharp fighting, and then proceeding more to the left by Gainesville, he crossed the Catharpin and Little River, struck into the turnpike below Al-

die, and proceeded to the rear of Frying Pan, where a regiment of infantry was encountered and attacked. Desultory skirmishing consumed some hours, when, having ascertained that the Sixth corps was encamped there, and industriously intrenching to defend itself from General Lee's army, (then retiring from Warrenton toward the Rappahannock,) General Stuart withdrew, and marched back without pursuit or molestation by the badly frightened enemy. This expedition induced the enemy to retire his whole force from Centreville to Fairfax Court-House, under the impression that General Lee had gotten into his rear, and was about to attack him! This may be called one of the best practical (cavalry) jokes of the war.

As our cavalry fell back from Gainesville, on the next day, the great "Buckland Races" took place. General Kilpatrick came down from Bull Run, as furious as a wild boar at finding that the circumventing force which had appeared at Frying Pan was only a portion of Stuart's cavalry. He declared to a citizen, at whose house he stopped, that "Stuart had been boasting of driving him from Culpeper, and now he was going to drive Stuart." He was about to sit down to an excellent dinner as he made the observation, when, suddenly, the sound of artillery attracted his attention, and he was obliged to get (dinnerless) into the saddle. General Stuart had played him one of those tricks which are dangerous. He had arranged with General Fitz Lee, whose division was still toward Manassas, to come up on the enemy's flank and rear, as they pursued, and when he was ready, fire a gun as a signal. At the signal, he (Stuart) would face about and attack. Every thing took place as it was planned. The signal roared, and General Stuart, who, until then, had been retiring before the enemy toward New-Baltimore, faced around and charged. At the same moment Fitz Lee came up on the enemy's flank, and the "Buckland Races" took place. Poor Kilpatrick was completely ruined. His command was killed, captured, or dispersed. When last heard from, he was at Alexandria, where he is supposed to have opened a recruiting-office for the enlistment of his command. To add to his misery, the confederates have caught his race-horse. General Kilpatrick is fond of racing, and had a thoroughbred mare, called "Lively," which he ran on every occasion. The other day "Lively" flew the track, and took to the woods, where some of Moseby's men took possession of her. Two soldiers were sent after her; and these, too, were gobbled up.

It would thus appear that the campaign, taken altogether, has been unfavorable to General Kilpatrick. Driven out of Culpeper, ruined at Buckland's, the loss of his favorite mare must appear to him the "unkindest cut of all."

At Buckland's, General Stuart captured a number of wagons and mules, and the headquarter baggage of General Custer; his papers, clothes, every thing. The papers reveal many interesting facts connected with their cavalry, and show a heavy loss in the recent engagements at Jack's Shop, James City, etc.

A few unimportant skirmishes followed the "Buckland Races," but that amusing occurrence may be regarded as the termination of the cavalry campaign.

I think you will agree with me that the cavalry have "done well for the Republic" in this campaign. They have met and fought the enemy all along the roads from the Rapidan to the Rappahannock, advancing on the Federals by two routes. They guarded the flank of General Lee as he marched to intercept Meade, doing the work so perfectly that the Federal General never at any time could ascertain a single fact in relation to Lee's movements. They drove the enemy, after a fierce and final struggle at Brandy, clear across the Rappahannock. They did the same on the next day at Warrenton Springs. They damaged the retreating columns seriously, to say the least, at Auburn. They drove them across Bull Run, and took possession of the fords in front of Centreville. They penetrated to the enemy's rear at Frying Pan, and made them fall back from Centreville to Fairfax Court-House, and intrench, under the impression that the "rebel army" was in their rear. They got Kilpatrick "between two fires" at Buckland's, and broke to pieces his entire command — killing, capturing, or driving back on their heavy infantry reserves the best cavalry in the whole Federal service. They effected these results, besides furnishing General Lee with thorough and reliable information of every movement and design on the part of the enemy.

And yet these services of the cavalry have not been more important than upon other occasions. The high reputation for courage and efficiency which they have received has not been the result of better generalship on the part of the commanders, or greater gallantry on the part of the men. It has all resulted from a circumstance already alluded to. The infantry of the army were held in reserve, and had an opportunity to see the cavalry at work and observe the results. I am disposed to think that some of the most intelligent and candid men in the infantry honestly adopted the old prejudice, and believe that the cavalry did all the straggling and none of the fighting. Far from the field of cavalry operations, which are generally off on the flanks of the army, or in the rear or the front, these honest and sensible men repeated the sneers handing from regiment to regiment, and ended by believing every calumny which was circulated. This is the only explanation I can think of for the naïve and enthusiastic applause which greeted the charge at Warrenton Springs. A gallant and dashing little affair, it is true; but only one of a thousand such which occur on every expedition of the cavalry. The infantry broke out into rapturous plaudits on that occasion, and evidently thought that such things rarely occurred—that the cavalry had "turned over a new leaf."

I repeat that the misfortune has been heretofore that the brave boys of the infantry did not see their comrades of the cavalry at work; and not finding them prominent in the middle of the big battles, believed they preferred the rear and did no fighting. It is fortunate that this hallucination is exploded. The gallant blood of noble hearts which flows in every cavalry fight cries aloud against this cruel calumny. While the infantry are resting after their toils, the cavalry are fighting; and it would astound some of those who have been in the habit of repeating the sneers alluded to, if they could know how much precious blood —of field officers, company officers, and noble men in the ranks — is shed in almost every skirmish which occurs upon the outposts. But, enough. I am glad the infantry have seen the cavalry at work.

P. S.—One incident of the late campaign has been omitted through inadvertence, though well worthy of notice. On the evening of the fight for possession of the Warrenton Springs ford, the enemy, puzzled to death at our movements, and determined to use every means to penetrate Lee's designs, advanced from Rappahannock Station by Brandy toward Culpeper Court-House, with two divisions of cavalry and some infantry. Our army had, of course, gone on, by the upper fords, and General Stuart had deserted that part of the field of operations for one more attractive beyond the Rappahannock. He had, however, left Colonel Rosser with a force of less than two hundred cavalry and one piece of artillery at Brandy, to repel any advance in that direction. The enemy appeared suddenly, in the evening, as I have said, and commenced a furious attack upon Rosser. He dismounted his command, and deployed them as sharp-shooters; and with these and his single gun received the assault. He was speedily forced, of course, to fall back; but this was done gradually, his piece retiring from hill to hill, and continuing to fire upon the enemy. The only hope which Colonel Rosser had was in Colonel Young, commanding the South-Carolina cavalry, and his own Cobb legion, Butler's brigade. Young was above Culpeper Court-House when he received Rosser's message, and immediately pushed on, and threw himself into the affair with the dash and gallantry which are a matter of course with him. He dismounted his entire brigade, scattered them over a front of a mile, advanced upon the Federals, and kept up such a hot fire upon them that they were completely checked and driven back. Night had now come, and ordering his men to build camp-fires along his entire front, Colonel Young brought up his brass band to the front and made it play "Dixie" and the "Bonnie Blue Flag" till midnight.

The consequence of this unique proceeding, on the part of the gallant Colonel, was pleasing. A mile and a half of camp-fires, and a brass band playing "Dixie," defiantly, could be accounted for upon no other hypothesis than the presence of a strong force of General Lee's army; and having reconnoitred the heavy body of troops evidently in their front, the enemy concluded that their expedition was "no go." When morning came they had fallen back beyond the Rappahannock.

Such is one of the many amusing incidents which wreathe with a smile the features of "grim-visaged war."

Doc. 189.

REBEL RAID ON GLASGOW, KY.

REPORT OF MAJOR MARTIN.

HEADQUARTERS UNITED STATES FORCES, }
GLASGOW, KY., October 9, 1863. }

Brigadier-General E. H. Hobson, Munfordville, Kentucky:

I now proceed to give you the particulars of the recent raid made on Glasgow, Ky., by the rebel Colonel John M. Hughse.

On the evening of the thirtieth of last month, I was ordered by Brigadier-General J. T. Boyle to send scouts into the border counties of Kentucky, on the Kentucky and Tennessee State line, to learn if the enemy was there, and what he was doing, etc., etc.

Previous to the reception of this order from General Boyle, I had ordered a scout of ninety men to go to the border, for the purpose which he desired, and on the morning of the ninth instant, I started the ninety men for that purpose. Lieutenant J. Kerigan was ordered to Cumberland county, Kentucky, with thirty men, with orders to go to Marrowbone Store, then to Centre Point and Tompkins', and from there to return to this place. Captain J. W. Roark, with thirty men, was ordered to Tompkinsville, with instructions to meet Captain Stone, at Gamalia, in Monroe county, Kentucky, which is near the State line. Captain G. B. Stone was ordered, with thirty men, to Jamestown, Monroe county, Kentucky, then to join Captain Roark at Gamalia; there Captain Roark was to take command of both companies, and proceed to Lafayette, Tennessee, and to return from there to this place—each company reporting to me as it returned. Lieutenant Kerigan was the first to return and report, which was done on the evening of the third instant. Captain Roark returned and reported on the evening of the fifth instant, reporting no rebels in the country; and that Captain Stone was in the country a short distance from town, and would be in that evening or early next morning. From these reports I telegraphed to General Boyle that my scouts had just returned and reported no rebels in the country. I should have said that Captain Stone returned on the evening of the fifth instant, but failed to report to me, and I was not apprised of his return until the sixth instant, when I saw him at Fort Hobson, near Glasgow, about twelve o'clock in the day. The town was attacked on the morning of the fifth instant, about daylight. I was in bed and heard the rebels passing through town, and in the direction of the fort, where my men were camped— I supposing as they passed through town that they were Captain Stone's men returning. I lay still until my father looked out the window, and said they were rebels, and while he was telling it to me firing commenced in the square. I had Captain J. O. Nelson's company as provost-guards in the court-house yard. They numbered about fifty men present. As soon as the firing commenced in the square, I sprang from my bed, loaded my Henry rifle, dressed myself, went to the window, and saw fifteen or twenty rebels ordering Captain Nelson's men into line, under guard. I asked them whose command they belonged to. Receiving no reply, myself and Lieutenant Chenoweth fired on them, both about the same time; they returned the fire, some of their balls passing through the window into our room. We fired six or eight times at them from the windows, wounding three or four rebels on the square. Here I will mention one of my orderlies, (Frank Clairborne.) We had shot a rebel off of his horse. I ordered Clairborne to go down and get on the horse and try to get to the fort and rally my men, then myself supposing that the rebels had not reached there. As quick as the order was given it was obeyed, and I saw him gallop off from the rebels in the square toward the fort, and I learn since that he was captured by them. Our fire from the windows was too severe, and the rebels left the square; then myself, Lieutenant Chenoweth, and William Griffith, (an orderly,) went down stairs to go to the stable to get our horses. When we got down stairs I saw Captain Nelson in the court-house yard by himself, and I told him to follow me to get a horse, which he did not do. When we turned the corner of the square to go to the stable where our horses were, we saw that it was surrounded by rebels catching them. We fired several times, and they left the stable, leaving in it four horses and saddles. We soon mounted three of them, and rode back through town and started toward the fort. At that time I heard firing and a hallooing at the fort. We went within two hundred yards of the fort, where we could see it well, and there I sat on my horse and saw the rebels sacking my camp and driving my men into line. I again lowered my gun to fire on them, but was prevailed on by Lieutenant Chenoweth not to do so. We were there helpless, only three of us with arms, and I considered the greater portion of my command captured. We sat here about two minutes, when we were discovered by the rebels, and about thirty of them started after us, but we kept out of their way and succeeded in collecting a few of my pickets who were yet at their posts. I stopped on the pike near town, and heard the rebels marching back to town, with a shout that told well that my men were captured. I then retreated five miles on the pike, and sent Lieutenant Chenoweth to Cave City to despatch to General Boyle, and return to where I was, which he did in a surprisingly short time. We left our post about eleven o'clock A.M., and started back for Glasgow, having twenty men at this time. We reached Glasgow about twelve o'clock that day, and found the rebels all gone.

Here I remained gathering up my men and the guns which had been scattered. I shipped a wagon-load of guns to Cave City that evening, and was reënforced about four o'clock P.M., by Captain Beck, from Munfordville, with twenty-five men, mounted, he having come by Cave City. After giving time to feed his men and rest, we started with sixty men in pursuit of the enemy. Moving out on the Columbia road one mile, we crossed to the Burksville road. This is the road on which the enemy retreated. We struck this road about two miles from Glasgow. It was then dark and raining, but we pressed on, hoping to overtake and surprise them before day. They left the Burksville road seven miles from Glasgow, and took the Tompkinsville road. We reached Tompkinsville one hour before day, dismounted the men, and hitched our horses in a dense thicket near town; then marched the men into an open field, and when we came to count our men, we found, to our great surprise and mortification, only thirty men to answer to their names, the balance having fallen out of ranks and got lost on the road. But we were determined to make the attack if the enemy was there. We formed our men in line to command the public square. There we waited until near daylight, when we learned that the rebels had not stopped in Tompkinsville, but had passed through there about dark the evening before. Here we gave up the chase, and remained in Tompkinsville until sun up, then started to return to Glasgow. About this time we were informed that two wagons had been left near Tompkinsville. We returned and found them as stated, with two mules, seventy guns, and various other articles, which were captured by the rebels of my command at Glasgow; the mules were tied near the wagons. This gave indication that the rebels intended returning for them. We set to work and soon had the two wagons wheeled about and off for Glasgow. But while we were hitching our teams I had pickets placed on the road the rebels had travelled, and twelve rebels came upon them; but the pickets drove them back by firing on them. We supposed the rebels were not far off, and had we had more men and fresh horses we would have followed after them, but our horses were rode down —Captain Beck having rode all the way from Munfordville via Cave City that day with his men, and my horses had been in constant use ever since daylight the morning before; so we turned our course for Glasgow, reaching there on the morning of the eighth instant, with our recaptured prize.

I will now give the particulars of the fight: On the morning of the sixth instant, when the town was attacked, the Provost-guards were all asleep, except those on duty at the guard-house, and the patrols about town. Captain George S. Nun was in command of the camp at the fort, and only a few of the men there were up. Some were on guard in the fort when the rebels got in sight of it. They charged right into camp and up to the fort. The men inside the fort discharged their guns promptly at the rebels, and one rebel fell mortally wounded. But the dash into camp was so sudden that the men were thrown into confusion; in fact, were panic-stricken, they being new recruits. The officers, so far as I can learn, did their duty as well as they could. Colonel Hughse asked who was in command of the camp, and Captain Nun told him that he was. Hughse then ordered him to surrender the whole command to him. Captain Nun told him that he would have to get the men like he (Hughse) got him; that was, by fighting. The men were then running in every direction, many without their arms or clothes. One of my men was shot three times. He had no arms, and was standing in the fort. Another one of my men was shot in the court-house yard. He was unarmed, and was not trying to get away. The rebels paroled one hundred and forty-two of my men and officers. They captured over two hundred horses and horse equipments, carried off all the clothing I had on hands unissued, and loaded two of my wagons with goods. They destroyed a great many of my commissary stores, and burnt a large building at the fort, which was built for government use. They carried off about one hundred guns, mostly carbines. They had thirteen wounded; four of them have since died. My wounded were three; one of them has since died; the other two are getting well. They also robbed the bank of about nine thousand dollars; most of the money had been deposited there by citizens for safety. They robbed one store of about four hundred dollars' worth of goods, and took horses and buggies from citizens to carry off their wounded in. They crossed Cumberland River into Turkey Neck Bend, and, hearing that I was pursuing them, they passed on to Kittle Creek, where they stopped and paroled the men. As soon as they crossed Cumberland River, they commenced scattering. My officers state that the rebel officers told them that they had over two hundred men with them when they attacked Glasgow, yet other reports say that there were not exceeding one hundred rebel soldiers in Glasgow. I am, General, your obedient servant,

SAMUEL MARTIN,
Major Thirty-seventh Kentucky Mounted Infantry.

Doc. 190.

THE BAXTER SPRINGS MASSACRE.

GENERAL BLUNT'S LETTER.

BAXTER SPRINGS, Sixty-three miles below Fort Scott, October 7, 1863, 10 o'clock P.M.

Captains Tholen and Loring:

. . . .

Every thing in the staff wagons is lost; the wagons were burned with most of their contents.

. . . . . .

We have just found the body of Major Curtis. (Major Curtis's body, as also that of Judge-Advocate Lieutenant Farr, arrived in Leavenworth on the eleventh instant.) When I wrote to Major Blair last night it was supposed he was a prisoner, as we had searched the ground over near where his horse fell, and could not find him. Moreover, Quantrel's Adjutant, or a person representing himself as such, who came into Lieutenant Pond's camp with a flag of truce, said they had my Assistant Adjutant-General a prisoner. To-day he was found near where he was thrown from his horse, shot through the head, evidently murdered after being taken prisoner.

I shall start his body, with that of Lieutenant Farr, to Fort Scott this evening. You will probably have heard some of the particulars of the affair here yesterday, before you receive this. The escort, company I, Third Wisconsin, and company A, Fourteenth Kansas, consisting of one hundred men, behaved disgracefully, and stampeded like a drove of frightened cattle. I did not anticipate any difficulty until we got below this point. We arrived near this camp about twelve M., and halted on the hill almost in sight of the camp, and not more than four hundred yards distant, to wait for the escort and wagons to close up. The escort came up and dismounted, to wait for the train, which was but a short distance behind. At this time my attention was called to a body of men, about one hundred, advancing in line from the timber of Spring River, on the left, which you will recollect is not more than three or four hundred yards from the road. The left of the line was not more than two hundred yards from Lieutenant Pond's camp at the spring. They being nearly all dressed in Federal uniforms, I supposed them at first to be Lieutenant Pond's cavalry, (two companies,) on service. At the same time my suspicions were aroused by some of their movements. I ordered the wagons, which had come up, to the rear, and formed the escort in line, with their carbines unslung, while I advanced alone toward the party fronting us, to ascertain if they were rebels. I had advanced but a short distance when they opened a fire, at the same time firing was heard down in Pond's camp. Turning around to give the order to the escort to fire, I discovered them all broken up, and going over the prairie to the west at full speed. They did not even discharge the loaded carbines they had in their hands, except in a few cases. Had the escort stood their ground, as soldiers should have done, they could have driven the enemy in ten minutes. I endeavored in vain, with the assistance of Major Curtis, to halt and form a portion of them. When the escort stampeded, the enemy discovering it, rushed on with a yell, followed by another line of about two hundred that emerged from the edge of the timber. Being better mounted than our men, they soon closed in on them. The men of the escort were much scattered, and with them it was a run for life.

After going a mile, I succeeded in halting fifteen men, including Lieutenant Pierce, company A, Fourteenth Kansas, who has done his duty well and nobly throughout. As soon as I got them in line and commenced advancing on the pursuing enemy, they fled and fell back to the wood, when their whole command (six hundred)

formed in line of battle. The balance of the escort that had escaped were all out of sight in the advance. Major Curtis had been seen to fall from his horse, which had been wounded and stumbled in crossing a ditch. About one o'clock I sent Lieutenant Tappan (who had kept with me all the time) with four men to Fort Scott, while with the other nine I determined to remain until the fate of those that had fallen could be ascertained, and whether the post at the spring had been captured, which I much feared was the case. As they fell back to the road, I followed them up over the ground we had come, to look for the wounded, but all, with two or three exceptions, (who had escaped accidentally,) were killed—shot through the head. All the wounded had been murdered. I kept close to them and witnessed their plundering the wagons. At one time they made a dash at me with about one hundred men, endeavoring to surround me, but failed in their purpose. As they moved off on the road leading south, I went down to the spring and found them all O. K.

Lieutenant Pond, of the Third Wisconsin, and also his command, are entitled to great credit for the manner they repulsed the enemy and defended the post. The colored soldiers fought with great gallantry. All of the wounded were shot through the head, and thus murdered. The band wagon was captured, and all of the boys shot in the same way after they were prisoners. The same was the case with the teamsters and Mart., my driver. O'Neill (artist to Frank Leslie) was killed with the band-boys. All of the office-clerks, except one, were killed; also my orderly, (Ely.) Major Henning is with me. But few of the escort who escaped have come in. I suppose they have gone to Fort Scott. The dead are not all buried, but the number will not fall short of seventy-five. The enemy numbered six hundred—Quantrel's and Coffey's commands. They are evidently intending to go south of the Arkansas. I have scouts on the trail. Two have just come in, and report coming up with them at the crossing of the Neosho River. Others are still following them up. Whether they will go directly south on the Fort Gibson road, or cross Grand River to Cowski Prairie again, I cannot determine. When they came in they crossed Spring River, close by Baxter. I have sent messengers to the Arkansas River, and, if they succeeded in getting through safe, our forces will be put on the alert and may intercept them. I am now waiting the arrival of troops from Fort Scott. If I get them, (which is doubtful, as the Fourteenth Kansas is not armed,) I will follow the hounds through the entire Southern Confederacy as long as there is a prospect of overtaking them. And I will have it well understood that any man of this command who again breaks from the line and deserts his post, shall be shot on the spot; and there shall be no quarter to the motley bands of murderers. . . .

I was fortunate in escaping, as in my efforts to halt and rally the men, I frequently got in the rear and became considerably mixed up with the rebels, who did not fail to pay me their compliments. Revolver bullets flew around my head thick as hail—but not a scratch. I believe I am not to be killed by a rebel bullet.

Yours truly,   JAMES G. BLUNT.

BAXTER SPRINGS, October 7—8 P.M.

CAPTAIN: Since I wrote you this morning, the body of Major Curtis has been found, near where he was thrown from his horse. He was shot through the head, and was evidently murdered after he was a prisoner, as were all the rest. His body, with that of Lieutenant Farr's, will leave here to-night for Fort Scott, on their way to their friends. Major Henning will accompany them to Iowa and Wisconsin. Have wooden coffins made by the time they arrive at Fort Scott. At Leavenworth they can be transferred to metallic coffins.

I also send the bodies of two soldiers of the Third Wisconsin, at the request of their wives, who are here, to be buried at Fort Scott. Have coffins ordered for them.

Some of my scouts, who have just come in, have trailed the enemy five miles south of Neosho Crossing, on the Fort Gibson road. There is also a trail leading into the creek below here, which indicates that they have been joined, since leaving here, by another party. I have sent messengers to the Arkansas River, and, if they get through in safety, our forces will be on the alert and may intercept them.

Our loss yesterday in killed, including this command at this post, will not be short of seventy-five. There are but five or six wounded. All the wounded and prisoners that fell into their hands were murdered.

The death of Major Curtis will not only be a severe loss to his wife and other relations, but also to the service.

Major-General JAMES G. BLUNT.

Doc. 191.

THE PURSUIT OF WHEELER.

CHATTANOOGA, October 18, 1863.

Major-General Halleck, General-in-Chief:

The following despatch has been received from Brigadier-General George Crook, commanding the Second cavalry division, dated Rogersville, Alabama, October tenth, 1863:

I have the honor to inform you that I have had three fights with the enemy since I left the Sequatchie valley, whipping them very badly each time. The last battle ended at Farmington Farm, where I fought Wheeler's entire command with only two brigades. I cut his force in two, scattering a large portion of it, capturing four pieces of artillery, one thousand stand of arms, two hundred and forty prisoners, besides the wounded.

As I pushed on after the enemy immediately, I have not been able to ascertain the number of their killed and wounded—but it was very heavy. They were scattered over a distance of fifteen miles from this, and their retreat was a perfect

rout, their men deserting and straggling over the country.

I pursued with great vigor, but their horses being better than mine, I was only able to come up with a couple of regiments at Sugar Creek, left to detain me. I made a charge on them, capturing some fifty of them and scattering the remainder in the mountains. When within eight miles of the river I struck the gallop, but when I reached the river I found they had all crossed at a ford some three miles above Samp's Ferry, where they could cross twelve abreast. I never saw troops more demoralized than they were. I am satisfied that their loss in this raid was not less than two thousand. No fears need be entertained of their making another raid soon.

GEORGE CROOK,
Brigadier-General Commanding.

W. S. ROSECRANS,
Major-General.

Doc. 192.

BATTLE AT BLUE SPRINGS, TENN.

GENERAL BURNSIDE'S REPORT.

KNOXVILLE, TENNESSEE, October 17, 1863.

Major-General H. W. Halleck, General-in-Chief:

On the eighth instant the enemy held down as far as Blue Springs, and a cavalry brigade of ours held Bull's Gap, supported by a small body of infantry at Morristown. I accordingly despatched a brigade of cavalry around by Rogersville to intercept the enemy's retreat, and with a considerable force of infantry and artillery moved to Bull's Gap.

On Saturday, the tenth, I advanced a cavalry brigade to Blue Springs, where they found the enemy strongly posted and offered a stubborn resistance. The skirmishing continued till the arrival of the infantry at about five o'clock A.M., when I sent in a division of infantry, who charged and cleared the woods gallantly, and drove the enemy, in confusion, till dark.

During the night the enemy retreated precipitately, leaving their dead on the field and most of the wounded in our hands. We pursued them in the morning with infantry and cavalry. The intercepting force met them at Henderson's, but, owing to some misunderstanding, withdrew and allowed them to pass with only a slight check. The pursuit was continued till evening, when I withdrew most of my infantry and returned to this place.

General Shackleford, with his cavalry and a brigade of infantry, continued the pursuit, the enemy making a stand at every important position. But he has driven them completely from the State and captured the Fort at Zollicoffer, burning the long railroad bridge at that place and five other bridges, and destroying three locomotives and about thirty-five cars. His advance is now ten miles beyond Bristol.

Our loss at Blue Springs and in the pursuit was about one hundred killed and wounded.

That of the enemy was considerably greater. About one hundred and fifty prisoners were taken.

A. E. BURNSIDE,
Major-General.

Doc. 193.

THE BATTLE AT HENDERSON'S MILL.

CAMP OF FIFTH CAVALRY,
EAST-TENNESSEE, Nov. 14, 1863.

BEFORE day had fairly dawned on Sunday, October eleventh, 1863, our advance-guard, consisting of two companies, suddenly met the entire force of the enemy, two thousand seven hundred strong. A contest followed, in which the Fifth Indiana cavalry alone engaged the foe, and bore a part of which their friends may well feel proud. It was no long-contemplated battle, in which every possible movement of the enemy was anticipated and guarded against, but a sudden coming together of two unequal forces, with at least five to one in favor of the enemy. It is not the practice of Colonel Graham to bring on such an unequal fight where every advantage accrues to the enemy—a thorough knowledge of the ground and every avenue of approach to it, a force of five times our number, and well-matured preparations for the engagement; but on the morning of the battle we found ourselves surrounded by such unfavorable circumstances, and in justice to our respected commander, the public should be made acquainted with some of the facts connected with this movement.

The Second brigade, Fourth division, Twenty-third army corps, commanded by Colonel Foster, left Knoxville on a forced march, under orders to bear to the left, pass around and intercept a force of rebels on the Blountville road. After a fatiguing march of four days, we reached the road at Rheatown at two o'clock on Sunday morning. Here a halt was made, for the purpose of gaining some information relative to the whereabouts and strength of the rebels. It was ascertained that General Williams was in command of from two to four thousand, back on the road to Knoxville a few miles, coming toward Rheatown. A short consultation was held, when it was decided that as Colonel Graham with his regiment had been on outpost duty here two weeks previous to this time, and was better acquainted with the country than the others of the brigade, he should take the advance and move down to meet the enemy, with the positive agreement by Colonel Foster to follow with the brigade.

Relying on the certainty of support from Colonel Foster, the Fifth cavalry advanced in direction of the enemy. Three hours more and day would dawn—perhaps ere daylight appears we meet the stealthy villains in their secret hiding-places. With such reflections as these, our never-faltering Colonel, with not more than five hundred men, cautiously felt his way through open fields and dark woods, confident that soon the entire rebel force would be in his possession, from the fact that General Shackleford was press-

ing them in the rear, and Colonel Foster had definitely agreed to support us n their front. The time had now come when the qualifications of a good general were needed, when action immediate and decisive was required. The enemy lay between two brigades, completely in our trap. It now remained to touch the spring and finish the work. It is an easy matter to lead a brigade from point to point, to command when not in front of danger, but when the crisis of a contemplated encounter approaches, then is the time when the commander of the forces should feel himself called upon to exert every energy and use vigorously every talent at his command. The lives of thousands who have volunteered in their country's cause are depending upon him; the work of weeks, perhaps months, is about to be terminated as gained or lost: he holds the fortunes of the day.

The brigade, unknown to Colonel Graham, remained at Rheatown, and the Fifth Indiana moved on. Two miles from town, Colonel Graham ordered a halt to reconnoitre. We found ourselves at Henderson's Mills. It was now four o'clock, Sunday morning; the men took their last meal, and the horses their last half hour's rest, early Saturday morning, but the undoubted prospect of capturing the enemy strengthened and encouraged them for the work. Company C and I were ordered one mile in advance, where they halted in sight of the camp-fires of the enemy. It was now ascertained that Colonel Foster, instead of coming forward, had remained in town. A request was immediately sent by Colonel Graham, urged on by Colonel Butler, that he come on as soon as possible, as the fight would shortly commence, and we alone were too weak for the heavy force before us. The messenger returned, bringing the report that Colonel Foster, instead of either coming to our assistance, or taking a commanding position at town, had moved away from the road two miles, leaving us four miles in front, with orders to engage the enemy; and on reading the message from Colonel Graham, he coolly replied: "My men want sleep. They cannot go." Oh! exemplification of kind humanity—"My men need sleep"—listen! "My men need sleep and cannot go." How, with the five hundred under Colonel Graham, about to engage with five times their number—must they be sacrificed at this important crisis, because "My men want sleep"? Must my men have their regular meals and sleep, and let General Williams pass on to Rheatown with a prospect of escaping? Oh! no; "my men" were all ready and willing to help strike the final blow, but were sworn to obey their commander. No help came, and the Fifth Indiana was forced to contend alone with this large force; nor did it wait long for Colonel Graham to arrange his comparatively small number. They came pouring down the road, flanking us on the right and left, yelling like a set of demons. Colonel Butler was ordered to take the rear and contest to the last every foot of ground, giving way only as overpowering necessity compelled him to. The ambulances were ordered to fall back to the brigade, under the protection of company L, Lieutenant Elliott. Companies F, Lieutenant Greer; M, Lieutenant Clegg; B, Captain Leuson; A, Captain Stretch—were ordered to take the right. Companies K, Captain Lea; E, Lieutenant Meneaugh, were ordered to the left. The fighting was becoming general all along the lines, but our men stood bravely up to the work, and reluctantly did they fall back. Colonel Graham, still clinging to the vague belief that Colonel Foster would be awakened from his sleep by the roaring of the artillery, drink another cup of the milk of human kindness, and conclude to come to our relief, ordered a charge. Colonel Butler, with companies H, Captain Souper; G, Lieutenant Armstrong; D, Sergeant Bronson, dashed forward, completely routed the enemy and retook the ground. Charge after charge was made upon the several companies forming our line of battle, but each time the rebels were handsomely repulsed. For four miles Colonel Graham contested every foot of the ground back to the brigade. Major Lyle, Captain Thompson, and Captain Loomis, the commanders of the several battalions, were all active in the performance of every duty devolving upon them. The heavy booming of the cannon and the sharp firing of the musketry told to all within hearing that a fearful contest was being waged. Anxious hearts were beating in the breasts of the brave five hundred as they slowly gave way to this large force; hopes would rise and fall, as if tossed about on ocean's waves. At times it seemed as though we were completely surrounded, but as often Colonel Graham would order a movement that cleared the way, and our hopes would brighten again. The infuriated enemy seemed determined to surround and capture our battery; all hearts beat low as they saw its critical situation; but the guns which had so effectually held them at bay were not to be taken. The whole command "fought like brave men, long and well," fighting at times hand to hand with their foes.

The firing now became broken, and finally ceased. I looked at my watch—we had been fighting two hours, and were now within sight of the brigade, where we saw Colonel Foster bravely sitting on his horse, surprised at our return, having heard that we were all captured.

Colonel Graham had performed nobly his part in this well-planned effort to capture General Williams, but the grand object was not accomplished. The road was left open, and the enemy went on to Rheatown.

In the afternoon the Indiana brigade attacked them at this place. The Fifth Indiana bore an active part. The particulars I will give at some future time.

The result of the battle Sunday morning is as follows:

Rebel loss in killed, thirty. We captured ten prisoners, among whom were the Adjutant-General and Inspector-General of General Jackson's staff.

Our loss was none killed, eleven wounded, and eight missing.

Wounded: William Thomas, company D, in the head, slightly; Andy Johnson, F, in face and hand, slightly; William Kinnick, F, in shoulder, slightly; William Derren, G, in hip, slightly; John A. Sammons, H, in left hip, flesh wound; Samuel G. Kingdon, H, in right side, slightly; John O. Spears, H, left leg broken; Thomas C. Waterson, H, in left hand, slightly; Matterson Sourd, I, in arm, flesh wound; Corporal L. Ball, L, in groin; Thomas Curren, L, breast and right arm, mortally.

Missing: John Hiatt, company B; Sergeant A. Becht, C; Jacob Jonas, C; Samuel E. Smith, C; Henry C. Veach, C; David T. Hamilton, E; David R. Badgley, F; Moses Lour, M.

Yours, respectfully, R.

Doc. 194.

THE BATTLE OF COLLIERSVILLE, TENN.

HEADQUARTERS C. B. DEPT., THIRTY-NINTH O. V. I.,
MEMPHIS, TENN., Oct. 14.

LAST Sunday morning, about eleven A.M., as I have told you before, General Sherman, staff, horses, baggage, and eight companies of the Thirteenth regular infantry, left here on one of the longest and heaviest trains that has gone out of Memphis for some time. At noon I had just gone up to camp to dinner when General Webster sent up word that he wanted me down at the depot immediately, with every available man not then on duty, armed, and with forty rounds of ammunition apiece. We supposed that there must be some disturbance or riot in the neighborhood which we were required to quell, and in a very short time we reported to the General. He told us that General Sherman had been attacked at Colliersville with artillery by a superior force, and had telegraphed for a special train to bring General Corse's brigade to his relief, who were then en route for this place on foot. He had telegraphed to send platform cars, on which to load the artillery, for that of it he stood particularly in need, as he had none, and that if we had not that kind of cars, to construct them, (by cutting the tops off of box-cars, I suppose.) We were required to accompany this train as a guard, with orders to return at the earliest opportunity. We jumped aboard, and at White's Station, about nine miles from here, came in sight of the rear of General Corse's brigade, and at Germantown caught up with the head of the column. Here we took aboard the Ninety-third Illinois, commanded by Colonel O'Meara, and three pieces of artillery belonging to Captain Cheeney's Illinois battery, and, with orders from General Corse to proceed cautiously, as the enemy were known to be between us and Colliersville, then only nine miles distant, continued on our way.

After going a few miles Colonel O'Meara, who is an Irishman, and appears to be a genuine fighting man, threw out skirmishers ahead of the train, whom we followed slowly. We picked up first two negroes, who reported that General Sherman was taken prisoner; next three citizens, who said that the enemy had possession of the place, and that General Sherman was hid, but that they were hunting for him, and had probably found him; then two more citizens, who said that the rebels had left. Two miles this side of Colliersville we came to the first obstruction, a large culvert that had been burnt. Here Colonel O'Meara disembarked his force, and after distributing one hundred and fifty rounds of ammunition to each man, we advanced. Arrived at the place, we found the report of the citizen last picked up to be the correct one. Before this, just after the cartridges were distributed, Colonel O'Meara, who had his sleeves rolled up, slaughter-house style, and was mounted on a very fine horse, and had his sword drawn—an ugly looking weapon, looking more like an elongated bowie-knife than a field-officer's sabre—made us a short speech, telling us that General Sherman had sent for his regiment to come to his relief, and that, with the assistance of the brave fellows on his left, (that was, my boys,) and Captain Cheeney's battery, he was going to do it, let there be what there might in the way. This quite took with the men, and they cheered him.

At Colliersville he ordered me to report in person to General Sherman, and receive his commands relative to my two companies. I did so, telling General Sherman what my orders were with regard to returning by the first train, but he told me that he could not let us do so yet, that we knew more about railroads than his men, and must first repair the damages to the road behind us. Now this was something about which I knew about as much as a cow does about dancing; but as he requested me to first go down and see what damage was done and report, in company with Captain York of his staff, I started. It was a long way, and growing dark very rapidly; but Captain York being confident that the rebels had all left, we thought we could venture it alone. On the way he gave an account of the whole affair.

The attack commenced on the train just as it had passed the station, about ten o'clock. The telegraph operator there had run out with his gun in one hand, and motioning with the other for the train to stop. The conductor hurried to General Sherman to inquire whether he should or not, and the latter ordered him to back up to the station. This was no easy task, the train being unusually long and heavy, and the grade backward up hill; but after a little time it was accomplished, the rebels all the while continuing their firing.

"When the train stopped," said my informant, "I never saw line of battle formed so quick from off the tops of cars. It was a mystery to me how the men got off so quick."

They fought for some time without the fort or earth-work, and then retreated inside, where Colonel Anthony's regiment, the Sixty-sixth Indiana, which garrisoned the post, already were.

Here the rebels sent in a written demand to surrender, signed, it was said, by General Pemberton's Adjutant. One of General Sherman's staff asked what reply they were to make to it. "Tell them 'No,' of course," said the General.

The attack was then renewed, and continued without intermission for some three hours—till after three o'clock—when a gallant lieutenant of the Thirteenth regulars, whose name I am sorry to have forgotten, made a charge upon them with thirty men, drove them like sheep, and they finally disappeared. They were all mounted, but fought part of the time on foot. They had several pieces of artillery, and we had none; but their practice was miserable—the poorest, General Sherman said, that he had ever witnessed on their part.

Our loss was fifteen killed and thirty wounded, about equally divided between the Thirteenth regulars and Sixty-sixth Indiana, and the loss of the rebels was supposed to be about the same, though it could not be got at exactly, as they were seen carrying off their dead and wounded. Right on the railroad track two were laying dead as we passed. One was a genuine type of the Butternut, dressed in a suit of that color, with a sallow complexion, long beard, and a ghastly wound in the side; the other was an old man, with his cartridge-box on, who was a resident in the neighborhood, had received protection papers from our Government, and, only a few days before, had been in the place, selling articles to the soldiers.

Of the conduct of the telegraph operator, Edw. F. Butler, I must speak in terms of the highest praise. Entirely unsolicited, he had taken his gun and fought gallantly at the breastworks till he was disabled by a shot in the left arm, when he turned over his gun to one who, he said, could then use it better than he. It was in excellent contrast to that of a brakesman on the train, who, after he had taken refuge and was cowering in the fort, was ordered by one of the officers to take up a musket, go to the breastworks, and fight for his life, but refused, saying that the Government paid him forty-five dollars a month to brake on that road, and that he had all that he could do to take care of his life now.

Of the colored servants belonging to the two regiments I must also speak. An Irish captain of the Thirteenth said: "I have always talked against the 'damned' niggers, and against making them soldiers; but, since I have seen what I have to-day, those brave fellows, to a man, without an officer saying a word to them, pick up guns and fight like devils at the breastworks, I have not a word to say."

Another brakesman took refuge under a bridge, but the rebels making a charge in that direction, he made a "break" for the fort, but in passing the depot saw a darkey's woolly head sticking out of a hole underneath, and thinking that a more secure place of refuge, made a dive for it, and found himself securely ensconced among cobwebs, between four stone walls, where, in event of the rebels capturing the place, he determined to remain till they left, unless by burning the depot they should compel him to come out.

One of General Sherman's negroes remained

on the train with the horses. The rebels came up and asked him which the General's horse was, and he replied falsely that he did not know. They then asked him which was a certain other officer's horse; to which question he made a like reply. They then commenced to select them out on their own judgment, and happened to get the General's mare among them. They were obliged to jump them from out of the cars on to the ground, and this feat of coming up right in front of the fort, all the while under a very hot fire, was spoken of as a very brave deed. They also rummaged the General's car, taking from it his coat, and a number of articles of baggage belonging to the members of his staff, and tried to set it on fire, but in this they did not succeed.

Throughout the fight General Sherman maintained his position in the centre of the fort, giving every move his personal superintendence, as calm and unconcerned as though he was standing in a ball-room, instead of in the most exposed position in the works, and by his example infusing coolness and courage into all around him. The conductor on the train said to me: "I was somewhat frightened at first, but when I saw such a great man as he, so unconcerned amid all the balls flying around him, I did not think it worth while for me to be scared."

A house close by the fort, filled with commissary stores, obstructed the range and gave shelter to the enemy. "Sixty days' furlough for the man who sets it on fire," said General Sherman; and one of the Sixty-sixth Indiana did it. I wish I knew the brave fellow's name.

One of his staff, Lieutenant James, his acting ordnance officer, whom I have seen passing into the depot yard on business connected with his department, every day, for several days past, was very severely injured — shot through the breast, while doing his utmost, with a musket.

But to return to the culverts. We found three of them burned—two small and one large one—and returned and reported the facts. Colonel Anthony furnished a detail to mend the former, and with my two companies we repaired the latter, and by seven o'clock in the morning had the road again in running order to Colliersville. General Sherman told us that we had done so well, that he now wished us to go to Lafayette, with the construction train which had just arrived, and repair the road to that point; after which we might return, according to our orders, to Memphis.

We did so; mending the telegraph wire in four places where it had been cut, and replacing one rail which the rebels had taken up and carried off some one hundred yards and hid among some weeds, and at Lafayette found the road and telegraph in good working order the rest of the way to Corinth.

On my return to Colliersville, General Sherman proceeded with his train on his way to Corinth, leaving us deeply impressed with his qualities as a gentleman and an officer.

As we were backing down again to Memphis, we struck with the tender and ran over a young heifer; without, however, throwing any thing off

the track, which completed our adventures on this expedition. The force of the enemy was estimated at two thousand five hundred; ours was about six hundred. Your affectionate son,

E. O. HURD,
Captain Company B, Thirty-ninth O. V. I.,
Commanding Detachment.

Doc. 195.

FIGHT AT MERRILL'S CROSSING, MO.

OFFICIAL REPORT OF GENERAL BROWN.

HEADQUARTERS IN THE FIELD, }
MARSHALL, MO., October 13, 1863. }

GENERAL: I have the honor to report that, after following the enemy through Cole Camp, Syracuse, and Boonville, skirmishing with his rear all the distance, he was forced to make a stand at Merrill's Crossing of Salt Fork, a point eight miles south-west of Arrow Rock, and about the same distance from Marshall, and commenced a skirmishing fight at six o'clock on the evening of the twelfth, in the midst of a cold, driving rain. We fought him as long as we could see, and lay down on our arms in the rain during the night.

At three o'clock this morning I detached Lieutenant-Colonel Lazear, with about nine hundred men, with orders to move to the south, avoiding the route of the enemy, and intercept him, if possible, at Marshall, and bring on an engagement, while I followed him (the enemy) with the balance of my command. The result was as I had hoped—Lieutenant-Colonel Lazear drove in the advance of the enemy, and an engagement commenced at eight o'clock A.M. The enemy had possession of the ford on my arrival, and checked my advance for a few moments, but by making a detour to the left, I found one of these crossings and gained position in their rear, on the bank of the creek along which they were formed. They soon gave way, and broke through the dense timber and brush which for a mile and a half fringed the borders of the creek. By throwing a force through their centre their forces were divided, part being driven east toward Arrow Rock, and part, under Shelby, to the north-west — both bodies pursued by our victorious troops.

I was misinformed when I reported to you by telegraph to-day that the enemy's artillery had been captured. We got his best gun, an iron ten-pounder, (Parrott pattern,) originally in Bledsoe's battery; but he succeeded in getting away with one piece, a brass six-pounder, (since captured,) that was captured at Springfield on the eighth of January.

I am unable to give you a correct account of the killed and wounded. Ours, including all our losses from Cole Camp to the place and the fight of to-day, will not exceed thirty. Of the enemy, I am officially advised that fifty-three dead have been found in the brush, and seventy wounded, who have been left at the hospitals here and at the houses on the road in the vicinity. They lost a considerable number in the different attacks we made on the march. At Merrill's we found sixteen dead in the morning after the skirmish. At Lamine Crossing they lost nine killed. We have taken a number of prisoners, and they are coming in hourly. A portion of their train was captured. I think they are effectually broken up, and I shall not give them time to rally or concentrate. The pursuit and fighting have been done by the M. S. M. and the E. M. M. I can only point to the result of their efforts as the best commentary on their gallantry and endurance. For the past three days they have followed and engaged the enemy night and day in the rain without subsistence, except that gathered by the wayside, or protection from the storm.

The enemy numbered nearly two thousand men. My own force was about one thousand six hundred. I am, very truly, your obedient servant,

E. B. BROWN,
Brigadier-General Volunteers, Commanding.

To Major-General J. M. SCHOFIELD,
Commanding Department of the Missouri, St. Louis.

Doc. 196.

FIGHTS ALONG THE RAPIDAN.

A NATIONAL ACCOUNT.

HEADQUARTERS ARMY OF THE POTOMAC,
Sunday, October 11, 1863.

For some days past it has been evident that this army would not long remain in the vicinity of Culpeper, and every one who knows any thing of our own and the rebel forces, understood that it would be impossible for us to advance. Hence, the only question for General Meade to solve was how to get his immense trains and stores away in safety.

On Wednesday, the seventh instant, General Meade received information that led him to believe that an extensive rebel raid was contemplated upon his right and rear—information since verified. It was also ascertained that on Thursday night the rebel cavalry under Stuart, and infantry under Ewell, were crossing the Rapidan in the vicinity of Robertson's River, and making toward Springville, via James City, and I presume it was this information which led to the strategy of the last two days.

General Meade was fully apprized of the rebel strength, and knew that by making a demonstration on their right and centre he would compel them to abandon their enterprise in order to protect their lines of communication with Gordonsville and Richmond.

Consequently a strong force of cavalry, under Buford, appeared at daylight on Saturday at Germania Ford, ten miles below Raccoon Ford, while infantry and cavalry appeared in force at the fords in the vicinity of Cedar Mountain. Kilpatrick was also sent out to the right to attract and engage the advance of the enemy at James City, ten miles south-west of Culpeper. It is said that General Buford crossed at Germania Ford.

On Friday night the First and Sixth corps, who had been encamped along the base of the Cedar Run Mountains and extending down to Raccoon Ford, built fires and advanced their lines to the river. They had previously been strengthened by two divisions; so that at the break of day on Saturday a most formidable array of Union soldiers appeared, ready to cross the river at several points simultaneously.

General Kilpatrick had also during Friday night moved to the right, and at daylight on Saturday morning engaged the enemy at James City. He was instructed not to bring on a general engagement, as the plan was to lure the rebels back to their right and centre by the demonstrations in those quarters—a plan which would be thwarted by bringing on a general engagement upon our right. Consequently, after a half hour's skirmishing, he fell back in the direction of Culpeper, and took position near Bethel Church, where a support of infantry was posted, and to which place they were followed by the rebels. Here a part of our cavalry dismounted and deployed as infantry, and for a short time the fight was brisk indeed; but the rebel force proving too strong, or abiding by his orders, Kilpatrick fell still further toward the main body of the corps, posted two miles west of Culpeper. In this movement a part of the One Hundred and Twentieth New-York volunteers was captured; but they did not long remain prisoners, for, watching their opportunity, a brigade of our cavalry, of which the Fifth New-York and Fifth Michigan were a part, dashed upon the guard having the captives in charge, and rescued all but some twelve or fifteen.

The ruse of threatening to cross the river by the First and Sixth corps had its desired effect. Immediately upon the discovery of our forces by the rebels, signals were displayed, calling upon the infantry to come back to check our advance. Accordingly Ewell recrossed the river during the forenoon, and took up his line of march toward the Orange and Alexandria railroad, where they had a series of works, leaving only Stuart to demonstrate upon our right, north of the river.

This, then, was the position of the forces on Saturday night at dark, with every prospect of a bloody fight on the coming day. Buford was at Germania, the First and Sixth corps extending from Raccoon Ford to Cedar Run; Kilpatrick, supported by the Second and Third corps, to the west of Culpeper, from three to four miles distant. Ewell had moved back from his position in the morning, and faced Newton and Sedgwick, while Stuart fronted French, Warren, and Kilpatrick in the vicinity of Bethel Church.

On Sunday morning at two o'clock our infantry force, both at the Rapidan and west of town, commenced moving toward the Rappahannock, their trains having all been sent back the night before, leaving the entire cavalry of Pleasanton to cover the retreat. Gregg had come up by forced marches during Saturday; so our cavalry force was by no means insignificant. Our infantry all reached their present camping ground in excellent order during the day, their pace accelerated a trifle perhaps by the sound of cannon in the direction of the town they had left in the morning.

But not so fortunate the cavalry; for they had a day of skirmishing by which to remember the inauguration of the second annual race over the Centreville course.

After the infantry had all passed over Mountain Run, a small stream just north of Culpeper, and the roads had become cleared, Kilpatrick and Gregg took up their line of march, and, skirmishing the while, advanced in the direction the infantry had taken. Kilpatrick came up by the way of Culpeper, while Gregg took the road toward Sulphur Springs. I do not learn that Gregg met with any enemy on the line of his march; but Kilpatrick did, and in his encounters with them confirmed his old reputation for dash and daring.

Kilpatrick retreated slowly from Bethel in the morning, Stuart's men showing themselves continually, and annoying him with their well-directed fire; but he met them with "tender in kind," until he had crossed Mountain Run, where the rebels ceased to trouble him. Here, at about twelve o'clock, he heard for the first time in the day heavy firing of artillery off to the eastward, in the direction of Germania Ford, and he knew that Buford was being hotly engaged. He immediately sent out scouts to open up communication with Buford, and learned that a junction was expected to be formed before night at Brandy Station, whither he bent his way, taking along his trains of ambulances leisurely, and not anticipating further molestation.

But upon reaching the hill just south of Brandy he discovered that a division, at least, of the enemy had slipped in between the rear of the infantry and his advance, and was strongly posted, waiting his coming. He halted but a moment, just long enough to take in the whole scene, when he shouted — and the word was carried back along the line, not a poetic burst or a devotional exclamation, but one suited to the times and the feelings of the rough, brave men he commanded—"Boys, yonder are the cusses." Turning to the Michigan brigade, who led his advance, and who glory not in euphonious appellatives, he called out, "Come on, you wolverines; now give them hell!" and, suiting his own action to his precept, he sprang to the head of his column and led such a charge as one does not see often, even in this age of valor.

Three regiments of rebels were drawn up by companies across the road, twelve platoons deep, flanked by a regiment on either side. It was upon this strongly posted force, directly at the centre, that our horsemen charged, while exposed upon the front and flank to a most murderous fire; but on they went, shouting, sabring, and trampling down the enemy with the fury of demons. To withstand such a charge was simply impossible, and the rebels broke in confusion and scattered in all directions. When once through the main body, our forces turned,

and with shot and shell poured upon the retreating rebels a very demoralizing testimonial of their high regard for the tools of this rebellion.

In this charge we lost a few in killed and wounded, and a few are missing; but we know also that the rebel surgeons will have to use the trepanning and amputating instruments, and will have to bury quite a number of their patients. Our own wounded are being brought in to-night, and are being sent to Washington per rail.

HEADQUARTERS, October 12—6 A.M.

The trains have all come in in safety, and in excellent order. Kilpatrick and Buford have also arrived at the river, and are in line of battle. Our forces are now in position to contest the further advance of the enemy, who appear in force south of the river. I do not think a general engagement will take place to-day, but in this I may be mistaken.

ANOTHER ACCOUNT.

WASHINGTON, October 14, 1863.

The whole of Gregg's division was ordered from Bealton Station on Saturday toward Culpeper, and arrived at Culpeper at four o'clock P.M. From thence the Second brigade of the Second division was ordered to Fox Mountain to support Kilpatrick, but finding that Kilpatrick did not need reinforcements, the brigade left them on Sunday morning and rejoined the division at Culpeper. On Sunday night Gregg moved to Sulphur Springs, arriving about nine o'clock.

On Monday morning two regiments — the Fourth and Thirteenth Pennsylvania—were sent forward to Jefferson, about five miles from Sulphur Springs, and the First Maine were sent out toward Little Washington to reconnoitre. The last-named regiment encountered a large force of the enemy just beyond Amosville, and were surrounded, but gallantly cut their way out, and crossed the river at Waterloo Ford, about twelve miles above Sulphur Springs.

About ten o'clock Monday morning, the enemy advanced on the Fourth and Thirteenth Pennsylvania, which were at Jefferson, with cavalry, showing heavy infantry supports in their rear, when our cavalry, seeing that they were being overpowered, fell back slowly, contesting the ground, to a large forest this side of Jefferson, where Gregg, who led these regiments in person, dismounted a portion of his men and sent them out as skirmishers, their horses having been sent back to Sulphur Springs.

After stubbornly contesting the ground for nearly two hours, they were ordered to fall back slowly, and as they were doing so a heavy infantry force of the enemy was discovered on each flank, and at the same time three regiments of cavalry, having made a wide detour, attacked them in the rear. At this time the Tenth New-York was sent to the support of Gregg, and Reed's battery (M, Second United States artillery) opened on the rebel cavalry, but owing to the short range of the guns, (which were brass Napoleons,) no serious damage was inflicted on the enemy by them.

The Fourth and Thirteenth were now pressed severely in the front and our centre broken, and at the same time they were attacked on each flank and in the rear. Our men cut their way through and escaped across the river with heavy loss.

The Eighteenth Pennsylvania was now dismounted and thrown out along the river-bank as skirmishers, whilst the Eighth was also dismounted, and ordered to support the battery, which had only four short-range guns, and the enemy opened on us with some twenty pieces of artillery, but our troops gallantly held the ground for several hours, repulsing the charges of the enemy, and gradually fell back on the Fayetteville road, the enemy following, but keeping at a respectable distance.

Colonel Gregg had but two aids with him—Lieutenants Martin and Cutler—and both were wounded; the former severely and the latter slightly. Lieutenant Adams, Fourth Pennsylvania; Major Wilson, Eighth Pennsylvania; Lieutenant-Colonel Kettler, First New-Jersey; Major Russell, First Maryland, were wounded; and the loss of the Second brigade, it is thought, will amount to about four hundred and fifty men in killed, wounded, and missing, the Fourth and Thirteenth Pennsylvania regiments suffering most severely.

Colonel Gregg is highly spoken of for the manner in which he fought his men, and it was owing to his skill and bravery that the Fourth and Thirteenth fought their way out of a precarious situation. He was at the head of his men in the thickest of the fight, and in several charges he took the lead.

During the engagement the rebels charged the battery and captured one of the guns; but the First New-Jersey cavalry gallantly charged back and recaptured the piece, which was immediately turned on them with good effect.

Our cavalry yesterday held the enemy in check, and there was some little skirmishing, one man being wounded while on picket last evening.

Doc. 197.

BATTLE OF BUCKLAND'S MILLS, VA.

GENERAL CUSTER'S REPORT.

HEADQUARTERS SECOND BRIGADE THIRD DIVISION CAVALRY CORPS, ARMY OF THE POTOMAC, October 24, 1863.

Captain L. G. Estes, A. A. G. Third Division:

In compliance with instructions received from the General commanding the division, I have the honor to submit the following report of the operations of my command, from October ninth to October twenty-third, 1863:

On the night of October ninth, my picket line, which extended along the north bank of Robertson River, in the vicinity of James City, was at-

tacked, and a portion of the line forced back upon the reserves; at the same time my scouts informed me that the enemy was moving in heavy column toward my right; this report was confirmed by deserters. In anticipation of an attack by the enemy at daybreak, I ordered my entire command to be saddled at three A.M. on the tenth. At daylight the enemy began by cautiously feeling my line; but seeing his inability to surprise us, he contented himself with obtaining possession of Cedar Mountain, which point he afterward used as a signal station. At one P.M. I received orders from the General commanding the division, to report with my command at James City. The head of my column arrived in the vicinity of that point at three P.M. The enemy had already obtained possession of the town, and had brought several guns to bear upon the position I was ordered to take. Battery M, Second United States artillery, under command of Lieutenant Pennington, was unlimbered, and succeeded in shelling the enemy out of the woods on the right of the town. At the same time, Colonel Alger, of the Fifth Michigan cavalry, who held the extreme left of my line, moved forward with one battalion of his regiment under the gallant Major Clark, and charged the battery. The charge, although daring in the extreme, failed for want of sufficient support. It was successful so far, however, as to compel the enemy to shift the position of his battery to a more retired point. Night setting in, prevented us from improving the advantage we had gained. Most of my command rested on their arms during the night. Early in the morning I retired on the road leading to Culpeper, which point I reached without molestation from the enemy. It was not until the rear of my column was leaving the town that the enemy made his appearance, and attempted, unsuccessfully, to harass my rear-guard. On the hills north of the town I placed my command in position to receive an attack. The enemy not feeling disposed to accept the invitation, I retired on the road leading to Rappahannock Station. My column had scarcely begun to march before the officer commanding the rear-guard—Colonel Mann, of the Seventh Michigan cavalry—reported the enemy to be pressing him closely. At the same time a strong column was seen on my outer flank, evidently attempting to intercept our line of march to the river. The vigorous attacks now being made upon my rear-guard compelled me to place my battery at the head of the column, and to employ my entire force to keep the enemy from my guns. My advance had reached the vicinity of Brandy Station, when a courier hastened back with the information that a brigade of the enemy's cavalry was in position directly in my front, thus cutting us completely off from the river. Upon examination I learned the correctness of the report. The heavy masses of the rebel cavalry could be seen covering the heights in front of my advance. When it is remembered that my rear-guard was hotly engaged with a superior force, a heavy column enveloping each flank, and my advance confronted by more than double my own number, the perils of my situation can be estimated. Lieutenant Pennington at once placed his battery in position and opened a brisk fire, which was responded to by the guns of the enemy. The Major-General commanding the cavalry corps at this moment rode to the advance; to him I proposed, with my command, to cut through the force in my front, and thus open a way for the entire command to the river. My proposition was approved, and I received orders to take my available force and push forward, leaving the Sixth and Seventh Michigan cavalry to hold the force in rear in check. I formed the Fifth Michigan cavalry on my right, in column of battalions; on my left, I formed the First Michigan in column of squadrons. After ordering them to draw their sabres, I informed them that we were surrounded, and all we had to do was to open a way with our sabres. They showed their determination and purpose by giving three hearty cheers. At this moment, the band struck up the inspiring air, "Yankee Doodle," which excited the enthusiasm of the entire command to the highest pitch, and made each individual member feel as if he was a host in himself. Simultaneously, both regiments moved forward to the attack. It required but a glance at the countenances of the men to enable me to read the settled determination with which they undertook the work before them. The enemy, without waiting to receive the onset, broke in disorder and fled. After a series of brilliant charges, during which the enemy suffered heavily, we succeeded in reaching the river, which we crossed in good order. From the eleventh to the fifteenth instant, my command was employed in picketing and guarding the flank and rear of the army. On the afternoon of the fifteenth, the brigade being posted on the Bull Run battle ground, I detailed Major Kidd with his regiment, the Sixth Michigan cavalry, to reconnoitre the position and strength of the enemy in the vicinity of Gainesville. The reconnoissance was entirely satisfactory, and showed the enemy to be in considerable force at that point. Sunday, the eighteenth instant, at three P.M., the entire division was ordered to move on the pike leading from Groveton to Warrenton. The First brigade moved on the pike, the Second moved on a road to the left of and parallel to the pike, but soon encountered the enemy, and drove him as far as Gainesville, where the entire command bivouacked during the night. The First Vermont cavalry, under Colonel Sawyer, deserves great credit for the rapidity with which they forced the enemy to retire. At daybreak on the morning of the nineteenth, my brigade took the advance and skirmished with the enemy's cavalry from Gainesville to Buckland; at the latter point I found him strongly posted upon the south bank of Broad Run. The position for his artillery was well chosen. After a fruitless attempt to effect a crossing in his front, I succeeded in turning his left flank so completely as to force him from his position. Having driven him more than a mile

from the stream, I threw out my pickets, and ordered my men to prepare their dinner. From the inhabitants of Buckland I learned that the forces of the enemy with whom we had been engaged were commanded by General J. E. B. Stuart in person, who, at the time of our arrival at that point, was seated at the dinner-table, eating; but, owing to my successful advance, he was compelled to leave his dinner untouched—a circumstance not regretted by that portion of my command into whose hands it fell. The First brigade took the advance. At this point I was preparing to follow, when information reached me that the enemy was advancing on my left from the direction of Greenwich. I had scarcely time to place my command in position to resist an attack from that direction before the enemy's skirmishers appeared. Pennington's battery opened upon them, while the Sixth Michigan cavalry, under Major Kidd, was thrown forward and deployed as skirmishers. One gun of Pennington's battery, supported by the First Vermont cavalry, was placed on my extreme left. The First Michigan cavalry, under Major Brewer, acted as a reserve, and as a support for the remaining five guns of the battery. The Fifth Michigan cavalry, under Colonel Mann, were engaged in the woods on my right. At first I was under the impression that the skirmishers were composed of dismounted cavalry, but later developments convinced me that it was a very superior force of infantry that now confronted me. After completing his dispositions for attack, the enemy advanced upon me. In doing so, he exposed a line of infantry of more than a mile in extent; at the same time he opened a heavy fire upon me from his artillery. Pennington's battery, aided by the Sixth Michigan cavalry, poured a destructive fire upon the enemy as he advanced, but failed to force him back. A desperate effort was made to capture my battery. Pennington continued to fire until the enemy was within twenty yards of his guns. He was then compelled to limber up and retire to the north bank of Broad Run. The other portions of the command followed. The First Michigan cavalry was intrusted with the duty of covering the movement—a task which was gallantly performed. My command being very exhausted, I retired to the vicinity of Gainesville, where I encamped for the night. Major Clark, Fifth Michigan cavalry, was detached from his regiment with one battalion. When the command retired to the north bank of Broad Run, he, with a small portion of his battalion, became separated from the rest of the command, and were captured by the enemy. Computing my losses from the ninth instant, I find them to be as follows:

	Officers.	Men.	Total.
Killed,	0	9	9
Wounded,	2	41	43
Missing,	8	154	162
Aggregate,			214

Before closing my report, I desire to make honorable mention of the highly creditable manner in which both officers and men of my command have discharged their duty during the long and arduous marches as well as the hard-fought engagements of the past few days. Too much praise cannot be given to the officers and men of battery M, Second artillery, for the gallantry displayed on more than one occasion. For the untiring zeal and energy, added to the unflinching bravery displayed in transmitting and executing my orders upon the field, my acknowledgments are due to the following members of my staff: Captain R. F. Judson, A. D. C., Lieutenant R. Baylis, A. A. D. C., Lieutenant William Colerick, A. D. C., and to Lieutenant E. G. Granger, A. A. A. G. Lieutenant Granger, while leading a charge at Brandy Station, had his horse shot in two places. Surgeon Wooster, of my staff, in addition to his professional duties, rendered me valuable assistance by aiding in transmitting my orders. Respectfully submitted,

(Signed) G. A. CUSTER,
Brig. Com. Second Brigade Third Division Cavalry Corps.

E. A. PAUL'S NARRATIVE.

HEADQUARTERS ARMY OF THE POTOMAC,
Wednesday, October 21, 1863.

The advance of this army — Lieutenant Whittaker and twenty of General Kilpatrick's cavalry division — entered Warrenton last evening, the enemy's cavalry, under Stuart, at the same time retiring toward Sulphur Springs.

The recent gallant cavalry fight of General Kilpatrick's division at Buckland's Mills and vicinity is still the subject of conversation throughout the army. Now that all the command is in, I am able to furnish a more reliable account of that affair than the first despatches, which were necessarily incomplete, owing to the absence of a portion of the command. The commander of the division received orders on Sunday last to move as far as possible toward Warrenton, under the supposition that nothing but cavalry would oppose his progress; and knowing that Kilpatrick had whipped Stuart alone on several well-contested fields, it was not thought worth while to advance infantry within immediate supporting distance. Notwithstanding this division has been constantly on active duty, and the men and horses were considerably the worse for wear, the order to march was obeyed with alacrity, and the command was moving by three o'clock P.M. on Sunday. But little progress had been made from Bull Run before the enemy's pickets were encountered and driven back upon their supports at Gainesville, where two regiments were found drawn up in line of battle. Night coming on, the command encamped. Early Monday morning the advance was sounded, and the enemy retired from Gainesville, fighting as they went, taking the Warrenton pike. From Gainesville General Kilpatrick took the precaution to send the First Virginia regiment, Major Farrable, to Haymarket and vicinity to guard the right flank, and the Seventh Michigan, Colonel Mann, to Greenwich and vicinity to guard the left flank, while the remainder of the division moved up the Warrenton pike. The enemy fled precipitately until they had crossed Broad Run, at Buckland's

Mills, where Hampton's and Jones's brigades, under the immediate command of Stuart, with two batteries, occupied a very strong position west of the run. The banks of Broad Run in this vicinity are very steep, and, therefore, are fordable only at a few places. Pennington's and Elder's batteries were opened with effect, compelling the enemy to move their batteries several times. After an artillery duel and skirmishing for nearly two hours, and the Commanding General having received word that there was no enemy near at hand on his right or left, under a concentrated fire of the artillery a crossing was effected in force by the pike bridge. The skirmishers, not to be left behind, boldly waded the river, and notwithstanding all the obstacles to such a movement, kept up an excellent line, the whole command pushing forward under a very heavy fire. The conflict, though comparatively brief here, was sharp, the enemy contending manfully for every foot of ground, but when they did give way, General Davies's brigade, which had before been held in hand while Custer's had the advance, moved rapidly forward, driving the enemy above New Baltimore. While General Custer's command was taking a nooning, a messenger came in out of breath to General Kilpatrick, with the information that a column of the enemy was threatening his left. Suitable disposition of the force was at once made to resist this unexpected danger by Major Cook, Chief of Staff, and Adjutant-General Estes. No sooner had this been done than a portion of the Seventh Michigan which had been stationed on their flank was forced back by a line of rebel infantry, acting as skirmishers, with a strong reserve, believed to have been at least one full division, with a brigade or more of cavalry. The extreme danger of the command as situated was seen at a glance by General Kilpatrick, and he despatched Lieutenant Hickey with orders to General Davies to fall back at once, as he was in danger of being cut off. General Davies had in part anticipated the order, for upon hearing firing at his rear, had fallen back to within one mile and a half of General Custer's brigade, and was there awaiting orders when the messenger arrived. While this was transpiring, the Fifth Michigan, Colonel Alger, was deployed as skirmishers to so far as possible fill up the gap between the two brigades and keep back a threatened movement of the enemy to divide the command. A severe struggle now took place for possession of the pike—our forces trying to hold it so as to enable Davies to pass and take up a new position, while the enemy were determined that the movement should not be made. Having both infantry and cavalry, in this they were successful — General Custer, however, succeeding in getting his command in safety across Broad Run after the most desperate fighting, in which Pennington's battery, (company M, Second artillery,) as usual, took a most important part, firing with great rapidity, and making their guns a terror to all massed forces with which the enemy threatened the retiring troops, though at one time they boldly came within a very short distance of the guns, intent upon capturing them.

Once across the river, the bridge was held, though some of the men were entirely out of carbine ammunition, and resort was had to Colt's revolvers, in which the officers took a conspicuous part. The enemy, however, succeeded in effecting a crossing some distance to the left, and the brigade fell back fighting to the vicinity of Gainesville, where the troops disappeared in a belt of timber, passing through a line of Sixth corps infantry skirmishers there concealed, whom the enemy, not seeing, made bold to charge, and were repulsed with great loss, the officer leading the charge being among the killed.

When General Kilpatrick saw that Custer's brigade was safe across Broad Run, he directed him to fall back slowly, and fighting if pursued, and then started, accompanied by an orderly only, to join General Davies, whom he had notified previously by an aid that he was cut off, and must make his way to the pike leading from Thoroughfare Gap to Gainesville. To many not acquainted with the circumstances this might seem a foolhardy errand, having to recross Broad Run, which he did at the bridge, and to run the gauntlet of skirmishers for more than a mile; but General Kilpatrick would rather have lost his own life on that field than to lose a brigade, the fate of which then hung in the balance; and while having the utmost confidence in the ability and coolness of General Davies, he at the same time realized the fact that his own presence would do something toward encouraging the troops, particularly as some of them had been associated with him for years. Providence permitting, he succeeded in reaching the command with ten or a dozen gallant spirits, both officers and men, who, seeing the noble conduct of their General, resolved to accompany him without orders. Fortunately, as the sequel will show, Dr. Capehart, Chief Surgeon of the brigade, was familiar with that section of country, and avoiding the main road leading to Thoroughfare Gap, reached the pike a short distance above the village of Haymarket. The difficulty of this movement will be understood when it is stated that this reduced brigade was attacked in the rear by both Hampton's and Jones's brigades, and that Fitz Lee was ready to confront it on the Thoroughfare Gap road, which they expected Davies would take when cut off. When General Kilpatrick reached the command, he at once ordered the Harris Light (Second New-York) to act as rear-guard. So hard pressed were they in rear and flank, that the choicest spirits—because the bravest, both officers and men—of the command joined the rear-guard, and nobly did they withstand the onsets of the enemy, and even mocked them—while exulting at the idea of even driving a moiety of Kilpatrick's command—in their beast-like yelp, and hurled them back on more than one occasion by the sword alone. At one time the rear-guard and the advance of the enemy were all mixed together. The enemy's advance wearing a uniform similar to that worn by our own troops, in the excitement of the moment it was not easy to distinguish one from the other. As an instance of this, I may state that a rebel urged Lieutenant Whittaker, of General Kilpatrick's staff, to press forward. Whittaker, supposing it was some of our own men, upbraided him for wishing, as he supposed, to press past and abandon the wagons. By half-past seven o'clock in the evening both brigades were in camp at Gainesville, having been engaged nearly all day fighting a combination of infantry and cavalry, with a loss, all told, as now appears — including killed, wounded, and missing — not to exceed one hundred men, instead of three hundred or four hundred, as was at first reported by stragglers. And instead of losing eight or nine wagons, the actual loss is only two, and one of these got mired, and the other broke down. No horses or mules were lost. In this retreat Elder's battery took a conspicuous part, and was handled with consummate skill.

General Kilpatrick, upon bringing his Second brigade into camp, reported personally at headquarters, and received the thanks of both Generals Meade and Pleasanton for the able manner in which he had discharged the important duty that had been intrusted to him, and the skill he displayed in extricating his command from the most trying positions in which a command can be placed. It is just such emergencies that test the capacity of a commanding officer, and General Kilpatrick, all through the trying scenes of Monday, showed that he was fully equal to the occasion, for nothing but cool judgment and discriminate action, with hard fighting, saved the division from the trap the enemy had laid for it. Generals Kilpatrick, Custer, Davies, Colonels Alger, Mann, Sawyer, and in fact a large majority of the officers and men, deserve particular mention for preserving intact, almost by superhuman exertions, the hard-earned reputation of the cavalry corps.

General Merritt reports that the enemy have so completely destroyed the Orange and Alexandria Railroad between Warrenton Junction and the Rappahannock River, that it will take two months to reconstruct it; and in the opinion of engineers, it will be much easier and save time to construct almost an entire new road than to attempt to repair the old one. They have filled the cuts—of which there are several—with trees and earth; burnt the culverts and bridges, blown up the abutments, destroyed the ties, and miles of rails, by heating and twisting them.

Doc. 198.

BATTLE NEAR BLOUNTSVILLE, TENN.

CINCINNATI "COMMERCIAL" ACCOUNT.

BRISTOL, TENN., October 16, 1863.

I WROTE you a few days ago from Brabson's Hill, giving an account of the battle of Blue Springs, on the tenth instant, and the chase after them to that point. General Shackleford, after recruiting his nearly worn-out horses for twenty-four hours, moved his command forward toward Blountsville, on the evening of the thirteenth. A reconnoitring party of the Seventh Ohio volunteer cavalry, under Captain Copeland, drove the rebel pickets in, and had a brisk skirmish for half an hour, losing one man, private James Barnes, company E, who was shot in the head and instantly expired.

Early on the morning of the fourteenth, the ball opened four miles from Blountsville, and the firing continued all day, the rebels making stands on all the hills, but they were driven from their positions and retreated through Blountsville at dark, toward Zollicoffer, on the East-Tennessee and Virginia railroad. Night coming on, we encamped near Blountsville for the night. The rebels becoming alarmed, evacuated their stronghold, Zollicoffer, during the night, and retreated toward Saltville, evidently thinking we were making for the Salt Works at that place. Our troops followed them up to within six miles of Abington, Va., when they returned to Bristol. We captured here three locomotives and thirty-four cars, all of which we destroyed, as well as five railroad bridges above Bristol. We also captured a large amount of salt, sugar, etc.

The rebels had thrown down the fences in the vicinity of Blountsville, and thrown up breast-works, and boasted that they intended to give the Yanks a good thrashing, and drive them from East-Tennessee; but, as usual, instead of their doing it, they did the tallest kind of running. Our loss in this engagement was small, consisting as follows:

Second Lieutenant Charles McBee, company G, Second East-Tennessee mounted infantry, wounded seriously in the head; private William G. Francis, company G, Second East-Tennessee mounted infantry, in the foot; Corporal John Little, company K, Fourteenth Illinois cavalry, in the foot; private Andrew Bishop, company H, Second Ohio volunteer cavalry, in the leg; Sergeant R. M. Bail, company C, Second Ohio volunteer cavalry, in the hip.

The rebels admit a loss of eight killed and twenty-six wounded. We also took ten prisoners.

Our boys, in the recent battles and skirmishes, have behaved most gallantly. They (General Shackleford's division) have been constantly on the move, and, in fact, have done all the work that has been done in East-Tennessee. Two brigades are in the neighborhood of Loudon, keeping the rebels, under Pegram, out of that section, while Colonels Foster's and Carter's brigades have been in the front here. The General is a working man, and will have none but that kind about him.

Doc. 199.

CAPTURE OF GILLMORE'S GUERRILLAS.

MARTINSBURGH, October 17, 1863.

AFTER the excitement incident to the anticipated Imbodenish raid had partially subsided here, our vigilant "citizen scout" reported at headquarters information in reference to the movements and whereabouts of Major Gillmore's predatory rebel band, "to villainy and to vandalism consecrate."

It appears this eminent and worthy bushwhacker had conceived a plan to destroy, on a moonless night, October fifteenth, the Baltimore and Ohio railroad bridge across Back Creek, and also to tear up generally the bridges and culverts above that point. With this intention Gillmore left his temporary encampments near a distillery, in the vicinity of Strasburgh, with his adventurous "knights of the order of rum-punch," consisting of about forty men, including two Captains and one Lieutenant. He followed in his line of march the narrow valley west of the North Mountain range, through which peacefully meanders the clear waters of Back Creek.

Now, Harry Gillmore is a thorough lady's man. That potent influence said to rule court and camp and grove controlled his movements in the present instance. En route to the point at which he intended to rendezvous until night set in, he halted to see a rebel maiden, "fair and all his fancy painted her," and she persuaded him to linger behind in her delightful society, and to intrust the business of bridge-burning to his senior Captain—Blackford. But for this circumstance Gillmore would not now be at large, as the reader will observe presently.

Leaving the Major with his Delilah, the Captain marched his men beyond the diminutive village of Tomahawk, within five miles of the railroad. He encamped—very secretly, he thought—in an almost inaccessible ravine in North Mountain. It was a capital hiding-place, covered with a thick growth of timber, and, like an African jungle, easier to get into than out of. Here the party awaited the approach of nightfall.

In this lair our citizen scout discovered the gang and reported the fact at headquarters. The post commandant immediately ordered out two small detachments of cavalry from the Twelfth Pennsylvania and First New-York regiments—one commanded by Captain Henry, the other by Captain R. S. Prendergast. To Captain Prendergast, by virtue of his seniority, was intrusted the management and command of the enterprise to capture the guerrillas. A small party of infantry was also directed to march to Tomahawk, to act in conjunction with the cavalry.

Captain Prendergast, accompanied by the scout, reconnoitred, unseen, the position of the rebels, and judiciously posted his cavalry force where they would entirely cut off every avenue of escape. He directed Captain Henry, with the men of the Twelfth, to occupy the road running by what is known as the "Old Stone Church," and himself and men held the main road through Tomahawk—infantry, in the mean time, by his directions, moving upon the bushwhackers from the direction of Hedgesville, with orders to dislodge them from the mountain ravine.

The infantry acted promptly. It was a complete surprise—a coup d'état; the graybacks were thunderstruck by the unexpected presence and sudden onset of "the boys in blue." Those of them who could get to their horses sprang into their saddles, and, with accelerated speed, fled from the ravine, only to encounter the New-York and Pennsylvania boys, who met them with sabre in hand. Others left their horses behind them and took to their heels, and ran in a style exceedingly creditable to chivalrous pedestrianism. We routed them, "foot, horse, and dragoon," capturing nearly the entire party. .

Captain Blackford and four men, hatless and terribly excited, spurred their horses desperately up a steep hill-side, but were overtaken and captured by the horsemen of the First New-York. The other Captain—Diggs, I believe they called him—with his Lieutenant, attempted to "dig out" and escape on foot, but were captured by the boys of the Twelfth; as I have been informed.

We captured in all, to sum up, two Captains, one Lieutenant, twenty-five men, thirty horses, besides pistols, sabres, and other weapons of offensive war "too numerous to mention." We have exterminated, so to speak, Gillmore's choice spirits, his select party, his picked band, his daring and reckless favorites.

The fortunate result of this affair is highly creditable to the genius and enterprise of Captain Prendergast, as well as to the courage and gallantry of the officers and men of the different detachments, whose effective coöperation was so essential to the complete success of the expedition. In this connection, it affords me great pleasure to state that General Kelley's son, visiting Martinsburgh to-day, paid a fine tribute to the energy, capacity, and remarkable success of Captain Prendergast, complimenting him for thus terminating, for the present time at least, the career of so many of Gillmore's lawless and ruffianly satellites.

Among the prisoners were several who were in the engagement near Smithfield with Captain Summer's company, when that gallant and lamented officer lost his life. They say Gillmore killed him, but they speak in terms of praise of his spirited conduct and bravery. Honorable and valiant in life, in death, as a warrior, he rests gloriously, peacefully, where the din of battle shall never more disturb him. "He lives in fame, that died in virtue's cause." The prisoners frankly admitted the irregular character of their military avocations. They had speculated in horses, (stolen ones, of course,) attacked our cavalry pickets at night, carried rebel mails, aided parties running the river "blockade" with goods, burned bridges, robbed Union people, and lived on the plunder thus obtained. One of them, an Irishman, boastingly remarked that he had read the Baltimore papers daily, for some time past; another, with an inward chuckle of delight, said he had crossed the Baltimore and Ohio railroad at night three times during the past three weeks, with contraband goods; while a third jocosely added that he had purchased, with "greenbacks," an india-rubber overcoat, which came from Goodyear's establishment in New-York City, only three weeks ago! These rebel assertions may or may not be true, but as regards "articles contraband of war," I think there is a screw loose somewhere along the Potomac.   GRAPESHOT.

Doc. 200.

DESTRUCTION OF BLOCKADE RUNNERS.

REAR-ADMIRAL BAILEY'S REPORT.

UNITED STATES FLAG-SHIP SAN JACINTO, }
KEY WEST, October 24, 1863. }

Hon. Gideon Welles, Secretary of the Navy:

SIR: I have to report the destruction of the blockade-running steamer Scottish Chief and the sloop Kate Dale, in Hillsborough River, by an armed expedition from the United States gunboats Tahoma and Adela.

Having learned that these vessels were loading with cotton and about to sail, and being apprehensive that by reason of their light load and draft they would escape the blockading vessel, I sent Lieutenant Commander Semmes to Tampa Bay to destroy them. It was planned between myself and Captain Semmes that he should, with the Tahoma, assisted by the Adela, divert attention from the real object of the expedition by shelling the fort and town, and that, under cover of the night, men should be landed at a port on old Tampa Bay, distant from the fort, to proceed overland to the port on the Hillsborough River, where the blockade-runners lay, there to destroy them.

The plan was successfully carried out, but not without considerable loss.

On the sixteenth instant the Tahoma and Adela ran in abreast of the batteries and shelled them slowly during the day. The firing was in an unusual degree accurate and precise. At dark, as soon as the moon went down, a force—consisting of Acting-Ensigns J. P. Randall and J. G. Kochler, with sixty men from the Tahoma, and of Acting-Ensigns Stomberg and Balch, and First Assistant-Engineer Bennett, with forty men from the Adela, and Acting Master's Mate Crane and Mr. J. A. Thompson, guides—was landed at Ballast Point.

The expedition was under the immediate command of Acting-Master T. R. Harris, executive officer of the Tahoma. The line of march was quietly taken up for the river, under the guidance of Mr. J. A. Thompson, who, being too ill to walk, was borne in a litter. A march of fourteen miles (rendered circuitous by the necessity of avoiding houses, creeks, etc.,) brought the party before daylight to the river-bank. As soon as it was light the vessels were discovered on the opposite bank. The force was, therefore, moved to a point opposite where they lay, and those on board brought under aim of the rifles and ordered to send a boat, which they did. A detachment was thereupon sent to bring over the vessels and to make prisoners of those on board.

At this time two men succeeded in escaping from the vessels, who carried the alarm to the garrison. The vessels, meantime, were fired effectually, and the force thereupon set out upon its return. Encountering an armed party near the beach, a charge was made and two rebels made prisoners. The beach, finally, was safely reached without loss, and pickets were stationed and the party rested, waiting the arrival of the boats then being despatched from the Tahoma and the Adela. While so resting, word was brought that a detachment of cavalry and one of infantry were advancing. The party was formed to resist an attack, and, the boats having arrived, the embarkation commenced.

While this was proceeding the rebels opened fire. The First and Second divisions, with seven prisoners, proceeded in an orderly manner to the boats, and the Third division, spread out that the rebels might not fire into a mass, returned the fire energetically and with great coolness and bravery. The Adela meantime shelled the woods (in which the rebels were concealed, and from which they fired) with shrapnel. The First and Second divisions having embarked, the rear-guard, on receiving the order to do so, followed. This rear-guard stood nobly to their post, protecting the retreat under an extremely severe fire from a concealed enemy, loading and firing with the coolness of target practice, and finally leaving quietly at the word of command, bearing with them their wounded.

The rebels were under the command of Captain (a son of the late United States Senator) Westcott, and were so-called "regulars."

The retreat to the boats was admirably conducted by Acting-Master Harris. The expedition throughout was characterized by a disciplined courage on the part of both officers and men. The force suffered severely at the beach, and both courage and discipline were called for. Our loss was as follows:

Killed — James Warrall, seaman, Tahoma; John Roddy, seaman, Adela; Joseph O'Donnell, seaman, Adela.

Ten were wounded, including Acting-Ensign Randall and Kochler, and two seriously. Five were made prisoners.

In reporting these losses, Lieutenant-Commander Semmes observes:

"I regret seriously our loss, yet I feel a great degree of satisfaction in having impressed the rebels with the idea that blockade-running vessels are not safe even up the Hillsborough River."

I am respectfully, your obedient servant,

THEODORUS BAILEY,
A. R. Admiral, Commanding E. G. B. Squadron.

A NATIONAL ACCOUNT.

KEY WEST, FLA., Oct. 23, 1863.

On the twelfth instant, the United States gunboat Tahoma, Lieutenant-Commander Semmes, after three months' repairing and preparation, and taking on board a two-hundred-pound Parrott rifle, left here for Tampa Bay, arriving on the evening of the thirteenth, where she found the United States steamer Adela, Acting Volunteer Lieutenant Stodder, and schooners Stonewall Jackson and Ariel, blockading.

The next morning both steamers started up for Tampa, the county seat of Hillsboro County, standing at the head of Tampa Bay. The town is defended on the water-side by a battery of five guns, built on one end of the United States parade ground, and formerly called Fort Brooke, used during the war with the Indians. To the right of this are the United States docks and warehouses, now occupied by the rebels as barracks. Behind these are some blacksmith and machine shops, used by the rebel army, and also for fitting out blockade-runners.

Before going far the Tahoma's engine gave out, causing a delay until the next morning. On the fifteenth they continued on their way, the Tahoma taking the lead, and the Adela following. While crawling along shore, off Gadson's Point, looking for a battery reported to be there, the Tahoma got aground three times, and was hauled off after some trouble and breaking of hawsers by the Adela. In the afternoon the Tahoma's engine again broke down, and the Adela started with her in tow, when her engine also gave out. On the sixteenth, the Adela being again in order, the Tahoma was lashed alongside, and towed into position before Tampa, where she came to anchor as near the battery as she could get. The Adela being of much lighter draft, cast loose, ran up nearer the works and opened on them, throwing shell after shell into the battery, barracks, and buildings adjoining. Captain Semmes, after going out in a small boat and planting stakes with flags attached, as if preparing to land on left side of bay, returned to ship, and opened fire from his pivot, and twenty-pound Parrotts, the shell from both vessels making dirt and splinters fly, driving the men from the works, and the people from the town.

In the evening forty picked men from the Adela—fifteen from the Engineer's division, under Chief-Engineer Bennett; fifteen from the First division of riflemen, under Acting-Ensign Strandberg; ten from Second division, under Acting-Ensign Balch; and sixty men from the Tahoma—thirty from the First division, under Acting-Ensign Kaeler; thirty from Second division, under Acting-Ensign Randall; the whole under command of Acting-Master Harris, executive officer of the Tahoma, answered to their names on the deck of the Tahoma. She then got under way, manœuvred about the bay, making feints of landing at several places, then ran some miles down the bay, and, at ten P.M., landed them at Gadson's Point, on the right-hand shore; the boats all returning to the ship, with the exception of one which the party carried with them. At three and a half A.M. of the seventeenth, they had made less than one half the distance necessary to travel before sunrise, and were much fatigued by dragging a heavy boat for some miles through swamps and thick underbrush. The boat becoming too much stove for use, was thrown in the bushes, the party pushing on and arriving near the bank of Hillsboro River, six miles above Tampa, at six A.M. There they divided into squads, each approaching the river by a different route to prevent communication with the troops below. Acting-Ensign Balch and men were the first to reach the river, where, near the opposite bank, lay the steamer Scottish Chief, loaded with one hundred and fifty-six bales of cotton, and also the sloop Kate Dale, with eleven bales. He hailed some men moving about the steamer, and ordered his men to cover them with their rifles, gave them three minutes to lower their boat to come over after him, which they immediately did. Turning them out, and leaving them prisoners under a guard ashore, he took possession of the boat, taking six men with him, boarded the steamer, capturing all on board, and informing the Captain that he took possession in the name of the United States Government. When the rest of the party arrived, the vessel was ready for firing. The order having been given, he started a fire in her fore-hold. The sloop was served in the same way, and in a few minutes they both were a mass of flames. Ten minutes from the time of first seeing the vessels, the whole object of the expedition was accomplished, and the party started on their way back by a more direct route to the bay, making short halts for rest, and carrying some of their number who gave out on the road. One of the Tahoma's men became so exhausted that, by his own request, he was left behind, after being carried some miles through swamp and bushes. When within a mile of the shore, small squads of rebel troops were seen dodging about in the scrub ahead, at first in squads of five or six, then by eight, ten, fifteen, until when near the beach a sharp fire was opened on the advance scouts. The main body coming up scattered them in all directions, and, taking a number of prisoners, the line of march was continued to the beach, down the beach to nearly opposite where the Adela lay aground. Here they made signal for boats and came to a halt, first throwing out pickets to prevent a surprise. So exhausted were some of the men that they would sink down anywhere, and would rather die than go further. The Adela, on seeing them, fired a lee gun, and made signals to the Tahoma, which, with all the boats with her, lay aground on the opposite side of the bay, some miles from them. On seeing the Adela's signals, she sent the boats after them in charge of an Acting Master's Mate.

In the mean time some horsemen had been seen flying about through the woods, as if arranging matters, while others were seen dodging about, behind trees and bushes, and apparently planting themselves in a half circle about them. Not appearing in any force or showing any disposition to make an attack, one of the men was sent out to half his depth in the water. When the boats got to him they were turned about. Acting-Master Harris ordered all, except the Tahoma's First division, to embark. No sooner had they got in the water some distance than the concealed enemy began to close up from all sides, and opened a rapid fire on them. Acting-Ensign Strandberg's division had not yet left. These

faced about with the Tahoma's First division, charged on the enemy, and compelled them again to seek refuge in the bushes. Captain Harris ordered the remainder to take to the boats, which were now some quarter of a mile out. Before they had got half way out, a fire was opened on them from the bushes along the beach for the space of a mile, and from some light artillery masked among the bushes. A party of riflemen and cavalry, before unseen, came around from behind a building below them, charged up the beach with a yell, some of the horsemen riding along into the water, to cut them to pieces as they got into the boats. The Adela was the first to see this movement. Having but one gun that would reach, she opened on the advancing column, Captain Stodder himself sighting the gun, and making some splendid shots, bursting shell among the horsemen, compelling most of them to put back and go around through the woods. This with the fire from the boats, and from those in the water, kept the rebels in check until all the boats got off, bringing the prisoners with them. Orders were given to turn back and capture the guns, and fight it out, when it was discovered that in wading and swimming to the boats, nearly all the arms and ammunition had become wet and useless; the project was therefore abandoned, the boats returning to their ships. Shortly after the Adela got off and ran over to the place of conflict, and opened on the rebels, driving them up toward Tampa. On Sunday, the eighteenth, Captain Semmes sent in a flag of truce to ascertain what had become of our missing men. From what we can gather, the Tahoma lost one man, James World, killed. Acting-Ensign Randall, and six men wounded, and two men, Collins and Hilton, taken prisoners. The Adela lost two men, Roddy and O'Donnald, killed, five men wounded; one man, Donnelly, taken prisoner. The rebels lost six killed, a number wounded, and seven taken prisoners.

On the night of the sixteenth the citizens of Tampa held a crowded meeting in the court-house, for the purpose of forming a military company, and electing a captain. Had Captain Semmes known it while they were balloting, he would have sent them several two hundred-pound black-balls, which they would not have stopped to count.

Some time after the boats had returned, a head was seen projecting above water at some distance from land, while a party of rebels were on the beach firing at it, and calling out for the man to come on shore. A boat was sent in charge of Acting-Ensign Garman, to ascertain who the head belonged to, when it was found to belong to the pilot of the Tahoma, who had waded out up to his neck in water, determined rather to drown than be taken prisoner. He was nearly dead from exhaustion.

Among the trophies were some cartridges. In place of balls there are twelve large buckshot or pistol-balls wrapped up in cloth. Some of our men were wounded with these. Doctor Gale, of the Adela, took from one of the wounded a home-made lead ball weighing four ounces. The wounded were taken to a Government building near the light-house, on Egmont Key, and left in charge of Doctor Gunning, of the Tahoma. Captain Westcott, commander of the post, (rebel,) and formerly of the United States Army, and representative from Florida, said that as our men who died on shore fought so bravely, they intended to give them the best funeral they could get up. The Adela raised a purse of one hundred and eight dollars and sent it to one of these men—Donoly, who is a prisoner. The Tahoma also sent money to these men to pay their way while travelling in Dixie. Most of the rebels engaged in this fight were old Indian hunters, who bushwhacked with the Indians but a few years ago, and beat them at their own game.

From the flag of truce and the prisoners taken, we learned many incidents connected with the fight. As the steamer approached the town, one of the garrison at the fort asked the others: "What are those two large steamers coming up here for?" The others answered: "They are coming here after oysters; I think you will soon see them throwing their shells over this way."

One of the Tahoma's mammoth shells entered a house, and burst; one of the pieces, weighing about forty pounds, swept the dinner-table, at which sat Miss Crane, daughter of formerly Colonel Crane, of the army, now an Acting Master's Mate on the Tahoma.

Our party were surprised on receiving a charge from so large a body of cavalry, not knowing that there were any in the place. The way in which this happened was this: A party of fifty cavalry had been sent about the country to pick up cattle and send them to Bragg's army; these by chance arrived at Tampa on the day of the bombardment, and (as they say) eagerly took a hand in the sport.

The light field-pieces used in the woods were made in Tampa, by the rebels, by boring out an engine shaft.

The *ruse de guerre* of Captain Semmes succeeded perfectly. The rebs watched him putting down the stakes near the southern entrance, guessed its meaning, and in the evening posted a strong body of men in the woods, ready to annihilate any party attempting to land there. The smoke from the burning vessels gave them the first notice that we had landed on the opposite side and given them the slip.

Yours,   PHŒNIX.

Doc. 201.
ADDRESS OF JEFFERSON DAVIS.

MISSIONARY RIDGE, Oct. 17, 1863.

THE following address from the President to the troops was published yesterday:

HEADQUARTERS ARMY OF TENNESSEE,
October 14, 1863.

SOLDIERS: A grateful country recognizes your arduous services, and rejoices over your glorious victory on the field of Chickamauga. When your countrymen shall more fully learn the adverse circumstances under which you attacked the enemy, though they cannot be more thankful, they may admire more the gallantry and patriotic devotion which secured your success. Representatives of every State of the Confederacy, your steps have been followed up with affectionate solicitude by friends in every portion of the country. Defenders of the heart of our territory, your movements have been an object of interest, anxiety, and hope.

Our cause depends on you, and happy it is that all can rely upon your achieving whatever, under the blessing of Providence, human power can effect.

Though you have done much, very much remains to be done. Behind you is a people providing for your support, and depending upon your protection. Before you is a country devastated by your ruthless invaders, where gentle women, feeble age, and helpless infancy have been subjected to outrages without parallel in the warfare of civilized nations.

With eager eye they watch for your coming to their deliverance, and homeless refugees pine for the hour when your victorious arms shall restore their family shelters from which they have been driven and forced to take up arms to vindicate their political rights, freedom, equality, and State sovereignty, which were a heritage purchased by the blood of your Revolutionary sires.

You have but the alternative of being slaves of submission to a despotic usurpation or of independence, which a vigorous, united, and persistent effort will secure.

All which fires a manly breast, moves a patriot, or exalts a hero, is present to stimulate and sustain you. Nobly have you redeemed your pledges, given in the name of freedom, to the memory of your ancestors and the rights of your posterity.

That you may complete the mission to which you have devoted yourselves, will require of you such exertions in the future as you have made in the past, and the continuous self-denial which rejects every consideration at variance with the public service as unworthy of the holy cause in which you are engaged.

When the war shall be ended the highest meed of praise will be due, and probably be given, to him who has claimed the least for himself in proportion to the service he has rendered. And the bitterest self-reproach which may hereafter haunt the memory of any one will be to him who has allowed selfish aspiration to prevail over his desire for the public good.

United as we are in a common destiny, obedience and cordial coöperation are essential. There is no higher duty than that which requires one to exert and render to all what is due to their station. He who sows the seeds of discontent and distrust prepares for a harvest of slaughter and defeat.

To your gallantry, energy, and fortitude you crown this harmony with due subordination and cheerful support of lawful authority.

I fervently hope that this ferocious war, so unjustly waged against our country, may soon end, and that, with the blessing of peace, you may be restored to your homes and useful pursuits, and I pray our heavenly Father may cover you with the shield of his protection in your battle, and endow you with the virtues which will close your trials in victory complete.

JEFFERSON DAVIS.

Doc. 202.

PRESIDENT LINCOLN'S PROCLAMATION.

October 17, 1863.

By the President of the United States:

Whereas, The term of service of part of the volunteer forces of the United States will expire during the coming year; and, whereas, in addition to the men raised by the present draft, it is deemed expedient to call out three hundred thousand volunteers, to serve for three years or the war—not, however, exceeding three years:

Now, therefore, I, Abraham Lincoln, President of the United States and Commander-in-Chief of the Army and Navy thereof, and of the militia of the several States when called into actual service, do issue this, my proclamation, calling upon the Governors of the different States to raise and have enlisted into the United States service, for the various companies and regiments in the field from their respective States, their quotas of three hundred thousand men.

I further proclaim that all the volunteers thus called out and duly enlisted shall receive advance pay, premium, and bounty, as heretofore communicated to the Governors of States by the War Department, through the Provost-Marshal General's office, by special letters.

I further proclaim that all volunteers received under this call, as well as all others not heretofore credited, shall be duly credited and deducted from the quotas established for the next draft.

I further proclaim that, if any State shall fail to raise the quota assigned to it by the War Department under this call, then a draft for the deficiency in said quota shall be made in said State, or on the districts of said State, for their due proportion of said quota, and the said draft shall commence on the fifth day of January, 1864.

And I further proclaim that nothing in this proclamation shall interfere with existing orders, or with those which may be issued for the present draft in the States where it is now in progress or where it has not yet been commenced.

The quotas of the States and districts will be assigned by the War Department, through the Provost-Marshal General's office, due regard being had for the men heretofore furnished, whether by volunteering or drafting, and the recruiting will be conducted in accordance with such instructions as have been or may be issued by that department.

In issuing this proclamation, I address myself not only to the Governors of the several States, but also to the good and loyal people thereof, invoking them to lend their cheerful, willing, and effective aid to the measures thus adopted, with a view to reënforce our victorious armies now in the field, and bring our needful military operations to a prosperous end, thus closing for ever the fountains of sedition and civil war.

In witness whereof, I have hereunto set my hand and caused the seal of the United States to be affixed.

Done at the city of Washington, this seventeenth day of October, in the year of our Lord one thousand eight hundred and sixty-three, and of the independence of the United States the eighty-eighth.   ABRAHAM LINCOLN.

By the President.
WILLIAM H. SEWARD,
Secretary of State.

Doc. 203.

FIGHT AT PHILADELPHIA, TENN.

A NATIONAL ACCOUNT.

LOUDON, TENN., October 27, 1863.

THE beautiful valley known as the "Sweetwater Valley," extending from Loudon, on the Holston, to Calhoun, on the Hiawassee Rivers, has lately been the scene of bloodshed and suffering.

Colonel Wolford is an exceedingly cautious man, and so excessively cautious in guarding against surprise, that the more fiery and incautious have regarded him faulty in this wise. While at Philadelphia, his pickets were well posted, and were kept vigilant by a system of visiting them often, which he himself inaugurated, and which he compelled his officers to pursue. In addition to detailed scouts, whom he constantly kept out, he had his picket posts so strong as to allow scouts from them to be out four or five miles, day and night.

On the morning of the twentieth instant, (the day of the fight,) a staff-officer from General Burnside arrived at headquarters, with a flag of truce to the enemy, and obtained an escort of ten men from Wolford, requesting the Colonel to immediately withdraw his scouts and send out no more until his return, assigning as a reason that his scouting parties might so provoke the enemy as to endanger the flag. The request was acceded to, except picket scouts and a scout at Sweetwater, a distance of six miles from Philadelphia. It was not long after the departure of the flag of truce, before an orderly announced the fact that a rebel column had come up to Sweetwater, and had taken a north-westerly direction, which threatened the safety of our foraging train. The Eleventh Kentucky cavalry, being on review, the commanding officer, Major Graham, was ordered to hasten to the train for its defence. But a short time had elapsed before another communication from Sweetwater announced a still heavier force of the enemy moving in the same direction. These two rebel forces, evidently sufficient to overwhelm the Eleventh Kentucky, the First Kentucky,

Lieutenant-Colonel Adams, was ordered to reenforce Graham.

Meantime, two hundred of the Twelfth Kentucky were sent to reconnoitre in the vicinity of Sweetwater, and endeavor to ascertain, if possible, the magnitude of the movements of the enemy, and endeavor to develop his designs. It was but a short time until the real animus of the enemy was disclosed, for a heavy column, moving up the main road from Sweetwater, announced the intention to be an attack. A courier was hurriedly despatched to recall Adams and Graham, but, unfortunately, was captured before reaching his destination. Soon the rebels swarmed in from every direction in overwhelming force—in front, in the rear, and on both flanks; and making no demands, and giving no warning for the women and children to leave the place, they commenced the attack with fury. It was now that the brilliancy of Wolford's qualities were called into requisition, for the rebel hosts had sworn that they would have Wolford and his entire command. Environed on all sides by such a force, was placing him in a position of unenviable character. The First and Eleventh Kentucky cavalry both gone, no information of their whereabouts could be obtained, and their fate no one was able to divine, which left but the Twelfth Kentucky cavalry and Forty-fifth Ohio mounted infantry to confront and battle an enemy, the lowest estimate of whose force was seven thousand picked and experienced warriors, with a battery of heavy guns. It was really a critical situation. The fight was inaugurated in front. Wolford, getting his battery of little mountain howitzers into position, and arranging his handful of men to the best advantage, opened with animation on the advancing foe, and by a desperate struggle, in which the Twelfth Kentucky cavalry and Forty-fifth Ohio mounted infantry distinguished themselves, the rebel column was checked, reeled, and finally gave way. This cheering result was quickly followed by the enemy advancing in every direction. The battle progressed for four hours, during which time our trusty Enfields and carbines were dealing death in the rebel lines, while our little battery, under the command of the gallant Lieutenant Allison, was in close and effective range. The anaconda began to tighten, and our little band were being gradually confined to more narrow limits; and, there being no hopes of reënforcements from Loudon, all began to feel their critical attitude, and that something must speedily be done, or defeat and capture were inevitable. Our men, wearied with four hours' exertion, and plainly seeing themselves surrounded by the rebel lines, began to settle down in the conviction that capture was unavoidable, and numbers so expressing themselves, Wolford told them never to think of surrendering, and straightening up his shattered ranks, as best he could, ordered a charge, leading it himself, and amid the huzzas of our cavaliers the rebels gave way, and could not be rallied until Wolford and almost his entire command were out of their clutches, coming off the field with fifty-one prisoners,

losing twenty-two out of fifty-four wagons, and losing his battery, but not until every round of ammunition had been exhausted. Thus ended the battle of Philadelphia. Now, I will sketch the whereabouts of the First Kentucky and Eleventh Kentucky cavalry, and I may say with propriety that the achievements of these two regiments add a distinguishing lustre to the whole affair. The Eleventh Kentucky, in the advance, had proceeded but four miles before they came upon the enemy in possession of the train, having captured it and the guard. Under the leadership of the gallant Graham, the rebels were soon put to flight, and the train and escort recaptured. Then commenced a running fight of twelve miles, in which severe punishment was inflicted on the enemy, for the rebel dead and wounded lay scattered along the road at short intervals, during the entire chase. They threw away blankets, saddle-bags and contents, and guns, evidently in order to facilitate their flight. According to the best information, the result of the pursuit sums up a mortality list on the part of the rebels of thirty killed, one hundred wounded, and seven hundred prisoners. This I regard as close figuring, without exaggeration. But, unfortunately, we were pursued by eighteen hundred rebels, who recaptured the most of them, together with the men guarding them. It was in this way, and not at Philadelphia, that we lost the most of our captured men. Hearing cannonading at Philadelphia, we discontinued the pursuit, knowing that our forces there were engaged. Ascertaining that Wolford was completely surrounded, we aimed to strike the road leading from Loudon to Philadelphia, which we succeeded in doing, and on arriving at the road, found the rebels, and under Adams attacked them, driving them near Philadelphia. In one charge, we captured twenty-five, and killed a number. Learning that Wolford had cut his way out safely, we withdrew to Loudon, bringing in sixty prisoners. The full and complete result of the day's proceedings exhibits our list in killed to be twenty; wounded, eighty; and missing, three hundred and fifty-four.

The rebels acknowledge a loss of one hundred and fifty killed, and three hundred and fifty wounded, and a loss of prisoners of one hundred and eleven, which we have in our possession. This acknowledgment is fully corroborated by the citizens of Philadelphia. With this result before us, we may claim the advantage of the fight. What occurred at Philadelphia I obtained from the most reliable source—from officers in whose statements the utmost confidence can be safely reposed; and of what happened, as narrated on the pursuit, I was an eye-witness.

"LOUISVILLE JOURNAL" ACCOUNT.

To the Editors of the Louisville Journal:

As you and your numerous readers may be interested about affairs in East-Tennessee, and many of our personal friends solicitous to learn the casualties of our late engagement, I therefore send you the following reliable account: We had been ordered back from Athens, some eighteen miles west to Philadelphia, which lies six miles from Loudon Bridge, in order to be in supporting distance of that strong position—had been constantly on the lookout there with scouts and patrols up till Tuesday morning of the twentieth instant, when a flag of truce passed through our lines from General Burnside to the confederates. On account of the usages of war, we sent no menacing force forward to a reconnoissance, but sent out some forage wagons for corn. They had gone out but a few miles when they were rushed upon and captured by the enemy. Colonel Wolford immediately sent the First and Eleventh Kentucky cavalry, and part of the Twelfth, to recapture them, which was accomplished, but was not all held. Just at this time an attack was fiercely made upon the town on the east, north, and west sides, including all the approaches, and was defended by the Forty-fifth Ohio, mounted men, on the west, and the Twelfth Kentucky cavalry on the east, and a small part of the First and Eleventh on the north, while the small howitzer battery, commanded by Captain Laws, was stationed on the high hill which sets in the south of the town. Picket skirmishing commenced at twelve o'clock, and in thirty minutes the lines engaged, and continued firing with more or less volume for an hour, when it was ascertained that two brigades at least surrounded our position, and cut off the return of the First and Eleventh. As our danger had been telegraphed to General White at Loudon, and our guns in hearing of his quarters, Colonel Wolford naturally expected reënforcements from there; hence he encouraged his men to a stubborn stand, which was responded to cheerfully and maintained with indomitable courage.. The Forty-fifth Ohio fought gallantly, more than once charging the rebel lines with fatal effect. The battery fought a Georgia regiment single-handed, who were five times repulsed by canister shot with fearful loss. The Twelfth, on the east, led by Major Delfosse, had several times broke the rebel lines and scattered their front, which was filled up by reserves, until it became a hand-to-hand affray, in many instances, of capturing and recapturing prisoners. Thus continued the contest of unequal numbers till four long hours had passed, our ammunition wagons captured, the cartridge-boxes depleted, while horses and men were fatigued, and yet no reënforcements came. In this dilemma, Colonel Wolford ordered his undaunted band to charge the eastern line with sabre and every available instrument, and taking the lead himself, they soon cut themselves out of their fearful surroundings, bringing off some eighty-three prisoners and many horses, yet not without the loss of some valuable lives and serious casualties. Major Delfosse, of the Twelfth, was shot dead just as he gave orders to charge.

Captain Harrison took command, and led the Twelfth in the gallant charge on double lines of reserves of the enemy, and, being assisted by the Forty-fifth Ohio and commandants of the battery, went through. While this was being done the First and Eleventh were fighting manfully a force some miles north of the town, and so moved as to join Colonel Wolford soon after cutting the rebel lines, when the whole brigade fell back slowly toward Loudon Bridge, fighting back the approaching foe, who checked pursuit when in about two miles of the bridge. Night coming on, every thing became quiet. It was ascertained that our whole brigade of over two thousand men had lost about four hundred and twenty-five men, and that of these the Forty-fifth Ohio had lost one hundred and eighty-one, the Twelfth Kentucky cavalry ninety-two, and the First and Eleventh Kentucky cavalry the balance, in killed, wounded, and missing. As the enemy held the battle-ground, our information is defective, but from the best sources we know of but eight were killed dead on the field, and about eighty wounded. The Forty-fifth lost about forty-five and the Twelfth Kentucky thirty of this number, they being subject most of the time to a strong enfilading fire, and occupying the most dangerous position as a body. The rebel loss was heavy, as we learned they buried thirty-seven, besides hauling off several wagon loads after filling all their ambulances. They also sent back from Sweetwater several wagons next morning to remove the disabled from the field. Colonel Wolford estimates their casualties at over six hundred in killed, wounded, and missing. Many of our wagons were destroyed with our camp and garrison equipage; most of our men, however, saved their horses and arms. It is some gratification in our loss to know that our enemy added little or no strength to himself by it. Our boys were cheerful and more than willing to go at them again, which they did in fine style in two succeeding days, driving the rebels several times back and reöccupying our old ground for at least a temporary season.

Doc. 204.

DESTRUCTION OF THE VENUS.

LIEUTENANT COMMANDING LAMSON'S REPORT.

UNITED STATES STEAMER NANSEMOND, OFF NEW-INLET,
WILMINGTON, N. C., October 21, 1863.

SIR: I have the honor to report the capture and entire destruction of the blockade-runner Venus, from Nassau to Wilmington, with a cargo of lead, drugs, dry goods, bacon, and coffee.

This morning at half-past twelve she attempted to run the blockade, but was discovered by this vessel, and after a short chase overhauled. When abeam I opened fire on her—one shot striking her foremast; another exploding in her wardroom; a third passing through forward, and killing one man; and a fourth striking under the guard near the water-line, knocking in an iron plate, and causing her to make water fast, she was run ashore. We boarded her at once, capturing her captain and twenty-two of her officers and crew.

The United States steamer Niphon, Acting-

Master J. B. Breck commanding, which was lying near where she went ashore, came immediately to my assistance. · I ran a nine-inch hawser to the Venus, and Captain Breck sent a seven-inch hawser to the Nansemond's bow; but all our efforts were unavailing, as the tide had turned ebb, and she was going at least fourteen knots per hour when she went ashore. Finding it impossible to move her, I ordered her to be set on fire, which was done in three places by Acting-Ensigns Porter and Henderson of this vessel. Our boats were for some time exposed to a sharp fire of musketry from the beach, and the vessel was within range of one of the batteries.

We had just commenced shelling her machinery when another vessel was seen off shore, and by the light of the burning steamer I was able to give him one shot and started in pursuit, but it was so cloudy and hazy that we lost sight of her almost immediately. I ran east at the rate of fourteen knots till seven o'clock, but did not get sight of him again, and ran back, making the land to the northward.

In the mean time Captain Breck, with the assistance of the Iron Age, Lieutenant Commander Stone, had completed the destruction of the Venus, her boilers having been blown up and her hull riddled with shell.

I have to express my thanks to Captain Breck for the prompt assistance rendered me by sending his boats to assist in carrying my heavy hawser, and by sending a hawser to the Nansemond's bows. His boats then reported to Acting-Ensign J. H. Porter, who was in charge of the Venus. The fire forward not burning as well as was expected, he sent a boat on board in the morning and re-kindled it.

The Venus was two hundred and sixty-five feet long and one thousand tons measurement, and is represented by her captain and officers to have been one of the finest and fastest vessels engaged in running the blockade. She had the finest engines of any vessel in this trade, and was sheathed completely over with iron. She drew eight feet of water, and when bound out last crossed the bar at low-water, with over six hundred bales of cotton on board. The wrecks of the Hebe, Douro, and Venus are within a short distance of each other.

Inclosed is a list of the officers and crew of the Venus, captured before they could escape.

I am, sir, very respectfully, your obedient servant,   R. H. LAMSON,
                Lieutenant Commanding.
Rear-Admiral S. P. LEE,
                Commanding N. A. B. Squadron.

Doc. 205.
THE BATTLE AT CHEROKEE STATION, ALABAMA.
MEMPHIS "BULLETIN" ACCOUNT.

MEMPHIS, October 26, 1863.

THE advance of the Union forces eastward from this point met with a sharp resistance on Wednesday, the twenty-first instant, at Cherokee Station, on the Memphis and Charleston railroad, about eight or nine miles this side of Tuscumbia. The troops of the gallant Fifteenth corps met the rebels with their usual bravery, however, and soon made themselves masters of the situation.

On the day previous a brisk cavalry fight took place near the same spot, between a considerable body of rebel mounted infantry and the Fifth Ohio cavalry, in which six rebels were killed, and fifteen wounded left on the field. Our gallant troops went into the rebels with a shout, cutting and slashing right and left, and cleaned them out in short order, losing only two men killed and five horses. The Third regular cavalry also went forward to participate, but the Ohio boys had completed the job. This was on Tuesday evening. The cavalry then fell back near the advance of General Osterhaus's division.

The next morning, Wednesday, broke dark and lowering, with rain and fog. The movement of the First division, General Osterhaus's, which was to have been at six o'clock, was delayed till eight. The Second division, General Morgan L. Smith, lay close up to the First division, waiting until they should move ahead before striking camp. Major-General Blair commanded both divisions. When General Osterhaus moved forward toward Tuscumbia, he had not proceeded far before his advance, consisting of the Fourth, Ninth, Twenty-fifth, Twenty-sixth, Thirtieth, (the Thirtieth in the advance,) and Thirty-first Iowa regiments, encountered a large force of rebels, estimated at between four and six thousand, under command of the rebel Generals S. D. Lee, Roddy, and Richardson. A heavy musketry fire was immediately opened, and the fight was furious for an hour; when the rebels fell back with heavy loss in killed and wounded. General Osterhaus hurried up several twenty-four-pounder Parrotts, which made havoc in their retreating columns, and our whole division was soon on the ground. The General managed his troops with great skill.

The loss on our side will not exceed one hundred in killed and wounded. The death of Colonel Torrence, of the Thirtieth Iowa, was the most serious disaster. This brave officer was killed while in advance of his men, in the midst of the fight. Mistaking a party of rebels, who were dressed in Federal uniforms, for our troops, he rode forward to ascertain who they were, and at half-range distance was shot down by them. The regiment seeing him fall, raised a yell and rushed forward, at a charge, regaining his body and scattering the rebels in all directions.

The loss in this regiment was twenty-nine killed and wounded. Captain H. Randall, of company D, was killed; Captain Hall, of company A, was severely wounded in the leg, which he will lose; Captain Clark, of company H, was seriously and probably mortally wounded in the back; Captain Smith, of company E, was also seriously wounded; Adjutant Clendenning was wounded in the head and thigh, and had six or seven bullets through his clothes. In company E three privates were killed. Several other regiments, including the Fourth and Twenty-Fifth Iowa, lost more or less, but we were unable to learn particulars.

The bodies of Colonel Torrence and Captain Randall arrived here last evening, where they were embalmed, and will be sent North to-day in charge of C. D. Gage, Sutler of the Thirtieth regiment. Colonel Torrence lived at Keokuk, Iowa. He served with distinction through the Mexican war, and was one of those men whose influence and character were almost without blemish. Tall and commanding in person, active, energetic, strict in discipline, kind of heart, he was held in great regard among the troops. Iowa has lost in him one of her most worthy and gallant sons.

Since the above was written, we have gathered a few additional items of interest, which are subjoined:

It appears that the rain and fog had delayed an early advance movement on Wednesday morning, and the first known of the proximity of the rebels was the driving in of our pickets and forage-teams, and their appearing in sight. The regiments above named were immediately ordered into line, and skirmishers thrown out to feel their position. The enemy did the same, except that a large portion of their force had dismounted and were lying in ambush. The advance of the enemy wore the United States uniform, and in the fog it became difficult for Colonel Torrence to distinguish friends from foes. He therefore ordered his men to cease firing, and approached the enemy dressed in blue, and when within a short distance they opened a galling fire upon him, piercing his body in many places, and killing him instantly. At the same time they opened a murderous fire upon our left flank, killing and wounding the Captain and Adjutant above named. For a few moments the Thirtieth regiment was thrown into confusion, but when Colonel Torrence's Orderly came back and announced that their Colonel was in the hands of the enemy, the men rushed forward with a yell, recovered his body and dispersed the rebels. They found, however, that his body had been searched, and all his money and watch stolen. Our troops pursued the fleeing rebels back to their fortifications.

The rebels are said to have very strong fortifications about one mile this side of Tuscumbia, on the railroad, and prisoners report that they expect to make a strong defence there. They say they had four thousand men there on Tuesday, and received reënforcements of one thousand cavalry on Wednesday morning, and that some twenty thousand more are expected there from Bragg's army. The following officers are said to be in command there: Generals Loring, S. D. Lee, Roddy, Richardson, and Forrest.

Colonel Torrence, who was in command of the Thirtieth Iowa, is said to have been an officer of rare excellence. He served with distinction in the Mexican war, and entered the service again as soon as the war commenced—first as Major of the First Iowa cavalry, and then Lieutenant-Col-

onel of the Thirtieth Iowa infantry. On the death of the gallant Colonel Abbott, in the charge on Vicksburgh, he assumed command of the regiment, and was an officer of substantial merit and a man of rare virtue.

Some of the prisoners taken at the Cherokee Station give as an explanation of their blue uniforms, that the rebel Government intends to clothe all their troops with blue overcoats. This statement may have been trumped up for the moment, but the fact that hundreds of their men appeared in the front rank of battle dressed in the uniform, would seem to give it some color of probability.

It is said that rebel despatches from Johnston have recently been captured, in which rebel officers have been conjured not to permit our forces to open up the road between Memphis and Decatur.

Tennessee River is reported to have risen in the vicinity of Eastport some nine feet, and is still rising fast. There have been heavy rains in that section, and, if necessary, we presume that gunboats can now ascend that stream to any point where their services may be effective.

An impression exists, induced by existing circumstances, to the effect that probably before this our forces have encountered the enemy and drove them from their fortifications. If such a conflict has not taken place, it is because the rains have prevented, or the enemy has run away.

Doc. 206.

IMPRESSMENT OF SLAVES.

REBEL GENERAL ORDER.

ADJUTANT AND INSPECTOR-GENERAL'S OFFICE, RICHMOND, Oct. 24, 1863.

GENERAL ORDER, No. 138:

The following instructions are published for carrying into effect the ninth section of the act of twenty-sixth of March, 1863: To regulate impressments in respect to labor on fortifications and other public works in States in which provisions have not been made on this subject:

1. The Commanding General, or the officer of Engineers in charge of the work, shall have power to decide upon the necessity for making impressments of slaves for this purpose, after making suitable efforts to secure the necessary labor by contract. He must be satisfied of the necessity of the measure before he resorts to it.

2. He may authorize the impressment of male slaves between the ages of seventeen and fifty years, but before the first day of December next shall abstain from impressing slaves from plantations exclusively devoted to the production of grain and provisions without the consent of the owner, except in cases of urgent necessity.

3. No impressments shall be made of the slaves employed in the domestic and family service exclusively, nor upon farms or plantations where there are not more than three slaves of the age specified, and not more than five per cent of

'the population of slaves shall be impressed in any county at the same time, unless the necessity is very great, and after consultation with this Department or the Governor of the State in which the impressment is to be made.

4. The ordinary period for impressment shall be sixty days, but if the owner of any slave shall fail to bring the slaves impressed to the place of rendezvous within five days after the time appointed, the slaves so withheld may be detained for ninety days, and for a longer term of ten days for every day of default, unless a reasonable excuse can be given for the delays that have occurred.

5. It shall be the duty of the Commanding General in charge of any lines requiring fortifications, to acquaint himself with the resources of slave labor within his department, and to consider with care the manner in which he may obtain the control of whatever is necessary for the public service by fair and equitable apportionment among the owners of such property. He will consult with the Governor of the State and other State authorities as to the best mode of proceeding, so that his impressment may cause the least embarrassment to the industrial pursuits of the community.

6. Notice shall be given of the number and character of the slaves required, the time and place of their delivery, the time for which the service is required, and of the arrangements made for the subsistence, management, and custody of the slaves so required; and if the masters of slaves shall agree to furnish subsistence for their slaves, and a suitable overseer or agent to superintend them, they shall have the privilege of so doing. But such overseers shall be subject to the control of the officer in charge, and may be dismissed for any misconduct by him.

7. The sum of twenty dollars per month for each slave delivered in pursuance to requisition, and fifteen dollars per month for each slave held in consequence of failure of his master to obey requisition made as hereinbefore provided, shall be paid by the Confederate States, and soldiers' rations, medicines, and medicinal attendance furnished, and the value of all such slaves, as may die during their time of service or thereafter from injuries received, or diseases contracted in such service, or may not be returned, shall be paid by the Confederate States. Such value shall be conclusively established by a formal appraisement by a Board of Experts, mutually agreed upon at the time the slaves are received into the confederate service. Compensation shall also be made for all injuries to slaves arising from the act of the public enemy, or from any injury arising from a want of due diligence on the part of the authorities of the Confederate States. But the Confederate States will not be liable for any slave not returned by reason of fraud or collusion on the part of his owner or his agent, or the overseer selected by him to superintend them, nor if his death should be caused by the act of God, or by disease existing when the slave is received by confederate authorities.

8. Subsistence and provisions furnished by the owner shall be commuted for at the rates allowed soldiers in service. All slaves sent voluntarily to the confederate authorities, and accepted by them without other special contract, shall stand on the same footing as those delivered under requisition, and the owners of all slaves delivered or taken under requisition shall be entitled to regard the Confederate States as contracting with them to comply with the obligations and conditions herein expressed.

9. In case there should be any disagreement on the subject of the value of any slave impressed, or in case the impressing officer shall not be satisfied of the accuracy of any valuation or valuations, the appraisement shall be referred to the appraisers appointed under the fifth section of the act concerning impressments according to the provisions of the act of Congress, approved twenty-seventh April, 1863, and published in Orders No. 53, current series.

By order, S. COOPER,
Adjutant and Inspector-General.

Doc. 207.

BATTLE OF PINE BLUFF, ARK.

OFFICIAL REPORT OF COLONEL CLAYTON.

HEADQUARTERS ARMY OF ARKANSAS, }
LITTLE ROCK, ARK., Nov. 3, 1863. }

MAJOR: I have the honor to inclose Colonel Clayton's report of his gallant defence of Pine Bluff, also Lieutenant-Colonel Caldwell's report of his pursuit of Marmaduke. Caldwell captured more property than fell into the possession of Marmaduke during his raid.

Very respectfully, Major,
Your obedient servant,
FREDERICK STEELE,
Major-General Commanding.

Major O. D. GREEN,
A. A. G., Department of the Missouri.

HEADQUARTERS POST OF PINE BLUFF, }
PINE BLUFF, Oct. 27, 1863. }

GENERAL: I respectfully submit to you the following report of the battle fought at this place October twenty-fifth, between General Marmaduke's forces and the garrison at this post.

About eight o'clock in the morning, I sent Lieutenant Clark, Fifth Kansas cavalry, with one company, out in the direction of Princetown. He did not go far before he met the enemy advancing in force. The enemy's skirmishers fired on him at once, but soon after an armed party, bearing a flag of truce, came forward, and the officer in command of this party insisted that he should be allowed to pass in immediately. Lieutenant Clark told him it was no way to first fire on him, and then insist on going in with a flag of truce. But he would give him half an hour for him (Clark) to send in to headquarters and get an answer. He rejected the proposition, and said he had despatches from General Marmaduke to the commanding officer, he supposed demanding a surrender of the place. The Lieutenant replied: "Colonel Clayton never surrenders, but is always anxious for you to come and take him, and you must get back to your command immediately, or I will order my men to fire on you." He fell back, and they commenced skirmishing again. Meantime the whole command was ordered out, and skirmishers sent in every direction; also three hundred negroes set to work rolling cotton-bales out of the warehouses. In less than half an hour I had all the streets leading into Court Square completely and very formidably fortified with cotton-bales, and my artillery — six mountain howitzers, and three small steel rifled guns — planted so as to command every street leading into the square; my sharp-shooters posted in all of the houses and other buildings on the square, so that the enemy could in no way approach the works only through the open spaces. I then had about two hundred negroes commence carrying water from the river up to the square, and fill all the barrels they could find, so that, if necessary, I could hold out two days, even though cut off from the river. The enemy succeeded in driving in my skirmishers about nine o'clock, and approached the works in three columns, as follows—on my right, centre, and left, the main one being in the centre—and opened on me with their artillery, twelve pieces, a part of which were twelve-pound rifle guns, throwing both the Hotchkiss and the James projectiles. The firing from both sides, from the artillery and the sharp-shooters, continued with great rapidity until two o'clock. Between twelve o'clock M. and one o'clock P.M., the enemy set fire to the buildings on my right, expecting thereby to rout me; but I put some two hundred negroes to carrying water and throwing it on the buildings immediately joining the square, and thus prevented the fire from doing me any damage. The enemy seeing that he failed in his efforts to drive me by fire as well as by force, planted another battery on my centre and kept up a heavy cannonading for a short time, then retreated, (about two o'clock P.M.,) leaving a great portion of his wounded and dead on the field. I followed him for about one mile, then returned and stationed my pickets as usual.

My loss was eleven killed, twenty-seven wounded, and one missing. There were also five negroes killed, and twelve wounded. The enemy's loss in killed and wounded, so far as ascertained, is about one hundred and thirty, and will probably reach one hundred and fifty. I have also three Lieutenants and thirty men prisoners, fifteen of whom are wounded. The buildings that were burned by the enemy were occupied by the Fifth Kansas cavalry as quarters, consequently their camp and garrison equipage, and their books and papers, were all burned. The train was also corralled in sheds in rear of the buildings that were burned. When the fire was raging the mules were cut loose to keep them from burning, and sixty-two of them are missing. The enemy also burned one warehouse, containing over two hundred bales of cotton. In setting fire to these buildings, General Marmaduke committed the gross and barbarous deed of burning some of his own wounded. Several of his own men who were wounded were burned to death, and almost entirely consumed by the flames that he kindled. The court-house, General James's, General Yell's, and John Bloom's houses, were all nearly destroyed by the enemy's artillery. There is scarcely a house in town that does not show the effects of the battle. The enemy plundered every house he could get to, and stole every horse and mule from the citizens that he could lay his hands on. The prisoners that I captured reported General Marmaduke's force from two to three thousand men, and twelve pieces of artillery. I think he had some two thousand five hundred men, and twelve pieces of artillery.

My force consisted of the Fifth Kansas cavalry, commanded by Major Thomas W. Scudder, and the First Indiana cavalry, commanded by Lieutenant-Colonel Thomas N. Pace, and one company of State militia, commanded by Captain Murphy, amounting in all to some five hundred and fifty men. Captain Murphy's company behaved like veterans. The officers and men both of the Fifth Kansas cavalry and of the First Indiana cavalry behaved most admirably. The fact that so small a force kept four times their number at bay for five hours, and finally drove them from the field, bespeaks for the whole command greater efficiency and gallantry than words can do; every officer and soldier in the whole command seemed determined to fight as long as there was a round of ammunition left. The negroes also did me excellent service, and deserve much praise therefor.

I am, General, very respectfully,

Your obedient servant,

POWELL CLAYTON,
Colonel Commanding.

Major-General STEELE,
Commanding Army of Arkansas.

CONGRATULATORY ORDER OF GENERAL STEELE.

HEADQUARTERS ARMY OF ARKANSAS,
LITTLE ROCK, ARK., Nov. 7, 1863.

GENERAL ORDERS, No. 41:

It is fit that the conduct of troops on the battle-field, especially gallant and heroic, should be publicly approbated by the commanding officer, and officially published for the emulation of the whole command.

Therefore, the Major-General commanding the army of Arkansas publishes to his command these facts:

On the twenty-fifth day of October last, the cavalry brigade, consisting of the Fifth Kansas and First Indiana cavalry, commanded by Colonel Powell Clayton, and numbering less than six hundred men, was attacked at Pine Bluff, Arkansas, by an army of rebels, twenty-five hundred in number, with twelve pieces of artillery.

Unawed by this overwhelming force, they fought them for five hours, and drove them, discomfited and with heavy loss, from the field. Retreat and surrender were words unknown to these brave men, and their determined heroism has inflicted a blow upon the rebel army not soon to be forgotten.

The Major-General Commanding hereby tenders to Colonel Powell Clayton and his brave command his sincere and earnest thanks, for their gallant conduct in the defence of Pine Bluff; and they can rest well-assured that their gallantry deserves, and will receive, the applause of their Government and the loyal people — the highest ambition of the true soldier.

By order of   F. STEELE,
Major-General.

F. H. MANTER,
Colonel and Chief of Staff.

CHICAGO "TRIBUNE" ACCOUNT.

PINE BLUFF, ARKANSAS, October 26, 1863.

The attack that the authorities here have been expecting for some time has at last come, and the roar of cannon and the rattle of musketry have subsided, and the smoke from a hard-fought battle-field, or rather battle-town, has disappeared enough to enable us to see where we are and what we have accomplished.

This place is situated on the south bank of the Arkansas River, about fifty miles from Little Rock, ninety from the Mississippi River, and sixty from Arkadelphia, (General Price's late headquarters.) It contained, before the war, some three thousand inhabitants, and was one of the finest and most business towns in Arkansas. For six or seven weeks it has been occupied by the Federals, during which time it has been garrisoned by the Fifth Kansas cavalry, and the First Indiana cavalry, under the command of Colonel Powell Clayton, of the Fifth Kansas cavalry. There is also here one company of State militia, which has been recruited since the Federals came here.

About two weeks ago, Colonel Clayton took three hundred and fifty men and four pieces of light artillery, and by making a circuitous route, and marching ninety miles in thirty-three hours, succeeded in surprising and completely routing Colonel Dobbin's cavalry brigade at Tulip, capturing one stand of colors, all his camp and garrison equipage, quartermaster and commissary stores, medical supplies, transportation, etc.

The rebel authorities feeling ashamed and aggrieved at this, began to concentrate General Marmaduke's cavalry force at Princeton, forty-five miles from Pine Bluff, Friday, (October twenty-third,) about noon, with about four thousand men and twelve pieces of artillery, mostly twelve-pound rifled guns, and started to take revenge on Colonel Clayton, who only had between five hundred and six hundred men, and nine pieces of light artillery. Sunday morning, about eight o'clock, Lieutenant Clark, of the Fifth Kansas cavalry, with one company, was sent out on the Princeton road, to see what he could discover, but did not go far before he met the enemy's advance, which fired on him at once. They did not skirmish but a few minutes before an armed party bearing a flag of truce came forward, and the officer commanding it said : "I must go to the commanding officer immediately." Lieuten-

ant Clark replied : "You cannot see Colonel Clayton. You have no right to be here with a flag of truce ; you have already been firing on me, but I will give you half an hour to wait here for me to send in and get an answer." He replied : "I will not wait. I have despatches from General Marmaduke, as I suppose, demanding a surrender of the post. I must go in immediately." Lieutenant Clark said : "You cannot go in. Colonel Clayton never surrenders, but is always anxious for General Marmaduke to come and take him ; and now, God damn you, get back to your place immediately, or I will order my men to fire on you." He fell back, and they commenced skirmishing again.

Meanwhile Colonel Clayton assembled his whole command and sent out skirmishers in every direction, and come the General Jackson on them by setting three hundred negroes to rolling cotton-bales out of the warehouses to barricade Court Square. In less than thirty minutes every street and opening leading into Court Square was completely and very formidably fortified, and the artillery planted so as to command every street and opening leading into the square, and sharp-shooters placed in every building adjacent thereto, so that the rebels could approach the square in no way except through the streets and openings that were commanded by our artillery. Thus did Colonel Clayton, with a few negroes and plenty of cotton-bales, almost "in the twinkling of an eye," convert a place apparently defenceless into a strong fort. Surely Cotton with his ebony sceptre is king. About nine o'clock the enemy had succeeded in driving in the skirmishers, and approached us in three columns, namely, on our right, centre, and left, the main one being in the centre, and commenced pouring in their shell and canister like hail. The first fire was greeted with loud cheers from our boys, shell and canister from the guns, and a Sharpe's rifle-ball from every man that could get his eye on a "Butternut." From this on there was a perfect tornado of shells, canister, and bullets flying from both sides for five hours. During all this time Colonel Clayton rode round the works and gave directions with as much coolness and composure as though he was directing the movements of some celebration instead of a battle. Every man also seemed determined to fight as long as he could get a round of ammunition. Between twelve o'clock M. and one o'clock P.M., the enemy set fire to the buildings on the right, expecting to be able to rout us by fire, though not able to do so by force. Two hundred negroes were set to carrying water and throwing it on the buildings on the right, adjacent to the square, and by thus doing prevented the fire from doing us any damage.

As soon as the enemy found that he could not rout us by fire, he changed a battery from the right to the centre, kept up a sharp cannonading for a short time, then retreated, leaving his wounded and dead on the field. We followed him for about two miles, then returned and put out pickets the same as usual. The battle was fought and won. Two regiments, the Fifth Kansas cavalry, the First Indiana cavalry, and one militia company—less than six hundred men in all—fought and kept at bay for five hours four thousand men, and finally made them beat an inglorious retreat.

> " Bravely they fought and well,
>   The gallant six hundred."

No words or comments to show the efficiency and gallantry of these two regiments are necessary. The battle they fought and won speaks for itself.

Our loss was seventeen killed and thirty-nine wounded, and one missing, of whom five of the killed and twelve of the wounded were negroes. The enemy's loss, as far as ascertained, fifty-three killed and one hundred and sixty-four wounded. We captured three officers and thirty men. General Marmaduke, in trying to burn us out, burnt several of his own wounded men. Oh! what an act of barbarity to men who, by taking the front of the battle, were wounded, and unable to get away. Their screams and groans, amid the crackling of the flames, and the thundering of the cannon, struck terror to our hearts, but it was impossible to rescue them. They were burned to death and almost entirely consumed by the fire that was kindled by his own ruthless and barbarous hand.

They plundered every house that they could get to, and stole from the citizens all of the mules and horses they could find.

The court-house was nearly demolished by the enemy's artillery; also so were several dwelling-houses. In fact, there is scarcely a house in town that does not show the effects of the battle. The women and children, by order of Colonel Clayton, went down under the river-bank, and not one of them was hurt. The negroes, the most of whom where employed during the battle in rolling cotton-bales and carrying water, though exposed most of the time to a heavy fire, did most admirable service, and behaved with a gallantry that will ever entitle them to be classed among the brave.

The enemy is in full retreat, and every thing is quiet again.   RALPH KAW.

LIST OF CASUALTIES.

Killed—Abraham Campbell, company B, Fifth Kansas cavalry; George W. Lucas, company C, Fifth Kansas cavalry; Brice W. Miller, company C, Fifth Kansas cavalry; V. Hinton, company D, Fifth Kansas cavalry; Geo. S. Cartwright, company D, Fifth Kansas cavalry; Chas. S. Perrin, company D, Fifth Kansas cavalry; Chas. E. Wate, company F, Fifth Kansas cavalry; Patrick McMahon, company K, Fifth Kansas cavalry; Sergeant Joseph Travoli, company B, First Indiana cavalry; Corporal John L. Whellen, company G, First Indiana cavalry; Charles H. Steel, company G, First Indiana cavalry.

Wounded—Thomas Archer, company A, Fifth Kansas cavalry; Abraham Manon, company A, Fifth Kansas cavalry; D. W. Boutwell, company A, Fifth Kansas cavalry; Corporal William Steele, company A, Fifth Kansas cavalry; George Cox, company B, Fifth Kansas cavalry; Sergeant James Clarke, company C, Fifth Kansas cavalry; Sergeant Arthur T. Perry, company C, Fifth Kansas cavalry; George W. Smith, company C, Fifth Kansas cavalry; Lewis N. Gibson, company C, Fifth Kansas cavalry; Thomas S. Fuller, company C, Fifth Kansas cavalry; Sergeant William Duncan, company D, Fifth Kansas cavalry; F. M. White, company D, Fifth Kansas cavalry; Andrew Rogers, company E, Fifth Kansas cavalry; Matthew Schaus, company F, Fifth Kansas cavalry; James Grooms, company F, Fifth Kansas cavalry; David N. Snook, company H, Fifth Kansas cavalry; Dennis Forrester, company K, Fifth Kansas cavalay; Corporal Wm. Bilderback, company A, First Indiana cavalry; Wm. Dean, company E, First Indiana cavalry; James L. Crawford, company F, First Indiana cavalry; George W. Clark, company F, First Indiana cavalry; L. D. Padget, saddler, company F, First Indiana cavalry; Michael Huzzy, company G, First Indiana cavalry; Corporal Stephen Hill, company H, First Indiana cavalry; John White, company H, First Indiana cavalry; Geo. H. Herring, blacksmith, company G, First Indiana cavalry; Robert S. Parker, State militia.

Missing—Corporal John Longer, company I, Fifth Kansas.

RECAPITULATION.

Killed—Fifth Kansas cavalry, eight; First Indiana, three. Total, eleven. Wounded—Fifth Kansas cavalry, seventeen; First Indiana, nine; State militia, one. Total, twenty-seven. Missing—Fifth Kansas cavalry, one. Total of casualties, thirty-nine.

Doc. 208.

ORDER OF GENERAL W. T. SHERMAN.

HEADQUARTERS AT IUKA, MISS., October 25.

ORDER No. 2:

First. Major-General Frank Blair takes command of the Fifteenth and a portion of the Sixteenth army corps now in the field.

Third. All officers in command of corps and fixed military posts will assume the highest military powers allowed by the laws of war and Congress. They must maintain the best possible discipline, and repress all disorder, alarms, and dangers in their reach. Citizens who fail to support the Government have no right to ask favors and protection, but if they actively assist us in vindicating the national authority, all commanders will assist them and their families in every possible way. Officers need not meddle with matters of trade and commerce, which by law devolve on the officer of the Treasury Department; but whenever they discover goods contraband of war being conveyed toward the public enemy, they will seize all goods tainted by such transactions, and imprison the parties implicated, but care must be taken to make full records and report such case. When a district is infested by guerrillas, or held by the enemy, horses and mules, wagons, forage, etc., are all means of war, and can be freely taken, but must be accounted for as pubic property. If the people do not want their horses and corn taken, they must organize and repress all guerrillas or hostile bands in their neighborhood.

Third. It is represented that officers, provost-marshals, and others in the military service, are engaged in business or speculation on their own account, and that they charge fees for permits and passes. All this is a breach of honor and law. Every salaried officer of the military service should devote every hour of his time, every thought of his mind, to his government, and if he makes one cent profit beyond his pay, it is corrupt and criminal. All officers and soldiers in this department are hereby commanded to engage in no business whatever, save their sworn duty to their government.

Fifth. Every man should be with his proper corps, division, brigade, and regiment, unless absent, sick, or wounded, or detached by written order of a competent commander. Soldiers when so absent must have their descriptive rolls, and when not provided with them the supposition is that they are improperly absent. Mustering officers will see that all absentees not away by a written order from their proper commander are reported on the muster-rolls as deserters, that they may lose their pay, bounty, and pensions, which a generous government and people have provided for soldiers who do their whole duty. The best hospitals in the world are provided for the wounded and sick, but these must not be made receptacles for absentees who seek to escape the necessary exposures and dangers of a soldier's life. Whenever possible, citizens must be employed as nurses, cooks, attendants, stewards, etc., in hospitals, in order that enlisted men may be where they belong—with their regiments. The medical inspectors will attend to this at once. The General Commanding announces that he expects the wounded and sick to have every care possible, but this feeling must not be abused to the injury of the only useful part of an army—a soldier in the field.

Sixth. In time of war and rebellion, districts occupied by our troops are subject to the laws of war. The inhabitants, be they friendly or unfriendly, must submit to the controlling power. If any person in an insurgent district corresponds or trades with an enemy, he or she becomes a spy, and all inhabitants, moreover, must not only abstain from hostile and unfriendly acts, but must aid and assist the power that protects them in trade and commerce.

The people who occupy this department had better make a note of this, and conduct themselves accordingly.

By order of   Maj.-Gen. W. T. SHERMAN.
R. M. SAWYER, A. A. G.

Doc. 209.

FIGHT NEAR TUSCUMBIA, ALA.

ST. LOUIS "UNION" ACCOUNT.

CANE CREEK, ALA., October 28, 1863.

My last was dated "Cane Creek, October twenty-eighth." Well, we are back in camp at Cane Creek. We have been to Tuscumbia, saw what was to be seen, suffered to the extent of about ten wounded and two killed, and left Tuscumbia this morning for this, our old camp of five days. But let me tell you. At daylight on the twenty-sixth, Osterhaus moved forward his first brigade in front. He had not proceeded over three miles before he came upon a strong picket of the enemy, which were soon driven away. About a mile further on (the summit of Graveyard Ridge, close by Barton Station) the enemy opened upon us with two pieces of artillery strongly posted upon a hill near a frame church. The Thirteenth Illinois, Seventy-sixth Ohio, and Fourth Iowa, were soon in line of battle on the left of the railroad; while the Twenty-seventh, Twenty-ninth, Thirty-first, Thirty-second, Third, and Twelfth Missouri were posted on the right. The Twelfth and Seventy-sixth, in their respective fronts, were deployed as skirmishers. On the extreme right were the Fifth Ohio cavalry. A section of Hoffman's battery (Fourth Ohio) was stationed immediately on the left of the railroad; while still farther to the left was Griffith's battery. On the right was the balance of Hoffman's Landgraeber's (Flying Dutchman) batteries. After exchanging a few cannon-shots, while our skirmishers were advancing, these batteries moved forward with the general advance, and the rebels at once skedaddled. General Blair then ordered Morgan L. Smith to keep his division closed up to Osterhaus, and the latter pushed forward rapidly. This advance was commenced at half-past eight A.M.

The forward movement was made cautiously and quietly until about nine o'clock, when our skirmishers again commenced firing. This time the action was severe in front of the Twelfth Missouri, (Colonel Wangelin,) which regiment, as skirmishers, advanced in splendid style, and never once halted in their onward march. Lieutenant Wangelin, nephew to the Colonel, and aid to General Osterhaus, was wounded while bearing an order from the General to the Colonel. I never saw such magnificent skirmishing as the Twelfth Missouri did in that advance. It was but a short time before firing ceased and we again advanced.

At five minutes past twelve our column was again halted, and Osterhaus deployed his battalions—Morgan L. Smith well closed up. The enemy in his new position had five pieces of artillery advantageously-posted, but they withdrew as our skirmishers on the right and left seemed about to close them in. Here, as at the first stand, the enemy left as soon as our bullets whizzed around their heads. Our line of skirmishers was composed of the Third, Twelfth, Seventeenth, and Twenty-seventh Missouri, Seventy-sixth Ohio, and Thirteenth Illinois. The troops of the Second brigade, Colonel Williamson, were close to our skirmishers, and where our skirmishers escaped the bullets of the enemy the Second brigade felt the inconvenience of their shells. At this second position the fight was of short duration. Artillery and cavalry of the enemy soon hastened away, and General Osterhaus, with the Fifth Illinois cavalry, moved forward in rapid pursuit. General Lightburn's brigade having been moved on the left flank of the enemy, was then recalled, and the whole force moved forward as rapidly as infantry can travel. Onward we moved until a quarter-past three P.M., when we were again thrown into position by the discovery of the fact that the enemy were drawn up in line in a formidable position some three miles outside of Tuscumbia. They appeared bold and defiant. Hoffman's two Parrotts failed to dislodge them after an hour's practice. Undoubtedly we did them some damage, and they injured some six or eight of our men. The Twenty-seventh Missouri lost one man killed and two wounded by a single shell. The Major of the Thirty-first Iowa barely escaped, a ball lodging in the ground immediately under his horse. Further than this, no damage was inflicted by the rebels upon our boys, and it being late in the day, all but our pickets were withdrawn, and our little army went quietly into bivouac.

From where I was quartered on the top of a hill, between which and the rebels, a mile off, flowed a narrow stream called Little Bear Creek, I could distinctly see the rebels manœuvring upon an extended plain, the front of which was protected by the steep banks of the Little Bear, and the upper and lower fords by strong squads of the enemy. They got themseves into certain positions and saucily remained there. No fires burned on that plain during the night, but on our side of the creek fence-rails went off by the thousand, and hot coffee, fresh beef, and good old hard tack made our boys quite comfortable. General Blair put up for the night at the house of a Mr. Hanson, whose two sons are in our own army. In the morning early the General sent Lightburn and Giles A. Smith by the upper ford, intending thereby to flank the enemy. Lightburn in the advance soon fought his way across the ford, which made the rebels in Osterhaus's front soon prepare for a march eastward. At this juncture General Blair sent Lieutenant De Grass with two Parrotts to the front of Osterhaus. De Grass planted two or three shells with the greatest precision immediately among the rebels, and a general stampede took place. The rebels ran in perfect panic, and had it not been for the difficulty in crossing the Little Bear, we would have got their every cannon. Lightburn threatening their flank, caused the enemy to rush in hot haste beyond Tuscumbia. So we moved on rapidly toward Tuscumbia. But I forget. When we arrived at the "last stand" of this squad of rebels, the latter attempted to turn our right flank, but, ignorant of the fact

that that flank was well protected, they rushed blindly on, until a volley from the Twenty-seventh and Third Missouri caused them to turn in wild confusion. It was here that, among others, Colonel Forrest was mortally wounded. We found him at the house of Mrs. Steele, wife of Captain Steele, of Forrest's own regiment. A man, calling himself Forrest's chaplain, a Captain Rosser, was in attendance upon him. Both took the parole, and were allowed to remain.

We marched into a town with plenty of houses, but with few inhabitants. Here, as elsewhere, we found plenty of women, old men, and children. Men between sixteen and fifty were scarce. Half the houses were deserted. In the numerous store buildings, not a living soul, not an article of goods. The three large hotels all vacant of any thing like human beings, save that in one corner of the Franklin Hotel lives, or seems to live, a man of fifty years, with his wife and young boy. Houses still occupied are wonderfully dilapidated.

Generals Blair and Osterhaus occupied the Franklin House. General Morgan L. Smith pitched his tent with his division west of the town. Very soon in came female after female, all wanting protection. These wicked "Yanks" would steal chickens, would shoot hogs. Colonel Coleman, (Eighth Missouri,) Provost-Marshal, gave them guards, and raids upon chickens ceased. In leaving Tuscumbia, the rebs burned up thirty-five bales of cotton, but inflicted no other damage upon the place. In truth, those thirty-five bales of cotton were all that was worth destroying in the town.

This morning we returned, and here we are in our old camps. We have lost some two killed and six wounded. The enemy, to our knowledge, has lost ten killed and over thirty wounded.

Forrest was shot through both legs. His wound was too severe to admit of his removal. Our surgeons think he will die. Inclosed I send you some rebel documents found on Forrest's person.

Osterhaus, in the whole affair, exhibited the greatest bravery—in fact, hazarding himself too much; but he answered all such suggestions by saying: "I must see for myself, and then I know what's going on." Morgan L. Smith had but little chance to get into the fight, as the rebels would give Osterhaus a feeble resistance. The small loss in our ranks was owing to the splendid management of the whole expedition.

October 29, 1863—11 A.M.

This morning early the rebels, under Lee, again attacked us, having closely followed on our rear. Osterhaus drove them back three or four miles, and fighting is still going on in front. We captured two prisoners this morning, and three wounded rebs. The rebs succeeded in carrying off several of their wounded. From those captured we learn that Colonel Forrest died of his wound, in Tuscumbia, yesterday. He was more of a scoundrel than a soldier, and had as much pity in him as you could crowd on the sharp point of a cambric needle.   MORE ANON.

Doc. 210.

OCCUPATION OF BROWN'S FERRY, TENN.

HEADQUARTERS SECOND BRIGADE, THIRD DIVISION,
FOURTH ARMY CORPS, BROWN'S FERRY,
NEAR CHATTANOOGA, October 30, 1863.

General W. F. Smith, Chief Engineer Army of the Cumberland:

I have the honor to report as follows of the part taken by troops under my command, in the occupation of the left bank of the Tennessee River, at this point.

On the morning of the twenty-fifth instant, I reported, by order of the commanding officer of the Fourth army corps, to the Chief Engineer of this army for instructions, and was then briefly informed for the first time of the duty to be assigned me, and the method of performing it, which was to organize fifty squads of one officer and twenty-four men each, to embark in boats at Chattanooga and float down the river to this point, a distance by the bends of the river of nine miles, and land upon its left bank, then occupied by the enemy, making thereafter immediate dispositions for holding it, while the remaining portion of my brigade and another one should be speedily sent over the river in the same boats to reënforce me. The movement was to be made just before daylight of the twenty-seventh. My brigade then consisted of the following regiments: Sixth Kentucky volunteer infantry, Ninety-third Ohio volunteer infantry, Fifth Kentucky volunteer infantry, First Ohio volunteer infantry, Sixth Ohio volunteer infantry, Forty-first Ohio volunteer infantry, One Hundred and Twenty-fourth Ohio volunteer infantry, Sixth Indiana volunteer infantry, Twenty-third Kentucky volunteer infantry, with an aggregate for duty of two thousand one hundred and sixty-six men.

The twenty-fifth was employed in organizing my parties, each being placed in charge of a tried officer.

On the morning of the twenty-sixth I, in company with the Chief Engineer, visited the place where it was desired to effect the landing, and, from the opposite bank, found the position as represented below.

It was desired that I should land and occupy the two hills to the left of the house.

There was a picket post at this point, also in the depression between the two hills.

It was thought best to organize a party of seventy-five men, who should be the first to land and at once push out upon the road that comes in at the house, clearing and holding it, while half the first organized force should be landed simultaneously at each of the two gorges, (A and B,) who should immediately push up the hills, inclining to the left and following the crest, till they were wholly occupied. Each party of twenty-five was to carry two axes, and as soon as the crest should be reached, a strong line of skirmishers was to be pushed out and all the axes at once put at work felling a thick abatis.

The remainder of the brigade was to be organized, and being ready on the opposite bank, armed and provided with axes, was to be at once pushed over and also deployed in rear of the skirmishers, were to assist in making the abattis.

Positions were also selected for building signal fires to guide us in landing.

I afterward selected tried and distinguished officers to lead the four distinct commands, who, in addition to being instructed fully as to the part they were to take in the matter, were taken to the spot, and every feature of the bank and landings made familiar to them.

They, in turn just before night, called together the leaders of squads, and each clearly instructed what his duties were, it being of such a nature that each had, in a great degree, to act independently, but strictly in accordance to instructions.

At twelve o'clock at night the command was awakened and marched to the landing and quietly embarked under the superintendence of Colonel T. R. Stanly, of the Eighteenth Ohio volunteers.

At precisely three o'clock A.M., the flotilla, consisting of fifty-two boats, moved noiselessly out. I desired to reach the point of landing, at a little before daylight, and soon learned that the current would enable me to do so without using the oars. After moving three miles, we came under the guns of the enemy's pickets, but keeping well under the opposite shore, were not discovered by them till the first boat was within ten feet of the landing, when the picket fired a volley, harmlessly, over the heads of the men. The disembarkation was effected rapidly, and in perfect order, each party performing correctly the part assigned it with so little loss of time, that the entire crest was occupied, my skirmish line out, and the axes working before the reënforcements of the enemy, a little over the hill, came forward to drive us back.

At this time they came boldly up along nearly our entire front, but particularly strong along the road, gaining the hill to the right of it, and would have caused harm to the party on the road, had not Colonel Langdon, First Ohio volunteers, commanding the remaining portion of the brigade, arrived at this moment, and after a gallant but short engagement, driven the enemy well over into the valley, gaining the right-hand hill. They made a stubborn fight all along the hill, but were easily driven away with loss.

General Turchin's command now came over, and taking position on the hills to the right, my troops were all brought to the left of the road. The enemy now moved off in full view up the valley.

The Fifty-first Ohio volunteers, Eighth Kentucky, Thirty-fifth Indiana volunteers, and two batteries of artillery, were subsequently added to my command, and the three points farther to the left occupied.

We knew nothing of the country previous to occupying it, excepting what could be seen from the opposite bank, nor of the force there to oppose us. We found the hill facing the river precipitous, and the face opposite less steep, but of difficult ascent. The top is sharp, having a level surface of from two to six feet in width, forming a natural parapet, capable of an easy defence by a single line against the strongest column. It is from two hundred and fifty to three hundred feet above the river. Beyond it is a narrow productive valley, and the higher parallel range of Raccoon Mountains is about one and one fourth mile distant. The entire opposite face of the hill now is covered with slashed timber.

The enemy had at this point one thousand infantry, three pieces of artillery, and a squadron of cavalry—ample force, properly disposed, to have successfully disputed our landing.

Our losses were five killed, twenty-one wounded, and nine missing. We buried six of the enemy, and a large number were known to be wounded, including the colonel commanding.

We captured a few prisoners, their camp, twenty beeves, six pontoons, a barge, and several thousand bushels of forage fell into our hands.

My thanks are especially due to Colonel A. Wiley, Forty-first Ohio volunteers, and Major Wm. Birch, Ninety-third Ohio volunteers, who commanded and led the party that took the heights, and to Lieutenant-Colonel Foy, Twenty-third Kentucky, commanding party that swept the road, and Lieutenant-Colonel Langdon, First Ohio volunteers, commanding the battalions formed of the residue of the brigade.

Had either of these officers been less prompt in the execution of their duties, or less obedient to the letter of their instructions, many more lives might have been lost, or the expedition failed altogether. The spirit of every one engaged in the enterprise is deserving of the highest commendation. My staff gave me the intelligent and timely assistance they have always done when needed, and to Lieutenant-Colonel Kimberly, Forty-first Ohio volunteers, and Lieutenant Ferdinand D. Cobb, same regiment, I am especially indebted for valuable service.

Very respectfully, your obedient servant,
W. B. HAZEN,
Brigadier-General.

COLONEL WILEY'S REPORT.

HEADQUARTERS, FORTY-FIRST REGIMENT,
OHIO VOLUNTEER INFANTRY,
BROWN'S FERRY, TENN., Oct. 30, 1863.

Jno. Crowell, Jr., Captain and A. A. G.:

In compliance with your order I have the honor to submit the following report of the part taken by the detachment under my command, in gaining possession of the ridge on the west side of the Tennessee River, at Brown's Ferry, on the morning of the twenty-seventh instant.

The detachment consisted of one hundred and fifty officers and men Forty-first Ohio volunteers, Captain W. W. Munn commanding; one hundred and seventy-five officers and men One Hundred and Twenty-fourth Ohio volunteers, Lieutenant-Colonel Jas. Pickands commanding; one hundred and fifty officers and men Sixth Ohio volunteers, Lieutenant-Colonel A. C. Christopher command-

ing; one hundred officers and men Fifth Kentucky volunteers, Lieutenant-Colonel J. L. Treanor commanding.

The detachments from each regiment were organized into companies consisting of twenty-four enlisted men and one commissioned officer each. The whole embarked on twenty-four pontoons. At three o'clock A.M. the fleet moved from the landing at Chattanooga in the following order:

The Forty-first Ohio volunteers, One Hundred and Twenty-fourth Ohio volunteers, Sixth Ohio volunteers, and Fifth Kentucky volunteers, and reached the landing at the ferry at five A.M.

The fleet was preceded by a detachment under Lieutenant-Colonel Foy, Twenty-third Kentucky, on a barge, which was not under my command. My orders were to land at the ferry and carry and hold the height on the left of the gorge. The eminence to be gained is a ridge about four hundred yards in length, parallel with the river, and about three hundred feet above it, the face next the river being very precipitous; the ascent at the end next the gorge not so difficult. The fleet proceeded without molestation until about five o'clock A.M. When the first boat, which was almost abreast of the barge containing Lieutenant Colonel Foy's detachment, was within about ten yards of the landing, it was fired on by the enemy's pickets stationed at the landing. The crew of the first boat delivered a volley and leaped ashore, followed instantly by the second boat, in which I myself had embarked. The first company, deployed as skirmishers to cover the flank of the column, were immediately pushed up the further slope of the ridge; the second company, covering the head of the column, advanced along the crest toward the left. The regiments effected their landing promptly in the order already indicated, and advanced in column by company up the height and along the crest, when the line was established as previously indicated in the following order: The Fifth Kentucky on the right, Forty-first Ohio on the left, Sixth Ohio on the right centre, One Hundred and Twenty-fourth Ohio on the left centre. Each regiment, as soon as it gained its position, threw out two companies as skirmishers to cover its front, and commenced felling the timber and constructed a parapet, each company having carried two axes for that purpose.

The enemy were encamped in the valley at the foot of the ridge, and at the first sound of the axes his skirmishers advanced up the hill and engaged our force vigorously for some time, when they were driven back to the road at the foot of the ridge. A section of artillery then opened on us, but without effect. No further effort was made to dislodge us. As soon as it became light, we discovered the enemy retreating to our left up the further side of the valley. He left five dead and one wounded in front of our line of skirmishers. The following is a list of casualties:

Killed: Privates Thomas Ladler, company A, Forty-first Ohio volunteers; Melvin F. Howard, company B, Fifth Kentucky volunteers. Wounded: Second Lieutenant C. W. Hills, company A,

Forty-first Ohio volunteers; Sergeant C. H. Bennett, company A, Forty-first Ohio volunteers; First Lieutenant A. S. Galbreath, company I, One Hundred and Twenty-fourth Ohio volunteers; Sergeant Samuel Gaynes, company I, One Hundred and Twenty-fourth Ohio volunteers; privates Jos. Sims, company K, One Hundred and Twenty-fourth Ohio volunteers; Wm. Clark, company K, One Hundred and Twenty-fourth Ohio volunteers.

I cannot commend too highly the gallantry and firmness of the troops engaged as skirmishers.

The enemy's line attacked vigorously, encouraged by the shouts of their officers to "drive the Yankees into the river," and only gave way within a few rods of our own line. I have also the pleasure of testifying to the promptness, skill, and efficiency of Lieutenant-Colonel Pickands, One Hundred and Twenty-fourth Ohio volunteers; Lieutenant-Colonel Christopher, Sixth Ohio volunteers; Lieutenant-Colonel Treanor, Fifth Kentucky volunteers, and Captain Munn, Forty-first Ohio volunteers, commanding detachments from their respective regiments.

The best evidence of the alacrity and skill with which they handled their troops, consists in the fact of their effecting a landing, gaining the crest of the height, and the position assigned them, and making all their dispositions for defences before the enemy, who had doubtless been alarmed by the firing at the landing, who not only knew the country, but could have gained it by a much less difficult slope.

I have the honor to be, very respectfully, your obedient servant,

AQUILA WILEY,
Colonel Forty-first Ohio Volunteers, Commanding Detachment.

Doc. 211.

THE BATTLE OF WAUHATCHIE.

MAJOR-GENERAL HOOKER'S REPORT.[*]

HEADQUARTERS ELEVENTH AND TWELFTH CORPS, ARMY OF THE CUMBERLAND, LOOKOUT VALLEY, TENNESSEE, November 6, 1863.

Lieutenant-Colonel C. Goddard, Assistant Adjutant-General, Army of the Cumberland:

COLONEL: I desire to submit the following report of the battle of Wauhatchie, and the operations of my command preliminary to that engagement:

In conformity with orders from the headquarters of the Department, I crossed the Tennessee by the pontoon-bridge, at Bridgeport, on the morning of the twenty-sixth of October, with the greater portion of the Eleventh corps, under Major-General Howard, a part of the Second division of the Twelfth corps, under Brigadier-General Geary, one company of the Fifth Tennessee cavalry, and a part of a company of the First Alabama cavalry, and at once took up line of march along the railroad, to open and secure it in the direction of Brown's Ferry. A regiment was left to defend the bridge head, when

* See Doc. 96, page 347, *ante.*

the column had crossed the river, and to take possession of and hold the passes leading to it through Raccoon Mountain.

Our route lay along the base of this mountain, until we reached Running Waters, when we followed the direction of that stream, and in the morning descended through the gorge into Lookout Valley. No event attended our first day's march deserving mention, unless it be that the enemy's pickets fell back as we advanced, and the leaving of two more of my regiments—one at Shellmound, with instructions to occupy a pass near Gordon's Mines, and another at Whitesides, to protect the route over the mountains through which we had passed.

After entering Lookout Valley, our general course lay along a creek of that name, until within a mile or more of its mouth, where the Brown's Ferry road leaves it to the left. This valley is, perhaps, two miles in width, and completely overlooked by the lofty crests of Lookout and Raccoon Mountains. All the movements and disposition of troops are easily descried from the heights of either, while the valley itself affords abundant opportunity for concealment from the observation of those within.

Another prominent feature in Lookout Valley requires mention, to a clear perception of its topography, and a correct understanding of our operations. This is a succession of hills two or three hundred feet high, with precipitous timbered slopes, and narrow crests, which penetrate three miles up the valley, and divide it, as far as they go, nearly in the centre. There are five or six of them in number, almost isolated, though in a direct line, on the left bank of Lookout Creek, with the railroad passing between the two summits; at the extreme of the range, and still lower down the valley, the road bears off to Chattanooga, about two miles distant through these hills, while the road to Brown's Ferry continues along the west base of the Tennessee River. The enemy held possession of these hills, as indeed of all the country through which we had passed after crossing at Bridgeport. They had also batteries planted on Lookout Mountain, overlooking them.

On the opposite side of the valley is Raccoon Range, and about three miles up is the gorge through which it leads to what is called Kelly's Ferry, three miles distant. As it was proposed to make this our new line of communications with Chattanooga, my instructions required me, if practicable, to gain possession of and to hold it. As the gorge debouches into Lookout Valley, the road forks, one leading to Wauhatchie, and up the valley, the other to Chattanooga, and down the valley.

It was known that a portion of Longstreet's command was in the valley, it is presumed, in part, for convenience in supplying themselves with rations and forage, but mainly for his sharpshooters to annoy our communications on the north side of the Tennessee, and compel our trains to make long detours over execrable roads in their transit from Chattanooga to our depots at Stevenson. From its proximity to the enemy's lines of investment around Chattanooga, and his facilities for detaching heavily from his masses, it was apprehended that the enemy would make unusual efforts to prevent the transfer of its possession, as a failure on our part to establish new communications involved a fact of no less magnitude than the necessity for the early evacuation of Chattanooga, with the abandonment of much of our artillery and trains.

To return to the column: it pushed on down the valley until arrested by an irregular fire of musketry, proceeding from the hill next the railroad, as it passes through the central ridge before described. As it was densely covered with forest, we had no means of ascertaining the number of the enemy, except by feeling. Howard's corps being in the advance, he was directed to throw a brigade to the right to turn the position, and a regiment, supported by the balance of another brigade, to the left, for the same purpose. No sooner had the brigade on the right deployed, than the enemy took to his legs and fled across the creek, burning the railroad bridge in his flight.

We lost a few men here, as well as from the shelling we received from the batteries on Lookout Mountain, whenever our column was exposed to them. The central ridge of hills afforded partial cover from these batteries. These, however, caused no serious interruption in the movement of the column, which, about six o'clock P.M., halted for the night, and went into camp a mile or more up the valley from Brown's Ferry. Here we learned that a pontoon-bridge had been thrown across the river, and that General Hargen's brigade held the heights on the south side of it.

Geary's division being in the rear, and being anxious to hold both roads leading to Kelly's Ferry, he was directed to encamp near Wauhatchie, three miles from the position held by Howard's corps. Pickets were thrown out from both camps on all of the approaches, though no attempt was made to establish a communication between them. The commands were too small to keep up a substantial communication that distance, and I deemed it more prudent to hold the men well in hand than to have a feeble one. In my judgment, it was essential to retain possession of both approaches to Kelly's Ferry if practicable, as it would cause us inconvenience to dispossess the enemy if he established himself on either.

Before night, Howard threw out three companies in the direction of Kelly's Ferry, to intercept and capture, if possible, the enemy's sharpshooters, who had been engaged in firing across the river into our trains, and had, in fact, compelled them to avoid that line entirely. A regiment was also sent toward the point where the Chattanooga road crosses Lookout Creek, and about twelve o'clock had a little skirmishing with the enemy. An hour after, the muttering of heavy musketry fell upon our ears, from the direction of Geary. He was fiercely attacked, first his pickets, and soon after his main force; but not before he was in line of battle to receive it.

Howard was directed to double-quick his nearest division (Schurz's) to his relief, and before proceeding far, a sheet of musketry was thrown on him from the central hills, but at long range, and inflicting no great injury. This was the first intimation that the enemy was there at all.

Directions were immediately given for one of the brigades *en route* to Geary (Tyndale's) to be detached, and assault the enemy in the hills on the left, and the other brigade to push on as ordered. Meanwhile, Howard's First division, under Steinwehr, came up, when it was discovered that the hill to the rear of Schurz's division was also occupied by the enemy in force, and Smith's brigade of this division was ordered to carry it with the bayonet. This skeleton but brave brigade charged up the mountain, almost inaccessible by daylight, under a heavy fire without returning it, and drove three times their number from behind the hastily thrown up intrenchments, capturing prisoners, and scattering the enemy in all directions. No troops ever rendered more brilliant service. The name of their valiant commander is Colonel Orlan Smith, of the Seventy-third Ohio volunteers. Tyndale, encountering less resistance, had also made himself master of the enemy's position in his front.

During these operations, a heavy musketry fire, with occasional discharges of artillery, continued to reach us from Geary. It was evident that a formidable adversary had gathered around him, and that he was battering him with all his might. For almost three hours, without assistance, he repelled the repeated attacks of vastly superior numbers, and in the end drove them ingloriously from the field. At one time they had enveloped him on three sides, under circumstances that would have dismayed any officer except one endowed with an iron will and the most exalted courage. Such is the character of General Geary.

With this ended the fight. We had repelled every attack, carried every point assaulted, thrown the enemy headlong over the river, and, more than all, secured our new communications for the time being, peradventure.

These several conflicts were attended with unusual interest and satisfaction, from the violence of the attack, the great alacrity displayed by the officers and men in springing to their arms on the first indication of the presence of the enemy, and the glorious manner in which they closed in on him for the struggle.

I regret that my duty constrains me to except any portion of my command in my commendation of their courage and valor. The brigade despatched to the relief of Geary by orders delivered in person to its division commander never reached him until long after the fight had ended. It is alleged that it lost its way, when it had a terrific infantry fire to guide it all the way, and also that it became involved in a swamp where there was no swamp or other obstacle between it and Geary, which should have delayed it a moment in marching to the relief of its imperilled companions.

For the instances of conspicuous individual daring and conduct, also of regiments and batteries most distinguished for brilliant service on this field, the attention of the Commanding General is respectfully called to the reports of corps and division commanders herewith transmitted. I must confine myself to an expression of my appreciation of the zealous and devoted services of Major-General Howard, not only on the battlefield, but everywhere and at all times. Of General Geary I need say no more. To both of these officers I am profoundly grateful for the able assistance they have always given me.

Our loss is four hundred and sixteen, among them some of the bravest officers and men of my command.

General Green was severely wounded while in the heroic performance of his duty. Colonel Underwood, of the Thirty-third Massachusetts volunteers, was also desperately wounded, and for his recovery I am deeply concerned. If only in recognition of his meritorious services on this field, his many martial virtues and great personal worth, it would be a great satisfaction to me to have this officer advanced to the grade of Brigadier-General.

For the many whose deaths the country will deplore, I must refer you to the reports of subordinate commanders.

Of the loss of the enemy, it cannot fall much short of one thousand five hundred. Geary buried one hundred and fifty-three rebels on his front alone. We took upward of one hundred prisoners, and several hundred stand of small arms. With daylight to follow up our success, doubtless our trophies would have been much more abundant.

The force opposed to us consisted of two of Longstreet's divisions, and corresponded in number to our corps. From the prisoners we learn that they had watched the column as it descended the valley, and confidently counted on its annihilation.

To conclude, I must express my grateful acknowledgments to Major-General Butterfield, Chief of my Staff, for the valuable assistance rendered me on the field; also to Major Lawrence, Captain Hall, Lieutenants Perkins and Oliver, Aids-de-Camp, for the faithful, intelligent, and devoted performance of all the duties assigned them.

Very respectfully, your obedient servant,
JOSEPH HOOKER,
Major-General Commanding.

COLONEL WOOD'S REPORT.

HEADQUARTERS ONE HUNDRED AND THIRTY-SIXTH N. Y. V., IN THE FIELD, LOOKOUT VALLEY, NEAR CHATTANOOGA, TENN., November 1, 1863.

Captain B. F. Stone, A. A. A. G., Second Brigade:

I have the honor to submit the following report of the operations of the regiment under my command, since and including the twenty-sixth day of October, ultimo.

On that day I was relieved from the duty of guarding the part of the Nashville and Chatta-nooga Railroad, and the bridges and wooden structures thereon, between Anderson and Tantalton, to which I had been assigned, by orders from brigade headquarters, bearing date eleventh October, ultimo.

The regiment marched from Anderson to Bridgeport, to join the brigade from which it had been detached while guarding the railroad. The march was made over the Cumberland Mountains by a steep and declivitous road or bridle-path, inaccessible to wagons, under the guidance of L. Willis, Esq., a firm and unconditional Union man, residing near Anderson. The regiment arrived at Bridgeport the evening of the same day, having marched a distance of sixteen miles. On arriving at Bridgeport, I learned that the brigade had marched the evening before to Shellmound, on the south side of the Tennessee River. I thereupon reported with my command to Brigadier-General A. Von Steinwehr, division commander, and encamped for the night.

During the evening I received orders to march with the Eleventh corps at sunrise the next morning, and to join my brigade on the march. In pursuance of the order, the regiment marched with the corps at the time designated, crossed the Tennessee River at Bridgeport, on pontoon-bridges, and took up the line of march on the Chattanooga road. At Shellmound the regiment came up with and joined the brigade. From this point the regiment with the Eleventh corps, of which it forms a part, marched to Brown's Ferry on the Tennessee River, in Lookout Valley, about three miles from Chattanooga, at which point it arrived near sunset, October twenty-eighth. Although the troops were on two occasions during the march massed in columns by divisions, preparatory to an engagement, in case the enemy attempted to dispute our progress, (of which it was reported there were indications,) and some skirmish firing was heard in our front, this regiment did not see, nor was it in any way molested by the enemy on this march, except that as soon as the marching column came within range of his artillery posted on Lookout Mountain, he opened upon it with shot and shell, and kept up the fire until the whole had passed. But such was the elevation of the mountain and necessary inaccuracy of aim, that the cannonade was entirely harmless. The shot and shell fell wide of the mark, and did not as much as create any sensible uneasiness among the men of my command.

I may be allowed to mention, that as I passed the point next exposed to the fire, I found Major-General Hooker stationed beside the road, notifying the men as they passed that there was no danger from the artillery firing, and testifying by his presence and position that he believed what he said.

It is unnecessary for me to say that this conduct of our Commanding General had the most inspiring influence on the officers and men of my command. On arriving at our place of destination, this regiment with the brigade encamped for the night.

About one o'clock of the morning of the twenty-ninth I was awakened by skirmish firing, which seemed to be a short distance back on the road over which we had marched. The firing, rapidly increased in intensity, and the report of artillery soon mingling with it, admonished us that some part of our forces were engaged with the enemy.

The regiment was immediately ordered to fall in under arms, and to march in the direction of the conflict. It was soon ascertained that the firing was occasioned by an attack made by the enemy upon the command of Brigadier-General Geary, of the Twelfth corps, who had been following us from Bridgeport, and was a few hours in our rear. His command, consisting of a part of his division, had encamped for the night at a place called Wauhatchie, about three miles from the position occupied by the Eleventh corps. General Howard ordered his command to march at once to the aid of General Geary. This regiment, at a double-quick, took up the line of march in rear of the brigade, being preceded by the Seventy-third Ohio, Thirty-third Massachusetts, and Fifty-fifth Ohio. When about one and a half miles from camp, it was ascertained that the enemy occupied the crest of a hill, at the foot of which the road on which we were marching passed, and it was regarded important to dislodge him. Colonel O. Smith, commanding the brigade, was ordered to do it. Preparatory to executing the movement, the brigade was halted in the road. Colonel Smith sent forward the Seventy-third Ohio and Thirty-third Massachusetts, and directed them to charge the hill and drive the enemy therefrom. In the mean time I was ordered by Brigadier-General Steinwehr, division commander, to march my regiment by file to the left, and form in line of battle west of and perpendicular to the road on which we had been halted. This was at the foot of another hill about two hundred yards north of the one occupied by the enemy, and similar in appearance to it, and from which it was separated by a "gap" or "pass." When I had completed the movement ordered, I was directed to send two companies to skirmish up the hill, at the foot of which our line of battle was formed, to ascertain if it was occupied by the enemy. I immediately detached companies H and K from the left of my left wing to execute the movement, and placed the force in command of Captain Eldredge of company K.

The Seventy-third Ohio and Thirty-third Massachusetts being hard pressed by the enemy on the hill which they had been ordered to charge, my regiment was ordered to their support. I marched to the base of the same hill, halted and formed in line of battle facing it. My centre was opposite the highest crest of the hill. Although it was a bright moonlight night, neither the height of the hill nor the obstacles to be encountered could be seen. I was ordered to charge in line of battle to the top of the hill, drive off the enemy, and form a junction with the Thirty-third Massachusetts on my right.

It should be borne in mind that the two companies detached as skirmishers had not at this time rejoined the regiment. I gave the command "Forward!" when the regiment advanced in line of battle at as quick a pace as the steep ascent of the hill would permit, moved steadily and firmly forward under a brisk and constant fire from the enemy, reached and crowned the crest of the hill, drove off the enemy, and took possession. Not a shot was fired by my men until the crest was gained, when one volley was discharged at the retreating enemy. At the time the charge was made the enemy was engaged in throwing up a line of rifle-pits. We captured their intrenching tools.

Having gained and occupied the crest of the hill, I deployed one company to the front as skirmishers. Moved by the right flank and formed a junction with the Thirty-third Massachusetts, which regiment had preceded me, charging up the hill on my right, and was vigorously engaged with the enemy when I reached the crest. The victory was complete. The crest of the hill is not more than six yards in width, from which there is a rapid descent, with a valley on the other side. Down this declivity the enemy precipitately fled in the utmost confusion. He staggered under the intrepid charges and deadly blows delivered to him by the braves of the Seventy-third Ohio and Thirty-third Massachusetts. His discomfiture was made complete by the vigorous and splendid charge of the One Hundred and Thirty-sixth New-York. The ground over which he retreated was strewn with rifles, swords, hats, caps, and haversacks. As daylight opened upon us, we were astonished by the audacity of our charge, and astounded at our success. The hill is over two hundred feet perpendicular height, and the distance from the road where I formed in line of battle to the crest of the hill is one hundred and eighty yards. Prisoners report (and the report is confirmed by other information, and may be regarded as reliable) that the force of the enemy occupying the hill consisted of Law's brigade of Hood's division, Longstreet's corps. This brigade was composed of six regiments, five of which were posted on the crest, the sixth being held in reserve in the valley below. The face of the hill is covered by a forest of wood and a thick coating of leaves, broken by gullies or ravines, and obstructed by bushes and upturned trees. Over and through these obstructions, up an ascent of over forty-five degrees, the men charged with a steadiness and precision that could not be excelled by the most experienced and veteran troops. At no time was there any confusion. At no time was there any wavering. From the commencement to the end of the charge the alignment of the line of battle was wonderfully preserved.

My hearty commendation and profound thanks are especially due to the officers and men of my command, for their brave and gallant conduct on this occasion. As I was deprived of the assistance of my able and energetic field-officer Lieutenant-Colonel Faulkner, being absent on detached service in the State of New-York, and

Major Arnold being detained at Bridgeport by an attack of illness, which rendered him unable to take the field, there is no occasion to make special mention of any officer or man of my command, for every one engaged seemed to perform his whole duty.

No one faltered—there were no stragglers. All are alike entitled to credit—all alike should receive the commendation of their superior officers, the gratitude of their country, and the friends of all may well feel proud of the bravery and gallantry which was exhibited.

Our casualties, it affords me pleasure to say, are slight, our loss being only two killed and four wounded. This exemption from disaster is due to the steepness of the hill up which we charged, the bullets from the enemy's rifles passing harmlessly over our heads. The casualties happened after we reached the crest. We captured five prisoners and forty rifles left on the field by the retreating enemy.

I have the honor to be, Captain,
Respectfully yours, etc.,
JAMES WOOD, Jr.,
Colonel Commanding.

HEADQUARTERS SECOND BRIGADE, SECOND DIVISION,
ELEVENTH CORPS, LOOKOUT VALLEY,
NEAR CHATTANOOGA, Oct. 31, 1863.

GENERAL ORDERS:

The Colonel Commanding, in adding to the testimony of others to the valor of his troops, renews his thanks to the officers and men of his command for their heroic conduct on the afternoon of October twenty-eighth and the morning of the twenty-ninth. The splendid deeds of that memorable morning need not to be recounted. The glory of the living and the dead is complete and sufficient for the most ambitious. To those brave comrades of all grades who so gallantly responded when called to breast the wall of fire from two thousand muskets, he cannot be too grateful. Yours is the credit—yours is the fame. Let its brilliant lustre never be tarnished either upon the battle-field or in the more quiet routine of duty. You are above jealousy of others or sinister discussions about the appropriation of praise. Your greatest satisfaction will be derived from the consciousness of a perilous duty heroically done.

You have won the title of gallant soldiers—add to it that of honorable and upright men, and your fame shall be perfect, and the most precious legacy you can bequeath to your loved ones at home.

Let us sympathize with the suffering wounded, and cherish the memory of our fallen comrades.
By order   Colonel SMITH.
B. F. STONE,
Captain and A. A. G.

SECOND DIVISION ELEVENTH CORPS,
CHURCH OF JOHN THE BAPTIST, Oct. 31, 1863.

GENERAL ORDERS:

The General Commanding division desires to express to his troops his appreciation of the valor shown by them in the action of the twenty-eighth and twenty-ninth instant.

This division formed the advance during the march from Bridgeport to this place—the First brigade, under Colonel A. Buschbeck, leading.

Their movements were marked by calmness and resolution. Whatever resistance was made by the enemy was quickly borne down.

During the night of the twenty-eighth to the twenty-ninth instant the rebels made a fierce attack upon the command of General Geary. Our corps was ordered out for his support. The division moved forward on the double-quick, the Second brigade, under Colonel O. Smith, in advance. On the left of the road by which the division must pass to support General Geary, a hill commanding the way was found occupied by two rebel brigades. The Second brigade was ordered to take and hold this position. The Seventy-third Ohio and Thirty-third Massachusetts formed line of battle, and with the greatest determination scaled the precipitous slope, moving over almost impassable ground in the face of rapid volleys.

The One Hundred and Thirty-sixth New-York was now ordered to support the left of the two advancing regiments, and advanced with heroic bravery, as did the Fifty-fifth Ohio, which was to support the right. On the crest a fierce hand-to-hand contest ensued. The enemy, although well fortified in a position almost impregnable by nature, could not withstand this most extraordinary bayonet attack, and were forced to inglorious flight, leaving many arms and intrenching tools behind their parapet.

The storming of this hill against such stupendous odds is a brilliant episode of the war, a feat of arms rarely surpassed in history.

Officers and soldiers! by your courage you have gained your badge, a proud distinction. Let your valor preserve unsullied the honor of the White Crescent. By command of
Brigadier-General A. VON STEINWEHR.
FREDERICK W. STONE, A. A. G.

HEADQUARTERS ELEVENTH CORPS, LOOKOUT
VALLEY, TENN., November 1, 1863.

GENERAL ORDERS, No. 5.

It is with extreme pleasure that the Major-General Commanding communicates to the troops composing the Eleventh corps, and to the Second division of the Twelfth corps, the subjoined letter from the Major-General commanding the army of the Cumberland, expressive of his appreciation of your distinguished services on the night of the twenty-eighth ultimo.

It is a noble tribute to your good conduct from a brave and devoted soldier.

The General hopes that it will inspire as much satisfaction in the hearts of his officers and men as it has in his own, and that we may all be stimulated by it to renewed efforts to secure the good opinion of our commander, while we also emulate the courage and valor of our companions in arms.

HEADQUARTERS DEPARTMENT OF THE CUMBERLAND,
CHATTANOOGA, October 30, 1863.

Major-General Hooker, Commanding Eleventh and Twelfth Corps:

GENERAL: I most heartily congratulate you

and the troops under your command at the brilliant success you gained over your old adversary (Longstreet) on the night of the twenty-eighth ultimo. The bayonet charge of Howard's troops made up the side of a steep and difficult hill over two hundred feet high, completely routing the enemy from his barricades on its top, and the repulse by Geary's division of greatly superior numbers, who attempted to surprise him, will rank among the most distinguished feats of arms of this war. Very respectfully, etc.,

(Signed)   GEORGE H. THOMAS,
Major-General Commanding.

By command of Major-General HOOKER.

(Signed)   H. W. PERKINS, A. A. G.
Official.

(Signed)   F. A. MEYSENBERY, A. A. G.
Official.

FRED. W. STONE, Capt. and A. A. G.

HEADQUARTERS SECOND BRIGADE, }
November 5, 1863. }

Official.

BENJ. F. STONE, Capt. and A. A. A. G.

CINCINNATI "GAZETTE" ACCOUNT.

CHATTANOOGA, October 29.

Last night, a little before one o'clock, we were startled, though not surprised, to hear volleys of musketry, interspersed with the booming of cannon at short intervals, off to the right of Chattanooga, seemingly about five miles. The sound came up from what is called Lookout Valley, which lies between that mountain and the Raccoon Ridge. It was known that troops had been sent across the new pontoon at Brown's Ferry, but had not gone as far down as the place whence the sound proceeded, and so the great secret, so long and faithfully guarded, must out. Hooker is there!

And this was the fact. "Fighting Joe" had come, even at the eleventh hour, to the help of the army not yet rested of Chickamauga.

We rejoiced, and yet shuddered, when the deep-mouthed cannon belched forth from Lookout, and the waves of musketry, the more terrible by night, crashed up through the valley and reëchoed from the mountain sides; for we could not believe that General Hooker had chosen this midnight hour for his attack.

It is not proper to state the various movements that brought about the battle, much less to give a full catalogue of the troops engaged. Sufficient that the afternoon of the twenty-eighth instant found Hooker in the Lookout Valley, with his forces present, arranged as follows:

General Geary, with a portion of the Twelfth corps, was at Wauhatchie Junction on the Memphis, Charleston, and Trenton Railroad, while certain portions of the Eleventh corps, under General Howard, marched further up the valley toward Brown's Ferry, where it was expected to unite with our troops that had been thrown across the river, thus making navigation safe, as the rebels would be entirely driven from it. They were permitted to march quietly up the valley and pitch their tents at leisure. The night wore silently till near twelve o'clock, when, like an eagle swooping on its prey, the rebels rushed down from Lookout Mountain and the plateau below, with the evident intention of wedging themselves into the space between our two corps, and thus cut them off by piecemeal. As they came they fired a deadly volley into Geary's ranks, and at the same time their batteries on Lookout opened and sent their shells crashing among the tree-tops above the heads of our men. Hooker was not long in seeing the necessities of the hour. Geary's men were fighting with that desperation which made brave men braver; but the rebels were three to their one, and it was evident they could' not long hold out against such fearful odds. "Forward to their relief, boys! charge the devils double-quick!" shouted fighting Joe, and his words flew like magic through the camp. "Fall in line!" and down they rushed through the valley, seemingly "into the jaws of death." But their danger, as it appeared, was not all, nor even half, in front; for as they passed along the foot of a ridge, some two hundred feet high, lying on their left, which, as it seems, they thought to be occupied by our forces, a furious volley of musketry was poured into them from its brow. This force must be dislodged, or here would be a second danger of being flanked. Estimating from the firing, it was thought that one brigade would be sufficient to' do the work, the strength of the position occupied by the enemy being as yet entirely unknown. Accordingly, the Seventy-third Ohio and Thirty-third Massachusetts, to be supported, if necessary, by the One Hundred and Thirty-sixth New-York, the whole under command of Colonel Smith, of the Seventy-third, which was commanded by Captain Thomas W. Higgins, Acting-Major. Colonel Underwood led the Thirty-third Massachusetts till he was wounded, mortally, it is feared.

At the word "Charge!" the two regiments, in all not more than five hundred men, rushed up the hill with fixed bayonets—rushed madly, it would seem, when it is remembered that they knew not how many reapers of death were on the top, waiting to mow them down.

But on they went; through the underbrush and trees, up a hill so steep, that even by daylight, when one can pick his way, nor fear a wily enemy, it is found very difficult to climb. The rebels held their fire till we had approached near the top, and then, accompanied by that demoniacal yell which only a rebel can utter, they poured a most deadly volley into our ranks.

Taken aback by the immensely superior numbers which the firing proved the enemy to have, staggered by the unexpected appearance of heavy rifle-pits which frowned like death itself, in the flash of the guns, many fallen, among whom was a large proportion of officers, it was not strange, nay, it could not but be, that our men should fall back to the foot of the hill to rally and arrange their broken lines.

It was now known that the enemy was four times their own number, that he had strong rifle-pits, and was elated and encouraged by the success of his first blow; but the hill was ordered to be taken, and the blood of their brothers who had already fallen cried out to our boys for revenge.

Again they came to the charge, and this time with that desperate determination that knows no retreat. Volley after volley was poured into them, and many fell, but none faltered. Yells and fiendish shouts that often before had been set up with terrifying effect, now swept over this noble remnant of two regiments, powerless as the winds that moaned the while through the pines above them. On they rushed—leaped into the rifle-pits. "Back, ye grayhounds!" And their flashing eyes still emphasized the words.

Confused and confounded by such bravery, ay, reckless daring, the rebels broke and rushed in every direction down the hill, except forty, who remained as prisoners, and left us in possession of the entire ridge. According to their own statements, there were on this hill five regiments, in all two thousand men, it being Lowe's brigade, Hood's, now Jenkins's division, Longstreet's corps.

The One Hundred and Thirty-sixth New-York is entitled to some honor in this most brilliant action, although it was not brought up till the eleventh hour. The loss in that regiment will probably amount to five or six in killed and wounded. It is due also to state that it was through no lack of desire on their part that they were not brought up sooner. To prove what desperate and almost unequalled fighting the other two did, it is but necessary to state that the Thirty-third Massachusetts lost one hundred and one men in killed, wounded, and missing, among whom is Colonel Underwood, wounded, a brave patriot, and Adjutant Mudges, killed, a gallant and very promising young officer; and that the Seventy-third Ohio lost one hundred killed and wounded, among whom are six commissioned officers.

In walking over the hill where this fight was, I could not but be surprised that any of our brave boys escaped. Scarcely a tree or a shrub could be seen that was not marred by some stroke of the fearful contest. Trees not more than ten inches through had, in some instances, as many as a dozen bullet holes.

While the contest was in progress on this ridge, General Geary, with his reënforcements from the Eleventh, was hotly engaged with the rebels a half mile below. Here victory seemed to perch awhile on one and then on the other side, but at length our fire got too warm for them, and they fled precipitately to Lookout Mountain, leaving us in possession of the field and their dead.

Our loss altogether, in killed, wounded, and missing, will foot up something near five hundred. The enemy's, perhaps, is not larger than ours, as all the advantages were on his side. The firing ceased about four o'clock this morning. The enemy, however, has been throwing shell from the batteries on Lookout nearly all day, but with little or no damage to us. Our guns have replied three or four times. According to count, the shells thrown by the enemy last night amounted to two hundred and forty. His entire force is estimated at about sixteen thousand, which was at least three times that of our own. General Green is reported dangerously wounded. Captain Geary, son of the General commanding, was instantly killed. One of the saddest losses Ohio sustained, is the death of Captain McGroarty, of the Sixty-first, who fell early in the fight.

Our men are in high spirits. Their confidence in Hooker is unbounded. In the thickest of the fight he was foremost among the men, cheering and waving them on to victory.

Doc. 212.

OPERATIONS OF THE REBELS IN TENNESSEE.

A REBEL REVIEW OF GENERAL BRAGG'S CAMPAIGN.

NORTH-GEORGIA, October, 1863.

To the Editor of the Whig:

The following *resumé* of the late operations of the army of the Tennessee may possess sufficient interest to the country to ask its publication:

It may be remembered that, in consequence of a flank movement on the right, and the threatened danger to its communications, toward the last of June, the army of Tennessee was put in retreat from Shelbyville and Tullahoma on or toward Chattanooga. The retreat was effected with slight or inconsiderable loss in men or transportation, and Chattanooga was occupied during the days of the first week of July. Polk's corps, except Anderson's brigade, of Withers's division, which was ordered to Bridgeport, where the Nashville and Chattanooga Railroad crosses the Tennessee River, for purposes of observation, was retained in and around Chattanooga, and Hardee's corps was distributed along the line of the Knoxville Railroad, with Tyner's Station as the centre, General Bragg establishing the army headquarters at Chattanooga. The work of fortifying was begun and prosecuted for some weeks, during which the army seemed to await the development of the enemy's plans, and at the end of which we had two guns in position. Beyond reconnoissances in some force at Bridgeport and the mouth of Battle Creek, the enemy made no demonstration until the twenty-first of August, when he succeeded in covering the town of Chattanooga with his artillery from the heights overlooking the Tennessee River and the town. This bombardment of our position, which was intended as a demoralizing *coup de main*, had the more pregnant significance of an inchoate announcement that the enemy's plans were completed, and were about being put in active operation. The effect of the bombardment was the official evacuation of the place to points beyond range outside, and the withdrawal of stores to points of convenience on the railroad to the rear, and the withdrawal of Anderson's brigade from Bridgeport. On the twenty-sixth or twenty-seventh of

August, or some five or six days after the surprise of Chattanooga, Burnside's advance into East-Tennessee was announced by the presence of his cavalry in the vicinity of Knoxville, and Major-General Buckner received orders to evacuate Knoxville, and occupy Loudon. In consequence of a demonstration, it is said, by a portion of Rosecrans's army at Blythe's Ferry, on the Tennessee River, opposite the mouth of the Hiawassee, he was ordered to fall back from Loudon to Charleston, and soon after to the vicinity of Chattanooga. Pending these movements above, which were to give East-Tennessee to the Federals, not only for occupation, but for coöperation with Rosecrans in his designs upon Chattanooga and the Army of Tennessee, Rosecrans was not idle below. On Tuesday morning, September the first, citizens living near Caperton's Ferry reported that the enemy was crossing the Tennessee River in force at that point, (Caperton's Ferry;) that on Saturday, the twenty-ninth of August, three days before, a Federal cavalry force had forded the river at some shallows above to the south side, had proceeded down the river to Caperton's, and in conjunction with another force, appearing contemporaneously on the opposite shore, had thrown a pontoon bridge across the river; and that the enemy commenced immediately to cross in force, and had been crossing for three days, Saturday, Sunday, and Monday, and were moving across Sand Mountain, in the direction of Wills's Valley and Trenton. This story, regarded at army headquarters as incredible, was soon after confirmed by reports of the occupation of Trenton by the enemy's cavalry, and its advance up the Wills's Valley railroad, in the direction of Chattanooga, as far as Wauhatchie, within seven miles, as a covering force to the advance of its infantry columns on Trenton.

In order to understand this movement of Rosecrans, and subsequent operations, a topographical *coup d'œil* is necessary.

Chattanooga is situated on the Tennessee River, at the mouth of the Chattanooga Valley —a valley following the course of the Chattanooga Creek, and formed by Lookout Mountain and Mission Ridge. East of Mission Ridge, and running parallel with it, is another valley—Chickamauga Valley—following the course of Chickamauga Creek, which, with the Chattanooga Creek, discharges its waters into the Tennessee River—the first above, and the last below the town of Chattanooga, and has with it a common source in McLemore's Cove—the common head of both valleys, and formed by Lookout Mountain on the west, and Pigeon Mountain to the east. Wills's Valley is a narrow valley lying to the west of Chattanooga, formed by Lookout Mountain and Sand Mountain, and traversed by a railroad, which takes its name from the valley, and which, branching from the Nashville and Chattanooga Railroad, where the latter crosses the valley, has its present terminus at Trenton, and future at Tuscaloosa, Alabama. The distance of Bridgeport from Chattanooga is twenty-eight

miles, of Caperton's Ferry about forty, and of Trenton something over twenty. Ringgold is eighteen miles from Chattanooga on the Georgia State road, and Dalton some forty, at the point where the Georgia State road connects with the East-Tennessee Railroad. Rome is sixty-five miles south-west of Chattanooga, on the Coosa River, at the point of confluence of the Etawah and Estanalsh. The wagon-road from Chattanooga to Rome, known as the Lafayette Road, crosses Mission Ridge into Chickamauga Valley at Rossville, and, proceeding in a south-westerly direction, crosses Chickamauga Creek, eleven miles from Chattanooga, at Lee and Gordon's Mills, and, passing to the east of Pigeon Mountain, goes through Lafayette, distant some twenty-two miles from Chattanooga, and Summerville within twenty-five miles of Rome. From Caperton's Ferry there is a road leading over Sand Mountain into Wills's Valley at Trenton, and from Trenton to Lafayette and Dalton, over Lookout Mountain, through Coopers's and Stevens's Gaps, into McLemore's Cove, and over Pigeon Mountain by Plug Gap. The road from Trenton, following Wills's Valley, exposed, by easy communications, Rome, and, through it, Western Georgia and Eastern Alabama, with easy access to the important central positions, Atlanta and Selma.

The General Commanding, believing a flanking movement to be the purpose of the enemy in his movement on the left, ordered Lieutenant-General Hill, on Monday, September seventh, to move with his corps toward Lafayette, and General Polk to Lee and Gordon's Mills, and Major-General Buckner, with the Army of East-Tennessee, and Major-General Walker, with his division from the Army of Mississippi, to concentrate at Lafayette, and Brigadier-General Pegram to cover the railroad with his cavalry. These dispositions having been made of the confederate forces, Major-General Crittenden, commanding the left wing of Rosecrans's army, which had not moved with the right and centre, but had been left in the Sequatchie Valley, crossed the Tennessee River at the mouth of Battle Creek, and moved upon Chattanooga. Major-General McCook, commanding the right wing, was thrown forward to threaten Rome, and the corps of Major-General Thomas was put in motion over Lookout Mountain, in the direction of Lafayette.

It will be perceived, from this distribution of the forces of both armies, that Rosecrans exposed himself in the hands of an adversary of capacity and vigor to the hazard of quick and certain destruction. The centre corps, under Thomas, being in McLemore's Cove, immediately opposite Lafayette, at and near which General Bragg had all his forces concentrated, was completely at the mercy of the latter. It was only necessary that General Bragg should fall upon it with such a mass as would have crushed it; then turn down Chattanooga Valley, thrown himself between the town and Crittenden, and crushed him; then passed back between Lookout Mountain and the Tennessee River into

Wills's Valley, and cut off McCook's retreat to Bridgeport; thence moved along the Cumberland range into the rear of Burnside, and disposed of him.

This campaign, which was so obvious to parties engaged in the general movements, and which was so feasible, would have gone far toward ending the war, and have added fresh lustre to our arms. But it was not perceived and acted upon by the mind directing the army. It is true that a force was thrown forward into McLemore's Cove, but the movement was inadequate, and by no means equal to the magnitude or the consequences suspended on its success. Various causes have been assigned for its failure; but among the best informed, it is set down to the score of the limited scale on which it was planned.

The movement upon Thomas, in McLemore's Cove, having failed, he having effected his escape up the mountain, the whole of the troops of Bragg were withdrawn to Lafayette. On their withdrawal, Rosecrans, who, by this time, had discovered Bragg's whereabouts, recalled McCook into Will's Valley, and ordered him to follow Thomas, who was again put in motion over the mountain into the cove. The two corps were thus concentrated on the east side of Lookout Mountain, in thirty-six hours after Bragg left it. In the mean time, Crittenden, who reached Chattanooga, and, finding no enemy there, did not stop to occupy and fortify it, but, strong in the general feeling of the Northern army, that the confederates were thoroughly demoralized, and would not fight, moved on toward Ringgold, to cut off Buckner, who was understood to be moving to the support of Bragg. On reaching the point on the Georgia Railroad at which Buckner crossed, he discovered he was too late, and turned toward Lafayette to follow him. He moved up the Chickamauga on its east side, in the direction of Lafayette, and was confronted by the cavalry under Generals Pegram and Armstrong. After skirmishes with them, in which there were some brilliant dashes on the part of our cavalry, the latter retired slowly before the enemy, falling back toward Lafayette. To meet this movement, General Bragg ordered a force of two divisions under Lieutenant-General Polk, to move to the front. These divisions, Cheatham's and Walker's, were put in motion, and were in line of battle before daylight, covering the three roads on which the enemy's three divisions were marching. Hindman came up after daylight, and Buckner was thrown forward as a supporting force to guard Polk's left against Thomas and McCook, in the cove. Crittenden finding himself confronted, declined battle, and retired during the night, falling back on the Chickamauga, which he crossed at Lee and Gordon's Mills. This placed the whole of Rosecrans's three corps on the east side of the Chickamauga and in easy supporting distance.

Now was presented once more a magnificent opportunity for the confederate General. There was no longer a doubt as to the position of the forces of the enemy. His whole army, with the exception of Granger, was before him. It was distributed from the head of McLemore's Cove, along and down the west side of the Chickamauga Valley, as far as Lee and Gordon's Mills, Chickamauga Creek separating it from the army of the confederates. A strong demonstration on the creek was all that was necessary to cover the proper movement. That movement was to march his whole army rapidly by the right flank, down as low as Reed's bridge and the contiguous fords, and at that point to throw it across the creek and valley, forming it at right angles to the Lafayette and Chattanooga road, and so covering the exit from the valley in the direction of Chattanooga. This movement would have been met by that of the Virginia troops landing from the railroad at Ringgold, and would have effectually blocked the Yankee army up in McLemore's Cove, cut it off from Chattanooga, and placed it at the mercy of the confederates. But the point was not seen. It was beyond the limited range of the usual strategic combinations of the confederate chief, and while he ordered a demonstration on the enemy's lines at Gordon's Mills, he failed to grasp the whole of the situation. Instead of throwing his whole army in a body across the Chickamauga and far down, he moved it by divisions and crossed it at several fords and bridges north of Gordon's Mills, up to which he ordered the Virginia troops which had crossed many miles below, and near to which he attempted to concentrate about half of his army. This was on Saturday, the nineteenth.

While he was engaged in discussing the precise position of the enemy, the latter relieved his embarrassment by an attack on Major-General Walker's corps. This attack was made with great vigor, and was sustained by the gallant men who compose that division in a style in keeping with their former reputation for the highest soldierly qualities. The attack was made simultaneously on front and flank by a part of Thomas's corps and Palmer's division of Crittenden's corps. In meeting the attack, the brigades of Walthall and Govan, under the command of Brigadier-General Liddell, commanding division, eminently distinguished themselves. The division of Major-General Cheatham was moved to the support of Walker, and was taken into the fight most opportunely; for while the greatly superior force by which Walker was attacked was not only held in check, but driven, at the outset—Walker running over several of the enemy's batteries—yet the strong reënforcements that came up caused Walker to hail Cheatham's approach as a seasonable relief. This veteran division, under its well-tried and skilful leader, threw itself upon the enemy's line, with its usual weight and force, capturing many of the enemy's guns, and driving him back, until he was met by heavy reënforcements. The enemy here crowded his troops down upon his left, and the fight became one of great desperation, being sustained by the enemy with the whole of Thomas's corps. The strength of his force being great enough to outflank Cheatham, he lapped around him on both right and left, and although his advance was met with heroic firmness, yet being so greatly outnumbered, he was compelled to fall back. This was not accomplished, however, until fearful sacrifices had been experienced, and no help was seen to be at hand. His line was maintained until the enemy, by a rapid flank movement on his left, had pushed close upon the battery of the gallant Captain Carnes, and slain most of its horses and men. The heavy loss in horses rendered it impossible to withdraw the guns, and they were therefore abandoned to the enemy. The division of Major-General Cleburn, of Lieutenant-General Hill's corps, which had held Lee and Gordon's Mills during the day, now came to Cheatham's support. It moved to the attack with its usual energy, and rolled back the tide of battle which was pressing with such weight on Cheatham's right. The fire with which it opened was terrific, and soon afforded relief to Cheatham, who, with the elasticity which belongs to that veteran division, resumed immediately the forward movement, uniting with Cleburn, and pressing the retiring lines of the enemy. This fight was continued until night, and it was just before the close that the gallant officer, Brigadier-General Preston Smith, with one or more of his Aids-de-Camp, fell under one of the volleys of the enemy's musketry.

The division of Major-General Hood and the corps of Major-General Buckner were prominently engaged in the operations of the day, and bore themselves most gallantly.

At the close of the day's work, the General Commanding issued an order, dividing the forces of his army into two wings.

The right wing was placed under Lieutenant-General Polk, and the left under Lieutenant-General Longstreet. The former was composed of Lieutenant-General Hill's corps, of two divisions, Major-General Cleburn's and Major-General Breckinridge's; of the division of Major-General Cheatham, of Lieutenant-General Polk's corps, and the division of Major-General W. H. T. Walker.

The left was composed of the divisions of Major-General Stewart, Brigadier-Generals Preston and Bushrod Johnson, of Major-General Buckner's corps; Major-General Hindman, of Lieutenant-General Polk's corps, and Benning's, Lane's, and Robertson's brigades, of Hood's division, and Kershaw's and Humphries's brigade, of McLaw's division, of his own (Lieutenant-General Longstreet's) corps.

The front line of the right wing consisted of three divisions—Breckinridge and Cleburn, of Hill's corps, and Cheatham, of Polk's corps—which were posted from right to left in the order named. Major-General Walker was here in reserve.

The left wing was composed of Major-General Stewart's division on the right, with Hood's on the left. On Hood's left was Hindman's division of Lieutenant-General Polk's corps, with Preston's division of Buckner's corps on the extreme left.

Orders were given to the Lieutenant-General commanding the right wing to attack at daylight next morning. These orders were immediately issued by him to his subordinate commanders, but, owing to circumstances beyond his control, the attack was not made until nine o'clock. Prior to giving the order to move forward to the attack, General Polk discovered that, owing to the want of precaution on the part of the proper authority in the formation of the general line of battle, a portion of the line of the left wing had been formed in front of his line, a portion amounting to a whole division, and that had the order to make the attack at daylight been obeyed, this division, from its position, must inevitably have been slaughtered. It was saved by an order to halt Cheatham's division, and by orders to the left of Cleburn, advising it of its whereabouts.

The battle then opened by a forward movement of Breckinridge, followed and accompanied by Cleburn. The enemy had, during the night, thrown up breastworks of heavy timber, cut down from the forest, behind which he had intrenched himself. These lay chiefly in Cleburn's front. He moved directly upon them, while Breckinridge swung round to flank them. The assault was a desperate one. General Polk being informed by General Hill that the enemy was threatening his right flank, Polk ordered Walker immediately to move to the right and form an echelon upon Breckinridge, overlapping his right. It was then ascertained that no enemy was there. But the forward movement of the front line had resulted in a severe conflict, desperately contested, which drove the enemy around on the extreme left a mile or more across the Chattanooga road. In this conflict those gallant officers, Brigadier-Generals Deshler and Helm were killed, and Brigadier-General Daniel Adams was severely wounded and taken prisoner. Heavy reenforcements being sent from the enemy's right to support his left, he was enabled to regain a portion of the ground he had lost. Cleburn's division, which had encountered the enemy behind his breastworks, after a firm onset and most gallant assault, was driven back with heavy loss. This veteran division returned slowly and in good order to a position just beyond the range of the guns in the enemy's works, which they occupied and held. Information of this fact having been communicated by General Sill to General Polk, the latter ordered Cheatham to replace Cleburn in the general line, and while this movement was being effected, another message from General Hill was received by General Polk, informing him that his right was again threatened, and he wanted support. General Polk examined the position of Cleburn, and finding he could hold it if he could not advance, moved Cheatham rapidly by the right flank to the extreme right to meet the reported movement of the enemy, which was ascertained to be one of the divisions of Granger's corps, approaching from Chattanooga, and was moving toward the centre, where Cleburn had made his attack. ,

The whole line was then revised and posted, and a forward movement in all its length ordered. The right swung round with an extended sweep, with its firm supports, and the left rallied once more to the charge of the works, before which it had suffered so severely in the morning. Never did troops move up to their work with more resolution; the daring Breckinridge with his Kentuckians and Louisianians, and Cleburn with his Arkansians and Alabamians, and Walker with his South-Carolinians, Mississippians, and Georgians, and Cheatham with his Tennesseeans, all moved forward in one mighty tide, amidst the thunders of some twenty batteries and the roar of thousands of muskets and rifles. The scene was one of surpassing sublimity and grandeur. Sweeping forward as the flood of a mighty river, it carried every thing before it, nothing being able to stand before it in the resistless line of its path. The enemy's works, which opposed such a stubborn resistance in the morning, succumbed before the onmoving torrent, and the brave men of Cleburn's division, which had been repulsed in the morning, had, by their extraordinary gallantry in the evening, the opportunity of avenging the experiences of the earlier part of the day. The whole field was carried triumphantly, and the enemy driven as chaff before the wind. He withstood as long as human powers of endurance could bear up against such a pressure, then yielded and fell back partly upon and into the hands of the right wing, where several hundred were captured, the residue crossing the Chattanooga road, and retreating in the direction of Mission Ridge. Night interposed, and though it brought with it a magnificent moon, no orders were received to pursue, and the troops were halted, giving expression to their sense of the glorious victory won, and unconquerable desire to pursue it to an absolute success in the enemy's utter annihilation, in such long, loud, and triumphant cheering, as would almost seem to rend the heavens. Such cheering has never been heard at the close of any battle, since the war began.

Such were the operations on the right wing. The battle beginning on the right, its tide ran from right to left, and reached Longstreet's extreme left about eleven o'clock, and was availed of and directed by that eminent chief — who very much resembles the Duke of Wellington in the aspects, moral and intellectual, of his character, as he has resembled him in the fortune of a uniform success — in a manner as prompt and energetic as it was wise and skilful. While Hood and others were ordered by him to make a vigorous assault in front, Buckner was made to execute a successful flank movement, the joint effect of which was to force the Federals to abandon that part of the field, and to seek a position on a high ridge. From this position they were driven, with heavy loss in killed,

wounded, prisoners, artillery, small-arms, and colors, after a desperate struggle, by the brigades of Kershaw and Humphries, under the command of Brigadier-General Kershaw, in the absence of Major-General McLaws, reënforced by Gracise's, Kelley's, and Trigg's brigades, of Major-General Preston's division, Major-General Hindman completing the general work of the line on the left, by driving the enemy on his front before him, along with those driven from the ridge by Preston and Kershaw. Rosecrans, perceiving what was taking place on his right, ordered up reënforcements from his left, to support his retiring, or, rather, frightened battalions, which, finding a good position, waited for their arrival, turning upon their pursuers with the fierceness of a temporary and desperate energy. Brigadier-General Law, commanding Hood's division, perceiving this movement, ordered a battery of ten guns to a position from which he could enfilade the reënforcing column as it advanced. The battery opened just as it was about wheeling into position, and, at the same time, Stewart's division, posted on the extreme right, was thrown forward on its flank.

These movements, made contemporaneously with the movements of Polk's wing, as mentioned above, led to the almost simultaneous rout of the whole Federal army, and ensued in the glorious victory described, one of the most absolute and decisive of the war. From this moment, panic, confusion, disorder became the condition of an army which had never before acknowledged defeat, and which for two days had been contesting every inch of ground with valor the most obstinate. And what did the confederate commander do? Did he pursue an enemy thus demoralized, and furnished, by his not forming his line of battle at right angles with his actual line, with opportunity of retreat upon Chattanooga, whose possession was the object of the campaign—an enemy not only demoralized, but encumbered with heavy trains, and no mode of exit save through two gaps of Mission Ridge, a mountain? No. Night had set in, and he deemed it prudent to halt, notwithstanding his men were eager for pursuit, and a brilliant moon furnished almost the light of day. Three hours were lost in the morning by Polk's failure to attack at daylight; and, therefore, the condition of the troops was such as to forbid the possibility of pursuit. But granting that reasons, substantive reasons, existed for not pursuing on Sunday night, what hindered the Commander-in-Chief from pursuing on Monday morning at daylight? Chattanooga was only ten miles from the battle-field, and, unfortified, our pursuing cavalry could see the head of their column, and urged General Bragg by repeated messages to pursue; that every hour's delay would be equal to the loss of a thousand men. Citizens along the road reported that many of their commands passed their dwellings in the utmost disorder, without arms or accoutrements, and many without hats, as a confused and routed mob, not as troops in column, every thing in Chattanooga and on the road inviting rather than forbidding attack. Even if they had good defensive works, with the condition as reported above, by a prompt pursuit our army would have gone into Chattanooga with theirs, and thus broken the effect of their fire; and if such would have been the result of good defensive works, what might not the result have been without them, and the enemy panic-stricken because of the knowledge that none such existed? What hindered him from pursuing is not known, but it is known that while pursuit seems to have been invited, he did not pursue, and not pursuing, what did he do on Monday morning? He first sent out detachments to the battle-field to gather up the fruits of victory, in arms, large and small, to be secured and sent to the rear, and caused the captured banners to be collected to be sent to Richmond, and prisoners to be counted and sent to the rear. He then ordered the troops under arms, and marched them down the Chattanooga road until they came near to Rossville, where Forrest and Pegram were thundering away with their batteries at the retreating enemy, there had them filed to the right, and thrown down the Chickamauga Creek, that they might rest from their fatigues and be in good position to move upon Burnside or flank Rosecrans, as future contingencies might dictate.

There the troops halted from Monday until Wednesday morning; the enemy, in the mean time, working like beavers, and fortifying night and day with all their might. On Tuesday night an order was issued for the whole army to move upon Chattanooga at six o'clock the next morning, Wednesday, twenty-third September.

The army moved up to and over Mission Ridge, where it was halted, and where it remains halted to this day, the twenty-eighth October!

That the campaign, so far, is a failure, and the battle of Chickamauga, though a victory, is not a success, are propositions too plain for denial. We have not recovered Chattanooga as yet, much less Tennessee, and it may be well for the country to inquire whether the fault lies with a subordinate officer, or is to be traced to the inefficiency and incompetency of one higher in rank, one who is presumed intellectually to direct the operations of the army of Tennessee.

HISTORICUS.

Doc. 213.

PRISON-LIFE IN RICHMOND.

JOURNAL OF A UNION SOLDIER.

ANNAPOLIS, MARYLAND, November 6, 1863.

You doubtless have heard a great deal about the way our prisoners are treated during their captivity in the land of Dixie, yet I feel sure you will do a soldier the kindness to give the following notes a space in your columns. These notes were taken while I was a prisoner, and are strictly correct. I desire the public to know how the boys that were wounded and captured in the battle of Chickamauga were treated by the chivalry:

STEWARD'S HOSPITAL, Sept. 20, 1863.—At nine A.M. this morning I was wounded and captured by the rebels. I was hurried to the rear as fast as possible, with quite a number of our wounded. We were taken to Steward's Hospital, which is situated some three miles from the battle-field. We were put out upon the ground, with no shelter whatever, and a great many of us had no blankets. There were some eighty of our wounded at this place. Dr. Hamilton (rebel) came round and examined our wounds; some of the worst cases were washed and partially dressed. Toward evening, all that were able were marched off. Captain McWilliams and Lieutenant Cole, of the Fifty-first Illinois infantry, were among them. About sundown we were forced to believe our troops were falling back. The rebels are jubilant. They say they have captured half of Rosecrans's army.

Sept. 21.—To-day the rebels have been so jubilant on what they term the "Yankee rout," that they have taken no notice of us whatever; the men are lying weltering in their blood, suffering beyond description.

Sept. 22.—To-day we had a man die. Dr. Story (rebel) has been put in charge of all the Yankee wounded. He appears to be a gentleman, but as yet there has been nothing done for the wounded, who are suffering intensely.

Sept. 23.—To-day the Doctor dressed most of the wounds. Many of the men have shattered limbs, and are suffering beyond description. We have had nothing to eat since we came here.

Sept. 24.—Two of our men died to-day. They had shattered limbs, and the worms had got into their wounds; had they had proper attention, they probably could have been saved.

Sept. 25.—The rebels say they have driven Rosecrans over the river, also Burnside out of East-Tennessee. The doctors are having a spree over it. No attention has been paid to us to-day. There are two or three hundred rebel wounded here that have to be attended to first. One man died to-day.

Sept. 26.—To-day we drew the first rations we have had since we came here. A ration consists of half a pint of corn-meal and two ounces of beef, a miserable pittance for a hungry man. No doctor has been near to-day. Some of the men are suffering intensely. The rebels don't seem to care how many of us die. Heavy firing in the direction of Chattanooga.

Sept. 27.—We lost one man by death to-day. Two of the boys have had limbs amputated; both will probably die. The boys are suffering a great deal from their wounds; mortification has taken place in many instances, while some have worms in their wounds. Many are very sick; no medicine to be had.

Sept. 28.—We lost two by death to-day; arteries burst; surgeon absent; bled to death. We have had nothing to eat to-day. I believe they mean to starve us to death. It is a pitiful sight to see the haggard countenances of the men. To-day they have sent two hundred rebel wounded to the hospitals.

Sept. 29.—Dr. Hamilton told us this morning that arrangements had been made to send us all through our lines. We drew rations to-day.

Sept. 30.—To-day the boys are trading their pocket-knives and every thing they can for rations. There is scarcely five dollars among us. The miserable thieves robbed us of every thing we had. To-day has been a day of intense suffering among our men. It has rained all day, and we have no shelter.

Oct. 1.—It rained all night last night. We look like a set of drowned rats. Some of the boys are very sick; many must die with such treatment. The sergeant of the guard procured a tent for eight of us. Dr. Story does all he can for us. We drew our pittance of corn-meal to-day.

Oct. 2.—We expect to leave here to-day. I sincerely hope we will. I long to be in God's country once more, and behold the good old flag again. The lice and filth here are intolerable.

Oct. 3.—No signs of leaving yet. Dr. Story is doing his best to make us comfortable, but we have no bandages to dress our wounds with. Two deaths to-day.

Oct. 4.—To-day is very cold. We have no blankets, hence there is a great deal of suffering from cold. Our rations have run out, and taking all things into consideration, it would be hard to embitter our condition.

Oct. 5.—Heavy cannonading has been going on in the front all day. The rebels say they are shelling Chattanooga. We learned to-day that the armistice was over, and that we would have to take a trip to Richmond. The trip will doubtless kill quite a number of us. We got our mush to-day. Intense suffering from cold nights.

Oct. 6.—We expected to leave here to-day for Atlanta, but for some reason the ambulances have not come. All we have to eat is mush, with little or no salt in it. Many are suffering from diarrhœa.

Oct. 7.—To-day we drew rations of flour. Captain Foster, Forty-second Illinois, is baking bread. One of our men died to-day. We have lost fourteen by death since we came here.

Oct. 8.—At nine A.M. this morning we were stowed in lumber-wagons and hauled to Ringgold, a distance of eight miles, over the roughest road I ever travelled. Many of the men were so sick that they could not raise their heads.

Oct. 9.—Last night they put one hundred and eighty of us into box-cars and brought us to Dalton, where we stopped for the night. We had to sleep in the cars, and they gave us no supper. The night was very cold. It was heart-rending to witness the suffering among the sick and wounded. This morning we left for Dalton without breakfast, and arrived at Atlanta, Ga., at six A.M. We were then taken to a military prison, where we now lie upon the ground with no shelter and no fires. Our wounds have not been dressed for three days; the stench is awful.

Oct. 10.—We are under the charge of our own doctors here, but the rebels won't furnish bandages to dress the wounds. I never suffered so from hunger in all my life. They have been promising us rations all day, and now they tell us they will be here early in the morning. The boys are selling their rings and every thing they have for something to eat.

Oct. 11.—We are a little more comfortable to-day; the surgeons have amputated several limbs and dressed all the wounds. One man died this morning. On the seventh instant, one of our men was shot by the guard for going too near the fence. One of our officers is here, carrying around a thirty-two pound ball and chain; several of the men are handcuffed.

Oct. 12.—Two men died last night. The wounded are doing pretty well under the treatment of our surgeons. We get a little better rations, but not half enough. Later: All the wounded that were able, were taken out of prison and put in tents; things are much more comfortable here.

Oct. 13.—This morning the names of all those who are able to travel were taken. We start for Richmond to-morrow. We drew five days' rations to-night—ten crackers and half a pound of pork to the man.

Oct. 14.—At two A.M. we fell in and marched down to the dépôt, a distance of one mile; many of us had to go on crutches. There were over two hundred of us, and we were put into five box-cars. Only those who experienced it know how we suffered on the train. For eight days we were jammed up in these cars. One of our number died, and we had to leave several at hospitals on the road. Our five days' rations lasted only two, and those who had no money had to share with the rest. Bread was a dollar a loaf, and pies sold as high as two dollars. The fifteenth, sixteenth, seventeenth, eighteenth, nineteenth, and twentieth were spent on the cars.

Oct. 21.—Arrived at Richmond and were put in Libby. Although we found this a miserable hole, it was much better than the filthy, lousy cars. When we got to Libby we were as nearly starved as men get to be, and navigate. We drew our rations here and got all our wounds dressed, although no surgeon was there.

Oct. 22.—To-day they have stopped our rations for punishment. Four men escaped from Castle Thunder last night. We get grub from our officers who are confined above, but we have to be very sly, as they allow no communications to be held between us and them.

Oct. 23.—They still keep our rations from us. The wounded are doing pretty well; but we are all so dirty and filthy it is a wonder we don't catch some contagious disease; we can get no soap to wash with.

Oct. 24.—This morning all the wounded were taken to the Alabama Hospital, and all those who were not wounded were sent to Belle Isle, to remain there until exchanged or starved to death, the latter the most probable.

Oct. 25.—We are much more comfortably situated than we were at Libby. We have a very good room, yet we have no blankets and have to sleep on the floor. There is no medicine even here.

Oct. 26.—Nothing of importance to-day.

Oct. 27.—To-day they took the names of one hundred and eighty-five of the worst wounded to exchange at nine P.M. We were put in a scow and started for City Point.

Oct. 28.—We are now on the flag of truce boat New-York. The Stars and Stripes float proudly above us, yet it is a sorrowful sight to see the poor boys, they look like skeletons. I venture not more than ten of our number will weigh one hundred pounds. I fear quite a number of the boys will die, they are beyond medical skill.

Oct. 29.—I feel like a white man now, the first time since I was captured. We are now in St. John's College Hospital. Each one of us had to take a good scrub, and was put into a clean shirt, after which, the most welcome of all things, came a beautiful roast. I trust our troubles are ended for a season.

Doc. 214.

BAXTER'S SPRINGS MASSACRE.

REPORT OF LIEUTENANT POND.

BAXTER'S SPRINGS, CHEROKEE NATION, Oct. 7, 1864.

COLONEL: I was attacked by Quantrell to-day with about six hundred and fifty men, and after one hour's hard fighting I am able to report to you that I still hold the camp, and the old flag floats over us as proudly as ever.

The attack was unexpected, as I had sent my cavalry out not more than an hour previous, to reconnoitre on the same road the enemy came in on. My men were at dinner when the attack was made, and most of them were obliged to break through the enemy's lines in order to get their arms, which were in camp. In doing this, four of my men were shot down. I was in my tent, about two hundred yards west of the camp, when I heard the first firing, (the reason of my tent being here was, that I had just arrived with reënforcements, and the camp was not large enough to accommodate the whole of my command, and I had just had the men at work extending the defences up to my quarters,) when I looked out and saw my camp surrounded by mounted men two ranks deep. I called what men were near me to get inside the fortifications if possible, at the same time I ran through the enemy's ranks myself, and got safely inside, where I found the enemy as numerous as my own men. In a moment every man was rallied, and we soon succeeded in driving the enemy outside the camp. This done, I called for men to get the howitzer, which stood just over the intrenchments, on the north side. Whether the men heard me or not I am unable to say, as the volleys of musketry and yells of the enemy nearly drowned every other noise. I got the howitzer at work myself, and after three shots into their ranks succeeded in repulsing their main force, which retreated in good order over the hill

north of the camp, where I heard firing, and supposed they had attacked my cavalry, which was then out; but on looking around, I discovered Major Henning, of our regiment, who had gallantly cut his way through the enemy and rescued three of my men who had been taken prisoners, and brought them safely to camp. The Major informed me that General Blunt was close by, and that the enemy were driving him, and called for cavalry to go to the General's relief. This I could not furnish him, as every effective man had been sent out in the morning, and all I had was twenty-five of my own company, C, and twenty of company D, Third Wisconsin cavalry, and fifty negroes, none of whom had serviceable horses. The Major thought that, under the circumstances, I could do no better than to hold my camp, while he went out in hopes to find General Blunt, and inform him that my camp was still in our possession. Shortly afterward I discovered that General Blunt's escort and band had been massacred, their wagons burned, and the bodies of the dead stripped of clothing and left upon the ground, and that the enemy had formed in line of battle on the prairie. At two o'clock a flag of truce approached; the bearer (George Todd) demanded the surrender of the camp, which being refused, he stated that he demanded, in the name of Colonel Quantrell, of the First regiment, First brigade, army of the South, an exchange of prisoners. I answered that I had taken no prisoners, as I had not been outside the intrenchments, and had no opportunity of taking any; that I had wounded some of his men, whom I had seen fall from their saddles, and would see that they were cared for, provided he would do the same by our men. He said he had twelve privates and the Adjutant-General (Major Curtis) prisoners, and that I had killed and wounded about fifty of his men, and if I would promise to take care of his wounded, and see that they were paroled after they were able to leave, he would promise me that no harm should befall Major Curtis or our men. This, I think, was intended as a blind, to find out what I had done, as they had already murdered Major Curtis and our prisoners. This evening, General Blunt came in accompanied by Mr. Tough, who, with six or eight men, had been following Quantrell on his retreat all the afternoon, and report that he crossed the Neosha at the Fort Gibson road, and went south. Is there a braver man living than the General? My loss is nine killed and sixteen wounded, (six of company C, Third Wisconsin cavalry,) Lieutenant Cook, of the Second colored, and John Fry, the express-rider, and one negro. As near as I can learn, the casualties of General Blunt are about eighty killed and six or seven wounded. Most of the killed are shot through the head, showing that they were taken prisoners and then murdered. Lieutenant Farr, Judge-Advocate, is among the murdered; also Henry Polloque, and the entire brigade band. Here allow me to make mention of some of the noble acts of some of my men. Sergeant McKenzie, of my company, exchanged eleven shots with a rebel officer, and succeeded in killing his horse. The man then dismounted and took to the timber; McKenzie followed him, and with but one shot in his revolver killed his man while his adversary was firing at him. Sergeant Smith, I think, was the coolest man on the ground, and did not fail to see that every order was obeyed to the letter. Sergeant Chestnut, company D, Third Wisconsin cavalry, commanded his company, and did nobly. The darkeys fought like devils; thirteen of them were wounded at the first round, and not one but that fought throughout the engagement. The number of the enemy killed, as far as I can learn, are eleven, and I know we wounded more than twice that number, which they carried off the field.

There are several other interesting items, which I will furnish you in a future report.

Very respectfully, your obedient servant,
JAMES B. POND,
First Lieut. Co. C, Third Wis. Cav., Com'd'g Post, Fort Blair.
To Lieutenant-Colonel C. W. BLAIR,
Commanding Post, Fort Scott.

MAJOR HENNING'S REPORT.

BAXTER'S SPRINGS, CHEROKEE NATION, Oct. 7, 1863.

COLONEL: I have the honor to report the following facts in regard to the fight at Baxter's Springs, Cherokee Nation, October 6, 1863.

On Sunday, the fourth, General Blunt, with the following members of his staff, namely, Major H. Z. Curtis, Assistant Adjutant-General, Major B. S. Henning, Provost-Marshal of District, Lieutenant Tappin, Second colored volunteers A. D. C., Lieutenant A. W. Farr, Judge-Advocate, together with the brigade band and all clerks in the different departments of district headquarters, and also an escort, consisting of forty men of company I, Third Wisconsin cavalry, under Lieutenant H. D. Banister, forty-five men of company A, Fourteenth Kansas cavalry, under Lieutenant Pierce, and the whole escort, under the command of Lieutenant J. G. Cavart, Third Wisconsin cavalry, and a train of eight wagons, transporting the effects of district headquarters, company effects, etc., left Fort Scott, for Fort Smith, Ark., and on that day marched six miles and camped. On the succeeding day marched thirty-four miles and camped on Cow Creek, and on Tuesday, the sixth instant, marched from Cow Creek to within a distance of eighty rods of a camp at Baxter's Springs, Cherokee Nation, and halted at twelve M., for the train to close up, as it had become somewhat scattered. The halt continued about fifteen minutes, and the command had just been given for the column to move, when horsemen were seen coming out of the woods, a distance of about eighty rods to the left, and forming in line. As we were so near Baxter's Springs, (although not in sight of it, by reason of an intervening ridge,) many supposed them to be our own troops drilling or returning from a scout. The General immediately ordered the two companies into line of battle, and the train to close up in rear of the line, which was done under the immediate direction of Major Curtis, Assistant Adjutant-General. At the same time a reconnoitre was made by Mr. Tough, a scout of the General's, who reported that the force were enemies, and that an engagement was going on at the Springs. I had ridden forward myself, and discovered that the force was large, and reported the same to the General, who then rode to reconnoitre for himself. At this time I discovered that the enemy were being reënforced from the south-west, on a line between us and the camp at Baxter's Springs, (the main body of the enemy being east of us,) and wishing to ascertain the condition of things in that quarter, I rode forward to the crest of the hill, where I saw that the camp was nearly surrounded by the enemy, and the fighting very brisk. While there, the stragglers of the enemy continued to pass from the south-west to their main body. Although within range of the camp, and receiving a straggling fire therefrom, I immediately commenced to fire upon these stragglers, and received their fire in return, and was seconded in this by Captain Tough and Stephen Wheeler, of company F, Third Wisconsin cavalry, both of whom acted with great bravery, and was just on the point of returning to our line, when I saw five mounted men (rebels) with three Federal soldiers prisoners, trying to pass as the others had done. I immediately recognized one of the prisoners as a private of company C, Third Wisconsin cavalry, one of the companies stationed at the Springs, (and belonging to my own regiment.) I determined to rescue them, and called to Tough and Wheeler to advance with me, but the former had just shot one rebel and was in close pursuit of another, in a direction taking him away from me. Wheeler advanced with me, and by pressing hard on the rebels and firing fast, we drove them, killing one, wounding another, and rescuing the prisoners, who all belonged to company C, Third Wisconsin cavalry. As the rebels escaped, they attempted to shoot their prisoners, and wounded one in the shoulder. As this was right under the fire of the camp, two of the prisoners made for the camp without stopping to say thank you; the other, and the one personally known to me, named Heaton, seemed so bewildered that I had to ride up to him, and force him to go in the right direction. All this had taken me over the brow of the hill, so that when I turned to go back, our forces were partially out of sight, but a few jumps of my horse brought them in sight again, and I saw them still in line of battle, while the enemy to the number of about four hundred and fifty were advancing upon them in line of battle, and firing very rapidly. I will here state that of the eighty-five men of our escort, twenty acted as rear-guard to the train, and did not form in line at all, leaving only sixty-five men in line, of which forty were of company A, Fourteenth Kansas cavalry, on the right; twenty-five, of company I, Third Wisconsin cavalry, on the left. At this time the distance between the two lines was not two hundred yards, and the enemy advancing at a walk firing, I had just time to notice these facts, when I saw two men in the centre of company A, Fourteenth Kansas, turn to run, but before they could fairly turn round, Major Curtis and the officers of the company forced them back, and I concluded the fight would be desperate, and was hopeful; but before the officers could get their places, the same two men and about eight more turned and ignominiously fled, which the enemy perceiving, the charge was ordered, and the whole line advanced with a shout, at which the remainder of company A, and despite the efforts of General Blunt, Major Curtis, Lieutenants Tappin and Pierce, could not be rallied. At this time a full volley was fired by company I, Third Wisconsin cavalry, which so staggered the right of the enemy, that I began to have hopes again; but as their left continued to advance, their right rallied, but were checked so much that their line, as seen by me, was crooked, their right being behind. The firing then became indiscriminate, and I saw that company I stood firing their revolvers until the enemy were within twenty feet, and then turned; but before any distance could be made the enemy were in their midst, and out of forty of the company, twenty-three were killed and six wounded, and left for dead upon the field. At this time my attention was attracted to my own danger, the enemy having advanced so fast as to cut me off from the rest, and after trying a couple of dodges, I succeeded in getting into camp at Baxter's Springs, all the while closely pursued; and found Lieutenant Pond, who was in command, busily engaged in firing a mountain howitzer outside his breastworks. The garrison at Baxter's Springs consisted of parts of two companies of Third Wisconsin cavalry, and one company of the Second Kansas colored regiment, the whole under the command of Lieutenant James B. Pond, of company C, Third Wisconsin cavalry. The camp had only been established a few days, and in that time Lieutenant Pond caused to be built a breastwork like a log-fence, on three sides of a square, in which were his tents and quarters. The attack on the camp had been a partial surprise, but the troops acted splendidly, and Lieutenant Pond, taking the exposed position outside the breastworks, loaded and fired the howitzer three times without any assistance, and the engagement was so close, that during this time some of the enemy had entered the breastworks; and at the time I entered the defences and got where Lieutenant Pond was, the bullets were pelting against the logs near by and all around him. As the fight with the force of General Blunt had been out of sight of the camp, Lieutenant Pond had been unable to tell what it meant, and very much surprised to see me, and in answer to my order for his cavalry, with which I hoped to be of some use to our scattered troops, told me, that he had that morning started out a forage train of eight wagons, and an escort of sixty men, who had gone in the direction from which the enemy had come, and he supposed they had been "gobbled up," and in response to his order only seven

men reported to me. With these I returned to the brow of the hill, in the direction of the first attack, and plainly saw the enemy engaged in sacking the wagons, and, while there, plainly saw the band brutally murdered. At the time of the attack the band-wagon, containing fourteen members of the brigade band, James O'Neal, special artist of Frank Leslie's Pictorial Newspaper, one young lad twelve years old, (servant of the leader of the band,) Henry Polloque, of Madison, Wis., and the driver, had undertaken to escape in a direction a little to the south of west, and made about half a mile, when one of the wheels of the wagon run off and the wagon sloped on the brow of the hill, in plain sight of where I stood. As the direction of the wagon was different from that in which most of the troops fled, it had not attracted such speedy attention, and the enemy had just got to it as I returned, giving me an opportunity to see every member of the band, Mr. O'Neal, the boy and the driver, shot, and their bodies thrown in or under the wagon, and it fired, so that when we went to them, all were more or less burned, and almost entirely consumed. The drummer-boy, a very interesting and intelligent lad, was shot and thrown under the wagon, and when the fire reached his clothes, it must have brought returned consciousness, as he had crawled a distance of thirty yards, marking the course by bits of burning clothes and scorched grass, and was found dead with all his clothes burned off except that portion between his back and the ground, as he lay on his back. A number of the bodies were brutally mutilated and indecently treated. Being satisfied that Lieutenant Pond could hold the camp against their force, I took two of the men and started out on the prairie in search of General Blunt, Major Curtis, or any other I could find, and in about an hour after, succeeded in hearing of the General's safety, and learned also that Major Curtis was supposed to be a prisoner, as his horse had been shot from under him. I learned this from a wounded soldier who had concealed himself in the grass, while the enemy had passed by him; and just then discovering a deserted horse and buggy, placed him in it with a man to take care of him, and they reached the camp in safety. The enemy were still in plain sight, and remained on the prairie till about four o'clock, when they marched south in a body. General Blunt and Major Curtis had tried to stop the flight of our troops from the start, and had several very narrow escapes in doing so, as the enemy were close upon them, and finally the General succeeded in collecting about ten men, and with these he worried the enemy, attacking them in small parties, and when pursued by too large a force, falling back until they turned, and then in turn, following them, so that at no time was he out of sight of the enemy, and most of the time close enough to worry and harass them. As they withdrew from the field, he searched for and took care of the wounded, and remained upon the ground till they were all taken in and cared for, and then went into camp. The ground on which the fight took place, is a rolling prairie, extending west a long distance, covered with grass and intersected with deep ravines, gullies, on the banks of which grow willow bushes, sufficient to conceal any difficulty in crossing, but not sufficient to protect from observation; and in retreating, many of our men were overtaken at these ravines, and killed while endeavoring to cross. Major Curtis had become separated from the General, and while riding by the side of Lieutenant Pierce, his horse was shot and fell. All supposed he was taken prisoner by the enemy, being close upon them, and Lieutenant Pierce saw him alive in their hands. The next day his body was found where his horse had fallen, and he was, without doubt, killed, after having surrendered. Thus fell one of the noblest of all the patriots who have offered up their lives for the cause of their country. Major H. Z. Curtis was a son of Major-General Curtis, and served with his father during his memorable campaign through Arkansas, and was present with him at the battle of Pea Ridge, where he did good service as aid to his father. When General Curtis took command of the Department of Missouri, the Major remained with him as Assistant Adjutant-General on his staff, and when General Curtis was relieved of that command, the Major sought for and obtained an order to report to General Blunt as Assistant Adjutant-General, and in that position had done much toward regulating and systematizing the business of district headquarters of Kansas and the Frontier; and on General Blunt determining to take the field, Major Curtis accompanied him with alacrity, parting with his young and affectionate wife at Fort Scott, on the fourth of October, and met his horrible fate at Baxter's Springs, on Tuesday, sixth October. All who knew Major Curtis, acknowledged his superior abilities, and in his particular duties he had no equal. Beloved by the General and all his staff, his loss has cast a gloom over us, "whose business is to die," unusual and heartfelt. In looking over the field, the body of Lieutenant Farr was found near to where the first attack was made, with marks of wounds by buck-shots and bullets. The Lieutenant was unarmed at the time of the attack, and had been riding in a carriage, but had evidently jumped therefrom and attempted to escape on foot. Lieutenant A. W. Farr was a prominent young lawyer, from Geneva, Wisconsin, and had been a partner of General B. F. Butler, at Worcester, Mass. At the time of the breaking out of the rebellion he took a patriotic view of the difficulty, and although a strong Democrat, like General Butler, had accepted a position where he thought he could be of service to his country, and has fallen in the good cause. Well does the writer of this, remember the night before his death, while we were lying on the ground with our blankets over us, the Lieutenant said, it was not ambition nor gain, that prompted him to enter the army, but only that he might do his mite toward crushing the rebellion; that he did not seek promotion, but was willing to serve where he could do the most good. Truly, a patriot was lost when Lieutenant Farr was killed. Other dead, many of them brave and true men, were scattered and strewn over the ground for over a mile or two, most with balls through their heads, showing that they were killed after having surrendered, which the testimony of the wounded corroborates. They were told in every instance, that if they would surrender and deliver up their arms, they should be treated as prisoners of war, and upon doing so, were immediately shot down. Sergeant Jack Splane, company I, Third Wisconsin cavalry, was treated in this way, and the fiend who shot him, after taking his arms, said: "Tell old God, that the last man you saw on earth, was Quantrell." Sergeant Splane is now alive, although he received five balls, one in his head, one through his chest, one through his bowels, and the other in his leg and arm. Private Jesse Smith was shot nearly as bad, and under the same circumstances; but he did not lose his consciousness, and says, that the rebel who shot him, and as he lay upon his face, jumped upon his back, and essayed to dance, uttering the most vile imprecations. Some unarmed citizens who were with us, were killed, and their bodies stripped of clothing. Take it all in all, there has perhaps not a more horrible affair (except the massacre at Lawrence, in Kansas) happened during the war, and brands the perpetrators as cowards and brutes. I will here also state that a woman and child were shot at the camp, but both will recover. It was done premeditatedly and not by random shots, and the brute who shot the child, was killed by a shot from the revolver of Sergeant McKenzie, company C, Third Wisconsin cavalry. I respectfully call your attention to the facts set forth in this report, in hopes that the Government will see fit to retaliate for the actions of this band of desperadoes, who are recognized and acknowledged by the confederate authorities, and whose report of this affair stated that the brutality of the beast, was exultingly published by the confederate papers, and approved by the confederate officials. Captain A. N. Campbell, Fourteenth Kansas volunteers, while a prisoner in the hands of the enemy, at Fort Smith, Arkansas, was in presence of this man Quantrell, and heard him say, that he never did and never would take any prisoners, and was boasting of the number of captured soldiers he had caused to be shot, stating particulars, etc. These facts should be published to the civilized world, that all may know the character of the people against whom we are contending. I would also respectfully call the attention of the General Commanding to the fact that passes in and out of the posts of Sedalia, Springfield, and Kansas City, signed by the commanders of the posts, and also permits to carry arms, were found on the bodies of a number of the rebels killed in the fight, and from them and other papers there is no doubt but that a portion of Quantrell's force was made up of persons belonging to the Missouri militia. I desire to take special notice of the bravery and coolness of Lieutenant James B. Pond, company C, Third Wisconsin cavalry, commanding the camp, Sergeant R. McKenzie, of company C, Third Wisconsin cavalry, and Sergeant R. W. Smith, of said company.

The number of the killed is as follows:

Major N. Z. Curtis, Lieutenant A. W. Farr, Lieutenant Cook, ...	3
Members of the brigade band, ...	14
Clerks and orderlies, ...	6
Company A, Fourteenth Kansas, ...	18
" I, Third Wisconsin cavalry, ...	23
" C, " " (in camp)	6
Citizens, ...	10
	80
Wounded, ...	18
Total, ...	98

The loss of the enemy, as far as known, is between twenty and thirty.

Very respectfully, your obedient servant,

B. S. HENNING,
Major Third Wisconsin Cavalry.

To COLONEL O. D. GREEN,
Assistant Adjutant-General, Department of Missouri, St. Louis.

LIEUTENANT-COLONEL BLAIR'S REPORT.

HEADQUARTERS FORT SCOTT, KANSAS, }
October 15, 1863. }

SIR: I have the honor to report to you, for the information of the Major-General Commanding, the following particulars, as far as they came to my knowledge, or under my observation, of the late disaster at Baxter's Springs.

On the fourth instant Major-General Blunt, his staff, consisting of Major B. S. Henning, Third Wisconsin cavalry, Provost-Marshal; Major H. Z. Curtis, Assistant Adjutant-General; Lieutenant J. E. Tappin, Second Colorado cavalry, A.D.C.; and Lieutenant A. W. Farr, Third Wisconsin cavalry, Judge-Advocate; his clerks and orderlies, the brigade band, and parts of two companies of cavalry, respectively under the command of Lieutenants Robert Pierce, Fourteenth Kansas, cavalry, and Josiah G. Cavart, Third Wisconsin cavalry, left this place for Fort Blunt, Cherokee Nation. About four o'clock on the morning of the seventh instant, Lieutenant Tappin returned, informing me that about one o'clock the day previous, General Blunt had been attacked, within a few hundred yards of Lieutenant Pond's camp, at Baxter's Springs, and the entire command, except the General himself and about ten men, either killed or taken prisoners, and the baggage and transportation captured and destroyed. He also informed me that the General could not be persuaded to come away, but remained with his few men, hanging near the enemy, to watch their movements, and succor any of the wounded who might be left alive, while he despatched him (the Lieutenant) to me to inform me of the circum-

stances. The Lieutenant further stated, that as the enemy came over the brow of the hill, just from the direction of Pond's camp, it seemed without a doubt, that his little force had been captured, and destroyed also. He was further under the impression that Majors Curtis and Henning, and Lieutenant Farr, were prisoners.

Within an hour I was *en route* to the General's relief, with three companies of the Twelfth Kansas infantry, two companies of the Second Kansas colored infantry, and about one hundred cavalry, under Lieutenants Josling and Clark. Twenty miles out, I met a despatch from General Blunt, that he was safe with Lieutenant Pond, who had been fortunate enough to repulse the enemy in their attack on his camp. I pushed on, however, without relaxation, and arrived at the Springs, a distance of seventy miles, in the afternoon of the second day, although it was the first heavy marching the infantry had ever attempted. On my arrival I found that the General had sent off every mounted man he could find, either as scouts or messengers, and had notified the officers in command on the line of the Arkansas River, of the disaster at the Springs, the direction in which the enemy was heading, and when he would probably cross the river.

The graves were being dug and the dead carried in for burial as I arrived. It was a fearful sight; some eighty-five bodies, nearly all shot through the head, most of them shot from five to seven times each, horribly mangled, and charred, and blackened by fire. The wounded, who numbered six or seven, were all shot at least six times, and it is a remarkable fact that with the exception of Bennett, of the Third Wisconsin cavalry, all who were alive when they were brought in, are in a fair way of final recovery.

The circumstances of the double conflict, as well as I can gather them on the spot, are about these:

Quantrell, with a force variously estimated at from six hundred to one thousand, was passing south, on the border line of counties in Missouri, and made a detour to attack the camp at Baxter's Springs, which up to that time had been defended by one company of colored men, under Lieutenant Cook, and a fragment of company D of the Third Wisconsin cavalry only. Fortunately, however, on the day before, I had sent Lieutenant James B. Pond, with part of another company of the Third Wisconsin cavalry, and a mountain howitzer. The cavalry was, however, all absent with a forage-train; but the blacks, the dismounted men of the cavalry, the howitzer, and Lieutenant Pond were still left. The first attack of the enemy, twelve M. of the sixth instant, was so sudden and impetuous, that he was inside the rude breastworks and firing pistol-shots into the tents before our forces recovered from the surprise into which they were thrown by the onset. They rallied, however, promptly and gallantly, under the directions of the Lieutenant, and after a severe struggle, repulsed the enemy, and drove him outside the fortifications. He then concentrated his forces for a more careful attack—formed in line of battle—but before the word could be given to charge, Lieutenant Pond opened upon them with the little howitzer, getting outside of his breastworks to operate it, which again threw them into confusion, and drove them over the brow of the hill. At this point, it seems, they first perceived General Blunt's little column, which had halted for the wagons and band to close up, and immediately formed in line to attack it. They formed in two lines, one on the prairie, and the other under the cover of the timber, and commenced the advance. Coming in the direction they did, the General of course, supposed it was Lieutenant Pond's cavalry, either on drill, or coming out to receive him. For safety, however, he formed his little force in line of battle, and sent the wagons, with the band, clerks, orderlies, cooks, and other non-combatants, to the rear, and then rode about fifty paces to the front, accompanied by his staff, to reconnoitre, and endeavor to ascertain to a certainty what the approaching force was. Whatever doubts he may have entertained were soon dispelled, for the front line, pouring a volley, and raising the guerrilla yell, charged forward at full speed. The General turning in his saddle to order his body-guard to advance and fire, saw with shame and humiliation, the whole of it in disgraceful flight over the prairie. There was nothing left for it then, but to follow and attempt to rally them ; he accordingly turned with his staff-officers, all except Major Henning, to endeavor to overtake the fugitives. By this time the enemy were upon and all around them, and their escape with life seemed almost a miracle.

At this time too, it seems to have struck Major Henning that the enemy approached from an angle which might miss Lieutenant Pond's camp, and that consequently, he might be safe. With this thought he determined to strike for the camp, and endeavor to bring Pond's forces to the assistance of the General. Accordingly, he charged straight forward at full speed, passing through a shower of bullets, and through the enemy's line ; deflecting a little to the right, he was over the brow of the hill before the enemy could recover from his astonishment at the daring feat. About half-way from the brow of the hill to the camp, he saw a party of five guerrillas, who had taken three of Lieutenant Pond's men prisoners, and were hurrying them off ; as they were directly in his way, and a much larger force behind him, he was cool enough to reflect that temerity was here discretion, and instantaneously charged them. He shot two of them, killing one, and frightening the others so badly that they abandoned the prisoners and took to flight. He then approached the camp at full speed, swinging his cap around his head, to announce that he was a friend, and after narrowly escaping being shot by our men, at length arrived there in safety. He here learned of the attack on the camp, and that not a cavalry man was left, all being absent with the forage-train.

The distant sounds of the battle showed already that infantry was useless ; and he again turned his horse's head in the direction of the field, and solitary and alone, forced his way through the scattered bands of the enemy back to the side of his chief and his little band of supporters. History should not fail to record such deeds of gallantry and devotion.

General Blunt, in his endeavor to rally his men as fast he could catch up with them, was frequently thrown behind, and several times almost surrounded, although mounted in a superior manner. He finally rallied some fifteen men, and charging his foremost pursuers, compelled them in turn to retire. He then started Lieutenant Tappin, with four men, to me, and determined with the balance to watch the enemy. They killed our men as fast as they caught them, sparing none. The members of the band were shot as they sat in the band-wagon, and it was then set on fire. They rifled all the trunks, boxes, etc., in the different wagons, and then set them on fire, with the bodies of the teamsters in them, and all others who happened to be in them when taken. The non-combatants were slaughtered as ruthlessly as the soldiers. Lieutenant Farr was killed early in the struggle. Major Curtis came very near escaping, although his full uniform and showy horse made him a conspicuous mark ; he was some distance in advance of his pursuers, when, just as his horse was gathering himself to spring over a deep ravine, he was struck on the hip with a ball, which so stung or frightened him, that he missed his leap, and falling short, threw the Major over his head. The horse gathered himself almost instantly and galloped wildly over the prairie. The Major was first taken prisoner and then brutally murdered. Thus died as gallant a soldier and as true a gentleman as ever drew a sword in defence of his country. It may well be said of him, as of Chevalier Bayard of old, "he was without fear and without reproach."

The enemy, seeing that General Blunt persistently kept them in view, keeping away if pursued, and returning as soon as the pursuit slackened, were no doubt forced to believe that a large force was approaching, of which he was only the advance. His persistent following them up, doubtless riveted this conclusion in their minds, as they hurried through their wholesale work of slaughter, and then moved off slowly to the South. General Blunt hovered near them till near night, and then returned to the melancholy work of caring for the wounded and collecting the dead. But few were left alive, as their evident intention was to kill all. The bodies of Major Curtis and Lieutenant Farr were not found until the next day.

Lieutenant Pond is entitled to great credit for his gallant defence of his camp ; and Lieutenant Pierce, who strove hard to rally the flying soldiers. But the men seemed struck by a sudden and uncontrollable panic, and I met many of them within ten miles of Fort Scott as I moved out with my force.

The enemy left between twenty and thirty dead on the field ; as their wounded were taken away with some ambulances and buggies they captured, it is impossible to state their number.

Disastrous as this engagement has been, it would undoubtedly have been as bad, if not worse, if General Blunt and his little force had not been near. In that event, a more careful and combined attack would have been made on Pond's camp, and with the force around it, must finally have succumbed, and every person there would undoubtedly have been put to death.

The names and number (accurately) of our killed and wounded will be forwarded in a subsequent report.

I have the honor to be, your obedient servant,
                                    CHAS. W. BLAIR,
                            Lieutenant-Colonel Commanding.
Colonel O. D. GREEN,
    Assistant Adjutant-General, Department Missouri, St. Louis.

Doc. 215.

ELECTION IN MARYLAND.

LETTER FROM GOVERNOR BRADFORD.

EXECUTIVE OFFICE, ANNAPOLIS, }
October 31, 1863. }

To His Excellency, President Lincoln:

SIR : Rumors are to-day current, and they reach me in such a shape that I am bound to believe them, that detachments of soldiers are to be despatched on Monday next to several of the counties of the State, with a view of being present at their polls on Wednesday next, the day of our State election. These troops are not residents of the State, and consequently are not sent for the purpose of voting, and as there is no reason, in my opinion, to apprehend any riotous or violent proceedings at this election, the inference is unavoidable that these military detachments, if sent, are expected to exert some control or influence in that election. I am also informed that orders are to be issued from this Military Department, on Monday, presenting certain restrictions or qualifications on the right of suffrage—of what precise character I am not apprised—which the Judges of Election will be expected to observe. From my knowledge of your sentiments on these subjects, as expressed to Hon. R. Johnson, in my presence, on the twenty-second instant, as also disclosed in your letter of instruction to General Schofield, since published, in reference to the Missouri election, I cannot but think that the orders above referred to are without your personal knowledge ; and I take the liberty of calling the subject to your attention, and invoking your interposition to countermand them. I cannot but feel that to suffer any military interference in the matter of our election, or to prescribe any test of oath to voters when all the candidates in the State—with the exception, perhaps, of two or three in one Congressional District, are all loyal men—would be justly obnoxious to the public sentiment of the State. There are other reasons why

such proceedings would appear as an offensive discrimination against our State. Our citizens are aware that highly important elections have recently taken place in other States, without, as it is believed, any such interference by the Government authorities ; and if votes by hundreds of thousands have been allowed to be cast there without objection, and with no limit upon the elective franchise other than the State laws prescribe, and where one, at least, of the candidates so supported was considered so hostile to the Government that for months past he has been banished from the country, certainly any such interference as between the loyal men now candidates in this State would, under such comparisons, be more justly objectionable, and finds nothing in the present condition of things here to justify it. I rely therefore upon your Excellency for such an order as will prevent it.

I have the honor to be, with great respect, your Excellency's obedient servant,
                                    A. W. BRADFORD

REPLY OF PRESIDENT LINCOLN.

WAR DEPARTMENT, WASHINGTON, }
November 2, 1863. }

To His Excellency A. W. Bradford, Governor of Maryland :

SIR : Yours of the thirty-first ultimo was received yesterday, about noon, and since then I have been giving most earnest attention to the subject matter of it. At my call General Schenck has attended, and he assures me that it is almost certain that violence will be used at some of the voting-places on election day, unless prevented by his provost-guards. He says that at some of those places the Union voters will not attend at all, or run a ticket, unless they have some assurance of protection. This makes the Missouri case of my action, in regard to which you express your approval.

The remaining point of your letter is a protest against any person offering to vote being put to any test not found in the laws of Maryland. This brings us to a difference between Missouri and Maryland, with the same reason in both States. Missouri has, by law, provided a test for the voter with reference to the present rebellion, while Maryland has not. For example, General Trimble, captured fighting us at Gettysburgh, is, without recanting his treason, a legal voter by the laws of Maryland. Even General Schenck's order admits him to vote, if he recants upon oath. I think that is cheap enough. My order in Missouri, which you approve, and General Schenck's order here, reach precisely the same end. Each assures the right of voting to all loyal men, and whether a man is loyal each allows that man to fix by his own oath. Your suggestion that nearly all the candidates are loyal I do not think quite meets the case. In this struggle for the nation's life, I cannot so confidently rely on those whose election may have depended upon disloyal votes. Such men, when elected, may prove true, but such votes are given them in the expectation that they will prove false. Nor do I think that to keep the peace at the polls, and to prevent the persistently disloyal from voting, constitutes just cause of offence to Maryland. I think she has her own example for it. If I mistake not, it is precisely what General Dix did when your Excellency was elected Governor. I revoke the first of the three propositions in General Schenck's General Order No. 53, not that it is wrong in principle, but because the military being, of necessity, exclusive judges as to who shall be arrested, the provision is liable to abuse. For the revoked part I substitute the following:

That all provost-marshals and other military officers do prevent all disturbance and violence at or about the polls, whether offered by such persons as above described, or by any other person or persons whatsoever.

The other two propositions of the order I allow to stand. General Schenck is fully determined, and has my strict order besides, that all loyal men may vote, and vote for whom they please.

Your obedient servant,
A. LINCOLN,
President of the United States.

Doc. 216.

THE PURSUIT OF SHELBY.

GEN. JOHN McNEIL'S REPORT.

HEADQUARTERS FRONTIER DISTRICT,
FORT SMITH, November 1, 1863.

GENERAL: I have the honor to report the following facts as the result of the expedition, to the command of which I was verbally ordered at St. Louis on the ninth of October:

I arrived at Lebanon on the twelfth, and finding that Lieutenant-Colonel Quin Morton had marched to Linn Creek with a detachment of the Twenty-third Missouri infantry volunteers, and another of the Second Wisconsin cavalry, and that he expected to be joined by a detachment of the Sixth and Eighth cavalry, Missouri State militia, I ordered Major Eno, in command, to fall back on Lebanon, and proceeded to Buffalo, where I found Colonel John Edwards, Eighteenth Iowa volunteers, in command, with a few cavalry and some enrolled militia. I at once addressed myself to the work of concentrating force enough for pursuit when the enemy should cross the Osage on his retreat south.

With about two hundred and sixty men and a section of Rabb's battery, I marched to Bolivar, where General Holland was in camp with part of two regiments enrolled militia, and a demi-battery under Lieutenant Stover. Leaving the General directions to observe and pursue Coffee and Hunter, if they should cross the Osage at Warsaw, I marched in the direction of Lamar, via Humansville and Stockton, to cut off Shelby, who was reported in full flight south of Snybar, with General Ewing in pursuit. At Stockton I was joined by Major King, Sixth cavalry, Missouri State militia, with three hundred and seventy-five men of the Sixth and Eighth Missouri State militia. The force had entered Humansville from the north, in pursuit of Hunter and Coffee, four hours after I had passed through it toward the west.

Major King attacked and drove this force through Humansville, capturing their last cannon.

Finding that Shelby had passed through Stockton in advance of me, I marched to Greenfield and Sarcoxie, via Bower's Mill, and on the night of the nineteenth camped at Keitsville, when I learned of scouts of Colonel Phelps, commanding at Cassville, that the enemy had crossed the telegraph road at Cross-Timbers that day about noon.

I kept up a rapid pursuit, following the trail of our flying foe via Sugar Creek and Early's Ferry, to Huntsville; our advance party, entering Huntsville with a dash, took quite a number of soldiers of Brooks's rebel command, with their horses and arms. I was there joined by Colonel Edwards, Eighteenth Iowa infantry, with three hundred men of his regiment, and Major Hunt, First Arkansas cavalry volunteers, one hundred and seventy-five men and two mountain howitzers. This gave me an effective force of six hundred cavalry and three hundred infantry, with four guns, two of these being twelve-pounder mountain howitzers; these last would have been a much greater acquisition to me than they proved had they been properly supplied with ammunition. They were sent from Fayetteville with only sixty-seven rounds for the two howitzers, and of course could not be relied upon for any length of time.

We had here information that Shelby and Brooks had united their forces on War Eagle Creek, and that Hunter and Coffee were also there; the combined force amounting to two thousand five hundred men. We marched toward this camp to attack, but found that the enemy had gone.

On the twenty-fourth, we marched across a tremendous mountain, called Buffalo Mountain, and found the enemy in camp in a snug little valley on the other side, attacked and drove him, at sundown dropping into his camp. The mountain on the other side was too steep and the passes too narrow for a night pursuit, and we had to content ourselves by waiting for the light of morning. At early dawn we struck again into the mountains; our advance under Major Hunt, First Arkansas cavalry, was skirmishing with the enemy all day, driving them before us. On the twenty-sixth, while engaged in an attack on the enemy's rear-guard, who were posted in a narrow pass, Lieutenant Robinson, of the First Arkansas cavalry, was mortally wounded; he was brought into camp, and died that night at ten o'clock.

On the twenty-seventh, we marched into Clarksville, and learned that Shelby had made good his escape, and crossed the river, and that Brooks had gone down into the valley of Big Piney, with about four hundred men, with instructions to pick up stragglers from the rebel army, and to cut off any train that might be coming to me from Fayetteville.

My cavalry and artillery horses were too badly used up to admit of pursuit across the river, so I turned my course toward Fort Smith. At a point four miles north of Ozark, I sent Colonel Catherwood, with the men of the Sixth and Eighth regiments Missouri State militia, and Major Hunt, with the men and howitzers of the First cavalry Arkansas volunteers, to Springfield and Fayetteville. I arrived in Fort Smith on the evening of the thirtieth. Although I have been disappointed in my earnest hope to attack and destroy the force under Shelby, I feel confident of having done all man could do under the circumstances. We have driven the enemy so that he had to stick to the road, and thus prevented a widely extended pillage, both in Arkansas and Missouri.

We have taken forty-four prisoners, besides discharging as many more, who were conscripts. We have killed and wounded many of his men, and driven numbers to the mountains, where he will not easily get them again. The captures in horses were also large.

My officers and men bore the fatigue and exposure of this campaign without tents and on small rations, in a manner to excite my admiration. Colonels Edwards and Catherwood were earnest in their coöperation in duty. Majors King, Eno, and Hunt, were always ready for any duty assigned them. Major King deserves special mention for his gallant attack on the enemy at Humansville, on the fifteenth, in which he captured the last cannon the enemy brought into Missouri with him—a six-pounder brass gun. Major Hunt, with his battalion of Arkansans, were, on account of their knowledge of the country, pushed forward in the advance from Huntsville to Clarksville; this duty was promptly and cheerfully performed by the Major and his gallant command, who drove the enemy from every position, killing and wounding many, and taking prisoners at every charge.

To Captain Rabb, Chief of Artillery, and Lieutenant Whicker, Rabb's battery, and Johnson's section of howitzers, I am under obligations for services which mark them as true soldiers. Lieutenant Baubie, Quartermaster of the Eighth Missouri State militia, acted as Chief Quartermaster of the expedition, and gave unqualified satisfaction. Lieutenant Sell, Commissary of the same regiment, acted as Chief Commissary, acquitting himself with great credit.

Captain Hopkins, First Arkansas cavalry, joined me at Clarksville with thirty-four men. I had sent him from Buffalo on the thirteenth toward Duroc, to observe the enemy and report his motions. While on this duty, he ran on to the enemy in force, killing six, and losing but two of his own men. The day after he joined me, he attacked a party belonging to Brooks, of one hundred and fifty strong, and drove them back upon a detachment of the Third Wisconsin cavalry, that had been sent from Van Buren in pursuit of this party, taking several horses, and killing and wounding six of the enemy. The Captain is a most active and efficient scout, and a brave soldier.

The health of the command has been uniformly good. We had but three sick men in all the troops.

I have the honor to be, General, your obedient servant,

JOHN McNEIL,
Brigadier-General Volunteers.

POETRY AND INCIDENTS.

OUR COUNTRY'S CALL.

BY JOHN PIERPONT.

Air—*Scots wha Hae.*

Men who plough your granite peaks,
O'er whose head the Eagle shrieks,
And for aye of *Freedom* speaks,
   Hear your Country's call!
Swear, each loyal mother's son,
Swear " Our Country shall be ONE !"
Seize your sword, or bring your gun,
   Bayonet and ball !

For the land that bore you—Arm !
Shield the State you love from harm !
Catch, and round you spread the alarm ;
   Hear, and hold your breath !
Hark ! the hostile horde is nigh !
See ! the storm comes roaring by !
Hear and heed our battle-cry :
   " VICTORY OR DEATH !"

Sturdy landsmen, hearty tars,
Can you see your Stripes and Stars
Flouted by the three broad bars,
   And cold-blooded feel !
There the rebel banner floats !
Tyrants, vanquished by your votes,
Spring, like bloodhounds, at your throats ;
   Let them bite your *steel !*

With no traitor at their head ;
By no braggart coward led,
By no hero caught abed,
   While he dreams of flight ;
By no " Young Napoleons,"
Kept at bay by wooden guns,
Shall our brothers and our sons,
   Be held back from fight !

Like a whirlwind in its course,
Shall *again* a rebel force,
Jackson's foot or Stuart's horse,
   Pass our sleepy posts ;
Roam, like Satan, " to and fro,"
And our Laggard let them go ?
No ! in thunder answer, " *No !*
   By the Lord of Hosts !"

With the Lord of Hosts we fight,
For his Freedom, Law, and Right—
Strike for *these,* and his all-might
   Shall with victory crown
Loyal brows, alive or dead,
Crush each crawling Copperhead,
And, in bloody battle, tread
   This rebellion down !

Talk of " Peace " in hours like this !
'Tis Iscariot's traitor kiss !
'Tis the Old Serpent's latest hiss!
   Foil his foul intrigue !
Plant your heel his head upon !
Let him squirm ! his race is run !
Now to keep your Country *one,*
   Join our Union League !

LIBERTY NOT DEAD.

Written in reply to a poem, " Liberty—Dead," which appeared in the *Cincinnati Enquirer,* by Mrs. Alice Key Pendleton, daughter of the author of The Star-Spangled Banner.

What though the daughter of a sire
   Who gave the noblest song
To grace a nation's poetry
   That echo shall prolong,
Whose matchless words and trumpet tones
   Make dying soldiers strong ;

What though she sing in cadenced verse
   That Liberty is dead,
And softly chides the gathered crowd
   By whom no tears are shed,
Though powerless seems the snowy hand,
   And marble-like the head—

She wrongs the men who, fearless, stood
   By dark Antietam's side,
And those whose patriot-blood, outpoured,
   The plain of Shiloh dyed,
And those who braved the iron hail
   On Mississippi's tide.

She wrongs the *fathers, mothers,* who
   Their children send to war ;
For *them* great Liberty still lives—
   Still shineth as a star,
Which passing clouds a moment hide,
   Without the power to mar.

What though a moment pallid *now,*
   And lustreless her eye,
The people's will her mighty breath,
   She cannot, *dare not die ;*
In homes like ours, her glorious lot
   Is *Immortality.*

Thus living, and to live for aye,
   On mountain or in hall,
In vain will rhythmic verse essay
   To spread her funeral pall,
And tell her children, Liberty,
   Alas ! is dead to all

Ah! no, her march o'er mountain-tops
  Shall be from sea to sea,
Her music as she sweeps along,
  The *glorious song* of KEY!
The patriot statesman's stirring song,
  The Anthem of the Free!   L. A. C.

GATEWOOD FARM, Kenton Co., Ky.

ONE VOICE.

BY MINNIE FRY.

One who sat at home in silence
  Saw the army hurrying by,
And her thoughts gave echo faintly
  To their eager battle-cry.

" Ah!" she sang, "some wrong is hidden
  Under all our high endeavor;
We shall fail, and fail forever,
  Till we work as we are bidden;
Till the last red chain we sever,
  Linking us to sin and wrong.
What although the tie be strong?
  Yet the spirit sword is stronger,
Keen to sever good from ill;
  Ready, when we doubt no longer,
All God's purpose to fulfil,
  Ready, waiting for our hand;
Shall our hands hang slack beside us,
  Idle till some good betide us
While the war-cloud glooms the land?"

" Rise, O youth, in strength and glory,
  Age with wisdom deep and calm;
Minstrel tune for lofty story;
  Women pour the healing balm.
Let the earth feel your upstarting;
  Shame on those who careless stand,
While the glory is departing
  From the threshold of our land;
Come with freedom for the nation,
  Freedom for *each man* therein;
Spread the glorious proclamation,
  Though it be accounted sin;
Though upon the lofty places,
  Where ambition spreads her lure,
There be pallid, fear-struck faces—
  Make the glorious end secure."

" Ah!" she sang, "so few are dreaming
  Of the perfect end of peace;
Ah!" she sang, "so many scheming
  How the strife may soonest cease;
Ah! so many name and station
  And the watchword of the nation
To ignoble purpose lend;
  Here and there a lofty spirit
Shall the hight of love inherit
  Faithful found unto the end."

But the end looks through the distance,
  Faint and far off, like a star;
Never, save through *upward climbing*,
  Reach we where its glories are.

PLEASANT RIDGE, O.

THE OLD SHIP OF STATE.

BY DAVID BARKER, OF EXETER, ME.

O'er the dark and gloomy horizon that bounds her,
Through the storm and the night and the hell that
  surrounds her,

I can see, with a faith which immortals have given,
Burning words, blazing out o'er the portals of Heaven—
        " She will live!"

But a part of the freight which our forefathers gave
  her
We must cast to the deep yawning waters to save
  her—
'Tis the *chain of the slave* we must fling out to light her,
'Tis the *brand* and the *whip* we must yield up to right
  her.
        She will live!

Clear the decks of the curse! If opposed by the
  owner,
Hurl the wretch to the wave, as they hurled over
  Jonah;
With a " Freedom to all!" gleaming forth from our
  banner,
Let the tyrant yet learn we have freemen to man her.
        She will live!

She will live while a billow lies swelling before her,
She will live while the blue arch of heaven bends o'er
  her,
While the name of a Christ to the fallen we cherish,
Till the hopes in the breast of humanity perish.
        She will live!

REPLY TO THE BONNIE BLUE FLAG.*

BY ISAAC M. BALL.

We're fighting for our Union,
  We're fighting for our trust,
We're fighting for the happy land
  Where sleeps our Fathers' dust.
It cannot be dissevered,
  Though it cost us bloody wars;
We never can give up the land
  Where float the Stripes and Stars.
    CHORUS—Hurrah! Hurrah!
          For equal rights, hurrah!
          Hurrah for the good old flag
          That bears the Stripes and Stars.

We trusted you as brothers,
  Until you drew the sword,
With impious hands at Sumter,
  You cut the silver cord.
So now you hear our bugles,
  We come, the sons of Mars,
To rally round the brave old flag
  That bears the Stripes and Stars.
      CHORUS—Hurrah! hurrah! etc.

We do not want your cotton,
  We care not for your slaves,
But rather than divide the land
  We'll fill your Southern graves.
With Lincoln for our chieftain,
  We wear our country's scars,
We'll rally round the brave old flag
  That bears the Stripes and Stars.
      CHORUS—Hurrah! hurrah! etc.

We deem our cause most holy,
  We know we're in the right,
And twenty million freemen
  Stand ready for the fight.

* See page 84, Poetry and Incidents, Vol. IV., REBELLION RECORD.

Our pride is fair Columbia,
　No stain her beauty mars ;
On her we'll raise the brave old flag
　That bears the Stripes and Stars.
　　　　Chorus—Hurrah, hurrah ! etc.

And when this war is over,
　We'll each resume our home,
And treat you still as brothers
　Wherever you may roam ;
We'll pledge the hand of friendship,
　And think no more of war,
But dwell in peace beneath the flag
　That bears the Stripes and Stars.
　　　　Chorus—Hurrah ! hurrah ! etc.

THE SECOND LOUISIANA.

MAY 27TH, 1863.

BY GEORGE H. BOKER.

Dark as the clouds of even,
Ranked in the western heaven,
Waiting the breath that lifts
All the dread mass, and drifts
Tempest and falling brand
Over a ruined land—
So, still and orderly,
Arm to arm, knee to knee,
Waiting the great event,
Stands the Black Regiment.

Down the long dusky line
Teeth gleam and eyeballs shine ;
And the bright bayonet,
Bristling and firmly set,
Flashed with a purpose grand,
Long ere the sharp command
Of the fierce rolling drum
Told them their time had come,
Told them what work was sent
For the Black Regiment.

"Now," the flag-sergeant cried,
"Though death and hell betide,
Let the whole nation see
If we are fit to be
Free in this land ; or bound
Down, like the whining hound—
Bound with red stripes of pain
In our old chains again !"
Oh ! what a shout there went
From the Black Regiment !

"Charge !" Trump and drum awoke ;
Onward the bondmen broke ;
Bayonet and sabre-stroke
Vainly opposed their rush.
Through the wild battle's crush,
With but one thought aflush,
Driving their lords like chaff,
In the guns' mouths they laugh,
Or at the slippery brands
Leaping with open hands,
Down they tear man and horse,
Down in their awful course ;
Trampling with bloody heel
Over the crashing steel,
All their eyes forward bent,
Rushed the Black Regiment.

"Freedom !" their battle-cry—
"Freedom ! or leave to die !"
Ah ! and they meant the word,
Not as with us 'tis heard,
Not a mere party-shout :
They gave their spirits out ;
Trusted the end to God,
And on the gory sod
Rolled in triumphant blood ;
Glad to strike one free blow,
Whether for weal or woe ;
Glad to breathe one free breath,
Though on the lips of death :
Praying—alas ! in vain !—
That they might fall again,
So they could once more see
That burst to liberty !
This was what "freedom" lent
To the Black Regiment.

Hundreds on hundreds fell ;
But they are resting well ;
Scourges and shackles strong
Never shall do them wrong.
Oh ! to the living few,
Soldiers, be just and true !
Hail them as comrades tried ;
Fight with them side by side ;
Never, in field or tent,
Scorn the Black Regiment !

BELLE MISSOURI.

Arise and join the patriot train,
　Belle Missouri ! my Missouri !
They shall not plead and plead in vain,
　Belle Missouri ! my Missouri !
The precious blood of all thy slain
Arises from each reeking plain ;
Wipe out this foul, disloyal stain,
　Belle Missouri ! my Missouri !

Recall the field of Lexington,
　Belle Missouri ! my Missouri !
How Springfield blushed beneath the sun,
　Belle Missouri ! my Missouri !
And noble Lyon, all undone,
His race of glory but begun,
And all thy freedom yet unwon,
　Belle Missouri ! my Missouri !

They called the craven to the trust,
　Belle Missouri ! my Missouri !
They laid the glory in the dust,
　Belle Missouri ! my Missouri !
The helpless prey of treason's lust,
The helpless mark of treason's thrust,
Now shall thy sword in scabbard rust ?
　Belle Missouri ! my Missouri !

She thrills ! her blood begins to burn,
　Belle Missouri ! my Missouri !
She's bruised and weak, but she can turn,
　Belle Missouri ! my Missouri !
So, on her forehead pale and stern,
A sign to make the traitors mourn,
Now for thy wounds a swift return,
　Belle Missouri ! my Missouri !

Stretch out thy thousand loyal hands,
　Belle Missouri ! my Missouri !
Send out thy thousand loyal bands,
　Belle Missouri ! my Missouri !

To where the flag of Union stands,
Alone, upon the blood-wet sands,
A beacon unto distant lands,
    Belle Missouri! my Missouri!

Up with the loyal Stripes and Stars,
    Belle Missouri! my Missouri!
Down with the traitor stars and bars,
    Belle Missouri! my Missouri!
Now by the crimson crest of wars,
And liberty's appealing scars,
We'll lay the demon of these wars,
    Belle Missouri! my Missouri!

AN APPEAL TO ARMS.

In earlier days, when war with fierce alarms
    Broke o'er our country's thinly peopled shores,
The stirring cry, "To arms! ye brave, to arms!"
    Around her standard brought indignant scores;
        The youth unbearded and the bending sire
        Went forth with arm of nerve and heart of fire!

From "city full" and mountain solitude
    In rallying thousands rushed the patriot throng;
In danger's front like sturdy oaks they stood
    And braved the tempest as it swept along;
        While from each true, undeviating eye
        Flashed out the firm resolve to do or die!

On many a hill, by forest and by stream,
    They met the foe and battled for the right;
Fearless of death, home, honor was their theme,
    For these they dared the thickest of the fight.
        How gloriously did they their cause maintain,
        And trample under foot a despot's reign!

Slumbers there not in veins of every son
    The zeal that nerved their sires to noblest deeds?
Along our border booms the foeman's gun!
    And precious blood for vengeance loudly pleads!
        Out from the noisy mart! desert the field!
        Nor rest until the foe is made to yield!

Our glorious banner, bathed in patriot's blood,
    Apostate legions ruthlessly assail;
By vengeful raid, by fiery 'whelming flood,
    They would o'er all our liberties prevail.
        Shall freemen pause, ignobly, basely wait,
        While perfidy adjusts the nation's fate?

What though the ties of kindred claim your stay,
    The stronger ties of country loudly call!
Brush off the trembling tear and haste away!
    Better that friends should grieve than honor fall;
        Urge back the foe!—defend our dear domains
        Till victory hovers o'er the embattled plains!
BALTIMORE.   G. W. M.

LEFT BEHIND.

BY MARY CLEMMER AMES.

Oh! hear the music coming, coming up the street!
Oh! hear the muffled marching of swift on-coming
    feet!
Oh! hear the choral drum beat — the bugle piercing
    sweet!

Our volunteers are coming, coming up the street;
Throw open wide the windows, beloved ones to greet—
We're ready waiting, eager, our bonny boy to meet.

Our volunteers are coming! They've lived through
    every fray—
Through marching, through fighting, through fever's
    cruel prey—
To be mustered out of service, the gallant boys to-
    day!

Your tattered battle-banner, unfurl it in the air!
I'm seeking one beneath it—I'll know him, bronzed or
    fair:
Oh! glad returning faces, our darling is not there!

The trumpets clash exultant, the bayonets flash me
    blind,
And still my eyes are seeking the one I cannot find;
Oh! tell me true, his comrades, have you left our boy
    behind?

Say, soldiers, did you leave him upon the battle-plain,
Where fiendish shell and canister pour fierce their
    fiery rain?
Did leave him with the wounded, or leave him with
    the slain?

Or, weary in the wasting camp, sore worn with sun
    and scar,
Did turn your faces to the North, to homes beloved
    afar,
And say, Good-by, we go, but _you_ enlisted for the
    war?

Be pitiful, O women! with pity softly kind!
You clasp your war-worn veterans; there are mother-
    eyes tear-blind;
There are women broken-hearted for boys left behind.

Can the hero crush the woman, and cry, Oh! let it be,
Let arms and homes be empty, for thy sake, Liberty?
O generation! perish! The land shall yet be free!

Oh! hear the music dying, dying on the wind,
And still my eyes are seeking the one I cannot find;
Oh! tell me not of "glory," our boy is left behind.

MOTHER, CAN I GO?

BY A. H. SANDS.

I am writing to you, mother, knowing well what you
    will say,
When you read with tearful fondness all I write to
    you to-day,
Knowing well the flame of ardor on a loyal mother's
    part,
That will kindle with each impulse, with each throb-
    bing of your heart.
I have heard my country calling for her sons that still
    are true;
I have loved that country, mother, only next to God
    and you,
And my soul is springing forward to resist her bitter
    foe:
Can I go, my dearest mother? tell me, mother, can I
    go?

From the battered walls of Sumter, from the wild
    waves of the sea,
I have heard her cry for succor, as the voice of God
    to me.
In prosperity I loved her—in her days of dark distress,
With your spirit in me, mother, could I love that
    country less?
They have pierced her heart with treason, they have
    caused her sons to bleed,

They have robbed her in her kindness, they have triumphed in her need ;
They have trampled on her standard, and she calls me
in her woe :
Can I go, my dearest mother ? tell me, mother, can I
go ?

I am young and slender, mother—they would call me
yet a boy,
But I know the land I live in and the blessings I en-
joy ;
I am old enough, my mother, to be loyal, proud, and
true
To the faithful sense of duty I have ever learned from
you.
We must conquer this rebellion ; let the doubting
heart be still ;
We must conquer it, or perish — we must conquer,
and we will !
But the faithful must not falter, and shall I be want-
ing ? No !
Bid me go, my dearest mother ! tell me, mother, can
I go ?

He who led his chosen people, in their effort to be
free
From the tyranny of Egypt, will be merciful to me ;
Will protect me by His power, whatsoe'er I under-
take ;
Will return me home in safety, dearest mother, for
your sake.
Or should this my bleeding country need a victim such
as me,
I am nothing more than others who have perished to
be free.
On her bosom let me slumber, on her altar let me lie ;
I am not afraid, my mother, in so good a cause to die.

There will come a day of gladness, when the people of
the Lord
Shall look proudly on their banner, which his mercy
has restored ;
When the stars in perfect number, on their azure field
of blue,
Shall be clustered in a Union, then and ever firm and
true.
I may live to see it, mother, when the patriot's work
is done,
And your heart, so full of kindness, will beat proudly
for your son ;
Or through tears your eyes may see it with a sadly
thoughtful view,
And may love it still more dearly for the cost it won
from you.

I have written to you, mother, with a consciousness
of right—
I am thinking of you fondly, with a loyal heart to-
night ;
When I have your noble bidding, which shall tell me
to press on,
I will come and see you, mother — come and kiss
you, and be gone.
In the sacred name of Freedom, and my Country, as
her due,
In the name of Law and Justice, I have written this
to you.
I am eager, anxious, longing, to resist my country's
foe :
Shall I go, my dearest mother ? tell me, mother, shall
I go ?

GO, MY BOY, WHERE DUTY CALLS YOU.

AN ANSWER TO "MOTHER, CAN I GO?"

Go, my boy, and Heaven bless you ! I have read each
precious line
Of your heart's responsive throbbings to a Higher
Call than mine.
God hath spoken—you have heard Him — and though
tears these eyes bedim,
Your affection for your mother shall not mar your
love for Him.
Could I bid you stay from fondness, when the ever-
ruling Hand
Marks your path to duty clearly for the safety of your
land ?
No ! 'tis yours to be a patriot, and 'tis mine to prove
as true ;
Go, my boy, where duty calls you, and my heart shall
follow you !

Go in faith, and feel protection in a Power Supreme,
Divine ;
Should a bullet pierce your body it will also enter
mine.
Do I think of this in sorrow ? Does my love sad fears
renew ?
Do I tremble at the prospect ? No, my son, no more
than you.
Dear to me is every pathway where your precious feet
have trod ;
But I give you fondly, freely, to my country and my
God.
You and I shall never falter in the work we have to
do ;
Go, my boy, where duty calls you, and my heart shall
follow you !

I shall pray for you—how often — with the waking
hour of morn,
Through the labors of my household, and when night
is coming on.
If a mother's prayers can keep you, 'mid the dangers
you incur,
God will surely bring you back again to happiness and
her.
I will never doubt the goodness that has kept you until now,
That has kept the evil from your heart, the shadow
from your brow ;
And I know that it shall keep you in the path you
must pursue ;
Go, my boy, where duty calls you, and my heart shall
follow you !

If my boy were less a hero, less the man in thought
and deed,
I had less to give my country in her trying hour of
need ;
And I feel a pride in knowing that to serve this cause
divine,
From the hearthstone goes no braver heart than that
which goes from mine.
I have loved you from the hour that my lips first
pressed your brow,
Ever tenderly, but never quite as tenderly as now.
All I have is His who gave it, whatsoe'er He bids me
do ;
Go, my boy, where duty calls you, and my heart shall
follow you !

I shall miss you through the spring-time, when the orchard is in bloom,

When the smiling face of nature bathes its beauty in perfume;

When the birds are sweetly singing by the door and on the wing,

I shall think of you who always loved to pause and hear them sing.

Long will seem the waning hours through the drowsy summer day,

With my boy exposed to dangers on a soil so far away.

But my spirit shall not murmur, though a tear bedim my view;

Go, my boy, where duty calls you, and my heart shall follow you!

You will come and see your mother, come and kiss her, as you say,

From her lips receive the blessing that shall cheer you on your way;

From her fond embrace go forward to resist your country's foe,

With the comforting assurance that your mother bade you go.

Heaven protect, and bless, and keep you; holy angels guard your way,

Keep your spirit from temptation, and your feet from going astray.

To your mother ever faithful, to your country ever true,

Go, my boy, where duty calls you, and my heart shall follow you!

A MIDNIGHT SCENE AT VICKSBURGH.

BY HORACE B. DURANT,

Company A, One Hundredth Regiment P. V., First Division
Ninth Army Corps.

By Mississippi's mighty tide, our camp-fires flick'ring glow,

O'er weary, tented, slumb'ring men, are burning dim and low;

Calm be their rest beneath the shade of bending forest bough,

And soft the night-wind as it creeps across the dreamer's brow;

The hot glare that to-morrow shines within this Southern land

May drink its draught of crimson life that stains the burning sand;

And some, alas! of this brave band their mortal course shall run,

And be but ghastly, mould'ring clay ere sets another sun.

'Tis midnight lone. The moon has climbed high up the eastern steeps,

While in her holy, pensive gaze the trembling dewdrop weeps;

Across the river's moaning flow, the bold, gray bluffs arise,

Like banks of rugged, slumb'ring clouds against the sapphire skies;

There Vicksburgh stands upon the slope and on the frowning height,

While spire and dome gleam strangely out upon the fearful night.

Ay, there is fear within the gloom, such fear as guilt may know,

When it has drawn upon its crimes the swift, avenging blow.

There comes no slumber to the eyes that gaze with horror dread

Upon the upturned, frightful face of all the mangled dead.

There is no peace to those who list the shriek of woe and pain

That, never ceasing, rises from the weeping and the slain.

Proud one, thy hour of doom is traced upon the burning wall,

And leaguered round with armed hosts, thy boasted might shall fall.

See, where the smoke of battle hangs, above the water's breast!

See how it wreathes the trodden height and winds along their crest!

Around, above, both friend and foe, the dead, the dying—all,

It floats and wraps the dreadful scene in one vast funeral pall!

Look there, that lightning flash, close by the lurid, winding shore!

See how the flaming shell mounts up! Hark to the awful roar!

The shell, up higher, higher still; the zenith reached at last,

Down, down it goes, with fiery curve, in thunder bursts, 'tis past;

Another—there, and there, with vengeful scream, and orb of fire,

They circle through the skies! Look there! it bursts above the spire!

List! list! Do ye not hear that cry, that shrieking comes away

Where fell that dreadful, burning bolt, to mangle and to slay?

Did you not hear that horrid crash of shivered timbers then,

As bursting down through roof and house, 'mongst women, children, men,

Upon the cowering throng it fell, and with sulphurous breath,

Spread fiery ruin all around within that house of death?

The ramparts answer. Flash on flash run all along their line,

And many a gleaming, hissing track athwart the heavens shine;

'Tis all in vain; their shot and shell fall short of every mark;

Or, wildly erring, sullen plunge beneath the waters dark.

'Tis all in vain; our marksmen true, with an unerring aim,

Behind their very ramparts lie, and bathe them red in flame;

No foeman bold above those works may show his daring form;

Down sentry, gunner, soldier, go beneath that leaden storm!

Thou frowning battlement, Rebellion's only, fondest trust,

With all their hopes, thy stubborn strength must topple to the dust;

These waters, mingling from afar, as they sweep to the sea,

Proclaim that they must still unite, that they must still be free!

The time shall come when these proud hills no more shall quake with dread;

Beneath their peaceful breast shall lie the heaps of gory dead;

Redeemed from slavery's blighting curse, the battle's war shall cease,
And all Columbia's broad domain shall smile in golden peace.

VICKSBURGH, MISS., June 21, 1863.

NEW-ENGLAND'S DEAD.

Oh! chant a requiem for the brave, the brave who are no more,
New-England's dead! in honored rest they sleep on hill and shore,
From where the Mississippi now in freedom proudly rolls
To waves that sigh on Georgia's isles a death-hymn for their souls.
Oh! first of all, the noble blood by traitorous hand was shed ;
It dyed the streets of Baltimore, New-England's heroes bled :
And still the mystic number "three" will live for aye in song
While history tells, with glowing pen, of Putnam, Shaw, and Strong.
Immortal names. O noble "three!" a nation's heart will throb
For ye who fell, in manly prime, for Freedom and for God!
And women's eyes grow dim with tears, and manhood bows its head
Before thy deeds of valor done, New-England's honored dead.
But not *alone* for those who die a soldier's death of glory :
Full many a brave, heroic soul has sighed its mournful story
Down in the sultry swamps and plains, where fever's subtle breath
Has drained the life-blood from their hearts, and laid them low in death—
As proud a memory yours, O ye who murmured no complaint!
Who saw Hope's vision day by day grow indistinct and faint ;
Who, far from home and loving hearts, from all yet held most dear,
Have died. O noble, unknown dead! ye leave a record here!
New-England! on thy spotless shield, inscribe thine honored dead,
Oh! keep their memory fresh and green, when turf blooms o'er their head ;
And coming nations yet unborn will read, with glowing pride,
Of those who bore thy conquering arms, and suffering, fought and died ;
Who, foremost in the gallant van, laid life and honor down—
Oh! *deck with fadeless bays their names who've won the martyr's crown.*

A REGIMENT OF GREYBEARDS.—The Thirty-seventh regiment of Iowa volunteers (known as the "Greybeard Regiment") left St. Louis on Monday for the South. A striking peculiarity of this regiment is, that nearly all its members, officers and men, are over forty-five years of age. Three fourths of them are grey-headed, and many have long white beards, giving them a venerable appearance. Many have sent their sons to the field, and are now following them.

ONE of the arts by which the Southern heart is fired is this : Soon after the battle of Murfreesboro, the rebel General Bragg caused to be printed and widely circulated in the army counterfeits of the *Nashville Union*, in which was conspicuously displayed "Startling News! Four States Seceded from the Old Government! Missouri, Indiana, Illinois, and Kentucky!" This was followed by an editorial bewailing the loss of these States. Of course the whole affair was a forgery, but the illiterate soldiery of the South, a large proportion of whom cannot read at all, could not detect it. While Buckner was in Kentucky, bogus copies of the *Louisville Journal* were freely circulated by the rebels, filled with all kinds of matter adapted to inflame and encourage the rebels, and discourage the loyal.

WILLIAM REID, an old sailor and man-of-war's man, who was on board the Owasco, was one of the heroes of the fight at Galveston. During the hottest moments of the battle between the Owasco and the rebel batteries, this man, who is forty-eight years of age, received a severe wound while in the act of loading his rifle. His two forefingers on his left hand were shot away, and the surgeon ordered him below, but he refused to go, and tying his pocket-handkerchief around his fingers, he remained on deck and did good execution with his rifle. Not more than thirty minutes after, another shot struck him in his right shoulder, and the blood spirted out through his shirt. Master's Mate Arbana then ordered him to go below, and have the surgeon dress his wounds. The brave old fellow said : "No, sir, as long as there is any fighting to be done, I will stay on deck!"

After the engagement was over the noble-hearted sailor had his wounds dressed and properly attended to. He is now on board the Owasco, and whenever they beat to general quarters you will see William Reid standing at his post ready for orders. He was told one day by the Captain to go below, as he was on the sick-list, and his place was in the hospital; he was displeased with this remark and replied : "No, Captain, my eyes are good and I can pull a lockstring as well as any on 'em!" The lockstring is a lanyard connected with the cap that fires the gun.

Master's Mate Arbana of the Owasco had a very narrow escape from death at the battle of Galveston, three shots having struck him in different places. One of the bullets passed completely through the crown of his cap, another penetrated his pantaloons just below the right knee, taking the piece of cloth with it. The third shot struck his sword just as he raised it in the air, and ordered his men to give a rousing cheer for "Yankee Doodle."   CICERONE.

BRAVERY OF CAPT. W. N. GREEN.—Among the interesting incidents of the battle of Chancellorsville, that of the capture of the colors of the Twelfth regiment, Georgia volunteers, during the battle of Sunday, May third, 1863, by Captain William N. Green, commanding the color company of the One Hundred and Second regiment N. Y. S. V., is worthy of commemoration, as evidence of the fighting qualities of the Nationals, and as an act of personal strength and bravery :

After several days' severe fighting between the United States forces under General Hooker, and the confederate forces under General Lee, the morning of Sunday, May third, 1863, found the One Hundred and Second regiment, N. Y. S. V., forming a portion of the Twelfth army corps, lying in the trenches on the extreme left of the Federal forces.

The battle commenced at five A.M., and the One Hundred and Second were for several hours subjected to a heavy fire from a battery of the rebels, situated on their right flank; at ten A.M., the enemy's infantry attacked the brigade of which the One Hundred and Second N. Y. S. V. was a part, and succeeded in driving the regiment which was on the right of the One Hundred and Second away in confusion; advancing up the trenches, the enemy charged the One Hundred and Second, and were repulsed. Soon after the One Hundred and Second was charged upon by the Twelfth regiment, Georgia volunteers, and immediately the men of each regiment were engaged in hand-to-hand conflicts.

The company of the One Hundred and Second N. Y. S. V., which Captain Green commanded, was especially singled out by the enemy for a fierce struggle, as they had charge of the National colors; the captain commanding the Twelfth regiment Georgia volunteers, rushed forward at the head of his men, and made a jump right at Captain Green, calling out to him, "Surrender," to which Captain Green replied, "Not yet;" then seizing the rebel captain by the throat with his left hand, he flung him violently to the ground, by tripping him up, and wrenched his sword from his grasp. Captain Green was then seized from behind by an ambulance-sergeant of the rebels, who, putting his knee in the middle of his back, flung him on the ground. Captain Green sprung to his feet, and putting both swords (his own and the rebel captain's) into his left hand, he knocked the ambulance-sergeant down with his right hand.

Captain Green then sprang forward some six feet, and grasped with his right hand the flag-staff of the rebel battle-flag, which the color-sergeant was holding, and said to the color-bearer, "Give me that flag," at the same time pulling the flag-staff away from the sergeant; he then tore the flag from the flag-staff, and flung the staff over the parapet, putting the flag inside the breast of his fatigue-jacket. Captain Green then went to two rebel privates who were a few feet off and demanded them to give up their muskets, which they did. Taking the muskets, he gave them to some of his own company to carry off, and taking the equipments of the two privates, he flung them into a puddle of water near by; then going to the rebel captain he pulled him up off of the ground, and putting him, together with the ambulance-sergeant, the color-sergeant, and the two privates, under charge of two of his company, sent them to the rear, to be placed in custody under the provost-guard.

Thus in the short space of five minutes, Captain Green disarmed one captain, one ambulance-sergeant, and two privates of the Twelfth Georgia volunteers, besides taking their color-sergeant, with his colors, and sending the whole of them, five in number, as prisoners, under guard to the rear.

The rebel flag was one of the confederate battle-flags, made of coarse red serge cloth, about four and a half feet square, having a blue Saint Andrew's cross running from each corner; three white stars were in each limb of the cross, and one star in the centre, making thirteen stars in all. The flag was sent to General Hooker by his order; the sword was presented to Captain Green by his brigade commander, for his good conduct during the battle.

A WIFE ON THE BATTLE-FIELD.—The following extract from a letter, dated at Corinth on the sixth of October, 1862, vividly portrays the fearful emotions and anxious thoughts which torture the mind of an observer during the progress of battle, and narrates but one of the many harrowing scenes of war:

"O my friend! how can I tell you of the tortures that have nearly crazed me for the last three days! Pen is powerless to trace, words weak to convey one tithe of the misery I have endured. I thought myself strong before. I have seen so much of suffering that I thought my nerves had grown steady, and I could bear any thing; but to-day I am weak and trembling, like a frightened child.

"But do not wonder at it. My dear husband lies besides me, wounded unto death perhaps. I have lost all hope of saving him, though I thank God for the privilege of being this moment beside him. And besides this, all around me the sufferers lie moaning in agony. There has been little time to tend them, poor fellows. True, the surgeons are busy all the time, but all the wounded have not yet been brought in, and it seems as if the time will never come when our brave men shall have been made comfortable as circumstances may permit. It is awful to look around me. I can see every imaginable form of suffering, and yet am helpless to aid them any of consequence.

"Since night before last, I have not left my husband's side for a moment, except to get such things as I required, or to hand some poor fellow a cup of water. Even as I write my heart throbs achingly to hear the deep groans and sharp cries about me. F—— is sleeping, but I dare not close my eyes, lest he should die while I sleep. And it is to keep awake, and in a manner relieve my overburdened heart, that I am now writing you under such sad circumstances.

"On the morning of the third instant the fight began. The attack was made on General McArthur's division, and we could plainly hear the roll of the artillery here, as it is about two miles and a half distant only from this place. Oh! the fearful agony of that awful, awful day! I had seen F—— a moment early in the morning, but it was only a moment, when he bade me good-by, saying hurriedly as he tore himself away: 'Pray for me, my wife, and, if I fall, God protect you!' There was something in his look and tone which struck a chill to my heart, and every moment after I knew the fight had begun I felt as if he had indeed fallen. I cannot tell how long it was before I heard that Oglesby's brigade was engaged, but it seemed an age to me. After that my agony was nearly intolerable. I never had a thought of fear for myself; I was thinking only of F——. Then I got the word that he had been hotly pursued by the rebels, and had fallen back.

"Late in the afternoon I succeeded in gaining a little intelligible information. Poor General Hackleman was shot through the neck, while giving a command, and fell mortally wounded. He died between ten and eleven o'clock the same night, I have since learned. Up to the time of receiving the wound he had acted with the greatest bravery and enthusiasm, tempered by a coolness that made every action effective. When dusk at last put an end to the first day's conflict, I learned that General Oglesby had been dangerously wounded, but could gain no intelligence of my husband. I could not bear the suspense. Dark as it was, and hopeless as it seemed to search for him then, I started out to the battle-field.

"Oh! how shall I describe the search of that night? It looked like madness. It was madness. But all night long I staggered amongst bleeding corpses, over dead horses, trampled limbs, shattered artillery — every thing that goes to make up the horrors of a' battle-field when the conflict is over. . They were removing the wounded all night. Oh! think how awful to stumble over the dead and hear the cries of the wounded and dying, alone, and in the night-time. I had to start off alone, else they would not have let me go.

"As you may suppose, I could not find him, either amongst the living or the dead. But the next morning, just after sunrise, I came to a little clump of timbers where a horse had fallen — his head shot off and his body half covering a man whom I supposed dead. His face was to the ground, but as I stooped to look closer, I perceived a faint movement of the body, then heard a faint moan. I stooped and turned the face upward. The head and face were both covered with blood, but when I turned it to the light I knew it in spite of its disfiguration. O God! the agony of that moment sickened me almost to suffocation. With a strength I thought impossible in me, I drew him crushed and bleeding from beneath the carcase of our poor old horse, whom we had both so loved and petted, and dipping my handkerchief in a little pool of water amongst the bushes, bathed his face, and pressed some moisture between his parched, swollen lips. He was utterly senseless, and there was a dreadful wound in his head. Both limbs were crushed hopelessly beneath his horse. He was utterly beyond the reach of human skill to save, but as soon as possible I had him conveyed to the hospital. I have nursed him ever since — hopelessly, and with a heart breaking with grief. Oh! how many wives, how many mothers are to-day mourning the dead and dying, even as I mourn my dying! He has not opened his eyes to look' at or spoken to me since he fell. Oh! could he but speak to me once before he dies, I should give him up with more resignation. But to die thus—without a look or word! Oh! my heart is breaking!"

THE FIRST RECRUIT.—On the sixteenth of April, 1861, when the Governor of Pennsylvania, just after the Fort Sumter affair, at the instance of President Lincoln, called for three companies of militia from the counties of Mifflin, Schuylkill, and Berks, the first recruit was a Philadelphian, who telegraphed his application. He served three months with the "Logan Guard," of Lewistown, Mifflin county, and is now in the Armory Square Hospital, under Surgeon George H. Mitchell's medical treatment. His name is John T. Hunter, and he is now attached to the Nineteenth regiment Pennsylvania volunteers.—*Philadelphia Inquirer, March 16.*

LAPORTE, PA., *Feb.* 4.—There may be but few persons outside of the army who are prone to credit the reports of atrocities which are perpetrated by the rebels upon the unsuspecting and innocent; but nevertheless there is much perpetrated that is almost too shocking to be brought before the public at home, of cruelties committed abroad by the rebel soldiery. The last and most demoniacal thing brought to our notice is a small instrument invented by them to cripple the horses of our cavalry. It is constructed of four pieces of rod-iron hardened, less than a quarter of an inch in thickness, and about two inches long. Four of the ends are made to centre together, and they project from the middle in the form of arms. To the ex-

treme end of each is welded out a very sharp point. These are intended to be sprinkled through the woods and over roads, to prevent the advance of cavalry. No matter how thrown, one of the points will stand perpendicularly, and when the horse treads upon it, it will enter his foot and disable him on the spot.—*Sullivan County Democrat.*

ANECDOTE OF STONEWALL JACKSON.—The night after the battle of Fredericksburgh a council of war was held by General Lee, to which all of his generals of division were invited. General Jackson slept throughout the proceedings, and upon being waked and asked for his opinion, curtly said: "Drive 'em in the river; drive 'em in the river!"—*Mobile Advertiser.*

ANOTHER "CROSS IN THE SKY." — A well-defined cross was seen in the sky a few nights since. A correspondent of the Wilmington (N. C.) *Journal*, writing from Kingston, N. C., gives the following description of the phenomena:

The moon rose cloudless. At a little before seven o'clock, two bright spots, some twelve degrees, (quarter in extent?) were visible, one north and the other south, and immediately thereafter a cross was seen in the heavens, the moon joining the four arms of the cross.

About half-past eight o'clock' the northern light went out, but the cross and the spot to the south remained until past ten, when I retired. Can any one tell when the cross has appeared before since the days of Constantine, when the letters of I. H. S. accompanied the sign?—*The Jackson (Miss.) Crisis, Feb.* 23.

LIEUTENANT PIKE, son of the editor of the Augusta (Me.) *Age*, lost a leg in the battle of Williamsburgh. He, however, remained in the field, and led his battery on horseback, carrying his crutches with him.

THE Chattanooga *Rebel* mentions the fact that the wife of General John C. Breckinridge has had prepared a magnificent stand of colors, constructed from the silk of the wedding-dress worn by herself upon the day of her marriage, to be presented through her husband to the most gallant and brave regiment of his division. The *Rebel* understands that this appropriate and valued present has been bestowed upon the Twentieth Tennessee regiment, commanded by Col. Tom Smith, and well known as the famous "Battle regiment," that did such gallant service in the disastrous battle of Fishing Creek.—*Jackson Crisis, Feb.* 25

ANECDOTE OF GENERAL GRANT.—The following is told by an officer of General Grant's staff:

The hero and veteran, who was citizen, captain, colonel, brigadier and major-general within a space of nine months, though a rigid disciplinarian, and a perfect Ironsides in the discharge of his official duties, could enjoy a good joke, and is always ready to perpetrate one when an opportunity presents. Indeed, among his acquaintances, he is as much renowned for his eccentric humor as he is for his skill and bravery as a commander.

When Grant was a brigadier in South-east Missouri, he commanded an expedition against the rebels under Jeff. Thompson, in North-east Arkansas. The distance from the starting-point of the expedition to the supposed rendezvous of the rebels was about one hundred and ten miles, and the greater portion of the route lay through a howling wilderness. The imaginary suffering that our soldiers endured during the first two days of their march was enormous. It was impossible to steal or "confiscate" uncultivated real estate, and not a hog, or a chicken, or an ear of corn was anywhere to be seen. On the third day, however, affairs looked more hopeful, for a few small specks of ground, in a state of partial cultivation, were here and there visible. On that day, Lieutenant Wickfield, of an Indiana cavalry regiment, commanded the advance-guard, consisting of eight mounted men. About noon he came up to a small farm-house, from the outward appearance of which he judged that there might be something fit to eat inside. He halted his company, dismounted, and with two second lieutenants entered the dwelling. He knew that Grant's incipient fame had already gone out through all that country, and it occurred to him that by representing himself to be the General he might obtain the best the house afforded. So, assuming a very imperative demeanor, he accosted the inmates of the house, and told them he must have something for himself and staff to eat. They desired to know who he was, and he told them that he was Brigadier-General Grant. At the sound of that name they flew around with alarming alacrity, and served up about all they had in the house, taking great pains all the while to make loud professions of loyalty. The lieutenants ate as much as they could of the not over sumptuous meal, but which was, nevertheless, good for that country, and demanded what was to pay. "Nothing." And they went on their way rejoicing.

In the mean time General Grant, who had halted his army a few miles further back for a brief resting spell, came in sight of, and was rather favorably impressed with, the appearance of this same house. Riding up to the fence in front of the door, he desired to know if they would cook him a meal.

"No," said a female, in a gruff voice; "General Grant and his staff have just been here and eaten every thing in the house except one pumpkin pie."

"Humph," murmured Grant; "what is your name?"

"Selvidge," replied the woman.

Casting a half-dollar in at the door, he asked if she would keep that pie till he sent an officer for it, to which she replied that she would.

That evening, after the camping-ground had been selected, the various regiments were notified that there would be a grand parade at half-past six, for orders. Officers would see that their men all turned out, etc.

In five minutes the camp was in a perfect uproar, and filled with all sorts of rumors; some thought the enemy were upon them, it being so unusual to have parades when on a march.

At half-past six the parade was formed, ten columns deep, and nearly a quarter of a mile in length.

After the usual routine of ceremonies the Acting Assistant Adjutant-General read the following order:

HEADQUARTERS, ARMY IN THE FIELD.

SPECIAL ORDER, No. ——.

Lieutenant Wickfield, of the —— Indiana cavalry, having on this day eaten every thing in Mrs. Selvidge's house, at the crossing of the Ironton and Pocahontas and Black River and Cape Girardeau roads, except one pumpkin pie, Lieutenant Wickfield is hereby ordered to return with an escort of one hundred cavalry and eat that pie also.   U. S. GRANT,
                                        Brigadier-General Commanding.

Grant's orders were law, and no soldier ever attempted to evade them. At seven o'clock the Lieutenant filed out of camp with his hundred men, amid the cheers of the entire army. The escort concurred in stating that he devoured the whole of the pie, and seemed to relish it.

SONGS OF THE REBELS.

THE SOUTHERN CROSS.

Fling wide each fold, brave flag, unrolled
   In all thy breadth and length!
Float out unfurled, and show the world
   A new-born nation's strength.
Thou dost not wave all bright and brave
   In holiday attire;
'Mid cannon chimes a thousand times
   Baptized in blood and fire.

No silken toy to flaunt in joy,
   When careless shouts are heard:
Where thou art borne all scathed and torn,
   A nation's heart is stirred.
Where half-clad groups of toil-worn troops
   Are marching to the wars,
What grateful tears and heartfelt cheers
   Salute thy cross of stars!

Thou ne'er hast seen the pomp and sheen,
   The pageant of a court;
Or masquerade of war's parade,
   When fields are fought in sport:
But thou know'st well the battle yell
   From which thy foemen reel,
When down the steeps resistless leaps
   A sea of Southern steel.

Thou know'st the storm of balls that swarm
   In dense and hurtling flight,
When thy crossed bars, a blaze of stars,
   Plunge headlong through the fight:
Where thou'rt unfurled are thickest hurled
   The thunderbolts of war;
And thou art met with loudest threat
   Of cannon from afar.

For thee is told the merchant's gold:
   The planter's harvests fall:
Thine is the gain of hand and brain,
   And the heart's wealth of all.
For thee each heart has borne to part
   With what it holds most dear;
Through all the land no woman's hand
   Has staid one volunteer.

Though from thy birth outlawed on earth,
   By older nations spurned,
Their full-grown fame may dread the name
   Thy infancy has earned.
For thou dost flood the land with blood,
   And sweep the seas with fire;
And all the earth applauds the worth
   Of deeds thou dost inspire!

Thy stainless field shall empire wield,
   Supreme from sea to sea,
And proudly shine the honored sign
   Of peoples yet to be.
When thou shalt grace the hard-won place
   The nations grudge thee now,
No land shall show to friend or foe
   A nobler flag than thou.

MONODY ON THE DEATH OF GENERAL STONEWALL JACKSON.

Spoken at the Richmond Varieties by Miss Wren.

BY THE EXILE.

Ay, toll! toll! toll!
  Toll the funeral bell!
And let its mournful echoes roll
From sphere to sphere, from pole to pole,
O'er the flight of the greatest, kingliest soul
  That ever in battle fell.

Yes, weep! weep! weep!
  Weep for the hero fled!
For death, the greatest of soldiers, at last
Has over our leader his black pall cast,
And from us his noble form hath passed
  To the home of the mighty dead.

Then toll! and weep! and mourn!
  Mourn the fall of the brave!
For Jackson, whose deeds made the nation proud,
At whose very name the enemy cowed,
With the "crimson cross" for his martial shroud,
  Now sleeps his long sleep in the grave.

His form has passed away;
  His voice is silent and still;
No more at the head of "the old brigade,"
The daring men who were never dismayed,
Will he lead them to glory that never can fade;
  Stonewall of the iron will!

He fell as a hero should fall;
  'Mid the thunder of war he died.
While the rifle cracked and the cannon roared,
And the blood of the friend and foeman poured,
He dropped from his nerveless grasp the sword
  That erst was the nation's pride.

Virginia, his mother, is bowed;
  Her tread is heavy and slow.
From all the South comes a wailing moan,
And mountains and valleys reëcho the groan,
For the gallant chief of her clans has flown,
  And a nation is filled with woe.

Rest, warrior! rest!
  Rest in thy laurelled tomb!
Thy mem'ry shall live through all of earth's years,
And thy name still excite the despot's fears,
While o'er thee shall fall a nation's tears,
  Thy deeds shall not perish in gloom.

PRAYER. *

Before thy throne, O God!
Upon this blood-wet sod,
  We bend the knee:
And to the darkened skies
We lift imploring eyes,
  We cry to thee.

The clouds of gloom untold
Have deepened fold on fold,
  By thy command;
And war's red banner waves
Still o'er the bloody graves
  That fill the land.

* These verses were written by a deaf and dumb girl of Savannah, Georgia, on the occasion of a fast-day.

Our trampled harvest fields,
No more their bounty yields
  Our corn and wine;
Thy suffering children see;
We crave no friend but thee,
  No help but thine.

Behold how few we stand,
To guard our native land
  From shame and wrong;
How weak without thine aid!
Yet by thy hand arrayed,
  We shall be strong.

Hark! through the vernal air,
The foemen's shout we hear,
  They come, they come!
From valley, hill, and coast,
They throng, a countless host,
  Around our home.

O God! save it from harm!
Stretch forth thy mighty arm,
  Thy glitt'ring spear!
We fight beneath thy shield,
We cannot fear nor yield,
  For thou art near.

And thou, O Christ! so fair,
Who didst our sorrows bear;
  O Prince of peace!
Breathe but thy love divine
Through all this world of thine,
  And war shall cease.

TO ——.

These lines were supposed to be written by a Southern girl to her betrothed, who refused to return and fight for his native State until self-interest compelled him. It is needless to say the engagement was broken off.

I have met thee once again—not a tear was in my eye,
In my heart no lingering tenderness, for all that had gone by;
I felt my spirits strength-girt, with more than common power,
And blest the welcome destiny that tested me that hour.

With eager eyes around me, who vainly hoped to see
Some portion of that feeling they deemed I *had* for thee,
With none to whisper one kind word, encouraging my heart,
And waken more of scorn and pride than manner dared impart.

Alone I met thy downcast eye; ah! well thou didst not raise
Thy guilty eye to meet the haughty welcome of my gaze;
'Twas coward-like to seek me beneath my sacred roof
When all things slumber—e'en the eye that might have flashed reproof.

Wise as *thou* wert, in knowledge of hypocrisy and guile,
Sorrow taught my woman's heart—I met thee with a smile;
But when thy hand sought mine with a friendly grasp and bold,
I felt the life-blood at my heart was turning sick and cold.

Yet watchful eyes were round us, they saw thy proffered hand,
And heard thy words of greeting — open, courteous,
bland ;
I met thy clasp as calmly as the rock the wavelet's
spray,
Then to more welcome guests as calmly turned away.
                                         S. A. D.
                      —Southern Literary Messenger.

THE DRUMMER-BOY OF THE RAPPAHANNOCK.—Recently, a bright boy, with dark eyes and ruddy cheeks,
came to my desk and gave me a brief history of his
adventures at the battle of Fredericksburgh. He was
neatly dressed in a military suit of gray cloth, and
carried in his hands a pair of drumsticks — his drum
was destroyed by the fragment of a shell immediately
after his landing on the river-bank, in that hurricane
of sulphury fire and iron hail on the twelfth of December, 1862.

The reader will distinctly remember that for several
days a curtain of thick fog rose up from the waters of
the Rappahannock, completely hiding from view the
artillery that crowned the opposite hills, and the infantry
that crowded the sheltering ravines : but the preparation for the great fight, so hopefully commenced, was
continued amid the thunder of cannon and the volcanic eruptions of exploding batteries.

The hazardous work of laying the pontoon-bridges
was frequently interrupted by the murderous fire of
rebel sharp-shooters, concealed in the stores and dwelling-houses on the bank of the river. To dislodge
these men, and drive them out of their hiding-places,
seemed an impossible task. At a given signal, our
batteries opened with a terrific fire upon the city,
crashing through the walls of houses and public buildings, not sparing even the churches in which treason
had been taught as paramount to Christianity. In
this storm of shot and shell, which ploughed the streets
and set the buildings on fire, the sharp-shooters survived, like salamanders in the flames, and continued
to pour a deadly fire upon our engineers and bridge-
builders.

In this dilemma it became evident that the bridges
could not be laid except by a bold dash. Volunteers
were called for to cross in small boats ; forthwith, hundreds stepped forward and offered their services. One
hundred men were chosen, and at once started for the
boats. Robert Henry Hendershot, the hero of our
sketch, was then a member of the Eighth Michigan —
acting as a drummer. Seeing a part of the Michigan
Seventh preparing to cross the river, he ran ahead,
and leaped into the boat. One of the officers ordered
him out, saying he would be shot. The boy replied
that he didn't care, he was willing to die for his country. When he (the boy) found that the captain would
not permit him to remain in the boat, he begged the
privilege of pushing the boat off, and the request was
granted. Whereupon, instead of remaining on shore,
he clung to the stern of the boat, and, submerged to
the waist in water, he crossed the Rappahannock.
Soon as he landed, a fragment of a shell struck his
old drum and knocked it to pieces. Picking up a
musket, he went in search of rebel relics, and obtained
a secesh flag, a clock, a knife, and a bone ring. On
opening a back-door in one of the rebel houses, he
found a rebel wounded in the hand, and ordered him
to surrender. He did so, and was taken by the boy-
soldier to the Seventh Michigan. When the drummer-
boy recrossed the river from Fredericksburgh, General

Burnside said to him, in the presence of the army :
"Boy, I glory in your spunk ; if you keep on this way
a few more years, you will be in my place."

Robert is a native of New-York, but moved with his
parents to Michigan when he was an infant. His
father died ten or twelve years ago, leaving his mother
in destitute circumstances, and with a family of four
children to support and educate. About fifteen months
ago, "our drummer-boy" went from Jackson (Michigan) to Detroit, with Captain C. V. Deland, in the capacity of waiter in the Ninth Michigan. With that
regiment he went to Louisville, West-Point, Ky., and
Elizabethtown, Ky.—at the last-named place he was
appointed drummer-boy. Since that time he has been
in six battles, as follows : Lebanon, Murfreesboro,
Chattanooga, Shelbyville, McMinnsville, and Fredericksburgh. At the battle of Murfreesboro, where the
Union forces were taken by surprise before daylight
in the morning, after beating the long-roll, and pulling
the fifer out of bed to assist him, he threw aside his
drum, and seizing a gun, fired sixteen rounds at the
enemy from the window of the court-house in which
his regiment was quartered, but our men were compelled to surrender, and they were all taken prisoners,
but were immediately paroled, and afterward sent to
Camp Chase, Ohio.

Soon as the news came from the Rappahannock
that Robert had lost his drum in that terrible tempest
of fire and iron, The New-York Tribune Association
promised to make good his loss and give him a new
drum.   GEORGE W. BUNGAY.

A FRIENDLY INTERVIEW BETWEEN PICKETS.—A correspondent writing from the Ninth army corps, opposite Fredericksburgh, Va., narrates the following,
which occurred on Christmas-day, 1862, while the
writer was out on picket with his company :

"After partaking of a Christmas dinner of salt
junk and hard tack, our attention was attracted by a
rebel picket, who hailed us from the opposite side of
the river : 'I say, Yank, if a fellow goes over there,
will you let him come back again ?' Receiving an
affirmative answer, he proceeded to test the truth of
it by paddling himself across the river. He was decidedly the cleanest specimen of a rebel I had seen.
In answer to a question, he said he belonged to the
Georgia Legion. One of our boys remarked : 'I met
quite a number of your boys at South-Mountain.'
'Yes, I suppose so, if you were there,' said the rebel,
while his face grew very sad. 'We left very many of
our boys there. My brother, poor Will, was killed
there. It was a very hot place for a while, and we
had to leave it in a hurry.' 'That's so, Georgia, your
fellows fought well there, and had all the advantage,
but the old Keystone boys were pressing you hard.
By the way, I have a likeness here (taking it out of
his pocket) that I picked up on the battle-field the
next morning, and I have carried it ever since.' He
handed it to the rebel, who, on looking at it, pressed
it to his lips, exclaiming : "My mother ! my mother !"
He exhibited considerable emotion at the recovery
of the picture ; but on regaining his composure,
he said that his brother had it in his possession,
and must have lost it in the fight. He then asked
the name of the one to whom he was indebted for
the lost likeness of his mother, remarking : 'There
may be better times soon, and we may know each
other better.' He had taken from his pocket a small
pocket-Bible, in which to write the address, when
Alex. ——, who had taken no part in the conversa-

tion, fairly yelled: 'I know that book! I lost it at Bull Run!' 'That's where I got it, Mr. Yank,' said the rebel, and he handed it to Alex. 'I am much obliged to you, Georgia Legion, for I wouldn't part with it for all the Southern Confederacy.' I was a little curious to know something further of the book, so I asked Alex. to let me see it. He passed it to me. I opened it, and on the fly-leaf saw written in a neat hand: 'My Christmas-gift, to Alex. ——, December 25th, 1860. Ella.' 'Well, Alex.,' said I, 'it's not often one has the same gift presented to him a second time.' 'True, Captain; and if I could but see the giver of that to-day, there's but one other gift I would want.' 'What's that, Alex.?' 'This rebellion played out, and my discharge in my pocket.'

"The boys had all been busily talking to our rebel friend, who, seeing a horseman approaching in the direction of his post, bid us a hasty good-by, and made as quick a trip as possible across the Rappahannock. Night came on, and those not on duty lay down on the frozen ground, to dream of other Christmas nights, when we knew not war."

ANECDOTE OF GEN. BUTLER.—The following story is told of Gen. Butler: "I will not go back to New-Orleans," says the General, "unless I can have more troops. Why can't you give me more?" "We haven't them to give," replied Mr. Lincoln. "Then why don't you raise more — put the draft upon New-York — raise that forty thousand who should have been raised in that State last fall?" "Mr. Seymour says it will not do to draft in New-York," answers Mr. Lincoln. "*Then I would draft Seymour!*" asserts Butler.

SOUTHERN CREDULITY.—The Mobile *Advertiser and Register* learns that a good many negroes in the region above Okalona, Miss., have found their way back to their masters, completely disgusted with Yankee freedom and its attendant hardships. With the propensity to embellishment for which the African race are so noted, they tell dolorous stories of the treatment they have experienced and that which they discovered was in store for them. One of them asserts that it is the custom of the Yankees to dispose of the surplus negro women and children by blindfolding them and driving them into the river.

THE PROPOSITIONS FOR AN ARMISTICE.

To THE EDITORS OF THE EVENING POST: At a meeting held at Stamford, Ct., on Tuesday evening last, I said "that propositions for an armistice or peace had been submitted to the President on the twelfth December last, which, had they been accepted, would have terminated this war by the first of April, upon a basis satisfactory to the people North and South." In referring to this statement, you ask: "Who made these 'propositions for an armistice or peace,' the adoption of which Mr. Wood pretends to believe 'would have settled the matter' by All-Fools' day? Were they made by Davis and his fellow-rebels? If so, how does Mr. Wood know any thing about them? Has he been in secret correspondence with the enemy? Or were they made by some of the anti-war men here? If so, who authorized them? And what are the terms of the propositions from which Mr. Wood hopes so much? If they are honorable to the nation; if they are such as patriotic Americans ought to favor, why not make them public at once?" To which I say in reply, that the statement referred to was made by me delib-

erately, with a full and personal knowledge of the facts, and that I am constrained from the publicity of them only by the request of one of the principal officers of the Government. When this interdiction shall be withdrawn, I will cheerfully gratify your curiosity. Very respectfully, etc.,
March 11, 1863.   FERNANDO WOOD.

A MAINE SECESSIONIST.—F. O. J. Smith, of the *Portland Advertiser*, and Member of the Maine Legislature, has just delivered himself of a tremendous speech of three days' length. He sees visions of commercial wealth and greatness in a union of Maine with the Canadas under British protection and government, and looks forward to the time when Maine can "mount the wings of hope and go back to the mother government."—*New-York Tribune, March 6.*

LOYAL AMERICANS IN CHILI.
OFFICIAL CORRESPONDENCE.
THE REV. MR. BELLOWS TO MR. SEWARD.
UNITED STATES SANITARY COMMISSION,
NEW-YORK AGENCY, No. 823 Broadway,
New-York, March 13, 1863.

Hon. Wm. H. Seward, Secretary of State:

SIR: I have the honor to acknowledge your letter of March eleventh, with an inclosure of your check for three thousand six hundred and fifty eight dollars and eighty-four cents. I have passed the money to the Treasurer of the Sanitary Commission, G. T. Strong, who will send you a formal receipt.

In thanking, through you, our countrymen in Chili for their generous thoughtfulness for our and their soldiers who may fall sick or be wounded in this greatest battle of humanity, it may be for their satisfaction to know that, contrary to all ordinary cases, devotion to our Government, Union, and cause has been proportioned to the distance of the unselfish position of our countrymen — those farthest from the seat of war being nearest in their sympathy and beneficence. The Pacific coast has given three times as much to the National Sanitary Commission as the Atlantic coast; and its most distant region — Washington Territory — more in proportion to its inhabitants than any other. Our countrymen in Vancouver's Island, Honolulu, and the Sandwich Islands, in England, France, Germany, and India, have shown that no seas, however wide, could shut their ears to the groans of their suffering patriots in the field.

Our countrymen in Chili may have the satisfaction of knowing that their contribution mingles in our treasury with the contributions of loving countrymen, from wherever an American has carried his country's enterprise, or followed her flag; and that from the resources thus accumulated succor and consolation will flow impartially to the national soldier, whether in Louisiana or North-Carolina, Virginia or Kentucky, Mississippi or Maryland. If he be anywhere under our flag, there the National Sanitary Commission will follow and find him.

I have the honor to be, gratefully, your obedient servant,   HENRY W. BELLOWS,
President.

MR. NELSON TO MR. SEWARD.
LEGATION OF THE UNITED STATES,
SANTIAGO DE CUBA, Feb. 1, 1863.

Hon. Wm. H. Seward, Secretary of State, Washington:

SIR: I have the honor to inclose a bill of exchange, dated January thirty-first, 1863, drawn by Messrs. Alsop & Co., of Valparaiso, upon Messrs. H. G. Enthom & Co., London, England, payable to my order, and indorsed by me, for the sum of four hundred and ninety-seven pounds sterling, which was purchased by the amount subscribed by loyal Americans in Chili, in aid of the sick and wounded soldiers of the Union army. The amount subscribed was two thousand six hundred and thirty-six dollars. I also inclose a list of the names of the subscribers and the amount paid by each. You will please appropriate the proceeds to the object indicated in such manner as you may deem most advisable.

This contribution, though not large, will, it is hoped, mitigate the suffering of the brave soldiers who have perilled their lives on the battle-field in behalf of our beloved country; while, at the same time, it has given to our citizens residing in Chili an opportunity of manifesting their patriotism in this hour of our utmost need in a substantial and unequivocal mode.

Other remittances for the same purpose will be made from time to time until the rebellion is crushed.

I have the honor to remain your obedient servant,
THOMAS W. NELSON.

MR. SEWARD TO MR. NELSON.

DEPARTMENT OF STATE, WASHINGTON, March 9, 1863.

SIR: I have read your despatch of the first ultimo, accompanied by a list of loyal citizens residing in Chili, who have subscribed to a fund for the relief of the sick and wounded soldiers of the Union army, and by a bill of exchange for four hundred and ninety-seven pounds sterling, remitting that fund for the purpose for which it was destined.

You will be pleased to inform the subscribers that their proceeding will be viewed at home with great sensibility, as doing honor alike to their benevolence and their patriotism. Care will be taken that their bounty shall be so disposed as to reach the most needy and worthy of those for whom it has been offered.

I am, sir, your obedient servant,
WM. H. SEWARD.
To THOMAS W. NELSON, Esq., etc., etc., Chili.

A COMPANY OF CHEROKEES.—Major Thomas, of the confederate States army in East-Tennessee, has in his command a full company of Cherokee Indians from the Indian settlements of North-Carolina. They make fine soldiers, obey orders promptly, make the best scouts in the world, have committed no depredations upon citizens, are perfectly orderly and docile, *and have done much to rid that modern Sodom of its abolition bushwhackers and assassins.* — *Columbus (Ga.) Sun.*

INCIDENT OF STONE RIVER. — In the rebel charge upon McCook's right, the rebel Third Kentucky was advancing full upon one of the loyal Kentucky regiments. These two regiments were brought from the same county, and consequently were old friends and neighbors, and now about to meet for the first time as enemies. As soon as they came near enough for recognition they mutually ceased firing, and began abusing, and cursing, and swearing at each other, calling each other the most outlandish names; and all this time the battle was roaring around them without much attention from either side. It was hard to tell which regiment would come off the victor in this wordy battle. As far as I could see, both sides were **terrible** at swearing; but this could not always last;

by mutual consent they finally ceased cursing, and grasping their muskets, charged into each other with the most unearthly yell ever heard on any field of battle. Muskets were clubbed, bayonet met bayonet, and in many instances, when old feuds made the belligerents crazy with passion, the musket was thrown away, and at it they went, pummelling, pulling, and gouging in rough and tumble style, and in a manner that any looker-on would consider a free fight. The rebels were getting rather the better of the fight, when the Twenty-third Kentucky succeeded in giving a flanking fire, when they retreated with quite a number of prisoners in their possession. The rebels had got fairly under weigh, when the Ninth Ohio came up on the double-quick, and charging on their now disordered ranks, succeeded in capturing all their prisoners, besides taking in return a great many of the rebels. As the late belligerents were conducted to the rear they appeared to have forgotten their late animosity, and were now on the best terms imaginable, laughing, and chatting, and joking, and, as the rebels were well supplied with whiskey, the canteens were readily handed about from one to the other, until they all became as jolly as possible under the circumstances.

AN EXPEDIENT TO ABATE SHINPLASTERS

HEADQUARTERS DISTRICT OF MEMPHIS,
MEMPHIS, Nov. 26, 1862.

To the Mayor and Common Council of the City of Memphis:

GENTLEMEN: I regret to notice that you propose to issue a species of currency of denominations as low as *ten* cents — "shinplasters" — to swell the amount of bad money with which your community is already afflicted. The issuing of bills of credit by way of money is, in my judgment, in direct violation of the Constitution of the United States; and I think Congress, at the last session, passed a bill prohibiting all issues below one dollar, and provided a species of currency called the "post-office currency," which will soon supplant the worthless trash which now is a disgrace to the name of *money.* As soon as possible, enough of this post-office money will come here, and suffice for the wants of the people.

Inasmuch as we seem to be imitating the example of Mexico, rather than those high models of ancient and modern times that we were wont to do in times past, I would suggest a simpler and better currency for the times. In Mexico soap is money, and the people do their marketing through the medium of cakes of soap. Why do you not use cotton for money? It has a very convenient price—fifty cents a pound. Put it up in pounds and fractions, and it will form a far better currency than the miserable shinplasters you propose. If cotton be king, it has the genuine stamp and makes money — is money. Therefore I suggest that, instead of little bits of paper, you set to work and put up cotton in little parcels of five, ten, twenty-five, and fifty cents.

If it be my last act, I wish to spare the people of Memphis from the curse of any more bad money.

Yours in haste,
W. T. SHERMAN,
Major-General Commanding.

AN INCIDENT.—Rev. Robert Colyer, chaplain to one of the Western regiments, in an address in Boston, Mass., related the following:

When I was in Jefferson City, Mo., I found the hospitals in the most fearful condition you can imagine.

I cannot stop to tell you of the scenes I saw; it is enough to say that one poor fellow had lain there sick on the hard boards, and seen five men carried away dead, one after the other, from his side. He was worn to a skeleton; worn through so that great sores were all over his back, and filthy beyond telling. One day, a little before my visit, old Hannah, a black woman who had some washing to do for a doctor, went down the ward to hunt him up. She saw this dying man and had compassion on him, and said: "O doctor! let me bring to the man my bed, to keep him off the floor." The doctor said: "The man is dying; he will be dead to-morrow." To-morrow came, and old Hannah could not rest. She went to see the man and he was still alive. Then she got some help, took her bed, put the man on it, and carried him bodily to her shanty; then she washed him all over, as a woman would a baby, and fed him with a spoon, and fought death hand to hand day and night, and beat him back and saved the soldier's life. The day before I went to Jefferson the man had gone on a furlough to his home in Indiana. He besought Hannah to go with him, but she could not spare time; there was all that washing to do. She went with him to the steamboat, got him fixed to her mind, and then she kissed him, and the man lifted up his voice as she left him and wept like a child. I say we have grown noble in our sufferings.

RICHMOND, VA., *July* 29. — From a gentleman recently from Strasburgh, we learn that there occurred a panic among the Yankees at that place on last Wednesday week. A hurricane sweeping from the south raised a great line of dust in the road leading from Front Royal. The Yankees, some two thousand in number, thought the army of the ubiquitous "Stonewall" was certainly upon them. Setting fire to all their tents and stores, they fled in confusion, the greater number of them not halting till they arrived in Winchester. The amount of property destroyed by them in this panic is estimated at between $30,000 and $40,000. — *Richmond Examiner, July 29.*

THE SPIRIT OF ILLINOIS. — A few days ago Gov. Yates of Illinois received a letter from a town in the south part of the State, in which the writer complained that traitors in his town had cut down the American flag, and asking what ought to be done in the premises. The Governor promptly wrote him as follows: "Whenever you raise the flag on your own soil, or on the public property of the State or country, or at any public celebration, from honest love to that flag and patriotic devotion to the country which it symbolizes, and any traitor dares to lay his unhallowed hand upon it to tear it down, then I say shoot him down as you would a dog, and I will pardon you for the offence." — *Boston Transcript, July 25.*

CHICAGO, *Thursday, July* 31. — The *Times* has a special despatch, dated Memphis, 28th instant, which says: "Late advices from the South by rebel sources are important. Ten iron-clad gunboats, built in England, and fully equipped, have arrived off Mobile harbor, and three more are on their way. These constitute a fleet ordered by the Southern Confederacy, and purchased in Europe. They mount from ten to thirty guns each, and are said to be mailed with six-inch iron. The blockade was run openly by the dint of superior strength and weight of metal. Mobile is now considered open to the commerce of the world, with the support of the newly-acquired power."

WHILE Mr. Buchanan was President, the Pottstown Bank came into existence, and out of compliment to him the notes contained his portrait. But of late the bank has received so many mutilated notes, with the words "traitor," "Judas Iscariot," etc., inscribed under the portrait, that it has resolved to call in all the notes bearing the likeness, and re-issue new ones. It must be done to abate a nuisance. — *Boston Advertiser, July 16.*

ORIGINAL NATIONAL ANTHEM.

BY DAVID B. SICKLES.

Dear land of our birth, by our fathers adored,
  Devoted to thee is each patriot heart;
Though blasted and scourged by cannon and sword,
  Thy spirit of Freedom shall never depart.
We'll love thee the more the greater thy woes,
  Assured that the Right shall triumphantly reign;
The Nation that conquered its earliest foes
  Can never be governed by tyrants again.

The cause that was won by the blood of our sires—
  The glorious emblem of Freedom they gave—
With holiest ardor each Freeman inspires,
  From the hills of the North to the home of the
    slave.
Undaunted by death, unmoved by defeat,
  The patriot ranks return to the field,
Prepared for the foes that in battle they meet—
  To bleed and to die, but *never* to yield.

In the God who espouses the cause of the Just,
  And reigns in all lands with omnipotent power,
The Nation will ever confidingly trust,
  And seek for his aid in its perilous hour.
When God by his might shall all fetters unbind,
  And the claims of the free shall be rightly esteemed,
The flag that we honor, unfurled to the wind,
  Forever shall float o'er the Nation redeemed.

MARCH ALONG.

BY GEORGE H. BOKER.

Soldiers are we from the mountain and valley—
  Soldiers are we from the hill and the plain;
Under the flag of our fathers we rally;
  Death, for its sake, is but living again.
      Then march along, gay and strong,
      March to battle with a song!
      March, march along!

We have a history told of our nation—
  We have a name that must never go down!
Heroes achieved it through toil and privation!
  Bear it on, bright with its ancient renown!
      Then march along, etc.

Who that shall dare say the flag waving o'er us,
  Which floated in glory from Texas to Maine,
Must fall, where our ancestors bore it before us,
  Writes his own fate on the roll of the plain!
      Then march along, etc.

Look at it, traitors, and blush to behold it!
Quail as it flashes its stars in the sun!
Think you a hand in the nation will fold it,
While there's a hand that can level a gun?
Then march along, etc.

Carry it onward till victory earn it
The rights it once owned in the land of the free;
Then, in God's name, in our fury we'll turn it
Full on the treachery over the sea!
Then march along, etc.

England shall feel what a vengeance the liar
Stores in the bosom he aims to deceive;
England shall feel how God's truth can inspire;
England shall feel it, but only to grieve.
Then march along, etc.

Peace shall unite us again and forever,
Though thousands lie cold in the graves of these
wars;
Those who survive them shall never prove, never,
False to the flag of the Stripes and the Stars!
Then march along, gay and strong,
March to battle with a song!
March, march along!

FAIL!

BY A. P. M'COMBS.

Fail! who dares to utter such a thought,
With heritage so dearly bought;
What! twenty millions freemen fail,
Who do and dare, whose hearts ne'er quail,
Whose cause is just and must prevail
O'er every foe?
Fail! with millions spent, with thousands slain,
With all our tears, with all our pains,
With all we've lost, with all we've won?
By Fredericksburgh! by Donelson!
By heaven, no!

Fail! never while a Bunker Hill,
Or Cowpens field is whispering still,
Or Saratoga's frowning peak,
Or Brandywine's red flowing creek,
With Yorktown battlements still speak
Of glorious deeds.
We cannot drop a single star,
While Italy looks to us afar,
While Poland lives, while Ireland hopes,
While Afric's son in slavery gropes,
And silent pleads.

Fail! never breathe such burning shame,
Sell not your birthright or your name,
He's sure a coward or a knave
Who'd heap dishonor on the grave
Of all the host of martyred brave,
For liberty.
What! twenty millions freemen fail,
Whose strength is borne on every gale,
Whose power is of such vast extent,
That it grasps in half the continent,
From sea to sea.

With plains so rich, the race can feed
Or starve their enemies if need;
With iron roads all o'er the land,
With cities stretched on every hand,
And flag unfurled from every strand,
Upon the gale.

And education as a dower,
Bringing knowledge that's always power,
While maid and matron, son and sire,
Are burning with the olden fire,
They cannot fail.

With forests deep and valleys wide,
With rattling wheels on every side,
With mines of gold, with iron hills,
With giant streams and massive mills,
With hands for toil, and master wills
To move the whole.
Whose art out-rivals every one,
Whose eagle soars in every sun,
Whose name and fame and wealth are known
In every land and clime and zone,
From pole to pole.

By all the grand historic names!
By all our fathers' heaven-born aims!
By the great name of Washington!
By all the past and present won!
By all the future yet to come!
We must not fail.
Fail! never breathe the word again,
'Twill make the bones of heroes slain,
Now bleaching on Antietam's plain,
Cry out in agony of pain,
To hear the wail.

What! shall a nation great and free,
Now blazoned bright in heraldry,
Be stranded and go down in night,
Forgotten, lost to human sight,
Too base to struggle for the right,
'Gainst tyranny.
No! banish ease, each pelfish god—
No! never stoop to kiss the rod—
What! shall a puny foe prevail,
And spirits of our sires bewail
Their progeny?

Fail! traitors only breathe the word;
Let those with love of country stirred
Rise in their strength, nor fail, nor falter,
But firm around their country's altar,
United stand.
Northmen! *you* feel the mighty throes
Of your nation struggling with her foes;
Rise in your strength! rise in your might!
Strike! for your country and the right!
Strike! for your flag, strike treason pale,
Strike! him who dares to utter fail,
Strike! for yourselves, your hearthstone fires,
Strike! with the nerve each hope inspires,
Strike! for your sons in battle torn,
Strike! for your children yet unborn,
Strike! for mankind blows that will tell,
On time's great stream responding swell,
Strike deadly blows, none else will do,
Strike traitors till they beg and sue,
Strike crushing blows, then war will cease,
And then will fall the dews of peace
All o'er our land.

JARRETTSVILLE, June 30, 1863.

BOSTON HYMN.

BY RALPH WALDO EMERSON.

The word of the Lord by night
To the watching Pilgrims came,
As they sat by the sea-side,
And filled their hearts with flame.

God said, I am tired of Kings,
I suffer them no more ;
Up to my ear the morning brings
The outrage of the poor.

Think ye I made this ball
A field of havoc and war,
Where tyrants great and tyrants small
Might harry the weak and poor ?

My angel—his name is Freedom—
Choose him to be your king ;
He shall cut pathways east and west,
And fend you with his wing.

Lo ! I uncover the land
Which I hid of old time in the West,
As the sculptor uncovers his statue,
When he has wrought his best.

I show Columbia, of the rocks
Which dip their foot in the seas,
And soar to the air-borne flocks
Of clouds, and the boreal fleece.

I will divide my goods,
Call in the wretch and slave :
None shall rule but the humble,
And none but Toil shall have.

I will have never a noble,
No lineage counted great :
Fishers and choppers and ploughmen
Shall constitute a State.

Go, cut down trees in the forest,
And trim the straightest boughs ;
Cut down trees in the forest,
And build me a wooden house.

Call the people together,
The young men and the sires,
The digger in the harvest-field,
Hireling and him that hires.

And here in a pine state-house
They shall choose men to rule
In every needful faculty,
In church, and state, and school.

Lo ! now, if these poor men
Can govern the land and sea,
And make just laws below the sun,
As planets faithful be.

And ye shall succor men ;
'Tis nobleness to serve :
Help them who cannot help again ;
Beware from right to swerve.

I break your bonds and masterships,
And I unchain the slave :
Free be his heart and hand henceforth,
As wind and wandering wave.

I cause from every creature
His proper good to flow :
So much as he is and doeth,
So much he shall bestow.

But, laying his hands on another
To coin his labor and sweat,
He goes in pawn to his victim
For eternal years in debt.

Pay ransom to the owner,
And fill the bag to the brim !
Who is the owner ? The slave is owner,
And ever was.   *Pay him!*

O North ! give him beauty for rags,
And honor, O South ! for his shame ;
Nevada ! coin thy golden crags
With Freedom's image and name.

Up ! and the dusky race
That sat in darkness long—
Be swift their feet as antelopes,
And as behemoth strong.

Come East, and West, and North,
By races, as snow-flakes,
And carry my purpose forth,
Which neither halts nor shakes.

My will fulfilled shall be,
For, in daylight or in dark,
My thunderbolt has eyes to see
His way home to the mark.

FORGIVEN.

"In a recent battle fell a secession colonel, the last remaining son of his mother, and she a widow. That mother had sold
eleven children of an old slave mother, her servant ; that servant went to her and said : 'Missus, we're even now ; you sold
all my children ; de Lord took all yours ; not one left to bury
either of us ; now I forgive you.'"

A Southern widow knelt beside the bier
Of her lifeless son,
They had brought him back from the battle-field,
The field that he died upon ;
And of all her children, this dead boy
Was the last remaining one.

Oh ! lonely through that silent house
The wide, deserted halls ;
Now never a sound of dancing feet
Across their pavement falls—
Nor the mother's voice through the summer air,
After her children calls.

One after one, from her home they went,
One after one, to the grave,
And their father was laid by the village kirk
Where the solemn cedars wave,
And this last one of her household band,
How she had hoped to save !

But that hope died out on the fatal day,
So sorrowful and black,
When strangers brought unto her door
That only darling back—
Not as he went, so strong and brave
And full of life, alack !

Oh ! sad it was to hear her mourn
In that wide, lonely home ;
Not a ray of comfort or of hope
To radiate the gloom,
Not a kindred step beside her own,
To follow to the tomb.

One came to her, but not of kin,
Only an aged slave,
And spoke, as she never spoke before—
Perhaps grief made her brave ;
The swelling tide of a mighty grief
Impulsive accents gave.

" Missus, you mourn, for your last boy
     Will never come back more.
You took my children, one by one,
     From the little cabin-door;
De Lord took yours, now I forgive—
     I never could before.

" I pity you in de lonesome house,
     For I knows how;
Not one left to bury either of us,
     We're even now !
But de good Lord helps sufferin' hearts
     Dat to him bow."   ERIE.
HOME, Feb. 27, 1863.

THE BLACK BRIGADE AT PORT HUDSON.

BY JOHN A. DORGAN.

Not fair, for they too long have borne
The badge of shame, the lash of scorn;
Not fair, for seamed with many a scar
Their spirits like their bodies are;
Nor learned in books, nor smooth in speech,
Whom tyrants made it crime to teach;
But strong of limb and true of heart,
Behold them in their manhood smart
For this their trial-day arrayed,
The soldiers of the Black Brigade.

Forward ! And with one pulse sublime,
And ringing tread of ancient rhyme,
They sweep; and forward as they sweep,
The thunders of the cannon leap
Upon them, and their bleeding host
Within the battle-cloud is lost;
Flash sword and bayonet, shot and shell
Fly screaming through that mist of hell,
But onward, onward, undismayed,
They hold their way—the Black Brigade.

And on, and on, and on they tread;
And all the field is heaped with dead,
And slippery grows the grass with gore,
But onward, onward, yet once more.
In vain ! In vain ! The moated wall
Mocks them, but valiantly they fall;
Anselmo dies, but to his breast
The flag he bore in life is pressed;
Or knave or fool who did not aid
The heroes of the Black Brigade.

Again, again, and yet again
They charge, but ah! too few, in vain.
The negro's courage is in vain,
Nor can atone the Saxon's brain;
The day is lost; on every side
Have Saxons fled; let none deride
Who mark *them*, as with footsteps slow
And eyes of rage they backward go;
And all who saw how few huzzaed
In honor of the Black Brigade.

But not for them was lost the day,
Who made like Winkelried a way,
And bridge-like o'er whose bodies dead
Shall Freedom to their brethren tread;
The sickle they shall grasp no more,
But harvest in the fields of war;
Their history shall keep the fame
Of these, who dying overcame;
Their poets in their songs shall braid
The memory of the Black Brigade.

ARM AND OUT.

BY PARK BENJAMIN.

Arm and out, ye Pennsylvanians;
     Leave your homesteads, arm and out !
Hear ye not the rebel foemen
     Coming with a mighty shout ?

In delay lose not a minute;
     This is not the time for doubt—
Beat your drums and load your muskets;
     Pennsylvanians, arm and out !

Lee is bringing on his cohorts,
     Ninety thousand strong, about;
Meet them, kill them, drive them backward
     Pennsylvanians, arm and out !

Young men, bid adieu to sweethearts,
     Though they whimper, scold, and pout;
Duty calls you now, not dalliance;
     Pennsylvanians, arm and out !

Husbands, quit your wives and children,
     Social cares and thoughts devout,
Pleasure, work, trade, occupation;
     Pennsylvanians, arm and out !

Take your hands from mines and forges,
     Where free labor made them stout;
March, resistless, to the battle;
     Pennsylvanians, arm and out !

Arm and out ! your country orders—
     Put the rebel ranks to rout;
Fight for love, and home, and Union—
     Pennsylvanians, arm and out !
NEW-YORK, June 16, 1863.

CAVALRY SONG.

BY ELBRIDGE JEFFERSON CUTLER.

The squadron is forming, the war-bugles play.
To saddle, brave comrades, stout hearts for a fray !
Our captain is mounted—strike spurs, and away !

No breeze shakes the blossoms or tosses the grain:
But the wind of our speed floats the galloper's mane,
As he feels the bold rider's firm hand on the rein.

Lo ! dim in the starlight their white tents appear !
Ride softly ! ride slowly ! the onset is near !
More slowly ! more softly ! the sentry may hear !

Now fall on the rebel—a tempest of flame !
Strike down the false banner whose triumph were
     shame !
Strike, strike for the true flag, for freedom and fame !

Hurrah ! sheathe your swords ! the carnage is done.
All red with our valor, we welcome the sun.
Up, up with the stars ! we have won ! we have won !

A BRAVE PENNSYLVANIAN.

Cairo, June 23, 1863.—Permit me to note to you
some of the incidents I witnessed at the siege before
Vicksburgh.

At the battle and capture of Port Gibson, Sergeant
Charles Bruner, a Pennsylvanian, of Northampton
County, with a squad of fifty men of the Twenty-third
regiment Wisconsin volunteers, was the first to enter

said fort. The flag-sergeant being wounded, Sergeant Bruner seized the colors, and, amid cheers and a rain of bullets, planted the Stars and Stripes upon the ramparts.

Again, at Champion Hill, the Twenty-third was about breaking, when Sergeant Bruner took the colors in his hand and cried, "Boys, follow! don't flinch from your duty!" and on they went, following their brave color-bearer; and the intrenchment was taken.

Again, at the battle of Big Black, company B, of the Twenty-third Wisconsin, got orders from General Grant to plant a cannon and try to silence a battery, which was bravely done, when the cannon was dismantled, captain and first lieutenant were gone and wounded. Sergeant Bruner again cheered on his men, and in a hand-to-hand fight the enemy were routed. The sergeant was made prisoner twice, but his captors were soon put *hors du combat* by his brave followers, who would die for their brave sergeant and now captain. The rebels were driven back, with lost colors.

Singular to say, Sergeant Bruner has now been leading on his men in more than thirteen battles, always in front, yet he has never been wounded. He captured with his own hands three rebel flags, which he handed over to General Grant.

Sergeant Bruner being the only Pennsylvanian in that regiment, he does the old Keystone State great honor.   J. H.

A REGIMENT SAVED BY TWO WOMEN.—In travelling on the cars from Bethel to Jackson, Tenn., the Twenty-seventh Iowa regiment was saved from a fearful loss of life by the heroism of a couple of Union women. The train was running in the night at a high rate of speed, and just before reaching a railroad bridge the engineer saw a couple of lanterns being waved in the distance, directly on the track. He stopped the locomotive, and men were sent ahead to ascertain the cause of the alarm. They found that the lanterns were held by two women, who explained to them that a party of guerrillas in that vicinity had been informed of the coming of the regiment, and at about eight o'clock that evening the villains had set the bridge on fire, and allowed the main timbers to burn so much that they could not bear the weight of the train, and then put out the flames and went away, hoping, of course, that the cars would run on the bridge, that it would break down with the weight, and thus kill and injure many of the soldiers, and prevent the regiment from going through. The noble women had learned of these intentions, and had walked ten miles through the darkness and mud to save the Union soldiers.

A MODEL SPEECH.—A captain in an Iowa regiment having been informed that his company had subscribed a handsome sum for the purpose of purchasing and presenting him with an elegant sash and sword, called his men together and delivered himself of the following model speech: "Boys, if you have any money to spare, send it home to your families if they need it; if not, keep it until you need it yourselves. I will buy my own sword. Should you do it, and should it come to disgrace in these hands, you could but regret the gift; or should I accept it from you, and some day find it my imperative duty to kick some one of the donors out of this company, it might be unpleasant to think that I was under obligations to that person as a contributor to the elegant sword fund. For these

reasons I must firmly and kindly decline the favor which your loyal hearts prompt you to bestow. Wait until the war is over; wait until the tide of battle shall have been stayed—till the raging billows of this cursed rebellion shall have been rolled back; wait until I have proved myself worthy to receive so noble a gift—until you have shown yourselves, by deeds of daring and feats of bravery worthy to bestow it upon me; then, perchance, I may be happy to accept at your hands some lasting testimonial of your confidence and esteem. Till then wait."

RICHMOND, *May* 13, 1863.—The Quebec *Journal* says that news had reached that city that fifteen regiments had been ordered from England to Canada, in consequence of the American (Yankee) Ambassador having notified the British government that, in case the iron-clad steamers now building for the "Emperor of China," should be allowed to depart, it will be considered an equivalent to a declaration of war against the United States. The Canadian journals also say that nine vessels had left England for Canada with arms, ammunition, and military stores, six of them being bound to Quebec, and three to Montreal.—*Charleston Mercury.*

ADVENTURE OF MAJOR KIERNAN.—A paragraph telegraphed from Cairo, regarding the unjustifiable seizure by the rebels of a train of five ambulances, which had been out to bring in a number of Federal wounded, contained several inaccuracies. Major Kiernan (formerly surgeon of the Sixty-ninth New-York and Third regiment M.S.M.) has arrived here and gives the following particulars:

Colonel Clark Wright, Sixth Missouri cavalry, was ordered out with three hundred men of the regiment, and four mounted howitzers, to recover them. He started on the sixth of May from Rock Spring, and passing through Port Gibson, reached on the same evening the place where the ambulances had been captured, which was at Oakland College, near Rodney. It was forty miles from Rock Spring, the starting-point of the expedition. There they drove in the enemy's pickets and pursued them for some time. But ascertaining that the enemy, in much superior force, were about surrounding them, they immediately took about ten prominent citizens prisoners as hostages and retreated. The prisoners included Dr. William L. Breckinridge, the President of the college, and his two sons. One of these was John Breckinridge, who a few years ago had a duel with one Leavenworth, of New-York, in Canada, whom he wounded, and at a later time, while editing the *Courier* in New-Orleans, had another duel with Nixon, the editor of the *Crescent*, and in which Breckinridge was wounded.

The detachment then fell back toward Port Gibson with the prisoners, traversing a broken country in the night, and skirmishing with the enemy all the way. About ten o'clock Major Kiernan, of Wright's regiment, was severely wounded in the shoulder and thrown from his horse. At two A.M. they reached Port Gibson. They held possession at ten A.M., when they ascertained that the enemy were about surrounding the town. The place being indefensible, Colonel Wright fell back to a hill beyond Bayou Pierre, two miles south of the town, toward the Federal army. About an hour after his departure the rebel cavalry dashed into town and captured Major Kiernan's orderly and nurse, and his horse and accoutrements. They offered a parole, which he declined. Skirmishing between Colonel Wright's command and the rebels (then in possession of the town) was kept up for some time, when both retired in opposite directions. That night the rebel cavalry again entered Port Gibson. The Major was a second time offered a parole, which was again declined. He was very kindly attended by a confederate surgeon. On the sixteenth ult., about daylight, from the open window of his room at the hotel, he heard a conversation between a rebel officer and a citizen, to the effect that about ten thousand rebels were concentrating at Port Gibson for the purpose of capturing trains going from Grand Gulf to Grant's army. A large commissary train, to leave the following day, of which they had heard through spies, was a particular object in view.

Roused by this information, he got up, and guided by further information given by negroes who were preparing to flee themselves, he went through back gardens unobserved and reached the brush. He crossed Bayou Pierre on a log, and at last reached Grand Gulf, eight miles distant. He was completely exhausted, and fainted on arriving there. He gave information of the designs of the rebels and it was forwarded to General Grant, thereby saving, probably, a most valuable train from the hands of the enemy. Major Kiernan has been warmly recommended by high officials of the army of the Tennessee and department of the Missouri to the President for promotion. Governor Gamble, Generals Grant, Blair, Schofield, Hurlbut, Sullivan, and half a dozen 'others of rank, bear testimony to the gallantry of his services, and unite in asking the Government to recognize them by his advancement.

Rev. Mr. Breckinridge, when taken to General Grant's headquarters, had an interview with that officer, which resulted in the unconditional release of himself and sons. Permission was also given him to return to Oakland, take the female members of his family and remove them to Kentucky, or to any place in the North he pleased. Mr. Breckinridge has never been a supporter of the rebellion, and he has remained South during the war wholly on account of his inability to get away with his family.

FREDERICKSBURGH, VA., *Dec. 25, 1863.*—We were driving Sedgwick's infidels across Banks's Ford, when a Yankee officer was seen making his way through the streets of Fredericksburgh, where we had no troops at the time, in order to gain the opposite side of the river. A number of ladies, standing on a porch at the time, saw the runaway and cried out, "Stop him! stop him!" when a Miss Philippa Barbour, a niece of Colonel Phil. Barbour, of Virginia, with a number of other ladies gave chase, and ran the Yankee officer nearly down, who, convulsed with laughter at the sport and the idea of being pursued by ladies, became nearly exhausted, and gave up on being hemmed in at the corner of a garden fence. The ladies took him prisoner and locked him up in a room until our troops again entered the city.— *Mobile Tribune.*

ABOU BEN BUTLER.

Abou Ben Butler (may his tribe increase!)
Awoke one night down by the old Belize,
And saw, outside the comfort of his room,
Making it warmer for the gathering gloom,
A black man shivering in the winter's cold.
Exceeding courage made Ben Butler bold,

And to the presence in the dark he said:
"What wantest thou?" The figure raised its head,
And with a look made of all sad accord
Answered: "The men who'll serve the purpose of
        the Lord."
"And am I one?" said Butler. "Nay, not so,"
Replied the black man. Butler spoke more low,
But cheerily still, and said: "*As I am Ben,*
You'll not have cause to tell me that again."

The figure bowed and vanished. The next night
It came once more, environed strong in light,
And showed the names whom love of freedom blessed,
And lo! Ben Butler's name led all the rest.

A GOOD CAMP STORY.—A correspondent attached to the army of the Potomac writes the following:

To show you how rumors will spread in the army, I will illustrate an incident. The lady friends of our fifth corporal sent him a box; among the many good things in the said box was a life-size doll, dressed in full Zouave uniform, which they won at a soldier's fair in your city. The corporal, after getting the box, was taken sick. The boys started the rumor that the corporal was a woman and gave birth to a boy. The rumor spread like wild-fire; hundreds flocked to our quarters to see the wonderful phenomenon—a newborn babe—but we guarded the tent with zealous care, only allowing pryers to catch a passing glimpse of the supposed mother and babe. We could find a number of men to swear they had seen both. But the cream of the joke was to come off; the corporal received a ten days' furlough; all thought it was the mother going home with her babe; some had it that she was a rich heiress escaping from a tyrant father; but hundreds believed in the mother corporal and young recruit of company I of the Zouaves d'Afrique.

NEW-ORLEANS, *April 18.*—Much interest is felt in the fortunes of Admiral Farragut by every loyal man in the country, and his assured safety is a source of congratulation among good men everywhere.

Not the least gratifying intelligence in this news is the fact that the renowned Colonel Ellet of the ramfleet is in command of the Switzerland, with Admiral Farragut. The rebel papers up the river trumped up a very ingenious theory some time ago, by which the writers proved—to their own great satisfaction—that Colonel Ellet was lost, with every body else on board the ram Lancaster, while attempting to pass the batteries at Vicksburgh.

On Tuesday morning, April fourteenth, Lieutenants H. B. Skinner and C. C. Dean of General Dudley's staff, and Lieutenant Tenney, Quartermaster of the Thirtieth Massachusetts volunteers, went up from Baton Rouge to Port Hudson in the Richmond, they having volunteered to go across the point opposite Port Hudson, and carry despatches from below to the Admiral, who was to be at the mouth of False River on Wednesday morning. Captain Roe and Lieutenant Herbert of the signal corps accompanied the expedition. During the sail up an additional mast was put above the main topmast of the Richmond, with a "crow's nest" in the top, from which it was proposed to signal over the trees covering the point with the Admiral, which plan proved entirely successful.

On the morning of the fifteenth, Lieutenants Skinner, Dean, Tenney, and Herbert went up the levee a couple of miles to reconnoitre. They found that the enemy were crossing cavalry over from Port Hudson,

Returning to the Richmond, the welcome signal-guns were heard from the Hartford, whose masts were plainly visible from the "crow's nest." They were quickly answered by Captain Alden, and in a few minutes the expedition started. Beside the above-mentioned officers, Mr. Shaw, Acting Master of the Richmond, and Mr. Gabandau, Private Secretary to Admiral Farragut, who came down a week ago, and returned to the Richmond from New-Orleans, put in here to accompany us over. Also Mr. Graves, Purser's Clerk of the Albatross, accompanied the expedition. A negro was taken along as a guide. The party was well armed, and started about noon.

They struck the woods some two miles below the river, embarked in two skiffs, and for five miles proceeded through the woods, overflowed with water to a depth ranging from three to thirty feet. It was a novel scene. Silently they paddled through the forest—the only noises heard were the voices of numberless birds and the low rustling of the leaves. Arriving near the False River, the boats were hid in the bushes, and the party waded waist-deep through the water a mile further in, where they struck the old State Levee, following which for a short distance, they came out into the open road in full sight of the enemy's batteries, which were no longer to be feared, for right ahead was the welcome sight of the flag-ship.

The Albatross, Captain Hart, came quickly down and took us on board. While waiting for her to reach us, the enemy fired a few shells at the party, which went harmlessly over. In a few moments we were alongside the Admiral's ship, who gave us a most cordial welcome. The officers vied with each other in making us comfortable, and eagerly asked numberless questions about the news below.

After a good night's rest, the party, decreased by the officers belonging above, early the next morning started to return, which was a much more dangerous matter than going, for the enemy having divined our intentions, had, during the night, sent a small force over, evidently with the intention of "gobbling" the party; but we struck a different road from the one we came on, and reached our boats in safety, having encountered but one of the enemy's pickets, who was mounted, and quickly fled on our firing at him. We got back to the Richmond at noon, having thus in twenty-four hours accomplished an object full of importance and danger, and one which Yankee pluck and perseverance alone could accomplish.

The Admiral is well, and has seen considerable service since passing the port. He reports heavy batteries erected at Grand Gulf, which fired on him in going up and coming down. There are batteries also at Warrenton, just below Vicksburgh. The ram Switzerland is with him. He is now blockading the mouth of Red River, down which a large amount of the enemy's supplies come. He reports that the rebels have only four days' provisions at Port Hudson, and is of opinion that there are not more than fifteen thousand troops there, and that if invested it must fall in a week's time at most.—*New Orleans Era.*

WASHINGTON, *April* 24, 1863.—Intelligence was received here to-day of an important arrest at Falmouth, the headquarters of the army of the Potomac. No doubt has existed for a long time that the rebels have had some secret means of knowing every thing that transpired within our lines, and that such information was instantaneously conveyed.

The orders for recent movements had not reached the circumference of the military circle formed by our army before the pickets on the opposite bank were calling out, in mocking tones: "How are *you*, Yank? An't those eight days' rations mouldy yet?" These facts have caused the deepest anxiety at headquarters, as, until now, the means adopted by the rebels have baffled the vigilance and labor expended to detect them.

General Patrick, the Provost-Marshal of the army of the Potomac, was, however, determined that the secret should be brought to light. The guards stationed along the river-bank, and in situations favorable for signals, have been constantly enjoined to use the utmost care and watchfulness to discover and expose the iniquitous system.

Yesterday their efforts were crowned with success. One of the guards in the town of Falmouth, stationed outside a dwelling adjoining the brick church on the river-bank, heard a clicking like that of a telegraph instrument. He advised his superior officers, and was directed to enter the house and investigate.

This was done, and on opening a door he discovered a party of four or five persons, one of whom was seated by a telegraph instrument, sending messages by a submarine wire across the Rappahannock. They were all arrested, and as their offence is of extraordinary atrocity, a just and speedy punishment will, doubtless, be at once meted out to them. This punishment, according to the laws of war, is death by hanging.

The danger that would have resulted from a continuance of this means of conveying information, it is, of course, impossible to estimate; but it must also be borne in mind that General Hooker has displayed the most extraordinary reticence with regard to his plans, so that any facts about a movement that could have been revealed by the wire, would, a short time later, be made known to the enemy by deep-throated cannon, announcing the "opening of the ball."—*Philadelphia Inquirer.*

WORSHIP OF THE NEGROES.—A correspondent at Port Royal, S. C., gives an interesting account of the religious meetings of negroes, in which singing is the favorite exercise. They have a great variety of sacred songs, which they sing and shout at the top of their voices, and never grow weary. A favorite melody is, "Roll, Jordan, roll:"

> Little children sitting on the tree of life,
>   To hear when Jordan roll;
>   Oh! roll, Jordan, roll; roll, Jordan, roll;
> We march the angel march; oh! march the angel march;
> On, my soul is rising heavenward, to hear when Jordan roll.
>   O my brother! sitting on the tree of life,
>   To hear when Jordan roll, etc.
>   Sister Mary, sitting on the tree of life,
>   To hear when Jordan Roll, etc.

The verses vary only in the recitative. If Mr. Jones is a visitor, he will hear, "Mr. Jones is sitting on the tree of life." All of the persons present are introduced to the tree of life—Nancy, James, and Sancho. There is no pause; before the last roll is ended, the one giving the recitative places another brother or sister on the tree, and then Jordan rolls again. It is a continuous refrain, till all have had their turn upon the tree.

A weird plantation refrain in a minor key is, "Down in the Lonesome Valley." This has also a recitative and chorus:

> My sister, don't you want to get religion?
> Go down in the lonesome valley,
> Go down in the lonesome valley,
> Go down in the lonesome valley, my Lord,
> To meet my Jesus there.

As the song goes on the enthusiasm rises. They sing louder and stronger. The one giving the recitative leads off with more vigor, and the chorus rolls with an increasing volume. They beat time at first with their feet, then with their hands. William cannot sit still. He rises, begins a shuffle with his feet, jerking his arms. Ann, a short, thick-set, pure-blooded black woman, wearing a checked gingham dress, and an apron which was once a window-curtain, can no longer keep her seat. She claps her hands, makes a short, quick jerk of her body on the unaccented part of the measure, keeping exact time. Catharine and Sancho catch the inspiration. We push the centre-table aside to give them room. They go round in a circle, singing, shuffling, jerking, shouting louder and louder. Those upon the seats respond more vigorously, keeping time with feet and hands. William seems in a trance; his eyes are fixed, yet he goes on into a double-shuffle. Every joint in his body seems to be hung on wires. Feet, legs, arms, head, body, jerk like a dancing dandy Jack. Sancho enters into the praise with his whole heart, clasping his hands, looking upward and outward upon the crowd as if they were his children and he a patriarch. His countenance beams with joy. He is all but carried away with the excitement of the moment. So it goes on till nature is exhausted. When the meeting breaks up, the singers go through the ceremony of shaking hands all round, keeping time to the tune, "There's a meeting here to-night."

WHIPPED BY WOMEN.—A correspondent informs us that in Lee County, Va., near the Tennessee line, a tory, who had slandered the widow of a deceased confederate soldier, was tied up by some half-a-dozen indignant women, and received twenty stripes. The women who administered this wholesome admonition were soldiers' wives and widows.—*Richmond Despatch.*

A DARING EXPLOIT.

SOMERSET, KY., *May* 11, 1863.—One of the most daring and successful exploits of this war was performed by four men on Saturday night, May first, on Rock Creek, in Wayne County. Benjamin Burke, a citizen, Hudson Burke, a discharged soldier, James Burke, of Wolford's cavalry, and another citizen, named James Davis, having received intimation of a band of twenty-eight men, under command of Captain Evans, of the famous band of rebel robbers that infest Wayne and Clinton counties, of this State, known as Champ Fergurson's men, having stopped at the house of Jonathan Burke, to spend the night, determined to attempt their capture. Four men against twenty-eight fiends, who had revelled in the blood of innocent neighbors for a year—think of it! It seemed like madness, yet the attempt was made. Coming to a sentinel, who stood watch over their thirty-one horses, Davis ordered him to surrender his gun, which the coward did, and received in return a blow from it which knocked his brains out. The way was now clear to the house, where the remainder of the party were asleep. Surrounding the dwelling, they at once raised a hideous yell, crying, "Wolford, Wolford!" at the top of their voices. The rebels, awakened by their noise, supposed at once that Wolford's cavalry, whom they dread as they do death, was upon them, sprang from their beds, leaving their clothes and guns behind, and rushed for the doors. Out they rushed, without any thing on but shirts and drawers; some without the latter, even,

rushed out to take leg-bail. Hudson Burke met Capt. Evans at the door; both fired at the same time. Burke was slightly wounded in the head, but the infamous Evans was instantly killed. Four others were slain, the remainder of the party escaping; but they abandoned every thing—all their horses, personal property, guns, and several thousand dollars in greenbacks, in addition to a considerable amount of confederate money. Nothing remained for the victorious few to do but gather up the fruits of their victory, which they divided with William Mulligan, a prisoner whom they had released from the clutches of the marauders.

REBEL BARBARITIES IN EAST-TENNESSEE.—The editor of the Memphis *Bulletin* communicated the following to his paper in reference to rebel rule in East-Tennessee. Col. Crawford, the gentleman from whom the facts were obtained, had a personal knowledge of some of the circumstances, and vouched for the truth of all of them:

In the month of January, 1863, at Laurel, N. C., near the Tennessee border, all the salt was seized for distribution by confederate commissioners. Salt was selling at seventy-five dollars to one hundred dollars per sack. The commissioners declared that the "tories should have none," and positively refused to give Union men their portion of the quantity to be distributed in that vicinity. This palpable injustice roused the Union men; they assembled together and determined to seize their proportion of the salt by force. They did so, taking at Marshall, N. C., what they declared to be their just share. Immediately afterward, the Sixty-fifth North-Carolina regiment, under command of Lieut.-Colonel James Keith, was ordered to Laurel to arrest the offenders.

Among those arrested were Joseph Wood, about sixty years of age; David Shelton, sixty; Jas. Shelton, fifty; Roddy Shelton, forty-five; Elison King, forty; Halen Moore, forty; Wade Moore, thirty-five; Isaiah Shelton, fifteen; Wm. Shelton, twelve; James Metcalf, ten; Jasper Channel, fourteen; Samuel Shelton, nineteen, and his brother, aged seventeen, sons of Lifus Shelton—in all thirteen men and boys. Nearly all of them declared they were innocent, and had taken no part in appropriating the salt. They begged for a trial, asserting that they could prove their innocence.

Col. Allen, who was with his troops, told them they should have a trial, but they would be taken to Tennessee for that purpose. They bid farewell to their wives, daughters, and sisters, directing them to procure the witnesses and bring them to the court in Tennessee, where they supposed their trial would take place. Alas! how little they dreamed what a fate awaited them!

The poor fellows had proceeded but a few miles, when they were turned from the road into a gorge in the mountain, and halted. Without any warning of what was to be done with them, five of them were ordered to kneel down. Ten paces in front of these five, a file of soldiers were placed with loaded muskets. The terrible reality flashed upon the minds of the doomed patriots. Wood (sixty years of age) cried out: "For God's sake, men, you are not going to shoot us! If you are going to murder us, give us, at least, time to pray." Col. Allen was reminded of his promise to give them a trial. They were informed that Allen had no authority, that Keith was in command, and that there was no time for praying. The order was given to fire; the old men and boys put their hands to their faces and rent the air with agonizing cries of despair; the soldiers wavered and hesitated to obey the command.

Keith said, if they did not fire instantly, he would make them change places with the prisoners. The soldiers raised their guns, the victims shuddered convulsively, the word was given to fire, and the five men fell pierced with rebel bullets. Wood and Shelton were shot in the head, their brains scattered upon the ground, and they died without a struggle. The other three lived only a few minutes.

Five others were ordered to kneel, among them little Billy Shelton, a mere child, only twelve years old. He implored the men not to shoot him in the face. "You have killed my father and brothers," said he, "you have shot my father in the face; do not shoot me in the face." He covered his face with his hands. The soldiers received the order to fire, and five more fell. Poor little Billy was wounded in both arms. He ran to an officer, clasped him around the legs, and besought him to spare his life. "You have killed my old father and my three brothers; you have shot me in both arms — I forgive you for all this — I can get well. Let me go home to my mother and sisters." What a heart of adamant the man must have who could disregard such an appeal! The little boy was dragged back to the place of execution; again the terrible word "fire!" was given, and he fell dead, eight balls having entered his body. The remaining three were murdered in the same manner. Those in whom life was not entirely extinct, the heartless officers despatched with their pistols.

A hole was then dug, and the thirteen bodies were pitched into it. The grave was scarcely large enough; some of the bodies lay above the ground. A wretch jumped upon the bleeding bodies, and said to some of the men: "Pat Juba for me, while I dance the d—d scoundrels down to and through hell." The grave was covered lightly with earth, and the next day, when the wives and families of the murdered men heard of their fate, searched for and found their grave, the hogs had rooted up one man's body, and eaten his head off.

Upon the return of Keith and his men to Laurel, they began systematically to torture the women of loyal men, to force them to tell where their fathers and husbands were, and what part each had taken in the said raid. The women refused to divulge any thing. They were then whipped with hickory switches; many of them till the blood coursed in streams down their persons to the ground—and the men who did this were called soldiers! Mrs. Sarah Shelton, wife of Esau Shelton, who escaped from the town, and Mrs. Mary Shelton, wife of Lifus Shelton, were whipped and hung by the neck till they were almost dead, but would give no information. Martha White, an idiotic girl, was beaten and tied by the neck all day to a tree. Mrs. Unus Riddle, aged eighty-five years, was whipped, hung, and robbed of a considerable amount of money. Many others were treated with the same barbarity. Mrs. Sallie Moore, seventy years of age, was whipped with hickory rods till the blood ran in streams down her back to the ground; and the perpetrators of this were clothed in the habiliments of rebellion, and bore the name of soldiers!

One woman, who had an infant five or six weeks old, was tied in the snow to a tree, her child placed in the door-way in her sight, and she was informed that if she did not tell all she knew about the seizure of the salt, both herself and the child would be allowed to perish.

All the women and children of the Union men who were shot, and of those who escaped, were ordered by Gen. Alfred E. Jackson to be sent through the lines by way of Knoxville. When the first of them arrived, the officer in charge applied to Gen. Donelson (formerly Speaker of the House of Representatives at Nashville) to know by which route they had been sent from there, whether by Cumberland Gap or Nashville. Gen. Donelson immediately directed them to be released and sent home, saying that such a thing was unknown in civilized countries. They were then sent home, and all the refugees met on the road were also turned back.

SONGS OF THE REBELS.

THE FEDERAL VANDALS.*

They come, they come—a motley crew,
    For rapine, rape, and plunder met;
From different realms, of every hue,
    The olive, yellow, white, and jet,
The princely loom-lord and his servile loot,
By sea and land they come, on horse, on foot.

Ye Southern freemen, who is he,
    By foes encompassed as thou art,
That will, that can deliver thee?
    That dares attempt to take thy part?
Hark ye! in loudest thunder from on high,
The great Jehovah answers—It is I.

Rise, then, ye freemen, old and young,
    Unsheathe your swords—be bold, be brave!
Away be every scabbard flung,
    In Federal blood your broadswords lave.
Arise, "arise and thresh"—'tis God's command,"†
And sweep Abe's cringing minions from your land.
                                    SENEX.

AN ACROSTIC.

IN MEMORY OF O. JENNINGS WISE.

Written in California, on reading an account of the battle of Roanoke Island.

            O'er his cold brow,
Just touched by time's soft, silvery tracing,
Entwine immortelles with the unfading laurel,
Nor fear the mildew of the grave will blight their fragrance,
Nor the rustle of the icy worm 'mid its green leaves
Impair the freshness of the dead soldier's coronal.

Not for the grave is the wreath woven, but,
Glorious dust! when the last loud reveille
Shall wake thee from thy slumbers, as one of those
Whose flitting wings reflect heaven's opening light,
In the full blaze of glory, shalt thou rise,
Soaring on high, with earth's long line of heroes,
Enwreathed with this, the patriot's fadeless crown.
                                    MIRIAM.

* The writer has taken the liberty to vary and apply to our Northern foes parts of an original poem in manuscript, written by himself.

† Micah 4:13: "Arise and thresh, O daughter of Zion; for I will make thine horn iron, and I will make thy hoof brass, and thou shalt beat in pieces many people; and I will consecrate their gain unto the Lord, and their substance unto the Lord of the whole earth."

HARP OF THE SOUTH.

A SONNET.

Harp of the South, awake! A loftier strain
Than ever yet thy tuneful strings has stirred,
Awaits thee now. The Eastern world has heard
The thunder of the battle 'cross the main,
Has seen the young South burst the tyrant's chain,
And rise to being at a single word—
The watchword, Liberty—so long transferred .
To the oppressor's mouth. Moons wax and wane,
And still the nations stand with listening ear,
And still o'er ocean floats the battle-cry;
Harp of the South, awake, and bid them hear
The name of Jackson; loud and clear and high,
Strike notes exultant o'er the hero's bier,
Who, though he sleeps in dust, can never die.

　　　　　　　　　　　　　　CORA.

A NORTH-CAROLINA CALL TO ARMS.

AIR—*The Old North State.*

BY LUOLA.

Ye sons of Carolina! awake from your dreaming!
The minions of Lincoln upon us are streaming!
Oh! wait not for argument, call, or persuasion,
To meet at the onset this treach'rous invasion!
　　Defend, defend, the old North State forever,
　　Defend, defend, the good old North State.

Oh! think of the maidens, the wives, and the mothers;
Fly ye to the rescue, sons, husbands, and brothers,
And sink in oblivion all party and section,
Your hearthstones are looking to you for protection!
　　Defend, defend, the old North State forever, etc.

Her name stands the foremost in Liberty's story,
Oh! tarnish not now her fame and her glory!
Your fathers to save her their swords bravely wielded,
And she never yet has to tyranny yielded.
　　Defend, defend, the old North State forever, etc.

The babe in its sweetness, the child in its beauty,
Unconsciously urge you to action and duty!
By all that is sacred, by all to you tender,
Your country adjures, arise and defend her!
　　Defend, defend, the old North State forever, etc.

The national eagle above us now floating,
Will soon on the vitals of loved ones be gloating;
His talons will tear, and his beak will devour;
Oh! spurn ye his sway, and delay not an hour.
　　Defend, defend, the old North State forever, etc.

The Star-Spangled Banner, dishonored, is streaming
O'er bands of fanatics; their swords are now gleaming;
They thirst for the life-blood of those you most cherish;
With brave hearts and true, then, arouse, or they
　　perish!
　　Defend, defend, the old North State forever, etc.

Round the flag of the South, oh! in thousands now
　　rally,
For the hour's departed when freemen may dally;
Your all is at stake; then go forth, and God speed
　　you!
And onward to glory and victory lead you!
　　Hurrah! hurrah! the old North State forever!
　　Hurrah! hurrah! the good old North State.

INCIDENTS OF. GRIERSON'S RAID.—While several of the Union scouts were feeding their horses at the stables of a wealthy planter of secession proclivities, the proprietor looking on, apparently deeply interested in the proceeding, suddenly burst out with : "Well, boys, I can't say I have any thing against you. I don't know but that on the whole I rather like you. You have not taken any thing of mine except a little corn for your horses, and that you are welcome to. I have heard of you all over the country. You are doing the boldest thing ever done. But you'll be trapped, though; you'll be trapped, mark me."

At another place, where the men thought it advisable to represent themselves as Jackson's cavalry, a whole company was very graciously entertained by a strong secession lady, who insisted on whipping a negro because he did not bring the hoecakes fast enough.

On one occasion, seven of Colonel Grierson's scouts stopped at the house of a wealthy planter to feed their jaded horses. Upon ascertaining that he had been doing a little guerrilla business on his own account, our men encouraged him to the belief that, as they were the invincible Van Dorn cavalry, they would soon catch the Yankees. The secession gentleman heartily approved of what he supposed to be their intentions, and enjoined upon them the necessity of making as rapid marches as possible. As the men had discovered two splendid carriage horses in the planter's stable, they thought, under the circumstances, they would be justified in making an exchange, which they accordingly proceeded to do.

As they were taking the saddles from their own tired steeds and placing them on the backs of the wealthy guerrilla's horses, the proprietor discovered them, and at once objected. He was met with the reply that, as he was anxious the Yankees should be speedily overtaken, those after them should have good horses. "All right, gentlemen," said the planter; "I will keep your animals until you return. I suppose you'll be back in two or three days at the furthest. When you return you'll find they have been well cared for." The soldiers were sometimes asked where they got their blue coats. They always replied, if they were travelling under the name of Van Dorn's cavalry, that they took them at Holly Springs of the Yankees. This always excited great laughter among the secessionists. The scouts, however, usually wore the regular "secesh" uniforms.

UNPOLITE RAIDERS.— . . . We are informed that at Okolona, in Mississippi, the Yankees, led by Grierson, set fire to and destroyed a female institute in a spirit of wanton and devilish destruction. "At Starksville," says a Southern paper, " they took from the stores such articles as they desired. They visited most of the houses, appropriating watches, jewelry, and money. They stated there and at other places that this was but an advance-guard, but that in two or three weeks an army was coming that would make a clean sweep, and burn every house in Columbus. They captured a team and wagon-load of hats going from the factory to Columbus. The hats they distributed among the negroes who were with them, and took the team along with them. They compelled a great many negroes to go with them." . . . They took all the good horses and mules, money, jewelry, and silver ware they could find. At one house in Lowndes County a portion stopped and called for milk. This was handed them in fine cut-glass goblets, which, when they had drank the milk, they dashed to pieces on the ground. A squad stopped at one house and demanded dinner. The lady said she would not cook for men acting as they were. They said : " You may think us bad, but we an't nothing, for you'll see —— along here in a few weeks." . . . A small body passed Garlandsville stealing mules and negroes. On their way there they used up and destroyed all the corn and meal of Mr. G. W. Howe, robbed him of two gold watches, all his horses and money. In Kentucky the conduct of the Yankee marauders, who are constantly spying out the land, is said to be that of licensed and uninterrupted outrage. We have had for some time on our file a copy of an unaffected letter from a lady in Kentucky ; and as it retains its interest as a simple and truthful evidence of the character of Yankee raids, we give it here : " I suppose you have heard of the raid made upon us by the Yankees. From ten to twenty caroused in the back porch all night, threatening to break in. Papa, never dreaming of such an occurrence, had remained at the farm, to protect our winter provisions, thinking food would be the only thing they would trouble. In vain we sent messenger after messenger to the officers. No help came. The fiends came about dark in the evening. The first thing they did was to carry off sister Lizzie's buggy. They broke into the store-room and took sister Lizzie's and sister Emilie's wine, which they drank and carried away next morning. They found a keg of blasting-powder, with which they threatened continually to blow us up. They were furious against papa, cursing him, saying they knew he was in the house, and if they could get hold of him they would kill him. We have heard of some being butchered in their own houses. I think it was the goodness of God that kept papa away that night. Henry and Charley (negro men) stood by us bravely, though the men were threatening their lives. Henry ran up once and took the keg of powder away from them, which they had over the candle, too drunk to know that, though they would have destroyed the house, they would have been the first to perish. Henry and Charley, who could talk a little Dutch, persuaded them, first one way and then another, not to break into the house, and got some to sleep in the cabin. They did not get in the house till morning. They got from the upper porch through the boys' room window. When ma found they were in the house she locked her room door. As we sat quietly awaiting our fate, still hoping that God — in whose care ma had in the beginning placed us, kneeling with us in earnest prayer—would yet save us, we heard them dancing, whooping, breaking, and plundering away over the house. At last the robbers scattered, carrying away every thing they could. Oh ! what a sight the house was ! Every thing scattered in confusion ; dresses, broken parasols, boxes, etc., in one incongruous mass. They stole all my jewelry—they broke all of sister Emilie's pictures. All of the silver was taken. Nan (servant) was very much distressed at their taking the blankets. Papa was arrested at the big gate, and not allowed to come to the house to tell us any thing about it. He and seven others were kept in an open tent, exposed to the chill of night and hot sun through the day, and were then carried off to Louisville."—*Richmond Examiner.*

June 1.--The sharp-shooters at Vicksburgh intersperse their crackling fire with frequent passages of polite conversation. One of the rebels three days since asked if he could have a drink of coffee if he came over and was allowed. His comrades calling to

him to return, he replied that the coffee was so tempting he intended to remain. This was the first coffee he had tasted in a twelvemonth.

A SINGULAR SPECTACLE IN BATTLE.—At the battle of Stone River, while the men were lying behind a crest waiting, a brace of frantic wild turkeys, so paralyzed with fright that they were incapable of flying, ran between the lines and endeavored to hide among the men. But the frenzy among the turkeys was not so touching as the exquisite fright of the birds and rabbits. When the roar of battle rushed through the cedar thickets, flocks of little birds fluttered and circled above the field in a state of utter bewilderment, and scores of rabbits fled for protection to the men lying down in line on the left, nestling under their coats and creeping under their legs in a state of utter distraction. They hopped over the field like toads, and as perfectly tamed by fright as household pets. Many officers witnessed it, remarking it as one of the most curious spectacles ever seen upon a battle-field.

THE GOVERNOR OF ST. CROIX AND THE ALABAMA.— An agent of the so-called " confederate States of America " at St. Croix purchased a large quantity of coal for the *Alabama*, whereupon the governor of the island informed him that it would not be permitted to be taken away by that vessel. The fire-eater's reply was that " Captain Semmes would come and take it." His Excellency's answer was an imperative order to immediately remove the coal three miles inland.

WHILE the rebel General Jenkins was in Hagerstown, Md., a lieutenant and five men, wearing the uniform of Union soldiers, crept out of some of the houses of the town where they had been hidden, and delivered themselves up. When they made their appearance before General Jenkins, the following conversation occurred :

Jenkins.—Halloo ! who are you, and where did you come from ?

Lieutenant.—We belong to the Union army, or did belong to it, but we don't wish to fight any longer against our Southern brethren ; so when our forces left here we staid behind, and to-day we came out to be paroled.

Jenkins.—What did you say about " Southern brethren " ? If I thought I had a twenty-fifth cousin who was as white-livered as you are, I would kill him and set him up in my barn-yard to make sheep own their lambs. I'll show you how I parole such pukes as you are. You are too miserable to be paroled in military style."

So saying, he ordered a detail of six men and a sergeant—"good lusty fellows, with thick boots "—who paroled the recreant Federals to the west border of the town, where the paroling process ceased, and the detail and crowd returned highly pleased with Jenkins's mode of paroling cowards.

AN ANGLO-REBEL.—The following is an extract from a private letter from an officer in the confederate army:

MY DEARLY BELOVED PARENTS : I wrote you a letter some three weeks ago, but do not know whether you have received it. Do try and write to me ; find out in London the name of some merchant in Nassau, (where all the steamers lay for a while before they run the blockade into some confederate port,) and write to me in care of that firm, and put on the envelope: "From yourself in England to a son in the confederate army in America." Oh! I do so long to hear from you all. I am in tolerably good health, and hope it will continue, and that my dear mother and sisters, Charlie, and all my relations, are alive and well, and that my dear father is also alive and well and knows no trouble; but I am afraid he has known too much since this war began. Provisions and clothing must be very high in England; in fact, I expect every thing, or nearly so, is. I wish with all my heart this war was over, and then you may be sure it would not be very long before I see the old cliffs of dear England. O England! how I love thee; never so much as when separated from thee. I love my country, but I had to join in this war, as we are in the right, and the North wants to crush us out entirely from off the face of the earth. We have now about four hundred thousand troops in the field, and the Yankees have twice as many, if not more, and yet they cannot whip us, and never will; for much as I love my dear old soil, England, never will I give up fighting for liberty and independence. We would all like this war to cease; but only on one condition — separation. No union any more for us. Why, the meanest beggar man lives better than we do. One pint of Indian corn-meal and three quarters pound fresh beef, or eight ounces of salt pork, constitute our daily meal, with a drink of water; no coffee or sugar. Coffee only costs (when there is any) twenty shillings a pound, and sugar five shillings; salt, four shillings a pound; shoes, six pound ten shillings; coat, twenty-eight pounds; trowsers, eight pound five shillings; boots, fifteen pounds; flour, seventeen pounds a barrel of two hundred pounds; eggs, four shillings a dozen; chickens, five shillings each; butter, five shillings and sixpence a pound; ink, eighteen shillings a pint; pens, sixpence each; common tallow candles, three shillings each; shirts, two pounds five shillings; and every thing else in proportion. The ladies cut up their carpets to make blankets for the soldiers. When you have something good to eat, just think of me in America, twenty-six years old this year, going on seven years since I left home. Oh! I do so long for the time to come for me to go home; and I hope God will spare my life until that end is attained.

ARMY OF TENNESSEE, TULLAHOMA, Tenn., Confederate States of America, April 5.

THE FIRST ATTEMPT TO ARM NEGROES.—A correspondent of the Memphis *Bulletin* shows the first attempt to arm negroes and put them in the field as soldiers was made by the rebels. He copies from the Memphis *Appeal* and the Memphis *Avalanche* of May ninth, tenth, and eleventh, 1861, the following notice:

ATTENTION, VOLUNTEERS: Resolved by the Committee of Safety, that C. Deloach, D. R. Cook, and William B. Greenlaw be authorized to organize a volunteer company composed of our patriotic free men of color, of the city of Memphis, for the service of our common defence. All who have not enrolled their names will call at the office of W. B. Greenlaw & Co.

F. TITUS, President.

F. W. FORSYTHE, Secretary.

GENERAL LEE'S WOOING.

"*My Maryland! My Maryland!*"

My Maryland! My Maryland!
  Among thy hills of blue
I wander far, I wander wide,
  A lover born and true;
I sound my horn upon the hills,
  I sound it in the vale,
But echo only answers it—
  An echo like a wail.

My Maryland! My Maryland!
  I bring thee presents fine—
A dazzling sword with jewelled hilt,
  A flask of Bourbon wine;
I bring thee sheets of ghostly white
  To dress thy bridal bed,
With curtains of the purple eve
  And garlands gory red.

My Maryland! My Maryland!
  Sweet land upon the shore,
Bring out thy stalwart yeomanry!
  Make clean the threshing-floor;
My ready wains lie stretching far
  Across the fertile plain,
And I among the reapers stand
  To gather in the grain.

My Maryland! My Maryland!
  I fondly wait to see
Thy banner flaunting in the breeze
  Beneath the trysting tree;
While all my gallant company
  Of gentlemen, with spurs,
Come tramping, tramping o'er the hills,
  And tramping through the furze.

My Maryland! My Maryland!
  I feel the leaden rain!
I see the winged messenger
  Come hurling to my brain!
I feathered with thy golden hair,
  'Tis feathered not in vain;
I spurn the hand that loosed the shaft,
  And curse thee in my pain.

My Maryland! My Maryland!
  Alas! the ruthless day!
That sees my gallant buttonwoods
  Ride galloping away;
And ruthless for my chivalry,
  Proud gentlemen, with spurs,
Whose bones lie stark upon the hills,
  And stark among the furze.   G.

AFTER THE BATTLE.

The drums are all muffled, the bugles are still;
There's a pause in the valley, a halt on the hill;
And bearers of standards swerve back with a thrill
  Where shreves of the dead bar the way;
For a great field is reaped, Heaven's garners to fill;
  And stern Death holds his harvest to-day.

There's a voice in the wind like a spirit's low cry;
'Tis the muster-roll sounding, and who shall reply,
For those whose wan faces glare white to the sky,
  With eyes fixed so steadfast and dimly,
As they wait that last trump which they may not delay!
  Whose hands clutch that sword-hilt so grimly;

The brave heads late lifted are solemnly bowed,
As the riderless chargers stand quivering and cowed,
As the burial requiem is chanted aloud,
　　The groans of the death-stricken drowning;
While victory looks on like a queen pale and proud,
　　Who awaits till the morning her crowning.

There is no mocking blazon, as clay sinks to clay;
The vain pomp of peace-time are all swept away
In the terrible face of the dread battle-day;
　　Nor coffins nor shroudings are here;
Only relics that lay where thickest the fray—
　　A rent casque and a headless spear.

Far away, tramp on tramp, peals the march of the foe,
Like a storm-wave retreating, spent fitful and slow,
With sound like their spirits that faint as they go
　　By the red glowing river, whose waters
Shall darken with sorrow the land where they flow
　　To the eyes of her desolate daughters.

They are fled—they are gone; but oh! not as they
　　came;
In the pride of those numbers they staked on the
　　game,
Nevermore shall they stand in the vanguard of fame,
　　Never lift the stained sword which they drew;
Nevermore shall they boast of a glorious name,
　　Never march with the leal and the true.

Where the wreck of our legions lay stranded and
　　torn,
They stole on our ranks in the midst of the morn;
Like the giant of Gaza, their strength it was shorn,
　　Ere those mists have rolled up to the sky;
From the flash of the steel a new day-break seemed
　　born,
　　As we sprung up to conquer or die.

The tumult is silenced; the death lots are cast;
And the heroes of battle are slumbering their last:
Do you dream of yon pale form that rode on the
　　blast?
　　Would ye free it once more, O ye brave!
Yes, the broad road to Honor is red where ye passed,
　　And of glory ye asked—but a grave!

OUR VOLUNTEER.

BY MARY CLEMMER AMES.

We gather round the twilight hearth,
　　Beneath the evening's pallid flame;
And softening every sound of mirth,
　　We murmur the beloved name.

We try to still the voice of care,
　　And cheerily say: "One year to-day
The dulcet drum and bugle blare
　　Allured our darling far away."

And stifling back the crowding tear,
　　We murmur, while our prayers ascend:
"Our Father's saved the boy a year—
　　He'll surely save him to the end."

His grand dog smooths sad, drooping ears
　　Along my hand, in mute regret;
His wistful eyes half read my fears—
　　"Old Boy, you miss your master yet!"

The ringing voice, the eye of fire,
　　The lithe young form, the step of pride,
That once made all your heart's desire,
　　Old pet, they're sundered from you wide.

Your gay bark in the hunt is hushed—
　　A dearer meaning now you take,
As every thing his hand has touched
　　Is cherished sacred for his sake.

Ah! does he think of home to-night,
　　And how we sit and talk of him—
Repeat his words with fond delight,
　　With voices low and eyelids dim?

We wonder when, with faces white,
　　Must be the next terrific fray;
And if the march began last night,
　　And where our army is to-day?

We listen to a dear young voice
　　Sing words of love to music wed;
So mournful, we may not rejoice—
　　He loved that song in summers fled.

It says: "Oh! take me home to die!"
　　What tender pains its rhythms yield;
Not thus, not thus, O Lord! we cry,
　　Send back our boy from war's red field!

Oh! leave us not, lest we repine,
　　If this the "glory" thou shalt mete;
To die for truth makes death divine,
　　To die for country, it is sweet!

We love thee 'neath the heavy rod;
　　We trust thee in the nation's night;
Our only help and hope is, God,
　　That thou at last will crown the right.

The paradise of spring-time hours
　　He loved. In all her azure space,
'Mid all the summer pomp of flowers,
　　We'll yearn in vain to see his face.

In wasting march, in bloody fight,
　　All, in love, yet half in fear,
We pray from morning until night,
　　That God will save Our Volunteer.

THE FORCED RECRUIT.

In the ranks of Rebellion you found him,
　　He died with his face to you all;
Yet bury him here where around him
　　You honor your bravest that fall.

Virginian—fair-featured and slender,
　　He lies shot to death in his youth,
With a smile on his lips over-tender
　　For any mere soldier's dead mouth.

No stranger, and yet not a traitor;
　　Though hostile the cloth on his breast,
Underneath it how seldom a greater
　　Young heart has a shot sent to rest!

By your enemy tortured and goaded
　　To march with them, stand in their file,
His musket (see!) never was loaded,
　　He facing your guns with that smile!

As orphans yearn on to their mothers
　　He yearned to your patriot bands;—
"Let me die for America, brothers,
　　If not in your ranks, by your hand!

"Aim straightly, fire steadily! spare me
　　A ball in the body which may
Deliver my heart here, and tear me
　　This badge of the traitor away!"

So thought he, so died he, this morning.
　What then?　Many others have died.
Ay, but easy for men to die scorning
　The death-stroke who fought side by side—

One tri-color floating above them;
　Struck down 'mid triumphant acclaims
Of America rescued to love them
　And blazon the brass with their names.

But he—without witness or honor,
　Mixed, shamed in his country's regard
With the traitors who march in upon her,
　Died faithful and passive: 'twas hard.

'Twas sublime.　In a cruel restriction
　Cut off from her guerdon of sons,
With most filial obedience, conviction,
　His soul kissed the lips of her guns.

That moves you?.　Nay, grudge not to show it
　While digging a grave for him here:
The others who died, says our poet,
　Have glory—let *him* have a tear.

A BATTLE POEM.

BY BENJ. F. TAYLOR.

Break up camp, drowsy World!
　For the SHROUDS are unfurled,
And the dead drummers beat the long roll through
　　the morn,
　And the bugle-blown orders
　Invade the dumb borders
Where the grave-digger dreamed he had laid them
　　forlorn.

　From old Saratoga,
　From old Ticonderoga,
From Bennington, Bunker, and Lexington Green,
　They have marched back sublime
　To the sentries of time,
And have passed on triumphant, unchallenged be-
　　tween!
　I can hear the flint-locks,—
　The old click of the clocks
That timed Liberty's step to no pendulum swing!
　When the bullets all sped,
　Woman smilingly said,
"Let us charm the dull weights till they fly and they
　　sing!"

　Ah! those old blackened ladles
　Where Glory's own cradles!
Rocked a red-coat to sleep with each birth from the
　　mould,
　And the old fashioned-fire
　Blazed hotter and higher,
Till it welded the New World and walled out the Old.

　By battalions they come,
　To the snarl of the drum!
Bleeding feet that turn beautiful, printing the snow,
　For roses seem blowing
　Where'er they are going,
As if June with her blushes were buried below.

　Hail, mighty Campaigners!
　The Lord's old retainers!
Eighty winters on furlough, the tidings ye bring,
　Of the old royal Georges
　And the old Valley Forges,
Our cannon are telling: the People are King!

　Clear and strong, far and near,
　Rings a Green Mountain cheer,
And they lower their dim colors all shivered and shred,
　And their swords red with rust,
　And their guns gray with dust,
And then shoulder to shoulder, the Living and Dead!

　The broad age is a line—
　Past and present entwine—
We will finish the work that the Fathers begun;
　Then those to their sleeping,
　And these to their weeping,
And one faith and flag for the Federal gun!

　Speak, Helmsman, the words
　Half battles, half swords—
Let the "President's March" be resounding abroad;
　With thy pen on the page
　Keeping time with the Age,
Till thy swords without scabbards flash grandly for
　　God!

Then the rattling roll of the musketeers,
And the ruffled drums, and the rallying cheers,
And the rifles burn with a keen desire,
Like the crackling whips of the hemlock fire,
And the singing shot, and the shrieking shell,
And the splintery fire of the shattered hell,
And the great white breaths of the cannon-smoke,
As the growling guns by batteries spoke
In syllables dropped from the thunder of GOD—
The throb of the cloud where the drummer-boy trod!
And the ragged gaps in the walls of blue
Where the iron surge rolled heavily through,
That the Colonel builds with a breath again,
As he cleaves the dim with his "Close up, men!"
And the groan torn out from the blackened lips,
And the prayer doled slow with the crimson drips,
And the beamy look in the dying eye,
As under the cloud the Stars go by!
But his soul marched on, the Captain said,
For the Boy in Blue can never be dead!

And the troopers sit in their saddles all,
As the statues carved in an ancient hall,
And they watch the whirl from their breathless ranks,
And their spurs are close to the horses' flanks,
And the fingers work of the sabre hand—
Oh! to bid them live, and to make them grand!
And the bugle sounds to the charge at last,
And away they plunge, and the front is past,
And the jackets blue grow red as they ride,
And the scabbards, too, that clank by their side,
And the dead soldiers deaden the strokes iron shod,
As they gallop right on o'er the plashy red sod:
Right into the cloud all spectral and dim,
Right up to the guns, black throated and grim,
Right down on the hedges bordered with steel,
Right through the dense columns, then "Right about,
　　wheel!"
Hurrah! a new swath through the harvest again!
Hurrah for the Flag!　To the battle, amen!

　O glimpse of clear heaven!
　Artillery riven!
The Fathers' old fallow God seeded with Stars—
　Thy furrows were turning
　When ploughshares were burning,
And the half of each "bout" is redder than Mars!

　Flaunt forever thy story,
　O wardrobe of glory!
Where the Fathers laid down their mantles of blue,

And challenged the ages,
O grandest of pages!
In covenant solemn, eternal, and true.

O Flag glory-rifted!
To-day thunder-drifted,
Like a flower of strange grace on the crest of a surge,
On some Federal fold
A new tale shall be told,
And the record immortal emblazon thy verge.

A WELCOME HOME.

Delivered at the Reception of the Framingham members of
the Massachusetts Forty-fourth regiment, South-Framingham,
June 11, 1863.

BY THOMAS F. POWER.

Rest! soldier, rest! Not now the trumpet pealing,
Rousing to arms, shall thrill the patriot breast,
For white-robed Peace shall now awhile enfold thee;
Rest! soldier, rest!

Rest! soldier, rest! the joyous cannon hail thee;
The singing trumpets' silvery tones attest
That all now bid the war-tried patriot welcome;
Rest! soldier, rest!

Not now the drenching rain—the weary marching;
No fierce besiegers now thy valor test;
No bursting shells—guerrilla raids at midnight;
Rest! soldier, rest!

Not here the flashing of the foeman's sabre;
Not here the wide ranks kneel to Death's behest;
Naught but the glance of bright eyes kindly beaming;
Rest! soldier, rest!

Not here the whistling of the leaden death-shots—
'Tis but the Oriole singing o'er her nest;
The waving tree-tops whispering peace and quiet;
Rest! soldier, rest!

See yon fair wife, a white-armed welcome waving!
No longer now by deadly fear opprest;
What heavenly music is that dear voice saying:
Rest! soldier, rest!

A mother's kisses greet her first-born darling;
O joy! how closely heart to heart is prest;
In home, sweet home, she bids the weary wanderer
Rest! soldier, rest!

Not all who answered to Columbia, calling
On her brave sons from North, and East, and West,
Can answer now—their voices hushed forever;
Rest! soldier, rest!

Loud let the bugle swell the note of triumph!
Sound, trumpets! praise our bravest and our best!
Thousands of voices bid each hero welcome;
Rest! soldier, rest!

FOR THE UNION.

BY CHARLES BOYNTON HOWELL.

Speak boldly for the Union,
Though traitorous foes are near!
Let not that flag trail in the dust
Our fathers held so dear;
Then victory's golden sunlight
Will break in the nation's sky,
And the starry folds of our banner
Will float triumphantly!

Fight bravely for the Union,
Ye soldiers in the field!
And though the hour of strife is dark,
Never to traitors yield!
Remember the bold defenders
Of our land in its infancy,
And strike for your country gallantly,
For God and Liberty!

Work, patriots, for the Union,
Till the hour of triumph comes!
When the lusty shouts of victory
Mingle with rolls of drums;
Till the shadowy clouds of treason
Have floated fore'er away,
And the sunrise beams of hope and peace
Tell of a brighter day.

THE EAGLE OF THE SEA.

BY W. H. C. HOSMER.

Rocked in the trough of waves—to-night
Aquila takes an eagle's flight;
In the wind's eye she walks ahead,
Ruled by a Chief who knows not dread.

He is a sailor, staunch and true,
Upholding the "Red, White, and Blue,"
And guides his vessel over waves
That roll above a million graves.

I love the thunder of the gale,
And pity those whose cheeks turn pale;
I love the broad, blue open sea,
Its billows have a charm for me.

We may go down, or strike a reef,
But the last anguish will be brief;
The resurrection trump from sleep
Can wake the dead ones of the Deep.

Oh! what is Greenwood to the sea,
A grander, nobler cemetery;
On its vast bottom lie the brave
Entombed in many a coral cave.

Let the storm whistle through the shrouds,
While over us are angry clouds;
Staunch is the bark that bears us o'er
Rough waters to a brighter shore.

Capped is the mountain surge with foam,
And grand is Father Neptune's home;
I wish his shell by dolphins drawn
Could bear the fiery poet on.

But canvas-winged, and cable-reined
Our ship her glory has maintained,
While shouts aloud the sailor boy,
She walks the waters in her joy.

At last her toughened bones may bleach
On ocean's gray and wreck-strewn beach;
But what a nobler fate could be
For the proud Eagle of the sea.

Let the wind howl, and roar the surge,
Aquila will her pathway urge,
And time, with swift, but easy motion,
Keep to the pulse-beat of the ocean.

Fear not, my comrades, going forth,
From the broad West and frowning North,
To crush upon a Southern shore
False traitors with the cannon's roar.

God rules by sea, as well as land,
Trust ever in his saving hand;
For man upon life's troubled seas
Must brave the battle and the breeze.

NATIONAL WAR-SONG.

AIR—*John Brown.*

Oh! say, and is the Union gone, O countrymen! for
　　aye?
Alas! the starry Flag is rent that floated once on high!
But shall the Southern rebel rag e'er mock our North-
　　ern sky?
　　　　O Northmen! answer, Nay!

Chorus.

　　To arms! ye heroes of the nation!
　　To arms! and stay the conflagration!
　　Come from high or lowly station!
　　To arms! we'll conquer yet!

We hold the forts that frown above the Mississippi's
　　tide.
Though Vicksburgh yet may mock us, we will soon
　　her strength deride.
Shall rebels keep our commerce from that current
　　strong and wide?
　　　　O Northmen! answer, Nay!

Shall we give up the city, friends, where Jackson
　　boldly fought?
Shall Farragut's wild gallantry be thrown away for
　　naught?
Shall New-Orleans belong to those who have our ruin
　　sought?
　　　　O Northmen! answer, Nay!

Louisiana is our own, we bought her with a price;
Ours her fields of sugar-cane; ours her swamps of
　　rice!
Shall rebels win her from us, friends, by any base
　　device?
　　　　O Northmen! answer, Nay!

A cry goes up to heaven above from Eastern Tennes-
　　see,
And Knoxville prays our conquering arms to set her
　　people free;
Shall we give up her patriot sons to Southern tyranny?
　　　　O Northmen! answer, Nay!

The noble West-Virginians foreswore the Richmond
　　yoke,
And braved the Old Dominion's power with sturdy
　　hearts of oak;
Shall Letcher and Jeff Davis, friends, their patriot
　　ardor choke?
　　　　O Northmen! answer, Nay!

Remember Sumter's fearful siege, and noble Anderson!
We kept our hands from brothers' blood—they fired
　　the fatal gun:
Shall we give up Virginia, the land of Washington?
　　　　O Northmen! answer, Nay!

Chorus.

　　To arms! ye heroes of the nation!
　　To arms! and stay the conflagration!
　　Come from high or lowly station!
　　To arms! we'll conquer yet!

SPIRITUALISM AT THE WHITE HOUSE.

WASHINGTON, April 23, 1863.

A few evenings since, Abraham Lincoln, President
of the United States, was induced to give a spiritual
soirée in the crimson room at the White House, to test
the wonderful alleged supernatural powers of Mr.
Charles E. Shockle. It was my good fortune, as a
friend of the medium, to be present, the party consisting of the President, Mrs. Lincoln, Mr. Welles, Mr.
Stanton, Mr. L—— of New-York, and Mr. F—— of
Philadelphia. We took our seats in the circle about
eight o'clock, but the President was called away shortly after the manifestations commenced, and the spirits,
which had apparently assembled to convince him of
their power, gave visible tokens of their displeasure at
the President's absence, by pinching Mr. Stanton's ears
and twitching Mr. Welles's beard. He soon returned,
but it was some time before harmony was restored,
for the mishaps to the secretaries caused such bursts
of laughter that the influence was very unpropitious.
For some half-hour the demonstrations were of a physical character—tables were moved, and the picture of
Henry Clay, which hangs on the wall, was swayed
more than a foot, and two candelabras, presented by
the Dey of Algiers to President Adams, were twice
raised nearly to the ceiling.

It was nearly nine o'clock before Shockle was fully
under spiritual influence, and so powerful were the
subsequent manifestations, that twice during the evening restoratives were applied, for he was much weakened; and though I took no notes, I shall endeavor to
give you as faithful an account as possible of what
took place.

Loud rappings, about nine o'clock, were heard directly beneath the President's feet, and Mr. Shockle
stated that an Indian desired to communicate.

"Well, sir," said the President, "I should be happy
to hear what his Indian majesty has to say. We have
recently had a visitation from our red brethren, and it
was the only delegation, black, white, or blue, which
did not volunteer some advice about the conduct of
the war."

The medium then called for pencil and paper, and
they were laid upon the table in sight of all. A handkerchief was then taken from Mr. Stanton, and the
materials were carefully concealed from sight. In less
space of time than it has required for me to write this,
knocks were heard and the paper was uncovered. To
the surprise of all present it read as follows:

"Haste makes waste, but delays cause vexations.
Give vitality by energy. Use every means to subdue.
Proclamations are useless; make a bold front and
fight the enemy; leave traitors at home to the care of
loyal men. Less note of preparation, less parade and
policy talk, and more action. HENRY KNOX."

"That is not Indian talk, Mr. Shockle," said the
President. "Who is Henry Knox?"

I suggested to the medium to ask who General
Knox was, and before the words were from my lips
the medium spoke in a strange voice: "The first Secretary of War."

"Oh! yes, General Knox," said the President; who,
turning to the Secretary, said: "Stanton, that message
is for you; it is from your predecessor."

Mr. Stanton made no reply.

"I should like to ask General Knox," said the President, "if it is within the scope of his ability, to tell us
when this rebellion will be put down."

In the same manner as before, this message was received:

"Washington, Lafayette, Franklin, Wilberforce,

Napoleon, and myself have held frequent consultations on this point. There is something which our spiritual eyes cannot detect which appear well formed. Evil has come at times by removal of men from high positions, and there are those in retirement whose abilities should be made useful to hasten the end. Napoleon says, concentrate your forces upon one point; Lafayette thinks that the rebellion will die of exhaustion; Franklin sees the end approaching, as the South must give up for want of mechanical ability to compete against Northern mechanics. Wilberforce sees hope only in a negro army.—KNOX."

"Well," exclaimed the President, "opinions differ among the saints as well as among the sinners. They don't seem to understand running the machines among the celestials much better than we do. Their talk and advice sound very much like the talk of my cabinet—don't you think so, Mr. Welles?"

"Well, I don't know—I will think the matter over, and see what conclusion to arrive at."

Heavy raps were heard, and the alphabet was called for, when "That's what's the matter," was spelt out.

There was a shout of laughter, and Mr. Welles stroked his beard.

"That means, Mr. Welles," said the President, "that you are apt to be long-winded, and think the nearest way home is the longest way round. Short cuts in war times. I wish the spirits could tell us how to catch the Alabama."

The lights, which had been partially lowered, almost instantaneously became so dim that I could not see sufficiently to distinguish the features of any one in the room, and on the large mirror over the mantlepiece there appeared the most beautiful though supernatural picture ever beheld. It represented a sea view, the Alabama with all steam up flying from the pursuit of another large steamer. Two merchantmen in the distance were seen, partially destroyed by fire. The picture changed, and the Alabama was seen at anchor under the shadow of an English fort—from which an English flag was waving. The Alabama was floating idly, not a soul on board, and no signs of life visible about her. The picture vanished, and in letters of purple appeared: "The English people demanded this of England's aristocracy."

"So England is to seize the Alabama finally?" said the President. "It may be possible; but, Mr. Welles, don't let one gunboat or monitor less be built."

The spirits called for the alphabet, and again "That's what's the matter," was spelt out.

"I see, I see," said the President, "Mother England thinks that what's sauce for the goose may be sauce for the gander. It may be tit, tat, too, hereafter. But it is not very complimentary to our navy, anyhow."

"We've done our best, Mr. President," said Mr. Welles. "I'm maturing a plan which, when perfected, I think, if it works well, will be a perfect trap for the Alabama."

"Well, Mr. Shockle," remarked the President, "I have seen strange things and heard rather odd remarks; but nothing which convinces me, except the pictures, that there is any thing very heavenly about all this. I should like, if possible, to hear what Judge Douglas says about this war."

"I'll try to get his spirit," said Mr. Shockle; "but it sometimes happens, as it did to-night in the case of the Indian, that though first impressed by one spirit, I yield to another more powerful. If perfect silence is maintained, I will see if we cannot induce General Knox to send for Mr. Douglas."

Three raps were given, signifying assent to the proposition. Perfect silence was maintained, and after an interval of perhaps three minutes Mr. Shockle rose quickly from his chair and stood up behind it, resting his left arm on the back, his right thrust into his bosom. In a voice such as no one could mistake who had ever heard Mr. Douglas, he spoke. I shall not pretend to quote the language. It was eloquent and choice. He urged the President to throw aside all advisers who hesitate about the policy to be pursued, and to listen to the wishes of the people, who would sustain him at all points if his aim was, as he believed it was, to restore the Union. He said there were Burrs and Blennerhassetts living, but that they would wither before the popular approval which would follow one or two victories, such as he thought must take place ere long. The turning-point in this war will be the proper use of these victories. If wicked men in the first hours of success think it time to devote their attention to party, the war will be prolonged; but if victory is followed up by energetic action, all will be well.

"I believe that," said the President, "whether it comes from spirit or human."

Mr. Shockle was much prostrated after this, and at Mrs. Lincoln's request it was thought best to adjourn the dance, which, if resumed, I shall give you an account of. Yours as ever, MELTON.

THE HERO OF THE DRUM.

BY GEO. W. BUNGAY.

The drummer with his drum,
Shouting, "Come! heroes, come!"
  Forward marched, nigher, nigher;
When the veterans turned pale,
And the bullets fell like hail;
In that hurricane of fire,
  Beat his drum,
  Shouting, "Come!
      Come! come! come!
      And the fife
      In the strife
    Joined the drum, drum, drum—
And the fifer with his fife and the drummer with his drum,
Were heard above the strife and the bursting of the bomb;
        The bursting of the bomb,
            Bomb, bomb, bomb.

Clouds of smoke hung like a pall
Over tent, and dome, and hall;
  Hot shot and blazing bomb
Cut down our volunteers,
Swept off our engineers;
  But the drummer beat his drum—
    And he beat
    "No retreat!"
      With his drum;
        Through the fire,
        Hotter, nigher,
        Throbbed the drum, drum, drum,
In that hurricane of fame, and the thunder of the bomb!
Braid the laurel-wreath of flame for the hero of the drum.
        The hero of the drum,
            Drum, drum, drum.

Where the Rappahannock runs,
The sulphur-throated guns
    Poured out hail and fire;
But the heroes in the boats
Heeded not the sulphur-throats,
    For they looked up higher, higher;
        While the drum,
        Never dumb,
        Beat, beat, beat,
            Till our oars
            Touch the shores,
            And the feet, feet, feet,
Of the soldiers on the shore, with the bayonet and
    gun,
Though the drum could beat no more, made the dastard
    rebels run,
        The dastard rebels run,
                    Run, run, run.

"GREENBACKS."

The following was written across the back of one of those bills.

Green be thy back upon thee!
    Thou pledge of happier days,
When bloody-handed treason
    No more its hand shall raise;
But still, from Maine to Texas,
    'The Stars and Stripes shall wave
O'er the hearts and homes of freemen,
    Nor mock one fettered slave.

Pledge—of the people's credit
    To carry on the war,
By furnishing the sinews
    In a currency at par—
With cash enough left over,
    When they've cancelled every note,
To buy half the thrones of Europe,
    With the crowns tossed in to boot.

Pledge—to our buried fathers,
    That sons of patriot sires,
On Freedom's sacred altars,
    Re-light their glorious fires—
That fortune, life, and honor
    To our country's cause we give—
Fortune and life may perish,
    Yet the Government shall live.

Pledge—to our unborn children,
    That, free from blot or stain,
The flag hauled down at Sumter
    Shall yet float free again—
And, cleansed from foul dishonor,
    And re-baptized in blood,
Wave o'er the land forever,
    To Freedom and to God!

"SHOULDER ARMS!"

There's a cry sweeps o'er the land—
                    Shoulder arms!
Who would not a coward stand—
                    Shoulder arms!
When one's country cries for aid,
Only fools hang back afraid.
There's a cry sweeps o'er the land—
                    Shoulder arms!

Who's afraid to meet the foe—
Who would see the flag laid low
In the dust by traitors base—
Let him hide his face!
Who would win a soldier's fame—
                    Shoulder arms!
Who would bear a hero's name—
                    Shoulder arms!
Let him march with purpose high,
Now to conquer or to die!
Who would win a soldier's fame—
                    Shoulder arms!

There's a cry falls from the sky—
                    Shoulder arms!
Through the air 'tis sweeping by—
                    Shoulder arms!
Armies of the patriot dead
Fill the heaven above your head,
There's a cry falls from the sky—
                    Shoulder arms!
"Ye, our children," hear them say,
"Ye are born in evil day;
    But the evil stout withstood
    Turneth into good.
For the country we made free—
                    Shoulder arms!
For the world that free shall be—
                    Shoulder arms!
Europe eager watches you;
Bring the great Republic through!
For the world that free shall be—
                    Shoulder arms!"

Onward! onward to the van!
                    Shoulder arms!
Forward like a loyal man!
                    Shoulder arms!
Stand not like one deaf and dumb,
While you hear th' appealing drum!
Onward! onward to the van!
                    Shoulder arms!
    See the rebels ranks advance!
    Wake, man, from your guilty trance!
    'Tis the time for action deep,
    Not the hour for sleep.
God will bless the work you do—
                    Shoulder arms!
He will bring you safely through—
                    Shoulder arms!
Fearless of the issue, fight,
Fighting on the side of Right!
God will bless the work you do!
                    Shoulder arms!

OUR COUNTRY'S CALL.

TO THE PATRIOTIC WOMEN OF ST. LOUIS.

Come, sisters! in this noble strife
    Join every heart and hand!
There's work for each and every one—
    And shall we listless, idly stand?
List to the widow's piercing shriek!
    Oh! hear the orphan's piteous cry!
Watch the pale wife as o'er his couch
    She bends to catch the parting sigh.

Shall we, Columbia's daughters, sit,
    With hearts unmoved and listless air,
Nor aid our brothers, husbands, sons,
    Our country's flag to nobly bear?

Forbid it, heaven! on thee we call
  In this dark hour of deep distress!
Oh! give us true and loyal hearts,
  And words of cheer and tenderness.

We cannot wear the glittering sword,
  And gain the laurel wreath of fame,
Or raise upon some gory field,
  For warlike deeds, a deathless name;
But we can go with gentle words,
  With acts of kindness and of love,
To some brave heart—some suffering one—
  And point him to a home above.

Our hands can soothe the aching brow,
  And wipe the tears which freely flow
From manly eyes, unused to weep—
  'Tis ours the feeling heart to show.
Our country calls! We join this league,
  And pledge ourselves with earnest zeal—
With loyal hearts and lifted hands,
  To firmly stand—come woe or weal.

Oh! never can we see that Flag
  Which our forefathers proudly bore,
Through years of dark and deadly strife,
  Through fields red with their brave heart's
    gore,
Torn from its place, and 'neath the feet
  Of traitors vile, trailed in the earth,
Disgraced, abused, by those who've lived
  Beneath its folds from earliest birth.

Next to our God, our country's cause
  Demands our aid—our earnest care—
In her defence we'll ever stand;
  In all her sorrows we will share.
Then, when the storms of war are o'er—
  When Peace resumes her gentle sway,
We'll join to raise our voices high
  To Him who led us on our way.

O God of Nations! hear our prayer
  For our brave soldiers in this fight;
Protect them in each fearful hour;
  Defend them with thy arm of might,
We look to thee, and humbly bow,
  Chastened, subdued, we meekly cry,
"Thy will, O, God! not ours, be done!"
  Oh! hear us, from thy throne on high.
                  VIOLA.

THE CAVALRY SCOUT.

A BALLAD OF THE SECOND WISCONSIN, WRITTEN
AMONG THE TOMBS.

"Spare man nor steed, use utmost speed; before the
  sun goes down,
Thou, sir, must ride," the Colonel cried, "unto
  Helena town."

"Colonel!" the stern Lieutenant said, "to hear is to
  obey!
Comrades! the path is fringed with death; who rides
  with me to-day?"

Instant a gallant Sergeant spoke: "I ride with thee
  to-day."
Along the ranks a wild shout broke: "We follow!
  lead the way!"

Out sprang a little trumpeter, and clasped the courier's
  knees;
"I'll sound the charge, I'll call the halt—me, too! let
  me go, please!"

"Nay, boy! I want nor trumpet-note, nor arm nor
  sword so small;
The ranger's ball shall sound the charge, the halt but
  death shall call."

To horse! the steeds impatient neigh; to horse! the
  way is long.
Brave hearts are light, keen sabres bright, and willing
  arms are strong.

The clatter of hoofs! the clash of steel! the day is
  nearly done;
There will be need of armed heel ere the far off goal
  be won.

Lo! the entrance to Cyril's Wood gapes like the
  mouth of hell;
The dauntless courier mutters, "Good! the rebel dogs
  watch well!"

No rein is drawn at the line of flame; tally, a score
  and six.
"My place to lead" is the sergeant's claim; "Ho for
  the River Styx!"

"Thou follow!" rings the quick reply; "for God and
  liberty!"
And the well-closed column dashes by—tally, a score
  less three.

"Comrades!"—the courier turned his head—"if I
  fall, pass me by,
'Whom the gods love, die young,' 'tis said; it is no
  shame to die."

The sunless swamp is near at hand; gleameth each
  hostile tree;
Eyes to the front, the lessening band, reckless, ride
  rapidly.

"Help ho! the sergeant!" (One hath seen whence
  the death-bearing sped;
Aimeth the ranger's eyes between, pierceth the ranger's head.)

Under the giant cypress him the rough hands gently
  place;
Give water to cool the fevered lips, to lave the burning face.

Not here! his thoughts are far away in the home he
  loved so well;
Like a sleepy child he murmurs: "Hark! do you
  hear the vesper-bell?"

Hid in his bosom, bathed in blood, is a cherished lock
  of hair;
He snatches it forth from the welling flood, and takes
  of his own so fair,

And puts them into his comrade's hand—"You know
  the happy spot;
Give her who waits these tresses twain, and say I
  ne'er forgot."

Away! away! think not to stay! no bootless vigil
  keep,
Give little heed to a comrade's need—a soldier may
  not weep.

Away! away! the passing day warns to use utmost
speed;
Hark to the shouts of the rebel scouts! Away!
away! good steed!

Come hither and see the glory with me—are thine
eyes so weak, my love?
Sunlit mountains stand on either hand, and a purple
sky above:

"There's a path goes out at the golden west," trod
by the parting day,
That leads to the fabled home of the blest, "over the
hills away:"

The sun swells big in a last fond gaze, big with the
light of love—
Come hither and see, it will not daze, for the purple
grows misty above.

Drive home the spur! a riderless horse into the night
leads on;
Follow! faint not! his master's corpse is many a mile
by-gone.

On! on! deem not the danger passed till the wished-
for goal be won.
—"WHO GOES?"—"Thank God! the lines, at
last!" and the hard race is done.

"Boys! who is here?" a trooper cried; "How many
are alive?"
And the stern courier's voice replied: "BRAVE COM-
RADES, WE ARE FIVE!"

   EDMUNDUS SCOTUS, Ninth Illinois Cavalry.
CYRIL'S WOOD, ARK.

THE "OLD CONCERN."

A NEW SONG BY UNCLE SAM.

The "Old Concern," which has so long
 Its banner bright unfurled—
In honor, truth, and glory strong—
 The pride of all the world!
Ah! cowards, if one spark of shame
 Can in your bosom burn,
Reflect how much you owe the name
 Of that good "Old Concern."

Through long, long years, your happy lot
 It made for you; and then
It gave—what else you ne'er had got—
 A station among men;
Without its aid which of you, pray,
 An honest cent would earn?
And yet you wish to run away,
 And leave the "Old Concern."

Remember Bunker! Lexington!
 The Delaware! Yorktown!
Fields where our fathers fought and won
 Their glory and renown!
To Vernon go, and thoughtfully
 Gaze on yon sacred urn,
Then think what caitiffs you must be,
 To curse the "Old Concern!"

You're rich, because you robbed my till,
 And cotton makes you great;
You'd shut up shop against my will,
 But cotton you can't eat;

And when your negroes run away,
 You then, perhaps, will learn
It had been wiser far to stay
 And mind the "Old Concern."

When anarchy's dread wings unfurl
 Upon that shore so dark,
To which ambitious fiends would hurl
 Your frail and happy bark,
Ah! then, perhaps—but when too late—
 You'll hopelessly discern,
How happier was your former state
 When in the "Old Concern."

O madmen! time will surely come
 When you, in grief, will learn
To taste again the sweets of home,
 Within the "Old Concern."
Ah! yes, you'll come before not long,
 In penitent return,
To strive and wipe out all the wrongs
 You've done the "Old Concern!"

A VOICE FROM CAMP.

"As we approached the battery, he fell, waving his sword,
and shouting: 'We are men from Massachusetts! Don't fire
on us!'"

We are men of Massachusetts! And from Berkshire
to Cape Ann.
We will rally for the Union of our fathers, man to
man!
The beacon-light of Sumter gleamed o'er our hills of
pine,
And lighted up a war-path for the Massachusetts line,
And now, we wave our starry flag along your South-
ern sky,
Beneath its folds to conquer, or in its shroud to die;
No coward in our rear guard, no braggart in our van,
While we battle for the Union of our fathers, man to
man.

We are men of Massachusetts! and we cannot soon
forget
The leaguered wall of Sumter, and its broken parapet;
We saw the clouds roll outward and upward to the
sun,
We heard your empty boasting, one hundred men to
one;
We stumbled in the gloaming, on our dead at Baltimore;
But our wives forgot their weeping, and from fare-
wells we forebore,
As, from hearthstone unto hearthstone, the hurried
summons ran,
Up! and battle for the Union of our fathers, man to
man!

We are men of Massachusetts! Your brothers until
now;
But, to your shrines of damning wrong, our free
knees cannot bow.
Ye have plucked our banner from the stars, and trailed it in the dust,
Till our swords will sleep no longer in their beds of
ancient rust;
Ye have dared to brand us cowards, ye have called us
peddling knaves,
Ye have proffered us "a welcome to inhospitable
graves!"

But the old Flag still is waving, and we spurn your
bloody ban,
While we battle for the Union of our fathers, man to
man.

We are men of Massachusetts! And we live not in
the Past,
But from the furnaced Present, our histories we cast;
We boast no defunct heraldry, nor of perished glory
prate,
While war's red shuttle glitters through the web and
woof of fate:
No vaunting words we utter, nor bitter taunt for
scorn,
But stand, as stood our pioneers in Freedom's stormy
morn,
With no pride of state or section, no hate of class or
clan,
To give battle for the Union of our fathers, man to
man.

We are men of Massachusetts! along whose rugged
shore,
The surges to the beaches sing of Freedom evermore;
Across whose sun-trod valleys, adown whose rock-
ribbed hills,
The flowers bloom in freedom, in freedom laugh the
rills.
No slaver ploughs our waters, no bondman tills our
soil,
Nor tawny mother wakes to weep o'er unrequited
toil,
Yet we leave our hills and homesteads, to strike as
best we can,
In the battle for the Union of our fathers, man to
man.

We are men of Massachusetts! Oh! stay this ghastly
strife!
Ye but stab, with matricidal hand, the breast that
gave you life!
Ye but quench the holy altar-fires of Justice and of
Truth,
And plant Death's gory chaplet on the brow of Free-
dom's youth!
And would ye tear, with bloody hands, the glory-
wreaths that twine
Round Yorktown's ancient ruin and the shades of
Brandywine!
No! no! It cannot, shall not be! Give back, ye
traitor-clan!
In this battle for the Union of our fathers, man to
man!

We are men of Massachusetts! O shades of mighty
dead!
Awakened from your sleeping by the thunder of our
tread!
Do ye marvel at the striving of your sons above your
graves?
Do ye ask, what means this reddening clash of bayonets and glaves?
They would pluck the stars from out the flag, and
break the corner-stone,
And in Freedom's sacred altar-place erect a reeking
throne!
But we are sworn to finish what you so well began,
While we battle for the Union of our fathers, man to
man.   S. P. D.
23d Mass. Vols., Newbern, N. C.

SONGS UPON THE BATTLE-FIELD.—A brave and godly
captain in one of our Western regiments, told us his
story as we were taking him to the hospital. He was
shot through both thighs with a rifle-bullet—a wound
from which he could not recover. While lying on the
field he suffered intense agony from thirst. He supported his head upon his hand, and the rain from
heaven was falling around him. In a little while a
little pool of water formed under his elbow, and he
thought if he could only get to that puddle he might
quench his thirst. He tried to get into a position to
suck up a mouthful of muddy water, but he was unable
to reach within a foot of it. Said he: "I never felt so
much the loss of any earthly blessing.

"By and by night fell, and the stars shone out clear
and beautiful above the dark field, and I began to
think of that great God who had given his Son to die
a death of agony for me, and that he was up there—
up above the scene of suffering, and above those glorious stars; and I felt that I was going home to meet
him, and praise him there; and I felt that I ought to
praise God, even wounded and on the battle-field. I
could not help singing that beautiful hymn:

"'When I can read my title clear,
To mansions in the skies;
I'll bid farewell to every fear,
And dry my weeping eyes.'

"And," said he, "there was a Christian brother in
the brush near me. I could not see him, but I could
hear him. He took up the strain, and beyond him another and another caught it up, all over the terrible
battle-field of Shiloh. That night the echo was resounding, and we made the field of battle ring with
hymns of praise to God."

THE WAR OF CAVALRY AND NEGROES.—It is announced in the Northern telegrams that one hundred
thousand cavalry are soon to be armed and equipped
for our destruction. Simultaneously we hear from
every quarter that regiments and brigades of negroes
are also being impressed into the ranks of our foes.
The cause of these new movements is clear; our enemies, despairing of conquest by armies of infantry,
and unwilling longer to expose their own precious persons to the privations, suffering, and death resultant
from a fair and equal conflict, are resolved to burn up
our cities, bridges, depots, and dwelling-houses, by
raids in the interior, and to add the horrors of a St.
Domingo massacre to their own plundering and brutal
warfare.

Such elements of darkness do not mean reünion;
they do not even stop at the idea of conquest and subjugation; they can only portend utter desolation and
extermination. We feel profoundly touched at the
sad and solemn picture of the future that is thus weaving in the womb of fate, but we are not sure that it is
to be deplored as an unmixed evil; thousands of innocent, helpless, and noble hearts will fall crushed and
bleeding under the wheels of this Juggernaut of fanaticism, but from the blood of the martyrs will spring
the seed of the Church, and the temple of hope and
freedom will be rebuilt and reconsecrated. We cannot thus be subdued. We shall rise higher, more intact and united as these ten-fold furies, thus turned
loose, have to be met and confronted.

Our government must develop its reserved energies, cast away forbearance, and humbly imitating the
course said by Milton to have been pursued by our
Creator when the devils heaved up volcanic mountains and tartarean pitch to overwhelm his angels and

desolate heaven, we, too, must gather the two-edged sword, and pour out a consuming fire that will deluge the East with destruction, burning, and the horrors of despair.

We can arm and equip fifty thousand of our veterans, who never fled from the face of an enemy, and can move unhurt, and almost unchallenged, from Cincinati to Boston. They can lay in ashes the richest and most populous of Northern cities, leaving behind them a belt as broad and as burning as the elliptic. They can run a burning plough-share over the hot-beds of puling fanaticism, from which sprang the Ate turned loose on the South.

If our President will but announce and permit such a policy, he will be justified in the eyes of the civilized world, and will evoke a new spirit in the South that has never yet been called into action. Thousands of men are just now thrust out with cruelty and ignominy from Louisiana, Tennessee, Kentucky, and Maryland, and they are thirsting to go back with fire and sword. Thousands more of our people, who have felt that mere defence of our own land was not the true policy, would be stirred to their inner depths by the trumpet-call of invasion. We believe firmly that myriads at the North are prepared to take refuge in our ranks from the storm of despotism that is darkening around them.

If it be necessary, in order to save ourselves from cavalry raids and negro massacres, that we should raise the war-cry of "Blue bonnets over the border," so be it. We have struggled long and faithfully to meet the exigencies of this contest in a fair, open, and manly fight; but when the demons of hell are to be turned loose on our beautiful land, and its civilization choked amid blood and flames, we must, in self-defence, pour back the fell tide of ruin on our barbarian foes and make them sing, amid the falling glories of their once-thriving cities, the song of the Persian poet:

"The spider has woven his web and the owl hath sung in the towers of Apasiab."

We shall meet the truculent Yankees as the Indian Conanchet did when they sought his alliance after murdering his people and devastating his land. He raised himself proudly to his full height and replied: "The fire that consumed the lodges of my people turned the heart of Conanchet to stone."—*Chattanooga Rebel.*

AN INSULT TO THE FLAG AVENGED.—A butternut meeting was held at Barnesville, Belmont County, Ohio, and before the speeches were made the "faithful" had a procession, in which they carried a flag with seven stars, and a string of butternuts appended. A soldier belonging to the Third Ohio infantry, named Brackley Machanna, upon seeing this, armed himself with a large butcher knife, and cut the flag in pieces, and daring any man to speak against the National Government, also inflicting a severe wound on the side of the face of the man carrying the disloyal emblem. The mass of the people there assembled were completely terrified by the threats of the brave fellow. This man deserves high promotion for his deed of valor, and we hope that he may be justly rewarded.— *Columbus (O.) Fact.*

June 8.—A medal of honor was awarded to private Samuel Johnson, of company G, Ninth Pennsylvania reserves, for having, by individual bravery and daring, captured from the enemy two colors, at the battle of Antietam, September seventeenth, 1862, and received, in the act, a severe wound. He was transferred to the Invalid Corps as a commissioned officer.

AN EXTRAORDINARY CASE OF WOUNDS.

NASHVILLE, *June* 1.—The most extraordinary case of surviving apparently mortal wounds that has ever come under my observation is that of John W. Vance, company B, Seventy-second regiment of Indiana mounted infantry, commanded by Colonel Miller.

Early in April I made a brief report of the case from Murfreesboro; but at that time I had no idea of the severity of the wounds. The demoniacal malignity that could have induced any one bearing the human form to have inflicted such wounds under the circumstances, seems almost beyond conception.

While the regiment to which young Vance belonged was scouting near Taylorsville, Tennessee, he and a companion were taken prisoners. During the next twenty-four hours their captors treated them kindly. They neither saw nor heard any thing to lead them to suspect that any different treatment was in store for them till they came within a mile or two of Lebanon. Here the rebels wished to be free from the care of their prisoners. They therefore tied them to a tree. A Captain French, of the rebel army, objected to the plan of leaving them thus pinioned, and at once coolly and calmly drew his revolver and fired three shots through the head of each as they were pinioned to the trees. His companion was at once despatched; but as Vance was unfastened he fell forward on his face, and another of the rebel band, named Cartwright, fired the fourth shot through the victim's head.

Vance assures me that he did not at any time lose his consciousness. He heard all they said and knew all they did. Here he lay twenty-six hours, during the fourth and fifth of April, when he was discovered by some of our troops and brought into camp, and his wounds dressed by a surgeon of one of the Ohio regiments. Nothing was done for him till thirty-two hours after he was wounded. These are the facts. Now for the nature of the wounds:

They were inflicted by the large revolver used by our cavalry, and the cold-blooded murderers fired within a yard of the prisoned victim's head.

The first shot took effect about an inch back and below the right cheek-bone, and came out on the opposite side, about the same distance from the left cheek-bone.

The second ball entered about an inch and a half below, and a little nearer the ear than the first, and passing through in the same line as the first, breaking the jaws and loosening the teeth.

The third entered the neck just below and in a line vertical to the lower tip of the ear. This lodged in the opposite side of the neck, from whence the surgeon removed it.

The fourth—the one that had been inflicted by Cartwright, after he had been thrown on his face—entered back of his ear, about the centre of combativeness, and escaped through his left eye, completely destroying it.

And yet John W. Vance lives and looks well and hearty. He is an intelligent, fine-looking young man, just arrived at his majority. I sat half an hour on the adjoining cot, and conversed with him and examined his wounds while he was eating his dinner; and he ate with the relish of a man who loves life and desires to prolong it. The loss of his left eye will be his only real disfigurement.

But how it was possible for four leaden messengers

of death to pass through the parts they did without proving mortal, is a marvellous problem. But such are the facts, and they are of sufficient importance to be perpetuated.—*Cincinnati Gazette.*

PLEASANT BEDFELLOWS.—A diary of a prisoner of war contains the following suggestive incident : " Becoming drowsy, I borrowed a blanket, went into the depot, and finding a vacant place between two prostrate forms, dropped down to rest and was soon lost in forgetfulness. I have no knowledge of how long I slept, but getting cold, I partially awoke, and hunching my right-hand partner, requested him to roll over and spoon. He made no reply, and giving him a tremendous thump, I again besought him to spoon, but it was no go. Turning on my other side I shook my other bedfellow, and made the same request. He too paid no heed to my desire. Exasperated at what I considered his unaccommodating spirit, I determined to bring matters to a crisis. Drawing up my left leg, I gave him a most unmerciful kick, but he was as immovable as the rock of ages. I was now thoroughly awake. Jumping up, I turned down the blankets, first on one and then on the other, and by the dim fire-light beheld on either hand a corpse. My nap was finished. In the morning I learned that they were rebel dead, brought down from Murfreesboro for burial at Chattanooga.

June 4.—The *Richmond Despatch* relates, that, " a few days since, in Lee County, Virginia, near the Tennessee line, a tory who had slandered the widow of a deceased confederate soldier, was tied up by some half-dozen indignant women, and received twenty stripes." As Mr. Macbeth remarked to Mrs. Mac, such women " should bear only male children."

KNOXVILLE, TENNESSEE, *June* 4.—Never within the memory of the " oldest inhabitant " have there been more beautiful fields of wheat than bless East-Tennessee to-day. We heard it said when stampeding was going on that there would be no labor in the country to plant a crop. The *Register*, it was said, by its ultra course was driving the Lincolnites out of East-Tennessee and when the Lincolnites were driven out there was no labor left to plant a crop for this season. The result is, that there has been more wheat planted in East-Tennessee, and, by the blessing of providence, a greater crop, than ever was known. On every plain, on every hill, the grain stands up healthful and heavy—the big ears are crying for the reapers. Now, all through our land there is going up a wail that there is not labor enough to save this great crop which God has vouchsafed us. General Beauregard has been addressed in Georgia, has been solicited to let the soldiers go home to reap their wheat, that their wives and children may not starve. General Beauregard, as far as we can learn, has not responded to the cries of the soldiers' wives.

In East-Tennessee we are more fortunate. We have a large force here in our nitre and mining bureau ; good, trusty fellows, who under Captain Finnie's direction, have been digging villainous saltpetre out of the bowels of the earth. In consideration of their delving in caves and boiling nitrous earth, they have been exempted from conscription. They have done good service for the Confederacy. Captain Finnie, through their aid, has shipped innumerable barrels of nitre to the confederate powder-mill. But now the question arises, how is our great crop of wheat to be saved ? It was suggested to the commander of this department that the nitre brigade might render essential service in this matter. General Buckner, being a practical man as well as a valiant soldier, has consented that the nitre men shall have a furlough during harvest, not only to gather their own crops, but to assist their neighbors, and especially the wives and children of soldiers who are in the army.

We have no doubt that under the regulation which Captain Finnie will adopt, the nitre brigade will do good service in the ensuing harvest.

Some of our tory friends, whose wheat-fields, contrary to their expectations, give promise of an enormous yield, have raised the cry that there is no labor to reap the unprecedented crop that blesses the land, and therefore have turned their stock into their wheat fields. They have the right to do as they please in regard to their own fields ; we have only to say that we think they have not acted prudently or wisely. There was labor enough in the country to plant a great crop in spite of all the croakers, and we venture to say there is labor enough to save the crop in East-Tennessee, great as it is.

General Buckner has acted very promptly in view of the emergency, and we have reason to believe that the measures he has taken will be ample to meet all the requirements of the season.

A GALLANT DEED AND A CHIVALROUS RETURN.

In the movement of Stoneman's cavalry the advance was led by Lieutenant Paine, of the First Maine cavalry. Being separated by a considerable distance from the main body, he encountered unexpectedly a superior force of rebel cavalry, and his whole party were taken prisoners. They were hurried off as rapidly as possible, to get them out of the way of our advancing force, and in crossing a rapid and deep stream Lieutenant Henry, commanding the rebel force, was swept off his horse. As none of his men seemed to think or care any thing about saving him, his prisoner, Lieutenant Paine, leaped off his horse, seized the drowning man by the collar, swam ashore with him and saved his life, thus literally capturing his captor. He was sent to Richmond with the rest of the prisoners, and the facts being made known to General Fitz-Hugh Lee, he wrote a statement of them to General Winder, the Provost-Marshal of Richmond, who ordered the instant release of Lieutenant Paine, without even parole, promise, or condition, and, we presume, with the compliments of the Confederacy. He arrived in Washington on Saturday last. This act of generosity as well as justice must command our highest admiration. There is some hope for men who can behave in such a manner.

But the strangest part of the story is yet to come. Lieutenant Paine, on arriving in Washington, learned that the officer whose life he had thus gallantly saved had since been taken prisoner by our forces, and had just been confined in the Old Capitol Prison. At the last we heard of him he was on his way to General Martindale's headquarters, to obtain a pass to visit his beneficiary and benefactor. Such are the vicissitudes of war. We could not help thinking, when we heard this story, of the profound observation of Mrs. Gamp : "Sich is life, vich likeways is the hend of hall things hearthly." We leave it to casuists to determine whether, when these two gallant soldiers meet on the battle-field, they should fight like enemies or embrace like Christians. For our part, we do not believe their swords will be any the less sharp, nor their zeal any the less determined, for this hap-hazard exchange of soldierly courtesy.

"YANKEES."

BY JAMES S. WATKINS.

It is the "chivalry's" delight
  To "Yankee" every loyal man,
And I, just here, but think them right
  In calling "Yankees" all they can!
For who are "Yankees" but "the brave,"
  The noble and the daring free?
Who'd rather moulder in the grave,
  Than bow to tyrant's slavery!

Who but the "Yankees" dared to break
  The bonds of George, the tyrant king?
And who but they, ne'er feared to stake
  Upon their cause their every thing?
Who but the "Yankees" justly brought
  Destruction on the British tea,
And then against the tyrant fought
  The battles of our LIBERTY?

And who but they, with iron will—
  A sabre and a trusty gun—
Earned laurels bright at Bunker Hill,
  At Concord, and at Lexington?
Who but a "Yankee" dared to stand
  Before Ticonderoga's wall,
And, in Jehovah's name command,
  "This night thou shalt surrender all"?

Call me a "Yankee!"—who but they,
  O'er Delaware's proud but frosty tide,
With frozen feet, once pushed their way,
  Led on by WASHINGTON, their pride!
Who but a "Yankee" forced to yield
  Cornwallis' trembling Hessian horde,
And, as the victor of the field,
  Received that British tyrant's sword?

Who but the "Yankees" fiery hot,
  Rushed to the battle-field and plain,
And, led on by their beloved Scott,
  Won laurels, too, at Lundy Lane?
Who but the "Yankees" forced to wave,
  Not very many years ago,
Our banner, emblem of the brave,
  High o'er the walls of Mexico?

Who but the "Yankees" dared to say
  To rebels, who can never joke,
"Fort Hatteras," now, this very day,
  Surrender must, with Roanoke!
Brave BURNSIDE, "Yankee" to the end,
  Thrice honored shall thy name e'er be,
For on that Island's burning sand
  Stacked arms three thousand chivalry!

Who but the "Yankees," brave and free,
  Upon the fierce contested field,
Forced the usurping "chivalry"
  Their boasted battle-ground to yield?
Who but the "Yankees" did compel
  The rebels from Pea Ridge to flee,
Leaving their wounded where they fell,
  To hear the shouts of victory?

Who but the "Yankees" braved the tide
  Of battle, when its heat begun,

And stormed the frozen, rocky side
  Of that stronghold, Fort Donelson?
And who but "Yankees" captured there
  Full "thirteen thousand" daring men,
While "seven thousand" still prepare
  To stack their arms, at Number Ten?

Who but the "Yankees" faced the heat,
  Where death's relentless missiles sped;
To Zollicoffer's band defeat,
  And shoot the vile arch-traitor dead?
Call me a "Yankee!"—it was they
  Who brought Antietam's battle on,
And forced the traitors, in a day,
  To cross again the rubicon!

At Gettysburgh, 'twas "Yankees" too,
  That memorable triumph gained;
And there the victor's trumpet blew,
  While o'er them shell in torrents rained!
'Twas "Yankees" there, who forced to flee,
  With over "thirty thousand" loss,
Their best and ablest General, Lee,
  And back to Jeff's dominions cross!

'Twas "Yankees," too, boldly attacked
  The Mississippi's strongholds well,
Where two score thousand arms were stacked,
  When Vicksburgh and Port Hudson fell!
'Twas "Yankees" there—all "Yankees" brave!
  The rebels' great domain did sever,
And planted, on its wreck to wave,
  Their flag, forever and forever!

Call me a "Yankee!"—who but they
  Tore down the vile oppressor's rag!
And hoisted there—auspicious day!
  O'er New-Orleans the freeman's flag!
And who but they, pray tell me ye
  Who know, perhaps, the future more,
Will keep it spread, till unity
  Shall bless our land as heretofore?

Then call me, friends, a "Yankee"—ay,
  O'er earth and sea that name proclaim;
I cannot better live, to die,
  Than by so proud, so brave a name!
I am a "Yankee" first and last!
  No other name to mine affix—
Call me a "Yankee" loud and fast,
  And place beside it '76!

BORDER WAR,

AS SEEN AND EXPERIENCED BY THE INHABITANTS OF CHAMBERSBURGH, PA.

I.

A wandering hunter spied the spot,
  Where the Falling Spring, a limpid stream,
  Which glides on its course like a fairy dream,
A moment's joy and then forgot,
Rolls laughing over its rocky bed;
  A moment pure and a moment free,
A lagging moment forever sped,
  Then hurried onward toward the sea.
Swept off, the victim of wild intrigue,
'Twixt the ripples and waves of the Conococheague.

On that spot now rests a quiet town,
  Called after a man attracted there
  By the hunter's tale, bewitching fair,
Of the water-fall which tumbles down

In foamy spray o'er its rough-hewn stair ;
The spot I have learned to love so well,
  Where fancy can revel without restraint,
And her creations are wont to dwell,
  And fill the mind with pictures quaint ;
And there I muse on a thousand things,
Which come on Imagination's wings,
And the well-known legends fondly trace,
That are told of the Indian-haunted place.

'Twas on this spot stood free and wild,
  The Shawanese and the Delaware savage,
Ere Indian warrior taught his child
  To scalp and murder, burn and ravage.
And as I stood by the stream one day,
  A thousand visions flitting o'er me,
I thought of times long passed away,
  And buried chieftains rose before me ;
But vain are the dreams we would fain recall,
For oblivion's mantle is over them all.

And then I thought of the old-time fort,
  With its blunderbuss and its swivel gun,
Its cracking fire-arms' loud report,
  And the name its bold defender won ;
How the savage ventured not too near
Its stockade sides, from a wholesome fear
Of the bull-dogs laid at rest within,
But oping their mouths with a ghastly grin :
And how when the governor's mandate came,
"Forthwith to deliver up the same,"
Old Colonel Chambers bristled with pride,
And declared that "the guns should stay by his side,
For his guns had stood by him, and he
Would stand by his guns, as they should see."
Then followed visions of trouble and strife,
Of the tomahawk and the scalping-knife,
The war-whoop wild and the scene of slaughter,
And of human blood in the limpid water.

And then from the buried past we fly
  To the living present which vividly seems
  The realization of mystic dreams
That are wont to fleck our dream-land's sky.
From the time on freedom's natal day,
When Craighead urged the youth away,
And our patriot sires, a martial band,
Shoulder to shoulder and hand to hand,
Marched forth to consecrate the land
  At liberty's shrine and on freedom's altar ;
Up to the day when marched the son
To end the work the sire begun,
  And not a man was known to falter.
From the fields where Steele and Chambers fought,
  At the nation's first baptismal,
To the gory spot where Easton wrought
  And died 'midst the deep swamps dismal ;
And from where our patriot fathers bled,
And their comrades moaning, " dead, dead, dead,"
  Consigned them to God's own keeping,
To the far-off hillside's thorn-bush shade
Where the gallant Kerns to rest is laid,
  As one who is gently sleeping.

The past, the present, the future, all
  We have known in life or loved in story ;
The dead the living, the great, the small,
Obscurity's son and the child of glory
In vision arise before our eyes,
  And troop through brain in wild disorder,
And we look in the stream with strange surprise,
  When we recollect we're on the " border."

II.

And thus again as I lay by the stream
  Which murmuring rolls its waters along,
  And drips o'er the Falls in rippling song,
My fancies were shaped and this my dream,
Minerva-like, sprang out of my brain,
  And bore away the triumphal car
  Of terrible, glorious " border war ;"
While rose to my ears a swelling strain,
Which seemed like the voices of heroes slain,
And this was the burden of what they were singing,
Its cadence wild with the waters ringing.

  Away to the border, away,
    Where your brethren are calling.
  Away and take part in the fray,
    Where your children are falling.
Fall in, men, fall in, and forward in order,
Do you not hear the cry coming up from the border ?

  Away to the border, away,
    Where stout hearts are contending.
  Away, and take part in the fray,
    Your own hearth-stones defending.
Fall in, men, fall in, and forward in order,
The foe's at your doors almost, his foot on the border.

  Away, to the border away,
    Where brave men are dying.
  Away, and take part in the fray,
    Where your kinsmen are lying.
Fall in, men, fall in, and forward in order,
The blood of the slain is calling, " Come to the border."

III.

Then quickly before my astonished eyes—
For dreams are like clouds in summer skies—
Passed visions of men in warrior's guise,
  Of men who were going to battle :
And mixed and mingled with my dream,
Was sabre-thrust and bayonet-gleam,
  And the fierce artillery's rattle ;
There was the Home Guard's steady line,
  The "State Militia's" martial front,
The "Anderson Troop," in clothes so fine,
  And men who had borne the battle's brunt.

The Home Guards marched like men who knew
  Their dinners were safely cooking behind them,
And like men who felt quite conscious, too,
  Of where the dinner hour would find them ;
And I marched along with my gun by my side,
  And I praised my captain so kind and clever,
Who looked at " the boys " with a soldier's pride,
  And called time, RIGHT, RIGHT, whenever
        He meant the left foot
        On the earth should be put ;
  But hurrah for our captain forever.

I can never forget, nor could I desire
  That a scene like that which is certainly worth
  A life-long pilgrimage here on this earth
From my memory should ever expire.
  When our sergeant led out our squad in the night,
  Our homes to defend, for our hearth-stones to fight,
And instructed us thus : "If the foe comes don't fire,
For you see if you should, and a rebel ' bites dirt,'
  It would end our organizations ;
For you know that in case there were ' somebody hurt,'
  'Twould conflict with the regulations."
Then behind a stone fence we were placed where we
  Till we heard the approaching relief,   [slept

When we marched back to camp, and like soldiers we
    stept,
    Only stopping to drink to our chief,
The provost, who'd shut up the bars, though by stealth
We still had enough to drink to his health.

The provost (I dreamed) I could never forget,
    And his aids I would always remember,
How from morning till night they were sorely beset
    In that terrible month of September;
When the foe in Middletown Valley was seen,
    As the sun went down in the west,
And at dark had advanced already between
    Greencastle and Marion at least.

But the provost (I dreamed) was a man who would
    have
    His will and his way in his station,
And to show that the town he would certainly save,
    He issued a strict proclamation:
"No citizen armed for the common defence,"
    His bitters could get of a morning;
But the citizen-soldiers scorned abstinence,
    As their mode of attack was by *horning*.
"In case the foe approaches the town,"
    The command was, "Destroy all the brandy,"
But it did not say *how*, so my friend Mr. Brown,
    Thought to drink it were far the most handy;
"And guards will be placed," it was thus ran the text,
    "At every approach to the Borough."
So away trooped a crowd, exceeding perplexed
    Lest they should bear arms on the morrow.

I can never forget what the Guards have achieved,
    And how closely they looked at the "passes"
Of honest old farmers who "spies" were believed,
    While they kissed and passed out all the lasses.

Then the "Anderson Troop" came riding along,
    On horses impressed from the farmers;
Their clothes were new and their sabres were strong,
    So they thought themselves "perfect charmers."
And I looked at their steeds when I saw the mark,
    Uncle Sam puts on all of his forces;
And I "laughed in my sleeve," as cried out some gay
    lark,
    "They've been branding borrowed horses."

These "Anderson fellows" had drilled for a while,
    And moreover were splendid blowers;
So with sabres like scythes they came in style,
    To show rebels some excellent mowers.
And I saw in my dream, I can't vouch for its truth,
    That with dauntless and terrible blows
They mowed forty thousand rebs down, forsooth,
    When at least thirty miles from their foes.

Thus ended this part of my dream, when behold,
    As the danger was past and as bloodshed was over,
The "State Militia," in numbers untold,
    The "War on the Border" began to discover.
So away they marched with but little persuasion,
To protect "the line" from threatened invasion.

Unluckily for the "Militia," their fate,
'Twas to be right in time to be too late;
Unless they meant not to fight where my rhyme
Will bring them just in the nick of time.

Thus peace again reigned, not so much, I suppose,
    That the rebels were fearful we'd beat 'em,
As from a deep-seated conviction that rose
    In their minds on the banks of Antietam.

IV.

The quiet town in its still repose,
    Not a whisper heard from the whispering trees,
    Not a rumor borne on the passing breeze,
But little recked of the coming foes.

The clouds were lowering, and pattering rain
Began to plash on the window-pane,
And darkness to veil all scenes from the light,
O'ercasting the earth with the mantle of night.

An anxious horseman with panting steed,
Rode into the town at his utmost speed,
    With the word that "the rebels were coming!"
Bells rang and drums beat in that hour of need,
    But all smiled at the ringing and drumming.
'Twere absurd, men argued, that here, so far
    From the army that lay on the river away,
    The rebels should come in a single day,
With all the paraphernalia of war,
Yet while they argued, the guns of the foe
Oped their mouths with a grin on the town below.

"They're here, they're here!" was borne on the air,
    Through street and alley, "The rebels are here;
Don't you see them down in the Diamond there?
    I heard their trumpet-tones calling clear."

And I walked the streets, and I felt the pain
Of "surrender" thrill me through every vein
When I heard a heroic woman declare,
"The dirty rebels, they won't fight fair,
    But come when they know we can't beat them,
Instead of giving us time to prepare,
    As we do with them ere we meet them."

Then into the town incessant poured
The hateful stream of the rebel horde;
"They had now just come," they deigned to say,
"A hasty visit the place to pay;"
And kindly promised for hurry this once,
To come again and stay for months.
We told them no doubt 'twas well designed,
But still we were sure they were quite too kind;
And assured them one thing was very clear,
We were not at all fond of "butternuts" here.

And General Stuart, the rebel chief,
Whom the farmers call "the great horse-thief,"
Who captured "the city without delay,"
(Or "quiet village," as Harpers say,)
Inquired next morning with pride: "If his men
    Were bad as was represented."
"But the devil ne'er," he was answered then,
    "Was black as he was painted."

But up and away with the early morn
Were these defiant rebels borne,
    As fast as *our* horses could carry them.
As the flame and smoke to heaven arose,
We declared our purpose to follow our foes,
To strike them hard, and as to their blows,
    We swore long and loud we would parry them.

So we shouldered our guns and went out to see
Where the infernal rebels might be,
    But the devil himself couldn't find them.
For "over the river and far away,"
They had gone, as they hadn't "the time to stay,"
    Leaving "flaming regrets" behind them.

V.*

The autumn bleak and the winter cold
Passed slowly by, while afar off rolled
    War's tide and train of desolation.
On the Rappahannock's blood-stained shore,
Where the Yazoo's darksome waters pour,
Or Stone River's waves are mingled with gore,
    Stood the bulwarks of the nation.

Our fathers, brothers, sons were there,
While a sister's sigh or a mother's prayer,
Went up to heaven, "O Father, spare!"
The rifle-flash and bayonet-thrust,
The ranks of men, the columns of dust,
The musketry crash, the cannon's roar,
And all the ominous sound of war,
Was the only answer the lightning brought,
From where contending thousands fought.

The only answer—Ah! no, the rod
    Upraised to punish a nation for sin,
Is felt in the cry, "My son, O God!"
    At the one little name in the bulletin;
And this is answer enough for her,
    Whose hopes and all that she loved on earth,
Are borne to a soldier's sepulchre,
    And buried afar from the place of his birth;
Or brought in sorrow and laid to sleep,
Where its vigils affection may silently keep.

The dreadful sounds of WAR, WAR, WAR,
Still smote on the ear, yet while we bore
Our loved ones home and mournfully laid
    Their bodies at rest in the earth at our feet,
Mourned over their graves and solemnly played
    Funereal dirges for heroes meet;
Men black as Erebus sprung forth,
    And I saw them spring at their country's call,
Raised up the banner of the North,
    And placed it high on Wagner's wall.

From the dens where burrow a subject race,
Methought I saw them face to face
With the monster Death on Wagner's towers,
Exclaiming: "THE FORT IT MUST BE OURS."
And I turned and pointed where heroes lay,
    And pronounced a benediction of sorrow:
"Sleep sweetly, brave men, for ye this day
    Have gained for your children a glorious to-morrow."

VI.

But again the rumor is borne on the breeze,
(We often before had rumors like these,)
    That Lee is moving, intent on invasion.
But we heeded it not until it was clear
That Jenkins had come unpleasantly near,
And Lee himself would surely be here
    Before his head had many more days on.
Then away the "prominent citizens" hurried,
Excited, frightened, flustered, flurried,
In wagons, carriages, sulkies, carts,
On horseback, "on foot," by all manner of arts
    And devices;
And all kinds of people—Smith, Jones,
Roberts, Robinson, Brown, and Bones,
    And the Rices.

* This Part refers to the young men of Chambersburgh, Pa., who were killed in the battles of Stone River and Frede'ck'sburgh, and to the colored men of the same place who belonged to the Massachusetts Fifty-fourth regiment, which displayed so great bravery at the attack on Fort Wagner.

While away in advance of the headlong race,
    Was a carriage that looked like R——n's,
Which seemed "like he gwine to leab de place,"
    Through fear of the mighty Jenkins.

'Mid shriek, and yell, and cry, and shout,
    And peals of wicked laughter,
On, hurried on, the rabble rout,
    With Milroy's wagons after.
        Pell-mell,
        Helter-skelter,
        Hurry-skurry,
    Toss and tumble,
    Roll and rumble,
And dust to make us blind, most;
    Thus Milroy's trains
    Came over plains,
    And rills and ridges,
    Brooks and bridges,
    Let worst be worst,
    The best man first,
And devil take the hindmost.
And sure enough, when all had gone,
And night put her sable garments on,
Came Jenkins, the guerrilla chief,
And arrant traitor, and braggart, and thief,
    To pay us that long-threatened visit.
His rebs were dirty as dirt could make 'em,
And Jenkins himself may have been a sachem,
A man or gorilla, a monkey or fairy,
    Or p'rhaps the famous "What is it?"
Which usually goes with "travelling shows."
But whatever he was, no one I suppose,
Will deny he was wretchedly dirty and hairy.

Now Jenkins put up at the best hotel,
And as every thing looked uncommonly well,
    He grew quite communicative;
No foe on his front, no foe on his rear,
Though he found on his flanks two glasses of beer,
    He soon threw them off like a "native."

'Tis wondrous to tell how he soon sought his way,
    From the house with the sign of the Eagle,
A bird which he found he could ne'er lead astray,
    However he tried to inveigle,
To that spot on the Spring whose waters are clear,
Transparent and lucid as lager or beer,
Where our good friends the Dutch delight overmuch,
To hear their mugs jingle and "smile" at the touch,
    While they fight o'er their battles "mit Sigel."

"Dear Harmon," says Jenkins, "I'm glad to be here,
    And to know you's a great delight, sir,
I confess I'm remarkably fond of your beer,
    And relish your 'kase' and your 'Sweitzer.'
Your people shall all be treated as well
As I this day have been 'treated;'
I'll see they are paid for all that they sell,
    And will suffer no one to be cheated;
But then they must all be content to receive
Such money as we are able to give."

Impressed, no doubt, with this honest feeling,
(For Jenkins was morally hostile to stealing,)
He ordered all business men open their doors,
And he would send officers round to their stores,
And these, he assured them, "would carefully make
    A correct catalogue of their stock;
Such things as they wanted were all they would take,
    And the balance erase from the book;

Except whatever ' the men' might find
To tickle the fancy or please the mind."
Thus pleasantly chatting, when all was "took down,"
He looked at the bills and bought out the town.

Still Jenkins had terrible griefs to bear,
And as Jenkinses never were known to swear,
    He affirmed: "He'd be d—d if he'd stand 'em."
And so he launched forth in a speech at the rate
Of Phœbus's horses when Phæton sate
    On the box and drove 'em tandem.

" In a peaceable way he had entered the town,
Yet we had a hostile spirit shown ;"
If he had said " horse steal " to me it appears,
The kettle had had the pot by the ears—
" Had stolen his horses and tried to shoot down
His men in a charge inoffensively made,
Which greatly displeased his entire brigade ;
Who swore that unless we paid all their losses,
Or begging their pardon returned them their ' hosses,'
The d—d little town should in ashes be laid.
He felt for his men, he was bound to confess it,
And whatever their wrong was compelled to redress it,
And to settle the matter desired to call
    Our worthy Town Fathers together."
Such was the substance of what he " let fall "—
From the " change in the wind " we augured a
    " squall,"
    And not wishing a " change in the weather,"
Concluded to send our Burgess right down,
With the onerous duty of " saving the town,"
Who managed the business he found to be done,
In a mode that " did credit " in more ways than one,
    To our ancient and goodly Borough ;
To the knowledge of these if you wish to attain,
Go ask certain lenders of scrip to explain—
Now, gentlemen, please don't become so profane,
    You all shall be paid—to-morrow.

Now Jenkins determined to leave us awhile,
    But first thought it best to disarm us.
Believing perhaps our powder might spoil,
    Or that pistols and guns might harm us.
And hence he issued an order requiring
All persons within the precincts of the town,
All rights being forfeited by them by firing
    (And oh! how we trembled at Jenkins's frown)
Upon the benignant confederate forces,
And wickedly stealing the best of their horses,
At once to deliver all arms and munitions
    To officers named to make proper disposal,
On pain of reprisal for any omissions,
    And punishment dire for every refusal.

But whether compliance was honestly made,
Or a feigned respect to the order was paid,
We all were swift his commands to obey,
    And have our names on his books " put down,"
'Twas really a laughable farce to play,
    Though done, of course, " to preserve the town."

Such a motley collection of arms I swear,
Has never before been exhibited here.
There were swords without hilts and guns without
    locks,
Stocks without barrels and barrels without stocks ;
Pistols as big as your finger, and e'en
A two-ounce vial of powder was seen.
And I stood and looked on as my friends passed by,
And to whate'er they carried I gave " half an eye."

" Hollo, dear N——, what is that you have there ?"
    " Oh! nothing—or only a trifle."
I caught a slight glimpse, and it was, I declare,
    A telescopic rifle.
And then friend F—— came along and got booked
    For a load that would break down a mason ;
Five muskets—two sabres—astonished I looked
    For howitzer, cannon, and caisson.

VII.

But Jenkins now returns again,
And Lee and his army following them,
    Grief, terror, and desolation
Throughout our lovely valley fling,
And nearer, nearer, nearer bring
    Destruction to the nation.

The first to come over the roads was Rhodes,
    And then brigade, division, and corps
Into the town with clatter and roar,
    In one unceasing current pour ;
    Divisions almost half a score :
Johnson's, Anderson's, Picket's, and Hood's,
    On, and on, and onward still,
    McLaw's, and Pender's, and Heath's, until
    The corps of Ewell and A. P. Hill,
And " Bull-dog" Longstreet, all were found
Encamped throughout the neighborhood round.

These rebels were flushed with insolent pride,
Believing an irresistible tide
    Like the waves of a deep-flowing river,
Was sweeping the nation far and wide,
    Engulfing us 'neath it forever.
"We're back in the Union again," they cried
    And endless their boasting and vaunting ;
"You'll in it remain," was all we replied,
    Though endless their gibes and their taunting.

While Hood's division was passing through,
A lady sporting the " Red, White, and Blue,"
    From a bosom whence traitor ne'er won it,
Was hailed by an insolent reb, who cried,
As he our own loved emblem spied,
    " A breastwork, lady, please bear in mind,
Hood's boys delight to storm, when they find
    The Yankee colors on it."

These rebs were an ignorant set, to be sure,
Nor was their language always pure ;
For reading, and writing, and such little arts,
Are not esteemed " essential parts,"
    Among our Southern cousins ;
And one of them asked, in a drawling tone,
A dirty, lousy son of a gun,
    " What fur do yo'ns fight us'ns ?"

A lady, Blackwood says and knows,
    Cried out as the rebs passed by,
" To the Red Sea Pharaoh's army goes,"
    But things since veered awry.
For when old Pharaoh led before,
His army to the Red Sea's shore,
    Moses was passing through ;
But this time " Moses " might be seen
On Pharaoh's side, sufficiently " green,"
    To enter the Red Sea too.

Now Moses (I dreamed) went round to see
That all our merchandise might be
    (In Blackwood find the text)

Carefully packed and marked "supplies,"
While we looked on with sad surprise,
   To see our goods "annexed."

But I suddenly from my dreams awoke,
As a distant sound of thunder broke
   Upon my startled ear;
And I looked around, but the foe was gone,
My dream of "Border War" was done;
While the Falling Spring went singing on,
   O'er the Falls in accents clear.

BLACK SOLDIERS.—A Western colonel, in a private letter, dated June, 1863, from General Rosecrans's army, to a friend, says:

"I want to say a word about darkey soldiers. You probably know more about their fighting than I do, but I am satisfied they *will* fight like tigers when properly managed; but a more useful attachment to a post than a regiment of them was never made. We have a regiment here, First Mississippi, and without them it would have been *impossible* for us to do all the guarding and fatigue. They relieve us of the fatigue duty entirely, and have built some fine breastworks besides. When soldiers see them hard at work in the hot sun, doing what *they* would otherwise have to do, the 'opposition' and 'prejudice' to the plan of organizing and enlisting them soon disappear. It is a wise movement of the Government. Never did any thing give the army more pleasure than the conscription act."

THE INDUSTRY OF THE WOMEN OF THE SOUTH.—A letter from Lincoln County, Tenn., says:

"I witnessed many a scene in this rural district, which the gay ladies of our fashionable cities may well ponder on, with the reflection of surprise, of how little they know of the hardships which their sex are forced to undergo to sustain and support their families, while their husbands and brothers are absent fighting the battles of our country. On the small farms throughout this section all is life, activity, and industry. Many a woman who never before held a plough is now seen in the corn-field; many a young girl who would have blushed at the thought of handling a plough-line, now naturally and unconsciously cries, 'Gee up!' to Dobbin, to the silvery tones of which the good brute readily responds, as if a pleasure to comply with so gentle a command. Many a Ruth as of old, is seen to-day, binding and gleaning in the wheat-fields; but alas! no Boaz is there to console or to comfort. The picture of the rural soldier's home is at this time but a picture of primitive life. Throughout the country, at every farmhouse and cottage, the regular sound of the loom, as the shuttle flies to and fro, with the whirl of the spinning-wheel, is heard, telling of home industry. Cotton fabrics, of neat, pretty figures, the production of home manufactory, are now almost wholly worn in Tennessee, instead of calicoes. But it is a sad thought, that while these exertions of thriving industry are being made for the support of the soldier's family, his little cottage home, of which he nightly dreams, is to be abandoned and left unprotected by the falling back of our troops, and subject to the pillage and plunder of the vandal infidels. Such, at least, I fear will be the case in the counties of Bedford and Coffee, from which we have fallen back."—*Charleston Courier, July 24.*

ABLE TO DEFEND "THE FLAG."—On the sixteenth of June, a Copperhead meeting was held near Plainfield, N. J. In the immediate vicinity resided an old couple named Jenks, the old gentleman, aged sixty-seven, being a soldier of the war of 1812. During the meeting, Mrs. Jenks, whose age is seventy-one, indignant at the proceedings, got out an old American flag which had seen service, and hoisted it on her house, her husband being absent. The base wretches who participated in the meeting, seeing the flag, determined it should come down, and they forthwith proceeded to the house and demanded of Mrs. Jenks that she should take it down. With all the patriotic indignation of a matron of '76, she refused. They then threatened to tear it down. Seizing her husband's old, rusty musket, she dared them to try it. Cowed by her resolution, and feeling as much shame as such cattle can feel, they sneaked away, leaving the old Stars and Stripes "still full high advanced" in all its proud splendor. Some gentlemen of New-York City, hearing of the circumstance, came up and took Mr. Jenks down to that city, purchased for him a magnificent American flag, and bade him give it into Mrs. Jenks's hand, to be hoisted on the Fourth of July ensuing, saying, as they gave it, that they were sure "she was able to defend it and keep it flying."—*Newark Mercury.*

BARBARITY OF THE YANKEES.

TREASURY DEPARTMENT C. S.,
SECOND AUDITOR'S OFFICE, July 28, 1863.

GENTLEMEN: I have this day received at my office a series of Yankee returns of our soldiers and citizens, who have been murdered by cold, starvation, and the most cruel and intentional neglect, in the Yankee prisons all over Yankeedom, numbering many thousands. A perusal of these lists is enough, and ought to fire the hearts of every confederate man, woman, and child with the deepest hatred, fury, and the desire of speedy vengeance. Any one desiring to inspect these lists, comprising the bravest and the best soldiers and citizens from all the confederate States, and of the latter especially, from Missouri, Kentucky, and Tennessee, can do so by calling at my office, at the corner of Ninth and Grace streets, from eight A.M. to four P.M.

I am, very respectfully, your obedient servant,

W. H. S. TAYLOR,
Second Auditor, C. S.

—*Richmond Enquirer, August 11.*

REBEL LETTERS WRITTEN ON NORTHERN SOIL.

Hanover, Pa., July 1, 1863.—The rebel cavalry left this vicinity last evening or this morning, and passed on by the way of Duke's Mill, Jefferson, and Seven Valleys.

The following correspondence from rebel soldiers to their friends in Dixie was captured this morning:

York, Pa., June 20, 1863.—I arrived here yesterday, about eight P.M., finding General Early with his headquarters at the Court-House. York was surrendered by the authorities without a struggle, and ere this reaches you we expect to witness the fall of Harrisburgh. There was a small fight at or this side of Columbia Bridge yesterday, which resulted in driving the Yankees across the river, when they fired the bridge and burned it. The boys are a jovial set of fellows, confident of being able to take Philadelphia.

York, Pa., June 29, 1863.—The "rebels" arrived

here yesterday and took possession, and now hold this place. I, by strategic movements, brought up the rear about eight o'clock P.M. yesterday. No doubt you will be surprised to hear that I am here.

. . . . .

General Early has demanded one hundred thousand dollars from the citizens as their portion of the levy for the support of the troops. The confederates are a brave set of men, anxious at all times to engage the Yankees.

York, Pa., June 29, 1863.—My Still Remembered and Dearly Beloved: How long has it been since I saw you and listened to your sweet voice? And when about to leave you, the clasp we gave each other's hands, the kiss, the last fond look, and thus we parted. This is all fresh to memory, and will be until I behold you again, in the same way that true friends are known to meet. What I have suffered and gone through since I left you I cannot describe. It appears like a long time to me, and you are ever present in mind, and I hope I am still remembered by my dearest love.

After a difficult and very perilous route I arrived at this place about eight o'clock last night, and found the rebels in full command of the city. They have been skirmishing about the neighborhood this morning. They destroyed some of the railroad track at Hanover on Saturday, captured a good many horses, but they were returned, the men not being authorized by the officers to do it.

I had to give my horse, "General Lee," to a man to pilot us. I hated to part with him; but I will soon get another one, a better one than I have now.

George and I have temporarily joined the Seventeenth Virginia cavalry; that is, until we can get with the Maryland companies, which are not very many miles distant. . . It is very likely we will be in a battle before to-morrow morning at Harrisburgh, if it is not surrendered.

York, Pa., June 29, 1863.—After a long and round-about wild goose chase, we arrived here about eight o'clock last night, and found Jackson's foot cavalry in full possession of the town. . . . .

The notorious rebels are under the command of General Early. They are in high spirits, well dressed, and all they want is to fight. . . . .

We expect to be ordered to Harrisburgh every minute. The pickets drove back a large force of the Yankees just below Columbia, yesterday evening, and I expect long ere you get this you will hear of the fall of Harrisburgh.

The General has demanded one hundred thousand dollars from the Yankees of this place. Already preparations are being made for the desired amount. As there is no money in the bank, there has been a committee of the citizens appointed to raise it, which I think can be done, as they are terribly scared. . . . .

Good by. Rest assured that I will never disgrace myself by running from a black Yankee, but, on the other hand, fight till I die or conquer. This is my motto, actuated by pure motives and principles.

York, Pa., June 29, 1863.—We are in strong force, numbering about eight thousand. There are about sixty thousand to eighty thousand rebels in Pennsylvania. We will march on Harrisburgh, I expect, to-night. About six hundred cavalrymen were at Hanover Saturday night. They destroyed the railroad for a few miles, took what horses they wanted, and then made back. I expect we will make an attack on Baltimore after Harrisburgh.

THE FIGHT AT WILTOWN.

"Honor to whom honor is due."

MESSRS. EDITORS: In your issue of the eighteenth instant, I noticed an account of the engagement of our forces and the enemy at Wiltown, on the Edisto River. I do not wish to detract a single iota of the glory that now covers the heroes of that combat. We are all engaged in a common cause, and the defeat of an unprincipled enemy is our only aim, our highest ambition. That attained, we are a happy, free, and independent people. We would not have serious contentions over small matters. But, at the same time, let us "share and share alike" the brilliant deeds as they transpire—give "honor to whom honor is due." We would not pluck a single twig that would cause to wither the laurel that crowns a fellow-soldier.

The "Ranger" is perfectly correct in his account of the progress of the enemy up the river in the direction of Jacksonboro Bridge. The Sixth regiment of cavalry fought gallantly and bravely, encountering all the difficulties of an ambushed enemy at every step—they having gained possession of a thick wood, lay concealed behind every log and in every thick cluster of trees. Like a "snake in the grass," one heard their bullets when he least expected them. But, like "old soldiers," our men rushed onward, driving the Vandals before them like a herd of sheep, even to the very water's edge. Virginia's heroes could not have taken a plume from their hat. Now, in consequence of the dense fog, the sudden and unexpected approach of the enemy's boats, a section of Captain Schultz's battery at Wiltown were forced to make a hasty retreat, to prevent being captured. The cavalry had not as yet reached the scene of action. This move left the enemy in quiet possession of the river at that point. Hence they proceeded forthwith to remove the obstructions that had checked their progress; after which they passed with ease and without molestation up the river, within two miles of the railroad bridge on the Charleston and Savannah Road — the object of their raid.

Here they came in unexpected contact with Captain George H. Walters's battery, who gave the enemy a warm reception with salutes of shot and shell. This certainly surprised them very much, for they did not anticipate any danger so high up the river and on the opposite side. But with a mighty demonstration of courage, the enemy turned her broadside, fired several rounds and retired, Captain Walters shaking hands with her stern as she left—as the poet says, a "long, lingering farewell," for he knew she would never venture there again. It was at this point, (if any,) and not Wiltown, that she was death-stricken. Suffice it to say, that it was here she was stopped in her diabolical career. The Jacksonboro Bridge was saved! Huzza! for the Washington artillery. On their return, a section of Schultz's battery and Captain Parker's took a beautiful position at Mr. Gibb's house, one mile above Wiltown Bluff, and rapid cannonading ensued, which continued about ten minutes. She may have been hit, I will not say, but steamed along down the river until she struck the obstruction again, and failed to pass through the clearance she had made in the morning. Our guns had then ceased to fire on her. Giving up in despair, her bottom being tightly wedged on the *piles* driven in the river, she threw her guns overboard, to make it lighter, that she might pass over. The men embarked on the other boat, and left this in flames. The wreck still stands high up out of the water, on top of the piles, which proves clearly that if she is dead she *committed suicide.*

ANOTHER RANGER.

—Charleston Courier, July 24.

INCIDENTS OF VICKSBURGH.—A Vicksburgh letter, describing the meeting of General Grants and Pemberton, on the day before our occupation of the rebel stronghold, says:

"Thousands of soldiers looked upon the strange scene. Two men who had been lieutenants in the same regiments in Mexico now met as foes, with all the world looking upon them—the one his country's glory, the other his country's shame. When they had approached within a few feet there was a halt and silence. Colonel Montgomery spoke: 'General Grant, General Pemberton.' They shook hands politely, but Pemberton was evidently mortified. He said: 'I was at Monterey and Buena Vista. We had terms and conditions there.' General Grant here took him aside, and they sat down on the grass and talked more than an hour. Grant smoked all the time; Pemberton played with the grass and pulled leaves. It was finally agreed to parole them, allowing the officers each his horse. It was a politic thing. The dread of going North and fear of harsh treatment had deterred them from capitulating sooner.

"Our men treated the rebels with kindness, giving them coffee, which some had not tasted for a year. The city is much dilapidated, and many houses are injured. The Vicksburgh paper of July second admits the eating of mule meat and the pilfering of soldiers.

"In private houses there seems to be much suffering from sickness and our missiles.

"The river batteries at Vicksburgh are composed of thirty-six guns of the Blakely, Whitworth, and Brooks pattern. All these fell into our hands."

PERRY'S REBEL BRIGADE AT THE BATTLE OF GETTYSBURGH.

The following is a copy of a communication addressed to the editors of the *Richmond Enquirer* in relation to the conduct of Perry's brigade at the battle of Gettysburgh, which we cheerfully lay before our readers as an act of justice to the brave men of Colonel Long's command:

HEADQUARTERS ANDERSON'S DIVISION,
THIRD ARMY CORPS, August 6, 1863.

EDITORS RICHMOND ENQUIRER: In the letter which I addressed to you a few days ago, correcting the statements made of P. W. A., the correspondent of the *Savannah Republican*, I omitted to take notice of the following sentence: "Perry's brigade advanced a short distance, but did not become fully engaged." This is quite as incorrect as the other statements which I have contradicted.

Perry's brigade, under the command of Colonel David Long, advanced as bravely, as perseveringly, and as far any troops could have done in the same situation.

They were hotly engaged. Suffered heavier loss in killed and wounded, in proportion to their numbers, than any brigade in the army, and did not retire until compelled, like all the others, to do so by the superior force of the enemy and the great strength of his position.

By giving this communication a place in your columns, you will render an act of justice to brave men, whose honor and reputation I take pleasure in defend-

ing against the incorrectness of the statement, and the inferences which might be drawn from my omission to notice it. I am, very respectfully,
Your obedient servant,
R. H. ANDERSON,
Major-General.

In this connection, we publish the annexed letter, which appeared in our evening's edition of yesterday, previous to the receipt of General Anderson's communication correcting the mistake which our correspondent, unintentionally, had fallen into, in relation to the part borne by Perry's brigade in the Gettysburgh fight. The letter will speak for itself:

HEADQUARTERS WRIGHT'S BRIGADE,
ORANGE C. H., VA., August 5, 1863.

MR. EDITOR: I desire to make a correction of the statement in my letter of the seventh ult., and published in your issue of the twenty-third, as to the conduct of Perry's brigade in the charge upon the enemy's lines at Gettysburgh on the second of July. From information received from several officers of that brigade, and who were in the charge, I am satisfied that the brigade (which is very small) acted well—that it advanced along with Wilcox's and Wright's brigades until it was overwhelmed by vastly superior numbers, and that even then it only fell back in obedience to orders, and when it was apparent that the day was lost. I learn, also, that it was engaged again on the third, when Pickett's charge was made, and that it suffered severely in this latter charge.

This correction and explanation is due to those gallant soldiers, and I trust that all the papers that published the original letter, as a matter of simple justice will publish this also. Just after a battle there are so many reports and rumors of particular commands, that it is not at all surprising that grave errors should be made by those who write hurriedly, and not alone from what they see, but from what is talked of in the camps.—*Georgia Constitutionalist, August* 12.

MUNCHAUSENIANA.—Mr. J. D. Howe, of the First Missouri regiment, informs us that on the second inst. two regiments, one from Kentucky and the other from Indiana, rebelled at Rienzi, Miss., and started South with their arms. Four regiments of Wisconsin troops were sent to intercept them, when a fight ensued, lasting from Saturday morning until night. The Kentuckians and Indianians drove the Wisconsin regiments six miles in the direction of Corinth. At sundown the Federals were reenforced by two Illinois regiments, who came up in the rear of the rebels and compelled them to surrender. They were arrested and sent to Chicago.

An eye-witness who walked over the field says he counted three hundred and fifty-three killed; and another, who spent more time, says he counted over six hundred dead.—*Jackson Mississippian, August* 25.

SPERRYVILLE, *Thursday, August* 7, 1862.—Out of one hundred and twenty citizens of Sperryville who have taken the oath of allegiance within the past two days, there are fifty who cannot write their names. The poor whites as a rule are loyal, and but few of them will be sent South.—*N. Y. Tribune, August* 8.

WHAT WAS FOUND IN A PRAYER-BOOK.—The following was found written on the fly-sheet of a prayer-book in one of the churches in Louisville:

"Hurrah for John Morgan! The Marion of the

South, following his footsteps as much so as the Apostles followed the footsteps of Christ."

"There shall be a Southern Confederacy, so saith the Apostle Paul. See third verse, chapter fourth, Acts of the Apostles."

"Hurrah for Jeff Davis! and the Southern Confederacy! —— the Lincoln hordes and Hessians; polluting the homes and lands of Southern men! Hurrah for Stonewall Jackson, the Deliverer of the Southern Soil, to our Southern Brethren."

"P. P. FIELDS."

A SUBSTITUTE.—I will serve as a substitute in the confederate service for two thousand five hundred dollars, or in the militia for one thousand five hundred dollars. For further information, apply to THOMAS ALLEN, Dépôt Agent at Duck Hill.

WANTED.—Any one wishing to act as a substitute for a man subject to the conscript act, will receive the following compensation: a likely negro boy and five hundred dollars. Address B., *Appeal* Office.—*Vicksburgh Whig, August 6.*

AN ANECDOTE. — The rebel General Stuart and General Milroy had a conversation, in which General Milroy censured the system of guerrilla warfare practised by the rebels at that time, in the most severe terms. General Stuart remarked that this species of warfare was practised by our troops in Mexico. General Milroy asked him where he obtained his information.

General Stuart—"I read of it."

General Milroy—"You are mistaken, sir! 'Twas not done, sir! I was in Mexico myself."

In the course of conversation, General Stuart feigned impatience at the time consumed in burying the dead, and said he was in a hurry, as he intended to sup in Culpeper that evening. The conference ended by General Milroy remarking: "You may sup there, sir; *but I will sit at the head of the table.*"

CERTIFICATE OF AN "EXEMPT."—Doctor G. H. Burrell, of North Hyde Park, Vermont, gives the following certificate to one G. C. Lowther:

"August, the 19 1862

"this may Surtify that I george H Burell of North Hide park as a Fisian do surtify that gardner C Lother is not Liable to do Military duty having a pain in the Left Side and the Liver Bing a fected and a Kidney efected and one hand efected   G H BURRELL"

MUNCHAUSENIANA.

RICHMOND, *September 8.*—Yesterday being Sunday, the usual variety of rumors were afloat. Those which gained most credence were the following: That Generals Jackson and Longstreet had crossed the Potomac at Edward's Ferry, and were at the Relay House on Friday morning last. There may be some truth in this rumor, as the account published in another column from a Yankee journal shows that the greatest panic prevailed in the Yankee capital; and old Abraham doubtless has his Scotch cap at hand, ready to make his exit.

If Generals Jackson and Longstreet have really reached the Relay House, all communication between Washington and Baltimore and the West is thereby entirely cut off.

The reported blowing up of the Long Bridge is now generally believed. A lady who came through to this city from near Washington states that she was an eye-witness to the affair.

The enemy, before evacuating Acquia Creek, destroyed a large amount of stores and provisions.

Later intelligence gives us the gratifying assurance that General Jackson has entered Maryland by the route above indicated, and is now on a tour to the most important and inviting point between Baltimore and Washington. It is now useless to speculate upon probabilities. The war has assumed a new phase, and our citizens must expect hereafter to hear news that will startle amidst both good and bad report. The tables have been turned, and the confederate army is now an army of invasion.

LOYAL DISCIPLES.—The Disciples, "Campbellites," of Ohio, had been holding a tent meeting at Bedford, in Cuyahoga County. On the morning of the eighth of September, just before commencing religious exercises, Dr. Robinson arose and offered the following resolution:

"*Resolved,* That in the present condition of our country it becomes us as a people professing Christianity, to remember our Government before God in our prayers, to give of our substance in support of the same most freely, and our lives in every emergency, when called upon by the 'powers that be,' which powers are ordained of God; remembering that our duty to our God and to ourselves requires this at our hands."

INCIDENTS OF PORT HUDSON. — Adjutant Howard Cooke, One Hundred and Fifty-sixth regiment N. Y. V., at Port Hudson, related the following incidents of the battle of the fourteenth of June:

"Drummer Alex. Clearwater especially distinguished himself by his exertions in carrying off the wounded. He took charge of a squad of four negroes, and went through the field in discharge of his duties unmindful of the balls which were flying around thick as rain. He was wounded while trying to rescue General Paine—the same fate that met all others who attempted it.

"Wouldn't you like to hear of Col. Lew. Benedict? He led a charge down on the left, and with his color-bearer reached the top of the parapet. Here the sergeant was killed by a shell, and the Colonel seized the color, when his regiment being forced back, he was compelled to retire, which he did without injury."

The following is an extract of a letter from Adjutant S. B. Meech, of the Twenty-sixth Connecticut, written after the battle:

"I saw Colonel Benedict standing just in front of me, where I was wounded on the edge of the ravine, looking intently at the rebel works, while bullets and shells were flying about very thick. He walked to the rear as composedly as if he was out for a stroll. I think he is a fine officer. One of his officers died in this hospital this A.M. Lieutenant Haven, I think, was his name."

SQUIRREL-SKIN SHOES.—Squirrel skins tacked down to a board, the hair next to the board, with hickory ashes sprinkled over them, for a few days, to facilitate the removal of the hair, and then placed in a strong decoction of red-oak bark, will, at the end of four days, make excellent leather, far stronger and tougher than calf skin. Four skins will make a pair of ladies' shoes. We hear that the ladies of some of the interior counties are wearing these shoes, and find them equal in softness and superior in durability to any others. The longer the skins are left in the decoction of bark the better the leather. By this plan any body may have a tan-yard, and make their own leather, as the skins are easily and cheaply procured, and any vessel holding a gallon will serve as a vat. Our readers will do well to try it.—*Richmond Whig, August* 21.

GENERAL LEE ON INVASION.—A correspondent writing from Gettysburgh, June seventh, relates a talk between General Lee and a mill-owner of this State, during the recent invasion:

General Lee's confiscation of paper at the mills near Mount Holly Springs has been mentioned. Mr. Givin, one of the sufferers, at whose house the General breakfasted, gives me some facts of interest. "It is not that we love the Pennsylvanians," observed Lee, "that we refuse to let our men engage in plundering private citizens. We could not otherwise keep up the *morale* of the army. A rigid discipline must be maintained, or the men would be worthless." "In fact," adds Mr. G., "I must say that they acted like gentlemen, and, their cause aside, I would rather have forty thousand rebels quartered on my premises than one thousand Union troops. The colonel of one of the New-York regiments (militia) drove his horse into the engine-room of my mill, a place which must be kept as clean as a parlor; the men broke all the locks, and defiled every apartment from basement to garret. Yet all this time I have been quartering sick officers at my house, and my new hotel is thrown open to the men to sleep in free of charge."

"I told General Lee," continued Mr. Givin, "that the South must give it up; that the North would fight it out rather than see the country broken in two, and that their invasion of Pennsylvania was a great mistake." "What would you do," replied the General, "if you were in our place?" Here he produced copies of the Richmond papers, which complained so bitterly about the war being waged in the South, while it ought to be carried into the Free States. One of the motives to this inroad was, therefore, the pressure of public opinion brought to bear on the confederate government by means of the newspapers. The circumstance shows that uncle Jeff's throne is not so stable as has been supposed.

If the insurgents acted somewhat humanely by the way, they exacted an ample recompense from the citizens of Gettysburgh. After getting possession on Wednesday, they advised the people to leave. Those who did so had their houses broken into and robbed without mercy. Every thing was carried off that could be made use of, and what could not be was torn, soiled, defaced, or rendered useless. With the influx of strangers, the destruction of property, and the railroad in the hands of Government agents, it is positively difficult to get enough to eat, except "hard tack," and even that is not easily come-at-able by civilians. As to sleeping accommodations, blessed is he that expecteth nothing, for he shall not be disappointed. Yet I have good reason to believe the people kind and hospitable to strangers to a degree that Harrisburgh has never attained and never may.

"CHIVALRY."—We find in the New-Orleans *Era* the following horrible story related by a speaker at a Union association. It is given as authentic, and was told by an eye-witness of the occurrence in Texas:

"A Union man, or Yankee as he was called, had been taken out by the Texans and hanged before the very eyes of his family. They then cut him down, cut off his legs, his head; cut him open, took the fat, tried it out and put it in the vials to oil their revolvers; took out his heart, put it into a jar, took the scalp from his head; then boiled the head till the meat was removed, then nailed the skull to a board fence, and putting a candle in each eye, in the evening they had a dance in front of it, and as they promenaded up to it, the chivalrous gentlemen would ask their partners how they liked the Yankee candlestick."— *Council Bluffs Nonpareil, August* 1.

YANKEE VILLAINY AND FLUNKEYISM.—In the late raid to Rocky Mount, N. C., says the Raleigh *State Journal*, the Yankees entered the dwelling of ex-Gov. Clark, and took from his wife the wedding present of jewelry her husband had given her, and which of course she highly prized. One of the men remarked he thought it hard; but, said he, though our officers profess otherwise, in stealing these things, *we are strictly under orders*—we must obey.

We learn from the *Philadelphia Inquirer*, the most sycophantic of all Lincoln's lick-spittles, that the betrothal ring ordered by ex-Governor Sprague for his intended bride, Miss Kate Chase, is a diamond *solitaire*, set in enamel and not chased. It is described as a beautiful and tasteful ornament, worthy of the *beautiful* young lady who is the happy possessor of the token. The price of the ring was four thousand dollars.—*Savannah News, August* 14.

A WOMAN'S APPEAL FOR VOLUNTEERS.

BY MRS. FIELDS.

While Autumn lustre peaceful dies down in the yellow West,
  For thee, my country, I would plead!
  For thee, who art my life, my creed,
I would forego this beauty of the West
And its sweet rest.

Is she then quite bereaved, has love of glory fled the land?
  Do men forget, who wear the scars,
  They, and they only, win the stars?
For them the undying laurels of the land
Drop from each hand?

Have the forgotten days of Christ then past so far away?
  He knew not where to lay his head!
  You shall lie soft on Glory's bed,
If in clear faith you walk the patriot's way,
Nor longer stay.

Is God's own image sunk so low that money stands for man?
  Where are the arms of will and brawn?
  Where is the strength we cannot pawn?
Do piles of gold wear dignity like man,
In this our plan?

Men, fathers, brothers, hear you not our strong beseeching cry?
  O lovers! Women have grown proud!
  They learn to look upon a shroud,
But will not face a man who dares not die
For liberty!

Mothers and sisters, sitting by the quiet twilight
    hearth,
  We are not lonely, though alone,
  Each patriot soldier is our own,
Our prayers arise beside the silent hearth,
  To bless their worth.

Is high ambition dead, and every fresh desire of
    praise?
  With him who makes a patriot's choice,
  With him shall all the hours rejoice,
He shall be rocked by breezes joy can raise
  On beds of praise!

In ancient days, the nobly brave 'twas said should win
    the fair.
  Now, tears shall bathe victorious feet,
  Falling, as fell the ointment sweet:
To wipe these wounds, the noblest of the fair
  Unbinds her hair.

Is human life so vast a thing, subject to no decay?
  Do we forget the dying leaves?
  Are we unlike the garnered sheaves?
That we can dare to let God's right decay,
  In life's short day!

Go! thou shalt follow Honor, Mercy calling thee
    to go!
  The lamp of Glory shall not pale,
  The holiest love shall never fail,
To light the way thy blessed feet may go
  With Victory's glow!

HYMN

FOR THE EIGHTY-SEVENTH ANNIVERSARY OF AMERICAN
INDEPENDENCE.

BY GEORGE H. BOKER.

Lord, the people of the land
  In thy presence humbly stand;
On this day, when thou didst free
Men of old from tyranny,
We, their children, bow to thee.
    Help us, Lord, our only trust!
    We are helpless, we are dust!

All our homes are red with blood;
Long our grief we have withstood;
Every lintel, each door-post,
Drips, at tidings from the host,
With the blood of some one lost.
    Help us, Lord, our only trust!
    We are helpless, we are dust!

Comfort, Lord, the grieving one
Who bewails a stricken son!
Comfort, Lord, the weeping wife,
In her long, long widowed life,
Brooding o'er the fatal strife!
    Help us, Lord, our only trust!
    We are helpless, we are dust!

On our nation's day of birth,
Bless thy own long-favored earth!
Urge the soldier with thy will!
Aid their leaders with thy skill!
Let them hear thy trumpet thrill!
    Help us, Lord, our only trust!
    We are helpless, we are dust!

Lord, we only fight for peace,
Fight that freedom may increase.
Give us back the peace of old,
When the land with plenty rolled,
And our banner awed the bold!
    Help us, Lord, our only trust!
    We are helpless, we are dust!

Lest we pray in thoughtless guilt,
Shape the future as thou wilt!
Purge our realm from hoary crime
With thy battles dread, sublime,
In thy well-appointed time!
    Help us, Lord, our only trust!
    We are helpless, we are dust!

With one heart the nation's cries,
From our choral lips arise;
Thou didst point a noble way
For our fathers through the fray;
Lead their children thus to-day!
    Help us, Lord, our only trust!
    We are helpless, we are dust!

In His name, who bravely bore
Cross and crown begemmed with gore;
By his last immortal groan,
Ere he mounted to his throne,
Make our sacred cause thy own!
    Help us, Lord, our only trust!
    We are helpless, we are dust!

THE CONSTITUTION.

BY ALEXANDER H. MORRISON.

Hail!—thou eternal platform of the right!
  Whose planks are battle-fields of old renown,
Where justice gained bright victories over might,
  And hurled defiance at a tyrant's crown.
Yes, crushed and beat the bold oppressor down;
  And the young States, whose liberty was bought
Unconquered, and unshrinking from the frown
  Of Europe's monarchs, nobly, faithful wrought
  Their blood-bought rights into this pyramid of
    thought.

And who will raise his eyes and look afar
  O'er the broad plains and rivers of our land,
And see for every State a blazing star
  Gemming our flag, that waves on every strand—
Sees binding all the Constitution's band
  Into one mighty whole—will dare to say
One word, and much less raise his impious hand
  Against that glorious sun, whose livening ray
  Sheds o'er Columbia's sons the light of freedom's
    day.

Thou mighty fortress of a people free!
  A rock upon whose solid front may break
The billows of oppression ceaselessly,
  And never cause its firm-set base to shake.
Kingdoms may tumble, monarchies may quake,
  And revolutions rend the very earth,
Yet all the while, if freedom's sons awake,
  Will guard their sacred rights of bloody birth,
  Will this, their potent shield, protect each peaceful
    hearth.

Thou "Bow of Promise" on oppression's cloud!
  Down-trodden millions gaze on thee with eyes
That thence draw lightning to confuse the proud
  Oppressor, who beholds thy arch with sighs,

And feels the weakness of his prophecies
  Of failure of free government—and long,
Yes, long before the tyrant struggling dies,
  Will innovation's cheering, strengthening song,
From his own people rise, a liberated throng.

O solid keystone of the Union's arch !
  Will any dare to scoff or scorn at thee ?
Where are the warriors whose victorious march
  Secured for us our sacred liberty ?
Hark !—call them from their resting-place to be
  The judges of the man who dares deny
Unto this useful code supremacy ;
  From Bunker Hill and Yorktown they pass by,
  And blast the traitorous wretch, with lightning in
    each eye.

Thou art the heart of all this mighty land !
  Thou art the soul of freedom and of right !
Thou art our ruler ; at thy high command
  The people raise their voice to praise or blight.
Thine is the arm of law and warring might,
  The all that is American thou art !
And if in foreign war or civil fight,
  Columbia's arm will shield her noble heart,
The fierce and bloody strife will but new strength
    impart.

Where art thou, mighty one, whose noble form
  At Valley Forge, was bowed in fervent prayer ?
That never bowed before the battle's storm,
  But humbly sought the God of battles there ;
Then sought the British lion in his lair ?
  And when at Princeton, on the cheeks of those
Thy countrymen—thou saw'st by morning's glare
  A blanching ! Then thy mighty form uprose,
With flaming eye and cheek, and led them to their
    foes.

Dost thou not from the spirit-land above,
  Watch thy proud child of freedom, and behold,
With kind remembrance and undying love,
  Thy Government's strong principles unfold,
Wherever our bright banner is unrolled,
  Causing the hearts of the oppressed to burn
With fervent zeal, that never will grow cold,
  Until the groaning millions rise and spurn
The tyrant's yoke, and gain the power for which
    they yearn ?

O thou—and those who girt thy form around—
  In battle and in council not too soon
Your warning voices thunder from the ground,
  And shake the silence of Columbia's noon :
Oh ! tell thy heirs, the precious, cherished boon
  Of liberty to them to guard is given,
While beam the stars on high, or shines the moon
  Upon the land so favored of high heaven ;
For which that Constitution from tyrant's hands was
    riven !

And tell them, too, that that old Ship of State
  Must pass the rocks and shoals of civil war ;
And if it sinks, then freedom shares its fate,
  And darkness soon must cover every star.
Hark ! hear the wail of millions from afar !
  And mark the tears of sons of Washington.
Cursed be the hand that's ever raised to mar
  The title to our birthright—let the sun
Ne'er rise to witness such destruction if begun.

And let the cannon's awful thunder sound,
  Now beating in wild ways through freedom's air,
Startle the people to a thought profound,
  To watch the brazen war-cloud's sullen glare.
And let not souls be sinking with despair ;
  For twice before the cannon's fearful roar
Omened the breaking of a day more fair
  Of constitutional liberty—what more
  Should stir the ruler's soul who sways upon this
    shore ?

For this, our fathers fought, and bled, and died ;
  And this is ours by dying testament.
And if for this our soldiers side by side
  Are shedding blood, and living in the tent,
Then victory to our armies will be sent.
  But if a vile ambition sheds our gore,
In vain are noble hearts asunder rent !
  In vain our fathers' graves are trampled o'er !
  Since God has never owned the wrong upon this
    shore.
East-Springfield, Ohio.

THE REBEL PRESS ON THE GETTYSBURGH BATTLE.

General Lee's magnificent victory at Gettysburgh has, doubtless, cost us very dear, as many of us will know too well when the sad details come in. At present we have only the great and glorious result — the greatest army of the Yankee nation swept away, trampled under foot, and all but annihilated upon its own soil—the best part of Pennsylvania laid under contribution to sustain our army, and, in some small measure, make good our heavy losses ; the second city on the continent open to our armies, and already reckoning up the number of millions it must pay to ransom it from pillage and conflagration ; our own city of Baltimore waiting its deliverance with a passionate but secret joy ; and Washington, that foul den of thieves, expecting the righteous vengeance of heaven for the hideous crimes that have been done within its walls. In Philadelphia, how the Quakers quake this day ! In Washington, how the whole brood of Lincoln and his rascal ministers turn pale — how their knees smite together, as they hear from afar off the roar of their grand army of the Potomac rolled back in bloody rout and dismay, and see flashing through their guilty dreams the avenging bayonets of those they dared to call " rebels !" Ha ! does their monstrous crime weigh heavy on their souls to-day ? Mingling with the cheers that greeted the sweet perorations of their Fourth of July " orators of the day," do their ears hear the wail of the homeless and the fatherless whose houses they have laid in ashes, whose pride and strength they have laid low in the graves of a hundred battle-fields ? Yes, they begin to feel that they were in the wrong ; that there was some mistake somewhere ; and for the first time they pray for peace.

But this is only their first lesson. It is probable that our peace commissioners will have several other such to administer before the enemy shall be perfectly satisfied that there is no possible peace for him until he withdraws every soldier from the soil of every State, including Missouri, Kentucky, Maryland, and Delaware, and yield up to their lawful owners every town and fort he holds all around our borders. *Cincinnati, for example, would, we are assured, burn well.*

The *Dispatch* has the following :

" In the present instance the very enormity of the loss in prisoners attributed to the enemy excites incredulity, although no man doubts that the reporter stated accurately the prevalent belief in Martinsburgh at the time. We feel as well assured that General Lee, if he has met the enemy in a pitched battle, has inflicted a terrible blow upon them, as we do that we are living, breathing, sentient beings. Whether the details be precisely such as the telegraph gives us is another matter. If General Lee has, after a hard-fought battle, taken forty thousand prisoners, he has gained one of the most complete victories on record. He has utterly destroyed the only obstacle that stood between him and Baltimore, and we can see no reason why he should not be in that city to-morrow night. The force to defend it consists entirely of militia, many of them but ill-affected; and they have within the city a deadly enemy, as numerous as themselves, panting for revenge, and ready to rise on the first opportunity. In the panic which must follow such an astounding overthrow, nothing can be easier than to march in and take possession."

EPITAPH FOR GENERAL MEADE.—The following epitaph, from the grave-stone of an infant, should be placed upon the monument of Meade:

"If so soon I'm done for,
Wonder what I was begun for."
—*Richmond Enquirer.*

A HERO OF GETTYSBURGH.—The following thrilling incident was related to the editor of the Bradford *Argus*, by B. D. Beyea, who spent several days on the battle-field in search of the body of Captain C. H. Flagg, who fell in that terrible fight:

In the town of Gettysburgh lives an old couple by the name of Burns. The old man was in the war of 1812, and is now nearly seventy years of age, yet the frosts of many winters has not chilled his patriotism or diminished his love for the old flag, under which he fought in his early days. When the rebels invaded the beautiful Cumberland Valley, and were marching on Gettysburgh, Old Burns concluded that it was time for every loyal man, young or old, to be up and doing all in his power to beat back the rebel foe, and if possible, give them a quiet resting-place beneath the sod they were polluting with their unhallowed feet. The Old Hero took down an old State musket he had in his house and commenced running bullets. The old lady saw what he was about, and wanted to know what in the world he was going to do? "Ah!" said Burns, "I thought some of the boys might want the old gun, and I am getting it ready for them." The rebels came on. Old Burns kept his eye on the lookout until he saw the Stars and Stripes coming in, carried by our brave boys. This was more than the old fellow could stand; his patriotism got the better of his age and infirmity—grabbing his musket he started out—the old lady halloaed to him. "Burns, where are you going?" "Oh!" says Burns, "I am going out to see what is going on." He immediately went to a Wisconsin regiment and asked them if they would take him in. They told him they would, and gave him three rousing cheers.

The old musket was soon thrown aside and a first-rate rifle given him, and twenty-five rounds of cartridges.

The engagement between the two armies soon came on, and the old man fired eighteen of his twenty-five rounds, and says he killed three rebs to his certain knowledge. Our forces were compelled to fall back and leave our dead and wounded on the field, and

Burns having received three wounds, was left also not being able to get away. There he lay in citizen's dress, and if the rebs found him in that condition, he knew death was his portion. So he concluded to try strategy as his only hope. Soon the rebels came up, and approached him, saying: "Old man, what are you doing here?" "I am lying here wounded, as you see," he replied. "Well, but what business have you to be here, and who wounded you, our troops or yours?" "I don't know who wounded me, but I only know that I am wounded and in a bad fix." "Well, what was you doing here—what was your business?" "If you will hear my story, I will tell you. My old woman's health is very poor, and I was over across the country to get a girl to help her, and coming back before I knew where I was, I had got right into this fix, and here I are." "Where do you live?" inquired the rebels. "Over in town, in such a small house." They then picked him up and carried him home and left him. But they soon returned, as if suspecting he had been lying to them, and made him answer a great many questions, but he stuck to his old story, and they failed to make any thing out of old Burns, and then left him for good.

He says he shall always feel indebted to some of his copperhead neighbors for the last call, for he believes some one had informed them of him. Soon after they left, a bullet came into his room and struck in the wall about six inches above where he lay on his sofa, but he don't know who fired it. His wounds proved to be only flesh wounds, and he is getting well, feels first-rate, and says he would like one more good chance to give them a rip.

Old Burns is the great hero of the battle; his home is thronged with visitors. Governor Curtin and many other distinguished men have called on him, and have made him valuable presents.

Now mark the contrast between Burns, who had risked his life to save his country, and lay there on his couch wounded and bleeding from three different wounds, and his copperhead neighbors, who, no doubt, sent the rebels back to cut his throat; and if they had been the one hundredth part as mean as their sympathizers, would have done it. He has but little doubt that after the rebels left him for good, those fiends in human shape, finding the rebels had some pity for suffering humanity and spared his life, tried to kill him themselves by firing at him in his own home.

A REBEL BILL OF FARE.

J. H. Early, Surgeon of the Seventeenth Iowa regiment, found the following copy of a bill of fare in the rebel camps at Vicksburgh. While it is a capital specimen of burlesque, it is no less a melancholy specimen of burlesque upon the rebel rations of mule flesh indulged in by them during the last day of the siege:

HOTEL DE VICKSBURGH.

Bill of Bare for July, 1863.

SOUP.

Mule Tail.

BOILED.

Mule bacon with poke greens.
Mule ham canvassed.

ROAST.

Mule sirloin.
Mule rump stuffed with rice.

VEGETABLES.

Peas and rice.

ENTREES.

Mule head stuffed à la mode.
Mule beef jerked à la Mexicana.
Mule ears fricasseed à la gotch.
Mule side stewed, new style, hair on.
Mule spare ribs plain.
Mule liver hashed.

SIDE DISHES.

Mule salad.
Mule hoof soused.
Mule brains à la omelette.
Mule kidney stuffed with peas.
Mule tripe fried in pea-meal butter.
Mule tongue cold à la Bray.

JELLIES.

Mule foot.

PASTRY.

Pea-meal pudding, blackberry sauce.
Cottonwood berry pies.
China berry tart.

DESSERT.

White oak acorns.
Beech nuts.
Blackberry leaf tea.
Genuine confederate coffee.

LIQUORS.

Mississippi Water, vintage of 1492, superior, $3.
Limestone Water, late importation, very fine, $2.75.
Spring Water, Vicksburgh brand, $1.50.
Meals at all hours. Gentlemen to wait upon themselves. Any inattention on the part of servants will be promptly reported at the office.

JEFF DAVIS & Co., Proprietors.

CARD.—The proprietors of the justly celebrated Hotel de Vicksburgh, having enlarged and refitted the same, are now prepared to accommodate all who may favor them with a call. Parties arriving by the river or Grant's inland route, will find Grape, Canister & Co.'s carriages at the landing or any dépôt on the line of intrenchments. Buck, Ball & Co. take charge of all baggage. No effort will be spared to make the visit of all as interesting as possible

---

THE SURRENDER OF VICKSBURGH.

A Vicksburgh correspondent of the Cincinnati *Commercial* gives the following interesting particulars of the surrender of the city:

As melancholy a sight as ever man witnessed, for brave men conquered and humbled, no matter how vile the cause for which they fight, present always a sorrowful spectacle, and these foes of ours, traitors and enemies of liberty and civilization though they be, are brave, as many a hard-fought field can well attest. They marched out of their intrenchments by regiments upon the grassy declivity immediately outside their fort; they stacked their arms, hung their colors upon the centre, laid off their knapsacks, belts, cartridge-boxes and cap-pouches, and thus shorn of the accoutrements of the soldier returned inside their works, and thence down the Jackson road into the city. The men went through the ceremony with that downcast look so touching on a soldier's face; not a

word was spoken; there was none of that gay badinage we are so much accustomed to hear from the ranks of regiments marching through our streets; the few words of command necessary were given by their own officers in that low tone of voice we hear used at funerals. Generals McPherson, Logan, and Forney, attended by their respective staffs, stood on the rebel breastworks overlooking the scene never before witnessed on this continent. The rebel troops, as to clothing, presented that varied appearance so familiar in the North from seeing prisoners, and were from Texas, Alabama, Mississippi, Louisiana, Georgia, and Missouri; the arms were mostly muskets and rifles of superior excellence, and I saw but very few shot-guns, or indiscriminate weapons of any kind; it was plain that Pemberton had a splendidly-appointed army. Their flags were of a kind new to me, all I saw being cut in about the same dimensions as our regimental colors, all of the single color red, with a white cross in the centre.

The ceremony of stacking arms occupied little over an hour upon that part of the lines, and when it was concluded, the glittering cavalcade of officers, Federal and rebel, mounted and swept cityward on the full gallop, through such clouds of dust as I hope never to ride through again. A few minutes fortunately, brought us to a halt at a house on the extreme outskirts of the city, built of stone in the Southern fashion, with low roof and wide verandahs, and almost hidden from view in an exuberance of tropical trees, and known as Forney's headquarters.

And here were gathered all the notables of both armies. In a damask-cushioned armed rocking-chair sat Lieutenant-General Pemberton, the most discontented looking man I ever saw. Presently there appeared in the midst of the throng a man small in stature, heavily set, stoop-shouldered, a broad face, covered with a short, sandy beard, habited in a plain suit of blue flannel, with the two stars upon his shoulder, denoting a Major-General in the United States army. He approached Pemberton and entered into conversation with him; there was no vacant chair near, but neither Pemberton nor any of his generals offered him a seat, and thus for five minutes the conqueror stood talking to the vanquished seated, when Grant turned away into the house and left Pemberton alone with his pride or his grief—it was hard to tell which. Grant has the most impassive of faces, and seldom, if ever, are his feelings photographed upon his countenance; but there was then, as he contemplated the result of his labors, the faintest possible trace of inward satisfaction peering out of his cold gray eyes. All this occupied less time than this recital of it, and meantime officers of both armies were commingled, conversing as sociably as if they had not been aiming at each other's lives a few hours before. Generals McPherson and Logan now turned back toward our camps to bring in the latter's division, and a party specially detailed galloped cityward, about a mile distant for the purpose of hoisting the flag over the Court-House.

Lieutenant-Colonel William E. Strong, assisted by Sergeant B. F. Dugan, fourth company Ohio independent cavalry, and followed by a numerous throng of officers, soldiers, and civilians, ascended to the cupola of the court-house, and at half-past eleven o'clock on the Fourth of July, 1863, flung out our banner of beauty and glory to the breeze.

In addition to the arms borne by the captives, fifteen thousand Enfield rifles, intended for the use of Kirby Smith's army, fell into our possession. Kirby's men are badly off for shooting-irons, I am told, and Pemberton was to have made an effort some time since to send the English rifles to him.

We have taken twenty-seven eight-inch and ten-inch guns, and several pieces of English manufacture—Brooks, Armstrong, and Whitworth. One hundred and nine pieces of light artillery have already come to light. We captured twelve of their field-batteries at Black River and Champion Hills. They had on hand at the time of surrender, fifteen tons of cannon-powder, besides what was in the different service magazines. Their rifle cartridges were nearly exhausted. Rebel officers told me that at the rate they had been firing they had ammunition enough to last them for two weeks.

The following paragraphs are from the Vicksburgh correspondence of the St. Louis *Republican:*

Pemberton was of course the chief attraction. He is in appearance a tall, lithe built and stately personage. Black hair, black eyes, full beard, and rather a severe if not sinister expression of countenance, as of one who had great trials of the soul to endure. He is, you know, a native of Philadelphia, who is said to have been enamored early in life of the charms of a Southern lady, and since then has cast his lot with her friends. He is a trusted friend of the President, who, it is thought, would have spared nothing of men or means to aid him in this extremity.

The greatest curiosities are the caves hewn into the banks of earth, in which the women and children and non-combatants crept during the heat of the bombardment. At night, and sometimes during an entire day, the whole of these people would be confined to these caverns. They are constructed about the height of a man and three feet wide, a fork Y shaped into the bank. There are perhaps five hundred of these caves in the city around the works. As many as fifteen have been crowded into one of them.

AN INCIDENT AT THE BATTLE OF GETTYSBURGH.— General Schimmelfennig escaped capture by resorting to a dodge worthy of the sharpest Yankee. When he found his retreat cut off, he seized the coat of a private and buttoned it closely over his uniform; he was knocked known and run over by a gang of rebels who were after plunder. He then stumbled away into a cellar, and lay there concealed and without food for two days, but when he heard the boys playing "Yankee Doodle" in the streets, he thought it safe to come out. He is now in command of his brigade and ready for work.

COLONEL C. F. TAYLOR.

KILLED AT THE BATTLE OF GETTYSBURGH, JULY SECOND.

He fell as many a hero falls,
  Untimely, in the fearful fray,
Who only asks where duty calls,
  Then bravely leads the ordered way.

Undaunted by the battle storm,
  "Come on, come on, my boys!" he cried;
Dismayed they saw his reeling form,
  But conquered where their leader died.

And now he sleeps the endless sleep;
  Naught shall disturb that blest repose.
Though friends may sigh and kindred weep,
  His heart no pain nor sorrow knows.

Young hero, rest! thy strife is o'er,
  And thou hast gained a sweet release;
The bugle's blast, the cannon's roar,
  No more shall break thy spirit's peace.
WESTDALE, Delaware County, Pa.   D. B. S.

THE DEAD AT VICKSBURGH.—They lay in all positions; some with musket grasped as though still contending; others with the cartridge in the fingers just ready to put the deadly charge where it might meet the foe. All ferocity had gone. Noble patriots! uninhabited tenements! ye rest here now in security! Your portals whence the spirits fled are as calm and pale as moonlight upon snow—as though no sweet love had ever woven for ye myrtle wreaths, nor death draped your hearts in ivy—as though mirth had never smiled nor sorrow wept where all is now silent. War with its dangers, earth with its perplexities, neglect and poverty with their pangs, slander with its barb, the dear heart-broken ones at home—all fail to call ye back to strife. A dark and fearful shadow has crept over the land and gathered ye in its gloom. O the tears that will be shed! O the hearths that will be desolated! Eyes will look in vain for your return to the hearths that ye once gladdened, while Fame crowns ye with its laurels, and the land of the hereafter welcomes ye as "they who saved the land."

A remarkably sweet and youthful face was that of a rebel boy. Scarce eighteen, and as fair as a maiden, with quite small hands, long hair of the pale golden hue that auburn changes to when much in the sun, and curling at the ends. He had on a shirt of coarse white cotton, and brown pants, well worn; while upon his feet were a woman's shoes of about the size known as "fours." Too delicate was his frame for war; perchance some mother's idol. His left side was torn by a shell, and his left shoulder shattered. Poor misguided boy! Hyacinth was scarce more delicately beautiful than he. Mayhap he had his Apollo too.

Two men who had caught at a fig tree to assist them up a steep embankment lay dead at its feet slain in all probability by an enfilade fire from their right; the branch at which they caught was still in their grasp. Some could not be recognized by their nearest friends. Several were headless—others were armless; but the manner of their death was always plain. The Minié left its large, rather clear hole; the shell its horrid rent; the shrapnel and grape their clear, great gashes, as though one had thrust a giant's spear through the tender, quivering flesh.

In one trench lay two, grasping the same weapon—friend and foe. Across their hands fell a vine, the end upon the breast of the rebel, where it had fallen with them from an elevation above; the roots still damp with the fresh earth; upon it was a beautiful passion flower in full bloom and two buds; the buds were stained with blood—the flower as bright as was the day when the morning stars sang together. On the faces of both was the calm that follows sleep—rather pale, perhaps, but seeming like him of old, of whom it was said, "He is not dead, but sleepeth." But ah, the crimson! All is not well where earth is stained with blood. In some places the dead were piled, literally, like sacks of grain upon the shore.

It is remarkable with what patience the fatally wounded, they who already stood upon the shore, bore their sufferings. Some knew that they could not recover, but bore it manfully. Sometimes a tear, and a low voice would say, "My sweet wife," or "Darling," "Mother," "God forgive"—a quiver, then all was over. Let us hope that friend and foe alike found favor in His sight where all is well.

Death is life's mystery—that undiscovered country whence none return—in no place so great and marvellous a study as here.

One would think that war would develop ferocity in hard natures; perhaps it does; but it is not shown in the faces of the dead. They enter the silent land with eyes open; a stare of surprise is in them; the lines of care are softened upon the brow, and the cheek, when untorn, shows determination, as though they slept where doubt is unknown, where all mystery is revealed; where the reason of our creation, to bear the myrtle leaf of joy or the habiliments of mourning, to reap the golden sheaves of content or gather the mildew of misery, is known.

They have been sent, rather than gone, to the garner where all shall be gathered.

This is the work of treason! This it is to unroof the temple of law and order, and let loose the demon of discord. A people more than prosperous have fallen upon evil times. Murder, arson, theft, all kinds of injustice, follow in the footsteps of war. Nor is the end yet. When shall spears and swords be beaten into ploughshares and pruning-hooks? "How long, O Lord?"—*Cincinnati Gazette.*

HURRAH!

BY ALFRED B. STREET.

Vicksburgh is ours,
　Hurrah!
Treachery cowers,
　, Hurrah!
Down reels the rebel rag!
Up shoots the starry flag!
High, like a beaconed crag,
Let its light flash around
All through the Union's bound!
Flash, till the welkin gleams!
Flash, till the hills and streams,
Cities and hamlets, throw
Back a responsive glow!
Let the red rocket soar!
Let the deep cannon roar!
Bonfires their torrents pour!
Let the bells o'er and o'er
Clang the joy, peal the glee,
Waking one jubilee!
While the heart sends the shout,
Lengthening in thunder out,
　Triumph is ours,
　　Hurrah!

Vicksburgh is ours,
　Hurrah!
　Rain the wreathed flowers,
　　Hurrah!
Where the great river-band
Links the bright States that stand
Filling the valley grand,
See now that mighty land,
Stretching out either hand,
From where his river flows,
Out of its urn of snows
To the perennial rose!
Never to know again
On its free wave a chain;
But, while the waters wind,
Know them a bond to bind

Firm the great UNION: shout
All the broad Nation then!
Let the joy ring about,
So to be known of men
Wherever men shall see
Glory in Liberty.
　Triumph is ours,
　　Hurrah!

Vicksburgh is ours,
　Hurrah!
　Arch the green bowers,
　　Hurrah!
Arch o'er the hero, who
Nearer and nearer drew,
Letting wise patience sway,
Till, from his brave delay,
Swift as the lightning's ray,
Bounded he to the fray
Full on his fated prey;
Thundering upon his path,
　Swerving not, pausing not,
　Darting steel, raining shot,
　In his fierce onset, hot
With his red battle-wrath;
Flashing on, thundering on;
　Pausing then once again,
　Curbing with mighty rein,
　All his great heart, as vain
Writhed the fierce foe, the chain
Tighter and tighter wound—
Till the reward was found,
Till the dread work was done,
Till the grand wreath was won.
　Triumph is ours,
　　Hurrah!

Haughty Lee cowers,
　Hurrah!
Doubt no more lowers,
　Hurrah!
Swell the full pean shout
Over the rebel rout!
Over the traitor horde
In our free valleys poured!
Coming with sworded might
All the wide North to smite;
Coming with blazing torch
All her green fields to scorch;
Fleeing now, scathed and broke,
At the red lightning-stroke
Liberty wrathful woke;
Reeling in dazzled flight
At the grand sunburst light
Liberty woke to sight.
Bells ring out! banners fly!
Festal flames seek the sky!
　Triumph is ours,
　　Hurrah!

Haughty Lee cowers,
　Hurrah!
Triumph is ours,
　Hurrah!
Arch too his sweeping way,
He who in full array
Sprang from bright Fortune's head
Armed for the conflict dread,
Armed in proud freedom's right,
Hurling his martial might
　On the foe's serried files;

Once, twice, and thrice the fight
  Hurling; red battle-piles,
Torn in his mighty wrath,
Heaping his thunder-path.
Smiting on, smiting on,
Till the fierce field was won;
And the foe, wild with fear,
Plunged in his back career,
Wild for the river near,
Wild to hide there the drear
Change from the onset, bright
With his hope's fickle light;
  Triumph is ours,
    Hurrah!

  Victory ours,
    Hurrah!
  Proudly Meade towers,
    Hurrah!
Banks, too, whose starry brain
Shines over war's domain
Bright as in civic reign;
Who, with unyielding strain,
Rent the Port Hudson chain,
Last of the bonds that vain
Flung the mad foe across
Mississippi's mighty path.
Have ye seen torrents toss
  Off their ice-bands in wrath?
So, when the moment came,
Did the strong River claim
All his grand liberty.
Fools, did ye deem to see
  Fettered the Conqueror?
He whose majestic sweep
Holds the world's climates? Soar,
  Eagle, in rapture! leap
Echoes, as high and bold,
All round the shout is rolled!
As on each roof and hold
Banners from every fold
Flash joy in sunny gold.
As in tones uncontrolled,
Still is the gladness told,
Shouted o'er wood and wold,
In the bell's music knolled,
  Vicksburgh is ours,
    Hurrah!
  The valley is ours,
    Hurrah!
  Grant, Banks, and Meade ours,
    HURRAH!

THE NORTHERN INVASION OF LEE.

What means this invasion of Lee?
  This Northern invasion by Lee?
Can any one tell the extent of his lines?
And why he cuts up such impertinent shines?
And where it is going? Has any one guessed?
On a frolic up North, or a raid in the West,
  This great rebel army of Lee?

Some say that this army of Lee,
  This half famished army of Lee,
Has invaded the North to secure the relief
Of old Pennsylvania's bread, butter, and beef,
And horses and blankets, and shirts, boots and shoes,
And that her choice whisky they will not refuse,
  These tatterdemalions of Lee.

Some guess that this army of Lee,
  This penniless army of Lee,
Is destined to play us some ruinous pranks,
To surprise Philadelphia, and clean out her banks
And Uncle Sam's mint, and their treasures untold
In "greenbacks" and nickel, and silver and gold,
  This vagabond army of Lee.

And others will have it that Lee,
  Or a part of this army of Lee,
Is moving North-West, and to Pittsburgh is bound,
To sack it, and blow up, or burn to the ground
Its factories of great guns, and gunboats—that all
Its warlike establishments surely must fall
  To the wrath of this army of Lee.

And others are certain that Lee,
  And the savage battalions of Lee,
Are moving for Baltimore, there, in the name
Of pious Jeff Davis, to kindle the flame
Of a roaring rebellion—that this is the game,
The grand calculation and object and aim,
  Of these terrible Tartars of Lee.

Some think that these movements of Lee,
  And these raids from the army of Lee,
Are only deceptions, the tricks and the show
Of a Northern invasion, to cheat "Fighting Joe,"
And then to push on, without pausing to rest,
To a junction with Bragg to recover the West,
  By these bold Carthaginians of Lee.

Some think that abandoning Lee,
  The Cotton State Legions of Lee,
Care little for Richmond—that Davis & Co.
Have packed up their traps and are ready to go
To some safer refuge down South—that, in fine,
In Georgia they next will establish their shrine,
  And leave old Virginia to Lee.

But it is our impression that Lee,
  And this wonderful army of Lee,
Are moving with Washington still in their eyes,
Looming up as the grand and desirable prize
Which will gain the alliance of England and France,
And bring in John Bull to assist in the dance,
  Hand in hand with the army of Lee.

'Tis the last chance remaining to Lee,
  And the last to this army of Lee,
And the last to Jeff Davis; for, sure as they fail
In this desperate game, nothing else will avail.
To keep their frail craft and its masters adrift,
Or to rescue from ruin, disastrous and swift,
  This grand rebel army of Lee.

All these Border State movements of Lee
  Are but the diversions of Lee
To divide our main army which holds him at bay,
To divide it, and crush it, and open the way
To "Old Abe's" headquarters; for, these once pos-
    sessed,
King Jeff will retrieve his misfortunes out West,
  As he thinks, by this triumph of Lee.

But this Northern invasion of Lee,
  With the loss of this army of Lee,
To Richmond so strongly invites us that way,
That we are expecting the tidings some day
That Dix has gone in, and that Davis has saddled
His steed, and has over the river skedaddled
  To hunt up the army of Lee.

And we think in these movements of Lee,
 With this hide and seek army of Lee,
The occasion has come when his game may be foiled,
And we hope that his schemes will be thoroughly,
 spoiled
By our war-chiefs at Washington waiting the day
To bring our whole army *en masse* into play
 On the broken battalions of Lee.

KING COTTON.

When, tempted by Satan, Jeff Davis would try
 To imitate Louis Napoleon,
When oaths and allegiance like chaff he made fly,
 And trampled whatever was holy on;
To give him a character in the world's eyes,
 And bolster his plans misbegotten,
He called on the strongest of all his allies,
(A better than Memminger, Stephens, or Wise,)
 His pal and his comrade King Cotton,
 King Cotton,
 His pal and his comrade King Cotton.

"Hurra, mighty Cotton! our scheme is a-foot,
 So get up your prettiest figure;
For travelling dress take your best royal suit,
 (Dyed *gules* with the blood of a nigger;)
Go round to the nations and ask for their aid,
 And teach them much more than they wot on;
Go, make all your brothers, the monarchs, afraid
Their kingdoms must perish if 'reft of our trade."
 "By Plutus, I will," says King Cotton,
 King Cotton,
 "By Plutus, I will," says King Cotton.

Then off goes King Cotton to find Johnny Bull,
 And deep in his counting-house found him;
(Of idols and opium the top shelves were full,
 With Bibles and prayer-books just round him.)
"Your help or your life, Master Johnny!" says he;
 "Up, arm, and bring Paddy and Scot on!
For if you don't aid such good fellows as we,
Your mills shall be stopped, and then where will you
 be?
 "Put that in your pipe," says King Cotton,
 King Cotton,
 "Put that in your pipe," says King Cotton.

Then Johnny looked up with his pen in his hand,
 Says he: "My dear Cotton, I tell you,
In the way of fair business, as you understand,
 A pirate or two I can sell you.
But to go without corn is quite out of my line,
 A Yankee war's not to be thought on;
And though for employment our workingmen pine,
'Twere cheaper to feed them on venison and wine."
 "You and they may be—blessed!" says King Cotton,
 King Cotton,
 "You and they may be—blessed!" says King Cotton.

King Cotton goes off with a flea in his ear;
 Away to Napoleon he hies him:
"I'm sure *you* will help us, O Emperor dear!"
 And then he with flattery plies him.
"My brother and yours ever prays for your weal,
 That your glory there be not a spot on;
He sends you an envoy extremely genteel,
The Marquis of Faro and Duke of Sly-deal,
 He's one of your set," says King Cotton,
 King Cotton,
 "He's one of your set," says King Cotton.

Says Louis, says he: "Live forever, O king!
 And long may your pal live in clover!
His mission and mine are to do the same thing—
 Crush liberty all the world over.
But though to assist you my spirit inclines,
 A year or two first I must plot on;
Just wait till I've pillaged those Mexican mines,
And then I may help you to cut up some shines."
 "I wish you'd make haste," says King Cotton,
 King Cotton,
 "I wish you'd make haste," says King Cotton.

King Cotton goes off with two fleas in his ear,
 He goes to those sons of —— their mothers,
The copperhead reptiles, who bother us here,
 Vallandigham, Wood, and the others;
"Once more, my brave fellows, be true to your kind,
 And stay the war-storm that comes hot on!
Bewilder our foe with your fire from behind,
And go it for Davis and slavery blind!
 Come give us a lift," says King Cotton,
 King Cotton,
 "Come give us a lift," says King Cotton.

The copperheads said: "To our kind we are true,
 We lie and we hiss as we used to,
But the people have found they can do without you,
 And sad are the straits we're reduced to.
Our necks feel already a kind of a twist,
 Our schemes tyrant Lincoln sits squat on;
We try to dissuade those who want to enlist,
But as to *our* fighting—we daren't resist."
 "You cowardly scum!" says King Cotton,
 King Cotton,
 "You cowardly scum!" says King Cotton.

King Cotton goes off with three fleas in his ear;
 He goes back to Jefferson Davis.
Says Jeff, "How is this? What! are you again here?
 And could you do nothing to save us?
Our great institutions are at their last kick,
 And all our confederacy rotten;
Up in Pennsylvania I took my best trick,
But Meade was at hand, and he trumped me too quick.
 "We *are* up a tree," says King Cotton,
 King Cotton,
 "We *are* up a tree," says King Cotton.

King Cotton he took off his (sham) royal crown,
 He took off his robe that was gay;
His palmetto sceptre he sadly laid down,
 And bade an adieu to his glory.
"Since I must confess that my subjects are free,
 So well they without me have got on,
I'll give up to Corn, for too plainly I see
That he is the ruler they own and not me.
 I'll abdicate here," says King Cotton,
 Poor Cotton!
 "I'll abdicate here," says King Cotton.
 CARL BENSON.

"VICKSBURGH IS OURS!"

BY J. O. BLYTHE, M.D.

Hark! borne upon the Southern breeze,
As whispers breathed above the trees,
Or as the swell from off the seas,
 In summer showers,
Fall softly on the ears of men
Strains sweetly indistinct, and then—
Hist! listen! catch the sound again—
 "Vicksburgh is ours!"

O'er sea-waves beating on the shore,
'Bove thunders e'en the storms are o'er,
O'er cataract in headlong roar,
    High, high it towers.
O'er all the breastworks and the moats
The Starry Flag in triumph floats,
And heroes thunder from their throats:
    "Vicksburgh is ours!"

Spread all your banners in the sky,
The sword of victory gleams on high,
Our conquering eagles upward fly,
    And kiss the stars;
For Liberty the gods awake,
And hurl the shattered foes a wreck,
The Northern arms make strong to break
    The Southern bars.

The flaunting flag, the rebels' trust,
Lies trailing in the bloody dust,
With sword and halberd there to rust
    And rot to shreds;
No more from its dishonored grave
To flout defiance to the brave,
Who proudly our broad banners wave
    High o'er their heads.

All honor to the brave and true
Who fought the bloody battles through,
And from the ramparts victory drew
    Where Vicksburgh cowers;
And o'er the trenches, o'er the slain,
Through iron hail and leaden rain,
Still plunging onward, might and main,
    Made Vicksburgh ours.

Wave, wave your banners in the sky,
The glory give to God on high,
In lofty praises far outvie
    All other powers,
Who nerved the arms that struck the blow,
Which, in defeat o'erwhelmed the foe,
And laid his frowning bulwarks low,
    Made Vicksburgh ours!

SONG OF THE BORDER.

Air—Bonnie Dundee.

To the heart of the nation the booming guns spoke,
While the true flag went down in the fire and the
    smoke;
And the grim walls of Sumter yet echoed the fray
When the loyalists rushed where the Stars led the way.
  CHORUS—Then fight for the Stripes, boys, and fight
      for the Stars!
        Confounded be treason! torn down be the
         Bars!
        Let foul traitors tremble, and rebels grow
         pale,
        As the Banner of the Union floats out on
         the gale!

Though the land of the cypress its vandals sends forth,
They are met in the path by the hosts of the North:
Toward the troopers that spring from the cotton-bank-
    ed stream,
With the fires of just vengeance our bayonets gleam.
  CHORUS—Then fight, etc.

They may flaunt in the breeze their famed rattlesnake
    flag;
They may sneer at the Banner and call it a rag;
But by all we hold sacred, above or below,
We solemnly swear that their flag shall lie low!
  CHORUS—Then fight, etc.

They may boast of their chivalry, boast of their blood;
We stand by our fathers' faith, bow but to God:
Let them come in their pride; they shall grievously
    feel
The firmness and keenness of loyalists' steel.
  CHORUS—Then free let the Stripes wave, bright shine
      the Stars!
        Confounded be treason! despised be the
         Bars!
        The false hearts of rebels shall falter and
         quail,
        As the Banner of Union floats out on the
         gale.

THE BATTLE OF GETTYSBURGH.

The days of June were nearly done;
The fields, with plenty overrun,
Were ripening 'neath the harvest sun,
      In fruitful Pennsylvania!

Sang birds and children—"All is well!"
When, sudden, over hill and dell,
The gloom of coming battle fell
      On peaceful Pennsylvania!

Through Maryland's historic land,
With boastful tongue and spoiling hand,
They burst—a fierce and famished band—
      Right into Pennsylvania!

In Cumberland's romantic vale
Was heard the plundered farmer's wail;
And every mother's cheek was pale,
      In blooming Pennsylvania!

With taunt and jeer, and shout and song,
Through rustic towns, they passed along—
A confident and braggart throng—
      Through frightened Pennsylvania!

The tidings startled hill and glen;
Up sprang our hardy Northern men,
And there was speedy travel then
      All into Pennsylvania!

The foe laughed out in open scorn;
For Union men were coward-born,
And then—they wanted all the corn
      That grew in Pennsylvania!

.   .   .   .   .   .

It was the languid hour of noon,
When all the birds were out of tune,
And Nature in a sultry swoon,
      In pleasant Pennsylvania!

When—sudden o'er the slumbering plain,
Red flashed the battle's fiery rain—
The volleying cannon shook again
      The hills of Pennsylvania!

Beneath that curse of iron hail,
That threshed the plain with flashing flail,
Well might the stoutest soldier quail,
    In echoing Pennsylvania!

Then, like a sudden, summer rain,
Storm-driven o'er the darkened plain,
They burst upon our ranks and main,
    In startled Pennsylvania!

We felt the old, ancestral thrill,
From sire to son, transmitted still;
And fought for Freedom with a will,
    In pleasant Pennsylvania!

The breathless shock—the maddened toil—
The sudden clinch—the sharp recoil—
And we were masters of the soil,
    In bloody Pennsylvania!

To westward fell the beaten foe—
The growl of battle hoarse and low
Was heard anon, but dying slow,
    In ransomed Pennsylvania!

Sou' westward, with the sinking sun,
The cloud of battle, dense and dun,
Flashed into fire—and all was won
    In joyful Pennsylvania.

But ah! the heaps of loyal slain!
The bloody toil! the bitter pain!
For those who shall not stand again
    In pleasant Pennsylvania!

Back through the verdant valley lands,
East fled the foe, in frightened bands;
With broken swords and empty hands,
    Out of Pennsylvania!
        HOWARD GLYNDON.

A BEAUTIFUL LETTER.—Some time since a rebel by the name of Hardin was captured near Vicksburgh, with a letter written by a lady of one of the "first families" in Mississippi, residing near Lake Providence, which letter he was conveying to Mrs. Amy Anderson in a neighboring State. The writer of the letter speaks of her husband as "Mr. P.," and it appears that he was a man of considerable influence and standing. I send you the letter with extracts marked, in order that readers may see what spirit pervades the "high-bred dames" of this region. If any one imagines that the language used by the writer of this letter is unusual with high-born Southern ladies, let him inquire of the first returned officer or soldier he meets, and he will doubt no longer. The italics are mostly my own.

"DEAREST AUNT: Mr. P. could not attend to Rob's business for the same reason that he dissuaded him from going, as Rob neglected to bring his proper papers, and without them, Mr. P. felt certain he could have gone no further than Canton, as our laws are decidedly more rigid, at least the conscript law, and carried out to the very letter, than in your State or any other. So Mr. P. assisted Rob in getting the services of our old friend Mr. J. I fear to tell any names, as the unprincipled demon foe prides himself upon discovering important information through intercepted letters, which have been extracted from the poor, affrighted negro, child, or unprotected female, whom they may

chance to meet or discover in their murdering, thieving, devil-like travels. I wish they could see all that I have written of them, and wish still more fervently that every line and desire of my heart could fall upon them to place them in situations I would designate. If there is an hereafter, a heaven or hell, I pray to go to perdition ere my soul would be joined or rest in heaven with the fiendish foe. But God has ever shown himself a just, true Father, and will ere long mete out to them their proper punishment. Heaven would not be the place described to us were it filled with spirits so foul, so hellish, (excuse the expression.) Words are too weak, too trite, too feeble, to convey even the slightest idea of feeling which our refined, elegant, high-toned, principled, chivalrous people feel or look upon such an offcast, degenerate set. It would be some solace to us when we lose our husbands, fathers, sons, and friends, to know they were fighting an enemy civilized or refined to a great degree. But oh! the thought is killing, is too painful, to see our men, the choicest, most refined specimens of God's work, destroyed and even forced to take up arms against the offscourings, outcast dregs of creation; for every man they lose is a blessing, a god-send to humanity and society. But enough of such stuff. I might write ten thousand pages and then fail to pen one idea correctly.

"If ever I had one lady-like feeling or wish for a Northern man, even before this bloody war, I was not aware of it, and I pray to live just to raise my son and daughter, to despise the whole race, and our boy must shoot them down as he would the most ferocious wild beast whenever they cross his path. So extreme is my disgust, that if I once thought my children would ever countenance—not a Yankee, but a Northerner, (for they are the same,) I could and would plunge a dagger into their hearts, and laugh to see their life's blood oozing. They must notice them only to murder and poison."

It appears that every thing in Secessia does not suit the writer's ideas of propriety, and that the rights of private property, in other words, of private niggers, are not invariably respected in the dominions of Jeff Davis, as bear witness the following:

"The overseers and managers treat the property of private patriotic men at Vicksburgh more like the Yanks than I thought a Southern man could do. They are not only cruel but worse. They neglect them in sickness, whereas an hour's attention would save hundreds; but we must stand it, even if we lose all we have. Say not a word—the laws of State so order. I see not why Mississippi cannot remunerate our losses as easily as other States, but we run some things into the ground and entirely neglect other items equally as important. I pray the hated foe will all be sent to perdition, vessels and all, ere they gain one inch more foothold on any property of any kind that can benefit them. I would joyously see every thing we own crumble to ashes ere it should fall into the hands of the devils. ANNA."
August, 1863.

COLONEL WILDER AT CHICKAMAUGA.—Colonel Wilder's position was such as to enable him to know not only the movements of the troops preceding the battle of Sunday, but to bring from the field the very last news that could be gathered there. In Saturday's fight, he was on the left or left centre. That night the greater portions of McCook's and Crittenden's corps moved past him to strengthen Thomas on the extreme left, leaving him on the extreme right. Between his brigade and Thomas, in the centre, instead of two corps, as represented by the *Herald* writer, there were but two divisions, Sheridan's and Jeff C. Davis, of these corps. Here the line was necessarily very weak, and the rebels failing in the desperate attack upon Thomas, and in a fierce but not persistent dash upon the right, took the opportunity of some movement in the centre to strike there. They massed a column six or eight deep against our thin line and broke through it, scattering the divisions more by main strength and pressure than by their fire, into the hills and hollows of Mission Ridge behind them, where the nature of the ground made it difficult to keep them together or rally them. This was the only real reverse of the day. It embraced but two divisions, as already stated, and of these, Sheridan and Davis, who, Wilder says, did all that human daring and coolness could, rallied a considerable number, and returned to the fight. Not many were killed or captured, as the rebels were prevented from using their advantage by a deadly flanking fire thrown into them by Wilder's seven-shooting rifles and artillery as they passed him in pursuit. He says they did not go a half-mile beyond his line, and soon fell back. After this he held his ground *five hours without molestation.* How Thomas held the left, or rather the main body of the army, is known to every body. On both flanks the rebels were stopped and beaten back. In the centre they broke up two divisions, but with a less fatal result than might have been expected. This is the sum of the matter. On Sunday night Wilder distributed his brigade so as to protect the roads from the right to Chattanooga, and on Monday joined the main body in good order and good spirits, entirely unconscious of any defeat. Thomas came in on Monday at his own pleasure, with more than two thirds of the whole army, and any thing but a defeat to report, as the most dispiriting accounts show. Our line was held, except at the right of the centre, till we chose to leave it, as Rosecrans would have done before the fight, if the rebels had let him. They fought to break him up before he could get back to the impregnable position at Chattanooga, and only succeeded in breaking up two divisions. As Wilder came in he gathered up and brought with him a very large amount of stores and material, supposed by those in Chattanooga, and of course by the *Herald* writer, to have been lost. Among these were two guns, one hundred ambulances, sixty beef cattle, and a large number of ammunition wagons and caissons. Similar recoveries were doubtless made by other portions of the army, but the correspondent had hurried off to publish his description of the fight, and knew nothing of this rather important variation of the state of facts behind him. Our loss in prisoners, in both days, the Colonel says, will not exceed two thousand five hundred, including the wounded. In artillery, it will be less than Colonel Barnett supposed, as guns were recovered and brought in, of which he could know nothing when he gave his estimate to the correspondent. We captured about two thousand prisoners, of whom Wilder brought one thousand five hundred and thirty with him to Stevenson. The distance of the battle-field from Chattanooga has not been fully understood, and the supposition that Rosecrans was driven back twenty or thirty miles has added a gloomy shade even to the most cheering aspect of the fight; but the distance was small, our extreme right, which was farthest away on Sunday, being less than twelve miles off, and the left, after falling back to Mission Ridge, being hardly more than half of it.

On Monday, immediately after the return from the field, Wilder was sent off up the Tennessee to guard fords and passes for Burnside's benefit, and took with him despatches from Rosecrans with full news of the "situation." These despatches were safely delivered, as the courier taking them got back just as Wilder started home. This assures the country that Burnside will not be caught unprepared. When the courier reached him he was moving toward Chattanooga, at what point or with what strength it would probably be improper to state, but we may state that by this time he is past all danger of being intercepted by the rebels, and has force enough to make good all Rosecrans has lost, and something over. At Stevenson Wilder heard a rumor that Grierson's cavalry from the Mississippi were within ten miles, and that Sherman's whole corps was within two days' march, coming up from Decatur, Alabama, but the rumors were undoubtedly false, as Grierson was in Springfield, Illinois, on Friday, and Sherman could not have got to the point stated, from the Big Black, in the time that has elapsed since the battle, and we know that he had not started before.

Among the incidents of the battle of Saturday, Colonel Wilder described the frightful slaughter of Longstreet's men at the time they were driven back by our left wing. This celebrated corps, as desperate soldiers as ever lived, attacking two divisions, Van Cleve's and Davis's, to the right, and a little in front of Wilder, separated them and pushed on through the open space yelping—the rebel shout is a yelp, instead of a civilized hurrah—and confident of victory. A portion of them had to cross a small field, behind which, in the bordering woods, Wilder lay, and through which ran a ditch five or six feet deep to carry off the water of an adjacent stream or swamp. As the rebels entered this field, in heavy masses fully exposed, the mounted infantry, with their seven-shooting rifles, kept up a continuous blast of fire upon them, while Lilly, with his Indiana battery, hurled through them double-shotted canister from his ten-pounder rifles, at less than three hundred yards. The effect was awful. Every shot seemed to tell. The head of the column, as it was pushed on by those behind, appeared to melt away or sink into the earth, for, though continually moving, it got no nearer. It broke at last, and fell back in great disorder. It was rallied and came on again, and with desperate resolution pushed through the solid fire to the ditch. Here all who could get in took shelter. Instantly, Lilly whirled two of his guns and poured right down the whole length of the ditch his horrible double canister. Hardly a man got out of it alive. "At this point," said Wilder, (who has been seasoned to slaughter by being two hundred times under fire,) "it actually seemed a pity to kill men so. They fell in heaps, and I had it in my heart to order the firing to cease to end the awful sight." But the merciless seven-shooters and canister would not stop, and again the boasted flower of Lee's army was crushed into a disorderly mob, and driven off. When the firing ceased one could have walked for two hundred yards down that ditch on dead rebels without touching the ground. Of course Colonel Wilder doesn't claim that his brigade defeated Longstreet. His statement refers only to that portion of the corps which entered the field in his front. He thinks that not less than two thousand rebels were killed and wounded in this field. It was probably the most disastrous fire of the two days' fight on either side.

On Sunday, Colonel Edward A. King, of the Sixty-eighth Indiana, then commanding a brigade, was killed by a rebel sharp-shooter concealed in a tree.

The shot struck him in the forehead, killing him instantly. Colonel Grose, reported killed, was not hurt.

In a skirmish of Wilder's brigade with Forrest, a few miles from Dalton, Georgia, three days before the battle, Forrest was so badly wounded that he was unable to take his command during the battle. General Joe Johnston accompanied Forrest's brigade, and narrowly escaped being captured. The same day Lee, Johnston, Bragg, and other rebel generals, were in Dalton in consultation.—*Indianapolis Journal.*

SONGS OF THE REBELS.

NO UNION MEN.

BY MILLIE MAYFIELD.

"On the twenty-first, five of the enemy's steamers approached Washington, N. C., and landed a hundred Yankees who marched through the town playing 'Yankee Doodle,' hoisted their flag on the Court-House, and destroyed gun-carriages and an unfinished gunboat in the ship-yard. The people preserved a sullen and unresisting silence. The Yankees then left saying they were disappointed in not finding Union men."—*Telegram from Charleston, March 29th, 1862.*

"*Union men.*" O thrice-fooled fools!
 As well might ye hope to bind
The desert sands with a silken thread
 When tossed by the whirling wind;
Or to blend the shattered waves that lick
 The feet of the cleaving rock,
When the tempest walks the face of the deep,
 And the water-spirits mock;
As the severed chain to reünite
 In a peaceful link again.
On our burning homesteads ye may write:
 "We found no Union men."

Ay, hoist your old dishonored flag,
 And pipe your worn-out tune,
The hills of the South have caught the strain
 And will answer it full soon;
Not with the sycophantic tone
 And the cringing knee bent low—
The deep-mouthed cannon shall bear the tale
 Where the sword deals blow for blow;
Our braying trumpets in your ears
 Shall defiant shout again:
"Back, wolves and foxes, to your lairs,
 Here are no Union men."

Union, with tastes dissimilar?
 Such Union is the worst
And direst form of bondage that
 Nations or men has cursed!
Union with traitors? Hear ye not
 That cry for vengeance deep,
Where hand to hand and foot to foot
 Our glittering columns sweep?
Our iron-tongued artillery
 Shouts through the bristling glen,
To the war-drum echoing reveille,
 "Here are no Union men."

Oh! deep have sunken the burning seeds
 That the winged winds have borne,
That for all your future years must yield
 The thistle and prison thorn.
Our soil was genial—ye might have sown
 A harvest rich—'tis too late!
To our children's children we leave for you
 But a heritage of hate!

Ye have opened the wild flood-gates of war
 And we may not the torrent pen,
But ye seek in vain on our storm-beat shore
 For the myth called "Union Men."

WHAT THE SOUTH WINDS SAY.

Faint as the echo of an echo born,
 A bugle note swells on the air;
 Now louder, fuller, far and near
It sounds a mighty horn.

The noblest blast blown in our time
 Comes from the South on every breeze,
 To sweep across the shining seas
In symphony sublime!

'Tis Freedom's *reveille* that comes
 Upon the air, blent with a tramp
 Which tells that she now seats her camp
With trumpets and with drums.

When first I heard that pealing horn
 Its sounds were faint and black in the night;
 But soon I saw a burst of light
That told of coming morn!

When first I heard that martial tread
 Swell on the chilly morning breeze,
 'T was faint as sound of distant seas—
Now, it might rouse the dead!

Ay, it has roused the dead! They start
 From many a battle-field, to teach
 Their children noble thoughts and speech—
To "fire the Southern heart!"

Not only noble thoughts, but deeds
 Our fathers taught us how to dare;
 They fling our banners on the air
And bring our battle-steeds!

While louder rings that mighty horn—
 Whose clarion notes on every gale
 Tell history's latest, greatest tale—
A nation now is born!

And as that trump's inspiring peal,
 Within time's lists I see it stand,
 A splendid banner in its hand,
Full armed from head to heel!

Long ages in their flight shall see
 That flag wave o'er a nation brave—
 A people who preferred one grave
Sooner than slavery.
   —*Richmond Dispatch.*

WILL YOU GO?

BY ESTELLE.

Will you go! will you go!
Where the foeman's steel is bright
In the thickest of the fight,
For God and for right.
 Will you go! will you go!

Will you stay! will you stay!
And let eternal blame
Mark with finger-point of shame
Your deep dishonored name.
 Will you stay! will you stay!

Will you go! will you go!
For freedom's struggling cry,
In the name of God most high,
To rescue her or die.
 Will you go! will you go!

Will you stay! will you stay!
While the coil is tighter bound,
And the tyrant on our ground
Plants his foot with dismal sound.
 Will you stay! will you stay!

Will you go! will you go!
Where our dying brothers call,
As they bleed and bravely fall,
To free us from this thrall.
 Will you go! will you go!

Will you stay! will you stay!
And let the silent grave
Reproach you for the brave,
Who have died our land to save.
 Will you stay! will you stay!

Will you go! will you go!
The brow of boyhood bared,
With the old and hoary-haired,
Have the darkest perils dared.
 Will you go! will you go!

Will you stay! will you stay!
Slaves of a tyrant's chain,
Slaves ever to remain,
In dishonor's deepest stain.
 Will you stay! will you stay!

Will you go! will you go!
Answer YES or answer NO,
For soon the fatal blow
Will descend for weal or woe.
 Will you go! will you go!

Will you stay! will you stay!
Then may eternal gloom,
Draped by the hand of doom,
For ever shroud your tomb.
 CAN you stay! CAN you stay!

HEART VICTORIES.

BY A SOLDIER'S WIFE.

There's not a stately hall,
 There's not a cottage fair,
That proudly stands on Southern soil,
 Or softly nestles there,
But in its peaceful walls
 With wealth or comfort blest,
A stormy battle fierce hath raged
 In gentle woman's breast.

There Love, the true, the brave,
 The beautiful, the strong
Wrestles with Duty gaunt and stern,
 Wrestles and struggles long;
He falls—no more again
 His giant foe to meet,
Bleeding at every opening vein,
 Love falls at Duty's feet.

O daughter of the South!
 No victor's crown be thine,
Not thine, upon the tented field
 In martial pomp to shine;
But with unfaltering trust
 In Him who rules on high,
To deck thy loved ones for the fray,
 And send them forth to die.

With wildly throbbing heart—
 With faint and trembling breath—
The maiden speeds her lover on
 To victory or death;
Forth from caressing arms
 The mother sends her son,
And bids him nobly battle on,
 Till the last field is won.

While she, the tried, the true,
 The loving wife of years,
Chokes down the rising agony,
 Drives back the starting tears,
" I yield thee up," she cries,
 In the country's cause to fight;
Strike for our own, our childrens' home,
 And God defend the right.

O daughter of the South!
 When our fair land is free,
When peace her lovely mantle throws
 Softly o'er land and sea,
History shall tell how thou
 Hast nobly borne thy part,
And won the proudest triumphs yet—
 The victories of the heart.

BEHOLD He performeth that which is appointed me.—JOB 23 : 14.

'Twas in the month of April last,
When flowers were springing all so fast,
A dream I had I'll tell to you,
A dream 'twould seem an omen true.

Methought I saw in sombre yew,
An eagle cowering from the view
His ruffled plumage, soiled and torn;
In plight he was most sad, forlorn.

And close beside an evergreen
Of brilliant foliage there was seen
A mocking-bird, with cheerful song,
Was skipping gay the leaves among.

Nor was the bird alone, I ween,
For many little ones were seen,
As gay, as joyous, glad and free,
As family of birds would be.

The eagle's plumage, ruffled, soiled,
You'd think he'd through the waters toiled;
Nor pride nor valor he displayed,
But trembled in the yew tree's shade.

The mocking-bird unconscious seemed,
That by the eagle she was deemed
An object rare, of terror drear,
Or that she could inspire fear.

Her sole employment was to sing,
To hail with joy the new-born spring,

To spend her days in thankful lays,
In hymning forth her Maker's praise.

I give this dream as omen true,
Of what of good's in store for you;
The eagle cowering, trembling, hides,
The mocking-bird on high abides;

With grateful heart she pours her song,
The evergreen the leaves among,
My dream unfolds a future bright—
The mocking-bird still soars in light.

Take courage, then, nor shrink in fear;
Your wives, your children, homes are dear;
The God of nations be your trust;
The High, the Holy One and Just.

He setteth up and pulleth down,
And each in turn abide his frown;
The eagle here in cowering fear,
Betrays a want of conscience clear.

Take courage, friends, and as you see
The mocking-bird so joyous, free,
Still hope that God is on our side,
And let your trust in him abide.

He speaks, and at his sovereign will,
The storm is laid, the sea is still;
He weighs the cause 'tween man and man,
And clasps the nation with a span.

Then go to him with praying heart,
Oh! be but faithful on your part,
To God and to yourselves be true,
Your battles he will fight for you.

East Baton Rouge, March 5, 1862. L. F.

GREEK FIRE.—The rebel General Beauregard protests against the Federal General Gillmore's use of "Greek fire" against Charleston, as an outrage against humanity, unworthy of civilized nations, etc.

The name "Greek fire" is applied to a peculiar compound of bitumen, naphtha, and pitch that burns on the surface or under water. It is composed largely of what the chemists call "arsenical alcohol," most destructive in its effects, and, in course of its discharge, emitting a most offensive odor. "Greek fire" has frequently been employed in European wars, but not often in modern times. The secret of its preparation and use was derived from a native of Heliopolis, Syria, about a thousand years ago.—*New-York Express.*

BARBARISM.—The following, from the Chicago *Post*, on the authority of Lieutenant Cole, of the Mississippi Marine Brigade, is suggestive of the superiority of rebel civilization:

"The day after the battle of Milliken's Bend, in June last, the Marine Brigade landed some ten miles below the Bend, and attacked and routed the guerillas, who had been repulsed and routed by our troops and the gunboats the day previous. Major Hibbard's cavalry battalion of the Marine Brigade followed the rebels to Tensas Bayou, and were horrified at the finding of skeletons of white officers commanding negro regiments, who had been captured by the rebels at Milliken's Bend. In many cases, these officers had been nailed to the trees, and crucified; in this situation a fire was built around the tree, and they suffered slow death from broiling. The charred and partially burned limbs were still fastened to the stakes. Other instances were noticed of charred skeletons of officers who had been nailed to the slabs, and the slabs placed against a house, which was set on fire by the inhuman demons; the poor sufferers having been roasted alive; nothing was left but charred remains."

ONE OF A HUNDRED.—A rural conscript appeared before the Eastern Board of Enrolment, and desired to be exempted forthwith, that he might return to his country home. "What are your claims?" demanded the Doctor. "*I'm entirely dependent upon my mother for support,*" was the innocent reply. Whereupon, thus the Doctor, while a smile faintly illumined the face of the Board: "I am happy to assure you, my honest-hearted friend, that the Government is prepared at once to relieve your mother of so unsuitable a burden, and assume your entire charge and expense during the next three years, without the slightest recourse to the maternal fount for support or succor." The young draftee appeared a little bewildered, and referred to the papers to ascertain what was the matter.—*Providence Journal.*

THE SCHOOLS OF FERNANDINA.—From correspondence dated Fernandina, Fla., July twenty-first, of the *Wisconsin State Journal*, we extract:

The colored schools, which have been in successful operation here for the past eight months, closed on Wednesday for a vacation of two months. The progress made by the pupils more than equals the expectations of the most sanguine friends of the race. The children have evinced an aptitude to learn and a capacity fully equal to white children at the North, and in all the better characteristics they are in no way behind them. . . . . None who have witnessed the grateful expressions of fathers and mothers, and the daily tributes of flowers, and other evidences of affection of the children for their teachers, will ever question the natural susceptibility of this people to cultivation and a prompt response to the ordinary appliances which make mankind respectable. Corporeal punishment has been so rare that I question whether, during the entire term, among three hundred children, there have been more than half a dozen cases; and I have never seen uneducated children anywhere exhibit more sensibility to the dishonor of a banishment from school, or other similar infliction, than these children of slavery.

Some of the girls and boys had committed pieces, which were properly spoken; and one little ebony, only eight years old, showed extraordinary aptness at declamation in a little piece he had learned. True, he was in rags, and his skin was coal-black, but a more intelligent and happy face I never saw. If permitted, that boy will yet shame many a "pale-face" by his superior intellectual power.

At the close of the exercises, a little book or primer was presented to each scholar as a present for their attendance and good conduct; and it was pleasing to see with what eagerness and satisfaction each received this first testimonial of scholarship. Nearly three hundred presents were distributed, which were furnished principally through the liberality of Hon. Joseph Hoxie, of New-York, who had visited the schools a few months since, and whose judicious selections were universally commended and his generosity fully appreciated. These children will never forget this occasion.

Among the songs by the school, interspersed throughout the exercises—and *every* child sings in these schools—was the following, which, aside from its intrinsic merit and affecting pathos, was particularly interesting from the fact that just before the rebellion, a congregation of slaves attending a public baptism on Sunday, at Savannah, were arrested, imprisoned, and punished with thirty-nine lashes each for singing the song of spiritual freedom—now a crime since slavery had become a " divine institution :"

SLAVE SONG.

"My mother! how long! Mothers! how long! mothers! how long!
    Will sinners suffer here?
CHORUS—It won't be long! It won't be long! It won't be long!
    That sinners 'ill suffer here!

" We'll walk de golden streets! we'll walk de golden streets! we'll walk de golden streets!
    Where pleasures never die!
CHORUS—It won't be long! etc.

" My brother! do sing! my brother! do sing! my brother! do sing!
    De praises ob de Lord!
CHORUS—It won't be long! etc.

" We'll *soon* be free! we'll *soon* be free! we'll *soon* be free!
    De Lord will call us home!
CHORUS—My brother! do sing! my brother! do sing! my brother! do sing!
    De praises ob de Lord!" ·

And these verses, so expressive and pathetic, are added to almost indefinitely in the same style by the interested singers. Now where this and the hundred kindred songs sung by the slaves came from, or who amidst the darkness of slavery inditeth them, I cannot of course say, but it is easy to determine the source of the inspiration. In patient faith and enduring hope these " Songs of Zion" have been sung by generations of these bondmen, as the only relief for bleeding hearts and lacerated bodies, and now God comes in judgment to requite the nation for the wrongs inflicted upon his oppressed and suffering poor.

Another interesting and significant event connected with the people here, occurred on Monday. The women called a meeting at the church, to consider the propriety of presenting Colonel Littlefield's regiment, now enlisting here, a stand of colors. Like the great dinner and celebration on the Fourth, all was arranged by the colored women, and $50 was contributed on the spot, by these poor fugitives, from the hard earnings of their brief freedom—contributed to purchase an American flag to be borne by their colored brethren—the flag which had been to them till now the emblem of oppression! They cherish no feelings of malignity for the wrongs which have been inflicted, but hail the new era of freedom with joy, and rally to the country's standard with pride and satisfaction, now that the country is prepared to respect their humanity and protect their rights. Among the contributors was one slave woman, who has five sons and a husband in the army, while she remains at home to care for younger children.

Ned Simons, an old negro belonging to the Dungenness estate of General Nathanael Greene, on Cumberland Island, and who was left by the rebel inheritor, Nightingale, on his evacuation of the place, died here last week, at the house of the lady teachers of the schools, who have kindly cared for him since their arrival here. Ned was over one hundred years old, and remembered General Washington well, and was one of the number who assisted in carrying him through the streets of Savannah on his last visit to that place. Old Ned took a lively interest in the affairs of the nation, and rejoiced in the prospect of the freedom of his race. He was deeply interested in the cause of education, and, though partially blind with age, he desired, himself, to learn to read. On being asked why he wished to learn, when he could not expect to live much longer, he replied, " As the tree falls, so it will lay;" his attainments on earth would contribute to higher attainments on high; and the ladies yielded to his request, and during the last months of his life he, with much labor and effort, acquired a knowledge of his letters and syllables. Poor old Ned! After a long life of unrequited toil and slavery, he has " gone where the good negroes go;" where no slave-driver will ever follow; where he can sing " de praises ob de Lord " in freedom and safety.

A BRAVE IRISHMAN.—One of the Indiana regiments was fiercely attacked by a whole brigade, in one of the battles in Mississippi. The Indianians, unable to withstand such great odds, were compelled to fall back about thirty or forty yards, losing, to the utter mortification of the officers and men, their flag, which remained in the hands of the enemy. Suddenly, a tall Irishman, a private in the color company, rushed from the ranks across the vacant ground, attacked the squad of rebels who had possession of the conquered flag, with his musket felled several to the ground, snatched the flag from them, and returned safely back to his regiment. The bold fellow was, of course, immediately surrounded by his jubilant comrades, and greatly praised for his gallantry. His captain appointed him to a sergeancy on the spot; but the hero cut every thing short by the reply: "Oh! never mind, captain—say no more about it. I dropped my whisky-flask among the rebels, and fetched that back, and I thought I might just as well bring the flag along!"

BEAUREGARD AND GILLMORE.

At midnight, in his blackguard tent,
" Old Beau" was dreaming of the hour
When Gillmore, like a suppliant bent,
    Should tremble at his power.
In dreams, through camp and street he bore
    The trophies of a conqueror.
He sported Gillmore's gold-laced hat—
His red-topped boots, his gay cravat,
    As wild his fancy as a bat,
        Or " any other bird."
An hour passed on—" Old Beau" awoke,
Half strangled by a villainous smoke,
    Enough the very devil to choke,
While all around the " stink-pots" broke
    And blinded him with smoke.
He cursed the villainous compound,
    While stunk the pole-cats far around;
        Then roared with wild, demoniac shriek:
" Lord! what a stink! the Greek! the Greek

Put out this villainous Greek fire !
Or in the last red ditch expire.
'Tis sweet to draw one's dying breath
For one's dear land, as Horace saith,
But dreadful to be stunk to death."
—*Nashville Union.*

INCIDENTS OF FORT WAGNER.—Sergeant-Major Lewis
H. Douglas, a son of Fred. Douglas, who, by both white
and negro troops, is said to have displayed great courage
and calmness, was one of the first to mount the parapet, and with his powerful voice shouted—" Come on,
boys, and fight for God and Governor Andrew," and
with this battle-cry led them into the fort.

But above all, the color-bearer deserves more than
a passing notice. Sergeant John Wall, of company
G, carried the flag in the first battalion, and when near
the fort he fell into a deep ditch, and called upon his
guard to help him out. They could not stop for that,
but Sergeant William H. Carney, of company C, caught
the colors, carried them forward, and was the first
man to plant the Stars and Stripes upon Fort Wagner.
As he saw the men falling back, himself severely
wounded in the breast, he brought the colors off,
creeping on his knees, pressing his wound with one
hand, and with the other holding up the emblem of
freedom. The moment he was seen crawling into the
hospital with the flag still in his possession, his wounded companions, both black and white, rose from the
straw upon which they were lying, and cheered him
until, exhausted, they could shout no longer. In response to this reception the brave and wounded standard-bearer said : " Boys, I but did my duty ! the dear
old flag never touched the ground."

GENERAL STUART'S DINNER EATEN BY GENERAL
BUFORD.—A correspondent of the *Philadelphia Press,*
writing from Brandy Station, Va., on the sixth of August, says :

Some people have contended that Stuart no longer
had command of the Rebel cavalry, but that Fitz-Hugh
Lee was the chief of that branch of the army. Whether this be so or not, as I before stated, Stuart fought
Buford last Saturday, for Buford ate his dinner in a
cosy little house, nestled among pines, cedars, and jes-
samine about one and a half miles from Culpeper,
where General Stuart and staff were going to dine.
Every luxury and delicacy that could be procured in
this poor ransacked country was smiling on the white,
spotless linen which covered the table. The chairs
were placed, the wine ready to be uncorked, the piano
in the dear little parlor open as it was left but a few
minutes before. The fair occupant of the stool (I hope
I am not slandering her features when I call them
fair) had no doubt hurried on a sun-bonnet and slipped off to Culpeper. The " Bonnie Blue Flag " would
not sound so well in the old parlor, and she feared
General Buford and staff could not appreciate her selection of songs.

However, the dinner was appreciated ; and if smack-
ing of lips and looks of regret at the fragments they
could not eat was of any significance, the dishes prepared by these kind people met with the appreciation
of all the partakers.

REBEL RAIDS.—The following extracts from the diary of a rebel prisoner captured in Kentucky, are suggestive :

" 24th da of juli 1863, crossed mountain at big
Crick gap.
" 25th juli. To Williamsborg, driv in piket found
they was the dam 44th O.
" 26th juli. To loudon, skirmished sum with
enemy.
" 27th. Crosst big Hill driv in some more pickets
attakt enemy near Richmond at daylite drove them
from position.
" 28th Juli, got to Winchester, picked up several
mules and a few horses.
" 29th, 9 o'clock, was captured ; conclude to add
that raids into Kentucky don't pa, no how."—*Boston
Advertiser.*

August 14.—General Grant don't please the rebels
in Mississippi any better than he pleases their allies up
this way. When sugar, cotton, or molasses is discovered within his lines, he don't let the rebel owners sell
it to the Government on the easily manufactured assurance that they are loyal, but takes it all away and
gives them receipts to be paid at the end of the war,
on proof of the loyalty of the holder.—*Indianapolis
Journal.*

SCOUTING AMONG THE INDIANS.—From the Indian
expedition, Shayenne River, Dacotah, the correspondent
of the *Springfield Journal* writes at date of July eleventh :

There are many, doubtless, who imagine that the
thrilling tales of the experiences and adventures of
scouts, as related in books of romance and in newspaper
columns, have no counterpart in actual life at the present time. But such an idea is far from the truth.
From the narratives almost daily of the scouts connected with this expedition, I could weave many a
story of reality that would be quite as exciting as some
of the fictitious monstrosities that are agonized into
the weekly literary journals. Probably no scout organization for Indian warfare was ever more complete
than that now employed in the Sioux war by General
Sibley. The force numbers seventy, one half of whom
are whites, and the other half Indians and half-breeds.
If an Eastern man wanted to see a motley company
of the oldest traders, most experienced hunters, and
most cunning and daring Indians in the North-West, he
could find them nowhere so well as in this very camp
of scouts. They are men who never speak of danger,
and who look upon a horseback ride of one hundred
miles on the prairies as a mere common-place trip.
Major Joseph Brown, the most noted Indian trader in
all this region of country, and a well-known politician,
editor, and adventurer in the North-west, is in command of the force, and most skilfully he conducts the
operations. There are two companies of scouts, which
are on duty on alternate days and nights. One of
them is commanded by a man whose entire family
was massacred by the Sioux Indians last fall, and the
man who begged the privilege, which was granted, of
cutting the rope at the execution of the thirty-eight
Indians at Mankato last winter. He told me his story
with tears in his eyes, and concluded by pledging his
life even to the avenging of the murder of his family.
The other division is commanded by an adventurous
and shrewd frontiersman, a man who knows every war-
path or Indian trail in all the territory.

Among the Indians are some of the most sagacious
Chippewas, Sioux, and half-breeds in the Indian territory. Some of them have been captured at different

times by our troops, and some are of the friendly or farmer Indians. Scouting is no child's play with them, as they are sure of a terrible death if captured by the hostile Sioux. Two of them are men who helped Mr. Riggs and the families of the mission at Yellow Medicine to escape from the savages last fall. Other-day, who was formerly a leading chief of the Sioux, and who is now a farmer near St. Paul, was expected to join the force, but failed for some reason. The scouts camp in low tents just high enough to creep into, and are constantly at work at their dangerous and tedious tasks.

I said that they had wild experiences. A few days ago, four of them had wandered over on to the Coteau Ridge, twenty miles from camp, expecting to find Indian lodges there, by reason of a war-club which had been found and interpreted. After they left camp, another party of twenty left for another locality, intending to be gone through the night. While the smaller company was wandering through the bushes, they suddenly came upon the remains of a recent fire, and near by were fresh moccasin tracks. They did not doubt the presence of Indians, and moved cautiously. At last, in the distance, they heard the tread of horses' feet, and then the crackling of bushes. They put spurs to their horses and started for the heights of the Cotteau Ridge. Finally they dismounted in an open space, got their carbines in readiness, and awaited the approach. But instead of one direction, their pursuers seemed to be coming in from every side, and to be constantly increasing. Fearing lest they should be overpowered by numbers, four took to flight again, and then there was a long and sharp chase of miles through the darkness. But the pursuers gained, and the four dismounted again and waited for the worst. The party soon came up, and fortunately there was a recognition before shots were exchanged. The men of both companies were scouts, and had thus been manœuvring for Indian warfare. Such meetings are not infrequent.

The scouts have found quite a number of bodies of persons who were massacred last fall. A few days since they found a body with a purse of gold upon it. They have all sorts of experiences, dodging about in Indian style, leaving fictitious and deceitful signs, meeting herds of buffalo and elk, and hunting for forage and water. They bring in all sorts of trophies. One night they discovered an old Indian pack ox, that looks some as I imagine the infernal bovines ought to, and yesterday a nest of young eagles, a pemican and wolf were brought in. Their life is a hard one, but they enjoy it. It is a rich treat to hear their stories of experience and adventure while engaged as fur traders and hunters on the prairies. One of the Indian scouts, Antoine by name, has offered to carry the mail to and from the expedition throughout the campaign, whether it be one hundred or three hundred miles, and however dangerous the venture. He wants the privilege of killing one horse to every trip, and good pay for his labor, which he will be sure to get. He cannot be induced to speak of any danger. It is to his pluck that I am indebted for this opportunity to send a letter. He is an old Red River Indian, and came into camp in a genuine Pembina cart a few days since.

ARKANSAS TACTICS.—An Arkansas colonel has the following order for mounting his men:

First Order—Prepare fer terr git onto yer creeters.
Second Order—GIT!—Leavenworth Conservative.

GOOD WORK.—A correspondent sends an account of the gallant conduct of Henry Shaler, of Indianopolis, Indiana, at the battle of Gettysburgh, written by a son of Daniel Noble, to his mother, which deserves wide publicity. Young Shaler has more than equalled the mythical performance of the Irishman who "surrounded" a half-dozen of the enemy and captured them. We are proud of him. His parents live on South-Alabama street, in Indianapolis. They are Germans. Young Noble says: "Harry is a brick; he did more, that is, he took more prisoners, in the battle of Gettysburgh, than any other man in the army. He took in all twenty-five men; one lieutenant and eighteen men at one time; he took them by strategy that was strategy; "he surrounded them," and they had to give up. On the morning of the fourth he went out with his poncho over his shoulders so that the rebs couldn't see his coat, so they thought he was one of their own men; he went up and told them to lay down their arms and come and help carry some wounded off the field; they did so; when he got them away from their arms he rode up to the lieutenant, and told him to give up his sword; the lieutenant refused at first, but Harry drew his pepper-box, and like Crockett's coon the lieutenant came down without a shot. Harry then took them all into camp. He took a captain and five men at another time, making twenty-five in all, which is doing pretty well for a little Dutchman; and he deserves to be remembered for it."—Indianapolis Journal.

A YANKEE SPELLING-BOOK.—We have received from the publishers, Messrs. Toon & Co., of Atlanta, Georgia, a spelling-book, which we regret to be compelled to denounce as unworthy of public favor. It is, as the author, Mr. Fleming, admits, a revised edition of Webster's Spelling-Book—in other words, it is a Yankee school-book. It is the duty of the Southern press to unite in putting it down.

Mr Fleming tells us in his preface that "no better spelling-book than Dr. Webster's has ever been presented to the American people," ample proof of which he finds in the Yankee test of the unparalleled extent of its circulation. He goes on to add that "his (Webster's) dictionary may be found in almost every family, occupying, as it deservedly does, a preëminence over all others." This statement discloses an amount of ignorance on the part of the author which should deter him from rehashing any more Yankee school-books for Southern use. Webster is not the standard of the best Southern scholars; but Johnson, Walker, and Richardson. Webster's orthography is the detestation of every cultivated Southern gentleman, and this orthography, Mr. Fleming tells us, he has invariably retained. Centre he spells "center," theatre, "theater," and, doubtless, ton, "tun." The retention of these execrable Yankee innovations is enough of itself to damn the book and drive it out of circulation.

Mr. Fleming says further, that "in very few instances Webster's pronunciation has been rejected. The flat or Italian sound of a, as heard in the word father, should not be heard in the words grass, mass, glass, bass, etc. The flat sound of the letter a in these instances is a New-England provincialism." Here, again, Mr. Fleming displays gross ignorance. To this day, the flat, or, as we should say, the third sound of a in grass, mass, glass, etc., is used by the educated and well-bred classes in England, and by those on this continent who have preserved the English language in its greatest purity—the tide-water Virginians.

We dislike extremely to speak harshly of literary labor of any kind. But Mr. Fleming has labored very little in reproducing this bit of Yankee clap-trap, and he is poisoning the very fountain-head of Southern literature. His book should be suppressed at once, for it is to all intents and purposes a Yankee spelling-book, slightly and easily altered by the introduction of Bible readings on the subject of slavery. We do not dwell upon numerous typographical errors, because they can be corrected in subsequent editions, if any should be called for, which we trust will not be the case.

We must get rid of Yankee orthography and pronunciation at all hazards. If we begin by spelling "centre" "center," we shall end by pronouncing "dew" "doo," and "cow" "keow." In truth, it would be well for us to have an entirely new language, unknown and unpronounceable in Yankee land. We must have new coins, new weights, new measures, as unlike Yankee coins, weights, etc., as possible. We must be a distinct people in every thing, or else we will never be independent. At all events, we must not be duped with a Yankee spelling-book, such as Mr. Fleming and Messrs. Toon and Co. are attempting to palm upon us.—*Richmond Whig.*

BALLAD OF VICKSBURGH.

Two years the tide of war had rolled
  In restless fury on—
Hearts growing prematurely old
  In grief for loved ones gone!

Two years the burdened land had groaned
  Beneath the martial train;
With bitter, scalding tears bemoaned
  Its argosy of pain!

Two years had brothers met as foes
  On many a field and flood—
Had fathers drained the cup of woes
  Their sons had steeped in blood!

The haughty rebel striving hard
  To fill a land with slaves;
The gallant freeman still to guard
  The home of patriot graves!

Both had at times successes won
  And both reverses met;
Both captured city, fort, and gun,
  And lost them with regret!

Yet closer draws the circling coil
  Around the stubborn foe;
The freemen fight on sacred soil,
  And on, still on they go!

A stronghold by the river side,
  The key to needed stores,
Stands like a kingdom in its pride,
  To guard opposing shores.

On this is fixed their eagle eye,
  And this, they say, must fall;
They dare the rebel hosts defy,
  And thrust them to the wall!

What though the fronting water-bluff
  Is mounted, steep and high?

What though the circling rear is rough,
  And frowning forts defy?

What though so many times before
  In vain the mortars bayed;
While gunboats rained their hail on shore,
  And land assaults were made?

Many the plans that failed to raise
  The dear old banner there;
Many the long and weary days
  That mocked at toil and care!

But dauntless still that armored host
  The rebel hordes defy.
They bide their time at duty's post,
  Hope kindling every eye.

The brave commander speaks the word
  And on it goes once more;
Again the hostile guns are heard
  Along the river shore.

The gauntlet of the plunging fire
  Is run with little harm;
Ne'er fails such resolute desire
  To brave the wild alarm!

A fleet above, a fleet below,
  Is ready for the strife,
Ready to strike a telling blow
  For freedom and for life!

The fleet below pours forth its host
  Of brave and gallant men,
Like waves upon the white sea-coast
  To storm the land again!

Like the wild rushing avalanche
  Armed with resistless might,
To crush rebellion root and branch,
  They hurry to the fight.

The circling path is rough and long
  To gain the stronghold's rear;
The foe they meet is fierce and strong,
  But wakes no coward fear.

They boldly meet him on the way
  In many a bloody fight;
In all they nobly win the day,
  As triumph for the right!

They reap a large and worthy spoil
  Of cannon and of men,
The fruit of Hope's heroic toil
  Inspiring hope again!

On, on they press their winding way,
  A strong and valiant host;
And still they keep the foe at bay,
  Despite his wonted boast!

They reach at last the waiting goal,
  The frowning forts invest;
The thunders of their cannon roll
  To mar the city's rest.

All avenues of flight they guard
  With strong and jealous care,
Cut off supplies and press them hard
  With burdens hard to bear.

They boldly make the fierce assault,
　The moated walls to scale,
Nor is it yet the heroes' fault
　Once and again they fail.

Too steep, too high, too strong, the walls,
　Too hot the cannon's breath,
Too thickly fly the deadly balls,
　Too many fall in death !

The spade and shovel here must win
　If triumph ever come ;
Their song must mingle with the din
　Of cannon and of drum !

So through the sultry summer days
　They onward dig their way ;
Vain all attempts the siege to raise,
　Or long their work delay !

The heroes labor long and well,
　Slowly the stronghold near,
While day and night fly shot and shell
　To keep the foe in fear !

The city proudly bears its scars,
　The people hide in caves,
And cursing still the Stripes and Stars,
　There many find their graves !

But closer draws the giant coil,
　Want stares them in the face,
In vain is all their arduous toil,
　They cannot hold the place.

And Vicksburgh by the river side
　So long the rebel boast,
Falls from its dizzy height of pride
　Before the loyal host.

And on that joyful summer morn,
　The great day of the year
That symbols still a nation born,
　There waves the flag so dear !

And many a shout goes up that day
　In pæans loud and grand,
Long peals of joy to find their way
　In echoes through the land ;

As for a nation born again
　On this its natal day,
Born for a gift of nobler men
　Through Freedom's larger sway !

A CURSE FOR A NATION.

BY MINNIE FRY.

" I heard an angel speak last night,
　And he said : ' Write,
Write a nation's curse for me,
　And send it over the Western Sea.' "
　　　　　　—E. B. BROWNING.

O Woman crowned with motherhood,
　And sphered in song ! How couldst thou send
That curse against a kindred blood
　With Heaven's long garnered wrath to blend !
A mother's curse the strong man fears
　Through all the glory of his years ;

But we have cause for deeper dread,
　When she who lifts denouncing hands
A priestess at Love's altar stands,
　A priestess bound by holiest vows,
A woman's crown upon her head,
　A poet's glory on her brows.

O woman poet ! In the dust
　We lay our pride—our hearts are sad—
　We walked abroad among the glad
Free nations of the earth—more just,
　More noble we than all beside—
Till suddenly our triumph died,
　And a great awe stole o'er the land.
As one who sees his ship's command
Torn from him by the fateful winds,
As one whom sudden lightning blinds,
　We gazed aghast at destiny,
And in our dread remembered thee.

O poet heart of love and light !
Thy curse is just and pure and right,
Approved even in Heaven's own sight.
We can but bear the chastening sign,
And drink the blood poured out for wine,.
With patience, till the storm goes by—
And if we perish utterly
We perish. 'Tis no more than meed ;
But if in our extremest need,
When sinking just beneath the wave,
We cry to Love, Love yet shall save,
And with soft fingers on shut eyes,
The darkness of the soul surprise,
As once of old in Galilee
He healed the blind and hushed the sea.

My Country ! O my lovely Land,
Outspread 'neath heaven by Love's own hand !
How is it with thee ? Wilt thou bear
Heaven's wrath till wrath has waked despair !
Too proud to listen love's own call,
Till even love triumph in thy fall—
While other lands redeemed shall rise,
With foreheads lifted to the skies,
With stainless hands and fearless mien,
All thou wert not yet mightst have been—
Whose sons shall speak beneath their breath
Of her who sold her life for death !

Forbid it, Heaven—forbid it, Love—
Forbid it, all ye powers above—
Forbid it, thou who spok'st that curse
Before a listening universe.
Our blessed Land shall rise again—
Let all the people say, AMEN !

CINCINNATI, O.

LENOX.

BY C. K. TUCKERMAN.

Soft summer sounds salute the air,
　Cool country colors greet the eye ;
Around the wide piazza chair
　The hay-blown breezes swoop and sigh.

The level lawn of gracious green,
　The odorous line of gay parterre,
The clear cut paths that run between—
　Content the claims of cultured care.

Near by, the neat New-England town,
　In latent strength of thrifty ease,

Scatters its squares of red and brown
   Beneath the old familiar trees.

The white church gleaming on the hill
   Beside its patch of village graves,
Lifts, like a lighthouse, calm and still,
   Above the dark green swell of waves.

Beyond the vale the landscape looms
   In mountain masses, crowned with firs,
Save where the golden chestnut blooms,
   Or where the silver birch tree stirs.

Low at their feet, in sweet surprise,
   Repeating every varied hue,
The " Mountain Mirror " scoops the skies,
   And laughs in sunshine and in blue.

And over all sublimely broods
   The spirit, by Nature only taught;
And all is peace, save where intrudes
   One dark, deep shade of human thought.

Embraced within her mountain arms,
   Few fairer scenes the eye have met :
Would that the soul knew no alarms—
   Would that the gazer could forget!

Forget the far-off strife, that shakes
   His country's glory into shame ;
Forget the misery that makes
   A by-word of the nation's name !

Forget that she, who years ago,
   Brought Freedom forth, in throes and tears,
Now lies in second labor low,
   Convulsed in agony and fears.

God grant swift safety to the land :
   God haste the peace-returning morn
When our great Mother yet shall stand
   Triumphant with her second born !

Then, like this fair and favored place,
   Shall the Republic's grandeur be ;
For she shall look from heights of grace,
   And undiminished glory see.

Like this, shall glow her atmosphere
   Bannered by day with blue and white,
While all her stars shall reäppear
   To shame the shadows of her night.

THE SERGEANT'S COT.

The door-stone fowl affrighted fly,
For the wary hawk with thievish eye,
Gloats eddying in the morning sky.

With wide, fell swoop, the airy king
Drops cruelly on one poor thing,
Denied the cover of its mother's wing.

One piteous flutter and a plaint—no more !
Two wondering faces from the cottage door
Peer as the victor with his prey sails o'er.

There were bitter tears and tenderness
Within that cot, for little Bess
Could hardly brook one chick the less.

The kitten gambolled, the pet linnet sung ;
All day old Monument's shadow swung—
She mused and sobbed—her heart was wrung.

The mother took her to her arms, and said:
" Thy chick my child, is gone, is dead,
But a kind All-Father rules o'erhead.

" Such little chastenings are meant
   To probe the secrets in our being pent,
Like sun and storm in rainbow blent.

" Your father, Bess !" 'twas hard to see
His parting look for you and me ;
His country called—such things must be.

" But 'twas a pang we felt we owed
For all the land on us bestowed ;
We faltered—but we've borne the load."

Just then the post-train screeched in sight,
Glimpsed on its way with throbbing light,
With tidings fraught—shall they be of blight ?

'Twas farmer John came up the road
He drove his oxen with restless goad ;
He left a pallor on that drear abode.

'Twas said : " The Tenth had suffered most,
And one brave Sergeant of the host,
Fell with the colors at his bloody post."

The kitten gambolled, the pet linnet sung ;
The orphaned Bessie at her girdle hung ;
The widow sank—_her_ heart was wrung.

THE FOLLOWING LINES

Were found in a bundle of Socks, sent by a " Lively Old Lady,"
in Amherst, N. H., to the U. S. Hospital, corner of Broad and
Cherry streets, Philadelphia.

By the fireside, cosily seated,
   With spectacles riding her nose,
The lively old lady is knitting
   A wonderful pair of hose.
She pities the shivering soldier,
   Who is out in the pelting storm ;
And busily plies her needles,
   To keep him hearty and warm.

Her eyes are reading the embers,
   But her heart is off to the war,
For she knows what those brave fellows
   Are gallantly fighting for.
Her fingers as well as her fancy
   Are cheering them on their way,
Who, under the good old banner,
   Are saving their Country to-day.

She ponders, how in her childhood,
   Her grandmother used to tell—
The story of barefoot soldiers,
   Who fought so long and well.
And the men of the Revolution
   Are nearer to her than us ;
And that perhaps is the reason
   Why she is toiling thus.

She cannot shoulder a musket,
   Nor ride with cavalry crew,
But nevertheless she is ready
   To work for the boys who do.
And yet in " official despatches,"
   That come from the army or fleet,
Her feats may have never a notice,
   Though ever so mighty the _feet !_

So prithee, proud owner of muscle,
Or purse-proud owner of stocks,
Don't sneer at the labors of woman,
Or smile at her bundle of socks.
Her heart may be larger and braver
Than his who is tallest of all,
The work of her hands as important
As cash that buys powder and ball.

And thus while her quiet performance
Is being recorded in rhyme,
The tools in her tremulous fingers
Are running a race with Time.
Strange that four needles can form
A perfect triangular bound;
And equally strange that their antics
Result in perfecting "the round."

And now, while beginning "to narrow,"
She thinks of the Maryland mud,
And wonders if ever the stocking
Will wade to the ankle in blood.
And now she is "shaping the heel,"
And now she ready is "to bind,"
And hopes if the soldier is wounded,
It never will be from behind.

And now she is "raising the instep,"
Now "narrowing off at the toe,"
And prays that this end of the worsted
May ever be turned to the foe.
She "gathers" the last of the stitches,
As if a new laurel were won,
And placing the ball in the basket,
Announces the stocking as "done."

Ye men who are fighting our battles,
Away from the comforts of life,
Who thoughtfully muse by your camp-fires,
On sweetheart, or sister, or wife;
Just think of their elders a little,
And pray for the grandmothers too,
Who, patiently sitting in corners,
Are knitting the stockings for you.
                                        S. E. B.

'CUTENESS OF A CONTRABAND SCOUT.—A private letter from West-Point, Va., narrates an exciting adventure which befell a negro scout in the employ of the Union forces, and his shrewdness in escaping from the rebels. His name is Claiborne, and he is a full-blooded African, with big lips, flat nose, etc. He has lived in the vicinity all his life, and is therefore familiar with the country, which renders him a very valuable scout. On Claiborne's last trip inside the enemy's lines, after scouting around as much as he wished, he picked up eight chickens and started for camp. His road led past the house of a secesh doctor named Roberts, who knows him, and who ordered him to stop, which, of course, Claiborne had no idea of doing, and kept on, when the doctor fired on him and gave chase, shouting at the top of his voice. The negro was making good time toward camp, when all at once he was confronted by a whole regiment of rebel soldiers, who ordered him to halt. For a moment the scout was dumbfounded, and thought his hour had come, but the next he sung out:

"The Yankees are coming! the Yankees are coming!"

"Where? where?" inquired the rebels.

"Just up in front of Dr. Roberts's house, in a piece of woods," returned Sambo. "Dr. R. sent me down to tell you to come up quick, or they'll kill the whole of us."

"Come in, come into camp," said the soldiers.

"No, no," says the 'cute African, "I have got to go down and tell the cavalry pickets, and can't wait a second." So off he sprang with a bound, running for dear life, the rebs, discovering the ruse, chasing him for three miles, and he running six, when he got safely into camp, but minus his chickens, which he dropped at the first fire.

INCIDENTS OF CHICKAMAUGA.

CHATTANOOGA, TENN., September 24, 1863.

The two armies are now confronting each other in the immediate vicinity of the town of Chattanooga. After the two days' battle of the nineteenth and twentieth, the line of the Federal army occupied a position eight miles from the town—the left, with General Thomas, maintaining its former front, while the right and centre had fallen back some two miles from its former position.

From the superior force of the rebels in our front, and the great extent of line which the Federals were necessarily forced to defend, after holding the enemy at bay for forty-eight hours, our lines were withdrawn within the support of the works which had been thrown up by the enemy previous to their evacuation of this place. The enemy having been so severely punished in the late conflict, were slow in following us to our present established line.

They held back as if to give us full opportunity for a successful recrossing of the Tennessee River. But General Rosecrans did not see proper to take advantage of these favorable designs of the enemy. On retiring to Chattanooga, instead of placing the Tennessee between his forces and those of the rebels, he immediately called around him his generals, and in a few words explained to them his future intended plans.

"This place is to be held at all hazards; we here make the big fight, be the strength of the enemy what it may. Beyond this point the army of the Cumberland will not retire while there is a foe to menace it!" General St. Clair Morton, Chief of Engineers, immediately set about to put the place in a defensible condition for the warm welcome of the enemy.

The Nationals at present occupy the works previously constructed by the rebels to prevent the approach of the Yankees. The former strength of these works the enemy know full well.

But they have now been made more complete, enlarged and improved upon by those whose approach they were first intended to resist.

The enemy have been constantly moving around us since our retirement to this place. Large bodies of cavalry, infantry, and artillery are to be seen moving along the heights and through the valleys and plains beyond our present limits. They have been trying the range of their guns upon our position, but have not as yet succeeded in the accomplishment of any advantage to themselves or injury to the Nationals. Their shot and shell have all fallen harmless to the earth. They are distinctly to be seen in very strong force, in successive lines of battle, on the hillsides and in the bottoms.

The dense woods in our immediate front are also swarming with them, but they thus far have shown but little disposition to advance and again try their strength and fortune with the little army of despised *menials* with which they are at present confronted.

For the purpose of a more perfect range in our immediate front, it has been our painful duty to burn all the dwellings between the Federal lines and those of the enemy. More than fifty buildings have thus been levelled to the ground, some of which were quite valuable, and the premises most beautifully ornamented with all the surroundings of comfort and pleasure.

But all is now a complete waste; every thing has been levelled and destroyed. Houses, trees, shrubbery, fences, and all are gone — made to give way to the result of rebellion and the curse of war. Over this now desert waste the guns of the Federals have complete control.

On the twenty-third, the enemy were observed in the attempt of getting into position with their batteries.

From this the Federals opened upon them with a few of the guns of General Negley's command, from their powerful and commanding "Star Fort," the design and partial erection of the rebels, which work has been fully completed and improved upon by the Nationals. This introductory soon had the desired effect, the enemy withdrawing with their pieces to a more secure position. As the enemy had been observed in taking up their position in line of battle, a few shells were thrown in among them to notify them of the Yankee objection to their close proximity. From these pesky annoyances they hastily retired. Large bodies of the enemy were seen moving to our right, but feeling fully prepared for them at all points, no diversion was made from our lines to counteract the rebel movements.

On the right some picket-firing occurred with the enemy's skirmishers, but no further aggressive movements were indulged in. During the day considerable enthusiasm was manifested along the rebel lines. Great cheering at the remarks of orators was indulged in. At the outpost pickets they were heard to exclaim, while haranguing the soldiers, "that the fate and success of the Southern Confederacy now depending upon the crushing of the present army of the Cumberland." But that they have found to be a game that more than themselves can indulge in. The day of the twenty-third closed with nothing of particular importance transpiring along the lines. Toward evening the Star-Spangled Banner was raised to the top of a long staff erected on the Star Fort, in honor of its completion, and expression of thanks to the enemy for their unintended favors in the planning and labor bestowed upon this strong work. The flag now floats where the enemies of their country can have a plain and distinct view of its stars and stripes, waving over the battlements of their former possessions.

Some picket-firing was indulged in during the night of the twenty third. The enemy seemed quite desirous of advancing their lines under cover of darkness, but they found the Unionists in sufficient force and strength to successfully dispute any encroachments upon their established lines. From some hostile demonstration on our centre, a battery was opened upon the enemy, which soon made all quiet again in that quarter. Rockets were to be seen in the air during the night, with which the Federal pickets had been furnished for the conveyance of information, should the enemy make any demonstrations of advance or other movements.

Toward morning a heavy fog hung over the ground in our front, completely screening the position of the enemy from view. In anticipation of the rebels taking advantage of this circumstance to advance and post their batteries, a fire was opened upon their lines, and

continued until all was known to be safe. The enemy have not replied to our batteries for the last two days. What may be their present or future intentions cannot be well conjectured.

During the day of the twenty-third, the enemy were known to be moving cavalry, infantry, and wagon-trains along the south side of the Tennessee, toward Knoxville. Whether they are intending another invasion of Kentucky is more than your correspondent can correctly determine.

But it is to be presumed that our military authorities here are fully aware of all the demonstrative movements of the foe, and will make all the necessary changes consequent to the occasion. The rebels will, no doubt, make great efforts to interrupt our line of communication with the North, and thus cut off our army supplies; but in this they will be mistaken, as there is now a large supply of provisions here for future consumption, sufficient to prevent any inconvenience that might occur from the designs of the enemy.

Nearly all of the sick and wounded of our army have been removed from this place to Stephenson, from which point they will be taken farther north as rapidly as the facilities of the railroad will admit.

THE NATION.

BY ALFRED B. STREET.

Union! it draws from heaven its birth,
  Linking the pine-tree with the sod,
The unseen atom with the earth,
  The systems with the throne of God.
The eagle, soaring to the sun,
  Joins with the bee that seeks the flower;
  The ocean with the drop of dew,
  The bubble with the boundless blue,
The stars in endless course that run
  With fire-fly sparks of twilight's hour.

And in the wondrous world of man,
  Strongest this mystic web is twined;
What soul can live in lonely ban?
  Heart leaps to heart, and mind to mind—
Deed vibrates unto deed—the chain
  Joins with another's weal or woe;
The father's sins, in lengthened reign
  Of influence dire, the son shall know.
His virtues, too, the child shall bless;
  And thus a touch shall yield its meed
Of misery or of happiness
  In this electric web of deed.

Union the car of progress speeds—
  By it the steamship lords the deep;
It drives the railway's thundering steeds—
  Along the wire its lightnings leap.

My native land, to thee was given
A Union blest by favoring heaven!
Our fathers wrought with direst toil
  The chain in fortune's fiercest flame;
From battle's fearfullest turmoil
  Our glorious young Republic came.
Nobly they dared the dangerous deep,
  Spurning the cultured joys of life;
And in the forest's boundless sweep
  Existence linked to endless strife.
But though the ambush gleamed with death,
  Disease and famine aimed the dart,

They faced their fate with tranquil breath,
    And wrought their work with trusting heart.
For tireless hope and energy,
    And faith sublime, and lofty pride,
That bent to naught but Heaven the knee,
    Were in those souls personified.

And so they grasped the magic ax,
    And swept the forest as they went;
Wherever shone their living tracks,
    The hamlet rose—the harvest bent.
Theirs too was high, far-reaching thought;
    Knowledge and godly wisdom swayed—
Thus, while with sinewy hand they wrought,
    An empire's corner-stone they laid.
Not one to fear a despot's frown—
    To wither in a sceptre's blight;
Justice alone should wear the crown—
    The only sceptre, Human Right.

And, vital pulse of every heart,
One principle played mightiest part—
Taught by the crag's cloud-piercing form,
    The cataract thundering down the rock,
The eagle dashing through the storm,
    The frenzied flood, the whirlwind's shock,
The boundless sweep of forest-sea—
It was the love of Liberty

O Liberty! gift celestial,
    Twined deep in the Deity's plan!
Thy glorious life is immortal,
    And yields the best blessings to man.
Thou art twin to the chainless lightning,
    The maddened tornado's flight;
Thou dancest in bound of the billow
    And glancest in gleam of the light.

No blossom art thou of the garden,
    To breathe in the sunshine warm;
Thou swingest upon the pine top,
    To the roar of the grappling storm.
The strength that would challenge the whirlwind
    Dissolves in the valley of flowers;
The voice that sounds mate to the thunder
    Would sink in soft melody's bowers.

A warrior, grim and frowning,
    Thou springest upon thy steed,
Armed for the battle to conquer
    Or die in the moment of need.
When the battle is ended, thou leanest
    Ever thine ear to the ground,
And ready to clutch thy falchion
    To danger's most far-away sound.

O Liberty! gift celestial,
    What glorious joys are thine?
Yet to few of the earth is given
    To watch o'er thy holy shrine.
Oh! many the hearts that are fettered
    In tyranny's cruel gyves;
But among them the seed is scattered
    Where Liberty's germ survives.

And sometimes the seed springs upward
    To wildest and fiercest life;
Ah! how the world has tottered
    In the quake of the dreadful strife!
The earth has turned red with slaughter,
    And Liberty, torn and stained,

Down to the dust has been cloven;
    But its life—its life remained.

And again, to its feet upleaping,
    Again it has dared the fight;
And as long as earth stands will the battle
    Rage on between Might and Right.
O Liberty! born of heaven!
    Not always the despot's ban
Will darken the light of thy glory—
    Thy light is immortal in man.

And such the light our fathers knew;
    Thus, when Oppression stealthy came,
Up to the sun their front they drew,
    With voice of storm and eye of flame.
At the Virginian's trumpet-breath
Of "Give me Liberty or death!"
Bounded our nation to the fray,
As from night's shadow bounds the day.
On went the words, winged fierce with ire,
Like the dread tongues of cloven fire.
Bear witness, blazoned battle-fields,
What bolts an uproused nation wields!
A living lustre flashes forth—
Fields, bounded not by South or North,
But scattered wide, in every part—
Sword joined to sword, and heart to heart;
Where Hudson rolls its lordly tide,
    And where the broad Potomac flows,
Where Susquehanna's waters glide,
    And where St. Mary's silver glows.

Then to the struggles of the free
Kind heaven vouchsafed the victory.
Sheathing the lightnings of her brand,
    And sharpening ax, and guiding plough,
Swift onward went our happy Land,
    With flowery feet and starry brow.
A continent was ours to bless
With Liberty's own happiness;
A happiness of equal right—
    Of government to rest on all—
Of law, whose broad and steadfast light
    On each obedient heart should fall.
In Union's sacred bond they reared
    A Union temple, and the sun
Never a fairer fabric cheered;
    Our starry flag, with trophies won
In many a fight on sea and shore,
Waved in its blazoned beauty o'er.
From where the half-year sleeps in snow
To where Magnolian breezes blow,
Our eagle flew, and saw no break
In the expanse that God had joined.
Ours was some sheltered, happy lake,
Which, though the transient breeze might shake,
    Yet by the sun again was coined
To peaceful gold, and upward sent
Its grateful smile of blest content.
Then came the storm—the darkness fell—
    Dashed the wild billows to the blast;
And, staggering on the foaming swell,
    With shivering sail and quivering mast,
Fierce breakers crashing on her lee,
    In the red lightning's angry glare,
    Kindling alone the blackened air,
Our once proud Ship of State we see.
And, bearing down, a phantom bark,
    In lurid light its trappings wound—
Sides darting fires along the dark,
    Terrific thunders roaring round—

Comes flashing through the awful gloom
With threatening of impending doom.
Heaven save the Ship! in godly care
　The stately mould our fathers wrought;
Her sails of States, in Union, caught—
Union alone—the favoring air.
Our fathers' blood her firm cement,
　Their hearts the planks that formed the pile,
Their prayers the blue above it bent,
　Their virtues the surrounding smile.

And shall that Ship, in hopeless shock,
Be dashed upon Disunion's rock?
Shall we not, on the severing sky,
　See some gray tinge of softness cast,
Prophetic of the crimson dye,
　The glorious sunburst throws at last?

Ye stately shades—O glorious sires!
　Bend from the clouds of darkness now
With memory-waking battle-fires,
　Flashing from every awful brow!
Throughout the realm hath shone your blade,
Throughout the realm your bones are laid!
For the whole realm ye fought and died;
Descend! march round on every side!
Come Sumter, Marion, Greene, and Wayne!
　And thou, O stateliest WASHINGTON!
Lead through the land the mighty train—
　The lovely land the heroes won.
Touch every heart with kindly flame,
　Sweep every barrier-cloud away,
And rear again the Union's frame
　The brighter from its new array.
Let our broad banner stream to view
　Without a stain, without a rent—
With every star in brightened blue,
　With every stripe more beauteous blent.

Dear flag of our fathers! how wildly
　It streams to the hurricane's might!
Yet no more shall be quenched in the darkness
　Than the sunshine be swept from the sight.

It was born in the tumult of battle,
　When the land rocked with wrath at the foe,
And Liberty, striving and reeling,
　Rained blood at each terrible blow.

There was naught on the yoked earth to render
　Fit emblems that flag to adorn;
So the sky—the grand symbol of freedom—
　Sent gifts from its night and its morn.

The stars shone for hopes to be kindled
　Anew from dark tyranny's sway;
And the stripes beamed for courage and patience,
　Fresh dawning to lead up the day.

Thus favored above, changing fortune
　Came smiling our banner to join;
And the first its bright folds were expanded,
　It waved over conquered Burgoyne.

Though it trembled at times to the tempest,
　And clouds o'er its blazonry passed,
Our eagle thence wafted it onward,
　Till proudly 'twas planted at last.

And now, as we gaze on its splendors,
　In the heart what starred memories rise!
Of worthies with feet in our pathways,
　But glorified brows in the skies.

High lifted—the foremost among them—
　Our Nation's great Father is seen,
With figure in mould so majestic,
　And face so benign and serene.

And Jefferson, Adams, and Franklin
　There shine in the stately array;
And there the wreathed forehead of Jackson,
　And there the grand presence of Clay.

And battle-fields, trophied in honor,
　On the breast of the banner are rife—
The evergreen summit of Bunker,
　And Trenton's wild winter-tossed strife.

And proudly our own Saratoga,
　Where the first of our triumphs was won;
And Yorktown—that height of our glory,
　Where burst our victorious sun.

Then, hail to our sky-blazoned banner!
　It has brightened the shore and the sea;
And soon may it wave o'er one nation,
　The starred and striped FLAG OF THE FREE!

TREACHERY OF THE REBELS.

CAMP OF FIFTH PENNSYLVANIA CAVALRY, }
WILLIAMSBURGH, VA., June 6, 1863. }

During the last few days there appeared a flag, purporting to be a sign of distress, on Hog Island, opposite King's Landing, on the James River. The matter, as soon as reported to Major C. Kleinz, received due attention by an examination by the Major in person, who, after satisfying himself of the existence of the flag, ordered Lieutenant James Smith, of company A, to take a small boat and visit the island, to ascertain the object of the parties displaying the flag of truce. Lieutenant Smith took one man (and two contrabands to row the boat) with him, and started for the Island. When coming within two hundred yards of the east end of the island, he could distinguish a camp in a clump of trees, also a flag floating in the air; he then drifted his boat westward along the island, without being able to see any thing more than the white flag, which was constantly displayed in an inviting manner.

By the aid of a field-glass he could see every object about the houses, barns, and sheds, with the exception of a long tobacco warehouse, which is situated on lower ground, but, getting to a favorable position, he did distinguish three soldiers, partially concealed from view. On a nearer approach and closer examination, he saw a man sitting on the stairway loading a musket. Still, the white flag was displayed by a single person. On getting within fifty yards of the shore the flag was taken down, and near the flag-bearer sixteen men suddenly made their appearance. On Lieutenant Smith asking the object of the flag of truce, they ordered him to land his boat, and immediately the rebel flag was hoisted over their heads. Lieutenant Smith, aware of their treacherous intent, headed his boat from the shore, encouraging the colored men to pull for their lives, and began to beat a hasty retreat.

As soon as the rebels saw the boat headed off they were ordered to fire; they did so, but their fire fell about six yards short of the boat; another squad about three times as large, from the tobacco warehouse, fired, but their fire went too high; a third as large, and from the same place, fired, filling the air round the little boat with bullets. Fortunately Smith and his party escaped uninjured, owing to the precautionary preparation after the first fire, which was to stoop down in the boat, and work her out, exposing nothing more than their arms and heads. Many other shots were fired by small squads running along the shore to head the boat off, but injuring nothing. As soon as Smith got beyond the range of their pieces there was a black flag displayed for over an hour. Lieutenant H. E. Whittlesey, who first reported the appearance of traitors on the Island, had seen signal lights on the Island, on Jamestown Island, and on the south bank of the James River, both east and west of Hog Island.

June 7.—The following is from the Raleigh *State Journal*, a secession paper:

"We fear that the same conflict between the State authorities and the confederate government which was witnessed in this State at the session of the last Legislature is to be renewed. The Governor has assumed the position of an avowed advocate of the supremacy of the State judges, and has in advance decided all cases against the claims of the confederate government. We have observed with regret a recent order of the Governor, by which he commands the officers of the State to resist by force the arrest of any person claimed as a conscript, who has once been discharged by the decision of a State judge. We look with alarm upon these unsettled and conflicting claims. The only honest course for a State of the Confederacy is to give her all to the contest now raging, or to quit the field at once. There can be no divided service compatible either with honor or safety."

BURNSIDE.—The Louisville *Journal* gives the following judgment up against the flood of abuse poured out upon him:

"Burnside looks and acts like a great man; and the manner in which he has managed the affairs of this department shows him to be a statesman as well as a General. The more we see of Burnside the more we like him. He has done much for Kentucky. His Order No. 38 has worked like a charm, and has given peace, quiet, and security to many portions of the State which have been invested by rebel sympathizers and marauders. Previous to its publication, many parts of the State were invested by Morgan's men and other rebels, whose presence brought fear and terror, but since the enforcement there are none to be found within our lines, except a few desperate characters, who come and go secretly, to act the spy—and those are caught whenever found and executed."

HOW GENERAL GRANT CARES FOR HIS SOLDIERS. — General Grant, says the Cleveland *Herald*, has issued a special order forbidding steamboat men to charge more than five dollars to enlisted men, and seven dollars to officers, as fare between Vicksburgh and Cairo. Immediately after Vicksburgh had fallen, a large number of steamboats cleared from Northern ports for that place, and were in the habit of charging soldiers going home on furlough from fifteen to thirty dollars fare to Cairo. A friend relates to us that the steamer Hope was compelled by General Grant to disgorge its ill-gotten gains the other day, under the following circumstances: This boat had about one thousand enlisted soldiers, and nearly two hundred and fifty officers, aboard, *en route* for home on short leave of absence, after the fatigues of their protracted but glorious campaign. The captain of the Hope had charged these men and officers from ten to twenty-five dollars apiece, as fare to Cairo. Just as the boat was about to push off from

the wharf at Vicksburgh, an order came from General Grant requiring the captain to pay back to his passengers all money received by him as fare in excess of five dollars to enlisted men, and seven dollars to officers, or submit to imprisonment for disobedience and have his boat confiscated. The order was an astonisher to the captain, but the presence of a guard rendered it useless to refuse, and so, amid the shouts of the soldiers over General Grant's care of their interests, he complied with as good grace as possible, and paid back the money. Our informant, himself a passenger on the Hope, was present when General Grant issued the order above referred to. The General, upon being informed of the impositions being practised upon furloughed men and officers, by steamboat men, was very indignant. "I will teach them, if they need the lesson," said the gallant General, "that the men who have perilled their lives to open the Mississippi River for their benefit cannot be imposed upon with impunity." No wonder that the soldiers of the army of the Mississippi fairly worship their General.

INCIDENTS OF PICKET LIFE ON THE RAPIDAN.—The pickets indulge in the usual badinage of the outposts. One—a Louisianian—asked why we did not throw up some rifle-pits. The answer was: "What for?" "Why, because we might come over and attack you." "Oh! is that all?" was the sentry's answer; "come along; we wouldn't throw any thing in your way; it's what we want. Come over and bring all your friends; we shall not stop you. Did you throw up that dirt to prevent our advance? O pshaw! when we advance we'll walk right round them." One of the rebel artillerymen was anxious to know whether a soldier's pay was good for any thing now. He was told that it would buy thirteen dollars' worth of goods, the same as ever. "Well, I'll tell you what we do with ours," said he. "We tell off the battery into fives, and play poker till one man out of five gets the money. The winners tell off into fives again, and so at last somebody has enough money to treat his friends." General Early's headquarters are in a white house near the ford. His portly form, in white shirt and an enormously high-crowned hat, with a feather, is occasionally seen about the opposite shore. It is stated, on the authority of a sergeant, who was down at the river-bank arranging a little matter, in which coffee, tobacco, and a Richmond *Examiner* figured prominently, that the General himself came down and made this offer: "If any of you Yanks want to trade a first-rate pair of high boots, good leather, and so forth, I'll pay for them in gold." Whether he has yet achieved the boots, is a matter upon which no testimony has been offered.

COLONEL MORROW'S RECOLLECTIONS.—Colonel Morrow, the brave leader of the famous Twenty-fourth Michigan, lately made a long war-speech to his fellow-citizens of Detroit. Among other things he told them the following:

One of the rebel officers captured by us afterward met me in Gettysburgh, where I was a prisoner. A man came up to me in the street and said: "Colonel, how do you do? You don't know me, and think I don't know you. (I had cut off my straps to prevent my being recognized as a colonel.) Come and take a drink." Of course, I drank with him, and then asked who he was. He took me one side from the rebel officers, and said: "Your regiment captured me at Fitz-Hugh's Landing, d—n you!" Said I: "Glad of it. Didn't they treat you well?" "Bully," was his reply. "Then treat me the same." "We will; where are your straps?" "I have lost them for the time being." "All right, I shan't say a word." He kept his promise, and when I left the rebels, they took me for a surgeon.

Twenty-four hours after crossing at Fitz-Hugh's Landing, we recrossed and went to Chancellorsville. There we were stationed at a separate space, and guarded two roads, a position of honor, given, as I was assured by General Hooker, as a compliment to the regiment. We were unsuccessful at Chancellorsville, but through no fault of General Hooker's. It would have been a glorious victory, had it not been for the defection of an army corps, and this was due to the bad conduct of its officers, and not to any lack of courage among the men. The Eleventh corps occupied a position directly in front of the enemy, and was, nevertheless, allowed by its officers to lay down its arms and make coffee. It was then attacked by the rebels with those unearthly shouts of theirs. The rebels beat any people out shouting. One half the battles in that neighborhood were fought by power of the lungs rather than the bayonet. The lungs of the rebels are not so strong as ours, but they have a boy-like scream, which is much shriller. (Colonel Morrow then related an amusing anecdote of the counter-cheering of the rebels and the Twenty-fourth at Fitz-Hugh's Landing.) General Hooker, at Chancellorsville, exhibited splendid generalship. I was told by a prisoner, a rebel colonel—a fact never before printed, I believe—that General Hooker succeeded in transporting thirty thousand men across the Rappahannock and Rapidan, and right into the centre of the rebel position, without their obtaining the least knowledge of it. In fact, General Hooker succeeded in dividing the rebel army, cutting off Stuart from Lee, and obliging the former to cut his way through in order to reach headquarters. However, we lost the battle, and fell back into our old camp.

At Gettysburgh, with my assistant surgeon, Dr. Collar, indefatigable in season and out of season, I visited the hospitals and the battle-field—the latter at twelve o'clock in the night on the third, determining the names of those that had fallen. In a barn, among two hundred others, I found a little Irish boy from this city, Patrick Cleary, a bright boy, and a brave little fellow. I said to him: "Patrick, how do you feel?" He said: "Pretty well, but the doctor says I can't live." I looked at his wounded leg and saw that mortification had set in. I said: "I don't know; the doctor is the best judge. If he says you can't live, you had better prepare to die." Said he: "Colonel, if you'll have the leg taken off, I'll be with the regiment in a week." I told him that was impossible. He then said: "Colonel, an't you proud of the Twenty-fourth? Won't the people of Wayne County be proud?" God bless that boy. He is dead now. [A voice: "He is alive yet."] I am glad to hear it. He is a credit to his native and adopted country. The last thing the boys think of is what those at home think of them. They feel proud of themselves, and they want you to feel proud too. Write them cheering letters. Encourage your soldiers. Bid them God speed. Tell them they are fighting in a just and holy cause, as they certainly are.

INCIDENTS OF THE RAPPAHANNOCK.—Quietness still reigns on the Rappahannock, and there seems an absence of certain infallible indications which foreshadow a general movement. The weather is fine, with just enough airiness to render camp-life at this season of the year agreeable. Lee's rumored movement up the river is still the subject of much speculation, and there are good reasons for believing that he has transferred a part of his force to the vicinity of Banks's Ford. The river-pickets report that trains of artillery and wagons are heard nightly wending their way up the river, and the balloonist, stationed at present near the Wrotton House, one mile below Banks's Ford, discovers a large rebel encampment opposite that point. He also reports a large force still confronting our left wing, and opposite "Washington's Farm." This camp is, perhaps, three or four miles from the river, and is discernible only from the balloon. But four or five small rebel camps are visible below and above Fredericksburgh from our side of the river. The secretiveness of the rebels is quite remarkable. Not a single rebellious ensign can be seen up or down the river; but why, is a matter of conjecture. Possibly, the price of bunting in Dixie is incompatible with the rebels' idea of economy.

Yesterday morning a party of rebels approached the river opposite Falmouth with a seine, and immediately commenced preparations for a little piscatorial recreation. The officer of our picket, acting in compliance with orders, called out his guard, and ordering the men to prime their pieces, hailed the would-be fishermen after the following manner:

"Hello, over there! What are you going to do?"

"Fish," was the brief response from one of the party.

"Don't you know that General Hooker has forbidden fishing in the river?" inquired the officer.

"Yes, but we thought you'd have no objection as long as we kept on our side."

"But we do object," replied the officer, "and if you put that seine in the river I'll order my guard to fire on you." A short consultation among the rebel party ensued, and in a few moments they withdrew, taking their seine with them. Communication between the pickets is no longer allowed, but occasionally a brief conversation is indulged in. A picket informed your correspondent, yesterday, that, when last on picket, a rebel on the other side held up a paper as if to say: "Don't you wish you may get it!" The Union picket beckoned him to come over, and finally the rebel waded to the middle of the river, but would come no further. Finding that he could not induce the blue-jacket to meet him half-way, he returned to the other side. On inquiring of the picket what course he would have pursued had the rebel ventured over, he replied: "I should have taken him prisoner." The vaunted discipline of the rebels is scouted by our men who can observe the movements of their pickets. The sentries are relieved with any thing but military precision, and the relief goes shambling along like "the whining schoolboy unwillingly to school." With coats off, and with an air of lazy indisposition, they lounge, with their muskets behind them, along the other shore, gazing listlessly on our soldier-like pickets pacing with regular and steady step their respective "beats." Two deserters forded the river this morning below Banks's Ford, and were received by the pickets of the Third corps. They told the usual story of destitution and suffering on the other side.

UNION LEAGUE SECRETS.—A correspondent of the Ohio *State Sentinel*, who assumes to have penetrated to the mysteries of the order, sends the following as a portion of the instructions given to the initiated:

When you first meet a member, present your left hand and say:

"How are you, Major?"

Answer: "Comfortably well."

"Are you a member of our Union League?"

Answer: "Prove me."

"How shall I prove you?"

Answer: "By positions."

Here comes in what might be called a command, for the person asking the questions above set forth says: "Take positions, and I'll call them."

The person who answers the questions then raises his left hand perpendicularly over his head, at which time you say: "Washington." He then drops his arm to a horizontal position and you say: "Jefferson." He then drops his hand on his left thigh, and you say: "Jackson." He then raises his left hand to his breast and you say: "Union." He then joins the thumb and third finger of his left hand; at this time you must also join the thumb and third finger, as he does; then both of your hands meet, and you put your thumb and third finger inside of his and you say: "League." All this is done in a shorter time than I can tell you.

When a member is going into the lodge, the password at the first door is, "Eternal Vigilance;" at the second door, "Is the Price of Liberty." When a member enters the lodge, he salutes the President by holding up his left-hand forefinger. When he leaves the lodge, he holds up his right-hand two forefingers.

When a Union League man gets into a fight at night he cries out: "I, I." If any of the brothers are around and willing to assist him they cry out: "What, what."

SONGS OF THE REBELS.

UNLAURELLED HEROES.

Oh! praise not those supremely blest
  With honor, talents, life, and beauty,
But let your high encomiums rest
  On those who fall at posts of duty;
On those who bravely meet their fate,
  With hearts of oak and souls of iron,
And leave those bright homes desolate,
  Where hope to love sang like a syren.

'Tis not for those the trump of fame
  Salutes with flattery's warm caresses,
Who bear through life a splendid name,
  That all the world admires and blesses;
But oh! for those, our tears we shed,
  Who fall uncrowned with rays of glory,
And come back like the Spartan dead,
  On shields that tell their own sad story.

Look where brave Zollicoffer fell,
  To music of the death-shot's rattle;
And where young Peyton's final knell
  Swept o'er him in disastrous battle—
For such the heart in anguish bleeds,
  And pours out all its warmest praises;
They went forth on their fiery steeds,
  So soon to sleep beneath the daisies!

While life was young and manhood bright,
  And honors clustered fast and faster,
They went forth, armed with truth and might,
  To meet defeat and dark disaster;
Theirs was the martyr's dreary doom,
  When, to their brows, a thorn-crown pressing,
They dimly saw, beyond the tomb,
  The prize they sought—their country's blessing.

Then weep for the unlaurelled brave
  Who fell undecked with victory's splendors,
And place upon each martyr's grave,
  "Most loved, most blest of our defenders;"
For each shall be a holy shrine,
  And pilgrim's tears, upon them falling,
Shall rise, like frankincense divine,
  Their hero-martyr lives recalling.   GUY

DIXIE ALL RIGHT.

Sunny South we trust will be—hurrah! hurrah! hurrah! ·

Ere long from Northern rulers free—hurrah! hurrah! hurrah!

With lead and powder, sword and gun, they will him to the —— run!

They will him to the —— run! Hurrah! hurrah! hurrah!

Then hang the fiddle on the wall,
With fife and drumsticks lead the ball;
We'll teach them dancing fine and neat
With cannon, sword, and bayonet.

We bought the dry goods from the North,
Now all our clerks are going forth
To do the job of measuring—
With swords, not yards, they do the thing.

Our doctors found a remedy
For every Northern malady;
They cure all fevers, pains and chills,
With bombshells and with leaden pills.

Thus men throughout the South are armed,
Their hearts by freedom steeled and warmed;
And should one man refuse to fight,
The ladies will their courage slight.

TRUST TO LUCK, ALABAMA.

Trust to luck, Alabama! prolong the loud shout:
Three cheers for our State, boys; she is out! she is out!

We have cut ourselves loose from the huckstering knaves,
Who whine about negroes and make white men slaves.
Though enriched by the South, rankest traitors they stand,
Who swore to befriend us, basest foes to our land.
Trust to luck, Alabama! prolong the loud shout,
Three cheers for our State, boys; she is out! she is out!

Trust to luck, Alabama! and end as it may,
Better death than submit to fanatical sway;
No compromise now, the solemn words have gone forth
Which declare we are free from the traitorous North.
We seek no revenge, and would part without strife,
But if war they must have, why, then war to the knife!
Trust to luck, Alabama! prolong the loud shout,
Three cheers for our State, boys; she is out! she is out!

Trust to luck, Alabama! and heed not the boast
Of superior numbers—our cause is a host;
We fight for the homesteads our fathers bequeathed,
Who died to defend them, with victory wreathed.

Like our sires, we will venture our all on the fight.
Trust to luck, Alabama! God sides with the right!
Trust to luck, Alabama! prolong the loud shout!
Three cheers for our State, boys; she is out! she is
out!

BANNER SONG.

BY WILLIAM H. HOLCOMBE, M.D.

See! our banner floating high,
Star in freedom's shining sky;
Soldiers! follow it or die—
    Star of death or victory!

Beauty's hands its tissues wove,
Glory lends its aid to love;
Honor, truth, and God approve;
    Comrades! follow it or die!

At the tyrant's call arrayed
Hireling troops our land invade;
Dear Virginia cries for aid!
    Answer, cheering to her cry!

Forward! spirits brave and true!
Forward! till the foe's in view!
Death is the invader's due;
    Death to hateful tyranny!

Soldiers! march at duty's call,
Meet the bayonet and the ball;
Front the cannon, scale the wall,
    Shouting, Death or liberty!

Nations watch with eager eyes;
He who lives shall share the prize;
He is doubly crowned who dies.
    Free or dead, be this our cry!

Fame! inspire us with thy charm;
Angels! shield our souls from harm;
Just our cause and strong our arm;
    Forward, comrades! Do or die!

INCIDENTS OF THE FIGHT WITH MOSBY.

FAIRFAX COURT-HOUSE, June 2, 1863.

THE sun glistens on a twelve-pound brass howitzer, which, with its limber, occupies a position directly in front of General Stahel's headquarters. The story of the gun is this: Made in the year 1859, it was used by the Union troops at Ball's Bluff, where it fell into the hands of the rebels, and since that time has done service in the rebel army. After Mosby had been whipped several times by Stahel's cavalry, this gun was furnished him to redeem his laurels. On Friday night last, Mosby, with about one hundred and seventy-five men and the howitzer, camped at Greenwich. Early Saturday morning they made a hurried march toward the Orange and Alexandria Railroad, which they struck about one and a half miles this side of Catlett's Station. Here they concealed themselves in the woods, placed the howitzer in position, and awaited the arrival of the train from Alexandria, carrying forage and stores to Bealton. As the cars came opposite the ambuscade, a rail adroitly displaced caused the locomotive to run off the track. At this moment a ball from the gun went through the boiler and another pierced the smoke-stack. The guard upon the train were scared by hearing artillery, and beat a hasty retreat, leaving the train at the disposition of the rebels. Had any

resistance been offered, it is believed that the train could have been saved and all the rebels captured. As it was, the guerrillas destroyed the cars, ten in number, and then, anticipating a visit from Stahel's cavalry, made off in the direction of Auburn. Meanwhile, Colonel Mann, of the Seventh Michigan cavalry, who was in command of the portion of Stahel's cavalry at Bristow, hearing the firing, started with portions of the Fifth New-York, First Vermont, and Seventh Michigan, to learn the cause. Taking the precaution to send the Fifth New-York, Captain A. H. Hasbrouck commanding, across the country to Auburn to intercept the retreat, he followed up the railroad until the sight of the burning train told that portion of the story. Leaving the burning train, Colonel Mann followed the track of the retreating foe, and soon heard the sound of cannon toward Greenwich, indicating that Captain Hasbrouck, with the Fifth New-York, had either intercepted or come up with the enemy. As it afterward proved, they had come upon their rear, and had been fired upon from the howitzer. Owing to the nature of the ground, the Fifth New-York was unable to deploy, so as to operate effectively, and the enemy again started on the run, closely followed by Captain Hasbrouck and his command. Colonel Mann pressed on to reach the scene of the firing. Learning the particulars of their escape, he divided his force, sending Lieutenant-Colonel Preston, with part of the First Vermont cavalry, to reënforce the Fifth New-York, and with the balance he struck across the country, again hoping to intercept them.

Finding themselves so hotly pressed, the enemy, when near Grapewood Farm, about two miles from Greenwich, took position at the head of a short narrow lane, with high fences on either side, placing the howitzer so as to command the lane, strongly supported by his whole force. The advance of the Fifth New-York, about twenty-five men, under Lieutenant Elmer Barker, coming up, the Lieutenant determined to charge the gun, fearing if he halted the rebels would again run away. Gallantly riding up the narrow lane, with almost certain death before them, these brave men, bravely led by Lieutenant Barker, dashed with a yell toward the gun. When within about fifty yards the rebels opened fire with grape upon them. The result was three men were killed and seven wounded. The rebels immediately charged, led by Mosby himself. Lieutenant Barker, twice wounded in the leg, continued with his handful of men to contest every inch of the ground, and himself crossed sabres with Mosby. But numbers told, and several of the Fifth New-York were made prisoners. This gallant fight of Lieutenant Barker afforded Colonel Preston an opportunity to come up with the First Vermont. Lieutenant Hazleton was in advance, with about seventy-five men, and charged bravely up the lane, the few boys of the Fifth New-York, who were left, joining the Vermonters. Again and again the gun dealt destruction through the ranks, but nothing could check their impetuosity, and the brave fellows rode over the gun, sabring the gunners, and captured the piece. Sergeant Carey, of the First Vermont, was shot dead by the side of the gun; his brother, a corporal in the same regiment, although his arm was shattered, struck down the gunner as he applied the match for the last time. Mosby and his men fought desperately to recover the gun, but in vain.

Meanwhile Colonel Preston had charged across the fields upon their flank, and the enemy fled in all directions, taking refuge in the thickets, with which they are so familiar. One party attempted to take away the limber, but it was speedily captured and brought in. The long chase in the hot sun, the desperate fight, and the jaded condition of the horses, prevented further pursuit, which, with the enemy so widely scattered, and with their knowledge of every by-path and thicket, would have been almost fruitless. Captain B. S. Haskins, an Englishman, and formerly a Captain in the Forty-fourth Royal Infantry, who was with Mosby, was so badly wounded that he has since died. Lieutenant Chapman, formerly of the regular army, who was in charge of the gun, was also dangerously wounded and paroled on the field, as he could not be removed. Our loss was four killed and fifteen wounded. The rebels had six killed, twenty wounded, and lost ten prisoners. All the Fifth New-York who were taken by the rebels were re-captured.

The result of this fight is more disastrous to the rebels than the previous engagements. The Southern Confederacy will not be apt to trust Mr. Mosby with other guns if he cannot take better care of them than he has of this one. The enemy was beaten by about the same force, in a position chosen by themselves, and defended by a howitzer. Their killed and wounded outnumber ours, and the howitzer is ready to be turned against them at the earliest opportunity. The conduct of officers and men is highly commended by Colonel Mann in his official report to General Stahel, and the gallantry of the charges of the Fifth New-York and the First Vermont is deserving mention.

REBEL LETTERS CAPTURED.—A rebel mail-bag was found on board the blockade runner Calypso, from which the following letters were taken:

A GEORGIA MERCHANT TO HIS PARTNERS.

NASSAU, Sunday, June 7.

DEAR BROTHER: . . . If I am not mistaken, some of the blockade-runners will lose a pile of money, as confederate money is becoming at such a discount they cannot get price enough on the goods to pay the difference of exchange, as all goods have to be paid in gold or sterling exchange, and all freights prepaid, and then take all chances of getting them through, besides paying duties on them at Charleston. Some of the blockade men think the next steamer from Dixie will bring bad news, and there will be a much greater discount on confederate money—say seven hundred dollars or eight hundred dollars for one hundred dollars in gold, and my opinion is it will soon be worthless. Yesterday I bought here (Nassau) five hundred dollars in confederate money at four cents on the dollar, and some was sold here for even a greater discount. So you can see what the people here think of Dixie money, and in fact no one here will take it at any price for goods or for freight money; and if I had a million of gold dollars I would not invest one dollar here and take the chances of getting through and take confederate money.

If you have any confederate money on hand when you receive this, get clear of it on the best terms you possibly can, and in future do not take any more confederate money, only at what you can sell it for gold, and turn it into gold as soon as you receive it. The best investment of confederate money is good sterling exchange, the next is gold or silver, and the next is cotton, for, sooner or later, I am confident confederate money will not be worth the paper it is made on, although I may be mistaken.

Yours truly,   S. B. JAQUES.

A RICHMOND AGENT'S TESTIMONY.

NASSAU, June 3, 1863.

William E. Simons, Richmond, Va.:

DEAR FRIEND: . . . I have not been able to find sale of the bonds, though there have been sales heretofore, but now no one seems ready to buy. I could sell at forty-five cents, but am not willing to sell at that figure. I have concluded to deposit them in a house here, to be disposed of at a fair price, and proceed myself to New-York, as we talked of before my departure from Richmond. Until my return I shall not be able to make any shipment to you. [Probably intends to buy goods in New-York.]

The feeling here by residents seems to be in favor of the South, but I do not think it exists any further than dollars and cents are concerned. They are all making money out of the war, and do not care, in my opinion, how long it may last. As to England herself, from what I can see and hear, she is in favor of the South, on account of the gallantry shown by Southern soldiers, and would be willing to recognize her, providing she would emancipate her slaves, which can never be done.   Yours, very truly,

HENRY WOODWARD.

THE EXPEDITION UP THE YAZOO.—The following extracts are from a letter of an officer dated Haines's Bluff, Miss., June 1, 1863, and which to-day was received in this city:

"We reached here yesterday, after a week's march up between the Black and Yazoo Rivers. The object of the expedition was to destroy the resources of the country, to prevent the enemy from subsisting their armies, and to drive out any force he might have in that region, and if possible to ascertain if the enemy was concentrating in any considerable force for the purpose of raising the siege of Vicksburgh. We had six brigades, numbering something over ten thousand men.

"We have marched over one hundred miles in a week, during the hottest kind of weather. We destroyed all the forage, and supplies, and cotton, and drove off all the cattle, horses, and mules between the two lines for a distance of fifty miles. We met no considerable body of the enemy, and had only one or two slight skirmishes, but we ascertained where the enemy were concentrating, and gained much valuable information, which may be of use hereafter.

"The Commanding General having reported to General Grant, the latter came this morning to Haines's Bluff, and seemed well satisfied with our operations. It was made our painful but imperative duty to destroy every thing, corn, cotton, meat, mills, and cotton-gins, that we could find, sparing only dwellings, and a small supply of provisions for each family.

"This is bringing the war home to their people, and making them realize their own crime in bringing its calamities upon the country. The command will rest here for a day or so, and then return to Vicksburgh, which cannot hold out very long against our forces. They can raise no force to make us give up the siege."

MUNCHAUSENIANA.

HOUSTON, TEXAS, May 23.—A reliable officer of Colonel Bates's regiment, who arrived last evening, brings the information that before he left Columbia a courier arrived from Corpus Christi with information that General Magruder had fitted out several small steamers at that place and attacked the blockading fleet. He succeeded in sinking two of the enemy's vessels, capturing fifteen prisoners, and raising the blockade. Hurrah for the horse marines! Hurrah for Magruder!—*Houston Telegraph, May 26.*

HEROISM OF MISS SCHWARTZ.

GENERAL BROWN'S ORDER.

HEADQUARTERS, DISTRICT OF CENTRAL MO., }
JEFFERSON CITY, August 9, 1863. }

GENERAL ORDERS No. 42.

On the night of the sixth inst. a party of bushwhackers, some three in number, visited the house of a Mr. Schwartz, about twelve miles from Jefferson City, in Cole County, and on demanding admittance they were refused by Miss Schwartz, a young lady of fifteen. They replied they would come in, at the same time trying to break down the door. While this was going on, the other inmates of the house, namely, Mr. Schwartz, John Wise, Captain Golden, Government horse-dealer, and a young man in his employ, all left, taking with them (as they supposed) all the arms and ammunition. In their hasty retreat they left behind a revolver, which Miss Schwartz appropriated to her own use. She went to the door, and on opening it presented the pistol to the leader of the gang, telling them to "Come on, if they wanted to, and that some of them should fall, or she would." They threatened to kill her if she did not leave the door. She replied: "The first one who takes one step toward this door dies, for this is the home of my parents, and my brothers and sisters, and I am able to and shall defend it." Seeing that she was determined in her purpose, and after holding a consultation together, they left.

Here is an instance of true courage; a young girl of fifteen years of age, after all the inmates of the house, even her father, had fled, leaving her alone to her fate, with a courage worthy a Joan of Arc, boldly defended her native home against three blood-thirsty and cowardly ruffians, and by her coolness and heroic daring succeeded in turning them from their hellish designs.

It is with feelings of no ordinary pride and pleasure the Commanding General announces this act to the citizens and soldiers in his district. On the other hand, those miserable cowards who deserted this brave girl in the hour of danger, flying from the house, leaving her to her fate, are unworthy the name of men, deserve the scorn and contempt of the community at large, and whose society should be shunned by every one who has the least spark of honor or bravery with them. By order of Brigadier-Gen. BROWN.

HEROES OF GETTYSBURGH.

HARRISBURGH, PA., Nov. 3, 1863.

FRANK MOORE, ESQ.: DEAR SIR: Perhaps this is too late. Perhaps it is not good enough to appear in the REBELLION RECORD. It is nevertheless *true,* and although its author does not pretend to be a poet, he would wish to record the instance, the singularity of which may attract readers to it, and cause it to be remembered. The hero, Weed, was a citizen of New-York. Of Hazlett I know nothing except that he was a dear friend of Weed's, and in the same regiment, the Fifth United States artillery, a First Lieutenant, and appointed from Ohio.

AN INCIDENT AT GETTYSBURGH.

"On to the Round Top!" cried Sykes to his men;
"On to the Round Top!" was echoed again;
"On to the Round Top!" said noble Steve Weed;
Now comes the hour for the Southron to bleed.

Weed's fierce artillery foremost in fight;
Rebels! prepare ye for death or for flight:
Weed's fierce artillery, dreaded of old,
Belching destruction—refulgent as gold.

On toward the Round Top, revolve the strong wheels,
Spurned is the ground by the war-horses' heels;
Ploughed is the furrow with shrapnel and ball,
Little avails them the field's friendly wall.

Lee's serried ranks are mowed down as the corn
Falls 'neath the cradle on-hot harvest morn.
Bold Mississippians, pause and take breath,
Weed is before you—beside him is death!

On to the Round Top! the Round Top we gain!
Falls gallant Weed from a ball—is he slain?
Prone on the earth he lies heavily sighing,
Near him lie gallant men wounded and dying.

"Hazlett, come hither," sighed Weed as he lay;
"Hither, my friend—I have something to say."
Hazlett rushed forward, bent down, raised his head—
Whistles a minié-ball—Hazlett is dead!

Dead ere Weed uttered the words he would speak;
Dead are both heroes on field, cheek to cheek;
Mingling their dying thoughts—their dying breath;
Grasped by each other—united in death.

Thus fell the gallant artill'ry men twain
In the supreme hour of victory slain,
Just as the Round Top was won from the foe,
And rebels shall never recover that blow.

Long may History's muse her fair pages adorn
With the names of the heroes who fell on that morn;
Who fell for the Union—for Freedom who fell—
Let Fame sound her trumpet proclaiming who fell.

ANONYMOUS.

The verses are not worth having a name affixed to them. For the facts, however, I am responsible, they having been related to me by an officer of the United States army, in whom I have entire confidence.

I am respectfully yours, JAMES WORRALL.
HARRISBURGH, PA.

DRUM.

BY J. R. G. PITKIN.

I.

Drum!
Drum! drum! drum! drum!
Drum!
On they come.
While throbs a stern, responsive beat
Of martial lines of measured feet,
Down, down the stony street.
And thousands wait
At door and gate,
To bless each form
Who dares the storm,
And every tie
Can waive, to die
When Treason's hand
Assails his land:
And thus to greet
Brave souls, they meet,
While horrid fears
Rouse abject tears,
And all
Appall!

God's will be done—
    God bless them all!
For such have won
    Half, ere their call!

There woman stands
With clonic hands!
Such woes infest
Her tender breast ;
Her eyelids drip,
While the dumb lip
Essays in vain
To crush its pain
'Neath smiling mask—
Self-cruel task!

In vain, in vain—
Hearts cannot feign
When their full swell
Bursts with farewell !
That buried face,
That shrieking phrase,
That dismal chill
As horrors thrill—
All, all confess
A keen distress!
And while thus wildly quakes her woe
    Drum, drum, drum!
    On they go!
    Drum!
And loudly throbs that solemn beat
Of martial lines of measured feet
Down, down the stony street ;
And to every ear and every heart
There throbs a truth, with subtle art,
A truth, the patriot's sacred trust,
That nerves his arm till brought to dust,
" Pledge cordial hand, true heart and all,
United stand ; divided fall !"
    Drum!

                II.

        Drum!
Drum! drum! drum! drum!
        Drum!
    On they come.
Here where the foe in grim array
Await the van to hew and slay,
Theirs the gory way !
    And the horrid yell
    And fearful hell
    Of shot and shell
    Begin the fight
    Of Wrong and Right !
    Hot flame and fire,
    Wild rancor, ire,
    Convulsive breath
    And swifter death !
    Austere endeavor
    Or now or never
    With fiendish will
    To mar and kill !
    God's image, cheap
    In frequent heap,
    Is rent and torn
    And wildly borne
    Piece, piece from piece,
    With hell's caprice !

    Oh ! how shells shiver !
    And torn trunks quiver !

    From lip and breast
    With frightful zest
    The curse and gore
    Their tides outpour ;
    The hands now clutch
    Breasts, that too much
    Of anguish bear—
    As 'twere to tear
    Their pulses out,
    While torrents spout
    Anew—the tone
    'Twixt sigh and moan—
    The dismal fear
    That death is near—
    The mental strife
    'Gainst waning life—
    The sudden bound
    Up from the ground—
    The choking gasp,
    The loosened grasp—
    And the cold eye
    Glares 'gainst the sky !

    Drum ! drum ! drum !
    On they go !
    Blow on, blow !
    Drum !
Yet livelier beat for the devils yield !
God ! in whom we win the field !
Be with us still our arms to wield !
    On they fly,
    Fast they die !
    On, on, on,
    They're gone !
    And the throbbing drum
    Beats far on
    Like the peaceful hum
Of a dim cathedral's holy psalm,
In murmur pure, august and calm,
Full of Earth's meek, prayerful truth,
Rich of Heaven's benignant ruth !
" Pledge cordial hand, true heart and all,
United stand ; divided fall !"
    Drum !

                III.

        Drum !
Drum ! drum ! drum ! drum !
        Drum !
    Back they come !
And slowly throbs the solemn beat
Of martial lines of weary feet
Down, down the stony street !
Slow as a mighty soul it throbs,
Too sore and deep for tears or sobs,
And far too spent by lethal woes
For aught but slow and pond'rous throes !
        Drum !
    On they come !
    And at each door
    Fast throng a score
    Of anxious souls,
    Whom Hope condoles—
    Who forward cast
    Eyes half aghast,
    And though tear-wet
    Still rainbow-set.

    O sore suspense !
    A choking sense
    Of loss, delight,
    Of stars—but night !

Drum! drum!
Ha! here they come;
And now how peer
All, fraught with fear,
With eager signs,
Along the lines!
And crave to trace
Therein the face
Of him they kissed,
And through the mist
Of tears, saw fade
In sombre shade!

Drum! drum!
God! what a shriek!
A poignant beak
Of vulture hath
In mystic wrath
Pierced one poor heart!
Keen with the smart,
She blankly stares
With fickle glares,
Her palm close-pressed
Against her breast,
And dumbly reels!
She knows or feels
Not now the blow
Of death and woe!
Nay, do not wake
Her now, the ache
Of sore regret
She feels not yet.
The awful shock
Hath stunned to rock!
God stay the fang!
God help the pang!

God bless them all!
Who dared to fall
Face to the foe
When blow on blow
In death crushed low,
Yet with a front
No foe could daunt,
Still looked with proud
White face to God!
Laud high their deed—
Crowns are their meed!

Ah! few remain
To tell the pain,
The frenzied strife
And wasted life
Of that red day!
In sad array
They pass along
With silent tongue,
And brows sublime
With scars and grime!

And slowly throbs that solemn beat
Of martial lines of weary feet
Down, down the stony street!
And loud reverb'rant from the ground,
The city's walls exultant sound
The lordly metre, deep and strong,
That proudly wakes the awe-struck throng;
Till on their beats from heart to heart
The truth sublime with subtle art—
"Pledge cordial hands, true hearts and all,
United stand; divided fall!"
    Drum!

REQUIEM.

Requiem Æternam dona iis, Domine!

Give them eternal rest,
  Father, with thee,
On thy paternal breast,
  God of the free!

Dumb is the cannon's throat,
  Broken the brand,
Feebly the pennons float
  O'er the red land;
When, on the battle-field,
By the rude torch revealed,
  Slumber the brave,
Pillowed on foes o'erthrown;
While round them shriek and groan,
Blent with the night-wind's moan,
  Ceaselessly rave.

Them shall the thunder's roar.
Nevermore, nevermore
  Rouse up amain.
Theirs is that olden sleep,
Sacred and golden sleep,
  Free from all pain.
So sleep the dutiful,
Dreamless but beautiful,
  Their duty done;
Sinking in tranquil rest,
As in the purple west
  Sinketh the sun.

Fast closed the fight round them,
Vast rose the night round them,
  Night at noonday—
Night of the sulph'rous smoke,
Glad with the sabre-stroke,
Death-shot and thunder-roar,
Deluge of human gore,
  Dreadfullest fray!
Oh! they fought fearfully,
Bleeding, but cheerfully,
  On for the free,
Dealing their dying blows,
As o'er the flying foes
  Rose victory!

Close up each ghastly wound
  Gaping so wide;
Lift them up from the ground,
  Liberty's pride.
Wrap round each gory form,
  Torn though it be,
The star of the battle-storm,
  Flag of the free!
Calm is their slumber now;
Fame on each bloody brow
  Sits like a star,
Gleaming through death and night,
With a celestial light
  Streaming afar!

Drop no tears vain on them!
There is no stain on them;
  Earth shall now tell
How, glad with life to seal
Freedom and country-weal,
  Nobly they fell,
Leaving a story
  Of valor and doom
Wreathing with glory
  Their brows for the tomb!

Give them eternal rest,
    Father, with thee,
On thy paternal breast,
    God of the free !
Gather those ever thine
In thy fond arms divine,
Who for their country's laws,
God, and old Freedom's cause,
    Battle and fall !
Give them eternal youth,
Life in immortal truth !
    Flash wide o'er all
Their far-splendoring story,
    To stream on sublime—
Their sunshine of glory,
    To hallow all time !

                                    C. A. M.

A MOTHER'S STORY.

BY EUGENE H. MUNDAY.

Amid the throng that gathers where
The mail dispenses joy and care,
I saw a woeful woman stand—
A letter falling from her hand :
She spoke no word, she breathed no sigh ;
Her bloodless cheek, her sad, fixed eye,
And pallid, quivering lips apart,
Showed hopeless grief had seized her heart.
I spoke ; a word of kindness cheers
The heavy heart, and heaven-sent tears
Refresh the eye dry sorrow sears.

"Ah ! sir, my boy ! my brave, bright boy !"
    In broken voice, she said ;
"My only son ! my only joy !
    My brave, bright boy is dead !"

"Sorrow is sacred !" and the eye
That looks on grief is seldom dry :
I listened to her piteous moan,
Then followed to her dwelling lone,
Where, sheltered from the biting cold,
She thus her simple story told :

"My grandfather, sir, for freedom died,
    On Eutaw's bloody plain ;
My father left his youthful bride,
    And fell at Lundy's Lane.

"And when my boy, with burning brow,
    Told of the nation's shame—
How Sumter fell—oh ! how, sir, how
    Could blood like mine be tame !

"I blessed him ; and I bade him go—
    Bade him our honor keep ;
He proudly went to meet the foe ;
    Left me to pray and weep.

"In camp—on march—of picket round—
    He did his equal share ;
And still the call to battle found
    My brave boy always there.

"And when the fleet was all prepared
    To sail upon the main,
He all his comrades' feelings shared—
    But fever scorched his brain !

"He told the general, he would ne'er
    From toil or danger shrink,

But, though the waves he did not fear,
    It chilled his heart to think

"How drear the flowerless grave must be,
    Beneath the ocean's foam,
And that he knew 'twould comfort me
    To have him die at home.

"They tell me that the general's eye
    With tears did overflow :
GOD BLESS THE BRAVE MAN ! with a sigh
    He gave him leave to go.

"Quick down the vessel's side came he ;
    Joy seemed to kill his pain ;
'Comrades !' he cried, 'I yet shall see
    My mother's face again !'

"The boat came bounding o'er the tide ;
    He sprang upon the strand ;
God's will be done ! my bright boy died,
    His furlough in his hand !"

Ye, who this artless story read,
If Pity in your bosoms plead—
    And "Heaven has blessed your store "—
If broken-hearted woman meek,
Can win your sympathy—go, seek
    That childless widow's door !

PHILADELPHIA, February 3, 1862.

A SCOUTING EXPEDITION.

CAMP OF THE ELEVENTH CORPS,
VIRGINIA, June 8, 1863.

Scouting is a very pleasant business if one is fond of
novelty and adventure, and does not mind taking
the chances of the weather and of meeting the enemy
in too great force. I went out on an expedition of
this kind a short time since, and found it quite as
agreeable as I had anticipated. The object of our
foray was not to reconnoitre, but to pick up straggling rebel soldiers and guerrillas, of whom there are
many in the country, not far outside of our lines.
Secesh soldiers get furloughs to visit their friends
in this portion of the State, and many of them are
sent here to glean information regarding our army.
During the day they remain concealed, or play the *rôle*
of peaceful citizens ; but, when night arrives, they
often collect in squads and capture or shoot pickets,
or commit other depredations. Hence expeditions,
such as the one I accompanied, always go out in the
night. Small parties are the best for this purpose, and
ours consisted of four men besides Captain Newcomb
and myself.

The Captain had information that five men of the
Stafford Rangers were in the country, about ten miles
outside of our lines. All of these men had families or
friends in the neighborhood, and were stopping at their
own homes or at those of acquaintances. They were
mostly furloughed men, but were fond of amusing
themselves by getting together and capturing an occasional Yankee picket, for the sake of the spoils, such
as horses, arms, and equipments, which are important
to the ill-supplied rebels, and worth some trouble and
risk to obtain. Indeed, a poorly clad rebel will frequently risk life and liberty with the prospect of capturing a blanket or an overcoat.

We knew the rendezvous of the party we were after
and the residences or stopping-places of most of them.
Some of the same clan had already been captured by
Captain Newcomb. If it should be one of their gather-

ing nights, there was a chance that we might take the whole party together; otherwise, our design was to take the individuals from their abiding-places.

We were piloted by a scout named Hogan, one of those who became so efficient under Sigel's direction—than whom no general in the army appears so well to understand the business and the benefits of scouting. Hogan and all the privates of our party belong to the First Indiana cavalry, a detachment recruited as a body-guard, and which has acted as such under Rosecrans, in Western Virginia, Fremont, Sigel, and is now with General Howard.

Better soldiers than those of this guard do not exist, and their "story" is much more worthy of being told, while it would be more interesting, than that of the Missouri Guard to which Mrs. Fremont devotes a book. It was this guard, with some of the Sixth Ohio cavalry, that, led by Captain Dahlgren, made the famous raid into Fredericksburgh last fall, and which rebels even confess was the most daring feat of the war. The story is worth repeating. Fifty-two men, more than fifty miles from any support, pierced through the enemy's pickets, forded the Rappahannock, and dashed into Fredericksburgh, which was occupied by five hundred rebel cavalry, of whom they killed and wounded a number, and at one time captured one hundred and twenty, bringing off over forty, recrossing the river and returning with a loss of one man killed and one taken prisoner. The rebels were so badly scared that many of them did not pause in their flight until they reached another body of troops several miles below Fredericksburgh.

To return to the narrative of our expedition—which, however, will be found to amount to very little. We started at about four o'clock P.M., and travelled by unfrequented roads and paths through the woods, fording creeks, picking our way among trees and transcending fences in a rather aboriginal style. We did not find our nomadic friends at their rendezvous, and it was necessary to seek for them at their several places of abode. This is a rather unpleasant business for men of humanitarian feelings — as all of our party were — for one does not like to batter at doors in the dead of night, frightening women and children out of their wits when they peep out and behold armed men surrounding their domicil and hear them thundering for admittance. A soldier's duty in such a case is plain, for it will not do to let a house which may conceal a rebel soldier, or perhaps arms and supplies, remain unsearched. When a hastily dressed dame appears with a tallow candle and a supplicating air, her fears must be quieted in the most delicate manner, and if she assumes the indignant and hurls all sorts of epithets at the Yankee barbarians, a little pleasant raillery suffices; but, in either case, the search must be proceeded with. When these people find that they are treated with courtesy, and that all their rights are respected as much as is consistent with military necessities, they soon lay aside the one sort their demeanor of apprehension and the other of railing scorn. In most of these houses will be found supplies of provisions concealed in cellars and garrets, and in some cases arms and munitions of war.

We were not fortunate on this occasion, and it would seem that those we sought had information of our approach. We found but one rebel soldier comfortably sleeping in his bed, and his gun was discovered hid in a closet. Two horses were found in the stable, one of which had evidently been captured, as it was branded "U.S." We reached camp about sunrise the next

morning, having made a circuit of perhaps thirty miles during the night. Such is a scouting expedition, with less than average results.

INTERCEPTED REBEL MAIL.

June 16.—A day or two since Major Wheelan, of the First New-York Mounted Rifles, captured a large rebel mail near the North-Carolina State line, which was destined for Richmond. The greater number of the letters were written in Portsmouth and Norfolk. Many of them referred to the Union forces of the vicinity, and copious clippings from the columns of the Northern papers were included. The mail was delivered to General Peck. One of the letters which has been handed to your correspondent covers fifteen pages of closely written letter paper, and is extremely variegated in sentiment. From grave political questions it diverges into the most common household affairs. A few extracts will not be amiss, and here they are:

"My Dear Boys: The Yankees presume that we rebels have no rights. Even the market-carts and oyster-boats have to hoist the Yankee flag. The Yankees force their way into the houses of respectable citizens, under all sorts of false pretexts, and when they can't get in at the doors they come through the traps on the roof. The old white cow went dry last week, and the rest of the family are very well. Hoping that you are the same, I remain devotedly,

"S——."

Many other letters are as ridiculous as the above few sentences, which are copied from the lengthy epistle.

PETER APPLE, of Oakland, Marion County, was lately recruited for the Eleventh Indiana, and took part in the attempt to storm one of the Vicksburgh batteries. The rebel fire was so destructive that our army recoiled. Apple, the "raw recruit," "didn't see" the backward movement, and kept going ahead until he came right up to one of the rebel guns, caught a gunner by the collar, and brought him within our lines, saying: "Boys, why didn't you come on? Every fellow might have got one."

BALTIMORE, *June* 25, 1863.—Upward of two years ago, in these very streets, the Massachusetts volunteers, while marching to defend the national capital, were assaulted by a mob. To-day, an armed guard patrols every corner and square of the city; and for two whole years a rebellious population have been taught the bitter lesson of loyalty by the threatening guns of Fort McHenry.

Strolling along Eutaw, or any of the principal streets, of an evening, your ear will probably catch, as mine has already, some fragment of conversation like the following: Miss Blank is sitting upon her door-step, musing, with her large, dark eyes fixed absently upon the heavens above her. A gentleman in linen trowsers is directly ahead of you. The shadowy form of the sentry is about disappearing in the ill-lighted street a few yards further on. The gentleman recognizes Miss Blank, and inquires is she enjoying the breeze, or makes some other equally intellectual remark.

"Oh! no," Miss Blank replies in a subdued, melancholy tone, "I had not thought of the breeze; it is delicious; I am waiting for our dear Southern army."

This is the spirit that prevails in Baltimore this month of June, 1863.

Here, as in Alexandria, the streets are barricaded, and the pedestrian is often obliged to leave the sidewalk in his progress through the city. But the barricades are of the shallowest description, and would throw but little obstruction in the path of a resolute enemy. They consist of a number of barrels placed side by side, with beams resting on them. Only yesterday a lady, riding down Lombard street, touched her horse with her riding-whip, and cleared one with a bound. What possible defence could these be against a charge of cavalry?

On the outskirts of the city earth-works are being rapidly constructed, and guns of considerable calibre mounted commanding the Northern and Frederick roads. By order of Lieutenant-Colonel Fish, Provost-Marshal, no person is allowed to visit the fortifications without a proper pass. I must postpone, therefore, going more into detail, until I have had an opportunity of inspecting them.

General Halleck was here yesterday, but returned almost immediately to Washington. There is but little excitement in the city, law and order prevailing, without interruption even of the slightest kind.

N. G. S.

A SEVERE SUFFERER.—An old German gentleman, by the name of George Gerwig, who resides in Braxton County, arrived in this city yesterday, having in charge an insane daughter, en route for the insane asylum at Columbus, Ohio. Mr. Gerwig is seventy-two years of age, and is a thoroughly loyal man. He owns in Braxton County six thousand three hundred acres of land. During the last raid, the rebels robbed him of sixty head of cattle, nine horses, four hundred bushels of dried peaches, a large lot of hay, and, in fact, every thing he had. There is scarcely a good fence upon the farm, and the accumulated wealth of twenty-five years has been destroyed and cast to the winds. He has two sons in the Union army. The boy who was killed by Kuhl and others about a year ago was an adopted son of Mr. Gerwig's. It will be recollected that Kuhl and his companions caught the boy in a field, and cut his head off with a scythe, for which they were court-martialed and hung at Sutton. The daughter whom Mr. Gerwig brings with him lost her reason in consequence of the troubles to which we allude.—Wheeling Intelligencer, June 25.

CHATTANOOGA, Saturday, June 16, 1863.—The week has been characterized by a series of dreary rains which have continued up to this morning. At the present writing it is warm and clear, but lazy-looking clouds still hang heavily in the east, indicating that the "rainy term" is not yet over. The corn never yet promised a more abundant yield, but the wheat in some districts is slightly touched with the rust, produced by the late rains, and there is some difficulty in being able to save the immense crop in East and Middle Tennessee for want of hands to secure the harvest. The flour-mills in East-Tennessee last year principally supplied our whole South-Western army, and it is to be hoped that some means will be afforded to farmers to gather their crops before it is too late to save them.

The Board of Commissioners for this State under the impressment law has fixed the price of shelled corn at two dollars per bushel. This is complained of very much by the farmers, who think it is under the average price, corn in Virginia being fixed at four dollars per bushel. The Commissioners, however, promise to raise the schedule of prices according to circumstances. It would be desirable if the Commissioners in each State would agree on a uniform system of prices, which could be easily done.

The movements of our army toward Murfreesboro indicate that General Bragg is determined that General Rosecrans shall show his hand, and not keep up an appearance of strength under false pretences. We have, therefore, made an advance to feel of the enemy, and already several skirmishes have occurred. A portion of our forces have advanced to within five miles of Murfreesboro, and if Rosecrans will come out of his fortifications, an engagement will take place. But if not, it is supposed General Bragg will not attempt to storm the enemy's works without having learned his strength; in the latter case we may attempt to turn the enemy by a flank movement and gain his rear.

Last Sabbath, the thirty-first ultimo, General Bragg was confirmed in the Episcopal faith by Rev. Bishop Elliott, of Georgia. General Bragg has thus set an example to his army which will not be without its influences. On visiting General Lee's army of Northern Virginia, I was struck with the high moral character which prevailed among the officers and soldiers, as well as the deep religious feeling that pervaded, especially in the lamented General Jackson's corps. It will be a source of congratulation should General Bragg succeed in producing the same beneficial result. There is no occasion for men becoming reckless and demoralized on entering the army, but on the contrary, a different feeling should prevail. ORA.

A THREE DAYS' SCOUT OVER ELK RIDGE MOUNTAIN.

RED HILL, ELK RIDGE, June 29, 1863.

Messrs. Editors Baltimore American:

On Tuesday morning, twenty-second instant, Lieutenant Martindale, accompanied by Lieutenant New and eight men of company H, First New-York cavalry, made a reconnoissance of the enemy's position and progress from the crossing at Sheppard's Ford. The numerous camps that had the previous evening studded the hill-sides from Sharpsburgh back to the Ford, had now disappeared, and nothing was visible under the glass but a few solitary pickets and some four companies of cavalry, but on the road passing through Keedysville toward Boonsboro several horsemen were seen taking their onward course through the rich fair fields of "my Maryland."

Lieutenant Martindale conceived the idea of spoiling their sport, and sent down five or six from his little squad, who, descending on the unfortunate graybacks with that impetuosity which has ever characterized the men of the First New-York cavalry, returned each with a prisoner. Amongst the number was the son of Colonel Miller, of Sharpsburgh, belonging to the Twelfth Virginia cavalry, and a notorious scoundrel called Hill, who has acted as a guide to the invader since they set their feet on our soil. Four more were taken during the same evening, and of this number one was courier to General Lee, who had been returning to him with a message from Ewell.

On Wednesday morning we resumed our old position on Red Hill, which is one of the highest of the

Elk Ridge, overlooking Sharpsburgh and the pleasant village of Keedysville, situated on the Sharpsburgh and Boonsboro pike. Lieutenant Martindale, having learned from citizens the plunder of several stores in Keedysville by the straggling parties of the enemy, resolved to put a stop to it by the capture of some of their number. Accordingly, as soon as he observed them entering the village, he descended with a few of his men on whom he knew, from past experience, he could rely, and invariably returned with captives. We thus took four of the Seventh Virginia cavalry, horses, arms, and equipments, including an officer, who seemed grieved as the prospect of a rich harvest of plunder was suddenly taken from his view.

Soon after, four of our men descended, and directed their attention to a party, consisting of five or six, who, by their uniforms, looked like officers. This party was General Wright and staff, belonging to A. P. Hill's corps. They wheeled round, however, and our boys gave chase, and succeeded in capturing Lieutenant Wright, (the General's son and aid,) wounding one of the horses, and probably some more of the party. The General, having a fast horse, escaped with the loss of his hat, which is preserved as a memento of the chase after a live general. Five or six more were captured afterward.

Yesterday morning, about seven o'clock A.M., we were again on the lookout. Now we see more crossing the ford—looks at first like a brigade, but lengthens evidently into a division, and about noon was certainly a corps, supposed, from the report of prisoners, to be Longstreet's. It stretched — artillery, cavalry, infantry, and wagon-train—over a line of four miles, and as the last of their train disappears beyond the Dunkers church, where fell the gallant Mansfield, and where Hooker showed his bold front to the enemy last fall, another column appeared, coming from the river. Our captures to-day amounted to some twenty rebels and two sutler's wagons. We took infantrymen belonging to Eighth Florida, Sixteenth Mississippi, Third and Sixteenth Virginia. Thus you see, Messrs. Editors, we are getting along pretty well. I forward you these particulars as an eye-witness and participator in the honor of most of the captures. The line of the enemy's march for the last two days has been in the direction of Hagerstown. The previous days they had passed through Boonsboro and some toward Frederick, but since the main body has been moving on to Hagerstown—where next, heaven knows! unless we meet and repel the invader from our soil. This is no time for fireside talk on the probabilities of this grand raid. Now is no time for delay. Let us meet them when and where they be found, and teach them once for all the lesson that Maryland and Pennsylvania have no sympathies with their ruthless invaders.

Yours, as ever,   C. C.

INCIDENTS AT PORT HUDSON. — An officer with Banks's army relates, in a private letter, an incident which occurred during a temporary truce at Port Hudson on the twenty-seventh of May. He availed himself of the opportunity this afforded to ride up to the rebel works as close as he could, to get a good view of them, when he saw a regiment of the enemy throw down their arms, and heard them give three cheers and exclaim: "We surrender." The rebel officers at once approached them, and, with drawn swords and pistols, overpowered and controlled them, and compelled them to take up their arms and resume their position.

The same officer, at a truce entered into the next day for the purpose of looking after the dead and wounded, while riding as near to the rebel lines as he could get, was hailed by a confederate officer within the works with the question, whether he did not think, upon reflection, that he was coming nearer than was exactly proper. Our officer replied in the negative, saying that he had men wounded and killed as near the enemy as he himself then was. A conversation then ensued, in which the rebel officer spoke of Sherman's charge of the preceding day, and remarked that: "Inside they regarded it as the finest thing of the war." Our officer did not belong to Sherman's division.

PROPOSITION TO HANG THE DUTCH SOLDIERS.—*June 12.*—Of late, in all battles and in all recent incursions made by Federal cavalry, we have found the great mass of Northern soldiers to consist of Dutchmen. The plundering thieves captured by Forrest, who stole half the jewelry and watches in a dozen counties of Alabama, were immaculate Dutchmen. The national odor of Dutchmen, as distinctive of the race as that which, constantly ascending to heaven, has distended the nostrils of the negro, is as unmistakable as that peculiar to a pole-cat, an old pipe, or a lager-bier saloon. Crimes, thefts, and insults to the women of the South invariably mark the course of these stinking bodies of animated *sour-krout.* Rosecrans himself is an unmixed Dutchman—an accursed race which has overrun the vast districts of the country of the North-West. It happens that we entertain a greater degree of respect for an Ethiopian in the ranks of the Northern armies than for an odoriferous Dutchman, who can have no possible interest in this revolution. . . .

Why not hang every Dutchman captured? We will hereafter hang, or shoot, or imprison for life all white men taken in command of negroes, and enslave the negroes themselves. This is not too harsh. No human being will assert the contrary. Why, then, should we not hang a Dutchman, who deserves infinitely less of our sympathy than, Sambo? The live masses of beer, krout, tobacco, and rotten cheese, which, on two legs and four, on foot and mounted, go prowling through the South, should be used to manure the sandy plains and barren hill-sides of Alabama, Tennessee, and Georgia. . . . Whenever a Dutch regiment adorns the limbs of a Southern forest, daring cavalry raids into the South shall cease. . . . President Davis need not be specially consulted, and if an accident of this sort should occur to a plundering band like that captured by Forrest, we are not inclined to believe that our President would be greatly disgruntled.—*Knoxville Register.*

SONGS OF THE REBELS.

THE FLORIDA'S CRUISE.

BY A FORETOP MAN OF THE C. S. S. FLORIDA.

AIR—*Red, White, and Blue,* (Southern edition.)

One evening, off Mobile, the Yanks they all knew,
That the wind from the north'ard most bitterly blew;
They also all knew, and they thought they were sure,
They'd blocked in the Florida safe and secure.
   Huzza! huzza! for the Florida's crew!
     We'll range with bold Maffit the world through
      and through.

Nine cruisers they had, and they lay off the bar,
Their long line to seaward extending so far;
And Preble, he said, as he shut his eyes tight:
"I'm sure they're all hammocked this bitter cold night."

Bold Maffit commanded—a man of great fame,
He sailed in the Dolphin—you've heard of the same;
He called us all aft, and these words he did say:
"I'm bound to run out, boys; up anchor, away!"

Our hull was well whitewashed, our sails were all stowed,
Our steam was chock up, and the fresh wind it blowed;
As we crawled along by them, the Yanks gave a shout—
We dropped all our canvas, and opened her out.

You'd have thought them all mad if you'd heard the cursed racket
They made upon seeing our flash little packet;
Their boatswains did pipe, and the blue lights did play,
And the great Drummond light, it turned night into day.

The Cuyler, a boat that's unrivalled for speed,
Quick let slip her cables, and quickly indeed
She thought for to catch us, and keep us in play,
Till her larger companions could get under way.

She chased and she chased, till at dawning of day
From her backers she thought she was too far away;
So she gave up the chase, and reported, no doubt,
That she'd sunk us and burnt us—somewhere thereabout.

So when we were out, boys, all on the salt sea,
We brought the Estelle to, right under our lee,
And burnt her and sunk her, with all her fine gear,
And straight sailed for Havana the bold privateer.

'Twas there we recruited, and took in some stores,
Then kissed the senoras, and sailed from their shores;
And on leaving their waters, by way of a joke,
With two Yankee brigs, boys, we made a great smoke.

Our hull was well washed with the limestone so white,
Which sailors all know is not quite Christianlike;
So to paint her all ship-shape we went to Green Keys,
Where the Sonoma came foaming, the rebel to seize.

We put on all sail and up steam right away,
And for forty-eight hours she made us some play;
When our coal being dusty and choking the flue,
Our steam it slacked down, and nearer she drew.

"Oh! ho!" cried our captain, "I see what's your game!
Clear away the stern-pivot, the Bulldog by name,
And two smaller dogs to keep *him* companie,
For very sharp teeth have these dogs of the sea."

The Sonoma came up until nearly in range,
When her engines gave out!—now wasn't that strange?
—I don't know the truth, but it's my firm belief,
She didn't like the looks of the Florida's teeth.

She gave up the chase, and returned to Key West,
And told her flag-captain that she'd done her best;
But the story went round, and it grew rather strong,
And the public acknowledged that something was wrong.

We went on a cruising, and soon did espy
A fine lofty clipper, bound home from Shanghai;
We burnt her and sunk her in the midst of the sea,
And drank to old Jeff in the best of Bohea!

We next found a ship with a Quakerish name—
A wolf in sheep's clothing oft plays a deep game;
For the hold of that beautiful, mild, peaceful Star
Was full of saltpetre, to make powder for war.

Of course the best nature could never stand that—
Saltpetre for Boston's a little too fat;
So we burnt her and sunk her, she made a great blaze,
She's a star now gone down, and we've put out her rays.

We next took a schooner well laden with bread—
What the devil got into old Uncle Abe's head?
To send us such biscuit is such a fine thing,
It sets us all laughing, as we sit and sing.

We next took the Lapwing — right stuff in her hold,
And that was black diamonds, that people call coal;
With that in our bunkers, we'll tell Uncle Sam,
That *we* think his gunboats are not worth a damn.

The Mary Jane Colcord to Capetown was bound,
We bade her heave to, though, and swing her yards round;
And to Davy Jones's locker, without more delay,
We sent her afire, and so sailed on our way.
    Huzza! huzza! for the Florida's crew!
    We'll range with bold Maffit the world through and through.

GENERAL BUTLER.

A REBEL SONG.

Butler and I went out from camp,
    At Bethel to make battle,
And then the Southrons whipt us back,
    Just like a drove of cattle.
        Come, throw your swords and muskets down,
            You do not find them handy,
        Although the Yankees cannot fight,
            At running they're the dandy.

And then we got a monster gun,
    Which gives us satisfaction,
For seven miles are just the space
    That Yankees like in action.
        Come, throw your swords, etc.

Whenever we go out to fight
    The Southrons give us lickings,
But then we strive to get revenge
    By stealing all their chickens.
        Come, throw your swords, etc.

Old Butler stays in Fort Monroe,
   And listens to the firing,
And when his men have met defeat
   He then goes out inquiring.
     Come, throw your swords. etc.

To say that Butler will not fight
   Is certainly no scandal,
For not a trophy he has gained
   Except an old pump-handle,
     Come, throw your swords, etc.

WAR SONG OF THE MACON LIGHT DRA-GOONS.*

To horse! To horse! The standard flies!
   The bugles sound the call!
Your glittering sabres quickly seize;
The voice of battle's on the breeze;
   Arouse ye! one and all!

From Georgia's fertile plains we come,
   A band of brothers true;
Our casques the leopard's spoil surround,
Our neighing chargers paw the ground,
   We boast the red and blue.

And shall we bend the stubborn head,
   In Freedom's temple born?
Dress our pale cheeks in timid smile,
To hail a master in our Isle,
   Or brook a victor's scorn?

No! though destruction o'er the land
   Come pouring as a flood,
The sun that sees our falling day
Shall mark our sabres' deadly sway,
   And set that night in blood!

For gold let Scott's dull regions fight,
   Or plunder's bloody gain,
Unbribed, unbought, our swords we draw
To guard our country and our law,
   Nor shall their edge be vain.

And now, while breath of Northern gale
   Still fans the tri-color,
And footsteps of invader rude,
With rapine foul and red with blood,
   Pollute the happy shore.

Farewell, dear friends, and farewell homes,
   Adieu each tender tie,
Resolved, we mingle in the tide,
Where charging squadrons furious ride
   To conquer or to die!

To horse! To horse! Our sabres gleam,
   High sounds the bugle's call,
Combined with honor's sacred tie,
Our word is law and liberty—
   March forward, one and all!

ILLNESS OF THE EAGLE.

   The Eagle was sick.
He'd had too much physic of Abolition;
The blood in his veins was hot and thick,
The Eagle's pulse was fevered and quick,
   He was in a sad condition.

* See Poetry and Incidents, page 7, Vol. III. REBELLION RECORD.

They called a doctor to cure the bird:
   There came with the doctor General Scott.
The voice of Sir Fuss and Feathers was heard—
He could not set by without saying a word,
As the ire of the gallant old soldier was stirred!
   He proposed that the bird be shot.

Loud rose the voice of Greeley and Seward!
   Many their words—we're sorry to lose them—
They told how the Eagle might be cured,
Like a Duffield ham—and his life insured.
Raymond and Bennett added a word,
   And they hid him in Abraham's bosom.

Poor old Eagle, of Stars and Stripes,
   There was a nest for you, I said;
At the very thought my eyes I wipe,
Your talons I see take a firmer gripe.
The stars fade away, but you feel the stripe—
   Poor Eagle hangs down his head.

Better the fate proposed by Scott;
   Perhaps not better, but full as well;
Rather than live, so I would be shot,
Picked of my feathers, boiled in a pot;
Rather would list to my funeral knell,
   Be dead and be buried and go to — well,

Send me to climes where orange trees bloom,
   There let me rest my wearied head,
Fan my feathers with sweet perfume;
Let music of honest contentment come,
With manly hearts I find my home,
   And sleep in their shade when dead.

Bird of the broad and sweeping wing,
   They have swept your nest with a dirty broom,
Tarnished your glorious covering;
From Tammany Hall I hear them sing,
Weed and Morgan and Governor King,
Vanderbilt, Law, Beecher, and Tyng—
   Priest and pirate, together they come.

Arise, proud Eagle! thy bird of fame!
   Phœnix-like soar from thy burning nest;
Not wrong nor oppression thy spirit can tame,
   Or drive away truth from thy noble breast.
Come, proud Eagle! our old bird, come!
And live in an honest Southern home.
             CHARLES DULLNESS.
ST. CHARLES HOTEL, NEW-ORLEANS, May 10, 1861.

INFLAMMATORY PLACARDS.

NEW-YORK, *July 3.*—During this afternoon the following inflammatory placard was posted about the city and hung up in conspicuous positions in some of the hotels:

ATTENTION! MAJOR-GENERAL HALLECK: The people of the North, West, and East, who are numbered by millions, and who are firm friends of the Administration and Government, have been for months ardently wishing, hoping, praying, and expecting to see some signs of energy and capacity in their rulers, corresponding to the magnitude of the danger that threatens our glorious institutions. They have been disappointed. Being true patriots and idolizing their Government, they have believed the President, his Cabinet, and our generals were animated with the same burning patriotic desires. They have been astonished at the delay of the draft and the death-like torpor that seems to pervade the Administration. They formerly had implicit faith, especially in the patriotism of Secretary Stanton and President Lincoln. The people begin to inquire, to fear, and are perplexed. They suspect you, General Halleck, of imbecility, or something worse. They know that you are the Commander-in-Chief, and hold you responsible. Answer these questions if you can. Two immense armies have been confronting each other for months on the Rappahannock — preparing for a decisive struggle — a struggle which was, perhaps, to decide the fate of a great nation—a mighty empire—to determine whether a free Government could sustain itself. Did you do your whole duty upon that momentous occasion ? The people say, No, no. "Why in hell" did you not have the troops about Washington within striking distance ? Why were you not on the spot to support the brave General Sedgwick and his gallant troops when they carried the fortifications on the heights of Fredericksburgh ? With the assistance of Heintzelman's army thrown in at the right moment, the whole rebel army could have been completely annihilated and the nation saved from disgrace and humiliation. Instead of this, the rebel army is now invading and desolating the loyal and free States. If you had been equal to your duty and the occasion, the troops at Suffolk, Fortress Monroe, Norfolk, Baltimore, etc., etc., would have been on board of swift steamers — ready before the battle commenced—to have been concentrated and launched at the enemy like thunderbolts from avenging heaven. A few more such fatal mistakes as you made on that occasion and our Government is lost and will break up in anarchy. This is so. Our nation is in or at another fearful crisis. The audacious General Lee, having faith in your imbecility, has boldly invaded one of our most populous States. What are you doing ? The people fear you will do as before, and they call upon Abraham Lincoln, Salmon P. Chase, William H. Seward, Edwin M. Stanton, and ask what are you doing ? If you repose supinely as heretofore in your chair of office, and let Lee proceed, you ought to be damned, and you will certainly be damned, and you will be of that class whose sins go to judgment beforehand. The great and free people of the North, East, and West will not stand this humbugging any longer ! You must conquer Lee or resign ! Do you hear this ? The people have given you all the guns, ammunition, ships, and money that you can use. They expect and require that you will concentrate all the troops within five hundred miles of Lee's army within the next ten days (as you easily can) and plunge them at Lee on a given day, and the work is done. Unless you do this, you and the nation are undone. P. S.— If you had hung Vallandigham (as you ought to have done) and sent him to be Governor of the copperheads in the infernal regions, you would not have been troubled by the traitorous, cowardly, miserable sneaks and poltroons, who are boring you about him ; and who, when they visit Washington, should be impressed into the service of the Government, which they are endeavoring to overthrow—and all the people would say, Amen !

ONE OF THE PEOPLE.

NEW-YORK, June 30, 1863.

THE SOUTHERN DECLARATION OF INDEPENDENCE.

When, in the course of events, our plans were fully matured, and our determination to overthrow the Government had reached its culminating point—when we were ready to invoke foreign aid, and ask the recognition of our nationality, to which the institution of slavery and our hatred of freedom entitled us, a respect for ourselves would seem to require us to declare the causes which led us to desire a separation from the Northern people.

We hold these truths to be undeniable, that some men are born to command, and are possessed of certain inherent rights; that among these are, power, dominion, and the spread of slavery; that to secure those rights a form of government is instituted among us, deriving its only power from those who govern ; that whenever the people will not allow us to hold the reins of government, and absorb the funds of the treasury, to our own benefit, and for our own aggrandizement, we have the right to seize the Capital, overthrow the Government, and drench the land with blood. Prudence has caused us to wait till we got a good chance to accomplish our ends. But when at last an Administration was in power, which was completely at our control, and the people, by electing his successor, gave us to understand that our sceptre would depart, and the spoils of office would no more help to rivet the chains on those we could no longer control, the history of their forbearance and devotion has no parallel in any age or country. Let facts be submitted to a candid world.

They have for a long series of years submitted to our dictation.

They have not complained when the General Government was carrying our mails at an expense of some millions of dollars, in excess of receipts, in the Post-Office Department.

They have many times refused to give audience in some parts of the country, and sometimes maltreated abolition lecturers.

They have on several occasions furnished men and money to fight the battles of the country.

They have acquiesced in the purchase, by the General Government, of Louisiana and Florida for our benefit.

They sanctioned the annexation of Texas, by electing James K. Polk on that issue, thereby adding extensively to our domains.

They have accorded to us the right to hang John Brown and his abettors, when he frightened us almost out of our senses, by his raid upon our cherished and much-admired institution in the Old Dominion.

They have never insisted upon Congress passing laws for the abolition of slavery in the States, but they have prevented us from extending it into all the territories ; denying that the Constitution guarantees to us the right to do so.

They have insisted upon their right to denounce slavery.

They have protested against abridging the right of franchise, and establishing a censorship over the press.

They have contended for the right of free speech, and free and liberal education.

They have at last succeeded in electing a President upon these principles, thereby endangering the stability of our institutions, and depriving us of the power of ruling at will.

In every stage of these proceedings we have resisted.

We have labored to prove to them that slavery was better than freedom — that ignorance among the masses was better for us than a system of general education.

We have warned them from time to time of the danger of free institutions, and their attempts to enlighten all, without our consent.

We have reminded them of the circumstances of our emigration and settlement in the territories.

We have appealed to them to refrain from assisting free emigration from free States.

We have sought to gain the ascendency by inducing them to 'remain in *statu quo*, but they have been deaf to the voice of our dictation. We must, therefore, resort to arms, and hold them as enemies, until they are willing to acknowledge our pretensions as a superior race.

We, therefore, the self-constituted rulers of the Southern people, at Montgomery assembled, appealing to King Cotton, and relying upon the protection of masked batteries, and the ardor of our soldiers, declare that they are absolved from their allegiance to the General Government; and that these States are, and of right ought to be, wholly and solely devoted to slavery. And in support of these pretensions, we pledge ourselves to stand whan we can, and run when we must, to save our lives and our ammunition.

FREEDONIA.

SPEECH OF GEN. PEMBERTON AT BROOKHAVEN, MISS., JUNE, 1863.

SOLDIERS: In assuming the command of so brave and intelligent an army as that to which President Davis has assigned me, I desire at once to win your confidence by frankly declaring that I am a Northern man by birth; but I have married, raised children, and own negroes in the South, and as such shall never consent to see my daughters eating at the same table or intermarrying with the black race, as the Northern teachers of equality would have them. I take command of you as a soldier, who will not fear to lead where any brave man can follow—I am no *street scavenger*—no General Lovell. (Cheers.) If any soldier in this command is aggrieved, or shall feel himself aggrieved by any act of his superior officer, he must have no hesitation in applying to me personally for redress. The doors of my headquarters shall never be closed against the poorest and humblest soldier in my command. Come to me, if you suffer wrong, as fearlessly as you would charge the enemy's battery, and no orderly shall turn you off, or tell you, as has been too much the case in our army, that the General cannot see nor hear the complaints of his soldiers. (Applause.) In regard to the question of interference by Europe, we want no interference in our private quarrel. (Great applause.) We must settle the question ourselves, or fail entirely. The moment England interferes she will find us a united people, and she will have *to meet with the armies of the South as well as of the North*. (Cheers, and cries of "Yes, yes, yes," from every quarter; "No interference," "Let us settle it between us.") I am glad to see you thus united on this question; and, with a reliance on ourselves, and a firm trust in the God of battles, in a few days your General will again fling your banners to the breeze, and march forward to retrieve the recent disasters we have suffered in this department.

The General was loudly cheered as he closed his address to the troops, who appeared to be quite satisfied with their new commander. It is worthy of note that the two principal Generals in the rebel army immediately in our vicinity, on the east bank of the Mississippi, are Northern men, and, we believe, from Massachusetts—Pemberton and Ruggles. It is also worthy of note that the dislike of England is quite as strong in the rebel army as in the ranks of the defenders of the Union.

In the Third Wisconsin regiment it is a rule that no soldier can leave camp without a pass. The chaplain one day distributed tracts; among them was one headed: "Come, Sinner, Come!" Soon afterward, the tract was picked up in the camp, and under the heading was pencilled: "Can't do it; Colonel Rogers won't sign any pass!"

NEW-YORK, *July* 13.—About two years ago, Mrs. Mary Seizgle left this city for the seat of war, with the Forty-first regiment New-York volunteers, of which her husband was a member. She returned on Saturday night last, dressed in a soldier's uniform. The police took her into custody under the act which forbids a woman to walk the streets in male apparel. She was taken to the Twenty-seventh Precinct station-house, where it was satisfactorily shown that she had lost all of her clothing in the late battles of Gettysburgh, and that she had no other alternative but to put on a soldier's uniform. It further appeared that during her two years' absence she has rendered herself very useful as hospital nurse. She was sent to the residence of her husband's brother, No. 8 Spring street.

A CONSCRIPT'S EPISTLE TO JEFF DAVIS.—The following quaint epistle was furnished for publication by a member of the Mounted Rifles, who picked it up in a deserted rebel camp on the Chowan River, about thirty miles from Winton, while out on a scouting expedition.

The letter was addressed in this wise:

Read, if you want to, you thieving scalp-hunter, whoever you are, and forward, post-paid, to the lord high chancellor of the devil's exchequer (?) on earth,

JEFF DAVIS,

Richmond, Va.

HEADQUARTERS "SCALP HUNTERS," }
CAMP CHOWAN, N. C., January 11. {

Excellency Davis:

It is with feelings of undeveloped pleasure that an affectionate conscript intrusts this sheet of confiscated paper to the tender mercies of a confederate States mail-carrier, addressed, as it shall be to yourself, O Jeff, Red Jacket of the Gulf and Chief of the Six Nations—more or less. He writes on the stump of a shivered monarch of the forest, with the "pine trees wailing round him," and "Endymion's planet rising on the air." To you, O Czar of all Chivalry and Khan of Cotton Tartary! he appeals for the privilege of seeking, on his own hook, a land less free—a home among the hyenas of the North. Will you not halt your "brave columns" and stay your gorgeous career for a thin space? and while an admiring world takes a brief gaze at your glorious and God-forsaken cause, pen for the happy conscript a furlough without end? Do so, and mail it, if you please, to that city the windy, wandering Wigfall didn't winter in, called for short Philadelphia.

The Etesian winds sweeping down the defiles of the Old Dominion and over the swamps of Suffolk come moaning through the pines of the Old State laden with the music and sigh themselves away into sweet sounds of silence to the far-off South. Your happy conscript would go to the far-away North whence the wind comes, and leave you to reap the whirlwind, with no one but your father the devil to rake and bind after you. And he's going.

It is with intense and multifariously proud satisfaction that he gazes for the last time upon our holy flag

—that symbol and sign of an adored trinity—cotton, niggers, and chivalry. He still sees it in the little camp on the Chowan, tied to the peak of its palmetto pole, and floating out over our boundless confederacy, the revived relic of ages gone, banner of our king of few days and full of trouble. And that pole in its tapering uprightness typifying some of the grandest beauties of our nationality; its peak pointing hopefully toward the tropical stars, and its biggest end — run into the ground. Relic and pole, good-by. 'Tis best the conscript goes; *his* claim to chivalry has gone before him. Behind he leaves the legitimate chivalry of this unbounded nation centred in the illegitimate son of a Kentucky horse-thief.

But a few more words, illustrious President, and he is done—done gone.

Elevated by their sufferings and suffrages to the highest office in the gift of a great and exceeding free people, you have held your position without a change of base, or purpose of *any* sort, through weary months of war, and want, and woe; and though every conscript would unite with the thousands of loyal and true men in the South in a grand old grief at your downfall, so too will they sink under the calamity of an exquisite joy when you shall have reached that eminent meridian whence all progress is perpendicular.

And now, bastard President of a political abortion, farewell.

"Scalp-hunters," relic, pole, and chivalrous confederates in crime, good-by. Except it be in the army of the Union, you will not again see the conscript. NORM. HARROLD,
of Ashe County, N. C.

COLORED SOLDIERS AT PORT HUDSON.

PORT HUDSON, LA., June 24, 1863.
NORTHERN papers have come to hand giving accounts of the fight at Port Hudson on May twenty-seventh, and the part the negro regiments took in it. The description given in the *Times* of the thirteenth of June is in the main correct. The correspondent of that journal should have stated that some of the line officers of the First Native Guards are colored, instead of saying the field officers are black—the officers composing the field and staff are all white. The *Tribune* has a few paragraphs about the colored troops in its issue of June eleventh, but they are as far from being correct as the following, which for the sake of comment are extracted from the the *New-York Express*:

"CONDUCT OF THE NEGRO TROOPS.—While an occasional shot was being fired, before the battle commenced in its more deadly fury, speculations were rife as to the manner in which the Second Louisiana black troops would act during the conflict. They had been placed in the rear, with white troops leading them. General Banks, however, in order to test their military capacity, ordered them to the front. The negroes at once rushed to the assigned point, and in the midst of the battle they proceeded to storm the rebel position opposite to them. They rushed in a body over the parapets and siege-guns, and reached the interior of the fort, in despite of the opposition of a large number of rebels. The presence of the black soldiers inside, not less than the probability that the pass they had made into the stronghold, seemed to create a spirit of fury in the enemy. They left their guns at all points, and rushed to the quarter where the negroes had prepared to make a vigorous struggle. The whites and blacks in a moment had a hand-to-hand conflict unprecedented for its ferocity.

"The negroes in the conflict were soon disarmed, and in defending themselves they rapidly used the weapons of savage humanity. In every position in which the struggle placed them, they fought with their teeth, biting their assailants in every available part of the body, kicking and scratching them. Soon, however, they had to succumb; the bayonet, the trigger, the revolver, and merciless hands on their throats, doing the work for them with fearful fatality. It may be here noted, as a key perhaps to other battles, that the presence of the black troops made the rebels in the fort almost as ferocious as the blacks. In the attack, the enemy did not content himself in wounding the Africans; *of eight hundred, six hundred were at once killed;* when one was wounded, the assault was repeated till he died. Finding themselves thus overpowered, about two hundred of the negro troops rushed to the siege-guns, jumped headlong over the walls, and were saved."

Now to show how utterly false in every particular the statements of the correspondent of the *Express* are, I will say that the "Second Louisiana black troops" are on Ship Island, and their commander, Colonel Daniels, is or has recently been in New-Orleans under arrest. The Second regiment Louisiana Native Guards has never been near Port Hudson. The colored regiments in the fight spoken of were the First and Third regiments Native Guards, (the name of the organization has been changed, and these regiments are, by an order of General Banks issued since the fight, now called the First and Third infantry U. S. volunteers, Corps d'Afrique.) The colored soldiers were never placed in "the rear with white troops leading them." No soldiers, white or black, "rushed in a body over the parapets and siege-guns, and reached the interior of the fort." It is not true that they (the colored soldiers) "fought with their teeth"—"kicking and scratching."

To show that the correspondent of the *Express* was not present, and that he was ignorant of the actual facts, I will only add that the First regiment went into the fight with a few men short of five hundred. Of this number thirty-one are known to be killed, ninety missing, and one hundred and fifty wounded, most of them severely. The loss of the Third regiment was quite small, as it was not much exposed to the enemy's fire. The loss of both regiments is much smaller than it otherwise would have been, had they not been sheltered by the woods. From the time these colored regiments began to enlist men, last August, till the present, the Northern press has misrepresented the organization and the ability of colored men to become soldiers. No one who has been conversant with either of the four regiments composing the Native Guards, so far as I know, has ever lifted a pen to defend them from the malicious attacks that have been made upon them by many officers in this department, as well as the copperhead press of the North.

The colored soldiers have said from the first: "Let us go into the field, and by the use of arms prove that we are men, and that we are worthy to fight for the flag under which we were born!" Every man of them is a patriot. He does not count the number of days to the end of his enlistment. He has no sympathy with his former oppressor; he feels an honest pride in being a soldier, and has no desire to return to slavery. Any one can imagine the joy of the colored soldiers, after months of drudgery, building forts, repairing bridges, cleansing sinks for white regiments, carrying baggage for white officers, and all sorts of dirty work, when the command was given for them to leave Baton

Rouge and march to Port Hudson. The regiment (the First) broke out in cheers for General Butler and Colonel Stafford, and marched off singing the song, "John Brown."

The correspondent of the *Times* has told how these colored soldiers fought on the twenty-seventh, and I need not repeat the story here. The unflinching courage shown on that day has been exhibited nearly every day since, for they have had frequent skirmishes with the rebels, and in every instance the latter have been driven back with loss. Only last week one company of the First regiment charged upon a ridge where there was a company of rebels in a rifle-pit who had annoyed our soldiers very much. The rebels were put to flight and driven into their works, with a loss of two killed, and two or three wounded ; our loss was the same. The rebels left behind them their supper, canteens, blankets, etc. Our boys were much joyed with their success ; and it may be added that they have been constantly advancing on the rebel works, and have *never given up an inch of ground that they have once gained.* All honor to our brave colored soldiers !

General Banks has spoken in the highest terms of the fighting qualities of the negro soldiers, and it is probable that they will no longer be kept in the background for want of his confidence.

The unflinching courage of the black soldier, as displayed at Port Hudson, shows that we may depend upon him to do his part in the present contest.

The siege is progressing favorably, and will soon end in success to our arms.　　　　J. T. PAINE,
Surgeon-in-charge First and Third Infantry,
U. S. Volunteers, Corps d'Afrique.

A LETTER FROM PRESIDENT LINCOLN.

At the commencement of the rebellion Melancthon Smith was postmaster of the town of Rockford, Illinois, and his wife was acting as deputy-postmaster. Feeling it his duty to participate in the struggle, Mr. Smith raised a regiment, of which he was appointed Colonel, and entered service under General Grant, leaving Mrs. Smith to attend to the duties of the post-office. Colonel Smith distinguished himself on several occasions, and at the recent storming of the first redoubt at Vicksburgh, led the forlorn hope, and was shot through the head and killed. Application was then made for the appointment as postmaster of a gentleman who, under ordinary circumstances, would have been a proper person to fill the office. Counter applications to retain the widow were also sent in. The matter was brought before the President ; he indorsed the application for the widow, and afterward sent a letter to the Postmaster-General, of which the following is a copy :

EXECUTIVE MANSION, WASHINGTON, July 24, 1863.
Hon. Postmaster-General :

SIR : Yesterday little indorsements of mine went to you in two cases of postmasterships sought for widows whose husbands have fallen in the battles of this war. These cases occurring on the same day, brought me to reflect more attentively than I had before done as to what is fairly due from us here in the dispensing of patronage toward the men who, by fighting our battles, bear the chief burden of saving our country. My conclusion is, that other claims and qualifications being equal, they have the better right, and this is especially applicable to the disabled soldier and the deceased soldier's family.　　Your obedient servant,
　　　　　　　　　　A. LINCOLN.

WALTER S. NEWHALL.

OB. DECEMBER 18, ÆT. 22.

CAPTAIN WALTER S. NEWHALL, of Philadelphia, Acting Adjutant-General upon the staff of General Gregg, was lately drowned in a tributary of the Rappahanock. He was one of the earliest volunteers in the war, leaving all to serve his country. First distinguished in the famous charge of Zagonyi at Springfield in Missouri, he was afterward engaged in the most active and dangerous service ; and, always a hero, he never disappointed the fond faith of the hearts that loved him. He leaves two brothers in the service ; and at the time of Lee's invasion last summer we believe that his parents had five or six sons on active military duty. The following lines, by a mother whose son had been in Captain Newhall's company, have a truly lyrical fervor.

Not 'mid the cannon's roar,
Not 'mid red fields of gore,
When the fierce fight was o'er,
　His young life parted ;
But low beneath the wave,
No hand outstretched to save,
As in a hallowed grave
　Slept the true-hearted.

All seamed with noble scars
Won in his country's wars,
Battling 'neath Stripes and Stars
　For his land's glory.
One of a dauntless race,
Who each in foremost place
Still strive the foe to face,
　Here ends his story.

Stern was the strife and brief—
Death came with quick relief—
While watched each glorious chief
　Who went before him.
The waiting angel stood
Calm by the turbid flood,
And to that brotherhood
　Gently he bore him.

Once, in Rome's elder day
(So her old legends say,)
Across the Sacred Way,
　Wrath's fearful token,
Earth opened wide her breast ;
Nor might the land find rest
Till of her wealth the best
　There should lie broken.

Vainly poured gold and gem,
Rich robe with broidered hem,
Sceptre and diadem—
　Wealth's hoards uncoffered.
Wide yawned the gulf apart,
Till one brave Roman heart
Plunged in with shield and dart—
　Life freely offered.

Lord, in our hour of woe,
In our land's breach we throw
Riches whose treasures flow
　In streams unfailing :
Widows' and orphans' tears,
Sad days and nightly fears,
Long-garnered hopes of years—
　All unavailing.

Yes, purer offerings still—
Meek faith and chastened will,
All that, through good and ill,
　Thy mercy gave us :

Honor, and love, and truth,
Bright joys and dreams of youth,
Thou, Lord, in pitying ruth,
　Oh! let them save us!

Hear! for our cause is just
Hear! for our children's dust—
God of our fathers' trust,
　Bring thy salvation!
Hasten, O Lord! the day;
Point thou through clouds our way,
And by Truth's steadfast ray
　Lead home thy nation!

CHRISTMAS, 1863.

OPENING OF THE MISSISSIPPI.

Hail, Father of Waters! again thou art free!
And miscreant treason hath vainly enchained thee;
Roll on, mighty river, and bear to the sea
The praises of those who so gallantly gained thee!
　From fountain to ocean, from source to the sea,
　The west is exulting: "Our River is free."

Fit emblem of Freedom! thy home is the North!
And thou wert not forgot by the mother that bore thee;
From snows everlasting thou chainless burst forth,
And chainless we solemnly swore to restore thee!
　O'er river and prairie, o'er mountain and lea,
　The North is exulting: "Our River is free!"

'Twas midnight—in secret the traitor conclave
Had sworn: "We will throw off the bonds that unite us:
Our king shall be cotton, our watchword be slave!"
What ghostly intruder hath come to affright us!
　"I'm the god of the river, from source to the sea,
　I bear proudly onward the flag of the free!"

"Accursed is your treason—no power can break
The bond with which God hath united the nation,
And, thrice perjured ingrates, well may ye quake
At the certain approach of your dark condemnation!
　So long as my waters flow south to the sea
　Shall the flag of the Union float over the free!"

Glad River, thy bosom doth gratefully swell
Toward the heroes who bravely have fought to regain
　　thee,
And proudly thou bearest them onward where dwell
Their comrades, who, crescent crowned, fight to re-
　　tain thee!
　But hark! what echo comes over the sea?
　'Tis the Nation exulting: "Our River is free!"
　　　　　　　　　　　　CAPT. R. H. CHITTENDEN,
ST. PAUL, July 7, 1863.　　　　First Wisconsin Cavalry.

GRANT AT CHATTANOOGA.

BY JAMES B. EVERHART.

There went up a wail of sorrow
　From all the loyal land—
There went up a shout of triumph
　From every rebel band;
For the banks of Chickamauga
　Beheld our smitten host,
And the banks of Chickamauga
　Made good the rebel boast.

And trade through all our cities
　Was staggered by the blow,

And down, with its torn banner, fell
　The nation's credit low.
In the market and the warehouse,
　The pulpit and the press,
In the parlors and the highways
　Was seen the sore distress.

Good men beyond the ocean,
　The poor of every soil,
And the negro, like a culprit,
　Chained to his daily toil,
Felt, each, the dire disaster—
　Feared, each, a darker hour—
Feared, all, this cursed prestige
　Of fell barbaric power.

Now many a brave heart trembled;
　Many a weak one sighed;
Many a prayer was offered up
　To turn the battle's tide;
Will our God forsake his children,
　And turn away his face?
Will the cause of truth go under,
　And crime usurp its place?

Will the fields of so much glory,
　Will all the martyrs slain,
Will our history and altars
　And all our hopes be vain?
Oh! for a sign in heaven,
　Such as the Kaiser saw—
Oh! for some gifted hero,
　His conquering sword to draw!

So some doubted and debated,
　And marvelled and deplored—
With unswerving faith some waited
　The justice of the Lord.
Soon, brighter than the morning fire,
　His stately steps are seen—
Chariots, blazing with his ire,
　Amongst the clouds careen!

Now! GRANT girds on his armor,
　And leads his legions forth—
For in the fray that comes to-day
　Jehovah's with the North!
And he bids his trusty captains,
　That at the signal peal,
Their ranks shall scale, through iron hail,
　The mountain sides with steel.

The columns, swiftly formed in line,
　Move gaily o'er the field,
As if they know the haughty foe
　Is sure to fly or yield.
And, rebels, now look to your works,
　See that your aim be true,
For Grant commands those loyal bands,
　And this is no review.

Full fierce the mighty struggle swells;
　Death roars from every gun,
While through a flood of human blood
　The rifle-pits are won.
Our forces follow up the steep,
　Loud shouting as they go,
Nor heed the shot that, thick and hot,
　Come crashing fast below.

And when they gain the crested ridge,
   The clouds beneath them lie,
And down afar it seems a war
   Of demons in the sky.
Round them rolls the sulph'rous smoke
   That follows ball and bomb,
While thunders boom, as if the doom
   Of all the earth had come.

They reach the very last redoubt,
   Hell yawns at every fire;
Midst sword and lead, o'er piles of dead,
   The rebel hordes retire;
And routed, scattered, and dismayed,
   Far flee these lords of slaves,
While flashing bright, on every height,
   The flag of freedom waves!

All honor, then, to all our men,
   To leaders and to guard,
Who bared their life in mortal strife,
   Or who kept watch and ward;
And praises to the Lord of Hosts,
   Whom nations must obey,
That he did bide, all by our side,
   On Chattanooga's day!

Let holy tears bedew the graves
   Of those who fell in fight;
Let marble stones, above their bones,
   Salute the morning light;
Let history write in golden books;
   Let bards with song enshrine;
Let women chant the name of Grant,
   And the glory of the Line!
WEST-CHESTER, PA.

THE DOVE OF THE REGIMENT.

AN INCIDENT OF THE BATTLE OF CHICKAMAUGA.

"And the dove came into him in the evening, and lo! in her mouth was an olive leaf!"—BIBLE.

It will be remembered that, during the battle of Chickamauga, stragglers from our army spread extravagant reports of disaster and defeat, and that the enemy, supposing the destruction of our army complete, exultingly announced that the road was clear to Nashville.

After the retreat, while placing Chattanooga in a state of defence, General Rosecrans ordered groves levelled and houses burned, when so situated as to afford shelter to the enemy, or interfere with the range of the artillery. A dove escaped from a burning building, and took shelter in the tent of an officer of the Forty-first Ohio regiment. It remained with its protector during the siege, which terminated in the rout of Bragg's army at Lookout Mountain and Mission Ridge. When the regiment marched with Granger's corps to the relief of the beleaguered army, at Knoxville, it accompanied it, and when the Forty-first reënlisted, this "dove of the regiment" came with it to Cleveland.

The Sabbath day—toward Welden bridge slow stoops
   the autumn sun;
As when by prophet's mandate stayed, he paused on
   Gideon.
Above the crest of Mission Ridge the shifting cloud
   we see
Is not the fleeting morning mist that shrouds the Tennessee.
A hundred thousand freemen pale struggle beneath its
   shade;
While, from old Lookout's rugged front, echoes the
   cannonade.
"Now glory the stars and bars, what may not valor
   do?
Our foe, in Georgia's dread defiles, has met his Waterloo!

Here, on the soil long consecrate to Indian hardihood,
We have met the rude invader, and spilled his richest
   blood.
While nations celebrate their birth, or venerate their
   slain,
Shall live the heights of Mission Ridge and Chickamauga's plain.
Now let the hated Yankee seek again his native sod,
And feel, in this last fearful stroke, the hand of
   Israel's God;
Let him tame his flowing rivers, let him quell the restless lake,
Whose billows on his northland in sullen grandeur
   break,
But never let him think to bind, and fetter at his will,
The Southern mind, while Southern hands can wield
   the sabre still."

So spake a haughty Southern lord, with stern and
   flashing eye,
Gazing upon a recent throng that slowly straggled by.
Cease, babbling fool, your soul to soothe with this delusive strain;
Though *stragglers* flee the field of death, the *soldiers*
   yet remain.
When storms assail the rugged oak, its giant form
   may rock,
But withered leaves and worthless boughs alone yield
   to the shock.

The fight is done, and from the field, the rebels on
   their track,
A weary host, our scattered bands come marching
   slowly back.
"Now fire the dwellings, fell the groves, these sylvan
   bowers lay low,
That o'er the plain our guns may speak a welcome to
   the foe!
Though driven from the bloody field we almost won,
   and lost,
Back from this mountain citadel we'll hurl the rebel
   host;
As, after Cannæ's fatal day, the Roman armies bore
Their standards from Tiber's banks to Afric's hated
   shore;
As when the northern bear waned weak, in Borodino's
   fight,
Napoleon's host recoiled before the vengeful Muscovite;
So yet from Chattanooga's walls we'll spring, the foe
   to meet—
The army of the Cumberland shall never know defeat!"

As from doomed Sodom's sin-cursed town to Zoar Lot
   trembling crossed,
So from the tumult flees a dove, and cowers amid our
   host;
A message to that war-worn band it bears upon its
   wing,
Though not the olive-leaf of Peace, Hope's grateful
   offering.
"Be firm," its language seems to be, "though right
   may yield to wrong,
Hope's brightest omens cheer the souls that suffer and
   are strong."
Responsive to the Tennessee its songs no longer
   break,
But mingled with the hoarser roar of Erie's sleepless
   lake.
HAYFIELD, O., April 7, 1864.

TO ROBERT GOULD SHAW.

Buried by South-Carolinians under a pile of twenty-four negroes.

On Alaric, buried in Busento's bed,
  The slaves, the stream who turned, were butchered
      thrown,
  That, so his grave eternally unknown,
No mortal on the Scourge of God might tread.
Thou, nobler hero, nobler grave hast won,
  In Wagner's trench, beneath brave freemen hid,
  By Vandals on thee piled—a pyramid,
That to all coming time shall make thee known.
In death, as life, round thee their guard they keep;
  And, when next time they hear the trumpet's sound,
Will they, with thee, on heaven's parapet leap:
  The four-and-twenty elders on the ground
Their crowns before thy lowly comrades lay,
While "Come up higher, Friend!" thou hearest God
      say.

                                   L. HOLBROOK.

THE MERCEDITA.

AIR—*The Battle of Bull Run.*

Come all you loyal seamen, a song I'll sing to you,
It's of a gallant steamer, now on the ocean's blue;
Her name's the Mercedita, rigged as a barquentine,
A bully ship and a bully crew as ever yet was seen.

Stellwagen is our captain, his knowledge none can
      doubt,
The prizes we have taken have shown that he's about;
And there's Lieutenant Abbot, beloved by us all,
Then Wilder, Gover, Baldwin, we hope they ne'er
      will fall.

The next is Mr. Dwyer, no braver man can be;
And then comes Doctor Mason, no kinder man he;
Then Steine and Rogers, they come next, both good
      men and brave;
A better group of officers ne'er crossed the ocean
      wave.

The engineers are all the same, just what we seamen
      like;
There's Doig, Martin, and Munger, who always keep
      us right.
Another name I'll give you now, none bolder or more
      sound,
It's Rockefeller puts us through when we are home-
      ward bound.

The gallant Mercedita, with all her gallant crew,
She hoists her flag up to her mast—the red, the white,
      the blue—
And when the rebel ram struck her, and split her boil-
      er through,
"How are you, Mercedita, and all your noble crew?"

Now here's to the "blue jackets," the Mercedita's
      crew,
A nobler lot of sailors ne'er crossed the ocean blue,
And if we meet the enemy, with any chance to win,
We'll go down like the Cumberland, and let our col-
      ors swim.

Now to conclude this ditty, and not to detain you
      long,
We'll all fight for our country, our country right or
      wrong;

A toast I'll give, to finish, it will please you all, I
      know,
It's "champagne" to our real friends, and "real pain"
      to our foe.

MUSTERED OUT.

BY REV. WILLIAM E. MILLER.

·Let me lie down,
Just there in the shade of this cannon-torn tree,
Here, low on the trampled grass, where I may see
The surge of the combat; and where I may hear
The glad cry of victory, cheer upon cheer!
      Let me lie down!

Oh! it was grand!
Like the tempest we charged the triumph to share:
The tempest—its fury and thunder was there;
On, on, o'er intrenchments, o'er living and dead,
With the foe under foot and our flag overhead;
      Oh! it was grand!

Weary and faint,
Prone on the soldiers' couch, ah! how can I rest
With this shot-shattered head and sabre-pierced breast?
Comrades, at roll-call, when I shall be sought,
Say I fought till I fell, and fell where I fought,
      Wounded and faint.

Oh! that last charge!
Right through the dread host tore shrapnel and shell,
Through without falt'ring—clear through with a yell,
Right in their midst, in the turmoil and gloom,
Like heroes we dashed, at the mandate of doom
      Oh! that last charge!

It was duty!
Some things are worthless; some others so good,
That nations who buy them pay only in blood;
For Freedom and Union each man owes his part,
And here I pay my share all warm from my heart;
      It is duty!

Dying at last!
My mother, dear mother, with meek, tearful eye,
Farewell! and God bless you, for ever and aye!
Oh! that I now lay on your pillowing breast,
To breathe my last sigh on the bosom first prest;
      Dying at last!

I am no saint!
But, boys, say a prayer. There's one that begins:
"Our Father," and then says: "Forgive us our sins:"
Don't forget that part; say that strongly, and then
I'll try to repeat it, and you'll all say, "Amen!"
      Ah! I'm no saint!

Hark! there's a shout!
Raise me up, comrades! We have conquered, I know!
Up, up on my feet, with my face to the foe!
Ah! there flies the Flag, its Star-spangles bright,
The promise of glory, the symbol of right!
      Well may they shout!

I'm mustered out!
O God of our fathers! our freedom prolong,
And tread down rebellion, oppression, and wrong!
O land of earth's hope! on thy blood-reddened sod
I die for the Nation, the Union, and God!
      I'm mustered out!

GENERAL JOE HOOKER.

Supposed to be sung by one of his Division, on the summit of Look-Out Mountain, subsequent to its capture, November, 1863.

THE camp fire burns bright and the cider is sound:
Come, comrades, attention, let us gather around:
In the gloom of my tent when we'd taken Look-Out,
With heart fired with vict'ry, foot-sore from a scout,
I just jingled these rhymes and I'll sing them to you;
They're of one whom true soldiers acknowledge True
    Blue,
'Tis of one who ne'er shunned to encounter the foe,
You must know whom I mean, it's our own "Fighting
    Joe."
Come, fill every cup—for a fight he's the cooker,
With three cheers and a tiger, we'll drink to Joe
    Hooker.

The old proverb it'runs, "Every dog has his day,"
But some dogs have two chances when dog's work's
    to play,
And the people at home, when the truth comes to
    light,
Will accord second chance to the dog who *can* fight:
And, whatever backbiters and stay-at-homes say,
If Joe's last at the feast he's e'er first at the fray.
And while some love champagne, toothsome sweets,
    and good mutton,
It is only for fighting that Hooker's a glutton;
And with him, at no hardship should private repine,
For though tempting the meats and enticing the wine,
He'll not see his men suffer and sit down to dine.
Rat-ta-tat, Tra-la-la, fill we out a full can,
We'll both drink to the Hero, and drink to the Man,
And the General too, who 'mong bold ones will stand,
Who dared put into practice what head-work had
    planned.

Listen, comrades, we Yankees are most reading men,
And something of history and generals ken.
Which commanders are those that a soldier will men-
    tion,
Who's studied his books with delight and attention?
Why, Gustavus, and Fred'rick, Charles, Blücher, and
    Saxe,
And the like, who trod ably in Hannibal's tracks,
'Mong our own, Greene, "Mad Anthony," Schuyler,
    and Lamb,
And Montgomery, dead near the field of Montcalm—
That field where Wolfe died, all content as victorious—
Leaving names that are watchwords—whole nation's
    themes glorious.
Well! who most in this war showed a spirit like
    theirs?
Grant and Farragut truly have done their full shares;
But the two, who *at outset*, the foremost will show
Were Phil Kearny *in coffin;* alive, "Fighting Joe."

Do you know why true soldiers *will* talk "Fighting
    Joe,"
Because he's a game-cock will fight well as crow,
And like Taylor no responsibility shirk
If the country would win though he lost by the work.
"As well hang for a sheep as a lamb," so he said,
When the orders to back out from Richmond were
    read;
And at Look-Out, when counted all out of the fight,
'Twas Hooker who triumphed, 'twas Joe stormed the
    height.
"If a man's got fight in him, laughed 'ruddy-faced Joe,'
When a fight's to come off he'll in stirrup get toe:"
Then three cheers and a tiger for him who will plan
And then try to accomplish his thoughts like a man.

Some generals' sole thought is a well-secured base;
The great forte then of others intrenchments to trace
I've e'en heard of commanders "skedaddled" out
    right,
And 'mong these, once, great Fred'ric, if read I aright
Some, like Oliver Twist, are e'er calling for "more"—
By the way, that's not only the case in this war;
Even Nap used to say, Never leave back a corps,
But to "Field of Decision" bring up every man,
For exactly what's needed who calculate can?
Some generals, in practice, worth not even a "red,"
Dream of catching Naps napping, get "gobbled" in-
    stead;
Or, at newspaper clamor, send thousands to die,
Without caring a "hard-tack" for you boys or I!
"On to Richmond" speech-makers, who, deep in the
    mire
Of political strategy keep out of fire,
Incorruptible Brutuses, devoured by the thirst
To see, who, for fat office, can sell himself first;
Sly political schemers may worship a sham,
But the soldier will never be quit with a flam,
For the generals true soldiers look up to as "some"
Are not those who say, "Go on!" but those who say,
    "Come!"
And the rank and file scout a political plan,
For a soldier knows soldier, a man loves a man!
Then to him who of fighting ne'er yet got his fill;
To that general who e'er found a way for his will;
To that one when most wronged chose then most to
    obey;
And in stern path of duty, showed, led on, the way;
Three cheers and a tiger! 'Tis Joe Hooker, the man
Who as chief or corps leader will do all he can,
And as long as he serves our dear country we know
Just the spot where to find him, Joe Hooker, our Joe.
                     ANCHOR.

INCIDENTS OF THE OCCUPATION OF HAGERSTOWN.

July 7.—During the stay of the confederates in town, the boys ranging from twelve to sixteen reaped quite a harvest by confiscating all the revolvers that were left in the holsters upon the backs of officers' horses, which they (the boys) were holding. Our informant was shown some sixty revolvers thus captured, and the Union boys are making good use of them.

Business has been suspended for nearly three weeks at Hagerstown, and the streets are continually crowded with men, women, and children. The Union men congregate in front of the Hagerstown Bank—at times numbering hundreds—all bearing a cheerful look and discussing the prospects of the war. On the other hand, the secesh make their headquarters at the Washington House, immediately opposite the Bank, where they can be heard vowing vengeance upon the loyal portion of the community.

A pleasing incident occurred during Ewell's stay in town. The Fourth North-Carolina, Colonel Grimes, was encamped in the public square, doing provost duty. Attached to this regiment was an excellent brass band, and on the first evening of their arrival they enlivened the town by playing rebel airs. At last they struck up "Dixie;" immediately some twenty young ladies, headed by Miss McCameron and Miss Emma Wantz, joined in singing the "Star-Spangled Banner," which soon drowned the rebel horns. This created intense feeling, and the Union boys sent up shout after shout.

Another incident, worthy of note, occurred after a portion of the rebel army had passed into Pennsylvania. Four Union prisoners, captured near Carlisle, were brought into town under guard, when the two young ladies above named stepped into the street and presented each prisoner with a bouquet, tied with red, white, and blue.

In passing through Maryland the rebel army lost large numbers by desertion, the most of them being Virginians and North-Carolinians, while some few were Northern men and foreigners. When the Union cavalry entered the town several rebel soldiers came in and gave themselves up.

After the passage of Longstreet's corps every thing remained quiet until Sunday, when, about six o'clock in the evening, thirteen cavalrymen belonging to a New-York regiment made a dash into town, and, with the assistance of the Union boys of the town, who ran to the confederate hospital and seized the muskets there stored, they succeeded in capturing quite a number of prisoners, among them a rebel mail-carrier and his mail. Chaplain Dabney Ball, (formerly pastor of Wesley Chapel in Washington,) who was in town, made his escape by jumping from his horse and taking to the fields. His horse was secured by a smart little fellow named Richard Boward, who rode the horse to Frederick, and handed it over to the military.

Again, on Monday last, twenty men of the Fifth regulars made a dash into town and captured eleven stragglers, two carbines, four muskets, and four horses. This command took breakfast at the Washington House, kept by Harry Yingling, a well-known rebel sympathizer, and who has been taking rebel scrip from the confederates for bills contracted. It was suggested to the officer in charge that he should pay his bill with the same kind of money, and the "gray-backs" being furnished him by a citizen, he paid Harry off in his own coin.

And again, on Tuesday morning, our men made another dash, and captured eleven prisoners and two horses. The rebels, hearing of this, came over in force from Williamsport, but our men had made their escape with their prisoners.

NEGROES TAKEN IN ARMS.—On this very important subject, in reply to some strictures of the Charleston Mercury, (made under misapprehension,) the Chief of Staff of General Beauregard addressed to that journal the following letter:

HEADQUARTERS, DEPARTMENT OF S. C., GA., AND FLA.,
CHARLESTON, S. C., August 12, 1863.

Colonel R. B. Rhett, Jr., Editor of Mercury:

In the Mercury of this date you appear to have written under a misapprehension of the facts connected with the present status of the negroes captured in arms on Morris and James Islands, which permit me to state as follows:

"The Proclamation of the President, dated December twenty-fourth, 1862, directed that all negro slaves captured in arms should be at once delivered over to the executive authorities of the respective States to which they belong, to be dealt with according to the laws of said States."

An informal application was made by the State authorities for the negroes captured in this vicinity; but as none of them, it appeared, had been slaves of citizens of South-Carolina, they were not turned over to the civil authority, for at the moment there was no official information at these headquarters of the Act of Congress by which "all negroes and mulattoes, who shall be engaged in war, or be taken in arms against the confederate States, or shall give aid or comfort to

the enemies of the confederate States," were directed to be turned over to the authorities of "State or States in which they shall be captured, to be dealt with according to the present or future laws of such State or States."

On the twenty-first of July, however, the Commanding General telegraphed to the Secretary of War for instructions as to the disposition to be made of the negroes captured on Morris and James Islands, and on the twenty-second received a reply that they must be turned over to the State authorities, by virtue of the joint resolutions of Congress in question.

Accordingly, on the twenty-ninth July, as soon as a copy of the resolution or act was received, his Excellency Governor Bonham was informed that the negroes captured were held subject to his orders, to be dealt with according to the laws of South-Carolina.

On the same day (twenty-ninth July) Governor Bonham requested that they should be retained in military custody until he could make arrangements to dispose of them; and in that custody they still remain, awaiting the orders of the State authorities. Respectfully, your obedient servant,

THOMAS JORDAN,
Chief of Staff.

SECESH SYMPATHY.—The following incident occurred at Salem, Indiana, during the raid of John Morgan. Some of his men proceeded out west of the town to burn the bridges and water-tank on the railroad. On the way out they captured a couple of persons living in the country, one of whom was a Quaker. The Quaker strongly objected to being made a prisoner. Secesh wanted to know if he was not strongly opposed to the South. "Thee is right," said the Quaker, "I am." "Well, did you vote for Lincoln?" "Thee is right; I did vote for Abraham."

"Well, what are you?"

"Thee may naturally suppose that I am a Union man. Cannot thee let me go to my home?"

"Yes, yes; go and take care of the old woman," said secesh.

The other prisoner was taken along with them, but not relishing the summary manner in which the Quaker was disposed of, said: "What do you let him go for? He is a black Abolitionist. Now, look here, I voted for Breckinridge, and have always been opposed to the war. I am opposed to fighting the South, decidedly."

"You are," said secesh; "you are what they call around here a Copperhead, an't you?"

"Yes, yes," said the Butternut, insinuatingly; "that's what all my neighbors call me, and they know I an't with them."

"Come here, Dave!" hallooed secesh. "There's a Butternut. Just come and look at him. Look here, old man, where do you live? We want what horses you have got to spare, and if you have got any greenbacks, just shell 'em out!" and they took all he had.

ORGANIZED RESISTANCE TO THE CONFEDERACY IN LOUISIANA.—Many persons are disposed to doubt the correctness of the published statements of the condition of affairs at the South—such as the marked change of sentiment in North-Carolina, the wholesale desertions from the rebel armies, the banding together of conscripts to resist any attempt to force them into the confederate ranks, etc., etc. We now have positive proof of the fact however, that as long ago as last

February, conscripts in Louisiana formed together and defied the Government of Jeff Davis. The following is a copy of a letter found in Port Hudson, after the surrender of that place:

"PORT HUDSON, February 9, 1863.
"*Lieutenant-Colonel James H. Wingfield:*

"COLONEL: In obedience to Special Order No. 27, I proceeded to the Parish of Washington, and immediately commenced notifying all men belonging to my command to come to camp, when they promised to do so, and I find nine of them here on my return.

"Others I saw belonging to my command, and some of company C, who positively refused to do so, saying at the same time that they would prefer to die at home. The absentees from this command, together with the conscripts, have formed themselves into a company for mutual protection and resistance of confederate authorities. They number some seventy-five men, and meet in their camp once or twice a week, and the depredations carried on by them are fearful. The citizens are intimidated, and dare not speak their mind in the neighborhood of these men.

"I applied to Lieutenant-Colonel Miller, the nearest confederate authority at Ponchitoula, for force sufficient to arrest these men. Answer is herewith inclosed. I also beg leave to submit the following facts: That the entire lake coast of St. Tammany, over sixty miles in width, is left unguarded, and daily communication is kept up with the enemy in New-Orleans; that cotton and other contrabands are shipped to the enemy to any extent the people may see proper. I saw many loads of cotton being hauled for shipment to New-Orleans.

"There is a steamer by the name of the Charles Rust, Captain J. Johnson, plying between the lower landings of Pearl River and some of the counties in the State of Mississippi. Upon the return trip she brings cotton to the lower landings, from thence it is shipped to New-Orleans.

"Negroes are constantly leaving Washington and Fort Tammany Parishes, Louisiana, and Hancock and Pike counties, Mississippi, and the people think they will all leave if there is not sufficient force sent to protect the coast.

"I find the people much exposed to the depredations of this band, and I ask in behalf of the citizens of the Parish of Washington, in which companies A, C, and K of this battalion were raised, that some force be sent to protect the families of the men who are now in the service of their country.

"With the above facts, I beg leave to submit myself your obedient servant, J. J. SLOCUM,
"Captain Co. A, Ninth Battalion P. R."

The above letter was brought home by a Massachusetts soldier.—*Boston Traveller.*

THE REBEL DESPOTISM IN GEORGIA.—Mr. J. Harford, a refugee from Atlanta, Georgia, sends to the Nashville *Union* the following account of the sufferings of the people of Georgia under the rebel rule:

"When this war commenced I was engaged in the dry-goods business; have subsequently kept a dining-saloon, with a license for the sale of liquors. In Atlanta citizens are compelled to obey military rules which they do not recognize as law, and which rules even that government (through Alexander A. Stephens) pronounced to be illegal, arbitrary, and unjust, yet for refusing to obey which I have been seven times imprisoned—my property forcibly carried away without compensation. My family thus robbed, I was sent into another State for trial, and there imprisoned in Chattanooga to satisfy the malice of the military authorities in Atlanta, whose acts of despotism caused the death of peaceable citizens, and murdered even the babe in my wife's arms. During my imprisonment my family became sick, one of my children died, and my wife's recovery was for some time regarded as hopeless. Sir, these are facts which many respectable citizens of Atlanta can corroborate.

"For defending the character of Michael Myers, a respectable citizen, who was arrested on suspicion of Union principles—and when visited by his friends on the following day, was found senseless, with a fracture in his skull about three inches long, from the effects of which he died in less than forty-eight hours from the time of his arrest—I was again made to suffer. Having dared to call for an investigation into the cause of his death, and accusing the provost-guards of at least some knowledge of his murder, has been, I well believe, the indirect cause of my repeated arrests, until deprived of all that could constitute a home. I was then, as if in mockery of my situation, called on to defend my home from 'Yankee' invasion too — regardless of the certificates of two eminent doctors, proving my exemption from military service. These conscript officers have endeavored to force me to fight for their benign government. Military law having ignored all civil law, left me no means of redress. My wife, therefore, wrote an appeal to the military authorities, but the newspapers of Atlanta refused to publish it, stating that it was too personal."

SONGS OF THE REBELS.

BEYOND THE POTOMAC.

BY PAUL H. HAYNE.

They slept on the fields which their valor had won!
But arose with the first early blush of the sun,
For they knew that a great deed remained to be done,
When they passed o'er the River!

They rose with the sun, and caught life from his light—
Those giants of courage, those Anaks in fight—
And they laughed out aloud in the joy of their might,
Marching swift for the River:

On! on! like the rushing of storms through the hills—
On! on! with a tramp that is firm as their wills—
And the one heart of thousands grows buoyant and thrills
At the thought of the River!

Oh! the sheen of their swords! the fierce gleam of their eyes
It seemed as on earth a new sunlight would rise,
And king-like flash up to the sun in the skies,
O'er the path to the River.

But, their banners, shot-scarred, and all darkened with gore,
On a strong wind of morning streamed wildly before,
Like the wings of death-angels swept fast to the shore,
The green shore of the River.

As they march—from the hill-side, the hamlet, the
　　stream—
Gaunt throngs whom the foeman had manacled, teem,
Like men just roused from some terrible dream,
　　　To pass o'er the River.

They behold the broad banners, blood-darkened yet
　　fair,
And a moment dissolves the last spell of despair,
While a peal as of victory swells on the air,
　　　Rolling out to the River.

And that cry, with a thousand strange echoings spread,
Till the ashes of heroes seemed stirred in their bed,
And the deep voice of passion surged up from the
　　dead—
　　　Ay! press on to the River!

On! on! like the rushing of storms through the hills
On! on! with a tramp that is firm as their wills,
And the one heart of thousands grows buoyant and
　　thrills
　　　As they pause by the River.

Then the wan face of Maryland, haggard and worn,
At that sight, lost the touch of its aspect forlorn,
And she turned on the foeman full statured in scorn,
　　　Pointing stern to the River.

And Potomac flowed calm, scarcely heaving her breast,
With her low lying billows all bright in the West,
For the hand of the Lord lulled the waters to rest
　　　Of the fair rolling River.

Passed! passed! the glad thousands march safe
　　through the tide.
(Hark, Despot! and hear the wild knell of your pride,
Ringing weird-like and wild, pealing up from the side
　　　Of the calm flowing River!)

'Neath a blow swift and mighty the Tyrant shall fall,
Vain! vain! to his God swells a desolate call,
For his grave has been hollowed, and woven his pall,
　　　Since they passed o'er the River!

KING SCARE.

The monarch that reigns in the *warlike* North
　An't Lincoln at all, I ween;
But old King Scare, with his thin, fast legs,
　And his long sword in between;
The world has not for many a day
　Seen merrier king or lord;
But some declare, in a playful way,
　　Scare should not wear a sword.
　　　　Yes, I have heard, upon my word,
　　　　　And seen in prose and rhyme,
　　　　That if old Scare no sword would wear,
　　　　　He'd make much better time.

I cannot tell why he put it on,
　Nor tell where he got the heart,
But guess he intended it all for fun,
　And not for a tragedy part;
But well made up with his togs and wear-
　With his boots, and sword, and gun—
Not one of us knew it was old King Scare
　Till we saw the monarch run.
　　　　It did us good to see him scud,
　　　　　And put the miles behind him;
　　　　His friends now say: "Put your sword
　　　　　away!"
　　　　But old Scare doesn't mind 'em.

He is ruler of twenty terrible States,
　With ships and soldiers and tin;
But the State that all of these outrates
　Is the terrible state he is in—
With just nowhere for his ships to move,
　With his tin most terribly rare,
With his soldiers on every field to prove
　True subjects of old King Scare.
　　　　The English *Times* and *Punch* in rhymes
　　　　　Both say the Republic's *nil*;
　　　　That after the war, just as before,
　　　　　Scare will be despot still.

Scare rides a horse in his "own countrie,"
　And a high horse rides King Scare,
And a mighty host in his train there be
　Who no gun nor falchion wear;
Now these be the freedom-shriekers bold
　Who keep off the war-gine's track,
Who shut on the white race dungeon-doors,
　And send "braves" to steal the black.
　　　　For abolition is but a mission
　　　　　Of white-skinned niggers, to pray
　　　　And steal, and make the blacks they take
　　　　　As free and as mean as they.

This monarch Scare is imperious quite,
　And he loves to swear and chafe
At the "rebel" foe that, in every fight,
　He can always run from—safe;
And all his gazettes in great round words
　His "brave volunteers" bepraise,
Whom Scare drives up against "rebel" swords,
　And the swords drive otherways.
　　　　Thus into battle, driven like cattle,
　　　　　Come his "brave volunteers,"
　　　　When from the fight, with all their
　　　　　might,
　　　　Each gallantly—disappears.

Hurrah for the land of old Scare, then—
　Hurrah for the Yankee land!
What a grand old war were this if their men
　Could only be made to stand;
How the guns would roar, and the steel would ring,
　And the souls up to heaven would flare,
If all the Yankees had now for king
　Old Courage, and not old Scare.
　　　　But never they that lie and pray,
　　　　　And steal and murder too,
　　　　Have pluck to fight, for only the Right
　　　　　Is the soldier to dare and do.
　　　　　　　　　　　　　　　　　　H.

UP! UP! LET THE STARS OF OUR BANNER

BY M. F. BIGNEY.

Respectfully dedicated to the Soldiers of the South.

Up! up! Let the stars of our banner
　Flash out like the brilliants above;
Beneath them we'll shield from dishonor
　The homes and the dear ones we love.
　　　"With God and our Right!"
　　　　Our cry in the fight,
　　　　　We'll drive the invader afar
　　　　And we'll carve out a name
　　　　In the temple of Fame
　　　　　With the weapons of glorious war

Arise with an earnest endeavor—
　A nation shall hallow the deed;

The foe must be silenced for ever,
Though millions in battle may bleed.
   Chorus: With "God and our Right!" etc.

Strong arms and a conquerless spirit
We bring as our glory and guard:
If courage a triumph can merit,
Then Freedom shall be our reward.
   Chorus: With "God and our Right!" etc.

Beneath the high sanction of Heaven,
We'll fight as our forefathers fought;
Then pray that to us may be given
Such guerdon as fell to their lot.
   Chorus: With "God and our Right!" etc.

SONG OF THE SOUTHERN SOLDIER.

BY P. E. C.

Air—Barclay and Perkins' Drayman.

I'm a soldier you see, that oppression has made,
  I don't fight for pay or for booty;
But I wear in my hat a blue cockade,
  Placed there by the fingers of beauty.
The South is my home, where a black man is black,
  And a white man there is a white man;
Now I'm tired of listening to Northern clack—
  Let us see what they'll do in a fight, man.

The Yankees are 'cute, they have managed somehow
  Their business and ours to settle;
They make all we want from a pin to a plough,
  Now we'll show them some Southern metal.
We have had just enough of their Northern law,
  That robbed us so long of our right, man,
And too much of their cursed abolition jaw—
  Now we'll see what they'll do in a fight, man!

Their parsons will open their sanctified jaws,
  And cant of our slave-growing sin, Sir;
They pocket the *profits*, while preaching the laws,
  And manage our cotton to spin, Sir.
Their incomes are nice on our sugar and rice,
  Though against it the hypocrites write, Sir.
Now our dander is up, and they'll soon smell a mice,
  If we once get them into a fight, Sir.

Our cotton-bales once made a good barricade,
  And can still do the state a good service—
With them and the boys of the blue cockade,
  There is power enough to preserve us.
So shoulder your rifles, my boys, for defence,
  In the cause of our freedom and right, man;
If there's no other way for to learn them sense,
  We may teach them a lesson in fight, man.

The stars that are growing so fast on our flags,
  We treasure as liberty's pearls;
And stainless we'll bear them, though shot into rags:
  They were fixed by the hands of our girls.
And fixed stars they shall be in our national sky,
  To guide through the future aright, man;
And young Cousin Sam, with their gleam in his eyes,
  May dare the whole world to fight, man.

NOTE.—The foregoing lines were written on the eighth of January, 1861, for a friend who had intended to sing them in the theatre, but thought at the time to be too much in the secession spirit. Cousin Sam, or C. S. Confederate States.—*Richmond Examiner.*

THE BLUE COCKADE.

BY MARY WALSINGHAM CREAN.

God be with the laddie who wears the blue cockade!
  He's gone to fight the battles of our darling Southern land;
He was true to old Columbia, till more sacred ties forbade—
  Till 'twere treason to obey her, when he took his sword in hand.
And God be with the laddie who was true in heart and hand,
To the voice of old Columbia, till she wronged his native land!

He buckled on his knapsack—his musket on his breast—
  And donned the pluméd bonnet—sword and pistol by his side;
Then his weeping mother kissed him, and his aged father blessed,
  And he pinned the floating ribbon to his gallant plume of pride.
And God be with the ribbon, and the floating plume of pride!
They have gone where duty called them, and may glory them betide!

He would not soil his honor, and he would not strike a blow,
  For he loved the aged Union, and he breathed no taunting word;
He would dare Columbia, till she swore herself his foe,
  Forged the chains for freemen, when he buckled on his sword.
And God be with the freeman when he buckled on his sword!
He lives and dies for duty—and he yields no inch of sward.

The foes they come with thunder, and with blood and fire arrayed,
  And they swear that we shall own them, they the masters, we the slaves;
But there's many a gallant laddie who wears a blue cockade,
  Will show them what it is to dare the Blood of Southern braves!
And God be with the banner of those gallant Southern braves,
They may nobly die as freemen—they can never live as slaves!

THE RIGHT ABOVE THE WRONG.

BY JOHN W. OVERALL.

In other days our fathers' love was loyal, full, and free,
For those they left behind them in the island of the sea:
They fought the battles of King George, and toasted him in song,
For then the Right kept proudly down the tyranny of Wrong.

But when the King's weak, willing slaves laid tax upon the tea,
The Western men rose up and braved the island of the sea:

And swore a fearful oath to God, those men of iron
    might,
That in the end the wrong should die, and up should
    go the right.

The King sent over hireling hosts, Briton, Hessian,
    Scot,
And swore in turn those Western men when captured
    should be shot,
While Chatham spoke with earnest tongue against the
    hireling throng,
And mournfully saw the Right go down, and place give
    to the Wrong.

But God was on the righteous side, and Gideon's sword
    was out,
With clash of steel, and rattling drum, and freemen's
    thunder-shout;
And crimson torrents drenched the land through that
    long, stormy fight:
But in the end, hurrah! the Wrong was beaten by the
    Right!

And when again the foeman came from out the North-
    ern Sea,
To desolate our smiling land, and subjugate the free,
Our fathers rushed to drive them back with rifles keen
    and long,
And swore a mighty oath, the Right should subjugate
    the Wrong.

And while the world was looking on, the strife uncer-
    tain grew,
But soon aloft rose up our stars amid a field of blue.
For Jackson fought on red Chalmette, and won the
    glorious fight,
And then the Wrong went down, hurrah! and triumph
    crowned the Right!

The day has come again, when men who love the beau-
    teous South,
To speak, if needs be, for the Right, though by the
    cannon's mouth;
For foes accursed of God and man, with lying speech
    and song,
Would bind, imprison, hang the Right, and deify the
    Wrong.

But canting knave of pen and sword, nor sanctimoni-
    ous fool,
Shall never win this Southern land to cripple, bind,
    and rule;
We'll muster on each bloody plain thick as the stars
    of night,
And through the help of God, the Wrong shall perish
    bv the Right.   —N. O. True Delta.

THE SOUTH IN ARMS.

BY REV. J. H. MARTIN.

Oh! see ye not the sight sublime,
Unequalled in all previous time,
Presented in this Southern clime,
        The home of Chivalry?

A warlike race of freemen stand
With martial front and sword in hand,
Defenders of their native land,
        The sons of Liberty.

Unawed by numbers, they defy
The tyrant North, nor will they fly,
Resolved to conquer or to die,
        And win a glorious name.

Sprung from renowned heroic sires,
Inflamed with patriotic fires,
Their bosoms burn with fierce desires,
        The thirst for victory.

'Tis not the love of bloody strife—
The horrid sacrifice of life;
But thoughts of mother, sister, wife,
        That stir their manly hearts.

A sense of honor bids them go
To meet a hireling, ruthless foe,
And deal in wrath the deadly blow,
        Which vengeance loud demands.

In Freedom's sacred cause they fight,
For Independence, Justice, Right,
And to resist a desperate might.

And by Manassas' glorious name,
And by Missouri's fields of fame,
We hear them swear, with one acclaim,
        We'll triumph or we'll die.

THE LANDING ON MORRIS ISLAND, S. C.—Captain
S. H. Gray, commanding two companies of the Seventh
Connecticut regiment, in the landing upon Morris
Island, on the ninth of July, 1863, gives the following
account:

"Early on the ninth we received orders to be ready
by sundown for a fresh start. To prevent any mistake
in the night, each officer and man had on his left arm
a white badge three inches wide. General Strong was
to embark two thousand men in boats, and take them
up Folly River in the Lighthouse Inlet; and at sunrise
the batteries that had been erected (there were over
forty guns and mortars in position) were to open, and
the gunboats to engage the batteries on the opposite
side of the island. The boats arrived with the troops
in good time, preceded by eight boat-howitzers from
the gunboats; the first boat contained General Strong
and staff, and then came the battalion of the Seventh
Connecticut volunteers.

"General Gillmore told Colonel Rodman that the
General had concluded that our battalion was the
most reliable, and could be trusted, and was selected
for that reason. The batteries opened at daylight,
and in a short time the enemy discovered the boats,
and threw shell and solid shot, trying to sink them.
The shot and shell struck and burst all around us, but
only one boat was struck, containing some of the
Sixth Connecticut volunteers, killing one, and wounding two or three.

"The General's boat got two discharges of grape.
Just at this moment, Lieutenant-Colonel Rodman said
to the General: 'Let me land my command and take
that battery.' The General hesitated at first, and
then said: 'Go!' Colonel Rodman stood up in the
stern of his boat, and gave the command—as the boats
were all in line and in good order—'Seventh Connecticut! man your oars and follow me.' We had
previously detailed fifty men as oarsmen, leaving us
about one hundred and seventy-five effective men and
officers. At the order, we all headed for the shore;
and, as the boats struck, every man sprang as if by
instinct, and in an instant the men were in line.

"We advanced rapidly to the first line of rifle-works; our skirmishers cleared it with a bound, and advanced to the second line. Our main forces moved to the first line; the foe retired, firing. Lieutenant-Colonel Rodman now sent word back for the General to land his whole force, as we could hold the line we occupied. After exchanging a few shots, and the brigade being landed and ready to advance, the enemy began to give way. Lieutenant Jordan, with a detachment of company I, pushed right up into their batteries on our right, and not finding the first gun in working order—it having been disabled by a shot—he pushed forward to what is now called Battery Rodman, in which there was an eight-inch sea-coast howitzer, and turned it on the retreating foe, bursting several shells over their heads before they reached Fort Wagner.

"Our forces captured eight single-gun batteries and three mortars, and not far from two hundred prisoners."

REMARKABLE PHENOMENON.—A writer in the Staunton *Spectator*, dating at Lewisburgh, Greenbrier County, Virginia, September fifteenth, writes to that paper a description of a remarkable atmospheric phenomenon witnessed in that town. It was seen by our pickets, a few miles from the town. The same scene has been described in several respectable papers, the editors of which all vouch for the reliability of their informants. The writer says:

"A remarkable phenomenon was witnessed, a few miles west of this place, at the house of Mrs. Pearcy, on the first day of this month, at about three o'clock P.M., by Mr. Moses Dwyer, her neighbor, who happened to be seated in her porch at the time, as well as by others at or near the house.

"The weather was quite hot and dry; not a cloud could be seen; no wind even ruffled the foliage on the surrounding trees. All things being propitious, the grand panorama began to move. Just over and through the tops of the trees, on the adjacent hills on the South, immense numbers of rolls, resembling cotton or smoke, apparently of the size and shape of doors, seemed to be passing rapidly through the air, yet in beautiful order and regularity. The rolls seemed to be tinged on the edge with light green, so as to resemble a border or deep fringe. There were apparently thousands of them, and were, perhaps, an hour in getting by. After these had passed over and out of sight, the scene was changed from the air above to the earth beneath, and became more intensely interesting to the spectators, who were witnessing the panorama from different stand-points.

"In the deep valley beneath, thousands upon thousands of (apparently) human beings (men) came in view, travelling in the same direction as the rolls, marching in good order, some thirty or forty in depth, moving rapidly, 'double-quick,' and commenced ascending the sides of the almost insurmountable hills opposite, and had the stoop peculiar to men when they ascend a steep mountain. There seemed to be a great variety in the size of the men; some were very large, whilst others were quite small. Their arms, legs, and heads, could be distinctly seen in motion. They seemed to observe strict military discipline, and there were no stragglers to be seen.

"There was uniformity of dress—loose white blouses or shirts, with white pants, wool hats, and were without guns, swords, or any thing that indicated 'men of war.' On they came, through the valley and over the steep hill, crossing the road, and finally passing out of sight, in a direction due north from those who were looking on.

"The gentleman who witnessed this is a man with whom you were once acquainted, Mr. Editor, and as truthful a man as we have in this county, and as little liable to be carried away by 'fanciful speculations' as any man living. Four others (respectable ladies) and a servant-girl witnessed this phenomenon.   W.

"P. S.—On the fourteenth instant, the same scene, almost identical, was seen by eight or ten of our pickets at Bunger's Mill, and by many of the citizens in that neighborhood; this is about four miles east of Pearcy's. It was about one hour passing."—*Richmond Dispatch*, October 2.

JENNIE WADE.

Beside a little streamlet that sparkled clear and bright,
Reflecting back in beauty the morning's rosy light,
There stood a little cottage, so humble, yet so fair,
You might have guessed some fairy had found a refuge
    there;

There bloomed the sweet syringos, there blushed the
    roses red,
And there the stately lily its rarest perfume shed;
Within that humble cottage there dwelt a maiden fair,
And those who knew pronounced her the fairest flower there.

But to that lowly dwelling there came one summer's
    morn,
The muttering of the thunder, which told the coming storm:
"Fly to your country's rescue!" the rousing tocsin
    said,
"And sweep the base invaders to slumber with the
    dead."

And Jennie's father heard it—her lover heard it too;
And those intrepid freemen asked not what they
    should do,
They had no thought of keeping a coward watch at
    home,
While sweeping through their country the rebel foes
    did come.

So calling to his daughter, the hardy yeoman said:
"I hear, my darling Jennie, the rebel foemen's tread;
And I must go to meet them; they will not harm you
    here;
Else I should deem my duty to guard a life so dear."

"Yet war is dark and bloody," with quivering lips he
    said,
"And ere the strife is ended, I may be with the dead:
May God in mercy keep you, and every blessing send,
And should I fall, in William you'll find a faithful
    friend."

"And I, my darling Jennie," the gallant William said,
"May in the coming conflict be numbered with the
    dead,
And yet," with trembling accents, and misty eyes,
    said he,
"I only fear, my treasure, lest harm should come to
    thee."

"Fear not for me," she answered, "but I will breathe
    a prayer
That God will guide and cherish the lives to me so
    dear,

And when the conflict's over, come to this home so
      dear,
And I will wait to welcome and bless your coming
      here."

The father's arms a moment were folded round his
      child,
Whose fair and gentle presence his weary hours be-
      guiled,
And mingled tears and kisses were rained upon her
      cheek,
While William looked the parting his lips refused to
      speak.

The summer days went gliding in golden circles by,
And Lee's impetuous army to Gettysburgh drew nigh ;
The fierce and bloody conflict swept through that re-
      gion fair,
Yet still heroic Jennie dwelt in the cottage there.

And while her heart was aching, lest those she loved
      were dead,
Her plump and rosy fingers moulded the soldiers
      bread.
"Fly ! fly ! heroic maiden," a Union soldier said,
"For through this vale there sweepeth a double storm
      of lead."

Then spoke the fearless Jennie : "I fear not for my
      life,
My father and one other are in that deadly strife :
I may not fight beside them, but ne'er shall it be said,
While they were battling for me, I feared to bake
      their bread."

Loud and more loud thundered the crimson tide of
      war,
And thick and fast the bullets swept through the sum-
      mer air,
And one (some fury sped it) pierced Jennie's faithful
      breast,
And laid its throbbing pulses for evermore at rest.

      .   .   .   .

The bloody day was over, and thousands slept there
      dead,
Who on that summer morning swept by with martial
      tread ;
Among them Jennie's father in death's embraces lay,
But William passed unwounded through all that fear-
      ful day :

And so with hurried footsteps he sought the cottage-
      door,
But oh ! no Jennie met him with welcome, as of yore.
He crossed the humble threshold, then paused in hor-
      ror there :
There lay his heart's best treasure—so cold, so still, so
      fair !

"O God !" he cried in anguish, "what fiend hath done
      this deed ?
Would I had died in battle, ere I had seen her bleed :

Alas, alas, my darling ! no words of welcome come,
For cold in death sweet Jenny awaits for me at home.

"For this, (oh ! hear me, heaven,) my eye shall never
      fail,
My hand be true and steady to guide the leaden hail :
A force more strong than powder, each deadly ball
      shall urge—
The memory of the maiden who died at Gettysburgh."

And now, all bravely battling for freedom and for life,
Whene'er the bugle soundeth to call him to the strife,
He remembers that fair maiden, all cold and bloody—
      laid,
And strikes with dread precision, as he thinks of Jen-
      nie Wade.   E. S. T.

HOME ON THE HILL, Jan. 28.

SHE COMES FROM ST. LOUIS !

BY EDNA DEAN PROCTOR.

"On the sixteenth of July, 1863, the steamboat Imperial arrived at New-Orleans from St. Louis, the first boat between the
cities for more than two years."

She comes from St. Louis ! Hurrah and hurrah !
She lies at the levee unmarred by a scar !
No cursing guerrillas could frighten her back,
Though longing, like bloodhounds, to leap on her
      track ;
Nor cannon to sink her, nor chain set to bar—
She comes from St. Louis ! Hurrah and hurrah !

She comes from St. Louis ! Who now will deny
That Vicksburgh, Port Hudson, in ruins must lie ?
The good boat Imperial laughed them to scorn
As bold to our levee she rounded at morn,
And brought with her freedom and wealth from afar—
She comes from St. Louis ! Hurrah and hurrah !

She comes from St. Louis ! The river is free !
What tidings of glory, New-Orleans, for thee !
Oh ! welcome her ! herald the holiday time—
Fling out all your banners now—let the bells chime
Of sunny days dawning, the harbinger star,
She comes from St. Louis ! Hurrah and hurrah !

She comes from St. Louis ! Our torpor is o'er ;
We breathe the fresh air of the Northland once more ;
Life wakes at the wharves again, stirs in the street,
Beams bright in the faces that smile as they greet ;
No traitor our triumph can hinder or mar—
She comes from St. Louis ! Hurrah and hurrah !

She comes from St. Louis ! Away with the plea
That river or people divided may be !
One current sweeps past us, one likeness we wear ;
One flag through the future right proudly we'll bear ;
All hail to the day without malice or jar !—
She comes from St. Louis ! Hurrah and hurrah !

INDEX.

—◆◆◆—

EXPLANATIONS OF ABBREVIATIONS IN THE INDEX.

D. stands for *Diary of Events;* Doc. for *Documents;* and P. for *Poetry, Rumors, and Incidents.*